The Dictionary of Art · volume four

The Dictionary of Art

4

Biardeau
TO
Brüggemann

GROVE

The Dictionary of Art

edited by JANE TURNER, in thirty-four volumes, 1996

Reprinted with minor corrections, 1998

This edition is distributed within the United Kingdom and Europe
by Macmillan Publishers Limited, London, and within the United States and Canada by
Grove's Dictionaries Inc., New York.

Text keyboarded by Wearset Limited, Sunderland, England
Database management by Pindar plc, York, England
Imagesetting by William Clowes Limited, Suffolk, England
Printed and bound by China Translation and Printing Services Ltd, Hong Kong

British Library Cataloguing in Publication Data	*Library of Congress Cataloging in Publication Data*

The dictionary of art
  1. Art - Dictionaries 2. Art - History -
    Dictionaries
  I. Turner, Jane
  703
 	
ISBN 1-884446-00-0
	The dictionary of art / editor, Jane Turner.
	    p. cm.
	    Includes bibliographical references and index.
	    Contents: 1. A to Anckerman
	    ISBN 1-884446-00-0 (alk. paper)
	    1. Art—Encyclopedias.
	    I. Turner, Jane, 1956–
	  N31.D5 1996 96–13628
	  703—dc20 CIP

Contents

List of Colour Illustrations   vi

General Abbreviations   vii

A Note on the Use of *The Dictionary*   xiii

The Dictionary, volume four:
Biardeau–Brüggemann   1

Illustration Acknowledgements   926

List of Colour Illustrations

PLATE I. **Beadwork**

1. Beaded pouch, 206×206 mm, probably made by the Native American Seminoles of Florida or the Creeks of Georgia or Oklahoma, early to mid-19th century (Washington, DC, National Museum of Natural History/Photo: Department of Anthropology, cat. no. 358247, Smithsonian Institution photo no. 76–6580)

2. Bead and shell decoration on a rattan basket, h. 435 mm, made by the Kayan people of the Baram River district, Sarawak, Malaysia, *c.* 1905 (London, British Museum/Photo: Trustees of the British Museum)

3. Beadwork sculptural group, h. 255 mm, made by the Yoruba people of south-west Nigeria, before 1912 (London, British Museum/Photo: © Margret Carey)

PLATE II. **Beadwork**

Beads and sequins on a printed voile evening dress made by Callot Soeurs, Paris, *c.* 1922 (London, Victoria and Albert Museum/Photo: Board of Trustees of the Victoria and Albert Museum)

PLATE III. **Bookbinding**

Book cover of the Sion Gospels, beechwood, overlaid with gold, enamels and precious stones, 254×220 mm, from Germany, possibly Trier, 11th century with 12th-century additions (London, Victoria and Albert Museum/Photo: Board of Trustees of the Victoria and Albert Museum)

PLATE IV. **Bookbinding**

1. Book cover (interior) of a bound manuscript, painted with lacquer, 230×140 mm, from Kashmir, India, early 19th century (London, Victoria and Albert Museum/Photo: Board of Trustees of the Victoria and Albert Museum)

2. Book cover of a manuscript, ivory, possibly from the 9th-century Codex Aureus of St Emmeram, 10th-century Byzantine enamels, cloisonné enamel and gold, 425×315 mm, Regensburg or Bamberg, early 11th century (Munich, Bayerische Staatsbibliothek/Photo: Bayerische Staatsbibliothek)

3. Book by Paul Bonet (1889–1971) for *La Treille Muscate* by Colette, inlays of leather with gold-tooling, 325×250 mm, 1942 (private collection/Photo: © Jean-Loup Charmet, Paris/© ADAGP, Paris, and DACS, London, 1996)

General Abbreviations

The abbreviations employed throughout this dictionary, most of which are listed below, do not vary, except for capitalization, regardless of the context in which they are used, including bibliographical citations and for locations of works of art. The principle used to arrive at these abbreviations is that their full form should be easily deducible, and for this reason acronyms have generally been avoided (e.g. Los Angeles Co. Mus. A. instead of LACMA). The same abbreviation is adopted for cognate forms in foreign languages and in most cases for plural and adjectival forms (e.g. A.= Art, Arts, Arte, Arti etc). Not all related forms are listed below. Occasionally, if a name, for instance of an artists' group or exhibiting society, is repeated within the text of one article, it is cited in an abbreviated form after its first mention in full (e.g. The Pre-Raphaelite Brotherhood (PRB) was founded...); the same is true of archaeological periods and eras, which are abbreviated to initial letters in small capitals (e.g. In the Early Minoan (EM) period...). Such abbreviations do not appear in this list. For the reader's convenience, separate full lists of abbreviations for locations, periodical titles and standard reference books and series are included as Appendices A–C in vol. 33.

A.	Art, Arts	Anthropol.	Anthropology	Azerbaij.	Azerbaijani
A.C.	Arts Council	Antiqua.	Antiquarian, Antiquaries	B.	Bartsch [catalogue of Old Master prints]
Acad.	Academy	app.	appendix		
AD	Anno Domini	approx.	approximately	*b*	born
Add.	Additional, Addendum	AR	Arkansas (USA)	BA	Bachelor of Arts
addn	addition	ARA	Associate of the Royal Academy	Balt.	Baltic
Admin.	Administration			*bapt*	baptized
Adv.	Advances, Advanced	Arab.	Arabic	BArch	Bachelor of Architecture
Aesth.	Aesthetic(s)	Archaeol.	Archaeology	Bart	Baronet
Afr.	African	Archit.	Architecture, Architectural	Bask.	Basketry
Afrik.	Afrikaans, Afrikaner	Archv, Archvs	Archive(s)	BBC	British Broadcasting Corporation
A.G.	Art Gallery				
Agrar.	Agrarian	Arg.	Argentine	BC	Before Christ
Agric.	Agriculture	ARHA	Associate of the Royal Hibernian Academy	BC	British Columbia (Canada)
Agron.	Agronomy			BE	Buddhist era
Agy	Agency	ARIBA	Associate of the Royal Institute of British Architects	Beds	Bedfordshire (GB)
AH	Anno Hegirae			Behav.	Behavioural
A. Inst.	Art Institute	Armen.	Armenian	Belarus.	Belarusian
AK	Alaska (USA)	ARSA	Associate of the Royal Scottish Academy	Belg.	Belgian
AL	Alabama (USA)			Berks	Berkshire (GB)
Alb.	Albanian	Asiat.	Asiatic	Berwicks	Berwickshire (GB; old)
Alg.	Algerian	Assist.	Assistance	BFA	Bachelor of Fine Arts
Alta	Alberta (Canada)	Assoc.	Association	Bibl.	Bible, Biblical
Altern.	Alternative	Astron.	Astronomy	Bibliog.	Bibliography, Bibliographical
a.m.	ante meridiem [before noon]	AT&T	American Telephone & Telegraph Company	Biblioph.	Bibliophile
Amat.	Amateur	attrib.	attribution, attributed to	Biog.	Biography, Biographical
Amer.	American	Aug	August	Biol.	Biology, Biological
An.	Annals	Aust.	Austrian	bk, bks	book(s)
Anatol.	Anatolian	Austral.	Australian	Bkbinder	Bookbinder
Anc.	Ancient	Auth.	Author(s)	Bklore	Booklore
Annu.	Annual	Auton.	Autonomous	Bkshop	Bookshop
Anon.	Anonymous(ly)	Aux.	Auxiliary	BL	British Library
Ant.	Antique	Ave.	Avenue	Bld	Build
Anthol.	Anthology	AZ	Arizona (USA)	Bldg	Building

Bldr	Builder
BLitt	Bachelor of Letters/Literature
BM	British Museum
Boh.	Bohemian
Boliv.	Bolivian
Botan.	Botany, Botanical
BP	Before present (1950)
Braz.	Brazilian
BRD	Bundesrepublik Deutschland [Federal Republic of Germany (West Germany)]
Brecons	Breconshire (GB; old)
Brez.	Brezonek [lang. of Brittany]
Brit.	British
Bros	Brothers
BSc	Bachelor of Science
Bucks	Buckinghamshire (GB)
Bulg.	Bulgarian
Bull.	Bulletin
bur	buried
Burm.	Burmese
Byz.	Byzantine
C	Celsius
C.	Century
c.	circa [about]
CA	California
Cab.	Cabinet
Caerns	Caernarvonshire (GB; old)
C.A.G.	City Art Gallery
Cal.	Calendar
Callig.	Calligraphy
Cam.	Camera
Cambs	Cambridgeshire (GB)
can	canonized
Can.	Canadian
Cant.	Canton(s), Cantonal
Capt.	Captain
Cards	Cardiganshire (GB; old)
Carib.	Caribbean
Carms	Carmarthenshire (GB; old)
Cartog.	Cartography
Cat.	Catalan
cat.	catalogue
Cath.	Catholic
CBE	Commander of the Order of the British Empire
Celeb.	Celebration
Celt.	Celtic
Cent.	Centre, Central
Centen.	Centennial
Cer.	Ceramic
cf.	confer [compare]
Chap., Chaps	Chapter(s)
Chem.	Chemistry
Ches	Cheshire (GB)
Chil.	Chilean

Chin.	Chinese
Christ.	Christian, Christianity
Chron.	Chronicle
Cie	Compagnie [French]
Cinema.	Cinematography
Circ.	Circle
Civ.	Civil, Civic
Civiliz.	Civilization(s)
Class.	Classic, Classical
Clin.	Clinical
CO	Colorado (USA)
Co.	Company; County
Cod.	Codex, Codices
Col., Cols	Collection(s); Column(s)
Coll.	College
collab.	in collaboration with, collaborated, collaborative
Collct.	Collecting
Colloq.	Colloquies
Colomb.	Colombian
Colon.	Colonies, Colonial
Colr	Collector
Comm.	Commission; Community
Commerc.	Commercial
Communic.	Communications
Comp.	Comparative; compiled by, compiler
Concent.	Concentration
Concr.	Concrete
Confed.	Confederation
Confer.	Conference
Congol.	Congolese
Congr.	Congress
Conserv.	Conservation; Conservatory
Constr.	Construction(al)
cont.	continued
Contemp.	Contemporary
Contrib.	Contributions, Contributor(s)
Convalesc.	Convalescence
Convent.	Convention
Coop.	Cooperation
Coord.	Coordination
Copt.	Coptic
Corp.	Corporation, Corpus
Corr.	Correspondence
Cors.	Corsican
Cost.	Costume
Cret.	Cretan
Crim.	Criminal
Crit.	Critical, Criticism
Croat.	Croatian
CT	Connecticut (USA)
Cttee	Committee
Cub.	Cuban
Cult.	Cultural, Culture
Cumb.	Cumberland (GB; old)

Cur.	Curator, Curatorial, Curatorship
Curr.	Current(s)
CVO	Commander of the [Royal] Victorian Order
Cyclad.	Cycladic
Cyp.	Cypriot
Czech.	Czechoslovak
$	dollars
d	died
d.	denarius, denarii [penny, pence]
Dalmat.	Dalmatian
Dan.	Danish
DBE	Dame Commander of the Order of the British Empire
DC	District of Columbia (USA)
DDR	Deutsche Demokratische Republik [German Democratic Republic (East Germany)]
DE	Delaware (USA)
Dec	December
Dec.	Decorative
ded.	dedication, dedicated to
Democ.	Democracy, Democratic
Demog.	Demography, Demographic
Denbs	Denbighshire (GB; old)
dep.	deposited at
Dept	Department
Dept.	Departmental, Departments
Derbys	Derbyshire (GB)
Des.	Design
destr.	destroyed
Dev.	Development
Devon	Devonshire (GB)
Dial.	Dialogue
diam.	diameter
Diff.	Diffusion
Dig.	Digest
Dip. Eng.	Diploma in Engineering
Dir.	Direction, Directed
Directrt	Directorate
Disc.	Discussion
diss.	dissertation
Distr.	District
Div.	Division
DLitt	Doctor of Letters/Literature
DM	Deutsche Mark
Doc.	Document(s)
Doss.	Dossier
DPhil	Doctor of Philosophy
Dr	Doctor
Drg, Drgs	Drawing(s)
DSc	Doctor of Science/Historical Sciences
Dut.	Dutch
Dwell.	Dwelling
E.	East(ern)

EC	European (Economic) Community	figs	figures	Heb.	Hebrew
Eccles.	Ecclesiastical	Filip.	Filipina(s), Filipino(s)	Hell.	Hellenic
Econ.	Economic, Economies	Fin.	Finnish	Her.	Heritage
Ecuad.	Ecuadorean	FL	Florida (USA)	Herald.	Heraldry, Heraldic
ed.	editor, edited (by)	*fl*	*floruit* [he/she flourished]	Hereford & Worcs	Hereford & Worcester (GB)
edn	edition	Flem.	Flemish	Herts	Hertfordshire (GB)
eds	editors	Flints	Flintshire (GB; old)	HI	Hawaii (USA)
Educ.	Education	Flk	Folk	Hib.	Hibernia
e.g.	*exempli gratia* [for example]	Flklore	Folklore	Hisp.	Hispanic
Egyp.	Egyptian	fol., fols	folio(s)	Hist.	History, Historical
Elem.	Element(s), Elementary	Found.	Foundation	HMS	His/Her Majesty's Ship
Emp.	Empirical	Fr.	French	Hon.	Honorary, Honourable
Emul.	Emulation	frag.	fragment	Horiz.	Horizon
Enc.	Encyclopedia	Fri.	Friday	Hort.	Horticulture
Encour.	Encouragement	FRIBA	Fellow of the Royal Institute of British Architects	Hosp.	Hospital(s)
Eng.	English	FRS	Fellow of the Royal Society, London	HRH	His/Her Royal Highness
Engin.	Engineer, Engineering			Human.	Humanities, Humanism
Engr., Engrs	Engraving(s)	ft	foot, feet	Hung.	Hungarian
		Furn.	Furniture	Hunts	Huntingdonshire (GB; old)
Envmt	Environment	Futur.	Futurist, Futurism	IA	Iowa
Epig.	Epigraphy	g	gram(s)	ibid.	*ibidem* [in the same place]
Episc.	Episcopal	GA	Georgia (USA)	ICA	Institute of Contemporary Arts
Esp.	Especially	Gael.	Gaelic		
Ess.	Essays	Gal., Gals	Gallery, Galleries	Ice.	Icelandic
est.	established	Gaz.	Gazette	Iconog.	Iconography
etc	*etcetera* [and so on]	GB	Great Britain	Iconol.	Iconology
Ethnog.	Ethnography	Gdn, Gdns	Garden(s)	ID	Idaho (USA)
Ethnol.	Ethnology	Gdnr(s)	Gardener(s)	i.e.	*id est* [that is]
Etrus.	Etruscan	Gen.	General	IL	Illinois (USA)
Eur.	European	Geneal.	Genealogy, Genealogist	Illum.	Illumination
Evangel.	Evangelical	Gent.	Gentleman, Gentlemen	illus.	illustrated, illustration
Exam.	Examination	Geog.	Geography	Imp.	Imperial
Excav.	Excavation, Excavated	Geol.	Geology	IN	Indiana (USA)
Exch.	Exchange	Geom.	Geometry	in., ins	inch(es)
Excurs.	Excursion	Georg.	Georgian	Inc.	Incorporated
exh.	exhibition	Geosci.	Geoscience	inc.	incomplete
Exp.	Exposition	Ger.	German, Germanic	incl.	includes, including, inclusive
Expermntl	Experimental	G.I.	Government/General Issue (USA)	Incorp.	Incorporation
Explor.	Exploration			Ind.	Indian
Expn	Expansion	Glams	Glamorganshire (GB; old)	Indep.	Independent
Ext.	External	Glos	Gloucestershire (GB)	Indig.	Indigenous
Extn	Extension	Govt	Government	Indol.	Indology
f, ff	following page, following pages	Gr.	Greek	Indon.	Indonesian
		Grad.	Graduate	Indust.	Industrial
F.A.	Fine Art(s)	Graph.	Graphic	Inf.	Information
Fac.	Faculty	Green.	Greenlandic	Inq.	Inquiry
facs.	facsimile	Gr.-Roman	Greco-Roman	Inscr.	Inscribed, Inscription
Fam.	Family	Gt	Great	Inst.	Institute(s)
fasc.	fascicle	Gtr	Greater	Inst. A.	Institute of Art
fd	feastday (of a saint)	Guat.	Guatemalan	Instr.	Instrument, Instrumental
Feb	February	Gym.	Gymnasium	Int.	International
Fed.	Federation, Federal	h.	height	Intell.	Intelligence
Fem.	Feminist	ha	hectare	Inter.	Interior(s), Internal
Fest.	Festival	Hait.	Haitian	Interdiscip.	Interdisciplinary
fig.	figure (illustration)	Hants	Hampshire (GB)	intro.	introduced by, introduction
Fig.	Figurative	Hb.	Handbook	inv.	inventory

Inven.	Invention	m	metre(s)	Moldov.	Moldovan
Invest.	Investigation(s)	m.	married	MOMA	Museum of Modern Art
Iran.	Iranian	M.	Monsieur	Mon.	Monday
irreg.	irregular(ly)	MA	Master of Arts; Massachusetts (USA)	Mongol.	Mongolian
Islam.	Islamic			Mons	Monmouthshire (GB; old)
Isr.	Israeli	Mag.	Magazine	Montgoms	Montgomeryshire (GB; old)
It.	Italian	Maint.	Maintenance	Mor.	Moral
J.	Journal	Malay.	Malaysian	Morav.	Moravian
Jam.	Jamaican	Man.	Manitoba (Canada); Manual	Moroc.	Moroccan
Jan	January	Manuf.	Manufactures	Movt	Movement
Jap.	Japanese	Mar.	Marine, Maritime	MP	Member of Parliament
Jav.	Javanese	Mason.	Masonic	MPhil	Master of Philosophy
Jew.	Jewish	Mat.	Material(s)	MS	Mississippi (USA)
Jewel.	Jewellery	Math.	Mathematic	MS., MSS	manuscript(s)
Jord.	Jordanian	MBE	Member of the Order of the British Empire	MSc	Master of Science
jr	junior			MT	Montana (USA)
Juris.	Jurisdiction	MD	Doctor of Medicine; Maryland (USA)	Mt	Mount
KBE	Knight Commander of the Order of the British Empire	ME	Maine (USA)	Mthly	Monthly
		Mech.	Mechanical	Mun.	Municipal
KCVO	Knight Commander of the Royal Victorian Order	Med.	Medieval; Medium, Media	Mus.	Museum(s)
kg	kilogram(s)	Medic.	Medical, Medicine	Mus. A.	Museum of Art
kHz	kilohertz	Medit.	Mediterranean	Mus. F.A.	Museum of Fine Art(s)
km	kilometre(s)	Mem.	Memorial(s); Memoir(s)	Music.	Musicology
Knowl.	Knowledge	Merions	Merionethshire (GB; old)	N.	North(ern); National
Kor.	Korean	Meso-Amer.	Meso-American	n	refractive index of a medium
KS	Kansas (USA)			n.	note
KY	Kentucky (USA)	Mesop.	Mesopotamian	N.A.G.	National Art Gallery
Kyrgyz.	Kyrgyzstani	Met.	Metropolitan	Nat.	Natural, Nature
£	libra, librae [pound, pounds sterling]	Metal.	Metallurgy	Naut.	Nautical
		Mex.	Mexican	NB	New Brunswick (Canada)
l.	length	MFA	Master of Fine Arts	NC	North Carolina (USA)
LA	Louisiana (USA)	mg	milligram(s)	ND	North Dakota (USA)
Lab.	Laboratory	Mgmt	Management	n.d.	no date
Lancs	Lancashire (GB)	Mgr	Monsignor	NE	Nebraska; Northeast(ern)
Lang.	Language(s)	MI	Michigan	Neth.	Netherlandish
Lat.	Latin	Micrones.	Micronesian	Newslett.	Newsletter
Latv.	Latvian	Mid. Amer.	Middle American	Nfld	Newfoundland (Canada)
lb, lbs	pound(s) weight	Middx	Middlesex (GB; old)	N.G.	National Gallery
Leb.	Lebanese	Mid. E.	Middle Eastern	N.G.A.	National Gallery of Art
Lect.	Lecture	Mid. Eng.	Middle English	NH	New Hampshire (USA)
Legis.	Legislative	Mid Glam.	Mid Glamorgan (GB)	Niger.	Nigerian
Leics	Leicestershire (GB)	Mil.	Military	NJ	New Jersey (USA)
Lex.	Lexicon	Mill.	Millennium	NM	New Mexico (USA)
Lg.	Large	Min.	Ministry; Minutes	nm	nanometre (10^{-9} metre)
Lib., Libs	Library, Libraries	Misc.	Miscellaneous	nn.	notes
Liber.	Liberian	Miss.	Mission(s)	no., nos	number(s)
Libsp	Librarianship	Mlle	Mademoiselle	Nord.	Nordic
Lincs	Lincolnshire (GB)	mm	millimetre(s)	Norm.	Normal
Lit.	Literature	Mme	Madame	Northants	Northamptonshire (GB)
Lith.	Lithuanian	MN	Minnesota	Northumb.	Northumberland (GB)
Liturg.	Liturgical	Mnmt, Mnmts	Monument(s)	Norw.	Norwegian
LLB	Bachelor of Laws			Notts	Nottinghamshire (GB)
LLD	Doctor of Laws	Mnmtl	Monumental	Nov	November
Lt	Lieutenant	MO	Missouri (USA)	n.p.	no place (of publication)
Lt-Col.	Lieutenant-Colonel	Mod.	Modern, Modernist	N.P.G.	National Portrait Gallery
Ltd	Limited	Moldav.	Moldavian	nr	near

Nr E.	Near Eastern
NS	New Style; Nova Scotia (Canada)
n. s.	new series
NSW	New South Wales (Australia)
NT	National Trust
Ntbk	Notebook
Numi.	Numismatic(s)
NV	Nevada (USA)
NW	Northwest(ern)
NWT	Northwest Territories (Canada)
NY	New York (USA)
NZ	New Zealand
OBE	Officer of the Order of the British Empire
Obj.	Object(s), Objective
Occas.	Occasional
Occident.	Occidental
Ocean.	Oceania
Oct	October
8vo	octavo
OFM	Order of Friars Minor
OH	Ohio (USA)
OK	Oklahoma (USA)
Olymp.	Olympic
OM	Order of Merit
Ont.	Ontario (Canada)
op.	opus
opp.	opposite; opera [pl. of opus]
OR	Oregon (USA)
Org.	Organization
Orient.	Oriental
Orthdx	Orthodox
OSB	Order of St Benedict
Ott.	Ottoman
Oxon	Oxfordshire (GB)
oz.	ounce(s)
p	pence
p., pp.	page(s)
PA	Pennsylvania (USA)
p.a.	per annum
Pak.	Pakistani
Palaeontol.	Palaeontology, Palaeontological
Palest.	Palestinian
Pap.	Paper(s)
para.	paragraph
Parag.	Paraguayan
Parl.	Parliament
Paroch.	Parochial
Patriarch.	Patriarchate
Patriot.	Patriotic
Patrm.	Patrimony
Pav.	Pavilion
PEI	Prince Edward Island (Canada)
Pembs	Pembrokeshire (GB; old)

Per.	Period
Percep.	Perceptions
Perf.	Performance, Performing, Performed
Period.	Periodical(s)
Pers.	Persian
Persp.	Perspectives
Peru.	Peruvian
PhD	Doctor of Philosophy
Philol.	Philology
Philos.	Philosophy
Phoen.	Phoenician
Phot.	Photograph, Photography, Photographic
Phys.	Physician(s), Physics, Physique, Physical
Physiog.	Physiognomy
Physiol.	Physiology
Pict.	Picture(s), Pictorial
pl.	plate; plural
Plan.	Planning
Planet.	Planetarium
Plast.	Plastic
pls	plates
p.m.	post meridiem [after noon]
Polit.	Political
Poly.	Polytechnic
Polynes.	Polynesian
Pop.	Popular
Port.	Portuguese
Port.	Portfolio
Posth.	Posthumous(ly)
Pott.	Pottery
POW	prisoner of war
PRA	President of the Royal Academy
Pract.	Practical
Prefect.	Prefecture, Prefectural
Preserv.	Preservation
prev.	previous(ly)
priv.	private
PRO	Public Record Office
Prob.	Problem(s)
Proc.	Proceedings
Prod.	Production
Prog.	Progress
Proj.	Project(s)
Promot.	Promotion
Prop.	Property, Properties
Prov.	Province(s), Provincial
Proven.	Provenance
Prt, Prts	Print(s)
Prtg	Printing
pseud.	pseudonym
Psych.	Psychiatry, Psychiatric
Psychol.	Psychology, Psychological
pt	part

Ptg(s)	Painting(s)
Pub.	Public
pubd	published
Publ.	Publicity
pubn(s)	publication(s)
PVA	Polyvinyl acetate
PVC	polyvinyl chloride
Q.	quarterly
4to	quarto
Qué.	Québec (Canada)
R	reprint
r	*recto*
RA	Royal Academician
Radnors	Radnorshire (GB; old)
RAF	Royal Air Force
Rec.	Record(s)
red.	reduction, reduced for
Ref.	Reference
Refurb.	Refurbishment
reg	*regit* [ruled]
Reg.	Regional
Relig.	Religion, Religious
remod.	remodelled
Ren.	Renaissance
Rep.	Report(s)
repr.	reprint(ed); reproduced, reproduction
Represent.	Representation, Representative
Res.	Research
rest.	restored, restoration
Retro.	Retrospective
rev.	revision, revised (by/for)
Rev.	Reverend; Review
RHA	Royal Hibernian Academician
RI	Rhode Island (USA)
RIBA	Royal Institute of British Architects
RJ	Rio de Janeiro State
Rlwy	Railway
RSA	Royal Scottish Academy
RSFSR	Russian Soviet Federated Socialist Republic
Rt Hon.	Right Honourable
Rur.	Rural
Rus.	Russian
S	San, Santa, Santo, Sant', São [Saint]
S.	South(ern)
s.	solidus, solidi [shilling(s)]
Sask.	Saskatchewan (Canada)
Sat.	Saturday
SC	South Carolina (USA)
Scand.	Scandinavian
Sch.	School
Sci.	Science(s), Scientific
Scot.	Scottish
Sculp.	Sculpture

SD	South Dakota (USA)	suppl., suppls	supplement(s), supplementary	Urb.	Urban
SE	Southeast(ern)			Urug.	Uruguayan
Sect.	Section	Surv.	Survey	US	United States
Sel.	Selected	SW	Southwest(ern)	USA	United States of America
Semin.	Seminar(s), Seminary	Swed.	Swedish	USSR	Union of Soviet Socialist Republics
Semiot.	Semiotic	Swi.	Swiss		
Semit.	Semitic	Symp.	Symposium	UT	Utah
Sept	September	Syr.	Syrian	*v*	*verso*
Ser.	Series	Tap.	Tapestry	VA	Virginia (USA)
Serb.	Serbian	Tas.	Tasmanian	V&A	Victoria and Albert Museum
Serv.	Service(s)	Tech.	Technical, Technique	Var.	Various
Sess.	Session, Sessional	Technol.	Technology	Venez.	Venezuelan
Settmt(s)	Settlement(s)	Territ.	Territory	Vern.	Vernacular
S. Glam.	South Glamorgan (GB)	Theat.	Theatre	Vict.	Victorian
Siber.	Siberian	Theol.	Theology, Theological	Vid.	Video
Sig.	Signature	Theor.	Theory, Theoretical	Viet.	Vietnamese
Sil.	Silesian	Thurs.	Thursday	viz.	*videlicet* [namely]
Sin.	Singhala	Tib.	Tibetan	vol., vols	volume(s)
sing.	singular	TN	Tennessee (USA)	vs.	versus
SJ	Societas Jesu [Society of Jesus]	Top.	Topography	VT	Vermont (USA)
Skt	Sanskrit	Trad.	Tradition(s), Traditional	Vulg.	Vulgarisation
Slav.	Slavic, Slavonic	trans.	translation, translated by; transactions	W.	West(ern)
Slov.	Slovene, Slovenian			w.	width
Soc.	Society	Transafr.	Transafrican	WA	Washington (USA)
Social.	Socialism, Socialist	Transatlant.	Transatlantic	Warwicks	Warwickshire (GB)
Sociol.	Sociology	Transcarpath.	Transcarpathian	Wed.	Wednesday
Sov.	Soviet	transcr.	transcribed by/for	W. Glam.	West Glamorgan (GB)
SP	São Paulo State	Triq.	Triquarterly	WI	Wisconsin (USA)
Sp.	Spanish	Tropic.	Tropical	Wilts	Wiltshire (GB)
sq.	square	Tues.	Tuesday	Wkly	Weekly
sr	senior	Turk.	Turkish	W. Midlands	West Midlands (GB)
Sri L.	Sri Lankan	Turkmen.	Turkmenistani		
SS	Saints, Santi, Santissima, Santissimo, Santissimi; Steamship	TV	Television	Worcs	Worcestershire (GB; old)
		TX	Texas (USA)	Wtrcol.	Watercolour
		U.	University	WV	West Virginia (USA)
SSR	Soviet Socialist Republic	UK	United Kingdom of Great Britain and Northern Ireland	WY	Wyoming (USA)
St	Saint, Sankt, Sint, Szent			Yb., Y.-b.	Yearbook, Year-book
Staffs	Staffordshire (GB)	Ukrain.	Ukrainian	Yem.	Yemeni
Ste	Sainte	Un.	Union	Yorks	Yorkshire (GB; old)
Stud.	Study, Studies	Underwtr	Underwater	Yug.	Yugoslavian
Subalp.	Subalpine	UNESCO	United Nations Educational, Scientific and Cultural Organization	Zamb.	Zambian
Sum.	Sumerian			Zimb.	Zimbabwean
Sun.	Sunday	Univl	Universal		
Sup.	Superior	unpubd	unpublished		

A Note on the Use of the Dictionary

This note is intended as a short guide to the basic editorial conventions adopted in this dictionary. For a fuller explanation, please refer to the Introduction, vol. 1, pp. xiii–xx.

Abbreviations in general use in the dictionary are listed on pp. vii–xii; those used in bibliographies and for locations of works of art or exhibition venues are listed in the Appendices in vol. 33.

Alphabetization of headings, which are distinguished in bold typeface, is letter by letter up to the first comma (ignoring spaces, hyphens, accents and any parenthesized or bracketed matter); the same principle applies thereafter. Abbreviations of 'Saint' and its foreign equivalents are alphabetized as if spelt out, and headings with the prefix 'Mc' appear under 'Mac'.

Authors' signatures appear at the end of the article or sequence of articles that the authors have contributed; in multipartite articles, any section that is unsigned is by the author of the next signed section. Where the article was compiled by the editors or in the few cases where an author has wished to remain anonymous, this is indicated by a square box (□) instead of a signature.

Bibliographies are arranged chronologically (within section, where divided) by order of year of first publication and, within years, alphabetically by authors' names. Abbreviations have been used for some standard reference books; these are cited in full in Appendix C in vol. 33, as are abbreviations of periodical titles (Appendix B). Abbreviated references to alphabetically arranged dictionaries and encyclopedias appear at the beginning of the bibliography (or section).

Biographical dates when cited in parentheses in running text at the first mention of a personal name indicate that the individual does not have an entry in the dictionary. The presence of parenthesized regnal dates for rulers and popes, however, does not necessarily indicate the lack of a biography of that person. Where no dates are provided for an artist or patron, the reader may assume that there is a biography of that individual in the dictionary (or, more rarely, that the person is so obscure that dates are not readily available).

Cross-references are distinguished by the use of small capital letters, with a large capital to indicate the initial letter of the entry to which the reader is directed; for example, 'He commissioned LEONARDO DA VINCI . . .' means that the entry is alphabetized under 'L'.

B

[continued]

Biardeau, Pierre (*b* Le Mans, 4 Dec 1608; *d* Angers, Oct 1671). French sculptor. Like his father René Biardeau (*fl* 1614–34), he was principally a sculptor in terracotta, working in the tradition of such sculptors from the Maine region as Mathieu Dionise (*fl* 1581–1613), Gervais Delabarre (*fl* 1593–1642) and Charles Hoyau (*d* 1644). His brother, also named René Biardeau, sculpted statues of the *Virgin* (*c.* 1638) to be set above the city gates of Le Mans. But Pierre's large output was dominated by pious images intended for Baroque retables.

Biardeau first settled in Laval, where from 1632 he collaborated with the architect Pierre Corbineau (1600–78) on statues decorating the retable in the parish church at Piré-sur-Seiche (Ile-et-Vilaine). He moved *c.* 1637 to Angers, where he worked on the altar of the Augustinian chapel and then on the altar and the tomb of *Hercule de Charnacé* (destr.) in the Carmelite church. In Paris, between 1647 and 1650, he worked on a major contract for the Petits Augustins, executing statues and reliefs for their high altar. Returning to Angers in 1650, he was entrusted with the high altar at the priory of Breuil-Bellay, Cizay-la-Madeleine, which included a statue of *St Stephen of Muret* (*in situ*). Around 1652 or 1653 he sent an *Annunciation* group (destr.) to Mayenne, and in 1654 undertook to make the retable (destr.) for Notre-Dame des Ardilliers, Saumur. Between 1657 and 1659 he worked on the decoration of the Chapelle de la Barre in the St Jacques district of Angers. The high altar, decorated with the figures of the *Virgin and Child*, *St James* and *St John*, is perhaps the most impressive work in terracotta. He worked on the reconstruction of Notre-Dame des Ardilliers until his death and during the same period produced a retable (destr.) for the convent of the Calvairiennes, a reformed Augustinian order, in Mayenne. Other works include an *Annunciation* for the Visitandines, another such order, in Saumur and an altar in the Palais des Marchands, Angers. Two depictions of the *Virgin and Child* (Poitiers Cathedral) and a *Virgin* in Nozay (Faculté catholique d'Angers) are convincingly attributed to Biardeau.

Biardeau brought a profoundly meditative quality to the stereotyped iconography of the Counter-Reformation. His stay in Paris probably brought him in contact with Jacques Sarazin, the leading sculptor of the period. Both artists managed to combine in their works a feeling of calm with strength in a way reminiscent of the paintings of their contemporaries Simon Vouet, Laurent La Hyre and Eustache Le Sueur.

BIBLIOGRAPHY

P. Beclard: 'Recherches sur le sculpteur Biardeau', *Mém. Soc. Agric., Sci. & A. Angers*, n.s. 2, i (1850), pp. 43–50
P. Belleuvre: 'La Vierge de Nozé', *Mém. Soc. Agric., Sci. & A. Angers*, n.s. 2, v (1854), pp. 133–43
C. Port: *Les Artistes angevins* (Paris, 1881), pp. 25–41
J. Denais: 'La Chapelle de la Barre et les sculptures de Pierre Biardeau (1659–1664)', *Réun. Soc. B.-A. Dép.*, xx (1896), pp. 359–67
M. Brillant: 'Pierre Biardeau et la statuaire angevine en terre cuite au XVIIe siècle', *Correspondant*, n.s., ccxlvi (1921), pp. 464–88
M. M. Aldis: *La Statuaire en terre cuite dans les provinces du Maine et de l'Anjou*, 10 vols (diss., Paris, Ecole du Louvre, 1938)
Y.-J. Riou: 'Réflexions sur l'attribution à propos de deux tableaux de Berthélémy et une statue de Biardeau conservés à la cathédrale de Poitiers', *Bull. Soc. Antiq. Ouest*, n.s. 4, xvi (1982), pp. 430–39

GENEVIÈVE BRESC-BAUTIER

Biasino, Cipriano (*b* Lanzo d'Intelvi, 1580; *d* Krems, 2 June 1636). Italian architect, active in Austria. In 1606 he was engaged on reconstructing the bridge over the River Mur near Kapfenberg in Styria. During 1610–11 he was involved in building work at Seckau Abbey, and in 1613 there are records of him in both Graz and Bruck. He subsequently moved to Lower Austria, settling in Krems, where he was in charge of building the parish church of St Veit (from 1616), probably to his own designs. This is one of the earliest Baroque churches in Austria of the wall pillar type, with a four-bay nave, narrower apsidal choir and single tower. Between 1624 and 1627 Biasino, as one of the representatives of Italian builders working in Vienna and Lower Austria, successfully took part in negotiations over admission into the masons' guild, which was controlled by 'German' masters. In 1631–4, together with Johann Jakob Spazio and Antonio Canevale, he supervised the building of the Dominikanerkirche in Vienna, to the designs of Giovanni Giacomo Tencalla (*fl* 1631–71). He was commissioned to repair the dilapidated vaulting of the parish church at St Michael in der Wachau in 1631 and that year began alterations to the north aisle of Göttweig Abbey Church, to give it a Baroque appearance (later rebuilt after a fire). The design of the Jesuit College in Krems, which was not executed until after his death, has also been attributed to him, but this attribution remains questionable. Biasino was one of the most respected building contractors in Austria in the 17th century and

1

was to a large extent responsible for the dissemination of Early Baroque architecture in Lower Austria.

BIBLIOGRAPHY

DBI; Thieme–Becker

L. Koller: 'Die Comasken Cipriano Biasino und Domenico Sciassia', *Waldviertel*, iv/4–5 (1955), pp. 97–101

H. Kühnel: 'Die Baumeister Cipriano Biasino und J. B. Spazio der Ältere', *Mitt. Krems. Stadtarchvs*, ii (1962), pp. 53–66

PETER FIDLER

Biauneveu, Andrieu. *See* BEAUNEVEU, ANDRÉ.

Bibbiena, Bernardo [Dovizi, Bernardo] (*b* Bibbiena, nr Arezzo, 4 Aug 1470; *d* Rome, 9 Nov 1520). Italian cardinal and patron. He was from an obscure family and moved at an early age to Florence, where his elder brother Pietro was serving as secretary to Lorenzo de' Medici. Bernardo, too, entered Medici service and quickly became secretary to Cardinal Giovanni de' Medici, whom he served loyally and followed into exile in 1494. When Cardinal de' Medici was elected Pope Leo X in 1513, he made Bernardo treasurer general and then Cardinal. Generally known as Cardinal Bibbiena, from 1513 he lived in the Vatican Palace and during the first years of Leo's pontificate was the Pope's main adviser, even being called *alter papa*. Around 1515, however, his influence began to decline, as Leo increasingly relied on the advice of his cousin, Cardinal Giulio de' Medici (the future Clement VII). In 1516 Cardinal Bibbiena was sent as papal legate to the Holy Roman Emperor, Maximilian I, and in 1518 to Francis I. His influence further diminished as he showed increasing sympathy with the French. At the end of 1519 he returned to Rome, where he died the following year and was buried in S Maria d'Aracoeli.

In addition to his diplomatic skills Cardinal Bibbiena was admired for his amiability and wit. He is represented as the leader in the discussion on humour in Baldassare Castiglione's *Il cortegiano* (Venice, 1528). A learned man well versed in the arts and literature, he corresponded with many prominent contemporaries. He was also active as an author, writing one of the first Italian comedies based on Classical models, *La calandria* (played first at Urbino, 1513). He was in contact with such artists as Michelangelo and Raphael, with whom he was on especially good terms. Bibbiena offered Raphael the hand of a relative, Maria (the marriage, however, never took place), and on Raphael's death in 1520 he inherited Raphael's house in Rome. A portrait of Bibbiena by or after Raphael is in Florence (Pitti). Raphael and his assistants decorated the *stufetta* (bathroom; 1516) and *loggetta* (1519) of Bibbiena's apartment in the Vatican. From Pietro Bembo's correspondence with the Cardinal it appears that Bibbiena chose the subjects depicted, which were derived from Classical mythology and are mildly erotic. This, together with the sometimes coarse humour in *La calandria* and some of his letters, has given rise to an image of Bibbiena as a worldly man, unworthy of his office. Erotic scenes were not uncommon for bathroom decoration, however, and the humour of *La calandria* is paralleled in contemporary comedies.

BIBLIOGRAPHY

DBI

A. M. Bandini: *Il Bibbiena o sia il ministro di stato* (Livorno, 1758)

L. von Pastor: *Geschichte der Päpste* (Freiburg im Breisgau, 1886–1933), IV/i

G. L. Moncallero: *Il cardinale Bernardo Dovizi da Bibbiena umanista e diplomatico (1470–1520)* (Florence, 1953)

D. Redig de Campos: 'La stufetta del cardinale Bibbiena in Vaticano e il suo restauro', *Röm. Jb. Kstgesch.*, xx (1983), pp. 221–40

J. L. DE JONG

Bibiena. *See* GALLI-BIBIENA.

Bible. Term meaning 'the books', derived via Latin from Greek, used to refer to the sacred writings of Judaism and Christianity. The Bible is composed of two parts: the Hebrew scriptures or Old Testament, written originally in Hebrew (with some parts in Aramaic), which consists of the writings of the Jewish people; and the New Testament, composed in Greek, which records the story of Jesus and the beginnings of Christianity. The stories, moral teachings and theological doctrines in the Judeo-Christian Bible have provided subjects for an immense body of visual art. Although predominantly a Christian art form (*see* §I below), a significant body of Jewish imagery has been inspired by the Old Testament (*see* §II below). For Christians, a canon of biblical books was established in the Early Christian period, although many apocryphal books continued to circulate; from the late medieval period onwards poetic and dramatic reinterpretations of biblical narratives were popular. Much of this extra-canonical literature contributed to the development of such important subjects in Christian art as the PIETÀ. Events only hinted at in the Bible, the Last Judgement for example, were expanded through commentaries and pictorial tradition into complex iconographical forms; the same is true of abstruse theological concepts, such as the Holy Trinity.

In its broadest sense, Bible illustration has been a central force in Western art from the catacomb paintings and sarcophagi of the Early Christian period up to the profound interpretations of the great Baroque artists; and it has continued to have a place, if only occasionally, in the work of many 19th- and 20th-century masters. The present article is limited to Bible illustration found in books, both manuscript and printed, where it is directly linked to the scriptural texts. Yet this relatively narrow field is more diverse than it might seem since the texts, and thus their illustration, are not confined to the canonical scriptures. The variety of biblical imagery ranges from the literal to the symbolic, and in some important instances the decoration of biblical volumes has scarcely any perceptible relation to the biblical content; such are the dazzling pages of abstract pattern in Insular Gospel books or the fantastical drolleries in the margins of Gothic Psalters. Throughout the Middle Ages the decoration of books was a leading art form in which the various biblical manuscripts held an important position. With the introduction of the printed book in the 15th century, book illustration rapidly declined in art historical significance, becoming only a marginal part of the great range of the pictorial arts. Moreover, the gradual waning of the role of religion in post-medieval society has led to a much diminished share for Bible illustration in the proliferating arts of the book. Although in the late 20th century talents as diverse as Gustave Doré and Salvador Dalí have on occasion prepared illustrations for new editions of the Bible, these are rare exceptions.

I. Christian. II. Hebrew.

I. Christian.

Over its lengthy history, Christian biblical art has obviously not maintained any continuity of style or illustrative method. It is a remarkable fact that some of the oldest known biblical manuscripts have the most thorough picture cycles. The Cotton Genesis fragment, probably dated to the late 5th century AD, originally contained over 300 miniatures illustrating its single biblical book (*see* §1(i) below). Such a high ratio of image to text was scarcely ever approximated in later times. Early Psalters, Gospel books and manuscripts of the Apocalypse had similarly complete illustrative programmes, closely related to the texts. There is an impressive ambitiousness in the epic pictorial sequences of the Early Christian manuscript tradition, apparently made possible by the illustration of discrete sections of the Bible rather than the complete Bible. The Early Christian illustrative tradition was maintained, in some measure, in Byzantine works; an 11th-century Byzantine Gospel book, for example, might have as many as 350 images (*see* EARLY CHRISTIAN AND BYZANTINE ART, §V, 2(iii)).

In the West, during the Romanesque period, there was a heightening of aesthetic refinement in biblical art but, in general, a decrease in the density of illustrative cycles (*see* ROMANESQUE, §IV, 2(iii)). At the same time there were signs of a new tendency to reduce the link between illustration and the accompanying biblical text. Some 12th-century biblical manuscripts were illustrated with typological miniatures, which presented analogies between the Old Testament and New Testament as derived from exegetical thought (*see* TYPOLOGICAL CYCLES). In the Gothic period a more radical departure from conventional Bible illustration was seen in the *Bible moralisée*, a huge illustrated compendium of scriptural extracts and moralizing commentary (*see* §3(i) below). In a comparable vein were such illustrated volumes of typological texts as the *Biblia pauperum* (*see* §3(ii) below) and the *Speculum humanae salvationis*. Another variant on the biblical text was the *Historia scholastica* and its French translation, the *Bible historiale*, in which biblical history and legend were combined (*see* §3(iii) below). These projects required the creation of complex new iconographic programmes, some of which were repeatedly copied for several centuries. Thus, over the course of the medieval period an original concern with literal Bible illustration was increasingly displaced by illustrations of an indirect nature. Furthermore, types of illustrated biblical manuscripts that had been important for religious practice in the early Middle Ages, most notably Gospel books and Psalters, became widely replaced during the Gothic period by new kinds of liturgical and devotional books—the Missal, the Book of Hours—in which biblical texts were unimportant and in which there could be little question of directly illustrating the biblical content.

Early in the history of printed books (*see* §2 below), works of an exegetical nature, such as the *Biblia pauperum*, continued to be broadly popular in the form of the woodcut BLOCK-BOOK. With the decline of this type of biblical publication in the 16th century, biblical art was largely given over to the illustration of narrative biblical events. Although to some extent Bible illustration had returned to its earlier, literal principles, the forms of illustration were decreasingly bound by iconographic tradition, and artists often inclined towards individual readings and representations of biblical narrative, frequently depicted in a picturesque and genre-like fashion. In the modern period the publication of illustrated biblical literature has been subject to an increase in volume, much of it involving ephemeral, popular paraphrases for use by missionary agencies or Sunday schools—or, at an opposite extreme, special publications of severely limited circulation.

1. Manuscript. 2. Printed. 3. Variants.

1. MANUSCRIPT. Bibles were an important type of illustrated manuscript throughout the Middle Ages. Their decoration and illustration was not confined to manuscripts of the complete Bible but included individual biblical books, particularly the Book of Psalms (*see* PSALTER), the Apocalypse (*see* APOCALYPSE, §1) and, less frequently, such narrative books of the Old Testament as Genesis or the Book of Job. Certain groups of biblical books might be incorporated in separate manuscripts, the most significant being the GOSPEL BOOK. Common groupings from the Old Testament were the Pentateuch (the first five books) and the Octateuch (the first eight books). Also sometimes richly illustrated were manuscripts in which the biblical text was rearranged for liturgical purposes—for example Evangeliaries (Gospel lectionaries; *see* SERVICE BOOK)—or manuscripts of commentaries on particular biblical books; the iconographical content of such volumes is at times closely related to that of Bibles. This article will focus on complete Bible manuscripts and groups of biblical books not covered elsewhere in this *Dictionary*. The treatment of biblical illustration in both the Byzantine East and in the West shows some common features, but there is often a different emphasis in the type of biblical books illustrated. Thus, for example, complete Bible manuscripts are virtually unknown in the East, while Octateuchs and the Book of Job are fairly common, but the latter is rare in the West.

(i) Early Christian and Byzantine. (ii) Western medieval.

(i) Early Christian and Byzantine. Most extant illustrated biblical manuscripts from the 6th to the 8th century are fragments of single biblical books or groups of books (*see* EARLY CHRISTIAN AND BYZANTINE ART, §V, 1 and 2(ii)–(iv)). These show that it was common practice in this period to accompany the biblical narratives with lengthy picture cycles of a literal nature. The Quedlinburg Itala fragment (second quarter of the 5th century; Berlin, Staatsbib., MS. theol. lat., fol. 485) comprises only a few leaves from the first three books of Kings, with painted scenes from the *Lives of Samuel and Saul*. Another fragment, the COTTON GENESIS (?late 5th century; London, BL, Cotton MS. Otho B. VI), written in Greek, originally contained about 340 miniatures. These may have been the iconographic prototype for such later medieval Genesis cycles as the 13th-century mosaics in the narthex

1. Biblical illustration showing *Joseph and Potiphar's Wife*, miniature from the Vienna Genesis, 333×270 mm, 6th century (Vienna, Österreichische National-albibliothek, Cod. theol. gr. 31, p. 13)

Little is known of Bible illustration during the early Byzantine period due to the extreme scarcity of preserved examples. After the iconoclastic controversy (726–843), with the renewed production of manuscripts, there was a major revival of biblical illustration. Illustrated complete Bibles were, however, rarely produced at any time, the only such surviving book being the 9th- or 10th-century LEO BIBLE (Rome, Vatican, Bib. Apostolica, MS. Reg. gr. 1); even in this case it is possible that the work was not originally planned to contain imagery, for its full-page paintings were inserted well after the completion of the text. The best of the paintings are accomplished examples of the neo-classical style favoured in the Macedonian Renaissance.

Extensive sections of Old Testament narrative are illustrated in Byzantine manuscripts of the Octateuch (*see* EARLY CHRISTIAN AND BYZANTINE ART, §V, 2(iv)(b)); six copies dating from the 11th to the 13th century are known, all but one containing closely similar picture cycles (e.g. second half of the 13th century; Mt Athos, Vatopedhi Monastery, Cod. 602). The full cycle runs to about 370 framed miniatures, placed within the text and literally related to its content (see fig. 2). The explicitness and completeness of the illustrative method is reminiscent of such Early Christian manuscripts as the Vienna Genesis, although precise links between the mid-Byzantine Octateuchs and Early Christian art have not been traced. More numerous are illustrated manuscripts of the Book of Job, of which some 15 are preserved (*see* EARLY CHRISTIAN AND BYZANTINE ART, §V, 2(iv)(d)). Probably the oldest of these (Patmos, St John the Divine Monastery, Treasury Lib., MS. 171) may have been produced as early as the 9th

of S Marco, Venice. The VIENNA GENESIS (6th century; Vienna, Österreich. Nbib., Cod. theol. gr. 31), also written in Greek, is about a quarter of its original length; its pages are stained purple, with the illustrations arranged in strip compositions across the bottom of each page (see fig. 1). The Ashburnam Pentateuch (?early 7th century; Paris, Bib. N., MS. nouv. acq. lat. 2334), its text in the Latin Vulgate, was possibly made in Spain or North Africa. Of an estimated original 68 illustrations, 19 are preserved. Most of these colourful and complex paintings fill an entire page and include several narrative episodes. The sources of inspiration for these lengthy Early Christian picture cycles have been much debated: the existence of models in elaborately illustrated Jewish Bibles from the Roman period has been suggested, but no such manuscripts have survived.

Two complete Bibles are of more limited artistic content. A 6th- or 7th-century Syriac Bible (Paris, Bib. N., MS. syr. 341) has a single modest miniature at the beginning of each book, representing the author or a principal figure of the narrative. The Codex Amiatinus (*c.* 700; Florence, Bib. Medicea-Laurenziana, MS. Amiatinus 1), a large Bible made in Northumbria and believed to be closely based on a 6th-century Italian model, contains only two major illustrations: full-page paintings of the Old Testament scribe *Ezra* and, at the beginning of the New Testament, *Christ in Majesty*.

2. Biblical illustration showing *Joshua at the Walls of Jerico*, miniature from the Vatopedhi Octateuch, second half of the 13th century (Mt Athos, Vatopedhi Monastery, Cod. 602, fol. 343*r*)

century. The Job manuscripts, like the Octateuchs, contain large numbers of pictures in a modest scale and immediately related to the sequence of narrative action.

Another frequently found type of Byzantine Old Testament manuscript is that containing the books of the major and minor prophets (e.g. mid-10th century; Rome, Vatican, Bib. Apostolica, MS. Chisi. R. VIII. 54); since the prophetic texts have little narrative matter, the volumes are illustrated with stately full-length portraits of each of the prophets (*see* EARLY CHRISTIAN AND BYZANTINE ART, fig. 58). Unique in several respects is the JOSHUA ROLL (Rome, Vatican, Bib. Apostolica, MS. Pal. gr. 431), now generally dated to the mid-10th century. The scroll has complex illustrations to the Book of Joshua with only brief selections from the text, which serve as captions. The relation of this manuscript to antique sources has long been a subject of debate.

(ii) Western medieval.

(a) c. 700–c. 1070. With the uncharacteristic exception of the Codex Amiatinus (*see* §(i) above), no decorated complete Insular Bible has survived, despite the rich flowering of manuscript production in Irish and Northumbrian monasteries during the 7th and 8th centuries. The main emphasis was, rather, on the making of Gospel books, works from which narrative illustration is almost entirely absent (*see* INSULAR ART, §3). Although Gospel books also make up the principal form of decorated manuscript in the early stages of the Carolingian period (*see* CAROLINGIAN ART, §IV, 3), in the scriptorium at St Martin, Tours, there was a significant production of illustrated complete Bibles (*see* TOURS, §2(i) and fig. 2). The large manuscripts include both full-page miniatures and numerous tiny decorations and illustrations worked into the initial letters. The oldest of the illustrated Tours Bibles is the Montier-Grandval Bible (*c*. 840; London, BL, Add. MS. 10546), which contains four full-page miniatures: the *Story of Adam and Eve*, in horizontal strip compositions, as a frontispiece to the Book of Genesis; *Moses Receiving the Tablets of the Law*, as the frontispiece to Exodus (see fig. 3); *Christ in Majesty*, introducing the Gospels; and the *Throne Set in Heaven*, before Revelations. This is a more elaborately illustrated work than any earlier extant full Bible. Although it had been argued that the four illustrations were copied in their entirety from a lost 5th-century Italian Bible, it is more likely that their sources were varied.

Another contemporary Tours Bible (Bamberg, Staatsbib., MS. Bibl. 1), includes only two full-page paintings—the *Story of Adam and Eve* and *Christ in Majesty*—executed in a delicate style quite different from the monumental spirit of the Grandval Bible illustrations. The slightly later Vivian Bible (Paris, Bib. N., MS. lat. 1) approximately repeats the style and iconography of the four Grandval Bible compositions, with four additional full-page miniatures: scenes from the *Life of St Jerome*, the translator of the Vulgate text, as a frontispiece to the entire volume; *David and his Musicians*, placed before the Book of Psalms; scenes from the *Life of St Paul*, before the Pauline Epistles; and, at the end of the book, an image of a ruler, probably *Charles the Bald*, being presented with the manuscript.

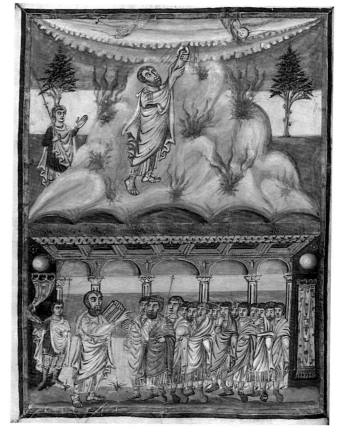

3. Biblical illustration showing (top) *Moses Receiving the Tablets of the Law* and (bottom) *Moses Addressing the Israelites*, miniature from the Montier-Grandval Bible, *c*. 840 (London, British Library, Add. MS. 10546, fol. 25*v*)

This sequence of Carolingian Bibles reaches its peak in the BIBLE OF SAN PAOLO (Rome, S Paolo fuori le Mura), made *c*. 870, possibly at Reims. The S Paolo Bible draws on the imagery of the Tours Bibles but has a larger cycle of 23 (originally 24) full-page miniatures (*see* CAROLINGIAN ART, fig. 8), many of them remarkably expansive and dynamic in design.

The most noteworthy Bibles of the following period are those from Spain. One of these (920; León Cathedral, MS. 6) includes few narrative miniatures but a considerable amount of symbolic imagery and abstract pattern, executed in the bold, flattened, colourful forms of Mozarabic style. Another Bible (960; León, Mus.-Bib. Real Colegiata, S Isidoro, MS. 2) is similarly illustrated but with more narrative content, the painted scenes interspersed among the text; this Bible is perhaps a distant relative of the Ashburnam Pentateuch (*see* §(i) above). Two 11th-century Catalan Bibles are less dramatic in style but far more thoroughly illustrated than the León Bibles. Indeed, the Ripoll Bible (Rome, Vatican, Bib. Apostolica, MS. lat. 5729) is one of the most extensively illustrated of all early medieval complete Bibles; it includes, most unusually for such manuscripts, a lengthy, complex series of Christological scenes. The Roda Bible (Paris, Bib. N., MS. lat. 6) is only slightly less extensively illustrated.

There are no richly illustrated complete Bibles from the Ottonian period. Only one Bible is known (Hildesheim, Diözmus. & Domschatzkam., Cod. 61), thought to have been made in the early 11th-century for Bishop Bernward of Hildesheim and containing a single painted full-page frontispiece. Much more significant in this period was the production of Gospel books and Evangeliaries (*see* OTTONIAN ART, §IV, 2). Gospel books were also much produced at this period in the monasteries of northern France and the Netherlands, but complete Bibles were rare. The only ambitiously illustrated Bible in this field is the St Vaast Bible (early 11th century; Arras, Bib. Ville, MS. 559), a three-volume work, which is badly mutilated but still contains several large illustrations. No illustrated complete Bibles are known to have been created in Anglo-Saxon England, but some highly interesting illustrated manuscripts of Old Testament narrative in vernacular paraphrases were produced. The most remarkable of these is a paraphrase of the five books of Moses and the book of Joshua, the Old English 'Hexateuch' (London, BL, Cotton MS. Claud. B. IV), which has over 400 lively scenes, a cycle that in terms of quantity is comparable to those in the approximately contemporary Catalan Bibles.

(b) c. 1070–c. 1450. During the later decades of the 11th century there was a revival of illustrated complete Bibles throughout much of Western Europe, although the reasons for this are not well understood. The typical Romanesque Bible is a massive, two-volume work; less thoroughly illustrated than some of its predecessors, the Romanesque Bible shows a more carefully controlled sense of format and a more polished aesthetic (*see* ROMANESQUE, §IV, 2(iii)(a) and (vi)).

It is clear that the Umbro-Roman region was a particularly active centre of production of the numerous Romanesque Bibles made in Italy. The earliest examples, from the late 11th century (e.g. before 1084; Munich, Bayer. Staatsbib., Clm. 13001), are principally illustrated with small paintings of isolated standing figures, a simple arrangement recalling the 6th-century Syriac Bible (*see* §(i) above). In the course of the 12th century the illustrative programmes became more sumptuous and descriptive, as in the Pantheon Bible (*c.* 1125; Rome, Vatican, Bib. Apostolica, MS. Vat. lat. 12958), which contains sequential narrative illustrations to accompany several of the Old Testament books.

From the Mosan region (the diocese of Liège) the Lobbes Bible (1084; Tournai, Bib. Sémin. Episc., MS. 1) is decorated at the beginning of each book with historiated initials, many involving narrative subjects; it is the earliest surviving Bible to have a complete set. A related manuscript, the Stavelot Bible (1097; London, BL, Add. MSS 28106–7), is similarly illustrated with historiated initials but also includes a single impressive full-page miniature of *Christ in Majesty* introducing the New Testament. A later Mosan manuscript, the Floreffe Bible (?*c.* 1153; London, BL, Add. MSS 17737–8), is illustrated in a different way, with large schematic images of typological content (*see* ROMANESQUE, fig. 59). The important Salzburg school of manuscript illumination produced the Walther Bible (*c.* 1120–30; Michaelbeuern, Stiftsbib., MS. perg. 1), sparsely illustrated with Old Testament scenes

placed within the pages of text, and the Admont Bible (*c.* 1130–40; Vienna, Österreich. Nbib., Cods s.n. 2701–2), with a somewhat more extensive Old Testament cycle in a similar style and layout. From the Rhineland, the Arnstein Bible (1172; London, BL, Harley MSS 2798–9) has elaborately decorated and historiated initials in a Late Romanesque style.

The wide variety of Romanesque biblical art is exemplified by such French manuscripts as a Bible (*c.* 1100; Paris, Bib. N., MS. lat. 8) produced at St Martial, Limoges, in which the illustrative emphasis is on author portraits with additional Old Testament scenes in framed headpieces; the early 12th-century Bible of Stephen Harding (1109; Dijon, Bib. Mun., MSS 12–15), made at Cîteaux, with vigorous, lightly sketched narrative scenes and grotesque motifs; and, from the end of the 12th century, the Souvigny Bible (Moulins, Bib., MS. 1), with numerous full-page compositions of an epic character in several tiers. In an imposing series of English Romanesque Bibles the most outstanding works are the BURY ST EDMUNDS BIBLE (*c.* 1135; Cambridge, Corpus Christi Coll., MS. 2; *see* ROMANESQUE, fig. 64) with historiated initials and larger,

4. Biblical illustration showing (top) *Abraham and the Three Angels*, (bottom) the *Sacrifice of Isaac* and *Jacob's Ladder*, miniature from the Lambeth Bible, 378×583 mm, *c.* 1135 (London, Lambeth Palace Library, MS. 3, fol. 6*r*)

tiered illustrations of deep colour and magnificent crafts-manship; the mid-12th-century LAMBETH BIBLE (London, Lambeth Pal. Lib., MS. 3; Maidstone Mus. & A.G.), in a similar format but with a more distinctively expressive drawing style (see fig. 4); and the WINCHESTER BIBLE (*c.* 1160–90; Winchester, Cathedral Lib.; *see* MANUSCRIPT, colour pl. V, fig. 1). As with most Romanesque Bibles, the narrative cycles of English Bibles were largely confined to Old Testament history, while the life of Christ was not depicted. This is particularly striking in the English works, since English Psalters of the same period regularly included elaborate Christological cycles.

During the 13th century biblical manuscripts underwent a drastic change in form. Bibles became single volumes of portable size, with their script and illustrations greatly reduced in both number and size; illustrations were confined to small historiated initials introducing the bibli-cal books. This type of Bible originated in Paris, where copies were produced in large quantity by secular ateliers, working in a rather routine way (e.g. London, BL, Add. MS. 15253). The minimalism of such Bible illustration is in remarkable contrast to the huge volume of images included in the contemporary *Bibles moralisées* also made in Paris (*see* §3(i) below). The single-volume Parisian Bibles clearly influenced later 13th-century English Bibles, such as the Bible of William of Devon (London, BL, Royal MS. D.I), but are less directly reflected in contemporary Italian Bibles (e.g. New York, Pierpont Morgan Lib., MS. G. 38). In contrast, during the 14th century picture Bibles became popular; these contained immense and complicated cycles of imagery, with only brief biblical passages as captions (e.g. the Holkham Bible Picture Book, London, BL, Add. MS. 47682).

Towards the end of the medieval period illustrated Bibles were scarce. Individual commissions, often for secular patrons, produced some impressive Bibles. Some of these were variants on the biblical text, such as the *Bible historiale* of Charles V (1371; The Hague, Rijksmus. Meermanno–Westreenianum, MS. 10.B.23; *see* §3(iii) be-low). A *tour de force* of Bohemian manuscript production is the WENCESLAS BIBLE (*c.* 1390–95; Vienna, Österreich. Nbib., Cods 2759–64), its text a German translation. The pictorial programme, even though only half finished, comprises about 600 miniatures (see fig. 5), representing one of the most extensive biblical cycles. In 15th-century Italy, where manuscript painting assumed the classicizing forms of the early Renaissance style, illustrated Bibles were also relatively uncommon. The most elaborate extant example is the two-volume BIBLE OF BORSO D'ESTE (1455–61; Modena, Bib. Estense, MS. V.G. 12 [lat. 422–23]), made at Ferrara, with over 1000 illuminated leaves.

BIBLIOGRAPHY

W. Neuss: *Die katalanische Bibelillustration um die Wende des ersten Jahrtausends und die altspanische Buchmalerei* (Leipzig, 1922)
B. Smalley: *The Study of the Bible in the Middle Ages* (Oxford, 1952/R 1970)
G. Folena and G. L. Mellini: *Bibbia istoriata padovana* (Venice, 1962)
M. Rickert: *Painting in Britain: The Middle Ages*, Pelican Hist. A. (Harmondsworth, rev. 1965)
C. R. Dodwell: *Painting in Europe, 800 to 1200*, Pelican Hist. A. (Harmondsworth, 1971)
K. Weitzmann: 'The Illustration of the Septuagint', *Studies in Classical and Byzantine Manuscript Illumination*, ed. H. L. Kessler (Chicago, 1971), pp. 45–75

5. Biblical illustration, showing scenes from the *Creation*, historiated initial I from the Wenceslas Bible, 530×565 mm, *c.* 1390–95 (Vienna, Österreichische Nationalbibliothek, Cod. 2759, fol. 2*v*)

C. R. Dodwell and P. Clemoes: *The Old English Illustrated Hexateuch: British Museum, Cotton Claudius B.IV* (Copenhagen, 1974) [facs]
J. J. G. Alexander, ed.: *A Survey of Manuscripts Illuminated in the British Isles* (London 1975-)
R. Branner: *Manuscript Painting in Paris during the Reign of Saint Louis* (Berkeley, 1977)
H. L. Kessler: *The Illustrated Bibles from Tours* (Princeton, 1977)
W. Dynes: *The Illuminations of the Stavelot Bible* (New York, 1978)
W. Oakeshott: *The Two Winchester Bibles* (Oxford, 1981)
W. Cahn: *Romanesque Bible Illumination* (Ithaca and New York, 1982)
C. de Hamel: *Glossed Books of the Bible and the Origins of the Paris Booktrade* (Woodbridge, 1984)
I. Levin: *The Quedlinburg Itala* (Leiden, 1985)
P. Huber: *Hiob, Dulder oder Rebell? Byzantinische Miniaturen zum Buch Hiob* (Patmos, 1986)
K. Weitzmann and H. Kessler: *The Cotton Genesis* (Princeton, 1986)

DON DENNY

2. PRINTED. The advent of printing with movable type in the mid-15th century brought new aesthetics to Bible publication; combined with woodcuts, engravings and etchings, it transformed the appearance of Bibles. The capabilities for mass production that made the Bible widely available also tended to emphasize textual and functional over artistic aspects of the Bible. In a consideration of the art of printed Bibles two groups emerge: Bibles without illustrations, which rely on book design, including layout,

TYPOGRAPHY and ornament; and illustrated Bibles, in which subject-matter, graphic techniques and artistic impression play an important role (*see also* BOOK ILLUSTRATION).

(i) Unillustrated Bibles. The first major book printed with movable metal type, the Gutenberg Bible (*c.* 1455; *see* GUTENBERG, JOHANN) is one of the great monuments of the art of the book. The high-quality materials, the geometrically proportioned layout and justified two-column text give it a harmonious appearance (see fig. 6). The typography, which includes special characters that allow for subtle spacing of adjoining letters, reproduces formal Gothic (*textura*) script. With added, illuminated initials for each book and chapter, the folio-size 42-line Bible creates a magnificent impression.

By the early 16th century, printing had not only spread rapidly through Europe but had also undergone certain technological refinements. This early phase of printing coincided with interest in vernacular translations and scholarly editions of the biblical text. Some printed Bibles continued to emulate the most beautiful manuscript Bibles (*see* §1 above) as seen in the Venetian Jenson Bible of 1476 (*see* VENICE, §III, 1). Others experimented with Roman typeface, for example the Vulgate printed in Rome in 1471 by Konrad Sweynheim (*d* 1477) and Arnold Pannartz (*d* 1476). The creation of fonts for Hebrew and Greek facilitated scholarly work on biblical editions. The Complutensian Polyglot directed by Cardinal Francisco Jiménez de Cisneros (1436–1517) at the University of Alcalá in Spain between 1514 and 1517, which placed Latin, Greek and Hebrew texts of the Bible in parallel columns, was a significant typographical achievement. The 16th century is considered a highpoint in Bible printing for both the number and the quality of texts and for the refinement of visual features. One printer, Robert Estienne, working in Paris and Geneva, was at the forefront of Bible printing. His folio Latin Vulgates of 1532 and 1540 rank among the most beautiful printed Bibles. Although they differ in detail, both editions feature long lines, varying sizes of Roman type for text and headings and delicate ornamental initials. Later, Estienne returned to double columns as he standardized the use of verse divisions. Other outstanding Bibles were printed in Lyon by Jean de Tournes (1504–64) and in the Netherlands by Christoph Plantin; especially so the latter's great Polyglot Bible, the *Biblia regia*, of 1569–72.

From the 17th century until the end of the 19th few printed Bibles matched the standards set by the early printers. One exception is the folio English Bible printed at Cambridge by John Baskerville and completed in 1763. It displays the characteristics of his excellent presswork, including readable type, deep black ink and smooth paper. In the late 19th century the revival of fine printing produced some beautiful Bibles. The Doves Press Bible, published in England (1903–5) in five columns, drew inspiration from earlier monuments of printing with its Roman type and display capitals set in long lines. The American printer Bruce Rogers successfully merged artistic and commercial printing in two folio Bibles, the Oxford Lectern Bible (Oxford, 1935) and the World Bible (Cleveland and New York, 1949). In both Bibles well-designed typography, ornament and layout were used.

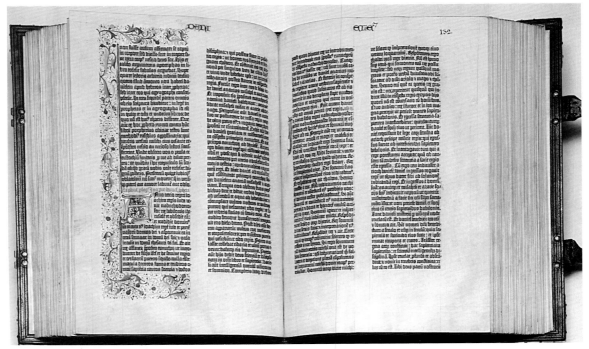

6. Printed Bible, incipit to the Book of Daniel, from the Gutenberg Bible, 295×500 mm, published in Mainz, *c.* 1455 (New York, Pierpont Morgan Library)

(ii) Illustrated Bibles. A tradition of illustrated printed Bibles also began with the earliest period of printing (*see also* PRINTS, §II and WOODCUT, §II). Following precedents from medieval manuscripts, illustration was most common in vernacular Bibles, in picture Bibles with textual excerpts or in books or sections of the Bible printed separately. Apart from the typological *Biblia pauperum* (*see* §3(ii) below), two German Bibles printed *c.* 1475 in Augsburg are the first illustrated printed Bibles: in the Bible published by Günther Zainer (*fl* 1468–78) woodcut historiated initials introduce biblical books, while in the version printed by Jodocus Pflanzman (*fl* 1475–6) framed pictures are inserted into the two-column text. These early woodcuts display a simple, linear style. During the late 15th century and the early 16th, Bible illustration became more elaborate. Two Cologne Bibles printed *c.* 1478 by Heinrich Quentel (*d* 1501) contain more than 100 double-column illustrations. The fine, linear woodcuts capture a sense of action and emotion. An edition of the Malermi Bible, named after its Italian translator, was printed in Venice in 1490 by Lucantonio di Giunta (1457–1538) with 386 woodcuts. While some of the scenes depend on prototypes in the Cologne Bible, all show Italian Renaissance architectural perspective and landscape.

The activity in Bible printing that the Reformation fostered affected illustrated Bibles. In Germany the publication (1522–34) in sections of Martin Luther's translation utilized the talents of several graphic artists including Lucas Cranach the younger, whose designs reflect a High Renaissance style. The Swiss printing centres, Basle and Zurich, produced illustrated Bibles, the illustrators of which included Hans Holbein the younger. His best-known Bible illustrations appeared in a picture Bible published by Johannes Treschel (*fl* 1488–98), the *Historiarum veteris testamenti icones* (Lyon, 1538). Holbein's woodcuts were also used in or influenced illustrations of English translations by William Tyndale (*c.* 1494–1536) and Miles Coverdale (*c.* 1488–1565), as well as the Great Bible in the 1530s and 1540s. During the 17th and 18th centuries, engraving became the favoured technique for book illustration. In Bible printing, imagery was concentrated on elaborate title-pages. Picture Bibles capitalized on the theatrical Baroque style to dramatize biblical scenes with accompanying moralizing passages from the Bible. The Bible of Royaumont by Nicholas Fontaine (1625–1709), 'sire de Royaumont', became a popular example of this genre. In this book, first published in Paris in 1670, a large engraving precedes and vividly illustrates each Bible story.

Industrialization brought changes to printing processes in the 19th century. Mass production made printed materials available at lower cost to a wider audience, and new techniques such as chromolithography for colour printing were exploited for illustrations. Illustrated family Bibles, often issued in installments, were published in Europe and America. The illustrations, which could number over 1000, as in the Bible published by John Cassell (1817–65) in England, were eclectic in technique and style. Some 19th century artist–illustrators, such as Gustave Doré, contributed original designs, while others reproduced images by such artists as Rubens. Gospel books, Psalters and prayerbooks, in which colour printing evoked Gothic ornamentation from medieval illuminated manuscripts, were also fashionable.

In the modern period several artists explored the interaction of illustration and biblical text. During the early 19th century, William Blake's poetic fusion of word and image, for example in the *Book of Job* (published 1826), presents a unique personal vision of the Bible (*see* BLAKE, WILLIAM). In France the tradition of grand-scale picture Bibles continued. Romanticism pervades Gustave Doré's mid-19th-century biblical scenes, while realism of the Middle Eastern setting characterizes James Tissot's illustrations published in Paris in 1904 (*see* TISSOT, JAMES). The mid-20th-century lithographic Bible images by Edouard Léon Louis Edy-Legrand (1892–1970) reflect a search for religious meaning during the turmoil of World War II. For *In Our Image* (Oxford, 1949), Guy Rowe (1894–1969), an American artist, produced striking portraits of 32 characters drawn from everyday life to illustrate Old Testament stories. While these works emphasize image over text, Eric Gill, the British sculptor and designer, balanced the arts of book design and illustration. His *Four Gospels of Our Lord Jesus Christ*, published by the Golden Cockerel Press in 1931 (see fig. 7), in which the wood-engraved illustrations inhabit initials that begin textual sections, exemplifies his concept that illustration should 'grow from the text'. His approach demonstrates the continuing potential of the printed Bible to present its text with beauty, dignity and visual impact.

7. Illustrated printed Bible showing the *Adoration of the Shepherds* by Eric Gill; wood-engraving from his *Four Gospels of Our Lord Jesus Christ*, published in Waltham St Lawrence, 1931

BIBLIOGRAPHY
P. d'Espezel: *Les Illustrateurs français de la Bible* (Paris, 1950)
J. Strachan: *Early Bible Illustrations* (Cambridge, 1957)
M. H. Black: 'The Evolution of a Book-form: II. The Folio Bible to 1560', *The Library*, xviii (1963), pp. 191–203
——: 'The Printed Bible', *The Cambridge History of the Bible*, iii (Cambridge, 1963), pp. 408–75
W. Eichenberger and H. Wendland: *Deutsche Bibeln vor Luther* (Hamburg, 1977)

KAREN GOULD

3. VARIANTS. During the Gothic period several new types of manuscript consisting of variations on the biblical text were developed. These were all richly illustrated, with the text often appearing to be of secondary importance.

(i) *Bible moralisée*. (ii) *Biblia pauperum*. (iii) *Bible historiale*.

(i) *Bible moralisée* [Fr.: 'moralized Bible']. Type of illustrated book, conceived in the early 13th century, that presents visual and literary commentaries on the Bible. It contains lavishly illustrated biblical excerpts and paraphrases combined with illustrated commentaries that provide moral, allegorical and anagogical interpretations. The *Bible moralisée* represents the most complete and systematic visual exegesis of the Bible produced during the Middle Ages. There are 15 extant manuscripts of the *Bible moralisée* dating from *c.* 1220–30 to *c.* 1460–70. The four earliest examples were made in Paris during the first half of the 13th century. They represent the characteristic form of the *Bible moralisée* and appear to be closest to its original conception. Of these, the two earliest (Vienna, Österreich. Nbib., Cods 2554 and 1179) are in French and in Latin respectively. The other two, both in Latin, are dispersed in various libraries: one between Oxford (Bodleian Lib., Bodley MS. 270b), Paris (Bib. N., MS. lat. 11560) and London (BL, Harley MSS 1526–7); the other, mostly in Toledo (Archv & Bib. Capitulares, MSS 1–3), with eight leaves in New York (Pierpont Morgan Lib., MS. M.240).

These manuscripts are large folio-size picture books. Each leaf is illustrated on one side only, and originally illuminated pages consistently faced each other. The illustrations take precedence over the text, which is relegated to a few short lines in the margins. Each illustrated page contains eight painted medallions divided into two columns (see fig. 8). In all but one of the early manuscripts the medallions are read in pairs from top to bottom in the left column and then in the right-hand column. The first medallion in the upper left illustrates a biblical passage. Directly beneath, the second medallion illustrates the explanatory commentary on the biblical text.

In these 4 manuscripts there are altogether over 13,000 images. The completion of such an enormous undertaking would have required a large scriptorium with a tradition of manuscript production and illumination, and with a library and exegetical tradition able to supply the material necessary for the formulation of such a text. It would also have needed skilled theologians capable of choosing and arranging the biblical images and providing the appropriate explanations for them. Based on these requirements, it has been suggested that either of the Parisian monastic houses St Victor or St Germain-des-Prés might be the source of the *Bibles moralisées*. All four Bibles were painted in what is generally termed the *Muldenfaltenstil* ('depressed fold style') of painting. Its most characteristic feature is seen in the treatment of drapery, in which pronounced shading

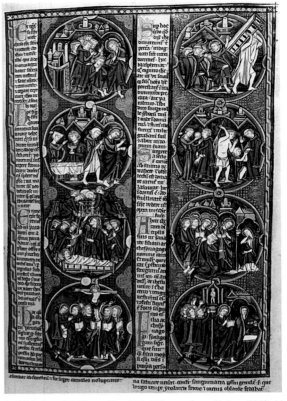

8. *Bible moralisée* illustration, 395×275 mm, from Paris, *c.* 1240–46 (London, British Library, Harley MS. 1527, fol. 27*r*)

defines long, deep folds, dramatically falling along the forms of the figures and ending in shapes resembling hairpin loops. The colours most often used are red and blue. Thus the layout of the pages, with rows of circular medallions, and the predominance of blues and reds have led to their comparison with contemporary stained-glass windows.

The ateliers, comprising several artists, that illuminated the *Bibles moralisées* worked on other books, including Bibles, biblical commentaries, Psalters, Missals, prayerbooks and literary works. On the basis of comparisons with other dated manuscripts painted by the same artists, it is possible to localize the *Bibles moralisées* to Paris and to assign them approximate dates. These evaluations together with iconographic comparisons between the *Bible moralisée* manuscripts themselves indicate that they were executed between *c.* 1220 and *c.* 1246, beginning with the Latin manuscript in Vienna, followed by the Vienna volume in French, the version in Toledo and, finally, the dispersed Oxford, Paris and London manuscript. In view of their obvious expense and luxury, it is generally believed that the *Bibles moralisées* were made for members of the aristocracy and very likely for members of the French royal family. The connection to royalty is also suggested by the image of a king at the end of one of the two Vienna codices (Cod. 1179) and of a king and queen pictured on the last folio of the Toledo manuscript (New York,

Pierpont Morgan Lib., MS. M. 240, fol. 8*r*; *see* GOTHIC, fig. 72). Philip II Augustus, Louis VIII, Blanche of Castille and Louis IX have all been suggested as possible patrons, but none of the manuscripts has yet been conclusively linked to a particular individual.

The ten later copies of the *Bible moralisée* are all either derived from or closely related to one of the four 13th-century versions. They follow their models more or less closely in terms of content and format, but there are some important differences. For example, a *Bible moralisée* (1350–55; Paris, Bib. N., MS. fr. 167) made for John the Good, King of France, and another (Paris, Bib. N., MS. fr. 166) for Philip the Bold, Duke of Burgundy, worked on from *c.* 1402 to 1404 by the brothers Pol and Jean de Limbourg, both stem from the manuscript divided between Oxford, Paris and London (*see* LIMBOURG, DE, and fig. 1). The formats of the two later books are close to the original except that every page is illuminated, and rectangles are used instead of medallions; they also have French translations accompanying the Latin texts in the margins. There are even more striking variations, such as the *Bible moralisée* found in the margins of leaves without full-page miniatures (*c.* 1430–33; Paris, Bib. N., MS. lat. 9471). Other later versions contain only the text, without its illustrations: for example three mid-15th-century manuscripts produced in the workshop of Willem Vrelant (London, BL, Add. MS. 15248; Paris, Bib. N., MS. fr. 897; The Hague, Kon. Bib., MS. 76. E. 7).

BIBLIOGRAPHY

Comte A. de Laborde: *La Bible moralisée illustrée conservée à Oxford, Paris, et Londres*, 5 vols (Paris, 1911–27)

B. Blumenkranz: 'La Représentation de Synagoga dans les Bibles moralisées françaises du XIII au XV siècle', *Proc. Israel Acad. Sci. & Human.*, ii (1970), pp. 70–91

F. Avril: 'Un Chef-d'oeuvre de l'enluminure sous le règne de Jean le Bon: La Bible moralisée manuscrit français 167 de la Bibliothèque Nationale', *Mnmts Piot*, lviii (1972), pp. 91–125

R. Haussherr: '*Sensus litteralis* und *sensus spiritualis* in der Bible moralisée', *Frühmittelalt. Stud.*, vi (1972), pp. 356–80

——: *Bible Moralisée: Faksimile-Ausgabe im Originalformat des Codex Vindobonensis 2554 der Österreichischen Nationalbibliothek*, Codices selecti, xl, 2 vols (Graz, 1973)

——: 'Eine Warnung vor dem Studium von zivilem und kanonischen Recht in der Bible moralisée', *Frühmittelalt. Stud.*, ix (1975), pp. 390–404

R. Branner: *Manuscript Painting in Paris during the Reign of Saint Louis* (Berkeley, Los Angeles and London, 1977)

R. Haussherr: 'Drei Texthandschriften der *Bible moralisée*', *Festschrift für Eduard Trier*, ed. J. Müller Hofstede and W. Spies (Berlin, 1981), pp. 35–65

M. HEINLEN

(ii) Biblia pauperum [Lat.: 'Bibles of the poor']. Term coined by modern scholars for a category of medieval manuscripts and early prints that focuses on the typological connection between the Old Testament and the New Testament, demonstrated through texts and images. Typology is a method of interpreting certain events, persons and prophecies of the Old Testament as foreshadowing the deeds of Christ related in the New Testament (*see* TYPOLOGICAL CYCLES). Accordingly, in the *Biblia pauperum* a scene from the Gospels (the 'antitype') is set against two corresponding events from the Old Testament (the 'types') and further elucidated by pertinent quotations from four of the Prophets. The oldest copies contain a cycle of 34 such typological groups of pictures, starting with the Infancy of Christ and ending with Pentecost and the Coronation of the Virgin. In later manuscripts and editions of block-books and early prints this cycle is extended to 40 or more groups of pictures by increasing the number of scenes from the Life of Christ and by inserting at the end the Last Judgement.

The oldest surviving *Biblia pauperum* manuscripts all date to the early 14th century. Although they represent different variants, they can all be traced back to a common prototype, which must have appeared around the mid-13th century in south Germany or Austria; the author was presumably a Benedictine monk or an Augustinian canon. Schmidt was able to demonstrate that the prototype was constructed according to a systematic programme, which the earliest of the surviving copies still adhere to. The *Biblia pauperum* began on the *verso* of the first leaf; on it and every subsequent page two typological groups of pictures were shown beneath one another. Accordingly, when the book was open four such groups could be viewed simultaneously and each of the total of eight groups of four covered a certain episode from the Life of Christ: 1. The Incarnation (the Annunciation, the Nativity, the Adoration of the Magi and the Presentation in the Temple as the antitypes); 2. The Flight from Herod (the Flight into Egypt, the Fall of the Egyptian Idols, the Massacre of the Innocents and the Return from Egypt); 3. and 4. The Temptation and the Ministry of Christ (the Baptism, Temptation and Transfiguration of Christ, the Repentance of Mary Magdalene, the Raising of Lazarus,

9. *Biblia pauperum* illustration, 335×240 mm, *c.* 1310 (Stiftsbibliothek, St Florian Abbey, MS. III, 207, fol. 7*r*)

the Entry into Jerusalem, Christ Driving the Money-changers from the Temple and the Last Supper); 5. The Betrayal of Christ (the Conspiracy of the Jews, Judas Accepting 30 Pieces of Silver, the Kiss of Judas, Christ before Pilate); 6. The Passion (the Crowning with Thorns, Christ Carrying the Cross, the Crucifixion and the piercing of Christ's side); 7. The first three days after Christ's death (the Entombment, the Descent into Limbo, the Resurrection and the Three Marys at the Tomb); 8. The Appearances of Christ (*Noli me tangere*, the Supper at Emmaus, the Incredulity of Thomas and the Ascension). Two final groups of pictures (with Pentecost and the Coronation of the Virgin as antitypes) again appear on a *verso* page; they no longer belong to the narrative of the Life of Christ but relate to the Church founded by him, its inspiration by the Holy Spirit and its exaltation as the Bride of Christ.

This strict structuring of the content of the *Biblia pauperum* was originally matched with an equally clear layout for the individual groups of pictures (see fig. 9): the antitype generally appeared in a central medallion, which was surrounded by the busts of four Prophets, with the types on either side. Accompanying them were explanatory texts in Latin: two prose 'lessons' clarifying the two Old Testament types and their relation to the antitype; four prophecies foreshadowing the antitype; and three *tituli* in Leonine hexameters, which also served as captions to the scenes portrayed. In the case of the *Crucifixion*, for example, the *titulus* reads 'Eruit a tristi baratro nos passio Christi' ('The suffering of Christ delivers us from the dark abyss'). The scene is flanked by the *Sacrifice of Isaac* with the *titulus*, 'Signantem Christum puerum pater imolat istum' ('Foretokening Christ this boy is sacrificed by his father'), and by the *Brazen serpent* with its *titulus*, 'Lesi curantur serpentem dum speculantur' ('Those that are injured are cured when they look at the serpent'). Then there are the four sayings by the Prophets, for example the words of Isaiah (53:7), 'Oblatus est quia ipse voluit' ('He was sacrificed because he himself desired it'). The two 'lessons' appear above the pictures giving a brief description of the event depicted and also a typological interpretation of it; thus the lesson for the *Sacrifice of Isaac* is 'Abraham stands for our Father in Heaven who sacrificed his son, Christ, on the Cross for us all, in token of his love for us.'

As early as the second quarter of the 14th century there were various departures from the original formula, involving either an increase in the number of picture groups or their rearrangement in less meaningful groupings, or the depiction of only one group of pictures on each page. Often the types were no longer ranged on either side of the antitype but placed above or below it. German translations were provided alongside the Latin texts, and the amount of text was generally increased. This may be seen as a reaction to the appearance of such later typological illustrated manuscripts as the *Speculum humanae salvationis* produced *c.* 1300 and the *Concordantiae caritatis* of *c.* 1355, both of which contained far more extensive picture cycles and texts. Around 80 complete or fragmentary copies of the *Biblia pauperum* are known, originating at first from Germany and Austria only but from the early 15th century also from the Netherlands. Unillustrated versions are relatively rare.

BIBLIOGRAPHY

LCI; *RDK*: 'Armenbibel'
P. Heitz and W. L. Schreiber: '*Biblia pauperum*': *Nach dem einzigen Exemplar in 50 Darstellungen* (Strasbourg, 1903)
H. Tietze: 'Die typologischen Bilderkreise des Mittelalters in Österreich', *Jb. Ksr.-Kön. Zent.-Komm. Erforsch. & Erhaltung Kst- & Hist. Dkml.*, n. s. 2, ii (1904), cols 21–88
C. Dodgson: *The Weigel–Felix Biblia pauperum* (London, 1907)
H. Cornell: *Biblia pauperum* (Stockholm 1925) [fundamental]
J. Lenhart: 'The *Biblia pauperum* or Medieval Biblical Mnemonics', *Eccles. Rev.*, lxxiii (1925), no. 4
G. Schmidt: *Die Armenbibeln des XIV. Jahrhunderts* (Graz and Cologne, 1959)
H. T. Musper: *Die Urausgabe der holländischen Apokalypse und Biblia pauperum* (Munich, 1961)
G. Schmidt and F. Unterkircher: *Die Wiener Biblia pauperum*, 3 vols (Graz, Vienna and Cologne, 1962) [facs.]
K.-A. Wirth: '*Biblia pauperum*', *Die deutsche Literatur des Mittelalters: Verfasserlexikon*, 2/i (1978), cols 843–52 [bibliog.]

GERHARD SCHMIDT

(iii) Bible historiale. French translation (*c.* 1295) by Guiart des Moulins of a compilation of biblical history and legend, the *Historia scholastica*, written by Peter Comestor (*d* 1179). The work is based on the Bible but includes apocryphal legend, historical material (mainly derived from Flavius Josephus) and theological commentary. Both Latin and French versions were widely read, and the earliest copies of the *Bible historiale* were often illustrated. For the wealthier members of late medieval society this became one of their main sources of biblical knowledge, and the apocryphal elements in it came to be viewed as inseparable from the biblical text itself. It is significant that the title of the early printed version of Guiart des Moulins's text was the *Bible en françoys*. It was only at the time of the Reformation that such legendary glosses to the established text of the Bible were discouraged.

In the 14th and 15th centuries, above all in France, many luxury copies of the *Bible historiale* were made, with considerably richer illustration than that devoted to contemporary texts of the Latin Vulgate Bible. The earliest versions, from the early years of the 14th century, have square, framed miniatures at the beginning of most of the textual divisions (e.g. *c.* 1310–20; Oxford, Bodleian Lib., MSS Douce 211–12 and 1317; Paris, Bib. Arsenal, MS. 5059). This format continued to be popular throughout the history of the text's decoration. It is used in the copy with 136 miniatures illustrated by Jean Pucelle and his workshop (*c.* 1330; Geneva, Bib. Pub. & U., MS. fr. 2). During Charles V's reign in France several copies were made with more elaborate decoration, with half-page miniatures at the beginning of some of the books divided into four or more scenes (e.g. Hamburg, Ksthalle, MS. fr. 1; Paris, Bib. Arsenal, MS. 5212; see fig. 10). These are some of the most elaborately illustrated copies of the *Bible historiale* (for further illustration *see* BOUDOLF, JAN), which are rivalled only by some versions made early in the 15th century for Jean, Duc de Berry (e.g. London, BL, Royal MS. 15. D. III; Paris, Bib. Arsenal, MSS 5057–8; and Paris, Bib. N., MSS fr. 9–10). Although the *Bible historiale* continued to be read throughout the 15th century, richly illustrated versions are rare after the first quarter of the century. It is significant that from the great period of Burgundian patronage, *c.* 1440–80, there are very few copies.

The *Historia scholastica* was also adapted into a Dutch version by Jacob van Maerlant, the *Rijmbijbel*, and another version, the *Historiebijbel*, which exists in two editions. In the 14th century and more frequently in the 15th these were produced in illustrated versions. They usually have small rectangular miniatures set at the beginning of some of the books (e.g. London, BL, Add. MS. 38122; Munich, Bayer. Staatsbib., Cgm.1102; and Vienna, Österreich. Nbib., Cods 2771–2). Apart from France and the northern Netherlands, picture Bibles were made in Germany with paraphrases of the Bible partly derived from the *Historia scholastica*. In the 15th century, in particular, many copies of such vernacular biblical texts in German were produced, illustrated with coloured pen drawings.

BIBLIOGRAPHY

S. Berger: *La Bible française au moyen âge* (Paris, 1884), pp. 157–99, 281–91, 325–36

B. Gagnebin: 'Une *Bible historiale* de l'atelier de Jean Pucelle', *Genava*, iv (1956), pp. 23–65

M. W. Evans: 'Boethius and an Illustration to the *Bible historiale*', *J. Warb. & Court. Inst.*, xxx (1967), pp. 394–8

M. Meiss: *French Painting in the Time of Jean de Berry: The Late Fourteenth Century and the Patronage of the Duke*, 2 vols (London and New York, 1967, rev. 1969)

F. Avril: 'Une *Bible historiale* de Charles V', *Jb. Hamburg. Kstsamml.*, xiv–xv (1969–70), pp. 45–76

S. Hindman: 'Fifteenth Century Dutch Bible Illustration and the *Historia scholastica*', *J. Warb. & Court. Inst.*, xxxvii (1974), pp. 131–44

M. Meiss with S. O. Smith and E. Beatson: *French Painting in the Time of Jean de Berry: The Limbourgs and their Contemporaries*, 2 vols (New York and London, 1974)

S. Hindman: *Text and Image in Fifteenth-Century Illustrated Dutch Bibles* (Leiden, 1977)

R. P. McGerr: 'Guyart Desmoulins, the Vernacular Master of Histories and his *Bible historiale*', *Viator*, xiv (1983), pp. 211–42

NIGEL J. MORGAN

II. Hebrew.

1. Manuscript. 2. Printed.

1. MANUSCRIPT. The oldest surviving decorated codices of the Hebrew Bible, which came from Egypt, Palestine and perhaps Syria and Babylonia, date from the 10th, 11th and 12th centuries. A few were executed in Persia at the end of the 13th century and in the 14th, while in the Yemen almost all date from the 15th century. A single example, dated 1225, is undoubtedly from North Africa, but the greatest number originated in Europe, from France, Spain, the Germanic countries and Italy, between the first quarter of the 13th century and the beginning of the 16th. Although these manuscripts reflect the different milieux in which they were produced, both in terms of decorative vocabulary and style, their decoration nearly always retains certain common structural and functional characteristics and certain techniques that are responsible for its remarkable originality. Likewise, the illustrations sometimes associated with this decoration retain a certain degree of independence, particularly in their iconography (*see also* JEWISH ART, §IV, 1(ii)).

(i) *Decoration.* The placing of the decoration in the earliest known Middle-Eastern manuscripts (10th–11th century) was devised in a very elaborate way: outside the text, in purely decorative, full-page panels at the beginning and/or the end; in association with appended texts, at both beginning and end of the volume; and within the text, at the main and secondary divisions. (Unless otherwise

10. *Bible historiale* frontispiece, 283×192 mm, mid-14th century (Paris, Bibliothèque de l'Arsenal, MS. 5212, fol. 1*r*)

stated, the following examples in §(i) are in St Petersburg, Saltykov-Shchedrin Pub. Lib.).

The full-page panels were sometimes painted to look like false bindings (e.g. AD 929; MS. Evr. II B 17) or like carpets, with the same motif endlessly repeated (e.g. 951; MS. Evr. II B 8); some have compositions with a radiating pattern (e.g. 1008–10; MS. Evr. I B 19a; see fig. 11) or with an architectural form, arches on columns with capitals, bases and tympana (e.g. *c.* 925–50; MS. Evr. II B 267). The pages might have quotations from the psalms or dedications written in monumental letters on painted bands (e.g. MS. Evr. II B 17), at times under an arcade (examples, 10th century; MSS Evr. II B 267 and Evr. II B 262). On the pages usually placed at the end of the biblical text, the decoration frames the appended texts with arcades (e.g. MS. Evr. II B 17); or emphasizes the columnar structure of the text with motifs placed between, above and below the columns (e.g. MS. Evr. II B 262; and 988–9; Evr. II B 39). Decoration within the text itself,

11. Egyptian Hebrew Bible, illumination with radiating design including, in its centre, the name of the patron Mevorakh ben Yoseph, from Fustat (Old Cairo), 1008–10 (St Petersburg, M. E. Saltykov-Shchedrin Public Library, MS. Evr. I B 19a, fol. 489*v*)

deliberately subordinated to the text, assumes precise functions: it emphasizes the division of the text into books by frames with lateral *ansae* around the final notes (e.g. MS. Evr. II B 17), and division into pericopes for weekly reading by ornamented marginal indicators (e.g. MS. Evr. II B 8). The presence of decoration in the margins might also highlight particularly noteworthy passages: Exodus 15: 1–18, Deuteronomy 22: 1–43 (e.g. MS. Evr. II B 17).

The colour schemes of this sumptuous decoration are extremely sober and are dominated by the use of unburnished flat gold usually outlined with brown ink, worked with highly delicate motifs and highlighted with notes of red, blue, brown and green. Remaining areas of parchment ground were strewn or carpeted with motifs executed in

ink of the same tones of sepia, blue–black and, in the 11th century, red as well. Few decorated pages are without the most remarkable element of this type of decoration, indeed the distinguishing feature of the Hebrew Bible: the calligram, in which script is used not to fill in motifs (as found in other types of calligram), but to trace the outline of designs.

Bible decoration in Spain did not fully develop until the second half of the 13th century. Spanish Bibles have the same structure and the same dominant use of gold as those produced in the East, although these were applied to new decorative schemes, and the range of inks, pigments and the use of burnished gold are closer to Western illumination. Here from the 13th century onwards the decorative, full pages are found not only at the beginning and end of the text (e.g. 1266; Haverford College, PA, MS. Rogers 1), but also marking its divisions, both major (e.g. 1260; Jerusalem, Jew. N. & U. Lib., MS. heb. 4° 790) and minor: small panels at the end of biblical books (examples, *c.* 1300 and 1476; Oxford, Bodleian Lib., MS. Kenn. 2 and MS. Kenn. 1) and marginal motifs for pericopes and psalms (e.g. 1299/1300; Lisbon, Bib. N., MS. Iluminando 72).

On the other hand, in the Bibles of northern Europe, France and the Germanic countries, from as early as the second quarter of the 13th century, certain characteristics of the ornamental structure of contemporary Latin books were borrowed. In most cases, as there are no capital letters in Hebrew, the whole of the first word of each book is emphasized by larger black ink or more often burnished gold lettering and is placed on an ornamental panel, which is either painted (e.g. 1237–8, U. Wrocław Lib., MS. M 1106; e.g. from *c.* 1320, Jerusalem, Schocken Lib., MS. 14940; e.g. from early 15th century, Parma, Bib. Palatina, MS. Parm 2823–De Rossi 893), or decorated in pen and coloured inks (e.g. Berlin, Staatsbib. Preuss. Kultbes. Orientab., MS. or. quart. 1). Alternatively, the word itself might be written in monumental decorated letters (e.g. Karlsruhe, Bad. Landesbib., MS. Reuch. 1).

Decoration using lines of text, so characteristic of the Jewish book, spread to both northern Europe and to Spain; more frequently than in the East, this type of decoration came to occupy the horizontal margins, where was copied the *masora magna* (the principal marginal notes in Bibles), the long lines of which it used, especially those in the bottom margin. Its animal and plant motifs were condemned in the north at the turn of the 13th century, but examples even with human figures may be seen in Bibles from *c.* 1230 (e.g. 1233–4; Berlin, Staatsbib. Preuss. Kultbes. Orientab., MS. or. quart. 9). This micrographic decoration was also used, from about the middle of the 13th century, for large initial words panels (e.g. 1264; Toronto, Friedberg priv. col., Ashkenazi Bible; 1294, Vatican, Bib. Apostolica, Cod. Urb. Ebr. 1; end 13th century, Berlin, Staatsbib., Preuss. Kultbes. Orientab., MS. or. fol. 1212; see fig. 12). This decoration disappeared, however, after the second half of the 14th century. In Sephardic Bibles it is rare until the second half of the 13th century, and is restricted to simple designs. Yet it was here that geometric interlace framing the page was created (e.g. 1232; Paris, Bib. N., MS. hébr. 25), and, around the 1260s, full-page panels appeared with interlacing or stylized plant motifs highlighted with gold and colours, which were unknown in northern Bibles (examples, MS. Evr. II B 53; Marseille, Bib. Mun., MS. 1626/2–3). Ornaments in the vertical margins also began to appear in the last third of the 13th century, in the form of stylized, tree-like shapes, known as 'candelabra' (e.g. 1278; Parma, Bib. Palatina, MS. Parm. 3214–De Rossi 304). This last type of decoration flourished in the 14th century, while, retaining the customary geometric forms, the repertory of the horizontal margins displays much more complex interlacing, with plant shapes only by way of accessory and rarely with animal forms (e.g. 1299–1300; Lisbon, Bib. N., MS. Iluminado 72; e.g. dated 1300, Paris, Bib. N., MS. hébr. 20). In the 15th century this decoration reached its

12. Ashkenazi Hebrew Bible, initial page of Genesis with micrographic decoration, from Germany, late 13th century (Berlin, Staatsbibliothek Preussischer Kulturbesitz, Orientabteilung, MS. or. fol. 1212, fol 1*v*)

apogee, as is seen in some 17 extant manuscripts and particularly in their full-page panels usually executed with lines from the Psalms (e.g. Paris, Bib. N., MS. hébr. 1314–15). It is this type of decoration that has contributed most towards securing for the Jewish book a unique place in the history of the decorated book.

In Eastern codices and 13th century Ashkenazi Bibles the dimensions of the books and the size of the texts' script dictated a small, but not microscopic, script for the ornamental lines. In the Ashkenazi Pentateuchs of small format and in Sephardic codices, which were much smaller than their northern counterparts, a tiny and, particularly in the 15th century, genuinely microscopic script was used. It is particularly in its Western form that this decoration may be accurately designated 'micrographic decoration' (*see* MICROGRAPHY). This marginal decoration was sometimes combined with other forms of painted or pen decoration, although in other instances micrographic decoration tended to be used to the almost complete exclusion of all other types, as in, for example, German Bibles of the late 13th, Catalan Bibles of the 14th and Andalusian

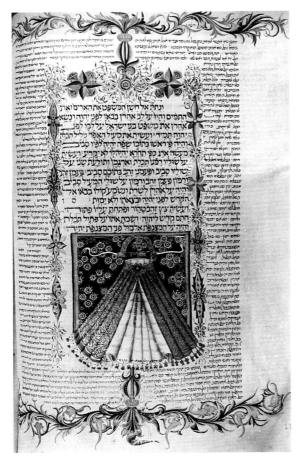

13. Italian Hebrew Bible, miniature of *Aaron's Holy Garments*, illustrating Exodus 28: 30–37, and marginal commentaries by Rashi and Abraham ibn Ezra, from Ferrara, 1396 (Florence, Biblioteca Medicea-Laurenziana, MS. Plut. II, 1, fol. 111*v*)

and Castilian Bibles of the late 15th century. Nevertheless, some Spanish Bibles borrowed Latin forms of organization of book decoration, with painted panels of initial words and, exceptionally, initial letters (e.g. 1480; Genoa, Bib. Universitaria, MS. D. IX. 31), the same motifs and floral margins used in contemporary non-Jewish books (e.g. Parma, Bib. Palatina, MS. Parm. 1994–95–De Rossi 346).

Italian biblical manuscripts were the most quickly and completely, even for minor divisions, Latinized. In the late 13th century and early 14th, besides the decorated pericopes signs (e.g. Parma, Bib. Palatina, MS. Parm. 3216–De Rossi 1261), there appeared decorated initial words (e.g. Parma, Bib. Palatina, MS. Parm. 2169–De Rossi 291 and MS. Parm. 1870–De Rossi 510). The *masora*, moreover, was usually not copied in the margin of the biblical text, and thus micrographic decoration had no opportunity to develop, except when used by refugees from northern Europe or Spain (e.g. Florence, Bib. Medicea–Laurenziana, MS. Plut. 3.10 and MS. Plut. 2.1). Hebrew Bibles in Italy from the last decades of the 13th century until the 16th thus generally reflected all the decorative styles of other Italian books (see fig. 13).

(ii) Illustration. In medieval Bibles illustration was rarely given a special place in the book. Images were not integrated into the text and were rarely freely placed in the margins in relation to the text. Illustration was always an integral part of the decoration, whether the latter was painted, drawn or micrographic, and was found in all positions traditionally occupied by ornament: as full-page pictures (see fig. 14), between each book and in the margins at pericopes signs and catchwords, in initial words panels (*see* JEWISH ART, fig. 19) and *masora*. The development of illustration was halted by the constraints imposed by its close relationship to decoration. It may be, however, that such restraints were intentionally sought in order to maintain the image in the background. Illustrations representing a real scene with figures are rare in all periods and in several cases reveal recourse to non-Jewish models and artists (e.g. London, BL, Add. MS. 11639; *see* LONDON MISCELLANY). The dominant type of image is gloss-like, representing or interpreting just one element, figure or object from the text, rarely two or three. Narration is thus eschewed in favour of allusion. The position of images at the principal and secondary *initia*, that is at some distance from each other within the text, worked against the creation of consistent series. Exceptions were few and included some Bibles (e.g. Jerusalem, Schocken Lib., MS. 14940: 50 images, 46 of which on same initial page; e.g. 1340, Oxford, Bodleian Lib., MS. Opp. 14: 76 images mostly in outer margins) and Psalters (e.g. Parma, Bib. Palatina, MS. Parm. 1870–De Rossi 510: 103 illustrations). On the other hand, micrographic illustrations lent themselves more easily to series parallel to the text (examples, Rome, Vatican, Bib. Apostolica, Cod. Vat. Ebr. 14: 50

14. Sephardi Hebrew Bible, miniature of the *Vision of Zechariah*, from Cervera (Catalonia), Tudela (Navarre) and Soria (Castile), 1299–1300 (Lisbon, Biblioteca Nacional, MS. Iluminado 72, fol. 316*v*)

illustrations; London, BL, Add. MS. 21160: 15 illustrations), although few were produced. Half of some 200 Hebrew biblical manuscripts with illustrations do not offer more than one image and a third no more than two to five.

The most striking aspect of the development of medieval illustration is its extreme diversity and unevenness. Thus in both Ashkenazi and Sephardic Bibles even of the same date and from neighbouring areas there is little correspondence between subjects chosen for the *initia* of the books or the choice of illustrated *initia*. Even fewer parallels are found in Bibles of different periods and from different regions. During the period there is no tendency towards progressive enrichment of the iconography; on the contrary, the greatest creative momentum and the longest series of illustrations occur early on: in the 13th century in Ashkenazi works, at the end of the 13th century and throughout the 14th in Italy, and in the 14th century in Sephardic examples. One constant theme, however, that of the Sanctuary, is present from the 10th century, but subject over the centuries to completely different treatment and interpretation (*see* JEWISH ART, fig. 16); only in Spain, in the approximately 30 extant images of this subject, is there any proper iconographic interrelation.

In general the images in Bibles, as is also the case with the biblical cycles in the Haggadot, were the late and localized products of the medieval West, rather than offshoots of an ancient Jewish iconographic tradition. Unity, standardization and traditional continuity were absent, nor was any proper programme of illustration devised for the Bible itself. Contrary to the processes of decoration, illustration seems to have remained a personal affair, reinvented almost every time. Moreover, it appears not to have been the main preoccupation of illuminators, concerned above all to honour and beautify their books to the best of their ability. No doubt, because of the specifically Jewish approach to the biblical text, which was not open to a visual equivalent, their images continued to be mere ornaments and failed to attain the prime status accorded to illustration in the Christian Bible. However modest and however reliant on borrowed elements these images are, they bear striking witness to the artists' experimentation with an unfamiliar mode of expression, the freshness of discovery and the originality of the results.

BIBLIOGRAPHY

D. Kaufmann: 'Zur Geschichte der jüdischen Handschriftenillustration', *Die Haggadah von Sarajevo* (Vienna, 1898), i, pp. 255–311 [on Bibles, pp.255–62, 295–303]

D. Gunzburg and W. Stassof: *L'Ornement hébreu* (Berlin, 1905)

Z. Ameisenowa: *Biblja Hebrajska xivgo wieku w Krakowie i jej dekoracja malarska* [A 14th-century Hebrew Bible in Kraków and its painted decoration] (Kraków, 1929)

——: 'Bestiariusz w Biblji hebrajskiej z xiii wieku, studjum ikonograficzne' [A bestiary in a 13th-century Hebrew Bible: An iconographic study], *Miesięcznik Żydowski*, iii (1933), pp. 79–110

——: 'Das messianische Gastmahl der Gerechten in einer hebräischen Bibel aus dem XIII. Jahrhundert: Ein Beitrag zur eschatologischen Ikonographie der Juden', *Monatsschrift Gesch. & Wiss. Judentums*, lxxix (1935), pp. 409–22

——: 'Eine spanisch-jüdische Bilderbibel um 1400', *Monatsschrift Gesch. & Wiss. Judentums*, lxxxi (1937), pp. 193–209

J. Leveen: *The Hebrew Bible in Art* (London, 1944/R New York, 1974) [on illuminated Bibles, pp. 66–90, 104–117]

B. Narkiss: *Hebrew Illuminated Manuscripts* (Jerusalem, 1969, 3/1978, Heb. trans., rev. and enlarged, 1984) [good pls, 21 from Bibles]

T. Metzger: 'Les Objets du culte, le sanctuaire du désert et le Temple de Jérusalem dans les bibles hébraïques médiévales enluminées, en Orient et en Espagne', *Bull. John Rylands Lib.*, lii (1970), pp. 397–436; liii (1970), pp. 167–209; extract rev. (1970), pp. 1–83

G. Sed-Rajna: *Manuscrits hébreux de Lisbonne* (Paris, 1970) [good colour pls, 3 from Bibles]

T. Metzger: 'La Masora ornementale et le décor calligraphique dans les manuscrits hébreux espagnols du moyen âge', *La Paléographie hébraïque médiévale. Colloques internationaux du Centre national de la recherche scientifique, no. 547: Paris, 1972*, pp. 87–116

——: 'Les Illustrations d'un psautier hébreu italien de la fin du XIIIe siècle, le Ms. Parm. 1870-De Rossi 510 de la Biblioteca Palatina de Parme', *Cah. Archéol.*, xxvi (1977), pp. 145–62

J. Gutmann: *Hebrew Manuscript Painting* (New York, 1978/R London, 1979)

L. Avrin: *Micrography as Art* (Paris, 1981) [pls 6–42, 49–72, 74 from Bibles]

B. Narkiss and A. Cohn-Mushlin: *The Kennicott Bible* (London, 1985) [facs.]

T. Metzger: 'La Décoration de la Bible hébraïque au moyen âge: De l'Orient à l'occident', *Proceedings of the XXXII International Congress for Asian and North African Studies: Hamburg, 1986*, pp. 24–38

——: 'Ornamental Micrography in Medieval Hebrew Manuscripts', *Bib. Orient.*, xliii (1986), cols 377–88

G. Sed-Rajna: *La Bible hébraïque* (Fribourg, 1987; Eng. trans., 1987), review by T. Metzger and M. Metzger in *Echos-Unir*, 61 (1988), pp. 12–15

T. Metzger: 'L'Illustration biblique dans la bible hébraïque Ms. Iluminado 72 de la Biblioteca Nacional de Lisbonne', *Rev. Bib. N.*, 2nd ser., v (1990), pp. 61–108

M. Garel: *D'une main forte: Manuscrits hébreux des collections françaises* (Paris, 1991)

T. Metzger: 'L'Iconographie de la Bible hébraïque médiévale', *Die Juden in ihrer mittelalterlichen Umwelt* (Vienna, Cologne and Weimar, 1991), pp. 151–67

——: 'Les Arts du livre (calligraphie, décoration, reliure) en Espagne à la veille de l'Expulsion', *L'Expulsion des Juifs d'Espagne (1492) et ses conséquences. Colloque international: Paris, 1992* (in preparation)

——: *Facsimiles from an Illuminated Hebrew Bible of the Fifteenth Century in the Library of the Hispanic Society of America* (New York, 1993)

——: 'The Iconography of the Hebrew Psalter from the Thirteenth to the Fifteenth Century', *The Visual Dimension: Aspects of Jewish Art*, ed. C. Moore (Boulder, San Francisco and Oxford, 1993), pp. 47–81

——: *Die Bibel von Meschullam und Josef Qalonymos, Ms. M 1106 der Universitätsbibliothek Breslau*, Quellen and Forschungen zur Geschichte des Bistums and Hochstifts Würzburg, xlii (Würzburg, 1994)

——: 'A History and Analysis of the Manuscript, Ms. Parm. 1870–Cod. De Rossi 510', *The Parma Psalter: A Thirteenth Century Illuminated Hebrew Book of Psalms with a Commentary by Abraham Ibn Ezra*, facs. and intr. vol., ed. J. Schonfield (London, 1996)

——: *Corpus de la décoration de la bible juive médiévale* (in preparation)

——: *Index raisonné de l'illustration biblique juive médiévale* (in preparation)

2. PRINTED. Up to the second half of the 19th century, no attempt was made to introduce illustrations in the text of the Bible itself, the only exception being, since the late 17th century, the Yiddish biblical paraphrase *Tsene-U'rene*. Aesthetic pursuit concentrated on typography and page layout, as well as on the purely decorative ornamentation of pages and initial words. From the first, Jewish printers were independent of illuminators, using either no decoration or merely initial letters and engraved borders. Illustration appeared in Bibles only late, in the 17th century, and then only rarely, in the form of title-page vignettes, chosen to pay homage to the printer or to patrons, while also illustrating the content of the book. Full-page illustrations at the beginning of a biblical book were quite exceptional. In the modern period the Hebrew Bible has provided Jewish artists with subjects, isolated or in series (those of Marc Chagall being among the best-known), but no more than in the past has there been an attempt to turn it into an illustrated book.

(i) Decorated. Decorated incunabula Bibles were all printed in Italy, Spain or Portugal. Introduced by Joshua Soncino in Italy in 1483 in his Hebrew books, printed decoration was present in his first biblical edition, the *First Prophets* of 1485, as woodcut initial words in decorative frames (*see* SONCINO). In his later biblical editions (Bible, 1488; Psalms, Job, Proverbs in 1490; Pentateuch, 1490–91; Bible, *c.* 1492) he added beautiful borders with *putti* and *rinceau* backgrounds to initial words and frames. The first decorated Hebrew Pentateuch from Iberia was printed by Eliezer Alantansi in Híjar, Aragón, between 1486 and 1489. Besides very beautiful typography, it had engraved initial letters in reserve against a very fine plant decoration, and a delicate border ornamented with foliage and fauna. They were executed by the Christian goldsmith, Alfonso Fernández de Córdoba. Brought to Lisbon, border and letters were used in the printing shop of Eliezer Toledano (who was very likely the same person as Eliezer Alantansi who had himself emigrated to Portugal), but the only decoration in his Pentateuch printed there in 1491 is the beautiful initial for Genesis. Woodcut decoration was used by Portuguese Jewish printers and appears as a large ornamented initial for Genesis in the Faro Pentateuch, in 1487, and as decorative frames in the Leiria Former Prophets of 1495.

No forms of decoration were devised specifically for biblical editions in the 16th century. At Pesaro, Gershom Soncino framed the title-pages of his Former (1511) and Latter Prophets (1515) with the borders he had used since 1507, enriched with masks, vases, garlands and *rinceau* borrowed from ornamental sculpture. In the Bible that he printed in 1524–5 in Venice and in his rabbinical Bible of 1546–8, Daniel Bomberg placed the initial words in lavish cartouches and enclosed the title-pages in architectural frames with the portal, arch, cornices and columns that he had already used in his Talmud Yerushalmi in 1522–3. This type of architectural frame, introduced also by Gershom in his publications of 1525, found such great favour that it was copied, adapted into later styles and used from then on by almost all printers of Hebrew books, Jewish and non-Jewish, not only in Italy but in central Europe, Germany and Holland. Most of the biblical editions contained no other ornament worth noting.

(ii) Illustrated. In Amsterdam, in the second half of the 17th century, biblical scenes were introduced on the title-page. The first example was the Bible of Joseph Athias, printed in 1659–61, on which the first title-page in Hebrew contained five vignettes with biblical scenes framing the title, date and name of the printer. On the second title-page, which is repeated at the head of the Former and Latter Prophets and Hagiographa, the meeting of Jacob and Joseph in Egypt is figured. The title-page of David de Castro Tartas's Pentateuch of 1666 illustrated the four crowns (of law, priesthood, kingship and good name) and four scenes from the lives of David and Solomon. In their Yiddish Bibles, Uri Phoebus ha-levi (1676–8) and Athias (1679) were the first to introduce biblical scenes and motifs at the top and bottom, and monumental figures at the sides in their copper-engraved title-pages: in Uri's Bible, Moses and Aaron, very likely borrowed from German engravings (Hanau, 1610, 1614; Augsburg, 1644);

in Athias's, Moses and David, flanking the coat of arms of the king of Poland, of which Athis had been granted the use. In 1726 Bernard Picart (1673–1733) engraved for a Pentateuch a title-page, which recalled that of 1666 in its subject-matter, although its execution is more elegant. In the second half of the 18th century only variants on established formulae were used, for instance in Proops's Pentateuch of 1762. The title-page of the Pentateuch (1768) by Leib Soesmans, however, although associated with the old portal motif, has some novel interest, its vignettes depicting the ritual reading of the Law in the synagogue.

German presses had no wholly original formulae to offer, although a few beautiful pages were executed, such as in the Pentateuch of 1726, printed at Sulzbach, in which a columned central bay in an architectural composition is flanked by figures of *Moses* and *Aaron*, with angels bearing palm leaves. Four vignettes show *David Harping* and three scenes from the *Life of Jacob*. A Bible printed by Bragadin in Venice from 1739 to 1746 is the only known one to have contained full-page copper engraved illustrations at the head of the four parts of the text (Pentateuch, Former Prophets, Latter Prophets, Hagiographa).

BIBLIOGRAPHY

A. Freiman: *Thesaurus typographiae hebraicae saeculi XV* (Berlin, 1924–31/*R* Jerusalem, 1967–9)

A. M. Habermann: 'The Jewish Art of the Printed Book', *Jewish Art*, ed. C. Roth (London, 1961), cols 455–92

I. Adler: *Les Incunables hébraïques de la Bibliothèque nationale* (Paris and Jerusalem, 1962)

A. M. Habermann: *Title Pages of Hebrew Books* (Safed, 1969)

J. Bloch: *Hebrew Printing and Bibliography* (New York, 1976)

M. Heyd: 'Illustrations in Early Editions of the Tsene-U'rene: Jewish Adaptations of Christian Sources', *J. Jew. A.*, 10 (1984), pp. 64–86 [40 figs]

A. K. Offenberg: 'The Spread of Hebrew Printing', *The Image and the Word: Jewish Tradition in Manuscripts and Printed Books* (Amsterdam and Leuven, 1990), pp. 23–32

T. Metzger and M. Metzger: *L'Illustration gravée des imprimés hébraïques du XVe au XIXe siècle* (in preparation)

THÉRÈSE METZGER

Bible of Borso d'Este. Italian illuminated manuscript, made in Ferrara between 1455 and 1461. The manuscript (Modena, Bib. Estense, MS. V.G. 12–13, lat. 422–3) consists of two full-folio volumes of 311 and 293 leaves respectively and contains more than 1000 individual illuminations; it has been termed an encyclopedia of 15th-century Ferrarese illumination. The text is written in two columns in a fine Renaissance hand by the Bolognese scribe Pietro Paolo Marone. The contract for illumination of the Bible was given to TADDEO CRIVELLI and Franco dei Russi in 1455. Two rates of payment were specified, one for normal pages and one for 'principii' or incipits. The contract, known from two 18th-century copies, also stipulated that the incipits should be 'as magnificent as the manuscript deserves', a phrase that seems to reflect the aesthetic ambitions of the patron, Borso d'Este. On every page of the manuscript is at least one figurative illumination as well as dense border decorations. The incipits for each book of the Bible are much more elaborately illuminated (see fig.), with larger and more numerous miniatures. At the beginning of the project Taddeo and Franco were lent a French Bible, probably the Bible of Niccolò III d'Este

Bible of Borso d'Este: Genesis incipit by Taddeo Crivelli, 375×265 mm, 1455–61 (Modena, Biblioteca Estense, MS. V.G. 12, lat. 422, fol. 5ν)

(Rome, Vatican, Bib. Apostolica, MS. Barb. lat. 613; *see* BELBELLO DA PAVIA). This may have been to provide a standard of magnificence that the illuminators were expected to emulate. At least five different hands can be discerned in the Borso Bible. This is borne out by the documents, which indicate that both the principal illuminators found it necessary to employ assistants and/or to subcontract individual gatherings. In addition to Crivelli and dei Russi, Marco dell'Avogaro, Giorgio d'Alemagna, Malatesta Romano and several other minor artists worked on the project. The manuscript was completed in 1461. The cost of the illuminations alone came to almost 5000 lire, a staggering sum.

In 1598, with the reversion of Ferrara to the papacy and the transfer of the Este court to Modena, the entire ducal library including the Bible was moved to the new capital. It remained in Modena until 1859, when it was taken to Vienna by Francesco V d'Este, the last Duke of Modena. The Bible subsequently passed into the private collection of the Archduke Franz Ferdinand of Este-Austria. With his assassination (1914), the Bible became part of the imperial library in Vienna. In 1918, when the Austro-Hungarian empire fell, Charles, the former emperor, took the Bible with him into exile in Switzerland. At his death (1922), the manuscript was offered for sale in Paris, where it was purchased by the Milanese industrialist Giovanni Treccani. Treccani then gave the Bible to the Italian state, which, in turn, returned it to the Biblioteca Estense.

The Bible is one of the most lavishly illuminated Italian manuscripts of the period and, in that respect, reflects the pinnacle of mid-15th-century courtly taste and the particular predilection for exaggerated public magnificence, which its patron, Borso d'Este, consciously cultivated.

BIBLIOGRAPHY
A. Venturi, ed.: *La Bibbia di Borso d'Este* (Milan, 1937) [facs.]
M. Salmi: *Pittura e miniatura a Ferrara nel primo rinascimento* (Milan, 1961)
C. Rosenberg: 'The Bible of Borso d'Este: Inspiration and Use', *Cultura figurativa ferrarese tra XV e XVI secolo* (Venice, 1981), pp. 51–73
CHARLES M. ROSENBERG

Bible of Queen Christina. See LEO BIBLE.

Bible of San Paolo [Bible of San Callisto]. Illuminated manuscript (Rome, S Paolo fuori le Mura), probably made at Reims *c*. 870. It is the most extensively illustrated of all extant Carolingian Bibles. A dedicatory poem by *Ingobertus referens et scriba fidelis* and the verses accompanying an image of a ruler establish that it was made for a King Charles, now identified as Charles the Bald, who when he was crowned Emperor in Rome in 875 probably gave it to Pope John VIII.

The manuscript contains 337 parchment folios measuring 448×355 mm. The decoration consists of 92 initials, of which 36 occupy full pages, four canon tables and 24 frontispiece miniatures (*see* CAROLINGIAN ART, fig. 8). The initials represent the finest work in the calligraphy of the Reims school and are, despite their variety, of one cast. The miniatures, however, show variations in style and technique in which it is possible to distinguish the work of three separate artists who reassembled and translated shared pictorial sources into their own idioms. These sources were a mid-9th century Tours Bible and Gospel Book (untraced) and a cycle of Bible illustrations from an imperial atelier at Constantinople of the later 4th to the mid-5th century. Of the three artists, the so-called Evangelist Master made the most use of this late Hellenistic source to provide a last flowering of these trends in the Carolingian West. The 'Master of the Throne Images', in his episodal narrative work, gave a two-dimensional firmness to the illusionistic character of the Reims style of painting of the previous generation, whereas the St Paul Master reduced this illusionistic corporeality to an essentially 'medieval' form of expression.

BIBLIOGRAPHY
H. Schade: 'Studien zu der karolingischen Bilderbibel zu St Paul vor den Mauern in Rom', *Wallraf-Richartz-Jb.*, xxi (1959), pp. 9–40; xxii (1960), pp. 13–48
J. E. Gaehde: 'The Bible of San Paolo fuori le Mura in Rome: Its Date and Relation to Charles the Bald', *Gesta*, v (1966), pp. 9–21
——: 'Studies on the Pictorial Sources of the Bible of San Paolo', *Frühmittelalt. Stud.*, v (1971), pp. 359–400; viii (1974), pp. 351–84; ix (1975), pp. 359–89
La Bibbia di San Paolo fuori le Mura: Commentario (Rome, 1989) [facs. edn]
JOACHIM E. GAEHDE

Bibliography of art. Term applied to the compilation of the literature on an art subject; it can also refer to the study of art historiography or to the study of artistic book production (such as *livres d'artistes*). Art bibliographies usually take the form of sources cited at the end of scholarly treatises or of such lists presented as books or other formats (e.g. computer disk, optical disk or microform). This article is restricted to the intellectual compilation and classification of printed material about art. Art bibliography differs fundamentally from bibliography in the other humanities, such as music or literature. In these fields bibliography includes both the description and study of the primary texts, such as manuscripts or first editions, and the classification of the secondary sources. The first of these, the descriptive level, is almost absent from the bibliography of art. There the primary document is the work of art, which, other than manuscripts, *livres d'artistes* or printed architectural plans, is not textual. The bibliography of art thus consists almost entirely of books or other texts about art rather than the description of unique books that are works of art in themselves, although there are some significant exceptions, such as T. Besterman's *Old Art Books* (1977).

I. Introduction. II. Cataloguing and classification. III. Bibliographies.

I. Introduction.

1. TYPES. All bibliography, regardless of subject discipline, can be divided into three genres: systematic, enumerative and descriptive. Some bibliographies combine more than one type. Systematic bibliography organizes material by or within a subject: for example, the Carnegie Library's *Index to Handicraft Books* (1986) lists the books broken down into specific subdivisions. A sub-type of systematic bibliography is the critical or annotated bibliography. Usually written by scholars, such bibliographies are both selective and evaluative: thus Johannes Molanns's

critical bibliography on Chartres Cathedral (1989), subdivided into sections on the archaeology of the site, iconographic studies, monographic studies etc, is both selective, in that it does not attempt to cite every piece of writing about Chartres, and evaluative, describing through annotation the merits of each cited work. Enumerative art bibliographies are simply lists of holdings, book-auction inventories or library shelf-lists: examples are printed library catalogues or auction catalogues. Descriptive bibliography is less concerned with the arrangement of citations and more with the description of a book's appearance in order that it can be identified. Although descriptive cataloguing is a component of the catalogue of most art libraries, descriptive bibliography is a less common form of printed art bibliography; it is most frequently associated with rare or special art collections, an example being *The Fowler Architectural Collection of the Johns Hopkins University Catalogue* (1961).

2. HISTORY. Specialized bibliographies of art are a relatively recent phenomenon, the result of developments in subject bibliography, art history and the book trade. The earliest subject bibliographies were German printers' lists of the second half of the 15th century, which organized entries roughly by subject for the buyer's convenience. Art had not previously been considered as a topic for book production or bibliographic organization, because it was not a part of the liberal arts canon. In 1548–9 Konrad Gesner (1516–65) issued the *Pandectarum sive partitionum universalium*, the second part of his larger bibliographic classification *Bibliotheca universalis*; his rejection of much traditional book-title arrangement allowed him to create subject headings that could embrace books on art. His innovation was matched about the same time by the commercial *Messkataloge*, sales catalogues produced for book fairs. These frequently included sections under such headings as entertainment or technology that for the first time listed books specifically devoted to art practice.

The development of a bibliography within an art book is first documented in 1593, when Antonio Possevino annotated the biographical section of his *Tractatio de poesi et pictura ethnica, humana et fabulosa* by printing book-title citations in the margin. It was not until the 17th century, however, that the first separately compiled art bibliography appeared: in 1651 Raphaël Trichet du Fresne, in his *Trattato della pittura di Leonardo da Vinci*, an edited version of Leonardo's treatise on painting, devoted a separate section to 'recommended reading', an organized list of art books. Although he prefaced this with an apology about wasting space, it is considered the first true bibliography in the history of art. Several other art-bibliographical genres were initiated in the 17th century, when the great libraries of the Casante, Capponi and Chigi families, containing exquisite art volumes, were amassed and catalogued. The Barbarini library catalogue (1681) was widely circulated, setting a bibliographical precedent for art book entries. In popular art literature, guidebooks, which often describe and comment on paintings, introduced the bibliography as part of their service (*see* GUIDEBOOK). Luigi Pellegrino Scaramuccia's *Le finezze dei pennelli italiani* (1674) has a separate title-based *catalogo*, derived from du Fresne's list, as an appendix.

Modern art bibliography took shape in the 18th century. The Enlightenment zeal for the classification of knowledge and the increasing variety of published art books created the elements of modern art bibliography: detailed subject classification, precise criteria for book selection and accurate bibliographic description. Art dictionaries, such as Pellegrino Antonio Orlandi's *Abecedario pittorico* (1704), devoted separate sections to books on art. Around the middle of the century art bibliographies began to be published as separate books. The *Bibliothek der schönen Wissenschaften und der freyen Kunste*, published in Leipzig by the firm of J. Dyck in 1757 (ed. C. F. Nicolai), is a series of anonymous volumes devoted entirely to art bibliographies, which proclaimed as their mission the advancement of the fine arts, grouping together aesthetics, histories and practice.

Enlightenment bibliographers whose work was seminal to art bibliography include Christoph Gottlieb von Murr, an art scholar who in 1770 issued a comprehensive assessment of art bibliography, the *Bibliothèque de peinture, de sculpture, et de gravure*, the precursor of modern critical art bibliography. This was the result of personal examination and selection of titles, not simply the conflation of older lists; it also gives the modern scholar a glimpse of the changing view of art history (e.g. there are 20 times as many entries on mosaics as on oil painting). Also important is Angelo Comolli's *Bibliografia storico-artistica* (1788), the first art bibliography to use the term; although incomplete, it represents a form of bibliography written completely from the scholar's point of view. Comolli's work, expensively printed and bound, competes not with other bibliographies but with art books themselves.

The earliest bibliographer to assemble the various elements of art bibliography into a work of truly modern bibliography, still consulted by scholars, was Johann Samuel Ersch (1766–1828), who in his *Allgemeines Repertorium* (1793), the first union catalogue (*see* §II, 4 below), included an art section that closely matches modern bibliographical organization. It includes all languages and historical periods. Ersch divided and subdivided areas of the arts and included in his *Bücherkunde* what was perhaps the earliest section on books devoted to the history of art. In 1821 Leopoldo Cicognara, a Venetian art scholar and collector, published what is still the basic retrospective bibliography of art. 'Cicognara', as art historians refer to his *Catalogo ragionato*, is a discriminating selection from his personal library; it became the core of the Vatican Library's modern art-book collection. It includes books on Classical art, as well as the art of other periods, which made it the first general-purpose art bibliography, and it was eruditely annotated by the author, with remarks on such subjects as engravings, maps and errors of fact. Cicognara's work continued to be translated and reprinted long after his collection ceased to be a personal library.

Historical art bibliography is important not simply because it presents another view of the development of the history of art, but also because it documents the hierarchy of knowledge about art. Because art history builds on the work of earlier scholars, the consultation of old bibliographies is essential in order to document a work of art adequately.

II. Cataloguing and classification.

1. Introduction. 2. Types.

1. INTRODUCTION. In contradistinction to a bibliography, which is a theoretical or ideal grouping of material, a CATALOGUE is a list of the actual holdings of an institution or event; cataloguing is the term used for describing such holdings so that individual items can be identified. Art material in English-language libraries has been standardized according to the Anglo-American Cataloging Rules, now in their second revision (known as AACR2). With minor variations, these rules are accepted throughout Great Britain and North America. It is important for users of art libraries to become familiar with the system: for example, AACR2 requires an institution, such as a museum of art, to be entered under the name by which it is known in its own country's language, rather than a standardized form or translation of the name or the name of its city. Books or exhibition catalogues published by that museum will be found under its name and further identified, if necessary, by the city's name (e.g. MOMA, New York). This practice requires the researcher to know the institution's indigenous name. Exhibition catalogues devoted to one artist are catalogued under the artist's name, not that of the author or editor of the catalogue, nor those of contributing essayists or that of the museum or gallery.

Classification is the sub-system of cataloguing, according to which books or items are arranged, both physically on the shelves and in a printed shelf catalogue. Most art libraries use one of the universal classification systems, but a considerable number employ a system of their own; this is due partly to the interdisciplinary nature of art history, which makes it difficult to assign some books to a single subject, and partly to the unsatisfactory manner in which universal classification systems treat material on visual subjects.

In the USA the system developed c. 1900 by the Library of Congress in Washington, DC, and known as LC, has gained acceptance by most academic libraries and more recently established museum libraries. Its art subdivision (classified as 'N') divides the arts first by medium and then, where possible, by the artist's country. 'N' stands for art in general (e.g. surveys, handbooks), 'NA' for architecture, 'NB' for sculpture, 'NC' for drawing, 'ND' for painting, and so on. Librarians consider LC to be a pragmatic system since it is not underpinned by any theory of knowledge. Older, more established art libraries in the USA and many libraries in Britain use the Dewey Decimal System (DDS), devised by Melvil Dewey (1851–1931). Its wholly numerical code divides all knowledge into 10 decimally numbered classes. The 700s—the 'fine arts'—include all of art and art history, as well as music, dance, sport and theatre. Like LC, the DDS subdivides art material by medium and then by country of origin.

Several major art libraries have developed their own classification systems. The Metropolitan Museum of Art, New York, has devised a decimal system that applies solely to art. The most idiosyncratic system is probably that used by the Warburg Institute Library, London. It was devised by Aby Warburg to be an accurate representation of his individual approach to art history; the classification begins with religion, natural science and philosophy, then moves to language and literature, followed by fine arts and finally social and political life.

2. TYPES.

(i) Art library catalogues. Manuscript catalogues existed in the Middle Ages, but the first printed art library catalogue was that of Cicognara's personal library (see §I, 2 above). Since the 1960s most of the largest art libraries have published printed catalogues of their holdings. Some, such as the New York Public Library or the library of the Metropolitan Museum of Art, have continued to update them; other libraries ceased to publish once their holdings had been included in a national cataloguing database (see §4 below).

Because most art libraries are dedicated to a specific purpose, their catalogues can serve as retrospective subject bibliographies. For serious retrospective bibliography, at least five of the major art library catalogues should be consulted. Among the most comprehensive are those of the world's largest art library, the National Art Library at the Victoria and Albert Museum, London; its detailed holdings catalogues constitute retrospective subject bibliographies. The library's first catalogue, the *Universal List* (1870), represents not just the library's holdings at that period, but all the books its curators considered necessary for an art library; it remains a powerful document for 19th-century art bibliography. In 1972 the full book catalogue was published in 10 volumes, with a supplement for exhibition catalogues. Like many European library catalogues, the National Art Library has separate listings for author/title and for subject. The absence of a subject index from the printed volumes limits their usefulness to scholars; the microfiche index does not wholly rectify this.

The catalogue (1960, rev. 1980) of the Metropolitan Museum of Art Library, New York, remains the most extensive general art catalogue. Like most American library catalogues, it combines author, title and subject into a single list; it also makes no distinction between exhibition catalogues, books or periodical articles, providing a handy and reasonably comprehensive index to the literature of art. Periodical articles ceased to be cited in 1929, and since 1980 sales catalogues are accessed through the SCIPIO (Sales Catalog Index Project Input Online) database (see §5 below). This library, like the museum itself, has endeavoured to collect in all areas, but it remains particularly excellent in Far Eastern, Classical and American art literature. The New York Public Library (NYPL) issues an annual update to its retrospective *Dictionary Catalog* (1975): the *Bibliographic Guide* (1975–), which is virtually a world publication list of books on art in European languages and is often used by the bibliographers of collections as a purchase list. However, being a yearly publication, it cannot be sufficiently cumulative and must be supplemented by on-line database searching; NYPL is a member of RLIN (Research Libraries Information Network; see §4 below). Its holdings are particularly strong in costume design, architecture (with subject headings for architectural elements) and ephemera, such as pamphlets and newspaper items. Being a general collection, the NYPL holds a wider variety of books than can be found in specialist art libraries.

Other library catalogues provide unusual pockets of retrospective holdings. Harvard University's *Catalogue of the Harvard University Fine Arts Library* (1971) is perhaps the finest university art library catalogue, with strengths in Romanesque sculpture, Italian primitives and historiography. The printed catalogue (1974, 1986) of MOMA, New York, is notable for early 20th-century books and documentary material. The *Catalog of the Avery Memorial Architectural Library* (1968) of Columbia University, New York, is one of the oldest published library catalogues of architecture.

The Archives of American Art in Washington, DC, a collecting body of primary and some secondary source material of American artists, has produced several important catalogues. A catalogue of its exhibition catalogues (*see* §III, 6(vi) below) was issued in 1979. The *Card Catalog of the Manuscript Collections* (1980) lists scrap-books, printed announcements and other material donated to the Archives since their foundation in the 1940s. The holdings lists of the Archives are more than location catalogues, since the Archives have much of their collection on microfilm, which is available for loan.

(ii) Union, national and on-line catalogues. Conglomerate catalogues are a key source for the verification of citations. Union catalogues—the holdings of several libraries combined into a single catalogue—are particularly useful, because they supply the locations of a number of copies. Originally developed to locate volumes for loan purposes, national catalogues, which list all the books received by a country's national library during some period, often function as union catalogues and often provide an instant, comprehensive bibliography of an author or subject. Particularly for researchers working in smaller libraries, union and national catalogues provide accurate descriptive information on specific editions and locations. The most useful union catalogues are the retrospective ones, listing older editions that are less likely to be on modern bibliographic databases. The *National Union Catalog: Pre-1956 Imprints* (1968–81) provides citations by author (or main entry) to any book printed before 1956 that is held in the participating academic, museum and larger public libraries in the USA and Canada. The *British Library General Catalogue of Printed Books to 1975* (1979–84) is notable for its rare Western European and British material. Likewise, the *Catalogue général des livres imprimés de la Bibliothèque nationale* (1960) in Paris is strongest for titles of French and Italian publications. The Biblioteca dell'Istituto Nazionale d'Archeologia e Storia dell'Arte in Rome issues a yearly acquisition catalogue, the *Annuario bibliografico di storia dell'arte*, a subject index of books, journal articles and exhibition catalogues.

Among conglomerate catalogues solely of books on art, *Art Books* (1979–84), covering the years 1876–1984, offers access by subject to complete library-cataloguing entries; it is limited to material that has become available on American computer records, with very little foreign-language coverage, and is complemented by Schimmelman's *American Imprints on Art through 1865* (1990), a union catalogue and national imprint index in one.

Most large art libraries now use some version of computer-retrieval catalogue. On-line catalogues, originally developed by individual libraries to save space and to yield information faster, now also form part of record-sharing consortium databases. Scholars routinely search local on-line catalogues and consortium catalogues, thus effectively consulting a union catalogue. Of the two most important consortium catalogue databases, RLIN is the richest for art sources. It was begun in 1974 by the libraries of Columbia, Yale and Harvard universities and the New York Public Library, and it represents the on-line holdings of most of the larger American art-museum and rare-book libraries. In addition to databases of books and periodicals, it also contains several special files (separate databases) useful to art researchers: these include the ESTC (Eighteenth-century Short Title Catalog); the RIPD (Research-in-Progress Database); and SCIPIO, which lists sale catalogues (*see* §5 below). The other outstanding national cataloguing database, OCLC (Ohio College Library Center), is the largest (22 million records in 1990); it represents most academic and public libraries in the USA, as well as the National Gallery of Art Library in Washington, DC. OCLC is more available than RLIN and easier to use, being particularly useful for searching broad areas and recorded-media works. Subject-heading and key-word searching is available via a subsystem called EPIC. There are also several smaller library consortia, such as the University of Toronto Library Automation System (UT-LAS), primarily in Canadian libraries, and the Washington Library Network (WLN) in the western USA, which may also be useful for regional art libraries. Academic libraries and the larger art libraries usually belong to RLIN for cataloguing purposes and maintain reference-searching facilities with OCLC.

(iii) Catalogues of auction catalogues. The documentation provided when art objects are sold has become an increasingly valuable tool in art research (*see* CATALOGUE, §5). Auction catalogues often provide the only documentation of an object's existence as it passes between private collections; they thus help to establish provenance and provide a bibliographic reference to the object. Reitlinger's *The Economics of Taste* (1961–70), which provides significant auction bibliography in addition to a commentary on collecting, excited contemporary interest in auction records. Bibliography on auctions takes the form of indexes to individual auction catalogues or of union lists of catalogues. Auction houses usually provide summary indexing of their own sales. *Christie's Review of the Season* (1928–), Drouot's *L'Art et les enchères en France* (1988–) and Sotheby's *Art at Auction* (1963–) catalogue the auction houses' own holdings and publish signed articles on various aspects of the sales year. Auction indexes allow the researcher to locate an object sold and then trace it back to its auction catalogue. Mayer's *International Auction Records* (1967–) cross-refers works to auctions in chronological order. Theran's *Leonard's Index of Art Auctions* (1980–) is useful for smaller auctions and minor artists, and Hislop's *Art Sales Index* (1968–) is useful for the broadest country coverage.

Looking up an auctioned work under its title will not necessarily provide all the bibliographic information required; often works must be sought under the subject of the auction at which they were sold, by means of a union catalogue of auction catalogues. The paramount catalogue of sales catalogues is Lugt's *Répertoire des catalogues de ventes publiques* (1938–87), covering the years 1600–1925. It gives the international locations of sales catalogues, a great number of which are in the USA or Britain. This series is indispensable for tracing owners of items, kinds of sale items and libraries holding the catalogues. Other union catalogues include the Bibliothèque Forney's *Catalogue des catalogues de ventes d'art* (1972), which is especially useful for decorative arts material. The Harvard *Catalogue of Auction Sales Catalogues* (1971) is a supplement to its library catalogue. Lancour's *American Art Auction Catalogues, 1785–1942* (1944) indexes American sales catalogues in over 150 libraries, with an index of owners of the objects sold. SCIPIO, a combined union-list and auction-index database available through RLIN, indexes international auction catalogues by their title-page information (collector's name, subject of the auction and date). It comprises selected American art-museum collections belonging to RLIN and also identifies catalogue citations from Lugt and Lancour. Because it is a purely bibliographic database, it does not index individual works of art.

III. Bibliographies.

1. General art bibliographies. 2. Reference bibliographies and study guides. 3. Commentaries on art historiography. 4. Bibliographies of bibliographies. 5. On-line databases. 6. Specialized formats.

1. GENERAL ART BIBLIOGRAPHIES. Many of the separate-book bibliographies published in the late 20th century—on nearly every conceivable art subject—are massive, unannotated compilations of citations. Thanks to computer information-retrieval, they are easy to compile but are of questionable value, since bibliographies are supposed to save readers' time by screening out irrelevant material. By far the best bibliographies are those that accompany a book or article, because these have actually served to produce the text they follow. Reviews in periodicals, in which scholars select and comment on the relevant literature of a subject, are also excellent sources of bibliography. Art history gives rise to fewer such articles than other disciplines; however, the *Art Bulletin* publishes the 'State of Research', a series of thoughtful essays on the literature of art and historiography of individual art topics, which began in 1986 with B. S. Ridgway's essay on ancient art.

Bibliography in art monographs is a comparatively recent development and one that is still not always considered essential; thus Carrier's *Principles of Art History Writing* (1991) has no separate bibliography, and very often the bibliographies of monographs do not match the texts in quality. Bibliographies included in historical surveys are generally better sources. The Pelican History of Art (1953–), which was published by Yale University Press after 1992, is a series of commissioned volumes that can be relied on for well-organized bibliographies. Its German counterpart, the Propyläen Kunstgeschichte (1923, 1966), is slightly richer in subject bibliography. The Arts of Mankind series, another set of individual histories (up to the Renaissance), has excellent selective bibliographies on the topics covered in each volume. All three series should be consulted in compiling the initial bibliography of a period.

Most scholarly encyclopedias on arts and culture provide excellent bibliographies. The *Enciclopedia universale d'arte* (1958–67) and its English translation, the *Encyclopedia of World Art* (1959–68), remain a fundamental source for bibliography, especially for topics bridging traditional art-historical periods too general to be covered by separately published bibliographies. The *Lexikon der Kunst* (1987) is more up to date but has far fewer bibliographic citations. It is especially good for German-language articles and dissertations. Among special-subject encyclopedias, the *Enciclopedia dell'arte antica* (1958) stands out as a major contribution to general bibliography on ancient art.

2. REFERENCE BIBLIOGRAPHIES AND STUDY GUIDES. A handful of general bibliographies of art books, known as reference bibliographies, are central to art-history research. Because the literature of art never goes entirely out of date, recent art reference bibliographies have wisely attempted not to supersede but to update older bibliographies. Chamberlin's *Guide to Art Reference Books* (1959) remains the principal critical source; it is a retrospective (to 1957) English-language art bibliography, compiled with the assistance of art historians at Columbia University, New York, and other institutions, published under the auspices of the American Library Association. It was augmented by Arntzen and Rainwater's *Guide to the Literature of Art History* (1980), in which art literature is reorganized into sections on general reference works and then primary and secondary sources. Also useful in the early stages of research are the series of books by Ehresmann. The general *Fine Arts* (1989) should be consulted first: the multi-volume series includes *Decorative Arts* (1977) and *Architecture* (1977). Each volume has its own bibliography, classified by medium.

Modern art bibliographies increasingly adopt a 'study-guide' format, because of the variety of bibliographic formats and ways of accessing art information. A satisfactory bibliography-cum-study guide is *Art Information: Research Methods and Resources* (1990) by L. Jones, who has merged a study-guide format with extensive bibliography to create the most elaborate single-volume inventory of essential tools for art history (both reference and monographic). Most other study guides restrict their scope to particular methodological interests or to a historical period. The American Library Association's excellent research series, of which van Keuren's *Guide to Research in Classical Art and Mythology* (1991) is an example, discusses a core group of books in detail, devoting chapters to the decorative arts and other areas that are difficult to locate by traditional library subject headings. Kleinbauer and Slavin's *Research Guide* (1977) is organized methodologically to conform to mainstream approaches to art history, but nevertheless provides a unique selection of fundamental books.

3. COMMENTARIES ON ART HISTORIOGRAPHY. Such commentaries offer unique selections of evaluative bibliography, which, since they adopt a particular point of view, tend to be more controversial than study guides; but their opinionated nature makes them more valuable than the traditional reference manual. Johnson's *Art History: Its Use and Abuse* (1988), for example, has chapters on bibliography and cataloguing theory that discuss the often ignored question of how the form and availability of art information determines art-historical scholarship. Dilly's *Kunstgeschichte als Institution* (1979) provides another rarefied selection of texts forming the basis of modern scholarly research. The archetypal work of commentary on art historiography is Julius von Schlosser's *Die Kunstliteratur* (1923). Schlosser's concern was with the textual sources of art; his book is most often cited in discussions of the sources and documents of art. He was, however, equally concerned with the transmission of ideas; the programme of his book starts with each historical period in art and traces the written record of its genesis to its origins. Schlosser subdivided these broad periods according to the distinctive trends in the art-writing of the period or place, for example legacies of Vasari's art theory in the Renaissance or the topographic literature of Spain in the Baroque period. He considered nearly all forms of literature that affected art interpretation as art literature and in his first German edition attempted to follow these sources back to their origin. The 1964 edition, revised, edited and translated into Italian by Otto Kurz, neglected to carry out Schlosser's intention of updating the literature on the sources.

4. BIBLIOGRAPHIES OF BIBLIOGRAPHIES. Art historians often need to consult general, cross-disciplinary bibliographies, especially where art is linked to another subject, such as women's studies; when other methodologies, such as literature or anthropology, need to be employed; or when other disciplines (e.g. archaeology, museum studies) need to be consulted. They should therefore be familiar with the most important general bibliographies of bibliographies. Sheehy's *Guide to Reference Books* (1986), annotated and cross-indexed, is an excellent universal reference bibliography. Another is *Walford's Guide to Reference Material* (1980). Older general reference bibliographies with strength in the humanities occasionally help scholars to reconstruct the knowledge of a subject as it was during a particular period or to refer to sources that current bibliographies consider outdated. Besterman's *World Bibliography of Bibliographies* (1965) is a rich collection of both obscure and standard subject bibliographies (its art section was published separately). Likewise Malclès's *Les Sources du travail bibliographique* (1950–58) is still useful.

5. ON-LINE DATABASES. The distinction in bibliography between on-line information (computer retrieval) and 'hard copy' (printed sources) is fading. The databases of many printed sources are being reconstituted to serve on-line retrieval; many libraries are unable to support the cost of providing both hard copy and computer access; and the printed versions of bibliographical sources are

increasingly being discontinued. Researchers should therefore think in terms of information systems, choosing between them according to their particular strengths and their availability. This does not mean that computer retrieval and hard-copy retrieval are the same thing. Broad-topic searches are generally less successful by computer, because it is unable to sort out nuances that will appear obvious to the scholar. For example, a computer search starting with the name of an artist or movement may result in hundreds of citations, many of little relevance, from just a few years—a waste of time and money, especially when charged per citation. However, when the subject is complex, either because it is specific (e.g. Ambulatory and Reims Cathedral) or because it is hybrid (e.g. ecology and painting), computer searching is essential. It is also of significant value when the specific terms searched for are ambiguous or interchangeable. Although such projects as the Getty Art History Information Program's *Art and Architecture Thesaurus* (1990) have been developed to standardize art terms in bibliographies and elsewhere, researchers whose subjects have multiple or foreign names have greater success with computer searches. Many institutions have computer-file subject bibliographies for art and other subjects, as part of local networks. Since almost all printed books now published pass through a stage of being computer files, it should be possible in the future to offer researchers traditional bibliographies in computer form.

On-line art bibliographies include indexes of journal articles, books and other published records. Some remain essentially journal indexes, while others were developed to contain all published documentation on art. Whatever their origin, literature indexes, searched together with relevant subject catalogues, are the primary bibliographic search method for modern scholarship. The extent to which databases overlap depends on the age of the index and the specific aim of its producer; some databases, such as *Artbibliographies Modern*, have changed their indexing profiles over time.

RILA, the *Répertoire international de la littérature de l'art*, covers books, journals, *Festschriften*, conference proceedings and essays for the years 1973–89; it does not cover African, Islamic, Far Eastern, Native American, prehistoric or ancient art. It is available both on-line and in book form and is particularly good for finding books, *Festschriften*, museum literature and dissertations. Because it was created to be an on-line retrieval system, it has a wide variety of access points, including time-period, the person honoured (for *Festschriften*) and article type. *RAA*, the *Répertoire d'art et d'archéologie*, covers 1910 to 1989 (1973–89 on-line); it is essentially a periodicals index that also includes exhibition catalogues and *Festschriften*. Its importance lies in the length of its publication history and its representation of Classical-period titles.

BHA, the *Bibliography of the History of Art*, which combines *RAA* and *RILA* but has wider coverage of journals, became the most comprehensive on-line literature bibliography in 1990. It offers an analysis of each entry in French and English, supplying an abstract and descriptors (standardized subject headings) for each citation. It collects in one database books, journal articles, *Festschriften*, conference proceedings and essays and also appears in book form. It excludes the same areas as *RILA*. Its recent origin limits its usefulness; *RILA* and *RAA* must still be consulted for retrospective citations, and, what is perhaps worse, the elaborate indexing means that *BHA* citations are published at least two years later than the literature they describe.

For the scholar of 19th- and 20th-century subjects, *Artbibliographies Modern* (from 1969) is particularly useful, because it limits its artistic topics to that period, so reducing the likelihood of inappropriate citations. The on-line database was started in 1984 (the printed volumes extending to 1993); since 1989 it has covered only subjects from 1900 onward. The database is particularly rewarding for researchers in design and contemporary art. *Art Index*, the most popular art citation index, limits book citation to the books reviewed in the periodicals it indexes; the same criteria govern exhibition catalogues. Its inclusion of ancient and indigenous art subjects, its long indexing history (from 1929; on-line from 1984) and its general availability make it a worthwhile, if not comprehensive, bibliographic source.

A humanities database that should be consulted almost as routinely as any art bibliography is the *AHCI* (*Arts and Humanities Citation Index*), available both in printed version and on-line. This massive bibliography of books and periodicals indexes 1300 humanities journals by the author's last name and by title; it allows the researcher to trace books by journal articles that have cited them. As the history of art looks more closely at its own literature in order to reveal methodology, or as it becomes ever more interdisciplinary, the *AHCI* becomes increasingly essential.

Until the rather expensive process of retrospective conversion—adding older citations to on-line databases—has been completed, printed bibliographies of older material will remain essential. Even subsequently, retrospective bibliographies will continue to be necessary, particularly for the specialized areas for which no computer database exists or where the information is buried in a text unretrievable by key words.

6. Specialized formats.

(i) Catalogues raisonnés. This is a catalogue of all of an artist's works. The better catalogues raisonnés include a reproduction and a bibliography for each work, its provenance and a scholarly essay on each period of the artist's life. These primary research tools are often difficult to locate in libraries; frequently, particularly in older library cataloguing, catalogues raisonnés are listed simply under the artist's name, or with the qualifier 'catalogue', so that it is not clear whether it is an exhibition catalogue, a checklist or a catalogue raisonné. Freitag's *Art Books: A Basic Bibliography of Monographs on Artists* (1985) indicates catalogues raisonnés by CR next to the citation. Most of the artists included are painters, and the citations are not annotated; Freitag's work is principally useful in identifying titles. Arntz's *Verzeichnis der seit 1945 erschienenen Werkkataloge* (1975) concentrates on a small group of 20th-century artists; similarly, Riggs's *Print Council Index to Oeuvre-Catalogues of Prints by European and American*

Artists (1983) focuses on books on graphic artists from the 15th century onwards.

(ii) Bio-bibliographies. Other information on particular artists can be found in bio-bibliographies. Biographical dictionaries of artists abound in art literature, and almost every western European country has a biographical reference book of its artists. Bio-bibliographies, where literature and biography intermingle, are less common. Some principally biographical sources contain significant bibliographical citations: outstanding in this respect is Thieme and Becker's 37-volume *Allgemeines Lexikon der bildenden Künstler* (1907–50), updated by Vollmer (1953–62). Each biographical entry is followed by an invaluable bibliographical section in abbreviated form. A revised edition of 'Thieme–Becker' (as it is generally known) began to be published in 1983.

(iii) Festschriften. One common source for art research is commemorative essays collected in the form of a *Festschrift*. The difficulty in locating these is that such a collection, usually cited under the titles of the individual essays, may be very disparate and catalogued only under the broadest of subject headings or under the name of the dedicatee. Furthermore, *Festschriften* may appear in a great variety of formats. Some appear as special issues of periodical publications, others as monographs, and yet others may form part of conference proceedings. Recent bibliographical indexes such as *RILA* and the *BHA* have addressed the need to catalogue *Festschriften* both as a whole and under individual titles. For retrospective years, however, the main bibliography is Rave's *Kunstgeschichte in Festschriften* (1962), which indexes individual essays by subject, author and the person honoured. An English-language supplement by Lincoln, *Festschriften in Art History* (1988), covers the years up to *RILA*'s first appearance. The New York Public Library's *Guide to Festschriften* (1977) and Leistner's *International Bibliography of Festschriften* (1976) provide limited indexing to such collections of essays.

(iv) Dissertations. These offer another useful source of information that is similarly difficult to locate in a library catalogue, for several reasons. First, since dissertations frequently represent the newest areas of research, traditional subject headings may not characterize them accurately. Second, few libraries can afford to collect a wide range of copies of dissertations. Third, although recent art bibliographies, such as *BHA* or *Artbibliographies Modern*, do index dissertations, many that relate to art may be written under the auspices of non-art departments, such as philosophy or Classical studies, and may be missed by traditional art indexes. Separate bibliographies of dissertations can provide special points of access. *Dissertation Abstracts International* (1938–) is both a series and an on-line database, indexing American and (from 1970) select foreign dissertations. Dissertations from participating universities are searchable on-line by key word from the abstract or subject headings. *Dissertation Abstracts* also sells copies of the theses that it holds. There also exist indexes to dissertations in other languages, such as the dissertation section of the *Deutsche Nationalbibliographie* (1968–) for German dissertations or the *Inventaire des*

thèses de doctorat soutenues devant les universités françaises (1981–) for French theses. Master's theses, although usually less important in art, are also searchable, either through their own indexes or as part of a dissertation series.

(v) Special subject series. The 'information explosion' has encouraged the publication of series of critical bibliographies on art topics, indexed in most libraries under the series title. Reference Publications in Art History, published by G. K. Hall, has provided a forum for scholars to select and comment on the literature of a subject. The scope of this series has been defined broadly, ranging from Glass's *Italian Romanesque Sculpture* (1983) to Biebuyck's *Arts of Central Africa* (1987). Other valuable series are the Garland Press's extended Garland Library of the History of Art, with slightly less fully annotated bibliographies than those in Hall; Greenwood Press's Art Reference Collection; and the older Art and Architecture Information Guide Series of the Gale Information Guide Library. Van de Waal's *Iconclass* (1973–84) was written as a classification system for image collections and is better known to picture researchers than to bibliographers. Each of its seven divisions (e.g. religion and magic, nature, the Bible) is followed by a general bibliography of the subject. These are particularly useful because they end at approximately the point when major on-line bibliographies began (late 1960s to mid-1970s); they thus represent a useful complement to computer retrieval.

(vi) Exhibition catalogues. Bibliographies of exhibition catalogues present some problems, as does locating individual catalogues. Most libraries treat exhibition catalogues as monographs, having a title, author (often corporate) and collation. However, the number of copies printed is often very small, the information highly topical and the essays very short, so that they tend to be used more as a periodical article than a book and are often cited as such, with the barest date information and the title of a particular essay. Newer and more comprehensive on-line bibliographies have tried to include as many points of access as possible to these publications; however, exhibition catalogues remain ephemeral, making it necessary to use special bibliographic resources, especially for retrospective subjects.

The *Art Exhibition Catalogs Subject Index* (1978–), devoted exclusively to contemporary exhibition catalogues, is a catalogue of the collection of the University of California at Santa Barbara. It has some 70,000 entries and provides access by subject, city of exhibition, collation and authors. Parts of the collection are available for loan. The quarterly *Worldwide Art Catalogue Bulletin* (1963–) is the sales catalogue of Worldwide Art Catalogues, a major dealer in exhibition catalogues. It supplies useful reviews of the catalogues and publishes an annual index of the firm's holdings. Exhibition catalogues from museum and commercial galleries are classified by medium and topical terms (e.g. women artists).

Retrospective bibliography of exhibition catalogues is extensive. Such bibliographies generally specialize by subject. The more notable retrospective catalogues include Gordon's *Modern Art Exhibitions, 1900–1916* (1974), which covers the rich period of German Expressionism;

the *National Museum of American Art's Index to American Art Exhibition Catalogues* by Yarnall and Gerdts (1986), which lists American and Canadian exhibitions held before 1876; and the Archives of American Art's *Collection of Exhibition Catalogs* (1979), available on RLIN and microfiche. Graves's *A Century of Loan Exhibitions, 1813–1912* (1913–15) covers major exhibitions in England and Scotland. Many more British exhibitions, whether or not a catalogue was issued, are traceable through Graves's series of dictionary catalogues, such as the eight volumes of the *Royal Academy of Arts* (1905–6).

Because of the relative scarcity of exhibition catalogues, reprint collections have been produced, the indexes of which are catalogue bibliographies in themselves. Notable examples are Reff's *Modern Art in Paris, 1855 to 1900* (1981), covering the important periods of Impressionism and Symbolism, and *Art Exhibition Catalogues on Microfilm*, covering private and museum shows of several centuries.

(vii) Artists' comments and manifestos. Modern art history often appears to be a series of manifestos and critical reactions to a work's initial presentation, and such fragments of text can be difficult to locate. Textual primary sources are often elusive, because exhibition reviews, especially from the 19th century, are not topically indexed in many newspaper indexes. Until recently, artists' statements were neglected as ancillary documents. The specialized bibliographies for textual documentation are perhaps particularly important for contemporary scholars. *Twentieth-century Artists on Art* (1985) is a useful bibliography of artists' statements and quotations and such reliable reprint sources as exist. There are also a few special subject-area bibliographies, such as Spalek's *German Expressionism in the Fine Arts* (1977) and Fredeman's *Pre-Raphaelitism: A Bibliocritical Study* (1968). Collections of artistic texts also sometimes carry significant bibliographies, which are necessarily less comprehensive than bibliographies alone. Holt's *Documentary History of Art* (1966) and Motherwell's series of *Documents of Twentieth-century Art* (New York, 1944–) both contain some additional bibliography.

(viii) Image collections. 'Visual information', finding a reproduction of a known picture or searching for images to support a thesis, is a vital part of art research. Some image collections, such as the Marburger Index and the Index Iconologus, are indexed themselves and designed to work without the use of bibliographies. Specialized bibliographies that index reproductions in art books can also act as art picture archives for smaller libraries. Havlice's *World Painting Index* (1977) indexes nearly 1200 books on painting by artist and title; because few paintings before the 20th century had exact titles, researchers must be flexible when searching by title and subject alone. Similar reference works include Thomson's *Index to Art Reproductions in Books* (1974) and Korwin's *Index to Two-dimensional Art Works* (1981). For prints, Parry and Chipman's *Print Index* (1983) lists reproductions of prints in books by artists from the 18th century to the 20th.

(ix) Art librarianship. The bibliography and literature of art librarianship can be of great value to the art researcher.

Knowing how art information is organized can often be the key to making the most of a collection. Pacey's *Art Library Manual* (1977) outlines the literature of the profession, while his *Reader in Art Librarianship* (1985) updates and expands the earlier book. The publications of the Art Libraries Societies of North America (ARLIS/NA) and of Great Britain (ARLIS/UK) provide critical analysis of art material in a manner different from that of art-history periodicals. *Art Documentation*, a publication of ARLIS/NA, regularly features pithy reviews of books. The *Art Libraries Journal*, from ARLIS/UK, is known for literature reviews on topics of art-information access.

See also ARCHIVES, CATALOGUE, ENCYCLOPEDIAS AND DICTIONARIES OF ART and PERIODICAL.

BIBLIOGRAPHY

TYPES

L. Fowler: *The Fowler Architectural Collection of the Johns Hopkins University Catalogue* (Baltimore, 1961)

W. Freitag: 'Art Libraries and Collections', *Encyclopedia of Library and Information Science*, i (New York, 1968), pp. 571–621

E. L. Lucas: 'Art Literature', *Encyclopedia of Library and Information Science*, i (New York, 1968), pp. 621–6

T. Besterman: *Old Art Books* (London, 1977)

Index to Handicraft Books, 1974–1984, Pittsburgh, Carnegie Lib. (Pittsburgh, 1986)

J. van der Meulen: *Chartres: Sources and Literary Interpretation: A Critical Bibliography* (Boston, 1989)

HISTORY

K. Gesner: *Pandectarum sive partitionum universalium . . . libri xxi*, 20 vols (Zurich, 1548–9)

A. Possevino: *Tractatio de poesi et pictura ethnica, humana et fabulosa collata cum vera, honesta et sacra* (Lyon, 1593)

R. Trichet du Fresne: *Trattato della pittura di Leonardo da Vinci* (Perugia, 1651)

L. P. Scaramuccia: *Le finezze dei pennelli italiani ammirate e studiate da Girupeno sotto la scorta e disciplina del genio di Raffaello d'Urbino* (Padua, 1674)

P. A. Orlandi: *Abecedario pittorico de' professori più illustri in pittura, scultura, ed architettura* (Bologna, 1704, rev. 1719) [numerous subsequent editions]

C. G. von Murr: *Bibliothèque de peinture, de sculpture, et de gravure*, 2 vols (Frankfurt am Main, 1770)

A. Comolli: *Bibliografia storico-artistica dell'architettura civile ed arti subalterne*, 4 vols (Rome, 1788)

J. S. Ersch: *Allgemeines Repertorium der Literatur für die Jahre 1785 bis 1790*, 3 vols (Jena, 1793)

L. Cicognara: *Catalogo ragionato dei libri d'arte e d'antichità posseduti da conte Cicognara*, 2 vols (Pisa, 1821)

L. Sorensen: 'Art Bibliographies: A Survey of their Development, 1595–1821', *Lib. Q.*, lvi (1986), pp. 31–55

ART LIBRARY CATALOGUES

Universal Catalogue of Books on Art, London, S. Kensington Mus. [V&A], 2 vols (London, 1870/*R* New York, 1963)

Catalog of the Avery Memorial Architecture Library, New York, Columbia U., 19 vols (Boston, 1958, 1968, 2/1972)

Library Catalog of the Metropolitan Museum of Art, 25 vols (Boston, 1960, rev. in 48 vols, 2/1980)

Catalogue of the Harvard University Fine Arts Library, the Fogg Art Museum, 15 vols (Boston, 1971)

National Art Library Catalogue: Author Catalogue, London, V&A, 10 vols (Boston, 1972)

Catalogue of Exhibition Catalogues, London, V&A (Boston, 1972) [suppl.]

Dictionary Catalog of the Art and Architecture Division, New York, Pub. Lib., 30 vols (Boston, 1975)

Bibliographic Guide to Art and Architecture, New York, Pub. Lib. (1975–) [annual]

Catalog of the Library of the Museum of Modern Art, 14 vols (Boston, 1976)

Annual Bibliography of Modern Art, New York, MOMA (Boston, 1986–)

The Victoria & Albert Museum Library: Subject Catalogue (London, n.d.) [microfiche]

UNION, NATIONAL AND ON-LINE CATALOGUES

Annu. Bibliog. Stor. A.

Catalogue général des livres imprimés de la Bibliothèque nationale, 231 vols (Paris, 1960)

The National Union Catalog: Pre-1956 Imprints, 754 vols (Chicago, 1968–81)

Art Books, 1950–1979 (New York, 1979)

British Library General Catalogue of Printed Books to 1975, 360 vols (London, 1979–84)

Art Books, 1876–1949 (New York, 1981)

Art Books, 1980–1984 (New York, 1984)

J. Schimmelman: *American Imprints on Art through 1865: Books and Pamphlets on Drawing, Painting, Sculpture, Aesthetics, Art Criticism and Instruction: An Annotated Bibliography* (Boston, 1990)

AUCTION CATALOGUES

F. Lugt: *Ventes: Répertoire des catalogues de ventes publiques* (1938–87)

H. Lancour: *American Art Auction Catalogues, 1785–1942* (New York, 1944)

G. Reitlinger: *The Economics of Taste*, 3 vols (New York, 1961–70)

E. Mayer: *International Auction Records* (Paris, 1967–) [annual]

R. Hislop, ed.: *Art Sales Index* (Weybridge, Surrey, 1968–)

Catalogue of Auction Sales Catalogues, Cambridge, MA, Harvard U. (Boston, 1971)

Catalogue des catalogues de ventes d'art, Paris, Bib. Forney, 2 vols (Boston, 1972)

S. Theran, ed.: *Leonard's Index of Art Auctions* (Newton, MA, 1980–) [annual]

GENERAL ART BIBLIOGRAPHIES

A. Reigl: *Stilfragen: Grundlegungen zu einer Geschichte der Ornamentik* (Berlin, rev. 2/1923)

Enciclopedia dell'arte antica, 7 vols plus supplements and index (Rome, 1958)

Enciclopedia universale dell'arte, 15 vols (Rome, 1958–67); Eng. trans. as *Encyclopedia of World Art* (New York, 1959–68)

B. S. Ridgway: 'The State of Research on Ancient Art', *A. Bull.*, lxviii (1986), pp. 7–23

Lexicon der Kunst, 12 vols (Basle, 1987)

D. Carrier: *Principles of Art History Writing* (University Park, PA, 1991)

REFERENCE BIBLIOGRAPHIES

M. Chamberlin: *Guide to Art Reference Books* (Chicago, 1959)

D. Ehresmann: *Fine Arts: A Bibliographic Guide to Basic Reference Works, Histories and Handbooks* (Littleton, CO, 1975, rev. 3/1989)

W. E. Kleinbauer and T. P. Slavin: *Research Guide* (Chicago, 1977)

L. Jones: *Art Research Methods and Resources* (Dubuque, IO, 1978); rev. as *Art Information: Research Methods and Resources* (Dubuque, IO, 1990)

E. Arntzen and R. Rainwater: *Guide to the Literature of Art History* (Chicago, 1980)

F. van Keuren: *Guide to Research in Classical Art and Mythology* (Chicago, 1991)

COMMENTARIES ON ART HISTORIOGRAPHY

J. von Schlosser: *Die Kunstliteratur* (Leipzig, 1923; It. trans., Florence, 3/1964)

H. Dilly: *Kunstgeschichte als Institution: Studien zur Geschichte einer Disziplin* (Frankfurt am Main, 1979)

W. Johnson: *Art History: Its Use and Abuse* (Toronto, 1988)

BIBLIOGRAPHIES OF BIBLIOGRAPHIES

L.-N. Malclès: *Les Sources du travail bibliographique*, 3 vols (Geneva, 1950–58)

T. Besterman: *A World Bibliography of Bibliographies and of Bibliographical Catalogues, Calendars, Abstracts, Digests, Indexes and the Like* (Lausanne, 1965)

A. Walford: *Walford's Guide to Reference Material*, 3 vols (1980)

W. Sheehy: *Guide to Reference Books* (Chicago, rev. 10/1986)

ON-LINE DATABASES

RAA: Répertoire d'art et d'archéologie (1910–89; on-line, 1973–89)

Art Index (1929–; on-line, 1984–)

RILA: International Repertory of the Literature of Art/Répertoire international de la littérature de l'art (1973–89)

Art and Architecture Thesaurus, Getty Art History Information Program, 3 vols (New York, 1990)

BHA: Bibliography of the History of Art/Bibliographie d'histoire de l'art (1990–) [combines *RAA* and *RILA*]

SPECIALIZED FORMATS

Catalogues raisonnés

W. Arntz: *Verzeichnis der seit 1945 erschienenen Werkkataloge zur Kunst des 20. Jahrhunderts* (Haag, Oberbayern, 1975)

T. Riggs: *The Print Council Index to Oeuvre-catalogues of Prints by European and American Artists* (Millwood, NY, 1983)

W. Freitag: *Art Books: A Basic Bibliography of Monographs on Artists* (New York, 1985)

Bio-bibliographies

U. Thieme and F. Becker, eds: *Allgemeines Lexikon der bildenden Künstler von der Antike bis zur Gegenwart*, 37 vols (Leipzig, 1907–50)

H. Vollmer, ed.: *Allgemeines Lexikon der bildenden Künstler des XX. Jahrhunderts*, 6 vols (Leipzig, 1953–62)

G. Meissner, ed.: *Allgemeines Künstler-Lexikon: Die bildenden Künstler aller Zeiten und Völker* (Leipzig, 1983–)

Festschriften

P. Rave: *Kunstgeschichte in Festschriften* (Berlin, 1962)

O. Leistner: *International Bibliography of Festschriften* (Osnabruck, 1976)

Guide to Festschriften, New York, Pub. Lib., 2 vols (Boston, 1977)

B. Lincoln: *Festschriften in Art History, 1960–1975: Bibliography and Index* (New York, 1988) [suppl. to Rave, 1962]

Dissertations

Dissertation Abstracts International (1938–)

Deutsche Nationalbibliographie (1968–)

Inventaire des thèses de doctorat soutenues devant les universités françaises (1981–)

Special subject series

H. van de Waal: *Iconclass: An Iconographic Classification System*, 17 vols (Amsterdam, 1973–84)

D. Glass: *Italian Romanesque Sculpture: An Annotated Bibliography* (Boston, 1983)

D. Biebuyck: *The Arts of Central Africa: An Annotated Bibliography* (Boston, 1987)

Exhibition catalogues

A. Graves: *The Royal Academy of Arts*, 8 vols (London, 1905–6)

——: *A Century of Loan Exhibitions, 1813–1912*, 5 vols (London, 1913–15)

Worldwide Art Catalogue Bulletin (New York, 1963–)

D. Gordon: *Modern Art Exhibitions, 1900–1916*, 2 vols (Munich, 1974)

Art Exhibition Catalogs Subject Index: Collection of the Arts Library at Santa Barbara (New York, 1978–) [microfiche]

Collection of Exhibition Catalogs, Washington, DC, Smithsonian Inst., Archvs Amer. A. (Boston, 1979) [microfiche]

T. Reff: *Modern Art in Paris, 1855 to 1900*, 47 vols (New York, 1981)

J. Yarnall and W. Gerdts: *National Museum of American Art's Index to American Art Exhibition Catalogues*, 6 vols (Boston, 1986)

Art Exhibition Catalogues on Microfilm (New York, n.d.) [microfiche]

Artists' comments and manifestos

E. G. Holt: *Documentary History of Art*, 3 vols (Garden City, NJ, 1966)

W. E. Fredeman: *Pre-Raphaelitism: A Bibliocritical Study* (Cambridge, MA, 1968)

J. Spalek: *German Expressionism in the Fine Arts* (Los Angeles, 1977)

D. Ashton, ed.: *Twentieth-century Artists on Art* (New York, 1985)

Image collections

E. Thomson: *Index to Art Reproductions in Books* (Metuchen, NJ, 1974)

P. Havlice: *World Painting Index* (Metuchen, NJ, 1977)

Y. Korwin: *Index to Two-dimensional Art Works*, 2 vols (Metuchen, NJ, 1981)

P. Parry and K. Chipman: *Print Index* (Westport, CT, 1983)

Art Librarianship

Art Libraries Journal, ARLIS/UK (1976–)

P. Pacey: *Art Library Manual* (London, 1977)

Art Documentation, ARLIS/NA (1982–)

P. Pacey: *A Reader in Art Librarianship* (Munich, 1985)

LEE SORENSEN

Biccherna. A small painted panel, initially created as a cover for official documents of the civic government of Siena between the 13th and 17th centuries. The Italian word derives from the chief financial office of Siena, the Biccherna, a name that first appears at the beginning of the 13th century; it was supposedly inspired by the imperial treasury of the Blachernae Palace in Constantinople. The term has also been extended to designate painted covers and small panels connected with other Sienese civic offices and institutions, such as the tax office (Gabella), the hospital of S Maria della Scala, the Opera del Duomo and various lay confraternities. Most *biccherne*, however, are from the office of the Biccherna itself.

The officials of the Biccherna comprised a *camarlingo*, charged with expenditure on behalf of the Comune, and four *provveditori*, responsible for revenues and for approving disbursements. All officials were appointed for six-month terms, at the end of which the working accounts were transferred to parchment registers to be presented to the Consiglio Generale of Siena for inspection. Initially these were prepared as two distinct volumes: the *Entrata* of the *provveditori*, showing revenues received, and the *Uscita* of the *camarlingo* showing expenditures. For the official presentation to the council each volume received a painted wooden cover. During the 13th century the *Uscita* cover bore an image of the *camarlingo* at his task and the *Entrata* cover had the names and arms of the four *provveditori*. The earliest surviving *biccherna* dates from the second term of 1258 and depicts a certain Ugo, monk of the Cistercian abbey of San Galgano and *camarlingo* for that period. After the beginning of the 14th century the two volumes were united in a single parchment register and the imagery was combined, so that both the figure of the *camarlingo* and the names and arms of the *provveditori* were shown (e.g. *biccherna* for 1329; Berlin, Tiergarten, Kstgewmus.; see fig.). Such representations continued

Biccherna cover for the *Entrata/Uscita* register of July–December 1329, 385×245 mm (Berlin, Tiergarten, Kunstgewerbemuseum)

until the mid-15th century, but the subject-matter then became more varied including, for example, an *Allegory of the Plague* (1437; Berlin, Schloss Köpenick), attributed to Giovanni di Paolo, and the *Coronation of Pope Pius II* (1460; Siena, Pal. Piccolomini, Archv Stato) with a view of Siena, attributed to il Vecchietta. At the same time, as a result of damage done to the covers, the practice of attaching panels to the financial registers was replaced by the creation of small panels to hang on the walls of the Biccherna. Because dimensions no longer had to accord with the size of the registers, the *biccherne* grew in size. The last surviving example is dated 1682.

The *biccherne* are more valuable as historical than artistic documents: the arms of the *provveditori* provide information on the civic activities of Sienese families and, as the panels are dated, they form important documents for the history of palaeography. Those dating from the mid-15th century to the 17th also often include views of the city. Most examples of *biccherne* are in Siena (Pal. Piccolomini, Archv Stato).

Generally the artistic quality of the surviving *biccherne* is not high. There are panels attributed to Ambrogio Lorenzetti (1344), Bartolommeo Bulgarini (1329, 1353), Giovanni di Paolo (1436, 1437, 1440, 1445), the Master of the Osservanza (1441, 1444), Sano di Pietro (1451, 1457, 1471, 1473 and two undated panels), il Vecchietta (1460) and Domenico Beccafumi (1526, 1548), but these attributions are often optimistic. Duccio di Buoninsegna executed a series of lost covers for the office of the Biccherna itself (1279, 1285, 1287, 1291, 1292, 1294, 1295), as did Bartolommeo Bulgarini (1338, 1341, 1342). The surviving documents relating to payments for covers of the *Entrata* and/or the *Uscita* registers have not been completely published, but items in the *Uscita* representing payments for them normally either fail to name the artist or cite painters otherwise unknown. The *Uscita* volumes for 1280–1350 suggest that the earlier commissions at least were considered minor decorative projects and largely assigned to minor artists, a conclusion borne out by the retardataire style of the works themselves.

For further discussion and illustration *see* SIENA, §II and fig. 3.

BIBLIOGRAPHY
U. Morandi: *Le biccherne senesi* (Siena, 1964)
L. Borgia and others: *Le biccherne: Tavole dipinte delle magistrature senesi* (Rome, 1984)

H. B. J. MAGINNIS

Bicci di Lorenzo (*b* Florence, 1373; *d* Florence, 6 May 1452). Italian painter and architect, son of LORENZO DI BICCI. He continued the workshop founded by his father. Though not attracted to the artistic ideals and innovations of the Renaissance, he developed the productive capacities of the workshop by inaugurating a remarkable series of partnerships and collaborations with other painters.

1. Life and work. 2. Style and workshop.

1. LIFE AND WORK.

(i) To 1430. Bicci's first artistic work was naturally done in the paternal workshop. No doubt because of the similarity between the names of father and son, Vasari assigned works to Lorenzo that were actually painted by Bicci. Moreover, he attributed to Lorenzo a second son, NERI DI BICCI, whereas Neri was in fact the only son of Bicci.

Between 1385 and 1408 Bicci enrolled in the Arte dei Medici e Speziali (Doctors' and Apothecaries' Guild), to which painters in Florence were required to belong. Over a period of nearly 40 years he produced a huge number of paintings inscribed with the year of production or recorded in documents. In his first dated work, a triptych of the *Annunciation with Saints* (1414; Porciana, nr Stia in Casentino, S Maria Assunta), the style is still reminiscent of the late 14th century, that is, the style learnt in his father's workshop, but with more attention paid to Gothic lines and modulations. The readiness of Bicci's workshop to take on any work connected with painting is recorded in an archive note dated 1416, when Bicci gilded chandeliers and benches for the Florentine charitable organization of the Compagnia Maggiore di S Maria del Bigallo.

In 1417 Bicci married Benedetta d'Amato d'Andrea Amati, with whom he had three daughters, Andrea, Maddalena and Gemma. The son who was to carry on the activity of the workshop, Neri di Bicci, was born in 1418. In that year Bicci seems to have begun a fruitful period of activity for the hospital complex of S Maria Nuova, Florence, which also employed him as an architect. He provided the modelli for the construction of the church of S Egidio, included within the old hospital building. In 1420 he frescoed the façade of the church with the *Consecration of St Egidio* (*in situ*), a composition that has often been cited as echoing Masaccio's *Festival of the Carmine* (untraced). In 1420–21, for the same church, Bicci painted an altarpiece (untraced) commissioned by Bartolommeo di Stefano of Poggibonsi, known as Ghezzo.

Bicci's pupil Stefano d'Antonio Vanni (?1407–1483) collaborated with him in his fresco painting. Much of his production was in this medium. In the first decade of the 15th century he had probably worked alongside his father in the monumental frescoed tabernacle known as the *Madonnone*. He painted frescoes (1421–*c.* 1425) for Ilarione de' Bardi in the Florentine church of S Lucia de' Magnoli. Of these all that remain are small fragments, no longer clearly visible in the church.

A predella with scenes from the *Lives of the Saints* (Berlin, Gemäldegal.) is dated 1423, a significant year in the development of Bicci's style (see Paolucci). Influenced by Gentile da Fabriano, who was then in Florence painting the *Adoration of the Magi* (ex-Florence, Santa Trìnita; Florence, Uffizi) for Palla Strozzi, he introduced some strongly gothicizing elements, though Gentile's passages of shade and the richness of his materials and expression were very different from the precise backgrounds and bright colours of Bicci's painting. In 1423 Bicci also began the panel of the *Virgin and Child with Saints* (Empoli, Mus. S Andrea) for the church of the Collegiata, Empoli, commissioned by Simone da Spicchio. This work was finally paid for in 1426.

In 1424 Bicci was enrolled as a member of the Compagnia di S Luca. At the same time he continued to work in S Egidio, where he produced some statues of *Apostles* (untraced) and a terracotta relief of the *Coronation of the Virgin* (Florence, Arcisp. S Maria Nuo.; copy *in situ*). An altarpiece with the *Virgin and Child with Six Saints* for S Niccolò sopr'Arno, Florence (*in situ*), dates from 1425. In 1427 Bicci painted a fresco cycle (untraced) for Niccolò da Uzzano (1359–1431) in S Lucia de' Magnoli, Florence. Frescoes, documented in 1427, 1433 and 1441, for Santa Croce, Florence, are also untraced. From 1428 to 1432 he continued his fresco painting in S Marco, Florence, in collaboration with Stefano d'Antonio Vanni, with whom he had formed an official partnership in 1426. This relationship continued until 1434 with the addition of another painter, Buonaiuto di Giovanni.

During this period countless commissions were received by Bicci's active workshop. In 1429 he executed frescoes in the Camaldolese Monastery, Florence, and in the same year he produced the panel with *SS Cosmas and Damian*, commissioned by Antonio Dalla Casa for Florence Cathedral. The altarpiece with the *Virgin and Child Enthroned with Four Saints* (Siena, Pin. N.) for the church of Vertine near Gaiole in Chianti dates from 1430, the date at one time inscribed on the fresco depicting the *Virgin and Child with SS Leonard and George* in the lunette over the Porta S Giorgio in the city wall of Florence.

(ii) 1430 and after. The influence of Gentile da Fabriano's painting, first evident in Bicci's work around the mid-1420s, re-emerged, at least superficially, in the polyptych (1433; centre panels, Parma, G.N.; see fig. 1; side panels, Grottaferrata, Mus. Abbazia S Nilo, and New York, Met.) for the Benedictine convent of S Niccolò di Cafaggio (destr.), Florence. This was modelled almost slavishly on the Quaratesi polyptych (1425; dispersed), which Gentile painted for S Niccolò sopr'Arno, Florence. The frescoes with *Sacred Scenes* in the baptistery of S Martino a Gangalandi, near Lastra a Signa, are documented to 1433.

In 1434 in Santa Trìnita, Florence, Bicci worked with Stefano d'Antonio Vanni on the fresco decoration of the Compagni Chapel. The scenes of the *Slaying of the Brother* and the *Pardon of St John Gualberto* remain visible on the entrance arch; the altarpiece, also a product of the collaboration, is now in Westminster Abbey, London. Bicci's patrons thus also included some of the noble (or at least upper-class) families of Florence, as well as those from the surrounding countryside from whom he received a constant flow of commissions for altarpieces.

Bicci's son Neri has been credited with a role in the execution of the triptych showing the *Virgin and Child with SS Hippolytus, John the Baptist, James and Christopher* (1435; Bibbiena, SS Ippolito e Donato; see fig. 2). By the age of 20, Neri was managing the workshop alongside his father and his name began to appear in official documents next to that of Bicci. In this they repeated the procedure whereby Bicci had succeeded his father Lorenzo.

For the consecration (1435–6) of Florence Cathedral Bicci was appointed, together with Lippo di Buono, Rossello di Jacopo Franchi and Giovanni dal Ponte, to decorate the chapels of the tribune with frescoes depicting the *Apostles* (*in situ*). This was a prestigious commission for the city's most important church and was entrusted to a stylistically homogeneous group of painters. The figures were repainted between 1439 and 1440 by Bicci himself, because the haste of the original execution led to their deterioration. In 1437 he was again working at Santa

1. Bicci di Lorenzo: *Virgin and Child*, tempera on panel, 1710×817 mm, 1433 (Parma, Galleria Nazionale); central panel of an altarpiece for the Benedictine convent of S Niccolò di Cafaggio, Florence

Trìnita, painting the altarpiece for the Scali Chapel (untraced). This had first been commissioned from Giovanni dal Ponte, who had left the work unfinished. On 7 June 1438 Bicci was a witness, with his son Neri, in a dispute between a gold-beater called Bastiano di Giovanni and Domenico di Giovanni Lapi. In 1439–40 Bicci received payment for the *trompe-l'oeil* funerary monument to *Luigi Marsili* (1342–94) frescoed on the right wall of the cathedral, although Neri appears to have played a large part in the execution of this work.

Bicci updated his style only with regard to decorative or accessory elements, inserting passages in classicizing taste into a repertory that depended essentially on the Gothic tradition. It is hard to say to what extent these elements were borrowed from the new Renaissance language and to what extent they were inherited from the

2. Bicci di Lorenzo: triptych with the *Virgin and Child and SS Hippolytus, John the Baptist, James and Christopher*, 1435 (Bibbiena, SS Ippolito e Donato)

tradition of ornamental expression going back to Giotto. In 1441, with a commission from the church of S Egidio at the Ospedale di S Maria Nuova, Florence, the 68-year-old Bicci was working alongside some of the most advanced painters of the day, Domenico Veneziano and Andrea del Castagno. By that time, however, his art had crystallized immutably and no great stimulus resulted to modify the compositional schemes that he repeated in so many works. His figures with their motionless features and his decorative repertory were favoured by many classes of patrons. This gave him a central role in the production of Florentine art and put him at the head of a workshop that employed many painters, albeit most were of modest standing.

From this point on, biographical information on Bicci becomes more scarce. In 1442 it was Neri who drew up the *catasto* (land registry declaration) in his father's name. There Bicci's age is given as 67; however, such inconsistencies are not rare in these declarations of income made by Florentine citizens to the government of the Republic. The workshop was evidently still operating in S Maria Nuova (works untraced), and receiving payments in 1443–6 and 1447. The altarpiece depicting *St Nicholas of Tolentino Protecting Empoli from the Plague* (Empoli, Mus. S Andrea) for the Augustinian church of S Stefano, Empoli, was completed on 5 October 1445.

Despite his age Bicci continued to receive commissions for important works: in Arezzo the Bacci family appointed him to fresco the main chapel of S Francesco, and he worked in the town sporadically from 1445 to 1447, when he was forced to leave Arezzo either because of an epidemic or because his own health was poor. In the angels of the triumphal arch, scholars have detected the less refined, more archaic style of Neri, who by that time seems to have been definitely in charge of the workshop. Yet another project, the fresco decoration of the Lenzi Chapel in the church of the Ognissanti, Florence, was commissioned by Bartolommeo Lenzi and begun by Bicci in 1446. It was completed in 1451 by Neri and other workshop collaborators.

In the *catasto* of 1446–7 Neri di Bicci, in his father's name, gave the address of the workshop as Via S Salvadore, in the district of Santo Spirito, declaring that it was bought from the abbot of the Camaldolese Monastery. Bicci's last *catasto* of 13 August 1451, drawn up as usual by Neri, gives his age as 82, and that of his son as 31. Bicci, perhaps the most prolific and long-lived painter of the early 15th century, died the following year and was buried in S Maria del Carmine. It was not, however, the end of the workshop: this had been solidly managed, perhaps since the mid-1440s, by his son Neri, who expanded both its operative capacity and its range of activities.

Almost all of Bicci's most important works are documented. There are many others without documentation, including the frescoed tabernacle from Ponte a Greve, a suburb of Florence, depicting the *Virgin and Child* (Florence, Sopr. B.A. & Storici Col.); the altarpiece depicting the *Nativity* in the building known from 1551 as S Giovannino de' Cavalieri, Florence; the *Coronation of the Virgin* (ex-oratory of S Apollinare, Florence; Florence, Santa Trinita); the polyptych of the *Virgin and Child with Saints* in S Maria Cetica in the Pratomagno; a *Virgin and Child with St Catherine of Alexandria and Other Saints* frescoed in a private house, the Casa Bandinelli Gradi, Cerbaia, near San Casciano Val di Pesa; and the tabernacle with the *Virgin and Child Enthroned with Saints* at the Canto alla Cuculia in the district of Santo Spirito, Florence, near the church of S Maria del Carmine. All these works were painted after 1440.

2. STYLE AND WORKSHOP. Bicci's work retained coherence during his more than 40 years of documented activity. Indeed it became so distinctive, with the figures posed like cutouts against the gold backgrounds of the panels, and the thrones, tabernacles and chairs supported by little twisted columns decorated with rigid carved patterns or those inspired by Cosmati work, that the term Biccism is sometimes used in connection with the spread of his style (Frosinini). The extraordinary activity of Bicci's workshop required a large number of collaborators, with some of whom the master would on occasion go into partnership, as he did with Stefano d'Antonio Vanni and Buonaiuto di Giovanni. Other painters in the workshop were, from the 1420s, Masaccio's brother, Scheggia, Antonio di Maso, Marco da Montepulciano (with whom, according to Vasari, Bicci worked in Arezzo in S Bernardo) and Giovanni di Cristofano. During the 1440s he collaborated with Buono di Marco and Antonio di Lorenzo (*fl* 1391–*c*. 1440/50). The painter known as the Maestro di Signa left, in the church in Signa, frescoes whose formal characteristics are very close to those of Bicci. This anonymous artist worked in the town until the 1460s, and also painted numerous murals in both town and country

churches. The tabernacle of the Canto alla Cuculia has also been assigned to him.

Although Bicci came into contact with the most important painters of the early 15th century, the figurative spirit of the Renaissance did not attract him even superficially, as it would later attract his son Neri. Nevertheless, his paintings were in great demand until the mid-century and not only in the countryside where outdated taste might be expected to linger on, but also in the city of Florence itself. Traditionalism, it would seem, was quite persistent, and Bicci its perfect, if unwitting, representative.

BIBLIOGRAPHY

Bolaffi; Colnaghi; *DBI*

G. Vasari: *Vite* (1550, rev. 2/1568); ed. G. Milanesi (1878–85), ii, pp. 49–60

O. Sirén: 'Di alcuni pittori fiorentini che subirono l'influenza di Lorenzo Monaco: Bicci di Lorenzo', *L'Arte*, vii (1904), pp. 345–8

G. Poggi: 'Gentile da Fabriano e Bicci di Lorenzo', *Riv. A.*, v (1907), pp. 86–8

R. Van Marle: *Italian Schools* (1923–38)

F. Zeri: 'Una precisazione su Bicci di Lorenzo', *Paragone*, 105 (1958), pp. 67–71

R. Caterina Proto Pisani: 'Tre casi d'intervento nel territorio toscano', *Boll. A.*, lxxii/6 (1984), pp. 3–6

C. Frosinini: 'Un contributo alla conoscenza della pittura tardogotica fiorentina: Bonaiuto di Giovanni', *Riv. A.*, xxxvii/4 (1984), pp. 107–31

——: 'Il trittico Compagni', *Scritti di storia dell'arte in onore di Roberto Salvini* (Florence, 1984), pp. 227–31

A. Padoa Rizzo and C. Frosinini: 'Stefano d'Antonio Vanni "dipintore" (1405–1483): Opere e documenti', *Ant. Viva*, xxiii/4–5 (1984), pp. 5–33

U. Procacci: 'Lettera a Roberto Salvini con vecchi ricordi e con alcune notizie su Lippo d'Andrea modesto pittore del primo quattrocento', *Scritti di storia dell'arte in onore di Roberto Salvini* (Florence, 1984), pp. 213–26

A. Paolucci: *Il Museo della Collegiata di S Andrea in Empoli* (Florence, 1985), pp. 62–3

C. Frosinini: 'Il passaggio di gestione in una bottega pittorica fiorentina del primo rinascimento: Lorenzo di Bicci e Bicci di Lorenzo', *Ant. Viva*, xxv/1 (1986), pp. 5–15

——: 'Il passaggio di gestione in una bottega fiorentina del primo '400: Bicci di Lorenzo e Neri di Bicci', *Ant. Viva*, xxvi/1 (1987), pp. 5–14

B. Santi: 'Pittura minore in S Trinita: Da Bicci di Lorenzo a Neri di Bicci', *La chiesa di S Trinita* (Florence, 1987), pp. 132–42

C. Frosinini: 'A proposito del "San Lorenzo" di Bicci di Lorenzo alla Galleria dell'Accademia', *Ant. Viva*, xxix/1 (1990), pp. 5–7

BRUNO SANTI

Bîchâpour. *See* BISHAPUR.

Bichitr [Vicitra] (*fl c.* 1615–50). Indian miniature painter. Bichitr's career spanned the reigns of the Mughal emperors Jahangir (*reg* 1605–27) and Shah Jahan (*reg* 1628–58). What are apparently his earliest works show the same accomplished technique and surface brilliance that characterize those from the end of his career. Only three examples have inscribed dates: two paintings of 1631 (see below) and a drawing of 1645 (untraced). His remaining works are dated by external evidence, usually the estimated age of the personages depicted or the probable chronological limits of a historical event.

In *Jahangir Preferring a Sufi Shaykh to Kings* (*c.* 1615–20; Washington, DC, Freer, 42.15; *see* INDIAN SUBCONTINENT, fig. 267) Bichitr apparently depicted himself immediately below the two kings whom the Emperor is spurning. The unparalleled prominence of this self-portrait led Ettinghausen (1961) to propose a royal Hindu identity for the figure, but the act of tendering a painting is now recognized as a convention reserved for artists (*see* INDIAN

SUBCONTINENT, §VI, 4(i)(c) for an alternative view). The remarkable rendering of the Emperor's diaphanous garments, the exquisitely tooled goldwork, the highlights on jewels and the hour-glass throne, and the crisp edges of every form are hallmarks of the artist's style. This precision of detail continued throughout all of Bichitr's work, but other features changed subtly over time. The limited tonal modelling of the bolster and the foreign kings' clothing was soon abandoned in favour of still purer colours and flatter surfaces; conversely, the meticulous delineation of hair in orderly rows ultimately yielded to a more granular treatment of hair and beards in later works.

The chronology of Bichitr's work is anchored by two paintings dated to 1631: a portrait of *Shah Jahan* (London, V&A) and *Akbar Transferring the Timurid Crown to Shah Jahan* (Dublin, Chester Beatty Lib., MS. 7, fol. 19), which is dated to year 3 of Shah Jahan's reign (1630–31) by a faint inscription on the footstool of the Emperor's throne. The formality of this latter image of dynastic succession is enhanced by the stiff poses of the impassive emperors and their chief ministers as well as by the unrelenting clarity of detail in the dais, carpet, jewel-encrusted thrones, and canopies. Bichitr seldom returned to this dry, hieratic landscape for his portraits, preferring instead to use a dark, abstract background or a bluish backdrop filled with rows of sketchy retainers, as in *Shah Jahan in Majesty* (*c.* 1630; Dublin, Chester Beatty Lib., MS. 7, fol. 16). Such backgrounds invite the viewer to dwell on the precise contours of the figure and the richly burnished surfaces of his embellishment. The Emperor's bright orange *jāma* ('robe') not only removes him from the surrounding ethereal world, but also serves as a foil for strands of wondrously tangible gems gleaming with light.

Bichitr's extreme formal elegance discourages the perception of personality in many of his portraits, a feature considered by some scholars to indicate a lack of empathy and lauded by others as admirable restraint. Bichitr's work seems to embody a much less modern conception of a portrait, one that seeks not to reveal an individual's common humanity by suggesting an ephemeral physical or mental state, but to define his enduring social identity by means of an immutable countenance and real or symbolic attributes. His predilection for taut linear forms and polished surfaces was particularly well-suited to imperial subjects, whose inherent aloofness is underscored by an ostentatious display of material wealth.

See also INDIAN SUBCONTINENT, §V, 4(i)(c) and (d).

BIBLIOGRAPHY

P. Brown: *Indian Painting under the Mughals* (Oxford, 1924)

T. W. Arnold and J. V. S. Wilkinson: *The Library of A. Chester Beatty: A Catalogue of the Indian Miniatures*, 3 vols (London, 1936)

R. Ettinghausen: 'The Emperor's Choice', *De artibus opuscula, xl: Essays in Honor of Erwin Panofsky*, ed. M. Meiss (New York, 1961), pp. 98–120

S. C. Welch: *Imperial Mughal Painting* (New York, 1978)

The Grand Mogul: Imperial Painting in India, 1600–1660 (exh. cat. by M. C. Beach; Williamstown, MA, Clark A. Inst.; Baltimore, MD, Walters A.G.; Boston, MA, Mus. F.A.; New York, Asia House Gals; 1978–9)

The Indian Heritage (exh. cat. by R. Skelton and others; London, V&A, 1982)

S. C. Welch and others: *The Emperors' Album* (New York, 1987)

JOHN SEYLLER

Bichvinta, 10th-century church; restored 1860s

Bichvinta [anc. Gr. Pitsunda; Lat. Pitiunt]. Town on the Black Sea coast, *c.* 400 km north-west of Tbilisi, in the republic of Georgia. The name, in use by the early 4th century AD, derives from *pichvi* (Georg.: 'pine tree'). Excavations begun in 1952 have shown that the site was settled between the late 2nd millennium BC and the early 1st BC. By the 2nd century BC a Hellenistic city had been established, and from the 2nd century AD it served as a Roman fortress, remains of which include residential, religious and commercial buildings within the stone wall, together with a water-supply system. It was a bishopric by AD 325, and remained under Byzantine control until the 780s when the west Georgian kingdom of Abkhazeti was created; the Catholicos-patriarch of Abkhazeti continued to reside there even after the decline of the united Georgian State in the 15th century. Bichvinta was under Turkish rule in the 17th–18th centuries, and became part of Russia in the early 19th century.

Among the richest archaeological finds are the remains of a 5th-century AD three-aisled basilica that replaced a 4th-century church on the outskirts of the settlement. Parts of the 5th-century mosaics were uncovered in the chancel and baptistery, showing a fountain of life, figures of animals and birds, geometric designs and a cross motif. The flattened forms, motionless figures and tendency to arrange motifs in decorative patterns recall mosaics in Syria and Palestine, but they were executed by local craftsmen. Near the seashore the remains of a double-apsed church (6th century) have been excavated.

A 10th-century church (see fig.), heavily restored in the 1860s, stands in the centre of a fortified enclosure outside the town. It has a two-storey cross-in-square plan (42.3×22 m) with a dome resting on a low drum and two piers, three apses and a western narthex; its walls are built of alternating rows of stone and brick. Only fragments of the 16th-century frescoes survive, as the interior surfaces were largely painted over and whitewashed in the 19th century. The ruins of three small churches (8th–9th century) and other utilitarian buildings lie near by.

BIBLIOGRAPHY
A. Apakidze, ed.: *Didi Pitiunti: Arkeologiuri gatkhrebi Bichvintashi* [Great Pitiunt: archaeological excavations in Bichvinta], i (Tbilisi, 1975)
V. Beridze and others: *The Treasures of Georgia* (London, 1984)
V. BERIDZE

Bickham, George, the elder (*b* London, *c.* 1684; *d* London, 4 May 1758). English engraver. A son of John Bickham the elder, he was taught writing and copperplate engraving by John Sturt (1658–1730). He engraved many frontispieces and portraits of contemporary worthies, such as *Sir Isaac Newton* or the poet *Stephen Duck*, but he made his name as the finest engraver of writing copybooks of his day. At least 18 titles are known, most of them made up solely of engravings after examples of Bickham's own calligraphy.

Bickham advertised that he boarded and taught youths writing, drawing, engraving and accounts. In the early 18th century these subjects were still relatively interdependent, and it was not at all unusual to find a writing master capable of intricate Baroque penwork flourishes or a mathematician (who could more easily understand the rules of perspective) offering lessons in drawing. Thomas Weston (*d* 1728), Assistant Astronomer Royal and Master of the Academy at Greenwich, employed Bickham to engrave and provide examples for his *Writing, Drawing and Mathematics* copybook in the 1720s.

On 23 November 1723 a notice in the *London Gazette* announced that Bickham had been imprisoned as an insolvent debtor; nevertheless, by the end of the decade he managed to publish *The Drawing and Writing Tutor: or an Alluring Introduction to the Study of Those Sister Arts*. The book contains a unique combination of calligraphic examples in the centre of each of its 12 plates, surrounded by drawings for copying, presented in the usual progression from parts of the face to nude and finally clothed figures. Later reissues by his son George Bickham the younger (*d* 1771) and other print-sellers include additional plates, but none contains Bickham's unique combination of writing and drawing, which had underlined the interdependence of these two skills.

In 1733 Bickham began his most important contribution to calligraphic engraving with the first of 52 issues of *The Universal Penman*, a folio series completed in 1741. He was aided in this massive undertaking by George Bickham the younger, who assisted with the embellishments (the introduction states that these are included to assist students of drawing), as did John Bickham the younger (*fl* 1730–50), either a brother or son of Bickham himself.

One of Bickham's most interesting contributions was in colour printing. A large portion of the 81 folio-sized plates he issued in *The Museum of the Arts: or the Curious Repository* (*c.* 1745) consists of line-engravings with superimposed counterproofs of colour line-engravings, a method he appears to have devised to make new use of surplus prints from his calligraphic books (see 1980 exh. cat., pp. 8–9). He superimposed blue, green, red and yellow impressions of engravings after Old Masters, flowers, animals, birds and so forth, in reverse over the top of old plates bearing examples of penmanship.

WRITINGS

The Drawing and Writing Tutor: Or an alluring Introduction to the Study of Those Sister Arts (London, [*c.* 1730], later edn *c.* 1750 with add. pls by G. Bickham the younger and others)
The Universal Penman, 52 issues (London, 1733–41)
The Museum of the Arts: or the Curious Repository (London, [*c.* 1745])

BIBLIOGRAPHY
A. Heal: *English Writing Masters and their Copy-books, 1570–1800* (Cambridge, 1931)
Colour Printing in Britain (exh. cat. by J. Friedman, New Haven, CT, Yale Cent. Brit. A., 1980)
M. Snodin: 'George Bickham Junior', *V & A Mus. Album*, ii (London, 1983), pp. 354–60

KIM SLOAN

Bicknell, Elhanan (*b* Southwark, London, 21 Dec 1788; *d* Herne Hill, London, 27 Nov 1861). English merchant, patron and collector. His successful business as a merchant of refined sperm whale oil enabled him to collect works by painters and sculptors of the modern British school, either commissioning works from them or buying directly from the studio. He did not 'give a damn' for the work of Old Masters, as his taste was primarily for landscape paintings. His collection was displayed at his house at Herne Hill, London, where he entertained most of the leading artists of his day. His closest friend was David Roberts, whose daughter Christine married Bicknell's son. J. M. W. Turner and John Ruskin were also frequent visitors. Bicknell's collection was dispersed at auction at Christie's from 25 April to 1 May 1863 and from 7 to 8 May. There were landscapes by Roberts, Clarkson Stanfield, Augustus Wall Callcott and Edwin Landseer as well as ten oils and eighteen watercolours by Turner, including *Palestrina* (exh. RA 1830; London, Tate) and *Blue Riga: Lake of Lucerne—Sunrise* (1842; priv. col., see Bicknell and Guiterman, p. 37). A portrait of Bicknell (*c.* 1830) by T. Phillips is in the Vintners Hall, London.

DNB   BIBLIOGRAPHY
G. F. Waagen: *Treasures of Art in Great Britain*, ii (London, 1854), pp. 349–54
W. Roberts: *Memorials of Christie's: A Record of Art Sales from 1766 to 1896*, i (London, 1897), pp. 198–207
A. S. Bicknell: *Five Pedigrees* (London, 1912)
P. Bicknell and H. Guiterman: 'The Turner Collector: Elhanan Bicknell', *Turner Stud.*, vii/1 (1987), pp. 34–44

PETER BICKNELL

Bidar [Bīdar]. City in Karnataka, India. Once the capital of the Bahmani and Barid Shahi dynasties, it flourished in the 15th and 16th centuries. Bidar displaced GULBARGA as the capital of the BAHMANI dynasty when Shihab al-Din Ahmad (*reg* 1422–36) shifted his headquarters there shortly after acceding to the throne. Under this ruler, royal palaces were laid out and the fort was strengthened. Bidar's outstanding personality and most notable builder in the second half of the 15th century was Mahmud Gawan, minister of Shams al-Din Muhammad III (*reg* 1463–82). After Mahmud Gawan's murder in 1481, the Bahmani kingdom disintegrated rapidly. A former slave of Turkish origin, Qasim Barid, declared himself chief minister; his son, Amir Barid (*reg* 1527–43), after raising a succession of puppet rulers to the throne, established the BARID SHAHI dynasty. Under Amir Barid, Bidar once again experienced prosperity, and the fort was renovated. In 1619 Bidar and its territory fell to the 'ADIL SHAHI dynasty.

It was captured by forces of the MUGHAL dynasty in 1656, and in 1724 it was annexed by the Asaf Jahis of Hyderabad.

Bidar is built at the head of a promontory that rises gradually to the north. The fort and town are both roughly circular and of almost equal area, each contained within a complete circuit of fortifications. The crenellated walls of the fort are set within a triple moat, partly hewn out of laterite, on the south and west. Many of the defences were rebuilt in the 15th century on the orders of Mahmud Gawan; other improvements, including the mounting of large cannons, are of the Baridi period. The walled perimeter of the fort has numerous bastions, mostly polygonal. There are seven gates, three linking the fort to the town; the Sharza Darvaza has tigers sculpted in the spandrels above the pointed-arched entrance; the Gumbad Darvaza has sloping walls and is surmounted by a dome.

Inside the fort stands the Solahkhamba Masjid, the earliest Muslim building at Bidar. The long prayer-hall is severely plain, with massive circular columns. The mosque overlooks a long garden with a central water channel. At the south end of the garden are the private apartments of the harem, including the Tarkash Mahal and Rangin Mahal, the latter with carved woodwork and mother-of-pearl inlays; both were substantially rebuilt during the Barid Shahi period. At the north end is a hammam, or bathhouse. Two great royal complexes to the west have spacious internal courts surrounded by high walls. The Diwan-i 'Am ('hall of public audience') has a reception hall on the south side of the court, but only the stone column bases, presumably for timber columns, are preserved. The surrounding chambers are decorated with panels of polychrome tilework in intricate arabesque and geometric patterns. The Takht Mahal has a formal throne room entered through a lofty portal with traces of tiger and sun emblems in tilework.

The monuments of the town face two main streets running at right angles to each other; at the intersection stands the Chaubara, a massive tower (h. 39.6 m) built as an observation post. The Takht-i Kirmani (*c.* 1430) is a celebrated shrine with an entrance façade decorated with intricate plasterwork. The Madrasa of Mahmud Gawan (1472–3; *see* INDIAN SUBCONTINENT, fig. 95) is the most perfect example in India of a Persian theological college. Student rooms are arranged symmetrically between four arched portals that face inwards to a spacious court. High minarets, one now fallen, flanked a façade enlivened with brilliantly coloured tilework in the Timurid style. The Jami' Masjid is a plain but elegant structure dating from the 15th century.

The Bahmani royal necropolis is situated at Ashtur, 2.5 km north-east of the city, with the tombs arranged in a long line. The earliest mausoleums, those of Shihab al-Din Ahmad and 'Ala al-Din Ahmad (*reg* 1436–58), are also the largest; their imposing square, domed chambers have arched recesses on their outer walls, ornamented in places with tilework. The tomb of the Sufi saint *Khalil'ullah Kirmani* (*d* 1460), known as the Chaukhandi, has an unusual octagonal curtain wall with arched recesses on two levels; a small domed chamber stands freely inside the court. The calligraphy of the verses of the Koran inscribed on the basalt lintel over the entrance is of exceptional quality. The tombs of the Baridi rulers are west of the city. The group is dominated by the tomb of *'Ali Barid* (*reg* 1543–80). Its lofty domed chamber, open on four sides, is situated in the middle of a formal garden.

Bidar has given its name to the inlaid damascened metalwork known as bidri ware (*see* INDIAN SUBCONTINENT, §VII, 15(v)).

See also INDIAN SUBCONTINENT, §III, 6(ii)(f) and 7(ii)(a).

BIBLIOGRAPHY
Enc. Islam/2: 'Bahmanīs: Monuments, Bīdar', 'Barīd Shāhīs: Monuments', 'Bīdar'
G. Yazdani: *Bidar: Its History and Monuments* (Oxford, 1947)
H. K. Sherwani and J. Burton-Page: 'Bīdar', *Enc. Islam/2* (Leiden, 1954–)
Z. A. Desai: 'Architecture—The Bahmanis' and 'Architecture—Bahmani Succession States', *History of Medieval Deccan (1295–1724)*, ed. H. K. Sherwani and P. M. Joshi, ii (Hyderabad, 1974), pp. 227–304
G. Michell: 'Bidar', *Islamic Heritage of the Deccan*, ed. G. Michell (Bombay, 1986), pp. 42–57
GEORGE MICHELL

Bidau, Nicolas (*b* ?Reims, 1622; *d* Lyon, 17 Nov 1692). French medallist and sculptor. He was working in Lyon by 1657, when he produced a medallion of *Archbishop Camille de Neuville de Villeroi*. Further medallions worked in wax and cast in wax or lead, in the manner of Jean Warin, show members of the Consulat of Lyon and some members of their families and date from 1658–65 (e.g. Paris, Bib. N.; Lyon, Mus. B.-A.). Bidau also carved stone sculptures for buildings in Lyon, including a *Virgin* (before 1658), *David and Goliath* (1660), an *Annunciation* (1665) and *St Catherine* (1678). His relief for the Hôtel de Ville celebrating the Peace of the Pyrenees (1660–61; *in situ*) was made in collaboration with the local sculptor Jacques Mimerel (*fl* 1649–70); in addition Bidau provided the model for a fountain (1661) in the Place des Terreaux.

In 1671 Bidau joined the team of sculptors working for Louis XIV at Versailles, returning to Lyon next year as Sculpteur du Roi. He then began intensive production of religious sculptures in Lyon. He decorated the apse and the high altar of the abbey of St Pierre with a relief of *St Peter Imprisoned* (1675–7; destr.). In 1678 he provided reliefs of the *Visitation* and the *Burial of the Virgin* (both Lyon, Mus. B.-A.) for the church of the Pénitents du Gonfalon, and in 1681 he was commissioned by Nicolas de Villeroi, brother of the archbishop and governor of Lyon (1642), Marshal of France (1646) and Duke of Villeroi (1651), to execute statues of *St Elijah, St Elisha* and *St Teresa* (all untraced) for the high altar of the Carmelite convent, as well as a *Virgin of Pity* for the portal. Bidau also provided allegories in polished stucco for the great staircase of the abbey of St Pierre (1681–2; Lyon, Mus. B.-A.). These were based on designs by the painter Thomas Blanchet, as was Bidau's most ambitious tomb, that of *Nicolas de Villeroi* (1685–7; destr.), which included marble figures of the deceased flanked by Prudence and Religion. Bidau, employed in the productive milieu of Lyon, is a good example of a sculptor working in the grand style of Versailles.

Lami
BIBLIOGRAPHY
N. Rondot: *Nicolas Bidau, sculpteur et médailleur* (Lyon, 1887)
M. Audin and E. Vial: *Dictionnaire des artistes et ouvriers d'art du Lyonnais* (Paris, 1918), pp. 85–6
J. Tricou: *Médailles lyonnaises du XVe au XVIIIe siècle* (Paris, 1958)
GENEVIÈVE BRESC-BAUTIER

Bidauld, Jean-Joseph-Xavier (*b* Carpentras, 10 April 1758; *d* Montmorency, 20 Oct 1846). French painter. He was apprenticed in Lyon for six years with his brother Jean-Pierre-Xavier Bidauld (1745–1813), a landscape and still-life painter. Subsequently, they left Lyon to travel together in Switzerland and Provence. In 1783 he moved to Paris, where he met Joseph Vernet (from whom he received valuable advice), Joseph-Siffred Duplessis and Jean-Honoré Fragonard. In 1785 he went to Rome with the assistance of Cardinal de Bernis and his patron, the dealer and perfumer Dulac. He stayed there for five years, travelling through Tuscany, Umbria and Campania and painting such works as *Roman Landscape* (1788; Basle, Kstmus.). Bidauld was closely involved with the circle of French Neo-classical painters in Rome in the 1780s. He was friendly with Louis Gauffier, Nicolas-Antoine Taunay and especially with Guillaume Lethière, who became his brother-in-law and with whom he occasionally collaborated. On his return to Paris in 1790 he travelled extensively in France, visiting Brittany, the Dauphiné and in particular Montmorency, where he stayed in the Mont-Louis house that had been the home of Jean-Jacques Rousseau.

Bidauld was, with Pierre-Henri de Valenciennes, among the best of the few exponents of Neo-classical landscape painting (*see* LANDSCAPE PAINTING, fig. 9). During his travels in Italy he developed his own distinctive style, working up in his studio studies made directly from nature into numerous landscapes, which sometimes included diminutive figures added by artists such as Lethière, Carle Vernet, François Gérard and Louis-Léopold Boilly. Bidauld's *Landscape with Waterfall* (1800; Compiègne, Château) epitomizes Neo-classical historical landscape painting, the genre for which he became famous: the composition is strict and rigorously ordered and the bucolic subject served merely as a pretext for the vast landscape setting, which is treated with precise brushwork and clear lighting. During the same period he received a commission for four landscapes for the Casita del Labrador, an annexe of the palace of Aranjuez in Spain. Between 1804 and 1812 many commissions for landscapes and Troubadour subjects from the French imperial family and the aristocracy followed. Under Louis XVIII he continued to enjoy official patronage and was commissioned to paint two large works on subjects from French history for the Galerie de Diane in the château of Fontainebleau, the *Departure of the Chevalier Bayard from Brescia* (1821; Valence, Mus. B.-A. & Hist. Nat.) and *View of the Plain of Ivry*, commemorating Henry IV (1822; Toulouse, Pal. Maréchal Niel).

Bidauld exhibited regularly in the Paris Salon between 1791 and 1844, winning a gold medal in 1812. He was the first landscape painter to be admitted to the Académie des Beaux-Arts, in 1823. His most important pupil was Edouard-François Bertin.

BIBLIOGRAPHY
Jean-Joseph-Xavier Bidauld (1758–1846): Peintures et dessins (exh. cat. by S. Gutwirth, Carpentras, Mus. Duplessis, 1978)
A. DAGUERRE DE HUREAUX

Biddulph Grange. English garden in Staffordshire. It was laid out from 1849 by its owner, James Bateman (1811–97), in collaboration with the painter Edward

William Cooke and the sculptor Waterhouse Hawkins (*fl* 1830s–1850s). Bateman, a noted amateur orchid-grower, purchased a farmhouse on Biddulph Moor in 1842 and began his major landscaping work there about seven years later. An Italianate parterre was laid out immediately in front of the house, but beyond this terrace the grounds were subdivided into a network of irregular compartments, each devoted to a different architectural style or manner of planting, the whole bounded by a walk planted as a pinetum. These compartments were to provide 'a suitable home for nearly all the hardy members of the great plant family', according to the garden designer Edward Kemp, thus necessitating 'the production of an unusual number of separate and independent areas, each of which has a character of its own'. The two most important compartments were an Egyptian garden, having stone sphinxes and high walls of shaped yew hedging, and 'China', a garden planted with Chinese plants and ornamented with chinoiserie garden buildings designed by Cooke and sculptures by Hawkins. These disparate areas at Biddulph Grange were screened from one another by a variety of rockworks, walls, tunnels and mounds, so planted (noted Kemp) as to seem from the house 'an irregular wavy sea of shrubs and trees in which there is nothing incongruous'.

In the 1850s and 1860s Biddulph Grange was successfully promoted as a model for the reconciliation of unity and variety in garden design, and its compartmental principle became influential, although Bateman himself sold the estate in 1871 and moved away. After a period of dereliction in the mid-20th century it was acquired by the National Trust in 1986.

BIBLIOGRAPHY
E. Kemp: *Description of the Gardens at Biddulph Grange* (London, 1862) [ser. of articles in the period. *Gardeners' Chronicle*]
M. Hadfield: *A History of British Gardening* (London, 1960, 2/1985), pp. 351–5
B. Elliott: *Victorian Gardens* (London, 1986), pp. 102–6, 121–3
P. Hayden: *Biddulph Grange: A Victorian Garden Rediscovered* (London, 1989)

BRENT ELLIOTT

Bidermanas, Izis (Israel). *See* IZIS.

Bidjogo. *See* BIJOGO.

Bidlake, William Henry (*b* Wolverhampton, 12 May 1861; *d* Wadhurst, E. Sussex, 6 April 1938). English architect. He was the son of a Midlands architect, George Bidlake (1830–92). After some experience in his father's office, he worked as assistant to Robert Edis, Bodley & Garner and Rowand Anderson. He began working in Birmingham *c.* 1888; most of his work, which consists mainly of churches and houses, was done in and around that city. He designed and built nine churches, all but one of which belong to the late phase of the Gothic Revival: they are late Perpendicular in inspiration and inventive in detail. Each has the nave and chancel united in a single airy space. The finest is St Agatha's (1898–1901), Sparkbrook, Birmingham.

Bidlake's skill as a domestic architect is seen in the middle-class houses he designed on leafy suburban sites. His own home, Woodgate (1897), 37 Hartopp Road, Four Oaks, Sutton Coldfield, and Garth House (1900–01), Edgbaston Park Road, Birmingham, are good examples.

Composed with careful but relaxed asymmetry and built of good materials, they recall earlier English vernacular building. They show how the English Domestic Revival of the late 19th century was intensified by the Arts and Crafts Movement. Bidlake was personally involved in the movement which flourished in Birmingham at the turn of the century. He also played an important part in the development of architectural education in Birmingham. His practice diminished after World War I, and he retired to Sussex.

BIBLIOGRAPHY
S. Webster: 'W. H. Bidlake, 1862–1938', *Archit. W. Midlands*, xxvi (1976), pp. 17–25
A. Crawford, ed.: *By Hammer and Hand: The Arts and Crafts Movement in Birmingham* (Birmingham, 1984)

ALAN CRAWFORD

Biduino [Biduinus] (*fl c.* 1173–94). Italian sculptor. He was possibly from Bidogno in Val, near Lugano. The lintel above the central portal of S Cassiano a Settimo, near Cascina, representing *Christ Healing the Two Blind Men of Jericho*, the *Raising of Lazarus* and the *Entry into Jerusalem*, bears the date 1180 and the inscription 'Hoc opus quod cernis Biduinus docte peregit'. Indeed, Biduino is considered responsible for the entire architecture and decoration of the church. The only documented reference to Biduino records him in Lucca on 27 November 1181, and one signed (but undated) work survives there: a lintel with a *Miracle of St Nicholas* at the Chiesa della Misericordia (formerly S Salvatore). Another lintel in the same church, illustrating the same saint's life, is also attributed to him. Other signed works include a lintel with *St Michael* and the *Entry into Jerusalem* (Lucca, Col. Mazzarosa) from the nearby S Angelo in Campo (destr.) and a strigillated tomb (Pisa, Camposanto), imitating Roman sarcophagi, with reliefs of *Lions Devouring Stags*.

The autograph works allow the attribution to Biduino of other carvings with differently spelt or less legible signatures, for example a well with animal reliefs in the church of Sorbano del Vescovo at Capannori, near Lucca, and a pulpit with scenes from the *Infancy of Christ* (1194; S Michele in Groppoli, nr Pistoia). Important attributions on stylistic grounds include several friezes with animal motifs and the capitals of the lowest storey (*c.* 1173–4) of the campanile of Pisa Cathedral (e.g. monkey capital, Berlin, Schloss Kleinglienicke, Klosterhof). Also attributed to him is the main portal (New York, Cloisters) from S Leonardo al Frigido, near Massa. Biduino's name has been proposed for numerous other works, such as the lintel of the portal of S Micheletto, Lucca; the lintel of the main portal of S Maria at Diecimo, near Borgo a Mozzano; the tombstone of the parish priest Lieto in SS Jacopo e Maria Assunta at Lammari, near Lucca; and the façade decoration of the parish church in Pieve San Paolo, near Lucca. Together with his workshop, Biduino appears to have been one of the most prolific artists active in western Tuscany in the late 12th century. His characteristic style, exploiting strong contrasts of light and shade, recalls the works of such sculptors active during the period of his training as Guglielmo and Robertus.

BIBLIOGRAPHY
A. Bertolani: 'Un'opera ritrovata di Biduino?', *Prov. Lucca* (1965), pp. 87–9

F. Kobler: 'Das Affenkapitell in Berlin-Glienike', *Munuscula discipulorum: Kunsthistorische Studien Hans Kaufmann zum 70sten Geburtstag* (Berlin, 1968)
F. Redi: *La pieve di San Michele in Groppoli* (Pistoia, 1976)
G. Dalli Regoli: *Dai maestri senza nome all'impresa dei Guidi* (Lucca, 1986)
G. De Angelis d'Ossat, ed.: *Il Museo dell'Opera del Duomo a Pisa* (Milan, 1986) [section by C. Baracchini]

ANTONIO CALECA

Bidyugo. See BIJOGO.

Bid Zard. See ELYMAIS, §4.

Bie, Cornelis de (*b* Lier, nr Antwerp, 10 Feb 1627; *d* after 18 Feb 1711, before 1716). Flemish writer and lawyer. He was the son of the painter Adriaan de Bie (1594–1668) and Clara van Bortel and spent most of his life in his birthplace, where he practised as a notary. He married twice and had 14 children. His fame rests on his authorship of 50 or more books, particularly *Het gulden cabinet vande edele vry schilder const* ('The golden cabinet of the noble and free art of painting'), published by Johannes Meyssens in Antwerp in 1661. The starting-point and one of the sources for this was a series of artists' portraits that Meyssens had published in 1649.

The book is in three sections, dealing respectively with deceased artists, contemporary living painters, and 17th-century engravers, sculptors and architects. Much of the information was provided by de Bie's patron Anthonie van Leyen, by Hendrick ter Brugghen's son Richard, by de Bie's father and by Erasmus Quellinus II and Luigi Primo. These last three artists had visited Italy at different times, which may account for the wealth of information on the foreign travels of Netherlandish artists and the inclusion of some French and Italian painters. With this material, and with the help of visits to local art collections, de Bie broadened the scope of his work, which otherwise concentrated mainly on painting in the southern Netherlands. In cases where portraits were available, these accompany the biographies. Many of the artists were favoured with laudatory verses by de Bie, a traditional practice originating with Paolo Giovio's series of portraits and including Domenicus Lampsonius's *Pictorum aliquot celebrium Germaniae Inferioris effigies* (Antwerp, 1572) on Netherlandish artists. Other entries are true biographies, following the model of Karel van Mander's *Schilder-boeck* ([1603]–1604). In de Bie's sectional introductions and a number of other passages on art-theoretical and moral *topoi* he borrowed freely, with variations, from van Mander, Philips Angel's *Lof der Schilder-konst* (Leiden, 1642) and Franciscus Junius's *De pictura veterum libri tres* (Dutch trans., Middelburg, 1641).

For a long time *Het gulden cabinet* was not generally understood or appreciated by art historians, largely because its contents are difficult to grasp; also the quality of the information about artists is variable and the literary standard undistinguished. However, de Bie's most important contribution was to provide theoretical conclusions informed by his appreciation of (then) less valued forms of painting: still-lifes, *bambocciate* (low-life subjects), portraits and landscapes. He praised unreservedly the artists who specialized in these genres. He made manuscript additions to his own copy of the book for a projected, but never achieved, second edition.

WRITINGS
Het gulden cabinet vande edele vry schilder const (Antwerp, 1661); facs. of 1st edn with intro. by G. Lemmens (Soest, 1971); projected 2nd edn (Lier, 1675); Brussels, Bib. Royale Albert 1er, MS. 14648); with intro., commentary and index by C. Schuckman (in preparation)
Den spiegel vande verdrayde werelt [The mirror of the topsyturvy world] (Antwerp, 1708), pp. 270–77 [on Hendrick ter Brugghen]

BIBLIOGRAPHY
J. A. Emmens and S. H. Levie: 'The History of Dutch Art History', *Criticism and Theory in the Arts* (Paris, 1963), pp. 1–14; also in *Kunsthistorische Opstellen 2—Verzameld Werk*, pt 4, ed. J. A. Emmens (Amsterdam, 1981), pp. 35–50
C. H. Schuckman: *Cornelis de Bie* (diss., Utrecht U., 1984)
——: 'Did Hendrick ter Brugghen Revisit Italy? Notes from an Unknown Manuscript by Cornelis de Bie', *Hoogsteder-Naumann Mercury*, iv (1986), pp. 7–22
E. S. de Villiers: 'Flemish Art Theory in the Second Half of the 17th Century: An Investigation of an Unexploited Source', *S. Afr. J. A. Hist.*, ii, pp. 1–11

CHRISTIAAN SCHUCKMAN

Biederman, Charles (Karel Joseph) (*b* Cleveland, OH, 23 Aug 1906). American painter and theorist. He worked as a graphic designer for several years before studying art at the School of the Art Institute of Chicago from 1926 to 1929. A week after his arrival he saw a painting by Cézanne that greatly influenced his subsequent thought. He lived in New York from 1934 to 1940, except for a nine-month period in 1936–7 when he lived in Paris. He began to make reliefs in 1934. His visits in Paris to the studios of Mondrian, Georges Vantongerloo, César Domela and Antoine Pevsner made him aware of De Stijl, Neo-Plasticism, Abstraction-Création and Constructivism. He also met Léger, Miró, Arp, Kandinsky, Robert Delaunay, Alberto Giacometti, Picasso and Brancusi.

Shortly before returning to New York in 1938, Biederman made his first abstract reliefs, which he termed 'non-mimetic'. In the same year, while visiting Chicago, he attended a seminar given by the Polish-born writer Alfred Korzybski, founder of the General Semantics Institute, which strongly influenced his later theories about history as an evolutionary process. He moved to Red Wing, near Minneapolis, MN, in 1942 to work on an army medical project. Although he did not make art again until 1945, when he returned to painted aluminium reliefs of geometric elements (e.g. *Structurist Relief, Red Wing No. 20*, 1954–65; London, Tate), he began work on his first book, *Art as the Evolution of Visual Knowledge* (1948), in which he explained how art could reflect the structure of nature without imitating its outward appearances. His beliefs, formally referred to as Structurism, were espoused in other books and were influential on other Constructivist artists such as Victor Pasmore, Kenneth Martin, Mary Martin and Anthony Hill.

WRITINGS
Art as the Evolution of Visual Knowledge (Red Wing, 1948)
Letters on the New Art (Red Wing, 1951)
The New Cézanne: From Monet to Mondriaan (Red Wing, 1958)
An Art Credo (Lanark, 1965)
Search for New Arts (Red Wing, 1979)
Art–Science–Reality (Red Wing, 1988)

BIBLIOGRAPHY
G. Rickey: *Constructivism: Origins and Evolution* (New York, 1967), pp. 59, 86, 100, 118–21, 243, 275
Charles Biederman: A Retrospective Exhibition with Especial Emphasis on the Structurist Works of 1936–69 (exh. cat., foreword R. Denny, essay J. van der Marck; ACGB, 1969)

ROY R. BEHRENS

Biedermann, Johann Jakob (*b* Winterthur, 7 Oct 1763; *d* Aussersihl, Schwyz, 10 April 1830). Swiss painter and engraver. He studied under Johann Rudolf Schellenburg in Winterthur and then, in 1778, with Heinrich Rieter (1751–1818) in Berne, where he was also influenced by the topographical landscapes of Johann Ludwig Aberli. He was adept at executing such sharply detailed engravings of Swiss cities as *View of Lucerne* (*c.* 1790; e.g. Lucerne, Zentbib.), which he sold to tourists. In 1802 he published an important series of views of Switzerland, which were widely circulated. His skill as a painter of animals was sometimes combined with his rendering of the landscape, as in *View of the Lake of Bienne* (*c.* 1800; Winterthur, Kstmus.). In 1807 he taught drawing in Basle and in 1814 was active in the area around Lake Constance. His paintings are often characterized by warm colours and frequently capture the atmosphere of late afternoon, as in *Murg on the Lake of Walen* (*c.* 1820; St Gall, Kstmus.). Many of his landscapes are straightforward depictions of the Swiss countryside, stressing the romantic nature of the scene, as in *View of the Area of Bex* (1821; Winterthur, Kstmus.). He painted in Zurich in 1827 and was known to have travelled to Munich and Dresden. His works are important visual documents of an image of the pastoral countryside frequently propagated by Swiss artists in accordance with the philosophical ideals of Jean-Jacques Rousseau (*see* PRINTS, colour pl. VII, fig. 2).

BIBLIOGRAPHY
Gedächtnis Ausstellung für J. J. Biedermann (exh. cat., ed. P. Fink; Winterthur, Kstver., 1930)
J. J. Biedermann (exh. cat., ed. W. Hugelshofer; Lucerne, Kstmus., 1938)
WILLIAM HAUPTMAN

Biedermeier. A term applied to bourgeois life and art in Germanic Europe, an extensive area embracing such cities as Copenhagen, Berlin, Vienna and Prague, from 1815 (the Congress of Vienna) to the revolutions of 1848. It originated as a pseudonym, Gottlieb Biedermeier, created by Ludwig Eichrodt (1827–92) and Adolf Kussmaul (1822–1902) for publishing poetry in the Munich journal *Fliegende Blätter* between October 1854 and May 1857. The connotations of the German adjective *bieder*—plain, solid, unpretentious—pointed to the gently parodic function of these poems, which were based on the work of Samuel Friedrich Sauter (1766–1846), a Swabian schoolmaster and amateur versifier.

The Biedermeier period may very generally be divided into two phases, with the years around 1830 marking the moment of transition between a more restrained, cooler and more severe style (purer lines and more affinity to Neo-classicism in design, sparsely furnished interiors, and greater objectivity in painting) to a more complex, catholic and emotional one (greater historicism and eclecticism in design, more pattern and upholstery in interiors, and a more fluid style, greater sentimentality and the rise of anecdotal genre in painting). However, regional variation was very marked: the colour and drama of such Viennese genre scenes as Josef Franz Danhauser's *Indulgence* (1836; Vienna, Belvedere), which echoed the local Baroque heritage, is very distant from the calm of such interiors as *At the Mirror* (1827; Kiel, Christian-Albrechts U.,

Ksthalle) by the Dresden painter Georg Friedrich Kersting, which is more akin to the precise, severe and linear style of Berlin and Hamburg. The identity of Biedermeier is further confused by the fluid borders between it and the concurrent styles of Neo-classicism and Romanticism; it is best distinguished from either by a stronger link between the fine and the applied arts. Many artists worked in both areas, and such standards derived from craftsmanship as technical expertise were often applied to the appraisal of paintings.

Biedermeier painters were ideologically opposed to academic and religious painting; while establishment critics regarded their work as inferior, it was much appreciated and eagerly bought by a large middle- and upper-class public which, in turn, did much to establish its major characteristics. Biedermeier pictures were, on the whole, small and biased towards conveying specific content, documentary or narrative: in this, their close connection to both contemporary book illustration and the popular diorama is evident. Accordingly, Biedermeier titles for paintings, as for novels and plays, were often essential to the ironic or moralistic points being conveyed. Formally and technically, the most common traits were the use of separate, clear tones and a high degree of finish. The most popular subjects were portraits, landscapes and genre scenes, with still-lifes, especially of flowers, serving as a strong link to the decorative arts in designs for glass, porcelain and for textile patterns.

In portraiture, groups, especially families, were very popular, with the 18th-century English conversation piece often serving as a model. Portraits often approached genre; figures were shown in detailed interiors or in garden settings, as in Carl Julius Milde's *Pastor Rautenburg and his Family* (1833; Hamburg, Ksthalle). Characterization stressed an individual's interests, but little attempt was made at deeper psychological exploration. Landscape scenes often included identifiable monuments and stressed human and domestic associations; views were chosen to heighten a sense of enclosure through framing devices, as in *View of the Salzburg* (1837; Dresden, Grünes Gewölbe) by Julius Schoppe (1795–1868). Similar techniques were employed in architectural scenes documenting both the official side of a city as well as its back streets and the sites of human interaction in business transaction: for example Erdmann Hummel's *Corner Shop on the Schlossfreiheit* (1830; ex-Berlin, N.G.; destr.). Interiors were frequently shown, often as character portraits of the absent owner, as in *Studio Window* (1836; Vienna, Albertina; see fig.) by Jakob Alt (1789–1872). Industrial architecture also became an interesting new theme with views of factories, mills and railroads, such as in Alfred Rethel's *Harkort Factory at Burg Wetter* (*c.* 1834; Düsseldorf, Demag AG priv. col., see Geismeier, p. 183). Genre scenes were especially popular and documented many aspects of middle-class life both at home and at places of public entertainment such as concerts or cafés or in parks, as in Hummel's *Granite Bowl in the Lustgarten in Berlin* (1831; Berlin, Neue N.G.). Military and peasant subjects, especially popular in Munich and Vienna, were invariably idealized, as in the *Five 'Kreuzer' Dance* (1829; Vienna, Hist. Mus.) by Michael Neder (1807–82).

Jakob Alt: *Studio Window*, watercolour, 512×415 mm, 1836 (Vienna, Graphische Sammlung Albertina)

Although the term Biedermeier has also been used to refer to painters outside Germanic Europe, such as Pavel Fedotov in Russia, Wouter Johannes van Troostwijk in Holland, Louis-Léopold Boilly in France and George Caleb Bingham in America, they are probably better described in terms more relevant to their various and very distinct social and artistic contexts. No accepted definition of Biedermeier architecture and sculpture has yet been established. Both were primarily Neo-classical throughout the period and associated with public and representational purposes, for example the façades of the large housing blocks (1835–45) designed by Joseph Kornhäusel in Vienna, although many of the country villas of the period might well qualify as examples of Biedermeier style.

The Biedermeier period is best known for its furniture design which was determined by concern for comfort and practicality and reduced economic circumstances. It was influenced by both English Sheraton furniture and the early classicism of Louis XVI. The strongest influence, however, was the French Empire style, from which it took Neo-classical symmetry, a preference for simple geometric shapes and flat surfaces and an architectural vocabulary of columns, mouldings and pediments. It rejected ornate decoration, costly materials and aristocratic references. The aesthetic dimension came from the skills of fine craftsmanship: proportion, simplicity, formal clarity and the natural beauty of the materials. Favourite materials included fruitwoods, walnut and ash, with ebonized wood for accent. Comfort dictated the introduction of upholstery and new curved shapes for chair legs and backs (*see* HUNGARY, fig. 17). The most popular furniture types were those used for daily life: the sofa, chair, desk (especially secrétaire), cabinet, *étagère*—used to display collections of

Biedermeier porcelain and glass—and such smaller pieces as plant-stand, night-table, wine cooler, wastebasket and needlework holder. Regional variations ranged from the elegant, delicate and imaginative Viennese designs typified by the work of Joseph Ulrich Danhauser (e.g. sofa, *c.* 1820; Vienna, Bundesmobiliensamml.; *see* AUSTRIA, fig. 32) to the massive architectural forms of Berlin furniture under the influence of Karl Friedrich Schinkel. Furniture produced after 1830 had more historicizing ornamentation and more opulent materials, reflecting the increased prosperity of the middle classes.

The concern for comfort and convenience also dominated the design of the Biedermeier interior. Furniture was no longer aligned against the wall but was used to create groupings known as *Wohninsel*. These arrangements, usually composed of sofa-table-chair combinations, established small informal areas sympathetic to family life and abandoned the formality of Empire room design. From 1815 to 1830 furnishings were sparse; subsequently wallpaper, textile hangings, parquet floors and carpets became the norm. Floral arrangements and floral motifs in fabrics were especially popular, just as the garden itself became an extension of the interior living-space.

By the 1880s Biedermeier had come to be used pejoratively to characterize the reactionary bourgeois elements in society in the period and region concerned and, more specifically, to describe its furniture, interior decoration and fashions which were often seen as a provincial offshoot of the French Empire style. In 1896, however, with the Congress of Vienna exhibition, Biedermeier furniture and design began to receive positive reappraisal, largely motivated by the admiration of *Jugendstil* artists for products of the Biedermeier era. The application of the term to the fine arts began with the Berlin Centennial Exhibition of 1906; and its validity as a stylistic term for literature, music and philosophy was examined in the 1920s and 1930s. The more dogmatic definition of Biedermeier bourgeois society as one that deliberately withdrew into the private sphere and remained indifferent to social problems has subsequently been questioned. Certain aspects of the traditional view of the period have endured: celebration of the domestic realm, cultivation of a sense of order, sobriety and cheerfulness and rejection of heroic drama in favour of lyricism or of gentle humour poised between the sentimental and the ironic.

See also GERMANY, §V, 4 and fig. 39, and AUSTRIA, fig. 38.

BIBLIOGRAPHY
M. von Boehn: *Biedermeier: Deutschland von 1815–1847* (Berlin, [*c.* 1911–13])
P. F. Schmidt: *Biedermeiermalerei* (Munich, 1921)
K. Gläser: *Das Bildnis im Berliner Biedermeier* (Berlin, 1932)
K. Simon: 'Biedermeier in der bildenden Kunst', *Dt. Vjschr. Litwiss. & Geistesgesch.*, xiii (1935), pp. 59–90
A. T. Leitich: *Wiener Biedermeier* (Leipzig, 1941)
R. Feuchtmüller and W. Mrazek: *Biedermeier in Österreich* (Vienna, 1963)
L. Schrott: *Biedermeier in München* (Munich, 1963)
P. Pötschner: *Genesis der Wiener Biedermeierlandschaft* (Vienna, 1964)
Wien, 1800–1850 (exh. cat., Vienna, Hist. Mus., 1969)
I. Wirth: *Berliner Biedermeier* (Berlin, 1972)
Berliner Biedermeier (exh. cat., ed. G. Bartoschek; Potsdam, Schloss Sanssouci, 1973)
G. Himmelheber: *Biedermeier Furniture* (London, 1974)
W. Geismeier: *Biedermeier* (Leipzig, 1979)
R. Krüger: *Biedermeier: Eine Lebenshaltung zwischen 1815 und 1848* (Vienna, 1979)

Vienna in the Age of Schubert: The Biedermeier Interior 1815–1848 (exh. cat., London, V&A, 1979)

H. Kretschmer: *Biedermeier* (Munich, 1980)

Berlin zwischen 1789 und 1848: Facetten einer Epoche (exh. cat., Berlin, Akad. Kst DDR, 1981)

M. Bernhard: *Das Biedermeier: Kultur zwischen Wiener Kongress und Märzrevolution* (Düsseldorf, 1983)

R. Waissenberger, ed.: *Vienna in the Biedermeier Era, 1815–1848* (New York, 1986)

A. Wilkie: *Biedermeier* (Cologne, 1987)

Biedermeiers Glück und Ende . . . die gestörte Idylle 1815–1848 (exh. cat., Munich, Stadtmus., 1987)

Bürgersinn und Aufbegehren: Biedermeier und Vormärz in Wien 1815–1848 (exh. cat., Vienna, Hist. Mus., 1987)

G. Himmelheber: *Kunst des Biedermeier 1815–1835* (exh. cat., Munich, Bayer. Nmus., 1988)

MARSHA L. MORTON

Biegas, Bolesław [Biegalski, Boleslas-Biegas] (*b* Koziczyn, nr Ciechanów, 29 March 1877; *d* Paris, 30 Sept 1954). Polish sculptor, painter and writer, active in France. Between 1896 and 1901 he studied at the School of Fine Arts in Kraków under the sculptors Alfred Daun and Konstanty Laszczka. In 1901 he went to Paris on a scholarship and remained there until his death. He exhibited from 1897 throughout Europe (especially at the Salon National des Beaux-Arts, the Salon d'Automne and the Salon des Indépendants in Paris), and he took part in the competitions for the Kościuszko monument for Washington, DC, and the Chopin monument for Warsaw.

Initially, Biegas's sculptures were inspired by folk art, but towards the end of the 1890s naturalistic traits verging on expressionism and a certain geometrization of form are evident in his compositions. His most characteristic sculptures, mostly heads of women with long hair in the style of the Secession, appeared in the early 20th century. These works, often simplified and geometrical in form (e.g. *Eternity*, *Life*, *Presentiment* and *Sphinx*), make him one of the leading representatives of Secessionist sculpture. He was also well known as a portraitist.

Encouraged by Stanisław Wyspiański, Biegas started painting *c*. 1900. His compositions show the obvious influence of Arnold Böcklin. In the course of time sculpture gave way to painting in Biegas's work, and his one-man exhibition of 1925 consisted solely of paintings. Nothing is known of Biegas's later years. The largest collection of his sculptures is to be found in the Polish Historical-Literary Society in Paris.

SAP

BIBLIOGRAPHY

Boleslas Biegas, sculpteur et peintre (Paris, *c*. 1906)

M. Domański: 'Z zagadnień treści i formy rzeźby Bolesława Biegasa do 1914' [Selected aspects of the form and content of the sculpture of Bolesław Biegas to 1914], *Biul. Hist. Sztuki* (1970), no. 3–4

WOJCIECH WŁODARCZYK

Bielorussia [Bielarus']. *See* BELARUS'.

Biemann [Bimann], **Dominik** (*b* Harrachsdorf, 1 April 1800; *d* Eger, 29 Sept 1857). Bohemian glass-engraver. He was the son of a carpenter and patternmaker at the Harrachsdorf glassworks and received his training as a glass-engraver at the Nový Svět glassworks on the estate of the counts of Harrach, which was then one of the largest in Bohemia. His teacher was Franz Pohl (1764–1834), the glass-engraver and stone-carver, and Biemann's skill was such that he was nominated First Glass-engraver.

Despite his success, in 1825 he went to Prague where he studied painting and anatomy at the academy from 1826. From 1827 he earned his living as an independent stone-carver both in Prague and in the popular spa town of Franzenzbad (now Františkovy Lázně) in western Bohemia in the summer months, where he soon took up permanent residence. At first he primarily depicted landscapes, hunting scenes and mythological and religious scenes on glasses and cups for affluent guests. He also worked for the wholesale glass dealers Muttoni and Steigerwald. In 1826 he tried for the first time a *tiefschnitt* (deep-cut) portrait and soon became an outstanding master of this technique. In 1829 and 1831 he exhibited several works at industrial exhibitions in Prague, including a plaque (Prague, Mus. Dec. A.) decorated with a portrait of *Count Kaspar Maria von Sternberg* (1761–1838) and a glass (1826; Gustav Schmidt priv. col., see Streit and Lauer, fig. 1), the earliest documented work of Biemann, decorated with Raphael's *Seated Madonna*. On the invitation of prominent figures, Biemann travelled for portrait commissions to Gotha and Coburg (1830–31), Berlin (1834) and Vienna (1839–40), where he executed profile portraits of members of the different ruling houses and the court entourage, an example of which is a beaker with a portrait of *Duke Ernst I von Saxe-Coburg-Gotha* (Coburg, Veste Coburg). At the end of the 1830s the demand for wares with engraved portraits declined. Because of the lack of commissioned work, Biemann became depressed; he never recovered and even attempted suicide in 1855. Of the several hundred glasses and plaques on which Biemann worked, it is difficult to identify many of them with any certainty as his work as they are often not signed. One of his brothers, Vincenz Biemann (1811–48), was also a glass-engraver, and a cup with a lid decorated with a representation of *Apollo and the Muses* (Berlin, Tiergarten, Kstgewmus.) has been attributed to him.

UNPUBLISHED SOURCES

Prague, N. Tech. Mus. [Biemann's memoirs and a manuscript, *Anmerkungen über Gesichts-Physiognomie*, 1841]

BIBLIOGRAPHY

G. E. Pazaurek: 'Dominik Bimann (1800–1857): Der erste Glasschneider der Biedermeierzeit', *Kst & Ksthandwk*, xxiv (1921), pp. 221–32

J. Streit and O. Lauer: *Dominik Biemann: Lebensbericht und Meisterarbeiten des besten Porträtgraveurs* (Schwäbisch Gmünd, 1958)

S. Pesatová: 'Dominik Biemann', *J. Glass Stud.*, vii (1965), pp. 83–106

G. E. Pazaurek and E. von Philippovitch: *Gläser der Empire- und Biedermeierzeit* (Brunswick, 1976)

R. von Strasser and W. Spiegl: *Dekoriertes Glas: Renaissance bis Biedermeier, Meister und Werkstätten: Katalog raisonné der Sammlung Rudolf v. Strasser* (Munich, 1989)

FREYA PROBST

Bienaimé, Luigi (*b* Carrara, 2 March 1795; *d* Rome, 17 April 1878). Italian sculptor. In 1818 he won the Rome Prize at the Accademia di Belle Arti e Liceo Artistico in Carrara and then went to Rome, where he entered Bertel Thorvaldsen's studio, a centre for the production of sculpture and an important attraction for foreign visitors and clientele. He soon became a popular exponent of his master's style and, in addition to taking his own commissions, he finished many of Thorvaldsen's pieces and made authorized copies of his work, for example six copies of *Tsar Alexander I* (1822). By 1827 he was in charge of the studio. After Thorvaldsen's death in 1844 he taught at the

Accademia Nazionale di San Luca and continued to work in both Rome and Carrara, frequently collaborating with his brother Pietro Antonio Bienaimé (1781–1857). In 1839 Prince Alexander of Russia (later Tsar Alexander II) acquired from him his series of figures of *Telemachus*, *Andromeda*, *Andromache*, *Diana* and *Zephyr*, which were installed in the Winter Palace (now the State Hermitage Museum) in St Petersburg. Duke Alessandro Torlonia commissioned a *Venus* (1842; Rome, Pal. Corsini) for his palazzo and Victor Amadeus, Prince of Carignano, also ordered a *Venus* (*c.* 1842; Turin, Gal. Civ. A. Mod.). William Spencer Cavendish, 6th Duke of Devonshire, commissioned copies of the Classical figures for the gardens at Chatsworth House, Derbys. Other works in public collections are *St John the Baptist* (1820; New York, Met.), *Innocence* (1821; Cadenabbia, Villa Carlotta) and a portrait bust of *Napoleon* (*c.* 1843; Rome, Protomoteca Capitoline) after Thorvaldsen. Much of Bienaimé's sculpture in both marble and plaster is preserved at various sites in Carrara, including the Casa Bienaimé, a museum set up in his brother's former house. All of his marble sculpture is markedly derived from Thorvaldsen's, being highly polished with a clear, clean line, and using Classical subjects and poses that are explicit and decorous, if not direct copies of the Greco-Roman.

BIBLIOGRAPHY
DBI; Thieme–Becker
A. M. Ricci: *Sculture di Luigi Bienaimé da Carrara* (Rome, 1838)
J. B. Hartmann: 'L'Erma di Napoleone nella Protomoteca Capitolina', *Capitolium*, xxxi (1956), pp. 40–42
——: 'Lettere di Luigi Bienaimé ad A. M. Ricci', *L'Urbe*, xxii (1959), pp. 11–16
G. Hubert: *La Sculpture dans l'Italie napoléonienne* (Paris, 1964), pp. 418, 426, 456
                                        GRETCHEN G. FOX

Bieninc. *See* BENING.

Biennais, Martin-Guillaume (*b* Lacochère, Orne, 29 April 1764; *d* Paris, 26 March 1843). French cabinetmaker and silversmith. The silver and silver-gilt produced in his workshop rivals that of his contemporaries Henri Auguste and Jean Baptiste Claude Odiot. By 1789 Biennais had established himself at 283, Rue Saint-Honoré, Paris, as a cabinetmaker and *tabletier* (a dealer in and maker of small objects). After 1797 Biennais, no doubt encouraged by the dissolution of the guild system, expanded his business to include the manufacture of silver. During the Consulate Biennais became Napoleon's personal silversmith, although he may have provided Napoleon with silver as early as 1798, when it is said that he supplied him with a *nécessaire de voyage* prior to his Egyptian campaign (1798–1801) and trusted him to pay for it on his return.

Biennais produced large amounts of silver for Napoleon and his family, including, in 1804, the crown and sceptre for his coronation and a number of *nécessaires* of different types, remarkable for the combination of forms of varying shapes and sizes that are ingeniously accommodated in a restricted space. One (*c.* 1800; Edinburgh, Royal Mus. Scotland) supplied to Napoleon's sister, Pauline Bonaparte, Princess Borghese, contains 97 items in a case 570×400×185 mm. Much of the silver in these cases was made by independent goldsmiths working to Biennais's specifications, including Jean-Charles Cahier (*b* 1772; *d*

after 1849), Marie Joseph Gabriel Genu (*fl* after 1788) and Pierre-Benoit Lorillon (*fl* after 1788). Biennais also provided silver for a number of other European monarchs including those of Russia, Austria and Bavaria. Increased demand for his work led him to expand his workshop, where he employed possibly as many as 600 workers. Many of Biennais's best designs for both silver and furniture were supplied by Percier and Fontaine.

Biennais continued to make furniture on a limited basis, occasionally for Napoleon, even after the success of his silver business. His furniture, generally small in scale and often based on antique models (e.g. Egyptian Revival coin cabinet, *c.* 1800–14; New York, Met.), is of great sophistication and elegance. An *athénienne* (*c.* 1804–10; New York, Met.) is after a design by Percier (Paris, Mus. A. Déc.). Biennais retired in 1819, leaving his silver business to his assistant, Cahier.

BIBLIOGRAPHY
S. Grandjean: *L'Orfèvrerie du XIXe siècle en Europe* (Paris, 1962)
D. Ledoux-Lebard: *Les Ebénistes parisiens, 1795–1870* (Paris, 1965)
S. Grandjean: *Empire Furniture* (London, 1966)
                                        DONNA CORBIN

Bierbauer, Virgil. *See* BORBIRÓ, VIRGIL.

Bierbaum, Otto Julius (*b* Grüneberg, 28 June 1865; *d* Dresden, 1 Feb 1910). German writer and publisher. From 1892 to 1894 he edited the *Freie Bühne* (later renamed *Neue deutsche Rundschau*), the Berlin-based magazine that acted as the chief mouthpiece of literary naturalism. He took up the cause of modernist painting in his very first publication, *A. Böcklin* (1891), a text introducing 15 heliographs of the artist's work, and this was followed by publications on *Fritz von Uhde* (1893; 1908) and on *Hans Thoma* (1904). In 1894, with Julius Meier-Graefe, Bierbaum founded *Pan*, which was to become the leading avant-garde journal of the period in Germany, notable for its typography and for the inventive integration of text and illustration. There were also reproductions of paintings, drawings and sculpture, and the list of contributors included Franz von Stuck, Thoma, von Uhde, James Abbott McNeill Whistler, Henri de Toulouse-Lautrec, Max Klinger, Arnold Böcklin, Paul Signac, Georges Seurat, Félix Vallotton, Max Liebermann, Walter Leistikow and Käthe Kollwitz. Many of these artists also served on the supervisory board of the journal, as did Edward Burne-Jones.

The graphic quality of *Pan* was carried over into a new journal, *Die Insel*, which Bierbaum co-founded with writer and publisher Alfred Walter Heymel (1878–1914) and writer Rudolf Alexander Schröder (1878–1962) in 1899 and co-edited until 1902. He was also editor of *Der moderne Musenalmanach* (1891; 1893–4) and the *Goethe-Kalender* (1905–9). In addition to his activities as a journalist and editor Bierbaum revived literary cabaret with the *Überbrettl*, which he and Ernst von Wolzogen (1855–1934) established in Berlin in January 1901. In the late 19th century and the early 20th Bierbaum was one of the most widely read German poets; his most successful collection, *Irrgarten der Liebe* (Leipzig, 1901), sold 86,000 copies between 1901 and 1923. He also wrote novels, notably *Stilpe* (Berlin, 1897), about a gifted bohemian with an exotic circle of friends (modelled on celebrated Berlin characters), and *Prinz Kuckuck* (Leipzig, 1907), which, in three volumes, develops the biographical model of *Stilpe* in describing the flamboyant life of an illegitimate prince. Although bordering on the trivial, *Prinz Kuckuck* was highly successful and ran to 33 editions in the 14 years following its publication.

WRITINGS

A. Böcklin (Munich, 1891)
Fritz von Uhde (Munich, 1893)
Kaktus und andere Künstlergeschichten (Berlin and Leipzig, 1898)
Hans Thoma (Berlin, 1904)

BIBLIOGRAPHY

A. von Klement: *Otto Julius Bierbaum Bibliographie* (Vienna, 1957)
D. Stankovich: *Otto Julius Bierbaum: Eine Werkmonographie* (Berne, 1971)
W. H. Wilkening: *Otto Julius Bierbaum: The Tragedy of a Poet—A Biography* (Stuttgart, 1977)

IAIN BOYD WHYTE

Biermann, Aenne [née Sternefeld, Anna Sibilla [Änne]] (*b* Goch, 3 March 1898; *d* Gera, 14 Jan 1933). German photographer. After her marriage in 1920 she took her husband's surname and at the same time changed her first name. She took her first photographs in 1921, without any training, but it was not until 1926 that she devoted herself seriously to the medium. Soon after this she produced a series of botanical photographs, such as *Rubber Plant* (*c.* 1927; Essen, Mus. Flkwang), taken in close-up to reveal the details of texture and structure. She also produced a number of images of crystals in a similar vein, such as *Scheelite with Quartz* (*c.* 1929; Essen, Mus. Flkwang), on the suggestion of the geologist Rudolf Hundt, who wanted them for his scientific work; these reflected her own interests as a collector of rocks and minerals. Her concern in such works with the detailed rendering of objects, closely linked to the Neue Sachlichkeit movement, showed the influence of photographs produced during the same period by Albert Renger-Patzsch.

About 1928 Biermann met the German photographer and writer Franz Roh (1890–1965); he became her first supporter and the author of the first monograph on her work. Soon afterwards her photographs appeared in several exhibitions and were commented on in photographic criticism. She continued to produce close-ups of objects as well as landscapes and images of people (e.g. *Portrait, c.* 1929; Essen, Mus. Flkwang). Although she generally avoided experimental techniques because of her commitment to 'straight' photography, she did occasionally make use of multiple exposures and photomontage; in *Untitled* (*c.* 1931; Essen, Mus. Flkwang), for example, the image of a woman's face is superimposed over a street scene. Biermann's early death was due to a liver disease contracted in 1932.

BIBLIOGRAPHY

F. Roh: *Aenne Biermann: 60 Fotos* (Berlin, 1930)
U. Eskildsen: *Aenne Biermann: Photographs 1925–33* (London, 1988)

Biermann, Peter. *See* BIRMANN, (1).

Bierpfaff, Jan Chrystian (*b* Dithmarschen, Holstein, after 1600; *d* Toruń, *c.* 1690). Polish goldsmith and metalworker of German birth. He is known to have been an apprentice in Toruń in 1623 and from *c.* 1640 he worked for the royal court in Kraków. In 1653 he adopted Toruń citizenship and entered its goldsmiths' guild as a master. From the beginning of his career he exhibited a fondness for the Dutch auricular style, particularly the designs of the van Vianen family. This was probably a result of his friendship and, possibly, his studies with Andrzej MACKENSEN I, to whom he dedicated his pattern 'alphabet' *Libellus Novus Elementorum Latinorum*, engraved by Jeremias Falck and published in the mid-17th century in Hamburg. The 27 copperplates represent letters composed of shell-like ornaments with masks and entangled figures of putti, animals and fantastic creatures. Bierpfaff executed gilt-copper sheets for the coffins of King Vladislav IV (*reg* 1632–48) and Queen Cecily (1611–44) in the crypt of Kraków Cathedral. They are composed of coats of arms, ornaments, trophies, and scenes of the King's victories on the King's coffin and Old Testament themes on the Queen's. Bierpfaff was commissioned by Chancellor Jerzy Ossoliński to produce silver ornaments and figurines of four angels for the ebony altar of the chapel of Our Lady of Częstochowa in the Paulite monastery at Jasna Góra in Częstochowa, although the large figures are the work of other Augsburg and Gdańsk goldsmiths. After the mid-17th century the mingling of Mannerist and Baroque traditions can be observed in his work. Some of his engraved tankards (examples in Budapest, N. Mus.; Nuremberg, Ger. Nmus.) and a cup (Warsaw, N. Mus.) are decorated with abstract Mannerist ornament, while another tankard (London, E. Raczyński priv. col.) in the Baroque style has a repoussé relief representing sea deities.

BIBLIOGRAPHY

E. von Czihak: *Westpreussen* (1908), ii of *Die Edelschmiedekunst früherer Zeiten in Preussen* (Leipzig, 1908), p. 132
M. Woźniak: *Sztuka złotników toruńskich okresu manieryzmu i baroku* [The art of Torunian goldsmiths in the Mannerist and Baroque periods] (Warsaw, 1987), pp. 53–62
T. Chrzanowski and M. Kornecki: *Złotnictwo toruńskie* [Goldsmithing in Toruń] (Warsaw, 1988), pp. 59–65, 115–16

TADEUSZ CHRZANOSWKI

Bierstadt, Albert (*b* Solingen, Germany, 7 Jan 1830; *d* New York, 18 Feb 1902). American painter of German birth. In a career spanning the entire second half of the 19th century he emerged as the first technically sophisticated artist to travel to the Far West of America, adapt European and Hudson River School prototypes to a new landscape and produce paintings powerful in their nationalistic and religious symbolism.

Bierstadt spent his early years in New Bedford, MA, where his family settled two years after his birth. Lacking funds for formal art instruction, he spent several years as an itinerant drawing instructor before departing in 1853 for Düsseldorf, Germany, where he hoped to study with Johann Peter Hasenclever, a distant relative and a celebrated member of the Düsseldorf art circle. Hasenclever's death shortly before Bierstadt's arrival altered the course of his study, for rather than finding German mentors, he responded to the generous assistance offered by fellow American artists Emanuel Gottlieb Leutze and Worthington Whittredge. After four years of study and travel in

Germany, Switzerland and Italy, he had achieved a remarkable level of technical expertise. In 1857, his apprenticeship complete, he returned to New Bedford. The following year he made his New York début contributing a large painting, *Lake Lucerne* (1858; Washington, DC, N.G.A.), to the annual exhibition at the National Academy of Design.

The turning-point in his career came in 1859 when he obtained permission to travel west with Frederick W. Lander's Honey Road Survey Party. Bierstadt accompanied the expedition as far as South Pass, high in the Rocky Mountains, not only making sketches, but also taking stereoscopic photographs of Indians, emigrants and members of the survey party. On his return east Albert gave his negatives to his brothers Charles Bierstadt (1819–1903) and Edward Bierstadt (1824–1906), who shortly thereafter opened their own photography business. Albert himself, after taking space in the Tenth Street Studio Building in New York, set to work on the first of the large western landscapes on which he built his reputation. In 1860 he exhibited *Base of the Rocky Mountains, Laramie Peak* (untraced) at the National Academy of Design and thereby laid artistic claim to the landscape of the American West. Of all the paintings he produced following his first trip west, none drew more attention than *The Rocky Mountains, Lander's Peak* (1863; New York, Met.; see fig.). A huge landscape combining distant mountain grandeur with a close-up view of Indian camp life, *The Rocky Mountains* was seen by some as the North American equivalent of Frederic Church's *Heart of the Andes* (1859; New York, Met.).

In 1863 Bierstadt made his second trip west, accompanied by the writer Fitz Hugh Ludlow. Travelling by stagecoach and on horseback, the pair reached San Francisco in July, spent seven weeks in Yosemite Valley and then rode north as far as the Columbia River in Oregon before returning east. Following this trip, Bierstadt produced a series of paintings that took as their subject the awesome geography and spiritual power of Yosemite Valley. Such images of undisturbed nature served as welcome antidotes to the chaos and carnage of the Civil War then ravaging the eastern landscape. In 1865 Bierstadt sold *The Rocky Mountains* to James McHenry, an English railroad financier, for £25,000. The sale marked not only the artist's economic ascendancy but also his entry into European and American society. At the peak of his fame and wealth, Bierstadt built a magnificent home, Malkasten, on the banks of the Hudson River. He continued to produce large paintings of western mountain scenery including *Storm in the Rocky Mountains, Mount Rosalie* (1866; New York, Brooklyn Mus.) and *Domes of the Yosemite* (1867; St Johnsbury, VT, Athenaeum).

In June 1867 Bierstadt and his wife departed for Europe, where they spent two years travelling and mixing with potential patrons among the wealthy and titled. In Rome during the winter of 1868 he completed *Among the Sierra Nevada Mountains, California* (Washington, DC, N. Mus. Amer. A.; *see* LANDSCAPE PAINTING, colour pl. IV, fig. 1), a key example of the mythic rather than topographical paintings that would occupy much of his time during the 1870s. In 1871 he returned to California and Yosemite, but the transcontinental railroad had flooded the valley with tourists and he turned his attention to less accessible

Albert Bierstadt: *The Rocky Mountains, Lander's Peak*, oil on canvas, 1.86×3.06 m, 1863 (New York, Metropolitan Museum of Art)

and still pristine areas such as Hetch Hetchy Valley, Kings River Canyon and the Farallon Islands. Returning east in 1873 he began work on a new series of paintings of California as well as a commissioned work for the US Capitol, the *Discovery of the Hudson* (1875; *in situ*). In 1877, when his wife's health required a warmer climate, he began regular trips to Nassau. The island's lush landscape and tropical light offered new subject-matter and encouraged him to adopt a brighter palette. In the following decade he travelled constantly, returning to Europe, California, Canada and the Pacific Northwest. In 1881 he visited Yellowstone Park and eight years later Alaska and the Canadian Rockies.

The growing American taste for paintings exhibiting French mood rather than German drama, on an intimate rather than a panoramic scale, had begun to affect Bierstadt's reputation as early as the mid-1870s, but the most painful blow came in 1889 when his ambitious western canvas, the *Last of the Buffalo* (1888; Washington, DC, Corcoran Gal. A.) was rejected by an American selection committee for the Paris Exposition Universelle. Declaring the canvas too large and not representative of contemporary American art, the committee reinforced the view that Bierstadt was an outmoded master. The revival of interest in Bierstadt's work in the 1960s was sparked not by the large studio paintings celebrated during the 1860s and 1870s, but rather by the fresh, quickly executed sketches done as preparatory works for the larger compositions.

BIBLIOGRAPHY
R. Trump: *Life and Works of Albert Bierstadt* (diss., Columbus, OH State U., 1963)
E. Lindquist-Cock: 'Stereoscopic Photography and the Western Subjects of Albert Bierstadt', *A.Q.*, xxxiii (1970), pp. 360–78
G. Hendricks: *Albert Bierstadt: Painter of the American West* (New York, 1973)
M. Baigell: *Albert Bierstadt* (New York, 1981)
G. Carr: 'Albert Bierstadt, Big Trees, and the British: A Log of Many Anglo-American Ties', *Arts*, lx (1986), pp. 60–71
N. Anderson and L. Ferber: *Albert Bierstadt: Art & Enterprise* (New York, 1991)
NANCY ANDERSON

Biesa. *See* BAEZA.

Biffi, Gian Andrea (*b* Milan, ?*c*. 1581; *d c*. 1630). Italian sculptor. His first documented works are an *Abraham* (1595) and *David* (1596) executed for Milan Cathedral; their dates cast doubt on the evidence for his date of birth. Apart from some minor works for S Maria presso S Celso (1601, 1603) in Milan and for the Certosa di Pavia (1605), his activity was concentrated on Milan Cathedral, where his work is richly documented, although it is not always easy to identify. For the exterior he produced a series of documented statues of *Joshua* (1605), *David* and *Moses* (all 1606), *Tobias* and the *Archangel* (both 1608). Between 1612 and 1629 he executed eight of the relief sculptures of the scenes from the *Life of Christ* together with figures of prophets for the external wall of the cathedral. In 1616 he was asked to provide 40 red wax models of angels for the altar of the Madonna dell'Albero, and from 1617 he worked on modelli for the ceiling of the crypt of S Carlo. Under the direction of Cerano, who provided the drawings (Milan, Mus. Duomo), he prepared modelli for trophies

and for the scene of *Esther and Ahasuerus* for one of the cathedral portals (1629).

In 1621 Biffi's importance as a sculptor was officially recognized by his appointment as the first professor of sculpture in the Accademia Ambrosiana, which was founded in that year. In 1626 he became chief sculptor of the cathedral. His art was rooted in the traditions of late Mannerism, and he never entirely freed himself from the resulting academicism. He was reluctant to indulge in the drama of the new art of the Baroque and maintained a rigorous classicism and a sense of balance and symmetry that was only superficially affected by the stimuli of such painters as Cerano and Giulio Cesare Procaccini, with whom he was in contact on various occasions.

BIBLIOGRAPHY
DBI [with bibliog.]
R. Bossaglia: *Il Duomo di Milano* (Milan, 1973), ii, pp. 109–18
R. Bossaglia and M. Cinotti: *Tesoro e Museo del Duomo* (Milan, 1978), ii, pp. 8, 13, 27–8
G. Anedi: 'Biffi, Gian Andrea', *Il Duomo di Milano: Dizionario storico artistico e religioso* (Milan, 1986)
G. Grigioni: 'Biffi, Gianandrea', *Dizionario della chiesa ambrosiana*, i (Milan, 1987)
MARIA TERESA FIORIO

Bigaglia, Nicola (*b* Venice, 1852; *d* Venice, 8 Oct 1908). Italian architect, teacher and designer, active in Portugal. Little is known of his early life and work before the 1880s, when he was one of several Italian architects invited by the Portuguese State to teach in the recently founded schools of industrial design set up in Portugal as part of the reform of art education there, which was carried out by the Minister of Public Works, Emídio Navarro. Bigaglia divided his time in Portugal between teaching in the Escola Industrial Afonso Domingues, Lisbon, and designing many single-family houses or small residential blocks in Lisbon and other parts of Portugal. Bigaglia was a versatile architect and adapted well to the variations in Portuguese middle-class taste of the time, designing decorative façades that incorporated the fashionable style of Art Nouveau in wrought-iron railings, *azulejo* (glazed tile) friezes, and door- and window-mouldings, but which retained traditional structural design and volume. The most original examples are in Lisbon: Casa Lima Mayer (1902), Avenida da Liberdade, which won the Valmor Prize, and Casa José Pinto Leitão (1904), Avenida Marquês da Fronteira, in which he made elegant use of an Italianate colonnade motif. His architectural activity was complemented by landscape design and interior design and decoration, including staircases, stuccowork, furniture and tableware; this attempt to embrace all aspects of design echoed the basic principles of the Arts and Crafts Movement. Bigaglia was also responsible for the restoration and modernization of several 18th-century palaces, such as the Palácio do Burnay at Junqueira.

BIBLIOGRAPHY
Viterbo
J.-A. França: *A arte em Portugal no século XIX*, ii (Lisbon, 1966)
RAQUEL HENRIQUES DA SILVA

Bigarelli, Guido di Bonagiunta. *See* GUIDO DA COMO.

Bigari, Vittorio (Maria) (*b* Bologna, 1692; *d* Bologna, 1776). Italian painter and stuccoist. He was largely self-taught yet gifted with exceptional talent—'such praiseworthy qualities not the fruit of long toil but of gifts with which the painter was endowed' (Zanotti)—and thus able to establish a position among the most highly reputed artists in Bologna of his time. He was chosen four times (1734; 1748; 1767; 1773) to be the director of the prestigious Accademia Clementina of Bologna. He began his career as a stuccoist. However, impressed by the art of the *quadraturista* Marcantonio Chiarini (1652–1730), whose large perspective paintings he saw while working at the Palazzo Almandini, he himself began to specialize in painting perspective effects. He studied Ferdinando Galli Bibiena's *L'architettura civile* (Parma, 1711) and, profiting also from his experience as an assistant to a scenery designer, Carl Antonio Buffagnotti (1660–after 1715), soon became expert in this art and began to assist the established *quadratura* specialist Stefano Orlandi (*b* 1681). Yet soon he also developed his talents as a figure painter, becoming a stylist of 'unsurpassed elegance' (Zanotti) whose late Baroque idiom (*Barocchetto*) was closer than that of any of his contemporaries to the style of the Rococo.

In this new capacity, Bigari entered a partnership with Orlandi that endured for several decades and produced some of the most attractive fresco decorations created by Bolognese artists of the first half of the 18th century. In this kind of collaborative enterprise the *quadraturista* provided a sumptuous fictive architectural setting through which the aerial vision, created on the vault by the figure painter, can be seen. The effect was one of singular richness. In 1722 Bigari and Orlandi worked together, with brilliant results, in the Palazzo Aldrovandini (now Montanari), Bologna, where they frescoed the vault of the grand staircase with *Mercury Presenting Astrea to the Gods on Olympus* (*in situ*). There followed a grand ceiling decoration (1724–5) in the senatorial palace of Vincenzo Ferdinando Ranuzzi (now the Palazzo di Giustizia, Bologna): the two artists created an enchanting visual allegory, based on a scenario prepared by the poet Pier Jacopo Martelli, concerning the salubrious properties of the mineral waters and baths of Porretta, near Bologna, located on land owned by the Ranuzzi family. These successful enterprises led to a succession of major commissions, including an impressive series of huge scenes from Roman history in grisaille that Bigari, working alone, painted (1727) for a room in the Palazzo Pubblico at Faenza, Emilia-Romagna. In 1731 the two artists worked at the Palazzo Archinto, Milan, where Tiepolo was also employed, and in 1738–40 they were in Turin. Four monochrome figures of the *Four Parts of the World* (1739) survive from Bigari's decoration in the Sala del Caffè in the Palazzo Reale, Turin. Bigari and Orlandi returned to the Palazzo Aldrovandini in 1748, where their most notable work was a glowing fresco of *Aurora Abandoning Tithonus*; in 1754 they decorated another room with scenes glorifying the Aldrovandini family (all *in situ*; see BOLOGNA, fig. 4).

Bigari also painted some altarpieces (e.g. the *Immaculate Conception*, *c.* 1732; Bologna, S Eugenio Papa) and easel paintings of devotional subjects and mythological scenes.

The imposing and fantastic architectural settings of the *Sacrifice to Venus* and its pendant, *Belshazzar's Feast* (Bologna, Pin. N.), demonstrate his skill and imagination in architectural perspective painting. He also produced elegant figure compositions, on a small scale, in landscapes or architectural vistas painted by specialists in these categories, as in two pictures of *Ruins* (Bologna, Pal. Montanari, see Zucchini, pls 6 and 7) painted in collaboration with il Mirandolese, a ruin specialist.

UNPUBLISHED SOURCE
Bologna, Bib. Com. Archiginnasio, MS. B 131 [M. Oretti: *Notizie de' professori del disegno . . .*, pp. 123–35]

BIBLIOGRAPHY
DBI
G. Zanotti: *Storia dell'Accademia Clementina di Bologna* (Bologna, 1739), ii, pp. 285–92
G. Zucchini: *Paesaggi e rovine nella pittura bolognese del settecento* (Bologna, 1947), p. 8, pls 6–7
P. Galimberti: *Vittorio Maria Bigari* (diss., U. Bologna, 1955–6)
C. Volpe: 'Per Vittorio Bigari', *A. Ant. & Mod.*, v (1962), pp. 104–5
D. Miller: 'Vittorio Bigari and Francesco Monti: Two Decorative Painters of the Bolognese Settecento', *A. Q.* [Detroit], xxxi/4 (1968), pp. 421–32
R. Roli: *Pittura bolognese, 1650–1800: Dal Cignani ai Gandolfi* (Bologna, 1977), pp. 60–62

DWIGHT C. MILLER

Bigaud, Wilson (*b* Port-au-Prince, 29 Jan 1931). Haitian painter and draughtsman. He was introduced to the Centre d'Art in Port-au-Prince by Hector Hippolyte, his neighbour at the time, when he was only 15; his seriousness and tenacity were already apparent. From the first his drawings were densely detailed. Working towards a mastery of colour as well as an illusion of volume modelled in light and dark, Bigaud demonstrated a mature command of his art in the great *Terrestrial Paradise* (1952; Port-au-Prince, Mus. A. Haït.), painted when he was just 21. He has been called a popular realist, as he delighted in the festivals of Carnival and Rara, representing them in full action and colourful detail. His *Self-portrait in the Carnival Costume of the Fancy Indian* (WI, Flagg priv. col.) demonstrates his love for lush detail and the golden colours that suffuse many of his paintings. His genre scenes are material rather than dream-like, solid and respectful of the limitations of naturalism. The ritual and mystery of Vodoun are presented as he observed them in reality. His masterpiece in Ste Trinité Episcopal Cathedral in Port-au-Prince, the *Marriage at Cana*, anthologizes many of the themes he had treated previously and introduces numerous details of Vodoun ritual into the Christian subject. Between 1957 and 1961 Bigaud suffered a series of breakdowns that affected his work, but he continued to paint in his little house in Petit-Goâve.

BIBLIOGRAPHY
Haitian Art (exh. cat. by U. Stebich, New York, Brooklyn Mus., 1978)
S. Rodman: *Where Art is Joy* (New York, 1988), pp. 113–21
M. P. Lerrebours: *Haïti et ses peintres*, ii (Port-au-Prince, 1989), pp. 79–90, 382

DOLORES M. YONKER

Bigg, William Redmore (*b* London, 6 Jan 1755; *d* London, 6 Feb 1828). English painter. In 1778 he entered the Royal Academy Schools in London. His master there was Edward Penny, who was among the first English artists to paint genre scenes depicting virtuous and charitable actions, and Bigg followed the older painter's example. His first two exhibited paintings, *Schoolboys giving Charity to a Blind Man* (1780) and *A Lady and her Children Relieving a Distressed Cottager* (1781; both untraced), are typical subjects, which recur throughout his career. Bigg was a prolific exhibitor, showing at the Royal Academy almost annually until his death and, from 1806, at the British Institution. He was elected ARA in 1787 and, after an exceptionally long gap, RA in 1814. When not concerned with specifically moral themes, he painted small portraits in oil and pastel, conversation pieces and, most commonly, rustic genre paintings. The latter were frequently pendants; *Girl at a Cottage Door, Shelling Peas* and *Girl Gathering Filberts* (both 1782; Plymouth, City Mus. & A.G.) and *Woman in a Cottage Interior* and *Man with a Cottage Exterior* (both 1793; London, V&A) are typical. Bigg's style is less elegant and refined than that of Francis Wheatley but more delicate than that of George Morland, although in 1825 John Constable was asked to inspect three paintings by Morland that proved to be coloured and varnished engravings by Bigg, Morland and Wheatley respectively. Edward Dayes described Bigg's colouring as 'sometimes chalky and feeble', adding, perceptively, 'nor has he the power, but seldom, to interest beyond the subject', but his genre paintings and portraits have charm, and his repertoire of kind schoolboys, distressed sailors and the virtuous poor was very popular in his lifetime and often engraved.

BIBLIOGRAPHY
Redgrave; Waterhouse: *18th C.*
E. Dayes: *The Works of the Late Edward Dayes* (London, 1805/*R* 1971)
DAVID RODGERS

Bighordi [Bigordi]. *See* GHIRLANDAIO.

Bigio, Nanni di Baccio [Lippi, Giovanni] (*b* Florence, 1512–13; *d* Rome, Aug 1568). Italian architect and sculptor. He was the most productive member of an architectural family. His father, Baccio Bigio (Bartolomeo di Giovanni Lippi), was active in Florence in the early 16th century; his sons, Annibale Lippi (*fl* 1563–81) and Claudio Lippi, were active in Rome in the 1560s and 1570s. Nanni himself trained first as a sculptor in association with Raffaelo da Montelupo, enrolling in the Compagnia di S Luca in Florence in 1532. With Montelupo he travelled to Rome, where he entered the workshop of Lorenzo di Lodovico di Guglielmo Lotti (Lorenzetto), under whom he carved the first of two well-received copies (1532; marble; Rome, S Maria dell'Anima; and mid-1540s; Florence, Santo Spirito) of Michelangelo's early *Pietà* in St Peter's in Rome and the tomb effigy of *Clement VII* (1540; Rome, S Maria sopra Minerva).

About 1540 Nanni turned to architecture, finding employment with Lorenzetto on the fabric of St Peter's, then under the direction of Antonio da Sangallo the younger. He was active with the 'Setta Sangallesca' on projects for the Farnese family and their circle in Rome and Lazio. He learnt to build in the manner of Sangallo: plain walls with strengthened corners and weighty cornices, and repeated standard details. He developed a taste for the Doric order, columnar loggias, oculi and blind windows that would characterize his mature work. After the death of Sangallo in 1546, Nanni emerged as spokesman for the 'Setta', attacking Michelangelo's alteration of Sangallo's designs at St Peter's and the Palazzo Farnese, and thus commenced his independent career as a significant architect in the Sangallo tradition.

Nanni built fortifications, bridges and roads in Rome (1556–68), Fano (1559), Civitavecchia (1567) and Ostia (1568). Beginning with the Villa Rufina (now Villa Falconieri; 1548; rebuilt 1667–8), FRASCATI, he designed numerous villas and gardens, especially in Rome and Frascati. He also expanded and transformed a number of major palaces. His buildings are sober, practical and substantial; they display his taste for brick construction (he patented a brickmaking process in 1551), for making the principal floor and mezzanine into a single façade unit and for articulating wall-planes with string courses and rhythmic placing of the windows. This suited the tastes of a circle of important patrons, particularly Cardinal Giovanni Ricci of Montepulciano (1497–1574), for whom Nanni designed a Vatican apartment (1551–2); Palazzo Ricci (1550s), Montepulciano; Palazzo Ricci–Sacchetti (1552–7), Rome; the Villa Ricci (now Villa Vecchia; 1550s; rebuilt 1568–9; destr. and rebuilt 20th century), Frascati, and the Villa Ricci–Medici (1564–8), Rome. Other patrons included the Mattei family (Palazzo Mattei–Paganica (1540s), Rome; first projects for Il Gesù (1550), Rome), Julius III (Vatican apartment, 1551–2; Ponte S Maria, 1551; expansion of the Palazzo del Monte (1552), Monte Sansovino), the Salviati family (Palazzo Salviati alla Lungara (1556–68), Rome), Pius IV (exterior of the Porta del Popolo, Rome, 1562–5), Pius V (the Casaletto, 1566–7; S Martino degli Svizzeri (1568), Vatican) and Bernardino Cirillo (1500–75), for whom Nanni designed the Palazzo del Commendatore (1567–8), Rome, and a master-plan for the Ospedale di S Spirito (1567), Rome.

Ironically, Nanni is most generally remembered for his ill-fated Ponte S Maria, which collapsed in 1557, and for his hubristic but almost successful campaign (on grounds of structural expertise and economy) to supplant Michelangelo at St Peter's. (He was briefly appointed to supervise the basilica in 1563.) This earned him the ire of Vasari, who recorded incidents to cast Nanni in a bad light, thus misleading subsequent historians. The lack of information about his work is compounded by extensive alterations to most of his buildings, making stylistic analysis difficult.

BIBLIOGRAPHY
Thieme-Becker
G. Vasari: *Vite* (1550, rev. 2/1568); ed. G. Milanesi (1878–85), vii, pp. 234–5, 551–2
G. Giovannoni: *Antonio da Sangallo il Giovane* (Rome, 1959)
R. Wittkower: 'Nanni di Baccio Bigio and Michelangelo', *Festschrift Ulrich Middeldorf* (Berlin, 1968), pp. 248–62
C. Frommel: *Der römische Palastbau der Hochrenaissance* (Tübingen, 1973)
G. Andres: *The Villa Medici in Rome* (New York, 1976)
D. R. Coffin: *The Villa in the Life of Renaissance Rome* (Princeton, 1979)
La Villa Medici, Académie de France à Rome, ii (Rome, 1991)
GLENN M. ANDRES

Bigot, Alexandre (*b* Mer, nr Blois, 5 Nov 1862; *d* Paris, 1927). French ceramics manufacturer. He was initially a physics and chemistry teacher and in 1889 visited the Exposition Universelle in Paris, where he saw Chinese porcelain with opaque glazes that enhanced the ground colours and emphasized the forms of the body. He transferred this technique to stoneware, a less expensive material that has the advantage of being able to withstand great variations of temperature when fired. In this way, with one type of ceramic body, it is possible to vary the degree to which enamels are fused in order to obtain dull, oily or crystalline finishes in the greatest possible variation of colours.

Bigot exhibited his work in the Salons from 1894 and through Siegfried Bing in 1897. In 1900 he won a major prize at the Exposition Universelle, for which he made a frieze of animals in low relief, after the design by the sculptor Paul Jouve (*b* 1880), for the monumental gateway to the exhibition designed by René Binet (1866–1911). The catalogue produced by Bigot's firm in 1902, *Les Grès de Bigot*, placed the greatest value on one-off, made-to-order objects, which were fired directly from clay models without passing through a casting stage. This was the procedure he followed for the windows, door, doorframes and balcony of 29, Avenue Rapp, Paris, designed by JULES LAVIROTTE. Bigot concluded that it was no more expensive to decorate a façade with high-fired stoneware than it was to do so with sculpted stone; furthermore, by this method one obtained everlasting colours. He embellished numerous buildings both inside and out, with ornaments in fired stoneware, including Henri Sauvage's Villa Majorelle (1898) in Nancy, and, in Paris, Héctor Guimard's Castel Béranger (1894–5), Anatole de Baudot's church of St Jean (1897–1904) in Montmartre and Auguste Perret's block of flats (1903) at 25, Rue Franklin (*see* PARIS, fig. 11). Like his predecessor, Emile Muller, Bigot also mass-produced objets d'art, vases and statues, from bathtubs to teapots, and such architectural ornaments as friezes, tiles, decorative bosses and balusters, based on the designs of the greatest architects associated with the Art Nouveau style, including Guimard, Jean-Camille Formigé and Henri Van de Velde. With the decline in popularity of the Art Nouveau style, Bigot's firm in Rue des Petites Ecuries, Paris, closed in 1914.

WRITINGS
'Emaux pour grès', *Moniteur Cér. Verrerie* (1894), pp. 88

BIBLIOGRAPHY
R. Borrmann: *Modern Keramik* (Leipzig, *c.* 1902)
Grès de Bigot: Cheminées et poëles à bon marché à partir de 40 francs (Beaugency, 1908)

HÉLÈNE GUÉNÉ-LOYER

Bigot [Bigotti; Trofamonti; Troffamondi; Trufemondi], **Trophime** [Teofilio] (*b* Arles, *c.* 1579; *d* Avignon, Feb 1650). French painter. He was first recorded in Provence in *1605* as a *maître peintre*, having presumably served his apprenticeship in a studio in Arles. In 1623 in Provence a cousin claimed his property, on presumption of his death; but from 1620 to 1629 a French painter, Trophime Bigot or Teofilo Bigotti, was documented in the records of the Accademia di S Luca as working in Rome. The same records mention in 1624 one Teofilo Troffamondo, and a painter called Trufemondi appears in the Roman *Stati d'anime* of 1630. Sandrart mentions a Languedoc painter named Trufemondi who specialized in nocturnal half-length Caravaggesque compositions. In 1690 an inventory of the Giustiniani collection in Rome assigned two paintings that fit this description, the *Virgin and Child with St Joseph* and *Soldiers Dicing for Christ's Garment*, to Teofilo Trofamonti. It is generally agreed that Trufemondi (and all its variant forms), as well as Teofilo Bigotti can be identified with Trophime Bigot, and that while living in Rome in the 1620s he painted nocturnal half-length figures (all of which are untraced) in the manner of Caravaggio.

In 1634 Bigot reappeared in Arles and then established himself in Aix-en-Provence (1638–42); he subsequently worked in Arles and Avignon. A number of his large-scale altarpieces, signed and with dates from 1635, are preserved in churches in and around Arles and Aix-en-Provence: they include *St Lawrence Condemned to Torture* (1635; Arles, church of La Roquette), executed for the high altar of St Laurent in Arles; and the altarpiece of the *Assumption of the Virgin* (1639; Notre-Dame, La Tour d'Aigues, Vaucluse; *in situ*). Caravaggesque elements are not always apparent in these Provençal *tableaux*, which reflect the traditions of French provincial monumental altar paintings of the early 17th century, but a link between Bigot's Roman painting style, as documented by Sandrart, and his later work is provided by an engraving (1708; Paris, Bib. N.) by Jacobus Coelemans (1654–*c.* 1731) of a painting by Bigot, the *Virgin and Child in St Joseph's Workshop*, which was in the Boyer d'Eguilles collection in Aix-en-Provence at the end of the 17th century. The half-length figures and artificial lighting correspond to Sandrart's description. Another painting, *St Joseph's Workshop* (Aix-en-Provence, priv. col.) has been attributed to Bigot; the figure types correspond to the Provençal canvases, while the soft chiaroscuro effects point to Caravaggesque influences. A fragment of a wall painting discovered *c.* 1978 in the Carmelite convent in Aix-en-Provence may also be attributed to Bigot. The painting, probably executed between 1639 and 1641, represents either the *Last Supper* or the *Supper at Emmaus*, with half-length figures and artificial lighting.

The engraving of the Boyer d'Eguilles painting and the other nocturnal compositions attributed to Bigot, with their soft chiaroscuro effects and static compositions, show clearly that Bigot was influenced by Gerrit van Honthorst; while, to a lesser extent, the Provençal canvases reveal a familiarity with the Roman works of both Honthorst and Carlo Saraceni. Obviously, the nature of the commissions that Bigot received in Provence demanded grand, large-scale, diurnal compositions; in such paintings Bigot reverted to a traditional type of iconography and to a style of painting that was common to the French provinces in the early 17th century, where a vigorous realism was employed to temper the excesses of the Mannerist style.

Nicolson (1960 and 1963) made an attempt to attribute a large number of nocturnal paintings first to the Candlelight Master and then to Bigot. This group bears little stylistic relation to the later Provençal work and forced Nicolson to invent the existence of a younger and an older Bigot, to explain the discrepancy between the two groups of paintings. This hypothesis was rejected by Cuzin (1979), who argued that there was only one Trophime Bigot, who had painted in Rome and was the author of a few nocturnal half-length compositions, as well as of the Provençal canvases.

BIBLIOGRAPHY

J. von Sandrart: *Teutsche Academie* (1675–9); ed. A. R. Peltzer (1925), p. 259

B. Nicolson: '"The Candlelight Master": A Follower of Honthorst in Rome', *Ned. Ksthist. Jb.*, xi (1960), pp. 121–64

——: 'Un Caravaggiste aixois: Le Maître à la chandelle', *A. France*, iv (1963), pp. 116–39

J. Boyer: 'Nouveaux documents inédits sur le peintre Trophime Bigot', *Bull. Soc. Hist. A. Fr.* (1964), pp. 153–8

Valentin et les Caravagesques français (exh. cat., ed. A. Brejon de Lavergnée and J.-P. Cuzin; Paris, Grand Pal., 1974), pp. 3, 5–7, 9–22, 39, 44

La Peinture en Provence au XVIIe siècle (exh. cat., ed. H. Wytenhove; Marseille, Mus. B.-A., 1978), pp. 3–9

J.-P. Cuzin: 'Trophime Bigot in Rome: A Suggestion', *Burl. Mag.*, cxxi (1979), pp. 301–5

B. Nicolson: *The International Caravaggesque Movement: Lists of Pictures by Caravaggio and his Followers throughout Europe from 1590 to 1650* (Oxford, 1979), rev. in 3 vols as *Caravaggism in Europe*, ed. L. Vertova (Turin, 1989), i, pp. 59–64; ii, pls 829–83

J. Boyer: 'The One and Only Trophime Bigot', *Burl. Mag.*, cxxx (1988), pp. 355–7

☐

Biguerny [Bigarne], **Felipe.** *See* VIGARNY, FELIPE.

Bihzad [Kamāl al-Dīn Bihzād; Behzad] (*b c.* 1450; *d* Tabriz, 1535–6). Persian illustrator. The most famous master of Persian painting, he is important both for the paintings he executed and for the wider influence of the style associated with his name. Evidently orphaned at a young age, Bihzad is said to have been raised and trained by MIRAK, a painter and calligrapher employed in Herat by Husayn Bayqara (*see* TIMURID, §II(8) and ISLAMIC ART, §III, 4(v)(d)) and his minister 'ALISHIR NAVA'I. The earliest literary reference to Bihzad's work is contained in the *Khulāṣat al-akhbār* ('Essences of the eminent'), a history of the Timurid dynasty composed by Khwandamir in 1499–1500 but recounting events before 1471. Khwandamir described Bihzad as one of several skilled painters associated with these two patrons. The senior artist among them was Bihzad's teacher, Mirak, but greatest praise was reserved for another painter, QASIM 'ALI. By 1524, when Khwandamir completed his general history, *Habīb al-siyar* ('Beloved of careers'), Bihzad had become more prominent. He was praised as the most skilled of painters, the equal of Mani, who was eulogized in Persian literary sources as the paragon of painters.

Bihzad may have spent the years 1507–10 at Bukhara in the employ of Muhammad Shaybani (*reg* 1500–10) before moving to the court of the Safavid dynasty at Tabriz. His reputation continued to grow during the Safavid era, although few concrete details about this period in his life are known. A series of documents assembled by Khwandamir entitled *Nāma-yi nāmī* (The Illustrious Book; Paris, Bib. N. MS. supp. pers. 1842) contains a decree of Isma'il I dated AH 928 (1522) appointing Bihzad head of the royal manuscript workshop. The authenticity of this document, however, was questioned by Ganjei, who stated that Khwandamir's text is dated by chronogram to AH 925 (1519). Other anecdotes linking Bihzad with Isma'il given in later sources, such as Mustafa 'Ali's *Manāqib-i hunarvarān* (1587), appear quite fanciful. 'Ali claims that fear of an Ottoman victory led Isma'il to hide Bihzad and the calligrapher Shah Mahmud Nishapuri in a cave during the Battle of Chaldiran in 1514. The Ottoman scholar extols Bihzad's skill in vague superlatives, which shows how his historical personality had become obscured by an almost mythical status.

In contrast to the uncertainty over Bihzad's association with Isma'il, the artist is clearly linked with Tahmasp (*reg* 1524–76). Several Safavid authors, such as Dust Muhammad, Qazi Ahmad and Iskandar Munshi, describe Bihzad as one of Tahmasp's painters. An album assembled for Tahmasp (Istanbul, U. Lib., MS. 3818) contains a painting (fol. 1) of a thin, slightly stooped man with a grey beard and typical Safavid turban; it is labelled as the portrait of the master Bihzad. Bihzad's nephew, the calligrapher Rustam 'Ali, and his two grand-nephews, the painters Muhibb 'Ali and Muzaffar 'Ali, are all said to have been trained at Tabriz, so Bihzad was probably accompanied by his family when he moved to the Safavid court.

Only one manuscript contains paintings with signatures by Bihzad that are accepted as genuine by modern scholars: a copy (Cairo, N. Lib., Adab Farsi 908) of Sa'di's *Bustān* ('Orchard') produced for the library of Husayn Bayqara. The four illustrations in the text are signed by Bihzad within the architectural decoration (see fig.) or in inconspicuous places, and the frontispiece bears traces of his signature. The colophon is signed by SULTAN 'ALI MASHHADI, the scribe, and dated 1488, and two of the paintings are dated 1489. Six other manuscripts have paintings

Bihzad: *Seduction of Yusuf*, opaque colour on paper, 305×215 mm, from Sa'di: *Bustān* ('Orchard'), 1489 (Cairo, National Library, Adab Farsi 908, fol. 52*v*)

plausibly ascribed to Bihzad or his close associates in Herat: a copy (Baltimore, MD, Johns Hopkins U., Garrett Lib.) of Sharaf al-Dīn ʿAli Yazdi's *Zafarnāma* ('Book of victory') dated 1467 and dedicated to Husayn Bayqara; a copy (New York, Met. 63.210) of ʿAttar's *Manṭiq al-ṭayr* ('Conference of birds') dated 1483 (*see* ISLAMIC ART, fig. 123); a copy (divided, Oxford, Bodleian Lib., Elliott 287, 317, 339, 408 and Manchester, John Rylands U. Lib., Turk. 3) of ʿAlishir Navaʾi's *Khamsa* ('Five poems') dated 1485 and dedicated to Husayn Bayqara's son Badiʿ al-Zaman; a copy (A. Soudavar priv. col., ex-Paris, Roths-child priv. col.) of Saʿdi's *Gulistān* ('Rose-garden') dated 1486; and two copies of Nizami's *Khamsa*, one (London, BL, Or. MS. 6810; *see* MANUSCRIPT, colour pl. VI) dated 1495–6 and the other (London, BL. Add. MS. 25900) dated 1442 with paintings added *c.* 1490.

Significantly, three of these manuscripts, the *Zafarnāma*, the *Gulistān* and the copy of Nizami's *Khamsa* dated 1495–6, contain notes by the Mughal ruler Jahangir (*reg* 1605–27). He ascribed all the paintings in the *Zafarnāma* to Bihzad, as well as 16 of the 21 paintings from the Nizami manuscript, but he did not specify who executed the paintings of the *Gulistān*. Most modern scholars have accepted Jahangir's comments about the *Zafarnāma*, but opinions vary about the Nizami manuscript because its paintings are also attributed to Mirak, ʿAbd al-Razzaq and Qasim ʿAli. Unfortunately there are no known works signed by these painters that would allow their style to be differentiated from that of Bihzad. Whatever the merits of Jahangir's attributions, these three manuscripts were important sources of inspiration for Mughal court painters. The *Zafarnāma* manuscript was probably the principal model for illustrated dynastic histories of the Mughals, such as the *Akbarnāma* ('Book of Akbar'), and other Mughal manuscripts contain paintings derived from compositions in the *Khamsa* of 1494–5 (*see* INDIAN SUBCON-TINENT, §VI, 4(i)).

Discussion of Bihzad's personal style is usually based on an examination of the Cairo *Būstān* and a comparison of it with other manuscripts from Herat. Bihzad shares with his contemporaries a style where linear precision and compositional balance are more important than the depiction of space or corporeal substance. Buildings, usually rendered as flat surfaces, are covered with calligraphy and decorative patterns rendered in meticulous detail. Yet Bihzad does create a palpable sense of space in which his figures appear to move with ease. Many figures are differentiated by age and physical type, and some are so individualized that they may have been portraits. The *Būstān* paintings are also characterized by the high quality of their execution and their intricately structured compositions in which each line and nuance of colour is calibrated to produce a sense of harmony and balance. Princely iconography has been expanded to include everyday activities such as grave digging, gathering firewood and constructing buildings.

Bihzad's legacy to Safavid painting (*see* ISLAMIC ART, §III, 4(vi)(a)) is evident in the copies made for Tahmasp of Firdawsi's *Shāhnāma* ('Book of kings'; ex-Houghton priv. col.) and Nizami's *Khamsa* (London, BL. Or. MS. 2265). Several paintings from each manuscript are similar in composition and execution to Bihzad's *Būstān* paintings.

Khwandamir and Qazi Ahmad mentioned that Bihzad also produced single paintings. Numerous single works bear attributions to him, but only two are widely accepted as authentic: a roundel depicting a youth and an older man (before 1524; Washington, DC, Freer 44.48), and a folio (Tehran, Gulistan Pal. Lib.), removed from an album assembled for Jahangir, showing two fighting camels and their keepers. Both may date from Bihzad's residence in Bukhara as they exhibit stylistic features later used by Bukharan painters. Manuscript paintings produced in Central Asian centres controlled by the Shaybanids (*see* ISLAMIC ART, §III, 4(vi)(c)) have strong compositional affinities with the works of Bihzad and his contemporaries but are usually coarser in execution.

While it is possible to suggest the specific qualities that characterize Bihzad's style, most of its features are also present to varying degrees in the paintings of his contemporaries. In later periods the name of Bihzad was identified in a generic way with paintings from late 15th-century Herat. Conversely, the appreciation of these paintings was probably heightened by the prestige accorded to his skill. The shadowy nature of the historical Bihzad does not detract from the importance of his mythical persona for the evolution of painting in Iran, Central Asia and Mughal India.

BIBLIOGRAPHY

Enc. Iran.; *Enc. Islam/2*

Ghiyāth al-Dīn Khwāndamir: *Fadl-i az khulāsat al-akhbār* [Essences of the eminent] (1499–1500), ([Kabul], AH 1345/1926), pp. 63–4

——: *Makārim al-akhlāq* (1501); facs. ed. T. Ganjei (Cambridge, 1979), p. x [panegyric biography of ʿAlishir Navaʾi; with Eng. intro.]

——: *Habib al-siyar* [Beloved of careers] (1523–4); ed. J. Humaʾi, iv (Tehran, Iran. Solar 1333/1954), p. 362; Eng. trans., ed. W. M. Thackston in *A Century of Princes: Sources on Timurid History and Art* (Cambridge, MA, 1989), p. 226

Zahīr al-Dīn Muhammad Bābur: *Bāburnāma* [Book of Babur] (*c.* 1530); Eng. trans., ed. A. S. Beveridge, 2 vols (London, 1922), pp. 272, 291, 329

Dūst Muḥammad: *Preface to the Bahram Mirza Album* (1544); Eng. trans., ed. W. M. Thackston in *A Century of Princes: Sources on Timurid History and Art* (Cambridge, MA, 1989), p. 347

Muṣṭafā ʿAlī: *Manāqib-i hunarvarān* [Virtues of artists] (1587); ed. M. Cunbur as *Hattatların ve kitab sanatçılarının destanları (Menakib-i hunervarān)* [Legends of calligraphers and book artists (virtues of artists)] (Ankara, 1982), pp. 21, 73, 112, 114, 116, 118

Qāżī Aḥmad ibn Mīr Munshī: *Gulistān-i hunar* [Rose-garden of art] (*c.* 1606); Eng. trans. by V. Minorsky as *Calligraphers and Painters* (Washington, DC, 1959), pp. 135, 147, 159, 179–81, 183, 186

Jahāngīr (*d* 1627): *Tūzuk-i jahāngīrī* [Regulations of Jahangir], Eng. trans. by A. Rogers, ed. H. Beveridge (London, 1909/*R* Delhi, 1968), ii, p. 116

Iskandar Munshi: *Tarīkh-i ʿalamārā-yi ʿabbāsī* [History of the world-adorning ʿAbbas] (1629); i, ed. I. Afshar (Tehran, Iran. Solar 1350/1971), p. 174; Eng. trans. by R. M. Savory as *The History of Shah Abbas the Great*, i (Boulder, 1978), pp. 270–71

M. M. Qazwini and L. Bouvat: 'Deux documents inédits relatifs à Behzad', *Rev. Monde Musulman*, xxvi (1914), pp. 146–61

A. Sakisian: *La Miniature persane du XIIe au XVIIe siècle* (Paris and Brussels, 1929), pp. 62–80, 103–5

T. W. Arnold: *Bihzad and his Paintings in the Zafar-namah MS.* (London, 1930)

L. Binyon, J. V. S. Wilkinson and B. Gray: *Persian Miniature Painting* (Oxford, 1933/*R* New York, 1971), pp. 81–92, 105–6, 109–12, 114–16, 190–91

I. Stchoukine: *Les Peintures de manuscrits tîmûrides* (Paris, 1954), pp. 19–27, 68–86

Timur and the Princely Vision (exh. cat. by T. W. Lentz and G. D. Lowry, Washington, DC, Sackler Gal.; Los Angeles, CA, Co. Mus. A., 1989)

T. W. Lentz: 'Changing Worlds: Bihzad and the New Painting', *Persian Masters: Five Centuries of Painting*, ed. S. R. Canby (Bombay, 1990), pp. 39–54

PRISCILLA P. SOUCEK

Bijan Island. *See under* HADITHA REGION.

Bijapur [anc. Vijayapura: 'City of victory']. City in Karnataka, India. Set in the arid tract between the rivers Bhima and Krishna, it was the capital of the 'Adil Shahi dynasty and flourished from the late 15th century to the late 17th. Bijapur was one of the centres of Yadava power that fell to Muslim forces under 'Ala al-Din of the KHALJI dynasty in 1294. That there must have been extensive building at the site before the conquest is evident from the stone pillars and slabs from earlier structures incorporated into the city's numerous mosques and tombs. The importance of Bijapur increased after 1347, when the BAHMANI dynasty took control of the Deccan. In the reorganization of the Bahmanid kingdom carried out in the 15th century by its chief minister Mahmud Gawan, Bijapur was constituted as a separate province with its own governor. After Mahmud Gawan's murder in 1481, the governorship of the city fell to Yusuf 'Adil Khan (*reg* 1489–1509), who proclaimed independence, thereby founding the 'ADIL SHAHI line of sultans. Bijapur became the capital of an increasingly powerful state, and after the defeat of the Vijayanagara kingdom in 1561 the city's wealth increased markedly. In 1636 forces of the Mughal empire besieged Bijapur, but the city was not finally absorbed until 1686, thereafter losing all importance.

The massive city walls completed under 'Ali I (*reg* 1557–79) were laid out in an irregular circle with the royal citadel in the middle, itself contained within a circuit of fortifications. The walls (h. *c.* 10 m) had semicircular bastions and were protected by a moat. Five main gates, each with a lofty arched entrance, determined the layout of the city's streets; many of the principal mosques and tombs were built near a prominent east–west thoroughfare. The citadel was entered by drawbridges over a moat (now filled in). The residence of the 'Adil Shahis inside the citadel was laid out by 'Ali I but added to by later rulers. The nucleus of the royal complex is a vast quadrangle with arcades on four sides. The court is overlooked from the north-west by the Sat Manzil (1583), a multi-storey palace with only five of its original seven levels still standing. The paintings that adorned the interior walls and domes have faded. Immediately to the north is the Gagan Mahal (1561), its lofty arched portal facing an open parade-ground (now a garden). The earliest mosque within the citadel is the Karim al-Din Masjid (1320). The building, which has a colonnaded prayer chamber with raised central bays, was constructed with reused temple pillars and lintels. The finely finished Mecca Mosque, surrounded by high walls, belongs to the reign of 'Ali II (*reg* 1656–72).

Immediately outside the citadel walls to the east is the Athar Mahal, originally the Dad Mahal, or Hall of Justice, of Ibrahim II (*reg* 1579–1626). This building was later converted into a shrine to house a relic of the Prophet Muhammad. Mural paintings are preserved in the upper chambers. The building stands next to the dilapidated Jahaz Mahal. The Anda Mosque (1608) on the south side of the citadel is another project from the time of Ibrahim II. The mosque is raised above a rest-house, or caravanserai, and is crowned by a ribbed dome. The Jami' Masjid in the south-east quadrant of the city was started by 'Ali I in 1576, financed by spoil from the destruction of Hampi,

Bijapur, Ibrahim Rauza complex, 1627

but, despite the addition of the eastern gateway during the Mughal occupation, the mosque was never finished. The inventive vaulting of the interior, with intersecting squares supporting the octagonal drum of the dome, was imitated in the tomb known as Gol Gumbaz (1656; *see* INDIAN SUBCONTINENT, fig. 110). This imposing monument, with what is reputed to be the largest dome in India (external diam. *c.* 44 m), was built as the mausoleum of Muhammad (*reg* 1627–56), the most powerful of the later 'Adil Shahis. Its dome and corner minarets still dominate the city's skyline. Immediately in front of the tomb is a gateway with the Naqqar Khana ('Drum house'; now the Archaeological Museum) above.

Among the other important religious monuments within Bijapur's walls are the complexes of 'Ali Shahid Pir and Yaqut Dabuli, Malika Jahan's Mosque (1587) and the Jor Gumbaz. One of the finest ensembles, despite its modest scale, is the Mihtar Mahal (early 17th century), consisting of a multi-storey gateway and adjacent mosque, both exquisitely decorated. The mausoleum of 'Ali II was begun directly north of the citadel, but only the arcades of its lower storey were completed. Evidence of an extensive hydraulic system includes traces of aqueducts and subterranean channels, the latter with regularly spaced water-towers. Several large reservoirs, or tanks, were dug within the walls, including the Taj Bauri and Chand Bauri, both with monumental arched entrances.

As the city expanded, building work extended beyond its walls. A short distance outside the Mecca Darvaza, the principal western gateway, stands the Ibrahim Rauza (1627; *see* fig.), the funerary monument of Ibrahim II. This superlative architectural conception with its finely executed decoration is one of the outstanding achievements of the 'Adil Shahi period. The monument consists of a tomb and a mosque, both elevated on a high plinth, set in a formal walled garden and facing each other across a small ornamental pond. Each has an arcaded lower storey with slender minarets marking the corners, surmounted by a bulbous dome springing from a prominent lotus-petal base. To the west of the tomb is the suburb of Nauraspur, with its own fortifications, which was laid out by Ibrahim II; the area was abandoned after 1626. To the east was another suburb, Aynapur, where several large-scale monuments still stand, among them the unfinished tomb of Muhammad's queen, Jahan Begam, obviously intended to rival the Gol Gumbaz in scale. Some 16 km east of Bijapur is Kumatgi, a favourite resort of the 'Adil Shahis, built on the banks of a large reservoir. One of the palaces has an octagonal tower standing in a small pond. Near by is a vaulted hall with poorly preserved wall paintings depicting courtly subjects.

See also INDIAN SUBCONTINENT, §§III, 7(ii)(j), and V, 4(vi)(b).

BIBLIOGRAPHY
J. Fergusson and M. Taylor: *The Architecture at Beejapoor* (London, 1866)
H. Cousens: *Bijapur and its Architectural Remains*, Archaeol. Surv. India, New Imp. Ser., xxxvii (Bombay, 1916/*R* New Delhi, 1976)
R. M. Eaton: *Sufis of Bijapur* (Princeton, 1978)
K. Rotzer: 'Bijapur: Alimentation en eau d'une ville Musulmane du Dekkan aux XIVe–XVIIe siècles', *Bull. Ecole Fr. Extrême-Orient*, lxxiii (1984), pp. 125–95
J. Burton-Page: 'Bijapur', *Islamic Heritage of the Deccan*, ed. G. Michell (Bombay, 1986), pp. 58–75

GEORGE MICHELL

Bijlert [Bylert]**, Jan (Hermansz.) van** (*b* Utrecht, ?1597–8; *d* Utrecht, *bur* 12 Nov 1671). Dutch painter. He was the son of the Utrecht glass painter Herman Beerntsz. van Bijlert (*c.* 1566–before 1615). Jan must have trained first with his father but was later apprenticed to the painter Abraham Bloemaert. After his initial training, he visited France and travelled to Italy, as did other artists from Utrecht. Jan stayed mainly in Rome, where he became a member of the Schildersbent; he returned to Utrecht in 1624. In Rome he and the other Utrecht artists had come under the influence of the work of Caravaggio; after their return home, this group of painters, who became known as the UTRECHT CARAVAGGISTI, adapted the style of Caravaggio to their own local idiom. The Caravaggesque style, evident in van Bijlert's early paintings, such as *St Sebastian Tended by Irene* (1624; Rohrau, Schloss; see fig.) and *The Matchmaker* (1626; Brunswick, Herzog Anton Ulrich-Mus.), is characterized by the use of strong chiaroscuro, the cutting off of the picture plane so that the image is seen close-up and by an attempt to achieve a realistic rather than idealized representation. Van Bijlert continued to paint in this style throughout the 1620s, a particularly productive period.

Probably inspired by Gerard van Honthorst, who had already turned from Caravaggism to classicism, around 1630 van Bijlert adopted a more classicizing style. His paintings became clearer and the colours lighter, sometimes demonstrating a strong affinity to the work of Simon Vouet. Van Bijlert painted elegant subjects such as the *Virgin and Child* and personifications of *Charity* (e.g. Quimper, Mus. B.-A., and Sibiu, Brukenthal Mus.). During the 1630s he also painted compositions with small figures. The most important example of this is the history piece depicting the *Banquet of Alexander and Cleitos* (1625; Berlin, Bodemus.). There is a small number of paintings

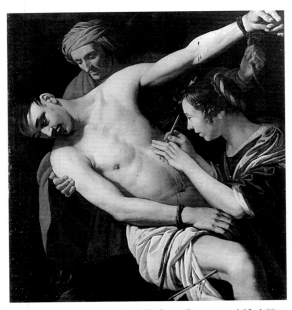

Jan van Bijlert: *St Sebastian Tended by Irene*, oil on canvas, 1.13×1.00 m, 1624 (Rohrau, Graf Harrach'sche Familiensammlung, Schloss Rohrau)

in which the Italianate style of Cornelis van Poelenburch is evident. However, van Bijlert generally used this small-figure format for genre scenes of brothels or musical gatherings, similar to those being painted in Utrecht by Jacob Duck. From 1632 to 1636 van Bijlert was dean of the Guild of St Luke in Utrecht. At this time his pupils included Ludolf de Jongh, Bertram de Fouchier (1609–73) and Abraham Willaerts; Matthias Wytmans was a later pupil in the 1660s.

Patrons of van Bijlert included burgomasters and nobles in Utrecht, for instance members of the Strick van Linschoten family, whose portraits he painted over the years (examples in the family's former country seat, Huis te Linschoten). Jan van Bijlert painted some 200 pictures, the best collection of which is in the Centraal Museum, Utrecht.

BIBLIOGRAPHY

G. J. Hoogewerff: 'Jan van Bijlert, schilder van Utrecht (1598–1671)', *Oud-Holland*, lxxx (1965), pp. 2–33 [incl. list of works]

Nieuw licht op de Gouden Eeuw: Hendrick ter Brugghen en tijdgenoten [New light on the Golden Age: Hendrick ter Brugghen and his contemporaries] (exh. cat., ed. A. Blankert and L. J. Slatkes; Utrecht, Cent. Mus.; Brunswick, Herzog Anton Ulrich-Mus.; 1986–7), pp. 194–207

P. Huys Janssen: *Jan van Bijlert (1597/8–1671), Painter in Utrecht* (Amsterdam and Philadelphia, 1996) [inc. cat. rais.]

PAUL HUYS JANSSEN

Bijlivert [Bilivert; Bylivert]. Family of artists of Dutch origin, active in Italy.

(1) Jacques Bijlivert [Jacopo [Giacomo] Biliverti] (*b* Delft, 17 Nov 1550; *d* ?Florence, between Jan and April 1603). Goldsmith. He served his apprenticeship in Delft or Augsburg and travelled to Florence in 1573 to head the workshops of Grand Duke Francesco I de' Medici, supervising small groups of goldsmiths from various countries. It is said that he received his first commission, a pendant (untraced) for the Duke, six days after his arrival. In 1576 he married Fiametta Mazzafiri who was probably related to the goldsmith Michele Mazzafiri of the Medici workshops. In 1577 Bijlivert began work on the new Medici ducal crown (destr.), completed in 1583: a gold circlet with 17 gem-set rays and the red fleur-de-lis of Florence at its centre. It is depicted in several Medici portraits, including Scipione Pulzone's portrait of *Cristina di Lorena* (1590; Florence, Pal. Medici-Riccardi), and an 18th-century drawing, perhaps by Giovanni Cassini, inscribed *Corona di Casa Medici* (London, V&A). The Rospigliosi Cup (New York, Met.), previously attributed not only to Bijlivert but to Benvenuto Cellini, has been identified as a 19th-century fake. Bijlivert is known to have created the gold mounts for the sculpted lapis lazuli urn (*c.* 1583; Florence, Pitti; *see* ITALY, fig. 95), which was designed by Bernardo Buontalenti. The neck of the urn is flanked by two attenuated human necks of enamelled gold, terminating in female grotesque heads. The foot, neck and lid are also ornamented with enamelled gold bands.

BIBLIOGRAPHY

Y. Hackenbroch: 'Jacopo Bilivert and the Rospigliosi Cup', *Connoisseur*, clxxii (1969), pp. 174–81

C. W. Fock: *Jacques Bylivert aan het hof van Florence* (diss., Leiden, Rijksuniv., 1975)

J. F Hayward: *Virtuoso Goldsmiths and the Triumph of Mannerism, 1540-1620* (London and New York, 1976)

(2) Giovanni Bilivert (*b* Florence, 25 Aug 1585; *d* Florence, 16 July 1644). Painter and draughtsman, son of (1) Jacques Bijlivert. He probably first studied painting with Alessandro Casolani (1552/3–1607) in Siena. After his father's death in 1603, Giovanni entered the studio of Lodovico Cigoli, following him in April 1604 to Rome, where he remained for most of the next three years. In 1609 Bilivert enrolled in the Accademia del Disegno, Florence. His first documented painting, the *Martyrdom of St Callistus* (1610; Rome, S Callisto in Trastevere), is indebted both to Cigoli and to naturalistic painting. Bilivert was employed by Cosimo II de' Medici, from 1611 until the Grand Duke's death in 1621, as a designer for works in pietra dura.

In 1611 Bilivert painted an unadventurous *Annunciation* and shortly afterwards *St Carlo Borromeo Adoring the Crucifix* (both Pisa, S Nicola). There followed one of his most famous and most copied works, the *Archangel Raphael Refusing Tobias's Gifts* (1612; Florence, Pitti) and the brilliantly coloured and meticulously detailed *Miracle of St Zenobius* (London, N.G.). In 1618 he painted the figures of *SS Cosmas and Damian* on the doors of a cabinet (Florence, Pitti) and in 1619, for Cardinal Carlo de' Medici, *Joseph and Potiphar's Wife* (Florence, Pitti), with sumptuous fabrics and setting and rich, exotic colour. The canvas of *Michelangelo and the Turkish Ambassadors* (Florence, Casa Buonarroti) was completed in 1620. With the *Finding of the True Cross* (1621; Florence, Santa Croce) Cigoli's influence gave way to freer brushwork and warmer effects of light and shade indebted to 16th-century Venetian painting, especially the work of Veronese. Both *Susanna and the Elders* (1622; Florence, Depositi Gal.) and *Roger and Angelica* (1624; Florence, Pitti) were painted for Cardinal Carlo de' Medici. The latter painting, Bilivert's first secular work, suggests a response to the *sfumato* style of Francesco Furini. In the *Guardian Angel* (1625; Florence, Certosa del Galluzzo, Pin.) Bilivert united a naive and touchingly simple interpretation of the story with highly sophisticated and elegant figures, and his extravagant temperament can be seen in his inclination towards popular subject-matter (mentioned by Fidani; see Barocchi, pp. 73–4) and in the few examples of his unconventional portraiture, for example the portrait of *Neri Corsini* (*c.* 1620–25; ex-Corsini Gal., Florence; see Contini, 1985, fig. 17). There followed *Daniel and Habakkuk* (1626; Pisa Cathedral), *St Agatha* (1627; Florence, priv. col., see Contini, 1985, fig. 93b), commissioned by Michelangelo Buonarroti the younger, *Leo X Standing up to Meet Francis I, King of France* (1627; ex-Broomhall, Fife), which was one of a series of paintings by different artists commissioned by Marie de' Medici to commemorate Medici family history, and *St Mary Magdalene at the Sepulchre* (1627; Florence, P. Bigongiari priv. col., see Contini, 1985, fig. 23), distinguished by its psychological introspection. In 1628 Bilivert painted a series of altarpieces: *Christ Carrying the Cross*, the *Agony in the Garden* (both Pistoia, S Filippo) and the *Assumption of the Virgin* (Pecciolo, S Verano). These works, together with a *Crucifixion* (1629; Pisa Cathedral), are painted in a soft, *sfumato* style with strong contrasts of light and shade.

In the 1630s Bilivert concentrated on mythological and courtly subjects and Old Testament stories that lent themselves to a secular treatment. Examples are *Apollo and Daphne* for Lorenzo de' Medici (1630; Stuttgart, Staatsgal.), *Cleopatra* (1630; Florence, Depositi Gal.), *Salome* (Florence, Marchese E. Pucci priv. col., see Contini, 1985, fig. 49, XIV), *Venus, Cupid and Pan* (Dresden, Gemäldegal. Alte Meister) and *Echo and Narcissus* (1633; Schleissheim, Neues Schloss), the latter also painted for Lorenzo de' Medici. *Thetis Giving Arms to Achilles* (1634; Florence, P. Bigongiari priv. col., see fig.) is an example of Bilivert's opulent treatment of such subjects. In 1636, however, while working on the *Stigmatization of St Francis* (Pisa, S Giusto dei Cappuccini), Bilivert suffered a serious illness and on recovering underwent a sort of religious conversion. From then on he devoted himself almost exclusively to sacred themes. For the left wing of the altarpiece in S Giusto he painted an opulent and richly coloured *St Donnino*, in contrast to the anguished and almost monochromatic *St Bernard* on the right wing (both on dep. Pisa, Pal. Reale). Around this time he also painted the wide-eyed *St Bruno* (Florence, Certosa del Galluzzo, Pin.) and the portrait of *Father Pietro Bini* (Florence, S Firenze), the co-founder of the Congregazione Filippina di Firenze, who died in 1636. Bilivert had been working on *St Helena and the Finding of the True Cross* and *Heraklios Carrying the Cross* (both Florence, S Gaetano)

since 1632, and he delivered the *St Helena* late in 1636 or early in 1637 and the *Heraklios* in 1641. The latter is a large, richly picturesque canvas, still close to Cigoli and reminiscent of the earlier altarpiece of *Christ Carrying the Cross* (1628). It contrasts sharply with the *Mystic Marriage of St Catherine* (1642; Florence, SS Annunziata), which has the soft shadings reminiscent of Furini. This work was executed in collaboration with Agostino Melissi (?1616–83), Bilivert's most gifted pupil.

About 300 of Bilivert's drawings, many in red chalk, survive (e.g. Florence, Uffizi). These are mainly compositional works (e.g. *Apollo and Daphne*), in which the artist explored movement and the effects of light and shade.

BIBLIOGRAPHY
F. Baldinucci: *Notizie* (1681–1728); ed. F. Ranalli (1845–7), iv, pp. 301–11
G. Ewald: 'Studien zur Florentiner Barockmalerei', *Pantheon*, xxiii (1965), pp. 302–18
A. Matteoli: 'Una biografia inedita di Giovanni Bilivert', *Commentari*, xxi (1970), pp. 326–66
P. Barocchi: *Appendice alle 'Notizie dei professori del disegno' di F. Baldinucci* (Florence, 1975), pp. 65–78 [transcriptions of F. Bianchi: *Vita del Bilivert* (before 1656) and O. Fidani: *Vita del Bilivert* (before 1656)]
C. Monbeig Goguel and C. Lauriol: 'Giovanni Bilivert: Itinéraire à travers les dessins du Louvre', *Paragone*, xxx/353 (1979), pp. 3–48
R. Contini: *Bilivert: Saggio di ricostruzione* (Florence, 1985) [with full bibliog.], review by M. Chappell, *Master Drgs*, xxix (1991), pp. 198–207

Giovanni Bilivert: *Thetis Giving Arms to Achilles*, oil on canvas, 1.74×2.18 m, 1634 (Florence, P. Bigongiari private collection)

——: 'Apocrifi bilivertiani, e altro', *Paradigma*, vii (1986), pp. 53–69
Il seicento fiorentino: Arte a Firenze da Ferdinando I a Cosimo III (exh. cat., ed. P. Bigongiari and M. Gregori; Florence, Pal. Strozzi, 1986), i, pp. 218–29; ii, pp. 226–30; iii, pp. 34–6
F. Moro: 'In margine al seicento fiorentino: Un'aggiunta per il Bilivert', *Paragone*, xl/471 (1989), pp. 102–06

ROBERTO CONTINI

Bijogo [Bidjogo; Bidyogo; Bidyugo; Bijago]. Semi-Bantu-speaking people living in the Arquipélago dos Bijagós off the coast of Guinea-Bissau, West Africa. The Bijogo are especially famous for their zoomorphic masks and also have rich traditions of figure sculpture, painting and woodcarving. Their origins are unknown, although some observers (e.g. Rogado Quintino), having noted Nilotic traits in their culture, believe they came from East Africa. Despite 19th-century rivalry between European powers, as a result of which the Arquipélago dos Bijagós was colonized by the Portuguese in 1884, the island geography largely preserved the archipelago from outside influences until Guinea-Bissau's independence in 1976. Some changes, however, occurred during the 20th century. The formerly dominant role of women declined, and the production of certain artefacts ceased, notably the long canoes hollowed out from the trunk of a mangrove tree and adorned at the prow with the figure of an ox or hippopotamus head. Examples of Bijogo art are held by many European museums (e.g. Lisbon, Mus. Ethnol. Ultramar and Mus. Zool. & Antropol.; Vienna, Mus. Vlkerknd.) and have been quite widely illustrated (see bibliography).

1. ARCHITECTURE AND WALL PAINTING. The houses of the Bijogo, traditionally built by women, are circular mud dwellings (diam. *c.* 5–6 m) with conical thatched roofs supported by a roof-post and a framework of mangrove branches. Windowless walls are erected on a low, stone platform (h. *c.* 300 mm). The surrounding verandah is used as a granary and storage area. In the eastern islands a corridor between the verandah and the central room serves as a guest-room and shelter for statues and carvings of family spirits. The granary, also with a conical roof, is a box (area *c.* 12 sq. m) raised on blocks of wood or on large stones. It is always kept secured with highly complex external locks, the sliding parts of which are particularly elaborate. They depict such strong animals as oxen or hippopotami, symbolizing the importance of safeguarding this vital structure in the household economy.

Shrines belong to a single family or to the village as a whole. Formerly these consisted of a windowless, circular double wall with staggered openings surrounding the space to which the public were admitted. In the southern islands a painted mud-built altar is set against the inner wall. It is often framed by engaged columns and contains a hollow, the dwelling-place of Orebok Ocoto ('Great Spirit'; *see* §3 below). Sculptures and offerings are placed on the floor in front of the altar. An earthenware vessel for water and a plaited bed for the priestess are the only other furnishings.

Both the outer and inner wall surfaces of granaries and shrines are covered with coloured designs painted on a coating of pure white sand. These pigments are applied with twigs, feathers, vegetable sponges or with the hand, and they include red ochre from the shores of the northern islands, brown made from the sap of the mangrove tree, green from palm-leaves, black from charcoal and white from crushed shells. Women paint the external walls of buildings with such primarily geometrical motifs as chevrons, chequered patterns, stylized human figures, opposed triangles and crosshatched patterns of broken or wavy lines. These patterns, particularly conspicuous on shrines, have been in use since at least 1940, and such figurative designs as boats and helicopters later began to appear on the outside of granaries. Figurative scenes cover the inner walls of granaries and shrines. On the latter they are more expressive, depicting sorcerers and such animals as sharks, crocodiles and, especially, serpents, which are closely connected with the divine and evoke respect for the shrine. These objects are painted by men since it is they who protect the community from these animals.

2. MASKS AND MASQUERADES. Among the Bijogo initiation takes place in several stages that mark the transformation of the adolescent, through a series of age-grades, from an unformed creature at the mercy of his instincts to a mature, responsible man. Spectacular masquerade performances are held for initiations and as considered necessary by the council of elders. Each age-grade is distinguished by its own dress code. Young uninitiated boys (*canioca*) wear a light headdress surmounted by the snout of a hammer-headed shark or the delicate horns of a young ox, and they may have a dorsal fin or a painted wooden bird fixed to their backs. They also wear large, round or flat armlets with engraved or painted decoration, a wide leather belt and braided palm fibres around their ankles and chest. When the adolescent boy has reached physical maturity but has not yet completed initiation (*cabaro*), he wears a heavy mask representing either a wild bull with eyes of frosted glass or a large sawfish. Engraved wooden hoops hug his lower back, and he carries a stick with many bronze bells attached (see fig.). An enormous, red hippopotamus mask has been

Bijogo masker, Ile d'Urucane, Arquipélago dos Bijagós, Guinea-Bissau; from a photograph by Danielle Gallois Duquette, 1978

worn in the northern islands. The maskers imitate the sounds and movements of the animals, bellowing like cattle or wriggling like fish.

The headdresses, back ornaments and other paraphernalia are extremely varied. They are made mainly of wood and may be carved, painted, studded with nails or decorated with horsehair, vegetable fibre, seashells or mirrors. Nylon or cotton thread, beads, seeds, leather, tortoiseshell and bits of scrap metal are also used, as are animal bones and teeth, fish-bones, animal skulls and, especially, horns. All of this masking gear is the work of initiated men who are fully conversant with the symbolism and imagery specific to their island.

3. RELIGIOUS SCULPTURE. The Bijogo supreme deity (Nindu) is not worshipped directly but through the cult dedicated to the Great Spirit, Orebok, who has a number of attributes including fertility, peace and protection against theft. Orebok may be manifested in a wooden sculpture or in various kinds of sacred potions mixed with earth. Anthropomorphic sculptures used in the cult are not easily identified by outsiders. On Bubaque and Canhabaque the figures usually represent Orebok, but on Orango Grande the spirit is venerated in the form of a sphere or as a potion conserved in a special dish, and it is the secondary family spirits that are rendered in human form. Anthropomorphic sculptures may depict a man sitting stiffly on an elder's stool, his arms resting on the upper edge of the curved seat. His shoulders are broad, the neck is long, and often encircled by rings, and he wears a hat. The oldest-known pieces (for illustration see Bernatzik, p. 146; Gallois Duquette, p. 167) from the northern islands show a seated figure with a shaven head, his hands placed on his knees. These statues are carved from very hard, termite-resistant wood, of which the durability honours the spirit. Red ochre may be rubbed on scarification patterns that adorn the torso and back and resemble those of initiated men. The eyes, set beneath arched, protruding eyebrows, are often covered with metal. The ears are pierced, and a collar surrounds the neck. Another type of figure is characterized by a very small head, covered by one or more hats, with a very long neck attached to a hollowed-out wooden cylinder split longitudinally and covered on the front with red and black cloth. During sacrifices sacred medicines are placed in the hollow while others are spat directly on to the Orebok. Together with the smoke of sacrificial fires these give a dark patina to the wood. Some sculptures, carved from a single piece of wood, have a stylized head with a prominent chin and a neck that is wider at the top than at the bottom. The body is trapezoidal and stands on a broad base resembling an eggcup or three or more rings stacked above each other. The figure is set back on the base so that the area in front may serve as a receptacle for offerings.

4. OTHER WOOD-CARVING. A variety of ritual and everyday objects are produced on request by part-time carvers. The tools they use include machetes, saws, mallets, two types of adze, knives, scrapers, awls and coarse tree-leaves for polishing. The most striking objects they produce are the low stools with U-shaped seats used by old men. The supports of these stools are highly varied and include single cylindrical forms, two or more non-figural carvings, anthropomorphic legs and a full-length figure resembling the body of a pachyderm.

Spoons up to 1 m long are used in ceremonies for stirring and serving rice. The most characteristic have a female bust carved below the scoop, while on others an animal is represented standing on the handle, its back being used as the grip. Wooden bowls are engraved with animal figures and the same sorts of geometric motifs as are used in wall paintings (see §1 above). Elaborate, lidded bowls were used formerly by elders for storing their personal possessions. These are surrounded or supported by male or female figures, and their lids surmounted by the figure of a dog, monkey or hippopotamus (e.g. Basle, Mus. Vlkerknd.; Stockholm, Etnog. Mus.; Tervuren, Kon. Mus. Mid.-Afrika).

Young girls carry special axes during their initiation dances, in the course of which they become possessed by the soul of a boy who died before undergoing his own initiation. In a sense the girl completes the dead boy's initiation for him, accordingly playing the part of a male and carrying a warrior's attributes. The highly decorated handles of these axes are much shorter than the ordinary type: the upper part comprises the body of a female figure, and the blade is fitted into her tall hairstyle.

Other types of carvings still being produced into the 1990s included cylindrical dolls with widely spread legs, which little girls carry on their hips, box lids, combs and statuettes of women pounding rice and of mothers with babies.

BIBLIOGRAPHY

H. A. Bernatzik: *Im Reich der Bidyogo* (Innsbruck, 1944)
A. J. de Santos Lima: *Organização económica e social dos Bijagós* (Lisbon, 1947)
F. R. Rogado Quintino: 'Sobrevivências da cultura etiopica no ocidente africano', *Bol. Cult. Guiné Port.*, xvii/65 (1962), pp. 5–40; no. 66 (1962), pp. 281–343; xix/73 (1964), pp. 5–35; xxi/81 (1966), pp. 5–27
Escultura africana no Museu de Etnologia do Ultramar (Lisbon, 1968) [col. cat.]
F. Galhano: *Esculturas e objectos decorados da Guiné portuguesa no Museu de Etnologia do Ultramar* (Lisbon, 1971)
R. C. Helmholz: 'Traditional Bijagó Statuary', *Afr. A.*, vi/1 (1972), pp. 52–7
People and Cultures (exh. cat., Lisbon, N.G. Mod. A., 1972)
A. T. da Mota: 'Actividade marítima dos Bijagós nos séculos XVI e XVII', *In memoriam António Jorge Dias*, iii (Lisbon, 1974), pp. 243–77
D. Gallois Duquette: 'Informations sur les arts plastiques des Bidyogo', *A. Afrique Noire*, 18 (1976), pp. 26–43
A. Gordst: 'La Statuaire traditionelle Bijago', *A. Afrique Noire*, 18 (1976), pp. 6–21
Modernismo e arte negro-africana (exh. cat., Lisbon, Mus. Etnol., 1976) [colour illus.]
D. Gallois Duquette: 'Woman Power and Initiation in the Bissagos Islands', *Afr. A.*, xii/3 (1979), pp. 31–5, 93
——: '1853: Une Date dans l'histoire de l'art noir?', *Antol. B.A.*, v/17–20 (1981), pp. 69–82
——: *Dynamique de l'art Bidjogo (Guinée-Bissau): Contribution à une anthropologie de l'art des sociétés africaines* (Lisbon, 1983)

DANIELLE GALLOIS DUQUETTE

Bijvoet & Duiker. Dutch architectural partnership founded by Bernard Bijvoet (*b* Amsterdam, 1889; *d* Haarlem, 1979) and Johannes Duiker (*b* The Hague, 1890; *d* Amsterdam, 1935) in 1913 and active until 1935. They met at secondary school and studied architecture together at the Technische Hogeschool in Delft. Both graduated in 1913 and worked until 1918 in Rotterdam in the office of

Henri Evers, one of their teachers at Delft; during this period they entered several competitions. The first in 1913 was for a village church, and their strong, simple vernacular design won first prize, as did their project of 1918–19 for the Karenhuizen home for the elderly in Alkmaar, which reflected the ideas of H. P. Berlage; it was their first executed building. Their next project, again awarded first prize, was for an academy of fine arts in Amsterdam (1917–19; unexecuted); the new influence of Frank Lloyd Wright is evident in both the plan and the interior perspectives. Their striking entry in the competition for the *Chicago Tribune* Tower (1922; *see* COMPETITION, fig. 3) in Chicago also paid homage to Wright, with a series of balconies cantilevered far out over the window bands of the lower stories, and suggests as well an interest in De Stijl.

From 1919 to 1921 Bijvoet & Duiker built a number of semi-detached houses in The Hague, and from 1919 to 1925 at nearby Kijkduin they executed an ensemble of brick villas in the Prairie school idiom of horizontally extended planes defined by spreading hip roofs. In a small house (1924–5) in Aalsmeer, however, they declared their independence from Wright. The house is framed and clad in wood, a traditional local material used here with wit and originality; its single-slope roofs and projecting cylindrical stairhall give it a unique silhouette. Duiker's change from a Wrightian style to a functionalist vocabulary is illustrated perfectly when the initial project for a trade school (1921) in Scheveningen is compared with the constructed building (completed 1931). Massive walls topped by projecting slabs were replaced by taut volumes and slender steel details.

The last and best-known phase of Duiker's work began with a laundry (1924–5) at Diemen; the steel-framed sash and stuccoed walls, the spare detailing and the focus on an efficient plan make the building an early example of the developing International Style. The laundry was for the Diamond Workers Union, a social democratic group that commissioned another major work, Zonnestraal Sanatorium (1926–8; see fig.), completed primarily by Duiker. The sanatorium, which was located in a wooded area outside Hilversum, was innovative in its approach as well as in its radial layout. Intended not only to heal the inmates but to teach them new skills, it incorporated workshops as well as light-filled individual rooms for the patients and medical and administrative facilities housed in separate pavilions. Zonnestraal's exposed reinforced concrete structures with elegantly detailed glass walls embodied Duiker's announced goal of 'a light, sunny architecture executed with a minimum of materials' (1932). The same concept guided the designs for the Open-Air School (1929–30), Cliostraat, the Cineac film theatre (1934), Reguliersbreestraat, and the Winter department store (1934; destr.), Weteringschans and Vijzelstraat, all in Amsterdam.

Duiker's last project, the Hotel Gooiland in Hilversum, begun in 1934, was completed in 1936 by Bijvoet, who had been working with Pierre Chareau in Paris from 1925 (e.g. the Maison de Verre, 1928–32; *see* GLASS, fig. 7). Bijvoet went back to Paris and worked with Eugène Beaudouin and Marcel Lods from 1937 to 1940. He later returned to the Netherlands and in 1945–6 established a

Johannes Duiker: Zonnestraal Sanatorium, near Hilversum, 1926–8

partnership with G. H. M. Holt. Many of Duiker's buildings were done in association with the engineer Jan Gerko Wiebenga (1886–1974), a specialist in concrete construction with whom Duiker made a study of high-rise housing that led to one of the first executed tall blocks of flats in the Netherlands, the Nirwâna Flats (1927–30) in The Hague, as well as an important book, *Hoogbouw*. Duiker was also editor of the functionalist magazine *De 8 en Opbouw*.

WRITINGS
Hoogbouw (Rotterdam, 1930; *R* Amsterdam, 1981)

BIBLIOGRAPHY
G. Fanelli: *Architettura moderna* (1968), pp. 148–57
R. Vickery: 'Bijvoet and Duiker', *Perspecta*, 13 (1971)
P. Bak and others, eds: *J. Duiker bouwkundig ingenieur* (Rotterdam, 1982)
M. Casciato: *Johannes Duiker, 1890–1935* (Rome, 1982)
R. Zoetbrood: 'J. Duiker, an "Elder of the Young Generation"', *Het Nieuwe Bouwen* (Delft, 1982)
P. Bak and J. Molena: *Jan Gerko Wiebenga: Apostel van het Nieuwe Bouwen* (Rotterdam, 1987)
J. Molena: *Ir. J. Duiker* (Rotterdam, 1989)

HELEN SEARING

Bikaner. City in northern Rajasthan, India. It was founded in AD 1488 by Rao Bhika, sixth son of Rao Jodha, founder of JODHPUR. Bhika's fort (1485) outside the city's southern wall is now in ruins but contains the royal cenotaphs: domed pavilions of sandstone and marble. A second, larger fort (Junagarh Fort) was built by Raja Rai Singh (*reg* 1571–1611) between 1583 and 1593. This immense complex houses palaces built between the 16th century and the early 20th. As at Jodhpur, their sandstone façades consist of lattice screens (*jālīs*) punctuated by projecting balcony forms. The main entry into the complex is the Suraj Pol (Sun Gate) of 1593. The palace apartments are notable for their sumptuous interiors, such as that at the Lal Niwas (late 16th century), which has floral wall paintings and lacquer doors, a ubiquitous feature at Bikaner. The Karan Mahal (1631–9), a hall of public audience (*dīvān-i 'ām*), has arcades of cusped arches and fluted columns, imitating the architecture of Shah Jahan (*reg* 1628–58), while the Anup Mahal, a lavish private audience chamber (*dīvān-i khāṣ*), is decorated with red and gold paint, mirror work and inlaid coloured glass. In the Gaj Mandir (1745–87), a suite of five small chambers above the Karan Mahal, lattice screens filled with coloured glass create a jewel-like effect; it also has lacquer doors painted with scenes from the life of Krishna.

Bikaner has several Hindu and Jaina temples dating to the 16th–19th centuries and combining western Indian features with Mughal architectural forms. The Laxmi Narain (1505–26) is the principal Hindu temple; the major Jaina monuments are the Parsvanatha and Neminatha temples (16th century). The latest architectural activity at Bikaner dates to the reign of Maharaja Ganga Singh (1887–1944), who added a reception hall, the Ganga Niwas, and a range of palaces to earlier structures within Junagarh Fort, combining European technology with classical artistic vocabulary, for example in the finely carved façade of the Ganga Niwas. He also built the Lalgarh Palace, designed by SAMUEL SWINTON JACOB and located north of Bikaner. Built of red sandstone, and rich with carved screens, pavilions and a wealth of ornamental detail, it represents a blend of Rajput and European elements in its overall design and its architectural details.

The Ganga Golden Jubilee Museum houses stone sculptures, Gupta terracottas, miniature paintings and examples of folk art and local crafts. The royal collection of miniature paintings (Bikaner, Lalgarh Pal.) is rich in examples of Deccani painting (*see* INDIAN SUBCONTINENT, §V, 4(vi)), part of the spoils of war between the Deccani kingdoms and the Mughals, whom the Bikaner kings served as generals. In Bikaner painting itself, strong Deccani and Mughal elements are synthesized with a Rajasthani artistic sensibility (*see* INDIAN SUBCONTINENT, §V, 4(iii)(d)).

BIBLIOGRAPHY

H. Goetz: *Art and Architecture of Bikaner State* (Oxford, 1950)
K. K. Sehgal: *Bikaner*, Rajasthan District Gazetteers (Jaipur, 1972)
D. Barrett and B. Gray: *Indian Painting* (Geneva, 1978)
G. H. R. Tillotson: *The Rajput Palaces* (New Haven, 1987)
K. Singh: *Bikaner* (New Delhi, 1988)

Bikkavolu. Temple site in north-western Andhra Pradesh, India. The village's name is a corruption of Bikkanavrol, or Birudankavrolu, which was derived from Birudankabhima—an epithet of the Eastern Chalukya king Gunaga Vijayadita III (*reg* AD 848–92). It has been suggested that Bikkavolu was the Eastern Chalukya capital (*see* INDIAN SUBCONTINENT, §I, 2(iii)) before the move to Rajamahendri (Rajamahendrapura). The Bikkavolu temples date from *c.* 850–950. Three of them, located in fields just outside the village, are southern (*drāviḍa*) in style, with square, tiered superstructures and very little sculptural ornamentation (*see* INDIAN SUBCONTINENT, §III, 5(i)(h)). Within the village are three more elaborate temples, the Golingeshvara, Rajaraja and Chandrashekhara, which are attributed to the time of Gunaga Vijayaditya or slightly later. Their carved images of the various forms of Vishnu and Shiva, mother goddesses and Surya are iconographically interesting, as they exhibit a combination of Pallava, Western Chalukya and Orissan influences (*see* INDIAN SUBCONTINENT, §V, 7(vi)(d)). In the Golingeshvara Temple, for example, the image of Surya is essentially Orissan in iconography (i.e. booted rather than bare-legged), as are the mother goddesses and Durga. The Vishnu image, however, combines iconographic elements from both north and south. The technique of setting rectangular slabs carved with high-relief images within the niches of the temple walls also suggests Orissan influence.

BIBLIOGRAPHY

M. Rama Rao: *Eastern Chalukyan Temples of Andhradesha* (Hyderabad, 1964)
C. Sivaramamurti: *The Art of India* (New York, 1977)
N. Ramesan: *East Godavari*, Andhra Pradesh District Gazetteers (Hyderabad, 1979)

WALTER SMITH

Bílá Hora ['White Mountain']. Hill near the village of Liboc, 14 km from PRAGUE. It was the site of the defeat in 1620 of the Czech forces in revolt against the Habsburgs. One km south is the former game park of Hvězda (star), in which a villa ('Star Castle') was built (1555–6), with a ground-plan shaped like a six-pointed star, and set in a sham defensive enceinte with projecting towers by Hans Tirol and Bonifaz Wolmut to the designs of Giovanni Maria Aostalli and Giovanni Luchese. Rhomboidal chambers are located in the points of the star at ground- and first-floor level, separated in each case by a peripheral corridor from a polygonal central hall. The top floor, however, is given over to a single star-shaped hall. The roof comprises six steeply pitched hips, which converge at the apex. This idiosyncratic design is a centrally planned caprice of a type often designed (sometimes with symbolic implications), but rarely executed, by Italian Mannerist architects. A brilliant stucco cycle (1556–61), probably the work of Antonio Brocco (*fl c.* 1550–1600) and others, inspired by Roman frescoes of the 1st and 2nd centuries AD, accentuates the Mannerist contrast with the austere exterior. The villa is the only survivor of its kind from the 16th century in central Europe. Somewhat to the south of the villa a chapel to the Virgin was erected in 1622–4 to commemorate Ferdinand II's victory of 1620. It was later (1704–15) incorporated into a Baroque pilgrimage church (Panna Maria Vítězná) of cruciform plan, with three domes that were subsequently frescoed by Václav Vavřinec Reiner, Cosmas Damian Asam and J. A. Schöpf respectively. A cloister with corner chapels was built round the church in 1710–29.

BIBLIOGRAPHY

J. Morávek: 'Ke vzniká Hvězdy' [The rise of the Star], *Umění*, ii (1954), pp. 119–211
P. Preiss: *Václav Vavřinec Reiner* (Prague, 1970), pp. 50, 88, 113
J. Krčálová: *Centrální stavby české renesance* [Centrally planned buildings of the Renaissance in Bohemia] (Prague, 1974), pp. 51–7
J. Neumann: *Český barok* [The Baroque of Bohemia] (Prague, 1974), pp. 15–17, 54, 180–81
J. Krčálová: 'Arts in the Renaissance and Mannerist Periods', *Renaissance Art in Bohemia* (London, New York, Sydney and Toronto, 1979), pp. 49–147
B. Hamacher: 'Fresken: Prag: Weisser Berg (Bílá Hora)', *Cosmas Damian Asam, 1686–1739: Leben und Werk*, ed. B. Bushart and B. Rupprecht (Munich, 1986), pp. 246–7
P. Preiss: 'Zu den Werken der Asam in Böhmen und Schlesien', ibid., pp. 69–75
M. Vilímková: 'Archivalien zur Tätigkeit der Brüder Asam in Böhmen und Schlesien', ibid., pp. 76–82

J. KRČÁLOVÁ

Bilbao. *See* SANTA LUCÍA COTZUMALHUAPA.

Bilcoq, L(ouis-)M(arc-)A(ntoine) (*b* Paris, 27 July 1755; *d* Paris, 24 Jan 1838). French painter. At the age of 13 he became the pupil of Louis Lagrenée and later studied with Pierre-Antoine Demachy (1723–1807). On 24 September 1785 he was approved (*agréé*) by the Académie Royale de Peinture et de Sculpture, Paris, with his *Fortune-teller*, and on 27 June 1789 he was received (*reçu*) as a member, his *morceau de réception* being *The Naturalist* (both untraced). He exhibited at the Salons between 1787 and 1812, specializing in interior scenes of everyday life, generally in oil on wood panels. Bilcoq created a poetic pictorial language, influenced by 17th- and 18th-century Dutch, Flemish and French genre painters. He liked to contrast rays of golden light with sombre shadows in a manner reminiscent of Rembrandt's chiaroscuro (e.g. *The Soothsayer*, 1785; priv. col., see Florisoone, p. 127, fig. 91). His compositions, conceived according to classical academic canons, were characterized by harmonious tones of grey and brown and highlighted with vivid colours that he reserved for major details and persons. A profusion of objects, depicted with still-life precision, recalls the art of David Teniers the younger and Gerrit Dou and suggests an allegorical reading of the scene, as in *The Store-room* (*c.* 1795; priv. col., see Bergström and others, p. 177). Bilcoq's portraits depict individuals with naturalistic realism, whether in the silence of their personal worlds, as in *Woman Reading* (*c.* 1787; Paris, Mus. Cognacq-Jay), which is inspired by Chardin, or against a neutral background rapidly coloured with large, visible brushstrokes. His paintings were engraved by Jean-Jacques Le Veau and Géraud Vidal (1742–1801; Paris, Bib. N., Cab. Est.).

BIBLIOGRAPHY

M. Florisoone: *La Peinture française, le dix-huitième siècle* (Paris, 1948), p. 127, fig. 91

I. Bergström and others: *Natura in posa: La grande stagione della natura morta europea* (Milan, 1977), p. 177

C. Bell-Carrier: *Recherches sur la peinture de genre au temps de la révolution française, 1789–1799: L'Exemple de L. M. A. Bilcoq* (MA thesis, 2 vols, U. Paris IV, 1987)

CHERYL E. BELL-CARRIER

Bilders, (Albertus) Gerard(us) (*b* Utrecht, 9 Dec 1838; *d* Amsterdam, 8 March 1865). Dutch painter. He received his first training from his father, the Romantic landscape painter Johannes Warnardus Bilders (1811–90). At the age of 17 he accepted the patronage of Johannes Kneppelhout (1814–85), a Dutch writer who did much to advance his career. Kneppelhout—who was notoriously meddlesome with his protégés—sent Bilders to The Hague, where for four years he learnt French and took drawing classes under Simon van den Berg. In addition he made studies after plaster casts at the Hague Academie and copied paintings in the Mauritshuis, for example Paulus Potter's *The Bull*. In 1857 Bilders went to paint in Oosterbeek (a place known as the 'Dutch Barbizon' and already very familiar to his father). In Geneva the following year he took lessons with the landscape and animal painter Charles Humbert (1813–81), who transmitted to Bilders his special interest in the cattle pieces of the Dutch 17th-century masters and the French animal painter Rosa Bonheur. Humbert's influence is particularly apparent in the freely painted cattle in Bilders's large *Swiss Landscape* (*c.* 1859; The Hague, Gemeentemus.). On his return from a long walking tour of Switzerland, Bilders lived in Leiden for a year; in 1859 he moved permanently to Amsterdam. Around that time Kneppelhout, who was unhappy with the way Bilders's work was developing, withdrew his financial support.

After his Swiss journey, Bilders became primarily interested in mixing colours to produce an overall grey tonality, which gave to his paintings a distinctive effect of light. In 1860 he went to Brussels, where, according to his diary, he was deeply impressed by the work of the Barbizon painters Constant Troyon, Gustave Courbet, Narcisse Diaz and Jules Dupré. In their paintings he saw harmony, peace, gravity and an intimate bond with nature. Although Bilders remained a melancholy man, his landscapes, mostly painted on a wide canvas, assumed a more cheerful and sunny character, and the compositions became freer and less contrived. *Polder Landscape with Cows* (The Hague, Gemeentemus.) was probably painted shortly after his visit to Brussels in 1860 and must have inspired Anton Mauve's early cattle paintings. *The Herdswoman* (*c.* 1864; Amsterdam, Rijksmus.) was an equally informal and influential reinterpretation of the Barbizon aesthetic. He also produced a substantial number of landscape drawings.

After the death of his mother in 1861, Bilders went once again to Switzerland. By that time his tuberculosis had already reached a fairly advanced stage. His health rapidly declined and he died aged 27. In 1868 Bilders's letters and diaries were published by Kneppelhout, who subsequently destroyed all the original manuscripts. Bilders was a forerunner of the second generation of HAGUE SCHOOL painters, although he himself had little experience of the first generation. Paul Joseph Gabriël, Anton Mauve and Willem Maris were particularly influenced by his work. Bilders's relative obscurity can be explained partly by the fact that he was overshadowed by his father and partly by his early death.

FRANSJE KUYVENHOVEN

WRITINGS

J. Kneppelhout, ed.: *A. G. Bilders: Brieven en dagboek* [A. G. Bilders: letters and diary], 2 vols (Leiden, 1868, 2/1876)

W. Zaal, ed.: *Vrolijk versterven: Een keuze uit zijn dagboek en brieven* [Withering away cheerfully: a selection from his diary and letters] (Amsterdam, 1974)

Scheen

BIBLIOGRAPHY

H. F. W. Jeltes: 'Gerard Bilders', *Elsevier's Geïllus. Mdschr.*, xlv/89 (1935), pp. 72–96; xlvii/93 (1937), pp. 80–97

Gerard Bilders, 1838–1865: Enkele voorgangers en tijdgenoten [Gerard Bilders, 1838–1865: some predecessors and contemporaries] (exh. cat., Amsterdam, Fodor Mus., 1938)

H. F. W. Jeltes: *Gerard Bilders: Een schildersleven in het midden der 19de eeuw* [Gerard Bilders: a painter's life in the middle of the 19th century] (The Hague, 1947)

The Hague School: Dutch Masters of the 19th Century (exh. cat., The Hague, Gemeentemus.; London, RA; 1983), pp. 161–5

GEERT JAN KOOT

Bílek, František (*b* Chýnov, Bohemia [now in Czech Republic], 6 Nov 1872; *d* Chýnov, 13 Oct 1941). Czech sculptor and printmaker. He studied at the Academy of Fine Arts in Prague (1887–8, 1890) under Maximilián Pirner, at the School of Applied Arts in Prague (1888) under Josef Mauder (1854–1920) and at the Académie Colarossi in Paris (1892) under Antoine Injalbert. From the outset of his career Bílek displayed an almost fanatical zeal in using his religious art to rouse mankind to avert a moral decline. While he was in Paris, the dramatic naturalism of his first important statues treating Christological themes was greeted with indignation by the Prague scholarship commission.

In Bílek's over life-size woodcut of the *Crucifixion* (1896–9; Prague, St Vitus Cathedral), Symbolism prevailed over his initial naturalism and he was inspired by the work of William Blake and the Pre-Raphaelites. Bílek's imagination was excited by the neo-Platonic symbolism of light, which he interpreted in an original way in both his woodcuts and prints. When he was criticized by the Catholic Moderns for exaggerated individualism, he turned to the tradition of the medieval Bohemian Hussite movement and began to foster their ideals. This is reflected in his mystically conceived statue of the heretic and leader of the movement, Jan Hus, entitled a *Tree Struck by Lightning, which Burned for Ages* (1901; Prague, N.G., Zbraslav Castle). He enlarged this into a 12 m high statue for the town of Kolín, east of Prague, just before World War I.

Bílek also wrote books (e.g. *Cesta*, 'Pilgrimage', 1909), in which he described projects for a grand collection of themes symbolizing the spiritual development of man, a scheme he was able to realize only in part. He designed his own studio–house in Prague in an Art Nouveau style and, while he rejected the mere aestheticism of the style, he made a significant impact on the spiritual tendencies of Czech art and became the most eminent representative of turn-of-the-century Czech Symbolist sculpture.

BIBLIOGRAPHY
F. Kovárna: *František Bílek* (Prague, 1941)
František Bílek: Výbor z díla [František Bílek: selected works] (exh. cat., Prague, Mun. Gal., 1966)

PETR WITTLICH

Bilibin, Ivan (Yakovlevich) (*b* Tarkhovka, St Petersburg, 4 Aug 1876; *d* Leningrad [now St Petersburg], 7 Feb 1942). Russian graphic artist and stage designer. The son of a naval doctor, Bilibin was educated in St Petersburg, studying law at the University (1896–1900) and art at the school of the Society for the Encouragement of the Arts (1895–8); then, under Il'ya Repin, he studied at both Princess Maria Tenisheva's Art School (1898–1900) and the Academy of Arts (1900–04). From 1899 he exhibited with the group known as the WORLD OF ART (Mir Iskusstva) and was elected chairman of its reconstituted exhibition society in 1916. He also contributed to the *Mir Iskusstva* journal. Meanwhile he taught graphic art at the school of the Society for the Encouragement of the Arts (1907–17).

Bilibin had a strong interest in Russian medieval and folk art and became famous for his book illustrations of Russian fairy tales, especially those by Pushkin. His most celebrated theatrical works were his set and costume designs for operas by Nikolay Rimsky-Korsakov, for example his designs (1909; St Petersburg, A. S. Pushkin Apartment Mus. and Moscow, Barkrushin Cent. Theat. Mus.; see also Golynets, pl. 97–106) for the production in Moscow of *The Golden Cockerel*. His style was highly individual and much imitated, with flat washes of vivid colour, foreshortened perspective and intricate draughtsmanship related to Art Nouveau. His designs (1928;

Oxford, Ashmolean) for *The Legend of the Invisible City of Kitezh and the Maiden Fevroniya* are typical of his work.

After the Revolution, Bilibin lived in the Crimea (1917–20), then continued his painting and theatre design work in Egypt (1920–25) and France (1926–36). He returned to Leningrad in 1936 to become professor of graphic art at the Academy of Arts.

BIBLIOGRAPHY
S. V. Golynets, ed.: *I. Ya. Bilibin: stat'i, pis'ma, vospominaniya o khudozhnike* [Articles, letters, reminiscences about the artist] (Leningrad, 1970)
G. E. Klimov: *Poiski pera zhar-ptitsy: zhizn' i tvorchestvo russkogo khudozhnika I. Ya. Bilibina po materialam sobraniya E. P. Klimova* [Searching for the firebird's feather: the life and work of the Russian artist I. Ya. Bilbin using material from the collection of E. P. Klimov] (Moscow, 1981)

KENNETH ARCHER

Bilivert. *See* BIJLIVERT.

Bilkahīyya, Farīd. *See* BELKAHIA, FARID.

Bilkis. *See* ASPENDOS.

Bill, Max (*b* Winterthur, 22 Dec 1908; *d* Zurich, 9 Dec 1994). Swiss architect, sculptor, painter, industrial designer, graphic designer and writer. He attended silversmithing classes at the Kunstgewerbeschule in Zurich from 1924 to 1927. Then, inspired by the *Exposition Internationale des Arts Décoratifs et Industriels Modernes* (1925), Paris, by the works of Le Corbusier and by a competition entry (1927) for the Palace of the League of Nations, Geneva, by Hannes Meyer and Hans Wittwer (1894–1952), he decided to become an architect and enrolled in the Bauhaus, Dessau, in 1927. He studied there for two years as a pupil of Josef Albers, László Moholy-Nagy, Paul Klee and Vasily Kandinsky, mainly in the field of 'free art'. In 1929 he returned to Zurich. After working on graphic designs for the few modern buildings being constructed, he built his first work, his own house and studio (1932–3) in Zurich-Höngg; although this adheres to the principles of the new architecture, it retains echoes of the traditional, for example in the gently sloping saddle roof.

In his studio Bill first made pictures and sculptures intended as 'laboratory pieces', preparing the way for the design of utilitarian objects, sometimes even of buildings. In 1932 he became a member of the Abstraction–Création artists' association in Paris, where he first exhibited his work. As a theorist and a painter he was an important exponent of art based on rational principles with reference to mathematics; building on the ideas of Theo van Doesburg, who died in 1931, Bill narrowed down the concept of CONCRETE ART in 1936, becoming a protagonist of the Zürcher Konkreten art group (see also COLD ART). But whereas van Doesburg spoke only of the elements of Concrete art, Bill explicitly included the relationships between them. In 1936 he designed the Swiss pavilion at the Triennale in Milan, where the principles of Concrete art were extended for the first time to architectonic design. During this period he also took part in several architectural competitions held by the city of Zurich, and he became a member of CIAM in 1938.

After World War II Bill worked increasingly in the field of applied art. This is also reflected in his writings, especially the essay 'Schönheit aus Funktion und als

Funktion' (1949), which introduced ideas that were further detailed in his exhibition *Die gute Form* (1949) at the Swiss Industries Fair, Basle, as well as in the book *Form* (1952): the aesthetic component of an object was defined not only as arising from a function but as being the actual function of form. The concept of 'good form' was substantially adopted by the Deutscher Werkbund and similar movements in different countries. Through his personal contacts with the circle around Otl Aicher (1922–91) and Inge Scholl, Bill collaborated in founding the Hochschule für Gestaltung in Ulm. He designed its buildings on a hillside in Ulm in 1950 and set up the curriculum for a school of creative design that was intended to link up with the work of the Bauhaus and pursue similar objectives. The buildings for the Hochschule (1950–55; see fig.) were his most important architectural works, and his design is based on complex relationships between a number of unobtrusive, geometrically elegant structures. Seen from outside, the buildings are embedded in the sloping site; in the interior, however, individual units or 'containers' are grouped around two central areas. This is similar to Bill's competition entry for the monument to the *Unknown Political Prisoner* (1953; unexecuted), London. Bill was principal of the Hochschule until 1955 and head of the departments of architecture and industrial design. Internal tensions forced him to resign and to leave the college in 1957.

There followed a period when Bill was able to realize most of his architectural projects, working in collaboration with others; examples include the Cinevox cinema and residential complex (1957–8) at Neuhausen, near Schaffhausen; two detached houses near Cologne, the Lichtdruck factory at Dielsdorf, near Zurich, and the Imbau administration building in Leverkusen (all in 1960–61). He designed several major exhibition displays and in 1960 he was awarded the important commission to design the pavilion for the Bilden und Gestalten sector of the Swiss National Exhibition held in Lausanne in 1964. This

building, now mostly dismantled, consisted of a group of modules spread over a large area; two elements, the box with the theatre and the square with the 'Hof der Künste', stood out of this carpet of modules, forming a contrast of 'solid' and 'void' in a neutral grid. Bill was also commissioned to extend the radio studio in Zurich (1964–74); he worked on the design for the bridge over the Lavina-Tobel (1966–7; with Aschwanden & Speck) near Tamins, and in 1967–8 he built a second house and studio for himself at Zumikon.

In 1968 Bill was awarded the city of Zurich art prize and elected a member of the Swiss Federal Parliament. He held the chair of environmental design at the Hochschule für Bildende Künste in Hamburg from 1967 to 1974 as well as several other public appointments. He was a prolific writer on art, architecture and design, producing several books and exhibition catalogues, as well as numerous contributions to art and architecture journals around the world. He continued to produce architectural designs, such as those for a museum of contemporary art (1981; unexecuted) in Florence and for the Bauhaus archive (1987; unexecuted) in Berlin. In 1982 he also entered a competition for an addition to the Neue Nationalgalerie in Berlin, built to a design by Mies van der Rohe. In the 1980s Bill was able to realize two of his most important, constantly recurring ideas in the field of sculpture on a large scale. The Pavillon-Skulptur (1979–83) in Bahnhofstrasse, Zurich, goes back to a prototype made in 1968 and consists of 64 parallelepipedals out of polished granite, which are arranged together to create a three-dimensional meander. For Kontinuität (1983–6), on the square in front of the Deutsche Bank in Frankfurt am Main, he reverts to the theme of the Möbius-strip in the *Unendliche Schleife* ('unending loop'; 1935; *see* SWITZERLAND, fig. 11), giving it a new interpretation: there are two strips of granite that as a result of several turns become entwined with one another. Bill's work was exhibited regularly at museums

Max Bill: Hochschule für Gestaltung, Ulm, 1950–55

and galleries all over Europe and in the USA; however, his influence as an architect, as opposed to an artist, was limited, perhaps due to the subtlety of the design principles behind his simple architectural forms.

WRITINGS

with others: *Zeitprobleme in der Schweizer Malerei und Plastik* (exh. cat., Zurich, Ksthaus, 1936)
with others: *Modern Swiss Architecture* (Basle, 1942)
with others: *Konkrete Kunst* (exh. cat., Basle, Ksthalle, 1944)
Die gute Form (exh. cat., Zurich, Kstgewmus.; Basle, Schweiz. Mustermesse; Cologne, Werkbundausstell.; 1949)
'Schönheit aus Funktion und als Funktion', *Werk*, xxxvi/8 (1949), pp. 272–4
Form: Eine Bilanz über die Formentwicklung um die Mitte des XX Jahrhunderts (Basle, 1952) [with an Eng. text]
Die gute Form (Winterthur, 1957)
with R. Wehrli and M. Staber: *Konkrete Kunst: 50 Jahre Entwicklung* (exh. cat., Zurich, Ksthaus, 1960)

BIBLIOGRAPHY

Max Bill (exh. cat., Ulm, Ulm. Mus., 1956)
M. Staber: *Max Bill* (London, 1964)
Max Bill (exh. cat. by L. Alloway and J. N. Wood, Buffalo, NY, Albright–Knox A.G., 1974)
E. Hüttinger: *Max Bill* (Zurich, 1977; rev. 3/1987)
V. Anker: *Max Bill ou la recherche d'un art logique: Essai d'une analyse structurale de l'oeuvre d'art* (Lausanne, 1979)
H. Frei: *Konkrete Architektur? Ueber Max Bill als Architekt* (Baden, 1991)

HANS FREI

Billant, Pierre du. *See* PIERRE DU BILLANT.

Billarderie d'Angiviller, Comte de la. *See* ANGIVILLER, Comte d'.

Bille, Ejler (Kristian Torbensen) (*b* Odder, nr Århus, 6 March 1910). Danish sculptor, painter and writer. He trained at the Kunsthåndværkerskole in Copenhagen with Bizzie Høyer from 1930 to 1932 and at the Kongelige Danske Kunstakademi (1933). Bille made his début as a sculptor at the Kunstnernes Efterårsundstilling (Artists' Autumn Exhibition) in Copenhagen in 1931. He became interested in abstract art very early in his career; in 1933, with the artist Vilhelm Bjerke-Petersen, he was one of the first artists in Denmark to exhibit abstract sculptures and paintings. In 1934 Bille was a founder-member with Richard Mortensen and Bjerke-Petersen of the artists' group Linien (The Line), whose journal of the same name he also co-edited. During Bille's many trips abroad in the 1930s he was particularly stimulated by the work of Alberto Giacometti, Hans Arp and Max Ernst. His originality was nevertheless clearly apparent in the early sculptures, which often used animals as subjects, for example *Marten* (1931) and *Walking Form* (1933–6; both Copenhagen, Stat. Mus. Kst).

As a painter Bille developed in a non-figurative direction characterized by a spontaneous sense of fantasy. His involvement with the COBRA group (1949–51) changed his use of colour. In paintings from these years appear swarms of miniature forms, people and bird-like creatures drawn in light green, yellow and grey. Bille made many trips to Bali and drew much inspiration from Balinese art for his sculpture and paintings. Among his larger projects were the decoration of the Jerne Seminary (1964) in Esbjerg, and of Danmarks Tekniske Højskole (1966–8), Copenhagen. He wrote many articles, in particular for the journal *Helhesten* between 1941 and 1944, and several books on art.

WRITINGS

Picasso, surrealisme, abstrakt kunst (Copenhagen, 1947)
Mine notater: Om billedkunst [My notes: about pictorial art] (Copenhagen, c. 1948)
'Kommentarer til mine skulpturer', *Signum*, i/3 (1961)

BIBLIOGRAPHY

P. Vad: *Ejler Bille* (Copenhagen, 1962)

MICHAEL FLINTHOLM

Biller [Bühler]. German family of goldsmiths, furniture-makers and engravers. Lorenz Biller (i) (*fl c.* 1664–85) achieved prominence with works for Emperor Leopold I, for whom he made a centrepiece with a knight on a horse (1680–84; Moscow, Kremlin, Armoury) that was sent to Moscow as an ambassadorial gift. Lorenz Biller (i)'s sons, Johann Ludwig Biller (i) (1656–1732), Albrecht Biller (1663–1720) and Lorenz Biller (ii) (*fl c.* 1678–1726), supplied silverware of the highest quality to several German courts, especially that of Prussia, for which Albrecht made large wine-coolers and 'pilgrim' bottles (1698; Berlin, Schloss Köpenick). The strongly sculptural style of these pieces suggests familiarity with the work of Andreas Schlüter. Albrecht Biller's abilities as a sculptor are also evident in his reliefs and in seven splendid silver vases he supplied to the court of Hesse-Kassel (*c.* 1700; Kassel, Hess. Landesmus.). The silver vases ordered by the court usually followed French fashions, yet the form and lavish decoration of these pieces are quite different. A pair of vases by Lorenz Biller (ii) (Florence, Pitti) with views of Hungarian forts are similarly overdecorated. In 1716 Albrecht also published designs for embossed silver and furniture in the style of Jean Berain I. Johann Jacob Biller (*d* 1723), descended from Lorenz (ii), was a goldsmith and engraver of ornament.

Johann Ludwig (i)'s sons, Johann Ludwig Biller (ii) (1692–1746) and Johannes Biller (1696–1745), also achieved renown as goldsmiths. Johann Ludwig (ii)'s French-influenced style is clear in the four *pots à oille* and a number of platters that are strictly classical in style (1721; priv. col.). He received commissions from several courts: he supplemented the 17th-century gold service of the court of Bavaria, for example, with two large *pots à oille*, and in 1731 he supplied George II, King of England and Elector of Hanover (*reg* 1727–60), with a silver table decorated with a relief of *Hercules Supporting the Vault of Heaven* (Nordstemmen, Schloss Marienburg). For King Frederick William I of Prussia, Johann Ludwig (ii) made a pair of tureens and a pair of enormous pâté tins (1731–3; Berlin, Schloss Köpenick). The three-dimensional eagles and lions on this piece may have been designed by a sculptor. About the same time Johann Ludwig (ii) produced part of the Riga Service, commissioned by the Russian court for William Augustus, Duke of Cumberland (St Petersburg, Hermitage). One of Johann Ludwig (ii)'s outstanding works is the gold service that he made for Anna, Empress of Russia (1736–40; St Petersburg, Hermitage). It comprises a toilet mirror, a ewer and basin, a covered bowl, various boxes, candlesticks, covered beakers and tea and coffee utensils. The forms show French influence; the decoration—*Bandelwerk* (ornament in the style of Jean Berain I) with interwoven cartouches and monograms—is more elaborate than that of most German plate of this period.

The surviving work of Johannes Biller is less extensive. He also supplied several courts with silverware and worked as a silver trader. In 1738 he was appointed court gold- and silversmith to the Prussian royal family. Four pedestal tables (Nordstemmen, Schloss Marienburg) with the coat of arms of the Braunschweig-Wolfenbüttel family were supplied with the table by Johann Ludwig (ii) to King George II. A mounted chalcedony bowl by Johannes was kept in the *Kunstkammer* of the Dukes of Württemberg (Stuttgart, Württemberg. Landesmus.). Johannes's son Johann Martin Biller appears to have worked only as a dealer of silver.

BIBLIOGRAPHY
S. Rathke-Kohl: 'Geschichte des Augsburger Goldschmiedegewerbes vom Ende des 17. bis zum Ende des 18. Jahrhunderts', *Schwäbische Geschichtsquellen und Forschungen*, vi (Augsburg, 1964)
H. Seling: *Die Kunst der Augsburger Goldschmiede, 1529–1868* (Munich, 1980)

FABIAN STEIN

Biller [née Allen], **Olive Allen** (*b* Ormskirk, Lancs, 17 Oct 1879; *d* Vancouver, 15 Oct 1957). Canadian painter and illustrator of English birth. She briefly attended the Liverpool Art School, the Lambeth School of Art, London, and finally, from 1900, the Slade School of Art, London, where she studied with Henry Tonks and others. From 1901 Biller was a successful illustrator of children's magazines, books and Christmas annuals, chiefly for T. C. & E. C. Jack of London. Many titles were translated into German, and they enjoyed wide circulation in Europe. After marrying John Biller (1912), she emigrated to Canada. While her commercial work virtually ceased there, she never stopped illustrating her life and surroundings in letters and sketchbooks. After her husband's death in World War I, Biller settled with her two children on James Island (near Victoria) in 1919. In 1927 she moved to Victoria, where she was an active member of the (Vancouver) Island Arts and Crafts Society, founded by Josephine Crease. Biller's watercolours often appeared in the Society's exhibitions. Relocation to Vancouver in 1934 gave her the opportunity of studying oils with Fred Varley and Jock Macdonald at the British Columbia College of Arts; she also took life drawing with Plato (Tonshik) Ustinov (1903–90) at the Vancouver School of Art. The college failed, but many of the artists who attended continued to work together. Biller's work is dominated by landscapes in an expressionistic manner; the lyricism differentiates it from the harsh intensity of the work of her contemporary Emily Carr. Biller exhibited at the Vancouver Art Gallery and other local venues; examples of her paintings are in the British Columbia Archives and Records Service, the Art Gallery of Greater Victoria and private Canadian collections.

UNPUBLISHED SOURCES
Victoria, BC Archvs & Rec. Serv., Dept Vis. Records [doc. and rec. of the Vancouver Island Arts and Crafts Society, 1909–41]

BIBLIOGRAPHY
E. Johnson: *Fact and Fable* (London, 1901) [illus. by Olive Allen]
M. Edgeworth, retold and illus. by O. Allen: *The Birthday Present* (London, 1908)
C. Sinclair, retold and illus. by Olive Allen: *Holiday House* (London, [?1908])
E. M. Whitaker: *Bee, Paul and Babs* (London, n.d.) [illus. by Olive Allen]

C. Johnson-Dean: *Josephine Crease and the Island Arts and Crafts Society* (MA thesis, U. Victoria, BC)

MICHAEL D. WILLIS

Billet. Ornamental device used extensively in the Romanesque period, particularly in the 12th century. It is formed of small blocks, either flat and square or cylindrical, spaced out in horizontal bands (see fig.). Billets in a single band occur frequently (e.g. the nave string course at Ely Cathedral; early 12th century), but are found less often in double bands (e.g. an impost in the crypt of Worcester Cathedral; from 1084). Their most common arrangement is in three bands: the blocks in the two lower bands are placed under the voids in the band above to give a chequerboard effect (e.g. the interior east windows of Paray-le-Monial Priory, France). Where there are more than three bands (e.g. the north portal of Charlieu Priory, France) the billets are tiny. Occasionally, as in the north portal of Fontgombault Abbey, billets are placed without voids, side by side.

Examples of billet ornament survive from the 6th century AD on the nave arcade of S Apollinare Nuovo, Ravenna, and on a capital from the north gate at Rusafa, Syria. Viollet-le-Duc dated a billeted impost from Poissy

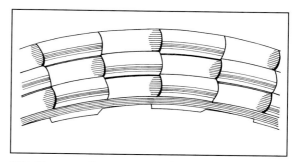

Billet, Norman or Romanesque type, formed by cylindrical blocks arranged in three bands

(France) to the Merovingian period. Lasteyrie believed the billet to be a debased form of the Classical dentil, and its ultimate prototype may have been the termination of roof timbers left exposed on the wooden structures that preceded stone temples. Billets went out of use as an architectural ornament after the 12th century.

Billets are also heraldic charges, dispersed across the field in rows (semés), the row beneath being placed under the spaces in the row above (e.g. the Deincourt shield, *c.* 1255: 'azure billety a dance or').

BIBLIOGRAPHY
E.-E. Viollet-le-Duc: *Dictionnaire raisonné de l'architecture française du XIe au XVIe siècle* (Paris, 1854–68), ii, pp. 208–10
R. de Lasteyrie: *L'Architecture religieuse en France à l'époque romane* (Paris, 1911, rev. 2/1929), pp. 574–6
A. Wagner: *Heraldry in England* (London and New York, 1946), p. 32, pl. xv
R. Krautheimer: *Early Christian and Byzantine Architecture*, Pelican Hist. A. (Harmondsworth, 1965), pl. 45A

FREDA ANDERSON

Billi, Antonio (*fl* 1500–?1530). Italian connoisseur. He was possibly the owner and perhaps also the compiler of a collection of notes about the lives and works of the artists of Florence in the Renaissance. The text of this collection, first published in 1891 by CORNELIUS VON FABRICZY, has survived in two versions in two different manuscripts in the Biblioteca Nazionale, Florence: the so-called Codice Strozziano (Cod. Magliabechiano cl XXV 636) and the Codice Petrei (Cod. Magliabechiano cl XIII 89). The first of these seems to be in fragments but is more accurate, the second somewhat careless but more complete; the two texts may be compared in the edition of 1892 by Karl Frey. The association of the texts with Billi was first made in writings by Fabriczy and Frey following Gaetano Milanesi's 1872 citing of Billi's name after an investigation of the Codice dell'Anonimo Magliabechiano (Florence, Bib. N. Cent. Cod. Magliabechiano cl XVII 17). Billi was a member of a distinguished family in Florence, who owned a chapel in SS Annunziata, for which, according to Vasari, they commissioned from Fra Bartolommeo in 1516 a painting of the *Salvator mundi* (Florence, Pitti); and it seems that the compiler of these notes, whether Billi or not, was someone like him, a connoisseur of the history of art who knew much about works in Florence but was limited in the vocabulary of criticism. The record begins with Cimabue and ends with Michelangelo; it contains reminiscences of phrases in the commentary of Cristoforo Landino (1424–1504) on Dante, and a reference to the recently made model of the New Sacristy in S Lorenzo by Michelangelo suggests a date for the notes of after 1481 and about 1529 or just after. Frey suggested that these notes were put together between 1516 and 1535. The record is in three parts, the first containing 27 names (28 if Andrea Tafi is included from the Codice Petrei) from Cimabue to Alesso Baldovinetti; the second, Florentine sculptors and architects from Brunelleschi to Antonio del Pollaiuolo, contains 10 names; the third, from a certain 'Bernardo dipintore' to Leonardo da Vinci and Michelangelo, mentions another 10 names. The text, composed of lists of works of art, anecdotes and notes on style, is interesting not only for the material it contains but also as a reflection of earlier sources—Filippo Villani, Landino and the life of Brunelleschi by Antonio di Ciaccheri Manetti; it seems that another source, now untraceable, was used for the trecento artists. It is clear this text was known to later writers, not only to the Anonimo Gaddiano but to Giovanni Battista Gelli and GIORGIO VASARI, yet something of the measure of Vasari's achievement can be gauged in how he was able to translate the brief accounts here into rich, coherent and reflective descriptions of the artists and their art. Crude though it is, the so-called 'Libro di Antonio Billi' stands as an interesting pointer to the interest in the visual arts among a certain class in Florence in the early years of the 16th century.

BIBLIOGRAPHY

G. Milanesi: 'Documenti inediti riguardanti Leonardo da Vinci', *Archv Stor. It.*, xvi (1872), pp. 219–21

C. von Fabriczy: 'Il libro di Antonio Billi e le sue copie nella Biblioteca Nazionale di Firenze', *Archv Stor. It.*, ser. 5, vii (1891), pp. 299–368

C. Frey: *Il libro di Antonio Billi esistente in due copie nella Biblioteca Nazionale di Firenze* (Berlin, 1892)

J. Schlosser-Magnino: *La letteratura artistica*, It. trans., F. Rossi, ed. O. Kurz (Florence, 1967), pp. 189–90, 198

G. Tanturli: 'Le biografie d'artisti prima del Vasari', *Il Vasari storiografo e artista: Atti del congresso internazionale nel IV centenario della morte: Arezzo, 2–8 settembre 1974*, pp. 275–98

Il libro di Antonio Billi (MS., 1516–35); ed. F. Benedettuci (Rome, 1991)

DAVID CAST

Billing, Hermann (*b* Karlsruhe, 7 Feb 1867; *d* Karlsruhe, 2 March 1946). German architect and teacher. He came from a family of building craftsmen established in Karlsruhe and studied there (1883–4) at the Kunstgewerbeschule, which, under the directorship of Hermann Götz (1848–1901), had become a focus of progressive tendencies in the applied arts in Germany. After a year's military service he moved on to study architecture at the Technische Hochschule, Karlsruhe, but did not graduate. Feeling little affinity with the doctrinaire Renaissance Revival ideas promoted by his teacher Josef Durm, he was more influenced by study tours in Germany, France, Italy, the Netherlands, Switzerland and Scandinavia. In 1888–92 he lived in Berlin and Aachen, where he worked in leading architectural practices and encountered the emerging stylistic movements of the day.

In 1892 Billing set up his own practice in Karlsruhe and produced some competition entries that attracted considerable attention, for example the design (1893) of a bridge over the River Weser at Bremen. Private commissions for houses, residential buildings and industrial developments followed. His work before 1899 is marked by an irreverent historicism, as he deployed elements of the most disparate styles in pursuit of a picturesque overall effect. After 1900 historical precedents gave way to freer, more individual forms influenced by *Jugendstil*. He designed a succession of buildings notable for their variety of façade articulation and their unconventionality of plan. Among these were the Hofapotheke building (1900–01) and the Baischstrasse development (1900–03), both in Karlsruhe, which were featured in German art and architecture periodicals. After 1904, when a music room designed by him attracted much attention at the Louisiana Purchase Exhibition, St Louis, he was mostly engaged on official commissions for large public buildings: the Kunsthallen at Mannheim (1905–7) and Baden-Baden (1906–9); the Kollegiengebäude (1907–11) at the Universität Freiburg im Breisgau; and the Rathaus (1907–11), Kiel. Stylistically these have more restful forms and an almost sculptural quality in the treatment of mass. These works won him official recognition and a number of honours, enhancing his reputation as one of the most important architects of this period in south-west Germany.

Billing worked with the assistance of a well-organized studio, occasionally running branch offices in other German cities and working in partnership with other architects, although they exerted virtually no artistic influence on him. In 1901 he began to teach architectural drawing at the Akademie der Bildenden Künste, Karlsruhe, where he became a professor in 1903. From 1906 to 1937 he also taught at the Technische Hochschule, Karlsruhe, becoming a professor of building construction and design in 1907. After 1911, and especially after World War I, Billing concentrated more on teaching, and in 1919 he was placed in charge of the reorganization of the Akademie der Bildenden Künste and Kunstgewerbeschule, both in Karlsruhe, which he joined together under the name Landeskunstschule. His architectural designs of the 1920s and 1930s, including the few that were actually built (e.g. the hospital, 1925–9, at Singen and the fire station, 1924–6, and Kolpingplatz development, 1927–35, both in Karlsruhe) show him trying to keep pace with recent changes in architecture. He incorporated influences from Neo-classicism, Expressionism and *Neues Bauen*, but never succeeded, as he had in the pre-war period, in imposing a style of his own. After the Nazis came to power in 1933, Billing withdrew more into private life; he was able to complete only one part of the Ettlinger-Tor-Platz development, Karlsruhe, which he had first planned in 1924: this was the postal headquarters building.

WRITINGS
Architekturskizzen (Stuttgart, 1904)

BIBLIOGRAPHY
K. Widmer: *Der Musikraum in der Weltausstellung St Louis von Professor Hermann Billing* (Stuttgart, [1904])
K. Martin: *Hermann Billing* (Berlin and Vienna, 1930)
D. V. Lafrenz: *Die Architektur des Kieler Rathauses von Hermann Billing (1867–1946)* (diss., U. Kiel, 1978)
G. Kabierske: 'Hermann Billings Kunsthalle und die Jubiläumskunstausstellung von 1907', *Jugendstil: Architektur um 1900 in Mannheim* (exh. cat., Mannheim, Städt. Ksthalle, 1985), pp. 225–47
——: 'Tempel oder Stall? Das Gebäude der Kunsthalle Baden-Baden', *Kunsthalle Baden-Baden: Ausstellungen, Inszenierungen, Installationen, 1909–86* (exh. cat., Baden-Baden, Staatl. Ksthalle, 1986), pp. 9–19, 140–01
——: *Der Architekt Hermann Billing (1867–1946): Leben und Werk* (diss., U. Freiburg im Breisgau, 1993)

GERHARD KABIERSKE

Billingsley, William (*b* Derby, *bapt* 12 Oct 1758; *d* Coalport, 16 Jan 1828). English ceramic artist and porcelain manufacturer. In 1774 he was apprenticed to William Duesbury at the DERBY porcelain factory, where his father, William Billingsley (*d* 1770), was a flower painter. He became one of their chief flower painters and some ten years later developed a new, soft, naturalistic style of painting flower petals on ceramics that came to be widely, though poorly, imitated at other English factories. His innovative technique involved painting with a heavily loaded brush, and then wiping away much of the paint with a virtually dry brush to produce more delicate colours and highlights (e.g. two-handled tray, *c.* 1790; Derby, Mus. & A.G.). Though particularly famous for his 'Billingsley roses', he also painted landscapes, buildings and other botanical subjects. In 1795 he helped John Coke (1776–1841) to set up a porcelain factory at Pinxton, Derbys. By 1799 he was working as a decorator of blanks, first in Mansfield, then moving in 1802 to Brampton-in-Torksey, Lincs, and in 1808 to Worcester. In 1813 he and his son-in-law, Samuel Walker (*fl* 1813–35), established a porcelain factory at Nantgarw, near Cardiff. Production difficulties caused financial problems and in 1814 they joined L. W. Dillwyn (1778–1855) at his larger and better equipped factory in Swansea. In 1817 they returned to Nantgarw where they succeeded in producing a popular soft-paste porcelain ware with deep green, turquoise and claret grounds and lavishly decorated with highly burnished gilding. Production continued until 1819 when the moulds were bought by the COALPORT PORCELAIN FACTORY, with which Billingsley remained associated until his death.

BIBLIOGRAPHY
W. D. John: *William Billingsley, 1758–1828: His Outstanding Achievements as an Artist and Porcelain Maker* (Newport, 1968)

JOHN MAWER

Billson, Edward (Fielder) (*b* Melbourne, 1892; *d* 17 April 1986). Australian architect. He was the first recipient of Melbourne University's diploma in architecture, which had been instituted in 1906 but not brought immediately into operation: he completed the course in 1913 and the diploma was granted two years later. In 1916 he entered the office of American architect Walter Burley Griffin, as his first Australian assistant. While with him, Billson designed his own father's house (1918) in Toorak in a chunky manner reminiscent of Griffin's American work and much influenced by Frank Lloyd Wright; and the Margaret Armstrong house (1919), Caulfield. A year later Billson and a fellow employee, Roy Lippincott, were successful in the competition for the Arts building (completed 1926; for illustration *see* AUCKLAND), University of Auckland, New Zealand. Lippincott left for New Zealand late in 1921, and Billson resigned from Griffin's office in 1922 but remained in Melbourne. In 1922 Billson and Lippincott received an honourable mention for their entry in the *Chicago Tribune* Tower Competition.

Billson's solo work in the late 1920s was not remarkable. An example is the Woodlands Golf Club (1925–9), Mordialloc, but he returned from a world tour in 1930 and asserted that the Spanish Mission style was dead and Australian architecture was lagging behind European Functionalism. A more adventurous phase of his practice ensued. He introduced a brick style reminiscent of W. M. Dudok in his extensive remodelling of the C. Werner & Co. building in 1933, several blocks of flats and two adjoining buildings at Warburton, for the Signs Publishing Co. (1936) and for the Sanitarium Health Food Co. (1936–7), Melbourne; the latter was awarded the Street Architecture Medal of the Royal Victorian Institute of Architects. In the post-war period Billson was responsible for grandstands for racecourses in Adelaide and Melbourne and, in 1960–61, for the renovation of William Butterfield's St Paul's Cathedral, Melbourne.

WRITINGS
'A Life in Architecture', *Architect* [Australia], ii (Sept 1968), p. 22

BIBLIOGRAPHY
R. Haddon: *Australian Architecture: A Technical Manual* (Melbourne, 1908)
D. L. Johnson: *Australian Architecture, 1901–51: Sources of Modernism* (Sydney, 1980)
P. Goad: 'Obituary: Edward Fielder Billson, 1892–1986', *Archit. Australia*, lxxv/5 (1986), p. 23

MILES LEWIS

Bimah [bema]. Raised pulpit in a synagogue from which the Torah is read (*see* JEWISH ART, §II, 1(iii) and fig. 8). □

Bimann, Dominik. *See* BIEMANN, DOMINIK.

Bimbi [del Bimbo], **Bartolomeo** (*b* Settignano, Florence, 1648; *d* Florence, 1730). Italian painter. He studied in Rome with Mario dei Fiori (1603–73), then with Lorenzo Lippi, Onorio Marinari (1627–1716) and Agnolo Gori (1610/20–78). He was employed at the Medici court, particularly under Ferdinand II and Cosimo III de' Medici and by Cosimo's daughter the Electress Palatine Anna Maria Luisa, and specialized in painting from nature animals or vegetables that had some extraordinary or freakish aspect; he classified these by species, season or place of origin. Some of his works are initialled and dated. His style, which remained constant throughout his long career, is distinguished by its scientific accuracy, and he must have had close contact with scientists and naturalists, such as Francesco Redi and Pier Antonio Micheli, who frequented the court of Cosimo III. No drawings have survived.

His flower paintings form a small part of his oeuvre yet perhaps best reveal his personality; they are touched with melancholy, in the manner of Willem van Aelst, whose works Bimbi may have seen in the Medici residences. His most important series of paintings, commissioned by the Medici from 1685 for the Villa dell' Ambrogiana and the Villa della Topaia, are two compositions entitled *Basket of Grapes*, four entitled *Basket of Citrus Fruits* and other paintings featuring various specimens of cherries, plums, figs and peaches (all Florence, Pitti). These large canvases are enclosed in frames decorated with accurately represented plant motifs; each displays many different fruits, all numbered with reference to an inscription in which the various species are listed with their scientific names. A series of paintings of vegetables, which includes *Beets*, *Spanish Thistle*, *Bean Plants* and *Truffle*, all of extraordinary size (Florence, Mus. Botan.), are each labelled with the date and place of discovery and often with the weight and dimensions of the subject. Similar information accompanies the *Two-headed Calf* and the *Two-headed Lamb* (Florence, Pitti, see 1985 exh. cat.).

BIBLIOGRAPHY

DBI
F. S. Baldinucci: *Vite* (1725–30); ed. A. Matteoli (1975), pp. 239–53
La natura morta italiana (exh. cat., ed. S. Bottari; Naples, Pal. Reale; Zurich, Ksthaus; Rotterdam, Boymans–van Beuningen; 1964), pp. 82–4
M. Gregori: 'Gli specchi dipinti della Galleria Riccardi', *Paragone*, xxiii/267 (1972), pp. 74–82
M. L. Strocchi: 'Bartolomeo Bimbi pittore naturalista alla corte Cosimo III de' Medici', *Agrumi, frutta e uve nella Firenze di Bartolomeo Bimbi pittore mediceo* (Florence, 1982), pp. 7–16
Natura viva in casa Medici (exh. cat., ed. M. Mosco; Florence, Pitti, 1985), pp. 33–63
Floralia (exh. cat., ed. M. Mosco; Florence, Pitti, 1988), pp. 92–106
M. L. Strocchi: *La natura morta in Italia*, 2 vols (Milan, 1989), pp. 592–6

MARIA LETIZIA STROCCHI

Binant (*d* Paris, *c.* 1857). French dealer. He was one of the first dealers in contemporary paintings to attempt to exploit the shortcomings of the annual Salons in Paris, which, during the 1820s, were becoming exclusive and infrequent. In 1827 he took over operation of the Galerie Lebrun, where in the previous year the dealer Charles Paillet had organized two large independent exhibitions. Binant organized a more modest exhibition there, made up of paintings refused by the jury of the 1827 Salon. By 1829 he was advertising a permanent exhibition of paintings by contemporary avant-garde artists at 7, Rue de Cléry (adjacent to the Galerie Lebrun), the location that would become his permanent address. He offered his paintings for hire in provincial towns, as well as abroad; this was a distinctive practice later to be particularly associated with his gallery. In addition to selling works from exhibitions, he held auctions periodically from the late 1820s. In a preface to a catalogue of one held in 1829, he stressed the advantage of investing in contemporary painting, using the popular argument that it avoided the risks of buying dubious Old Masters. His stock showed a bias towards English artists, particularly watercolourists; the works of the Fielding family, Thomas Shotter Boys and William Callow, and those of their French or Anglo-French friends Louis Francia, Charles Arrowsmith (*b* 1798) and Richard Parkes Bonington were all represented. The paintings in his gallery continued to reflect tastes in art during the 1820s and 1830s; the sale (Paris, Gal. Petit, 19 Jan 1857) held after his death featured works by such French Romantic painters as Tony Johannot and Eugène Devéria rather than those by English artists. Landscapes by Jules Coignet (1798–1860), a painter much favoured by dealers in the 1830s, were also sold.

LINDA WHITELEY

Binasco, Francesco. *See* MASTERS, ANONYMOUS, AND MONOGRAMMISTS, §III: MASTER B.F.

Binbirkilise [Turk.: 'The Thousand and One Churches']. Group of late Roman and Byzantine sites on the Karadağ, an isolated mountain in the plain north of the Taurus Mountains in the modern province of Karaman in south-central Turkey (Roman and Byzantine Lykaonia). The mountain has been convincingly identified as the site of Barata, a minor city attested as a bishopric from the 4th century AD to the 12th. On the mountain there are the remains of over 40 churches and associated buildings. These are concentrated in two groups: a lower settlement now known as Maden Şehir and an upper settlement called Değler (see fig.). There are also numerous other remains on the Karadağ, including some Hittite rock carvings,

Binbirkilise, view of the upper settlement of Değler

several churches built on the peaks of the mountain and several medieval fortifications.

Although known to scholars since 1826, the first and only survey of the Karadağ was that carried out by Sir William Ramsay (1851–1939) and GERTRUDE MARGARET LOWTHIAN BELL in 1905 and 1907. Much had disappeared between 1826 and 1905, and the destruction has continued so that Bell's photographs (U. Newcastle upon Tyne, Dept. Archaeol.) are an essential record of what has been lost. Most of the churches are stone built, vaulted basilicas with aisles and a narthex. Other types include a small number of centrally planned churches, the most important example being a small domed octagon with four projecting arms (Ramsay and Bell, no. 8) that corresponds to Gregory of Nyssa's late 4th-century description of a martyrium at Nyssa in Cappadocia; a group of cruciform burial chapels; and some cross-in-square plans. Church no. 7 in Maden Şehir is notable for a free-standing exedra set to its east, while the large basilica (no. 32) in Değler with a two-storey narthex and galleries above the nave is reminiscent of such churches as Hagia Sophia at Thessaloniki (*see* THESSALONIKI, §III, 5(i)) or the Koimesis (probably early 8th century; destr. 1922) at Nicaea (now İznik). In general the architecture has affinities with that of Syria (*see* EARLY CHRISTIAN AND BYZANTINE ART, §II, 2(i)(d), (ii)(c) and (iii)(c)) and Armenia (*see* ARMENIA, §II, 1), for example the widespread use of horseshoe-shaped arches in windows, nave colonnades and apses. There is little architectural sculpture other than simple lintels and string courses. Decorative brickwork is rare and limited to doors and windows. As a result the buildings have been described as 'village churches', but this impression of poverty and lack of sophistication is misleading. Almost all the churches bear the traces of wall plaster, and their impact must have been very different when covered with wall paintings in the manner of the Cappadocian rock-cut churches (*see* CAPPADOCIA, §2(ii)). As a whole they are evidence of relative prosperity. Without an adequate modern study the nature of the settlement and the source of its wealth remains obscure. Ramsay and Bell thought that the Karadağ was a holy mountain akin to Mt Athos or Sinai; another hypothesis would link the church building to the profits from nearby silver mines. Equally they may reflect the prosperity of a town serving the surrounding countryside in the Early Christian and Byzantine periods.

The dating of these churches is also difficult. At Maden Şehir the presence of churches convincingly dated by their plans to the 5th and 6th centuries AD and the signs of a later phase involving substantial rebuilding support the hypothesis that it was occupied up to the early 7th century, when the main settlement moved to Değler in search of greater security during the Arab invasions, and was then reoccupied from the mid-9th century until the Turkish conquest in the late 11th. A particularly obvious example of rebuilding is church no. 1, the largest basilica on the mountain, where a new vault was erected and the former nave columns replaced by piers. Eyice has suggested that the rebuilding at Maden Şehir reflects no more than earthquake damage and that there was no 7th-century break. At Değler, however, later building types (e.g. domed basilicas, cross-in-square churches and churches with galleries) and techniques (e.g. decorative brickwork, blind

arcading and niches) seem to predominate, with no clear example of a building from the 4th to the 6th century. None of the churches can be dated any later than the 11th century.

RBK

BIBLIOGRAPHY

W. M. Ramsay and G. L. Bell: *The Thousand and One Churches* (London, 1909) [essential photographs]
S. Eyice: *Karadağ (Binbirkilise) ve Karaman çevresinde arkeolojik incemeler/Recherches archéologiques à Karadağ (Binbirkilise) et dans la région de Karaman* (Istanbul, 1971) [Fr. summary]
K. Belke and M. Restle: *Galatien und Lykaonien* (1984), iv of *Tabula Imperii Byzantini* (Vienna, 1976–), pp. 138–43

MARK WHITTOW

Binck, Jakob [Jacob] (*b* Cologne, *c.* 1500; *d* Königsberg [now Kaliningrad], *c.* 1569). German painter, engraver and designer, active in Denmark and Sweden. While he worked as a court painter in Denmark *c.* 1530–50, he also served the Swedish court temporarily (1541–2) under Gustav Vasa, of whom he executed a portrait: this is untraced but is known through an old copy (Uppsala, U. Kstsaml.). Binck's picture, according to the copy, belonged to the so-called South German portrait school, showing the King half-figure against a neutral background. It is dominated more by the mass of the body and costume than by the impassive, three-quarter-profile face. Binck's picture has long since been widely distributed, represented on Swedish banknotes. A similar bust portrait of Christian III was engraved by Binck in 1535 (see fig.) Later, when he returned to Denmark from Sweden, he was influenced by the Dutch art of portraiture, with its more penetrating depiction of character. This can be seen in the portrait of

Jakob Binck: *Christian III, King of Denmark*, copperplate engraving, 1535

the Danish chancellor *Johan Friis* (1550; Hillerød, Frederiksborg Slot). Woodcuts after Binck's drawing of *Christian III* and the Danish state coat of arms, in a framework in the style of Cornelis Floris (Hollstein, nos 246, 263), were made for the Danish translation of the Bible in 1550. Binck probably collaborated on the exterior and interior decoration of Johan Friis's castle at Hesselagergaard on Fyn, where parts of the wall paintings with battle and chivalric motifs (?1549–51) have survived.

SVKL

BIBLIOGRAPHY
K. E. Steneberg: *Vasarenässansens porträttkonst* [Portraiture of the Vasa renaissance] (Stockholm, 1935)
O. Norn: *Hesselagergaard og Jacob Binck* (Copenhagen, 1961)

TORBJÖRN FULTON

Bindesbøll. Danish family of artists.

(1) (Michael) Gottlieb (Birkner) Bindesbøll (*b* Ledøje, Zealand, 5 Sept 1800; *d* Frederiksberg, Copenhagen, 14 July 1856). Architect. In 1819 he finished his apprenticeship as a mill-builder; his training had included instruction at the Kongelige Danske Kunstakademi in Copenhagen. In 1820, when he was given the opportunity of further education, he chose to study mathematics and physics with H. C. Ørsted, the discoverer of electromagnetism. Ørsted took him as a travelling companion on a tour through Germany, France and England in 1822. The journey was of great importance to Bindesbøll; in Paris he met H. C. Gau (1790–1853), who aroused his interest in Pompeii and in polychromy in Classical architecture. On his return to Denmark in 1823 he began to study architecture, at the same time acting as clerk of the works to Jørgen Hansen Koch (1789–1860), the court architect. Bindesbøll won the academy's Gold Medal in 1833 for a design for a Protestant cathedral in a medieval style, which constituted an abrupt break with the Neo-classical tradition prevailing in Denmark. The prize included a travelling scholarship, and in 1834 Bindesbøll began a lengthy study tour, visiting Greece, Asia Minor and Rome. He stayed in Rome until 1836.

While in Rome, Bindesbøll discussed plans with BERTEL THORVALDSEN for a museum in Denmark to house the latter's sculptures. Bindesbøll's first sketches (Copenhagen, Kon. Dan. Kstakad.) for the museum, in a templar, Greek Revival style, were not to the taste of Thorvaldsen, who wanted a modest building that would not overshadow the sculptures. The two subsequently worked together on the project. In 1839 Frederick VI assigned a building adjoining Copenhagen's Christiansborg Slot to the museum committee. The ground-floor of this structure, built under Christian VI (*reg* 1730–46), was being used as a store for royal carriages. Bindesbøll won the competition for the new museum in fierce rivalry with G. F. Hetsch and with his employer, Koch. Thorvaldsens Museum (1839–47; see fig.) was opened in 1848 and confirmed Bindesbøll as Denmark's most creative architect. He had planned a multicoloured building from the beginning; the result was much admired throughout Europe and constituted an important contribution to the largely theoretical contemporary discussions about architectural polychromy.

Although the proportions of the building were determined by the rectangular form of the old coach-house, the museum's plan was a clever adaptation of Bindesbøll's Roman projects. At the front of the building, a transverse barrel-vaulted ceiling gives the vestibule a spatial self-containment; the room is balanced, at the rear of the building, by the hall centred on Thorvaldsen's statue of *Christ*. Rows of small alcoves along the long sides of the building are decorated with the painted and stuccoed motifs then associated with the Pompeian style; all the rooms in the museum are covered with coffered barrel vaults and painted with 'Pompeian' colours that set off Thorvaldsen's plaster and marble sculptures.

The geometrical severity of the building's exterior is tempered by the decoration designed and executed by Bindesbøll and his painter associates. The structural elements are painted white, green and blue in contrast to the dominant yellow ochre. The portal motifs that run around the exterior and courtyard walls of the building are, in their rhythmic repetition, more decorative than functional. With their battered sides, they suggest an Egyptian character, but the motif's design was based on Bindesbøll's studies of ancient and Renaissance Roman architecture. They frame a frieze, executed by Jørgen Sonne in a special stucco intarsia, showing the transport of Thorvaldsen's sculptures from Rome to Copenhagen at the behest, and with the help of, ordinary men and women. The courtyard with Thorvaldsen's grave constitutes the most striking element of the design. Here the dark walls are enlivened by palms, laurels and oak-trees beautifully painted by Henrik Christian From (1811–79).

Despite Thorvaldsen's expressed fear that the building might become Bindesbøll's museum rather than his own, the finished work complements his sculptures and collections most beautifully. The museum was built in a period of stylistic transition, when Neo-classicism was losing adherents in Denmark but historicism had not yet gained a firm footing. For Bindesbøll's contemporaries, the museum's significance lay in its break with Neo-classical aesthetics and in its free interpretation of historical sources.

Bindesbøll stayed in Copenhagen during the museum's construction. Although he was appointed inspector of buildings in Holstein, then part of Denmark, in 1839, he did not move there until 1847. He was based in Århus as

Gottlieb Bindesbøll: Thorvaldsens Museum, Copenhagen, 1839–47

inspector of buildings for Jutland between 1849 and 1851, afterwards returning permanently to Copenhagen. The free historicism characteristic of Bindesbøll's work immediately after the completion of Thorvaldsens Museum is represented by the church (1850–52) at Hobro, Jutland. With its placement on an elevated site, the church is as much a romantic interpretation of a medieval castle as it is an example of the revival of Danish late medieval ecclesiastical architecture. This impression is accentuated by the pinnacles on the tower (unconventionally placed at the east end of the church), which resemble crenellations. Pinnacled gables top the west end and the three chapel-like projections on each side of the nave's exteriors. Red and yellow bricks are alternated in layers; in conjunction with the decorative placement of the bricks themselves, this gives an impression of fluidity to the church's exterior surfaces.

At the insane asylum Jyske Asyl (1850–51), north of Århus, style was subordinated to function. Bindesbøll formulated the plan in close collaboration with Harald Selmer (1814–79), the director of the hospital and a pioneer of Danish psychiatric research. The accommodation of the practical requirements of the institution contributed to an impression of simplicity. Wings for male and female patients extend from the main block, containing the assembly hall, chapel and staff quarters. The buildings are plain and uniform, the only ornament being the semicircular gables. The building materials are yellow and red bricks and red roof tiles. The hospital derives its aesthetic impact from the massing of the buildings and from Bindesbøll's ability to harmonize architecture with landscape. With such projects as the unrealized plan for St Hans Insane Asylum (1852–3) near Roskilde, Zealand, and Oringe (1854–7), the posthumously built insane asylum near Vordingborg, Zealand, the concept is fully developed. Bindesbøll created a continuing Danish tradition of functional construction for institutional building. An example of his domestic architecture is the residence built for the Physicians' Association in Østerbro, Copenhagen, in 1853. This two-storey block of flats was built after a cholera epidemic ravaged the oldest, central part of the city. The influence of foreign, particularly English, models is evident in the philanthropic impetus behind the building, in its organization and its terrace design.

Bindesbøll was professor at the Kongelige Danske Kunstakademi, Copenhagen, for three years before his death but never taught, and his importance to his own generation and later ones lay in his executed buildings, particularly Thorvaldsens Museum.

BIBLIOGRAPHY
C. Bruun and L. P. Fenger: *Thorvaldsens Museums historia* (Copenhagen, 1892)

H. Bramsen: *Gottlieb Bindesbøll: Liv og arbejder* [Gottlieb Bindesbøll: life and works] (Copenhagen, 1959)

K. Millech: 'Bindesbøll's museum', *Meddel. Thorvaldsens Mus.* (1960), pp. 1–136

L. Balslev-Jørgensen: 'Thorvaldsens Museum: Symbol og fortolkning' [Thorvaldsen's Museum: symbol and interpretation], *Meddel. Thorvaldsens Mus.* (1970), pp. 7–15

——: 'Thorvaldsen's Museum: A National Monument', *Apollo*, n. s., xcvi/127 (1972), pp. 198–205

WIVAN MUNK-JØRGENSEN

(2) Thorvald Bindesbøll (*b* Copenhagen, 21 July 1846; *d* Copenhagen, 27 Aug 1908). Architect and designer, son of (1) Gottlieb Bindesbøll. Having finished his studies at the Kongelige Danske Kunstakademi, Copenhagen, in 1876, he travelled to Italy in 1882 and 1897. His modest architectural career began with two historicizing manor houses in southern Sweden, Hjuleberg (1875) and Mostrop (1880). The well-proportioned red-brick institution, 'Bombebøssen' (1891), in Christianhavn, Copenhagen, is an example of classical simplicity, while the house built for Georg Bestle (wine dealer and titular councillor of state) in 1897 in Vedbæk, Zealand, is in the 17th-century revival white-plastered mansion style popular during this period. About 1900 the easy curves of the Art Nouveau style began to appear in his work, including his decorations (1905–7) on Skagen Fish Warehouses, which were also influenced by old Norse architecture. He also produced monuments and designs for fountains.

Bindesbøll's chief achievement was the rejuvenation of the Danish applied and decorative arts. The fine vigorous lines of his decorative work were applied with inexhaustible variety to every sphere of design and all types of interior. The best of his Art Nouveau designs were pioneer works, forerunners of much 20th-century abstract art. Most noteworthy were his ceramics (e.g. enamelled earthenware plate, 1901; Paris, Mus. A. Déc.), inspired by Italian *sgraffito* techniques and produced between 1883 and 1906. His style developed from classical neatness through the vogue for Japanese motifs towards liberated, asymmetrical and forceful abstraction, often characterized by tautly rounded and hard-edged contrasting forms. He produced book designs and other graphic work from the 1880s, and the clean lines of his labels for Carlsberg Pilsner (1897–1904) became world-famous. At the Exposition Universelle in Paris in 1900 his silverware received international recognition. From about 1890 he designed furniture in three distinct styles: he continued to work in the style of his father; he revived traditional Danish designs; and he created Art Nouveau pieces covered with metal inlay or upholstery based on the embroidery designs of his childhood (e.g. white lacquered pine chair, exh. Exposition Universelle, Paris, 1900; Copenhagen, Kstindustmus.). It was only with the Council of Europe exhibition *Les Sources du XXe siècle* in Paris (1960–61) that Bindesbøll's importance was properly recognized.

BIBLIOGRAPHY
K. Madsen: *Thorvald Bindesbøll* (Copenhagen, 1943)

Les Sources du XXe siècle (exh. cat., Paris, Mus. N. A. Mod., 1960), pp. 286–9

Thorvald Bindesbøll (exh. cat., Copenhagen, Kstforen., 1982)

I. Brown: *Thorvald Bindesbølls møbler* [Thorvald Bindesbøll's furniture] (diss., U. Copenhagen, 1983)

——: 'Thorvald Bindesbøll', *Herculanum paa Sjælland: Klassicisme og nyantik i dansk møbeltradition* [From Herculanum to Sjælland: classicism and Neo-classicism in the Danish furniture tradition], ed. M. Gelfer-Jørgensen (Copenhagen, 1988), pp. 266–79

IBEN BROWN

Binding medium. *See* VEHICLE.

Bindo, Benedetto di. *See* BENEDETTO DI BINDO.

Bindon, Francis (*b c.* 1690; *d* 2 June 1765). Irish painter and architect. He was the only Irish artist other than

Charles Jervas to study at Godfrey Kneller's Academy of Painting and Drawing, London. Bindon's family held an estate in Co. Clare, and, like his father and brother, he was MP for Ennis, Co. Clare. He travelled in Italy, had a notable library and was a friend of Jonathan Swift, whom he painted four times between 1735 and 1740. During his lifetime he enjoyed a high reputation as a painter, probably based more on lack of competition than on his skill.

The buildings most securely attributed to Bindon are houses in Co. Kilkenny: Bessborough (c. 1744; rebuilt), Woodstock (mid-1740s; ruined) and Castle Morres (partially destr.). They are related in style to the houses of Richard Castle, with whom Bindon collaborated in the 1740s (he probably completed Russborough, Co. Wicklow, after Castle's death in 1751). The houses confirm Bindon's status as a gentleman–amateur rather than an innovative and imaginative professional. The routine rhythms of his façades are enlivened by rusticated detail (Gibbs surrounds and quoins), features that suggest Bindon's presence or influence at undocumented contemporary houses such as Sopwell, Co. Tipperary, Altavilla, Co. Limerick, and Carnelly, Co. Clare, and also at St John's Square (begun 1751), Limerick. The forecourt at Curraghmore, Co. Waterford, sometimes attributed to Bindon, is probably by John Roberts of Waterford (1712–96).

BIBLIOGRAPHY
Strickland
G. Faulkner: Obituary, *Dublin J.*, 3977 (4–8 June 1765)
The Knight of Glin: 'Francis Bindon (*c.* 1690–1765)', *Bull. Irish Georg. Soc.*, x/2–3 (1967), pp. 1–36
A. Crookshank and the Knight of Glin: *The Painters of Ireland* (London, 1978)

EDWARD McPARLAND

Binellus (*fl* 1195–1201). Italian sculptor and architect. He is first recorded in an inscription of 1195 set to the right of the main portal of S Silvestro, Bevagna (Umbria). With Rodulfus he signed the portal on the more important church of S Michele in the same square in Bevagna, but the inscription is undated. The portals on both churches have an archivolt with rich foliate decoration, but that at S Michele is further enriched by an inlaid marble guilloche on the outer order and large impost blocks bearing reliefs of flying angels. The portal of the north façade of Foligno Cathedral, which is dated 1201, is still more refined and is again signed by both Binellus and Rodulfus, the last work that can be firmly associated with these sculptors. The portal bears foliate decoration on the archivolt and an inlaid marble motif on the outer order, but it is also decorated with couchant lions at the base of each column, beautifully carved inhabited scroll-work on the jambs and an inner archivolt with panels bearing the Signs of the Zodiac on the outer face and Symbols of the Evangelists, carved almost in the round, projecting from the soffit; reliefs of the Holy Roman Emperor Frederick I ('Barbarossa') and Bishop Anselm are set on the inner face of the doorposts. The intricately rendered foliate and figurative relief-carving on these portals seems to be derived from such Umbrian sources as the leaf-carving on the portals of S Salvatore, Spoleto, while the inlaid marble patterns are characteristic of Roman marble-work (*see* COSMATI).

The sculptors named on the inscriptions may also have been responsible at least for the façades of these buildings,

which are typical of late Umbrian Romanesque churches: plain ashlar, articulated only by a bold horizontal cornice or corbel-table separating the lower zone from the upper and pierced by symmetrically placed window-openings; similar but simpler examples, no doubt connected to the workshop of these sculptors, may be seen at S Eufemia, Spoleto, and at S Felice, Giano.

BIBLIOGRAPHY
M. Faloci Pulignani: *Una pagina di arte umbra* (Foligno, 1903)
U. Tarchi: *L'arte nell'Umbria e nella Sabina*, ii (Milan, 1937) [pls]
E. Hutton: *The Cosmati: The Roman Marble Workers of the XIIth and XIIIth Centuries* (London, 1950), pp. 40, 52
A. Prandi and others: *Ombrie romane*, Nuit Temps (La Pierre-qui-vire, 1980), pp. 233–45

PAUL WILLIAMSON

Bing, Ilse (*b* Frankfurt am Main, 23 March 1899). German photographer, active in France and the USA. Self-taught, she used only the small format Leica camera throughout her career. She produced photographic essays for German magazines and, inspired by Florence Henri, she went to Paris in 1930, where she produced fashion photography for *Vu* and *Harper's Bazaar*. Bing incorporated photojournalist techniques into images about motion and, influenced by abstract painting and by Surrealism, she built up geometric compositions using real objects, as in her photograph of *Paris, Eiffel Tower Scaffolding with Star* (1931; Chicago, IL, A. Inst.). She moved to New York in 1941. Bing experimented with night photography, cropping and enlarging, solarization and, briefly, with colour before she gave up photography completely in 1959.

BIBLIOGRAPHY
N. Barrett: *Ilse Bing: Three Decades of Photography* (exh. cat., New Orleans, LA, Mus. A., 1985)

SHERYL CONKELTON

Bing, S(iegfried) (*b* Hamburg, 26 Feb 1838; *d* Vaucresson, nr Paris, 6 Sept 1905). French art dealer, critic and patron, of German birth. Often misnamed Samuel, he was a major promoter of Japanese art and ART NOUVEAU. From a wealthy, entrepreneurial Hamburg family, he trained as an industrial decorator for ceramics under the guidance of his father and independently in Paris during the Second Empire (1852–70). After the Franco-Prussian War (which he spent in Belgium) Bing established a thriving Oriental trading business, primarily of Japanese arts, the success of which permitted the opening of his Oriental crafts shop in Paris in the late 1870s. Following a trip to Japan, he expanded the business in the 1880s, selling both contemporary and ancient Japanese objects, to meet the demand for Oriental merchandise. At the end of the 1880s, as JAPONISME developed, Bing founded a monthly periodical, *Le Japon artistique* (pubd simultaneously in Eng., Fr. and Ger., 1888–91), and organized a series of exhibitions of rare Japanese art, featuring ceramics and *ukiyoe* prints. Through Bing's sponsorship, the taste for Japanese art escalated; he became one of the main collectors of Japanese ceramics and prints, and his private collection was a mecca for international artists.

Tired of being seen solely as a merchant of Japanese art, Bing accepted a commission from the French government in 1894 to investigate artistic culture in the USA. His report, eventually published as *La Culture artistique en Amérique* (Paris, 1896), received considerable attention on both sides of the Atlantic. This trip fired Bing's interest in design, giving rise in December 1895 to the reopening of his gallery as the first Salon of international Art Nouveau. The controversial exhibition was openly criticized by many in the press; only a few advocates of modernism came to Bing's aid. He found support among designers who recognized that his commissions for entire room ensembles, such as those given to the Belgian artists Henry Van de Velde and Georges Lemmen, were pioneering. These interiors, along with stained-glass windows commissioned from the Nabis painters Edouard Vuillard, Paul Ranson, Pierre Bonnard, Henri-Gabriel Ibels and Félix Vallotton, as well as Toulouse-Lautrec (Paris, Mus. d'Orsay), and executed by Louis Comfort Tiffany in America, were installed in Bing's redesigned Art Nouveau galleries, the creation of Louis Bonnier. The Salon of 1895 also demonstrated that all the arts were equal in helping to professionalize the new field of interior design. Subsequently, small exhibitions such as that of the paintings and prints of Edvard Munch in 1896, did much to galvanize the avant-garde behind Bing as well as to separate his concepts from the conservative tendencies in France.

At the end of the 1890s Bing's success as an arbiter of taste was further enhanced by his shift from selling such items as fabrics and wallpapers by William Morris, silks from Liberty & Co., London, and metalwork by the English Arts and Crafts designer W. A. S. Benson, towards producing pieces by artisans working solely for his own workshops. By 1898–9 Bing had renovated an unused storage area behind his gallery to establish studios where plans for furniture, ceramics and jewellery were made. In 1899 he exhibited examples of his jewellery in the Grafton Galleries, London, where they were either ridiculed or ignored by the press and public. Bing's ultimate success among devotees of design reform climaxed with the construction and opening of his own pavilion, Art Nouveau Bing (destr.), at the Exposition Universelle in Paris in 1900. This building, financed solely by Bing's fortune, was prepared by the young architect André-Louis Arfvidson, who was inspired by Bonnier's work, and incorporated modern rooms as sample environments of how a modern home could be furnished. Designed by Georges de Feure, Edouard Colonna and Eugène Gaillard, the rooms excited comment internationally, although there was little press coverage in Paris. Examples of the sitting-room furniture designed by de Feure were sold to the Danske Kunstindustrimuseum in Copenhagen; pieces from Gaillard's dining-room were secured by the Museum für Kunst und Gewerbe, Hamburg. These samples were in turn displayed in applied arts museums where young craftsmen studied them as models of contemporary design. Bing contributed to the Esposizione Internazionale d'Arte Decorativa in Turin (1902); examples of his ceramics designed by Colonna and de Feure and produced by the firm of Porcelaines GDA of Limoges were well received, and Bing received a prestigious award.

In 1904 Bing sold his gallery and auctioned his Art Nouveau pieces, ending his effective leadership in French design reform. He ceded the Oriental side of his business to his son Marcel Bing, a talented Art Nouveau jeweller. A major sale of Bing's private Oriental art collection was held in 1906 in Paris, bringing estimable prices and further adding to the prestige of his connoisseurship. The Art Nouveau aspect of his entrepreneurial acumen languished until re-examinations of the period in the 1970s and 1980s demonstrated his vital significance as a promoter and innovator.

BIBLIOGRAPHY

R. Koch: 'Art Nouveau Bing', *Gaz. B.-A.*, n. s. 6, liii (1959), pp. 179–90

G. P. Weisberg: 'Samuel Bing: International Dealer of Art Nouveau', *Connoisseur*, clviii (1971), pp. 200–05, 275–83; clix (1971), pp. 49–55, 211–19

——: 'Siegfried Bing, Louis Bonnier et la Maison de l'Art Nouveau en 1895', *Bull. Soc. Hist. A. Fr.* (1982–3), pp. 241–9

——: 'S. Bing's Craftsmen Workshops: A Location and Importance Revealed', *Source* (Autumn 1983), pp. 42–8

——: *Art Nouveau Bing: Paris Style, 1900* (New York, 1986)

——: 'Félix Vallotton, Siegfried Bing and l'Art Nouveau', *A. Mag.*, lx (Feb 1986), pp. 33–7

——: 'On Understanding *Artistic Japan*', *J. Dec. & Propaganda A.* (1986), pp. 6–19

——: 'S. Bing, Edvard Munch and l'Art Nouveau', *A. Mag.*, lxi (Sept 1986), pp. 58–64

C. Denney: 'English Book Designers and the Role of the Modern Book at l'Art Nouveau', *A. Mag.*, lxi (May 1987), pp. 76–83; (Summer 1987), pp. 49–57

G. P. Weisberg: 'S. Bing and *La Culture artistique en Amérique*: A Public Report Re-examined', *A. Mag.*, lxi (March 1987), pp. 59–63

——: 'Siegfried Bing and Industry: The Hidden Side of l'Art Nouveau', *Apollo*, cxxviii/321 (1988), pp. 326–9, 379

GABRIEL P. WEISBERG

Bingham, George Caleb (*b* Augusta County, VA, 20 March 1811; *d* Kansas City, MO, 7 July 1879). American painter. Raised in rural Franklin County, MO, Bingham experienced from an early age the scenes on the major western rivers, the Missouri and the Mississippi, that inspired his development as a major genre painter. During his apprenticeship to a cabinetmaker, he met the itinerant portrait painter Chester Harding, who turned Bingham's attention to art. Teaching himself to draw and compose from art instruction books and engravings, the only resources available in the frontier territories, Bingham began painting portraits as early as 1834. The style of these works is provincial but notable for its sharpness, clear light and competent handling of paint.

Bingham travelled to Philadelphia in 1838, where he saw his first genre paintings. He spent the years 1841 to 1844 in Washington, DC, painting the portraits of such political luminaries as *Daniel Webster* (Tulsa, OK, Gilcrease Inst. Amer. Hist. & A.). His roster of impressive sitters later enabled him to attract many portrait commissions. He settled back in Missouri at the end of 1844 and, although portraits would always form the greater portion of his work, it was over the next seven years that he made the outstanding contribution of his era to American genre painting. On the East Coast, Bingham's slightly older contemporary William Sidney Mount had been exhibiting genre scenes of farmers since 1830. In the 1840s, however, the major focus of national concern shifted to westward expansion and its meaning for American society. Bingham's work stunningly interpreted these concerns with three major motifs.

The first was that of the fur trader, which he developed in his painting *Fur Traders Descending the Missouri* (1845; New York, Met.). Against an imposing background of golden light and towering clouds, he placed a fur trader and his half-breed son (so identified in the original title of the painting), along with their chained bear cub, in a canoe floating downstream. Looking out at the viewer, the men seem thoughtful and cleanly dressed—not at all the uncivilized creatures described in contemporary literature. The surface of the water is mirror-like; reflections of the canoe, the oar and other details lock the scene into place. It is a romantic vision, transforming into a peaceful idyll the very terms of commercial gain in which the continent had been explored. The painting pays tribute to a vanishing phenomenon, for soon after the Panic of 1837 the market for pelts dropped disastrously and never recovered. As such it epitomizes Bingham's role in preserving, and reinterpreting, the vanishing West. *Fur Traders* is moreover characteristic of his style. His clearly delineated figures derive from character studies of frontier people that he had sketched on paper. He created a formal design, which conveyed an ordered, inviolate world (there exist no studies for his works other than drawings of individual figures); he painted smoothly, with an absence of brushstroke; and his tonalities were light, dominated by areas of bright colour and often, as in this painting, luminous.

Bingham's second motif explored the life of the Mississippi raftsman. His *Jolly Flatboatmen* (1846; Detroit, MI, Manoogian Mus.; see fig.), again dominated by a clear light, is even more tightly organized than *Fur Traders*, with a number of figures balancing one another. This predilection for order, fundamental to Bingham's very energies as an artist, contributed crucial meanings to his renderings of the West. These are often ironical meanings. No group of men on the western rivers seemed less responsible to society than the violent, fun-loving, gambling flatboatmen. He painted the flatboatmen in several versions, including scenes of dancing and cardplaying, for example *Raftsmen Playing Cards* (1847; St Louis, MO, A. Mus.), attracting audiences in St Louis and other western cities as well as in the East. His paintings transformed the terms in which frontier life had been understood, negating the threat of the rough frontiersman to civilized life. The American Art-Union, acting on a demand for this vision in the East during a period in which the nation was aggressively expanding westward, became Bingham's major patron. In 1847 it engraved *Jolly Flatboatmen* for an audience of about 10,000 subscribers.

The final motif that Bingham explored was that of the election. No longer near the river (and the river's associations with commerce and movement), these scenes take place in a village. Clearly influenced by Hogarth, but inspired by his own experience in politics, they show politicians arguing their point in *Stump Speaking* (1854), citizens casting their vote in *County Election* (1851 and

George Caleb Bingham: *Jolly Flatboatmen*, oil on canvas, 969×1232 mm, 1846 (Detroit, MI, Alex and Marie Manoogian Museum)

1852; one version in St Louis, MO, A. Mus.) and the electorate gathered to hear election results in *Verdict of the People* (1855; all three in St Louis, MO, Boatmen's N. Bank). In each painting Bingham shows the wide range of social class, economic standing and apparent intellectual capability in the electorate; he chronicles political abuses as well—such as drinking at the polls and electioneering at the ballot box. Bingham exhibited *County Election* widely and painted a second version that was engraved by the Philadelphia engraver John Sartain (1808–97).

Although the genre scenes are Bingham's major achievement, he also painted landscapes. His *Emigration of Daniel Boone* (1851; St Louis, MO, George Washington U.), while inspired by the popularity of the theme rather than his own experience, pictured the early Western scout leading a caravan of settlers over the Cumberland Gap. Bingham went to Düsseldorf in 1857, where he painted several large historical portraits on commission, notably a *Thomas Jefferson* (destr. 1911). His angry historical painting protesting against the imposition of martial law in Missouri during the Civil War, *Order No. 11* (1865–8; Cincinnati, OH, A. Mus.), is full of quotations from earlier works of art. Although Bingham was increasingly involved in state and local politics, he continued his work as a portrait painter. The major repositories for his paintings and drawings are the St Louis Art Museum and the Boatmen's National Bank of St Louis.

BIBLIOGRAPHY
C. Rollins, ed.: 'Letters of George Caleb Bingham to James S. Rollins', *MO Hist. Rev.*, xxxii (1937–8), pp. 3–34, 164–202, 340–77, 484–522; xxxiii (1938–9), pp. 45–78, 203–29, 349–84, 499–526
J. F. McDermott: *George Caleb Bingham: River Portraitist* (Norman, OK, 1959)
J. Demos: 'George Caleb Bingham: The Artist as Social Historian', *Amer. Q.*, xvii/2 (1965), pp. 218–28
E. M. Bloch: *George Caleb Bingham: The Evolution of an Artist*, 2 vols (Berkeley, 1967) [with cat. rais.]
R. Westervelt: 'Whig Painter of Missouri', *Amer. A. J.* [New York], ii/1 (1970), pp. 46–53
E. M. Bloch: *The Drawings of George Caleb Bingham* (Columbia, MO, 1975)
B. Groseclose: 'Painting, Politics, and George Caleb Bingham', *Amer. A. J.*, x/2 (1978), pp. 5–19
M. Shapiro and others: *George Caleb Bingham* (St Louis, MO, and New York, 1990)
W. Truettner and others: *The West as America: Reinterpreting Images of the Frontier* (Washington, DC, 1991)

ELIZABETH JOHNS

Binket. *See* TASHKENT.

Binnenhuis, 't. Interior design cooperative and retail store established in Amsterdam in 1900. The architect and designer H. P. Berlage and the designer Jacob van den Bosch (1868–1948) set out to provide well-designed, reasonably priced furniture and products for mass consumption. They received financial backing from a number of wealthy friends and were joined in the venture by Willem Hoeker (*b* 1862), director of the Amstelhoek earthenware factory. Many artists working in different specialities also joined the venture, among them WILLEM PENAAT and JAN EISENLÖFFEL, who were respectively directors of a furniture workshop and metal workshop attached to the Amstelhoek workshop. The vision of a cooperative serving a mass public foundered, however, and many of the artists left 't Binnenhuis in January 1902.

Although van den Bosch and Berlage stayed on, the latter left in 1913. The early production of 't Binnenhuis was seen as representative of the rationalist trend in the Nieuwe Kunst, and in the early years there was considerable interest in the group's interiors. Around 1907 the severity of rationalism was tempered by a more decorative and comfortable style adapted to the taste of the period by van den Bosch, who was responsible for the commercial side of the business; the original ideal of producing good, affordable design for a mass public had long since been abandoned. Nevertheless, the financial situation continued to be precarious, and in 1936 't Binnenhuis went into liquidation.

BIBLIOGRAPHY
L. Gans: *Nieuwe Kunst: De Nederlandse bijdrage tot de Art Nouveau: Dekoratieve kunst, kunstnijverheid en architektuur, omstreeks 1900* [Nieuwe Kunst: The Dutch contribution to Art Nouveau: The decorative arts, the applied arts and architecture, *c.* 1900] (Utrecht, 1966)
Jac. van den Bosch en de vernieuwing van het Binnenhuis [Jac. van den Bosch and the renovation of 't Binnenhuis] (exh. cat., ed. M. Boot and others; Haarlem, Vleeshal, 1976)
F. Leidelmeijer and D. van der Cingel: *Art Nouveau en Art Deco in Nederland* (Amsterdam, 1983)
C. Schoemaker: 'Meubels en interieurontwerpen' [Furniture and interior designs], *Jac. van den Bosch, 1868–1948* (exh. cat., ed. J. J. Heij; Assen, Prov. Mus. Drenthe, 1987), pp. 44–85

PETRA DUPUITS

Binnink. *See* BENING.

Binns, Charles Fergus (*b* Worcester, UK, 4 Oct 1857; *d* Alfred, NY, 4 Dec 1934). American potter and teacher of English birth. As the son of Richard William Binns (1819–1900), director of the Worcester Royal Porcelain Co. Ltd, he was exposed at an early age to the pottery industry. After holding various positions in the Worcester firm, he resigned. In 1897 he settled in the USA, where he was appointed director of the Technical School of Arts and Sciences in Trenton, NJ, and superintendent of the Ceramic Art Co., also in Trenton. In 1900 he became the first director of the New York College of Clayworking and Ceramics at Alfred University, NY. In this capacity and as a founder-member and officer in the American Ceramic Society, he greatly influenced the development of American ceramics. He frequently contributed articles to *Craftsman*, *Keramic Studio* and the *Transactions* and *Journal* of the American Ceramic Society, and he was the author of several books. His own technically exquisite stoneware, produced at Alfred, was inspired by early Chinese ceramics and emphasized the interrelationship of classical shape and finely textured glazes. His students included Maija Grotell, Arthur Eugene Baggs and R. Guy Cowan, who became important potters and teachers.

WRITINGS
Ceramic Technology (London, 1897)
The Story of the Potter (London, 1898)
The Potter's Craft (New York, 1910, rev. 4/1967)

BIBLIOGRAPHY
S. R. Strong: 'Charles Fergus Binns: The Searching Flame', *Amer. Cer.*, i (1982), pp. 44–9

ELLEN PAUL DENKER

Binyinyiwuy (*b* 1928; *d* 1982). Australian Aboriginal painter. He was a leader of the Ngaladharr Djambarrpuyngu clan, Dhuwa moiety, who lived at Milingimbi mission (later Milingimbi township) for most of his adult life. His clan country was at Djarraya, Napier Peninsula, and the totemic ancestor to which he had particular affiliation was Ḏa:rrpa, King Brown Snake. According to Wells (pp. 229–30), Binyinyiwuy originally visited the mission only to raid the store or to 'make havoc among the young women', and he declared that he wanted nothing of white people or their ways. He was persuaded to settle when offered cash in return for bark paintings. He had a reputation among Yolngu of the Milingimbi region as a man of great knowledge. Together with his younger brother Djatijiwuy (*b c.* 1934), whose death in 1975 was a great blow, he was very active in the ritual life of the township and mainland community. The topics of Binyinyiwuy's bark paintings between 1960 and 1982 included those belonging to the Djambarrpuyngu group: Ḏa:rrpa (King Brown Snake), Milkmilk (Mosquito) and Baṉumbirr (Morning Star); the last appears to have been his favourite subject. Baṉumbirr is an exchange ceremony involving an exchange of gifts between two clan groups. Djambarrpuyngu people at Milingimbi performed this ceremony almost every year during the early 1970s, the years of Binyinyiwuy's maturity as an elder. He also painted other topics belonging to his mother's clan, Daygurrgurr Gupapuyngu, including Birrkuḏa (Honeybee), Dhupiḏitj (the male ancestral 'boss' of the Honeybee and the Nga:rra ceremony), Wurrpaṉ (Emu) and Waṉ'kurra (Bandicoot). Topics belonging to his maternal grandmother's clan, Liyagalawumirr (Dhuwa moiety), included the Ngulmarrk ceremony and Wititj or Yulunggur (Olive Python). His paintings are represented in the collection of the Australian National Gallery, Canberra.

BIBLIOGRAPHY

A. E. Wells: *Milingimbi: Ten Years in the Crocodile Islands of Arnhem Land* (Sydney, 1963)

H. Groger-Wurm: *Australian Aboriginal Bark Paintings and their Mythological Interpretation*, Australian Aboriginal Studies, xxx (Canberra, 1973), pp. 48, 61, 85, 119, 129, 172

L. A. Allen: *Time before Morning: Art and Myth of the Australian Aborigines* (New York, 1975), pp. 23, 136, 139, 230

IAN KEEN

Binyon, (Robert) Laurence (*b* Lancaster, 10 Aug 1869; *d* Reading, 10 March 1943). English writer and critic. He studied Classics at Trinity College, Oxford. From 1893 he worked at the British Museum, London, first in the Department of Printed Books and later in the Department of Prints and Drawings. Throughout his life he worked as both a poet and art historian. At the turn of the century he was part of a group of intellectuals and artists who met at the Wiener Cafe in New Oxford Street; among them were William Rothenstein, Charles Ricketts, Charles Shannon, Lucien Pissarro, Edmund Dulac (1882–1953) and Walter Sickert. Many of Binyon's poetic works were illustrated by artists, and his play *Attila* (1907) had sets by Ricketts. Rothenstein and William Strang painted portraits of him, and Dulac produced a fine caricature of him dressed as a Japanese actor.

Binyon produced major scholarly catalogues for the British Museum, as well as popular books on Botticelli and on Dutch and British art; his work on William Blake and his followers was particularly extensive. By *c.* 1910 he had developed a special interest in Chinese and Japanese art and in 1913 was put in charge of the new Department of Oriental Prints and Drawings at the British Museum. Two of his books, *Painting in the Far East* (1908) and *The Flight of the Dragon* (1911), the latter a study of Eastern aesthetics, were pioneering works on their subject in English, and he was instrumental in fostering an appreciation of Far Eastern art in Great Britain; his writings on the subject influenced both the paintings of Wyndham Lewis and the poetry of Ezra Pound and helped to lay the foundations for later academic study.

WRITINGS

Dutch Etchers of the Seventeenth Century (London, 1895)
John Crome and John Sell Cotman (London, 1897)
Catalogue of Drawings by British Artists and Artists of Foreign Origin in Great Britain Preserved in the Department of Prints and Drawings at the British Museum, 4 vols (London, 1898–1907)
The Life and Work of J. S. Cotman (London, 1903)
Painting in the Far East, 2 vols (London, 1908)
The Flight of the Dragon (London, 1911)
The Art of Botticelli (London and Glasgow, 1913)
The Followers of William Blake (London and New York, 1925)
The Spirit of Man in Asian Art (Cambridge, MA, 1934)
Art and Freedom (Oxford, 1939)

BIBLIOGRAPHY

DNB
Laurence Binyon and Lancaster (exh. cat. by D. Steel, Lancaster, City Mus., 1979)

RICHARD HUMPHREYS

Biomorphism. Term derived from the Classical concept of forms created by the power of natural life, applied to the use of organic shapes in 20th-century art, particularly within SURREALISM. It was first used in this sense by Alfred H. Barr jr in 1936. The tendency to favour ambiguous and organic shapes in apparent movement, with hints of the shapeless and vaguely spherical forms of germs, amoebas and embryos, can be traced to the plant morphology of Art Nouveau at the end of the 19th century; the works of Henry Van de Velde, Victor Horta and Hector Guimard are particularly important in this respect.

From 1915 biomorphic forms appeared in wood reliefs, ink drawings and woodcuts by HANS ARP. By representing ovoid forms shifting into one another, he indicated the unity of nature in conscious opposition to the mechanization and dislocation of modern life. Biomorphic forms were also featured in the *Improvisations* painted around the beginning of World War I by Vasily Kandinsky, who had met Arp while living in Munich. At the end of the 1920s, apparently stimulated by the work of Yves Tanguy (*see* SURREALISM, fig. 1), Arp began to use more rounded and modelled shapes. He remained committed to biomorphism throughout his life, using it to express metaphors of cyclical transformation (*see* METAMORPHISM), cosmic harmony and the mystical union of human beings with the form-giving powers of nature.

JOAN MIRÓ was also influential in promoting the concept of biomorphism in his work, particularly from the mid-1920s, when he came into contact with Surrealism. He developed arabesque contours and a flux of coloured spaces, from which the shapes seem to surface, to convey a sense of creation and evolution and a range of human archetypes, by turns humorous and aggressive. Similar strategies of deformation were developed in the mid-1920s by Picasso, for instance in his *Three Dancers* (1925; London, Tate) and in his series of bathers of the late

1920s. In these and related works he explored ideas of perpetual movement, and through human and animal associations he used the formal language of biomorphism to suggest psychological truths. The application of biomorphism to the human figure in the sculpture of Henry Moore from the early 1930s was, in principle, also rooted in formal concerns linked to Surrealism. In his case abstract rhythms and an organic interdependence of form and space were used to express the relationship between human and landscape forms.

The example of these artists, and especially the impersonal, pantheistic biomorphism of Miró and Moore, had a liberating effect on many others in the 1930s and 1940s. In particular Miró's use of biomorphism stimulated Alexander Calder, Isamu Noguchi, Willi Baumeister and painters associated with Abstract Expressionism, notably Willem de Kooning, Arshile Gorky, Jackson Pollock and Robert Motherwell. While biomorphism never resulted in a style as such, it remained an important tendency through the 1940s in unifying otherwise diverse stylistic innovations.

BIBLIOGRAPHY

L. Glózer: *Picasso und der Surrealismus* (Cologne, 1974)
S. Poley: *Hans Arp: Die Formensprache im plastischen Werk* (Stuttgart, 1978)
C. Lichtenstern: *Picasso 'Tête de Femme': Zwischen Klassik und Surrealismus* (Frankfurt am Main, 1980)
——: 'Henry Moore and Surrealism', *Burl. Mag.*, cxxiii/944 (1981), pp. 645–58
B. Rose: 'Miró aus amerikanischer Sicht', *Joan Miró* (exh. cat. by R. S. Lubar and others, Zurich, Ksthaus; Düsseldorf, Städt. Ksthalle; New York, Guggenheim; 1986)
J. Mundy: *Biomorphism* (diss., U. London, Courtauld Inst., 1987)

CHRISTA LICHTENSTERN

Biondo, Flavio (*b* Forlì, 1392; *d* Rome, 4 June 1463). Italian scholar, writer and administrator. He trained as a notary—perhaps in Lombardy—and served as an administrator in various north Italian states, including for a time as secretary to the Venetian humanist and statesman Francesco Barbaro. In 1432 he became an apostolic notary and shortly thereafter a papal secretary in the service of Eugenius IV (*reg* 1431–47). This appointment brought him into the mainstream of the humanist movement too late to acquire the literary graces apparent in the work of his contemporaries at the Curia, but an immense curiosity and the inspiration of Rome itself enabled him to take new and fertile directions in the study of history. His *Decades ab inclinatione imperii* (completed 1453), which filled a gap hitherto unperceived in historiography, is an objective account of the history of political power, from the fall of Rome to the flourishing Italian states of his own day. He was necessarily limited by the diverse aims and quality of his literary sources, but in putting the emphasis on human capacities, Biondo disengaged his narrative from his sources' concentration on the role of providence or fortune, which led them to promote moralizing or propagandistic points. The same unifying intent is found in his *Italia illustrata* (1453), a historical survey of the regions of Roman Italy (excluding the far south), which relates their ancient division to contemporary circumstances, covering such cultural features as eminent men of the distant and recent past, surviving ancient monuments and contemporary churches and libraries. The synoptic approach of these works, important in the long run, made little impression in the 15th century, where readier advancement was achieved through sponsored histories of states and princes. More immediately influential was Biondo's handbook to the monuments of Rome. *Roma instaurata* (1446) was the first methodical reconstruction of the ancient city (although it also included notable modern buildings), arranged both topographically and by building type. Taking as a basis the map of the imperial urban areas, Biondo brought to bear on this work a wide range of ancient and medieval sources, tested against his own intimate knowledge of the remains. Personal examination of structures and the use of archaeological, epigraphic and even archival evidence led to the rejection of many current identifications, of the learned literature and of the legendary traditions enshrined in the medieval pilgrim's *Mirabilia*. When Biondo discusses the Theatre of Pompey, for example, a precise citation of Classical authors is followed by an almost successful attempt to locate it with reference to a recently found inscription. His careful handling of all accessible information and an eye for the significant made Biondo the true founder of the scientific study of antiquities, and his work remained unsurpassed in range and depth for a century. His last major work, *Roma triumphans*, comprised a systematic account of Roman public and private life and its development. Biondo was buried in the heart of Rome, at S Maria in Aracoeli on the Capitol.

WRITINGS

Roma instaurata (Rome, 1446)
Italia illustrata. Blondi Flavio Forliuensis de Roma instaurata (Rome, 1453; rev. Venice, 1503; 1470 edn London, BL); ed. J. Bremius, with comment. by R. Maffei (Turin, 1527)
Roma triumphans (n.p., n.d.)
Decades ab inclinatione imperii (Venice, 1483; London, BL)
Scritti inediti e rari di Biondo, Flavio (Rome, 1484; London, BL), ed. B. Nogara (Vatican City, 1927)

DBI   BIBLIOGRAPHY
R. Weiss: *The Renaissance Discovery of Classical Antiquity* (Oxford, 1969, rev. 1988)

M. C. DAVIES

Biondo, Giovanni del. *See* GIOVANNI DEL BIONDO.

Biow, Hermann (*b* Breslau, ?1803/4; *d* Dresden, 20 Feb 1850). German photographer. Son of the painter Raphael Biow (1771–1836), he was initially a painter, lithographer and writer. He opened the first photographic studio in Hamburg in 1841 and worked with Carl Ferdinand Stelzner from 1842 to 1843. A series of 46 daguerreotypes (3 extant) of the Great Fire of Hamburg in 1842 has been attributed to Biow (Kaufhold, 1989) and forms an early example of photographic reportage. Travelling to cities such as Berlin, Frankfurt and Dresden, he took portraits of the famous, including *Jakob and Wilhelm Grimm*, *Alexander von Humboldt* (1847) and *Friedrich Wilhelm IV, King of Prussia* (all Hamburg, Mus. Kst. & Gew.). In 1848 he photographed the members of the Frankfurt National Assembly for his portfolio work *Deutsche National-Gallerie*, containing lithographic reproductions of his daguerreotypes. Kempe describes Biow as the 'first photographer to collect people'. The essential quality of his photographs is their monumental unity. He used larger formats than other daguerreotypists; his plate size ranged from 216×162 mm to 270×320 mm.

PHOTOGRAPHIC PUBLICATIONS

Deutsche Zeitgenossen: Herausgegeben nach H. Biows gesammelten Lichtbildern (Leipzig, 1850) [engraved reproductions of photographs with biographical text]

BIBLIOGRAPHY

W. Weimar: 'Die Daguerreotypie in Hamburg, 1839–1860: Ein Beitrag zur Geschichte der Photographie', *Jb. Hamburg. Wiss. Anstalten*, xxxii (1914) [suppl.]; *R* in *The Daguerreotype in Germany: Three Accounts*, ed. R. Sobieszek (New York, 1979)

F. Kempe: *Daguerreotypie in Deutschland: Vom Charme der frühen Fotografie* (Seebruck, 1979)

E. Kaufhold: 'Hermann Biow und Carl Ferdinand Stelzner in Hamburg: Legenden, Fakten, Umschreibungen, Wahrscheinlichkeiten', *Silber und Salz*, ed. B. von Dewitz and R. Matz (Cologne, 1989)

HANS CHRISTIAN ADAM

Birago, Giovanni [Giovan] **Pietro** [Giampietrino] (*fl c.* 1471/4–1513). Italian illuminator and engraver. In 1894 he was tentatively associated with his principal work, the Hours of Bona Sforza (London, BL, Add. MSS 34294, 45722 and 62997), and became known as the Master of the Sforza Book of Hours or the Pseudo-Antonio da Monza; in 1956 he was conclusively identified by his signature PSBR IO PETR BIRAGVS FT on the frontispiece of a copy (Warsaw, N. Lib., Inc. F. 1347) of Giovanni Simonetta's life of Francesco Sforza, the *Sforziada*, published first in Latin and then in Italian translation at Milan in 1490.

Three choir-books from Brescia Cathedral dated *c.* 1471–4 (Brescia, Pin. Civ. Tosio-Martinengo, nos 22, 23 and 25) are the earliest known works signed by Birago. It has been suggested that he was active in Venice during the 1480s. Miniatures attributed to him appear in a Breviary of the Venetian Barozzo family, printed on parchment by Nicolas Jenson at Venice in 1481 (Vienna, Österreich. Nbib., Inc. 4. H 63), and in a Pontifical of the Hungarian Cardinal Johannes Vitéz of Veszprém (Rome, Vatican, Bib. Apostolica, MS. Ott. lat. 501). Birago also contributed two miniatures of *Apollo* to a small volume of Italian sonnets and songs (Wolfenbüttel, Herzog August Bib., Cod. 277 4 Extr.). By 1490 he was the leading illuminator at the Sforza court in Milan, and most of his important works are of around this date. The principal of these, the Hours of Bona Sforza, was executed for the mother of Duke Giangaleazzo Sforza (*reg* 1476–94). Unfinished at the Duke's premature death when Ludovico Sforza seized the duchy, the book accompanied Bona into retirement in her native Savoy in 1495. It was completed by Gerard Horenbout in the Netherlands in 1519–21 for Margaret of Austria, widow of Bona's nephew (for illustration *see* HORENBOUT, (1)). Birago participated in the decoration of a *Life of St Iosaphat* (Milan, Bib. N. Braidense, MS. AC XI, 37), also for Bona Sforza.

For Ludovico, Birago executed ornate illuminated frontispieces in a series of de luxe copies, printed on parchment, of the Italian translation of the *Sforziada*. Several copies survive: Ludovico's own copy (London, BL, Grenville MS. 7251); that presented to his nephew Giangaleazzo (Paris, Bib. N., Imp., rés., vél. 724); and the signed one in Warsaw, which was a gift to General Galeazzo da Sanseverino, who married Ludovico's illegitimate daughter Bianca in 1496. Nine fragments of the frontispiece of a fourth book (Florence, Uffizi) include one signed AVTORE IO PE BIRA. There is also a copy of the second Latin edition (1486) of the *Sforziada* with a frontispiece and a full-page miniature of *Francesco Sforza on Horseback* by Birago; this book (Florence, Bib. Riccardiana, ed. v. 428) was probably presented to Maximilian I, Holy Roman Emperor, on his marriage to Ludovico's daughter Maria Bianca (1472–1510) in 1494. Maria Bianca may have owned the Wolfenbüttel volume of sonnets, which was in Germany by the beginning of the 16th century. Birago also contributed to the decoration of two books for Massimiliano Sforza, one of Ludovico's sons: a copy of Aelius Donatus's *Ars minor* and the *Liber Iesus* (both Milan, Bib. Trivulziana, Cods 2167 and 2163). He also executed a small Book of Hours (Venice, Fond. Cini, Bib., MS. 4) presented by Ludovico to Charles VIII of France. About 1497 Birago illuminated a volume of biographies of French kings by Alberto Cattaneo of Piacenza, destined for Charles VIII, but probably presented after his death to Louis XII (Paris, Bib. Arsenal, MS. 1096). In 1506, as Duke of Milan, Louis granted Birago a copyright. The artist was still alive on 6 April 1513, the date of an autograph letter.

Birago's workshop was responsible for the mutilated Hours of Francesco Maria Sforza (1491–4; London, BL, Add. MS. 63493), a Book of Hours probably for a Cremonese patron (Cambridge, U. Lib., Add. MS. 4104) and a decorated copy (London, BL, Add. MS. 21413) of Ludovico's marriage grant of 1494 to his wife, Beatrice d'Este. Six engravings of religious subjects, two of putti and a series of twelve upright ornamental panels, have also been attributed to Birago. One large woodcut records a lost Birago composition, probably also an engraving, but a recent attempt to add two small paintings to his oeuvre is unconvincing.

Like the classicizing details of architecture and armour in his work, Birago's predilection for landscapes composed of rocky heaps of striated boulders interspersed with formalized trees and distant buildings reveals his ultimate dependence on Mantegna, whose style had been introduced to Lombardy by Vincenzo Foppa in 1456. At the Sforza court Birago came into contact with Leonardo da Vinci, from whom he derived the technique of depicting hair as a mass of wiry curls. Grotesque facial types in the Bona Hours suggest a knowledge of Leonardo's celebrated caricatures. The equestrian figure of *Francesco Sforza* in Maximilian's *Sforziada* probably reflects Leonardo's lost plaster for the Sforza monument, which was exhibited on the occasion of the Emperor's betrothal to Ludovico's daughter. Probably the most distinctive element in Birago's own repertory of figures is a particular sort of chubby putto, which frequently appears in miniatures and decorative borders.

Birago customarily employed a limited but distinguished colour range, composed primarily of deep blues and greens and dark reds, in both miniatures and borders. These colours are sometimes taken up in small pebbles scattered in the foreground of miniatures. Gold was employed sparingly, as often to suggest illumination as for decorative purposes. His full-page miniatures are bordered with simple, moulded gold frames, like those of panel paintings. Opening lines of prayers often appear in cartellini, which stand free within the pictorial space of miniatures or rest on their frames, like attached labels. In Birago's *Sforziada* frontispieces, the ornate borders surround the text with a superabundance of sphinxes, putti, mermaids, cornucopiae, vases and jewels, as well as arms, mottoes, imprese, portraits and political allegories. In the London *Sforziada*, the frontispiece text is transformed into the appearance of a pasted-down leaf of parchment, bending at the top under the weight of a putto who appears to lie on it. This perspectival capriciousness is in harmony with the witty and rich profusion of images that frames the page. As an ingenious response to the fundamental irreconcilability between the flat lines of text and the pictorial space of the miniatures, Birago's borders are comparable with the fictive architecture framing Mantegna's frescoes in the Camera Picta in the Palazzo Ducale, Mantua. Possibly Birago's greatest achievement is his series of *Sforziada* frontispieces, which brings to life the last decade of Sforza Milan in a pageant of emblems and allegories.

DBI

BIBLIOGRAPHY

G. F. Warner: *Miniatures and Borders from the Book of Hours of Bona Sforza, Duchess of Milan, in the British Museum* (London, 1894)
J. C. Robinson: 'The Sforza Book of Hours', *Bibliographica*, i (1895), pp. 428–36
F. Malaguzzi Valeri: *La corte di Ludovico il Moro: La vita privata e l'arte a Milano nella seconda metà del quattrocento*, i (Milan, 1913), pp. 164, 450, 584; iii (Milan, 1917), pp. 157–75, 200, 225, 227
E. Calabi: 'Giovanni Pietro da Birago e i corali miniati dell'antica cattedrale di Brescia', *Crit. A.*, iii (1938), pp. 144–51
A. Cutolo: '*L'Officium Parvum Beatae Mariae Virginis*' donato da Ludovico il Moro a Carlo VIII Re di Francia* (Milan, 1947)
E. Pellegrin: *La Bibliothèque des Visconti et des Sforza, ducs de Milan au XVe siècle* (Paris, 1955), pp. 364–5, 382, 396–7
B. Horodyski: 'Birago, miniaturiste des Sforza', *Scriptorium*, x (1956), pp. 251–5
Arte lombarda dai Visconti agli Sforza (exh. cat., Milan, Pal. Reale, 1958), pp. 141–5
A. Bertini: 'Un'ipotesi sull'attività pittorica di Giovan Pietro Birago', *Arte in Europa: Scritti di storia dell'arte in onore di Edoardo Arslan* (Milan, 1966), pp. 471–4
G. M. Canova: *La miniatura veneta del rinascimento, 1400–1500* (Venice, 1969), pp. 136–40
J. A. Levenson, K. Oberhuber and J. L. Sheehan: *Early Italian Engravings from the National Gallery of Art* (Washington, DC, 1973), pp. 272–80
J. J. G. Alexander: *Italian Renaissance Illumination* (London, 1977), pp. 96–103
G. Bologna: *Milano e gli Sforza Giangaleazzo Maria e Ludovico il Moro, 1476–1499* (Milan, 1983), pp. 71–5
A. C. de la Mare: 'Script and Manuscripts in Milan under the Sforzas', *Atti del Convegno internazionale: Milano dell'età di Ludovico il Moro: Milan, 1983*, pp. 399–407
T. Kren, ed.: *Renaissance Painting in Manuscripts* (New York and London, 1983), pp. 107–22
M. L. Evans: 'A Newly Discovered Leaf of *The Sforza Hours*', *BL J.*, xii/1 (1986), pp. 21–7
——: 'New Light on the *Sforziada* Frontispieces of Giovan Pietro Birago', *BL J.*, xiii/2 (1987), pp. 232–47
——: *The Sforza Hours* (London, 1992)
The Painted Page: Italian Renaissance Book Illumination, 1450–1550 (exh. cat., ed. J. J. G. Alexander; London, RA, 1994)

M. L. EVANS

Birch, Thomas (*b* Warwicks, 26 July 1779; *d* Philadelphia, PA, 14 Jan 1851). American painter of English birth. He was one of the most important American landscape and marine painters of the early 19th century. He moved to America in 1794 with his father William Birch (1755–1834), a painter and engraver from whom he received his artistic training. The family settled in Philadelphia, where William, armed with letters of introduction from Benjamin

Thomas Birch: *Fairmount Waterworks*, oil on canvas, 511×764 mm, 1821 (Philadelphia, PA, Pennsylvania Academy of the Fine Arts)

West to leading citizens of that city, became a drawing-master. Early in their American careers both Birches executed cityscapes, several of which were engraved. Thomas contributed a number of compositions to *The City of Philadelphia in the State of Pennsylvania, North America, as it Appeared in the Year 1800* (1800), a series of views conceived by the elder Birch in obvious imitation of comparable British productions. An English sensibility is also apparent in the many paintings of country estates executed by father and son in the early 19th century (e.g. *Eaglesfield*, 1808; priv. col., see 1986 exh. cat., p. 26). These compositions, along with such portrayals of important public edifices in and near Philadelphia as *Fairmount Waterworks* (1821; Philadelphia, PA Acad. F.A.; see fig.), emphasize the cultural progress and commercial prosperity of the young United States as well as its almost Edenic natural beauty. Birch is also known for his representations of winter landscapes (examples in Shelburne, VT, Mus.).

Among Birch's most accomplished landscapes from the 1810s are his two views of Point Breeze, the country seat of Joseph Bonaparte outside Bordentown, NJ. The sweeping view of the Delaware River as seen from the elegant terrace of this villa, decorated with classical sculpture and populated with fashionably dressed men and women (1818; priv. col., see 1986 exh. cat., p. 146), is perhaps unique in American art of this period. Its pronounced French flavour seems particularly appropriate for a composition probably commissioned by Napoleon's brother or by one of the prince's admirers. The collection of Old Masters and contemporary European works at Point Breeze was a major artistic attraction and a source of inspiration to many American painters, including Birch.

At the time of the war of 1812 with Britain, Birch took up marine painting. Although he continued to paint landscapes, particularly with river views (e.g. *View on the Delaware*, 1831; Washington, DC, Corcoran Gal. A.) and country estates, many of his works from the second half of his career are naval scenes that reflect his familiarity with the Anglo-Dutch tradition of marine painting. While these compositions frequently depict shipping on the Delaware and in New York harbour (several in Boston, MA, Mus. F.A.), he also executed a series of important canvases chronicling major naval engagements of the war (Philadelphia, PA, Hist. Soc.; New York, NY Hist. Soc.). His seascapes with shipping along rocky coasts buffeted by storms, such as *Shipwreck* (1829; New York, Brooklyn Mus.), recall the compositions of Claude-Joseph Vernet, whose work Birch knew first hand and through prints, and those of Vernet's followers in England, such as Philippe de Loutherbourg. Birch was a frequent exhibitor at the Pennsylvania Academy, where he served as keeper from 1812 to 1817, as well as at other artistic institutions in Philadelphia and New York.

BIBLIOGRAPHY
D. J. Creer: *Thomas Birch: A Study of the Condition of Painting and the Artist's Position in Federal America* (MA thesis, Newark, U. DE, 1958)
Thomas Birch (exh. cat. by W. H. Gerdts, Philadelphia, Mar. Mus., 1966)
J. Wilmerding: *A History of American Marine Painting* (Boston, 1968), pp. 102–18
M. Hutson: 'The American Winter Landscape, 1830–1870', *Amer. A. Rev.*, ii (Jan–Feb 1975), pp. 60–78
Views and Visions: American Landscape before 1830 (exh. cat. by E. J. Nygren and others, Washington, DC, Corcoran Gal. A., 1986)

EDWARD J. NYGREN

Bird, Edward (*b* Wolverhampton, 2 April 1772; *d* Bristol, 2 Nov 1819). English painter. He was the son of a carpenter, also named Edward Bird, and his wife Elizabeth. Educated at the Free Grammar School, Wolverhampton, he was then apprenticed as a decorator with the firm of Taylor & Jones, manufacturers of japanned wares made of papier mâché or tin coated with black varnish in imitation of Oriental lacquer and sometimes painted with elaborate scenes. This training was probably responsible for his rapid painting technique and the impure colour and inadequate finish frequently remarked on by contemporary writers. At the age of 22, after unsuccessfully attempting to establish himself as an independent artist, he left Wolverhampton for Bristol at the invitation of the amateur artist Thomas Corser. Following a brief period in the Bristol japanned goods industry, he set up a practice as a drawing-master, which he continued to his death. About 1794 he married Martha, daughter of the engraver John Dodrell.

In Bristol Bird became friendly with a group of amateur artists including George Cumberland (1754–1848), through whom he met Francis Chantrey and Thomas Stothard. Probably in 1813 a drawing society, mostly of amateurs, was formed around Bird; during his lifetime the other professional members comprised Edward Villiers Rippingille, Francis Gold (*fl c.* 1813–20), George Holmes (*fl c.* 1799–1843) and possibly Francis Danby.

It seems likely that from the beginning Bird's work was concentrated on the themes of domestic life with which he subsequently established his artistic reputation. However, he also painted portraits, landscapes, and historical, literary and fancy subjects. Much of his work was purchased by merchants from Bristol, his most consistent patron being the banker Benjamin Baugh.

Bird probably first exhibited in 1807, at the Bath Institution, prompted by the artist Denis Brownell Murphy (*d* 1842). In 1809 he sent the painting *Good News* (untraced), depicting domestic life, to the Royal Academy, where it was considered a serious rival to the work of David Wilkie. In 1810 Sir George Beaumont and others persuaded Wilkie to withdraw his exhibits to avoid being overshadowed by Bird's *Village Choristers* (British Royal Col.), which was purchased for 250 guineas by the Prince Regent (later George IV).

In subsequent years, however, Bird came to be regarded more as a follower of, rather than as a rival to, Wilkie. In 1812 he exhibited his first historical picture, the *Day after the Battle of Chevy Chase* (untraced; sketch in Wolverhampton, A.G.). Its success secured him an appointment in 1812 as Historical Painter to Princess Charlotte; the same year he was elected ARA and in 1815 he became an RA. In 1814 he had begun his most ambitious project, a pair of large-scale paintings depicting the return of Louis XVIII to France from England following the defeat of Napoleon. The pictures took several years to complete, and Bird was disappointed by the Prince Regent's refusal to buy *The Embarkation* (Bristol, Mus. & A.G.), though he was able to sell two versions (one Burton Constable,

Humberside) of *The Landing* (Wolverhampton, A.G.) to Sir Thomas Clifford and Lord Bridgewater for large sums. In later years Bird became increasingly ill and would exhibit only sombre religious subjects. He died bankrupt. His influence was principally felt in the subjects of domestic life by Rippingille, Danby and other artists of the Bristol school. Collections of his work are in the City of Bristol Museum and Art Gallery and the Wolverhampton Art Gallery.

BIBLIOGRAPHY

J. Eagles: 'The Sketcher', *Blackwood's Edinburgh Mag.*, xxxiv (1833), pp. 879–84

'Memoir of Edward Bird', *Lib. F. A.*, n. s., i (1833), pp. 257–65

A. Cunningham: *Lives of the Most Eminent British Painters* (London, 1830, 2/1879–80), ii, pp. 26–39

Edward Bird, R.A. (exh. cat. by S. Richardson, Wolverhampton, A.G., 1982)

S. Richardson: *Edward Bird, R.A.* (diss., U. Birmingham, 1986)

SARAH RICHARDSON

Bird, Francis (*b* London, 1667; *d* London, Feb 1730–31). English sculptor. He was born in the parish of St Martin-in-the-Fields and was sent to Flanders to the studio of a sculptor named Cozins (perhaps a member of the family of sculptors named Cosyns) and later to Rome. Back in England by *c.* 1689, he was employed by both Grinling Gibbons and Caius Gabriel Cibber, but he returned to Rome some years later, perhaps from 1695, and worked in the studio of Pierre Legros (ii). These journeys equipped him particularly with a knowledge of the Baroque in Rome and the works of Bernini. On his return to England, by 1700, after the death of Cibber, he was appointed by Sir Christopher Wren to undertake the major sculptural decoration of St Paul's Cathedral, notably the pediment of the west front (*see* LONDON, fig. 25) with its boldly dramatic representation of the *Conversion of St Paul*, for which he was paid £650 in 1706. He may have derived the pediment from Bernini or Legros but, since no drawings or models survive, this remains conjecture. He also carved the figures of the Evangelists and Apostles, over three and a half metres high, on the west and south fronts, receiving more than £2000, and the statue of *Queen Anne* with her attendant figures of England, Scotland, Ireland and France in front of the west façade (now St Mary's Place, Holmhurst, E. Sussex) *c.* 1711. Together with other artists, among them Sir James Thornhill and Louis Laguerre, Bird was appointed a director of the academy founded by the painter Sir Godfrey Kneller.

Bird's major output, like that of most sculptors at this time, was in the provision of funerary monuments, many of them innovative, such as that commemorating *Sir Orlando Gee* (*d* 1705), with its half-length frontal effigy, in All Saints, Isleworth. The monument to *Thomas Shadwell* (*d* 1708), in Westminster Abbey, has possibly the earliest pyramidal background in England. The most dramatic and original of his monuments is to *Elizabeth Benson* (*d* 1710) in St Leonard's, Shoreditch; this depicts two finely carved skeletons tearing apart a living oak tree. Bird's monument to *Admiral Henry Priestman* (*d* 1712), in Westminster Abbey, introduced a new motif into English monumental design, the profile portrait medallion suspended from a ribbon, and this greatly influenced other sculptors during the 18th century. Also attributed to him is the monument

to *William Hewer* (*d* 1715), St Paul's, Clapham, which is a very close copy of Bernini's memorial to *Maria Raggi* of 1643 in S Maria sopra Minerva, Rome. His other major sculptures in Westminster Abbey include the monument to *Dr John Ernest Grabe* (*d* 1711; see fig.), the enormous monument to *John Holles, Duke of Newcastle* (*d* 1711), erected in 1723, for which John van Nost (i) had earlier produced a design, but which was eventually designed by the architect James Gibbs, and the monument to the dramatist *William Congreve* (*d* 1729), which incorporates a portrait relief based on a painting by Kneller.

Among statues by Bird are those of *Henry VIII* (1703), over the gateway to St Bartholomew's Hospital, London; *Henry VI* (1719), at Eton College, Windsor; and, of the same date, *Cardinal Wolsey*, at Christ Church College, Oxford.

Bird, whose yard was in Lincoln's Inn Fields, was buried in St Andrew's, Holborn. The sale of his possessions by Langford started on 30 April 1751 and lasted five days. It included casts after Bernini (*Neptune* and a *Diana and Apollo*), models of a boy, and hands, by Legros, 'flying boys' and a *Minerva* by Algardi, other works by or after Michelangelo and drawings by Wren. The sculptor Henry Cheere bought from the sale. Bird's son, Edward Chapman Bird (*b c.* 1716), was a mason, but he became bankrupt in 1770, and his stock was auctioned by Christie's in the following year.

BIBLIOGRAPHY

R. Gunnis: *Dictionary of British Sculptors, 1660–1851* (London, 1953)

M. D. Whinney: *Sculpture in Britain, 1530–1830*, Pelican Hist. A. (Harmondsworth, 1964, rev. by J. Physick, 1988)

JOHN PHYSICK

Francis Bird: monument to *Dr John Ernest Grabe* (*d* 1711), marble, h. *c.* 1.5 m (London, Westminster Abbey)

Bird, William. *See* BYRD, WILLIAM.

Bird's-eye view. Prints, drawings or paintings that incorporate high-level perspective: the viewer has the sensation of looking at the ground from the clouds. Views taken from just above roof-level and map-views—pictorial maps that have a consistent scale—fall outside this category. Bird's-eye views have also been called 'aeronautical views', 'balloon views' and 'aero-views'. The advantage of the high angle is that more detail can be displayed, as the foreground does not obscure the background. This has made the bird's-eye view the ideal medium for representing battlefields, a purpose for which it was first used in the Classical period (*see* ROME, ANCIENT, §IV, 1(iv)(b)). It has also been found useful for depicting proposed urban developments, such as estates, docks and railways, and for landscape garden plans. It has been widely used for depicting palaces and country houses and, in the 19th century, for individual factories, the choice of the bird's-eye medium being motivated by landlords' and capitalists' pride of ownership. Civic pride has contributed to the even more widespread use of the method for depicting towns and cities.

Although there are some 15th-century bird's-eye views of towns (e.g. the images of *Rome, Florence* and *Jerusalem* in the *Nuremberg Chronicle*, 1493), the first significant town view was a six-sheet woodcut view of *Venice* (1500) by Jacopo de' Barbari. In its wake came a view of *Constantinople* (1559) by Melchior Lorck; *Bruges* (1562) by Marcus Gheerhaerts the elder; *Ancient Rome* (1574) by Etienne Dupérac; and a view of *Amsterdam* (1638) by Jan Christaensz. Micker (*c.* 1600–64), in which passing clouds cast shadows over the townscape. Such views were generally considered cartographic; mapmakers published them to supplement or substitute for town plans. Consequently many such views are to be found in town atlases such as the six-volume *Civitates orbis terrarum* (1572–1618) of Georg Braun (1541–1622) and Franz Hogenberg.

Bird's-eye views of palaces and their gardens seem to have originated in France, where Jacques Androuet Du Cerceau *l'aîné* produced a series of such engravings for the first volume (1576) of his *Les Plus Excellents Bastiments de France*. In the 17th century the genre continued to flourish in France. Pierre Patel *l'aîné*, for instance, painted a bird's-eye view of the *Château of Versailles* (1668; Versailles, Château), and drew a bird's-eye view of the *Château of Fontainebleau* (*c.* 1670), which was engraved. The genre was also established in the Netherlands; the foreground of the Dutch views frequently featured an imaginary hill, with tree stumps, gesticulating figures or a carriage heading for the subject of the image.

The bird's-eye view portrayal of houses with their estates was introduced to England by Dutch artists working there in the last quarter of the 17th century. Jan Siberechts's output included oil paintings of *Wollaton Hall and Park* (New Haven, CT, Yale Cent. Brit. A.), the *Grove at Highgate* (see Harris, p. 73) and *Cheveley Park* (1681; Belvoir Castle, Leics). His compatriot Jacob Knijff, with his brother Leonard Knijff, embarked in the 1690s on an ambitious project of drawing and engraving noblemen's and gentlemen's seats, beginning with those of John Holles, Duke of Newcastle (1662–1711): *Nottingham Castle, Bolsover* and *Haughton*. Soon afterwards he produced views of the royal palaces of *Whitehall, St James's, Hampton Court* and *Windsor Castle*. In 1701 Knijff announced that he had drawn 60 seats to date and that his series of engravings would eventually total 100. A large number of them appeared in *Britannia Illustrata or Views of Several of the Queen's Palaces, as also of the Principal Seats of the Nobility and Gentry of Great Britain (1707)*. This work was reissued in several volumes at various dates by a variety of publishers, sometimes with the title *Nouveau théâtre de la Grande Bretagne* (see fig. 1), and the engravings were simultaneously marketed as independent prints. Knijff produced oil paintings of a few of the seats, including one of *Windsor Castle* (Windsor Castle, Berks, Royal Col.), but most of the bird's-eye view paintings attributed to him are copies after engraved originals. Many of Knijff's plates were engraved by Johannes Kip, who also drew and engraved bird's-eye views of seats in Gloucestershire for the *Ancient and Present State of Gloucestershire* (1712) by Sir Robert Atkyns (1647–1711). Kip engraved many of the views of seats for the *History of Kent* (1719) by John Harris (*c.* 1666–1719) and drew, engraved and, in 1720, published the largest of all British bird's-eye views: a 12-sheet representation of London, looking east from a point above St James's Park. English followers of the Dutch topographical artists included Thomas Badeslade (*fl* 1712–*c.* 1742), John Stevens (*d* ?1722), John Harris the elder (*fl* 1693–1719) and John Harris the younger (1715–55), whose finest paintings are a suite of four bird's-eye views of *Dunham Massey Hall* (1751), Cheshire, the seat of George Booth, 2nd Earl of Warrington (1675–1758).

In the 1750s the bird's-eye view declined in popularity. Printed general views of towns now tended to be accommodated on single rather than multiple sheets, and most views of necessity were distant ones. The first manned hot-air balloon flight in 1784 and the invention of the panorama around 1785 led in the early 19th century to a revival of the use of bird's-eye perspective. It was used to show proposed urban developments, such as the Brighton developments of Kemp Town and Brunswick Square (1824), a number of cemetery layouts (e.g. the design by Francis Goodwin (1784–1835) for a *Grand National Cemetery*) and towns, such as the *Aeronautical View of London* (1831) by Robert Havell jr, which showed the city from a point 402 feet above the Thames. Lithographs of balloon views were especially popular in France; French artists, engravers and publishers produced views of many European cities and some North American ones. In the 1840s Jules Arnout (*b* 1814) issued *Excursions aériennes*, a series of remarkably accurate town views, on each print of which a small balloon features just above the horizon. In the 1850s A. Appert (*fl c.* 1840) and Alphonse Testard (*b* 1810) published a series of *Vues générales*, which included views of *Paris, Rome, Naples, London* and *St Petersburg*. The most prolific of the Parisian bird's-eye-view artists was Alfred Guesdon (1880–76), who was a non-practising architect from Nantes. His lithographed views of towns appeared in several series: *Voyage aérien sur la Loire et ses bords* (*c.* 1846), *L'Italie à vol d'oiseau*

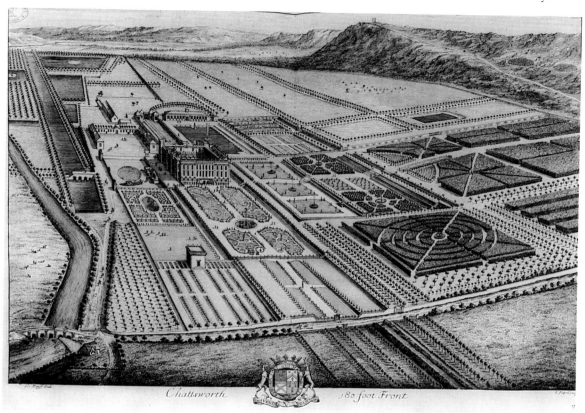

1. Bird's-eye view of *Chatsworth*, engraving by Leonard Knijff and Johannes Kip, 327×480 mm, from *Nouveau théâtre de la Grande Bretagne*, London, 1708 (London, Guildhall Library, Print Room)

(1849) by Hippolyte Etiennez, *L'Espagne à vol d'oiseau* (*c.* 1854–5) and *La Suisse à vol d'oiseau* (*c.* 1858). The trade in such prints was less developed in London than in Paris, but in 1847 Ackermann & Co. published attractive bird's-eye-view steel engravings of *Liverpool* and *Birmingham*, as did J. H. Banks a *Cosmoramic View of London* (1843) and a *Balloon View of London* (1851). Nathaniel Whittock (1791–1860) published lithographic bird's-eye views of *Oxford, London, Hull* and *York* and of *Melbourne*, Australia, while wood-engraved views appeared in the illustrated journals, particularly the *Illustrated London News* and its rival *The Graphic*. Some of the finest *Graphic* views were the work of W. L. Wyllie. During the Crimean War bird's-eye views of the battlefields appeared regularly, many of them published by Stannard & Dixon.

After the American Civil War bird's-eye views of towns became very popular in the United States and Canada. From the 1840s Edwin Whitefield (1816–92) had been producing town views, but most of these were taken from a low altitude. In the 1850s Edward Sachse (1804–73) and John Bachmann (*fl* 1849–85), printmakers of German origin, adopted a higher angle in their views. Sachse's firm produced at least 73 views and Bachmann's 53. Albert Ruger (1828–99), who began drawing town views in 1866, produced over 250. Thaddeus Mortimer Fowler (1842–1922), originally Ruger's assistant, issued 426 views, the

last in 1922. Oakley Hoopes Bailey (1843–1947), at one time Fowler's associate, issued 374, the last in 1926. Most of the North American views were of new communities, frequently quite small towns; they were intended to demonstrate that these communities were well served by railways and enjoyed the expected range of facilities, such as banks, hotels, churches and schools (see fig. 2). These views thus became a useful tool for land speculators, helping to encourage migration to the West. Most of them were single sheets, measuring typically 340×500 mm, but some striking multi-sheet views were published for major cities, including J. C. Laas's *Bird's-eye View of Syracuse, New York* (8 sheets), Sachse's *National Capital, Washington* (3 sheets) and *Bird's-Eye View of Baltimore* (12 sheets), Galt and Hoy's *City of New York* (4 sheets) and that of *St Louis* (118 sheets) drawn by Camille N. Dry (*fl* 1871–1904).

No comprehensive manual exists to explain how a bird's-eye town view was drawn, but it is possible to derive a notion of the process from artists' notes, advertisements and the few surviving preparatory sketches. The normal practice was for the artist to make general sketches from one or more elevated points, usually church towers, town halls, public monuments or neighbouring hills, though very seldom from balloons. The artist would then make sketches of the façades of buildings; a sketchbook of

2. *Perspective Map of the City of Laredo, Texas*, hand-coloured lithograph by Henry Wellge, 500×841 mm, 1892 (Fort Worth, TX, Amon Carter Museum of Western Art)

Whitefield's survives in a North American private collection, and the sketchbooks of Cecil Brown (1903–83) for the *Tribute to London* (1945) are in the Guildhall Library, London. These sketches were used to make the preliminary drawing, the information being adjusted if necessary to make it seem that the scene was being viewed from above. Separate, more detailed drawings were usually made of important landmarks—from the 1860s reference photographs of landmarks were frequently used—and this information was also transferred to the general view. The final watercolour drawing was passed to the engraver or lithographer, while another copy of it might be exhibited in the publisher's premises. Advertisements were then placed inviting the public to inspect the drawing and take out a subscription; further advertisements would appear on publication.

Despite their realism, bird's-eye views did not necessarily show the scene precisely as it was. Since the information in the background was as important to the user as that in the foreground, atmospheric perspective could be kept to a minimum or totally dispensed with. Maps were used as an aid at more than one stage of production, but, in order to accommodate everything the purchaser expected, topographical information sometimes had to be grossly distorted. Some North American views show cities more as it was hoped they would become rather than as they actually were on the date of publication. Nevertheless, the majority of bird's-eye views carry a vast amount of dependable information and represent an important historical source.

BIBLIOGRAPHY

C. Marrionneau:'Alfred Guesdon', *Rev. Bretagne & Vendeé* (June 1876)
Inventaire du fonds français après 1800, Paris, Bib. N. (Paris, 1955)
F. Bachmann: *Die alten Städtbilder* (Stuttgart, 1965)
J. R. Reps: *Cities on Stone: Nineteenth-century Lithographic Images of the Urban West* (Fort Worth, 1976)
J. Harris: *The Artist and the Country House* (London, 1979)
J. R. Hébert and P. E. Dempsey: *Panoramic Maps of Cities in the United States and Canada* (Washington, DC, 1984)
J. R. Reps: *Views and Viewmakers of Urban America* (Columbia, MO, 1984)
Gilded Scenes and Shining Prospects: Panoramic Views of British Towns, 1575–1900 (exh. cat. by R. Hyde, New Haven, CT, Yale Cent. Brit. A., 1985)
Ciudades del globoïal satélite (exh. cat., Barcelona, Cent. Cult. Contemp., 1994)

RALPH HYDE

Birdwood, George (Christopher Molesworth) (*b* Belgaum, India, 8 Dec 1832; *d* Ealing, England, 28 June 1917). English historian of Indian art and culture. After growing up in India, he was sent to Britain at the age of seven to be educated, first in Plymouth, then at the Dollar Academy, Dollar, after which he studied medicine at Edinburgh University. In 1854 he joined the medical staff of the East India Company in Bombay and later held professorships of anatomy and physiology, and of botany and materia medica at the Grand Medical College there. His interest in Indian art developed when he became curator of the Government Central Museum in Bombay. He returned to Britain in 1868 suffering from ill-health and found employment as assistant to John Forbes Watson in arranging exhibits from India for the annual international exhibition held in London from 1871 to 1874. In 1874 he became curator at the India Museum in London. When its collections were transferred to the South Kensington Museum (now the V&A) in 1880, he was appointed art referee to the Indian section. From 1878 he was also a special assistant in the Statistics and Commerce Department of the India Office, in which capacity he took charge of the Indian sections at international exhibitions up to the World's Columbian Exposition in Chicago in 1893. He was knighted in 1881 and retired from official work in 1902.

Birdwood was a prolific writer on many subjects connected with India, including art, philology, etymology, folklore and botany, and an accomplished Sanskrit scholar. In *The Industrial Arts of India* (1880), which incorporated information from his *Handbook to the Indian Court* written for the Exposition Universelle at Paris in 1878, he made an important contribution to the reappraisal of Hindu art. He was also concerned that the introduction of machinery into India was destroying principles of design established over thousands of years. His outlook, however, was conditioned by the emphasis on 'industrial' arts advocated by the South Kensington Museum and propagated at the schools of art in India, and in the early 20th century he was accused by a new generation of scholars of denying the existence of 'fine' art in India (*see also* INDIAN SUBCONTINENT, §XIII).

WRITINGS

The Industrial Arts of India, South Kensington Museum Art Handbooks (London, 1880/*R* 1971)

DNB   BIBLIOGRAPHY
R. Desmond: *The India Museum 1801–1879* (London, 1982), pp. 140–41

S. J. VERNOIT

Biretta. *See under* VESTMENTS, ECCLESIASTICAL, §1(iii).

Birger (Petterson), Hugo (*b* Stockholm, 12 Jan 1854; *d* Helsingborg, 17 June 1887). Swedish painter. He studied at the Konstakademi in Stockholm from 1871 to 1877. In 1877 he went to Paris and then spent the summer of 1878 at Barbizon with Carl Larsson, among others. There he painted several spontaneous *plein-air* paintings, such as *Rue Gabrielle* (1879; Göteborg, Kstmus.), in which the grey tones are contrasted realistically with exquisite colours. He also painted scenes of Parisian life, such as *The Toilette* (1880; two sketches in Stockholm, Nmus.), which aroused the interest of his contemporaries when it was exhibited at the Salon that year. Birger's art was always conventional in style, allied to French salon painting. He was a master of technique and a brilliant subject painter, creating such scenes as *In the Bower* (*c.* 1880; Stockholm, Nmus.).

In 1881 Birger visited Spain with Christian Skredsvig and again in 1883, taking in Granada, from where he travelled to Morocco. During these visits his treatment of colour grew more strongly contrasted, with sharper light and more stress on local colours. He painted a number of pictures of meals *al fresco*, for example *Holiday Lunch in Granada* (1882; Göteborg, Kstmus.). In Tangiers he produced *The Exiles* (1884; Göteborg, Kstmus.), a masterly work that was later considered too literary and

sentimental. In spring 1883 he was again in Paris and then went for the summer to Grez-sur-Loing, a place favoured by Scandinavian artists. When early in 1885 Birger returned to Paris after his travels to Spain and Morocco, he produced his last large painting, *Scandinavian Artists' Lunch at the Café Ledoyen on Opening Day 1886* (1886; Göteborg, Kstmus.). The painting is notable for its natural but intricately planned composition and delicate grey tones, but the theatrical poses of the figures create a wooden effect. On his way back to Stockholm in 1887, Birger died of tuberculosis in Helsingborg.

SVKL   BIBLIOGRAPHY
S. Strömbom: *Hugo Birger* (Stockholm, 1947)

HANS-OLOF BOSTRÖM

Biringucci. Italian family of artists.

(1) Vannuccio [Vannoccio; Vanuccio] **Biringucci** (*b* Siena, 20 Oct 1480; *d* ?Rome, before 30 April 1539). Metallurgist and architect. He may have trained with his father, Paolo di Vannuccio Biringucci, who was a mason and a member of one of Siena's noble families. Biringucci was subject to conflicting pressures in the city's unstable political environment and he was exiled three times for sedition and conspiracy. In 1507 he travelled to Germany and northern Italy, in 1517 to Rome, Naples and Sicily, and in 1526–9 to Germany and the Romagna. In 1524 he was given permission to manufacture saltpetre throughout Sienese territory. He went to Rome in 1536 and may have served as Master of the Papal Mint and artillery captain to Pope Paul III. He also served the Sienese Republic as an architect, designing arches (1513) for the triumphal entry of Bishop Gurgense, and succeeding Baldassare Peruzzi as architect to the republic and to the cathedral works (1535). His treatise, *De la pirotechnia* (1540), is one of the key works in the history of metallurgy, and covers the nature of ores and their location, the casting and fusing of metals, and mining techniques. It also deals extensively with artillery and ammunition. The importance of the work lies in its accurate and careful description of metallurgical practice and in its reliance on experimentation and observation. It is the first printed work to cover the entire subject of metallurgy and it had a wide-ranging influence in western Europe and the New World.

WRITINGS

De la pirotechnia: Libri X (Venice, 1540); ed. C. S. Smith, Eng. trans. by M. T. Gnudi as *The Pirotechnia of Vannoccio Biringucci* (New York, 1943, rev. Cambridge, MA, 2/1959)

BIBLIOGRAPHY
E. Romagnoli: *Biografia cronologica de' bellartisti senesi, 1200–1800*, vi (Siena, 1835, rev. Florence, 2/1976), pp. 289–342

(2) Oreste Vannocci Biringucci [Vannocci, Oreste; Vannoccio; Vanuccio] (*b* Siena, 1558; *d* Mantua, 8 July 1585). Architect, engineer and festival designer, grandson of (1) Vannuccio Biringucci. His father was the architect Oreste Vannocci. His early artistic contacts were in Rome and Florence, where he worked with Giovanni Giacomo della Porta and Bernardo Buontalenti. He was first noted as a translator of a commentary on Aristotle's *Mechanics* (Rome, 1582), and he later translated Heron of Alexander (1592; Siena, Bib. Com. Intronati, MS. L.VI.44). In 1583 he was appointed Prefetto delle Fabbriche to the Gonzaga court in Mantua, where he was primarily responsible for the design of festival decorations, such as those for the marriage of Vincenzo Gonzaga and Margherita Farnese in 1584. He coordinated the entire spectacle, including poetry, music and design.

Vannocci's importance rests on a small sketchbook (140×200 mm; Siena, Bib. Com. Intronati, MS. S.IV.1) of 149 folios. Entitled *Architettura, fortificazione e macchine di Oreste Vannocci*, it is a collection of drawings of buildings erected in Rome and Florence between 1540 and 1582. Included are copies of drawings by Jacopo Vignola—plans for Il Gesù in Rome and drawings after St Peter's—as well as drawings after Filippo Brunelleschi and the Antique. One important source was the Lille Sketchbook of Aristotele da Sangallo and Giovanni Battista da Sangallo. This work provides a record of various lost drawings and projects and is important for the method of presentation of the material. At times, Vannocci used a kind of comparative method (contemporary versus early Renaissance architecture). The manuscript was possibly to have formed part of an architectural treatise conceived on historical lines.

BIBLIOGRAPHY

E. Romagnoli: *Biografia cronologica de' bellartisti senesi, 1200–1800*, viii (Siena, 1835/R Florence, 1976), pp. 365–82
L. H. Heydenreich: 'Über Oreste Vannocci Biringucci', *Mitt. Ksthist. Inst. Florenz*, iii (1931), pp. 434–40
J. S. Ackerman and W. Lotz: 'Vignoliana', *Essays in Memory of Karl Lehmann*, i (Locust Valley, NY, 1964), pp. 1–24
G. Scaglia: *Francesco di Giorgio Checklist and History of Manuscripts and Drawings in Autographs and Copies from c. 1470 to 1687 and Renewed Copies* (Bethlehem, PA, 1992), pp. 136–9

NICHOLAS ADAMS

Birkás, Ákos (*b* Budapest, 26 Oct 1941). Hungarian painter, photographer and conceptual artist. He studied under Géza Fónyi at the Fine Art College in Budapest and then from 1966 to 1972 produced portraits, in which the influence of Expressionism was noticeable. From 1973 to 1979, however, he moved in a different direction, producing films, photographic sequences and textual conceptual works, all based on structuralist analysis of pictorial representation and of the institutions of the exhibition and the museum (e.g. the photographic sequences *Inquiries on the Exterior Wall of the Museum of Fine Arts*, 1975–6; and *Reflections*, 1976). From 1975 to 1980 he was involved in the Indigo project led by MIKLÓS ERDÉLY, but in 1980 he returned to oil painting, producing abstract works divided into two or three sections and often symmetrical in composition. At first these were vividly coloured, using bold brushstrokes and inspired by the Hungarian landscape, but later works were dominated by schematic representations of the human face, reduced after 1986 to an oval shape that served as a metaphor for the human intellect. From 1966 to 1984 Birkás was also a teacher at the Secondary School of Fine and Decorative Arts, and his lectures and writings, especially in the early 1980s, played an important part in promoting the appreciation of post avant-garde art in Hungary.

WRITINGS

'What is to be done?', *Apool Lett.* (1982)
'Die Budapester Szene', *Apool Lett.* (1986)

BIBLIOGRAPHY

Ákos Birkás: Fejek/Köpfe (exh. cat., Graz, Neue Gal., 1987) [incl. essays by W. Skreiner and L. Hegyi]

C. NAGY

Birkat Habu. *See* THEBES (i), §XII.

Birket Foster, Myles. *See* FOSTER, MYLES BIRKET.

Birmann. Swiss family of painters, publishers and art dealers. Although the family home was in Basle, both (1) Peter Birmann and his eldest son (2) Samuel Birmann spent part of their careers painting and sketching in and around Rome, principally landscapes in watercolour, bistre and wash. Peter Birmann established his own publishing company in Basle, as did Samuel Birmann; they were also art dealers. Peter Birmann's younger son Wilhelm Birmann (1794–1830) was also a painter and art dealer.

BIBLIOGRAPHY

B. Trachsler: 'Das Markgräflerland im Werk der beiden Basler Landschaftsmaler Peter und Samuel Birmann', *Markgräflerland*, xxxvi (1974), pp. 44–55

(1) Peter Birmann [Biermann] (*b* Basle, 14 Dec 1758; *d* Basle, 18 July 1844). He began his career as a portrait painter in Basle and Pruntrut but in 1775 moved to Berne, where he took up landscape painting. From 1777 to 1781 he worked with Johann Ludwig Aberli and was also a colour-printer with the publisher Abraham Wagner (1734–82). In 1781 he went to Rome, where he remained for ten years working for Louis Ducros and for Giovanni Volpato. While in Rome he painted landscapes in watercolour and drew in bistre, using a soft brush and making little use of the pen. He also sketched in the Alban Hills, being particularly attracted to the waterfalls at Tivoli and Terni. He became a member of Goethe's circle in Rome, and, under the influence of its members, he adopted Claude as his model. His watercolours and bistre drawings, enlivened by Greco-Roman or contemporary staffage, became more tranquil, more classical in style and increasingly strengthened with pen outlines. In 1792 he returned to Basle to teach. He soon became an art dealer, opened his own shop and set up his own publishing house, and in 1802 he printed his best-known work, a series of aquatints of *Voyage pittoresque de Basle à Bienne par les vallons de Mottiers-Grandval*. From 1802 to 1804 he showed at the annual exhibitions of the Künstlergesellschaft in Zurich, and in 1804 and 1810 in Berne he exhibited work in oils, a medium that was becoming increasingly important for him. In 1805 he was commissioned by the publishing house of Artaria & Co. in Vienna to sketch the scenery in the region of the north Italian lakes. For the next 30 years he continued to paint and draw, but after 1834 he tended to repeat the locales and compositions of his earlier landscapes.

WRITINGS

Voyage pittoresque de Basle à Bienne par les vallons de Mottiers-Grandval (Basle, 1802)

BIBLIOGRAPHY

Thieme–Becker
G. Lendorff: 'Der Landschaftsmaler Peter Birmann', *Baselbiet. Heimath.* (1943), pp. 179–94
L. Fromer-Im Obersteg: *Die Entwicklung der schweizerischen Landschaftsmalerei im 18. und 19. Jahrhundert*, Stud. Kstgesch., iii (Basle, 1945), pp. 42–52

(2) Samuel Birmann (*b* Basle, 11 Aug 1793; *d* Basle, 27 Sept 1847). Son of (1) Peter Birmann. From about 1811 he worked in his father's studio, where he drew mainly landscapes in pencil, pen, watercolour and bistre (e.g. *Rigi*, 1814; Basle, Kstmus.). In 1815 he went to Rome with the landscape painters Jakob Christoph Bischoff (1793–1825) and Friedrich Salathé (1793–1858). He executed a few oil paintings and also studies and detailed landscapes, usually in the hills around Rome, for which he employed pen, pencil, watercolour and wash. In 1817 he visited Sicily and produced drawings of luminous horizons in a Romantic vein, precisely delineated, yet with an economy of detail. In late 1817 he returned to Basle and worked in his father's business while sketching in the Alps each summer. In 1818 he exhibited in Berne and in 1820, 1821 and 1825 in Zurich. In 1822, together with a group of other Swiss artists that included his brother Wilhelm Birmann, he went to Paris to work on an edition of *Voyage pittoresque en Sicile* (Paris, 1822, rev. 1826) for the publisher Jean Frédéric Ostervald (1773–1850); while there he exhibited at the Salon. He set up his own publishing house in Basle and issued *Souvenirs de l'Oberland bernois* (n.d.) and *Souvenirs de la vallée de Chamonix* (1826). In his studies of trees, as well as in his larger landscapes of the Alps from 1829 (e.g. *Sawmill in the Lauterbrunn Valley*, 1843; Basle, Kstmus.), there is an increased interest in a Romantic vision of the forces that animate nature. In the 1830s periods of depression began to impede his artistic creativity, and he committed suicide in 1847.

WRITINGS
Souvenirs de l'Oberland bernois (Basle, n.d.)
Souvenirs de la vallée de Chamonix (Basle, 1826)

BIBLIOGRAPHY
Y. Boerlin-Brodbeck: *Alpenlandschaften von Samuel Birmann* (Basle, 1977)
——: 'Frühe "Basler" Panoramen: Marquard Wocher (1760–1830) und Samuel Birmann (1793–1847)', *Z. Schweiz. Archäol. & Kstgesch.*, xlii (1985), pp. 307–14
A. Esch and D. Esch: 'Die römischen Jahre des Basler Landschaftsmalers Samuel Birmann (1815–17)', *Z. Schweiz. Archäol. & Kstgesch.*, xliii (1986), pp. 353–61

Y. BOERLIN-BRODBECK

Birmingham. English city in the west Midlands. It is the second largest city in Britain, with a population of *c.* 1,000,000. Originally a small medieval town, it was transformed from the 17th century into a major industrial centre after the discovery of iron and coal. It now serves as a commercial and financial centre for the surrounding industrial towns. In 1974 Birmingham was absorbed into the metropolitan county of West Midlands. The city is an important centre for the production of metalwork (*see* §3 below), and its artistic life reflects its main concerns.

1. History and urban development. 2. Art life and organization. 3. Centre of metalwork production.

1. HISTORY AND URBAN DEVELOPMENT. From the 17th century Birmingham's economy and growth were based on the manufacture of metal wares. The liberal traditions of the town—it had no guilds, and the apprenticeship system was only practised to a limited degree—encouraged settlers and, despite its poor location from the point of view of transport, its population expanded steadily from approximately 5,500 in 1650 to 50,000 in 1780. Growth was encouraged by the encircling of the town by navigable canals (there is no large river near by) in the late 18th century and the opening of the railway to London in 1838. Industry was located close to the centre—even today the shopping area is remarkably constricted—and large areas of workers' housing, mostly in courts of back-to-backs, surrounded it. Concurrently more affluent suburbs, notably Edgbaston, were developed to the south. The population grew from 147,000 in 1831 to 344,000 in 1871.

In the early 19th century civic ambitions were modest: the main architectural landmarks were the Market Hall (1834; destr. 1957) by Charles Edge (*d* 1867) and the Town Hall (from 1834) by Joseph Aloysius Hansom, both Neo-classical in style. Birmingham did, however, become a significant early centre of the Gothic Revival, with work by Thomas Rickman (St George's Church, 1819–22, destr., and the Bishop Ryder Memorial Church, 1837, destr.). Rickman was followed by A. W. N. Pugin (*see* PUGIN, (2)) who, from 1837, had an influential position at the Roman Catholic seminary of St Mary's College, Oscott, just outside the city. In Birmingham Pugin built the fine Roman Catholic cathedral of St Chad (1839–41), and his designs for metalwork and stained glass were manufactured there by his friend and colleague, John Hardman (1812–67). Local architects Julius Alfred Chatwin (1821–1907), Yeoville Thomason (1826–1901) and J. H. CHAMBERLAIN worked in Gothic Revival styles throughout the 19th century, though Thomason's best-known buildings are neo-classical.

From 1866 the Georgian Colmore Estate was redeveloped as a business quarter, producing the fine neo-classical stone façades on Colmore Row, facing Thomas Archer's Baroque St Philip's church (1710–25; now the Anglican cathedral). In 1873 Joseph Chamberlain (1836–1914), the radical politician, became mayor, and a period of flourishing municipal enterprise began. Architecturally eminent were the Free Library (1866; rebuilt 1882; destr. 1974) by William Martin (*d* 1899) and J. H. Chamberlain, and the Council House and Museum and Art Gallery (1879 and 1885), by Yeoville Thomason. These formed a fine civic group in Chamberlain Square (see fig. 1) with the Town Hall and the Chamberlain Memorial (Martin and Chamberlain, 1880). Joseph Chamberlain's 1876 Improvement Scheme, which developed into Corporation Street, envisaged 'a great street, as broad as a Parisian boulevard' (Briggs, ii, p. 19). Six hundred buildings, including many slums, were destroyed, but the surveyors (Martin and Chamberlain) lacked the singlemindedness that Baron George-Eugène Haussmann displayed in Paris; Corporation Street was a patchwork of eclectic buildings on a curving route. One significant landmark at its northern end was the terracotta Victoria Law Courts (completed 1891) by Aston Webb and Ingress Bell. From the 1880s the red brick and terracotta of buildings like this became the predominant material and colour in Birmingham. Webb and Bell also designed the new campus (1900–09) for the University of Birmingham (founded as the Mason Science College 1880), a semicircle of brick buildings in a Byzantine style around a prominent campanile. A key event in urban planning history was George Cadbury's decision in 1879 to move his chocolate factory from the crowded town centre to rural Bournville, then a hamlet four miles to the south-west, where he also created a

1. Birmingham, aerial view of Chamberlain Square, looking towards the Museum and Art Gallery (1885; by Yeoville Thomason), with the Town Hall (from 1834, by Joseph Aloysius Hansom), right, and the Central Reference Library (1972; by J. H. D. Madin), bottom left

model village of small houses in gardens. Open space in Birmingham was until the 1880s the result of private benefaction; Adderley Park (1856) was the first of many such gifts.

The city expanded to incorporate other urban areas in 1891 and again in 1911, when the Greater Birmingham Bill tripled the city's size to 44,000 acres (*c.* 17,800 ha); it grew largely to the north and south. The Harborne Tenants' Estate, to the south, promoted by John Sutton Nettlefold (1866–1906), who was prominent in the urban planning movement, was an eminent example of the currently influential vision of the garden suburb. This idea later hardened into a formula that created vast areas of largely monotonous housing in the inter-war years in such estates as Kingstanding: between 1919 and 1939, 50,268 municipal houses were built. The post-1945 period was dominated by road-building and the removal of slums. Sir Herbert Manzoni, the powerful City Engineer and Surveyor, replanned much of Birmingham with A. G. Sheppard Fidler (1910–90), Birmingham's first City Architect, appointed in 1951. Thirty thousand houses, over half of which were back-to-backs, were destroyed in five Comprehensive Redevelopment Areas ringing the centre. They were replaced by mixed development devised according to Le Corbusier's theories. An inner ring-road had been planned since 1910, and the road finally built between 1957 and 1971 was an enormous stimulus to city centre development. The Council's flexible attitude towards developers facilitated rapid building but resulted in erratic design standards. In the vital anarchy of its city centre Birmingham is the most American of English cities. The Central Reference Library (1972; by J. H. D. Madin; see fig. 1) is the most orderly contribution, part of a civic

development sadly uncompleted. It replaced the huge neo-classical Civic Centre designed in the 1930s but abandoned after World War II with only a fragment (Baskerville House, 1936–40) built. After 1971 urban development was more restrained, with an emphasis on pedestrian precincts and conservation. Compensation for industrial decline in the surrounding areas has been sought in the urban fringe by the construction of the National Exhibition Centre (1976) near the airport; in the centre the International Convention Centre, Broad Street (1987–91; by Convention Centre Partnership), and the new urban space of Centenary Square have successfully moved the city centre beyond the Inner Ring Road.

BIBLIOGRAPHY
A. Briggs and others: *History of Birmingham*, 3 vols (London, 1952–74)
B. Little: *Birmingham Buildings* (Newton Abbot, 1971)
N. Borg: 'Birmingham', *City Centre Redevelopment*, ed. J. Holliday (London, 1973)
J. MacMorran: *Municipal Public Works and Planning in Birmingham, 1852–1972* (Birmingham, 1973)
V. Skipp: *The Making of Victorian Birmingham* (Birmingham, 1983)

JOE HOLYOAK

2. ART LIFE AND ORGANIZATION. In the 18th century the rapidly increasing manufacture of metal wares was creating enough wealth to sustain at least one portrait painter, James Millar (*fl* 1763; *d* 1805), and a still-life painter, Moses Haughton (1734–1804). The portrait of *John Freeth and his Circle* (1792; Birmingham, Mus. & A.G.) by John Eckstein testifies to a developing interest in the arts. By 1800 standards in commercial art in Birmingham had risen. This was reflected in the metalwork products of Matthew Boulton and others (*see* §3 below), and it led to the establishment of two drawing academies run by Joseph Barber (1757–1811) and Samuel Lines (1778–1863). Lines is remembered for his panoramic topographical drawings of Birmingham and also for founding the town's first Society of Artists in 1809, which was re-launched in 1842 and achieved royal recognition in 1868.

David Cox, a pupil of Barber, exhibited at the Society; one of his scenes of local life is the *Birmingham Horsefair* (before 1856; Birmingham, Mus. & A.G.). His contemporaries included the landscape painters Frederick Henry Henshaw (1807–91), Joseph Paul Pettitt (1812–82) and Charles Thomas Burt (1823–1902). Thomas Creswick also trained in Birmingham. They worked in oil and watercolour, although there were watercolour specialists in Birmingham, such as the antiquary Allen Edward Everitt (1824–82), John Steeple (*fl* 1846; *d* 1887), Henry Martin Pope (1843–1908) and Bernard Walter Evans (1848–1922). The leading Victorian portrait painters were William Thomas Roden (1817–92) and Henry Turner Munns (1832–98); the chief architectural sculptors were Thomas Roddis and his son John Roddis, who were active in 1840–90. In 1863 Peter Hollins's bust of *David Cox* was one of the first exhibits in the Birmingham Museum and Art Gallery. Among the genre painters were Edward Coleman (?1800–67), Samuel Cogford (1820–96) and, later, William John Wainwright (1855–1931), one of several Birmingham artists who painted at Newlyn. Important private art collections were put together during the 19th century, notably those of Edwin Bullock (*d* 1870) and Joseph

Gillott (the pen-nib manufacturer), whose Edgbaston gallery boasted many oil paintings by Turner.

The importance of the metalwork industry in the city produced a great number of medallists and engravers; major firms (e.g. Vaughton's) employed such artists as Joseph Moore (1817–92). In the mid-19th century John Pye, William Radclyffe, James Tibbetts Willmore (1800–63) and John Brandard (1812–63) were all dominant figures in the art of reproductive engraving.

A School of Design was established in 1842, but its influence on industrial manufacture was limited, as the prominent firms, such as Elkington & Hardman, trained their own designers. Edward Burne-Jones attended evening classes at the school in the 1850s, and in the 1860s Helen Allingham and Walter Langley were among its pupils. Edward Richard Taylor (1838–1912) was Head Master from 1877; he revolutionized the school's teaching by introducing practical training in the crafts. Its particular strengths lay in black-and-white illustration (see fig. 2), stained glass, metalwork and enamel. Arthur Joseph Gaskin (1862–1928), Henry Albert Payne (1868–1940) and Sidney Harold Meteyard (1868–1947) were teaching at the school when it won a corporate gold medal at the Paris Exposition Universelle (1900). After 1890 the school worked in conjunction with the Birmingham Guild of Handicraft, designing such products as stained glass. The decoration of the chapel at Madresfield Court, Worcs (1908–12), remains the finest example of the school's style.

The Birmingham Group, headed by the painter Joseph Southall (1861–1944), flourished in the years before 1914. Southall was also the leading figure in the revival of the use of tempera, as in his *Corporation Street, Birmingham, in March 1914* (1915–16; Birmingham, Mus. & A.G.). The painter Charles Gere (1869–1934) followed Southall

in his use of tempera. Henry Rushbury (1889–1968) and Gerald Leslie Brockhurst were the first of several notable painter-etchers; they were followed by Hubert Andrew Freeth and Raymond Teague Cowern. During the interwar years, a colour woodcut school led by Alice Margaret Coats (1905–78) was formed. John Melville (1902–86) and Conroy Maddox (*b* 1912) formed a provincial branch of the Surrealists. Sculpture again came to the fore with William James Bloye (1890–1975) and Gordon Herickx (1900–53). After World War II, important Birmingham painters included Bernard Fleetwood-Walker (1893–1963), Gilbert Mason (1913–72) and William Gear (*b* 1915).

The city's Museum and Art Gallery opened in 1885, and under its first Keeper Sir Whitworth Wallis (1855–1927) it amassed a remarkably wide-ranging collection. The Old Master collection is strong in 17th-century Italian paintings. The Print Room is especially rich, with a representative number of modern prints as well as Pre-Raphaelite drawings and an extensive holding of British watercolours. The University of Birmingham's Barber Institute, founded in 1932, has a small, high-quality collection of Old Masters. The Ikon Gallery, opened in 1966, was one of the first centres in Birmingham to exhibit contemporary art.

BIBLIOGRAPHY
J. Hill: *The Artists and Art Workers of Birmingham* (Birmingham, 1897) [Presidential address, Midland Art Club]
J. Hill and W. Midgley: *The History of the Royal Birmingham Society of Artists* (Birmingham, [1928])
R. Ormond: 'Victorian Painters and Patronage in Birmingham', *Apollo*, lxxxvii (1968), pp. 240–51
S. Morris and K. Morris: *A Catalogue of Birmingham & West Midlands Painters of the 19th Century* (Stratford-upon-Avon, 1974)
A. Crawford, ed.: *By Hammer and Hand: The Arts and Crafts Movement in Birmingham* (Birmingham, 1984)
S. Davies: *By the Gains of Industry: Birmingham Museums and Art Gallery, 1885–1985* (Birmingham, Mus. & A.G. cat., 1985)

STEPHEN WILDMAN

2. Edmund Hort New: *Birmingham School of Art*, pen and ink, 91×86 mm, 1894; from a book of drawings presented to Arthur Gaskin (Birmingham Museum and Art Gallery)

3. CENTRE OF METALWORK PRODUCTION. Birmingham has been a major producer of domestic metal wares since the 16th century. Originally it was known for ironwork, followed in the 17th century by the expansion of brass and copper manufacture and in the 18th century by small silverware. The growth of Birmingham's brass industry in the second half of the 17th century was largely a result of the ban on imported buttons in 1662 and the prohibition of trade with France in 1688. By the 18th century it was established as the main centre of production of small metalwork or 'toys', and Edmund Burke described it as the 'toy shop of Europe'. Production peaked in the third quarter of the 18th century with goods, about 80% of which were exported, to the value of £600,000 being produced in 1759, and with about 20,000 people working in the trade. Manufacture was organized by piecework, with each craftsman concentrating on one aspect of production or decoration. Labour costs, therefore, were kept to a minimum.

The 'toy' manufacturers made increasing use of silver during the 18th century, although the history of large-scale silver production begins with MATTHEW BOULTON. Boulton inherited his father's business but ambitiously extended his activities once his Soho factory was completed.

In 1764 he began the production of Sheffield plate, expanding later into ormolu and silver for the luxury market. The last was virtually impossible without an assay office at Birmingham and, until this was opened in 1773 through Boulton's lobbying of Parliament, all goods had to be sent to London or Chester for hallmarking (*see* MARKS, fig. 2). Boulton's ormolu products tried to compete with those from the finest French workshops and were intended for wealthy patrons (e.g. ice pail, *c.* 1775; London, V&A). Ormolu involved substantial manual work and was consequently expensive, with costs frequently exceeding estimates. Production ceased by the mid-1780s. His silverwork, by contrast, made innovative use of die-stamping machinery that could have reduced costs once the initial capital investment had been recovered. Problems with production and poor management, however, ensured that this side of his business also failed to be profitable in the long term.

The output of silver in Birmingham expanded steadily in the 19th century, although the industry was still largely based on small workshops. The manufacture of Sheffield plate also grew, and the leading makers were Waterhouse & Ryland and Edward Thomason (1769–1849). The latter in particular competed with some success with the London retailers Rundell, Bridge & Rundell. The brass industry also expanded, as new developments in the smelting of zinc led to a reduction in manufacturing costs. Small objects—chimney ornaments, boxes and inkstands—were made by casting or die-stamping.

The mid- and late 19th century was dominated by the huge firm of G. R. ELKINGTON & Co. In 1836 it took out patents in electrogilding, a cheaper and safer substitute for traditional fire gilding (*see* GILDING, §1, 3). These were followed by others for depositing silver by electrolysis (*see* ELECTROPLATING), a process that within a decade had rendered Sheffield plate obsolete. Most of their designs were available in silver, brass and electroplate, and the firm placed great emphasis, as did their London competitors, on design. Among their leading artists were Albert Wilms (*c.* 1830–*c.* 1900) and Léonard Morel-Ladeuil (1820–88). At the height of their success Elkington & Co. had showrooms in London, Manchester, Liverpool and Calcutta and employed more than 1000 people. Other important firms in the second half of the 19th century were Hardman & Co. and Hukin & Heath. Hardman's, whose chief designer was A. W. N. Pugin, dominated the market for church furnishings in silver and brass and also produced innovative domestic silver in Gothic Revival designs. Hukin & Heath's products could hardly have been more different as they promoted the severe minimalist electroplate designed by CHRISTOPHER DRESSER.

The most productive period for the Birmingham silver industry was the turn of the century, when assayed silver rose from 1 million ounces in 1890 to 4.2 million in 1912. Although remaining the leading centre of manufactured silverware in England, the 20th-century industry has never fully recovered from the reversal of trade caused by World War I. The War was followed by the merging of many firms and most production concentrated on relatively cheap reproductions of antique forms. The role of designers in most firms was reduced, with a few exceptions such as W. H. Haseler, who produced silver for Liberty's, and A. Edward Jones. In more recent years innovative and original designs have tended to be limited to specific commissions rather than production lines.

BIBLIOGRAPHY
Birmingham Gold and Silver, 1773–1973 (exh. cat., Birmingham, Mus. & A.G., 1973)
N. Goodison: *Ormolu: The Work of Matthew Boulton* (London, 1974)
K. Crisp Jones, ed.: *The Silversmiths of Birmingham and their Marks, 1750–1980* (London, 1981)

TIMOTHY SCHRODER

Biro. *See* PEN, §3.

Birolli, Renato (*b* Verona, 10 Dec 1905; *d* Milan, 3 May 1959). Italian painter. He moved to Milan in 1929 after being expelled from the Accademia Cignaroli in Verona. He was influenced by the critic Edoardo Persico, who adopted a pan-European style based on a return to French Impressionism. In 1932 Birolli participated in a collective organized by Persico at the Galleria Il Milione, Milan, which prefigured the orientation of the Corrente movement. There he exhibited the key work of his early period, *St Zeno the Fisherman* (1931; Milan, Gal. A. Mod.), which owed much to the colour of the Milanese Chiaristi group and the manner of Tullio Garbari (1892–1931).

After his dissociation from Persico in 1933, Birolli began to paint canvases such as *Eldorado* (1935; Milan, Gal. A. Mod.), with more strident colours and agitated brushwork. His deliberately anachronistic expressionism, inspired by van Gogh and James Ensor, served as a stylistic reaction to the Neo-classicism of the Novecento Italiano group. The *Metamorphoses* (1936–7), a series of some 70 drawings, document the evolution of his nervous calligraphy and amorphous forms. He was a founder-member of the group CORRENTE (1938–43), which eventually opposed the Fascist regime, and he contributed regularly to the group's journal and to its two exhibitions in 1939. Birolli's aesthetic and political views were documented in a series of diaries, his *Taccuini*, begun in 1936.

From 1943 to 1945 Birolli painted a series of portraits of peasants, such as *Peasant among the Sunflowers* (1945; Milan, Birolli priv. col.), which allude to the anti-Fascist movement in the countryside. Birolli was in the Resistance from 1943 to 1945 and depicted the horrors of human suffering in his cycle *Drawings of the Resistance* (e.g. *Una madre*, 1944; Turin, Gal. Civ. A. Mod., see 1976 exh. cat., no. 134). After World War II he adhered to the short-lived Fronte Nuovo delle Arti. Although of the political left, Birolli engaged in a polemic against the realism advocated by the Communist Party. In the 1950s he painted landscapes of the Ligurian coast in a Cubist–biomorphic style, which, in his final years, evolved into pure abstraction close to French *Art informel* painting.

WRITINGS
Metamorfosi (Milan, 1937)
Taccuini, 1936–1939, ed. E. Emanuelli (Turin, 1960)

BIBLIOGRAPHY
Renato Birolli (exh. cat. by G. C. Argan, V. Fagone and M. Mussini, U. Parma, Cent. Studi & Archv Communic., 1976)
Z. Birolli and others: *Renato Birolli* (Milan, 1978)

EMILY BRAUN

Birs Nimrud. *See* BORSIPPA.

Biscaino, Bartolomeo (*b* Genoa, *bapt* 14 April 1629; *d* Genoa, 1657). Italian painter, draughtsman and etcher. He was taught by his father, Giovanni Andrea Biscaino, a mediocre landscape painter, and entered the workshop of Valerio Castello (ii), probably at the end of the 1640s. The chronology of his oeuvre, truncated by his early death in a plague, is hard to reconstruct. Only two paintings bear early documentation: *St Ferrando Imploring the Virgin* (Genoa, Pal. Bianco) and an untraced *Flaying of Marsyas* (see Manzitti, 1971, pl. 31). However, his graphic work had a continuing reputation: he was called a 'great draughtsman' by Pellegrino Orlandi in his *Abecedario pittorico* (1704), and his etchings, of which over 40 are catalogued in Bartsch, were 'very favourably received', according to Antoine-Joseph Dezallier d'Argenville (1762). About half the etchings are signed or initialled, and two are dated (*Nativity*, 1655, B. 22; *St Mary Magdalene in the Desert*, 1656, B. 38). From them it is possible to attribute further works, mostly small canvases, to Biscaino, and to characterize his development.

The compositional simplicity of the *Triumph of David* (Genoa, priv. col., see Manzitti, 1971, pl. 22) and the *Drunken Silenus* (Genoa, priv. col., see Manzitti, 1972, no. 178) suggests that they are early paintings. *St Ferrando* likewise seems early, given its closeness to Castello, but already shows the curving draperies and sweetness of expression that is characteristic of Biscaino's works. They tend to be gentler in style, with a softening of forms through a broader brushstroke and a more delicate palette than the light touch and fiery colour of Castello. The example of Giovanni Benedetto Castiglione is important for Biscaino's later work. It influences the rendering of animals, figures and naturalistic settings in the *Vision of St Eustace* (Genoa, priv. col., see Manzitti, 1971, pl. 37) and in the *bozzetti* of the *Adoration of the Magi* (linked to a drawing; Florence, Uffizi, n.13323) and *Moses Striking the Rock* (both Genoa, Pal. Spinola). It also influences the iconography and technique of the etchings, which are mainly religious in theme, and can be seen in the play of light and shade in the complex *Nativity with Angels* (London, BM, B. 7; see fig.).

The grace and refinement of Biscaino's *Nativity* also suggest a study of Parmigianino. Further stylistic sources include Tuscan and Roman Mannerism, represented in Genoa by Perino del Vaga, Domenico Beccafumi and subsequently by Pietro Sorri (1556–1621) and Francesco Vanni. The sources record that Biscaino, apart from drawing from the nude, copied Giulio Romano's *Martyrdom of St Stephen* (Genoa, S Stefano) and Guido Reni's *Assumption* (Genoa, Il Gesù).

Other important works by Biscaino, difficult to place chronologically, include the *Holy Family with Grapes* (Genoa, Mus. Accad. Ligustica B.A.; cf. etching of same subject, B. 16), reminiscent of both Castello and van Dyck; two versions of the *Adoration of the Magi* (both Genoa, priv. col.; for one see 1947 exh. cat., p. 45); and three paintings of the *Finding of Moses* (all Genoa, priv. col., see Podesta, p. 252, and Bonzi, 1959, pp. 4 and 12), a subject that he repeated in two etchings (B. 182.1 and 183.2) and several drawings (e.g. Genoa, Pal. Rosso, 1767 and 1776).

Bartolomeo Biscaino: *Nativity with Angels*, etching, 395×279 mm (London, British Museum)

BIBLIOGRAPHY

DBI [with bibliog.]

Mostra della pittura del '600 e del '700 in Liguria (exh. cat. by A. Morassi, Genoa, 1947), p. 54, no. 60

M. Bonzi: 'Un bozzetto del Biscaino', *Liguria*, x (1959), p. 12

——: *Pellegro Piola, Bartolomeo Biscaino* (Genoa, 1963), pp. 30–54

E. Gavazza: 'Il momento della grande decorazione', *La pittura a Genova e in Liguria*, ii: *Dal seicento al primo novecento* (Genoa, 1971, rev. 1987), pp. 200–01, 260–61

C. Manzitti: 'Per Bartolomeo Biscaino', *Paragone*, xxii/253 (1971), pp. 38–46

A. Podesta: 'Inediti genovesi e fiammingo olandesi in raccolte liguri', *Studi di storia dell'arte in onore di Antonio Morassi* (Venice, 1971), pp. 36–44, 252, fig. 4

C. Manzitti: *Valerio Castello* (Genoa, 1972)

Genoese Baroque Drawings (exh. cat. by M. Newcome, Binghamton, SUNY; Worcester, MA, A. Mus.; 1972)

M. Newcome: 'Some Preparatory Drawings for Prints by Biscaino', *Paragone*, xxix/345 (1978), pp. 81–7

V. Belloni: 'Bartolomeo Biscaino, un prezioso pennello troncato a venticinque anni', *La Squilla*, lvii/3 (1981), pp. 12–13

P. Bellini: *Italian Masters of the Seventeenth Century* (1983), 47 [XXI/ii] of *The Illustrated Bartsch*, ed. W. Strauss (New York, 1978–), pp. 303–51 [with bibliog.] [B.]

F. Boggero: 'Mose fa scaturire l'acqua dalla roccia', *Galleria Nazionale di Palazzo Spinola: Interventi di restauro*, ed. G. Rotondi Terminiello (Genoa, 1983)

V. Belloni: *Scritti e cose d'arte genovese* (Genoa, 1988), pp. 97–102

FEDERICA LAMERA

Bischof, Werner (*b* Zurich, 26 April 1916; *d* Andes Mountains, Peru, 16 May 1954). Swiss photographer. He studied photography from 1932 to 1936 with Hans Finsler at the Kunstgewerbeschule in Zurich. From 1936 he worked as a freelance photographer and graphic artist, until obtaining a post with the Graphis publishing house in Zurich in 1938. Between 1942 and 1944 he published photographs of war damage in Europe in the magazine *Du*. His first collection *24 Photos von Werner Bischof* was published shortly afterwards. He won success in 1948 with his coverage of the winter Olympic Games in St Moritz for *Life* magazine: he was awarded contracts by *Picture Post*, *Weekly Illustrated* and the *Observer* and became a member of the Magnum agency. Thereafter until his death in 1954 he travelled as a photojournalist through Europe, Asia and South America, reporting on famine, war and daily life in the Third World.

In the photographs of this period, he abandoned the single shot and began to use the thematically linked series. His images of famine in India, published later as *Indios*, were notable in developing this technique, and his style had a particularly strong influence on many younger colleagues.

Bischof never abandoned his commitment to the perfection of the image as an appropriate vehicle for expressing his compassion towards other people. His striving for a valid and structured picture led him, however, mainly in his photographs of children, to turn from human suffering to less sombre subjects. Some of these photographs, such as the flute-playing South American Indian boy (1954; see Capa, 1969), became world famous through exhibitions and publications. An unexplained car accident in the Andes brought his work to a premature end.

PHOTOGRAPHIC PUBLICATIONS

24 Photos von Werner Bischof (Berne, 1946)
Japan (Zurich, 1954)
Unterwegs (Zurich, 1957)
Indios (Paris, 1961)
Werner Bischof: Querschnitt (Zurich, 1961); rev. as *The Photographs of Werner Bischof* (New York, 1968)

BIBLIOGRAPHY

C. Capa, ed.: *The Concerned Photographer* (New York, 1969)
Documenta 6, ii (exh. cat. by K. Honnef and E. Weiss, Kassel, Mus. Fridericianum, 1977), pp. 94–5
H. Loetsche: *Werner Bischof*, I Grandi Fotografi (Milan, 1983)
M. Bischof and R. Burri: *Werner Bischof* (London, 1990)

REINHOLD MISSELBECK

Biscia, Lelio (*b* 1573; *d* Rome, 1638). Italian lawyer, cardinal and patron. He purchased the office of Prefect of the Grain Supply of Rome and served Pope Paul V as chief urban planning official, superintending the building and maintenance of innumerable streets, sewers, bridges and squares in the city. He built a collecting basin for the Acqua Felice scheme (1587–90; see FONTANA (iv), (1)) and directed the construction of Paul's new aqueduct with its fountain on the Janiculum—the Acqua Paola. He enlarged the Piazza del Quirinale for the Pope and improved the street system connecting it with the Subura and Dataria districts of Rome and with the area around Trajan's Column. He also opened up the Piazza di S Sabina and other roads on the Aventine and built or improved those roads connecting S Maria ai Monti with the newly urbanized Pantani area, as well as those leading to the Forum Romanum by way of the Basilica of Maxentius and the Arch of Titus. Under Biscia's direction, the processional route along the Via della Scrofa was widened and the area around Palazzo Borghese dignified; the Via Flaminia was improved up to Ponte Milvio. The bridges, banks and stairs near the River Tiber were repaired, and a new straight street, the Via di S Francesco, was laid out from the heart of the Trastevere district to the church of S Francesco a Ripa. In 1626 Biscia was made cardinal by Pope Urban VIII. Allacci compares his burning ardour for the creation of a new Rome to the fire under Nero, which had transformed Rome into a city of straight streets.

BIBLIOGRAPHY

L. Allacci: *Romanae aedificationes curatae a Laelio Biscia* (Padua, 1644)
G. Moroni: *Dizionario di erudizione storico-ecclesiastica*, v (Rome, 1840–79), p. 251
A. R. De Amicis: 'Studi su città e architettura nella Roma di Paolo V Borghese (1605–1621)', *Boll. Cent. Stud. Stor. Archit.*, xxxi (1984), pp. 1–97

JOSEPH CONNORS

Bishan Das [Bishan Dās; Viṣṇudāsa] (*fl c.* 1583–1645). Indian miniature painter, nephew of NANHA. He is known mainly for his portraits, in the finest of which he not only conveyed a likeness of the people he painted but also showed an interest in the psychological penetration of his subjects and the exploration of the emotional currents and interactions among figures, even minor ones. He worked on several imperial commissions at the end of the reign of the emperor Akbar (*reg* 1556–1605) but came to maturity under the emperor Jahangir (*reg* 1605–27), his skill at portraiture being particularly responsive to the new emperor's taste. Jahangir stated in his memoirs, the *Tūzuk-i Jahāngīrī*, that Bishan Das had no equal as a portraitist.

1. EARLY WORKS. Bishan Das's early works show the gradual development of his talents. As a young artist he worked with his uncle, who was also known for his portraits. In an illustration for a *Bābarnāma* ('History of Babar'; *c.* 1589; London, V&A, IM. 260 to 276–1913), commissioned by Akbar, Nanha completed the portrait studies in a work otherwise by his nephew. Bishan Das's figural studies in other early works are tentative, as for example in the illustrations in an *Anvār-i Suhaylī* ('Lights of Canopus') manuscript begun in 1604 (London, BL, Add. MS. 18579) and possibly in a *Rāj kunvār* ('King's son') manuscript of the same year (Dublin, Chester Beatty Lib., MS. 37). The latter volume was certainly commissioned by Jahangir before he became emperor when, in rebellion against his father, he had established a separate court at Allahabad. It is possible that Bishan Das was recruited to work there, which would explain the artist's absence from most of the major imperial manuscripts commissioned by Akbar. By the early years of Jahangir's reign he had achieved sufficient eminence to be included among major painters whose portraits are found in the *Muraqqa'-i gulshan* (Tehran, Gulistan Pal. Lib., MSS. 1663–4), an album formed by the Emperor.

The first dated painting by Bishan Das is a portrait of *Raja Suraj Singh* (1608; Berlin, Staatsbib. Preuss. Kultbes., Orientabt.; see fig.). The *House of Shaykh Phul* (Varanasi, Banaras Hindu U., Bharat Kala Bhavan), with an inscription naming him as the artist, is one of his finest works.

Bishan Das: *Raja Suraj Singh*, opaque watercolour on paper, 140×71 mm, 1608 (Berlin, Staatsbibliothek Preussischer Kulturbesitz, Orientabteilung)

In its compositional simplicity and its ability to represent a carefully observed scene of daily life convincingly, it embodies the new direction that Mughal painting took under Jahangir. Figures are shown in informal poses or even mid-movement, and colour is applied lightly. The illustration has the effect of a coloured drawing, increasing the sense of the painter's spontaneity. Nonetheless, the work is experimental, and not everything is successful.

In a later attributed work, the *Birth of a Prince* (c. 1612; Boston, MA, Mus. F.A.), probably representing the birth of Jahangir himself and most likely intended for a manuscript of the *Jahāngīrnāma* ('History of Jahangir'; dispersed), the artist shows far greater control and expertise. Moreover, his ability to distinguish and animate individual facial expressions is by now far more sophisticated. The sensitive *Rai Bahrah and Jassa Jam Sitting on a Terrace* (London, V&A), inscribed with Bishan Das's name, shows

his fully developed skills as a portrait artist. Perhaps because of these skills, Bishan Das was sent to Iran in 1613 with an official embassy. On his return seven years later, he presented several portraits of the Iranian ruler Shah 'Abbas I to Jahangir (*see* INDIAN SUBCONTINENT, fig. 266) and was rewarded with the gift of an elephant. From 1613 to 1620, when he was absent from India, only portraits and studies of the Iranian court can be attributed to his hand.

2. LATE WORKS. Bishan Das's later works show disturbing changes in style. These are already evident in a second illustration to the *Jahāngīrnāma*, a *Processional Scene* (Rampur, Raza Lib.) that, though lacking an inscription naming him, is certainly by Bishan Das. In illustrations attributed to the artist in the great *Pādshāhnāma* manuscript ('History of the emperor'; Windsor Castle, Royal Lib., MS. HB.149, fols 120*v*–121*r*), covering the reign of the emperor Shah Jahan (*reg* 1628–58), proportions of individual figures become increasingly awkward, and the relationship between single and grouped figures laboured.

The final illustrations attributable to Bishan Das are paintings in a *Masnavī* (a poetical text) of Zafar Khan (London, Royal Asiat. Soc., Pers. MS. 310). The manuscript contains verses composed by the noble Zafar Khan accompanied by paintings of scenes from his life probably executed in the 1640s. The paintings are not signed but are in Bishan Das's characteristic style and seem to provide evidence that the painter was eventually released from imperial employment and sought patronage elsewhere.

See also INDIAN SUBCONTINENT, §V, 4(i)(c).

BIBLIOGRAPHY
A. K. Das: 'Bishan Das', *Chhavi, Golden Jubilee Volume: Bharat Kala Bhavan, 1920–1970*, ed. A. Krishna (Varanasi, 1971), pp. 183–91
B. W. Robinson: 'Shah Abbas and the Mughal Ambassador Khan Alam: The Pictorial Record', *Burl. Mag.*, cxiv (1972), pp. 58–63
The Grand Mogul: Imperial Painting in India, 1600–60 (exh. cat. by M. C. Beach, Williamstown, MA, Clark A. Inst.; Baltimore, MD, Walters A.G.; Boston, MA, Mus. F.A.; New York, Asia Soc. Gals; 1978–9)

MILO CLEVELAND BEACH

Bishapur [Bîchâpour; Pers. Bīshāpŭr]. Site of Sasanian city 21 km east of Kazerun in south-west Iran. It was founded by the Sasanian king Shapur I (*reg* AD 241–72) and flourished in the early and middle Sasanian periods (*see* SASANIAN). A relatively small area of the large, approximately rectangular city was cleared by Ghirshman in the 1930s, together with some of the defensive walls.

The purpose of the excavated buildings is disputed. They were once identified as a temple and associated palaces, but the whole area may have had a religious function. One structure, built of fine, ashlar masonry, is semi-subterranean and consists of a central square cella or court surrounded by an ambulatory. A series of subterranean stone channels linked the structure to the river, enabling the cella to be flooded when required. The building was once considered to be a fire temple (*see* ZOROASTRIANISM, §§1–3), but was more probably dedicated to the goddess Anahita. Another building consists of an enormous hall with four iwans opening on to it; its roofing and that of the stone temple are conjectural. The walls were decorated with simple painted stucco, and the pavements of some floors were covered with mosaics,

Bishapur, Tang-i Chogan, rock relief showing investiture of Bahram I (*reg* AD 273–6) by Mithra, h. *c.* 5 m (*in situ*)

almost certainly the work of Roman mosaicists. The geometric motifs and ornamental details in these mosaics are Greco-Roman, but there are also distinctively Iranian scenes with subjects such as dancers and harpists. Shapur's greatest military successes were achieved against the Romans, whom he defeated three times, finally capturing the unfortunate Emperor Valerian alive. Many prisoners were settled in Iran, and their influence is much in evidence at Bishapur, in its orthogonal plan, in the ashlar masonry used for the temple and for the commemorative monument erected at the intersection of the city's two main axes, and in the mosaics.

Shapur's victories provided the principal sculptural impetus for the rock reliefs carved in the nearby gorge, the Tang-i Chogan. The two earliest reliefs occupy the sites nearest the city. The first, which is poorly preserved, illustrated both Shapur's investiture by Ahura Mazda, the supreme god of the Zoroastrian pantheon, and his early successes against the Romans. Opposite is a most unusual sculpture. This abandons the standard formula in rock reliefs of relatively few large figures carved on a massive scale, and replaces it with five registers of small figures. The design must reflect Roman influence, and it seems probable that the relief was sculpted by a Roman working within a strict Sasanian vocabulary. Other novel features include the choice of a curved panel so that the figures seem to step out of the stone, a taut design with overlapping figures, and the introduction of the winged Victory motif. The relief commemorates both Shapur's Roman victories and his successes in the east of the empire. In another version of the same theme at the far end of the

gorge the designer used a more Iranian mode of expression, although, as the relief is unfinished, it appears misleadingly crude. Work stopped at an even earlier stage on the two-register relief opposite, with neither the outlines of all the figures nor the King's crown completed; it may also belong to Shapur I. It is possible that work on these two reliefs was in progress when the King died and had to be completed in plaster in time for his funeral, said to have been held at Bishapur.

The last two reliefs are elegantly carved in high relief and worked to a fine matt finish. One shows Shapur's son and successor, Bahram I (*reg* AD 273–6), being invested by Mithra in a beautifully balanced and symmetrical scene (see fig.), while the other shows Shapur's grandson, Bahram II (*reg* AD 276–93), receiving a delegation. In this scene the King is mounted, while the delegation, introduced by a Persian usher, is on foot and arranged in two rows, one above the other. The calm grace of the King balances the mass of people on the right. These two reliefs were carved within a short space of time and are so close in style that they were probably by the same team of sculptors. One of the most remarkable works of the early Sasanian period, carved from a massive stalactite in a cave on top of a hill near Bishapur, is a monumental statue of *Shapur I*, closely similar in style to his representations on the reliefs. It was unfortunately broken in an earthquake, although it has since been re-erected.

BIBLIOGRAPHY

E. Herzfeld: *Iran in the Ancient East* (Oxford, 1941)
R. Ghirshman: *Bîchâpour*, 2 vols (Paris, 1956–71)
——: *Iran: Parthians and Sasanians* (London, 1962)

V. Lukonin: *Persia*, ii (Geneva, Paris and Munich, 1967)
——: *Des Séleudes aux Sassanides* (1967), i of *Iran* (Geneva, 1967–)
G. Herrmann: *The Iranian Revival*, The Making of the Past (Oxford, 1977)
——: *Iranische Denkmäler*, ix–xi (Berlin, 1981–3)
L. Vanden Berghe: *Reliefs rupestres de l'Iran ancien* (Brussels, 1984)

G. HERRMANN

Bishkek [formerly Pishpek; Frunze]. Capital city of Kyrgyzstan. Located in the centre of the Chu Valley, the town was founded in 1878 as Pishpek on the site of several medieval settlements (Klyuchevskoye, Pishpekskoye, Karadzhigachskoye gorodischa), a Kokand fortress and the Russian outpost of Pishpek. In 1926 it was renamed Frunze in honour of the Red Army commander M. V. Frunze, who was born there. This industrial town, covering 12,352 ha, is divided into four administrative districts and built along a network of streets, boulevards and public gardens. The old town comprised one- and two-storey mud-brick buildings in the Russian style and single-storey pisé structures with thatched or flat adobe roofs in the style of Turkestan. The town centre was renovated from the 1930s to the 1950s, following general trends in Soviet architecture, and again in the 1960s, when high-rise residential zones were added to the south and industrial zones in the east and west. Many memorials, sculptural groups and monuments to military, political, academic, labour and literary figures were erected throughout the city. In the 1970s dilapidated buildings were replaced by multi-storey blocks, new residential quarters added and the administrative centre formed around Lenin Square (renamed Ala-Tau in 1993). In these buildings modern techniques of construction were synthesized with traditional motifs of Central Asian architecture. The cultural centre of Kyrgyzstan, the city (renamed Bishkek in 1991) is home to the Academy of Sciences of Kyrgyzstan, the Kyrgyzstan History Museum and the Kyrgyzstan Museum of Fine Arts, which houses Russian paintings of the 19th and 20th centuries and paintings and sculptures by Kyrgyz artists.

BIBLIOGRAPHY
V. V. Kurbatov and Ye. G. Pisarskoy: *Arkhitektura goroda Frunze* [Architecture of the city of Frunze] (Frunze, 1978)
Frunze (Frunze, 1984)

V. D. GORYACHEVA

Bishnupur [anc. Viṣṇupura]. Town in Bankura District, West Bengal, India. It flourished in the 17th and 18th centuries as the capital of the Malla rulers. Bishnupur is protected by earthen ramparts built in the second half of the 17th century by the ruler Bir Singh; two stone gateways of the old fort remain. The temples of Bishnupur, of which about 30 are preserved, have curved roofs with down-turned eaves, a form copied from the thatched huts of Bengal. As the region lacks stone, the buildings are predominantly brick and are typically decorated, both inside and out, with terracotta panels. These represent a high point of terracotta art in Bengal. As the Mallas were devotees of Vishnu, the terracottas often show events in the lives of Krishna and Rama, themes explored by contemporary Bengali authors. In addition to religious subjects, scenes from Bengali life were illustrated. Local craftsmen were evidently employed for the work; a modest community of artists still lives in the town.

The earliest structure at Bishnupur is the Rasa Mancha, built by Bir Hambir (*reg c.* 1597–1616) in the early 17th century for the Rasa Lila festival. The building is octagonal and has a domed central space surrounded by vaulted passages; externally it is surmounted by a stepped pyramidal spire of masonry. The Shyama Raya Temple (1643) is the most decorated at Bishnupur. It is surrounded by vaulted porches and has a pinnacle over the central chamber and smaller detached pinnacles on the corners, a configuration termed five-pinnacled (Skt *pañcaratna*). The Keshta Raya Temple (1655; *see* INDIAN SUBCONTINENT, fig. 120) has two vaulted chambers edged with the characteristic down-turned eaves; above are small chambers with pyramidal roofs. The terracotta panels with courtly and hunting scenes are noteworthy. The Madana Mohana (1694) is a single-pinnacled (*ekaratna*) temple. The principal façade is covered with terracotta panels illustrating epic stories and scenes of Krishna at play (*Kṛṣṇalīlā*). The 19th-century Shridhara Temple has nine pinnacles (*navaratna*) on two levels. The sculptural decoration, executed in plaster, illustrates Krishna and Radha, Shiva, Brahma and other gods. Dancers and musicians are shown on the temple base.

BIBLIOGRAPHY
Z. Haque: *Terracotta Decorations of Late Mediaeval Bengal: Portrayal of a Society* (Dacca, 1980)
G. Michell, ed.: *Brick Temples of Bengal from the Archives of David McCutchion* (Princeton, 1983)
K. K. Biswas: *The City of Temples: Bishnupur* (Bishnupur, n.d.)

G. BHATTACHARYA

Bishop, Isabel (*b* Cincinnati, 3 March 1902; *d* New York, 19 Feb 1988). American painter, draughtsman and etcher. She moved to New York in 1918 to study at the New York School of Applied Design for Women and from 1920 at the Art Students League under Guy Pène du Bois and Kenneth Hayes Miller. During these years she developed lifelong friendships with Reginald Marsh, Edwin Dickinson and other figurative painters who lived and worked on 14th Street, assimilating these influences with those of Dutch and Flemish painters such as Adriaen Brouwer and Peter Paul Rubens, whose work she saw in Europe in 1931.

From the early 1930s Bishop developed an anecdotal and reportorial Realist style in pictures of life on the streets of Manhattan such as *Encounter* (1940; St Louis, MO, A. Mus.), in which an ordinary-looking man and woman are shown meeting under a street lamp. Throughout her long career Bishop concentrated on the subtleties of fleeting moments in the daily routine of people who lived and worked in and around Union Square, giving these simple occasions a sense of timelessness: shopgirls seated at a lunch counter, tramps gathered under the horse's tail of the equestrian statue of *George Washington*, travellers waiting on a subway platform, children scrambling at play or students walking quietly through the park. She worked in a cautious and painstaking manner, often spending a year or more on a single picture and thus producing fewer than 175 paintings over a period of nearly 60 years. She also produced drawings and, from 1925, etchings on related subjects, for example *Office Girls* (1938) and *Encounter* (1941; both London, BM), the latter based directly on the painting of the same name.

BIBLIOGRAPHY
Isabel Bishop: Prints and Drawings, 1925–1964 (exh. cat., New York, Brooklyn Mus., 1964)
Isabel Bishop (exh. cat., essay S. Reich; Tucson, U. AZ Mus. A., 1974)
K. Lunde: *Isabel Bishop* (New York, 1975)
H. Yglesias: *Isabel Bishop* (New York, 1988)

MARTIN H. BUSH

Bisilliat, Maureen (*b* Surrey, England, 16 Feb 1931). Brazilian photographer and film maker. Having moved to Brazil, she studied painting with André Lhote in Paris (1953–4) and with the American painter Morris Kantor (*b* 1896) at the Art Students' League in New York (1954–6), before deciding to become a photographer; after 1962 she worked as a freelance photojournalist and film maker. In 1970 a Guggenheim Fellowship enabled her to go to Brazil, where she settled. She began to take an interest in the Indian inhabitants, and as a result spent years working with the Xingu in the Amazon region, creating an important visual record of the Amazon Indians at a time when their culture was increasingly threatened. In 1975 this work brought her the Critics' Prize at the São Paulo Biennale. In 1979 her illustrated book *Xingu Tribal Territory* appeared. Among her films were *A João Guimarães Rosa* (1986) and *Xingu Terra* (1980).

PHOTOGRAPHIC PUBLICATIONS
Xingu Tribal Territory (London, 1979) [texts by O. and C. Villas-Bôas]

ERIKA BILLETER

Bisitun [Pers. Bīsutūn; anc. Bagastāna: 'Site of the gods'; Behistan, Behistun]. Site in Iran on the eastern edge of the Zagros Mountains, situated on the Great Khorasan Road, the ancient Silk Road, which leads from southern Mesopotamia to Kirmanshah and eastern Iran. Set high on a cliff overlooking the road is the famous rock-relief of the Achaemenid king Darius I (*reg* 521–486 BC; *see* ACHAEMENID, fig. 1), which commemorates his victory over Gaumata, the false Smerdis, and nine rebel kings. Work on the relief took from 520 to 519 BC. The relief is accompanied by a trilingual inscription in Elamite, Babylonian and Old Persian. This describes Darius's royal descent and lineage, his campaigns and his victories over his opponents.

The relief, measuring 3.0×5.5m, shows Darius followed by a spear-bearer and a bow-bearer. He is depicted in profile wearing a crown and a long robe. In triumphant gesture he puts one foot on the defeated Gaumata, who is lying on the ground, pleading to the king of kings. Darius's right hand is raised towards the figure in a winged disc set above. Behind Gaumata is the row of captured kings roped together at the neck, with their hands tied behind their backs. They include the Persian Martya, the Sagartian Chissantakhma, the Persian Vahyazdata, the Armenian Arakha and the Median Fravartish. The final figure, that of the Scythian Skunkha, was added to the relief at a late stage. The theme, with the king stepping with one foot on the body of an outstretched captive, is similar to that on a relief of King Anubanini of the 3rd millennium BC found further west at Sar-i Pul-i Zuhab near Qasr-i Shirin.

The cuneiform inscriptions on the relief at Bisitun were carved in different stages, the first being the short Elamite inscription above the head of Darius. There followed the main Elamite inscription to the right of the relief panel, the Babylonian version to the left of the relief and the Old Persian text below the relief, carved in that order. Subsidiary inscriptions describing the rebel kings appear within the panel, squeezed into small spaces such as on garments. When in 519 BC the Scythian king was added at the far right, the original Elamite inscription was partly destroyed and had to be repeated below the relief and next to the Old Persian version. The inscriptions at Bisitun were copied between 1836 and 1847 by Sir Henry Creswicke Rawlinson (1810–95), and the availability of these texts led directly to a more complete decipherment of cuneiform scripts.

After the collapse of the Achaemenid empire further reliefs were added to the rock face at Bisitun. During the Seleucid period a reclining Herakles in high relief, accompanied by a Greek inscription of 148 BC, was carved over a relief showing a lion which is probably earlier, and has been re-used as the skin of the Nemean lion. In the following Parthian period two rock-carvings were cut below the relief of Darius. The earlier of these was badly damaged by an 18th-century inscription. It shows a row of standing figures in profile and a Greek inscription above the panel mentions the personal name of the ruler Mithradates, accompanied by his title 'king of kings'. The relief is generally regarded as a depiction of Mithradates II (*reg* 123–88 BC) receiving homage from the satrap Gotarzes. Set to the right of the relief of Mithradates is a badly eroded relief with only a few details surviving, though it is possible to recognize a combat scene with three mounted figures. Just above the head of the leading figure, who is generally identified as the victorious king, a Greek inscription mentions the name 'Gotarzes Geophotros' (Gotarzes the son of Gev). The relief is usually interpreted as showing the victory of Gotarzes II over his rival Meherdates in AD 49–50.

A third Parthian relief was found on a slope to the east of the reliefs of Mithradates and Gotarzes. Here, a central figure is shown beside an altar offering a sacrifice, flanked by an attendant on either side. An inscription carved on the altar mentions a 'Vologases, king of kings'. The fact that six Arsacid kings of this name are known from numismatic evidence makes it difficult to identify the central figure with certainty, but a date around the mid-2nd century AD is generally accepted. The fortification walls of a settlement, probably of the Parthian period, were discovered at Bisitun on the so-called Parthian slope.

BIBLIOGRAPHY
L. W. King and R. Campbell-Thompson: *The Sculptures and Inscription of Darius the Great on the Rock of Behistun in Persia* (London, 1907)
R. G. Kent: *Old Persian Grammar, Texts, Lexicon* (New Haven, 1953)
H. Luschey: 'Studien zu dem Darius-Relief in Behistun', *Archäol. Mitt. Iran*, n.s. 1 (1968), pp. 63–94 [best illustrations of relief]
W. Hinz: *Neue Wege im Altpersischen* (Wiesbaden, 1973)
——: *Darius und die Perser* (Baden-Baden, 1976)
M. A. R. Colledge: *Parthian Art* (London, 1977)
T. S. Kawami: *Monumental Art of the Parthian Period in Iran*, Acta Iran. 26 (Leiden, 1987)

VESTA SARKHOSH CURTIS

Biskupin. Site in Poland, near Gniezno, *c*. 230 km west of Warsaw. It was originally on an island, but is now part of a peninsula on a lake. An Iron Age fortified settlement at Biskupin flourished from the 8th century BC to the 6th.

Excavation of the site began in 1933 under the direction of J. Kostrzewski and continued until the outbreak of World War II, when much of the documentation and material from the site was destroyed, the excavation team dispersed and the site filled in. After the war excavations recommenced, combining new work with attempts to reconstruct the lost records. Finds of material from the Late Upper Palaeolithic (*c.* 20,000–*c.* 10,000 BP) and Mesolithic (*c.* 12,000 BP–*c.* 6500 BC) periods, together with evidence of settlement during the Neolithic (*c.* 6500–*c.* 2300 BC) period, Bronze Age (*c.* 2300–*c.* 750 BC), Iron Age (*c.* 750–*c.* 50 BC) and early medieval period, demonstrated continual reoccupation of the site over an extended time. However, the main period of occupation was during the 8th–6th centuries BC, when Biskupin served as a heavily fortified island settlement. Because of waterlogged conditions at the site, the organic materials there were exceptionally well preserved, enabling remarkable reconstruction work to be carried out.

There were two major phases of occupation during the Iron Age, differing little in their nature and extent: one spanned the 8th–7th centuries BC, the other the 6th century BC. Throughout this period the site was enclosed by a box-framed timber rampart filled with earth and measuring 3 m wide×6 m (max) high. This was surrounded by a defensive breakwater measuring 6.8 m wide and made of timbers set at a 45° angle. A gateway in the southern side measured 8 m long×3 m wide on the inside, less on the outside, and was linked by a causeway to the lake shore 120 m distant. It has been estimated that some 7155 cubic m of timber and 10,000 cubic m of earth and clay were used in the construction of Biskupin's defences and the roads and houses they enclosed. Running round the entire site within the rampart was a road measuring 417 m long and constructed of 3 m-wide logs laid side by side; 12 more of these 'corduroy' roads crossed the site, forming streets between rows of houses. There were between 104 and 106 of these houses, each laid out to a standard plan comprising a main room with a hearth and a porch; in some houses the main room was subdivided, with a small sleeping area separated from the rest of the room. The houses shared common walls, the longest terraces consisting of ten houses and the shortest, at the curved northern end of the site, of three. In the earlier phase the area around the entrance gate was clear of houses, and appears to have been left as a sort of open square; for the later phase, when the settlement contracted a little, losing a street and some houses, there is evidence of some structures in the 'square'.

At Biskupin a broad-based economy involving agriculture, farming and fishing was supplemented by many types of specialist crafts, including metalworking, leatherworking and weaving, the evidence for which was concentrated in certain houses. The astonishing aspect of this site is the coherence of the overall plan of the settlement, which is estimated to have housed a population of 700–1000. The roads, houses and defences were clearly laid out and constructed at the same time, implying either a dominant central authority (for which there is no archaeological evidence) or a communal decision-making process of exceptional strength, perhaps reacting to outside circumstances: there is no doubting the defensive nature of the

ramparts. The spectacular survival of the organic remains and the skill applied to their investigation add to the importance of this extraordinary site.

BIBLIOGRAPHY

J. Kostrzewski: *III Sprawozdanie z prac wykopaliskowych za lata 1938–1939 i 1946–1948* [Report of excavations for the years 1938–9 and 1946–8] (Poznań, 1950)

Z. Rajewski: *Biskupin: Osiedle obronne wspólnot pierwotnych sprzed 2500 lat* [Biskupin: Defensive settlement of primitive communities of 2500 years ago] (Warsaw, 1970)

SARA CHAMPION

Bisschop. Dutch family of traders, collectors and patrons. The brothers Jan Bisschop (*b* Rotterdam, 1680; *d* 5 March 1771) and Pieter Bisschop (*b* 1689; *d* 1 June 1758) of Rotterdam continued their father's haberdashery trade and amassed a fortune, which they invested in a collection of art and natural objects that gained an international reputation. It included paintings, drawings, prints, books, Japanese porcelain, Japanese and Chinese lacquerwork, glass, coins, ivories, miniatures, shells etc. In 1767, following a false rumour that Jan Bisschop had died, the Duc de Choiseuil, a French minister, attempted to acquire the collection, but it was dispersed only after Jan's actual death in 1771: the books were auctioned on 5 June 1771, the prints and drawings on 24 June and the porcelain and lacquerwork on 15 July. The 230 paintings, mainly by Dutch and Flemish artists, were transferred under the terms of the will to Bisschop's friends, the bankers and collectors John Hope (1737–84) and Adrian Hope (1709–81), for 65,000 guilders; among these were Gerard ter Borch (ii)'s *Two Officers* (Philadelphia, PA, Mus. A.) and Paulus Potter's *Cattle and Sheep in a Stormy Landscape* (London, N.G.). Gerard Hoet (ii) published a description of 110 of the paintings in 1752. Jan Bisschop left his fortune to the Baptist church authorities, who built a church in Rotterdam in 1773–5. Cosmo Alexander (*fl* 1750–70) painted *Jan Bisschop*, Jan Stolker (1724–85) painted a double portrait of *Jan and Pieter Bisschop* and Aert Schouman a triple portrait of *Jan and Pieter Bisschop with Olivier Hope* (1753; Blair Castle, Tayside).

BIBLIOGRAPHY

NNBW

G. Hoet: *Catalogus of naamlyst van schilderijen* (The Hague, 1752), ii, p. 527

E. Wiersum: 'Het schilderijen-kabinet van Jan Bisschop te Rotterdam' [Jan Bisschop of Rotterdam's collection of paintings], *Oud-Holland*, xxviii (1910), pp. 161–86 [incl. complete inv.]

F. Lugt: *Ventes*, i (1938), nos 1937, 1942, 1945

J. W. Niemeijer: 'De Kunstverzameling van John Hope', *Ned. Ksthist. Jb.*, xxxii (1981), pp. 158–60, 171–204

FEMY HORSCH

Bisschop, Jan de [Episcopius, Joannes] (*b* Amsterdam, 1628; *d* The Hague, 7 Nov 1671). Dutch draughtsman and etcher. He was a lawyer by profession and a skilled amateur draughtsman. At the Amsterdam Latin school his teacher was the humanist Hadrianus Junius (1511–75), under whose supervision he wrote a poem about the Atheneum Illustre and Collegium Auriacum in Breda, published by Johannes Blaeu in 1647. From 1648 to 1652 he read law at Leiden University. In 1653 he married Anna van Baerle, daughter of the famous professor and theologian Caspar van Baerle (1584–1648), and throughout his life he moved in prominent intellectual circles. One of his closest friends was Constantijn Huygens the younger, who

Jan de Bisschop (after Guido Reni): *Drawing and Painting*, brush and brown ink, 223×244 mm, ?1650s or 1660s (Turin, Biblioteca Reale di Torino)

was also an amateur draughtsman, with a very similar drawing style (especially in landscapes), and who was probably a member—with Jacob van der Does (1623–73) and Willem Doudijns (1630–97)—of the small drawing academy that de Bisschop founded in The Hague. Although de Bisschop lived for a while in a house adjoining Claes Moeyaert's in Amsterdam, it was probably Bartholomeus Breenbergh, also living in Amsterdam at the time, rather than Moeyaert who most influenced his style of drawing. De Bisschop made two large etchings after paintings by Breenbergh: *Joseph Selling Corn to the People* (1644; untraced) and the *Martyrdom of St Lawrence* (1647; Frankfurt am Main, Städel. Kstinst.).

Besides landscape drawings, the earliest of which show views of Amsterdam, Bergen op Zoom and Hoogstraten (e.g. *Beckeneelshuisje (Nieuwe Kerk), Amsterdam*, 1648; Amsterdam, Rijksmus.), de Bisschop made numerous figure studies (e.g. *Jacobus Ewijk Reading*; Amsterdam, Rijksmus.) and drawings after Classical sculptures and famous paintings (mostly by Italian artists). The latter drawings, which Houbraken called 'imitations', were carried out in a particularly fluid technique using brush and luminous wash (see fig.). De Bisschop also designed a number of title-pages for books, mostly by Classical authors, and there are some drawings from 1660 recording the *Departure of King Charles II from Scheveningen* (e.g. Amsterdam, Rijksmus.).

Almost all of de Bisschop's drawings, whether drawn in pen or with the brush, were executed in a warm golden-brown ink, known as 'bisschops-inkt' after the artist. According to Willem Goeree in his *Inleiding tot de algemeene teyken-konst* ('Introduction to the general art of drawing', Amsterdam, 1697, p. 91), de Bisschop mixed Indian ink with a bit of copper red to obtain this 'modest colour of charm and beauty'. As did Breenbergh, de Bisschop drew over a preliminary sketch in black chalk, a technique imitated by Jacob van der Ulft (1627–89) and Jan Goeree

(1670–1731), some of whose drawings are virtual copies of those of de Bisschop. Wallerant Vaillant made several mezzotints based on de Bisschop's drawings of paintings; de Bisschop's brush and wash technique in these drawings was strongly determined by the use of chiaroscuro, which made it easy for Vaillant to translate the images into mezzotint. Other artists who made prints of his drawings include Hendrick Bary (*b* 1640), David Philippe and Petrus Philippe.

Although de Bisschop's drawings include a considerable number of Italianate landscapes (e.g. *View of Rome*, ?1650s; New York, Pierpont Morgan Lib.), he may not have been to Italy himself, and his Italian views could have been composed with the help of prints and drawings by others who had, such as Willem Doudijns, Adriaen Bakker (*b* 1635–6), Jacob Matham and Dirck Ferreris (1639–93). He certainly depended on drawings by other artists as well as the illustrations from François Perrier's *Icones* (Paris, 1645) for his two influential series of prints in book form, the *Signorum veterum icones* (1668–9), with 100 prints after Classical sculptures, dedicated to Johannes Wtenbogaard and Constantijn Huygens, and the *Paradigmata graphices variorum artificum* (1671), with prints after Old Master drawings and dedicated to Jan Six. Some of the Classical sculptures reproduced in de Bisschop's *Icones* were from the 17th-century collections of Gerrit Uylenburgh and Hendrik Scholten, to which de Bisschop had direct access; most of the Old Master drawings in the *Paradigmata* were based on works by Italians: Annibale Carracci, Domenichino, Francesco Salviati, Cavaliere d'Arpino, Giulio Romano and others. The sequence of the *Icones* adhered strictly to the Classical tradition: first the individual parts of the body were illustrated (this section was left unfinished at de Bisschop's premature death), then complete figures, followed by poses and suggestions for compositions with more than one figure. The prints were intended to provide artists with examples of ideal poses. From the paintings of Adriaen van der Werff and Nicolaes Verkolje, it is clear just how influential these studies were in the development of Dutch classical painting during the late 17th century.

PRINTS

Signorum veterum icones, 2 vols (The Hague, 1668–9)
Paradigmata graphices variorum artificum (The Hague, 1671, rev. Amsterdam, 2/[1671])

BIBLIOGRAPHY

Thieme–Becker: 'Episcopius'
A. Houbraken: *De groote schouburgh* (1718–21), iii, p. 212
J. G. van Gelder: 'Jan de Bisschop, 1628–1671', *Oud-Holland*, lxxxvi (1971), pp. 201–8
——: 'De ongenoemde "inventor"', *Bijdragen tot de geschiedenis van de grafische kunst opgedragen aan Louis Lebeer . . .* (Antwerp, 1975), pp. 115–33
J. G. van Gelder and I. Jost: *Jan de Bisschop and his Icones and Paradigmata* (Doornspijk, 1985)
Episcopius: Jan de Bisschop (1628–1671), advocaat en tekenaar/Lawyer and Draughtsman (exh. cat. by R. E. Jellema and M. Plomp, Amsterdam, Rembrandthuis, 1992)

GER LUIJTEN

Bisschop-Robertson, Suzanne. *See* ROBERTSON, SUZE.

Bissen, Hermann Wilhelm (*b* Schleswig, 13 Oct 1798; *d* Copenhagen, 10 March 1868). Danish sculptor. He studied at the Kongelige Danske Kunstakademi, Copenhagen, from 1816. Originally intending to become a painter, he decided after a few years to devote himself to sculpture, partly as a result of seeing the works of Bertel Thorvaldsen in Copenhagen in 1819. In 1823 Bissen gained the academy's grand gold medal and a travelling bursary, and he left for Rome in 1824, making several stops in Germany and Italy en route. He stayed in Rome for over ten years, and as well as making a number of small trips to southern Italy with his friend the sculptor Hermann Ernst Freund, Bissen got the chance to work in Thorvaldsen's studio in Rome. He eventually became one of Thorvaldsen's most trusted collaborators, and in 1833–4 he even carried out a commission in Thorvaldsen's name, the monument to *Johannes Gutenberg* in Mainz. After Thorvaldsen's death in 1844 he completed several of his master's works.

The foundation for Bissen's enormous production was laid in Rome. He worked in the same genres as Thorvaldsen: statues, bas-reliefs and portrait busts. Stylistically they are close to Thorvaldsen's classicism, but Bissen had to work hard to acquire the technique of carving marble. One of his major works from this period is the *Flower Girl* (1828–9; Copenhagen, Ny Carlsberg Glyp.), which in its delicate simplicity shows that Bissen could overcome the strict ideals of Thorvaldsen. Bissen was influenced by the move at that time towards a greater realism. He never attained the level of Thorvaldsen, but the educational years in Rome were to prove a useful background for his further work in Copenhagen. Immediately on his return to Denmark in 1834, he received several commissions for decorative works for Christiansborg Slot, Copenhagen, including a frieze representing *Bacchus and Ceres* that he modelled for the banqueting hall and that was lost when the palace burnt down in 1884. After Thorvaldsen's death Bissen became one of the country's leading sculptors. In 1840 Freund died, and Bissen took over his professorship at the Kunstakademi, becoming Director in 1850–53. Bissen ran a large studio and workshop in the spirit of Thorvaldsen, to which his pupils came, and this contributed to Thorvaldsen's continued strong influence on Danish sculpture well into the 19th century.

After 1850 there was a noticeable change in Bissen's style. Already in Rome he had got to know the art historian Niels Lauritz Høyen, who played a very prominent role in Danish artistic life at this period and was an eager spokesman for contemporary nationalist tendencies. In Rome Bissen had moved towards realism, and this was confirmed in the statue of the *Danish Soldier after the Victory* (1850–58; Fredericia, junction of Danemarksgade and Norgesgade), erected in memory of the battle of Fredericia in 1849, an important event in the Danish–German war of 1848–51. The work is remarkable in its use of a common soldier to symbolize a national event, and Høyen doubtless had some influence. In 1850 Bissen produced another war memorial, the *Isted Lion* (Copenhagen, Tøjhusmus.). He became a great sculptor of nationalist sentiment with these monuments, and the national, popular spirit of liberty also comes out in his statue of *King Frederick VI* (1855–8; Copenhagen, Frederiksberg Park). In addition Bissen carried out a large

number of portrait busts of the period's leading personalities (many in Copenhagen, Stat. Mus. Kst). At first glance they can seem somewhat similar in expression, but Bissen nevertheless managed to convey individual features and character.

BIBLIOGRAPHY

H. Rostrup: *Billedhuggeren H. W. Bissen* [The sculptor H. W. Bissen] (Copenhagen, 1945)

ELISABETH CEDERSTRØM

Bissier, Julius (*b* Freiburg im Breisgau, 3 Dec 1893; *d* Ascona, 18 June 1965). German painter and draughtsman. He registered at the Karlsruhe Academy of Fine Arts in 1914 but remained there for only a few months, preferring to work alone. In 1927 he met the sinologist Ernst Grosse, who in introducing him to ancient Chinese thought enabled him to familiarize himself with a form of art completely outside the European tradition. Among the few surviving works of this period are *Zurich Landing Stage* (1927) and *Self-portrait* (1928; both Düsseldorf, Kstsamml. Nordrhein-Westfalen). In 1930 he began to make ink paintings, in the same year meeting in Paris with Constantin Brancusi, who taught him that art was rooted in meditation. Bissier then began to question the abstract painting he practised at the time, to such an extent that when a fire destroyed almost all his works in 1934 he started again from scratch and began to paint in a style influenced by Chinese monochrome ink paintings. From then on he concentrated on the technique of wash drawing in black India ink. Strongly influenced by Taoism, he combined spontaneity and mastery in a single gesture, as in *Masculine–Feminine Unity Symbol* (1934; Düsseldorf, Kstsamml. Nordrhein-Westfalen). He lived quietly at Hagnau on Lake Constance, working in isolation, and did not exhibit his pictures under the Nazi regime. The monochrome ink paintings he executed throughout this period, such as *Penetration* (1939; Düsseldorf, Kstsamml. Nordrhein-Westfalen), were seen by the public only after World War II, making his reputation. From 1950 he took part in many major international exhibitions, including Documenta in Kassel (1959) and the Venice Biennale in 1960. While continuing to work on paper, he also began to paint on panel from 1953 (all destr.) and from 1956 on canvas. In these paintings, such as *30 July 1959* (1959; Düsseldorf, Kstsamml. Nordrhein-Westfalen), he developed a technique of egg-and-oil tempera that allowed him to use several washes on the canvas while retaining coloured contours to define his forms. He called these small pictures 'miniatures', but they might also be referred to as microcosms, because of the wealth of their symbolism. During the 1950s, Bissier left Germany for Ascona in Switzerland, where he continued to lead a quiet life in conditions favourable to the meditation on which his painting depended. Like Mark Tobey, he was one of the first modern western painters to have sought inspiration from the art of the Far East.

BIBLIOGRAPHY

K. Leonhard: *Julius Bissier* (Stuttgart, 1947)

W. Schmalenbach: *Julius Bissier* (Stuttgart, 1963; Fr. trans., Paris, 1963; Eng. trans., New York and London, 1964)

D. Vallier: *Julius Bissier Brush Drawings* (London, 1966)

Julius Bissier, 1893–1965 (exh. cat. by W. Schmalenbach and P. Cannon-Brookes, ACGB, 1977)

DORA VALLIER

Bissière, (Jean-Edouard-)Roger (*b* Villeréal, Lot-et-Garonne, 22 Sept 1886; *d* Boïssiérettes, Lot, 2 Dec 1964). French painter. Son of a lawyer, he attended the Ecole des Beaux-Arts in Algiers in 1904 before enrolling at that of Bordeaux the following year. He moved to Paris in 1910 and passed briefly through the atelier of Gabriel Ferrier (1884–1916) at the Ecole Nationale des Beaux-Arts. Bissière became a journalist in 1912 but by 1914 had exhibited a design for a fresco of *Daphnis and Chloe* at the Salon des Indépendants. From 1919 he exhibited regularly at the Paris salons, becoming an accepted figure among both the Salon Cubists and the adherents of the later 'rappel à l'ordre' that advocated a return to Classical values. He wrote the first monograph on Georges Braque (1920) for Léonce Rosenberg's Galerie de l'Effort Moderne, where he was offered a contract and one-man show in 1921, and published articles on Seurat (Oct 1920), Ingres (Jan 1921) and Corot (June 1921) for the Purist periodical *L'Esprit Nouveau*.

Bissière's work at this time ranged from landscapes inspired by Braque and André Lhote (e.g. *Landscape*, 1925; Paris, Pompidou) to interiors with monumental figures that bear similarities to Picasso's Ingres-influenced period. In 1923 he accepted a five-year contract with the Galerie Druet and succeeded Maurice Denis as professor of painting at the Académie Ranson, where his pupils included Maria Elena Vieira da Silva, Alfred Manessier, Jean-Louis Le Moal (*b* 1909) and Jean Bertholle (1909–70). He remained there until 1938.

Bissière's almost abstract landscape paintings of 1927–8, despite their green and brown palette, clearly anticipate the works of the so-called Jeunes Peintres de Tradition Française of the 1940s. By the mid-1930s, however, a humorous, ironical streak offset Bissière's debt to Braque with classical parody, as in *Nude with Baby Angel* (*c.* 1935–6; Paris, priv. col., see 1986–7 exh. cat., p. 32). A certain deliberate gaucheness and violent colouring appeared in his portraits. The influence of Matthias Grünewald's Isenheim altarpiece (Colmar, Mus. Unterlinden) became explicit in *Crucifixion* (1937; Paris, Gal. Gianna Sistu). From 1935 Bissière was involved with the Art Mural movement, which was working towards a renaissance of fresco painting in France, and, besides his own projects, he directed teams of his students in the execution of frescoes for the Air and Railway Pavilions at the *Exposition Internationale des Arts et Techniques dans la Vie Moderne* of 1937 in Paris in conjunction with Manessier and Robert Delaunay.

Bissière left Paris in 1939 for the seclusion of his family property at Boïssiérettes, where his prolonged isolation brought about a complete renewal of his art. The growing interest in Romanesque art among the circle of Henri Focillon was reflected in the cruder colours and more direct expression of Bissière's own contemporary work, for example the *Crucifixion* fresco at Boïssiérettes (see Abadie, pp. 178–9). In 1942 Manessier asked Bissière to participate in a group showing of the Jeunes Peintres de Tradition Française at the Galerie de France. Their use of reds, blues and oranges superimposed on a grid-like, post-Cubist framework encouraged Bissière to brighten his palette. After the exhibition of the Bayeux tapestry at the Louvre in 1944 and the opening of the Musée de la Fresque in June 1945 at the Palais de Chaillot, Bissière began his series of 'tentures', wall hangings in the tradition of medieval tapestry, with themes ranging from *Chartres* (1947; Colmar, Mus. Unterlinden) to *Hiroshima* (1947; untraced, see 1986–7 exh. cat., p. 14). Employing the rectangular structures and simple images of frescoes, they were made up from scraps of cloth and wool, roughly stitched together by Bissière's wife Mousse, evoking the rural tradition of patchwork. Bissière's rustic sculptures, assemblages of iron machinery and pieces of wood, such as the *Crucified Christ* (*c.* 1942; France, priv. col., see Abadie, p. 53), used abandoned materials in the same way, exemplifying the 'bricolage' aesthetic of the deprived Occupation years, also demonstrated by Gaston Chaissac.

In 1947, at Bissière's first major exhibition for over ten years, thirty paintings and seven tapestries were shown at the Galerie René Drouin, where the new wave of '*informel*' painters, Jean Fautrier, Wols and Jean Dubuffet, had been launched. Dubuffet quickly became a friend, and elements of both his graffiti-based work and Klee's pictographic art entered Bissière's work. After 1947 Bissière used smaller formats, initially because of a deteriorating eye condition, cured in 1950. From *c.* 1945 until 1954 he painted almost exclusively in egg tempera on cardboard, wood and paper. *Homage to Angelico* (1950; Amsterdam, Stedel. Mus.), with its predella structure and simple red, blue and yellow touches, demonstrates this Quattrocento-inspired primitivism, which probably influenced Nicolas de Staël's last figurative phase. In 1954 Bissière created the series of eleven coloured woodcuts, *Hymn to our Brother Sun, St Francis of Assisi*, hand-printed by the engraver Marcel Fiorini (*b* 1922), a high point of post-war French illustrated books.

In the late 1950s he returned to oil painting (e.g. *Composition with Green Tonalities*, 1955; Paris, Pompidou) and designed stained-glass windows for the transepts of Metz Cathedral in 1960–61. Mousse's death in 1962 led to the series of small paintings, each titled with a date, exhibited as *Journal 1962–1964* (see 1986–7 exh. cat., pp. 74, 76, 98–102) at the Galerie Jeanne Bucher. Bissière won an honourable mention when he represented France at the Venice Biennale in 1964, but the award of the Grand Prix to Robert Rauschenberg signalled the definitive triumph of New York over the Ecole de Paris.

BIBLIOGRAPHY

M.-P. Fouchet: *Bissière* (Paris, 1955)
Roger Bissière (exh. cat., Hannover, Kestner-Ges.; Lübeck, St-Annen-Mus.; 1957)
Bissière (exh. cat., Eindhoven, Stedel. Van Abbemus.; Amsterdam, Stedel. Mus.; 1957–8)
Bissière: Artisan de la cathédrale (exh. cat., Metz, Mus. A. & Hist., 1959)
Bissière (exh. cat., Paris, Mus. N. A. Mod., 1959)
Bissière (exh. cat., Paris, Mus. A. Déc., 1966)
Bissière: Peinture, 1945–1964 (exh. cat., Les Sables d'Olonne, Mus. Abbaye Sainte-Croix, 1977)
D. Abadie: *Bissière: Ides et calendes* (Neuchâtel, 1986)
Bissière, 1886–1964 (exh. cat. by P. Le Nouëne, Paris, Mus. A. Mod. Ville Paris; Dijon, Mus. B.-A.; Calais, Mus. B.-A.; 1986–7)

SARAH WILSON

Bissinger, Georges (*b* Hanau; *fl* Paris, second half of the 19th century). French gem-engraver of German birth. He worked in cameo in the Renaissance Revival style. Many of his gems are copies of English and French royal portraits dating from the 16th century. The cutting is very sharp and refined, often more so than in the original, and his gems are characterized by the frequent use of a raised line cut from the pale layer of the stone to border the main subject in imitation of the 16th-century Italian engravers from whom he derived his models and style. Bissinger's skill was demonstrated by a series of 112 gems, copied from examples in the Cabinet des Médailles in Paris, which he exhibited at the Exposition Universelle of 1878 in Paris. His work had already featured in the Exposition Universelle in Paris in 1867 and was noted in the London *Art Journal* (1868, p. 38). In 1873 he exhibited at the Weltausstellung in Vienna. After the 1876 Philadelphia Exhibition, Alexis Falize, the Parisian jeweller, remarked in his Jury Report on the extraordinary technique employed by Bissinger to create the effect of lace, using a lathe. Although his career was spent in Paris, several of the rare surviving signed examples of his work are set in jewelled mounts from English workshops, including a portrait cameo of Marie de' Medici (London, V&A), in an enamelled pendant setting by Carlo Giuliano (1831–95). Another signed example, an onyx cameo of Elizabeth I (sold Geneva, Sotheby's, 11–13 Nov 1981, lot 933), has a frame of emeralds and diamonds by Mrs Newman (*fl* before 1866– *c.* 1910).

BIBLIOGRAPHY

L'Exposizione universale di Vienna illustrata (Milan, 1873), p. 586
E. Babelon: *Histoire de la gravure sur gemmes en France* (Paris, 1902)
Shirley Bury: *Jewellery, 1789–1910*, 2 vols (Woodbridge, 1991)

CHARLOTTE GERE

Bissolo [Bissuolo], Francesco (*b* ?Treviso, ?*c.* 1470–75; *d* Venice, 20 July 1554). Italian painter. At least eight signed works by Bissolo are known; one of the most important of these, the *Coronation of St Catherine of Siena* (1513; Venice, Accad.), is also documented with a contract. On this basis a considerable number of other altarpieces and devotional half-lengths may be attributed to him with a reasonable degree of confidence. Bissolo is first recorded as an assistant of Giovanni Bellini at the Doge's Palace, Venice, in 1492, and his works demonstrate a stylistic dependence on his master throughout his long life (apparently spent entirely in Venice). Individual motifs are frequently borrowed directly from Bellini, as with the God the Father of the *Coronation*. Hallmarks of his own manner include a softness of modelling, tending towards formlessness, and a greater sentimentality of facial expression than usual in the work of Bellini's other followers.

In works that must belong to his later career, such as the *St Euphemia with Saints and a Donor* (Treviso Cathedral), Bissolo was evidently responding to the more advanced styles of younger contemporaries such as Paris Bordone and Bonifazio Veronese, without, however, abandoning the Bellinesque basis of his art. Bissolo was employed by distinguished men such as Pietro Barozzi, Bishop of Padua, and Bonino de' Bonini, printer and canon of Treviso Cathedral. Although as late as 1545 he enjoyed sufficient professional reputation to be asked to value a picture by Lorenzo Lotto, his rather low recorded fees confirm that his contemporaries did not overrate his essentially modest talents.

BIBLIOGRAPHY

DBI; Thieme–Becker
A. M. Zanetti: *Della pittura veneziana* (Venice, 1771), pp. 82–3
G. Ludwig: 'Archivalische Beiträge zur Geschichte der venezianischen Malerei', *Jb. Kön.-Preuss. Kstsamml.*, xxvi (1905), pp. 41–9 [docs]
L. Coletti: 'Intorno a Francesco Bissolo', *Boll. A.*, viii (1928–9), pp. 325–34
B. Berenson: *Venetian School* (1957), i, pp. 39–40
M. Palmegiano: 'Opere inedite di Francesco Bissolo', *A. Veneta*, xiii–xiv (1959–60), pp. 198–201
F. Heinemann: *Giovanni Bellini e i Belliniani*, i (Venice, 1962), pp. 90–97
L. Montobbio: 'Nuovi documenti su Francesco Bissolo', *Atti & Mem. Accad. Patavina Sci., Lett. & A.*, lxxxv (1972–3), pt iii, pp. 237–46
P. Carboni: 'La pala di Francesco Bissolo nel Duomo di Treviso', *A. Veneta*, xli (1987), pp. 128–30
P. Humfrey: 'Fra Bartolomeo, Venice and St Catherine of Siena', *Burl. Mag.*, cxxxii (1990), pp. 476–83

PETER HUMFREY

Bisson. French family of photographers. Louis-Auguste Bisson (Bisson aîné, Bisson fils; *b* Paris, 1814; *d* Paris, 1876) studied under Louis Daguerre and began to photograph professionally in 1840. He made 200 daguerreotypes of human types and in 1849–51 produced portraits of 900 members of the Assemblée Nationale. He also photographed Classical monuments and sculpture. He was a founder-member of the Société Française de Photographie and became official photographer to Pope Pius IX. His brother Auguste-Rosalie Bisson (Bisson jeune, Bisson fils; *b* Paris, 1826; *d* Paris, 1900), with whom Louis-Auguste worked (as Bisson frères) on many projects, frequently worked in Switzerland, where he made magnificent photographs during the first and second photographic ascents of Mont Blanc (e.g. *The Ascent of Mont Blanc: The Passage des Echelles*, 1862; see Berger-Levrault, pl. 24). He travelled in Egypt in 1869, producing 450 photographs in nine months. He photographed the siege of Paris in 1871 and exhibited throughout Europe.

PHOTOGRAPHIC PUBLICATIONS

L.-A. Bisson: *L'Oeuvre d'Albert Dürer photographiée* (Paris, 1854)
A.-R. Bisson: *Le Mont Blanc et ses glaciers* (Paris, 1860)

BIBLIOGRAPHY

Regards sur la photographie en France au XIXe siècle, Berger-Levrault (Paris, 1980)
H. Gernsheim: *The Rise of Photography, 1850–1880: The Age of Collodion* (London, 1988)

PATRICIA STRATHERN

Bissone, Elia de. *See* GAGINI, (2).

Bissucio, Leonardo (de' Molinari) da. *See* LEONARDO DA BESOZZO.

Bistam [Basṭām; Besṭām; Bisṭām]. Town in the province of Khurasan in eastern Iran, 6 km north of Shahrud. Its foundation has been attributed to Bastam, the maternal uncle of the Sasanian emperor Khosrow II Parviz, at the end of the 6th century AD, but no pre-Islamic remains have been discovered. The town is best known for the architectural complex that surrounds the tomb of the great Muslim mystic Abu Yazid (Bayazid) al-Bistami (*d* AD 874), one of the most important complexes of this kind in Iran. The oldest mosques date from his lifetime; they were restored in 912–13 and rebuilt as one unit in 1120–21. The last Ghurid prince, 'Ala' al-Din Muhammad, had his own mausoleum constructed next to the mystic's burial place *c.* 1215. Under the Mongol rulers Ghazan (*reg* 1295–1304) and Uljaytu (*reg* 1304–17; *see* ILKHANID), other important structures were added, including a tomb over the presumed grave of Muhammad, the son of Ja'far, the sixth Shi'ite Imam, and an entrance iwan dated 1313–14. The work was supervised by the architect–engineer, master mason and stucco-carver Husayn ibn Abi Talib Damghani and his son Muhammad. The iwan opens on to the Madrasa Shahrukhiyya, probably commissioned by the Timurid prince Shahrukh (*reg* 1405–47). To the south of the madrasa stands the congregational mosque. The only parts remaining from the original building are four pier bases. The most interesting elements date from the Mongol period: the decoration of the south wing (1306–7) and the Kashana tomb tower (1301–9).

BIBLIOGRAPHY

Enc. Iran.: 'Besṭām'
S. S. Blair: 'The Inscription from the Tomb Tower at Basṭām', *Art et société dans le monde iranien*, ed. C. Adle (Paris, 1982), pp. 263–86
R. Hillenbrand: 'The Flanged Tomb Tower at Basṭām', *Art et société dans le monde iranien*, ed. C. Adle (Paris, 1982), pp. 237–61
C. Adle: 'Recherches archéologiques en Iran sur le Kumes médiéval', *Acad. Inscr. & B.-Lett.: C. R. Séances* (1984), pp. 271–99
——: 'Katība'yi naw-yāfta dar Basṭām' [A newly discovered inscription in Bistam], *Āthār*, x–xi (Iran. Solar, 1364/1986), pp. 175–83

CHAHRYAR ADLE

Bisti, Dmitry (Spiridonovich) (*b* Sevastopol, 27 June 1925). Russian illustrator and printmaker. He studied at the Polygraphic Institute in Moscow (1947–52). From the 1960s he was counted as one of the leading Soviet book illustrators. He combined in his work both keen attention to the techniques of 20th-century foreign graphic artists and the tradition of the Russian school of book design. He was particularly impressed by the style of the Taller de la Gráfica Popular founded in Mexico by Leopoldo Méndez. In his book illustrations Bisti combined expressive succinctness in the use of image and symbol, rough emotionalism and a perfection of rhythm, achieving a fine understanding of the poetic style of the authors he illustrated. Among his best works are the woodcut illustrations to Vladimir Mayakovsky's poem *V. I. Lenin* (Moscow, 1967) and to the *Iliad* (Moscow, 1978). Bisti also made independent prints.

PRINTS

D. S. Bisti: Grafika [D. S. Bisti: graphics], text by M. P. Lazarev (Moscow, 1978)

BIBLIOGRAPHY

D. S. Bisti (exh. cat., Washington, DC, Corcoran Gal. A., 1988)

M. N. SOKOLOV

Bisticci, Vespasiano da. *See* VESPASIANO DA BISTICCI.

Bistolfi, Leonardo (*b* Casale Monferrato, 15 March 1859; *d* Turin, 2 Sept 1933). Italian sculptor, painter and writer. The leading Art Nouveau sculptor in Italy, he was the son of Giovanni Bistolfi, a wood-carver. Bistolfi first studied (1876–9) at the Accademia di Brera, Milan, under Giosué Argenti (1819–1901), transferring to the Accademia Albertina, Turin, in 1880 for more advanced work under Odoardo Tabacchi. In 1881 Bistolfi received a commission for the Braida family tomb (Turin cemetery), for which he carved the marble figure the *Angel of Death*, a commission enabling him to open his own studio. During the 1880s Bistolfi worked mainly on small bronze groups, in which he sought to communicate sentiments that had hitherto been expressed only in painting. Like the artists

of I Scapigliati, he depicted literary subjects, such as his bronze *Washerwomen* (Italian priv. col.), inspired by Emile Zola's novel *L'Assommoir* (1877). While influenced by Impressionism and by such artists as Daniele Ranzoni, Tranquillo Cremona and Giuseppe Grandi, Bistolfi produced his *Lovers* (1884; Casale Monferrato, Mus. Civ.), *Rain* (Rome, Pal. Braschi) and *Twilight* (1892; Turin, Gal. Civ. A. Mod.), the last of which is characterized by a certain brutal realism. In 1888 he entered the competition for a monument to Garibaldi to be erected in Milan. Although he did not win, his model was cast in bronze by the Associazione degli Artisti Milanesi and donated to the city (Milan, Castello Sforzesco).

Around 1890 Bistolfi began to frequent intellectual circles in Turin, making friends with leading Divisionism painters such as Angelo Morbelli and Giuseppe Pellizza da Volpedo. His works over the following decade were undertaken in the atmosphere of intellectual ferment that prevailed at the end of the century; Bistolfi himself was particularly sympathetic to the nascent trend for exploring ideas concerning humanitarian socialism. As an artist he was drawn to Symbolism, which influenced him as early as his work on the Braida tomb's *Angel of Death*, and in the later 1880s this emerged more fully still. His marble *Sphinx* (1889–92) for the tomb of the Pansa family (Cuneo cemetery) was followed by a number of works that earned him the soubriquet the 'poet of death'. They include his marble relief of the *Brides of Death* (1895) for the Vochieri tomb (Frascarolo Lomellina cemetery), the marble *Beauty of Death* (1895) for the Grandis tomb (Cuneo, Borgo S Dalmazzo cemetery), the bronze relief depicting *Grief Comforted by Memories* (1898) for the Durio tomb (Turin, cemetery of Madonna di Campagna), for which he won a gold medal at the Turin Exposition in 1902, and the marble Bauer-Toscanini tomb (1909–11; Milan, Cimitero Monumentale; see fig.). Bistolfi's idealized and increasingly graphic female figures for these tombs have their origin in the Pre-Raphaelite style popularized in mid-19th-century England.

As a faithful follower of William Morris's ideas on the arts, crafts and society, Bistolfi took part in reforming Italian art according to the new aesthetic canons of the Art Nouveau style and was among the organizers of the Mostra Internazionale di Arte Decorativa Moderna held in Turin in 1902. Together with Davide Calandra, Enrico Thovez and others he was also a founder-member of the periodical *L'arte decorativa moderna* (published in Turin), whose contributors vigorously supported Art Nouveau and showed themselves to be well informed about the modern movement elsewhere in Europe. Bistolfi's leading position was recognized in 1905, with the first one-man exhibition devoted to an Italian sculptor to be held at the Venice Biennale. By this time his work had begun to reveal a renewed attention to the human figure and his return to a more traditional type, though he never abandoned his innate decorative sense or linear bias. This new direction in his work was largely under the influence of Auguste Rodin, whose works Bistolfi had seen at the early Venice Biennale exhibitions, but it was also in response to the renewed interest in Renaissance artists, notably Michelangelo, which characterized Italian figurative art from 1895. During this phase Bistolfi produced a number of

Leonardo Bistolfi: Bauer-Toscanini tomb, marble, 1909–11 (Milan, Cimitero Monumentale)

significant monumental groups which still betrayed his Symbolist roots. Thus the individuals being commemorated are not represented in the form of a portrait sculpture in the round but are relegated to an appearance in a relief medallion on the side of the tomb, while the dominating figure above it is an idealized or allegorical female. These features can be seen in numerous works, including the gigantic group in gilded bronze, the *Sacrifice*, for the monument to *Victor Emanuel II* (1907; Rome, Piazza Venezia) and the marble monument to *Camillo Benso di Cavour* (1913; Bergamo).

After 1905 Symbolist imagery, though not always understood, became more widespread in Italy through the work of Bistolfi's many pupils and imitators, who dominated the fields of civic and memorial sculpture until the 1920s. There was criticism of his work, however, notably from the Futurists, who accused him of producing works that were excessively decorative and lacking in form. This was at a time when Bistolfi's participation in various juries and commissions provided him with considerable influence in matters of official sculpture.

While continuing to work on many funerary monuments and public sculptures, among which is the marble relief monument to *Giosuè Carducci* (1908–26; Bologna, Piazza Carducci) and the bronze equestrian monument to *Giuseppe Garibaldi* (1912–28; Savona, Piazzale dell'Eroe dei Due Mondi), with the end of World War I Bistolfi was also active as a maker of monuments—particularly in Piemont—to those killed in the course of the war. This work would have culminated in his ambitious monument *To the Fallen* for Turin, which he began in 1926, but the

project was never completed. Towards the end of his life Bistolfi was also active as a landscape painter in oils in the style of Antonio Fontanesi (examples in Turin, priv. col.; for illus. see 1984 exh. cat., pp. 157–62); he continued to write articles on art and took up writing poetry as well. His sculptural works in the 1920s include the seated bronze and marble monument to *Cesare Lombroso* (1922) in the Giardino di S Giorgio (*in situ*) in Verona and that *To the Fallen* (1928; Casale Monferrato), a marble exedra with caryatids enclosing the bronze figure of an infantryman, several steps below which stands the artist's bronze of *Spring*. The bust, also in bronze, of *Guido Gozzano* set in a marble monument in the grounds of a chapel (Agliè, S Anna), which Bistolfi had begun in 1926, was completed after his death by G. Giorgis, a one-time pupil.

DBI

BIBLIOGRAPHY
E. Lavagnino: *L'arte moderna* (Turin, 1956), ii, pp. 682–5
G. Anzani and L. Caramel: *Scultura moderna in Lombardia, 1900–1950* (Milan, 1981), pp. 38–57
M. De Micheli: *La scultura del novecento* (Turin, 1981), pp. 14–26
Bistolfi, 1859–1933: Il percorso di uno scultore simbolista (exh. cat. by R. Bossaglia and S. Berresford, Casale Monferrato, Pal. Langosco, 1984) [full bibliog.]
G. Panazza: 'La scultura', *Brescia postromantica e liberty, 1880–1915*, ed. F. O. Grafo (Brescia, 1985), p. 173
V. Terradoli: 'Leonardo Bistolfi', *Disegno e scultura nell'arte italiana del XX secolo*, ed. C. Pirovano (Milan, 1994), pp. 26–33

VALERIO TERRAROLI

Bistre. Warm brown, transparent pigment obtained by boiling the soot from a wood fire. It may also have been produced by burning resin or peat. Its history is uncertain, as references to the use of soot, even if they imply a brown colouring rather than a black, are often too vague to be associated with bistre. As well as being used as a watercolour, bistre tended to be used alone as a monochrome wash, and its name is associated with the shading of drawings in that way; however, the extent of its use is unclear because Van Dyck brown, Cologne earth, sepia and various inks all produce effects that are difficult to differentiate from bistre. It was listed by name in the 17th century by Sir Théodore Turquet de Mayerne (London, BL, MSS Sloane 1990 and 2052), although it was not mentioned with any frequency in England until the following century, when watercolour methods began to develop. Around the beginning of the 19th century it was eclipsed by sepia.

See also DRAWING, §III; INK, §I, 1(ii)(a); and PIGMENT, §IV.

BIBLIOGRAPHY
R. D. Harley: *Artists' Pigments, c. 1600–1835: A Study in English Documentary Sources* (London, 1970, rev. 2/1982)

JONATHAN STEPHENSON

Bite. Printmaking term used to describe the chemical action of acid etching or 'eating' into a metal plate. Backbiting describes the irregular and sideways action of acid on an etched line (*see also* ETCHING and FOUL-BITING).

□

Bitolj [Bitola; Herakleia Lynkestis; Turk. Manastir, Monastir]. Town on the Pelagonian plain in the Republic of Macedonia, at the foot of Mt Pelister. The ancient city of Herakleia Lynkestis, strategically situated on the River Siva

Reka, 3 km south of Bitolj, was probably founded by Philip II of Macedon (*reg* 359–336 BC). Under Roman rule from 148 BC, it became a major military and commercial centre on the Via Egnatia and continued to flourish throughout the early Byzantine period until the settlement of the Slavs in the late 6th century AD. In the 5th and 6th centuries Herakleia was also an important ecclesiastical see. The site was excavated in 1935–8 and 1957–80, and 14 early Byzantine mosaic floors were uncovered. The sculptural and archaeological finds from the site are kept in Bitolj (Archaeol. Mus.), Skopje (Archaeol. Mus. Macedonia) and Belgrade (N. Mus.).

Only the western part of the site has been explored, revealing six buildings, including the Roman theatre (2nd century AD), portico and baths, which together formed part of the city's ancient nucleus and surrounded what was probably the forum. The three other excavated buildings adjoin the baths to the west and belong to a 5th- and 6th-century ecclesiastical complex: the Small Basilica (*c.* 8.5×16 m), the Large Basilica (16×34 m) and the episcopal residence. Both churches, which are three-aisled basilicas with a western narthex, were erected over earlier public buildings. The Large Basilica probably functioned as the cathedral, while the Small Basilica probably served the clergy.

The mosaic pavements (early 5th century AD to the late 6th) found in the ecclesiastical complex are of special interest. The earlier mosaics mostly consist of geometric patterns inset with geometric or figural motifs (*see* EARLY CHRISTIAN AND BYZANTINE ART, §III, 3(i)). By the early 6th century, when the largest and most impressive of the mosaics was laid in the narthex of the Large Basilica, this ornamental style had given way to one invested with greater symbolic meaning. A row of trees, interspersed with animals and plants, stretches the full length of the narthex floor, and in the centre a pair of roebucks stand on either side of a kantharos with a branching vine of life. The whole composition is an ideal representation of the cosmos. Elsewhere in the complex, the pavements are divided into square fields containing a variety of compositions: terrestrial and marine scenes, individual animals and combinations of geometric and figural motifs. In style, technique and iconography they closely resemble mosaics from the Balkan sites of STOBI, Amphipolis and CARIČIN GRAD. A Latin votive inscription set in one of the mosaics in the Large Basilica refers to a certain 'Vinica domesticus', who contributed towards the church's decoration. It seems that Herakleia's own highly skilled mosaicists worked alongside imported craftsmen, an artistic collaboration that is also evident in the few fragments of architectural sculpture from the site.

The location of medieval Bitolj following its capture by the Bulgars in the 8th century is uncertain. Mentioned in the documentary sources as a fortified site and briefly the court of Gavrilo Rodomir (*reg* 1014–15), it probably lay north-west of the modern city. It was later taken by the Serbian Tsar Dušan (*reg* 1331–55). In 1382 it fell to the Turks and was renamed Monastir after the nearby monastery of Bukova. The later principal monuments in Bitolj are the 16th-century mosques of Hajda Kaddi, Jeni and Isak, the 17th-century Bezistan (covered market) and Sahat Kula (clock tower).

BIBLIOGRAPHY

Héraclée, 3 vols (Bitolj, 1961–7)

G. Cvetković-Tomašević: *Ranovizantijski podni mozaici: Dardanija, Macedonija, Novi Epir* [Early Byzantine floor mosaics: Dardania, Macedonia, New Epirus] (Belgrade, 1978), pp. 29–38

G. Filipovska and P. Srbinovski: 'A Review of the Archaeological Investigations of the Medieval Period in Bitola (1978–1981)', *Zbornik Trudovi*, ii–iii (1980–81), pp. 111–21

K. Balabanov, A. Nikolovski and D. Kornakov: *Spomenici na kulturata na Makedonija* [Reflections on Macedonian culture] (Skopje, 1980), pp. 194, 200

R. Kolarik: 'The Floor Mosaics of Eastern Illyricum: The Northern Regions', *Ellinika*, xxvi (1980), pp. 173–203; also in *Actes du Xe congrès international d'archéologie chrétienne: Thessalonique, 1980*, i, pp. 445–79

K. Hattersley-Smith: *Byzantine Public Architecture, from the Fourth to the Early Eleventh Centuries AD, with Special Reference to the Towns of Macedonia* (diss., U. Oxford, 1988), pp. 162–92, 346–7

SRDJAN DJURIĆ

Bitte [Bitti], il. *See* CAPORALI, (2).

Bitti, Bernardo (*b* Camerino, the Marches, Italy, 1548; *d* Lima, Peru, 1610). Italian painter, active in South America. He joined the Society of Jesus in Rome in 1568. The origins of his style lie in late Roman Mannerism, which was influenced by Giorgio Vasari and Francesco Salviati, while his figures are indebted to Raphael. The Jesuits in Peru sent a request to the General of the Order for a painter, which resulted in Bitti travelling first to Lima (1571) and later to America (1575). His journey took him through Seville, where he saw the work of Luis Morales, whose influence is also evident in his paintings. In Peru, Bitti worked in Lima and Cuzco, where he executed some wall paintings in the Capilla de Indios in La Campanía (damaged in 1650 earthquake), and he also executed several commissions for the city of Arequipa. From there he went to the Bolivian cities of La Paz, Potosí and Chuquisaca. He established his reputation in 1600 in Chuquisaca with his painted retable for the church of S Miguel (Chuquisaca, Mus. Cat.), of which the canvas of the *Investiture of St Ildefonsus* is outstanding. The *Virgin and Child with the Young St John* (Chuquisaca, Mus. Cat.) is probably not part of the same retable. His great canvas of the *Coronation of the Virgin* and the painting of *Candlemas* (Purification of the Virgin), characterized by the elegant and elongated figures typical of Roman Mannerism, are also preserved (Lima, S Pedro).

Bitti was sent to Juli, the town of Aymara Indians on the shores of Lake Titicaca, where the Jesuits had a missionary centre. Most of the work he painted there (1585–91, 1601–4) was produced in the large workshop he ran for the indigenous population, and this led to his having numerous followers. Among his collaborators were the Andalusian Jesuit Pedro de Vargas (*b* 1533), who worked with him in Lima, and the Ecuadorean Dominican friar Pedro Bedón, who founded a painting school for the native inhabitants of the city of Quito.

BIBLIOGRAPHY

R. Vargas Ugarte: *Ensayo de un diccionario de artífices coloniales de la América Meridional* (Lima, 1947)

M. Soría: *La pintura del siglo XVI en Sudamérica* (Buenos Aires, 1956)

J. Mesa and T. Gisbert: *Bitti, un pintor manierista en Sudamérica* (La Paz, 1974)

TERESA GISBERT

Bitumen. Dark brown solution of asphalt, a naturally occurring petroleum residue, dissolved in oil or turpentine and used as a brown oil paint from the 17th century to the 19th. It shows undesirable characteristics on ageing, as it never completely dries and, when applied in thick films, forms a network of broad cracks resembling an alligator's skin, revealing the ground colour below. The use of bitumen is evident in many paintings by Joshua Reynolds and his contemporaries.

RUPERT FEATHERSTONE

Bizarre silks. Name applied to a group of silks woven in Italy, France, England, and probably other countries, in the late 17th century and early 18th. The bizarre style had its origins in the rich mix of images provided by the goods imported into Europe from the Near and Far East by the Levant Company and the East India companies of France, Holland and England. An insatiable market for novelty and richness had been established at the courts of Louis XIV and Charles II, and other monarchs who followed their lead. The silks woven to satisfy that demand began to appear in the late 1680s; chinoiseries and vegetable forms derived from Indian textiles began to be mixed with European floral sprigs. By the mid-1690s, the plant forms, although still small, were becoming more angular and elongated, with an increasingly vigorous left-right movement. The patterns, typically asymmetrical, were brocaded with metal threads on damask grounds, which were already patterned with even stranger motifs.

From c. 1700 to 1705 the designs were at their most bizarre, incorporating strange gourds, serpentine vegetable stems, intertwined plants and unidentifiable shapes, some angular and others reminiscent of sea creatures or rock formations. They were brocaded with gold and silver threads and coloured silks on damask grounds and had repeats measuring as much as one metre. This exaggerated length suited the elongated lines of womens' dress in the early 18th century, and the silks were also used for covering furniture and wall panels.

The earliest English silk designs made by James Leman (1688–1745) in Spitalfields, London, from 1706 are in the bizarre style. They are the first of an unbroken line of designs that make it possible to follow the development of the style through a less bizarre phase, when clearer, but still strange, chinoiserie and japonaiserie motifs were combined with images derived from architecture and others taken from Indian floral filling patterns (e.g. of c. 1709; London, V&A). The repeats became shorter and, by c. 1712, vertical bands and more naturalistic flowers began to be introduced, ushering in what has been called 'the luxuriant bizarre period' (Thornton). Abundant foliage became the dominant feature; it was controlled by various forms of band or serpentine line, arranged symmetrically, in place of the asymmetrical plan of most bizarre silks. By c. 1720, the bizarre elements had virtually vanished.

BIBLIOGRAPHY

V. Slomann: *Bizarre Designs in Silks: Trade and Tradition* (Copenhagen, 1953)

P. Thornton: 'The "Bizarre" Silks', *Burl. Mag.*, c (1958), pp. 265–70

M. King and D. King: *European Textiles in the Keir Collection* (London, 1990)

N. Rothstein: *Silk Designs of the Eighteenth Century* (London, 1990)

C. Buss: *Silk, Gold and Silver: Eighteenth-century Textiles in the Collection of Antonio Ratti* (Milan, 1992)

□

Bizen. Japanese centre of ceramics production. High-fired ceramic wares were manufactured from the end of the 12th century in and around the village of Inbe, Bizen Province (now Okayama Prefect.). This region had been a centre for manufacturing Sue-style stonewares and Haji-style earthenwares from the 6th century AD (see JAPAN, §VIII, 2(ii)(a)). At the end of the Heian period (794–1185) the potters moved from the old Sue-ware sites around Osafune village to Inbe, just to the north. In response to increased agricultural development, the new kilns manufactured kitchen mortars (*suribachi*), narrow-necked jars (*tsubo*) and wide-necked jars (*kame*). During the 13th century the wares show less of the grey-black surfaces typical of the old Sue tradition and more of the purple-reddish colour characteristic of Bizen. In the 14th century Bizen-ware production sites shifted from the higher slopes to the foot of the mountains. Kilns expanded in capacity, ranging up to 40 m in length. Vast quantities of Bizen wares, particularly kitchen mortars, were exported via the Inland Sea to Kyushu, Shikoku and numerous points in western Honshu, establishing Bizen as the pre-eminent ceramics centre in western Japan. By the 15th century the Bizen repertory had expanded to include agricultural wares in graded sizes; wares then featured combed decoration and such functional additions as lugs and pouring spouts. Plastic–forming was assisted by the introduction of a fusible clay found 2–4 m under paddy-fields. This clay, which fires to an almost metallic hardness, is still in use today.

That Bizen adjusted quickly to demands from cultural centres is seen in its early manufacture of tea ceremony wares (see JAPAN, fig. 147), particularly water jars (*mizu-sashi*) and flower vases (see JAPAN, §XIV). Bizen teaware is first mentioned in the diary of the tea master Tsuda Sōtatsu in 1549. Tea practitioners were particularly fond of the decorative accents that occurred in the long, high-temperature firing: *hidasuki*, red scorch marks left by the straw cords in which the pots were wrapped for kiln packing; *hibotan*, blush marks created by the irregular play of the fire on the pots; *botamochi*, resist patterns created when wares are stacked one on top another; *goma*, a speckled pattern created by a shower of ashes on the pots. These effects were produced deliberately from the 17th century onwards. Also from the 17th century, in response to competition from the nascent porcelain industries, the Bizen potters manufactured a crisply formed product called *Inbede*. A line of decorative earthenware and stoneware figurines, variously known as *Ao Bizen* ('blue Bizen'), *Shiro Bizen* ('white Bizen') and *Saishiki Bizen* ('coloured Bizen'), began to be produced a century later. Some of these were exported to the West. The Bizen kilns declined in the Meiji period (1868–1912) but revived in the tourism and ceramic boom that began after World War II. The area now has about 300 potteries.

BIBLIOGRAPHY

M. Katsura: 'Bizen to sono shūhen' [Bizen and surrounding regions], *Nihon yakimono shūsei* [Collection of Japanese ceramics], ed. C. Mitsuoka, S. Hayashiya and S. Narasaki, ix (Tokyo, 1981), pp. 104–15

S. Uenishi: 'Kodai-chūsei no Bizen gama' [Bizen kilns in the ancient and medieval periods], *Nihon yakimono shūsei* [Collection of Japanese ceramics], ed. C. Mitsuoka, S. Hayashiya and S. Narasaki, ix (Tokyo, 1981), pp. 98–102

Nihon no tōji [Japanese ceramics] (exh. cat., ed. Y. Yabe; Tokyo, N. Mus., 1985)

RICHARD L. WILSON

Bizuti, Filippo. *See* RUSUTI, FILIPPO.

Bizzacheri, Carlo Francesco (*b* Rome, 13 April 1655; *d* Rome, Feb 1721). Italian architect. According to Missirini, he trained in the studio of Carlo Fontana (iv). There is also reason to suppose that Bizzacheri was associated early in his career with the late work of Carlo Rainaldi, such as S Maria di Montesanto, Rome, executed at a time when the elderly Rainaldi had himself repudiated the livelier style of his earlier years. In spite of these formative experiences Bizzacheri's work seems relatively unencumbered by the exacting academic style of either Fontana or the late work of Rainaldi. Instead, in early commissions such as the Vivaldi Chapel (1679) in S Maria di Montesanto or the convent of S Maria Maddalena (1680–84), both in Rome, there are echoes of the works of Francesco Borromini. Bizzacheri was one of the first architects to adopt the freely handled pediments and rich ornamental vocabulary of Borromini's Oratory of S Filippo Neri or S Carlo alle Quattro Fontane—motifs that eventually achieved widespread popularity among Rococo architects of the 18th century. In the corridor leading to the convent of S Maria Maddalena, Bizzacheri demonstrated his fondness for penetrating solids and moulding space with superimposed arches, curved walls and stucco in a manner equally prophetic of the Rococo. His perforated and imaginatively embellished screen wall (mid-1690s) at the Villa Aldobrandini, Frascati, is another example of his ability to infuse utilitarian structures with a sprightly character.

Among Bizzacheri's mature works, one or two commissions clearly stand out for their inventiveness. In 1704–5 he ingeniously transformed the stark and flat early 17th-century façade of S Isidoro, Rome, making it into a gentle but lively surface of apparently shifting planes and delicate relief. He did so by overlaying the harsh existing pilaster arrangement with a shallow layer of stucco relief, which, in characteristic manner, combines and virtually obscures the traditional distinction between architectonic and sculptural ornament. The façade also incorporates statues of *St Patrick* and *St Isidoro* (1704) by Simone Giorgini (*fl* 1686–1706). The result is a graceful and lively composition, which, while only a remodelling, was undeniably among the most progressive designs of its time and probably his masterpiece.

In 1709 work began on Bizzacheri's most ambitious undertaking, the convent of S Luigi de' Francesi, Rome. The principal façade of this grand palazzo is 17 bays long. Each of its three storeys is surmounted by a deep mezzanine level. The sobriety of the basic articulation of the façade is consonant with its monastic function, but Bizzacheri again presaged the Rococo by embellishing the doors and windows with stucco enframements of the utmost imagination and refinement. Through his numerous designs for chapels and monastic buildings, including an unexecuted scheme for S Carlo al Corso (Rome, Accad.

N. S Luca), or in his most appealing public monument, the Fontana dei Tritoni (1717–19) in the Piazza della Bocca della Verità, Rome, Bizzacheri was instrumental in sustaining the Baroque spirit of Borromini and others until the prevailing orthodoxy of his own generation was supplanted by the more zestful attitudes of the Rococo.

BIBLIOGRAPHY

M. Missirini: *Memorie per servire alla storia della romana Accademia di San Luca* (Rome, 1823), p. 226

A. Daly: *S Isidoro* (Rome, 1971)

A. N. Mallory: 'Carlo Francesco Bizzacheri, 1655–1721', *J. Soc. Archit. Historians*, xxxiii (1974), pp. 27–47 [with an annotated cat. by J. L. Varriano]

M. Carta: 'Carlo Francesco Bizzacheri e la Cappella del Monte di Pietà', *Boll. A.*, lxv (1980), pp. 49–56

——: 'Il muro di cinta di Villa Aldobrandini a Frascati: Un momento della produzione artistica di Carlo Francesco Bizzacheri', *Boll. A.*, lxvii (1982), pp. 89–96

——: 'Un architetto collezionista: Carlo Francesco Bizzacheri', *Paragone*, xxxiv (1985), pp. 112–30

JOHN VARRIANO

Bjarnason, Sveinn Kristján. *See* CAHILL, HOLGER.

Bjerke-Petersen, Vilhelm (*b* Copenhagen, 24 Dec 1909; *d* Halmstad, 13 Sept 1957). Danish painter and writer. He was the son of the art historian and museum director Carl V. Petersen (1868–1938), who introduced him to the visual arts at an early age. His extensive knowledge of art history had a considerable influence on the development of his paintings and artistic theories. He had private painting lessons before beginning studies at the Kunstakademi in Oslo in 1929. In 1930–31 he studied with Paul Klee, Vasily Kandinsky and Oskar Schlemmer at the Bauhaus in Dessau, after which he returned to Denmark inspired by new conceptions of a completely abstract art. He became a central figure in Danish artistic life in the 1930s. He was a founder-member of the Danish artists' group Linien (The Line) in 1933, at that time an association of abstract and Surrealist artists, and he edited the group's journal of the same name.

Bjerke-Petersen was an active artistic experimenter. He favoured Constructivist abstraction at the beginning of the 1930s. His ideas, based on first-hand knowledge of the newest international developments in the art of the time, as for example in the Bauhaus-influenced *Sensible Lines* (1931; Stockholm, Gal. Bel-Art), inspired Danish artistic practice. He assumed a pioneering role, but his artistic sense and working methods distinguished him from his Danish colleagues. While they developed their works with the aid of preliminary studies, Bjerke-Petersen's works were completely thought out before execution. For him, adherence to a definite style took precedence over any mark of individuality.

In 1933 Bjerke-Petersen published his first theoretical book, *Symboler i abstrakt kunst* ('Symbols in abstract art'), in which he introduced symbols as fundamental concepts of pictorial language. With this book he anticipated 30 years of Danish artistic debate. His conflation of symbol and abstract form found expression in the series of works he showed in Linien's exhibition of 1934. For Bjerke-Petersen, this event marked the end of several years' work with paintings conceived around form and space. He began to avoid pure form, producing a more dream-like and fantastic art. In 1934–5, under the influence of contemporary psychological theories, he turned away from formally and spatially determined picture composition and sought to express himself directly through objects and their associations. Greatly influenced by the ideas of André Breton, he began to attempt to depict dreams. His painting evolved towards a Surrealism reminiscent of the work of Salvador Dalí, to which he added an erotic romanticism to create a sensual Surrealist world, as in the *Animal in the Woman Belongs to the Night* (1934; Silkeborg, Kstmus.). In 1934 he published *Surrealismen* ('Surrealism'), in which he broke away from the Danish Symbolists. In 1935 he arranged the international exhibition *Kubisme–Surrealisme* in Copenhagen, in which many of the European avant-garde participated. In 1937 he published *Surrealismens billedverden* ('Surrealism's pictorial world'). He took part in the international Surrealist exhibitions in London (1936) and Paris (1938).

During World War II Bjerke-Petersen fled to Sweden, where he continued to work. At this time he began to employ more intense colours, which by 1945 were appearing with glowing force in his paintings (e.g. the *End of Power*, 1949; Stockholm, Gal. Bel-Art). He also returned to painting more concrete forms. After the war he lived for a year in the USA, afterwards returning to Sweden, where he lived first in Stockholm and later in Halmstad. In 1956 he published *Konkret konst* ('Concrete art'). He founded the Moderna Konstskolan in Stockholm in 1949.

WRITINGS

Symboler i abstrakt kunst (Copenhagen, 1933, repr. Silkeborg, 1974)
Surrealismen (Copenhagen, 1934)
Surrealismens billedverden (Copenhagen, 1937)
Konkret konst (Stockholm, 1956)

BIBLIOGRAPHY

G. Jespersen: *De abstrakte* (Copenhagen, 1967), pp. 17–24, 28–9
T. L. Larsen: 'Maleren Vilhelm Bjerke-Petersen', *Fynske minder* (1976), pp. 81–94
O. Mogensen: 'Vilhelm Bjerke-Petersen', *Sønderjyllands kunstmuseums samlinger/Nordslesvigske museer* (Tønder, 1982), pp. 58–78
Vilhelm Bjerke-Petersen (exh. cat., Silkeborg, Kstmus., 1986)

RIGMOR LOVRING

Björck, (Gustaf) Oscar (*b* Stockholm, 15 Jan 1860; *d* Stockholm, 5 Dec 1929). Swedish painter. He studied at the Konstakademi in Stockholm from 1877 to 1882. In the summer of 1882 he made the first of several visits to the artists' colony at Skagen in Denmark. In 1883 he was awarded a scholarship from the Konstakademi and travelled again to Skagen, then to Paris. His early paintings show the influence of the Skagen colony's *plein-air* Realism, for example *Distress Signal* (1883; Copenhagen, Nmus.), which is in the style of Christian Krohg, and *Boat Putting out to Sea* (1884; priv. col., see Hedberg, p. 23). Björck also painted some school interiors at Skagen, including *School for Girls* (1884; Stockholm, Nmus.), a realistic and intimate rendering of the school-house atmosphere.

Björck spent the spring of 1884 at Grez-sur-Loing on the outskirts of the Fontainebleau Forest, where many Scandinavian artists congregated, but he returned to Skagen in the summer of the same year. During the next few years he visited Berlin, Munich, Venice and Rome. In Munich in 1885 he painted a large, psychologically penetrating portrait of his wife Isaria (Stockholm, Nmus.), and in Rome in 1886 he completed *Susanna*, a brilliant nude study in the salon tradition (Göteborg, Kstmus.).

In Venice Björck was fascinated by the colourful life of the streets, markets and canals, and he depicted these in *Venetian Market Hall* (1877; Stockholm, Nmus.) and the chiaroscuro study *Vespers in St Mark's* (1887; priv. col., see Hedberg, p. 47). He stayed in Rome for almost three years; there he painted *Roman Blacksmiths* (1887; Washington, DC, Corcoran Gal. A.; preparatory study in Göteborg, Kstmus.). With its skilfully controlled chiaroscuro effects, it is one of the best Swedish Realist depictions of working life in the 1880s.

In the autumn of 1888 Björck returned to Stockholm and worked as a portrait painter. Like Anders Zorn, he produced a great many portraits of leading citizens, the nobility and the royal family. The great number of Björck's portraits led to a somewhat uneven quality, with little effort made towards deeper interpretation of character. More impressive are some of the portraits of his wife (*The Artist's Wife*, 1891; Göteborg, Kstmus.) and friends, and a few studies of the leading cultural personalities of the time, including one of the poet and statesman *Gunnar Wennerberg* (1889; priv. col., see Hedberg, p. 61) and the great heroic and idealizing portrait of the Symbolist poet *Verner von Heidenstam* (1900; Göteborg, Kstmus.). Björck painted the poet in romantic pose on a verandah overlooking a bay on the Baltic, in a pensively lyrical twilight scene that marks the painting as one of the most typical portraits in Scandinavian mood painting at the turn of the century. He also painted pure landscapes, sometimes reminiscent of those of Prince Eugen, for example *Haycocks* (1892; Stockholm, Prins Eugens Waldemarsudde).

During 1894 and 1895 Björck painted ten decorative works (*in situ*) for the Operakällare restaurant in Stockholm, depicting frenzied, naked bacchantes, nymphs and fauns, inspired by Arnold Böcklin and Franz von Stuck. These pictures caused one of the most heated debates on morality in Sweden in the 1880s, between the Free Church, parliament and art historians. Together with Per Hasselberg, whose sculpture was also under debate at that time, Björck was responsible for bringing about a more unprejudiced view of the nude in art in Sweden. Another monumental painting by Björck was *View of the Park*, an idealized pastoral landscape for the Theatre of Dramatic Art in Stockholm (1907; *in situ*).

Björck's best work shows a virtuosity of technique and solid excellence of the level of Zorn, but no innovation; he lacked boldness and independence of spirit. He never joined the protest movement against the outmoded teaching methods of the Konstakademi, nor the Artists' Union that arose in 1886 from the revolt. He agreed with the union on various matters, however, and furthered its aims through reforms he was able to carry through as a teacher at the Konstakademi. He was professor at the Konstakademi from 1898 to 1925.

SVKL

BIBLIOGRAPHY

K. Fåhraeus: 'Oscar Björck', *Konstrevy* (1930), pp. 41–9
T. Hedberg: *Oscar Björck* (Stockholm, 1930)

HANS-OLOF BOSTRÖM

Bkra shis lhun po. *See* TASHILHUNPO.

Blaas, Karl [Carl] **von** (*b* Nauders, Tyrol, 28 April 1815; *d* Vienna, 19 March 1894). Austrian painter. Starting life in a peasant family, he studied at the Accademia di Belle Arti in Venice between 1832 and 1837, under Ludovico Lipparini (1800–1856). He won a five-year grant to go to Rome for his painting *Moses on Mount Sinai*, travelling there via Florence, where he studied the works of Raphael and early Renaissance religious painting. In Rome he encountered the circle around Friedrich Overbeck, and he began to produce paintings in a pious spirit such as *Jacob's Journey through the Desert* (1841; Vienna, Belvedere).

Blaas's paintings are typically open and simple, with clear forms, strong lines and cool colours. His feeling for colour, however, sometimes emerges in a brilliant, miniature-like use of paint, as in *St Catherine Carried by Angels* (1850; Vienna, Belvedere). His work suited the taste of the time, and he had commissions for his religious paintings from patrons in Vienna, Hungary, Paris, England and America. Through his patron Lord Shrewsbury he became the favourite portrait painter of Roman society. He also painted many small genre pictures, contrasting in spirit with the earnest vision of the Nazarenes.

In 1850 Blaas returned to Vienna, where he became a professor at the Akademie der Bildenden Künste. He worked on Joseph von Führich's decorative scheme for the Altlerchenfelder Kirche in Vienna, between 1854 and 1858, producing 24 frescoes in a style reminiscent of the Nazarenes and the early Renaissance. He continued to be a popular society portrait painter, producing a full-length portrait of *Emperor Francis Joseph* in 1853 (priv. col., see 1985 exh. cat.). The theatrically posed *Emperor Karl the Great in the Boys' School* (1855; Vienna, Belvedere) won a medal at the Exposition Universelle in Paris in 1855. Between 1858 and 1866 he followed Ludovico Lipparini as professor at the Accademia in Venice, where he attempted to make the teaching less restrictive and more modern. He was also in charge of the restoration of the mosaics in S Marco in Venice. In 1866 he returned to the Akademie der Bildenden Künste in Vienna. He worked on a series of frescoes for the Waffenmuseum (now Heeresgeschichtliches Museum) in the Arsenal in Vienna, designed by Theophilus Hansen. After the completion of these works he was knighted by Emperor Francis Joseph.

WRITINGS
Selbstbiographie des Malers Karl Blaas (Vienna, 1876)

BIBLIOGRAPHY
ÖKL
E. Vancsa: 'Überlegungen zur politischen Rolle der Historienmalerei des 19. Jahrhunderts', *Wien. Jb. Kstgesch.*, xxviii (1975), pp. 145–59
R. Feuchtmüller: 'Das Gebetsbuch der Kaiserin Elisabeth', *Alte & Mod. Kst*, 160–61 (Vienna, 1978)
W. Kitlitschka: *Die Malerei der Wiener Ringstrasse* (Wiesbaden, 1981)
Carl von Blaas (exh. cat. by B. Wild, Vienna, Belvedere, 1985)
Aus Österreichs Vergangenheit: Entwürfe von Carl von Blaas (exh. cat., Vienna, Ambrosi Mus., 1991)
MARIANNE FRODL-SCHNEEMANN

Blaauw, C(ornelis) J(onke) (*b* 1885; *d* 1947). Dutch architect and teacher. As instructor and then director of the School for Architecture, Decorative Arts, and Crafts, in Haarlem (1914–26), he taught that 'constructional form and architectural form, which must always be considered in relation to each other, transcend their purely constructive nature in the ultimate artistic form' (1917). In this stress on formal over practical values, Blaauw reflected the attitude of the Amsterdam school, a group he served and fostered through his membership of the editorial board of its organ, *Wendingen*, from 1918 to 1919 and again from 1927 to 1931. The most fertile period of Blaauw's career was from 1917 to 1925, when he produced such works as the three villas (1917–18) at Park Meerwijk in Bergen, and the laboratories (1921) of the Landbouwhogeschool in Wageningen. These buildings are characterized by individualistic, hand-crafted details, expressive plastic form and extensive use of such traditional materials as brick, tile, thatch and wood. Despite the dramatic manipulation of the external envelopes through sweeping roof forms and polygonal projections, however, the basic plans of these buildings remain fairly conventional, and Blaauw was criticized by functionalists for failing to integrate interior space and exterior massing. The same disparity may be seen in his housing on the Minervalaan (1931–2) in Amsterdam, where he attempted to disguise the standardization of the dwelling units through exterior diversity. Ultimately, Blaauw's design philosophy made it impossible for him to come to terms with the increasing rationalization of architectural practice after 1925.

BIBLIOGRAPHY
G. Fanelli: *Architettura moderna in Olanda* (1968)
A. Ringer: 'De School voor Bouwkunde te Haarlem/The School of Architecture in Haarlem', *Het Nieuwe Bouwen: Voorgeschiedenis/Nieuwe Bouwen: Previous History*, eds W. A. L. Beeren and others (Delft, 1982), pp. 111–17 [Dut. and Eng. text]
W. de Wit, ed.: *The Amsterdam School: Dutch Expressionist Architecture, 1915–1930* (London and Cambridge, MA, 1983)
HELEN SEARING

Blacas d'Aulps, Pierre-Louis-Jean-Casimir, Duc de (*b* Château de Vérignon, Var, 10 Jan 1771; *d* Prague, 17 Nov 1839). French patron and collector. A leading ultraconservative political figure, he engaged in restoration of French royal properties. As Ministre de la Maison du Roi (March–June 1815) he tried to initiate the restoration of Versailles. As ambassador to Rome (1816–22) he restored the Spanish Steps and Domenichino's frescoes (1612–15) in S Luigi dei Francesi. His Trinità dei Monti project involved Charles-François Mazois, Ingres, Pietro Tenerani and pensioners of the French Academy in Rome. He was the patron of JEAN-AUGUSTE-DOMINIQUE INGRES, Eugène Delacroix, Horace Vernet and Vincenzo Camuccini as well as of artists of lesser renown such as François-Xavier Fabre, Pietro Tenerani, Auguste-Jean-Baptiste Vinchon (1789–1855), Auguste Forestier (1780–1850) and Louis-Vincent-Léon Pallière (1787–1820). Blacas's extensive collection of ancient art (London, BM) comprised 950 gems, over 500 Greek vases, terracotta and bronze sculpture, Roman mural paintings, Greek and Roman glass, papyrus inscriptions, jewellery, over 400 Egyptian artefacts, Islamic vessels and over 2,000 Greek and Roman coins. He supported scholarly research that resulted in *Monumens arabes, persans et turcs du cabinet de M. le duc de Blacas et d'autres cabinets* (Paris, 1828) by Joseph-Toussaint Reinaud, *Les Ruines de Pompei* (Paris, 1824–38) by Mazois, *Musée Blacas: Monumens grecs, étrusques et romains* (Paris, 1830) by Théodor Panofka and *Lettres à M. le Duc de Blacas d'Aulps, premier gentilhomme de la chambre, pair de France, etc, relatives au Musée royal égyptien de Turin.*

Première lettre: Monuments historiques (Paris, 1824) by Jean-François Champollion. Blacas was also influential in founding the Louvre's Musée Egyptien (1826).

DBF

BIBLIOGRAPHY
L. Neis: *Ultra-Royalism and Romanticism: The Duc de Blacas's Patronage of Ingres, Delacroix and Horace Vernet* (diss., U. WI, Madison, 1987)

LAURA HICKMAN JONES

Black, Dorrit (Foster) (*b* Burnside, Adelaide, 23 Dec 1881; *d* Adelaide, 13 Sept 1951). Australian painter and printmaker. She worked in an undistinguished tonal Impressionist style following her studies at the South Australian School of Art and Crafts, Adelaide, from *c.* 1909 and from 1915 at Julian Ashton's Sydney Art School. Between 1927 and 1929 she learnt a more modern style and philosophy at the Grosvenor School of Art, London, and André Lhote's academy in Paris, supplemented by lessons with Albert Gleizes: paintings such as the mildly Cubist *Mirmande* (*c.* 1928; Adelaide, A.G. S. Australia) were the result. Black was particularly influenced by the artistic theories of Clive Bell and at the Grosvenor School by the linocut teacher Claude Flight (1881–1955). In 1929 she returned to Sydney, where she attempted to promote the linocut as an original art form that the ordinary person could afford. Black's most notable linocuts were produced between 1927 and 1937, for example *Music* (1927).

After holding her first solo show at the Macquarie Galleries in Sydney in 1930, which included a major oil, *The Bridge* (1930; Adelaide, A.G. S. Australia), Black began the Modern Art Centre in Sydney with the aim of exhibiting and promoting modernism. Between 1932 and 1933 exhibitors included Ralph Balson, Grace Crowley (1897–1979) and Roland Wakelin. Black became foundation vice-chairman of the Contemporary Arts Society, South Australian branch (1942), and in 1944 founded Group 9. Her work of the 1940s (mainly landscapes) is uneven, sometimes taking on Surrealist and Expressionist qualities, although it includes some of her most powerful works; for example, the *Olive Plantation* (1946; Adelaide, A.G. S. Australia).

Black died following a road accident. Like a number of the prominent Australian women artists of her generation, she was supported (modestly) throughout her life by family money. Perhaps her most notable achievement was to break out of the trap of formalistic modernism to a more directly powerful form of expression. She is well represented in the Art Gallery of South Australia, Adelaide, and the Australian National Gallery in Canberra.

BIBLIOGRAPHY
I. North: *The Art of Dorrit Black* (Melbourne, 1979)

IAN NORTH

Black American art. *See* AFRICAN AMERICAN ART.

Blackburn, James (*b* Upton, Essex, 1803; *d* Melbourne, 3 March 1854). Australian architect of English birth. He was employed in London as an inspector for the commissioners of sewers for Holborn and Finsbury, until his transportation to Hobart Town, Van Diemen's Land (now Tasmania), with his wife and daughter in 1835, after forging a cheque. He was immediately employed in the Department of Roads and Bridges and was responsible for a great proportion of the colony's road building, surveying and engineering work. When the department was merged into the Department of Public Works (1839), he began designing important government buildings; he was also able to operate privately in partnership with James Thjomsonn, as both architects and building contractors.

Although his buildings show the influence of John Claudius Loudon, Blackburn was also a powerful and innovative designer in his own right and was the first major exponent of the PICTURESQUE in the Australian colonies (e.g. the Italianate extension of Rosedale of 1848–50 nr Campbell Town). His knowledge of published sources is confirmed by his son's library, which seems mostly to have been acquired by the father, and which is one of the first extensive architectural collections in Australia. Blackburn was one of the first Greek Revivalists in Tasmania, as exemplified by the Doric temple design of the Lady Franklin Museum (1842–3), Hobart. His Gothic Revival churches were influenced by those of John Lee Archer, but his Norman style churches are more distinctive and are advanced even by British standards. Of the latter, the distinctive raking arcades of St Mark's, Pontville, derive from Benjamin Ferrey's published design for a chapel at Cardiff. The economic depression in Tasmania in the late 1840s led Blackburn and his family to emigrate to Melbourne (1849), where he formed a company to sell purified water. In 1850 he was appointed the city surveyor and designed the Town Hall.

AUDB

BIBLIOGRAPHY
Catalogue of the Library of James Blackburn (Melbourne, 1888)
E. G. Robertson: *Early Buildings of Southern Tasmania*, 2 vols (Melbourne, 1970)
J. Broadbent: 'James Blackburn, 1803–1854', *Architects of Australia*, ed. H. Tanner (Melbourne, 1981)
J. Grove: *James Blackburn* (diss., U. Melbourne, 1981)

MILES LEWIS

Blackburn, Joseph (*b c.* 1730; *d* after 1778). English painter, active in the American colonies. He first appeared in Bermuda in August 1752, where in a matter of months he painted many of the island's leading families. Approximately 25 of these portraits (e.g. *Mrs John Harvey*, Paget, Bermuda, priv. col.) survive; these demonstrate considerable skill in the painting of lace and other details of dress. Because of these abilities it is thought he probably began his career in one of the larger studios in London as a drapery specialist.

By the end of 1753 Blackburn set out for Newport, RI. His portrait of *Mrs David Chesebrough* (New York, Met.), signed and dated 1754, is the earliest mainland portrait to survive. In the following year he proceeded to Boston where, with John Smibert dead and Robert Feke and John Greenwood departed, only two younger painters, Nathaniel Smibert (1735–56) and John Singleton Copley, were in competition. Blackburn's grandest picture, *Isaac Winslow and his Family* (1755; Boston, MA, Mus. F.A.), a stylish and sizeable group portrait, indicates the level of success Blackburn achieved in Boston; however, not accustomed to painting group compositions, he employed three single portrait formats, tentatively linked by outstretched hands.

Over the next four years Blackburn painted more than 30 portraits for the upper levels of Boston society. He used a light, pastel palette that recalled that of Joseph Highmore, although Blackburn's handling of paint is not as fresh. He was not concerned with expressing the character of his sitters, but rather their chalky flesh-tones with fashionably rouged cheeks, artful gestures and exquisite trappings. Part of Blackburn's overt success may be attributable to his willingness to enhance his sitters' appearance. His attention to meticulously rendered lace, diaphanous neckerchiefs and delicate bows, in addition to attractive likenesses, enchanted his female sitters. Unfortunately for Blackburn, John Singleton Copley was a fast learner and within a year was skilfully emulating the visitor's success with such portraits of his own as *Ann Tyng* (Boston, MA, Mus. F.A.). By 1758 Copley was threatening Blackburn's pre-eminence, which may have influenced the latter's decision to move to Portsmouth, NH, that year. After five years there, Blackburn returned to England. His signed and dated English portraits range from 1764 to 1778. A Mr Blackburn, possibly the same artist, exhibited three history pictures at the Free Society of Artists in 1769.

BIBLIOGRAPHY

L. Park: *Joseph Blackburn: A Colonial Portrait Painter with a Descriptive List of his Works* (Worcester, MA, 1923)
J. H. Morgan and H. W. Foote: 'An Extension of Lawrence Park's Descriptive List of the Work of Joseph Blackburn', *Proc. Amer. Antiqua. Soc.*, xlvi (1936), pp. 15–81
C. H. Collins Baker: 'Notes on Joseph Blackburn and Nathaniel Dance', *Huntington Lib. Q.*, ix (1945), pp. 33–47
W. B. Stevens jr: 'Joseph Blackburn and his Newport Sitters, 1754–1756', *Newport Hist.*, xl (1967), pp. 95–107
A. Oliver: 'The Elusive Mr Blackburn', *Colon. Soc. MA*, lix (1982), pp. 379–92
W. Craven: *Colonial American Portraiture* (Cambridge, 1986), pp. 296–304

RICHARD H. SAUNDERS

Blackburn, William (*b* Southwark, London, 1750; *d* Preston, 28 Oct 1790). English architect. Of humble birth, he was apprenticed to a surveyor, became a student at the Royal Academy Schools in London and was awarded a silver medal in 1773. In 1782 he won the first prize in a public competition for the design of a prison. This was offered by commissioners appointed by Parliament to erect two new model prisons in the neighbourhood of London. In the event these prisons were never built, but Blackburn became known as an architect who had studied prison design and who had the confidence of John Howard, the prison reformer. He soon became the leading British prison architect and was employed to build a new generation of county gaols. These embodied the latest ideas in prison design, including radial planning on the panopticon principle, solitary confinement and the segregation of different sorts of offenders. The earliest example of these prisons was at Ipswich (1786–90), followed by others at Salford (destr. *c.* 1872), Bristol (destr. 1831), Gloucester, Monmouth, Preston, Limerick, Lewes (destr. 1967), Dorchester, Exeter (destr. 1853) and Stafford (*c.* 1789–93).

His few other works included the Watermen's Hall in London (1778–80) and the Unitarian Chapel at Lewin's Mead in Bristol (1788–91), both Neo-classical buildings of considerable merit. Blackburn was surveyor to St Thomas's and Guy's Hospitals in London and carried out alterations to the buildings of the latter.

Colvin; *DNB*

BIBLIOGRAPHY
HOWARD COLVIN

Blacket, Edmund (Thomas) (*b* London, 25 Aug 1817; *d* Sydney, 9 Feb 1883). Australian architect, of English birth. He was the son of James Blacket, a London cloth merchant, and he initially worked in his father's office and in a linen mill in Yorkshire before becoming a surveyor for the Stockton and Darlington Railway, where he must have obtained a knowledge of building. Blacket also sketched and measured old buildings in his spare time. In 1842 he moved to Sydney, where he obtained an appointment as a 'valuator' and perhaps also as an inspector of buildings. He received his first architectural commission in 1843 (All Saints, Singleton; destr.) and went on to become one of the leading architects in New South Wales in the mid-19th century. Appointed Diocesan Architect by 1847, he is known particularly for his Gothic Revival churches, mostly traditional in manner, of which he designed more than 50. Among them are simple country churches (e.g. at Berrima, Picton, Greendale and Wollombi); elegant city buildings (e.g. at Sydney: St Philip's, 1848, Church Hill, and All Saints, 1874, Woollahra); and cathedrals: St Andrew's, Sydney (from *c.* 1847; begun by James Hume); Bathurst (begun *c.* 1848; later rebuilt); Goulburn (begun 1874); and St George's, Perth (begun 1879). In 1849 Blacket was appointed to succeed Mortimer Lewis as Colonial Architect. He resigned in 1854, however, to take up the commission to design the main building and Great Hall of the University of Sydney, which are generally considered to be the finest collegiate Gothic Revival buildings in Australia (completed *c.* 1860). Built in local sandstone, the Great Hall is modelled on the medieval Westminster Hall in London, with a hammerbeam roof structure and traceried windows set with English stained glass. Blacket also designed St Paul's College (1856) at the university, again in the Gothic style; his wing extensions (1856) to Sydney Grammar School, on the other hand, are competent essays in classicism. He was a prolific architect, designing a large number of houses and commercial buildings in the 1850s and after, many of the latter in classical styles. Several young architects trained in his office, including John Horbury Hunt in the 1860s. Blacket's son Cyril Blacket (1857–1937) joined him in partnership in 1880. After Blacket's death the practice was continued by Cyril and his elder brother Arthur Blacket (*b* 1848) and later descendants of the family until the 1930s.

UNPUBLISHED SOURCES
Sydney, Mitchell Lib. [E. Blacket: *Journal of a Voyage to Sidney*, 1842; Blacket's plans; Colonial Architect's papers]

BIBLIOGRAPHY
G. M. Blacket: 'The Life and Work of Edmund Thomas Blacket', *J. Proc. Royal Austral. Hist. Soc.*, xxxii (1946), pp. 145–72
M. Herman: *The Early Australian Architects and their Work* (Sydney, 1954, rev. 1970), pp. 113–15, 182
——: *The Blackets: An Era of Australian Architecture* (Sydney and London, 1963)
G. L. Fischer, ed.: *The University of Sydney, 1850–1975* (Sydney, 1975)

VALERIE A. CLACK

Blackfriars. *See* DOMINICAN ORDER.

Blackjack. Drinking vessel made of treated and stitched leather, in common use in England from the Middle Ages until the 18th century. Surviving examples, which date mainly from the 17th and 18th centuries, are sometimes mounted and, more rarely, lined with silver or pewter. They were made in various sizes and were usually bottle- or cylinder-shaped with a characteristic bulge around the centre of the body and stamped decoration. In 1635 it was reported that after the French first saw blackjacks in use, they returned home claiming that the English drank from their boots.

Black lead. *See* GRAPHITE.

Blackman, Charles (*b* Sydney, 12 Aug 1928). Australian painter. An itinerant, largely self-taught young artist in the late 1940s, he was inspired by the depth of feeling of Picasso's pink and blue periods, and by the Melbourne painters of the Angry Penguins group, especially their efforts to see intuitively and compose freely, as children might be supposed to do. In a profoundly disturbing series of drawings and paintings produced during the early 1950s, Blackman elaborated the theme of innocence within danger as thoroughly as any of his key sources of inspiration—William Blake, Giorgio De Chirico, Sidney Nolan and Joy Hester, and the Australian poet Shaw Neilson. The urban settings of such works seem especially threatening: in still factoryscapes, vacant lots and suburban streets empty of all but screaming billboards, schoolgirls walk, run, lie prone, even float, as if lost in the open desert. Deceptively simple, such paintings as *Prone Schoolgirl* (*c.* 1953; Melbourne, Heide Park A.G.) were striking metaphors, not just of Australia's cultural isolation from Europe and of the consequent invasion of American consumerism, but also of the psychological impact of Hiroshima and the Cold War. In the 1957 *Alice in Wonderland* series, all-seeing Alice, shocked by the adult monsterworld around her, but protected by the wisdom of common sense, became the artist's signature-figure, paralleling Nolan's use of Ned Kelly. Related paintings formed part of his contribution to the 1959 Manifesto exhibition of the ANTIPODEAN GROUP.

After 1959 Blackman's art diversified and sought echoes in other cultures, especially that of France. He became a sympathetic, exceptionally insightful chronicler of the worlds of women. He painted the elusive figments of imperfect sight, even of blindness. His intense alertness to the suggestive glimpse, the sounds of something seen and the aura of someone else's feelings evolved in useful opposition to the masculine heroics much celebrated in Australian art since the 1940s. In the 1980s his range broadened to encompass major environmental issues: a series of paintings of 1987 celebrates the beauties of Australia's threatened rainforests.

BIBLIOGRAPHY

T. Shapcott: *Focus on Charles Blackman* (St Lucia, Queensland, 1967)
R. Mathew: *Charles Blackman* (Melbourne, 1969)
N. Amadio: *Charles Blackman: The Lost Domains* (Sydney, 1980)
——: *Paris Dreaming: A Celebration of the City of the Imagination, the Paris Drawings of Charles Blackman* (French's Forest, NSW, 1982)
A. Alvarez: *Rainforests/Charles Blackman* (Melbourne, 1988)
T. Shapcott: *The Art of Charles Blackman* (London, 1989)

TERRY SMITH

Black Mountain College. Experimental liberal arts college at Black Mountain, NC, open from 1933 to 1957. In the 1940s and early 1950s it was a centre for a group of painters, architects, musicians and poets associated particularly with the development of performance and multimedia work, crossing many disciplines. It was founded by John Andrew Rice (1888–1968) and a group of students and staff from Rollins College, Winter Park, FL. It was located in the Blue Ridge Assembly Buildings, *c.* 29 km east of Asheville, NC, until 1941, when it moved to nearby Lake Eden until its closure. The progressive ideas of John Dewey influenced the interaction of formal education with community life, the absence of conventional grades and credits and the central importance accorded to the arts. The college was owned and administered by the staff. The setting was modest, and fewer than 1200 students attended in 24 years.

In the founding year Josef Albers, the first of many European refugees to teach at Black Mountain, came from Germany to teach art; through his activities the college disseminated Bauhaus teaching methods and ideas into American culture. The visual arts curriculum included courses in design and colour that later became a standard part of art education, as well as workshops in weaving, wood-working, printing, photography and bookbinding. Anni Albers, a former Bauhaus student, developed a weaving course that emphasized designing for industrial production. Xanti Schawinsky (1904–79), who studied with Oskar Schlemmer at the Bauhaus, taught art and stage studies from 1936 to 1938 and directed *Spectodrama: Play, Life, Illusion*, one of the earliest performances of abstract theatre in the USA.

In 1944 Black Mountain College sponsored its first summer arts programme, which attracted many major artists for intense periods of teaching and participation in concerts, exhibitions, lectures and drama and dance performances. Among the European artists who taught were Lyonel Feininger, Walter Gropius, Leo Lionni (*b* 1910), Amédée Ozenfant, Bernard Rudofsky (1905–88) and Ossip Zadkine. Other summer staff included Leo Amino (*b* 1911), John Cage, Mary Callery (1903–77), Merce Cunningham, Willem de Kooning, Buckminster Fuller, Jacob Lawrence (*b* 1917), Barbara Morgan (*b* 1900) and Robert Motherwell. Ilya Bolotowsky taught from 1946 to 1948.

After Josef Albers left in 1949, the central figure in the community was the poet and critic Charles Olson (1910–70), who taught at the college in 1948–9 and returned in 1951. Under his direction the college became a centre for the formulation of a new poetics based on open form and 'projective verse'. The *Black Mountain Review*, edited by Robert Creeley (*b* 1926), was one of the most influential small-press journals of the period, and the college played a formative role in the revival of the small-press movement in the USA. Creeley, Joseph Fiore (*b* 1925), M. C. Richards (*b* 1916) and Robert Duncan (1919–88) were among the members of the young American staff. A ceramics course was added to the curriculum and the faculty included Robert Turner (*b* 1913), Karen Karnes (*b* 1925) and David Weinrib (*b* 1924). The summer sessions in the arts brought many artists to the campus, including Harry Callahan,

Shōji Hamada, Franz Kline, Bernard Leach, Ben Shahn, Aaron Siskind, Jack Tworkov and Peter Voulkos (*b* 1924).

Albers and the other European artists brought the spirit of modernism to the progressive, experimental spirit of the founders, and the fusion of these two movements culminated in a creative atmosphere and an intense, intellectual community, receptive to experimental ventures in the arts. It was at Black Mountain College that Buckminster Fuller attempted to raise his first dome in 1948, that John Cage staged his first work of performance art in 1952, and that the Cunningham Dance Company was founded in 1953. Through the work of its students, among them Ruth Asawa (*b* 1926), John Chamberlain, Ray Johnson, Kenneth Noland, Robert Rauschenberg, Dorothea Rockburne (*b* 1929), Kenneth Snelson, Cy Twombly, Stanley Vanderbeek (1927–84) and Jonathan Williams (*b* 1929), the college played a formative role in the definition of an American aesthetic and identity in the arts during the 1950s and 1960s.

UNPUBLISHED SOURCES
Raleigh, NC State Archvs [Black Mountain College papers]

BIBLIOGRAPHY
F. Dawson: *The Black Mountain Book* (New York, 1970)
M. Duberman: *Black Mountain College: An Exploration in Community* (New York, 1972)
M. E. Harris: *The Arts at Black Mountain College* (Cambridge, MA, 1987)
MARY EMMA HARRIS

Black Sea colonies. Ancient colonies that flourished along the coasts of the Black Sea. In the late 8th century BC Greeks from Miletos in Ionia (Turkey's western coast) first sailed into the Black Sea and founded Sinope, midway along the Pontus, Turkey's northern littoral. This settlement was soon destroyed by Kimmerian marauders from southern Russia but was recolonized when that menace receded (?632 BC). New settlements were planted at Istros by the Danube delta (?657 BC) and at Borysthenes Olbia (now Ol'viya) on the Bug–Dneper estuary (?647 BC). Milesians went on to found Apollonia (now Sozopol) and Odessos (now Varna) on the Bulgarian coast, and Tomis (now Constanţa) and Tyras (now Belgorod) on the coasts of Romania and western Ukraine respectively. Far to the north-east, by the Kimmerian Bosporos (Kerch Straits), they settled Pantikapaion, Theodosia and Kepoi, while Phanagoria was founded from another Ionian city, Teos (*c.* 545 BC). These cities by the early 4th century BC formed part of the strong Bosporan state, which was ruled by dynasts of Thracian origin until *c.* 110 BC. Meanwhile Amisos (now Samsun in northern Turkey), a colony east of Sinope sent out from Phokaia in northern Ionia, had been sited to secure access to the hinterland of Anatolia (*c.* 564 BC). Four years later Dorian Greeks, Megarians from the Greek mainland, moved into Pontus, founding Herakleia, and much later settled Mesembria (now Neseběr in Bulgaria), a colony of refugees from the Persians (*c.* 510 BC). Herakleia, in time growing strong on her exploitation of native peoples, looked across the Black Sea for further opportunities and founded Chersonesos near Sevastopol', in the south-west Crimea (5th century BC), and Kallatis (now Mangalia) south of Tomoi on the coast of the Romanian Dobrudzha (date uncertain, but in existence by the early 4th century BC). Tanais at the mouth of the River Don was founded in the 3rd century BC.

BIBLIOGRAPHY
A. J. Graham: 'Pontus', *Cambridge Anc. Hist.*, iii (2/1982), pp. 122–30
J. G. F. Hind: 'Greeks and Barbarian Peoples around the Black Sea', *Archaeol. Rep.: Council Soc. Promotion Hell. Stud. & Managing Cttee Brit. Sch. Archaeol. Athens*, iii (1983–4), pp. 71–97; xxxix (1992–3), pp. 82–112
J. Bouzek: *Studies of Pottery in the Black Sea Area* (Prague, 1990)
M. J. Price: *The Black Sea* (London, 1993), ix/1 of *Sylloge Nummorum Graecorum* (1986–)
JOHN HIND

1. Northern. 2. Western and southern.

1. NORTHERN. The art of the Greek colonies on the northern Black Sea coast developed from the second half of the 7th century BC to the 4th century AD under the influence of the local barbarian tribes (Scythians, Sindians, Sarmatians etc), whose own artistic traditions became influenced by the colonists' to an even greater degree (*see* SCYTHIAN AND SARMATIAN ART). Residential areas with a grid plan (the so-called Hippodamian system) have been excavated; at Pantikapaion (later Kerch) there was a radial circular plan and an acropolis. Tyritaka, Myrmekion and Nymphaion had irregular plans. The material of construction was local limestone laid as polygonal mortarless masonry (sometimes with clay mortar); imported marble was used for columns and entablatures. In the 5th–4th century BC walls with towers were erected (ruins of these are preserved at OL'VIYA and CHERSONESOS); peristyle houses have been found, as well as the foundations of public buildings, such as the remains of a theatre at Chersonesos. Burial mounds (kurgans) with a corridor-dromos leading to a stone burial chamber formed distinctive monuments of religious architecture; the vaults were stepped, as at Tsarsky Kurgan and Yuz Oba near Pantikapaion (both 4th century BC), or semicircular, as at Vasyurinsky Kurgan on the Taman Peninsula. From the early 1st century AD architecture was influenced by the Roman tradition; for example in the Crimea the Romans built the fortress of Charax, complete with *thermae*.

Mosaics have been uncovered, for example at Chersonesos; most of the wall paintings (generally executed on plaster; *in situ*) that have been discovered are in the tombs of the kingdom of Bosporos (5th century BC–4th century AD), with its capital at Pantikapaion. In the 5th–2nd century BC wall painting had a predominantly decorative character, representing masonry, socles, cornices and other features, as in the 'Tomb of 1908' on Mt Mithridates, Pantikapaion. In the mound of Bol'shaya Bliznitsa (4th century BC) a monumental bust of Demeter or Kore within a garland of leaves and flowers, painted directly without a priming layer, was depicted on the slab that caps the stepped vault. The representation of the head of Demeter on the ceiling of the 'Tomb of Demeter' near Pantikapaion (1st century AD) seems less monumental but more Hellenistic in expression. The multi-figural paintings in the lunettes of the Tomb of Demeter and other Bosporan tombs, the 'Tomb of Anthesterios', the paintings of which are preserved only in sketches, the Stasov Tomb and the Tomb of 1891 (all 1st century BC–2nd century AD) depict mythological subjects, ritualized genre scenes from the life of the Bosporites and battle scenes, among others. They are executed on thin plaster with size paints. The local style is characterized by flatness (people are shown frontally, animals in profile) and by the hieratic nature of its images. The decorative painting in the same tombs is executed in the 'Flower style' peculiar to the Hellenistic period: flowers, garlands, boughs and leaves are scattered unsystematically or border the painted area. Sometimes the Flower style was combined with the 'Incrustational style', an imitation in paint of the incrustation of a wall with mounts of multicoloured stones etc. Painted decoration reminiscent of the wall paintings in the tombs was discovered on the inside walls of a sarcophagus (St Petersburg, Hermitage) of the 1st century AD from Pantikapaion; it includes an interesting scene showing an encaustic artist at work in his workshop.

In a tomb near Nymphaion limestone reliefs (St Petersburg, Hermitage) were discovered on the entrance wall of the burial chamber: a half-length depiction of Athena with the Gorgoneion on her breast and busts of Pan and Silenos in the corners. Distinctive funerary sculpture of the Black Sea colonies are limestone stelai bearing the name of the deceased. Early stelai (5th–4th century BC) are crowned with a cornice and an anthemion of vegetal motifs and palmettes. From the 3rd century BC stelai topped by pediments with acroteria became widespread; below these were placed niches with images in relief. In the 2nd century BC a form of stele originating in Asia Minor appeared, which has an arch above the niche. The traditional subjects of the reliefs were depictions of a seated woman and a female slave standing before her with a casket, as on the Stele of Hellas (London, BM), wife of Menodoros, at Kerch (1st century BC); of the deceased represented as an idealized knight, as on the dedicatory relief of Tryphon from Tanais (see fig. 1); and of a funerary feast, as on the Stele of Dionysios and Aristeides from Kerch (limestone, early 1st century AD; Kerch, Historical and Archaeological Museum). A tendency to deviate from Classical forms—the 'barbarization' of the sculpture—is evident in the manner of representation.

The metalwork of the 4th century BC produced for the Scythian nobility ranks among the masterpieces of Classical art from the northern Black Sea coast. It includes the silver amphora from the Chertomlyk burial mound (see SCYTHIAN AND SARMATIAN ART, fig. 3), the gold comb from the Solokha burial mound, the electrum vessels from the mounds at Kul' Oba (all St Petersburg, Hermitage) and from the Gaymanovaya Mogila mound, and the pectoral from the Tolstaya Mogila mound. The images worked in repoussé on these depict scenes of Scythian life (or, more exactly, subjects from Scythian epic) with ethnographic precision. On a gold pendant (St Petersburg, Hermitage) from Kul' Oba the head of *Athena Parthenos* of Pheidian type was reproduced in repoussé with engraving. The finest stamped images are represented by gold coins of the 4th century BC from Pantikapaion that bear the head of a satyr on the obverse and a guardian-griffin on the reverse.

Imported types, such as the marble stelai from Pantikapaion with reliefs depicting athletes that were produced by an Ionian craftsman (5th century BC; St Petersburg, Hermitage and elsewhere), predominated in the sculpture

1. Marble relief of Tryphon, from Tanais, 2nd century AD–early 3rd (St Petersburg, Hermitage)

of the northern Black Sea coast in the 6th–1st century BC. A head of *Herakles* from Chersonesos (marble, 4th century BC; St Petersburg, Hermitage) and a head of *Asklepios* from Ol'viya (marble, 4th century BC; Moscow, Hist. Mus.) were created under the influence of the work of Skopas. An acroterion of palmettes and acanthus leaves from Phanagoria (marble, 4th century BC; Moscow, Pushkin Mus. F.A.) has been ascribed to the work of Attic craftsmen, while the 'Taman Sarcophagus' (marble, 4th or 3rd century BC; Moscow, Hist. Mus.), which has a gabled cover and ornamented acroteria and antefixes, is also regarded as Greek. Three marble heads of a bearded god (?Asklepios), a goddess and cupid (3rd century BC; St Petersburg, Hermitage) belong to the Alexandrine school.

Several masterpieces of moulded pottery—polychrome figured vases from Phanagoria depicting a *Sphinx*, a *Siren* and *Aphrodite* (5th century BC; St Petersburg, Hermitage)—are Attic work. In the first centuries AD, side by side with imported sculpture, such as the marble statue of a Roman from Charax (Moscow, Pushkin Mus. F.A.), local sculpture appeared, such as male and female portrait statues in marble from Kerch (1st century AD; St Petersburg, Hermitage), a marble statue of the ruler of Gorgippia with local peculiarities in his appearance and clothing (2nd century AD; Moscow, Pushkin Mus. F.A.) and a statue, perhaps funerary, of a Sindian from the outskirts of Phanagoria (Moscow, Hist. Mus.).

Unique types of wood-carving have been found in the northern Black Sea colonies: reliefs with depictions of Hera and Apollo in a High Classical style on a sarcophagus from the burial mound of Zmeiny Kurgan (4th century BC; St Petersburg, Hermitage) and the openwork reliefs by local craftsmen on a sarcophagus from Kerch representing Niobids and lions, among others (2nd century AD; St Petersburg, Hermitage). Terracottas are numerous and include grotesque examples connected with the Eleusinian mysteries, found in the burial mound of Bol'shaya Bliznitsa (late 5th century BC–early 4th; St Petersburg, Hermitage), and protomes of Demeter, Kore and Aphrodite made locally.

In vase painting imported forms of the East Greek Wild Goat style and Attic Black-figure vases predominated, especially in the early period, followed by Red-figure vases, including those in the Kerch style of the 4th century BC, which have subjects taken from legends set in the northern Black Sea area (Amazons etc). There are also luxury vases with polychrome relief decoration, such as those from the workshop of Xenophantos the Athenian. From the 4th–3rd century BC local production of painted pottery developed, predominantly of the 'watercolour' vases that are decorated with vegetal motifs in mineral colours.

The Classical culture of the northern Black Sea coast was destroyed at the beginning of the period of the barbarian migrations (3rd–4th century AD). Its traditions were preserved principally in wheelmade ceramic production and metalwork; some ornaments produced by Bosporan workshops were set with hardstones in the polychrome style.

BIBLIOGRAPHY

Archaeol. Rep. Soc. Promot. Hell. Stud.
G. Kieseritzky and C. Watzinger: *Griechische Grabreliefs aus Südrussland* (Berlin, 1909)
M. Rostovtzeff: *Iranians and Greeks in South Russia* (Oxford, 1922)
K. Schefold: *Untersuchungen zu den kertschen Vasen* (Berlin, 1934)
A. P. Ivanova: *Iskusstvo antichnykh gorodov severnogo Prichernomor'ya* [The art of the ancient cities of the northern Black Sea coast] (Leningrad, 1953)
———: *Skul'ptura i zhivopis' Bospora* [The sculpture and painting of Bosporos] (Kiev, 1961)
N. I. Sokol'sky: *Antichnyye derevyannyye sarkofagi severnogo Prichernomor'ya* [The ancient wooden sarcophagi of the northern Black Sea coast] (Moscow, 1969)
Terrakoty severnogo Prichernomor'ya [Terracottas of the northern Black Sea coast], 4 vols (Moscow, 1970–74)
V. F. Gaidukevic: *Das bosporanische Reich* (Berlin, 1971)
M. M. Kobylina: *Antichnaya kul'tura severnogo Prichernomor'ya* [The ancient culture of the northern Black Sea coast] (Moscow, 1972)
G. I. Sokolov: *Antichnoye Prichernomor'ye: Pamyatniki arkhitektury, skul'ptury, zhivopisi i prikladnogo iskusstva* [The ancient Black Sea coast: monuments of architecture, sculpture, painting and applied art] (Leningrad, 1973); Eng. trans. as *Antique Art of the Northern Black Sea Coast: Architecture, Sculpture, Painting, Applied Arts* (Leningrad, 1974)
M. M. Kobylina: *Divinités orientales sur le littoral nord de la Mer Noire* (Leiden, 1976)
———: *Izobrazheniya vostochnykh bozhestv v severnom Prichernomor'ye v pervyye veka nashey ery* [Depictions of eastern deities in the northern Black Sea coast in the first centuries AD] (Moscow, 1978)
Antichnyye gosudarstva severnogo Prichernomor'ya [The Antique states of the northern Black Sea coast] (Moscow, 1984)
Kul'tura i iskusstvo Bospora: Pantikapey [The culture and art of Bosporos: Pantikapaion] (Moscow, 1984)
Ancient Civilizations from Scythia to Siberia: An International Journal of Comparative Studies in History and Archaeology, i/1 (1994)

V. YA. PETRUKHIN

2. WESTERN AND SOUTHERN. After generations of Hellenic superiority over the weakly organized barbarian tribes, these latter began to form powerful kingdoms: the Odrysae in Thrace (*see* THRACIAN AND DACIAN ART) and the 'Royal Scythian' nomads in the steppes between the Danube and the Don (*see* SCYTHIAN AND SARMATIAN ART). On the southern, Pontic, coast Cappadocians first threatened, then swallowed up, Sinope (183 BC) and Amisos (*c.* 250 BC), which became capital cities of the Mithridatid dynasty. For over two centuries the Persian empire under the Achaemenids exercised great political and cultural influence on the region, which is partly to be explained by the large numbers of Persians there but also by their immense wealth, power and cultural prestige (*c.* 550–330 BC). Architecture, objects of daily use, religious dedications and grave monuments all display Greek, local, and Achaemenid Persian elements, whether in pure imported or local mixed styles. In the regions annexed by Rome (Pontus after 63 BC and Thrace and the Danube area between AD 6 and 46) a provincial variant of the common Hellenistic and Roman styles prevailed.

The earliest significant artefacts found in these Black Sea cities are the Wild Goat style wine jugs and stemmed dishes made in Miletos and other East Greek cities during the early period of the colonies' existence (*see* GREECE, ANCIENT, §V, 4(iv)). These have been found at Sinope, Istros and Apollonia. In the 5th and 4th centuries BC Sinope and Istros struck attractive silver coins displaying on their reverse a sea-eagle-on-dolphin motif, which perhaps hints at their participation in a maritime league and a shared cult of Apollo Delphinios. Apollonia, Mesembria, Trapezous and Herakleia also minted silver coins at this time with unique types struck with high-quality dies (anchor, helmet, bankers' table with coins, warrior nailing up a trophy). Apollonia commissioned a colossal statue of *Apollo*, made by Kalamis in the mid-5th century BC (Pliny: *Natural History* XXXIV.18), which was carried off to Rome by M. Lucullus in 72 BC (Strabo: *Geography* VII.vi.1). Also from Apollonia but still extant (Sofia, N. Archaeol. Mus.) is the grave stele of Anaxandros, a bearded man exchanging soulful glances with his pet dog (first half of the 5th century BC). Sinope too had large-scale statues, including one of its mythical founder Autolykos, made by Sthennis of Olynthos, which was likewise looted by the more famous brother of Lucullus, Lucius, in 70 BC (Strabo: XII.iii.11). This city had once possessed another statue, which was taken to Ptolemaic Egypt to be the focus of the new world-wide cult of Serapis (Tacitus: *Annals* IV.lxxxiii).

Fine silverware is represented on this Pontic coast by a few scattered finds. A silver omphalos bowl from Ünye, east of Sinope, has been attributed to the Kimmerians; it incorporates elements of the nomads' Animal style. A fine silver amphora-rhyton (4th century BC) is in the Achaemenid Persian style (priv. col.) and has its best analogues in the gold example from the treasure at Panagyurischte (Bulgaria) and the silver-gilt amphora from Chertomlyk, Ukraine (*see* §1 above). Jewellery (earrings, necklaces, wreaths of leaves, berries), bronze hydriai and a series of Red-figure pottery kraters and amphorae come from the city necropoleis at Apollonia, Mesembria and Odessos and from nearby Thracian tumuli. Terracottas in their thousands were found at Kallatis. Several Hellenistic and Roman reliefs representing 'horseman heroes' have been found at Thracian shrines, while at Sinope two grave monuments of the late 5th century–4th BC reproduce rather crudely the Classical motif of servants tending their dead mistress (Kastamonou Mus.). Thracian tombs, such as those at Kazanlŭk and Sveshtary, have interior decoration with Hellenic-looking charioteers or pilasters in the form of caryatids. The size of the exterior mounds betrays a wealth beyond that of colonial Greeks and is only outdone by the royal burials of Lydia or Macedon. The

2. *Glykon*, the snake-god, promoted by Alexander of Abonouteichos, marble, h. 660 mm, 2nd–3rd centuries AD (Constanţa, Museum of National History and Archaeology)

royal tombs at Amaseia and Sinope in Pontus (Strabo: XII.iii.39) clearly retained features of Greek culture even after the cities had fallen subject to more powerful masters.

Under the Romans, a common Classical, but provincial, style continued. Outstanding pieces are the full-size *Fortuna*, accompanied by Pontus (the 'Black Sea') personified as a diminutive bearded figure by her left side. A unique figure of the snake-god Glykon promoted by Alexander of Abonouteichos (see fig. 2) was found in the same cache of sculpture dating to the 2nd and 3rd centuries AD (Constanţa, Mus. N. Hist. & Archaeol.). Roman sculpture has been found at Amisos, including a full-size bronze *Arringatore* figure (Istanbul, Archaeol. Mus.), and there is an excellently preserved floor mosaic depicting Achilles and Thetis surrounded by anthropomorphic heads of the Four Seasons (Samsun, Archaeol. Mus.). The street plans of these cities are hardly known, all but Istros being under modern towns. A striking common arrangement of acropolis, harbour, city and rows of burial-mounds on the hills above can be noticed, as at Pantikapaion and Amisos, though they are separated by the width of the Black Sea. The present, still imposing, walls of several cities (Amastris, Istros, Mesembria, Sinope and Trapezus) owe much to Late Roman and Byzantine construction with some Genoese rebuilding.

BIBLIOGRAPHY
Catalogue sommaire des musées Ottomans: Bronzes et bijoux (Constantinople, 1911), p. 3, no. 3
M. I. Rostovtzev: 'Pontus, Bithynia and Bosporus', *Annu. Brit. Sch. Archaeol. Athens*, xxii (1918), pp. 1–22
E. Akurgal and L. Budde: 'Vorläufige Bericht über die Ausgrabungen in Sinope', *Türk Tarih Kurumu Basimevi*, 5th ser., xiv (1956), pp. 27–41
P. Amandry: 'La Toreutique achémenide', *Ant. Kst*, ii (1959), pl. 24
E. Akurgal: *Die Kunst anatoliens* (Berlin, 1961), pp. 270–73
I. Venedikov and others: *Apolonia* (Sofia, 1962)
V. Canarache and others: *Tezareul de sculpturi de la Tomis* [Sculptural treasures of Tomoi] (Bucharest, 1963)
E. Akurgal: 'Kimmerische Schale', *Ant. Kst*, x (1967), pp. 32–8
C. Scorpan: *Cavalerul Trac.* [The Thracian horseman] (Constanţa, 1967)
V. Canarache: *Masks and Tanagra Figurines Made in the Workshops of Callatis–Mangalia* (Constanţa, 1969)
I. Venedikov and others: *Nesebre*, i–ii (Sofia, 1969–80)
I. Venedikov and T. Gerassimov: *Trakiiskoto iskustvo* [Thracian art treasures] (Sofia, 1975)
M. Tsaneva: *Craters from Apollonia* (Sofia, 1982)
M. Chichikova: 'Découverte d'une tombe royale thrace', *Archéologie*, cxc (1984), pp. 17–24
V. Velkov: 'Mesembria', *Die bulgarische Schwarzmeerküste in Altertum*, ed. W. Schuller (Konstanz, 1985), pp. 29–49
V. Velkov and others: *Mesambria, Mesemvria, Nessebur* (Sofia, 1986)
P. Alexandrescu and W. Schuller, eds: *Histria: Eine Griechenstadt an der rumänischen Schwarzmeerküste* (Konstanz, 1990), pp. 95–232

JOHN HIND

Bladder colours. Ready-mixed oil paints, prepared commercially and contained in a bladder of animal membrane. The bladder was pierced and resealed with a tack of metal or bone, and the paint remained usable for several months. Bladder colours were available from the mid-17th century until the 1840s, when they were superseded by metallic tubes.

RUPERT FEATHERSTONE

Bladelin, Pierre [Bladelijn, Pieter; Bladelinus, Petrus] (*b* ?Bruges, ?1400; *d* Middelburg, 8 April 1472). South Netherlandish patron. He came from an established wealthy family of Bruges; his property was considerably enlarged through his marriage to Margriet van de Vageviere (1414–76). From 1436 to 1440 he was treasurer of the city of Bruges. He subsequently worked as a bailiff in the service of Philip the Good, Duke of Burgundy, until 1446, when he became steward to the Duke and treasurer of the Order of the Golden Fleece; he also carried out many diplomatic missions for the Duke. He was known as the 'Leestmaker'.

Bladelin spent a large part of his fortune on the foundation of the city of Middelburg. The castle was begun in 1448, the church in 1452 (ded. 1460), and the walls were built in 1464, although the town was said to be largely completed in six years. He is primarily known through the triptych of the *Nativity* (also known as the Bladelin triptych; Berlin, Staatl. Ksthalle), attributed to Rogier van der Weyden and made for the church at Middelburg; a 17th-century replica can still be seen there. The centre panel shows Bladelin on his knees with a townscape in the background. Bladelin also commissioned a painting of the *Pietà*, which may originally have hung over the high altar of the church in Middelburg, and a silver reliquary with an image of St Helena (both untraced).

BIBLIOGRAPHY
BNB
K. Verschelde: *Geschiedenis van Middelburg in Vlaanderen* [A history of Middelburg in Flanders] (Bruges, 1876)
M. J. Friedländer: *Early Netherlandish* (1967–76)
E. d'Haenens: 'Nieuwe gegevens betreffende het Bladelin-retabel, toegeschreven aan Rogier van der Weyden (*c.* 1445)' [New facts about the Bladelin altarpiece, attributed to Rogier van der Weyden (*c.* 1445)],

Bijdr. Gesch. Kst Nederlanden (1981), pp. 45–52 [issue in honour of J. Steppe]

L. VAN MEERBEEK

Bladen, Ronald (*b* Vancouver, 13 July 1918; *d* New York, 3 Feb 1988). Canadian sculptor and painter. He studied at the Vancouver School of Art and at the California School of Fine Arts in San Francisco. While living in San Francisco in the 1950s, he produced paintings related to the Abstract Expressionism of Clyfford Still, using mythic and pictographic forms (e.g. *Untitled, c.* 1956–9; New York, Met.). In the early 1960s he turned to sculpture, abandoning the subjectivity of his previous work in favour of large, simple structures, such as *Three Elements* (painted aluminium, 1965; New York, MOMA), that demanded to be appreciated in formal terms alone, without explanation, interpretation or evaluation. Nevertheless, the anthropomorphic qualities seen by some critics in his massive solid forms separated his sculpture from the more geometric forms of Minimalism practised by sculptors such as Tony Smith, Donald Judd or Sol LeWitt. In the mid-1980s Bladen again created visual drama by reflecting light from aluminium sheets attached to skeletal wood constructions.

BIBLIOGRAPHY
W. Berkson: 'Ronald Bladen: Sculpture and Where We Stand', *A. & Lit.*, xii (Spring 1967), pp. 139–50
S. Ellis: 'Expanded Pictograms', *A. America*, lxxv/4 (1987), pp. 204–9
S. Westfall: 'Ronald Bladen at Washburn', *A. America*, lxxvii/8 (1989), pp. 141ff
Ronald Bladen: Early and Late (exh. cat. by W. Berkson, San Francisco, CA, MOMA, 1991)

DANIEL E. MADER

Blaeser, Gustav (Hermann) (*b* Düsseldorf, 9 May 1813; *d* Stuttgart-Bad Canstatt, 20 April 1874). German sculptor. He studied drawing in Cologne under the painter Egidius Mengelberg (1770–1849) and in 1828 embarked on three years of training as a wood-carver with Christoph Stephan (1797–1864). From 1831 he worked in the studio of the Mainz sculptor Joseph Franz Scholl (1796–1842), before moving to Berlin in June 1834 as a student of Christian Daniel Rauch. As well as working on small pieces of his own, Blaeser collaborated with Rauch on various monumental projects. His apprentice years ended with work on the enlargement of the small model for the full-size equestrian statue for Rauch's Berlin monument to *Frederick II (The Great)* (Berlin, Unter den Linden). Blaeser's statues of his brother *Julius Blaeser* (1834; Düsseldorf, Kstmus.), the *Tsarina Aleksandra Feodorovna* (1836; Berlin, Schloss Charlottenburg), and the painters *Friedrich Wilhelm Schadow* (1838; Düsseldorf, Kstmus.) and *Carl Friedrich Lessing* (1838–9; Berlin, Alte N.G.; see fig.) reveal that he had assimilated Rauch's idealizing manner, despite a partially narrative, independent realism. Such works brought Blaeser a reputation beyond Berlin's artistic circles, and he was thus guaranteed a constant flow of commissions for busts and portrait reliefs as well as for sculpture for private and public buildings. From the 1840s he made numerous small-scale figures with genre and symbolic content, such as the *Christmas Child* (1855; Berlin, Märk. Mus.), commissioned both by wealthy citizens and by the Prussian court.

Gustav Blaeser: *Carl Friedrich Lessing*, bronze, h. 400 mm, 1838–9 (Berlin, Alte Nationalgalerie)

Blaeser's first work to be recognized as a masterpiece was the *bozzetto* of 1842 for *Athena Supporting the Young Warrior in Battle*, one of the eight mythological groups for Karl Friedrich Schinkel's design for the Schlossbrücke over the Spree, Berlin. The group was finished in marble in 1854 at the Berlin workshop that Blaeser had set up after returning from a journey to Italy in 1845. During the 1850s Blaeser became one of the leading artists to represent Prussian sculpture at international exhibitions in London and Paris. Along with other honours, he was elected, in 1855, to the Berlin Kunstakademie, where he had exhibited since 1836. In the years 1851–7 he made the monument to Bürgermeister *August Wilhelm Francke* (Magdeburg, Bei der Hauptwache Platz), his first public statue of an individual. In contrast to the lively images of his portrait figurines, he aimed at the monumental style established by Rauch that was widely accepted by this period, where the aim was to unite the individual appearance with an idealized, classical concept of the figure. Blaeser's success in this respect is reflected in the large number of commissions won for monuments to sovereigns in contrast to only two busts to great thinkers (*Alexander von Humboldt*, 1869, New York, Central Park, West Central Park/77th Street; and *Georg Friedrich Wilhelm Hegel*, 1870, Berlin, Hegelplatz).

In 1864 Blaeser completed a bronze equestrian statue of *Frederick William IV* (see 1990 exh. cat., p. 159) for the Rheinbrücke in Cologne. By adapting Andreas Schlüter's baroque *Great Elector* monument he achieved a vivid and sophisticated interpretation of the genre. In the same year, however, Rauch's influence is detectable in Blaeser's design for the monument (completed in 1878) to *Frederick William III* (see 1990 exh. cat., p. 161) in Cologne (destr. 1939–45; recently rest.), built for the 50th anniversary of the annexation of the Rheinland by Prussia in 1815. This was the largest of Blaeser's works and was completed by Alexander Calandrelli and Rudolf Schweinitz (1839–96). It derived from Rauch's monument to *Frederick II*, although less in the figure of the horseman than in the tall pedestal, surrounded by over life-size, high-relief figures. These, however, show both greater naturalism and a leaning towards Baroque models.

Attempts to integrate realistic representation and classical form occupied Blaeser throughout his life. Without finally overcoming Rauch's formal understanding or creating a separate style of his own, his work progressed in the area of tension between idealistic tradition and modern development, and so left an oeuvre that embraces realistic representations of contemporary subjects, such as the figure group of an *Inventor, Engineer and Worker* (1862; Berlin, Maschinenfabrik Borsig; destr.), as well as classical, symbolic and allegorical figures, such as *Hospitality* (marble, 1856–68; Heidelberg, Kurpfälz. Mus.).

BIBLIOGRAPHY
AKL
P. O. Rave: 'Gustav Blaeser und sein Kölner Heumarkt-Denkmal', *Wallraf-Richardtz-Jb.*, v (1928), pp. 119–55
P. Bloch and W. Grzimek: *Das klassische Berlin: Die Berliner Bildhauerkunst im 19. Jahrhundert* (Frankfurt am Main, Berlin and Vienna, 1978), pp. 125–7, 146–9
Rheinland-Westfalen und die Berliner Bildhauerschule des 19. Jahrhunderts (exh. cat., ed. P. Bloch; Berlin, Skulpgal., 1984), pp. 63–72
E. Trier and M. Puls: 'Berlin und die Rheinlands: Tendenzen und Konstellationen', *Ethos und Pathos: Die Berliner Bildhauerschule, 1786–1914* (exh. cat. by P. Bloch and others, Berlin, Skulpgal., 1990), pp. 141–68

M. PULS

Blain, Jean-Baptiste. *See* BELIN, JEAN-BAPTISTE.

Blake, Peter (*b* Dartford, Kent, 25 June 1932). English painter, printmaker and sculptor. He studied at Gravesend Technical College and School of Art from 1946 to 1951, and from 1953 at the Royal College of Art, London, where he was awarded a First-Class Diploma in 1956. He then travelled through Europe for a year on a Leverhulme Research Award to study the popular and folk art that had already served him as a source of inspiration. While still a student Blake began producing paintings that openly testified to his love of popular entertainment and the ephemera of modern life, for example *Children Reading Comics* (1954; Carlisle, Mus. & A.G.), and which were phrased in a *faux-naif* style that owed something to the example of American realist painters such as Ben Shahn. In these works Blake displayed his nostalgia for dying traditions not only by his preference for circus imagery

Peter Blake: *Got a Girl*, enamel on hardboard with wood, photo-collage and gramophone record, 0.94×1.55×0.04 m, 1960–61 (Manchester, University of Manchester, Whitworth Art Gallery)

but also by artificially weathering the irregular wooden panels on which he was then painting. His respect for fairground art, barge painting, tattooing, commercial art, illustration and other forms of image-making rooted in folkloric traditions led him to produce some of the first works to which the term Pop art was later applied. His attitude to his source material was consistently that of the fan, to the extent that he literally wore his allegiances on his sleeve in *Self-portrait with Badges* (1961; London, Tate).

Blake's virtuosity as a draughtsman was largely directed to naturalist and academic traditions, giving this side of his work an old-fashioned air tempered by the contemporaneity of his subject-matter. From the late 1950s, however, he also produced works far more radical in conception by eliminating the personal touch. *Fine Art Bit* (1959; London, Tate), *Got a Girl* (1960–61; U. Manchester, Whitworth A.G.; see fig.) and *Toy Shop* (1962; London, Tate) typify the collage paintings and constructions composed only of patterns of bright colour and of ready-made materials such as postcards, photographs, book illustrations, toys and other objects, and brutally presented without mediation. The acts of selection and retrieval in these works, generally made in alliance with references to pop music and mass entertainment, including Hollywood films, wrestling, pin-ups and strip-tease, are presented as equivalent to the painstaking recording of observations.

Blake's devotion to illustration and to Victorian art, clearly avowed in his watercolours for Lewis Carroll's *Through the Looking-glass* (1970–71; priv. col., see 1983 exh. cat., nos. 153–60), which were also reproduced as screenprints, dominated his work between 1975 and 1979. At that time he was living in Wellow, near Bath, and painting with like-minded artists who styled themselves the Brotherhood of Ruralists. Blake's work of this period, on such 19th-century themes as fairy painting, was at its most effete and sentimental. A slow and painstaking technician, Blake demonstrated little stylistic development after this ruralist phase but continued to produce small-scale paintings and drawings of great refinement and popular appeal. To the general public, however, he remains best known as the designer of the record cover for *Sergeant Pepper's Lonely Hearts Club Band* by the Beatles (1967), a fitting tribute to his genuine enthusiasm for the popular icons of his time.

BIBLIOGRAPHY

R. Coleman: 'A Romantic Naturalist: Some Notes on the Paintings of Peter Blake', *Ark*, xviii (1956), pp. 60–61
Peter Blake (exh. cat., ed. F. Greenacre; Bristol, Mus. & A.G., 1969)
Peter Blake: Souvenirs and Samples (exh. cat. by P. Blake, London, Waddington Gals, 1977)
Peter Blake (exh. cat., ed. M. Compton; London, Tate, 1983) [retro.]
M. Vaizey: *Peter Blake* (London, 1986)

For further bibliography see POP ART.

MARCO LIVINGSTONE

Blake, William (*b* London, 28 Nov 1757; *d* London, 12 Aug 1827). English printmaker, painter and poet. His reputation as a visual artist increased during the 20th century to the extent that his art is as well known as his poetry. Yet in his own mind Blake never completely separated the two, and his most original work is to be found in hand-printed books of prophecy, which developed a personal mythology of limitless intellectual ambition. In these books, text and design are completely integrated in what he called 'illuminated' printing. He also made many pen and watercolour drawings, prints in various media and a small number of tempera paintings, but even in these his broader aims were primarily theological and philosophical: he saw the arts in all their forms as offering insights into the metaphysical world and therefore potentially redemptive of a humanity he believed to have fallen into materialism and doubt.

1. Early years. 2. The illuminated books. 3. Patronage and commissions. 4. 'Milton', 'Jerusalem' and the exhibition of 1809–10. 5. Last years.

1. EARLY YEARS. The son of a Soho hosier, Blake was trained as an engraver and continued to practise as one until almost the end of his life. The unusual nature of his ambitions and achievement owes much to this fact. At the age of ten, he entered the drawing school of Henry Pars (*c.* 1733–1806) in the Strand; between 1772 and 1779 he was apprenticed to the engraver James Basire I, learning traditional techniques that fitted him for a modest career in etching and engraving prints and book illustrations after the designs of others. His profound political and theological radicalism was largely derived from his London artisan background, but, unlike many of his contemporaries who rose from similar circumstances to become established artists, he never sought to escape from it. His training as an engraver also meant that a livelihood was assured (or so he thought), even if he failed to find customers for his imaginative works. As a consequence he felt himself free of the need to compromise with the prevailing demand for landscape, portraits and classical subject-matter. It also meant that his attitude towards his art was, in a social sense, quite alien to those found in the Royal Academy, which he entered briefly after his apprenticeship; many of its senior members were nonetheless remarkably willing even in later years to give credit to his gifts. He continued throughout most of his life to exhibit at the Royal Academy, and his pursuit of an art of high seriousness is not far in intention from that of Joshua Reynolds, whom Blake professed to despise (as indicated in his annotated copy (London, BL) of Reynolds's *Discourses*, 2/1798). By the mid-1780s Blake was reasonably successful, exhibiting watercolours of historical and biblical subjects, most notably the series of three watercolours of the *Story of Joseph* (exh. RA 1785; Cambridge, Fitzwilliam). He was admired both as an artist and as a poet by some contemporaries, especially John Flaxman, who was partly responsible for financing publication of his first collection of poems, *Poetical Sketches* (1783). A note of submerged radicalism can be discerned in his choice of apocalyptic and British historical subjects, which foreshadow some of his prophetic themes of the 1790s; but his artistic vocabulary was still dominated by the work of Royal Academy painters such as James Barry and Benjamin West, though he seems never to have attempted to paint in oils.

2. THE ILLUMINATED BOOKS. During 1787–8 there was a complete change in Blake's work, and by the end of the decade he had perfected his method of illuminated printing. This required an intense period of experimentation, almost certainly provoked by the tragic death in

February 1787 of his favourite brother Robert Blake (*b* 1767), a talented artist, who had lived with him as a pupil from 1784 and whose spirit, Blake claimed, had helped him solve the problems of the new printing techniques. The other contributory factor was a religious crisis that led him nominally to take up the doctrines of the Swedenborgian Church. Blake's objective in developing his method of illuminated printing was to combine text and design on one plate in a way that was not possible with the usual methods of intaglio engraving and letterpress printing. His concern on the one hand was to unify his poetry and painting, a desire that reflected his dissatisfaction with such works as the unfinished narrative poem *Tiriel* (*c.* 1786–9; London, BL), which was to have included illustrations—12 sepia drawings survive (e.g. New Haven, CT, Yale Cent. Brit. A.). On the other hand he was also seeking a means of bringing the production of illustrated texts under his own control so that he could become his own publisher, independent of commercial publishers and letterpress printers. His solution to both problems was to develop between 1787 and 1789 a unique method of 'relief etching', enabling him to produce durable copperplates that could be printed off in his own workroom in as few or as many copies as he liked. The *Approach of Doom* (*c.* 1787–90; London, BM) is probably one of his first experiments in the technique. This method was not fully elucidated until the 1940s by Ruthven Todd and others. Blake combined the techniques of etching and relief printing, drawing his designs probably in reverse in stopping-out solution on the surface of the copper, so that the parts of the copper that were not to be printed were eaten away by the acid. The method, although ingenious, had some disadvantages: it was extremely difficult to control the acid and thus ensure even biting and a clean outline; and as Blake invariably added pen and wash to the final printing, as well as colour, the method is unlikely to have saved him much labour.

Blake's earliest experiments in illuminated printing are three small and incomplete prose tracts: *All Religions Are One, There Is No Natural Religion* and a third whose title is lost. In these he sought to demonstrate the logical impossibility of 'natural religion', which he tendentiously reduced to a purely empirical explanation of the universe. He first achieved complete success with his new printing method in the *Songs of Innocence* (title-page dated 1789), a series of poems addressed to children, which are also complex meditations on the presence of the divine in the state of childhood. In 1794 they appeared jointly with *Songs of Experience*; the latter, by contrast, are meditations on the fallen state of the material world. The illuminations to each poem in *Songs of Innocence* usually consist of an illustration to the text; but Blake also added decorative borders and interlinear designs, often with tiny or barely legible figures and scenes that counterpoint the text. Almost every known copy has been delicately painted in watercolour by Blake himself, or possibly by his wife Catherine (whom he married in 1782); the colouring varies from the spare tinting of early copies to the medieval-style opulence of those coloured in the 1820s. The designs reveal not only the influence on Blake of medieval illumination but also conventions of 18th-century music printing.

As with his two books of *Songs*, the delicately illuminated poem *The Book of Thel* (1789) is pastoral in genre, but Blake could apply himself equally to epic themes. The dramatic progress of the French Revolution in the years after 1789 excited his sympathies and led to his association with the radical circle of the publisher Joseph Johnson (1738–1809). This circle included Henry Fuseli and Mary Wollstonecraft, and in 1791 Blake illustrated the second edition of Wollstonecraft's *Original Stories from Real Life*, a progressive book on the bringing-up of children. In 1790 or 1791 he began a poem entitled *The French Revolution*, apparently completing only a fragment of what was intended to have been a much larger work. In 1791 Johnson printed Book I but did not publish it (only one set of proofs is known: San Marino, CA, Huntington Lib.). Blake also began an immense epic, or series of epics, in which the Revolution would be seen as arising inevitably from the troubled history of the human spirit and as an apocalyptic stage in the redemption of mankind. Some of these ideas are foreshadowed in his illuminated book *The Marriage of Heaven and Hell* (see fig. 1), an ironic mixture of parable, aphorism and prophecy, towards the end of which (pl. 24) Blake proclaimed 'I have also: The Bible of Hell: which the world shall have whether they will or no'. This seems to be a reference to the series of prophetic books of varying lengths that emerged in 1793–5. Some look more to the present and future—*America: A Prophecy* (1793; *see* ETCHING, RELIEF), *Europe: A Prophecy* (1794)

1. William Blake: *The Marriage of Heaven and Hell*, hand-coloured etching, 150×100 mm, 1793, pl. 2 (Cambridge, Fitzwilliam Museum)

and *The Song of Los* (1795); others—*The [First] Book of Urizen* (1794), *The Book of Ahania* (1795) and *The Book of Los* (1795)—look back to the early history of Man and the original divisions leading to his mental and physical enslavement.

As physical objects, these prophetic or 'Lambeth' books (named after the London suburb where Blake lived at the time) are unique. The meanings of both text and design seem opaque at first: Blake evidently intended them to be seen as mysterious objects that would yield their meaning only after prolonged and sympathetic study (which, even within his own circles, few were prepared to give at the time). The illuminations are not always related to or integrated with the text, yet the general effect is of a liberating sublimity, in which visions of horror and beauty vie with one another. In addition to relief etching, Blake used the compatible technique of white-line engraving and a form of monotype colour printing, probably applied by copperplate and then finished with pen and watercolour. This he seems to have associated symbolically with primeval and fallen worlds, although he colour-printed a great many of his designs, even such engravings as his exultant *Albion Rose* ('*Glad Day*', *c.* 1800; e.g. London, BM), as samples of his method.

Each of the prophetic books of the 1790s is best understood as a psychomachia, in which the main characters represent aspects of the human mind. At the same time these books make up a syncretic myth, drawing together elements from the Bible, Greek mythology and British legend. The old and corrupt order is realized in Urizen, a tyrannical god embodying aspects both of Jehovah and Jupiter as well as of the repressive British state. Urizen's dominance is challenged in *America*, which describes the outbreak of the American Revolution as the emergence of Orc, the embodiment of energy, who stands for both destructive and creative aspects of revolution. The third major figure of these books is the eponymous Los, who represents the creative artist. His desperate task, like that of Urizen and Orc, is to give form to the inchoate forces of the universe, and, like the artist in any age, he is doomed to be imprisoned in his own creations. 'The strife of blood' making up the action of Blake's prophecies seems to parallel, in ways not easy to discern, the unfolding tragedy of the French Revolution and the increasingly belligerent British response to it.

Despite the uncertainties concerning the chronological order of these books, they seem to reveal an increasing emancipation of pictorial elements at the expense of text,

2. William Blake: *Elohim Creating Adam*, monotype, watercolour and wash, 431×536 mm, 1795; from the series '*Large Colour Prints*', 1795 and *c.* 1804 (London, Tate Gallery)

3. William Blake: *Newton*, monotype, 1795; from the series *'Large Colour Prints'*, 1795 and *c.* 1804 (London, Tate Gallery)

and a greater use of colour printing. In *The [First] Book of Urizen*, for instance, about a third of the 28 plates are without text (some copies have as few as 24 plates), and in another third the design predominates. In *The Song of Los* the text is closed in by the magnificent and densely printed illuminations, while *The Book of Los* and *The Book of Ahania*, both small books, show Blake preferring intaglio to relief-etching for his printing of the text. The series of 12 large monotypes known as the *'Large Colour Prints'* (1795 and *c.* 1804), which are without any accompanying text, seem strikingly purposeful in technique when compared with the prophetic books of 1795, though their overall theme, if there was one, has never been satisfactorily elucidated. Much of their subject-matter is derived from the Bible (e.g. *Elohim Creating Adam*; see fig. 2), but some is from Milton and Shakespeare (e.g. *Hecate, c.* 1795; London, Tate) or illustrates ideas from Blake's own prophecies. One example of this is the extraordinary representation of the supposed arch-rationalist *Newton*, seated naked in his cave, absorbed in reducing the universe with his compasses to a mathematical diagram (see fig. 3).

3. PATRONAGE AND COMMISSIONS. For Blake, the years 1788–95 had provoked a sustained burst of creative energy, stimulated mainly by external events. In 1796 or 1797 he began work on an epic (later abandoned), which survives as a much revised manuscript known as *Vala* or the *Four Zoas* (London, BL). He also started a series of 537 watercolour illustrations for the text of Edward Young's poems *Night Thoughts*, to be published in four volumes. One volume appeared (1797), using only 43 plates of the 156 designs for that section of the text (London, BM). They are among the least inspired of Blake's designs, but in the course of making them he realized the potential for using visual illustration to comment critically upon a text, by reinforcing its truths and 'correcting' its errors. They are, therefore, the forerunners of his great series of watercolour illustrations of later years for the Bible and the works of Thomas Gray, Milton, John Bunyan and Dante. Despite his political radicalism, Blake achieved modest success and some prosperity during the 1790s; by the end of the decade he had secured a loyal patron, Thomas Butts (1757–1845), a minor civil servant, as well as commissions from others.

Butts commissioned 50 small biblical paintings from Blake (about 35 survive). Blake executed these in a defective glue-based 'tempera' technique of his own devising, which he misleadingly called 'fresco'. The series was conceived as a typological cycle and appears to have placed a strong emphasis on Christ's role in the redemption of man. It also shows an unexpected openness to the influence of earlier European painting, especially of the

Italian Renaissance, examples of which Blake would have seen in the Orléans collection displayed for sale in London in 1798–9. Butts followed up this commission, which seems to have been completed in 1800, with a more open-ended one, for Blake to make watercolours, when he was able, of biblical subjects at a price of one guinea each. Until *c.* 1809 he continued to supply Butts with watercolours; these provide a useful index to his stylistic development and reveal a determination on Blake's part to tackle abstract and symbolic subjects thought (since the Middle Ages, at least) to lie beyond any artist's powers. This is especially true of the remarkable designs for the Book of Revelation (e.g. Philadelphia, PA, Rosenbach Mus.), in which he attempted to give a coherent form to such ineffable beings as the 'Great Beast', while at the same time suggesting the immensity of the crowds that bow down before him. One group of watercolours illustrating the mourning over the dead Christ (e.g. London, V&A) is notable, however, for their solemnity and rigorous symmetry of composition, suggesting a renewed appreciation of Gothic sculpture. Nevertheless, the generous commission from Butts did not prevent Blake from experiencing financial difficulties, mainly caused by a decline in engraving commissions. He decided to accept a post, obtained for him by John Flaxman, as assistant to the poet William Hayley in Felpham, Sussex, moving there in September 1800 and remaining exactly three years. His employment was largely menial (it included decorative interior work for Hayley's house), and Hayley, at Flaxman's urging, seems to have deliberately discouraged Blake (who described his employer as 'a corporeal friend and spiritual enemy') from the pursuit of imaginative work. Even so, the Felpham period was to prove seminal for the great works of his later years: while there, Blake began conceiving his final illuminated books, *Milton* and *Jerusalem*. At the same time, his letters reveal a sense of personal alienation, which was to intensify almost to insanity in the years after his return to London.

Blake's three-year break at Felpham perpetuated his inability to pick up engraving work, and he entered a period of increasing poverty. This was not helped by his growing irascibility, vividly expressed by scurrilous verse in his Notebook (London, BL) and by bitter annotations in books by others, especially Reynolds's *Discourses*. Butts remained loyal and, in addition to watercolours of biblical subjects, commissioned illustrations of Milton's poems. The series of Milton watercolours (1801–*c.* 1816), illustrating *Paradise Lost* and several other poems, are usually of 12 designs; there are often two sets for each series, one commissioned by the Rev. Joseph Thomas and the other by Butts. It has become clear that these illustrations, built on the basis of a literal rendering of the original text, are in fact complex commentaries on Milton's life and art, which Blake believed had been full of unresolved conflicts. This can be seen in *Paradise Lost* (e.g. Boston, MA, Mus. F.A.; San Marino, CA, Huntington Lib.) and more clearly in *L'allegro* and *Il penseroso* (*c.* 1816; e.g. New York, Pierpont Morgan Lib.), in which Milton's pastoral poems are transformed into a kind of spiritual biography, beginning with his carefree youth and continuing through troubled manhood to contemplative old age.

4. 'MILTON', 'JERUSALEM' AND THE EXHIBITION OF 1809–10. Between 1805 and 1810 Blake worked on more ambitious projects than ever, including a large painting of the *Last Judgement* (untraced), which he did not complete, though a detailed description by Blake (in his Notebook) and several drawings survive (e.g. Washington, DC, N.G.A.). He also took up work in earnest on two final prophetic books. The first, *Milton: A Poem* (title-page dated 1804), consisting initially of 45 illuminated pages, was probably not completed until 1809. It tells of Blake's spiritual struggle with the inheritance of Milton, the greatest of English poets, and how this period of psychological combat brought him the strength to continue his own redemptive mission. *Milton* was the prelude to his richest and most complex work, *Jerusalem* (100 pages in its final form), which occupied him until the early 1820s. Baldly stated, the theme of *Jerusalem* is Man's fall to his present divided state, and it ends with a vision of redemption. Unlike the prophecies of the 1790s, *Jerusalem* is more unified in structure through its central symbols: Albion, standing for humanity, and Jerusalem, representing the British nation alienated from the spirit. Albion is in thrall to Vala (goddess of Nature) and dominated by his own wayward children (the people of Britain), who pursue the false gods of materialism; he seeks redemption through the mercy of Christ and freedom from the dominant spectre of reason, achieving these in the exultant vision of the poem's last pages. Nevertheless, the final plate suggests Blake's belief that much remains to be done towards the building of Jerusalem.

The text of *Jerusalem* is interspersed with a great variety of designs, ranging from full-page plates to border and interlinear designs. In some cases their meaning in relation to the text is relatively clear, but in others they remain resistant to interpretation. This is so particularly in the case of the beautiful and mysterious scenes that act as headpieces to each of the four chapters. Both *Milton* and *Jerusalem* contain direct references to Blake's own life and mental struggles, and they also reflect his increasing sense of rejection by others, including his friends. A number of misunderstandings concerning commissions occurred at this time. The most notable was with Robert Hartley Cromek (1770–1812) over a series of engravings to illustrate a new edition of Robert Blair's *The Grave*. Publication in 1808, after Luigi Schiavonetti had engraved Blake's designs, was followed by a scornful attack in *The Examiner* (7 Aug 1808) by Robert Hunt. This led Blake to make public his artistic ideas: he organized a retrospective exhibition of his work, held from May 1809 to the summer of 1810 in the house in which he had been born (then occupied by his brother James). This exhibition was accompanied by *A Descriptive Catalogue* of 72 pages containing his own invaluable accounts of some of his most notable paintings, including the tempera *Canterbury Pilgrims* (Glasgow, Pollok House). Although full of idiosyncratic attacks on other artists, it includes a cogent defence of his concern with vision rather than with the representation of the exterior world. He also made a strong case for the primacy of outline ('the hard, wiry line of Rectitude') over colour, and his work of 1809–10 (e.g. the *Milton* illustrations) shows a more emphatically linear approach than at any other period. Predictably, the exhibition was a failure, although it was visited in April 1810 by Henry Crabb Robinson, who reported on it for the first issue of *Vaterländisches Museum*, a Hamburg magazine. It marked the beginning of a period of obscurity for Blake that was to last until 1818. He seems to have had just enough engraving work to keep him from absolute destitution, although his production of imaginative work continued unabated. He worked in his rooms in South Molton Street on *Milton* and *Jerusalem*, and also on the *Last Judgement*. In 1815 George Cumberland the younger, the son of his lifelong friend, remarked 'he has been labouring . . . till it is nearly as black as your Hat'. Blake also continued to perfect his watercolour technique, achieving in *L'allegro* and *Il penseroso* a radiance of colour and sensitivity to natural light that suggests he gradually became less dogmatic in his insistence on the primacy of outline.

5. LAST YEARS. In 1818 George Cumberland the younger introduced Blake to John Linnell; he in turn introduced him to a circle that included Samuel Palmer, George Richmond and Edward Calvert. To this group, who later called themselves THE ANCIENTS, Blake was a heroic figure who had proclaimed the necessity for a spiritual art in a materialistic age—one that they hoped had now ended. In their protective friendship he found a group of people who had real sympathy for his vision. Linnell bought one copy of *Jerusalem* (priv. col.) and

encouraged Blake to publish his own designs in line-engraving, without etching, in the early Italian manner. He also found commissions for Blake, including one for 17 tiny wood-engravings of pastoral life. This was for a school edition of Robert Thornton's *The Pastorals of Virgil* (known as '*Thornton's Virgil*'), first published in 1812. Blake's wood-engravings were published in the edition of 1821, and they became a major influence on Palmer. Although landscape as a genre was, in a theoretical sense, anathema to Blake, he seems to have preserved an easy relationship with the landscape painters in Linnell's circle, confining to a prophetic voice his strictures upon those (including Wordsworth) who sought God through nature.

In the 1820s Blake began two major works. Both were commissioned by Linnell: 22 engravings of the *Book of Job*, published in 1826 (*see* ENGRAVING, fig. 8), and the series of 100 watercolours of Dante's *Divine Comedy* (see fig. 4). These, with other engravings, remained unfinished at Blake's death. The *Job* engravings were worked up from a set of watercolours of 1805–10 (New York, Pierpont Morgan Lib.), which remained in the possession of Butts, with the addition of freely engraved borders containing complementary designs and texts. Their 'gothic' style of engraving made them appear quaint to contemporaries, but to others they must have seemed a return to order after the complexity of his illuminated books. In fact, thematically, their underlying narrative has parallels with

4. William Blake: *Dante and Virgil Penetrating the Forest*, watercolour, pen, ink, chalk and pencil, 371×527 mm, 1824–7 (London, Tate Gallery)

Jerusalem: Job is an Everyman who begins by defining his universe in terms of a satanic, vengeful conception of Jehovah yet, by artistic celebration of the divine, ultimately achieves redemption through recognition of the Christ within himself. The Dante series is perhaps more difficult to interpret because it remains substantially unfinished and also because Blake's attitude towards Dante was equivocal, as it was also towards Milton. Dante, in Blake's view, was open to several charges: that he was more concerned with the world than the spirit; that the *Divine Comedy* was an act of vengeance, not of Christian forgiveness; and that the end of his quest was a return to the Catholic Church. Despite these problems, the watercolours are remarkable for their atmospheric depiction of Hell, Purgatory and Heaven and show a freedom of handling that suggests Blake had learnt from the British watercolour school.

On his death, Blake was mourned by a small but devoted circle of admirers, but his work received little public recognition over the following years. His rediscovery in the middle of the 19th century was due to the Pre-Raphaelites, especially Dante Gabriel Rossetti, and their interest culminated indirectly in the first full-length biography of Blake (Gilchrist, 1863), subtitled '*Pictor ignotus*'. To Victorian admirers Blake represented variously the exemplary Christian life, a devotion to art that foreshadowed 'Art for art's sake', a 'gothic' sincerity worthy of the Italian Primitives, and the ideal of the humble artist–craftsman. Behind these conceptions lay the assumption that Blake stood wholly apart from his age. Throughout the 19th century his prophetic books, except for *Songs of Innocence and Experience*, were regarded almost universally as incomprehensible and irrational, and where his poetry was admired it was entirely apart from its setting in the illuminated books. During the 20th century there was a sustained effort, mainly by American literary scholars, to reveal the intellectual coherence of the prophetic books and to place them at the centre of his achievement. At the same time, further research into 18th-century Dissenting religion continues to demonstrate that, despite the unique forms his art took, Blake's religious and political attitudes were not alien to the thought of his era.

ILLUMINATED BOOKS

Places and/or dates in quotation marks are those engraved by Blake on the title-page. High-quality facsimiles of the illuminated books (and several of Blake's other works) have been produced by the William Blake Trust (1949–95).

All Religions Are One; *There Is No Natural Religion* [2 versions: series a and b] (1788) [14 sets known, consisting of 8 to 14 pls]

The Book of Thel ('1789') [17 copies known]

Songs of Innocence ('1789') [21 copies known]

America: A Prophecy ('Lambeth 1793') [13 copies known, plus 1 untraced and 3 posth. printed]

The Marriage of Heaven and Hell ('1793 . . . Lambeth') [9 complete copies known]

Visions of the Daughters of Albion ('1793') [15 complete copies known]

The [First] Book of Urizen ('Lambeth 1794') [7 copies known]

Europe: A Prophecy ('Lambeth 1794') [12 copies known, 10 without the prefatory poem]

Songs of Innocence and Experience: Shewing the Two Contrary States of the Human Soul ('Lambeth 1794') [28 copies known]

The Book of Ahania ('Lambeth 1795') [1 complete copy known: Washington, DC, N.G.A.]

The Book of Los ('Lambeth 1795') [1 complete copy known: London, BM]

The Song of Los ('Lambeth 1795') [5 copies known]

Jerusalem: The Emanation of the Giant Albion ('1804') [5 complete copies known; also 3 posth. printed]

Milton: A Poem in 2 Books ('1804') [4 copies known]

WRITINGS

Notebook (London, BL); facs. ed. D. V. Erdman (Oxford, 1973, rev. 2/1977)

A Descriptive Catalogue of Pictures, Poetical and Historical Inventions by William Blake (London, 1809)

G. Keynes, ed.: *The Letters of William Blake* (London, 1956, rev. Oxford, 3/1980)

——: *The Complete Writings of William Blake* (Oxford, 1957, rev. 2/1966)

D. V. Erdman, ed.: *Poetry and Prose of William Blake* (Garden City, NY, 1965, rev. 2/1982 as *The Complete Poetry and Prose of William Blake*)

T. Bindman, ed.: *Blake's Illuminated Books* (London, 1995)

BIBLIOGRAPHY

MONOGRAPHS

A. Gilchrist: *Life of William Blake: 'Pictor ignotus'*, 2 vols (London, 1863); ed. R. Todd (London, 1942, rev. 2/1945)

S. Foster Damon: *Blake: His Philosophy and Symbols* (Boston, 1924, rev. London, 1969)

N. Frye: *Fearful Symmetry: A Study of William Blake* (Princeton, 1947, R 4/1969)

G. L. Keynes, ed.: *Blake Studies: Essays on his Life and Work* (Oxford, 1949, rev. 1971)

D. V. Erdman: *Blake: Prophet against Empire* (Princeton, 1954, rev. 3/1977)

A. Blunt: *The Art of William Blake* (Oxford, 1959)

S. Foster Damon: *A Blake Dictionary* (Providence, 1965/R 1973)

M. D. Paley: *Energy and the Imagination* (Oxford, 1970)

D. Bindman: *Blake as an Artist* (Oxford, 1977)

W. J. T. Mitchell: *Blake's Composite Art* (Princeton, 1978)

COLLECTIONS AND CATALOGUES

G. Keynes and E. Wolf: *William Blake's Illuminated Books: A Census* (New York, 1953)

H. D. Willard: *William Blake: Water-color Drawings*, Boston, Mus. F.A. cat. (Boston, 1957)

G. E. Bentley jr: *Blake Records* (Oxford, 1969)

D. Bindman, ed.: *William Blake: Catalogue of the Collection in the Fitzwilliam Museum* (Cambridge, 1970)

M. Butlin: *William Blake: A Complete Catalogue of Works in the Tate Gallery* (London, 1971)

R. Easson and R. N. Essick: *William Blake: Book Illustrator* (Normal, IL, 1972)

D. V. Erdman: *The Illuminated Blake* (Oxford, 1974, 3/1978)

William Blake (exh. cat., ed. W. Hofmann; Hamburg, Ksthalle, 1975)

G. E. Bentley jr: *Blake Books* (Oxford, 1977)

D. Bindman: *The Complete Graphic Works of William Blake* (London and New York, 1978)

William Blake (exh. cat. by M. Butlin, London, Tate, 1978)

M. Butlin: *The Paintings and Drawings of William Blake*, 2 vols (London, 1981)

William Blake: His Art and Times (exh. cat. by D. Bindman, New Haven, Yale Cent. Brit. A.; Toronto, A.G. Ont.; 1982–3)

R. N. Essick: *The Separate Plates of William Blake* (Princeton, 1983)

——: *The Works of William Blake in the Huntington Collections* (San Marino, 1985)

SPECIALIST STUDIES

J. H. Wicksteed: *Blake's Vision of the Book of Job, with Reproductions of the Illustrations: A Study* (London, 1910, rev. 2/1924)

A. S. Roe: *Blake's Illustrations to the 'Divine Comedy'* (Princeton, 1953)

G. E. Bentley jr: *William Blake: Vala or the Four Zoas* (Oxford, 1963)

Blake Newsletter (1967–77); cont. as *Blake: An Illustrated Quarterly* (1978–)

Blake Studies (1968–)

I. Tayler: *Blake's Illustrations to the Poems of Gray* (Princeton, 1971)

B. Lindberg: *William Blake's Illustrations to the Book of Job* (Abo, NM, 1973)

P. Dunbar: *Blake's Illustrations to the Poetry of Milton* (Oxford, 1980)

D. V. Erdman and others: *Blake's Designs for Edward Young's 'Night Thoughts'* (Oxford, 1980)

R. N. Essick: *William Blake: Printmaker* (Princeton, 1980)

M. Eaves: *William Blake's Theory of Art* (Princeton, 1982)

R. Essick and M. D. Paley: *Robert Blair's 'The Grave' Illustrated by William Blake* (London, 1982)

D. Bindman, ed.: *William Blake: Illustrations of the Book of Job and Colour Versions of Blake's Book of Job Designs* (London, 1987)

J. Viscomi: *Blake and the Idea of the Book* (Princeton, 1993)

DAVID BINDMAN

Blakelock, Ralph Albert (*b* New York, 15 Oct 1847; *d* Elizabethtown, NY, 9 Aug 1919). American painter. One of the most important visionary artists in late 19th-century America, he was self-taught as a painter. From 1867 he was exhibiting landscapes in the style of the Hudson River school at the National Academy of Design in New York. Rather than going abroad for advanced training, like most of his contemporaries, he spent the years 1869–72 in the western United States. Back in New York, Blakelock evolved his personal style during the 1870s and 1880s. Eschewing literal transcriptions of nature, he preferred to paint evocative moonlit landscapes such as *Moonlight* (Washington, DC, Corcoran Gal. A.). These paintings, almost never dated, often included camp-fires or solitary figures; but such elements were absorbed into the setting rather than being the painting's focus, as in *Moonlight Indian Encampment* (Washington, DC, N. Mus. Amer. A.). Blakelock's images, imbued with a melancholy that had been evident even in his early work, drew on his deeply felt response to nature.

Blakelock's technique was as individual as his subject; the surfaces, sensuously textured, were built up of layers of thick pigment, although his use of bitumen has disfigured some of his work. Blakelock's unconventional paintings were not well received, and he sold them for meagre sums to a few private patrons and through minor New York auction houses and art dealers to support his nine children. Financial distress led to mental breakdown, and in 1899 Blakelock was confined to a mental institution, where he spent most of the rest of his life. Ironically, Blakelock's unique artistry soon gained appreciation and brought substantial prices, from which neither he nor his family benefited. The popularity of his work has also encouraged numerous forgeries.

BIBLIOGRAPHY

E. Daingerfield: 'Ralph Albert Blakelock', *A. America*, ii (Dec 1913), pp. 55–68; rev. as *Ralph Albert Blakelock* (New York, 1914); rev. *A. America*, li (Aug 1963), pp. 83–5

Ralph Albert Blakelock Exhibition (exh. cat. by L. Goodrich, New York, Whitney, 1947)

Ralph Albert Blakelock, 1847–1919 (exh. cat. by N. A. Geske, Lincoln, U. NE, Sheldon Mem. A.G.; Trenton, NJ State Mus.; 1975)

LAURETTA DIMMICK

Blakstad & Munthe-Kaas. Norwegian architectural and furniture design partnership formed in 1922 by Gudolf Blakstad (*b* Gjerpen, 19 May 1893; *d* Oslo, 1986) and Herman Munthe-Kaas (*b* Christiania [now Oslo], 25 May 1890; *d* Oslo, 5 March 1970). Blakstad was awarded his diploma as an architect at the Norwegian Institute of Technology in Trondheim in 1916. He collaborated with Jens Dunker on the New Theatre, Oslo, from 1919 to 1929. After a preliminary training in Christiania, Munthe-Kaas finished his education at the Royal Institute of Technology in Stockholm in 1919.

From the beginning of their careers Blakstad and Munthe-Kaas played a leading role in Norwegian architecture. After studying in Italy in the early 1920s, they advocated Neo-classicism in architectural projects, furniture designs and writings. In 1922 they won the competition for the new Town Hall in Haugesund (1924–31), a major work of 20th-century Norwegian Neo-classicism. Above a powerfully rusticated basement, the long office wing with its regular fenestration contrasts with the higher City Council Hall, accentuated by pairs of monumental, free-standing columns. In general the effect is of robust strength and an exciting interplay of horizontals and verticals.

In 1928 Blakstad and Munthe-Kaas went to the Netherlands to study modern Dutch architecture. On their return they designed the House of Artists (1928–30), an exhibition building in Oslo. Their classical background emerges in the symmetry of the main façade with its central portal, but, with its concrete structure and smooth walls faced in patterned brickwork, the building is clearly Modernist. In the Odd Fellow building (1931–4) in Oslo, the fundamental elements of Modernism are evident: a recessed supporting skeleton, a 'free' plan and continuous strip windows separating layers of concrete wall-surfaces covered in glittering stucco. Important works by Blakstad & Munthe-Kaas in Oslo later in the 1930s include such office buildings as that at Roald Amundsens Gate 4, containing the fine Klingenberg cinema (1938), and the Oslo Business College (1936–41), which fulfils the period's ideal of democratic and less formal schooling. The attractive development of eight houses on Observatorie terrasse (1932–6) of concrete with red brick façades was clearly inspired by Ernst May's work in Frankfurt am Main. After World War II Blakstad & Munthe-Kaas abandoned Functionalism for buildings incorporating historical and national motifs. Characteristic examples are the Cathedral (1947–56) and Town Hall (1953) in Bodø, a city reconstructed after the war: the results of this laudable attempt were not altogether successful.

NKL

BIBLIOGRAPHY

C. Norberg-Schulz: *Modern Norwegian Architecture* (Oslo, 1986)

CHRISTIAN NORBERG-SCHULZ

Blanc, (Auguste-Alexandre-Philippe-)Charles (*b* Castres, Tarn, 15 Nov 1813; *d* Paris, 17 Jan 1882). French writer, arts administrator and engraver. The younger brother of the journalist and politician Louis Blanc, he settled in Paris around 1830 to study engraving under Luigi Calamatta and Paolo Mercuri (1804–84). He engraved a series of portraits in the 1830s of famous contemporary figures such as François-Pierre-Guillaume Guizot and the composer and conductor Philippe Musard. However, his interest lay principally in art criticism: between 1836 and 1840 he wrote reviews of the Salons and articles on art for journals such as *Bon Sens* and *Le Progrès* and also contributed to *Courrier français*, *L'Artiste* and *Journal de Rouen*. By this time he had already joined the Republican opposition to Louis-Philippe and was running *Propagateur de l'Aube*.

Blanc's experience as an art critic and his support for the Republican–Socialist cause, as well as the protection of his elder brother (who became a member of the provisional government after the Revolution of February 1848), contributed to his appointment as head of the

Bureau des Beaux-Arts in February 1848. He was very active in this important position, in particular opposing the reduction of funds allocated to the national museums. He published 'Rapport sur les arts du dessin et sur leur avenir dans la République' in *Le Moniteur* (10 Oct 1848), which promised a new golden age in state patronage of public art. The results were meagre; in particular, the competition to paint a symbolic figure of the new Republic ended in failure. Blanc had more success as a patron of landscape and genre painting, buying Charles-François Daubigny's *Banks of the Seine* (Limoges, Mus. Mun.) from the Salon of 1849. His foray into the senior ranks of government was short-lived: he was dismissed from his post after the *coup d'état* of 1851 because of his Republican views.

Blanc returned to his career as an art critic; he visited museums and art collections throughout Europe and wrote numerous articles on exhibitions and museums both in France and abroad, including *Les Trésors de l'art à Manchester* and *De Paris à Venise: Notes au crayon* (both 1857). In 1859 he founded the *Gazette des beaux-arts* and became its chief editor. With the assistance of several colleagues, he returned to the project of publishing his monumental *Histoire des peintres de toutes les écoles* (1853–75). He also wrote *Grammaire des arts du dessin* (1867).

With the fall of the Second Empire in 1870 and the return of the Republic, Blanc was reappointed head of the Bureau des Beaux-Arts in November 1870, but before long he was the object of criticism from the conservative and royalist majority elected in February 1871; the victory of the Ordre Moral was at the root of his dismissal on 24 December 1873. Once again, Blanc was free to travel (see his *Voyage en Haute-Egypte*, Paris, 1876) and to write. A member of the Académie des Beaux-Arts from 1868, he was elected to the Académie Française in 1876. After the defeat of the Ordre Moral and the Republican victory of 1877, he was appointed a teacher at the Collège de France, where he taught aesthetics and art history from 1878. He wrote on the Italian Renaissance and such artists as Leonardo da Vinci, Veronese and Rembrandt. He also contributed art criticism to the newspaper *Le Temps* and finished writing his *Grammaire des arts décoratifs* (1882).

Despite his radical political beliefs, Blanc held fairly conservative views on art, preferring Ingres to Courbet. He expressed his devotion to the Old Masters in *Histoire des peintres de toutes les écoles*, which became a standard text for French teachers of art history, and he was convinced of the benefits of artists copying the masterpieces of the past. His grander dreams for public patronage were never realized, and as an aesthetician he had his most lasting influence. In *Grammaire des arts du dessin* and at the Collège de France he advanced a scientific interpretation of aesthetics and proposed general laws on the expression of beauty, which proved of central importance to Seurat and Neo-Impressionism.

WRITINGS

Histoire des peintres au XIXe siècle (Paris, 1845) [vol. ii never completed]
L'Oeuvre de Rembrandt (Paris, 1853)
Histoire des peintres de toutes les écoles, 14 vols (Paris, 1853–75)
Grammaire des arts du dessin (Paris, 1867)
Ingres: Sa vie et ses ouvrages (Paris, 1870)
Les Artistes de mon temps (Paris, 1876)
Grammaire des arts décoratifs (Paris, 1882)

For a complete list of Blanc's Salon criticism (1852–70), see M. Ward and C. Parsons: *A Bibliography of Second Empire Salon Criticism* (Cambridge, 1986).

BIBLIOGRAPHY

L. Fiaux: *Portraits politiques contemporains: Charles Blanc* (Paris, 1882)
T. Massarani: *Charles Blanc et son oeuvre* (Paris, 1885)
'Hommage à Charles Blanc', *Rev. Hist. & Lit. Languedoc*, xix (1948) [whole issue]
P. Vaisse: 'Charles Blanc und das "Musée des Copies"', *Z. Kstgesch.*, xxxix/1 (1976), pp. 54–66
M. Song: *Art Theories of Charles Blanc (1813–1882)* (diss., University Park, PA State U., 1981)
W. Drost: 'Materialgerechtigkeit und absolute Kunst: Zu Charles Blancs Ästhetik der Vasenmalerei', *Wallraf-Richartz-Jb.*, xliv (1983), pp. 367–74

PAUL GERBOD

Blanc, (Paul) Joseph (*b* Paris, 25 Jan 1846; *d* Paris, 5 July 1904). French painter. He was a pupil of Emile Bin (1825–97) and Alexandre Cabanel at the Ecole des Beaux-Arts in Paris and in 1867 won the Prix de Rome with the *Murder of Laius by Oedipus* (1867; Paris, Ecole N. Sup. B.-A.), which opened up an official career to him. He painted religious and mythological subjects (e.g. *Perseus on Pegasus*, 1869; Nîmes, Mus. B.-A.) and also worked on numerous decorative projects in both Paris and the provinces. Between 1873 and 1883 he worked on the huge mural compositions the *Vow of Clovis at the Battle of Tolbiac* and the *Baptism of Clovis* for the Panthéon in Paris, executed in an academic style. He produced a series of 14 panels depicting the *Passion of Christ* for the church of St Peter at Douai. He executed four grisailles for the cupola of the church of Saint-Paul-Saint-Louis in Paris, which were commissioned in 1873 and finished in 1875 and depicted *St Louis, Charlemagne, Robert the Pious* and *Clovis*. He painted four panels for the corridor of the foyer of the Opéra Comique in Paris, showing *Music, Comedy, Song* and *Dance*. In 1882 he was commissioned to decorate the staircase leading to the 'Comité des Maréchaux' room in the Ministère de la Guerre [now Ministère de la Défense], Paris, with three panels depicting *The Departure, The Charge* and *Salve Patria*. His tapestry cartoons for the Gobelins included one for the *Arms of the Town of Paris* (1892) for the Tribunal de Commerce in Paris; he contributed a large decorative frieze for the Palais des Beaux-Arts at the Exposition Universelle in Paris in 1900. He also participated in the enormous enterprise of decorating the new Hôtel de Ville in Paris, producing five compositions influenced by Luc Olivier Merson. Destined for the north landing of the Escalier des fêtes, they represent the *Republican Months, Dawn, Day, Evening* and *Night* and were finished in 1903.

BIBLIOGRAPHY
Bénézit; *DBF*; Thieme–Becker

A. DAGUERRE DE HUREAUX

Blanchard. French family of painters. (1) Jacques Blanchard was a contemporary of Simon Vouet, whose style as a history, religious and decorative painter was marked by his experience of Italian art, both the colourism of the Venetian school and the classicism of the Bolognese. Before his relatively early death, he took part in many of the major decorative schemes of mid-17th-century France. He is, however, best known for his easel paintings of the

Holy Family and *Charity*, of which he painted numerous variations. His brother (2) Jean Blanchard was also highly esteemed as a decorative painter, but his few surviving works are mostly genre scenes in the manner of Jan Miel and Pieter van Laer. (3) Gabriel Blanchard, son of Jacques, had a successful career as a religious and decorative painter in the service of Louis XIV.

(1) Jacques Blanchard (*b* Paris, 1 Oct 1600; *d* Paris, Nov 1638). He trained with his maternal uncle Nicolas Bollery (*c.* 1550/60–1630) from 1613 to 1618. He then set off for Italy but stopped at Lyon to work in the studio of Horace Le Blanc. Le Blanc left for Paris in 1623, and Blanchard is known to have finished a number of his works left in Lyon, including perhaps the *Virgin and Child with a Bishop and a Woman Holding a Baby* (Lyon, St Denis). At the end of October 1624 he reached Rome in the company of his brother Jean Blanchard, remaining there until April or May 1626. He was then in Venice until 1628, when he returned to Lyon via Turin. All that is known of his work in Italy is the mention by Félibien and Perrault of scenes from Ovid's *Metamorphoses* painted in Venice, and pictures of the *Loves of Venus and Adonis* executed for Charles-Emanuel I, Duke of Savoy, in Turin. Blanchard's earliest surviving work, the *Virgin with the Christ Child Giving the Keys to St Peter* (Albi Cathedral), painted in Lyon in 1628, shows the influence of Bolognese painting in such details as the faces, but the work as a whole reveals his knowledge of 16th-century Venetian painters such as Titian, Veronese, Tintoretto and Jacopo Bassano: Perrault called him the 'Titian of France', and Félibien stated that the principal quality of his work was colour. Blanchard was to oscillate between these two tendencies—the Bolognese, cool in colour and polished in handling, and the Venetian, warm, sensuous and colouristic—throughout his career.

In 1629 Blanchard returned to Paris and embarked on a successful and prosperous career as a history and decorative painter: his subject-matter covered mythology, Classical history, literature and religious themes. He also produced occasional portraits. Around 1630 he was received into the Académie de St Luc with *St John on Patmos* (untraced; engraved by Pierre Daret), a work indebted to the art of Giovanni Lanfranco. The Bolognese influence is also visible in the *Assumption of the Virgin* (?1630; Cognac, St Léger). In another early commission, the *ex-voto* commemorating the plague of 1628–9, *Pierre Tullier, Mayor of Bourges, Presented to the Virgin and Child by St Stephen* (Bourges, Mus. Berry; once attributed to Jean Boucher), it is the Venetian elements that predominate. In 1631 Blanchard painted his only known signed portrait, the brooding, Titianesque *Portrait of a Man Aged 27* (Detroit, MI, Inst. A.). It is apparent, however, from such works as *St Jerome* (1632; Budapest, Mus. F.A.) that he was also sensitive to the work of contemporary artists working in Venice during his stay, including the Roman Domenico Feti and the German Johann Liss; he owned a picture of a *Lute Player* by Liss.

In 1632–4 Jacques Blanchard painted a series of 21 decorative works on the theme of the *Loves of the Gods* for the gallery of the Hôtel Le Barbier (later Hôtel Perrault), Paris. Of these only one painting survives:

Diana and Endymion (France, priv. col.). The success of the scheme brought him in 1634 the prestigious commission to decorate the lower gallery of the Paris hôtel of Claude de Bullion, where he painted mythological scenes corresponding to the months of the year (destr.). He worked for a number of other high-ranking officials, including Pierre Puget de Montauron (after 1591–1664), for whom he painted a series of scenes from the *Life of the Virgin* for the Château de Chevrette near Paris. Also in 1634 he received from the Goldsmiths' Corporation of Paris the important commission for that year's May for Notre-Dame. The altarpiece he painted, representing *Pentecost*, is still *in situ*; the architectural background would seem to be, as was usual in his works, the result of a collaboration with his brother. In 1636 Blanchard was appointed Peintre du Roi, and in the same year he signed and dated a *Bacchanal* (Nancy, Mus. B.-A.), possibly part of the decoration of the Hôtel Morin, Paris, that Perrault described as among Blanchard's most beautiful works. The *Allegory of Charity* (U. London, Courtauld Inst. Gals; see fig.) dates from 1637 and is known in other versions (St Petersburg, Hermitage; Paris, Louvre). The *Holy Family* is another theme on which he painted a number of variations (e.g. Paris, Louvre; Chicago, IL, A. Inst.; Cherbourg, Mus. Thomas-Henry). His last important work was a *Holy Family* (untraced; engraved by Daret) inspired by Raphael's *Madonna of Loreto* (Chantilly, Mus. Condé), which he may have seen in Rome.

BIBLIOGRAPHY
A. Félibien: *Entretiens* (1666–8; rev. 1725)
C. Perrault: *Les Hommes illustrés qui ont paru en France*, ii (Paris, 1700), pp. 93–4

Jacques Blanchard: *Allegory of Charity*, oil on canvas, 1.06×0.83 m, 1637 (London, University of London, Courtauld Institute Galleries)

A.-J. Dézallier D'Argenville: *Abrégé de la vie des plus fameux peintres* (1745–52, 2/1762), iv, pp. 49–53
C. Sterling: 'Les Peintres Jean et Jacques Blanchard', *A. France*, i (1961), pp. 77–118
P. Rosenberg: 'Quelques nouveaux Blanchard', *Etudes d'art français offertes à Charles Sterling* (Paris, 1975), pp. 217–25
J. Thuillier: 'Documents sur Jacques Blanchard', *Bull. Soc. Hist. A. Fr.* (1976), pp. 81–94
R. Beresford: 'Deux inventaires de Jacques Blanchard', *Archvs A. Fr.*, n. s. 1, xxvii (1985), pp. 107–34

(2) Jean [Jean-Baptiste] **Blanchard** (*b* after 1602; *d* Paris, 5 April 1665). Brother of (1) Jacques Blanchard. He probably trained with his uncle Nicolas Bollery in Paris and joined his brother in Lyon *c.* 1623–4. They travelled to Rome together, arriving in October 1624. Jean Blanchard returned to Paris in 1634. In 1637 he was appointed Peintre du Roi and in 1656 was working on the decoration of the Louvre, though what part he played is not known. In 1663 he was received (*reçu*) as a member of the Académie Royale de Peinture et de Sculpture, Paris, but he died before submitting his *morceau de réception*.

Jean Blanchard's surviving works are few: two genre scenes, *Company of Guards in a Ruin* (Reims, Mus. St Denis) and the signed *Beggars among Ruins* (priv. col., see Sterling, p. 102), and a signed and dated religious work, *Holy Family with SS John the Baptist and Simeon* (1640; Paris, Louvre), which is in fact a copy with variants of a work by his brother. These pictures reveal an artist influenced by the work of Jacques Callot, by the Bamboccianti (whom he could have known in Rome), such as Jan Miel and Pieter van Laer, as well as by the architectural painter Viviano Codazzi. He was one of those rare French painters, among them the Le Nain brothers, Sébastien Bourdon and Jean Tassel, in whose low-life scenes realism does not exclude a vein of poetry. His contemporary reputation seems to have been as high as that of his brother, and he was entrusted with a number of important decorative schemes, including those executed *c.* 1644–5 for the great collector Louis Hesselin in his Paris hôtel and at his château of Chantemesle, near Essonnes, and *c.* 1645–7 for Pierre Viole (1600–67), President of the Paris Parlement, in Paris and at the château of Guermantes, Seine-et-Marne. None of this work survives. The inventories of his possessions taken after the death of his first wife in 1645 and after his own death indicate an artist working in all the genres from history to landscape and from allegory to still-life. The two surviving genre scenes demonstrate his interest in architecture and perspective, and he seems to have collaborated with his brother on the architecture in the latter's paintings.

Thieme–Becker
BIBLIOGRAPHY
C. Sterling: 'Les Peintres Jean et Jacques Blanchard', *A. France*, i (1961), pp. 77–118

(3) Gabriel Blanchard (*b* Paris, 26 Dec 1630; *d* Paris, 30 April 1704). Son of (1) Jacques Blanchard. He trained with his uncle Jean Blanchard and was received (*reçu*) as a member of the Académie Royale in 1663 with an *Allegory of the Birth of Louis XIV* (Versailles, Château), which shows the influence of Charles Le Brun both in the style and in its use of allegory. In 1670 he was awarded the prestigious commission to paint the May of Notre-Dame by the Paris Goldsmiths' Corporation; his altarpiece, *St Andrew Trembling with Joy at the Sight of his Torture*, survives *in situ*. He went on to have a successful official career, receiving numerous decorative commissions from the Bâtiments du Roi. The only work of this kind still extant is the Salon de Diane (1674–80) at the château of Versailles, where he collaborated with Claude Audran II and Charles de La Fosse. Blanchard's contribution was *Diana and Endymion* and the central compartment of the ceiling (*Diana Presiding over Navigation and the Hunt*) and four grisaille overdoors. In 1686 he contributed to the decoration of the high altar at Notre-Dame in Paris, painting a *Holy Family* (Tours, Mus. B.-A.) influenced by Anthony van Dyck's *Virgin with Donors* (Paris, Louvre), which had been bought by Louis XIV the year before. Two other paintings by Blanchard are known to survive: a *Purification of the Virgin* (Toulouse, Mus. Augustins) and an *Annunciation* (Lyon, St Polycarpe). From 1672 Blanchard was a professor at the Académie Royale, and he delivered a number of lectures, including the influential *Discours sur le mérite de la couleur, sur la disposition des couleurs et leurs propriétés* (1672), in which he took the side of the pro-colourist Rubénistes in the debate on the relative merits of drawing and colour. His own painting demonstrates his theoretical allegiances, combining the early influence of Le Brun with the family tradition of colourism and the taste of his generation for the art of Flanders and Holland. In 1684 he was sent by Louis XIV to acquire pictures in recently conquered French Flanders.

Thieme–Becker
BIBLIOGRAPHY
G. Brière: 'Le Replacement de peintures décoratives aux "Grands appartements" de Versailles', *Bull. Soc. Hist. A. Fr.* (1938), pp. 197–216

THIERRY BAJOU

Blanchard, Auguste (Thomas Marie), III (*b* Paris, 18 May 1819; *d* Paris, 23 May 1898). French engraver. He first studied with his father, Auguste Jean-Baptiste Marie Blanchard II (1792–1849), and then in 1836 enrolled at the Ecole des Beaux-Arts, Paris. In 1838 he took part in the competition for the Prix de Rome and won second prize, which enabled him to study in Italy. In 1840 he made his début in the Salon in Paris with an engraving of *Spartacus* after the painting by Domenichino. His first major plate was a portrait of the architect *Jean Nicolas Huyot* (1842) after the painting by Michel-Martin Drolling, in which he displayed complete mastery of the medium. Its success brought him the patronage of two major publishers, Adolphe Goupil in Paris and Ernest Gambart in London. In his later engravings he adopted the fashionable contemporary calligraphic style, although he also produced some luminous plates in the new technique of *taille douce* (Fr.: 'smooth-cut'). He also specialized in reproducing the work of Ernest Meissonier (e.g. the *Chess Players*, 1873) and Lawrence Alma-Tadema (e.g. the *Parting Kiss*, 1884).

BIBLIOGRAPHY
Bellier de La Chavignerie–Auvray; Bénézit; Thieme–Becker
J. Laran and J. Adhémar: *Inventaire du fonds français après 1800*, Paris, Bib. N., Dépt Est. cat., 3 vols (Paris, 1930–42)

ATHENA S. E. LEOUSSI

Blanchard, María (*b* Santander, 6 March 1881; *d* Paris, 15 April 1932). Spanish painter. She was marked from birth by a physical deformity, which determined her bitter destiny. In 1903 she moved to Madrid to become a painter, studying successively under the painters Emilio Sala (1850–1910), Fernando Alvarez de Sotomayor (1875–1960) and Manuel Benedito (1875–1963). She won a grant in 1909 to pursue her studies in Paris, where she attended the Académie Vitti; she was taught by Hermengildo Anglada Camarasa and later by Kees van Dongen, whose example helped free her from the constraints of her academic training in Spain. During this period she came into contact with Cubism, meeting Juan Gris and Jacques Lipchitz, both of whom influenced her later work. Until 1916, however, her work remained academic in spirit, with an emphasis on firm draughtsmanship and sombre tonalities.

On her return to Madrid in 1914, Blanchard participated in *Pintores integros*, an exhibition organized by the writer Ramón Gómez de la Serna, in which works by Lipchitz and Diego Rivera were also included. After teaching drawing for a short period in Salamanca, in 1916 she returned definitively to Paris, where in works such as *Woman with Guitar* (1917) and *Woman with Fan* (both Madrid, Mus. A. Contemp.) she enthusiastically adopted the methods of Cubism; the former painting, with its decorative arrangement of interlocking flat shapes, is close in style to works by Gris. In 1920 she returned to a more traditional figurative idiom, her colours becoming more poetic and her characters appearing in a sad, melancholy world. Although she achieved notable success in 1921 with the presentation of her picture *The Communicant* (1914) at the Salon des Indépendants in Paris, the last years of her life were submerged in great sadness and financial penury.

BIBLIOGRAPHY
W. George: *María Blanchard* (Brussels, 1927)
C. de Campo Alange: *María Blanchard* (Madrid, 1944)

PALOMA ALARCÓ CANOSA

Blanche, Jacques-Emile (*b* Auteuil, Paris, 1 Jan 1861; *d* Paris, 20 Sept 1942). French painter and writer. His father, a fashionable nerve specialist, owned a clinic where many of Blanche's sitters had been patients. As a painter he had both talent and charm, and he enjoyed a great vogue in his day. His work lacks originality and was much influenced by such contemporaries as James Tissot and John Singer Sargent. The loose brushwork and subdued colouring of his portraits are also reminiscent of Edouard Manet and English 18th-century artists, especially Thomas Gainsborough. Except for a few lessons with Henri Gervex and Ferdinand Humbert (1842–1934), he had no formal training, and many of his paintings have deteriorated because of poor technique. He worked best on a small scale, and some of his less ambitious oils and small sketches (e.g. *Head of a Young Girl*, 1885; priv. col., see *Post-Impressionism*, exh. cat., London, RA, 1979–80, p. 46) are among his most appealing works. The few pastels he executed during the 1880s and 1890s are also of high quality, as exemplified by the dramatic portrait of the poet *Georges de Porto-Riche* (?1890–95; London, F.A. Soc.).

As much at home in England as in France, Blanche visited London every year from 1884 with great success. His chief patrons there were Mrs Saxton Noble and Violet Manners, Duchess of Rutland. Among the many portraits he painted of English sitters are those of *Mrs Holland* (1885; untraced) and the *Saville Clark Sisters* (*c*. 1890; Leeds, C.A.G.), both of which have a panache worthy of Sargent. His ability to capture a sitter's personality is particularly apparent in his portrait of *Aubrey Beardsley* (1895; London, N.P.G.), for whose novel, *Under the Hill*, Blanche wrote the preface. He also painted the artist *Charles Conder* (1904; London, Tate), *James Joyce* (1934; Dublin, N.G. and 1935; London, N.P.G.), *Violet Trefusis* (1926; London, N.P.G.) and *Virginia Woolf* (1927; Providence, RI, Sch. Des., Mus. A.).

Blanche regularly spent his summers at his family house in Dieppe, playing host to many of his artist friends, including Walter Sickert and Sargent, and popularizing Dieppe as an artistic colony. There he painted his masterpiece, the large group portrait of the Norwegian landscape painter *Frits Thaulow and his Family* (1907; Paris, Mus. d'Orsay). He made a generous bequest of his own paintings, and those he had collected, to the nearby Musée des Beaux-Arts in Rouen.

Blanche's closest connections, however, were with Paris. He exhibited at the Salon from 1882 to 1889 and at the Société Nationale des Beaux-Arts from 1890. Although he quarrelled irrevocably with his patron Comte Robert de Montesquiou in 1889, he remained part of the social and cultural life of Paris. Many of his friends were painters—among them Edgar Degas, Paul Helleu and Giovanni Boldini. He painted portraits of the composer *Claude Debussy* (untraced), the poet *Anna de Noailles* (1912; Rouen, Mus. B.-A.) and the dancer *Vaclav Nijinsky* (1910; London, priv. col.), depicted life-size in Diaghilev's production *Les Orientales*. His portrait of *Marcel Proust* (1892; Paris, priv. col.), whom he had met in the salon of a fashionable hostess in 1891, depicts the author as a young dandy on the threshold of society. The two became good friends; Proust helped Blanche with his writing and corrected the proofs of his *Cahiers d'un artiste*, a series of letters about the activities of their mutual friends (under pseudonyms) during World War I. Proust also wrote the preface to *Propos de peintre*, a group of essays in which Blanche discussed many painters from Jacques-Louis David to his own time. Blanche was unhappy about Proust's remark in his introduction that the artist when young had been known as one whose 'sole ambition was to be a much sought-after man of the world'; but this criticism is born out by his own memoirs, which recount his life in society and often compromise accuracy for entertainment.

WRITINGS
Cahiers d'un artiste, 6 vols (Paris, 1914–17)
Propos de peintre, 3 vols (Paris, 1919–29)
Portraits of a Lifetime (London, 1937)
More Portraits of a Lifetime (London, 1939)

BIBLIOGRAPHY
Exposition Jacques Emile Blanche, 1861–1942 (exh. cat. by D. Halévy, Paris, Mus. Orangerie, 1943)
A. Ferrier: 'Jacques-Emile Blanche, peintre et mémorialiste', *L'Oeil*, viii (1962), pp. 58–65, 108

JANE ABDY

Blanchefort de Créquy, Charles de. *See* LESDIGUIÈRES, Ducs DE, (2).

Thomas Blanchet: *Roman Apotheosis*, oil on canvas, 2.65×2.43 m, 1658–63 (Lyon, Musée des Beaux-Arts)

Blanche of Burgundy, Countess of Savoy. *See under* SAVOY, §I, 1.

Blanche of Castile, Queen of France. *See* CAPET, (1).

Blanchet, Louis-Gabriel (*b* Paris, 1705; *d* Rome, 17 Sept 1772). French painter, active in Rome. He won second place in the Prix de Rome competition in 1727 and thereafter settled in Rome, where he enjoyed the patronage of Nicolas Vleughels, Director of the Académie de France, and the Duc de Saint-Aignan (1684–1776), who at that time was French Ambassador to the Holy See. In 1752 Blanchet painted the *Vision of Constantine* (Paris, Louvre), a copy of Giulio Romano's fresco in the Sala di Costantino in the Vatican. He was, however, principally a portrait painter. His portrait of *Tolozan de Montfort* (1756; Lyon, Mus. B.-A.) is a fine example of his elegant, rather nervous style and his distinctive use of colour. In the same year Blanchet executed a portrait of the contemporary painter *Johann Mandelberg* (1730–86; Copenhagen, Kon. Dan. Kstakad.). Other surviving works of his include *St Paul* (signed and dated 1757; Avignon, Mus. Calvet) and his full-length portrait of *P. P. Lesueur and E. Jacquier* (1772; Nantes, Mus. B.-A.). His last documented work was an allegory of *Painting and Sculpture* (1762; untraced). His work as a portrait painter has been compared with that of his Roman contemporary Pompeo Girolamo Batoni.

BIBLIOGRAPHY
Thieme–Becker
L. Gonse: *Les Chefs d'oeuvre des musées de France*, i (Paris, 1900), pp. 175, 245
I. H. Nielsen: 'Richard Wilson and Danish Artists in Rome in the 1750s', *Burl. Mag.*, cxxi (1979), pp. 439–43

Blanchet, Thomas (*b* ?Paris, 1614; *d* Lyon, 21 June 1689). French painter, draughtsman, architect, sculptor and printmaker. He trained in Paris, where he came into contact with Jacques Sarazin, who advised him to study painting rather than sculpture. He probably studied (*c.* 1637–45) with Simon Vouet, becoming familiar with perspective, the Mannerism of the School of Fontainebleau and the Baroque, then newly introduced to Paris. Around 1645 he arrived in Rome; during his stay there (which ended in 1653) he worked with artists who were members of Nicolas Poussin's circle and frequented the studios of Andrea Sacchi, Pietro da Cortona and Gianlorenzo Bernini (who thought highly of him). He executed paintings for Niccolo Guido di Bagno (1584–1663). His engravings of antique tombs and his *prospettive* were much admired. In 1654 he created a mausoleum for *René de Voyer d'Argenson*, Ambassador of France in Venice, in S Giobbe, Venice.

In 1655 Blanchet returned to Lyon, having been summoned to carry out the decoration, both painted and sculpted, of the Hôtel de Ville. In 1658 he was appointed Peintre Ordinaire to the city of Lyon, which he made his home. He was in charge of numerous important decorative projects, both ephemeral and permanent, as well as producing many paintings, on both religious and secular subjects, such as *Roman Apotheosis* (1658–63; see fig.). In 1662 he executed decorations for the *Réjouissances de la Paix*, and in 1664, ephemeral triumphal arches for the ceremonial entry into the city of Cardinal Flavio Chigi. In 1666–7 he painted the *Invincible Glory of Lyon* for the Escalier d'Honneur of the Hôtel de Ville. Between 1675 and 1684 he decorated the abbey of the Dames de St Pierre (now the Musée des Beaux-Arts); he also decorated the Palais de Roanne (now the Palais de Justice) and the Carmelite convent (destr.) in Lyon. In 1676 he was approved (*agréé*) by the Académie Royale in Paris, and was appointed professor and Peintre du Roi; in 1681 he was received (*reçu*) as a member, with a painting of *Cadmus and Minerva* (Semur-en-Auxois, Mus. Mun.) as his *morceau de réception*. In 1685 he executed the funerary monument of *Nicolas de Neufville, Maréchal de Villeroi* in a chapel of the Carmelite convent. In the course of his career he exhibited considerable eclecticism: having in Rome painted chiefly *vedute*, he exhibited in his decorative work in Lyon a notably broad, energetic and fluent style. Much of this is to be seen *in situ* in Lyon. His paintings *Alexander at the Tomb of Achilles* and the *Finding of Moses* are in the Musée du Louvre, Paris, which also has a major collection of his drawings; another collection, in the Nationalmuseum in Stockholm, was assembled by an admirer of his work in Lyon, Nicodemus Tessin the younger, architect to Charles XII of Sweden. The Kunstmuseum in Basle has a collection of engravings after Blanchet by Johann Jakob Thurneysen.

BIBLIOGRAPHY
J. von Sandrart: *Teutsche Academie* (1675–9); ed. A. R. Peltzer (1925), pp. 339–40
J. Montagu: 'Thomas Blanchet: Some Drawings in the National Museum, Stockholm', *Gaz. B.-A.*, n.s. 5, lxvi (1965), pp. 105–11
L. Galactéros-de Boissier: 'Thomas Blanchet: La Grande Salle de l'Hôtel de Ville de Lyon', *Rev. A.* [Paris], xlvii (1980), pp. 29–42
J. Montagu: 'Le Maître de *Cléobis et Biton* de la collection Corsini, le jeune Thomas Blanchet?', *Bull. Soc. Hist. A. Fr.* (1985), pp. 85–104

L. Galactéros-de Boissier: *Thomas Blanchet: Peintre, architecte, sculpteur, graveur (1614–1689)* (Paris, 1991)

LUCIE GALACTÉROS-DE BOISSIER

Blanching of paint. Cloudy discoloration of an oil paint film caused by the breakdown of the binding medium or the pigment. The effect may occur within the film or on the surface below the varnish. Blanching is the result, among other things, of the action of moisture and heat (e.g. during lining), the action of solvents during cleaning or the chemical instability of certain pigments in oil.

RUPERT FEATHERSTONE

Blanes, Juan Manuel (*b* Montevideo, 8 June 1830; *d* Pisa, 15 April 1901). Uruguayan painter and draughtsman. He came from a humble background and as a child suffered the separation of his parents, a disrupted schooling, poverty and the social upheavals of Montevideo under siege by General Manuel Oribe during Uruguay's *Guerra grande* of 1839–51. From an early age he showed talent as a draughtsman, making life drawings and oil paintings while working as a typographer for *El defensor de la independencia americana*, a daily newspaper run by the besieging army.

The work produced by Blanes from 1850 to 1860 established him as one of the outstanding portraitists in South America as well as a distinguished painter of murals on historical themes. He supported himself through commissions while living in Montevideo with his wife and children and by teaching painting at the Colegio de Humanidades in Salto after settling there in 1855. His own formal training was limited to that of local artists and to the basic guidelines established by foreign academic and naturalist portrait painters. During these years he did eight paintings of the military victories of the Argentine General Justo José de Urquiza, some paintings on religious themes for the chapel at Urquiza's palace and *Yellow Fever* (1857; untraced), in which he commemorated the epidemic that struck Montevideo.

Thanks to a study grant he was able to move with his family to Paris in 1860 and to Florence in 1861, where he was taught painting by Antonio Ciseri, who introduced him to academic disciplines of rigorous drawing, perspective, composition, local colour and tonal modelling. A group of drawings sent as his first shipment to Uruguay in 1862 was lost in a shipwreck, but when he returned to Montevideo in 1864 he was in great demand as a portraitist; the President of Paraguay, Francisco Solano López, was among his eminent sitters. Following the failure of his proposal in 1866 to the Uruguayan government to create an Escuela de Bellas Artes, he travelled to Argentina and Chile, where he treated such episodes of Latin American history as the *Review at Rancagua* (1871; Buenos Aires, Primer Mus. Hist. Argentina) and *Last Moments of General José Miguel Carrera* (1873; Montevideo, Mus. N.A. Plást.). Through such works and related portraits, including the *Thirty-three Uruguayan Patriots* (1878; Montevideo, Mus. N.A. Plást.), he confirmed his reputation in Latin America.

From 1879 to 1883 Blanes again lived in Florence, where his two sons, Juan Luis Blanes (1856–95) and Nicanor Blanes (*b* 1857), received their training as painters. On his return to Montevideo in 1883 he painted the *1885 Review* (Montevideo, Mus. Mun. Blanes) on commission from the President of Uruguay, Máximo Santos, and portraits of *General José G. Artigas* (Montevideo, Mus. Hist. A.) and *Carlota Ferreira* (Montevideo, Casa Gobierno): the latter, one of his most successful works, depicts the woman whose marriage to Nicanor did much to disrupt the relationship between father and son. In 1890 Blanes travelled to Europe and the Far East with his sons, returning to Argentina in order to undertake his most important commission, the *Rio Negro Review* (3.53×7.04 m, 1891; Buenos Aires, Mus. Hist. N.). After the death of Juan Luis in a road accident, he returned to Europe to look for Nicanor, who had disappeared after conflicts with his wife. He was unsuccessful in his search but established himself in Pisa where he remained until his death.

BIBLIOGRAPHY

E. de Salterain y Herrera: *Blanes: El hombre, su obra y su época* (Montevideo, 1950)
J. P. Argul: *Proceso de las artes plásticas del Uruguay* (Montevideo, 1975)
F. García Esteban: *El pintor Juan Manuel Blanes* (Montevideo, 1977)
Seis maestros de la pintura uruguaya (exh. cat., ed. A. Kalenberg; Buenos Aires, Mus. N. B.A., 1985), pp. 21–42

Blanes Viale, Pedro (*b* Mercedes, 19 May 1878; *d* Montevideo, 22 June 1926). Uruguayan painter. He first studied painting and drawing as a child with the Catalan painter Miguel Jaume i Bosch. As an adolescent he moved with his family to Spain, where he studied at the Real Academia de Bellas Artes de San Fernando in Madrid and frequented the workshop of Santiago Rusiñol. After studying in Paris with Benjamin Constant, he visited Italy and Mallorca, where he first developed his talents as a landscape painter before returning briefly to Uruguay in 1899. During another prolonged visit to Europe from 1902 to 1907 he enthusiastically studied the work of Pierre Puvis de Chavannes, Lucien Simon, Henri Martin, Claude Monet and James Abbott McNeill Whistler. After his return to Montevideo in 1907 he painted shimmering Impressionist-influenced landscapes such as *Palma de Mallorca* (1915; Montevideo, Mus. N. A. Plást.) and treated local rural and urban scenes in which he established himself as a remarkable colourist. He also commemorated subjects from Latin American history in works such as *Artigas Dictating to his Secretary Don José G. Monterroso* (*c.* 1920; Montevideo, Mus. Hist. N.), the equestrian portrait of *General Galarza* (1909; Durazno, Mus. Mun.) and *Artigas in el Hervidero* (Palacio Legislativo, Montevideo). He exhibited at the Paris Salons and in 1910 was awarded the Gold Medal at the *Exposición Internacional del Centenario de la Independencia Argentina* in Buenos Aires for his portrait of Galarza.

BIBLIOGRAPHY

G. Peluffo: *Historia de la pintura uruguaya* (Montevideo, 1988–9), iii, pp. 43–57
Pedro Blanes Viale (exh. cat., ed. A. Kalenberg; Buenos Aires, Mus. N. B. A., 1991)

ANGEL KALENBERG

Blanquart-Evrard, Louis-Désiré (*b* Lille, 2 Aug 1802; *d* Lille, 28 April 1872). French photographer. A chemist by training, he learnt about William Henry Fox Talbot's negative/positive calotype process in 1846 and devoted himself to perfecting the technique. An early example of his work is the picture of a *Young Woman Knitting in a Drawing Room* (before 1847; see Berger-Levrault cat., no. 25a). He did research into ways of improving darkroom techniques and processes, and he was the first to propose developing the positive print and printing on albumen paper, in 1851 (*see* PHOTOGRAPHY, §I). That same year, with his associate Hippolyte Fockedey, he founded the Imprimerie Photographique in Lille, the first large-scale photographic printers. At a time when photographic albums and books illustrated with photographs were very popular in Europe, his business was a great success. The first work to be produced was a series of 36 photographic albums, with three issues a month. He published albums of his own work as well as that of famous contemporary photographers such as Maxime Du Camp (1852–4). A founder-member of the Société Française de Photographie (1854), Blanquart-Evrard exhibited at the Great Exhibition, Crystal Palace, London, in 1851, at the Exposition Universelle in Paris in 1855 and in Brussels in 1856. Colour photography and colour phototypographic printing were his main interests and field of research from 1870 until his death. In 1871 he donated his entire collection of prints to the Musée Industriel et Commercial in Lille.

WRITINGS

Traité de photographie sur papier (Paris, 1851)

PHOTOGRAPHIC PUBLICATIONS

Album photographique d'archéologie religieuse (Paris, 1857)

BIBLIOGRAPHY

R. Lecuyer: *Histoire de la photographie* (Paris, 1945), pp. 55-69

Regards sur la photographie en France au XIXe siècle, Berger-Levrault (Paris, 1980)

I. Jammes: *Blanquart-Evrard et les origines de l'édition photographique française: Catalogue raisonné des albums photographiques édités 1851–1855* (Geneva and Paris, 1981)

PATRICIA STRATHERN

Blarenberghe, Louis-Nicolas van (*b* Lille, 1716; *d* Fontainebleau, 1794). French painter. He was the son of the Flemish battle painter Jacques-Wilhelm van Blarenberghe (*c.* 1679–1742), and he moved to Paris in 1750. In 1769 he was appointed battle painter to the War Department in Paris by his patron Etienne-François, Duc de Choiseul. The following year he was commissioned to paint a set of 14 gouache overdoors representing the capital cities of Europe for the Hôtel de la Marine, et des Affaires Etrangères (now Bibliothèque Municipale) at Versailles (13 *in situ*). In 1773 he was appointed painter to the Ministry of Marine, of which Choiseul was in charge, and he painted a number of views of the port of Brest in conjunction with his son Henri-Joseph van Blarenberghe (1741–1826). From 1779 to 1790 he was occupied on a series of 22 large gouache scenes representing sieges and battles of the reign of Louis XV (Versailles, Château).

Van Blarenberghe is best known, however, as a miniature painter. In 1767 he painted a series of six miniature views (New York, Met.) of the exterior and gardens of Choiseul's country seat at the Château de Chanteloup, near Amboise. The 'Choiseul Box' (1770; Paris, Baron Elie de Rothschild priv. col.) shows interiors of his patron's Paris residence in the Rue de Richelieu; although it only measures 80×60×37 mm, the people and pictures portrayed are clearly recognizable. These outstanding works are in gouache on vellum and mounted under crystal glass in small gold snuff-boxes. Three further boxes by van Blarenberghe are known, one with views of Mme de Pompadour's Château de Bellevue (1764; Paris, Louvre); a second, unsigned, depicts Versailles and other French royal palaces (*c.* 1765; Paris, Louvre); and a third shows the marriage of Grand Duke Paul of Russia to Princess Nathalia of Hesse-Darmstadt (1774; St Petersburg, Hermitage).

Both van Blarenberghe's son, Henri-Joseph, and his brother Henri-Désiré van Blarenberghe (1734–1812) worked in a manner almost indistinguishable from van Blarenberghe's own.

BIBLIOGRAPHY

Thieme–Becker

F. J. B. Watson: *The Choiseul Box*, Charlton Lectures on Art (London, 1963)

F. J. B. Watson and C. Dauterman: *The Wrightsman Collection Catalogue*, New York, Met. cat., 5 vols (New York, 1970)

JOSHUA DRAPKIN

Blashfield, Edwin Howland (*b* Brooklyn, NY, 15 Dec 1848; *d* New York, 12 Oct 1936). American painter. He began to study art seriously in 1867 in Paris under Léon Bonnat, with whom he remained (except between 1870 and 1874) until 1880. Blashfield's mural style was significantly influenced by Pierre Puvis de Chavannes, Jean-Paul Laurens and Paul Baudry, whose decorations he had studied in the Panthéon while in Paris. He made a trip in 1887 to England, where he became briefly associated with the Anglo-American artists' colony in Broadway, Glos, which included Edwin Austin Abbey, John Singer Sargent, Lawrence Alma-Tadema and Frederic Leighton.

Coming to prominence as a muralist at the World's Columbian Exposition (Chicago, 1893), Blashfield soon won the reputation of 'dean' of American muralists. Among his best works is the mural representing the *Evolution of Civilization* (1895–6), which decorates the dome of the main reading-room in the Library of Congress, Washington, DC. Here a group of 12 allegorical figures representing historical culture and human achievement—from 'Egypt and written records' to 'America and science'—encircles the lantern, where 'Human Understanding' sits with lifted veil, gazing upwards. Blashfield's subsequent decorations reflect the same humanist conception of art. His designs and subject-matter reflect the monumental character of the architecture they adorn. He decorated state capitols (Minnesota, Iowa, Wisconsin, South Dakota), courthouses (e.g. New York City Appellate Court and Baltimore Courthouse), churches (e.g. St Matthew the Apostle, Washington, DC) and private residences (e.g. the W. H. Vanderbilt mansion, New York; *see* VANDERBILT, WILLIAM HENRY). Blashfield was president of the National Academy of Design and of many other societies.

UNPUBLISHED SOURCES

New York, Brooklyn, Hist. Soc. [Blashfield's papers]

WRITINGS

with E. W. Blashfield: *Italian Cities* (London, 1901)

Mural Painting in America (New York and London, 1914)

BIBLIOGRAPHY

R. Cortissoz: *The Works of Edwin Howland Blashfield* (New York, 1937)

The Mural Decorations of Edwin Howland Blashfield (exh. cat., ed. L. N. Amico; Williamstown, MA, Clark A. Inst., 1978)

IRMA B. JAFFE

Blasset, Nicolas (*b* Amiens, 8 May 1600; *d* Amiens, 2 March 1659). French sculptor. He was the son of the sculptor Philippe Blasset (*b* 1565/70; *d* 1624). He became a master sculptor in 1625 and was appointed Architecte et Sculpteur Ordinaire du Roi in 1637. As well as an architect, he was a mason. He became famous when, as a result of losing a lawsuit, he was obliged to execute a statue of a *Weeping Angel* (marble, 1636; Amiens, Cathedral) for the funerary monument of *Canon Lucas*. Blasset's altars, retables and statues of the Virgin, such as *Notre-Dame de Bon Secours* (marble, *c.* 1632) and the *Assumption* (marble, 1637; both Amiens, Cathedral), manifest the spirit of the Counter-Reformation. His favourite theme, childhood, is treated with astonishing mastery and unusual sensitivity, as in the funerary monument of his eight-year-old son *Jean-Baptiste Blasset* (polychromed stone, *c.* 1647–8; Amiens, Mus. Picardie). His funerary sculpture also displays his readiness for innovation. He was among the first in France to introduce the allegory of death, in the tomb of *Jacques Mouret* (stone, 1641; destr.; drawing, Berlin, Kstbib. & Mus.). The allegory of death is also seen in the tomb of *Jean de Sachy* (marble, *c.* 1643; Amiens, Cathedral). Blasset's successful career in Picardy, his considerable productivity and his style characterize his workshop as one of the most prosperous and, from the point of view of art history, one of the most interesting of the provincial workshops of the first half of the 17th century. He was a man of original personality, whose work reflected both the centralizing force of Paris (e.g. funerary monument of *Nicolas de Lannoy*, marble, *c.* 1631; Amiens, St Remi) and that of the provincial workshops, which looked for inspiration to Rubens and Northern Baroque art; as in the monument to *Claude Pierre* (marble, 1651; Amiens, Cathedral). A series of seven *Epitaphs Devised by N. Blasset of Amiens* were engraved by Jean Lenfant *c.* 1645 after a set of drawings (untraced) by Nicolas Blasset (*see* EPITAPH, fig. 2).

Nicolas Blasset's cousin, Pierre Blasset (1610–63), became a master sculptor in 1641. In 1649 he left Amiens for Provins, where the church of St Ayoul contains the sole remaining examples of his work, a fine ensemble of panelling.

BIBLIOGRAPHY
C. Debrie: 'Pierre Blasset: Un Sculpteur natif d'Amiens qui termina sa carrière à Provins (1610–1663)', *Bull. Soc. Hist. & Archéol. Provins*, 129 (1975), pp. 39–67
——: *Nicolas Blasset: Architecte et Sculpteur ordinaire du Roi, 1600–1659* (Paris, 1985)
CHRISTINE DEBRIE

Blathwayt, William (*b* ?1649; *d* Dyrham, Glos [now in Avon], Aug 1717). English patron and collector. He first held office in 1668 as one of Sir William Temple's secretaries at The Hague. In 1683 he became Secretary-at-war and three years later Clerk of the Privy Council. Under William III he was invaluable as an experienced administrator, continuing as Secretary-at-war until 1704, when he was made Secretary-at-state and Commissioner of Trade and Plantations. In 1686 Blathwayt married Mary Wynter, the heiress of Dyrham Park, Avon, NT (where all works of art mentioned in this article remain). At some time between then and her death in 1691 he commissioned portraits of himself and his wife from Michael Dahl. In 1692 he employed the Huguenot architect Samuel Hauduroy to design a fine new west front for Dyrham, and in 1698 he commissioned a more richly articulated east front from William Talman. He also began to lay out fine new gardens, with pools and a cascade. He fitted out the house interiors with oak wainscotting by local craftsmen and purchased delftware and Flemish verdure tapestries and contemporary Dutch pictures, for example *Fisherman on a Quay* by David Teniers (ii) and *Horsemen Halting in a Wood* by Barend Gael (*c.* 1620–87). Blathwayt's taste in paintings was sound rather than adventurous and that in architecture retardataire; his real enthusiasm was for books, which he collected avidly and with scholarly discrimination.

BIBLIOGRAPHY
G. A. Jacobsen: *William Blathwayt: A Late Seventeenth-century Administrator* (New Haven, 1932)
M. Girouard: 'Dyrham Park, Gloucestershire', *Country Life*, cxxxi (15 Feb 1962), pp. 335–9; (22 Feb 1962), pp. 396–9
J. Lees-Milne: *English Country Houses: Baroque 1685–1715* (Feltham, 1970), pp. 85–94
M. Archer: 'Delft at Dyrham', *NTYb.* (1975–6), pp. 12–18
A. Mitchell: 'The Park and Garden at Dyrham', *NTYb.* (1977–8), pp. 83–108
A. E. C. Simoni: 'The Books at Dyrham Park', *Bk Colr*, xxxii (1983), pp. 171–88, 283–95
CHARLES SAUMAREZ SMITH

Blauen Vier. *See* BLUE FOUR.

Blaue Reiter [Ger.: 'Blue Rider']. German group of artists active in Munich from 1911 to 1914. The principal members were Vasily Kandinsky, Franz Marc, Gabriele Münter, Alfred Kubin, Paul Klee and August Macke. The group's aim was to express the inner desires of the different artists in a variety of forms, rather than to strive for a unified style or theme. It was the successor to the NEUE KÜNSTLERVEREINIGUNG MÜNCHEN (NKVM), founded in Munich in 1909.

1. FOUNDATION AND EXHIBITIONS, 1911–*c.* 1912. The conservatism of certain members of the NKVM led to the resignation of Kandinsky, Münter, Marc and Kubin in 1911. At the instigation of Kandinsky and Marc, the four organized the first exhibition of the editorial board of *Blaue Reiter* (see below), held from 8 December 1911 to 1 January 1912 in the Galerie Thannhauser in Munich. According to Kandinsky in 1930 ('Der blaue Reiter Rückblick', *Das Kunstblatt*, 14), the name of the Blaue Reiter had come up spontaneously in coffee-table talk with Franz and Maria Marc: 'We both liked blue, Marc liked horse and I liked rider'. However, this explanation seems too trivial to be exhaustive. From all Kandinsky's written statements it can be seen with hindsight that the claims attached to the name were considerable. It was linked to diverse traditions rooted in German history, and associated the masculine virtues of medieval knights and Christian warrior saints, including those of Russian Orthodox Christianity, with the group's romantic idea that the essence of things can be revealed to mankind through works of art. The horse was used as a subject by Franz Marc in many works, for example *Blue Horse 1* (1911; Munich, Lenbachhaus; see fig.), and in Kandinsky's woodcut of St George for the cover of the almanac *Blaue Reiter* of 1912.

Blaue Reiter painting by Franz Marc: *Blue Horse 1*, oil on canvas, 1120×845 mm, 1911 (Munich, Städtische Galerie im Lenbachhaus)

Kandinsky prefaced the catalogue list of the group's first show with the following text: 'In this small exhibition we do not seek to propagate a precise or special form, but aim to show in the diversity of the forms represented how the inner desire of artists shapes itself in manifold ways'. In keeping with this stance, the exhibition presented a heterogeneous picture. It contained 43 works by 14 artists, including Marc, Kandinsky, David Burlyuk, Vladimir Burlyuk, Robert Delaunay and the recently dead Henri Rousseau. At Marc's request August Macke, Heinrich Campendonk and Jean Bloé Niestlé (1884–1942) took part, while at Kandinsky's instigation his companion Gabriele Münter and his former pupil Elisabeth Epstein (1879–1956) showed works. Albert Bloch (1882–1961) was also invited by Kandinsky, while two works by his dead friend Eugen von Kahler (1882–1911) and, finally, pictorial visions by the composer Arnold Schoenberg were displayed.

The pluralism proclaimed at this exhibition attracted unexpectedly strong support from artists. Some, such as Hans Arp, who visited Munich in 1912, and Paul Klee, developed strong personal contacts with the group. Many others contributed to a second exhibition, devoted exclusively to graphic works. This show of 315 works by 31 artists was held from February to April 1912 in the art showroom of Hans Goltz (1873–1927). The best-known names included Klee, Kubin, Georges Braque and Pablo Picasso, as well as Emil Nolde, Max Pechstein, Ernst Ludwig Kirchner and Erich Heckel of Die Brücke. Klee, in particular, shared the concern of his Blaue Reiter

colleagues for the spiritual in art, emphasizing the qualities of popular and primitive art, as well as that produced by the mentally ill and children.

Among the public and critics the two exhibitions produced an almost entirely negative response. As with the earlier exhibitions of the NKVM, people felt they were being mocked and confused. Where new forms of expression appropriate to new subject-matter were being revealed, the public and critics saw only incompetence and the scurrilous outpourings of sick minds. Despite this opposition, the exhibition went on tour, first to the Gereonsclub in Cologne, and in March 1912 Herwarth Walden opened his Sturm-Galerie in Berlin with this collection. Exhibitions in Bremen, Hagen and Frankfurt am Main followed. Somewhat later a different selection of the works was to be seen at the exhibition of the Sonderbund in Cologne in 1912, and the following year, again in Berlin, they appeared in Herwarth Walden's Ersten Deutschen Herbstsalon, and even, on his initiative, in Sweden in 1914.

2. THE 'BLAUE REITER' ALMANAC AND LATER DE-VELOPMENTS, *c.* 1912–14. In order to explain to the public the difference between the intentions and practice of 19th-century painting and the entirely different expressive means of the new generation of artists, an almanac was produced in May 1912 by Piper-Verlag of Munich. Entitled *Der Blaue Reiter* and edited by Kandinsky and Marc, it was originally intended to be a periodical, but went through only one edition, which was reprinted in 1914. The almanac contained essays written exclusively by artists on subjects related to the fine arts. The carefully produced volume proved in retrospect to be the most significant programmatic writing on art of the 20th century. Kandinsky and Marc set out in individual essays their conceptions of the subject-matter of art and its formal expression. They reproduced works of art of very diverse styles, epochs and cultures, such as medieval book illustrations, religious paintings on glass, child art, and carvings and other objects from non-European cultures, juxtaposed with illustrations of their own works (e.g. Marc's *The Steer*, 1911; New York, Guggenheim). In this way they reminded the reader that the endeavour to achieve a particular means of expression had always determined artistic form, not only for the artists of the Blaue Reiter. Their principal aim, however, was to explain the new subject-matters and means of expression used by the artists of their own group. On this point Kandinsky wrote: 'None of us seeks to reproduce nature directly … We are seeking to give artistic form to inner nature, i.e. spiritual experience'. He then went on to stress that as the artists' souls were different, so their motifs varied. However, they had in common the quality of bringing into their pictures only those details of nature that served 'the inner purpose of the particular work'. In 1912 Kandinsky also expounded his ideas in *Über das Geistige in der Kunst*.

Meanwhile, Alexei Jawlensky and Marianne Werefkin left the NKVM in 1912 and began contributing works to Blaue Reiter exhibitions. They had initially remained loyal to the circle in the NKVM headed by Adolph Erbslöh (1881–1947). However, after the publication of the group's *Das neue Bild*, which also came out in 1912 as a kind of counterblast to the almanac, disagreements within the NKVM sealed its fate. Its proposed fourth exhibition failed to materialize, and with Werefkin and Jawlensky, Wladimir von Bechtejeff (1878–1971) also announced his resignation. Jawlensky's work, in particular, exemplified the Blaue Reiter's use of form and colour to represent the artist's inner state as well as the subject depicted (e.g. *Head of a Woman*, 1912; Berlin, Alte N.G.).

As compared to other associations of artists at the beginning of the 20th century, the Blaue Reiter was marked by a sense of a spiritual mission. However, the painters of the Blaue Reiter were indebted to such other avant-garde movements as Futurism, Fauvism and Cubism; for example, the Futurist depiction of sequences of movement influenced Macke and Marc. Contemporary French developments, in particular the Orphism of Delaunay, had a decisive influence on Klee, Marc and Macke, who visited him in Paris in 1912. The French art that Klee saw was reflected in his graphic art (e.g. *Garden of Passion*, etching, 1913; e.g. New York, MOMA). Delaunay's depiction of interpenetration of forms influenced such works as Marc's *The Tiger* (1912; Munich, Lenbachhaus; for illustration *see* MARC, FRANZ). Such influences were not merely stylistic but helped to express in their art the deep convictions of Kandinsky's analytical spirituality and Marc's pantheistic philosophy.

The desire to represent inner experience was exemplified by Kandinsky's gradual advance towards abstraction. He first studied the laws inherent in forms and colours through contemplation of nature before the Blaue Reiter period. Finally he produced painted compositions without any link to objective reality that consisted of a pure play of colours and forms analogous to music. This was Kandinsky's highest goal, achieved in such works as *Composition VII* (1913; Moscow, Tret'yakov Gal.; *see* KANDINSKY, VASILY, fig. 4). Marc represented animals, whom he saw as beings less distorted by culture than man: he depicted them as embedded in surrounding nature, even producing compositions in which the subject was broken up almost entirely into prismatic structures. He thus attempted to create images whereby man too might again feel his unity with the cosmos. His thesis in the almanac, 'that art is concerned with the deepest things, that renewal cannot be a formal matter but a rebirth of thought', clearly expresses his concerns. With this conception Marc took his place in the tradition of mysticism, pursuing no lesser goal than to produce through his work 'symbols which belong on the altars of the coming intellectual religion, behind which the technical producer vanishes'. His final work before the outbreak of World War I consisted of almost entirely abstract paintings such as *Playing Forms* (1914; Essen, Mus. Flkwang).

It goes without saying that such aims and works made heavy demands on the beholder. However, the strength of the Blaue Reiter artists remained their openness to different forms of communication. They realized that the widespread need for spiritual renewal in a materialistic age sought expression in the most diverse ways. The group saw themselves as developing a spiritual principle that would draw together these various forces to give them the greatest possible impact on the outer world. Admittedly the reaction of the public did not meet the hopes and expectations of Kandinsky and Marc. In the preface to the second edition of the almanac a hint of resignation can be discerned. Kandinsky wrote: 'One of our aims—in my eyes one of the main ones—has hardly been attained at all. It was to show, by examples, by practical juxtaposition and by theoretical demonstration, that the question of form in art is secondary, that the question in art is predominantly one of content . . . Perhaps the time is not yet ripe for 'hearing' and 'seeing' in this sense'. Moreover, Marc quoted a dictum of Theodor Däubler: 'Everything in this world can only be a beginning'.

The outbreak of World War I put an end to the common endeavours of the Blaue Reiter. Kandinsky had to leave Germany and returned to Russia via Switzerland. Macke was killed in the Champagne region in the first weeks of the war. Marc, whose search for 'pure form' in his sketchbook from the battlefield had also led to abstraction, died at Verdun in 1916. Klee served in the rear of the Front, Münter lived in Sweden, and only Kubin stayed above the mêlée in his refuge at Zwickledt near Wernstein am Inn. Although the Blaue Reiter did not survive World War I, the BLUE FOUR group was formed in 1924 as its successor by Kandinsky, Jawlensky, Klee and Lyonel Feininger.

WRITINGS
V. Kandinsky: *Über das Geistige in der Kunst: Insbesondere in der Malerei* (Munich, 1912)
V. Kandinsky and F. Marc, eds: *Der Blaue Reiter Almanach* (Munich, 1912, rev. 1965)

BIBLIOGRAPHY
L. G. Buchheim: *Der Blaue Reiter und die Neue Künstlervereinigung München* (Feldafing, 1959)
O. Neigemont: *Der Blaue Reiter* (Munich and Milan, 1966)
Il Cavaliere Azzurro/Der Blaue Reiter (exh. cat. by L. Carluccio and L. Mallé, Turin, Gal. Civ. A. Mod., 1971)
R. Gollek: *Der Blaue Reiter im Lenbachhaus München: Katalog der Sammlung in der Städtischen Galerie* (Munich, 1974, rev. 3/1985)
A. Cavallaro: *Il Cavaliere Azzurro e l'orfismo* (Milan, 1976)
P. Vogt: *Der Blaue Reiter* (Cologne, 1977)
A. Hüneke, ed.: *Der Blaue Reiter: Dokumente einer geistigen Bewegung* (Leipzig, 1986)
Der Blaue Reiter (exh. cat., ed. H. C. von Tavel; Berne, Kstmus., 1986–7)
M. M. Moeller: *Der Blaue Reiter* (Cologne, 1987)
R. Gollek: *Brennpunkt der Moderne: Der Blaue Reiter in München* (Munich, 1989)
A. Zweite, ed.: *The Blue Rider in the Lenbachhaus, Munich* (Munich, 1989, Ger. trans., 1991) [with commentaries by A. Hoberg]

ROSEL GOLLEK

Blavatsky, Vladimir (Dmitriyevich) (*b* St Petersburg, 12 Sept 1899; *d* Moscow, 10 Nov 1980). Russian archaeologist and art historian. He graduated from the social sciences department at Moscow University in 1923 and joined the staff of, first, the Pushkin Museum of Fine Arts and then the State Academy of Art Sciences (later the Research Institute for the Theory and History of Fine Art), taking part in several archaeological expeditions. From 1925 to 1929 he was a postgraduate student at the Russian Association of Social Sciences Research Institutes and took part in excavations of Ol'viya under the direction of Boris Farmakovsky. In the 1930s he was on the staff of the State Academy for the History of Material Culture, teaching and conducting excavations at the ancient cities of Charaxes, Panticapaeum (now Kerch) and Phanagoreia. His general works on Classical architecture and Greek sculpture were published in this period. In 1943 he defended his doctoral thesis on the techniques of Classical sculpture and became a professor of archaeology at Moscow University. In 1944 he was appointed director of the Classical archaeology section of the Institute for the History of Material Culture (later the Institute of Archaeology) and a corresponding member of the Academy of Architecture. From the late 1940s to the 1970s he directed numerous archaeological excavations of Classical monuments at Panticapaeum, Sindica and Apollonia (in Albania). He also directed underwater research and published works on the Classical archaeology and art of the northern Black Sea region and Greek vase painting.

WRITINGS
Arkhitektura drevnego Rima [The architecture of ancient Rome] (Moscow, 1938)
Arkhitektura antichnogo mira [The architecture of the Classical world] (Moscow, 1939)
Grecheskaya skul'ptura [Greek sculpture] (Moscow, 1939)
Iskusstvo Severnogo Prichernomor'ya antichnoy epokhi [The art of the northern Black Sea region during the Classical era] (Moscow, 1947)
Istoriya antichnoy raspisnoy keramiki [The history of Classical painted ceramics] (Moscow, 1953)
Antichnaya arkheologiya Severnogo Prichernomor'ya [The Classical archaeology of the northern Black Sea region] (Moscow, 1961)
Pantikapey: Ocherki istori stolitsy Bospora [Panticapaeum: essays on the history of the capital of Bosporus] (Moscow, 1964)

BIBLIOGRAPHY
A. Boltunova, ed.: *Kul'tura antichnogo mira* [The culture of the Classical world] (Moscow, 1966)
M. Kobylina, ed.: *Istoriya i kul'tura antichnogo mira* [The history and culture of the Classical world] (Moscow, 1976)
'Pamyati Vladimira Dmitriyevicha Blavatskogo' [Recollections of Vladimir Dmitriyevich Blavatsky], *Sovet. Arkheol.*, iv (1981), pp. 296–8

V. YA. PETRUKHIN

Blažíček, Oldřich Jakub (*b* Prague, 8 Nov 1914; *d* Munich, 28 June 1985). Czech art historian. The son of the painter Oldřich Blažíček (1887–1953), he was a student of the art historian Antonín Matějček (1889–1950) and his successor designate at the university in Prague. He was associate professor at Charles University 1947–51, subsequently working at the Institute for Protection of Monuments in Prague and from 1966 a senior member of staff at the National Gallery in Prague.

Throughout his life his studies were devoted to Baroque art, above all sculpture, as one of the scholars relating Bohemian Baroque to an historical period of religious and social oppression, often with modern political allusions. Initially he built up a firm base of information data in *Pražská plastika raného rokoka, Rokoko a konec baroku v Čechách* and *Sochařství baroku v Čechách*. On this data he based his understanding of Baroque in Bohemia as an organic expression reflecting the events that took place in the country, as outlined in his book *Baroque Art in Bohemia*. He illustrated his concept by preparing exhibitions of Bohemian Baroque art that were shown throughout Europe. Among his many writings the monograph on *Ferdinand Brokof* is outstanding. The exhibitions Blažíček organized in the National Gallery in Prague deepened national understanding of Bohemian Baroque sculpture, and through him Bohemia's Baroque art was ideologically rehabilitated in Czechoslovakia and popularized abroad.

WRITINGS
Pražská plastika raného rokoka [Prague sculptures of the early Rococo] (Prague, 1946)

Rokoko a konec baroku v Čechách [Rococo and the end of Baroque in Bohemia] (Prague, 1948)
Sochařství baroku v Čechách [Baroque sculpture in Bohemia] (Prague, 1958)
Baroque Art in Bohemia (London, 1968)
Ferdinand Brokof, xlvii of České Dějiny (Prague, 1976); *R* lxiv of České Dějiny (Prague, 1986)

BIBLIOGRAPHY
I. Kořán: 'Šedesát let O. J. Blažíčka' [Sixty years of O. J. Blažíček], *Umění*, xxiii (1975), pp. 180–82
——: 'Oldřich J. Blažíček pět let po šedesátce' [Oldřich J. Blažíček five years after his 60th birthday], *Umění*, xxvii (1979), pp. 534–7
M. Horyna: 'Významné životní jubileum Oldřicha J. Blažíčka' [Important anniversary of Oldřich J. Blažíček], *Umění*, xxxiii (1985), p. 83
I. Kořán: 'In memoriam Oldřicha J. Blažíčka', *Umění*, xxxiv (1986), pp. 543–4

IVO KOŘÁN

Blázquez, Casiano Alguacil. *See* ALGUACIL BLÁZQUEZ, CASIANO.

Blechen, Karl [Carl] (*b* Cottbus, 29 July 1798; *d* Berlin, 23 July 1840). German painter.

1. EARLY LIFE AND WORK. Despite early artistic inclinations, he trained as a bank clerk and then worked as one from 1814 to 1822 before studying at the Akademie der Künste in Berlin. Here Heinrich Anton Dähling (1773–1850) sharpened his interest in Romantic and poetic subjects, while Peter Ludwig Lütke (1759–1831) encouraged his eye for the potential expressiveness of observed language. Blechen was also strongly influenced by the paintings of Caspar David Friedrich, which he was able to study in Berlin at this time. In 1823 he travelled to Dresden, where he visited Johann Christian Clausen Dahl and probably also met Friedrich, who shared the same house. Here Dahl impressed Blechen with his impulsive style of oil sketching. Studies (Berlin, Alte N.G.) of Meissen, especially of the cathedral, and of the dramatic landscape of the surrounding parts of Saxony reveal the early development of Blechen's tendency to perceive landscape and architecture, especially ruins, as allegories of his own usually rather depressed moods. This passionately subjective use of imagery distinguishes Blechen from Friedrich, whose work shows a far more level-headed deployment of landscape symbols as religious allegory.

Blechen was also strongly attracted to Berlin theatre life, and in 1824, when he finished his studies at the Akademie, Karl Friedrich Schinkel helped him to obtain work as a designer and painter of stage sets at the Königstadt Theatre, a post he retained until 1827. Approximately 90 sketches for set designs from this period survive (Berlin, Alte N.G.). In 1824 Blechen exhibited paintings at the Akademie and in 1826 was accepted into the Verein Berliner Künstler. In his *Ruin of a Gothic Church* (1826; Dresden, Gemäldegal. Neue Meister; see fig. 1) the sleeping pilgrim in the foreground indicates that Blechen still shared Friedrich's view of the visible world as religious allegory. Connected motifs, such as ruins and hermits, are also to be found in 3 etchings (1823–6) and 14 lithographs (1825–30).

In 1827 Blechen resigned from his post at the theatre and embarked on a career as an independent artist in Berlin. The almost demonic melancholy evinced in his pictures ensured that his work was noticed but also often criticized for gratuitous indulgence in a sense of dread. More significant, however, in view of his subsequent development, is his interest in composition as pure landscape, as revealed in his use of a title describing the precise view shown in what was ostensibly a history painting of patriotic implications: *View from the Müggelberge Looking South towards Köpenick; Accessories: The Semnones Preparing to Repel the Onrush of the Romans* (1828; ex-Staatl. Museen, N.G., Berlin, destr. 1945, see Heider, 1970, p. 44). In the summer of 1828 Blechen travelled to the Baltic and to Rügen, his *Stormy Sea with Lighthouse* (1828; Hamburg, Ksthalle) anticipating his next destination in its central image of a motif taken from scenes of Genoa. At the end of September Blechen left Germany and travelled south, staying away for 13 months in Rome, Naples and various cities in central Italy.

2. LATER WORK. Blechen's Italian journey was the central event of his brief creative life, though the frequent claim that it changed the very basis of his artistic vision fails to take account of the compulsive and personal traits seen in his work both before and afterwards. It is also significant that he only seems to have paid real attention to some aspects of the Italian scene: the famous buildings of Italy, for example, barely occupied him, and, where he did depict them, their situation in the landscape is more important than the architecture itself. The south of Italy—especially Capri, the Gulf of Salerno and the area around Amalfi—made the strongest impression on him: for here the contrasts of dazzling, harsh light and deep shadow stimulated him and appealed to his inclination to make the experience of a painted landscape almost physically real to the viewer as if he too were a traveller coming suddenly upon such a scene. While travelling, Blechen made sketches rather than paintings, and during his journey his style of drawing evolved, moving from the linear manner common at that period in Germany to the use of blunter, often violent strokes. Increasingly he restricted himself to brush and watercolour, using the unpainted white of the paper to convey the harshness of the light.

A good many of the works painted after Blechen's return to Berlin in late 1829 were based on Italian motifs he had sketched on the spot. It is difficult to establish an exact chronology of these paintings as Blechen did not date his work, but exhibitions provide some clues. In 1830 he showed *Cività Castellana* and the lyrical *Shepherds at Narni* (both ex-Staatl. Museen, N.G., Berlin, destr. 1945, see Heider, 1970, pp. 69–70) and in 1832 *Afternoon in Capri* (Vienna, Neue Gal. Stallburg) and *Villa d'Este* (Berlin, Alte N.G.). In this last, the architecture prompted him to add imaginary figures in 16th-century costume, just as the shepherds were added to the Narni scene. At the Berlin Akademie where, in 1831, Blechen succeeded Lütke as Professor of Landscape Painting, such works inspired many students to imitation. A further imaginative elaboration on an architectural setting is to be seen in the two views of 1834 showing the interior of the *Palm House* on the Pfaueninsel near Potsdam, which were painted for King Frederick William III of Prussia (Potsdam, Schloss Sanssouci). While reproducing precisely the interior and the vegetation, and even evoking the sultry atmosphere, Blechen attempted to increase the exotic charm of the

1. Karl Blechen: *Ruin of a Gothic Church*, oil on canvas, 1.30×0.97 m, 1826 (Dresden, Gemäldegalerie Neue Meister)

image by adding figures in Indian costume. A second version of his *Ruin of a Gothic Church* (lost 1944) has a decidedly visionary tone: a pilgrim discovers that the floor of the church he has just entered has turned into a lake, making it impossible to continue his journey.

In the summer of 1835 Blechen travelled to Paris with the art dealer Louis Sachse (1798–1877), who was attempting to promote French art in Berlin. Blechen was compared at this time to contemporary French artists in the sureness of his technique and the clarity of content in his paintings. Blechen himself particularly admired Théodore Gudin and made a copy (Schweinfurt, Samml. Schäfer) of one of his seascapes. In 1836 the first signs of Blechen's mental illness became apparent, and this forced him to resign from his teaching post at the Akademie. His progressive deterioration is seen in the late drawings in increasing effusiveness and a shorthand simplification of the strokes and in the paintings of this period in the use of harsher colours and increasingly abstract forms. The oddities of this final phase, however, were anticipated in aspects of earlier work: in the portrait drawings from 1831 (Berlin, Berlin Mus.), for example, the artist's own agitation is projected on to the faces of his sitters, and in his most successful painting, *Girls Bathing* (1835; Berlin, Neue N.G.), of which there are four large and five small versions, an apparently idyllic scene is disturbed by some sudden

2. Karl Blechen: *Gulf of La Spezia*, oil on canvas, 0.93×1.43 m, *c*. 1830 (Berlin, Schloss Charlottenburg)

but unspecified shock. In 1837 Blechen was admitted to a mental institution and is recorded as producing his last drawing on 7 March 1838. Earlier works, however, were shown at the Berlin Akademie exhibitions of both 1838 and 1839, including the *Gulf of La Spezia* (*c*. 1830; Berlin, Schloss Charlottenburg; see fig. 2), a painting believed to have been one of the first of his great Italian views.

3. REPUTATION. At the time of his death in 1840, Blechen had received such recognition that almost all of his unsold work was bought by the State and some of it given to the Akademie for use as study material, his oil sketches being especially admired and copied by students almost as if they were finished works. (Many of these copies are now passed off as originals in various collections.) It is, in fact, often unclear whether particular studies by Blechen were made as sketches from nature or as subsequent preparatory work for specific paintings. The further difficulty of defining what, in Blechen's view, constituted a finished work has increased misunderstanding of his role in the development of 19th-century approaches to observing and recording nature. Although Blechen has frequently been regarded as a forerunner of Impressionism, this is a misleading view of his achievement, as it fails to recognize the overriding symbolic significance of his subjects—both in terms of traditional religious themes and as a more personal expression of emotions and states of mind.

BIBLIOGRAPHY

Marie von Parmentier, *Karl Blechen, Adolf Schrödter und August Bromeis* (exh. cat., Berlin, N.G., 1881)

L. von Donop: *Der Landschaftsmaler Carl Blechen mit Benutzung der Aufzeichnungen Theodor Fontanes* (Berlin, 1906)

G. J. Kern: *Karl Blechen: Sein Leben und seine Werke* (Berlin, 1911)

P. O. Rave: *Karl Blechen: Leben, Würdigungen, Werk* (Berlin, 1940)

A. Paul-Pescatore: *Karl Blechen: 60 Bilder* (Königsberg, 1944)

Daniel Chodowiecki, Johann Gottfried Schadow, Karl Blechen (exh. cat., Berlin, Akad. Kst. DDR, 1960)

Der Maler Carl Blechen, 1798–1840 (exh. cat., Cottbus, Bezirksmus, 1963)

G. Heider: *Carl Blechen* (Leipzig, 1970)

Karl Blechen (exh. cat., ed. L. Brauner; E. Berlin, N.G., 1973)

H. Börsch-Supan: *Die Werke Carl Blechens im Schinkel-Pavillon*, Aus Berliner Schlössern: Kleine Schriften, iv (Berlin, 1978)

G. Heider: *Carl Blechen: Italienische Skizzen* (Leipzig, 1979)

H. Börsch-Supan: 'Kopien nach Carl Blechen: Überlegungen zur Revision seines Oeuvrekataloges', *Festschrift für Martin Sperlich* (Tübingen, 1980), pp. 245–58

J. Sarn: 'Angst in der Natur', *Z. Kstgesch.*, x/iii (1980), pp. 181–95

Carl Blechen: Zwischen Romantik und Realismus (exh. cat., Berlin, Neue N.G., 1990)

HELMUT BÖRSCH-SUPAN

Bleed (i). Term used in printing to describe that part of an image that extends beyond the intended edge or trimline of a page. An illustration that is 'bled-off' has no margin.

Bleed (ii). Seeping and spreading of one colour into another. Bleeding occurs with watercolour washes, when two colours are applied next to each other. In other forms of painting, bleeding can take place when an under layer of paint seeps through to the upper surface. It is in order to prevent this phenomenon that pigments used in oil painting must be insoluble in oil.

Blegen, Carl (William) (*b* Minneapolis, 27 Jan 1887; *d* Athens, 24 Aug 1971). American archaeologist. From 1911 to 1927 he held posts at the American School of Classical Studies, Athens; from 1927 onwards he was Professor of Classical Archaeology at the University of Cincinnati. Early surveys and soundings around Corinth led to excavations at Korakou (1915–6), which established a full Bronze Age sequence for the Greek mainland, a sequence then confirmed at Zygouries (1921–2). Excavations at Nemea (1924–6) and Acrocorinth (1926) dealt mainly with Classical periods. But at Prosymna in the Argolid (1925–8) Blegen exposed a large Middle and Late Helladic cemetery. Further study of burial customs and of the distribution of prehistoric sites convinced him that Greek-speakers entered Greece *c.* 1900 BC, a view long influential but now doubted. His excavations at Troy (1932–8) greatly refined previous findings by Heinrich Schliemann and Wilhelm Dörpfeld and suggested that Troy VIIa, not VI, was destroyed in the Trojan War (*see* TROY). Study of the Mycenaean pottery here and elsewhere helped him, with A. J. B. Wace, to overturn (1939) Sir Arthur Evans's theory of a Cretan colonization of the mainland. During World War II he lived in Washington, DC (1942–5), and then became US cultural attaché to Athens (1945–6). His excavations at Pylos (1939, 1952–64) yielded a full picture of a late 13th-century BC Mycenaean palace, fine but fragmentary frescoes and Linear B tablets, which helped confirm Michael Ventris's simultaneous decipherment. His meticulous excavations, wide knowledge and cautious judgements laid much of the basis for the study of Greek prehistory.

WRITINGS

with A. J. B. Wace: 'Pre-Mycenaean Pottery of the Mainland', *Annu. Brit. Sch. Athens*, xxii (1916–8), pp. 175–89

Korakou: A Prehistoric Settlement near Corinth (Boston and New York, 1921)

Zygouries: A Prehistoric Settlement in the Valley of Cleonae (Cambridge, MA, 1928)

Acrocorinth: Excavations in 1926 (1930), III/i of *Corinth* (Cambridge, MA and Princeton, NJ, 1929–)

Prosymna: The Helladic Settlement Preceding the Argive Heraeum, 2 vols (Cambridge, 1937)

Troy: Excavations Conducted by the University of Cincinnati, 1932–1938, 4 vols (Princeton, NJ, 1950–58)

The Palace of Nestor at Pylos in Western Messenia, 3 vols (Princeton, NJ, 1966–73)

BIBLIOGRAPHY

Obituary, *Gnomon*, xlv (1973), pp. 222–4; *The Times* (26 Aug 1971)

DONALD F. EASTON

Blender. Flared brush, often of badger hair, used dry, with a vertical stippling action, to blend two areas of freshly applied oil paint.

RUPERT FEATHERSTONE

Blenheim Palace. English country house near Woodstock, Oxon, designed by John Vanbrugh for JOHN CHURCHILL, 1st Duke of Marlborough. It was begun in 1705 and completed *c.* 1725. The gardens, initially laid out by Vanbrugh and Henry Wise, were largely redesigned in 1764–74 by 'Capability' Brown. Blenheim Palace is regarded as one of the finest examples of English Baroque architecture. It was a gift to the Duke from a grateful Crown and nation to commemorate his victory in 1704 over the French and Bavarians at Blenheim (now Blindheim) during the War of the Spanish Succession (1701–14). The intention was to create a public monument symbolizing the glory of Britain and a palace fit for a hero, rather than a building on a domestic scale. This is reflected in Vanbrugh's dramatic and monumental design, inspired by both English and French architecture, which developed the style he had begun to formulate in his earlier work at Castle Howard, N. Yorks. In both undertakings he was assisted by NICHOLAS HAWKSMOOR.

The plan of Blenheim Palace consists of a main block approached on the north by a great forecourt flanked by two huge wings, the kitchen and stable courts, which are linked to the main block by colonnades (see fig.). The façade (total width *c.* 146 m) and the courtyard (depth *c.* 90 m) create an impressively framed approach to the main block. The central entrance is a massive portico surmounted by a pediment. The vast scale of the exterior is balanced by prominent towers or belvederes at the four corners of the main building, each with sculptured finials (h. 9 m) carved in 1708–16 by Grinling Gibbons. They are echoed by similar towers at the sides of the kitchen and stable courts. The elaborate roof-line is further embellished by gilded and painted statues of men and beasts. Giant Corinthian pilasters and Doric half columns decorate the walls, with free-standing loggias at the corners. Considerable variety was achieved through the use of contrasting recessions and projections: the whole has been described as a piece of sculpture (for further discussion and illustration of main front *see* VANBRUGH, JOHN, and fig. 2).

The palace is entered through a clerestoried Great Hall (h. *c.* 20 m), from where the staircase leads to the upper floors. Beyond the Hall is the Saloon (h. *c.* 12 m), with a musicians' gallery above. To either side of it extend symmetrical suites of state apartments consisting of antechamber, drawing-room and bed-chamber; together with the Saloon, these occupy the entire south front. Along the west front of the house runs the Long Gallery (intended as a picture gallery but completed as a library); to the east were the family apartments, designed on a more domestic scale. The interior decoration and fittings were lavishly executed. Door- and window-frames are of marble, with architectural carvings by Gibbons in an uncharacteristically restrained classical style appropriate to the great proportions of the rooms. The ceiling of the Great Hall was painted with an allegory of the Duke presenting a plan of the Battle of Blenheim to Britannia (1716) by James Thornhill in his continental Baroque style. The walls and ceiling of the Saloon were decorated (*c.* 1720) by Louis Laguerre, the former painted as an illusionistic composition of a colonnade open to the sky, from behind which figures representing the four continents look into the room. In the Gallery and Hall hung works by Titian, Rubens and Raphael, while the state suites were hung with Brussels tapestries, including a set of ten 'Victories' depicting the Duke's campaigns (*in situ*). There are said to be 187 rooms in the main building. The relationship of the building to the landscape was a crucial part of the design. Vanbrugh and HENRY WISE created formal gardens and turned the surrounding forest into parkland to provide a more appropriate frame for the house; Vanbrugh also sought (unsuccessfully) to retain the nearby medieval ruins

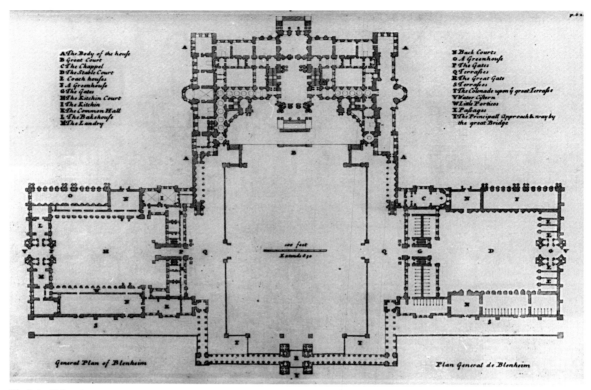

Blenheim Palace, by John Vanbrugh, 1705–24; plan from Colen Campbell: *Vitruvius Britannicus*, i (1715), pl. 62

of Woodstock Manor. His triple-spanned Grand Bridge in front of the palace originally crossed three canals but now spans the lake created by 'Capability' Brown when he redesigned the landscaping (*see* GARDEN, fig. 4).

Blenheim Palace represents the culmination of the English Baroque, but it was regarded as being out of date even before it was finally completed. It remains the finest expression of Vanbrugh's theatrical style, combining dramatic quality and a sense of mass and volume with the more intricate details and complex skyline that heralded a more picturesque and Romantic approach. Among the many influences that inspired him were English medieval fortifications (he originally wished the building to be called Blenheim Castle), the classical rhythms of Wren and the exuberance of the great Italian and French Baroque palaces. The building was first projected to cost around £100,000, but at least three times that amount was spent during the main building phase (1705–12), with 1500 workmen employed at one time. Work was halted in 1712 when the Marlboroughs lost favour with Queen Anne and went into exile. After the accession of George I, construction resumed (1716), but Vanbrugh resigned almost immediately after disputes with the Duchess, who had always wanted Wren as the architect and a comfortable home rather than a monument. She employed the cabinetmaker James Moore (1670–1726) to advise her, and in 1722, after the death of the Duke, recalled Hawksmoor (who had departed with Vanbrugh) to complete the work. When Vanbrugh attempted to visit the building in 1725, the Duchess refused him entrance. Later modifications were made by William Chambers, who redecorated the palace in the 1760s and 1770s.

BIBLIOGRAPHY

G. Scharf: *Catalogue Raisonné; or a List of the Pictures in Blenheim Palace* (London, 1862)

H. A. Tipping and C. Hussey: *The Work of Sir John Vanbrugh and his School*, iv/2 of *English Homes* (London, 1928)

D. Green: *Blenheim Palace* (London, 1951)

N. Pevsner and J. Sherwood: *Oxfordshire*, Bldgs England (Harmondsworth, 1974)

M. Fowler: *Blenheim: Biography of a Palace* (Harmondsworth, 1991)

CAROLA HICKS

Blérot, Ernest (*b* Brussels, 21 Feb 1870; *d* Brussels, 19 Jan 1957). Belgian architect and designer. He studied architecture at the Ecole Saint-Luc in Brussels and during his very brief career as a practising architect (1899–1903) he became one of the most interesting protagonists of the Art Nouveau style in Brussels. His work included a total of 17 houses in Saint-Gilles and 11 houses in Saint-Boniface, Ixelles, Brussels, where he acted as both architect and builder and sold the houses on completion. To suit the individual tastes of the purchasers he created a different façade for each house based on virtually identical plans, and these buildings remain as examples of Art Nouveau ensembles that are unique in their architectural variety. During the same period he built some 15 houses in the new districts to the south of Brussels, for which he also designed some remarkable wrought ironwork. From 1902 to 1908 he concentrated on building his own house (destr. 1962; see exh. cat., p. 98), one of the most interesting corner buildings in Brussels whose decorative detail showed a desire to go beyond Art Nouveau. However, the difficulty of finding a transition between Art Nouveau and a different style led Blérot to abandon his professional practice almost entirely. For several years he devoted himself to rebuilding the Elzenwalle château near Ypres, which belonged to his wife's family and had been destroyed during World War I; his passion for machinery led him ultimately into the design of motor vehicle prototypes.

BIBLIOGRAPHY
Antoine Pompe et l'effort moderne en Belgique, 1890–1940 (exh. cat., ed. M. Culot and F. Terlinden; Brussels, Mus. Ixelles, 1969)

ANNE VAN LOO

Bléry, Eugène(-Stanislas-Alexandre) (*b* Fontainebleau, 3 March 1805; *d* Paris, 10 June 1887). French printmaker and draughtsman. At the age of 20 he became a mathematics tutor to Charles Montalivet in Berry and during his three years in the post began the first of his long series of tours of France commemorated in a set of 12 lithographs of 1830, which marked his decision to concentrate on landscape art. The etchings of Jean-Jacques de Boissieu, which he encountered in Lyon, appear to have confirmed him in this vocation by 1836, when he exhibited with increasing popular success under the initial patronage of the Montalivet family. Worked either directly from nature or from his own drawings, his etchings (frequently combined with drypoint, burin or roulette) are meticulous, delicate and highly wrought, although superficially they often seem uneventful and repetitious. They usually appeared in series, concentrated particularly between 1838 and 1868. Although his subjects owe a little to Claude, they are principally a skilful and well-integrated compendium of Rococo motifs; picturesque Boucher-like watermills and farm buildings inhabited by elegant peasants underline the 18th-century mood. Despite their occasional Romantic overtones of transience, the formal topography of his landscapes and tree portraits belongs essentially to Barbizon naturalism. He also produced many closely focused botanical studies gracefully composed with an acute realization of species. The strongest influence on him (perhaps initiated by the example of Jean-Jacques de Boissieu) was that of Dutch 17th-century art, in particular Antoni Waterlo and contemporary etchers, as well as Meindert Hobbema and Jacob van Ruisdael, both of whom Bléry copied. The finest collection of his work is in the Bibliothèque Nationale, Paris.

BIBLIOGRAPHY
C. Le Blanc: *Manuel de l'amateur d'estampes*, i (Paris, 1854/*R* Amsterdam, 1970), pp. 359–71 [incorporates Bléry's own cat. rais. of his prints]
H. Béraldi: *Les Graveurs du XIXe siècle*, ii (Paris, 1885), pp. 94–131

HARLEY PRESTON

Bles, David Joseph (*b* The Hague, 19 Sept 1821; *d* The Hague, 3 Sept 1899). Dutch painter and printmaker. He received his first training at the drawing academy in The Hague. He then worked in the studio of Cornelis Kruseman from 1838 to 1841, at the same time as Alexander Hugo Bakker Korff. Bles studied under Joseph Robert-Fleury in Paris in the following two years. Back in The Hague in 1843, he quickly attracted attention with his submissions to exhibitions. He specialized in the playful depiction of the well-to-do middle classes in domestic settings, often with a coquettish young woman as the main character.

Like Bakker Korff, Bles bacame highly renowned for his lightly satirical genre scenes with elegant, usually 18th-century, accessories; he may have developed his preference for frivolous 18th-century costume after attending a masked ball shortly after 1843. He had earlier painted some historical subjects but from then on he painted moralizing scenes, often with a mischievous double meaning, and subjects derived from literature and everyday life. Among the best-known examples are *Poverty and Wealth* (1848; Haarlem, Teylers Mus.), the *Consolable Widow* (1856; Amsterdam, Hist. Mus.) and '*The way you hear it is the way you sing it*' (1869; Amsterdam, Rijksmus.). His small, meticulously painted panels belong to the anecdotal genre tradition of Jan Steen, Cornelis Troost and Hogarth, all interpreters of interior scenes with a narrative element.

Bles also painted portraits, again with a narrative overtone, such as *Return from Heemstede of Mr J. L. van den Berch* (1847; Nijmegen, Mus. Commanderie St Jan). He was a competent draughtsman and watercolour painter (*c.* 200 examples; The Hague, Gemeentemus.) and produced etchings and lithographs. He also took an active part in the artistic life of The Hague (he was chairman of the Pulchri Society from 1863 to 1866 and from 1869 to 1872).

Scheen
BIBLIOGRAPHY
H. C. de Bruijn: 'De interieurstukken van David Bles en A. H. Bakker Korff', *Op Uitkijk: Christ. Cult. Mabl.* (Nov 1961), pp. 83–7

WIEPKE F. LOOS

Bles [Blesio, Blesius, Blessio; de Dinant, de Patinir], **Herri met de** [Henri, Henrico; Herry (met de)] [Civetta] (*b* Bouvines, *c.* 1510). Flemish painter. Both van Mander and Lampsonius recorded Bouvines as his birthplace, although Guicciardini gave it as Dinant. The identification of Herri met de Bles with Herry de Patinir, who was a master of the Antwerp Guild of St Luke in 1535, is generally accepted. He may have been related to Joachim Patinir, possibly a nephew. In the *Pictorum aliquot celebrium Germaniae Inferioris effigies* (Antwerp, 1572) of Domenicus Lampsonius, *Henricus Blesius Bovinati pictori* is portrayed aged 40, sporting the type of clothing and beard that were fashionable in 1550. He may have visited Italy, although this is not documented. His work was undoubtedly popular in Italy, where he was known as 'Civetta' because of the little owl that often appears in his paintings (usually in a hollow tree or in a cavity between some rocks), a motif regarded by van Mander as his signature. However, other painters used similar owls too, so this is not a reliable basis for attributions. No signed paintings are known by Herri met de Bles or Herry de Patinir. An *Adoration of the Magi* (Munich, Alte Pin.), which used to bear the false signature HENRICVS BLESIVS F and thus served as a basis for many attributions, is no longer considered to be by him; it and the paintings assembled around it constitute the so-called PSEUDO-BLES group (*see* MASTERS, ANONYMOUS, AND MONOGRAMMISTS, §I).

Herri met de Bles and Joachim Patinir are two of the earliest landscape painters of the southern Netherlands;

after Patinir died in 1524, Herri met de Bles became the genre's most outstanding practitioner. They both painted landscapes characterized by a high viewpoint and dominated by imposing rocky masses, their aim being to create a spectacular rather than realistic view. Herri met de Bles always included a few small figures, enacting his favourite themes of mining activities or religious episodes (e.g. Christ Carrying the Cross, the Journey to Emmaus or St John the Baptist Preaching), alongside which he represented such everyday activities as agriculture or trade. His paintings are distinguished from Patinir's by their extensive foreground landscapes, less structured composition and profuse detail. They lack the planes and horizontal lines that structure Patinir's pictures. The rocks, for example in the *Landscape with the Journey to Emmaus* (Vienna, Ksthist. Mus.), with their soaring peaks, projections and archways, are often more fantastic than Patinir's, yet better integrated in the landscape, rising from hills and linked with mountain ranges, not standing in isolated clumps. His choice of colours is on the whole less rich than Patinir's, the backgrounds thinly painted with grey tones to unify the composition and to enhance its atmospheric quality.

The *Landscape with the Good Samaritan* (Namur, Soc. Archéol.; see fig.) is typical: on the left is a tree truncated by the picture frame and a rock, on the right a view over low-lying farmland, towns and villages. The quantity of detail, especially in the middle plane, together with the unnatural structure of the rock formation create a rather confused overall effect. The painting bears a date, probably added later, that used to be read as 1511 but has been reinterpreted on stylistic grounds as 1531 (Courtoy), 1541 (Hoogewerff) or 1551 (Franz). A similar, though less fragmented composition, *Merchant with Monkeys* (Dresden, Gemäldegal. Alte Meister), is almost certainly the picture described by van Mander as in the collection of Maerten Papenbroeck in Amsterdam; here the rocks are more natural and details are sparser. A comparison between Herri met de Bles's *Landscape with St John the Baptist Preaching* (Brussels, Mus. A. Anc.) and Patinir's *Landscape with St Jerome* (Madrid, Prado) further demonstrates the similarities and differences between the two painters. The rock formation is almost insignificant in Patinir's broad panorama, with its high horizon, though it dominates the other composition, in which the horizon is less important. Patinir's rocks rise unnaturally from the ground, while those in the Brussels picture seem almost organically related to their surroundings. Moreover, Patinir's work has two different viewpoints: frontal for the group of rocks in the foreground and elevated for the panorama. The viewpoint is unified in Herri met de Bles's painting.

Figures, which are few in these works, are more prominent in a series of paintings depicting *Christ Carrying*

Herri met de Bles: *Landscape with the Good Samaritan*, oil on panel, 840×1135 mm, 15[?]1 (Namur, Société Archéologique de Namur)

the Cross. The series contains two compositional types: traditional and static, in which the vertical lines of the architecture, trees and rocks are balanced by the horizontal lines of the procession and of the bushes (e.g. Princeton U., NJ, A. Mus.), or modern and dynamic, in which there is a sustained movement leading into the picture, achieved by the inward-winding roads and by the countless figures seen from behind (e.g. Rome, Gal. Doria-Pamphili).

BIBLIOGRAPHY
L. Guicciardini: *Descrittione di. . .tutti Paesi Bassi* (1567)
K. van Mander: *Schilder-boeck* ([1603]–1604), fol. 219*r*
M. J. Friedländer: *Die altniederländische Malerei* (Berlin, 1924–37), xiii, pp. 36–45, 146–9; rev. Eng. edn (1975), pp. 23–7, 78–82, 110–11
E. Larsen and L. Larsen: 'Quelques notes à propos de Herry de Patinir et Herry Bles', *Oud-Holland*, lvii (1940), pp. 21–8
F. Courtoy: 'H. Blès de Bouvignes: Son tableau de *Bon Samaritain* au Musée de Namur', *Namurcum*, xxii (1947), pp. 49–59
G. J. Hoogewerff: *Het landschap van Bosch tot Rubens* (Antwerp, 1954), pp. 28–34
E. Gérard: *Dinant et la Meuse dans l'histoire du paysage* (Lammersdorf, 1960), p. 86
H. G. Franz: *Niederländische Landschaftsmalerei im Zeitalter des Manierismus*, 2 vols (Graz, 1969), i, pp. 78–92; ii, pp. 47–52, 54–6, 58
A. Piron: *Joachim le Patinier et Henri Blès* (Gembloux, 1971)

HANS DEVISSCHER

Blijenberch, Abraham van. *See* BLYENBERCH, ABRAHAM VAN.

Blin, Jean-Baptiste. *See* BELIN, JEAN-BAPTISTE.

Blind arcade. Series of arches supported on columns or pilasters and set against a wall, with no openings beneath the arches. Blind arcading is a decorative device or means of articulation, which often has the effect of creating overall architectural consistency in a composition by spreading a motif or group of forms across an elevation, whether an opening—a window or portal—is involved or not, to produce an intelligible, harmonious whole. In Romanesque architecture it is common to find a series of oversailing arches (they have no columns or pilasters to support them but 'hang' in mid-air) either rising up a gable or set horizontally beneath a principal course or demarcation, for example on the west façades of S Zeno Maggiore (from *c.* 1138), Verona, and Lund Cathedral (from *c.* 1080). A development of this, and a true blind arcade, with shafts supported on corbels, can be seen on the west façade (after 1160) of S Michele, Pavia (*see* PAVIA, fig. 3). In addition, many Romanesque buildings have series of arches and columns, set immediately in front of a solid wall, which might articulate a whole façade or even run around an entire building. Often these aedicules—as they effectively become—are totally blind, but in other examples they are pierced by a small window of a different shape. Blind arcades can also be set beside real arcades: Pisa Cathedral (begun 1064) has examples of these different features (*see* PISA, fig. 5). In Gothic architecture, blind arcades again perform the role of articulating a structural system or of decorating or enhancing a composition. The insides of aisle walls in great churches are often provided with a blind arcade, of which the shafts and arches may be fully three-dimensional, projecting from the wall behind (see fig.). The height is approximately that of a person, which has the effect of relating the elevation to a human scale. Such an arcade can also be

Blind arcade, north aisle of nave, Beverley Minster, early to mid-14th century

used to fill the wall space below a major window. Other Gothic blind arcades (though in many cases used for decorative effect) are situated above the main arcades and give the impression of a triforium, even if there is no passage. In both Romanesque and Gothic architecture there are series of superimposed blind arcades where the arches interlace (e.g. Cefalù Cathedral; 1240). Blind aedicules and niches often occur in Renaissance, Baroque and Neo-classical architecture, but long series of blind arcading are not generally found.

See also ARCADE.

JOHN THOMAS

Blind-blocked [blind-stamped; blind-tooled]. Method in which a design on a block (or die or tool) is impressed into a surface without the use of any ink (*see* BOOKBINDING, EMBOSSING and LEATHER).

□

Blinder, Olga (*b* Asunción, 1921). Paraguayan painter and engraver. She studied under the painters Ofelia Echagüe, João Rossi and Lívio Abramo, and her work contributed fundamentally to the revival of Paraguayan art in the 1950s. Until then representational art was still tied to 19th-century Naturalism, but in 1954 the Arte Nuevo group, founded by Blinder, Josefina Plá, Lilí del Mónico and José Laterza Parodi, organized the Primera Semana de Arte Moderna, which helped bring to a head the struggle with entrenched academicism. She began by painting still-lifes and landscapes that emphasized structure, but she soon turned to thematic and expressive content centred on the human condition; later her work was concerned as much with intensity of meaning as with the severity of formal arrangement. Sensitive and intellectual, subjective and socially aware, her work turned into an individual lyrical expressionism, enlivened by tension but carefully formal. This complexity can be seen in the techniques she used at different stages: the severe images that she developed in paintings and wood-engravings during the 1960s, the engravings made with zincograph blocks in the 1970s that incorporate conceptual analysis based on her existential and social preoccupations; and finally painting, which she resumed in the 1980s.

BIBLIOGRAPHY
Guggiari, Blinder, Colombino (exh. cat. by L. Abramo, Asunción, Paraguay, Mis. Cult. Bras., 1969)
J. Plá: *Treinta y tres nombres en las artes plásticas Paraguayas* (Asunción, 1973)
T. Escobar: *Una interpretación de las artes visuales en el Paraguay* (Asunción, 1984)
TICIO ESCOBAR

Bliss. American collectors. Robert Woods Bliss (*b* St Louis, MO, 5 Aug 1875; *d* Washington, DC, 19 April 1962) and his wife, Mildred Bliss (née Barnes) (*b* New York City, Sept 1879; *d* Washington, 17 Jan 1969), developed their interest in art while living abroad, where Robert Bliss served as a diplomat until his retirement in 1933. They were particularly concerned with the then neglected areas of Pre-Columbian and Byzantine art. Their Byzantine collection included coins, icons, ivories, mosaics, jewellery and textiles; their Pre-Columbian collection was similarly wide-ranging. In 1920 Robert and Mildred Bliss purchased Dumbarton Oaks, a large house in the Georgetown area of Washington, DC. Although they lived there intermittently for only seven years, they extensively renovated the house and 16-acre garden. Frederick H. Brooke (*d* 1960) was the architect responsible for removing the Victorian accretions and adding the music room; from 1922 to 1933 the landscape architect BEATRIX JONES FARRAND worked on the garden. Robert Bliss was a Harvard graduate, and in 1940 the couple donated Dumbarton Oaks and their collection to Harvard University. They continued to enrich the collection until Robert Bliss's death. Dumbarton Oaks became a centre for Byzantine studies in the United States and also serves as a research facility in the areas of landscape architecture and Pre-Columbian civilization.

BIBLIOGRAPHY
H. Cairns: *Robert Woods Bliss* (Washington, DC, 1963)
W. Whitehill: *Dumbarton Oaks* (Cambridge, MA, 1967)
ANNE MCCLANAN

Bliss, Lillie [Lizzie] **P(lummer)** (*b* Boston, MA, 11 April 1864; *d* New York, 12 March 1931). American collector, museum founder and patron. She was born into an affluent family and discovered modern art through her friendship with the painter Arthur B. Davies. In 1907 she purchased her first painting by Davies and eventually had the largest private collection of his work. Bliss toured galleries with Davies and at the Armory Show (1913) purchased, on his advice, two paintings by Redon, two by Renoir, and an oil and a pastel by Degas. She later turned to more avant-garde modernism, acquiring 27 works by Cézanne, and became a great supporter of modern art during the next 15 years, although she was asked by her family not to display her collection in public.

Bliss was one of the co-founders of MOMA, New York, in 1929, and was Vice-President at the time of her death. She bequeathed paintings to the Metropolitan Museum of Art, New York, and the Corcoran Gallery, Washington, DC, but principally to MOMA, which celebrated the acquisition of over 150 works with a memorial exhibition. Her collection became the core of the museum's extensive holdings of works by Cézanne, Matisse and other pioneering French modernists.

BIBLIOGRAPHY
Memorial Exhibition of the Collection of the Late Miss Bliss (exh. cat., New York, MOMA, 1931)
M. W. Brown: *The Story of the Armory Show* (New York, 1963)
DAVID M. SOKOL

Blister. Raised area of paint that has become detached from the ground or support due to faulty technique or to unfavourable environmental conditions, such as extremes of humidity. Blistering, also known as cleavage, may develop into flaking and the loss of paint fragments.
RUPERT FEATHERSTONE

Bloch, Carl (Heinrich) (*b* Copenhagen, 23 May 1834; *d* 22 Feb 1890). Danish painter and etcher. He studied under Wilhelm Marstrand at the Kunstakademi in Copenhagen. His early work includes genre scenes, prompted by the art historian Niels Laurits Andreas Høyen, who called for painting representing the everyday life of the people. Bloch depicted farm life, as in a *Boy Waking a Girl with a Feather* (1856), and the life of the fishermen, as in *Fisher Families Awaiting the Return of the Men in an Impending Storm* (1858; both Copenhagen, Hirschsprungske Saml.). From 1859 to 1866 Bloch lived in Italy, and this stay provided him with a rich source on his return, as in such humorous scenes of daily life as a *Monk with Toothache* (1871; untraced; see Magnussen, p. 66).

Bloch's stay in Italy was particularly important for his history painting. He was influenced by contemporary examples of the genre, and he produced large-scale historical works there. He achieved his greatest success when *Prometheus Unbound* (1864; ex-Royal Pal., Athens) was exhibited in Copenhagen in 1865. The painting shows Hercules freeing Prometheus; and in the political context of Denmark's recent defeat by Prussia, the Danish public did not fail to see the stirring implications of Danish resistance to tyranny and the hope for national reconstruction. After the death of Wilhelm Marstrand, Bloch finished the decoration of the ceremonial hall at the University of Copenhagen (*in situ*). His largest public commission was for 23 paintings for the Frederiksborg Palace Chapel (1865–79; *in situ*).

In his later years, landscape painting, based on *plein-air* studies made during the summers, came to play a central part in Bloch's work, which reveals a keen interest in the treatment of light. This is also a feature of Bloch's many etchings, almost all of which date from the 1880s (e.g. *View of the Beach at Hellebaek in Mild Weather*, 1881). Bloch also produced some able portrait etchings and some striking etched compositions with imaginary figures (e.g. the *Young Man and Death*, 1880).

BIBLIOGRAPHY
J. R. Thiele: *Beskrivende fortegnelse over Carl Blochs raderinger* [Descriptive cat. of Carl Bloch's etchings] (Copenhagen, 1898)
R. Magnussen: *Carl Bloch, 1834–1890* (Copenhagen, 1931) [with cat. of works]
GITTE VALENTINER

Bloch, Martin (*b* Neisse, Silesia [now Nysa, Poland], 16 Nov 1883; *d* London, 19 June 1954). British painter and teacher of German birth. The son of a Jewish factory-owner, Bloch studied architecture in Berlin in 1902, aesthetics with Heinrich Wölfflin in Munich in 1905 and drawing with Lovis Corinth in Berlin in 1907. As a painter he was largely self-taught. His first one-man exhibition (1911) took place at the Paul Cassirer Gallery, Berlin. In 1912 he went to Paris, where he worked in Montparnasse and became a friend of Jules Pascin. The years 1914–18 were spent in Spain. In 1923 he founded the Bloch–Kerschbaumer school in Berlin with Anton Kerschbaumer, whose place was later taken by Karl Schmidt-Rottluff. In 1933 Bloch was declared a 'degenerate artist' by the Nazis, and in 1934 he fled with his family to Denmark, and thence to London, where, with Roy de Maistre, he opened his School of Contemporary Painting. In later years he taught at Camberwell School of Art.

Bloch left Germany as a mature and established artist, but in England had to struggle for recognition. His only one-man exhibition to be held in England during his lifetime took place in 1939 at the Alex Reid & Lefèvre Gallery, London. Architecture, portraits, still-lifes and, above all, landscape formed Bloch's staple subject-matter. Although he shared the heightened palette and subjectivity of the German Expressionists, his lyrical humanism and classical sense of composition allied him with the modern French tradition. He was widely respected as a tolerant teacher who stressed the importance of sound craftsmanship.

BIBLIOGRAPHY
Martin Bloch (exh. cat., ed. C. da Costa; London, S. London A.G., 1984)
MONICA BOHM-DUCHEN

Block. In printing, a solid material, usually wood (rather than a metal plate), which can be engraved or cut and used to print on to a surface.

☐

Block, Der. German association of architects formed in Saaleck early in 1928, in reaction to the avant-garde group Der Ring and to the emerging Modern Movement in general. The most prominent members were Paul Schultze-Naumburg, Paul Schmitthenner, German Bestelmeyer and Paul Bonatz. Bonatz and Schmitthenner were both supposed to take part in the exhibition of the Deutscher Werkbund in Stuttgart in 1927, and even prepared a layout plan for the Weissenhofsiedlung, the showpiece of the exhibition. Their design was, however, rejected in favour of the modernist design by Mies van der Rohe. Schultze-Naumburg from the early years of the century had propagated a return to organic and traditional forms of architecture, for example in his series of books *Kulturarbeiten* (1902–17). He was the leading theorist of the Heimatschutz movement, which advocated the preservation and continuation of German traditions and values. Bestelmeyer, Schmitthenner and Bonatz were among the most prominent architects of southern Germany, all holding influential teaching posts in Munich and Stuttgart. Der Block wanted to retain traditional skills and lifestyles and rejected functional, modern architecture with its emphasis on internationalism. Their 'Manifesto' appeared in *Baukunst 4* (v (1928), pp. 128–9; repr. in Teut, p. 29); its polemic, enriched with an emphasis on 'German-ness', was eventually to evolve into the fierce opposition and persecution by the Third Reich of the 'cultural bolshevism' of the architecture and architects of the Modern Movement. As a group, however, Der Block was shortlived, active only into 1929.

BIBLIOGRAPHY
A. Teut, ed.: *Architektur im Dritten Reich, 1933–1945* (Berlin, 1967) [incl. repr. of manifesto]
K. Kirsch: *Die Weissenhofsiedlung: Werkbundausstellung 'Die Wohnung'* (Stuttgart, 1987)
CLAUDIA BÖLLING

Block-book. Type of book, the pages of which are printed from single blocks of wood. Both picture and words are carved from the block, which is inked and printed by hand-rubbing on a dampened sheet of paper. When dry, the sheet could not be printed on the reverse side because of an indented surface caused by the rubbing.

1. Origins. 2. The Netherlands. 3. Germany.

1. ORIGINS. The earliest extant records of woodblock printing date to between AD 764 and 770, in China. In AD 868 one of the oldest preserved block-printed books appeared, in scroll form, the Diamond Sutra (London, BL, Sir Aurel Stein Col.). The earliest block-books from the heartland of northern Europe date probably from the middle of the 15th century. Around this time Johann Gutenberg in Mainz was perfecting printing by means of movable type that was cast in metal. Thus the uneven alignment of letters in the hand-cut line of text in the block-book was corrected by the typographic page, printed in a press. By the late 1470s Gutenberg's method gained total ascendancy, and the making of block-books ended, after only about 25 years. Thus the block-book was not the precursor of the modern book but rather evolved with it. With its emphasis on images, it betrays origins and purposes different from those of the text-oriented printed book.

There has been much controversy about the time when block-books in general were produced, for all the early and most important ones are without dates. Some think they began as early as 1420–30; others believe in an origin of 1450 to 1460. It seems likely that the earliest block-books were produced in the Netherlands and Germany no earlier than *c.* 1450, hence concurrently with the development of movable type and the printing press. At this time the first block-book as a fully developed type, the *Apocalypse*, appeared in the Netherlands. In Germany there was a slower development during the 15th century: first woodcuts were pasted into handwritten manuscripts; next came the chiro-xylographic block-book in which the text was added by hand to the areas within or below the woodcut; and finally the xylographic, or wholly woodcut, page appeared.

The dating of all block-books in the West later than the 1420s and probably not until 1450 at the earliest is strongly supported by two technical factors. The first is the similarity of the woodcut style of the block-book images to that of the single-leaf woodcut print developed during the 15th century. Less subjective is the technique of dating watermarks in paper by beta-radiography and thereby determining the correct sequence of the editions of a block-book. This method seems to prove that block-books were not created before the middle of the century and that they reached their peak in both quality and popularity *c.* 1465–75.

The block-book in the West was devised to spread stories from the Bible and legends of a moralizing nature to semi-literate people. The pictures usually had explanatory captions and brief texts, generally in Latin, and it is thought that most of the block-books served as aids for preachers, to illustrate or dramatize their sermons; thus all block-books were devoted to the propagation of the faith through images and text. The main centre of production of the finest block-books was the Netherlands. Germany produced an almost equal number, but few of these were of great significance and many were based on Netherlandish originals. France apparently produced no block-books, and only a single example of significance is known from Italy: *Minabilia Romae*, Rome, *c.* 1475 (London, BL).

2. THE NETHERLANDS. In his standard catalogue of block-books (Berlin, 1891–1910) Wilhelm Ludwig Schreiber attempted the complex task of sorting the different editions of the six major Netherlandish block-books. He divided them into groups under each title and gave their locations in public and private collections in Europe and North America. Having no dates with which to work, he relied mainly on the quality of the cutting of the blocks, stating that it was almost impossible to determine their

2. Block-book page from *Ars moriendi*, woodcut, 219×156 mm, from the Netherlands, *c.* 1450 (London, British Library)

chronological order. (A few scholars have since tried to do this; the most successful attempt it would seem is the method of watermark examination by Stevenson.)

Schreiber grouped the Netherlandish block-books into two categories: the first, 'meditations on the Bible', includes four of the five most popular titles, to judge by the number of editions: the *Biblia pauperum*, the *Speculum humanae salvationis*, the *Canticum canticorum* and the *Apocalypse*; the second category Schreiber entitled 'catechism texts': *Ars moriendi* and *Exercitium super Pater Noster*.

The earliest of all surviving block-books is the chiroxylographic edition of the *Exercitium super Pater Noster* (Paris, Bib. N., XYL. 31; see Schreiber, vol. viii, pl. lxxvii). It has ten woodcuts and survives in a single but defective copy, with manuscript text in Flemish. A second edition is entirely xylographic, with texts in Flemish and Latin. Arthur Hind dated the first edition to *c.* 1430–40, using as a criterion for judgement the costumes in the Netherlandish paintings of that decade. Schreiber proposed as the author of the *Exercitium* a member of the Brotherhood of the Common Life, perhaps Hendrik van den Bogarde (1382–1469), prior of their community at Groenendael, near Brussels.

Manuscripts of the *Apocalypse*, the Book of Revelation of St John the Divine, were widespread throughout the Middle Ages, illustrated copies dating from as early as the 8th century. The block-book was based on an as yet unidentified manuscript, although a single prototype was

1. Block-book page from the *Apocalypse*, woodcut, 250×190 mm, 4th edition, probably German copy, *c.* 1465 (Princeton, NJ, Princeton University, Art Museum)

common to all (*see* APOCALYPSE, §2). Most scholars have agreed that the *Apocalypse* is the oldest completely xylographic block-book, although opinions differ as to the date of the earliest edition and range from the early 15th century to *c.* 1450; the latter seems more probable. There are six editions, the first three Netherlandish, the others German (see fig. 1 and *see* BOOK, fig. 6). The first edition has 24 sheets, each printed with two block-book pages side by side, which when folded create 48 leaves, printed on only one side. For a second edition, signatures were added, starting with 'a', to indicate the sequence of the pages.

The best reason for according the *Apocalypse* priority among the block-books is stylistic: the forms are described only in outline, with no shading and no background landscape; the scenes were designed to be coloured by hand, and in fact almost all the copies that have survived, in whole or in part, have been tinted.

Colouring is very much less frequent in the editions of the *Ars moriendi* (written *c.* 1450) because the forms are now shaded in short parallel or hatched lines (see fig. 2). The first (*c.* 1465) of 20 known editions of this most popular of all block-books is thought by many to be also the finest in quality. Its great popularity was surely due in large part to the fear of death from the many plagues that devastated Europe from 1347; the book was used by the clergy and others as a manual in comforting or counselling the sick at their bedside. As is the case for most block-books, its author is not known, although the text was evidently inspired by the writings on death by Jean Gerson (1363–1429). The compositions adapt 11 small engravings of *c.* 1450 by one of the earliest German engravers, Master E.S. The *Ars moriendi* comprises 11 full-page woodcuts; banderole inscriptions in abbreviated Latin occur by each of the speakers. Scenes depict the struggle between Virtue and Vice: alternately, on one page demons try to incite vice in the infirm (the sins of Infidelity, Despair, Impatience, Vainglory and Avarice), on the next angels comfort or instruct the dying man; on the last page Virtue triumphs over all temptations, in the hour of his death.

Editions of the *Biblia pauperum*, both Netherlandish and German, were widespread, indicating a popularity almost equal to that of the *Ars moriendi*: their scheme paralleled events in the Old Testament with the life of Christ (*see* TYPOLOGICAL CYCLES, §2). Many manuscripts of the *Biblia pauperum* were illustrated in the 14th and 15th centuries, although they were not known by a collective title until the 18th century. Ten surviving xylographic Netherlandish editions have 40 pages and depend on a single prototype, none of the 10 being the first, according to Schreiber. A single chiro-xylographic copy (*c.* 1460; Heidelberg, Ubib.) has survived that has only 34 pages; it is probably German. There is also a unique 50-page xylographic edition (Paris, Bib. N.) that copies the 40-page one, with texts added on banderoles throughout the images. The scheme of illustration of all copies of the *Biblia pauperum* (manuscript, block-book or typeset with woodcuts) is the same: the pictorial layout presents a central New Testament subject flanked by two scenes of Old Testament prefigurations, with portraits of four prophets with their prophecies on each page (*see* BIBLE, §I, 3(ii)). The earliest of the popular 40-page Netherlandish

3. Block-book page from *Speculum humanae salvationis*, woodcut, 200×105 mm, from the Netherlands, *c.* 1474 (London, British Library)

editions can be securely dated to shortly after 1460; it may have originated in a Carthusian studio in or near Utrecht (see Schreiber, vol. viii, pl. lxxv).

The *Canticum canticorum* is an allegorical treatise on the Song of Solomon. Among the books of the Old Testament, apart from the Apocalypse, the Song of Solomon was the subject of most theological commentary, despite being only eight chapters in length. The *Canticum canticorum* was produced in a North or South Netherlandish workshop *c.* 1465, possibly in Leuven (Louvain), since the figure style suggests that of the Leuven painter Dieric Bouts the elder. There are 32 compositions, two together on each page, with the Latin text given on banderoles (see Schreiber, vol. vii, pl. lviii). The first of two editions is beautifully designed and cut, with elegant figures, tranquil and dreamlike in arrested movements. A second edition was copied from the first but is decidedly inferior. Many accessories were omitted or simplified, for example tufts of grass replace the picturesque plants of the original.

The latest of the Netherlandish block-books is the *Speculum humanae salvationis* (see fig. 3). The original text was probably written by a Carthusian monk, Ludolphus of Saxony (*c.* 1300–77) in Strasbourg in *c.* 1320, and many illustrated manuscript copies of this popular work exist. Like the *Biblia pauperum* it is a typological treatise intended as a manual for poor preachers, as is clearly stated in its preface. Three Old Testament parallels, or types, follow a New Testament scene, the antitype, across two open pages. There are 26 of these, from the *Annunciation* to the *Resurrection*, and as an introduction the book begins with eight scenes from Genesis relating the story of *Creation* and the *Fall of Man*; it ends with two illustrations of the *Last Judgement* with its types. In all, 58 blocks were employed. Below each picture is printed a lengthy explanatory text; there are both Latin and Dutch editions. Except for 20 pages in one edition (Schreiber's second Latin edition, of which he notes 20 extant copies), the text was not cut out of the block but was printed with movable type, in black ink. In a separate operation the woodcuts were printed in sepia; thus the page is normally both xylographic and typographic (for illustration see Wilson and Wilson, pp. 122–3). The quality of the drawing and cutting of the wood blocks varies, with those at the end being markedly inferior. These blocks were later cut apart and used as book illustrations by the printer Jan Veldener (*fl* 1474–84) at Utrecht between 1481 and 1484. Hind believed that the best blocks could be by the hand that cut the *Canticum canticorum*, and he dated the work to *c.* 1470–75. Although in all but one edition (*c.* 1474) the *Speculum* is printed entirely with movable type, it is nonetheless considered to be a block-book as it follows the tradition in being printed on only one side of the paper.

3. GERMANY. Numerous block-books were produced in Germany between about 1450 and 1475, but none is as fine or important as those done in the Netherlands. Four are especially notable: the *Symbolum apostolicum* (Vienna, *c.* 1450), which presents 12 subjects based on the Apostles' Creed; the *Decalogus*, each page giving one of the Ten Commandments in Latin, together with the German translation and the Devil's answer in German; the *Dance of Death*, compromising 27 leaves with German text; and the *Fable of the Sick Lion* (Basle, *c.* 1458). There were several editions of the *Planets*, a lively series illustrating their influence on humanity; *Defensorium virginitatis Mariae* was written by Franciscus de Retza (*d* 1425) and first printed in 1470 by Friedrich Walter (*fl* 1470) in Nördlingen; *Mirabilia Romae* was the first printed edition as a block-book of a popular guide-book, probably issued by a German printer in Rome.

See also WOODCUT, §II, 2.

BIBLIOGRAPHY

W. L. Schreiber: *Manuel de l'amateur de la gravure sur bois et sur métal au XVe siècle*, 8 vols (Berlin, 1891–1910)
J. J. Schretlen: *Dutch and Flemish Woodcuts of the Fifteenth Century* (New York, 1925/*R* 1969), chap. 2
A. M. Hind: 'Block-books', *An Introduction to a History of Woodcut*, 2 vols (New York, 1935/*R* 1963), pp. 207–72
A. Stevenson: 'The Quincentennial of Netherlandish Blockbooks', *BM Q.*, xxxi (1966–7), pp. 83–7
R. Field: *The Fable of the Sick Lion: A Fifteenth-century Blockbook* (Middletown, CT, 1974)
R. Koch: 'New Criteria for Dating the Netherlandish *Biblia pauperum* Blockbook', *Studies in Honor of Millard Meiss*, i (New York, 1978), pp. 283–9
A. Wilson and J. Wilson: *A Medieval Mirror: Speculum humanae salvationis, 1324–1500* (Berkeley, 1984)

ROBERT A. KOCH

Blocke [Block], **van den** [dem]. Flemish family of artists, active throughout the Baltic countries. (1) Willem van den Blocke took Netherlandish Italianate Mannerist styles of monumental sculpture to the Baltic towns, where he and his workshop were responsible for several civic commissions. His eldest son, (2) Abraham van den Blocke, worked mainly in GDAŃSK (Danzig) as a sculptor and architect, employing a large workshop. Willem's second son, (3) Izaak van den Blocke, a painter, is best known for his ceiling paintings (1608) in Gdańsk Town Hall (now Mus. Hist.) and a third son, Jakob van den Blocke (1576–1653), for his tower domes in Gdańsk.

(1) Willem van den Blocke (*b* Mechelen, *c.* 1545–50; *d* Gdańsk, 28 Jan 1628). Sculptor and architect. After training under Cornelis Floris in Antwerp, he went in 1569 with other members of the workshop to the Prussian court in Königsberg (now Kaliningrad), where they executed the monument of *Albert I, Duke of Prussia* (from 1569; destr.). Independently he sculpted the monument of *Margravine Elizabeth* (1578–82; destr.), wife of George Frederick of Brandenburg-Auspach (*d* 1603), repeating the kneeling figure and architectonic composition with superimposed orders of the Floris idiom. In 1582 he granted a commendatory letter from the Margrave on completing 14 years' service. Subsequently Stephen Bathory, King of Poland (*reg* 1576–86), commissioned him to execute a monument for his late brother, *Christopher Bathory, Prince of Transylvania* (1583; Alba Julia Cathedral; destr.). In 1584 van den Blocke settled in Gdańsk, where he ran a workshop until his death; safeguarded by royal privilege, he did not have to belong to the guild. On the town council's commission he designed and executed the stone façade of the city's High Gate (1586), modelled after that of St George in Antwerp.

However, van den Blocke was best known for his monuments, as the main representative of the Italianizing Netherlandish Mannerism in the Baltic area. They are characterized by clarity and variety of arrangements and by contrasted colours, whether incrusted or polychromed. He frequently applied classical orders with fluted columns, caryatids and herm pilasters. In relief decoration he combined rich acanthus arabesques *all'antica* with the ornaments typical of Netherlandish Mannerism. He presented the deceased realistically. Most frequently he was commissioned to produce wall monuments in the style of Andrea Sansovino: the figure of the deceased reclining on his side, head supported on hand, the legs bent and crossed. A notable example is the monument of *John III Vasa, King of Sweden* (1594–6; ex-Zeughaus, Gdańsk; Uppsala Cathedral) commissioned by Sigismund III Vasa, King of Sweden and Poland, and the Swedish senate. For the tomb of *Cardinal Andrew Bathory, Bishop of Varmia* and his brother *Balthazar Bathory* (1598; Barczewo, nr Olsztyn, St Andrew; see fig.) van den Blocke produced a two-tiered composition: a full-length kneeling figure of the Cardinal, with his brother recumbent. It combined Floris's type with the format of Roman cardinals' tomb monuments and initiated a series of similar tombs of Polish ecclesiastics.

Willem van den Blocke: tomb of *Cardinal Andrew Bathory, Bishop of Varmia* and his brother *Balthazar Bathory*, black marble and alabaster, 1598 (Barczewo, St Andrew)

Notable among van den Blocke's later works are the monuments to *Piotr Tarnowski* (1603–4; Łowicz, Collegiate Church) and *Stanisław Radziwiłł, Grand Marshal of Lithuania* (1618–23; Vilnius, St Michael Archangel). Works attributed to van den Blocke and his workshop include the portal of the Red Granary in Toruń (1600) and the portal of the Pelplin Abbots' House in Gdańsk (1617).

BIBLIOGRAPHY

SAP; Thieme–Becker

G. Cuny: *Danzigs Kunst und Kultur im 16. und 17. Jahrhundert* (Frankfurt am Main, 1910), pp. 75–9

L. Krzyżanowski: 'Plastyka nagrobna Willema van den Blocke' [Sepulchral sculpture of Willem van den Blocke], *Biul. Hist. Sztuki*, xx (1958), nos 3/4, pp. 270–98

Z. Hornung: 'Gdańska szkoła rzeźbiarska na przełomie XVI i XVII w.' [The Gdańsk school of sculpture at the turn of the 16th century], *Teka Kom. Hist. Sztuki*, i (1959), pp. 103–39

(2) Abraham van den Blocke (*b* Königsberg [now Kaliningrad], 1572; *d* Gdańsk, 31 Jan 1628). Sculptor and architect, son of (1) Willem van den Blocke. Trained in his father's studio, in 1597 he became a master and a member of the artists' guild. His first important work was the main altar (1598–1611) in St John, Gdańsk, after a presented design. His style slowly evolved from the polychrome, ornamental forms of northern late Mannerism to early Baroque plain and severe architectonic forms in black marble. In tomb sculpture of complex architectonic framing he applied the motif of a kneeling figure, for example in the free-standing monument of *Justyna and*

Szymon Bahr (1614–20; Gdańsk, Our Lady) and those of *Henryk Firlej, Archbishop of Poland* (1627–8; Łowicz, Collegiate Church; completed by W. Richter) and *Mikołaj Działyński, Voivode of Chełmno* (after 1604; Nowe Miasto Lubawskie).

Van den Blocke was appointed town sculptor in Gdańsk in 1610 and town architect in 1611, running a large workshop of sculptors and builders. In 1606–8 he built the Royal Granary for Sigismund III. He also designed and built the Golden House at 41 Długi Targ (1606–13) and the Golden Gate (1612–14), and he remodelled the façade of the Artus Court (1616–18).

BIBLIOGRAPHY

SAP; Thieme–Becker

JERZY KOWALCZYK

(3) Izaak van den Blocke (*fl* Gdańsk, 1608; *d* Gdańsk, 1628). Painter, son of (1) Willem van den Blocke. His most important work is the ceiling (completed 1608) of the Great Chamber of the former main town hall in Gdańsk (now Mus. Hist.), composed of 25 oil paintings on oak panels. The subjects of the oblong paintings, tondi and ovals are scenes from Classical mythology, the history of ancient Greece and Rome, and the Old Testament. The ceiling surfaces between them are covered with small compositions of irregular shape and emblematic derivation. The content of all these works extols the council's piety and authority as the promoter of the town's prosperity. The ceiling's central painting is the *Apotheosis of Gdańsk* (see fig.), showing a triumphal arch over the River Vistula with an outline of the town on the cornice, above genre scenes depicting trading. Its symbolism denotes the town and its council's submission to God, the path of life (the avenue with the fountain of eternal life) and marine perspectives on the world (see Iwanoyko). The style of the paintings evidences van den Blocke's Dutch training, especially the influence of the architectonic inventions of Hans Vredeman de Vries, with whom he may have worked in Gdańsk. The gaps between the perspectives are filled in with airy, freely painted landscape details, so that the ceiling imparts an illusory spaciousness. The figures, in manneristic poses, are set in intense colour schemes, with an emphasis on contour intended to facilitate the viewing of the high panels.

From the five paintings (1611–14) intended for the Small Chamber of the town hall, only the *Allegory of Punishment and Reward* (*in situ*) has survived. Nine paintings on canvas, depicting allegories of Virtues and Vices and scenes from the Old and New Testament (*c*. 1610–14; Nuremberg, Ger. Nmus.), undoubtedly formerly constituted part of the ceiling of the church in Różyny, near Gdańsk; they are characterized by the same compositional principle found in fantastic architecture. The paintings *Before the Deluge*, *The Deluge* and the *Building of the Tower of Babel* (*c*. 1616; Gdańsk, hall of the Town Treasury, in the Town Hall) present a different phase of van den Blocke's creativity: the scenes from *The Deluge*, almost free of the didactic ostentation of the ceiling paintings of the town hall, are naturally integrated into the spatial plans of the landscape, with a fluidity that reveals his experience of Dutch Mannerist landscape in which biblical themes harmonize with decorative views of nature. He is attributed with other works in the same style:

Izaak van den Blocke: *Apotheosis of Gdańsk*, oil on panel, 3.31×2.37 m, 1608 (Gdańsk, Museum of the History of Gdańsk)

Animals in the Forest and *Noah in the Vineyard* (Gdańsk, Mus. Hist.).

Izaak van den Blocke also executed religious works, such as the paintings (1611) surrounding the main altar of St Katherine, Gdańsk, and he is attributed with the same church's *Allegory of the Choice of Life's Path* (?1616), the *Last Supper* (1613; Gdańsk, St Barbara) and the *Agony in the Garden* (1617; Gdańsk, St Bartholomew), as well as some paintings (1616) on the pulpit of St John. He was also recorded as having painted and gilded the façades of several houses. His work is hallmarked by Mannerist figure compositions and by depiction of intricate symbolic themes in spatially unified scenes.

BIBLIOGRAPHY

SAP; Thieme–Becker

E. Iwanoyko: *Apoteoza Gdańska* [The Apotheosis of Gdańsk] (Gdańsk, 1976)

BOŻENA STEINBORN

Block group [Pol. Blok]. Polish avant-garde group active in Warsaw between 1924 and 1926. Group members included Henryk Berlewi, J. Golus, W. Kajruksztis, Katarzyna Kobro, K. Kryński, Maria Nicz-Borowiak (1896–1944), Aleksander Rafałowski (1894–1981), Henryk Stażewski, Władysław Strzemiński, Mieczysław Szczuka, M. Szulc, Teresa Żarnower (*d* after 1945). Most members of the group had already exhibited together in some of the numerous exhibitions of the avant-garde in Poland in the

early 1920s. They shared an enthusiasm for Soviet Constructivism, but there were already significant divisions within the group when it was formally founded in early 1924, holding its first official exhibition in the showroom of the car manufacturer Laurent-Clément in Warsaw in March of that year. The first issue of the group's own magazine, *Blok*, appeared at the same time.

The members of Block proclaimed their adherence to the ideas of 'absolute constructivism', the rigour of the composition, the concept of collective work as opposed to the individual creative effort and 'the maximum economy of the means of artistic expression'. However, their lack of a unified artistic programme resulted in a marked division within the group in 1925. Kobro and Strzemiński, Nicz-Borowiak and Stażewski followed pure 'laboratory' Constructivism, while Szczuka and Żarnower adhered to the principle of the artist as a creator, engineer and manufacturer, thus unifying the artistic, social and political aspects of art. The 11 issues of *Blok* contained members' reviews of artistic events and articles by foreign contributors with reproductions of European works of art, and the group participated in a number of exhibitions, including the first Warsaw International Exhibition of Architecture. The Block group ceased its artistic activity in March 1926, and many members subsequently joined the PRAESENS GROUP.

BIBLIOGRAPHY

Constructivism in Poland, 1923–1936 (exh. cat., ed. R. Stanisławski and others; Essen, Mus. Flkwang, 1973)

Z. Baranowicz: *Polska avangarda artystyczna, 1918–1939* [The Polish artistic avant-garde, 1918–1939] (Warsaw, 1975), pp. 87–130

A. Turowski: *Konstruktywizm polski: Próba rekonstrukcji nurtu, 1921–1934* [Polish Constructivism: an attempt to reconstruct its development, 1921–1934] (Wrocław, 1981)

EWA MIKINA

Blocklandt [van Montfoort], **Anthonie** [Anthonis] (*b* Montfoort, 1533–4; *d* Utrecht, 1583). Dutch painter and draughtsman. A portrait medallion (lead pencil; Leiden, Rijksuniv., Munt- & Penningkab.) made by Steven van Herwijck in 1560 gives Blocklandt's age as 26. His father was a burgomaster in Montfoort, and he first trained in Delft with his uncle Hendrick Sweersz., a portrait painter. From *c.* 1550 to 1552 he was one of Frans Floris's many pupils in Antwerp. After his marriage in 1552 to Geertgen Cornelis Meynertsdr., Blocklandt moved to Delft. He is then unrecorded until April 1572, when he travelled from Utrecht to Rome in the company of a goldsmith from Delft. He returned in September of the same year, going first to Montfoort and later to Utrecht, where in 1577 he entered the saddlemakers' guild, to which painters then belonged. In 1578 he was married for the second time, to Susanna Anthonis Reversdr. van Vreeswijk, who bore him three children. He lived the last years of his life in the monastery of St Catharine, which belonged to the Knights of St John in Utrecht. He was a friend of Willem Danielsz. van Tetrode, the Delft sculptor; among his pupils were Cornelis Ketel in Delft and Michiel van Mierevelt in Utrecht.

Blocklandt's small oeuvre, which was formerly thought to comprise only six paintings (Jost, 1960), none from before the 1570s, has since been extended. The *Adoration of the Shepherds* (Amsterdam, Rijksmus.), probably his earliest known work and very obviously influenced by Floris, is ambitious in design but somewhat parochial in conception. The *Beheading of St James* (c. 1570; Gouda, Stedel. Mus. Catharina Gasthuis), another work executed before Blocklandt went to Italy, was made for the altar of the Guild of St James in Gouda's St Janskerk and must have been painted before 1573, when the altarpieces were removed from that church. It, too, reveals a strong dependence on Floris's example. The composition is related to work by artists, such as Federico Zuccaro and Jacopo Bertoia, who decorated the oratory of S Lucia del Gonfalone in Rome.

Several remarkable compositions by Blocklandt were engraved by various artists. Oil sketches dated 1574 (Utrecht, Cent. Mus.) apparently served as designs for Philip Galle's engravings of the *Four Evangelists*. There are several series of mythological subjects, including some of the earliest illustrations to be found in the Netherlands of Ovid's *Metamorphoses*, a theme that later became very popular. A series of engravings by Galle after Blocklandt's designs of the *Life of Adonis* (1570s; Hollstein: *Dut. & Flem.*, vii, nos 287–90) is characterized by tall elegant figures, with limbs often left unmodelled and impassive faces. The elegance of the figures is reminiscent of Parmigianino, while some of the compositions recall the graphic work of Andrea Schiavone. The influence of the former is also strong in the painting *Venus and Cupid* (Prague, N.G., Šternberk Pal.). Blocklandt composed his images with great precision. He made careful studies of heads, sometimes in an oil sketch, and came to use a few standard types, for example the frequently recurring image of a woman in *profil perdu* who bends her head slightly forward.

Blocklandt's greatest work is a large altarpiece dedicated to the Virgin (Bingen am Rhein, St Martin), comprising an *Assumption of the Virgin* (central panel; see fig.), an *Annunciation* and an *Adoration of the Shepherds* (inner wings) and the *Virgin as the Woman of the Apocalypse with an Anonymous Donor and St Michael* (outer wings). Probably made for a church in Utrecht in 1579, it was never installed because of the town's official conversion to Protestantism. The survival of a panel from another monumental altarpiece, with the *Baptism of Christ* on one side and *St Philip the Deacon* on the other (Lille, Mus. B.-A.), indicates that Blocklandt probably fulfilled further commissions of this kind. Two late paintings come from a series of the *Life of Joseph: Joseph Interpreting the Dreams of Pharaoh* (large fragment, Utrecht, Cent. Mus.) and *Joseph's Brothers Showing his Bloody Robe to Jacob* (Freising, Diözmus.). This was the unfinished series in Amsterdam mentioned by van Mander.

BIBLIOGRAPHY
K. van Mander: *Schilder-boeck* ([1603]–1604), fols 253*v*–5*r*
I. Jost: *Studien zu Anthonis Blocklandt* (diss., U. Cologne, 1960)
——: 'Ein unbekannter Altarflügel des Anthonis Blocklandt', *Oud-Holland*, lxxxii (1967), pp. 116–27
K. Johns: ' "Het leven van Ioseph den Patriarch": The Final Work of Anthonis Blocklandt', *Ned. Ksthist. Jb.*, xxxvii (1986), pp. 241–58
Kunst voor de beeldenstorm: Noordnederlandse kunst, 1525–1580 [Art before the iconoclasm: North Netherlandish art, 1525–1580] (exh. cat., ed.

Anthonie Blocklandt: central panel of the *Assumption of the Virgin*, altarpiece, oil on panel, 2.85×2.45 m, ?1579 (Bingen am Rhein, St Martin)

J. P. Filedt Kok, W. Halsema-Kubes and W. Th. Kloek; Amsterdam, Rijksmus., 1986), pp. 341, 419–28

WOUTER TH. KLOEK

Block statue. *See* EGYPT, ANCIENT, §IX, 2(i)(c).

Bloem, Hans. *See* BLUM, HANS.

Bloemaert. Dutch family of artists. Cornelis Bloemaert I (*b* Dordrecht, *c.* 1540; *d* Utrecht, *bur* 1 Nov 1593) was an architect, sculptor and teacher, whose pupils included Hendrick de Keyser I. In 1567 he visited 's Hertogenbosch in order to repair the city gates and the pulpit of the St Janskerk, which had been damaged in 1566 during the Iconoclastic Fury. From 1576 he lived in Utrecht, where in 1586 he collaborated on decorations for the ceremonial entry of Robert Dudley, 1st Earl of Leicester and self-styled Governor General of the United Provinces. From 1591 to 1593 Bloemaert was master builder of Amsterdam. His son (1) Abraham Bloemaert (*b* 1566) was the most gifted member of the family and became one of the most important painters working in Utrecht in the first half of the 17th century. Four of Abraham's sons also worked as artists, all of them receiving their initial training from their father. The eldest son, Hendrick Bloemaert (*b* Utrecht, 1601–2; *d* Utrecht, 30 Dec 1672), was a painter and poet. Hendrick travelled to Italy and was in Rome in 1627; he returned to Utrecht *c.* 1630. His oeuvre includes religious works, mythological and genre scenes and portraits. His best works are those in which he combined the style of the Utrecht Caravaggisti with the decorative manner of his father. As a poet, Hendrick is best known for his rhymed translation of Guarini's *Il pastor fido* (Venice, 1590). Abraham Bloemaert's second son, Cornelis Bloemaert II (*b* Utrecht, 1603; *d* Rome, ?1684), studied with his father, Gerrit van Honthorst and Crispijn de Passe I, but although he was originally trained as a painter, he devoted himself primarily to printmaking (see Hollstein, nos 1–321). In 1630 Cornelis the younger travelled to Paris and then to Rome, where he made prints after paintings and sculptures in major collections. He also made engravings after works by his father (e.g. six *Pastorals*, Hollstein, nos 212–15). Another of Abraham's sons, Adriaen Bloemaert (*b* Utrecht, *c.* 1609; *d* Utrecht, 8 Jan 1666), was a painter, draughtsman and perhaps also an engraver. He travelled to Italy and worked for a time in Salzburg, where in 1637 he painted eight canvases: the *Mysteries of the Rosary* (all U. Salzburg, Aula Academica). The landscapes signed *A. Blommaert*, which are attributed to him, are now believed to be the work of Abraham Blommaert (*fl* 1669–83) from Middelburg (see Bok and Roethlisberger). Frederick Bloemaert (*b* Utrecht, *c.* 1616; *d* Utrecht, 11 June 1690) worked exclusively as an engraver; almost all his prints were after his father's compositions. These include the engravings for his father's *Konstryk tekenboek* ('Artistic drawing book'), which was reprinted many times up to the 19th century.

PRINTS
Oorspronkelyk en vermaard konstryk tekenboek van Abraham Bloemaert, geestryk getekend, en meesterlyk gegraveert by zyn zoon Frederik Bloemaert (Amsterdam, 1711)

BIBLIOGRAPHY
Hollstein: *Dut. & Flem.*; Thieme–Becker; Wurzbach
K. van Mander: *Schilder-boeck* ([1603]–1604), fol. 297
M. G. Roethlisberger and M. J. Bok: *Abraham Bloemaert and his Sons: Paintings and Prints*, 2 vols (Doornspijk, 1993)
M. J. Bok and M. Roethlisberger: 'Not Adriaen Bloemaert but Abraham Blommaert (of Middelburg), Landscape Painter', *Oud-Holland*, cix (1995)

(1) Abraham Bloemaert (*b* Gorinchem, 24 Dec 1566; *d* Utrecht, 13 Jan 1651). Painter, draughtsman, writer and teacher. His long, successful career and many prominent pupils, especially among the Utrecht Caravaggisti, made him one of Utrecht's principal painters in the first half of the 17th century. During his lifetime he enjoyed high esteem for his paintings of religious and mythological subjects and for his numerous drawings. At first he worked in a Mannerist style, then in a Caravaggesque manner, finally adopting a distinctive, decorative synthesis of both approaches.

1. LIFE AND PAINTED WORK. According to van Mander, as a child Bloemaert moved with his family from Gorinchem to 's Hertogenbosch and from there to Utrecht. He began to draw in Utrecht, under the direction of his father, Cornelis Bloemaert I, copying works by Frans Floris. He was apprenticed to the painter Gerrit Splinter (*fl* 1569–89) but remained with him for only two weeks. His second teacher, Joos de Beer (*d* 1599), was a mediocre painter in van Mander's view, although he possessed an excellent collection of paintings, including works by Dirck Barendsz. and Anthonie Blocklandt. In preparation for an apprenticeship with Blocklandt (then the most important painter in Utrecht), Bloemaert was sent by his father to study with an unnamed bailiff at Hedel Castle, but the bailiff used Bloemaert as a house

servant rather than instructing him, and Bloemaert returned home empty-handed after 18 months. Then, *c.* 1582, he travelled to Paris, where he studied first with Jehan Bassot, later with a 'Maître Herry' and finally with Hieronymous Francken. (In later years Bloemaert complained bitterly of his fragmented training, under no fewer than six masters.) Before leaving Paris, he came in contact with French Mannerist works from the school of Fontainebleau. By 1585 he was back in Utrecht, where he probably worked with his father. In April 1591 he accompanied him to Amsterdam, of which he became a citizen on 13 October. In May 1592, the banns proclaimed in both Utrecht and Amsterdam, he married Judith van Schonenburgh (*d* 1599), a wealthy spinster 20 years his senior; this marriage remained childless. A year later he returned to Utrecht, where he remained for the rest of his life.

Two circular paintings, *Bacchus* and *Ceres* (both Buscot Park, Oxon, NT) were recognized by Roethlisberger as probably the earliest known works by Bloemaert (see Roethlisberger, 1994). They show a strong influence of the work of Frans Floris and the Fontainebleau school. The earliest known dated paintings, the *Death of the Children of Niobe* (1591; Copenhagen, Stat. Mus. Kst; see fig. 1) and *Apollo and Daphne* (1592; ex-Schles. Mus. Bild. Kst., Breslau; ? destr.), were executed in Amsterdam in a style strongly related to the late Mannerist style influenced by Bartholomäus Spranger that was current in Haarlem at that time. In works of this period one part of the scene, often the principal subject, takes place in the background, while the foreground is filled with large, usually nude, figures, who are presented in unnaturally twisted poses. The distinction between foreground and background is emphasized by colour: warm foreground colours, such as brown and red, contrast with the cooler greens and greywhites of the background. Although the muscular figures betray the considerable influence of Cornelis Cornelisz. van Haarlem's characteristically Mannerist works of the late 1580s, they are distinguished by their lyrical character: strong emotion and violence are alien to Bloemaert, and his modelling of the muscles is softer. Several of Bloemaert's Mannerist works before *c.* 1600 represent religious and mythological subjects not previously depicted in Dutch art, such as the *Death of the Children of Niobe* and the *Burning of Troy* (Frankfurt am Main, Städel. Kstinst. & Städt. Gal.). The latter is one of several loosely painted nocturnes executed *c.* 1593; these small panels, which also include two versions of *Judith* (Vienna, Ksthist. Mus., and Frankfurt am Main, Städel. Kstinst. & Städt. Gal.), reveal a combination of brilliant lighting effects and bright acidic colours.

After 1595 the transition between the foreground and background in Bloemaert's works became less abrupt. He deployed the figures more evenly within the picture space, as in *Moses Striking Water from the Rock* (1596; New York, Met.). Landscape elements became more important after 1596, as can be seen, for example, in *St John the Baptist Preaching* (Amsterdam, Rijksmus.) and the *Baptism* (Ham House, Surrey, NT); powerful tree formations in particular are prominent in his work of this period. The attitudes of the figures remain unnatural, however, and the musculature is still exaggerated.

1. Abraham Bloemaert: *Death of the Children of Niobe*, oil on canvas, 2.04×2.49 m, 1591 (Copenhagen, Statens Museum for Kunst)

After the death of his first wife, Bloemaert married Gerarda de Roij, the daughter of a local brewer, on 12 October 1600; they had many children, four of whom became artists. Around this time his work manifested a development that had occurred earlier in Haarlem, influenced by Hendrick Goltzius's journey to Italy. The exaggerated poses used by Bartholomäus Spranger began to give way to more relaxed, natural figures who move freely, usually within more naturalistic surroundings, giving the paintings of these years, such as the *Baptism* (1602; Ottawa, N.G.), a more subdued Mannerism. At the same time he painted his first landscapes with picturesque ruined cottages, in which the religious or mythological figures play a subordinate role, such as the *Parable of the Sower* (1605; print by Jacob Matham after Bloemaert, Hollstein, xi, p. 221) and *Tobias and the Angel* (St Petersburg, Hermitage). Country life was to remain a favourite subject, which he depicted with an increasing naturalism; however, as van Mander recommended, he drew such motifs as peasant cottages, dovecotes and trees from life ('*naer het leven*') and then in his studio composed them into imagined scenes ('*uyt den geest*').

Between 1610 and 1615 the Catholic Church awarded several important commissions to Bloemaert, who was a devout Catholic. In 1612 he painted an *Adoration of the Shepherds* (Paris, Louvre) for the convent of the Poor Clares in 's Hertogenbosch, where his sister Barbara was a nun, and in 1615 *Christ and the Virgin before God the Father* for the new high altar of the St Janskerk in the same town. In 1611 he was one of the founders of the Utrecht Guild of St Luke.

Bloemaert's career reached a peak in the 1620s; influenced by his pupil Gerrit van Honthorst, who had returned from Italy in 1620, and other Utrecht Caravaggisti, he painted several Caravaggesque pieces c. 1623, some of which are notable for their use of candlelight effects, as in the *Supper at Emmaus* (Brussels, Mus. A. Anc.) and the *Adoration of the Shepherds* (Brunswick, Herzog Anton Ulrich-Mus.), and others for the half-length figures, such as *The Flute-player* (Utrecht, Cent. Mus.). He also made large altarpieces for clandestine Catholic churches, including an *Adoration of the Shepherds* (1623; The Hague, St Jacobskerk) and an *Adoration of the Magi* (Utrecht, Cent. Mus.). In 1625 Bloemaert was commissioned by Frederick Henry, Stadholder of the Netherlands, to paint two scenes from the *Story of Theagenes and Chariclea* for Honselersdijk: *Theagenes, Chariclea and the Robbers* (1625; Potsdam, Schloss Sanssouci) and *Theagenes Receiving the Prize from*

Chariclea (1626; The Hague, Mauritshuis). Still under the influence of the Utrecht Caravaggisti, he also painted several small pastoral landscapes with peasants and shepherds (e.g. Hannover, Niedersächs. Landesmus.), as well as half-length shepherds and shepherdesses (e.g. Karlsruhe, Staatl. Ksthalle; Toledo, OH, Mus. A.). Bloemaert's large figural works of the 1620s, such as the *Adoration of the Magi* and *Theagenes Receiving the Prize from Chariclea*, are characterized by an extremely rich palette, with colours varying from citron yellow and bright blue to penetrating reds, acidic greens and pinks. This multicoloured mixture enhances the decorative character of the paintings. The pastoral landscapes of the same period, with shepherds and peasants, were painted in lighter pastel tints; these found great favour during the 18th century, notably with François Boucher.

Bloemaert's interest in peasant life was expressed in the 1630s mainly in studies of heads of old men and women (e.g. Stockholm, Nmus.; Dresden, Gemäldegal. Alte Meister). These reveal Bloemaert as a keen observer, though they lack the psychological depth of similar studies by Jan Lievens or Rembrandt. Bloemaert's *Rest on the Flight to Egypt* (1632; Amsterdam, Rijksmus.) is set, most unusually, in a peasant hut. In 1635 Frederick Henry commissioned another painting from Bloemaert for Honselersdijk, this time the *Wedding of Amarillis and Mirtillo* (Berlin, Jagdschloss Grunewald), a scene from Guarini's *Il pastor fido* (Venice, 1590).

Bloemaert's last paintings, executed in the 1640s when he was in his eighties, show his technical skill undiminished; their style is still decorative and their subjects increasingly recall his earlier works, as in *Mercury, Argus and Io* (1645; Vaduz, Samml. Liechtenstein) and *Leto and the Peasants* (1645; Utrecht, Cent. Mus.). In the background of his *Landscape with a Farmhouse* (1650; Berlin, Gemäldegal.) is a Mannerist scene of Tobias and the Angel.

2. DRAWINGS. Bloemaert was also a talented draughtsman. His enormous output, more than 1500 drawings, covers not only figure drawings, peasant cottages, nature studies and preparatory studies for paintings, but also countless detailed drawings that served as models for prints (see fig. 2). According to van Mander he had 'a very nice manner of drawing and handling the pen, and he obtained an unusual effect by adding a few succulent touches of colour'. His drawings are characterized by the great variety of both the techniques he applied and especially the styles he used. The latter is not surprising, as he had a long professional life and probably continued drawing until the last year of his life. His early landscape drawings can be considered as belonging to the best ever made in this genre. On the one hand they still show influence of such predecessors as Pieter Bruegel the elder and Hendrick Goltzius, but on the other they stand out because of a very precise observation of nature. Compositions from his Mannerist period were made into prints by, among others, Jan Saenredam, Jan Muller and Jacques de Gheyn II, and later by his sons Cornelis and Frederick, which greatly facilitated the dissemination of his oeuvre. His drawings were extremely popular and were frequently copied. His *Konstryk tekenboek* ('Artistic drawing book'),

2. Abraham Bloemaert: *Landscape at Sunrise with a Gnarled Tree, Shepherd and Sheepcote*, pen and brown ink, blue-green wash, over black chalk, 148×231 mm, *c.* 1600–10 (Amsterdam, Rijksmuseum)

a pattern book for young artists, was engraved by Frederick Bloemaert and appeared in numerous editions up to the 19th century.

3. INFLUENCE AND POSTHUMOUS REPUTATION. As a teacher, Bloemaert played an important role in the formation of a distinctive Utrecht style of painting. Not only were such Utrecht Caravaggisti as Gerrit van Honthorst, Hendrick ter Brugghen and Jan van Bijlert his pupils, but the Dutch Italianates Cornelis van Poelenburch, Jan Both and Jan Weenix also studied with him, as did Jacob Gerritsz. Cuyp. The great Flemish master Peter Paul Rubens visited him in 1627. Bloemaert's early style had a significant influence on the work of Joachim Wtewael, but his son Hendrick Bloemaert was the only artist who continued to work in his mature manner. Although Abraham Bloemaert enjoyed high esteem in his own day, his reputation has, for a long time, up to 1993, suffered from the lack of an up-to-date catalogue raisonné of his entire oeuvre.

BIBLIOGRAPHY

Hollstein: *Dut. & Flem.*; Thieme–Becker
K. van Mander: *Schilder-boeck* ([1603]–1604), fols 297*r*–298*r*
G. Delbanco: *Der Maler Abraham Bloemaert* (diss., U. Strasbourg, 1928)
M. A. Lavin: 'An Attribution to Abraham Bloemaert', *Oud-Holland*, lxxx (1965), pp. 123–5 [rosailles]
M. Röthlisberger: 'Abraham Bloemaert', *Gemälde bedeutender niederländischer Meister des 17. Jahrhunderts* (exh. cat., Vienna, Gal. Friederike Pallamar, 1967), pp. 15–26
Abraham Bloemaert, 1564–1651: Prints and Drawings (exh. cat., New York, Met., 1973)
G. Vikan: 'Notes on Princeton Drawings, 10: Abraham Bloemaert', *Rec. A. Mus., Princeton U.*, xxxiii (1974), pp. 2–17
R. S. Slatkin: 'Abraham Bloemaert and François Boucher: Affinity and Relationship', *Master Drgs*, xiv/3 (1976), pp. 247–60
J. Bolten: *Method and Practice: Dutch and Flemish Drawing Books, 1600–1750* (Landau, 1985)
Nieuw licht op de Gouden Eeuw (exh. cat., ed. A. Blankert and L. J. Slatkes; Utrecht, Cent. Mus.; Brunswick, Herzog Anton Ulrich-Mus., 1986–7), pp. 208–17
R. Ruurs: 'The Date of Abraham Bloemaert's Birth', *Hoogsteder-Naumann Mercury*, 9 (1989), pp. 4–5
J. Bolton: 'Abraham Bloemaert (1564–1651) and his *Tekenboek*', *Delineavit & Sculp.*, 9 (March 1993), pp. 1–10
M. G. Roethlisberger and M. J. Bok: *Abraham Bloemaert and his Sons: Paintings and Prints*, 2 vols (Doornspijk, 1993)
Dawn of the Golden Age: Northern Netherlandish Art, 1580–1620 (exh. cat., ed. G. Luijten and others; Amsterdam, Rijksmus., 1993–4), pp. 300–01 and *passim*
M. G. Roethlisberger: 'Early Abraham Bloemaert', *Tableau*, xvii/3 (1994), pp. 44–51

C. J. A. WANSINK

Bloemen [Blommen; Bloms], **van.** Flemish family of painters and draughtsmen, active also in Italy and France. While still in their native Antwerp, (1) Pieter van Bloemen was the first teacher of his brother (2) Jan Frans van Bloemen—who later also studied with Antoine Goubau—and probably also of his younger brother Norbert van Bloemen (*b* Antwerp, 10 Feb 1670; *d* Amsterdam, *c.* 1746). From 1667 Pieter had himself trained with Simon van Douw (*c.* 1630–*c.* 1677), and in 1673 he became a master in the Antwerp Guild of St Luke. The following year he travelled to Rome. He is recorded in Lyon about a decade later (*c.* 1684) in the company of the Dutch artists Adriaen van der Cabel and Gillis Weenix. At about the same time (*c.* 1684–5) Jan Frans was in Paris, until he was summoned by his brother to Lyon. There Jan Frans apparently worked

with van der Cabel. The two brothers were not happy in Lyon, however, and went to Rome. They travelled via Turin, staying there for some time. From 1686–7 they were in Rome, where they were both members of the Schildersbent, the confraternity of Dutch and Flemish artists active in Rome. Pieter was given the bent or nickname Standaart (or Stendardo), undoubtedly a reference to the banners and standards that he depicted in his scenes of soldiers; Jan Frans's facility for producing panoramic landscapes earned him the nickname Orizzonte (It.: 'horizon'), which had previously been applied to Claude Lorrain. Jan Frans did not leave Rome again, apart from an eight-month journey to Naples, Sicily and Malta, from which he returned with a large number of drawings. Pieter left in 1692, after having had the Flemish painter Frans Vanier as his assistant (1689–92); he was back in Antwerp in 1694 and became dean of the Guild of St Luke there in 1699. Norbert also apparently joined his brothers in Rome, where he too was a member of the Schildersbent (which gave him the nickname Cephalus). After failing to succeed as an artist in Italy, however, Norbert returned to Antwerp. His fortunes were no better there, and he set off again, eventually settling in Amsterdam, where he painted history subjects, interior genre scenes and portraits, for instance that of the art dealer and collector *Jan Pietersz. Zoomer* (Amsterdam, Rijksmus.).

(1) Pieter van Bloemen (*b* Antwerp, *bapt* 17 Jan 1657; *d* Antwerp, before 6 March 1720). His production of paintings was prolific; most are landscapes with figures and animals, caravan scenes with camps and resting travellers and animals, military and genre scenes and horse markets. He was at his best painting animals, which he also provided for works by other artists. His period in Italy was the most successful of his career, and his work continued to bear traces of its influence to the end of his life. Characteristic of van Bloemen's style are carefully grouped 'still-lifes' of animals, open, Italianate landscapes with one or two monuments to convey the 'Roman' atmosphere and the lively colouring of the figures' costumes contrasted to the more sombre greys and browns of the herds and ruins. Typical works include a *Herd of Cattle in the Ruins of the Roman Forum* (Karlsruhe, Staatl. Ksthalle); a *Blacksmith* with a pendant *Drinking-place* (both Rome, Zingone priv. col.); *Riders in a Roman Landscape* (1700; Dresden, Gemäldegal. Alte Meister); a *Caravan* (1704; Madrid, Prado); a *Cavalry Camp* (1708; Rome, Pal. Barberini); and the *Market between Roman Ruins* (1710; Dresden, Gemaldegal. Alte Meister.). His drawings are mainly landscapes and figure and animal studies from life.

BIBLIOGRAPHY

A. Busiri Vici: 'Pieter van Bloemen, detto "Stendardo"', *Stud. Romani*, viii/3 (1960), pp. 279–88
D. Bodart: *Les Peintres des Pays-Bas méridionaux et de la principauté de Liège à Rome au XVIIe siècle*, i (Brussels and Rome, 1970), pp. 455–60
N. Smolskaya: 'Pieter van Bloemen', *Trudy Gosudarstvennogo Ermitazha*, xxv (1985), pp. 62–7

CHRISTINE VAN MULDERS

(2) Jan Frans van Bloemen [Orizzonte] (*b* Antwerp, *bapt* 12 May 1662; *d* Rome, 13 June 1749). Brother of (1) Pieter van Bloemen. He was married in Rome in 1693,

Jan Frans van Bloemen: *Landscape with the Colosseum*, oil on canvas, 1.19×1.65 m, 1741 (Rome, Galleria Pallavicini)

and the Dutch artist Caspar van Wittel, known as 'Vanvitelli', was godfather to the couple's first child, baptized in 1694. Although patronized by aristocratic Roman families, Orizzonte's artistic career was marred by his prolonged confrontation with the Accademia di S Luca. The precise reasons for the difficulties are unknown, but he was only finally accepted by the Accademia at the age of 80, after his third application for membership.

Orizzonte was inspired by the classicizing landscape paintings of Gaspard Dughet, as well as by the beauty of Rome and the surrounding campagna. With the Flemish landscape tradition as his foundation he easily absorbed Dughet's dynamic and analytic style, producing such works as *Landscape with Ruins, Nocturnal Landscape* and the *Storm* (all Rome, Pal. Doria-Pamphili). Some of Orizzonte's views, painted at the end of the 17th century, anticipate the *vedute* (view paintings) of the 18th century and mark a shift from the classically orientated Roman landscapes of his French predecessors in Rome. In pictures such as *Landscape* (Attingham Park, Salop, NT), the *View of Gardens with Statues* (Schloss Wörlitz, nr Dessau) and the *Landscape with the Colosseum* (Rome, Gal. Pallavicini; see fig.), there is a more realistic representation of views, and the paintings show characteristics close to those of Andrea Locatelli, Giovanni Paolo Panini and Paolo Anesi. Around 1730 Orizzonte began to adapt his delicate and sensitive style towards a calmer and more synthetic artistic vision, some features of which were borrowed directly from Poussin, as in the *Landscape with the Belvedere of the*

Vatican (Rome, Gal. Pallavicini) and the *Landscape with Temple* (Tivoli, Villa d'Este). Among the painters who provided figures for his landscapes were Carlo Maratti, Placido Costanzi and Pompeo Batoni.

Considered a great artist by his contemporaries, Orizzonte produced some of the finest classical landscape painting in Rome during the first half of the 18th century. His numerous Italianate landscapes are distributed in museums and private collections throughout Europe, many being in England. His pupils, for example Francesco Oelefe, known as 'Bavarese', Gabriele Ricciardelli and Nicolo Bonito, all imitated his style.

BIBLIOGRAPHY
F. J. Van den Branden: *Geschiedenis der Antwerpsche schilderschool* (Antwerp, 1883), p. 1081
J. A. F. Orbaan: *Bescheiden in Italië omtrent Nederlandsche kunstenaars en geleerden*, i (The Hague, 1911), p. 260
W. Bombe: 'Ein uneditierte Lebensbeschreibung des Malers Jan Frans Van Bloemen', *Repert. Kstwissen.*, lxvi (1925)
D. Coekelberghs: 'J. F. Van Bloemen et le paysagisme romain du XVIIIe siecle', *Annales du Congrès de Liège: Liège, 1968*
A. Zwollo: *Hollandse en Vlaamse veduteschilders te Rome, 1675–1725* (Assen, 1973)
D. Coekelberghs: *Les Peintres belges à Rome, de 1700 à 1830* (Brussels, 1976)
ALAIN JACOBS

Bloemfontein. South African city in the Orange Free State. Established on the site of a former farm in 1848, it later became the state capital (1854) and seat of the South African judiciary (1910). Following modest development from the late 1860s, in the 1880s a number of churches and other public buildings were built, such as the Dutch Reformed Church (1880) by the local architect Richard Wocke (1831–90). The new Presidency (1885) and the fourth Raadzaal (1893), in Greek Revival style, were designed by F. Lennox Canning (?1856–95). Building in the 1890s was dominated by the Dutch architects J. E. Vixseboxse (1863–1943) and D. E. Wentink (*fl* 1891–1903), who worked in a Dutch and Flemish Revival style, and the English architects WILLIAM HENRY STUCKE and John Edwin Harrison (1870–1945). In 1893 the Orange Free State Fine and Industrial Arts Association was founded under the chairmanship of D. B. O. Kellner (1836–1918), and it organized exhibitions. After the Anglo-Boer War (1899–1902), in the period of the Orange River Colony (1902–10), there was an influx of British immigrants and a marked strengthening of British influences as seen in the architecture of such figures as HERBERT BAKER and FRANCIS MASEY. Their partner F. K. KENDALL supervised (1902–5) work on the new government offices. Other notable buildings from the first half of the 20th century include the Grand Theatre (1906; destr.) by E. C. Choinier, St Patrick's Church (1908–23; destr.) by the untrained architect Edgar Rose, the Appeal Court (1929) and the City Hall (1934). Various art schools and institutes were set up in this period: the short-lived Association of Arts and Crafts (1907, revived 1925), the School of Art (1921), founded by John Muff-Ford (1884–1981), and the South African Institute of Art (1926). In the 1920s the artist Sydney Carter (1874–1945) briefly settled in the city, and in 1958 the loose association of local artists, the Bloemfontein Group, was founded under the leadership of Alexander Podlashuc (*b* 1930) and lasted several decades. Public sculpture flourished in the 20th century, leading to such works as the Vrouemonument (Women's Monument; 1913) by Anton van Wouw (1862–1945) and the equestrian statue of *General C. R. de Wet* (1954) by Coert Steynberg (1905–82). Other notable sculpture was made by the local artists Laurika Postma (1903–87), Frieda Ollemans (*b* 1915) and Laura Rautenbach (*b* 1932). Rapid economic development and expansion, which began in the 1960s, led to the destruction of many old buildings, which were replaced by largely unremarkable new ones. Two public art galleries were, however, founded: the A. C. White Art Gallery (1960) and the Oliewenhuis Art Museum (1989).

BIBLIOGRAPHY
E. Berman: *Art and Artists of South Africa* (Cape Town, 1970, rev. 1983)
K. Schoeman: *Bloemfontein: Die ontstaan van 'n stad, 1846–1946* [Bloemfontein: the development of a city, 1846–1946] (Cape Town, 1980)
——: *Vrystaatse erfenis* [Free State heritage] (Cape Town, 1982)
——: *Boukunsskatte van die Vrystaat/Free State Heritage* (Roodeport, 1985) [bilingual text]

KAREL SCHOEMAN

Blois, château of. French royal château, dominating the town of Blois, Loir-et-Cher, on the spur of land above the River Loire on the old Chartres–Bourges road. In its present form it consists mainly of buildings undertaken in the 16th century by Louis XII and Francis I and in the 17th century by Gaston d'Orléans (1608–1660), brother of Louis XIII.

Records of a castle belonging to the counts of Blois on this site go back to AD 903. Of the early buildings, whose disposition shaped the irregular quadrilateral courtyard around which the present château stands, there survive the twin-aisled, arcaded Great Hall (or Salle des Etats-Généraux) built by Theobald VI (*reg* 1205–18), the round Tour du Foix and part of the north wall of the fortifications. In 1391 the château passed to the Orléans family and thence to Louis XII, who had been born at Blois in 1462. On succeeding to the throne in 1498, Louis immediately set about rebuilding the château, to which his father, Charles, Duke of Orléans, had made some modifications (destr.) after 1440. Louis's principal contribution is the north-east wing (1498–1508), which forms the principal entrance to the courtyard. The design has been attributed to Colin Biart; François de Pontbriant (?1451–1521) is recorded as Clerk of Works. It consists of a two-storey elevation of red brick with a lozenge pattern of black bricks. The dressings to the quoins and the irregularly spaced mullioned windows with drip mouldings are of stone, as are the elaborately decorated dormer windows in the steep slate roof with its tall brick chimneys. The entrance, which is placed off-centre, is surmounted by an equestrian statue of *Louis XII* (a poor 19th-century replica of the original, destroyed in the French Revolution), set into a carved niche of late medieval form. The royal device of a porcupine is much in evidence in the sculptural decoration, which also incorporates stiff Italian Renaissance elements alongside more graceful medieval ones. The courtyard elevation has an open arcade of basket arches at ground-floor level, with an enclosed gallery above. There are square, enclosed staircase turrets at each end.

The chapel of St Calais (consecrated 1508), of which only the three bays of the choir remain, and the octagonal garden pavilion (*c.* 1503) of Anne of Brittany also belong to Louis XII's building campaign. The extensive gardens designed for him by the Neapolitan Pacello da Mercogliano (*d* 1534) no longer survive.

The most impressive part of the château is the north-west wing (1515–24), built against the medieval ramparts for Francis I. Here the rich decoration of the ashlar-faced, three-storey inner and outer elevations, with pilasters, entablatures and other classicizing elements, is Italianate. The irregular disposition of the parts is, however, dictated by the site and the sequence of rooms within. It is possible that the Italian influence is due to Domenico da Cortona, though construction before 1519 was probably the responsibility of Jacques Sourdeau (*c.* 1460–1522), Master Mason to the King, who moved to the château of Chambord at that date. The main feature of the courtyard elevation is the great open polygonal staircase turret (see fig.) that originally occupied its centre; it is monumental in conception and festive in its decoration. The garden front, thrown out from the ramparts, consists of three superimposed arcades (the lowest closed in) below an openwork balustrade around the attic storey.

Work on the château came to a halt with Francis I's Italian campaign (1524–5); it was not resumed until 1635, when Gaston d'Orléans, eager to establish a rival court to that of his brother, employed François Mansart (*see* MANSART, (1)) to rebuild the south-west wing (1635–9).

Château of Blois, north-west wing, staircase turret, 1515–24

In 1638 Cardinal Richelieu cut off funds for the project, which was left incomplete. The courtyard façade is majestically articulated by the slightly projecting central staircase bay, and this main block is tied to two short projecting wings by segmental colonnades. The elevation to the gardens, which is on a different axis, is raised on battered ramparts and flanked by two boldly projecting pavilions. Internally, the well of the grand staircase is lit through a rectangular opening by an oval dome crowned by a lantern. The staircase itself (*see* STAIRCASE, fig. 2) was built in 1932 to a design based on that by Mansart at the château of Maisons (Maisons-Laffitte, near Paris).

During the 18th century the château of Blois was neglected, and after 1788 it was used as a barracks. In 1810 it was given to the town of Blois, and in 1840 it was listed as a historic monument. Extensive restoration was carried out from 1845 to 1869 by Félix-Jacques Duban and others. It suffered damage, since repaired, from German bombardment in 1944.

BIBLIOGRAPHY

J.-A. Du Cerceau: *Les Plus Excellents Bastiments de France*, ii (Paris, 1579/*R* London, 1972)
F. Lesueur and P. Lesueur: *Le Château de Blois* (Paris, 1914–21, rev., shortened, 2/1970)
A. Betgé: 'Les Constructions de Gaston d'Orléans au château de Blois', *Mém. Soc. Sci. & Lett. Loir-et-Cher*, xxx (Blois, 1938), pp. 61–168
A. Braham and P. Smith: *François Mansart* (London, 1973)
A. Cospérec: 'L'Aile François 1er du château de Blois, une nouvelle chronologie', *Bull. Mnmtl*, cli (1993), pp. 591–603
——: *Blois, la forme d'une ville: Etude topographique et monumentale* (1994)

JEAN MARTIN-DEMÉZIL

Blois, Henry of. *See* HENRY OF BLOIS.

Blok, Aleksandr (Aleksandrovich) (*b* St Petersburg, 28 Nov 1880; *d* Petrograd [now St Petersburg], 7 Aug 1921). Russian poet and critic. Italian Renaissance painting and the work of contemporary Russian and foreign artists of the modern school greatly influenced Blok's poetry, which in turn was exceptionally suggestive for masters of the fine arts as well as for many Symbolist poets. Blok belonged to the second generation of Russian Symbolist poets, who saw literature as a powerful theurgic force, capable of revealing the true, ideal world through temporal symbols. Symbolism in Russia was strongly influenced by the mystical philosophy of Vladimir Solovyov (1853–1900), who initiated the cult of the divine Sophia—the image of Eternal Woman as the soul of the universe and the link between the human and the divine. Blok reflected this cult in his *Stikhi o prekrasnoy dame* ('Verses about the beautiful lady'). The beautiful lady whom Blok described is both a real woman and a transcendental figure, unattainable Beauty, the Ideal. She assumes an unearthly aspect, revealing herself to the poet in an atmosphere of dreams that are like fairy tales or medieval visions.

Blok's ethereal images of the Eternal Feminine recur in the paintings of the Symbolist artist Viktor Borisov-Musatov and in the works of the artists of the Blue Rose group. Borisov-Musatov's works, haunted as they are by a nostalgic longing for the grace of a bygone age and a remote feminine beauty, are paradigmatic. Such retrospection and evocation of mood, where spiritual and physical wholeness are identified in another 'time', characterized Symbolist poetry and painting alike, and the function of art was seen in terms of transporting the individual from the quasi-real to the much more real world. Blok's links with the art world were strengthened as a result of his critical articles in the magazines *Mir Isskusstva* (World of art) and *Zolotoye Runo* (Golden fleece). Apart from Borisov-Musatov's work, Blok's poetic pictures share many features in common with the painting of Mikhail Vrubel'. Blok's poem *Dvenadtsat'* ('Twelve'; 1918) in particular attracted illustrators, notably Yurii Annenkov whose illustrations (1918) were the fruit of a creative dialogue with the poet.

WRITINGS
Sobraniye sochinenii [Collected works], 8 vols (Moscow, 1960–63)

BIBLIOGRAPHY
V. Alfonsov: *Slova i Kraski: Ocherki iz istorii tvorcheskikh svyazey poetov i khudozhnikov* [Words and paint: essays from the history of creative links between poets and artists] (Moscow and Leningrad, 1966)
J. E. Bowlt: 'Russian Symbolism and the Blue Rose Movement', *Slav. & E. Eur. Rev.*, li/123 (1973), pp. 161–81
A. Pyman: *The Distant Thunder, 1880–1908*, i of *The Life of Alexandr Blok* (Oxford, 1979)
M. Z. Dolinsky: *Iskusstvo i Aleksandr Blok* [Art and Aleksandr Blok] (Moscow, 1985)
A. M. Gordin and M. A. Gordin: *Aleksandr Blok i russkiye khudozhniki* [Aleksandr Blok and Russian artists] (Leningrad, 1986)

CHARLOTTE HUMPHREYS

Blom. *See* BLUME.

Blom, Piet(er) (*b* Amsterdam, 8 Feb 1934). Dutch architect. He attended the Academie van Bouwkunst, Amsterdam, in the evenings from 1956 to 1959 and won the Prix de Rome in 1962. He became internationally known through his final examination project, 'Dorpsgewijs bewonen van steden' ('Village-style living in towns'), presented at the CIAM congress in Otterlo in 1959. His ideas are related to those of Aldo van Eyck, a prominent member of Team Ten and a representative of Dutch structuralism. During the 1960s Blom was very active in the Provo protest movement, which denounced conventional society and increasing bureaucracy. Like van Eyck, Blom wanted to give form to the interplay between private and public life, between a single room and the building as a whole. By means of varied combinations of the same basic constructional unit, as in the De Bastille refectory building (1964–7) for the Technische Universiteit near Enschede, he strove to establish a visual relation between an individual space and the whole. In the 'Academie Minerva' building (1976–84) for the Academie voor Beeldende Kunsten, Groningen, symmetry of diagonals was the governing principle. His best-known works are the residential district De Kasbah (1967–70) in Hengelo and extensions to Blaak (1978–84), Rotterdam, in both of which the distinction between architecture and urban planning was diminished. In the Rotterdam project he designed houses, shops and an academy building as one unit over an important trunk road, like a 20th-century Rialto Bridge. The houses comprise large hexagonal blocks that surmount the walkway on concrete stairways. Blom's design is very craftsmanlike in its use of wood, concrete and brick, but he expanded the playfulness of his architecture by the bold use of colour.

WRITINGS

with R. Brouwers: 'Piet Blom: De vormgever van het alternatief', *Tijdschr. Archit. & Beeld. Kst*, 22–3 (1969), pp. 540–58, 564–90

BIBLIOGRAPHY

S. Hiddema: *Piet Blom en de kunst van het bouwen* (Groningen, 1984)
M. Sack: 'Piet Blom', *Mag. Int. Wohnen*, 2 (1986), pp. 59–70

JOUKE VAN DER WERF

Blomfield, Sir Reginald (Theodore) (*b* Bow, Devon, 20 Dec 1856; *d* Hampstead, London, 27 Dec 1942). English architect and writer. He was educated at Haileybury College, Herts, and then read Classics at Oxford University. In 1881 he entered into articled pupillage with his uncle, Arthur W. Blomfield (1829–99), a Gothic Revival architect, and attended classes at the Royal Academy schools under R. Phené Spiers (1838–1916).

Blomfield set up his own practice in 1884, with early commissions coming from church, school and family connections. This work is mainly in the OLD ENGLISH STYLE. Through E. S. Prior he met the circle of R. Norman Shaw's young pupils and assistants, who were the main instigators of the ART WORKERS' GUILD and the Arts and Crafts Exhibition Society. Blomfield became a leading member of both organizations and in 1890 was a founder of Kenton & Co., a furniture manufacturing company established in London and based on Arts and Crafts principles. Although he eventually became unsympathetic to some of the more simplistic dogmas of the ARTS AND CRAFTS MOVEMENT, he always maintained that architecture should be at the head of the arts rather than at the foot of the professions and that art should not be segregated into narrow and exclusive compartments. During the 1880s Blomfield began to write articles, mainly concentrating on an exploration of the English

Renaissance. From these works sprang his first two great literary successes, *The Formal Garden in England* (1892), illustrated by F. Inigo Thomas, and *A History of Renaissance Architecture in England, 1500–1800* (1897). These books began a literary career that lasted almost up to his death and also gave a great boost to his practice. Blomfield believed that the garden should be designed by the architect to complement the house, and he supported a return to more formal, geometric, garden designs. Typical is the garden at Apethorpe Hall, Northants (1904), which combines grand avenues and vistas with more intimate spaces. Commissions for the restoration and design of country houses and gardens came his way. In 1892 he began the garden restoration at Chequers Court, near Wendover, Bucks. The house was also gradually altered so that by the time it was presented to the nation in 1917 as the prime minister's country residence, it had been completely reorganized. The country seat of Charles Pelham, the 4th Earl of Yarborough, Brocklesby Park, Lincs, a mainly 18th-century house with 19th-century additions, was remodelled along with its gardens after a fire in 1898, with Blomfield's interior decoration mainly in a late 17th-century style. Most new houses were smaller in scale, though grand and classical in concept, and built of red brick and stone, such as Moundsmere Manor, Nutley, Hants (1908), and Wittington, Medmenham, Bucks (1897, 1909). For these commissions Blomfield borrowed features from Christopher Wren and late 17th-century architecture. He also found this style ideal for some of the larger institutional and commercial buildings he designed, such as the London and County Bank (1909; now National Westminster Bank), King's Road, Chelsea, London. Blomfield's style later evolved into a grander but more severe and restrained classicism, which he championed through both his writing and his designs.

This purer classical style was suitable for large-scale urban developments; since it had rules and could be taught, it gained widespread acceptance in the new full-time schools of architecture. Blomfield believed that greater coordination among teaching centres was needed and supported the movement for the reform of architectural education. He was a member of the Board of Architectural Education from its inception in 1904. Mainly through this involvement in education, he consolidated his position as an establishment figure in the first decade of the 20th century. He was elected an ARA in 1905, an RA in 1914 and was Professor of Architecture at the Academy from 1907 to 1911. He joined the RIBA in 1906 and was President 1912–14. His RA lectures, outlining his approach to classicism, were published in 1908 and the first two volumes of his *History of French Architecture* appeared in 1911. World War I interrupted his career as a leading architect of country houses, but despite his age Blomfield did not retire and started a new phase in his career. He was knighted in 1919.

Before the war Blomfield had served on a committee concerned with the completion of the Quadrant, Regent Street, London, left unfinished on R. Norman Shaw's death in 1912. He produced the design that was eventually built in the years 1923–27 and suggested extending his scheme to remodel the whole of Piccadilly Circus (see fig.), but this was unrealized. This opened the way for his

Reginald Blomfield: projected design for Piccadilly Circus, London, with (left) his buildings completing the Quadrant (1923–7) and (right) buildings proposed *c.* 1929 (unexecuted); from a drawing by Cyril Farey, 1936 (private collection)

choice as architect for the Headrow, Leeds (1924–37), a dignified new urban thoroughfare, and as assessor for other large-scale projects. He continued his interest in urban schemes, participating from 1916 in the lengthy deliberations over the future of London's bridges and producing in 1925 the first design for Lambeth Bridge (1926–32) in conjunction with the London County Council architect and engineer George Humphreys (1865–1948).

The second strand of his new career was his work for the Imperial War Graves Commission. Appointed one of three principal architects in 1918 with Herbert Baker and Edwin Lutyens, he had responsibility for the design of many cemeteries in northern France and Belgium. He also designed the War Cross, an austere stone cross which was used as a standard feature for all cemeteries. The Menin Gate, Ypres (1922), placed at a main entry to the town, has a large vaulted interior where stone tablets record the names of the missing. It is one of Blomfield's major works, and he was responsible for the choice of the building's location as well as its form.

Although he continued to practise with his son, Austin Blomfield (1892–1968), Blomfield's declining years in the 1930s were marred by controversy. His book *Modernismus* (1934) was a merciless and indiscriminate attack on the Modern Movement, which alienated virtually the whole of the succeeding generation. His plan to replace John Nash's Carlton House Terrace with a scheme of his own brought the opprobrium of almost the entire artistic establishment in early 1933. Blomfield, who had long been seen as an arbiter of taste, was gleefully discredited. His aggressive manner often made him unpopular, and some of his design work appears stilted, but he was a man of considerable and versatile ability, with talent as a draughtsman, writer and scholar. He was proficient as a designer of a range of building types and was at the forefront of professional politics and architectural movements of the Edwardian period.

WRITINGS

The Formal Garden in England (London, 1892)
A History of Renaissance Architecture in England, 1500–1800, 2 vols (London, 1897)
A Short History of Renaissance Architecture in England, 1500–1800 (London, 1900)
Studies in Architecture (London, 1905)
The Mistress Art (London, 1908)
A History of French Architecture from the Reign of Charles VIII till the Death of Mazarin, 1494–1661, 2 vols (London, 1911)
Architectural Drawing and Draughtsmen (London, New York, Toronto and Melbourne, 1912)
A History of French Architecture from the Death of Mazarin till the Death of Louis XV, 1661–1774, 2 vols (London, 1921)
The Touchstone of Architecture (London, 1925)
Byways: Leaves from an Architect's Notebook (London, 1929)
Memoirs of an Architect (London, 1932)
Modernismus (London, 1934)
Six Architects (London, 1935)
Three Hundred Years of French Architecture, 1494–1794 (London, 1936)
Sébastien le Prestre de Vauban, 1633–1707 (London, 1938)
Richard Norman Shaw, RA, Architect, 1831–1912: A Study (London, 1940)

BIBLIOGRAPHY

C. H. Reilly: *Representative British Architects of the Present Day* (London, 1931)
M. S. Briggs: 'Voysey and Blomfield: A Study in Contrast', *Builder*, clxxvi (1949), pp. 39–42
R. A. Fellows: *Sir Reginald Blomfield: An Edwardian Architect* (London, 1985)

RICHARD A. FELLOWS

Blommendael [Bloemandael]**, Johannes** [Jan] (*b* ?The Hague, before 1650; *d* Amsterdam, 1707). Dutch sculptor. He was probably a pupil of Rombout Verhulst. He is first heard of in 1671, when he paid the Guild of St Joseph for the rights of his shop. In 1675 he joined Pictura, the Hague guild of painters; he must already have been an experienced sculptor, as he was asked to pay the highest entrance fee and was called 'Monsieur'. Like Verhulst, he made a great number of funerary monuments, several of which have survived. They include that of *Jacob de Brauw* (signed and dated 1684; Ketel, Dutch Reformed Church); *Admiral Johan van Brakel* (signed and dated 1691; Rotterdam, Grote (St Laurens) Kerk); and *Pieter de Huybert* (signed and dated 1697) and *J. de Huybert* (signed and dated 1701; both Burg, Dutch Reformed Church). Such monuments usually consist of portraits in relief or busts, set in an architectural frame. In the case of the monument of *Johan van Brakel*, Blommendael used a new iconographical type, which was to become very popular in the 18th century; it had an obelisk rising out of the centre and a portrait bust or medallion placed against it.

Blommendael worked for a number of German patrons, including Johann Kramprich von Kronefeld (*d* 1693), the imperial ambassador in The Hague, for whom he made a wall tomb (Koblenz, Liebfrauenkirche). Blommendael's inventory included, moreover, a small clay or terracotta portrait of the *'Duke of Brunswick'*. The Schloss Museum in Gotha has a bust by Blommendael (*c.* 1700) of *Herzog Frederik II von Sachsen-Gotha-Altenburg*. A marble portrait bust of *Don Antonio Suasso* (Amsterdam, Mus. Willet-Holthuysen) has been ascribed to him.

Blommendael also made coats of arms in stone. He executed one for the Arsenal in Delft, and one for *James Campbell, 2nd Earl of Loudoun* (*d* 1684) in the Anglican church, Leiden. He produced garden vases and garden sculptures, including a marble group of four putti, representing the *Four Winds* and forming the base of a celestial globe (untraced).

Among the other commissions that Blommendael executed for William III, Stadholder of the Netherlands and later King of England, were two portraits of him (1676 and 1699; both The Hague, Mauritshuis); he also made portrait medallions of *King William III* and *Queen Mary*, one of them signed (*c.* 1700; ex-art market, London, 1966). Blommendael also worked on panelling designed by Daniel Marot I in the Trèveszaal in the Binnenhof, The Hague. After William III's death in 1702 Blommendael probably followed Marot to Amsterdam. A portrait of *Stonemason Blumenthal*, attributed to the painter Noël Jouvenet III (*d* 1698) in the Landesgalerie, Hannover, may be a portrait of Johannes Blommendael. His son, François Blommendael, was also a sculptor.

BIBLIOGRAPHY
Thieme–Becker
D. S. van Zuiden: 'De beeldhouwer Johannes Bloemmendael', *Oud-Holland*, xxx (1912), pp. 31–6
A. Bredius: *Künstler inventare*, vi (The Hague, 1919), pp. 1894–7
A. E. Brinckmann: *Barockskulptur: Entwicklungsgeschichte der Skulptur in den romanischen und germanischen Ländern seit Michelangelo bis zum Beginn des 18. Jahrhunderts* (Berlin, 1919), pp. 313–14
F. Michel: *Die kirchlichen Denkmäler der Stadt Koblenz*, xx/1 (Düsseldorf, 1937), pp. 11, 190–91
E. Neurdenburg: *De zeventiende eeuwsche beeldhouwkunst in de noordelijke Nederlanden* [Seventeenth-century sculpture in the northern Netherlands] (Amsterdam, 1948), pp. 227–30
G. von der Osten: 'Zur Barockskulptur im südlichen Niedersachsen', *Niederdt. Beitr. Kstgesch.*, i (1961), pp. 246–51
A. Staring: 'Een onbekend werk van Johannes Blommendael' [An unknown work by Johannes Blommendael], *Delftse Studien: Ein bundel historische opstellen over de stad Delft voor Dr. E. H. ter Kuile* [A collection of historical essays about the city of Delft in honour of Dr E. H. ter Kuile] (Assen, 1967), pp. 250–54
P. M. Fischer: '"Koninklijke Beelthouwer" Johannes Blommendaal: Zijn verblijf in Amsterdam en zijn sterfdatum' ['Royal sculptor' Johannes Blommendaal: his residence in Amsterdam and the date of his death], *Bull. Kon. Ned. Oudhdknd. Bond*, lxxxvii (1988), pp. 134–8

WILHELMINA HALSEMA-KUBES

Blommér, Nils Jakob (Olsson) (*b* Blommeröd, Skåne, 12 June 1816; *d* Rome, 1 Feb 1853). Swedish painter. After training as an artisan painter, in 1839 he began studying at the art academy in Stockholm of which he quickly became the outstanding student, winning numerous prizes. Having received the academy's travel scholarship in 1847, he went to Paris via Germany; more important than the period he spent as a student in Léon Cogniet's atelier was his contact with Moritz von Schwind's Romantic painting in Germany. This style of painting—full of fairies, nymphs and creatures from nature—particularly appealed to Blommér, who aspired to create an identifiably Nordic art, with subjects drawn from local folktales rather than Classical mythology. Blommér was a member of the artists' guild in Stockholm, which had first promoted this type of subject-matter in protest at the art academy's preference for classicism. In Paris Blommér painted *Meadow Fairies* and *Nacken and Agir's Daughters* (1850; both Stockholm, Nmus.). He intended to include them in a series of the *Four Seasons* that was never completed. *Meadow Fairies*, representing Spring, shows particularly strongly the influence of Moritz von Schwind, although it has a quiet, melancholy atmosphere characteristic of Blommér; the fairies are also set in a realistic Nordic landscape.

From Paris Blommér proceeded to Italy. In Rome he painted *Freja Searching for her Husband* (1852; Stockholm, Nmus.). He tried to absorb the example of Italian masterpieces of the past, such as Annibale Carracci's *Triumph of Bacchus* in the Palazzo Farnese, Rome, while asserting his own national identity in the Nordic physiognomy of Freja. His technique is distinguished here, as in other works, by a smooth surface without a trace of brushwork. While copying in the Doge's Palace in Venice, Blommér contracted a lung inflammation that brought about his death the following year in Rome.

BIBLIOGRAPHY
G. Thomaeus: 'Blommér i Rom', *Tidskr. Kstvet.*, iii (1919), pp. 147–50
A. Gauffin: 'Blommérs ängsälvor' [Blommér's meadow fairies], *N. Mus. Årsbok* (1921), pp. 38–44
G. Thomaeus: *Nils Jakob Blommér* (diss., Lund U., 1922)
S. Stjerncreutz: 'Ur Nils Blommérs fästmansbrev' [From Nils Blommér's love letters], *Ord & Bild*, xxxvi (1927), pp. 23–34

TORSTEN GUNNARSSON

Blommers, Bernard[us] **(Johannes)** (*b* The Hague, 31 Jan 1845; *d* The Hague, 15 Dec 1914). Dutch painter and printmaker. He was already an accomplished lithographer when he went to study with Christoffel Bisschop (1828–1904) in The Hague. Until 1868 he was taught by Johan Philip Koelman at the Hague Academie where he met Willem Maris. In 1870 he visited Paris and stayed with Jacob Maris. His work from this period—interiors of fishermen's cottages, usually with two figures, such as the *Fisherman's Breakfast* (1872; The Hague, Gemeentemus.)—is strongly reminiscent of the early work of Jozef Israëls. Critics thought it showed a search for truth and colour. In the early 1870s Blommers constructed a Scheveningen fisherman's interior in his studio in which he painted half-length figures of muscular fishermen's wives, presumably based on his own wife, who came from Scheveningen. His *Where Are the Little Doves?* (*c.* 1875; untraced), which shows a mother lifting up her child to look at the doves, was particularly successful. The critic Jacobus van Santen Kolff (1848–96) described it as 'deeply poetical through an intensity of feeling and truth'. Van Santen Kolff also appreciated the artist's broad touch, rich use of colour and clear drawing.

Blommers's bravura technique is particularly well illustrated by his beach scenes from the 1880s, such as the *Fish Auction* (Munich, Neue Pin.) and the *Pinks Sailing Out* (Detroit, MI, Inst. A.). These works are characterized by a broad landscape format and by crowding with large groups of figures. Blommers was presumably following the example of the Flemish artist Henri Bource (1826–99), who had painted similar subjects in the previous few years. In about 1890 Blommers's style changed: his brushstrokes became broader, the outlines tentative and the colours paler. In the early 1890s Blommers painted a series of peasants eating, in which he was undoubtedly indebted to Israëls's successful *Frugal Meal* (1876; Glasgow, A.G. & Mus.). Another favourite theme was that of children playing on the beach (e.g. the *Little Shrimp Fishers*; Amsterdam, Stedel. Mus.).

During his lifetime Blommers enjoyed a considerable reputation among painters of the HAGUE SCHOOL. From 1868 he was a member of the executive committee of the Hague artists' society, the Pulchri Studio. In 1911 he became chairman of the Hollandsche Teeken-Maatschappij (Dutch Drawing Society). Through art dealers his paintings and watercolours were sold to English, Scottish and American collectors, who particularly appreciated his figure paintings.

BIBLIOGRAPHY

J. van Santen Kolff: 'Een blik in de Hollandsche schilderschool onzer dagen' [A look at the Dutch school of painting of our times], *De Banier*, ii (1875), pp. 328–30

J. Gram: 'Scheveningen in Blommers' atelier' [Scheveningen in Blommers's studio], *Kunstkronyk*, n. s. 17 (1876), pp. 65–6

A. G. G. van Duyl: 'B. J. Blommers', *Elsevier's Geïllus. Mdschr.*, iii (1892), pp. 317–32 [repr. in M. Rooses, ed.: *Het schildersboek*, ii (Amsterdam, 1898), pp. 158–75]

J. de Gruyter: *De Haagse school*, i (Rotterdam, 1968), pp. 107–8

D. A. S. Cannegieter: 'Blommers: Een schilder uit de Haagse school' [Blommers: a painter of the Hague school], *Antiek*, vii (1972/3), pp. 446–61

The Hague School: Dutch Masters of the Nineteenth Century (exh. cat., Paris, Grand Pal.; London, RA; The Hague, Gemeentemus.; 1983), pp. 167–9

DIEUWERTJE DEKKERS

Blomstedt. Finnish family of architects, critics and designers.

(1) Pauli (Ernesti) Blomstedt (*b* Jyväskylä, 1 Aug 1900; *d* Helsinki, 3 Nov 1936). On graduating from the University of Technology in Helsinki (1922), he worked in a number of offices, including that of his influential teacher, Armas Lindgren, and in the Helsinki City Building Office under the direction of Gunnar Taucher. Blomstedt's influence in Helsinki is seen most clearly in the refined neo-classicism of the Workers' College (1927) and the flats at Mäkelänkatu 37–43 (1924–6). In 1926 he set up his own office and immediately began to attract attention by winning prizes in architectural competitions. From these early commissions Blomstedt's most important assistant was his wife, the architect Märta Blomstedt (1899–1982). Trips around Europe and study of the architectural theory of historical periods directed him away

from the classicism that was then dominant throughout the Nordic countries. By winning competitions for new offices for the Liittopankki (Allied Bank) in 1926 and the Suomalainen Säästöpankki (Finnish Savings Bank) in 1928, he won further commissions. These two new banks in the centre of Helsinki (completed in 1930 and 1932) introduced a new American-influenced Modernism to Finland.

Blomstedt's later works are characterized by an elasticity of composition using simple geometrical shapes and an unusual dynamism in clear articulations of space. The austere funeral chapel (completed 1931) at Jyväskylä was a key transitional work: its architecture is both a mature synthesis of the classical tradition and a breakthrough to Functionalism. The Suomalainen Säästöpankki (1935) in Kotka is a small three-storey building, the structural and spatial solutions of which, down to the last detail, comprise a perfect expression of the then current, predominantly French-influenced, spirit of Modernism. The Pohjanhovi Hotel (1935–6) in Rovaniemi, Lapland, was a monument to the new architecture of the modern form of sporting tourism. War damage and intensive renovation and extension later altered its character. The church (1933–8) at Kannonkoski is one of the few religious buildings in the mature functional style in Finland. Blomstedt was also influential as a writer on many subjects and as a critic. Most of his architectural articles were published in the magazine *Arkkitehti*, while others appeared in the daily newspaper *Uusi Suomi*. He also wrote articles on industrial arts for *Domus*, a short-lived journal of the early 1930s. In the mid-1930s he suggested that the grid plan of the historic centre of Helsinki should be complemented with pedestrian pathways cutting diagonally across the blocks, but the proposal was taken up only in the late 1980s.

BIBLIOGRAPHY

P. E. Blomstedt, arkkitehti (Helsinki, 1951) [col. of Blomstedt's writings, incl. those pubd in *Arkkitehti*, *Uusi Suomi* and *Domus*; with Fr. summary]

RIITTA NIKULA

(2) Aulis Blomstedt (*b* Jyväskylä, 28 July 1906; *d* Espoo, 21 Dec 1979). Brother of (1) Pauli Blomstedt. After qualifying in 1930 at the Technical University, Helsinki, he entered several architectural competitions, but with little immediate success. From 1941 to 1945 he was editor-in-chief of *Arkkitehti*, the Finnish architectural review, and in 1948 he designed the Villa Salonen at Espoo. Around this time he was also researching industrially prefabricated cell construction systems in connection with post-war reconstruction. He also devised his own theoretical basis for proportion in architecture, which was first displayed at the Saimanhori Club Building (1950), Imatra, in groups of domestic buildings designed for artists. In the Kolmirinne group of ten flats (1954), Tapiola, he employed an innovative diagonal planning grid. He also produced experimental designs (1954) for an aluminium house.

In 1958 Blomstedt attracted attention for his extension to the neo-classical Workers' College (1927; by Gunnar Taucher and Pauli Blomstedt), Helsinki. Here his excavation of the rock face behind the building creates a dramatic frame for the inner courtyard and main entrance, while the functional, well-proportioned extension, including an auditorium, is located subtly behind the main building. In the late 1950s he developed a system of modular dimensioning, based on the dimensions of the human body as correlated with the musical harmonies. This was first expounded in the journal *Le Carré Bleu* (1961), and Blomstedt developed its application in subsequent projects, for example the two blocks of flats (1961) at Riistapolku, Tapiola, and other group housing schemes there (1962; 1964; 1966). Underlying this system was Blomstedt's belief that architecture should be both 'natural' and 'intellectual'. From 1960 he designed several major exhibitions on Finnish architecture and also worked as a designer of graphics and jewellery. From 1958 he was a professor at the Technical University, Helsinki, and in 1971 he was appointed a professor at the University of Washington, Seattle, WA.

WRITINGS
Regular contributions to *Arkkitehti* (1943–78)

BIBLIOGRAPHY
Aulis Blomstedt: Architecte: Pensée et forme (exh. cat., ed. Juhani Pallasmaa; Helsinki, Mus. Fin. Archit., 1977)
J. Pallasmaa: 'Aulis Blomstedt, 1905–1979', *Carré Bleu*, 1 (1980)

MICHAEL SPENS

Blon, Jacob Christoph Le. *See* LE BLON, JACOB CHRISTOPH.

Blondeel, Lanceloot [Lancelot] (*b* ?Poperinghe, 1488; *d* Bruges, *bur* 4 March 1581). South Netherlandish painter, draughtsman, designer, architect, civil engineer, cartographer and engraver. He is said to have trained as a bricklayer, and the trowel he used to add as his housemark next to his monogram LAB testifies to this and to his pretensions as an architectural designer. In 1519 he was registered as a master painter in the Bruges Guild of St Luke, where he chose as his speciality painting on canvas. The following year he collaborated with the little-known painter Willem Cornu in designing and executing 12 scenes for the Triumphal Entry of Emperor Charles V into Bruges. From then onwards Blondeel received regular commissions, mainly as a designer and organizer. Records of legal actions show that he was sometimes late with commissions; he took seven years to execute a *Last Judgement* ordered in 1540 for the council chamber at Blankenberge, and in 1545 the Guild of St Luke summoned him for his failure to supply their guild banner on time. Blondeel was married to Kathelyne, sister of the wood-carver Michiel Scerrier; of the two daughters of this marriage, the eldest, Maria, married the tapestry-weaver Andries Hansins before 1542 and the younger, Anna, married Blondeel's pupil, the painter Pieter Pourbus, before 1545.

Blondeel was highly regarded in his day and mentioned by Guicciardini and Vasari. He was a friend of Jan van Scorel, met Jan Gossart in Mechelen and received commissions from such leading humanists as Pieter Moscron, city treasurer of Bruges, and Filips van Ravenstijn, who owned many of his works at his castle in Wijnendaele. In 1534 Blondeel designed a series of tapestry cartoons for Jan Adornes, Lord of Nieuwenhove and Nieuwenvliet. The same year he designed cartoons for tapestries commissioned by Louis de Valle, called Passay, commander of Flanders, in the monastery of the Knights of Jerusalem at Slijpe. Lucas Munich, abbot of St Bavo Abbey, Ghent, ordered two paintings from him in 1559, which later passed to Jean Perrenot de Granvelle.

Blondeel is best known for designing the monumental mantelpiece honouring Charles V in the council chamber of the Landhuis van het Vrije (now Vrije Mus.), Bruges (*in situ*), a commission he received in 1528 after winning the competition for it. Earlier he had supplied a tapestry cartoon (1523) for the Stadhuis in Bruges, and in 1528 he began, but did not finish, a wall painting of the *Battle of Pavia* and the *Peace of Madrid*. In the same year he also designed a *Virgin and Child* for the municipal authorities. In 1546 he was appointed topographical expert in connection with the Zuid-Leie and supplied the Bruges town council with a remarkable plan (Bruges, Rijksarchf) for laying out a new sea harbour to replace the silted-up Zwinhaven; this suggests that he had considerable experience as an engineer. The plan reveals many pentimenti and is incomplete. Through public tender he was responsible for the town decorations for the Triumphal Entry of Prince Philip of Spain and Emperor Charles V into Bruges in 1549, which perhaps led to the commission for the mausoleum of Margaret of Austria in the convent of the Annunciation outside Bruges. In 1550 he and Jan van Scorel cleaned Hubert and Jan van Eyck's *Adoration of the Lamb* from the Ghent Altarpiece (*c.* 1423–32; Ghent, St Bavo). This was not the only time he was involved in restoring old paintings. Other documented commissions include designs for façade sculptures for the Chapel of the Holy Blood in Bruges in 1542; the design for a new organ for the St Donaaskerk in Bruges in 1559; paintings on heraldic shields for the Guild of St George in 1555–8; and other commissions in 1558 for schools and churches.

Of Blondeel's very diverse oeuvre, little survives that is signed or well documented, which explains why he is not accorded the recognition he deserves. The literature has focused mainly on his earlier works on paper or canvas, such as the well-documented canvas of *SS Cosmas and Damian* (1532; Bruges, St Jacobskerk) for the guild of barbers and surgeons, the *St Luke Painting the Virgin* (1545; Bruges, Groeningemus.) and the *Virgin and Child with SS Luke and Giles* (1545; Bruges, St Salvatorskerk; see fig.) for the altar of the Guild of St Luke, a painting connected with the commission for the guild banner. The only monogrammed and dated panel painting by him is the *Martyrdom of a Saint* (1588; Doorn, heirs of the priv. col. of H. de Beaufort van Riemsdijk, see Friedländer, pl. 190), and the only known monogrammed drawing is that of *Ruins* (1557; Weimar, Ksthalle): it is markedly picturesque, with mobile chiaroscuro effects that confirm Vasari's opinion of Blondeel as a specialist in landscapes with lighting effects. The sheet recalls the recurrent theme of ruins in his work; the *Landscape with a Burning Building* (New York, Met.) is clearly by the same hand. In Blondeel's canvases the viewpoint is dominated by an intricate, virtuoso, decorative construction built up from grotesques, scrollwork and antique building elements worked out in grisaille on a ground of gold leaf. This gives his works the appearance of *trompe l'oeil* painted screens that dominate the space both in front and behind, while leading the eye to scenes in the far distance.

Lanceloot Blondeel: *Virgin and Child with SS Luke and Giles*, canvas, 1.36×0.95 m, 1545 (Bruges, St Salvatorskerk)

Blondeel was a committed Renaissance artist, who completely mastered the repertory of the antique grotesque (which favours Weale's supposition that he travelled to Italy before 1519). He certainly employed an architectural scheme and proportions originally associated with Renaissance developments in Lombardy, though he may have become familiar with these through prints. Blondeel used a restrained tonal palette for his figures, with a preference for dramatic highlights. His refined picturesque style is closely related to that of van Scorel, while his contrived perspectives and busy landscapes with antique ruins are distinctive. These stylistic features can be seen in other works attributed to him, such as the triptych with the *Story of the Holy Cross* (Veurne, St Nicolaaskerk) and the design (Berlin, Kupferstichkab., and London, BM) for a triptych with the *Martyrdom of St George* (perhaps for the Bruges archers' guild). Wescher's attribution of the *Good Samaritan* (Bruges, Memlingmus.) also deserves serious consideration. There are still many works by Blondeel given to followers of van Scorel. Hymans and Hollstein connected a number of woodcuts with Blondeel.

BIBLIOGRAPHY

Hollstein: *Dut. & Flem.*; Thieme–Becker; Wurzbach
G. Vasari: *Vite* (1550, rev. 2/1568); ed. G. Milanesi (1878–85), vii, pp. 584–5
K. van Mander: *Schilder-boeck* ([1603]–1604), fol. 204*v*
A. Sanderus: *Flandria illustrata* (Cologne, 1641), i, p. 210; ii, pp. 169
D. Van de Casteel: *Keuren, 1441–1744, et autres documents inédits concernant la Ghilde de Saint-Luc de Bruges* (Bruges, 1867), p. 259
H. Hymans: 'Lanceloot Blondeel als Graphiker', *Graph. Kst.*, xxvii (1904), p. 1
W. H. J. Weale: 'Lancelot Blondeel', *Hand. Genoot. Gesch. 'Soc. Emul.' Brugge* (1908), pp. 277–301, 373–80
——: 'Lanceloot Blondeel', *Burl. Mag.*, xiv/11 (1908), pp. 96–101; xiv/12 (1908), pp. 160–66
P. Clemen: *Belgische Kunstdenkmäler*, ii (Munich, 1923), pp. 1–40
F. Winkler: *Die altniederländische Malerei* (Berlin, 1924), p. 376
M. J. Friedländer: *Die altniederländische Malerei* (Berlin, 1924–37), xi (1933), pp. 108–15; Eng. trans. as *Early Netherlandish Painting* (1967–76), xi (1974), pp. 108–12, 148
A. Schouteet: 'Documenten in verband met de Brugge schilders uit de XVIe eeuw, IV: Lanceloot Blondeel', *Rev. Belge. Archéol. & Hist. A.*, xxvii (1958), pp. 173–91
J. Duverger and E. Roobaert: 'Lanceloot Blondeel (1498–1561): Zijn rol en betekenis', *Gent. Bijdr. Kstgesch. & Oudhdknd.*, xviii (1959–60), pp. 95–105
P. Wescher: 'Zu zwei niederländischen Bildern der Berliner Museen', *Berlin. Mus.: Ber. Staatl. Mus. Preuss. Kultbes.*, xii/2 (1962), pp. 55–9
Le Siècle de Bruegel (exh. cat. by G. Marlier, Brussels, Mus. A. Anc., 1963), no. 29
G. T. Faggin: 'Nuove opere di Lancelot Blondeel', *Crit. A.*, n. s. 1, xv/1 (1968), pp. 37–54

PAUL HUVENNE

Blondel. French family of artists. They came from Rouen, but (1) Jean-François Blondel was also active in Switzerland and Paris and produced engravings for a number of important architectural treatises that were published in Paris in the first half of the 18th century. His nephew (2) Jacques-François Blondel is better known as an architectural theorist and teacher than as a practising architect, and he was a highly influential advocate of a rationalist approach to architectural design in the mid-18th century. Jacques-François had two sons who also followed the family traditions: Georges-François Blondel (*c.* 1730–*c.* 1790), who was an engraver, and Jean-Baptiste Blondel (1764–1825), who was an architect and worked for the city of Paris.

(1) Jean-François Blondel (*b* Rouen, 1683; *d* Paris, 9 Oct 1756). Architect and engraver. He travelled in Switzerland from 1721 to 1723 and helped to spread French architectural ideas through his buildings executed there. This is evident in his design for the Hôtel Mallet in Place St Pierre, Geneva, where Blondel used the traditional French courtyard plan, enabling him to construct a double range of rooms lit by windows on both the outer and inner elevations. The main façade of the hôtel is impressive, consisting of a series of Doric columns at ground-floor level, which is echoed by pilasters on the *piano nobile*. In 1723 Blondel designed a lakeside house for Aimé Lullin; such houses were then fashionable in Geneva. The house was set in farmland and was approached by a long driveway. The main façade is divided into three bays by four giant Doric pilasters; the middle bay is capped by a pediment and projects slightly to give additional emphasis. A balustrade runs around the top of the façade. The original design provided for a flat roof but the patron, Aimé Lullin, had a pitched roof built instead, which caused Blondel much disquiet: he remarked in a letter to Lullin that any deviation from his plan would deprive the house of its beauty. These designs were considered so typically French that Jean Mariette included them in his *L'Architecture française* (Paris, 1727–38), in which other examples of Blondel's designs may also be found. Of particular note is a series of plates of a country house (probably unexecuted) near Geneva, designed on a grand scale with much decorative detail.

After returning to France, Blondel designed a house (1724; destr.) at Grand Charonne, near Paris, which is also illustrated in *L'Architecture française*. He was elected a member of the Académie d'Architecture in 1728, and in 1732 he enlarged the house of M. Rouille on the Rue des Poulies-Saint-Honoré, Paris. During the 1730s he executed a project for the church of Ste Madeleine at Besançon as well as La Maison des Consuls (1732–9) at Rouen. Blondel's work in Paris continued into the 1740s, when he designed the high altar and communion chapel of the church of St Jean-en-Grève. Alongside these architectural designs, which provided fine examples of the Régence style in France, Blondel proved himself a skilled draughtsman and produced many engravings for several important contemporary architectural treatises.

PRINTS
J. Mariette: *L'Architecture française*, 5 vols (Paris, 1727–38/*R* 1927–9)
C.-E. Briseux: *L'Art de bâtir les maisons de campagne* (Paris, 1743/*R* Farnborough, 1966)
G. Boffrand: *Livre d'architecture* (Paris, 1745)

BIBLIOGRAPHY
L. Blondel: 'L'Influence de l'architecture française à Genève au XVIIIe siècle: Les Oeuvres de J. F. Blondel', *Actes du congrès d'histoire de l'art: Paris 1921*, ii, pp. 219–25
J. Lejeaux: *Jean-François Blondel, professeur d'architecture* (Paris, 1927)
L. Hautecoeur: *Architecture classique*, iii (1950)

(2) Jacques-François Blondel (*b* Rouen, 8 Jan 1705; *d* Paris, 9 Jan 1774). Architect, theorist, teacher and writer, nephew of (1) Jean-François Blondel. Although he was also a practising architect (*see* §2 below), Jacques-François Blondel made a considerable contribution to the development of architectural theory in France in the latter part of the 18th century and was arguably the most outstanding teacher of architecture of the period.

1. EARLY TRAINING, TEACHING AND WRITINGS. He received his early training in architecture from his uncle and continued his studies under Gilles-Marie Oppenord, from whom he acquired a knowledge of the Rococo. His earliest published writings were his contributions to Jean Mariette's practical manual *L'Architecture française* (Paris, 1727–38). His earliest independent publication, *De la distribution des maisons de plaisance et de la décoration des édifices en général* (1737–8), is essentially a compendium of the early phases of the Rococo, addressing the question of style and including the work of Robert de Cotte and Jean-François Blondel.

In 1742 Blondel received permission from the Académie d'Architecture in Paris to open his own private school, the Ecole des Arts, which was the first school of architecture in France that was independent of the Académie. Blondel publicized it effectively by publishing his opening lectures under the title *Discours sur la manière d'étudier l'architecture et les arts qui sont relatifs à celui de bastir* (1747), which outlined his teaching methods. These deviated considerably from those of the Académie. Initially his course lasted three years, beginning with the study of modern principles of architectural theory and practical drawing. Most radical of all was the inclusion in the syllabus of a study of contemporary buildings in both

Paris and the regions, which included site visits led by Blondel. Later, in an attempt to increase the school's fee income and attract a wider range of scholars, Blondel offered shorter courses covering specific aspects of the syllabus. In 1750 the school received royal patronage in the form of six student scholarships, which Blondel immediately increased to twelve. The school provided a complete architectural education for both the interested layman and the next generation of French architects, among them Claude-Nicolas Ledoux and Charles de Wailly. Blondel did not break his ties with the Académie; he was elected a member in 1755 and became a professor of architecture there in 1762.

Blondel's theories continued to develop with the appearance in 1752–6 of new editions of *L'Architecture françoise*, which included Mariette's original engravings accompanied by a text by Blondel in which he compared contemporary architecture unfavourably with the stricter classicism of 17th-century architecture in France. His dislike of excessive architectural decoration resulted in a declared preference for the work of that period by Claude Perrault, François Mansart and Louis Le Vau. This text also provides an insight into the different styles of architecture then current in France. These ranged from the *style rocaille* (*see* ROCAILLE) to a form of Gothic and even the introduction of orientalizing elements, all regarded by Blondel as manifestations of a lack of direction in French architecture due to the absence of any true rational principles of design. He was not alone in recognizing this problem: his ideas were influenced by Germain Boffrand's *Livre d'architecture* (Paris, 1745), in which it is argued that the character of architecture is comparable to that of music. Boffrand also rejected fashion as the arbiter of taste and warned against excessive decoration.

Blondel's theories and approach were typical of the Enlightenment, and their importance was recognized by the French *philosophes* Denis Diderot and Jean le Rond d'Alembert (1717–83), who invited him to write the section on architecture for the *Encyclopédie ou dictionnaire raisonné des sciences, des arts et des métiers* (Paris, 1750–76), a work that epitomizes the philosophical outlook of the 18th century. Although the first volume of illustrations to the *Encyclopédie*, which included architectural drawings, was not published until 1761, Blondel's influence on professional and lay architectural thinking through this work alone was enormous.

Blondel explored the dilemma of French architecture further in his lectures, which were published in several volumes as the *Cours d'architecture* (1771–7; see fig. 1), the last two written by Pierre Patte. In these lectures, which were written over a period of 20 years, Blondel praised the virtues of symmetry and proportion but rejected anthropomorphism in architecture on the grounds that it was not rational. He argued that the logic of art should be reinstated and that architecture should become a more rational discipline. The central problem of the relationship between architecture and decoration had already been discussed in Blondel's previous writings, but here he proposed a solution based on compromise, and the Vitruvian principles of 'commodity, firmness and delight' are presented as a triple unity that should exist within a design. Even here, however, the flaws in his argument

1. Jacques-François Blondel: ceiling designs form his *Cours d'architecture* (Paris, 1771–7), pls XXV and XXVII

became apparent as Blondel recognized the rationalist viewpoint that these three ideals cannot co-exist. Nevertheless, he argued that 'commodity and delight' could be reconciled, either by emphasizing the importance of aesthetic considerations on the outside of a building and practicalities inside, or by giving precedence to aesthetic considerations for public buildings and to practicalities for private ones. Such compromises were unworkable but they show Blondel to be a sensitive observer of the problems of 18th-century architecture, which intensified as the century progressed.

2. ARCHITECTURE. From early in his career Blondel was occupied more as a teacher of architecture than as a practising architect. Few of his buildings survive although his writings contain much evidence of his projects, whether or not they were actually realized. According to *De la distribution des maisons . . . en général*, Blondel laid out a park and terrace on the outskirts of Paris in 1727 and a few years later provided designs for a château and orangery near Florence and for a château north-west of Paris, but these designs show little originality, with their bulbous domes, complicated interior plans and applied statuary typical of contemporary design. His Hôtel Petit de Marivat (before 1736), Besançon, however, demonstrates greater

originality and a move towards the simpler, bolder forms advocated in his teaching.

Once his Ecole had been established, Blondel built very little. He decorated the new lecture theatre at the Collège Louis le Grand (*c.* 1745) for the Jesuit fathers, but it was more than 15 years before he had the opportunity to put into practice his theories on architecture and town planning. Blondel's work at Metz (1762–75; *see* METZ, §1) is perhaps best known, although little of it remains intact. He was initially summoned to the town in September 1761 to produce designs for the newly formed Collège Royal et Séculier de St Louis. These were never realized, but Blondel took the opportunity to use them as teaching examples in his *Cours d'architecture*. The design for the chapel is of particular interest, as here Blondel felt he had fused all the most successful elements of the churches known to him in a design that reconciled centralized planning with a directional nave. During Blondel's stay in Metz, the governor, the Maréchal de Belle-Isle, decided to develop the Place des Armes to the south-east of the cathedral. His successor, the Maréchal d'Estrées, continued the project and employed Blondel to design the Hôtel de Ville, which was to be constructed in the square. The façade of the Hôtel de Ville (1764–75) is not articulated by orders; instead, an arcade running the length of the ground floor is surmounted by a *piano nobile* with regularly spaced rectangular windows, below each of which runs a balustrade. The mezzanine windows are plain squares. This scheme set the tone for the whole square, as can be seen in Blondel's design for the façade of the Corps de Garde. For the sake of unity, he continued the arcades around the square and along the south side of the cathedral. Blondel also created the Place de la Cathédrale, a smaller square in front of the cathedral, together with a new façade for the cathedral (see fig. 2), the new Bishop's Palace and the parliament building. Blondel's ideas about urban planning developed further when, in 1765, he was invited to Strasbourg to advise on the urban development of the town. He recommended a complete redevelopment based on a central axial road along which new municipal buildings were to be built. As with so many of Blondel's visionary ideas, however, this project exists only in the engravings in his *Cours d'architecture*, the work for which he is best remembered.

WRITINGS

De la distribution des maisons de plaisance et de la décoration des édifices en général, 2 vols (Paris, 1737–8/R Farnborough, 1967)
Discours sur la manière d'étudier l'architecture, et les arts qui sont relatifs à celui de bastir (Paris, 1747)
L'Architecture françoise, 8 vols (Paris, 1752–6/R 1904–5) [with original engrs from Mariette's *L'Architecture française* of 1727–38]
Discours sur la nécessité de l'étude de l'architecture (Paris, 1754)

2. Jacques-François Blondel: west portal of the cathedral of St Etienne, Metz, 1764 (destr. 19th century); from a 19th-century photograph

with P. Patte: *Cours d'architecture, ou traité de la décoration, distribution & construction des bâtiments; Contenant les leçons données en 1750, & les années suivantes*, 8 vols (Paris, 1771–7)
L'Homme du monde éclairé par les arts (Paris, 1774/R Geneva, 1973)

BIBLIOGRAPHY

J. Lejeaux: 'Jacques-François Blondel, professeur d'architecture', *Architecture* [Paris], xl (1927), p. 23
E. Kaufmann: 'The Contribution of Jacques-François Blondel to Mariette's "Architecture française"', *A. Bull.*, xxxi (1949), p. 58
L. Hautecoeur: *Architecture classique*, iii (1950)
E. Kaufmann: *Architecture in the Age of Reason* (Cambridge, MA, 1955, rev. New York, 2/1968)
E. Schlumberger: 'L'Art de bâtir à la campagne selon Jacques-François Blondel', *Conn. A.* (1967), p. 74

DANA ARNOLD

Blondel, (Nicolas-)François (*b* Ribemont, Somme, 1628; *d* Paris, 21 Jan 1686). French engineer, architect, teacher and writer. He was born to a newly ennobled member of the household of the queen-mother, Marie de' Medici. He joined the army and became a military engineer, attaining the rank of Maréchal de Camp by 1652. In that year he was seconded by one of the secretaries of state for foreign affairs, the Comte de Brienne, to accompany his son on a comprehensive Grand Tour of Europe. On his return in 1655 Blondel was equipped with an unrivalled range of first-hand experience that recommended him for a diplomatic career, although the following year he was appointed Professor of Mathematics at the Collège de France. Diplomatic missions took him to Prussia, Sweden and Turkey and, while waiting on the Sultan, he visited Greece and Egypt. He was ambassador to Denmark in 1659–63. Thereafter he rejoined the armed services and was assigned to the navy as an engineer responsible for port and coastal defences in Normandy and Brittany, most notably transforming Saintes and constructing the new port and arsenal of Rochefort.

Blondel was elected to the Académie des Sciences in 1669 as a mathematician and was appointed mathematics tutor to the Dauphin in 1673. Meanwhile, in 1671 he was a founder-member and first director of the Académie Royale d'Architecture. Apart from his fortifications, as a builder he is best remembered for his contribution to the great campaign of civic improvement in Paris initiated by Jean-Baptiste Colbert in the mid-1660s. From 1671 he was involved in the rebuilding of the Porte St Denis as a grand triumphal arch and the refurbishing of the Porte St Bernard, Porte St Antoine and Porte St Martin, overseeing the work of his pupil Pierre Bullet (*see* BULLET, (1)) on the latter at least. The daring scale and monumental virility, if not austerity, of the Porte St Denis owe much to Blondel's mastery in the field of military engineering. He is reputed to have provided plans for an armoury in Berlin, which were much modified by his pupil Jean de Bodt in executing the Arsenal there over 30 years later.

In the early part of his career, Blondel wrote on the Roman calendar, on Pindar and Horace, on mathematics and on fortification, but his greatest claim to fame was his *Cours d'architecture* (1675), based on the lectures he gave at the Académie. The rationalist doctrine of this, the first course in architecture taught under state auspices in France, is marked by Blondel's admiration of the Antique, acquired at first-hand, and by the approach of the mathematician, in sharp contrast to the empiricism of Claude 'Perrault the doctor'. For Blondel, Rome's great masterpieces are the pre-eminent models, and analysis of the orders, involving the comparison of practice and all the great 16th-century theorists in particular, is fundamental. As the 'noble elements of architecture', the orders demonstrate that beauty depends on proportion as the key to coherence. Their rules discipline the imagination, essentially and beneficently, by establishing mathematical limits to its field of operation. Within these limits, faced with diverse possibilities, artistic genius is led by experience to 'grace'. In pursuing the ideal proportions of the orders, guided by the concept of the harmony of the cosmos appreciable in music, Blondel led the Académie in the search for an objective standard of beauty. When the Academicians debated the ideas expounded by Perrault in his *Ordonnance*, the polarization of the 'Ancients' and the 'Moderns' had the majority siding with Blondel in opposing empiricism and custom with dialectic and principle.

WRITINGS

Résolution des quatre principaux problèmes d'architecture (Amsterdam, 1673)
Cours d'architecture enseigné dans l'Académie royale d'architecture (Paris, 1675)
Cours de mathématique contenant divers traitez composez et enseignez à Monseigneur le Dauphin (Paris, 1683)

BIBLIOGRAPHY

C. Mauclair and others: *Nicolas-François Blondel* (Laon, 1938)
L. Hautecoeur: *Architecture classique*, ii (Paris, 1948)
W. Bronner: *Blondel–Perrault* (diss., Bonn, Rhein. Friedrich-Wilhelms-U., 1972)
W. Herrmann: *The Theory of Claude Perrault* (London, 1973)
F. Fichet: *La Théorie architecturale à l'âge classique* (Brussels, 1979)

CHRISTOPHER TADGELL

Blondel, Merry-Joseph (*b* Paris, 25 July 1781; *d* Paris, 12 June 1853). French painter. After an apprenticeship at the Dihl et Guerhard porcelain factory in Paris, where he was taught by Etienne Leguay (1762–1846), Blondel moved to Jean-Baptiste Regnault's atelier in 1802. He won the Prix de Rome in 1803 with *Aeneas and Anchises* (Paris, Ecole N. Sup. B.-A.) but did not go to Rome until 1809, when he stayed there for three years. After gaining a gold medal in the Salon of 1817 for the *Death of Louis XII* (Toulouse, Mus. Augustins), Blondel embarked on a wide-ranging and successful career as official decorative painter. In addition to the decoration of the Salon and of the Galerie de Diane at Fontainebleau (1822–8) and the ceiling of the Palais de la Bourse (*Justice Protecting Commerce*, sketch, 1825; Dijon, Mus. Magnin), he received commissions for several ceilings in the Louvre, of which the earliest and most remarkable is in the vestibule to the Galerie d'Apollon (*The Sun* or the *Fall of Icarus*, exh. Salon, 1819; *in situ*). The ceiling painting in the Salle Henri II (the *Dispute between Minerva and Neptune on the Subject of Athens*, exh. Salon, 1822) was removed in 1938, while those in the Salles du Conseil d'Etat, *France Victorious at Bouvines* (1828) and *France Receives the Constitutional Charter from Louis XVIII* (1827), are still in place. These monumental allegorical compositions belong to the tradition of David, which by the 1820s had become academic, and display more learning than originality.

Blondel adhered to classicism in most of his works: *Maternal Tenderness* or *Hecuba and Polyxena* (exh. Salon,

1814; Dijon, Mus. B.-A.; reduced version, Los Angeles, CA, Co. Mus. A.); *Philippe Auguste before the Battle of Bouvines* (exh. Salon, 1819, for the Galerie du Duc d'Orléans); the *Assumption of the Virgin* (exh. Salon, 1824, commissioned by the State for the church of St Amand at Rodez). However, in pictures such as *Elisabeth of Hungary Placing her Crown at the Feet of the Image of Jesus Christ* (exh. Salon, 1824; Paris, St Elisabeth) he revealed greater originality in his emphasis on theatrical effects of lighting and gesture. Blondel received the Légion d'honneur after the 1824 Salon and became a member of the Institut in 1832. He executed *Ptolemaïs Delivered to Philippe Auguste and Richard the Lionheart* for the Musée Historique in Versailles (exh. Salon, 1841; Salle des Croisades). The orientalist figures in the foreground and the contrasts between light and shadow prefigured the art of Eugène Fromentin and Alexandre-Gabriel Decamps.

In 1839 Blondel spent several months in Rome as the guest of Ingres, who valued his talent. After 1841 Blondel took part in the ornamental painting movement inspired by Ingres. He worked on the Salle des Séances in the Senate and decorated the cupola above the crossing and the chapel of St-Vincent-de-Paul in St-Thomas-d'Aquin, Paris (1851). In this, Blondel's last work, the influence of David was less ponderous, the style more flexible and eclectic. His murals in the cupola show an animation and a mastery of *trompe l'oeil* drawn from the 17th-century Italian masters. Only the Apostles against gilded backgrounds on the pendentives recall the taste for early Italian painting advocated by the school of Ingres.

Blondel was also a portrait painter. The *Portrait of his Daughter at the Age of Five* (*c.* 1839; Gray, Mus. Martin) shows the influence of the English school. Among the many portraits he executed for the Musée Historique in Versailles, the portrait of *Percier* (exh. Salon, 1839; Versailles, Château) has a genuine psychological acuity.

BIBLIOGRAPHY

G. Guillaume: 'Merry-Joseph Blondel et son ami Ingres', *Bull. Soc. Hist. A. Fr.*, i (1936), pp. 73–91
P. Grunchec: *Le Grand Prix de peinture: Les Concours des Prix de Rome de 1797 à 1863* (Paris, 1983), p. 135
T. W. Gaehtgens: *Versailles: De la résidence royale au Musée Historique* (Paris, 1984), pp. 142–3
B. Foucart: *Le Renouveau de la peinture religieuse en France (1800–1860)* (Paris, 1987), pp. 358, 369, 407

PASCALE MÉKER

Blondel d'Azincourt, Barthélémy-Augustin. *See* AZINCOURT, BARTHÉLÉMY-AUGUSTIN BLONDEL D'.

Blondel de Gagny, Augustin (*b* Paris, March 1695; *d* Paris, 10 July 1776). French administrator and collector. His early career is obscure, but by 1737, when he was one of the major purchasers at the sale of the collection of Jeanne-Baptiste d'Albert de Luynes, Comtesse de Verrue, he possessed a considerable fortune. At the beginning of 1750 he was appointed Trésorier Général des Amortissements des Dettes du Roi, and two years later became Intendant des Menus Plaisirs du Roi. He collected chiefly Dutch and Flemish paintings; during the 1760s and 1770s, his gallery was one of the best known and most frequented in Paris. His collection was depicted in a drawing, *View of Blondel de Gagny's Picture Cabinet* (Paris, Louvre, Cab. Dessins) by Augustin de Saint-Aubin, and described by

Hester Thrale, later Mrs Piozzi (1741–1821). The paintings were hung in panels, juxtaposed to complement each other and reflect the display on the opposite wall; paintings on similar themes by the same or different artists were hung as pendants on either side of mirrors or of paintings that complemented them. Schools and subjects were often intermingled. In addition to purchasing works from sales in Paris, Blondel sponsored picture-buying trips abroad by the picture dealer Edmé-François Gersaint. The catalogue of Blondel's posthumous sale (Paris, Pierre Remy, 10–24 Dec 1776 and 8–22 Jan 1777) listed 1141 items, including paintings, drawings, busts, vases, lacquer, porcelain from the Orient, Sèvres and Saxony, and Boulle furniture, as well as many other objects. Blondel's son BARTHÉLÉMY-AUGUSTIN BLONDEL D'AZINCOURT also became a noted collector.

UNPUBLISHED SOURCES
Paris, Archvs N., Minutier, Paris LVII/529 [Inv. of the col. of Augustin Blondel de Gagny (27 July 1776); copy Santa Monica, CA, Getty Provenance Index]

BIBLIOGRAPHY
A. J. Dezallier d'Argenville: *Voyage pittoresque de Paris* (Paris, 1757), pp. 277–82
C. Blanc: *Le Trésor de la curiosité*, i (Paris, 1857), pp. 333–46 [contains summary of Blondel's sale cat.]
C. de Ris: *Les Amateurs d'autrefois* (Paris, 1877), pp. 342–58
M. Tyson and H. Guppy, eds: *The French Journals of Mrs Thrale and Doctor Johnson* (Manchester, 1932), pp. 112–13

Blondelu, Constance Marie. *See* CHARPENTIER, CONSTANCE MARIE.

Blonder, Sasza [Blondel, André] (*b* Czortków, Podolia, 27 May 1909; *d* Paris, 22 June 1949). Polish painter. He studied at the Ecole des Beaux-Arts in Paris (1926–9) and at the Academy of Fine Arts in Kraków (1929–34). As a student he joined the Kraków group. His early work was clearly influenced by Chagall and Chaïm Soutine. He produced many watercolours and drawings, views of his native Czortków and studies of Kazimierz, the Jewish quarter of Kraków. In his oil paintings (still-lifes and landscapes) he employed excessively synthetic form and bold outline, which divides the composition into an arrangement of fields filled with saturated colour, as in *Landscape with Dwellings and a Tree* (1934). In time he turned to abstract compositions, for example *Yellow Triangle* (1934). In the drawing entitled *Demonstration* (1935) the crowd attacked by the policemen changes into a two-dimensional arrangement of interwoven lines. After leaving Kraków in 1935, Blonder ran a Jewish children's theatre in Bielsko. He then moved to Warsaw and in 1937 settled permanently in Paris. In 1937 he was expelled from the Union of Polish Plastic Artists for his Communist activities. In France during World War II he adopted the name Blondel and in 1940 joined the Resistance. After the war he lived in Paris and Sète, in southern France. He became a member of the Artistes Méridionaux group. In his post-war works (landscapes of Sète and abstract pictures) the former bold outline and forceful, static composition are replaced with light strokes and a subtle, unforced field of colour.

BIBLIOGRAPHY
Sasza Blonder—André Blondel, 1909–1949 (exh. cat., ed. H. Blum; Kraków, N. Mus., 1970)
Słownik artystów polskich: Malarze, rzeźbiarze, graficy [Dictionary of Polish artists: painters, sculptors and graphic artists], i (Wrocław, 1971)
J. Pollakówna: *Malarstwo polskie między wojnami, 1918–1939* [Polish painting between the wars, 1918–39] (Warsaw, 1982)

EWA MIKINA

Blondus, Michael. *See* LE BLON, MICHEL.

Bloodworth [Bloodsworth; Blodworth], **James** (*b* Middlesex, *c*. 1760; *d* New South Wales, 1804). Australian architect of English birth. He was probably no more than a master-builder's assistant by 1785 when he was sentenced to transportation. In January 1788 he arrived with the first fleet in the new colony of New South Wales at Port Jackson, Sydney, and as an experienced brickmaker he was immediately put in charge of the brickworks at Brickfield Hill, producing the first bricks for the colony three months after arrival. He became Australia's first architect when Governor Arthur Phillip put him in charge of permanent building projects, including the first Government House (completed 1789; destr.), erected on a hill overlooking Sydney Cove. This two-storey building was the first in the colony to have architectural pretensions; built of brick with stone dressings and a hipped roof, it had glazed sash windows brought from England and a projecting gabled frontispiece, the central doorway surrounded by glazed sidelights and a semicircular fanlight. Although simple, the building embodied the principles of Georgian design in which Bloodworth was well grounded. Later extended and constantly under repair, it served as Government House for 56 years. Other buildings designed by Bloodworth in 1788–90 included the stone King's Warehouse, the timber hospital, Surgeon-General White's residence, military barracks and houses for the civil officers (all destr.). He served the colony so well that Phillip pardoned him in 1790, several years before the end of his sentence, and he remained in Sydney as the first official Superintendent of Works and also became a successful farmer at Petersham Hill. His later works under Governor Hunter included a tall clock-tower (destr.) on Church Hill, Sydney, and probably Old Government House (1800) at nearby Parramatta, another simple Georgian building (*see* AUSTRALIA, fig. 2; portico added by Francis Greenway in 1816); this replaced Bloodworth's earlier Parramatta Government House (1790), a charming building but constructed of materials that quickly perished. Bloodworth's work, although not abreast with leading British designers, can be compared with houses by James Paine and with contemporary North American designs.

BIBLIOGRAPHY
J. M. Freeland: *Architecture in Australia* (Harmondsworth, 1972), pp. 12–15, 24
S. Evans: *Historic Sydney as Seen by its Early Artists* (Sydney, 1983), p. 66
J. F. Millar: *A Handbook on the Founding of Australia, 1788* (Williamsburg, VA, 1987), pp. 47–59

JOHN FITZHUGH MILLAR

Bloom. Misty surface coating that occurs on certain oil paintings with natural resin varnish films, especially of mastic. It diminishes the transparency of the varnish but can be removed in water. Bloom is apparently the result of atmospheric pollution. It is no longer a major problem, owing to the widespread use of synthetic varnishes.

RUPERT FEATHERSTONE

Bloom, Barbara (*b* Los Angeles, CA, 11 July 1951). American sculptor. She studied at the California Institute of the Arts, Los Angeles, with John Baldessari, Robert Irwin and James Lee Byars. In 1974 Bloom moved to Amsterdam; she later divided her time between New York and Berlin. She became known for her installations, through which she questioned the relationship between vision and desire. In several groups of works she uses photographic images of parapsychological events to bring issues of the uncanny and unconscious into the realm of the viewers' perception and reception of art. Absence, which establishes the conditions for desire, is symbolized by photographs of seances, UFOs or infra-red images. The photographic medium enhances the effect of historical record, while highlighting the absence inherent in the attempt to document events and objects that do not exist. In a well-known work, *The Collection: The Reign of Narcissism* (mixed-media installation, 1989), Bloom meticulously recreated a very bourgeois interior with furnishings and accessories to examine the home and how it structures our understanding of ourselves and the world. In dealing with the home, the familiar or the native (*heimlich*), it complements other work exploring the uncanny (*unheimlich*) and also questions how identity is created. Bloom was known as an artist who questioned and explored how the fictions of identity and desire are created.

BIBLIOGRAPHY
Ghost Writer (exh. cat., Berlin, daad gal., 1988) [incl. essays and stories by Bloom and others]
D. Rimanelli: 'Barbara Bloom and her Art of Entertaining', *Artforum*, xxviii/2 (1989), pp. 142–6

☐

Bloom, Hyman (*b* Brinoviski, Latvia, 29 March 1913). American painter of Latvian birth. He went to the USA when he was seven and received his early artistic training at the West End Community Center in Boston. He studied art with Denman Ross (1853–1935) of Harvard University, as a fellow pupil of Jack Levine. Among the paintings that he saw at the Museum of Fine Arts in Boston, he was particularly attracted to the thickly painted and richly coloured works of Georges Rouault and Chaïm Soutine. The first recognition of his expressionistic canvases came with his inclusion in the *Americans 1942* exhibition at the Metropolitan Museum of Art, New York.

Although superficially similar to Abstract Expressionism in their use of strong colours, thickly applied paint and large scale, Bloom's paintings took as their subject the human form, as a means of commenting on the human condition, for example *Apparition of Danger* (1951; Washington, DC, Hirshhorn). His interest in mysticism was influenced by William Blake and by the philosophy of Spinoza, Kant and Ouspensky. He also produced paintings of Judaic religious life, such as *Synagogue* (1940; New York, MOMA). In later years his work became much brighter and richer in colour, his interest in aspects of Abstract Expressionism more clearly grafted on to recognizable forms.

BIBLIOGRAPHY
Contemporary American Painting (exh. cat. by A. Weller, Urbana, U. IL, 1952)
Hyman Bloom (exh. cat. by F. Wight, Buffalo, Albright–Knox A.G., 1954)
Hyman Bloom: Paintings and Drawings (exh. cat., New York, Kennedy Gals, 1986)

DAVID M. SOKOL

Bloomsbury Group. Name applied to a group of friends, mainly writers and artists, who lived in or near the central London district of Bloomsbury from 1904 to the late 1930s. They were united by family ties and marriage rather than by any doctrine or philosophy, though several male members of the group had been affected by G. E. Moore's *Principia Ethica* (Cambridge, 1903) when they had attended the University of Cambridge. Moore emphasized the value of personal relationships and the contemplation of beautiful objects, promoting reason above social morality as an instrument of good within society. This anti-utilitarian position coloured the group's early history. It influenced the thinking of, for example, the biographer and critic Lytton Strachey (1880–1932) and the economist John Maynard Keynes (1883–1946) and confirmed the position of conscientious objection maintained by some members of the group in World War I. Before 1910, literature and philosophy dominated Bloomsbury; thereafter it also came to be associated with painting, the decorative arts and the promotion of Post-Impressionism in England. This was mainly effected by the introduction into Bloomsbury of Roger Fry in 1910 and his close friendship with Vanessa Bell and Duncan Grant, with Clive Bell and with the writers Leonard Woolf (1880–1969) and Virginia Woolf (1882–1941). Fry, helped by the literary editor Desmond MacCarthy (1877–1952), Clive Bell and the Russian artist Boris Anrep (1883–1969), was chiefly responsible for the two large Post-Impressionist exhibitions held in London at the Grafton Galleries in 1910 and 1912. Bloomsbury's swift identification with radical tendencies in the arts was realized by Vanessa Bell's Friday Club (founded 1905) and the Grafton Group exhibiting society (1913–14); by Fry and Clive Bell's association with the newly founded Contemporary Art Society (1910); and by the publication of Bell's *Art* (London, 1914). This pre-eminence as apologists for new movements in art was soon challenged by Wyndham Lewis, T. E. Hulme and others, and by *c.* 1920 Bloomsbury painting and art criticism can be characterized as increasingly conservative.

While Fry's greatest admiration was reserved for Cézanne, whose work profoundly influenced his own painting from 1910 onwards, Vanessa Bell and Duncan Grant gained greatly from Matisse and, to a lesser extent, Picasso. From *c.* 1912 to 1920 they were among the most innovative artists in England in both their easel painting (espousing abstraction in 1914–15) and their decorative work and applied design. The latter was chiefly carried out for Fry's Omega Workshops, of which they were both co-directors. Professional and personal links with the Paris art world were curtailed by the restrictions of World War I and from then on England was the centre of their activities and influence. They were variously involved in the London Group, the London Artists' Association and in fostering a closer association between art and commercial design.

Duncan Grant: *Vanessa Bell at Charleston*, oil on canvas, 1.27×1.02 m, *c.* 1917 (London, National Portrait Gallery)

Other figures in Bloomsbury maintained an interest in the arts: Keynes, for example, as a patron and collector, and Virginia Woolf as a financial backer in 1938 of the Euston Road School. Keynes's later ideas on the public funding of the arts led to the foundation of the Arts Council of Great Britain in 1946.

Between the two World Wars, Grant and Vanessa Bell developed a rich, mainly figurative style of decoration, which had some influence in England and which may be described as a Bloomsbury style. In their (and Fry's) easel paintings are found consistent qualities of unemphatic realism and a pacific contemplation of their immediate surroundings, for example in Grant's *Vanessa Bell at Charleston* (*c.* 1917; London, N.P.G.; see fig.). Characteristic subjects include still-lifes, English, French and Italian landscapes, and portraits of their family and friends, usually informal in pose and setting. The classic Mediterranean tradition was preferred to Northern European art, with fluency preferred to laborious detail and formal values to illustrative content.

BIBLIOGRAPHY
J. K. Johnstone: *The Bloomsbury Group* (London, 1954)
Q. Bell: *Bloomsbury* (London, 1968, rev. 3/1986)
R. Shone: *Bloomsbury Portraits: Vanessa Bell, Duncan Grant and their Circle* (Oxford and New York, 1976, rev. London, 1993)
D. A. Laing: *Roger Fry: An Annotated Bibliography of the Published Writings* (New York and London, 1979)
——: *Clive Bell: An Annotated Bibliography of the Published Writings* (New York and London, 1983)

RICHARD SHONE

Bloore, Ronald (Langley) (*b* Brampton, Ont., 29 May 1925). Canadian painter, teacher and gallery director. He received his BA from the University of Toronto in 1949 and studied at the Institute of Fine Arts, New York, from 1949 to 1951. He obtained his MA from Washington University, St Louis, MO, in 1953 and also studied at the Courtauld Institute in London, England (1955–7).

Bloore taught at Regina College, University of Saskatchewan, from 1958 to 1966. He served concurrently as director of the Norman Mackenzie Art Gallery, bringing a number of national and international exhibitions to Regina. In 1961 he organized the *May Show*, which became the basis for the National Gallery of Canada's landmark exhibition *Five Painters from Regina* in that year. The exhibition documented the significant development of abstract painting in Regina and included the work of artists who became known as the 'Regina Five': Bloore, Kenneth Lochhead (*b* 1926), Art McKay (*b* 1926), Douglas Morton (*b* 1926) and Ted Godwin (*b* 1933). In 1966 Bloore was appointed Professor at York University, Toronto.

Dedicated to total non-figuration, Bloore has worked in a variety of media. These include sculptures made from wooden spoons ('sploores'), strongly influenced by the simplified forms of Africa and the Mediterranean, and later a series of free-flowing automatic paintings in ink. He is known principally for the powerful non-objective paintings, such as *Painting, June 1960* (1960; Ottawa, N.G.), often white on white, which have been the focus of his work from the 1960s.

WRITINGS
Five Painters from Regina/Cinq peintres de Regina (exh. cat., Ottawa, N.G., 1961)
Ronald Bloore, Sixteen Years: 1958–74 (exh. cat., Windsor, Ont., A.G.; Montreal, Mus. A. Contemp.; Vancouver, A.G.; and elsewhere, 1975)
BIBLIOGRAPHY
R. L. Bloore—Drawings 1960–1988 (exh. cat. by I.-M. Tamplin, Peterborough, Ont., A.G., 1988)

JOYCE ZEMANS

Bloosaerken. *See* NEVE, FRANS VAN DER.

Blooteling, Abraham (*b* Amsterdam, *bapt* 2 Dec 1640; *d* Amsterdam, *bur* 20 Jan 1690). Dutch engraver, draughtsman and printseller. He was the son of a shopkeeper and the pupil and eventual heir of Cornelis van Dalen (1636–64). His dated prints commenced in 1665, and, as well as portraits, they include biblical, mythological and genre subjects, as well as six views of Amsterdam after Jacob van Ruisdael, and two of the Jewish burial-ground there (1670; also after van Ruisdael). During this period he produced many exceptional line-engravings, such as his sensitive portrait of *Govaert Flinck* and the equestrian *Pieter Schout Muylman* (see Hollstein, pp. 167, 179). Blooteling went to London in 1672, probably at the suggestion of David Loggan, whose plumbago miniatures he emulated in such works as the signed *Noah Bridges* (London, BM). He met Peter Lely and Mary Beale and engraved portraits after them. During his stay he became increasingly involved in mezzotint engraving and, in collaboration with his brother-in-law Gerard Valck, significantly advanced its technique through fully grinding the plate with the rocker in order to achieve a solid black ground; this produced controlled and intense contrasts by use of the scraper and burnisher alone. His large plates of *Charles II, James, Duke of York* and *James, Duke of Monmouth* (all after

Lely; see Hollstein, pp. 223, 237, 244) are among the early masterpieces of the mezzotint, and his influence on the later English practitioners of the medium was immeasurable. He was again in Amsterdam by September 1678, when he acted as godfather to his nephew Abraham Valck, but he kept up his contacts with London. During his later years he concentrated on the business side of his activities, particularly the publication and sale of prints and maps. However, he still found time to engrave 265 plates for Agostino Lionardo's *Gemmae et sculpturae antiquae* (Amsterdam, 1685).

BIBLIOGRAPHY

Hollstein: *Dut. & Flem.*; Thieme–Becker; Wurzbach
H. Walpole: *Anecdotes of Painting in England* (1762–71); ed. R. N. Wornum (1849), iii, pp. 939–41
J. E. Wessely: *Abraham Blooteling: Verzeichnis seiner Küpferstiche und Schabkunstblätter* (Leipzig, 1867)
J. C. Smith: *British Mezzotinto Portraits*, i (London, 1883), pp. 64–70
'The Note-books of George Vertue', *Walpole Soc.*, xvii (1930), xx (1932), xxii (1934), xxiv (1936)
Darkness into Light: The Early Mezzotint (exh. cat. by J. Bayard and E. D'Oench, New Haven, CT, Yale Cent. Brit. A., 1976), pp. 10, 22–4; nos 26–9

RICHARD JEFFREE

Blore, Edward (*b* Stamford, Lincs, 1787; *d* London, 4 Sept 1879). English architect. He was the eldest son of Thomas Blore, an antiquarian and lawyer of Stamford. He began as a topographical artist preparing illustrations for his father's *History of Rutland* (1811) and several other early 19th-century county histories. By this means he came to the notice of Sir Walter Scott, who employed him in 1816 to improve William Atkinson's design for Abbotsford (Borders), making it more 'in the old fashioned Scotch stile'. Blore made an easy transition from topographical artist to architect, but it is not clear how he received his practical training. Certainly by the 1820s he had built up a large architectural practice as a purveyor of Tudor Gothic country houses and Gothic or Norman revival churches. In these he used his unrivalled knowledge of original details, derived from his studies as an antiquarian draughtsman, but he lacked the flair and originality to breathe life into his creations. His churches in particular are competent but dull, and several have been demolished. Some of them, however, were interesting from the structural point of view: St John's (1835; destr. 1972), Potters Bar, near London, for instance, was built of 'Rangers stone', a type of concrete. A characteristic example of Blore's country-house work is Capesthorne, Cheshire, which he remodelled in 1839–42 for Edward Davies Davenport as a grand Jacobean mansion. Its elaborate gabled silhouette is impressive from a distance but close-up it is disappointing: 'a grand concept executed lamely' (Pevsner). Where he was adding to an existing Gothic building Blore's quiet antiquarian literacy is acceptable enough; for instance in the residential ranges at Lambeth Palace, London, reconstructed in 1829–48 for Archbishop William Howley. His work as Surveyor to Westminster Abbey, including the decorative Gothic rood screen, is also sensitive and appropriate.

Blore's best-known but least characteristic work was the completion of Buckingham Palace in 1832–50 following the dismissal of George IV's architect, John Nash, for extravagance. This is one of only two classical works, the other being Haveringland Hall, Norfolk, designed in 1839–43 (destr. 1946) for Edward Fellowes. Blore was given the Buckingham Palace commission by the Office of Works because of his reputation for cheapness. The *Builder* (28 Aug 1847) remarked of his new front '[it] does not pretend to grandeur, and magnificence, scarcely to dignity' and few regretted its refacing by Aston Webb in 1912–13. Albert, the Prince Consort, entrusted the south-west wing to James Pennethorne. Blore was so upset by his failure to please his royal clients that he refused the knighthood offered him on the completion of the work. He was awarded an honorary doctorate of civil law from Oxford in 1834.

UNPUBLISHED SOURCES

48 volumes of Blore's antiquarian drawings are in London, BL, Add.MSS 42000–42047

BIBLIOGRAPHY

Colvin
Obituary, *Builder*, xxxvii (1879), p. 1019
Obituary, *Proc. Soc. Antiqua.*, n.s. 2, viii (1879–81), pp. 347–52
N. Pevsner and E. Hubbard: *Cheshire*, Bldgs England (Harmondsworth, 1971/R 1978), p. 125
RIBA Drawings Collection: B (Farnborough, 1972), pp. 90–93
H. M. Colvin, ed.: *History of the King's Works*, vi (London, 1978), pp. 277–92

JOHN MARTIN ROBINSON

Blossfeldt, Karl (*b* Schielo, 13 June 1865; *d* Berlin, 9 Dec 1932). German photographer. He studied as a sculptor and modeller in the ironworks and foundry at Mägdesprung from 1882 to 1884 and then at the Kunstgewerbeschule in Berlin (1884–90). Between 1890 and 1896 he travelled to Italy, Greece and North Africa with Professor M. Meurer (1839–1916), who had a theory that natural forms were inherently reproduced in art. With funds from the Prussian government, Blossfeldt made a series of plant photographs for use in education. In 1898 he was given a teaching post at the Kunstgewerbeschule in Berlin, where he set up an archive for plant photographs. In the 1920s his photographs became very popular, and a collection, *Urformen der Kunst*, was published. They were seen as forerunners of Neue Sachlichkeit. It was not only the clearcut quality of the reproductions that won him esteem, but also the way in which the plant was revealed as the basis for a formal language of construction that could also be applied to objects and architecture. More of his photographs were published in *Wundergarten der Natur*. This depiction of basic forms provoked a variety of responses among artists, from a Neo-Romantic longing for nature, to alienation from the surreal enlargement of subject-matter. They were rejected by the avant-garde in Cologne as superficially aestheticizing. Exhibitions in Bonn and Kassel in 1976 and 1977 renewed public awareness of Blossfeldt's work.

PHOTOGRAPHIC PUBLICATIONS

Urformen der Kunst (Berlin, 1928/R Munich, 1981)
Wundergarten der Natur (Berlin, 1932/R Munich 1981); Eng. trans. as *Art Forms in Nature* (New York, 1932)

BIBLIOGRAPHY

Karl Blossfeldt: Fotografien, 1900–1932 (exh. cat. by K. Honnef, Bonn, Rhein. Landesmus., 1976)
Documenta 6, ii (exh. cat. by K. Honnef and E. Weiss, Kassel, Mus. Fridericianum, 1977), pp. 134–5

REINHOLD MISSELBECK

Blot drawing. Technique described by Alexander Cozens (*see* COZENS, (1)) in his book *A New Method for Assisting the Invention in Drawing Original Compositions of Landscapes* (1786), whereby a blot or accidental mark can be developed and incorporated into a composition. Cozens's title may have been inspired by Leonardo da Vinci's description of a method of 'quickening the spirit of invention' by observing in damp walls and stones 'strange landscapes', 'figures in violent action', 'expressions of faces' and 'an infinity of things'.

See also AUTOMATISM.

☐

Blouet, Guillaume Abel (*b* Passy, 6 Oct 1795; *d* Paris, 17 May 1853). French architect and theorist. He began studying architecture in 1817 under Pierre-Jules-Nicolas Delespine (1756–1825) at the Ecole des Beaux-Arts, Paris, and in 1821 he won the Prix de Rome. While in Rome, Blouet became the protégé of Antoine Quatremère de Quincy and executed restoration drawings for a series of ancient monuments. With Quatremère's support, the Académie Royale d'Architecture published his *Restauration des thermes d'Antonin Caracalla à Rome*. The support given to Blouet is said to have encouraged Henri Labrouste to proceed with his own controversial study of the temples at Paestum. Blouet's interest in archaeology and building construction continued after his return to France. He became associated with the Académie des Inscriptions et Belles-Lettres in Paris and in 1828 joined its expedition to the Peloponnese, which was to excavate at Olympia and Aegina. His subsequent publication *L'Expédition scientifique de Morée* included polychromatic reconstructions of major Greek monuments but also featured comparative examples from the Byzantine era in this region.

On returning to Paris, Blouet was immediately appointed to succeed Jean Nicolas Huyot as architect of the Arc de Triomphe. He was joined on this commission by E.-J. Gilbert, who served as superintendent of construction. Blouet's contribution to the monument consisted of completing the upper part of the arch, providing for the interior spaces and supervising the sculptural decoration. His design for the attic level reveals a shift in style from the Empire aesthetic of Jean-François-Thérèse Chalgrin to a more energetic, plastic classicism. Shortly after the dedication of the Arc de Triomphe in July 1836, Blouet was dispatched by the French government to the USA to study American prison architecture. Travelling with the magistrate F.-A. Demetz, he was assigned to follow the work of Alexis de Tocqueville, who had made a similar journey in 1830. In his investigation Blouet was particularly impressed by the work of John Haviland, whose innovative radial plan for the Eastern State Penitentiary (1823–9), Philadelphia, was one of 14 plates included in the report on the American trip that Blouet and Demetz published in 1837.

The impact of the American report was such that in 1839 Blouet was appointed Inspecteur Général des Prisons, and in the same year he was given the commission to design an agrarian and penal colony at Mettray (Indre-et-Loire). The ground-plan for the complex at Mettray was organized formally through strict Beaux-Arts symmetry, with a series of pavilions flanking a garden court and a chapel situated at the far end of the entry axis. However, perhaps reflecting Blouet's architectural liberalism, the chapel took its inspiration from Romanesque and Gothic forms, with round-arched openings and a stepped spire. Blouet's influence in the field of prison architecture continued with his treatise *Instruction et programmes pour la construction de maisons d'arrêt et de justice*. Ideal designs by Blouet, along with those by Romain Harou (1796–1856) and Hector Horeau, thoroughly explored the possibilities of the radial cellular configuration for the penitentiary, ideas that were used by Gilbert in the Prison de la Nouvelle Force (1843–50), Paris. In 1846 Blouet was appointed professor of architectural theory at the Ecole des Beaux-Arts, a position he held until his death. Among his students were members of the next generation of rationalist architects, including Joseph-Auguste-Emile Vaudremer. During this time Blouet published his *Supplément au traité théorétique et pratique et l'art de bâtir de Jean Rondelet*, the theoretical expression of his long-standing interest in architectural construction. His last architectural project was the restoration of the Château de Fontainebleau, where he was responsible for work on the Cour du Cheval Blanc, the Pavillon de Sully and the Galerie François I.

WRITINGS

Restauration des thermes d'Antonin Caracalla à Rome (Paris, 1828)
L'Expédition scientifique de Morée, 4 vols (Paris, 1831–8)
Instruction et programmes pour la construction de maisons d'arrêt et de justice (Paris, 1841)
Supplément au traité théorétique et pratique et l'art de bâtir de Jean Rondelet, 2 vols (Paris, 1847–8)

BIBLIOGRAPHY

L. Hautecoeur: *Histoire de l'architecture classique en France*, 7 vols (Paris, 1943–57)
D. van Zanten: 'A French Architect in America in 1836', *J. Soc. Archit. Hist.*, xxix (1970), pp. 255
B. Foucart: 'Architecture carcérale et architectes fonctionnalistes en France au XIXe siècle', *Rev. A.* [Paris] (1976), pp. 37–56
P. Saddy: *Henri Labrouste: Architecte, 1801–1875* (Paris, 1977)
R. Middleton and D. Watkin: *Neoclassical and 19th-century Architecture* (New York, 1980)

LISA B. REITZES

Blow, Detmar (Jellings) (*b* 24 Nov 1867; *d* Painswick, Glos, 7 Feb 1939). English architect. He was articled to Wilson & Aldwinckle in 1883. In 1888, when he was sketching Abbeville Cathedral in France, he met John Ruskin and they toured Italy together. Ruskin persuaded Blow to give up his architectural training to learn about building, and in 1891 Blow was apprenticed to a working mason in Newcastle upon Tyne. In 1892 he won the RIBA Pugin Scholarship, the same year that he was elected to the Art Workers' Guild.

In 1897 Blow acted as clerk of works for Ernest Gimson in the construction of Lea and Stoneywell cottages in Charnwood Forest, Leics. Built among rocky outcrops in hilly country, Stoneywell Cottage (1898) blends with its surroundings and is an extreme manifestation of the ARTS AND CRAFTS MOVEMENT style, which exerted considerable influence on Blow.

In 1900 he built Happisburgh Manor, Cromer, Norfolk, on a butterfly plan, a variation on the X-plan. This striking house, with gables, thatched roof and large chimneys, draws on the Arts and Crafts tradition of incorporating local building techniques and materials, in this case flint, used to form patterns. In 1904–6 he built Wilsford Manor, near Salisbury, Wilts, his finest house in the Arts and Crafts style. In 1900–10 he had a practice designing country houses and was also involved in the sympathetic repair of churches for the Society for the Protection of Ancient Buildings.

In 1905 Blow went into partnership with the French architect Fernand Billerey (1878–1951), and his style became influenced by 18th-century French classicism. He married into the aristocracy in 1910, moved in wealthy circles and did considerable work for the Grosvenor Estate. In 1916 he became a full-time agent to Richard Grosvenor, the 2nd Duke of Westminster, and largely gave up his architectural practice. However, in 1933 the Duke made serious, and largely unfounded, financial accusations against Blow, who retired a broken man to his country house Hilles, near Painswick, Glos, an Arts and Crafts house that he had built between 1914 and 1917.

BIBLIOGRAPHY

F. H. W. Sheppard, ed.: *The Grosvenor Estate and Mayfair—Part 1* (1977), xxxix of *The Survey of London* (London, 1900–)
R. Gradidge: *Dream Houses: The Edwardian Ideal* (London, 1980)
A. S. Gray: *Edwardian Architecture: A Biographical Dictionary* (London, 1985/*R* 1988)
G. Stamp and A. Goulancourt: *The English House: 1860–1914* (London, 1986)

RODERICK GRADIDGE

Blue-and-white ceramic. Category of ceramics defined by the use, on a white surface, of blue derived from cobalt oxide, the most powerful of the colouring oxides in tinting strength. Depending on its concentration, colours range from a pale blue to a near blue-black. Cobalt produces good colours on all ceramic bodies, from low-fired earthenwares to high-fired porcelains (*see* CERAMICS, §I, 4). It was used as a colourant on figures found in Egyptian

1. Blue-and-white, tin-glazed earthenware dish, diam. 365 mm, Iznik, *c.* 1525 (Oxford, Ashmolean Museum)

tombs of the 5th Dynasty (*c.* 2465–*c.* 2325 BC), and glass beads coloured with cobalt and dating to *c.* 2250 BC have been discovered in north-west Iran. Its use in ceramic glazes is datable to 1200 BC from tomb objects found in Ethiopia, Mycenae and Tiryns, which probably originated in Egypt or Phoenicia. Persian and Syrian potters used cobalt on earthenwares for several centuries before they introduced it to China, where it was first used as an underglaze colour on earthenware during the Tang period (AD 618–907) and then later on porcelain.

1. Islamic world. 2. East Asia. 3. The West.

1. ISLAMIC WORLD. The opaque white, tin-glazed earthenware that originated in Mesopotamia during the 9th century AD or early 10th should be considered the first blue and white (*see* ISLAMIC ART, §V, 2(ii)). The technique was later introduced into Europe during the Arab conquests of North Africa and Spain. Merchants from Persia (now Iran) established communities on the coast and in the large cities of China, so it is logical that they would have had an effect on the production of ceramics and constituted one of the earliest and largest markets for Chinese blue-and-white decorated porcelains (*see* §2(i) below); blue-and-white porcelain was first really appreciated in the Middle East, which was unable to produce its own high-fired ceramic due to the lack of appropriate materials and techniques. Illustrations in Persian books of the 15th century (*see* ISLAMIC ART, fig. 121) occasionally show large numbers of Chinese blue-and-white wares, which attest to their popularity in Persia, as do the existing collections at the Topkapı Palace Museum in Istanbul (10,358 pieces from the Yuan to the Qing dynasty) and the Ardabil Shrine in ARDABIL, Iran, which was dedicated in 1611 to Shaykh Safi and holds 1162 pieces dating from the 14th to 16th centuries.

In the Ottoman empire, a general indebtedness to Chinese blue-and-white porcelains is visible in the hexagonal tiles decorating the mosque of Murad I (1436) in Edirne or the ceramic vessels attributed to the reign of Mehmed I (*reg* 1444–81). By the 1520s close imitations of Chinese blue-and-white wares were produced at Iznik in western Anatolia (*see* IZNIK, §2). They were copied from porcelains the Ottomans had acquired as booty at Tabriz in 1514 and at Damascus and Cairo in 1517. These copies incorporated Chinese shapes influenced by 15th-century designs and such motifs as the lotus, peony, dragon and phoenix (see fig. 1).

In Kashan and Meshhed the use of cobalt on pottery produced a smeared effect, which was minimalized with the use of a black outline. This technique was used during the 17th century at the kilns in Kirman, which produced blue-and-white pottery decorated with dragons and flowers closely imitating Chinese wares.

The Safavid monarch 'Abbas I (*reg* 1588–1629) is said to have brought Chinese potters and great quantities of Ming wares to his capital in Isfahan, from where the Chinese influence filtered throughout the pottery industry. 'Kubachi' wares, made in the 17th century and named after the small town in the Russian republic of Dagestan where they were found, were directly inspired by Chinese porcelains. They are decorated in blue without the black outline frequently found on other Persian wares. 'Kubachi' wares were frequently decorated with pagodas and high hills, imitating 17th-century Chinese porcelain (see §2(i) below), and were marketed in Europe but not in quantity. One of the motivating factors in the production of Chinese-style wares was the placing of orders by the Dutch in an effort to fill the void caused by the destruction of kilns in China at the fall of the Ming dynasty (1644). Records from the Dutch East India Company show that these blue-and-white wares were shipped from Gombroon (Bandar Abbas; now Bandar Khomeini) in the Persian Gulf nearly every year between 1652 and 1682.

2. EAST ASIA.

(i) China. The introduction of blue and white represents 'the most revolutionary technical and decorative innovation of the Mongol regime in China, if not in the whole of Chinese ceramic history' (Medley, 1969). Initially the cobalt oxide for making blue and white was imported from Persia, probably from the Kashan area and possibly in a cake form, which was ground into a powder. The cobalt was called *wu ming yu* ('nameless rarity'), *sunibo* ('Sumatra') or *hui hui qing* ('Muhammadan blue'). Local Chinese cobalt was at first difficult to obtain, and what was available invariably contained too much manganese, which blackened the colour; a refined form of cobalt from Chinese sources was not perfected until *c.* 1520 (see also CHINA, §VII, 2).

It is uncertain when the systematic production of blue-and-white wares began in China. Three porcelain figures decorated in underglaze blue were excavated in 1978 from a tomb dated 1276 at Hangzhou in Zhejiang Province, but the first blue-and-white wares appear to have been made during the early 14th century; of more than 18,000 pieces of ceramics found in 1975 on a Sinan shipwreck of 1323, there were no blue-and-white wares. The first dated blue-and-white porcelains are the David Vases, two temple vases inscribed and dated to 1351 (see CHINA, fig. 208). The mastery of the blue-and-white decoration on these vessels indicates that the use of cobalt was well understood by this date.

Large-scale production of good-quality blue and white began *c.* 1328 and became well established in JINGDE-ZHEN, Jiangsu Province. The Mongol rulers of the Yuan dynasty (1279–1368) had a particular predilection for monochromatic whitewares; there were some blue-and-white porcelains used in temples and for burials, but only one piece has been found at the site of the Yuan capital, Dadu (now Beijing). Blue and white was considered vulgar by the Chinese literati and was therefore mostly exported (see CERAMICS, §II): the Mongol rulers were chiefly interested in this ware as a means of raising revenues.

Large dishes, derived from Islamic metalwork or glass forms, comprised the major export from China to the Middle East in the 13th and 14th centuries (see §1 above). Wares were densely decorated with designs based on the mathematical complexity of decorative schemes found in Islamic architecture, a Near-Eastern aesthetic alien to the Chinese (see CHINA, §VII, 4(iii)). The few 14th-century blue-and-white wares made for the Chinese markets are decorated with scenes from Yuan plays and such motifs

from the established Chinese repertory as clouds, dragons, prunus and pine trees, phoenix birds, waves and lappets; these designs were, however, framed by forms and elements derived from the Near East.

An edict of 1368 by the Ming Hongwu emperor (*reg* 1368–98) disrupted trade routes, and with the loss of the Islamic market the exportation of blue and white temporarily ceased. The subsequent loss of Islamic influence led to the production of more wares decorated with underglaze red, which Hongwu preferred. When blue and white was produced in this period the cobalt used was a mixture of Persian—of which supplies were scarce—and native sources, which contained iron impurities and therefore lacked the clarity and depth of the later blue and white of the Yuan dynasty; the hues ranged from a pale silver to a dark grey-blue (see CHINA, §VII, 3(vi)).

In 1403 the Yongle emperor (*reg* 1403–24) sent diplomatic missions overseas for trade; these were described by Feixian and Ma Huan, the latter a translator to Zheng He, the Muslim eunuch who commanded the naval expedition for the Emperor. Ma Huan listed 'blue porcelain' as one of the products traded and reported that it was popular in Dai Viet (now Vietnam), Java, Sri Lanka and Dhofar (now the province of Ẓufār, Oman). He also included comments on Jingdezhen blue and white as highly valued in foreign countries (see CHINA, §VII, 4(iv)).

During the Xuande reign period (1426–35) imperial interest in blue and white increased, and the palace placed large orders for it. This period is considered the apogee in the development of blue-and-white wares. The *Ming shu* (official history of the Ming dynasty) records that in 1426, 1430, 1433 and 1434 Muhammadan blue was brought as tribute from Sumatra. One of the results of the use of cobalt at this time is known as the 'heaped and piled' effect, where the cobalt occasionally burnt black through the glaze. The period is also noted for the subtle, pitted surface of its wares, which was known as 'orange peel', and a more exuberant style of decoration. The exact sources for the motifs then found on blue-and-white porcelains is not fully understood, although they ultimately derive from traditional scroll paintings, reflecting scholarly interest in ornamental rocks and gardens (see fig. 2).

During the Chenghua reign period (1465–87) the execution of motifs outlined and filled in with blue became more refined and delicate. The purity of the porcelain body and the fineness of potting became highly important. During the reign of the Zhengde emperor (*reg* 1506–21) there were major changes in the production of blue and white, among which was the beginning of the use of purely local cobalt, which was only occasionally mixed with imported cobalt.

Between 1573 and 1661, during the last four imperial reigns of the Ming dynasty and the first of the Qing, there was a style of blue-and-white porcelain produced first for the South-east Asian market and later exported to Europe; it is generally identified by its thinness, brittle edges, pale and uneven blue colouring and decoration of divided panels with a central scene (see CHINA, fig. 228) and is known as 'Kraak' ware (see §3(iii) below). The forms and decorations also followed those used for the local and South-east Asian market, but these were modified to suit the tastes of the new European market.

2. Blue-and-white porcelain charger, diam. 430 mm, Chinese, probably Xuande reign period, 1426–35 (Salem, MA, Peabody Essex Museum)

Artistic vitality was rekindled during what is termed the Transitional period (1620–83). With a lack of direction from the imperial kilns in Jingdezhen, which were destroyed during civil disturbances in 1673 and 1675, the decorators painted motifs taken from popular poetry, myth, history and paintings. Jars decorated with the 'prunus on cracked ice' motif, sometimes called the 'Hawthorn' pattern, were one of the most popular and enduring forms and decorations of this period related to the production of blue and white.

The kilns at Jingdezhen were rebuilt in the 1680s. By the Kangxi reign period (1662–1722), the cobalt had become a clear and translucent blue, sometimes running to a bright violet under a thick glaze, which prompted the descriptive phrase 'violets in milk'. Trade was re-established with the European market, and the production of 'Chinese Imari' was introduced, a combination of underglaze blue with overglaze iron-red and gilding, a palette borrowed from the Japanese.

Wares produced during the reign of the Yongzheng emperor (reg 1723–35) imitated early blue-and-white Ming. Although he preferred wares decorated with polychrome enamels, Yongzheng's son, Qianlong (reg 1736–96), did retain a reverence for earlier wares, which led to an imitation of the 'heaped and piled' effect of the Xuande reign period. It had been the introduction of opaque, overglaze enamels of a palette called famille rose during the reign of Qianlong's grandfather that led to the decline of interest in blue and white. The production of blue and white, however, never completely ceased, especially for the export market.

In the mid-18th century a renewed interest in blue and white of Western manufacture occurred with the introduction of transfer-printing (see §3(v) below). The development in the West of less expensive porcelain and pottery

led to the decline of Chinese porcelain exportations. Nevertheless, blue and white remained an important trade commodity for Europe and America during the 18th and 19th centuries. Nineteenth-century blue-and-white wares, which were popular then and have remained so with 20th-century collectors, include patterns with such names as 'Fitzhugh', 'Nanking' and 'Canton'. Chinese hand-painted blue-and-white wares continued to be produced until the 1930s.

(ii) Korea. The gift to King Sejong by the Chinese Ming Xuande emperor (reg 1426–36) in 1428 is the first recorded instance of Chinese blue and white being introduced into Korea. By 1456 Korean potters were reproducing Chinese wine cups in hwa chagi (blue and white). Cobalt was, however, extremely difficult to find, and in 1461 its use was limited by decree; porcelain decorated with cobalt was to be used only by the warrior class and only for wine vessels, a strict control that lasted for about 100 years. The first official reference to blue and white is in the Sejo sillok, or annals of King Sejo's reign (1455–68), which states that in 1464 cobalt was discovered near the southern coastline of Korea. In 1469 prizes were offered for further discoveries of cobalt. No other references to sources of Korean cobalt exist, and the only mentions of cobalt in official records are complaints about the expense and difficulty of obtaining it. A Korean publication of 1591 states that Muhammadan blue was priced at 'double that of gold'.

The Japanese invasions of 1592 and 1597 destroyed the Korean potteries. Little, if any, blue and white was produced from this period until c. 1618. When production resumed, the style had changed from a direct imitation of Chinese originals to a wholly Korean style reflecting the aesthetics of restraint and simplicity; the scarcity of cobalt played into this. The standard form of decoration consists of floral or scenic designs within a circular or polygonal frame. The blue and white produced during this period was much appreciated and was collected by the Japanese tea masters.

Official potteries were established in 1718 at the Punwon kilns in Kwangju district, south-east of Seoul. The production of blue and white was confined to these potteries, which sold their surplus implements for the writing-table to scholars and artists (see fig. 3). As late as 1754 restrictions concerning the use of cobalt existed, although production continued in a much diminished artistic mode until 1883, when the state subsidy was terminated.

(iii) Japan. From the 16th to the 17th century three types of Chinese blue-and-white porcelains had been brought into Japan by independent Japanese merchants, as well as by Portuguese, Dutch and Chinese merchants: ko-sometsuke (old blue and white), tenkei (named after the Tianqi Emperor, reg 1621–8) and shonsui (refined, mid-17th-century, blue-and-white porcelain ordered by tea masters). When Japanese traders were restricted by an edict in 1633 from trading with China, the Dutch, Portuguese and Chinese continued to supply them with blue-and-white porcelains.

The end of the Ming dynasty (1644) resulted in—among other calamities—the destruction of kilns and the disruption of trade between China and Europe. The Japanese were called upon to supply the orders from the Western traders, which they did as early as the 1640s by producing porcelain in imitation of blue-and-white 'kraak'. The Dutch East India Company records first mention their importation into Japan of 'porcelain paint' (cobalt) in 1650, and they began exporting enormous quantities of blue and white from Japan. The first ship loaded with Japanese porcelain (2200 gallipots) for the Western market left Nagasaki in 1653 for Batavia (now Jakarta) on Java. This was the start of a short-lived but world-wide trade of Japanese porcelain, not only to the Netherlands but through the Dutch to India, Persia, Sri Lanka, Siam, Vietnam and other parts of South-east Asia. Among the most notable blue and white exports of the second half of the 17th century are apothecary bottles bearing monograms within wreaths, and flatware with the VOC (Verenigde Oostindische Compagnie) monogram. Tall, cylindrical vases (known as *rolwagens*), jugs and tankards, all decorated with blue, Chinese-style motifs, were also common (*see* JAPAN, §VIII, 3(iii)).

The re-establishment of the kilns in China during the 1680s led to the decline of the ceramic industry in Japan. The Dutch returned to their sources in China, which were better equipped to provide cheaper ceramics in larger quantities. Japanese blue-and-white porcelain, however, continued to be made on a limited scale throughout the 18th and 19th centuries, especially at Hirado.

3. THE WEST.

(i) Portugal, Spain and Mexico. The Portuguese were the first Europeans to arrive in China by sea (1517) and to begin direct trade with China. They were the major exporters of Chinese blue-and-white wares throughout the 16th century and were therefore the first Europeans to be directly influenced by these porcelains. By the 1520s shipments of mostly blue-and-white porcelain to Portugal amounted to between 40,000 and 60,000 pieces, many of which were re-exported to the Netherlands. One outstanding example of the mania for Chinese blue and white is the Santos Palacio (now the French Embassy) in Lisbon: in what an inventory of 1704 calls the 'Casa das Porçolanas', a pyramidal ceiling was covered with 261 Chinese blue-and-white dishes and plates dating from the 16th century to the early 17th.

Portuguese imitations of Chinese blue and white are not well documented until the 1580s, when Chinese blue-and-white 'kraak' was the most imitated ware in the production of tin-glazed earthenware; even then they reflected an inevitable leaning towards Islamic, Italian, Spanish and Flemish styles. At first the products were direct copies of the Chinese, although by the 1650s the styles became increasingly European and by the 1680s tin-glazed wares were far more European in style, with only the most oblique references to China. Blue decoration was used on such Western forms as *albarelli* (drug jars) rather than on Chinese forms.

Although Spain ruled Portugal from 1580 to 1640, different ceramic traditions existed in each territory. Blue-and-white decorated ceramics were not as influential in Spain as they were in Portugal. The first influences came through the blue-and-white tin-glazed wares made by the

3. Blue-and-white porcelain brushpot, h. 160 mm, Korean, probably Punwon kilns, 18th century (Seoul, Ho-am Art Museum)

Arabs, whose caliphates extended through most of the Iberian Peninsula. Imitations of Chinese blue and white did, however, occur, at Talavera de la Reina and Puente del Arzobispo (*see* SPAIN, §VII, 3). Familiar late Ming designs, especially those on 'kraak' ware, were the favoured motifs. By the late 17th century and the early 18th blue and white had been replaced by polychrome decoration.

Mexican tin-glazed earthenware reflects the influence of the Spanish Conquest (1519–21) and of Spain's trade with China. Spanish galleons sailed from Manila in the Philippines to Acapulco on the Pacific coast. Wares were carried across Mexico to Puebla (if not sent to Mexico City) and then to Veracruz on the Gulf of Mexico, from where they were shipped across the Atlantic to Seville. The presence of Chinese blue and white in Puebla exerted an influence that, when mixed with native pottery styles, produced an exuberant Mexican version of Chinese blue and white. Potters were first working in Puebla between 1550 and 1570, at about which time native potters were being retrained by friar-potters from Talavera de la Reina; Pueblan pottery of this style is known as Talavera de Puebla. The Ordenanzas (est. 1653) stipulated that 'in making the fine wares the colouring should be in imitation of the Chinese ware, very blue, finished in the same style and with blue relief work, and on this style of pottery there should be painted black dots and grounds in colours'. The speciality of Pueblan potters was large, Chinese-style, blue-and-white jars decorated with landscapes, birds, deer or flowers painted in an ebullient manner (*see* MEXICO, fig. 14).

(ii) Italy. Because of Venice's early efforts in maritime trade, the importation of silk and other luxuries from Asia made Italy a viable location for the introduction of Chinese porcelain to the European Continent. In 1461 the Sultan of Egypt presented 20 pieces of Chinese blue-and-white porcelain to Doge Pasquale Malipiero of Venice and later even more to Lorenzo the Magnificent in Florence. Francesco I, Grand Duke of Tuscany, was the first to develop a close replica of Chinese porcelain; a soft-paste porcelain was made in his court workshops (est. *c.* 1565) in Florence *c.* 1575 using clay from Vicenza, which contained some kaolin (*see* FLORENCE, §III, 1). Only 57 pieces are recorded and all are decorated with blue winding stems and coiled foliage resembling similar decoration on Chinese porcelain of the 15th and 16th centuries (*see* ITALY, fig. 88). Similar Chinese motifs had already been used on Italian maiolica in a style known as *alla porcellana*. At the end of the 16th century Italian potters dispersed the technique of maiolica production, including the blue-and-white palette, throughout Europe.

(iii) The Netherlands. The Dutch established their own East India Company in 1602, after Philip II, King of Spain, closed Lisbon to the Dutch. In the same year the Dutch captured two Portuguese ships (*carracks*) containing approximately 200,000 pieces of Chinese export porcelain (hence the name 'kraak' ware). In 1609 the Dutch were granted permission to establish a trading post at Hirado in Japan, and in July 1610 the first ship arrived in the Netherlands from Japan carrying Chinese blue-and-white porcelains, which had previously been brought by Portuguese ships. In 1636, 259,000 pieces of 'kraak' were shipped from Batavia, and the passion for blue and white in the Netherlands was thus established.

From the second quarter of the 17th century the declining Delft breweries became the site for a pottery industry where tin-glazed earthenware was produced in such profusion that the name of the town has become synonymous with its product, Delftware (*see* DELFT, §3). The enormous quantities of Chinese blue and white imported by the Dutch East India Company affected the local ceramics industry to the extent that at first they directly copied the imported blue-and-white porcelain and only later introduced Dutch motifs and designs. In the Netherlands wares were covered with a clear lead glaze to resemble more closely the finish of the Chinese porcelains. Plates, chargers, ewers and tiles were decorated with designs in cobalt in the Chinese style. The Dutch East India Company records show requests for Delftwares by Japanese warlords and wealthy merchants from 1634 until 1668, when Japanese sumptuary laws prohibited the importation of foreign pottery. These wares were thought to be especially suitable for the tea ceremony, and a set of small, irregularly shaped dishes (*mukozuke*) for this ceremony, made in Delft and decorated by Frederik van Frytom (1632–1702), have been found in Japan.

(iv) Germany. Centres for the production of tin-glazed wares were established at Hamburg, Frankfurt am Main and Jannau in the late 17th century in order to compete with Dutch imports. The first fine earthenware factory established in Frankfurt am Main in 1666 was influenced by Chinese blue and white, either directly or through the Dutch wares. As with the Dutch tin-glazed wares, these were covered with a clear lead glaze.

Under the auspices of Frederick-Augustus I, Elector of Saxony (also Augustus II, King of Poland; known as Augustus the Strong), a method of imitating Yixing ware, called *Jaspis Porzellan*, was discovered at Meissen in 1706–7, and a hard-paste 'true' porcelain, using kaolin from Colditz, was made from 1710 (see fig. 4). By March 1720 David Köhler (*d* 1723) and Johann Gottfried Mehlhoun

4. Blue-and-white chinoiserie porcelain, Meissen, 18th century (Berlin, Schloss Charlottenburg)

had discovered a method of decorating the white ground in blue enamels at Meissen, and examples were exhibited that year at Leipzig and Naumberg. The technique, however, was lost after Köhler's death and was not rediscovered until some years later. The *Zwiebelmuster* ('blue onion' pattern), a highly stylized pattern derived from the Chinese, was originally introduced at Meissen on tableware *c.* 1735 and continued to be popular into the late 20th century.

(v) England. Early examples of Chinese blue and white in Britain suggest that blue and white was rare in the 16th century: William Cecil, Lord Burghley, Lord Treasurer to Elizabeth I, owned a blue-and-white Wan li dish with silver-gilt mounts, and another dating to between 1580 and 1600 was a gift from the Queen to her godchild Thomas Walsingham.

After the accession of William III to the English throne in 1688, the stylistic influences from the Dutch court were strong and included the extensive use of blue and white, especially in interior design (*see* DISPLAY OF ART, fig. 10). The display of blue-and-white wares became one of the primary styles of interior decoration (*see* CABINET (i), §4(i)), mainly through the work of the Huguenot Daniel Marot (*see* MAROT, (2)), who had worked for Queen Mary II in the Netherlands (*see* ORANGE NASSAU, (6)).

This passion for blue and white naturally led to its being imitated by English potters producing tin-glazed earthenwares, especially at the London potteries of Southwark and Lambeth. In the 18th century the production of tin-glazed wares—mostly tablewares—was particularly centred in Bristol (*see* BRISTOL, §3(i)) and Liverpool (*see* LIVERPOOL, §3). Soft-paste porcelain was first produced at the CHELSEA PORCELAIN FACTORY in London *c.* 1745. Other porcelain factories were established in England, including the Bow Porcelain Factory in London's East End, which, after 1749, specialized in the production of blue and white decorated with chinoiseries. Not until the New Hall Factory in New Hall, Staffs, was established in 1781 were blue-and-white, hard-paste porcelains produced in quantity. By 1800 Josiah Spode (ii) had perfected bone china at Stoke-on-Trent, Staffs, making blue-and-white ware less expensive and thus available to a wider public.

In the 1750s transfer-printing was introduced at such factories as Worcester; the designs from an engraved copper plate were transferred with tissue paper on to the ceramic object. One of the most ubiquitous patterns in this category of ceramic ware is the so-called 'Willow' pattern. 'Flow blue', a category of transfer-printed blue and white, was an early 19th-century development that, by firing in an atmosphere containing volatile chlorides, created a soft appearance resulting from the diffusion of the pigment into the glaze.

(vi) France. The production of blue and white first began in France when Chinese-style faience was produced at Nevers (*see* NEVERS, §1). Made between 1650 and 1680, typical pottery of this type is decorated with a deep-blue ground and yellow and orange motifs; it was erroneously known as *bleu persan*. It was imitated at Rouen as well as in the Netherlands and England. The French East India Company was established in 1664, after which many French ceramics reflected an increased interest in Chinese

wares. From *c.* 1700 factories in Normandy began to produce blue-and-white faience in the *style rayonnant*, identified by blue lacy borders sometimes accented by red, yellow and green (*see* ROUEN, §III). A similar style was developed at the factory of Pierre Clérissy (1651–1728) in MOUSTIERS in southern France.

BIBLIOGRAPHY
T. Volker: *Porcelain and the Dutch East India Company* (Leiden, 1954)
——: *The Japanese Porcelain Trade of the Dutch East India Company after 1683* (Leiden, 1959)
G. St. G. M. Gompertz: *Korean Pottery and Porcelain of the Yi Period* (London, 1968)
M. Medley: *The Chinese Potter* (Oxford, 1969)
M. Yoshida: *In Search of Persian Pottery* (New York, 1972)
M. Lerner: *Blue and White: Early Japanese Export Ware* (New York, 1978)
C. J. A. Jorg: *Internations in Ceramics: Oriental Porcelain and Delftware* (Hong Kong, 1984)
D. Lion-Goldschmidt: 'Les Porcelaines chinoises du palais de Santos', *A. Asiatiques*, xxxix (1984), pp. 5–72
S. Little: *Chinese Ceramics of the Transitional Period, 1620–1683* (New York, 1984)
Blue and White: Chinese Porcelain and its Impact on the Western World (exh. cat. by J. Carswell, U. Chicago, IL, Smart Gal., 1985)
N. Atasoy and J. Raby: *Iznik: The Pottery of Ottoman Turkey* (London, 1989)
M. Rinaldi: *Kraak Porcelain* (London, 1989)

WILLIAM R. SARGENT

Blue Four [Blauen Vier]. Name applied to a group of German painters, founded at the Bauhaus in Weimar, Germany, on 31 March 1924. The group consisted of Vasily Kandinsky, Paul Klee, Alexei Jawlensky and Lyonel Feininger, who were formerly associated with the BLAUE REITER group. The idea for founding the Blue Four came from Galka Scheyer, a former pupil of Jawlensky, who sought to make the work and ideas of these artists better known in the USA through exhibitions, lectures and sales. While the Blue Four was not an official association, its name was chosen to give American audiences an idea about the type of artists involved and also to allude to the artists' previous association with the Blaue Reiter group. In May 1924 Scheyer travelled to New York, where the first Blue Four exhibition took place at the Charles Daniel Gallery (Feb–March 1925). Scheyer then moved to California, where the first of many Blue Four exhibitions in the San Francisco and Los Angeles areas took place at the Oakland Museum in autumn 1925. Further exhibitions, often with lectures by Scheyer, were held in Portland, OR (1927), Seattle, WA (1926, 1936), Spokane, WA (1927), Mexico City (1931) and in Chicago, IL (1932), as well as at the Ferdinand Möller Gallery in Berlin (1929).

BIBLIOGRAPHY
The Blue Four (exh. cat. by R. Haas, Pasadena, CA, Norton Simon Mus., 1975)
S. Campbell, ed.: *The Blue Four Galka Scheyer Collection* (Pasadena, 1976)
P. Weiss: 'The Blue Four', *The Blue Four—Feininger, Jawlensky, Kandinsky, Paul Klee* (exh. cat., New York, Leonard Hutton Gals, 1984), pp. 7–12
Theme and Improvisation: Kandinsky and the American Avant-Garde, 1912–1950 (exh. cat. by G. Levin and M. Lorenz, Dayton, OH, A. Inst., 1992), pp. 156–9
P. Weiss: *The Blue Four: A Dialogue with America. The Correspondence of Lyonel Feininger, Alexei Jawlensky, Wassily Kandinsky and Paul Klee with Galka Scheyer* (in preparation)

MARIANNE LORENZ

Bluemner, Oscar [Florianus] (*b* Prenzlau, Germany, 21 June 1867; *d* South Braintree, MA, 12 Jan 1938). American painter and architect of German birth. He emigrated to the USA in 1892, after receiving his diploma and an award for a painting of an architectural subject from the Königliche Technische Hochschule, Berlin. He first worked as a draughtsman at the World's Columbian Exposition, Chicago, and later designed New York's Bronx Borough Courthouse (1902). Around 1910 his professional focus moved to painting under the aegis of Alfred Stieglitz, who gave him a one-man exhibition at the 291 gallery in 1915, published his writings in *Camera Work* and recommended his inclusion in the *Forum Exhibition of Modern American Painters* (1916).

Bluemner's prismatically structured early landscapes (e.g. *Expression of a Silktown*, 1915; Newark, NJ, Mus.) reflected his lasting interest in colour theory and familiarity with the work of Paul Cézanne and Vincent van Gogh and with Neo-Impressionism. During the 1920s he concentrated on watercolours (e.g. *Eye of Fate*, 1927; New York, MOMA), whose dramatic forms and enriched palette followed his study of oriental art, Symbolist painting and such thinkers as Johann Wolfgang von Goethe, Arthur Schopenhauer, Henri Bergson and Oswald Spengler. His late pictures, painted in oil or casein, were produced in part while he was employed by the Public Works of Art Project and were conceived as a series of *Compositions for Color Themes* (e.g. *Situation in Yellow*, 1933; New York, Whitney); they were formally inspired by classical music and iconographically influenced by Freud's ideas on the subconscious. After 1933 Bluemner signed his paintings FLORIANUS, a Latin idealization of his own surname.

WRITINGS
'Audiator et Altera Pars: Some Plain Sense on the Modern Art Movement', *Camera Work* (June 1913), pp. 25–38

BIBLIOGRAPHY
Oscar Bluemner: American Colorist (exh. cat. by C. Coggins, M. Holsclaw and M. Hoppin, Cambridge, MA, Fogg, 1967)
F. Gettings: 'The Human Landscape: Subjective Symbolism in Oscar Bluemner's Painting', *Archv Amer. A. J.*, xix/3 (1979), pp. 9–14
Oscar Bluemner (exh. cat. by J. Zilczer, Washington, DC, Hirshhorn, 1979)
J. Hayes: 'Oscar Bluemner's Late Landscapes: The Musical Color of Fateful Experience', *A. J.*, xxxiv/4 (1984), pp. 352–60
Oscar Bluemner: Landscapes of Sorrow and Joy (exh. cat. by J. Hayes, Washington, DC, Corcoran A.G., 1988)
J. Hayes: *Oscar Bluemner* (Cambridge, 1991)

JEFFREY R. HAYES

Blueprint. *See under* PHOTOGRAPHY, §I.

Blue Rider. *See* BLAUE REITER.

Blue Rose [Rus. Golubaya Roza]. Group of second-generation Russian Symbolist artists active in Moscow between 1904 and 1908. The term derives from the title of an exhibition that they organized at premises in Myasnitsky Street, Moscow, in 1907. The group originated in Saratov, when in 1904 Pavel Kuznetsov and Pyotr Utkin (1877–1934) organized the exhibition *Crimson Rose* (Rus. *Alaya Roza*), which included the work of the two major Symbolist painters Mikhail Vrubel' and their teacher Viktor Borisov-Musatov. Later that year, at the Moscow School of Painting, Sculpture and Architecture, they attracted artists of a similar persuasion such as Anatoly Arapov (1876–1949), Nikolay Krymov, Nikolay Milioti, Vasily Milioti, Nikolay Sapunov, Martiros Saryan and Sergey Sudeykin. An important member of the group was the wealthy banker, patron and artist Nikolay Ryabushinsky, who publicized Blue Rose in his magazine GOLDEN FLEECE (Rus.: *Zolotoye Runo*). By 1907 most of the group had become co-editors, but a group statement or manifesto was never published. Ryabushinsky also contributed to the stability of the group by purchasing works from Kuznetsov, Sapunov, Saryan and Sudeykin.

During the years of their collaboration, the group shared a common philosophy and approach to painting. Inspired principally by the Symbolist poets Andrey Bely and Aleksandr Blok, Blue Rose artists believed that it was the function of art to transcend reality and communicate with the beyond. To this end the group adopted a common symbolism and a common stylistic approach. Pregnancy, foetal life and flowing water were familiar themes, as in Kuznetsov's *Blue Fountain* (1905; Moscow, Tret'yakov Gal.), where the cool blue, grey and green tones convey a feeling of melancholy, and the indistinct outlines of the distorted human forms overlap in transparent veils to create a psychologically disturbing effect.

The unusual title of the exhibition was chosen for its evocative otherworldly qualities and recalled the imaginary flowers in the paintings of Odilon Redon. Flower symbolism was important for the Blue Rose group, and the exhibition was decorated with hyacinths, lilies and daffodils. It contained over a hundred works and attracted varied reviews. Igor' Grabar', for instance, assumed a mocking tone, calling on Blue Rose artists to surrender their symbols to the playwright Maurice Maeterlinck and to come out into the sunlight. However, Sergey Makovsky was entranced: 'The pictures are like prayers . . . a spring flower of mystical love.'

A few months after their exhibition, Blue Rose disintegrated. There was a feeling that Symbolism had come to the end of its useful life and the artists developed in different directions. Saryan journeyed to Armenia and Kuznetsov to Kyrgyzstan, where both began to use brighter and more vivid colours. Krymov and Sudeykin developed greater solidity of form in their work, while Arapov and Sapunov moved into stage design.

BIBLIOGRAPHY
I. Grabar': 'Golubaya Roza', *Vesy*, 5 (1907), pp. 93–6
S. Makovsky: 'Golubaya Roza', *Zolotoye Runo*, 5 (1907), p. 25
Golubaya Roza (exh. cat., Moscow, 1907)
J. E. Bowlt: 'Russian Symbolism and the Blue Rose Movement', *Slav. & E. Eur. Rev.*, li/123 (1973), pp. 161–81
D. Sarabyanov: *Pavel Kuznetsov* (Moscow, 1975)
J. E. Bowlt: 'The Blue Rose: Russian Symbolism in Art', *Burl. Mag.*, cxviii (1976), pp. 566–74
P. Stupples: *Pavel Kuznetsov: His Life and Work* (Cambridge, 1990)

ANTHONY PARTON

Blum [Bloem; Bloome], **Hans** (*b* Lohr, *c*. 1525). German architect, engraver and writer. After training as an architect in his native town, Hans Blum left Lohr because two architects were already working there: Peter Volckner (*fl* 1539–48) and Jost Wenzel (*fl* 1548–70). He then moved to Zurich, where he married Ragali Kuchymeister in 1550. Their eldest son Christoffel Blum (*bapt* 21 Jan 1552) was named after the publisher Christoffel Froschauer (?1490–1564), who later published Hans Blum's treatises on architecture.

Hans Blum is primarily known as the author of *Quinque columnarum exacta descriptio atque delineatio cum symmetrica* (1550), a book on the five orders of architecture (*see* PATTERN BOOK, fig. 3). He based his work on the fourth volume of Serlio's *Regole generali di architettura* (Venice, 1537), a German edition of which was published in 1542. The second source for Blum's book was Gualtherus Rivius's edition of Vitruvius, published in 1548 and illustrated by Peter Flettner (1485–1546). Treating temple and column as a unity, Vitruvius had distinguished five types of temple on the basis of a system related to the spacing and proportion of the columns. During the Renaissance the use of columns was extended to various kinds of buildings other than those of a religious purpose. The columns were designed on the basis of a unit of measurement known as the module, which could be calculated in two ways. According to Vitruvius, the module was either one half or a whole column diameter (used also by Alberti and Palladio); with others (e.g. Jacopo Vignola) the module depended on the total height of the column. For Hans Blum the module had lost its function as a unit of measurement; instead, he took the height of the column as a starting point and divided this into equal parts. In this way, he arrived at the following seven types: Tuscan, Doric, Ionic I, Ionic II, Corinthian I, Corinthian II, Composite. The Tuscan column was divided into 9 parts with 2 for the pedestal; the Doric into 8 with 2 for the pedestal; the Ionic I into 7.2 with 3 for the pedestal; the Ionic II into 7.2 with 3 for the pedestal; and the Corinthian I into 8 with 1 for the base (this column has no pedestal). The Corinthian II consisted of 9 parts with 2 for the pedestal and the Composite had 13 parts with 3 for the pedestal. Vitruvius's columns have no pedestals, while those of Serlio do; Blum combined the two in Ionic and Corinthian I and II.

In 1560 Christoffel Froschauer published a sequel to Blum's book, in which Blum deals with the elements of architecture and the use of columns (Ionic superimposed on Doric); it is based on Serlio's third book *Delle antichità* (Venice, 1540). Of the illustrations, only the title page, which carries the monogram HB, can be attributed to Blum. It shows an attic with two pairs of columns. The foremost columns have a pedestal; a cartouche with scrollwork is crowned by the head of a faun, which connects two volutes. Through the attic can be seen a landscape with ruins, and to the right an obelisk with the monogram HB.

After 1558 a third volume was added comprising a collection of palaces, temples and triumphal arches based on designs by Bramante and Antonio Sangallo II. The book was published by Jacopo Gessner and Thobias Gessner, and is illustrated with woodcuts signed RW, IW and WI. RW is the monogram of the draughtsman and engraver Rudolph Wyssenbach (*fl* 1546–60); IW might refer to Ieremias Wyssenbach. All the illustrated designs are of imaginary schemes.

WRITINGS

Quinque columnarum exacta descriptio atque delineatio cum symmetrica, earum distributione (Zurich, 1550) [ded. to Andreas Schmid, city architect of Zurich]

Ein Kunstrych Buoch von allerley Antiquiteten, so zum verstand der fünf Sülen, der Architekten gehörend (Zurich, 1560)

Architectura antiqua, waarhaften Contrafacturen etlich alt und schöner Gebauden (Zurich, 1562)

BIBLIOGRAPHY
Hollstein: *Ger.*; Wasmuth

G. K. Nagler: *Monogrammisten*, iii (Munich, 1863)

E. von Mey: *Hans Blum, ein Bautheoretiker der deutschen Renaissance* (Strasbourg, 1910)

A. Haupt: *Baukunst der Renaissance in Frankreich und Deutschland* (Berlin, 1923)

O. Schmidt: *Reallexikon zur deutschen Kunstgeschichte*, i (Stuttgart, 1937)

M. J. T. M. STOMPÉ

Blum, Robert Frederick (*b* Cincinnati, OH, 9 July 1857; *d* New York, 8 June 1903). American painter and illustrator. The son of German-American parents, he probably became interested in magazine illustration while an apprentice at Gibson & Co., lithographers in Cincinnati, during 1873 and 1874. He began drawing lessons at the McMicken School of Design (now the Art Academy of Cincinnati) *c.* 1873, transferring to the Ohio Mechanics Institute in 1874. Blum visited the Centennial Exposition (1876) in Philadelphia and was impressed with paintings by Giovanni Boldini and Mario Fortuny y Carbó and by Japanese art. He remained there for about nine months, studying at the Pennsylvania Academy of the Fine Arts.

Blum moved to New York in 1878, where he contributed illustrations to such magazines as *St Nicholas* and *Scribner's Magazine*. In 1880 he took the first of numerous trips to Europe. In Venice he met James Abbott McNeill Whistler and Frank Duveneck and under their influence took up etching. He travelled frequently with William Merritt Chase, with whom he founded the Society of Painters in Pastel, New York, which held four exhibitions, the first in 1884. Sketchy pastels made in the Netherlands (1884) and relatively large, detailed and compositionally intricate paintings such as *Venetian Lace-makers* (1887; Cincinnati, OH, A. Mus.) demonstrate his stylistic range.

In May 1890 Blum was sent to Japan by *Scribner's Magazine* to make illustrations for articles by Sir Edwin Arnold. He remained there for about two years, making both small sketches and ambitious works such as *The Ameya* (1892; New York, Met.), which depicts a crowded Japanese street scene.

In New York in 1893 Blum began the large murals for Mendelssohn Hall, *Mood to Music* and the *Vintage Festival* (both New York, Brooklyn Mus.). He was working on murals for the New Amsterdam Theater when he died of pneumonia.

WRITINGS
'Technical Methods of American Artists, vi: Pen and Ink Drawing', *The Studio*, iii (3 May 1884), pp. 173–5

'An Artist in Japan', *Scribner's Mag.*, xiii (April–June 1893), pp. 399–414, 624–36, 729–49

BIBLIOGRAPHY
Robert F. Blum 1857–1903: A Retrospective Exhibition (exh. cat., ed. R. J. Boyle; Cincinnati, A. Mus., 1966)

B. Weber: *Robert Frederick Blum (1857–1903) and his Milieu* (diss., New York, City U., 1985)

CAROLYN KINDER CARR

Blumbergs, Ilmārs (*b* Riga, 6 Sept 1943). Latvian painter, stage designer and graphic designer. After a childhood spent in Siberian exile, he studied decorative art and trained as a painter in the Latvian Art Academy (1963–72), preparing for a career as a stage designer. Stage design and the applied arts were less constrained by Socialist Realist dictates during the 1970s, and he quickly became one of Latvia's most innovative artists. His fluency with process art and installation, for example, was already evident in his designs for a 1973 Riga production of *Žanna d'Arka* (Joan of Arc) by Andrej Upīts, the stage metamorphosing from Minimalist cavity to an assemblage in Arte Povera style. Abandoning the theatre in 1987, Blumbergs continued his prolific output. His compositions, sometimes abstract, often figurative and allegorical, are notable within Latvian art for their spare elegance and uncontrived expressiveness, successfully combining grand literary allusion and subtle metaphysical content. His graphic virtuosity earned him a degree of international celebrity rare among his Latvian peers. Exceptional, too, for his political candour, he was a harbinger of *glasnost* with his illustrations for a translation (Riga, 1988) of the tragedies of Lucius Annaeus Seneca the younger (*c.* 5 BC–AD 65), in which he updated imagery of brutality with Soviet motifs, made more explicit in his two-volume book *Via dolorosa: Staļinisma upuru liecības* ('Testimony of the victims of Stalinism', Riga, 1990–93), written with Anda Lice (Litsa; *b* 1941). These works have an immediacy and profundity for Latvians, who are represented in an untitled series of paintings (from 1993) as complicit in their fate as a subjugated people.

BIBLIOGRAPHY
V. Berjozkins: *Ilmārs Blumbergs: Scenografija* (Riga, 1983)
Ilmārs Blumbergs (exh. cat., Riga, Mus. Latv. & Rus. A., 1993)
                                    MARK ALLEN SVEDE

Blume [Blom]. German family of sculptors and stonemasons active in Sweden. Henrik [Heinrich] Blume (*b* Bremen; *d* Stockholm, July 1648) arrived in Sweden *c.* 1621. He was responsible for the south portal (1644) of the church of St Jakob in Stockholm, in which he combined a classical columnar arrangement with a rich figure programme and the almost organic scrolls characteristic of contemporary German patterns. He also contributed (1637) to the sculpture at the Royal Palace, Stockholm, and executed (from the designs of other artists) portals and mixed sculpted work at the castles of the Oxenstierna family at Tidö in Västmanland and Fiholm in Södermanland (1638–43; *in situ*). Henrik Blume's brother Didrik Blume (*b* Bremen; *d* Stockholm, Feb 1668) arrived in Sweden in the early 1630s and contributed decorative work to the Stockholm palaces of Jakob De la Gardie (1583–1652; *see* DE LA GARDIE, MAGNUS GABRIEL) and Lennart Torstensson (1603–51). Of the two portals (*c.* 1647–8; *in situ*) of the Torstensson building, one is a martial composition of banded Doric columns surmounted by lions and heraldic shields.

BIBLIOGRAPHY
SVKL
G. Axel-Nilsson: *Dekorativ stenhuggarkonst i yngre vasastil* [Decorative sculpture in the early Vasa style] (Lund, 1950)
——: *Makalös Fültherren greve Jakob De la Gardies hus i Stockholm* [The peerless palace: the Stockholm house of the field marshal Count Jakob De la Gardies] (Stockholm, 1984)
                                    TORBJÖRN FULTON

Blume, Peter (*b* Smorgon, Russia, 27 Oct 1906; *d* New Milford, CT, 30 Nov 1992). American painter and sculptor. His parents emigrated to the USA and settled in Brooklyn, New York, *c.* 1912. He studied art from the age of 13 at evening classes, then at the Educational Alliance, the Beaux-Arts Institute of Design and the Art Students League. By 1926 he had a studio in New York. Blume's admiration for Renaissance technique largely inspired his working method: making drawings and compositional cartoons and then painstakingly transferring the images to canvas, a craftsmanlike approach that resulted in a surprisingly small body of work.

Blume's early work shows the influence of the Precisionists and was exhibited by Charles Daniel (one of the first to exhibit modernist American painting). In 1934 Blume won first prize at the Carnegie International Exhibition with the surreal *South of Scranton* (1930–31; New York, Met.). A year in Italy on a Guggenheim grant (1932) inspired his only political painting, *Eternal City* (1934–7; New York, MOMA), in which Mussolini is characterized as a garish jack-in-the-box.

The figurative and literary elements of Blume's work continued into his later career despite the ascendancy of Abstract Expressionism. His pervading themes deal with discontinuity caused by destruction, distance, time and chance, and with man's attempt to unite, repair and rebuild from the fragments that remain. Stones, rocks and girders recur as iconographic motifs, for instance in *Tasso's Oak* (1956; New York, Dintenfass Gal.). *Recollection of the Flood* (1969; New York, Dintenfass Gal.) shows victims of the floods in Florence (1966) seeking shelter in a hall where restorers are already at work. This painting was followed by Blume's first sculpture, *Bronzes about Venus* (1970; New York, Dintenfass Gal.), whose deliberate references to antiquity and Mannerist art are reiterated in the painting *From the Metamorphoses* (1979; New York, Dintenfass Gal.). The latter depicts the legend of Deucalion and Pyrrha, who repopulated the world by throwing stones that turned into men, a further indication of Blume's preoccupation with the role of the artist in restoring the world through the ability to transform materials.

BIBLIOGRAPHY
Peter Blume: Paintings and Drawings in Retrospect, 1925–1964 (exh. cat., intro. C. E. Buckley; Manchester, NH, Currier Gal. A., 1964)
Peter Blume: A Retrospective Exhibition (exh. cat. by D. Adrien and P. Blume, Chicago, Mus. Contemp. A., 1976)
                                    RINA YOUNGNER

Blumenfeld, Erwin (*b* Berlin, 26 Jan 1897; *d* Rome, 4 July 1969). American photographer of German birth. In 1918, in exile in the Netherlands, he met George Grosz, Howard Mehring and Paul Citroen. Working already as a photographer, painter and writer, he set up a photographic business in Paris in 1936 after the bankruptcy of his leather-goods shop in the preceding year. In 1941 he emigrated to the USA, and within two years he was one of the best-paid freelance photographers, working for *Vogue*, *Life* and *Harper's Bazaar*. In 1955 he began the text of his autobiography, *Blumenfeld: Meine 100 Besten Fotos* (1979), on which he worked for the rest of his life. Blumenfeld's personal photography showed the influence of Dada. He experimented unflaggingly with the technical possibilities of photography: solarization, multiple exposures, distortions. The dominant themes throughout his work were women and death. His international reputation was based not only on his experimental photography but also on his fashion photography, which he had begun as early as 1936 in France, and with which he very quickly established himself in the USA. He did not, however, choose any of his fashion or glamour photographs for the 100 in his autobiography. The images that were important to him were those in which he tried to 'realize visions and penetrate unknown transparencies'. The laboratory work, at which he was supremely skilled, helped him to enhance the refinement of the chosen visual angle in order to achieve a state of suspension of the real and the unreal.

PHOTOGRAPHIC PUBLICATIONS
Blumenfeld: Meine 100 Besten Fotos (Berne, 1979)

BIBLIOGRAPHY
Contemp. Phot.
P. Mahassen: 'Les Collages de Blumenfeld', *Tribune A.* (13 June 1981)

ERIKA BILLETER

Blumenthal, George (*b* Frankfurt am Main, 7 April 1858; *d* New York, 26 June 1941). American financier, collector, museum official and philanthropist of German birth. He entered banking in Germany and emigrated to New York as a young man, becoming a partner in 1893 in Lazard Frères. He retired in 1925 to devote his time to art collecting and philanthropy, favouring causes connected with the arts, medicine and Jewish social services. His wife Florence, née Meyer (1872–1930), whose family were noted philanthropists, was his partner in these activities. After World War I they formed a foundation for the support of French artists, a model for 20th-century arts funding. A longtime finance officer of the Metropolitan Museum in New York, Blumenthal became its seventh president in 1934, guiding it through the Depression. He and his wife maintained collections in their château near Grasse and in a sizeable home in Paris. Their showplace mansion at 50 E 70th Street (dem. 1943) housed their New York collections. Its central feature was a 16th-century Spanish castle courtyard (now New York, Met., Blumenthal Patio); particularly notable objects from the collection were Justus of Ghent's *Adoration of the Magi*, the Charlemagne tapestry (*c.* 1500) and a 10th-century Ottonian carved ivory altarpiece.

UNPUBLISHED SOURCES
Washington, DC, Smithsonian Inst., Archvs Amer. A. [Blumenthal's correspondence with Jacques Seligman, dealer]

BIBLIOGRAPHY
Catalog of the Collection. . .Blumenthal, New York (Paris, 1926)
'Blumenthal Collection', *Bull. Met.* (Oct. 1941), pp. 193–8 [house described]
Masterpieces from the Collection of George Blumenthal (exh. cat., New York, Met., 1943)
M. Gauthier: *La fondation americaine Blumenthal pour la pensée et l'art français* (Paris, 1974)

GRETCHEN G. FOX

Blumenthal, Hermann (*b* Essen, 31 Dec 1905; *d* Russia, 17 Aug 1942). German sculptor. He began an apprenticeship as a sculptor in stone in 1920 and attended evening classes at the Folkwang-Schule in Essen for five years. From 1925 to 1931 he continued his studies at the Kunsthochschule in Berlin. His earliest sculptures, mainly torsos, reveal the influence of his teacher Edwin Scharff, although even as a student he had developed a recognizable style, specializing in very slender youths in expressive rather angular poses, for example *Large Male Figure of a Thinker* (1929; Duisburg, Lehmbruck-Mus.) and *Large Kneeling Male Figure* (Berlin, Neue N.G.). These gentle human figures share the qualities of Wilhelm Lehmbruck's late male figures.

Blumenthal won early recognition as a sculptor, including prizes and a scholarship to study at the Villa Massimo, Rome (1931–2). On his return he worked in Essen and near Potsdam and from 1934 in the Klosterstrasse studio co-operative. Under the influence of Ludwig Kasper his figures became larger and more tectonic. A second period in Italy (1936–7) reinforced Blumenthal's orientation towards a classical repertory of form; this is evident in the large male figures created between 1935 and 1937, for example *Large Striding Male Figure* (Hamburg, Ksthalle) and *Standing Male Figure with Raised Arms—Roman Man* (Essen, Mus. Flkwang). In 1940 he was called up for military service and was shot by partisans. Despite his early death his works had a great influence on the younger generation of sculptors in the post-war period. A number of works from his estate are on loan to the Georg Kolbe Museum in Berlin.

BIBLIOGRAPHY
C.-A. Isermeyer: *Der Bildhauer Hermann Blumenthal* (Berlin, 1947)
H. Blumenthal, W. Gilles (exh. cat., foreword A. Hentzen; Hannover, Kestner-Ges., 1949)
Hermann Blumenthal (exh. cat., foreword G. Busch; Bremen, Marcks-Haus, 1981)
G. Schmidt: *Ateliergemeinschaft Klosterstrasse, 1933–1945* (Berlin, 1988)
C.-A. Isermeyer: *Hermann Blumenthal* (in preparation)

URSEL BERGER

Blundell, Henry (*b* Ince Blundell, Lancs, 1724; *d* Ince Blundell, 28 March 1810). English landowner, collector and patron. The Blundell family, of Ince Blundell Hall, near Liverpool, was Roman Catholic, and so Henry Blundell was educated in France, at St Omer, Douai and Paris. He continued to visit Paris periodically, buying pictures such as his important Sebastiano Ricci, the *Marriage of Bacchus and Ariadne*, but he did not make his first Italian tour until 1776–7, when he joined his Lancashire neighbour Charles Townley in Rome and through him was introduced to a broad circle of dealers and antiquarians. Thereafter he began to form a vast collection of sculptures and pictures; it was eclectic and of uneven quality. While in Italy, Blundell also patronized various contemporary painters, and he purchased sculptures from Carlo Albacini (*fl c.* 1780–1807), Giuseppe Angelini (1735–1811) and, later, Antonio d'Este (1754–1837). More importantly, he began to acquire substantial numbers of antique marble sculptures through dealers such as Thomas Jenkins, Bartolomeo Cavaceppi and Giovanni Battista Piranesi; subsequently, however, he used as his principal agent the former Jesuit John Thorpe (1726–92). At home in England Blundell bought pictures by, among others, Richard Wilson and George Stubbs. He revisited Italy in 1782–3, in 1786, when he acquired the Ince *Athena* from the Palazzo Lante, and in 1790. He was one of Antonio Canova's first English patrons and commissioned from him the important *Psyche* (1792). Having augmented his collection at the Cawdor sale (1800) and the Bessborough sale (1801), Blundell built in 1801–5 the circular Pantheon, adjoining Ince Blundell Hall, as a sculpture gallery. His son Charles Blundell continued to purchase paintings and drawings, particularly Flemish primitives. The Ince Blundell marbles were presented to the Liverpool Museum in 1959.

BIBLIOGRAPHY

DNB
An Account of the Statues, Busts, Bass-Relieves, Cinerary Urns, and other Ancient Marbles and Paintings at Ince, Collected by H.B. (Liverpool, 1803)
Engravings and Etchings of the Principal Statues, Busts, Bas-Reliefs, Sepulchral Monuments, Cinerary Urns etc. in the Collection of Henry Blundell, Esq. at Ince, Liverpool, 1809, 2 vols (Liverpool, 1810)
G. Waagen: *Treasures of Art in Great Britain*, iii (London, 1854), pp. 242–60
A. Michaelis: *Ancient Marbles in Great Britain* (Cambridge, 1882), pp. 333–414
B. Ashmole: *A Catalogue of the Ancient Marbles at Ince Blundell Hall* (Oxford, 1929)
G. Vaughan: 'Henry Blundell's Sculpture Collection at Ince Hall', *Patronage and Practice: Sculpture on Merseyside*, ed. P. Curtis (Liverpool, 1989), pp. 13–21
J. Fejfer and E. Southworth: *Ince Blundell Collection of Classical Sculpture*, i (Liverpool, 1991)

GERARD VAUGHAN

Blunt, Anthony (*b* Bournemouth, Hants, 26 Sept 1907; *d* 26 March 1983). English art historian. After graduating in 1930 from Trinity College, Cambridge, he became art critic for *The Spectator*. In 1939 he was appointed Reader in the History of Art at London University and Deputy Director of the Courtauld Institute. In 1945 he was made Surveyor of the King's Pictures and in 1947 Director of the Courtauld Institute, posts he held until 1972 and 1974 respectively. In 1939 Blunt published *The Drawings of Poussin*, the first of *c.* 25 books he wrote over the next 40 years. French art of the 17th century occupied much of his early career; his later studies of the Italian Baroque and Rococo reflected a turn from the principles of Cartesian classicism to more intuitive, and sometimes less rational, modes of expression. In 1956 he was knighted, but in 1964 he confessed that he had acted as a Soviet agent, and when this revelation was made public in 1979 his knighthood was annulled. The relationship between his interests in art and his political interests remains a matter of debate.

WRITINGS

The Drawings of Poussin (London, 1939)
Artistic Theory in Italy, 1450–1600 (Oxford, 1940, rev. 1994)
François Mansart and the Origins of French Classical Architecture (London, 1941)
Art and Architecture in France, 1500–1700, Pelican Hist. A. (Harmondsworth and Baltimore, 1953)
Philibert de L'Orme (London, 1958)
The Art of William Blake (New York, 1959)
The Paintings of Poussin, 2 vols (London, 1967–8, rev. 1995)
Sicilian Baroque (New York, 1968)
Neapolitan Baroque and Rococo Architecture and Decoration (London, 1975)
Baroque and Rococo: Architecture and Decoration (New York, 1978)
Borromini (Cambridge, 1979)
Guide to Baroque Rome (New York, 1982, rev. London, 1995)
with J. M. Merz: *The Architecture of Pietro da Cortona* (in preparation)

BIBLIOGRAPHY

G. Steiner: 'The Cleric of Treason', *New Yorker* (8 Dec 1980), pp. 158–95
D. S. Pepper: 'Is Academic Art History Controlled by the KGB?', *J.A.* [USA], i/5 (1989)

JOHN VARRIANO

Bluntschli, Alfred Friedrich (*b* Zurich, 29 Jan 1842; *d* Zurich, 27 July 1930). Swiss architect and writer. He attended the Zurich Polytechnikum (1860–63), studying under Gottfried Semper, and then studied (1864–6) under Charles-Auguste Questel at the Ecole des Beaux-Arts, Paris. Between 1870 and 1881 he was in partnership with Karl Jonas Mylius (1839–83) in Frankfurt am Main, before becoming a professor at the Zurich Polytechnikum. His intensive work on town halls gave rise to a number of prize-winning designs (for Munich, 1866; Vienna, 1872; Hamburg, Berne and Berlin), although none of them was executed, and to his *Compendium von Rathäusern* (1887), which became a popular reference work. His special interest was in internal planning and in matching the form of a building to its type, as in the chemistry building of the Zurich Polytechnikum (1886). He also produced prestigious houses, in the asymmetrical style of the Renaissance Revival, with picturesquely irregular silhouettes (e.g. Schloss Langenzell, 1880; and the Villa Bleuler, Zurich, 1885–8), as self-contained structures with domed vestibules (e.g. the Villa Wegmann, Zurich, 1886–90), or as symmetrical buildings in the Baroque Revival style (e.g. the Villa Stehli-Hirt, Zurich, 1895–6). One of his most influential works was the Renaissance Revival church (1892–4) at Enge, a cruciform centralized building faced in volcanic limestone, with a prominent dome over the crossing. His work also includes the Zentralfriedhof (1870–74), a cemetery in Vienna, and several tombs. Much influenced by Semper, Bluntschli designed imposing Renaissance Revival buildings, his particular hallmark being external decoration in disparate materials, for example at the Villa Rieter (1885–6), Zurich, where he juxtaposed yellow limestone and red brick, adding colourfully glazed tiles, wrought-iron gratings and painted wooden friezes.

WRITINGS

Compendium von Rathäusern (1887)

BIBLIOGRAPHY

SKL

CORNELIA BAUER

Blyenberch [Blijenberch], **Abraham van** (*fl* 1617–22). Flemish painter, active in England. He worked in London from *c.* 1617 and lived in the parish of St Martin-in-the-Fields. He worked on designs for tapestries woven at the royal tapestry factory at Mortlake and was one of the painters who provided the physician Sir THEODORE TURQUET DE MAYERNE with information on pigments and technique. He also painted a number of portraits of prominent figures at the Jacobean court: the *Prince of Wales*, later Charles I (*c.* 1617–20; London, N.P.G.), *Ben Jonson* (*c.* 1620; London, N.P.G.), *Count Gondomar*, the Spanish Ambassador (probably 1622; Brit. Royal Col.), and two of the most enlightened members of the court circle, *William Herbert, 3rd Earl of Pembroke* (1617; Powis Castle, Powys, NT) and *Robert Ker*, later 1st Earl of Ancram (1618; Newbattle Abbey Coll., Lothian). The portraits are in the Anglo-Netherlandish style, in which Daniel Mijtens (i) and Paul van Somer were working at the same time in London. However, the characterization in van Blyenberch's portraits is more lively, the settings sometimes more arresting and the handling more direct, perhaps more palpably Netherlandish, than in the work of these contemporaries. He was recorded in Antwerp in 1621–2, where he was the master of Theodoor van Thulden.

BIBLIOGRAPHY
O. Millar: *The Tudor, Stuart and Early Georgian Pictures in the Collection of H.M. the Queen* (London, 1963), p. 83
The Age of Charles I (exh. cat., ed. O. Millar; London, Tate, 1972), p. 20
M. K. Talley: *Portrait Painting in England: Studies in the Technical Literature before 1700* (London, 1981), pp. 84–6

OLIVER MILLAR

Blyth, Benjamin (*bapt* Salem, MA, 18 May 1746; *d* ?1787). American painter. He began his professional career in the 1760s and may have been encouraged by his older brother, Samuel, who was an heraldic and commercial painter. He worked primarily in pastels, or 'crayons', as he advertised in the *Salem Gazette* (May 1769), and he capitalized on their increasing popularity around Boston during this decade.

Approximately 30 pastels are now attributed to Blyth, and of those the best known is *John Adams*, the earliest portrait of the diplomat and second President of the United States, together with a pendant of his wife, *Abigail Smith Adams* (both 1766; Boston, MA, Hist. Soc.). The Adams pastels are typical of Blyth's works: smoothly drawn, restrained in colour and highly finished. They are slightly lighter than their counterparts by John Singleton Copley but possess neither the dramatic lighting nor the masterful foreshortening of that artist's work. Blyth's sitters are frequently stiff and have a fixed, impenetrable gaze.

The Salem diarist Rev. William Bentley dismissed Blyth as a 'wretched dauber' but noted he had 'much employment from the money of the privateer men'. Despite this criticism, Blyth was able to remain in Salem completing pastels and oil portraits until 1786, at which point he moved to Richmond, VA.

BIBLIOGRAPHY
R. Townsend Cole: 'Limned by Blyth', *Antiques*, lxix (1956), pp. 331–3
H. W. Foote: 'Benjamin Blyth, of Salem: Eighteenth-century Artist', *Proc. MA Hist. Soc.*, lxxi (1959), pp. 82–102

RICHARD H. SAUNDERS

Blythe, David Gilmour (*b* Wellsville, nr East Liverpool, OH, 9 May 1815; *d* Pittsburgh, PA, 15 May 1865). American painter and sculptor. He began his career as an itinerant portrait painter in the early 1840s and became one of the leading satirical artists in America by the beginning of the Civil War. Self-taught, from 1840 to 1850 he worked in East Liverpool, OH, and Uniontown, PA, and nearby towns and villages, painting rather stiff likenesses of the local gentry. He also carved a monumental polychrome wooden statue of *Marie-Joseph, Marquis de Lafayette* (*in situ*) for the Uniontown courthouse and painted a landscape panorama (destr.) of the Allegheny mountains, which he took on tour through Maryland, Pennsylvania and Ohio. The death of his wife in 1850 and the commercial failure of his panorama in 1852 led to a period of wandering; the bitterness he felt at his misfortune came to be reflected in his poetry and in his growing involvement with social and political issues.

Following his move to Pittsburgh, PA, in 1856, Blythe began to specialize in humorous genre scenes, attacking a broad range of human follies in paintings whose treacly palette, wealth of narrative detail and grotesque distortions

of anatomy and facial expression form a distinctive contrast to the sentimental realism of most American genre painting of the period. Blythe drew from a variety of sources: the paintings of Adriaen Brouwer, David Teniers (ii) and Bartolomé Esteban Murillo, the caricatures of William Hogarth, Thomas Rowlandson and George Cruikshank, the lithographs of Honoré Daumier and contemporary periodical illustration. *Trial Scene* (1860–63; U. Rochester, NY, Mem. A.G.) is typical of Blythe's mature genre painting in both choice of subject and style. It depicts a kangaroo court being held inside a tavern by the 'Molly Maguires', a secret society of Irish-American miners known for their violence. The dramatic lighting and lurid colour of the scene, the exaggerated gestures of the figures and the surfeit of weapons scattered about the room graphically convey the participants' travesty of justice. During the Civil War the content of Blythe's paintings became even more topical. In political cartoons and allegories, often large-scale, he advanced Abraham Lincoln's efforts to preserve the Union while attacking obstructionists and extremists on both sides of the conflict. *Lincoln Crushing the Dragon of Rebellion* (1863; Boston, MA, Mus. F.A.) shows the President raising his log-splitting maul to crush a cloven-hoofed dragon, the artist's symbol for the evils of secession. Lincoln, however, is impeded in his assault by the gnarled figure of Tammany, the Democratic Party organization of New York, which had fought Union efforts to raise an army.

Unlike his contemporaries Thomas Nast, David Claypoole Johnston and Adalbert J. Volck (1828–1912) of Baltimore, whose primary medium was the print, Blythe worked almost exclusively in oil; only one of his paintings was reproduced for general circulation. Instead, he chose to display his barbs in the window of his Pittsburgh dealer, J. J. Gillespie. His audience was therefore entirely local, while his patrons were drawn from the city's new industrial class, which was predominantly Scots-Presbyterian, Republican and reformist. Blythe also painted some memorable images of the Civil War, including *Libby Prison* (1863) and the *Battle of Gettysburg* (both Boston, MA, Mus. F.A.), as well as a few landscapes and still-lifes. He died of 'delirium from drink', apparently the result of a depressive binge caused by the assassination of Lincoln a month earlier.

BIBLIOGRAPHY
D. Miller: *The Life and Work of David G. Blythe* (Pittsburgh, 1950)
Works by David Blythe, 1815–1865 (exh. cat., Columbus, OH, Mus. A., 1968)
B. W. Chambers: *The World of David Gilmour Blythe* (Washington, DC, 1980)

BRUCE W. CHAMBERS

Bo, Lina Bardi. *See* BARDI, LINA.

Bo & Wohlert. Danish architectural partnership formed in 1957 by Jørgen Bo (*b* Copenhagen, 8 April 1919) and Vilhelm Wohlert (*b* Copenhagen, 27 May 1920). Both studied at the school of architecture of the Kongelige Danske Kunstakademi in Copenhagen, Bo from 1936 to 1941 and Wohlert until 1944. Wohlert was a pupil of the architect and furniture designer Kaare Klint, with whom he designed the F. A. Thiele shop (completed 1957), Copenhagen. Bo & Wohlert's first and best-known work is the Louisiana Museum (1958), Humlebæk, near Elsinore, a gallery for modern art incorporated into the park of a former country house (*see* MUSEUM, fig. 8). It consists of low wings planned in a varied sequence that exploits the contrasts between the buildings and the rural setting. The buildings themselves are composed of a few simple but carefully designed elements: white-painted brick, glass façades, wooden beams and flat roofs. The partnership enlarged the museum in the 1960s and 1980s, mainly adding closed brick cubes lit from above. The austere yet informal and intimate architecture of the Louisiana Museum is reflected in numerous housing projects by Bo & Wohlert, such as the terraced housing at Piniehøj (1962), Rungsted, and Kirstineparken (1964), Hørsholm. The partnership's later work includes the cabinetmakers' training centre (1967), Monastir, Tunisia, the Danish Embassy (1973), Brasília, and, after a competition, the Museum Bochum (1977–83) in Germany.

Jørgen Bo, in his various partnerships and independently, created buildings that are characteristic of post-war Danish architecture with their qualities of clarity, simplicity and meticulous execution. A notable example is the IBM Training Centre (1969–75), Brussels, with Anders Hegelund (*b* 1938). Other architects with whom he collaborated include Karen Clemmensen (*b* 1917) and Ebbe Clemmensen (*b* 1917). He also worked on the restoration of several historic Danish buildings, including, from 1966, the Thorvaldsens Museum (1839–47; by Gottlieb Bindesbøll), Copenhagen. From 1960 he was a professor at the Kongelige Danske Kunstakademi, Copenhagen. Vilhelm Wohlert, outside the partnership with Bo, was responsible for a number of churches, the Institute of Technology (1973), Tåstrup, near Copenhagen, and the training centre (1978–82) in Ksar El Boukhari, Algeria, with Hans Munk Hansen (*b* 1929). He specialized in restoration, in which he had an international reputation; an example of such work is the cathedral of Our Lady, Copenhagen (1979), rebuilt by C. F. Hansen in 1829. A professor in the school of architecture at the Kongelige Danske Kunstakademi from 1968 to 1986, he was also a consultant with UNESCO.

WRITINGS
Jørgen Bo: 'Danmarks ambassade i Brasilien', *Arkitektur DK*, xx/3 (1976), pp. 81–8

BIBLIOGRAPHY
K. Fisker: 'Louisiana: Museum for moderne Kunst', *Arkitektur*, ii/5 (1958), pp. 145–65
K. Dirckink-Holmfeld: 'Museum Bochum Tyskland', *Arkitektur DK*, xxviii/3 (1984), pp. 88–103

JØRGEN SESTOFT

Boada, Francisco Javier Parcerisa y. *See* PARCERISA I BOADA, FRANCESCO XAVIER.

Board. Flat panel on which paper may be rested during drawing or painting, on which a painting or drawing may actually be executed (*see also* PANEL PAINTING), or on or with which a completed artwork is mounted. In these uses the board is of thin, rigid material such as natural wood or, more probably, processed and reconstituted wood or of a substance similar to or evolved from paper. Before *c.* 1700 artists were often depicted resting their work on a stout folder, but drawing boards are shown in use in the *Drawing Academy* (Segovia, Pal. Granja de San Ildefonso)

by Michel-Ange Houasse, and a variant form with legs appears in *Time and Death* (1814; San Marino, CA, Huntington Lib. & A.G.) by Thomas Rowlandson. Since the 19th century, the commercial production of various types of boards has increased the range of potential supports. Millboard, a stiff card of pulp or paper sheets pasted together, frequently used in book covers and sometimes heavily impregnated with size, was used for oil sketching by J. M. W. Turner and for several nude studies by William Etty. Cardboard, a packaging material related to millboard, was used extensively by Henri de Toulouse-Lautrec and features in the work of several artists active *c.* 1900, notably Pierre Bonnard and Edouard Vuillard. By 1900 Academy Board (pasteboard or millboard primed with a white ground) had become popular as an inexpensive support, and it has evolved during the 20th century into a range of commercial painting boards that are either embossed in imitation of canvas or covered with a thin layer of primed cloth or primed and embossed paper; these are known as canvas boards or panels. Various artists' papers are also mounted on boards to give them increased stability or to permit a specialized application (e.g. strippable airbrush board). More robust types of board, including hardboard (Masonite), chipboard (particle board), blockboard (lumber-core plywood), plywood and fibreboard, are made from wood or wood pulp. These sheet materials have significant practical advantages over natural wood, but none is specifically intended for artistic use. As their suitability is dependent upon the exact specification and mode of employment, they have been exploited with various degrees of wisdom by painters at both amateur and professional level. Potential problems are well illustrated by the case of mount board (matt board), used to mount and display works on paper within their frames. Made from wood pulp, with various chemicals involved in its manufacture, it has proved to be self-destructive and to harm the artwork it houses; in consequence, the specification of such boards has been altered to take account of their art-related use. Museum board, conservation board and acid-free board are products now supplied as mount board with the necessary archival qualities.

See also PAPER, §VI and SUPPORT, §§1 and 2.

BIBLIOGRAPHY
J. Stephenson: *Graphic Design: Materials and Equipment* (London, 1987)
——: *The Materials and Techniques of Painting* (London, 1989)
S. Fairbrass: *Learn to Frame* (London, 1990)

JONATHAN STEPHENSON

Boari (Dandini), Adamo (*b* Ferrara, 1863; *d* Rome, 1928). Italian architect and engineer, active in Mexico. He graduated as an engineer at the Università di Bologna in 1886 and completed his architectural training in the USA in 1899. He was then appointed to design and oversee the building of the Teatro Nacional (now Palacio de Bellas Artes; *see* MEXICO, fig. 5) in Mexico City. During the preparatory stages he travelled widely to study current ideas of theatre architecture and he also made an urban study of the streets and open spaces around the site. His original plans show the influence of Art Nouveau derived from the Exposition Universelle of 1900 in Paris and incorporate Mexican national features, such as mascarons of coyotes, monkeys and eagles. The design included a glass-enclosed garden instead of a foyer, a dome over the garden rather than the auditorium and a safety curtain of opalescent glass. The structure was of iron. Construction began in 1904 and lasted several years. Meanwhile Boari also undertook the construction of the Edificio Central de Correos (1902–7), Mexico City, the first building in Mexico to use reinforced concrete. The exterior was faced in white stone, and the decorative details show a hybrid revival of Italian Renaissance and Hispano-Flemish style. It is an early example in Mexico of a large project given a specific functional role. Work on the Teatro Nacional was eventually halted by financial problems, and in 1916 Boari returned to Italy. The building was completed in 1934 under other architects, including Géza Maróti, who modified the original plan.

BIBLIOGRAPHY
El Palacio de Bellas Artes: Album histórico (Mexico City, 1934)
J. Urquiaga and V. Jiménez: *La construcción del Palacio de Bellas Artes* (Mexico City, 1984)

MÓNICA MARTÍ COTARELO

Boas, Franz (*b* Minden, Westphalia, July 1858; *d* New York, 21 Dec 1942). American anthropologist and art historian of German birth. Trained as a physical scientist at the University of Kiel, he became interested in anthropology soon after receiving his doctorate in 1881. He emigrated to the USA in 1888 and became curator of ethnology at the American Museum of Natural History in New York in 1895. The following year he also began to teach at Columbia University, where he worked full-time from 1905 until his retirement in 1936.

Boas's first publications on art consisted largely of descriptions of artefacts made by the native population of the north-west coast of North America (*see* NATIVE NORTH AMERICAN ART, §XVII), but by 1888 he had begun to reconstruct the history of this art. Between 1896 and 1900 he demonstrated the inadequacy of the then-prevalent evolutionistic theory that art degenerated from realism to abstraction and proposed that conventionalization in the art of the north-west coast resulted from attempts to represent as many characteristics of an animal as possible even if this resulted in a distortion of the image, as, for example, when an animal was split down the middle and flattened out so that both sides could be depicted in a two-dimensional medium. After 1900 he began to use examples from other regions in his attempt to substitute history for evolutionism and to show that the psychology of the individual artist was as important in primitive art as it was in Western art: whatever differences there were between the two were not due to the inferiority of the primitive artist but to the constraints imposed on him by his culture. Boas's research culminated in his book *Primitive Art*, in which he dealt with African and Asian as well as Native American art.

WRITINGS
'The Development of Culture of Northwest America', *Science*, xii (1888), pp. 194–6
'The Decorative Art of the Indians of the North Pacific Coast', *Bull. Amer. Mus. Nat. Hist.*, ix (1897), pp. 123–76
'Facial Paintings of the Indians of Northern British Columbia', *Pubns Jesup N. Pacific Expedition*, i (1898), pp. 13–24
'The Decorative Art of the North American Indians', *Pop. Sci. Mthly*, lxiii (1903), pp. 481–98
'Decorative Designs of Alaskan Needlecases: A Study in the History of Conventional Designs, Based on Materials in the U.S. National Museum', *Proc. US N. Mus.*, xxxiv (1908), pp. 321–44
'Representative Art of Primitive Peoples', *Holmes Anniversary Volume* (Washington, DC, 1916), pp. 18–23
Primitive Art (Oslo, 1927)

BIBLIOGRAPHY
A. Jonaitis: *A Wealth of Thought: Franz Boas on Native American Art* (Seattle, 1995)

ALDONA JONAITIS

Boas, Manuel Cenaculo Vilas. *See* VILAS BOAS, MANUEL CENÁCULO.

Bobadilla, Jerónimo de (*b* Seville, *c.* 1620; *d* Seville, 1709). Spanish painter. He probably learnt to paint in Seville *c.* 1640 and was influenced by Zurbarán. He married in 1654 in Antequera but continued to paint in Seville, where from 1660 he was included in the roll of members of the Academia de Pintores. He was one of the most respected artists in that city during the second half of the 17th century.

Only four paintings by him are known (all Málaga, priv. col., see Clavijo, pp. 72–80): two versions of the *Adoration of the Magi*, a *Circumcision* and a *Flight into Egypt*. From these paintings, datable to *c.* 1650, his style can be characterized as undemanding and sentimental, remote from the austere forcefulness of Zurbarán yet undeniably influenced by him. Although no late paintings survive, it would seem from the evidence of his drawings (e.g. *St Luke*, London, priv. col., see Clavijo, p. 81, and *St Joseph and the Christ Child*, Hamburg, Ksthalle) that stylistically he moved towards Murillo at the end of his career.

BIBLIOGRAPHY
A. Clavijo: 'Un zurbaranesco olvidado: Jerónimo de Bobadilla', *Bética*, 6 (1983), pp. 49–82

ENRIQUE VALDIVIESO

Boberg, (Gustaf) Ferdinand (*b* Falun, 11 April 1860; *d* Stockholm, 7 May 1946). Swedish architect, draughtsman and painter. After studying at the Kungliga Tekniska Högskolan and the Kungliga Akademien för de fria Konsterna (1878–84), with his artist-wife Anna Boberg (*b* 1864) he made extensive journeys in Italy, France, Spain and the rest of the Mediterranean region, also visiting Britain. Early on he was impressed by the work of H. H. Richardson, and this was reinforced by his visit to the World's Columbian Exposition in Chicago (1893) and to the studio of Louis Sullivan. Boberg's highly personal style amalgamated these American influences with impressions from Italy, Spain and North Africa, and his ornamentation in particular is connected both to Sullivan and to the Moorish and Byzantine. Gävle Fire Station (1890) shows clearly the Richardsonian use of the Romanesque with round-arched doorways in heavy granite, picturesque asymmetry and colonette motifs. Industrial buildings for the Stockholm Gas and Electricity Works in the 1890s demonstrate Boberg's effective use of colourful brick and stone. The surviving portal of an electricity station (destr.) in central Stockholm is decorated by ornamentation of electric light-bulbs with a Sullivanesque sharpness, and postal motifs of a similar nature adorn the Central Post Office (1898–1905), Stockholm. Boberg designed the architecture for several large exhibitions (e.g. the Stockholm Exhibitions of 1897 and 1909, and the Baltic Exhibition in Malmö in 1914). The pavilions were always rich in surface decoration, like many of his buildings, for example the Rosenbad office, bank and restaurant complex (1900; now Government headquarters), a series of princely villas on Djurgården, all in Stockholm, and the unexecuted project for a Nobel Festivity Hall (1912). Plain, white plaster surfaces inlaid in parts with colourful tiles dominate the symmetrical front of the Thielska Galleriet (1904) in Djurgården, a combined residence and picture gallery with toplighting. Boberg's later production has a more heavy massing, usually in dark brick and granite (e.g. Malmö Post Office, 1905, and Saltsjöbaden Church, 1913). Also in granite are the façades of the Nordiska Kompaniet department store (1912) in Stockholm, which otherwise is a steel structure with a grand toplit hall. Boberg was a skilful draughtsman, watercolourist and etcher, and from 1914 on he devoted his efforts to the documentation of the Swedish architectural and industrial heritage in sketches, often in charcoal or crayon. In this capacity he was a representative of National Romanticism and its striving to capture the atmosphere of past centuries. His designs for furniture and other items demonstrate his preference for graphic effects and quasi-filigree patterning in a style similar to Art Nouveau.

BIBLIOGRAPHY

J. Nihlén, ed.: *Bobergiana* (Stockholm, 1958)

E. Stavenow-Hidemark: *Svensk Jugend* (Stockholm, 1964)

L. K. Eaton: *American Architecture Comes of Age: European Reaction to H. H. Richardson and Louis Sullivan* (Cambridge, MA, and London, 1972)

H. O. Andersson and F. Bedoire: *Swedish Architecture Drawings, 1640–1970/Svensk arkitektur ritningar* (Stockholm, 1986) [bilingual text]

Bobić [Bubich; Budich], **Bernardo** (*fl* 1680; *d* Zagreb, 1694/5). Croatian painter. Between 1680 and 1692 he was painting in Zagreb, and he executed several altarpieces for churches in Zagreb and the surrounding area. He painted and gilded the altarpiece of *St Dionysius* for the church of St Catherine, Zagreb, in 1680, and for the altar of the Apostles he painted his only known oil paintings on canvas, the *Ascension of the Holy Ghost* and *Judith and Holofernes*. His other identified paintings are oil on wooden panels. Three other paintings have been attributed to him; they were executed for the altarpiece of *St Mary* in Zagreb Cathedral and depict scenes from her life. It has been assumed that Bobić was directly influenced in Venice by the work of Titian, Tintoretto and Palma Giovane, but it is fairly certain that he assimilated the influence of Venetian 16th-century painting indirectly through Austria and Slovenia. His most important work is the cycle of 12 paintings for the altarpiece of *St Ladislas* in Zagreb Cathedral (now Zagreb, City Mus.); they represent scenes in the life of King Ladislas, founder of the diocese of Zagreb. Despite some notable imperfections, Bobić's work displays undeniable talent, with a tendency towards free expression within mainstream Baroque mannerism.

BIBLIOGRAPHY

I. Kukuljević-Sakcinski: *Prvostolna crkva zagrebačka* [Zagreb Cathedral] (Zagreb, 1857)

I. Kugli: 'Bernardo Bobić', *Bull. Inst. Likovne Umjetnosti JAZU* (1957)

M. Veža: 'Bobić Bernardo', *Enciklopedija likovnih umjetnosti* [Encyclopedia of arts], i (Zagreb, 1959), pp. 409–10

BORIS VIŽINTIN

Böblinger. German family of architects. They exerted a decisive influence on building activities and architectural decoration in south-west Germany for at least three generations. The family emerged as architects and masons from the second quarter of the 15th century, holding leading positions on such important building projects as Konstanz Cathedral and Ulm Minster. At times, notably in Esslingen (Frauenkirche, Spitalkirche St Katharina), several members of the family worked together for several decades. (1) Hans von Böblingen I had at least five sons—(2) Hans Böblinger II, (3) Matthäus Böblinger, (4) Marx Böblinger, (5) Lux Böblinger and (6) Dionysius Böblinger—and a daughter, Ursula Böblinger; her husband Stefan Waid (*fl* 1487–1504) was included in the close professional relationships between members of the family, working with his brothers-in-law in Esslingen and employed in Konstanz as successor to Lux Böblinger. The buildings to which the Böblingers substantially contributed survive only in part, but the sketches and diagrams left by Hans I, Matthäus and his son (7) Hans Böblinger III are notable examples of Late Gothic architectural drawing. The scope and content of their accompanying notes make them exceptionally important sources for the study of building practices.

BIBLIOGRAPHY

Macmillan Enc. Architects; Thieme–Becker

K. Pfaff: *Die Künstler-Familie Böblinger: Ein Beitrag zur deutschen Kunstgeschichte* (Esslingen, 1862)

K. D. Hassler: 'Urkunden zur Baugeschichte des Mittelalters', *Jb. Kstwiss.*, ii (1869), pp. 114–25

A. Klemm: 'Württembergische Baumeister und Bildhauer bis zum Jahr 1750', *Württemberg. Vjhft. Landesgesch.*, v (1882), pp. 87–90

H. Klaiber: 'Der Ulmer Münsterbaumeister Matthäus Böblinger', *Z. Gesch. Archit.*, suppl. 4 (Heidelberg, 1911/*R* Nendeln, 1978), pp. 7–10

A. Seeliger-Zeiss: *Lorenz Lechler von Heidelberg und sein Kreis*, Heidelberger Kunstgeschichtliche Abhandlungen, n. s., x (Heidelberg, 1967)

F. Bucher: *Architektor: The Lodge Books and Sketchbooks of Medieval Architects*, i (New York, 1979), pp. 375–411

W. Bernhardt: 'Die Quellen zur Geschichte der Esslinger Frauenkirche', *Essling. Stud.*, xix (1980), pp. 47–71

H. Koepf: 'Die Esslinger Frauenkirche und ihre Meister', *Essling. Stud.*, xix (1980), pp. 2–46

V. Segers: *Studien zur Geschichte der deutschen Steinmetzbruderschaft* (diss. U. Berlin, 1980), pp. 175, 195, 198

H. Koepf: 'Die Bauten des Esslinger St. Katharinenhospitals', *Essling. Stud.*, xx (1981), pp. 41–58

——: 'Die Böblinger-Planrisse', *Essling. Stud.*, xxi (1982), pp. 7–18

N. Nussbaum: *Deutsche Kirchenbaukunst der Gotik: Entwicklung und Bauformen* (Cologne, 1985), p. 200

(1) Hans [Hanns] **von Böblingen I** [Hans von Boeblingen; Hans von Ess(e)lingen] (*b* ?Böblingen; *fl* 1435; *d* Esslingen, 4 Jan 1482).

1. Life and works. 2. Working drawings in the Leaf-pattern Book.

1. LIFE AND WORKS. The first reference to him appears on a collection of drawings of foliage patterns, the so-called Leaf-pattern Book (1435; Munich, Bayer. Nmus., 3604; *see* §2 below), which is inscribed, under his mason's mark, 'I, Hans of Böblingen, a stonemason'. A study on parchment (Ulm, Stadtarchv, 11), dating from the same year and inscribed 'sketched in Konstanz', is also signed with the mason's mark and names Konstanz as his place

of domicile at the time. From the detailed tituli and the drawings, which resemble specimen pages and designs, Hans seems to have been still relatively young, and although he does not characterize himself as 'master', he was perhaps already at the end of his training as a master mason. Assuming the usual period of apprenticeship to be approximately five years, Hans must have been born at the beginning of the second decade of the 15th century. The frequent presumption that the young mason had occasionally worked in Esslingen during his apprenticeship or as a journeyman cannot be verified. He may have been employed within Württemberg by Count Ludwig I (*reg* 1419–50) and Count Ulrich V (*reg* 1441–80). A letter of 6 April 1439 from the Council of Esslingen to Matthäus Ensinger, master mason of the Frauenkirche there, proposes Hans for the post of warden (or undermaster) of the building. The Council wrote to Hans on 1 June informing him of the negotiations, and he was eventually appointed on 22 April 1440, on the recommendation of Matthäus Ensinger. On 21 April 1456 he received a permanent contract together with many other privileges. Hans had already taken over supervision of the Frauenkirche project in 1440, although it passed to him officially only on the death of Matthäus Ensinger in 1463. He remained master mason of the Frauenkirche until his death, and his gravestone, bearing a detailed inscription and his master's mark, is preserved in the church.

In 1440 Hans married Ursula Koch, the daughter of an Esslingen citizen, and seems to have become wealthy, as in 1448 the family sued a fellow citizen, Oswald Schultheiss, for the considerable sum of 600 pound hellers. Under the name of 'Master Hans of Esslingen' he was one of the most important signatories of the Regensburg Ordinance (*see* MASON (i), §III, 1) of 1459 and its revision at Speyer in 1464. As a leading member of his profession, he acted with other masters as mediator in a dispute involving Hans von Mingoldsheim (*d* 1473), a mason from Heilbronn.

The planning and completion of the spire of the Frauenkirche at Esslingen is Hans von Böblingen I's most important work. From the mid-14th century this building, a chapel of ease belonging to the city, had been converted at considerable cost to the existing fabric, particularly the tower, begun by Ulrich von Ensingen in 1395, to compete with the original parish church, St Dionys, which belonged to the chapter of Speyer. The start and progress of building work at the Frauenkirche under Hans I are marked by a chiselled master's emblem with his mason's mark of 1440 on the interior of the spiral staircase at the third stage of the tower, together with a further series of marks and details of dates on the tower itself. The comparison of a sketch of a tower (Munich, Bayer. Nmus., 1023) with a plan that Hans may have produced early in his career at Esslingen shows most clearly his own contribution to the design of the octagon and the openwork tracery spire, which remained uncompleted at his death. The motifs of the asymmetrical structure, following the architectural and decorative forms of the 15th century, probably reflect earlier designs in the style of Ulrich von Ensingen and the precedent of the spire of Freiburg im Breisgau Cathedral.

Reliable evidence of Hans's activities outside Esslingen exists only for 1460, when he took over the construction of a spire of the Martinskirche, Möhringen. The suggestion of his involvement from 1456 in the former Benedictine abbey of St Walburgis, near Haguenau, in Alsace, is based on the occurrence of his mason's mark on a keystone. Dated 1479 and confirmed as the work of Hans von Böblingen by his symbol is a stone ciborium now in the south aisle of the Frauenkirche at Esslingen, but probably originally intended as an altar canopy. This example of decorative architecture shows his exceptional skills, particularly in the elaborately double-layered net vault and the outstanding detail in the foliage on the capitals.

2. WORKING DRAWINGS. Hans von Böblingen's working drawings are of particular significance. In two instances his work can clearly be identified on the grounds of his autograph inscriptions, the immense detail of which is highly unusual for the time. Apart from the sketch of the Esslingen spire in Munich and that in Ulm of 1435, which is possibly the design for a spire at Konstanz Cathedral (Hecht) or a design for a micro-architecture (Koepf, 1990), the so-called Leaf-pattern Book, dated 1435, gives the best insight, as a unique testimony of his drawing ability, into the training of the late medieval master mason. The ten-page booklet consists of 31 drawings of fruit and foliage motifs (see fig.), which were to serve as models for capitals and decorative elements of Late Gothic architectural ornament. The leaf designs, some of great virtuosity, must have served as models for such later engravings as those produced above all in the

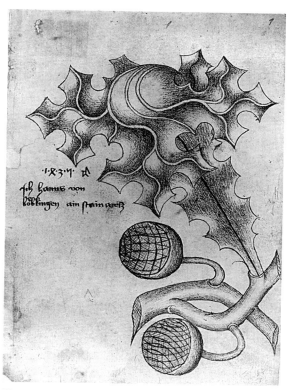

Hans von Böblingen I: foliage motif, drawing on paper, 216×154 mm; opening page from the Leaf-pattern Book [Laubhauerbüchlein], 1435 (Munich, Bayerisches Nationalmuseum, 3604)

Upper Rhine by the Master E. S. and Martin Schongauer. Hans von Böblingen I's foliage designs show his close affiliation to the regions of the Upper Rhine and Lake Constance, where he had spent his apprentice and journeyman years. The extent to which he was influenced by the work of the leading master Hänslin Jörg (*c.* 1380–*c.* 1450) while working near Stuttgart is still not sufficiently elucidated.

BIBLIOGRAPHY

Beschreibung des Oberamts Stuttgart, Königliches topographisches Bureau (Stuttgart, 1851/*R* Neudruck Magstadt, 1966)

L. Schneegans: 'Der Werkmeister Peter von Algesheim und dessen Siegel', *Anz. Knd. Dt. Vorzt*, n. s., iv (1857), pp. 105–10

H. Klaiber: 'Hans Böblingers Entwurf zum Turm der Esslinger Frauenkirche im Bayer. Nationalmuseum', *Münchn. Jb. Bild. Kst*, v (1910), pp. 163–8

H. Rott: 'Oberrheinische Meister des 15./16. Jahrhunderts: Namen und Werke', *Oberrhein. Kst*, ii (1928), p. 59

M. Barth: *Handbuch der elsässischen Kirchen im Mittelalter* (Strasbourg, 1960–63/*R* Brussels, 1980), col. 1209

P. Pause: *Gotische Architekturzeichnungen in Deutschland* (diss., Bonn, Rhein. Friedrich-Wilhelms-U., 1973), pp. 193–8, 301–2

H. Koepf: *Die gotischen Planrisse der Ulmer Sammlungen*, Forsch. Gesch. Stadt Ulm, xviii (Ulm, 1977), p. 105

W. Supper: 'Der Baldachin in der Esslinger Frauenkirche', *Essling. Stud.*, xx (1981), pp. 37–9

F. Bucher: 'Hans Böblingers Laubhauerbüchlein und seine Bedeutung für die Graphik', *Essling. Stud.*, xxi (1982), pp. 19–24

K. Hecht: 'Hans Böblingers Konstanzer Pergamentriss', *Ulm & Oberschwaben*, xliv (1982), pp. 253–66

H. Koepf: 'Die Stellung des Esslinger Böblingerbaldachins im Rahmen der gotischen Altarbaldachine', *Essling. Stud.*, xxi (1982), pp. 25–30

Glanz der Kathedrale: 900 Jahre Konstanzer Münster (exh. cat., Konstanz, Rosgtnmus., 1989), pp. 101–3, 106–7

H. Koepf: 'Hans Böblingers Konstanzer Pergamentriss', *Ulm & Oberschwaben* (1990), pp. 227–37

(2) Hans Böblinger II [Hannss von Esslingenn; Hans von Esslingen] (*b* Esslingen; *fl* 1459; *d* ?1532). Son of (1) Hans von Böblingen I. He is first mentioned in 1459 as 'Hannss von Esslingenn' in the list of apprentices employed in the masons' brotherhood of Regensburg. There is only one more dated reference to him, on 22 November 1475, when he requested a certificate of his legitimate birth, which he needed in order to set up business 'abroad'. The document describes Hans as a master craftsman who had learnt his trade in Esslingen and elsewhere. It is still uncertain whether Hans had undergone part of his training in Regensburg and can be identified as the wood-carver referred to as 'Hans ernst von Beblingen' in an inscription on the choir-stalls of the Hospitalkirche in Stuttgart, as has been suggested (Bucher). The latter is described as a carpenter until 1506, and in 1509 as a *Baumeister*. Promoted in 1510 to be Master of the Works to the court at Stuttgart, this master died in 1532.

BIBLIOGRAPHY

F. Bucher: 'Hans Böblingers Laubhauerbüchlein und seine Bedeutung für die Graphik', *Essling. Stud.*, xxi (1982), p. 22

(3) Matthäus Böblinger [Matheus Beblinger; Matthäus von Esslingen; Mattheus von Esselingen] (*b* Esslingen, *c.* 1450; *d* Esslingen, 1505). Son of (1) Hans von Böblingen I. He was the most important of Hans I's sons and probably the second eldest. He is first mentioned between 1459 and 1472 in a list of members of the masons' brotherhood in Strasbourg, where he is reported in ?1468 to be an apprentice to his father. A sketch (Ulm, Ulm. Mus.), signed with his mason's mark, for the stone Mount

of Olives (destr. 1807; fragments in Ulm, Ulm. Mus.) that was to be built in front of the west façade of Ulm Minster, contains a detailed accompanying text, which states that Matthäus produced the design for the Mount of Olives in 1474 in Esslingen, where he was living at the time.

In 1477 Matthäus was appointed Master of the Works of Ulm Minster. In 1480 he obtained a permanent contract, which obliged him to settle in Ulm. He had earlier, perhaps in 1477, taken over a building project in 'Zell' (perhaps the church of the Assumption at Radolfzell am Bodensee), which he was able to supervise with the approval of the trustees during his period of office in Ulm. Despite his exclusive contract with the authorities of Ulm Minster, which lasted until 1493 or 1494, Matthäus undertook other non-local commissions during the same period. In 1483 he was paid the considerable sum of 20 florins for a project (perhaps providing expert evidence for the completion of the spire) in connection with the collegiate church (now cathedral) of St Bartholomäus in Frankfurt am Main. On 2 May 1482 the City Council of Esslingen had requested his services for building a hospital chapel, but although Matthäus had issued preliminary building instructions in June 1483, he was formally contracted for the work only in May 1485, with the permission of Ulm Council. In May 1494, following the appearance of a structural fault in the spire of Ulm Minster (for which Matthäus can hardly be blamed), he mysteriously disappeared from Ulm, to be replaced as Master by Burkhard Engelberg. Matthäus returned to Esslingen, and by 1495 or 1496 he is thought to have become Master of the Works at the Frauenkirche in succession to his brother-in-law, Stefan Waid. It was in this capacity that he was summoned as an expert to Schwäbisch Gmünd. According to a letter of the Council of Memmingen of 6 May 1496, Matthäus was also appointed to supervise the building of a parish church there. His master's mark, the date and the monogram MB, appears on the south-west choir buttress of the Martinskirche. The authorities in Memmingen had already asked for him in 1489, while he was still active in Ulm.

Despite the incidents connected with the building of Ulm Minster, Matthäus went on to become much sought after in his profession. In 1501 he was consulted as an expert witness of Duke Ulrich VI of Württemberg (*reg* 1504–19, 1534–50) in a dispute with master mason Peter von Koblenz (*fl* 1481–1501) over the building of St Amandus, Urach. In a letter to the Council of Esslingen of 4 August 1503, there is a fleeting reference to projects planned for Margrave Christopher I of Baden (*reg* 1475–1527), although no further details are known.

Matthäus was probably trained primarily by his father at the Frauenkirche of Esslingen. Alleged visits to Cologne and Milan, mainly suggested in early studies, are unsubstantiated. The scarce evidence of his financial situation indicates that he was exceptionally business-minded and may have acquired a great fortune, not only through his work as a mason. On several occasions, for example in 1486 and 1494, he was in touch with property and financial businesses. In 1487 he sought an advance of 400 florins with 5% interest from the Council of Esslingen. In 1495 he lent 1000 gold florins to the brothers Hans and Jacob von Wernau against a security from the town and castle of Wernau. His gravestone in the Frauenkirche of Esslingen bears his master's mark and the date of his death.

The Mount of Olives sketch of 1474 in Ulm is thought to be Matthäus Böblinger's earliest surviving work. The perspective drawing of a hexagonal structure with openwork tracery represents one of the most original creations of late Gothic micro-architecture. Particularly noteworthy are the pinnacled buttresses marking the hexagon and the nodding ogee arches between the buttresses and halfway up the spire. A font in the parish church of Langenau, which must date from after 1474 and bears Matthäus's mason's mark, also demonstrates his highly developed artistry. The elegance of the design is seen particularly in the strongly indented, star-shaped shaft and the branch and foliage decoration of the octagonal bowl. Similar decorative elements are adopted in the architectural frame of a figural relief (destr.) in the Besserer Chapel of Ulm Minster, which Matthäus marked and dated 1485.

The beginning of Matthäus's building activities at Ulm Minster is marked by the so-called Böblinger Pillar at the south-west end of the nave; originally embellished with elaborate pinnaclework, it bears his emblem and the date 1478. For the completion of the spire he produced c. 1480 a sketch on parchment ('Drawing C'; Ulm, Ulm. Mus.; see fig.). He modified the finished parts to the level of the bell stage. Compared to earlier designs, 'Drawing C' in particular harmonizes the transition both from rectangular to octagonal plan and to the octagonal tracery spire. The main decorative motif used to enrich the openwork tracery spires is a series of intersecting nodding ogee arches, which also characterizes the Mount of Olives sketch of 1474. Only the second floor of the spire with the rectangular gallery was completed under his supervision, which was abruptly interrupted in 1493 or 1494, but the tower (see ULM, fig. 2) was finished in the 19th century closely following his designs.

The planning and construction of the Spitalkirche St Katharina in Esslingen (destr. early 19th century) are documented in a perspective drawing of 1501 by Matthäus's son Hans III (see (7) below); it is a side view that probably shows the original design dating from 1485. The building was, however, completed in 1495 following extensive alterations made in 1486 to the original plan. A highly original feature that occurs in the drawing was the south portal, with a four-centred arch and surmounted by three gabled and pinnacled canopies; the portal would have been inserted between the nave buttresses. In contrast to his work in Ulm and Esslingen, however, his new choir for the Martinskirche in Memmingen (1496–1500) dispensed with all decorative elements.

Although most of Matthäus's verified works are lost, and even though his contribution to Ulm Minster ended abruptly owing to the structural failure caused by his predecessors, he must be rated as one of the most important master masons of the last quarter of the 15th century. His sketch of the Mount of Olives in Ulm and the design of the spire of Ulm Minster are a testimony above all to his virtuosity, principally in the field of decorative micro-architecture. His particular preferences were evidently for *Astwerk* and nodding ogee gables. These characteristic forms, together with the vesica or bladder shapes that occur frequently in his tracery designs,

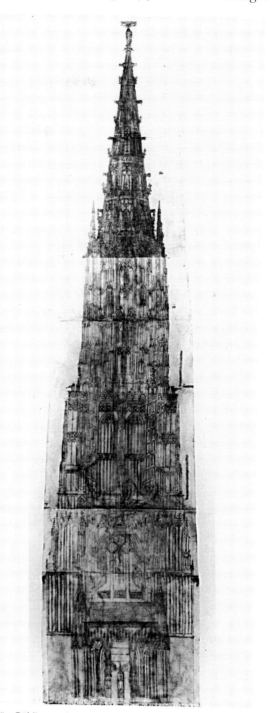

Matthäus Böblinger: elevation of west tower, Ulm Minster, 'Drawing C', parchment, h. 3 m, c. 1480 (Ulm, Evangelischen Gesamtkirchengemeinde, on deposit Ulm, Ulmer Museum)

show that he was precisely familiar with a wealth of forms favoured by the circle of Jodok Dotzinger, Master of the Works at Strasbourg Cathedral from 1452. They imply that Matthäus was partly trained in the workshops of Strasbourg and the Upper Rhine.

BIBLIOGRAPHY

W. K. Zülch: *Frankfurter Künstler, 1223–1700* (Frankfurt am Main, 1935/*R* 1967), p. 227

N. Lieb: *Die Fugger und die Kunst im Zeitalter der Spätgotik und frühen Renaissance*, Studien zur Fuggergeschichte, x (Munich, 1952), p. 423

R. Wortmann: *Das Ulmer Münster* (Stuttgart, 1972)

P. Pause: *Gotische Architekturzeichnungen in Deutschland* (diss., Bonn, Rhein. Friedrich-Wilhelms-U., 1973), pp. 280–86

W. Müller: 'Ein Gewölberiss des Ulmer Ölbergs', *Das Münster*, xxviii (1975), pp. 242–3

H. Koepf: *Die gotischen Planrisse der Ulmer Sammlungen*, Forsch. Gesch. Stadt Ulm, xviii (Ulm, 1977)

E. Schmitt: 'Münsterbibliographie', *Das Münster in Literatur und Buchillustration* (exh. cat., ed. E. Schmitt and B. Breidenbach; Ulm, Stadtbib., 1977); rev. and enlarged by E. Schmitt as *Münsterbibliographie: Kommentiertes Gesamtverzeichnis aller Schriften über das Ulmer Münster* (Weissenhorn, 1990)

J. Julier: *Studien zur spätgotischen Baukunst am Oberrhein* (Heidelberg, 1978)

B. Bushart and G. Paula: iii: Schwaben, iii of *Bayern*, Dehio-Handbuch (Munich, 1989), p. 689

Les Bâtisseurs des cathédrales Gothiques (exh. cat., ed. R. Recht; Strasbourg, Musées Ville, 1989), pp. 438–9

(4) Marx [Markus; Marxs] **Böblinger** [Marx von Esselingen] (*b* ?Esslingen, ?after 1450; *d* Esslingen, before 4 March 1492). Son of (1) Hans von Böblingen I. He is mentioned as 'Marxs, master Hannsens son, of Esslingen' alongside Matthäus as an apprentice to his father in a list of members of the brotherhood of masons in Strasbourg between 1459 and 1472. He was probably the third son and probably lived most of his life in Esslingen, close to his father; responsibility for building the Frauenkirche may have passed to him after the latter's death. He was mainly involved in the completion of the spire and the tracery gallery surrounding the nave. His mark occurs with the date 1484 on a pinnacle on the south-west gable of the nave. The letter of 1483 from the Council of Esslingen concerning the appointment of Matthäus to the construction of the Spitalkirche St Katharina (*see* (3) above) refers to a brother, undoubtedly Marx, working in Esslingen. Matthäus's contract as Master of the Works confirms this: in connection with further negotiations concerning the appointment of a warden (or foreman), in which Matthäus had obviously involved his younger brother, it is made very clear that Marx should retain his post at the Frauenkirche. The only later reference to Marx, who must have worked on the Frauenkirche for his entire career, appears in a letter of 4 March 1492, in which Matthäus approached the Council of Esslingen on behalf of his brother-in-law Stefan Waid as possible Master of the Works at the Frauenkirche; the former holder of the position, Marx Böblinger, is referred to as deceased. Artistically, Marx was greatly influenced by his father and his brother Matthäus.

(5) Lux [Lukas] **Böblinger** (*b* Esslingen; *fl* 1482; *d* Konstanz, before 7 Oct 1502). Son of (1) Hans von Böblingen I. He is first documented in a report of 11 January 1482, which appoints him warden to (3) Matthäus Böblinger at Ulm Minster, with a yearly stipend of 43 florins. Previously he was probably working at the Frauenkirche, Esslingen, where his mason's mark was discovered on the spire, begun in 1477. Lux, the fourth son of Hans I, is first named as Matthäus's brother in a letter from the

Council of Esslingen of January 1485, concerning the negotiations for building the Spitalkirche St Katharina at Esslingen (*see* (3) above). In the contract drawn up with Matthäus on 10 May, Lux is established as warden of the building works at the Spitalkirche, after (4) Marx Böblinger was not released from his post at the Frauenkirche. It is not stated whether Lux actually took up the position, and a letter of 26 May 1487 refers to Stefan Waid, and not Lux, as Matthäus's colleague.

By 22 February 1488 Master Lux Böblinger had undertaken to become warden at the Konstanz Cathedral works, whereby he was promised the position of Master of the Works should a replacement be required. Following the dismissal of Vincenz Ensinger on 22 October 1489, Lux must have been appointed to the position at the beginning of 1490, for Matthäus calls him 'mins Herrn von Constennz Werkmaister' in a letter of March 1492 to the Council of Esslingen. On 22 June 1492, while in the service of the chapter of Konstanz Cathedral, Lux is mentioned as owning a house, but an inquiry made on 7 October 1502 by the Council of Esslingen to the chapter of Konstanz establishes that he was already dead.

Lux probably planned the central tower of Konstanz Cathedral, the foundation stone of which was laid in 1497. Work is thought to have begun under his instruction on the so-called Welser-Kapelle at the north tower, the elaborate decorative stonework on the exterior of which was restored in 1988. The extent of his contribution to the decoration, mainly on the inside, is controversial, as is the attribution to him of the architectural frame of a niche for a piscina of 1490 (perhaps originally a receptacle for the Sacrament) in the so-called lower sacristy. The filigree vegetation and curved branches, showing a marked similarity to goldsmiths' work, the finely chiselled web of arches and curved pinnacles reveal a high standard of technical skill, but as a whole the work appears roughly executed. Lux's decorative work shows dependence on the designs of Matthäus, for example the south portal of the Spitalkirche St Katharina at Esslingen, as shown in the design by (7) Hans Böblinger III.

BIBLIOGRAPHY

M. Krebs: 'Die Protokolle des Konstanzer Domkapitels', *Z. Gesch. Oberrheins*, c (1952), pp. 128–257; ci (1953), pp. 74–156

H. Reiners: *Das Münster Unser Lieben Frauen zu Konstanz*, Die Kunstdenkmäler Südbadens, i (Konstanz, 1955)

F. W. Fischer: 'Ein neu entdeckter spätgotischer Turmriss und die letzte mittelalterliche Bauphase am Münster zu Konstanz', *Jb. Staatl. Kstsamml. Baden-Württemberg*, iii (1966), pp. 7–50

A. Knoepfli: *Kunstgeschichte des Bodenseeraumes*, ii (Sigmaringen, Stuttgart and Munich, 1969), pp. 86, 99–104, 114

Glanz der Kathedrale: 900 Jahre Konstanzer Münster (exh. cat., Konstanz, Rosgtnmus., 1989), pp. 65–6

(6) Dionysius [Dionisen; Nisi] **Böblinger** (*b* ?Esslingen; *fl* 1501; *d* ?1515 or 1516). Son of (1) Hans von Böblingen I. He is documented only from 1501, when he was involved first as a journeyman (*Knecht*) and, from 1502, intermittently as a warden under his brother-in-law Stefan Waid at the parish church of Köngen, near Esslingen. The name of Dionysius Böblinger, probably the youngest of Hans I's sons, appears in connection with a lengthy legal dispute fought from 1505 to 1513 with Dionysius's support by Waid's widow Ursula against a client of the deceased. Dionysius must, however, have lived mainly in Esslingen, where he might have worked first with his brothers and then as Master on the Frauenkirche project. On 29 July 1506, as a citizen of Esslingen and also in his capacity of Master of the Works to the free city, he acted as a witness in a lawsuit involving the theft of some sketches that had come into his hands on the death of his parents. On 17 December 1506, on the recommendation of the Esslingen Council, he applied unsuccessfully for the post of Master of the Works to the city of Schwäbisch Gmünd. On 17 March 1514, again supported by the city of Esslingen, he was appointed master mason of St Ulrich, Stockheim. Unlike his brothers Matthäus and Lux, Dionysius can lay claim only to a regional significance.

BIBLIOGRAPHY

Beschreibung des Oberamts Brackenheim, Königliches topographisches Bureau (Stuttgart, 1873/*R* Neudruck Magstadt, 1976), p. 437

F. Piel: *Baden-Württemberg,* Dehio-Handbuch (Munich, 1964), pp. 253, 462

D. Zimdars and other: *Baden-Württemberg, I: Die Regierungsbezirke Stuttgart und Karlsruhe,* Dehio-Handbuch (Berlin and Munich, 1993), pp. 202, 204, 732

(7) Hans Böblinger III (*fl* 1501; *d* Strasbourg, before 22 Aug 1511). Son of (3) Matthäus Böblinger. He represents the third generation of the Böblinger 'dynasty' of masons. In a letter from Esslingen to Strasbourg dated 22 August 1511, in which his brother Matthäus and a sister lay claim to his inheritance, he is referred to as having recently died in Strasbourg. He was probably trained primarily in Esslingen, perhaps under his father. A drawing of the Spitalkirche St Katharina in Esslingen (Vienna, Akad. Bild. Kst., 16829; see fig.) is authenticated as his work from the accompanying notes, which are dated 1501 and bear his mason's mark. Hans had therefore recorded in detail his father's original plan, obviously in his possession in 1501. It is uncertain whether Hans was living in Esslingen or in Vienna at the time (the latter suspected merely on the grounds that the drawing is now in Vienna).

Hans von Böblingen III: oblique view of the south façade and choir, Spitalkirche St Katharina, Esslingen, pen and ink, 581×633 mm, 1501 (Vienna, Kupferstichkabinett der Akademie der Bildenden Künste, 16829); after the design by Matthäus Böblinger, 1485

He was, however, definitely in south Germany between 1508 and 1510: according to a contract drawn up on 21 December 1508, he was to receive 45 florins for a sacrament house for the parish church (formerly St Blasius) of Bopfingen. The work, bearing his mark, is dated 1510 above the shrine. He is thought to have moved to Strasbourg shortly afterwards.

The most puzzling question is where and for what reason Hans made the perspective view of the south façade of the Spitalkirche in Esslingen. The sketch, clumsy in places, most probably represents the building as planned by his father but shows the latter's ideas only in single decorative details. Despite the quality of the masonry work, even the badly damaged Bopfinger sacrament house hardly matches the unique and creative design of the sketch, which relies heavily on earlier traditions. The individual forms employed by Hans were obviously greatly influenced by (3) Matthäus.

BIBLIOGRAPHY
W. Irtenkauf: 'Miszellen zur Bopfinger Kirchengeschichte: Vom Sakramentshäuschen in der Bopfinger Stadtkirche', *Ellwanger Jb.*, xix (1960–61), pp. 120–24
H. Koepf: *Die gotischen Planrisse der Wiener Sammlungen*, Studien zur österreichischen Kunstgeschichte, iv (Vienna, Cologne and Graz, 1969), p. 37
V. Frebel: 'Das Ulmer Sakramentshaus und sein Meister', *Ulm & Oberschwaben*, xliv (1982), pp. 246–7
H. Koepf: 'Die Böblinger-Planrisse', *Essling. Stud.*, xxi (1982), pp. 8, 15–16

FRANZ BISCHOFF

Bobo. Mande-speaking, agricultural people of Burkina Faso and neighbouring regions of Mali. Their self-ethnonym is Bobo, though they are often referred to in African art literature as 'Bobo-Fing'. They are best known for their masks and masquerades (well illustrated in the various works of Le Moal). Examples of Bobo art are held in many private and public collections of African art.

1. INTRODUCTION. The Bobo, numbering about 110,000, are an ancient amalgamation of several peoples who have assembled around a number of core clans that do not preserve any oral traditions of immigration into the area. The major Bobo community in the south is Bobo-Dioulasso, the second city of Burkina Faso and the sometime French colonial capital. Farther north are such large towns as Fo and Kouka, as well as Boura in the extreme north in Mali.

Bobo villages are compact, with large flat-roofed buildings of moulded mud or dried clay brick. Buildings were often two or even three storeys high, but the damage to many old Bobo villages by French artillery during the Bobo uprising in 1914 was so extensive that few buildings over one storey remain.

The Bobo creator-god Wuro cannot be described and is not represented in sculpture. Bobo cosmic myths describe the creation of the world by Wuro and the ordering of his creations, which are placed in basic opposing pairs: man/spirits, male/female, village/bush, domesticated/wild, culture/nature, cold/hot, farmer-/blacksmith. The balances between forces as they were created by Wuro are precarious, and it is easy for man, through the simplest daily acts, to pollute his world and throw these forces out of balance. Even farming, in which crops are gathered in the bush and brought into the village, can upset the precarious equilibrium between culture/nature, village/bush. Wuro is an otiose god. After creating a perfect world he saw he could not improve upon it. To avoid confrontations with man, the most difficult of his creatures, he withdrew from the world, leaving behind part of his own vital material, his son Dwo, the mask, to help mankind. Dwo is the materialization of one form of Wuro and his principal manifestation. Wuro also left behind his two other sons: Soxo, the spirit of the bush, of vital force, and Kwere, the spirit that punishes with lightning and thunder. As the representative of men to their creator, Dwo remains the major spiritual being through whom communication between man and Wuro is possible and desirable. Wuro's creations are celebrated in the rapid swirling rotation of masks. Dwo is revealed to man in the form of a mask made of leaves or of cultivated fibres, or sometimes as a bull-roarer or other object kept near the cult shrine.

2. MASKS AND MASQUERADES. The Bobo produce masks in leaves, fibres, wood and cloth. Each mask type is used by one or more segments of Bobo society in a range of traditional contexts. The many types are distinguished by the name of the leaves or fibres used, the colours of the fibres, or the shape of the head of the mask. Each is a manifestation of Dwo.

Masks with wooden heads are often called Syêkele. The heads must be carved by smiths, and stylistically they are indistinguishable from the older and more important wooden smiths' masks. One cannot easily tell by looking at a wooden mask in a museum if it was used by farmers or smiths.

The basic Syêkele is characterized by a long, trapezoidal face bisected vertically by a thin, straight nose. The head is a large, spherical helmet surmounted by thin, straight horns. The eyes are high, at the intersection of the planes of the cheeks and the brow, and the mouth is placed very low on the chin. Large, rounded, convex semicircles represent the eyebrows. Farmers' Syêkele occur in many variations on the same basic forms. The most common variation is the addition of a long, rectangular plank. Two additional characters are represented by Syêkele: Buffalo (Tu), with large vertical, flat, spreading horns; and Hornbill (Kuma), with a massive curving beak that projects from the face, and horn shapes that may curve forward or back depending on their village of origin.

Smiths use masks made of leaves, fibres and cloth, but they most commonly use wooden face masks, which they also carve for farmers. Among wooden masks, the most important types are sacred masks (Molo and Nwenke), escort masks (Nyâga) and entertainment masks (Bole). The sacred masks are representative, rather than representational, and do not represent any living, tangible being, human or animal. As a result, they are abstract and stylized. Because it represents a character of Dwo that does not take human or animal form, a mask with human features may have added to it both forward-curving antelope horns and a great bird's beak. Similarly, animal shapes do not mean that the mask represents an animal, rather they recall the spirit of an animal that saved the founding ancestor of the clan.

Molo masks are carved of the wood of the sacred tree *lingué* (*Afzelia africana*). These have a long, rectangular or trapezoidal face. The head is a spherical helmet with a sagittal crest. Two thick, long horns project dramatically upward from the helmet, and there is no frontal plank above the face. A small handle of plaited fibre beneath the chin permits the masks to be held on the head during acrobatic performances. The mouth is placed far down very near the chin and is broad and protuberant. The face is marked by slanting tribal scars (Le Moal, 1980, p. 224, fig. 18).

Nwenke masks (sing. Nwenka) are less important to smiths than Molo masks. They are composed of a very elongated trapezoidal face with a narrow chin, surmounted by a frontal plank (i.e. a plank that is seen fully from in front of the mask). The intersection of the nose and brow forms a 'T', and the brow is protuberant, with the small eyes high in the angle of nose and brow. The nose is long and bisects the face vertically; the mouth is small and always very low on the face. The heavy helmet-shape is surmounted by a sagittal ridge. The frontal plank is complex and is pierced frequently with triangles so that it appears to be built up of a vertical series of triangular wings that spread horizontally. The plank is the determining characteristic of the Nwenke type (Le Moal, 1980, p. 217, fig. 16). Nwenke maskers wear fibre costumes.

The mask called Nyâga (see fig.) represents the large kob antelope (*Hipportragus koba*). Enormous horns curve backwards from a large, rounded forehead. The snout is

Bobo Nyâga mask, representing kob antelope, dancing at a funeral, Dofigso village, southern Bobo, Burkina Faso; from a photograph by Christopher D. Roy, 1984

elongated and curves forward and down in dramatic balance to the horns. The mouth is open and is studded with real antelope teeth. The horns are banded and the eyes hooded with protruding lids. There are several regional styles, the most spectacular being from Muna village, though the village itself retains no examples, all having been stolen.

Bobo leaf masks never 'dance'; fibre masks may do so, but always individually, in turn. Wooden masks also perform in turn. Only such animal masks as the Nyâga imitate the movements of the animals they represent; other masks do not imitate natural characters—their dances are abstract, like the beings they represent.

In the region around Bobo-Dioulasso, wooden masks spin wildly, seeming to be almost out of control, from one side of the open dance area to the other and then back. The climax of each mask's performance is a *tour de force* rotation of the solo mask. The performer plants his feet firmly and twists his torso and neck, grasping the small handle that protrudes from the chin of the mask or a band of fibre knotted inside the chin. The mask's wooden head rotates two or three times, then returns, in such a way that the mask may leave the master's head and is only kept from flying across the performance area by the dancer's tight grip on it. It is quite common for spectators to be able to see clearly the masker's head and torso. In the south, the performances of fibre masks are very athletic. Unencumbered by a heavy wooden mask, the maskers leap across the dance area like gymnasts, executing forward flips, cartwheels and somersaults.

The Bobo use masks in three major contexts: at annual harvest rites (Birewa Dâga), during male initiation rituals (Yele Dâga), their major function, and in burial (Syebi) and funeral rites (Syekwe) of people who have been killed by Dwo or who are elder priests of Dwo. Masks seem to participate in funerals much more frequently in the Syankoma area in the south, near Bobo-Dioulasso, than in the north.

Leaf masks representing the initial and universal form of Dwo serve to integrate the individual into human society and to link the community of man with the natural world; fibre masks fix the individual in a social grouping, dedicated to one of the later forms of Dwo. These masks are important agents of socialization. The significance of the lessons they import is impressed on each new generation in the major institution of initiation.

Each mask is considered to embody the spirit of Dwo and serves during sacrifices as a sort of portable altar of Dwo. Sacrifices are placed directly on the head of the mask as offerings to the spirits they incarnate.

The different levels of knowledge of life, the world and the universe are explained to Bobo boys in several steps over a period of 15 years. Masks play an essential role in initiation because they re-establish and reinforce the cosmic order created by Wuro and restore the balance and the rhythms of the natural world and of the community. Each step in initiation is punctuated by important ceremonies at which the initiates dance with several types of masks.

At funeral ceremonies, masks have two functions: they escort the deceased to the tomb and they send the spirit on the road to the world of ancestors. In southern Bobo country, Syêkele wooden masks appear at funerals of all elders, male and female. They destroy the wooden biers that represent the deceased, freeing their souls to travel the long, smooth road to the Black Volta, the Bobo equivalent of the River Styx.

BIBLIOGRAPHY

G. Le Moal: 'Notes sur les populations Bobo', *Bull. Inst. Fr. Afrique Noire*, ser. B, xix/3–4 (1957)

——: 'Poisons, sorciers et contre-sorcellerie en pays Bobo (haute Volta)', *Systèmes de pensées en Afrique noire* (Paris, 1975)

——: 'Rites de purification et d'expiation', *Systèmes de signes: Textes réunis en hommage à Germaine Dieterlen*, Actualités scientifiques et industrielles, 1381 (Paris, 1978)

——: *Les Bobo: Nature et fonction des masques* (Paris, 1980)

C. D. Roy: *The Art of the Upper Volta Rivers* (Meudon, 1987)

CHRISTOPHER D. ROY

Bobrun. *See* BEAUBRUN.

Bocanegra, Pedro Atanasio (*b* Granada, 1638; *d* Granada, 1689). Spanish painter. By 1668 he was established as the major painter active in Granada and from that date began to receive important commissions. In 1670 he painted a series of canvases (*in situ*) on the *Life of the Virgin* for the lateral walls of the church of the Charterhouse in Granada, and these constitute the most important part of the decorative programme in the building. The large paintings are lively in colouring and dynamic in composition; their Baroque illusionistic effect can best be seen in the *Assumption of the Virgin* in the centre of the chancel wall. Almost immediately after finishing these works, he painted two more small compositions for the chancel depicting the *Adoration of the Shepherds* and the *Adoration of the Magi* (*in situ*). He followed this commission with several large works, whose exact titles are unknown, painted in 1672–3 for the convent of the Discalced Trinitarians, also in Granada. Documents testify that four paintings represented the *Mysteries of the Virgin*

Boccaccio Boccaccino: *Birth of the Virgin*, fresco from the *Life of the Virgin* series (1514–18), Cremona Cathedral

and eight represented the *Life of St John of Matha*. Two portraits of *Members of the Trinitarian Order* (Granada, Pal. Carlos V) may have formed part of this commission. Bocanegra's prospering career made him the favourite painter of the archbishops of Granada, and he was appointed painter to the cathedral church and also an honorary *Pintor del Rey* under Charles II. Though a much less talented artist, Bocanegra derived his style from that of Alonso Cano. His best works are those of female figures, which are always depicted as charming, graceful and delicate, with rather childish features and meditative poses. His output was prolific but uneven, including carelessly executed and incomplete works as well as very accomplished ones. He was a mediocre draughtsman but contrived to conceal this defect with harmonious colouring and a reasonable talent for composition. Red and blue tones frequently predominate in his paintings. An example of his draughtsmanship can be seen in the drawing of *St Jerome* (Florence, Uffizi).

BIBLIOGRAPHY

E. Orozco Díaz: *Pedro Atanasio Bocanegra* (Granada, 1937)

A. E. Pérez Sánchez: *Pintura barroca española* (Madrid, 1992), p. 384

ENRIQUE VALDIVIESO

Boccaccino [Boccacci]. Italian family of painters.

(1) Boccaccio Boccaccino (*b* Ferrara, before 1466; *d* Cremona, 1525). He is first recorded in 1493 in Genoa, where he contracted to paint the high altarpiece (untraced) for S Maria della Consolazione. In 1497 he was extracted from prison in Milan by the agent of Ercole I d'Este, Duke of Ferrara, and worked for the Duke in Ferrara until 1500. Perhaps as a consequence of having killed his common-law wife he then left, presumably for Venice, where he is recorded as residing in 1505. A fresco in Cremona Cathedral is dated 1506, and Cremona was his principal workplace thereafter.

Boccaccio's early works (e.g. *Death of the Virgin*, Paris, Louvre; fragmentary frescoes from S Maria degli Angeli, Ferrara, now Ferrara, Pin. N.) show an uncertainty of orientation common to Ferrarese painters in the 1490s. Reminiscences of Ercole de' Roberti are overlaid, in different paintings, with elements from Lombard painting (especially Bramantino), Lorenzo Costa the elder and other Emilian artists, Perugino, Dürer's prints and the Bellinesque painters of Venice. In his most impressive early work, the *Road to Calvary* (London, N.G.), those elements are amalgamated into an expressive personal style.

Boccaccio's stay in Venice was decisive for his development. In his numerous Madonnas and *sacre conversazioni* (e.g. Venice, Correr; Boston, MA, Mus. F.A.) he appears as a highly resourceful convert to the contemporary style of Giovanni Bellini, emulating him in format, sentiment, in a harmonious but daringly variegated palette, and in the fluidly impressionistic rendering of landscape. He was also influenced by Benedetto Diana, Pier Maria Pennacchi and Giorgione at this time. Boccaccio's monumental altarpiece (*in situ*) for S Zulian, Venice, reflects both Bellini's S Zaccaria Altarpiece (1505; *in situ*) in Venice and Giorgione's Castelfranco Altarpiece (Castelfranco Cathedral). Also from this Venetian period, though dated later by some, is the idyllic *Mystic Marriage of St Catherine* (Venice, Accad.), which exemplifies the translucent harmony of colour and magical delicacy in the evocation of landscape.

In 1506 Boccaccio frescoed the half-dome of the apse of Cremona Cathedral with a huge *Christ in Glory among Saints*, and for the next ten years he dominated painting in Cremona, working in the cathedral (the *Annunciation*; 1507) and other churches. Puerari suggests that he returned to Venice and Ferrara during this decade, and certain paintings such as the *Nativity* (Naples, Capodimonte) or the *Virgin with Shepherds* (Modena, Gal. & Mus. Estense) evince renewed contacts with the younger generation of Ferrarese painters: Ludovico Mazzolino, Ortolano and Garofalo. Vasari mentions a trip to Rome, possibly in 1513–14, during which Boccaccio spoke slightingly of Michelangelo.

Between 1514 and 1518 Boccaccio painted eight large scenes (e.g. the *Birth of the Virgin*; see fig.) from the *Life of the Virgin* in the nave of Cremona Cathedral, initiating a fresco cycle continued by Altobello Melone, Gian Francesco Bembo, Girolamo Romanino and Pordenone. These, his most ambitious surviving works, combine panoramic Venetian landscapes, elaborate architectural scenography, startlingly vivid portraits and anecdotal episodes, restlessly swirling patterns of drapery and motion and, on occasion, classical fixity of composition into paradoxical but not incoherent wholes. Boccaccio's late altarpieces (e.g. the *Virgin Enthroned with Saints*, 1518; Cremona, Mus. Civ. Ala Ponzone) are quieter and more intensively atmospheric in effect, but they, too, show his responsiveness to German prints and to the work of his younger colleagues.

Boccaccio successfully assimilated a wide range of influences into a personal style that served as a point of departure for other painters. In Ferrara, Garofalo was apprenticed to him, and Boccaccio's adoption of a Venetian style *c.* 1500 was probably instrumental in the turning of a whole generation of Ferrarese painters (Garofalo, Mazzolino, Ortolano, Dosso Dossi) towards Venetian models. In Venice and Cremona his particular synthesis of Venetian and Lombard elements influenced Andrea Previtali, Romanino, Altobello Melone and Gian Francesco Bembo. After 1500 Boccaccio incorporated elements of Giorgione's style into his own, but, earlier, he may well have been among the Emilian artists to whom Giorgione looked when forming his art.

BIBLIOGRAPHY
DBI: 'Boccacci, Boccaccino'; Thieme–Becker
G. Vasari: *Vite* (1550, rev. 2/1568); ed. G. Milanesi (1878–85), iv, pp. 581–4; vi, pp. 459–60
G. B. Zaist: *Notizie storiche de' pittori, scultori, ed architetti cremonesi*, 2 vols, ed. A. M. Panni (Cremona, 1774/*R* 1976), i, pp. 63–90
C. Bonetti: *Note e appunti di storia cremonese* (Cremona, 1923), pp. 63–6
G. Gronau: 'Unveröffentliche Bilder des Boccaccio Boccaccino', *Belvedere*, viii (1929), pp. 250–55
A. Puerari: *Boccaccino* (Milan, 1957) [standard monograph; chronology occasionally questionable]
M. Calvesi: 'Nuovi affreschi ferraresi dell'Oratorio della Concezione', *Boll. A.*, xliii (1958), pp. 141–238
S. Zamboni: 'Ludovico Mazzolino: Una primizia e altri inediti', *Prospettiva*, 15 (1978), pp. 53–2
E. Sambò: 'Per l'avvio di Ludovico Mazzolino', *Paragone*, 395 (1983), pp. 40–45
——: 'Sull'attività giovanile di Benvenuto Tisi da Garofalo', *Paragone*, 395 (1983), pp. 17–34
I Campi e la cultura artistica cremonese del cinquecento (exh. cat., ed. M. Gregori; Cremona, Mus. Civ. Ala Ponzone, 1985), pp. 51–63, 270–72, 457–8

FRANCIS L. RICHARDSON

(2) Camillo Boccaccino (*b* Cremona, 1504–5; *d* Cremona, 1546). Son of (1) Boccaccio Boccaccino. He probably received his initial training from his father, but was influenced at an early stage by Pordenone's Cremonese works, and also by Titian, whom he evidently came to know during his long sojourn in Venice (documented until 1525). His earliest known works show these influences and that of contemporary Brescian painters. They include the *Virgin and Saints* altarpiece from S Maria del Cistello (1527; Prague, N.G., Šternberk Pal.), the imposing organ shutters of *David and Saul* from S Maria di Campagna in Piacenza (1530; Piacenza, Mus. Civ.) and the *Annunciation* (Piacenza, S Maria di Campagna), which was cut down to fit the church's apse. These works show a remarkable maturity and originality in the use of colour and chiaroscuro to create illusionistic effects.

Although Camillo Boccaccino produced very few paintings, several stylistic phases can be distinguished in his oeuvre. In 1532 he painted the altarpiece of the *Virgin and Child in Glory with SS Bartholomew, John the Baptist, Albert and Jerome*, formerly in S Bartolomeo, Cremona (Milan, Brera), a carefully constructed composition showing the influence of Pordenone, Raphael and Correggio. From 1535 to 1537 he frescoed the vault, semi-dome and entablature of the apse of S Sigismondo in Cremona with *Christ in Glory* and the *Four Evangelists*, biblical scenes and decorative friezes. While influenced by Correggio, Pordenone and Giulio Romano, the frescoes demonstrate the variety of Boccaccino's inventions and the novelty and boldness of some of his figurative solutions which inaugurated a new stylistic and decorative language in the Cremonese school of painting at this date.

During the 1530s Boccaccino moved stylistically closer to Parmigianino, with his extreme refinement, sinuously elegant forms and imaginative compositions; he was in close contact with Parmigianino, whose ideas he reinterpreted with originality, sometimes reaching his own eccentric solutions. These traits are evident in the altarpiece, commissioned in 1533 and probably painted in the late 1530s, for the altar of S Marta in Cremona Cathedral. It was never installed (at the artist's death it was still in his studio), but is known through an engraving by Niccolò Vicentino, numerous preparatory studies and some *bozzetti*. Camillo Boccaccino was a prolific and attractive draughtsman.

The frescoes of the *Resurrection of Lazarus* and *The Adultress* (1540) in the presbytery of S Sigismondo, Cremona, are notable for their bold use of colour and their disconcertingly novel mannerist solutions. These stylistic tendencies were developed further in the frescoes of the *Life of the Virgin* painted in 1545 for S Sigismondo and in the altarpiece of the *Virgin and Child with St Michael and the Blessed Ambrogio Ansedoni* formerly in S Domenico (1544; Cremona, Mus. Civ. Ala Ponzone).

BIBLIOGRAPHY
DBI; Thieme–Becker
G. Vasari: *Vite* (1550, rev. 2/1568), ed. G. Milanesi (1878–85), iv, pp. 583–4
G. P. Lomazzo: *Idea del tempio della pittura* (Milan, 1590)

A. M. Panni: *Distinto rapporto delle dipinture che trovansi nelle chiese della città e sobborghi di Cremona* (Cremona, 1762)

G. B. Zaist: *Notizie istoriche de' pittori, scultori ed architetti cremonesi* (Cremona, 1774)

G. Aglio: *Le pitture e le sculture della città di Cremona* (Cremona, 1794)

F. Sacchi: *Notizie pittoriche cremonesi* (Cremona, 1872)

A. Venturi: *Storia* (1904–40, R/1966), IX, vi

M. Gregori: 'Traccia per Camillo Boccaccino', *Paragone*, iv/37 (1953), pp. 3–18

G. Bora: 'Note cremonesi, I: Camillo Boccaccino, le proposte', *Paragone*, xxv/295 (1974), pp. 40–70

I Campi e la cultura artistica cremonese del cinquecento (exh. cat., ed. M. Gregori; Cremona, Mus. Civ. Ala Ponzone, 1985)

GIULIO BORA

Boccaccio, Giovanni (*b* ?nr Florence, 1313; *d* Certaldo, 21 Dec 1375). Italian writer. He was the natural child of an unknown mother and Boccaccino di Chellino, a merchant banker. At the age of 14 Boccaccio was sent to Naples and apprenticed to a Florentine counting house; subsequently he attended the University of Naples, where he studied canon law and met many of the city's leading scholars and humanists, including Paolo da Perugia, Andalo del Negro and Cina da Pistoia. Boccaccio's desire to pursue a literary career eventually supplanted all other interests. One of the most influential writers of the 14th century, he is now known primarily for his works in Italian, in particular the *Decameron*. During his lifetime, however, such works in Latin as *De claris mulieribus* (1361), *De casibus virorum illustrium* (1355–60) and the immensely influential encyclopedia *De genealogia deorum gentilium* (written 1350–60; revised 1371–4) were the major sources of his fame and were often the subject of manuscript and book illustrations, especially in the 15th century.

Boccaccio began the *Decameron* in 1350 and completed it *c.* 1353. In 1370 he revised it, and this second version exists in an autograph manuscript (Berlin, Staatsbib. Preuss. Kultbes., Hamilton MS. 90), which has both literary importance and artistic merit; it contains a series

of 13 whimsical bust portraits ascribed to Boccaccio. These small sketches, executed in pen and watercolour, appear at the end of each quire and represent the work's major characters. Boccaccio was greatly influenced by Petrarch, whom he met in 1350, and by Dante, on whose life and works he delivered a series of lectures. Undeniably, the *Decameron* owes much to Dante. It is written in the vernacular, like the *Divine Comedy*, and comprises 100 tales, which contain references to many recognizable, contemporary individuals. The stories are drawn from a wide variety of sources, including the literature of France, Provence, Spain, the Near East, Byzantium and Italy. Throughout, the theme of love in all its guises predominates, but there are also tales of adventure and buffoonery.

Set in Florence in 1348 at the height of the Black Death, the story begins when seven young women and their three male companions decide to flee the disease-ridden city for a sojourn in the Tuscan countryside, filling their time with storytelling, singing and dancing. Six of the tales are concerned with contemporary Florentine artists. Giotto is the central character of VI.5, while the stories of VIII.3, 6 and 9, and IX.3 and 5 relate the scurrilous, fictional escapades of Buffalmacco, Bruno di Giovanni d'Olivieri (*fl* 1301–20) and the less talented Calandrino (Giovannozzo di Perino, *fl c.* 1301–18). Boccaccio's much-quoted comments regarding Giotto's fame, his humility, and the extraordinary illusionistic realism of his art were based on Pliny the elder's observations in *Natural History* XXXV (AD 77) on the genius of Classical art. Underlying the pranks of Buffalmacco and his colleagues is an equally serious allusion to the creative artist's power to reconstruct the world according to the dictates of his own imagination.

The *Decameron* soon attracted the interest of artists, as its concrete imagery and ribald humour afforded excellent subjects for manuscript illumination as well as monumental art. The earliest extant illustrations are found in a late 14th-century Florentine manuscript (Paris, Bib. N., MS. it. 482). The work was translated into French by Laurent de Premierfait in 1414, under the title *Cent nouvelles*, and enjoyed a particular vogue in France and England. The first known illuminated manuscript of the French translation (Rome, Vatican, Bib. Apostolica, MS. Pal. lat. 1989) dates from the second decade of the 15th century. The *Decameron* achieved its greatest literary and artistic success during the 15th century and the early 16th, beginning with the first printed edition produced in Venice by Giovanni and Gregorio de' Gregoriis in 1492, which had 104 high-quality woodcuts (see fig.) executed by two artists; the illustrations were reused in the two later Venetian publications of 1498 and 1504. Subsequently such artists as Pesellino and Sandro Botticelli depicted stories from the *Decameron* on cassoni (*see* CASSONE, §1). The tale of patient Griselda (*Decameron* X) is one of the most popular subjects for illustration, as in the cycle of frescoes (probably 15th century) in the Castello Roccabianca near Parma, for example. In the 20th century interest in the *Decameron* by artists as stylistically diverse as Giorgio de Chirico and Marc Chagall testified to the enduring appeal of Boccaccio's masterpiece.

WRITINGS

Decameron (MS.; 1350–*c.* 1353); ed. D. Wallace (Cambridge, 1991)

V. Branca, ed.: *Tutte le opere de Giovanni Boccaccio*, 7 vols (Milan, 1964–92) [further five vols planned]

The *'Brigada' Seated in a Garden*, woodcut, frontispiece to Giovanni Boccaccio: *Decameron* (Venice, 1492) (Florence, Biblioteca Nazionale Centrale)

BIBLIOGRAPHY

G. von Terey: 'Boccaccio und die niederländische Malerei', *Z. Bild. Kst*, xxx (1919) [whole issue]

G. S. Purkis: 'A Bodleian Decameron', *Medium Aevum*, xix (1950), pp. 67–9

M. Meiss: 'The First Fully Illustrated Decameron', *Essays in the History of Art Presented to Rudolph Wittkower* (London, 1967), pp. 56–61

Omaggio a Giovanni Boccaccio degli artisti contemporanei (exh. cat., Certaldo, Pal. Pretorio, 1967)

M. Meiss: 'The Boucicault Master and Boccaccio', *Stud. Boccaccio*, v (1968), pp. 251–63

R. O'Gorman: 'Two Neglected Manuscripts of Laurent de Premierfait's *Decameron*', *Manuscripta*, xiii (1969), pp. 32–40

M. Ferrari: 'Dal Boccaccio illustrato al Boccaccio censurato', *Boccaccio in Europe. Proceedings of the Boccaccio Conference: Leuven, 1975*, pp. 111–34

P. M. Gathercole: *Tension in Boccaccio: Boccaccio and the Fine Arts*, University of Mississippi Romance Monographs (Oxford, MS, 1975)

Boccace en France. De l'Humanisme à l'érotisme: VI centenario della morte del Boccaccio (exh. cat. by F. Avril and F. Callu, Paris, Bib. N., 1975)

F. B. Salvadori: 'L'incisione al servizio del Boccaccio nei secoli XV e XVI', *An. Scu. Norm. Sup. Pisa*, 3rd ser., vii/2 (1977), pp. 596–734

E. Callmann: 'The Growing Threat to Marital Bliss as Seen in Fifteenth-century Florentine Paintings', *Stud. Iconog.*, v (1979), pp. 73–92

V. Branca: 'Boccaccio illustratore del suo *Decameron* e la tradizione figurativa del suo capolavoro', *It. Q.*, xxi/79 (1980), pp. 5–10

——: *Boccaccio medievale e nuovi studi sul 'Decameron'* (Florence, 1981)

P. F. Watson: 'Gatherings of Artists: The Illustrators of a *Decameron* of 1427', *Text*, i (1981), pp. 147–56

M. Arese Simicik: 'Il ciclo profano degli affreschi di Roccabianca: Ipotesi per una interpretazione iconografica', *A. Lombarda*, 65 (1983), pp. 5–26

Tales Retold: Boccaccio's 'Decameron', 17th Century to 19th Century (exh. cat. by C. Gordon, Buxton, Mus. & A.G., 1983)

P. F. Watson: 'The Cement of Fiction: Giovanni Boccaccio and the Painters of Florence', *Mod. Lang. Notes*, xcix/1 (1984), pp. 43–65

V. Branca and others: 'Boccaccio visualizzato', *Stud. Boccaccio*, xv–xvi (1985–6) [whole issues]

JOAN ISOBEL FRIEDMAN

Boccador. *See* DOMENICO DA CORTONA.

Boccara, Charles (*b* Sousse, Tunisia, 21 Dec 1940). French architect, active in Morocco. He studied at the Ecole des Beaux-Arts in Paris, concentrating his studies on urban development and craft traditions. In 1968 he received his diploma and became a registered architect. He left France in 1969 and travelled in several countries, working in Casablanca before settling in Marrakesh in 1971, where he established his own practice. This remained a small one, allowing him as designer to retain control of every detail of his work. In both layout and design, Boccara's architecture is rooted in the traditions of Islamic architecture in Morocco (*see* ISLAMIC ART, §II, 7(v)), which is characterized by refined decoration. His built works are not numerous but have been influential in developing a vocabulary for Moroccan architecture. They vary from the small Abtan House (1984), located in a palm grove outside Marrakesh, to the large, incomplete Opera House there (begun 1984), and some tourist projects. Three of Boccara's projects in or around Marrakesh provide a clear illustration of his concerns. The first, Assif middle-income housing (1978), is part of a complex of 300 semi-detached houses and blocks of flats conceived to answer the needs of large families, and Boccara designed a house type that responded to traditional lifestyles and allowed for future modification or extension. In the second project, he designed the Military Hospital in 1978, mainly on the existing foundations of a 1930s plan, with low-rise buildings organized around planted courtyards (Arab. *riyād*)

allowing easy access for patients and their families. Much effort was devoted to humanizing the environment by the use of patterns, materials and landscape. The third project, the Hotel Tichka (1986), evokes an atmosphere of the hospitality of Moroccan nobility at the end of the 19th century by defining spaces of medium scale, five storeys high, and 'home-like' rooms. The simple arcaded façades with their contrasting wood balconies and trellises and the rich interior design give the visitor an immediate appreciation of Moroccan architecture.

BIBLIOGRAPHY

B. B. Taylor: 'Profile: Charles Boccara', *Mimar: Archit. Dev.*, xv (1985), pp. 41–61

Contemporary Houses, Traditional Values (exh. cat. by B. B. Taylor, London, Zamana Gal., 1985)

C. Boccara: 'Hotel Tichka, Marrakesh', *Mimar: Archit. Dev.*, xxii (1986), pp. 30–36

HASAN-UDDIN KHAN

Boccardi, Giovanni (di Giuliano) [Boccardino the elder] (*b* Florence, 1460; *d* Florence, 1 March 1529). Italian illuminator. His activity is documented through Florentine records of payment by the Badia, the Opera del Duomo and the church of S Lorenzo. From payments dated 1477, 1479 and 1480 it appears that Boccardi was enrolled in the Compagnia della Purificazione e di S Zanobi. In 1480 he was an apprentice in the bottega of the bookseller Bastiano, but he may have begun working as early as 1475 in the bottega of Francesco di Antonio del Chierico.

Boccardi worked on Classical and humanist subjects as well as religious books. In 1485 he illuminated for a Book of Hours (Munich, Bayer. Staatsbib. Clm. 23639) a page that is particularly close to the work of Gherardo di Giovanni del Foro in the Netherlandish treatment of landscape and figures. Eight miniatures for the Psalter of S Egidio, dated 1486, are lost. In a Book of Hours illuminated by several artists (Attavante Attavanti, Mariano del Buono di Jacopo and Stefano Lunetti) for Lorenzo de' Medici's daughter-in-law Laudomia (1502; London, BL, Yates Thompson MS. 30), the use of the cameo is characteristic of Boccardi; its Classical iconography is sometimes abandoned in favour of a portrait. A Breviary (*c.* 1500; Paris, Bib. N., MS. lat. 6869) that Boccardi illuminated for an unidentified bishop reflects the strong influence of Domenico Ghirlandaio's bottega in its landscape vignettes, while the picturesque scenes from urban, suburban and country life are reminiscent of Gherardo. In 1512 the artist collaborated with Monte di Giovanni del Foro on a Choir-book (Florence, S Marco, MS. 542) for the Badia. Among his contributions to humanist codices for Matthias Corvinus, King of Hungary, is a Philostratus manuscript (Budapest, N. Széchényi Lib., Cod. lat. 417).

Boccardi's work shows a consistent interest in the Antique, using Classical motifs and decorative elements. His style before 1490 reflects close links with the del Foro bottega. Despite considerable enrichments, it is also recognizable in late documented works, showing affinities with the type of illustration typical of an ex-voto or of the predella of a panel painting: minuteness of detail, figures with faces narrowed towards the chin, astonished expressions and mannered attitudes.

BIBLIOGRAPHY

M. Levi d'Ancona: *Miniatura e miniatori a Firenze dal XIV al XVI secolo* (Florence, 1962), pp. 149–54

A. Garzelli: *Miniatura fiorentina del rinascimento, 1440–1525: Un primo censimento*, i (Florence, 1985), pp. 80–81, 341–6

PATRIZIA FERRETTI

Boccati (da Camerino), Giovanni (di Pier Matteo) (*b* Camerino, Marches, *c.* 1420; *d* after 1480). Italian painter. He was granted citizenship of Perugia in 1445, and it seems likely that he received at least part of his artistic training there. In 1447 he painted the *Madonna del pergolato* (*Virgin and Child with Saints*; Perugia, G.N. Umbria) for the Confraternità dei Disciplinati of S Domenico, Perugia. It is an eclectic work: the composition is based on altarpieces of the later 1430s by Fra Angelico (who was in Perugia in 1437) and Filippo Lippi; the Virgin's face is derived from Angelico, those of the Child, the saints and the angels from Lippi, while the pageantry of the predella, showing scenes from the *Passion of Christ*, may reflect the work of Domenico Veneziano, who had also been in Perugia in 1437. By 1448 Boccati was in Padua, but he may have been there earlier given the dominant influence of Filippo Lippi, who had worked there in the mid-1430s.

In 1451 Boccati left Camerino for Florence with the painter Giovanni Angelo di Antonio, also of Camerino. He may not have reached the city but have turned instead for Urbino, as at about this time he probably painted the frescoes (partly destr.) in the Appartamento dell'Iole, Palazzo Ducale, Urbino. The walls and vaults of the frescoed room, possibly originally an audience chamber, were covered with huge figures of heroes and soldiers, putti, coats of arms, medallions and damask hangings. In style the figures are similar to those of the *Madonna del pergolato*, and their monumentality perhaps reflects Boccati's recent stay in Padua.

By 1458 and again in 1462 he was in Camerino, where he appears to have remained until at least 1470. To this period belongs the Belforte Polyptych, with the *Virgin and Child with Saints* (Belforte sul Chienti, nr Camerino, S Eustachio), which is signed and dated 1468. This is a compartmentalized polyptych of the type produced by contemporary Venetian artists working in the Marches, such as Bartolomeo Vivarini and Carlo Crivelli. The gold ground and rich gold brocade of the Virgin's mantle are Venetian in origin, but the draperies and blonde light pervading the predella scenes recall Domenico Veneziano, and the physiognomy of the saints is reminiscent of Filippo Lippi. The figures of SS Eustace and Venanzio suggest that Boccati had been influenced by Mantegna's work in the Ovetari Chapel in the church of the Eremitani, Padua.

The altarpiece of the *Virgin and Child with Saints* for the chapel of S Savino in Orvieto Cathedral (Budapest, Mus. F.A.) is signed and dated 1473. Stylistically, it is similar to the Belforte Polyptych, although the rendering of the draperies is more linear and the conception of the bodies underneath is less firm, leading to some flatness in the figures. The two surviving predella panels, showing scenes from the *Life of St Savino* (sold London, Sotheby's, 11 March 1964 and 24 March 1971), with their clothed but weightless figures and inaccurately constructed architecture, confirm this tendency. Boccati's last surviving dated work, the *Pietà* (1479; Perugia, G.N. Umbria), is in

poor condition; it has the same flat figures, but the lyrical mood and the clear light are still present. Boccati was last recorded in Perugia in 1480, when he was paid for two altarpieces (untraced).

BIBLIOGRAPHY

G. Vitalini-Sacconi: *La scuola camerinese* (Trieste, 1968), pp. 107–15

M. Bacci: 'Il punto su Giovanni Boccati', *Paragone*, xx (1969), no. 231, pp. 15–33; no. 233, pp. 3–21

P. Zampetti: *Giovanni Boccati* (Milan, 1971)

M. Cionini Visani: 'Un libro sul Boccati', *A. Ven.*, xxvii (1973), pp. 321–5

Urbino e le Marche, prima e dopo Raffaello (exh. cat., ed. M. G. Ciardi, Duprè dal Poggetto and P. dal Poggetto; Urbino, Pal. Ducale, 1983), pp. 35–9

JEANNETTE TOWEY

Bocchi, Francesco (*b* Florence, 1549; *d* Florence, 31 March 1613/18). Italian scholar and writer. His literary output (only partly published) was immense: largely speeches and other occasional works, but also many historical writings. In the field of art literature he wrote (in 1571) *Eccellenza della statua del San Giorgio di Donatello*. Dedicated initially to Cosimo I de' Medici, it was published in 1584 with a new dedication to the Florentine Accademia del Disegno. Also significant is *Le bellezze di Firenze* (1591), the first Renaissance guide to Florence. The treatise on Donatello's sculpture is an important academic document on the theory of art in Florence in the 16th century. His *Discorso sopra l'eccellenza dell'opere del Andrea del Sarto, pittore fiorentino* (1567; Florence, Bib. Uffizi, MS.9, ins. 1) and *Oratio . . . de laudibus Michaelis Angeli fiorentini pictoris, sculptoris atque architecti nobilissimum* (London, BL, MS. 1978, fols 1–25) were also written for the Accademia del Disegno.

UNPUBLISHED SOURCES

London, BL [MS. of F. Bocchi: *Oratio . . . de laudibus Michaelis Angeli fiorentini pictoris, sculptoris atque architecti nobilissimum*]

WRITINGS

Eccellenza della statua del San Giorgio di Donatello (Florence, 1584)

Le bellezze di Firenze (Florence, 1591)

BIBLIOGRAPHY

DBI [with bibliog.]

P. Barocchi: *Trattati d'arte*, iii (Bari, 1966), pp. 125–94, 393, 408–11, 471–500

R. De Mattei: 'Francesco Bocchi', *Archv Stor. It.*, cxxiv/1 (1966), pp. 3–30

M. Komorowski: 'Donatello's St George in a Sixteenth-century Commentary by Francesco Bocchi: Some Problems of the Renaissance Theory', *Ars Auro Prior: Studia Ioanni Białostocki sexagenario dicate* (Warsaw, 1981), pp. 61–6

Z. Waźbinski: 'Il "modus" semplice: Un dibattito sull'arte sacra fiorentina intorno al 1600', *Studi sul Raffaello. Atti del congresso internazionale di studi: Urbino e Firenze, 1984*, pp. 625–48

R. Williams: 'A Treatise by Francesco Bocchi in Praise of Andrea del Sarto', *J. Warb. & Court. Inst.*, 52 (1989), pp. 111–39

Z. WAŹBIŃSKI

Boccioni, Umberto (*b* Reggio Calabria, 19 Oct 1882; *d* Sorte, Verona, 17 Aug 1916). Italian sculptor, painter, printmaker and writer. As one of the principal figures of FUTURISM, he helped shape the movement's revolutionary aesthetic as a theorist as well as through his art. In spite of the brevity of his life, his concern with dynamism of form and with the breakdown of solid mass in his sculpture continued to influence other artists long after his death.

1. Early work, to 1909. 2. Birth of Futurism, 1910–11. 3. Sculptures and later paintings, 1912–16.

1. EARLY WORK, TO 1909. Boccioni spent his childhood years in Forlì, Genoa and Padua, then finished his studies in Catania and began to involve himself with literature. In 1899 he moved to Rome, where he developed a passionate interest in painting and frequented the Scuola Libera del Nudo. In Rome he met Gino Severini, with whom he made visits to the studio of Giacomo Balla, who taught them the basic principles of the divisionist technique and encouraged them to experiment with the application of colour in small overlapping brushstrokes. Inspired by his own pictorial experiments, Balla also urged them to develop a compositional method using angles and foreshortening analogous to photographic techniques. It was Balla who first introduced them to the use of complementary colours, which Boccioni later expressed in increasingly dramatic and violent ways, and it was Balla who instilled in him the love of landscape and nature that remained a constant feature of all his painting. In his first years of activity, closely following his master's teaching, Boccioni produced oil paintings, sketches, pastels, studies in tempera and advertising posters.

In the spring of 1906 Boccioni grew tired of the provincial life he was living and went to Paris. The French metropolis had an extraordinary impact on him; he was astonished and fascinated by its modernity. That sensation accounts for the more rapid rendering of his palette and the more complex spatial structure of the pictures he made in the following years. In late August 1906 he went to Russia with a Russian family he had met in Paris. Few works are known from that period, and there is no documentation that might throw light on his interests and contacts with artistic circles in France and Russia. He returned to Italy in December 1906, settling in Padua (where his mother and sister lived), but very soon he felt suffocated by the life of that small provincial city. His thoughts and anxieties in that period were recorded in a diary that provides an exceptionally rich fund of information. In its pages he raised questions about the meaning of his painting and expressed the desire to seek new forms, abandoning the styles and subjects of the past.

In this feverish search Boccioni felt the need to move away from Balla's teaching and from divisionistic verism, which no longer seemed to him to offer anything new. The search for artistic 'truth' was really blocking his progress towards a more contemporary pictorial vision and preventing him from finding more modern solutions. These he now found in the intensification of light contrasts.

In Venice, between April and August 1907, Boccioni learnt how to etch and produced numerous prints (e.g. *Maria Sacchi Reading*, drypoint, 1907; see 1988 exh. cat., p. 33). After this brief episode he decided to move to Milan, and in October he spent a week in Paris to see the exhibition *Salon des peintres divisionnistes italiens* organized by the Galerie d'Art Moderne Italienne A. Grubicy. His first months in Milan were difficult and full of problems. In his diary entry of 27 September 1907 (Birolli, ed., 1971, p. 264) he wrote: 'I don't know if I ought to transform a literary or philosophical vision into a pictorial one. Yesterday I wondered whether I had lost my love for colour, as I find I keep drawing without thinking of my brushes.'

In his attempt to find new solutions Boccioni now moved towards the painting of Gaetano Previati. He retraced the path of divisionism and Expressionism, accentuating the linear quality of his paintings and loading his subjects with heavy colour. His oscillation between the poles of Neo-Impressionism and Expressionism explains the very diverse and discontinuous results achieved in the period between 1907 and 1909 in such works as *Portrait of the Sculptor* (1907; Milan, Col. Italia Assicur.), *Mourning* (1909; ex-Shultz priv. col., New York, see Ballo, p. 175) and *Stage Mistress* (1909–10; priv. col.).

2. BIRTH OF FUTURISM, 1910–11. Boccioni's meeting with Filippo Tommaso Marinetti in late 1909 or early 1910 led him to make a more decisive break from traditional models. Futurism, which was proclaimed as a literary movement in February 1909, was now reborn as a movement in painting; the *Manifesto dei pittori futuristi*, issued in the form of a pamphlet dated 11 February 1910, was signed by Boccioni, Carlo Carrà, Luigi Russolo, Gino Severini and Giacomo Balla. This violent declaration against the dead wood of the past embedded in Italian art was followed by a further proclamation on 11 April 1910, *La pittura futurista—Manifesto tecnico*, illustrating the Futurist idea: to make the dynamic sensation of the modern age live in paintings, to involve the spectators by drawing them inside the picture. The movement's expressive maturity, however, came more gradually than would appear from the glib verbal aggressiveness that marked the group's early activity. In fact Boccioni's first one-man exhibition, at the Ca' Pesaro in Venice in the summer of 1910, still showed strong links with the past and in particular to 19th-century figurative styles. When he and the rest of the Futurist group exhibited together in the spring of 1911 at the *Mostra d'arte libera*, held in Milan in the former workshops of the Ricordi factory, they were violently accused by Ardengo Soffici of not having managed to express an idea of modernity. The episode developed into a bitter quarrel with the Florentine literati, but this was soon resolved in a solid union that lasted until 1914. The review *Lacerba*, edited by Soffici and Giovanni Papini, became one of the most important propaganda organs of Futurism.

Boccioni had become familiar with Cubist syntax, through articles in journals such as *La Voce* and especially through a trip to France in the autumn of 1911. This new experience helped him to achieve a more autonomous artistic language in which the fragmentation of colour was combined with a deeper perception of space. From the swirling vision of the *City Rises* (1910; New York, MOMA), a work built from pure colour contrasts and still filled with Symbolist references, Boccioni moved to a more formal but still richly hued meditation on the possibility of using lines and signs to express sensations. These intentions are particularly evident in two sets of three paintings entitled *States of Mind*, notably in the second series (all New York, MOMA), painted on his return to Italy from France (e.g. *States of Mind II: Those Who Go*; see fig. 1).

1. Umberto Boccioni: *States of Mind II: Those Who Go*, oil on canvas, 708×959 mm, 1911 (New York, Museum of Modern Art)

It was in these works that Boccioni first applied the theories of simultaneity and dynamism that he had expounded in April 1910 in the 'technical manifesto' on painting. Rejecting the concept of continuity of space and time, he explained (in his catalogue introduction to an exhibition at Bernheim-Jeune, Paris, in February 1912) that he sought to create a 'synthesis of what is remembered and what is seen', of 'that which moves and lives beyond the densities . . . that surround us left and right' (Drudi Gambillo and Fiori, eds, p. 106). He conceived of such a synthesis as a visual representation of the sensation 'of the internal and the external, of space and movement in all directions'. In his paintings of 1911, such as the *Street Comes into the House* (Hannover, Kstmus.) and *Simultaneous Visions* (Wuppertal, von der Heydt-Mus.), Boccioni shattered the traditional view of space, mixing elements of consciousness and reality in a single revolving image. The very rapid dynamic trajectories, or lines of force, intersect one another to express contrasts of energies within the subject itself, thus developing an intense dynamic content.

3. SCULPTURES AND LATER PAINTINGS, 1912–16. In 1912, thanks to the vitality of Marinetti who wanted to spread the Futurist movement on an international scale, the group exhibited in the major European capitals, including Paris, London, Brussels and Berlin. From that

same year Boccioni began to show a serious interest in sculpture. In April 1912 he published 'La scultura futurista' (Drudi Gambillo and Fiori, eds, pp. 67–72), a 'technical manifesto' in which he expressed scathing contempt for traditional sculptural notions:

Sculpture must make objects live by rendering their extension in space sensible, systematic and plastic, for no one can any longer imagine that one object ends where another begins; and there is nothing that surrounds our bodies—bottle, automobile, house, tree, street—that does not cut and section them with curves and straight lines. . . . We proclaim that the environment must become part of the plastic block like a world unto itself, with its own laws; that the pavement can rise up on to our table and that your head can cross the street, while between one house and the other your lamp spins its web of plaster rays.

In this context Boccioni produced his first sculptures in a variety of materials, inserting fragments of substances such as glass, wood or horsehair into the basic plaster structure. *Head+House+Light* and *Fusion of a Head and a Window* (both 1912, destr.; see 1988 exh. cat., p. 202) were his first such works, through which he sought to transform the object into a tactile form conceived as the sum of its mass and the space it encompasses. By contrast *Unique Forms of Continuity in Space* (plaster, 1913; U. São

Paulo, Mus. A. Contemp.), later cast in bronze (London, Tate; *see* FUTURISM, fig. 2), resulted from a long process of synthesis of form in motion and in relation to the surrounding environment. The striding figure is wedged into the atmosphere; its inner energy is unleashed and fragmented through its own action, forming a unitary complex with the space that surrounds it. The sculpture *Development of a Bottle in Space* (bronze, New York, MOMA; see fig. 2) executed a year earlier manifests the same preoccupations.

During this period Boccioni explored similar concerns in his paintings but arrived at different spatial solutions, achieving an ever greater degree of formal abstraction but still accepting the possibility of creating subjects that are identifiable through their lines of dynamic tension. Making reference to the concept of the FOURTH DIMENSION, he asserted: 'The dynamic form is a sort of fourth dimension in painting and sculpture, which cannot live perfectly without the complete affirmation of the three dimensions that determine volume: height, width and depth' (*Pittura e scultura futuriste*, p. 197). In paintings such as *Matter* (1912; Milan, Dr Gianni Mattioli priv. col., see 1988 exh. cat., p. 139), *Horizontal Volumes* (1912; Munich, Staatsgal. Mod. Kst) and *Elasticity* (1912; ex-Brera, Milan) Boccioni accentuated the play of volumes in the figures. In the series of *Dynamisms*, on the other hand, such as *Dynamism of a Footballer* (1913; New York, MOMA) and *Dynamism*

of a Human Body (1913–14; Milan, Civ. Mus. A. Contemp.), the main interest lies in the increasingly brilliant and violent colours.

Boccioni was extremely active at this moment and participated in many exhibitions in Rome, Florence, Rotterdam, Paris and Naples. From the beginning of 1914, however, he passed through a more meditative phase, as can be judged from his numerous articles and in the typographic works (in the *parole in libertà* idiom devised by Marinetti) published in *Lacerba*. In late 1913 Boccioni had withdrawn into a reflective isolation and had worked out some acute and profound theoretical observations; these were published in book form as *Pittura e scultura futuriste* (Milan, 1914). In this text he analysed the relationship between Futurist and Cubist painting and emphasized the desire to overcome what he considered the static vision of the French through the dynamism and simultaneity of forms. During this time he also wrote a manifesto on architecture, though this remained unpublished until 1972. After the publication of his book Boccioni passed through a period of profound crisis that coincided with a broader questioning of Futurism itself and a divergence of ideas between him and the other exponents of the group. At the same time he was actively involved in Italian political events: in fact he took part with great fervour in anti-Austrian demonstrations and was imprisoned, together with Marinetti, for burning an Austrian flag. He

2. Umberto Boccioni: *Development of a Bottle in Space*, bronze, h. 381 mm, 1912 (New York, Museum of Modern Art)

supported the interventionists in favour of Italy's entry into World War I.

In his paintings Boccioni now tended towards more volumetric solutions, almost in the manner of Picasso, as in *Dynamism of a Woman's Head* and *Dynamism of a Man's Head* (both 1914; Milan, Gal. A. Mod.). In the works that followed he showed a renewed interest in light and in chromatic decomposition, as in the *Two Friends* (Rome, Assitalia priv. col.). In July 1915 Boccioni joined the Battaglione dei Volontari Ciclisti, together with Marinetti, Mario Sironi, Achille Funi, Carlo Erba (1884–1917) and Antonio Sant'Elia. On returning to Milan a few months later he began painting again. He abandoned his heavy palette of strident colours and returned to a figurative mode linked to the French Post-Impressionist tradition and particularly to Cézanne, as in his last work, a portrait of *Ferruccio Busoni* (1916; Rome, G.N.A. Mod.). In July 1916 Boccioni enlisted in the Italian army and was assigned to the field artillery; he died after falling from a horse.

WRITINGS

Pittura e scultura futuriste (Milan, 1914)
F. T. Marinetti, ed.: *Opera completa* (Foligno, 1927)
Z. Birolli, ed.: *Gli scritti editi e inediti* (Milan, 1971) [incl. diary entries]
——: *Altri inediti e apparati critici* (Milan, 1972)

BIBLIOGRAPHY

M. Drudi Gambillo and T. Fiori, eds: *Archivi del futurismo*, i (Rome, 1958)
The Graphic Work of Umberto Boccioni (exh. cat., ed. J. C. Taylor; New York, MOMA, 1961)
G. Ballo: *Boccioni* (Milan, 1964, rev. 1982)
G. Bruno: *L'opera completa di Boccioni*, intro. by A. Palazzeschi (Milan, 1969)
R. De Grada: *Boccioni: Il mito del moderno* (Milan, 1972)
J. Golding: *Boccioni: Unique Forms of Continuity in Space* (London, 1972, rev. 1985)
Boccioni e il suo tempo (exh. cat., Milan, Pal. Reale, 1973–4)
L. Tallarico, ed.: *Boccioni: Cento anni* (Rome, 1982)
Boccioni a Milano (exh. cat., ed. G. Ballo; Milan, Pal. Reale; Hannover, Kstmus.; 1982–3)
M. Calvesi and E. Coen: *Boccioni: L'opera completa* (Milan, 1983)
Boccioni prefuturista (exh. cat., ed. M. Calvesi, E. Coen and A. Greco; Reggio Calabria, Mus. N.; Rome, Pal. Venezia; 1983)
Boccioni a Venezia (exh. cat. by E. Coen, L. Magagnato and G. Perocco, Verona, Gal. Scudo and Castelvecchio; Milan, Brera; Venice, S Staè; 1985–6)
Boccioni (exh. cat. by E. Coen, New York, Met., 1988)
For further writings and bibliography *see* FUTURISM.

ESTER COEN

Boch, William, & Bros. *See under* UNION PORCELAIN WORKS.

Bochner, Mel (*b* Pittsburgh, PA, 23 Aug 1940). American conceptual artist, draughtsman, painter and writer. He studied painting at the Carnegie Institute of Technology, Pittsburgh (BFA, 1962). In 1964 Bochner moved to New York. His first exhibition (1966), described by Benjamin Buchloch as the first conceptual art exhibition, was held at the Visual Arts Gallery, School of Visual Arts, New York, and titled *Working Drawings and Other Visible Things on Paper Not Necessarily Meant To Be Viewed as Art*. In his work he investigated the relation between thinking and seeing. In his first mature works (1966), which are both conceptual and perceptual in basis and philosophical in content, he was interested to eliminate the 'object' in art and to communicate his own feelings and personal experience, and he did not wish to accept established art-historical conventions. He also experimented with word-drawings and number systems. For his *Measurement* series (late 1960s) he used black tape and Letraset to create line drawings accompanied by measurements directly on to walls, effectively making large-scale diagrams of the rooms in which they were installed. Bochner continued to make series of installational line drawings into the 1970s and 1980s, but from 1983 he made paintings on irregular shaped canvases that can be interpreted as meditations on drawing and the interrelation between the mind, eye and hand. They display vigorously made marks, all tracing the hand's movement across specific surfaces. From the 1990s he was dealing with the visual and perceptual systems of perspective.

WRITINGS

with R. Smithson: 'Domain of the Great Bear', *A. Voices*, v/4 (1966), pp. 44–51
Ten Misunderstandings: A Theory of Photography (New York, 1970)

BIBLIOGRAPHY

Mel Bochner: Number and Shapes (exh. cat. by B. Richardson, Baltimore, MD, Mus. A., 1976) [excellent essay on development of Bochner's work]
Mel Bochner, 1973–1985 (exh. cat., essay by E. A. King; Pittsburgh, PA, Carnegie–Mellon U. A.G., 1985) [incl. interview with Bochner]
B. Buchloch: 'Conceptual Art, 1962–1969', *October*, 55 (1991), pp. 105–43

Bocholt, Franz von. *See* MASTERS, ANONYMOUS, AND MONOGRAMMISTS, §III: MASTER FVB.

Bocion, François (-Louis-David) (*b* Lausanne, 30 March 1828; *d* Lausanne, 12 Dec 1890). Swiss painter. He studied drawing in Vevey and Lausanne before going to Paris in 1845 to study with his compatriots Louis Grosclaude (1784–1869) and Charles Gleyre. An attack of typhoid fever forced him to return to Lausanne, where he became professor of drawing at the Ecole Industrielle, a post he held for 41 years. Bocion's earliest artistic efforts were illustrations and caricatures for local satirical journals, as well as history paintings. When he first went to Italy, in 1852, he admired the landscape more than works of Classical art; he developed a particular interest in Jean-Baptiste-Camille Corot's paintings. His first important landscapes date from the late 1850s and reveal a remarkable insight into the atmospheric effects of the region around Lake Geneva, a subject Bocion explored in endless variations, notably in *Stormy Evening at Ouchy* (Lausanne, priv. col.).

Bocion's style in the 1860s shows an independent approach to landscape painting in which colour and light play a greater role than geographical accuracy. This can be seen in *The Tow Ship* (1867; Lausanne, Pal. Rumine), in which the glowing sunset and smoky atmosphere recall J. M. W. Turner's work. Although not specifically associated with the French Impressionists, Bocion showed affinities with their paintings in the free use of colour, the importance of direct observation and the sketch-like finish of his canvases. This tendency was further developed during frequent trips to Venice and San Remo in the 1870s, when his paintings became even more divorced from the traditional patterns of Swiss landscape representation. Bocion's works were little appreciated during his lifetime and were exhibited only rarely. He was nevertheless admired by such contemporaries as Gleyre, who saw in his work a faithful record of the atmospheric effects particular to Lake Geneva, and Courbet, who settled in Switzerland in 1871 and became familiar with Bocion's work.

BIBLIOGRAPHY
P. Budry: *F.-L. Bocion: Le Peintre du Léman* (Lausanne, 1925)
B. Aubert-Lecoultre: *François Bocion* (Lutry, 1977)

WILLIAM HAUPTMAN

Bock, Théophile (-Emile-Achille) de (*b* The Hague, 14 Jan 1851; *d* Haarlem, 22 Nov 1904). Dutch painter and printmaker. He began his career as a clerk for the Dutch Railway Company, but he was dismissed for devoting too much time to his hobbies of painting and drawing. He trained with J. W. van Borselen (1825–92) and later with Jan Hendrik Weissenbruch and Jacob Maris. He worked first in Bergen op Zoom, then Delft, The Hague, Barbizon (1878–80; 1904) and Paris (1880–83), again in The Hague, then Renkum and finally in Haarlem, where he remained until his death.

De Bock painted primarily landscapes, mostly views of forests and wooded countryside, for example *View in the Woods* (Amsterdam, Rijksmus.). During his stay in Paris and Barbizon he was influenced by the style of Corot; other artists he admired greatly were Millet and Rousseau (he copied a painting by the latter). De Bock's work stands halfway between Romanticism and Realism and is generally thought to be decorative, but lacking in substance. Besides oil paintings—characterized by broad brushstrokes and restrained colour—this minor master of the Hague school made etchings, lithographs and drawings. De Bock was also responsible for painting a large part of the dune landscape in the *Panorama Mesdag* in The Hague (1881).

De Bock taught and advised many professional and amateur painters—van Gogh was a close friend when he was living in The Hague (1882–3). He also played an important part in the contemporary Dutch art world, serving as the first chairman of the Haagsche Kunstkring, a society of young progressive artists who wished to counterbalance the more established Pulchri Studio society. His estate was auctioned by F. Muller & Co. in Amsterdam on 7–10 March 1905.

FRANSJE KUYVENHOVEN

BIBLIOGRAPHY
Scheen
M. Rooses, ed.: *Het schildersboek: Nederlandsche schilders der negentiende eeuw, in monographieën door tijdgenoten* [The book of painters: Dutch painters of the 19th century, in monographs by contemporaries], iii (Amsterdam, 1900), pp. 25–48
J. Wesselink: *Schilders van den Veluwezoom* [Painters of the Veluwe region] (Amsterdam, 1946), pp. 59–63
W. J. de Gruyter: *De Haagse school*, ii (Rotterdam, 1969), pp. 90–91 [with Eng. summary]
G. A. Schilp: 'Théophile de Bock: Een sympathiek talent en bijzondere persoonlijkheid' [Théophile de Bock: A sympathetic talent and exceptional personality], *Antiek*, iii/8 (1977), pp. 7–9
J. H. de Bock: *Théophile de Bock, schilder van het Nederlandse landschap* (Waddinxveen, 1991)

GEERT JAN KOOT

Bock, Tobias. *See* POCK, TOBIAS.

Bockhorst, Johann. *See* BOECKHORST, JAN.

Böckler, Georg Andreas (*b* Cronheim, *c*.1617; *d* Ansbach, 22 Feb 1687). German architect and writer. He was recorded in Strasbourg, as a student in 1641 and as teaching in 1654, and was active there and in Nuremberg and Frankfurt am Main between 1644 and 1687. In 1679 he entered the service of Johann Friedrich, Markgraf von Ansbach (*reg* 1672–86), for whom he designed several buildings. Details of his work as architect and fortifications engineer are unknown: the only recorded work was the gate-tower at Herried (1684–5; destr. 1750–51), a sketch of which was published in *Neue Auslag in Ansbach* (1686). He probably built a theatre at Ansbach in 1679, which has been identified with a summer-house that was pulled down in 1726 to be replaced by an Orangerie. However, Böckler published numerous books on architectural theory and mechanical arts, especially hydraulics, as well as handbooks on military building techniques and economics. An *Ars heraldica* (Nuremberg, 1687) has also survived. His most important literary achievement was the translation (1684) of Palladio's first two books. Böckler's compendia faithfully reflect contemporary knowledge in the fields of architecture, military building and mechanics.

WRITINGS
Compendium architecturae civilis/Compendium architecturae militaris (Frankfurt am Main, 1648)
Theatrum machinarum novum . . . (Nuremberg, 1661/*R* 1673)
trans.: H. Schmitz: *Theatrum machinarum novum, exhibens aquarias, alatas, iumentaris, manuarias* (Cologne, 1662/*R* Nuremberg, 1686)
Architectura civilis, nova & antiqua . . . (Frankfurt am Main, 1663)
trans.: J. C. Sturm: *Architectura curiosa nova* (Nuremberg, 1664/*R* 1701)
Architectura curiosa nova . . . (Nuremberg, 1666/*R* 1673, 1704)
Schola militaris moderna oder neu vermehrte Kriegs-Schule (Frankfurt am Main, 1668/*R* Nuremberg, 1685)
Nützliche Hauss- und Feld-Schule . . . (Nuremberg, 1678/*R* 1683, 1699)
Ars heraldica, das ist: Die hoch-edle teutsche Adelskunst (Nuremberg, 1687)
trans.: A. Palladio: *I quattri libri dell'architettura*, i, ii (Venice, 1540) as *Die Baumeisterin Pallas oder der in Deutschland entstandene Palladius* (Nuremberg, 1698)
Theatrum machinarum novum . . . (Nuremberg, 1703)

BIBLIOGRAPHY
NDB; Thieme–Becker
B. Vollmer: *Die deutsche Palladio-Ausgabe des Georg Andreas Böckler, Nürnberg, 1698: Ein Beitrag zur Architekturtheorie des 17. Jahrhunderts*, Mittelfrankische Studien, iii (Ansbach, 1983)
K. Fischer: *Städtische und topographische Beschreibung des Fürstentums Brandenburg Ansbach*, 2 vols (Ansbach, 1786)
G. K. Nagler: *Monogrammisten*, ii (Munich, 1835), p. 558
F. H. Hofmann: *Die Kunst am Hofe der Markgrafen von Brandenburg* (Strasbourg, 1901)
A. Bayer: *Die Ansbacher Hofbaumeister beim Aufbau einer fränkischen Residenz* (Würzburg, 1951)
M. Krieger: 'Die Ansbacher Hofmaler des 17. und 18. Jahrhunderts', *Jb. Hist. Ver. Mittelfranken*, lxxxiii (1966), pp. 51–8
W. Bürger: 'Georg Andreas Böckler: Architekt, Ingenieur und hochfürstlicher Baumeister', *Ansbach: Gestern und Heute* (Ansbach, 1978), xiii, pp. 315–21; xiv, pp. 328–35
W. Stadler, ed.: *Lexikon der Kunst*, ii (Freiburg im Breisgau, Basle and Vienna, 1987), p. 215
H. Günther, ed.: *Deutsche Architekturtheorie zwischen Gotik und Renaissance* (Darmstadt, 1988)

ANDREAS KREUL

Böcklin, Arnold (*b* Basle, 19 Oct 1827; *d* San Domenico, nr Fiesole, 16 Jan 1901). Swiss-German painter. He was one of the most celebrated and influential artists in central Europe, particularly Germany and Switzerland, in the later 19th century, notable for his imaginative and idiosyncratic interpretation of themes from Classical mythology.

1. Early landscapes and first mythological works, to 1859. 2. Expansion of repertory, 1860–74. 3. Idealist and Symbolist works, 1875–84. 4. Large-scale religious and mythological polyptychs, 1885–1901.

1. EARLY LANDSCAPES AND FIRST MYTHOLOGICAL WORKS, TO 1859. In Basle, while still at school, Böcklin attended the Zeichenschule of Ludwig Adam Kelterborn (1811–78). He then trained (1845–7) at the Kunstakademie in Düsseldorf, where he studied principally in the landscape painting class of Johann Wilhelm Schirmer. Among Böcklin's fellow students in Düsseldorf were Carl Friedrich Lessing and Anselm Feuerbach. Böcklin's early works were largely landscapes marked by a strong sense of atmosphere akin to that in the work of Lessing. This was the case both in daytime scenes, such as the bleak, overcast *Dolmen* (1847; Basle, Kstmus.), and also in several dramatic nocturnal subjects, such as *Ruined Castle* (1847; Berlin, Tiergarten, N.G.).

After travelling in Belgium, where he was impressed by early Netherlandish painting in public collections, and working briefly in Switzerland with the Swiss landscape painter Alexandre Calame, Böcklin went to Paris. He remained for several months, throughout the turbulence of the February and June revolutions of 1848, studying the work of both Old Masters and contemporary artists. He felt particular admiration for the bravura and control of Thomas Couture's large figure composition *Romans of the Decadence* (1847; Paris, Mus. d'Orsay) and for the treatment of light and colour in the landscapes of Jean-Baptiste-Camille Corot. On his return to Basle Böcklin produced his first works with a distinctive personal style: a number of landscape scenes going beyond the essentially realist Düsseldorf tradition to suggest an understanding of nature as the embodiment of unseen supernatural powers. Typical of this approach are the curiously glowing sky and rearing silhouettes of the group of trees in *Proud Firs* (1849; Basle, Kstmus.).

In February 1850 Böcklin travelled to Rome, where he soon came to know various members of the German artists' group, the Tugendbund, spending the summer at Olevano in the Alban Hills outside Rome with Heinrich Dreber, Ludwig Thiersch (1825–1909) and others. Among Böcklin's first paintings from Italy, *Landscape from the Alban Hills* (1851; Karlsruhe, Staatl. Ksthalle) clearly reveals the influence of Dreber's landscape style in its combination of careful attention to detail with a certain lyricism of mood. A work from the next year, *Roman Landscape* (1852; New York, Brooklyn Mus.), is bolder in its response to the lush vegetation of the region and is significant in its addition of the imaginary figure of a bathing woman, in the manner of Karl Blechen and of Böcklin's teacher, Schirmer.

While maintaining strong links with Basle through his friend the historian Jacob Burckhardt, Böcklin strengthened his ties with Italy in 1853 by marrying an Italian, Angela Pasucci, the daughter of a papal guard. Böcklin continued to record the contemporary reality of life in Italy, as in *Goatherd in the Campagna* (1855; Winterthur, Stift. Oskar Reinhart), but he turned increasingly to themes from Classical mythology. From this time the imaginary rather than the observed is the dominant element in most of his work.

Böcklin's paintings embrace both specific episodes and anonymous but characteristic scenes. With the subject from Ovid's *Metamorphoses*, *Syrinx Fleeing Pan* (1854; Dresden, Gemäldegal. Neue Meister), an important aspect of Böcklin's emerging style is seen in the strong contrast of cool and warm tones and of light and shadow to underline the theme of sexual conflict. In another erotically charged composition, *Edge of a Wood with a Centaur and Nymph* (1855; Berlin, Alte N.G.), figures and landscape are revealed as alternative embodiments of the same vital force. Though found shocking on its first exhibition, in Rome, this subject proved popular enough for Böcklin to produce a second version (1856; Göteborg, Kstmus.) for a collector in Hannover, Consul Carl Wilhelm Wedekind.

Despite such success, Böcklin found himself in financial difficulties and was forced to paint scenes of Classical Roman sites for the tourist market. Encouraged by the possibility of a commission to decorate the dining-room of Wedekind's Hannover house with scenes illustrating the theme of the *Relations of Man to Fire* (1858; *in situ*; Hannover, Georgplatz; see Andree, 1977, pp. 230–36, pls 110.1–5), Böcklin left Rome in the summer of 1857. The arrangement with Wedekind, however, ended in dissatisfaction with the work and disagreement concerning the fee, and Böcklin moved on to Munich.

At the Munich Kunstverein in 1859 Böcklin exhibited the second version of a composition started in Rome, *Pan in the Reeds* (1856–8; Munich, Neue Pin., see fig. 1). The work encapsulates his approach to the world of Classical mythology in its compelling physical presence, its hint of melancholy and weariness and its element of mocking

1. Arnold Böcklin: *Pan in the Reeds*, oil on canvas, 1.99×1.53 m, 1856–8 (Munich, Neue Pinakothek)

irony, in this case with the inclusion of a group of croaking frogs in the foreground. The picture was acquired by King Maximilian II of Bavaria, thus bestowing instant celebrity on the artist. Further reassurance came with an introduction to the important Munich art collector, Graf Adolf Friedrich von Schack, and an appointment to teach landscape painting at the Weimar Kunstschule.

2. EXPANSION OF REPERTORY, 1860–74. Although not unhappy in the new post and in the company of artists who became and remained his friends, such as Franz von Lenbach and Reinhold Begas, Böcklin longed to return to Italy, and in 1862 he left again for Rome. During his second Italian period he paid less attention to landscape than to the example of the art of the past, making careful studies of both the Raphael *stanze* in the Vatican and of wall paintings at Pompeii, which he visited for the first time in 1863. A portrait of Böcklin's wife, *Angela Böcklin as a Muse* (1863; Basle, Kstmus.), is set against a refined and sumptuous décor clearly influenced by Pompeian examples. The various versions of the composition *Villa by the Sea* (e.g. 1864; Munich, Schack-Gal.) combine the Düsseldorf tradition of the atmospheric treatment of setting with the lessons of balance and simplicity derived from the example of antiquity and the High Renaissance. The haunting subject, to which Böcklin continued to return until the late 1870s, anticipates several aspects of his later composition the *Island of the Dead*.

Böcklin went back to Basle in 1866 in order to carry out a commission for fresco and secco decorations for the staircase of the museum in Augustinergasse, now the Museum für Natur- und Völkerkunde (1868–70; *in situ*). At the same period he also carried out several sculptural works, including six sandstone masks for the Basle Kunsthalle (1871; *in situ*). A particularly striking work from this time was Böcklin's treatment of a religious theme, *Mary Magdalene Bewailing the Dead Christ* (1867–8; Basle, Kstmus.), notable for its lack of a sense of consolation and its relentless objectivity in the treatment of the uncontrolled sorrow of the woman.

In 1870 Böcklin went briefly to Paris, where his picture *Murderer Pursued by Furies* (1870; Munich, Schack-Gal.) was exhibited. It is possible that he was hoping to establish himself in Paris, but with the advent of the Franco-Prussian War (1870–71) this idea became far less feasible and he returned to Basle. The war was reflected in a number of Böcklin's paintings from this time, both scenes with a northern setting, such as the *Ride of Death* (1871; Munich, Schack-Gal.), and those with a Classical subject, such as *Battle of the Centaurs* (e.g. 1872–3; Basle, Kstmus.), exhibited to great acclaim at the Weltausstellung in Vienna in 1873.

Böcklin moved again to Munich in 1871 and was close to artists in the circle around Wilhelm Leibl, particularly Hans Thoma, on whom his work had a strong influence. Two self-portraits from this period suggest a new degree of self-confidence: *Self-portrait with Death Playing the Fiddle* (1872; Berlin, Neue N.G.), inspired by a work by Hans Holbein (ii) in the Alte Pinakothek but showing the artist at work and as if attentive to the apparition, and an idealized *Self-portrait* (1873; Hamburg, Ksthalle) posed against marble columns and a laurel bush. With the

outbreak of cholera in Munich in 1874, the time seemed ripe for a return to Italy. Böcklin made his last sale to Graf von Schack, *Triton and Nereid* (1873–4; Munich, Schack-Gal.), one of the first of many scenes of mythological sea creatures in his oeuvre. He then rented a house in Florence and left Germany.

3. IDEALIST AND SYMBOLIST WORKS, 1875–84. Böcklin joined the Florentine circle of German artists and scholars that included the painter Hans von Marées, the sculptor Adolf von Hildebrand and the art historian Hugo von Tschudi. He now increasingly shared with many of this group a commitment to idealism in art, and his works from the following years reflect this in their marked element of artifice. This is especially notable in the religious composition *Mourning at the Foot of the Cross* (1876; Berlin, Neue N.G.), with its incongruously neat flowered hilltop setting and stiff figures, and above all in a large picture commissioned by the Nationalgalerie in Berlin, the *Elysian Fields* (1877–8; untraced; see Andree, 1977, p. 401, pl. 320). The negative criticism that such works received in some quarters, in particular for their garish colour and their excess of detail, seems to have been taken into account by Böcklin in view of his generally more restrained and simpler compositions of the following years.

From the late 1870s Böcklin's fame drew a great many visitors to his Florentine studio, including the German Prince William, the future emperor William II. Among the more advantageous meetings of these years was that with the Berlin art dealer Fritz Gurlitt (1854–93), whose regular exhibitions of Böcklin's work from 1880, in Berlin and then in Dresden, brought an assurance of sales and fame and thus of freedom from financial or professional insecurity. Böcklin's marked independence from contemporary artistic developments was certainly further encouraged by this arrangement. A notable change in his working methods was the sharp increase during the 1880s and 1890s in his use of panel rather than canvas supports for his paintings.

While convalescing on the island of Ischia after contracting influenza on a sketching trip to Naples, Böcklin seems first to have had the idea on which he based five versions of the composition the *Island of the Dead* (1880–86; two versions 1880, Basle, Kstmus., see fig. 2, and New York, Met.; one version 1883, Berlin, Staatl. Museen, Neue N.G.; 1884, untraced; 1886, Leipzig, Mus. Bild. Kst.). The composition was initially devised in response to a request from Marie Berna (later Gräfin von Oriola) for a picture to induce dreams; and the various versions were made on request from other enthusiasts. The uncertainty as to the precise subject of the work is as important in achieving its intended effect as is the anxiety induced by the image of the rocky mausoleum-island or of the figures in the small boat approaching it. Of all Böcklin's works, this composition did most to secure an international revival of his popularity in the late 20th century.

A similar combination of the imprecise and the monumental is found in many of Böcklin's compositions from the early 1880s, for example the *Coming of Spring* (1880; Zurich, Ksthaus), notable for its paradoxically sombre mood, *The Adventurer* (1882; Bremen, Ksthalle), with its figure of the fearless mounted warrior setting off into the

2. Arnold Böcklin: *Island of the Dead*, oil on canvas, 1.11×1.55 m, 1880 (Basle, Kunstmuseum)

unknown, and the two versions of the *Sacred Grove* (1882; Basle, Kstmus.; 1886; Hamburg, Ksthalle), with their suggestion of a secret rite carried out by mysterious, robed figures. Extreme simplicity also adds to the impact of one of Böcklin's later treatments of a more specifically Classical theme, *Odysseus and Calypso* (1882; Basle, Kstmus.), where the use of tonal contrast between the male and female elements in the picture is exaggerated to an almost diagrammatic degree. A good deal of Böcklin's energy in these years went, sometimes reluctantly, into reworking earlier compositions to meet market demand.

4. LARGE-SCALE RELIGIOUS AND MYTHOLOGICAL POLYPTYCHS, 1885–1901. In 1885, concerned for the education of his now large family, Böcklin returned to Switzerland, settling in Zurich where he had a studio built. While the title, the local setting and the emotive use of colour in a work such as *Homecoming* (1887; priv. col., see Andree, 1977, p. 477, pl. 406) suggest a positive response to this move, Böcklin's most significant compositions from this time are more ambiguous. *Look, the Meadow is Smiling* (1887; Darmstadt, Hess. Landesmus.) quotes from the libretto of Richard Wagner's music drama *Parsifal* in its title but sets female figures, recalling the work of Veronese, against a Tuscan landscape. The monumental *Vita Somnium Breve* ('Life is but a short dream', 1888; Basle, Kstmus.) combines figures from a northern Dance of Death with those from a classical idyll.

Böcklin's enduring technical prowess was evident in his ability to convey the sensual reality of increasingly bizarre imaginary worlds, as in his sumptuously coloured scene of mythological sea-creatures at rest, *Calm Sea* (1887; Berne, Kstmus.); but his preoccupations and his ambitions were clearly changing. An unassuaged longing for commissions for large-scale fresco work found an outlet in a series of large polyptychs on religious and mythological themes, the first of which, *Legends of the Virgin Mary* (untraced; see Andree, 1977, p. 492, pl. 424), was completed in 1890. Despite generous and enthusiastic recognition of his achievements from the authorities in Zurich, Böcklin longed to return again to Italy. At the end of 1890, with the onset of a period of illness (which culminated in a stroke in 1892), he left Switzerland, going first to Viareggio and then moving south.

While working on his second polyptych, *Venus Genetrix* (1891–5; Zurich, Ksthaus), a work notable for its serenity, Böcklin produced a number of paintings marked by irony and despair. *In the Arbour* (1891; Zurich, Ksthaus) shows an aged couple at the end of a walled garden, which they have entirely deadened in their zeal for symmetry. With the figures from Dante's *Divina Commedia*, *Paolo and Francesca* (1893; Winterthur, Stift. Oskar Reinhart), Böcklin eschews the familiar love scene in favour of the medieval iconography of the subject and shows the couple drifting through the dark void of the Inferno.

In a *Self-portrait* of 1893 commissioned by the Kunst-museum in Basle (*in situ*) Böcklin affirms his return to good health, showing himself at his easel, brush in hand, wearing fashionable, brightly coloured clothes. His popularity throughout German-speaking Europe reached an unprecedented level during the last ten years of his life, partly due to the publication of four volumes of reproductions of his works by Bruckmann in Munich. It was also during these years that Heinrich Alfred Schmid (1863–1951) embarked on the first catalogue raisonné of Böcklin's work.

In 1894 Böcklin acquired the Villa Bellagio in San Domenico near Fiesole. After repairs and some rebuilding, Böcklin and his son Carlo (*b* 1870) carried out wall decorations in the style of those at Pompeii (1896; *in situ*; see Andree, 1977, pp. 514–15, pls 450.1–3), using the encaustic technique, in which they were instructed by Ernst Berger (*b* 1857). While Böcklin's fame reached a peak with his 70th birthday celebrations in Switzerland and Germany, he himself expressed little enthusiasm for these. The works from this period, notably the two versions of *War* (1896; Dresden, Gemäldegal. Neue Meister; 1897; Zurich, Ksthaus) and the horrifying vision of universal destruction, *The Plague* (1898; Basle, Kstmus.), suggest a mind overcome with the prospect of imminent extinction.

On Böcklin's death in 1901 his work was celebrated as distinctly German in spirit, but his reputation declined swiftly after compelling negative criticism from the modernist and anti-nationalist Julius Meier-Graefe, writing in 1905. While appreciated for incidental qualities by the Surrealists and in particular by Giorgio de Chirico, and celebrated once more as a national asset in both Switzerland and Germany on the centenary of his birth, Böcklin did not again receive serious consideration until the 1960s and 1970s.

BIBLIOGRAPHY

H. A. Schmid: *Arnold Böcklin: Eine Auswahl der hervoragendsten Werke des Künstlers in Photogravüre*, 4 vols (Munich, 1892–1901)
——: *Böcklins Leben und Schaffen* (Munich, 1902)
——: *Verzeichnis der Werke Arnold Böcklins* (Munich, 1903)
——: 'Meier-Graefe contra Böcklin', *Die Kunst: Mhft. Freie & Angewandte Kst*, xi (1904–5), pp. 432–6
A. J. Meier-Graefe: *Der Fall Böcklin und die Lehre von den Einheiten* (Stuttgart, 1905)
H. Thode: *Böcklin und Thoma* (Heidelberg, 1905)
E. Berger: *Böcklins Technik* (Munich, 1906)
A. Grabowsky: *Der Kampf um Böcklin* (Berlin, 1906)
H. A. Schmid: 'Böcklin und die Alten Meister', *Die Kunst: Mhft. Freie & Angewandte Kst*, xxxvii (1918), pp. 126–37, 237–49
G. de Chirico: 'Arnold Boecklin', *Il Convegno*, iv (1920), pp. 47–53
H. A. Schmid: *Arnold Böcklins Handzeichnungen* (Munich, 1921)
H. Floerke: *Böcklin und das Wesen der Kunst* (Munich, 1927)
H. A. Schmid: 'Der junge Böcklin', *Ernte: Schweizer. Jb.*, viii (1927), pp. 49–72
Arnold Böcklin (1827–1901): Ausstellung zur Feier des 100. Geburtsjahres (exh. cat., Basle, Kstmus., 1927)
Gemälde und Zeichnungen von Arnold Böcklin, ausgestellt zur Feier seines 100. Geburtstages (exh. cat., Berlin, N.G., 1927–8)
M. Bryner-Bender: *Arnold Böcklins Stellung zum Porträt* (diss., U. Basle, 1952)
R. Andree: *Arnold Böcklin: Beiträge zur Analyse seiner Bildgestaltung* (Düsseldorf, 1962)
J. Wissmann: *Arnold Böcklin und das Nachleben seiner Malerei: Studien zur Kunst der Jahrhundertwende* (diss., Westfälische Wilhelms-U., Münster, 1968)
G. Kleineberg: *Die Entwicklung der Naturpersonifizierung im Werk Arnold Böcklins (1827–1901)* (diss., U. Göttingen, 1971)
Arnold Böcklin, 1827–1901 (exh. cat., London, Hayward Gal., 1971)
Arnold Böcklin, 1827–1901 (exh. cat., Düsseldorf, Kstmus., 1974)
P. Betthausen: *Arnold Böcklin* (Dresden, 1975)
R. Andree: *Arnold Böcklin: Die Gemälde* (Basle and Munich, 1977) [catalogue raisonné]
Arnold Böcklin, 1827–1901 (exh. cat., Darmstadt, Ausstellhallen Mathildenhöhe, 1977)
Arnold Böcklin 1827–1901: Gemälde, Zeichnungen, Plastiken (exh. cat., Basle, Kstmus., 1977)
E. B. Putz: *Classical Antiquity in the Painting of Arnold Böcklin* (diss., U. CA, 1979)
W. Ranke: 'Le "Cas Boecklin": Un épisode toujours actuel de l'art en Allemagne', *Rev. A.*, xlv (1979), pp. 37–49
Arnold Böcklin e la cultura artistica in Toscana (exh. cat., Fiesole, Pal. Mangani, 1980)

ELIZABETH CLEGG

Böckmann, Wilhelm. *See under* ENDE & BÖCKMANN.

Bocksberger. Austrian family of artists. The Salzburg painter Ulrich Bocksberger (*fl* 1490–1518) probably trained his son (1) Hans Bocksberger I. The son of the latter, Hans Bocksberger II (*fl* 1564–79), has been confused with (2) Melchior Bocksberger, leading to the composite coinage of 'Johann Melchior Bocksberger'. Melchior was in fact probably the nephew of Hans Bocksberger I. Hans II, who is documented in Vienna by 1579, is best known for the woodcut plates he made for Jost Amman.

NDB

BIBLIOGRAPHY

M. Goering: 'Die Malerfamilie Bocksberger', *Münchn. Jb. Bild. Kst*, n. s. 1, vii (1930), pp. 185–280

(1) Hans Bocksberger I (*b* Salzburg, *c.* 1510; *d* Salzburg, before 1569). Painter, designer and woodcutter. He is chiefly known for his Renaissance-style decorative wall and ceiling paintings executed for the state rooms of princes, but he presumably also worked as a painter of façades and of portraits. The painting (1536) of the great hall in Goldegg Castle near Radstatt, Salzburg (*see also* AUSTRIA, §III, 2), is ascribed to him purely on grounds of style. In 1542–3 he painted the interior of the (Protestant) Schlosskapelle at Neuburg an der Donau for Elector Otto Henry of the Palatinate. In the same period he worked with Ludwig Refinger and Hermann Posthumus on the interior decoration of the Residenz at Landshut, being the best-paid painter. The decorative forms and the style of the figures are indebted to Giulio Romano's paintings in the Palazzo del Te at Mantua (he may also have visited Rome). Though his approach was very laboured, he showed himself a dedicated disciple of the Raphael school, then the height of modernity.

In 1548 Bocksberger worked with Jakob Seisenegger on an altar panel (untraced) for St Vitus's Cathedral in Prague. Here he was commissioned by King Ferdinand I to produce mural 'ancestral portraits' (untraced) for a room in the Hradčany. The possibility of further royal commissions in 1553, for the newly built Hofkirche at Innsbruck, did not materialize. Bocksberger is recorded in Salzburg at this time, then again in Landshut in 1555; in 1557–8 he is reported as working for Duke Albert V of Bavaria and for Schloss Freisaal, near Salzburg. The ceiling paintings (1559–60) for the Lusthaus (destr.) in Munich would have been his work rather than that of (2) Melchior Bocksberger. Woodcut prints by him are also known. Among his few other surviving works are *Poseidon's Triumphal Procession* (Munich, Alte Pin.) and a drawing of

Animals Fighting (1557; Vienna, Albertina). In his lifetime his reputation was high. His ceiling paintings, using a foreshortened perspective, are among the earliest of their kind to be found north of the Alps.

(2) Melchior Bocksberger (*b* Salzburg, *c.* 1530–35; *d* Regensburg, 1587). Painter and draughtsman, probably the nephew of (1) Hans Bocksberger I, but possibly his much younger brother. Like Hans Bocksberger II, with whom he has been confused, he served his apprenticeship with the elder artist, and thus the two men's styles are similar. Melchior is principally known for his façade paintings, praised by Sandrart; numerous preliminary drawings for them survive. In 1559 he settled in Munich as a master craftsman and a member of the guild and was often commissioned by the Bavarian court. In 1560 Christoph Schwarz started his apprenticeship with him. He was employed by Duke Albert V in 1570 to do work in his castle of Isareck near Landshut, and in 1572 at Dachau Castle, presumably to decorate rooms. In 1573–4 he designed a cartoon (Regensburg, Städt. Gal.) for painting the façade of the town hall and the market tower at Regensburg with scenes from Classical mythology and Roman history. In 1579 he purchased admission to the infirmary at Salzburg and in 1581 gave up citizen's rights in Munich; but *c.* 1585 he returned to Regensburg, there to die. His abilities as an artist can be judged almost solely from his design drawings, often depicting scenes from the Old Testament (e.g. the *Three Young Men in the Furnace*; Berlin, Kupferstichkab.) or processions with Poseidon accompanied by tritons—always refreshingly original and full of narrative verve. The splendid theatricality and graphic effectiveness of his pictorial approach express an essentially Bavarian character, more marked than in Hans Bocksberger's work.

BIBLIOGRAPHY

T. Herzog: 'Neues über die Landshuter Stadtresidenz: Ein Beitrag zur Bocksberger-Forschung', *Verhand. Hist. Ver. Niederbayern*, lxxiii (1940), pp. 21–42

F. Kaess and H. Stierhoff: *Die Schlosskapelle in Neuburg an der Donau* (Weisshorn, 1977), pp. 7–20

Zeichnung in Deutschland: Deutsche Zeichner, 1540–1640, i (exh. cat., ed. H. Geissler; Stuttgart, Staatsgal., 1979–80), pp. 8–9

HEINRICH GEISSLER

Böckstiegel, Peter August (*b* Arrode, nr Bielefeld, 7 April 1889; *d* Arrode, 27 March 1951). German painter and printmaker. After an apprenticeship he began to study at the Kunstgewerbeschule in Bielefeld. In 1912 he saw the works of Vincent van Gogh at the *Sonderbund* exhibition in Cologne. He moved to Dresden to study at the Kunstakademie, and he exhibited with growing success. In 1915 he was drafted into the army, and he remained a soldier until 1919, when he moved back to Dresden. There he became the friend (and brother-in-law) of Conrad Felixmüller, joining his Dresdner Neue Sezession Gruppe 1919. Although he disliked the strong political undercurrent of the group, he remained a friend while his own career began to unfold. In 1921 he received the Rome Prize of the Dresden Academy and in 1928 the Dürer Prize of the city of Nuremberg. By then he had moved to Arrode, but he continued to visit Dresden frequently.

Böckstiegel's themes did not change: everyday life and people, especially in agricultural areas, for example *Farmer Torlümke* (1925; Münster, Westfäl. Landesmus.), the landscapes of Westphalia, and still-lifes. The influence of van Gogh and strong expressionistic tendencies, particularly in his graphic works such as *Women Workers at the Glass Works* (lithograph, 1915; see 1989 exh. cat., p. 187), diminished to give way to a strong colouristic approach. He was declared a 'degenerate artist' by the Nazis (*see* ENTARTETE KUNST); many of his works were confiscated and some burnt. The bombing raid on Dresden in 1945 destroyed a large number of paintings and nearly all of his graphic works, the blocks and plates.

BIBLIOGRAPHY

Peter August Böckstiegel (exh. cat., Dresden, Staatl. Kstsammlungen, 1950)

P. A. Böckstiegel: Gemälde, Aquarelle, Zeichnungen, graphische und plastische Werke, foreword by H. Becker (Bielefeld, [1970])

G. Söhn, ed.: *Conrad Felixmüller: Von ihm—über ihn* (Düsseldorf, 1977), pp. 135–8

Peter August Böckstiegel: Retrospective zum 100. Geburtstag (exh. cat., Münster, Westfäl. Landesmus., 1989)

PETER W. GUENTHER

Bockstorffer, Christoph (*b* ?Memmingen; *fl c.* 1511; *d* Mulhouse, 1553). German painter, draughtsman and etcher. The son of a Memmingen artist, he was in Lucerne in 1512–13 and was taxed in Konstanz from 1515 to 1544. Leaving Konstanz in 1543, he stayed briefly in Colmar, then worked in Montbéliard (1544–6). From 1552 until his death he was employed painting the town hall (built 1551) of Mulhouse. His principal work was the high altar (1523–4; destr. 1529) of the church at St Gall Abbey. His surviving work was formerly thought to include the triptych (1524) in the cathedral at Konstanz, and the etchings of the Augsburg monogrammist Master CB were also attributed to him, but the triptych is now known to be the work of Matthäus Gutrecht II (*fl* 1517–24), and the monogrammist CB has been identified as Conrad Bauer (*fl* 1525–31). Thus Bockstorffer is no longer seen as a painter of Augsburg training who had a lasting influence on, and introduced significant innovations to, the painting of the Bodensee area. His oeuvre, of which only a few samples survive (along with the St Gall altarpiece, all the murals were lost), shows him as an artist of slight originality. A winged altarpiece (1516; Wil, St Peter), a *Death of the Virgin* (1523; Lucerne, priv. col.), a group of drawings and a few other works show the typical Bockstorffer figures with broad, disc-like faces, stocky bodies, exaggeratedly truncated limbs and stiffly, distortedly draped garments.

BIBLIOGRAPHY

Hollstein: *Ger.*

H. Rott: *Quellen und Forschungen zur. . .Kunstgeschichte im XV. und XVI. Jahrhundert. I. Bodenseegebiet* (Stuttgart, 1933), pp. 40–44 [sources], 80–90 [text]

B. Konrad: 'Das Triptychon von 1524 in der Konradi-Kapelle des Münsters zu Konstanz und die Christoph-Bockstorffer-Frage', *Jb. Staatl. Kstsamml. Baden-Württemberg*, xxv (1988), pp. 54–84

MICHAEL EISSENHAUER

Bod. *See* TIBET.

Bode, Wilhelm (von) (*b* Calvörde, nr Magdeburg, 10 Dec 1845; *d* Berlin, 1 March 1929). German museum official and writer. In the 30 years preceding World War I he (von Bode after 1914) was one of the most respected and powerful figures in the European art world. As a scholar his expertise was highly regarded in a wide range of fields and backed by a vast number of publications. As the leading light of the Berlin Museum (now the Altes Museum) he represented an institution of considerable intellectual prestige. His determined approach and unflagging energy earned him the nicknames 'Kunstkaporal' and 'Bismarck of the arts', though he did not match the uncompromising and humourless caricature promoted by his detractors.

Bode's family was prosperous and distinguished. He studied law at the Universität Göttingen and served for a short time as a court auditor before overcoming paternal resistance to his studying art history. His doctoral thesis (1870) at the Universität at Leipzig was entitled *Frans Hals und seine Schule*. A period of travel preceded his appointment to the staff of the Altes Museum in 1872, first as assistant in the Department of Sculpture, then as assistant to Dr Julius Meyer (1825–1913), Director of the Gemäldegalerie. It was an opportune moment to join the museum, which was being reorganized following the political upheavals of 1871. From the beginning Bode enjoyed the open patronage of the Prussian royal family. This helped him to rise, despite his many enemies within the museum, to become Director of the Skulpturen-Abteilung (1883), then of the Gemäldegalerie (1890), before being appointed Director General by Emperor William II in 1905, a post that he held until 1920. During his career the museum rose from obscurity to be one of the most important in Europe. The improvement of several different collections was largely due to his combination of formidable visual skills and a genius for business. The building of the Kaiser-Friedrich-Museum (opened 1905, now the Bodemuseum) was also due to his efforts.

Bode had spectacular success in the earlier part of his career in the acquisition of paintings and sculpture from Italy, despite the fierce opposition of a circle of Italian art historians led by Giovanni Morelli and the indecisiveness of his superiors. He corresponded directly with dealers all over Italy and was consistently better informed about movements in the art market than his rivals. Crucial to his activities was the Florentine dealer Stefano Bardini, through whom he negotiated important purchases from the Strozzi, Capponi and Torrigiani collections. He perceived the opportunities presented in England by the break-up of great private collections and purchased paintings from, amongst others, those of the Duke of Marlborough, the Earl of Dudley and the Earl of Ashburnham. These acquisitions bred resentment. The repeated intervention of the Italian government after *c.* 1900 blocked the export of important works of art to Berlin. In England the National Art Collections Fund was formed in 1904 partly in reaction to Bode's activities. During his term as Director General he concentrated on buying Islamic and Byzantine art. He also used his expertise to advise collectors such as Prince John II of Liechtenstein, Alfred Beit, Otto Beit and Oscar Huldinsky, who in return donated works of art to the museum or money to Bode's other projects, such as the Kunsthistorisches Institut in Florence.

The volume of Bode's scholarly output was prodigious: he published *c.* 50 books (including catalogues) and ten times as many articles in Italian, German, French and English periodicals. He had two specialist fields: Dutch 17th-century painting, in which his works are now regarded as out of date, and Italian Renaissance sculpture, in which they are still of some importance. His *Italienischen Bronze-statuetten der Renaissance* (Berlin, 1906–12) pioneered studies in this notoriously difficult field. His short books on carpets from the Near East and 15th-century Florentine maiolica were also pioneering works and are still in use.

Bode's reputation was damaged in 1909 by the affair of the bust of *Flora* (ex-Skulpgal., Dahlem). This had been bought by the Altes Museum in London and was attributed by Bode to Leonardo or his circle. A claim that it was in fact the work of an English Neo-classical sculptor, Richard Cockle Lucas (1800–83), was widely believed when a piece of cloth of mid-Victorian design was found within it. Bode maintained that Lucas had repaired rather than made the bust, which he was certain was Italian of the early 16th century. It is now generally agreed that Bode was right and his adversaries wrong.

WRITINGS
Fünfzig Jahre Museumsarbeit (Bielefeld, 1922)
Mein Leben (Berlin, 1930) [highly detailed autobiography, often prejudiced but generally reliable on dates and figures]

NDB   BIBLIOGRAPHY
J. D. Draper: 'Wilhelm von Bode, attributeur', *Rev. A.*, xlii (1978), pp. 32–6
Jb. Preuss. Kultbes. (1979) [various articles]
Wilhelm Bode: Stadtdirektor, Historiker, Sammler (exh. cat. by M. R. W. Garzmann, Brunswick, Städt. Mus., 1979)

RUPERT SCOTT

Bodegón. Term used up to *c.* 1650 in Spain with reference to genre paintings; in modern Spanish it means still-life (*see* STILL-LIFE, §III). Sebastián de Covarrubias Horozco's dictionary, *Tesoro de la lengua castellana o española* (1611), explains that a *bodegón* was a rough public eating-place where offal was consumed. Some Spanish genre paintings (*see* GENRE) appear to be set in actual *bodegones*, the most notable being the *Tavern Scene* (untraced; see Jordan, p. 115) painted in Madrid by JUAN VAN DER HAMEN Y LÉON, probably in 1627. However, by association, the work lent itself to a wide range of genre paintings depicting figures of humble origin, often with food and drink. As early as the 1590s Flemish and Italian kitchen and market scenes were referred to as *bodegones* in Spanish inventories. Such paintings were imitated by Spanish artists: three 'bodegones de Italia' were painted in 1592 by the court portrait painter JUAN PANTOJA DE LA CRUZ. The earliest known examples are the *Market Scene* (Granada, Pal. Carlos V) signed by Juan Esteban at Ubeda in 1606 and the *Kitchen Scene* (*c.* 1604) by a Spanish hand after Vincenzo Campi (*see* CAMPI, (3)), which forms part of the ceiling decoration of the Prelate's Gallery of the Palacio Arzobispal in Seville.

In his *Arte de la pintura* (1649), Francisco Pacheco described *bodegones* as the naturalistic genre paintings of his pupil and son-in-law, DIEGO VELÁZQUEZ. These were all painted by the young artist in Seville between *c.* 1617 and *c.* 1623 and form a relatively homogeneous group in terms of subject-matter, style and range of artistic interests. In the early 18th century Palomino described a kitchen scene with a boy counting money that was unique in being signed by Velázquez. Today, nine *bodegones* are generally accepted as the work of Velázquez. The *Negro Kitchen Maid* (Chicago, IL, A. Inst.) is Velázquez's copy of his religious painting *Supper at Emmaus* (Dublin, N.G.). The only dated pictures are both from 1618, the year in which Velázquez passed his guild examination and married: *Christ in the House of Martha and Mary* (London, N.G.) and *Old Woman Frying Eggs* (Edinburgh, N.G.; see fig. 1). *Three Musicians* (Berlin, Gemäldegal.), *Two Men and a Boy at Table* (St Petersburg, Hermitage) and *Two Men and a Girl at Table* (Budapest, Mus. F.A.) are considered early works. Despite its consistency of style and the presence of a Seville orange, *Two Young Men Eating at a Humble Table* (London, Apsley House) has sometimes been dated to the period after Velázquez's move (1623) to the court of Philip IV, King of Spain. *The Waterseller* (London, Apsley House) is generally considered the artist's masterpiece in this genre.

Only *The Waterseller* has a complete provenance. The painting was not sold in Seville but kept by the artist and taken to court in 1623. It was given or sold to the royal chaplain Juan de Fonseca, a Sevillian friend and amateur painter, and mentioned in the inventory of his collection in Madrid in 1627; it then entered the royal collection. Two *bodegones* by Velázquez were listed in 1637 at the Casa de Pilatos in Seville in the collection of the 3rd Duque de Alcalá (*see* RIBERA (i), (4)). One was probably *Two Young Men Eating at a Humble Table* and the other a small painting of a woman crushing garlic with similarities to *Christ in the House of Martha and Mary* (Brown and Kagan, p. 249, III, no. 12; p. 251, VI, no. 4). However, there is no evidence that Alcalá commissioned these or encouraged the young Velázquez to paint them; nor is it clear that this type of painting was pitched at an educated and aristocratic taste. Rather, *bodegones* appealed to connoisseurs of painting, including members of the civic government of Seville. It is fitting that the Flemish merchant Nicolas Omazur, one of the greatest collectors of the 17th century in Seville, owned two, perhaps three, *bodegones* by Velázquez, including *Old Woman Frying Eggs*.

Although Pacheco claimed that Velázquez's *bodegones* inspired many artists to paint similar subjects, this may be an exaggeration. Painted in Madrid *c.* 1628–9, Velázquez's *Triumph of Bacchus* (Madrid, Prado) did inspire one anonymous masterpiece, the *Bodegón Keeper* (Amsterdam, Rijksmus.), in which a drunkard is shown in a tavern and

1. *Bodegón* by Diego Velázquez: *Old Woman Frying Eggs*, oil on canvas, 0.99×1.17 m, 1618 (Edinburgh, National Gallery of Scotland)

Velázquez's brown earthenware jug appears. Evidence from inventories drawn up in Seville and Madrid in the first half of the 17th century suggests that genre was of limited popularity and that still-lifes were always more numerous in contemporary collections. Spanish artists generally were not specialists in any one genre, although the staple of painters, especially in Seville, was religious painting. Artists occasionally worked in all the genres, as the small number of high-quality *bodegones* shows. No school of genre painters formed and no major personality emerged in genre between Velázquez and Bartolomé Esteban Murillo. Literary sources mention *bodegones* by the talented Sevillian painter Francisco de Herrera the elder (*see* HERRERA, (1)) that probably postdated those of Velázquez, but none is known today.

Only one signed Sevillian *bodegón* has been identified: *Kitchen Scene* (Barcelona, priv. col.; see fig. 2) by Francisco López Caro (1598–1661), which depicts a young *pícaro de cocina* (kitchen hand). This is also the only known painting by López Caro. He was apprenticed in 1608, was a boyhood friend of Velázquez and enjoyed a reputation as a portrait painter. Clearly he fell under Velázquez's spell. The horizontal, rectangular shape of the picture, the figure of the young *pícaro* and some of the still-life objects follow his younger colleague's example. In fact, the picture may derive directly from an untraced painting by Velázquez described in 1724 by Palomino (p. 156); this included the same still-life arrangement with a portable stove, but in it the boy wore a hat and cut a humorous figure. While López Caro's *bodegón* rises above the generally mediocre quality of other pastiches, he did not share Velázquez's gift for composition and drawing, nor his intense realism.

Recent interpretations of Velázquez's *bodegones* as symbolic are not convincing. The early *Three Musicians* and *Two Men and a Boy at Table* are 'merry companies', genre scenes staged in *bodegones* or taverns with humorous overtones. Although these have been related to the Italian tradition of *pitture ridicole*, comic genre scenes depicting such vices as gluttony, drunkenness and lust, it is difficult to detect any overt moralizing. Velázquez's *bodegones* are free from the vulgarity and salaciousness of much foreign genre; nor do they appear to contain any hidden eroticism.

Velázquez's palette of earth tones in the *bodegones* is appropriate to their earthy realism, akin to the *grosero estilo* of some contemporary realistic fiction. The main protagonist of *Two Men and a Boy at Table* is the *pícaro* in the centre, grinning and saluting the viewer with a flask of wine. This comic character was familiar from popular Spanish picaresque novels, the earliest and best-known of which was *Lazarillo de Tormes* (1554; anon.), although the painting does not illustrate any particular literary episode. Some genre pictures cited in the inventories of 17th-century collections show the figure of the young boy as a *pícaro* but do not give him one of his literary names. While hunger and poor food is the source of crude humour in picaresque novels, this is not the tone of Velázquez's *bodegones*. However, collectors of the pictures might have been amused by the humble tables depicted, perhaps showing the wretched fare served in real *bodegones*. In *Two Men and a Boy at Table*, both the parsnip, if this is the vegetable depicted, and the bowl of mussels were the food of the poor, and commonly represented as such in Northern European painting.

Velázquez's two religious *bodegones*, *Christ in the House of Martha and Mary* and the *Supper at Emmaus*, are serious

2. *Bodegón* by Francisco López Caro: *Kitchen Scene*, oil on canvas, 585×980 mm (Barcelona, private collection)

in tone and imply another, deeper level of meaning. They are re-interpretations of the 16th-century Flemish paintings of Pieter Aertsen and Joachim Beuckelaer. While their small size and shape might suggest a print as their source, paintings of this type could have been seen by Velázquez in the collections of Flemish merchants in Seville and in the collection of the 3rd Duque de Alcalá. Velázquez clearly distinguished between the contemporary and the historical, the 'real' from the biblical event, watched by the servants from the kitchen. In the *Supper at Emmaus* the maid pauses to listen at the moment of the Risen Christ's revelation to his followers. Since she is black, and probably a slave, the picture might contain a reference to the nearness and accessiblity of Christ to the humble and the converted.

In *Christ in the House of Martha and Mary*, Velázquez brilliantly characterized the disgruntled expression of the young woman preparing a Lenten meal. An older woman points to her counterpart in the biblical story of Martha, resentful of her sister Mary's inactivity as she listened to Christ. Christ judged Mary to have chosen the better part, the story exemplifying the greater importance of the contemplative over the active life. However, Velázquez did not denigrate Martha's part; his visual emphasis is on the contemporary scene and the cooking and serving of food.

Bodegones were generally regarded as inconsequential, even disreputable, paintings and were openly ridiculed by Velázquez's rival at court Vicente Carducho, in his *Diálogos de la pintura* (1633). Pacheco, however, justified Velázquez's genre in his *Arte de la pintura* by citing antique precedents and claimed that through his *bodegones* and portraits, Velázquez 'found the true imitation of nature'. These are images of everyday life only in the sense that they were painted from life, with models and props posed and studied in the artist's studio. Although some of the still-life objects appear in more than one of the *bodegones*, they were each time studied afresh and from life. Some of the models, too, can be recognized in more than one of the pictures, among them the figure of the young boy and the old woman who appear in *Christ in the House of Martha and Mary* and *Old Woman Frying Eggs*, both painted in 1618. The example of Caravaggio probably influenced Velázquez's approach and his practice of painting from models, although there are no obvious formal similarities between their work.

Velázquez's naturalism is calculated. The theme of the Senses may lie behind the *Three Musicians* and other *bodegones*. In *Two Men and a Boy at Table*, *Old Woman Frying Eggs* and *The Waterseller* the figures are not only portraits, but contrasted types of youth and age, their heads depicted in full face, three-quarters and profile views. Unlike contemporary Flemish and Italian genre paintings known to Velázquez, his *bodegones* are spare and carefully ordered; the composition of *Old Woman Frying Eggs* is based on interlocking diagonals of a simple X pattern, while in *The Waterseller* the figures and still-life are related and integrated with great visual sophistication.

With his *bodegones* Velázquez learned to paint. He chose original subjects, possibly close to his own experience, and demonstrated increasing mastery of his art. These are virtuoso paintings in which the young painter set himself the artistic challenge of the imitation of visual reality, seen most dramatically in such details as the coagulating eggs in the *Old Woman Frying Eggs* and the glass of water in *The Waterseller*. The generally monochromatic palette of the *bodegones* emphasizes relief and volume, and in *The Waterseller* the illusionistic treatment of the jug is a startling *tour de force*. Velázquez's concentration on a dispassionate and objective description paradoxically renders the representation of figures comparable to still-life, and the character of these two *bodegones* is somewhat dour and expressionless. However, it is this quality of seriousness that makes the *bodegones* so distinctive and raises them above the generally trivial nature of the genre painting of Velázquez's day.

BIBLIOGRAPHY

V. Carducho: *Diálogos de la pintura* (Madrid, 1633); ed. F. J. Calvo Serraller (Madrid, 1979)

F. Pacheco: *Arte de la pintura* (Seville, 1649); ed. B. Bassegoda i Hugas (Madrid, 1990)

A. A. Palomino de Castro y Velasco: *Museo pictórico* (1715–24)

J. López Navío: 'Velázquez tasa los cuadros de su protector Don Juan de Fonseca', *Archv Esp. A.*, xxxiv (1961), pp. 53–84

I. Bergström: *Maestros españoles de bodegones y floreros* (Madrid, 1970)

M. Haraszti-Takács: *Spanish Genre Painting in the Seventeenth Century* (Budapest, 1983)

Pintura española de bodegones y floreros de 1600 a Goya (exh. cat. by A. E. Pérez Sánchez, Madrid, Prado, 1983)

W. B. Jordan: *Spanish Still-life in the Golden Age, 1600–1650* (Fort Worth, 1985)

D. Kinkead: 'The Picture Collection of Don Nicólas Omazur', *Burl. Mag.*, cxxviii (1986), pp. 132–44

J. Brown and R. L. Kagan: 'The Duke of Alcalá: His Collection and its Evolution', *A. Bull.*, lxix (1987), pp. 231–55

B. Wind: *Velázquez' 'Bodegones': A Study in Seventeenth-century Genre Painting* (Fairfax, 1987)

N. Bryson: *Looking at the Overlooked: Four Essays on Still-life Painting* (London, 1990)

P. Cherry: *Still-life and Genre Painting in Spain during the First Half of the Seventeenth Century* (diss., U. London, Courtauld Inst., 1991)

PETER CHERRY

Bodendick, Jacob (*b* Limburg an der Lahn; *fl* London, 1664–88). English goldsmith of German birth. He appears to have come to England in the entourage of Charles II at the Restoration of 1660 and was naturalized in 1661. The first mark attributed to Bodendick (IB over a crescent between two pellets) was entered in 1664, the year Bodendick and WOLFGANG HOWZER presented a letter from the King to the Wardens of the Goldsmiths' Company commanding the Company to assay and mark their wares. His mark is found on a number of objects that show a strong Germanic influence, for example a tankard of 1674 (Madrid, Mus. Thyssen-Bornemisza). His work is noted for a variety of technical and stylistic innovations, for example the use of pierced and embossed cagework, and sculptural, cast handles in the Auricular style (e.g. porringer and cover, 1668; Al-Tajir priv. col.). A number of tankards and trays by Bodendick have cartilaginous handles, showing the continuing appeal of the grotesque. Other surviving work includes a pair of candlesticks (1673; Oxford, Ashmolean) and a ginger jar (1674; Copenhagen, C. L. David priv. col.).

BIBLIOGRAPHY

H. Muller: *The Thyssen-Bornemisza Collection: European Silver* (London, 1970)

C. Oman: *Caroline Silver, 1625–1688* (London, 1970)
T. Schroder: *The Gilbert Collection of Gold and Silver* (Los Angeles, 1988)

EMMA PACKER

Bodhgaya and Gaya [Bodhgayā and Gayā]. Pilgrimage centres and towns located on the Phalagu (Niranjana) River in Bihar, India. From an early date Gaya has been a site for the performance of *śrāddha*, rites for recently deceased parents. This ancient tradition and the general sanctity of Gaya in the 5th century BC probably drew Siddhartha Gautama to its outskirts, to the place now known as Bodhgaya, where, following profound meditation, he became a Buddha (Enlightened One). The tree under which he meditated (the *bodhi* tree) became an object of veneration; initially it was surrounded by a hypaethral temple (Pali *bodhighara*), the general form of which is known from relief sculptures of the 2nd–1st centuries BC at Bodhgaya and other sites (*see also* INDIAN SUBCONTINENT, §III, 3). A stone slab (Skt *vajrāsana*) at the site, dating to the 3rd century BC, carries motifs similar to those found on contemporary Mauryan pillars (*see* INDIAN SUBCONTINENT, §V, 3). Parts of a stone railing (1st century BC) demarcating a path for circumambulation around the temple also survive (*see* INDIAN SUBCONTINENT, fig. 148). The railing is decorated with reliefs depicting scenes from the life of the Buddha, his previous incarnations and other subjects (see Coomaraswamy). As devotion to deities through anthropomorphic images became customary, the temple was converted into an image shrine. By the end of the 6th century the form of the building closely anticipated that of the present Mahabodhi temple (*see* INDIAN SUBCONTINENT, fig. 50), with a towering brick superstructure and miniature shrines at the corners of an elevated terrace. Stone sculptures, mostly depicting the Buddha, are placed in the temple's niches; others are gathered at small shrines in the temple courtyard. While some are as early as the 4th century, most of the images date to between the 8th and 12th centuries. The Mahabodhi temple, subject to many repairs over time, was completely renovated in the late 19th century.

Bodhgaya continued to be an important site of Buddhist pilgrimage, but others, particularly Hindu worshippers of Shiva, also built shrines there, as evidenced by an early 9th-century relief bearing an inscription commemorating the dedication of a linga. The Shaiva role at Bodhgaya resulted in a modern legal dispute regarding the ownership of the Mahabodhi temple. The Shaiva authority, the Mahant, no longer controls the building, but he remains an important presence at Bodhgaya, and his compound contains many sculptures.

Gaya, 6 km north from Bodhgaya, is an important city with commercial and administrative functions. Dozens of temples are found in Gaya, but none is older than the 17th century. Many images in the temples, however, date from the 8th to 12th centuries, and surviving inscriptions indicate the present buildings replaced older structures. The largest and most important temple is the Vishnupad, a late 17th-century building enshrining representations of Vishnu's footprint. Nearby are the Surya temple and Krishna Dvarka temple, both containing sculptures much older than the present shrines. The Mangala Gauri temple contains some of Gaya's earliest sculptures.

BIBLIOGRAPHY
R. Mitra: *Buddha Gayā: The Great Buddhist Temple, the Hermitage of Śakya Muni* (Calcutta, 1878/*R* Delhi, 1972)
A. Cunningham: *Mahābodhi or the Great Buddhist Temple under the Bodhi Tree at Buddha-Gayā* (London, 1892/*R* Delhi, 1969)
R. A. N. Singh: *A Brief History of the Bodh Gayā Math, District Gayā* (Calcutta, 1893)
B. Barua: *Gayā and Buddha-Gayā*, 2 vols (Calcutta, 1931–4/*R* 1975)
A. Coomaraswamy: *La Sculpture de Bodhgayā* (Paris, 1935)
S. K. Sarasvathi and K. C. Sarkar: *Kurkihār, Gayā and Bodh-Gayā* (Rajshahi, 1936)
P. Meyer: 'The Great Temple at Bodh Gayā', *A. Bull.*, xl/4 (1958), pp. 25–34
D. Paul: 'Antiquity of the Viṣṇupada at Gayā, Tradition and Archaeology', *E. & W.*, xxxv (1985), pp. 103–41

FREDERICK M. ASHER

Bodhnath [Skt Bodhnāthā; Newari Khāstu; Tib. Byarung-kha-shor]. Stupa site 7 km east of Kathmandu, Nepal. The stupa (h. 45 m, diam. 90 m) is the largest of its kind in the Kathmandu Valley. Its great plinth consists of three broad terraces of intersected squares and rectangles forming a platform of 20 angles (Skt *vimśatikona*), one of the canonical forms prescribed by the *Kriyāsamgraha*. The dome has a hemispherical shape; its base is decorated by a series of stone images framed in small niches.

Newar chronicles ascribe the construction of the stupa at Bodhnath to the Lichchhavi king Manadeva I (*reg c.* AD 464–505). The original mound subsequently fell into a state of neglect and, according to later Tibetan tradition, the site became a cemetery. The stupa is mentioned again in the 14th-century Tibetan religious epic *Padma thang-yig* in connection with events taking place in the second half of the 8th century AD. It was excavated and entirely rebuilt by the Tibetan master Rig-'dzin Shakyabzang-po from Helambu (Helmu; Tib. Yol-mo; a mountain area north of the Kathmandu Valley) some time in the second half of the 15th century or the first half of the 16th. The same master also prepared the current edition of the Tibetan guide to the stupa, a legendary account originally compiled in the 12th century. Tibetan exiles have virtually taken over Bodhnath since the Chinese occupation of Tibet in 1959, renewing their ancient bond with this site by erecting a number of monasteries in the area.

Five kilometres west of Bodhnath, on the way to Kathmandu, is a smaller stupa at the site of Cha-bahil, which is popularly known as Little Bodhnath. This site is particularly important for its sculpture; a number of fine stone reliefs and statues of the Lichchhavi period are still extant in the area.

See also NEPAL, §III, 1.

BIBLIOGRAPHY
K. Dowman: *The Legend of the Great Stupa and the Life Story of the Lotus Born Guru* (Berkeley, 1973)
A.-M. Blondeau: 'Religions tibétaines', *Annu. Ecole Pratique Hautes Étud., Ve Sect., Sci. Relig.*, xci (1982), pp. 123–30
F.-K. Ehrhard: 'The Stupa of Bodhnath: A Preliminary Analysis of the Written Sources', *Anc. Nepal*, cxx (1990), pp. 1–9

ERBERTO F. LO BUE

Bodiansky, Vladimir (*b* Kharkiv, 25 March 1894; *d* Paris, 10 Dec 1966). French engineer of Ukrainian birth. He trained as a civil engineer in Moscow and worked on the construction of the Bukhara–Kabul railway before serving as a pilot in the tsarist army. The October Revolution of 1917 forced him to emigrate to Paris, where he received a degree in aircraft engineering from the Ecole Nationale Supérieure de l'Aéronautique (1920). After three years in the Belgian Congo (now Zaire), Bodiansky worked as a designer for various aircraft builders and also established his own aircraft company in 1930. He then went into private civil engineering practice in 1931, adapting his previous experience with aerodynamics, lightweight materials and prefabrication techniques to building projects; this marked the beginning of his significant but underestimated contribution to the development of modern architecture in France. He worked with Eugène Beaudouin and Marcel Lods on the prefabricated housing development of the Cité de la Muette (1932–4; destr.), Drancy, where the 15-storey towers were constructed of a light steel framework enclosed by reinforced concrete components, a process that became popular in France after World War II. It was also used in the Quarry Hill flats (1937; with R. A. H. Livett) in Leeds, 950 prefabricated units that Bodiansky built during his period as managing director of Mopin & Company (1933–9). Other work with Beaudouin and Lods included an entry to a competition sponsored by the Office Technique de l'Utilisation de l'Acier, an innovative design in steel and glass for a circular Palais des Expositions (1933; unexecuted) in La Défense, and the Maison du Peuple (1936–9; with Jean Prouvé), Clichy, an assembly hall and market building clad in metal panels. Bodiansky also served as technical consultant for Paul Nelson's unexecuted projects for a 'Maison Suspendue' (1936–8) and a 'Palais de la Découverte' (1938; with Oscar Nitszchké). After World War II, when he met Le Corbusier, Bodiansky's reputation and practice expanded considerably. In 1945–6, as a member of the French technical study mission, he travelled for several months in the USA. Upon his return he founded ATBAT (Atelier des Bâtisseurs), a multi-disciplinary group of architects, planners and engineers set up on Le Corbusier's initiative originally to supervise the construction of the Unité d'Habitation (1945–52), Marseille, and which Bodiansky directed until his death. Through ATBAT-Afrique he also worked with Georges Candilis and Shadrach Woods on low-cost housing projects in Morocco. In 1947 he was technical consultant for the United Nations headquarters in New York, designed by a team including Le Corbusier and Oscar Niemeyer. He was a regular participant in the post-war meetings of CIAM and proposed a Habitat Charter at the congress held in Aix-en-Provence in 1953; he also taught at the Ecole des Beaux-Arts in Paris. His last major work was the Olympic Stadium (1961–3), Phnom Penh, Cambodia.

WRITINGS
'Quelques Opinions sur la préfabrication et l'industrialisation du bâtiment', *Archit. Aujourd'hui*, n. s., 4 (1946), pp. 13–15

BIBLIOGRAPHY
M. Tournon-Branly: 'The Work of Vladimir Bodiansky', *Archit. Des.*, xxxv/1 (1965), pp. 25–8

ISABELLE GOURNAY

Bodley, G(eorge) F(rederick) (*b* Brighton, 14 March 1827; *d* Water Eaton, 21 Oct 1907). English architect. He was the leading British church architect of the late 19th century, and with George Gilbert Scott (ii) jr and J. D. Sedding he was one of the three architects principally responsible for undermining the hegemony of High Victorian Gothic, a style principally based on 13th-century, usually French examples, in favour of later, and English styles of medieval architecture. He was also responsible for setting the dominant tone for Anglican church architecture until well into the 20th century and built up a large practice, designing both new buildings and church furnishings.

A descendant of the founder of the Bodleian Library in Oxford, Bodley was the first pupil taken by George Gilbert Scott (ii) sr, with whom he served a five-year apprenticeship from 1845. Upon setting up in independent practice, Bodley began to enjoy patronage from the Anglo-Catholic wing of the Church of England, while his work soon followed the move towards French and Italian precedents set by G. E. Street. The church of St Michael (1858–62), Brighton, employed heavy plate tracery and bands of stone in its red brickwork and was later dismissed by its architect, in 1896, as 'a boyish, antagonistic effort. Not believing in what one saw at Scott's one went in for a violent reaction' (Warren, 1910). In fact, Bodley produced some of the most imaginative and austere examples of the so-called 'Muscular' Gothic, that abstracted Gothic manner closely dependent upon French precedents. These included the church of St John the Baptist (1855–7), France Lynch, and All Saints' (1861–2), Selsley, both in Glos, and St Martin's (1861–2), Scarborough, Yorks. The Scarborough and Brighton churches are also notable for patronage of the firm newly founded by William Morris. In the early 1870s, however, Bodley was instrumental, with Thomas Garner (1839–1906) and George Gilbert Scott jr, in setting up the firm of Watts & Co. to supply 'ecclesiastical and domestic furniture', fabrics and decoration, while for stained glass Bodley tended to employ the firm of Burlison & Grylls to supply the lighter-toned glass his Late Gothic style churches needed.

The seminal change in Bodley's style, from 13th- to 14th-century Gothic, and depending upon English rather than continental precedents, may be seen in the successive designs for All Saints (1861–71), Cambridge, and St Salvador's (1865–7), Dundee, but the significant monument is the church of St John the Baptist (1867–70), Tue Brook, Liverpool. This building, with its stencilled wall decoration, represented a return to the ideals of A. W. N. Pugin after the High Victorian experiment and reflected the dominating influence of Garner, who became Bodley's partner in 1869 and seems to have replaced Philip Webb in his affections around this time. Charles L. Eastlake, in his *History of the Gothic Revival* (1872), considered that in this building 'the genuine grace of Mediaeval art seems at length to have been reached'. The mature style of Bodley & Garner may be seen in two churches of the early 1870s: St Augustine (1870–74; see fig.), Pendlebury, built in an industrial suburb of Manchester and notable for being an unbroken vessel from east to west with internal buttresses cut through by passage aisles in the manner of Albi Cathedral, and the church of the Holy Angels (1871–6), Hoar Cross, Staffs, an expensive estate church that is more pedantically medieval in character. Both buildings are conspicuous for the use of a Late Decorated style with flowing tracery. Bodley came to

G. F. Bodley: St Augustine, Pendlebury, Manchester, 1870–74; interior, looking east

believe that the 14th century was 'the golden age of Architecture in England', and he attempted in his own work to develop English Decorated Gothic as it might have continued if not cut off by the Black Death. Both churches also exemplify Bodley's belief in the importance of 'Refinement in Design'.

The style established at Pendlebury and Hoar Cross was used by Bodley as an elegant formula for ecclesiastical design that became increasingly etiolated. Only in smaller, urban works, such as St Luke's (1892–3), Warrington, Lancs, with its unusual central nave arcade, did Bodley show more abstraction in treatment and originality in planning. Typical works include two aristocratic estate churches: that at Clumber, Notts (1886–9), and St Mary's (1899), Eccleston, Ches. The chapel at Clumber was one of the architect's favourites and marked the end of the active partnership with Garner, although the formal separation came only in 1898 with Garner's reception into the Roman Catholic Church. Towards the end of his long life, Bodley prepared the first designs for cathedrals in the United States, at Washington, DC, and San Francisco, but he never had the opportunity to build a large church. He was disappointed in the first Liverpool Cathedral competition of 1886, but as assessor in the second competition (1901–2) he was able to select the design by the son of his old friend George Gilbert Scott jr, Giles Gilbert Scott, with whom he unhappily collaborated on the design for the Lady Chapel until his death.

Bodley was primarily an ecclesiastical designer, but he was also responsible for domestic work. This included pioneering Queen Anne Revival style vicarages at Scarborough, Yorks (1866–7), and Valley End, Surrey (1866),

and the remarkable villas he built (1868–89) at Great Malvern, Worcs, which are among the earliest examples of Neo-Georgian in Britain. His London School Board Offices (1872–6; destr.), Victoria Embankment, London, and River House (1876–9), Chelsea, London, are more conventional expressions of the contemporary Queen Anne Revival. Bodley was a devout High Churchman, a poet and a musician, whose work showed an attention to detail and colour that verged on preciousness. He remained loyal to the ideals of Ruskin and the Pre-Raphaelites, although after the 1870s he became estranged from earlier friends such as Philip Webb. His pupils included C. R. Ashbee, Ninian Comper and Robert S. Lorimer, and his practice was continued after his death by Cecil Greenwood Hare (1875–1932). When awarded the Royal Gold Medal of the RIBA in 1899, Bodley answered that 'I feel it to be an honour done to my beloved old Gothic rather than to what little I may have done'.

WRITINGS
'On Some Principles and Characteristics of Ancient Architecture, and their Application to the Modern Practice of Art: A Paper Read before the Students of the Royal Academy of Arts', *Builder* (28 Feb 1885)
English Architecture of the Middle Ages: A Paper Read before the Students of the Royal Academy of Arts (London, 1886)

BIBLIOGRAPHY
DNB
E. Warren: 'Thomas Garner: Architect', *Archit. Rev.* [London], xix (1906)
F. M. Simpson: 'George Frederick Bodley, RA, FSA, DCL', *J. RIBA*, 3rd ser., xv (11 Jan 1908)
E. Warren: 'The Life and Work of George Frederick Bodley', *J. RIBA*, 3rd ser., xvii (19 Feb 1910)
D. Cole: *Handlists of the Works of British Architects, i: G. F. Bodley, T. Garner & C. G. Hare* (London, 1972)
A. N. R. Symondson: 'G. F. Bodley and St Salvador's, Dundee', *Bull. Scot. Georg. Soc.*, 1 (1972), 2 (1973)
D. Verey: 'George Frederick Bodley: Climax of the Gothic Revival', *Seven Victorian Architects*, ed. J. Fawcett (London, 1976)
G. Stamp and A. Symondson: *Clumber Chapel* (London, 1982)
S. C. Humphrey: *The Victorian Rebuilding of All Saints' Church, Cambridge* (London, 1983)

GAVIN STAMP

Bodmer, Karl [Carl] (*b* Riesbach, Switzerland, Feb 1809; *d* Barbizon, Seine-et-Marne, 30 Oct 1893). Swiss painter and graphic artist, active in America. His earliest exposure to art probably came from his uncle, the landscape painter and engraver Johann Jakob Meyer (1787–1858). When he was 22 Bodmer moved to Paris, where he studied art under Sébastien Cornu. In Paris he met his future patron, Prince Maximilian of Wied-Neuwied, who was planning an ambitious scientific expedition to North America. Bodmer was engaged to accompany the expedition and to provide sketches of the American wilderness. After touring the East Coast, the party made their way westward via the Ohio and Mississippi rivers to St Louis, MO, and in 1833 travelled up the Missouri River into country scarcely inhabited by white men. On the journey north to Fort MacKenzie, WY, Bodmer recorded the landscape and the groups of Indians they encountered. Having wintered in Fort Clark, ND, they returned to New York and then Europe in 1834.

Bodmer's paintings of Indians are full of carefully observed anthropological detail. His delicate, linear style and subdued palette give a savage splendour to such works as *Two Ravens* (Omaha, NE, Joslyn A. Mus.). In his masterpiece, *Bison Dance of the Mandan Indians* (known only in engraving), Bodmer shows a skill in dramatic composition unmatched by his contemporary George Catlin. His watercolour sketches were exhibited in Europe to admiring audiences. The journals of the expedition were published in 1839 with aquatint illustrations based on Bodmer's watercolours. In 1849 he established himself in the Barbizon colony in France, where he painted such works as *Forest Scene* (1850; Paris, Pal. Luxembourg), exhibited regularly at the Paris Salons and was associated with Jean-François Millet. The Joslyn Art Museum, Omaha, NE, has an important collection of his paintings.

BIBLIOGRAPHY
F. Weitenkampf: 'A Swiss Artist among the Indians', *Bull. NY Pub. Lib.*, lii (1948), pp. 554–6
America through the Eyes of German Immigrant Painters (exh. cat., ed. A. Harding; Boston, MA, Goethe Inst., 1975)
H. Läng: *Indianer waren meine Freunde: Leben und Werk Karl Bodmers (1809–1893)* (Berne, 1976)
Pictures from an Expedition: Early Views of the American West (exh. cat. by M. A. Sandweiss, New Haven, Yale Cent. Amer. A., 1978–9)
Views of a Vanishing Frontier (exh. cat. by J. C. Ewers and others, Omaha, Joslyn A. Mus., 1984)

LESLIE HEINER

Bodmer, Walter (*b* Basle, 12 Aug 1903; *d* Basle, 3 June 1973). Swiss painter and sculptor. He studied in the arts and crafts department of the Allgemeinenen Gewerbeschule in Basle from 1919 to 1923 and then went on a series of long study trips to Paris, Collioure in southern France, Spain and Italy. His early paintings, such as *Fishing Harbour at Collioure* (1931; Basle, Kstmus.), were executed in a Post-Impressionist style. From 1932 his work became increasingly abstract, though initially retaining a figurative base, as in *Composition* (1934; Basle, Kstmus.); such works are similar in style to synthetic Cubism, although their imagery is even less legible. Bodmer was a founder-member of GRUPPE 33 in 1933 and took part in their first exhibition in the following year. By 1935, under the influence of Constructivism, his work became entirely abstract and was characterized by broadly geometric arrangements of lines and colour planes, as in *Construction* (1935; Basle, Kstmus.). He quickly extended this style into reliefs and free-standing sculptures made of wire and metal plate, for example *Wire Picture* (1936; Basle, Kstmus.), a relief mounted on a wooden base in a frame. In 1937 Bodmer helped found another Swiss group, ALLIANZ, participating in their group exhibitions, and from 1939 to 1968 he taught drawing and anatomy at the Allgemeinenen Gewerbeschule in Basle.

Bodmer's later work, including reliefs such as *White Wire Relief on Black* (1953; Basle, Kstmus.), remained consistent in style over the succeeding years, forming part of the flourishing Constructivist current in Swiss art that included, amongst others, Max Bill. He also produced numerous drawings and monotypes that were often highly abstracted images of animal and human forms, as in the monotype *Bull's Head* (1953; Basle, Kstmus.). Some of his sculptures of the late 1960s are of solid geometric forms constructed from metal sheets, for example *Metal Sculpture* (1969; see 1973 exh. cat.). Having executed abstract paintings with centralized compositions of linear and solid elements, in his paintings of the 1970s he explored the possibilities of 'all over' composition using

intricate abstract patterns, as in *Without Beginning and End* (1972; Basle, Kstmus.).

BIBLIOGRAPHY
Walter Bodmer (exh. cat. by D. Christ and others, Basle, Ksthalle, 1973)
Walter Bodmer im Kunstmuseum Basel (exh. cat. by L. Klotz, C. Geelhaar and D. Koepplin, Basle, Kstmus., 1978)

□

Bodnant Garden. Garden in Gwynedd, Wales. It was laid out from 1874 by Edward Milner (1819–84) for Henry Davis Pochin, an industrial chemist, with further improvements undertaken in the early 20th century by Pochin's descendants. Milner's initial design confined Bodnant's formal and architectural features—most notably a laburnum archway and beds of flowering shrubs—to the curtilage of the house, while an extensive lawn, artificial rockworks by James Pulham (*c.* 1820–98) and a conifer collection filled the rest of the grounds. Between 1905 and 1914 Pochin's grandson, Henry Duncan McLaren, 2nd Baron Aberconway (1879–1953), carved the lawn into a series of five Italianate terraces of individual character (including one with a buttressed wall and formal water-lily pool) and a canal terrace. This last terrace was provided with trelliswork and an open-air stage backed by yew hedges, and it was further supplemented in 1938 by the Pin Mill, a small industrial building of *c.* 1740, which was dismantled where it had stood at Woodchester, Glos, and re-erected at Bodnant to serve as a summerhouse at one end of the canal. Beyond the terraces (which provide panoramic views of Snowdonia), in the woodland gardens that fall towards the River Hiraethlyn's rocky gorge, the emphasis shifts from conifers to flowering trees, especially rhododendrons. For much of the 20th century Bodnant has been held up as a model for woodland gardening. In 1949 it was given to the National Trust.

BIBLIOGRAPHY
A Guide to the Gardens at Bodnant (1936)
Bodnant, NT Guidebook (London, 1975)
D. Ottewill: *The Edwardian Garden* (London, 1989), p. 57

BRENT ELLIOTT

Bodon, Alexander (*b* Vienna, 6 Sept 1906). Dutch architect of Austro-Hungarian birth. He began his training at the Magyar Iparmüvészeti Iskolában (Applied Arts School), Budapest (1924); in 1926 he became an apprentice with Jan Wils in the Netherlands, where he met Cor van Eesteren who was managing Wils's office. This experience introduced Bodon directly to the theories of De Stijl and functionalism. He returned to Budapest and produced some Constructivist designs, which were not enthusiastically received, and in 1929 he settled permanently in the Netherlands, working for various firms including Buijs and Lürsen in The Hague and Amsterdam until 1932. His first major work was the renovation and design of the Schröder and Dupont bookshop (1932) on the Keizersgracht, Amsterdam, a functionalist design based on a single, open space, incorporating colour and metal railings, which attracted much attention. During 1934–9 he was office manager for Benjamin Merkelbach and Charles Karsten (1904–79) in Amsterdam, assisting on their AVRO Radio studio building (1934–6), Hilversum. He was a member of the functionalist group Architectengroep De 8 and of CIAM (1932–56) and worked on many study groups in the 1940s and 1950s, such as the Post-war Housing Committee formed by the Dutch architects' association, as well as teaching in Amsterdam. In 1955 he joined the architectural partnership Drexhage, Sterkenburg, Bodon and Venstra. His work continued to reveal functionalist concerns for practicality and objectivity, and he became much sought-after for complex projects, many of which nevertheless manifest a refined simplicity externally. Well-known examples include the RAI exhibition and conference centre (1951–64), Amsterdam, with high-level glazing on steel space frames; the extension of the Museum Boymans–van Beuningen (1963–72), Rotterdam; and the headquarters (1974–6) of Estel NV in Nijmegen, a stepped, steel and glass composition on a cross-shaped plan, for which he won the European Steel Prize in 1979.

BIBLIOGRAPHY

L. Juhasz: *Alexander Bodon* (Budapest, 1977)
M. Kloos: *Alexander Bodon* (Rotterdam, 1990)

PIETER SINGELENBERG

Bodoni, Giambattista (*b* Saluzzo, 16 Feb 1740; *d* 29 Nov 1813). Italian typographer. He was born into a family of typographers and at the age of 18 moved to Rome, where he was introduced to Cardinal Spinelli. In 1766 Bodoni set out for England, but illness forced him to return home. He started printing and received some local commissions; then, through the offices of Cardinal Spinelli's librarian, Paolo Maria Paciaudi (1755–1829), he was employed as head of the Stamperia Reale of the dukes of Parma. His early books show the influence of the types used by Pierre-Simon Fournier. He developed a dramatic, bold style, exemplified by the *Epithalamia* (1775), which celebrates the wedding of the sister of the French king Louis XVI. His mature style achieved a stark brilliance and Neo-classical purity, and from the 1780s he worked with his brother Giuseppe Bodoni (*d* 1825) to produce his own types. Bodoni made three main innovations in type design: he gave a vertical alignment to the sloped swellings in the bowls of the letters that derive from the down strokes in handwriting; he made all the horizontal serifs on the upper and lower parts of the letters very thin and uniform; and he increased the contrast between stems and serifs. His most celebrated books include *Q. Horatii flacci opera* (Rome, 1791) and the two-volume *P. Virgilii maronis opera* (Rome, 1793), whose giant-folio format complemented his typography. Bodoni cut a total of *c.* 300 fonts of type. In 1806 he exhibited 14 of his books at the Exhibition of National Industry in Paris, where he was awarded gold medals. In 1810 he was granted a pension by Napoleon and awarded the Order of the Réunion. Notable late works include *La Gerusalemme liberata* (2 vols, Parma, 1794), the *Iliad* (3 vols, Parma, 1808) and *Fénelon* (2 parts, Parma, 1812). His major work on printing was the *Manuale tipografico* (Parma, 1788/*R* as 2 vols, 1818).

BIBLIOGRAPHY

R. Bertieri: *L'arte di Giambattista Bodoni* (Milan, 1913)
G. Giani: *Catalogo delle autentiche edizioni Bodoniane* (Milan, 1948)
J. Barr: *The Officina Bodoni* (London, 1978)
A. de Margerie: *Giambattista Bodoni: Typographe italien, 1740–1813* (Paris, 1985)

G. de Lama: *Vita del Cavaliere Giambattista Bodoni tipografo italiano: Ristampa del testo di Giuseppe de Lama a cura di Leonardo Farinelli e Corrado Mingardi* (Parma, 1989)

LAURA SUFFIELD

Bodrum. *See* HALIKARNASSOS.

Bodson, Fernand (Lucien Emile Marie) (*b* Liège, 6 June 1877; *d* Madison, OH, 4 March 1966). Belgian architect, urban planner and critic. He began his studies in architecture in 1893 at the Ecole St-Luc in Liège but quickly abandoned them in favour of training with an architectural firm. From 1901 to 1906 he trained with Eduard Cuypers in Amsterdam, where he met P. L. Kramer and was influenced by H. P. Berlage, whose urban planning manifesto *Kunst en maatschappij* (1910) he later published in French. A socialist in politics and a Rationalist in architecture, Bodson was in partnership with Antoine Pompe from 1910 to 1920, and notable projects include the Ferme–Ecole pour Enfants Anormaux (1913), Waterloo; the Maison du Peuple (1914; with Pompe; unexecuted), Liège; and the Batavia complex (1919; with Pompe and Raphaël Verwilghen), Roeselare. With Pompe he also experimented with the industrially based prefabrication of low-cost housing. In 1928 he completed eight residential blocks for old people at Homborch, Brussels, and at the end of the 1930s he retired from architectural practice. His interest in urban planning is reflected in the technical journals he founded and edited with Verwilghen: *Tekhné* (1912–13) and *Art et Technique* (1913–14; renamed *La Cité*, 1919). He was a founder-member of the Société des Urbanistes Belges in 1919. A forceful and acerbic critic of conventional turn-of-the-century architectural attitudes, Bodson was one of the first generation of Belgian modernists, for whom the solutions of the later Functionalists were to seem too extreme.

WRITINGS

Dictionnaire des termes récents, symboles et abréviations: Architecture, art de construire, génie civil (Brussels, 1948)

BIBLIOGRAPHY

M. Culot: 'Mon ami Fernand Bodson', *Bull. Inf. Mens. Archvs Archit. Mod.*, ix (1976)
M. Culot and A. Van Loo, eds: *Musée des archives d'architecture moderne: Collections* (Brussels, 1986), pp. 94–9

MAURICE CULOT

Bodt, Jean de (*b* Paris, Oct 1670; *d* Dresden, 3 Jan 1745). French architect and engineer, active in the Netherlands and Germany. He trained as a civil and military architect in Paris, although it is not known who taught him. As a Protestant he left France after the revocation of the Edict of Nantes (1685) and went to the Netherlands, where he entered the service of William III, Prince of Orange (*reg* 1672–1702). After William's accession to the throne of England he followed him there (1689) and became a captain in the artillery and engineering corps, in which capacity he was present at the Battle of the Boyne (1690); he also devoted himself to the study of civil architecture and produced a scheme for Greenwich Hospital (?1694–5; unexecuted) influenced by Libéral Bruand's plan for the Hôtel des Invalides (1671–6), Paris.

In 1699 de Bodt accepted an invitation to serve Frederick III, Elector of Brandenburg, who became Frederick I, King of Prussia, in 1701. From 1700 de Bodt was court architect in Berlin, supervising all civilian and military buildings. His patron's love of pomp provided him with many occasions for display. To commemorate the elevation of Prussia to a kingdom in 1701 he replaced a doorway (1679) at the Potsdam Stadtschloss with the Fortunaportal, a round-headed doorway two storeys high set in a powerfully rusticated wall on which he placed a belvedere; a dome capped by a finial with the figure of *Fortune* was supported by heavy piers faced with Ionic pilasters. For this invention, which shows how de Bodt could adapt his style to conform with Prussian Baroque, he was hailed as an 'héros en bâtiments'. Between 1701 and 1704 he built the Palais Podewils (now Klosterstrasse 68), the elevation of which features a niche over the main entrance framed by double pilasters and running through two storeys. In 1704 he built the Palais Schwerin (now Molkenmarkt 3), the broad central section of which, framed between plaster quoins, is crowned by a pediment enclosing an exuberant achievement of arms. Two balconies serve to distract the eye from the asymmetrically disposed entrance under one of them. De Bodt also produced a scheme for a hospital for disabled soldiers (1702; unexecuted) slightly smaller than that for Greenwich, completed Johann Arnold Nering's Arsenal (1706) in Berlin and supplied Lord Raby, the British Ambassador in Berlin, with a design for Stainborough House (1709; now Wentworth Castle), Yorkshire, which was built under the supervision of Thomas Archer, who modified it.

De Bodt's work was increasingly centred on military buildings and fortifications. After being promoted to the rank of major-general in 1715 he was appointed commander of the fortress of Wesel in 1719. He renewed the fortifications at Wesel and probably designed the Protestant church (1729; destr. World War II; exterior rest.); all that remains of the defences after destruction by war is the Berliner Tor (1718–22) of the citadel. In 1728 de Bodt entered the service of Augustus II, King of Saxony and Poland, as general director of civilian and military buildings, besides being given command of the engineering corps. Working under him at the head building office in Dresden were such important architects as Matthäus Daniel Pöppelmann, Zacharias Longuelune and Johann Christoph Knöffel. De Bodt went to Dresden as an architect with international experience; like Longuelune, he had been moulded by late 17th-century classical French architecture. Although he was mainly concerned with military tasks, he was nonetheless involved in an advisory and competitive capacity in major building projects. His classicism may be clearly detected in the central pavilion of the north front of the Japanisches Palais (1730), where four pairs of coupled columns standing on a rusticated ground floor as a base run through a *piano nobile* and a mezzanine floor to support an entablature and pediment. Of the alterations and extensions carried out at Schloss Moritzburg between 1723 and 1736, the new main staircases are his work. He also built the barracks (1732–6; destr. 1891) in Dresdner Neustadt and the well house (1735–6) at Königstein Fortress. Throughout his career de Bodt represented the structurally severe French aspects of Baroque architecture. This classicizing stance effectively countered the influence of the south German type of Baroque and prepared the way for the early breakthrough of classicism in Dresden. While his building regulations did not make much of an impact on domestic architecture, his influence on the architectural history of court Baroque in Saxony was significant, although his status declined after the accession of Augustus III in 1733.

BIBLIOGRAPHY

LK; Thieme–Becker
P. Du Colombier: *L'Architecture française en Allemagne au XVIIIe siècle* (Paris, 1956)
J. Harris: 'Bodt and Stainborough', *Archit. Rev.* [London], cxxx (July 1961), pp. 34–5
N. Pevsner: 'John Bodt in England', *Archit. Rev.* [London], cxxx (July 1961), pp. 29–34
F. Löffler: *Das alte Dresden* (Leipzig, 1981), p. 462
K. L. Thiel: *Staatsbauentwürfe J. de Bodts für Friedrich I* (diss., U. Cologne, 1985)

VOLKER HELAS

Body art. *See* PERFORMANCE ART.

Bodycolour. *See* GOUACHE.

Boeblinger. *See* BÖBLINGER.

Boeckel, Pieter van. *See* BOUCLE, PIERRE.

Boeckhorst, Jan (van) [Bockhorst, Johann; Lange Jan] (*b* Münster or Rees, *c.* 1604; *d* Antwerp, 21 April 1668). Flemish painter and draughtsman of German birth. Around 1626 he moved to Antwerp. According to de Bie and Filips Rubens (*Vita Petri Pauli Rubenii*, 1676), he became a pupil or assistant of Jacob Jordaens and Peter Paul Rubens; the style of his work bears this out. A document of 1655 reveals that Boeckhorst painted a 'Silenus', which was subsequently retouched by Rubens and which must have been made under his supervision (i.e. Rubens's typical workshop practice). Boeckhorst must have had a good relationship with Rubens during the 1630s, as he was one of those who contributed to the large series of paintings Rubens was then working on for the decorations of the *Pompa Introitus Ferdinandi* (1635; destr., see Martin, p. 134) and for the Torre de la Parada (1637–8; see Alpers, p. 218). Between 1635 and 1637 he toured Italy, and in 1639 he returned there especially to visit Rome. As an independent painter he also executed a number of commissions in the 1630s, such as the 26 scenes, mostly biblical, for the Falcon Monastery in Antwerp, commissioned by a merchant named Gaspar Roomer.

Early in his career Boeckhorst often added staffage to the paintings of others. In the 1630s, for instance, he collaborated with Frans Snyders, as in *The Pantry* (Dumfries House, Strathclyde, Lord Bute priv. col., see 1990 exh. cat., fig. 42) and *Peasants on their Way to Market* (Antwerp, Rubenshuis, see 1990 exh. cat., pl. 34); Snyders in turn added still-life elements to some of Boeckhorst's works. Boeckhorst also assisted Jan Wildens, and after Rubens's death he finished and touched up some of his master's paintings. Most of Boeckhorst's recorded commissions date from after *c.* 1650, the majority for churches and monasteries outside Antwerp. During this period he also made altarpieces for churches in Münster (e.g. *Crucifixion*, 1664; Münster, St Mauritz) and executed several history paintings with Old Testament and mythological subjects for private individuals and art dealers in Antwerp, as well as tapestry designs with mythological themes and drawings for the Plantin–Moretus publishing firm.

Boeckhorst's extant oeuvre can be divided into two periods: until *c.* 1650 his figure types and compositions closely follow the late work of Rubens and are characterized by a compact structure and rather solid style, as in *Calvary* (*c.* 1639–44; Lo, St Pieterskerk), based directly on Rubens's version of that subject (*c.* 1635; Toulouse, Mus. Augustins). A number of his monumental group portraits, such as *Portrait of a Family* (Munich, Alte Pin.), follow the tradition established *c.* 1620 by Cornelis de Vos. Unlike de Vos's rather static, descriptive style, Boeckhorst's impressions of his sitters are lively and spontaneous, qualities that characterized his oeuvre from the outset. The most striking elements are the agitated rendering of the drapery, with broken and angular lines, unmistakably related to the style of Jordaens, and subtly varied transparent grey shadows, which add a sense of melancholy to the faces. These elements are also present in Boeckhorst's works painted after 1650. The numerous altarpieces, including the *Adoration of the Magi* (*c.* 1655–8; Bruges, St Jacobskerk), *David's Vision* (*c.* 1655; Ghent, St Michielskerk) and the *Martyrdom of St James* (1659; Ghent, St Jacobskerk; see fig.), express the post-Tridentine triumphalism in a theatrical, typically Baroque way. Equally dramatic in conception are the history paintings, usually in wide format, such as *Mercury and Herse* (before 1659;

Vienna, Ksthist. Mus.). Boeckhorst's later style is characterized by a sense of pathos, particularly noticeable in the highly emotive and turbulent compositional scheme, the rather weak interplay of facial expression and gestures, freer brushwork and a bright Venetian tonality. The influence of Anthony van Dyck in the figure types and dramatic structure is an important feature.

A number of drawings by Boeckhorst are also known, mainly of subjects found in his larger compositions. Apart from painted modellos on panel or on canvas, he also used coloured drawings for the same purpose, a practice that he probably borrowed from Jordaens. It is possible that through Jordaens too he learnt to make large-format tapestry cartoons, such as the series of four cartoons illustrating the *History of Aeneas* (Cardiff, N. Mus.; also attributed by some scholars to Rubens).

BIBLIOGRAPHY
C. de Bie: *Het gulden cabinet* (1661), p. 254
J. S. Held: 'Jan van Boeckhorst as Draughtsman', *Bull. Mus. Royaux B.-A. Belgique*, xvi (1967), pp. 137–54
S. Alpers: *The Decoration of the Torre de la Parada* (1971), ix of *Corpus Rubenianum Ludwig Burchard* (Brussels, London and New York, 1968–)
J. R. Martin: *The Decorations for the Pompa Introitus Ferdinandi* (1972), xvi of *Corpus Rubenianum Ludwig Burchard* (Brussels, London and New York, 1968–)
M.-L. Hairs: *Dans le sillage de Rubens: Les Peintres d'histoire anversois au XVIIe siècle* (Liège, 1977), pp. 63–98
H. Lahrkamp: 'Der "Lange Jan": Leben und Werk des Barockmalers Johann Bockhorst aus Münster', *Westfalen: Hft. Gesch., Kst & Vlkesknd.*, lx (1982), pp. 3–184
J. Held: 'Case against the Cardiff Rubens Cartoons', *Burl. Mag.*, cxxv (1983), pp. 132–6
M. Jaffé: 'Rubens's Aeneas Cartoons at Cardiff', *Burl. Mag.*, cxxv (1983), pp. 114–23
H. Vlieghe: 'The Identity of the Painter of the Cardiff Cartoons: A Proposal', *Burl. Mag.*, cxxv (1983), pp. 350–53
J. S. Held: 'Nachträge zum Werk des Johann Bockhorst (alias Jan Boeckhorst)', *Westfalen: Hft. Gesch., Kst & Vlkesknd.*, lxiii (1985), pp. 14–37
'Beiträge zum internationalen Colloquium "Jan Boeckhorst—Maler der Rubenszeit" im Westfälischen Landesmuseum Münster, November 1990', *Westfalen: Hft. Gesch., Kst & Vlkesknd.*, lxviii (1990), pp. 127–83
Jan Boeckhorst (exh. cat., Antwerp, Rubenshuis and Münster, Westfäl. Landesmus., 1990)

HANS VLIEGHE

Jan Boeckhorst: *Martyrdom of St James*, oil on canvas, *c.* 5.0×3.0 m, 1659 (Ghent, St Jacobskerk)

Boeckl, Herbert (*b* Klagenfurt, 3 June 1894; *d* Vienna, 20 Jan 1966). Austrian painter. After an initial period of study at the Technische Hochschule in Vienna, he turned, self-taught, to painting in 1914. He served during World War I, subsequently studying in Berlin (1921–2) and Paris (1923), and coming into contact with the classicism of the *rappel à l'ordre* and Cubism. Between 1935 and 1939 he was professor of the general painting school of the Akademie der Bildenden Künste in Vienna, running the evening life-drawing classes there, before becoming principal.

Boeckl's works are distinguished by their spontaneous, broad brushstrokes, strong internal structure and dominant colour. Figures and objects are often placed close to the viewer by the barely connected background, so that the material structure of skin, hair and clothing is experienced almost tangibly (e.g. *Anatomy*, 1931; Vienna, Hist. Mus.). Influenced by Cézanne, he generally used a formal reduction over geometrical background shapes, giving the paint a rather flat effect, particularly in his landscape paintings. Boeckl's portraits are especially interesting, showing an extreme delicacy and sensitivity, despite concise forms and a powerfully expressive choice of colours, for example *Self-portrait* (1948; Paris, Pompidou). The works after 1945 show the influence of new Austrian analysis of abstraction. As well as oil paintings, Boeckl made a series of mostly abstract watercolours, along with large murals, such as the decoration of the Engelskapelle in Seckau (1952–60; *in situ*; e.g. *Apocalyptic Vision*; *see* AUSTRIA, fig. 18).

BIBLIOGRAPHY
O. Benesch and others: *Herbert Boeckl* (Vienna, 1947)
C. Pack: *Der Maler Herbert Boeckl* (Vienna and Munich, 1964)
G. Frodl: *Herbert Boeckl* (Salzburg, 1976)
Herbert Boeckl, 1894–1966: Gemälde (exh. cat., Graz, Neue Gal., 1979)
ULRIKE GAISBAUER

Boeckstuyns, Jan-Frans [Jean-François] (*b* Mechelen, *c*. 1650; *d* Mechelen, 1734). Flemish sculptor and architect. He was a pupil of Lucas Faydherbe, from whom he absorbed the influence of Rubens. Boeckstuyns became a master in the Mechelen Guild of St Luke in 1680 but may have continued to collaborate with Faydherbe. Among his commissions for Mechelen churches are three wooden confessionals with allegorical figures (1690) and the wooden gable (1712) for Faydherbe's earlier high altar for the basilica of Onze-Lieve-Vrouw van Hanswijk and numerous works for the Begijnhof Church, including the north interior portal (*c*. 1700), the communion rails (1710) and the wooden confessionals (also attributed to Faydherbe). In 1690 he collaborated with the Mechelen sculptors Frans Langhemans and Adam Frans van der Meulen on the wooden high altar of Onze-Lieve-Vrouw-over-de-Dyle. Boeckstuyns was perhaps responsible for the wooden pulpit in St Rombouts (also attributed to Michiel van der Voort I) as well as the wooden tabernacle for the altar of the Holy Sacrament (1704). In 1723 he made a wooden pulpit with an image of St Norbert for the former chapel at Leliendael (now Mechelen, St Rombouts). Boeckstuyns produced a number of small-scale works, including a palmwood crucifix (Mechelen, Stadsmus. Hof van Busleyden), the fine carving and dramatic presentation of which can be compared with Faydherbe's ivory works, and a signed terracotta *Cupid* (Mechelen, Stadsmus. Hof van Busleyden). Boeckstuyns's plans (1728; destr.) for the gable with a figure of St Sebastian for the headquarters of the Mechelen archers' guild reveal his skills as an architect. His most important pupil was Theodoor Verhaegen.

BIBLIOGRAPHY
I. Leyssens: 'De predikstoelen uit de Sint-Romboutskerk' [The pulpit from the church of St Rombouts], *Hand. Kon. Kring Oudhdknd., Lett. & Kst Mechelen/Bull. Cerc. Archéol., Litt. & A. Malines*, liii (1949), pp. 74–88
G. Derveaux-van Ussel: 'Jan-Frans Boeckstuyns', *De beeldhouwkunst in de eeuw van Rubens* [Sculpture in the century of Rubens] (Brussels, 1977), p. 33
CYNTHIA LAWRENCE

Boehm, Joseph Edgar (*b* Vienna, 4 July 1834; *d* London, 12 Dec 1890). English sculptor and medallist of Austrian birth. He was the youngest son of Joseph Daniel Boehm (1794–1865), court medallist and director of the Imperial Mint at Vienna; Joseph Daniel formed a major art collection, which he used as a basis for teaching such protégés

as Victor Tilgner and Anton Scharff (1845–1903) as well as his son. From 1848 to 1851 Joseph Edgar attended Leigh's art academy (later Heatherley's) in London and drew the Parthenon marbles in the British Museum. On his return to Vienna he enrolled at the Akademie der Bildenden Künste, where he won first prize at the Modellierschule in 1855. By 1858 he had forsaken medal design for sculpture and exhibited statuettes at the Österreichischer Kunstverein. Around 1858–9 he visited Italy, where he developed a lasting admiration for early Renaissance sculpture. From 1859 to 1862 he worked in Paris and was influenced by the work of Paul Gayrard (1807–55).

Boehm settled in London in 1862, when he made his Royal Academy début, and befriended John Leech and John Everett Millais, both of whom he portrayed in statuettes in 1863 (plaster, R. Dimsdale priv. col.; bronze, ex-Sir Ralph Millais priv. col.; plaster, London, N.P.G.). A statuette of *William Makepeace Thackeray* (1864; London, N.P.G.) led to an edition of 70 plaster casts. Thackeray is shown with his hands in his pockets and bespectacled. The inelegant pose and modern costume immediately distinguish Boehm's realism from the Neoclassical mainstream. Other early works include the bronze statuette of the racehorse *Johnny Armstrong* (1863; Newmarket, N. Horseracing Mus.), which shows the influence of Pierre-Jules Mène, and the bust of *Adeline, Countess of Cardigan* (1869; Deene Park, Northants), which shows that of Jean-Antoine Houdon. Boehm frequently worked in terracotta, a material common in French sculpture but less familiar in English. It suited his sketchy spontaneity.

Queen Victoria's admiration of Boehm's statuettes led to an association with the royal family that lasted from 1869 until his death. He received over 40 royal commissions, took on Princess Louise (1848–1939), the Queen's daughter, as a pupil, was appointed Sculptor-in-Ordinary in 1880 and was created a baronet in 1889. Royal favour was, however, a mixed blessing; it made other sculptors jealous, and sometimes the work involved was artistically futile—such as the life-size marble statue of the Queen's collie, *Noble* (1884; Osborne House, Isle of Wight, Royal Col.).

Most of Boehm's works are portrait busts. He effectively cornered the market of the famous and the fashionable: his sitters included John Ruskin, W. E. Gladstone, Herbert Spencer and Franz Liszt. His masterpiece is a life-size statue of *Thomas Carlyle* (plaster, 1875, destr. 1940; bronze, 1882, London, Chelsea Embankment Gardens). It combines realism with intelligent use of precedent (Houdon's *Voltaire*; Paris, Comédie Française) and his personal admiration for the sitter. Other works that approach the *Carlyle* in quality include the classicizing statue of *Louisa Stuart, Marchioness of Waterford* (1875–6; Christchurch, Dorset, Druitt Lib.) and the monument to *Arthur Penrhyn Stanley* (1882–4; London, Westminster Abbey). Two late works were prominent failures, the Jubilee Coinage effigy of Queen Victoria (1879–87) and the equestrian monument to *Arthur Wellesley, 1st Duke of Wellington* (1884–8; London, Hyde Park Corner). The effigy, with its small crown in danger of slipping from the

Queen's head, met with public derision. Its long history reveals Boehm's constant dithering over details of design. In the *Wellington*, the central group fails to cohere with the corner figures, attached as an afterthought. More successful was the *Cupid and Mermaid* (1889–91; Woburn Abbey, Beds), which shows the influence of the NEW SCULPTURE. However, Boehm neither received sufficient commissions for ideal sculpture nor had enough artistic courage to execute many such works.

Boehm was immensely prolific: some 360 different works are documented, a huge total even allowing for the part played by Boehm's talented studio assistants, who included Alfred Gilbert (for whom he secured the commission for the Shaftesbury memorial, 1886–93; London, Piccadilly Circus), Alfred Drury, Edouard Lanteri, John Willis Good (*d* 1879) and Robert Glassby (*d* 1892). Boehm was a highly consistent sculptor, rarely deviating from his brand of realism. He was modest about his immense popularity and aware of his imaginative shortcomings.

BIBLIOGRAPHY
W. Meynell: 'Our Living Artists: Joseph Edgar Boehm, A.R.A.', *Mag. A.*, iii (1880), pp. 333–8
B. Read: *Victorian Sculpture* (London and New Haven, 1982), pp. 194–5, 296–8, 335–7
G. P. Dyer and M. Stocker: 'Edgar Boehm and the Jubilee Coinage', *Brit. Numi. J.*, 54 (1984), pp. 274–88
M. Stocker: 'Joseph Edgar Boehm and Thomas Carlyle', *Carlyle Newslett.*, 6 (1985), pp. 11–22
——: *Royalist and Realist: The Life and Work of Sir Joseph Edgar Boehm* (New York and London, 1988)
——: 'The Church Monuments of Joseph Edgar Boehm', *Ch. Mnmts*, 2 (1988), pp. 61–75
MARK STOCKER

Boeken, Albert (*b* Amsterdam, 1 Feb 1891; *d* Amsterdam, 5 May 1951). Dutch architect and writer. He studied civil engineering at the Technische Hogeschool, Delft, graduating in 1916. For a period he was editor of the architectural periodical *Bouwkundig Weekblad*, his articles revealing an admiration for Le Corbusier and Ernst May, particularly the latter's efficient manner of working. He left the journal in 1924 because of its insufficient coverage of Functionalism. Between 1919 and 1926 he worked for the Department of Public Works in Amsterdam, mainly in the idiom of the AMSTERDAM SCHOOL, for example a telephone exchange (1923) in East Amsterdam. His later projects, for example the houses (1927–8) in Aalsmeerderstraat and Sassenheimstraat, Amsterdam, are simpler, more rigid and make more use of glass. In 1928 Boeken joined the Amsterdam Functionalists of ARCHITECTENGROEP DE 8, but he left before 1931. As a member of the main Dutch architectural society, Architectura et Amicitia, he supported Arthur Staal, who tried to push the society in the direction of Functionalism. In 1932 this led to the founding of Groep 32, an independent movement within Architectura et Amicitia that included Staal, Boeken and Harry Elte. From the start there was a certain amount of contact between Groep 32 and Architectengroep de 8, and in 1934 they merged. Boeken remained with Groep 32 when it split from de 8 in 1938, and he helped publicize its approach, namely a modified Functionalism with more emphasis on form than technique. His most important work is generally thought to be the Apollo Hall (1934–5)

on the corner of the Apollolaan and the Stadionweg, Amsterdam.

WRITINGS
'Drie Renaissance gebouwen in het noorden' [Three Renaissance buildings in the north], *Onze Kst*, i (1912), p. 21
'Over den architect Le Corbusier', *Bouwknd. Wkbld*, xlviii (1927), p. 243
Architectuur (Amsterdam, 1936)
with W. M. Dudok and J. de Meyer: *Bouwen en restaureren in Oud Amsterdam* (Amsterdam, 1940)

BIBLIOGRAPHY
G. Fanelli: *Architettura moderna* (1968)
B. Rebel: *Het nieuwe bouwen* (Utrecht, 1980)
DIANNE TIMMERMAN, FRANK VAN DEN HOEK

Boel [Bol], **Cornelis** (*b* Antwerp, *c.* 1576 or 1580; *d c.* 1621). Flemish draughtsman and engraver. He may have been a pupil of Jan Sadeler (i), whose genre he adopted. In Antwerp he engraved plates for works by Otto van Veen, including *Amorum emblemata* (1608) and *Vitae D. Thomae Aquinatis* (1610). A visit to England is deduced from his signature on the frontispiece of a Bible: *C. Boel fecit in Richmont, 1611*. In Flanders he produced portraits of kings and important persons, dated up to 1614. Boel was one of the first generation of Flemish engravers who established themselves in Spain in the first decades of the 17th century. He engraved the title-pages of the *Discursos consolatorios . . .* (Madrid, 1616) by Francisco Márquez Torres and the *Hechos de D. García Hurtado de Mendoza* (Madrid, 1616) by Cristóbal Suárez de Figueroa. The latter contains a fine portrait of its subject, the structure of which, in the form of a triumphal arch, was widely imitated in Madrid.

BIBLIOGRAPHY
Bénézit; Thieme–Becker
J. Ainaud Lasarte: *Grabado*, A. Hisp., xviii (Madrid, 1962), p. 276
A. Gallego: *Historia del grabado en España* (Madrid, 1979), p. 149
E. Paez Rios: *Repertorio*, i (Madrid, 1981), p. 148
J. Carrete, F. Checa and V. Bozal: *El grabado en España (siglos XV al XVIII)*, Summa A., xxxi (Madrid, 1987), pp. 252, 255, 308
BLANCA GARCÍA VEGA

Boel, Pieter (*b* Antwerp, *bapt* 22 Oct 1622; *d* Paris, 3 Sept 1674). Flemish painter, draughtsman and etcher. He came from an artistic family: his father Jan Boel (1592–1640), was an engraver, publisher and art dealer; his uncle Quirin Boel I was an engraver; and his brother Quirin Boel II (1620–40) was also a printmaker. Pieter was probably apprenticed in Antwerp to Jan Fyt, but may have studied previously with Frans Snyders. He then went to Italy, probably visiting Rome and Genoa, where he is supposed to have stayed with Cornelis de Wael. None of Boel's work from this period is known. In 1650 he became a master in the Antwerp Guild of St Luke (having given his first name as Jan, not Pieter). His marriage to Maria Blanckaert took place at about the same time. Boel dated only a few of his paintings, making it difficult to establish a chronology. He is best known for his hunting scenes, some of which clearly show his debt to Snyders, but the dominant influence on his work was that of Fyt, particularly evident in his emphatic brushwork. However, Boel was more restrained both in his treatment and in his handling of outline. He also borrowed the theme of open-air hunting still-lifes (e.g. *Feathered Game with Three Dogs*; Madrid, Prado) from Fyt, but he painted other subjects as

Pieter Boel: *Study of a Bird and Raccoon*, black and coloured chalk on beige paper, *c*. 290×435 mm, late 1668 or after (Paris, Musée du Louvre)

well, such as the monumental *Vanitas Still-life* (e.g. 1633; Lille, Mus. B.-A.). Certain compositional schemes, such as caravans of animals, enriched with still-life elements (e.g. Kassel, Gemäldegal.), were apparently adapted from the Genoese painter Castiglione, and a number of works by Boel are still attributed to Castiglione (see de Mirimonde). Boel occasionally collaborated with others, for example Erasmus Quellinus (ii), Pieter Thijs, Jacob Jordaens, Abraham van Diepenbeeck and Gaspar de Crayer.

Boel is mentioned in Antwerp in 1663 and on 13 October 1668. Shortly thereafter he must have moved to Paris, where he became Peintre Ordinaire to Louis XIV and produced tapestry designs for the Gobelins. (He had already worked on tapestry cartoons in Antwerp.) In Paris, he made studies of the animals in the royal menagerie, intended for use in the tapestry series of the *Months, or Royal Buildings*, for which Charles Le Brun was in charge of the designs. The first payment to Boel is dated 4 October. He was mentioned in Paris once again in 1671. Many of Boel's animal studies for the Gobelins have been preserved; there are some 260 drawings in the Louvre, Paris, and an extensive series of oil sketches scattered throughout 24 French museums (see Brejon de Lavergnée). The rediscovery of this material necessitated a revision of the established view of the artist; originally seen as no more than a lesser follower of Fyt, he must now be considered one of the great animal painters of his time, who was remarkably successful in capturing the characteristic postures of animals and evoking the texture of fur and feathers (see fig.). He had a considerable influence on such French animal painters of the 18th century as François Desportes and Jean-Baptiste Oudry.

Boel published a number of original etchings, including several of the Gobelins animal studies.

Boel's eldest son Jan Baptist Boel (*d* 1689) became a painter; the few documented or signed works by him show that he completely assimilated his father's style, which has sometimes led to attribution problems (see Greindl). Boel's second son Balthazar Lucas Boel (1651–1702/3) was also a painter, but none of his work is known. The only one of Boel's students to have achieved any reputation was David de Coninck (1638–99).

BIBLIOGRAPHY

Hollstein: *Dut. & Flem.*; Thieme–Becker; Wurzbach
T. Van Lerius: *Biographies d'artistes anversois*, 2 vols (Antwerp, 1880–81), i, pp. 107–21 [still the basic biog.]
F. Lugt: *Inventaire général des dessins des écoles du Nord: Ecole flamande*, Paris, Louvre cat. (Paris, 1949), i, pp. 3–6, nos 17–228; suppl. by E. Starcky (Paris, 1988), pp. 107–24, nos 123–67
E. Greindl: *Les Peintres flamands de nature morte au XVIIe siècle* (Brussels, 1956, rev. 1983), pp. 112–6, 147, 339–40
A. P. de Mirimonde: 'Les Natures mortes à instruments de musique de Peter Boel', *Jb.: Kon. Mus. S. Kst.* (1964), pp. 107–43
M. Díaz Padrón: *Catálogo de pinturas, I: Escuela flamenca siglo XVII*, Madrid, Prado cat., 2 vols (Madrid, 1975), pp. 27–30, pls 15–7 [best col. of his still-lifes, unfortunately not exh.]
M. Jarry: 'A propos de la tenture des Maisons Royales: Peter Boel, peintre d'animaux', *Bull. Liaison Cent. Int. Etud. Textiles Anc.*, xlv/1 (1977), pp. 19–24
F. Robinson: *Netherlandish Artists* (1979), 5 [iv] of *The Illustrated Bartsch*, ed. W. L. Strauss (New York, 1978–), pp. 190–96
A. Brejon de Lavergnée, J. Foucart and N. Reynaud: *Catalogue sommaire illustré des peintures du Musée du Louvre, I: Ecoles flamande et hollandaise* (Paris, 1979), pp. 27–9
S. A. Sullivan: *The Dutch Gamepiece* (Totowa and Montclair, NJ, 1984), pp. 21–2
J. P. De Bruyn: 'De samenweking van Peter Boel en Erasmus II Quellinus' [The collaboration of Peter Boel and Erasmus Quellinus II], *Jb.: Kon. Mus. S. Kst.* (1985), pp. 277–87
H. Robels: *Frans Snyders: Stilleben- und Tiermaler (1579–1657)* (Munich, 1989)
M. Pinault: *Le Peintre et l'histoire naturelle* (Paris, 1990), pp. 165–7, 170, 275
The Age of Rubens (exh. cat., ed. P. C. Sutton; Boston, MA, Mus. F.A.; Toledo, OH, Mus. A.; 1993–4), pp. 572–5

ARNOUT BALIS

Boeswillwald, Emile (*b* Strasbourg, 2 March 1815; *d* Paris, 20 March 1896). French architect and restorer. After training as a mason, he visited Munich in 1836 and then studied architecture at the Ecole des Beaux-Arts, Paris, in the studio of Henri Labrouste. He soon joined the group of Gothic Revival architects that formed around Jean-Baptiste-Antoine Lassus and Eugène-Emanuel Viollet-le-Duc, and from 1843 he worked for the Commission des Monuments Historiques, with which he spent a large part of his career. He built very little, apart from the church of Ste Eugénie at Biarritz, but restored a large number of buildings, including the cathedrals of Toul and Laon (*see* LAON, §1(i)) and the churches at Montiérender, Avioth (Notre-Dame), Chaumont (St Jean-Baptiste) and Guebwiller (St Léger). Boeswillwald began his career in the administration of diocesan buildings as Inspecteur (1845) at Notre-Dame, Paris, with Lassus and Viollet-le-Duc. He was successively appointed diocesan architect to Luçon (1846), Bayonne (1852), Soissons and Orléans (both 1855). In 1857, when Lassus died, Boeswillwald took over the restoration of the Sainte-Chapelle, which he completed, and became diocesan architect of Chartres and Le Mans. He also worked on the Ducal Palace (from 1871) at Nancy and the château of Coucy-le-Château. In 1860 he was appointed Inspecteur Générale des Monuments Historiques and a member of the Commission des Monuments Historiques.

BIBLIOGRAPHY

R. Echt: *Emile Boeswillwald als Denkmalpfleger: Untersuchungen zu Problemen und Methoden der französischen Denkmalpflege im 19. Jahrhundert* (Bonn, 1984)

JEAN-MICHEL LENIAUD

Boethos of Chalkedon (*fl* ?2nd century BC). Greek sculptor and metalworker. His signature occurs on a bronze archaistic herm (Tunis, Mus. N. Bardo) from the Mahdia shipwreck that supported a statue of a winged youth identified as Eros or as Agon, the personification of athletic contests. Though the lettering of the inscription suits a date in the 3rd century BC, the eclectic classicizing features of the youth and the one-sidedness of the group favour a century later, when 'Boethos of Chalkedon' signed the bases of a portrait of *Antiochos IV* (reg 175–164 BC) on Delos and a portrait at Lindos (*c.* 184 BC; see Marcadé, p. 28). This Boethos was probably also the famous engraver mentioned by Pliny (*Natural History* XXXIII.lv.155) and Cicero (*Against Verres* IV.xiv.32), and the sculptor of a bronze group of a *Boy Strangling a Goose* (Pliny: *Natural History* XXXIV.xix.84). This work is probably reproduced by various Roman copies (e.g. Rome, Mus. Capitolino; *c.* 150 BC), since their light-hearted mood and realistic depiction of soft youthful forms typifies the 'rococo' style of some later Hellenistic sculpture. True, their pyramidal arrangement may have been a feature of a 3rd-century BC composition referred to by Herondas (*Mimes* iv.31), but three-dimensional groups persisted into the 2nd century BC. This sculptor may also have been the Boethos of 'Charkedon' responsible for a gilded image of a youth at Olympia (Pausanias: *Guide to Greece* V.xvii.4), though the latter was perhaps Boethos Charkedonios, son of Apollodoros, whose signature has been found at Ephesos and who may have sculpted another group, perhaps of the 2nd century BC, showing a *Boy with a Goose*, which is reproduced by a Roman copy from Ephesos (Vienna, Ksthist. Mus.). Finally, at least two other sculptors called Boethos are mentioned in ancient sources, though without details of their origins.

BIBLIOGRAPHY

J. Overbeck: *Die antiken Schriftquellen zur Geschichte der bildenden Künste bei den Griechen* (Leipzig, 1868), nos 1596–9, 2167, 2184

A. Rumpf: 'Boethoi', *Jhft. Österreich. Archäolog. Inst. Wien*, xxxix (1952), pp. 86–9

J. Marcadé: *Recueil des signatures de sculpteurs grecs*, ii (Paris, 1957), pp. 28–36

W. Fuchs: *Der Schiffsfund von Mahdia* (Tübingen, 1963), pp. 12–14

J. J. Pollitt: *Art in the Hellenistic Age* (Cambridge, 1968), pp. 128, 140–41

MARK D. FULLERTON

Boetti, Alighiero (*b* Turin, 16 Dec 1940; *d* Rome, April 1994). Italian conceptual artist and writer. According to his own mythologized account, his fascination with the qualities of ordinary materials began during childhood. Although the extent of any orthodox artistic training remains unrecorded, by 1964 he was making objects and silhouette paintings of familiar items, influenced by such Turinese contemporaries as Michelangelo Pistoletto and Mario Merz. His first one-man show (1967; Turin, Gal.

Stein) included large objects made from materials such as corrugated cardboard, whose very ordinariness undermined orthodox notions of art. From the outset he participated in ARTE POVERA exhibitions and Happenings, in which a generation of Italian conceptual artists reinvented a world then in political turmoil. Boetti's self-reflexive brand of Arte Povera was typified by his notional 'twinning': by cutting a second image of himself into a photographic self-portrait (*Twins*, 1968; see 1986–7 exh. cat., p. 19) and by inserting 'e' ('and') between his names, stimulating a dialectic exchange between these two selves. Boetti's major project of the 1970s was *The 1000 Longest Rivers of the World*. He published the randomly poetic results in a catalogue and inscribed them on a related canvas (1970–77; see Boetti, 1978, p. 41). Several other alphabetical or sequential pieces explored esoteric signs and language as classifier. International travels broadened his vision, reflected in *Map* (1971; see Boetti, 1978, p. 37), with countries filled with their flags, and in the group of brightly coloured tapestry squares, each containing a letter, made by traditional means in Afghanistan. The random massing of the 100 versions of *ORDINE DISORDINE* (each 175×175 mm, 1973; artist's col.) was most effective in summarizing a world vision of polarities. During the 1980s the chaos of mass culture was suggested in larger tapestries crammed with heterogeneous details.

WRITINGS

Manifesto (Turin, 1968)
The 1000 Longest Rivers of the World (Milan, 1978)

BIBLIOGRAPHY

Alighiero e Boetti (exh. cat. by A. Boatto, Milan, Padiglione A. Contemp., 1983)

Alighiero & Boetti (exh. cat. by T. Trini, Genoa, Gal. Chisel, 1983) [It. and Eng. text]

Alighiero e Boetti (exh. cat. by G. B. Salerno and F. Kaiser, Villeurbanne, Nouv. Mus.; Nice, Villa Arson; Eindhoven, Stedel. Van Abbemus.; 1986–7)

MATTHEW GALE

Boeyermans, Theodor [Theodore] (*b* Antwerp, *bapt* 10 Nov 1620; *d* Antwerp, Jan 1678). Flemish painter. In 1634 his mother was granted a free passage to Holland and moved to Eindhoven, presumably with the 14-year-old Theodor. In April 1640 he was granted permission in Antwerp for another visit north, where he probably finished his studies. From the autumn of 1648 he was back in Antwerp permanently, living in De Gulden Pers (The Golden Press), the house where he was born. He remained a bachelor and at the relatively late age of 34 became an apprentice and joined the Guild of St Luke. He was also a member of the Sodaliteit der Bejaarde Jongmans (Society of Bachelors) and, from 1664, the rhetoricians' chamber known as De Olijftak (The Olive Branch).

Boeyermans's work is generally compared with that of Rubens and van Dyck, and undoubtedly he was influenced by them, although his pictures are on the whole more sombre in colour. He portrayed both artists in the allegory of *Antwerp as Foster Mother of the Arts* (Antwerp, Kon. Mus. S. Kst.). In 1665 he presented this work to the members of the Guild of St Luke for the ceiling of their new *schilderskamer*, or academy, in the Beurs; it was hung with works by Jacob Jordaens (Antwerp, Kon. Mus. S. Kst.), which together formed a *Homage to the Poet*. Boeyermans was rewarded with a silver-gilt head and a laudatory poem. He also painted the figures in Theodor van Delen's *Allegory of Painting and Poetry* (Antwerp, Kon. Mus. S. Kst.), which was also presented to the Guild. Boeyermans's religious works include two painted for the St Jacobuskerk in Antwerp: the *Ascension* (untraced) and the *Assumption of the Virgin* (1671; *in situ*). Marcus Forchoudt, son of the art dealer Guillaume Forchoudt, was Boeyermans's pupil in 1670. A letter dated September 1677 suggests that they maintained contact even after Marcus had gone to Vienna as an art dealer. Of the paintings attributed to Boeyermans, 33 are either signed or are firmly documented; 20 of these are also dated (1660–77). His last known work, the *Kalydonian Boar Hunt* (1677; ex-art market, Brussels; see Coekelberghs and Vautier, figs 31–4), is based on and somewhat imitative of Rubens's *Boar Hunt* (*c.* 1620; Vienna, Ksthist. Mus.), though it is simpler. In Boeyermans's version, the technique is free and swift.

BIBLIOGRAPHY
Thieme–Becker
P. Rombouts and T. van Lerius: *De liggeren en andere historische archieven der Antwerpsche Sint Lucasgilde*, ii (Antwerp and The Hague, 1872), pp. 248, 249, 253
M. Rooses: *Geschiedenis der Antwerpsche schilderschool* (Antwerp and The Hague, 1879), pp. 217, 511–13, 592, 659, 661
F. J. Van den Branden: *Geschiedenis der Antwerpsche schilderschool* (Antwerp, 1883), pp. 927–31
F. Donnet: *Het jonstich versaem der Violieren: Geschiedenis der Rederijkkamer de Olijftak sedert 1480* (Antwerp, 1907), pp. 324–7, 339–40, 347
J. Denucé: *Kunstuitvoer in de 17e eeuw te Antwerpen: De firma Forchoudt* (Antwerp and Amsterdam, 1931), pp. 112, 189, 201–2
L. Van Puyvelde: 'La *Décollation de Saint Paul* d'Aix-en-Provence, non de Rubens mais de Boeyermans', *Rev. Belge Archéol. & Hist. A.*, xxvii (1958), pp. 29–37
L. Van Puyvelde and D. Van Puyvelde: *De Vlaamse schilderkunst ten tijde van Rubens* (Hasselt, 1970), pp. 170–71
M. L. Hairs: *Dans le sillage de Rubens: Les Peintres d'histoire anversois au XVIIe siècle* (Liège, 1977), pp. 251–63, figs 71–6
D. Coekelberghs and D. Vautier: '*The Hunt of the Calydonian Boar* (1677): A Rediscovered Work by Theodore Boeyermans', *Burl. Mag.*, cxxiv (1982), pp. 755–7

TRUDY VAN ZADELHOFF

Boffrand, Germain (*b* Nantes, 16 May 1667; *d* Paris, 19 March 1754). French architect and writer. He maintained the tradition of the Grand Style in France between Jules Hardouin Mansart, who was born in 1646, and Ange-Jacques Gabriel, who died in 1782. His work also provided an important bridge between that of Louis Le Vau in the mid-17th century and those of the architects of the Piranesian generation of Neo-classicists in the mid-18th century, such as Etienne-Louis Boullée, whom he influenced.

1. BEFORE 1720. His father, Jean Boffrand, was a minor architect and sculptor. Germain Boffrand came to Paris at the age of fourteen to study sculpture, working for three years in the studio of François Girardon. From 1685 he worked as a draughtsman in the Bâtiments du Roi under Jules Hardouin Mansart. Through his uncle, the court poet Philippe Quinault, Boffrand met important artists and aristocrats, who were to prove useful connections later. By the late 1690s he was supervising architect of the new Place Vendôme, Paris, but in 1700 he left the Bâtiments du Roi to pursue an independent career. His first commission, for a nephew of the late court painter Charles Le Brun, was a hôtel particulier (1700) in Paris, a rather bare block with entablature and pediments. In 1702 Mansart may have sent him to Nancy, the capital of Lorraine, which at this period was still an independent state within France. Although Boffrand was always based in Paris, where he built a number of town houses, from at least 1708 onward and over the next 20 years he designed and built several important buildings in or near Nancy for Leopold, Duke of Lorraine (*reg* 1697–1729), to whom he was appointed Premier Architecte in 1711. These works included the château of Lunéville (begun 1708; various works there continued until 1722; for further discussion and illustration *see* LUNÉVILLE); the château of Malgrange (1712–17; destr.); and the Palais Ducal in Nancy itself (1715–22; not completed; destr. 1745). Boffrand's layout for the château of Lunéville, for which he drew upon the model of Versailles, features two great courtyards, connected through a cross wing punctuated by the Baroque device of a four-column pedimented portico surmounted by an old-fashioned steep French pavilion roof, in turn topped by a balustraded platform (see fig.1). At Malgrange he employed ideas derived from Le Vau's Château de Vaux-le-Vicomte, particularly the projecting central salon on the garden front. The palace in Nancy was based loosely on the Palais du Louvre, Paris, and was intended to surround a courtyard. The façades combined details from the Place Vendôme with Bernini's second design

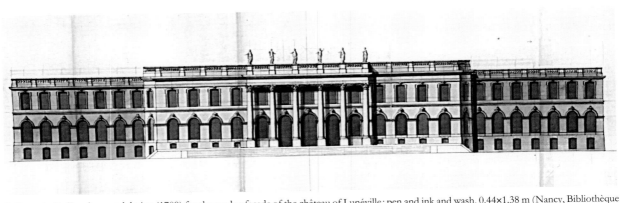

1. Germain Boffrand: second design (1709) for the garden façade of the château of Lunéville; pen and ink and wash, 0.44×1.38 m (Nancy, Bibliothèque Municipale)

2. Germain Boffrand: staircase of the Petit Luxembourg, Paris, 1709–11

(1665; unexecuted) for the Louvre. Only parts of the east wing were completed before the funds ran out. Boffrand also designed buildings for local aristocrats, including the central pavilion (1712) of the château of Commercy for the Prince de Vaudémont, a cousin of the Duke of Lorraine, and the Hôtel de Craon (1714) in Nancy for the Prince de Beauvau-Craon. Away from Nancy, he worked at the Château de Tervuren (1705; destr.), built a hunting-lodge at Bouchefort, near Brussels, for Maximilian II Emanuel of Bavaria (*reg* 1679–1726), during the Elector's exile (1704–9) from Bavaria. It was an octagonal building, with a tetrastyle portico on four sides. The rooms inside, variously square, round, octagonal or wedge-shaped, surrounded a central saloon, which rose through two storeys and was capped by a lookout structure. It was a Baroque variation upon Andrea Palladio's Villa Rotonda, Vicenza.

Meanwhile in Paris, Boffrand was also building *hôtels particuliers*, first to commission and from 1710 as speculative ventures. At the Hôtel d'Argenton (1704–5; destr.), built for the mistress of the Duc d'Orléans, Boffrand employed his 'annular' plan for the first time, disposing apartments around the core of the house, thus allowing varying room shapes. Other work in Paris included a new hôtel (1704) for Jean-Antoine de Mesme, who in 1712 appointed him architect for the Palais de Justice (1712–14; destr.); modernization of the Hôtel de Mayenne (1707) for the Prince de Vaudémont and the Hôtel de Soubise

(1707) for the Prince de Rohan, for whom he also completed the façade (1709; destr.) of the church of La Mercy opposite to improve the view from the Prince's windows; he also built the Petit Luxembourg (1709–11; see fig. 2) for Anne de Bavière, Princesse de Condé. At the same time (1709), following Mansart's death the previous year, Boffrand was received into the first class of the Académie Royale d'Architecture. He was later appointed architect for the Arsenal in Paris (1712), working under the Princesse de Condé's son-in-law the Duc de Maine, an illegitimate son of Louis XIV. There he built the river wing (1715–25) and designed the Pavillon de la Duchesse de Maine (1729; destr.).

Boffrand's speculative building in Paris, which was highly significant in the development of the faubourgs Saint-Germain and Saint-Honoré, included the Hôtel d'Amelot (1712–14) and Hôtel de Duras (1713–18), and the hôtels de Torcy (1713–14; now the German Embassy) and de Seignelay, adjacent houses in the Rue de Lille that were both sold to members of the Colbert family. The plan of the Hôtel d'Amelot was one of Boffrand's most ingenious. The court is a perfect oval, and inside the house pentagonal, square and apsed room shapes are formed around the internally assimilated curve. In 1718 Boffrand began his largest speculative gamble, with proposals for an extensive building scheme in the grounds of the Hôtel de Soissons, but this was interrupted by the financial collapse of John Law's speculative Mississippi Scheme, and the stockmarket crash that followed (1720) virtually ruined him. At the same time his ambitious plans for rebuilding at Lunéville (following a serious fire in 1719) were abandoned, apart from the chapel (1720–23).

2. 1720 AND AFTER. The year of 1720 marked a major break in Boffrand's career, although he did continue working during the 1720s on the completion of Jules Hardouin Mansart's Primatiale (now the cathedral) at Nancy (dome and upper façade, various designs 1721–8, not executed; towers, completed 1723 and high altar, completed 1728). For some years his architectural commissions were far fewer, and he never recovered his former practice in Nancy, where Leopold's successors Francis III (*reg* 1729–36) and Stanislav I Leszczyzński (*reg* 1736–66) did not employ him. He did not contribute to the next building boom in Paris, and such building projects as he did obtain tended to be for public works. He was consulted by Johann Philipp Franz von Schönborn on the design of his new Residenz at Würzburg, and he suggested alterations to the plans of Balthasar Neumann (particularly important was his scheme for the chapel). His only major private project, however, was his extension (1735–9) to the Hôtel de Soubise in Paris, in a two-storey pavilion, in which he housed oval salons (*see* ROCOCO, fig. 2). In the Salon de la Princesse on the first floor, he formed the walls into eight arches that frame the windows, mirrors and door. Between them are panels and gilt putti, with scenes painted on canvases of freely curved form in the spandrels. The division between walls and ceiling is dissolved in the zone of continuous undulation made by the curved frames, and one feature merges into another.

During the 1720s and 1730s Boffrand was invested in large capitalist enterprises, including the Canal de Picardie and a factory processing lead for the construction industry. These enterprises were linked to his technical interests—Boffrand was the inventor of a steam pump—and his most important professional posts were a reflection of this aspect of his career. In 1723 he entered the Corps des Ponts et Chaussées (reaching the rank of Premier Ingénieur and then Inspecteur Général by 1743), while in 1724 he joined the board and became architect of the Hôpital Général, Paris, which was the administrative body responsible for most of the capital's hospitals. For the first body he renewed or rebuilt several bridges (e.g. Bray-sur-Seine, 1730; Pont-sur-Yonne, 1738; and Sens, 1739–42). For the second body he drew up new designs for the Salpêtrière (1729). He also designed a magnificent reservoir for the Hospice de Bicêtre (1733; extant). The design for an unexecuted project (1738) for the Arsenal at Lyon survives (Paris, Bib. N.).

During the 1730s Boffrand became increasingly involved in the Académie Royale d'Architecture. From 1734 he was the leading campaigner for resuming the production of a 'model work' by each student (*see also* PARIS, §VI, 2). In 1745 he published his *Livre d'architecture*, illustrated with engravings of his own works. In it he set out his design philosophy, which advocated common sense based on good taste as the ultimate criterion and noble simplicity as the ideal. He thus decisively rejected the extreme forms of the contemporary Rococo style, while other parts of the book demonstrated that he could think historically and had an understanding of the Gothic style. He also implied the concept of *architecture parlante*, in which 'buildings should proclaim their purpose to the viewer'. The book was influential.

Although ecclesiastical work was a small proportion of Boffrand's output, apart from the few examples already mentioned he also designed in Notre-Dame, Paris, the Noailles chapel (1718–21; destr.) and restored the cathedral's vaults and the south rose window (1725–7). His interest in stereotomy or the stonecutting tradition was demonstrated particularly by his vaults in the kitchen of the Petit-Luxembourg and the reservoir of the Hospice de Bicêtre. He also designed the Chapelle de la Communion (1743–4) in St Merri and the choir of St Esprit (1745; destr.), both Paris.

Boffrand produced some significant late works, some of which show him to have been an innovator in the field of urban design. His last built work was the Hôpital des Enfants Trouvés (1746–51; destr. 1865), which had a pair of temple fronts flanking an axial road, returning as a colossal order of pilasters embracing three storeys. This scheme, which was criticized by Marc-Antoine Laugier as being too sumptuous for its purpose, was intended to stand on the west side of a square to be created by clearing old buildings that stood before the west front of Notre-Dame, with a Hôtel Dieu facing it on the south side. Boffrand submitted four projects in the competition (1748) for the new Place Louis XV (now Place de la Concorde), Paris, while in the second competition of 1753, his solution for laying out this difficult space provided a decisive impetus to the scheme, which was realized by Ange-Jacques Gabriel.

Boffrand always maintained an interest in the monumental tradition of French architecture, exemplified by Le Vau and Mansart, whilst demonstrating an awareness of the developments in Italy of Bernini and his circle. His design for Malgrange derives, as has already been pointed out, from Le Vau's Vaux-le-Vicomte, but a rejected design was for an extraordinary X-shaped building with a saloon at the crossing of the four wings, probably derived from a circle of Bernini through the Palais Althann (1690–93) by Johann Bernhard Fischer von Erlach (*see* FISCHER VON ERLACH, (1)) and similar to the later Palazzina di Stupinigi (1729–35) near Turin by FILIPPO JUVARRA. Although Boffrand never visited Italy, he was the most Italianate architect of his generation, and there is a clear debt to Andrea Palladio. Boffrand was also an important but untypical Rococo artist. His work exhibits a clear distinction in treatment between the interior and exterior of a building, and, thinking architectonically, he arrived equally and earlier than the decorators, at the complete fusion of forms that characterized Rococo interiors. Although he did not invent any architectural forms, he was gifted in their application, employing first-class painters and workmen in their execution. He was a master of planning, taking 17th-century French precedents and developing from them new and complex room shapes, most famously exemplified by the Hôtel d'Amelot. In particular he was very fond of round and oval rooms and used rounded corners in interiors, both in new buildings (Bouchefort) and in his insertions into old ones, such as the château of Croismare (1710–12) in Lorraine.

WRITINGS

Livre d'architecture (Paris, 1745)

BIBLIOGRAPHY

J.-F. Blondel: *L'Architecture françoise*, 8 vols (Paris, 1752–6/*R* 1904–5)
P. Patte: 'Abrégé de la vie de Monsieur Boffrand', *Discours sur l'art* (Paris, 1754)
P. Palte: *Monumens érigés en France à la gloire de Louis XV* (Paris, 1765)
A.-N. Dézallier d'Argenville: *Vies des fameux architectes et sculpteurs* (1788)
P. Morey: *Notice sur la vie et les oeuvres de Germain Boffrand* (Nancy, 1866)
L. Hautecoeur: *Le Style Louis XV* (1950), v of *Architecture classique* (Paris, 1943–57)
E. Kaufmann: *Architecture in the Age of Reason* (Cambridge, MA, 1955)
J. Garms: 'Der Grundriss des Malgrange I von Boffrand', *Wiener Jb. Kstgesch.*, xxii (1969), pp. 184–8
W. Kalnein and M. Levey: *Art and Architecture of the Eighteenth Century in France*, Pelican Hist. A. (Harmondsworth, 1972)
F. Boudon: 'Urbanisme et spéculation à Paris au XVIIIe siècle, le terrain de l'hôtel de Soissons', *J. Soc. Archit. Historians*, xxxii (1973), pp. 267–307
Germain Boffrand (exh. cat., ed. M. Gallet and J. Garms; Paris, 1986)
J. Garms: 'Les Nouveaux Dessins lorrains de Boffrand, leur place dans l'architecture de leur temps', *Bull. Soc. Hist. A. Fr.*, (1990), pp. 81–93

JÖRG GARMS

Bofill (Levi), Ricardo (*b* Barcelona, 5 Dec 1939). Spanish Catalan architect. The son of an architect, he studied at the Escuela Técnica Superior de Arquitectura in Barcelona (1955–6) and at the Université de Genève (1957–60). He worked first in his father's studio before founding the Taller de Arquitectura in Barcelona (1962) and Paris (1971); these multi-disciplinary studios, which included other environmental and design professionals as well as architects, sought an alternative to modernism in their approach to the meaning and form of urban complexes. Bofill's early work falls within the Neo-Expressionism and

Neo-Realism of the Barcelona School: outstanding examples include the Rubiol residential buildings (1960–62) and the Schenkel House (1963–5), both in Barcelona.

The Barrio Gaudí (1964–8) in Reus was a complex of 600 private dwellings that aimed to provide greater complexity and formal richness as an alternative to the more rational, rectilinear blocks of flats; its geometric groups of dwellings have four-storey projections in brick and concrete that give the five-storey blocks a powerful Neo-Realist image. This geometric morphology, reminiscent of popular Mediterranean forms, was continued in the leisure architecture that followed. In the El Castell group of flats (1966–8) at Sitges, Bofill used the modular possibilities of the cube as a generator of habitable spaces, creating a symbolic form that crowns the mountain like a medieval castle. At La Manzanera, Calpe, Alicante, the Taller built several groups of flats with recreational facilities. In the first of these, Xanadu (1966–8), a group of projecting pitched-roof modules was used, their gables and terraces piled high to produce a fantastic overall shape. Le Plexus (1967–8) is a more conventional line of houses in traditional masonry out of which arise cube-shaped volumes of various colours, but La Muralla Roja (1968–73), with its prismatic, superimposed shapes and intense red colouring, moved away from the vernacular images and underlined the provocative intentions of Bofill's architecture. All these buildings indicate the primacy of the architectural idea in Bofill's work.

In the 1970s the Taller de Arquitectura undertook large-scale urban projects that had a Utopian appeal. La Ciudad en el Espacio (1970–72; unexecuted) was an ambitious project for a residential complex of 1500 flats with community facilities that involved an experimental, community-led approach to architecture. A completed development was the first phase of Walden 7 (1970–75), comprising 400 flats, in Sant Just Desvern, near Barcelona. Severe 12-storey concrete structures like triumphal arches or Egyptian pylons are cleft to a height of ten floors to admit light to internal gardens and fountains, where it is reflected from brightly coloured ceramic finishes. The flats, of various sizes, some arranged on split levels, offered multiple-use areas that could be adapted to give either greater individual privacy or more communal space. On external walls were placed semicircular canopied balconies, looking like pieces of large-diameter pipe slotted to allow an outward view. Their arrangement, ostensibly random, gives the building a massive, turreted, fortified appearance.

Two unexecuted projects by the Taller in the early 1970s had clear historic connotations. For La Petite Cathédrale (1971) in the new town of Cergy-Pontoise, Bofill proposed a re-creation of monumental Gothic forms; and La Citadelle (1973) in the new town of Saint-Quentin-en-Yvelines was based on the renovation of an old military fortress to house a hotel and a cultural and commercial centre, together with 1200 luxury flats around them. Other projects incorporated historic references in a more abstract manner. For example, in parallel with Walden 7 and next to it, the Taller remodelled an old cement factory (1973–5) to include offices for their own use. The dream complex they created combined the industrial remains and silos, now with applied medieval details and roof gardens, with new structures. The house (1973) for Emilio Bofill in Montras, Gerona, is also a scenographic complex with separate pavilions in the shape of prisms built in rough red brick. The Parque de la Marca Hispánica (1974–6), commissioned by the French road transport authorities, lies adjacent to the Autoroute La Catalane at Le Perthus near the border with Spain and celebrates Catalonia's historic past. It takes the form of a monumental pyramid backing on to rising ground. The triangular face presented to the road is a formal landscaped garden bisected by a ceremonial staircase that rises in apparently heightened perspective to a roofless tempietto with four incomplete Gaudiesque red brick columns—a reference to the Catalan regional symbol. In the sanctuary of Meritxell (1974–8), Andorra, Bofill used round arches in naves and a bell-tower, but the shapes refer only vaguely to tradition and transmute established forms to a point at which the resulting spaces begin to seem culturally alien.

From this time on, reference to historical styles began to appear in all Bofill's projects. The Taller's winning competition entry for Les Halles (1974–5), Paris, for example, was based on a formal Beaux-Arts plan and was an early example of the reintroduction of classicism in Post-modernist architecture. It provoked a lively polemic and political in-fighting and, after various modifications, was eventually dropped. For this scheme Bofill proposed a monumental architecture featuring an elliptical colonnade, evocative of the great urban spaces in the French classical tradition. The same desire to recreate great urban spaces is combined with the consistent precedence of the architectural idea in a series of major residential developments in France over the next two decades. In these well-known monuments of Post-modernism, the stylistic links with the historic past became more prominent, both in composition and detail. Les Arcades du Lac and Le Viaduc (1972–5), Saint-Quentin-en-Yvelines, is a complex of 674 dwellings classically planned around and on a lake. Les Espaces d'Abraxas (1978–83), a theatrical urban complex in the new town of Marne-la-Vallée, contains a similar number of dwellings in buildings whose shapes reflect their names: constructed on an axis, the U-shaped Le Palais and semicircular Le Théâtre (see fig.) enclose a central open space in which the triumphal arch L'Arc is located. In Les Echelles du Baroque (1979–85) in the 14th arrondissement of Paris, dwellings are contained in seven-storey walls enclosing three interlinked plazas. L'Amphithéâtre Vert (1981–5) in Cergy-Pontoise comprises a crescent and two square plazas. Antígone (1979–83), Montpellier, is a new, axial city centre enclosing monumental volumes of Baroque scale and variety.

The design of these multi-storey residential complexes, whose enclosed plazas are the antithesis of the fluid, abstract spaces of modernist urban planning, was based on classical rules, but interpreted with an absolute freedom that constantly transgressed the language, proportion and scale of canonical classicism, producing elements that are often distorted and enlarged to create a disturbing colossalism. The blocks were increasingly built with the use of industrialized construction techniques such as prefabricated concrete and curtain walling systems. Bofill's re-creation of classical urban space with its emphasis on monumentality made him one of the most important

Ricardo Bofill: Le Théâtre, Les Espaces d'Abraxas, Marne-la-Vallée, 1978–83

exponents of Post-modernism; the architecture of his residential complexes has more to do with meaning than with other architectural values. Bofill's most recent works, such as the Institute of Physical Education in the Olympic Complex (1991) in Barcelona, the extension of Barcelona Airport (1992) and the 50-storey office tower (1992) at 77 West Wacker Drive, Chicago continue to be labelled 'modern classicism', though their incorporation of new technologies and attention to aspects of efficiency and function should not be overlooked.

WRITINGS
Hacia una formalización de la ciudad en el espacio (Barcelona, 1968)
L'architecture d'un homme (Paris, 1978)
Los espacios de Abraxas (Paris, 1981)
Taller de Arquitectura: City Design, Industry and Classicism (Barcelona, 1984)

BIBLIOGRAPHY
J. A. Goytisolo: *Taller de Arquitectura* (Barcelona, 1977)
Taller de Arquitectura: Ricardo Bofill (exh. cat., London, Archit. Assoc., 1981)
A. Drexler: *Ricardo Bofill and Léon Krier: Architecture, Urbanism and History* (New York, 1985)
Y. Futagawa, ed.: *Ricardo Bofill, Taller de Arquitectura*, intro. C. Norberg-Schulz (Tokyo, 1985)
'Ricardo Bofill', *Rev. N. Arquit.*, 258 (1986), pp. 41–66
W. A. James, ed.: *Ricardo Bofill, Taller de Arquitectura: Buildings and Projects, 1960–1984* (New York and Barcelona, 1988)
A. d'Huart: *Ricardo Bofill: Taller de Arquitectura* (Paris, 1989)
Ricardo Bofill: Taller de Arquitectura (exh. cat., Brussels, Mus. Ixelles, 1989)

JORDI OLIVERAS

Bogaert, Martin van den. *See* DESJARDINS, MARTIN.

Bogardus, James (*b* Catskill, NY, 14 March 1800; *d* New York, 13 April 1874). American inventor, engineer, designer and manufacturer. He trained first as a watchmaker's apprentice in Catskill and then worked as an engraver in Savannah, GA. About 1830 he moved to New York to promote his inventions. He secured many patents for small devices, such as new types of clock, an eversharp pencil, a dry gas meter and a meter for measuring fluids. His most original and successful invention was a widely useful eccentric type grinding mill (patented 1831); this was to provide a steady source of income throughout his life. During years spent in England (1836–40) he was granted an English patent for a postage device and won £100 in a competition for his proposal for a pre-paid postal system.

In 1847 Bogardus displayed a model of a prefabricated iron factory and attracted an order from Dr John Milhau (1785–1874) for an ornamental five-storey iron façade for his drug store on Broadway in lower Manhattan, New York. This first iron-fronted structure (1848; destr.) introduced what was to become a widespread building type for commercial architecture in the USA in the 19th century. Early in 1849 Bogardus completed the five unified iron-fronted Laing Stores (destr.) in Manhattan. Later in the same year he finished his own factory (destr.) at Duane and Center streets, virtually all made of iron—frame, trusses, walls, floor and roof. A US patent was granted to him in 1850 for his construction system. In 1850–51 he erected the five-storey *Sun* newspaper building (destr.) in Baltimore, MD, and further orders soon came in. During the next decade he erected prefabricated iron buildings in Baltimore, Charleston, SC, Chicago, Philadelphia and Washington, DC, and even a huge iron sugar warehouse in Cuba. After a fire in 1853 destroyed the offices and printing plant of America's largest publisher, Harper & Brothers, in Manhattan, Bogardus and others built on its site a large iron-framed structure. With exposed ornamental interior cast-iron columns and trusses, a floor system incorporating America's first successful roll of lengthy wrought-iron beams, and a long, ornate cast-iron façade, the Harper Building was reported as the first example of a new fire-proof building type. In 1856 Bogardus erected a large commercial building for inventor–printer George Bruce in Canal Street, Manhattan, and the same year he published the first of two editions of a pamphlet extolling the merits of cast-iron architecture. The following year he began construction of the virtually all-iron three-storey Thompkins Market (completed 1860; destr.).

During the 1850s Bogardus also erected unprecedented cast-iron towers. His first was a fire watch-tower (1851; destr.); built for the City of New York, this skeletal, iron-framed look-out rose to an impressive 30.5 m. Other iron towers built between 1851 and 1856 included a second fire look-out for New York (1855; destr.), a lighthouse for San Domingo, and two towers in Manhattan for manufacturing shot, one of which was 65 m high. Brick infill walls were added to the shot towers to keep out the wind; these formed curtain walls that were carried by the frame, an early demonstration of the principle of metal-framed curtain walls that would later be used for skyscraper construction. In addition, he produced many small iron-fronted buildings; two survive in Manhattan and a third, completed in 1863, in Cooperstown, NY. With DANIEL D. BADGER, Bogardus was a pioneer in skeletal iron construction; his innovative structural use of metal led to its employment in ever-larger buildings until, with the development of the lift, the skyscraper became possible.

WRITINGS
Cast Iron Buildings: Their Construction and Advantages (New York, 1856, rev. 1858); *R* in *The Origins of Cast Iron Architecture in America. Including . . . Cast Iron Buildings: Their Construction and Advantages*, intro. W. K. Sturges (New York, 1970)

DAB

BIBLIOGRAPHY
T. C. Bannister: 'Bogardus Revisited', *J. Soc. Archit. Hist.*, xv/4 (1956), pp. 12–33; xvi/1 (1957), pp. 11–19
W. R. Weismann: 'Mid-19th-century Commercial Building by James Bogardus', *Monumentum*, ix (1973), pp. 63–75
M. Gayle: *Cast-iron Architecture in New York: A Photographic Survey* (New York, 1974)
M. Gayle and C. Gayle: *James Bogardus: Pioneer of Cast-iron Architecture in America* (in preparation)

MARGOT GAYLE

Bogart [van den Boogaart], **Bram** (*b* Delft, 12 July 1921). Belgian painter of Dutch birth. He trained to be a decorator, which gave him his knowledge of painting techniques. His first works as a painter date from 1946–50, when he spent considerable time in southern France and Paris. Attracted by the French landscape, with its weather-beaten walls, he started to produce virtually monochrome abstract paintings allied to matter painting from the early 1950s. He was the first Dutch artist to work in this manner. Between 1951 and 1960 Bogart lived and worked in Paris. He exhibited regularly in the Netherlands, for example with the Nederlandse Informele Groep (formed in 1957), and he was the only artist among them to remain faithful to its principles. He continued to develop his paintings from the material textures, giving special attention to the calligraphic nature of the brushwork.

In 1960 Bogart moved to Brussels, where his work changed considerably. He started to apply more thickly painted primary colours on larger surfaces, laid flat on the floor; after 1962 he used jute stretched over a wooden support (e.g. *Yellow Young*, oil and watercolour, 1962; Ostend, Prov. Mus. Mod. Kst). After moving in 1964 to Ohain, near Braine-l'Alleud, he used geometric shapes and a restricted range of colours: he confined his paintings to a maximum of three colours, placed in fields alongside each other. After 1970 he began to work again in a more playful manner. He began to apply the paint in thicker layers, allowing it to drip over the edge of the panel. He used pastel shades based on the colours of the houses in Ohain. In the 1980s the signs returned, but this time they marked the basic shape of the painting, for example a circle or an oval.

WRITINGS
'Sculptural Paintings', *Leonardo*, xix/2 (1986), pp. 113–16
with F.-C. Legrand: *Bram Bogart* (Tielt, 1988)

BIBLIOGRAPHY
Bram Bogart: Schilderijen, 1950–83 (exh. cat., ed. W. Beeren and T. Schoon; Rotterdam, Boymans-van Beuningen, 1984)
Bram Bogart: Les Bleus de Delft (exh. cat., ed. I. Spaander; Delft, Stedel. Mus. Prinsenhof, 1984)
Bram Bogart: Retrospectieve (exh. cat., ed. W. van den Bussche; Ostend, Prov. Mus. Mod. Kst, 1995)

INEKE SPAANDER

Bogayevsky, Konstantin (Fyodorovich) (*b* Feodosiya, Ukraine, 12 Jan 1872; *d* Feodosiya, 17 Feb 1943). Ukrainian painter and graphic artist. He studied at the Academy of Arts, St Petersburg, from 1891 to 1897 under Arkhip Kuindzhi, and he was profoundly influenced by Kuindzhi's ideas of national romantic landscape. Bogayevsky was a member of the World of Art (Rus. Mir Iskusstva) Society and of the Union of Russian Artists (Soyuz Russkikh Khudozhnikov). Most of his work was devoted to the Eastern Crimea, and he became a master of the epic historical landscape. He was dedicated to depicting 'Kimmeriya' (the poetic name for the Crimea, after 'Kimmerians', ancient tribes that inhabited the peninsula in 8–7 BC), as was his friend, the poet and artist Maksimilian Voloshin (1877–1932).

On a number of occasions Bogayevsky approached a fine stylization in his work in the spirit of the Italian quattrocento (e.g. *Memories of Mantegna*, 1910; Moscow, Tret'yakov Gal.), but he usually worked from the motif, which he made monumental in the tradition of 'heroic landscape' (e.g. *Feodosiya*, 1930; Feodosiya, Ayvazovsky Pict. Gal.). In the period following the Revolution of 1917, Bogayevsky also painted a number of monumental industrial landscapes, including over 30 from the series *Dneprostroy* (1930; Moscow, Tret'yakov Gal. and elsewhere). He died in a bombing raid during World War II.

BIBLIOGRAPHY
R. D. Vashchenko: *K. F. Bogayevsky* (Moscow, 1984)

M. N. SOKOLOV

Boğazköy [Boğazkale]. Village in central Anatolia, Turkey, adjoining the site of ancient Hattusa, capital of the HITTITE kingdom, *c.* 1650–*c.* 1200 BC. Most of the remains belong to the Hittite empire period, *c.* 1400–*c.* 1200 BC. Excavations have recovered extensive ruins of walls and gates, a citadel and temples, and thousands of clay tablets inscribed in cuneiform that formed the royal library and archives of the Hittites. With interruptions for World Wars I and II, formal excavations have been conducted under H. Winckler, Kurt Bittel and P. Neve since 1906; the site continues to be highly productive. Finds are in the Pergamonmuseum, Berlin, the Museum of Anatolian Civilizations, Ankara, and the Archaeological Museum, Boğazköy.

1. ARCHITECTURE. Traces of settlement stretching back to the Chalcolithic have been identified, but no substantial remains have been found earlier than the Assyrian Colony period (*c.* 1920–*c.* 1740 BC), attested by a number of houses and some Old Assyrian cuneiform tablets and ended by a historically and archaeologically known destruction. The Hittite Old Kingdom period (*c.* 1650–*c.* 1500 BC), which saw the establishment of the Hittite state at Hattusa, is poorly represented, perhaps because its remains were largely obliterated by the later massive building works. The violent end of the empire is visible in the destruction and burning of the site, which seems to have been abandoned until a lesser rebuilding

and refortification by Phrygian settlers *c.* 900–*c.* 500 BC. Except for occasional, largely insignificant buildings, the site was not reoccupied before the rise of the modern village.

The site is imposing. Approached from the north along a wide, fertile valley, it rises steeply to the south with a series of craggy outcrops. Its north-east side is marked by the gorge (Turk. *boğaz*) that gives the site its modern name and borders the high rocky citadel, Büyükkale (Turk.: 'great citadel'). A comparatively flat area at the north end of the site at the foot of Büyükkale was occupied by the Lower Town, the site of the earliest settlement. South of the Lower Town and Citadel area, the site slopes up past an area of rocky outcrops and a flatter Upper Town to a high point, Yerkapı. The whole site was surrounded by a circuit of fortification walls that has been traced and excavated for most of its length. The walls were built of massive cyclopean masonry to the height of one storey with frequent towers and gateways, entered through corbelled arches of huge monoliths, many carved with protective figures. The superstructure of the walls and towers would have been of mud brick, all of which has collapsed and disappeared. The steep south face of the city fortifications was protected by an enormous glacis now impressively restored, and deep under the battlements ran long corbel-vaulted posterns, of which at least one, known as Yerkapı, is completely preserved (*see* ANATOLIA, ANCIENT, fig. 6).

The principal building of the Lower Town and the finest monument of Hattusa is the Great Temple, seat of the storm-god, and its extensive surrounding magazines and administrative quarters. The temple itself is built on the usual Hittite plan, entered through an elaborate chambered gatehouse into a courtyard surrounded by rows of rooms and with the inner shrine leading off the back of the courtyard. The wall-footings survive in the form of great blocks of dressed basalt, but here too the mud-brick superstructures have collapsed into debris cleared in the course of excavation. Similarly, the surrounding magazines are preserved only in their enormous foundations and huge dressed limestone thresholds. Many of the great pithoi (storage jars), which would have held grain, oil or wine, are preserved *in situ*. The temple precinct is intersected by paved streets and a number of large carved stone water-basins were found. A building covering a spring or well was excavated near by.

The Royal Citadel, Büyükkale, has been completely excavated but was found to be very much eroded down to the foundations of the buildings or even the bedrock. It was surrounded by its own system of fortifications connecting with the main city defences, and it was reached through only one or possibly two gates at its south-west end. The buildings were grouped as individual units round a series of courts: Entrance, Lower, Middle and Upper. They may be inferred to have had upper storeys, and they appear to have constituted a series of palaces or royal residence buildings. In one, a very large columned hall has been hypothetically reconstructed and designated the royal audience chamber.

More than twenty temples, all of the usual plan, have been found in the Upper Town. Most of the rocky peaks that dot the site show signs of building, rock-cut wall footings or, in places, surviving masonry. The purpose of these buildings is not generally clear, but one, Nişantaş, has a long but eroded rock inscription attached to it and may be an 'eternal peak' mentioned in a funerary context (*see* YAZILIKAYA (i)).

2. ARTEFACTS. The sack of Hattusa *c.* 1200 BC was thorough, and few items of portable wealth have been found, but the recovery of the royal library and archives has provided ample compensation. The thousands of clay tablets are inscribed in the cuneiform script borrowed from Mesopotamia. They were found principally in the foundations of the buildings on Büyükkale, in the magazines surrounding the Great Temple, in a house on the slope between the two (perhaps a scribal school) and in some of the temples of the Upper Town. They are written in a number of languages, principally in the Hittites' own and in Akkadian (Babylonian), which served as the diplomatic *lingua franca* of the Ancient Near East. The languages of the Hittites' neighbours are preserved in small groups of specialized texts: Hattian (the language of the pre-Hittite population of Hatti), Hurrian (that of the Hittites' eastern neighbours) and Luwian and Palaic (Anatolian languages closely related to Hittite). The library and archives contain texts typical of such collections: state documents, edicts, treaties, letters and laws; historical documents, royal annals; administrative texts, protocols for officials, land donations and records of court cases; poetic texts, myths and epics, both Anatolian and foreign; and numerous religious texts, the prayers, rituals and festivals that played such a prominent part in Hittite court life. Besides writing in cuneiform on clay tablets, the Hittites employed their own hieroglyphic script, which survives mainly on monumental stone inscriptions such as those of Nişantaş and of the 'tomb' of Suppiluliuma (discovered in 1988) and on seals. In cuneiform texts there are references to wooden documents and 'scribes on wood'. Although none of these documents has survived, it is likely that these too would have been inscribed in hieroglyphic.

There are many references in the texts to the immense wealth of gold, silver and precious artefacts accumulated in Hattusa, very little of which has survived. Temple inventory texts describe in detail the composite statues of gods made in gold, silver and ivory etc. Tablets and seals of gold, silver and bronze are mentioned, and in 1986 a magnificent bronze tablet was discovered containing the text of an entire treaty.

Some of the finest Hittite relief sculpture has come from Hattusa, notably the figure of the portal deity from the inner jamb of the King's Gate (see fig.), the sphinxes from the Sphinx Gate (*see* ANATOLIA, ANCIENT, fig. 7), the lions from the Lion Gate and a small stele of Tudhaliya IV (*reg c.* 1260–1230 BC). In these, carved on an accommodating stone, the figures are well rendered in fine detail, whereas other Hittite sculpture, carved on more intractable stone or badly eroded, may not illustrate so well the sculptor's proficiency. The carving of monumental hieroglyphic inscriptions also demanded a skill with detail.

The monumental sculpture is closely associated with the small-scale work of engraving seals. Comparatively few actual seals have been found, but the seal-carver's art is well known from impressions surviving on clay. Unlike

Boğazköy, relief of a portal deity, h. 2 m, 13th century BC (Ankara, Museum of Anatolian Civilizations)

Mesopotamia, with its characteristic cylinder seals, the Hittite kingdom favoured seals in the form of a stamp, lentoid in shape, or an oval signet. The finest of these are, naturally, royal seals, typically showing a central scene with figures of god and king, who has his name written in the centre in hieroglyphic surrounded by outer circles giving the name and titulary in cuneiform.

Hittite texts refer to an enormous number of vessels, many of precious metals, also many in strange, often theriomorphic shapes for cultic use. Few survive, but two magnificent silver rhyta, one in the form of a stag (New York, Met., Norbert Schimmel Col.), the other of a bull (Boston, MA, Mus. F.A.), display the skill of Hittite metalworkers. The humbler craft of pottery is also well represented, typically in a glossy red burnished ware in a wide range of elegant shapes, such as jugs, bowls, cups and enormous pithoi. Also common are vessels with appliqué animal forms and complete theriomorphic vessels. Perhaps the most dramatic type is represented by

fragments of large vases decorated with bands of relief figures with polychrome slip, showing the performances of Hittite festivals: a complete example was found at INANDIKTEPE.

BIBLIOGRAPHY
'Archaeology in Asia Minor', *Amer. J. Archaeol.*, lix– (1955–) [annual summary reports by M. Mellink]
K. Bittel: *Hattusha: The Capital of the Hittites* (New York, 1970) [extensive bibliog.]
R. M. Boehmer: *Die Kleinfunde von Boğazköy* (Berlin, 1972)
U. Seidl: *Gefässmarken von Boğazköy* (Berlin, 1972)
R. M. Boehmer: *Die Kleinfunde aus der Unterstadt von Boğazköy* (Berlin, 1979)
A. von den Driesch and J. Boessneck: *Reste von Haus- und Jagdtieren aus der Unterstadt von Boğazköy-Hattuša* (Berlin, 1981)
P. Neve: *Büyükkale: Die Bauwerke* (Berlin, 1982)
R. M. Boehmer: *Die Reliefkeramik von Boğazköy* (Berlin, 1983)
P. Neve: 'Boğazköy-Hattuša 1985 Kazı mevsiminin sonuçları' [Results of the 1985 season of the excavations at Boğazköy-Hattusa], *VIII Kazı Sonuçları Toplantısı* [Eighth meeting on excavation reports]: *Ankara, 1986*, i
R. M. Boehmer and H. G. Güterbock: *Glyptik aus dem Stadtgebiet von Boğazköy* (Berlin, 1987)
P. Neve: 'Die Ausgrabungen in Boğazköy-Hattusa 1986/1987/1988/1989', *Archäol. Anz.* (1987–90)

J. D. HAWKINS

Bogdanov [Malinovsky], **Aleksandr (Aleksandrovich)** (*b* Sokolka, Grodno province, Russia [now Sokółka, Białystock province, Poland], 22 Aug 1873; *d* Moscow, 7 April 1928). Russian theorist and writer. A physician by training, Bogdanov was also a political activist. Attributing the failure of the Revolution of 1905 to the cultural unpreparedness of the proletariat, he, together with Anatoly Lunacharsky and Maksim Gor'ky, sought to hasten the necessary Russian cultural development by organizing the Bolshevik Forward (Vperyod) group and training schools at Capri and Bologna in 1909–10. He developed the ideas of working man as a 'God-building' force and of the Party as an expression of that force. He envisaged the mystical and religious unity of the proletariat enabling man through revolution and Socialism to realize fully his potential and become like a god. Positing a path for Socialism that was three-fold (political, economic and cultural), he became the leading theoretician of PROLET-KUL'T in 1917: this mass working-class organization, with complete autonomy in the cultural sphere, was highly influential in orientating post-Revolutionary Russian Futurism towards an art of social utility. However, Bogdanov came into conflict with V. I. LENIN for his ideological independence. As a result he was dropped as a member of Proletkul't's central committee in 1920 and in the following year returned to medicine. He died performing a medical experiment on himself.

Bogdanov, who published a great variety of works, including science fiction novels, outlined his idea of proletarian art in the journal *Proletarskaya kul'tura* ('Proletarian culture'; Moscow, 1918–21), of which he was co-editor, as well as in other publications. Rejecting the notions of 'pure art' and 'civic art', he proclaimed art to be the 'organization of living images' and that the organizational principles controlling the effect of the art-work were more important than the actual content. Thus he introduced the notion of art as an organizer of the psyche. In this the avant-garde found justification for their refusal to reflect life through art and turned to the involvement of the audience in the active process of analysing the construction of the work of art.

WRITINGS

Iskusstvo i rabochiy klass [Art and the working class] (Moscow, 1918)

O proletarskoy kul'ture [On proletarian culture] (Moscow and Leningrad, 1924)

Voprosy Sotsializma: Raboty raznykh let [Questions of socialism: works from various years] (Moscow, 1990)

BIBLIOGRAPHY

D. Grille: *Lenins Rivale: Bogdanov und seine Philosophie* (Cologne, 1966)

JEREMY HOWARD

Bogdány [Bogdani], **Jakob** [Jacob; Jakab; James] (*b* Eperjes, *c.* 1660; *d* London, 11 Feb 1724). Hungarian painter, active in the Netherlands and England. He was born into a Protestant gentry family and by 1684 was working as a still-life painter in Amsterdam, where he may have gone to escape Catholic persecution. His earliest works (e.g. *Still-life with Apples and Other Fruit on a Ledge*; London, Rafael Valls) are austere groupings of fruit in the Dutch manner. By 1 June 1688 he was in London, settling at Tower Street, St Giles in the Fields. In 1691 he described his pattern of work: '[I] paint in the Spring flowers & in the Somer flowers & Fruits when they are out Lobsters and oyster pieces, In the Winter pieces of Fowell & plate' (MS., Chatsworth, Derbys). In 1694 he painted flower decorations for Mary II's Looking-glass Closet in the Water Gallery at Hampton Court, London. A number of flower paintings done for William Cavendish, 1st Duke of Devonshire, survive at Chatsworth House, Derbys, including *Flowers on a Draped Ledge with a Red-faced Parrot* (1698), in which the clarity of Dutch flower painting is combined with the baroque drama of the elaborate brass vase and swirling drapery. The parrot indicates Bogdány's interest in bird painting, which increased from *c.* 1703, when he had access to the aviary owned by Admiral George Churchill (1653–1710). Bogdány executed several large bird pictures for the Admiral (three at London, Hampton Court, Royal Col.). Bogdány's works show ensembles of farm, wild and exotic birds, often with a background of classical architecture (e.g. *Still-life with Birds*; Budapest, N.G.). He became the leading exponent of this genre in England, much in demand among aristocratic patrons. Prosperity allowed him to acquire property at Finchley, London, and Spalding, Lincs, and he became Lord of the Manor of Hitchin, Herts.

BIBLIOGRAPHY

L. Orsagh: 'James Bogdani, Magyar festö III. Vilmos és Anna királynö udvarában' [James Bogdani, a Hungarian artist in the court of William and Mary], *Studies in English Philology*, ii (Budapest, 1937) [with Eng. résumé]

A. Pigler: *Bogdány Jakab* (Budapest, 1941)

Jacob Bogdani, c. 1660–1724 (exh. cat., ed. M. Rajnai; London, Richard Green, 1989)

SUSAN MORRIS

Boggio, Emilio (*b* Caracas, 21 May 1857; *d* Auvers-sur-Oise, 7 May 1920). Venezuelan painter, active in France. He travelled to France in 1864 and studied at the Lycée Michelet in Paris until 1870. He returned to Caracas in 1873 but made a second journey to Paris in 1877, where he was a student of Jean-Paul Laurens at the Académie Julian. In 1889 Boggio was awarded the bronze medal at the Exposition Universelle in Paris. Between 1907 and 1909 he lived in Italy, where he painted seascapes. Boggio excelled in landscape painting, and Claude Monet and Camille Pissarro were decisive influences on the Impressionist style of his work. In 1919 he stayed briefly in Caracas and held an exhibition at the Academia de Bellas Artes, which greatly influenced local artistic circles. Notable among his works was *End of the Day* (1912; Caracas, Gal. A. N.).

BIBLIOGRAPHY

J. Calzadilla: *Emilio Boggio* (Caracas, 1968)

A. Junyent: *Boggio* (Caracas, 1970)

MARÍA ANTONIA GONZÁLEZ-ARNAL

Bogolyubov, Aleksey (Petrovich) (*b* Pomeran'ye, nr Novgorod, 28 March 1824; *d* Paris, 7 Nov 1896). Russian painter, collector and teacher. He was the foremost marine painter of the Realist group of Russian artists, the WANDERERS, and his work shows the influence of Ivan Ayvazovsky. A graduate of the Russian Navy School, Bogolyubov began to serve in the Russian fleet in 1839, where his outstanding ability at drawing attracted attention. He studied at the Academy of Arts in St Petersburg (1850–53) under Maksim Vorob'yov (1787–1855) and Bogdan Villeval'de (1819–1903). In 1853 he was appointed artist to the Naval General Staff and began to work on sea-battle scenes (including, from 1856 to 1860, depictions of events in the Crimean War). He received stipends from the Academy for study abroad between 1854 and 1860 and worked in Turkey, Greece, Italy, Holland, France and Germany. During this period he worked in Eugène Isabey's studio in Paris, where he was influenced by the Barbizon school, and in the studio of Andreas Achenbach (1815–1910) in Düsseldorf, where he became attracted to romantic landscape (e.g. *Seashore at Scheveningen*, *c.* 1859; St Petersburg, Rus. Mus.). In 1858 he was made an academician for his views of Constantinople, Rome and Lake Geneva. He gained a professorship at the St Petersburg Academy in 1861. He joined the Wanderers in 1872 and contributed to their exhibitions until his death. After 1872 he frequently worked abroad, especially in Paris (e.g. *Ecouen*, 1882; Moscow, Tret'yakov Gal.). Despite his extensive foreign travels Bogolyubov's mature work also reflects an interest in life within the Russian empire (e.g. *View of Nizhny Novgorod*, 1878; St Petersburg, Rus. Mus.).

The bulk of Bogolyubov's collection of Western European fine and applied arts was acquired in the 1870s, although some date from *c.* 1858. The collection includes paintings, tapestries, furniture, glass and ceramics; in painting he mainly collected contemporary French artists, and especially those whose technique and subject-matter related to his own, such as Daubigny, Corot and the Barbizon school. In 1885 he created the Radishchev Museum of Art in Saratov, formed on the basis of his own collection and named after his grandfather, the writer Aleksandr Radishchev (1749–1802). He also planned the Saratov Arts School, which opened in 1897.

BIBLIOGRAPHY

M. Andronikova: *Bogolyubov* (Moscow, 1962)

JEREMY HOWARD

Bogolyubovo. *See under* VLADIMIR–SUZDAL'.

Bogomazov, Aleksandr. *See* BOHOMAZOV, OLEKSANDR.

Bogotá, Santa Fe de. Capital and largest city of Colombia, located in the centre of the country on the Sabane, a plateau in the Andes 2600 m above sea level. The population in the late 20th century was *c.* 6 million. The city's name probably derives from that of the village of Bacatá, the seat of El Zipa, chief of a group of Muisca tribes that populated the region at the time of the Spaniards' arrival. (For a discussion of Pre-Columbian art and architecture in the region, *see* SOUTH AMERICA, PRE-COLUMBIAN, §II, 1).

1. TO 1819. In 1536 Gonzalo Jiménez de Quesada was commissioned to undertake an expedition to discover the mouth of the Magdalena River and to search for an alternative route to Peru. After an arduous year-long journey, he arrived in the Zipa lands; in 1538 he officially founded the city and proceeded to build a church and 12 straw houses, followed by Spanish-style constructions in more permanent materials. The city spread out on a grid, characteristic of Spanish rules of urban planning for the New World colonies, interrupted only by the San Francisco and San Agustín rivers. The central district of La Candelaria was developed around the Plaza Real and Calle Real (now the Plaza de Bolívar and Carrera 7). Of the houses, constructed around central patios and with hallways connecting the public and private spaces, a notable example is the home of the Marqués de San Jorge (now the Museo Arqueológico del Banco Popular); built on two storeys, it was one of the most complex houses in its adaptation to the uneven land.

Various religious orders established cloisters, including the Augustinians (1575; destr.), the Dominicans (1577; destr.) and the Jesuits (San Ignacio, 1604; now the Museo de Arte Colonial). Their churches were characterized by exquisite *Mudéjar* panelling on the ceilings and rich Baroque ornamentation, as in S Clara, decorated (1630) by Matías de Santiago; the altarpiece (1623) of S Francisco (1569–1622) by Ignacio García de Asucha (1580–1629); and the exuberant woodwork of the church of the Veracruz, left in its natural colour to highlight the beauty of the local woods. The Jesuit brick-built church of S Ignacio (1625–41; see fig.) by Giovanni Battista Coluccini (1569–1641) introduced such innovations as the Latin-cross plan, barrel-vaulted central nave and cupola. The wealth of architectural decoration was complemented by the painting and sculpture produced in local workshops, which inherited the traditions of Seville. The most prestigious painting of the so-called Santa Fe school was undertaken in the workshops of the families of Gáspar de Figueroa (*d* 1658) and Gregorio Vázquez de Arce y Ceballos (1638–1711), the latter being the most prolific artist of the period; his realistic treatment of mystical themes is exemplified in *Holy Family* (Bogotá, S Ignacio).

In 1717 Santa Fe de Bogotá became capital of the viceroyalty of Nueva Granada. Baroque gradually gave way to Mannerist and Rococo tendencies in painting, these coinciding with the move away from religious topics in the 18th century. In architecture Fray DOMINGO DE PETRÉS, with his Neo-classical style a representative of the Enlightenment, arrived from Spain in 1792 to undertake both civil works and plans for the cathedral (begun 1807; incomplete on Petrés's death in 1811).

Bogotá, S Ignacio, by Giovanni Battista Coluccini, 1625–41

2. 1819 AND AFTER. Following independence in 1819 English and French Neo-classicism appeared increasingly, as did Romanticism; the new styles came to be known as 'republican' architecture. New materials such as steel were introduced, although brick retained its popularity. Important exponents of these eclectic trends included the British architect Thomas Reed (1810–78), who built the Capitolio Nacional (1847) and the Panóptico (1851, now the Museo Nacional), and Pietro Cantini (1850–1929), who designed the Teatro Colón (1885).

For the exhibition of 1910 celebrating the centenary of the struggle for independence, the city underwent significant transformations in appearance as electric light was introduced and tree-lined avenues and parks with railings were created. The city also grew in density, with new construction backing on to former colonial sites. Among the most significant works of the period is the Palacio Echeverry (1905) by the Frenchman Gaston Lelarge (1852–1934). In the 1930s international Functionalism became popular in Colombia. Among those who played a major role in the transition from historicism to Modernism were Karl Brunner, who planned the Universidad Nacional, Leopoldo Rother (1894–1978) and Bruno Violi (1909–71), who designed the Faculty of Engineering (1938–42) at the Ciudad Universitaria. The embracing of these new trends resulted from various factors, including the need to meet the massive demands on housing made by the growing immigrant population, the creation of a faculty of architecture at the Universidad Nacional, the enthusiasm surrounding Le Corbusier's visit (1947) and his elaboration of the regulating plan (unrealized) for the city, and the need to rebuild areas destroyed by fire in the revolt of 1948.

In the 1950s, while the first International-style skyscrapers were being built, an organic style was developing, with the use of such traditional local materials as brick. An early example of this was the government-built multi-level Centro Antonio Nariño (1950–53; by Violi, Pablo Lanzetta (1933–85) and Gabriel Seranno Camargo (1909–82)). One of the first successful solutions to mass-housing, the scheme is notable for the way green areas are integrated and the buildings are adapted to the topography.

In the late 20th century a local architecture of formal richness was created from a versatile use of brick and occasionally masonry and wood, along with adaptation to the uneven land and to the landscape. Examples of this are the works of Rogelio Salmona (b 1929), such as the Residencias El Parque (1965–70; see COLOMBIA, fig. 4), the brickwork of which interprets the changing light of the Sabane and the mountains. Housing complexes such as the Sante Theresa Complex at Usaquen (1977–8) by Jorge Rueda, Enrique Gomez Grau and Carlos Morales also followed the organicist trend and with commercial centres contributed to raising the profile of other parts of the rapidly spreading city.

Sculpture and painting at the end of the 19th century were dominated by Academicism, due to the establishment of schools of art such as the Academia Gutierrez (1883) and the Instituto de Bellas Artes (1882). This art of the schools, which fulfilled the demand of local patrons for portraiture and landscape painting—the most popular genre in the early 20th century—evolved to produce the intimate and realistic renderings of the artists of the Escuela de la Sabana, who concentrated on the changing light and quiet landscapes surrounding Bogotá.

In the 1940s Bogotá came under the influence of international modernism, and the sculptures of Constructivists Edgar Negret and Eduardo Ramirez exemplify the abstract and rational tendencies that since then have characterized the city, in contrast to the figurative and subjective art of popular culture that prevailed elsewhere in Colombia.

The importance of Bogotá as an artistic centre is reflected in a number of major museums, including the Museo del Oro, the Museo Nacional, the Museo de Arte Colonial and the Museo de Arte Moderno. The Escuela de Conservación y Restauración de Colcultura has played an important part in salvaging the country's artistic heritage. There are a number of institutions teaching art and architecture, including the Universidad Nacional de Colombia, the Universidad de los Andes and the Pontificia Universidad Javeriana. The city hosts the Salón Nacional for Colombian artists (although this has also twice been held in Cartagena) and the Bienal de Bogotá.

BIBLIOGRAPHY
E. Pulecio Marino: *Museos de Bogotá* (Bogotá, 1889)
C. Martínez: *Bogotá: Sinopsis sobre su evolución urbana* (Bogotá, 1976)
M. Traba: *Mirar en Bogotá* (Bogotá, 1976)
G. Tellez: *Aspectos de la arquitectura contemporánea en Colombia* (Bogotá, 1977)
S. Arango de Jaramillo: *Historia de la arquitectura de Colombia* (Bogotá, 1980)
G. Franco Salamanca: *Templo de Santa Clara de Bogotá* (Bogotá, 1987)
B. Villegas, ed.: *Historia de Bogotá*, 3 vols (Bogotá, 1988)
NATALIA VEGA

Boguet, Nicolas-Didier (*b* Chantilly, 18 Feb 1755; *d* Rome, 1 April 1839). French painter and draughtsman, active in Italy. Sent to Paris at the age of 23 as a protégé of the Prince de Condé, he was admitted to the Académie on the recommendation of Augustin Pajou to study history painting. In 1783 he went to Rome, where he began to concentrate on landscape, spending the summer months outdoors in the Roman Campagna. These trips resulted in hundreds of drawings (Rome, Pal. Farnesina), the best of which have been compared to those of Claude Lorrain. In the 1790s Boguet painted views for European aristocrats staying in Rome, in particular Frederick Augustus Hervey, 4th Earl of Bristol, for whom he painted a *View of Lake Albano* (Grenoble, Mus. Peint. & Sculp.) in 1795. The following year Boguet was introduced to Napoleon, who persuaded him to paint a number of works celebrating his Italian campaigns, including the *Battle of Castiglione* (Versailles, Château).

In 1800, the year Boguet made his Salon début, he also began to paint such mythological scenes as the *Triumph of Bacchus* (1803; Naples, Capodimonte). From 1825 a new note of naturalism emerged in Boguet's Roman views, as seen in the *Grounds of the Palazzo Chigi, Arriccia* (signed and dated 1825; oil on canvas, 610×736 mm; sold London, Christie's, 25 June 1982, for £8,500). This tendency may be explained in part by the presence in Rome at that time of Boguet's friend the painter François Granet. Boguet's son, also named Nicolas-Didier (1802–after 1861), was painting by this date and there are several works that show evidence of collaboration between the two artists; however, the *View of the Villa Aldobrandini at Frascati* (1824; Aix-en-Provence, Mus. Granet) is probably the son's work alone.

BIBLIOGRAPHY
L'Italia vista dai pittori francesi del XVIII e XIX secolo (exh. cat., ed. G. Bazin; Rome, Pal. Espos., 1961)
M. M. Aubrun: 'N.-D. Boguet (1755–1839): Un Emule du Lorrain', *Gaz. B.-A.*, lxxxiii (1974), pp. 319–36 [cat. of paintings]
De David à Delacroix: La Peinture française de 1774 à 1830 (exh. cat., Paris, Grand Pal.; Detroit, MI, Inst. A.; New York, Met.; 1974–5), pp. 319–21 [mainly about Boguet's son]
LORRAINE PEAKE

Bogusz, Marian (*b* Pleszew, 25 April 1920; *d* Warsaw, 2 Feb 1980). Polish painter, sculptor and stage designer. He studied at the Academy of Fine Arts, Warsaw, in the studios of Jan Cybis (*b* 1897) and Jan Seweryn Sokołowski (1904–53) between 1945 and 1948. He was a co-founder and later head of the Painting Section of the Club of Young Artists and Scientists (Klub Młodych Artystów i Naukowców), an interdisciplinary avant-garde institution that flourished in Warsaw between 1947 and 1949. In 1955, together with Zbigniew Dłubak and Kajetan Sosnowski he founded Group 55, which took a stand against the ideas of the exhibition at the Arsenal, Warsaw (see ARSENALISTS), and which formulated a programme of modern art. From 1956 to 1965 he ran the Galeria Krzywe Koło in Warsaw, which showed innovative work by Polish artists. Bogusz staged the First Koszalin *Plein-air* Art Session in Osieki (1963) and jointly organized the First Biennial of Spatial Forms in Elblag (1965), both very important events shaping Polish art of the 1960s. He took part in many other symposia and exhibitions at home and abroad.

Bogusz's abstract paintings and sculptures (he also designed architecture and stage sets) evolved only slightly during the 30 years of his artistic career. During the 1940s he produced figurative compositions in a clearly defined space (e.g. *Joy of New Constructions*, 1948). In the mid-1950s Bogusz painted several pictures almost realistic in character, but with the same spatial concept (e.g. *Berlin*, 1955). In the late 1950s and early 1960s the influence of matter painting and *Art informel* is evident in his paintings, while in the mid-1960s there is a return to literally spatial constructions built from geometric shapes, using aluminium and the technique of collage. Bogusz's work belongs to the mainstream of modern Polish art and, despite its rationality, is far removed from the Polish 'Neo-avant-garde' of the second half of the 1960s.

BIBLIOGRAPHY
Marian Bogusz, 1920–1980: Wystawa monograficzna [Marian Bogusz, 1920–80: Monographic exhibition] (exh. cat., Poznań, N. Mus., 1982)

WOJCIECH WŁODARCZYK

Bohemia. *See under* CZECH REPUBLIC.

Bohigas, Oriol. *See under* MARTORELL, BOHIGAS, MACKAY.

Böhm (i). *See* BEHAM.

Böhm (ii). German family of architects and teachers. (1) Dominikus Böhm's career was devoted to the design of Roman Catholic churches in Germany, where his progressive understanding of the role of the laity in worship and his willingness to use new building technologies made him one of the most influential religious architects of his generation. From 1952 until his death he collaborated with his son (2) Gottfried Böhm, who worked both on churches and on a broader range of projects and was particularly interested in the use of space and the social function of buildings.

(1) Dominikus Böhm (*b* Jettingen, 23 Oct 1880; *d* Cologne, 3 Aug 1955). He attended the Bauschule, Augsburg, and the Technische Hochschule, Stuttgart, where he studied under Theodor Fischer. In 1908 he began teaching at the Technische Staatslehranstalt, Offenbach am Main. From the start of his career he was primarily interested in religious architecture. Early projects show him experimenting with Early Christian, Baroque and other formulae for church design. The church of St Johann (1921–7) in Neu-Ulm is the best of his early realizations. Here traditional forms are restated in an unornamented vocabulary generated by the methods of construction. Alternating bands of brick and stone give texture and colour to the broad narthex and the squat central tower of the austere façade (see fig.). Inside, jagged concrete vaults give an Expressionist interpretation of Gothic structure. Centrally planned chapels, also dramatically vaulted, reinforce the sense of detachment from the world.

In 1922 Böhm settled in Cologne, where he taught in the department of Christian art at the Werkschulen. Throughout the 1920s concrete vaults and brick arcades remained his favourite means of demarcating space. In the late 1920s he turned, however, to simpler interior plans for unvaulted, often aisleless, hall churches, and in the

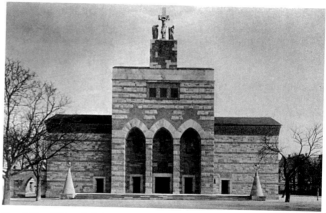

Dominikus Böhm: St Johann, Neu-Ulm, 1921–7

early 1930s the expressiveness that had characterized the internal arrangements of his earlier churches began to appear in his exterior treatments. St Englebert's (1930–33) in Cologne-Riehl, a circular church with a projecting apse and sacristy and an attached bell-tower, dramatically illustrates this shift. Each of the eight segments of the circle is roofed with a parabolic barrel vault radiating from the church's centre. During the Nazi era he was ousted from his teaching post but was able to build a handful of radical abstractions of early medieval German church prototypes. The churches he built after World War II rephrase the quest for spatial unity in terms of the International Style, tempered by the organic shapes and textures associated with Alvar Aalto. The church of St Maria Königin (1951–4) in Cologne-Marienburg is distinguished by the stained-glass curtain wall of its south façade, which also wraps around the projecting circular baptistery. In his last decade Böhm also restored a number of churches damaged during the war. Many of the characteristic features of Böhm's church designs, particularly the elimination of transepts and choirs that separated the congregation from the laity and the placement of unostentatious altars so that priests could face the congregation, anticipate the changes made in Roman Catholic liturgy by the Second Vatican Council (1962–5).

BIBLIOGRAPHY
R. Schwarz: 'Dominikus Böhm und sein Werk', *Mod. Bauformen*, xxvi (1927), pp. 226–40
J. Habel, ed.: *Dominikus Böhm: Ein deutscher Baumeister* (Regensburg, 1943)
A. Hoff, H. Much and R. Thoma: *Dominikus Böhm* (Munich, 1962)
R. Maguire and K. Murray: *Modern Churches of the World* (New York, 1965)
G. Stalling: *Studien zu Dominikus Böhm* (Berne, 1974)

KATHLEEN JAMES

(2) Gottfried Böhm (*b* Offenbach am Main, 23 Jan 1920). Son of (1) Dominikus Böhm. He studied architecture at the Technische Hochschule, Munich, from 1942 to 1947 and sculpture at the Kunstakademie, Munich. He then worked with his father as well as for a year with Rudolf Schwarz in Cologne, and for six months in the USA. After his father's death in 1955 he took over his office in Cologne, which was principally involved in church construction.

Böhm began by designing churches consisting of several geometric shapes united in an architectural framework such as a perimeter wall, for example the parish church (1958) at Schildgen. His projects later became more concentrated and less spontaneous. The pilgrimage church of Maria, Königin des Friedens (1965–8), at Neviges, near Velbert, built in the form of an Expressionist sculpture, typifies Böhm's work: he brings together different parts of the building and their function and skilfully combines interior and exterior areas—a concept that he later intensified—using an expressive architectural language. The town hall (1967–71) in the old castle area in Bensberg was characterized by his typical rhythmic style on a scale accessible to the public and sensitive to its historic location (*see* GERMANY, fig. 13). Böhm loved to accentuate his buildings with vivid rooms, varied walls and symbolic towers, preferring to work in concrete and brick.

In the 1980s, as a result of the more commercial nature of the building industry, his style became more technical and controlled, as in the Züblin administration building (1984) in the Stuttgart suburb of Möhringen. He was able to realize his lifelong concern to provide people with a sympathetic working environment with the Arbed-Stahl headquarters in Luxembourg (1994). Böhm's sketches show that his artistic goals in the form and decoration of all his projects remain an important part of his work. His tendency towards harmony and symmetry is also evident in his proposals to solve urban development problems. Böhm was professor of town planning and training at the Technische Hochschule in Aachen from 1963 to 1985.

BIBLIOGRAPHY
V. Darius: *Der Architekt Gottfried Böhm: Bauten der sechziger Jahre* (Düsseldorf, 1988)
S. Raèv, ed.: *Gottfried Böhm: Vorträge, Bauten, Projekte* (Stuttgart, 1988)
THOMAS SPERLING

Böhme, Lothar (*b* Berlin, 26 July 1938). German painter and graphic designer. He studied at the Werkkunstschule, Charlottenburg, Berlin, from 1957 to 1961, and thereafter worked on a freelance basis in Berlin. He soon became distanced from the propagandist formulae and stylistic narrowness of the Socialist Realism decreed by the Staatspartei and officials of the Künstlerverbandsfunktionären in the DDR in the 1950s and 1960s. The 'Cézannism' that spread into art in East Berlin *c.* 1962 had a strong influence on him. His awareness of the sensuality of the painting material and the universality of the simple object resulted in a long course of internal exile. Because he refused to allow art to be misused to illustrate ideological or social concepts, he remained in the shadows of official art in the DDR for *c.* 20 years, his work being a far cry from historical painting, representation of the working class and approval of Socialist society.

With almost obsessive concentration, Böhme aimed for his artistic goal through the standing, sitting or kneeling female figure with a strong pictorial quality and colours confined to earthy brown tones (darkening to black) and grey, with green and red for accentuation. He occasionally painted self-portraits, still-lifes and landscapes. Again and again, however, he found emotional support in the female nude, which appears not as a sensual erotic reflection but exclusively as a problem of the form of the sensuous

fullness of existence or as a pictorial representation of intoxicated rapture. The series of this pronounced artistic figure elaborated by Böhme gives the impression of a silent battery of silhouettes emerging out of nature and then flowing back into it again. It frequently looks angular in outline and the impasto makes it look modelled. Böhme used colour to intensify his figures through to their core. The figure itself is usually shrouded in darkness, but this cover opens up at the edge of the picture to reveal the white of the canvas or the paper background. Stillness, persistence and melancholic reticence radiate from this art, which speaks of intellectual awareness and thus also of emotional conflicts.

BIBLIOGRAPHY
Lothar Böhme: Der Maler und sein Motiv (exh. cat., W. Berlin, N.G., 1982)
CHRISTOPH TANNERT

Bohnstedt, Ludwig. *See* BONSHTEDT, LYUDVIG.

Bohomazov, Oleksandr (Konstyantynovych) [Bogomazov, Aleksandr Konstantinovich] (*b* Yampol, 26 March 1880; *d* Kiev, 3 June 1930). Ukrainian painter. He studied at the agricultural school in Kherson (1896–1902), then at Kiev Art School (1902–05). In the summer of 1906 he painted *en plein air* in the Crimea, then he worked in Moscow in the studios of Fyodor Rerberg and Konstantin Yuon (1907–08). Initially, his art was influenced by Symbolism, particularly by the work of Viktor Borisov-Musatov. By 1912 Bohomazov had become involved in Futurist pictorial theory and practice, and in 1914 he wrote a treatise on painting and its elements, constituting his formulations of the new Futurist art. In that year, with Aleksandra Exter, he organized an exhibition of Ukrainian modernist art, to which he contributed 88 paintings. In 1915–17 he taught in the provincial school at Heriusy (now Nagornyy Karabakh), where his Expressionist sensibilities were aroused by the mountainous surroundings and blended with his Futurist focus on quantitative and qualitative rhythms, the core idea of his treatise of 1914. In 1916 he participated in the annual exhibition at the Kiev Museum and was commended by the critic Yakov Tugendkhol'd. In 1917 Bohomazov became professor of drawing at the Commercial School and the Jewish School in Kiev. With the political upheaval of 1918, he assumed an active role in the many newly formed artistic organizations and at the first Congress of Plastic Art in Ukraine. In 1919, together with Exter and others, he helped to decorate Kiev's streets and agitprop trains with Futurist designs. He taught at Kiev's first Free Studio of Easel Painting and Decorative Art and, during 1921, illustrated children's books. In 1922 he became a professor of easel painting at the newly formed Institute of Plastic Arts in Kiev, but to combat tuberculosis he had to spend prolonged periods in the Crimea (1923–6). He continued to teach at the institute until 1930; it was the last bastion of modern art before the onslaught of SOCIALIST REALISM. By 1927 his work had become more figurative, culminating in *Sawyers* (Kiev, Mus. Ukrain. A.), for which he prepared a number of sketches, and in which he sought to arrive at a synthesis of figurative and Futurist art. The painting was displayed at the major retrospective of modern art in Ukraine, *Ten Years of October, 1917–1927*. In 1927 his

1914 treatise was accepted as a manual for artistic instruction at the Kiev institute. For many years his work was considered unacceptably 'formalist', and it was not until 1966 that the first retrospective of his paintings was held in Kiev.

UNPUBLISHED SOURCES
Kiev Lesya Ukrain. Lit. Mus. [MS. of *Zhivopis' i elementy* [Painting and elements] (1914)]

BIBLIOGRAPHY
Tatlin's Dream: Russian Suprematist and Constructivist Art, 1910–1923 (exh. cat. by A. Nakov, London, Fischer F.A., 1973), pp. 58–9
M. M. Mudrak: *The New Generation and Artistic Modernism in the Ukraine* (Ann Arbor, 1986)
Alexandre Bogomazov (Jampol, 1880–Kiev 1930) (exh. cat., Toulouse, Mus. A. Mod. and Mus. Jacobins, 1991)
Ukrajinska avangarda, 1910–1930 (exh. cat., ed. M. Susovski; Zagreb, Gal. Contemp. A., 1991), pp. 179–88

MYROSLAVA M. MUDRAK

Bohrmann, Horst Paul Albert. *See* HORST.

Bohun. English family of patrons. Between the 1340s and the 1390s the Bohun earls of Hereford and their relations were the most significant patrons of manuscript illumination in England. There was a tradition of book-collecting in the family. An Apocalypse in French of *c.* 1280 (Oxford, New Coll., MS. 65) was probably made for Joanna de Bohun (*d* 1283). Humphrey de Bohun IV (*c.* 1276–1321/2) commissioned the Longleat Breviary (Longleat House, Wilts, MS. 10) and had additions made to the Alfonso Psalter (London, BL, Add. MS. 24686), partly by the so-called Subsidiary Queen Mary Artist (*see* QUEEN MARY PSALTER), probably after the death of his wife Princess Elizabeth in 1316. In the 1340s Elizabeth (*d* 1355), wife of William de Bohun, Earl of Northampton, commissioned a Dominican Psalter-Hours (ex-Astor priv. col., Ginge Manor, Berks), the chief illuminator of which can be associated with Cambridge.

The first member of the family who is known to have retained an illuminator in his household, at Pleshey Castle, Essex, was Humphrey de Bohun VI (*c.* 1309–61), who succeeded his brother John as Earl of Hereford and Essex in 1336. In his will he named the illuminator as Brother John de Tye, and also referred to a resident painter named Peter. John de Tye was an Augustinian friar, of an order particularly favoured by Humphrey VI, who financed the rebuilding of their London church in 1354. In 1384 John de Tye was granted permission to train Brother Henry Hood for a year in the art of illumination, and the terms of the dispensation indicate that he was still living outside the convent.

The development of this school of illumination was occasioned by the Black Death. In the late 1340s Cambridge artists had begun work on a Psalter for Humphrey VI (Vienna, Österreich. Nbib., Cod. 1826*), but none of them apparently survived after 1348/9. It was in order to complete this book that John de Tye's services were first enlisted. When illuminating the calendar he was assisted by another miniaturist, with whom he also collaborated at this time on a Psalter (London, BL, MS. Royal 13.D.i*). This second artist was of South Netherlandish origin. His style indicates that he was trained in the Tournai region, and his hand can be identified in two South Netherlandish manuscripts: a Book of Hours (Oxford, Bodleian Lib.,

Lat. MS. liturg. f.3) and an Antiphonary (Brussels, Bib. Royale Albert 1er, MS. 6426), both executed before his emigration in the 1350s.

John de Tye's style is rooted in East Anglian miniature painting of the 1340s, but is tempered by the influence of Bolognese illumination, most probably mediated through imported canon law books. His work is characterized by sculptural forms modelled in subtly gradated tones, ovoid heads with small, dainty features and heavy eyelids. The South Netherlandish artist's approach is more linear, and makes greater use of architectural ornament and other decorative elements. His style matured as a result of his association with John de Tye and contact with Parisian illumination, probably in the French books in the library at Pleshey Castle.

Many of the Bohun manuscripts were illuminated in several campaigns, reflecting the circumstances of the family. The most extreme example is a Psalter (Oxford, Exeter Coll., MS. 47; see fig.), begun in the late 1350s for Humphrey VI, continued in the 1380s, but not completed until the 1390s. A Psalter-Hours (London, BL, MS.

Bohun Psalter, page reproducing Psalm 52, 'Dixit insipiens', late 1350s–1390s (Oxford, Exeter College, MS. 47, fol. 34*r*)

Egerton 3277) was probably written *c*. 1360, but most of the illumination was not carried out until the mid-1380s. Several pages are by a close follower of John de Tye, probably Henry Hood. He also overpainted two miniatures in a *Lancelot du Lac* (London, BL, MS. Royal 20.D.iv). Three of the books (Cambridge, Fitzwilliam, MS. 38–1950 (datable between September 1371 and 1372/3; Oxford, Bodleian Lib., MS. Auct. D.4.4; and Pommersfelden, Schloss Weissenstein, MS. 2934(348)) were executed, or at least begun, for Humphrey de Bohun VII (1342–72/3), Humphrey VI's nephew and heir. After Humphrey VII's death, the chief patrons of the workshop appear to have been his elder daughter, Eleanor (1366–99), and her husband, Thomas of Woodstock, Duke of Gloucester (1355–97), who built up an extensive library of which an inventory was taken after his death. Other possible patrons were Humphrey VII's younger daughter, Mary (1369–94), who married Henry, Earl of Derby (later Henry IV, *reg* 1399–1413), and his widow, Joan (*d* 1419). A Sarum Book of Hours and Lives of Saints (Copenhagen, Kon. Bib., MSS Thott.quarto 547 and Thott.quarto 517), which contain some of the latest work of John de Tye, dating from the early 1380s, were executed for a female member of the Bohun family, probably Mary.

A remarkable feature of several of the central Bohun manuscripts (Oxford, Exeter Coll., MS. 47; London, BL, MS. Egerton 3277; Cambridge, Fitzwilliam, MS. 38–1950 and Oxford, Bodleian Lib., MS. Auct. D.4.4) is their extensive cycles of Old and New Testament illustration, which in their literal approach to the biblical text reflect the theology of the Augustinian friars. Nearly all the Bohun manuscripts incorporate elaborate displays of heraldry referring to family alliances and their royal connections.

After the demise or departure of their resident miniaturists, the Bohuns turned to commercial illuminators. The last campaign in the Psalter (Oxford, Exeter Coll., MS. 47) can be linked with books produced for other patrons (e.g. Oxford, Bodleian Lib., MS. Laud. Misc. 165 and Hatfield House, Herts, MS. 290). A Psalter-Hours executed for Eleanor shortly before her husband's murder in 1397 (Edinburgh, N. Lib., MS. Adv. 18.6.5) was illuminated by a London artist who also worked on the Carmelite Missal (London, BL, Add. MSS 29704–5) and had links with the artists of the Lytlington Missal (London, Westminster Abbey, MS. 37). A copy of Higden's *Polychronicon* (Oxford, Bodleian Lib., MS. Bodley 316), presented by Thomas of Woodstock to the college he founded at Pleshey, was possibly executed in Norwich. The style developed by the Bohun illuminators was widely imitated by these and other professional miniaturists of the late 14th century.

BIBLIOGRAPHY

G. E. C[okayne]: *The Complete Peerage*, ed. V. Gibbs and others, vi (London, 1926), pp. 457–77; ix (London, 1936), pp. 664–8
M. R. James and E. G. Millar: *The Bohun Manuscripts: A Group of Five Manuscripts Executed in England about 1370 for Members of the Bohun Family* (Oxford, 1936)
L. Dennison: '"The Fitzwarin Psalter and its Allies": A Reappraisal', *England in the Fourteenth Century: Proceedings of the 1985 Harlaxton Symposium: Evansville, IN*, pp. 42–66
——: 'The Artistic Context of Fourteenth Century Flemish Brasses', *Trans. Mnmt. Brass Soc.*, xiv (1986), pp. 1–38
L. F. Sandler: *Gothic Manuscripts, 1285–1385*, 2 vols (London, 1986)
L. E. Dennison: *The Stylistic Sources, Dating and Development of the Bohun Workshop, c. 1340–1400* (diss., U. London, 1988) [full bibliog.]
——: 'Oxford, Exeter College MS 47: The Importance of Stylistic and Codicological Analysis in its Dating and Localization', *Medieval Book Production: Assessing the Evidence: Proceedings of the Second Conference of the Seminar in the History of the Book to 1500: Oxford, 1988*, pp. 41–59

L. E. DENNISON

Boichot, Guillaume (*b* Chalon-sur-Saône, 30 Aug 1735; *d* Paris, 9 Dec 1814). French sculptor, draughtsman and painter. He probably first trained in Chalon, under the sculptor Pierre Colasson (*c*. 1724–70); later he studied in Paris at the school of the Académie Royale, under Simon Challes. In 1766 he travelled to Italy, remaining there until 1770. The art of Raphael and his school and the Fontainebleau school influenced Boichet's art (e.g. *Agrippina Bearing Germanicus's Ashes*, Lille, Mus. B.-A.) from an early date by giving his work a Neo-classical character. Boichot next worked in Burgundy, where he was responsible for architecture, sculpture and paintings at the château of Verdun-sur-le-Doubs (destr.). He also produced decorative work for the salon of the Académie de Dijon, of which he was a member; for the refectory of the abbey of St Benigne, Dijon, he executed a painting of the *Triumph of Temperance over Gluttony* (Dijon, Mus. B.-A.). In Paris his studio was in the Passage Sandrier off the Chaussée d'Antin. Introduced by Augustin Pajou, he was approved (*agréé*) by the Académie Royale in 1788.

During the French Revolution, Boichot participated in the decoration of the Panthéon, Paris, including the sculpture of the *Declaration of the Rights of Man*, drawings of which are preserved in the Bibliothèque Nationale and in the Musée Denon, Chalon-sur-Saône; a plaster model has been rediscovered. He also produced *Strength under the Emblem of Hercules*, known from a bronze reduction (Los Angeles, CA, Co. Mus. A.). For the church of St Roch, Paris, he executed a statue of *St Roch*, as well as the *Four Evangelists* (plaster, 1823) for the pulpit and a painting in grisaille of *Jesus Shown to the People by Pilate*. Boichot was an excellent draughtsman and contributed to the illustrations for Jean-Baptiste Gail's translations of works by Theocritus, Xenophon, Thucydides and Herodotus and also to illustrations for the 1803 edition of Chateaubriand's *Génie du Christianisme*. He also sculpted a number of portraits, including busts of *Vivant Denon* (1802; Chalon-sur-Saône, Mus. Denon) and of *Bernardin de Saint-Pierre* (1806; Versailles, Château). Boichot regularly exhibited sculptures and drawings at the Salons from 1789 to 1812.

BIBLIOGRAPHY

Bellier de la Chavignerie–Auvray; Lami
L. Armand-Calliat: 'Sculptures et dessins de Guillaume Boichot', *Rev. A.* [Paris], 5 (1958), pp. 229–34
S. Laveissiere: *Dictionnaire des artistes et ouvriers d'art de Bourgogne*, i (Paris, 1980), pp. 53–4
Autour de David: Dessins néo-classiques du Musée des Beaux-Arts de Lille (exh. cat., Lille, Mus. B.-A., 1983), pp. 25–6
Le Panthéon: Symbole des révolutions, de l'église de la nation au temple des grands hommes (exh. cat., Paris, Hôtel de Sully; Montreal, Can. Cent. Archit.; 1989), pp. 234, 242
Nouvelles acquisitions du département des sculptures, 1988–1991, Paris, Louvre cat. (Paris, 1992), pp. 91–4

PHILIPPE SOREL

Boijen, William Bouwens van der. *See* BOUWENS VAN DER BOIJEN, WILLIAM.

Boijmans, F(rans) J(acob) O(tto). *See* BOYMANS, F. J. O.

Boileau. French family of architects.

(1) Louis-Auguste Boileau (*b* Paris, 24 March 1812; *d* Paris, 14 Feb 1896). The son of a clockmaker, he began his career as a journeyman carpenter, particularly skilled in making neo-Gothic church furnishings. These included a bishop's throne (1834–7) in St Antoine, Compiègne, and an organ (1839) for the choir of St-Germain l'Auxerrois, Paris. He then began to study architecture. Largely self-taught, he received some education from his friend Louis-Alexandre Piel (1808–41) and chose to specialize in designing churches. Between 1843 and 1848 Boileau built in a neo-Gothic style his first church at Mattaincourt, Vosges. His subsequent project in 1850 for a church at La Chapelle St-Denis, Paris, 'with the lower support piers in cast iron and the framework of the vaulting in iron', marked the beginning of his interest in the use of iron in architecture. That same year he exhibited a maquette of his so-called 'synthetic cathedral', a project that baffled both the public and the ecclesiastical world and united both Gothic Revivalists and the supporters of architectural eclecticism in severe condemnation. In particular, it provoked a controversy between Boileau and Viollet-le-Duc on the appropriate building materials for Gothic architecture. Boileau aimed at creating a style of his own, one that was free from the constraints of archaeology but that also avoided the pitfalls of eclecticism. He insisted that he wished to improve on Gothic vaulting. In his view, 13th-century cathedrals (dear to Viollet-le-Duc) displayed certain constructional drawbacks, particularly in their use of buttresses and flying buttresses and, for Boileau, there were other anomalies such as roofing superimposed above vaulting. His own project was for a church 272 m long, 128 m wide and 168 m high at its topmost point. The plan was a Latin cross, and the progressive elevation of each of the arms of the cross towards the central dome was intended to provide a novel lighting effect. This arithmetical progression would make it possible for all parts of the building to be well lit, particularly the dome; this comprised three recessed levels, the third forming a lantern. Although it was striking and original, Boileau was too eclectic in his widely ranging stylistic references, and since the outer form of his 'synthetic cathedral' exactly imitated the form of the interior, public opinion was divided. Originally intended to have been built in stone, the design was constantly reworked; after 1853 he proposed relacing the traditional frame by iron and cast iron.

Boileau succeeded in including certain aspects of his 'synthetic cathedral' in his designs for St Eugène in Paris. Built between 1854 and 1855 on a very small site, a metal frame was used since the parish was a relatively poor one and finances were limited. The church had a rectangular plan divided into five aisles, without a transept. An apse and two chapels terminated the three main aisles. Since it had adjoining buildings on two sides, the church was able to accommodate a large number of parishioners only by using a metal framework in its construction, which made buttresses unnecessary. By dispensing with the ambulatory and side chapels, Boileau brought the plan of the church

nearer to that of a utilitarian building—a rational use of available space that was more akin to the ideal basilican plan. His metal framework was designed to reproduce the decorative forms of the Gothic style; this included cast-iron columns of extreme delicacy, rounded vaulting with multiple ribs over the nave, intersecting ribs on the side aisles and broken barrel-vaulting supported by special pierced braces (reproducing those of the lower chapel of the Sainte-Chapelle). Together they constituted an unusual and original effect. The exceptional quality of the lighting at St Eugène depended largely on its windows; these offered the only flat, continuous surfaces in the building, which, enhanced by stained glass, displayed the church's religious imagery. With its self-bearing framework and masonry surfaces acting purely as a curtain wall, St Eugène remains Boileau's major work. He built several churches more or less directly influenced by this Parisian experiment: St Germain (1862) at Marencennes, Charente-Maritime; St Paul (1863–9) at Montluçon, Allier; Juilly (1869), Seine et Marne; Gua (1868), Aveyron; Abergement-Clemenciat (1866–8), Ain; Notre-Dame-de-France (1868; destr. 1944), Leicester Square, London; and the chapel of the civic hospital at Clermont, Oise.

Between 1867 and 1876 Boileau and his son (2) Louis-Charles Boileau built the Bon Marché department store in Paris, designed by Jean-Alexandre Laplanche (1839–1910). In collaboration with Gustave Eiffel they created one of the earliest 'grands magasins'. It was one of the first department stores where the usual metal-framed glazing (in which condensation tended to accumulate) was replaced by a glass lantern with a double shell (for illustration *see* DEPARTMENT STORE). Beneath the lantern is a monumental staircase surrounded by galleries on all sides. The store's reconstruction was completed in 1887, and (3) Louis-Hippolyte Boileau inherited the post of architect of the Bon Marché stores.

WRITINGS
La Nouvelle Forme architecturale (Paris, 1853)
Histoire critique de l'invention en architecture (Paris, 1886)

(2) Louis-Charles Boileau (*b* Paris, 26 Oct 1837; *d* Bordeaux, 17 Sept 1914). Son of (1) Louis-Auguste Boileau. His major work was the Gothic Revival church at Le Vésinet (1863–5), Yvelines. Designed in collaboration with his father, this church was built with an iron framework and masonry of reinforced concrete, the latter having been developed by François Coignet in the 1840s and 1850s. Between 1867 and 1876 he worked with his father on the Bon Marché in Paris; during the Commune (1871) Boileau was a member of the board of the Fédération des Artistes, alongside Gustave Courbet and others. He also contributed regularly to the review *L'Architecture*. He built a town house in the Rue du Bac, Paris, and a château in the country at Fontenay for Aristide Boucicaut. He also built the Pont du Midi at Lyon, the bridge and public buildings at Verjux and the presbytery at L'Isle-Adam. At Etampes both the town hall and the façades for the church of St-Martin were built to his designs.

JEAN-FRANÇOIS PINCHON

(3) Louis-Hippolyte Boileau (*b* Paris, 1878; *d* 6 Nov 1948). Grandson of (1) Louis-Auguste Boileau. He was a student of Gaston Redon at the Ecole des Beaux-Arts, graduating in 1907. Shortly thereafter he designed the Hotel Lutetia (1910; with Henri Tauzin), Paris, with façades and reception rooms that successfully combine Baroque ornamentation, characteristic of turn-of-the-century eclecticism, with a touch of Art Nouveau. He inherited from his father, (2) Louis-Charles Boileau, the position of architect of the Bon Marché department stores and built for them an annexe (1924) at the corner of the Rue du Bac and Rue de Sèvres, Paris, the Pavilion Pomone at the Exposition Internationale des Arts Décoratifs et Industriels Modernes (1925), and several stores in other French cities. In his interior designs for the Prunier restaurant (1925) on the Rue Traktir and the Café des Capucines (1928), both in Paris, Boileau appears as a major proponent of a classicizing, rich but not stuffy version of Art Deco. In the 1930s his style became more sober, as demonstrated by his Maison de France (1932), Avenue des Champs-Elysées, Paris. He was also involved in the transformation of Gabriel Davioud's Palais du Trocadéro into the Palais de Chaillot (with Jacques Carlu and Léon Azéma) for the Exposition Internationale des Arts et Techniques dans la Vie Moderne (1937) in Paris, an austerely neo-classicist building whose terraces form a strong perspective across the Seine to the Eiffel Tower and the Champ-de-Mars. His technical competence brought him a particularly active role on the construction site. Just before his death he was selected to direct the reconstruction of the town of Beauvais following World War II.

BIBLIOGRAPHY

'Hotel de voyageurs, Rue de Sèvres et Boulevard Raspail', *L'Architecture* [Paris], xxiv/18 (1911), pp. 156–8

M. Roux-Spitz: 'La Nouvelle Annexe des magasins du Bon Marché', *L'Architecte*, n. s., i/6 (1924), pp. 41–8

'Restaurant Boulevard des Capucines à Paris', *L'Architecte*, n. s., vii/4 (1929), p. 32

L. Hautecoeur: *Architecture classique* (1943–57), vi, vii

C. Beutler: 'Saint-Eugène et la Bibliothèque Nationale: Zwei Eisenkonstruktionen und ihr Ideegehalt', *Miscellanéa pro arte Hermann Schnitzer* (Düsseldorf, 1966)

B. Foucart: 'La Cathédrale synthétique de Louis-Auguste Boileau', *Rev. A.* [Paris], iii (1969), pp. 49–69

M. Emery: *Un Siècle d'architecture moderne en France, 1850–1950* (Paris, 1971)

B. Marrey: 'La Pensée fouriériste et l'architecture', *Profil*, xliv (1981), pp. 44–8

ISABELLE GOURNAY
(bibliography with JEAN-FRANÇOIS PINCHON)

Boileau [Boileau; Boiliaue; Boillesve; Boyleaux; Boylesve], **Etienne** [Estienne] **de**, Provost of Paris (*b c.* 1200; *d* Paris, April 1270). French official and writer. He belonged to a family of mayors and magistrates from Orléans. His marriage to Marguerite de la Guesle is recorded in 1225, but the date of his appointment as Provost of Paris is uncertain. In the *Histoire de Saint Louis* (*c.* 1305), Louis IX's chronicler, Jean de Joinville, recounted that after the King's return from the Crusade (1254) he made Boileau his chief magistrate and administrator of law. In 1260, however, Boileau was still Provost of Orléans, and it seems more likely that he took up office in Paris at the end of that year or early in 1261. The *Livre des métiers*, for which Boileau is famous, was compiled during his administration at Châtelet and is a register of the trade organizations in Paris, describing their practices

and regulations as well as the tariffs levied on their commodities. The earliest known manuscript of the work was destroyed by fire (1737) at the Chambre des Comptes, but notes taken from it and the survival of later manuscripts (several in Paris, Bib. N.) have allowed it to be reconstructed. The *Livre* covers various trades, from suppliers of provisions to craftsmen working in different media, including metal, ivory, wood, leather and fabric. Its importance for art historians lies in the information it provides about craft organizations in Paris in the second half of the 13th century. Goldsmiths, for example, were to work only for the court or the Church, and were granted privileges, such as permission to keep their shops open on Sundays and on certain feast days; sculptors, also highly regarded, were required to carve their sculpture from a single block (crucifixes alone could be made from three pieces); among tapestry-makers, the term 'tapissiers de tapis sarrasinois' possibly refers to the Arabic origins of the technique, and the craft as a whole is described as closed to women, for whom it was considered too arduous. Although such customs and rules had existed long before Louis IX's reign, Boileau's *Livre* gave them legal sanction, recording them in one place with uniformity and clarity.

WRITINGS

Le Livre des métiers (MS.; *c.* 1261–70); ed. G.-B. Depping as *Réglemens sur les arts et métiers de Paris, rédigés au XIIIe siècle, et connus sous le nom du livre des métiers d'Etienne Boileau* (Paris, 1837)

BIBLIOGRAPHY

Jean de Joinville: *Histoire de Saint Louis* (MS.; *c.* 1305); ed. N. de Wailly (Paris, 1874); Eng. trans. by M. R. B. Shaw in *Chronicles of the Crusades* (London, 1963/*R* 1982)

A. Lévis Mirepoix: 'Les Métiers de Paris au temps de Saint Louis, d'après *Le Livre des métiers* d'Etienne Boileau', *Saint Louis, roi de France* (Paris, 1970), pp. 277–368

TANYA ALFILLÉ

Boileau [Boileau-Despréaux], **Nicolas** (*b* Paris, 1 Nov 1636; *d* Paris, 13 March 1711). French writer. His influence on art was indirect: although he made no claim to knowledge of art, he unwittingly played a part in the development of historical painting during the second part of Louis XIV's reign and particularly in the development of the theory of art in the 18th century. At the beginning of the personal reign of Louis XIV he was at first excluded from the distribution of pensions awarded through the mediation of the Académie des Inscriptions et Belles-Lettres, the particular function of which was to lay down the iconography to be used in works that the King had commissioned; through Charles Perrault, it to some degree dominated the Académie Royale de Peinture et de Sculpture. In 1683, after Boileau had finally obtained admission to the Académie des Inscriptions, it ceased to deal with iconography, and from then on artists working for the King enjoyed greater freedom.

However, Boileau's main influence on French art was through his didactic poem *L'Art poétique* (1674), in which he set out the fundamental rules for writing a successful poem or play: the necessity for genuine talent, the requirement for self-knowledge in choosing an appropriate genre, the need for naturalism in style and subject-matter and the importance of respecting artistic conventions. This work soon came to be greatly admired, and its standards were generally accepted throughout the 18th century. It was used by classicist painters and art critics as a source of advice, in which it vied with Charles-Alphonse Dufresnoy's *L'Art de peinture*, and it became part of the canon of French writing on art.

WRITINGS
L'Art poétique (Paris, 1674)

BIBLIOGRAPHY
E. Magne: *Bibliographie générale des oeuvres de N. Boileau-Despréaux* (Paris, 1928)
J. R. Miller: *Boileau en France au XVIIIème siècle* (Baltimore, 1942)
J. Chouillet: *L'Esthétique des lumières* (Paris, 1974)
A. Becq: *Genèse de l'esthétique française moderne, 1680–1814* (Pisa, 1984)

CHRISTIAN MICHEL

Boilly, Louis-Léopold (*b* La Bassée, nr Lille, 5 July 1761; *d* Paris, 4 Jan 1845). French painter and printmaker. The son of a wood-carver, Arnould Boilly (1764–79), he lived in Douai until 1778, when he went to Arras to receive instruction in *trompe l'oeil* painting from Dominique Doncre (1743–1820). He moved to Paris in 1785. Between 1789 and 1791 he executed eight small scenes on moralizing and amorous subjects for the Avignon collector Esprit-Claude-François Calvet (1728–1810), including *The Visit* (1789; Saint-Omer, Mus. Hôtel Sandelin). He exhibited at the Salon between 1791 and 1824 and received a gold medal at the Salon of 1804. From the beginning his genre subjects were extremely popular with the public and collectors. In 1833, at a time when his popularity was declining, he was admitted to the Légion d'honneur and the Institut de France.

His early works (1790–1800) show a taste for moralizing, amorous and sentimental subjects inherited from Jean Honoré Fragonard and Jean-Baptiste Greuze that combine anecdote and a delight in the tactile qualities of textiles. Boilly sought the 'sensibilité' and the 'émotion' dear to Jean-Jacques Rousseau and Denis Diderot. His mannered colouring and precise techniques are almost those of a miniaturist, and recall such Dutch 17th-century genre painters as Gabriel Metsu and Gerard Terborch (ii); Boilly owned an important collection of their work (sold Paris, 13–14 April 1824). The *Thoughtful Present* (Paris, Mus. A. Déc.) is typical of his early period, mannered and tinged with a gentle sentimentality. In the same vein, but with a more erotic emphasis, is the *Lovers and the Escaped Bird* (Paris, Louvre). Because of this picture Boilly was condemned by the Comité du Salut Public in 1794, at the height of the Terror and at the instigation of his fellow artist Jean-Baptiste-Joseph Wicar, for painting subjects 'd'une obscénité révoltante pour les moeurs républicaines' (*J. Soc. Pop. & Républicaine A.*, April/May 1794, pp. 381–3). To refute these accusations he painted the more patriotic *Triumph of Marat* (1794; Lille, Mus. B.-A.), a compromise between history and genre painting. Generally, however, he had little interest in politics.

After 1800 Boilly's compositions became smaller and more complex, with more figures and animation. He turned to scenes of popular and street life noted down spontaneously and depicted with great refinement of colouring, for example the *Arrival of a Stagecoach in the Cour des Messageries* (1803; Paris, Louvre). He still studied human feelings but preferred the observation of popular customs, positioning the figures and recording their facial details meticulously. Paintings such as the *Game of Billiards*

(exh. Salon 1808; Norfolk, VA, Chrysler Mus.), executed with the virtuosity of a Dutch 17th-century domestic scene, reveal a genuine concern to provide an objective chronicle of daily life, albeit tinged with sentimentality. Boilly showed a great sense of humour and capacity for the theatrical organization of space in such works as *Entrance to the Ambigu Comic Theatre* (1819; Paris, Louvre). The pursuit of a humorous description of reality led to caricature in his *Study of 35 Facial Expressions* (Tourcoing, Mus. Mun. B.-A.).

Boilly's taste for group portraiture led him to depict the artistic world in such pictures as *Gathering of Artists in the Studio of Isabey* (1798; Paris, Louvre) and the *Amateurs of Prints* (1810; Paris, Louvre; see DRESS, §VIII, and fig. 49). His concern for veracity encouraged him to produce an increasing number of grisailles, such as *Galeries du Palais-Royal* (1809; Paris, Carnavalet), and *trompe l'oeil* works, for example *Christ* (1812; Oxford, Magdalen Coll.). Boilly also depicted historical events, interpreting them in domestic terms (e.g. the *Emperor's Mercy*; Paris, Bib. Thiers). The *Departure of the Volunteers in 1807* (Paris, Carnavalet) is not a heroic or patriotic picture but a study of the emotions aroused by conscription. In *Napoleon Bestowing the Légion d'honneur on Cartellier* (exh. Salon 1808; Arenenberg, Napoleonmus.) he played on the contrast between the faces of the artists and the graceful poses of the women, with a correspondingly subtle use of colours. He produced many portraits of the middle classes (e.g. series, Paris, Mus. Marmottan) and of his famous contemporaries (e.g. *Robespierre*; Lille, Mus. B.-A.). The composition of these works is extremely sober, the use of colour harmonies equally delicate (e.g. *Lucile Desmoulins*; Paris, Carnavalet).

Boilly was also a skilled painter in watercolour and active as an engraver and lithographer. He published a series of 94 plates in an album entitled *Recueil de grimaces*, which demonstrates his capacity for observation and sense of humour. His ability to seize on the comic aspect of a situation places him in the tradition of 19th-century caricaturists.

PRINTS
Recueil de grimaces (Paris, 1823–8)

BIBLIOGRAPHY
A. Dinaux: 'Boilly', *Archv Hist. N. France & Midi Belgique*, iv (1849), pp. 194–5
C. Blanc: *Histoire*, viii (1861–76), pp. 38–40
H. Béraldi: *Les Graveurs du XIXe siècle*, ii (Paris, 1885), pp. 144–6
H. Harrisse: *L.-L. Boilly, peintre, dessinateur et lithographe: Sa vie et son oeuvre, 1761–1845* (Paris, 1898)
P. Marmottan: *Le Peintre Louis Boilly (1761–1845)* (Paris, 1913)
J. Monneraye: 'Documents sur la vie du peintre Louis Boilly pendant la Révolution', *Bull. Soc. Hist. A. Fr.* (1929), pp. 15–30
A. Mabille de Poncheville: *Boilly* (Paris, 1931)
M.-C. Chaudonneret: 'Napoléon remet la Légion d'honneur au sculpteur Cartellier, par Boilly', *Thurgau. Beitr. Vaterländ. Gesch.*, cxviii (1981), pp. 185–92
J. S. Hallam: 'The Two Manners of Louis-Léopold Boilly and French Genre Painting in Transition', *A. Bull.*, lxiii (1981), pp. 618–32
Louis Boilly (exh. cat. by M. Delafond, Paris, Mus. Marmottan, 1984)
The Charged Image: French Lithographic Caricature 1816–1848 (exh. cat. by B. Farwell, Santa Barbara, CA, Mus. A., 1989), pp. 38–46
The Art of Louis-Léopold Boilly: Modern Life in Napoleonic France (exh. cat., Fort Worth, TX, Kimbell A. Mus.; Washington, DC, N.G.A.; in preparation)

MARIE-CLAUDE CHAUDONNERET

Boilvin, Emile (*b* Metz, 7 May 1845; *d* Paris, 31 July 1899). French painter and engraver. He was a pupil of Isidore-Alexandre-Augustin Pils and of Edmond Hédouin. He entered the Ecole des Beaux-Arts in Paris on 5 April 1864 and began his career as a painter of genre scenes (e.g. *Francesca da Rimini*, 1866), which he exhibited at the Salon. In 1868 he first experimented with etching, the medium for which he became famous, and from 1871 he abandoned painting entirely in favour of this. He reproduced the work of such major contemporary artists as Courbet and Ernest Meissonier and of such Old Masters as Frans Hals and Rubens. He also illustrated such books as Gustave Flaubert's *Madame Bovary* (Paris, 1874) and an edition of Rabelais's works, *Les Cinq Livres de F. Rabelais* (Paris, 1876–7).

BIBLIOGRAPHY

Bellier de La Chavignerie–Auvray; Bénézit; DBF; Thieme–Becker

Valabrègue: 'Le graveur E. Boilvin', *L'Oeuvre d'art* (November 1899)

ATHENA S. E. LEOUSSI

Bois, Guy Pène du. *See* PÈNE DU BOIS, GUY.

Boisbaudran, Horace Lecoq de. *See* LECOQ DE BOISBAUDRAN, HORACE.

Boissard, Jean-Jacques (*b* Besançon, 1528; *d* Metz, 30 Oct 1602). French antiquarian, artist and neo-Latin poet. After beginning his education with his uncle, the itinerant Classical scholar Hugues Babel, Boissard studied in Leuven and then in Germany and northern Italy, settling in Rome in 1556. Here he began to study and draw the monuments and collections of antiquities in and around the city. He returned to Besançon in 1559 but, because of his Protestant faith, soon moved to Metz, leaving most of his drawings at Montbéliard where they were later destroyed. Boissard collaborated with the goldsmith Jean Aubry (*fl* 1600) and the Frankfurt engraver and publisher Theodor de Bry (*see* BRY, DE, (1)) in the production of illustrated books to which he contributed texts and drawings. The *Emblematum liber* (1593) differs from the usual emblem format by including explanatory prose texts. This idea was developed in the *Theatrum vitae humanae* (1596), a collection of biblical and mythological vignettes with long, moralizing commentaries. Boissard also produced collections of portraits and a book on national costumes. His most ambitious work was the compendious *Romanae urbis topographia* (4 vols, Frankfurt, 1597–1602), one of the most important works of Renaissance antiquarianism to appear outside Italy. The work mainly consists of illustrations of statues, monuments and inscriptions, often imaginatively restored. Some of these engravings were based on Boissard's drawings, others were simply copied from existing engravings.

BIBLIOGRAPHY

E. Haag and E. Haag, eds: *La France protestante*, ii (Paris, 1879), cols 704–19

C. Callmer: 'Un Manuscrit de Jean-Jacques Boissard à la Bibliothèque royale de Stockholm', *Opuscula Romana*, iv (1962), pp. 47–59

RUTH WEBB

Boisserée. German family of collectors, museum curators and writers. Sulpiz (Melchior Damiticus) Boisserée (*b* Cologne, 2 Aug 1783; *d* Bonn, 2 May 1854) and Melchior (Hermann Josef Georg) Boisserée (*b* Cologne, 23 April 1786; *d* Bonn, 14 May 1851) were born into a rich, old family of Cologne and spent their youth under the French occupation (1794–1815) of that city. The monasteries had all been closed, and the property of the church sold by auction. This deterioration of the artistic heritage and the ruin of many German and Dutch pictures from the late Middle Ages troubled the two brothers, who were particularly interested in works of the school of Cologne. Their meeting with Johann Baptist Bertram, a passionate student of the aesthetic writings of Ludwig Tieck, Wilhelm Heinrich Wackenroder and Friedrich von Schlegel, increased their appreciation of a type of art that was then little valued, but which to their eyes symbolized the specific nature of German genius. In 1803 the Boisserée brothers and Bertram went to Paris where they visited the Musée Napoleon, then the largest museum in Europe. After seeing the galleries, enriched by the spoils of conquered countries and carefully arranged according to the different schools, Sulpiz and Melchior Boisserée decided to establish their own systematic collection.

Sulpiz assumed responsibility for the general organization of the collection and carried out academic research; Melchior was responsible for acquisition of the works. In 1810 they set up their collection in Heidelberg, conceived as a public place dedicated to study. It was visited by numerous artists and scholars, including Caroline von Humboldt, Wilhelm von Humboldt, Peter Cornelius, Karl Friedrich Schinkel and Antonio Canova. Schlegel was enthusiastic about the collection, and Goethe came to see it in 1814 and 1815, though his classical taste initially prevented him from appreciating its true value. Melchior and Sulpiz had hoped to entrust their paintings to the keeping of the Universität zu Köln to be used for the teaching of aesthetics and art history but the project failed. Ludwig I of Bavaria purchased the entire collection in 1827 for the Alte Pinakothek in Munich where it was installed in 1836. Sulpiz and Melchior were appointed keepers of the collection.

To the Boisserée brothers, their collection illustrated a problem of art history. In their view, up to the 15th century painting was dominated by what they called the 'modern Greek-Byzantine style'. The realism of Jan van Eyck and Hubert van Eyck liberated painting from this restrictive model. An investigation of this transition would lead to a better understanding of how Greek art had evolved out of Egyptian art and then become autonomous.

The collection, containing 218 paintings, was at that time divided into four groups. The first, called the 'Byzantine school of the Lower Rhine', comprised works from the 13th century to the early 15th, many of which were anonymous. The second group illustrated 'Jan van Eyck and his school, from its beginnings until the end of the 15th century'. This was the most precious section of the collection and included the triptych of the *Adoration of the Magi* by Rogier van der Weyden, *Cardinal Charles of Bourbon, Archbishop of Lyon* (*c.* 1480) by the Master of Moulins and the *Seven Joys of the Virgin* by Hans Memling (all Munich, Alte Pin.). Several of these works were attributed to Jan van Eyck by the two brothers. The third group covered the 'Masters of the 16th century and their pupils, up to the evolution of the new style at the end of the century', that is to say, Jan Gossart, Joos van Cleve and Bernard van Orley. The fourth group, called 'the school of Upper Germany', comprised the work of Dürer, Lucas Cranach (i) and Albrecht Altdorfer.

Contemporaneously with the development of the collection, Sulpiz Boisserée dedicated a large part of his life to the study and restoration of Cologne Cathedral, which, with its Gothic architecture, he thought symbolized the grandeur of German culture. The reconstruction of its ruins was not only a return to the origins of a little-known period of art and of a neglected style but it also promoted a national cultural renaissance, at a time when Prussia and the German states were humiliated by France.

Sulpiz succeeded in winning the interest of Goethe for his project and was hopeful that the latter's support would permit him to obtain public funding. At the fall of Napoleon I, Prince Frederick William of Prussia (later Frederick William IV) expressed enthusiasm for Sulpiz's plan and requested a report on the monument, which was drawn up by Schinkel. Excavations around the cathedral were carried out in 1815, while Sulpiz patiently researched the structure of the building. He visited the cathedrals of Châlons-sur-Marne and Metz, which, in his opinion, were modelled on that at Cologne. This reaffirmed his belief in the artistic superiority of Germany and resulted in the publication of the *Geschichte und Beschreibung des Doms von Köln, nebst untersuchungen über die alte Kirchenbaukunst* (1823). This work can be considered one of the earliest monographs on the history of architecture. Despite being self-taught, Sulpiz was an extremely accomplished architect. He successfully disseminated his ideas on Gothic architecture abroad. During his three visits to France (1820, 1823–4, 1825), he presented his research on Cologne Cathedral, even at the Académie des Beaux-Arts in Paris, thanks to the intervention of Antoine Quatremère de Quincy. When Frederick William became king, he gave instructions for the restoration of the cathedral to begin in 1842, though it was not finished until the end of the 19th century.

WRITINGS

Unless otherwise stated, all books cited were written by Sulpiz Boisserée.

S. Boisserée, M. Boisserée and J. Bertram: *Die Sammlung Alt-, Nieder- und Ober-Deutscher Gemälde der Brüder Sulpiz und Melchior Boisserée und Johann Bertram, lithographirt von Johann Nepomuk Strixner mit Nachrichten über die altdeutschen Malern von den Besitzern*, 2 vols (Stuttgart, 1821)

Geschichte und Beschreibung des Doms von Köln, nebst Untersuchungen über die alte Kirchenbaukunst, 2 vols (Stuttgart and Paris, 1823)

'Mémoire sur l'architecture du moyen-âge', *Rev. Enc.*, xxiv (1824), pp. 577–88

Denkmale der Baukunst von 7ten bis zum 13ten Jahrhundert am Niederrhein (Stuttgart, 1833)

'Ueber die Beschreibung des Tempels des heiligen Grales in dem Heldengedicht: Titurel Kap. III', *Abh. Philos.-Philol. Kl. Kön. Bayer. Akad. Wiss.*, i (1835), pp. 307–92

Mathilde Boisserée, ed.: *Sulpiz Boisserée*, 2 vols (Stuttgart, 1862) [autobiography and letters]

H.-J. Weitz, ed.: *Tagebücher, 1808–1854*, 4 vols (Darmstadt, 1978–85)

BIBLIOGRAPHY

O. Seiler: *Die Brüder Boisserée in ihren Verhältnis zu den Brüdern Schlegel* (diss., U. Zurich, 1915)

E. Firmenich-Richartz: *Die Brüder Boisserée, i: Sulpiz und Melchior Boisserée als Kunstsammler: Ein Beitrag zur Geschichte der Romantik* (Jena, 1916)

K. K. Eberlein: 'Schinkel und Boisserée', *Berlin. Mus.*, lii (1931), pp. 39–45

P. O. Rave: 'Anfänge preussicher Kunstpflege am Rhein', *Wallraf-Richartz-Jb.*, ix (1936), pp. 181–204

G. Poensgen: 'Die Begegnung Goethes mit der Sammlung Boisserée in Heidelberg', *Goethe und Heidelberg* (Heidelberg, 1942)

P. Moisy: *Les Séjours en France de Sulpiz Boisserée (1820–25): Contribution à l'étude des relations intellectuelles franco-allemandes* (Paris and Lyon, 1956)

A. Moisy: 'Sauveurs de chefs-d'oeuvre: Wallraf et les frères Boisserée', *L'Oeil*, lxiii (1960), pp. 36–47

R. Eichholz: 'Sulpiz Boisserée und der Dom zu Köln: Versuch einer Biographie', *Der Kölner Dom im Jahrhundert seiner Vollendung* (exh. cat., ed. H. Borger; Cologne, Josef-Haubrich-Ksthalle, 1980–81), ii, pp. 17–23

G. Leinz: 'Ludwig I und die Gothik', *Z. Kstgesch.*, xliv (1981), pp. 399–443

G. Goldberg: 'History of the Boisserée Collection', *Apollo*, cxvi (1982), pp. 210–13

PASCAL GRIENER

Boisset, Paul Randon de. *See* RANDON DE BOISSET, PAUL.

Boissieu, Jean-Jacques de (*b* Lyon, 30 Nov 1736; *d* Lyon, 1 March 1810). French printmaker, draughtsman and painter. Apart from studying briefly at the Ecole Gratuite de Dessin in Lyon, he was self-taught. His first concentrated phase as a printmaker was 1758–64, during which he published three suites of etchings. Boissieu spent 1765–6 in Italy in the company of Louis-Alexandre, Duc de la Rochefoucauld (1743–93), returning to Lyon via the Auvergne with a cache of his own landscape drawings. He remained in Lyon, where he published further prints at intervals, making occasional trips to Paris and Geneva. Boissieu's prints earned him the reputation of being the last representative of the older etching tradition—he particularly admired Rembrandt van Rijn—at a time when engraving was being harnessed for commercial prints, and lithography was coming into use. For his landscape etchings Boissieu drew upon the scenery of the Roman Campagna, the watermills, windmills and rustic figures of the Dutch school (notably Salomon van Ruysdael) and the countryside around Lyon. He also engraved *têtes d'expression* and genre scenes. His work as a printmaker was intermittent, covering the periods 1758–64, 1770–82 and after 1789, although his skill was such that he was much sought after as a reproductive engraver; one example of his work is the *Landscape with Huntsmen and Dogs* after a painting (San Francisco, CA Pal. Legion of Honor) by Jan Wijnants.

Boissieu's drawings (of which over 700 survive) are widely scattered (examples in Darmstadt, Hess. Landesmus.; Florence, Uffizi; Frankfurt am Main, Städel. Kstinst.; London, BM; Paris, Louvre; Vienna, Albertina; and elsewhere). The best-known are his large landscapes enhanced by grey wash, in which he specialized from 1780 to 1800; they include *Cart in a Farmyard* (after 1765; Paris, Louvre; see fig.), a *plein-air* drawing in which a workaday setting is transformed by Boissieu's pale washes of sky. His portraits drawn in red or black chalks show an acute sensitivity to individual psychology, for example the *Artist's Brother* (Berlin, Kupferstichkab.). Some 20 or so small paintings (oil on panel) comprise Boissieu's extant undertakings in this medium, many of which are after the subjects of his best-known prints. They appear to be little more than the productions of a diligent amateur, however, and include portraits (e.g. *Mme Boissieu Playing the Mandolin*, Lyon, Mus. B.-A.), landscapes strongly influenced

Jean-Jacques de Boissieu: *Cart in a Farmyard*, pen and ink and wash with traces of graphite, 179×246 mm, after 1765 (Paris, Musée du Louvre)

by the Dutch tradition (e.g. *Animal Market*, Lyon, Mus. B.-A.) and several genre scenes (e.g. *Children's Dance*, Paris, Petit Pal.).

Boissieu taught several amateur artists in Lyon as well as Jean-Michel Grobon (1770–1853), who studied both etching and painting under him. The generation of Lyon artists after Grobon was also influenced by Boissieu's bias towards Dutch art, and one of them, Antoine Duclaux (1783–1868), held up Boissieu's works in turn as models from which to learn. Eugène Bléry, Joseph Guichard and, most notably, Félix Bracquemond all benefited from this, as, independently, did Adolph Friedrich Erdmann Menzel and Félix Vallotton. The wide distribution of Boissieu's prints in the 19th century played a significant part in the dissemination of a taste for works whose style and subject-matter derive from Dutch 17th-century art.

PRINTS

Livre de griffonnements (Paris, 1758)
Paysages dessinés et gravés (Paris, 1759)
Suite de dix paysages à l'eau-forte (Paris, 1763)

BIBLIOGRAPHY

Mariette
[A. de Boissieu]: *Jean-Jacques de Boissieu: Catalogue raisonné de son oeuvre* (Paris and Lyon, 1878); rev. ed. by R. M. Mason and M.-F. Pérez (Geneva, 1994)
——: *Notice sur la vie et l'oeuvre de Jean-Jacques de Boissieu* (Paris and Lyon, 1879)
Jean-Jacques de Boissieu (exh. cat. by F. Baudson, Bourg-en-Bresse, Mus. Ain, 1967)
De David à Delacroix: La Peinture française de 1774 à 1830 (exh. cat., ed. F. Cummings, R. Rosenblum and A. Schnapper; Paris, Grand Pal.; Detroit, MI, Inst. A.; New York, Met.; 1974), pp. 325–8
M.-F. Pérez: *Jean-Jacques de Boissieu (1736–1810): Artiste et amateur lyonnais du XVIIIe siècle* (diss., U. Lyon, 1982)
——: 'Pour Jean-Jacques de Boissieu peintre', *Trav. Inst. Hist. Art Lyon*, xiv (1991), pp. 103–23

MARIE-FÉLICIE PÉREZ

Boit, Charles (*b* Stockholm, *bapt* 10 Aug 1662; *d* Paris, 5 or 6 Feb 1727). Swedish miniature painter, active in England. He was first apprenticed to a goldsmith and jeweller in Stockholm. He became adept at miniature painting in enamel, a method that had been introduced into Sweden by Pierre Signac (*d* 1684), and he is said to have studied the enamels of Jean Petitot I and Jacques Bordier (1616–84) when he spent three months in Paris in 1682. He arrived in England in 1687 at the invitation of John Sowters, a merchant who had earlier invited the portrait painter Michael Dahl to England. After spending some years in provincial English towns, including Lincoln and Coventry (1693), Boit was appointed Court Enameller to William III. He travelled in Europe, visiting the Netherlands, Germany, Austria and France, from 1699 to 1703; the most notable product of this period was his large enamel on copper of the *Emperor Leopold I and his Family* (Vienna, Ksthist. Mus.; *see* MINIATURE, fig. 6). On his return to England, Boit embarked upon a yet more ambitious project, a very large enamel intended to commemorate the Battle of Blenheim (1704). He proved unable to complete this task, and when in 1714 the Treasury pressed for a return on the large sums advanced to him, Boit fled the country leaving his debts unpaid. He settled in Paris, where he continued to enjoy important patronage, for example by Philippe, Duc d'Orléans, whose enamel portrait he painted (Paris, Louvre). He was insolvent when he died.

One of Boit's most successful large enamels is his double portrait of *Queen Anne and Prince George of Denmark* (1706; Windsor Castle, Berks, Royal Col.), but he excelled in the more usual format of the head and shoulders portrait of a size suitable for a locket or for holding in the hand. Many of his English portraits were copied from Dahl or from Godfrey Kneller, but he also worked from life. He painted enamel portraits of *Peter the Great* (London, V&A; St Petersburg, Hermitage; Windsor Castle, Berks, Royal Col.), whom he met in London in 1698 and again in Paris in 1717. Among his pupils was Christian Friedrich Zincke, who continued the practice of painting enamel portrait miniatures in England until the mid-18th century.

BIBLIOGRAPHY
W. Nisser: *Michael Dahl and the Contemporary Swedish School of Painting in England* (Uppsala, 1927) [with a list of works by Boit]
G. Cavalli-Bjorkman: *Svenskt miniatyrmaleri* (Stockholm, 1981)

GRAHAM REYNOLDS

Boitac [Boytac], **Diogo** (*fl* 1498; *d* ?Batalha, ?1528). Architect and engineer, active in Portugal. His nationality is unknown, and his effective role in the many works associated with him is not clear. The earliest documentary reference is dated 1498, when Manuel I, King of Portugal, granted him an annual payment for expenses and work at the Franciscan convent church, Igreja de Jesus, Setúbal. Formerly his only known signature was on a document of 1514, but 12 autograph manuscripts, dated between 1515 and 1521, have been found in the archive of the Misericórdia of Batalha Abbey, where he was judge of the confraternity (Gomes). In these his name is always written as *Boytac*, which suggests a French origin, whereas other documents that name him use the Portuguese form; this would appear to confirm that he was a foreigner. His first name only appears in a list of the members of the expedition to Mamora (now Mehdiya, Morocco) in 1515.

Although formerly there were doubts that the present monastery of Jesus (*c.* 1494–8) was designed and executed by Boitac, the attribution has been confirmed by Vieira da Silva and Ferreira de Almeida. Here Boitac introduced the concept of the total unification of space, with aisles of the same height as the nave, and innovative formal elements that were developed in later Portuguese architecture (*see* MANUELINE STYLE), such as twisted piers in the nave, a wide triumphal arch with niches, a complex system of rib vaults in the chancel and arches with a variety of profiles (see fig.).

Boitac's influence is apparent on some of the most important buildings executed in Portugal in the early 16th century. His next known work was at the Hieronymite monastery at Belém (*see* BELÉM (i) and PORTUGAL, fig. 3), where from 1501 he may have been responsible for the

Diogo Boitac: Franciscan convent church, Igreja de Jesus, Setúbal, *c.* 1494–8; interior of the nave looking east

general plan of the building, which resembles that at Setúbal. In 1507 he was directing the renovation of the monastery of Santa Cruz at Coimbra. He altered the division of space within the church, reducing it to a single nave, and erected over the nave and the chancel, which is almost as long, a low vault, the ribs of which rise from twisted pilasters resting on corbels; he signed a new contract in 1513 to complete the first stage of work. He was also documented in 1507 at Sintra, where the Hieronymite church and cloister (now part of the Palácio da Pena) resemble the work at Coimbra, especially the vaults. In 1509 he was registered as living at Batalha, where he married Isabel Henriques, the daughter of Mateus Fernandes I, in 1512. It is not certain that he was ever Master of the Works at the abbey, although he was further documented in 1514 and settled there from 1516; according to Francisco de São Lu, Cardinal Saraiva, he died at Batalha and was buried in the church, near his father-in-law's tomb.

Boitac also executed commissions for the municipality of Coimbra to site and build the abbatoirs (1511) in collaboration with Mateus Fernandes, to improve the Ponte de S Clara (altered) and to canalize the River Mondego. In 1510 he was knighted for his services at Arzila (now Asilah, Morocco) by Vasco Menezes Coutinho, Conde de Borba. He left for Morocco again on 25

May 1514, as Valuer of Works. In 1515 he built the fortress (destr.) at Mamora: Manuel increased Boitac's salary from 8000 reis to 12,000, but the site was to prove ill-chosen.

The number of works with which Boitac was involved simultaneously in different parts of Portugal and North Africa is striking. It is often impossible to determine his precise role in each, although he seems to have held a position as royal architect, similar to that of Diogo de Arruda. He adapted his knowledge of Late Gothic architecture to satisfy the taste of his foremost patron, the king. The design for the vault of the Setúbal chancel was influential in the spread of a type of vault that was characteristic of Late Gothic but had been used in Portugal only rarely in the 15th century, despite Huguet's work at Batalha. Boitac may also have been responsible for completing the carved tracery decoration in the Claustro Real at Batalha with naturalistic ornament in a perfectly assimilated Manueline style, including symbols of the Order of Christ and armillary spheres.

BIBLIOGRAPHY
F. de São Lu: *Lista de alguns artistas portugueses* (Lisbon, 1839)
R. Santos: *O estilo manuelino* (Lisbon, 1952)
J. C. Vieira da Silva: *A igreja de Jesus de Setúbal* (Setúbal, 1987)
P. Dias: *A arquitectura manuelina* (Oporto, 1988)
C. A. Ferreira de Almeida: *A igreja de Jesus de Setúbal* (Oporto, 1990)
S. A. Gomes: *Mestre Boytac* (Setúbal, 1991)

JOSÉ CUSTODIO VIEIRA DA SILVA

Boitchuk, Mikhail. *See* BOYCHUK, MYKHAYLO.

Boito, Camillo (*b* Rome, 30 Oct 1836; *d* Milan, 28 June 1914). Italian architect, teacher, restorer and writer. Boito was an important figure in many ways in the cultural life of Italy, and especially Milan, in the second half of the 19th century. He not only taught at the Accademia di Brera and the Istituto Tecnico Superiore for nearly 50 years but also took part in competitions (both as competitor and adjudicator), wrote articles on architecture and restoration for newspapers and periodicals, as well as numerous reports for private individuals and the government, and was active in numerous professional associations. He also served on numerous commissions, particularly after his appointment as Director of the Accademia di Brera in 1897.

1. TRAINING AND ARCHITECTURAL CAREER. Boito entered the Accademia di Belle Arti in Venice in 1850 and won a prize there in 1852. In 1854 he entered the Studio Matematico at the Università degli Studi in Padua, and in 1855 he qualified as a professional architect. In 1856 he began teaching at the Accademia in Venice, under the directorship of Pietro Selvatico, but a scholarship award enabled him to leave Venice and visit Tuscany and Rome. Around this time he also became involved with cultural and social circles in Milan. His mother, who was Polish, and his brother, the librettist and composer Arrigo Boito (1842–1918), moved there in 1854 in order for Arrigo to attend the Conservatoire, and in 1855 Camillo exhibited some of his designs at the Accademia di Brera. He also began publishing articles in such Milanese journals as *Giornale dell'ingegnere, architetto ed agronomo* and *Crepuscolo*. These led to his appointment in November 1860 as Professor of Higher Architecture at the Accademia di Brera, where he taught until 1908. Among the many artistic associations with which Boito became involved in Milan was the Scapigliatura movement (*see* SCAPIGLIATI, GLI), which sought to revitalize and reform the arts, especially literature. Under the influence of the movement he wrote many short stories, published as *Storielle vane* (Milan, 1876) and *Senso: Nuove storielle vane* (Milan, 1883).

Camillo Boito: Casa di Riposo per i Musicisti, Milan, 1899

Boito's first works as an architect in Lombardy were the chapels (1865) forming the perimeter of the cemetery at Gallarate, where he also built the Ponti Mausoleum. These reflect the influence of central Europe, which he visited during the trips he made to his mother's native Poland. He continued to have links with the Veneto region, however: in 1873 he won the competition for the Palazzo delle Debite in Padua, which was much criticized, and in 1879, again in Padua, he designed the entrance building and main staircase of the Museo Civico. The following year he adopted a more straightforward approach for the elementary schools at nearby Reggia Carrarese, then returned to the use of expensive, refined materials in his design for the main staircase (begun 1882) of the Palazzo Franchetti, Venice. His mature style was also exemplified by several works in Lombardy that both embodied his theory that the style should illustrate the functional structure of the building and included innovative features in the balance of the design. These include the Ospedale Civico (1869–74) at Gallarate, the elementary school (1888) on the Via Galvani in Milan and the Casa di Riposo per i Musicisti, founded by Giuseppe Verdi (1899; partly destr.; see fig.), also in Milan.

2. EDUCATIONAL CAREER AND THEORY. During his 48 years at the Accademia, Boito was involved in every area of artistic education, and he organized the courses of study rationally, stressing their boundaries while keeping a constant element of experimentation. He promoted the creation of the School of Civic Architecture (from 1865), using the syllabuses of the Istituto Tecnico Superiore and the Accademia di Brera, and was involved in numerous educational reforms. In 1884 he sat on commissions considering the creation of professional schools of industrial art and strongly supported the setting up of a periodical devoted to this subject (out of this developed the journal *Arte italiana decorativa e industriale*, which he ran). From 1861 he was involved in the debate on the setting up of higher schools of architecture, and in 1912 he proposed the formation of a school for picture restoration, which was, however, never implemented.

The articles Boito published from 1856 in such periodicals as *Spettatore*, *Rivista veneta* and *Crepuscolo* put forward his ideas for a reorganization of academic teaching. He condemned the emphasis placed on the historical styles (despite recent interest in medieval Venice expressed by Pietro Selvatico and in Milan by Friedrich von Schmidt), and he pointed out the scarcity and inadequacy of funding for the architecture and design schools. His method of teaching, partly inspired by his time in Venice working under Selvatico, involved the explanation of the formal and static aspects of each style, through an analysis of its fundamental links with a particular historical context. He was thus opposed to a simplistic eclecticism and advocated the use of detail in allied medieval styles so as to create a new direction of work. Experimentation was a central idea in Boito's teaching, where it was explicitly linked to the problems of contemporary architectural practice. His best-known pupils were LUCA BELTRAMI, Giuseppe Brentano and Gaetano Moretti, but others included Gaetano Landriani (1837–99), Luigi Broggi, Ruggero Berlam (1854–1921) and Giuseppe Sommaruga.

Boito's inquiry of 1859 in *Crepuscolo* into the state of contemporary architecture suggested a close interrelationship with the problems of teaching and prompted Boito to write several texts on the subject. Initially the theme of the search for a new image of architecture was in keeping with the political mood of change, but soon the call to adhere to the requirements of the moment became paramount. In 1872 Boito maintained that, 'with buildings serving new purposes created by modern civilization, a new style, or at least a need for one, has been born'. In his introduction to the *Architettura del medioevo in Italia* (1880) he claimed that architecture gave shape to beauty in an intimate fusion of its technological, scientific and formal aspects. He also maintained the indissolubility of the link between the 'organism', or the functional structure and the 'symbolism', or the aesthetic ornament. Grassi (1959) was the first to discern in Boito's theoretical and professional activity 'the fertile antecedents of the first phase of the Modern Movement'. In *Questioni pratiche di belle arti* (1893) Boito once more broached contemporary topics relevant to the professions of architect and engineer, such as restoration, competitions and legislation, and he did not conceal his disappointment at the failure to solve certain problems.

GIULIANA RICCI

3. IDEAS ON RESTORATION. Boito's theories on restoration were particularly important, as they were the first to be systematically formulated in Italy. They exemplified the historically orientated culture of the time and had a crucial influence on the state organization of conservation, and they provided a basis for the ideas of Gustavo Giovannoni later on. Boito's ideas were given their first and most complete expression during the fourth Congresso degli Ingegneri ed Architetti Italiani (1883). There, approval was given, with only minor alterations, to a document that summed up Boito's principles: the priority of maintenance and consolidation (i.e. the replacement of missing features); the obligation to carry out such completions only if necessary, and according to contemporary forms, if they were innovations or renovations of parts whose forms were not known with any certainty; fidelity to the original design, where there was any precise documentation, but with allowance for recognizably new materials or treatment, unless the building was of mainly archaeological importance; respect for the picturesque quality inherent in decorations, environmental conditions and the traces of the passage of time, even in buildings that were in ruins; and the maintaining of historical stratifications (at the expense of stylistic homogeneity), except in cases of particular historical or artistic interest. Other articles by Boito suggested ways of providing exact documentation of restoration projects, both to give accurate information to the public and scholars, and to the state conservation bodies. These ideas had formed the basis of the guidelines enunciated by the Ufficio del Ministero della Pubblica Istruzione per la Conservazione dei Monumenti in 1882. Boito's influence in the ministry was also evident in the latter's approval of his demand that specialized regional restoration bodies should be set up, under the control of the central office. This allowed for the withdrawal of civil engineers who lacked the requisite historical skills from restoration projects.

Boito's approach gave precedence to historical truth, a concept that played a large part in his theory of architecture, although aesthetic problems were also important. He regarded buildings as products of history rather than of style. Historical judgement underlaid decisions about restoration, and Boito thus believed he had eliminated the arbitrariness typical of stylistic intervention. However, he has been accused of self-contradiction on the basis of stylistic interventions that he himself is said to have carried out or encouraged as member of numerous competition boards. It should be remembered, though, that his only real work of restoration, the 12th-century Porta Nuova or posterngate of the Porta Ticinese, Milan, dates back to 1861–5 when, at a time of architectural historicism, the idea of a contemporary approach was far from clear. A typical case was the hurried completion of Milan Cathedral (1806–13) by Carlo Amati, which Boito wanted to replace. Accused of contradicting his principle of retaining the historical phases of a building, Boito said that the pressure of economic and practical needs had prevented Amati from expressing himself completely. As a result the work was 'lacking in the genuine feel' of its period, and thus was historically irrelevant regarding architectonic criticism. Boito supported the emotional values produced by the overall perception of the work rather than those that derived from stylistic or constructional analysis.

AMEDEO BELLINI

WRITINGS

'L'architettura odierna e l'insegnamento di essa', *Crepuscolo* (1859)
Scultura e pittura d'oggi (Turin, 1877)
Architettura del medioevo in Italia (Milan, 1880)
Ornamenti di tutti gli stili classificati in ordine storico (Milan, 1881)
Stoffe, intarsi ed altri ornamenti piani (Milan, 1881)
I principii del disegno e gli stili dell'ornamento (Milan, 1882)
Gite di un artista (Milan, 1884)
I restauratori (Florence, 1884)
'I nostri vecchi monumenti: Conservare o restaurare?', *Nuova Antol.* (1 June 1885), pp. 480–506
Il Duomo di Milano e i disegni per la sua facciata (Milan, 1889)
Questioni pratiche di belle arti (Milan, 1893)
Arte utile, decorazione policroma (Milan, 1894)
Relazione sul disegno di restauro per la Porta Pila (Genoa, 1896)
Relazione sul progetto di riduzione dell'interno del Palazzo della Loggia in Brescia (Brescia, 1896)
Il palazzo ducale di Venezia (Rome, 1896)

BIBLIOGRAPHY

B. A. Deon: *Camillo Boito* (Reggio Emilia, 1915)
C. Macchi: 'Le opere di Camillo Boito', *Rass. Gallara. Stor. A.*, iv (1933), pp. 11–16
L. Ragghianti: *Profilo della critica d'arte in Italia* (Florence, 1945)
C. Perogalli: *Monumenti e metodi di valorizzazione* (Milan, 1954)
L. Grassi: 'L'intuizione moderna nel pensiero di Camillo Boito', *Casabella-continuità*, 208 (1955), pp. 70–78
A. Barbacci: *Il restauro dei monumenti in Italia* (Rome, 1956)
L. Grassi: 'Architettura romantica', *Motivi per una storiografia dell'architettura* (Milan, 1956)
C. Ceschi: *Il restauro dei monumenti* (Rome, 1957, 2/1970)
L. Grassi: *Camillo Boito* (Milan, 1959)
—: 'Il restauro dei monumenti: Teorie e problematiche', *Storia e cultura dei monumenti* (Milan, 1960)
F. Borsi: *L'architettura dell'unità d'Italia* (Florence, 1966)
E. Giacheri and G. Miano: 'Boito Camillo', *DBI*, xi (Rome, 1969), pp. 237–41
G. Rocchi: 'Camillo Boito e le prime proposte normative del restauro', *Restauro*, 15 (1975), pp. 5–88
L. Santoro: 'Il contributo italiano alla definizione concettuale e metodologia del restauro', *Restauro*, 43 (1980), pp. 5–76
V. Fontana: 'Camillo Boito e il restauro a Venezia', *Casabella* (1981), pp. 48–53
—: 'La scuola speciale di architettura, 1861–1915', *Il Politecnico di Milano, 1863–1914* (Milan, 1981), pp. 228–46
O. Selvafolta: 'L'Istituto Tecnico Superiore di Milano: Metodi didattici e ordinamento interno, 1863–1914', *Il Politecnico di Milano, 1863–1914* (Milan, 1981), pp. 87–118
P. Torsello: *Restauro architettonico, padre, teorie, immagini* (Milan, 1984)
G. Ricci: 'Il dibattito culturale e legislativo per l'istituzione delle scuole superiori d'architettura', *Il Politecnico di Milano nella storia italiana (1914–1963)*, *Rivista milanese di economia* (1989), pp. 585–612 [suppl. to issue 18]
A. Grimoldi, ed.: *Omaggio a Camillo Boito* (Milan, 1991)

AMEDEO BELLINI, GIULIANA RICCI

Boizot, Louis-Simon (*b* Paris, 9 Oct 1743; *d* Paris, 10 March 1809). French sculptor. He was the son of Antoine Boizot (1704–82), a designer at the Gobelins, and a pupil of René-Michel Slodtz. He studied at the Académie Royale, Paris, winning the Prix de Rome in 1762, and after a period at the Ecole Royale des Elèves Protégés he completed his education from 1765 to 1770 at the Académie de France in Rome. He was accepted (*agréé*) by the Académie Royale in 1771, presenting the model (untraced) for a statuette of *Meleager*, but was not received (*reçu*) as a full member until 1778, when he completed the marble version (Paris, Louvre). He exhibited regularly at the Paris Salon until 1800.

The first years of Boizot's career were dedicated primarily to decorative sculpture, such as the model for the elaborate allegorical gilt-bronze clock known as the 'Avignon' clock (*c.* 1770; London, Wallace; see FRANCE, §IX, 2(iii)(a), figs 82 and 83), some caryatids for one of the chimney-pieces at the château of Fontainebleau (marble and bronze, 1772; now Versailles, Château) and various works for the château of Louveciennes, Yvelines. In 1773, perhaps at the instigation of Mme Du Barry, for whom he worked at Louveciennes, he was appointed artistic director of the sculpture studio at the Sèvres porcelain manufactory, and during his time there he made more than 150 models that were reproduced in biscuit porcelain. In addition to models for official portrait busts such as those of *Louis XVI* and *Marie-Antoinette* (both 1774–5) and numerous allegorical groups, he executed some unusual and prestigious pieces, for example the *surtout de table*, the 'Russian Parnassus' (1778; Sèvres, Mus. N. Cér.), a toilet set (1782; Pavlovsk Pal.) for the Comtesse du Nord (later the Tsarina) and the so-called large 'Medici' vases (1783; Paris, Louvre). The style of the models he made for Sèvres shows the influence of his predecessor there, Etienne-Maurice Falconet, though Boizot favoured softer modelling and somewhat contrived poses and drapery; characterizing his entire oeuvre, these derive from his large-scale work, a bas-relief representing a *Nymph* (stone; 1775–6) for the Fontaine de la Croix-du-Trahoir (now the Fontaine de l'Arbre Sec, intersection of the Rue de l'Arbre Sec and the Rue St-Honoré), Paris.

The most fruitful period of Boizot's career was in the 1770s and 1780s. He produced portrait busts of high quality, paying great attention to detail in such works as *Marie-Antoinette* (marble, exh. Salon 1781; untraced), *Louis XVI* (marble, exh. Salon 1777; untraced) and *Joseph II of Austria* (marble, 1777; Versailles, Petit Trianon), while his less formal busts, such as that of *Claude-Joseph Vernet* (marble, 1806; Paris, Louvre), show a more relaxed attitude and are generally more sympathetic. In his plaster reliefs (1777) for the Chapelle des Fonts Baptismaux at St Sulpice, Paris, he tried to adopt a more rigorous, classicizing style, although his statue of *St John the Baptist* (marble, 1785) and his large relief of the *Baptism* (plaster, 1781; both St Sulpice, Paris) look more to his teacher, Slodtz, and to Roman Baroque sculpture. In 1785–7 Boizot executed a marble statue of *Jean Racine* (Paris, Louvre) to contribute to the series of *Illustrious Frenchmen* commissioned by the Bâtiments du Roi.

During the French Revolution Boizot professed Republican views and played an important role in the Commission des Monuments, which advised on the preservation of the artistic heritage. Around 1800 he executed four large marble reliefs for the monument to *Gen. Lazare Hoche* (Versailles, Château), thereby demonstrating his continuing attachment to the descriptive relief style of the French school of the 17th century. Despite his difficulties in adapting his sculpture to the prevalent Neo-classical style, Boizot received official commissions under the Consulate (1779–1804) and Empire (1804–14), including bronze reliefs for the Colonne de la Grande Armée (1806–7), Place Vendôme, Paris, a statue of *Militiades* (plaster, c. 1806; untraced) for the Senate in the Palais du Luxembourg, Paris, decorative sculpture (bronze and stone, 1806; *in situ*) for the Fontaine du Palmier, Place du Châtelet, Paris, and numerous portrait busts.

Although he was a first-class craftsman working in an elegant and eclectic style, Boizot never really developed as an artist. He tended to couple his taste for beautiful forms with a weakness for complicated draperies and accessories, and his sense of grace with a rather chilly severity. His portrait busts are perhaps his most successful works.

BIBLIOGRAPHY

Lami

P. de Nolhac: 'Les Sculpteurs de Marie-Antoinette: Boizot et Houdon', *Les Arts* [Paris], clx (1917)

E. Bourgeois: *Le Biscuit de Sèvres au XVIIIe siècle* (Paris, 1919)

THÉRÈSE PICQUENARD

Bokkei. *See under* SOGA.

Bokurin. *See* NUKINA KAIOKU.

Bokusai. *See* SHŌTŌ BOKUSAI.

Bol, Cornelis (i). *See* BOEL, CORNELIS.

Bol, Cornelis [Cornelius] **(ii)** (*b* ?Antwerp, ?1589; *fl* 1636–*c*. 1666). Painter, etcher and draughtsman, active in London. He was probably from a family of painters originating in Mechelen who later settled in Antwerp. Bol and his wife were members of the Dutch Church in London in 1636. An etching of an *Action between the Dutch and Spanish Fleets* (Oxford, Bodleian Lib.) is signed and dated 1639, and a set of etchings by him after Abraham Casembrot (*fl c.* 1650–75) includes a view of *Lambeth Palace* as well as four imaginary Mediterranean seaports. A signed drawing of the *Blockhouse at Gravesend* is in the British Museum, London. George Vertue saw at Wotton House, Bucks, 'three views of London from the River side Arundel House Somersett house Tower Lond. painted before the fire of London by Cornelius Boll: a good free taste'. They were probably commissioned by John Evelyn, the diarist, around 1660 and descended in the Evelyn family. Their attribution to Bol is confirmed by a signed version of *Somerset House* (London, Dulwich Pict. Gal.). Although Bol was only moderately accomplished, he was able to reproduce the distinctive light and character of the River Thames and to render the riverside and its landmarks with much topographical detail; his pictures make pleasing visual documents. The handling of the naval craft is identical in a small signed oil panel of an *Action between Dutch and Spanish Ships* (Amsterdam, Rijksmus.) and in other marine subjects that have appeared in London salerooms. According to Immerzeel, Bol was still working in London at the time of the Great Fire in 1666.

BIBLIOGRAPHY

H. Walpole: *Anecdotes of Painting in England (1762–71)*, ed. R. N. Wornum (1849), ii, p. 432

K. Immerzeel: *De levens en werken der Hollandsche en Vlaamsche kunstschilders* (Amsterdam, 1842–3), p. 71

F. C. Willis: *Die niederländische Marinemalerei* (Leipzig, 1911), p. 21

'The Note-books of George Vertue', *Walpole Soc.*, xxix (1947), p. 22

E. Croft-Murray and P. Hulton: *Catalogue of British Drawings*, i: *XVI and XVII Centuries*, London, BM cat. (London, 1960), pp. 201–2

The Age of Charles II (exh. cat., London, RA, 1960–61), pp. 67–8, 71, 73

I. J. Bol: *Die holländische Marinemaler des 17. Jahrhunderts* (Brunswick, 1973), pp. 52–3

RICHARD JEFFREE

Bol, Ferdinand (*b* Dordrecht, *bapt* 24 June 1616; *d* Amsterdam, *bur* 24 July 1680). Dutch painter and draughtsman. He was a pupil and prominent follower of Rembrandt in Amsterdam. His reputation and fame are based on his history paintings, which, though successful at the time, lack originality, and on his portraits, a genre for which he showed more talent.

1. LIFE AND CAREER. His father, a surgeon, belonged to the prosperous middle class. Ferdinand received his initial training as a painter in Dordrecht from Jacob Gerritsz. Cuyp. It is possible that he, like Cuyp, worked for a short time in Utrecht, for his earliest signed work, *Vertumnus and Pomona* (c. 1635; London, Cevat priv. col., see Blankert, 1982, pl. 1), exhibits influences of the Utrecht school. Unlike many of his contemporaries, Bol did not travel to Italy, but left for Amsterdam in 1637, at the age of nearly 20, to study in Rembrandt's workshop. The older painter's influence profoundly affected the whole of his subsequent career. It is not known how long he remained with Rembrandt; however, there is no surviving signed and dated work before 1642. This would suggest that he had set up around this time as an independent painter.

Bol received his first major commission in 1649, a group portrait of the *Four Regents of the Amsterdam Lepers' House* (Amsterdam, Hist. Mus.). His reputation increased quickly, and he subsequently received commissions from outside Amsterdam, for instance for the group portrait of the *Officers of the Doelen in Gouda* (1653; Gouda, Stedel. Mus. Catharina Gasthuis). Although Bol had already lived for some time in Amsterdam, he became a citizen of the city suddenly in 1652, probably in connection with the decoration of Amsterdam's new town hall, for which the only candidates eligible were natives of the city. The following year he married Lysbeth Dell (*d* 1660), whose father, Elbert Dell, occupied a number of public offices, including ones at the Admiralty and the Wine Merchants' Guild. Bol received commissions from these institutions, probably through the intervention of his father-in-law. Bol lived with Lysbeth Dell on the Fluwelenburgwal, in the prosperous part of the city. Their only child to survive to adulthood, Elbert Bol, was born the following year.

Among Bol's later commissions is a series of portraits of *Admiral Michiel de Ruyter*, painted between 1661 and 1663 on the occasion of the journey to Chatham. In 1669 Bol married Anna van Arckel (*d* 1680), the wealthy widow of the treasurer of the Admiralty. One of the witnesses at the wedding, which was held in the Zuiderkerk, Amsterdam, was Bol's brother-in-law from his first marriage, Elbert Dell the younger. After this marriage Bol moved to the Herengracht and apparently stopped painting; there is no surviving work after 1669.

2. WORK.

(i) History subjects. Bol was clearly very dependent on Rembrandt in his early paintings and drawings; he copied compositions by his master almost literally, such as the biblical scene that probably depicts *Rachel Being Shown to Jacob* (*c.* 1640; Brunswick, Herzog Anton Ulrich-Mus.), for which Rembrandt's *Danaë* (1636; St Petersburg, Hermitage; *see* REMBRANDT VAN RIJN, fig. 3) served as the model. The *Three Marys by the Tomb* (1644; Copenhagen, Stat. Mus. Kst) is one of Bol's earliest dated paintings. Bol's talent was not at its best in this or his other narrative scenes. In general, they are rather statically conceived. Nevertheless, he received many such commissions for history paintings throughout his career, and he adapted his style over the years to conform to prevailing fashions.

After 1650 Bol turned away from Rembrandt's influence and adopted a new style of history painting, one that was more classicizing and elaborate and had recently been employed with great success in the decoration of the Huis ten Bosch near The Hague. The new town hall (now the Koninklijk Palais) in Amsterdam, the construction of which began in 1648, led to more commissions for this style of decorative painting, which suited the majestic character of the classicizing architecture. Bol was commissioned along with Govaert Flinck, another leading Amsterdam history painter, to decorate the burgomaster's office, one of the most important rooms in the new Stadhuis. Each was asked to design an overmantel that would express the burgomaster's status, prestige and incorruptibility. Opposite Flinck's *Marcus Curtius Dentatus Refusing the Gifts of the Samnites* (1656; *in situ*) hangs Bol's *Pyrrhus and Fabricius* (1656; *in situ*; see fig. 1).

The combination of *Pyrrhus* and *Dentatus* in a single room is unique in Netherlandish painting. Plutarch (*Fabricius Luscinus*, 21.20) recorded how the Roman consul Fabricius remained unmoved by the bribery of King Pyrrhus, who even tried to buy him off with the offer of an elephant. In an age when ancient culture was being revived, the burgomasters of Amsterdam were fond of comparing themselves to Roman consuls, whom they saw as prototypes of citizen–administrators of a republic. Bol's first compositional sketches are still fairly Rembrandt-esque, and the standing figure at the extreme right of the final composition is derived from a figure in Rembrandt's '*Hundred Guilder Print*' (*c.* 1643–9; B. 74; *see* REMBRANDT VAN RIJN, fig. 9). The large figures and clear colours in

1. Ferdinand Bol: *Pyrrhus and Fabricius*, oil on canvas, 4.85×3.5 m, 1656 (Amsterdam, Stichting Koninklijk Paleis)

this complex composition combine with surface divisions to achieve a spacious effect that was entirely to the taste of the commissioning body. An explicatory poem by Joost van den Vondel (1587–1679) is written on the wall under the two paintings. For another room in the Stadhuis, the aldermen's chamber, where trials were conducted, Bol painted another overmantel, *Moses with the Tablets of the Law* (*c.* 1664; *in situ*).

Bol was commissioned by the Admiralty to portray its guiding principles of reward and punishment in the same manner as he had done in his paintings for the new Stadhuis. For their council chamber he designed two overmantels: *Aeneas Distributing Prizes* (The Hague, Dienst Verspr. Rijkscol., on loan to Utrecht, Rijksuniv.) and *Consul Titus Manlius Torquatus Beheading his Son (Imperia Manliana)* (The Hague, Dienst Verspr. Rijkscol., on loan to Amsterdam, Rijksmus.). In 1661, instead of another group portrait, the regents of the Lepers' House commissioned a painting of a biblical theme to illustrate the regents' care for the sick. Instead of using the traditional comparison of Dives and Lazarus, Bol chose the Old Testament story from 2 Kings 5) of the *Prophet Elisha Refusing the Gifts of Naaman the Syrian* (Amsterdam, Hist. Mus): the regents could identify with the incorruptible prophet Elisha, and his greedy servant Gehazi provided an example for the institution's attendants of behaviour to avoid.

Bol's *Offering of Gifts at the Building of Solomon's Temple* (1669; Amsterdam, Ned. Hervormde Gemeente), dating from the year of his second marriage, may have been painted to encourage churchgoers to emulate his own generosity: Bol made this large canvas, apparently his last work, a gift to the congregation. The work is not distinguished for its originality and is a variation on an earlier sketch that probably represents the *Incorruptibility of Fabricius* (1656; Amsterdam, Hist. Mus.).

(ii) Portraits. Bol's earliest signed and dated portraits, from 1642–4, include a series of portraits of women, dressed according to the prevailing fashion, with large lace ruffs (e.g. 1642; Berlin, Gemäldegal.). These early portraits are a continuation of the style of Rembrandt but without his ability to convey the individuality of the sitter. For this reason, the attribution to Bol of the vivid portrait of *Elisabeth Bas* (Amsterdam, Rijksmus.) cannot be correct.

Like Rembrandt, Bol painted many *tronies* (character heads) and also imitated Rembrandt's custom of portraying men in a hat or beret. Not until 1649, with his first major commission for a group portrait, did Bol's work become somewhat more independent: the *Four Regents of the Amsterdam Lepers' House* is less in the manner of Rembrandt than in the tradition of earlier painters such as Thomas de Keyser. Although it initially seems to be a completely natural group of people, it is actually a composed tableau. The Regents' duty to care for lepers is underlined by the presence of a little boy with leprosy and an inmate of the institution at the extreme left.

Bol's individual portraits follow prevailing trends, influenced especially by the elegant portraits of van Dyck and other Flemish artists. By the 1650s Bol's palette included considerably more red, and several portraits from this period, such as the *Portrait of a Young Man* (1652; The Hague, Mauritshuis), were painted against a landscape background. The sitter is painted in the Flemish manner; the background landscape is pure Rembrandt. More of Bol's portraits, however, are set in an interior rather than against a landscape background. Most of these show the

sitter in three-quarter length, on a chair, with a table just visible and a curtain at the back. Examples include the *Self-portrait* and its pendant portrait of *Elisabeth Dell* (both 1653; Dell Park, Surrey, B. Schroeder priv. col., see Blankert, 1982, pl. 163). The best known of Bol's numerous self-portraits is his last (*c.* 1669; Amsterdam, Rijksmus.), with a frame embossed with sunflowers. It was probably painted on the occasion of his second marriage. The sleeping Cupid and the column are symbols of chastity, and the sunflower is meant to symbolize his honourable love for his second bride. The only one of Bol's many portraits that can be said to have an originality entirely its own is the *Portrait of a Boy* (1652; Castle Howard, N. Yorks; see fig. 2). It is without a trace of Rembrandt's influence, and in it Bol showed a surprising talent, which was never further developed, for still-life in the fruit and glass vessels at the lower right. Bol's later portraits became repetitious, in the same way as his history paintings. He made more portraits of men in berets and returned to Rembrandt's manner. In fact, Bol had little style of his own; he adapted to every new or changing fashion and to the taste of his patrons.

BIBLIOGRAPHY

A. Blankert: *Kunst als regeringszaak in Amsterdam in de zeventiende eeuw: Rondom schilderijen van Ferdinand Bol* (Lochem, 1975)
W. Sumowski: *Drawings of the Rembrandt School*, i (New York, 1979)
E. de Jongh: 'Bol vincit amorem', *Simiolus*, xii (1981–2), pp. 147–62
A. Blankert: *Ferdinand Bol (1616–1680): Rembrandt's Pupil* (Doornspijk, 1982)
W. Sumowski: *Gemälde der Rembrandt-Schüler*, i (Landau, 1983)
B. Haak: *The Golden Age: Dutch Painters of the Seventeenth Century* (New York, 1984)

MARIJKE VAN DER MEIJ-TOLSMA

Bol, Hans (*b* Mechelen, 16 Dec 1534; *d* Amsterdam, ?*bur* 20 Nov 1593). Flemish painter and draughtsman. He received his training as a painter from two of his uncles, Jacob Bol I and Jan Bol (*fl* 1505). After two years in Heidelberg, he was made a master in the Mechelen Guild of St Luke. After the annexation of the city by the Spanish troops in 1572, Bol settled in Antwerp, where he became a master in 1574. A decade later he left Antwerp, arriving in Amsterdam after travelling to Bergen-op-Zoom, Dordrecht and Delft. Van Mander's statement that he was buried in Amsterdam on 20 November 1593 is disputed by some sources because of a supposedly signed *Adoration of the Shepherds* dated 1595 (see Wurzbach, i, p. 130). Bol's most important students included his stepson Frans Boels, Jacob Savery and Joris Hoefnagel.

Bol began his career primarily as a watercolour painter; the technique of *waterschilderen* was very common in Mechelen, where, instead of the far more expensive wall tapestries, large-scale scenes were painted on canvas using opaque watercolour or tempera. While in Antwerp he also executed numerous fine miniature landscapes in gouache on parchment, richly populated with human figures. He was a gifted draughtsman, and many of his drawings were made into prints by such engravers as Hieronymus Cock and Phillip Galle. Prints after his work include series devoted to *Landscapes* (1562) and the *Story of Tobias* (1565). Some of his landscape drawings and paintings clearly show the influence of the imaginary panoramas of

2. Ferdinand Bol: *Portrait of a Boy*, oil on canvas, 1.75×1.50 m, 1652 (Castle Howard, N. Yorks)

Joachim Patinir and Cornelis Massys. Others are more naturalistic: for instance, Bol executed a number of topographical drawings (e.g. the *View of Antwerp*, Los Angeles, CA, Co. Mus. A.) and towards the end of his life produced several drawings of wooded landscapes.

BIBLIOGRAPHY

Hollstein: *Dut. & Flem.*; Wurzbach

H. G. Franz: 'Hans Bol als Landschaftszeichner', *Jb. Ksthist. Inst. Graz*, i (1965), pp. 19–67

——: *Niederländische Landschaftsmalerei im Zeitalter des Manierismus* (Graz, 1969), i, pp. 182–97; ii, pls 286–324

——: 'Beiträge zur niederländischen Landschaftsmalerei des 16. Jahrhunderts, II: Baumlandschaft und Waldlandschaft bei den Brüdern Valckenborch und Hans Bol', *Jb. Ksthist. Inst. Graz*, xv–xvi (1979–80), pp. 151–74

The Age of Bruegel: Netherlandish Drawings in the Sixteenth Century (exh. cat. by J. O. Hand and others, Washington, DC, N.G.A.; New York, Pierpont Morgan Lib.; 1986–7), pp. 71–4

HANS DEVISSCHER

Boldini, Giovanni (*b* Ferrara, 31 Dec 1842; *d* Paris, 11 Jan 1931). Italian painter and printmaker. He received his earliest training from his father, the painter Antonio Boldini (1799–1872). From 1858 he may have attended courses given by Girolamo Domenichini (1813–91) and Giovanni Pagliarini (?1809–78) at the Civico Ateneo di Palazzo dei Diamanti, where he assiduously copied Old Masters. At 18 he was already known in Ferrara as an accomplished portrait painter. In 1862 he went to Florence, where he sporadically attended the Scuola del Nudo at the Accademia di Belle Arti. He frequented the Caffè Michelangiolo, a meeting-place of progressive artists, where he came into contact with the MACCHIAIOLI group of artists.

Boldini's taste for wealth and elegance brought him into association with the established portrait painter Michele Gordigiani (1830–1909), who gave him a share of his numerous commissions; with the sophisticated Telemaco Signorini; and especially with the wealthy Cristiano Banti (1824–1904), with whom he travelled to Naples in 1866. Stimulated by the Macchiaioli, Boldini painted a number of landscapes, but distinctly preferred portraits. The numerous small portraits of his friends, including *Cristiano Banti with Cane* (1865–6), *Alaide Banti in White* (1866) and *Diego Martelli* (*c.* 1867; all Florence, Pitti), display a revolutionary approach to this genre that was to influence its development in Tuscany. Structured in broad areas of tone and colour, of light and dark patterns according to the *macchia* technique that was used by the Macchiaioli, they introduced a low vantage point, a darker palette of greys and browns—peculiar to Boldini's later work—and a novel treatment of the background as an ambience displaying the sitter's milieu and interests.

Between 1866 and 1868 Boldini enjoyed the patronage and the hospitality of Isabella (*c.* 1809–69) and Walter Falconer, members of the expatriate community living in Florence, who were introduced to Boldini by Signorini, from whom Isabella took painting lessons. Boldini decorated a room at their villa, La Falconiera, near Pistoia, with the only mural paintings of his career: eight large-scale compositions in dry tempera (1868; Pistoia, Cassa di Risparmio, see 1989 exh. cat., pp. 26–9), depicting rural scenes and seascapes. The motif was inspired by his *plein-air* experience, gained while working in 1867 alongside Giuseppe Abbati (1836–68) and Giovanni Fattori, but was handled in a grand manner and with a dynamism that was to become characteristic of his art. In 1870 and 1871 Boldini travelled to London as a guest of the English patron William Cornwallis-West, a friend of the Falconers; he was inspired by the great 18th-century English portrait painters and was also impressed with Turner's work.

In 1871 Boldini settled in Paris, having previously visited the Exposition Universelle in 1867, but continued to maintain close ties with his Florentine artist-friends. Almost immediately he became celebrated. Under contract with the art dealer Adolphe Goupil he painted landscapes and particularly genre subjects that met the market's demand for small, bright, lightly executed, 18th-century costume pieces (e.g. *Gossip*, 1873; New York, Met.), in the manner of Jean-Louis-Ernest Meissonier and Mariano José Bernardo Fortuny y Marsal. Also popular were his views of Parisian life, such as *Place Clichy* (1874; Rome, priv. col., see 1989 exh. cat., no. 20), the silvery tones of which reveal his enthusiasm for Jean-Baptiste-Camille Corot. He used the same motifs to express boldly his incipient fascination with dynamic movement. In *Leaving a Masked Ball in Montmartre* (*c.* 1875; Ferrara, Gal. Civ. A. Mod.), horses, a recurring favourite subject, people and even buildings are transformed into an unprecedented centrifugal explosion of frenetically applied pigment.

In 1874 Boldini exhibited for the first time at the Salon du Champ-de-Mars, winning public acclaim. In 1876 he travelled to Germany, where he met Adolph Friedrich Erdmann von Menzel, and to the Netherlands, where he admired the work of Frans Hals; he was much inspired by their pictorial styles. Around this time Boldini began to paint portraits of beautiful society women, peculiar to which is the contrast between the carefully rendered and illuminated face and the loosely painted, undefined surroundings; one such is the painting of his close friend and frequent model *Comtesse Gabrielle de Rasty Seated in an Armchair* (*c.* 1878; New York, Stair Sainty Matthiesen, see 1984 Grey A.G. exh. cat., p. 17). Boldini became friends with other fashionable portrait painters: James McNeill Whistler, Paul César Helleu and John Singer Sargent, whose *Madame X* (Mme Pierre Gautreau, 1884; New York, Met.) inspired some of Boldini's later works.

Boldini also found an affinity with Edouard Manet and established an enduring friendship with Edgar Degas. Around 1878–80 he began to experiment with engraving, producing a small number of etchings and drypoints (53 titles). Degas's influence is apparent in some of his choices of theme, composition and technique, as in the subject and configuration of his first etching, *At the Paris Opera* (*c.* 1878–80; Ferrara, Gal. Civ. A. Mod.), which displays strong contrasts between very dark and brightly illuminated areas. In the 1880s Boldini, like Degas, began to use pastel for large, often full-scale portraits; the different effects he achieved demonstrate his virtuoso command of the medium. In the delicate *Emiliana Concha de Ossa* ('The White Pastel', 1888; Milan, Gal. A. Mod.), pastel in various tones of white enhances the progressive dematerialization of the image, while in the forceful *Giuseppe Verdi* (1886; Rome, G.N.A. Mod.) the composer's powerful presence is immortalized in tones of grey and black.

In 1889 Boldini travelled with Degas to Spain, where they admired the work of Velázquez, and to Morocco. In the 1880s and 1890s Boldini travelled extensively in Italy and Spain and visited London and New York; he made Venice, which held a particular attraction for him, the subject of many evocative images that recalled Turner. In 1890, at the Exposition Universelle in Paris, he was inspired by the grand manner and dynamism of Anders Zorn's portraits. While continuing to paint still-lifes, views of Venice, horses and portraits of women, often in provocative poses, Boldini in the 1890s specialized in portraits of the beautiful and the famous. By the end of the century he was, along with Sargent, the most sought-after portrait painter in Paris. He recorded a whole era—

Giovanni Boldini: *Mme Charles Max*, oil on canvas, 2.05×1.00 m, 1896 (Paris, Musée d'Orsay)

the *fin-de-siècle* in France, the world of Marcel Proust—conveying in his nervous, swift, fluid brushwork the artificial splendour of an ephemeral world. Exaggerated movement distorted the figures; *Mme Charles Max* (1896; Paris, Mus. d'Orsay; see fig.) exemplifies the characteristics of Boldini's development. The sophisticated, artificial curvatures and elongations, the *figura serpentinata* and the greyish palette of Parmigianino reflect Boldini's Emilian Mannerist tradition, which he reconciled with the contemporary fashion of elongated forms and the undulating line of Art Nouveau, thus conferring on the figures a new dynamic movement, described by fluid clothes that accentuate sensual overtones. Boldini applied the same distorted movement to portrayals of men and children, effectively revealing and underscoring different aspects of the sitters' personalities.

Around 1900 Boldini's style became more dynamic. In *Consuelo, Duchess of Marlborough, and her Son, Lord Ivor Spencer-Churchill* (1906; New York, Met.) the poses, seen from a very high vantage point, are increasingly awkward, and there is a stronger contrast between the mask-like faces and turbulent bodies. Boldini's female sitters seem all of the same *femme fatale* model, typical of the *fin-de-siècle*.

Boldini became more concerned around 1910–15 with the process of bravura painting that translated reality into vigorous whirling movement. Thus *Marchesa Luisa Casati* (1914; Rome, G.N.A. Mod.) is a virtuoso performance of frenetic energy that transcends female characterization; a prelude to the configurations of Futurism. These seemingly spontaneous executions were based on many studies: audacious drawings, closely related to the revolutionary expressions of modern artistic movements.

Extremely prolific in different media (including watercolour), Boldini was active to the end of his life. In 1916 his eyesight began to deteriorate, and from 1927 he executed only charcoal drawings, many of them portraits of his future wife, the journalist Emilia Cardona.

BIBLIOGRAPHY
E. Cardona: *Vie de Jean Boldini* (Paris, 1931)
——: *Lo studio di G. Boldini* (Milan, 1937)
E. Camasesca and C. Ragghianti: *L'opera completa di Boldini* (Milan, 1970)
G. Sari: *Boldini a Parigi* (Alghero, 1980)
F. Farina: *Boldini: I cavalli* (Ferrara, 1981)
Giovanni Boldini: Opera incisoria (exh. cat., Ferrara, Gal. Civ. A. Mod., 1981)
E. Piceni: *Giovanni Boldini: L'uomo e l'opera* (Busto Arsizio, 1981)
S. Bartolini: *Giovanni Boldini: Un macchiaiolo a Collegigliato* (Florence, 1982)
Dessins parisiens de Giovanni Boldini (exh. cat., ed. F. Farina and V. Doria; Paris, Carnavalet, 1982)
Giovanni Boldini (exh. cat., ed. P. Dini; Pistoia, Convent of S Domenico, 1984)
Giovanni Boldini and Society Portraiture, 1880–1920 (exh. cat., ed. G. A. Reynolds; New York U., Grey A.G., 1984)
P. Mauries and A. Borgogelli: *Boldini* (Milan, 1987) [beautiful illustrations]
Boldini (exh. cat., ed. E. Camasesca and A. Borgogelli; Milan, Pal. Permanente, 1989) [excellent illustrations and bibliog.]
P. Dini: *Boldini macchiaiolo* (Turin, 1989)
Giovanni Boldini, 1842–1931 (exh. cat., Paris, Mus. Marmottan, 1992)

EFREM GISELLA CALINGAERT

Boldrini, Nicolò (*b* ?Vicenza, *c.* 1500; *fl* Venice, *c.* 1530–70). Italian wood-engraver. He is known only by his signed prints drawn from the designs of various artists. The inscription TITIANVS INV/*Nicolaus Boldrinus/Vicenti[n]us* *inci/debat. 1566* on the chiaroscuro woodcut of *Venus and Cupid* (see Muraro and Rosand, p. 317) testifies to its derivation from a Titian model as well as to its date. Boldrini was long considered the engraver of Titian's work *par excellence* and his direct collaborator, but today critical opinion (Oberhuber) tends to see such collaboration only in the famous woodcut of the *Six Saints* (Landau, p. 335, n. P34). Stylistic and historical considerations lead to the conclusion that some landscape prints, such as *Landscape with a Milkmaid* and *St Jerome in the Wilderness*, are not the product of a direct relationship between Boldrini and Titian but rather the work of the German Giovanni Britto (see 1993 exh. cat., pp. 563–4). Of around 30 works of very different style and engraving quality that have been assigned to Nicolò Boldrini, among the most famous, also known in chiaroscuro forms, are the *Caricature of Laokoon* (Muraro and Rosand, no. 49) and *Marco Curzio* by Pordenone (Muraro and Rosand, no. 79).

BIBLIOGRAPHY
M. Muraro and D. Rosand: *Tiziano e la silografia veneziana del cinquecento* (Vicenza, 1976), pp. 102–7, 110–14, 134–41
K. Oberhuber: 'Titian Woodcuts and Drawings: Some Problems', *Tiziano e Venezia*, ed. F. Benvenuti (Vicenza, 1980), pp. 523–8
M. A. Chiari: *Incisioni da Tiziano: Museo Correr* (Venice, 1982), pp. 31–5, 40–41
D. Landau: 'Printmaking in Venice and the Veneto', *The Genius of Venice, 1500–1600* (exh. cat., ed. J. Martineau and C. Hope; London, RA, 1983), pp. 303–54
M. A. Chiari: 'La fortuna dell'opera pordenoniana attraverso le stampe di traduzione', *Il Pordenone: Atti del convegno internazionale di studio: Pordenone, 1985*, p. 184
W. R. Resrick: 'Titien, la maturité et les dernières années: Dessins et gravures', *Le Siècle de Titien* (exh. cat., Paris, 1993), pp. 559–94

FELICIANO BENVENUTI

Bole. Fine red clay tinted with iron oxides to a red or yellow colour. When mixed with size, it is used as a base for gilding, since it takes a fine polish when burnished. It was widely employed on panel paintings up to the mid-15th century and is still used for picture frames. The red colour is often visible below worn areas of gilding. White bole is a synonym for raslin or china clay.

RUPERT FEATHERSTONE

Bolea, Pedro Pablo Abarca de. *See* ARANDA.

Boleslas–Biegas. *See* BIEGAS, BOLESŁAW.

Bolfgangus of Crngrob (*fl* 1453–71). Slovenian painter. He has been identified by the damaged signature 'Bolfgangus de . . . cz . . .' on a fresco cycle of the *Nativity, Adoration of the Magi, Virgin and Child* and several saints (1453; Crngrob, Church of the Annunciation). He is generally seen as the first representative of the new naturalistic style in Carniola (now Slovenia) and the head of a large workshop that produced the finest wall paintings of the late 15th century. He seems to have drawn inspiration primarily from German printed graphics, such as the work of the Master of the Playing Cards (which explains the affinity with Konrad Witz) and Master E.S. A softened, elaborated fold style of German origin formed the basis of his art, adapted to suit the traditional, central Slovenian preference for a simplified, popularized prettiness. He is attributed with the painting (1465) of the presbytery of St John's in Mirna, Lower Carniola. A few later wall paintings

(1467, Mače nad Preddvorom, St Nicholas; *c.* 1465–70, Bled-Otok, Church of the Assumption; 1471, Žminj, Istria, Trinity Chapel of the parish church) are ascribed to his circle. Master Leonard, the Master of St Andrew at Krašce (*fl c.* 1490–1510), can be seen as the last representative of this workshop tradition. In all these works, models not only from German graphic art but also from the 40-page *Biblia pauperum* (*c.* 1450) from the Netherlands were often used.

BIBLIOGRAPHY
J. Höfler: 'Meister Bolfgangus und die Rolle der deutschen Druckgraphik in der Wandmalerei der zweiten Hälfte des 15. Jahrhunderts in Slowenien', *XXV. Internationaler Kongress fuer Kunstgeschichte CIHA: Vienna, 1983*, ix, pp. 91–3
——: *Stensko slikarstvo na Slovenskem med Janezom Ljubljanskim in Mojstrom sv. Andreja iz Krašc* [Wall painting in Slovenia between Johannes of Ljubljana and the Master of Sv. Andrej at Krašce] (Ljubljana, 1985), pp. 22–5, 64–79

JANEZ HÖFLER

Bolgi, Andrea [il Carrarino] (*b* Carrara, 22 June 1605; *d* Naples, 1656). Italian sculptor. He first trained under Pietro Tacca in Florence. In 1626, together with Francesco Baratta, he moved to Rome, where he entered the studio of Gianlorenzo Bernini and was put to work on the models for the angels on top of the baldacchino in St Peter's. In 1629, at the age of 24, Bolgi was well enough respected to be given one of the most important commissions in Rome, the execution of the statue of *St Helena*, one of the four colossal marble statues in the piers under the cupola of St Peter's; the other three were executed by Bernini, Francesco Du Quesnoy and Francesco Mochi (all *in situ*). Bolgi spent almost ten years (1629–39) on this statue, but it was very poorly received. Offended by the criticism, he moved to Naples (before 1653), where he sculpted a number of marble portrait busts, including *Francesco Antonio de Caro* and *Giovanni Camillo Cace* (both Naples, S Lorenzo Maggiore). Bolgi's style, much influenced by his study of antique sculpture, is conservative and classicizing, characterized by a relentless precision. His work in Naples, however, has certain Baroque qualities that seem to represent a forced attempt to emulate Bernini's vigour.

BIBLIOGRAPHY
Thieme–Becker
L. Pascoli: *Vite de' pittori, scultori ed architetti moderni*, ii (Rome, 1730), p. 436
A. Riccoboni: *Roma nell'arte: La scultura nell'evo moderno dal quattrocento ad oggi* (Rome, 1943), pp. 168–70
R. Wittkower: *Bernini* (London, 1955); rev., enlarged as *Gian Lorenzo Bernini: The Sculptor of the Roman Baroque* (London, 1966)
——: *Art and Architecture in Italy, 1600–1750*, Pelican Hist. A. (London, 1958, rev. 4/1982), pp. 305–6
V. Martinelli: 'Contributi alla scultura del seicento: Andrea Bolgi a Roma e a Napoli', *Commentari*, x (1959), pp. 137–58
A. N. Cellini: 'Ritratti di Andrea Bolgi', *Paragone*, xiii/147 (1962), pp. 24–40

ROBERT H. WESTIN

Bolivia, Republic of. South American country that shares borders with Brazil to the north and east, with Paraguay and Argentina to the south, and with Chile and Peru to the west (see fig. 1). The Spanish arrived in Bolivia in 1534. During colonization, as part of the Viceroyalty of Peru, the territory of Bolivia was called Charcas or Upper Peru. The name derives from the Charcas Indians who lived to the north of Potosí, where the Spanish established the main political and administrative body of the region, the Audencia de Charcas. The region remained under the control of Lima until 1776, when it became the most northerly region of the Viceroyalty of Rio de la Plata. The Republic of Bolivia (founded 6 August 1825) was named after the Venezuelan revolutionary Simón Bolívar. It is divided into nine departments, which are further divided into provinces and cantons. Each department has a canton, usually the largest city. Sucre is the legal capital, and La Paz is the administrative capital.

Although the nation is identified with the Andean *meseta* (high tablelands or plains), more than half of its territory consists of low-lying tropical lands, largely unpopulated because of the rugged terrain and the difference in level (*c.* 3400 m) between high- and low-lands. After the 19th century Bolivia lost large tracts of territory through international wars and diplomatic agreements. The climatic variety of the country allows for a great diversity of plant and animal types. Some species, including pumas, condors, jaguars and caymans, have been the subject of myths and blends of religions. Animal skins were used ritually, and the multicoloured plumes of tropical birds are still used for festive decoration. Cattle, horses and sheep, some imported by the Spanish, have aided in the cultivation of land, in transport and in providing fine wools. The harsh nature of the topography, however, has also been one of the factors that has most forcefully limited development because of the difficulty of establishing and maintaining communication routes. Bolivia's mineral wealth led to the development of metallurgy in copper and bronze in Pre-Columbian times, a decisive factor in the supremacy of Tiahuanaco, an ancient city state on the southern shores of Lake Titicaca. In the colonial period exploitation of these minerals and metals continued for craft products of daily use, silver for minting and the creation of works of art. The wooded valleys and plains provided materials, particularly cedar and pine, for the construction of the missions and for architectural wood-carving, wooden sculptures and the production of altarpieces and furniture. In the 20th century new access to more humid zones, previously unexploited, facilitated the use by artists of various precious woods.

For a discussion of the art and architecture of Bolivia before colonization *see* SOUTH AMERICA, PRE-COLUMBIAN, §III.

I. Introduction. II. Architecture. III. Painting and graphic arts. IV. Sculpture. V. Gold and silver. VI. Textiles. VII. Patronage, collecting and dealing. VIII. Museums and photographic collections. IX. Art education.

I. Introduction.

Within a short period after their arrival, the Spaniards took over the whole country, concentrating on the occupation of the highlands and attracted by the availability of cheap labour and mineral wealth. At this time the indigenous population's economic basis lay in farming and cattle-breeding. Pre-Columbian practices of food storage and distribution of goods and services persisted despite their lack of recognition by the Spanish, and other Pre-Columbian cultural features continued with the influence of mestizos (people of mixed Indian and European ancestry),

1. Map of Bolivia; those sites with separate entries in this dictionary are distinguished by CROSS-REFERENCE TYPE

of which the textile art of the Andes is especially noteworthy (*see* §VI below). The city of POTOSÍ was founded officially in 1572, although it had been established unofficially in 1545; other 16th-century cities were La Plata (founded in 1540; now SUCRE), COCHABAMBA (1542), LA PAZ (1548), Santa Cruz (1560) and Tarija (1574). Oruro was founded in 1606, following the discovery of silver mines there. The low tropical and jungle lands were colonized in the 17th and 18th centuries through the Jesuit and Franciscan missions. The ecclesiastic hierarchy was based mainly in La Plata, where the episcopate (established in 1565) was elevated to an archbishopric in 1605. (For discussion of the role of religious missionaries in Bolivia *see* FRANCISCAN ORDER and JESUIT ORDER, §4(ii).)

Charcas was divided up among Spanish *encomenderos* (colonists granted Indian labourers by royal decree), some of the lands remaining in the hands of native Indians in the form of *reducciones* (settlements of native Indians). The *reducciones* obliged the Indians to gather together in towns and better facilitated control of the Indians who lived in the countryside but did not belong to any *encomienda*. The discovery of silver mines in Porco, Potosí and Oruro enhanced Charcas's importance, and the subsequent need for a large labour force was met by a system of forced labour on a rotating basis for all Indians, known as *mita*.

On its foundation the Republic proclaimed the abolition of the *mitá*, the *encomienda*, taxes on the natives and enslavement. It favoured the élites of landholders, businessmen and creole (people of European ancestry born in the New World) bureaucrats. With the economic decline in the 19th century, the government had to face the harsh reality that the Spanish administration had created no industries, basing its hopes solely on agricultural development and on mineral wealth. In 1879 Bolivia was engaged in a war with Chile, as a result of which it lost its outlet to the sea. In the late 19th century there was a revival of silver mining, and in the early 20th century a boom in tin mining created a new Bolivian aristocracy, perhaps more attached to foreign interests. In the 1940s the oil industry began to develop and became one of the most important sources of foreign currency. The most significant historical event of the 20th century was the National Revolution of April 1952, which led to nationalization of the mines, land reform and universal suffrage. It also brought the Indians and mestizos into the economic, political and cultural activity of the nation.

BIBLIOGRAPHY
J. E. Fagg: *Latin America: A General History* (London and New York, 1963, rev. 3/1977), pp. 426–30, 679–90
R. Villaroel Claure: *Bolivia* (Washington, DC, 1963)
A. Arguedas: *Historia general de Bolivia: El proceso de la nacionalidad, 1809–1921* (La Paz, 1967)
W. E. Carter: *Bolivia: A Profile* (New York, 1971)
J. Fellman Velarde: *Historia de la cultura boliviana* (La Paz, 1976)
H. Klein: *Historia general de Bolivia* (La Paz, 1980)
J. de Mesa and T. Gisbert: *Manual de historia de Bolivia* (La Paz, 1983)

LAURA ESCOBARI

II. Architecture.

1. 1534–1825. 2. After 1825.

1. 1534–1825. When the Spanish arrived in the region that became Bolivia, they found traditions of planning, building and architecture that dated back to pre-Inca cultures, such as that at Tiahuanaco (*c.* AD 500 onward). The grid plan, for example, existed here long before it was reintroduced from Spain, and other architectural elements had been rigidly formalized and related to location and climate.

(i) Urban planning and building techniques. (ii) Historical survey.

(i) *Urban planning and building techniques.* Only rarely did the Indians of the Pre-Columbian period settle in great urban centres. Their concept of a city was in reality a ceremonial site; for all other purposes they lived in rural communities. All the towns and cities of modern Bolivia, therefore, date from after the arrival of the Spanish, who forced the Indians to gather in *reducciones* and new towns. The latter were laid out in grid plans with precise specifications for street blocks, width of the streets and water courses, and assigned spaces for places of worship, monasteries and hospitals. The Pre-Columbian tradition of building open-air temples was influential in determining the standard layout of churches. Typically, these consist of large, walled atria or courtyards on to which usually face an open chapel (*capilla abierta*) and small open shrines (*posas*) as well as an enclosed church.

Traditional Indian building methods continued under the Spanish throughout the colonial period and after, especially for residential buildings. Wattle, adobe and thatch, for example, were used to construct enclosures for everyday use, including churches at first. However, local skills also included the more sophisticated rubble and fieldstone methods handed down from the Pre-Columbian Chavín period and the accurately fitted dry-stone masonry

of the Incas. These techniques were combined by the Spanish with the stylistic complexities in structure and decoration that were common in Spain. There the transition from Gothic to Renaissance in the last quarter of the 15th century coincided with the introduction of the Plateresque manner of overall low-relief surface decoration and was further complicated by continuing use of MUDÉJAR references. Consequently, colonial architecture shows putative Renaissance forms, Gothic vaulting and other medieval remnants, together with *Mudéjar* building in brick and timber, including coffered ceilings. Once absorbed by tradition-bound local craftsmen, these new forms tended to persist longer than in Spain: for example Gothic vaulting continued well into the 18th century. Architecture with European pretensions was in the hands of the architects and engineers who came from Europe, while construction was executed by masons assisted by both Indian and mestizo craftsmen.

(ii) *Historical survey.*

(a) Renaissance, Plateresque and early Baroque, 1534–1690. (b) Mestizo Baroque to Neo-classicism, 1690–1825.

(a) Renaissance, Plateresque and early Baroque, 1534–1690. Buildings of this period, of which churches are the best examples, mirror the contemporary stylistic transition from Gothic to Renaissance architecture in Spain. Exteriors are simple, and imported styles affected principally the design of portals. These are Plateresque in character in early examples and more purist after the mid-16th century, when the so-called classical period had begun in Spain. Ground-plans are elongated rectangles with apsidal-ended single naves and usually octagonal chancels. Walls were reinforced with thick buttresses, and roofs were coffered or rib-vaulted in timber. Examples include the early church (1560) at Caquiaviri, which helped to set the trend for rich interior decoration, the adobe church (1590) at Corque, with a brick and ceramic tiled portal, and the simple stone church (1612) at Tiahuanaco, its classicizing portal framed in a delightful, locally devised Ionic order. All have characteristic atria, with four small open shrines and, unique to Bolivia and Peru, centrally placed miserere chapels. At Copacabana, near Lake Titicaca, which was a place of pilgrimage in Pre-Columbian times, the first Christian sanctuary was built by the Augustinians (warrant issued in the mid-1580s) and a chapel followed (1614–18). From this period dates the unusual, *Mudéjar*-influenced cloister (see fig. 2), which is roofed with flat domes concealed from the courtyard by a narrow entablature above the piers of the arcade. A larger new church was begun by the architect Francisco Jiménez de Singüenza in 1668. It is built mainly in brick and, like some other Augustian foundations, has crenellated walls around an atrium with four open shrines: here the open chapel also has an open dome. *Mudéjar* influence is apparent in the local jade-green tiling of the main dome and cupolas. Building continued into the 18th century.

At La Plata (now Sucre), the cathedral was begun in 1561 by Juan Miguel de Veramendi, and the earliest phase of building was completed in 1572. The vaulted nave and side aisles (1683–92) of the present building are by José González Merguelete; although the cathedral was not

2. Cloister in the sanctuary at Copacabana, early 17th century

completed until 1712, it remained unaffected by the regional Mestizo Baroque style that was developing around it. The flat roof emphasizes the horizontality: above the smooth stone walls is a continuous balustrade, broken only by terminal urnlike features on pedestals above each buttress. Unusually, one of the long sides of the cathedral faces the main square, providing the spacious background for a magnificent retable portal. Other significant churches built in La Plata include S Lázaro (already in use by 1544, though it continued to develop well into the 17th century) and S Francisco (1581–1619), the latter by Martín de Oviedo, both of which were closely based on Andalusian models; the *Mudéjar*-style brick and timber church of S Miguel (1612), its tower later painted to resemble stonework; and the groin-vaulted churches of S Domingo (1583–1628) and S Augustín (1590–1632). Among civil buildings constructed in La Plata are the famed Casa de Moneda (1592), the spacious Casa Consistorial (*c.* 1600), the Casa del Gran Poder (1630) and some early buildings of the Universidad Boliviana Mayor, Real y Pontificia de S Francisco Xavier, founded in 1624.

The influence of the Baroque was apparent from *c.* 1630 in Latin-cross ground-plans, frequently with timber domes at the crossing. Building methods remained largely unchanged, although adobe churches became less frequent. Single Roman barrel-vaulted naves, Gothic cross-vaulting (especially for subsidiary naves of three-naved churches)

and *Mudéjar* coffered roofs all continued but with less inventiveness from the middle of the century. Surfaces other than stone were whitewashed or painted in earthen colours, but from the beginning simplicity of construction or spatial expression was accompanied by highly decorated interiors, with altarpieces, panels, framed pictures and pedestals, all in painted and gilded timber often enriched with precious metals. Such exuberant expression of evangelical success is heralded but rarely matched by the exterior splendours of the portal ensembles, which became increasingly expressive of the Baroque spirit. The most notable examples were also in La Plata, including the transitional monastery churches of S Clara (1639) and S Teresa (1665), the latter by the architect–friar Pedro de Peñaloza, and the church of the Hospital de S Bárbara (*c.* 1663), perhaps the finest regional example in the early Spanish Baroque tradition. The Universidad de S Francisco Xavier retains its two-storey cloister of 1697 with typical Doric and Ionic orders, in which the rhythm of the upper-storey arcade is doubled, a lightness of touch not seen in earlier buildings. Spandrel panels show the persistence of *Mudéjar* influence on Spanish models. Civil buildings built in La Plata at the end of the 17th century include the Palacio Torre Tagle and the Palacio Arzobispal, both with two-storey stone portals with sculptural decoration.

(b) Mestizo Baroque to Neo-classicism, 1690–1825. By the late 17th century regional culture and techniques had

so overlaid the imported early Baroque trends as to produce, along a strip from Arequipa in Peru to Lake Titicaca and right across the Bolivian highlands, a recognizable regional style, the Mestizo Baroque, which was derived from the synthesis of European, particularly Spanish, culture with resurgent indigenous traditions. Towards the end of the 17th century the indigenous taste for low-relief decoration received greater impetus through the influence of the Churrigueresque style from Spain. Largely disposed in surface decoration, the motifs of Mestizo Baroque combine elements of the Christian pre-Renaissance and Mannerist traditions with the non-figural geometrical patterns of *Mudéjar* origin and images of tropical flora and fauna. Unlike European Baroque, there is no concern with innovative ground-plans nor any attempt at chiaroscuro effects in the decoration, which is archaicizing in character and largely planiform. Rather, it is the *horror vacui* of the Baroque that makes for the near filigree effects of the characteristic style.

Bolivian Mestizo Baroque developed and reached its apogee in the silver-mining town of Potosí. At the height of its prosperity the town boasted *c.* 30 churches and monastic establishments. The Carmelite church of S Teresa (founded 1685), Potosí, is one of the earliest of the Mestizo Baroque churches: the archaic pedimented tympanum above the door to its nunnery is dated 1692, although the brick and stone whitewashed façade of the church is probably a little later. It is a fine example of a 'flying façade', in which a two-storey belfry with three arches, framed by single twisted columns, stands atop the façade of the church itself. In the same category is the church of La Compañía (1700–07), Potosí, by the Indian stonecutter Sebastián de la Cruz, one of the most notable of Bolivian colonial buildings. The vigorous decoration of the portal and coupled spiral columns flanking the niche above it stands boldly against the plain surface of rose-coloured stone. A finely hewn façade with a bold two-storey belfry surmounting it together rise to 35 m above street-level. The works of de la Cruz, who also began the church of S Francisco (1704–14), Potosí, were completed after his death by Indian craftsmen colleagues Joseph Augustín and Felipe Chavarria. S Bernardo (1725–31) and El Belén (1725–50), both in Potosí, are by the local architect Fernando de Rojas Luna, who also influenced the design of S Benito (1711–44), one of many Latin American buildings of the period inexplicably decorated with classical figures. S Lorenzo (1728–44), Potosí, by an anonymous architect, has been acclaimed as the ultimate expression of the Mestizo Baroque: cruciform in plan, it has a dome at the crossing and half-domes over transepts and apse. Its façade consists of two towers and a central pediment (restored late 19th century), below which the portal (see fig. 3) is sheltered under an arch of great depth that spans the area between the towers, seeming to continue the vault of the nave. The highly original portal decoration includes 'Indiatids' and mermaids playing the *charango*, a mestizo stringed instrument, on either side of a niche above the entablature.

Notable contemporary and somewhat later churches remain in La Paz: S Francisco (1744–84) is similar to churches in some of the nearby Titicaca settlements but, unlike them, is on a rectangular (three-aisled basilican)

3. Portal of S Lorenzo, Potosí, 1728–44

plan: plates of alabaster used in the original windows are still preserved in the church; slightly earlier, mid-18th century S Domingo served throughout the 19th century as the city's cathedral. In Sucre (formerly La Plata) the only extant portal in the Mestizo Baroque style is that of the church of Las Monicas (*c.* 1740). Elsewhere, well-known examples include the church at Arani (1745) in the Cochabamba Valley, designed by Lucas Cabral, and churches at Sicasica (1725) and Guaqui (1784) in the highlands.

With the notable exception of the early Casa Vicaria (1615), Potosí, distinguished civil architecture is mainly later in date. The monumental Casa de Moneda (1759–72), Potosí, by Salvador Villa and Luis Cabello, has domes, high-arching roofs, three large courtyards and many out-buildings. The many fine mansions and houses are usually of two storeys and intimate in scale; they form a continuous streetscape but have spacious patios behind. Notable examples of secular architecture in Potosí, all from the last quarter of the 18th century, include the portal and bold decoration of the Casa de Otavi (1750–85; now the Banco Nacional de Bolivia); the filigree surface decoration matching the dignity of its official occupant of the Casa del Corregidor; and the lacelike carving around the neo-*Mudéjar* portal of the Casa de Herrera (now part of the university). The manorial houses of La Paz, such as the Casa Villaverde (*c.* 1755), built for the marquis of the same name, and the three-storey Palacio de Diez de Medina (1775), have particularly fine courtyards.

The mid-18th-century architecture of the Jesuit *reducciones* in the regions inhabited by the Moxos and Chiquitanos Indians, in the eastern and north-eastern plains respectively, was much influenced by the designs of the corresponding missions to the Guarani Indians in Paraguay and Argentina, where Giovanni Battista Primoli worked in the 1730s. The principal buildings, typically a church with free-standing belfry, a college and a miserere chapel, face on to a square with a monumental central cross and a subsidiary cross or open shrine at each corner. Churches follow the Jesuit rectangular plan and here have a nave and two aisles with adobe walls set back inside the outer rows of timber columns, which support the wide eaves necessary in areas of heavy rainfall. The most important of these are the mission buildings of the Chiquitanos group, designed by the Jesuit architect–priest Martin Schmid, who came to Bolivia in 1730, including S Javier (1749–53), Concepción (1768) and S Rafael (1749–53), all showing the influence of Schmid's native Bavarian Rococo.

By the late 18th century, there were signs of a move away from the exuberance of the regional style in churches such as S Teresa, Cochabamba, and S Felipe Neri, Sucre, both of transitional Neo-classical design. The Mestizo Baroque disappeared from the cities, but classicizing designs were still much affected by the strong Baroque tradition, and portals and other features retained their Baroque character in both form and decoration well into the 19th century. Under the influence of France, however, there was a return in the new century to the High Renaissance models of Jacopo Vignola and Palladio, precisely coinciding with the turbulent events surrounding Bolivian independence.

BIBLIOGRAPHY

Fernandez: *Relación historial de las misiones de Indios Chiquitos* (Madrid, 1726)

A. Ramos and R. Sans: *Historia de Copacabana* (La Paz, 1860)

V. Martinez: *Anales de Potosí* (Potosí, 1925)

J. Rosquellas: 'La arquitectura en el Alto Perú', *Bol. Soc. Geog. & Hist. Sucre*, xii (1925)

G. Angel: 'El estilo mestizo o criollo en el arte de la colonia', *Congreso internacional de historia de America: Buenos Aires, 1938*, iii, pp. 474–94

M. J. Buschiazzo: *Impresiones sobre Bolivia* (Buenos Aires, 1939)

E. Harth-Terré: 'La obra de la Compañía de Jesus en la architectura virreinal peruana', *Mercurio Peru.*, xxx (1942), pp. 57–8

M. de Castro: 'La arquitectura barroca del virreinato del Peru', *Rev., U. La Habana*, xvi–xviii (1943–4) [special issues]

P. J. Vignale: *La Casa Real de Moneda de Potosí* (Buenos Aires, 1944)

E. Harth-Terré: *Artifices en el virreinato del Peru* (Lima, 1945)

H. Velarde: *Arquitectura peruana* (Mexico City, 1946)

A. Neumeyer: 'The Indian Contribution to Architectural Decoration in Spanish Colonial America', *A. Bull.*, xxx (1948), pp. 104–21

P. Kelemen: *Baroque and Rococo in Latin America* (New York, 1951), pp. 186–91

H. E. Wethey: 'Hispanic Colonial Architecture in Bolivia', *Gaz. B.A.*, n. s. 5, xxxix (1952), pp. 47–60

——: 'La ultima fase de la arquitectura colonial en Cochabamba, Sucre y Potosí', *A. América & Filipinas*, ii/4 (1952), pp. 21–42

D. Angulo Iniguez and others: *Historia del arte hispano-americano* (Barcelona, 1956), iii, pp. 471–574

H. E. Wethey: *Arquitectura virreinal en Bolivia* (La Paz, 1960)

L. Castedo: *A History of Latin American Art and Architecture* (New York and London, 1969)

T. Gisbert and J. de Mesa: *Monumentos de Bolivia* (La Paz, 1978)

L. Castedo: *Precolombino: El arte colonial* (1988), i of *Historia del arte iberoamericano* (Madrid, 1988), pp. 271–80

2. AFTER 1825.

(i) Neo-classicism to Eclecticism, 1826–1952. (ii) Modern to Post-modern, after 1952.

(i) Neo-classicism to Eclecticism, 1826–1952. Development in Bolivia was set against an unstable political background for more than half a century after independence (1825). Neo-classicism came relatively late and by the early 19th century had developed characteristics more typical of 17th-century Italian Baroque: plain surfaces remained, though sometimes touched with an element of the Rococo in the style and distribution of decoration. This is well exemplified in the early work of Manuel de Sanahuja, the Franciscan architect–friar who went to Bolivia in 1808 to design Potosí Cathedral, which was completed in 1838 after his death. Although Sanahuja's name is associated with Neo-classicism, the façade owes little to classical principles. Severe square towers are drawn up into tall octagonal towers with ogee cupolas of neo-Gothic origin and are linked by a Rococo gable. The plain surface of the gable is pierced by three deeply arched portals, each with a simple lunette above it. In 1830 Sanahuja was in La Paz working on a new retable for the church of La Merced and was commissioned to design the city's new cathedral (for illustration *see* LA PAZ). This is in a purer Neo-classical style, though still reminiscent of Baroque: only the first storey of the façade was completed before his death. Santa Cruz Cathedral was begun in 1832 under the direction of the French engineer Philippe Bertrés, in local bricks with a timber vault. Within the limits of the materials it is Neo-classical in form, but it retains vestiges of Mestizo Baroque in the cutting of stone and the decoration, as do a number of contemporaneous churches built near cities in that decade, such as that at Viacha, near La Paz. The monastery of the Tercera Orden Franciscana (1833), La Paz, by Vicente Loayza has been described as *arquitectura crucista*, after Andrés de Santa Cruz, who was the Bolivian leader between 1829 and 1839. It is an elegant Neo-classical design, with more stylistic interest than later, more academicist buildings. The period of the 1830s is also rich in civil buildings, for example the Casa del Mariscal Andrés de Santa Cruz (now the S Calixto College), the Casa del Repositorio Nacional and the triumphal arches dedicated to Santa Cruz, all in La Paz, and the commemorative column at Potosí. In 1832 Bertrés with José Núñez del Prado established the first school of architecture in La Paz, disseminating a somewhat sober French Neo-classicism. Among its early manifestations are Núñez del Prado's Teatro Municipal (1834–45) and the three-storey Palacio del Gobierno (1845–52), both in La Paz. Both architects also continued work on La Paz Cathedral.

The Neo-classical style persisted up to and beyond the middle of the century: the commemorative Capilla Redonda (1850), Sucre, for example, is firmly based on Palladian models. Thereafter Bolivian architecture slowly began to mirror the eclecticism of the European architecture, as is evident in the Banco Nacional, Sucre, by the Swiss-born Antonio Camponovo, who came to Sucre from Argentina in 1872 to carry out the project: it is in the manner of the early Renaissance though with Gothic overtones. A little later Eulalio Morales introduced a full-blown Gothic Revival style in La Paz in the churches of S

Calixto (1882) and La Recoleta (1884–94). Camponovo worked on the Palacio de Gobierno (begun 1892), Sucre, one of the more successful revivals of French urban Louis XV style. As in Paris, the neo-Baroque style was used in Sucre for its opera and *zarzuela* (musical comedy) house, the Teatro Gran Mariscal Sucre; a scaled-down version of the Eiffel Tower was erected in the capital's Alameda pleasure gardens as tribute to French engineering, alongside the obelisks, triumphal arches and artificial lakes. The century ended with the French academic style in the ascendancy: it is exemplified by Eduardo Doynel's Banco Argandoña, Sucre, and in country houses (*quintas*) outside the capital, such as La Florida, Ñucchu and Camponovo's El Guereo, all with their formal landscaped gardens. Throughout the 19th century Franciscans from Potosí and Tarija continued to build missions among the Chiriguano Indians in the southern and eastern plains.

By 1900 Camponovo had completed the Palacio de la Glorieta, the finest residence in Sucre and a virtuoso demonstration of eclectic design with elements of the Romanesque, Renaissance and *Mudéjar* as well as Neoclassical. At La Paz Cathedral he was appointed as Eulalio Morales's successor; he reverted to the spirit of Sanahuja's original design: he added the second storey to the façade and finished the interior, using a Corinthian order, and he constructed the cupola over the crossing, completing the cathedral but for the upper parts of the towers by 1905. At the same time he built the Palacio Legislativo (1900–08), La Paz, a work of academic Neo-classicism elegantly articulating the principal elements of Senate and Chamber of Deputies. In 1909 he redesigned the façade and interior of the Teatro Municipal, La Paz. The first manifestation of the search for a national architecture also dates from this time, the La Paz house (1909) built by the archaeologist Arturo Posnansky (1878–1946) for himself in the style of the Pre-Columbian site of Tiahuanaco (now Museo Nacional de Arqueología). At this time also the earliest architectural uses of iron occurred: wrought-iron balconies and windows appeared in houses in La Paz, as did iron-framed glazing over inner circulation areas in residential blocks. Prefabricated iron buildings, such as the Aduana Nacional (1915–20), La Paz, erected by Miguel Nogué, and the modular Colegio Militar, La Paz, were imported from abroad, the former from Philadelphia, the latter from France.

French academicism continued in La Paz and elsewhere in such buildings as Adán Sánchez's Palacio de Justicia (1919), in the Palais Concert theatre (1930), Oruro, and, perhaps more importantly, in the earlier work of Emilio Villanueva, the most distinguished mid-20th-century Bolivian architect. In La Paz Villanueva designed the Banco Central de Bolivia, the Hospital General (late 1920s and early 1930s) and the Alcadía Municipal, with its mansard roofs and towers of 17th-century French influence. Although Villanueva's spatial design displays an incipient mid-century European rationalism, his continuing eclectic attitude led him also to seek a national style in the culture of Tiahuanaco, seen in such buildings as the Universidad Boliviana Mayor de 'S Andrés' (1940–48), La Paz, for which he adopted a sculpturesque concept based on the monoliths of Tiahuanaco. Villanueva founded the first Faculty of Architecture in the country, at the University of La Paz in 1943. A nostalgic return to neo-colonial and Hispanic models is revealed in such buildings as the Estación de Ferrocarril (1947) by Mariaca Pando and Mario del Carpio's contemporary Caja Nacional de Seguro Social, both in La Paz.

(ii) Modern to Post-modern, after 1952. There was a hiatus in architectural activity following the successful left-wing revolution in 1952. Industries were nationalized, and rural migrants settled in self-built *ranchos* around the expanding cities, Santa Cruz in particular. The consequent need for extensive building programmes created a growing economic dependence on North America. The result was rapid urban development with anonymous international Modernist buildings designed outside Bolivia. Triumphal revolutionary zeal eventually found expression in the Monument to the National Revolution (1960), La Paz, an impressive work by the sculptor–architect Hugo Almaraz, inspired by Pre-Columbian architecture. Design in the 1960s, however, followed European Rationalist ideals in buildings such as La Papelera and the headquarters of Yacimentos Petroliferos Fiscales Bolivianos, both in La Paz and both by Luis Perrin and Luis Iturralde. By 1970 a more contextual organic architecture had been developed by graduates of the post-revolutionary years; one such was Marco Quiroga, whose Casa Kyllman, La Paz, is an early example; another was the American-trained Juan Carlos Calderón, who has designed many major buildings: the HANSA headquarters building (1975), the Plaza Hotel (1976), the Illimani and S Teresa residential blocks (1979 and 1980) and such major government buildings as the Edificio Nacional de Correos (1983) and the Ministerio de Transportes y Comunicaciones (1975–90), all in La Paz.

The best-known member of this school is Gustavo Medeiros, although his work leans towards a late Brutalist expression in brick and board-marked concrete. It began with his own highly original house (1970), La Paz, and other unique houses, such as the Casa Buitrago (1982; see fig. 4), La Paz, a double-coded, almost Post-modernist design, in response to his client's wish for a neo-Georgian house. The commission is brilliantly interpreted in a multi-layered angular composition, in brick and concrete with steep, tiled roofs, backing almost directly on to a canyon wall above La Paz. His most widely discussed work is the

4. Gustavo Medeiros: Casa Buitrago, La Paz, 1982, view from the north-west

Ciudad Universitaria (begun 1970; Faculty of Engineering completed 1982), Oruro, on a flat riverside site near Lake Poopo. Here Medeiros's aim was to combine innovation with tradition while subscribing to a clear contextualist relationship between the low brick and concrete buildings, with their oblique references to Pre-Columbian models, and the view across the river to the city. Post-modernism tinges the later work of both Calderón and Medeiros and was also more self-consciously adopted in the 1980s by such younger architects as Roberto Valcárcel (*b* 1951), for example in his Casa Morales (1985), La Paz.

BIBLIOGRAPHY
E. Villanueva: *Urbanistica: Practica y tecnica* (La Paz, 1967)
L. Castedo: *A History of Latin American Art and Architecture* (New York, 1969), pp. 202–16
G. Medeiros: *Oruro: Su ciudad universitario como factor del desarollo regional y urbano* (La Paz, 1975)
T. Gisbert and J. de Mesa: *Monumentos de Bolivia* (La Paz, 1978)
R. Gutierrez: *Arquitectura y urbanismo en Iberoamerica* (Madrid, 1983)
C. D. Mesa: *Emilio Villanueva: Hacia una arquitectura nacional* (La Paz, 1984)
G. Medeiros: 'Bolivia: Inovación y adaptación', *Summa*, 232 (1986), pp. 334–9
L. Castedo: *Siglo xix, siglo xx* (1988), ii of *Historia del Arte iberoamericano* (Madrid, 1988), pp. 37–9, 219–21
M. Cuadra: *Arquitectura y proyecto nacional: Los siglos XIX y XX en los paises andinos* (Buenos Aires, 1989)
Cien años de arquitectura Paceña, Colegio de Arquitectos (La Paz, 1990)

III. Painting and graphic arts.

1. 1534–1825. 2. After 1825.

1. 1534–1825. During the Viceroyalty (1572–1825) there were three major influences on painting in Bolivia: the Italian, which was very intensive during the 16th century and the early 17th and which regained strength in the late 18th century through Neo-classicism; the Flemish, an enduring influence from the beginning through the importation of paintings and drawings; and the Spanish, in the 17th-century Baroque period, through the school of Seville and in particular the school of Potosí. This period can be divided stylistically into the following stages: Renaissance to Mannerism (*c*. 1534–*c*. 1630); Baroque (*c*. 1630–*c*. 1700); Mestizo Baroque (*c*. 1700–*c*. 1790); and Neo-classicism (*c*. 1790–*c*. 1825). This division does not mean, however, that particular features did not survive and develop from one period to another. In the first stage Spanish, Italian and Flemish paintings and such materials as canvas, panel and copper-sheeting were imported in substantial quantities. Graphic art, imported in the form of large series of European and especially Flemish prints and illustrated books, circulated throughout the country and was important in the dissemination of subject-matter. No local workshops are known in the Audencia de Charcas however, although there is a painting on a printing plate in Potosí by the Italian Mateo Pérez de Alesio, who was active in Lima. The characteristics of Mannerism, such as elongated, elegant figures, bright, cool colours and centralized compositions, can be seen in such works as the *Adoration of the Shepherds* (*c*. 1590; Sucre Cathedral) by Bernardo Bitti and the *Magdalene* (1582; Sucre, Charcas Mus.) by Antonio Bermejo (*b* 1588) and in the works of Gregorio Gamarra and Montufar (both *fl* 1601–42).

The Baroque period was characterized by the enduring Flemish influence in its rich colouring, refined pictorial technique, large compositions and grandiose settings. The Spanish influence, however, as defined by Zurbarán's work, was also evident in the choice of subject-matter and in such stylistic features as the introduction of tenebrism and realism, the interest in the figure and the sobriety and warm chromatic range of the school of Seville, a tendency evident, for example, in the *St Michael* (1634; La Paz, Mus. N.A.) by Diego de la Puente (1586–1663). The schools formed during this period defined the particular spirit of each region and town: they included the school of Cuzco, which had a great influence on Bolivian Mestizo Baroque; the school of Lake Titicaca (also known as the school of Collao), which encompassed La Paz, the surrounding towns and the shores of Lake Titicaca; the school of La Plata, in what is now Sucre; and the school of Potosí. There was also the religious art of the Jesuit missions of Moxos and Chiquitos. Wall painting underwent a great development in the Mestizo Baroque period, featuring decorative themes and religious and pagan history. Examples of this are in the churches in Callapa and Carabuco, in the department of La Paz, in Curahuara de Carangas, department of Oruro, and the church of SS Michael and Raphael in Chiquitos, department of Santa Cruz. Mestizo Baroque was a conceptual style full of symbolism, which did not treat space and perspective realistically. In the school of Lake Titicaca, South American originality became prominent for the first time. Its main exponents included Leonardo Flores (*fl* 1665–83), José López de los Ríos (*fl* 1670) and the Master of Calamarca (*fl* 1670–1700), all of whom painted large-scale works and treated their subjects in an individualistic manner. In the *Last Stages of Man* in the church in Carabuco, López de los Ríos drew inspiration from Baroque allegorical religious plays (*autos sacramentales*). In *Archangels Armed with Arquebus* in the church at Calamarca, the Master of Calamarca presented the forces of nature in the form of angels, dressed as army officers and knights of the period.

The work of the school of Potosí, with its characteristic tenebrism and realism and themes centering on the human figure, shows the marked influence of Spanish art. Important 17th-century painters there included Francisco de Herrera Velarde (*fl* 1650–70), who painted *St Francis Solano* (Potosí, S Francisco), and Francisco López de Castro (*fl* 1674–84), known for the *Immaculate Virgin* (Sucre, Charcas Mus.). Melchor Pérez de Holguín was a major figure during the late 17th century and the first third of the 18th, painting such works as the *Nativity* in the church of S Teresa, Potosí. Exponents of the Mestizo Baroque in Potosí included Gaspar Miguel de Berrio (1706–62) and Luis Niño (*fl c*. 1720), to whom is sometimes attributed the *Virgin of the Hill* (see fig. 5), in which the Virgin's spreading skirts are depicted both as a hill of silver mines and as the fertile land of Pachamama. There was a simultaneous interest in the depiction of cities, as in *Potosí* (1758; Sucre, Charcas Mus.) by Berrio and *La Paz* (1781; La Paz, Alcaldia) by Olivares. Although there are no known prints from this period, at Potosí copperplates survive from members of the school of Lake Titicaca at Juli, where the Jesuits had a press. These, however, have been re-engraved and used as supports for painting. The only copperplate to have been preserved from this period

5. Luis Niño (attrib.): *Virgin of the Hill*, oil on canvas, 1.37×1.05 m, *c.* 1720 (Potosí, Museo Nacional de la Casa de Moneda)

is the *Virgin of Cocharcas* (*c.* 1700; La Paz, Mus. N. A.), by an anonymous indigenous local artist.

Neo-classicism in Bolivia mixed elements of metropolitan Baroque with Rococo, especially in the centres of La Plata (now Sucre), Cochabamba, Potosí and La Paz, but this did not reach rural areas. The important painters of this period were Manuel Gumiel, Oquendo, the Master of Moxos and La Plata, Balcera in Potosí and Diego del Carpio in La Paz.

2. AFTER 1825. The quality of artistic production in Bolivia declined following independence. In official quarters attempts were made to deny the past of the Viceroyalty, and French academic art was taken as a model. This soon led to a cultural division between those in positions of social or economic power and the middle and lower classes, who maintained a cultural tradition linked to the Baroque period of the Viceroyalty with which they identified. The academic painters included Manuel Ugalde, Antonio Villavicencio and José García Mesa. Popular art took the form of small-scale images, votive offerings and domestic items, made by such artists as Joaquín Castañón (*fl* 1853). In this period Melchor María Mercado was exceptional. A self-taught painter, he produced more than 100 watercolours depicting his environment, in particular the customs of the Indians and mestizos.

Little change occurred in the first decade of the 20th century. When La Paz became the capital and the seat of government it was, like Sucre, the location for urban and cultural renewal. Mural paintings of romantic scenes drawn from European photographic prints became a fashionable feature of interior decoration. Angel Dávalos (1871–1953)

and Arturo Borda were active in this bohemian atmosphere, and Avelino Nogales worked for a period in Potosí and Cochabamba, where the same kind of activity was taking place as in Sucre and La Paz but on a smaller scale. Landscape as subject-matter was gradually introduced into Bolivian painting, as in the urban scenes of José García Mesa and the colourful patios full of flowers and rural scenes of Nogales. The reinterpretation of history and the depiction of moralistic allegories were other recurrent subjects from the end of the 19th century, particularly in the work of Dávalos, who painted portraits of all the national heroes and liberators. Dávalos also designed the emblems of Bolivia and all its departments, which were then lithographed and officially adopted. His other works included urban landscapes and delightful still-lifes, in which he was influenced by contemporary literature. In the early 20th century Borda was an influential figure; although self-taught, he achieved great success as a painter of technical accomplishment and stylistic versatility. While his portraits of members of his family show affinities with Hyperrealism and Surrealism, and while he also depicted native and social themes, another of his great concerns was landscape, in particular Illimani, the snow-covered mountain of La Paz, which he painted many times (see fig. 6).

In the 1920s and 1930s local artists were influenced by the many foreign painters who went to Bolivia, notably Juan Rimsa, a Lithuanian who arrived there in 1937 and stayed until 1950 (when he went to Mexico, before settling in California, USA). He helped to introduce Expressionism, and he was prolific in his dramatic depictions of the Andean landscape and people. He also trained a whole generation of painters in Sucre, Potosí and La Paz. There were also developments in the graphic arts in the 1930s, although the only outstanding figure was the engraver Genaro Ibáñez. The Bolivian artist whose work best represents the first half of the century was Cecilio Guzmán de Rojas, who studied painting first under Nogales and then in Europe, where under the influence of Julio Romero Torres (1880–1930) he began depicting Bolivian native themes in a style that combined Art Nouveau, Art Deco and indigenous Bolivian realism. After returning to Bolivia, Guzmán de Rojas held several official positions, through which he helped to establish Indigenism as the official style of Bolivian art. Indigenism became popular among high society and the wealthy classes, who ignored the social and economic problems that lay behind it. It nevertheless played a part in the slow process of national awareness that characterized Bolivian art in the 20th century. Armando Jordán, a self-taught painter active in Santa Cruz, painted landscapes and depicted the customs and people of the region in the 1940s and 1950s, when it was comparatively isolated. He invented a technique of retouching photographs of his paintings to produce *fotoleos* (oil-photos), which he valued more highly than the original paintings.

In the 1950s a period of renewal began, heralded by the deaths of Guzmán de Rojas and Borda in 1950 and 1953 respectively and by political and economic changes instigated by the National Revolution. The generation of artists that began working in this decade is known as the Generación del '52. This grew out of the Anteo group,

6. Arturo Borda: *Illimani*, 1932 (La Paz, Museo Tambo Quirquincho)

formed in 1950 in Sucre, which comprised artists, writers and intellectuals under the overall sponsorship of the Universidad de Chuquisaca, where many of the young artists of the new generation received their training. Another influence was the work of Rimsa. The group's aesthetic and ideological postulates were embodied in the 1950s and 1960s in government programmes promoting the fine arts as well as representing their personal artistic principles. A vigorous mural-painting movement arose that had undeniable connections with the Mexican movement (*see* MURAL, §2) and expressed Marxist political doctrines. Allegorical murals of moral, pedagogical content, which depicted the Pre-Columbian period as an era of untroubled peace and happiness, were painted on the walls of public buildings, universities and schools. The leading proponents were members of the Anteo group: Solón Romero (*b* 1925), Gil Imaná, Lorgio Vaca Duran (*b* 1930) and other independent artists in La Paz, such as Miguel Alandia (1914–75). Their principal subject-matter was the social and economic defence of the factory worker, the miner and the Indian, and they depicted figures en masse with grandiloquent gestures, using distorted perspective to emphasize the historical, revolutionary message, as in Lorgio Vaca Duran's triptych *Public Demonstration* (1963; La Paz, Mus. N. A.).

At the same time another group of artists sought to achieve a more universal language for Bolivian art, trying to open it up to international trends, notably the Abstract Expressionism of the New York school. They became known as 'abstract' painters despite their wide range of responses and varying degrees of abstraction. Artists associated with this movement include Armando Pacheco (*b* 1913) and María Luisa Pacheco, who was greatly influenced by her period of study in Europe but whose gradual evolution towards stylization and abstraction were reaffirmed in her participation in the São Paulo Biennales and, later, in her move to New York. The first exhibition of abstract art was held in La Paz in 1956. Most Bolivian artists, however, including those termed 'abstract', showed a strong feeling for their native land, which was incorporated into their paintings with varying degrees of subjectivity. María Luisa Pacheco created a lyricism of colour, structure and material that recalls the light and landscape of the Andes, while Oscar Pantoja (*b* 1925) pursued a poetic use of subtle colours in abstract, mystical works that often include reminiscences of ancestral Andean cultures.

A third tendency sought to deal with characteristic national themes such as the Bolivian landscape, the urban dweller and the Indian in a style that was not ideologically committed to the revolution nor sufficiently unconventional or stylized to be considered abstract. Its adherents included numerous artists of very different aesthetic and ideological positions who wanted to find points of contact with other Latin American art. Many of them oscillated between the polarized trends of abstraction and social realism. Although apparently stifled at first by the vigorous activity and production of the followers of these other movements, this third trend slowly gained ground, especially in the late 1960s, and gradually became dominant. Artists associated with it include Fernando Montes (*b* 1930), Luis Calderón Zilveti (*b* 1941) and Enrique Arnal, whose subject-matter included the stony landscape of the Andes, mines, the inns and markets of La Paz, condors and, later, female nudes. In La Paz a large group of artists depicted the landscape of the towns of the highlands, distant mountains and displaced people, while in such cities as Cochabamba, Sucre and Potosí landscape painting became rather bucolic. Herminio Pedraza (*b* 1935), working in Santa Cruz, made expressive use of colour in his paintings, while other artists idealized the landscape, and still others used signs and symbols in interesting reformulations of the spatial concepts implicit in indigenous textiles and of the symbolism of the *munachis*, the magic amulets with which the Indians sought to secure good fortune. A little later, within the same movement, an interest in mestizo cultural expressions, popular traditions and folklore developed, resulting in portrayals of a fantastically distorted reality in which ordinary people were suddenly transformed into the heroes of a magical, dramatic universe.

In the 1980s there was a sense of exhaustion at the diatribes of the social realists and at the proposals of the abstract painters, most of whom had turned to figurative art or disappeared from view. Changes in the social and economic situation gradually led to economic depression; cities increased dramatically in size while rural areas were depopulated. New industries arose, and previously remote areas such as Santa Cruz rose to prominence. In this context art also sought new directions. There was a feeling of disillusionment with the annual art competitions, while art galleries increased in number. The biennial exhibitions organized from the second half of the 1970s by INBO (Inversiones Bolivianas) gave encouragement and impetus to those seeking new artistic ideas. Many artists of this new generation trained outside Bolivia and gained a fresh inspiration for their work, and there was a great development in techniques and materials as artists worked with new processes to produce experimental art using *objets trouvés* and other non-traditional materials. Forms of conceptual art and Arte Povera developed alongside happenings and performances, drawing was re-evaluated as a medium in its own right, and photography developed significantly. However, because of limited access to advanced technical means, artists were somewhat timid in making use of modern technology. The generation that succeeded the Generación del '52 took as its subject-matter everyday urban themes, such as passengers on public transport, seated mestizos selling their wares in the markets, the despair of the Indian who had moved to the city and lost a sense of identity, victims of political persecution, students, prostitutes, cocaine sellers and their victims. The aim was still a criticism of society but more subtle than in the work of the Generación del '52. A notable artist of this period was Roberto Valcárcel (*b* 1951), whose social analysis and criticism were deeply probing. Gastón Ugalde (*b* 1946) reformulated Indigenism, while Fernando Rodríguez-Casas (*b* 1946) was concerned with the third and fourth dimensions and problems of perspective.

For bibliography *see* §IV below.

IV. Sculpture.

The three main stylistic periods of sculpture are Mannerism (*c.* 1534–*c.* 1630), Realism (*c.* 1630–*c.* 1680) and Hyperrealism (*c.* 1680–*c.* 1790), the last two originating in Seville and being roughly contemporaneous with the Baroque and Mestizo Baroque periods in painting and architecture. With the arrival of Neo-classicism, sculpture declined and became comparatively undistinguished. The importation during the Viceregal period of Spanish carved, polychromed works such as the *Virgin of La Paz* (1550; La Paz Cathedral), by an unknown artist, or the *Immaculate Virgin* (*c.* 1620; Oruro Cathedral), by Juan Martínez Montañés, provided models, especially for Indian sculptors. Sculpture workshops were formed, in which artists worked on techniques that became characteristic of each region, such as the pasteboard made of agave fibre combined with cloth and glue that was used in the workshops of Copacabana and La Plata (now Sucre). The majority of master craftsmen in the Mannerist period were Spanish, such as the Galván brothers, who executed the main retable (1582) of the church of La Merced in Sucre, and Diego Ortiz, the sculptor of *Christ of La Recoleta* (1580) in Cochabamba. Italian artists such as Bernardo Bitti and Angelino Medoro were also active in this period, as were the Copacabana sculptors Francisco Tito Yupanqui, who carved the *Virgin of Copacabana* (1582) in the shrine there, and Sebastián Acosta Tupac Inca, who made the retable of Copacabana (1618).

The two principal centres of Realism were La Plata and, in particular, Potosí, where the Sevillian sculptor Gaspar de la Cueva produced such works as the *Christ of S Lorenzo*, still in Potosí, and another Spaniard, Luis de Espíndola, made the retable of St Anthony (Potosí, S Francisco). After their deaths, sculpture remained entirely the work of anonymous indigenous and mestizo artists, one of whom made the *St Michael of Chiquitos* (*c.* 1760; Santa Cruz). They formed semi-industrial workshops, which in the Hyperrealist period produced numerous articulated works with clothing, glass eyes, natural wigs and other details. These works included the images of St James that are found in many churches. During the Mestizo Baroque period Hyperrealist sculptures of groups or scenes were common, for example the Christmas crèches with miniature figures and those representing the events of Holy Week. The same period also featured the development of large-scale retables, richly decorated in gilt or polychrome, which covered the main walls of churches and which at times were extended laterally, forming an ensemble with the pulpits and the frames of the large canvases on the side walls. Examples of this are the main retable (*c.* 1700) at Copacabana, the *Calvary* retable (*c.* 1765; Sucre, S Miguel) by the Indian Juan de la Cruz and the main retable (*c.* 1775) in Arani (Cochabamba) by the Master of Arani.

In the 19th century mainly popular sculpture was produced. By the early 20th century French and Italian works in marble and bronze were imported for the decoration of public buildings, residences and offices. The establishment in 1926 of the Academia de Bellas Artes in La Paz was of major importance in the development of modern Bolivian sculpture. Such sculptors as Alejandro Guardia (*b* 1897), Emiliano Luján (1910–74) and Marina Núñez del Prado all studied there and trained in the style of Indigenism. They later developed personal idioms, for example the traditional realism of Luján, who executed some of the most important monumental sculptures in Bolivian art and some of the most notable portrayals of the condor and of death. Marina Núñez del Prado developed from Indigenism to abstraction, working in a great variety of materials, most notably precious tropical wood

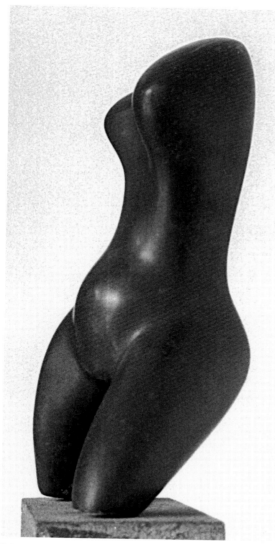

7. Marina Núñez del Prado: *Venus negra*, basalt, 1958 (La Paz, Museo Nacional de Arte)

from the Amazon region and Andean stones. Her subject-matter centred on the female figure (see fig. 7) and symbolic animals and birds. Ted Carrasco, an artist of the Generación del '52, was greatly inspired in his choice of subject-matter by ancestral cultural expressions, imbuing his portrayals with a totemic character. Marcelo Callaú (*b* 1946), active in Santa Cruz, was of the generation that succeeded the Generación del '52. His sculptures in precious tropical wood portray the human figure in harmony with the tropical environment and incorporate geometric optical illusions. These sculptors were all inspired by a feeling for their native soil, by ancestral and mestizo Bolivian cultures and their myths, the mountains, condors, the mystery of life and death and the exuberant and luxuriant world of the tropics.

BIBLIOGRAPHY
P. Kelemen: *Baroque and Rococo in Latin America* (New York, 1951)
R. Villarroel Claure: *Arte contemporáneo: Pintores, escultores y grabadores bolivianos* (La Paz, 1952)
R. Carpani: *Arte y revolución en América Latina* (Buenos Aires, 1960)
T. Gisbert and J. de Mesa: *Pintura contemporánea, 1952–1962* (La Paz, 1962)
M. Chacón Torres: *Pintores del siglo XIX* (La Paz, 1963)
T. Gisbert and J. de Mesa: *El arte en Perú y Bolivia, 1800–1840* (La Paz, 1966)
Art in Latin America since Independence (exh. cat. by S. L. Catlin and T. Grieder, New Haven, CT, Yale U. A.G.; San Francisco, CA, Mus. A.; New Orleans, LA, Mus. A.; and elsewhere; 1966)
G. Chase: *Contemporary Art in Latin America: Painting, Graphic Art, Sculpture, Architecture* (New York, 1970), pp. 115–20
T. Gisbert and J. de Mesa: *Escultura virreinal en Bolivia* (La Paz, 1972)
M. Chacón Torres: *Arte virreinal en Potosí: Fuentes para su historia* (Seville, 1973)
M. Traba: *Dos décadas vulnerables en las artes plásticas latinoamericanas, 1950–1970* (Mexico City, 1973)
D. Bayón: *Aventura plastica de Hispanoamerica: Pintura, cinetismo, artes de la acción, 1940–1972* (Mexico City, 1974), pp. 172–91
T. Gisbert and J. de Mesa: *Holguin y la pintura virreinal en Bolivia* (La Paz, 1978)
D. Bayón, ed.: *Arte moderno en America Latina* (Madrid, 1985), pp. 330–31
G. G. Palmer: *Sculpture in the Kingdom of Quito* (Albuquerque, 1987)
L. Castedo: *Historia del arte iberoamericano*, 2 vols (Madrid, 1988), i, pp. 315–17, 346–50; ii, pp. 221–4
P. Querejazu: *La pintura boliviana del siglo XX* (Milan, 1989)
D. Bayón and R. Pontual: *La Peinture de l'Amérique latine au XXe siècle* (Paris, 1990)

PEDRO QUEREJAZU

V. Gold and silver.

The wealth of silver and gold that, from the 16th century, was extracted from the mines, most significantly those at Porco and Potosí, is difficult to quantify, although a study of historical documents in 1971 indicated that between 1556 and 1800 over 22,000 tonnes of silver were mined at Potosí alone. The extravagant displays of the rich merchants and mine operators of the region are legendary: the streets of Potosí were paved with silver bullion in 1658, for the celebrations for the birth of a Habsburg prince, while as late as 1813, when mining was in decline, the Argentine general Manuel Belgrano (1770–1820) found that the fronts of the houses of Potosí were decorated with gold and silver. In 1737 Juan de Santelices gave the city of Potosí a great silver *carro* (cart) to carry the Host through the streets on the feast of Corpus Christi; it was surmounted by an architectonic canopy and flanked by statues of saints and angels.

Surviving 18th- and 19th-century objects, while not on this scale, are evidence of the great wealth of the region.

Baroque foliage and scrolls, often combined with Indian motifs, cover the surfaces of altar fronts and tabernacles, for example those of *c.* 1700 in the church of the Carmine, La Paz, and of *c.* 1700–40 in the parish church at Calamarca. Arrangements of liturgical furnishings such as that in Calamarca, when seen with its statues in place, show the splendour that was intended to impress the visitor. The elaborate foliage decoration of these works is compartmentalized yet nevertheless presents a continuous pattern, broken only by roundels containing figures of saints. As in the silverwork of coastal Peru, Baroque elements continued to be used throughout the 18th century, and the only Rococo influence tended to be the addition of bold rocaille scrolls, based on German printed sources, during the fourth quarter of the 18th century (e.g. altar plaque depicting the *Last Supper, c.* 1780; Sucre, Mus. Catedral). On the other hand, silverwork produced in the 18th century for the Jesuits shows much greater influence of European fashions in design and craftsmanship: an early 18th-century tabernacle, which was acquired by Sucre Cathedral after the Jesuits' expulsion in 1767, has cast and applied figures of clambering putti and winged horses that show little Indian influence.

BIBLIOGRAPHY

A. Taullard: *Platería sudamericana* (Buenos Aires, 1941)
J. A. de Lavalle and W. Lang: *Platería virreynal* (Lima, 1974)
A. L. Ribera and H. H. Schenone: *Platería sudamericana de los siglos XVII–XX* (Munich, 1981)

CHRISTOPHER HARTOP

VI. Textiles.

Bolivian textiles remain firmly linked to the traditions of Bolivia's past, both Pre-Columbian and the period of the Viceroyalty (1534–1825). Dyes were traditionally obtained from vegetable, animal and mineral sources, and cochineal dye, *magnum*, still enjoys the greatest prestige. The looms used are those that were known before the arrival of the Spanish (*see* SOUTH AMERICA, PRE-COLUMBIAN, §III, 6).

8. Pouch (*chuspa*) for holding coca, Bolívar style, alpaca wool, 180×170 mm, from Cochabamba, 19th century (Buenos Aires, private collection)

To these were added, among others, the wooden, foot-operated pedal loom. During the Viceroyalty woven tapestries and carpets were produced, while liturgical embroidery, festive clothing and knitted fabrics underwent significant developments. These last two types of textiles were highly popular in the late 20th century because of their fine quality. Although it is difficult to distinguish between Bolivian and Peruvian tapestries produced in the Viceroyalty, from the 19th century onwards republican themes make it possible to identify a specific area of origin. Until the late 20th century woven tapestries were produced in Villa Rivero for quilting and carpeting.

The finest expression of textile art in Bolivia is to be found in dress. Native dress still derives, for the most part, from the Pre-Columbian period. Clothing worn by men comprises the *llacota* (cloak), the poncho, the *uncu* (a short shirt or tunic, fast disappearing from common use), the *chullu* (woven hood) and the *chuspa* (a bag or pouch worn by both men and women; see fig. 8). Women's dress consists of the *lliclla* (cloak), the *acsu* (a rectangular piece of fabric wrapped around the body like a dress) and the *ahuayo* (a quadrangular piece of fabric used for carrying children). In the cities of Bolivia, the clothing worn by the *cholas* (mestizo women) draws its inspiration from the period of the Viceroyalty: skirts, blouses and various forms of hat are worn, especially the embroidered silk shawl (*mantón de Manila*).

Decoration on native dress is divided into two main areas: the *pallai* (the area filled with decoration) and the *pampa* (the area left plain). Decorative motifs comprise those from the pre-Inca traditions—hooks, s motifs and zigzags that refer to the snake, and fantastic animals in the Paracas style (*see* SOUTH AMERICA, PRE-COLUMBIAN, §III, 6(ii)(c) and fig. 39); those from the Inca traditions—such geometric motifs as rectangles or squares, eight-pointed stars (*see* INCA, §3(iii)); Christian motifs and motifs used in the period of the Viceroyalty, including crosses, double-headed eagles, floral ornament and the portrayal of European breeds of cattle; contemporary motifs reflecting the industrial age—trucks, aeroplanes and helicopters; and dedications and inscriptions common to all Andean textiles.

The production of textiles in Bolivia can be classified according to eight ethnographical areas: Charazani, Aymaras, Oruro, Charcas, Central Area, area of Incaic influence, Tarabulo, Potosí. In the Charazani area three substyles are found: the *Charazani*, the *Ulla-ulla* and the *Amarete*. The *Charazani* style is produced by a group of weavers living to the north-west of Lake Titicaca, who maintain Pre-Columbian traditions that bear testimony to the relationship between artefacts and belief systems. The Callahuayas, ancestral herbalists of the Aymara Indians, transport their medicinal herbs in bags on which the s motif refers to ancient myths, and their clothing still marks their social status. Women's cloaks indicate the place of origin and the resources of their lands: green identifies those who reside in the corn belt, reddish backgrounds indicate those residing in areas where red potatoes are cultivated, and brown indicates those residing in the *punas*, the high Andean plateaus. Crops do not, however, appear in the decoration of the textiles, although such symbolic motifs as condors, birds and dancers do. In the *Ulla-ulla* substyle, textiles are decorated by warp ikat weaving (*see* TEXTILES, §III, 1(ii)(a)), and in the *Amarete* substyle, textiles are predominantly red in colour with the decoration in white. The distinct style produced by the Aymara Indians in the environs of Lake Titicaca includes the Juli, *Pacaje* and *Omasuyos* substyles. Until the mid-20th century fine-quality fabrics similar to shot silk were made in Juli, and the fabrics produced there are still considered to be the finest examples of spinning and workmanship. The Aymara cloaks display a range of black and brown shades with thin strips of geometric designs that make up a sober *pallai*. In the Oruro area, the archaic *chipaya* weavers are deemed among the best spinners of the high plateaux, producing work in the little-known Oruro style. One of the most attractive substyles of the Charcas area is produced north of Potosí in Llallagua, a mining area, and reflects the surrounding contemporary technology, incorporating such motifs as trucks and motorcycles.

In the Central area, a number of different styles are produced around Cochabamba. One of the most distinct is the Bolívar style (see fig. 8), with its prevalent colours of pinks and sky-blues. The lace edging that borders the stripes and lace designs are notable, as are the *lymi linku* flowers. This style is thought to have disappeared in the 19th century. The *Kurti* style is based on four motifs: condors with spread wings, snakes, *intis* (suns) and rhombuses, which represent lagoons. Pre-Inca ornament, rhombuses, birds and mythological animals are predominant in the *Leque* style. The Tapacarí substyle found in Cochabamba itself reflects the movement of displaced peoples in the Inca period. In colour and design the textiles are similar to some produced in Cuzco. To the south-east, the Tarabuco style is found in the environs of Sucre. The Yamparaes Indians make ponchos with Spanish motifs and, to a lesser degree, Pre-Columbian designs. The ceremonial textiles are highly coloured, with a predominance of reds, oranges and yellows. The mourning fabric is predominantly black in colour.

Textiles from the Potosí area are produced in a number of different substyles. The *Macha* style is characterized by its marked Pre-Columbian heritage. The *pampa* is black or brown, and the *pallai* yellow, red, pink, burgundy or white. The designs are abstract in nature. In the *Pocoata* substyle, the *pallai* consists of linear designs ranging in colour from red to yellow to purple, while the *pampa* is reddish. The *Potolo* substyle produces *acsus* with fantastic animals, generally in purple tones. The *pampa* is usually black or brown. A characteristic of this style is that the colour of the design does not contrast with that of the background. The designs are loose, irregular and asymmetrical, the motifs zoomorphic. The Calcha substyle is characterized by ponchos with decoration of coloured stripes, achieved by the ikat technique.

BIBLIOGRAPHY

L. Girault: *Textiles boliviens: Région de Charanazi* (exh. cat., Paris, Mus. Homme, series H: Amérique, 1969)
A. P. Rowe: *Warp-patterned Weaves of the Andes* (Washington, DC, 1977)
T. Waserman and J. S. Hill: *Bolivian Indian Textiles: Traditional Designs and Costumes* (New York, 1981)
L. Adelson and A. Tracht: *Aymara Weavings: Ceremonial Textiles of Colonial and 19th-century Bolivia* (Washington, DC, 1983)
T. Gisbert, S. Arce and M. Cajías: *Arte textil y mundo andino* (La Paz, 1987)
C. Gravelle Le Count: *Andean Folk Knitting: Traditions and Techniques from Peru and Bolivia* (St Paul, MI, 1990)

RUTH CORCUERA

VII. *Patronage, collecting and dealing.*

During the Viceroyalty artistic patronage was essentially provided by the Crown and the Church. Wealthy and powerful mining industrialists and landowners also acted as patrons and financed the construction of some religious buildings, retables and paintings, in which the portraits of the donors were frequently included. Often there was recourse to alms to contribute towards the costs of construction and maintenance or alterations of buildings. Collecting in the period of the Viceroyalty was mainly the pursuit of these industrialists and landowners, some of whom managed to assemble substantial collections, which were dispersed by the 20th century. A few bishops had important collections, which they passed on to their respective churches and which were later housed in the museums of the cathedrals of Sucre, Potosí, La Paz and Santa Cruz. Other important collections are in convents such as S Teresa and S Monica in Potosí, S Teresa and S Clara in Sucre and S Teresa in Cochabamba; in monasteries such as La Recoleta and those of S Francisco in Potosí and La Paz; and in country churches in the highlands and in valley and mission churches, especially in Chiquitos.

The period between 1825 and 1900 was marked by a cultural dichotomy between the upper classes and ruling political and economic groups on the one hand, who were partisans of European and especially French culture, and the middle and lower classes on the other, who continued the aesthetic tradition of the 18th-century Mestizo Baroque. Patronage was reduced to the commissioning of portraits of the ruling class and officials. Of the few public buildings constructed, all were in the academic style, which did not allow for artistic innovation. Moreover, because the Church lacked political power, few religious buildings were erected. The cultural division between the upper classes with their admiration for European art and the middle and lower classes meant there were few important developments in collecting during this period, even in the last 20 years of the 19th century, when an economic boom brought increased prosperity. The wealthy classes travelled to Paris and other European cities where they acquired paintings, sculptures and other works of official, academic art and bought imitation Baroque or Neo-classical furniture and mass-produced *objets d'art* of little artistic value.

In the early 20th century liberal governments concentrated on such works as road and railway construction rather than on local culture. In their attraction to European ideals, however, they did seek to transform Bolivian cities, especially La Paz, through the Modernist urban-planning ideas embodied in Le Corbusier's concept of the *ville radieuse*. By the 1940s the art of the Viceroyalty had been rediscovered in Potosí, where, due largely to Cecilio Guzmán de Rojas and the Indigenist movement, the population began to be aware of its own cultural values: small collections of Baroque art appeared, while at the same time people started collecting works by such contemporary Bolivian artists as Juan Rimsa, Arturo Borda, Jorge de la Reza, Genaro Ibáñez and Guzmán de Rojas himself.

The formation of several private collections gave rise to the first museums (*see* §VIII below).

It was not until the National Revolution of 1952 and the government that followed it, however, that there was substantial official art patronage, channelled through such national institutions as the Ministry of Education, offering a national prize for culture and national art awards, and through the various municipalities and universities. The Mayoralty of La Paz was particularly notable for establishing the Salón Anual de Artes Plásticas and other artistic awards. During the same period impetus was given to all the arts, from public building and increased production in the visual arts to collecting, with government and national organizations commissioning and acquiring works by contemporary artists and colonial and Republican items, now housed mainly in public museums. Prize-winning entries in the Salón Anual de Artes Plásticas in La Paz began to be collected and are now in the Museo Tambo Quirquincho.

In the late 1960s the economic and political situation changed drastically, and public patronage dwindled. The Church now saw its role as being the spiritual and material care of the dispossessed, and with almost no tradition of artistic patronage by individuals, it was only in the 1970s that private patronage developed, above all in La Paz and especially through the banks. Particularly noteworthy was Inversiones Bolivianas (INBO), which in 1975, 1977 and 1980 organized important biennales of Bolivian art, with large prizes and international juries. These exhibitions were suspended, however, after the last one was censored by the military government. Thereafter patronage was applied to rescuing works of the art heritage of the country, helping art museums, publishing the first complete history of Bolivian art and establishing the Fundación BHN, a foundation dedicated to the propagation and dissemination of Bolivian art. The difficult economic and political circumstances after the 1960s also militated against the development of private collections. Another important factor has been the Law of Artistic Patrimony, which states that any Pre-Columbian material or object is state property, the private collection of which is prohibited. Moreover, the same law decrees that any cultural item dating from before 1900 is national patrimony and cannot be exported. While recognizing the right to private ownership of some types of art objects, the law has discouraged private collecting, which is considered intrinsically contrary to the interests of the state. Zealous state control has led, moreover, to the break-up and looting of a large number of those private collections of art that had been kept in churches and monasteries over the previous 400 years, resulting in much smuggling of the national art heritage into Brazil, Argentina, Paraguay, the USA and elsewhere. Special mention should be made, however, of the collection of the Banco Central de Bolivia, which has important works of Viceregal and contemporary art in its offices and on loan to museums.

For the same historical reasons, there has been very little art dealing in Bolivia, what little there has been occurring since the 1960s, when the Galería ARCA played an important role in promoting the new trends and the artists of the Generación del '52, who could not rely on official support. By the 1990s the Galería Empresa Minera Unificada Sociedad Anonima (EMUSA) was the oldest and most consistent in dealing in contemporary *objets d'art*. Its rivals included Arte Unico in La Paz and the Galería de la Casa de la Cultura in Santa Cruz. There have been many others at different times, which were short-lived.

BIBLIOGRAPHY
P. Querejazu: *La pintura boliviana del siglo XX* (Milan, 1989)

VIII. Museums and photographic collections.

The first museum of artistic and cultural objects (including natural history items) was established in 1845 by Melchor María Mercado, although the collection was dispersed soon after the artist's death. Others followed in the 20th century, including those associated with, or part of, religious buildings. A Museo Publico was established in La Paz in 1911, with natural history, ethnographical and archaeological objects. In time this developed into what is now the Museo Nacional de Arqueología. Another public museum, the Casa de la Libertad in Sucre, was founded in 1925 under the sponsorship of the Banco Central de Bolivia. This is a historical museum in a former Jesuit college, the chapel of which was used in 1825 for the ceremony of the founding of the Republic and thereafter as the seat of the National Congress. The museum houses the largest collection of portraits of Bolivian presidents and many paintings of important battles among its more than 1000 works of art from the Viceroyalty and the Republican periods. The Museo Charcas was founded in 1939 as part of the Universidad Boliviana Mayor, Real y Pontificia de S Francisco Xavier in Sucre. Located in the old Casa del Gran Poder (1630), where the Tribunal of the Inquisition performed its functions in the 17th century, it is Bolivia's most wide-ranging museum, with works of art from the early Renaissance to the present day, including a collection of 16th- and 17th-century Flemish works, examples by the school of Potosí and an important collection of popular and official 19th-century portraits. It also has a notable collection of furniture and musical instruments. The Museo Casa de Murillo, La Paz, another public museum that is under the auspices of the mayoralty of the city, was founded in October 1948. It is principally a historical museum, with more than 2000 works of art from before and after independence.

The Pinacoteca Colonial, which Cecilio Guzmán de Rojas organized in 1945, later became the art collection of the Museo Nacional de la Casa de Moneda in Potosí, while the collection formed by him in 1948 grew into the Museo Nacional de Arte, La Paz. The building (1759–72) housing the Museo de la Casa de Moneda was constructed as the Mint. Implements used for casting, testing and minting are exhibited along with examples of coins. The modern museum, which is financed by the Banco Central de Bolivia, was founded in April 1942. Works originally in the Pinacoteca Colonial were added later; as well as over 4000 paintings and sculptures dating from the Viceroyalty onwards, the museum has assembled a diverse collection of minerals, fossils, furniture and silverware. The Museo Nacional de Arte is housed in an old Mestizo Baroque mansion in La Paz, built in 1775. After restoration, it was established as a public museum in 1964 and is financed by the Instituto Boliviana de Cultura. Although it includes interesting works of art from the 19th and 20th centuries in its collection, its most important works date from the period of the Viceroyalty, in particular paintings by Melchor Pérez de Holguín and artists of the school of Lake Titicaca. Two other museums were set up in the 1960s: the Museo Catedralicio (1962), Sucre, a private foundation dependent on the Church and designated for religious art, with 400 items of Viceregal and Republican painting, sculpture, metalwork and ecclesiastical vestments; and the Pinacoteca de Arte Colonial (1967), Cochabamba, a public museum financed by the Casa de la Cultura of the mayoralty of Cochabamba, which has a collection of contemporary art and paintings from the Viceroyalty.

Among the museums established in the 1970s are the Museo Ricardo Bohorquez (1974), for art and archaeology and attached to the Universidad Autónoma 'Tómas Frías' in Potosí, with a collection of local contemporary art, and the Museo de la Casa de la Cultura (1975), Oruro, attached to the Universidad Técnica de Oruro, with an interesting collection of regional art. The Museo Costumbrista Juan de Vargas and the Museo del Litoral Boliviano in La Paz (both 1978) were founded as museums of local history, although they also have small art collections.

More significant, however, was the establishment of a number of privately funded museums. Institutions financed by the Church include the Museo de S Clara (1971) and the Museo de La Recoleta (1972), both in Sucre, the Museo del Convento de S Teresa (1976) and the Museo S Francisco (1979) in Potosí and the Museo S Francisco (1978), Tarija. All have collections of work from the period of the Viceroyalty and the Museo S Francisco in Potosí and its namesake in Tarija also have collections from the period after independence. The Museo Sacro (1982), La Paz, and the Museo de Arte Sacro S Lorenzo Martir (1983), Santa Cruz, are among later examples of Church-funded museums of religious art, the former having a collection of fine art, metalwork and ecclesiastical vestments. The Casa Museo Núñez del Prado (1982) in La Paz, was founded by the Fundación Marina Núñez del Prado in 1982, and it has a fine collection of the sculptor's work from 1925 to 1971 as well as works by other artists, including some in gold and silver by Nilda Núñez del Prado, Marina's sister. In addition, public finances continued to be used to establish new institutions, such as the Museo de la Casa Dorada (1985), Tarija, a historical museum with over 400 works of contemporary art, and the Museo de Arte Contemporáneo (1991) in Santa Cruz. In 1992 there were 49 museums in Bolivia.

Although there are no museums in Bolivia devoted exclusively to photography, there are some notable collections, the largest of which is in the Biblioteca y Archivo Nacional in Sucre, which has a good-sized archive of photographs taken between 1860 and 1940. The Archivo Histórico of Potosí in the Museo de la Casa de Moneda has another important collection of photographs relating to local history, and the archives of La Paz in the Universidad Boliviana Mayor de 'San Andres' in La Paz has a photographic section, most of it relating to the period between 1900 and 1940. The only notable private photographic collection is that of Núñez del Arco in La Paz, which is important for its 19th-century Bolivian photographs. The Mesa–Gisbert collection has negatives and photographs of the art of the Viceroyalty and Republic in Bolivia and of the Andean region.

BIBLIOGRAPHY
M. Gimenez Carrazana: *Museo Charcas* (La Paz, 1962)
T. Gisbert and J. de Mesa: *Museos de Bolivia* (La Paz, 1969)
Diagnóstico de los museos de Bolivia (La Paz, 1989)
P. Querejazu: *150 años de fotografía en Bolivia* (La Paz, 1990)
T. Gisbert and J. de Mesa: *La pintura en los museos de Bolivia* (La Paz, 1991)

IX. Art education.

During the Viceroyalty artists were trained in the guilds, based on medieval European prototypes, which were brought to the Audiencia de Charcas by the Spanish. Evidence of apprenticeship in workshops under this system includes numerous teacher–apprentice contracts and other testimonies, such as the autobiography of the sculptor Francisco Tito Yupanqui. There followed an academic type of training, in which the participants were no longer treated as master craftsman and workshop apprentice but as teacher and pupil. The first academy was founded in San Pedro de Moxos, where the painter Oquendo was appointed Master Painter of the Province of Moxos in 1790 in order to 'direct an Academy' in which he 'taught drawing and painting to a group of Indians', with the aid of a drawing book by Charles Lebrun. There was another school in Concepción de Moxos and still others in the Chiquitos region that were very active until 1820. After the foundation of the Republic, various attempts were made to offer a firm academic training, but they were all short-lived. In 1848 there was a Chair of Drawing in the Colegio de Ciencias in La Paz. In the early 1850s the Prefect of Potosí created a Sala de Dibujo Popular, and in 1858 President Linares established in La Paz the Escuela Popular de Dibujo Lineal. Some years later the painter José García Mesa founded the Academia de Dibujo y Pintura as part of the Instituto Nacional de Ciencias y Letras in La Paz. In the early 20th century a further attempt was made to establish schools that would endure. Many artists taught privately, and in 1905 a privately run Academia Particular de Pintura was established in La Paz, while other organizations set out to encourage the visual arts. These included the Círculo de Bellas Artes of La Paz (active from 1910), the Atheneum in Sucre, the Círculo de Bellas Artes in Potosí and the Sociedad de Artistas Plásticos in Cochabamba.

A third period of development began in 1926, when the Academia de Bellas Artes was founded in La Paz, with regular five-year programmes and courses. It has functioned continuously since then, although it subsequently changed its name to the Escuela Superior de Bellas Artes. In 1939 schools were established in Sucre and Potosí. The Atheneum in Sucre sponsored the school there and the Museo Colonial Charcas, both of which became subsidiaries of the Universidad Boliviana Mayor, Real y Pontificia de S Francisco Xavier in Sucre in 1950. The school operated until 1972. The school in Potosí was established in 1939 as the Academia Man Césped, teaching music and the visual arts. In 1948 it was separated from the music academy and remained as the Escuela de Artes Plásticas before being incorporated into the Universidad Autónoma

'Tomás Frías' in Potosí. In 1948 the schools of Oruro and Cochabamba were founded, and in 1960 two other important schools were established: the Escuela de Artes Plásticas of the Universidad Boliviana Mayor de 'S Andrés' in La Paz, in which architecture was taught from 1969, and the Escuela de Bellas Artes of Santa Cruz, which closed and reopened several times but continued to be active as a Taller de Artes Visuales. In the 1960s other schools were founded in Tarija and Tupiza and later in the city of Trinidad. These schools offered training in drawing, painting, especially in watercolours and oil, engraving, modelling, sculpture, ceramics and such theoretical subjects as the history of art, aesthetics and anatomy. The schools of La Paz, Sucre, Potosí and Cochabamba played an important role in the training of the artists of the Generación del '52 and their followers. In the late 20th century difficulty in obtaining good, affordable materials and the scarcity of large, well-equipped premises, combined with problems in the teaching programmes and systems connected with low teachers' salaries, meant that many of the best-known contemporary artists received their training outside the country. Attempts began to be made to establish private schools with modern pedagogical systems and an emphasis on creativity.

Although there are no specialist art libraries in Bolivia, there are sections on art in major libraries such as the Biblioteca Nacional de Bolivia in Sucre, although this essentially deals only with Bolivian art. The central library of the Universidad Boliviana Mayor de 'S Andrés' in La Paz contains a good section on world art, and the university also has a small arts section in the library of the Faculty of the Humanities. A similar situation exists in the libraries of the universities in Sucre, Cochabamba, Oruro, Potosí and Santa Cruz. The art museums lack libraries of note, and although there are some small private libraries with books on world art, public access to them is limited. The most important library in the art field in Bolivia is the Biblioteca Mesa–Gisbert, put together by the art historians José de Mesa and Teresa Gisbert. It has the most complete series of essays on architecture and art of the colonial and republican periods. The recently established Fundación BHN has a bibliographic and documentary centre for Bolivian art.

BIBLIOGRAPHY
P. Querejazu: *La pintura boliviana del siglo XX* (Milan, 1989)
PEDRO QUEREJAZU

Bollé, Hermann (*b* Cologne, 18 Oct 1845; *d* Zagreb, 17 April 1926). German architect, active in Croatia. He was educated in Cologne, then continued his architectural studies in Vienna, where he entered the studio of Friedrich von Schmidt, and was later in Rome. Under Schmidt he worked on the restoration of the Stephansdom in Vienna, and in 1876 he was put in charge of similar work in Croatia, implementing Schmidt's designs (1875–82) for the cathedral at Đakovo and his project (1876–82) to restore St Mark's, Zagreb. His most notable restorations were at the church of Marija Bistrica (1878–83) and at Zagreb Cathedral (1879–1902), but his rather purist approach often failed to respect the organic accretions of later periods, and he destroyed many provincial Baroque buildings, for example in the Gornji Grad and Kaptol

districts of Zagreb (and elsewhere). An earthquake in Zagreb in 1880 gave Bollé his greatest opportunities in terms of both architecture and urban planning. In addition to further restoration work and a number of new neo-Gothic and neo-classical churches he built several urban housing blocks and public buildings in a Renaissance Revival style reminiscent of works in Vienna. Of these the city's Crafts School (1888–92; now the Museum of Arts and Crafts), is outstanding, as are the long domed arcades (1917) fronting the Mirogoj Cemetery, perhaps his finest work in the city, which are in a similar style. As Director of the Crafts School in Zagreb from 1882 to 1914, organizer of the Croatian exhibition at the Exposition Universelle in Paris in 1900 and chief conservator for historical monuments in Croatia and Slavonia, Bollé was an influential figure. Thoroughly German in outlook, however, he played no part in the revival of Croatian national consciousness.

BIBLIOGRAPHY
V. Lunaček: 'Hermann Bollé', *Obzor*, (1926), no. 104, pp. 2–3
Život Umjetnosti, xxvi/xxvii, (1978) [special issue devoted to Bollé]
FRANK ARNEIL WALKER

Bologna [Etrus. Felsina; anc. Rom. Bononia]. Northern Italian city and capital of the province of Emilia-Romagna. It lies in the north-eastern foothills of the Appenine range betwen the rivers Reno, Savena and Aposa and a system of canals, at the heart of a rich agricultural basin, and has a population of *c.* 401,000. It is the principal railroad terminus of Italy. Prominent since Roman times, the city straddles the Roman Via Emilia linking Rome and Ravenna, which formed the *decumanus maximus*, its main east–west street. The Roman street plan survives clearly in the central city. It has one of the oldest universities in Europe (founded 1088), famous as a centre of jurisprudence. The site's numerous waterways served the city's main industries, including production of silk, wool and hemp, which peaked during the Renaissance; the city was also known for its production of ceramics (*see* §III below). In the 17th century Bologna became an outstandingly important artistic centre (*see* §II, 2 below), and the achievements of Bolognese artists, the CARRACCI in particular, were fundamental to the creation of the early Baroque. Architecturally Bologna is noted for its arcaded streets, and it largely retains the works of builders from the late 14th century to the 16th, enhanced by 18th-century additions and embellishments.

I. History and urban development. II. Art life and organization. III. Centre of ceramics production. IV. Buildings.

I. History and urban development.

1. Before *c.* 1400. 2. *c.* 1400–*c.* 1600. 3. After *c.* 1600.

1. BEFORE *c.* 1400. There is archaeological evidence of habitation from the Bronze and Iron ages and of necropolises indicating Villanovan settlement from *c.* 1050 to 500 BC. The Etruscans called the city Felsina; the Romans established a Latin colony there in 189 BC, which became Bononia, named after the Gallic Boii. In AD 53 a fire destroyed the city. Around 500 the Roman city was encircled by walls of selenite. Bologna came under Byzantine rule in the 6th century, before passing to the

Lombards and then, in 765, to the Papacy. In the 10th century it became a free city. Between 1055 and 1070 the city boundaries were enlarged by a second circuit, and a century later the city was divided into four administrative quarters, and the wall became the circle of *torresotti* (gate towers) as habitations replaced original defensive functions.

An agreement among the local population in 1123 may mark the beginning of the Commune. The university, with its emphasis on legal studies, contributed much to the city's prosperity, especially from 1158, when Emperor Frederick I (*see* HOHENSTAUFEN, (1)) granted special privileges to students. Although conflicts with the Papacy caused Bologna to decline in the early 14th century, the re-establishment of an independent Comune in 1376 led to major civic improvements. The main city walls were built in the 13th and 14th centuries and lasted until the 19th century, when work began on the circumferential boulevard (*see* §3 below). The programme of urban improvements also included paving roads, providing drainage and ordinances for the maintenance of arcades, streets and canals. The focal points of the medieval extension were the Piazza di Porta Ravegnana in the east and the Piazza Malpighi in the west. From the former, six broad, arcaded streets fan outwards from the central nucleus to the principal gates of the city. With the *cardo* and *decumanus* of the Roman city, they lead to the twelve gates of the third wall.

The character of the city is determined by its towers, its porticoes, and by the russet and pink-toned local sandstone and red brick and tile, which dominate the urban fabric. In the early 14th century Bologna boasted more than 170 towers. The highest, the Torre degli Asinelli (h. 97.5 m; 1109–10), was joined to the contemporary Torre Garisenda in the mid-14th century, the two towers representing the city in frescoes (see fig. 1) and paintings from the 14th century to the 17th and present in modern logos. The 34 km of arcaded streets, an amenity maintained by proprietors for the benefit of the public, were to reach their ultimate expression in the Portico Meloncello, designed by Carlo Francesco Dotti in 1714. The first cathedral of Bologna, S Pietro Metropolitana, founded in AD 910, was rebuilt in the Romanesque style in 1161–5 but has since undergone Gothic and Baroque remodelling. Similar treatment has been accorded to S Domenico, begun *c.* 1235 (*see* §IV, 1). It is one of the most prominent of the belt of monasteries and convents formed on the periphery of the city as the orders proliferated. The Palazzo del Podestà, the residence of the chief officer of the city, was started in 1201, although the present structure, except for the tower, is the outcome of a rebuilding of 1492–4 in the Renaissance mode. To its rear, abutting the present Piazza Nettuno, is the Palazzo di Re Enzo (1245); facing this, and running south into the adjoining square, is the enormous complex of the Palazzo Comunale, begun in 1245. This southern extension of the Palazzo Comunale, together with the Palazzo del Podestà, constitute two sides of the Piazza Maggiore, the heart of the city (see fig. 2). On the third side Church confronts State in the shape of the north front of S Petronio (oriented north–south). This was begun in 1390 and intended to outdo Florence

1. View of Bologna in the lower part of the *Madonna del Terremoto* (1505), by Francesco Francia, fresco, Palazzo Comunale, Bologna

Cathedral and even St Peter's in Rome, but only the nave was completed (*see* §IV, 2 below).

2. *c.* 1400–*c.* 1600. Growth occurred particularly during the rule of the Bentivoglio in the 15th century, especially under Giovanni II (1463–1506). Conspiracies against the ruling family led to control by papal authority, sealed by the entry of Julius II into the city in 1506. Following the Sack of Rome (1527), Bologna became the second city of the Papal States. The city's days of glory were in 1530 when it acted as host for the coronation by Clement VII of Charles V as the Holy Roman Emperor. Papal ties were further reinforced by Pius IV, who initiated an extensive scheme of urban renewal, focused on the area in the vicinity of the Piazza Maggiore. The see of Bologna was raised to an archbishopric in 1582. In the late 15th century the Bentivoglio began a far-reaching programme of public works, paving streets, building new porticoes and opening the Canal Naviglio to Corticello. The most prominent of the Bentivoglio buildings was the family palace (destr. 1507), built from 1460 according to the designs of the Florentine Pagno di Lapo Portigiani, with its residential tower and the loggia on the Via S Donato near their church of S Giacomo Maggiore. The Bentivoglio also supervised the transformation by Aristotile Fieravanti (1415–?1485) of the Podestà into a Renaissance palace. Its huge corner piers are appropriate to a

2. Bologna, Piazza Maggiore, showing (from left to right) S Petronio, Palazzo Comunale and the Palazzo del Podestà; from an engraving by L. Carlini after a drawing by Ciro Ferri

centre of civic rule, with its open loggia and grand hall providing easy access. A Florentine style is more noticeable in the finely carved low reliefs of S Giacomo Maggiore, a huge aisleless church founded in 1267 and vaulted with four shallow domes in 1493; however, the loggia along the south front (1477–81) is unmistakably Bolognese. From 1486 to 1496 the cloth-makers' guild built an imposing headquarters opposite the two towers; the decorative details of the Casa dei Drappieri supposedly derived from the Palazzo Bentivoglio, which owed much to Florentine precedents.

The private domain also expanded, particularly after the fall of the Bentivoglio, when an assembly of prominent citizens governed Bologna, and their palaces served as ornaments to the city. Façades, salons and courtyards often provided ceremonial backdrops for festivities and receptions staged by the governing bodies. Whereas most of these senatorial palaces were subsumed in the dominant arcaded structure of the city, there are notable exceptions, such as the Palazzo Fantuzzi (1517–32), by Andrea da Formigine, with its heavy masonry and heraldic sculpture, and the Palazzo Albergati (?1523; attrib. Baldassare Peruzzi), the irregular shape of which is determined by its site.

Pope Pius IV contributed a development scheme around the Piazza Maggiore, with the Piazza Nettuno created for the view, from the Via Emilia, of the Fountain of Neptune (1563) by Giambologna (*see* FOUNTAIN, fig. 3) within it. Balancing this square opposite the unfinished transept of S Petronio was built the Palazzo Archiginnasio (1562–3) by ANTONIO TERRIBILIA, a single structure to unite all the university faculties (*see also* UNIVERSITY PALACE). Few buildings are as indicative of the political and religious situation of the time as the Archiginnasio, the first structure specifically designed to accommodate the activities of the university, which, since its foundation, had prospered in makeshift quarters throughout the city. To complete the new design for the square, JACOPO VIGNOLA designed the Facciati dei Banchi (1565–8), a masterpiece of classical stagecraft, to harmonize with the rest of the Piazza and to provide the type of urban backdrop familiar in the works of Sebastiano Serlio and Andrea Palladio. He was also responsible for a number of other projects in the city and had taken Bolognese citizenship in February 1549. In the last decades of the 16th century the completion of the façade of S Petronio constituted the principal architectural debate: 'Gothic' or 'modern' became a barometer for changing attitudes towards classicism. Vignola, Palladio and Terribilia, among others, submitted designs, continuing the controversy begun by Peruzzi and Giulio Romano in the first half of the century.

3. AFTER *c.* 1600. Civic building declined in the 17th century as a result of a weak economy, although the Bolognese school of painting flourished. The leading families extended their palaces and constructed villas outside the city, strengthening the links between town and country. On the façade of the Palazzo Davia-Bargellini (1638–58) by Bartolemeo Provaglia (*d* 1672) atlantes flanking the portico support the balcony, imparting a note of fantasy and recalling currents popular in Rome and Milan.

During this time many churches were built or remodelled, notably the cathedral, begun in 1605 by Floriano Ambrosini (*fl* 1596–1615) on the ruins of the Gothic church. His huge nave features arcades with alternate high and low arches, while the chapels have lofty galleries; Alfonso Torreggiani added the façade in 1743–50. In the first half of the 18th century one of the most important architects active in the city was CARLO FRANCESCO DOTTI, whose major works there included the Arco del Meloncello (1718–32) and the sanctuary of the Madonna di S Luca (1723–57), linked by a lengthy arcade; the scenographic features of these works may be due to the involvement of the stage designer Francesco Galli-Bibiena. Torreggiani designed the façade of Palazzo Montanari, one of the many splendid palaces in the Via Galleria, the staircase of the Malvezzi de Medici (1725) and the Accademia di Belle Arti (1727). The oval dome of S Maria della Vita (1787) by Giuseppe Tubertini (1759–1831) gives the Piazza Maggiore a somewhat theatrical air, while the rectangular plan with bevelled corners and shallow chapels (1687–90) by Giovan Battista Bergonzoni (1628–92) indicates its Roman Baroque derivation. The Palazzo Hercolani (1792) by Angelo Venturoli (1749–1821) has a restrained Neoclassical exterior that contrasts with the exuberance of the cortile, stairway and gardens.

After the Napoleonic invasion (1796) the role of the Church in Bologna declined, and the city was transformed from the northern capital of the papal states and a leading industrial city into the centre of an agrarian province. Ecclesiastical property was demolished, and the influence of the church and aristocracy declined. During the 19th century a lack of speculative enterprise led to the preservation of medieval monuments in a romantic wish to recreate the past. Restoration work, frequently inaccurate and ignoring the changes of later historical periods, often bore the imprimature of terracotta as a local colour. The railway station opened in 1858, transforming Bologna into the hub of Italy, and 30 years later the Via Independenza linked it to the city centre. New urban spaces were created with the Piazza Cavour (1861) and the Piazza Minghetti (1893). Grand avenues, such as the Via Farini, the Via Garibaldi and the Viale XII Giugno, were designed to meet new urban regulations. The accompanying buildings were generally undistinguished replicas of past styles forming monotonous rows of housing. At the turn of the 20th century, the city expanded to the north, and the third circle of walls was demolished. The old town sustained many changes, notably the destruction of the Artenisi, Riccadonna and Guidagagni towers in 1917–18 to make way for a wide boulevard, the Via Rizzoli. In 1924 the Via Ugo Bassi was enlarged, contributing to the changed appearance of the town centre. Bologna suffered severe damage in World War II. In 1958 the *piano regolatore* incorporated the plan of 1942; halted by the war, it had encouraged building speculation, and was marked by structures such as the Faculty of Economics and Business (Trenti and Vignali, 1955). The plan of 1969 to preserve the historic city centre has been a model for the rehabilitation of other cities with similar problems. Urban planning is determined by a more conservationist policy than in the past, one in which respect for the city's patrimony is deemed an essential component for the city's future.

BIBLIOGRAPHY
L. Alberti: *Historie di Bologna*, i (Bologna, 1541/*R* 1979)
P. Lamo: *Graticola di Bologna* (Bologna, 1560); ed. G. Roversi (1977)
P. C. Ghirardacci: *Della historia di Bologna*, 3 vols (Bologna, 1596–1657)
G. Guidicini: *Case notabili della città di Bologna*, 5 vols (Bologna, 1868–73)
G. Gozzadini: *Delle torri gentilizie di Bologna* (Bologna, 1875)
F. Cavassa: *Le scuole dell'antico studio bolognese* (Milan, 1896)
F. Malaguzzi Valeri: *L'architettura a Bologna nel rinascimento* (Bologna, 1899)
L. Sighinolfi: *L'architettura bentivolesca in Bologna e il Palazzo del Podestà* (Bologna, 1909)
G. Zucchini: *Il Palazzo del Podestà di Bologna* (Bologna, 1912)
G. B. Comelli: *Piante e vedute della città di Bologna* (Bologna, 1914)
E. Sulze: 'Gli antichi portici di Bologna', *Atti & Mem. Regia Deput. Stor. Patria Prov. Romagna* (1928), pp. 305–411
G. Zucchini: *Edifici di Bologna: Repertorio bibliografico e iconografico*, 2 vols (Rome, 1931)
A. Foratti: *Aspetti dell'architettura bolognese della seconda metà del secolo XVI alla fine del seicento* (Bologna, 1932)
C. Ady: *The Bentivoglio of Bologna: A Study in Despotism* (London, 1937)
A. Raule: *Architetture bolognesi* (Bologna, 1952)
R. Renzi: *Bologna: Una città* (Bologna, 1960)
G. Fasoli: 'Momenti di storia urbanistica bolognese nell'alto medio evo', *Atti & Mem. Regia Deput. Stor. Patria Prov. Romagna*, xiii–xiv (1960–63), pp. 313–43
G. Rivani: *Le torri di Bologna* (Bologna, 1966)
G. Cencetti: *Il Palazzo dei Notai in Bologna* (Bologna, 1969)
A. M. Matteucci: *Carlo Francesco Dotti e l'architettura bolognese del settecento* (Bologna, 1969)
G. Cuppini: *I palazzi senatorii a Bologna: Architettura come immagine del potere* (Bologna, 1974)
A. Barbacci: *Monumenti di Bologna: Distruzioni e restauri* (Bologna, 1977)
F. Bergonzoni: *Venti secoli di città: Note di storia urbanistica bolognesi* (Bologna, 1980)
M. Fanti: *La fabbrica di S. Petronio in Bologna dal XIV al XX secolo* (Rome, 1980)
G. Ricci: *Bologna* (Rome, 1980)
G. Roversi: *Palazzi e case nobili del 500 a Bologna* (Bologna, 1986)
N. Miller: *Renaissance Bologna*, University of Kansas Humanistic Studies, lvi (New York, 1989)

NAOMI MILLER

II. Art life and organization.

1. Before *c.* 1400. 2. After *c.* 1400.

1. BEFORE *c.* 1400. Traces of the Etruscan period in Bologna have been found (e.g. vases, bronzes and carved commemorative steles), but few from the Gallic Boii. The development of the University by the end of the 12th century gave the legal, medical and academic professions a central role in Bologna's economic and cultural growth. The immediate effect on the arts of the University, centred on the Benedictine abbey of S Procolo, was to lead the mendicant orders to set up schools and major churches.

(i) Manuscript illumination. (ii) Sculpture and painting.

(i) Manuscript illumination. The presence of the University led *c.* 1250 to the development of the most important centre of manuscript illumination south of the Alps. Its works are conventionally classified into two streams. The 'First Style' encompasses a wide range of styles, incorporating Romanesque, French Gothic and sometimes Byzantine elements (usually older Byzantine styles), embracing some very fine and probably costly Bibles, but also all the more cheaply produced manuscripts and the work of old-fashioned artists. This group includes most 13th-century Bolognese manuscripts and some early 14th-century ones, particularly university texts and all the earlier statute books of secular corporations. Many of its features reflect the presence of artists from Umbria (e.g. Oderisio da Gubbio

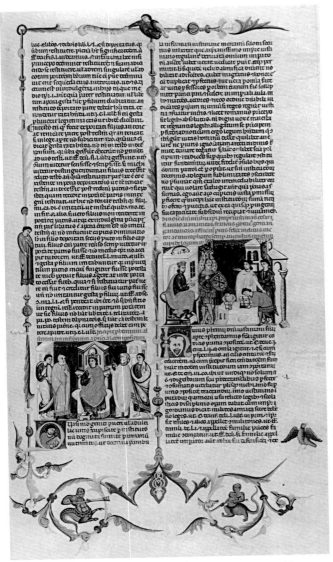

3. Bolognese *Tribunal Scenes*, miniatures from a legal textbook, late 13th century (Oxford, Bodleian Library, MS. Holkham misc. 47, fol. 254*r*)

(*fl* 1268–71)) and Tuscany (numerous scribes from Arezzo are recorded, some of whom may also have been illuminators), as well as others from southern Italy after the collapse of the Hohenstaufen dynasty, including Jacobellus (*fl* late 13th century), called Muriolus of Salerno, who illuminated an Antiphonal (Malibu, CA, Getty Mus., MS. Ludwig VI. 1).

The 'Second Style' (sometimes associated, though without any historical basis, with Franco Bolognese) is reserved to describe manuscripts of high quality in their materials and execution, often Bibles, Psalters and choir-books, rarely the principal legal texts or other academic books. Little is currently known of the original owners of such manuscripts. The earliest examples include the *Statutes* of the Flagellant Company of 1260 and the devotional texts

bound in with their founder's life (Bologna, Bib. Com. Archiginnasio, Fondo Ospedali MSS 1–2), but no other guild statutes and registers are of this quality or idiom. The first practitioner of the Second Style, the GIRONA MASTER (*see* MASTERS, ANONYMOUS, AND MONOGRAMMISTS, §I), was probably the single most important source of the diffusion of contemporary Palaiologan art in Italy *c.* 1260. The leading later artist was probably Jacopino da Reggio, who signed a copy of Gratian's *Decretum* (*c.* 1269–86; Rome, Vatican, Bib. Apostolica, MS. Vat. lat. 1375). Not only the Byzantine features of such Tuscan artists as Cimabue and Duccio but also most of the more advanced Bolognese illumination of the early 14th century is derived from the Second Style, although its refined pigments and exquisitely classicizing execution were greatly simplified by such 14th-century illuminators as Nerio Bolognese (*fl c.* 1305–before 1320), the Master of B 18 (*fl c.* 1310–30) and other illuminators working on the choir-books (1307–26 with later additions) of S Francesco and S Domenico. While one illuminator's workshop produced major manuscripts in this style in Hungary, the Gherarduccio Master (dates unknown), working mainly in Padua, and the 1328 Master in Bologna developed its pictorial features to incorporate Giotto's spatial innovations and his compositions too, probably as early as 1306.

From the end of the 13th century it became normal to divide the gatherings of a manuscript to be illuminated among several masters, often of quite different styles and with assistants of their own. This enabled the manuscript to be completed more rapidly, just as university texts were written from parts (*pecie*) hired one or two at a time to allow several scribes to work from a single copy (*see* MANUSCRIPT, §II, 1). The Vatican copy of Gratian's *Decretum* signed by JACOPINO DA REGGIO already exemplifies such a division of labour before 1300. Some illuminators were also scribes (e.g. Bartolomeo da Modena (*fl* 1265), Jacopino da Reggio) or notaries (e.g. Gerardo di Pietro (*fl* 1234–84), Jacopo di Bonapreso Aspettati (1284–94), Paolo di Jacopino Avvocato (*fl* 1269–94)). The illuminator and painter Andrea de' Bartoli was brother to a leading calligrapher, Bartolomeo de' Bartoli (*fl c.* 1345–84). The scribe Galvano di Rinaldo da Vigo (*fl* 1314–47) founded a dynasty of illuminators, as did his contemporary, the illuminator NERIO. The tendency of many illuminators to develop similar styles between 1300 and 1340 probably derived both from collaboration and such family ties. With the emergence of the ILLUSTRATORE MASTER as the dominant illuminator between 1335 and 1345 (*see* MASTERS, ANONYMOUS, AND MONOGRAMMISTS, §I), and his successors NICCOLÒ DI GIACOMO DA BOLOGNA and Stefano degli Azzi (*fl* 1354–1402) between 1348 and 1400, Bolognese illumination was concentrated in fewer hands and with much greater unity of style.

The decline of the University after schisms and papal interdicts, and probably the abundance of second-hand copies of the main academic texts, led on one hand to decreasing production of legal texts and Bibles, but on the other to an increasing production of commentaries by Giovanni d'Andrea and other jurists on the texts themselves, of lavish choir-books for the local churches and illuminated guild statutes and registers. Bolognese legal texts acquired a characteristic iconography featuring tribunals (see fig. 3), detailed landscapes referring to legal rights and obligations, particular subjects of dispute such as trees encroaching on neighbouring properties, papal courts issuing decretals or adjudicating disputes, baptismal rights, sorcery and the killing of heretics. The *Distribution of Imperial and Papal Powers*, derived from the partly surviving 9th-century mosaics of the triclinium of the Lateran Palace in Rome, provided the frontispiece of Gratian's *Decretum*, the most important canon law text, which had widespread influence on 14th-century art (*see* DECRETAL).

Little is known of any guild organization for illuminators, although some would have had rights as notaries. In general the university students and their nations exercized control over conditions of trade. There appears to have been a rising scale of payment, very modest for routine rubrication and modest for minor decorative initials, but considerably higher for frontispieces. The jurist Benvenuto da Imola considered the confrontation of Cimabue and Giotto with Oderisio da Gubbio and Franco Bolognese in Dante's *Divine Comedy* to be an ironic comment on the illuminator's lowly status, but Dante's own words and the lavish commissions secured by Bolognese illuminators throughout the 14th century in Padua and (by the Master of the Brussels Initials) in Paris suggest a much higher standing with patrons elsewhere. The lack of surviving contracts may be assumed, by analogy with painting, to show that they were rarely drawn up, rather than that they fell below the minimum fee paid for their obligatory recording in the city's registers: the illumination of the finest Bibles and *Decretals* almost certainly cost more than £25.

(ii) Sculpture and painting. Most important Bolognese sculpture was commissioned from Tuscan or Venetian sculptors: the Shrine of St Dominic by Nicola Pisano, the high altar of S Domenico by Giovanni di Balduccio, the high altar of S Francesco by the dalle Masegne brothers of Venice. Bettino da Bologna, however, carved the tomb-slab of the knight, *Colaccio Beccadelli* (signed and dated 1341; now in Imola, S Domenico) and probably that of *Bonifacio Galluzzi* (1346; Bologna, Mus. Civ. Med.). The finest of the tombs, that of *Giovanni d'Andrea Calderini* (*c.* 1348; Bologna, Mus. Civ. Med.), may also be the work of a local artist. This type of tomb replaced free-standing monuments with pyramidal canopies, probably evoking imperial prototypes in celebration of the imperial authority of Bolognese lawyers: most notable is that of *Rolandino Passaggeri* (*d* 1300), the 'dictator' of the popular government, outside S Domenico.

Whereas most 14th-century illumination in Florence appears to be the work of painters, in Bologna the two professions were largely separate throughout the period, although there were exceptions: the painters Pseudo-Jacopino, Andrea de' Bartoli and Jacopo di Paolo all illuminated manuscripts. In the 13th century painting in Bologna appears to have been a fairly modest occupation, although a few ruined fragments of fine wall painting survive in S Stefano, from the tomb arches along the flank of S Giacomo and a fragment of a young saint's face on a pier of S Francesco. Most of the major panel paintings were commissioned from Tuscan painters: Giunta Pisano's Crucifix (*c.* 1235–40) for S Domenico (*in situ*), which may have led him to form a local workshop that produced others for S Francesco; the *Virgin and Child* (Bologna, S Maria dei Servi) by an associate of Cimabue; and Giotto's polyptych of the *Archangels* (*c.* 1327–30; Bologna, Pin. N.) for S Maria degli Angeli. Major altarpieces were commissioned for S Giacomo Maggiore from Paolo Veneziano (1344; *in situ*; *see* PAOLO VENEZIANO, §1(ii)) and Lorenzo Veneziano (untraced) in 1368. In 1382 the Società dei Notai chose to replace their paintings with new commissions from Venice if a suitable painter could not be found in Bologna.

From *c.* 1320 the Bolognese Pseudo-Jacopino began to produce panels as well as wall paintings. His art reflects a strong influence of the Riminese school, and, indeed, Francesco da Rimini signed the wall paintings (?1320s) in the refectory (rest. 1949) of S Francesco. Vitale da Bologna established a large workshop with commissions (e.g. *St George and the Dragon*, *c.* 1340–45; Bologna, Pin. N.; for illustration *see* VITALE DA BOLOGNA) that led to an immense dissemination of his own style throughout Friuli, Carinthia and Slovenia over the period 1350–1420, as well as maintaining a dominant influence on Bolognese painting from 1340 to the 1370s. From 1350 most Bolognese artists worked mainly for local patrons. Until his death in 1399 Simone dei Crocefissi dominated the profession, marrying the sister of the painter Dalmasio Scannabecchi and living next door to his son. Simone was wealthy and a prominent citizen, becoming a member of the government in 1380. Lippo di Dalmasio also held important civic offices up to the level of judge. Simone was a close friend of the illuminator Niccolò and probably trained his nephew Jacopo di Paolo, who became in turn one of the leading artists in the city. Although his own son Orazio was less prominent, his daughter married the leading artist active between 1410 and 1469, Michele di Matteo da Bologna. The dominance of this pair of families, together with the distinctive political and social character of the city, was probably responsible for the extreme conservatism of Bolognese art for much of the 15th century. In the late 14th century Bolognese painters were incorporated into the Società delle Quattro Arti: the four crafts (or guilds) were predominantly workers with leather and steel, the makers of sheaths, swords and knives, shield-makers and painters (together), and saddlers. Statutes, undated but known to be of the 1370s, are largely concerned with the control of apprentices and journeymen, the exclusion of non-members and non-citizens unless enrolled and the observation of feast-days; the statutes of 1382 exclude non-citizens, perhaps reflecting the closing of Bolognese art and the citizens after the populist revolt against papal authority in 1376. In 1410 Jacopo di Paolo was enrolled in both the Quattro Arti and the goldsmiths' guild.

The signories of the Pepoli and Visconti families left little mark on the city as patrons of art. Cardinal Egidio Albornoz (*reg* 1360–76), however, appears to have considered Andrea de' Bartoli as his court artist, sending him to Pavia to work for the Visconti and also commissioning him (1368) to paint his tomb chapel's frescoes in the lower church of S Francesco, Assisi. A painter of even greater artistic stature, Jacopo Avanzi, appears to have worked mainly for signorial patrons outside Bologna: the Malatesta of Rimini and the Carrarese and Lupi in Padua. Most Bolognese commissions appear, however, to reflect the interests of the academic community in dramatic and often original iconography; for example the Pseudo-Jacopino's depiction of *Christ among the Doctors* as an academic dispute in his polyptych of the *Dormition* (Bologna, Pin. N.) and Dalmasio Scannabecchi's *Crucifixion with Prophets and Fleeing Jews* (Bologna, Pin. N.). Papal overlordship (and also the popularity of an exceptionally admirable pontiff) is reflected by a series of representations of Urban V, of which two examples by Simone survive (Bologna, Pin. N.). His patrons were often academics or prosperous students: the widow of the doctor of medicine Alberto Zancari commissioned a Crucifix in 1367 (Bologna, S Giacomo Maggiore), while the student Giovanni da Piacenza left a bequest for his *Virgin and Child* for the shrine of the Madonna del Monte (now Bologna, Pin. N.). This site close to the earlier execution ground appears to have been popular with students and with patrons of devotional art: most surviving 14th-century frescoes are from the shrine or the church of S Apollonia at Mezzaratta, lower down the hill. Simone was paid £ Bolognese 25 to paint five Old Testament narrative frescoes at Mezzaratta in 1366 and, if the testator's wishes were followed, £ Bol. 150 for the S Giacomo Maggiore Crucifix, 10 florins (*c.* £ Bol. 15) for Giovanni da Piacenza's *Virgin* and £ Bol.6 for a complex but probably small panel including Urban V in 1378. He also painted a Crucifix (*c.* 1375) for S Stefano (*in situ*; for illustration *see* SIMONE DEI CROCEFISSI).

The re-establishment of the Commune in 1376 appears to have been matched by repetitive commissions and overtly expressive imagery, as seen in Simone's versions of the *Coronation of the Virgin* (one version now Bologna, Pin. N., on dep. Budrio, Pin. Civ. Inzaghi). Most of the recorded and surviving art of the period from 1390 to 1420 was created for or frescoed within the basilica of S Petronio (commissioned by the Commune in 1390; *see* §IV, 2 below), including a lost model of the design in wood and card by Jacopo di Paolo in 1402. No rival source of patronage nor major Renaissance tradition was created until Sante Bentivoglio established the Bentivoglio signory in Bologna during the 1450s.

BIBLIOGRAPHY

I. Supino: *L'arte nelle chiese di Bologna*, 2 vols (Bologna, 1932)
F. Filippini and G. Zucchini: *Miniatori e pittori a Bologna: Documenti dei secoli XIII e XIV* (Florence, 1947)
——: *Miniatori e pittori a Bologna: Documenti del secolo XV* (Rome, 1968)
F. Arcangeli: *Pittura bolognese del '300* (Bologna, 1978)
A. Conti: 'Problemi di miniatura bolognese', *Boll. A.*, ii (1979), pp. 1–28
R. Gibbs: 'Two Families of Painters at Bologna in the Later Fourteenth Century', *Burl. Mag.*, cxxi (1979), pp. 560–68
A. Conti: *La miniatura bolognese: Scuole e botteghe* (Bologna, 1982)
R. Grandi: *I monumenti dei dottori e la scultura a Bologna, 1267–1348* (Bologna, 1982)
W. Schenkluhn: *Ordines Studentes: Aspekte zur Kirchenarchitektur der Dominikaner und Franziskaner im 13. Jahrhundert* (Berlin, 1985)
R. D'Amico and R. Grandi, eds: *Il tramonto del medioevo a Bologna: Il cantiere di S Petronio* (Bologna, 1987)
R. Gibbs: *Tomaso da Modena* (Cambridge, MA, 1989) [esp. pp. 26–49, 221–3]
R. D'Amico, R. Grandi and M. Medica, eds: *Francesco da Rimini e gli esordi del gotico bolognese* (Bologna, 1990)
M. Medica: 'Un San Domenico per l'altare bolognese di Giovanni di Balduccio', *A. Bologna*, 1 (1990), pp. 11–20

ROBERT GIBBS

2. AFTER *c.* 1400. In 1401 Giovanni I Bentivoglio established his family's pre-eminence in Bologna, facilitating the rise of a new aristocracy, who shared with the merchant classes and humanist intellectuals an antiquarian and mythographical interest in collecting antiquities. In the early years the presence of foreign artists and works of art remained isolated episodes: Paolo Uccello's fresco the *Nativity* (Bologna, S Martino) dates from 1437; a large-scale polyptych (now Bologna, Pin. N.) by Bartolomeo and Antonio Vivarini arrived for the Certosa in 1450; Marco Zoppo returned from a period in Venice in 1461. Yet the culmination of a long era of Bentivoglio rule with Giovanni II (*see* BENTIVOGLIO, (2)), a godson of Lionello d'Este, Marchese of Ferrara, encouraged the influx of many artists from Ferrara, among them ERCOLE DE ROBERTI and FRANCESCO DEL COSSA. In the 1470s Bologna became an important artistic centre. Lorenzo Costa was the favoured artist of Giovanni II Bentivoglio, and he headed a busy studio, which carried out a series of important public commissions in Bolognese churches. At the turn of the 16th century local artists acquired similar prominence, and Costa, Francesco Francia and Amico Aspertini collaborated on a major commission of the period, the fresco cycle (1506) in the oratory of St Cecilia in S Giacomo Maggiore, funded by Giovanni II Bentivoglio (for illustration *see* ASPERTINI, AMICO). Sculptors were less prominent in Bologna, and the major figures were the Apulian NICCOLÒ DELL'ARCA, who rented a shop from the Fabbrica of S Petronio in 1462, and the Tuscans Francesco di Simone Ferrucci and Jacopo della Quercia. Michelangelo stayed in the Bolognese house of Giovanni Francesco Aldrovandi in 1494, when he carved the small statues for the Arca di S Domenico.

With the fall of the Bentivoglio their favoured artists fled, and in the 16th century, when Bologna was governed by papal legates, artistic links with Florence and Rome became increasingly important. In 1515 the arrival of Raphael's *St Cecilia* altarpiece (Bologna, Pin. N.) introduced a model of Roman classicism, and in the 1530s Giorgio Vasari and Francesco Salviati worked in the city. High churchmen decorated their palaces with frescoes of scenes from mythology and ancient history, such as those painted by Nicolo dell'Abate in the Palazzo Poggi and the Palazzo Torfanini (1548–52); by Prospero Fontana (who moved between Rome and Bologna) in the Palazzina della Viola (1550); and by Pellegrino Tibaldi in the Palazzo Poggi (*see* TIBALDI, PELLEGRINO, fig. 1). Cardinal Giovanni Poggi had met Tibaldi at the Roman court of Julius III, with which Bologna enjoyed a close relationship.

The Council of Trent held two sessions in Bologna, from 1547 to 1549; its demands for a clear and persuasive religious art were articulated by GABRIELE PALEOTTI, Bishop of Bologna from 1566, in his treatise *Discorso intorno alle immagini sacre e profane* (1582), which influenced the move away from Mannerist abstruseness of such Bolognese artists as Bartolomeo Cesi, Bartolomeo Passarotti and Prospero Fontana. Paleotti's ideal of truth to nature was supported by the naturalist Ulisse Aldrovandi, whose museum of natural history was visited by many artists. Most art of the period remained religious, but such artists as Passarotti and Lavinia Fontana also painted portraits and some genre scenes. In the studios of

4. Vittorio Bigari and Stefano Orlandi: *Restoration of Bologna to the Vatican* (*c.* 1754), fresco, Palazzo Montanari, Bologna

Denys Calvaert, and of Passarotti, the study of prints by north European artists was popular.

Artists became increasingly concerned to raise their social status and to establish painting as a liberal art and a profession. In 1569 painters separated from the Società delle Quattro Arti (*see* §I above), and they became associated with the Compagnia dei Bombasari. In 1600 the Compagnia de' Pittori separated from the Bombasari, and the painters were thus finally released from the old artisans' guilds. This redefinition of the role of the artist was accompanied by an increasing emphasis on an academic education. Calvaert ran a school for artists, and BERNARDINO BALDI opened the Accademia degli Indifferenti, which emphasized life drawing. In 1582 Agostino and Annibale CARRACCI founded the Accademia degli Incamminati, which emphasized the study of nature yet also stressed that painting was a profession. In 1646 Ettore GHISILIERI opened an academy in his house, where such artists as Guercino and Alessandro Tiarini studied; in 1686 another member of the Ghisilieri family established an academy known as the Ottenebrati.

In the 17th and 18th centuries Bologna was dominated by the classical tradition founded by the Carracci, which passed from Guido Reni and Francesco Albani to the decorative painters Carlo Cignani and Marcantonio Franceschini, both of whom presided over vast studios. The city became a pre-eminent artistic centre, whose challenge to the supremacy of Florence was championed by the Bolognese art historian Carlo Cesare Malvasia; it was celebrated for great decorative fresco cycles, in both private palaces and churches. Painting was more important

than sculpture; Alessandro Algardi worked mainly in Rome. In the 17th century *quadratura* illusionistic architectural painting, was popular, and *quadratura* specialists often collaborated with figure painters; Angelo Michele Colonna and Agostino Mitelli were one such celebrated partnership. Many painters, not always from the same workshop, collaborated on the most grandiose undertakings. Entire families of artists, such as the Galli-Bibiena, the Quaini and the Orlandi, made careers as architectural painters. Stucco surrounds became popular in the 18th century and Vittorio Bigari, painter and stuccoist, worked with Stefano Orlandi (see fig. 4). There was also a demand for vast altarpieces, while history paintings and small cabinet pictures of pastoral themes were popular with private collectors. Pastoral themes, introduced by Albani, were developed by Cignani, Franceschini, Lorenzo Pasinelli and Giovan Gioseffo dal Sole. An outstanding Bolognese art collection, at its height in the 18th century, was formed by the ALDROVANDI family.

A number of academies were formed during the Enlightenment. The Accademia Clementina, the first official Bolognese academy of art, was established in 1710 and had a close relationship with the Istituto delle Scienze (est. 1714). New kinds of genre painting were introduced by Donato Creti and by Giuseppe Maria Crespi. In the 19th century Napoleonic legislation brought about great changes: most convents and churches were suppressed, and the artistic world became stagnant. The engraver Antonio Basoli (1774–1848) and the painter Pelagio Pelagi (1775–1860) were two of the few active artists of the period, as literary activities gained artistic pre-eminence.

The period following the Unification of Italy in 1864 was dominated by Leonardo Bistolfi and Adolfo De Carolis. In the 20th century the pictorial tradition was continued by such influential artists as Giovanni Romagnoli (1893–1976), Ercole Drei, (1886–1973) VIRGILIO GUIDI and GIORGIO MORANDI, whose work remained closely preoccupied with naturalistic themes, but who abstracted and synthesized form in his still-lifes. All of these artists trained at the Accademia di Belle Arti, an institution descended from the Accademia Clementina.

BIBLIOGRAPHY

F. Malaguzzi Valeri: 'L'arte dei pittori a Bologna nel secolo XVI', *Archv Stor. A.*, 3 (1897), pp. 309–14
P. Prodi: 'Sulla teoria delle arti figurative nella riforma cattolica', *Archv It. Stor. Pietà*, iv (1965), pp. 121–212
E. Battisti: 'Un documento sull'Accademia dei pittori in Bologna', *L'Arte*, 57 (1968), pp. 96–105
Il Liberty a Bologna e nell'Emilia Romagna (exh. cat., Bologna, 1977)
C. Dempsey: 'Some Observations on the Education of Artists in Florence and Bologna during the Later 16th Century', *A. Bull.*, (1980), pp. 552–69
A. Ghirardi: 'Per una lettura di due ritratti di famiglia di Bartolommeo Passerotti', *Itinerari: Contributi alla storia dell'arte in memoria di M. L. Ferrucci*, ii (Florence, 1981), pp. 57–65
R. Grandi: *Dall'Accademia al vero: La pittura a Bologna prima e dopo l'unità* (exh. cat., Bologna, 1983)
G. Fasoli and M. Saccenti: *Carducci e Bologna* (Bologna, 1985)
A. Baccilieri and S. Evangelisti: *L'Accademia di Bologna: Figure del novecento* (Bologna, 1988)
R. Barilli: *Il secondo '800 italiano: Le poetiche del vero* (exh. cat., Milan, 1988)
G. Cammarrota: 'Cronache della compagnia dei pittori', in *Dall'avanguardia dei Carracci al secolo barocco* (Bologna, 1988), pp. 56–68

ELENA DE LUCA

III. Centre of ceramics production.

The history of Bolognese ceramic manufacture remains somewhat unclear, due to the lack of documentary evidence; production is known to have been established, however, by the early 14th century. Clearly, it was well under way by the mid-16th century, when Cipriano Piccolpasso referred to the clay used by the city's artists in *I tre libri dell'arte del vasaio* (1556–9). In addition to the northern Italian cities of Ferrara and Padua, Bologna was also a major centre for the production of lead-glazed, incised slipwares, the finest of which competed with the colourful tin-glazed earthenwares of Faenza and other maiolica centres for the luxury market. Signed and dated *sgraffito* pieces are extremely rare, and attribution is often difficult. However, excavations in Bologna have provided evidence for production there in the late 15th century and the 16th, patronized by such prominent local families as the Bentivoglio, whose arms appear on certain pieces (e.g. inkstand, *c.* 1500; London, V&A, cat. 1332). Among the best works are elaborate, large plates, tazze and modelled inkstands decorated with putti, figures of youths, portrait busts, animals and occasional genre, allegorical or religious scenes, bordered by patterns of stylized, Gothic-influenced leaves. The typical restrained palette is comprised of a whitish slip, through which a design was scratched to reveal the red earthenware beneath; the designs were then heightened with yellow, green, brown, purple and blue pigments and finally covered with a transparent glaze. Unlike the decoration of maiolica, which is characterized by a painterly quality and complex colour range, incised

slipwares rely on the linear directness of the artist's draughtsmanship for their effect. Maiolica was frequently imported into Bologna from Florence, Venice and Faenza. The tile-pavement (1487) in the Vaselli Chapel in the church of S Petronio, Bologna (*see* TILE, fig. 12), for example, bears the name of the Faentine potter Petrus Andrea (*fl* 1493–1526). By 1595, however, maiolica workshops were established in Bologna and production of both types of wares continued. During the late 19th century the factory of Angelo Minghetti (1822–92) was known for its excellent reproductions of Renaissance maiolica.

BIBLIOGRAPHY

F. Malaguzzi Valeri: 'Su l'origine della fabbricazione delle maioliche a Bologna', *Faenza*, vi/2 (1918), pp. 25–6
W. B. Honey: 'Bologna Pottery of the Renaissance Period', *Burl. Mag.*, xlviii (1926), pp. 224–35
B. Rackham: *Catalogue of Italian Maiolica*, 2 vols (London, 1940, rev. 2/1970)
La ceramica graffita in Emilia-Romagna dal secolo XIV al secolo XIX (exh. cat., ed. G. Reggi; Modena, Pal. Musei, 1971)

WENDY M. WATSON

IV. Buildings.

1. S Domenico. 2. S Petronio. 3. S Stefano.

1. S DOMENICO. Church dedicated by Innocent IV in 1251 to St Dominic. It has been enlarged several times, and the present interiors are the work of CARLO FRANCESCO DOTTI, who remodelled (1728–32) the church in the early 17th-century Bolognese style. It is notable chiefly as the home of the tomb of St Dominic, the Arca di S Domenico (*see* DOMINICAN ORDER, fig. 1). St Dominic died in Bologna in 1221; in 1234 he was canonized, and *c.* 30 years later the Dominicans of S Domenico commissioned a tomb for their founder. The design of the tomb is generally credited to Nicola Pisano (*see* PISANO (i), (1), §3), partly on stylistic grounds and partly on the evidence of a passage in the *Chronicle of the Convent of St Catherine in Pisa*, compiled *c.* 1400 but based on much earlier authorities, which refers to the body of St Dominic being placed in a tomb that had been sculpted by 'Nichole di Pisis'. The carving seems to have been under way by 1265, for at the General Chapter of the Dominicans held at Montpellier in that year, the friars recommended that funds should be allocated for the completion of the sepulchre.

The tomb no longer survives in its 13th-century form. The original shrine comprised a rectangular sarcophagus borne on caryatid figures. In 1411 it was relocated at the centre of the church, and later in the 15th century its originally flat top was modernized with the present pitched roof, and its statuary was supplemented with figures by Niccolò dell'Arca and Michelangelo. Probably at the same time, the caryatid supports were dispersed. Some of these have since been hypothetically identified in the archangels *Michael* and *Gabriel* in London (V&A); a statue of *Faith* in Paris (Louvre); a statue of three deacons holding liturgical objects in Florence (Bargello); and a similar group in Boston, MA (Mus. F.A.). Several attempts have been made to determine the original appearance of the shrine. Pope-Hennessy's reconstruction (1951), endorsed by Moskowitz (1987), would require two groups of three figures supporting the long sides of the sarcophagus (the two archangels and probably a third unidentified archangel on one side and the Louvre *Faith* and possibly two other virtues on the other side). Along the central long axis would have been the two deacon groups in Florence and Boston. The sarcophagus is divided into six panels that recount significant events of St Dominic's life. On what is now the front are (i) *St Dominic Restoring Napoleone Orsini to Life after a Fall from his Horse* and (ii) the *Miracle of the Unburnt Books at Fanjeaux*; on the back, (iii) the *Profession and Vision of Reginald of St Gilles*, and (iv) the *Confirmation of the Dominican Order*; and on the short sides, (v) the *Apparition of SS Peter and Paul to Dominic* and *Dominic Sending his Followers out on their Mission*; and, (vi) *Dominic and his Disciples Fed by Angels*. The reliefs are separated from each other by statuettes. A *Virgin and Child* occupy a central position on the front; *Christ the Redeemer* is centrally located on the back; and the *Four Doctors of the Church* stand at the corners.

Compositionally, all of the reliefs show a single approach to space, suggesting the same designer. The figures are ranged in neatly organized rows that completely fill the frame. However, scholars have long recognized the diversity of handling in the actual carving. At least five different hands have been identified: Nicola Pisano; Arnolfo di Cambio; Fra Guglielmo da Pisa, who designed a pulpit in S Giovanni Fuorcivitas in Pistoia *c.* 1270; Lapo; and an anonymous sculptor whom Gnudi (1948) christened the Fifth Master. This conforms perfectly with what is known about medieval sculptural practice, where groups of carvers were co-ordinated to work on large-scale commissions. The Arca di S Domenico, with its historiated sarcophagus carried on statuettes, became the model for other tombs. The commission for the shrine of *St Peter Martyr* in S Eustorgio in Milan requested specifically that it should be like the tomb of St Dominic in Bologna. Other comparable monuments are the shrine to *St Luke* (1316) in S Giustina, Padua, and the tomb of the *Beato Bertrando* (*c.* 1334–50) in Udine.

BIBLIOGRAPHY

C. Gnudi: *Nicola, Arnolfo, Lapo: L'arca di S Domenico in Bologna* (Florence, 1948)
J. Pope-Hennessy: 'The Arca of St Dominic: A Hypothesis', *Burl. Mag.*, xciii (1951), pp. 347–51; repr. in *Essays on Italian Sculpture*, (London, 1968), pp. 11–15
S. Bottari: *L'arca di S Domenico in Bologna* (Bologna, 1964)
A. F. Moskowitz: 'The Arca di San Domenico Caryatids: Support for a Hypothesis', *Source: Notes Hist. A.*, vi/3 (1987), pp. 1–6

BRENDAN CASSIDY

2. S Petronio. Bologna's votive and civic basilica located on the south side of the central Piazza Maggiore (see fig. 2 above) is dedicated to Bologna's patron saint. The Gothic-style church was erected by the Commune between 1390 and the third quarter of the 17th century. Although unfinished, it dominates the skyline and ranks among the largest ecclesiastical buildings in Italy (60 m wide, 132 m long, 44.27 m to the crowning of the vaults). Here Charles V was crowned Holy Roman Emperor by Clement VII in 1530. St Petronius was the eighth bishop of Bologna (*reg* AD 431–50). His cult was of minor importance until the later Middle Ages, when he began to be venerated as a rebuilder of the city, founder of Bologna University—a popular but erroneous legend—and defender of communal liberty. By the mid-14th century he

was the principal symbol of municipal patriotism, legitimizing local power and political autonomy against imperial and papal claims. On 1 January 1389 a popular government headed by artisans, merchants and intellectuals declared that a church be built in his name on the main civic square. A board of works, the Fabbricieri, was created, and the local master builder Antonio di Vincenzo (*c.* 1350– ?1401/2) was appointed architect. In consultation with the head of the Servite Order, Andrea Manfredi da Faenza, the architect built an enormous model (destr. 1402) in wood and brick. The church was intended to be the largest in Christendom. For its site the city fathers expropriated and destroyed many houses and towers, as well as eight churches. The cornerstone was laid on 7 June 1390, and work proceeded southwards from the façade. In the course of the 15th century members of the ruling Bentivoglio family promoted uninterrupted construction: by 1401 the first two bays of the nave with a provisional apse, vaulted aisles and eight vaulted chapels (see fig. 5); by 1446 the third bay, a second apse, aisles and chapels; by 1450 the fourth bay, aisles and chapels; by 1462 the fifth bay, aisles and chapels; by 1469 a new apse at the fourth bay; in 1479 the founding of the final two of 22 chapels; and by 1492 a campanile. At the end of the 15th century the basilica had nearly reached its present configuration.

After Antonio di Vincenzo's large model was destroyed, Jacopo di Paolo prepared a small wood and paper model, which has disappeared along with all graphic evidence of the architect's original intentions for the church as a whole.

5. Bologna, S Petronio, interior of the nave and north aisle, by Antonio di Vincenzo, begun 1390

Modern reconstructions of the first plan have not been conclusive. From the contract for the large model it is known that the church was to have been 183 m long and 137 m wide at the transepts. Only the six-bay nave was built, but it makes clear that Antonio di Vincenzo was guided by Tuscan and Lombard precedents. The structure and dimensions of the nave and aisle bays were taken directly from Florence Cathedral, as was the general design of the piers. The inclusion of lateral chapels, two to each bay, was inspired by such monastic churches in and around Milan as S Maria del Carmine in Pavia. Yet what Antonio di Vincenzo envisioned beyond the nave, especially for the crossing, remains enigmatic.

From the early 16th century onwards the Fabbricieri grappled with three major problems: laying out the crossing, transepts and choir; vaulting the nave; and decorating the façade. In each case they consistently sought stylistic congruity with the existing Gothic structure. In 1509–15 Arduino Arriguzzi (1460–1531) founded two piers for the crossing following a plan elaborated in a wooden model (c. 1513–16, Bologna, Mus. S Petronio). The model, often mistaken as representing the original 14th-century scheme, features deep, square transepts and a roundheaded choir ringed with chapels and an octagonal cupola on a high drum. Arriguzzi's project was soon abandoned, and all hope of completing S Petronio was effectively buried in 1563 with the erection of the Palazzo dell'Archiginnasio along the left flank of the church. Attention turned to covering the nave when Francesco Terribilia (see TERRIBILIA, (2)) vaulted the fifth bay (1587–9) to a height of c. 38 m. Terribilia's work was judged too low and was destroyed when the present quadripartite rib vaults were constructed over six metres higher along the entire nave (1646–58) by Girolamo Rainaldi. The choir was then closed by the present polygonal apse and vaulted. Illuminated by large windows in the nave, aisles and chapels, and articulated throughout by architectural members of buff sandstone and red brick against off-white walls, the vast and harmonious interior is remarkable above all for its spatial clarity.

The problem of the great façade (66 m wide, 51 m high) has never been fully resolved. The present marble socle goes back to Antonio di Vincenzo (1391–4), while Jacopo della Quercia decorated the Porta Magna with 10 marble relief scenes from Exodus on the flanking pilasters, 18 busts of *Prophets* on the jambs, five New Testament scenes on the lintel and statues of the *Virgin and Child* and *St Petronius* in the lunette (1425–30; see JACOPO DELLA QUERCIA, fig. 4). DOMENICO AIMO added the figure of *St Ambrose* (1510) to the lunette, above which Michelangelo installed his colossal bronze portrait statue of *Pope Julius II* (1506–8; destr. 1511). In 1518 Aimo drew up a masterplan for the façade (Bologna, Mus. S Petronio), which was followed for the decoration of the two existing lateral portals embellished with Old and New Testament scenes (1524–30). The marble reliefs were carved by teams of sculptors under the direction of Ercole Seccadenari (d 1540). The artists included Alfonso Lombardi, Amico Aspertini, Niccolò Tribolo, Girolamo da Treviso, Zaccaria Zacchi da Volterra (1473–1544) and Properzia de' Rossi. The lunette over the left portal contains a figural tableau of the *Resurrection* (1527) by Lombardi, the lunette over

the right portal the *Deposition* by Aspertini, Tribolo and Seccadenari. The pinnacles are adorned by reliefs (1567–9) by Giacomo Silla, Teodosio de' Rossi (*fl* 1560–1613) and Lazzaro Casario (*fl* 1568–88).

Dissatisfaction with Aimo's façade design induced the Fabbricieri to solicit outside opinions, some from leading architects who submitted their own original proposals for clothing the Gothic building. The majority of the surviving drawings are still preserved in the museum at S Petronio. Among them are three vivid and varied Gothic designs (1521–2) by Baldassarre Peruzzi, two austere projects by JACOPO VIGNOLA, architect to the basilica between 1543 and 1550, and a collaborative scheme (1545) by Giulio Romano and Cristoforo Lombardo. The debate continued: later 16th-century projects include those by Domenico Tibaldi (1571), Andrea Palladio (1572–9), who sought a purely classical solution and Terribilia (1580). From the 17th century is a proposal by Girolamo Rainaldi (1626) and from the 18th, Gothic and 'modern' designs by Mauro Antonio Tesi (1749) and CARLO FRANCESCO DOTTI (1748 and 1752). The drawings represent an extensive sampling of critical and creative meditations by classically inspired designers on the nature and value of an obsolete and discredited style, and thus they constitute a small, but significant, chapter in the history of artistic theory. In 1887 and again in 1933 open competitions were held to finish the façade, but without effect.

BIBLIOGRAPHY
A. Gatti: *La fabbrica di S. Petronio: Indagini storiche* (Bologna, 1889) [doc.]
M. Fanti: *La fabbrica di S. Petronio in Bologna: Storia di un'istituzione* (Rome, 1980)
M. Fanti and others: *La Basilica di San Petronio in Bologna*, 2 vols (Bologna, 1983–4) [excellent illus.]
M. Fanti and Carlo De Angelis, eds: *Sesto centenario di fondazione della Basilica di San Petronio, 1390–1990: Documenti per una storia* (Bologna, 1990)
M. Fanti and D. Leuzi, eds: *Una basilica per una città: Sei secoli in San Petronio* (Bologna, 1994)

RICHARD J. TUTTLE

3. S STEFANO. This group of monastic buildings dates chiefly from the Romanesque period, although the complex originated much earlier, and fragments of earlier buildings survive. The complex as a whole is documented from the 9th century with the title 'Santo Stefano detto Gerusalemme', or 'Sancta Gerusalemme'. None of the surviving churches now bears the name of S Stefano, and their early history is obscure. Here, or near by, was originally a temple dedicated to Isis, and the site was later a Christian burial ground at the end of the 4th century. The church of S Stefano may have been founded by St Petronius, Bishop of Bologna (*reg* AD 431–50), who is buried here. Probably by the 10th century the basic components of the group were in existence. From around the 12th century the buildings came increasingly to be seen as an imitation or interpretation of the Holy Sepulchre complex in Jerusalem (see SEPULCHRE CHURCH) and acquired numerous symbolic references to reinforce the connection. The church of S Stefano itself also became an important local pilgrimage goal. From the 9th to the 10th centuries S Stefano housed a Benedictine monastery, which was then run by Celestine monks until 1797. Restoration work, begun in 1880 and continued into the early 20th century, has destroyed much of the early aspect

6. Bologna, S Stefano monastery complex, showing (left) SS Vitale e Agricola, rebuilt 8th century, (centre) San Sepolcro, 11th century, and (right) the church of the Crocifisso, 11th century

of the complex, which now comprises four churches, a cloister, several courtyards and chapels and a campanile. Three of the churches face on to a central courtyard, the 12th-century Cortile di Pilato (see fig. 6), at the centre of which stands a 9th-century marble basin with an inscription commemorating the Lombard kings Luitprand and Ilprand (*reg* 736–44). The church of the Crocifisso was built in the 11th century, and it retains parts of the original walls of nave and crypt. The polygonal church of San Sepolcro (*see* JERUSALEM, fig. 10) may have been founded in the 5th century, although the present edifice dates from the 11th century. Fragments of Romanesque wall paintings were transferred in 1803 to the museum and cloisters. Sections of the basilical church of SS Vitale e Agricola may date back to the 5th century; the church was rebuilt in the 8th century with remains of Roman stone, and again in the 11th century in the Lombard Romanesque style. At one end of the courtyard is the church of the Trinity or Martyrium, with 13th-century walls and façade reconstructed in 1911. Its cruciform Cappella della Croce is flanked by small apses and square rooms, all of which were rebuilt over the original 9th–12th century foundations in 1927. The Romanesque cloister adjoining the Cortile di Pilato was built in two phases; the lower colonnade is 11th century, and the upper gallery dates from the 12th century.

BIBLIOGRAPHY
M. Fanti: 'Sulla simbologia gerosolimitana del complesso di Santo Stefano di Bologna', *Il Carrobbio*, x (1984), pp. 121–33
G. Fasoli, ed.: *Stefaniana: Contributi per la storia del complesso di S Stefano in Bologna*, Deputazione di Storia Patria per le Provincie di Romagna: Documenti e studi, xvii (Bologna, 1985)
L. Serchia, ed.: *Nel segno di S Sepolcro* (Vigevano, 1987)
Sette colonne e sette chiese: La vicenda ultramillenaria del complesso di Santo Stefano (exh. cat., ed. F. Bocchi; Bologna, Mus. Civ. Archeol. and Mus. S Stefano, 1987)

□

Bologna, Andrea dà. *See* ANDREA DEI BRUNI.

Bologna, Cristoforo di Jacopo Biondi da. *See* CRISTOFORO DI JACOPO BIONDI DA BOLOGNA.

Bologna, Giovanni. *See* GIAMBOLOGNA.

Bologna, il. *See* DOMENICO AIMO and TOMMASO VINCIDOR.

Bologna, Niccolò di Giacomo da. *See* NICCOLÒ DI GIACOMO DA BOLOGNA.

Bologna, Vitale da. *See* VITALE DA BOLOGNA.

Bolognini Amorini, Antonio, Marchese (*b* Bologna, 7 Feb 1767; *d* Bologna, 18 June 1845). Italian art historian. He studied art and architecture independently and in 1786 and 1789 travelled around Italy recording his impressions of monuments and works of art. Concerned about the artistic patrimony of Bologna during the French occupation, he executed drawings and descriptions of the works of art and architecture in risk of removal or destruction and in 1816 celebrated the restitution by the French of 18 paintings with the booklet *Descrizione de' quadri restituiti a Bologna*. He was appointed an honorary member of the Accademia di Belle Arti, Bologna, in 1805, academician in 1818 and acting president in 1824, with the title of Propresidente in 1831. *Elogio di Sebastiano Serlio: Architetto bolognese* (1823) was the first of 15 biographical studies written by Bolognini. These formed the basis of his principal achievement: *Vite dei pittori ed artefici bolognesi*. The work describes 184 painters, sculptors, architects and engravers who lived in or originated from Bologna between 1090 and the 1730s. Intended as a sequel and revision of Carlo Malvasia's *Felsina Pittrice* (1678), the *Vite* has none of the Baroque verbosity of the earlier work. He worked on revising it for a second edition until the end of his life. An articulate and erudite speaker, Bolognini delivered a number of important lectures at the academy, especially in defence of the Bolognese school against the ideas promulgated by the Puristi (*see* PURISMO).

WRITINGS

Vite dei pittori ed artefici bolognesi, 2 vols (Bologna, 1841–3)

'Elenco degli scritti del Marchese Antonio Bolognini Amorini', *Prose e poesie in morte del Marchese Antonio Bolognini Amorini* (Bologna, 1845), pp. 29–33 [a complete list of Bolognini's published and unpublished writings with biographical notes by V. Davia]

BIBLIOGRAPHY

DBI

EFREM GISELLA CALINGAERT

Bolotowsky, Ilya (*b* St Petersburg, 1 July 1907; *d* New York, 22 Nov 1981). American painter and sculptor of Russian birth. Having moved first to Constantinople (now Istanbul) and then in 1923 to New York, he studied at the National Academy of Design (1924–30). Inspired both by Surrealist biomorphic forms and geometric abstraction, he painted his first non-objective work in 1933 and was a founder-member of American Abstract Artists in 1936. During the Depression of the 1930s he painted numerous abstract murals under the auspices of government-sponsored art programmes. By the late 1940s, when he taught for two years at Black Mountain College, he was concentrating on a colouristically diverse variant of Piet Mondrian's Neo-plasticism, the style that characterized both the painted columns Bolotowsky began to make in the 1960s (e.g. *Metal Column 1966*, 1966; Minneapolis, MN, Walker A. Cent.) and the paintings of the rest of his career.

WRITINGS

'On Neoplasticism and my Own Work', *Leonardo*, ii (1969), pp. 221–30

'Adventures with Bolotowsky', *Archvs Amer. A. J.*, xxii/1 (1982), pp. 8–31

BIBLIOGRAPHY

Ilya Bolotowsky (exh. cat., New York, Guggenheim, 1974) [includes interview by L. A. Svendsen and M. Poser]

S. Larsen: 'Going Abstract in the Thirties: An Interview with Ilya Bolotowsky', *A. America*, lxiv/5 (1976), pp. 70–79

NANCY J. TROY

Bolswert. Family of Dutch engravers and publishers. Both (1) Boetius Bolswert and (2) Schelte Bolswert began their careers in Amsterdam but moved south *c.* 1617–18, working as book illustrators in Antwerp and Brussels and producing religious prints (e.g. the joint work on *Saints of the Order of the Jesuits*, Hollstein, p. 85, nos 278–82). The brothers are chiefly known for the excellence of their reproductions of paintings by Rubens, which they began to produce *c.* 1630.

(1) Boetius [Boëthius] **(Adamsz.) (à) Bolswert** (*b* Bolsward, *c.* 1580; *d* Brussels, 25 March 1633). His first dated engraving, *Interior of the Exchange in Amsterdam* (1609; Hollstein, no. 362), was published by the Amsterdam publisher Michiel Colyn (*fl c.* 1609). Boetius Bolswert executed four engravings of the *Horrors of the Spanish War* after David Vinckboons (1610; Hollstein, nos 314–17) and several series after Abraham Bloemaert, with whom he must have had a close relationship (e.g. *Pastorals*, 1611; Hollstein, nos 324–37, and *Saints and Hermits*, 1612; Hollstein, nos 96–119). In his technique, he conscientiously conveyed the sketchy and mannered style of Bloemaert. In large landscapes after Vinckboons and Gillis van Coninxloo III, Bolswert used a denser, more diffuse style (e.g. *Village Fair on a Market-place*, Hollstein, no. 321). In 1615 and 1616 the Dutch States-General licensed Boetius to produce portraits after Michiel Mierevelt.

Boetius Bolswert moved to the southern Netherlands *c.* 1618, when he produced an engraving in Brussels of the *Bed of State of Prince William of Orange* (Hollstein, no. 386). In 1620 he became a member of the Antwerp Guild. He worked mainly on illustrations for religious books, among which was his own composition: *Duyfkens ende Willemynkens Pelgrimagie* [Duyfkens and Willemynkens's pilgrimage] (Antwerp, 1627; Hollstein, nos 286–312). Between 1630 and 1633 he executed five engravings after Rubens's works: the *Judgement of Solomon* (Hollstein, no. 3), the *Raising of Lazarus* (Hollstein, no. 6), *Christ on the Cross between the Two Thieves* (1631; Hollstein, no. 9), the *Last Supper* (*c.* 1632–3; Hollstein, no. 7) and the *Emperor Julius Caesar* (Hollstein, no. 380). The engravings, produced under the supervision of Rubens and to his designs, show a considerable refinement in Boetius's somewhat dry technique; their fine, muted style with soft transitions and shimmering effects sets them among the best of the Rubens prints.

(2) Schelte [Schelderic] **(Adamsz.) (à) Bolswert** (*b* Bolsward, *c.* 1586; *d* Antwerp, 12 Dec 1659). Brother of (1) Boetius Bolswert. He was probably a pupil of his brother in Amsterdam. He engraved a number of prints after such artists as Vinckboons (e.g. *Christ Entering Jerusalem*, 1612; Hollstein, no. 14), Gillis van Coninxloo III and Abraham Bloemaert. He moved to the southern Netherlands and in 1617 was working for the publishers Plantin–Moretus in Antwerp. Schelte devoted himself mainly to religious prints (e.g. the *Life of St Augustine* series, 1624; Hollstein, nos 201–28) and became a master in the Antwerp Guild of St Luke in 1625–6. Until 1627 he worked in Brussels and Antwerp on Gérard Thibault's *Académie de l'espée* (Leiden, 1628; Hollstein, no. 327).

Schelte Bolswert's career as an engraver of Rubens's work began with the *Lion Hunt* (?1628; Hollstein, no. 298), but the majority of this reproductive work was executed after 1630. In all, Schelte made about eighty engravings after Rubens, of which only four, however, were authorized by Rubens: the *Lion Hunt*, the *Conversion of St Paul* (1630–33; Hollstein, no. 196), the *Miraculous Draught of Fishes* (after 1633; Hollstein, no. 11) and

Landscape with Sunset (1638; Hollstein, no. 316). Martin van den Enden the elder (*fl c.* 1630–45) published many of Schelte's religious engravings after Rubens (principally representations of the Virgin) and his set of *Small Landscapes* after Rubens (*c.* 1640–45; Hollstein, nos 305–25, with the exception of no. 316 (above)). A set of *Large Landscapes* (Hollstein, nos 299–304) was published by Gillis Hendricx (*fl c.* 1643–4). Schelte Bolswert's technique was extremely painterly; he used fine, curved cross-hatching and dots to achieve sculptured and shimmering light effects. He became one of the most brilliant reproductive engravers of Rubens, surpassing even his brother Boetius in his ability to re-create the spirit of Rubens's painting.

Schelte Bolswert also made engravings after such artists as Abraham van Diepenbeeck, Anthony van Dyck, Jacob Jordaens I, Erasmus Quellinus (ii), Theodoor Rombouts and Gerard Seghers. Quellinus noted that Schelte only had one eye.

BIBLIOGRAPHY

BNB; Hollstein: *Dut. & Flem.*; Thieme–Becker; Wurzbach

E. Dutuit: *Manuel de l'amateur d'estampes*, iii (Paris, 1885/*R* Amsterdam, 1972), iv, pp. 21–274

T. Levin: 'Handschriftliche Bemerkungen von Erasmus Quellinus', *Z. Bild. Kst*, xxiii (1888), p. 173

A. Rosenberg: *Die Rubensstecher* (Vienna, 1893), pp. 97–133

F. van den Wijngaert: *Inventaris der Rubeniaansche Prentkunst* (Antwerp, 1940), pp. 13, fols 30–37

Graphisch werk van Boetius en Schelderic a Bolswert (exh. cat., ed. L. Lebeer; Bolsward, Stadhuis, 1951)

J. Müller Hofstede: 'Beiträge zum zeichnerischen Werk des Rubens', *Wallraf-Richartz-Jb.*, xxvii (1965), pp. 338–40

——: 'Rubens' Grisaille für den Abendmahlstich des Boetius à Bolswert', *Pantheon*, xxviii/2 (1970), pp. 108–16

K. Renger: 'Planänderungen in Rubensstichen', *Z. Kst*, xxxvii (1974), pp. 5–9

——: 'Rubens dedit dedicavitque', *Jb. Berlin. Mus.*, xvi (1974), pp. 148–52

Rubens e l'incisione: Nelle collezioni del Gabinetto Nazionale delle Stampe (exh. cat., ed. D. Bodart; Rome, Gab. Stampe, 1977)

J. Pohlen: *Untersuchungen zur Reproduktionsgraphik der Rubenswerkstatt*, Beiträge zur Kunstwissenschaft, vi (Munich, 1985), pp. 83–107, 182–98

HELLA ROBELS

Boltanski, Christian (*b* Paris, 6 Sept 1944). French sculptor, photographer, painter and film maker. Self-taught, he began painting in 1958 but first came to public attention in the late 1960s with short avant-garde films and with the publication of notebooks in which he came to terms with his childhood. The combination in these works of real and fictional evidence of his and other people's existence remained central to his later art. As well as presenting assemblages of documentary photographs wrenched from their original context, in the 1970s he also experimented inventively with the production of objects made of clay and from unusual materials such as sugar and gauze dressings. These works, some of them entitled *Attempt at Reconstitution of Objects that Belonged to Christian Boltanski between 1948 and 1954* (1970–71; see 1990 exh. cat., p. 11), again included flashbacks to segments of time and life that blurred memory with invention.

In the 1970s photography became Boltanski's favoured medium for exploring forms of remembering and consciousness, reconstructed in pictorial terms. After 1976 he handled the medium as if it were painting, photographing slices of nature and carefully arranged still-lifes of banal everyday objects in order to convert them into grid compositions that reflected the collective aesthetic condition of contemporary civilization in a stereotyped way. In the early 1980s Boltanski ceased using *objets trouvés* as a point of departure. Instead he produced 'theatrical compositions' by fashioning small marionette-like figures from cardboard, scraps of materials, thread and cork, painted in colour and transposed photographically into large picture formats. These led to kinetic installations in which a strong light focused on figurative shapes helped create a mysterious environment of silhouettes in movement (e.g. *The Shadows*, 1984; see 1990 exh. cat., p. 20).

In 1986 Boltanski began making installations from a variety of materials and media, with light effects as integral components. Some of these consisted of tin boxes stacked in an altar-like construction with a framed portrait photograph on top, for example the *Chases School* (1986–7; Ghent, Mus. Hedendaag. Kst). Such assemblages of objects again relate to the principle of reconstruction of the past. Such works, for which he used portrait photographs of Jewish schoolchildren taken in Vienna in 1931, serve as a forceful reminder of the mass murder of Jews by the Nazis. In the works that followed, such as *Reserve* (exh. Basle, Mus. Gegenwartskst, 1989), Boltanski filled whole rooms and corridors with items of worn clothing as a way of prompting an involuntary association with the clothing depots at concentration camps. As in his previous work, objects thus serve as mute testimony to human experience and suffering.

BIBLIOGRAPHY

Christian Boltanski: Reconstitution (exh. cat., ed. A. Franzke and M. Schwarz; Karlsruhe, Bad. Kstver., 1978)

Boltanski (exh. cat., ed. B. Blistène; Paris, Pompidou, 1984)

Christian Boltanski: Lessons of Darkness (exh. cat., ed. L. Gumpert and M. J. Jacob; Chicago, IL, Mus. Contemp. A., 1988)

Christian Boltanski: Reconstitution (exh. cat., essay L. Gumpert; London, Whitechapel A.G.; Eindhoven, Stedel. Van Abbemus.; Grenoble, Mus. Grenoble; 1990) [includes box with reprints of earlier publications]

ANDREAS FRANZKE

Boltraffio [Beltraffio]**, Giovanni Antonio** (*b* Milan, *c.* 1467; *d* Milan, 15 June 1516). Italian painter and draughtsman. A pupil of Leonardo da Vinci, he was active mainly in Milan and was particularly noted as a portrait painter.

1. TRAINING AND WORKS BEFORE *c.* 1500. Boltraffio belonged to a noble Milanese family; he did not paint from financial necessity and did not pursue his career in a systematic way. His birth date is calculated from the inscription on his tomb (Milan, Castello Sforzesco; ex-S Paolo in Compito, destr. 1547). No signed painting by him survives, and the documentation records only three works of secure attribution and date and provides little biographical information. His reconstructed oeuvre has been expanded unduly by some writers and restricted too rigorously by others. Vasari stated that he trained with Leonardo; he is probably the 'Gian Antonio' mentioned by Leonardo in a note of 1491 (Paris, Bib. Inst. France, MS. C, fol. 15v), when Boltraffio was about 24. Some writers suggest that before he entered Leonardo's workshop Boltraffio had a phase of work influenced by Vincenzo Foppa and Bernardo Zenale, when he may have painted two panels with *Saints and Devotional Figures*

(Milan, Castello Sforzesco). The execution is too crude, however. According to Suida, they should be ascribed to a painter greatly influenced by him, whom Suida called the 'Pseudo-Boltraffio'.

Boltraffio's contract with Marco d'Oggiono, another pupil of Leonardo, for an altarpiece of the *Resurrection with SS Leonard and Lucy* (Berlin, Gemäldegal.) for the oratory of S Leonardo in S Giovanni sul Muro in Milan also dates from 1491 (Shell and Sironi). The work is the most secure example of Boltraffio's style in the 1490s. Marco was probably responsible for the entire upper part; Boltraffio painted the kneeling figures of the saints, in poses based on balanced oppositions. The finely painted surface and light shadows show the influence of Leonardo, to whom this altarpiece was once attributed. It was probably executed under Leonardo's supervision and perhaps even based on his drawings. Other works datable to the same years confirm Boltraffio's adherence to Leonardo's approach in his early period. The *Madonna of the Flower* (Milan, Mus. Poldi Pezzoli) is modelled on Leonardo's dynamic counterposition of movements; the *Portrait of a Lady* (Milan, Mattioli priv. col.) follows Leonardo's style in the *Portrait of a Musician* (Milan, Bib. Ambrosiana), although its dark background and pyramidal figure also recall the works of Antonello da Messina. In the *Madonna of the Bowl* (Budapest, Mus. F.A.) a new interest in Bramantino appears. Early writers indicate that Leonardo often intervened in paintings begun by his pupils. This has led to doubts about the attribution to him of such works as the *Madonna Litta* (St Petersburg, Hermitage) and the *Belle Ferronière* (Paris, Louvre), both of which have been linked to Boltraffio. The *Madonna Litta*, datable to the early 1490s, is undoubtedly from Leonardo's workshop; in fact it corresponds to autograph drawings by Leonardo, for instance the *Head of the Virgin* (Paris, Louvre). It is likely that Leonardo was responsible for the compositional scheme and that he intervened with corrections and alterations during its execution by a pupil (Brown, 1991). Although it has been proposed that this pupil was Marco d'Oggiono, the picture's many affinities with Boltraffio's style, and its indisputable technical excellence, suggest it may be his work. The *Belle Ferronière* is now usually attributed to Leonardo alone, but the fact that writers have suggested intervention by Boltraffio in a work of such quality indicates how highly his work has been regarded.

Boltraffio was known for his skill as a portrait painter. In 1498, Isabella of Aragon (1470–1524), widow of Gian Galeazzo Sforza, Duke of Milan (*reg* 1476–94), asked him to copy a portrait of her brother Ferrante (1469–96) in the Gonzaga collection in Mantua, and the poet Gerolamo Casio also praised his ability in that field, commenting that he 'made every man more handsome'. Certainly in his portraits, unlike painters in the Lombard realist tradition, he tended to idealize his subject. In the famous *Portrait of a Young Man* (Chatsworth, Derbys), the ambiguous beauty that Boltraffio conferred on the sitter (Casio, according to the inscription on the back) has led to the suggestion that the portrait is that of a woman. The identification of her as Costanza Bentivoglio (*c.* 1490–after 1525) of Bologna, from the initials C B on the cuff (Reggiani Rajna), however, has been generally rejected. There are two other autograph versions of this work (Moscow, Pushkin Mus.; San Diego, Timken priv. col.). All three are linked to Boltraffio's friendship with Casio, who was responsible for his commission for an altarpiece in Bologna that Vasari dated from 1500 (see §2 below). Thus the portraits thought to be of Casio, including a fourth (Milan, Brera), should be dated around that time. Stylistically they are datable before 1500, both in their courtly tone and in their dependence on Leonardo's style in the *Portrait of a Musician*: this suggests that Boltraffio's relationship with Casio began before he went to Bologna.

Boltraffio also executed numerous drawings during the 1490s (Bora), mainly done with metalpoint on prepared paper (generally blue), a technique Leonardo introduced in Milan. These are distributed widely (e.g. Milan, Bib. Ambrosiana; Chatsworth, Derbys; Turin, Bib. Reale; Paris, Louvre; London, BM; Florence, Uffizi), although many attributions are uncertain.

2. WORKS AFTER *c.* 1500. Boltraffio later made drawings in coloured chalks or pastels, which can be dated after 1500, the year he painted the *Virgin and Child with SS John the Baptist and Sebastian and Two Donors* (Paris, Louvre; see fig. 1) for S Maria della Misericordia in Bologna, the altarpiece commissioned by the Casio family and mentioned by Vasari. The artist's time in Bologna gave him new interests that tempered his basic adherence to Leonardo: the Casio altarpiece is set in a luminous landscape with echoes of Pietro Perugino and Francesco Francia. His stay was short: in 1502 he was commissioned by the congregation of S Maria presso S Satiro in Milan to produce an altarpiece of *St Barbara* (Berlin, Gemäldegal.). The altarpiece combines the ideas developed in Bologna

1. Giovanni Antonio Boltraffio: *Virgin and Child with SS John the Baptist and Sebastian and Two Donors*, oil on panel, 1.86×1.84 m, 1500 (Paris, Musée du Louvre)

with a strong interest in Bramantino and Andrea Solario. It is related to a splendid charcoal and pastel drawing (Milan, Bib. Ambrosiana) that signals the change in Boltraffio's graphic style. The subject of another well-known drawing, *Portrait of a Young Man* (Milan, Bib. Ambrosiana), has been identified by some writers as Ferrante d'Aragona (Cogliati Arano, 1982). Boltraffio's permanent return to Milan is confirmed by a document of 1503, in which he is named among the experts appointed to judge models submitted for the door of the north transept (the Porta verso Compedo) of Milan Cathedral.

A fresco cycle commonly associated with Boltraffio is that depicting 26 figures of saints in fictive *oculi* in the loggia of S Maurizio al Monastero in Milan. Datable shortly after 1503, the cycle was worked on by various artists, some closer to Zenale and others to Boltraffio. It is unlikely, however, that Boltraffio ran a workshop, given his aristocratic origins and wealth. He may simply have provided models to be elaborated by other painters. Other figures of saints attributed to him include those frescoed in medallions in the Certosa di Pavia (transverse arches over the side aisles).

It was probably in the early 16th century that Boltraffio painted such portraits of very high quality as the *Lady in Grey* and the *Portrait of a Man* (both Isola Bella, Mus. Borromeo) and the *Portrait of a Man* (Florence, Uffizi), which show a renewal of his usual portrait formula. While the *Portrait of a Gentleman* (London, N.G.; see fig. 2) still follows the model of the profile against a dark background,

derived from portrait medals, and the *Portrait of a Youth* (Berne, Kstmus.) has a composition reminiscent of the Casio portraits, in the later works the figure is depicted with broad forms against a light background; the contours are less distinct, and there is a keener sense of psychological introspection.

It has been suggested that Boltraffio made a journey to Rome before the end of 1506, when he might have painted the fresco of the *Virgin and Child with the Donor Francesco Cabañas* in S Onofrio. There is no documentation of such a journey, however, and the fresco was more probably painted by Cesare da Sesto. Leonardo mentioned Boltraffio in 1507 in a brief note on the back of a drawing (Windsor Castle, Berks, Royal Col., 19092v), an indication that their relationship continued. The identification of him as the Giovanni who accompanied Leonardo to Rome in 1513 is extremely unlikely, however. Boltraffio's works show none of the elements later adopted by those Lombard artists who were fascinated by the Roman cultural climate, and the antiquarian taste and the influences of Raphael and Michelangelo remained foreign to his art.

Boltraffio's last documented work, an altarpiece of the *Virgin and Child with SS John the Baptist, Sebastian and Donor* (Budapest, Mus. F.A.) for the da Ponte Chapel in Lodi Cathedral, was commissioned in 1508. The rocky landscape, the Child and the pointing gesture of St John the Baptist all derive from Leonardo's *Virgin of the Rocks* (London, N.G.; see LEONARDO DA VINCI, fig. 2). Thus Boltraffio reaffirmed his fidelity to his master and returned to the models he had used earlier. The St Sebastian recalls a prototype by Perugino, indicating that Boltraffio gathered ideas outside the Lombard tradition. It is significant, however, that during Leonardo's second Milanese period (1506–13) Boltraffio returned to his artistic roots. In the Lodi altarpiece only the application of paint lacks his usual refinement. The central motif recurs in the tondo of the *Virgin and Child* (Bergamo, Gal. Accad. Carrara).

It is difficult to reconstruct Boltraffio's activity after the Lodi altarpiece, although he is documented in 1509 and 1510 as living in the parish of S Paolo in Compito in Milan. He may have accepted only occasional commissions. Perhaps Leonardo's departure from Milan in 1513 left him with no incentive to paint. The catalogue of Boltraffio's works is far from definitive either for paintings or drawings. The works of the Pseudo-Boltraffio should be excluded. These are probably not by a single imitator but indicate a wider influence. A large altarpiece fragment with *Two Devotional Figures* (Milan, Brera), once considered essential to Boltraffio's catalogue, is now generally rejected (Fiorio).

2. Giovanni Antonio Boltraffio: *Portrait of a Gentleman*, oil on panel, 565×425 mm, *c.* 1500 (London, National Gallery)

DBI

BIBLIOGRAPHY

G. Casio: *Cronica* (Bologna, 1525)

G. Vasari: *Vite* (1550, rev. 2/1568); ed. G. Milanesi (1878–85), iv, p. 51

P. Lamo: *Graticola di Bologna* (Bologna, 1560/*R* 1844), p. 14

W. Suida: *Leonardo und sein Kreis* (Munich, 1929)

M. Reggiani Rajna: 'Un po' d'ordine fra tanti Casii', *Rinascimento*, ii (1951), pp. 337–83

L. Cogliati Arano: *Disegni di Leonardo e della sua cerchia alle Gallerie dell'Accademia* (Milan, 1980)

——: 'I disegni di Leonardo e della sua cerchia', *Leonardo all'Ambrosiana* (Milan, 1982), p. 92

M. T. Fiorio: *Leonardeschi in Lombardia* (Milan, 1982)

E. Rama: 'Un tentativo di rilettura della ritrattistica di Boltraffio tra quattrocento e cinquecento', *A. Lombarda*, 64 (1983), pp. 79–86

D. A. Brown: 'Leonardo and the Idealized Portrait in Milan', *A. Lombarda*, 67 (1983–4), pp. 102–16

O. Magnabosco: 'Un'ipotesi per la ritrattistica di Boltraffio', *A. Lombarda*, 73–5 (1985), pp. 45–50

G. Bora: 'Per un catalogo dei disegni dei Leonardeschi lombardi', *Rac. Vinc.*, xxii (1987), pp. 139–82

L. Cogliati Arano: 'Un Boltraffio inedito alla Biblioteca Ambrosiana', *Rac. Vinc.*, xxii (1987), pp. 61–9

M. T. Fiorio: 'Boltraffio', *Scuole lombarda e piemontese, 1300–1530*, Milan, Brera cat. (Milan, 1988), pp. 116–18, 415–19

L. Cogliati Arano: 'Un disegno del Boltraffio', *Arte Doc.*, iii (1989), pp. 128–9

J. Shell and G. Sironi: 'Giovanni Antonio Boltraffio and Marco d'Oggiono: The Berlin *Resurrection of Christ with Sts Leonard and Lucy*', *Rac. Vinc.*, xxiii (1989), pp. 119–54

D. A. Brown: 'The Master of the *Madonna Litta*', *Leonardeschi a Milano: Fortuna e collezionismo*, ed. M. T. Fiorio and P. C. Marani (Milan, 1991), pp. 25–34

V. Markova: 'Il *San Sebastiano* di Giovanni Antonio Boltraffio e alcuni disegni dell'area leonardesca', *Leonardeschi a Milano: Fortuna e collezionismo*, ed. M. T. Fiorio and P. C. Marani (Milan, 1991), pp. 100–107

MARIA TERESA FIORIO

Bolzano [Ger. Bozen]. Italian city, capital of the Alto Adige. It stands at the confluence of the Tálvera and Isarco rivers and has a population of *c.* 106,000. Until 1276 possession of the region was disputed by the counts of Tyrol and bishops of Trent, and it was ceded to the Habsburgs in 1363. From 1810 to 1813 it belonged to the Napoleonic Kingdom of Italy and was then returned to Austria until 1918. The cathedral of the Assumption was built as the town parish church in the 12th century on the site of an Early Christian cemetery; its façade survives as part of the present west end. The building was replaced by an Early Gothic basilica (1300–40), but soon after completion its interior was converted by German masons into a hall church with a star vault (1380–1420) by Martin Schiche of Augsburg (*d* before 1420). Italian masons, and later Swabian masters, worked on the sculptural decoration. The simple façade is pierced by a rose window (early 14th century), beneath which stands a portal (1499) incorporating a Romanesque porch supported by two stylized lions. The roof of the cathedral is decorated with polychrome tiles arranged in a striking geometric pattern. The interior and parts of the exterior are decorated with numerous frescoes, including a *Crucifixion*, flanked by donors (late 13th century) on the exterior of the apse, a *Virgin and Child* (*c.* 1475) by Michael Pacher and scenes from the *Life of St Christopher* (1498) by Friedrich Pacher. HANS VON JUDENBURG made the influential Bolzano Altarpiece (1421–4) for the cathedral; it is now dispersed (Cologne, Schnütgen-Mus.; Nuremberg, Ger. Nmus.; elsewhere). In 1499 the bell-tower (h. 65 m) was partially destroyed by fire; the upper part was rebuilt (1500–09) in sandstone in an elaborate Late Gothic style under the supervision of HANS LUTZ to a design (*c.* 1500) by Burkhard Engelberg. The tower is incorporated into the main structure of the building and rises on the north side alongside the choir. Lutz also executed some high quality sculpture, including the sandstone pulpit (1513–14; rest.). Baroque work in the cathedral includes the marble high altar (1710–20), executed by Giovanni Battista Ranghieri (1646–1718), and the polygonal Grazie Chapel (1743–5) by Giuseppe Delai (*c.* 1658–1766), which opens into the apse and is decorated with frescoes (1771) by Carlo Henrici (1737–83) in the vault. The cathedral was badly damaged in World War II and was subsequently restored.

BIBLIOGRAPHY

H. von Klebelsberg: 'Die Restaurierung des bozner Pfarrturms', *Schlern: Illus. Mhft. Heimat- & Vlksknd.*, lix/1 (1985), pp. 8–28

E. Kreuzer Eccel: 'Zu den Figuren am bozner Pfarrturm', *Schlern: Illus. Mhft. Heimat- & Vlksknd.*, lix/1 (1985), pp. 55–69

E. Egg: 'Die bozner Architektur am Ende der Gotik', *Festschrift Niccolò Rasmo: Scritti in onore* (Bolzano, 1986), pp. 217–46

Bomarzo, Sacro Bosco [Villa Orsini]. Italian estate below the hill town of Bomarzo, near Viterbo. The popular name derives from an inscription in the wood, which refers to it as a 'sacro bosco', an allusion to *Arcadia* (1504) by Jacopo Sannazaro. The Sacro Bosco, built for Pier Francesco ('Vicino') Orsini (*d* 1585) from *c.* 1552, was dedicated by him to his deceased wife, Giulia Farnese. Called a *boschetto* (little wood) by Orsini, the site is hilly with untouched terrain, although there are also level terraces and rectilinear enclosures. Much was done by 1564; sculpture was added during the 1570s, and work continued until Orsini's death in January 1585.

The original planting plan is unknown, and since the rediscovery of the site in the 1940s much has been replanted. The stream may have been dammed to form a lake in the areas of the present entrance and the path lined with heads (moved there in the modern restoration). The original entrance was probably near the Leaning House, the former location of the sphinxes, as their inscriptions address the entering visitor. The hypothesis of a formal garden contemporary with the Sacro Bosco on the hillside above must be rejected without further evidence.

The Sacro Bosco is filled with garden architecture and sculpture, some of which were originally fountains. Much of the architecture is in a classical style, although the principal structure, the tempietto dedicated to Giulia Farnese, imitates an Etruscan temple. The other major architectural works include the Leaning House (see fig.), dedicated to Cardinal Cristoforo Madruzzo, the theatre, inspired by the exedra of Bramante's Belvedere Court in the Vatican, Rome, and the *all'antica* nymphaeum adjacent to it. The sculpture is for the most part carved of volcanic outcroppings and is colossal in size; in late 1574 it was coloured. The sculpted figures are strikingly novel and enigmatic, although many belong to conventional categories of garden ornaments. The animals—common in 16th-century woods—include a stylized dragon fighting lions, a life-size African war elephant bearing a castle on its back and a soldier in its trunk, a giant tortoise supporting a statue of fame, an orc and the three-headed dog Cerberus. Other garden ornaments include a fountain of Pegasus, a river god, a sleeping nymph, a siren and grotesque heads; the giant grotesque head supporting a sphere with a castle on top and the colossal head called the *Mouth of Hell* are unparalleled, as are the seated female figure with a huge vase on her head and siren-like creatures holding an upended male figure at her back. Orsini was involved in the creation of the garden, which extended over a long period. Among the many architects whose names have been suggested in connection with the site are Jacopo Vignola, Bartolomeo Ammanati and Pirro Ligorio. The

Bomarzo, Sacro Bosco, the Leaning House, from *c.* 1552

colossal figures of the mid-1570s have been attributed to Simone Mosca Moschino.

A number of architectural and sculpted elements bear carved inscriptions, which during the modern restoration were painted over, some inaccurately. Sources have been noted in literary texts by such writers as Dante, Petrarch and Ariosto.

Many and widely different interpretations of the garden have been suggested, although its unusually personal character is widely agreed. The themes of history, time and artistic deception are evident in several feigned Etruscan funerary monuments as well as feigned evidence of destruction in the pseudo-Roman nymphaeum and the Leaning House. The Etruscan civilization—important to both regional and Orsini family history—is alluded to throughout. Sources have been uncovered for many of the ornaments, in Etruscan and Roman antiquities, engravings, emblems and woodcuts from the *Hypnerotomachia poliphili* (Venice, 1499) as well as influences from India, China and the New World. Disagreement remains about the significance and relationship of individual elements: some see a narrative development corresponding to Orsini's own biography or to such literary texts as Ariosto's *Orlando furioso* (1516, 1521, 1532), others a more general unifying theme in Vicino's devotion to his wife. The layout, diversity of ornaments and long period of creation instead suggest several overlapping themes including the pastoral ones of love and death.

BIBLIOGRAPHY
A. Bruschi: 'Il problema storico di Bomarzo', *Palladio*, xiii (1963), pp. 85–114
——: 'Nuovi dati documentari sulle opere orsiniane di Bomarzo', *Quad. Ist. Stor. Archit.*, 55–60 (1963), pp. 13–58
J. von Hennenberg: 'Bomarzo: Nuovi dati e un'interpretazione', *Stor. A.*, xiii (1972), pp. 43–55
J. Theurillat: *Les Mystères de Bomarzo et des jardins symboliques de la Renaissance* (Geneva, 1973)
L. Quartermaine: 'Vicino Orsini's Garden of Conceits', *It. Stud.*, xxxii (1977), pp. 68–85
E. G. Dotson: 'Shapes of Earth and Time in European Gardens', *A. J.* [New York], xlii (1982), pp. 210–16
M. J. Darnell and M. S. Weil: 'Il Sacro Bosco di Bomarzo: Its 16th-century Literary and Antiquarian Context', *J. Gdn Hist.*, iv (1984), pp. 1–91
H. Bredekamp: *Vicino Orsini und der heilige Wald von Bomarzo*, 2 vols (Worms, 1985)
J. B. Bury: 'Review Essay: Bomarzo Revisited', *J. Gdn Hist.*, v (1985), pp. 213–23
C. Lazzaro: *The Italian Renaissance Garden: From the Conventions of Planting, Design and Ornament to the Grand Gardens of Sixteenth-century Central Italy* (New Haven, 1990)

CLAUDIA LAZZARO

Bombay [Mumbai]. Indian city, port, manufacturing centre and, since 1960, administrative capital of the state of Maharashtra. It is located on a peninsula, originally a group of seven islands, projecting into the Arabian Sea from the western coast of India. Known as the Gateway of India because its port was the main entrance to the subcontinent for Western contacts, Bombay was ceded to England in 1661. Its prosperity has been built on shipbuilding, industry and international trade, and the entrepreneurial genius of its booming cosmopolitan population. The city retains a fine colonial legacy of Indo-Saracenic styles, set within a context of indigenous buildings.

1. History and urban development. 2. Art life and organization.

1. HISTORY AND URBAN DEVELOPMENT.

(i) Early history, before 1803. (ii) 1803–*c.* 1900. (iii) After *c.* 1900.

(i) Early history, before 1803. Occupied since prehistoric times, Bombay formed part of the kingdom of Gujarat from 1348 to 1534, when the Sultan Bahadur Shah (*reg* 1526–37) ceded the districts of Bassein, Salsette and Bombay to the Portuguese in exchange for their assistance against the Mughals. The Portuguese did little to develop its potential, devoting their efforts to religious conversion. Settlement was concentrated in the castle or fort on the harbour front, now engulfed by the government dockyard; a few fragments of early Portuguese fortifications survive embedded in later construction.

In 1661 Bombay passed to England peacefully as part of the marriage dowry of Catherine of Braganza to Charles II. On 23 September 1668 it was made over to the British East India Company at an annual rent of £10. Notwithstanding the insalubrious climate, Bombay replaced Surat as the trading headquarters of the Company on the west coast of India in 1708. By 1720 the town had a total population of 50,000, including about 1000 Europeans. It was protected by a fortified wall, inside which lay the principal buildings, including a mint and the Anglican church of St Thomas, now the cathedral. The latter, which survives in a much altered form, was begun by Governor Gerald Aungier in 1672 and completed in 1718.

Bombay was the only coastal settlement in the region where the rise of the tide permitted the construction of large-scale docks. In 1736 a Surat Parsi, Lavji Nasarvanji Wadia, established the government dockyard adjacent to the fort. This laid the foundations of the city's future maritime supremacy and further enhanced Bombay's use as a naval base from 1755.

Throughout the 18th century the economy of the town was consolidated, but Bombay remained small and isolated from contact with the rest of India by the Maratha tribes, who formed a formidable bulwark against further expansion inland across the Deccan. As a result, a valuable if limited commerce was maintained in raw silks, pearls, dates and perfumes with Muscat and Arabia, and in cotton, bullion, sugar and spices with Java and China.

(ii) 1803–c. *1900.* On 17 February 1803 the town was devastated by a huge fire. This induced the authorities to build outside the walls, which surrounded the core of the modern city centre. Between 1809 and 1816 annual trade in raw cotton trebled from 30 million lbs to 90 million. Most important of all, in 1817 Maratha power was broken at the Battle of Kirkee, and the long-standing barrier to transcontinental trade was lifted. By 1830 the road to the Deccan had been opened and improved, encouraging a two-way flow of goods and produce across the interior. The town became the commercial centre of the Arabian Sea. Under the guidance of Governor Mountstuart Elphinstone (1779–1859), the administrative framework of the Bombay Presidency and its capital was laid down between 1819 and 1827.

The Town Hall was begun in 1820 to the designs of Colonel Thomas Cowper (1781–1825) of the Bombay Engineers and was completed in 1835 at a total cost of £50,000. The finest Neo-classical building in India, faced with white chunam, a form of local stucco, and raised high on a podium with an octastyle Doric portico, it was a potent symbol of burgeoning civic pride. In 1824–7 a new Mint was erected near by by Major John Hawkins (1783–1831); also faced with chunam and with a fine Ionic portico that complemented the Town Hall. In 1835 a bishopric was established, and three years later the church was raised to cathedral status. In 1836 the Chamber of Commerce was founded.

The following decades were years of steady consolidation. The formation of the Bombay Bank in 1840 and the construction of the Great Indian Peninsula Railway, which reached Thana to the north of the city in 1853, facilitated expansion, fuelled by competition from the rival Bombay, Baroda & Central India Railway, which opened in 1860 and reached Bombay four years later. With the abolition of Company rule in 1858, a huge boost was given to the development of a modern rail network, which reinforced the city's role as a regional trading centre.

In the 1860s economic activity was stimulated by a slump in the supply of cotton to the Lancashire mills at the outbreak of the American Civil War. Bombay immediately became a vast clearing-house for the cotton fields of India. By 1864 there were 31 private banks, 16 financial associations, 8 land corporations, 10 shipping companies and 62 joint stock companies. In 1862 a major reclamation project linked the seven islands into a continuous peninsula and released new areas for urban development. This influx of unprecedented wealth coincided with the arrival of Sir

Bartle Frere (1815–84), who, as Governor in 1862–7, continued the transformation of the city begun by his predecessor Sir George Clerk (1800–89), who was Governor in 1846–8 and 1860–62. From about 1860 Clerk had planned the layout of Elphinstone Circus, the first example of civic planning on a grand scale in Bombay. It incorporated Cowper's elegant Town Hall into a circus of arcaded four-storey Italianate buildings set around central gardens. Frere maintained this impetus, determined to give the city a series of buildings worthy of its wealth, location and emerging pre-eminence as the Gateway of India. By 1866 the population had risen to over 800,000. Frere personally stipulated the highest standards of design, with conscious thought given to civic impact and artistic presence.

One of the first major municipal improvements was the removal of the walls of the old fort in 1864 and the reconstruction of the city to a generous new plan devised by James Trubshawe (*fl* 1860–75), architect to the Ramparts Removal Committee. The first truly Gothic Revival building was the unpretentious but influential Afghan Memorial Church of St John the Evangelist in the Early English style at Colaba, on the tip of the peninsula. Conceived by Henry Conybeare (*fl* 1845–73) in 1847 and consecrated 11 years later, it generated enthusiasm for Gothic Revival architecture. Taking ideas from such architectural publications as *The Builder* and from contemporary buildings in London, this movement resulted in a large group of secular public buildings that transformed the townscape of Bombay into one of the finest High Victorian Gothic cities in the world.

The most cohesive group of Gothic Revival buildings was that erected along the Esplanade (now Mayo Road). They were built in buff-coloured Coorla sandstone from Salsette and embellished with a variety of local building stones. The old Secretariat (1867–74) by Captain Henry St Clair Wilkins (1828–96), in Venetian Gothic style enriched with structural polychromy, was followed by the Public Works Office (1869–72), also by Wilkins, the Telegraph Office (1871–4) by W. Paris (*fl* 1865–75), the Post Office (1869–72) by Trubshawe and Paris, and the Law Courts (1871–9) by Lt-Col. James Augustus Fuller (1823–1902). The most accomplished composition in the group was by Sir George Gilbert Scott (*see* SCOTT (ii), (1)), who designed the Convocation Hall (1869–74) and Library (1869–78) of the university from his London office. Dominated by the soaring Rajabai clock-tower, which is named after the mother of its benefactor Premchand Roychand and derived from the cathedral campanile in Florence, the University Hall and Library are among Scott's finest works, little known in his own country. The City Improvement Trust was created in 1898 to replan the overcrowded slums and to provide new housing, with an ambitious programme including sanitary schemes, 50,000 one-roomed tenements for the poor, major land reclamation in the Back Bay area and the planned development of outlying industrial estates.

The popularity of the Gothic style was linked with the availability of good local building stone as well as the growth of a workforce well versed in Western techniques of carved masonry. This was largely due to the enterprising guidance of John Lockwood Kipling (1837–1911) of the Bombay School of Art (founded 1857), who laid the basis for a creative resurgence of Indian arts and crafts. Another crucial factor was the presence of two rich and influential ethnic minorities, the Parsis and the Sephardic Jews. This social élite provided enlightened patronage for a whole range of ambitious philanthropic ventures, funded by Sir Jamsetjee Jejeebhoy (1783–1859), Sir Cowasjee Jehangir Readymoney (1812–78), the Sassoon family and others. Watson's Hotel (now Watson's Building) on the Esplanade was in 1867 the first iron-framed building to be erected in Bombay; it also stood out because of its classical details, as did the Victoria and Albert Museum (1862), Bycullah, by William Tracey (*fl* 1860–65). Virtually the entire triangle of land bounded by Cruikshank Road, Carnac Road and Hornby Road, north-east of the central Maidan, was lined with buildings united by the use of Gothic Revival styles. Other notable examples are the Crawford Markets (1871; by William Emerson), with relief sculpture over the entrance by John Lockwood Kipling, the delightful Mechanics or Sassoon Institute (1870; by Fuller) and Elphinstone College (1871; by Trubshawe), Bycullah.

During this volatile and creative period a distinguished Bombay-based architect, FREDERICK WILLIAM STEVENS, developed a synthesis of Gothic and indigenous styles that produced some of the most exuberant buildings in British India. Following the Royal Alfred Sailors' Home (1872–6; now the Council Hall), in 1878 Stevens won the commission for a new city terminus for the Great Indian Peninsula Railway. The Victoria Terminus (1878–87; see fig. 1), known as VT, is the finest Victorian Gothic building in India. Inspired by Scott's St Pancras Station in London, it is a monumental affirmation of Victorian civic and imperial pride and an effective measure of the economic stature of the city. Crowned by a huge dome and interwoven with eclectic Indo-Saracenic details, it is an exuberant display of polychromatic stone, decorated tiles, marble and stained glass. In 1888 Stevens won the commission for the new Municipal Buildings, which were completed in 1893 in an Indo-Saracenic style of exoticism and vigour. Crowning the main gable is a great winged statue, *Urbs Prima in Indis*, a reflection of the supreme self-assurance of the age. In 1894–6 Stevens designed a second great terminus, Churchgate, for the Bombay, Baroda & Central India Railway. During the late 19th century and into the early 20th, the principal commercial docks were also expanded and modernized: the Victoria Dock in 1885–8, Prince's Dock in 1875–9, Merewether Dry Dock in 1891 and the Alexandra Dock in 1905. These transformed the eastern foreshore from a swamp into valuable commercial property linked to the mainline railway system.

(iii) After c. 1900. Among early 20th-century buildings, the vast Taj Mahal Hotel (1903) by William Chambers (*fl* 1895–1905) on Apollo Bunder, built for J. N. Tata, the Parsi multi-millionaire, became one of the great hotels of the British Empire. In 1903–9 a huge new General Post Office was built by John Begg in an incisive and scholarly Indo-Saracenic style. Civic improvements, assisted by private philanthropy, continued with schemes such as the Institute of Science by GEORGE WITTET, begun in 1911, which owed its inception to Lord Sydenham as Governor (1907–13) but was funded by leading Jewish and Parsi families. George Wittet also designed the colossal Prince

1. Bombay, Victoria Terminus, by Frederick William Stevens, 1878–87

of Wales Museum of Western India (1914; extended 1937; *see* MUSEUM, fig. 6) in a scholarly interpretation of the 15th- and 16th-century Islamic styles of the Deccan, in particular the Bahmani tombs at Bijapur. The museum contains a fine collection of European paintings, as well as Mughal and Rajput miniatures, oriental arms and galleries devoted to archaeological and natural history collections. The last great imperial building to be raised in the city was the triumphal Gateway of India (1927; see fig. 2) on Apollo Bunder; designed by George Wittet, it was modelled on Gujarati architecture of the 16th century. Built of local honey-coloured basalt, with pierced stonework from Gwalior in the side aisles, it commemorates the visit of George V and Queen Mary in 1911.

The inter-war period was architecturally highly inventive, as European Art Deco styles were adapted for use on many domestic, commercial and office buildings throughout the city. Good examples survive in Marine Drive and in Churchgate Street. The first detailed master-plan for the city was prepared by the Bombay City and Suburbs Post-War Development Committee. This was superseded in 1948 by the Modak–Meyer plan, which encouraged expansion to the northern suburbs as far as Bassein, with new north–south highways and two new satellite towns across the bay. In 1964 the Development Plan for Greater Bombay reinforced decentralization with the aim of reducing population densities in the centre to between 250 and 600 persons per acre.

In the post-war period the distinctive skyline of Bombay was eroded by intrusive development in the International Style (*see also* §2 below). Although decentralization diverted pressure away from the historic centre to such areas as Narriman Point, new buildings such as the Share Market and the Reserve Bank of India altered the Victorian skyline. Few good modern buildings have been produced. In New Bombay a middle-class apartment block at Vashi and a small artists' enclave at Belapur by Charles M. Correa are of interest among otherwise mediocre developments. In the central area of the city many narrow streets and bazaars survive with some wooden houses in the Gujarati style. They are decorated with carving and some have projecting storeys. Also in the centre, the infill adjacent to the

2. Bombay, the Gateway of India by George Wittet, 1927; built to commemorate the visit in 1911 of George V and Queen Mary

Municipal Buildings is a brave attempt at continuing the Victorian Gothic tradition in a modern, but sympathetic, arcuated form.

See also INDIAN SUBCONTINENT, §III, 8(i).

BIBLIOGRAPHY
J. Murray: *Handbook to the Bombay Presidency* (London, 1881)
S. M. Edwardes: *The Rise of Bombay* (Bombay, 1902)
G. Claridge: *Old and New Bombay* (Bombay, 1911)
S. Jackson: *The Sassoons* (London, 1968)
G. Tindall: *City of Gold: The Biography of Bombay* (London, 1982)
P. Davies: *Splendours of the Raj: British Architecture in India, 1660–1947* (London, 1985)
                                              PHILIP DAVIES

2. ART LIFE AND ORGANIZATION. The explosive growth of Bombay that followed the outbreak of the American Civil War, together with the consolidation and expansion of British rule after 1857, gave an impetus to the development of art life in the city. One of the institutions founded in the 1850s was the Sir J. J. College of Art and Architecture. This pioneering school trained many generations of artists in the academic tradition of British painting. The Bombay Art Society, started *c.* 1888, promoted art and artists by giving awards; its greatest triumph was the recognition of the genius of AMRITA SHER-GIL.

The genesis of the contemporary Indian art movement following independence from British rule in 1947 came with the formation of the Progressive Artists Group in 1947–8. Its six founder-members—FRANCIS NEWTON SOUZA, MAQBOOL FIDA HUSAIN, H. A. Gade (*b* 1917),

K. H. Ara (1914–85), S. K. Bakre and SAYED HAIDER RAZA—were instrumental in formulating modern Indian art and giving it direction. Their aim was a modernism that incorporated tradition by interpreting it according to present conditions and not by harking back to the past in an artificial manner. They were influenced by Rajput, Basohli and Jain miniature paintings, folk and tribal art, Gupta sculpture, Chola bronzes and reproductions of modern Western art, in particular the works of van Gogh, Picasso, the School of Paris, the German Expressionists and Paul Klee. The group met at the Bombay Art Society premises, which comprised a room in the Jehangir Art Gallery and a larger room on nearby Rampart Row. The first collective exhibition was held in July 1949; in 1952 the group was formally closed down, having served its purpose. However, artists such as GEORGE KEYT, VASU-DEV S. GAITONDE, Ram Kumar (*b* 1924), AKBAR PADAM-SEE, KRISHEN KHANNA and TYEB MEHTA, who had been closely associated with the Progressive Artists Group, subsequently contributed to the flowering of the modern art movement in Bombay.

These artists were first encouraged by European expatriate artists and patrons living in Bombay—such as Emanuel Schlesinger, Rudolph van Leyden and Walter Langhammer—and later by the scientist Homi Bhabha, who founded the Tata Institute of Fundamental Research and who was responsible for creating one of the best collections of modern Indian art. The Tata Trusts also started *Marg* (founded 1946), India's foremost magazine of art, architecture, heritage and culture; its first editor, from 1946 to 1981, was the erudite and innovative author Mulk Raj Anand. The establishment of the Bhulabhai Desai Institute by Soli Batliwala and Madhuri Desai in 1952 was another milestone in the history of the Bombay art movement. The Institute was a unique place where artists, sculptors and musicians could interact creatively and rent studios at a nominal rate. Gaitonde, Husain and the musician Ravi Shankar were all regular attenders at the Institute, which perpetuated the work of the Progressive Artists Group. The Jehangir Art Gallery (opened 1952) was one of the first to provide a venue for art exhibitions. Later, a number of successful private galleries such as the Chemould Gallery (1963), the Pundole Gallery and Framing Centre (late 1950s), the Taj Art Gallery and the Cymroza Art Gallery (1971) made major contributions to the appreciation of art and artists in Bombay, while newer, more innovative art galleries led to a greater awareness of the nuances of contemporary Indian art, for example Gallery 7 (1984), the Designscape Gallery (1985), the Sophia Duchesne Gallery (1986) and the Sakshi Art Gallery (1992). Auctions held by Sotheby's and Christie's in the late 1980s also stimulated art in Bombay by giving artists much-needed publicity. Bombay's pioneering role in the modern art movement was nurtured in the 1990s by a number of very talented and committed artists such as Jehangir Sabavala (b 1922), Akbar Padamsee, Gieve Patel (b 1940), Imtiaz Dharkar (b 1955), NALINI MALANI, Navjot Altaf (b 1949) and B. Prabha (b 1931). Of the original members of the Progressive Artists Group, Raza moved to France and Souza to New York, while Husain remained in Bombay. In keeping with his position as India's foremost artist, Husain extended the frontiers of his own work, while building institutes to display the best of Indian art.

The contribution of Bombay to contemporary Indian sculpture is best seen in the works of Pilloo Pachkhanwalla (1923–86) and B. Vithal (1932–92), who revitalized and reinterpreted the legacy of ancient Indian sculpture. In architecture, the architects and buildings of Bombay have been influenced since 1947 by two major factors—Le Corbusier and commercialism. The influence of Le Corbusier was strongest during the late 1950s and early 1960s, and phenomenally high land values continue to dictate the parameters of the city's architecture. The most important Indian architect of the post-war period, CHARLES CORREA, lived and worked in Bombay, while among younger architects the lively and unorthodox architecture of Hafeez Contractor (b 1950) stood out in the Post-modernist 1990s.

BIBLIOGRAPHY

Contemporary Indian Art from the Collection of Chester and Davida Herwitz (exh. cat. by G. Patel, T. W. Sokolowski and D. A. Herwitz, New York, Grey Gal. & Stud. Cent.; Lewisburg, PA, Bucknell U., Centre A. Gal.; Burlington, U. VT, Robert Hull Fleming Mus.; 1986)
Indian Art Today: Four Artists from the Chester and Davida Herwitz Family Collection (exh. cat. by P. Mitter and D. A. Herwitz, Washington, DC, Phillips Col., 1986)
'Contemporary Art: Syntheses and Polarities', Marg, xxxviii/4 (1987) [whole issue]
M. R. Anand: Amrita Sher-Gil (New Delhi, 1989)

RASHMI PODDAR, ASIT CHANDMAL

Bombelli, Sebastiano (b Udine, bapt 15 Oct 1635; d Venice, 7 May 1719). Italian painter. He was perhaps the most influential Italian portrait painter of the later 17th century. His early style was formed by his father, Valentino Bombelli, a painter in Udine, and his godfather, the Mannerist artist Girolamo Lugaro. In the early 1660s he was in Venice (Boschini; Sansovino), where he responded passionately to the brilliant colour, painterly freedom and naturalism of 16th-century Venetian artists, particularly Veronese, whose works he copied. According to Sandrart, who in 1683 provided the first significant report of Bombelli's earliest activities, the artist was initially known as a history painter in the manner of Veronese, although no such painting by him has been identified.

Bombelli is thought to have studied c. 1663–5 with Guercino in Bologna, where he also saw portrait paintings by Cesare and Benedetto Gennari and Pier Francesco Cittadini. Sandrart wrote that at around this time Bombelli dedicated himself exclusively to portrait painting, and perhaps the earliest work that may be attributed to him is a portrait of Giovanni Bonatti of Ferrara (known through an engraving by Giuseppe Zauli, which may have been painted in Bologna. It was once thought to be by Guercino, and the attribution to Bombelli was made by Baruffaldi in 1834.

In early 1665 Bombelli probably visited Udine and then Florence, where he encountered the work of Giusto Suttermans. He established himself in Venice late in 1665, but during the late 1660s and the 1670s travelled widely, according to Sandrart, working in European courts, including Vienna, Mantua and Parma, and executing commissions from, for example, the Dukes of Lüneburg and Brunswick. No paintings immediately associated with these sojourns are known, although a portrait of the Grand Elector of Brandenburg (d 1688) (ex-Wrocław, N. Mus.) might have been executed during such an excursion.

Around 1669 Bombelli began a series of portraits of his most notable patrons, the brothers Gerolamo Querini (1648–1709) and Polo Querini (1654–1728), which included two half-length depictions (both c. 1669–70), as well as the dazzling full-length representations of Gerolamo Querini, Procurator of Citra (c. 1669; Venice, Fond. Querini-Stampalia) and Polo Querini, Procurator of Ultra (1670; Venice, Fond. Querini-Stampalia; see fig.), both of which demonstrate the refined formula of official portrait painting for which Bombelli became celebrated. The faces are lucidly rendered and the sitters' attitudes commanding yet naturalistic; the gestures are formal, yet humanely disposed, and there is a sudden, theatrical emergence of exquisitely textured garments from the muted background.

Works of the earlier 1670s include the portrait of Isabella del Sera (1671; Florence, Uffizi) and a series of official portraits, in which he achieved a particularly delicate balance between the pictorial assessment of his sitters' temperaments and the rhetorical objectives of the painting: the Censors Carlo Contarini and Lunardo Donà (1673; Venice, Doge's Pal.), Procurator Lunardo Donà (1673; Venice, Lorenzo Donà della Rose priv. col., see Pallucchini, fig. 1041), and the triple portrait showing the Avogadori of the Seminary of Rovigo (c. 1674; Rovigo, Pin. Semin.). Bombelli's earliest known Self-portrait (1675–6; Udine, Mus. Civ.) is remarkable for a new depth of

Sebastiano Bombelli: *Polo Querini, Procurator of Ultra*, oil on canvas, 2.13×1.52 m, 1670 (Venice, Fondazione Querini-Stampalia)

domestic intimacy in portrait painting of this type, while the triple portrait of the *Avogadori Diedo, Donà and Bembo* (*c.* 1677; Venice, Doge's Pal.) is notable for its hint of companionable humour.

In 1682 Bombelli was nominated for office in the Coronello of Venetian artists, and in 1683–4 executed the double portrait of *Avogadori Pietro Garzoni and Francesco Benzon* (Venice, Doge's Pal.). In 1685 and 1686 respectively he painted two more self-portraits (Florence, Uffizi; Udine, Mus. Civ.), and in 1687 and 1689 was registered in the Venetian Fraglia dei Pittori. Paintings assigned to the 1680s include a *Magistrate* (Faenza, Pin. Com.), an unknown *Gentleman* (Vicenza, Bertagnoni priv. col., see Pallucchini, fig. 1045), a *Senator* and a *Magistrate* (both Venice, Fond. Querini-Stampalia).

In 1692 Vittore Ghislandi, known as Fra Galgario, began his 12-year tenure in Bombelli's studio. Around the same year the master began to produce a group of portraits that betray an increasingly acute psychological observation of his subjects; they include *Count Bullo di Chioggia* (1693; San Vito al Tagliamento, Mainardis priv. col., see Pallucchini, fig. 1048) and the unusual depiction in oval format of a *Gentleman Taking a Pinch of Snuff* (early 1690s; ex-John Maxon priv. col., Chicago, see Pallucchini, fig. 1046). The portrait of *Frederick Walter* (1649–1718) (Hillerød, Frederiksborg Slot), among the most interesting of Bombelli's depictions of men-at-arms, has been dated to the period 1670–80, but is more likely to have been executed

during or just after 1692–3, when the sitter was first in Venice, or perhaps during his second journey to the city in 1708–9.

Bombelli was recorded in the Fraglia dei Pittori again in 1700, and in 1705 executed the portrait of *Count Nicolò di Valvasone* (Padua, priv. col., see Pallucchini, fig. 1049). On his admission to the Accademia di S Luca that year he presented the quite remarkable depiction of *Rosalba Carriera* (1705; Rome, Accad. N. S Luca). Many paintings have been attributed to his final period, including that of *Bernardo Frangipane* (1708; Ioannis (Udine), Strassoldo-Frangipane priv. col., see Pallucchini, fig. 1050) and, while numerous pictures produced by him are untraceable, a large number of these were recorded in engravings (see Rizzi, 1964 and 1969).

BIBLIOGRAPHY

DBI

M. Boschini: *La carta del navegar pitoresco* (Venice, 1660), p. 548

F. Sansovino: *Venetia città nobilissima. Descritta in 14 libri . . . con aggiunta di cosi notabili dal 1580 sino al 1663* (ed. G. Martinioni; Venice, 1663), pp. 21–2

J. von Sandrart: *Academia nobilissimae artis pictoriae* (Nuremberg, 1683), p. 400

G. Baruffaldi: *Vite de' pittori e scultori ferraresi* (1834), 2 vols (Ferrara, 1844–6), ii, p. 248

M. del Bianco: *Opere di Sebastiano Bombelli al Museo Civico di Udine* (Udine, 1951)

Mostra del Bombelli e del Carneo (exh. cat., ed. A. Rizzi; Udine, S Francesco, 1964), pp. xlv–lvii

F. Cessi: 'Il ritratto di Rosalba Carriera dipinto da Sebastiano Bombelli per l'Accademia di S Luca', *A. Ven.*, xix (1965), p. 174

Mostra della pittura veneta del seicento in Friuli (exh. cat., ed. A. Rizzi; Udine, S Francesco, 1968), pp. 14–22

A. Rizzi: *Storia dell' arte in Friuli: Il seicento* (Udine, 1969), pp. 72–4

M. Dazzi and E. Merkel: *Catalogo della Pinacoteca della Fondazione Scientifica Querini-Stampalia* (Vicenza, 1979), cat. nos 103–12; pp. 20–21, 70–73

R. Pallucchini: *La pittura veneziana del '600* (Milan, 1981), pp. 305–9

G. Perusini and T. Perusini: 'Un ritratto inedito del Bombelli in Friuli', *Ce fastu?*, ii (1982), pp. 229–35

A. Rizzi: 'Bombelli, Carneo e Carlevarijs: Tre grandi udinesi per la cultura figurativa veneta', *Udine* (1983), pp. 319–23

F. Vizzutti: 'Una proposta bombelliana', *A. Ven.*, xxxix (1985), pp. 156–7

M. Gregori and E. Schleier, eds: *La pittura in Italia: Il seicento*, 2 vols (Milan, 1988, rev. 2/1989), ii, pp. 644–5

□

Bomberault, Benoît (*fl* 1515–28). French sculptor. He was established at Orléans, producing architectural, religious and tomb sculpture that is now destroyed or untraced. Among his works were the carved stone doorway of the chapel at the château of Thouars, Deux-Sèvres (destr.) and a group of three statues (*c.* 1520; destr. 1820) for the chapel of St Saviour at the collegiate church of Cléry-Saint-André, near Orléans. One of his most ambitious works, for which he inherited the contract from Martin Claustre in 1525, was the marble and alabaster tomb of *Guillaume de Montmorency and Anne Pot* (destr. 1808 but known from an engraving of 1624) in the church of St Martin at Montmorency, Val-d'Oise. It followed a common pattern for French tombs in the early 16th century, with a base in the form of a sarcophagus, surrounded by statues of the 12 Apostles in shell-headed niches separated by pilasters in the antique manner. On top of this were the recumbent effigies of the deceased in contemporary dress.

A Mathurin Bomberault, presumably the son of Benoît Bomberault, was active as a sculptor at the château of Oiron, Deux-Sèvres, in the mid-16th century. In 1551 he carved 8 of the 34 marble medallion portraits of Roman emperors that still survive on the courtyard façade of the north wing. It is possible that he was also responsible for the Italianate white marble fountain in the courtyard at Oiron, fragments of which survive in the parish church, incorporated in the font and the lectern.

BIBLIOGRAPHY

Lami

M. Dumolin: *Le Château d'Oiron* (Paris, 1931)
R. Baillargeat: 'Etude critique sur les monuments funéraires élevés par les seigneurs de Montmorency', *Bull. Soc. Hist. A. Fr.* (1952), pp. 102–12

PHILIPPE ROUILLARD

Bomberg, David (*b* Birmingham, 5 Dec 1890; *d* London, 19 Aug 1957). English painter. The fifth child of a Polish immigrant leather worker, he spent his earliest years in Birmingham and then grew up in the Whitechapel area of London. He suffered considerable financial hardship while studying at evening classes given by Walter Bayes (1869–1956) at the City and Guilds Institute from *c.* 1905 to 1908

and by Walter Sickert at Westminster Art School from 1908 to 1910. With the help of John Singer Sargent and the Jewish Education Aid Society, he secured a place at the Slade School of Fine Art, London, in 1911. It was a period of dramatic change, stimulated in part by Roger Fry's two Post-Impressionist exhibitions and the display of Italian Futurist works at the Sackville Gallery, London, in 1912. Bomberg was the most audacious painter of his generation at the Slade, proving in works such as *Vision of Ezekiel* (1912) and *Ju-jitsu* (*c.* 1913; both London, Tate) that he could absorb the most experimental European ideas, fuse these with Jewish influences and come up with a robust alternative of his own. His treatment of the human figure, in terms of angular, clear-cut forms charged with enormous energy, reveals his determination to bring about a drastic renewal in British painting.

The direction taken by his art brought him into contact with Wyndham Lewis and the Vorticists, but Bomberg resisted Lewis's attempts to enlist him as a member of the movement. He refused to let his work be illustrated in *Blast* magazine and appeared only in the 'Invited to show' section of the Vorticist Exhibition held in London in June

David Bomberg: *In the Hold*, oil on canvas, 1.96×2.31 m, 1914 (London, Tate Gallery)

1915. His precocious confidence did not require group solidarity. Bomberg's two great canvases of 1914, *In the Hold* (see fig.) and the *Mud Bath* (both London, Tate), take as their starting-point the East End of London, which Bomberg knew well, but he certainly did not produce documentary images of Whitechapel life. *In the Hold*, based on the subject of men at work on a ship moored at the docks, is dramatically fragmented by a grid that Bomberg has imposed on the figures, ladders and floor-boards. The result is a flickering, darting canvas that conveys through its fractured elements the restless dynamism of the monumental labourers. The *Mud Bath* translates the spectacle of bathers at Schevzik's Vapour Baths, Whitechapel, into a harsh and strident painting. Half-human and half-mechanical, the blue and white figures hurl themselves around the red rectangle of water. The *Mud Bath* celebrates their energy in a taut and bracing manner but also reflects Bomberg's awareness that 'I look upon *Nature* while I live in a *steel city*'. He made that assertion in the foreword to the catalogue of his first one-man show, held in July 1914 at the Chenil Gallery, London, where the *Mud Bath* was displayed outside the building and festooned with Union Jacks. 'I APPEAL to a *Sense of Form*,' Bomberg proclaimed in the same militant statement, insisting: 'My object is the *construction of Pure Form*. I reject everything in painting that is not *Pure Form*.'

The Chenil Gallery exhibition marked the triumph of Bomberg's early career and earned him the admiration of many experimental artists both in London and abroad. The show was reviewed enthusiastically in *The New Age* (9 July 1914) by T. E. Hulme, whose views about machine-age art coincided in many respects with Bomberg's vision of the new century. With the advent of World War I, everything changed dramatically. By November 1915 Bomberg had enlisted in the Royal Engineers, and his harrowing experiences at the Front brought about a profound transformation in his outlook. It can be seen most clearly in the large painting of *Sappers at Work*, which he carried out as a commission for the Canadian Government. The first version (1918–19; London, Tate) retains much of the freedom of colour and structure he had developed in the pre-war period, but it introduces recognizable figures that no longer conform to the mechanistic vision of the *Mud Bath*. When this version was rejected by the Canadian committee, Bomberg painted a far more realistic alternative (1919; Ottawa, N.G.), which introduced an almost photographic style in the treatment of the men working underground.

Bomberg never again returned to this dogged and limiting idiom, but he did explore a radically different path during the 1920s. His disillusion with the destructive power of the machine at war led to a few years spent experimenting with ways of making his stark pre-war style more rounded and organic. He travelled to Jerusalem in 1923 and concentrated on landscape painting. At first his paintings of Palestine were very tight and almost topo-graphical in character. By the time he returned to London in 1927, however, his determination to base his art on first-hand experience of nature had led to a looser and more expressive approach. He developed an outspoken and impassioned language during a visit to Toledo in 1929, where he began to use the loose, gestural brushmark that

characterized his later work. The nature of the landscape itself, his admiration for the work of El Greco and his profound dissatisfaction with the work he had recently produced in Palestine were all contributory factors.

Throughout the 1930s Bomberg's art became broader and more impassioned as he sought to convey the essence of his response to landscapes in Scotland and Spain. At Cuenca and Ronda and in the Asturian mountains, in works such as *Valley of la Hermida: Picos de Europa, Asturias* (1935; Sheffield, Graves A.G.), Bomberg allowed his vigorously handled paint a life of its own—even as he continued to depict the natural world around him. This work met with little approval in Britain, and during World War II his outstanding series of *Bomb Store* paintings did not lead to further commissions from the War Artists Committee, despite his repeated requests. While continuing to suffer from appalling neglect in the post-war years, Bomberg was an influential teacher at the Borough Poly-technic, London. His students included Frank Auerbach and Leon Kossoff. His painting reached a climax at the same time with work done during expeditions to Devon and Cornwall and above all Cyprus (e.g. *Castle Ruins at St Hilarion*, 1948; Liverpool, Walker A.G.), where his search for 'the spirit in the mass' resulted in fiery masterpieces charged with an exhilarating apprehension of the landscape he scrutinized. In 1954 he returned to Ronda with his wife Lilian and attempted to found a school of painting there, but the plan failed. His last years were darkened by the realization that his art remained overlooked and even belittled in Britain. His final landscapes and figure paint-ings, most notably the tragic *Last Self-portrait* (1956; London, C. St John Wilson priv. col., see Cork, pl. c65), include some of his most powerful works.

WRITINGS
'The Bomberg Papers', *X: Q. Rev.*, i/3 (1960), pp. 183–90

BIBLIOGRAPHY
David Bomberg, 1890–1957 (exh. cat. by A. Forge, W. Lipke and D. Sylvester, ACGB, 1967)
W. Lipke: *David Bomberg: A Critical Study of his Life and Work* (London, 1967)
Bomberg: Paintings, Drawings, Watercolours, Lithographs (exh. cat. by J. Drew and D. Sylvester, London, Fischer F.A., 1973)
R. Oxlade: *David Bomberg, 1890–1957*, Royal College of Art Papers, 3 (London, 1977)
David Bomberg: The Later Years (exh. cat. by J. Spurling, London, Whitechapel A.G., 1979)
David Bomberg in Palestine, 1923–1927 (exh. cat. by R. Cork and S. Rachum, Jerusalem, Israel Mus., 1983)
R. Cork: *David Bomberg* (New Haven and London, 1987)
David Bomberg (exh. cat. by R. Cork, London, Tate, 1988)
David Bomberg: Poems and Drawings from the First World War (exh. cat., London, Gillian Jason Gal., 1992)

RICHARD CORK

Bombois, Camille (*b* Vénarey-les-Laumes, Côte d'Or, 3 Feb 1883; *d* Paris, 11 June 1970). French painter. As a child he lived on a barge. After working in various rural trades, he became a fairground wrestler in order to live near Paris, moving there to work as a typographer by night so that he could paint by day. In 1922 he exhibited for the first time at the Foire aux Croûtes in the open air at Montmartre. His work was noticed in 1924 by Wilhelm Uhde, who bought nearly all his production and who exhibited his work in the Galeries des Quatre Chemins in 1927. Bombois's pictures were included in the important exhibition *Les Maîtres populaires de la réalité* (1937) and in 1944 he was given his first one-man show at the Galerie Pétridès; by the 1960s he had an international reputation as a naive artist.

Bombois was a robust Burgundian proud of his athletic prowess, and he expressed his admiration for physical strength in his bold drawing, in his handling of space and in his use of colour. Among his subjects were scenes of fairground life based on personal experience, for example *Arms of Steel* (1920; Paris, Pompidou) and *Before the Entry into the Ring* (c. 1930; New York, MOMA). His still-lifes are violently coloured and concisely painted and simplified in composition, but it was in the carnal energy of his nudes that Bombois excelled, often choosing only a partial view of the body to concentrate the focus of attention and containing its mass within a continuous curve by which the pale pink mounds of smooth flesh stand out against a sombre background.

BIBLIOGRAPHY

Les Maîtres populaires de la réalité (exh. cat., Paris, Salle Royale, 1937)
W. Uhde: *Fünf primitive Meister: Rousseau, Vivin, Bombois, Bauchant, Séraphine* (Zurich, 1947)
Bauchant, Bombois, Séraphine, Vivin (exh. cat., Basle, Ksthalle, 1956)
Bombois: Memorial Exhibition (exh. cat. by K. Perls, New York, Perls Gals, 1972)
Camille Bombois (exh. cat. by D. Vallier, Paris, Gal. Dina Vierny, 1981)
For further bibliography *see* NAIVE ART.

NADINE POUILLON

Bon. *See* BUON (i) and (ii).

Bon, Christof. *See under* CHAMBERLIN, POWELL & BON.

Bonaccorsi, Raimondo. *See* BUONACCORSI, RAIMONDO.

Bonadura [Bandura; Bondura; Bundura; Penadura; Petradura], **Cristoforo** (*b* ?1582; *d* Poznań, between 22 Sept 1667 and 25 Jan 1670). Italian architect, active in Poland. His presence is first recorded *c.* 1622 in Wielkopolska, where he supervised the rebuilding of the Dominican friary in Poznań (partially destr.). He built churches and palaces (the latter destr.), particularly for various members of the landowning Opaliński family. His first important work, the Minorite church in Sieraków (1624–39), owes its cruciform plan and dome to its function as the Opaliński family mausoleum. The articulation of the church develops the post-Renaissance stylistic tradition brought to central Europe by Lombard master masons. Bonadura's most distinguished work, the church in Grodzisk Wielkopolski, is Mannerist in style; it was founded in 1626 by the politician and intellectual Jan Opaliński (*d* 1637), consecrated in 1649 and completed in 1672. The nave is flanked by pairs of domed side chapels, all of equal height, and there is a huge octagonal dome over the chancel. The latter's shape and figured finials have Venetian and Paduan antecedents. The interior is lent additional dynamism by means of giant pilaster-herms set against the piers. These derive from Netherlandish and north German types and frequently recur in Bonadura's works. There is a single west tower. In 1658 Bonadura moved from Grodzisk Wielkopolski to Poznań, where in 1667 he was elected Elder of the Masons' Guild. In his later works, while continuing to use expressive forms typical of Mannerism as regards layout and façade design, he began to imitate early Baroque models. It is difficult to determine the extent of the contribution made to his work by his son Cristoforo Bonadura the younger (*fl* 1662–97) and his partner Giorgio Catenazzi (*fl* 1664; *d* before 1692).

Bonadura's style is characterized by heavy, often excessive and grotesque decoration employing Mannerist forms, occasionally massed together to such an extent that they approach the Baroque; such motifs as deep recesses afford strong chiaroscuro effects to his façades. He is undoubtedly one of the most original among those architects deriving from the guild tradition who were active in Poland in the 17th century, and his work continued to influence local architects as late as the 18th century.

BIBLIOGRAPHY

J. Białostocki: 'Kościół Św. Jadwigi w Grodzisku Wielkopolskim' [The Church of St Jadwiga in Grodzisk Wielkopolski], *Biul. Hist. Sztuki*, xx (1958), pp. 124–5
A. Miłobędzki: *Architektura polska XVII wieku* [17th-century Polish architecture] (Warsaw, 1980), pp. 268–77

ADAM MIŁOBĘDZKI

Bonafous, Louis-Abel. *See* FONTENAI.

Bonaguida, Pacino di. *See* PACINO DI BONAGUIDA.

Bonaiuto, Andrea di. *See* ANDREA DA FIRENZE (i).

Bonamico. *See* BUFFALMACCO.

Bonampak. Site of a MAYA ceremonial centre in the tropical rain-forest of the Chiapas, Mexico, that flourished around the end of the 8th century AD. Bonampak is best known for its colourful and complex wall paintings, which are the most complete indigenous examples in Pre-Columbian Mesoamerica. The paintings, brought to modern attention by Giles Healey in 1946, are preserved *in situ* on the walls of a fragile three-room building known as Structure 1. There are colour copies of the paintings in the Museo Nacional de Antropología, Mexico City. The rest of the site is still largely unexcavated, but several fine sculptures have also been found.

The paintings in Structure 1 were commissioned between AD 790 and 800 to celebrate various events—particularly the selection of a child as heir—in the reign of the last known Bonampak king, Chaan-muan (*reg* AD 775–?792). Bright pigments were applied to damp stucco on walls, vaults, benches and doorjambs by a team of painters following the programme of a single master. Black-and-white pigments were used last, for outlines, highlights and hieroglyphic writing. The positions of such architectural features as benches partly determine the reading order of the scenes. The text and image work together, neither subordinate to the other. In no other work of Maya art do so many individuals appear; they are painted throughout at about two-thirds life-size.

There are three scenes in Room 1, beginning on the upper registers of the east, south and west walls with the presentation of a child by the royal family to a court of nobles. Scholars generally agree that the text records a date for the event in the Maya Long Count system (*see* MESOAMERICA, PRE-COLUMBIAN, §II) corresponding to 14 December 790. The child's name, itself obliterated, is linked to his maternal uncle, king of Yaxchilan. The text then records a second event that took place on 15

November 791. This was a celebration with music, dance and costume and is depicted in the lower register of all four walls. That scene is preceded by the surprisingly intimate painting of lords donning ritual attire on the upper register of the north wall; this—like all the paintings in the same area—would only have been visible to a person seated on the built-in bench. The east wall of Room 1 is lined with paintings of fine-featured musicians playing drums, turtle carapaces, rattles and trumpets, as well as mummers in costumes of aquatic and terrestrial creatures. On the opposite wall, *sahals* (subject governors) are depicted in procession. At the centre of the south wall Chaan-muan, the Bonampak king, dances with two attendants. Although the heir is not depicted in these scenes, the presentation of the child in the upper register is echoed in the lower with the display of young maize by two of the masked performers (*see* COLOUR, colour pl. I, fig. 1).

The scenes on the east, south and west walls of Room 2 depict a battle involving warriors led by Chaan-muan. A boustrophedon reading order is indicated, beginning at the upper left, and the narrative is sequential; some individuals occur twice. The text records a war that was astronomically determined for 2 August 792 by a heliacal rising of Venus, a time chosen by all Mesoamerican peoples for warfare. On the north wall victorious Bonampak lords present and torture captives on stairs under representations of the astronomical signs associated with that particular rising of Venus (see fig.). The figures of naked captives are considered the finest representations of the human form in Maya art.

On the east, south and west walls of Room 3, the paintings show the sacrifice of captives, while Bonampak lords, in elaborate feathered costumes, dance in celebration on the steps of a pyramid. On the north wall is a depiction of nobles performing self-sacrifice and, in the upper east vault, the royal family perforating their tongues with spines. A painting of the little royal heir sitting in a woman's lap brings the narrative back to the point at which it began. (For further discussion of painting at Bonampak *see* MESOAMERICA, PRE-COLUMBIAN, §V.)

The sculptures at Bonampak date mainly to the Late Classic period (*c*. AD 600–*c*. 900). There is, however, an unprovenanced Early Classic-period (*c*. AD 250–*c*. 600) panel (ex-Wray priv. col.) that carries the Bonampak emblem glyph (a type of sign indicating place or lineage). This panel is among the first Maya sculptures to represent two persons facing one another. Three carved stelae, four carved lintels and five miscellaneous sculptures remain at the site. The stelae all date to the reign of Chaan-muan. Stele 1, set on the plaza, depicts the king over a large basal panel of maize gods emerging from the earth, represented as a creature known as the *huitzac* monster. Stele 2 shows the king undergoing a bloodletting ritual in the company of his wife and mother, in commemoration of his accession to office. No other Maya sculpture of the Classic period

Bonampak, wall painting from Structure 1, Room 2, depicting the presentation and torture of captives; copy by Antonio Tejeda from the original of *c*. AD 790–800 (original *in situ*; copy in Mexico City, Museo Nacional de Antropología)

shows a man with two women. On Stele 3 Chaan-muan, dressed in war costume, humbles a captive.

The three doorways of Structure 1 have carved lintels bearing traces of stucco pigments. Each shows a warrior pressing a captive to the ground. Lintel 4 from Structure 6 is an archaistic representation of a king also named Chaan-muan but from a previous era. The positions of the hands on this monument appear typically early, but it must actually be of a later date, judging from the representation of a human bust, unknown in the Early Classic period. Miscellaneous sculptures 1 and 5 are wall panels that each depict an enthroned king at his accession receiving offerings from lesser lords. On Miscellaneous sculpture 2 a deity within a full lunar cartouche holds a rabbit. Sculptures 1, 2 and 5 are all finely incised stones. Miscellaneous sculpture 3 is a roughly carved, life-size representation of a segmented cayman, similar to those found at the neighbouring city of YAXCHILÁN. Miscellaneous sculpture 4, carved in relief, records the death of an early 7th-century king also named Chaan-muan, depicted posthumously in the guise of a god.

BIBLIOGRAPHY
K. Ruppert, J. E. S. Thompson and T. Proskouriakoff: *Bonampak, Chiapas, Mexico* (Washington, DC, 1955)
R. E. W. Adams and R. C. Aldrich: 'A Re-evaluation of the Bonampak Murals: A Preliminary Statement on the Paintings and Texts', *The Third Palenque Round Table*, ii (Austin, 1980), pp. 45–59
P. Mathews: 'Notes on the Dynastic Sequence of Bonampak, Chiapas, Mexico', *The Third Palenque Round Table*, ii (Austin, 1980), pp. 60–73
F. G. Lounsbury: 'Astronomical Knowledge and its Uses at Bonampak, Mexico', *Archaeoastronomy in the New World*, ed. A. F. Aveni (New York, 1982), pp. 143–68
M. E. Miller: *The Murals of Bonampak* (Princeton, 1985)
The Blood of Kings: Dynasty and Ritual in Maya Art (exh. cat. by L. Schele and M. E. Miller, Fort Worth, TX, Kimbell A. Mus., 1986)

MARY ELLEN MILLER

Bonanos, Georgios (*b* Kephallinia, 1863; *d* Athens, 1939–40). Greek sculptor. He studied sculpture in Athens during the late 1870s at the School of Fine Arts and in the workshop of Demetrios Philippotis and then at the Reggio Istituto in Rome. Influenced by the school of Canova, he based his work on Classical Greek principles; throughout his career he copied and restored Classical statues in marble, a medium which he used almost exclusively for his own work. In his sculpture he blended a realist approach with academic classicist forms. His very active Athenian workshop produced funerary monuments and tombstones (e.g. *Sleeping Woman*, 1911; Athens, First Cemetery, S. Stamboltzi tomb), busts, monuments and statues of eminent Greeks (e.g. *Admiral Miaoulis*, 1885–8, erected 1889, Syros Mus.; and *Ioannis Capodistrias*, 1930–33, U. Athens).

BIBLIOGRAPHY
S. Lydakes: *E ellenes glyptes* [The Greek sculptors] (Athens, 1981), pp. 92–100, 401–4
C. Christou and M. Koumvakali-Anastasiadi: *Modern Greek Sculpture, 1800–1940* (Athens, 1982), pp. 62, 184
F. Markatou: *O glyptis Georgios Bonanos (1863–1940): I zoi kai to ergo tou* [The sculptor Georgios Bonanos (1863–1940): his life and work] (Thessaloniki, 1992)

EVITA ARAPOGLOU

Bonanus of Pisa (*fl c.* 1179–86). Italian sculptor. He made three pairs of bronze doors: at Pisa Cathedral for the Porta Regia of the west façade and for the Porta di S

Ranieri of the south transept, and in Sicily, for the west portal of Monreale Cathedral. The latter is signed and dated 1186 (1185, Roman calendar). The doors from the west façade at Pisa were destroyed by fire in 1595, and their subject-matter is unknown; but their inscription, recorded in 1590, names Bonanus as the artist and dates them to 1180 (1179). The transept doors are probably close in date. Vasari also attributed the building of the bell-tower (begun 1173) to Bonanus and Guglielmo, but there is no other evidence to support this.

The extant doors at Pisa (4.70×3.02 m) and Monreale (7.8×3.7 m) are composed of a series of panels cast in high relief and separated by borders of rosettes. Each door has a wide horizontal panel across the top and bottom, framing smaller panels arranged in pairs in the middle registers. In both cases, the iconographic programme covers the theme of salvation: scenes from the life of Christ from the *Annunciation* to the *Ascension* (Pisa ends with the *Death of the Virgin*), read chronologically from left to right and from bottom to top, surmounted by the figures of *Christ and the Virgin Enthroned* in the top horizontal panels. In addition, the larger doors at Monreale have on the lower registers an extensive series of scenes from Genesis, and in the middle registers there are figures of patriarchs and prophets. The figures of 12 prophets separated by palm trees are ranged across the bottom horizontal panels at Pisa, while at Monreale these are filled by lions and griffins. The scenes are identified by inscriptions written in a mixture of Latin and Tuscan vernacular.

The iconography of the individual scenes on both sets of doors is predominantly Byzantine in origin, taken directly from or inspired by objects of eastern Christian manufacture. Close parallels can be seen in other doors and in portable objects such as manuscripts and ivories. At Pisa, in the lower left-hand corner of the panel depicting the *Journey of the Magi*, a small frieze representing the *Expulsion of Adam and Eve from Paradise* is very close both stylistically and iconographically to such examples of this subject in ivory as the 11th- or 12th-century casket in Pesaro (Bib. & Mus. Oliveriani). The source material for the themes Bonanus treats is transformed by the artist's strong sense of plastic form and compositional pattern, producing a style of great clarity and directness, deftly adjusted to the requirements of the narrative. Figures are characteristically in very high relief, with heads and limbs frequently in the round and projecting from the surface. Their posture and gesture are stiffly angular, while draperies are elongated and tubular. These figures are set against wide, often unadorned, stretches of panel. Otherwise, backgrounds are formed by attaching rudimentary landscape elements to horizontal or arched strips of ground. This treatment of form seems to be a direct result of the artist's manipulation of clay and wax and an expression of his working methods; it also clearly reflects many of the formal solutions of such contemporary Tuscan, especially Pisan, stone-carving as the work of Guglielmo and his school.

BIBLIOGRAPHY
G. Vasari: *Vite* (1550, rev. 2/1568); ed. G. Milanesi, i (1878), p. 274
W. Biehl: *Toskanische Plastik des frühen und hohen Mittelalters* (Leipzig, 1926), pp. 55–7
M. Salmi: *La scultura romanica in Toscana* (Florence, 1928), pp. 99–121

V. Martinelli: 'Bonanno Pisano scultore', *Belle A.*, i (1946–8), pp. 272–97

A. Boeckler: *Die Bronzetüren des Bonanus von Pisa und des Barisanus von Trani* (1953), iv of *Die frühmittelalterlichen Bronzetüren*, ed. R. Hamann (Berlin, 1926–53); review by A. Grabar in *Kunstchronik*, vii/1 (1954), pp. 10–20

F. Bartolini: 'La data del portale di Bonanno nel duomo di Monreale', *Studi medievali in onore di Antonio De Stefano* (Palermo, 1956), pp. 39–41

H. M. von Erffa: 'Das Programm der Westportale des Pisaner Domes', *Mitt. Ksthist. Inst. Florenz*, xii (1965–6), pp. 55–106

U. Götz: *Die Bildprogramme der Kirchentüren des 11. und 12. Jahrhunderts* (Bamberg, 1971), pp. 149–59, 160–68

DAVID A. WALSH

Bonaparte [Buonaparte]. French family of rulers, collectors and patrons. The family was descended from Charles-Marie Bonaparte (1746–85), an advocate in Ajaccio, Corsica, who in 1764 married Maria-Letizia Ramolino (1750–1836); her half-brother JOSEPH FESCH, a churchman who rose to be cardinal, was an art lover who built up a magnificent collection. Four years after the Bonapartes' marriage, Corsica was ceded by Genoa to become part of metropolitan France; consequently the second of their eight surviving children, (1) Napoleon Bonaparte, became a military cadet in France. It was he who was the founder of the family's fortunes. His army career developed slowly at first; but once he had achieved command, his astonishing succession of brilliant campaigns (most notably in Italy and Egypt), in the course of which he inflicted defeat on most of the major European powers, gave France the overlordship of a vast proportion of Europe, including Italy, Spain, the Low Countries and parts of Germany. Napoleon became commander of the French army and, by coup d'état in 1799, First Consul, finally crowning himself Emperor of the French (1804–14). The period of his rule saw, and to a considerable extent, fostered, the flowering of Neo-classicism; his patronage, which was primarily intended to serve political ends, extended to most of the visual arts. He was forced to abdicate in 1814 and exiled to Elba, but in 1815 he returned and mounted a short-lived campaign to regain his former greatness (the 'Hundred Days'). He was finally defeated that year at the Battle of Waterloo.

In 1796 Napoleon married (2) Josephine (née Marie-Joseph-Rose Tascher de la Pagerie), widow of General Alexandre de Beauharnais; she shared in her new husband's rise, becoming Empress of the French. As well as being a collector of every sort of art object and setting styles in dress and interior decoration, she extended patronage to numerous contemporary artists.

As master of much of Europe, Napoleon was able to confer kingdoms and principalities on his siblings (see fig.). His elder brother, (3) Joseph Bonaparte, was created King of Naples (1806–8) and of Spain (1808–13). He amassed a large collection of Old Master paintings; following his overthrow in 1813, this was dispersed, through capture or sale. Napoleon's next brother, (4) Lucien Bonaparte, in the course of a political career played an important part in the coup d'état that gave Napoleon supreme power. After the Emperor's fall, Lucien settled in Italy, being made Prince of Canino by the Pope; his magnificent collection, much of it later dispersed through

sale, included both Old Masters and the work of contemporary artists, and he was also a noted collector of antiquities.

The eldest of Napoleon's three sisters, (5) Elisa Bonaparte, was granted numerous dignities, becoming Grand Duchess of Tuscany in 1809. She did much to encourage the productivity of the marble quarries of Carrara, one of her possessions; during her reign in Tuscany, which ended in 1813, she exercised considerable artistic patronage. Of Napoleon's remaining siblings, (6) Louis Bonaparte was created King of Holland in 1806, abdicating in 1810; he was both a patron and a collector but on a modest scale. His wife, Hortense de Beauharnais (1783–1837), the Empress Josephine's daughter, was herself an artist and was distinguished as collector and patron, as well as being the joint inheritor, with her brother EUGÈNE DE BEAUHARNAIS, of their mother's extensive collections. Napoleon's second sister, (7) Pauline Bonaparte, in 1803 married, as her second husband, Prince Camillo Borghese (1755–1832); in 1806 Napoleon made her Duchess of Guastalla. Her beauty was celebrated by many artists, notably Antonio Canova; her taste was reflected also in her patronage of architecture and the decorative arts. Napoleon's third sister, Caroline Bonaparte (1782–1839), married in 1800 General JOACHIM MURAT, who was King of Naples from 1808 to 1815. The youngest of Napoleon's siblings, Jérôme Bonaparte (1784–1860), was created King of Westphalia (1807–13); during the Second Republic he became a Marshal of France in 1850.

In the next generation, Louis-Napoléon Bonaparte, youngest son of Louis and Hortense, became President of the French Republic (1848–52); in 1851 he seized supreme power, and the following year he made himself Emperor as Napoleon III. Not himself a noted collector, he encouraged the patronage of the arts by the state; but the greatest artistic achievement of his reign was the programme of urban development that transformed Paris into the most magnificent of European capitals. Two of his cousins, the children of Jérôme by his second wife, exhibited an active interest in the arts: (9) Princess Mathilde Bonaparte was a collector and the generous patron of numerous artists, as well as an amateur painter in watercolours, and her brother (10) Prince Napoléon Bonaparte established a collection of antiquities and contemporary works, some of which reflected his antiquarian interests. He was one of the authors of the 1855 Exposition Universelle in Paris.

BIBLIOGRAPHY

J. Valynseele: *Le Sang des Bonaparte* (Paris, 1954)

A. Castelot, A. Decaux and G. Koenig: *Le Livre de la famille impériale* (Paris, 1969)

A. Chaffanjon: *Napoléon et l'univers impérial* (Paris, 1969)

B. Chevallier: *La Généalogie des Bonaparte* (Paris, 1986) [folding leaflet pubd by the Musées Nationaux]

(1) Napoleon I, Emperor of the French (*b* Ajaccio, Corsica, 15 Aug 1769; *reg* 1804–14 and 1815; *d* Saint Helena, South Atlantic, 5 May 1821). French monarch and patron. His period in power as First Consul, from 1799, and as Emperor, from 1804, coincided with the zenith of Neo-classicism in Europe. Works of art created in France between 1800 and 1815 are usually classified under the headings CONSULATE STYLE and EMPIRE STYLE.

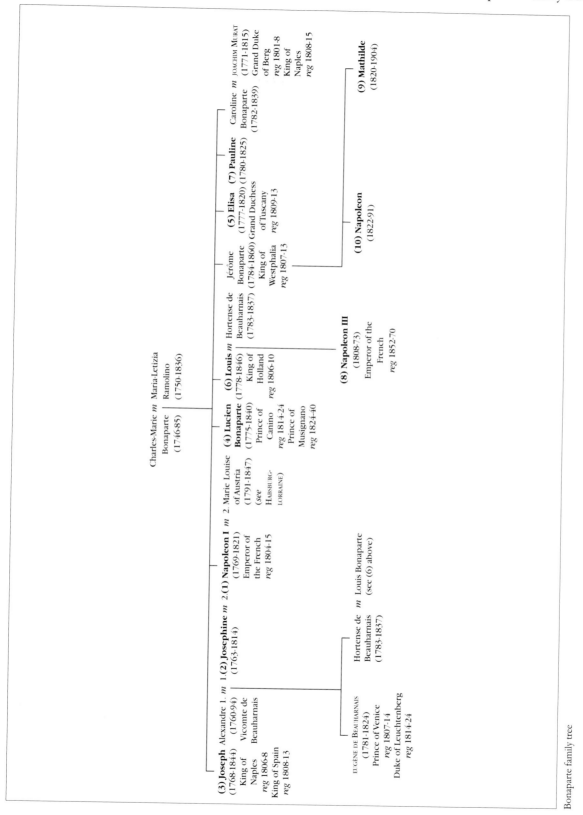

Charles-Marie *m* Maria-Letizia
Bonaparte   Ramolino
(1746-85)   (1750-1836)

(3) Joseph Alexandre 1. *m* 1.**(2) Josephine** 2.**(1) Napoleon I** 2. Marie Louise
(1768-1844) (1760-94)   (1763-1814)   (1769-1821)   of Austria
King of   Vicomte de   Emperor of   (1791-1847)
Naples   Beauharnais   the French   (*see*
reg 1806-8   *reg* 1804-15 HABSBURG-
King of Spain   LORRAINE)
reg 1808-13

EUGÈNE DE BEAUHARNAIS   Hortense de *m* Louis Bonaparte
(1781-1824)   Beauharnais   (see (6) above)
Prince of Venice   (1783-1837)
reg 1807-14
Duke of Leuchtenberg
reg 1814-24

(4) Lucien   **(6) Louis** *m* Hortense de   Jérôme   **(5) Elisa** **(7) Pauline** Caroline *m* JOACHIM MURAT
Bonaparte   (1778-1846)   Beauharnais   Bonaparte   (1777-1820)   (1780-1825)   Bonaparte   (1771-1815)
(1775-1840)   King of   (1783-1837)   (1784-1860) Grand Duchess   (1782-1839) Grand Duke
Prince of   Holland   King of   of Tuscany   of Berg
Canino   *reg* 1806-10   Westphalia   *reg* 1809-13   *reg* 1801-8
reg 1814-24   *reg* 1807-13   King of
Prince of   Naples
Musignano   *reg* 1808-15
reg 1824-40

(8) Napoleon III   **(10) Napoleon**   **(9) Mathilde**
(1808-73)   (1822-91)   (1820-1904)
Emperor of the
French
reg 1852-70

Bonaparte family tree

Although lacking fine discrimination in matters of the visual arts, Napoleon appreciated its propaganda value, and his regime commissioned many works and revived old institutions or established new mechanisms concerned with state patronage.

1. Aims and institutions. 2. Painting. 3. Sculpture. 4. Architecture and urban planning. 5. Decorative arts. 6. International influence.

1. AIMS AND INSTITUTIONS. Napoleon's training had been military, scientific, technical, literary and historical and thus did not incline him towards the visual arts. From the time of his earliest victories in Italy (1796–7) and the Egyptian Expedition (1798), however, his all-embracing curiosity impelled him to preserve ancient monuments, add to public collections, commission new artistic creations, win the loyalty of such renowned artists as Antonio Canova and Jacques-Louis David and leave behind the most flattering portraits of himself. He enjoyed the company of artists, gladly playing host to Vivant Denon, David, Jean-Baptiste Isabey, Antoine-Jean Gros, Canova and the architect Pierre-François-Léonard Fontaine, and listened to their opinions. He paid lengthy visits to official exhibitions and had pictures shown to him; if he called for alterations, the reasons were generally political.

Without imposing an aesthetic code, Napoleon saw himself as a patron, seeking to revive the kingly tradition of large-scale projects and to make Paris the artistic capital of the world. Nor did he neglect the major cities of his vast empire. The instruments he used to implement his policies were education, state commissions, competitions, awards and efficient administration. In 1806 he moved the Académie des Beaux-Arts and the Ecole des Beaux-Arts into new quarters at the Collège des Quatre-Nations in Paris, the same year in which the re-established Académie de France in Rome was moved to the Villa Medici. The latter institution admitted, as well as French students, citizens of the then recently conquered Belgium, Holland and Switzerland. He created academies in Italy and elsewhere and instigated the foundation of galleries in Amsterdam, Milan, Venice and Madrid. In France he continued the efforts begun by the Directory government to fill the newly established provincial museums with representative works of art. He established the Decennial Prizes, which were judged only once, in 1810, but never awarded. Perhaps his greatest institutional creation was the Musée Napoléon, founded in 1803 (largely dispersed 1815) and housed in the Palais du Louvre, to which the artistic plunder of the Netherlands, Italy, Austria and the German states was sent (see FRANCE, §XIV). This remarkable gallery proved highly influential on the rising generation of French artists. In all these endeavours he relied on the guidance of VIVANT DENON, who was appointed Director-general of the Imperial Museums in 1802, and who accompanied Napoleon on his campaigns as artistic adviser.

2. PAINTING. Although Napoleon had firm literary opinions and a love of theatre and music, his poor eyesight was undoubtedly a disadvantage for him in the judgement of art objects, particularly paintings. His guarded judgements were often dictated by Denon. Nevertheless, Napoleon revealed likes and dislikes that, taken as a whole, reflect his individual taste, if not a coherent aesthetic philosophy. For a long time JACQUES-LOUIS DAVID was one of his most favoured painters; yet his disapproval of Neo-classical themes dominated by mythology and allegory made him force David to delete the figure of Victory hovering above the soldiers in the *Distribution of the Eagle Standards* (1810; Versailles, Château), one of a series of monumental paintings commissioned to record the great ceremonial events of the Emperor's reign. More than anything else Napoleon valued truthfulness and accuracy in representing the 'national' subjects that he favoured. In this respect he had a particularly high regard for ANTOINE-JEAN GROS, who managed to combine colour and vigour with precision in his historical scenes from the Napoleonic 'epic'. Napoleon ordered that drawings and sketches made on the battlefield by Denon himself or by such artists as Giuseppe Pietro Bagetti (1764–1831) and Louis-Albert Bacler d'Albe (1761–1824), topographers of the Grande Armée, be handed over to painters. He was fond of the works of Louis-François Lejeune (1775–1848), an officer in the Engineers as well as a painter. Napoleon sometimes rejected commissioned works, judging them inadequate, as in the case of an official portrait that David and his assistants had executed too hastily. As a rule, moreover, he refused to sit for portraits, seeking only to leave behind mementos of a calm hero and a gracious sovereign, whose likeness mattered little. The finest examples of such images are David's *Napoleon Crossing the St Bernard Pass* (1801; Malmaison, Château N.) and Jean-Auguste-Dominique Ingres's hieratic *Napoleon on the Imperial Throne* (1806; Paris, Mus. Armée; see REGALIA, fig. 5).

Napoleon's Romantic literary taste for the *Ossian* poems of James Macpherson led him to commission in 1800 two extraordinary canvases for the salon at the Château de Malmaison: Anne-Louis Girodet's *Apotheosis of the Heroes of France who Died for their Homeland in the War of Liberty*, which shows Ossian welcoming the heroes into Morven, the Warrior's Paradise; and François Gérard's *Ossian Conjures up the Ghosts of his Race on the Banks of the Lora* (both *in situ*). He dismissed domestic genre scenes as unworthy of painting, and he seems to have been uninterested in the facture or colouring of pictures.

It is tempting, where painting is concerned, to criticize Napoleon for intervening too forcefully. Like Louis XIV, he related everything to his own person; but his scorn for images of abstractions hastened the development of Neo-classicism and heralded the birth of Romanticism—indeed, even of Realism. In providing painters with abundant sources of inspiration in the remarkable events of his own career, he helped them break new ground. Through paintings of contemporary history and portraits, they were compelled to revert to nature and real life. David, Pierre-Paul Prud'hon, Ingres, Gérard, Girodet, Gros, Andrea Appiani and Pietro Benvenuti—diverse as their gifts were—all enjoyed the Emperor's favour; and such talented military painters as Lejeune, Bacler d'Albe, Jacques-François Swebach and Bagetti owed their survival to him.

3. SCULPTURE. Napoleon's regime generated a huge number of sculptural commissions. These included portraits of the Emperor and the imperial family and decorations for the numerous new buildings and restorations of

old ones, as well as free-standing monuments. Napoleon, whose preference in sculpture was for the Neo-classical style, planned to offer 20 years' work to sculptors in France and Italy. His sister (5) Elisa Bonaparte, Grand Duchess of Tuscany, was delegated to run the marble quarries at Carrara to produce sculpture, especially portraits of the imperial family, in order to disseminate the Napoleonic image throughout Europe. Even gem-engraving could be used as a vehicle for propaganda (see GEM-ENGRAVING, §I, 12 and fig. 17). With some difficulty, Napoleon insisted that in portraits imperial notables should be shown dressed in contemporary civilian clothes or military uniform, rather than antique costume.

Among French sculptors, Joseph Chinard and François-Joseph Bosio produced notable portraits of members of the imperial family. Jean-Antoine Houdon, the best portrait sculptor of the older generation, modelled a classicizing herm bust of the Emperor (1806; Dijon, Mus. B.-A.), but the widely distributed official sculpted portrait of the Emperor was a modified version of Denis-Antoine Chaudet's bust of *Napoleon as First Consul*. Chaudet was also responsible for the colossal statue (destr.) of *Napoleon* that surmounted the Colonne de la Grande Armée in the

Napoleon I as Mars the Peacemaker by Antonio Canova, marble, h. *c.* 3.50 m, 1803–8 (London, Apsley House)

Place Vendôme, Paris (see CHAUDET, (1)). This monument, with reliefs designed by Pierre-Nolasque Bergeret, was erected to satisfy Napoleon's desire to record his victories in the manner of Trajan's column in Rome. Among the many sculptors who modelled reliefs for it was LORENZO BARTOLINI, who from 1807 directed the Accademia di Carrara and in 1810 began a colossal statue of the Emperor for Livorno (now at Bastia, Corsica). Napoleon's favourite sculptor was, however, ANTONIO CANOVA, among whose many and influential imperial commissions was that for the monumental marble statue of *Napoleon I as Mars the Peacemaker* (1803–8; London, Apsley House; see fig.). This figure, based on Hellenistic and Roman portrayals of rulers as deities, shocked Napoleon by its nudity.

4. ARCHITECTURE AND URBAN PLANNING. Napoleon, who was responsive to ensembles of buildings and massive forms, admired Egyptian architecture, the powerful structures of ancient Rome and the feigned simplicity and grandiose ideas of the architects of his own time; he was thus more at ease with urban planning, public buildings and civil engineering projects than with paintings or sculpture. He followed closely the projects he had commissioned and wanted the monuments that would immortalize his memory in Europe to be at once economical, useful, impressive and sturdy. He appeared as an innovator when he called for iron to be used in building the Pont des Arts and Pont d'Austerlitz in Paris and in the new roofing of the city's Halle au Blé (Corn Exchange) and Temple de la Gloire (church of the Madeleine). His principal architectural adviser was PIERRE-FRANÇOIS-LÉONARD FONTAINE, who, with his partner Charles Percier, was in charge of most of the imperial building projects, eventually being appointed Premier Architecte in 1813.

The Emperor's taste was apparent not only in his up-to-date and pragmatic approach to construction but also in his respect for tradition and the associations of old buildings. When churches or old palaces were due for restoration, additions or alterations, Napoleon ruled that their original design and conception should be respected: this applied in decorating the interior of the Tuileries, completing the Cour Carrée of the Louvre, restoring the châteaux of Saint-Cloud, Fontainebleau, Compiègne and Rambouillet and the Trianons at Versailles, as well as for projects in the conquered territories. Owing to inadequate information, he allowed some famous medieval buildings, such as Cluny and St Martin at Tours, to be destroyed, but whenever he could use old buildings by converting them into prefectures, schools, barracks, galleries or prisons, he did so.

Napoleon advocated long vistas, buildings that were clearly visible, well-planted avenues, monumental ensembles and fountains, as well as general improvements in urban sanitation and modernization in keeping with a classicizing aesthetic. Paris is notably indebted to him for the Arc de Triomphe du Carrousel, the foundations of the Arc de Triomphe de l'Etoile, the portico of the Palais Bourbon (housing the Assemblée Nationale), the Rue de Rivoli and many fountains embellished with statues (see PARIS, §II, 5).

5. DECORATIVE ARTS. The destruction or dispersal during the Revolution of much of the contents of the French royal palaces necessitated a great campaign of refurnishing, which continued throughout the years of the Empire. This, combined with the need to furnish imperial buildings in occupied Europe and to provide expensive diplomatic gifts, brought about a revival in the fortunes of the old royal, now imperial, factories and the workshops of Parisian furniture-makers and goldsmiths, which were flooded with official commissions. The Château de Malmaison, the most complete expression of the CONSULATE STYLE, owed more perhaps to the taste of (2) Empress Josephine than to Napoleon. As Emperor, however, he was aware of the political value of decorative iconography based on a combination of the symbols of the *ancien régime*, of imperial Rome and of his own conquests, in particular Egypt (*see* EGYPTIAN REVIVAL). He also liked accomplished workmanship, costly materials and the sometimes heavy forms of furniture that were hard-wearing enough for constant use. CHARLES PERCIER and Fontaine sought to satisfy these tastes, as they developed the Consulate style into the more grandiose and official EMPIRE STYLE. Napoleon often chose designs and colours himself and took a keen interest in porcelain from Sèvres, carpets and tapestries from the Gobelins and the Savonnerie, as well as silks from Lyon. He kept the plainest and most comfortable furniture for his own use. During his reign gilt-bronze, clocks, watches, jewellery and silverware reached a rare peak of perfection. The Jacob family of cabinetmakers, the clock and watchmaker Abraham-Louis Bréguet (1747–1823), the goldsmiths Henri Auguste and Jean Baptiste Claude Odiot and the supplier of furniture and plate Martin-Guillaume Biennais owed much to Napoleon's discerning commissions.

6. INTERNATIONAL INFLUENCE. As a patron and as the inspiration of a style Napoleon made an impact throughout Europe. In Belgium the palace of Laeken, near Brussels, was restored, with Gilles-Lambert Godecharle sculpting for it numerous statues, busts and reliefs; in Holland Jean-Thomas Thibault (1757–1826) restored the palaces of The Hague and Amsterdam, while François Verly from Lille built the Amsterdam Law Courts. In Germany (among other examples) Joseph Ramée erected the Stock Exchange and a theatre in Hamburg, Eustache de Saint-Far (1746/7–1822) constructed a new theatre and a bridge in Mainz, and Auguste-Henri Grandjean de Montigny completed or altered various official buildings in Kassel for the new King of Westphalia, the Emperor's brother Jérôme Bonaparte. Napoleon's influence reached as far as Russia: from 1809 Percier and Fontaine regularly sent to Alexander I drawings of the improvements being carried out in Paris, and Frenchmen such as the architect Thomas-Jean de Thomon, designer of the St Petersburg Bourse, worked there. Despite the Peninsular War, Spain and Portugal were not exempt from Napoleonic town planning.

It was in Italy, however, where he exercised personal power, that Napoleon was most active; it is there that the art of his reign has left its most conspicuous traces. In Turin ramparts were demolished, and a bridge was built. At Milan the Foro Buonaparte and the Arena, which revived the design of the Circus Maximus in Rome, were built around the Castello Sforzesco. The old city gates—the Porta Marengo and Porta Nuova—were modernized, and work began on the Arco del Sempione at the end of the new road to Simplon. In Venice, Napoleon created the Giardini Pubblici and commissioned the Ala Napoleonica (also known as the Fabbrica Nuova) to be constructed at the western end of the Piazza S Marco, in the style of the neighbouring Procuratie. In Rome the beautiful gardens on the Pincio were laid out by Giuseppe Valadier, while Ingres and Bertel Thorvaldsen helped in redecorating the Palazzo del Quirinale. Through his sister (5) Elisa, Grand Duchess of Tuscany, and his brother (2) Joseph, King of Naples, Napoleon also left his mark on Florence and Naples.

DBF   BIBLIOGRAPHY
G. Lefebvre: *Napoléon* (Paris, 1936)
G. Hubert: *La Sculpture dans l'Italie napoléonienne* (Paris, 1964)
S. Grandjean: *Empire Furniture* (London, 1966)
Napoléon (exh. cat., Paris, Grand Pal., 1969)
R. Huyghe: 'Napoléon et l'art', *Le Grand Livre de Napoléon*, ed. J. Mistler, ii (Paris, 1981)
C.-O. Zieseniss: *Napoléon et les peintres de son temps* (Paris, 1986)

(2) Josephine, Empress of the French [née Tascher de la Pagerie, Marie-Joseph-Rose] (*b* Trois-Ilets, Martinique, 23 June 1763; *d* Malmaison, nr Paris, 29 May 1814). Wife of (1) Napoleon I. She was a member of an aristocratic family originating from the Perche region, which farmed the modest plantation of La Pagerie in Martinique. In December 1779 she married Alexandre de Beauharnais, but although she gave birth to two children, the future Prince Eugène de Beauharnais and Hortense de Beauharnais, who was to marry (6) Louis Bonaparte, the couple separated, Alexandre de Beauharnais considering Josephine to be culturally and intellectually lacking. Both were imprisoned during the French Revolution, and General de Beauharnais was guillotined on 23 July 1794; Josephine was released on 6 August of that year. Penniless and widowed, she secured protection for herself and her two children from Paul, Vicomte de Barras, and other political leaders. On 9 March 1796 she married the young hero of the Italian Campaign, General Napoleon Bonaparte, and with her elegance, charm and connections became 'the matchless Josephine', at last able to gratify her expensive tastes for fashion, jewellery, interior decoration, paintings, antiques, sculpture and collecting. She evinced genuine ability in zoology and botany and managed to keep up a learned correspondence with scientists from France and other countries. Her mansion on the Rue Chantereine, Paris, was converted and furnished by the most progressive interior decorators, as was the Château de Malmaison at Rueil, which she purchased in 1799, the year in which Napoleon became First Consul of the Republic.

In Malmaison, Josephine created a showpiece of CONSULATE STYLE, admired even by travellers from England. She employed young artists, notably the architects PIERRE-FRANÇOIS-LEONARD FONTAINE and CHARLES PERCIER, whose *Recueil de décorations intérieures* (Paris, 1801) includes drawings showing the Council Chamber, the library and the frieze in the Consul's Bedchamber; the dining-room, drawing-room and music-room at Malmaison still bear witness to their talents and to Josephine's taste. She also took personal charge of laying out the grounds, which she treated as a landscape garden, with help from an English gardener called Howatson.

In May 1804 Bonaparte declared himself Emperor of France, and on 2 December 1804 Josephine was anointed by Pius VII and crowned Empress by Napoleon; in 1805 she was granted the title of Queen of Italy. Her apartments in the palaces of the Tuileries, Paris, Saint-Cloud, Fontainebleau, Compiègne and Strasbourg, though sumptuously furnished partly in accordance with her wishes, do not reflect her personality in the way that Malmaison does. There she continued to give her imagination free rein, surrounding herself with such advisers on the collections as Vivant Denon and Alexandre Lenoir and securing the services of the architect Louis-Martin Berthault (1770–1823), the botanists Charles-François Brisseau de Mirbel, Etienne-Pierre Ventenat and Aimé Bonpland, the flower painter Pierre-Joseph Redouté and the watercolourist Auguste Garneray. Redouté provided the drawings for Ventenat's admirable *Le Jardin de la Malmaison* (Paris, 1803–14), for Bonpland's *Description des plantes rares cultivées à Malmaison et à Navarre* (Paris, 1812–17) and for *Les Liliacées* (Paris, 1802–16), all published under Josephine's patronage. She also bought some fine flower paintings from Jean-François van Dael (including the *Tomb of Julie*, 1804; Malmaison, Château N.), Cornelis van Spaendonck (1756–1840) and others. She placed large orders with porcelain factories in Paris, such as those of Dagoty, Dihl and Guérhard, and bought unstintingly from goldsmiths, jewellers and so on, contributing to the success of, among others, the cabinetmaker François-Honoré-Georges Jacob-Desmalter, the goldsmith Jean Baptiste Odiot and the supplier of furniture and plate Martin-Guillaume Biennais.

Josephine was painted by the best portrait painters of the time, and there are many likenesses of her, both private and official. They include François Gérard's *Mme Bonaparte in her Drawing-room at Malmaison* (1801; St Petersburg, Hermitage; another version, Malmaison, Château N.; see fig.), and the *Empress Josephine in Coronation Robes* (Fontainebleau, Château); Pierre-Paul Prud'hon's *Empress Josephine at Malmaison* (1805; Paris, Louvre; unfinished portrait, Malmaison, Château N.); Antoine-Jean Gros's *Empress Josephine at Malmaison* (Nice, Mus. Masséna; sketch, Malmaison, Château N.); miniatures by Jean-Baptiste Isabey (*see* ISABEY, (1)), Daniel Saint (1778–1847), Louis-Bertin Parant (1768–1851) and Pierre-Louis Bouvier (1766–1836); and sculptures by Denis-Antoine Chaudet, Joseph Chinard (marble, 1805; Malmaison, Château N.), Jean-Antoine Houdon and François-Joseph Bosio (plaster, *c.* 1809; Malmaison, Château N.).

Josephine patronized many contemporary artists, particularly the exponents of the TROUBADOUR STYLE and painters taking as their subject light-hearted historical anecdotes, such as Pierre-Nolasque Bergeret, Marie-Philippe Coupin de la Couperie (1773–1851), Fleury Richard, Jean-Antoine Laurent, Alexandre-Millin Duperreux (1764–1843), Auguste Forbin, François-Marius Granet, Hippolyte Lecomte, Henriette Lorimier (*fl* 1800–14), Jeanne-Elisabeth Chaudet, Lancelot-Théodore Turpin de Crissé and Jean-Baptiste Vermay (*d* 1833). Such patronage

Mme Bonaparte in her Drawing-room at Malmaison (fragment) by François Gérard, oil on canvas, 1.73×1.66 m, *c.* 1800 (Malmaison, Musée de Malmaison)

was to encourage the development of ROMANTICISM in France. She was also a collector of contemporary Neoclassical sculpture, her taste tending towards the more graceful and refined works of such sculptors as Antonio Canova, Chaudet, Pierre Cartellier and Bosio. Among the pieces in Josephine's gallery at Malmaison were Canova's *Dancer with her Hands on her Hips* (marble, 1805–12) and *Paris* (marble, 1807–10; both St Petersburg, Hermitage). Her sculpture collection also included works by earlier French masters working in the classical tradition, among them a terracotta version (untraced) of Germain Pilon's *St Francis Receiving the Stigmata* (marble version, Paris, St Jean-St François); François Anguier's bas-relief of the *Deposition* (gilt-bronze, 1637; Rueil, St Pierre-St Paul); François Girardon's *Sorrow* (marble, *c.* 1672–5; New York, Met.); Jean-Baptiste Pigalle's *Flora, or a Nymph Removing a Thorn from her Foot* (marble, Paris, Mus. Jacquemart-André); Louis-Claude Vassé's *Cupid Playing with Venus's Doves* (marble, 1785; Paris, Louvre); and Jean-Pierre-Antoine Tassaert's *Cupid Preparing to Shoot an Arrow* (marble, Malmaison, Château N.). She also had an important collection of Greek and Etruscan vases and of antique bronzes.

In 1807 Josephine added to other works bought or otherwise acquired in Italy a collection of 36 paintings seized from William I, Elector of Hesse-Kassel; to house this collection, Berthault hastily constructed at Malmaison a large gallery, over 20 m in length and lit from above. The catalogue for the gallery for 1811 lists 252 pictures; some of the attributions appear questionable, but the canvases that have been traced are often of the finest quality, including paintings of the *Deposition* by Rembrandt and Rubens, Paulus Potter's *Farm near Amsterdam*, Claude

Lorrain's *The Hours* (all St Petersburg, Hermitage) and works by or attributed to Gerrit Dou, Gabriel Metsu, Philips Wouwerman, Anthony van Dyck and Salomon van Ruysdael; also Poussin, Giovanni Bellini and Correggio, Raphael and Leonardo, Titian and Veronese, the Carracci and a few Spanish painters. The last inventory for the gallery, drawn up in 1814, lists 345 paintings.

Josephine was unable to give Napoleon an heir, and on 15 December 1809 the couple were divorced. Josephine kept the titles of Queen and Empress, but in order to assuage the jealousy of the new empress, Archduchess Marie-Louise of Austria, she was obliged to retire to Malmaison, or the Château de Navarre, near Evreux; or else to travel, in Switzerland, Savoy and Italy. The Consular (later Imperial) Bedchamber at Malmaison was redecorated in red and gold, bearing witness to a change of style. Josephine continued to acquire châteaux—Bois-Préau and Lachaussée near Malmaison and Prégny, near Geneva—to house her new collections; she did not, however, survive Napoleon's first abdication. After her death her collections were divided between her children, Prince Eugène inheriting the Château de Malmaison. Several paintings and statues are now in the Napoleonmuseum in Arenenberg, Switzerland, and the Hermitage, St Petersburg, a number of important works having been acquired in 1814 by Alexander I of Russia.

BIBLIOGRAPHY

DBF
Apollo, cvi/1 (1977), pp. 2–59 [issue ded. to Josephine]
G. Hubert: *Malmaison* (Paris, 1980)

GÉRARD HUBERT

(3) Joseph, King of Naples and Spain (*b* Corte, Corsica, 7 Jan 1768; *d* Florence, 28 July 1844). Brother of (1) Napoleon I. He formed his first art collection as King of Naples from March 1806. It included a *Venus of Urbino* attributed to Titian (untraced). He was proclaimed King of Spain in 1808; during his short reign he gave away a number of works from the Spanish royal collections, among them Murillo's *Marriage of the Virgin* (London, Wallace). In 1813 he was defeated at the Battle of Vitoria by Arthur Wellesley, 1st Duke of Wellington, who captured a number of his baggage wagons loaded with pictures. These included such masterpieces as Correggio's *Agony in the Garden* and Velázquez's *Waterseller of Seville*; they entered Wellington's collection and are now at Apsley House, London. After the final defeat of Napoleon in 1815 Joseph fled to the USA. He took with him nearly 200 paintings, which were to enhance his property at Point Breeze on the Delaware. To provide an income, he gradually sold off the collection in New York—for instance Titian's *Tarquin and Lucretia* (Cambridge, Fitzwilliam) and a Murillo *Virgin* (Houston, TX, Mus. F.A.)—and in London, where he stayed in 1832 and 1835. He also sold some ten works to Alexander Baring, 1st Baron Ashburton, including a Titian *Mary Magdalene* (destr. 1873), Rubens's *Diana the Huntress* (ex-Smith priv. col., London) and a *Boar Hunt*, attributed to Velázquez (Madrid, Prado). On returning to Europe in 1839 Joseph brought back the principal works remaining in his collection. Having become heir to his uncle Cardinal JOSEPH FESCH, who died in that year, he negotiated the bequest of part of the Fesch collection to the town of Ajaccio, Corsica. Some 60

paintings still at Point Breeze at Joseph's death were sold there in August 1845.

BIBLIOGRAPHY

DBF
G. Bertin: *Joseph Bonaparte en Amérique* (Paris, 1893) [with inventories of the col. taken to USA]
G. Girod de l'Ain: *Joseph Bonaparte* (Paris, 1970)

GUY COUPET

(4) Lucien Bonaparte, 1st Prince of Canino (*b* Ajaccio, Corsica, 21 May 1775; *d* Viterbo, 29 June 1840). Brother of (1) Napoleon I. In April 1798 he was made a member of the Council of Five Hundred and played a decisive role in Napoleon's coup d'état of 18 Brumaire (9 November) 1799. In December 1799 he was appointed Minister of the Interior and of the Arts, and in November 1800 ambassador to Madrid. His second marriage, of which his brother disapproved, created a rift between them and prompted Lucien's departure for Rome. In 1810 he set off with all his family for the USA but was captured at sea by the English and spent four years as a prisoner in England. On his return, Pope Pius VII created Lucien's estate at Canino a principality. Reconciled with his brother, Lucien was in Paris during the Hundred Days (1815), but after Napoleon's final defeat he spent the rest of his life in retirement in Italy, devoting his time to literary and artistic projects.

Lucien's collection of paintings, both Old Masters and modern pictures, was one of the most famous formed in the early years of the 19th century. Among his works by contemporary artists was the *Repentance of St Mary the Egyptian in the Desert* (Norfolk, VA, Chrysler Mus.), commissioned from Jean-Baptiste Greuze, Jacques-Louis David's *Belisarius Begging Alms*, and the *Return of Marcus Sextus* by Pierre Guérin (Paris, Louvre). Unlike his uncle Cardinal Joseph Fesch, whom he accused of 'picture mania', Lucien limited the number of paintings in his collection and chose them with care, acting on professional advice: he took with him to Spain, for instance, the painters Guillaume Lethière and Jacques Sablet. Among the paintings formerly in his collection are Velázquez's *Lady with a Fan* (London, Wallace), Titian's *Allegory of Prudence*, Lorenzo Lotto's *Family Group*, Gerrit van Honthorst's *Christ before the High Priest* and Aert van der Neer's *Evening View near a Village with a Man and a Milkmaid* (all London, N.G.), as well as Bronzino's *Portrait of a Young Man* (New York, Met.), then thought to be by Sebastiano del Piombo, and Bernardino Luini's *Mary Magdalene* (Washington, DC, N.G.A.), formerly attributed to Leonardo da Vinci.

In 1815 a part of the collection of pictures was brought to England and offered for sale privately in London by the dealer William Buchanan. The following year, a continuing need for funds forced Lucien to put these pictures up for sale by public auction at Stanley's (14–16 May). Apart from paintings, he also formed a notable collection of antiquities, certain parts of which were published as *Le Museum étrusque* (Viterbo, 1829).

BIBLIOGRAPHY

DBF
Abate Guattini: *Galeria del Senatore Luciano Bonaparte* (Rome, 1808)
Choix de gravures d'après les peintures de la galerie de Lucien Bonaparte (Paris, 1812)
W. Buchanan: *Memoirs of Painting*, ii (London, 1824), pp. 269–94

T. Iung: *Lucien Bonaparte et ses mémoires* (Paris, 1882)
F. Pietri: *Lucien Bonaparte* (Paris, 1939)

BEATRICE EDELEIN-BADIE

(5) Elisa [Maria-Anna], Grand Duchess of Tuscany (*b* Ajaccio, Corsica, 3 Jan 1777; *d* Trieste, 7 Aug 1820). Sister of (1) Napoleon I. She was educated at Saint-Cyr and in 1797 married a Corsican officer, Félix-Pascal Baciocchi (1772–1841). Later she held an artistic and literary salon in Paris, first with her brother (4) Lucien Bonaparte, then at her own residence in the Rue de la Chaise. She was less interested in the arts for their own sake than in the possibility of influencing artists.

In March 1805 Napoleon gave her the principality of Lucca, and in the following year he added Carrara, with its marble quarries. Elisa expanded and modernized these, founding an academy of design, a school for sculptors and the Banco Elisiano, which was meant to finance the whole development. Her intention was that these establishments should increase the output of portrait busts of the Bonaparte family, with which to flood Europe. In 1807 she appointed LORENZO BARTOLINI as director of the sculpture school. He was also given responsibility for preparing models for production in the sculpture workshops. The French painter Jean-Baptiste Desmarais (1756–1813), a former Prix de Rome winner, directed the academy of design. Carrara so increased its output that Napoleon contemplated annexing the quarries to his empire. This form of patronage was perfectly suited to Elisa's organizational skill, with its tinge of propaganda.

In 1809 Elisa became Grand Duchess of Tuscany. Fully aware of being a successor to the Medici, she sought to restore the former glory of Florence. She furthered its cultural life by supporting a circle of local artists that included the gem engraver Giovanni Antonio Santarelli, from whom she commissioned many cameos, and Bartolini, who executed a marble group of her with her daughter Napoléone (completed 1813; Fontainebleau, Château) and a marble nude statue of *Napoléone* (Rennes, Mus. B.-A. & Archéol.). She also attracted to her court foreign painters, such as the Frenchman Joseph Franque (1774–1833) and the Genevan enamel painter Salomon-Guillaume Counis (1785–1859). The well-known Tuscan painter Pietro Benvenuti executed a portrait of her (Fontainebleau, Château) and, more notably, a large picture of *Elisa among the Artists* (Versailles, Château). More than a group portrait, this is an allegory of patronage as the Grand Duchess understood it—with herself as its centre and raison d'être. She was to be both the driving force of Florence's artistic life and its subject. When Antonio Canova visited the city, she commissioned a portrait bust and also a statue of herself with the idealized features of Polyhymnia (marble, 1812–17; Vienna, Hofburg-Schauräume). She also shielded from Napoleon a small opposition group centred on the painter François-Xavier Fabre, who had made Tuscany his home since the French Revolution. Most of the works commissioned by Elisa were portraits, for she had a highly reductive view of art as merely a medium for conveying absolutist or dynastic propaganda. She cared more for orthodoxy than for creativity and thus favoured institutions, such as the

Florentine Accademia degli Belli Arte, above individuals, as another means of governing.

In 1814, aware of Napoleon's precarious position, she cleared the Palazzo Pitti in Florence, her main residence, of her paintings, together with some mosaics and sculptures. After being held captive in Austria, she settled in Trieste. She maintained around her a small court that included the painter Louis Dupré (1789–1837), who depicted her entourage. Elisa herself took up watercolour painting, as witness her album (Paris, Mus. Marmottan). She became interested in archaeology, embarking on excavations in Apulia, where she contracted the fever that killed her.

BIBLIOGRAPHY

DBF
P. Marmottan: *Les Arts en Toscane sous Napoléon: La Princesse Elisa* (Paris, 1901)
Actes du colloque Florence et la France: Rapports sous la Révolution et l'Empire: Florence, 1977

(6) Louis, King of Holland (*b* Ajaccio, Corsica, 2 Sept 1778; *reg* 1806–10; *d* Livorno, 25 Sept 1846). Brother of (1) Napoleon I. In 1804 he was made a Prince of France and High Constable. Two years later he was appointed King of Holland, but poor health and disagreements with Napoleon led him to abdicate in 1810. Although not himself much drawn to collecting he endeavoured to act as a public patron, sending several of his subjects to study in Paris, as pupils of Jacques-Louis David, or in Rome. In 1807 he created a general directorate for the arts in the Netherlands. He also ordered the reorganization of the national museum in Amsterdam, which was renamed the Koninklijk Museum (now Rijksmuseum), stipulating that one room was to be reserved for living masters; a cabinet for safekeeping was to be established for the prize paintings of his *pensionnaires* from Paris and Rome; an exhibition of the work of living masters was to be held every year; a collection of plaster casts was to be assembled and a drawing school started. The museum's collections were moved on his orders to the Royal Palace and considerably enriched by purchases he made possible. He also instituted exhibitions of Living Masters, held in different major cities in turn, and established bursaries for artists.

While exiled in Germany and after 1815 in Italy, he collected a few paintings, including a *Landscape with Riders* by Jan Frans van Bloemen (untraced), an Adriaen van der Werff *Landscape with Venus* (ex-La Roche priv. col., Vienna) and François-Marius Granet's the *Choir of the Capuchin Church in Rome* (1815, New York, Met.). The latter was a gift from his sister Caroline Murat, Queen of Naples (*see under* MURAT, JOACHIM). In 1802 Louis had married Hortense de Beauharnais (*b* Paris, 10 April 1783; *d* Arenenberg, 5 Oct 1837), daughter by her first marriage of (2) the Empress Josephine. Queen Hortense was an amateur painter and watercolourist and patronized artists, especially those painting in the Troubadour style. An inventory of her collection (Paris, Bib. Thiers, MS. carton 64) includes works by Louis Ducis, Jean-Antoine Laurent and Fleury Richard. Some works of this kind are still at Schloss Arenenberg, near Lake Constance in Switzerland, where she lived from 1817. Among them are Ducis's *Story of Tasso* and Fleury Richard's *Francis I* and *Mlle de la Vallière as a Carmelite Nun*. She inherited part of her mother's collection.

DBF   BIBLIOGRAPHY
D. Labarre de Raillecourt: *Louis Bonaparte* (Paris, 1963)
F. de Bernardy: *La Reine Hortense* (Paris, 1968)
M.-C. Chaudonneret: *La Peinture troubadour* (Paris, 1980)
                                        GUY COUPET

(7) Pauline [Maria-Paoletta], Princess Borghese (*b* Ajaccio, Corsica, 29 Oct 1780; *d* Florence, 9 June 1825). Sister of (1) Napoleon I. She was a famous beauty and in 1797 married Victor Leclerc, one of Napoleon's most important generals. Leclerc died of yellow fever in 1802; the following year Pauline married Prince Camillo Borghese (1775–1832), inheritor of one of the most celebrated art collections in Italy. The marriage was not a success, and Pauline left Rome and returned to Paris in 1804. As the Emperor's sister, she had her own court at the château of St Cloud. With her considerable personal wealth she was also able to purchase the delightful early 18th-century Hôtel de Charost in Paris.

Pauline was a person of great taste, who participated in the development of the distinctive Empire style. For the Hôtel de Charost she employed the eminent architects Charles Percier and Pierre-François Fontaine and the furniture-maker François-Honoré-Georges Jacob-Desmalter. Even though she had a strong aversion to her sister-in-law (2) the Empress Josephine, Pauline copied her innovative dress in the troubadour style: the cult of historical romanticism can be seen in the superb portraits of Pauline painted by Robert Lefèvre (e.g. London, Apsley House). However, the commission for which she is best remembered is that which she gave to the Neo-classical sculptor Antonio Canova, whom she had known in Rome. Pauline summoned him to Paris to make a life-size marble portrait of her. The result was *Pauline Borghese Bonaparte as Venus Victorious* (1804–8; Rome, Gal. Borghese). It was her wish to be portrayed as Venus lightly clad in classical drapery and reclining on a couch. Even though it was in the prevailing Neo-classical style, the statue was nonetheless considered shocking, not least by Prince Borghese.

DBF   BIBLIOGRAPHY
B. Nabonne: *Pauline Bonaparte: La Vénus impériale, 1780–1825* (Paris, 1963)
P. Dixon: *Pauline: Napoleon's Favourite Sister* (London, 1964)
S. Grandjean: *Empire Furniture, 1800–1825* (London, 1966)
Le Style troubadour (exh. cat., Bourg-en-Bresse, Mus. Ain, 1971)
A. Spinosa: *Pauline Borghese née Bonaparte* (Paris, 1983)
A. Mackrell: *Dress in le style troubadour, 1774–1814* (diss., U. London, 1987)
                                    ALICE MACKRELL

(8) Napoleon III, Emperor of the French [Louis-Napoléon Bonaparte] (*b* Paris, 20 April 1808; *reg* 1852–70; *d* Chislehurst, Kent, 9 Jan 1873). Son of (6) Louis, King of Holland. He showed no marked personal interest in the arts, being more interested in the causes of social progress and industrial development, as is shown by his support for the French participants at the 1851 Great Exhibition in London. Nevertheless, he deemed patronage of the arts to be a duty, and during his period as President of the Republic (Dec 1848–52) a state policy for the arts was set up under the supervision of the Comte de NIEUWERKERKE, Directeur-Général des Musées from 1849. With the establishment of the Second Empire in 1852 the Emperor was able to combine his interest in progress with patronage of the arts, by inaugurating, under the supervision of GEORGES-EUGÈNE HAUSSMANN, a series of grandiose plans for the urban development of Paris, the completion of the Palais du Louvre and the rebuilding of the Opéra. By the end of the 1860s Paris was the most modern and elegant capital in Europe (*see* PARIS, §II, 5). Two of the principal residences of the Imperial Court, the Tuileries in Paris and the château of Compiègne, Oise, were the settings for lavish festivities.

Under the Second Empire the government nominated half the members of the jury of the annual Salon and awarded medals to the exhibitors. Napoleon III encouraged his arts ministry to buy works at the Salon, and to commission paintings and sculpture, without himself interfering in the decision-making. In 1855, on the initiative of the Empress Eugénie (1826–1920), artists were allowed to have retrospective exhibitions at the Exposition Universelle. Numerous paintings, many of them copies of works in the Louvre, were ordered for the decoration of the country's churches. In 1856 the idea of a museum to celebrate the great civil and military events of the Empire was conceived. Some of the paintings planned for the museum were carried out, among them, the *Installation of the Great State Institutions* by Charles-Louis Muller (1815–92), the *Taking of Malakoff* by Adolphe Yvon, the *Congress of Paris* by Edouard Dubufe and the *Completion of the Louvre* by Ange Tissier (1814–76) (all Versailles, Château). In 1863 the Emperor personally intervened in the increasingly affairs of the Salon, when he liberally allowed the Salon des Refusés (for those whose work was excluded from the official Salon) to be held (*see* PARIS, §VI, 3). It was there that Edouard Manet exhibited his scandalous *Déjeuner sur l'herbe* (Paris, Mus. d'Orsay). At this time the Emperor also encouraged moves by Nieuwerkerke, Prosper Mérimée (1803–70) and Viollet-le-Duc to reform the teaching of art (*see* FRANCE, §XV).

Although the Imperial Court employed official artists, such as the portrait painter Franz Xaver Winterhalter and the sculptor Jean-Baptiste Carpeaux (numerous examples of official works can be seen at the château of Compiègne), and although the variety of works acquired by the Ministère des Beaux-Arts is evidence of the Emperor's wish to help struggling artists, the rather modest personal acquisitions of the Emperor and Empress show that their intention was not to collect but simply to decorate their palaces. An idea of their taste can be derived from the catalogue of the sale held after Eugénie's death (London, Christie's, 1 July 1927). This includes *Evening Party at the Tuileries* by Pierre Henri Tétar van Elven (1831–1908) (Paris, Carnavalet), two views of the *Château of Pierrefonds* by Paul Huet, the *Emperor's Horse* by Alfred Dedreux, bouquets of flowers by Marie-Octavie Sturel-Paignée (1819–54) (all Compiègne, Château), and a few Old Masters by Jacob van Ruisdael, Philips Wouwerman, Canaletto and Francesco Guardi. Some of the pictures owned by the Empress, for example Winterhalter's portrait of *Empress Eugénie in 18th-century Costume* (New York, Met.), reveal her attachment to the memory of Queen Marie-Antoinette. This partiality explains her liking for the Louis XVI style and led her to acquire objects that had belonged to the Queen. These were exhibited at the Petit Trianon, Versailles, during the Exposition Universelle of 1867.

Napoleon III's most important action in the realm of the arts was to encourage the expansion of the national collections. In 1852 he created the Musée des Souverains at the Louvre, bringing together objects from the reign of Childeric to that of Louis-Philippe (it was disbanded by the Third Republic in 1872). The major artistic event of his reign was the purchase in 1861 of the huge collection of antiquities and early Italian paintings belonging to the Marchese GIAMPIETRO CAMPANA. The following year the collection was exhibited at the Palais de l'Industrie on the Champs Elysées under the name of the Musée Napoleon III. The paintings were subsequently divided between the Louvre (e.g. Paolo Uccello's *Rout of S Romano* and Lorenzo di Credi's *Annunciation*, originally attributed to Leonardo) and various provincial museums (since 1976 the latter group has been reunited at the Musée du Petit Palais in Avignon). The antiquities were housed together to make the Musée Campana, opened in the Louvre on 15 August 1863. The Emperor's interest in archaeology led him to encourage excavations to find the site of the battle of Alesia, Côte d'Or, and to the foundation of a small Gallo-Roman museum at Compiègne in 1862. Pieces from that museum found at Champlieu and other areas near Compiègne were later added to the Musée des Antiquités Nationales at Saint-Germain-en-Laye, also created in 1862. In 1863 the Empress created a Chinese museum at the château of Fontainebleau with objects brought back from the sacking of the Summer Palace in Peking, and with gifts

from the ambassadors of Siam. In 1867 the Emperor's notable collection of arms and armour was transferred from the Tuileries to the château of Pierrefonds, near Compiègne. After the fall of the Empire these last two collections became the property of the state: the weapons are now in the Musée de l'Armée, Paris, and the Musée Chinois remains at Fontainebleau. The dynastic ambitions of Napoleon III and some of the characteristic opulence of the SECOND EMPIRE STYLE are well represented in Claudius Popelin's enamel portrait of the Emperor (Paris, Mus. Frédéric Masson, on dep., Paris, Mus. d'Orsay; see fig.).

DBF

BIBLIOGRAPHY

Rapport de M. le comte de Nieuwerkerke sur la situation des musées impériaux pendant le règne de S. M. Napoléon III (1853–1860) (Paris, 1869)
E. Viollet-le-Duc: *Exposé des faits relatifs à la transaction passée entre le gouvernement français et l'ancienne liste civile. Musée des armes et Musée chinois* (Paris, [1874])
Marquis de Belleval: 'Napoléon III collectionneur', *Souvenirs de ma jeunesse* (Paris, 1895), pp. 269–92
S. Reinach: *Esquisse d'une histoire de la Collection Campana* (Paris, 1905)
P. Angrand: 'L'Etat mécène: Période autoritaire du Second Empire (1851–1860)', *Gaz. B.-A.*, n. s. 5, lxxi (1968), pp. 303–48
The Second Empire: Art in France under Napoleon III (exh. cat., Philadelphia, PA, Mus. A.; Paris, Grand Pal.; 1978–9)
J. F. McMillan: *Napoleon III* (Harlow, 1991)

(9) Princess **Mathilde** (*b* Trieste, 27 May 1820; *d* Paris, 2 Jan 1904). Niece of (1) Napoleon I. She spent the years 1823–31 in Rome, where her father Jérôme Bonaparte, the former king of Westphalia, lived in exile. Her first feelings for art were stimulated by the collection of paintings owned by her great-uncle Cardinal Joseph Fesch. In Florence, where her parents moved subsequently, she trained herself to draw by copying works at the Galleria degli Uffizi. In 1841 she married the rich Russian collector Anatole Demidov, Prince of San Donato. The marriage was a failure, and Mathilde moved to Paris, where she formed a relationship with the Comte de Nieuwerkerke, an amateur sculptor who became a museum official, and, in 1863, Surintendant des Beaux-Arts. Her first cousin, (8) Napoleon III, put at her disposal a town house at 24 Rue de Courcelles (destr.), where she lived from 1852 to 1870; after the fall of the Second Empire she moved to 20 Rue de Berri. She also owned a property at Saint-Gratien in the Val d'Oise, on the outskirts of Paris. In each of her homes she received many of the leading literary and artistic personalities of the day: the writers Charles-Augustin Sainte-Beuve, Gustave Flaubert, Théophile Gautier and in particular Edmond de Goncourt and Jules de Goncourt, were regular visitors, as were the sculptors Jean-Auguste Barre and Jean-Baptiste Carpeaux; the painters Eugène Giraud (1806–81) and Charles Giraud (1819–92), Ernest Hébert, Eugène-Emmanuel Amaury-Duval, Paul Baudry; and Auguste-Paul-Charles Anastasi (1820–89). The enamel painter Claudius-Marcel Popelin lived with her, taking the place of the unfaithful Nieuwerkerke.

Princess Mathilde surrounded herself with works of art and in 1867 had a gallery built at her Rue de Courcelles house, where she hung her 35 most beautiful Old Master paintings of the Flemish, French and Italian schools of the 17th and 18th centuries. Among them were the portrait of *Margareta de Vos*, attributed to Anthony van Dyck (Boston, MA, Mus. F.A.); Jean-Baptiste Perronneau's

Napoleon III by Claudius Popelin, enamel plaque in an ebonized wood frame with additional enamel portraits of *Charlemagne, Napoleon I, Clovis* and *Hugh Capet*, 950×743 mm, 1865 (Paris, Musée Frédéric Masson, on dep. Musée d'Orsay, Paris)

portrait of *Laurent Cars* (Ann Arbor, U. MI Mus. A.); the *White Coif* by Nicolas-Bernard Lépicié (Paris, Mus. Cognacq-Jay); *Piazza S Marco* by Francesco Guardi (Richmond, VA Mus. F.A.); the *Banquet of Cleopatra* by Giambattista Tiepolo (Paris, Mus. Cognacq-Jay); and the *Tooth-puller* and the *Minuet* by Giandomenico Tiepolo (Paris, Louvre). In conjunction with these, she assembled modern paintings bought either at the annual Salon or direct from artists; genre scenes and figure studies dominated this collection. Princess Mathilde prided herself on having recognized a number of future masters early in their careers, such as Léon Bonnat, Ferdinand Roybet, Gustave-Jean Jacquet (1846–1909) and Edouard Detaille. This moral and material encouragement became on occasions virtual charity, and earned her the nickname of 'Our Lady of the Arts'. However, the only one of her modern pictures that has been traced is *Retreat in the Tuileries Gardens* by James Tissot (Besançon, priv. col.).

Mathilde was herself a painter: in her studio in Paris, which was depicted by Charles Giraud (Compiègne, Château), and in that at Saint-Gratien she worked on watercolour portraits (e.g. *Comte de Nieuwerkerke*; Compiègne, Château) and genre figures (e.g. *Bust of a Young Girl*; Bayonne, Mus. Bonnat). From 1859 to 1867 she exhibited at the Salon as a pupil of Eugène Giraud. In 1861 she showed *A Fellah* (Nantes, Mus. B.-A.), and in 1865 she was awarded a third class medal. At her death she made bequests to the Louvre and the Bibliothèque Nationale, but the bulk of her various collections was sold at public auction at the Galerie Georges Petit 17–21 May 1904. A marble bust of *Princesse Mathilde* (1862) by Jean-Baptiste Carpeaux is in the Musée d'Orsay, Paris.

BIBLIOGRAPHY
DBF
F. Masson: 'La Princesse Mathilde: Artiste et amateur', *Les Arts* [Paris], 29 (1904), pp. 1–8
Catalogue des tableaux anciens, tableaux modernes, objets d'art et d'ameublement . . . de S.A.I. Madame la Princesse Mathilde (sale cat., Paris, Gal. Petit, 17–21 May 1904)
M. Castillon du Perron: *La Princesse Mathilde* (Paris, 1953)
E. de Goncourt and J. de Goncourt: *Journal*, 4 vols (Paris, 1956–9)
J. des Cars: *La Princesse Mathilde* (Paris, 1988)

(10) Prince Napoléon(-Jérôme) (*b* Trieste, 9 Sept 1822; *d* Rome, 17 March 1891). Brother of (9) Princess Mathilde. He spent the years 1823–31 in Rome, in a family environment where a taste for art was strongly cultivated, notably by his uncle (4) Lucien Bonaparte and also by his great-uncle Cardinal Joseph Fesch. His education was continued in Florence and at the military academy in Württemberg and was broadened by travels through Europe. He was receptive to modern social, economic and scientific ideas, as well as to the arts. He was in Paris during the 1848 Revolution and was a Republican deputy during the presidency (1848–52) of his cousin Louis-Napoléon Bonaparte. After the latter became Emperor as (8) Napoleon III in 1852, Prince Napoléon became a senator. He was President of the Imperial Commission for the 1855 Exposition Universelle in Paris.

After the exhibition closed Prince Napoléon built on part of its site a Pompeian-style house designed by the architect ALFRED NICOLAS NORMAND (1856–8; destr. 1891; drawings and photographs Paris, Bib. N.; Carnavalet; Mus. A. Déc.), based on the 'House of Diomedes' in Pompeii. The interior was decorated with brightly coloured murals by Charles Chauvin (1820–89), in the illusionistic Pompeian 'third style', and there were decorative canvases painted by Sébastien Cornu (Arenenberg Schloss) and Jean-Leon Gérôme (one panel, *The Odyssey*, France, priv. col.; others untraced). There were also sculpted portraits of the Imperial family by Eugène Guillaume (marble; Château de Prangins, nr Geneva, Prince Napoléon Bonaparte priv. col., on dep. Arenenberg Schloss). Bronze fixtures and fittings based on items in the Museo Archeologico in Naples were designed by Normand and furniture and tableware by Charles Rossigneux (1818–1907); some of the goldsmith's work was executed by Charles Christofle (1805–63).

Prince Napoléon's Pompeian house, designed for entertaining rather than habitation, also contained his collection of antiquities: this rich and eclectic collection of Greek vases, terracottas from Paestum, figurines found in Syria, fragments of Roman architecture, small Egyptian bronzes, stelae and other assorted pieces was augmented by objects discovered at Pompeii in 1862 and at Cumae in 1863. In 1858 and 1864 he offered some important Egyptian pieces to the Musée du Louvre. Napoléon's collection also included contemporary paintings; among them were a copy (Versailles, Château) of Jacques-Louis David's *Death of Marat*, a *Greek Interior* by Gérôme (untraced) and the *Self-portrait Aged 24* by the Prince's friend Jean-Auguste-Dominique Ingres (Chantilly, Mus. Condé). The sumptuous official opening of the house on 14 February 1860 is recorded in a painting by Gustave Boulanger (exh. Salon 1861; Versailles, Château).

In 1866, fearing that a political difference with the Emperor would force him to leave France, Prince Napoléon sold his house and then disposed of his collections. The antiquities were sold at the Hôtel Drouot on 23 and 26 March 1868; the paintings on 4 April. One of the most beautiful Greek vases in the Louvre, Paris, the cup of *Eos and Memnon* by the painter Douris, was among the items sold, as was the statue of *Amon Protecting Tutankhamun*, which entered the Department of Egyptian Antiquities at the Louvre in 1920.

BIBLIOGRAPHY
DBF
C. Ferri Pisani: 'Bronzes égyptiens tirés de la collection du Prince Napoléon', *Gaz. B.-A.*, i (1859), pp. 270–85
M. Fröhner: *Catalogue d'une collection d'antiquités* (sale cat., Paris, Drouot, 23–26 March 1868)
F. Berthet-Leleux: *Le Vrai Prince Napoléon* (Paris, 1932)
M.-C. Dejean de la Batie: 'La Maison pompéienne du Prince Napoléon avenue Montaigne', *Gaz. B.-A.*, n. s. 5, lxxxvii (1976), pp. 127–34
La Maison pompéienne du Prince Napoléon, 1856: Dessins de l'architecte Alfred Normand (exh. cat. by M.-N. de Gary, Paris, Mus. A. Déc., 1979)

FRANÇOISE MAISON

Bonasone, Giulio (di Antonio) (*b* Bologna, *c.* 1510; *d* Bologna, after 1576). Italian printmaker and painter. He was a pupil of Lorenzo Sabbatini and evidently a late follower of Marcantonio Raimondi. He is now credited with 410 prints (almost all Rome, Ist. N. Graf.), as against Adam von Bartsch's attribution of 354. They include reproductive as well as original prints, and his independence of vision makes him one of the most interesting interpreters of his time. His activity in this field began *c.* 1531, as is indicated by the date on the Raphaelesque *St*

Cecilia (B. 74). Parmigianino entrusted him with the copper engraving of his drawings, for example *Mercury and Minerva* (B. 168). While in Rome *c.* 1544–7 Bonasone interpreted works including Michelangelo's *Last Judgement* (B.80) and Raphael's *Toilet of Psyche* (B. 167). He often combined the techniques of etching and engraving in the same print.

In Bologna after *c.* 1547 Bonasone began his most important work, the illustration of the 155 symbols (B. 179–328) of the *Symbolicarum quaestionum de universo genere quas serio ludebat libri quinque* (Bologna, 1555) by Achille Bocchi (1488–1562), which show elements derived from Raphael, Michelangelo and Parmigianino, although they generally reproduce drawings (e.g. London, BM) by Prospero Fontana. The plates, first published in 1555, were completely retouched by Agostino Carracci and reprinted in 1574. They are unique among contemporary illustrations of such emblems in that, instead of being subordinated to the text, they actually add meaning to it. After 1560 Bonasone achieved new effects and greater freedom in his etchings, such as the *Adoration of the Shepherds* (B. 39), and in works modelled on Titian, for example *Rest during the Flight into Egypt* (B. 67), in which he anticipated the refined solutions of his later years, for example in *St George* (B. 77), his last dated engraving.

DBI

BIBLIOGRAPHY

S. Ferrara and G. G. Bertela: *Incisori bolognesi ed emiliani del secolo XVI* (Bologna, 1975), nos 1–122

M. Cirillo: *Iulio Bonasone and the Sixteenth-century Italian Printmaking* (diss., U. Wisconsin, 1978)

S. Boorsch: *Italian Masters of the Sixteenth Century*, 29 [XV/2] of *The Illustrated Bartsch*, ed. W. Strauss (New York, 1982), pp. 9–157

S. Boorsch and J. T. Spike: *Italian Masters of the Sixteenth Century*, 28 [XV/1] of *The Illustrated Bartsch*, ed. W. Strauss (New York, 1985), pp. 205–351

STEFANIA MASSARI

Bonatz, Paul (Michael Nikolaus) (*b* Solgne, Lorraine, 6 Dec 1877; *d* Stuttgart, 20 Dec 1956). German architect. He graduated from the Technische Hochschule in Munich (1900) and worked as an assistant to Theodor Fischer at the Technische Hochschule in Stuttgart (1902–6). When Fischer moved to Munich (1908), Bonatz was appointed as his successor. In 1911 he won the competition for the rebuilding of the main railway station in Stuttgart, and the modified design of 1913 was built in collaboration with F. E. Scholer (*b* 1874), with whom he shared a practice between 1913 and 1927. The station was finally completed in 1928, the design, in Bonatz's words, 'purified by the gravity of the war'. This paring down process took the project out of the realm of 19th-century historicism, and the resulting monumental, yet clear statement of the station's various functions anticipated the rationalist Modernism of the 1920s. Other important works from Bonatz's early career were the Henkel warehouses (1908–9) at Biebrich, the greatly admired university library (1910–12) at Tübingen and the Stadthalle (1912–14) at Hannover.

Bonatz appointed Paul Schmitthenner to the faculty at the Technische Hochschule in 1918; Heinz Wetzel (*b* 1882), another protégé of Theodor Fischer, joined them in 1921. Led by Bonatz, the three created the Stuttgart School of Architecture, which upheld the values of regional style, traditional materials and craftsmanship against the onslaught of international Modernism. Stuttgart became an important battlefield in the conflict between the traditionalists and Modernists, and the Werkbund's decision to build the programmatically modern Weissenhofsiedlung in the city in 1927 provoked Bonatz and his associates to compile the manifesto of DER BLOCK in 1928, in defence of *völkisch* architecture, and to build the Kochenhofsiedlung (1933), a project supported by the timber industry as a protest against the concrete and steel of the Weissenhofsiedlung. In his traditionalism, however, Bonatz was less dogmatic than Schmitthenner or Paul Schultze-Naumburg and, while his housing from the 1920s favoured Biedermeier models, his public and commercial buildings were conceived in strictly functional terms. This Functionalist tendency, already noted in Stuttgart station, led the Neckar Canal Authority to employ him as a consultant (1929–36), responsible for the design of an important series of locks, bridges and sluices at Heidelberg, Rockenau, Hirschhorn and Oberesslingen. His virtuosity as a bridge builder also led to commissions during Nazi rule, when he was attached to the Todt organization as an adviser to the Autobahn building programme and designed many outstanding Autobahn bridges. In spite of its impeccable pedigree as the scourge of Modernism and its great success in training architects on traditional lines, the Stuttgart School failed to achieve a power base in the Nazi architectural hierarchy. Bonatz's schemes for the Naval High Command in Berlin (1939–43) and for the main railway station in Munich (1939–42; see Frank, pp. 86–7) remained unexecuted, and his only public buildings from the Nazi era were the Stumm company building (1935; with F. E. Scholer) in Düsseldorf, a memorial chapel (1936) in Heilbronn and the Kunstmuseum (1936) in Basle, Switzerland. This lack of success and official recognition caused him to emigrate to Turkey in 1943, where he was appointed city architect in Ankara. A professorship at the Technical University in Istanbul followed in 1946, and the State Opera House at Ankara was built to his design in 1948. He returned to Stuttgart in 1954, where he was employed principally in repairing the war damage suffered by his earlier projects.

WRITINGS

Leben und Bauen (Stuttgart, 1950, 4/1958)

with Fritz Leonhardt: *Brücken* (Königstein im Taunus, 1951)

Paul Bonatz: Ein Gedenkbuch der technischen Hochschule Stuttgart (Stuttgart, 1957)

BIBLIOGRAPHY

G. Graubner, ed.: *Paul Bonatz und seine Schüler* (Stuttgart, 1930)

F. Tamms, ed.: *Paul Bonatz: Arbeiten aus den Jahren 1907 bis 1937* (Stuttgart, 1937)

N. Bongartz, P. Dübbers and F. Werner: *Paul Bonatz, 1877–1956* (Stuttgart, 1977)

H. Frank: 'Paul Bonatz: Public Works', *Lotus Int.*, 47 (1985), pp. 70–91

IAIN BOYD WHYTE

Bonaventura, Segna di. *See* SEGNA DI BONAVENTURA.

Bonavia, Carlo (*fl* Naples, 1751–88). Italian painter and draughtsman. He may have come from Rome. Although numerous paintings by him survive (many signed and dated), little is known about his life. The source of the dates for his career are drawn respectively from the *View of the Pier and the Lighthouse at Naples* (1751; sold London, Christie's, 11 March, 1983, lot 171) and the *View of the*

Castel dell'Ovo (1788; Honolulu, HI, Acad. A.), which seem to be his earliest and last surviving works. It seems highly likely that he trained in the Neapolitan tradition, whose leading figures were Salvator Rosa and Leonardo Coccorante (1680–1750), but the landscape paintings of Claude-Joseph Vernet (who worked in Naples between 1736 and 1746) exercised a stronger influence on his work. Bonavia borrowed from Vernet not only subject and viewpoint (sometimes to the extent of almost copying) but even the way in which he applied colour to the canvas. The resultant landscapes are full of chromatic tones and accents, emotional in feeling and far removed from the cold and analytical representations of such other *vedutisti* of the period as Antonio Joli and Pietro Fabris. The influence of Vernet is most evident in such works as the *Coastal Landscape* (1754), *The Waterfall* (1755; both Naples, Capodimonte) and the *Landscape with Waterfall* (1787; Honolulu, HI, Acad. A.). Also under the influence of Vernet is the *View of the Villa Firmian at Posillipo* (1756). Graf Karl Joseph Firmian (1716–82), Austrian ambassador to Naples 1753–8, was an enthusiastic patron. His inventory includes 17 works by the painter: landscapes, views, mythological subjects and subjects inspired by famous works of literature. Most remain unidentified.

There are a few known surviving drawings by Bonavia: five sheets depicting Neapolitan views (San Francisco, CA, Achenbach Found. Graph. A.) and a sheet depicting Roman ruins, signed in full (priv. col.). Although famous in his day and mentioned by Zani (1794) as a good painter of views and a history painter, Bonavia's renown faded quickly. He was not rediscovered until the 20th century.

BIBLIOGRAPHY

DBI

P. Zani: *Enciclopedia metodica ragionata delle belle arti* (Parma, 1794), viii, p. 30

All' ombra del Vesuvio: Napoli nella veduta europea dal quattrocento all'ottocento (Naples, 1990), pp. 366–7 [with full bibliog.]

MARCO CARMINATI

Bonavia, Giacomo [Santiago] (*b* Piacenza, 1705; *d* Madrid, 18 or 20 Sept 1759). Italian architect, painter, urban planner and stage designer, active in Spain. He was a pupil in Piacenza of the painters Bartolomeo Rusca (1680–1745), Andrea Galluzzi (*fl* 1700–1743) and Giovanni Battista Galluzzi (*fl c.* 1730–40). In 1728 he was one of a number of artists summoned to Spain by the Marchese Annibale Scotti to assist with the construction of royal projects that were already under way and to introduce an Italian influence in place of the French style that had been introduced by the Bourbon kings. He worked at the Aranjuez Palace with the French engineer Léandre Brachelieu (*fl c.* 1733–9) and then in 1735 became Director of Royal Works of Decoration. He specialized in *quadratura* painting and, in addition to his work at Aranjuez, where his fresco vault decorations provided fictive *trompe l'oeil* architectural settings for mythological figures executed by Rusca and F. Fedeli, he also worked at San Ildefonso and El Buen Retiro (*see* MADRID, §IV, 1). It was for the theatre at El Buen Retiro that he produced his first stage designs.

From the end of the 1730s Bonavia became increasingly active as an architect. In 1739 he was made Assistant Quartermaster and Curator of the Works at Aranjuez, and the same year he presented a new design for the church of SS Justo y Pastor (now S Miguel), Madrid: the elliptical nave of the church is articulated by diagonally placed piers, which rise to support heavy flat ribs that interlace in the vaults, recalling Guarino Guarini's design for S Maria della Divina Provvidenza (?1681), Lisbon. After a fire at Aranjuez, he designed the vestibule and the grandiose imperial staircase of the palace (*see* ARANJUEZ PALACE) and also drew up a new urban plan for the town, combining the traditional orthogonal layout of streets and squares with spacious avenues to form a trident in front of the palace, as at Versailles. He was also responsible for the small church of S Antonio (1748) at Aranjuez, built in the form of a rotunda, from which a cylindrical choir protrudes, and with an undulating façade facing the town's old square. However, his plans for the façade of the sanctuary of Alpagés, with two oblique towers in the manner of Johann Bernhard Fischer von Erlach, were rejected in 1749 in favour of a more conventional design.

As a painter Bonavia employed a Rococo style that incorporated some innovative ideas; he was skilled at creating illusion, theatricality and impressions of infinite depth by the use of soft ranges of colour. As an architect his work had similarities to other Spanish responses to the experiments of the Roman Baroque and of Filippo Juvarra, with the influence of Guarini being particularly evident in his plans and elevations. He played an active role in the foundation of the Real Academia de Bellas Artes de S Fernando and became Director of Architecture there in 1752.

BIBLIOGRAPHY

DBI

G. Kubler: *Arquitectura de los siglos XVII y XVIII*, A. Hisp. (Madrid, 1957)

F. Chueca Goitia: 'Guarini y el influjo del barrocco italiano en España y Portugal', *Guarino Guanini e l'internazionalità del barrocco*, ed. V. Viale, ii (Turin, 1970), pp. 523–48

V. Tovar Martín: 'Las pinturas de arquitecturas fingidas en los palacios españoles de Aranjuez y La Granja de San Ildefonso', *Bracara Augusta*, xxvii/64 (1973), pp. 571–84

J. U. Fernández: *La pintura italiana del siglo XVIII en España* (Valladolid, 1977)

Y. Bottineau: *L'Art de cour dans l'Espagne des lumières* (Paris, 1986)

A. Bonet Correa and others: *El real sitio de Aranjuez y el arte cortesano del siglo XVIII* (Madrid, 1987)

R. M. Aviza Achucarro: 'El trazado urbanístico de Aranjuez: Una obra de Santiago Bonavia', *Archv Esp. A.*, ccxlvi (1989), pp. 119–30

ALFONSO RODRÍGUEZ CEBALLOS

Bonazza. Italian family of sculptors. Active in Padua in the first half of the 18th century, the family was founded by (1) Giovanni Bonazza, a prolific artist who ran a busy workshop and was an important master for his sons. His eldest son, Tommaso Bonazza (*c.* 1696–1775), often collaborated with his father and with his brother, (2) Antonio Bonazza, his art remaining close to that of Giovanni. Among Tommaso's independent works are marble figures of *Elijah* and *Elisha* on the altar of S Teresa in the church of S Maria del Carmine, Padua, and the *Four Evangelists* and other saints (1741) for the parish church at Fratta Polesine. Francesco Bonazza (*d* Venice, 1770), who was probably born in Venice, worked as a sculptor and as a painter, mosaicist and engraver of cameos. He appears to have been the least involved in his father's workshop, although his style remains close to that of Giovanni and of his brothers. His most important works are the marble statues of the *Cardinal Virtues* on the upper part of the façade of S Margherita in Padua and the horses in *pietra tenera* (Trieste, Villa Sartorio Montebello) for the Villa Gradenigo, Terraglio, which reveal his interest in movement. (2) Antonio Bonazza was the most brilliant of Giovanni's sons and one of the most original 18th-century Venetian sculptors. The only documented activity of his brother Michelangelo Bonazza (1704–68) is his collaboration with Tommaso on statues on the portal of S Maria del Carmine, Padua. The Bonazza family had numerous pupils, who created a school at Padua that remained active until the end of the 18th century and influenced the young Antonio Canova.

(1) Giovanni Bonazza (*b* ?Venice, 1654; *d* Padua, 30 Jan 1736). He worked in Venice until 1696–7, and his early works include the statues of *St Peter* and *St Paul* for the façade of the parish church at Fratta Polesine (1682), the monument to *Alexander VII* in Treviso Cathedral (1689) and works in Venice. Initially his style was close to the heavy classicism of Josse de Corte, but the *Alexander VII* already reveals the influence of the more Baroque art of Filippo Parodi. In 1696–7 Bonazza settled in Padua with his family and between 1697 and 1710 contributed to the sculptural enrichment of the reliquary chapel at the Santo in Padua, initiated by Parodi. In 1703 Giovanni began carving the marble sections of the altar of the Addolorata in S Maria dei Servi at Padua, where vast marble volutes frame delicate bronze reliefs of the *Seven Sorrows of the Virgin*.

Among his other religious works are the marble figures of *St Anthony, Innocence, Patience* and *SS Zeno and Fidenzio with Angels* (1707–10) on the altar of S Antonio in Montagnana Cathedral; the delicate and tender marble angels (1710) on the high altar of the parish church at Bovolenta; the marble *St Mark* and *St Daniel* for the high altar of the parish church at Ponte dei Brenta (1714); the 15 saints in stucco (1722) in the niches of the nave crossing of the collegiate church of Candiana; and the marble high reliefs (1730–32) for the Cappella del Rosario of SS Giovanni e Paolo, Venice (*in situ*), where he collaborated with his sons, although the *Annunciation* is his own work.

Giovanni also made numerous garden statues, among which his most important are the marble figures of *Dawn, Noon, Evening* and *Night* (1719) for the Summer Garden at St Petersburg; the figures in *pietra tenera* of *Indians* for the Villa Breda at Ponte di Brenta; and the mythological figures, also in *pietra tenera*, for the Villa Pisani at Stra (*c.* 1720). The exotic *Indians* at Ponte di Brenta, which combine pathos with subtle humour, represent a highly original development in 18th-century Italian sculpture.

(2) Antonio Bonazza (*b* Padua, 23 Dec 1698; *d* Padua, 12 Jan 1763). Son of (1) Giovanni Bonazza. He is among the greatest and most original Venetian sculptors of the 18th century; his activity was widespread, and his art distinguished by its vivid and picturesque naturalism. He is first recorded working in collaboration with his father and brothers Tommaso and Francesco on the marble reliefs depicting the *Adoration of the Shepherds* (1730) and the *Adoration of the Magi* (1732) in the Cappella del Rosario of SS Giovanni e Paolo, Venice, which are

characterized by tender naturalistic detail. Later he produced the eight slightly rigid stucco *Virtues* (1741) in S Maria del Torresino, Padua, and the fourteen marble reliefs of the *Stations of the Cross* in the parish church at Cornegliana (Padua). In 1742 he created his masterpiece, a series of garden sculptures executed for the Villa Widman at Bagnoli di Sopra (*in situ*). Here, alongside mythological figures, are a soldier, an oriental, a Moor, a huntsman, a peasant, a gentleman and gentlewoman, and a quarrelsome old man and woman, engaged in a witty comedy reminiscent of Carlo Goldoni's contemporary plays; indeed Goldoni was a guest at the villa. Bonazza was also a gifted portraitist, as demonstrated in the portraits in *pietra tenera* of *Benedict XIV* and *Cardinal Rezzonico* (later Clement XIII) (both 1746; Padua Cathedral) and the vivid portrait in marble of the doctor *Alessandro Knis Macoppe* (U. Padua).

Antonio's mature religious works tend to be more conventional. His many saints and angels include the marble figures of *SS Peter and Paul* (1746) for the high altar of the parish church at Bagnoli di Sopra, the angels (1750s) for the church of S Tommaso dei Filippini, Padua, distinguished by their wonderfully rounded luminous surfaces, and the angels executed in a broader, freer style for the parish church at Valnogaredo (all *in situ*). His works in low relief include the slightly heavy, yet atmospheric reliefs (1753–5) for the altar of the Sacrament in Montagnana Cathedral, showing the *Sacrifice of Isaac, Elijah and the Angel* and the *Last Supper* (all *in situ*). In 1757 he completed a further series of garden sculptures, of *Flora, Pomona, Zephyr* and *Vertumnus*, for the Peterhof Garden at St Petersburg.

BIBLIOGRAPHY
A. Roncato: *Alcune notizie intorno agli scultori Bonazza fioriti in Padova nel secolo XVIII* (Rovigo, 1918)
G. Gurian: *Sopra sedici statue da giardino dello scultore padovano Antonio Bonazza* (Verona, 1931)
C. Semenzato: *Antonio Bonazza* (Venice, 1957) [with bibliog.]
——: 'Giovanni Bonazza', *Saggi & Mem. Stor. A.*, ii (1959)
——: *La scultura veneta del seicento e del settecento* (Venice, 1966), pp. 49–51, 53–5
A. Forniz: 'Note su alcune sculture settecentesche del Friuli Occidentale', *Noncello*, 27 (1968)

CAMILLO SEMENZATO

Boncompagni. Italian family of patrons. Pietro Boncompagni (*d* 1404), a reader in civil law from 1378 to 1391, was buried in a tomb in S Martino, Bologna, where a Boncompagni family chapel, outstanding for its works of art, was completed in 1534. Its richly carved decoration is attributed to Amico Aspertini, and it features an *Adoration of the Magi* (1532) by Girolamo da Carpi on the wooden altar (attrib. Bartolomeo Ramenghi Bagnacavallo I). A great-grandson of Pietro Boncompagni, Cristoforo Boncompagni (1470–1546) was a draper and financier. He built a palazzo (1538–45) near the cathedral of S Pietro; its decorations were completed by his sons after his death. Giacomo Barozzi da Vignola may have contributed to this elegant and dignified structure. Restored in 1845, the palazzo, now called Palazzo Benelli, stands at Via del Monte 8. Interior restoration work began in 1980.

Cristoforo Boncompagni's ten children included a son Ugo Boncompagni, who became GREGORY XIII. Ugo's grandson Francesco Boncompagni (1596–1641) became

Cardinal Archbishop of Naples. Francesco left a large library, partly to the Vatican and partly to the Collegio Germanico, and an important numismatic collection, which remained in the family. A descendant of Francesco Boncompagni, Giacomo Boncompagni (1653–1731), as Cardinal Archbishop of Bologna, laid the first stone of the church of the Madonna di S Luca (1723), Bologna, designed by Carlo Francesco Dotti. He also restored the family chapel in S Martino. His great-grandnephew Ignazio Boncompagni Ludovisi (1743–90) became a papal legate in Bologna and helped to solve the long-standing problem of the falling water-level in the area. He had 'superb intelligence, vast culture and great eloquence among the few who knew languages of northern Europe' (Litta). In the 19th century Ugo Boncompagni Ludovisi (1856–1935), Prince of Piombino, commissioned Gaetano Koch to build the Palazzo Margherita (1886–90; now US Embassy) on the Via Veneto in Rome. It is a T-shaped building with a three-storey, 13-bay elevation and a triple-arched portal, in a sober Renaissance style that diverges from the neo-Baroque tendencies of its day.

BIBLIOGRAPHY

P. Litta: 'Boncompagni di Bologna', *Famiglie celebri italiane*, xxxv (Milan, 1836)

S. Mazzetti: *Repertorio di tutti i professori antichi e moderni della famosa Università del celebre Istituto delle Scienze di Bologna* (Bologna, 1847), p. 64

C. Ricci and G. Zucchini: *Guida di Bologna*, ed. A. Emiliani (Bologna, 1968), pp. 123, 145, 188

GIORGIO TABARRONI

Boncampagni, Ugo. *See* GREGORY XIII.

Bond, Richard (*fl* 1820–50). American architect. There is evidence that Bond was trained by Solomon Willard. Certain of Bond's designs suggest the Greek Revival approach that Willard brought from Washington, DC. Bond's style moved between Gothic Revival and a Neo-classical heaviness. An example of Gothic Revival is St John's Episcopal Church and Rectory (1841), Devens Street, Boston, which has a rather heavy granite façade dominated by a square tower with a battlemented roof-line; there are large quatrefoil windows in the walls below. In the same year Bond was called to Oberlin College in Ohio to design First Church, which had to be a Greek Revival design. He worked on Lewis Wharf (1836–40; later remodelled), Boston, where certain walls reflect his attraction to boldly massed granite surfaces. Bond's best-known buildings during his life were at Harvard University, Cambridge, MA. These included Gore Hall (1838; destr. 1913), alterations to Harvard Hall (1842; later remodelled) and Lawrence Hall (1847; much modified). As a representative architect from Boston, Bond was present at a meeting in New York in 1838, which resulted in the formation of the National Society of Architects, the first professional architectural organization in the USA.

BIBLIOGRAPHY

Withey

DARRYL PATRICK

Bondarenko, Il'ya (Yevgrafovich) (*b* Ufa, 1870; *d* Moscow, 29 Jan 1946). Russian architect, architectural historian, restorer and exhibition organizer. He studied (1887–91) at the School of Painting, Sculpture and Architecture, Moscow, and then at the Technische Hochschule, Zurich, where he completed his studies in 1894. He designed the Russian craft pavilion at the Exposition Universelle (1900) in Paris with A. Ya Golovin and with the painter Konstantin Korovin. The work largely reflected the search for a distinct national style, particularly the revival of Russian timber architecture and tent-roofed churches (for illustration see *Mir Iskusstva*). His own churches, built for the Old Believers community, are in Bogorodsk (now Noginsk; 1900–02), Tokmakov Lane, Moscow, Gavrilov Lane, Moscow, and in Orekhovo-Zuyevo and Kuznetsy near Moscow, all built in 1906–9. Two later examples are at Kuznetsov (1911) near Kashin, near Moscow, and in Riga (1913–14). They are picturesque compositions, complex in form with expressive contrasts in texture and colour. Similar in approach are his country houses, including those for Baron Shteyngel' (1911) at Stantsiya Kubanskaya near Armavir, for Mironov (1913) near Stantsiya Kryukovo, outside Moscow, and the design (1912–15) for the Gus'kov House, near Moscow. At the other extreme are Bondarenko's industrial and practical buildings, for example his plan (1899–1900) for the industrial production of standard prefabricated, collapsible houses. He also designed the workshops (probably 1896–9) attached to Savva Mamontov's factory near Butyrskaya Zastava, and the mill and weavers' barracks (probably 1896–9) at both the Gorkinskaya Textile Works, near Ivanovo-Voznesensk (now Ivanovo). His designs for the Savvinskaya Textile Works in Moscow (1906–9) included a hostel for 1000 workers, a hospital and a surgery. Also in Moscow he built an orphanage (1913) on Prechistenskaya Embankment and the Shelaputin block of flats (1914) in Lefortovo district. Between these two poles of Bondarenko's work are his commercial buildings, built in the Russian style of Art Nouveau (Rus. *modern*), with vast windows and smooth walls of glazed brick, such as the Udin Commercial House (1900–02) and the Sokolov Arcade (1909), both in Ivanovo-Voznesensk. Similar are the grandiose interiors of the reading room (1911) of the library of the State Historical Museum in Moscow and the rebuilt interior (1911) of the church of the Exaltation of the Cross in Ivanovo-Voznesensk, both with broad concrete vaults.

Bondarenko was also one of the first scholars in Russia to study Moscow's post-Petrine architecture. He also wrote on the Neo-classical architects Matvey Kazakov and Osip Bove, and discovered the work of Domenico Gilardi (1788–1845) and Afanasy Grigor'yev, although references to this classical heritage appear rarely in his own designs, one instance being the Sokolov House in Ivanovo-Voznesensk. He also organized numerous exhibitions, including *Architecture and Artistic Production of the New Style* (1902; with Ivan Fomin) and *Red Moscow* (1922), which formed the basis of the Central Museum of the Revolution, Moscow. After the Revolution (1917) he virtually ceased practising as an architect but became president of the commission for the restoration of the architectural monuments of the Moscow Kremlin and of Yaroslavl'. He was also on the commission (1918) for recording and preserving the monuments in the monastery of the Trinity and St Sergius, Sergiyev Posad (formerly Zagorsk). In 1920–21 he was the founder and first director of the Bashkirian State Art Museum in Ufa, and founder of the department for the protection of artistic monuments and antiquities in the Polytechnic, Ufa. His last major work was his participation in the reconstruction of the Putevoy Dvorets (palace) (originally built 1763–7 by Matvey Kazakov) in Tver, after its destruction during World War II.

WRITINGS

Arkhitekturnyye pamyatniki Moskvy [Architectural monuments of Moscow], 3 vols (Moscow, 1904–6)
Matvey Fyodorovich Kazakov (Moscow, 1912)
'Arkhitektor Iosif Ivanovich Bove', *Ezhegodnik Inst. Istor. Ist.* (1914), pp. 11–18

BIBLIOGRAPHY

Ye I. Kirichenko: 'Il'ya Bondarenko', *Stroitel'stvo & Arkhit. Moskvy*, viii (1985), pp. 30–32
Mir Iskusstva iv (1990), nos 13–24, pp. 98–105, 108, 109

YE. I. KIRICHENKO

Bonde, Gustaf Trolle-. *See* TROLLE-BONDE, GUSTAF.

Bondol, Jean. *See* BOUDOLF, JAN.

Bone. The material that forms the skeletons of the higher animals. It consists of an organic portion composed mainly of the fibrous protein collagen and an inorganic portion formed by crystals of hydroxyapatite, a complex of tricalcium and calcium hydroxide. (For the identification of bone, *see* TECHNICAL EXAMINATION, §VIII, 8.) The combination of these two substances forms a material that is light and strong, especially longitudinally. It is fairly flexible and possessed of reasonable cross-sectional strength. It is readily available as a by-product of butchery and is easily worked with simple tools. It can be sawn, scraped, carved, filed and glued. The size and structure of even the largest bones tend to limit their utility to small objects. These artefacts tend to be utilitarian in nature, though they may be decorated to some extent, and bone was often used to adorn objects made from other materials. Bone has sometimes been used as a cheap substitute for ivory, but it cannot be so finely worked, and the grain is more prominent. For tools it was often the preferred material because of its greater strength in small sections.

Objects made from bone are among the earliest known artefacts made by man, and broken, worked and whole utilized animal bones are common on the sites of Stone Age occupation. The utility of even unmodified bone splinters and fragments is readily apparent. Numerous unworked bone fragments (*c.* 500,000–450,000 BC) were found in association with the remains of *Homo erectus* at Zhoukoudian, the home of Peking Man (*Sinanthropus*), located south-west of Beijing, China. Bone fragments and pendants (*c.* 30,000–20,000 BC) were also discovered together with the remains of *Homo sapiens sapiens* at the same site. Elsewhere, by the later Palaeolithic era spear throwers and bone tools, mainly simple points, harpoon heads and fish-hooks, were being carefully worked, polished and embellished with engraved ornament. Notable finds have been made in France, at Les Eyzies and La Madeleine in the Dordogne region, and in Britain at Starr Carr, S. Yorks, a Mesolithic site. Zoomorphic carvings have been found at Vogelherd in Germany, and anthropomorphic and zoomorphic figurines occur in the Brno

area of the Czech Republic. In Russia notable finds have been made at Kostyonki and Sunghir.

Later, the cultures of ancient Egypt, Mesopotamia and associated West Asian areas used bone as a decorative inlay on such wooden objects as furniture and boxes. They also used it to make sewing awls, spatulas, knife-handles and game-pieces, as well as more decorative objects, for example perfume bottles and cosmetic pallets. Ivory seems to have been the preferred material for all of the above, bone generally being a lower-quality substitute (*see* EGYPT, ANCIENT, §XVII, 9).

The Greco-Roman civilizations used bone in a similar manner, but metals gradually replaced bone for awls, needles, spatulas and similar objects. By *c.* 500 BC finely carved articulated dolls were being produced, alongside others made from only slightly modified portions of long bone (*see* COPTIC ART, §V, 1; ETRUSCAN, §VII; GREECE, ANCIENT, §X, 6; HELLADIC, §VI; and ROME, ANCIENT, §X, 4.)

In ancient East Asia similar small utilitarian objects were produced. Spatulas, chisels, harpoons, arrowheads, hairpins and needles (5th–4th millennium BC) were excavated in China at the Neolithic village site of Banpo, in

1. Inscribed oracle bone, l. 130 mm, from China, Shang dynasty, 12th century BC (London, British Library)

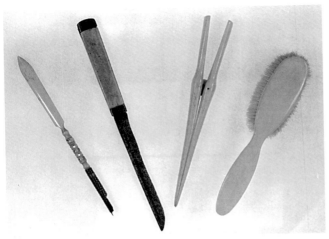

2. Bone objects (from left to right): souvenir pen, l. 177 mm, from the Great Exhibition of 1851, London; bone-handled knife, l. 213 mm, 18th century; glove stretchers, l. 185 mm, 19th century; baby's hairbrush, l. 155 mm, early 20th century (London, Museum of London)

Henan Province. Finds at the Shang-period (*c.* 1600–*c.* 1100 BC) site of Zhengzhou included arrowheads, knives and a piece of cut ox bone, the last being a left-over of bone-carvers' work. By the 2nd millennium BC ox scapulae were being used for divination (see fig. 1; *see also* CHINA, §IV, 2(i)). In more recent times bone was used in China instead of ivory for cosmetic pots, brush handles and scroll roller ends. Bone game-pieces were used for *mah-jong* in China and *go* in Japan. Since the late 18th century bone has been used as an inlay for furniture, notably in Japan, China and parts of South-east Asia, and as carved relief inlay on lacquerwares, lacquer screens and plaques, where it is often stained red, green or brown; it was frequently used for export pieces. Jewellery and small ornamental items are still made from bone in China in the absence of ivory.

In India, Nepal and West Asia bone continues to be used as an inlay for furniture and in the production of small figurines. Throughout the late 18th, 19th and early 20th centuries Indian craftsmen produced bone chess sets. In Tibet, parts of Nepal and those areas of China in which Tibetan Lamaist Buddhism was practised, human bones were used for such Buddhist ritual objects as drums, begging-bowls and cups, which were made from crania. Sets of monks' beads were made from epiphyses carved to resemble the human skull.

In North America bone is known to have been worked from the 5th millennium BC. Until the late 20th century the local people continued to use it much as their ancestors did, fashioning harpoon heads from long bones, sled runners from walrus ribs and snow shovels from various scapulae and larger whale bones, as well as a multitude of small, everyday objects. The plains and woodland tribes of North America appear to have used bone in much the same way as other pre-industrial societies.

In Mesoamerica the use of bone dates from the Pleistocene period (10,000–8,000 BC), when the material was used for tools and musical instruments. The first known

example of a ritual piece from this area is the sacrum of a fossilid llama (*c.* 8000 BC; Mexico City, Mus. N. Antropol.) worked to represent the head of a coyote. However, most extant bonework from this region dates from the 10th century AD onwards. In the 14th century, for example, the Aztecs made bone rattles, rasps and perforators for ritual bloodletting; they also used human skulls, overlaying them with turquoise mosaic work (*see* MESOAMERICA, PRE-COLUMBIAN, §IX, 2). In Central America most bonework is Maya in origin. Numerous tools and ritual objects have been found at pre-Classic (*c.* 2000 BC–*c.* AD 250) and Classic sites (*c.* AD 250–*c.* 900), and it is clear that the Maya, like the Aztec, attached particular significance to human bones (*see also* SOUTH AMERICA, PRE-COLUMBIAN, §VIII, 2).

In the Pacific, bone usage is limited to a few neck ornaments of whalebone and bird-leg bones from Hawaii, Tonga and Fiji, whalebone breast plates from Tonga and Fiji and whalebone meri and flutes from human femurs made by the New Zealand Maoris. The peoples of Papua New Guinea make daggers, arrowheads and nose and hair ornaments from cassowary and pig bones. Australian Aborigines use a magically charged 'pointing bone' to curse enemies.

In Sub-Saharan Africa the use of bone has been similarly limited. It is occasionally found in body ornaments; long bones are used for drumsticks, and ritual trumpets were made from human femurs decorated with mandibles by the Asante of Ghana; and various other African groups made bone spoons, votive masks and small zoomorphic carvings.

In Britain and elsewhere in Europe the use of bone was common up to the medieval period and peaked between 1820 and 1920 (see fig. 2), when a wide variety of artefacts, both decorative and utilitarian, was produced, ranging from the needleworker's crochet hook and the bookbinder and shoemaker's rubber to intricate miniature models of sailing ships and furniture.

For further information *see* country and style surveys on ivory and bone; *see also* EMBRIACHI and SCRIMSHAW.

BIBLIOGRAPHY
G. B. Hughes: *Living Crafts* (London, 1953)
R. J. Forbes: *Studies in Ancient Technology*, iii (Leiden, 1955)
J. P. Weinman and H. Sicher: *Bone and Bones* (St Louis, 1955)
J. F. Hayward: *English Cutlery of the 16th to 18th Centuries* (London, 1957)
R. C. Bell: *Board and Table Games from Many Civilisations* (London, 1960)
I. A. Crawford: 'Whalebone Artefacts', *Scot. Stud.*, xi (1967), pp. 88–91
N. K. Sanders: *Prehistoric Art in Europe*, Pelican Hist. A. (Harmondsworth, 1968, 2/1985), figs 34–6
J. D. Currey: 'The Mechanical Properties of Bone', *Clin. Orthopaedics*, lxxiii (1970), pp. 210–31
H. Wichmann and S. Wichmann: *The Story of Chesspieces from Antiquity to Modern Times* (London, 1970)
R. E. Chaplin: *The Study of Animal Bones from Archaeological Sites* (London, 1971)
B. Halstead and J. Middleton: *Bare Bones: An Exploration in Art and Science* (Edinburgh, 1972)
A. MacGregor: *Bone, Antler, Ivory and Horn: The Technology of Skeletal Materials since the Roman Period* (London, 1985)

FRANK MINNEY

Bône. *See* HIPPO REGIUS.

Bone, Sir (David) Muirhead (*b* Partick, nr Glasgow, 23 March 1876; *d* Oxford, 21 Oct 1953). Scottish draughtsman and etcher. The son of a journalist, he was apprenticed to an architect, but he took evening classes at the Glasgow School of Art. Two early ink studies of Glasgow were reproduced in the last issue of the *Yellow Book* in 1897. He began to study printmaking in 1898, and it was in the media of drypoint and etching that he produced his most distinguished work. The enduring influence of Piranesi, Charles Meryon and Whistler was already apparent in his first portfolio, *Six Glasgow Etchings* (Glasgow, 1899). In 1901 he moved to London, where he was promoted by Dugald Sutherland MacColl, William Strang, Alphonse Legros and Henry Tonks, and where he became a member of the New English Art Club. In 1916, at the suggestion of William Rothenstein, Bone was appointed the first Official War Artist, serving with Allied forces on the Western Front and for a time with the Navy, producing drawings such as *From the Bridge of a Battleship* (1917; London, Tate). He was instrumental in the commissioning of fellow artists such as William Orpen, Eric Kennington and Wyndham Lewis and became a War artist again in 1940. Bone exhibited frequently at P & D Colnaghi & Co. Ltd in London and M. Knoedler & Co. in New York and built up a considerable reputation between the World Wars. Of the many books he illustrated, several were by members of his family, such as D. W. Bone's *Merchantmen at Arms* (London, 1919) and James Bone's *The London Perambulator* (London, 1926). His subject-matter was often inspired by his foreign travels: in 1923 he executed three portraits of the novelist Joseph Conrad during an Atlantic crossing (e.g. *Joseph Conrad Listening to Music*, drypoint, 1923; U. St Andrews), and the luxurious folio-edition of *Old Spain* (London, 1936) arose from an extended visit to Spain in 1929. His most characteristic images, however, were of urban change: construction and demolition sites, shipbuilding yards (e.g. *Dry Dock*, 1899; see Dodgson, 1909, no. 48) and war-damaged cities provided the pretexts for large-scale, ambitious compositions and broad panoramas punctuated by minutely observed details, as in the *Demolition of St James's Hall* (1906; see Dodgson, 1909, no. 196).

WRITINGS
'From Glasgow to London', *Artwork*, v/19 (1929), pp. 143–6

BIBLIOGRAPHY
C. Dodgson: *Etchings and Drypoints of Muirhead Bone, 1898–1907* (London, 1909)
——: 'Later Drypoints of Muirhead Bone, 1908–1916', *Prt Colr Q.* (Feb 1922), pp. 173–200
Muirhead Bone: Portrait of the Artist (exh. cat. by P. Trowles, U. St Andrews, Crawford A. Cent., 1986)

DAVID COHEN

Bonechi, Matteo (*b* Florence, 8 Nov 1669; *d* Florence, 27 Feb 1756). Italian painter. He was a prolific artist, most successful as a fresco painter, who worked mainly in and around Florence. His early years are undocumented, and it is not clear with whom he trained; Gabburri (Florence, Bib. N. Cent., MS. E.B.9.5, iv, 62*v*-63) mentions Francesco Botti (1640–1710) as his teacher, while Luigi Lanzi specifies Giovanni Camillo Sagrestani. He was certainly strongly influenced by Sagrestani, from whom he may have found it difficult to free himself. The works of his maturity, however, are highly personal and reflect the carefree mood of 18th-century Florence, which responded to the lighter influences of the French Rococo. Apart from studies for wall decorations, the only works on canvas for which dates are documented are two tondi for S Jacopo Sopr' Arno, Florence: *Abraham with the Three Angels* and a scene from the *Life of St Francis* (both 1718). His documented frescoes are the dome of S Verdiana (1716) at Castelfiorentino, the domes of S Jacopo Sopr' Arno (1718) and the Conservatorio di S Agnese (1719–20), both in Florence, the *trompe l'oeil* ceiling in the shape of a sail for the Compagnia di S Agostino (1724) at Legnaia and the mural decoration of S Maria del Suffragio al Pellegrino (1734–5), near Florence.

DBI
BIBLIOGRAPHY
L. Lanzi: *Storia pittorica della Italia*, i (Bassano, 1795–6), p. 259
Painting in Italy in the 18th Century: Rococo to Romanticism (exh. cat., ed. J. Maxon and J. J. Rishel; Chicago, IL, A. Inst., 1970), pp. 146–9 [article by M. Gregori]
M. Chiarini: 'Nota sul Bonechi', *Ant. Viva*, x/6 (1971), pp. 7–16
S. Rudolph: 'Mecenati a Firenze fra sei e settecento: III: Le opere', *A. Illus.*, vii/59 (1974), pp. 279–98
The Twilight of the Medici: Late Baroque Art in Florence, 1670–1743 (exh. cat., ed. S. F. Rossen; Detroit, MI, Inst. A.; Florence, Pitti; 1974), pp. 192–7
C. Pizzorusso: 'Per Matteo Bonechi: La decorazione del Pellegrino', *Kunst des Barock in der Toskana: Studien zur Kunst unter den letzten Medici* (Munich, 1976), pp. 363–6
M. C. Improta: *La chiesa di Santa Verdiana a Castelfiorentino* (Pisa, 1986)
R. Contini and C. Ginetti, eds: *La pittura in Italia: Il settecento*, ii (Milan, 1990), pp. 301–48, 629, illustrations pp. 322–3

CHRISTINA IMPROTA ROMANO

Bonet, Antonio (*b* Barcelona, 2 June 1913; *d* Barcelona, 13 Sept 1989). Spanish architect, urban planner and designer, also active in Argentina and Uruguay. He graduated from the Escuela Superior de Arquitectura, Barcelona, in 1936, having also worked during 1932–6 in the offices of Josep Lluís Sert and, in Paris, of Le Corbusier. In 1938 he went to Buenos Aires and there became a founder member of Grupo Austral, together with (among others) Jorge Hardoy (*b* 1914) and Juan Kurchan, with whom he had worked in Paris. Bonet applied the rationalist principles of the group's manifesto *Voluntad y acción* (1939) in a wide range of architectural and urban-design projects in Argentina and Uruguay over the next two decades. He is perhaps most widely known for his individual houses, and especially for the Casa Berlingieri (1946) at Punta Ballena, Uruguay, and (with Jorge Vivanco and Valera Peluffo) for the four pavilions at Martínez, Buenos Aires, in a manner reminiscent of Le Corbusier's work of a decade or so earlier, although quite original in expression. As a planner Bonet was involved in the master-plans for Mendoza (1940) and the Casa Amarilla housing development (1943), Buenos Aires; he was a member of the San Juan reconstruction committee in 1944 and worked on the South Buenos Aires Urban Development Plan (1956). He was also a noted furniture designer, and he taught architecture as a visiting professor (1950) at Tucumán National University. Among many buildings in the 1950s, Bonet designed the Casa Oks (1955), part of a larger housing development at Martínez, the Galería Rivadavia and Terraza Flats (1957–9) and the Galería de las Américas (1958–62), all in Mar del Plata. In 1963 he returned to Spain to practise in Girona and Barcelona; his best-known building of this later period is the Urquinaona Tower (1971), Barcelona. He nevertheless continued periodic visits to Argentina, where he established the Bonet award for Argentine students of architecture.

BIBLIOGRAPHY
'Groupe de quatre pavillons à Martínez', *Archit. Aujourd'hui*, 18–19 (1948), pp. 64–5
F. Bullrich: *New Directions in Latin American Architecture* (London, 1969), pp. 13–14
F. Ortiz and M. Baldellon: *La obra de Antonio Bonet* (Buenos Aires, 1978)
E. Katzenstein and others: *Antonio Bonet* (Buenos Aires, 1985)
LUDOVICO C. KOPPMANN

Bonet, José Esteve. *See* ESTEVE, (1).

Bonevardi, Marcelo (*b* Buenos Aires, 13 May 1929). Argentine painter, sculptor and draughtsman. He studied architecture at the University of Córdoba in Argentina from 1948 to 1951 but later decided to devote himself to painting in which he was self-taught. Like other artists working in New York, where he settled in 1958 on being awarded a Guggenheim Fellowship, he reacted against Abstract Expressionism, in his case by developing a highly personal vocabulary and by incorporating sculptural elements within spaces hollowed out from the canvas support. These geometrical or enigmatic objects are presented as agents of revelation, emblems resonant with ancient significance, bringing together geometry, mathematics and astronomy in order to penetrate the secret labyrinths of the unconscious. *Supreme Astrolabe* (1973; New York, Guggenheim) is a good example of his extraordinarily rich work, as minutely detailed as that of a goldsmith. In other constructions he explored a psychologically intimate sense of space, as in *Trapped Angel III* (acrylic on canvas and wood, 1980; Buenos Aires, Mus. N. B.A.).

In his drawings Bonevardi abandoned the frontality of his reliefs, foreshortening images of disconcerting exteriors or useless, refined machinery, which he treated in a combination of graphic methods and techniques of dripping. Through his treatment of space and time he created irrational, enigmatic and dreamlike atmospheres.

BIBLIOGRAPHY
Marcelo Bonevardi Retrospective Exhibition (exh. cat., intro. D. Ashton; New York, Cent. Inter-Amer. Relations, 1980–81)
N. Perazzo: 'Constructivism and Geometric Art', *Latin American Presence in the United States, 1920–1970* (exh. cat., New York, Bronx Mus. A., 1988), pp. 106–7
NELLY PERAZZO

Bonfigli [Buonfigli], **Benedetto** (*b* Perugia, *c.* 1420; *d* Perugia, 8 July 1496). Italian painter. He was almost certainly trained in Perugia between 1430 and 1440, where a Late Gothic style was still dominant. Subsequently he was influenced by Fra Angelico, whose polyptych (Perugia, G.N. Umbria) for S Domenico, Perugia, was commissioned in 1437, and more importantly by Domenico Veneziano, who worked in that city *c.* 1438. The influence of Domenico Veneziano and of Gentile da Fabriano can be seen in Bonfigli's earliest surviving work, a polyptych (now dismembered), which had a central panel of the *Virgin and Child* (El Paso, TX, Mus. A.), shown against a densely wooded background, and *St Sebastian and a Bishop Saint* (Monserrat, Mus.) on one wing. Another wing (untraced) shows *St Bernardino of Siena* and *St Anthony Abbot*. Bonfigli is first documented on 7 March 1445, when he undertook to paint a *Virgin and Child with Two Angels* (untraced) for a chapel near S Pietro, Perugia. A votive fresco of *SS Catherine and Clement I* in S Cristoforo, Passignano, is dated 1446 and is very close to Bonfigli's style, but given its poor quality it should probably be attributed to one of his followers. It demonstrates, however, that by that date he was an established and imitated master.

An *Adoration of the Magi, and Christ on the Cross* (London, N.G.), which may either be a predella panel or a small altarpiece, and an *Adoration of the Child* (Florence, I Tatti) both show the influence of Domenico Veneziano; both have been plausibly attributed to Bonfigli and dated *c.* 1450.

Early in 1450 Bonfigli was in Rome working in the Vatican Palace; he was paid a salary of seven ducats per month, the same as Benozzo Gozzoli, which indicates that he was highly regarded at the court of Pope Nicholas V. Unfortunately, all his work in the Vatican has been destroyed. On 2 December 1454 Bonfigli was back in Perugia, where he contracted to paint a series of frescoes in the Priors' Chapel of the Palazzo dei Priori. Although in a bad state of preservation, this is his greatest work. Bonfigli painted a *Crucifixion with SS Francis and Ercolano* (later completely repainted by Hendrik van den Broeck) and scenes from the *Life of St Louis of Toulouse*, the patron of the palace, both of which were valued for payment by Filippo Lippi on 11 September 1461. The scenes from the *Life of St Ercolano* occupied Bonfigli for the rest of his life. In addition to the influence of Fra Angelico, Domenico Veneziano and Filippo Lippi, Bonfigli apparently also studied the work of Piero della Francesca and possibly Mantegna's frescoes in the church of the Eremitani, Padua. Bonfigli set these animated, anecdotal scenes in contemporary views of Rome and Perugia, as in *Totila Laying Siege to Perugia* (Perugia, G.N. Umbria; see fig.), in which the city is represented with archaeological and documentary precision. From 1450 to 1470 Bonfigli was at the height of his career. Also from this period are the *Annunciation with St Luke* (Perugia, G.N. Umbria), which shows the influence of Gozzoli, the exquisite small *Annunciation* (Madrid, Mus. Thyssen-Bornemisza) and the *Virgin and Four Saints* (Perugia, G.N. Umbria). In 1466 Bonfigli painted the altarpiece of the *Adoration of the Magi* with a predella of *Episodes from the Life of Christ and a Miracle of St Nicholas* (Perugia, G.N. Umbria) mentioned by Vasari. In this work Bonfigli confidently handles the depiction of space. The composition of the *Adoration* is derived from Gentile da Fabriano's altarpiece of the same subject (Florence, Uffizi). Stylistically it is influenced by Fra Angelico and Domenico Veneziano as well as Fra Filippo Lippi and Netherlandish painting, which would confirm that Bonfigli had travelled to Florence and possibly elsewhere in Italy. In 1467-8 for the chapel of S Vincenzo in S Domenico, Perugia, Bonfigli painted the *Virgin and Child with Music-making Angels* (Perugia, G.N. Umbria).

Bonfigli specialized in a typically Perugian art form: *gonfaloni* (banners or standards painted on canvas or linen, carried by confraternities). The *gonfalone* of *St Bernard Interceding for the Citizens of Perugia* (1465; Perugia, G.N. Umbria) contains anecdotal scenes but is poorly composed; that of *Christ Hurling Thunderbolts on Perugia with*

Benedetto Bonfigli: *Totila Laying Siege to Perugia*, detached fresco from the Priors' Chapel of the Palazzo dei Priori, Perugia, *c.* 1454–61 (Perugia, Galleria Nazionale dell'Umbria)

the *Virgin and Saints Interceding* (1472; Perugia, S Maria Nuova) and another of the *Virgin and Saints Interceding for Perugia* (1476; Perugia, S Fiorenzo) are both very beautiful and certainly autograph. The *gonfalone* of the *Madonna of Misericordia* (Perugia, S Francesco al Prato), made for the Cappella della Confraternità della SS Concezione, and two in the parish churches in the villages of Corciano (1472) and Civitella Benazzone, both near Perugia, are probably workshop productions made under Bonfigli's supervision. A small *gonfalone* (Perugia, Carmine) appears to be by a competent follower.

It is open to doubt whether Bonfigli played any part in the production of the series of eight small panels illustrating *Miracles of St Bernard* (1473; Perugia, G.N. Umbria), which have some similarity with the St Bernard *gonfalone* of 1465. Certainly they were influenced by Antonio del Pollaiuolo, Andrea Verrocchio and the art of Urbino. The influence of these artists represented a decisive turning-point in Perugian painting of the 1470s, and Bonfigli, although he lived for another 20 years, never adapted to the new style.

Vasari wrote that Bonfigli was the most highly esteemed painter in Perugia before Perugino; certainly he was a superior artist to his collaborator Bartolomeo Caporali and other contemporary Perugian painters; however, his influence hardly extended beyond his pupils.

BIBLIOGRAPHY
DBI; Thieme–Becker
G. Vasari: *Vite* (1550, rev. 2/1568); ed. G. Milanesi (1878–85), iii, pp. 505–6
L. Pascoli: *Vite de' pittori, scultori ed architetti perugini* (Rome, 1732), pp. 21–3
A. Mariotti: *Lettere pittoriche perugine* (Perugia, 1788), pp. 129–42
J. A. Crowe and G. B. Cavalcaselle: *A New History of Painting in Italy*, i (London, 1864), pp. 138–60
E. Muntz: *Les Arts à la cour des papes*, i (Paris, 1878), p. 129
L. Manzoni: 'Commentario di Benedetto Buonfigli', *Boll. Deput. Stor. Patria Umbria*, vi (1900), pp. 289–316
A. Venturi: *Storia* (1901–40), pp. 538–44
W. Bombe: *Benedetto Buonfigli* (Berlin, 1904)
V. Ansidei: *Di un documento inedito su Benedetto Bonfigli* (Perugia, 1912)
W. Bombe: *Geschichte der Peruginer Malerei* (Berlin, 1912), pp. 96–113
E. Jacobsen: *Umbrische Malerei des vierzehnten, funfzehnten und sechzehnten Jahrhunderts* (Strasbourg, 1914), pp. 46–51
U. Gnoli: *Pittori e miniatori nell'Umbria* (Spoleto, 1923), pp. 58–62
R. van Marle: *Italian Schools* (1923–38), xiv, pp. 99–128
C. Gamba: *Pittura umbra del rinascimento* (Novara, 1949), pp. xviii–xix
F. Zeri: 'Appunti nell'Ermitage e nel Museo Pusckin', *Boll. A.*, iv/46 (1961), pp. 226–31
B. Berenson: *Central and North Italian Schools*, i (1968), p. 58
F. Santi: *Gonfaloni umbri del rinascimento* (Perugia, 1976), pp. 23–7
F. Zeri: 'An *Annunciation* by Benedetto Bonfigli', *Apollo*, cviii (1978), pp. 394–5
F. Santi: *Galleria Nazionale dell'Umbria: Dipinti, sculture e oggetti dei secoli XV–XVI* (Rome, 1985), pp. 40–53
B. Toscano: 'Pittura del quattrocento in Umbria', *La pittura in Italia: Il quattrocento* (Milan, 1987), pp. 367–8
F. Todini: *La pittura umbra: Dal duecento al primo cinquecento* (Milan, 1989)
F. F. Mancini: *Benedetto Bonfigli* (Perugia, 1992)

P. SCARPELLINI

Bonfratelli, Apollonio de' (*b* Capranica, *c.* 1500; *d* Rome, 1575). Italian illuminator. He almost certainly studied under Giulio Clovio in Rome and later worked at the papal court, probably from 1523 to 1572; his name is entered in the Archivio di Stato Romano for the year 1568–9. A detached leaf from a choir-book, now in a book of cuttings, some of which are signed (London, BL, Add. MS. 21412, fols 36–43), bears the date 1564 and an inscription stating that Bonfratelli was *miniator* (miniaturist) to the Apostolic Chamber under Pope Pius IV. Its fine miniature of the *Adoration of the Shepherds* shows some influence of Raphael, while the borders, decorated with a frieze of festoons and architectural motifs, have small figures in the style of Michelangelo. Other works attributed to Bonfratelli include a small miniature of *St Luke* (Philadelphia, PA, Free Lib., Lewis MS. M. 27:7) and a single leaf (New York, Pierpont Morgan Lib., MS. M. 270) composed of fragments including the *Four Evangelists* and the arms of Pope Gregory XIII, for whom the book was probably made. The attribution of the latter to Bonfratelli has, however, been contested by Brown. Bonfratelli's work is characterized by a lively use of colour and a free compositional style. His borrowings (particularly in the marginal decorations) from contemporary trends in printed book designs show that he made attempts to modernize his repertory in the mid-16th century, at a time when manuscript illumination was already in decline.

BIBLIOGRAPHY
DBI; Thieme–Becker
J. W. Bradley: *A Dictionary of Miniaturists*, i (London, 1887), pp. 147–8
M. Harrsen and G. K. Boyce: *Italian Manuscripts in the Morgan Library* (New York, 1953), p. 58
T. J. Brown: 'Some Manuscript Fragments Illuminated for Pope Gregory XIII', *BM Q.*, xiii (1960–61), pp. 2–5
The Painted Page: Italian Renaissance Book Illumination, 1450–1550 (exh. cat., ed. J. J. G. Alexander; London, RA, 1994)

□

Bonheur, (Marie-) Rosa [Rosalie] (*b* Bordeaux, 16 March 1822; *d* Thomery, nr Fontainebleau, 25 May 1899). French painter and sculptor. She received her training from her father, Raymond Bonheur (*d* 1849), an artist and ardent Saint-Simonian who encouraged her artistic career and independence. Precocious and talented, she began making copies in the Louvre at the age of 14 and first exhibited at the Salon in 1841. Her sympathetic portrayal of animals was influenced by prevailing trends in natural history (e.g. Etienne Geoffroy Saint-Hilaire) and her deep affinity for animals, especially horses. Bonheur's art, as part of the Realist current that emerged in the 1840s, was grounded in direct observation of nature and meticulous draughtsmanship. She kept a small menagerie, frequented slaughterhouses and dissected animals to gain anatomical knowledge. Although painting was her primary medium, she also sculpted, or modelled, studies of animals, several of which were exhibited at the Salons, including a bronze *Study for a Bull* (1843; ex-artist's col., see Roger-Milès, p. 35) and *Sheep* (bronze; San Francisco, CA, de Young Mem. Mus.). In 1845 she attracted favourable notice at the Salon from Théophile Thoré. In 1848 she received a lucrative commission from the State for *Ploughing in the Nivernais* (1849; Paris, Mus. d'Orsay), which, when exhibited the next year, brought her further critical and popular acclaim. Typical of the Realist interest in rural society manifested in the contemporary works of Gustave Courbet and Jean-François Millet, *Ploughing* was inspired by George Sand's rustic novel *La Mare au diable* (1846). She exhibited regularly at the Salon until 1855. Her paintings sold well and were especially popular in Great Britain and the USA.

Bonheur's masterpiece, the *Horse Fair* (1853; New York, Met.; *see* PARIS, fig. 22), which is based on numerous drawings done at the horse market near La Salpetrière, was inspired by the Parthenon marbles (London, BM) and the works of Théodore Gericault. This immense canvas (2.45×4.07 m) combines her Realist preoccupation with anatomical accuracy and a Romantic sensitivity to colour and dramatic movement rarely found in her work. After its triumphant showing at the Paris Salon, the painting went on tour in Great Britain and the USA and was widely disseminated as a print. In 1887 Cornelius Vanderbilt purchased the *Horse Fair* for £53,000 and donated it to the newly founded Metropolitan Museum of Art, New York.

After 1860 Bonheur withdrew from the Paris art world and settled in the Château de By on the outskirts of the Forest of Fontainebleau with her companion, Nathalie Micas. Independent and financially secure, she painted steadily and entertained such celebrities as the Empress Eugénie and Buffalo Bill, whose portrait she painted in 1889 (Cody, WY, Buffalo Bill Hist. Cent.). In favour at court, Bonheur received the Légion d'honneur from the Empress Eugénie in 1865, the first woman artist to be so honoured. Although she enjoyed widespread renown during her lifetime, she was not universally admired by contemporary critics. Her spectacular success in Great Britain, her eccentric lifestyle and her militant feminism no doubt contributed to her mixed critical reception at home. Bonheur, who wore her hair short, smoked and worked in masculine attire, was a nonconformist who transcended gender categories and painted, according to various critics, like a man. After her English tour in 1856 she adopted a more detailed realistic manner, influenced perhaps by Edwin Landseer, though her style evolved little during her long career. She never abandoned her strict technical procedures and was unaffected by contemporary artistic trends. Her reputation declined after her death but has been revived in the 20th century by feminist art historians.

Bonheur was devastated by the death of Micas, her lifelong companion, in 1889. Her final years were brightened by Anna Klumpke (1856–1942), a young American portrait painter who was her biographer and her sole heir when Bonheur died in May 1899. In 1901 the town of Fontainebleau erected a monument in honour of Bonheur that was melted down during the German occupation of World War II. Her studio at the Château de By in Thomery has been restored and is open to the public.

WRITINGS
'Fragments of my Autobiography', *Mag. A.*, xxvi (1902), pp. 531–6

BIBLIOGRAPHY
L. Roger-Milès: *Rosa Bonheur: Sa vie, son oeuvre* (Paris, 1900)
A. E. Klumpke: *Rosa Bonheur: Sa vie, son oeuvre* (Paris, 1908)
T. Stanton, ed.: *Reminiscences of Rosa Bonheur* (New York, 1910/*R* 1976)
Women Artists: 1550–1950 (exh. cat. by A. Sutherland Harris and L. Nochlin, Los Angeles, CA, Co. Mus. A., 1976)
D. Ashton and D. Browne Hare: *Rosa Bonheur: A Life and a Legend* (New York, 1981)
A. Boime: 'The Case of Rosa Bonheur: Why Should a Woman Want to be more like a Man?', *A. Hist.*, iv (1981), pp. 384–409
C. Styles-McLeod: 'Historic Houses: Rosa Bonheur at Thomery', *Arch. Digest*, 43 (1986), pp. 144–50, 164
B. Tarbell: 'Rosa Bonheur's Menagerie', *Art and Antiques*, 15 (1993), pp. 58–64

HEATHER MCPHERSON

Bonhommé, (Ignace-)François (*b* Paris, 15 March 1809; *d* Paris, 1 Oct 1881). French painter, draughtsman and printmaker. His father painted scenes on carriages, and he provided his son with a rudimentary artistic training in an artisan's milieu of simple machinery and fellow workers. In 1828 Bonhommé entered the Ecole des Beaux-Arts in Paris under the aegis of Guillaume Lethière, whom he always listed first among his masters. Bonhommé drew from the model with Horace Vernet and studied further with Vernet's son-in-law, Paul Delaroche. Bonhommé's first Salon exhibit, in 1833, was a painting of a Newfoundland dog (untraced). In 1835 he showed a sequence of portraits in pastel and watercolour, owned by the writer Alexandre Dumas, who later published an article on Bonhommé in *L'Indépendance belge*. In 1835 Bonhommé also made two prints detailing the installation of the Luxor obelisk in the Place de la Concorde, Paris, on 25 October of that year, one made at noon and the other at 3 o'clock, an early manifestation of his facility for rapid and accurate description of machinery and topography. During the next year Delaroche chose Bonhommé to undertake a task he had himself declined, to paint the factories of Forchambault. Bonhommé claimed his first sight of molten metal being cast determined the course of his career. His Salon début as an industrial artist came in 1838, when he showed *Sheet Metal Manufacture in the Forges of Abbainville* (untraced). Two years later he exhibited another view of the Abbainville works, as well as a dramatic cross-section of the Forchambault factory, irregularly shaped to conform with the building. From then on Bonhommé executed almost exclusively industrial scenes, although he did occasionally exercise his talent as a portraitist, as in his portrait of M. Aubertot, the head of an iron manufactory (1847; Paris, Mus. d'Orsay). The 1848 Revolution excited Bonhommé as much as had that of 1830. He was commissioned by the Republican government to provide etched portraits of its major figures, as well as two important lithographs of key events, *Session of 15 May 1848, at the Constitutional Assembly* and *Barricade on the Saint-Martin Canal, 23 June 1848*, turbulent works reflecting his admiration for Delacroix.

In 1851, with the help of his neighbour Champfleury, Bonhommé won a state commission to produce pictures for the Ecole des Mines. During 1854–5 he worked for the same patrons on a more ambitious project, which included framed horizontal scenes on a large scale of metallurgical processes and crowds of workers. For the Exposition Universelle of 1855 Bonhommé assembled four of his past Salon works and received a third-class medal, his only such award. Later that year he executed a spectacular watercolour, *Fireworks set off at Versailles in Honour of Queen Victoria, 25 August 1855* (Paris, Carnavalet), which possesses the architectural sweep and cosmic chiaroscuro of John Martin's work. Bonhommé sent mining and factory scenes to the Salon intermittently until 1873, varying his perspective from that of the factory floor (e.g. *Workshop with Mechanical Sieves at the Factory of La Vieille Montagne, c.* 1859; Paris, Mus. N. Tech.) to an aerial viewpoint that recalls some of his teacher Vernet's battle scenes (e.g. *Coalpits and Clay Quarries at Montchanin*; Montchanin, Mairie). Bonhommé spoke of his intention to compile a project entitled *Soldiers of Industry*, in which

he could celebrate the 'peaceful conquests' of his favourite 'army'. His knowledge of professional dress was thorough and complete, and his impressive pen and ink drawings of individual workers can be equally exact in their description of occupational poses and gestures. In many of Bonhommé's works expressive power was subordinate to technical accuracy, but the best, like his nightmarish scene of a blindfolded white horse being lowered for work down a mine shaft (Jarville, Mus. Hist. Fer), have the descriptive poetry of Zola's *Germinal*. Bonhommé's mills are dark and satanic, but the artist, who signed his work 'François Bonhommé, called the Blacksmith', felt enthusiasm for industry and its magnates, as well as empathy for the workers.

Never prosperous, Bonhommé was saved from absolute indigence when Charles Lauth appointed him Professor of Drawing at the Sèvres Manufactory, through the intercession of supporters such as Jules Simon. Bonhommé was given a studio and associated with friends there, such as Bracquemond and Champfleury, director of the Sèvres Museum. However, his salary was low and his admirably consistent career ended sadly when he lost his mind and had to be committed to the Sainte-Anne Asylum, where he died shortly afterwards.

BIBLIOGRAPHY

H. Béraldi: *Les Graveurs du XIXe siècle*, ii (Paris, 1885), pp. 155–6

J. F. Schnerb: 'François Bonhommé', *Gaz. B.-A.*, n.s. 4, ix (1911), pp. 11–25, 132–42

Exposition François Bonhommé, dit le Forgeron (exh. cat. by B. Gille, Nancy, Mus. Fer, 1976)

L. Nochlin: *Gustave Courbet: A Study of Style and Society* (New York, 1977), pp. 111–14

P. Le Nouëne: '"Les Soldats de l'industrie" de François Bonhommé: L'Idéologie d'un projet', Les Réalismes et l'histoire de l'art, *Hist. & Crit. A.*, 4/5 (1977–8), pp. 35–61

G. Weisberg: 'François Bonhommé and Early Realist Images of Industrialization, 1830–1870', *A. Mag.*, 54 (April 1980), pp. 132–4

The Realist Tradition: French Painting and Drawing, 1830–1900 (exh. cat. by G. Weisberg, Cleveland, OH, Mus. A., 1981), pp. 71–9, 270–71

JAMES P. W. THOMPSON

Bonhomme, Léon(-Félix-Georges) (*b* Paris, 1870; *d* Saint-Denis, nr Paris, 1924). French painter. After studying with Jean-Jacques Henner, in 1890 he entered Gustave Moreau's studio, where he befriended Matisse, Albert Marquet, Jean Puy, Charles Camoin and especially Georges Rouault, all later associated with Fauvism. In a photograph of Moreau's studio taken shortly before Moreau's death, Bonhomme is seated in the front row next to Rouault, who later weighed so heavily on his own career that he gradually ceased to paint altogether. Painting generally in gouache and watercolour rather than oils in a technique clearly indebted to that of Rouault, he concentrated on subjects such as prostitution (as in the watercolour *Woman in Red on Chartreuse Couch*, 1913; see 1977 exh. cat., pl. 18), moral and physical poverty, and decadence. He was praised by writers fascinated by sin, such as Léon Bloy and Octave Mirbeau.

BIBLIOGRAPHY

Léon Bonhomme and Edouard Vuillard (exh. cat., London, Hanover Gal., 1948)

Léon Bonhomme, 1870–1924: Watercolours and Drawings (exh. cat., New York, Hammer Gals, 1977)

VANINA COSTA

Boni. *See* BUONO.

Boni, Giacomo (*b* Venice, 25 April 1859; *d* Rome, 10 July 1925). Italian archaeologist. He was educated in Venice at a time when there was great controversy over the conservation of original works of art, especially in connection with the restorations (1875) in S Marco. In 1888 he moved to Rome, where he became an inspector of monuments and advocated the establishment of a photographic archive and a catalogue of monuments as a basis for restoration programmes. Having collaborated on excavations inside the Pantheon in 1892, from 1895 he superintended new excavations in the Forum Romanum (*see* ROME, §V, 1); the latter uncovered fundamental evidence concerning the origins of Rome, including the Lapis Niger (1st century BC; *in situ*), an archaic Latin inscription (*c.* 500 BC; *Corpus inscriptionum latinarum*, Academia Litterarum Borussicae, Berlin, 1863–, vi, 36840) and 'pre-Romulan' burial grounds. He was influenced by John Ruskin's philosophy of art and argued that the prime function of restoration is to preserve original materials. In 1894 he condemned the mosaic restorations in Parenzo Cathedral, observing that 'authenticity does not constitute the main value of a monument, but it is a necessary condition for any value which the monument may have'. His dedication to the principle of preserving original material and his work on stratigraphic excavation made him a leading figure in the movement promoting a responsible approach to conservation, shaping attitudes to art history in late 19th-century Italy. However, because of his positivist view of archaeology, his racist theories on the decadence of Rome and his involvement with the Fascist authorities (who employed him to reconstruct the Classical lictor's fasces as their symbol), he was largely forgotten until the 1980s.

DBI

BIBLIOGRAPHY

L. Beltrami: *Giacomo Boni* (Milan, 1926)

E. Tea: *Giacomo Boni nella vita del suo tempo* (Milan, 1932)

A. Conti: 'Storia di una distruzione', *Via dei Fori Imperiali*, ed. L. Barroero and others (Venice, 1983), pp. 1–60 (32–6)

ALESSANDRO CONTI

Boni [Bona; Bono; del Bono; Buoni], **Giacomo Antonio** (*b* Bologna, 28 April 1688; *d* 7 Jan 1766). Italian painter. He was trained in the artistic climate of Emilia, as an apprentice to Marcantonio Franceschini and Donato Creti in Bologna and Carlo Cignani in Forlì. After visiting Genoa, Boni was influenced by the painting there, especially that of Lorenzo de' Ferrari, which contributed to a greater solidity and compositional equilibrium in his own work. In Bologna he belonged to the Accademia Clementina (1720), of which he was appointed director in 1721 and 1723. He was active, both as a painter of pictures for churches and as a decorator. His vast production in Genoa includes the *Agony in the Garden* and the *Deposition* in S Maria Maddalena; the fresco *Zephyr and Flora* (Pal. Bali-Durazzo, now Pal. Reale), painted in collaboration with the *quadraturista* Tommaso Aldrovandini (1653–1736), which, with its Rococo delicacy, is considered to be one of the painter's best works; and frescoes in aristocratic homes, such as the *Nurture of Jupiter* in the Palazzo Podestà. He also painted numerous works outside Genoa:

in Rome, the cupola of the Sacrament in St Peter's (1712), in collaboration with Franceschini; in Bologna, the decoration of the church of the Celestini (with Giacinto Garofalini (1661–1723) and Luca Antonio Bistega (1672–1732)); in Piacenza, the decoration of S Maria del Popolo (1717); in Parma, the decoration of the choir of the church of the Benedictines (1725)—both of the latter works were executed together with Franceschini; and others in Brescia and Milan. In addition he sent works to France and Spain and received commissions from Eugene, Prince of Savoy.

BIBLIOGRAPHY

DBI; Thieme–Becker

L. Crespi: *Vite de' pittori bolognesi non descritte nella 'Felsina pittrice'* (Rome, 1769), pp. 280–82

R. Soprani and C. G. Ratti: *Vite de' pittori, scultori, e architetti genovesi*, ii (Genoa, 1769), pp. 374–84

R. Roli: *Pittura bolognese, 1650–1800: Dal Cignani al Gandolfi* (Bologna, 1977), pp. 234–5 [with full bibliog.]

D. Puncuh: 'Collezionismo e commercio di quadri nella Genova sei-settecentesca', *Rass. Archv. Stato*, xliv (1984), pp. 164–218

E. Gavazza: 'Il momento della grande decorazione', *La pittura a Genova e in Liguria dal seicento al primo novecento*, ed. S. Editrice and E. Poleggi (Genoa, 1987)

M. Bartoletti: 'Boni, Giacomo Antonio', *La pittura in Italia: Il settecento*, ed. G. Briganti, ii (Milan, 1989), pp. 630–31 [with full bibliog.]

ANA MARIA RYBKO

Bonichi, Gino. *See* SCIPIONE.

Bonifacio, Martín Sanchez. *See* SANCHEZ BONIFACIO, MARTÍN.

Bonifás y Masó [Massó], **Luis** (*b* Valls, 1730; *d* Valls, 1786). Catalan sculptor. His great-grandfather and grand-father, respectively Luis Bonifás (*fl* 1676; *d* 1697) and Luis Bonifás y Sastre (1683–1765), settled in Valls and founded an academy of architecture and sculpture. His younger brother, Francisco Bonifás y Masó (1735–1806), was also a sculptor. Luis Bonifás y Masó himself worked in a Baroque style for both the architecture of his retables and for his sculptural compositions, as can be seen in the high altar at Cubells (1764), in which the figure of *St Peter* recalls the work of Bernini. In the previous year, however, he had successfully applied for full admission to the Real Academia de Bellas Artes de S Fernando, Madrid, and submitted a Neo-classical alabaster relief of *St Sebastian Succoured by St Irene* (*in situ*), clearly demonstrating that the extended Baroque strain in his work was due either to his own preference or to the demands of his clients. *St Sebastian* displays a poetic sentiment and pagan sensuality that is reminiscent of Poussin. Most of Bonifás y Masó's retables and Easter processional figures (*pasos*) have been destroyed. Two sculptural groups have survived, reliefs of the *Deposition* and the *Virgin of Solitude* (Valls, S Juan Bautista), both of which maintain the realistic expressive tradition of Spanish Baroque. The architectural frame and some of the decoration of the choir-stalls (1774–9; destr. 1936) for the new Lleida Cathedral were Neo-classical, while other more delicate motifs were Rococo. This important example of Catalan sculpture showed Bonifás y Masó's great ability as well as the moment of stylistic change from Baroque to Neo-classicism.

BIBLIOGRAPHY
C. Martinell: 'El escultor Luis Bonifás y Massó, 1730–86', *An. & Bol. Mus. A. Barcelona*, vi (1948), pp. 9–288
J. F. Rafols: *Diccionario biográfico de artistas de Cataluña* (Barcelona, 1951–3)
C. Martinelli: *Barroc Acadèmic, 1731–1810* (1963), iii of *Arquitectura i escultura barroques a Catalunya* (Barcelona, 1959–63)
J. Ainaud de Lasarte: *Cataluña* (Madrid, 1978)

GERMAN RAMALLO ASENSIO

Bonifazio de' Pitati. *See* PITATI, BONIFAZIO DE'.

Bonington, Richard Parkes (*b* Arnold, nr Nottingham, 25 Oct 1802; *d* London, 23 Sept 1828). English painter. His father, also called Richard (1768–1835), was a provincial drawing-master and painter, exhibiting at the Royal Academy and the Liverpool Academy between 1797 and 1811. An entrepreneur, he used his experience of the Nottingham lace-manufacturing industry to export machinery illegally to Calais, setting up a business there in late 1817 or early 1818. In Calais the young Richard Parkes Bonington became acquainted with Louis Francia, with whom he consolidated and expanded whatever knowledge of watercolour technique he had brought with him from England. Under Francia's direction Bonington left Calais for Paris where, probably not before mid- or late 1818, he met Eugène Delacroix. The latter's recollection of Bonington at this time was of a tall adolescent who revealed an astonishing aptitude in his watercolour copies of Flemish landscapes. Once in Paris Bonington embarked on an energetic and successful career, primarily as a watercolourist. In this he was supported by his parents who sometime before 1821 also moved to Paris, providing a business address for him at their lace company premises.

In Paris in 1818 Bonington enrolled at the atelier of Baron Antoine-Jean Gros, whose reputation was that of a skilled colourist and a progressive teacher. Bonington mastered the art of drawing *à la bosse*, as can be seen from the pencil and black chalk *Faun with Pipes* (New Haven, CT, Yale Cent.) and, in common with all Gros's pupils, engaged in *plein-air* sketching. From an early age Bonington was an extremely accomplished watercolourist as is revealed, for example, in his *View of Calais from La Rade* (*c*. 1818; Paris, Bib. N.), and he did much to encourage the vogue for the medium in the 1820s and 1830s among young Paris-based artists, from Ary Scheffer and Delacroix to Charles Gleyre and Gericault. He exhibited views of Lillebonne and Le Havre (untraced) at the Salon of 1821. Bonington left Gros's atelier in 1822; the teacher, after having been struck by the brilliant watercolours of his young pupil in a dealer's shop-window, declared: 'That man is a master.'

From that moment until his death six years later, Bonington was constantly on the move. He travelled the coasts of northern France and worked in Paris for the engraver J. F. d'Ostervald on the second volume of Baron Isidore-Justin-Severin Taylor's *Voyages pittoresques et romantiques dans l'ancienne France* (1825). He painted watercolours of the château of Rosny (1823–4; London, BM), which belonged to the anglophile Caroline, Duchess of Berry, and also travelled along the Seine, making numerous watercolour studies. He spent the spring and summer of 1824 in Dunkirk with Alexandre Colin (1798–1875). Here he visited members of the Morel family, to whom he had been introduced by Francia. The stay is recorded in a series of memorable pencil portrait studies of Bonington by Colin (Paris, Carnavalet), and also in a sequence of humorous pseudo-medieval letters by Bonington. While at Dunkirk he sketched at sea in a boat and must also have visited nearby Bergues and St Omer, whose ruined abbey appears in a number of his works. A sheet of small watercolour studies after Gerard ter Borch the younger, Rubens and others (Paris, Fond. Custodia, Inst. Néer.) shows how in Paris, during the winter months, Bonington supplemented his taste for TROUBADOUR STYLE painting (fanciful, mysterious and evocative recreations of historic interiors and balcony scenes) by freely copying Old Masters in the Louvre.

In 1825 Bonington went to London with several French artist friends including Delacroix, where they visited Westminster Hall and Sir Samuel Rush Meyrick's collection of medieval armour. The fruits of this study can be seen in Delacroix's *Murder of the Bishop of Liège* (1827–9; Paris, Louvre) and Bonington's *Quentin Durward at Liège* (Nottingham, Castle Mus.), both of which are based on Sir Walter Scott's novel *Quentin Durward*. With a letter of introduction from Francia to J. T. Smith, Keeper at the British Museum, Bonington and Colin were able to see the Elgin marbles; they also visited Carl Aders's collection of German and Flemish primitives. Following their return to Paris, Bonington and Delacroix shared a studio for a brief period, producing similar works, which were orientalizing or medievalizing in style and content.

In 1826 Bonington visited Venice in the company of Baron Charles Rivet. They travelled through Switzerland to Milan (where Bonington produced a dramatic watercolour of the interior of the church of S Ambrogio; London, Wallace) and then continued on to Bologna and Verona. Their visit profoundly affected Bonington, although Venice was not at this time a popular location among artists. Samuel Prout and Turner had visited the city before he had, but Bonington was the first to exhibit his oils publicly, showing *View of the Piazzetta* and the *Ducal Palace, Venice* (London, Tate) at the British Institution and the Royal Academy in 1828. Yet these oils, among them the *Piazza San Marco* (?1827; London, Wallace), appear laboured in comparison with the sparkling spontaneity and versatility of handling (ranging in treatment from liquid washes to dry brushstrokes) of his Italian watercolours such as *The Piazzetta, Venice* (?1826; London, Wallace).

In Venice Bonington had the opportunity of studying the work of Titian, Tintoretto and Veronese at first hand. His debt to them is evident both in the subject-matter and colour range of his Troubadour paintings, such as the oil version of *Henry IV and the Spanish Ambassador* (exh. Salon 1827–8; London, Wallace; see fig.). These pastiches were constructed from various sources: his familiarity with the work of van Dyck and Titian, his readings of Brugière de Barante and medieval chronicles, and his visits to the Paris theatres of the 1820s. Brilliantly executed, these small-scale fantasies parody and undermine the established meanings of historical pictures by artists such as Ingres and Paul Delaroche. The term *Ecole Anglo-Venetienne* was coined by Auguste Jal in 1827 to describe works in this

Richard Parkes Bonington: *Henry IV and the Spanish Ambassador*, oil on canvas, 384×524 mm, exhibited at the Salon of 1827–8 (London, Wallace Collection)

vein. This was a school that appealed not only to Delacroix (who told Bonington: 'Vous êtes roi dans votre domaine et Raphael n'eût pas fait ce que vous faites') but also to a variety of aristocratic collectors, such as Henry Fox, 3rd Baron Holland, and John Russell, 6th Duke of Bedford, in England, and Comte Turpin de Crissé in France. Bonington's most enthusiastic collector, however, was the Bordeaux wine-merchant John Brown, who acquired an outstanding collection of the artist's watercolours, a substantial part of which is now preserved in the Wallace Collection, London.

Bonington's career was suddenly and tragically cut short when he died of consumption at the age of 26. The brevity and brilliance of his working life have encouraged a sentimental appreciation of his work and a tendency to isolate him from such peers as Paul Huet, Alexandre Colin, THOMAS SHOTTER BOYS and the Fielding brothers.

BIBLIOGRAPHY

A. Cunningham: *The Lives of the Most Eminent British Painters, Sculptors and Architects*, v (London, 1832), pp. 295–311
A. Dubuisson and C. E. Hughes: *Richard Parkes Bonington: His Life and Work* (London, 1924)
A. Curtis: *Catalogue de l'oeuvre lithographié et gravé de R. P. Bonington* (Paris, 1939)
R. P. Bonington, 1802–1828 (exh. cat. by M. Spencer, Nottingham, Castle Mus., 1965) [based on author's diss., U. Nottingham, 1963]
Bonington: Un Romantique anglais à Paris (exh. cat. by P. Georgel, Paris, Mus. Jacquemart-André, 1966)
J. Ingamells: *Richard Parkes Bonington* (London, 1979)
C. Peacock: *Richard Parkes Bonington* (London, 1979)
M. Pointon: *The Bonington Circle: English Watercolour and Anglo-French Landscape, 1790–1855* (Brighton, 1985)
——: *Bonington, Francia and Wyld* (London, 1985) [cat. rais. of works in the V&A]
——: '"Vous êtes roi dans votre domaine": Bonington as a Painter of Troubadour Subjects', *Burl. Mag.*, cxxviii (1986), pp. 10–17
Richard Parkes Bonington: 'On the Pleasure of Painting' (exh. cat. by P. Noon, New Haven, CT, Yale Cent. Brit. A.; Paris, Petit Pal.; 1991–2)

MARCIA POINTON

Bonino, Giovanni di. *See under* MASTERS, ANONYMOUS, AND MONOGRAMMISTS, §I: MASTER OF THE FOGG PIETÀ.

Bonino da Campione. *See under* CAMPIONESI.

Bonis, Niccolo de' (*fl* 1574–92). Italian medallist. Although he worked in the papal mint from 1580 to 1592, virtually nothing is known about his life and career, which may say something about the relative unimportance of a die-engraver, a job that he is documented as having in 1591 (*'incisore della Zecca Romana'*). He seems to have moved with his brother, Emilio de' Bonis, from Venice to Rome and signed a medal in 1574 for the inauguration of the Collegio Germanico in Rome. Thereafter, virtually all of his medals were produced for his papal employers. According to Forrer, he struck medals for Gregory XIII

(1572–85), Sixtus V (1585–90; five variants), Gregory XIV (1590–91; eight variants), Innocent IX (1591; seven variants) and Clement VIII (1592–1605; four variants). As was usually the case with papal commemorative medals, an official portrait of the pontiff was established, coupled with a series of reverses devoted to significant acts or events that occurred during that particular papacy. Such medals were invariably struck and were relatively monotonous and dry in technique and style. Nonetheless, the medals of de' Bonis do possess certain distinctive qualities. The portraits of Sixtus V, for example, are quite vigorous and capture the gruff features of this former peasant. The medal struck to commemorate the building of the Ponte Felice over the Tiber in the Borghetto section of Rome (1589; see Panvini Rosati, no. 140) has a portrait executed in fine detail and in higher relief than is usual with these pieces. The pontifical cope is rendered with great delicacy and extraordinary attention to exact description. Few of Niccolò's portraits attain the same level of characterization, although his depiction of draperies is always precise and sensitive. The reverses also show a similar technical facility, as in the interesting perspective view of the Piazza del Popolo on a medal of Sixtus V (1589; see Pollard, no. 671) or the graceful figure of *Abundance* on a medal of Gregory XIV (1590–91; see Pollard, no. 686).

BIBLIOGRAPHY

Forrer

F. Panvini Rosati: *Medaglie e placchette italiane dal rinascimento al XVIII secolo* (Rome, 1968), pp. 43–4

Roma resurgens: Papal Medals from the Age of the Baroque (exh. cat., ed. N. T. Whitman and J. L. Varriano; Ann Arbor, U. MI, Mus. A., 1983), pp. 39, 44–5, 48, 187

G. Pollard: *Italian Renaissance Medals: Museo Nazionale del Bargello* (Florence, 1985), pp. 1156–8, 1170, 1175, 1189

STEPHEN K. SCHER

Bonito, Giuseppe (*b* Castellammare di Stabia, nr Naples, 1707; *d* Naples, 19 May 1789). Italian painter. A student of Francesco Solimena, Bonito became one of the most influential artists of the Neapolitan school in the 18th century. Throughout his career, but most notably during the latter part of the century when Rome was the arbiter of Neo-classicism, his style remained firmly within the rich painterly traditions of Naples. His earliest works, for example the *Archangel Raphael and Tobias* (1730; Naples, S Maria Maggiore), show an assimilation of elements derived from late Baroque artists working in Naples and a hesitant affinity to the tenebrism of Solimena. In other pictures of sacred subjects from *c*. 1730 onwards, however, he developed a personal neo-Baroque style characterized by sweeping movement, bold chiaroscuro and a saturated palette reminiscent of both Solimena and Luca Giordano. Paintings in this style, such as *St Vincent Ferrer* (1737; Barletta, S Domenico), *St Lazarus* (early 1740s; Portici, S Ciro) and *Charity* (1742; Naples, Pal. Monte di Pietà), show that Bonito's maturity was also characterized by delicacy and grace.

During the 1740s Bonito became a successful court portraitist, albeit in a style different from that of his other works. The *Turkish Ambassador in Naples in 1741* (1742; Madrid, Prado), probably his first royal portrait commission, exhibits the intense realism, carefully modelled light and naturalistic detail that thereafter distinguished his

portraiture from that of his court predecessors, notably Pompeo Batoni. Portraits from this period include the series of nine paintings representing the *Children of Charles III* (1748; Madrid, Prado).

Throughout the 1750s Bonito was also active as a designer and adviser on artistic matters to the Bourbon court. He was appointed *pittore di camera* in 1751, elected to the Accademia di S Luca, Rome, in 1752 and from 1755 onwards was director of the Accademia di Belle Arti in Naples. He executed a variety of royal commissions, including designs for commemorative medals and tapestries; among the latter are episodes from the *Story of Don Quixote* (designed 1758; tapestries, Naples, Pal. Reale). He also continued to produce portraits, including the *Portrait of a Neapolitan Gentlewoman* (*c*. 1754–5; Bergamo, priv. col., see 1981 exh. cat., p. 84) and the beguiling double portrait of *Prince Ferdinand and Prince Gabriel* (*c*. 1759; Naples, Mus. N. S Martino). His most acclaimed painting of the 1750s was the *di sotto in sù* vault fresco of the *Dedication of Solomon's Temple* (1752–8; Naples, S Chiara, destr. 1943; *bozzetto*, *c*. 1752–3; Naples, Capodimonte), which exhibited the rich colours and deeply shaded contours characteristic of his style throughout the middle part of the century.

In the late 1750s Bonito's religious paintings became more Rococo in style and spirit. The *Crucifixion* and the *Holy Family* (both *c*. 1757; Naples, SS Giovanni e Teresa) incorporated paler tones and more diffused contours than he had used previously. A further, late transition in Bonito's style is evident in the badly damaged *Immaculate Conception* of the 1780s (Caserta, Pal. Reale), which has the languid rhythms, pale luminosity and rich surface textures typical of the 18th-century Rococo style elsewhere in Europe. A late *Self-portrait* (1785–9) is also preserved (Florence, Uffizi). He is also thought to have executed a great number of genre pictures, but this aspect of his career remains uncertain and controversial.

BIBLIOGRAPHY

Bolaffi; *DBI* [excellent critical summary and bibliog. by R. Enggass]

N. Spinosa: 'Gli arazzi del Belvedere a Palazzo Reale', *Antol. B.A.*, ii/5 (1978), pp. 12–23

Pittura sacra a Napoli nel '700 (exh. cat., ed. N. Spinosa; Naples, Pal. Reale, 1980–81), cat. nos 3, 4, 49; pp. 26, 28, 98

The Golden Age of Naples: Art and Civilization under the Bourbons, 1734–1805, 2 vols (exh. cat., Detroit, MI, Inst. A., 1981), i, nos 8–10, pp. 82–5; nos. 8a, 213; ii, nos 127, 172, pp. 375–7 [entries by N. Spinosa]

Bonn. Cathedral city and capital of the Federal Republic of Germany from 1949 to 1991. It is situated on the River Rhine north of the Mittelrheinisches Schiefergebirge (the Siebengebirge), *c*. 25 km south of Cologne. Its population is barely 300,000. Although the earliest traces of habitation date from the Palaeolithic period, the town only began to take coherent shape under the Romans. A large legionary fortress, Castra Bonnensia, and an adjoining civilian settlement existed on the west bank of the Rhine from *c*. AD 30 to the mid-5th century; at its height the population was more than 20,000. During the MIGRATION PERIOD the region was settled by the Franks.

The medieval town, which achieved full legal status and its definitive size in the 13th century, developed around the Late Romanesque minster (11th–13th century), formerly a monastic church that can be traced back to an Early Christian chapel ('cella memoriae', *c.* 300). The minster has a typically Rhineland Romanesque choir with square towers decorated with Lombard bands, flanking a galleried apse. The polygonal transept terminations have similar decoration. The four-bay aisled nave has a three-storey elevation, with passages in both the triforium and the clerestory, and rib vaults over square bays. The cloisters (1126–89) are noteworthy. Bonn's other distinguished medieval buildings include the former Minoritenkirche (ded. 1317), now the parish church of St Remigius. Across the Rhine in the Beuel area are the former Benedictine monastic church of St Peter, Vilich (13th–17th century), and the mid-12th-century double church of St Klemens, Schwarzrheindorf, which was originally the castle chapel of the lords of Wied. Its cycle of contemporary wall paintings illustrating the book of Ezekiel make it a building of international significance. On the west bank, Bad Godesberg is dominated by the ruins of the Godesburg, a fortress of the archbishops of Cologne built in the early 13th century (destr. 1583).

From the 16th century until the end of the 18th, Bonn was the capital city and official residence of the Electors Palatine and archbishops of Cologne (*see* WITTELSBACH). Buildings from this period include the magnificent Baroque Rathaus (see fig.) on the Marktplatz, designed by Michel Leveilly; the Residenzschloss (1697–1725, by Enrico Zuccalli and Robert de Cotte; rebuilt 1926–30), which serves as the main building of the Rheinische Friedrich-Wilhelms-Universität (founded 1818); Schloss Clemensruhe in Bonn-Poppelsdorf (1715–40, by Robert de Cotte);

Bonn, Rathaus, by Michel Leveilly, 1737–8; in the background is one of the Baroque lanterns of the Residenzschloss (now the university)

the Baroque Namen-Jesu-Kirche (University church; 1688–1717); the pilgrimage church on the Kreuzberg (1628), with the holy stair extension (1746–51) built by Balthasar Neumann; and the surviving remains of the town wall. At the end of the 18th century Bad Godesberg also became an official residence; the Redoute, a late Classical ballroom and concert-hall (1790–92), is still used.

Although the street plan of the inner city largely follows the medieval plan, all the surviving buildings, except the medieval churches, date from the period after 1689, when Bonn was besieged for several weeks and all but destroyed. In 1815 the city became part of Prussia, with the rest of the Rhineland. Bonn developed into an affluent university town and the home of people of independent means; whole districts, such as 'Südstadt' in Bonn and 'Villenviertel' in Bad Godesberg, recall the character of this period. Among the most important 19th-century buildings are the Anatomiegebäude (1824), now the Akademische Kunstmuseum, and the observatory (1840–45), both built to the plans of Karl Friedrich Schinkel; a series of large Gothic Revival or Romanesque Revival churches; the Villa Hammerschmidt (1863–5), one of the residences of the president of the Federal Republic; the Palais Schaumburg (1858–60), formerly the residence of the chancellor of the Federal Republic; and the Zoologisches Museum Alexander Koenig, built in 1912–14 in Renaissance Revival style. After World War I the town became less prosperous, and the inner city area suffered heavy damage in World War II.

The granting of capital status in 1949 had far-reaching consequences. The Pädagogische Akademie (1930–33) was altered and extended to house the parliamentary committees, and in 1969 the Members' Building for the Bundestag, designed by Egon Eiermann, was completed; essentially a glass box (h. 114 m), it is the tallest building in Bonn. Other administrative buildings followed, and in 1969 the towns of Bonn, Bad Godesberg and Beuel, with a few smaller parishes, were combined to form the new city of Bonn; numerous villages near by had already been incorporated into the town in the 19th century and the early 20th.

The Beethovenhalle (1956–9), by Siegfried Wolske (*b* 1925), and the Oper (1962–5) were important cultural additions. Museums include the Rheinisches Landesmuseum, with its collection of painting, sculpture, applied arts and Roman remains connected with the region; and the Städtisches Kunstmuseum and the Bundeskunsthalle (both opened 1992), which contain important collections of German paintings and 20th-century works, the former with special emphasis on Expressionism, particularly the works of August Macke. The home of the historian Ernst Moritz Arndt (1769–1860), one of the first professors at Bonn University, specializes as the museum's exhibition area for Rhine Romanticism.

BIBLIOGRAPHY

E. Ennen and D. Höroldt: *Vom Römerkastell zur Bundeshauptstadt: Kleine Geschichte der Stadt Bonn* (Bonn, 1966, 4/1985)

D. Höroldt and M. van Rey, eds: *Geschichte der Stadt Bonn*, 4 vols (Bonn, 1989–)

NORBERT SCHLOSSMACHER

Bonnafé, A. A. (*fl* mid-19th century). ?French draughtsman and lithographer active in the USA and Peru. He lived briefly in the USA, where in 1852 he published a book containing 32 woodcuts depicting American working-class figures. Later he moved to Lima, the capital of Peru, where he published two albums of hand-coloured lithographs, *Recuerdos de Lima* (1856–7), of the city's people, clothing and customs.

PRINTS

Recuerdos de Lima (Lima, 1856–7)

BIBLIOGRAPHY

L. E. Tord: 'Historia de las artes plásticas en el Perú', *Historia del Perú*, ix (Lima, 1980)

C. Milla Batres, ed.: *Diccionario histórico y biográfico del Perú: Siglos XV–XX*, ii (Lima, 1986)

LUIS ENRIQUE TORD

Bonnard, Pierre (*b* Fontenay-aux-Roses, nr Paris, 3 Oct 1867; *d* Le Cannet, 27 Jan 1947). French painter, printmaker and photographer. He is known particularly for the decorative qualities of his paintings and his individual use of colour. During his life he was associated with other artists, Edouard Vuillard being a good friend, and he was a member of the NABIS.

1. Early development, the Nabis, and the literary world, until *c*. 1900. 2. Travels and stylistic changes, *c*. 1900–*c*. 1920. 3. International success and late work, after *c*. 1920.

1. EARLY DEVELOPMENT, THE NABIS AND THE LITERARY WORLD, UNTIL *c*. 1900. Bonnard spent some of his childhood at Grand-Lemps in the Isère, where his family owned a house surrounded by a large park. There was a farm adjoining the house, and from an early age he developed a love of nature and animals. After obtaining the baccalauréat at 18, he enrolled in the Law faculty in order to please his father, who wanted him to have a steady job. He graduated when he was 21, and he was sworn in as a barrister in 1889. In the meantime he was already drawing and painting, having enrolled at the Académie Julian, Paris, in 1887. In an attractive *Self-portrait* of 1889 (Paris, priv. col., see Zurich, 1984–5 exh. cat., p. 72) he depicted himself not in barrister's robes but as a young painter, holding a palette.

Bonnard's first paintings were landscapes of the Dauphiné, around Grand-Lemps, small-scale works in which the tonality is reminiscent of Corot. However, his technique was soon to change. At the Académie Julian he had met Maurice Denis and Paul Sérusier. The latter, who was the student in charge in his studio, had shown Bonnard, as well as his friends at the Ecole des Beaux-Arts, Ker-Xavier Roussel and Vuillard, the *Bois d'Amour at Pont-Aven* or *The Talisman* (Paris, Mus. d'Orsay), a small painting executed at Pont-Aven 'as dictated by Gauguin' (for illustration see SÉRUSIER, PAUL). Sérusier had revelled in the use of pure colour in flat areas with strong outlines. This revelation took place in October 1888. Bonnard himself said that he had been 'inspired by the magnificent example of Gauguin', after discovering his work in June 1889 at the exhibition at the Café Volpini. Sérusier decided to form a group, the Nabis, to proclaim to the world the new gospel of painting. The first members were Sérusier, Denis, Bonnard, Paul Ranson and Henri-Gabriel Ibels, and they were soon joined by Ker-Xavier Roussel and Vuillard. The first group exhibition took place in 1891 in the château of Saint-Germain-en-Laye.

Bonnard was also attracted by Japanese art, which he saw in 1890 in a large exhibition at the Ecole des Beaux-Arts. He was immediately captivated by the formal simplicity of the prints with their bold yet fluent strokes of colour, applied in strong flat tints interspersed with vibrant blacks on a monochrome ground. His fascination with this art was such that his friends called him 'the Japanesque Nabi'. During the period 1890–92 Gauguin and Japan were the major influences on Bonnard's work, affecting both the imagery and decorative character of his work, from *On Parade* (1890; priv. col., see Dauberville and Dauberville, i, p. 87), a humorous souvenir of a military period, up to the great composition of the *Croquet Party* (1892; Paris, Mus. d'Orsay), which depicts his family playing in the park at Grand-Lemps. This period also included the four *panneaux décoratifs* of *Women in the Garden* (oil on paper on canvas, each 1600×480 mm, 1891; Paris, Mus. d'Orsay). For S. Bing, a major promoter of Japanese art, Bonnard and other Nabis painters designed stained-glass windows (executed by Louis Comfort Tiffany in 1895) for his salon of international Art Nouveau.

Like a number of his friends Bonnard applied his decorative skills not only to paintings but also to such everyday objects used in ordinary houses as tapestries, furniture, decorated pottery, screens and fans. In the 1890s the term INTIMISME was first used to refer to paintings of daily life in domestic interiors, particularly those by Bonnard and Vuillard. In March 1891 Bonnard's *France-Champagne* poster (lithograph; New Brunswick, NJ, Rutgers U., Zimmerli A. Mus.) appeared on the walls of Paris. In strong contrast to the bright and colourful posters of Jules Chéret, *France-Champagne* was composed in three colours with black predominant. Its effect lay in the lettering, which was hand-drawn rather than produced from printed characters, and in the suggestive curves of the woman's extended arm. The only straight line was provided by a closed fan underlining the name of the brand of champagne being advertised. Toulouse-Lautrec was so impressed by this poster that he decided to enter this field himself. Bonnard introduced him to his own printer, Ancourt. After Toulouse-Lautrec won a competition to design a poster for the Moulin Rouge cabaret, which he had also entered, Bonnard deferred to his talent for the medium.

The 100 francs that Bonnard received for *France-Champagne* encouraged him to turn his back on his law studies and to try to make a living as a painter. He rented a studio at the foot of Montmartre, at the corner of Rue Pigalle and Rue La Bruyère, which he shared with Maurice Denis, Sérusier and Vuillard. The actor Aurélien Lugné-Poe, a friend and fellow student of Denis at the Lycée Condorcet, came to rehearse his roles there. The friendship strengthened the painters' links with the theatrical world. The Nabis designed sets for the poet and dramatist Paul Fort's Théâtre d'Art, for André Antoine's Théâtre Libre and for Lugné-Poe's own Théâtre de l'Oeuvre.

Sérusier, Bonnard, Vuillard, Paul Ranson and Toulouse-Lautrec collaborated in designing the sets, masks and costumes for Alfred Jarry's *Ubu-roi* when it was performed for the first time in 1896, at the Théâtre de l'Oeuvre. The music was composed by Claude Terrasse, who had married Andrée Bonnard, the painter's sister, in 1890. The artists also illustrated the programmes, a lucrative venture that led them to produce drawings and lithographs for books, newspapers and magazines, such as the *Revue blanche* established by Thadée, Alexandre and Alfred Natanson in Paris in 1891. At the magazine's offices they met such writers as Félix Fénéon, Jules Renard, Octave Mirbeau, Henri de Régnier and Léon Blum, and Thadée Natanson's wife, Misia, referred to by Lugné-Poe as 'radiant and sibylline', who frequently posed as a model for Bonnard and Vuillard. Bonnard's poster of 1894 for the *Revue blanche* (New York, MOMA), in grey and beige with touches of pink, depicting a warmly wrapped passer-by, evokes winter in the city with the 'fine Parisian mist' described by Gustave Geffroy. The woman's face in the poster was inspired by Maria ('Marthe') Boursin, a pretty model, whom he had met at the end of 1893. They later married. In Bonnard's paintings Marthe's slender, supple body never aged, remaining over the years just as it had appeared in his first nude studies. He also painted the children of the Claude Terrasse household: around the lamp, in front of the fire, surrounded by cats; or playing in the park and bathing in the lake at Grand-Lemps. In these works he captures a tenderness and an amusement at the games of his nephews and nieces. In other street scenes of the 1890s, such as the 12 lithographs and cover published by Vollard as *Quelques aspects de la vie de Paris* (1899), no part of the bustling life of Paris escaped his eye: the children on their way to school in their hooded cloaks; the policeman; the cabs waiting along the boulevard with their scrawny horses; the covert movements of those passing women who lift their long skirts before stepping up on to a pavement or adjust a beribboned hat.

Vollard had seen Bonnard's first one-man exhibition at Durand-Ruel in 1896, and he also commissioned 109 lithographs and 9 woodcuts as illustrations for Verlaine's *Parallèlement* (Paris, 1900) and 106 lithographs printed in black for *Daphnis and Chloe* (Paris, 1902). Vollard admired both the *Indolent Woman* (1899; Paris, Mus. d'Orsay), a sensual and voluptuous nude, and *Bourgeois Afternoon*, also known as the *Terrasse Family* (1900; Paris, Mus. d'Orsay), a large painting exhibited at the first Salon d'Automne in 1903. The irony of the title, which underlines the onlooker's amusement, should not be allowed to disguise Bonnard's new concern for order and for arrangement within the picture. The immediacy and imaginative composition of such paintings bear comparison with photographic snapshots. Bonnard had practised photography from the 1890s, using a small Kodak camera, which produced small-format negatives. Parallels can be seen in his photographs and his paintings, although he did not explore all the subjects of his paintings in his photographs. For the latter he restricted himself to the family or friendly setting: the majority of his photographs were taken during stays in the country, particularly when he was with the Terrasse family. Marthe was also the subject of his photographs.

2. TRAVELS AND STYLISTIC CHANGES, *c.* 1900–*c.* 1920. By the early years of the new century the Nabis had separated, and Bonnard travelled, visiting England, Belgium, Holland, Spain and Italy, often accompanied by Vuillard. Together they explored museums and new landscapes. This was a period of reflection, discovery and research. Although there were a number of new movements to observe in Paris alone (in 1905 Fauvism; from 1907–8 Cubism), Bonnard always maintained a distance and independence from them, though not out of hostility. His use of colour, in particular, distinguished his work at a time when the Fauves were applying it in almost violent hues, and the Cubists were treating it in greys and earth colours. In comparison with the avant-garde, Bonnard appeared to be reverting to Impressionism. In 1908 he painted *The Box* (Paris, Mus. d'Orsay) in apparent homage to Renoir and his painting of the same title (London, Courtauld Inst.). In *Nude in 'contre-jour'* (1908; Brussels, Mus. A. Mod.) in the interweaving of colours, like wools, he seemed to employ the techniques of Renoir and Monet. While these paintings take up the themes and sometimes the techniques of the Impressionists, they are very different in composition and treatment: *The Box* is organized around long vertical lines, with incandescent reds reminiscent of Fauvism; *Nude in 'contre-jour'*, like many of his later pictures, includes a small mirror, a device that allows him to represent space within a flat idiom. In the latter work Bonnard's concern with order in the composition bears witness to a deep reconsideration of his means of expression since the *Bourgeois Afternoon*. While acknowledging a debt to Impressionism, Bonnard said that he wanted to go beyond their practical interpretation of nature in art in favour of more expressive use of colour and stringency of composition.

Bonnard continued in developing his own style, often organizing compositions around strong verticals or horizontals determined by the framework of walls, doors, windows or pieces of furniture (see fig. 1). At the same

1. Pierre Bonnard: *The Dressing-table* (or *The Mirror*), oil on canvas, 525×455 mm, 1908 (Paris, Musée d'Orsay)

time that this evolution took place in his paintings, a similar change can be detected in Bonnard's photographic work. Around the time of *Marthe in the Tub* (*c*. 1908; see 1987–8 exh. cat., p. 75) he changed to a larger format of camera and negatives (85×55 mm). He took up the same subject in his paintings from *c*. 1912 to *c*. 1924, although in these, while using the same composition, he exaggerated the perspective. After his discovery in 1909–10 of the intense light of the Midi region he applied his colours with a luminescence expressive of decorative, sensual and emotional effects. However, he was aware that in his enthusiasm for colour, he must not let his drawing be sacrificed to it. Around the time that colour became the most important element in his painting, Bonnard seems to have lost interest in photography.

The difficulties that Bonnard faced in the years 1910–20 in seeking to synthesize these elements resulted in such masterpieces as *Summer in Normandy* (1912; Moscow, Pushkin Mus.) and *Country Dining-room* (1913; Minneapolis, MN, Inst. A.). Both were painted in the house Bonnard had bought near Vernon (Eure), not far from Giverny, where he visited Claude Monet. In the great decorative works that he undertook between 1916 and 1920, such as *Pastoral Symphony* (Paris, Bernheim-Jeune), he first defined masses by areas of colour, a technique that became a hallmark of his works. He also visited Renoir, also living in the Midi, finding support through friendship, as with Monet.

3. International success and late works, after *c*. 1920. From 1920 Bonnard enjoyed an uninterrupted string of successes. The painters and writers of Picasso's circle may not have appreciated the new quality in his work, but it was admired by such other artists as Signac, Matisse and Rouault. He was acclaimed in the USA, where his work was already being collected by Duncan Phillips; in 1926 he went to Pittsburgh, PA, to serve as a member of the jury of the Carnegie International exhibition, also visiting Philadelphia, Washington, DC, and New York. Bonnard's late landscapes and interiors looking through to gardens are notable for their luminosity. His most important later paintings include the *Breakfast Room* (1931–2; New York, MOMA; see fig. 2), *White Interior* (1932; Grenoble, Mus. Grenoble), *Nude in the Bath* (1936; Paris, Petit Pal.), the *Large Landscape of Le Cannet* (1945; Milwaukee, WI, A. Mus.) and *Studio with Mimosa* (1939–46; Paris, Pompidou), as well as a series of self-portraits executed in the last years of his life. Shortly before his death he finished *Almond Tree in Bloom* (1947; Paris, Pompidou).

Bonnard's innovative work as a printmaker continued in his later years, reflecting his increasing fluency and freedom as a draughtsman. A major project was his set of illustrations for Ambroise Vollard's text *Sainte Monique* (Paris, 1930), for which a variety of techniques was introduced 'to follow the rhythm of the text and break the monotony of a uniform technique', as Bonnard recalled in 1943 (quoted in Bouvet, p. 254). This series, begun in 1920 and not published until 10 years later, consisted of 29 drawings transferred on to stone, 17 etchings and 178 woodcuts. In later lithographs, such as *Woman Seated in her Bath* (nine-colour lithograph, 1942; see Bouvet,

2. Pierre Bonnard: *Breakfast Room*, oil on canvas, 1.61×1.12 m, 1931–2 (New York, Museum of Modern Art)

p. 291), Bonnard successfully adapted the glazing techniques of his paintings to subtle superimpositions of printed colours.

Bonnard's notebooks and jottings are full of very simple, spontaneous observations, both lighthearted and serious. He tells amusing anecdotes ('A house painter said to me one day: "Monsieur, the first coat always goes fine. When it comes to the second, I need you"'), and notes all the daily weather details ('Weather bright but cold; there is vermilion in the orange shadows and violet in the grey ones'). This precision demonstrates the keenness of his perception and reveals his urge to get back to the studio to paint the colours that only he had seen and only he knew how to transpose.

WRITINGS

Correspondance (Paris, 1944)
Bonnard-Matisse: Correspondance (Paris, 1991; Eng. trans., New York, 1992) [incl. texts by J. Clair and A. Terrasse]

BIBLIOGRAPHY

T. Natanson: 'Pierre Bonnard', *Rev. Blanche* (15 Jan 1896)
C. Roger-Marx: *Pierre Bonnard*, Les Peintres français nouveaux, 19 (1924)
C. Terrasse: *Bonnard* (Paris, 1927)
P. Courthion: *Bonnard: Peintre du merveilleux* (Lausanne, 1945)
F.-J. Beer: *Pierre Bonnard*, preface R. Cogniat (Marseille, 1947) [incl. text by L. Gillet]
J. Rewald: *Bonnard* (New York, 1948)
Pierre Bonnard (exh. cat. by J. Rewald and C. Terrasse, New York, MOMA, 1948)
Pierre Bonnard (exh. cat. by J. Leymarie, Zurich, Ksthaus, 1949)
C. Roger-Marx: *Bonnard* (Paris, 1950)

Exposition rétrospective Bonnard (exh. cat., preface C. Terrasse; Paris, Bernheim-Jeune, 1950)

T. Natanson: *Le Bonnard que je propose* (Geneva, 1951)

C. Roger-Marx: *Bonnard lithographe* (Monte Carlo, 1952)

Bonnard, Vuillard et les Nabis (1888–1905) (exh. cat., texts by B. Dorival and A. Humbert; Paris, Mus. N. A. Mod., 1955)

A. Terrasse: *Bonnard* (Geneva, 1964)

Bonnard and his Environment (exh. cat., texts by J. T. Soby, J. Elliott and M. Wheeler; New York, MOMA, 1964)

J. Dauberville and H. Dauberville: *Bonnard: Catalogue raisonné de l'oeuvre peint*, 4 vols (Paris, 1965–74) [incl. supplement]

Pierre Bonnard (exh. cat., texts by C. Wheeler and D. Sutton; London, RA, 1966)

A. Terrasse: *Pierre Bonnard* (Paris, 1967, 2/1988; Eng. trans., 1989)

Pierre Bonnard: Gemälde, Aquarelle, Zeichnungen und Druckgraphik (exh. cat., text by H. Platte; Hamburg, Kstver., 1970)

Pierre Bonnard (exh. cat., texts by R. Cogniat and C. Kunstler; Melbourne, N.G. Victoria, 1971)

Bonnard, Vuillard, Roussel (exh. cat., text by R. Cogniat; Brussels, Musées Royaux B.-A., 1975)

F. Bouvet: *Bonnard: L'Oeuvre gravé, catalogue complet*, preface A. Terrasse (Paris, 1981; Eng. trans., New York, 1981)

Bonnard (exh. cat. by A. Gonzalez García, Madrid, Fund. Juan March, 1983)

Bonnard (exh. cat., texts by J. Clair and others; Paris, Pompidou; Washington, DC, Phillips Col.; Dallas, TX, Mus. A.; 1984)

Bonnard (exh. cat., texts by J. Clair and others; Zurich, Ksthaus, 1984–5)

Drawings by Bonnard (exh. cat., texts by A. Terrasse and S. Mann; ACGB, 1984–5)

Hommage à Bonnard (exh. cat., texts by C. Freches-Thory and P. Le Leyzour; Bordeaux, Gal. B.-A., 1986)

Bonnard photographe (exh. cat., ed. F. Heilbrun and P. Neagu; Paris, Mus. d'Orsay, 1987–8)

Pierre Bonnard: The Graphic Art (exh. cat. by C. Ives, H. Giambruni and S. Newman, New York, Met.; Houston, TX, Mus. F.A.; Boston, MA, Mus. F.A.; 1989–90)

ANTOINE TERRASSE

Bonnassieux, Jean-Marie-Bienaimé (*b* Panissières, Loire, 19 Sept 1810; *d* Paris, 3 June 1892). French sculptor. He trained in Lyon with manufacturers of church furnishings, then in Paris at the Ecole des Beaux-Arts with Augustin Dumont. In 1836 he won the Prix de Rome and completed his education at the Académie de France in Rome under the directorship of Ingres. Though he exhibited only a few works at the Salon, including the classicizing *Cupid's Wings Clipped* (marble, 1842; Paris, Louvre), he received numerous commissions for decorative sculpture for the major public building projects of the second half of the 19th century, including the Louvre (1855, 1856, 1857, 1868, 1876), the Palais de Justice, Paris (1868), and the Lyon Bourse (1858, 1863). He also executed several public monuments, such as that to *Henry IV* (bronze, 1856; La Flèche, Sarthe, Place Henri IV).

Most of Bonnassieux's commissions, however, were for private patrons—often ecclesiastic—and included portrait busts and tombs such as the austerely classicizing *Duchesse Honoré de Luynes* (marble, 1866; Dampierre, Seine-et-Oise, parish church) and monuments such as that to *Ingres* (marble, 1868; Paris, Père Lachaise Cemetery). He executed the sculptural decoration of the church of La Madeleine in Tarare (Rhône) and contributed to the decoration of many churches in Paris, Lyon and his native Forez region of the upper Loire Valley. The most famous of his series of monumental statues of the Virgin is *Notre-Dame de France* (h. 16 m, cast iron, 1860), erected by public subscription at Le Puy. Sketch models of a number of his works are in the Musée d'Orsay, Paris.

BIBLIOGRAPHY

Lami

L. Armagnac: *Bonnassieux statuaire* (Paris, 1897)

A. Le Normand: *La Tradition classique et l'esprit romantique: Les Sculpteurs de l'Académie de France à Rome de 1824 à 1840* (Rome, 1981)

A. Le Normand-Romain: 'Six Esquisses du sculpteur Bonnassieux', *Rev. Louvre*, 5/6 (1982), pp. 366–72

La Sculpture française au XIXème siècle (exh. cat., ed. A. Pingeot; Paris, Grand Pal., 1986), pp. 29, 32–6, 47, 130, 235

ANTOINETTE LE NORMAND-ROMAIN

Bonnat, Léon(-Joseph-Florentin) (*b* Bayonne, 20 June 1833; *d* Monchy-Saint-Eloi, Oise, 8 Sept 1922). French painter, collector and teacher. He lived in Madrid from 1846 to 1853, where his father owned a bookshop, and there he studied with both José de Madrazo y Agudo and Federico de Madrazo y Küntz. After moving to Paris in 1854, he entered Léon Cogniet's atelier at the Ecole des Beaux-Arts and competed for the Prix de Rome in 1854, 1855 and 1857. He won second prize in 1857 with the *Resurrection of Lazarus* (Bayonne, Mus. Bonnat), a painting characterized by the jury as frank, firm and powerful, terms applied to his art throughout his career. His early paintings of historical and religious subjects gave way in the late 1860s to the less esteemed field of genre—scenes of Italian life and the Near East—based on sketches made during visits to Italy (1858–60) and the Near East and Greece (1868–70).

Bonnat's final change of career occurred in the mid- to late 1870s, when he became internationally renowned for his portraits, particularly of members of the European and American establishment. His highly realistic technique reflected his frequent use of photographs as models. The portraits, which cost 30,000 francs each, were so desirable that by the 1880s he had to schedule three to four sittings a day to accommodate his long waiting list.

Bonnat's portraits followed a pattern set by the monumental and elegant *Mme Pasca* (1874; Paris, Mus. d'Orsay), his first painting to be universally praised. His actress friend dominates a dark, amorphous space and is brightly lit to create a strong chiaroscuro effect. Bonnat's style was strongly influenced by Ribera and the portraits by Titian, Velázquez and van Dyck that he saw as a youth in the Museo del Prado in Madrid. In addition he owed a debt to Rembrandt, Courbet and Manet, the last of whom also loved Spanish painting, a fact that may account for Bonnat's support for Manet's Salon entries. Bonnat's portrait of *Adolphe Thiers* (1876; Paris, Mus. d'Orsay; see fig.), the first President of the Third Republic, established his fame. The portrait is serious and formal, full of the strength and dignity the audience expected of this contemporary hero. Bonnat adapted a pose from Titian's *Charles V* (Madrid, Prado), one of the first paintings to establish the pattern for state portraiture, which has been dominant ever since. His dour, stiff, implacable Thiers, portrayed as a confident national leader, became a model for every establishment figure desiring a portrait. Bonnat's approach in this and the innumerable portraits that followed distinguished him from his rival portrait painters, Carolus-Duran, John Singer Sargent and Jules Lefebvre.

Bonnat's work has a wide expressive range, though almost all his portraits flatter the sitters. Portraits of his close friends are full of energy and life (e.g. *Harpignies*, 1889; Paris, Petit Pal.). However, several portraits are dull and vapid (e.g. *Leland Stanford jr*, 1884; Stanford, CA, U. A.G. & Mus.), a result in part of the speed with which he worked to fulfil his many commissions. Contemporary critics mentioned that Bonnat's portraits of public officials enhanced their dignity, and in most of his portraits the subjects appear younger and more animated than in their contemporary photographs. The stiffness of many of the portrait figures reflects the cold, inexpressive public image that most 19th-century patrons cultivated. By generalizing the setting and minimizing attributes, features that might indicate profession or character, Bonnat diminished the personality of his sitters while emphasizing the idea of the importance of the individual. They form a telling document of a triumphant bourgeoisie, produced in a period when the focus on great individuals was yielding to the idea that broad social and economic forces were the significant factors shaping the world.

Bonnat was an important teacher and ran an active studio for over 30 years. In addition to supervising an independent studio from 1865, he taught the evening course at the Ecole des Beaux-Arts in Paris from 1883 until he became a *chef d'atelier* at the same institution in 1888, a post he held until he became Director in 1905. His best-known students included Thomas Eakins, Gustave Caillebotte, Raoul Dufy and Henri de Toulouse-Lautrec, although they did not stay with him long and soon rejected his guidance. He influenced artists from Scandinavia to the USA. Bonnat was also a popular Salon juror, as it was felt that he would be a sympathetic judge. He was a liberal teacher who stressed simplicity in art above high academic finish, as well as overall effect rather than detail. He encouraged strong chiaroscuro and heavy modelling as well as careful drawing, the hallmarks of his own work. In the 20th century he altered his technique and produced works that show the marks of the Impressionism and Neo-Impressionism that he had so long opposed (e.g. *George Cain*, 1909; priv. col.).

Bonnat's significance as an art collector dates from *c.* 1880, when he began collecting the Old Master drawings that form the basis of the Musée Bonnat in Bayonne (founded in 1924) and range from the Renaissance up to the 19th century.

Léon Bonnat: *Adolphe Thiers*, oil on canvas, 1.26×0.95 m, 1876 (Paris, Musée d'Orsay)

WRITINGS
Notes et dessins de Léon Bonnat (Paris, 1928)

BIBLIOGRAPHY
A. Fouquier: *Léon Bonnat: Première partie de sa vie et son oeuvre* (Paris, 1879)
H. Demesse: 'Léon Bonnat', *Gal. Contemp.*, v, pt a (1880)
L. Bénédite: 'Léon Bonnat, 1833–1922', *Gaz. B.-A.*, n. s. 4, vii (1923)
C.-M. Widor: *Notice sur la vie et les travaux de M. Léon Bonnat*, Acad. des B.-A. (Paris, 1923)
R. Cuzacq: *Léon Bonnat* (Mont-de-Marsan, 1940)
H. Jeanpierre: 'Une Correspondance inédite de Léon Bonnat', *Bull. Soc. Sci., Lett. & A. Bayonne*, 65 (1953)
——: 'Bonnat et l'art moderne', *Bull. Soc. Sci., Lett. & A. Bayonne*, 113 (1967), pp. 1–19
Dessins français du XIXe siècle du Musée Bonnat à Bayonne (exh. cat. by V. Ducourau and A. Serullaz, Paris, Louvre, 1979)
The Realist Tradition: French Painting and Drawing, 1830–1900 (exh. cat., ed. G. P. Weisberg; Cleveland, Mus. A.; New York, Brooklyn Mus.; St Louis, A. Mus.; Glasgow, A.G. & Mus.; 1980–81), pp. 164–6, 177–80, 271–3
H. Usselmann: 'Léon Bonnat, d'après les témoignages de ses élèves nordiques', *Ksthist. Tidskr.*, lv (1986), pp. 67–76

JULIUS KAPLAN

Bonne, François de, Duc de Lesdiguières. *See* LESDI-GUIÈRES, DUCS DE, (1).

Bonnemaison, Ferréol de, Chevalier (*b* Toulouse, 1766; *d* Paris, 1826). French dealer, restorer and painter. He may have begun his career as a protégé of Henri-Auguste de Chalvet, a collector and Associate Member of the Académie des Beaux-Arts in Toulouse. His first teachers were Pierre Rivalz and Lambert-François-Thérèse Cammas. He moved to Paris shortly before the French Revolution but went almost immediately to London, where he established himself as a portrait painter, exhibiting at the Royal Academy in 1794 and 1795. He returned to Paris in 1796 and that year sent three portraits to the Salon. In 1799, he exhibited the curiously Romantic *Girl Surprised by a Storm* (New York, Brooklyn Mus.). The following year he achieved popular success with *Woman of Property Begging* (England, priv. col.). His talents as a portrait painter were particularly admired: surviving examples are *Adrien Segond* (1812; Paris, Louvre) and *Dieudonné Jeanroy* (1812; U. Paris V, Fac. Médec.). His style of painting reflected contemporary admiration for highly finished works in the manner of 17th-century Dutch artists.

As a dealer, Bonnemaison helped to establish the picture collection of the piano- and harp-maker Erard, whose niece he married, so becoming related to Alexis Delahante

(1767–1837), one of the most eminent dealers of the early 19th century. When Delahante lived in England during the Napoleonic Wars, he facilitated Bonnemaison's international dealings with Thomas Penrice, whose collection was formed between 1808 and 1814. Delahante also acted for Bonnemaison when in 1811 he negotiated with David for his portrait of *Napoleon in his Study* (1812; Washington, DC, N.G.A.), commissioned by Alexander Douglas (later 10th Duke of Hamilton). Arthur Wellesley, 1st Duke of Wellington, acquired a number of Dutch paintings (e.g. Jan Steen's *A Wedding Party*, 1667; London, Apsley House) through Bonnemaison, who bid on his behalf at the La Peyrière sale (Paris, 14 April 1814) and the Le Rouge sale (Paris, 18 April 1818). In addition, Wellington bought several pieces of 18th-century French furniture from him, including a commode signed *Jacques Dautriche* and some furniture in the style of André-Charles Boulle by Etienne Levasseur (all Stratfield Saye House, Hants). After the Battle of Waterloo (1815), Wellington was entrusted with the return of works of art removed by Napoleon, and he commissioned Bonnemaison to restore five paintings (e.g. *The Visitation, c.* 1519; Madrid, Prado) attributed at that time to Raphael and to make copies of them (London, Apsley House) before returning them to Madrid. Bonnemaison had further dealings with the English market when in 1817 he negotiated the sale to William Buchanan of the Dutch and Flemish pictures in the collection of Charles Maurice de Talleyrand-Périgord (1754–1838). One of the best-known paintings that passed through his hands was Poussin's *Blind Orion Searching for the Rising Sun* (1658; New York, Met.), once owned by Reynolds. In 1815 he sold the collection of Vincenzo Giustiniani to Frederick William III of Prussia.

He also enjoyed success with French patrons. In 1814 Louis XVIII decorated him with the Croix de la Légion d'honneur and in 1816 he was appointed Director of Restoration for the Musée Royal, although much of his work was considered unacceptable by David and the Comte de Forbin, Minister of the King's Household. Together with Delahante, Bonnemaison advised Charles-Ferdinand, Duc de Berry, on the formation of his collection, and after the Duc's death in 1820, he became Keeper of the collection for Caroline, Duchesse de Berry, arranging to have lithographs of the works published. Such activities occupied him for the rest of his life, while at the same time he built up his own collection of Old Master paintings. At the sale (Paris, M. Henry, 17–21 April 1827) after his death, Forbin recommended that the Louvre buy five of his paintings by Correggio, Rubens, Murillo and Tintoretto, but no funds were available.

BIBLIOGRAPHY

D. Sutton: 'The Great Duke and the Arts', *Apollo*, xcviii (1973), pp. 161–9
De David à Delacroix: La Peinture française de 1774 à 1830 (exh. cat., ed. T. J. Cummings, R. Rosenblum and A. Schnapper; Paris, Grand Pal., 1974–5); Eng. edn as *David to Delacroix: French Painting, 1774–1830: The Age of Revolution* (Detroit, MI, Inst. A.; New York, Met.; 1975)
F. Haskell: *Rediscoveries in Art* (London, 1976), pp. 26, 34–5
A. Devries: 'Sébastien Erard, un amateur d'art du début du XIXe siècle, et ses conseillers', *Gaz. B.-A.*, 6th ser., xcvii (1981), pp. 78–86
C. M. Kauffmann: *Catalogue of Paintings in the Wellington Museum* (London, 1982), pp. 32–3

Toulouse et le néo-classicisme: Les Artistes toulousains de 1775 à 1830 (exh. cat., ed. J. Penent; Toulouse, Mus. Augustins, 1989–90), pp. 102–3

LINDA WHITELEY

Bonnet, Louis-Marin (*b* Paris, 1736; *d* Saint-Mandé, nr Paris, 20 Oct 1793). French engraver and publisher. He came from a family of artisans and owed his training in engraving to his brother-in-law, the engraver Louis Legrand (1723–1808). Through Legrand, Bonnet became the pupil of Jean-Charles François in 1756, a year before the latter discovered the CRAYON MANNER technique of engraving, designed to reproduce the effect of a coloured-chalk drawing. Around the end of 1757 Bonnet used the new technique to engrave a *Cupid* (see Hérold, no. 2A) after François Eisen. Gilles Demarteau, a rival of Jean-Charles François, enticed Bonnet to join his workshop and learnt the technique from him.

Bonnet engraved some 15 plates for Demarteau, and in 1760 he set up his own shop. During this period he strove to perfect the crayon manner by producing prints using several different plates, each inked with a different colour. Initially, he tried to reproduce drawings executed in black and white chalk on blue or buff paper; to do this he had to make a white ink that would not yellow with age. He was the first to use points of reference to print several plates one on top of the other. In 1764 he produced a *Head of Minerva* after François Boucher (H 53A) and two children's heads after Carle Vanloo (H 6A,2,3). He also experimented with aquatint-like techniques designed to reproduce wash drawings, and in 1763 he published the *Biscuit Seller* after Boucher (H 59A); this was dedicated to the Marquis de Bausset, who, when appointed ambassador to Russia, took Bonnet with him. There Bonnet remained until the end of 1766, making portrait engravings of the *Empress Catherine II* (H 56A) and of *Grand Duke Paul* (H 57A), as well as training several pupils.

On returning to Paris, Bonnet wished to establish his reputation. Unable to compete with Demarteau in crayon-manner engravings, he published aquatint prints, such as three plates for the Comte de Caylus's *Recueil de charges et de têtes . . . d'après Léonard de Vinci* (1767; H 62A); prints reproducing chalk drawings in several colours (*Première tête* after Boucher, 1767; H 9); and crayon-manner engravings in white on blue paper (*Cahier de têtes*) after Raphael (H 18,2). Above all, he published engravings employing his most famous discovery, pastel manner. His first important work in this area was a *Head of Flora: Portrait of Mme Baudion* (H 192; see fig.) after Boucher, printed using eight coloured plates. Having succeeded in generating considerable publicity for his discoveries, Bonnet established himself during the 1770s as an entrepreneur of engraving. Continuing to work himself, he also employed a group of young artists, and with their help he built up a considerable collection of work. At the time of his death this amounted to 1065 numbered engravings; the whole collection numbered 1600 examples, including the prints sold in book form.

Bonnet was a shrewd businessman who knew how to respond to changes in his public's taste. It was in his workshop that in 1772 Jean-François Janinet produced his first two coloured prints: the *Procurator* and the *Tailor* (both H 35,2) in the wash manner (*see under* GOUACHE

Louis-Marin Bonnet: *Head of Flora: Portrait of Mme Baudion* (after François Boucher), engraving in pastel manner, 407×327 mm, 1769 (London, Victoria and Albert Museum)

MANNER, §2), both after Clément-Pierre Marillier. He also invented a method of printing frames in gold ink around his works (e.g. *Woman Taking Coffee*, 1774; H 294). He exploited the contemporary fashion for things English by publishing stipple engravings with English titles and explanations and even went to the length of counterfeiting engravings by Francesco Bartolozzi (*Romeo and Juliet* after Gavin Hamilton, 1786; H 911). However, unlike the hand-coloured originals, these 'English prints' are for the most part printed from several plates.

So vast a production was bound to include works of uneven quality, but being an engraver who reproduced other artists' works, Bonnet brought about an unprecedented dissemination of drawings by most of his contemporaries, chiefly Boucher and Jean-Baptiste Huet but also van Loo, Louis Lagrenée, Joseph-Marie Vien and many others. His various *Cahiers pour apprendre à dessiner* (e.g. *Troisième cahier de principes de paysage*, Paris, 1777), which were widely available during the 1770s and 1780s, provided models for other artists.

BIBLIOGRAPHY
J. Hérold: *Louis-Marin Bonnet (1736–1793): Catalogue de l'oeuvre gravé* (Paris, 1935) [H]

CHRISTIAN MICHEL

Bonneuil, Etienne de. *See* ETIENNE DE BONNEUIL.

Bonnier, Joseph, Baron de la Mosson (*b* Montpellier, 6 Sept 1702; *d* Paris, 26 July 1744). French financier, patron and collector. In 1726 he resigned from a successful military career in order to succeed his father as Treasurer for the Etats du Languedoc. His marriage in 1740 temporarily put an end to a dissolute life. In 1742 Jean-Marc Nattier exhibited at the Salon a portrait of *Mme Bonnier as Diana* (Malibu, CA, Getty Mus.) and in 1746 a posthumous portrait of *Joseph Bonnier in his Study* (Washington, DC, N.G.A.). Bonnier divided his time between Paris and Montpellier. He completed the Château de La Mosson in Montpellier, begun for his father in 1723 by Jean Giral, a main block flanked by two wings and surrounded by a magnificent garden. Jean Raoux provided a series of decorative paintings of the *Four Ages of Man* (Montpellier, Mus. Fabre), and Nicholas-Sébastien Adam executed reliefs of *Cephalus and Aurora* and of *Diana and Endymion* (*in situ*), as well as numerous sculptures for the park, now dispersed. Of the château only the main block with its music room survives. Bonnier's Paris hôtel (destr.) in the Faubourg Saint-Germain, designed by Robert de Cotte, had been purchased by Bonnier's father in 1726. Bonnier undertook major redecorations, which included the commissioning from Jacques de Lajoüe of fantastical perspectival overdoors based on the interiors of the house (e.g. two at Russborough, Co. Wicklow). His collections of scientific instruments and specimens and of curiosities were arranged in the main rooms according to subject. They are known through drawings (U. Paris, Bib. Doucet) by Jean-Baptiste Courtonne (*c.* 1711–81) and the sale catalogue produced by Edmé Gersaint after Bonnier's death.

BIBLIOGRAPHY
E. F. Gersaint: *Catalogue raisonné d'une collection considérable de diverses curiosités en tous genres contenues dans le cabinet de feu Monsieur de la Mosson* (sale cat., Paris, 8 March 1745 and following days)
Turlubleu [pseud. of N. Ménin]: *Histoire grecque tirée du manuscrit gris-delin dans les cendres de Troyes* (Amsterdam, 1745)
Grasset-Morel: *Les Bonnier, ou une famille de financiers au XVIIIe siècle* (Paris, 1886)
M.-A. Roland-Michel: 'Le Cabinet de Bonnier de la Mosson et la participation de Lajoüe à son décor', *Bull. Soc. Hist. A. Fr.* (1975), pp. 211–21
B. Pons: 'Hôtel du Lude puis Bonnier de la Mosson puis de Grimberghem', *Le Faubourg Saint-Germain, la rue Saint-Dominique, hôtels et amateurs* (exh. cat., Paris, Mus. Rodin, 1984), pp. 150–63
M.-A. Roland-Michel: *Lajoüe et l'art rocaille* (Paris, 1984) [with cat. rais. with extensive bibliog.]

THIERRY BAJOU

Bonnier, Louis(-Bernard) (*b* Templeuve, nr Lille, 14 June 1856; *d* Paris, 16 Sept 1946). French architect and urban planner. Born to a staunchly republican peasant family in Flanders, in 1875 he entered the Ecoles Académiques, Lille, where he was initially attracted to painting. The death of his father in 1876 and the consequent need to support his family then directed him towards the more financially secure career of architecture. In August 1876 he entered the Ecole des Beaux-Arts, Paris; he also taught drawing and worked with various architects, notably Paul Sédille whom he greatly respected. In 1881 he married the daughter of Jean Deconchy (1827–1911), one of the architects employed by the city authorities of Paris, and in 1884 Bonnier himself joined the city administration as a trainee architect, working in the 19th arrondissement. In 1883 he won the competition for the construction of the town hall (1886–7) at Issy-les-Moulineaux on the southwest edge of Paris. He then built a series of villas, Les

Dunes, Les Oyats, Les Sablons, Les Algues and Robinson (1890–92; all destr. 1940 except Robinson), at Ambleteuse, near Boulogne-sur-Mer. Their layout, choice of materials and solidity of form revealed a combination of regional building traditions, a constructional rationalism inherited from Viollet-le-Duc and influences from the Arts and Crafts Movement. The furniture, which Bonnier designed himself, was very similar to that which Gustave Serrurier-Bovy later exhibited at the Salon de la Libre Esthétique, Brussels (1894).

After working on the design and construction of the town hall (1893–4) at Templeuve, Bonnier created the Salon de l'Art Nouveau (1895; destr. c. 1922) in Paris for the art dealer S. Bing. In less than six months and with a limited budget, he transformed Bing's small private mansion at 22 Rue de Provence, Paris, into a complete manifestation of the Art Nouveau style, and this project inspired André-Louis Arfvidson's Art Nouveau pavilion for Bing at the Exposition Universelle (1900), Paris. In 1897 Bonnier began to work on several projects for the Exposition, of which he was Directeur des Installations Générales; these included a 26-m diameter terrestrial globe (unexecuted) for the geographer Elisée Reclus (1830–1905) and a pavilion (destr.) for the Schneider Corporation, which, with its 45-m diameter reinforced dome, stood imposingly on the banks of the Seine. He was also coordinator of the commission responsible for revising the regulations for urban maintenance in Paris; the new regulations of 1902 included adjustments to the alignment of building façades, which made possible the construction of some of the finest Art Nouveau buildings in Paris.

In 1910 Bonnier became Directeur des Services d'Architecture, des Plantations et des Promenades for the city of Paris. His architectural work at this time included a school (1910–11) at Rue Rouelle, Paris, and in 1912 he drew up a report on the extension of Paris, which served as a basis for the planning and development competition of 1919 (see PARIS, §II, 6). During World War I he established the Casier Archéologique et Artistique de Paris, a detailed inventory of the architectural heritage of the city. He also founded the Ecole d'Art Public, which in 1919 became the Institut des Hautes Etudes Urbaines. In 1920 he was appointed Directeur des Services d'Architecture for the Exposition des Arts Décoratifs et Industriels Modernes, which took place in Paris in 1925.

Bonnier continued to build villas and houses for a limited private clientele, which included André Gide; other public works in the 1920s included the construction of a swimming-pool (1920–24), Place Paul Verlaine, Paris, and a block of low-cost flats (1922–6), Rue de Ménilmontant, Paris. In different ways according to budgetary allowances, these all reveal the rationalist impulse of Art Nouveau and Bonnier's quasi-pedagogical concern for decoration. He retired from public office on 1 January 1924. His career formed an important link between Viollet-le-Duc and the Modernists in the history of French architecture.

WRITINGS

with M. Poëte: *Aperçu historique: Considérations techniques préliminaires* (Paris, 1913) [on the planned extn of Paris]

BIBLIOGRAPHY

G. P. Weisberg: 'Siegfried Bing, Louis Bonnier et la Maison de l'Art Nouveau en 1895', *Bull. Soc. Hist. A. Fr.* (1983), pp. 241–9

B. Marrey: 'Des Rapports difficiles: Gide et Bonnier', *Mnmts Hist.*, clvi (1988), pp. 78–80

——: *Louis Bonnier, 1856–1946* (Liège, 1988); review by F. Hamon in *Bull. Mnmtl*, cxlvii/2 (1989), pp. 192–3

BERNARD MARREY

Bonnin & Morris. American porcelain manufacturer. Gousse Bonnin (*b* ?Antigua, *c.* 1741; *d c.* 1779) moved in 1768 from England to Philadelphia, where he established the first porcelain factory in America with money from an inheritance and with investments from George Morris (1742/5–1773). The land was purchased late in 1769, and in January 1770 the first notice regarding the enterprise was published. The first blue-decorated bone china wares were not produced until late in 1770. Newspaper advertisements noted 'three kilns, two furnaces, two mills, two clay vaults, cisterns, engines and treading rooms' and listed such wares as pickle stands, fruit baskets, sauce boats, pint bowls, plates, plain and handled cups, quilted cups, sugar dishes in two sizes, cream jugs, teapots in two sizes and breakfast sets (*see* UNITED STATES OF AMERICA, fig. 39). Well-established foreign competition, however, was too formidable for the new business, which had to charge high prices to meet large expenses; production ceased by November 1772.

BIBLIOGRAPHY

G. Hood: *Bonnin and Morris of Philadelphia: The First American Porcelain Factory, 1770–1772* (Chapel Hill, NC, 1972)

ELLEN PAUL DENKER

Bono. *See* BUONO.

Bono, Michele. *See* GIAMBONO, MICHELE.

Bono da Ferrara (*fl* 1450–52). Italian painter. An artist of this name is documented working in Siena Cathedral in 1442 and 1461, but he cannot be identified with certainty as the painter mentioned in the payments registers of the d'Este family for 1450–52, who frescoed a loggia in the *delizia* of Migliaro for Borso d'Este, 1st Duke of Ferrara and Modena, and who worked in the houses at Casaglia and in the *studiolo* of the Palazzo di Belfiore (all these works are untraced). The latter was certainly the painter whose signature OPVS BONI appears on the large fresco of *St Christopher* (destr. 1944) in the Ovetari Chapel in the church of the Eremitani, Padua, for which he received payments on 24 and 30 July 1451. The *St Jerome* (ex-Gal. Costabili, Ferrara; London, N.G.), signed BONVS FERRARIENSIS PISANJ DISCIPVLVS ('Bono da Ferrara pupil of Pisanello'), may reasonably be assigned to Bono on the basis of technical analysis and probably pre-dates the Paduan work. The undeniable mark of Pisanello in the painting led Venturi and Longhi, among others, to reject the signature and assign the painting to Pisanello himself. This argument is supported by a contemporary statement by Guarino Veronese documenting a painting of *St Jerome* by Pisanello in Ferrara. It seems preferable, however, to accept the attribution to Bono at a period when he was still strongly influenced by his master. The untraced painting cited by Guarino probably provided the basis for Bono's compositional scheme. The Paduan fresco and the *Virgin and Child* (*c.* 1450–60; Budapest, Mus. F.A.) strongly recall the works of Mantegna, the major figure involved in the decoration of the Ovetari Chapel, and also demonstrate Bono's marked interest both in the new Tuscan ideas then circulating among north Italian painters, in particular Piero della Francesca, and, still more strongly, in the powerful monumentality of Andrea del Castagno.

DBI   BIBLIOGRAPHY
T. Borenius: 'Bono da Ferrara', *Burl. Mag.*, xxxv (1919), p. 179
A. Venturi: 'Del quadro attribuito a Bono da Ferrara nella Galleria Nazionale di Londra', *L'Arte*, xxv (1922), pp. 105–8
R. Longhi: *Officina ferrarese* (Rome, 1934, rev. 1956), pp. 15, 16, 20, 95
M. Davies: *The Earlier Italian Schools*, London, N.G. cat. (London, 1951, 2/1961/R 1986), pp. 93–5

Bonolis, Giuseppe (*b* Teramo, 1 Jan 1800; *d* Naples, 2 April 1851). Italian painter. At an early age he enrolled in the Scuola di Disegno set up by the *comune* of Teramo and run by Muzio Muzii, a pupil of Vincenzo Camuccini. Bonolis taught calligraphy for a brief time at the Real Collegio in Teramo and in 1822 moved to Naples, where he was a pupil of Costanzo Angelini and Joseph-Boniface Franque at the Accademia di Belle Arti. Around 1830 he moved briefly to Rome in order to study the work of Raphael, Domenichino, Agostino Carracci and Annibale Carracci and to attend the classes of Camuccini, who had recently become director of the Roman branch of the Accademia in Naples.

Bonolis produced history paintings and portraits and showed his work at numerous exhibitions sponsored by the Bourbon court, by whom he was held in high esteem. About 1833 he painted portraits of members of the Bourbon household (all untraced) and also the *Prince of Fondi* (Naples, Mus. N. S Martino). Like other Neapolitan artists of the period Bonolis was influenced by the work of Francesco Podesti. Bonolis's painting, the *Death of Abel* (1837; Naples, Capodimonte), was shown at the Bourbon Biennale in the same year and acquired by Ferdinand II of the Two Sicilies (*reg* 1830–59). In the *Education of Bacchus* (1839; Naples, Pal. Reale) he reveals a greater interest in naturalism while still remaining faithful to a classically inspired aesthetic ideal. In 1841, for his *Marriage of Bacchus and Ariadne* (Naples, Capodimonte), he was nominated honorary professor at the Accademia in Naples. He also painted such religious subjects as the *Immaculate Conception* (Naples, S Spirito) and *St John* (Naples, S Maria di Caravaggio). At the end of the 1840s he opened a private painting school in Naples; the most successful of his pupils included Gennaro Ruo (1852–84) and Filippo Palizzi.

BIBLIOGRAPHY
V. Bindi: *Artisti abruzzesi* (Naples, 1883)
F. Bellonzi: *L'ottocento teramano* (1978)

ROSANNA CIOFFI

Bonomi, Joseph [Giuseppe] (*b* Rome, 19 Jan 1739; *d* London, 8 March 1808). English architect of Italian birth. A leading Neo-classical architect of the late 18th century, he studied at the Collegio Romano and trained (according to his son Ignatius) under Antonio Asprucci. He also studied under Girolamo Teodoli and may have received tuition from Charles-Louis Clérisseau. Around 1763 James Adam (i), then in Rome, saw some of Bonomi's student drawings and engaged him to draw Roman antiquities. In 1767 Robert Adam (i) and James Adam invited him to England, where he worked in their office until 1781. He became an independent architect in 1782 and prepared designs (none of which seem to have been executed) for several patrons, but in 1783 he was persuaded to return to Italy (probably by Angelica Kauffman, his wife's cousin). The following year he returned to London, practising there until his death. He was elected Associate of the Royal Academy in 1789 on Joshua Reynolds's casting vote as President; however, in spite of Reynolds's nomination in 1790, Bonomi was never elected to full membership of the RA nor made Professor of Perspective. He was consistently opposed by a group in the RA that included Joseph Farington. As a Roman Catholic he was excluded from public commissions. In 1800 he was appointed architect to the King of Naples, but was unable to take up the post because of political conditions in Italy.

Bonomi was a talented draughtsman and exhibited regularly at the Royal Academy from 1783. His exhibits, many of which have survived (London, RIBA), were highly finished and coloured and showed a firm handling of perspective and a feeling for light and shade. His design for the Great Room at Montagu House (destr.), Portman Square, London (exh. 1790), for Elizabeth Montagu, is perhaps the best known. In his designs and executed interiors he reacted against the elaborate delicacy of the Adam style, selecting and simplifying features of their decorative repertory to produce his own strong and chaste compositions. By contrast, many of his exteriors were blockish and severe, but some were enlivened with a bold and forceful feature, such as a *porte-cochère* (in the 1790s at Longford Hall, Salop, and at Laverstoke Park, Hants) or the open colonnaded belvedere on the roof of Rosneath (1806; destr. 1961), Strathclyde. At Packington Hall, Warwicks, where he worked from 1784 for Heneage Finch, 4th Earl of Aylesford, Bonomi designed most of the interiors, including the remarkable Pompeian Gallery in the late 1780s (*see* POMPEIAN REVIVAL). The source for this, N. Ponce's *Description des Bains de Titus* (Paris, 1786), may have been suggested by Lord Aylesford, who was a knowledgeable connoisseur of architecture. They collaborated closely, with Bonomi acting as Aylesford's tutor in drawing and perspective. Aylesford is also credited with the inspiration behind Bonomi's Packington Church (1789–90), a remarkable Neo-classical building having a Greek-cross plan, vaulting derived from the Roman Baths of Diocletian and Greek Doric columns; Bonomi translated this eclectic material into one solid form, producing a building as radical as any design by Friedrich Gilly or Claude-Nicolas Ledoux.

Bonomi's sources were Roman, not Greek: the pyramid of Caius Cestius in Rome inspired his pyramidal mausoleum (1793) at Blickling Park, Norfolk, for John Hobart, 2nd Earl of Buckinghamshire (1723–93). He had no affection for the Gothic style, but produced a few unexecuted designs in that style, for a gateway and a castellated summerhouse. Of his six children, Ignatius Bonomi (1787–1870) was his pupil and practised as an architect in Co. Durham, while Joseph Bonomi jr (1796–1878) was a sculptor, draughtsman of Egyptian antiquities and Curator of Sir John Soane's Museum, London, from 1862 to 1878.

Colvin

BIBLIOGRAPHY

W. Papworth: 'Memoir of Joseph Bonomi', *Transactions of the RIBA*, 1st ser. (1868–9), pp. 123–4
J. Cornforth: 'Longford Hall', *Country Life*, cxxxii (16 Aug 1962), pp. 354–8
M. Binney: 'Packington Hall, Warwickshire', *Country Life*, cxlviii (9 July 1970), pp. 102–6; (16 July 1970), pp. 162–6; (23 July 1970), pp. 226–9
——: 'A Pioneer Work of Neo-classicism', *Country Life*, cl (8 July 1971), pp. 110–15 [Packington Church]
D. Fitz-Gerald: 'A Gallery after the Antique: Some Reflections on "The Age of Neo-classicism"', *Connoisseur*, clxxxi (1972), pp. 2–13 [Pompeian Gallery, Packington Hall]
P. Meadows: *Joseph Bonomi Architect, 1739–1808* (London, 1988)
——: 'Drawn to Entice', *Country Life*, clxxxii (28 April 1988), pp. 128–33
P. Meadows and J. Cornforth: 'Draughtsman Decorator', *Country Life*, clxxxiv (19 April 1990), pp. 164–8

PETER M. MEADOWS

Bonomo, Jacobello di. *See* JACOBELLO DI BONOMO.

Bononi [Bonone], **Carlo** (*b* Ferrara, 1569; *d* Ferrara, 3 Sept 1632). Italian painter. He was among the last great painters of the Ferrarese school, his style uniting warm Venetian colour with the lyrical effects of light and elegant draughtsmanship of Ludovico Carracci. He was a pupil of Giuseppe Mazzuoli (*c.* 1536–89), but his early activity is little documented. The *Martyrdom of St Paul* (Pommersfelden, Schloss Weissenstein), which is indebted to Mazzuoli and combines elements of Ferrarese and Venetian traditions, may represent the earliest phase of his development. Later, through a study of the art of Ludovico Carracci, modified by a response to Dosso Dossi and to Correggio, he developed a more individual style. An altarpiece of the *Virgin with SS Maurilius and George* (Vienna, Ksthist. Mus.) is unanimously dated before 1600. It is probable that Bononi made study tours to Bologna, Parma, Verona and Venice. Between 1605 and 1610 he spent two years in Rome (Baruffaldi), a visit confirmed by three paintings of scenes from the *Life of St Paternian* in the church of S Paterniano in Fano; dated between 1610 and 1612 (Emiliani), these reflect a direct study of Caravaggio and of his early Roman followers, such as Orazio Borgianni.

Bononi is first securely documented in 1611, when he painted an *Annunciation* for S Bartolomeo in Modena (Campori), possibly the one now in the parish church at Gualtieri. In 1613 he was at Cento, where he worked with Guercino on the decoration of Santo Spirito. Around 1614 he developed a new treatment of space, and such works as the *Supper of Ahasuerus* (Ravenna, S Domenico) and the *Miracle of St Gualbert* (1614; Mantua, Pal. Ducale) show a deeper awareness of architectural perspective. In 1615 he established himself at Ferrara, and after the death of Ippolito Scarsellino (1620) he became the city's leading painter. He enjoyed a long and profitable relationship with the Este family, for whom he worked between 1616 and 1629 in the cities of Reggio, Carpi and Modena. He was also active in Bologna, where he painted the *Ascension* (1616–17) for the church of S Salvatore (*in situ*).

Bononi's most prestigious commission was to decorate the vault of the central nave (begun 1617; completed by 1621) and that of the apse (after 1622) of the Ferrarese church of S Maria in Vado. For the nave vault he painted huge canvases, among which are the *Visitation* and the *Miracle of the Blood*, and for the apse a vast fresco, the

Carlo Bononi: *Guardian Angel*, oil on canvas, 2.40×1.41 m, late 1620s (Ferrara, Pinacoteca Nazionale)

Exaltation of God's Name. These works are indebted to Correggio and foreshadow the Baroque in their dramatic contrasts of light and shade and in the complex poses of the figures. At this time Guercino was also in Ferrara, working for the papal legate Cardinal Serra; his admiration of Bononi is well known (Baruffaldi), and Bononi was influenced by his art. In 1621 Guercino was summoned to Rome by Pope Gregory XV, and Bononi took over the decoration of the Gabbi Chapel in the basilica of the Madonna della Ghiara in Reggio Emilia (1621–2). The decoration, in oil on plaster, comprises the *Church Fathers* on the pendentives and, on the vault, in intricate compartments divided by gilt stucco, female figures symbolizing the *Eight Beatitudes*. His softly naturalistic figures, and the play of ample and luminous planes, are stylistically similar to the work of Alessandro Tiarini, who in 1618 had decorated the adjoining chapel.

In 1622 Bononi was commissioned to paint large canvases of scenes from the *Life of the Virgin* for the choir of S Maria in Vado (*in situ*). During his final years he assimilated some of the characteristics of the late style of Guido Reni, evident in the still yet elegant poses and rigid modelling in such works as the *Guardian Angel* (Ferrara, Pin. N.; see fig.) and *St Margaret and Saints* (1627; Reggio Emilia, Pal. Vescovile). His last works, particularly the unfinished *St Louis of Toulouse Praying for an End to the Plague* (1632; Vienna, Ksthist. Mus.), reveal an increasingly melodramatic vein.

DBI

BIBLIOGRAPHY

G. Baruffaldi: *Vite di pittori e scultori ferraresi* (MS., 1697–1722; ed. Ferrara, 1844–6/*R* 1971), i, pp. 31, 345; ii, pp. 139, 142
G. Campori: *Artisti italiani e stranieri negli Stati Estensi* (Modena, 1855), p. 89
C. Volpe: 'Per il primo tempo di Carlo Bononi', *A. Ant. & Mod.*, v (1959), pp. 79–81
A. Emiliani: *Carlo Bononi* (Ferrara, 1962)
Dipinti 'reggiani' del Bononi e del Guercino (exh. cat., ed. N. Artioli and E. Monducci; Reggio Emilia, Basilica della Beata Vergine della Ghiara, 1982), pp. 19–84
E. Schleier: 'Carlo Bononi', *The Age of Correggio and of the Carracci: Emilian Painting of the 16th and 17th Centuries* (exh. cat., Washington, DC, N.G.A.; New York, Met.; Bologna, Pin. N.; 1986–7), pp. 379–84

MATILDE AMATURO

Bononia. *See* BOLOGNA.

Bononia, Baveram de. *See* BAVIERA.

Bonpō. *See* GYOKUEN BONPŌ.

Bonsai. *See* JAPAN, §XVI, 3.

Bonshtedt, Lyudvig (Lyudvigovich) [Bohnstedt, Ludwig] (*b* St Petersburg, 27 Oct 1822; *d* Berlin, 3 Jan 1885). Russian architect of German descent. He studied under Wilhelm Stier, both in the latter's private studio and at the Bauakademie in Berlin, and then travelled around Europe. He made his début in St Petersburg by completing several buildings by NIKOLAY YEFIMOV, such as the City Duma (1848–52), in Renaissance Revival style. In 1851–2 Bonshtedt built a house for Count A. Lamsdorf on Mokhovaya Street, using ideas from Berlin in the structure, in particular increasing the size of the central corpus at the expense of the wings. The influence of St Petersburg Baroque, particularly the work of Bartolomeo Francesco Rastrelli, is evident in one of Bonshtedt's most important commissions, the palace of Zinaida Yusupova (1852–8) on Liteyny Prospect. The façade is faced with Bremen sandstone, the luxurious interiors are in various styles, and the winter garden was one of the first in St Petersburg.

Most of Bonshtedt's other works have not survived. He actively participated in Russian and European architectural competitions, winning second prize in a competition (1854) for designs for the Rathaus in Hamburg. In his St Petersburg studio in 1862 he created the basis for a future architectural society that was eventually established with the help of his student Viktor Shreter. Seeking to reform construction practices in the capital, Bonshtedt came into conflict with the Academy of Arts, and in 1862, having received virtually no commissions, he moved to Gotha in Germany. There he worked on several commissions for building villas and banks. In 1872 he won first prize for his design for the Berlin Reichstag, an eclectic building that combined elements from Karl Rossi's St Petersburg arcades, the colonnade of Karl Friedrich Schinkel's Museum (1823–30; now the Altes Museum) in Berlin and the dome of Charles Garnier's Opéra (1860–75) in Paris. Bonshtedt's design was not executed, as Paul Wallot won the second, decisive competition for the design of the Reichstag.

BIBLIOGRAPHY

D. Dolgner: *Architektur im 19. Jahrhundert: Ludwig Bohnstedt, Leben und Werk* (Weimar, 1929)

SERGEY KUZNETSOV

Bonsignori [Monsignori], **Francesco** (*b* Verona, *c.* 1460; *d* Caldiero, nr Verona, 2 July 1519). Italian painter. His father, Albertus Bonsignori, was reputedly an amateur painter; and besides Francesco, the oldest and most talented of his children, three other sons, including Bernardino (*c.* 1476–*c.* 1520) and Girolamo (*b c.* 1479), are also recorded as painters. Barely 20 paintings and fewer than a dozen drawings have been attributed to Francesco Bonsignori. Documents from his time at the Gonzaga court in Mantua and Vasari's account of his life are the main sources for information on the artist.

Bonsignori's early career is the most fully documented period of his activity. His earliest signed work is a *Virgin and Child* (dated 1483; Verona, Castelvecchio), followed by the Dal-Bovo Altarpiece, depicting the *Virgin and Child Enthroned with Saints*, signed and dated 1484 (Verona, Castelvecchio), and the portrait of a *Venetian Senator* (London, N.G.), signed and dated 1487 (cartoon, Vienna, Albertina). The altarpiece depicting the *Virgin and Child Enthroned with Music-Making Angels and SS George and Jerome* in the Cappella dei Banda, S Bernardino, Verona, is signed and dated 1488. Another altarpiece that was signed and dated 1488 depicting the *Virgin and Child Enthroned with SS Anthony of Egypt and Onofrio* is known through a 19th-century copy (Florence, I Tatti). This group of works clearly indicates the characteristics and limitations of Bonsignori's art. Throughout his life he drew inspiration from other artists with regard to composition, form and colouring. His early models were Andrea Mantegna, Giovanni Bellini, Alvise Vivarini and Antonello da Messina. In spite of these identifiable influences, Bonsignori's style is unmistakably individual. His most successful genre is the devotional picture, where he is able to concentrate on the human figure. Because of this interest his portraits, too, are among his best works. Narrative details and landscape or architectural settings do not feature significantly in his paintings.

From 1492 Bonsignori was in Mantua in the service of the Gonzaga family, by whom he was employed as a portrait painter and in the decoration (destr.) of their palaces at Marmirolo and Gonzaga. In 1494 Francesco Gonzaga, 4th Marquis of Mantua, gave Bonsignori a piece of land in the Gonzaga region as a reward for his services as a painter. There is evidence from the same year that Bonsignori was then working on a portrait (untraced) of *Eleonora Gonzaga* (1493–1550). In 1495 Isabella d'Este, Marchioness of Mantua, planned to have her portrait painted by Bonsignori. This was delayed, however, by Francesco Gonzaga II's commission for a painting (untraced) to commemorate his victory as leader of the Italian states against Charles VIII, King of France, at Fornovo on 6 July 1495. In the autumn of 1495 Bonsignori travelled to the site of the battle with Francesco's court architect Bernardino Ghisolfi (*fl* 1483–1511) to make drawings of the area. A chalk drawing of *Francesco Gonzaga* (Dublin,

N.G.), datable to *c.* 1500, is one of Bonsignori's most expressive portraits and one of the most sympathetic portrayals of the ruler. It supports Vasari's remark that the relation between Francesco Gonzaga and Bonsignori was warm and affectionate. The high quality of the drawing is also apparent in the discussion of its attribution: Mantegna and Giovanni Bellini have also been considered as authors of the work.

From 1495 there is no documentary mention of Bonsignori until *c.* 1506–7, when he executed the *Last Supper* (untraced) for the monastery of S Francesco de' Zoccolanti, Mantua. The profile drawing of the *Young Federico Gonzaga, 5th Marquis of Mantua* (Vienna, Albertina) is probably a study for the painting, in which Federico was shown kneeling in front of his father Francesco and being commended to Christ through the intercession of St Francis; opposite this group, St Bernard commended Cardinal Sigismondo Gonzaga (1469–1525) and Eleonora Gonzaga. The painting of *SS Louis and Francis with the Insignia of Christ* (ex-S Francesco de' Zoccolanti, Mantua; Milan, Brera) was probably produced at the same time as the *Last Supper.*

Portraits of Francesco's sister, *Elisabetta Gonzaga* (1471–1526) (Florence, Uffizi), and of *Emilia Pia di Montefeltro* (1471–1528) (Baltimore, MD, Mus. A.) were probably produced in 1509, when the two women were in Mantua. Bonsignori usually made monochrome copies of his portraits, according to Vasari, who saw the artist's collection of portrait drawings in the possession of his heirs in Mantua. This collection included portraits of Francesco Gonzaga's family for use as gifts to foreign rulers as well as portraits of *Francesco Sforza, Duke of Milan, Massimiliano Sforza, Duke of Milan, Andrea Mantegna* and others.

Christ Carrying the Cross (*c.* 1510; Mantua, Pal. Ducale) not only recalls Mantegna but also reveals, in its colour and mood, the influence of Lorenzo Costa the elder, who succeeded Mantegna as court painter to the Gonzagas in 1507. That this position was not given to Bonsignori, whose talent, along with his reliability and his compliance with the wishes of the Gonzaga family, had made him the most highly esteemed painter after Mantegna among the group of artists employed by the court, may be because Bonsignori—who, Vasari wrote, led a life of exemplary piety—probably did not participate in the passionate reverence for antiquity that pervaded life at the Mantuan court and thus was not equal to the artistic requirements of Isabella d'Este in particular. Costa's use of form and colour had a decisive influence on Bonsignori's late style, as can be seen in the *St Sebastian* (1510–14; Curtatone, S Maria delle Grazie) and above all in the altarpiece depicting the *Virgin and Child in Glory with SS Blaise, Sebastian, Martial and Juliana* (1514–19) in SS Nazaro e Celso, Verona. In 1519 Bonsignori completed his last monumental work, an altarpiece depicting the *Adoration of the Blessed Osanna Andreasi* (Mantua, Pal. Ducale; see fig.). The nun is shown venerated by three Dominican nuns and two women in secular dress, one of whom, kneeling in the left foreground, can be identified as Isabella d'Este. A preparatory drawing for this figure (London, BM) shows the Marchioness dressed as a widow, indicating that the picture was completed after Federico Gonzaga's death on 29

Francesco Bonsignori: *Adoration of the Blessed Osanna Andreasi*, oil on canvas, 2.06×1.54 m, 1519 (Mantua, Palazzo Ducale)

March 1519. According to Vasari, Bonsignori died soon afterwards during a cure at Caldiero near Verona. The painting's old-fashioned compositional style provides a link with Bonsignori's first altarpiece of 1484. There are no landscape or architectural elements and no narrative details. The small group of pious women, probably all portraits, is the focus of attention. Bonsignori must have been familiar with the figure and facial features of the Blessed Osanna Andreasi (1449–1505), who had for decades been closely connected with the Gonzagas as a spiritual and political adviser. Thus in his final major work Bonsignori achieved a unique combination of the devotional picture and the portrait, genres that had from the beginning formed the twin focal points of his work.

BIBLIOGRAPHY

DBI; Thieme–Becker

G. Vasari: *Vite* (1550, rev. 2/1568); ed. G. Milanesi (1878–85), v, pp. 299–307

B. dal Pozzo: *Le vite de' pittori, scultori e architetti veronesi* (Verona, 1718), pp. 18–22

D. Zannandreis: *Le vite dei pittori, scultori e architetti veronesi* (1831–34); ed. G. Biadego (Verona, 1891), pp. 250–54

C. D'Arco: *Delle arti e degli artefici di Mantova*, i (Mantua, 1857), pp. 56–9

C. Bernasconi: *Studi sopra la storia della pittura italiana dei secoli XIV e XV e della scuola pittorica veronese dai medj tempi fino a tutto il secolo XVIII* (Verona, 1864), pp. 250–54

G. Biadego: 'La Cappella di S Biagio nella chiesa dei SS Nazaro e Celso di Verona', *Nuovo Archv Ven.* (1906), pp. 123–4

L. Venturi: *Le origini della pittura veneta* (Venice, 1907), pp. 266–8

E. Tea: 'La famiglia Bonsignori', *Madonna Verona*, iv/13–16 (1910), pp. 130–40

A. L. Mayer: 'Francesco Bonsignori als Bildnismaler', *Pantheon*, iv (1929), pp. 345–55

R. Brenzoni: 'Su l'origine della famiglia di F. Bonsignori', *L'Arte*, lvii (1958), pp. 295–300; lviii (1959), pp. 225–8

C. Perina: 'Francesco Bonsignori', *Mantova: Le arti* (Mantua, 1961), ii, 1, pp. 367–72

U. B. Schmitt: 'Francesco Bonsignori', *Münch. Jb. Bild. Kst* (1961), pp. 73–152

Andrea Mantegna (exh. cat., ed. G. Paccagnini; Mantua, Pal. Ducale, 1961), pp. 110–18

B. Berenson: *Central and North Italian Schools*, i (1968)

G. M. Sasso: *Venezia pittrice* (in preparation)

URSULA LEHMANN-BROCKHAUS

Bontecou, Lee (*b* Providence, RI, 15 Jan 1931). American sculptor and printmaker. She studied from 1952 to 1955 at the Art Students League in New York and made two prolonged visits to Rome in 1956 and 1958 on Fulbright scholarships. On her return to the USA she established her reputation with highly personal sculptural reliefs such as *Untitled* (1099×1309×305 mm, 1960; Buffalo, NY, Albright–Knox A.G.), which consists of a web-like arrangement of strips of canvas attached to a welded steel frame around a central oval void. One such work was included in the influential *Art of Assemblage* exhibition held at MOMA, New York, in 1961.

In the early 1960s Bontecou's reliefs became more aggressively three-dimensional, still based largely on the use of ovoid forms, as in *Relief* (welded iron and linen, 1.84×2.20×8.10 m, 1962; Basle, Kstmus.). Her importance was recognized through the commissioning of a wall relief for the Lincoln Center for the Performing Arts in New York in 1964 and by the first prize awarded to her in 1966 by the National Institute of Arts and Letters. In her later work she took up vacuum-formed plastic as a material for large structures, measuring as much as 3 m in extension, which incorporate natural forms such as fish and flowers of her own invention; she also produced plaster reliefs. After her marriage in 1967 and the birth of a daughter she restricted herself largely to drawing and printmaking.

PHOTOGRAPHIC PUBLICATIONS

Fifth Stone, Sixth Stone: Aquatints by Lee Bontecou (Long Island, NY, 1968) [text by T. Towle with an intro. by T. Grosman]

BIBLIOGRAPHY

Lee Bontecou (exh. cat. by A. Michelson, G. Dorfles and G. Gassiot-Talabot, Paris, Gal. Ileana Sonnabend, 1965)

Lee Bontecou (exh. cat., essays R.-G. Dienst, R. Wedewer, W. von Bonin and D. Ashton; Leverkusen, Schloss Morsbroich, 1968)

Lee Bontecou: Prints & Drawings (exh. cat. by R. S. Field, Middletown, CT, Wesleyan U., Davison A. Cent., 1974)

ALBERTO CERNUSCHI

Bontemps, Pierre (*b* ?Sens, *c.* 1512; *d* Verneuil-sur-Oise, *c.* 1570). French sculptor. He was one of the foremost French sculptors of the 16th century, along with his contemporary Jean Goujon. He was probably a native of Sens and may have been responsible for the four marble bas-reliefs (*c.* 1534; Sens, Palais Synodal) illustrating events from the life of Cardinal Duprat, Archbishop of Sens, that once decorated the base of the sarcophagus of the archbishop's tomb. These share many stylistic characteristics with Bontemps's documented reliefs decorating the base of the tomb of *Francis I* (marble, commissioned 1551; *in situ*) at Saint-Denis Abbey.

Bontemps is first documented in 1536 among the large team of artists and craftsmen working at the château of Fontainebleau under the direction of Francesco Primaticcio on the stucco decoration of the Chambre de la Reine (destr.). He remained associated with this work after 1540, when he established himself in Paris, executing a stone statue of *St Barbara* (untraced) for the church of St Victor. From 1540 to 1547 he repaired some of the items in the famous royal collection of coral carvings and had the task of repairing the moulds that Primaticcio had taken from antique statuary in Rome for Francis I. In 1543 he oversaw the casting and chasing of these influential works, five of which survive in the Galerie des Cerfs at Fontainebleau.

Among Bontemps's most important works is the sculpture for the tomb of *Francis I* in Saint-Denis Abbey, designed by the architect Philibert de L'Orme. In addition to the reliefs on the base recording the king's campaign in Italy, Bontemps contracted in 1549 in collaboration with François Marchand (*d* 1551) to supply the recumbent marble effigies of Francis and Queen Claude (*in situ*), and in 1551 he contracted for the marble kneeling statues of the King and Princess Charlotte (*in situ*). In 1550 he also received the commission for the magnificent classicizing monument for the *Heart of Francis I* (marble, completed 1556; Saint-Denis Abbey) intended for the Abbey of Les Hautes-Bruyères, near Rambouillet. It consists of an elaborately carved oval urn raised on paw feet and standing on a rectangular pedestal (see fig.). Its essentially secular decoration was inspired by Rosso Fiorentino's designs for a table service for Francis: four circular medallions representing *Astronomy*, *Music*, *Song* and *Lyric Poetry* adorn the pedestal, while four oval cartouches symbolizing *Architecture*, *Sculpture*, *Painting* and *Geometry* embellish the sides of the urn. The similarities between these subjects and Primaticcio's painted compositions for the Chambre des Arts at the château of Ancy-le-Franc, Yonne, reveal intimate familiarity with the art of the FONTAINEBLEAU SCHOOL, although the execution tends to the ponderous.

Bontemps received two further royal commissions in 1555 and 1556: a white marble relief of the *Four Seasons* (untraced) for a chimney-piece at Fontainebleau and a stone statue of *Francis I* (destr. 1618) for the Grand Salle of the Palais de la Cité, Paris. In 1557 he contracted to execute the tomb of *Charles de Maigny, Capitaine des Gardes de la Porte du Roi* for the church of the Célestins, Paris. The statue of the deceased (stone; Paris, Louvre) represents him seated and asleep in elaborate armour, his head resting on his hand. This documented work, with its powerfully modelled features and idiosyncratic handling of the beard and hair, has enabled a number of other surviving tomb effigies of the middle decades of the 16th century to be attributed to Bontemps. They include that of *Jean III d'Humières* (marble; Paris, Louvre), who died in 1550 and whose recumbent effigy lies on a sarcophagus decorated with reliefs of his seven sons; that of *Admiral Louis Malet, Sire de Graville* (marble, *c.* 1540–50; château of Malesherbes, Loiret); and that of *Guillaume du Bellay, Seigneur de Langey* (stone and marble, 1557; Le Mans Cathedral), who is shown dressed *all'antico*. Among Bontemps's documented but destroyed funerary monuments were those to *Etienne Poncher, Archbishop of Tours* (marble, contract 1555), formerly in the church of the Célestins at Esclimont, Eure-et-Loir, and *Antoine Duprat* (stone and

Pierre Bontemps: monument for the *Heart of Francis I*, marble, h. 2.1 m, 1550–56 (Saint-Denis Abbey)

Cleopatra; Rome, Mus. Pio-Clementino), which was among those works of which Bontemps cast a copy at Fontainebleau; a superb bronze relief of *Alexander Crossing the Granicus* (Paris, Louvre), which was cast in the workshops at Fontainebleau and which is very close in style to the reliefs on the tomb of *Francis I*; an *Adoration of the Magi* now in the chapel of the château of Anet, Eure-et-Loir, which is close to a painted version of the same theme (untraced but known through various copies, e.g. Frankfurt am Main, Städel. Kstinst. & Städt. Gal.) by Primaticcio for the chapel of the Hôtel de Guise (destr.), Paris; and a fine marble bust of *Guillaume Froelich, Colonel-General of the Swiss Guard* (Paris, Louvre), the only surviving fragment from his tomb in the church of the Cordeliers, Paris. The portrait, with its monumental structure and the realism of its features, recalls Bontemps's praying statue of *Francis I* on his tomb at Saint-Denis, but it also anticipates the magisterial funerary portraits of the first half of the 17th century. In 1566 Bontemps retired to Verneuil-sur-Oise, and in 1572 his widow remarried, which would suggest a date of around 1570 for his death.

BIBLIOGRAPHY
M. Roy: 'Le Sculpteur Pierre Bontemps', *Artistes et monuments de la renaissance*, ed. H. Champion (Paris, 1929), pp. 291–417
P. S. Wingert: 'An Adoration in the Cluny Museum', *A. Bull.*, xvii (1935), pp. 506–9
——: 'An Ecole de Jean Goujon Relief in the Louvre', *A. Bull.*, xix (1937), pp. 118–24
——: 'The Funerary Urn of Francis I', *A. Bull.*, xxi (1939), pp. 383–6
P. Vitry: 'Le Tombeau de Jean d'Humières et l'oeuvre de Pierre Bontemps', *Mnmts Piot*, xxxviii (1941), pp. 186–202
M. Beaulieu: 'Nouvelles attributions à Pierre Bontemps', *Rev. A.* [Paris] (1953), pp. 82–8
——: *La Renaissance française*, ii of *Description raisonnée des sculptures du Musée du Louvre* (Paris, 1978), pp. 75–86
——: 'Pierre Bontemps et les Cousin père et fils, artistes sénonais de la renaissance', *Mélanges Stiennon* (Liège, 1983), pp. 35–48
——: *Pierre Bontemps* (in preparation)

☐

Bontepaert, Dirck Pietersz. *See under* SANTVOORT, DIRCK.

Bonvicino, Alessandro. *See* MORETTO.

Bonvin. French family of painters. (1) François Bonvin and his younger half-brother (2) Léon Bonvin came from humble origins; their father was a constable in the Parisian suburb of Vaugirard. As artists they were largely self-taught.

(1) François (Saint) Bonvin (*b* Vaugirard, Paris, 22 Nov 1817; *d* Saint-Germain-en-Laye, 19 Dec 1887). François first trained as a printer and later briefly at the Gobelins. From 1828 to 1830 he was a student at the Ecole de Dessin, Paris, and later attended the Académie Suisse. In 1843 Bonvin showed some of his drawings to François Granet, whom he considered his only mentor.

In his earliest known canvas, *Still-life with a Beer Mug* (1839; Paris, priv. col., see Weisberg, 1979, p. 208), painted while working as a clerk for the Paris police, he displayed a predilection for still-lifes that he maintained throughout his career. By the mid-1840s Bonvin devoted more time to his painting, although he did not officially leave the police until February 1850. In 1844 Bonvin met his first patron, Laurent Laperlier (1805–78), an official in the War

marble, 1561) intended for the church at Nantouillet, Seine-et-Marne.

Bontemps's most famous and accomplished funerary monument for a private client was that to *Admiral Philippe de Chabot, Comte de Brion*, installed in the Célestins Convent, Paris, in 1565. Dismantled in the 1790s, its original appearance is recorded in a drawing by Roger de Gaignières (Paris, Bib. N., Cab. Est.), and it is probable that it was designed by Jean Cousin (i), which would explain the suppleness of pose of the semi-recumbent marble effigy of Chabot (Paris, Louvre), a quality not to be found in such a high degree in any of the other statues attributed to Bontemps. (For a different interpretation *see* COUSIN, (1).) Jean Cousin (ii) was responsible for the decorative sculpture of the tomb's setting, of which only three statuettes survive (marble; Paris, Louvre).

Four further works may be attributed to Bontemps with reasonable certainty: a marble relief of *Nymphs Awakening* (Paris, Louvre) with a central figure directly inspired by the antique statue of *Ariadne Sleeping* (formerly known as

Office, who bought some drawings that Bonvin showed under the arcades of the Institut de France, Paris. In 1847 he exhibited a portrait in the Salon and continued to show there until ill-health forced him to retire in 1880.

Through his friends, the novelist and art critic Jules Champfleury and the painter and writer Gustave Courbet, Bonvin joined the Realist movement. He had lengthy discussions with Amand Gautier, the writer Max Buchon (1818–69) and later the art critic Jules-Antoine Castagnary at the Brasserie Andler, Paris. These conversations probed the nature of Realism and the principles of truth and exactitude held by the artists in the group. François remained attached to the group until the mid-1860s.

In *La Silhouette* (1849) Champfleury singled out François's small *The Cook* (exh. Salon 1849; Mulhouse, Mus. B.-A.), comparing it with the work of Chardin, an artist whom François greatly admired. (Indeed, Bonvin convinced Laperlier to collect works by Chardin, from which he then borrowed motifs.) *The Cook* was awarded a third-class medal and won Bonvin a much-needed 250 francs. By the early 1850s François's dark-toned canvases were frequently exhibited and were sufficiently successful to win him a state commission to complete *The Girls' School* (exh. Salon 1850–51; Langres, Mus. St-Didier), which was awarded a second-class medal.

During the Second Empire (1852–70) François became well known for his small still-lifes and intimate genre scenes inspired by earlier painting. His *Interior of a Tavern* (1859; Arras, Mus. B.-A.) shows the influence of the Le Nain brothers. *Interior of a Tavern (Cabaret flamand)* (1867; Baltimore, MD, Walters A.G.; see fig.) is reminiscent of 17th-century Dutch painting, especially the work of Pieter de Hooch. Bonvin's preference was for thin tones of brown, grey and black, enlivened with red or yellow highlights. In 1859, when a number of young painters (including Whistler and Fantin-Latour) were rejected at the Salon, Bonvin held an exhibition of their work at his own atelier.

After his half-brother's death in 1866 François went to the Netherlands, where he studied Dutch painting in order to find inspiration for his images of 'an art for man' as expressed by the critic Théophile Thoré. Bonvin spent a year in London during the Franco-Prussian War (1870–71). When he returned to France he settled in the village of Saint-Germain-en-Laye, where, despite failing health and eyesight, he continued to create intimate Realist charcoal drawings and paintings of humble everyday objects and scenes.

(2) Léon Bonvin (*b* Vaugirard, Paris, 28 Feb 1834; *d* Meudon, Hauts-de-Seine, 30 Jan 1866). Half-brother of (1) François Bonvin, he first earned his living as an innkeeper but had artistic ambitions from an early age. He first executed small, sombre charcoal and ink sketches of his bleak environment, but by the end of his life he was producing luminous watercolour still-lifes (such as *Still-life: Containers and Vegetables*; 1863; Baltimore, MD, Walters A.G.) and studies of the countryside directly from nature, in a style that looked forward to Impressionism. When his watercolours were rejected by a Parisian art dealer, Léon committed suicide in a fit of despair by hanging himself from a tree in the forest of Meudon.

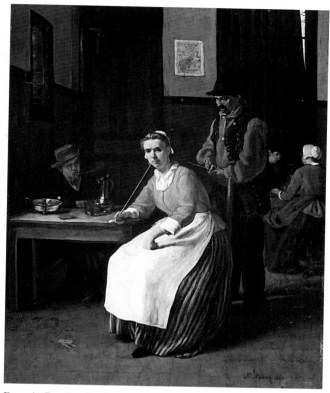

François Bonvin: *Interior of a Tavern (Cabaret flamand)*, oil on panel, 501×372 mm, 1867 (Baltimore, MD, Walters Art Gallery)

Although encouraged and supported by his half-brother, he was largely ignored during his lifetime; however, a sale of his watercolours after his death brought his destitute family over 8000 francs. The Walters Art Gallery in Baltimore, MD, has the largest collection of his work.

BIBLIOGRAPHY
E. Moreau-Nélaton: *Bonvin raconté par lui-même* (Paris, 1927)
G. P. Weisberg: 'François Bonvin and an Interest in Several Painters of the Seventeenth and Eighteenth Centuries', *Gaz. B.-A.*, lxxvi (1970), pp. 359–66
——: 'The Traditional Realism of François Bonvin', *Bull. Cleveland Mus. A.*, lxv (1978), pp. 281–98
——: *Bonvin: La Vie et l'oeuvre* (Paris, 1979)
——: 'Léon Bonvin and the Pre-Impressionist Innocent Eye', *A. Mag.*, liv/10 (1980), pp. 120–24
The Drawings and Watercolours of Léon Bonvin (exh. cat. by G. P. Weisberg, Cleveland, OH, Mus. A., 1980)
G. P. Weisberg: 'Small Works and Simplified Forms in the Art of Léon Bonvin', *A. Mag.*, lxiii/1 (1987), pp. 54-8

GABRIEL P. WEISBERG

Bonzagna [Bonzagni], **Gian Federigo** [Federigo Parmense] (*b* Parma, 1508; *d* after 1586). Italian medallist and goldsmith. His first signed medal was made in 1549 for Pope Paul III. Bonzagna is documented in 1554 working in the papal mint in Rome with his brother Gian Giacomo Bonzagna (1507–65) and Alessandro Cesati. He worked for the papal mint until 1575, when he prepared a medal for Pope Gregory XIII. He also worked in the mint at Parma, where he engraved the dies for medals of Pier Luigi Farnese, 1st Duke of Parma and Piacenza, Cardinal

Alessandro Farnese and Ottavio Farnese, 2nd Duke of Parma and Piacenza. Bonzagna also executed medals for Cardinal Federico Cesi and, in 1560, Gian Battista di Collalto. In 1561 Bonzagna worked as a goldsmith with Cesati and Gian Alberto de' Rossi on a silver-gilt pax for Milan Cathedral. Bonzagna was one of the most prolific medallists of the 16th century. Because many of his medals were unsigned, it is difficult to distinguish his dies from those of Cesati. In some medals the obverse is by Bonzagna and the reverse by another artist. These were produced when several medals were restruck by Mazio in the 19th century. Bonzagna's work is varied and shows considerable technical accomplishment, but his style is cold and academic.

Thieme–Becker

BIBLIOGRAPHY

G. F. Hill: *Medals of the Renaissance* (Oxford, 1920, rev. London, 1978), pp. 91, 178, no. 240
G. F. Hill and J. G. Pollard: *Renaissance Medals from the Samuel H. Kress Collection at the National Gallery of Art* (London, 1967), p. 70
F. Panvini Rosati: *Medaglie e placchette italiane dal rinascimento al XVIII secolo* (Rome, 1968), pp. 39–42
J. G. Pollard: *Medaglie italiane del rinascimento nel Museo nazionale del Bargello* (Florence, 1984–5), ii, pp. 990–95, 1056–64, 1075–6, 1086–91; iii, pp. 1333–4
C. Johnson and R. Martini: *Milano, civiche raccolte numismatiche: Catalogo delle medaglie*, ii (Rome, 1988), pp. 93–144

FRANCO PANVINI ROSATI

Bonzagni, Aroldo (*b* Cento, 24 Sept 1887; *d* Milan, 30 Dec 1918). Italian painter and draughtsman. In 1906 he moved to Milan with a scholarship and enrolled in the Accademia di Belle Arti di Brera in Milan. He soon joined the ranks of such Milanese avant-garde artists as Carlo Carrà, Umberto Boccioni and Luigi Russolo, whose admiration for Gaetano Previati he shared. Through the influence of the latter and through Boccioni he became familiar with modernism. In 1910 he signed the Futurist Manifesto and took part in the evening performances in which the Futurists declaimed their manifestos. However, he soon disassociated himself from the movement and turned his attention to the depiction of reality, which he interpreted and portrayed with a feeling of irony and caricature (e.g. *Exit from La Scala*, 1910; Cento, Gal. A. Mod. Aroldo Bonzagni). His numerous drawings were influenced by the work of Henri de Toulouse-Lautrec, Jean-Louis Forain and Théophile-Alexandre Steinlen, and above all by the style of the Munich and Vienna Secessions, known in Italy through the Venice Biennales of the early 1900s. In 1910–11 he created decorations for the Villa S Donnino (now Villa Leonardi) at San Donnino della Nizzola near Modena. In 1912, having participated in the *Mostra della pittura e della scultura rifiutata* organized by Boccioni at the Palazzo Cova, Milan, he exhibited at the Venice Biennale. In 1913 he participated in the *Mostra nazionale della caricatura* in Bergamo, leaving for Argentina the following year, after again exhibiting at the Venice Biennale. In Buenos Aires he painted some frescoes in the race-track (destr.) and worked for the humorous periodical *El Zorro*. After returning to Milan, he set up a show in 1915 in the Palazzo delle Aste. In his work he increasingly depicted the poorest sectors of society (e.g. *Beggars*, 1916–17; Milan, Gal. A. Mod).

DBI

BIBLIOGRAPHY

Aroldo Bonzagni (exh. cat. by M. Valsecchi, Ferrara, Gal. Civ. A. Mod., 1974)
G. C. Argan: *Aroldo Bonzagni, cento disegni* (Modena, 1986)

DANIELA DE DOMINICIS

Bonzanigo, Giuseppe Maria (*b* Asti, 6 Sept 1745; *d* Turin, 18 Dec 1820). Italian furniture-maker, sculptor and ornamentalist. He belonged to a family who owned a workshop of wood-carvers and organcase-makers in Asti. In 1773 he started working for the Savoy family and the following year gained admission to the Accademia di S Luca, Turin. In the accounts of the royal family he is recorded as having supplied numerous stools, chairs, armchairs, benches, sofas, screens, prie-dieux, beds and mirrors, as well as many ornamental panels and chests-of-drawers, for the Palazzo Reale in Turin and for royal residences at Moncalieri, Rivoli, Stupinigi, Venaria and Govone. His style is best expressed when, as part of a team of architects and assistants, he was commissioned to decorate and furnish entire rooms, such as the State Rooms of the Queen and King at Stupinigi. His work is characterized by its departure from the traditional school of Franco-Piedmontese inlay and marquetry cabinetmaking in favour of a more predominant use of carving. He adhered to Neo-classical forms in their most plastic, solid and vigorous, yet elegant, expression, in which the profusion of carvings always had a symbolic, allegorical and commemorative significance, with great use of garlands, emblems and trophies. In 1787 he was appointed wood-carver for Victor-Amadeus III and in 1793 was admitted *ad honorem* to the Accademia Clementina in Bologna. When Piedmont was conquered by Napoleon, the reputation of Bonzanigo—considered to be a collaborator—grew, overshadowing that of many of his colleagues, some of whose work may have been attributed incorrectly to him. In 1808 he exhibited at the Salon de Paris, and in 1815, on the return of the Savoy family, he was reinstated as royal sculptor; as a sculptor he is remembered for his *Military Trophy* (Turin, Pal. Madama), for the retable in the Sala del Trono (Turin, Pal. Reale), and especially for his small bas-relief portraits in light wood or ivory, which, set in their refined frames, evoke the cameo or wax silhouettes of the 18th century.

BIBLIOGRAPHY

R. Antonetto: *Minusieri ed ebanisti del Piemonte: Storia e immagini del mobile piemontese, 1636–1844* (Turin, 1985), pp. 354–77 [with further bibliog.]

DANIELA DI CASTRO MOSCATI

Bonzi, Pietro Paolo [Gobbo dei Carracci; Gobbo dei Frutti] (*b* Cortona, *c.* 1576; *d* Rome, 17 March 1636). Italian painter and printmaker. Perhaps because of his deformity (*gobbo* means hunchback in Italian), which would have made physical work difficult, his father, a carpenter, apprenticed him to a local painter. Bonzi left Cortona for Rome probably in the mid-1590s and, according to Malvasia, studied with Giovanni Battista Viola, a member of the Carracci circle who specialized in landscape painting. Bonzi was recorded at meetings of the Accademia di S Luca between 1621 and 1634, once as treasurer. Around 1620–24 he worked on his only major fresco commission, decorating the ceiling of a gallery in the

Palazzo Mattei di Giove, in the company of his younger compatriot Pietro da Cortona. Bonzi supplied the grisaille framework and coloured garlands of fruit and flowers surrounding the narrative scenes of the *Life of Solomon* and painted those of the *Marriage* and *Anointing*. His limitations as a figure painter were noted by Baglione.

Bonzi's distinctive style as a landscape painter has been isolated from that of Agostino Tassi, G. B. Viola and Domenichino. He painted trees and bushes in the middle distance to provide a layer of delicately textured tone and usually included tree stumps or dead trees as accents in the foreground. He favoured olive green, ochre and brown with a little blue (e.g. *Landscape with Shepherds and Sheep*, Rome, Mus. Capitolino, and *Landscape with a Roadside Shrine*, Rome, Gal. Doria-Pamphili). His small landscape paintings are appealingly evocative of the Roman countryside and reflect his appreciation of the work of Paul Bril, Adam Elsheimer, Annibale Carracci and Domenichino. A few signed still-lifes of fruit have also been discovered (e.g. a pair; Stockholm, Nmus.), which help to explain his second nickname, Gobbo dei Frutti. They have something of the luscious imagery characteristic of Neapolitan still-life of a later date. He also produced a few engravings (Battisti, 1954, figs 3, 11, 12) and at least one etching. Bonzi was not a major artist, but he was versatile and contributed to various significant trends in 16th-century Rome. Three etchings by him are known (see Battisti, 1954).

BIBLIOGRAPHY

G. B. Baglione: *Vite* (1642); ed. V Mariani (1935), p. 343
C. C. Malvasia: *Felsina pittrice* (1678); ed. G. Zanotti (1841), pp. 91–2
E. Battisti: 'Profilo del Gobbo dei Carracci', *Commentari*, v/4 (1954), pp. 290–302
J. Hess: 'Tassi, Bonzi e Cortona a Palazzo Mattei', *Commentari*, v/4 (1954), pp. 303–15
M. T. Pugliatti: 'Agostino Tassi a Palazzo Rospigliosi', *Atti Accad. Peloritana*, xli (1972–3)
——: 'Pietro Paolo Bonzi, paesista', *Quad. Ist. Stor. A. Med. & Mod.*, i (1975)
L. Salerno: *Pittori di paesaggio del seicento a Roma* (Rome, 1977–80), i, pp. 100–11; iii, pp. 902–94
Italian Still-life Paintings from Three Centuries (exh. cat. by J. Spike, New York, N. Acad. Des., 1983), pp. 15–16
A. Sutherland Harris: *Landscape Painting in Rome, 1595–1675* (exh. cat., New York, Richard L. Feigen, 1985), pp. 68–73

ANN SUTHERLAND HARRIS

Boogaart, Bram van den. *See* BOGART, BRAM.

Book. Portable object for storing information—usually a text of significant length—to be transmitted by means of scripts, notations, pictures or photographs, which are either inscribed by hand (*see* MANUSCRIPT, §I) or printed. This article is primarily concerned with the history and development of the book in the Western tradition. For

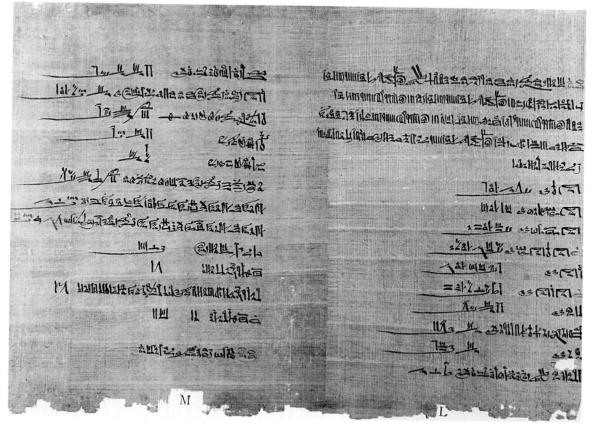

1. Papyrus roll, detail showing script in page-like columns, from the Great Harris Papyrus, from Egypt, *c.* 1166 BC (London, British Museum, EA 9999)

other traditions see under the heading for the relevant culture or civilization.

1. Origins. 2. Production. 3. Decoration and illustration.

1. ORIGINS. In the West the term 'book' is usually associated with the codex and is regarded as a collection of (folded) sheets of paper, all of the same size, printed on both sides and held together, between covers, by glue or string. Yet the codex gained dominance over previous book forms only around AD 400; paper was little used in western Europe before the 15th century (*see* PAPER, §III); and printing in Europe started as late as the middle of the 15th century (*see* §2 below). The form of the book that the codex replaced, having co-existed with it for some 400 years, was the roll, which dominated the cultural and literary life, first of Egypt (*see* EGYPT, ANCIENT, §XI, 3(i) and (v)) and later of Greece and Rome. The codex format was derived from the waxed writing tablets used in the ancient and Classical Mediterranean world and in the Ancient Near East. The material that helped the codex to evolve was parchment, known in Rome since the 1st century AD (*see* PARCHMENT, §2).

Rolls were made either from sheets of papyrus pasted together or from pieces of leather or parchment stitched together; in both cases the result was a continuous piece of writing material, normally inscribed only on one side

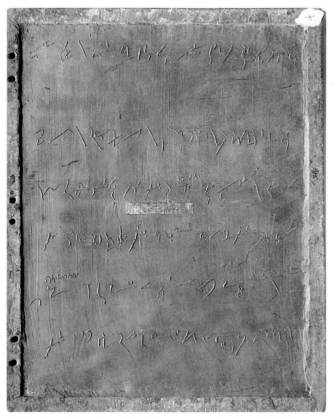

2. Waxed wooden writing tablet, 3rd century BC (London, British Museum, Add. MS. 33270)

and rolled up for storage (*see* ROLL and PAPYRUS). The writing could be arranged in a number of ways, but the most popular form, especially in (later) Greek and Roman times, was in columns, usually *c.* 70–80 mm wide, arranged from left to right and separated by a space of *c.* 10–20 mm (see fig. 1).

Writing tablets on the other hand, although for much of the time used simultaneously, fulfilled somewhat different needs. The majority consisted of one or more pieces of wood (sometimes ivory) held together by a clasp, hinge or leather cord passed through pierced holes (see fig. 2). Although physically more substantial than papyrus rolls, the nature of the material imposed certain restrictions: no more than 10 tablets could be laced together. Sometimes ink or chalk was applied directly to the tablets, but in most cases the boards were slightly hollowed out to allow for the application of wax, into which the script was impressed with the sharp end of a stylus—the other, flat, end was used for erasing. Often the edges and a small area in the centre of each tablet remained raised to protect the text when the tablets were closed together. Later on wood was sometimes replaced by thinner, lighter and more pliable materials such as papyrus or parchment. Parchment had certain advantages over papyrus: it was more durable, it did not crack when folded, and it could accommodate corrections more easily; it was also more expensive and more difficult to produce.

In Classical Greece writing tablets seem to have been as highly regarded as papyrus rolls, but they were later predominantly used for the storage of more mundane information such as letters, memoranda, bills, accounts, exercises and drafts of texts. In Rome, where writing tablets are documented from the earliest period, they also served as legal documents and official certificates. The Latin term 'codex', meaning a book not in roll form, was first used to describe a series of waxed tablets bound together. It had been assumed that writing tablets originated in Assyria, as a set of ivory tablets (*c.* 707 BC; London, BM, MS. 131952) found at Nimrud has traditionally been considered the earliest surviving example (*see* NIMRUD, §2(i)); subsequently, however, two small (50×80 mm), hollowed-out, wooden tablets held together by an ivory hinge were discovered by a team from the Institute of Nautical Archaeology, Texas, off the coast of Turkey in a ship sunk at the end of the 14th century BC.

The codex consists of sheets of parchment cut to the same size and (usually rectangular) shape, folded to form a unit known as a 'gathering'. These are stitched together and placed between thin wooden covers. Depending on the direction of the script, the binding is either on the left side (for Greek or Roman alphabets) or on the right (for Arabic or Hebrew scripts). Modern books made with paper pages follow this model.

Papyrus rolls, parchment rolls, papyrus codices, wooden tablets and parchment codices were all equally efficient forms of the book, often co-existing over long periods. It seems unlikely, therefore, that the transition from roll to codex was simply the result of changes in the materials used for writing. Practical considerations, technological innovations and cultural developments all combined to bring about the transition and to overcome the long-established conventions associated with the use of the roll.

3. *St Matthew Writing with a Quill Pen in a Codex*; miniature from the Lindisfarne Gospels, 343×248 mm, from Lindisfarne, *c.* AD 698 (London, British Library, Cotton MS. Nero D. IV, fol. 25*v*)

communication to spread the new faith and the new way of life all over Europe (see fig. 3).

The earliest reference to the codex comes from Martial (AD 40–104), who, in a number of somewhat controversial passages (*Epigrams* XIV.i.2), referred to literary publications in codex form (on parchment) although without mentioning the term codex itself. More decisive evidence is found in the writings of Roman lawyers, who, for the purpose of drawing up wills and bequests, had to define the difference between a book and a private manuscript. Paulus, who became Praetorian Prefect in AD 223, finally defined the book as a self-contained unit, independent of material or form (*Sententiae* III.vi.87). For the first time, the codex (now specifically mentioned) was given the official status of a book, a position previously reserved only for the papyrus roll. In Greek literature the codex is scarcely mentioned before AD 200; but having existed simultaneously with the roll for about a century, it eventually seems to have gained parity with it in about the 4th century. Extant early manuscripts or fragments are exceedingly rare, and, since the surviving examples are almost exclusively from Egypt, the evidence should be treated cautiously. The first extant parchment codex, an anonymous Latin work usually referred to as *De bellis Macedonicis* (London, BL, Papyrus 745 recto), dates from AD 100. About 172 fragments of Christian material from before 400 have survived; of these, only 11 belong to the 2nd century, all of them on papyrus and in codex form. Such manuscripts as the Codex Sinaiticus (London, BL, Add. MS. 43725; see fig. 4) and the Codex Alexandrinus (London, BL, Royal MS. 1.D.vi), written in the 4th century

The format of the codex offers several advantages over the roll: the size of the book can be increased to accommodate even the most lengthy text; since both sides of a folio are suitable for writing, production costs are reduced; the book is physically more compact and secure and thus more portable and more easily read. Other important factors were the end of a mode of life and an economy that had supported the large papyrus plantations of Egypt, the increased sophistication of parchment manufacture and the invention of the quill pen (*see* PEN, §2), which during the next millennium became firmly linked with the codex.

The main intellectual force behind the change from roll to codex was without doubt Christianity, a text- and book-orientated, proselytizing religion, which between *c.* AD 100 and *c.* 400 replaced the old, state-related, Roman cults and rituals. Apart from economic considerations and ease of textual accessibility, the codex offered Christianity other advantages: it clearly and visibly separated the new sect and the new social order from its Jewish ancestry (with its leather rolls of law) and from the more sophisticated Greek and Roman literary traditions (with their vast libraries of papyrus rolls). The parchment codex became a symbol of Christianity, and, after the destruction of Rome, Christian monks and missionaries took it, together with the split quill pen, along the old (Roman) routes of

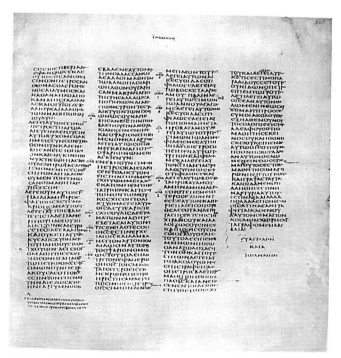

4. Codex Sinaiticus, parchment, 370×320 mm, from the monastery of St Catherine, Mt Sinai, Egypt, 4th century AD (London, British Library, Add. MS. 43725, fol. 260*r*)

and the 5th respectively, already represent an apex in the development of the new book form.

2. PRODUCTION. Between 400 and 1200, book production was largely in the hands of the Church. By the end of the 12th century, however, the Church's monopoly of scholarship and learning was beginning to decline, and gradually monastic scriptoria ceased to be the sole centres of book production. The secularization of society and the influence of Arab, Jewish and Greek scholarship encouraged the creation of new centres of learning and the foundation of universities without direct links with the Church.

The book market increased, catering for the needs of students and scholars and the new wealthy merchant class; simultaneously there was a demand for a wider range of books, including vernacular literature and those dealing with such subjects as philosophy, mathematics, music, astronomy, hunting, food and health. In the newly prosperous towns craftsmen established workshops and undertook specialized activities (for further discussion *see* MANUSCRIPT, §II, 1 and STUDIO, §II, 1).

The 42-line Bible printed in Mainz by JOHANN GUTENBERG from movable type in 1456 and the more securely dated Psalter (1457) of Johann Fust (*c.* 1400–1466) and Peter Schöffer (*c.* 1425–1502) inaugurated a new era in the history of European book production. Technically, the new process was less an invention than the fusion of already existing skills (*see* PRINTING). Physically the printed book differed little from the handwritten one. Indeed Gutenberg and the early printers took great care to cut type that imitated as closely as possible prevailing writing fashions; it was only after the punch cutters' skill increased that the closely woven text of the manuscript gave way to more widely spaced letters and a more open layout. In the early stages of printing, space was left for illumination, miniatures and the painting of capitals, which were often still executed by hand (*see* MANUSCRIPT, §III). Although printing developed at a different pace and in different ways in various parts of Europe, it developed with remarkable speed: by the end of the 15th century *c.* 40,000 incunabula had been produced. The effects of printing on the production, importance, position and distribution of the book were enormous. Printing was no longer merely a craft but also a trade, dependent on capital and functioning on a free enterprise basis.

3. DECORATION AND ILLUSTRATION. Since books store and disseminate textual information, they are closely connected with the history of writing, script, reading, words and language. From their earliest development, however, books have also been decorated and illustrated to create a visual impact designed to attract the widest possible audience. To the art of the scribe and the painter were in due course added those of the bookbinder, the maker of fine writing materials, the printer, typographer, layout artist and, eventually, that of the photographer. The art of the book, the concept of beautifying a written text, has been widely practised by most civilizations, during most periods.

One of the most obvious ways to make a written text aesthetically more pleasing is the use of calligraphy, which is practised primarily for Chinese script (*see* CHINA, §IV), Arabic script (*see* ISLAMIC ART, §III, 2) and Roman script (*see* SCRIPT). Further possibilities for beautifying the written text arise naturally from the process of writing:

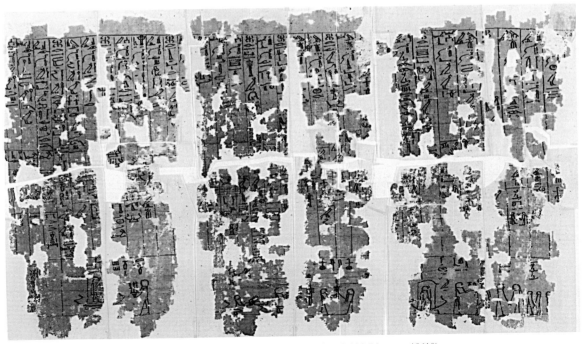

5. Ramesseum Papyrus with line drawing, from Egypt, 20th century BC (London, British Museum, 10610)

the enlargement and/or embellishment of letters, especially initials (*see* INITIAL, MANUSCRIPT), the use of calligraphic ornaments such as rosettes and other geometric designs and the use of different colours for particular letters. In addition, the text itself can be written in the shape of geometric or abstract patterns and designs. Picture-writing may be traced back to the Greek poet Simias who, in the 4th century BC, wrote poems in the shape of an egg, a double axe or the wings of a bird. Once established, the tradition continued and, in the 6th century AD, was introduced to Christian Europe by Venatius Fortunatus, Bishop of Poitiers (*fl c.* 530–610), who wrote his poem *De sancta cruce* in the form of a cross (*see* CARMINA FIGURATA).

Illustrations in books are not always directly related to the text; while they may be used to explain it, they are sometimes included purely to beautify. The text may be subordinated to the illustration, taking on the task of explanation, or the book may consist entirely of pictures with no text at all (for a detailed discussion of the history of illustrated books, *see* BOOK ILLUSTRATION). Illustrations may be positioned in various ways: they may form a band along the length of a roll or the page of a codex; they may be placed more or less haphazardly within the text or be planned so as to relate to the text; an illustration may be a framed picture within the text or it may occupy a full page.

Ancient Egyptian papyri contain illustrations to the text in the form of simple line-drawn (see fig. 5) or colour vignettes (*see* EGYPT, ANCIENT, §X, 4 and figs 75 and 76). This method of text-related illustration was passed on, probably in the 4th century BC and via Alexandria, into the Greek and Roman world. In Christian medieval Europe book illustration reached a high level of achievement (*see* MANUSCRIPT, §III, 2 and MINIATURE, §I), developing a number of distinct local and/or national styles (*see* EARLY CHRISTIAN AND BYZANTINE ART, §V, 2; INSULAR ART, §3; ANGLO-SAXON ART, §IV, 2; CAROLINGIAN ART, §IV, 3; OTTONIAN ART, §IV, 2; ROMANESQUE, §IV, 2; GOTHIC, §IV, 5).

Although printing brought an end to the medieval forms of illustration and decoration, it did not inhibit other forms of beautifying the book. Quite apart from the BLOCK-BOOK and its developments (see fig. 6) a third of all incunabula appear to have been illustrated (*see* WOODCUT, §II, 1). The TITLE-PAGE was adopted from the 1470s (see fig. 7) and by the end of the 15th century was very popular, soon becoming a focus for establishing the artistic aspirations of a particular publication. By the 17th century book illustrations were generally made by means of copper plates (*see* ENGRAVING, §II); at the end of the 18th century lithography was discovered. This process had far-reaching results for book illustration as well as for printing since it became the basis for offset printing. Another development was the discovery of the process of colour-printing (*see* LITHOGRAPHY, §§I and II). Printing has added another dimension to the art of the book, that of TYPOGRAPHY, an art form involving the design and selection of letter forms, their organization into words and sentences and their display in blocks of type as printing on a page; additional concern centres on the selection of paper, the method of printing and the design of the binding.

6. Xylographic book *Apocalypse*: detail showing Mary and the Lamb in Heaven, woodcut, probably from Haarlem, *c.* 1460–1470s (London, British Library, IB.14. Weigel Col. no. 253)

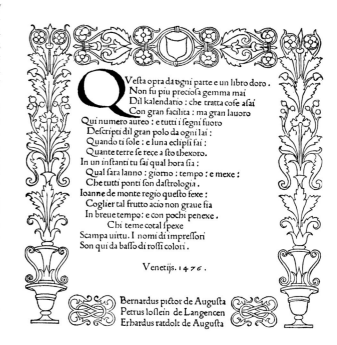

7. Title-page: woodcut, from Erhard Ratdolt's edition of *Calendarium* by Johann Müller, Venice, 1476 (Munich, Bayerische Staatsbibliothek)

The book continues to play an important role despite the rapid development of information technology. Nevertheless, a new element has been added to the possibilities of information storage: as the codex increased the ease of access to the information stored, and as printing guaranteed the authenticity of the mechanically copied text, so the computer has brought about the possibility of manipulating the information stored.

BIBLIOGRAPHY

T. Birt: *Das antike Buchwesen in seinem Verhältnis zur Literatur* (Berlin, 1882)

G. H. Putnam: *Books and their Makers during the Middle Ages: A Study of the Conditions of the Production and Distribution of Literature from the*

Fall of the Roman Empire to the Close of the 17th Century, 2 vols (London, 1896–7)

C. Davenport: *The Book: Its History and Development* (London, 1907)

W. Schubart: *Das Buch bei den Griechen und Römern* (Berlin, 1907, rev. E. Paul, Heidelberg, 3/1961)

D. McMurtrie: *The Book: The Story of Printing and Bookmaking* (London, 1938, rev. New York, 1943)

B. H. Newdigate: *The Art of the Book* (London, 1938)

H. A. Sanders: 'The Beginning of the Modern Book: The Codex', *U. MI Q. Rev.*, xliv/15 (1938)

K. Schottenloher: *Bücher bewegen die Welt: Eine Kulturgeschichte des Buches*, 2 vols (Stuttgart, 1951–2)

R. A. Pack: *The Greek and Latin Literary Texts from Graeco-Roman Egypt* (Michigan, 1952, rev. 1965)

C. H. Roberts: 'The Codex', *Proc. Brit. Acad.*, i/40 (1955), pp. 169–204

D. Diringer: *The Illuminated Book: Its History and Production* (Cambridge, 1958, rev. London, 1967)

S. H. Steinberg: *Five Hundred Years of Printing* (Harmondsworth, 1958, rev. 2/1979)

F. Wieacker: 'Textstufen klassischer Juristen', *Abha. Akad. Wiss. Goettingen*, Philos.-Hist. Kl, iii/45 (1960)

H. Hunger and O. Stegmueller: *Geschichte der Textüberlieferung der antiken und mittelalterlichen Literatur* (Zurich, 1961)

M. McLuhan: *Understanding Media: The Extensions of Man* (London, 1964, rev. 5/1987)

R. Hirsch: *Printing, Selling and Reading, 1450–1550* (Wiesbaden, 1967, rev. 1974)

T. Kleberg: *Buchhandel und Verlagswesen in der Antike* (Darmstadt, 1969)

H. D. L. Vervliet, ed.: *The Book through 5000 Years* (London, 1972)

E. Turner: *The Typology of the Early Codex* (Philadelphia, 1977)

P. A. Winckler, ed.: *Reader in the History of Books and Printing* (Englewood, 1978)

D. Jackson: *The Story of Writing* (London and New York, 1981)

C. H. Roberts and T. C. Skeat: *The Birth of the Codex* (London, 1983)

A. Gaur: *A History of Writing* (London, 1984, rev. 2/1992)

T. McArthur: *Worlds of Reference: Lexicography, Learning and Language from the Clay Tablet to the Computer* (Cambridge, 1986)

L. Avrin: *Scribes, Script and Books: The Book Art from Antiquity to the Renaissance* (London, 1991)

ALBERTINE GAUR

Bookbinding. Cover of a book and process of creating and attaching it by hand. This article is concerned with the Western tradition of bookbinding; for other traditions see under the relevant civilization or culture (e.g. *see* ISLAMIC ART, §III, 7). Mechanization of the various binding processes started in the 1820s, radically changing the traditional processes and turning the craft into an industry; handbinding continued in the late 20th century, but only as a small part of the luxury and collectors market.

I. Materials and techniques. II. Decoration. III. Conservation.

I. Materials and techniques.

Binding materials and the ways in which they have been deployed have varied over the centuries. The material on which a text is written or printed and its intended use have influenced the binding structure, as have economic and social circumstances. In the West the most important development in the history of the book before the age of printing was the change from roll to codex (*see* CODICOLOGY), which by the end of the 4th century AD had become the preferred format (*see* BOOK, §1). The codex consists of sections of folded leaves (gatherings), sewn through the fold of each section and protected by some form of cover. Binding materials may be divided into structural or support materials and covering materials. Structural or support materials are those that hold the leaves of the book together and form the structure of the binding. Covering materials cover this structure and form the book

cover itself; they provide the ground for decoration (*see* §II below).

1. Structural. 2. Covering.

1. STRUCTURAL. The structure of a binding comprises sewing thread and supports, boards, adhesives, end-bands and strengtheners (e.g. end-leaves and paste-downs, spine linings and joints); all these can be made of a variety of materials.

(i) Sewing thread and supports. (ii) Boards. (iii) Spines. (iv) End-bands. (v) Strengtheners.

(i) Sewing thread and supports. The sections or gatherings of Insular codices are linked together by a chain stitch, sewn through the fold of each gathering; the sewing thread may also be used to attach the boards to the textblock. An early Insular codex, the St Cuthbert Gospel of St John (*c.* 698; Stonyhurst, on dep. London, BL, Loan MS. 74; see fig. 1), is sewn in this way: a chain stitch links the gatherings and the boards have been sewn on. There is also evidence that early codices could be held together by some form of sewing around the spine. Unsupported sewing through the fold persisted for certain types of bindings. Stitching through holes stabbed in the inner margins of the text leaves occurs from the last two decades of the 16th century.

Sewing on supports with a herring-bone stitch occurs as early as the 8th century. In Carolingian bindings flax or

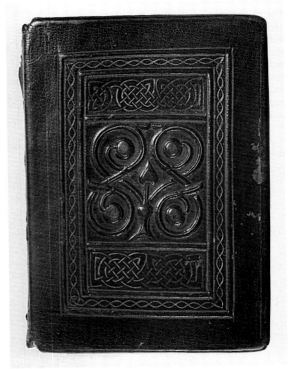

1. Upper cover of the St Cuthbert Gospel of St John, red-brown goatskin, moulded over gesso or cords, incised and decorated with paint, 137×95×35 mm, *c.* AD 698 (Stonyhurst, Lancs: on deposit at London, British Library, Loan MS. 74)

hemp cords were used for sewing supports. Sewing on a sewing frame may have been introduced during the 10th century, and sewing on supports remained the most common type of sewing in western Europe. From the second half of the 11th century tawed leather thongs, split across the width of the spine and sewn round in a variety of patterns (herring-bone, figure-of-eight, spiral, wrapped-round), were commonly used and continued to be used until the early 16th century. Tanned leather thongs were also used and cords were reintroduced in the 15th century. Thinner and single tawed and tanned thongs came into use during the 16th century, when parchment is also found as a sewing support. The number of sewing supports varied considerably, depending on the size of the textblock, but also on local traditions and on date. For example three sewing supports were usual for small books in Italy in the 16th century, while five were commonly used in England. Fewer supports were used for cheaper work. The thread could be of hemp, thin cord, linen, cotton or silk.

Thongs or cords could be used raised (lying on top of the backs of the gatherings) or recessed (lying in grooves cut or sawn into the backs of the gatherings). Recessed cords and thongs, producing a flat spine, were introduced during the 16th century and became common in France from the mid-16th century and in England from the late 16th century or the early 17th. Italian, Spanish and French bindings of the 16th century were sometimes sewn on flat (parchment) supports and the compartments between the supports were lined to form flat spines. Recessed cords were commonly used in France until c. 1650 and in England up to c. 1710. They were reintroduced at the end of the 18th century. Sewing on recessed cords saved time as the sewing thread could be passed over the cord instead of being wrapped around it. Later, recessed cords were combined with hollow spines (in France from c. 1770, in England from c. 1800, becoming widespread during the 1820s) to make the book open more easily. In the 19th century sewing on tapes made of canvas or linen came into use.

In the mid-16th century sewing took a variety of new forms. Instead of every thong or cord being circled by the sewing thread, every other cord could be bypassed, or two or more gatherings could be sewn at the same time. Quantity and economy forced binders to find ever quicker and ever cheaper methods of sewing. Sewing two gatherings at a time was widely used in retail binding in France in the last four decades of the 16th century and elsewhere early in the 17th century, but sewing three, four or even six gatherings at a time is not unknown. Overcasting, the practice of sewing single sheets together to make up gatherings that can then be sewn on to tapes, is found at the end of the 19th century and during the 20th, and earlier for volumes of plates or maps.

Decorative false bands (i.e. stuck-on cords, not proper sewing supports) are found in Italy and France in the 16th century. Many Italian bindings show alternating raised sewing supports and thin false bands. In France (as early as the late 1530s) there were bindings with three raised sewing supports and two false bands. Alternating double cords and false single bands are also occasionally found in Germany from the 1550s. False bands became increasingly common in inexpensive work, and by the 18th century

bindings sewn on recessed cords were given false bands for decorative purposes. In England in the 18th century false bands were used in pairs, but from the 1760s onwards smooth spines came back in fashion.

(ii) Boards. Not all bindings have solid boards. The structure and shape of the binding depend to a large extent on its function and on the way it is stored. When books were stored flat or on sloping shelves or lecterns there was less need for a fixed and rigid structure than when, from the mid-15th century, books were stored on shelves. Limp and semi-limp parchment bindings occur throughout the Middle Ages. Limp structures were frequently used for account-books and stationery bindings but also, from the 16th century onwards, as temporary bindings (in parchment or paper) or for inexpensive retail bindings. Paper wrappers were used for pamphlets and other thin publications, but paper was also used as a temporary cover for properly sewn books that could then later be bound in leather or parchment-covered boards (*see* BOOK JACKET and PAPER, §V, 3). Books in limp parchment bindings (without boards) could be made firmer by sewing through rigid plates of horn, wood or stiff leather. Sometimes metal rods were incorporated in the sewing of limp parchment bindings of the 16th century.

The boards of the earliest codices were made of papyrus or wood. Anglo-Saxon, Carolingian and later medieval boards are usually made of wood. Oak, beech, box, birch and poplar were all used. Scale-board or scaboard, very thin wooden boards, were already in use for cheap work in the 16th century. The thickness of wooden boards depended on the size and weight of the book, and the boards could be shaped (cushioned, chamfered, bevelled) in a variety of ways. Italian boards were normally bevelled only on the inside, while German boards were bevelled on the inside and outside. German boards were frequently partly bevelled, leaving the full thickness at the corners and at the fore-edge where the clasps would be fitted. Boards were also bevelled at the spine edge to accommodate the joints. Thick wooden boards were used well into the 17th century and in Germany well into the 18th. Thin wooden boards were used in America at the end of the 18th century and in the 19th. Wooden boards were occasionally used, especially in England but also in Germany, in the 19th century.

There are examples of leather boards in the 13th and 15th centuries, but these are rare. Boards made of sheets of parchment (sometimes from parchment manuscripts) pasted together were also sometimes used. In Europe, from the mid-15th century sheets of paper, often waste-paper, were pasted together to make boards, first in Italy but also elsewhere, and during the 16th century these pasteboards became more and more common. Couched laminated boards, made by pressing together sheets of paper straight from the papermaker's vat, were also used and were common in France from the 1530s. Pulpboard, made of pulped paper or paper shavings, was much used in England. Later in the 17th century pasteboard was replaced by rope-fibre millboard—at least for fine bindings—although pasteboard remained in use for inexpensive work until late in the 18th century. Rope-fibre millboard was made from rope fibres in a paper mill; it was particularly popular for better quality work in England in the 18th century. Strawboard appeared after the middle of the 19th century and had become the usual material by the 1880s.

Boards had to be cut to size. The amount by which the board extends beyond the textblock varied over the centuries. Early medieval boards were cut flush with the leaves of the book. Slight 'squares' (extension of the board beyond the leaves) emerged during the 15th century, now often only visible (because of shrinking of the boards) at head and tail; squares all round were widespread from the 16th century onwards. Board attachments also vary, depending on date and region. In Insular codices the boards were sewn on with the textblock. In Carolingian bindings the cord sewing supports enter the board through holes in the edge and are anchored in a loop. In Romanesque bindings the tawed leather thongs also enter through holes in the board, come out into a groove, re-enter the boards and are fastened with pegs or wedges. A great many different patterns have been found, largely on bindings in post-Conquest England: thongs entering the wood in a tunnel, emerging on the inside or on the outside of the board and being fastened with a peg; or thongs lying in grooves on the outside of the board, passing through holes and then lying in grooves on the inside of the board and being pegged. During the 13th century the thongs were sometimes taken over the outside of the board, then pulled through holes and pegged on the inside. The length and angle of the grooves can vary considerably. Sharply angled grooves forming triangles have been found in Anglo-Saxon bindings. Post-Conquest bindings appear to have grooves and tunnels of varying length perpendicular to the back edge of the board. During the 15th century the thongs were often brought over the outside of the boards, entered through holes and laid in grooves on the inside of the boards, secured by square or round pegs.

Single thongs were laced in using similar patterns, through holes punched or cut into pasteboards, often through two holes, either straight or at an angle. Lacing in through three holes appears to be characteristically French. In the late 16th century and the 17th not all thongs or cords were laced in. Books sewn on tapes were attached to the covers by inserting the tapes into split boards. There are medieval bindings where the leaves are held to the (limp) covers with tackets (short thongs), and limp and semi-limp bindings could be sewn through the fold of the gatherings with a longstitch. Covers could also be attached by the spine linings and the paste-downs, using adhesives. Case bindings, where the binding case (covers and spine) was made separately, were introduced in the mid-to-late 1820s (earlier in Germany); the textblock was attached to the case with adhesive and held firm by linings and paste-downs.

(iii) Spines. In bindings with boards, the shape of the spine is influenced by the shape of the boards, as well as by the thickness of the leaves (parchment, paper) and by the thickness or amount of sewing thread. The flat spine is a characteristic feature of Insular and Carolingian bindings. The rounding of the spine appeared as early as the 13th century and was the result of the swelling caused by the sewing thread in the centre fold of the gatherings: the

wooden boards, shaped or bevelled on the side nearest the leaves, pressed the backs of the gatherings into a gently rounded shape.

The flat spine survived in Italy until *c.* 1510–20, but elsewhere a rounded spine had become the most common form by the beginning of the 16th century. Later in the century the shaping of the spine was assisted by knocking the backs of the gatherings with a hammer (backing). The shape of the rounded spine varies. For example the use of thin sewing thread in France in the mid-16th century produced gently rounded spines. In England in the 16th and 17th centuries spines are smoothly rounded in shape. By the end of the 18th century more heavily shouldered, half-elliptical spines were introduced. At the beginning of the 19th century spines became flat once again and by *c.* 1820 hollow spines were in widespread use. Later in the 19th century very heavily rounded, glued-up and stiff spines became fashionable; they were strong but difficult to open. Against this trend T. J. COBDEN-SANDERSON introduced flat, barely rounded spines.

(iv) End-bands. End-bands draw the boards to the spine and prevent the boards from swivelling. There is little evidence of the materials of Insular end-bands. The spine leather of the Stonyhurst Gospels is turned over at head and tail and sewn through with a white thread that was tied down in the middle of each gathering; a blue thread that was worked with it is passed through the leather only. After the introduction of sewing on supports, the end-bands usually consisted of tawed or tanned leather thongs, or cores, laced into the boards, usually at an angle. End-bands were sewn, usually with white thread, sometimes also with a coloured thread, over the thongs or cores and tied down in the centre of each gathering. In the 12th century and the early 13th end-bands were often combined with semi-circular (or other-shaped) tabs, an extension of the spine leather or of the spine lining. They were sometimes lined with textile or stiffened by sewing them to the spine lining. The tabs were frequently sewn around the perimeter with coloured thread.

There are German and Netherlandish examples of complex plaited end-bands, while in the 15th and 16th centuries in Germany, Holland and England the spine leather is turned over the end-bands and sewn through. Already from the 13th or 14th century there is evidence of secondary, decorative sewing in coloured threads over the primary (structural) sewing. During the 16th century end-bands gradually lost their structural function and became purely decorative. They were no longer tied down in the centre of each gathering and were seldom laced into the boards.

End-band cores consisted of thongs, rolled leather, rope or cords, split lengths of cane (especially in England), flat strips or rolled pieces of parchment or rolled paper. The secondary, decorative sewing was almost always of coloured silk thread. At the end of the 15th century in Germany there were stuck-on end-bands, strips of tawed leather, folded over a core and sewn after they had been stuck on to the backs of the gatherings. The ends were either laced into or stuck on to the boards. (An early plaited German stuck-on end-band may date from the end of the 15th century.) These early stuck-on end-bands, also found in England in the late 16th century and the 17th and sometimes made of parchment, were not an economy measure, unlike the false end-bands of the late 18th and 19th centuries, which were manufactured separately and stuck on as a purely decorative device.

(v) Strengtheners. These were added to the basic structure of a binding to give it greater strength and to help maintain its shape. The principal materials for end-leaves are parchment, paper, either plain or decorated, and sometimes silk or leather. During the first few centuries of the codex, end-leaves consisted simply of two or four parchment leaves folded and sewn with the text leaves. When paper became the customary material for books (late 15th century), parchment end-leaves (still much in use in Italy and France in the 16th century) were gradually replaced with paper and were often strengthened at the fold with a strip of parchment (frequently a piece of manuscript waste). The use both of manuscript waste and of printed waste for end-leaves and paste-downs is not uncommon. For example parchment manuscript paste-downs are found in Oxford bindings of the end of the 15th century and throughout the 16th. A single leaf, folded, sewn through the fold and leaving a stub; a folded sheet, sewn through the fold forming two end-leaves, one of which could be pasted down; and multiple folded sheets are all found. Plain white paper was most commonly used during the 16th and 17th centuries, and for fine binding marbled paper was used from the end of the 16th century. Marbled end-leaves also appear in retail binding, more often in France and Holland, less frequently in Italy, Spain and England. In France in the 17th century books contain marbled paper paste-downs and plain white paper end-leaves. Marbled paper for end-leaves became more common during the 18th and 19th centuries, while for fine bindings other kinds of decorated paper were also used, such as paste paper (usually in German bindings), block-printed papers (in French, Italian and Dutch bindings) and embossed papers (most frequently in German bindings, often in Scottish bindings of the 18th century and, rarely, in English bindings). All these were first commonly used in the 18th century, reaching their peak of popularity during the first quarter of the century, and were less frequently employed during the 19th century. Marbled (or other decorated) paper and plain white paper could be pasted together after sewing to provide extra strength and hide the sewing thread.

Extra strength was sometimes provided by a leather joint, used as early as the 17th century in France but more often during the 18th century, especially in England. Thin leather joints could also be purely decorative. Cloth joints were in use in England at least as early as the 1840s. Leather *doublures* (linings) provided both extra strength and room for decoration. The earliest-known English leather *doublure* dates from *c.* 1550. *Doublures* were not much used in England until *c.* 1750, but they were popular for fine bindings in France during the 17th and 18th centuries. Silk or paper *doublures*, purely ornamental, are found in the 18th and 19th centuries. Spines, too, were reinforced in a variety of ways. Lining material (of parchment, thin leather, textile or paper) was used to hold the shape of the spine. In Italy, and also in Germany and France, spine liners were cut from single pieces of parchment so as to leave space for the sewing supports. The panels between the sewing supports could be lined separately. Spine linings could be glued or pasted into place or, occasionally, stabbed through with a bodkin. Sometimes only selected spine panels were lined. Spine liners could be used to reinforce the joints but were by no means always employed to do this.

2. COVERING. Materials used to cover a binding include leather, parchment, paper, textile, straw, metal, ivory (or whalebone), wood, tortoiseshell, plaster of Paris and perspex. Among these the most commonly used are leather, parchment, paper and, from the third decade of the 19th century, cloth. Leather and parchment are made of the skin of a variety of animals with different cell structures and different patterns of hair growth: goat, sheep, pig and calf are most frequently used, but leather made of deer, shark, seal and a variety of mammals, even human skin, has been used. Once cleaned, animal skins can be tawed or tanned (for the discussion of these processes *see* LEATHER, §2(i)). Parchment is made from animal skins that have been washed, soaked in lime water, stretched on a frame, scraped and dried under tension (for further discussion *see* PARCHMENT, §1).

Goatskin and sheepskin had been used in Egypt in the 4th and 5th centuries. The few Insular bindings that survive are also made of goatskin. Tawed skins, sometimes dyed pink, were most commonly used in Europe from the 12th century, alongside brown tanned calf during the 12th and 13th centuries. Parchment, calf, hide, pigskin, sealskin and chamois leather were all in use during the Middle Ages. Tawed pigskin was popular in Germany in the 15th, 16th and 17th centuries; tawed sheepskin and tawed calf were both frequently used. Tanned calf and sheep were used more frequently from the 15th century onwards and could be dyed or stained. Sprinkled calf was used from the 17th century; stained and marbled calf were common throughout the 18th century, especially in England. Diced calf (from a more mature animal), called Russia, came into use early in the 18th century and became more popular later in the century. Reversed calf was also used, especially in England and especially for law books and stationery bindings.

Shagreen or sharkskin was in use in the 17th and 18th centuries, frequently found on almanacks or on prayer-books. During the later Middle Ages tanned goatskin seems to have disappeared from use in Europe; it was reintroduced from the Middle East into Italy early in the 15th century. It remained a popular leather, especially for the more expensive bindings, and was tanned and dyed in a variety of colours. Marbled goatskin was used in France in the 1540s. Goatskins used in England were imported through Turkey, while goatskins from Morocco were not introduced there until the 1720s. Straight-grain morocco, an artificially grained goatskin, became popular in the 1770s. Limp and semi-limp parchment bindings were used on account-books at least as early as the 14th century and probably considerably earlier. Limp parchment bindings are found in Italy in the 16th century, and they became more widely used for inexpensive work throughout the 16th and early 17th centuries. Limp parchment remained in use in Italy and Spain until the 18th century. Parchment over boards is found in the second half of the 16th century in France, and it became common in Holland in the 17th century. It was also employed in England, even for fine work, in the 18th and 19th centuries and was frequently used in Italy in the 18th century.

Textile and embroidered bindings were already produced in the 14th century (possibly earlier) and became popular at the end of the 16th century and during the 17th. Such bindings continued in the 18th century, when canvas came into use for cheap books (especially school books). Bookbinders' cloth was introduced in the early 1820s, and both cloth and buckram were the most frequently used covering materials during the period following the mechanization of the various binding processes. (For the discussion of other, rarer, cover materials *see* §II below.)

To cover the boards and spine, leather was usually pasted and moulded over them; some kinds of parchment bindings were not pasted. Most 12th-century bindings had a chemise: a loose over-cover of leather or textile, with envelope pockets for the boards to slip into, sewn at the top and bottom of the covers and with flaps or skirts to wrap around the book. They were often held to the covers by bosses and by a long strap with a strap pull and a clasp that fitted over a pin protruding from the outer face of the opposite cover. In order to hold the leather to the covers and the spine, the binding was tied up with ropes or cords, either only at head and tail on smooth spines (in France) or at each spine band. The edges of the leather were turned in and pasted down. There are various methods of dealing with the accumulation of the leather at the corners, such as cutting off the corner or cutting a gap so that the edges when folded over would meet, cutting the corners so that they overlapped, or cutting the leather to leave a tongue. Many other methods have been used.

Straps, clasps and ties were employed to fasten the binding and to keep the book shut. Already on 10th-century German bindings clasps are found hinging on the lower cover. It appears that as a rule French and English clasps hinged on the upper cover and fastened on the lower cover, while in Germany and the Netherlands clasps fastened on the upper cover. Four pairs of clasps are common on Italian bindings. Metal bosses served to keep the bindings from rubbing on the surface of the lectern or sloping shelf. Chains to fasten the book to a reading desk or to rods above or below the shelves were used from the 14th to the 18th centuries.

BIBLIOGRAPHY
G. Pollard: 'Changes in the Style of Bookbinding, 1530–1830', *The Library*, 5th ser., xi (1956), pp. 71–94
B. C. Middleton: *A History of English Craft Bookbinding Technique* (London, 1978)
G. Pollard and E. Potter: *Early Bookbinding Manuals* (Oxford, 1984)
C. H. Roberts and T. C. Skeat: *The Birth of the Codex* (London, 1987)
F. A. Schmidt-Künsemüller: *Bibliographie zur Geschichte der Einbandkunst* (Wiesbaden, 1987) [bibliog. to 1985]
J. A. Szirmai: 'Old Bookbinding Techniques and their Significance for Book Restoration', *7th Internationale Arbeitsgemeinschaft der Archiv-Bibliotheks- und Graphikrestauratoren Congress: Uppsala, 1991*
B. van Regemorter: *Binding Structures in the Middle Ages*, Eng. trans. ed. J. Greenfield (Brussels and London, 1992)

II. Decoration.

Decorated bindings form only a small percentage of all books bound. They are collectors' items, presentation copies produced by top craftsmen, rather than the protective covers of books for daily and constant use. Bindings may be decorated in numerous ways, with metalwork, jewels, enamel (see colour pl. III), ivory, carved or painted wood, embroidery, painting, staining, stencilling, onlaying or inlaying with pieces of material in contrasting texture and/or colour, moulding or sculpting. The most widespread method of decorating leather bindings is by impressing them with engraved brass tools, either cold (obtaining a 'blind' impression) or heated through gold leaf (*see* LEATHER, §2(ii); GILDING, §II, 5).

1. Covers. 2. Fasteners and leaf edges.

1. COVERS.

(i) Before *c.* 1400. (ii) *c.* 1400–*c.* 1700. (iii) After *c.* 1700.

(i) Before c. *1400.* The most extravagant medieval bindings are of precious metals or ivory and are usually found on liturgical books. Silver or silver gilt covers were engraved (e.g. *see* GOTHIC, fig. 87) or show relief or filigree work, with or without precious stones or hardstones. Repoussé or separately cast figures often represent Christ, the Virgin, the four Evangelists or saints (e.g. for illustration *see* CODEX AUREUS OF ST EMMERAM). Carved ivory book covers were modelled on Late Antique diptychs. They too show saints or scenes from the Old and New Testaments

2. Blind-tooled binding, lower cover of Peter Lombard: *Sentences*, brown (mature) calf, from London, *c.* 1185 (Oxford, Bodleian Library, MS. Rawl. C. 163)

3. Blind-tooled binding by the Rood and Hunt Binder, upper cover of J. Nider: *Consolatorium timoratae conscientiae*, brown calf, from Oxford, *c.* 1480 (London, British Library, IA. 39102)

(*see* CAROLINGIAN ART, figs 13 and 15; see colour pl. IV, fig. 2). Book covers were sometimes enamelled, particularly from Limoges between *c.* 1180 and *c.* 1230. In Siena painted wooden covers were used to protect and adorn the local tax accounts from the 13th century to the 18th (*see* BICCHERNA). The earliest surviving embroidered binding, made in England, covers the early 14th-century Felbrigge Psalter. The upper cover shows the *Annunciation* and the lower cover the *Crucifixion*. Textile and embroidered bindings continued to be popular in England during the following centuries, especially for religious books. They were less common in Holland, France, Spain and Italy.

Very few medieval European decorated leather bindings are known. The earliest surviving European decorated binding, that on the Stonyhurst Gospel, was produced in England. It probably dates from the end of the 7th century and is covered in red–brown goatskin, decorated with a different design on each cover. The upper cover has an embossed floral design, surrounded by incised lines filled with coloured paint (see fig. 1 above); the lower cover has a much simpler incised step design, also showing traces of colour. During the 12th and early 13th centuries blind-tooled Romanesque bindings were produced in France, England, Germany and Austria. Several show stamps or tools depicting biblical subjects side by side with figures from Classical antiquity and mythology, monsters, dragons, birds and other animals (see fig. 2). The tools are

fairly large and their motifs bear strong resemblance to those found on Romanesque stone-carvings. They are usually arranged in circles, rows or concentric panels.

(*ii*) *c. 1400*–*c. 1700*. The monastic reforms on the Continent early in the 15th century contributed to a revival in book production, and the invention of printing gave a substantial boost to the book trade. An increase in the output of decorated leather bindings followed. In Germany, France and Italy and a little later in Spain, a large number of leather bindings decorated with small hand tools used in blind were produced, mainly in monasteries. Interlacing strapwork, effected with very few small rope or knot tools, were popular in Italy and Spain in the 2nd half of the 15th century and persisted well into the 16th. In France small animal, bird, insect and floral tools were used in vertical strips.

The earliest 15th-century English blind-tooled bindings were made in London. Other early centres were Oxford, Canterbury, possibly Salisbury, Winchester and, a little later, Cambridge. Small engraved tools showing animals, birds, stylized flowers, roundels, squares, triangles, monsters and fleurs-de-lis abound. Two designs, widely used on both sides of the Channel, show a frame of intersecting lines around a diamond and a saltire, or lines dividing the centre into smaller diamond-shaped and triangular compartments. Designs formed by arranging the tools in rows are frequently found in Oxford (see fig. 3) and sometimes

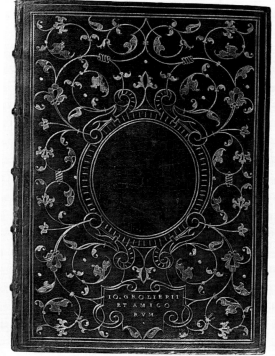

4. Gold-tooled binding by the Last Binder of Jean Grolier (with Grolier's name tooled), upper cover of Aeneas Vico: *Commentarium in vetera imperatorum Romanorum numismata*, brown goatskin, *c.* 1560 (London, British Library, C. 24.b.23)

in London, as well as in France. The influences of continental binding and tool design on English bookbinding of the last quarter of the 15th century and the first half of the 16th is marked. Rolls (engraved brass wheels) were introduced at the very end of the 15th century, while panels (engraved or, more probably, cast blocks) had been used in the Netherlands as early as the second half of the 13th century. They came into frequent use during the late 15th century and the early 16th, and are most commonly found in the Netherlands and England, but also in France and Germany. A technique that used a knife or other sharp instrument to draw a design into the leather or to cut or carve the leather away, leaving the decoration to stand out against the cut-away, sometimes punched, background, was popular in German-speaking countries between the end of the 14th and the beginning of the 16th centuries. Many of these cut-leather ('Lederschnitt') bindings have pictorial designs.

The technique of impressing heated brass tools through gold leaf into the leather is of Islamic origin (*see* ISLAMIC ART, §III, 7(ii); *see* GILDING, colour pl. II, fig. 1). Gold-tooled bindings were made in Morocco from the 13th century and the practice was well established by the 2nd half of the 14th century in the Mamluk empire and Iran. Gold-tooling reached Italy early in the 15th century, where by the third quarter of the century it was widely known. The technique came to Spain by the end of the 15th century and was used in Hungary, on bindings for Matthias Corvinus (*reg* 1458–90). Early in the 16th century gold-tooled bindings were produced in France. The best-known French binding collector of the 16th century, JEAN GROLIER, acquired his earliest bindings in Milan, but the pride of his collection was bound in Paris between 1520 and 1565 (see fig. 4). In France the binding trade was divided into forwarders (binders) and finishers (decorators) and it is frequently difficult to attribute French bindings purely on the basis of their finishing tools, the more so as the person who was paid for the bindings may well have been a bookseller or stationer who ordered rather than made them. The most stunning gold-tooled bindings were produced in Paris during the reign of Henry II (*reg* 1547–59), using a wide variety of designs showing linear frames, arabesques, or interlacing strapwork combined with solid, open and hatched tools. In the 1540s, 1550s and 1560s many famous collectors had their books bound in Paris, for example Thomas Mahieu (*fl* 1536–72) and the Englishman Thomas Wotton (1521–86). Thin pieces of onlaid leather in contrasting colour were combined with gold-tooling to produce the finest bindings of the period.

The technique of gold tooling came to England from France, the earliest example dating from 1519 (Oxford, Bodleian Lib., MS. Bodley 523). For the next ten years it was still largely an experimental technique, but from *c.* 1530 many fine gold-tooled bindings were produced, most of which show French or Italian influence. Gold-tooling was also practised in the Netherlands and in Poland. German binders continued tooling in blind, often on white-tawed pigskin, well beyond the mid-16th century. They also used rolls and panels longer than their colleagues in other countries and employed them either in blind or with low quality gold during the second half of the century. Italy continued to produce fine bindings. The bibliophiles

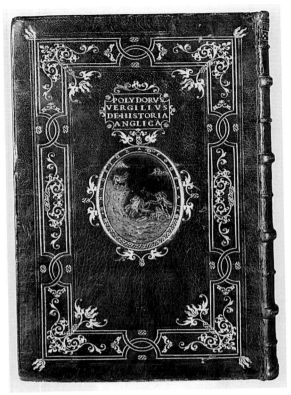

5. Gold-tooled binding attributed to Marcantonio Guillery, upper cover of Polydore Vergil: *Angelicae historiae*, with tooled device of G. B. Grimaldi, dark brown goatskin, *c.* 1545 (London, British Library, G. 4762)

Apollonio Filareto (*fl* 1537–50) and Giovanni Battista Grimaldi (*c.* 1524–*c.* 1612) used their own medallion-shaped devices (see fig. 5). Bindings with plaquettes modelled on antique coins or Classical intaglios and cameos were a typical Italian phenomenon, but they are also found in France, and to a lesser degree in England and Germany. During the reign of Elizabeth I (*reg* 1558–1603) fine gold-tooled bindings were made in England, the designs of many of which show French influence. Interlacing ribbons, combined with solid and hatched tools, as well as designs showing large corner and centre pieces prevailed. The latter continued to flourish during the reign of James I (*reg* 1603–25). The Dudley Binder (*fl* 1558), the Morocco Binder (*fl* 1571), the Initial Binder (*fl* 1562–3), Jean de Planche (*fl* 1567–80), the McDurnan Gospels Binder (*fl* 1566) and Matthew Parker's private bindery, among others, all produced first-rate work in London.

In France during the second half of the 16th century interlace developed into the fanfare style (see fig. 6). Echoes of this style are found in Holland and England in the 17th and 18th centuries and in Italy and Germany in the 18th. In France, later in the 17th century, this style developed into mosaic designs, when the compartments were frequently made of inlays or onlays of contrasting colours and filled with small dotted tools. At the end of the 16th century and during the 17th other designs that covered the whole of the boards in a regular way were also popular in France and a little later in Holland; they were effected by a sprinkling of small tools, sometimes as the background of a central arms block, or with drawer-handle tools and fleurons. The habit of sprinkling the covers with small tools was still current in England during the reign of Charles I (*reg* 1625–49). In the 1630s and 1640s dotted or pointillé tools became fashionable in France; they were much used in Holland later in the 17th century and continued in the 18th; they occur in Italy in the later part of the 17th century; and they first appeared in Cambridge in the 1640s and 1650s, soon to become one of the typical features of English Restoration binding. Characteristic designs, either circular or formed of concentric panels, and made with small tools, were prevalent in Cambridge in the first half of the 17th century.

Corner and centre designs, formed by whole or quarter fan shapes, were fashionable in Italy in the 1640s; they also occurred in Spain in the 17th century. The movement towards the use of smaller pointillé tools and polychrome leather onlays in England started early in the 1650s and developed into the splendours of the golden age of English bookbinding, the period following the restoration to the throne of Charles II. The cottage roof design (see fig. 7), typical of the Restoration binding, remained in use until

7. Gold-tooled and painted binding by Samuel Mearne, upper cover of the *Book of Common Prayer*, with the cypher of Charles II, red goatskin, 1666 (Durham, University Library, S.R.5.F.14)

6. Fanfare pointillé-tooled binding, upper cover of N. Guillebert: *Les Cent-cinquante Pseaumes de David paraphrasez*, tooled with the arms of Nicolas de Bailleul, light brown goatskin, *c.* 1647 (Oxford, Bodleian Library, Montague 508)

the early 18th century. The best-known binders of this period are John Houlden (*fl* 1631–*c.* 1670) in Cambridge, Stephen Lewis and Thomas Lewis (*fl* 1653–61), Charles Mearne (*fl* 1675–86) and Samuel Mearne (*fl* 1653–83), Robert Steel (*fl* 1677–1710), the Queen's Binders, the Naval Binder (*fl* 1670–90), the Centre Rectangle Binder (*fl* 1674–96), Richard Balley (*fl* 1680–*c.* 1711) and Alexander Cleeve (*fl* 1678–91), all in London, and Roger Bartlett (*fl c.* 1666–1711) and Richard Sedgley (*fl c.* 1680–1719) in Oxford.

(iii) After c. *1700.* During the first decade of the 18th century, the Geometrical Compartment Binder introduced some new designs to replace the cottage-roof style or 'all-over' designs of his predecessors and contemporaries; a number of his bindings recall the French fanfare style. The library founded by Robert Harley, Earl of Oxford, gave its name to a design formed by roll-tooled borders and a diamond-shaped centrepiece, built up of small tools. Developed by Thomas Elliott and Christopher Chapman (both *fl* 1719–25) for the Harleian Library, it persisted well into the 1760s in London and Cambridge. Bindings decorated with emblematic tools were made for Thomas Hollis and Jonas Hanway (1712–86) from the 1750s till the 1780s and are also found on Masonic bindings of the second half of the 18th century. Neo-classical bindings were designed by James Stuart and Robert Adam in the early 1760s.

In the second half of the 18th century numerous German binders immigrated to England and ran the fine binding trade in London, including Andreas Linde

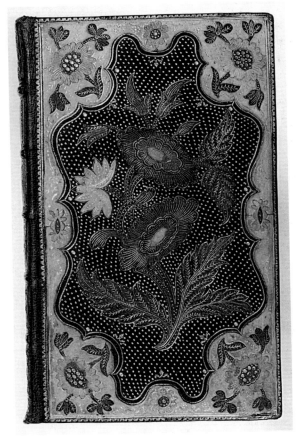

8. Mosaic binding by LeMonnier (signed), upper cover of the Bible, red goatskin onlaid in cream, brown and green, *c.* 1760 (London, British Library, C. 72.a.9)

sometimes painted or made of onlaid straw. Decorated paper bindings, already produced in Italy and Germany in the 16th century, became more popular during the 18th, especially on pamphlets, and survived well into the 19th century when they gradually lost their artistic merit. Printed woodblocks, marbling, coloured paste and embossed metal plates were all employed. Printed and painted silk bindings are found in France, Italy and the Netherlands in the 19th century, especially on almanacs.

During the first half of the 19th century a number of different styles were current: Neo-classical designs, simple panel designs, sometimes combined with elaborately tooled *doublures*, more complex designs effected with small tools, and designs making use of thick (sometimes double) boards with sunk panels, tooled and blocked in blind and gold. In the late 1820s, the process of embossing bindings was introduced in France and Germany, but it was soon practised in England where embossed designs often depicted cathedrals, although floral and chinoiserie designs were not uncommon. Painted parchment persisted, but black moulded papier mâché on a metal frame, often in elaborate Gothic designs, was also used. During the second half of the century pastiches of earlier periods were in vogue, both in France and in England. Breaking away from these traditional designs, Marius Michel produced bindings in Art Nouveau designs, while Thomas James Cobden-Sanderson designed his own (frequently floral) tools and used them in a variety of ways, always with great taste and restraint. He gave rise to the amateur school of English bookbinding which has dominated

(*fl* 1751–63), John Ernst Baumgarten (*fl* 1771–82), Christian Samuel Kalthoeber (*fl* 1780–1814), Henry Walther, L. Staggemeier (*fl* 1791–1804) and Samuel Welcher (*fl* 1791–1817), and Charles Hering. Native English binders working during the latter part of the 18th century include Roger Payne (*fl* 1757–97), who was an outstanding finisher and employed finely cut tools to comparatively simple designs, and the firm of Edwards of Halifax, best known for parchment bindings with scenes painted on the transparent under-surface and for so-called Etruscan bindings. Parchment bindings painted on the top surface were made in Italy in the 18th century and also in Hungary and Germany.

Very fine bindings were produced in Dublin in the 18th century with characteristic white onlays (made of paper, parchment or thin leather) and floral or fan tooling. During the 18th century in France two binding styles prevailed. One achieving a lace effect with the help of small tools (dentelle), the other using onlays and inlays to form colourful, often floral or pictorial, mosaics (see fig. 8). The best known Paris binders of this period were Derome, Monnier and Padeloup. Pictorial designs are also found in Germany, Austria and Italy, often tooled or blocked but

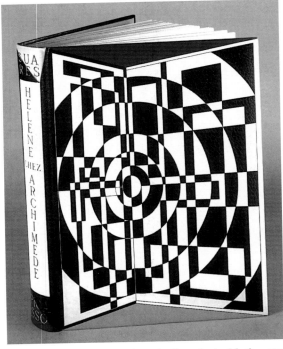

9. Onlaid binding in white and grey by Pierre-Lucien Martin, upper cover of André Suarès: *Hélène chez Archimède*, black box calf, 1962 (London, British Library, C. 108. eee. 18)

PLATE I

Beadwork

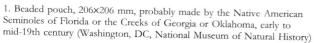

1. Beaded pouch, 206×206 mm, probably made by the Native American Seminoles of Florida or the Creeks of Georgia or Oklahoma, early to mid-19th century (Washington, DC, National Museum of Natural History)

2. Bead and shell decoration on a rattan basket, h. 435 mm, made by the Kayan people of the Baram River district, Sarawak, Malaysia, c. 1905 (London, British Museum)

3. Beadwork sculptural group, h. 255 mm, made by the Yoruba people of south-west Nigeria, before 1912 (London, British Museum)

Beads and sequins on a printed voile evening dress made by Callot Soeurs, Paris, *c.* 1922 (London, Victoria and Albert Museum)

PLATE III

Bookbinding

Book cover of the Sion Gospels, beechwood, overlaid with gold, enamels and precious stones, 254×220 mm, from Germany, possibly Trier, 11th century with 12th-century additions (London, Victoria and Albert Museum)

PLATE IV

Bookbinding

1. Book cover (interior) of a bound manuscript, painted with lacquer, 230×140 mm, from Kashmir, India, early 19th century (London, Victoria and Albert Museum)

2. Book cover of a manuscript, ivory, possibly from the 9th-century Codex Aureus of St Emmeram, 10th century Byzantine enamels, cloisonné enamel and gold, 425×315 mm, from Regensburg or Bamberg, early 11th century (Munich, Bayerische Staatsbibliothek)

3. Bookbinding by Paul Bonet (1889–1971) for *La Treille Muscate* by Colette, inlays of leather with gold-tooling, 325×250 mm, 1942 (private collection)

binding design in the 20th century both in the UK and in the USA.

Throughout the 20th century, but especially since World War II, binding design reached remarkable standards in France (see fig. 9 and colour pl. IV, fig. 3) and in England, although interesting work is also produced in Germany, Holland, the USA, and Japan. Styles have become more individual and designs tend to be determined by the book they embellish rather than by tradition. A wide variety of materials such as metal, stone, perspex and plastics have taken the place of or are combined with the more traditional leathers, parchment, paper or cloth. In some cases it is hard to draw the line between bookbindings and sculpture.

2. FASTENERS AND LEAF EDGES. Straps, clasps or ties, necessary to keep books shut, also offer scope for decoration. Medieval luxury bindings tend to have elaborate, often jewelled clasps. Finely chased, engraved, or otherwise decorated clasps occurred from the 12th century onwards and elaborately ornamented clasps are frequently found on textile bindings of the 15th and 16th centuries, as well as on leather work, or—in the 17th and 18th centuries—on tortoiseshell or as part of chased or repoussé metal covers, especially in Holland and Germany. Clasps were often combined with metal bosses or with metal corner and centre pieces and these are a typical feature of German bindings of the 15th century and later.

Decorated leaf edges may be stained, painted, marbled, sprinkled, gilt, or gilt and gauffered. Coloured edges seem to be as old as the codex itself and purple edges have been found on a 4th-century book. Edges painted with decorative designs are found at least as early as the 10th century. Marbled edges are most frequently found on 17th and 18th century books. Edge gilding started in Italy in the second half of the 15th century and gilt edges, sometimes also gauffered (decorated with heated finishing tools), were widespread from the 1530s in Italy, France, Spain, Holland and a little later in England, Germany and Scandinavia. The peak of elaboration, when paint was combined with gilding and gauffering, was reached during the second half of the 16th century, and continued in Holland, Germany and Scandinavia in the 17th and 18th centuries.

Stained edges are more common on retail bindings but are also found on finer work, especially in Germany and Holland, while sprinkled edges occur on English books of the 18th century and continued to be popular. The painting of designs underneath the gold of the edges dates back in England to the 1650s and was quite common during the Restoration Period. This practice continued in England during the first half of the 18th century and was much employed by Edwards of Halifax in the 1780s; it was still carried on in the first three decades of the 19th century and was revived early in the 20th century.

BIBLIOGRAPHY

L. Gruel: *Manuel historique et bibliographique de l'amateur de reliures*, 2 vols (Paris, 1887, 1905)
E. Thoinan: *Les Relieurs français, 1500–1800* (Paris, 1893)
H. Loubier: *Der Bucheinband von seinen Anfängen bis zum Ende des 18. Jahrhunderts* (Leipzig, 1926)
E. P. Goldschmidt: *Gothic and Renaissance Bookbindings*, 2 vols (London, 1928)
G. D. Hobson: *English Bindings before 1500* (Cambridge, 1929)
F. Hueso Rolland: *Exposición de encuadernaciones españolas* (Madrid, 1934)
H. Thomas: *Early Spanish Bookbindings* (London, 1939)
G. D. Hobson: *English Bindings in the Library of J. R. Abbey* (London, 1940)
E. Kyriss: *Verzierte gothische Einbände im alten deutschen Sprachgebiet* (Stuttgart, 1951)
L.-M. Michon: *La Reliure française* (Paris, 1951)
J. B. Oldham: *English Blind-stamped Bindings* (Cambridge, 1952)
L.-M. Michon: *Les Reliures mosaïquées du XVIIIe siècle* (Paris, 1956)
H. M. Nixon: *Broxbourne Library: Styles and Designs of Bookbinding* (London, 1956)
J. B. Oldham: *Blind Panels of English Binders* (Cambridge, 1958)
R. Devauchelle: *La Reliure en France de ses origines à nos jours*, 3 vols (Paris, 1959–61)
T. de Marinis: *La legatura artistica in Italia*, 3 vols (Florence, 1960)
G. Pollard: 'The Construction of English 12th-century Bindings', *The Library*, n. s. 4, xxvii (1962), pp. 1–22
H. M. Nixon: *Bookbindings from the Library of Jean Grolier* (London, 1965)
——: *Sixteenth-century Gold-tooled Bookbindings in the Pierpont Morgan Library* (New York, 1971)
——: *Restoration Bookbindings* (London, 1974)
A. R. A. Hobson: *Apollo and Pegasus* (Amsterdam, 1975)
G. Pollard: 'Some Anglo-Saxon Bookbindings', *Bk Colr*, xxiv (1975), pp. 130–59
J. Storm van Leeuwen: *De achttiende eeuwse Haagse boekband* [18th-century bookbinding] (The Hague, 1976)
H. M. Nixon: *Five Centuries of English Bookbinding* (London, 1978)
M. M. Foot: *The Henry Davis Gift*, 2 vols (London, 1978, 1983)
P. Needham: *Five Centuries of Bookbindings, 400–1600* (New York and London, 1979)
A. R. A. Hobson: *Humanists and Bookbinders* (Cambridge, 1989)
H. M. Nixon and M. M. Foot: *The History of Decorated Bookbinding in England* (Oxford, 1992)

MIRJAM M. FOOT

III. Conservation.

The basic concept of book conservation is to preserve the true nature of the book and to ensure that none of the bibliographic evidence is lost. It was and still is usual practice for books to be rebound, especially if the original binding was plain, dirty and worn as many early bindings often are. The practice of rebinding early books in a contemporary style is the cause of an enormous loss to the student of the history of bibliography; a more acceptable practice is for books to be kept as close to their original state as possible. Apart from rebinding, books may become damaged in a number of different ways and have to be repaired if they are to survive in a usable condition. Although the processes of conservation are easy to learn, the diagnosis and prescription of the correct treatment requires experience and a good knowledge of the history and structure of books and bindings.

Books covered in vellum, especially those in limp vellum, are usually able to resist the ravages of time provided they are kept away from excessive heat and moisture. Vellum covers without clasps tend to warp and lift away from the book. This problem can be overcome by expertly relaxing and flattening the vellum thereby returning the covers to their original position.

Most of the damage to leather bindings occurs at the back or spine or the corners of the board covers. Under normal storage conditions the spine is the area of the cover most exposed, and the hinge or joint where the boards meet the spine becomes either broken or seriously weakened by repeated flexing as the book is opened and closed. Invariably the cause is over-thinned and poor

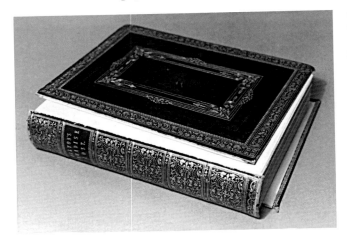

10. Leather bookbinding, showing (top) split joints and damaged corners and (bottom) the binding after conservation

quality leather. One of the tasks most frequently undertaken by the book conservator is that of reinforcing or replacing the spine or joints of a binding. The usual method is to place a layer of new leather over the spine and joints of a book in an operation known as rebacking. The original spine is removed by carefully cutting underneath the leather with a specially designed knife and lifting it from the spine. The leather on the sides along the outer joints is lifted by making an incision at a shallow angle parallel to the joints. The leather turn-ins and end-papers at the inside of the head and tail ends of the boards are also lifted. A new piece of matching leather is cut to size, stained with aniline dyes to match the exact colour of the original and pared to the correct thickness. The new leather is coated with adhesive, centred on the back of the book and drawn-on and moulded over the spine, and the original spine is reattached in position. Damaged, worn, cracked and broken corners are repaired by lifting the original leather cover, turn-ins and end-papers away from the corners of the boards and inserting and moulding a new piece of matching leather underneath the area of damage. Providing the matching of the leather and colour is successful and the repairs are sound, they should be

undetectable and will not disturb the aesthetic harmony of the binding (see fig. 10).

Publishers' edition bindings in paper and cloth, first introduced in the early 19th century, are not constructed to last and quickly show signs of wear. They become damaged at the joints along the edge of the spine. The conservator's task is to restore the binding to its original state without disturbing the cover decoration. This is usually achieved by attaching a strip of matching material underneath the cover to reinforce the weakness at the spine. The main cause of decay of modern books is acid paper. In the late 20th century processes for the deacidification of paper were successfully developed (see PAPER, §VI).

Much can be done to slow down the speed of deterioration of bindings. It is important that the books are stored on uncrowded shelves to permit a free circulation of air and to enable a book to be removed without damage. They should be kept in a constant temperature away from sources of heat such as radiators and fires. Bindings that are liable to damage by handling, especially those in paper wrappers, should be stored in a protective container made from acid-free board.

BIBLIOGRAPHY

B. C. Middleton: *A History of English Craft Bookbinding Technique* (London, 1963, rev. 1978)
——: *The Restoration of Leather Bindings* (Chicago, 1972, rev. 1984)
A. D. Baynes-Cope: *Caring for Books and Documents* (London, 1981, rev. 1989)
J. Greenfield: *Care of Fine Books* (New York, 1988)
A. W. Johnson: *A Practical Guide to Book Repair and Conservation* (London, 1988)

ROBERT C. AKERS

Book cover. *See* BOOKBINDING.

Book illustration. The relationship between an illustration and its text is varied. In the block-book the image dominates the text, but in most books the image is dependent on or explanatory of the text. In scientific, travel and other informative books images are didactic, even utilitarian, extending or complementing the verbal message. In fictional works they can act as interpretations or visual equivalents of scenes, or they can be iconic and symbolic, while in religious books they may be used to provoke piety. More generally, images may be present merely to enhance sales. Physically, the illustrations may be close to the corresponding text or might, instead, be employed to indicate textual subdivisions, in the manner of the historiated initial. Though a few incunabula were hand-illustrated, the woodcut (*see* WOODCUT, §II) dominated book illustration before 1600, as this allowed the simultaneous printing of both text and image. In the second half of the 16th century copper-engraving (*see* ENGRAVING, §II) grew in importance, and in the 17th century various other intaglio techniques were employed also. The difficulty of using movable type and intaglio plates on the same page led to the physical separation of text and image, a development compounded by the flourishing market for individual illustrations. In the 18th century ornate Rococo images were used for book illustration, the finest examples appearing in France. Wood-engraving (*see* WOOD-ENGRAVING, §2) also developed at this time through the work of Thomas Bewick. Colour-plate printing and lithography (*see* LITHOGRAPHY, §II) both came into use in the 19th century, and, at the end of the century, William Morris's Kelmscott Press spawned a renewed interest in book illustration in England and elsewhere. In the early years of the 20th century Ambroise Vollard helped to generate a market for luxury, illustrated books, and this led to a proliferation of private presses. Nevertheless, children's books constituted the main field for illustration in the 20th century.

This article is concerned primarily with the history and development of book illustration in the Western tradition. For information on other traditions *see* BURMA, §V, 2(ii); CENTRAL ASIA, §II, 5(ii); CHINA, §XIII, 3; INDIAN SUBCONTINENT, §VIII, 2; ISLAMIC ART, §III, 3 and 4; JAPAN, §IX, 2; KOREA, §VIII, 2; MONGOLIA, §IV, 2; and TIBET, §V, 1.

BIBLIOGRAPHY
H. Pitz: *A Treasury of American Book Illustration* (New York, 1947)
A. Lejard: *Le Livre* (Paris, 1949)
R. W. Ellis: *Book Illustration* (Kingsport, 1952)
D. Bland: *A History of Book Illustration* (London, 1958, 2/1969)
J. Carter and P. H. Muir, eds: *Printing and the Mind of Man* (London, 1967)
T. M. MacRobert: *Fine Illustrations in Western Printed Books* (London, 1969)
J. Lewis: *Anatomy of Printing* (London and New York, 1970)
J. Blumenthal: *The Printed Book in America* (Boston and London, 1977)
V. J. Brenni: *Book Illustration and Decoration: A Guide to Research* (Westport, 1980)
J. Harthan: *The History of the Illustrated Book* (London, 1981)
D. Roylance: *European Graphic Arts: The Art of the Book from Gutenberg to Picasso* (Princeton, 1986)
E. Hodnett: *Five Centuries of English Book Illustration* (Aldershot, 1988)

I. Before the 17th century. II. 17th century. III. 18th century. IV. 19th century. V. 20th century.

I. Before the 17th century.

1. BEFORE THE 1490s. Though the single woodcut print dates from the first quarter of the 15th century, in the years immediately following the invention of movable type (*c.* 1450) books did not include printed images. Nevertheless printed decorations of unsurpassed quality appeared in the two-colour wood- and metalcut initials of the Psalter printed in Mainz in 1457 by Johann Fust (*c.* 1400–1466) and Peter Schöffer (*c.* 1425–1502). Possibly printers recognized their inability to meet the standards set by illuminators (*see* MANUSCRIPT, §III), and, indeed, hand illustration, by illumination or pen and wash drawings, can be found in some incunabula. Assuming that the BLOCK-BOOK is contemporary with incunabula, the earliest printed book illustrated with woodcuts is probably Ulrich Boner's book of fables (*see* FABLES, §2), *Der Edelstein* (see fig. 1), which was printed by Albrecht Pfister in Bamberg in 1461. The text and image were not printed simultaneously in this work, though this process came very soon afterwards and constituted the most powerful reason for the woodcut's longevity in book illustration. In 1491 the *Meshal ha-Kuadmoni*—the first Hebrew illustrated book with illustrations printed in the text—was produced by Daniel Bomberg at Brescia (*see* JEWISH ART, §IV, 1(ii)). By contrast, intaglio techniques require lengthy inking processes and a press capable of much greater pressure. Nevertheless in 1476 the Bruges printer Colard Mansion

1. Book illustration, woodcuts hand-coloured in wash, from Ulrich Boner's *Der Edelstein* (Bamberg, 1461)

did use copper-engravings for his French edition of Boccaccio's *De casibus virorum illustrium*.

The hand illumination of incunabula (*see also* VENICE, §III, 1) was not the only way in which manuscript traditions were prolonged. Manuscript book artists may also have designed some woodcuts and devised other decorative methods to meet mass production needs, while scribes often designed typefaces and/or became printers and rubricators. Illumination was reserved for luxury, or special, copies, frequently printed on parchment and often presented to patrons (*see* MANUSCRIPT, §§II and III). Colour, which, with a few notable exceptions, was lacking from the printed woodcut, was often added after printing by methods ranging from rapid wash infill, in which the cut was treated as a crude outline, to careful overpainting using the cut as an underdrawing. It was probably intended that the earliest cuts, of simple black lines, should be hand-coloured, but modelling using parallel lines and cross-hatching soon developed. Albrecht Dürer (*see* DÜRER, (1)), often considered the greatest woodcut designer because of the wealth of detail and realism in his prints, was at work by the 1490s. The cuts for his famous *Apocalipsis cum figuris* (*see* DÜRER, (1), fig. 4 and APOCALYPSE, fig. 3) were issued separately, before their publication as a book with text in 1498. Even these may have been intended to be hand-coloured if, as Finlay suggests, the Harvard copy was coloured to Dürer's order. In common with other artists, Dürer designed, but probably did not execute, the woodcuts himself.

Illustration occurred in many types of Renaissance books but not the majority. Estimates of the proportion vary from a quarter to a third (see Sansy), but either figure depends on including the many editions with just one woodcut, on the title-page. Illustrations are often found in vernacular texts or translations, though these constitute only a quarter of incunabula and were still in the minority before 1600. Works of popular devotion and piety, medieval romances, some chronicles, some liturgical works and some science and travel books were illustrated. The first illustrated herbal (see HERBAL, §2) was the pseudo-Apuleius' *Herbarium*, printed in Rome (*c.* 1481–3) by Joannes Philippus de Lignamine (*fl* 1470–84). The *Herbarius zu teutsch* (*Gart der Gesundheit*; Mainz, 1485), another herbal, was printed by Schöffer and contained the first illustrations made from life, ushering in a new role for the print in scientific endeavour by virtue of its exact repeatability (see Ivins). In 1486 Erhard Reuwich illustrated and printed Bernhard von Breydenbach's *Peregrinatio in terram sanctam* in Mainz, and this was the first travel book with purpose-made illustrations.

The well-known distaste of the humanists for illustration was not an austere rejection of luxury or decoration, but a preference for words over pictures, a rejection of the role of illustration in instructing the illiterate. It was consequently not until 1493 that a Classical Latin text with woodcut illustrations was produced, when, in collaboration with the Netherlandish humanist Jodocus Badius Ascensius (1462–1535), Johann Trechsel (*fl* 1488–98) of Lyon printed an edition of Terence's *Comedies* (see Goldschmidt). Similarly, many vernacular editions of Boethius's *Consolation of Philosophy* are illustrated but not the Latin editions. Even university medical texts in Latin did without the diagrams often found in vernacular editions. Religious iconoclasm also affected book illustration, though there has been little investigation of this (see Camille, and Watt).

2. FROM THE 1490s TO 1600. From the 1490s to about 1550 the woodcut-illustrated book reached its peak. Dürer was joined by several other masters of the medium, among them Hans Burgkmair I, Hans Baldung, Hans Weiditz (ii), Lucas Cranach the elder and Hans Holbein the younger. Venice, the pre-eminent printing city (*see* VENICE, §III, 1), began to produce illustrated books, and in France many printed Books of Hours appeared. The Venetian book of most importance is the notorious *Hypnerotomachia Polifili*, a semi-erotic work printed in 1499 by Aldo Manuzio, who was not otherwise famous for illustrated books. The work was highly prized by antiquarians, artists and collectors, for a variety of reasons. The many Books of Hours printed by Phillipe Pigouchet (*fl* 1488–1518), Thielman Kerver (*fl* 1497–1524), Antoine Vérard (*fl* 1485–1514) and others represent the highest artistic development of the printed lay prayer book. Medieval in conception, characteristically every page of the Hours had a full border, often made up of many small wood- or metalcuts, the two being difficult to distinguish (see Hind). Some were printed on parchment and carefully illuminated. The movement from the dense, black medieval page to the lighter, grey Renaissance page is usually

seen as represented by Geofroy Tory's *Heures de la Vierge* (Paris, 1525), in which gothic types are replaced by roman and the woodcuts also reflect the new lightness. Tory's treatise on letter design, the famous *Champfleury* (Paris, 1529), further entrenched Italian influence in the golden age of French typography.

Great scientific endeavour was reflected in several illustrated books, notably the woodcuts, some of them thought to be by Jan Steven van Calcar, in Andreas Vesalius's *De humani corporis fabrica* (Basle, 1543; see fig. 2). The first botanical work with closely observed images to appear after the *Herbarius zu teutsch* of 1485 was the *Herbarium vivae eicones* (Strasbourg, 1530–36) by Otto Brunfels (1464–1534), which has woodcuts by Weiditz. This and *De historia stirpium* (Basle, 1542) by Leonhard Fuchs (1501–66) set the model for subsequent botanical illustration.

In the mid-16th century the EMBLEM BOOK emerged, the first being Andrea Alciato's *Emblematum liber* (Augsburg, 1531), which initiated a vogue that lasted throughout the 17th century. Here the relationship between text and image is of central importance, as text, image and motto interact in an elaborate intellectual game. The interest in emblems led to their encroachment on the title-page, which then became the principal, often sole, locus of illustration in the age of copper-engraving. The title-page, rare in manuscripts but relatively common by about 1500,

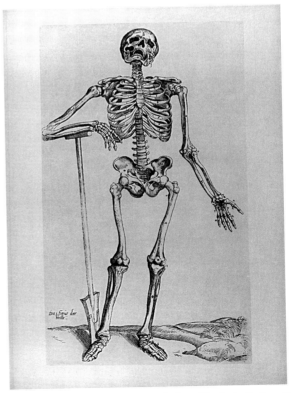

2. Book illustration, woodcut, from Andreas Vesalius's *De humani corporis fabrica* (Basle, 1543)

grew out of the unostentatious label-title into an advertisement for text, author and printer–publisher, attracting the decoration and images that had previously adorned the first page of text. Most common of all was the border composed of architectural and pseudo-architectural elements, reflecting a growing interest in architecture itself.

From about 1550 the woodcut, along with the printing industry in general, declined, and copper-engraving grew in importance. The woodcut had become a victim of its own increasing refinement, reaching a point where it could no longer be printed easily, thereby diminishing the relative difficulties of using engravings in books. The copper-engraving's superiority in achieving tonal effects and details led to its increasing use. This left the chief role of the woodcut in the late 16th century to popular literature, where woodcuts frequently appeared in books to which they had little textual relevance.

BIBLIOGRAPHY

R. Muther: *Die deutsche Buchillustration der Gothik und Frührenaissance, 1460–1530*, 2 vols (Munich, 1883–4; Eng. trans. by R. R. Shaw, Metuchen, 1972)

A. W. Pollard: *Early Illustrated Books: A History of the Decoration and Illustration of Books in the 15th and 16th Centuries* (London, 1893, 2/1917)

A. Schramm: *Der Bilderschmuck der Frühdrucke*, 23 vols (Leipzig, 1920–43)

A. M. Hind: *An Introduction to the History of Woodcut*, 2 vols (London, 1935/R 1963)

E. P. Goldschmidt: *The Printed Book of the Renaissance: Three Lectures on Type, Illustration, Ornament* (Cambridge, MA, 1950, rev. 1966)

W. Ivins: *Prints and Visual Communication* (London, 1953)

D. F. Bland: *A History of Book Illustration: The Illuminated Manuscript and the Printed Book* (London, 1958, 2/1969)

R. Mortimer: *Harvard College Library Department of Printing and Graphic Arts: Catalogue of Books and Manuscripts: Part I: French 16th-century Books*, 2 vols (Cambridge, MA, 1964)

R. Brun: *Le Livre français illustré de la Renaissance: Etude suivie du catalogue des principaux livres à figures du XVIe siècle* (Paris, 1969)

R. Mortimer: *Harvard College Library Department of Printing and Graphic Arts: Catalogue of Books and Manuscripts: Part II: Italian 16th-century Books*, 2 vols (Cambridge, MA, 1974)

H. Kunze: *Geschichte der Buchillustration in Deutschland: Das 16. Jahrhundert*, 2 vols (Leipzig, 1975)

S. Hindman, ed.: *The Early Illustrated Book: Essays in Honor of Lessing J. Rosenwald* (Washington, DC, 1982)

S. Hindman: 'The Illustrated Book: An Addendum to the State of Research in Northern European Art', *A. Bull.*, lxviii (1986), pp. 536–42

N. Finlay: *A Catalogue of an Exhibition of the Philip Hofer Bequest* (Cambridge, MA, 1988)

M. Camille: *The Gothic Idol: Ideology and Image-making in Medieval Art* (Cambridge, 1989)

D. Sansy: 'L'Illustration des incunables français: Enquête sur les bois gravées', *Gaz. Livre Méd.*, xiv (1989), pp. 8–11

T. Watt: *Cheap Print and Popular Piety, 1550–1640* (Cambridge, 1991)

II. 17th century.

Intaglio techniques of illustration had 15th-century roots and were increasingly used from the mid-16th century, but they dominated the 17th, when woodcuts mostly illustrated only cheaply produced works of popular literature issued as broadsides and chapbooks. Copper-engraving became the most common technique, but etching was favoured by the important English illustrators Francis Barlow and the Bohemian-born Wenceslaus Hollar. Some artists, for example Jacques Callot and Rembrandt, used both techniques, frequently in combination, and in 1642 the mezzotint was first used. Although engraving was late in becoming the principal illustration technique for books, it had already been thoroughly developed by the print trade, where its function was largely to reproduce, and thereby to help to market, the work of major artists in other media, especially that of painters and sculptors. This reproductive role affected book illustration, as the distinction between painting and illustration diminished. The engraved illustration had a potential market apart from its book, and this may have decreased the interest in tailoring image to text. In addition to this conceptual separation of text and image, a physical separation was forced by the very use of intaglio processes: as engraving and movable type required different printing presses, they appeared on the same page relatively rarely. Many 'illustrated' books of the period contained images only on the separately printed title-page, where the engraver assumed responsibility both for the text of the title and for the image.

Some scholars see the 17th century as the nadir of illustration, but its rehabilitation was begun in 1951 by the scholar–collector Philip Hofer, who focused on de luxe folios and quartos, especially those produced in France, Italy and the Netherlands. Under aristocratic and royal patronage, these books formed part of courtly collecting interests in architecture, horticulture, travel, military science, theatre and the arts. They had large plates, sometimes of exceptional quality, of battle scenes, city views and maps (e.g. *Topographia*, 29 vols, Frankfurt am Main, 1642–72) as well as elaborate ornamental designs (for lacemakers, goldsmiths, locksmiths, calligraphers etc) and views of theatrical, operatic and ceremonial occasions. Those portraying ceremonial occasions were sometimes infused with political meaning (e.g. *Eloges et discours sur la triomphante réception du Roy en sa ville après la réduction de La Rochelle*, Paris, 1629; see Jouhaud). Engraved portraiture reached its peak under such artists as Robert Nanteuil.

The pre-eminent artist of the engraved title-page was Rubens, who designed nearly 50 title-pages (see fig. 3) between *c.* 1612 and 1640 for Balthasar Moretus, grandson of and successor to the great 16th-century Antwerp printer Christoph Plantin. From 1640 Poussin designed titles for the Imprimerie Royale. An architectural framework continued to be the most common device around which to build a title-page, with the title itself worked into the image in ingenious ways: on a graven plaque or stone cartouche, on a hanging cloth attached to the arch by nails, or supported by cherubs. In the 16th century a woodcut of an architectural frame would surround a letterpress-printed title, the frame itself being re-usable and frequently re-used. In the 17th century, however, the engraved title was prepared for a specific edition and was not commonly re-used. It also became, in A. F. Johnson's words, 'a thing of emblems and allegories', tied symbolically to the meaning of its text (see Corbett and Lightbown). The vogue for emblem books continued, with nearly 350 17th-century editions appearing in the Low Countries alone. The supreme example of English emblem books is Francis Quarles's *Emblemes* (London, 1635).

Notable for their relative absence are illustrated editions of contemporary literature, the most important exception among English books being the engravings designed by John Medina for the 1688 edition of John Milton's *Paradise Lost* (London). The etcher Francis Barlow, father of the

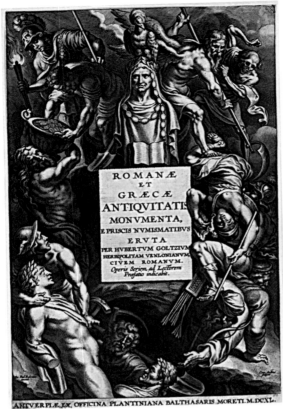

3. Book illustration by Peter Paul Rubens, engraved title-page for Hubertus Goltzius's *Romanae et graecae antiquitatis monumenta* (Antwerp, 1640)

British sporting print, was the first native-born English illustrator of note, justly famous for the illustrations for his polyglot *Aesop's Fables* (London, 1666) and for Edward Benlowes's *Theophilia: Or Love's Sacrifice, a Divine Poem* (London, 1652), on which Hollar and other artists also worked.

Illustrations figured in a number of major works that contributed to intellectual history: the first large sea atlas to contain maps and charts drawn on Gerardus Mercator's projections was Sir Robert Dudley's *Dell'arcano del mare* (Florence, 1646–7); Robert Hooke's *Micrographia* (London, 1665) was illustrated, with many of the plates designed by Hooke himself; Nicolaus Steno's *De solido* (Florence, 1669) contained the first attempt to represent geological sections in a diagram showing six successive types of stratification; and Sir Isaac Newton's *Philosophiae naturalis principia mathematica* (London, 1687) is replete with mathematical diagrams.

In the 17th century the first illustrated books specifically for children were produced, as educational reformers became interested in the didactic value of images. In 1659 Charles Hoole's translation of the Moravian-born educationalist Jan Amos Comenius's *Orbis pictus* appeared in London, with copper-engravings replacing the 150 woodcuts found in the 1658 Nuremberg edition. Numerous 17th-century editions followed in England and on the Continent. Imaginative illustrated literature for children was a later development, although moralizing literature did appear, for instance John Bunyan's *A Book for Boys and Girls* (London, 1686), which, however, was not illustrated until its third edition in London in 1707. Illustrated fairy tales were first produced on the Continent, beginning with *Histoires ou contes du temps passé, avec des moralitez* (Paris, 1697), a work attributed to Charles Perrault although issued in the name of his son Perrault d'Armancourt.

BIBLIOGRAPHY

J. Duportal: *Etude sur les livres à figures édités en France de 1601 à 1660* (Paris, 1914)
A. F. Johnson: *A Catalogue of Engraved and Etched English Title-pages down to the Death of William Faithorne, 1691* (Oxford, 1934)
P. Hofer: *Baroque Book Illustration: A Short Survey from the Collection of the Department of Graphic Arts of Harvard College Library* (Cambridge, MA, 1951)
D. Canivet: *L'Illustration de la poésie et du roman français au XVIIe siècle* (Paris, 1957)
Livres à figures du XVIIe siècle français, Bibliothèque de la ville de Lyon (Lyon, 1964)
E. Hodnett: *Francis Barlow, First Master of English Book Illustration* (London, 1978)
J. R. Judson and C. Van de Velde: *Corpus Rubenianum, Part xxi: Book Illustration and Title-pages*, 2 vols (London, 1978)
M. Corbett and R. W. Lightbown: *The Comely Frontispiece: The Emblematic Title-page in England, 1550–1660* (London, 1979)
C. Jouhaud: 'Printing the Event: From La Rochelle to Paris', *The Culture of Print: Power and the Uses of Print in Early Modern Europe*, ed. R. Chartier (Cambridge, 1989)
T. Watt: *Cheap Print and Popular Piety, 1550–1640* (Cambridge, 1991)

MARGARET M. SMITH

III. 18th century.

In the 18th century the grandeur of the Baroque was succeeded by the frivolities of the Rococo, which were soon reflected in the illustrated book. The charm of the illustrations was matched by the typography, which, later in the 18th century, included decorated typefaces and arabesques and other ornaments from the typefoundry of Pierre-Simon Fournier. Fashionable in France, illustrated books became the playthings of the court. In 1718 Philippe II, Duc d'Orléans, made the designs for a set of engraved illustrations for Longus' *Les Amours pastorales de Daphnis et Chloé* (Paris). In the following year Claude Gillot etched a number of vignettes for Antoine Houdard de la Motte's *Fables nouvelles*. François Boucher, well served by his engravers, illustrated a number of books, sometimes with other artists. These included *Les Métamorphoses d'Ovide* (Amsterdam, 1732; see fig. 4) and the *Oeuvres de Molière* (Paris, 1734). He also illustrated an edition of Corneille's work, which the Marquise de Pompadour engraved at her press in the north wing of Versailles. The popular book of the Rococo period was small in format. The first important one of this type was an octavo edition of Boccaccio's *Decameron*, issued in several volumes in London between 1757 and 1761, with illustrations by Boucher, Gravelot and others. In 1766 Denis-Pierre-Jean Papillon de la Ferté's *Traité historique et pratique de la gravure en bois* was published in Paris, an entrancing example of Rococo book work.

Published between 1781 and 1786, the Abbé de Saint-Non's *Voyage pittoresque ou description des royaumes de*

4. Book illustration after François Boucher, engraving from *Les Métamorphoses d'Ovide*, Amsterdam, 1732 (London, Victoria and Albert Museum)

Naples et de Sicile (Paris) set a new standard for topographical books with its illustrations by Jean-Honoré Fragonard and others. With the French Revolution in 1789 Rococo went out of fashion to be succeeded by the austerities of Neo-classicism. The printers Giambattista Bodoni in Italy and Pierre Didot in France were the first great exponents of this movement. Didot's *Quintus Horatius Flaccus* (Paris, 1799), with classical engravings after designs by Charles Percier, was a somewhat severe conclusion to the 18th century in France.

Apart from their title-pages, illustrated books in England in the first quarter of the 18th century showed little of the Baroque or the Rococo influences, although these were apparent in the engraved tradecards by Hogarth and other artists. Hogarth's first essay into book illustration was for an edition of Samuel Butler's *Hudibras* (London, 1726). Hogarth was a superb illustrator as his series of engravings *A Harlot's Progress* (1732), *A Rake's Progress* (1735) and *Marriage à la Mode* (1745) show, though these are not book illustrations. The Rococo was introduced into English book illustration by GRAVELOT, who came to London from Paris in 1732 or 1733. His illustrations usually have elaborate Rococo frames and are full of Gallic charm. In 1738 Gravelot illustrated John Gay's *Fables* (London) and in 1742 Samuel Richardson's *Pamela* (London). Various artists engraved these illustrations, including Charles Grignion (1717–1810), who had been trained by

Gravelot. In 1753 Thomas Gray's *Elegy Written in a Country Churchyard* (London) was published with engravings by Grignion after Gothick-Rococo designs by Richard Bentley (*d* 1782), a protégé of Horace Walpole. These illustrations (see fig. 5) are framed in crumbling Gothic arches decorated with Arcadian figures and romanticized garden implements.

The illustrations for technical treatises seemed to have a stronger Rococo element than those for fiction. In 1750 Robert Sayer's *The Ladies' Amusement or the Whole Art of Japanning Made Easy* was published in London, with chinoiserie decorations by Jean Pillement. This was followed a few years later by the *Gentleman and Cabinet-maker's Director* (London, 1754) by Thomas Chippendale (i), with engravings by Matthias Darly. In a different vein, in 1766 George Stubbs illustrated his *Anatomy of the Horse* (London) with a set of superbly engraved plates. The great change in the production of illustrated books was made by the Northumbrian engraver THOMAS BEWICK. He transferred the technique of intaglio metal-engraving on to the end grain of boxwood, thus producing illustrations that had much of the delicacy of copper- or steel-engravings yet which could be printed in a single operation with the type. Bewick's first important books were *Tommy Trip's History of Beasts and Birds* (Newcastle upon Tyne, 1779), *General History of Quadrupeds* (Newcastle upon Tyne, 1790; for illustration *see* BEWICK, THOMAS) and

5. Book illustration by Charles Grignion, engraving after a design by Richard Bentley, from *Elegy Written in a Country Churchyard* by Thomas Gray, London, 1753 (London, British Museum)

History of British Birds (2 vols, Newcastle upon Tyne, 1797–1804). The best printed of all his works were *Poems by Goldsmith and Parnell* (London, 1795) and William Somerville's *The Chase* (London, 1796), on both of which he collaborated with his brother John Bewick (1760–95) and others. These two books were printed by his fellow Northumbrian William Bulmer (1757–1830), who at the same time was engaged on John Boydell's grandiose edition of Shakespeare's plays (London, 1802), which had a superbly printed text but indifferent engravings after largely negligible paintings.

The finest 18th-century book illustration came from France, followed at some distance by England, with the rest of Europe lagging far behind, apart from some fine books on architecture from Germany. Notable among these was Paul Decker I's *Fürstlicher Baumeister* (3 vols, Augsburg, 1711–16) and *Entwurff einer historischen Architectur* (Vienna, 1721) by the Austrian architect Johann Bernhard Fischer von Erlach. Venice had been the home of fine printing since the 15th century, and some handsome books appeared there in the 18th century, including Torquato Tasso's *La Gerusalemme liberata* (1745) with elaborately bordered full plates and vignettes after Piazzetta. Pietro Antonio Novelli (1729–1804) illustrated an edition of Carlo Goldoni's *Comedies* in 1761 and Ariosto's *Orlando furioso* in 1772. By the 18th century the Netherlands was no longer a leader in European printing, although a few elegant books illustrated by French artists were published there, among them Boucher's *Les Métamorphoses d'Ovide* (Amsterdam, 1732; see above). In Spain

the one printer of great repute was Joachin Ibarra (1725–85), whose Spanish and Latin edition (Madrid, 1772) of Sallust is a masterly piece of work. The best known of his books was his *El ingenioso hidalgo Don Quixote de la Mancha* (Madrid, 1780, 1782), with illustrations by José del Castillo, Antonio Carnicero and others. The work of William Blake bestrides the late 18th century and early 19th. Although it lay outside the mainstream of European illustration, his relief-etched and hand-coloured illustrations to such books as his *Songs of Innocence* (London, 1789) have the mark of genius.

BIBLIOGRAPHY
R. Portalis: *Les Dessinateurs d'illustrations au 18e siècle* (Paris, 1877)
H. W. Singer: *Französische Buchillustration des achtzehnten Jahrhunderts* (Munich, 1923)
A. Ruemann: *Das deutsche illustrierte Buch des XVIII Jahrhunderts* (Strasbourg, 1931)
A. M. I. Lanckorońska and R. Oehler: *Die Buchillustration des XVIII Jahrhunderts in Deutschland, Österreich und der Schweiz*, 3 vols (Leipzig, 1932–4)
P. Hofer: *Eighteenth Century Book Illustrations* (Los Angeles, 1956)

IV. 19th century.

1. Great Britain. 2. France, the USA and elsewhere.

1. GREAT BRITAIN. The early and middle years of the 19th century were the heyday of the colour-plate book. With the exception of William Blake's relief-etched illustrations, early examples were usually aquatinted and were produced by such publishers as Rudolph Ackermann. Richard Ayton's *A Voyage Round Great Britain* (London, 1814–25) had hand-coloured aquatints by William Daniell and was considered the finest of all the topographical books. Thomas Rowlandson's series of *Tours of Dr Syntax* (London, 1812–22) also had coloured aquatints, with the plates etched by the artist. These amusing illustrations satirized William Gilpin's rather ponderous guidebooks. Colour-plate books covered both botany and ornithology. The *Temple of Flora* was published in London between 1797 and 1807 by Robert Thornton (c. 1768–1837); its plates were part aquatint, part mezzotint and richly hand-coloured. Edward Lear's *Illustrations of the Family of Psittacidae or Parrots* (London, 1830–32; see fig. 6) and John Gould's *Birds of Great Britain* (1862–73) were the most important of their genre and had lithographed and hand-coloured plates.

Though invented at the beginning of the 19th century, lithography was not immediately used in book work. In 1842 Thomas Shotter Boys lithographed *Original Views of London as It Is* (London), which was printed in colour by Charles Joseph Hullmandel. Chromolithography was most often seen in such imported German children's books as *Struwwelpeter* (Leipzig, 1848), written by Heinrich Hoffmann. The illustrations for most of these cheap little books had an unattractive oily quality; a better use of the medium was in Owen Jones's mammoth *Grammar of Ornament* (London, 1856). Etching was the process used for the illustration of most popular fiction. In his long career George Cruikshank etched the illustrations for many books, including *Sketches by Boz* (London, 1836) and *Oliver Twist* (London, 1837), both by Charles Dickens. Hablot Knight Browne (Phiz) illustrated most of Dickens's novels. An important factor in the popularity of *Mr*

Macmillan with illustrations by Linley Sambourne (1845–1910), another cartoonist for *Punch*.

Colour wood-engraving was a more attractive process than the reproductive black-and-white method. The two great printers of this medium were Benjamin Fawcett (1803–93) and Edmund Evans. Fawcett produced several natural history books and between 1860 and 1880 he printed *A Series of Picturesque Views of Seats of Noblemen and Gentlemen of Great Britain* (Driffield). Evans will always be associated with the children's books of Kate Greenaway, Randolph Caldecott and Walter Crane. The precision of the register and the softness of the colours in his printing were in happy contrast to contemporary chromolithography and greatly added to the charm of these books. The first Kate Greenaway book that Evans printed was *Under the Window* (London, 1878). The drawings were actually photographed on to the wood, an indication of the direction in which illustration reproduction was moving. Evans's skill is evident in his editions of Myles Birket Foster's work, in particular the delicate reproduction and printing of *Sabbath Bells Chimed by the Poets* (London, 1856). Hugh Thomson (1860–1920) was one of the first pen draughtsmen in England to benefit from process reproduction. Macmillan published his illustrations for such books as Oliver Goldsmith's *The Vicar of Wakefield* (London, 1891) and Mrs Gaskell's *Cranford* (London, 1892). Aubrey Beardsley was the first artist to see the possibilities of the process-line block with his use

6. Book illustration by Edward Lear: *Macrocercus Aracanga [Red and Yellow Maccaw]*, hand-coloured lithograph, from his *Illustrations of the Family of Psittacidae or Parrots* (London, 1830–32), pl. 7 (London, Victoria and Albert Museum)

Sponge's Sporting Tour (London, 1853) and *Handley Cross* (London, 1854), both by Robert Smith Surtees, was John Leech's hand-coloured etchings.

Reproductive wood-engraving dominated the market in the 1860s, not always with happy results. The family firm established by the Dalziel brothers was the most influential in this field. Between 1864 and 1865 they published an edition of *The Arabian Nights* (London) in parts, with illustrations by Arthur Boyd Houghton, G. J. Pinwell, John Tenniel and John Everett Millais. Millais illustrated a number of books including *Orley Farm* (London, 1862) and other novels by Anthony Trollope. He was one of the illustrators of Alfred Tennyson's *Poems* (London, 1857), published by Edward Moxon, and alone illustrated *The Parables of Our Lord and Saviour Jesus Christ* (London, 1864). John Tenniel, although a somewhat pedestrian cartoonist for the journal *Punch*, achieved immortality through his illustrations for *Alice in Wonderland* (London, 1865) and *Through the Looking-glass* (London, 1872), which, despite disagreements early in their collaboration, owed much to Lewis Carroll's guidance. In 1866 Charles Keene, generally acknowledged as the greatest of artists for *Punch*, illustrated Douglas Jerrold's *Mrs Caudle's Curtain Lectures* (London). *The Water Babies* (London, 1885) by Charles Kingsley was published by

7. Book illustration by Aubrey Beardsley, pen and ink, from *The Rape of the Lock* by Alexander Pope (London and New York, 1896)

of single, fine lines, white space and solid blacks, as in his drawings for Oscar Wilde's *Salomé* (London, 1894). For Alexander Pope's *The Rape of the Lock* (London and New York, 1896; see fig. 7) Beardsley also made use of textured patterns and stippled effects.

Despite its medievalism, William Morris's Kelmscott Press, which published books only from 1890 until 1898, had a profound effect on standards of printing in England, Germany and the USA. Yet the only notable piece of illustration from Kelmscott was the large folio *The Kelmscott Chaucer* (London, 1896), with illustrations by Burne-Jones and decorative borders by Morris. Archaic in a different way were the chapbooks published by Field and Tuer with lively woodcuts by Joseph Crawhall. These were later published in large volumes under such titles as *Olde ffrends wyth newe faces* (London and New York, 1883). William Nicholson worked in a comparable manner in his books *London Types* (London, 1898) by William Ernest Henley and *The Almanac of Twelve Sports* (London, 1898) by Rudyard Kipling, producing boldly cut illustrations on linoleum that were then coloured by hand.

2. FRANCE, THE USA AND ELSEWHERE. Book illustration in France in the 19th century began with such books as Jacques-Henri Bernardin de Saint-Pierre's *Paul et Virginie* (1806), with etchings after Isabey. Under the patronage of the Empress Josephine, between 1817 and 1824 *Les Roses* (Paris) was published in three volumes of coloured stipple engravings after paintings by Pierre-Joseph Redouté. In 1824 an edition of Goethe's *Faust* was illustrated with lithographs by Delacroix (*see* DELACROIX, EUGENE, fig. 2), so establishing this form of printing in France. No new advances were made in French book illustration until 1839 when La Fontaine's *Fables* was published with illustrations by J. J. Grandville. Grandville was an idiosyncratic but brilliant illustrator, and in 1842 his famous *Scènes de la vie privée et publique des animaux* appeared in Paris. In 1838 another immensely popular edition of *Paul et Virginie* (Paris) was issued by Léon Curmer, with illustrations by Ernest Meissonier, Isabey, Horace Vernet and Tony Johannot. Meissonier did over 100 drawings for this book and has been described as the inventor of modern illustration in France.

Paul Gavarni, a successful cartoonist, illustrated a number of books, such as *Gavarni in London* (1849), which was actually printed in England. In 1858 his version of *La Dame aux camélias* by Alexandre Dumas *fils* was illustrated with full-page, wood-engraved character studies. Gustave Doré was almost as famous in England as he was in France. In 1863 his edition of Cervantes's *Don Quixote* (Paris) appeared, followed by *The Holy Bible* (Tours, 1866). A few years later he visited England and produced two books, Alfred Tennyson's *Idylls of the King* (London, 1867) and *London: A Pilgrimage* (London, 1872), the latter being an interesting portrayal of squalor; there was, however, a certain mediocrity about Doré's work in London. Daniel Urrabieta y Vierge (1851–1904), one of the greatest of pen draughtsmen, was a Spaniard who worked in France. In 1882 his *Pablo de Segovia* (Paris) was published; it was a landmark in pen-drawn book illustration, filled with vivid Impressionist drawings of sun-baked scenes.

Towards the end of the 19th century there was a return to lithographic book illustration in France. Toulouse-Lautrec lithographed the illustrations for *Café-concert* (Paris) in 1893, followed in 1898 by his illustrations for *Au pied du Sinaï* (Paris), a book of satirical tales by Georges Clemenceau. In the same year he produced superb illustrations of animals for Jules Renard's *Histoire naturelle* (Paris). In 1893 Maurice Denis lithographed the illustrations for *Le Voyage d'Urien* (Paris) by André Gide, creating a masterpiece of Art Nouveau in which he took as much care with the book's design as he did with its illustrations. In 1896 Maurice Boutet de Monvel broke new ground in the children's book market with his delicately coloured lithographs for his book *Jeanne d'Arc* (Paris), skilfully printed by Draeger Frères.

No significant illustrated books had been printed in the USA in the 18th century. The first important illustrated book to appear there was John James Audubon's *The Birds of America* (4 vols, London, 1827–38), for which Audubon had the plates aquatinted and hand-coloured by Robert Havell jr in London. A powerful force in American publishing was the firm of Harper Brothers of New York with its magazine and book interests. The *Harper's Illuminated Bible*, fully illustrated with wood-engravings after designs by John Gadsby Chapman, was published in New York in 1846. In 1850 Washington Irving's *Knickerbocker's History of New York* (New York) was published with illustrations by Felix Octavius Carr Darley, who also illustrated Irving's *The Legend of the Sleepy Hollow* in 1875. Howard Pyle (1853–1911) was one of the most talented American illustrators, and he worked for many years for Harper Brothers. His early work, such as *The Merry Adventures of Robin Hood* (New York, 1883), was reproduced by wood-engraving. Working in many styles, he had a lasting influence on American illustrators. Edwin Austin Abbey, a contemporary of Pyle's, was also on the staff of Harper Brothers. His first important book was *Selections from the Poetry of Robert Herrick* (New York, 1882), which had a handsome Art Nouveau cover. Abbey was a fine pen draughtsman, whose pen work was possibly too fine for the process block.

In 1888 Frederic Remington's illustrations for Theodore Roosevelt's *Ranch Life and the Hunting Trail* (New York) were printed using both line and half-tone (see fig. 8). In 1885 Edward Windsor Kemble (1861–1933) did the drawings for Mark Twain's *Huckleberry Finn* (New York), and in 1892 Arthur Burdett Frost illustrated *Uncle Remus: His Songs and his Sayings* (London, 1895) by Joel Chandler Harris. All three artists were essentially American, their work evoking a feeling of the open air. While Remington concentrated on the last days of the cowboys of the Far West, Frost's backgrounds are of the mid-Western States and Kemble's are of the Mississippi and the Deep South. At the end of the 19th century this emphasis on outdoor life affected the illustrations for children's books through the work of Ernest Thompson Seton (1860–1946), who produced lively drawings of animals in such books as *Wild Animals I Have Known* (London, 1898) and *The Trail of the Sandhill Stag* (London, 1899). The animals jump and run down the wide margins of his books, the novel design and layout of which were conceived by his wife Grace Seton.

8. Book illustration by Frederic Remington, pen and ink, from *Ranch Life and the Hunting Trail* by Theodore Roosevelt (New York, 1888)

Joseph Pennell was an American artist and critic whose career was equally divided between England and the USA. While in England (1884–1917) he illustrated some of the volumes in the *Highways and Byways* series for Macmillan. In 1896 he illustrated Irving's *The Alhambra* (London) with lithographs. Pennell's great contribution to the art of book illustration was his huge *Pen Drawing and Pen Draughtsmen* (New York and London, 1889), which went through numerous editions. Charles Dana Gibson (1867–1944) was an extremely fluent pen draughtsman, whose intricate pen lines and cross-hatching could not have been reproduced without the process camera. Most of his work appeared in magazines, and in the 1890s he became a cult figure with his invention of the Gibson Girl character. Apart from some rather stilted drawings for *Rupert of Henzau* by Anthony Hope, he did little book illustration as such, but lavish landscape folios of his work, such as *Pictures of People* (New York), were published in the 1890s and well into the 20th century.

Although France, England and the USA seem to have dominated book illustration in the 19th century, some noteworthy books did appear elsewhere in Europe. The most important German illustrator was probably Adolph von Menzel, whose drawings for *Die Armee Friedrichs des Grossen in ihrer Uniformierung* (Berlin, 1851–7) were reproduced by lithography and coloured by hand. A superb edition of Cervantes's *Don Quixote* was published in Spain in 1853 with lithographs by J. J. Martinez, after drawings by the French artist Célestin François Nanteuil (1813–73). The Swiss artist Théophile-Alexandre Steinlen produced a set of beautiful drawings for Charles Nodier's *Histoire du chien de Brisquet*, which was published by Edouard Pelletan in Paris in 1900.

BIBLIOGRAPHY

J. Pennell: *Pen Drawing and Pen Draughtsmen* (New York and London, 1889)
G. White: *English Illustrators: 'The Sixties'* (London, 1897/*R* Bath, 1970)
A. Ruemann: *Die illustrierten deutschen Bücher des 19. Jahrhunderts* (Stuttgart, 1926)
J. Thorpe: *English Illustration: The Nineties* (London, 1935)
R. McLean: *Victorian Book Illustration* (London, 1963)
P. Muir: *Victorian Illustrated Books* (London, 1971)
R. V. Tooley: *English Books with Coloured Plates, 1790–1860* (1973)
G. Wakeman and G. D. R. Bridson: *A Guide to Nineteenth Century Colour Printers* (Loughborough, 1975)
G. Wakeman: *The Production of Nineteenth Century Colour Illustration* (Loughborough, 1976)
S. Houfe: *The Dictionary of British Book Illustrators and Caricaturists, 1800–1914* (Woodbridge, 1978)
G. Wakeman: *Victorian Colour Printing* (Loughborough, 1981)
Victorian Illustrated Books, 1850–1870: The Heyday of Wood-engraving (exh. cat., London, BM, 1994)

V. 20th century.

1. 'Editions de luxe' and private presses. 2. Commercial and children's books.

1. 'EDITIONS DE LUXE' AND PRIVATE PRESSES. In 1900 AMBROISE VOLLARD, a Parisian art dealer, published

Parallèlement (Paris) by Paul Verlaine (1844–96), illustrated by Pierre Bonnard with over a hundred lithographs printed in rose sanguine and nine wood-engravings printed in black. This exquisite book set a standard of book illustration rarely to be matched in France or anywhere else (*see also* LIVRE D'ARTISTE). Vollard was the most important figure in the *éditions de luxe* field at least until World War II and he financed these expensive productions by his art dealing. In 1903 he issued Longus's *Les Amours pastorales de Daphnis et Chloé* (Paris), again with lithographs by Bonnard, and over the following years Vollard published books illustrated by most of the significant painters of the Ecole de Paris, including Dufy, Chagall, Dunoyer de Segonzac, Rouault and Picasso. It is invidious to single out individual artists or titles but Rouault's *Cirque de l'étoile filante* (Paris, 1938), illustrated with both etchings and wood-engravings, is one of the most magnificent. Other publishers followed in Vollard's footsteps. Albert Skira in Lausanne produced a number of fine books, including Ovid's *Métamorphoses* (1931), illustrated by Picasso, and Matisse's first important essay in illustration, Stéphane Mallarmé's *Poésies* (1932). Matisse's *Jazz*, with collages and cut-outs, was published by Tériade in Paris in 1947. Among Picasso's most exciting illustrations were his sugar aquatints for Georges-Louis Leclerc, Comte de Buffon's *Histoire naturelle*, published in Paris by Martin Fabiani in 1942. The English publishers' nearest equivalent to the *éditions de luxe* were the Cresset Press limited edition of Jonathan Swift's *Gulliver's Travels* (London, 1930), with hand-coloured pen drawings by Rex Whistler, and Thomas Browne's *Urne Burial and the Garden of Cyrus*, published in London by Cassell and Co. in 1932 with stencil-coloured illustrations by Paul Nash. The private presses in England produced books on a more modest scale than their French counterparts. The Eragny Press was founded in 1894 by Lucien Pissarro and his English wife Esther Bensusan (1870–1951) and had its own printing press in Chiswick, London, from 1902. Together the couple produced a series of charming little books, many illustrated with coloured woodcuts executed by themselves. A typical example is *Riquet à la houppe* by Charles Perrault, which was published in 1907. The most commonly used method of illustration in the English private press books was wood-engraving, printed in a solemn black, a style established by William Morris at the Kelmscott Press and Charles Ricketts at the Vale Press.

The English illustrated private press book really came into its own in the 1920s. The Golden Cockerel Press was started in 1920 at Waltham St Lawrence, near Twyford, but it was not until 1925, when the Press was taken over by Robert Gibbings (1889–1958), that it made its reputation with a succession of handsome books with wood-engraved illustrations by, among others, Eric Gill, David Jones, Eric Ravilious and Gibbings. The magnum opus of the Press was an edition of the *Four Gospels* (1931) with decorations by Gill. Other books included *The Chester Play of the Deluge* (1927), with a set of powerful wood-engravings by Jones. The finest (literally) wood-engravings of that time were by Blair Hughes-Stanton (1902–81), who worked for some years at the Gregynog Press near Newtown, Powys, where he illustrated six books with wood-engravings composed of the finest of lines in a manner that was new to the craft. The handling of the drapery in John Milton's *Four Poems* (1933) is breathtaking in its precision and delicacy.

Such presses as the Golden Cockerel and Gregynog did their own printing. Other limited editions were produced by such publishers as the Nonesuch Press, which made use of commercial printers. In 1938 Eric Ravilious engraved a fine set of illustrations for the Nonesuch Press edition of *The Writings of Gilbert White of Selborne* (London). In the same year Ravilious illustrated *High Street* by J. M. Richards with a set of truly delightful lithographs, mainly of shop-fronts. In 1927 John Nash, the younger brother of Paul Nash and, like him, primarily a painter, engraved a memorable set of blocks for *Poisonous Plants* (London), which was printed by the Curwen Press and published by Etchells and Macdonald. Three years earlier he had done an amusing set of cuts for the Golden Cockerel's *Directions to Servants* (Waltham St Lawrence) by Jonathan Swift.

The Limited Editions Club of New York did more in furthering the art of the illustrated book than any other organization. The Club was founded by George Macy in 1929, with parallel commercial editions published by the Heritage Club. By the time Macy died in 1956 he had published 250 titles. He used many illustrators, including the English artist Barnett Freedman, who provided lithographs for a number of books. Among these was an edition of Leo Tolstoy's *War and Peace* (1938), of which Macy was justly proud. Macy employed many of the most important American illustrators of the period, including such designers as Bruce Rogers and artists who ranged from Boardman Robinson (1876–1952) to Edward Arthur Wilson (1886–1970). The English equivalent to the Limited Editions Club, on a rather less ambitious scale, was the Folio Society, which for many years run by Charles Ede. Among the illustrators used by the Society were Edward Bawden, John Buckland Wright (1897–1954), Joan Hassall (1906–88), Nigel Lambourne (*b* 1919), Mark Severin (1906–87) and Marcel Vertès (1895–1961).

In Germany and Austria at the beginning of the 20th century the major influence on book illustration was that of the Secessionist painters, in particular Max Slevogt and Lovis Corinth. In 1903 Bruno Cassirer published *Ali Baba und die vierzig Räuber* (Berlin), which had a mixture of Slevogt's lithographs and line drawings. Five years later Slevogt illustrated *Sinbad der Seefahrer* (Berlin) for the same publisher. Cassirer was among the first German publishers to use painter–illustrators. Among other distinguished 20th-century German illustrators were the Expressionist painters Oskar Kokoschka and Ernst Ludwig Kirchner, Max Ernst, a master of Surrealist collage, and George Grosz, who, in addition to the many portfolios of his cartoons, illustrated Alphonse Daudet's *Die Abenteuer des Herrn Tartarin aus Tarascon* (Berlin, 1921). In Weimar in 1913 Harry Graf Kessler (1868–1937) founded the Cranach Presse, which produced beautiful hand-printed books. The most distinguished of these was his edition of *Die tragische Geschichte von Hamlet* (1928), with woodcuts by Edward Gordon Craig. The Belgian artist Frans Masereel devoted much of his time to book illustration and produced a number of volumes consisting solely of woodcuts (e.g. *Le Soleil*, Geneva, 1919).

2. COMMERCIAL AND CHILDREN'S BOOKS. The *éditions de luxe* and the productions of private presses were very different from the commercial illustrated book. In the same year that *Parallèlement* was published in Paris, George Bell in London issued Thomas Carlyle's *Sartor Resartus*, with drawings by Edmund Joseph Sullivan (1869–1933). Sullivan was a very skilled pen draughtsman who taught at Goldsmiths' College School of Art in London and had as many followers in England as Howard Pyle (1853–1911) had in the USA. 'Gift books' formed an important part of commercial book illustration in England and involved such artists as Arthur Rackham, Edmund Dulac (1882–1953) and William Heath Robinson (1872–1944). Rackham was the most successful illustrator in this field. His grotesque drawings were combined with delicate watercolour tints, one of his most attractive books being Washington Irving's *Rip van Winkle* (London, 1905). Dulac's work has a fairy-tale charm, as shown in *Stories from the Arabian Nights* (London, 1911), which went through many editions. Heath Robinson, famous for his drawings of incredibly involved mechanical contrivances that were designed to solve the simplest problems, was a most prolific illustrator in his early years. One of the finest of his books was Shakespeare's *A Midsummer Night's Dream* (London, 1914), while his edition of Charles Kingsley's *The Water Babies* (London, 1915) was still being reprinted in the 1980s.

In the 1930s commercial publishers in England began to respond to the wood-engraving revival. In 1932 Constable published George Bernard Shaw's *The Adventure of the Black Girl in her Search for God* (London), with wood-engravings by John Farleigh (1900–65), whose skill as an engraver (see fig. 9) was enhanced by Shaw's art direction. Other prominent wood-engravers were Douglas Percy Bliss (1900–84), Agnes Miller-Parker (1895–1980), Clare Leighton (1898–1989), Eric Fitch Daglish (1894–1966) and, much later, Joan Hassall (1906–88), Reynolds Stone (1909–79), John O'Connor (*b* 1913) and David Gentleman (*b* 1930). After World War II the most prolific illustrator in England for the adult book market was Edward Ardizzone. The two works by Anthony Trollope that he illustrated for the Oxford University Press, *The Warden* (London, 1952) and *Barchester Towers* (London, 1953), were among his most successful, though he tackled some more ambitious projects for the Limited Editions Club, including stencil-coloured drawings for William Makepeace Thackeray's *The Newcomes* (New York, 1954). In 1950 Heinemann published a new edition of John Galsworthy's *The Forsyte Saga* (London) with most attractive line and colour illustrations by Anthony Gross. The Forsyte coloured illustrations introduced a new technique in which the colour separations were drawn by the artist on grained plastic sheets that were then printed down on to the lithographic plate. This process was known as plastocowell.

Before World War I the most successful illustrators in the USA were working for magazines and newspapers. When such artists as Maxfield Parrish and Edward Penfield (1866–1925), who both worked for magazines and advertising, turned to the colour-plate books as the natural outlet for their talents, they brought their journalistic mannerisms with them. Among the numerous other

9. Book illustration by John Farleigh, wood engraving, from George Bernard Shaw: *The Adventure of the Black Girl in her Search for God*, published by Constable (London, 1932)

talented American illustrators of the 20th century was James Daugherty (1889–1974), whose books include *Abe Lincoln Grows Up*, *Early Moon* and *The Knickerbocker History of New York*, all published in New York. Norman Rockwell, well-known for his *Saturday Evening Post* covers, did some highly realistic illustrations for Mark Twain's *Huckleberry Finn* (New York) for Heritage, and Donald Mackay drew an attractive set of two-colour drawings for Twain's *Tom Sawyer* (New York, 1930) for Random House. Warren Chappell was a typographer as well as an illustrator of such books as *Don Quixote* (New York, 1939) and *A Connecticut Yankee in King Arthur's Court* (New York, 1942). The outstanding American illustrator, however, is Rockwell Kent, who is particularly well known for his books about the sea, some of which—*Wilderness* (1919), *Voyaging* (1924) and *North by East* (1930; all pubd in New York)—he wrote himself. His greatest achievement was his edition of Herman Melville's *Moby Dick* for the Lakeside Press in Chicago and the smaller format volume that Random House published in New York in 1930. Not only were the illustrations vividly evocative, but the book itself was superbly designed by the artist himself.

10. Book illustration by Maurice Sendak, watercolour, from *Where the Wild Things Are* (New York, 1963)

By far the largest field for illustration in the 20th century was the children's book market, beginning with Beatrix Potter's *The Tale of Peter Rabbit* (London, 1902) in England, Maurice Boutet de Monvel in France with his illustrations to Anatole France's *Filles et garçons* (Paris, 1904) and—23 years after his first illustrations for children in *La France en zig-zags*—Florence K. Upton (1873–1922) and her Golliwog books in the USA. In 1919 Edouard Léon Louis Edy-Legrand (1892–1970) broke new ground in France with his *Macao et Cosmage* (Paris), a vividly hand-coloured large square book. In 1929 he illustrated two stencil-coloured landscape shaped books—*Bolivar* and *La Fayette*—for Tolmer in Paris. In the 1930s Feodor Rojankovsky, a Russian working in Paris, lithographed in a similar format some colour books of animal stories for Flammarion. These were the forerunners of the English Puffin Picture Books, which appeared during World War II. Another French artist, Jean de Brunhoff (1899–1937), enjoyed great success on both sides of the Atlantic with his books about Babar the elephant. In England Edward Ardizzone was one of the most successful writer–illustrators of children's books in the 20th century. The first of his books in this genre was *Little Tim and the Brave Sea Captain* (London) published by the Oxford University Press in 1936.

In the second half of the 20th century children's books were the area of book illustration that expanded most. It was led by such artists as the American Edward Gorey (*b* 1925) with his weird and doom-laden fantasies, for example *The Fatal Lozenge* (New York, 1960), the Brooklyn-born Maurice Sendak (*b* 1928), who first became famous with *Where the Wild Things Are* (New York, 1963; see fig. 10), and the English cartoonist Ralph Steadman (*b* 1936), who in 1967 illustrated the first notable edition of *Alice in Wonderland* (London) since that of John Tenniel. The horrors of *Cherrywood Cannon* (New York and London, 1978) by Steadman or *The Tin-pot General and the Old Iron Woman* (London, 1984) by Raymond Briggs (*b* 1934) are more than balanced by the calm of

such works as *The Tyger Voyage* (London, 1976) by Nicola Bayley (*b* 1949) or the *Brambly Hedge* stories (London, 1980) by Jill Barklem (*b* 1951).

In this short article it is impossible to list all the illustrators who have contributed to the modern children's book. Among the English artists who are also worth mentioning are Quentin Blake (*b* 1932), whose deceptively free style conceals a very real talent. His joyful collaboration with the author Roald Dahl (1916–90) can be seen in such books as *Roald Dahl's Revolting Rhymes* (London, 1982). John Burningham (*b* 1936) is another most successful illustrator. His *Borka: The Adventures of a Goose with no Feathers* (London, 1963) was the first of a series of children's books by this artist. Other illustrators of this period who are worth mentioning are Shirley Hughes (*b* 1927–9), Errol le Cain (*b* 1941) and Jan Pienkowski (*b* 1936). Notable books illustrated in the USA in the same period include Nancy Ekholm Burkert's *Snow White and the Seven Dwarfs* (New York, 1972), which remarkably owes nothing to Walt Disney, and *The Clown of God* (New York, 1978) by Tomie de Paola (*b* 1930), where the drawings are as good as the story, a good story being the vital element in all children's books.

BIBLIOGRAPHY
F. J. H. Darton: *Modern Book Illustration in Great Britain and America* (London and New York, 1931)
P. Muir: *English Children's Books* (London, 1954)
The Artist and the Book, 1860–1960 (exh. cat. by P. Hofer and E. N. Garvey, Boston, Mus. F.A., 1961)
J. Lewis: *The Twentieth Century Book: Its Illustration and Design* (London, 1967, rev. London and New York, 2/1984)
B. Peppin and L. Micklethwait: *Dictionary of British Book Illustrators: The Twentieth Century* (London, 1983)
C. Hogben and R. Watson, eds: *From Manet to Hockney: Modern Artists' Illustrated Books* (London, 1985)
M. Felmingham: *The Illustrated Gift Book, 1880–1930* (Aldershot, 1988)
JOHN NEWEL LEWIS

Book jacket [book wrapper; dust-cover; dust-jacket]. Loose cover for a book, usually made of paper and often decorated with a printed design, which functions as a protection for the binding and as a means of identifying and selling the book. Its antecedents may be seen in the temporary bindings of stiff paper or paper on board used by publishers in the days when books were usually bound in leather, after being sold, in a style chosen by the purchaser (*see* BOOKBINDING). By the mid-19th century many cloth-bound books, especially 'gift books', were elaborately decorated on the front, back and spine in gold and colours. Such books were wrapped in paper to protect them in transit to the bookseller. The need to identify the book on its paper covering was soon recognized, and the concept of the book jacket was born. Copies of *A History of British Butterflies* (London, 1853) and *A Natural History of British Moths* (London, 1861), both by Francis Orpen Morris and bound by the Yorkshire printer Benjamin Fawcett, have survived still with their blue paper jackets. These were folded round all three sides of the case front and back and printed in black with the same decorative pattern as that blocked in blind on the cloth; the book's title was shown only on the spine. These jackets are now extremely rare, since they would normally have been thrown away when the book was placed on the owner's shelves.

It is unclear when the idea of designing a jacket in a style completely different from the binding was developed. Books had been issued in decorated and colourful paper covers (exactly like later jackets) from the beginning of the 19th century, or even earlier. The 'yellow-back' style (books bound in yellow paper on boards with pictorial designs printed from woodblocks in colours) flourished from the 1850s until the end of the 19th century. They were cheap and popular, the exact counterpart of modern paperbacks. Another art form directly analogous with the book jacket is the poster, and it is therefore not surprising that the first great period of poster design, at the end of the 19th century in Paris, was also the time at which major artists first turned to book jackets and that the first to do so was Toulouse-Lautrec. In Britain Aubrey Beardsley designed magazine and book covers, for example that for the quarterly *Yellow Book* (London, 1894), but not, it seems, loose book jackets. In the 20th century British painters who designed distinguished jackets for books include Edward Bawden, Barnett Freedman, Duncan Grant, Lynton Lamb (1907–77), John Minton, John Piper, Kenneth Rowntree (*b* 1915), Graham Sutherland and Rex Whistler.

Apart from artist-designed jackets, there are those that employ existing artwork, which is adapted, often by selecting a detail. This method was brilliantly used by the designer Germano Facetti for Penguin Books in the 1960s and revived by George Mackie (*b* 1920) for the Edinburgh publisher Canongate's reprints of the Scottish classics in the 1990s. Typography has also played an important role in the design of book jackets. Hans Tisdall (*b* 1910), who had been taught lettering in Germany by Anna Simons (1871–1951), the pupil of Edward Johnston, made lettering the principal feature in a magnificent series of jackets he designed for the London publisher Jonathan Cape from the 1930s. The early use of photomontage in Germany by John Heartfield in the early 20th century resulted in his series of striking and often brutal jackets. This technique has been exploited on jackets by many designers since.

The work of the many brilliant American jacket designers is illustrated regularly in the publications of the American Institute of Graphic Arts (AIGA). Outstanding designers include Paul Rand, Herb Lubalin (1918–81), Milton Glaser and Seymour Chwast. Modern European jacket design may be studied in the numerous graphic design magazines, in particular *Gebrauchsgraphik*, *Graphis* and *Arts et métiers graphiques*.

BIBLIOGRAPHY

H. McAnally: 'Book Wrappers', *Bk Collector's Q.*, vi (1932), pp. 10–17
F. H. Ehmcke: *Broschur und Schutzumschlag am deutschen Buch der neuerer Zeit* (Mainz, 1951)
C. Rosner: *The Growth of the Book Jacket* (London, 1954)
G. K. Schauer: *Kleine Geschichte des deutschen Buchumschlages im 20. Jahrhundert* (Königstein im Taunus, 1962)
Paperbacks USA: An Exhibition of Covers (exh. cat., New York, Amer. Inst. Graph. A., 1962)
E. Berckenhagen: *Buchumschläge aus zwei Jahrhunderten* (Berlin, 1965)
K. Weidemann: *Book Jackets and Record Sleeves* (London, 1969)
G. T. Tanselle: 'Book Jackets, Blurbs and Biographers', *The Library*, 5th ser., xxvi (1971), pp. 91–134
Toulouse-Lautrec: Book Covers and Brochures (exh. cat., Cambridge, MA, Harvard U., Houghton Lib., 1972)
R. McLean: 'Book Jackets', *The Oxford Companion to the Decorative Arts*, ed. H. Osborne (Oxford, 1975, rev. 1985/*R* 1988), pp. 90–92
H. F. Kroehl: *Buch und Umschlag im Test* (Dortmund, 1984)
A. Hiersemann: *Lexikon des gesamten Buchwesens* (Stuttgart, 1987) [bibliog.]

RUARI MCLEAN

Book of Hours. Late medieval prayerbook containing, as its principal text, psalms and devotions (primarily invoking the Virgin Mary) for the eight canonical hours of the day: Matins, Lauds, Prime, Terce, Sext, None, Vespers and Compline. They were intended for private reading and meditation by the laity, forming a shorter version of the cycle of daily prayers and psalms recited from the BREVIARY by members of religious orders. Each office is usually no more than a few pages long, and the books are generally small and portable, often of octavo size. Most surviving Books of Hours were made in the 15th century and early 16th, and they were produced in such numbers that they still form the most common surviving group of European illuminated manuscripts.

1. Evolution and content. 2. Decoration. 3. Production, patronage and use.

1. EVOLUTION AND CONTENT. The offering of psalms eight times a day can be traced back to early monasticism, and parallel forms of worship are found in lay devotions (*see* SERVICE BOOK). By the 12th and 13th centuries Psalters had become common among the secular nobility, usually opening with a calendar of saints' days and often ending with a commemorative Office of the Dead. From *c.* 1200 they sometimes included early versions of the eight daily devotions to the Virgin placed before the Office of the Dead. During the 13th century these devotions, or hours, assumed greater prominence, reflecting the increased popularity of the cult of the Virgin. In the manuscripts they were described as the 'Cursus [or Horae] Beatae Mariae Virginis'. Copies with the psalms in full as well as the Hours of the Virgin are known as Psalter–Hours; many 13th-century examples are from the district of Liège and north-east France. One of the earliest manuscripts to have the Hours of the Virgin as a separate entity, detached from the Psalter, was produced in England

and illuminated by WILLIAM DE BRAILES (*c.* 1240; London, BL, Add. MS. 49999, fol. 47v; *see* GOTHIC, fig. 64). By the second half of the 13th century Psalter–Hours seemed unwieldy, and scribes began to write out the Hours of the Virgin, still sandwiched between the calendar and the Office of the Dead, as separate volumes. Thus by *c.* 1300 the Book of Hours became a devotional entity in its own right.

As Books of Hours were made for private use outside formal religious supervision, their content can vary immensely. The text is generally in Latin (although Netherlandish examples are usually in Dutch), with rubrics and other prayers frequently in the vernacular. In a typical mid-15th-century manuscript, the central text, the Office or Hours of the Virgin, is usually preceded by a calendar (often in French if produced in France), readings from the four Gospels, and a series of prayers to the Virgin, of which the two best-known open with the words 'Obsecro te' (I beseech you) and 'O intemerata' (O chaste one). The Hours of the Virgin might be followed by the seven Penitential Psalms and a litany of the saints, short cycles of eight abbreviated Hours of the Holy Cross and Hours of the Holy Ghost, the Office of the Dead (by the 15th century a much fuller text than in the earlier Psalter–Hours) and short prayers and hymns called Memorials or Suffrages of the Saints. To a great extent, the inclusion or omission of these or others of the many possible texts would have depended on the preferences and wealth of the manuscript's original owner and on local custom.

Even the central text and the Office of the Dead varied slightly according to local practices, and different dioceses, regions and even small towns might have their own 'use' of the Offices. These variations occur in the choice of antiphons and readings and can be of help in assigning provenances, particularly for French examples. Outside France, 'uses' were less prolific, and there was a greater degree of conformity: most Books of Hours for English owners follow the Use of Sarum, while those for use in the north Netherlands and the Rhineland are mainly of the Use of Utrecht, and almost all Italian and south Netherlandish manuscripts follow the Use of Rome.

2. DECORATION. Many Books of Hours are richly illuminated, and it is because of their decoration that they occupy such an important place in the study of medieval books. The extent of their illustration or ornament depended on the intended luxury and cost of the manuscript (records indicate that the provision of miniatures was the principal expense). Some copies were supplied with illuminated borders on every page and with miniatures for each section or even each subdivision within the text; others have only very simple decoration marking the three or four main openings within the volume; a very few have no illumination. Miniatures served both as devotional images in their own right and, because of their standardized subject-matter, as a means of helping readers of limited literacy to find their place within a volume of different Latin texts.

The choice of illustration originates in the 13th century with the earliest Books of Hours. The selection for the Hours of the Virgin was most often drawn from the *Infancy of Christ*. They almost invariably open with a

1. Book of Hours with miniature of *King David Praying*, opening to the Penitential Psalms, Ghent-Bruges school, 98×73 mm, *c.* 1490 (Oxford, Bodleian Library, MS. Douce 12, fol. 96*v*)

miniature of the *Annunciation* to mark Matins. If the Hours are fully illustrated, this is followed by scenes of the *Visitation* (Lauds), the *Nativity* (Prime), the *Annunciation to the Shepherds* (Terce), the *Adoration of the Magi* (Sext; *see* FRANCE, fig. 17), the *Circumcision* or *Presentation in the Temple* (None), frequently, but not always, the *Flight into Egypt* (Vespers) and the *Coronation of the Virgin* (Compline). A series of full-page miniatures showing these scenes is found in, for example, the Hours made for the Maréchal de Boucicaut (after 1401; Paris, Mus. Jacquemart-André, MS. 2) and illuminated by the BOUCICAUT MASTER (*see* MASTERS, ANONYMOUS, AND MONOGRAMMISTS, §I and fig. 1). In the Netherlands either Vespers or Compline is often illustrated by the *Massacre of the Innocents*. In north-west Italy scenes with saints are sometimes substituted. English examples often combined the entire cycle with the Hours of the Cross, and this was generally illustrated with scenes from the *Passion*, which were thought to have taken place at the same time as the devotions themselves were recited. An unusual example of the pairing of *Passion* scenes with the usual *Infancy* scenes is found, for example, in the Hours of Jeanne d'Evreux (1325–8; New York, Cloisters, MS. 54. 1. 2). Here the *Betrayal of Christ* is represented opposite the *Annunciation* accompanying Matins (fols 15*v*–16*r*; *see* PUCELLE, JEAN, fig. 2).

Miniatures marking the opening of the Penitential Psalms represent either *Christ in Judgement* (especially in early Books of Hours) or, more commonly, images of the psalmist King David. At first David was shown kneeling in prayer, either in the wilderness or, in later manuscripts, in or before his palace (see fig. 1). His harp usually lies before him, and God appears in the sky to hear his prayer. By the second half of the 15th century, however, miniatures for the Penitential Psalms sometimes depicted *David and Goliath* or, by *c*. 1500, *David Watching Bathsheba Bathing*, *David Sending Uriah into Battle* or multiples of these subjects. This text was recited in penance for sin, and thus the psalmist's own sin and atonement were suitable themes, incidentally giving scope for romantic and even mildly erotic imagery. The Office of the Dead was usually illustrated by a single miniature, the subject-matter of which evolved during the late Middle Ages. In early Books of Hours this shows a funeral taking place in a church with priests and mourners chanting around a bier (see fig. 2). The reader probably interpreted this as anticipating his own obsequies, death being a major theme in the 14th and 15th centuries. From *c*. 1410 the scene illustrated changed to the actual burial service in a churchyard. Sometimes angels and demons are shown fighting over the soul of the deceased. By the later 15th century the subject for the Office of the Dead changed completely to incidents from the *Life of Job*, reflecting the inclusion of readings in the text from the book of Job and his patience in the face of death and tragedy. Alternatively,

images of *Death* as a skeleton stalking his prey or the *Last Judgement* with the dead rising from their graves were used.

The most famous images of medieval secular life, often depicting events in contemporary settings, occur at the beginning of luxury Books of Hours, decorating the CALENDAR. They depict *Signs of the Zodiac* accompanied by activities appropriate to each month (the *Labours of the Months*), showing enchanting images of such events in the aristocratic and farming year as feasting, pruning, hawking, harvesting and feeding the pigs. The full-page calendar scenes in the TRÈS RICHES HEURES of Jean, Duc de Berry (*c*. 1411/13–16; begun before 1416; Chantilly, Mus. Condé, MS. 65), are probably the best-known European manuscript illustrations (for illustration *see* VALOIS, (3)). Most Books of Hours, however, are infinitely more humble, with small calendar scenes (if any) in margins or as half-page vignettes. Other optional texts had standardized illustrations, often reduced to a single image. At the Hours of the Cross, the *Crucifixion* was the most usual, although in the Voustre Demeure Hours (Madrid, Bib. N., MS. Vit. 25–5, fol. 14*r*), with illustrations by the MASTER OF MARY OF BURGUNDY (*see* MASTERS, ANONYMOUS, AND MONOGRAMMISTS, §I and fig. 4), multiple scenes from the *Flagellation* to *Christ Carrying the Cross* are found on a single leaf. The most frequent illustration for the Hours of the Holy Ghost is the *Pentecost* (for illustrations *see* MANUSCRIPT, colour pl. IV; MASTERS,

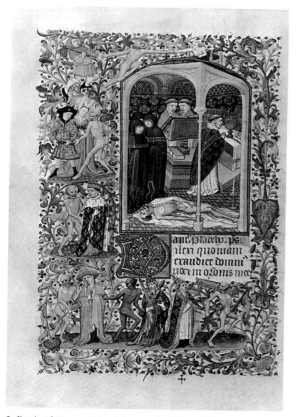

2. Book of Hours with miniature of a *Funeral Mass* and border scenes of *Death Stalking his Prey*, opening to the Office of the Dead, 212×148mm, *c*. 1430–40 (Paris, Bibliothèque Nationale, Rothschild MS. 2535, fols 108*v*–109*r*)

ANONYMOUS, AND MONOGRAMMISTS, §I: MASTER OF THE BRUSSELS INITIAL). Other texts were marked by an endless variety of traditional images of Evangelists and saints.

3. PRODUCTION, PATRONAGE AND USE. Books of Hours were made in most European countries. They were especially popular in France; Netherlandish, and English manuscripts are fairly common; Italian and Spanish books are usually not as richly illustrated; and German examples are extremely rare. Many manuscripts for English use were made in the south Netherlands for export and sale across the Channel, and by the early 16th century the workshops of Ghent and Bruges were making and marketing Books of Hours for customers throughout Europe. Generally, they were made by lay rather than religious craftsmen, although there are examples of north Netherlandish Books of Hours decorated by nuns. The evidence suggests that booksellers in Paris, Rouen, Bruges, London, Florence and other towns had active industries commissioning and selling them. In most cases the planning of the book was the task of the bookseller, perhaps by agreement with the customer who would eventually pay for the work, with the selection of the script and the actual copying itself under the bookseller's supervision. The provision of miniatures was often subcontracted to professional artists. Apparent collaboration by several illuminators in a single Book of Hours may mean no more than that the unbound leaves were distributed among several different artists, none of whom necessarily ever saw the completed book,

as the bookseller collected up the constituent parts and had the manuscript bound. In the south Netherlands, miniatures in Books of Hours were generally on single sheets, blank on the *verso*, and there is evidence that these single-sheet miniatures were traded among Bruges booksellers in the 1420s and could be bought and bound into the books at the appropriate places.

Most of the supremely great and luxurious Books of Hours were made for royal or aristocratic patrons. These books are rich with such emblems of ownership as coats of arms. In the so-called Bedford Hours, for example, John, Duke of Bedford, is pictured before St George, with his armorial bearings incorporated into the border (c. 1423; London, BL, Add. MS. 18850, fol. 256v; see MASTERS, ANONYMOUS, AND MONOGRAMMISTS, §I: BEDFORD MASTER, fig. 1). In the Hours of Margaret, Duchess of Clarence, a representation of the patron at prayer is included in the illustration to the Psalms of Degree, showing the *Presentation of the Virgin* (see fig. 3). The fame of these manuscripts eclipses the tens of thousands of more ordinary Books of Hours, most of which belonged to the only moderately wealthy, whose identification remains largely unknown. These lesser manuscripts resemble each other to an extraordinary degree. Books of Hours were the first books to be made in considerable quantities, and the workshops of Paris and elsewhere approached something like mass-production in supplying the demand, with miniatures reproduced industriously from pattern sheets or from other copies. The Book of Hours reached an audience that had never before owned books, and for many it was the only book they had ever handled. Treasured manuscripts were passed from one generation to another and were used for recording family dates and anniversaries and for teaching children to read. They were not only status symbols and luxury objects but also the focal points of lay piety.

Printed Books of Hours were first published in Paris c. 1488, and some 760 separate editions are known to have been produced by 1530. This attests to the enormous market for them and explains why their illustrations were among the most widely circulated pictorial images of the late Middle Ages.

BIBLIOGRAPHY

F. Madan: 'Hours of the Virgin Mary: Tests for Localization', *Bodleian Q. Rec.*, iii/2 (1920), pp. 40–44
V. Leroquais: *Les Livres d'heures manuscrits de la Bibliothèque nationale* (Paris, 1927)
——: *Supplément aux livres d'heures manuscrits de la Bibliothèque nationale: Acquisitions récentes et donation Smith-Lesouëf* (Macon, 1943)
L. M. J. Delaissé: 'The Importance of Books of Hours for the History of the Medieval Book', *Gatherings in Honor of Dorothy Miner* (Baltimore, 1974), pp. 203–25
J. Harthan: *Books of Hours and their Owners* (London, 1977)
C. de Hamel: *A History of Illuminated Manuscripts* (Oxford, 1986)
R. S. Wieck: *Time Sanctified: The Book of Hours in Medieval Art and Life* (New York, 1988)
C. Donovan: *The De Brailes Hours* (London, 1991)
A. Arnould and J. M. Massing: *Splendours of Flanders* (Cambridge, 1993)

CHRISTOPHER DE HAMEL

3. Book of Hours with miniature of the *Presentation of the Virgin*, including the patron praying below, opening to the Psalms of Degree, from the Hours of Margaret, Duchess of Clarence, 244×170 mm, England, c. 1421–30 (sold London, Sotheby's, 19 June 1989, lot 3018, fol. 65v)

Bookplate [Ex-libris]. Engraved or printed mark of ownership affixed to a book. The earliest, woodcuts from c. 1470, were for Hans Igler, called Knabensberg, with a hedgehog as a pun on his name, and two that recorded gifts to the Carthusian monastery of Buxheim by Wilhelm von Zell and Hildebrand Brandenburg (see fig.). Usage spread quickly in Germany, encouraged by the participation of Albrecht Dürer, Lucas Cranach (i), the Little Masters of copper-engraving and others. Their works inspired some fine bookplates of later centuries; but though many distinguished artists have subsequently lent their talents to bookplate-making, until the latter part of the 19th century most bookplates were the work of trade engravers.

In the 16th century, although western Europe adopted bookplates, significant contemporary styles emerged only as usage developed, from *c.* 1650 in France and *c.* 1700 in Britain and elsewhere in Europe. Earlier, notably in France, gold or blind stamping of bindings was more favoured. Many early British and 17th-century American bookplates were printed labels, often with ornamental borders. Labels have continued as a minority option, and engraved versions, common since the 18th century, have latterly been cut on wood with distinction. An armorial was, however, until recent times the most familiar bookplate form, engraved on copper or often in the 1800s on steel.

Among 17th-century British bookplates the terms Tudoresque and Carolean embrace the stylistic vagaries of some early examples. The few bookplates by William Faithorne are superb, and other armorials of the period echo their robust mantling, except where mantles are of cloth. William Jackson (*fl* 1698–1714), working near the Inns of Court in London, popularized bookplate usage. Concurrently using the Early Armorial and Jacobean styles,

he made bookplates for the nobility and for most English university colleges. Many others worked in these styles before Chippendale or Rococo became the vogue, *c.* 1745–80. Spade shield compositions with wreaths and festoons superseded them, giving way to plain armorials ('die-sinkers') for most of the 19th century. After 1860 an armorial renaissance was effected by Charles William Sherborn (1831–1912) and George W. Eve (1855–1914), and engravers including John Augustus Charles Harrison (1872–1955) and Robert Osmond maintained similar quality and prolific output from *c.* 1900 to *c.* 1950.

Pictorials or pictorial-armorials have, however, as old a history, their stereotyped styles overlapping and longer lived. The stolidly tiered bookpile, devised in 1698 by Samuel Pepys, long remained modestly popular. Allegories (showing gods, goddesses, cherubs and the like) appeared *c.* 1700, continental artists aiding their popularity. Their finest exponent was Francesco Bartolozzi, but many trade engravers used allegory, sometimes combined with 18th-century library interior subjects. Urn pictorials appeared from *c.* 1750, but though isolated landscape bookplates were used decades earlier, it was the wood engravings of Thomas Bewick and his followers that brought that style to its apogee.

After 1860 fresh impetus was afforded bookplate art in Europe and North America by the wide participation of book illustrators, engravers and artists. Diverse reproductive processes were exploited, bookplates were recognized as artistically significant, and the bibliographical and genealogical importance of their usage was recognized. Societies of collectors in many countries assisted their documentation, and bookplate production proliferated among Europe's printmakers and illustrators. Though less used in Britain in the 1990s, memorable wood-engraved bookplates were made by the inheritors of a tradition inspired notably by Eric Gill and Reynolds Stone (1909–79).

BIBLIOGRAPHY

P. E. A. Poulet-Malassis: *Les Ex-libris français* (Paris, 1874, rev. 1875)
J. Leicester Warren (Lord de Tabley): *A Guide to the Study of Bookplates* (London, 1880)
F. Warnecke: *Die deutschen Bücherzeichen* (Berlin, 1890)
E. Castle: *English Book-plates* (London, 1892, rev. and enlarged 1893)
W. Hamilton: *French Book-plates* (London, 1892, rev. 1896)
——: *Dated Book-plates*, 3 vols (London, 1894–5)
H. W. Fincham: *Artists and Engravers of British and American Book-plates* (London, 1897)
K. E. zu Leiningen-Westerburg: *German Book-plates* (London, 1901)
B. N. Lee: *Early Printed Book Labels* (London, 1976)
——: *British Bookplates* (Newton Abbot, 1979)

BRIAN NORTH LEE

Bookplate with donatory inscription for Hildebrand Brandenburg's gift of books to the Carthusian monastery of Buxheim, hand-coloured woodcut, angel h. 67 mm, *c.* 1470

Boom style. Term apparently coined by Robin Boyd in *Australia's Home* (1952) and loosely applied to highly ornate architecture in a classical idiom that was fashionable in the eastern states of Australia between the late 1870s and early 1890s. The style was made possible by, and is to some extent an expression of, the financial boom that followed the discovery of gold in 1851. The climax of the boom was in the 1880s in Victoria, where the richest goldfields were located. The buildings most commonly associated with the Boom style are the richly decorated Italianate villas and speculative terrace houses of Melbourne. The English picturesque Italianate fashion had been introduced to Australia by the early 1840s but only reached its sumptuous apogee in Victoria in the late 1880s. The architecture is characterized by asymmetrical towers, balustraded parapets, polygonal bay windows and round-arched openings and arcades, though the terrace houses often lack the more elaborate features. The buildings were usually stuccoed and enriched with mass-produced Renaissance-style elements in cast cement. They frequently incorporate cast-iron filigree verandahs, prefabricated in sections. A typical stuccoed villa is Wardlow (1888), Carlton, Melbourne, by John Boyes. Other Italianate Boom style work was carried out in rich polychromatic brickwork, which was characteristic of Melbourne. The other fashionable idiom commonly included in the Boom style category is French Second Empire, employed for example at Labassa (1890), a lavish house in Caulfield, Melbourne, by John A. B. Koch, and the town hall (1883–5) at Bendigo by W. C. Vahland. The Boom style rapidly declined during the depression of the 1890s.

BIBLIOGRAPHY
R. Boyd: *Australia's Home* (Melbourne, 1952, rev. Harmondsworth, 2/1978), pp. 52–65
M. Lewis: 'The Victorian House', *The History and Design of the Australian House*, ed. R. Irving (Melbourne, 1985), pp. 65–85

RORY SPENCE

Boon, Abraham. *See* JANSSEN, ABRAHAM.

Boonen, Arnold (*b* Dordrecht, 16 Dec 1669; *d* Amsterdam, 2 Oct 1729). Dutch painter. He began his training at the age of 13 with the painter Arold Verbuys (1673–1717) and in 1683 was apprenticed to the portrait and genre painter Godfried Schalcken (at that time working in Dordrecht), with whom he remained for six years. After working as an independent painter in Dordrecht, he travelled to Germany, where he had considerable success as a portrait painter in Frankfurt-am-Main, Mainz and Darmstadt. He settled in Amsterdam in 1696, shortly after his return to the Netherlands, and worked successfully as a portrait and genre painter.

Boonen was technically a highly accomplished, although somewhat stereotypical artist, who succeeded Nicolaes Maes as the most fashionable portrait painter in Amsterdam. His clientele included not only Amsterdam citizens but also important patrons from other cities and several visiting foreigners, including Tsar Peter the Great of Russia. Besides individual portraits, he produced a series of group portraits of the Amsterdam boards of regents (e.g. *Six Regents of the Oude Zijds Institute*, 1705; Amsterdam, Rijksmus.). In his genre pieces, dating mostly from before 1700 and in the tradition of the Leiden 'Fine' painters, he frequently made use of candlelight effects, in imitation of Schalcken, as in the *Girl with a Lantern* (1695; Dresden, Gemäldegal. Alte Meister). His students included Philip van Dijk, Jan Maurits Quinkhard and Cornelis Troost.

BIBLIOGRAPHY
Thieme–Becker
J. van Gool: *De nieuwe schouburg* (1750–51), i, pp. 294–309

W. Bernt: *The Netherlandish Painters of the Seventeenth Century*, i (London, 1970), pp. 141–2

RUDOLF EKKART

Boorne, W(illiam) Hanson (*b* Bristol, 1859; *d* Newcastle upon Tyne, 1945). English photographer, active in Canada. He emigrated to Canada in 1882, intent on buying a ranch at Bird's Hill, Manitoba, 12 miles north-east of Winnipeg. After two years he decided to move further west to the new and fast-growing town of Calgary, Alberta, a divisional point on the new railway line pushing westward to the Pacific. An amateur photographer, he recognized an opportunity to start a photographic business and returned to England in 1885 to purchase professional equipment and supplies. By spring 1886 he was back in Calgary working as a landscape photographer. In 1887 he and his cousin, Ernest May, became partners, operating as Boorne and May. May worked in the business for only two years and was largely responsible for darkroom work, correspondence and some portraits.

Boorne took many outstanding photographs of ranches and activities accompanying wheat farming and cattle-raising. He made frequent photographic trips to the mountains of Alberta and British Columbia along the Canadian Pacific Railway line. In summer 1888 he travelled from Victoria, British Columbia, to Calgary, photographing a great assortment of views of the burgeoning towns and cities, fish canneries, Native North Americans, ranches, railway construction and mountain scenery. His most widely known series is his documentation of the torture ceremony that took place in 1887 at the annual sun-dance on the Blood Indian Reserve near Fort McLeod, Alberta. The series won a gold medal at the World's Columbian Exposition in Chicago in 1893.

In the same year Boorne's business in Calgary collapsed. After unsuccessful attempts to establish branch studios in other cities, he was bankrupt and even had to forfeit his equipment and collections of glass negatives. He moved to Vancouver in an attempt to revive his business but by 1897 he had given up photography and moved to Toronto. Around 1900 he and his family moved back to England, where he remained for the rest of his life, engaged in mining promotion and invention.

UNPUBLISHED SOURCES
Manuscript by H. A. Dempsey: *W. Hanson Boorne, Photographic Artist*, Calgary, Glenbow–Alta Inst.
WRITINGS
'With Savages in the Far West', *Can. Phot. J.*, ii/11–12 (1893), pp. 372–3
BIBLIOGRAPHY
D. B. MacFarlane: 'Candid Camera of the 19th Century Enriches McGill Museum', *Royal Can. Mounted Police Q.*, vii (1940), pp. 352–6

STANLEY G. TRIGGS

Boos, (Georg Christian) Carl [Karl] (*b* Weilburg, 8 Sept 1806; *d* Wiesbaden, 18 July 1873). German architect. He studied in Karlsruhe from 1825 under Friedrich Weinbrenner, and after the latter's death in 1826 he continued his studies in Freiburg. Boos declined the promise of a chair at Karlsruhe and instead went to Heidelberg, where he sat his civil service examination in 1831. From 1835 he worked under Eberhard Philipp Wolff in Wiesbaden where he spent the rest of his career. His first independent building was an orangery in the Biebricher Schlosspark in

1836, the same year that he visited the Rhineland, Belgium and the Netherlands to study brick construction. In 1834 he had won a competition for a government building in the Luisenstrasse in Wiesbaden (now the Innenministerium). Built in the Romanesque Revival style (1838–42), it was the most important administrative building in the Duchy of Hesse-Nassau. Boos became chief planning officer in 1842, and it was in this capacity that he renovated and enlarged the medieval Schaumburg (1850–56) at Diez an der Lahn in English Gothic Revival style. Whilst working there, he was involved in the publication of a German edition of Augustus Charles Pugin's *Specimens of Gothic Architecture*. The Gothic Revival Marktkirche (1853–62) in Wiesbaden may be regarded as the first brick building in Hesse-Nassau, influenced by the churches of the Berlin school. It has five towers and terracotta ornamentation. The Marktkirche earned him several commissions, including one for a court chapel in Stuttgart (unexecuted). Less widely known is his renovation of the abbey church at Lahnstein (1856–7), and plans for the expansion of the Oldenburg Schloss (1856; built 1860–64 by Johann Heinrich Strack). Boos also worked as a surveyor, and in this capacity he tried to consider the city as an administrative seat, a garrison town and centre of trade, as well as a residence for prosperous burghers. He contributed surprisingly little to the development of the city as a health resort. His only known involvement was an unrealized project for a hydropathic establishment (1843). His general plan for Wiesbaden (1856), and in particular his ideas for the creation of a city district beyond the Rheinstrasse, were only partially realized, and other projects, such as the reorganization of the Schützenhof site, were never started. Although Boos retired in 1867, he continued to make designs, such as the Wilhelmsturm at Dillenburg (1867; unexecuted). He was invited to take part in the second competition (1873) for the Niederwald monument (in Rüdesheim), but he declined because of insufficient funds. Other work included a mausoleum (1856) for the Dowager Duchess Pauline in the Alter Friedhof, Wiesbaden (now parkland), and a monument to Duke William Albert (*reg* 1816–39) on the Geisberg (destr.).

BIBLIOGRAPHY

K. Boos: 'Die evangelische Haupt-Kirche in Wiesbaden', *Allg. Bauztg Abbild.*, xxxxiii (1878), pp. 51–7

W. Lotz: *Die Baudenkmäler im Regierungsbezirk Wiesbaden* (Berlin, 1880), pp. 400–01 and 438

C. Weiler: 'Romantische Baukunst in Nassau', *Nassau. An.*, lxiii (1952), pp. 232–66

G. Kiesow: 'Vom Klassizismus zur Romantik: Die baugeschichtliche Entwicklung in Nassau', *Kat. Herzogtum Nassau, 1806–66: Politik, Wirtschaft, Kultur* (exh. cat., Wiesbaden, Mus. Wiesbaden, 1981), pp. 305–29

W.-H. Struck: *Wiesbaden im Biedermeier* (Wiesbaden, 1981)

MICHAEL BOLLÉ

Boos, Roman Anton (*b* Bischofswang, nr Füssen, 28 Feb 1733; *d* Munich, 19 Dec 1810). German sculptor. He was the son of a farmer. He first trained as a sculptor in the leading workshop of the region, that of Anton Sturm (1690–1757) in Füssen. Boos then travelled as a journeyman to Munich, where he is believed to have worked for nine years with Johann Baptist Straub. By 1763 he had become a student at the Kaiserliche Kunstakademie in Vienna; he also studied at the Städtische Kunstakademie in Augsburg, where he worked at the studio of the brothers Placidus Verhelst and Ignaz Wilhelm Verhelst. In 1765 Boos returned to Munich. His earliest surviving works were executed the following year: over life-size statues at the entrance to the choir of the monastery church at Fürstenfeldbruck (1766), representing the monastery's founders, *Duke Ludwig II* and his son *Ludwig IV*. That same year Boos became one of the founders of a private school of drawing, which in 1770 developed into a modest academy of painting and sculpture. There he taught sculpture (without pay) and, from 1771, was the academy's business manager.

Between 1767 and 1768 Boos produced four stone figures, a large coat of arms and stucco reliefs for the façade of the Theatinerkirche, Munich, designed by François de Cuvilliés I. In this he succeeded Ignaz Günther, to whom the contract had first been awarded. Much the same thing happened in 1770, in connection with the stone statue (destr.) of *St Johann Nepomuk* for a well in front of the Jesuit college, Munich. Boos also carved oak figures (1770–71; untraced) for the palace garden at Schleissheim. Following the Theatinerkirche commission, he had been granted in 1769 the protection of the royal court, that is, a licence to pursue his profession without guild restrictions. In 1773 he travelled on the court's behalf to Mareit in the Tyrol, to obtain 13 marble blocks from a quarry discovered there by Christian Friedrich Wilhelm Beyer; these were to be used for garden statues for the Nymphenburg Palace, Munich. Boos thus became acquainted with Beyer and became involved in carving a series of statues under his direction for the garden of Schönbrunn Palace, Vienna. In 1775 Boos was appointed court sculptor in Munich.

The most important works by Boos include nine statues of ancient gods (1775–98) and 12 vases (1788–98) of Tyrolean marble in the ornamental garden of the Nymphenburg Palace. Of his pulpit (1780) for the Frauenkirche, Munich, there remain some reliefs (Munich, Bayer. Nmus.) and the crowning figure of the *Immaculate Conception* (Munich, Frauenkirche). In 1779–80 he produced for the arcades of the Hofgarten, Munich, seven groups in oak painted to resemble stone, representing the *Deeds of Hercules* (damaged World War II; some stored, Munich, Residenz; four terracotta models, Munich, Bayer. Nmus.; see fig.). For the Benedictine monastery church at Ettal, Boos produced in 1788 ten reliefs in gilded lead of scenes from the *Life of the Virgin* for the high altar and, in 1796, four gilded wood reliefs with scenes from the *Life of Christ* (*Baptism, Transfiguration, Crucifixion* and *Resurrection*). His works include the two funerary monuments of *Freiherr Aloys von Kreitmayr and his Wife* (1794) in the parish church at Offenstetten and wood figures of the *Four Evangelists* (1796) in the Stiftskirche at Altötting.

In the last quarter of the 18th century Boos succeeded Straub and Günther as the leading sculptor in Munich. He had made his mark as a sculptor in stone in the 1760s, outshining competitors who worked almost entirely in wood. His somewhat sober, bourgeois early Neo-classicism represents a distinct decline in quality in comparison with the imaginative Rococo creations of his predecessors. Among the models that he followed in striving for a monumental style were works of the High Baroque and

Roman Anton Boos: *Hercules and Atlas*, terracotta, h. 690 mm, 1779–80 (Munich, Bayerisches Nationalmuseum)

antiquity. Boos worked at a time of general economic depression, in which the number of commissions fell dramatically, compared to 1745–65. His art and character are aptly summed up by his *Self-portrait* from the 1790s, the marble bust from his tomb (Munich, Bayer. Nmus.).

BIBLIOGRAPHY

R. Johnen: 'Roman Anton Boos: Kurfürstlicher Hofbildhauer zu München, 1733–1810', *Münchn. Jb. Bild. Kst*, n. s. 1, xii (1937–8), pp. 281–320 [fundamental]
G. P. Woeckel: 'Drei unbekannte Holzbildwerke von Roman Anton Boos und ein neuentdecktes Bildnis des Künstlers', *Pantheon*, xxiii (1965), pp. 97–110
P. Volk: *Münchner Rokokoplastik*, Bayerisches Nationalmuseum Bildführer, vii (Munich, 1980)
U. Schedler: *Die Statuenzyklen in den Schlossgärten von Schönnbrunn und Nymphenburg* (Hildesheim, Zurich and New York, 1985)
——: *Roman Anton Boos (1733–1810): Bildhauer zwischen Rokoko und Klassizismus* (Munich and Zurich, 1985)
Bayerische Rokokoplastik: Vom Entwurf zur Ausführung (exh. cat., ed. P. Volk; Munich, Bayer. Nmus., 1985), pp. 234–44

PETER VOLK

Booth, Peter (*b* Sheffield, 2 Nov 1940). Australian painter of English birth. He attended drawing classes at the Sheffield College of Art from 1956 to 1957, and in 1958 he emigrated to Australia. There he worked as a labourer until 1962 when he entered the National Gallery School in Melbourne, studying painting until 1965. He then taught painting at the Prahran Technical College in Melbourne from 1965 to 1969. In 1969 he had his first one-man exhibition at Pinacotheca in Melbourne and exhibited in the same year at the Central Street Gallery in Sydney. He then gave up teaching and returned to labouring work. His early paintings were hard-edge abstract works, and slowly, within this style, black came to dominate his paintings. By 1971 they were wholly black, sometimes with coloured edges on three sides, as in *Painting* (1971; Melbourne, N.G. Victoria). He used black to signify social alienation and associated the colour with the industrial landscapes around his native Sheffield; he sought out similar areas in Melbourne.

In the late 1970s Booth's palette brightened and led to such works as *Painting* (1976; see 1976 exh. cat., pl. 14). He achieved a textural effect by the use of heavily impastoed paint and again framed the works by revealing the edges of the pulpboard base. After these transition paintings he turned to figuration in 1977, with alienation again an important theme. These menacing, apocalyptic works, such as *Painting* (1977; Melbourne, N.G. Victoria), are populated with magicians, carnival men and mutants. They are often rendered in black and burning reds and have their source in the paintings of Goya, Blake and Pieter Bruegel I.

BIBLIOGRAPHY

Project 12: Peter Booth (exh. cat. by F. McCarthy, Sydney, A.G. NSW, 1976)
Peter Booth: Recent Paintings (exh. cat. by M. Brenson, New York, CDS Gal., 1987)   □

Bopp, Sebald (*b* Bamberg; *d* Bamberg, 1503). German painter. Though he is first mentioned as a journeyman in Würzburg in 1474, his earliest known work remains in his native Bamberg: the *Sermon of John of Capistrano* (*c.* 1480; Bamberg, Neue Residenz, Staatsgal.), a scene of recent history packed with solid bourgeois figures, in a style modulated from the Netherlandish manner of the Master of the Bamberg Altar. After 1480 Bopp was seemingly in Nuremberg, to judge from the *Crucifixion* memorial plaque for Peter Volckamer and his wife Apollonia (*d* 1483; Bamberg, Neue Residenz, Staatsgal.)—an attribution on stylistic grounds—and from later elements in Bopp's style. A portrait of an *Elderly Man with a Rosary* (1483; Amer. priv. col.) shows the transition of Netherlandish portraiture into an East Franconian idiom.

In 1485 Bopp was made a citizen of Nördlingen, where documents suggest he became a well-respected painter. In 1486 he was commended in a letter by Sophie, Margravine of Brandenburg-Ansbach, wife of Margrave Frederick (*reg* 1486–1536): the work they had commissioned from him probably includes a portrait of a *Lady with the Brandenburg Order of the Swan* (Madrid, Mus. Thyssen-Bornemisza), which shows an originality of style—mannered, ornamented and precious. There is a comparable composition in a portrait of a *Citizen's Wife* (Munich, Bayer. Nmus.), though her apparel and sharp features translate the effect into a bourgeois idiom. From Nördlingen Bopp worked for the Öttingen-Wallerstein family: among them, Abbot Blasius of Hirsau commissioned a panel showing *Graf Adalbert II von Calw Presenting the Restored Monastery of St Aurelius to SS Aurelius and Benedict* (Calw, Mus. Stadt & Hermann Hesse-Gedenkstät.; lower half destr.), which incorporates portraiture in a rigid, antiquated composition, influenced by the Nördlingen painter Friedrich Walther (c. 1440–after 1494). The Counts of Öttingen also commissioned an altarpiece for their castle at Harburg, with wings showing the *Adoration of the Magi* (Nuremberg, Ger. Nmus.) in a packed, ingenious presentation. In Nördlingen itself there remain of Bopp only some undemanding murals (1497) in the vaulting of the Georgkirche; a similar commission is recorded in 1501. Also from 1497 are two altar wings showing *St Michael* and *St Elizabeth* (Füssen, Staatsgal. Hohen Schloss). Bopp brought to Nördlingen a new solidity of figure style and a refined sense of narrative; he was also one of the most original Franconian portraitists of his time.

BIBLIOGRAPHY

A. Stange: *Deutsche Malerei der Gotik*, viii (Munich, 1957), pp. 96–100
A. Stange, ed. N. Lieb: *Die deutschen Tafelbilder vor Dürer. Kritisches Verzeichnis*, ii (Munich, 1970), pp. 231–2, nos 1013–22

HANS GEORG GMELIN

Bor. *See* NOVÝ BOR.

Bor, Paulus (*b* Amersfoort, *c.* 1601; *d* Amersfoort, 10 Aug 1669). Dutch painter. He came from a prominent and wealthy Catholic family. In 1577 his grandfather Bor Jansz. was a member of the Treffelicxte, a group of the most exceptional citizens of Amersfoort. His father, also named Paulus Bor, was a textile merchant. Bor's style of painting shares elements with both the nearby Utrecht Caravaggisti and the so-called Haarlem classicists. The Haarlem architect and painter Jacob van Campen inherited a family estate in Amersfoort and was later in close contact with Bor, and some of his classicist works have been confused with those of Bor.

Bor's absorption of the influences of Caravaggio no doubt dates from when he studied in Italy. In 1623 he was recorded as living in a house in the Roman parish of S Andrea delle Fratte along with three other Netherlandish painters: Jan Hermans (*fl* 1623–59), possibly Willem Thins (Guglielmo Tens) and a certain Stefano Aipxi. In the same year Bor was one of the founder-members of the Schildersbent, the association of Netherlandish artists in Rome, which gave him the Bent-name 'Orlando'. His portrait appears under this name in a well-known drawing *Bacchus with Drinking Members of the Schildersbent* (*c.* 1625; Rotterdam, Boymans–van Beuningen). In Rome, Bor apparently followed the peripatetic life of most young foreign painters. In 1624 he was recorded as living on the Piazza di Spagna in the same house as Michelangelo Cerquozzi, Hermans and Thins. The same group of artists was documented as living in a house in the Strada dell'Olmo in 1625.

About 1626 Bor returned to Amersfoort, where he joined the Brotherhood of St Luke, the city artists' guild, in 1630. His earliest definite work is a group portrait of

the *Van Vanevelt Family Saying Grace* (1628), which was bequeathed by a member of the family to the St Pieter-en-Bloklands Gasthuis, Amersfoort, which still owns it. The next certain dated work is the signed *Vanitas Still-life* (1630; New York, art market, 1988). That Bor also had connections with Utrecht seems confirmed by his gift in 1631 of a bust-length painting of a 'devout woman' (untraced) to the St Jobsgasthuis in that city. The lost work must have resembled his somewhat unusual half-length portraits of women, for example *Female Allegorical Figure* (Rouen, Mus. B.-A.) and *Mary Magdalene* (Liverpool, Walker A.G.), both dated by Jansen (see 1987 exh. cat.) to the early 1630s. In his starkly lit *Christ among the Doctors* (1635–6; Utrecht, Cent. Mus.; see fig.), with its eccentric physiognomies, proportions and scale, Christ appears much too small. This work and paintings from the 1640s, with their dramatic chiaroscuro, suggest some possible contact with Rembrandt and his school in Amsterdam, which apparently tempered aspects of Bor's earlier style, derived from Haarlem and Utrecht sources.

In 1632 Bor married Aleijda van Crachtwijck, who also came from a prominent Amersfoort family. Despite her huge dowry and their combined wealth, Bor continued to work as a painter. In 1638, under the general supervision of van Campen, he painted decorations at Honselaarsdijk (destr.), one of the restored hunting palaces of Prince Frederick Henry of Orange-Nassau, for which a design for a ceiling showing musicians and other figures, attributed to Bor, survives in the Rijksprentenkabinet, Amsterdam. Unlike his collaborators on this project, Gerrit van Honthorst, Caesar van Everdingen and Christiaen van Couwenberg (1604–67), Bor did not contribute to the decoration of another important palace, the Huis ten

Paulus Bor: *Christ among the Doctors*, oil on panel, 1150×973 mm, 1635–6 (Utrecht, Centraal Museum)

Bosch, near The Hague. Nevertheless, he did remain in close contact with van Campen, with whom he apparently collaborated on individual paintings, until the latter's death; six paintings by Bor were listed in the 1657 death inventory of van Campen's estate. In 1656 Bor was elected one of the regents of the Amersfoort religious foundation for the poor, De Armen de Poth, to which he donated a still-life painting *Bread and Butter and other Objects*; it is still owned by the foundation.

BIBLIOGRAPHY

W. Croockewit: 'Paulus Bor', *Verslag van de werkzaamheden der vereeniging 'Flehite'* [Account of the activities of the 'Flehite' association] (1903), pp. 40, 74–7 [first study of Bor, who is neglected in early sources]
E. Plietzsch: 'Paulus Bor', *Jb. Preuss. Kstsamml.*, xxxvii (1916), pp. 105–15
G. J. Hoogewerff: *De Bentvueghels* (The Hague, 1952)
M. R. Waddingham: 'Notes on a Caravaggesque Theme', *A. Ant. & Mod.*, iv (1961), pp. 313–14
S. J. Gudlaugsson: 'Paulus Bor als portrettist', *Miscellanea I.Q. van Regteren Altena* (Amsterdam, 1969), pp. 120–22
D. P. Snoep: 'Honselaarsdijk: Restauraties op papier' [Honselaarsdijk: restorations on paper], *Oud-Holland*, lxxxiv (1969), pp. 270–94
J. W. von Moltke: 'Die Gemälde des Paulus Bor von Amersfoort', *Westfalen: Hft. Gesch., Kst & Vlksknd.*, lv (1977), pp. 147–61
B. Nicolson: *The International Caravaggesque Movement* (Oxford, 1979); review by L. J. Slatkes in *Simiolus*, xii (1981–2), pp. 167–83
Holländische Malerei im neuem Licht: Hendrick ter Brugghen und seine Zeitgenossen (exh. cat., ed. A. Blankert and L. J. Slatkes; Utrecht, Cent. Mus.; Brunswick, Herzog Anton Ulrich-Mus.; 1987), pp. 226–31 [entries on Bor by G. Jansen]

LEONARD J. SLATKES

Borbiró [Bierbauer], **Virgil** (*b* Nagyenyed [now Aiud, Romania], 6 March 1893; *d* Budapest, 25 July 1956). Hungarian architectural historian, architect, theorist and urban planner. He received his diploma in architecture in 1915 from the Technische Hochschule, Munich, where in 1920, as a student of Theodor Fischer, he was awarded a technical doctorate while also studying art history. His survey of the architectural history of Budapest, published the same year and emphasizing the influence of Neo-classicism, marked the beginning of a lifelong interest in the city. As editor (1928–42) of the journal *Tér és Forma*, he provided competent criticism and a forum for the young representatives of avant-garde architecture, in particular the Hungarian section of CIAM. He also argued for innovative methods in building residential blocks and was successful in urging the reform of outdated municipal building regulations. He often travelled abroad and, through his reports of the contemporary achievements of the European architectural avant-garde, including Le Corbusier and the Deutscher Werkbund, he helped to promote Modernism in Hungary.

Borbiró's own designs include the control centre (1930) of the Electricity Works, Budapest-Kelenföld, the façade of which has an unsettling combination of plastered brick surfaces, decorative bonds, square windows, arched entrances and balconies with thin iron railings. The reception building (1937; with László Králik) of Budaörs Airport, near Budapest, attests to his deepening understanding of the Modern Movement. Terraces underline the symmetry of the white plastered, two-storey building, and a glass roof covers the dominating central round hall on the upper level. After World War II, Borbiró proposed a project for the reconstruction of Budapest, and one for the improvement of housing conditions in villages. In 1953 he was among the first to suggest pedestrian zones for the centre of Budapest.

WRITINGS

A régi Pest-Buda építészete [The architecture of old Pest and Buda] (Budapest, 1920)
A magyar építészet jelen állapota, modern irányu fejlödésének szükségessége és akadályai [The present state of Hungarian architecture, the necessity for and the obstacles in the way of its modern development] (Budapest, 1928)
A magyar építészet története [The history of Hungarian architecture] (Budapest, 1937)

BIBLIOGRAPHY

N. Pámer: *Magyar építészet a két világháboru között* [Hungarian architecture between the two world wars] (Budapest, 1987)

ÁKOS MORAVÁNSZKY, KATALIN MORAVÁNSZKY-GYÖNGY

Borbón, Spanish House of. *See* BOURBON, §II.

Borbón y Braganza, Don Infante **Sebastián Gabriel** (*b* Madrid, 4 Nov 1811; *d* Pau, France, 14 Feb 1875). Spanish Infante, painter, collector and patron. He was the son of Pedro de Borbón and the Princessa de Braganza. He practised painting from the age of 12 under Bernardo López and Juan Ribera. In 1827 he was elected Académico de Mérito of the Academia de Bellas Artes de S Fernando, Madrid. He travelled for many years in Italy, copying works of art and painting landscapes. He was married first to Maria Amalia of Naples and then in 1860 to Maria Cristina (1833–1902), the sister-in-law of Isabella II (*see* BOURBON, §II(8)).

The Infante was a patron of contemporary artists; he supported Alejandro Ferrant (*b* 1844) in Italy with a pension and he commissioned paintings from José Ribelles (1778–1835), Rafael Tejeo and Juan Gálvez. The formation of his remarkable collection began with inheritances from his father and was augmented by his two wives and by the purchases he made through his friend, the painter José de Madrazo y Agudo, who acted as intermediary. An inventory made in 1835 reveals that by that early date his collection was almost complete. His preference was for 17th-century Spanish paintings, including such works as the *Annunciation* (1637; Madrid, Prado) and *Descent from the Cross* (Marseille, Mus. B.-A.), both by Antonio de Pereda; the *Miracle of the Porciuncula*, or *Plenary Indulgence* (*c.* 1655–65; Cologne, Wallraf-Richartz-Mus.) by Bartolomé Esteban Murillo; *The Dominican* (*c.* 1650; Munich, Alte Pin.) and *St Bernard and the Virgin* (Madrid, Prado), both by Alonso Cano; the portrait of *Charles II* (1673; Valenciennes, Mus. B.-A.) by Juan Carreño de Miranda; and *Doña Margarita* (*c.* 1655–60; San Diego, CA, Mus. A.) by Diego Velázquez. Only two 16th-century Spanish painters were represented in the Infante's collection: Juan de Juanes and El Greco. His acquisition of the latter's great *Assumption* (Chicago, IL, A. Inst.), purchased from the convent of S Domingo el Antiguo, Toledo, and *St Bernard* (Madrid, Prado) presaged the re-evaluation of this artist that took place in the 19th century. The Infante did not appreciate 18th-century painting, although he possessed several still-lifes by Luís Meléndez, from the royal Spanish collection, and some portraits by Anton Rafael Mengs. However, he did like the painting of Francisco de Goya and owned *Majas on the Balcony* (1808–12; New York, Met.), *The Monk* and *The Nun* (1827; Great Britain, priv. col., see Gudiol I Ricart, nos 763–4) and an important group of engravings including some of the painter's own first states. Netherlandish painting was well represented, including *Adoration of the Shepherds* (*c.* 1480; Berlin, Gemäldegal.) by Hugo van der Goes; *St Luke and the Virgin* (Boston, MA, Mus. F.A.) by Rogier van der Weyden; and *Saviour* (Aachen, Mus. B.-A.) by Quinten Metsys. There is a notable lack of Italian paintings of the 17th and 18th centuries, abundant in other Spanish collections, apart from a fine Mannerist work, the *Dead Christ between Two Angels* (Boston, MA, Mus. F.A.) by Rosso Fiorentino.

In 1837 the Infante's possessions were confiscated for political reasons, his immense library was given to the Biblioteca Nacional in Madrid, and his collection of paintings was exhibited in the Museo de la Trinidad, together with pictures acquired from the suppression of the religious orders. Shortly before his death his property was returned to him. After his death a first sale was held in Pau in 1876 and another in the Hôtel Drouot in Paris in 1890. When his widow died a final sale was held in Madrid in 1902; what was left remained in the possession of their heirs.

WRITINGS

De los aceites y barnices de que se hace uso en la pintura (Madrid, 1860)

UNPUBLISHED SOURCES

Madrid, Pal. Real, Archv, Sección Histórica, caja 123 [*Galería de Pinturas del Serenísimo Señor Ynfante Don Sebastián Gabriel*, 1835]

BIBLIOGRAPHY

J. Gudiol I Ricart: *Goya* (London, 1966)

M. Agueda: 'La colección de pinturas del Infante D. Sebastián Gabriel', *Bol. Mus. Prado*, iii/8 (1982), pp. 102–17

MERCEDES AGUEDA

Borch, ter [Terborch]. Dutch family of painters and draughtsmen. They came from Zwolle, capital of the province of Overijssel. In the 17th century Zwolle enjoyed only modest prosperity, but the ter Borchs, long influential in the professional and administrative life of the city, were comparatively well off. The head of the family, (1) Gerard ter Borch (i), fathered thirteen children by three wives. He gave up his career as an artist to assume the position of Master of Customs and Licences. Throughout his life he actively encouraged the artistic gifts of his children, providing a stimulating home environment and practical instruction for the more talented among them. The eldest and most gifted son, (2) Gerard ter Borch (ii), became one of the foremost Dutch genre and portrait painters. Anna ter Borch (*bapt* 27 Oct 1622; *d* 11/12 Nov 1679), the eldest surviving daughter, became interested in calligraphy as a child. The family preserved one writing book of hers containing quotations from well-known mythological and Christian texts. Another daughter, Gesina ter Borch (*b* 15 Nov 1631; *d* April 1690), though an amateur, actively engaged in calligraphy, drawing and watercolour from the 1640s to the 1670s. She entered many of her watercolours into albums, one of which, an anthology of favourite poems ranging from pastoral to drinking songs, she illustrated in a colourful miniaturist style. Another album became a scrapbook of family art and memorabilia. Gesina assumed the curatorship of the family collection of graphic art—numbering *c.* 700 sheets and 5 albums—which remained intact with descendants of the family until 1887, when it was auctioned and the majority purchased

by the Rijksmuseum, Amsterdam. Residing unmarried in the family home in Zwolle her whole life, she served frequently as Gerard (ii)'s model. Harmen ter Borch (*bapt* 11 Nov 1638; *d* before Oct 1677), though a prolific draughtsman in his youth, enjoyed only modest talent and chose to succeed his father as Licence Master in 1661. Jenneken ter Borch (*bapt* 3 Sept 1640; *d* 13 or 23 Aug 1675) left no artistic works, but her marriage to Amsterdam merchant Sijbrand Schellinger brought the family important contacts in the capital. The last-born, (3) Moses ter Borch, early exhibited a fine artistic sensibility, especially as a portraitist.

BIBLIOGRAPHY

A. Bredius: 'Die Ter Borch Sammlung', *Z. Bild. Kst*, xviii (1883), pp. 370–73 [report of the rediscovery of the ter Borch family estate in Zwolle]

J. J. van Doorninck: 'Het schildersgeslacht ter Borch', *Versl. & Meded. Ver. Beoefening Overijsselsch Regt & Gesch.*, xiii (1883), pp. 1–22

E. W. Moes: 'Gerard ter Borch en zijne familie', *Oud-Holland*, iv (1886), pp. 145–65

E. Michel: *Gérard Terburg et sa famille* (Paris and London, 1887)

A. Rosenberg: *Terborch und Jan Steen* (Bielefeld and Leipzig, 1897)

M. E. Houck: 'Mededelingen betreffende Gerard ter Borch en anderen, benevens aantekeningen omtrent hunne familieleden', *Versl. & Meded. Ver. Beoefening Overijsselsch Regt & Gesch.*, xx (1899), pp. 1–172

J. Verbeek: 'Tekeningen van de familie ter Borch', *Antiek*, i (1966), pp. 34–9

A. McNeil Kettering: *Drawings from the ter Borch Studio Estate in the Rijksmuseum* (The Hague, 1988)

For further bibliography *see* (2) below.

(1) Gerard [Gerhard] **ter Borch (i)** (*b* Zwolle, 1582–3; *d* Zwolle, 20 April 1662). He was trained in Zwolle, perhaps by Arent van Bolten (*fl* Zwolle, *c.* 1580–1600). At the age of 18 he went to southern Europe, staying until *c.* 1612; he spent seven years in Italy, mostly in Rome, but also in Naples. In Rome he lived in the Palazzo Colonna, from the gardens of which he drew the *Temple of the Sun* (1610; Rotterdam, Boymans–van Beuningen), an ancient ruin. Most of his drawings (often dated between 1607 and 1610) were contained in a sketchbook, which he brought back to Zwolle and dismantled (Amsterdam, Rijksmus.). Executed with fine parallel pen hatching with a lively sense of accent and contour, these sheets follow the tradition of 16th-century Roman topographical drawing established by Maarten van Heemskerck, Paul Bril and others. Like his forerunners, Gerard recorded ancient buildings and ruins, sometimes with archaeological exactitude, sometimes with a more picturesque intent (e.g. *View of the Pincio, Rome*, 1609; Amsterdam, Rijksmus.; see fig.). His most innovative drawings in terms of subject-matter depict scenes of everyday life and the landscape of the surrounding Roman Campagna. He also made intimate studies of the grounds of the Villa Madama outside Rome, to which he added watercolour washes for atmospheric effects. All the Roman drawings, even those executed solely in pen and ink, are characterized by subtlety of light and shadow. He also visited Naples, which he recorded in a view dated 1610. He had plans for a trip in 1611 from Naples to Spain in the company of the Spanish Viceroy, but he literally missed his boat (in the process losing a number of paintings on board). Several of his drawings indicate that while travelling en route to and from Italy he stayed in Nîmes and Bordeaux (possibly on his way south) and Venice (probably returning north).

Gerard ter Borch (i): *View of the Pincio, Rome*, pen and brown ink and grey wash, 136×275 mm, 1609 (Amsterdam, Rijksmuseum)

By mid-1612 he was back in Zwolle, where on 28 March 1613 he married Anna Bufkens, who gave birth to (2) Gerard ter Borch (ii) four years later. Dated drawings from this period have survived in some numbers: they represent Old and New Testament subjects, devotional pieces and Ovidian love stories, all subjects associated with Amsterdam and Utrecht history painting (most now in Amsterdam, Rijksmus.). He abandoned the fine draughtsmanship of his Italian work for experimentation in some sheets with a relatively expressive linear vocabulary and in others with a tighter manner characterized by firm contours, emphatic wash modelling and increasing abstraction. By the late 1610s his style began to harden and become mannered. His one painting to survive, *Abraham's Sacrifice of Isaac* (1618; Zwolle, Prov. Overijssels Mus.), shows a connection with Utrecht Mannerism. He may have made other paintings, but Gerard certainly limited his artistic activity after 1621, by which time he had succeeded his father, Harmen, in the position of Licence Master.

Despite his professional responsibilities, Gerard found time in the 1620s for some artistic activity. Most of his creative energy seems to have been devoted to supervising his first-born's efforts at drawing, but he also produced a number of colourful, witty and lively drawings which were entered into a hand-written amatory songbook (now in the Atlas van Stolk, Rotterdam, Hist. Mus.), to which Roeland van Laer (*d* Genoa 1635) and Pieter van Laer later contributed watercolour drawings. Perhaps responding to his own pedagogical theory, he returned to drawing from life in the 1630s in a handful of renderings of children and the local landscape, but generally he seems to have practised his art vicariously through his talented offspring.

BIBLIOGRAPHY

A. Bertolotti: *Artisti belgi ed olandesi a Roma nei secoli XVI e XVII* (Florence, 1880)
H. Egger: *Römische Veduten: Handzeichnungen aus dem XV–XVIII Jahrhundert* (Vienna, 1911)
J. M. Blok: 'Romeinsche teekeningen door G. Terborch, sr. en W. van Nieulandt II in 's Rijksprentenkabinet te Amsterdam', *Meded. Ned. Hist. Inst. Rome*, v (1925), pp. 128–9
J. Q. van Regteren Altena: *Vereeuvigde stad, Rome door Nederlanders getekend* [The eternal city of Rome drawn by Dutchmen] (Wormerveer, 1964)
D. P. Snoep: 'Een 17de eeuws liedboek met tekeningen van Gerard Ter Borch de Oude en Pieter en Roeland van Laer' [A 17th-century songbook with drawings by Gerard ter Borch the elder and Pieter and Roeland van Laer], *Simiolus*, iii (1968/69), pp. 77–134
J. Richard Judson: 'Jacob Isaacz. van Swanenburgh and the Phlegraean Fields', *Essays in Northern European Art Presented to Egbert Haverkamp Begemann* (Doornspijk, 1983), pp. 119–22

For further bibliography *see* (2) below.

(2) Gerard [Gerhard; Geraerdt; Geraert] **ter Borch (ii)** (*b* Zwolle, Dec 1617; *d* Deventer, 8 Dec 1681). Son of (1) Gerard ter Borch (i).

1. Life and work. 2. Critical reception and posthumous reputation.

1. LIFE AND WORK.

(i) Early training, 1625–35. (ii) Travel and residence abroad, 1635–48. (iii) Genre painting, 1648–mid-1660s. (iv) Portraiture, 1660s and 1670s.

(i) Early training, 1625–35. A precocious child, he responded quickly to his father's instruction. The first of his preserved drawings, *A Horseman Seen from Behind* (Amsterdam, Rijksmus., A 782), was executed before his eighth birthday, as his father proudly recorded on the sheet: *Anno 1625. den.25.September. G. T. Borch de Jonge inventur.* The second, a depiction of an officer (Amsterdam, Rijksmus., A 783), bears the inscription *nae[r] het leven* ('after life') and the date 24 April 1626. These two sheets illustrate the father's practice of annotating the youthful drawings of his children and retaining them for the family estate. Only one early history subject by Gerard survives: *Judith and Holofernes* (Amsterdam, Rijksmus., A 796). His father encouraged him to make exacting copies (all Amsterdam, Rijksmus.) of prints by Hendrick Goltzius, Pieter Quast and Jacques Callot, and even of sculpture casts, such as

the Farnese *Hercules*. But most of Gerard (ii)'s drawings depict scenes of everyday life.

In 1632 Gerard went to Amsterdam, presumably for an apprenticeship. He seems to have gone to Haarlem in 1633, then again in 1634 for an extended stay as apprentice to the landscape artist Pieter Molijn. The sketchbook Gerard kept from 1631 to 1634 (Amsterdam, Rijksmus., 1888: A 1797) charts his progress as he loosened the linear vocabulary he had inherited from his father, then added wash and finally abandoned pen altogether for chalk, in order to render the atmospheric effects of the Haarlem landscape. Separate sheets of 1633 and 1634 show Gerard expanding his subject-matter to include scenes of skaters, soldiers and markets, many perhaps made for sale, as few remained in the family estate. The *Market Scene* (Amsterdam, Rijksmus., A 825), for example, is distinguished by the subtle spatial relationships of just a few compact motifs, which, strengthened by accents in ink, stand out against the receding street sketched lightly in chalk. The association with Molijn proved strong, continuing into the 1640s when the two collaborated on a few landscape paintings. The first of Gerard's extant independent paintings, probably dating from *c.* 1634, is *Rear View of a Rider* (V. de Steurs priv. col., see Gudlaugsson, 1959–60, cat. no. 1), in which the figure seen from the back not only recalls his very first drawing but establishes a leitmotif of his painted oeuvre. His earliest dated painting, the *Consultation* (Berlin, Gemäldegal.) of 1635, was probably Gerard's entrance piece for the Haarlem Guild of St Luke which he joined that year.

(ii) Travel and residence abroad, 1635–48. Later in 1635 Gerard began a series of journeys lasting a decade and a half. First he went to London, where by the summer of 1635 he joined the studio of his uncle, the engraver Robert van Voerst (1597–1636), who was closely associated with Anthony van Dyck and presumably acquainted with other Netherlandish portrait painters in England such as Daniel Molyn and Cornelis Jonson van Ceulen I. Gerard's father sent a trunk to him in London full of painting supplies, clothes, a mannequin and a letter urging his son to continue drawing, especially lively figural compositions, and if he painted to produce the 'modern kind of figure group' that he had learnt in Pieter Molijn's studio. All that remains from Gerard's time in England is one drawing, a portrait of *Robert van Voerst* (Amsterdam, Rijksmus.), which was undoubtedly influenced by the linear style of van Dyck, but is miniaturist in its description of features and characterized by warmth and personal involvement with the sitter.

Documentary evidence indicates that Gerard was back home by April 1636 (either before or after his uncle's death that year), but about 1637 he departed for southern Europe, where he stayed until about 1639, travelling to Italy and probably to Spain. At the Spanish court he may have been commissioned to paint a portrait of *Philip IV* (Amsterdam, priv. col., see Gudlaugsson, 1959–60, cat. no. 9; ?copy after lost original). During the early 1640s Gerard resided in Holland, probably in Amsterdam, with visits to Haarlem, interrupted by stays in the southern Netherlands and France. He concentrated on portraits and genre paintings. The portraits were either bust-length

miniatures, such as the portrait of *Jan Six* (Amsterdam, Col. Six), or small full-length portraits of figures set in a barely defined, neutral space, a type he continued for the rest of his career. The genre pieces were guardroom scenes in the manner of the Amsterdam painters Pieter Codde and Willem Duyster, but characterized by a new subtlety of light and naturalism. The most impressive of these is *Soldiers Playing Trictrac* (Bremen, Ksthalle), in which the main figures are viewed from the back and side.

By late 1645 Gerard had moved to Münster to join the entourage of Adriaen Pauw, representative of the States of Holland to the peace negotiations between the Dutch Republic and Spain to end the Eighty Years War. Almost immediately he painted the *Entrance of Adriaen Pauw in Münster* (Münster, Westfäl. Landesmus.). He remained there throughout the signing of the Peace of Münster in May 1648, a ceremony he recorded in a fine, unusually small group portrait of over 70 delegates and their retainers (London, N.G.). By that time Gerard belonged to the household of the Spanish envoy, the Conde de Peñeranda, whose portrait he painted (Rotterdam, Boymans–van Beuningen). Despite Houbraken's assertion that Gerard journeyed to Spain immediately afterwards with Peñeranda, the count did not return to Madrid until 1650 and Gerard's trip probably took place a decade earlier.

(iii) Genre painting, 1648–mid-1660s. In the following years Gerard seems again to have spent some time in the southern Netherlands, but his normal place of residence was probably Amsterdam. Documents place him there in

1. Gerard ter Borch (ii): *Officer Writing a Letter, with a Trumpeter,* oil on canvas, 568×438 mm, 1658–9 (Philadelphia, PA, Museum of Art)

November 1648 but also indicate stays in The Hague (1649), perhaps Kampen (December 1650) and Delft (22 April 1653), where he signed a document with Johannes Vermeer. He must also have visited Zwolle frequently between 1648 and 1654, for he painted a portrait of the schoolmaster *Joost Roldanus* (1648; untraced), and in the same year his stepsister Gesina's art began to show his influence. On 14 February 1654 he married his stepmother's sister, Geertruyt Matthys, and settled permanently in Deventer in the province of Overijssel. A year later he became a citizen of Deventer and in 1666 was appointed common councillor (*gemeensman*), in which capacity he served for life. But he maintained close contact with his native Zwolle. Gesina had started appearing in his paintings *c.* 1648 and in the following years other members of the family served as his models.

With his return to Overijssel, Gerard matured as a genre painter. From the late 1640s he created small upright panels usually featuring several half- or three-quarter figures, selectively lit against dark backgrounds. The figures talk, drink, make music, attend to their ablutions or lose themselves in thought. Among the most successful of these pictures are the close-up depictions of women involved in domestic activities, such as *Woman Spinning* (*c.* 1652–3; priv. col. S. W. van der Vorm, on loan to Rotterdam, Mus. Boymans–van Beuningen) or *Woman Teaching a Child to Read* (*c.* 1653; Paris, Louvre). Gerard's pictures draw their special strength from an intimate knowledge of middle-class virtues, rituals and concerns,

as well as from his response to the expressive ordinariness of his own family's features. He may have used his stepmother as the model for the woman in these paintings and his stepbrother Moses for the child, but his stepsister Gesina was his favourite model. His genuine affection for her is evident in the sketches he made in the late 1640s and early 1650s (Amsterdam, Rijksmus.). In his paintings she usually assumed the guise expected of her class and situation, the most notable exceptions being the *Two Shepherdesses* (*c.* 1652–4; ex-London, Lady Baillie priv. col., see Gudlaugsson, 1959–60, cat. no. 85) and its variant, *A Shepherdess*, in Anholt (Fürst Salm-Salm, Mus. Wasserburg–Anholt). The pastoral subject of these paintings relates to Gesina's own literary and artistic interests.

The most innovative of Gerard's pictures of *c.* 1650 is the *Woman at her Toilet* (New York, Met.), representing the full-length forms of a stylish lady and her maid. The panel is often considered the earliest example of a new type of genre painting that was to become fashionable in the third quarter of the century, the high-life interior. Gerard's development of this type can be seen in his masterpiece of *c.* 1654, the '*Parental Admonition*' (Amsterdam, Rijksmus.; later version in Berlin, Gemäldegal.), with its well-to-do bourgeoisie in costly garments participating in a delicate and pschychologically nuanced exchange. Jean-Georges Wille's 18th-century engraving of the painting is responsible for the title, which was later adopted by, among others, Goethe for an episode in *Wahlverwandtschaften*. Later, in the 20th century, the characters were identified not as a daughter and parents, but as a courtesan, a procuress and a gentleman client enacting the old theme of bought love. Towards the end of the 20th century the work was reinterpreted as a Petrarchan courtship ritual that conveys the prevailing ideals of 17th century middle-class social and sexual behaviour.

Throughout the 1650s and into the early 1660s Gerard developed the high-life interior further, in paintings nearly as problematic to interpret as the '*Parental Admonition*' and no less formally rich and psychologically acute. Increasingly he chose subjects that allowed him to depict quiet figures caught in contemplative states of mind. His often solitary figures of women are shown writing letters (The Hague, Mauritshuis and London, Wallace), sealing envelopes (ex-Scarsdale, D. Bingham priv. col, see Gudlaugsson 1959–60, cat. no. 144), accepting letters delivered by messengers (Munich, Alte Pin. and Lyon, Mus. B.-A.) or contemplating the letter's content (Frankfurt am Main, Städel. Kstinst.). When the letter-writers are men they are always officers, waited on by trumpeters, and some clue is usually provided about the letter's amorous content (London, N.G. and Philadelphia, PA, Mus. A.; see fig. 1). In the latter two paintings, the colourfully dressed trumpeters function as love objects themselves.

The letter-writing theme reached its culmination in two paintings of *c.* 1660. The first, '*Curiosity*' (New York, Met.), depicts a woman craning to read a letter penned by her seated companion. Competing with this anecdotal action is a third figure, clad in a shimmering low-cut satin gown, who stands prominently at the side absorbed in her own thoughts. In the second, even more masterful canvas (London, Buckingham Pal., Royal Col., see fig. 2) a similarly clad woman (modelled by Gesina) commands

2. Gerard ter Borch (ii): '*The Letter*', oil on canvas, 795×680 mm, 1661–2 (London, Buckingham Palace, Royal Collection)

the viewer's attention by holding the letter and reading aloud from it to a woman and a boy. The figures are set in an exquisitely, though sparsely, appointed interior and are illuminated by sparkling light from a hidden source, which focuses on their subtly differentiated responses to the letter. This and other paintings of the early 1660s are distinguished from the works of the previous decade by elegant interiors, splendid fashions and the attractiveness of the figures. The change may indicate an increasingly affluent buying public, yet Gerard consistently maintains an economic formal vocabulary and an unusually delicate sense of narrative action. For example, in the *Interior with Musical Company* (c. 1662; Polesden Lacey, Surrey, NT), in which the relationship between lady and gentleman remains deliberately ambiguous and the action unresolved: the gentleman has been interpreted as the lady's client, her dance partner and as a suitor greeting her with elaborate, ritualized courtesy. While Gerard was producing such pictures, Gesina, the model for this and so many of the other ladies in satin, was collecting and illustrating Petrarchan love poetry. The attitudes and images in the poetry may well have provided the pictures' original frame of reference. At least one extant drawing by Gerard from the Deventer period (Amsterdam, Rijksmus., GJr 86) suggests his thorough familiarity with Petrarchan imagery.

(iv) Portraiture, 1660s and 1670s. Gerard produced relatively few genre paintings after the mid-1660s, concentrating instead on portraiture for the bourgeoisie of the increasingly prosperous eastern provinces. Compared with those by artists from the western province of Holland, Gerard's portraits focused less on his sitters' status and more on their individuality, honesty and sobriety, qualities associated with an older generation of artists and patrons. Nevertheless he sometimes relaxed this austere style to suit sitters with a taste for rich clothing, as in the *Portrait of a Man* (c. 1664; London, N.G.); the sitter, despite his exaggerated fashions, is still portrayed with straightforwardness. Gerard's only group portrait from his later years is the *Magistrates of Deventer* (1667; Deventer, Stadhuis). The artist's own appearance at this time can be seen in his *Self-portrait* (c. 1668; The Hague, Mauritshuis), which expresses a characteristic mixture of worldliness and reserve.

At the end of the 1660s and beginning of the 1670s, after a decade and a half of activity confined primarily to Deventer, Gerard began to spend more time in Amsterdam. This may have resulted from his wife Geertruyt's death (between 1668 and 1672) or from contact with his brother-in-law Sijbrand Schellinger, an Amsterdam merchant who had married his half-sister Jenneken in 1668. Around 1670 Gerard executed five portraits for Schellinger's relatives, the well-to-do Pancras family from Amsterdam's regent class. Perhaps the most influential of Gerard's patrons were members of the wealthy de Graeff family whom he painted in 1673–4. Their support may have been particularly welcome at this time, for Gerard had apparently fled Deventer in late spring 1672 on the eve of the invasion and subsequent two-year occupation by troops of the Archbishop of Cologne and Bishop of Münster, allies of Louis XIV. He left behind a portrait of the Dutch Stadholder Willem III, Prince of Orange Nassau

(later King William III of England), who had visited Deventer in May 1672. Gerard stayed in Amsterdam, returning to Deventer only in the summer of 1674. Two years later Cosimo III de' Medici, Grand Duke of Tuscany, commissioned a self-portrait of ter Borch for his collection of painters' self-portraits (autograph copy of lost original, Berlin, Staatl. Museen N.G.). Until the end of his life Gerard continued to execute portraits, most notably that of *King William III and Mary Stuart* (untraced), which confirm the esteem he enjoyed, despite his continued use of a more reserved portrait style.

2. CRITICAL RECEPTION AND POSTHUMOUS REPUTATION. Gerard's genre paintings, more than his portraits, exercised a considerable influence on such contemporaries as Gabriel Metsu, Pieter de Hooch, Frans van Mieris (i), Eglon van der Neer and even Johannes Vermeer. His works were valued for their technique, striking figural motifs and the elegant lifestyle they idealized. His reputation was furthered by the many copies produced by his pupils, the most distinguished being Caspar Netscher who worked with him in Deventer c. 1654 and 1658–9. But because ter Borch resisted the trend in the later 17th century towards exaggeratedly virtuoso surfaces, crowded, restless compositions and complicated light effects, his influence was limited. Yet few 17th-century Dutch artists focused so compellingly and subtly on their figures as individuals, and fewer still placed them in narratives that so successfully combined the substance of psychological insight with the forms of elegant decorum.

BIBLIOGRAPHY
A. Houbraken: *De groote schouburgh* (1718–21)
J. C. Weyerman: *De levens beschryvingen der Nederlandsche kunstschilders en kunstschilderessen*, ii (The Hague, 1729–69)
J. Smith: *A Catalogue Raisonné of the Works of the Most Eminent Dutch, Flemish and French Painters*, iv (London, 1833)
W. Bode: 'Der künstlerische Entwicklungsgang des Gerard Ter Borch', *Jb. Preuss. Kstsamml.*, ii (1881), pp. 144–5
C. Hofstede de Groot: *Holländischen Maler* (1907–28)
H. Leporini, ed.: *Handzeichnungen grosser Meister: Terborch* (Vienna, 1925)
J. G. van Gelder: 'Hollandsche etsrecepten voor 1645', *Oud-Holland*, lvi (1939), pp. 113–14
F. Hannema: *Gerard Terborch* (Amsterdam, [1943])
E. Plietzsch: *Gerard Ter Borch* (Vienna, 1944)
S. J. Gudlaugsson: 'Adriaen Pauw's intocht te Münster, een gemeenschappelijk werk van Gerard ter Borch en Gerard van der Horst', *Oud-Holland*, lviii (1948), pp. 39–46
——: 'De datering van de schilderijen van Gerard ter Borch', *Ned. Ksthist. Jb.* (1949), pp. 235–6
A. J. Moes-Veth: 'Mozes Ter Borch als sujet van zijn broer Gerard', *Bull. Rijkmus.*, iii (1955), pp. 36–7
——: 'Mozes of Gerard Ter Borch?', *Bull. Rijksmus.*, vi (1958), pp. 17–18
S. J. Gudlaugsson: *Gerard Ter Borch*, 2 vols (The Hague, 1959–60) [the principal monograph]
P. Pieper: 'Gerard Terborch in Münster', *Schöne Münster*, xxvi (1961), pp. 1–32
E. Haverkamp-Begemann, 'Terborch's *Lady at her Toilet*', *ARTnews* (Dec 1965), pp. 38–9
J. Q. van Regteren Altena: 'The Anonymous Spanish Sitters of Gerard Ter Borch', *Master Drgs*, x (1972), pp. 260–62
Gerard Ter Borch (exh. cat., ed. H. R. Hoetink and P. Pieper; Amsterdam, Rijksmus.; Münster, Westfäl. Landesmus.; 1974)
J. M. Montias: 'New Documents on Vermeer and his Family', *Oud-Holland*, xci (1977), pp. 267–87
S. A. C. Dudok van Heel: 'In Presentie van de Heer Gerard ter Borgh', *Essays in Northern European Art Presented to Egbert Haverkamp Begemann* (Doornspijk, 1983), pp. 66–71
A. McNeil Kettering: *The Dutch Arcadia: Pastoral Art and its Audience in the Golden Age* (Montclair, NJ, and Woodbridge, GB, 1983)
——: 'Ter Borch's Studio Estate', *Apollo*, cxvii (June 1983), pp. 443–51
Masters of Seventeenth-century Dutch Genre Painting (exh. cat., ed. P. Sutton; Philadelphia, PA, Mus. A.; Berlin, Gemäldegal.; London, RA; 1984)

A. McNeil Kettering: 'Ter Borch's Ladies in Satin', *A. Hist.*, xvi (1993), pp. 95–124

——: 'Ter Borch's Military Men: Masculinity Transformed', *Dutch Culture: Proceedings of the Symposium Sponsored by the Center for Renaissance and Baroque Studies, University of Maryland: College Park, 1993*

(3) Moses [Mosus; Mozes] **ter Borch** (*bapt* Zwolle, 19 Jun 1645; *d* Harwich, 12 July 1667). Son of (1) Gerard ter Borch (i). He showed a precociousness in art rivalling that of his eldest stepbrother, (2) Gerard (ii). By the age of seven he was drawing scenes from everyday life (e.g. Amsterdam, Rijksmus., A 1111), and he proved more responsive than his brothers to his father's traditional method of training by copying the work of earlier artists. Between 1659 and 1661 he made copies of sculptural casts, of his father's drawings and of prints by such artists as Jan Saenredam, Annibale Carracci, Albrecht Dürer, Adam Elsheimer and Rembrandt. Moses rarely made exact copies of the originals; instead he concentrated on composition and anatomy in his copies of Italian and German prints and on characterization of emotion and chiaroscuro effects in those after Rembrandt's etchings.

Moses's artistry and insight can be seen in his chalk portrait head studies of members of his family, dated 1660–61. He also executed many self-portraits. The quality of one of these (Amsterdam, Rijksmus., A 1047), an introspective rendering in smudged and stippled chalks, is so high that it was mistakenly attributed to Gerard (ii). Moses also experimented with oil painting in three portraits (Amsterdam, Rijksmus.), but his feeling for sculptural volumes, chiaroscuro and introspective facial expressions is seen at its best in the late series of sensitive chalk studies portraying single figures in military clothes (e.g. Berlin, Kupferstichkab.). These works originally came from a single sketchbook but were later sold or given away separately, presumably by Moses himself. They are thought to have been drawn in the mid-1660s, around the time Moses joined the Dutch fleet (by at least 1666). He was killed during one of the final engagements of the second Anglo-Dutch War.

BIBLIOGRAPHY
Dutch Figure Drawings from the Seventeenth Century (exh. cat. by P. Schatborn, Amsterdam, Rijksmus.; Washington, DC, N.G.A.; 1981–2), pp. 86–7, 131–2, cat. nos 22–3

For further bibliography *see* (2) above.

ALISON McNEIL KETTERING

Borcht, Pieter van der (*b* Mechelen, 1545; *d* Antwerp, 1608). Flemish painter, engraver and draughtsman. His identity is confused: it is known that a painter called Pieter van der Borcht worked in Mechelen for the Antwerp publisher Christoph Plantin from 1564 onwards. From 1552 until at least 1592 this artist—referred to as Pieter van der Borcht IV by Hollstein and as Pieter van der Borcht II by Bénézit—made etchings as well as woodcuts with the inscription FECIT PETRUS VAN DER BORCHT.

In addition, there was a Pieter van der Borcht active in Mechelen, who, after 1552, made woodcuts which he signed P.B. Thus, either one artist had a steady output of woodcuts and etchings over a long career (1552–*c.* 1600) or there were a number of artists with the same name. The second hypothesis seems the more likely. It is supported by other facts. In 1580 a 'Pieter Verborcht, painter' became a master in the Guild of St Luke in Antwerp, of which he served as dean in 1591 and 1592; the 'Pieter van der Borcht Jacopsz. of Mechelen, painter' who became a citizen of Antwerp was probably a different artist, since according to guild regulations it is doubtful that a non-citizen could have been a master in the guild from 1580 until 1597. There were two other painters in Brussels by the name of Pieter van der Borcht in the 17th century, one of whom may be identical with the Pieter van der Borcht IV described by Bénézit as an engraver active *c.* 1600.

The 16th-century Pieter van der Borcht who signed his name as the 'inventor' (designer) of prints contributed greatly to the spread of peasant weddings, country fairs and feasts as popular subjects. However, unlike the more sympathetic renderings of Pieter Bruegel I, those after van der Borcht's designs follow the German precedent of depicting the peasants as loud, carousing figures whose behaviour is ridiculed in the captions (e.g. *Great Flemish Fair*, 1559, Hollstein, no. 467). Besides peasant scenes, this artist engraved religious and mythological subjects and historical events. Many of his prints served as book illustrations (e.g. the series of 100 pictures for *Imagines et figurae bibliorum*, 1582; Hollstein, nos 1–100).

BIBLIOGRAPHY
Bénézit; Hollstein: *Dut. & Flem.*; Thieme–Becker

H. Miedema: 'Feestende boeren—lachende dorpers: Bij twee recente aanwinsten van het Rijksprentenkabinet' [Feasting peasants—laughing villagers: on two recent acquisitions of the Print Room of the Rijksmuseum], *Bull. Rijksmus.*, xxix/4 (1981), pp. 19–213

M. D. Carrol: 'Peasant Festivity and Political Identity in the Sixteenth Century', *A. Hist.*, x/3 (1987), pp. 289–314

JETTY E. VAN DER STERRE

Borda, Arturo (*b* La Paz, 14 Oct 1883; *d* La Paz, 1953). Bolivian painter and writer. He began painting in 1899 and was self-taught. He was a civil servant in various departments, and with his brother Héctor Borda he was a union organizer; together they founded the first workers' federation in Bolivia. His paintings contain a substantial modernist literary element and were largely done as illustrations to his autobiographical work *El loco*. He exhibited his work in La Paz on 14 occasions and twice in Buenos Aires (1920, 1950). From 1899 to 1920 he developed his style and technique in portraits of family members, such as *Héctor* (1915), *My Two Sisters* and *Yatiri* (1918; all La Paz, priv. cols), one of the first Bolivian paintings in which an Indian appeared as the main subject.

Between 1920 and 1940 Borda concentrated on literature, politics, public service and union activity and completed very few paintings, although he did paint landscapes, jungles and mountains, such as *Illimani* (1932; La Paz, Mus. Tambo Quirquincho; *see* BOLIVIA, fig. 6). From 1940 he began an intensive new period of painting, consisting of allegorical scenes with a strong content of social criticism, as in *Portrait of My Parents* (1943), which has Surrealistic elements, and the *Criticism of -isms and the Triumph of Classical Art* (1948; both La Paz, priv. cols). From 1950 to 1953 he executed several *Studies I, II* and *III*, full of light and colour, precursors of Op art.

BIBLIOGRAPHY
Borda (exh. cat., La Paz, 1966)
P. Querejazu: *La pintura Boliviana del siglo XX* (Milan, 1989)
                                        PEDRO QUEREJAZU

Bordalo Pinheiro. Portuguese family of artists. Manuel Maria Bordalo Pinheiro (1815–90) was a successful amateur painter, specializing in genre paintings on historical themes. The work of his son (1) Rafael Bordalo Pinheiro is sharp, graphic and witty, caricaturing intellectuals and politicians, while that of his younger son (2) Columbano Bordalo Pinheiro is more introverted, expressing in many portraits a notably sombre image of Portuguese life in the late 19th century. Rafael's son Manuel Gustavo Bordalo Pinheiro (1867–1920) continued his father's work, with less distinction.

(1) Rafael Bordalo Pinheiro (*b* Lisbon, 21 March 1846; *d* Lisbon, 23 Jan 1905). Draughtsman, caricaturist and ceramic designer. He attended drawing classes at the Academia de Belas-Artes in Lisbon. He also had a great and lasting passion for the theatre and a degree of acting talent that helped his early success as a caricaturist. His first humorous publication was the album *O Calcanhar de Aquiles* ('Achilles' heel'; Lisbon, 1870), which was followed by contributions to the periodicals *A Berlinda* ('Game of forfeits'; 1870–71) and *O Binóculo* ('The Opera-glass'; 1870). In his drawings of 1871–2, such as *Village Funeral* (Lisbon, Mus. Bordalo Pinheiro), he showed a tendency towards Realism that suggested that he might follow in the footsteps of Courbet and Proudhon. In 1873 he drew for the *Illustrated London News* as their correspondent in Spain during the Carlist War, but he returned to caricature with a series of nine lithograph portraits of celebrated actors published in 1873 and 1874. In 1874 he launched his first popular journal, *A Lanterna Mágica*. Its success won him a contract in Rio de Janeiro, Brazil, where he settled in 1875. There he contributed to *O Mosquito* and edited *Psit!!!* (1877) and *O Besouro* ('The Beetle'; 1878–9).

Homesick for Lisbon and its bohemian artistic and literary circles and subjected to death threats on behalf of personalities whom he had satirized, Rafael returned to Portugal in 1879. He launched a periodical, *O António Maria* (1879–85), named after his *bête noire*, the celebrated political leader A. M. Fontes Pereira de Melo. Rafael produced a vast volume of work with this journal and the further publications of *Pontos nos i i* ('Dots on the i's'; from 1885 until 1891, when it was banned by censorship), *O António Maria* (2nd series, 1891–8) and *A Paródia* (1900–06)—the last in collaboration with his son. He produced nearly 10,000 pages, accompanied by humorous, sharp or malicious articles signed by well-known writers, which illustrated every aspect of Portuguese social life of the period. This documentation, uniquely valuable for historical and sociological study, carries more proportional importance for its country of origin than the work of contemporary caricaturists in France, England or Italy. It secured for the artist an immense popular esteem that was manifested in national tributes, a public statue and the foundation of a museum of his work in 1915 (property of the Municipality of Lisbon).

From 1884 Rafael also worked as a designer of ceramics, founding a factory at Caldas da Rainha to produce popular pieces of humorous character in a highly decorative *fin-de-siècle* style. Rafael Bordalo Pinheiro is, however, mainly celebrated for his creation (in *A Lanterna Mágica* of 1875) of a personality symbolic of the Portuguese people, 'Zé Povinho', the Portuguese equivalent of John Bull or Uncle Sam, who still plays an important popular role in the national mythology. The eternal victim of the powers-that-be because of his poverty and credulity, yet capable of indignation and criticism by reason of his political and patriotic common sense, he is at the same time sentimental and heroic, paying for everything and yet laughing at everything. 'Zé Povinho' is the most typical creation of social Romanticism in Portugal.

BIBLIOGRAPHY
J.-A. França: *Rafael Bordalo Pinheiro: O português tal e qual* (Lisbon, 1980)

(2) Columbano Bordalo Pinheiro (*b* Cacilhas, nr Lisbon, 21 Nov 1857; *d* Lisbon, 6 Nov 1929). Painter, brother of (1) Rafael Bordalo Pinheiro.

1. TRAINING, TRAVELS AND EARLY CAREER. Columbano received his early training from his father. From 1871 to 1874 he attended the Academia de Belas-Artes in Lisbon under Miguel Ângelo Lupi for history painting and Tomás José da Anunciação for landscape, without distinguishing himself. In 1874 and 1876 he exhibited with some success genre paintings on historical themes at the Salão da Sociedade Promotora das Belas-Artes, for example *The Philosopher* (1876; untraced). He failed, however, in his attempts to win the Prix de Paris and then the Academia's history painting prize for 1880. In this year he exhibited in Lisbon some genre paintings, such as *Baptism* (1880; untraced), and a portrait of the critic *Ramalho Ortigão* (1880; untraced). These began a long series of portraits and paintings of humorous subjects that provided a novel commentary on the petit-bourgeois life of the city, with subjects such as *Invitation to the Waltz* (1880; Lisbon, Casa Mus. Gonçalves) and *Evening Out* (1880; Lisbon, priv. col., see de Macedo).

Columbano went to Paris that same year, owing to a personal scholarship from the Countess d'Edla, the morganatic wife of Ferdinand II, obtained through the intervention of his father, who was on friendly terms with the King. He was accompanied by his elder sister, Maria Augusta, a lacemaker, who was to be a second mother to him. He carried letters of introduction to Carolus-Duran, a portrait painter already renowned in Portugal, but never became his pupil, although Carolus-Duran is named as his master in the catalogue of the Salon of 1882. Here he exhibited the large *Soirée chez lui* or *Amateur Concert* (1882; Lisbon, Mus. N. A. Contemp.). Four singers are accompanied at the piano in a dimly lit middle-class drawing-room, the dedication of these amateurs being conveyed in rather melancholy caricature. The models were friends of the artist and included Maria Augusta. She also sat for the masterly *Grey Glove* (1881; Lisbon, Mus. N. A. Contemp.), inclining the sad head of an ageing spinster against the bare, soft skin of her shoulders in a composition focused on her glove. The final work of his Paris visit, exhibited at the 1883 Salon, is the portrait of the worldly journalist *Mariano Pina* (1882; Lisbon, Mus. N. A. Contemp.).

In 1883 Columbano returned to Lisbon, having derived little benefit from Paris on account of his timidity and lack of interest in Parisian artistic life. In Lisbon he became one of the founder-members of the Grupo do Leão (Lion Group), a gathering of the new generation of artists, joining more by reason of his age than through any sympathy with the *plein-air* painting, inspired by the Barbizon school, of José Malhoa, João Vaz and António Silva Porto, the mentor of the group. In 1884 Columbano submitted his *Soirée chez lui* to the Lisbon Salon. At first rejected by the jury because of its 'dangerously realist' originality, after its acceptance it received the authoritative praise of the best Portuguese critics, who invoked Goya and Velázquez and found in it a psychological insight worthy of Balzac.

2. WORK.

(i) Portraiture. Columbano's association with the Grupo do Leão painters (who included his brother (1) Rafael Bordalo Pinheiro) was crystallized when in 1885 he painted a collective portrait of his 12 companions, the *Grupo do Leão* (Lisbon, Mus. N. A. Contemp.; see fig. 1). They are seated around their usual table in the Cervejaria Leão de Ouro near the Rossio, Lisbon, with the proprietor and a servant. The enormous canvas was hung in the room in which it had been painted as an integral part of the decoration, together with works by each of the other artists of the Grupo. There is nothing solemn about this convivial conversation piece, which echoes another portrait group painted 30 years previously by João Cristino da

Silva, *Five Artists in Sintra* (1855; Lisbon, Mus. N. A. Contemp.), a manifesto in its time of the new Romanticism. Columbano's canvas proclaims the naturalism of the new generation along the lines of the famous compositions by Henri Fantin-Latour, *Homage to Delacroix* (1864) and *Atelier in the Batignolles* (1870; both Paris, Mus. d'Orsay). Columbano portrays himself standing at the back, wearing a hat as though about to leave, thus symbolizing his ambiguous attitude to the direct naturalism practised by his friends. The *Grupo do Leão* became the most famous work in contemporary Portuguese painting and established Columbano as the outstanding portrait painter of his generation.

Before 1885 Columbano's portraits (all, unless otherwise stated, in the Museu Nacional de Arte Contemporânea, Lisbon) were mostly small panel paintings in which the surrounding space is significant, often including symbolic decorative elements: those of the poet *Bulhão Pato* (1883), *Manuel Gustavo Bordalo Pinheiro* (1884), the writer *José Pessanha* and the actor *Augusto Rosa* (both 1885) belong to this group. Portraits of *Rafael Bordalo Pinheiro* (1881) and Rafael's wife *Elvira Bordalo Pinheiro* (1884) herald the more sober approach Columbano adopted after 1885, although the sophisticated pose and ironic formal refinement of *Amália da Silva Lima, Viscondessa de Sacavém* (1892; Lisbon, Visconde de Sacavém priv. col., see 1987 exh. cat.) harks back to his earlier, more varied compositions.

Columbano's sitters were principally men he considered of intellectual or artistic merit; he often contemptuously refused to paint rich bourgeois who did not interest him. Among the many portraits of poets and writers he

1. Columbano Bordalo Pinheiro: *Grupo do Leão* ('Lion Group'), oil on canvas, 2.0×3.8 m, 1885 (Lisbon, Museu Nacional de Arte Contemporânea)

executed, one of the most profound is that of *Antero de Quental* (1889), a poet who killed himself two years later. His cadaverous image, fading away among shadows in a red mist, is perhaps the most tragic in Portuguese painting. Columbano's attempt to paint *King Charles* (1892) had poor results, but his portraits of three presidents of the Republic, *Manuel Arriga* (1915), *Teófilo Braga* (1917) and *Teixeira Gomes* (1911 and 1925), commissioned for the Gallery of Presidential Portraits in Belem, are powerfully expressive; all three men had important roles in Portuguese intellectual life. Columbano also portrayed many actors, such as *João Rosa* (1890) and *Eduardo Brazão* (*c.* 1909).

Women sitting for Columbano came mostly from his family, e.g. *Two Nieces* (1910) and *Maria Cristina Bordalo Pinheiro* (1912). Infants, such as the *Children of the Conde de Arnoso* (1887), enter his work still more rarely. Temperamentally misogynistic, Columbano was nevertheless prompted by his sister to marry, in 1911, the model who had for many years posed for him; Maria Augusta feared she was getting too old to care for him. His wife appears anonymously in the small but beautiful composition *Cup of Tea* (1898; see fig. 2), one of the most widely exhibited of Portuguese paintings. An empty space in the unfinished *Self-portrait* of 1927 was to have been occupied by her. The portrait is the last in a series beginning with a *Self-portrait* of *c.* 1883. Other double portraits include *Raul Brandão and his Wife* (1928) and *Viana de Carvalho and his Daughter* (1928; ex-V. de Carvalho priv. col., see de Macedo).

(ii) Still-lifes, decorative and other later work. In 1872 Columbano painted his first still-life, a genre to which he returned in 1895 and to which he remained constant, since these unassuming compositions complemented his portraits, evoking the disquieting silence of objects in a hostile world. In 1917 the Palais du Luxembourg in Paris recognized this aspect of his work by buying *Still-life* (1917; Paris, Mus. d'Orsay). Columbano also practised large-scale decorative painting, for which he received many official commissions. These included the decoration of the ceiling of the Dona Maria II Theatre in Lisbon with *Apollo in his Chariot* (1894; destr. 1964). He painted a series of compositions related to Camões's *Lusiads* in the Museu Militar in Lisbon (1899–1904), portraits of celebrated medical men for the Escola de Medicina in Lisbon (1905–7) and portraits of famous politicians of the Liberal period for the Parliament building (1921–7). He also decorated private houses (the *Dance* series, 1891, Lisbon, Pal. Valenças; a series of putti, 1896, Lisbon, Pal. Foz).

In an unsuccessful bid to be appointed as the chair of history painting at the Lisbon Escola de Belas-Artes Columbano painted *Tullia Riding over the Corpse of her Father* (1897; Lisbon, Mus. N. A. Contemp.), but he was

2. Columbano Bordalo Pinheiro: *Cup of Tea*, oil on canvas, 340×260 mm, 1898 (Lisbon, Museu Nacional de Arte Contemporânea)

less at ease than his competitors in the observance of academic canons. His putti and his female nudes in the Camões series show his lack of taste for this kind of painting, though the realism of the drawing in his decorative painting goes far towards justifying the compositions. However, the great *Crucifixion* (Lisbon, Mus. N. A. Contemp.), which he painted slowly between 1898 and 1916, has an emotional realism suggestive of 17th-century paintings by Diego Velázquez.

Columbano was appointed professor at the Escola de Belas-Artes in 1901 and in 1914 Director of the Museu Nacional de Arte Contemporânea in Lisbon, established by the Republic in 1911. He received the Grand Cross of the Order of Santiago in 1919.

BIBLIOGRAPHY

D. de Macedo: *Columbano* (Lisbon, 1952)
J.-A. França: *Malhoâ (o português dos portuguêses) & Columbano (o português sem portuguêses), Colecção arte contemporânea* (Lisbon, 1987)
Soleil et ombres: L'Art portugais du XIXe siècle (exh. cat., Paris, Petit Pal., 1987), pp. 49–56, 223–41 [by J.-A. França]

JOSÉ-AUGUSTO FRANÇA

Bordeaux. French city, préfecture of the Gironde département and capital of Aquitaine. On the left bank of the River Garonne 100 km from the Bay of Biscay, it has a population of 211,200.

1. History and urban development. 2. Art life and organization. 3. Centre of faience production. 4. Buildings.

1. HISTORY AND URBAN DEVELOPMENT.

(i) Before *c.* 1700. (ii) *c.* 1700 and after.

(i) Before c. *1700.* In the 3rd century BC there was a Celtic settlement in a bend of the River Garonne, whence the Bituriges–Vivisques inhabitants regulated the tin trade from Armorica, creating a prosperous commercial crossroads. After the Roman conquest in 56 BC Burdigala—the origin of the name is still unknown—became the leading city in Aquitaine, made famous by the poet Ausonius (*c.* AD 310–95). The tin trade was replaced by wine, at first imported from Campania but later locally produced when a vine suited to the climate was discovered. The town, which spread over 125 ha, had a magnificent architectural ensemble (including the Gallo–Roman Piliers de Tutelle) but was largely destroyed by barbarians in AD 276. The population retired within a *castrum* for protection from the invasions and unrest that followed the fall of the Roman Empire. This walled enclosure, which also contained the Ombrière Palace (the fortified residence of the Dukes of Aquitaine) in a corner of the ramparts, was the principal habitation for 700 years. The ruins of the Palais Gallien, a 3rd-century Roman amphitheatre, survive.

In 1137 the marriage of Eleanor of Aquitaine (1122–1204) to the future Louis VII of France (*reg* 1137–80)

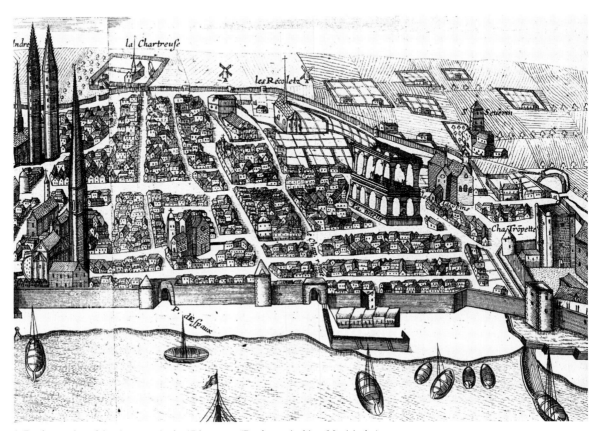

1. Bordeaux, plan of the city centre in the 17th century (Bordeaux, Archives Municipales)

briefly subjected Bordeaux to the Capetians, but in 1152 the couple's divorce and Eleanor's marriage to Henry II of England united Aquitaine with that country. Owing to the English taste for Bordeaux wine the region prospered and even survived the ravages of the Hundred Years War as the wine fleet continued to sail annually to England.

St Seurin was built from the 11th century onwards (*see* §4(ii) below). All that remains of the once powerful Sainte-Croix Abbey is its 12th–13th-century church. The development of Bordelais Gothic can be traced in the church of Ste Eulalie (12th century onwards). Notre Dame was once chapel to the nearby Dominican convent, and the Hôpital St André was founded in 1390. In new developments south of the Gallo–Roman ramparts the bourgeoisie built town houses and warehouses, notably for the salt-fish trade, the family business of the philosopher Michel de Montaigne (1533–92), who was mayor of the town in 1581. Jurats (aldermen), to whom municipal power had been granted by the English kings at the beginning of the 13th century, also resided in this area. In the 15th century the Grosse Cloche, a monumental belfry over a gateway, was built next to the Hôtel de Ville (destr.). The reabsorption of Bordeaux into the French kingdom in 1453 brought about the construction of the Château Trompette (destr.) and the Hâ Fort (1460; destr. apart from the Tour des Anglais) to deter rebellion by the anglophile population. The Ombrière Palace, which housed Parliament (1462), attracted the sons of rich merchants and created a new social class anxious to build large residences for themselves. The cathedral (*see* §4(i) below), begun in the 13th century, was completed in the 15th; the Tour Pey-Berland, originally a belfry, was erected (1440); and the university (1441; now the Musée d'Aquitaine) was built.

The basis of the city's prosperity in the 16th century continued to be trade in wine and pastel. The end of the 16th-century wars of religion encouraged a resurgence of building projects, led by the Duc d'Epernan's Baroque château of Cadillac. This 'Fontainebleau d'Aquitaine' impressed Bordeaux's archbishops and thus influenced the city's ecclesiastical architecture, as at the church of St Paul (1676) and Michel Duplessy's Notre Dame (1680s onwards; now a library).

In the 17th century, when drainage of the surrounding marshes began, Bordeaux turned towards the prospects offered by the Antilles, which in the following century would generate a new 'golden age' (see fig. 1). The city paid dearly for its rebellion against Louis XIV: the extension of the Château Trompette in 1677 brought about the destruction of Renaissance houses near the fortress and of the magnificent ruins of the Piliers de Tutelle. Only one of the King's orders was disobeyed: to demolish the tower and spire (1472–92) of St Michel. Its height of 114 m makes it the tallest spire in south-west France.

(ii) c. 1700 and after. Jean-Baptiste Colbert, in his role as Contrôleur Général des Finances, encouraged the Bordelais to prepare a merchant fleet to trade with Santo Domingo, Martinique and Guadeloupe; sugar, coffee, cotton, indigo and tobacco from these islands were then conveyed to the Baltic and North Sea ports. In the 18th century nearly 600 ships sailed to the Antilles, and some engaged in the African slave trade. The additional trade with the East Indies and the islands of the Indian Ocean made Bordeaux the leading port in France, a role secured by its contacts with northern Europe. This resulted in prosperity and a taste for luxury even among the important Protestant colony of foreign businessmen, who at this time still congregated in the suburb of Chartrons.

The arrival of the great Intendants (provincial administrators) radically altered the appearance of the town. Claude Boucher (*fl* 1720–43) made the first breach in the medieval enclosure and commissioned Jacques Gabriel V and Ange-Jacques Gabriel to design the Place Royale (1733), framed by a stock exchange (Palais de la Bourse) and a corn exchange (Hôtel des Fermes). Aubert de Tourny (1695–1760) followed suit, celebrating the town's 'golden age' by pulling down the *carcan* (iron collar) of the medieval walls and over about ten years designing the allées (avenues; see fig. 2) that, he said, 'would encircle the town' and connect Bordeaux to such major suburbs as Chartrons. Ange-Jacques Gabriel also designed a garden 'à la française' (1756; see GARDEN, §VIII, 4(ii)) of 15 ha and created several squares, including that of the Parlement (1754) and the Place Dauphine (now Place Gambetta) at the heart of the city. The medieval gates were replaced by arcs de triomphe, for example the gates of Dijeaux (1750), Aquitaine (1753) and Bourgogne (1755). Hôtels particuliers were built for businessmen and parliamentarians along the new allées and courtyards. Archbishop Mériadeck de Rohan (*reg* 1769–1815) commissioned François Bonfin (1730–1814) and Laclotte (*fl* second half of the 18th century) to build the Archbishop's Palace (1770; now the Hôtel de Ville). The Duc de Richelieu (1696–1788) employed Victor Louis to build the Grand-Théâtre (1773–80; for illustration *see* LOUIS, VICTOR), financed by the sale of part of the glacis of the Château Trompette, the destruction of which was now ordered. A promenade (1818) lined with trees ran along the central waterfront, and buildings along the embankment were decorated with a series of sculpted mascarons.

During the 18th century the population increased from 40,000 to more than 110,000, and Bordeaux became the third city in the kingdom after Paris and Lyon; but with the upheavals of the French Revolution and its aftermath the city was hit by an economic stagnation that particularly affected the port. In 1822, thanks to private enterprise, Claude Deschamps (1765–1843) built the 500 m-long Pont de Pierre (enlarged 1954), the first bridge over the Garonne. In 1865 part of the right bank was annexed to create a new quarter, La Bastide. The railway station was built in 1852, and the iron bridge (1856–60) over the Garonne by GUSTAVE EIFFEL allowed the Paris–Bordeaux railway line to be extended towards the south of France.

Under the Second Empire sanitation was improved in insalubrious districts of old Bordeaux. The town spread into the open countryside, although its western borders were fixed by the creation of peripheral boulevards. Around the new railway station and in the communities near the boulevards a typical style of house evolved, known as *l'échoppe*—a low stone house with a small garden. An *échoppe* is termed single if it has a corridor along one side and double if it has a central corridor; if it is double, the central corridor is flanked by three two-room units.

2. Bordeaux, the two allées designed by Aubert de Tourny, 18th century (Bordeaux, Archives Municipales)

There are nearly 15,000 *échoppes* in Bordeaux, and they give certain areas a distinctive character. Also characteristic are the large *chais* (warehouses) owned by wine-merchants, which line commercial sections of the waterfront; an example is the Entrepôts Lainés, built by Claude Deschamps in the 1820s (rest.; now an exhibition centre).

In the 19th century monumental civic buildings were constructed in a Neo-classical style redolent with nostalgia for the preceding century: the Hôpital St André (1829), the Palais de Justice (1846), various university departments (1873, 1874, 1880) and the rostral columns (1829). The Place des Quinconces, one of the greatest esplanades in Europe, was created, and the Monument des Girondins (by Victor Rich and Alphonse Jean Bumilâtre (*b* 1844)) added in 1902. The most notable early 20th-century project in the area is Le Corbusier's sensationally audacious housing development, Cité Frugès (1926), at Pessac, near Bordeaux. From 1960 Bordeaux became an industrial city, and in 1966 the 28 parishes of greater Bordeaux joined to form an urban community of 624,286 inhabitants. Bordeaux became capital of Aquitaine. Major developments were the creation on a marshy area of 600 ha of the Lac quarter, with an international exhibition park, and of the Cité du Grand Parc; the renovation of the Mériadeck quarter, covering 20 ha in the city centre, was one of the greatest urban planning projects in France. The universities moved to the suburbs, and an area of 150 ha was designated a protected zone, containing 5000 buildings of artistic or historic interest scheduled for restoration. Finally, a bypass was built leading to the Pont d'Aquitaine (1967), built two years after the Pont St Jean; the silhouette of the Pont d'Aquitaine rises more than 50 m above the Garonne. The French mint (Etablissement Monétaire) has been in Bordeaux since the 1970s.

BIBLIOGRAPHY
C. Jullian: *Histoire de Bordeaux* (Bordeaux, 1895)
J. Leroux: *La Colonie germanique de Bordeaux* (Bordeaux, 1918)
M. Lhéritier: *L'Intendant Tourny* (Paris, 1920)
P. Courteault: *La Place Royale de Bordeaux* (Paris, 1923)
X. Védère: *Les Allées de Tourny* (Bordeaux, 1929)
J. d'Welles: *Le Grand-Théâtre de Bordeaux* (Bordeaux, 1949)
R. Dion: *La Création du vignoble Bordelais* (Angers, 1952)
J. d'Welles: *Le Palais Rohan* (Bordeaux, 1954)
X. Védère: *Le Palais de la Bourse* (Bordeaux, 1955)
A. Rèche: *Naissance et vie des quartiers de Bordeaux* (Paris, 1979)
C. Higounet: *Histoire de Bordeaux* (Toulouse, 1980)
A. Rèche: *Bordeaux* (Bordeaux, 1988)
P. Butel: *Les Dynasties bordelaises, de Colbert à Chaban* (Paris, 1991)
ALBERT RÈCHE

2. ART LIFE AND ORGANIZATION. In the Middle Ages most artistic effort in Bordeaux was concentrated on church buildings. Many craftsmen and artists were from outside the city: most masons active between 1450 and 1530 came from neighbouring provinces, for example Mathurin Galopin (*fl* 1511–35) from Poitou and Jean Villetar (*fl* 1518–50) from the Loire. The jurats acted as patrons, commissioning the painter Jacques Gaultier in 1579. The sculptors Julien Rochereau (*fl* 1519–61) and Jean Baudoyn (*fl* 16th century) from the Loire produced statues and funerary monuments. There were many highly productive glass painters and embroiderers. About 1515 a guild of goldsmiths was established.

An important patron was the Maréchal Alphonse d'Ornano, who collected tapestries, pictures, silver coins and illuminated manuscripts. Cardinal François de Sourdis, archbishop of Bordeaux from 1599 to 1628, brought back from Italy sculptures and pictures, some of which can still be seen in the churches of Bordeaux, and middle-class professionals and merchants also collected pictures. The existence of a 'Bordeaux school' is doubtful: works of art were ordered from outside the city, and many artists working in Bordeaux were either foreign or came from other cities in France, notably Toulouse, which provided architects, painters and sculptors. By 1650 there was an important group of Parisian artists working in Bordeaux, including the sculptor Jean Langlois (*fl* late 16th century–1613), the architect Jacques Le Mercier and the painter Nivelon; artists from the second half of the 17th century included the architect Jacques Robelin, the sculptor François Mouflart (*fl* 1658–79) and the painters Philippe Deshayes (*d c.* 1665–6), Robert Larraidy (*fl* 1685–1734) and Antoine Le Blond de Latour (1630–1706). There were also such dynasties of local artists as the Ducuing family of goldsmiths, the Coutereau family of masons and the Dubois family of sculptors. The names are known of 20 engravers, and the existence of many marble-carvers and one ivory-carver are attested to.

In 1691 the efforts of Le Blond de Latour brought about the foundation of an Ecole Académique. Despite its connections with the Académie Royale in Paris, the Ecole Académique, still extant in 1727, gradually declined, as did local art. The mediocrity of local artists and the grudging support of the jurats were contributory factors. However, Nicolas Bazemont (1692–1770), head of a drawing school, helped to stimulate the artistic awakening of the 1770s. Among local sculptors were Jean Berquin and Pierre Berquin (*fl* late 17th century) and Pierre Vernet (1697–1787), but the best early 18th-century works of art executed in Bordeaux were by such non-Bordelais artists as the painter Frère Jean André and the sculptors Guillaume Coustou (ii) and Jean-Baptiste Péru II (1707–90). Official control over many aspects of artistic production passed from the Church and the jurats to the Intendants.

In 1768 a group of artists founded the Académie des Arts to provide a forum for lectures, papers and two annual public meetings; prizes were awarded at one of the latter. From 1771 to 1787 there was an annual exhibition of pictures and architectural projects. In 1783 the Musée de Bordeaux was founded, offering tuition in modern languages, mathematics and art. Both institutions closed *c.* 1793.

From 1770 to 1789 interest in the arts increased, and the Académie and city art collections were founded. The most important private collector was Bonaventura Journu (1717–81). Still-lifes and conversation pieces were fashionable, and the great demand for portraits attracted such painters and miniaturists as Jean-Baptiste Perronneau, Adolf Ulric Wertmüller and FRANÇOIS-LOUIS LONSING. Engravers were numerous but not outstanding. Decorative and religious sculpture, mainly by Parisian artists, flourished. The goldsmiths' guild was among the most important. The first local painter of distinction was Pierre Lacour (i) (1745–1814), known for fine portraits and landscapes. He taught at the Académie and was involved with the Musée de Bordeaux. An art collector himself, he was the centre of a circle of artists. Lacour continued to champion

art during the Revolution, founding the Musée (art museum) in 1794. He was succeeded as head of the Ecole des Beaux-Arts and of the Musée by his son Pierre Lacour (ii) (1778–1859). The royalist period was marked by renewed activity: the artistic and literary magazine *Musée d'Aquitaine* was launched by Lacour (ii) in 1823. In 1851 the art collector Charles-Jean Fieffé (1792–1857) founded the Société des Amis des Arts, which held annual exhibitions. Goya's presence in Bordeaux (1824–8) had little influence on local artists. Between 1850 and 1860 such miniaturists as Pierre-Edouard Gautier-Dagoty (1775–1871) were in demand. Gustave de Galard (1779–1841) and Léon Mousquet (1805–74) were popular portraitists. Several Bordelais painters attained fame in Paris, including Jacques-Raymond Brascassat, Adrien Dauzats, Virgilio Narcisso Diaz de la Peña (1808–76) and Rosa Bonheur. There was a group of landscape artists who were also interested in archaeology, notably Leo Drouyn (1816–96). Between 1895 and 1914 six students from the Ecole des Beaux-Arts were awarded the Prix de Rome. Nevertheless, there was no identifiable school. Artists tended to go to Paris (as did John-Lewis Brown) or to follow Parisian styles.

Gabriel Frizeau (1870–1938) was patron to such artists as Odilon Redon and ANDRÉ LHOTE. Albert Marquet, in Paris from about 1890, was another local painter who achieved fame. In the first half of the 20th century Bordeaux remained conventional in its artistic outlook and interests. The Atelier graphic arts association, founded in 1905 by Alfred de la Rocca (1855–1919), was equally traditional, but the Indépendants Bordelais (known as Indépendants d'Aquitaine from 1970) introduced modern art to the city. After 1945 various movements were represented by the groups Solstice, Regard, Les Isopolytes and La Palette. The painters F. E. Bonnet (known as Tobeen; *b* 1880) and Roger Bissière were at the forefront of the Bordeaux school of painting. Among sculptors active in Bordeaux were Lucien Schnegg (1864–1909), Jane Poupelet (1878–1932) and Joseph Rivière (*b* 1912), who tried to reconcile tradition and non-figurative art. The ceramicist René Buthaud (1886–1986), and Raymond Mirande (*b* 1932) with his enamels and stained glass, represent the vitality of Bordeaux's decorative arts. The municipal museums are supported by the Société des Amis des Musées de Bordeaux (established 1967) and by the magazine *Revue des Musées de Bordeaux*. Since 1951 there has been a music festival accompanied by an exhibition of pictures each May. Art galleries are flourishing, and the Sigma week of cultural research and exhibitions is devoted to contemporary art.

BIBLIOGRAPHY
C. Higounet, ed.: *Histoire de Bordeaux*, 5 vols (Bordeaux, 1965–72)
P. Roudié: *L'Activité artistique à Bordeaux en Bordelais et en Bazadais de 1453 à 1550*, 2 vols (Bordeaux, 1975)

MADELEINE BLONDEL

3. CENTRE OF FAIENCE PRODUCTION. Production of faience began in Bordeaux *c.* 1710 when a potter from Nevers, Jacques Fautier, settled there and continued in several workshops until the 1840s. However, the only really important factory, which operated from 1715 to 1780, was that of Jacques Hustin (1664–1749) and his son

Ferdinand Hustin (1696–1778), then of his wife Victoire. Hustin's factory was protected by a royal privilege, which entitled him to exclusive production rights until 1762. Utilitarian items included table-services, apothecary-style pots and tobacco jars, which were produced in large quantities and served a local and transatlantic market until other such factories were established. Most Bordeaux wares are thick and robust, decorated with high-fired colours including blue, azure, orange, almond-green and a pale or brownish mauve. Decoration was influenced by wares from other French centres of production including Nevers, which inspired the use of blue grounds with stylized flowers and palmettes; Rouen, from which came the idea of blue or multicoloured lambrequins, occasionally picked out in iron-red; Moustiers, which inspired the use of grotesques and arabesques by Jean Bérain I in blue monochrome, and later chinoiseries in green mono-chrome; and also Montpellier, whence came a more naturalistic, mainly floral, polychrome decoration, using a pinkish-mauve obtained from manganese. During the last years of production, designs and colours became stereo-typed and schematized. The finest Bordeaux pieces date from c. 1740 and include such items as water jugs, basins and tableware.

BIBLIOGRAPHY

J. du Pasquier: *Faïence de Bordeaux: Catalogue de faïences stannifères du XVIIIe siècle* (Bordeaux, 1980)

JACQUELINE DU PASQUIER

4. BUILDINGS.

(i) Cathedral. Little is known about the architecture of Bordeaux Cathedral, dedicated to St Andrew, before the 12th century. The single-aisled nave (w. 17.40 m) was rebuilt in the mid-12th century with an oblong bay at the west end followed by three square bays designed to carry domical vaults. These bays were subdivided by interme-diary responds and revaulted in the 13th century, giving the nave a total of seven bays. The Royal Portal, opening into the north side of the sixth bay, was probably associated with this campaign. It comprises one of the most important ensembles of monumental Gothic sculpture outside north-ern France and carries a *Last Judgement* programme. On the tympanum, Christ is enthroned with the Virgin, St John and numerous angels; the *Resurrection of the Dead* takes place beneath his feet. The four archivolts bear angels, Old Testament and female figures. In 1826–7 the column statues and trumeaux were removed, but at the end of the 19th century ten statues of the Apostles were reinstalled on the portal embrasures. Stylistic precursors for the Royal Portal are found in Paris as early as the 1240s (Apostles in the Sainte-Chapelle), but the workmanship of the Royal Portal is not of the same quality and was probably carved in the 1260s.

Later in the 13th century work began on the east end of the cathedral and continued, under a succession of master masons whose names are recorded, into the 15th century. The north and south transepts, which project by two bays, have impressive twin-tower façades pierced by figural portals and Flamboyant rose windows. These façades compensate for the extreme simplicity of the west front, which faced the Gallo-Roman city walls. The choir has four straight bays flanked by aisles that opened into

chapels. In the 19th century the partitions separating these chapels were removed, transforming them into second aisles. The inner choir aisles are continued into the ambulatory, which opens into five polygonal radiating chapels. North-east of the chevet is the Tour Pey-Berland, a detached bell-tower erected in the mid-15th century, with four square stages crowned by an octagonal stage and a 19th-century spire.

See also DESCHAMPS.

BIBLIOGRAPHY

P. Courteault: 'Cathédrale Saint-André de Bordeaux', *Congr. Archéol. France*, cii (1939), pp. 30–58

J. Gardelles: *La Cathédrale Saint-André de Bordeaux* (Bordeaux, 1963)

W. Sauerländer: *Gotische Skulptur in Frankreich, 1140–1270* (Munich, 1970; Eng. trans., London, 1972), pp. 510–11

(ii) St Seurin. The origins and early history of the collegiate church of St Seurin, dedicated to a 5th-century bishop of Bordeaux, are obscure. The oldest parts of the building, the crypt and the west porch, belong to the late 11th century, but Gallo-Roman, Merovingian and Carolingian fragments in the crypt may represent relics from an earlier church on the site. An important series of late 11th-century capitals, some figural, survives in the porch. Most of them are distantly based on the Corinthian form and are executed in deeply undercut relief.

The rebuilding of St Seurin, beginning with the chevet c. 1175, was largely completed by the mid-13th century, although additions and transformations continued into the 19th. The Gothic church comprised a square-ended choir of two bays, the western bay opening into a south transept, and a four-bay nave with quadripartite vaults, buttressed by narrow aisles with transverse barrel vaults. It is a hall church, without triforium or clerestory. In the 14th century the aisles enveloped the west porch; the west façade was rebuilt in 1828–9.

Opening into the second bay of the south aisle is an ambitious 13th-century portal flanked, following regional tradition, by two blind bays and preceded by a 16th-century porch. An inscription on the trefoil-headed en-trance arch refers to the death of 'Canonicus Ramundus de Fonte' in 1267, but the portal was in preparation long before that date. The lower embrasures belong to an initial campaign in which a continuous capital frieze was destined to carry arches and tympana in the traditional manner. From their style it is clear that the tympana and inner archivolts of the lateral bays also belonged to this project, which was abandoned c. 1250 when a workshop, trained in northern France, arrived and enlarged the design. This workshop added the column statues (representing *Ecclesia*, *Synagogue* and the *Twelve Apostles*), the archivolts, tympa-num and lintel of the central portal, the theme of which is the *Last Judgement*, and the outer archivolts of the lateral bays. The earlier blind tympana to left and right are carved, respectively, with the *Holy Women at the Tomb* and, probably, *St Severinus Received by St Amandus*. The figure style of the central portal, characterized by massive forms and heavy drapery, relates it to a group of monuments influenced by Reims Cathedral, including Semur-en-Aux-ois, Saint-Thibault-en-Auxois and Notre-Dame-de-la-Couture at Le Mans. This sculpture was carved c. 1250–70.

BIBLIOGRAPHY
G. Loirette: 'Eglise Saint-Seurin', *Congr. Archéol. France*, cii (1939), pp. 59–92
W. Sauerländer: *Gotische Skulptur in Frankreich, 1140–1270* (Munich, 1970; Eng. trans., London, 1972), pp. 509–10

KATHRYN MORRISON

Border, manuscript. The elaboration of the margins of a manuscript with decorative or figural motifs. The development of decoration for otherwise blank margins on a page with text is associated with the evolution of the decorated and historiated initial (*see* INITIAL, MANUSCRIPT; for borders accompanying full-page miniatures, *see* MINIATURE, §I). It forms part of a developing scheme of hierarchies in the decoration of the manuscript, which in turn is linked to the page design and punctuation of the text. In its earliest phase, border ornament was closely tied to the form of the initial, so that by the 12th century parts of the initial were elongated to the extent that they affected the design of the page. In the Gothic period, however, borders became a more independent form of decoration, and pages of lesser importance were also included in the decorative scheme.

Another factor in the development of border decoration was the use of penwork initials, particularly in the Canon law and theology books copied at the university towns of Bologna, Paris and Oxford in the Early Gothic period. In these textbooks, the decoration of initials of varying importance formed part of the visual organization of the page to enable easier reference. This hierarchical system of decoration for secular texts may have influenced the introduction of a similar system into the growing numbers of liturgical books owned by the laity. In addition, there seems to have been an association between the increased decoration of a text and its veneration, so that Psalters and Books of Hours, in particular, used as part of a programme of private devotion, were lavishly decorated both in a way that made them more accessible to the layman and in order to emphasize their sacredness. The amount of decoration used in a book can also help to gauge the cost of its production. This consideration, combined with the hierarchy of borders that had emerged by the end of the 13th century, was important in shaping the decorative programme of a manuscript; whether borders covered one or more margins on a page would depend on the amount of money spent and the relative importance of the text they framed.

The work of William de Brailes exemplifies the early development of border decoration in liturgical books. The combination of painted and penwork border extensions or bars, arranged over a double-page opening, frames the text, often leading the eye from one page to the other. Fully painted borders are sometimes used at the more important openings to different sections of the text and seem to have been regarded as more important than flourished ones; in the later part of the 13th century, however, the two techniques vie for prominence. The colours used in fully painted borders generally follow a standard formula of pink, blue and gold. Flourished decoration is usually in an alternating scheme of blue and gold or red and blue (or vice versa). The frequent use of these alternating, complementary colours in borders appears to have been influenced by French, especially Parisian, models. The inclusion of bars that form platforms on which stand figures, animals or grotesques is associated with the 'William of Devon group' of illuminators in England, who probably originated in France (perhaps Paris) and possibly migrated to Oxford. In the Bible of William of Devon (*c.* 1260–70; London, BL, Royal MS. 1. D. I; see fig. 1) painted borders mimic the angular extensions from the initials found in the penwork letters. This 'mixed' type of border and initial work is explored to its fullest in the double-page illuminated and penwork Beatus initial of the Windmill Psalter (*c.* 1290; New York, Pierpont Morgan Lib., MS. M. 102, fols 1*v*–2*r*) and related works (late 13th century; Baltimore, MD, Walters A.G., MS. W. 102; Oxford, Bodleian Lib., MS. Auct. D. 3. 2).

By the end of the 13th century certain formal relationships had developed between miniature, initial and border, contributing to the so-called *mis-en-page*, or characteristic layout of manuscripts. For border decoration the single most important of these developments was the placing of initials beneath illustration panels (rectangular images set above the text), with border extensions around the text. Frequently, a space was left at the bottom of the page, with the border forming a platform for subsidiary figures

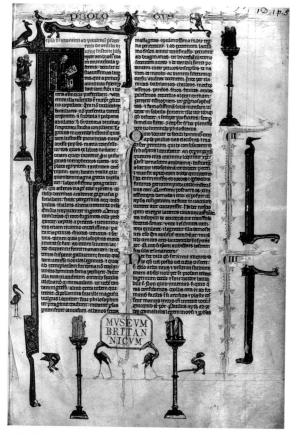

1. Border decoration of extended bars and penwork flourishes, with animals and grotesques; from the Bible of William of Devon, 314×200 mm, possibly from Oxford, *c.* 1260–70 (London, British Library, Royal MS. 1. D. I., fol. 1*r*)

2. Border decoration of foliage sprays with birds and butterflies, framing scenes of the *Miracle of the Leprous Pilgrim*, from the Saint-Denis Missal, 233×164 mm, Paris, *c.* 1350–51 (London, Victoria and Albert Museum, MS. 1346–1891, fol. 256*v*)

or scenes, known as the BAS-DE-PAGE. The creation of this area has important iconographical and conceptual implications. Set apart from the historiated initial and panel miniature, it was soon used to comment on the scene above, offering sometimes whimsical and humorous alternatives to the main narrative. Increasingly, fully integrated iconographical schemes, involving several cycles running through miniature, initial and border, became standard in expensive manuscripts.

Although these developments occurred throughout Europe, distinct regional types of border decoration can be detected by the end of the 13th century. These can help localize the material and an artist's training or whereabouts at the time of his contribution to a manuscript. Some of these regional types, however, are difficult to identify, since they may be derived from several, diverse traditions, both local and international. For example, the simple confronted, two-dimensional grotesques and short flowering tendrils found in Cologne borders of the early 14th century can be related to English and South Netherlandish manuscripts; it is the mixture of these elements that is specific to Cologne borders.

The development of borders in France is illustrated by a series of Evangeliaries executed for the Sainte-Chapelle in Paris over a period spanning *c.* 1250–75. The first (Paris, Bib. N., MS. lat. 8892) displays whirling spiral forms extending from the initials combined with flourishes that extend into the borders, often from penwork line endings. A second Evangeliary (Paris, Bib. N., MS. lat. 17326) displays elaborate border extensions that frame the upper and lower half of the two-column text. These are formed by angular and irregular spirals, which sometimes end in dragons or interlace or both. A third (London, BL, Add. MS. 17341) has thinner border extensions, often terminating in naturalistic leaf sprays (ivy and vine), inhabited by birds and animals. The seemingly random nature of the extensions found in the earlier books is absent, and more formalized platforms at regularly spaced intervals are used. The work associated with the illuminator Master Honoré in the late 13th century can be understood in the context of these developments. These characteristics are also found in other parts of northern France and the Netherlands.

Many of these basic formulae were used in English manuscripts, but in these much more emphasis was placed on drolleries and grotesques as well as observation from nature. One of the earliest formal organizations of all these elements is found in the Rutland Psalter (*c.* 1260; London, BL, Add. MS. 62925). Here, decorated initials are tied together by a vertical border bar, and scenes are placed at the bottom of the page. This may be compared with such later English manuscripts as the Gorleston Psalter (*c.* 1310–20; London, BL, Add. MS. 49622). This scheme is used for its minor two-line decorative initials but is further developed into full, inhabited borders (*see* LANDSCAPE PAINTING, fig. 2) for the leaves with historiated initials. Extremes of naturalism and realistic observation of incident combined with the grotesque are found here and in such other manuscripts as the Luttrell Psalter (*c.* 1330–40; London, BL, Add. MS. 42130). The vivacity of these English borders appears to have influenced French illuminators, for instance JEAN PUCELLE. The remarkably integrated page designs achieved in the Hours of Jeanne d'Evreux and the BELLEVILLE BREVIARY (1323–6; New York, Cloisters, MS. Acc. 54. 1. 2 and *c.* 1323–30; Paris, Bib. N., MSS lat. 10483–4, respectively) suggest some knowledge of developments in English border decoration.

French border decoration became progressively more conservative during the course of the 14th century. The formulae established by Pucelle and his workshop are used and reused in such manuscripts as the Saint-Denis Missal (*c.* 1350–51; London, V&A, MS. 1346–1891; see fig. 2). Their repetitiveness, however, masks a major development in which sparseness and naturalism are replaced by crowded luxuriousness, often with little interest in nature, even though naturalistic objects and animals are included. This shift of emphasis was partly caused by the new challenge of three-dimensional settings for figures within initials and miniatures, which Pucelle had explored in the first quarter of the century. In England, the evolution of the fully compartmentalized border surround for very expensive manuscripts heralds the direction in which solutions to the problem of space in manuscripts were developed in the early 15th century.

In Italy, the formal arrangement of borders does not differ radically in its *mis-en-page* from northern European manuscripts, but the forms and colouring are quite different. In the Early Gothic period, Bolognese manuscripts exemplify the type of borders that came to characterize Italian work in the 14th century: large acanthus-type leaves and thin tubular bars, placed in formal, often symmetrical, arrangements, are painted in bright blues and reds with gold balls. Even in the 13th century, *bas-de-page* scenes were exploited in a way more familiar in 14th-century northern European books (e.g. 13th century; Bologna, Bib. U., MS. 346). Byzantine influence is noticeable in Bologna after the Fourth Crusade of 1204; the use of scenes within borders, for example, is probably derived from the marginal scenes characteristic of the so-called Byzantine monastic Psalters. Roundels also feature in Italian manuscripts, often arranged in the lower margins and supplementing the figurative scenes found in the miniature panels and historiated initials, for example in the Justinian Codex (13th century; Turin, Bib. N. U., MS. E. 1. 8). In the 14th century, highly organized borders combining symmetrical sprays of leaves with birds, putti and narrative roundels suggest comparisons with such northern European manuscripts as the East Anglian St Omer Psalter (1325–30 and early 15th century; London, BL, Yates Thompson MS. 14), as does the use of grotesques.

By the end of the 14th century, border decoration in England had changed radically. Formal sprays of spoon-shaped leaves are symmetrically arranged on the page. Although such traditional elements as daisy buds are retained in the borders, few of the naturalistic elements that characterized English borders in the early 14th century remain. In France, experiments in the spatial relationship between the border and text elements on a page result in the distinction between borders on pages of different importance becoming formalized into a new hierarchy. The work of the de Limbourg brothers illustrates this change. Their miniatures in the Belles Heures of Jean, Duc de Berry (*c.* 1405–8; New York, Cloisters; *see* LIMBOURG, DE, fig. 3) often stand in contrast to the formal 'powdered' borders of gold ivy and vine leaves that were probably completed before the de Limbourgs contributed to the manuscript. In the TRÈS RICHES HEURES (*c.* 1411/13–16 and *c.* 1485–6; Chantilly, Mus. Condé, MS. 65) such openings as the *Procession of St Gregory* (fols 71*v*–72*r*) display a visual anomaly between border and text; the text block is treated as an illusionistic appendage to the page surface that is dominated by the border decoration. This is more systematically applied in the work of the Boucicaut Master and Bedford Master's workshop. On the important openings from the Sobieski Hours (Windsor Castle, Royal Lib.) the distinction between border and miniature is almost completely obscured. This type of border was taken to its logical conclusion by Jean Fouquet and his workshop in such manuscripts as the Hours of Louis de Laval (*c.* 1480–81; Paris, Bib. N., MS. lat. 9420), where only three lines of text hang like tapestries over framed miniatures.

During the 15th century in North and South Netherlandish illumination, the idea of the compartmentalized border, first explored in England in the early 14th century in such manuscripts as the Walter of Milemete Treatise (1326–7; Oxford, Christ Church Lib., MS. 92), takes on a new vitality. The problems being faced were again spatial and the solution illusionistic. Flowers, leaves, shells or even small narrative scenes are enclosed in compartments around the page, forming a frame to the text and often commenting on the miniature or initial. In the Soane Hours (*c.* 1500; London, Soane Mus., MS. 4, fol. 115*v*; see fig. 3), for instance, the *Noli me tangere* miniature is framed by a series of compartments showing detailed renderings of various objects of devotion. The minor pages in these books, however, usually continue to apply the 'powdered' field of leaves or flowers, which had been standardized in France by the end of the 14th century. The text block in these books begins to get smaller in the later 15th century and is often framed by two strips of decorative flowers and leaves in the outer margins, giving emphasis to the unilluminated border in the upper and lower margins.

Italian manuscripts show the most diversity in their solutions to problems of border decoration in the later 14th century. In northern Italy, influences from France, Bohemia and England come together in manuscripts made for the Visconti of Milan by such artists as Giovannino de Grassi. In his work in the Visconti Hours (before 1395; Florence, Bib. N. Cent., MSS Banco Rari 397 and Landau Finlay 22) almost every solution to problems of spatial design in borders is tackled. In some cases borders and historiated initials are integrated with text, in others strict divisions between frame and illustration are made. Visconti devices, often in bursts of colour and gold, suggest the influence of gold- and enamelwork. Contacts between Italy, France and Bohemia are clearly reflected in the appearance of 'national' styles in manuscripts on which visiting artists worked. The contribution of the Bolognese Master of the Brussels Initials to the Très Belles Heures of Jean, Duc de Berry (before 1402; Brussels, Bib. Royale Albert 1er, MSS 11060–61; *see* MASTERS, ANONYMOUS, AND MONOGRAMMISTS, §I: MASTER OF THE BRUSSELS INITIALS), demonstrates this type of interchange. Liturgical books in Italy, depending on the locality in which they were made, usually retain very conservative features throughout the 15th century. As the century progresses, references to the Antique in architecture, putti and displays of leaves and flowers become more frequent. In many manuscripts with humanist associations there is a curious revival of 12th-century *mis-en-page*, and flattened vine-scroll forms are transformed into the characteristic stylized, white-vine decoration of Italian work. This was probably caused by a misunderstanding of the antiquity of the texts being copied. The display pages of these manuscripts, for example in the Aristotle made for Matteo Acquaviva (Vienna, Österreich. Nbib., Cod. 4), explore many of the spatial problems that engaged French 15th-century illuminators. The minor pages also display wider blank margins, both as a sign of luxury and as a result of the influence of the 12th-century designs that were being revived inadvertently.

Many of the design solutions arrived at in the late 13th century and early 14th remained unchanged throughout the Gothic period. The subsequent introduction of illusionistic space into manuscript illustration, however, marks

3. Border showing objects of devotion in compartments, framing a *Noli me tangere*; miniature from the Soane Hours, 107×70 mm, Ghent-Bruges school, *c.* 1500 (London, Sir John Soane's Museum, MS. 4, fol. 115*v*)

a major shift in emphasis; pages with illusionistic miniatures or historiated initials could not be decorated with the two-dimensional decorative scrolls and tendrils of the 13th century. The integrated border–miniature designs that eventually predominate in the 15th century have the same spatial concerns as the miniatures within their frames.

BIBLIOGRAPHY

L. Randall: *Images in the Margins of Gothic Manuscripts* (Berkeley, CA, 1966)

N. J. Morgan: *Early Gothic Manuscripts*, 2 vols (1982–8), iv of *A Survey of Manuscripts Illuminated in the British Isles*, ed. J. J. A. Alexander (London, 1975–)

L. F. Sandler: *Gothic Manuscripts, 1285–1385*, 2 vols (1986), v of *A Survey of Manuscripts Illuminated in the British Isles*, ed. J. J. A. Alexander (London, 1975–)

M. A. MICHAEL

Bordon [Bordone; Padovano], **Benedetto** (*fl* 1488; *d* Padua, Feb 1530). Italian illuminator, printmaker and writer. He is first mentioned in Padua as an illuminator in 1488. He has been identified as the Benedetto Padovano who signed the *Digestum novum* (BENEDI[CTI] PATAV[INI]; see fig.) and the Decretals of Pope Gregory IX (BE[NEDICTI] PA[TAVINI]), published by Jenson in Venice in 1477 and 1479 respectively (Gotha, Landesbib., Mon. Typ. 1477; Mon. Typ. 1479). Both incunabula were

Benedetto Bordon: illumination from the *Digestum novum* (Venice, 1477) (Gotha, Landesbibliothek, Mon. Typ. 1477, *v* z.13, A.1.b)

commissioned by the German book dealer Peter Ugelheimer, for whom Girolamo da Cremona also worked, probably shortly after 1483; the apparent dependence of Bordon's style on Girolamo, particularly in his early works, may suggest that the Gotha incunabula were decorated after that date, during the years in which Bordon is documented in Padua. In the same period he probably also illuminated two folios (Munich, Staatl. Graph. Samml., 40198 and 40140), a Book of Hours (Vienna, Österreich. Nbib., Cod. 1970) and a Cistercian Breviary (Oxford, Bodleian Lib., MS. Canon. Lit. 343).

In 1492 Bordon moved to Venice, where he was noted also for his work as a scholar and writer. In 1494 he edited an Italian translation of the Dialogues of Lucian of Samosato, illustrating the text himself. The book (Vienna, Österreich. Nbib., Inc. 4.G.27) bears the coat of arms of the Mocenigo family, and its decoration reflects Bordon's fresh response to Venetian painting, especially the work of Giovanni Battista Cima. Evidence of Bordon's work as an engraver survives in his 'book in which we speak of all the islands of the world', the *Isolario* (Venice, 1528); in 1504 he requested a licence to print a *Triumph of Caesar*. This had long been thought to be lost, but in the 1970s it was traced back through a 19th-century record to the *Triumph* traditionally attributed to the Alsatian woodcutter Jacobus Argentoratensis (Massing, 1990), with whom it is thought Benedetto may have collaborated on more than one work. Nevertheless, the impression that provided the evidence for this claim, which referred to Jacobus as the publisher, is untraced. It has been suggested that Bordon may be identified with the 'Classical Designer', who was responsible for a number of Venetian woodcuts in the 1490s.

A contract of 1523 records that Bordon undertook to decorate a Gospel Book and an Epistles for the Benedictine monastery of S Giustina in Padua. These have been identified as the manuscripts held respectively in Dublin (Dublin, Chester Beatty Lib., MS. 107; signed BENEDETTO BORDONUS) and London (London, BL, Add. MS. 15815). Although they are years later than the Gotha incunabula, the works are homogeneous in style. This has supported Mariani Canova's emphasis on the identification of Bordon with Benedetto Padovano, which was accepted by the earliest critics but questioned by some later scholars, such as Levi D'Ancona (1967). The latter also attributed to Benedetto Padovano an Antiphonary (Padua, Mus. Civ., MSS C.M. 811–12) and other stylistically related works, including the Barozzi Missal (Padua, Bib. Capitolare, Inc. N. 260), but Mariani Canova has shown that these are the work of Antonio Maria da Villafora.

Bordon was the father of the humanist Giulio Cesare Scaligero, and he stands out as a truly eclectic personality with many interests, both literary and scientific. He was one of the principal masters of Paduan Renaissance illustration, strongly influenced by Mantegna but also open, in his mature years, to ideas from Venetian art and from contemporary Ferrarese illumination.

DBI

BIBLIOGRAPHY

R. Benson: *The Holford Collection: Dorchester House*, i (Oxford, 1929), pp. 32–3

M. Levi D'Ancona: 'Benedetto Padovano e Benedetto Bordone: Primo tentativo per un corpus di Benedetto Padovano', *Commentari*, xviii (1967), pp. 3–42

M. Billanovich: 'Benedetto Bordon e Giulio Cesare Scaligero', *Italia Med. & Uman.*, xi (1968), pp. 187–256

M. Levi D'Ancona: 'Precisazioni sulla miniatura veneta', *Commentari*, xvix (1968), pp. 268–72

G. Mariani Canova: 'Profilo di Benedetto Bordon miniatore padovano', *Atti Ist. Ven. Sci., Lett. & A.*, cxxvii (1968–9), pp. 99–121

J. J. G. Alexander and A. C. De La Mare: *The Italian Manuscripts in the Library of Major J. R. Abbey* (London, 1969), pp. 157–8

J. J. G. Alexander: 'Notes on some Veneto-Paduan Illuminated Books of the Renaissance', *A. Ven.*, xxiii (1969), p. 16

G. Mariani Canova: *La miniatura veneta del Rinascimento, 1450–1500* (Venice, 1969), pp. 68–74, 122–30

——: 'Manoscritti miniati veneti nelle biblioteche di Cambridge e Boston (Mass.)', *A. Ven.*, xxix (1975), pp. 97–104

U. Bauer Eberhardt: *Die italienischen Miniaturen des 13–16 Jahrhunderts* (Munich, 1984), pp. 26–7

J. M. Massing: '*The Triumph of Caesar* by Benedetto Bordon and Jacobus Argentoratensis: Its Iconography and Influence', *Prt Q.*, vii/1 (1990), pp. 2–21

The Painted Page: Italian Renaissance Book Illumination, 1450–1550 (exh. cat., ed. J. J. G. Alexander; London, RA; 1994)

MILVIA BOLLATI

Bordone [Bordon], **Paris** (*b* Treviso, *bapt* 5 July 1500; *d* Venice, 19 Jan 1571). Italian painter and draughtsman. He is best known for his strikingly beautiful depictions of women, both in portraits and in cabinet paintings. He also excelled in rendering monumental architectural settings for narrative, both religious and secular, possibly initiating a genre that would find great currency during the mid-16th century, especially in Venice, France and the Netherlands. His favoured media were oil and fresco, the latter being used on both interiors and façades. Although he was not generally sought after by Venetian patrons during his career, as his art was eclipsed by that of Titian, Paolo Veronese and Jacopo Tintoretto, Bordone was regarded in the mid-16th century as an accomplished artist (Pino; Sansovino). He worked for the moneyed élite of northern Italy and Bavaria, for the royalty of France and Poland, and had works commissioned to be sent to Spain and to Flanders. Despite knowledge of the important patrons for whom he worked, the chronology of Bordone's oeuvre is by no means clear. Dating on stylistic grounds is confounded by the diverse sources on which he drew, ranging from the Emilian, Lombard and Venetian to the French and northern European, depending on the patron. Due to the ease with which prints circulated during Bordone's career, it is difficult to ascertain whether influences were derived at first hand or from printed images. Such difficulties in assigning dates are further exacerbated by his use of the same figure study for numerous paintings evidently executed decades apart. Reliance on the testimony of Vasari, who interviewed Bordone in 1566, in conjunction with the extant documents, the few signed and dated paintings and, to a lesser extent, period fashion provides only a rough outline of his activity. Due to the lack of agreement among scholars regarding chronology, the following account is based mainly on the documentary evidence.

1. Training and early work in Venice, before 1538. 2. Middle period, 1538–*c*. 1550. 3. Late works, after *c*. 1550.

1. TRAINING AND EARLY WORK IN VENICE, BEFORE 1538. On the death of his father, Giovanni, in 1508, Paris moved with his mother, Angelica, to Venice. At school he excelled particularly in grammar and music and then entered the studio of Titian, probably in 1516. By 1518 he had become a master, although he had left Titian's studio prematurely, evidently due to Titian's hostility towards a student who so successfully imitated his style. The rift was apparently so great that Titian took for himself Bordone's first Venetian commission, the altarpiece (1523) of S Niccolò dei Frari. Giorgione's art also influenced Bordone early on, tempered by the example of other artists' work. *The Lovers* (early 1520s; Milan, Brera), for example, exhibits a Giorgionesque mood and attendant psychology; the lovers emerge from the dark ground bathed in a soft light, while a third figure is relegated to relative obscurity in the darkness. The figural composition evidently draws on Tullio Lombardo's marble relief of 1510 of the same subject, as well as Titian's own *Lovers* (Florence, Casa Buonarroti), but Bordone added a third party. Typically he took a delight in texture and attention to detail, evident particularly in the sumptuous fabrics and gems and the soft, supple skin of figures that are imbued also with a Raphaelesque elegance and grace. The subject-matter itself looks forward to the conflation of portraiture and allegory that characterizes much of his mature work.

In Bordone's early religious paintings comparable artistic influences are evident. Giorgione's *Virgin and Child with Saints* (*c.* 1500–05; Castelfranco Veneto Cathedral), executed for a condottiere (Tuzio Costanzo), provided Bordone with both a compositional and a stylistic guide for his *Virgin with SS Christopher and George* (*c.* 1524–6; Lovere, Gal. Accad. B.A. Tadini) for S Agostino, Crema, also commissioned by a condottiere, Giulio Manfron (*d* 1526). Typically, Bordone did not copy Giorgione slavishly; he enlivened the older master's composition in a manner evocative of both Titian and Pordenone, Titian's greatest rival in Venice. The figure of St George, a portrait of Giulio Manfron, stands in a relaxed but relatively static pose, while St Christopher, protector from violent deaths, such as Manfron was to suffer, emerges from the water with a forceful torsion reminiscent of Titian's and Pordenone's figures; the Virgin twists lest she let go of her son, recalling the sense of movement in Titian's figures of the Virgin; and the angels holding the cloth of honour evoke Raphael.

Bordone first achieved public recognition in 1534, when he won the competition of the Scuola Grande di S Marco to execute the *Presentation of the Ring to the Doge* (Venice, Accad.; see fig. 1). Nepotism may have played a part in his success; Zuan Alvise Bonrizzo, Guardian Grande of the Scuola in the 1530s, was his wife's uncle. With this painting Bordone reached artistic maturity; Vasari thought it the 'most beautiful and most noteworthy painting ever created by Paris'. The architecture is inspired by Books II and IV of his friend Sebastiano Serlio's unpublished treatise on architecture and follows a Venetian tradition of using detailed architectural backgrounds often not relevant to the narrative. It shows an ideal view of the renovations to the Doge's Palace and environs planned by Doge Andrea Gritti, who is represented as the 14th-century doge Pietro Gradenigo (*reg* 1289–1311), as well as a view of the tower of the Madonna dell'Orto, near where Bordone lived. Bordone's accomplished handling of the

1. Paris Bordone: *Presentation of the Ring to the Doge*, oil on canvas, 3.7×3.0 m, 1534–5 (Venice, Galleria dell'Accademia)

architecture may have prompted Titian's setting in the *Presentation of the Virgin* (1534–8; Venice, Accad.) of the Scuola Grande della Carità. No presentation drawing or modello survives for any painting by Bordone, although a sketch of a draped male figure seen from behind (Paris, priv. col., see Rearick in 1987 symposium, fig. 8) can be related to the *Presentation of the Ring*. Executed in black chalk, heightened with white, on blue paper, the artist's favoured method, the study relates to figures at the periphery of the canvas and exhibits the use of parallel hatching and the energetic touch that characterize much of Bordone's Titianesque draughtsmanship.

2. MIDDLE PERIOD, 1538–*c.* 1550. Success in the competition of 1534 did not lead to further important Venetian commissions for Bordone. In 1539 he lost a competition for a *Marriage of the Virgin* for the Scuola Grande della Carità to another follower of Titian, Gian Pietro Silvio (*d* 1552). He had already begun to look elsewhere for patrons. He was absent from Venice from March 1538 until April 1539, and, according to Vasari, he travelled to Fontainebleau in 1538 to work at the court of Francis I, where he executed a large number of paintings including portraits of women. Among these commissions Vasari mentioned a cabinet picture of *Venus and Cupid* (perhaps Warsaw, N. Mus.) executed for the Duc de Guise (?Claude I, 1496–1550); and an *Ecce homo* (untraced) and *Jupiter with Io* for Cardinal de Lorraine (?Jean de Lorraine 1498–1550), generally identified as the signed but undated *Jupiter with Io* (Göteborg, Kstmus.; see fig. 2). The work exhibits Bordone's synthesis of the Venetian, central Italian and French Mannerist sensibilities, probably inspired by such followers of Raphael as Luca Penni and Francesco Primaticcio, as well as the more Michelangelesque Rosso Fiorentino, who were also in the employ of the French king. The monumental figures of Jupiter and Io embrace amid the clouds, watched by Jupiter's eagle, while Juno rushes to the scene in her chariot. The soft, luminous flesh of the Brera *Lovers* is here given a more polished and pristine veneer, and the moody atmosphere, reminiscent of Giorgione, becomes a brighter, more refined ambience wholly in keeping with the courtly Mannerist style. Bordone's attention to detail and texture remains, but the glistening pearls on Io's tiara, her loosely flowing tresses (generally reserved for courtesans and maidens in 16th-century painting) and the delicacy and tactile quality of each fibre of her untied undergarment

2. Paris Bordone: *Jupiter with Io*, oil on canvas, 1.36×1.18 m, *c.* 1538–40 or *c.*1559 (Göteborg, Göteborgs Konstmuseum)

contribute to the preciosity and titillating nature of the scene.

On his return from France, Bordone embarked on an extensive fresco cycle for Santa Croce in Pialdier (Belluno) and continued to paint portraits, for which he was by this time apparently well known. The portrait of *Jerome Krafft*, signed and dated 1540 (Paris, Louvre), together with evidence of Bordone's absence from Venice from November 1540 to April 1543, has been used to date the artist's trip to Bavaria. The documents presented by Fossaluzza (1982), however, suggest that the portrait was painted in Venice and that Bordone was in Milan during the early 1540s in the employ of Carlo da Rho (*d* 1552). In the chapel of S Jeronimo in S Maria presso S Celso, Milan, Bordone painted the altarpiece of a *Holy Family with St Jerome and Angels*, with a predella of a *Sleeping St Roch Visited by Angels* as well as a frescoed lunette representing *God the Father Surrounded by Angels*, works that exhibit his continuing debt to Titian. Bordone received payment for work on the chapel in July 1542, and by 1543 he is again documented in Venice. He seems to have remained in the Veneto until the autumn of 1548, although the possibility that in the interim he travelled to Augsburg cannot be discounted altogether. On 22 November 1548 he is documented in Milan, where he remained until *c.* 1550–51. At this time he worked again for Carlo da Rho and his consort, Paola Visconti, and executed a group of paintings with secular and religious subjects as well as portraits. The portrait of Carlo has not been identified, but that of *Paola Visconti* (ex-Pal. Real, Sintra) exhibits a new influence from the Lombard school, particularly of Moretto. A debt to Lorenzo Lotto, with whom Bordone had in 1548 been in contact in Venice, is also evident. The narrative paintings of this period continue to manifest Bordone's synthesis of the Venetian, central Italian and French styles, especially of Raphael's school, and include *Venus and Mars under Vulcan's Net* (Berlin, Gemäldegal.) and its pendant, *Bathsheba Bathing* (Cologne, Wallraf-Richartz-Mus.), on the subject of adultery; a landscape with the *Holy Family and St John the Baptist* (Bonn, priv. col., see 1984 exh. cat., pl. 23), which, given the collocation of mythological and biblical subject-matter in the former pair, possibly formed a pendant to a pagan subject; as well as a nocturnal *Baptism of Christ* (Milan, Brera), possibly also a pendant to another unknown work. While in Milan, Bordone was also commissioned by Candiano, the Milanese physician to Mary, Queen of Hungary and Regent of the Netherlands, to execute a *St Mary Magdalene in the Desert with Angels* and a *Diana Bathing with Nymphs* (both untraced) as presents for the Queen. He also painted a number of Ovidian myths for the Marchese d'Astorga. These are thought to include a *Rape of Proserpina* (untraced), a *Rape of Europa* (Breda di Piave, Antonio Zangrando priv. col.) and a *Venus and Anchises* (Paris, Louvre). Bordone also seems to have painted a *Jupiter with a Nymph* for the King of Poland (either Sigismund I or II) at this time, or possibly slightly later, *c.* 1551–2, when he painted a portrait of the King's Veronese jeweller, *Gian Jacopo Caraglio* (Kraków, N. A. Cols) in Italy.

3. LATE WORKS, AFTER *c.* 1550. If Bordone did not go to Augsburg in the 1540s, he could not have travelled

there until, at the earliest, December 1552. About 1550 he executed an extensive fresco cycle at S Simon di Vallada, Venice, which exhibits an influence of Leonardo and his Milanese school; in 1551 he painted an altarpiece of the *Sacred Mysteries* for Treviso Cathedral, commissioned by Canon Andrea Salomon; he is documented as being in Treviso on 22–23 November 1552; and he executed several paintings, one on an extremely large scale, while in Bavaria at work for the Fugger family and an undocumented Prineri family, indicating a rather lengthy sojourn there. Garas dated the Bavarian stay to around 1550–60 and suggested that Bordone executed a series of six paintings for a room in the palace of one of his Bavarian patrons: a *Venus and Cupid* and its pendant, *Diana the Huntress with Nymphs* (both ex-Gemäldegal., Dresden); *Venus, Mars, Cupid and Victory* and *Mars Taking Cupid's Bow* with *Venus and Flora* (both Vienna, Ksthist. Mus.); *Apollo, Midas and Pan* (Dresden, Gemäldegal.) and an untraced panel with two unidentified female figures. The theme seems to concern love and marriage (e.g. Venus wears red, symbolizing love, and Victory holds the myrtle of marriage), yet the two figures of Mars differ substantially in age and appearance, suggesting either that there are problems in the reconstruction or that the paintings were intended to be viewed in pairs, rather than as a coherent programme. Vasari also mentioned that Bordone created a cabinet picture in the possession of the Cardinal of Augsburg, Otto Truchsess von Waldberg (1514–73), and 'a painting with all five orders of architecture' for the Prineri family, once identified as *Augustus and the Sibyl* (Moscow, Obraztsov Col., see Formicheva, 1971, fig. 45), but—given the French provenance of the latter work (traceable to the 17th century) and probable execution in France—now generally identified as the *Combat of Gladiators* (Vienna, Ksthist. Mus.) once attributed to Raphael's student Giulio Romano. For the *Combat* Bordone drew on Serlio once again, this time on Book III, but he accentuated the importance of the architecture by the use of diminutive figures; the painting probably has political overtones.

Of the many problems connected with the chronology of Bordone's works, the most contentious concerns a trip to the court of Francis II (*reg* 1559–60) at Fontainebleau in 1559. Federici (1803) found an encomium (untraced) written in 1559 by the Trevisan lawyer and humanist Prospero Aproino (*d* 1611) in honour of the departure of his city's most famed artist for France. Other peripheral documents have recently been used, with external evidence, to argue a case for a single French sojourn in 1559; for two French sojourns; and for a single trip in 1538. Were the trip to have occurred in 1559, then the *Venus and Cupid*, *Ecce homo*, *Jupiter with Io* and *Augustus and the Sibyl*, mentioned above, would all have to be dated some 20 years later than Vasari's testimony. Since documents reveal that from 1557–8 Bordone was at work on an altarpiece of the *Virgin Presenting St Dominic to the Saviour* (Milan, Brera), as well as a *Resurrection* and *Saints with Angels* (untraced) for the monastery of S Paolo in Treviso (destr. after 1810), and that in 1561 he was working for the monastery of Ognissanti in Treviso, then the possibility remains that in between Bordone was in France.

After 1560 Bordone worked at his Venetian studio, but his important commissions came from Treviso, not from Venice. This patronage derived from religious institutions, and, with the exception of portraits, he seems to have spent the remaining years of his life painting altarpieces exhibiting a somewhat repetitive formal repertory, a tendency to which he was inclined throughout his life, given his habit of repeating figure studies from his own model-book. In the signed and dated *SS Lawrence, Jerome, Peter, John the Baptist and Sebastian* (1562; ex-S Lorenzo, Treviso; now Treviso Cathedral), he not only repeated figures within the same composition, but reduced them to virtual petrifaction.

BIBLIOGRAPHY

DBI; Thieme–Becker

P. Pino: *Dialogo di pittura* (Venice, 1548); ed. R. Pallucchini and A. Pallucchini (Venice, 1946)

G. Vasari: *Vite* (1550, rev. 2/1568); ed. G. Milanesi (1878–85), vii, pp. 461–6

F. Sansovino: *Delle cose notabili che sono in Venetia* (Venice, 1561)

D. M. Federici: *Memorie trevigiare sulle opere di disegno*, ii (Venice, 1803), pp. 41–5

M. Muraro: 'Un ciclo di affreschi di Paris Bordone', *A. Ven.*, ix (1955), pp. 80–85

G. M. Canova: 'I viaggi di Paris Bordone', *A. Ven.*, xv (1961), pp. 77–88

——: *Paris Bordon*, Profili & saggi di arte veneta, ii (Venice, 1964); review by C. Gould in *Burl. Mag.*, cvii (1965), p. 583

——: 'Nuove note a Paris Bordon', *A. Ven.*, xxii (1968), pp. 171–6

T. Formicheva: 'An Architectural Perspective by Paris Bordone', *Burl. Mag.*, xciii (1971), pp. 152–5

B. Klesse: 'Studien zu italienischen und französischen Gemälden des Wallraf-Richartz-Museums', *Wallraf-Richartz-Jb.*, xxxiv (1972), pp. 175–262

K. Prijatelj: 'Le opere di una collezione veneziana della fine del seicento a Dubrovnik (Ragusa)', *A. Ven.*, xxxiii (1979), pp. 167–8

G. Fossaluzza: 'Una *Sacra Famiglia* di Paris Bordon ritrovata', *A. Ven.*, xxxvi (1982), pp. 197–9

G. M. Canova: 'Precisazioni su Paris Bordon', *A. Ven.*, xxxviii (1984), pp. 132–6

Paris Bordon (exh. cat., ed. E. Manzato; Treviso, Pal. Trecento, 1984); review by L. L. Crosato in *Kunstchronik*, xxxviii/5 (May 1985), pp. 166–73

S. F. Lake: 'A Pounced Design in *David and Bathsheba* by Paris Bordone', *J. Walters A.G.*, xlii–xliii (1984–5), pp. 62–5

S. Béguin: 'Deux dessins inédits du Musée de Rennes', *Paragone*, xxxvi/419–23 (1985), pp. 180–83

E. Coda: 'Un inedito ciclo di affreschi di Paris Bordon nel Bellunese', *A. Ven.*, xxxix (1985), pp. 132–9

P. Humfrey: 'The Bellinesque *Life of St Mark* Cycle for the Scuola Grande di San Marco in Venice in its Original Arrangement', *Z. Kstgesch.*, xlviii (1985), pp. 225–44

Paris Bordon e il suo tempo: Atti del convegno internazionale di studi: Treviso, 1985 [esp. articles by K. Garas and W. Rearick]

M. Rogers: 'The Decorum of Women's Beauty: Trissino, Firenzuola, Luigini and the Representation of Women in Sixteenth-century Painting', *Ren. Stud.*, ii/1 (1988), pp. 47–88

CORINNE MANDEL

Bordoni, Francesco di Bartolomeo [Bourdon, Francisque] (*b* Florence, 1580; *d* Paris, 15 Feb 1654). Italian sculptor and bronze-founder, active in France. He was the pupil and later the son-in-law of Pietro Francavilla and accompanied his master to Paris *c.* 1600–04. He was appointed sculptor to the King in 1606 and was active in the royal works at the Tuileries and at Fontainebleau, where in 1604 he cast two bronze vases (Paris, Louvre) for the Perseus fountain (destr.) and made ornaments for the Tiber Fountain (fragments, Paris, Louvre). He was naturalized in 1611, the year he married Francavilla's eldest daughter. From 1614 he assisted his father-in-law with the installation for the Pont Neuf, Paris, of the bronze equestrian statue of *Henry IV* (destr. 1792), begun by

Giambologna and completed by Pietro Tacca. On Francavilla's death in 1615 Bordoni inherited his royal salary and lodgings in the Tuileries. In 1618 he cast the four superb bronze slaves (Paris, Louvre) modelled by his father-in-law for the base of the Pont Neuf statue. He gave further proof of his outstanding skill as a bronze-founder when he cast Francavilla's three bas-reliefs for the base (destr.).

Bordoni's principal independent royal commission was the decoration of the chapel of the Trinité at Fontainebleau (begun 1628); he was responsible for the elaborate pavement of coloured marbles and for the high altar. The latter was in the form of a triumphal arch with life-size statues in marble of *Charlemagne* and of *St Louis* (depicted with the features of Louis XIII), and the whole was surmounted by four bronze angels in a robust Florentine Mannerist style. He also executed a number of commissions for private patrons and churches, including bronze decorations for the high altar at St Germain-l'Auxerrois, Paris (1613, destr.; an *Angel* survives in Paris, Ecole N. Sup. B.-A.) and in 1626 the remarkable twin life-size praying effigies in marble for the tomb of *Sister Mary of the Incarnation* (Madame Acarie), which are now in the Carmelite convents at Pontoise and Créteil. It seems likely that the bronze busts of *Henry IV* (Paris, priv. col.) and *Louis XIII* (Paris, Louvre) wearing the crowns and insignia of France and Navarre, currently attributed to Jean Warin, are by Bordoni. In 1659 materials destined for an altar for the Carmelite convent in the Rue Saint-Jacques, Paris, were still in Bordoni's studio, which had been inherited, along with his royal appointment, by his son Pierre (1612–84).

Jal

BIBLIOGRAPHY

'Chapelle du château de Fontainebleau', *Archvs A. Fr.*, ii (1862), pp. 349–62

Nouv. Archvs A. Fr. (1872), p. 13; (1876), pp. 31–2

R. de Francqueville: *Pierre de Francqueville, sculpteur des Médicis et du roi Henri IV, 1598–1616* (Paris, 1968)

J. Coural: 'Notes documentaires sur Francesco Bordoni', *Rev. des A.*, xx (1973), pp. 88–91

P. Chaleix: 'Madame Acarie fondatrice des Carmélites réformées de France, son tombeau à Pontoise par Francesco Bordoni', *Mem. Soc. Hist. & Archéol. Pontoise, Val d'Oise & Vexin* (1979), pp. 1–15

GENEVIÈVE BRESC-BAUTIER

Borduas, Paul-Emile (*b* Saint-Hilaire, Quebec, 1 Nov 1905; *d* Paris, 22 Feb 1960). Canadian painter. He studied with the artist Ozias Leduc and from 1923 to 1927 at the Ecole des Beaux-Arts, Montreal. After a short stay in Paris (1928–30), he lived in Montreal until 1941, when he moved to Saint-Hilaire. As a result of the Depression, Borduas was unable to continue the career of church decorator, for which his training with Leduc had prepared him, and found work as an art teacher. His appointment at the Ecole de Meuble, Montreal, in 1937 was a turning-point, making him an influential figure among a group of students, including Jean-Paul Riopelle, who were soon to be known as LES AUTOMATISTES.

Borduas's painting developed from a figurative mode, influenced at first by Maurice Denis and later by Cézanne, to a personal version of Surrealism inspired by the writing of André Breton. His Automatiste period is characterized by paintings in which 'objects' seem to float in space in front of an endlessly receding background, as in *Sous le vent de l'île* (1947; Ottawa, N.G.; *see* MONTREAL, fig. 2). The objects were often painted with a palette-knife and the background with a brush. Realizing the political implications of his art in a Catholic and conservative milieu epitomized by Quebec's premier, Maurice Duplessis, Borduas wrote the preface of a collective manifesto, REFUS GLOBAL (1948). Its anarchic proposals and denunciation of the Church scandalized Quebec. Borduas was immediately dismissed from his teaching post and had to attempt to support himself and his family by his painting. The stress led to his separation from his wife. In 1953 he moved to the USA, settling in New York, where he saw and was influenced by the work of the Abstract Expressionists, who at that time were practically unknown in Canada. Soon afterwards his painting began to reflect the impact of the New York School. His 'objects' exploded, and their fragments invaded the entire picture surface, while the backgrounds of his paintings tended to advance. Jackson Pollock's work encouraged Borduas to experiment with a dripping technique in watercolours of 1954, for example *Baguette joyeuse* (1954; Quebec, Mus. Québec).

Borduas thought that if he could succeed in Paris, recognition in New York would follow, as happened with his student Riopelle. He therefore moved to Paris in 1955 but did not manage to have a solo show there until 1959. During that time, however, his work was exhibited in Montreal, New York, London and Düsseldorf. In Paris his style changed again, and he began to paint balanced compositions such as *L'Etoile noire* (1957; Montreal, Mus. F.A.) in thick black and white impasto. Borduas died homesick for Canada and without the recognition that he sought in New York. In Canada he has been recognized as an influential figure both for his manifesto, *Refus global*, which was largely responsible for bringing modern culture to Quebec, and for his involvement with Les Automatistes.

WRITINGS

F.-M. Gagnon and D. Young, eds: *Ecrits/Writings, 1942–1958*, (Halifax, 1978)

BIBLIOGRAPHY

F.-M. Gagnon: *Paul-Emile Borduas: Biographie critique et analyse de l'oeuvre* (Montreal, 1978)

FRANÇOIS-MARC GAGNON

Boreads Painter. See VASE PAINTERS, §II.

Borenius, (Carl) Tancred (*b* Viipuri, Finland [now Vyborg, Russia], 1885; *d* Coombe Bissett, Wilts, 2 Sept 1948). Finnish art historian, dealer and archaeologist, active in England. After studying at Helsinki University, then in Berlin and Rome, he settled in London in 1906 and published *The Painters of Vicenza, 1480–1550* (1909), based on his doctoral thesis. Through his friendship with Roger Fry, he was introduced to the London art world. He revised (1912) *A History of Painting in North Italy* (1871) by J. A. Crowe and Giovanni Battista Cavalcaselle and the last two volumes (1914) of their *A New History of Italian Painting* (1864–6). Appointed lecturer in 1914 at the University of London, he served as Durning-Lawrence Professor of the History of Art (1922–47). He was a member of the Burlington Fine Arts Club and wrote on a wide range of subjects in the *Burlington Magazine*. A pioneer historian of early English art, he edited the

University College, London, monographs on English medieval art and started excavations at Clarendon Palace near Salisbury in 1932. He had a hand in 1925 in founding *Apollo*, for which he wrote copiously. He appreciated Cézanne and took an interest in such contemporary British artists as Sickert and Duncan Grant. He advised private collectors, notably Henry George Charles Lascelles, 6th Earl of Harewood, and was appointed adviser on paintings, drawings and prints at Sotheby's in 1924. During World War II he was acting editor of the *Burlington Magazine* (1940–45), attracting such contributors as Kokoschka and Augustus John and writing editorials that were frequently on the subject of collecting.

WRITINGS
The Painters of Vicenza, 1480–1550 (London, 1909)
ed.: J. A. Crowe and G. B. Cavalcaselle: *A History of Painting in North Italy: Venice, Padua, Vicenza, Verona, Ferrara, Milan, Friuli, Brescia; from the Fourteenth to the Sixteenth Century*, 3 vols (London, 2/1912)
ed.: J. A. Crowe and G. B. Cavalcaselle: *A History of Painting in Italy: Umbria, Florence and Siena*, v–vi (London, rev. 2/1914); rev. of *A New History of Painting in Italy from the Second to the Sixteenth Century*, 3 vols (London, 1864–6)
Forty London Statues and Public Monuments (London, 1926)
Florentine Frescoes (London, 1930)

BIBLIOGRAPHY
Obituary, *Burl. Mag.*, xc (1948), pp. 327–8
K. L. Strafford: 'Tancred Borenius Europe och viborgare', *Finland. Gestalt.*, xi (1976), pp. 7–13
D. Sutton: 'Tancred Borenius: Connoisseur and Clubman', *Apollo*, cvii (1978), pp. 294–309
F. Herrmann: *Sotheby's: Portrait of an Auction House* (London, 1980)
DENYS SUTTON

Bores, Francisco (*b* Madrid, 6 May 1898; *d* Paris, May 1972). Spanish painter. He began his training in Madrid in the studio of the painter Cecilio Plá (1860–1934) and as a copyist in the Museo del Prado; among the works he copied were paintings by Titian, Velázquez and Goya. In Madrid he became associated with intellectuals involved with the avant-garde and produced illustrations for journals such as *España*, *Alfar*, *Revista de Occidente* and *Cruz y Raya*. In 1925, after taking part in the important *Exposición de artistas Ibéricos* in Madrid, he settled in the Montparnasse district of Paris, where he became associated with Picasso, Gris and other Spanish artists. He also became friends with Derain and Matisse.

At his first one-man exhibition (Paris, Gal. Percier) Bores exhibited paintings in a late Cubist style, such as *Still-life with Rabbit* (1926; see Grenier, pl. 4), which he termed 'pseudo-collages'. Gradually he moved towards a more simplified language bordering at times on abstraction and reminiscent of the work of Matisse, for example *The Fitting* (1934; New York, MOMA). His later paintings, such as *Brown Interior* (1960; Paris, Pompidou), continued to be characterized by a rich sense of colour and by a synthetic treatment of space, especially in the relationship between figures and the landscape settings or interiors within which they are placed. In 1966, during André Malraux's tenure as French Minister of Culture, he was named an Officier of the Ordre des Arts et des Lettres.

BIBLIOGRAPHY
J. Grenier: *Borès* (Paris, 1961; Eng. trans., London, 1961)
Francisco Bores (exh. cat., Madrid, Min. Cult., 1976)
Bores (exh. cat., Madrid, Gal. Biosca, 1982)
PALOMA ALARCÓ CANOSA

Borg, Georg (*b* 1909; *d* 1983). Maltese sculptor. He studied modelling in Malta at the Government School of Art, and in Rome at the Regia Accademia di Belle Arti (1930–34). At the same time he attended classes at the British Academy of Arts, where in 1934 he received a special mention in a competition organized by the Selwyn Brinton a Calderon Competitions. Back in Malta he devoted most of his life to teaching. He excelled as a portrait artist and his bust of Malta's national poet, *Dun Karm Psaila* (1959; Valletta, N. Lib.), is one of the great Maltese works of the post-World War II period. He also produced deeply religious works, including a remarkable relief cast in bronze of *Jesus of the Sacred Heart*, commissioned in 1954 for the Auberge d'Aragon in Valletta (then the official residence of the Prime Minister of Malta). Among his secular works, worthy of note are his female nudes and *Dancing Girls*, which have a delicate sensuous appeal and an evocative linear grace. He remained consistently faithful to his academic formation, and all his works are distinguished by a Neo-classical refinement.

MARIO BUHAGIAR

Borges, Jacobo (*b* Caracas, 28 Nov 1931). Venezuelan painter. He studied at the Escuela de Artes Plásticas in Caracas from 1949 to 1951. In 1951 he was awarded a scholarship and moved to Paris, where he remained for four years, employing bright colours in a series of stylistic experiments that culminated in the Cubist-influenced *Fishing* (1956; Caracas, priv. col., see Ashton, pl. 3). In 1957 this painting won a prize at the Biennale in São Paulo. This success provoked a crisis of content and direction in Borges's work, from which emerged his first figurative paintings in an expressionist style and with a strong element of social criticism. In 1963 he won the national prize for painting, for the *Coronation of Napoleon* (Caracas, Gal. A. N.). The work of the mid-1960s, using bright colour, strong brushwork and grotesque distortions of the figure, bears comparison with that of de Kooning and Bacon. A retrospective of his work was held in 1976 at the Museo de Arte Moderno in Mexico City, and his reputation spread further when in 1983 he had his first one-man show in the USA, at the CDS Gallery in New York. In 1985 Borges was awarded a Guggenheim Fellowship, and the following year he was invited to work and exhibit in West Berlin by the Deutscher Akademischer Austauschdienst. By this stage his work had become more dramatic, with more realistic figures and a greater fluidity in the brushwork (e.g. *Swimmers in the Landscape*, 1986; New York, CDS Gal., see 1987–8 exh. cat., pl. 52).

BIBLIOGRAPHY
Jacobo Borges: Magia de un realismo critico (exh. cat. by J. Cortázar and R. Guevara, Mexico City, Mus. A. Mod., 1976)
D. Ashton: *Jacobo Borges* (Caracas, 1982)
Jacobo Borges: De la pesca . . . al espejo de aguas, 1956–1986 (exh. cat. by S. Imber and C. Ratcliff, Monterrey, Mus. Reg. Nue. León; Mexico City, Mus. A. Contemp. Int. Rufino Tamayo; W. Berlin, Staatl. Ksthalle; and elsewhere; 1987–8)
MELANÍA MONTEVERDE-PENSÓ

Borgherini, Pierfrancesco (*b* Florence, 4 April 1480; *d* Florence, 11 Nov 1558). Italian banker and patron. His main activities were in his family's Florentine banking business. His father, Salvi di Francesco Borgherini, presented him and Margherita Acciaiuoli on their marriage in 1515 with furnishings for their bedroom in the Palazzo Borgherini (now the Palazzo Rosselli del Turco) in the Borgo Santi Apostoli, Florence. These were produced by the workshop of Baccio d'Agnolo and were decorated with scenes by Andrea del Sarto (*Life of Joseph the Hebrew*; Florence, Pitti), Pontormo (London, N.G.), Bacchiacca (Rome, Gal. Borghese and London, N.G.) and Francesco Granacci (Florence, Uffizi; for illustration *see* GRANACCI, FRANCESCO), who also painted a *Trinity* (Berlin, Staatl. Museen, N. G.) that adorned the same room. The fireplace by Baccio d'Agnolo is *in situ*; the richly carved chimney-piece by Benedetto di Rovezzano is in the Bargello, Florence.

Michelangelo became a client at the family bank's branch in Rome from 1515 and became a friend of Pierfrancesco, who requested a painting from him that was never executed. On Michelangelo's advice, he commissioned SEBASTIANO DEL PIOMBO to paint frescoes (1516–24) in the family chapel at S Pietro in Montorio, Rome. The family also employed del Sarto again: Pierfrancesco commissioned a *Virgin and Child* (Florence, Pitti) and his brother Giovanni Borgherini the *Holy Family with St John the Baptist* (New York, Met.) on the occasion of his marriage to Selvaggia Capponi in 1526. While no portrait of Pierfrancesco is known, one of *Giovanni Borgherini and his Tutor* (Washington, DC, N.G.A.) is attributed to the circle of Giorgione.

BIBLIOGRAPHY
DBI
G. Vasari: *Vite* (1550, rev. 2/1568), ed. G. Milanesi (1878–85), vi, pp. 261–2, 455
A. Braham: 'The Bed of Pierfrancesco Borgherini', *Burl. Mag.*, cxxi (1979), pp. 754–65
A. Cecchi: 'Storie di Giuseppe Ebreo', *Andrea del Sarto 1486–1530: Dipinti e disegni a Firenze* (exh. cat., ed. M. Chiarini; Milan, D'Angeli-Haeusler; Florence, Cent. Di, 1986), pp. 105–11 [with bibliog.]
ALESSANDRO CECCHI

Borghese. Italian family of ecclesiastics, patrons and collectors. The family originated from Siena but came to settle in Rome. Camillo Borghese was elected (1) Pope Paul V in 1605 and the family's fortune greatly expanded during his pontificate. He undertook numerous architectural projects in Rome, including the completion of St Peter's. The most significant patron and collector of the family was his nephew (2) Scipione Borghese, who was raised by his uncle to the title and rank of Cardinal Borghese. Scipione came to hold numerous different posts, which gave him a considerable income and allowed him to increase the family properties as well as indulge his passion for collecting. In Rome, Scipione had the Villa Borghese built (1612–15), which he used to house his extraordinary collection of antique and contemporary sculpture. This included several pieces by Bernini, whose work he was one of the first to collect. His painting collection, originally housed in the Palazzo Borghese, consisted of works by such Old Masters as Titian as well as many by contemporary painters, including Caravaggio. (3) Marcantonio Borghese IV renovated both the Palazzo Borghese and the Villa Borghese, employing a number of Neo-classical artists to redecorate several of the rooms.

His son Camillo Borghese (1775–1832) married (1803) Napoleon I's sister Pauline and sold many of the antiquities to the Emperor, while the remaining sculptures and painting collection were sold to the State in 1902 and are now housed in the Galleria Borghese in the Villa Borghese.

BIBLIOGRAPHY
G. Borghezio: *I Borghese* (Rome, 1954)
L. Ferrara: *Galleria Borghese* (Novara, 1956)
P. della Pergola: *Galleria Borghese*, 2 vols (Rome, 1959)
I. Faldi: *Galleria Borghese: Le sculture dal secolo XVI al XIX* (Rome, 1964)

(1) Pope Paul V [Camillo Borghese] (*b* Rome, 17 Sept 1552; elected 1605; *d* Rome, 28 Jan 1621). He received his doctorate in law from the University of Perugia and then entered the priesthood, advancing rapidly in the Curia. Elected to the papacy in 1605 he took the name of Paul V in honour of Paul IV, under whom his father's fortune had been made. He enriched Rome with many monuments, churches, palaces, fountains and works of art. As a patron he was in essence a successor to Sixtus V, attracted by collective artistic enterprises and urban planning. Official taste remained predominantly eclectic and cautious, and the older generation of Late Mannerist painters and sculptors received important commissions. Yet where art under Sixtus V had been limited by the rigid dictates of the Council of Trent, Paul V's pontificate marked the beginning of a renewed freedom of expression; he recognized some more modern artists of higher quality.

Paul V was a frugal and charitable man who distributed huge amounts to the poor. Yet through his patronage he sought to add lustre to his name and almost immediately elevated his nephew Scipione Caffarelli to the rank and name of Cardinal Borghese, gave him lucrative posts and encouraged him to amass an enormous collection of antique and contemporary art. He also appointed his brothers to important positions and gave them the Palazzo Borghese in Rome, purchased in 1605 when he was still a cardinal. The conservative court architect Flaminio Ponzio was engaged to complete and enlarge it. Paul V's most grandiose architectural project was the completion of St Peter's (*see* ROME, §V, 14(ii)(a)). In 1605 he approved the demolition of the remainder of Constantine's basilica, with the proviso that its relics, papal tombs and works of art be transferred to the new building or, where this was impossible, recorded. He then supported the plans of the progressive architect Carlo Maderno to add a longitudinal nave to the Greek-cross church designed by Donato Bramante and Michelangelo, in order to better accommodate the vast crowds attending papal ceremonies. The façade (1608–12) included the huge papal coat of arms and inscription in honour of Paul V, *principis apostolorum*, which gave rise to the jest that Peter had given way to Paul. The vaults of the nave (1609–14) and the portico (1608–11) were decorated (1618) with stucco ornament and scenes from the *Acts of the Apostles* by Giovan Battista Ricci (1545–1620); over the central entrance Ambrogio Bonvicino (*c.* 1552–1622) carved the academic relief, *Christ Handing the Keys to St Peter* (1601). In 1615 Maderno designed a *confessio*, or chapel, under the high altar to facilitate public access to St Peter's underground tomb.

Paul V's taste is most clearly displayed in the Cappella Paolina, designed by Ponzio, in S Maria Maggiore (*see*

ROME, §V, 20), where he had been chaplain. Giovanni Battista Crescenzi was Superintendent of Works for the project (as he was of others commissioned by Paul V). The chapel houses an icon of the Virgin attributed to St Luke, and serves as a funerary chapel for Paul V's family and for the family of his predecessor Pope Clement VIII. It followed the design of the chapel of Sixtus V on the opposite side of the church, but surpassed it in the splendour and richness of its decoration (1610–13). Many ancient monuments were ransacked for its marble. Sculptors, predominantly Late Mannerists, included Ambrogio Bonvicino, Ippolito Buzio (d 1634), Antonio Peracca, Camillo Mariani, Nicolas Cordier, Pietro Bernini and the more modern Stefano Maderno and Francesco Mochi. The paintings were carried out under the direction of the Cavaliere d'Arpino; Lodovico Cigoli frescoed the dome, while the arches and lunette over the papal tombs were frescoed in a newer style by Guido Reni and Giovanni Lanfranco. In 1614 the Pope instructed Maderno to erect before the church a white marble column from the basilica of Maxentius; it was crowned with a gilt bronze statue of the *Virgin* by Guillaume Berthelot.

The transformation of the Palazzo del Quirinale (*see* ROME, §V, 26) was another of Paul V's major projects. In 1605 Ponzio began the construction of two new wings; on his death in 1613 they were completed by Maderno. The wing on the Via Pia (1614–15) contains the Cappella Paolina and the Sala dei Corazzieri (formerly the Sala Regia). The Sala dei Corazzieri was decorated (1616–17) by a team of artists that included Agostino Tassi, Lanfranco and Carlo Saraceni, an unusual combination of Bolognese and Caravaggesque artists, with frescoes showing delegations from the African Congo (1608) and Japan (1615) being received by the Pope. Through Scipione Borghese, Guido Reni won important papal commissions: in 1608 he decorated the Sala delle Nozze Aldobrandini with the *Story of Samson* as well as the vault of the Sala delle Dame in the Vatican (partially destr.), and in 1610 he decorated the Palazzo del Quirinale's private chapel, the Cappella Annunziata, with scenes from the *Life of the Virgin*.

Paul V's concern for the poor led him to build an aqueduct to bring water to Trastevere in Rome. In part this was a restoration of the aqueduct built by Trajan, but much of it was newly constructed, beginning in 1607, by Maderno and Pompeo Targone. The fountain of the Acqua Paola, which received the water on the Janiculum, was constructed by Giovanni Fontana and Ponzio, and its design competed with that of Sixtus V's Acqua Felice. Paul V had many other fountains erected in Rome, including one in the piazza of the synagogue in the ghetto, which had previously lacked good water. Maderno built three fountains in the Vatican gardens; the Fontana degli Specchi, Fontana delle Torri and Fontana dello Scoglio. Several new roads were also built, among them the Via delle Convertite, the Via della Propaganda towards Piazza di Spagna, an avenue linking S Maria in Trastevere and S Francesco a Ripa, and what is now the Via Garibaldi, to lead to the Acqua Paola.

In 1606 Paul V had summoned Pietro Bernini to Rome, and his son Gianlorenzo Bernini soon attracted his attention and that of Scipione Borghese: in 1618 Bernini carved a vividly naturalistic portrait bust of *Paul V* (Rome, Gal.

Borghese). Both the lavishness and the forms of Paul V's patronage were later emulated by successive 17th-century popes.

BIBLIOGRAPHY

L. von Pastor: *Geschichte der Päpste seit dem Ausgang des Mittelalters*, 24 vols (Freiburg, 1891–1924); Eng. trans., xxv (London, 1940), pp. 37–444

H. Hibbard: 'The Architecture of the Palazzo Borghese', *Mem. Amer. Acad. Rome*, xxvii (1962)

F. Haskell: *Patrons and Painters: A Study in the Relations between Italian Art and Society in the Age of the Baroque* (New York, 1963)

M. C. Dorati: 'Gli scultori della Cappella Paolina di Santa Maria Maggiore', *Commentari*, xviii (1967), pp. 231–60

C. Heilmann: 'Acqua Paola and the Urban Planning of Paul V Borghese', *Burl. Mag.*, cxii (1970), pp. 656–62

H. Hibbard: *Carlo Maderno and Roman Architecture, 1580–1630*, Stud. Archit., x (London, 1971)

T. Magnuson: *Rome in the Age of Bernini*, 2 vols (New Jersey, 1986) [extensive bibliog. and illus. regarding Paul V]

(2) Cardinal **Scipione Borghese** [Caffarelli] (*b* Rome, ?1576; *d* Rome, 2 Oct 1633). Nephew of (1) Paul V. He studied philosophy at the Jesuit Collegio Romano and then, subsidized by his uncle, law at the University of Perugia. When his uncle was elected Pope in 1605 he was made a cardinal and given the Borghese name and arms. Over the years he obtained many important and lucrative positions. No other cardinal had ever held so many offices and his resulting income was fabulous: in 1609 over 108,000 scudi and in 1619 over 189,000 scudi. With this wealth he began to increase the property and position of the Borghese family, purchasing large tracts of land in the Roman Campagna.

At the beginning of Paul's pontificate Scipione purchased his main residence (now Palazzo Torlonia) in the Borgo Leonino and in 1611 began to build a palace (now the Palazzo Rospigliosi–Pallavicini) on the site of the Baths of Constantine (land that was a gift from Paul V) so as to be near the Pope when the latter was at the Palazzo del Quirinale. Initially he employed the papal architect, Flaminio Ponzio, who worked in collaboration with Carlo Maderno. After Ponzio's death Giovanni Vasanzio took his place. The garden palace near the Quirinale was a sprawling collection of buildings decorated with frescoes of landscapes and pagan themes that convey the lighter taste of a new era. There was a casino (destr.) decorated by Lodovico Cigoli with paintings of the story of *Psyche* (1611–13; Rome, Pal. Braschi) and the Casino delle Muse, decorated by Agostino Tassi and Orazio Gentileschi with frescoes of muses and musicians within an illusionistic framework (1611–12; *in situ*; for illustration *see* TASSI, AGOSTINO). A third casino was adorned with landscape paintings of the *Four Seasons* (1613–14; *in situ*) by Paul Bril. The frescoed ceiling, depicting *Aurora* (1613–14; *in situ*), was painted by Guido Reni, who was part of Scipione's household for some years from 1608 and received commissions from the Pope on his patron's recommendation. Scipione apparently grew tired of the palace and in 1616, before it was finished, sold it to the Duke of Altemps, concentrating thereafter on the construction and decoration of his villa on the Pincio (now the Villa Borghese), which was also near the Quirinale. The project was started in 1612, again with Ponzio as architect and, after his death, Vasanzio (1613–15). It was intended as a rural retreat and to house the Cardinal's collection of antique and contemporary sculpture. His collection of antique sculpture was the most celebrated of his time. In 1607 he purchased 278 statues from the Ceuli, a Roman banking family, and in 1609 the collection of the sculptor Giovanni Battista della Porta (?1542–97), who also restored antiquities. Among the famous items in Scipione's collection were the BORGHESE GLADIATOR, discovered in 1611; the *Hermaphrodite*, excavated near S Maria della Vittoria, with its mattress added *c.* 1622 by Gianlorenzo Bernini; the *Centaur with Cupid*; the Borghese Vase; the *Silenus with Infant Bacchus*; and the *Dying Seneca* (all Paris, Louvre). They were purchased by Napoleon I from Prince Camillo Borghese in 1807. A relief of *Marcus Curtius*, a fragment heavily restored by Pietro Bernini in 1617, was positioned outside the Villa (now in the entrance hall). The collection was open to the public and many artists studied there, among them Gianlorenzo Bernini (*see* BERNINI, (2)), whose talent Scipione may have been the first collector to discover. His *Goat Amalthea with the Infant Jupiter and a Faun* (*c.* 1609; Rome, Gal. Borghese), which Scipione owned, was influenced by the realism of Hellenistic sculpture. Scipione also possessed the *Aeneas, Anchises and Ascanius Leaving Troy* (1618–19) and commissioned *Pluto and Proserpina* (1621–2; both Rome, Gal. Borghese), which he then gave to Ludovico Ludovisi, nephew of the new Pope, Gregory XV, as a gesture of goodwill. To replace it he commissioned *Apollo and Daphne* (1622–4; Rome, Gal. Borghese). *David* (1623; Rome, Gal. Borghese), a work which suggests Bernini's admiration for the Borghese *Gladiator*, was the last work commissioned before Bernini was employed by Urban VIII. In 1632 Bernini made two busts of Scipione (both Rome, Gal. Borghese; see fig.), which brilliantly suggest his pleasure-loving, vivacious personality. (The second was made because a flaw was discovered in the marble of the first when it was almost finished.) From MATTHIAS WALBAUM Scipione commissioned the impressive ebony and silver Borghese Altar (*c.* 1613; Rome, Gal. Borghese) for his private chapel.

As a collector of paintings Scipione broke with the austere taste of Counter-Reformation patrons, his wide-ranging and eclectic taste embracing Old Master paintings and works by contemporary artists, including the older generation of Late Mannerists and Bolognese and Caravaggesque painters. He was one of the earliest admirers of Caravaggio, among whose paintings he owned the *Madonna of the Serpent* (1605–6), commissioned by the papal grooms, the Palafrenieri, and *David with the Head of Goliath* (both Rome, Gal. Borghese). Scipione was also influential in launching the career not only of Guido Reni, but also of Giovanni Lanfranco, who decorated the vault of the loggia of the Villa Borghese with a fresco of the *Council of the Gods* (1624–5; *in situ*). His impressive array of Old Masters included Titian's *Sacred and Profane Love* (*c.* 1514) and *Education of Cupid* (*c.* 1565), Federico Barocci's *Aeneas's Flight From Troy* (1586–9; all Rome, Gal. Borghese) and pictures by Raphael, Veronese, Dosso Dossi, Domenichino and Cavaliere d'Arpino (Rome, Gal. Borghese). He could be utterly ruthless in satisfying his desire for works of art that appealed to him. Raphael's *Deposition* was stolen on his orders from the Baglioni family chapel in Perugia and brought by night to his

Scipione Borghese by Gianlorenzo Bernini, marble, over life-size, 1632 (Rome, Galleria Borghese)

collection. He confiscated 106 pictures from the Cavaliere d'Arpino, whom he had previously employed, when the artist was in trouble with the tax collector, and had Domenichino imprisoned for not selling him his *Diana with Nymphs at Play* (1618; Rome, Gal. Borghese), which had been commissioned by Cardinal Pietro Aldobrandini.

In addition to building his own collections, Cardinal Borghese was almost certainly Paul V's adviser in artistic matters and contributed to several public works in Rome. He commissioned Giovanni Battista Soria to build the façade of S Maria della Vittoria (1626) and to design the façade of S Gregorio Magno (begun 1629). In 1608 Reni was commissioned to decorate two chapels in the latter church: the chapel of S Silvia, in which he painted angelic musicians over the apse (1608–9; largely destr.), and the oratory of S Andrea, where he painted *St Andrew Led to Martyrdom* (1609), while Domenichino painted the *Flagellation of St Andrew* (both *in situ*). Lanfranco also worked in the oratory as an assistant. In his will Borghese left large bequests for restoration works to be carried out in the basilica of S Lorenzo in Lucina and in the Borghese Chapel at S Maria Maggiore, where he was buried.

See also FRASCATI and fig. 2.

BIBLIOGRAPHY
J. Manilli: *Villa Borghese fuori di Porta Pinciana* (Rome, 1650)
G. P. Bellori: *Vite* (1672); ed. E. Borea (1976), pp. 83, 223, 224, 317, 342, 365, 368, 395, 497, 499, 509, 539
F. Baldinucci: *Vita del Cavaliere Gio. Lorenzo Bernino scultore, architetto, e pittore* (Florence, 1682); Eng. trans., intro. R. Enggass (University Park, PA, 1966), pp. 11–12, 14, 113

L. von Pastor: *Geschichte der Päpste* (Freiburg, 1891–1924)
Catalogue des marbres antiques et des objets d'art formant le Musée du Pavillon à la Villa Borghese à Rome, provenant de l'héritage des princes Borghese (Rome, 1893)
I. Faldi: 'Note sulle scultore borghesiane del Bernini', *Boll. A.*, ser. 4, xxxviii (1953), pp. 140–46
H. Hibbard: 'Scipione Borghese's Garden Palace on the Quirinal', *J. Soc. Archit. Hist.*, xxiii (1964), pp. 163–92
H. Heilmann: 'Die Entstehungsgeschichte der Villa Borghese in Rom', *Münch. Jb. Bild. Kst*, xxiv/3 (1973), pp. 97–158
F. Haskell and N. Penny: *Taste and the Antique* (New Haven and London, 1981) [a thorough discussion of Scipione Borghese's collection of antique sculpture; excellent pls]
T. Magnuson: *Rome in the Age of Bernini*, 2 vols (New Jersey, 1986)

(3) Prince Marcantonio Borghese IV (*b* Rome, 14 Sept 1730; *d* Rome, 18 March 1800). Descendant of (1) Paul V. He was the first son of Prince Camillo Borghese (1693–1763) and Agnese Colonna and, by marrying Anna Maria Salviati in 1775, he brought the Salviati inheritance into the Borghese family. Around 1775, too, he began his renovations of the Palazzo Borghese and the Villa Borghese. Many artists from different countries were employed for *c.* 20 years at both locations, most of them working in the Neo-classical style and taking their subjects largely from Classical mythology.

At the Palazzo, home to the family collection of paintings, almost all the rooms of the ground floor were redecorated *c.* 1775. Gioacchino Agricola (1758–85) painted the *Chariot of Venus*; Mariano Rossi, *Venus and Cupid*; and Gaetano Lapis, *Venus Presented to Jupiter*. Ermenegildo Costantini (*fl* 1764–91) painted the *Triumph of the Borghese*, implying the family's inclusion in the company of mythical heroes. Francesco Caccianiga provided *Aurora* and Laurent Pécheux *Jupiter Marrying Cupid and Psyche* (1774). The redecoration of the Villa, supervised by the architects ANTONIO ASPRUCCI and his son Mario Asprucci (1764–1804), was aimed at giving the rooms of this early 17th-century building a more fashionable, classical look that would relate fittingly to the sculptures displayed in them. The relief panel of *Marcus Curtius*, restored by Pietro Bernini for Cardinal Scipione, was brought indoors and placed above the door in the entrance hall. On the hall's ceiling, Rossi depicted another saviour of Rome: *Marcus Furius Camillus Expelling the Gauls* (1776–9). Other ornamentation in the hall was undertaken by various artists and artisans, including Vincenzo Pacetti, Maximilian Laboureur (1739–1812), Pietro Antonio Rotari and Wenzel Peter (1745–1829). In Room III Pietro Angeletti (*fl* 1758–86) painted the *Metamorphosis of Daphne* to accompany Bernini's group of *Apollo and Daphne*. Room V, which contained the famous Borghese *Hermaphrodite* (Louvre, Paris), was decorated by Nicola Buonvicini with incidents from the myth of *Hermaphroditus and Salmacis*. Room XIX shows episodes from the *Life of Paris* (1782–4) by Gavin Hamilton, who also conducted excavations on the prince's property at Gabii, outside Rome, where he discovered the antique *Diane de Gabies* (Louvre, Paris).

The grounds of the Villa were also improved, largely to attract more visitors to the collections. The Asprucci designed a new main entrance on the Muro Torto, in grand Neo-classical style embellished with Borghese heraldic devices, and closer to the Piazza del Popolo and Piazza di Spagna, centres visited by aristocratic tourists from northern Europe. From this entrance the road led to the Casino del Muro Torto (now the Aranciera), probably also by the Asprucci, and then to an intersection with a grand avenue, at either end of which was built a temple in antique style: the Tempio di Escalupio (begun 1785; attributed to the Asprucci), set in a small artificial lake, and the Tempietto di Diana (1789), probably entirely by Mario Asprucci, raised on an artificial hill. Nearby the Asprucci created the Piazza di Siena, a hippodrome recalling both Roman tradition and the famous horse race, the *Palio*, of Siena, the Borghese family's town of origin. Other artists helped to transform the grounds: the Casino dell' Orologio (finished 1791) was built by Nicola Fagioli and in 1792 became home to many of the Borghese collection's antiquities, in particular those found at Gabii. Cristoforo Unterberger (1732–98) was responsible for the more Romantic Fountain of the Sea Horses, with horses sculpted in travertine by Luigi Salibeni (finished 1791). The mock ruin of the Tempio di Faustina (finished 1792) owes its sense of authenticity to Mario Asprucci and its picturesque quality to Unterberger.

On Marcantonio's death, his son Camillo Borghese (1775–1832) inherited his title and the collections, but in 1807, to ease his financial embarrassment, Camillo sold many of the prized antiquities to his brother-in-law, Napoleon I. This prompted his brother Francesco Borghese to create the Fidecomisso Borghese (1833), which eventually sold both the painting and the sculpture collections intact to the Italian State in 1902, and they are now held in the Galleria Borghese in the Villa Borghese.

BIBLIOGRAPHY
F. Haskell and N. Penny: *Taste and the Antique* (New Haven and London, 1981), pp. 191–3
B. di Gaddo: *Villa Borghese: Il Giardino e le Architetture* (Rome, 1985), pp. 111–52 [excellent text, bibliog. and pls]
C. Pietrangeli: *Palazzo Borghese e la sua decorazione*, Quaderni del Circolo della Caccia, i (Rome, 1985), p. 9
SHARON GREGORY, DAVID L. BERSHAD

Borghese, Maria-Paoletta, Princess. *See* BONAPARTE, (7).

Borghese, Michele. *See* CIAMPANTI, (1).

Borghese Gladiator [Borghese Warrior]. This statue (h. 1.99 m; Paris, Louvre) portrays a warrior lunging forward with his shield arm extended and his sword arm drawn back. Signed by Agasias of Ephesos, it is in the stylistic tradition of Lysippos and may be a copy of *c.* 100 BC of a work by his school. It was found in 1611 at Nettuno, near Rome, and by 1613 it formed part of the Borghese collection of antiquities. By 1650 it was on display in a ground-floor room of the Villa Borghese in Rome, but in 1807 it was sold to Napoleon Bonaparte along with a substantial part of the Borghese collection. In 1811 it was on display in the Salle d'Apollon at the Musée Napoléon in Paris, and by 1815 it had its own room, named in its honour. During the 17th century the statue was unanimously identified as a gladiator, originally holding a sword and/or a shield, and this interpretation is still broadly accepted. Later it was suggested that the figure might represent a boxer or discus thrower. Winckelmann believed that the work portrayed a specific hero or historical figure, and Carlo Fea proposed one of the two

Ajaxes or Leonidas; Ennio Quirino Visconti suggested Telamon. The *Gladiator* was the most admired of the ancient sculptures in the Borghese collection. The first bronze cast of it was one made for Charles I, King of England (*c.* 1630; Windsor Castle, Berks, Royal Col.), while in 1638 François Perrier devoted four plates to the work in his catalogue of engravings of the most beautiful statues in Rome (*Segmenta nobilium signorum et statuarum*). Bernini carved his *David* for the Villa Borghese in competition with the *Gladiator*. It was zealously studied by artists as an anatomical model: casts of the work appear in a view of the Académie Royale de Peinture et de Sculpture in Paris by Charles-Joseph Natoire (1745; Montpellier, Mus. Atger) and in the painting by Henry Singleton of the *Royal Academicians Assembled in their Council Chamber* (1795; London, RA).

BIBLIOGRAPHY

G. Winckelmann: *Geschichte der Kunst des Alterthums* (Dresden, 1764), rev. It. trans. by C. Fea as *Storia delle arti del disegno presso gli antichi*, ii (Rome, 1784), pp. 360–62

Frédéric, Compte de Clarac: *Description du Musée Royal des Antiques du Louvre* (Paris, 1830), p. 117

M. Robertson: *A History of Greek Art* (Cambridge, 1975), p. 543

F. Haskell and N. Penny: *Taste and the Antique* (New Haven and London, 1981), pp. 221–4

LUCA LEONCINI

Borghini, Raffaele (*b* Florence, *c.* 1537; *d* Florence, 26 Dec 1588). Italian writer. He was born into a noble Florentine family and epitomizes the courtly and literary world of Florence in the second half of the 16th century. As a young man he was connected with those Florentine nobles who opposed the Medici, but later he became a supporter of the powerful family. Most of his life was spent in Florence, except for a period (1572–5) in France, where he was perhaps forced to stay for economic reasons, and where he enjoyed the patronage of the Comte de Carcès and his wife Marguerite.

On his return to Florence, Borghini began his prodigious activity as a man of letters, poet and writer of comedies, producing *La donna costante* in 1575 and *L'amante furioso* in 1584. He also began to frequent the cultured society around the court of Francesco I de' Medici and moved in the circles of the Capponi, Vecchietti, Valori and Pitti families. In this milieu, under the influence of Francesco I, he assembled a collection that included not only works of art but also bizarre and curious natural objects, achieving a mixture of 'naturalia' and 'artificialia' that was typical of the German *Wunderkammer*. In 1584 he wrote his most celebrated book, *Il riposo di Raffaele Borghini in cui della pittura e della scultura si favella, de' più famose opere loro si fa menzione, e le cose principali appartenenti a dette arti s' insegnano* (Raffaele Borghini's 'Riposo', in which painting and sculpture are spoken of, the most famous works are mentioned and the main elements of those arts are taught). The work is divided into four books, the first two are of a theoretical nature, while the third and fourth contain important information on the artistic and cultural world of Florence. In the *Riposo* Borghini relied for information mainly on Vasari, and he may be considered Vasari's successor. Although much of the treatise lacks originality, it is useful as a source where it deals with artists contemporary with the author, such as those

who worked in the *studiolo* of Francesco I, or Federico Zuccari or sculptors such as Giambologna, who was also probably a friend of Borghini. The book is in the form of imaginary dialogues supposed to have taken place in a villa, Il Riposo (still in existence) near Florence, which belonged to the collector Bernardo Vecchietti, and which gave the book its name. The participants, who spend four spring afternoons discussing art, are Vecchietti, Baccio Valori (mentioned in other sources for his vast culture and his patronage of artists and writers), Girolamo Michelozzi and the sculptor Ridolfo Sirigatti (*fl* 1594–1601). They take as their point of departure Vecchietti's collections displayed in the villa and move on to discuss other important collections in Florence. The intended audience for the *Riposo* was a new one, that of the amateur, the refined and dilettante collector, the nobleman who, having abandoned his political interests, passed his time in the *studioli* and in cultivated conversation. Borghini's portrait (untraced) was painted by Sirigatti. He was buried in the church of Santa Croce in Florence.

WRITINGS

Il riposo di Raffaele Borghini . . . (Florence, 1584); facs., ed. M. Rosci (Milan, 1967), 2 vols [with essays, annotated bibliog. and good index]

BIBLIOGRAPHY

DBI [with bibliog. up to 1969]

A. Blunt: *Artistic Theory in Italy, 1450–1600* (Oxford, 1940)

P. Barocchi, ed.: *Scritti d'arte del cinquecento*, 3 vols (Milan and Naples, 1971–7), i, pp. 108–9, 674–90, 936–44; ii, pp. 1239–42, 1982–91

D. Heikamp: 'The Grotto of the Fata Morgana and Giambologna's Marble Gorgon', *Ant. Viva*, xx (1981), pp. 12–31

M. Rossi: 'Leonardo filosofo, Lomazzo e Borghini, 1584: Due linee di tradizione dei pensieri e precetti di Leonardo sull'arte', *Fra Risacimento Manierismo e realtà: Scritti di storia dell'arte in memoria di A. M. Brizio* (Florence, 1984), pp. 53–78

DONATELLA PEGAZZANO

Borghini, Vincenzo (Maria) (*b* Florence, 29 Oct 1515; *d* Florence, 18 Aug 1580). Italian philologist, historian and artistic adviser. On 20 June 1531 he entered the Benedictine Order at the Badia in Florence, took his vows a year later and was appointed a deacon in 1537. While there he was mainly concerned with studying Classical authors. After spending fairly brief periods in Perugia, Rome, Montecassino, Naples, Arezzo and Venice he settled in Florence in 1544 with the intention of devoting himself mainly to the study of literature and history. However, in 1552 Cosimo I de' Medici entrusted him with the time-consuming post of *spedaglino* (hospitaller) to the Ospedale di S Maria degl'Innocenti.

Borghini had become friendly with Giorgio Vasari and, along with Cosimo Bartoli and Pier Francesco Giambullari (1495–1555), he had corrected and provided plates for the first edition (1550) of Vasari's *Vite*. He collaborated with Vasari in several projects for Cosimo I: in 1563 he provided the programme for Vasari's ceiling decorations in the Salone dei Cinquecento in the Palazzo Vecchio, covering the history of Florence from its foundation until Cosimo I's rule (see MEDICI, DE', (14) and fig.). In selecting these scenes he was also contributing as a historian to the debate regarding the legend of how Florence had been founded. From 1563 to 1565 he was Luogotenente of the recently founded Accademia del Disegno (see FLORENCE, §V, 1), whose constitution he shaped, and in 1564 he stage-managed Michelangelo's funeral ceremony, establishing the ideal measurements for his tomb in Santa Croce. Subsequently he was employed as an iconographical adviser on staged festivities and public ceremonies. He designed a complicated piece of festive apparatus for the wedding (1565) of Francesco I de' Medici and Joanna of Austria. Borghini's abilities as an *inventore* (visualizer) are most evident in the programme for the *studiolo* that Vasari built in the Palazzo Vecchio in 1570 for Francesco I de' Medici (*see* MEDICI, DE', (16) and STUDIOLO, fig. 2), where he associated the sciences with the four elements. In 1574 he designed the décor for the funeral of Cosimo I de' Medici, who had been created Grand Duke of Tuscany in 1569, and three years later he staged the baptism of Filippo de' Medici.

Borghini was appointed to the Deputazione sopra i Monasteri of Florence and Siena in 1570, and in 1574 Cardinal Alessandro de' Medici requested his appointment as Archbishop of Pisa. Borghini declined the nomination as his true interests lay in the literary and artistic circles of Florence. His research into Classical authors resulted in the *Annotazioni e discorsi sopra alcuni luoghi del Decamerone.* He wrote several essays on Dante's *Divine Comedy* and published Franco Sacchetti's *Trecento novelle* and a new edition of the *Novellino.* His research into the history and language of Florence was published posthumously (Florence, 1584–5) under the title *Discorsi, raccolti e dati in luce dei Deputati per suo testamento.* These *Discorsi* include the first scholarly history of the Church in Florence, a study on the development of the Italian language and several essays on the origins of Florence.

WRITINGS

Discorsi, raccolti e dati in luce dei Deputati per suo testamento, 2 vols (Florence, 1584–5)

BIBLIOGRAPHY

M. Barbi: 'Degli studi di V. Borghini sopra la storia e la lingua di Firenze', *Propugnatore*, n. s. 2, x (1889), pp. 5–71

A. Lorenzoni, ed.: *I ricordi di Don V. Borghini* (Florence, 1909)

A. Legrenzi: *V. Borghini: Studio critico*, 2 vols (Udine, 1910)

P. G. Conti: *L'apparato per le nozze di Francesco de' Medici e di Giovanna d'Austria: Da lettere inedite di Vincenzo Borghini* (Florence, 1936)

S. J. Schaefer: *The Studiolo of Francesco I de' Medici in the Palazzo Vecchio in Florence* (diss., Bryn Mawr College, 1976), pp. 2–86

Lo stanzino del principe in Palazzo Vecchio (exh. cat., ed. M. Dezzi Bardeschi; Florence, Pal. Vecchio, 1980)

R. A. Scorza: 'Vincenzo Borghini and *invenzione*: The Florentine *apparato* of 1565', *J. Warb. & Court. Inst.*, xliv (1981), pp. 57–75

A. Cecchi: '"*Invenzioni per quadri*" di Don Vincenzo Borghini', *Paragone*, xxxiii/383–5 (1982), pp. 89–96

MARLIS VON HESSERT

Borgia [Borja]. Spanish and Italian family of patrons. They claimed descent from the kings of Aragon but probably originated from the Aragonese town of Borja. In return for their loyal service against the Moors during the 13th-century conquest of Valencia, they received land in and around the town of Játiva, henceforth becoming influential members of the local nobility. The elections to the papacy of Alfonso Borgia as (1) Calixtus III (1455) and Rodrigo Borgia as (2) Alexander VI (1492) marked a further rise in the family fortunes. Through nepotism the Borgias, among them Alexander's son, (3) Cesare Borgia, gained titles and possessions—both ecclesiastical and secular—in Italy, Spain and France. After the death of Alexander VI in 1503, the family was eclipsed but, as a consequence of skilful matrimonial alliances, including those of Alexander's daughter, (4) Lucrezia Borgia, survived within the Neapolitan, Ferrarese, Spanish and French nobility. Giovanni Battista Borgia, 3rd Prince of Squillace, built the village of Borgia on his southern Italian estates in 1547. In Spain, Maria Enríquez Borgia, widow of Alexander VI's son, Juan (Giovanni) Borgia, Duca di Gandía (?1474–97), embellished and endowed the collegiate church of Gandía and gave commissions to the Valencian sculptor Damián Forment and the Italian painter Paolo da San Leocadio, as well as initiating the family's patronage of the convent of the Poor Clares in Gandía. Later members of the family included Francisco Borja y Aragon (1510–72), who founded the city of S Francisco Borja, Mexico, and the National University of S Marcos (1551) in Lima, Peru, and the antiquarian and writer (5) Stefano Borgia.

BIBLIOGRAPHY

E. Bertaux: 'Monuments et souvenirs des Borgia dans le royaume de Valence', *Gaz. B.-A.*, xxxix/50 (1908), pp. 89–113, 198–220

M. Mallett: *The Borgias* (London, 1969)

DIANA NORMAN

(1) Pope **Calixtus III** [Alfonso Borgia] (*b* Játiva, 31 Dec 1378; elected 8 April 1455; *d* Rome, 6 Aug 1458). In Spain he patronized the Valencian painter Jacomart, from whom he commissioned a retable for the Colegiata in Játiva (1451–5; *in situ*), and initiated the construction of a chapel in Valencia Cathedral for the remains of St Louis of Toulouse (1430–86). During his pontificate Calixtus was obsessively preoccupied with organizing a crusade to recapture Constantinople, which had fallen to the Turks in May 1453. To this end he imposed taxes, sold gold- and silverwork and even rare bookbindings and halted the grandiose plan of his predecessor Nicholas V for the rebuilding of Rome. Humanists at the papal court criticized Calixtus for his apparent lack of interest in the arts, yet his passion for books was such that he himself made copies of manuscripts for his private library, while his accounts show large payments for bookbindings of velvet and silk and for plaques of gold and silver. He had an inventory made of the Latin manuscripts (both Rome, Vatican, Bib. Apostolica) collected and commissioned by Nicholas V, thus producing the first catalogue of the Vatican library. Calixtus also commissioned banners (untraced) for his galleys from painters and suits of armour (untraced) for his commanders from goldsmiths. He continued the programme of refurbishing Early Christian churches begun by Martin V, restoring the churches of SS Quattro Coronati, S Callisto, S Sebastiano, S Lorenzo fuori le Mura, S Prisca and the sancta sanctorum of St John Lateran. He also planned the present ceiling of S Maria Maggiore, which was installed by his nephew (2) Alexander VI.

BIBLIOGRAPHY

E. Muentz: *Les Arts à la cour des papes pendant le XVe et le XVIe siècle*, i (Paris, 1878), pp. 190–219

L. von Pastor: *Geschichte der Päpste seit dem Ausgang des Mittelalters*, i (Freiburg, 1885, 12/1955), pp. 655–794

S. Schueller-Piroli: *Die Borgia Päpste Kalixt III und Alexander VI* (Munich, 1980), pp. 13–82

(2) Pope **Alexander VI** [Rodrigo Borgia] (*b* Játiva, nr Valencia, 1 Jan 1431; elected 11 Aug 1492; *d* Rome, 18 Aug 1503). Nephew of (1) Calixtus III. His patronage reflected his love of sumptuousness and pomp. As a cardinal he built the palace opposite the Palazzo Piccolomini in the cathedral square at Pienza and the Palazzo Sforza Cesarini in Rome, which was his residence until his accession to the papacy and was compared to the Golden House of Nero. In 1473 he commissioned from Andrea Bregno for S Maria del Popolo a marble tabernacle, known as the Borgia Altar, that stood on the main altar of the church until the 17th century, when it was moved to the sacristy.

The reign of Alexander VI was governed by his vanity, sensuality and the promotion of his four illegitimate children, Juan, (3) Cesare, (4) Lucrezia and Gioffredo (b 1481/2). In 1501 he created Cesare Duke of Romagna, the largest province in the Papal States, and from then until the end of his reign pursued the aim of appropriating for his family the entire Papal States and all of central Italy. Enraged at the denunciations of papal corruption by the Florentine reformer Girolamo Savonarola, Alexander excommunicated him and had him tortured and burned at the stake.

Next to the wing of Nicholas V at the Vatican Palace Alexander built the tower known as the Torre Borgia. It was completed in 1494 and contains two of the six rooms, the Sala delle Sibille and the Sala del Credo, of the Pope's private apartment, the Appartamento Borgia, that Bernardino Pinturicchio and his assistants decorated with frescoes between 1492 and 1495 (see ROME, §V, 14(iii)). The Appartamento Borgia, which was virtually unknown before it was restored and opened to the public in 1897, is the culminating example of the taste for ornamental richness and narrative detail in art commissioned by the papacy that began with Martin V's employment of Gentile da Fabriano. The most conspicuous traits of the five rooms that preserve the work of Pinturicchio and his collaborators are the liberal use of gold and jewelled decoration and the profusion of personal or family insignia, for example the double crown of Aragon, the device of Alexander formed by pennant-like flames and the heraldic Borgia bull.

The Sala delle Sibille and the Sala del Credo, embellished with lunettes containing, in one, paired sibyls and prophets and, in the other, paired prophets and apostles, are austere in comparison with the three rooms in the wing of Nicholas V. Alexander's study, the Sala delle Arti Liberali, with personifications of the Liberal Arts on elaborate thrones, is mainly the work of Pinturicchio's assistant, Antonio del Massaro (fl 1489–1509), known as il Pastura. The most sumptuous room, and Pinturicchio's masterpiece, is the Sala dei Santi. On its ceiling, emulating ceiling decorations in the Golden House of Nero, are ornamental compositions of the legends of Isis and Osiris and the Egyptian bull-god Apis, to whom Alexander's ancestry had been supposedly traced by one of the humanists at his court. In the grand mural of *St Catherine of Alexandria Disputing with Pagan Philosophers before the Emperor Maximian*, the Arch of Constantine in the background is surmounted by the Borgia-Apis bull, and in the *Resurrection* in the Sala dei Misteri della Fede, which was Alexander's private dining-room, a portrait of Alexander was inserted next to the figure of the Risen Christ. The patronage of Alexander VI established Pinturicchio, who had already served Alexander's predecessors Innocent VIII and Sixtus IV, as the pre-eminent painter at the Vatican during the last quarter of the 15th century.

In 1497 Alexander began the Palazzo della Sapienza, which until 1935 housed the University of Rome, and visited the site in 1499. He rebuilt the ancient Roman Porta Settimiana at the end of the Via della Lungara. At S Maria Maggiore he installed the coffered wooden ceiling that had been planned by his uncle (1) Calixtus III. It was completed in 1498 and is said to have been gilded with the first gold brought from the New World (see ROME, §V, 20). At the Castel Sant'Angelo, Alexander commissioned the architect Antonio da Sangallo (i) to design a new tower that stood until the reign of Urban VIII (1623–44), and a new entrance portal. Following an explosion in 1497, he commissioned Sangallo to rebuild the residential chambers of the Castel Sant'Angelo and had them decorated by Pinturicchio with frescoes of episodes from his pontificate (destr.).

In preparation for the papal jubilee of 1500, Alexander laid out the Via Alessandrina (now part of Via della Conciliazione) between the Castel Sant'Angelo and the Vatican Palace, parallel to the Borgo Sant'Angelo built by Sixtus IV for the jubilee of 1475 (see ROME, §II, 3). At St Peter's Alexander completed the Benediction loggia that had been begun by Pius II in 1461. It was destroyed in the early 17th century, when Carlo Maderno built the present façade of the basilica, but it appears in the background of Raphael's fresco of the *Fire in the Borgo* in the Vatican *stanze* (see FRESCO, figs 1 and 4; SECCO PAINTING, fig. 1).

BIBLIOGRAPHY

L. von Pastor: *Geschichte der Päpste seit dem Ausgang des Mittelalters*, iii (Freiburg, 1895, 11/1955), pp. 339–656

E. Muentz: *Les Arts à la cour des papes Innocent VIII, Alexandre VI, Pie III* (Paris, 1898), pp. 139–267

P. de Roo: *Materials for a History of Pope Alexander VI: His Relations and his Times* (Bruges, 1924)

O. Ferrara: *The Borgia Pope* (London, 1942)

G. Soranzo: *Studi intorno a papa Alessandro VI* (Milan, 1950)

F. Saxl: 'The Appartamento Borgia', *Lectures* (London, 1957), pp. 174–88

G. Parker: *At the Court of the Borgia* (London, 1963)

R. N. Parker: 'On the meaning of Pinturicchio's "Sala dei Santi"', *A. Hist.*, ii (1979), pp. 291–317

S. Schueller-Piroli: *Die Borgia Päpste Kalixt III und Alexander VI* (Munich, 1980), pp. 83–394

A. Capriotti: 'Umanisti nell'appartamento Borgia: Appunti per la sala delle arti liberali', *Strenna Romanisti* (1990), pp. 73–88

HELLMUT WOHL

(3) Cesare Borgia, Duca di Valentino (*b* Rome, Sept 1475; *d* Viana, Navarre, 12 March 1507). Son of (2) Alexander VI. He received a succession of ecclesiastical titles, culminating in his creation as cardinal on 20 September 1493. After the murder of his brother Juan, Duca di Gandía, in 1497, Cesare renounced his ecclesiastical titles and embarked on a secular career. He sought the patronage of Louis XII, King of France, and acquired from him the title of Duca di Valentino and the hand of Charlotte d'Albret (1483–1514), sister of John III of Albret, King of Navarre. During Louis XII's campaign for Milan (1499), Cesare seized the chance to establish a feudal state for himself in Romagna. In a series of brilliant and ruthless campaigns, he captured many cities, which earned him the admiration of Niccolò Machiavelli (1469–1527) and formed the basis of his infamous reputation.

Although he was educated at the universities of Perugia and Pisa and was familiar with Renaissance humanist learning, Cesare's subsequent career, which was dominated by practical and military matters, left little time for scholarly pursuits. He nevertheless developed, consonant with his skills as a military leader, an abiding interest in architecture, particularly fortifications. Such interest is well illustrated by his employment of Leonardo da Vinci as his architect and engineer (1502–3). From Pavia on 18 August 1502 Cesare issued a patent that granted Leonardo free access to all the fortresses in his newly acquired possessions and gave the artist complete discretion to initiate improvements. During his period of employment Leonardo produced maps, urban plans—the finest of which is the map of *Imola* (Windsor Castle, Royal Lib.)—and designed a canal to connect Cesena with Porto Cesenatico, projections for systems of defence and a number of ingenious war machines. At this time Leonardo also sketched the head of *Cesare* from three angles (Turin, Bib. Reale). Cesare's entourage at this time also included the sculptor Pietro Torrigiano and the painter Bernardino Pinturicchio, but neither artist appears to have completed any work for him.

Contemporary descriptions of the ceremonial entries staged by Cesare refer to lavish displays of jewels, livery, musical instruments and harnesses. Similarly, his marriage gifts to Charlotte d'Albret included elaborately crafted jewellery, tableware and linen. Cesare's predilection for such items must have resulted in his patronage of skilled jewellers and metalworkers capable of producing such artefacts as the parade sword made for him in 1498, decorated with Borgia emblems and scenes from the life of his namesake, Julius Caesar. Despite looting the priceless Montefeltro collection at Urbino, however, Cesare apparently took little aesthetic interest in its contents. His ill-health, the death of Alexander VI and the accession of his family's implacable enemy, Giuliano della Rovere, as Julius II, led finally to the loss of his Italian strongholds and his French fiefs and to his imprisonment in Spain. Escaping from Medina del Campo, he was killed in a skirmish while in the service of the King of Navarre.

BIBLIOGRAPHY

DBI

W. H. Woodward: *Cesare Borgia* (London, 1913)

(4) Lucrezia Borgia, Duchess of Ferrara (*b* Subiaco, 18 April 1480; *d* Ferrara, 24 June 1519). Daughter of (2) Alexander VI. While her father's ambitions for (3) Cesare focused on the Church and the accumulation of wealth, property and titles, Alexander concentrated on securing for Lucrezia a series of advantageous marriages. After several aborted betrothals, in 1493 she married Giovanni Sforza (*d* 1510), ruler of Pesaro, in order to consolidate an alliance between the Borgias and the Sforzas of Milan. When this alliance was no longer politically expedient, Lucrezia obtained a divorce (1497) on grounds of non-consummation and subsequently (1498) married Alfonso, Duke of Bisceglie, illegitimate son of Alfonso II, King of Naples. On 18 August 1500 Lucrezia's second husband was murdered by a henchman of Cesare, undoubtedly with the connivance of her brother. Despite her genuine grief at her husband's death, Lucrezia apparently acquiesced in again being a pawn in her family's dynastic plans

and in 1502 duly married Alfonso I d'Este (i), the heir to the dukedom of Ferrara. She spent the rest of her life in Ferrara as Duchess, presiding over the court and bearing numerous children, only four of whom survived. She became increasingly pious, joining the Third Franciscan Order and founding the convent of S Bernardino in Ferrara (1510).

Although Lucrezia was not prominent amongst Renaissance women scholars and owned only a modest library of devotional texts, she nevertheless spoke a number of languages, wrote and composed poetry and, on the evidence of her surviving letters (examples, Milan, Bib. Ambrosiano), had a graceful epistolary style. The Ferrarese were also impressed by her skills as an embroiderer. As Governor of Spoleto and Nepi (1499) and the Vatican (1501) and as Duchess of Ferrara she demonstrated her administrative abilities. While Duchess of Bisceglie she presided over a small literary coterie of poets and writers. In Ferrara she was able to extend her literary patronage to include Ercole Strozzi (*d* 1508) and Pietro Bembo, who dedicated his masterpiece the *Asolani* (1505) to her. As a Renaissance princess, Lucrezia enjoyed an annual income that enabled her to commission works from a number of artists and craftsmen. These generally took the form of rich textiles, jewellery and tableware. She also offered employment to the painters Garofalo, who decorated her apartments in the Castello Estense, Ferrara, with murals on courtly themes (destr.), and Bartolomeo Veneto, who in 1507 painted her a *Madonna and Child* in a gilded frame (untraced). Several portraits of Lucrezia have been identified, including one from the collection of Paolo Giovio (Como, Nessi priv. col.) probably derived from a lost original. There is insufficient proof that Pinturicchio used Lucrezia as a model for the youthful St Catherine in the *Disputation of St Catherine* (*c.* 1492; Rome, Vatican, Appartamento Borgia). Other portraits are those on three medals, the first probably a matrimonial medal with *Alfonso d'Este* on the reverse, the second, as *Duchess of Ferrara*, identical to a third with *Amor* on the reverse. It is not known whether any of these were commissioned by Lucrezia.

BIBLIOGRAPHY

M. Bellonci: *Lucrezia Borgia* (Milan, 1939); rev. as *Lucrezia Borgia: La sua vita e i suoi tempi* (Milan, 1960); Eng. trans., abridged, by B. Wall as *The Life and Times of Lucrezia Borgia* (New York, 1953)

A. De Hevesy: 'Bartolomeo Veneto et les portraits de Lucrèce Borgia', *A. Q.*, ii (1939), pp. 233–49

N. Rubinstein: *Lucrezia Borgia* (Rome, 1971)

DIANA NORMAN

(5) Cardinal **Stefano Borgia** (*b* Velletri, Rome, 3 Dec 1731; *d* Lyon, 23 Nov 1804). His relationship to the earlier Borgias is unclear. Having completed his studies in philosophy, he turned his attention to antiquarian studies. While he was young, he became a member of the Accademia Etrusca in Cortona and of the Accademia Colombaria in Florence. His first published writing was *Monumento di Giovanni XVI* (Rome, 1750) on an inscription discovered in 1749. He graduated in theology in 1752, in canon law in 1757 and in 1758 was made rector of the monastery of Benevento, where between 1759 and 1764 he prepared one of his major works, the *Memorie istoriche della pontificia città di Benevento dal secolo VIII al secolo XVIII* (Rome,

1763–9), a historical and paleographical study. In 1765 he was ordained a priest, and on 30 March 1789 Pius VI elevated him to the rank of cardinal, with the title of S Clemente.

From the age of 19 Borgia collected manuscripts, medals and antiques, which he displayed in the rooms of his palace at Velletri; the collection became one of the richest and most famous private museums of the period and played an important role in the growing interest in ancient civilizations, especially in Etruri. Included in the Museo Borgiano were Egyptian, Italic, Etruscan, Greek, Roman and Christian, as well as Indian, Islamic, Celtic and Mexican antiquities. The collection included works of sculpture, ancient inscriptions, coins, religious objects, utensils, vases, gemstones, scarabs, paintings, archaeological finds and a wide variety of manuscripts. Borgia maintained many contacts with the scholars who visited the museum to study its collections. Among them was the Dane Georg Søga, who compiled a catalogue of Egyptian coins, *Numi Aegyptii Imperatorii prostantes in Museo Borgiano Velitris* (Rome, 1787), and Filippo Angelo Becchetti, who published *Bassi rilievi Volsci in terra cotta, dipinti a vari colori, trovati nella città di Velletri* (Rome, 1785). A few years after Stefano's death a sizable part of the museum, containing the Egyptian antiquities, was transferred through the intervention of Joachim Murat, King of Naples, to the then Palazzo dell'Accademia degli Studi di Napoli (now in Naples, Mus. N. S Martino). A large proportion of the manuscripts was transferred to the library of the Collegio di Propaganda Fide in Rome.

DBI

BIBLIOGRAPHY

B. Paulinus: *Vitae synopsis Stephani Borgiae S.R.E. cardinalis* (Rome, 1805), pp. 31–51 [notes on Museo Borgiano]

C. Borgia: *Notizie biografiche del Cardinale Stefano Borgia* (Rome, 1843)

LUCA LEONCINI

Borgianni, Orazio (*b* Rome, *c.* 1575; *d* Rome, 15 Jan 1616). Italian painter and etcher, also active in Spain. He was the son of a Florentine carpenter and stepbrother of the sculptor and architect Giulio Lasso. He accompanied Lasso to Sicily, and his earliest known work is a modest painting, in a Mannerist tradition, of *St Gregory in his Study* (1593; Catania, Villa Cerami, see Moir, pl. 48). He finished his training in Rome, and his study of the art of ancient Rome is evident in his early paintings, both in his use of Classical ruins and in the sculptural folds of his drapery. He must also have painted from nature and responded to the naturalism of Caravaggio. About 1598 Borgianni was in Spain and in 1601 he was in Pamplona. He stayed at least until June 1603, when he signed a petition for the establishment of an Italian-style academy of painting in Madrid. Among the other signatories was the Madrid-born Eugenio Cajés, whom Borgianni may have met in Rome, since Cajés was in Italy about 1595. Probably in this first Spanish period Borgianni painted, in a mood reminiscent of El Greco, the *Crucifixion* (Madrid, Prado, on dep. Cádiz, Mus. Pint.) set in a dark landscape with Roman ruins and stormy clouds. The *St Christopher* (Madrid, Prado), with a fantastic, rocky landscape, and the *Stigmatization of St Francis* (Madrid, Prado) are from the same period.

According to Baglione, Borgianni stayed in Spain for several years, married there and returned to Italy when he became a widower. The evidence suggests rather that he made two visits. He was in Italy in 1603, as evidenced by a dated portrait of *Tommaso Laureti* (1603; Rome, Accad. N. S Luca), and he was also there in February 1604, to witness a document that is now in the records of the Accademia di S Luca, Rome. From 1605 to 1607 he was in Spain, but he returned to Rome in 1607 and seems to have remained there until his death. He was elected a member of the Accademia dei Virtuosi in the Pantheon in 1610. His stay in Spain gave him Spanish friends and protectors and a continuing flow of commissions from Spanish patrons.

In the works painted after 1604, Caravaggio's influence on Borgianni became more apparent. Baglione related that there was personal rivalry between the two artists, which even brought them to blows. The horrific realism and violent contrasts of light and shade in Borgianni's *David Beheading Goliath* (Madrid, Real Acad. S Fernando) are indebted to Caravaggio, although the composition, with the fallen giant in a daringly foreshortened position, is based on one by Daniele da Volterra. Also indebted to Caravaggio are the *Death of St John the Evangelist* (Dresden, Gemäldegal.) and the *Christ among the Doctors* (Rome, Almagia priv. col., see Moir, pl. 53).

In 1608 Borgianni painted the *Virgin Appearing to St Francis* (ex-Pal. Com., Sezze). There followed an important group of pictures for the church of the monastery of Porta Coeli, Valladolid. The church was finished in 1613 and it is likely that the paintings were sent from Rome at this date. The high altar carries an enormous canvas of the *Assumption of the Virgin*, with an *Annunciation* and a *Birth of the Virgin* on the attics and other scenes from the *Life of the Virgin* on the predella. The two lateral altars are dedicated to *St Francis* and to *St Dominic*, their respective attics painted with the *Presentation of the Virgin* and the *Circumcision*. In all these works the complexity of the artist's training and his successful synthesis of the art of Caravaggio, Venetian tradition and knowledge of Giovanni Lanfranco is evident, most strikingly in the last two scenes. Borgianni's splendid *Birth of the Virgin* (*c.* 1612; Savona, Sanctuary of Nostra Signora della Misericordia) may be related to these works. It is spacious and brightly coloured, rich in tender genre details that suggest the influence of Jacopo Bassano. The intensely felt *St Carlo Borromeo in Adoration of the Trinity* (*c.* 1612; Rome, S Carlo alle Quattro Fontane) and the *St Carlo Borromeo and the Plague of Milan* (Rome, S Adriano, see Moir, pl. 89) are from the same period of outstanding creative achievement.

A more deeply meditated response to the art of Caravaggio is evident in a group of signed works of *c.* 1614–15. These include the *Holy Family with SS Elizabeth and John the Baptist* (Rome, Pal. Barberini; see fig.) and various versions of the *Holy Family* signed with Borgianni's monogram, O.B. (e.g. Vienna, priv. col., see Moir, pl. 86). The *Holy Family with SS Elizabeth and John the Baptist* unites a classical, Raphaelesque composition with intensely naturalistic detail, most striking in the painting of the covers in the cradle. The high background, dark and empty, is also reminiscent of Caravaggio. Borgianni's *Pietà*, in which the dramatically foreshortened body of Christ

J. M. J. Jurío: 'Martes de Carnestolendas en Pamplona (1601)', *Cuad. Etnol. & Etnog. Navarra*, xi (1979), pp. 277–93

A. E. Pérez Sánchez: 'La Academia Madrileña de 1603 y sus fundadores', *Bol. Semin. Estud. A. & Arqueol.*, xlviii (1982), pp. 281–90

ALFONSO E. PÉREZ SÁNCHEZ

Orazio Borgianni: *Holy Family with SS Elizabeth and John the Baptist*, oil on canvas, 2.26×1.74 m, *c.* 1614–15 (Rome, Palazzo Barberini)

echoes that of Andrea Mantegna's *Pietà* (Milan, Brera), must also date from the late years. Various versions of the work are preserved (e.g. Rome, Mus. Pal. Venezia, and Gal. Spada) and there are many copies. These were made after Borgianni's own etching of the composition (1615), dedicated to Francisco de Castro, Spanish ambassador in Rome. There are also several versions of his *St Christopher* (Edinburgh, N.G.; U. Würzburg, Wagner-Mus.; Gelves, nr Seville, S Maria de la Gracia). Borgianni also made an etching after this painting, this time dedicated to Juan de Lezcano, secretary to Francisco de Castro, and again the composition was much copied. Borgianni's *Self-portrait* (Rome, Accad. N. S Luca) is probably a late work. (None of the portraits mentioned in his will and in 17th-century inventories is known.) In this period he made his most important etchings, a series of 52 prints after Raphael's Vatican logge, which are signed with his monogram and dated 1615. Borgianni is buried in S Lorenzo in Lucina, Rome.

Borgianni's nephew, Pietro Cemfiglia, about whom nothing else is known, is documented as his pupil, and he also influenced the work of some Spanish-born painters, particularly that of Cajés.

DBI

BIBLIOGRAPHY

G. Baglione: *Vite* (1642), pp. 140–43; ed. V. Mariani (1935)

A. E. Pérez Sánchez: *Borgianni, Cavarozzi y Nardi en España* (Madrid, 1964)

H. E. Wethey: 'Orazio Borgianni in Italy and in Spain', *Burl. Mag.*, cvi (1964), pp. 147–59

A. Moir: *The Italian Followers of Caravaggio* (Cambridge, MA, 1967) [with pls]

Borgnis, Giuseppe Mattia [Maria] (*b* Craveggia, 23 Feb 1701; *d* West Wycombe, 12 Oct 1761). Italian painter, active in England. He trained in Bologna and Venice but returned to work in the Val di Vigezzo area of his native village. He painted both on panel and in fresco but preferred working in the latter, even decorating the ceilings of his own home. Among his earliest known works are the large signed and dated panel paintings for Craveggia parish church of scenes from the *Lives of SS Christopher, Roch and Lawrence* (1723–7; *in situ*). He also frescoed the church's main dome and side chapels (1739) and decorated the cupola of nearby S Maria Maggiore (1743). His only known student was Jean-Antoine Julien, with whom he was associated before 1748.

Around 1751 Borgnis left Italy for England at the invitation of Sir Francis Dashwood, who employed him thereafter. Two of his nine children went with him: Giovanni Borgnis (1728–?after 1783) and Pietro Maria [Peter] Borgnis (1739 or 1743–after 1810), both of whom made their careers as artists in England. Giuseppe Mattia decorated Dashwood's country house, West Wycombe Park, Bucks (1751–61), painting the staircase compartment and the ceilings of the dining room, salon, Blue Drawing Room and, most elaborately of all, the Music Room, with a rather unexpected mixture of frescoes after Raphael (from the Villa Farnesina), Annibale Carracci (from the Galleria Farnese) and Guido Reni, among others. He probably gleaned these images from prints. He also decorated portions of West Wycombe church and Medmenham Abbey, Bucks, the latter with images (destr.) bordering on the indecent. Other work included fresco interpretations of Reni's celebrated ceiling fresco of *Aurora* (1614; Rome, Pal. Pallavicini-Rospigliosi; see RENI, GUIDO, fig. 3) and of mythological subjects by Annibale Carracci on the ceiling of Thomas Duncombe's small Ionic temple (*in situ*; Duncombe Park, N. Yorks). There is no evidence of Borgnis's Venetian training in any of these frescoes. He was a talented imitator who occasionally altered his model's colour or composition, but created little original work. His ability to reproduce the Roman tradition was well suited to an English aristocratic milieu that continued to venerate Augustan taste.

BIBLIOGRAPHY

E. Croft-Murray: *Decorative Painting in England, 1537–1837*, ii (Feltham, 1970)

M. Chappell: 'Further Observations on Agostino Carracci's *Venus* in the Farnese Gallery', *Studies in Iconography*, iv (1975), pp. 161–5

O. Michiel: ' "Avoir tout ce qu'il y a de beau en Italie" ou quelques avatars de la Galerie des Carrache', *Carraches et les décors profanes. Actes du colloque organisé par l'Ecole française de Rome: Rome, 1986*, pp. 477–90

□

Borgo, Cristofano dal. *See* GHERARDI, CRISTOFANO.

Borgo, Francesco del. *See* FRANCESCO DEL BORGO.

Borgoña, Felipe de. *See* VIGARNY, FELIPE.

Borgoña, Juan de (*fl* from 1495; *d* Toledo, *c.* 1535). Spanish painter. His name indicates that he came from northern France, and he is first documented as working in the cloister of Toledo Cathedral in 1495. His arrival in Spain coincided with that of Juan de Flandes. Both painters were connected with Pedro Berruguete, which suggests that the three had met previously, in either Flanders or Italy. Borgoña's style indicates that he had studied painting in Italy, but it also contains traces of Flemish sensibility. The influence of Domenico Ghirlandaio and Gerard David is discernible, and Post (1956) has drawn attention to the influence of Piero della Francesca and Melozzo da Forlì in Borgoña's treatment of light. Castilian elements feature in his work, notably the use of gold backgrounds and a wealth of decoration. Borgoña's compositions are finely balanced, like those of the Italian High Renaissance, with skilfully drawn figures portrayed in elegant, tranquil poses. They are set against open spaces leading on to craggy landscapes reminiscent of Umbria or against gold embroidered drapery.

Borgoña's early works include the *Pietà* (Illescas, parish church), the *Last Supper* (Toledo Cathedral, sacristy) and the altarpiece of the Carboneras (Cuenca, Mus. Dioc.–Catedralicio). His most important work was executed in Toledo Cathedral, where he became the official painter. Between 1502 and 1504 he painted for the cathedral the altarpiece of the *Immaculate Conception* in the chapel of the Concepción, then the *Epiphany* altarpiece for the chapel of that dedication. He also worked in the provinces of Madrid, Cuenca and Guadalajara. In 1506 Borgoña and the painter Santa Cruz (*d* 1508) completed for Ávila Cathedral the altarpiece begun by Pedro Berruguete but left unfinished on his death.

Borgoña's greatest work was the series of frescoes (1509–1511) commissioned by Cardinal Francisco Jiménez de Cisneros for the chapter house of Toledo Cathedral. The frescoes feigned a gallery with widely spaced columns ending in *zapatas*, resembling that painted by Ghirlandaio for the choir of S Maria Novella, Florence. There are scenes from the *Life of the Virgin* on the lateral walls, scenes from the *Passion* on the altar wall and a *Last Judgement* on the entrance wall, which recall Luca Signorelli's fresco in Orvieto Cathedral. The mural paintings (1514) in the chapel of the Mozárabe, Toledo Cathedral, were also commissioned by Cisneros and commemorate the Cardinal's role in the capture of the town of Oran (1509). In 1517 Borgoña painted the altarpiece of *St John the Baptist* for the church of Camarena, near Toledo, and in 1518 he completed the altarpiece of the church of Pastrana, Guadalajara. From 1518 to 1523 he worked on the main altarpiece in the church of Villa del Prado, near Madrid, and began to use assistance from his workshop. In 1521 he painted the *Trinity* altarpiece in Toledo Cathedral. In 1531 he completed the altarpiece for the convent of S Miguel de los Angeles in Toledo (now in the Obispo Chapel, Madrid) as a dowry for his daughter when she entered the convent as a nun. In 1534 and 1535 he worked on the lateral altarpieces of the church of the Villa del Prado.

Borgoña had a large workshop, and it is often difficult to distinguish between his own work and that of his assistants. His last documented work dates from 1535, although he may have died later. He married in Toledo, and one of his children, Joan de Burogunga II (*fl* 1533; *d* 1565), became a painter. Among Borgoña's numerous pupils were Antonio de Comontes (*d* 1565) and Pedro de Cisneros (*d* 1548).

BIBLIOGRAPHY

L. de Saralegui: 'El retablo de la catedral de Ávila', *Museum* [Barcelona], vii/7, pp. 243–74
——: 'Un retablo de Juan de Borgoña en la iglesia de San Vicente de Toledo', *Toledo*, ii/57 (1916), p. 5
——: 'Notable descubrimiento en San Andrés: Un fresco de Juan de Borgoña', *Toledo*, iv (1918), p. 161
F. Darby: 'The Retable of Ávila', *Parnassus*, i/2 (1929)
Sierra: 'El convento de San Juan de la Penitencia', *A. Esp.*, iv/5 (1935), pp. 249–54
C. R. Post: *A History of Spanish Painting*, ix (Cambridge, 1947), pt 1
J. Ma. de Azcarate: 'Una traza de Juan de Borgoña', *Archv Esp. A.*, xxi (1948), p. 55
D. Angulo Iñiguez: *Juan de Borgoña* (Madrid, 1954)
——: *Pintura del siglo XVI*, A. Hisp., xii (Madrid, 1954)
C. R. Post: 'Juan de Borgoña in Italy and Spain', *Gaz. B.-A.*, xlviii (1956), pp. 129–42
A. Condorelli: 'Il problema di Juan de Borgoña', *Commentari*, xi/1 (1960), pp. 46–59
J. Ma. Caamaño Martínez: 'Sobre la influencia de Juan de Borgoña', *Bol. Semin. Estud. A. & Arqueol.*, xxx (1964), p. 292
P. Longhi: 'Per Juan de Borgoña', *Parnassus*, xvi (1965), pp. 65–71
J. Gómez Menor: 'Algunos documentos inéditos de Juan de Borgoña y otros artífices toledanos de su tiempo', *An. Toled.*, ii, iii (1968), pp. 162–83
J. Camón Aznar: *Pintura española del Renacimiento*, Summa A., xii (Madrid, 1970)
J. Gómez Menor: 'Un monumento artístico desaparecido: El convento de San Juan de la Penitencia', *An. Toled.*, iv, v (1971), pp. 7–83
M. C. González Muñoz: 'Un antiguo retablo de la Colegiata de Talavera: Posible obra de Juan de Borgoña', *Archv Esp. A.*, xlvii/85 (1974), pp. 53–66
F. Marías: 'Datos sobre la vida y la obra de Juan de Borgoña', *Archv Esp. A.*, xlix/194 (1976), pp. 180–82
J. M. Cruz Valdovinos: 'Retablos inéditos de Juan de Borgoña: Camarena y Pastrana', *Archv Esp. A.*, 209 (1980), pp. 27–56
I. Mateo Gómez: 'Juan de Borgoña, autor del retablo de San Miguel de los Angeles de Toledo', *Miscelanea de arte en honor de D. Diego Angulo* (Madrid, 1982), pp. 75–7

ISABEL MATEO GÓMEZ

Borisov-Musatov, Viktor (Yel'pidiforovich) (*b* Saratov, 14 April 1870; *d* Tarusa, 8 Nov 1905). Russian painter. He studied art in Saratov from 1890 to 1891 and then at the Moscow School of Painting, Sculpture and Architecture from 1893 to 1895. In the intervening years he attended the Academy of Art in St Petersburg and worked under Pavel Chistyakov (1832–1919). During three winters in Paris between 1895 and 1898 he attended the studio of the history and portrait painter Fernand Cormon. Cormon had little influence on his style, but the exposure to contemporary French art was crucial, and the first mature works of Borisov-Musatov date from this period. He produced landscapes and figure studies in the high-keyed colours of the French Impressionists, as in the oil painting *Boy with a Dog* (1895; Khar'kov, Mus. F.A.). In France Borisov-Musatov had also seen the murals of Pierre Puvis de Chavannes and he returned to Moscow hoping to produce monumental, decorative art based on a Symbolist rendering of nature. His many paintings of women in early 19th-century dress have a superficial resemblance to the retrospective paintings of the Russian World of Art (Mir Iskusstva) group, but add a new note of melancholy, of an imaginary past irretrievably lost. He came close in mood to the contemporary Russian Symbolist poets, Valery Bryusov (1873–1924) and Andrey Bely, who were his friends. Borisov-Musatov's oil and tempera *Self-portrait with Sister* (1898; St Petersburg, Rus. Mus.) is still Impressionist in the depiction of the landscape, but in the expressions on the faces it introduces a note of introspection that was to be characteristic of his oeuvre for the rest of his life. Increasingly he moved away from a direct transcription of nature towards a depiction of mood. His later works are premeditated exercises in colour, form and composition.

In the tempera painting *The Reservoir* (1902; Moscow, Tret'yakov Gal.) Borisov-Musatov no longer broke up the colours in the Impressionist manner and abandoned the depiction of the haphazard reflection of light on objects in favour of closed contours and large areas of a single muted colour. The figures of his sister and his fiancée take on the quality of symbols, as each exists in a separate self-contained world. The seated figure on the bank, resplendent in a blue dress and jewellery and with an elegant coiffure is contrasted with the plainer figure in a white shawl, who seems to float on the water of the pond that rises up to fill most of the picture plane. The predominating cold tones and static poses reinforce the dream-like quality of the scene. The circular forms of this painting, which express the closed world inhabited by the female figures, are unusual in Borisov-Musatov's oeuvre. Elsewhere he often used an elongated horizontal format, spreading his figures in a procession across the canvas, as if in a frieze. With trees and architectural features as vertical punctuation in the space, and using careful repetitions of lines and colours, he sought in his paintings to offer a pictorial counterpart to the rhythmic qualities of music. In the tempera paintings *Gobelin* (1901), *Phantoms* (1903) and the *Emerald Necklace* (1903–4; all Moscow, Tret'yakov Gal.) he used the real setting of a country estate of the late 18th century as the background for the frieze of figures in early 19th-century dress that float across the foreground space. Both figures and setting take on the character of a dream. Tempera, watercolour and pastel were Borisov-Musatov's preferred media since they suggested, better than oil, the fleeting qualities of mood he sought to express in his paintings. Although largely resident outside Moscow after 1898, he nonetheless exercised considerable influence on several Moscow artists, especially those associated with the Blue Rose group, including Pavel Kuznetsov and Martiros Saryan.

BIBLIOGRAPHY

A. Rusakova: *V. E. Borisov-Musatov* (Leningrad, 1966) [Eng. summary; colour illus.]
O. Kochik: *Zhivopisnaya sistema V. E. Borisova-Musatova* [The painterly system of V. E. Borisov-Musatov] (Moscow, 1980) [summary in Fr.]
I. M. Gofman, ed.: *V. Borisov-Musatov: Al'bom* [V. Borisov-Musatov: an album] (Moscow, 1989)

MARIAN BURLEIGH-MOTLEY

Borland, Kevin (*b* Melbourne, 1926). Australian architect. He began his architectural career at the age of 15 as office boy to Best Overend; in 1950, while completing his architectural thesis at Melbourne University, he was briefly employed by Harry Seidler. He entered practice as a protégé of Robin Boyd in association with Peter McIntyre. All three experimented in 1953 with the parabolic concrete 'Ctesiphon Arch' (*see* BOYD, (1)), the patent for which was held by a local building contractor. Meanwhile Borland and McIntyre, together with John and Phyllis Murphy, in 1952 won the competition for the Olympic Swimming Pool, Melbourne, and in 1953 formed a partnership that continued for three years. The pool was enclosed in a dramatic structure. Raked tiers of stands on either side were tied together at their highest points by elongated lozenge-shaped roof trusses. The structure was stabilized by ties running from the same points down to anchors in the ground. After 1956 Borland developed a practice of his own, largely in domestic and educational work, notably Preshil School (1962), Kew, Melbourne. The simple school buildings are loosely arranged around the site. A more urban image prevailed in the Harold Holt Pool (1969; with Daryl Jackson), and developed further in the Clyde Cameron College (1975), Wodonga, in which blocks are connected by tubular bridging corridors with porthole windows. Responsibility for the design was shared with a former employee, Bernard Brown, who rejoined the firm specifically for this project and was in partnership from 1980 to 1985. Borland was foundation professor of architecture at Deakin University, Geelong, from 1981 to 1984.

BIBLIOGRAPHY

J. Taylor: *Australian Architecture since 1960* (Sydney, 1986), pp. 83–5

MILES LEWIS

Borman [Borreman; Borremans]. South Netherlandish family of sculptors. Jan Borman II (*fl c.* 1479–1520) is first documented in Brussels in 1479, when he joined the guild of sculptors. His father, Jan Borman I, is recorded as deceased in the accounts of the Brussels chamber of rhetoric in 1498. Passchier Borman (*fl c.* 1491–1537), son of Jan II, became a master of the sculptors' guild in 1491, and a Jan Borman the younger, presumably Jan III (*fl c.* 1499–1522) and Passchier's brother, entered the guild in 1499.

In 1484–6 Jan II was commissioned to supply statues (destr.) for a stone altarpiece made by the Brussels sculptor Peeter Vogel for the parochial altar of Antwerp Cathedral. In 1489 a Jan Borman the elder and his son Jan (almost certainly Jan I and Jan II) stood surety for the bronzecaster Jan van Thienen (*fl* 1489–*c.* 1512) in the making of a door (untraced) for the St Pieterskerk, Leuven. Jan II entered the Leuven joiners' guild in 1491, when he restored a stone figure of *St John the Baptist* and carved a *St John the Evangelist* (both destr.) for the sacramental altar of the St Jacobskerk, Leuven. It has been suggested convincingly that Jan II made the wooden model for the tomb of *Mary of Burgundy* in the Onze Lieve Vrouwekerk, Bruges, cast in bronze by Renier van Thienen (i) or his son Renier van Thienen (ii) in 1491. He received payments from the St Sulpitiuskerk in Diest for a crucifix in 1492–4 (destr.). In 1493 Jan II signed and dated a wooden altarpiece comprising seven carved scenes from the *Life of St George* (Brussels, Mus. Royaux A. & Hist.; see fig.), commissioned by the Guild of Crossbowmen for the chapel of Onze Lieve Vrouwe buiten de Muren in Leuven. The altarpiece is said to have had polychromy, which apparently survived until 1813 but has since disappeared. The composition of

Jan Borman II: altarpiece with scenes from the *Life of St George* (detail), wood, h. 1.64 m, 1493 (Brussels, Musées Royaux d'Art et d'Histoire) each carved scene is ambitious, involving up to 12 large-scale figures arranged on a sloping ground, creating a strong illusion of space. The characterization of facial types is unusually varied, some idealized, many verging on the exotic or the grotesque. The meticulously carved decorative details of costume, hair and beards, characteristic of Jan Borman II, have led many to conclude, probably wrongly, that the *St George* altarpiece was never intended to be polychromed. Typical also is the agile, exaggerated sense of movement using twisting and swaying poses, the slender figures often placed with their backs to the viewer and swathed in heavy, angular, folded drapery. The second pair of wings originally belonging to the work are missing.

In 1508 Jan II produced carvings for a wooden altarpiece (destr.) for the brewers' altar in the St Pieterskerk, Leuven, collaborating with Jan Petercels, a Leuven joiner, who made the frame. The work was designed by the city architect Mathijs Keldermans (*d* 1526). In 1510 Jan II and his son Passchier, working again with Jan Petercels, produced a carved wooden altarpiece (destr.) for the Confraternity of the Holy Sacrament in Turnhout. In 1511, on the recommendation of court artists, Jan II was commissioned to provide wooden models of the Dukes and Duchesses of Brabant, designed by Jan van Roome, and of animals and birds; statues were to be cast from these by Renier van Thienen (ii) to decorate the grand esplanade of the Palais Royal (destr.) in Brussels. In the same year Jan II, who is stated in the royal accounts to be 'the best sculptor', carved a stone lion (destr.) for the façade of the palace (destr.). In an undated civic account, Jan II received an allowance for clothes, suggesting that he was at one time employed by the city of Brussels.

Passchier Borman is documented as an independent carver providing three scenes for an altarpiece (destr.) for the Confraternity of St Eligius in Brussels in 1509–10. Between 1517 and 1537 he is recorded doing a variety of sculptural work in the chapel of the hospital of St Pieter, Brussels, and he carved two funerary monuments in 1516 and 1534. His only surviving work is the signed wooden triptych (2.15×2.07 m) with seven carved scenes from the *Martyrdom of SS Crispin and Crispinian*. The wings and the polychromy have disappeared. A carved altarpiece (4.05×5.36 m) representing 13 scenes from the *Life of Christ*, signed with the name Jan Borman, was installed in the parish church of Güstrow, Germany, in 1522. The advanced date and the differing style suggest that this might be the work of Jan Borman III.

Many carved wooden altarpieces have been attributed to the Borman family. The quality of most is highly uneven, suggesting that the workshop rather than a single master was responsible. This heavy reliance on assistants is probably explained by Jan II's popularity and the consequent pressure of work; the royal accounts of 1511 state that he was occupied by many other works in addition to his royal commission. Three carved altarpieces in Swedish churches, one in Strängnäs Cathedral, a second from Skänela (now in Uppsala Cathedral) and a third in Vadstena, are convincingly attributed to the Borman family because they bear the mark of a head stamped in profile, which is usually associated with Brussels and which is found otherwise only on the Güstrow altarpiece. Further attributed altarpieces carved in Brussels include the first

altarpiece in Västerås Cathedral; another altarpiece in Strängnäs and those in the Swedish churches of Villberga, Jäder, Skepptuna, Bro, Veckholm and Ytter-selö; those in the German churches of St Nicholas, Orsoy, and the Stiftkirche, Aschaffenberg; and, in Belgium, the altarpiece in the church at Boendael and the Saluces Altarpiece (Brussels, Mus. Com.).

BIBLIOGRAPHY
G. J. Dodd: 'Notes relatifs à l'histoire des arts dans les Pays-Bas', *Rev. Hist. & Archéol.*, i (1859), pp. 425–8
M. P. D. Kuyl: 'Retable de l'ancien corporation des tanneurs dans l'église paroissale de Ste-Waudru à Herentals', *An. Acad. Royale Archéol. Belgique*, n. s., vi (1870), pp. 267–76
E. Van Even: 'L'Auteur du retable de 1493 du Musée de la Porte de Hal à Bruxelles', *Bull. Comm. Royales A. & Archeol.*, xvi (1877), pp. 581–98
——: 'Maître Jan Borman: Le grand sculpteur belge de la fin du xv siècle', *Bull. Comm. Royales A. Archéol.*, xxiii (1884), pp. 397–426
J. Roosval: *Schnitzaltäre in schwedischen Kirchen und Museen aus der Werkstatt des Brussler Bildschnitzer Jan Borman* (Strasbourg, 1903)
J. Duverger: *Brussel als kunstcentrum in de xiv en xv eeuw* (Antwerp, 1935), pp. 12, 87–8
J. Borchgrave d'Altena: 'Note au sujet de Jan Borman et Jan Borman le jeune', *Bull. Soc. Royale Archéol. Bruxelles* (1939), pp. 40–41
F. Prims: *Geschiedenis van Antwerpen*, vii/3 (Antwerp, 1940), p. 118
H. J. Duverger: 'De meesters van het grafmonument van Marie van Bourgondie te Brugge', *Jb.: Kon. Vl. Acad. Wet., Lett. & S. Kst. België*, viii (1946), p. 131
J. Borchgrave d'Altena: *Le Retable de St Georges* (Brussels, 1947)
A. G. B. Schayes: *Analectes archéologiques, historiques, géographiques et statistiques, concernant principalement la Belgique* (Antwerp, 1957), pp. 247–50
E. Fruendt: *Der Güstrower Altar* (Leipzig, 1964)
Aspekten van de Laatgotiek in Brabant (exh. cat., Leuven, Brouwerijmus., 1971), pp. 313–15, 382, 387–8
R. van de Ven: 'De Brusselse beeldsnijder Jan Borreman vervaardigde een triomfkruis voor de Sint-Sulpitiuskerk te Diest' [The Brussels sculptor Jan Borreman manufactured a triumphal crucifix for the church of St Sulpice in Diest], *Arca Lovan.*, iv (1975), pp. 361–9
B. D'Hainaut-Zveny: 'La Dynastie Borreman xv–xvi siècles: Crayon généalogique et analyse comparative des personalités artistiques', *An. Hist. A. & Archéol.*, v (1983), pp. 47–66
——: 'Le Retable de la *Passion* de Güstrow: Problèmes d'attribution et essais d'analyse', *Rev. Belge Archéol. & Hist. A.*, lv (1986), pp. 5–39

KIM W. WOODS

Bornebusch, Gehrdt (*b* Copenhagen, 15 April 1925). Danish architect. He studied at the Kunstakademiets Arkitektskole in Copenhagen, graduating in 1950. In the mid–1950s he began working with a highly successful competition team that included Max Brüel (*b* 1927), Jørgen Selchau (*b* 1923) and Henning Larsen. Among their buildings was Vangebo School (1960), Søllerød, the outcome of a competition in 1958. With its low, tightly knit, clustered forms and simple, rustically expressive use of materials, the school fulfilled the architectural aspirations of its period. Thereafter Bornebusch, Brüel and Selchau produced a number of harmonious and unconstrained projects, including the schools St Jørgensbjerg (1960), Roskilde, and Langemark (1964), Horsens, and seminaries in Holbæk (1967) and Esbjerg (1973). Bornebusch was individually responsible for the last two, as well as for the Danish Embassy (1974) in Beijing. The partnership's name was also behind one of the last large modernist works in Denmark, the Copenhagen County Hospital (1965) in Herlev: its central 23-storey ward tower must be attributed to Selchau, but Bornebusch designed the nursing school and service building. After the partnership's dissolution Bornebusch's designs included a nursing home in Tårnby

(1980), the Gymnasium (1981) in Vejen and the Central Library (1982) in Tårnby. A neo-rationalistic approach to form is revealed in the last and is also apparent in his prize-winning project for a new town quarter in Regensburg (1983), Germany.

BIBLIOGRAPHY

P. E. Skriver: 'Vangeboskolen i Søllerød', *Arkitektur DK*, v (1961), pp. 68–81
'Holbæk Seminarium', *Arkitektur DK*, xii/6 (1968), pp. 257–70
'Works by Gehrdt Bornebusch', *Arkitektur DK*, xix/1 (1975), pp. 1–40
'København Amtssygehus i Herler' [Copenhagen County Hospital in Herler], *Arkitektur DK*, xxi/5 (1977), pp. 169–208
C. Enevoldsen: 'Works by Gehrdt Bornebusch', *Arkitektur DK*, xxvii/6 (1983), pp. 217–56
'Danish National Museum', *Arkitektur DK*, xxxvi/8 (1992), pp. 389–407

JØRGEN SESTOFT

Bornemann [Borneman]. German family of painters. (1) Hans Bornemann, of Hamburg, a painter of altarpieces, was the first north German to adopt the realistic style of the Netherlands. His widow, Gerburg, married Hinrik Funhof, who took over the workshop and collaborated with his stepson (2) Henrik Bornemann, who also painted ecclesiastical works. On Funhof's death, Gerburg married Absalon Stumme (*fl* c. 1486–c. 1498), who became master of the workshop, and Henrik Bornemann opened his own workshop, which passed at his death to his third stepfather, WILM DEDEKE.

(1) Hans [Johann] **Bornemann** (*fl* c. 1440; *d* Hamburg, 1473–4). The Netherlandish style of his works presupposes an early journey to the southern Netherlands and a debt to Jan van Eyck, Robert Campin and the Master of Girart de Roussillon. Bornemann's small panel with the *Calvary* (c. 1440; Bremen, Roseliushaus) was the first north German work to follow the new realism of van Eyck. Instead of the usual gold ground, light plays around the figures, who are dressed in richly jewelled garments. The bodies are stocky, if somewhat two-dimensional, and Bornemann has attempted to create a three-dimensional landscape, even if the forms are still generalized. The same influences are shown in his four miniatures for the *Sachsenspiegel* (1442–8; Lüneburg, Rathaus) of Brand von Tzerstede (c. 1400–51) and in his high altarpiece for Heiligental Monastery in Lüneburg (after 1444; remains, Lüneburg, Nikolaikirche). The latter is dated from the view of Lüneburg in the panel of the *Fall of Aegeus*, in which the Gertrudenkapelle is shown under construction, while on the panel of the *Meeting of Abraham and Melchizedek*, on the outside of the altarpiece, the chapel, completed in 1447, is shown in its finished state. The two views of Lüneburg are innovative in that the view in the *Aegeus* scene is below a gold ground, and in the *Meeting of Abraham and Melchizedek* the town is shown as a detailed distant silhouette, separate from the large group in the foreground. Another panel of the Heiligental Altarpiece, the *Baptism of Maximilla by St Andrew*, bears witness to Bornemann's knowledge of van Eyck's *Virgin and Child in a Church* (Berlin, Gemäldegal.; *see* EYCK, VAN, (2), fig. 5) and works deriving from it. In the style of Campin's paintings, however, he showed a view into a cathedral with a section of the front. The *Baptism of Lucillus by St Lawrence* presents a diagonal view into a church interior

with a portal and cut-away stonework. There are carved reliefs of the *Passion* on the third view.

Although Hans Bornemann received important commissions from Lüneburg, he lived in Hamburg, where in 1448 he took over the house and workshop of Konrad von Vechta (*fl* 1425–44). In the same year he received payments for an untraced 'panel' on the rood altar of the Nikolaikirche, the church of the lepers' hospital near Lüneburg. After 1457 he produced a panel of *St Ansgar* (Hamburg, Petrikirche), and c. 1458 he completed work on an altarpiece (Lüneburg, Nikolaikirche) for the high altar of Lüneburg's Lambertikirche (destr. 1861). In both he followed the monumental style of Rogier van der Weyden, and the Lambertikirche altarpiece in particular presupposes a knowledge of the late works of that painter and his circle (indicating that Hans Bornemann had made a second journey to the southern Netherlands): instead of many small scenes, there are six large panels (showing the *Martyrdom of the Apostles Simon and Judas Thaddeus* and the *Martyrdom of St Lambert, Bishop of Liège*), and he renounced three-dimensionality in favour of symbolically determined proportions as regards space and figures. (As with the Heiligental Altarpiece, a third view, with carved reliefs, was completed at an earlier date.)

In 1467 Bornemann carried out various paintings (destr.) for the Rathaus at Stade, and subsequently he produced 17 panel portraits of kings for the Rathaus in Hamburg (destr. 1842). His style found no direct successors.

BIBLIOGRAPHY

H. Reinecke: 'Der Maler Hans Borneman', *Z. Dt. Ver. Kstwiss.*, v (1938), pp. 204–29
H. G. Gmelin: 'Hans Bornemans künstlerische Stellung in Nordwestdeutschland', *Niederdt. Beitr. Kstgesch.*, viii (1969), pp. 109–46

(2) Henrik [Hinrich; Hinrik] **Bornemann** (*fl* Hamburg, 1490; *d* Hamburg, 1499). Son of (1) Hans Bornemann. In 1490 he received payments from the town of Stade for completed works and in 1496 was established as a master in his own workshop. His *Calvary* panel (c. 1497; Hamburg, Ksthalle, ex-Katharinenkirche), painted for Tile Nagel (*d* 1491) and his wife Tibbeke Köting (*d* 1503), has background scenes of the *Passion*; the smoothly painted groups of figures seem to lack cohesion. On the wings of an altar of *St Luke* (1499; Hamburg, Jakobikirche), Bornemann's contribution was limited to the outsides of the wings showing the Virgin with the patroness, his mother Gerburg (later painted over by Absalon Stumme and changed to a representative image with angels), and the unusual picture of *St Luke Painting the Virgin*, to which Henrik Bornemann himself was added in miniature after his death, with an intercessional text, when the work was completed by Wilm Dedeke of Lübeck, who took over his workshop; the transition can be seen clearly.

BIBLIOGRAPHY

H. Reincke: 'Beiträge zur mittelalterlichen Geschichte der Malerei in Hamburg', *Z. Ver. Hamburg. Gesch.*, xxi (1916), pp. 112–54
Stadt im Wandel (exh. cat., Brunswick, Herzog Anton Ulrich-Mus.; Landesmus.; Cathedral; 1985), ii, no. 683

HANS GEORG GMELIN

Bornemisza, Thyssen-. *See* THYSSEN-BORNEMISZA.

Borobudur [Barabudur]. Indonesian monumental site, located in central Java, *c.* 40 km north-west of Yogyakarta. Indonesia's largest religious monument, Candi Borobudur was erected *c.* AD 800 to glorify the founder of the ruling Buddhist dynasty of the Shailendras. In addition to demonstrating high esteem for the ancestors, it was also intended to express in visual form the teachings of Mahayana Buddhism. This dual purpose accounts for its unique plan. The stepped pyramid surmounted by a stupa (see fig. 1) symbolizes the merit accumulated by the dynasty along the way shown by the Buddha. Candi Borobudur was constructed on a natural hill some 15 m above the extensive Kedu Plain. The construction required about two million blocks of volcanic stone. Rising from a redented square base 107×107×3.7 m, the monument is set back 6 m from its edge, so that a broad platform is created. Each of the five succeeding square terraces is set back just 2 m from the one below, forming narrow galleries that have balustrades on their outer sides. The superstructure, set on the uppermost square terrace, is composed of three circular platforms, each of which supports a ring of latticed stupas or dagobs (72 in total). Surmounting the whole edifice is an unlatticed central stupa, the top of which is more than 30 m above ground-level. Access to the upper part of the monument is by stairways on the axes that bisect the sides of the pyramid. They lead through a series of gates directly to the circular platforms, intersecting the corridors of the square terraces.

The three superimposed elements of the monument correspond with the Buddhist concepts of the three divisions of the universe. The base represents the *kāmadhātu* or sphere of desire. The square middle depicts the *rūpadhātu* or sphere of forms, where man has abandoned his desires but is still bound to name and form. The upper, circular part symbolizes the *arūpadhātu*, the highest sphere, where there is neither form nor name, only nothingness amid the eternal void. As if to emphasize this symbolism, the decoration of each of the three levels is different. The broad rim round the foot of the monument, which is not the actual base but an encasement (probably added to prevent sliding caused by the construction of the foundations on earth infill), conceals a series of over 160 reliefs (see fig. 2) carved on panels round the original base: Borobudur's 'hidden foot'. The reliefs illustrate the operation of *karma* or the law of cause and effect. They are based on the sacred Sanskrit work *Mahākarmavibhangga* ('Great Classification of Actions') and show how, on earth, good acts are rewarded and evil deeds punished. Although the encasement, which incorporates *c.* 11,500 cubic m of stone, covered these reliefs, it brought aesthetic and religious compensations. The broad platform smooths the monument's outline and also furnishes ample space for the pilgrim to perform the first circumambulations and to reflect deeply on the further steps to be taken without being disturbed by pictures of *karma*: indeed, the pilgrim is already literally above the *kāmadhātu* at the outset.

Abundant use is made of narrative reliefs to depict the *rūpadhātu* on the walls and balustrades of the galleries. The elaborately carved reliefs cover a total surface of 700 sq. m and are distributed over 1300 panels arranged in 10 rows round the monument, a total length of *c.* 2.5 km.

1. Candi Borobudur, *c.* AD 800; aerial view from the south-east

2. Candi Borobudur, stone relief of a coastal scene with a trading vessel, 9th century (*in situ*)

The first four series of reliefs in the first gallery, and the fifth series on the balustrade of the second gallery, depict the life of the historical Buddha, according to the *Lalitavistara* text, and his numerous former lives (*jātaka*s). There are also *avadāna*s, stories similar to *jātaka*s but recounting the meritorious deeds of characters other than the historical Buddha in his earlier incarnations. One, for example, recounts the story of the tireless wanderings of the rich merchant's son Sudhana, who renounced worldly life in quest of the highest wisdom, or the ultimate truth, as told in the *Gandavyuha* text and its sequel, the *Bhadracari*. The representation of the *rūpadhātu* is completed with 432 life-size stone statues in the round of the Dhyani or transcendental Buddhas of the cardinal points of the compass, each exhibiting a sublime craftsmanship that combines simplicity with subtlety. They are depicted in deep meditation, seated cross-legged on lotus cushions and facing outwards, under the shelter of arched niches arranged in rows above the narrative reliefs on the walls. These niches, each of which is surmounted by a set of small stupas, contribute in large part to the uneven but beautiful outline of the monument.

In striking contrast to the bewildering *rūpadhātu*, the circular terraces of the *arūpadhātu* have no ornaments, carvings or embellishments. The monotonous plainness is broken only by the 72 stupas that encircle the central stupa. Indeed, the idea of nothingness is perfectly conveyed by the total absence of any decorative element. Even the highest emanations of the Buddha, represented by statues similar to those of the *rūpadhātu*, are hidden from sight inside the latticed walls of the stupas. The central stupa, surmounting the entire monument, has an interior cavity, which may originally have contained the sacred temple deposit or the 505th statue, representing the omnipresent and omnipotent Adi Buddha or supreme Buddha, but was found empty when the monument was first described in the early 19th century.

For further discussion of the symbolic and ritual significance of Candi Borobudur and its place in the development of architecture and sculpture in Java, *see* INDONESIA, §§II, 1(i) and IV, 2.

BIBLIOGRAPHY
Beschrijving van Barabudur, 2 vols (The Hague, 1920–31)
C. Sivaramamurti: *Le Stupa de Barabudur* (Paris, 1961)
R. Soekmono: 'Notes on the Monuments of Ancient Indonesia', *Ancient Indonesian Art of the Central and Eastern Javanese Periods*, ed. J. Fontein (New York, 1971), pp. 13–17
C. Sivaramamurti: *Ageless Borobudur* (Wassenaar, 1976)
R. Soekmono: *Borobudur: A Monument of Mankind* (New York, 1976)
A. J. Bernet Kempers: *Herstel in eigen waarde: Monumentenzorg in Indonesie* (Zutphen, 1978), pp. 63–77, 212–22
J. Dumarçay: *Borobudur* (Singapore, 1978)
L. O. Gómez and H. W. Woodward jr, eds: *Barabudur: History and Significance of a Buddhist Monument* (Berkeley, 1981)
R. Soekmono: *The Restoration of Chandi Borobudur at a Glance* (Jakarta, 1983)
J. Miksic: *Borobudur: Golden Tales of the Buddhas* (Berkeley and Singapore, 1990)
R. Soekmono and others: *Borobudur: Prayer in Stone* (Paris, 1990)
R. Soekmono: 'Indonesian Architecture of the Classical Period: A Brief Survey', *The Sculpture of Indonesia*, ed. J. Fontein (Washington, 1990), pp. 67–95
——: 'Serat Centhini ungkap masalah arca Buddha dalam stupa induk Candi Borobudur' [*Serat Centhini* (early 19th-century Javanese enc.) reveals the presence of the unfinished Buddha statue in the main stupa of Candi Borobudur], *Saraswati: Esai-esai arkeologi* (Jakarta, 1993–4), ii, pp. 7–21
R. SOEKMONO

Borofsky, Jonathan (*b* Boston, MA, 1942). American sculptor, painter and draughtsman. As a child he accompanied his mother, a trained architect, to weekly painting classes, where he was encouraged to draw freely and not in a traditional manner. He studied at Carnegie-Mellon University, Pittsburgh, PA (BFA, 1962) and at Yale School of Art and Architecture, New Haven, CT (MFA, 1966), where his work was mainly sculptural. From the early 1970s his central concern was to diminish the boundaries between life and art. From 1973 he made use of dreams, in drawings, paintings, sculptures, projected images, prints, and finally combinations of these in multi-media installations. Borofsky first exhibited at the Artists' Space, New York (1973), showing *Counting* (1969–), a serial project comprising a stack of sheets of graph paper (220×280 mm), on which numbers from 1 to *c.* 1,800,000 were written in pencil and ink. An ongoing project, it continued to reappear in later shows under a tailor-made perspex box; by September 1993 the numbers reached 3,200,000 and the stack *c.* 1.28 m high. These characteristic numbers also appeared on the back of *Flags* (exh. 1988, New York, Paula Cooper Gal.), for which Borofsky painted the flags of the world, with the name of each country printed under its flag; the work also included a large (h. 3.65 m) sculpture of a man with a beating red perspex heart, his singularity contrasting with the numerous flags. One of his best-known images is the *Hammering Man*, which appeared in both two- and three-dimensional works, including a 3.65 m high sculpture with a motorized hammering arm.

BIBLIOGRAPHY

J. Simon: 'An Interview with Jonathan Borofsky', *A. America*, lxix/9 (Nov 1981), pp. 162–7
Jonathan Borofsky (exh. cat., essays by M. Rosenthal and R. Marshall; Philadelphia, PA, Mus. A.; New York, Whitney; Berkeley, U. CA, A. Mus., and elsewhere; 1984–5) [good photos of installations, some related by artist's notes to dreams]
Horizons: Jonathan Borofsky (exh. cat., with an essay by D. E. Scott; Kansas City, MO, Nelson–Atkins Mus. A., 1988)

Boronat, José Camarón y. *See* CAMARÓN, (1).

Borovikovsky, Vladimir (Lukich) (*b* Mirgorod, Ukraine, 4 Aug 1757; *d* St Petersburg, 18 April 1825). Russian painter of Ukrainian birth. Along with Fyodor Rokotov and Dmitry Levitsky, Borovikovsky is one of the three great Russian portrait painters of the second half of the 18th century. He was trained by his father and brothers, who were icon painters. His early works were also icons, such as the *Mother of God* (1784; Kiev, Mus. Ukrain. A.) and *King David* (1785; St Petersburg, Rus. Mus.); they are archaic in style and resemble portraits produced by Ukrainian folk artists. At the end of the 1780s Borovikovsky moved to St Petersburg and took up portrait painting. He was aided by advice from Levitsky and took lessons from Johann Baptist Lampi (i). He soon became established, gaining a reputation as a brilliant colourist, and he received many commissions. Throughout his career, however, he continued to paint icons from time to time. In 1795 he became a member of the St Petersburg Academy of Arts; he was also closely connected with many of the chief exponents of Russian culture in the city. The number of his surviving works is large (at least 400 portraits). He had his own workshop, and he would often rely on assistants to paint the less important parts of a portrait. His sitters included members of the imperial family, courtiers, generals, many aristocrats and figures from the Russian artistic and literary worlds. Most of his portraits are intimate in style. A particularly touching example is the portrait of *Ol'ga Filippova*, the wife of a close friend (*c.* 1790; St Petersburg, Rus. Mus.), who is seen in a white peignoir with a park in the background. The portrait is painted in a flowing style; the combination of light, subdued tones, typical of Borovikovsky, gives an impression of tender femininity and quiet contemplation.

Borovikovsky's skill as a portrait painter reached its height between the second half of the 1780s and the early 1800s. The vogue for sentimentality then pervading Russian art and literature influenced his work in many respects. Apart from the tenderness of feeling, however, most of his portraits depict the sitter in a truthful, sober fashion. For portraits of women, Borovikovsky developed a particular type, but introduced frequent variations. Most typical of his work at this time are his portraits of young women, half-length, with a thoughtful expression, seen against the background of a park or a family group, or making music. The portrait usually judged his most successful is that of

Mariya Lopukhina (1797; Moscow, Tret'yakov Gal., see fig.): she is shown standing under an oak tree, leaning on a garden parapet and surrounded by flowers. The portrait is remarkable for its softness and for the flowing contours of the figure, and for the delicate transition of shades: grey-blue, pink-lilac and light green. The endeavour to convey the sitter's emotional state is typical of Borovikovsky, who shared this aim with Rokotov but also with foreign artists such as the English painters Thomas Gainsborough and George Romney. Another strong work from this period is the portrait of the young *Yekaterina Arsen'yeva* (1795–9; St Petersburg, Rus. Mus.), shown wearing a shepherdess's bonnet and holding an apple. The lively face, with its snub nose and eyes slightly aslant, is full of ardour, a sense of mischief and genuine gaiety. In several portraits Borovikovsky strove to idealize his sitter's appearance, as in the double portrait of *Lizyn'ka and Dashenka* (1794; Moscow, Tret'yakov Gal.), two maids belonging to the L'vov household. Leaning towards each other in an affected manner, pretty and languid, dressed in fine clothes and jewels, they seem to personify the tenderness and true friendship frequently celebrated in the poetry of the day. Most of Borovikovsky's sitters were members of the nobility, their friends or those close to them; but he also painted simple peasants, continuing a practice of the painters Argunov and Levitsky. The small idyllic portrait of the peasant girl *Khristin'ya* (*c.* 1795; Moscow, Tret'yakov Gal.), who was nurse to the L'vov family, reflects not so much the sitter's social position as the charm, modesty and purity of heart of a simple countrywoman. Borovikovsky's portraits of men are more sensitive psychologically, and solve brilliantly the problems

Vladimir Borovikovsky: *Mariya Lopukhina*, oil on canvas, 720×535 mm, 1797 (Moscow, Tret'yakov Gallery)

of expressing feelings. The portrait of *Fyodor Borovsky* (1799; St Petersburg, Rus. Mus.) emphasizes the courage and resolution of a leading military figure; and the dominance of character, as well as the composition, anticipates the Romantic portraits of the 19th century.

Borovikovsky was also an outstanding painter of miniatures. The portrait of the poet *Vasily Kapnist* (1790–94; St Petersburg, Rus. Mus.) is among his best works of this type, elegant in drawing and colour and skilful in composition. Borovikovsky also painted ceremonial portraits. His portrait of *Prince Aleksandr Kurakin* (*c.* 1800; St Petersburg, Rus. Mus.) is especially impressive: the prince stands in a proud attitude, his coat covered in diamonds; thrown down on the left is the black cloak of a Knight of Malta; on the right is a bust of Paul I, indicating the prince's closeness to the emperor. The portrait is also very accomplished from a technical point of view; the range of colours is based on a harmonious combination of contrasting tones, which give the work a solemn and ceremonial air. The characterization is rich and complex: Borovikovsky conveys the sitter's pride and aristocratic hauteur, the cunning and yet also the intelligence and amiability of an enlightened aristocrat. A comparable work is the portrait of the Persian prince *Murtaza Kuli Khan* (1796; St Petersburg, Rus. Mus.), which shows the artist's fascination with an exotic sitter.

The portraits painted by Borovikovsky at the beginning of the 19th century reflect new intellectual and cultural trends, in particular a belief in the capacities of human reason. Borovikovsky put increased emphasis on his sitters' individuality, seeking to penetrate further into the fundamental character of each. Those portrayed appear generally self-contained and the use of bold and sombre local colour and stronger contrast established a serious air. The portrait of *Princess Margarita Dolgorukaya* (1811; Moscow, Tret'yakov Gal.) depicts a strong, reserved, somewhat cold woman, far from the languid dreamers of his previous period. The portrait of *Pyotr Dubovitsky* (1804; Moscow, Tret'yakov Gal.), however, has a captivating air of intelligence, nobility and inner dignity. During Borovikovsky's last years there was a decline in the quality of his work. He was attracted by religious mysticism and practically ceased painting.

BIBLIOGRAPHY

T. Alekseyeva: *Vladimir Lukich Borovikovsky i russkaya kul'tura na rubezhe 18–19 vekov* [Vladimir Lukich Borovikovsky and Russian civilization at the turn of the 19th century] (Moscow, 1975)

G. KOMELOVA

Borowski, Włodzimierz (*b* Kurów, 7 Sept 1930). Polish painter, sculptor and conceptual artist. In 1952–5 he studied art history at the Catholic University in Lublin. He was self-taught as an artist, and he made his first works at about the time of the formation of the group Zamek (Castle or Lock), which comprised young artists and theoreticians interested in the structural properties of works of art. His first pictures are abstracts with expressive subject-matter, usually executed in black (e.g. the *Feast of Nebuchadnezzar*, 1957; priv. col.).

In 1958 Borowski turned from pictures to objects. Using plastic odds and ends as ready-mades, he produced his first *Artony*—compositions from ikebana bowls, small

plates and pieces of wire joined together with the intention of giving them the autonomy of living organisms. He subsequently added movement, electric light, fluid circulating in transparent tubes, and smells. The *Manilusy* (1963) were environments of loosely hung pieces of mirror distorting spatial perception and drawing the viewer into a game of illusion. These were soon followed by a series of 'Syncretic Exhibitions', which by 1966–8 had the structure of Happenings, with controlled dramaturgy and pulsating light synchronized with sound and colour. At the same time he continued his defunctionalization of objects in series such as *Clothes-horse Collections*. During this period he increasingly shifted his concern from work to attitude and organized events that raised the problem of the artist's objectivity (e.g. *Dialogue*, 1970). In the manifesto *Sztuczna Sztuka* ('Artificial art', 1974) he expressed his disapproval of the objectification of art in the public sphere. He withdrew from official artistic life and took part in exhibitions on private property or in students' galleries and, from 1983, in churches. In the early 1980s echoes of his former waywardness transmuted into metaphysical concerns. In *I Was* (1983) and the *Magic Objects* series, he succeeded in capturing the emotions stirred up by the social tensions of the time using simple materials (loose canvas, rope, etc.).

BIBLIOGRAPHY

U. Czartoryska: *Od pop artu do konceptualizmu* [From Pop art to conceptual art] (Warsaw, 1973)

B. Kowalska: *Polska awangarda malarska 1945–1970* [Polish avant-garde painting 1945–1970] (Warsaw, 1975)

A. Wojciechowski: *Contemporary Polish painting: Trends, Goals, Works* (Warsaw, 1977) [also pubd simultaneously in Pol., Fr. and Ger.]

A. Kępińska: *Nowa sztuka—sztuka polska 1945–1978* [New art—Polish art 1945–1978] (Warsaw, 1981)

J. Bogucki: *Sztuka polski ludowej* [Art of the Polish people] (Warsaw, 1985)

ANDA ROTTENBERG

Borra, Giovanni Battista (*b* Dogliani, 27 Dec 1713; *d* ?Turin, Nov 1770). Italian architect, draughtsman and engineer. In 1733–6 he was a pupil of Bernardo Antonio Vittone, producing ten plates for Vittone's *Istruzione elementari per indirizzo de'giovani allo studio dell'architettura civile* (Lugano, 1760). In 1748 he published a practical handbook on the stability of buildings. Having met Robert Wood in Rome, he accompanied him as architectural draughtsman on an archaeological expedition to Asia Minor and Syria in 1750–51 (sketchbooks in London, Soc. Promot. Hell. & Roman Stud. Lib.), a trip financed by the young JOHN BOUVERIE. On getting to London in 1751, he prepared the drawings (London, RIBA) for Wood's books on Palmyra and Baalbek. In 1752–60 Borra undertook commissions for English patrons, creating Rococo interiors in 1755 for the residence of Edward Howard, 9th Duke of Norfolk, in St James's Square, London (destr. 1938; Music Room reconstr., London, V&A). At Stowe, Bucks, he was responsible for the interior decoration for Richard Grenville, 2nd Earl Temple. He altered and executed Robert Adam's design for the south front of Stowe and altered the garden buildings of John Vanbrugh and James Gibbs to conform with Grenville's Neoclassical tastes. Borra's principal work is his remodelling and extension in 1756–8 of Guarino Guarini's Castello dei Racconigi, near Turin (1676–83), which was commissioned by Prince Ludovico di Carignano. On the south façade and for the interior decoration of the Sala d'Ercole and Sala di Diana, on the *piano nobile*, Borra used antique decorative motifs from Baalbek and especially Palmyra, which were also becoming fashionable for ceiling decorations in England. He undertook work on Piedmontese palazzi, notably the Palazzo Isnardi di Caraglio in Turin (from *c.* 1766–7), collaborating with Benedetto Innocente Alfieri, and on churches. In 1763 he built the chapel of S Sudario with a Palladian façade for the senate of Nice. During his last ten years he designed fortifications at Alessandria and numerous hydraulic projects in the Piedmont region.

UNPUBLISHED SOURCES
London/Tisbury, Wilts [priv. col.]
London, V&A [watercolours of oriental towns and landscapes]
New Haven, CT, Yale Cent. Brit. A. [expedition drawings]

WRITINGS
Trattato della cognizione pratica della resistenze geometriche dimostrato (Turin, 1748)

Colvin; *DBI*

BIBLIOGRAPHY
R. Wood: *The Ruins of Palmyra, Otherwise Tedmor in the Desert* (London, 1753/R 1971)
———: *The Ruins of Balbec, Otherwise Heliopolis in Coelosyria* (London, 1757/R 1971)
A. Peyrot: *Torino nei secoli* (Turin, 1965), i, pp. 241–8
N. Gabrielli: *Racconigi* (Turin, 1972)
G. B. Clarke and M. J. Gibbon: 'The History of Stowe—xviii: Earl Temple and Giambattista Borra', *The Stoic*, xxv (1973), pp. 201–5
D. Fitz-Gerald: *The Norfolk House Music Room* (London, 1973)

O. ZOLLER

Borrassà, Lluís (*b* Girona; *fl* 1380; *d* Barcelona, between 19 Dec 1424 and 23 Feb 1425). Catalan painter. He was the second son of Guillem Borrassà (*fl* 1360–96), a painter of Girona, and is first mentioned on 21 January 1380, when he received payment for the repair of a stained-glass window in Girona Cathedral. Soon afterwards he moved to Barcelona, where in 1383 he was working on an important altarpiece (untraced) for the convent of S Damian, which was paid for by King Peter IV 'el Ceremonioso' of Aragon (*reg* 1336–87). Borrassà was already a citizen of Barcelona in 1385, and documents show clearly that his artistic gifts were soon recognized. In spite of his success, however, he maintained dual citizenship for several years and frequently returned to Girona to obtain commissions and payment for completed work; his elder brother Francesc (*fl* 1399–1422), who inherited the family workshop, often acted as his agent or partner. Lluís Borrassà evidently became the most outstanding and prolific painter in Catalonia of his time, carrying out important commissions not only in Barcelona and Girona but also in central Catalonia and in the area between Tarragona, Igualada and Vilafranca del Penedès. He exercised some influence in the area of Lleida as well, which was dominated in the first third of the 15th century by the painter Jaume Ferrer.

Eleven documented altarpieces by Lluís Borrassà survive, spanning practically his entire career from 1392 to 1423. It has thus been possible to establish the essential lines of his artistic development, an additional 20 works attributable to him being interspersed within this outline. Works such as the altarpiece of the *Virgin and St George* (Vilafranca del Penedès, S Francisco) and the altarpieces

for Santes Creus Abbey (1403–11; Tarragona, Mus. Dioc.; Barcelona, Mus. A. Catalunya), for S Pedro, Terrassa (1411–13; see fig.), for the convent of S Clara, Vic (1414–15; Vic, Mus. Episc.) and for San Miguel de Cruïlles Abbey (1416–17; Girona, Mus. A. & Mus. Dioc.) are excellent illustrations of his style. At the time of his arrival in Barcelona, the prevailing style was the Italianate, characterized by soft, harmonious colours and monumental compositions, with foreground groups of hieratic figures and backgrounds stripped of all anecdotal detail. Painters such as the Serra brothers had been active there for over 20 years, but they had lapsed into a routine decorative formalism. In this context the works of the young Borrassà must have made a profound impact. The new naturalism of the so-called International Gothic constituted a real revolution: bright, contrasting and sometimes arbitrary colours endow Borrassà's compositions with suggestive arabesques of colour; the narrative is enriched by the inclusion of numerous anecdotal details taken from everyday life; the figures are richly dressed in contemporary fashions and make graceful yet dynamic gestures; their postures are daringly foreshortened, and they move freely

Lluís Borrassà: *Fall of Simon Magus*, detail from the altarpiece of *St Peter*, tempera on panel, 1411–13 (Terrassa, S Pedro)

in a space already endowed with a certain depth of field; the variety of human types is increased, and a taste for the grotesque is noticeable, especially in the magnificent representations of devils.

BIBLIOGRAPHY

J. Gudiol i Cunill: 'Un document inèdit sobre el pintor Lluís Borrassà', *Veu Catalunya* (24 Aug 1911)
C. R. Post: *A History of Spanish Painting*, 12 vols (Cambridge, MA, 1930–66)
J. M. Madurell i Marimón: 'El pintor Lluís Borrassà: Su vida, su tiempo, sus seguidores y sus obras', *An. & Bol. Mus. A. Barcelona*, vii (1949); viii (1950) and x (1952) [issues dedicated to Lluís Borrassà]
J. Gudiol: *Borrassà* (Barcelona, 1953)
J. Gudiol and S. Alcolea Blanch: *Pintura gótica catalana* (Barcelona, 1986), pp. 75–85

SANTIAGO ALCOLEA BLANCH

Borrel. French family of medallists. Valentin Maurice Borrel (*b* Montataire, Oise, 24 July 1804; *d* Chevilly-Larue, Val-de-Marne, 29 March 1882) learnt his craft in the workshop of Jean-Jacques Barre (1793–1855). His first medal, of the dramatist *Louis-Benôit Picard*, was well received, and he pursued a successful and prolific career recording the main events of Louis-Philippe's reign, the Second Republic and the Second Empire. His son Alfred Borrel (*b* Paris, 18 Aug 1836; *d* 1927) trained under François Jouffroy at the Ecole des Beaux-Arts. Like his father, he exhibited regularly at the Salon, where his portrait medals and his allegorical figure compositions, notably that for the *Centenary of the Foundation of the School of Living Oriental Languages* (1895; Paris, Bib. N.), were admired. In 1906 he became a Chevalier of the Légion d'honneur.

BIBLIOGRAPHY

Bellier de la Chavignerie–Auvray
F. Mazerolle: 'V.-M. Borrel', *Gaz. Numi. Fr.* (1904), pp. 1–38
Catalogue général illustré des éditions de la Monnaie de Paris, iii (Paris, 1978), pp. 53–8

MARK JONES

Borromeo. Italian family of patrons. It is one of the oldest patrician families in Lombardy, descended from the Vitaliani family of Padua. Vitaliano I (*d* 1449) was the first member to abandon the surname Vitaliani and assume that of Borromeo in 1406. The name Borromeo derives from that of 'Bon Romano', first adopted by his forebear Vitaliani Giovanni (AD 553). While in the service of Duke Filippo Maria Visconti, Vitaliano I was created Duke of Arona (1445), and the Borromeo family was given Milanese citizenship. The Borromei were prominent in Milanese affairs and owned extensive properties throughout the duchy. They were benefactors of the church of S Carlo Borromeo (begun 1614), Arona, and the Borromeo Chapel in S Maria delle Grazie, Milan. Most notable patrons among the family members were (1) Carlo Borromeo and his cousin (2) Cardinal Federico Borromeo, both of whom were Archbishop of Milan (*see also* MILAN, §I, 3), and (3) Conte Vitaliano VI Borromeo. The Borromeo line has survived into the 20th century.

DBI

BIBLIOGRAPHY

P. Litta and others: *Famiglie notabili milanesi* (1875), ii of *Celebri famiglie italiane* (Milan and Turin, 1819–99)
Albero genealogico della famiglia Principesca Borromeo di Milano (Milan, 1935)

(1) Saint **Carlo** [Charles] **II Borromeo** (*b* Arona, 2 Oct 1538; *d* Milan, 3–4 Nov 1584; *can* 1 Nov 1610; *fd* 4 Nov 1610). Patron, collector, religious reformer and writer. He was one of the most influential figures of the Counter-Reformation and had a profound effect on Italian art and architecture. He was the son of Count Gilberto II Borromeo (*d* 1558) and Margherita de' Medici (*d* 1547). He was created Cardinal in 1560 and moved to Rome in that year, where he was instrumental in persuading Pope Pius IV, his maternal uncle, to convene the third session (1562–3) of the Council of Trent. As Secretary of State to the Pope, he played a significant role in formulating its decrees. In Rome in the 1560s, with his friend Filippo Neri, he explored the Early Christian remains, and his interest in the early Church, a response to Protestant attacks, informed his later writings. In 1562 he founded the Accademia delle Notti Vaticane, an academy of learned churchmen. He was appointed Archbishop of Milan in 1563 and returned to his diocese in 1565, where his austere way of life, practical charity and diocesan reform made him the model of the post-Tridentine pastor; he was particularly celebrated for his work among the sick and the poor of Milan during a severe famine (1570) and a plague (1576–8), which made him a folk hero.

Deeply influenced by the decrees of the Council of Trent, Carlo believed that religious art should be clear and direct, that it should educate the spectator and move him to penance. In his *Instructionum fabricae et supellectilis ecclesiasticae* (begun after 1572; Milan, 1577) he set out his proposals for the reform of church architecture and decoration. The first section, of 33 chapters, concerns the building and its interior; the second section, almost obsessively detailed, pertains to ecclesiastical furnishing. In Chapter 17, where he discusses the representation of sacred events, he stipulates punishments or fines for painters and sculptors who deviate from his proscribed guidelines for decorum. He believed that portraits should be as accurate as possible and that the depiction of animals, except in a biblical or hagiographic context, should be prohibited. His views influenced artists working in Milan; he supported Giulio Campi and Antonio Campi in the competition for the organ shutters in Milan Cathedral in 1564 and commissioned Antonio Campi to paint a *Crucifixion with Scenes from the Passion* (Monza, priv. col., variant of a picture now in Paris, Louvre) for his private chapel in the Palazzo Arcivescovile, a picture that perfectly expresses his belief, indebted to St Ignatius Loyola, in the value of meditating on religious images. Under his influence Paolo Camillo Landriani (*d* 1613), Simone Peterzano and Ambrogio Figino also developed clearer and more austere styles. It has been suggested that his religious ideals were also of fundamental importance to the art of Caravaggio (Calvesi). His collection, much of which he sold in 1569 for charitable purposes, included antique marbles, but remains ill-defined. An inventory of 1618 includes Titian's *Adoration of the Magi*, an *Agony in the Garden* by either Giulio or Antonio Campi and Jacopo Bassano's *Annunciation to the Shepherds* (all Milan, Ambrosiana). He asked Arrigo Fiammingo (?Hendrik van den Broeck) to make a copy of the highly venerated *Virgin and Child* in S Maria Maggiore, Rome, and may also have commissioned two portraits (?1585; Milan, Ambrosiana), executed after his death by Ambrogio Figino.

In the section of the *Instructionum* on architecture Carlo discusses the symbolic aspects of church buildings; the porticos, windows, octagonal-type baptistery doors and orientation. His aim was to fuse this symbolism with liturgical practicalities to produce buildings of simple design with a restrained use of the Classical orders. This new austerity did not preclude decoration altogether, as he declares, perhaps ironically, that churches could be embellished if such expenditure were balanced with the aid given to the poor. Instrumental in implementing these ideas was Pellegrino Tibaldi, who designed buildings for him in Milan and Pavia from 1564 to *c.* 1582, and whose *Discorso dell' architettura* (Milan, Bib. Ambrosiana) was strongly influenced by Borromeo's ideas (*see* TIBALDI, (1)). Works by Tibaldi include the Collegio Borromeo (1564–92) at Pavia, the Canonica del Duomo (1572–1604), the churches of S Carlo al Lazzaretto (1576–92) and S Sebastiano (begun 1577), and the courtyard of the Palazzo Arcivescovile, all in Milan. Tibaldi was succeeded by Martino Bassi as architect to the Fabbrica; Bassi was also commissioned to reconstruct the ancient church of S Lorenzo (shortly after 1575; for discussion and illustration *see* BASSI, MARTINO). Borromeo also owned many drawings by Tibaldi, including designs (unexecuted; Milan, Ambrosiana) for stained-glass windows for Milan Cathedral. Borromeo's views were also absorbed by such architects as Galeazzo Alessi and Andrea Palladio. The interior of Il Redentore (begun 1576), Venice, devoid of superfluous ornament with its separation of choir from presbytery, personifies this new simplicity (*see* PALLADIO, ANDREA, fig. 7). Borromeo may in turn have been inspired by the work of contemporary architects, for instance by Palladio's Latin-cross plan of S Giorgio Maggiore, Venice (Gábor). Carlo also appreciated the didactic possibilities of the Sacro Monte at Varallo; he made two visits (1578; 1584), encouraged the resumption of work, which had halted after the departure of Gaudenzio Ferrari, and modified Alessi's plans.

Carlo was canonized unusually soon after his death, and his life was celebrated by many painters and by the building of many churches and chapels dedicated to him in the first quarter of the 17th century in Milan, northern Italy and Rome (*see*, for example, MILAN, fig. 10). He was venerated as a protector against the plague and is often shown in the company of fellow plague saints, Sebastian and Roch. The Fabbrica of the Duomo commissioned an extensive cycle (Milan Cathedral) showing scenes from his life from leading Milanese painters, among them Cerano and Giulio Cesare Procaccini. In 1614 it was decreed that he was to be portrayed as a holy cardinal and not as an archbishop, thus emphasizing his overriding loyalty to Rome. The *Supper of St Carlo Borromeo* (Milan, S Maria della Passione; *see* CRESPI, DANIELE) movingly records his austerity, while a monumental bronze and copper statue known as *San Carlone* (completed 1694; h. 20.68 m), designed by Cerano in 1614 and erected near Arona by the Borromeo family to commemorate their illustrious native saint, suggests the heroic strength of the reformer.

WRITINGS
Instructionum fabricae et supellectilis ecclesiasticae libri duo (Milan, 1577); Eng. trans. and commentary by E. C. Voelker (Ann Arbor, 1981)
Acta ecclesiae Mediolanensis (Brescia, 1603); ed. A. Ratti (Milan, 1890)

BIBLIOGRAPHY
DBI
C. Marcora: 'Il Museo di S Carlo', *Mem. Stor. Dioc. Milano*, v/3 (1964), pp. 150–54
H. Gábor: 'Palladio e San Carlo Borromeo', *Boll. Cent. Int. Stud. Archit. Andrea Palladio*, xxii/2 (1980), pp. 205–11
G. Alberigo and others: *Il Grande Borromeo tra storia e fede*, ed. S. Lucioli (Milan, 1984)
San Carlo e il suo tempo: Atti del convegno internazionale nel centenario della morte: Milano, 1984, 2 vols
A. Crist., lxxiii/706 (1985) [whole issue]
R. de Maio: 'Michelangelo e San Carlo', *Prospettiva*, xliii (1985), pp. 56–60
I Campi e la cultura artistica cremonese del cinquecento (exh. cat., ed. M. Gregori; Cremona, Mus. Civ. Ala Ponzone, 1985)
Architettura a Roma e in Italia, 1580–1621: Atti del XXIII Congresso di storia dell'architettura: Roma, 1988, ii, pp. 153–221 [articles by M. L. Gatti Perer and others]
E. C. Voelker: 'Borromeo's Influence on Sacred Art and Architecture', *San Carlo Borromeo: Catholic Reform and Ecclesiastical Politics in the Second Half of the Sixteenth Century*, ed. J. M. Headley and J. B. Tomaro (Washington, DC, London and Toronto, 1988), pp. 172–87
R. Haslam: 'Pellegrino de' Pellegrini, Carlo Borromeo and the Public Architecture of the Counter-reformation', *A. Lombarda*, 94/5 (1990), pp. 17–30
For further bibliography *see* MILAN, §I, 3.

(2) Cardinal **Federico** [Federigo] **Borromeo** (*b* Milan, 18 Aug 1564; *d* Milan, 21 Sept 1631). Patron and art theorist, cousin of (1) Carlo Borromeo. He was the second son of Conte Giulio Cesare Borromeo and Margherita Trivulzio. After his father's death, Federico's education was entrusted to his elder cousin Carlo. He studied at the Studio di Bologna under the protection of Cardinal Gabriele Paleotti from 1579 to 1580 and graduated from the clerical Collegio Borromeo, Pavia, in 1585. Although he was profoundly influenced by his cousin, Federico's attitude towards religion and art was less austere, more humanistic. Like Carlo, he saw art as the tool of religion, but he combined this view with sensitive connoisseurship and relative leniency towards artistic licence.

Federico lived in Rome from 1586 to 1601; he was appointed Cardinal in 1587 and Archbishop of Milan in 1595. This period, when he mixed with scholars, theorists, patrons and artists, was crucial to the development of his views on art. He was fascinated by the inscriptions and paintings in newly discovered catacombs, which he explored with Filippo Neri, and in 1593 became the first Cardinal Protector of Federico Zuccaro's Accademia di S Luca, Rome. At this time he was more interested in Flemish still-life and landscape paintings than in historical subjects by contemporary Italian painters. In 1593 he met Paul Bril and Hans Rottenhammer I, and soon after formed a lasting friendship with Jan Breughel the elder, who became part of his entourage in both Rome and Milan (*see* BRUEGEL, (3)). In Rome he bought about 10 Flemish landscapes, and it was probably at this time that he acquired Caravaggio's *Basket of Fruit* (*c.* 1598–1601; Milan, Ambrosiana; *see* STILL-LIFE, fig. 4).

Borromeo moved permanently to Milan in 1601, where he was official overseer of ecclesiastical art in the diocese. The decoration of Milan Cathedral was then the city's major artistic project and he played an important role in commissioning the two cycles of paintings (1602–4; 1610) on the *Life and Miracles of Carlo Borromeo* (*see* MILAN, §II, 3 and fig. 10), taking a close interest in the choice of scenes and the clarity of their presentation. He also influenced the decoration of the cathedral's façade, yet his patronage is more clearly seen in the doctrinaire decoration of the Collegio Borromeo in Pavia, where Cesare Nebbia and Zuccaro painted scenes from the *Life of St Carlo Borromeo* (1602–4).

As a patron of architecture, Federico emulated his cousin, whose favourite architect, Pellegrino Tibaldi, was invited back to Milan but died the next year (1596) without executing anything. In 1602 Aurelio Trezzi (*fl* 1598–1616) was commissioned to design the courtyard of the Seminario Maggiore in Milan, which is based on Tibaldi's Collegio Borromeo, Pavia. Later the conservative Fabio Mangone became his preferred architect and designed the courtyard (1608) of the Collegio Elvetico, chaster and more classical than Trezzi's version. The classical façade of the Borromeo family church, S Maria Podone (1626) in Milan, was designed by Lelio Buzzi. The considerably more innovative Francesco Maria Ricchini, whom Borromeo had sent to Rome to be trained, also received commissions for Milan, including S Giuseppe (1607–30; *see* RICCHINI, FRANCESCO MARIA, §1(ii) and fig. 1) and the concave façade of the Collegio Elvetico (1627; *see* RICCHINI, FRANCESCO MARIA, §2 and fig. 2). Borromeo also patronized the Sacro Monte above Varese, and planned a similar scheme near Arona, dedicated to Carlo Borromeo, with 30 chapels leading to a colossal bronze statue (*see* (1) above).

In 1620 Borromeo founded the Institution for the Restoration and Construction of Parochial Churches, Milan's first historic preservation board. Although some of its records survive, nearly all of the buildings to which they relate have perished. His most enduring contribution was the founding of the Ambrosiana (see fig.) in Milan and the writing of two treatises, *De pictura sacra* (1624) and *Musaeum Bibliothecae Ambrosianae* (1625). The Ambrosiana, which now consists of the Biblioteca (founded 1607) and the Pinacoteca (founded 1618), at that time also included the Accademia del Disegno (active from *c*. 1613; formally founded 1620); Buzzi designed the classical façade of the Biblioteca Ambrosiana, and Mangone the Accademia del Disegno (1611–13).

As Borromeo explained in *De pictura sacra*, the Ambrosiana was founded in response to the Council of Trent's call for bishops to educate the faithful through images as well as words; it was thus dedicated to the city of Milan as a public resource. The Pinacoteca, which remains largely intact, although much augmented, consisted originally of many religious paintings by Italian Renaissance artists, landscapes and still-lifes by contemporary Flemish artists, drawings and prints, casts of antique sculptures and copies taken from famous Roman frescoes, Paolo Giovio's portrait collection and paintings by Leonardo da Vinci, Correggio, Bernardino Luini and Parmigianino. Among Borromeo's favourite works, described in *Musaeum*, were Titian's *Adoration of the Magi* (Milan, Ambrosiana), Luini's *St Mary Magdalene* (Washington, DC, N.G.A.), Caravaggio's *Basket of Fruit*, Breughel's series of the *Four Elements* (1608–21; *Fire* and *Water*, Milan, Ambrosiana; *Earth* and *Air*, Paris, Louvre) and Raphael's cartoon for the *School of*

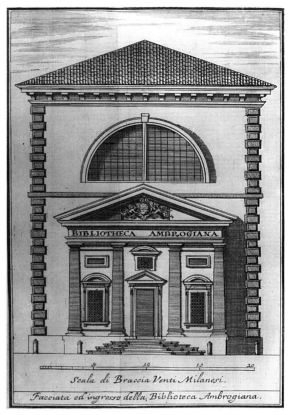

Lelio Buzzi: façade of the Biblioteca Ambrosiana, founded by Federico Borromeo in 1607; engraving from Serviliano Latuada: *Descrizione di Milano* (Milan, 1738) (Milan, Biblioteca Ambrosiana)

Athens (Milan, Ambrosiana). His writings indicate that the Ambrosiana collection was meant to intensify the viewer's religious experience: to instruct by telling stories or presenting historical information, to inspire by depicting virtue and heroism and to demonstrate God's wisdom and goodness by representing his creation, the natural world.

The Pinacoteca also served as a teaching aid for the Accademia del Disegno, of which Cerano was appointed director in 1621; the sculptor Gian Andrea Biffi and Mangone were also instructors. The programme of study, based on that followed at Florence, Rome and Bologna (*see* ACADEMY, §3), included art theory, religious history, anatomy and works of art in the museum. Borromeo desired students to turn away from the lascivious, abstruse and unnatural aspect of *maniera* art and create a more direct and emotionally appealing style. Drawing from the nude life model was encouraged as a means to give religious art more convincing naturalism.

Borromeo's two treatises are complementary. *De pictura sacra* emphasizes typically post-Tridentine concerns, including clarity and scriptural and iconographic accuracy in religious art. The most original aspect is the archaeologically correct discussion of Early Christian art, which was intended to assert the inveterate tradition of the Roman Church. *Musaeum*, organized as a walking tour of the finest items in the Ambrosiana collection, reveals his delight in art and his appreciation of various artists' talents. Both works testify, as does the collection, to his central importance as a patron in post-Tridentine Italy.

WRITINGS

De pictura sacra (Milan, 1624); ed. with It. trans. by C. Castiglione, intro. and notes by G. Nicodemi (Sora, 1932)
Musaeum Bibliothecae Ambrosianae (Milan, 1625); ed. with It. trans. by L. Grasselli, pref. and notes by L. Beltrami (Milan, 1901); Eng. trans. with intro. by A. Q. Platt as *Cardinal Federico Borromeo as a Patron and Critic of the Arts and his 'Musaeum' of 1625* (New York, 1986)

BIBLIOGRAPHY

DBI [with full bibliog.]
F. Rivola: *Vita di Federico Borromeo* (Milan, 1656) [the best and most comprehensive biog.]
G. Gabrieli: 'Federico Borromeo a Roma', *Archv Soc. Romana Stor. Patria*, lvi–lvii (1933–4), pp. 157–217
A. Peroni: 'Il Collegio Borromeo di Pavia: Architettura e decorazione', *IV Centenario del Collegio Borromeo di Pavia* (Pavia, 1961), pp. 111–61
A. Palestra: 'L'opera del Cardinal Federico Borromeo per la conservazione degli edifici sacri', *A. Lombarda*, xii (1967), pp. 113–20
S. Coppa: 'Federico Borromeo teorico d'arte; Annotazioni in margine al *De pictura sacra* ed al *Musaeum*', *A. Lombarda*, xv (1970), pp. 65–70
G. Melzi d'Eril: 'Federico Borromeo e Cesare Monti collezionisti milanesi', *Stor. A.*, xv–xvi (1972), pp. 293–306
D. Freedberg: 'The Origins and Rise of the Flemish Madonnas in Flower Garlands, Decoration and Devotion', *Münchn. Jb. Bild. Kst*, xxxii (1981), pp. 115–50
S. Bedoni: *Jan Breughel in Italia e il collezionismo del seicento* (Florence and Milan, 1983)
P. M. Jones: 'Federico Borromeo's Ambrosian Collection as a Teaching Facility for the Academy of Design', *Leids Ksthist. Jb.*, v–vi (1986–7), pp. 44–60
——: 'Bernardino Zuini's *The Magdalene* from the Collection of Federico Boromeo: Religious Contemplation and Iconographic Sources', *Stud. Hist. A.*, xxvi (1990), pp. 67–72
A. Morandotti: 'Il revival Leonardesco nell'età di Federico Borromeo', *I Leonardeschi a Milano: Fortuna e collezionismo Atti del convegno internazionale: Milano, 1990*, pp. 166–82
B. Agosti: 'Due amici de Federico Borromeo e il Medio Evo', *A. Lombarda*, xcvi–xcvii (1991), pp. 119–25
P. M. Jones: 'Defining the Canonical Status of Milanese Renaissance Art: Bernardino Luini's Paintings for the Ambrosian Accademia del Disegno', *A. Lombarda*, c (1992), pp. 89–92
——: *Federico Borromeo and the Ambrosiana: Art Patronage and Reform in Seventeenth-century Milan* (Cambridge and New York, 1993) [with complete cat. of original col.]

PAMELA M. JONES

(3) Conte **Vitaliano VI Borromeo** (*b* Milan, 5 April 1620; *d* Milan, 8 Oct 1690). Patron and collector. He was the son of Conte Carlo III Borromeo (1586–1652) and Isabella d'Adda. He was educated in Rome and, while pursuing a military and diplomatic career, was prominent in literary and scientific circles in Milan. He was involved in the completion of the villa–palazzo (1670) on Isola Bella, Lake Maggiore, begun in 1632 by his father. Between 1673 and 1685 he commissioned Filippo Abbiati (1640–1715) to paint episodes from the lives of notable members of the Borromeo family. Known as the *Fasti Borromei* (untraced), the two large paintings were destined for the Borromeos' *rocca* (castle) at Angera. Abbiati's canvas of *Vitaliano I Approving the Project for the Sepulchral Monument of St Giustina* (Isola Bella, Mus. Borromeo) was possibly also commissioned by Vitaliano. He assembled an impressive art collection, which included paintings by Bernardino Luini, Titian, Tintoretto, Leonardo da Vinci, Daniele Crespi and Paris Bordone. The richly furnished and decorated villa is now the Museo Borromeo and contains a tapestry gallery and paintings by Francesco Zuccarelli,

Antonio Tempesta, Bergognone, Paris Bordone, Giovanni Antonio Boltraffio and other Lombard masters.

BIBLIOGRAPHY

DBI
A. Cipollini: *Il conte Vitaliano Borromeo, 1620–1690* (Rome, 1913)
S. Zuffi: 'I dipinti per i Borromeo nell'evoluzione stilistica di Filippo Abbiati', *Paragone*, xxxvii/441 (Nov 1986), pp. 72–82

Borromini [Castelli], **Francesco** (*b* Bissone, nr Lugano, 25 Sept 1599; *d* Rome, 2 Aug 1667). Italian architect. His name, with that of his contemporary and rival Gianlorenzo Bernini (*see* BERNINI, (2)), is synonymous with the main phase of Roman High Baroque architecture between *c.* 1630 and 1665. Their working methods and perception of art were regarded as incompatible by their contemporaries, but later their work was synthesized to form the basis of late Baroque architecture in Rome and the Catholic areas of Central Europe (Austria, Bavaria, Bohemia and Silesia). In western Europe, on the other hand, a classical Baroque style evolved, and Borromini's style was rejected as odd and contrary to the rules.

I. Life and work. II. Character and personality. III. Architectural influence. IV. Critical reception and posthumous reputation.

I. Life and work.

1. Early work, 1619–33. 2. Palazzo Barberini. 3. S Carlo alle Quattro Fontane. 4. Oratory of S Filippo Neri. 5. S Ivo della Sapienza. 6. Lateran Basilica. 7. Piazza Navona. 8. Other palazzi. 9. Collegio di Propaganda Fide. 10. S Andrea delle Fratte.

1. EARLY WORK, 1619–33. Like most artists of the Baroque period who made their mark in Rome, Borromini was not a native Roman, but his career was confined to the city and its neighbourhood. While he was still a child he started a mason's apprenticeship at the cathedral workshop in Milan and moved to Rome in 1619. There, with the help of his numerous relations, he hoped to achieve the status of an independent architect. Born a Castelli, he took his mother's maiden name of Borromini to distinguish himself from numerous Castelli relatives. His family was part of a far-flung network of related families that provided Roman building sites with a constant source of trained building workers—masons, bricklayers, stuccoworkers and architects—from Ticino and Upper Italy. Members of the families who were already established in Rome had previously been instrumental in bringing to the city Domenico Fontana and Carlo Maderno, who had risen to become papal architects. It was only because his mother was related to Maderno that Borromini, as soon as he arrived in Rome, was able to work on the most prestigious building site in Europe, the façade and nave of St Peter's, where Maderno, working for Pope Paul V, was in charge. Borromini quickly rose from mason to architect, working alongside the aging Maderno and coordinating all the design and planning processes in his office. The sheer graphic brilliance and expressiveness of Borromini's drawings later gave him a clear advantage over all other architects: his soft lead pencil, its lines often smudged even further by his finger, imbued his precisely worked-out plans with an aura of mystery that aesthetically surpassed the hard, unyielding

penstrokes of other architects. His architectural drawings are rightly judged to be on a par with those of Michelangelo.

Initially, however, Borromini made his mark as a craftsman; he sculpted the angels' heads and carved the profiles for the frame of the Holy Door at St Peter's. The first mention of him as a designer was in connection with the iron grille that originally divided the canons' choir from the nave. Under the Barberini popes the grille was moved to its present position at the entrance to the chapel of the Holy Sacrament. Borromini's tireless working on drawings even during rest breaks led Maderno to take the young mason into his drawing office. From the early 1620s the fair copies of most of Maderno's designs were made by Borromini, and he was increasingly left to work out the details himself. Decorative details in Maderno's designs of 1621 for the waterfall at the Villa Ludovisi (later Villa Torlonia), Frascati, are attributed to Borromini. The completely individual touch of the emerging architect was revealed in the lantern (1623) for the dome of the Theatine church of S Andrea della Valle, Rome, which was to be completed by Maderno. In front of the areas of wall between the windows of the lantern Borromini placed the pairs of columns familiar from St Peter's, although here they are under a shared capital freely fashioned in the form of a winged angel's head with its pinions charmingly enfolding the columns. This decorative detail, which was barely visible owing to its elevated position, already showed Borromini's inner independence from conformity to the precise specifications for the orders laid down in the treatises of the day.

Borromini first emerged from the anonymity of the drawing office in 1624, when he was assigned to work alongside Bernini (who was then completely unversed in architectural matters) on the monumental bronze baldacchino commissioned by the Barberini pope Urban VIII to rise above the tomb of the Apostle at the crossing of St Peter's (see BERNINI, (2), fig. 2). This hybrid creation, in which architecture and sculpture were intended to merge into a new kind of art form, demanded specialists from both fields: Bernini was responsible for the designs and the bronze-casting, while Borromini and his staff produced the final drawings from the design sketches and supervised the structural aspects of the project. Here Borromini worked for the last time as a mason, carving the Barberini coat of arms on the marble base with Bernini's brother-in-law, Antonio Radi. Borromini was attached to Bernini in a similar capacity to that in which he had previously served Maderno. He could not have been better prepared for the task, for he had already been closely concerned with the problem of the crossing at St Peter's and the tomb; during the reign of Urban's predecessor, Paul V, Maderno had suggested that the makeshift canopy put up by him in 1606 should be replaced by a monumental structure, a hybrid form encompassing canopy and tabernacle.

The twisted bronze columns of the baldacchino were erected in the early summer of 1627, while the design and execution of the roof was not completed until 1633 (see ROME, §V, 14(ii)(b)). The extent of Borromini's artistic contribution is one of the most difficult problems of attribution in his career. While the baldacchino has traditionally been regarded as by Bernini alone, further research suggests that it was more of a team effort, with Maderno, Borromini and even Urban VIII playing a far greater role than had previously been thought. There is much to support the belief that Borromini's perspective sketches and calculations contributed substantially to making the baldacchino harmonize with the architecture of the basilica's crossing, and the suggestion for improving the coordination of the baldacchino with the height of the entablatures and with the arches of the crossing may well have come from him. This was achieved by means of impost blocks that further raised the crown of the bronze monument, so extending its proportions. Borromini is also credited with certain decorative details in the shafts and capitals of the columns. The scrolled ribs and the concave link-pieces between the columns may also have been his idea, although it is unlikely that positive proof will ever be found, and it is more probable that they were devised in collaboration with Bernini, so that their individual contributions can no longer be distinguished.

2. PALAZZO BARBERINI. The problem of distinguishing individual contributions also arises in relation to the collaboration between artists and architects on the Palazzo Barberini, where Maderno was in overall charge. Even more than the tabernacle at St Peter's, the new palace of the Barberini family has to be understood as a collective enterprise to which untrained amateurs among Urban VIII's erudite circle of friends also contributed (see ROME, §V, 24). It must have arrived at its present form in a very complicated design process involving not only Maderno but also the artists working under him, Bernini, Borromini and Pietro da Cortona. None of the distinguishing features of the building as a whole, the open, three-winged front, the loggia façade on three levels in the central block, the layout of the stairs and the diminishing widths of the entrance hall, can be ascribed with certainty to any one of the artists involved. The only clearly recognizable hand is Borromini's: as usual he made fair copies of all the design drawings.

Maderno died a year after building work began in December 1628. He was succeeded not by Borromini but by Bernini, who relied on Borromini's practical expertise. The latter's mark can be detected only in decorative aspects: the mezzanine windows on the bay linking the middle wing with the side wings at right angles show the individual touch of the young architect. He gave impact to the almost square windows, similar to the attic windows designed by Michelangelo and Maderno at St Peter's, by making the frames stand out from and become independent of the wall (to which frames had hitherto always run parallel) with the use of diagonally placed volutes, above which segmental cappings turned their ends out at 45°. Borromini also made the frames stand out from the walls on a grand scale in the doorways of the central *salone* (see ROME, fig. 61), but the sculptural decoration of their tympana was Bernini's contribution. This close collaboration came to a permanent end in 1631, when Borromini left the site after a Barberini family quarrel about the progress of the work. He also wanted to cut free from Bernini.

3. S CARLO ALLE QUATTRO FONTANE. In 1634 Cardinal Francesco Barberini helped Borromini to gain his first commission as an independent architect, the monastery and church of S Carlo alle Quattro Fontane (or S Carlino) for the Discalced Trinitarians, who had established themselves there in 1611. The monastic building, complete with cells, refectory and library, was finished by 1636, but work on the church could not begin until 1638. It was dedicated to S Carlo Borromeo in 1646, but the façade was not completed until 1677, ten years after Borromini's death. In this early masterpiece Borromini was faced with the conflicting demands of a strictly ascetic order with a severe shortage of funds that yet wished to create an impression on papal Rome. The monastic building with its small courtyard was created first to meet the Order's most pressing needs; the courtyard design is notable for the convex curvature of its corners and its pairs of monumental Doric columns. In his designs for the low upper storey of the courtyard, Borromini was apparently influenced by Bramante's cortile at S Maria della Pace, Rome (1500). He subsequently clad the stark external walls of the living-quarters with a spacious grid of flat pilasters.

The design of the church (see fig. 1) compresses into a very small area an almost impenetrably complex structure that cannot be traced back to any generally recognized formula. Some 20 different theories have been suggested to account for the putative geometric nucleus of the plan alone. The outcome of the debate is that the plan is a 'multiple form' based on a cross, an octagon and an oval, fused into an indivisible single entity. It may have been influenced by Carlo Borromeo's insistence, as a leader of the Counter-Reformation, on longitudinal church plans, as distinct from the Renaissance concept of a centralized plan (*see* CHRISTIANITY, §I, 3(ii)); the dilemma could be solved by stretching the ideal circle shape into an oval and its extension by two short cross arms, as at S Carlo. It is conceivable, moreover, that Borromini referred to Francesco Maria Ricchino's compromise formula at S Giuseppe, Milan (begun 1607), as a tribute to Borromeo.

However, the structure of S Carlo may simply have evolved by stages in the course of the design process. The first stage was a centralized plan with a circular dome above a square formed by four convex piers, possibly based on centralized late Classical buildings and the Santa Croce oratory (added to the Lateran Baptistery by Pope Hilarius (*reg* 461–8), destr. 1588). The second stage is thought to be a symmetrical, quatrefoil-shaped structure along the lines of Michelangelo's Sforza chapel (1560–73) at S Maria Maggiore, Rome. The final configuration would then have arisen through the elongation and sideways compression of the 'quatrefoil', which resulted in the oval form of the dome and the half-oval curves in the side chapels.

The origins of the structure are revealed neither in the building itself nor in the drawings (Vienna, Albertina), with their many and varied superposed design stages. The latter, however, reveal that one crucial aspect of Borromini's working methods was present even at this stage in his career. The module for all the measurements in the building was based on the triangle, a method practised in medieval 'constructive geometry' (*see* MASON (i), §IV, 2

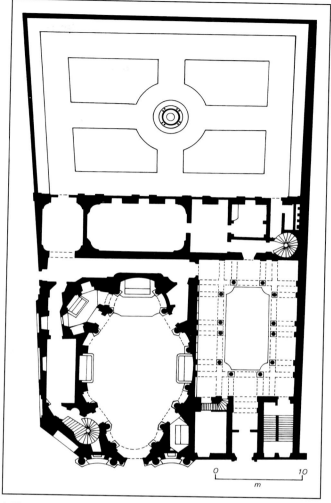

1. Francesco Borromini: S Carlo alle Quattro Fontane, Rome, begun 1638, plan

(i) and SETTING OUT), which was still in use in the Milan Cathedral building lodge where Borromini had been trained. It demonstrates that he had not adopted the Classical and Renaissance rule of proportion based on the human figure and practised by all his contemporaries, but was using a traditional system of design based on the division of a geometrical configuration.

The interior of S Carlo can be divided into three levels, the lowest of which extends to the main entablature, where curved and straight areas of wall alternate. The 16 monumental columns divide the space unevenly. Above the main entablature there is a low transitional area encompassing the dome pendentives, the half-domes of the chapels and their arches. The third level consists of the dome itself (see fig. 2), which is built in the traditional Lombard manner without a drum and seems to be suspended above the interior. This irrational impression is created by the use of a dome ring, which conceals the statical base of the coffered oval bowl.

2. Francesco Borromini: dome (1638–41) of S Carlo alle Quattro Fontane, Rome

The main artistic theme of the interior is the modelling of the walls beneath the main entablature and their articulation by the columns. Sections in the form of a semicircle or a half-oval are interspersed with flat surfaces. The slightly rounded lengths of wall frame the altar niches, the half-ovals lie at each end of the cross axis, while the semicircular sections are at either end of the longitudinal axis. The narrow, straight sections set between the rounded ones function as fronts for what must be regarded as bevelled wall piers. The wall system is given formal coherence by the columns, which can be grouped according to their function and decoration. The first, more important group acts as framing articulation in front of the dome piers while also supporting the arches of the chapel niches. This double purpose gives them markedly more importance than those in the second group, which merely frame the altars. Although they are identical in decoration and proportions, the two categories of column are subtly different: those that are associated with the piers have inverted scrolls on the capitals, whereas the others are formed in the conventional way. The restless movement of the walls and the sculptural volumes represented by the columns completely dominate the church interior, but the compactness of the small space is counteracted by an optical illusion of greater size, achieved particularly by the illusory perspectives of the oval dome

and the calottes above the altar recesses. The coffering on these is foreshortened to create an impression of greater height and breadth.

The façade of S Carlo (see fig. 3), delayed probably by lack of funds, is one of Borromini's final works, but it is likely that he designed the main artistic concept for the undulating movement of the wall as early as the 1640s. The lower part, up to and including the main entablature, had been completed by his death. The columns and walls stand in much the same relationship to each other as they do inside the building, but the façade is enhanced by the addition of small columns flanking the major order. The figures of saints in the niches were executed in the last quarter of the 17th century by pupils of Bernini. The upper level above the entablature was completed by Borromini's nephew, Bernardo Castelli, who clearly modified the original design, with the picture medallion supported by angels in the manner of Bernini and the division of the upper part of the wall into three concave bays. This arrangement does not occur elsewhere in Borromini's work, where he preferred to alternate concave and convex sections, although at S Carlo the effect is countered by the insertion of a feature resembling a sentry-box in the central bay. The height of the upper storey, which conceals the dome and lantern from the street, is also not authentic. Perhaps this drawback was accepted so that S Carlo would

3. Francesco Borromini: façade (completed 1677) of S Carlo alle Quattro Fontane, Rome

not appear less important than Bernini's neighbouring church of S Andrea al Quirinale, completed in 1670.

4. ORATORY OF S FILIPPO NERI. In 1637, while Borromini was still working on S Carlo, he was appointed by the Oratorians as chief architect for their community building, the Oratory of S Filippo Neri, near the Order's principal church, S Maria in Vallicella. On this occasion he was restricted not so much by the nature of the site as by the fact that he was supposed to execute the fully detailed design of his predecessor, Paolo Maruscelli, without substantially altering it. His main problem, however, was the petty-mindedness of the Fathers, who wanted to be consulted over every detail and were profoundly suspicious of his ideas. This unequal partnership endured for 13 years owing to the support and intervention of Virgilio Spada (*see* SPADA, (2)), who immediately recognized Borromini's genius and defended him when objections were raised by his fellow clergy. Yet in 1652 Borromini had to relinquish his unfinished building into the hands of the mediocre Camillo Arcucci.

The work required of Borromini was not so much practical as aesthetic. He was asked to provide the skeleton of the building designed by Maruscelli with an attractive outer skin that would convey something of the meaning and identity of the relatively new Oratorian Order. Borromini embellished the severe community building with motifs associated with the architecture of princely palazzi. The main staircase is modelled on that of the Palazzo Farnese (*c.* 1541, by Antonio da Sangallo (ii)), the large niches in the courtyard of the sacristy are derived from Jacopo Vignola's Palazzo Farnese in Piacenza (begun 1558), and the Giant pilasters on the façade of the clock-tower and the courtyard of the house are reminiscent of palazzi designed by Andrea Palladio and Michelangelo's façades for the Capitol in Rome (begun 1563).

Borromini's finest achievement here is the façade of the oratory hall. This room had special importance for the community because it was there that the form of devotion that typified their Order would be held: a sermon, discussion and exquisitely beautiful choral music. The main concern of the Fathers was that the elevation should not compete in height or richness with the adjacent church. They were particularly anxious to avoid the impression of matching twin fronts of equal importance. Thus the façade of the Oratory was lower and made from a cheap material (brick), with only a very sparing use of natural stone for decoration. Through his masterly handling of the brick, Borromini successfully achieved brilliant decorative effects, carrying on the tradition of elegant brickwork from the Roman Imperial period. The present appearance of the façade (see fig. 4) was created in several phases. The lower level, completed in 1638, was extended from five bays to seven, and a storey was added to it. In 1665

4. Francesco Borromini: façade of the Oratory of S Filippo Neri, Rome, 1637–40

Arcucci embedded the free-standing gable into a newly added mezzanine floor, thereby diluting the original effect of the gable.

Two qualities make the Oratory façade a masterpiece of Roman Baroque architecture: it is concave and has, on the middle bay at the lower level, a small concave projection. Except for Baldassare Peruzzi's Palazzo Massimo alle Colonne (begun 1532), built on a bend in the street, all Roman façades until then had been straight; at the Oratory, Borromini replaced their self-contained unity with a restrained turbulence, countering the cool objectivity of the High Renaissance with a current of subjectivity and emotion such as had not been experienced since the expressive architecture of Michelangelo. Borromini's second radical innovation was the loosening of the logical connection between the interior and exterior of the building. The façade gives the illusion that it is the narrow end of a building that extends further in depth, while in fact the oratory hall lies across the façade and extends beyond it at the sides. This optical illusion was chosen in order to bind together into a new entity the principal church of the Order and the house in which the form of devotional life that typified it took place.

5. S Ivo della Sapienza. Building work began on the university church of S Ivo della Sapienza in Rome in 1642 (for illustration *see* UNIVERSITY PALACE). Officially Borromini had been architect to the university since 1632, but the start of building work was delayed by lack of money. A plot of land, at the semicircular narrow end of the university court designed by Pirro Ligorio, succeeded by Giacomo della Porta, had been chosen as the site for the building. Della Porta had already designed a round church for this spot based on Michelangelo's unexecuted design (1559) for S Giovanni dei Fiorentini in Rome. Borromini also created a centralized, domed church, but he drew his inspiration from northern Italy, the dome designed without a drum and the vertical layering of the interior space and the junction of the exedrae showing parallels with Martino Bassi's renovation (after 1573) of the Early Christian church of S Lorenzo in Milan.

Borromini chose an original configuration for the ground-plan: a triangle with the apexes cut away in a concave curve, while the centres of the sides bulge out to form large semicircles. This plan soars upwards to the lantern with enormous momentum, uninterrupted by any transitional feature other than the horizontal barrier of the entablature. The variously shaped sectors ascend until the movement comes to rest under the lantern in a circle decorated with 12 stars (see fig. 5). The church was completed up to the cornice by 1644, but the accession that year of Pope Innocent X and preparations for the Holy Year in 1650 delayed work on the dome. The lantern and spiral were in place by 1652, but the stuccowork inside the dome was not completed until the early 1660s. The interior is lit solely from the dome, but the original lighting of the altar chapel reveals Borromini's familiarity with Bernini's manipulation of indirect sources of light in the Cornaro chapel (1645–52) in S Maria della Vittoria, Rome. At S Ivo, however, he refined this still further by using light reflected from steel mirrors (removed during 19th-century restorations) to illuminate the altar area.

5. Francesco Borromini: dome of S Ivo della Sapienza, Rome, completed early 1660s

The emblematic meanings associated with the shapes found at S Ivo have been the subject of much dispute. St Yves, patron saint of lawyers, seems to occupy a secondary position. To judge by the inscriptions on early designs (Vienna, Albertina), symbolism relating to wisdom, to the Temple of Solomon as the house of wisdom and to the traditional name of the university has a more important role. The inscription above the altar, 'The fear of the Lord is the beginning of wisdom' (Psalm 111:10), also emphasizes wisdom as a religious virtue. Alongside the Old Testament symbolism of wisdom, which is hard to grasp visually, Christian wisdom is depicted in the cupola in the form of the dove as one of the seven gifts of the Holy Spirit. The most puzzling question is the symbolism of the spirally shaped lantern on the dome. It has been interpreted as the tortuous path to wisdom, but others see the top of the dome as a symbol of the Pharos at Alexandria, the Tower of Babel as a symbol of wisdom or even as Dante's mountain of Purgatory from the *Divine Comedy*. In the absence of a written iconographic programme there can be no conclusions as to the meaning intended by Borromini himself.

6. Lateran Basilica. Borromini's largest commission came in 1644, when Innocent X entrusted him with the renovation of S Giovanni in Laterano (*see* ROME, §V, 15(ii)). The Pope wanted to restore the venerable but decrepit church of the Bishop of Rome for the Holy Year of 1650, so eliminating an old source of annoyance to pilgrims to Rome. Borromini was obliged to retain the

historic fabric of the nave as far as possible, cladding the old walls, which in places were leaning at a dangerous angle. The transepts, which had already been restored for the Holy Year of 1600, and the choir remained untouched, but the side aisles had to be completely reconstructed.

Borromini's proposals for renovating the walls of the nave easily prevailed over a competing design by Vincenzo della Greca. All three choices offered by Borromini divide the walls into two storeys linked by a Giant order of pilasters (see ORDERS, ARCHITECTURAL, §II). The Pope chose the most richly decorated concept, with a lower level featuring wide arches alternating with narrow segments of wall holding aedicule niches for the monumental statues of the *Apostles*. The surfaces above the niches are decorated with stucco reliefs of Old Testament and New Testament scenes attributed to the school of Alessandro Algardi, and above the arches are broad, boldly framed windows, the white light from which further emphasizes the coolness of Borromini's monochrome stucco and marble architecture. The strongest touch of colour is provided by the dark green marble columns of the aediculae, which bulge out from the walls like bent nibs, as if they were going to collapse under the lateral stress of the Giant pilasters flanking them. The columns are spolia recovered from the recently demolished side aisles. The niches for the statues are formed as fully developed aediculae with a doorway. Borromini not only gave them columns and a gable in front but also inserted a coffered oval roof and an illusionary door flanked by pilasters on the rear wall. The niches probably symbolize the 12 doors of the heavenly Jerusalem (Revelation 21:12).

The oval stucco medallions high on the walls between the windows on the upper stage have a special significance. Before the 18th century, when they were filled with the portraits of prophets, they opened directly through to the medieval masonry behind, so that the historic fabric of the building remained visible under the Baroque cladding. Thus the restoration preserved the remains of the Constantinian basilica in an outer skin that served as a form of reliquary.

Although Borromini completed the repair work on the nave by 1648, he was able only partly to achieve his artistic objectives. The nave in particular was deprived of its unified effect because the Pope was adamant that the flat, 16th-century wooden ceiling should be preserved at all costs, believing it to be the work of Michelangelo. The provisions made by Borromini for a vault, pier buttresses and vaulting brackets were to no avail; his designs for a new floor surface were also not implemented, nor his projects for a new façade: these designs were lost in the 18th century. Only two examples have been preserved of his indirectly lit chapels on the aisle walls; the others either were not built at all or had to make way for later additions that took no account of Borromini's scheme.

Borromini's final contribution to the decoration of the Lateran Basilica were the tombs in the side aisles commissioned by Alexander VII. They are a fanciful combination of medieval fragments and Baroque frames; mainly owing to the skilful handling of illusionistic perspectives these hybrid creations offer a spectacle of opposing forces crowded within the narrowest space. Alexander condemned them as being 'too Gothic'. This was not intended

as a comment on their style but rather implied that the innovative combination of classical elements produced an uncanonical ensemble alien to the conservative Pope.

7. PIAZZA NAVONA. Borromini's artistic and technical achievements at S Giovanni in Laterano prompted Innocent X to employ him for his ambitious building plans at Piazza Navona, on which the Pamphili family palazzo, the Pope's birthplace, was built. The gradual extension and reordering of the palazzo meant that a new façade was required to fuse the various parts of the building into a visual whole. Borromini's suggestions, which included Giant pilasters and a roof loggia in the form of a serliana, were rejected in favour of those by Girolamo Rainaldi, whose less exuberant conservatism and greater concentration on detail were more attuned to the Pope's taste. In 1646 Borromini added a large gallery to the palazzo, which was decorated with frescoes by Cortona. The gallery opens on to the Piazza Navona through a monumental serliana in which antique and Christian traditions are intermingled, referring both to the Imperial box at the circus and to the loggia from which the Pope gives his blessing in Raphael's fresco of the *Fire in the Borgo* (1514–17; Rome, Vatican, Stanza dell'Incendio). Both allusions acquired a special meaning at the Piazza Navona: it is built on the Stadium of Domitian (c. AD 86; destr.), the elongated form of which is still mirrored in the ground-plan of the piazza, while the reference to the fresco anticipated the subsequent transfer of the Curia to the Piazza Navona at the Pope's behest.

In 1653 Borromini received the greatest proof of confidence in his art when Innocent X dismissed Girolamo Rainaldi and his son Carlo Rainaldi as supervising architects of his favourite project, the church of S Agone, and entrusted Borromini with continuing the building. The new scheme was to incorporate the small Early Christian church as a crypt, to house the tomb of the Pope, and to serve as the chapel of his neighbouring family palazzo. When Borromini took over, the foundations and crossing piers were already in place. Carlo Rainaldi had also started on the façade, which had reached a height of 3 m; Borromini had it demolished, but his design retained the curved form envisaged by his predecessor to make room for the large flight of steps in front of the church without intruding on the piazza.

The most momentous proposal put forward by Borromini concerned the crossing piers. He wanted to make them convex and to swing into the crossing area, to engender the lively sense of movement that he had observed at the Piazza d'Oro of Hadrian's villa in Tivoli. Convex piers would also have required a different kind of dome, of the umbrella type with webs of varying width. Such bold ideas did not, however, appeal to the Pope's conservative taste. Borromini had to abandon them and settle for a conventional dome with a drum (see CHURCH, fig. 14). The crossing piers were bevelled to produce the effect of a regular octagon in the centre, the importance of which is stressed by the high drum and the dome with an elevated curve that soar above it. He had a freer hand with the exterior. By eliminating a vestibule that Rainaldi had planned, he was able to set back the façade of the church from the piazza, swinging out with a pair of short, concave link blocks to connect with the two west towers, which rise to an impressive height. He made room for these in turn by extending the façade sideways into the area of the adjoining palaces. He thus succeeded in presenting a dome between a pair of framing towers, which Michelangelo had wanted to do at St Peter's. Above the concavity of the façade rears the convexity of the drum, the same spatial reversal as at S Ivo.

The reckless haste with which the building work was pursued led to its partial collapse in 1655. The Pope died in the same year, and Prince Camillo Pamphili, with whom Borromini could find no common ground on an artistic or a human level, took over the project. Borromini was dismissed in February 1657, and the building was completed by Carlo Rainaldi at the head of a mediocre committee of architects, including Antonio del Grande and Giovanni Maria Baratta, who in 1663–6 completed the upper storeys of Borromini's bell-tower. In 1666 Bernini added a triangular pediment to the façade, which Borromini had completed up to the main cornice (*see* ITALY, fig. 16).

8. OTHER PALAZZI. Although Borromini's most outstanding achievements were in church building, he also left unmistakable traces of his innovative talent in the building of palazzi. His most ambitious project, the Palazzo Carpegna, remained largely unrealized, although the development stages have been preserved in a few drawings (Vienna, Albertina). In 1638 Conte Ambrogio Carpegna commissioned him to extend the Palazzo Vaini, near the Trevi Fountain, which his family had just bought. The dimensions and location of the plot forced Borromini to adopt a variety of irregular solutions, although he disguised them skilfully with curved walls, niches and illusionistic symmetrical effects that he had learnt from studying Hadrian's Villa. The most important of these designs is the magnificent oval court with arcading resting on coupled columns, as in the courtyard of the Palazzo Borghese (1586, by Martino Longhi the elder), although that is rectangular. The oval had never previously been used in the courtyard of a Roman palazzo. The project for an oval courtyard was extended by the suggestion that the street in front of the palace should be incorporated into it. The side of the palace would be shaped like a half-oval, with a similarly shaped configuration corresponding to it on the opposite side of the road; this was to be made possible by purchasing the requisite plots of land. The street would then have been the central axis of a huge oval courtyard with loggias running round it, becoming virtually a private road belonging to the Carpegna family. The death of Ambrogio Carpegna in 1643 meant that all these plans came to nothing, and his brother Cardinal Ulderico Carpegna (1595–1679) had the building completed by 1650 on a more modest scale. The most famous surviving element of the final concept is the stuccoed entrance arch at the end of the ground-floor loggia with two convoluted cornucopias and the head of the Medusa.

The building plans of the Florentine Falconieri family were less grand and more realistic. From 1646 to 1649 Borromini enlarged their newly acquired 16th-century palazzo on the banks of the Tiber behind the Palazzo Farnese by adding a framed doorway and three bays to the original seven. He paid tribute to the name of his client in the falcon herms on the angles of the façade. The garden side opened to form a U-shaped courtyard running down to the Tiber, and the river-front was topped by a roof loggia articulated in the manner of Palladio's basilica at Vicenza (*c.* 1550), with a degree of plasticity that increased rather than diminished with each ascending storey. In the interior Borromini used completely unconventional solutions to great effect for the ceilings, basing their symbolism on 16th-century emblem books. The delicacy and cool elegance of much of the stucco ornament bring to mind late 18th-century English interior decoration.

Borromini also worked at the Palazzo Spada in Piazza Capodiferro near the Palazzo Farnese. In the garden he created a folly known as the Prospettiva (1652); this was to become more famous than the actual palazzo, which had been altered by Paolo Maruscelli before 1649. With its slanted walls, floor and vault, this corridor conjures up the illusion of a Doric colonnade 20 m long, whereas its length is only 8.6 m. The ideas tried out in this small garden building were picked up in Bernini's Scala Regia (1663–6) at the Vatican. The mathematical basis for Borromini's witty little building was probably provided by an Augustinian mathematician, Giovanni Mario da Bitonto. Borromini emphasized the façade of the Palazzo Spada by placing on the opposite side of the road an illusionistic frontage (destr.), a wall that depicted a romantic landscape with a castle, the doorway of a villa with diamond-pointed rustication and a fountain of abundance.

9. COLLEGIO DI PROPAGANDA FIDE. A commission that involved Borromini as an architect of both churches and palazzi was the Collegio di Propaganda Fide, the headquarters of the Catholic missionary congregation. Although he took charge of building work in 1646, his greatest contributions to shaping the palazzo belong to his last creative years. The nucleus of the collegio was a small private palazzo on the southern edge of the Piazza di Spagna. It was extended in 1639 by Gaspare de Vecchi (*d* 1643), who added a long dormitory wing and provided the dilapidated building with a supporting façade of battered pilaster-strips. In 1644 Bernini added the travertine decoration and a monumental inscribed tablet with the arms of Urban VIII. Bernini had already built an oval chapel for the collegio in 1638, which had to make way for a new, larger building by Borromini *c.* 1660.

Borromini was first asked just to build a large extension wing on to de Vecchi's missionary college. Work did not really get under way until 1654, and the Cappella dei Re Magi was built in 1660–64; the stucco was executed after Borromini's death under the supervision of Carlo Fontana. The façade of the palazzo facing the Via di Propaganda was largely finished by 1662, and between 1665 and 1667 an attic storey was added to it at the request of the congregation. The chapel is hidden behind the west front of the palazzo, which makes its monumental effect all the more surprising: Borromini achieved this by using a Giant order of pilasters in the hall-like church with its low side chapels. The wall elevation exhibits the same structural framework as Borromini had aimed for at the Oratory of S Filippo Neri, where pairs of pilasters had been set diagonally into the corners; here at the Propaganda chapel they were replaced by slightly dished pilasters at the ends of the walls (see fig. 6). The roof is a very flat barrel vault with lunettes. The network of stucco lines forms a diamond-shaped pattern that is unusual in linking the wall articulations (i.e. the pilasters) through their projecting segments of entablature diagonally and not orthogonally. They and the subtly rounded corners endow this small church with the unified character of a typical Baroque space, the elements of which appear to circle round the onlooker in perpetual movement.

The key motif of the new street façade, the Giant pilasters, is the only element that the collegio shares with Bernini's façade for the Palazzo Chigi–Odescalchi, which was built at about the same time. Obviously both architects were inspired by the Palazzo Senatorio (1582–1605) on the Capitol by Michelangelo and Giacomo della Porta, but these two buildings produce a completely opposite effect: the seven window bays on the Borromini façade are full of great tension and an almost organic liveliness, as the window frames curve inwards, save for the central one, which is convex within a concave bay; Bernini's façade, on the other hand, has a truly classical peace and harmony.

10. S ANDREA DELLE FRATTE. While building the Collegio di Propaganda Fide, Borromini also worked on the neighbouring monastery church of the Minims, S Andrea delle Fratte. He began building the campanile, the only part of the project he was able to complete, in 1653. It has a high, square base supporting a small, almost completely open tempietto, with a storey above articulated alternately with deep recesses and pairs of angel herms. On top of the campanile is a device comprising four inverted scrolls that frame cartouches bearing the emblems of the Minimite Order and of their patron, Marchese Paolo del Bufalo, the whole surmounted by a spiky crown. In 1660 building work began on the dome, which remained unfinished, with no lantern or top storey, and retained the rough form of an unrendered brick building; the cupola was closed off inside with a temporary ceiling. There is a clear similarity between the drum of S Andrea delle Fratte and La Conocchia (first half of the 2nd century AD), a Roman mausoleum at Santa Maria Capua Vetere. In his last project Borromini again showed his fondness for the 'Baroque' forms found in late Roman architecture, which he always preferred to the Augustan Classicism extolled by the theorists.

II. Character and personality.

Borromini was remembered not only for his artistic inventiveness but also as the personification of unapproachable, melancholic genius in the same mould as Michelangelo and Caravaggio. The pathologically sombre outlook of his final years ultimately led him to commit suicide. His mental breakdown was certainly caused not solely by such external circumstances as the failure of the contemporary public and his clients to appreciate his artistic talent or by his rivalry with other architects but also by his introverted and unyielding character. Even as a young mason he used his breaks from work to practise

6. Francesco Borromini: Cappella dei Re Magi, Collegio di Propaganda Fide, Rome, 1660–64

drawing after antique originals or the works of Michelangelo, whom he admired inordinately, rather than to enjoy himself with his friends. He may even have modelled himself on Michelangelo in affecting melancholy and preferring solitude. But what had ranked as *terribilità* in Michelangelo, provoking awe and respect, was regarded by Borromini's associates more as crankiness and eccentricity. He always went about in a black Spanish suit that he never altered to conform to changing fashions, so that even the visual contrast between him and those around him became ever more marked as the years went by. On the other hand, his contemporaries noted with a certain respect that he lived a completely chaste life, devoting all his time and energy to his art.

It would be a mistake, however, to imagine Borromini as shy or boorish in his dealings with his fellow men. He was praised for his pleasant, aristocratic looks and polished manners. He successfully kindled the enthusiasm of those patrons who were congenial to him and kept it alive for over 20 years. He could persuade clients to accept his innovations, and he was equally skilful in eliminating troublesome rivals, as even the glib Bernini realized when Borromini's annihilating structural survey in 1644 literally brought about the downfall of both the bell-tower at St Peter's and its designer; the campanile was demolished in 1646, and Bernini fell from favour.

The loyalty of the building workers at the Lateran Basilica to their architect was so fanatical that they even killed a man whom they had surprised damaging freshly hewn marble capitals. Borromini's part in this attack was never satisfactorily clarified, because the Pope prevented a proper enquiry being held in the interests of carrying on with the building. A violent reaction would have been quite in keeping with Borromini's character; he called his buildings his children and could not bear to see them damaged or altered.

Beneath the aristocratic veneer, however, Borromini perhaps always remained a craftsman who lacked the self-confidence to become a true courtier. Although as a pure specialist architect he represented the modern type of professional, he always suffered from the preferential treatment accorded on both a social and a material level to such artists as Cortona and Bernini, who practised as painters and sculptors as well as being architects, and who had not worked their way up through the profession from the bottom. The fact that Borromini had specialized from the start prevented him from achieving the status of the universal genius so highly regarded at the papal court. Unlike Bernini, Borromini had not been accustomed to consort with rich patrons and courtiers from childhood, and he did not become professionally independent until he was over 30. He was 45 when he eventually penetrated Innocent X's court circle, and he never managed to adapt socially to the world of the papal court. His inability to make a social impression corresponding to his ambition and his rank as an artist produced in him exaggerated fears of plagiarism and intrigue. Mistrust and a feeling of inferiority prevented him from expressing himself openly regarding his art, and he became irritable and touchy.

Borromini was intellectually equipped to talk as an equal with the most distinguished of his contemporaries. As a well-read, if self-taught, scholar, possibly advised by his friend and patron Spada, he had acquired a wide general education as well as his specialist knowledge. There were about 1100 volumes in his unusually large private library, of which only 127 were architectural textbooks, the rest covering the customary fields of knowledge. His grasp of theology and philosophy was above average, and he seems to have had a special interest in Stoic philosophy: there was a bust of Seneca (*d* AD 65) in his house, and the manner of his suicide, using a sword, also suggests that he was a Stoic. In keeping with his reserved, suspicious character he had no pupils, and the career of his nephew Bernardo, whom he had employed along with Francesco Righi in his studio, was a complete failure.

III. Architectural influence.

Guarino Guarini (ii) employed some of Borromini's forms, although the spirit that imbued his approach was different. At the end of the 17th century and the beginning of the 18th there was a brief late flowering in Rome of forms inspired by Borromini's work, often relating less to structure than to decoration. The scenographic values of Alessandro Specchi's Porto di Ripetta (1704) have been seen as such an instance. Further afield in Italy, the interiors (1694) by Antonio Maria Ferri (*d* 1716) for the Palazzo Corsini, Florence, especially the central *salone*, display Borromini's influence, which may also be found in

Filippo Juvarra's Superga, near Turin (1717–31). Borromini's work exerted great influence on the nascent German Baroque. Johann Bernhard Fischer von Erlach recalled S Agnese in his façade for the Trinity Church in Salzburg (1694), and S Agnese's towers were emulated by Jean de Bodt at the Parochial Church in Berlin (1714). Borromini's work at the Lateran Basilica inspired Johann Dientzenhofer's rebuilding of Fulda Cathedral (1704–12), while Johann Conrad Schlaun adapted the plan of S Ivo for the Clemenskirche in Münster (1745–53). In Poland, the missionary church in Kraków (1719–28), designed by Kasper Barzanka (1680–1726), recalls the chapel in the Collegio di Propaganda Fide. In the 20th century Paolo Portoghesi, a profound Borromini scholar, reinterpreted some of the master's motifs in his own architecture, most notably at the Casa Baldi, Rome (1959–61).

IV. Critical reception and posthumous reputation.

Borromini's architecture was controversial in his own lifetime. His clients were generally delighted: the Procurator-General of the Discalced Trinitarians wrote of S Carlo, as reported by Fra Juan de S Bonaventura, 'In the opinion of everybody, nothing similar with regard to artistic merit, caprice, excellence and singularity can be found anywhere in the world.' Unfavourable reaction was not long in coming, however, and Borromini's contemporary Giovanni Baglione called his architecture 'ugly and deformed' and denounced him as 'a most ignorant Goth and corrupter of architecture, and the infamy of our century'. The rise of Neo-classicism was inimical to Borromini's reputation, and Francesco Milizia was particularly scathing. Sir John Soane could see little but 'chaotic confusion' in Borromini's work, while Jakob Burckhardt dismissed S Carlo with the remark that the only straight lines in it were in the window and door frames.

Borromini's reinstatement began with Cornelius Gurlitt's *Geschichte des Barockstils in Italien* (Dresden, 1887), although 40 years later Arthur Stratton could still write of S Carlo, 'Borromini should not be judged solely by this and other travesties of good taste which he certainly perpetrated.' Better progress in the appreciation of Borromini, however, had been made meanwhile by the 'Vienna school' led by Max Dvořák, with valuable studies by Oskar Pollak and Eberhard Hempel. In more recent years Borromini's oeuvre became the object of searching reassessment by Paolo Portoghesi and Anthony Blunt. Borromini's expressive and emotional handling of the Classical vocabulary of architectural forms had a powerful attraction for the late 20th-century generation, which was often drawn to the irrational.

WRITINGS

Opera del Caval. F. Borromini, cavata da suoi originali, cioè la chiesa, e fabrica della Sapienza di Roma (Rome, 1720); ed. P. Portoghesi (Rome, 1964)

Opus architectonicum: Opera del Cav. Francesco Borromini cavata da suoi originali, cioè l'Oratorio, e fabrica per l'abitazione dei PP. dell'Oratorio di S Filippo Neri di Roma (Rome, 1725) [Lat. and It. texts]; ed. P. Portoghesi (Rome, 1964)

BIBLIOGRAPHY

EARLY SOURCES

G. Baglione: *Vite* (1642); ed. V. Mariani (1935)

J. de S. Bonaventura: *Cronaca del convento e della chiesa di S Carlo* (*c.* 1665); ed. O. Pollak in *Die Kunsttätigkeit unter Urban VIII*, i (Vienna, 1928)

B. Farinacci: *La relazione della festa ed apparato della chiesa di S Agnese in Piazza Navona in occasione del nuovo aprimento di essa* (Rome, 1672)

GENERAL WORKS

F. Milizia: *Le vite de' piu celebri architetti d'ogni tempo* (Rome, 1768); rev. as *Memorie degli architetti antichi e moderni* (Bassano, 4/1785), ii, pp. 157–62

J. Burckhardt: *Der Cicerone: Eine Anleitung zum Genuss der Kunstwerke Italiens* (Basle, 1855; Eng. trans., London, 1873)

A. E. Brinckmann: *Die Baukunst des 17. und 18. Jahrhunderts in den romanischen Ländern*, Handbuch der Kunstwissenschaft, i (Berlin, 1915, 4/1919)

T. H. Fokker: *Roman Baroque Art: The History of a Style* (Oxford, 1938)

R. Wittkower: *Art and Architecture in Italy, 1600–1750*, Pelican Hist. A. (Harmondsworth, 1958, rev. 4/1980)

P. Portoghesi: *Borromini nella cultura europea* (Rome, 1964)

P. Marconi: 'La Roma di Borromini', *Capitolium* (March, 1968) [special issue]

MONOGRAPHS

A. Muñoz: *Borromini* (Rome, 1921)

M. Guidi: *Francesco Borromini* (Rome, 1922)

E. Hempel: *Francesco Borromini* (Vienna, 1924, rev. 2/1939)

H. Sedlmayr: *Die Architektur Borrominis* (Berlin, 1930; Munich, 2/1939)

G. C. Argan: *Francesco Borromini* (Milan, 1952)

F. Guzzi: *Borromini* (Palermo, 1960)

P. Portoghesi: *Borromini: Architettura come linguaggio* (Milan and Rome, 1967, 2/1984; Eng. trans. of 1st edition, London, 1968)

A. Blunt: *Borromini* (London, 1979)

ECCLESIASTICAL BUILDINGS

C. P. Ridolfi: *S Carlo alle Quattro Fontane* (Rome, n.d.)

H. Egger: 'Francesco Borrominis Umbau von S. Giovanni in Laterano', *Beiträge zur Kunstgeschichte Franz Wickoff gewidmet* (Vienna, 1903), pp. 154–62

K. Cassirer: 'Zu Borrominis Umbau der Lateranbasilika', *Jb. Preuss. Kstsamml.*, xvii (1921)

A. Castellucci: 'Le riparazioni del vecchio edificio e la costruzione del nuovo Collegio di Propaganda Fide nel secolo XVII', *Alma Mater*, iv (1921)

M. Guidi: 'Borromini e le fabbriche dei Filippini in Roma', *Rass. A. Ant. & Mod.*, xxi (1921), pp. 158–65

E. Re: 'La palomba della Sapienza', *Capitolium*, xviii/5 (1943), pp. 175–80

L. Benevolo: 'Il tema geometrico di S. Ivo alla Sapienza', *Quad. Ist. Stor. Archit.*, 3 (1953), pp. 1–10

A. Muñoz: 'Borromini alla Fabbrica di Propaganda Fide', *Strenna Romanisti*, xiv (1953), pp. 109ff

B. Zevi: 'San Carlino alle Quattro Fontane', *Archit.: Cron. & Stor.*, i/2 (1955), pp. 229–40

L. di Sopra, G. Garlatti and G. Vernier: 'Sant'Ivo della Sapienza', *L'Architettura*, iii (1957–8)

L. Montalto: 'Il drammatico licenziamento di Francesco Borromini dalla fabbrica di S Agnese in Agone', *Palladio*, viii (1958), pp. 139–88

H. Ost: 'Borrominis römische Universitätskirche S. Ivo', *Z. Kstgesch.*, xxx (1967), pp. 101–42

F. A. Salvagnini: *La Basilica di S Andrea delle Fratte* (Rome, 1967)

P. de la Ruffinière du Prey: 'Solomonic Symbolism in Borromini's Church of S Ivo della Sapienza', *Z. Kstgesch.*, xxxi (1968), pp. 216–32

G. Eimer: *La fabbrica di S. Agnese in Piazza Navona*, 2 vols (Stockholm, 1970–71)

G. Antonazzi: 'La sede della Sacra Congregazione e del Collegio Urbano', *Sacrae Congregationis de Propaganda Fide memoria rerum*, ed. J. Meller (Rome, 1971), i, pp. 306ff

F. Trevisani: 'La Fabbrica di S Agnese in Navona: Estate 1653', *Stor. A.*, xxiii (1975), pp. 61–72

V. Poulsen: *The Iconography of Francesco Borromini's Church of S Ivo della Sapienza in Rome* (diss., U. Oslo, 1976)

M. Heimbürger Ravalli: *Architettura, scultura e arti minori nel Barocco italiano: Ricerche nell'archivio Spada* (Florence, 1977)

L. Steinberg: *Borromini's S Carlo alle Quattro Fontane: A Study in Multiple Form and Architectural Symbolism* (New York, 1977)

M. Malmanger: 'Form as Iconology: The Spire of Sant'Ivo della Sapienza', *Acta Archaeol. & A. Hist. Pertinentia*, viii (1978), pp. 237–49

J. Connors: *Borromini and the Roman Oratory: Style and Society* (Cambridge, MA, 1980)

J. Beldon Scott: 'S Ivo della Sapienza and Borromini's Symbolic Language', *J. Soc. Archit. Hist.*, xli/4 (1982), pp. 294–317

SECULAR ARCHITECTURE

O. Pollak: 'Die Decken des Palazzo Falconieri in Rom und Zeichnungen von Borromini in der Wiener Hofbibliothek', *Jb. Ksthist. Inst. Ksr.-Kön. Zent.-Komm. Dkmlpf.*, v/3 (1911), pp. 111–41

D. Frey: 'Borrominis künstlerischer Anteil am Palazzo Pamphili auf der Piazza Navona', *Wien. Jb. Kstgesch.*, iii (1924–5), pp. 43–80

C. Cecchelli: 'Palazzo Spada', *Annuario della Associazione fra i cultori di architettura in Roma* (Rome, 1926), pp. 15ff

J. Genton: 'Palazzo Falconieri', *Magyar müvészet* (1929), pp. 406ff

G. Giovannoni: 'Il Palazzo Carpegna', *La Reale Accademia di S Luca nella inaugurazione della nuova sede* (Rome, 1934)

P. Portoghesi: 'L'opera di Borromini nel palazzo della Villa Falconieri di Frascati', *Quad. Ist. Stor. Archit.*, xiv (1956), pp. 7–20

E. Amadei: 'Il Palazzo Pamphili in Piazza Navona, oggi casa del Brasile', *Capitolium*, xxxvi/11 (1961), pp. 18–21

M. Tafuri: 'Borromini in Palazzo Carpegna', *Quad. Ist. Stor. Archit.*, xiv (1967), pp. 85–107

P. Waddy: 'The Design and Designers of Palazzo Barberini', *J. Soc. Archit. Hist.*, xxxv/3 (1976), pp. 151–85

G. Magnamini: *Palazzo Barberini* (Rome, 1983)

SPECIAL TOPICS

M. Dvořák: 'Borromini als Restaurator', *Kstgesch. Jb. Ksr.-Kön. Zent.-Komm. Erforsch. & Erhaltung Kst- & Hist. Dkml.* (1907), pp. 90–99; also in *Gesammelte Aufsätze zur Kunstgeschichte* (Munich, 1929)

A. Muñoz: 'La formazione artistica del Borromini', *Rass. A. Ant. & Mod.*, xix (1919), pp. 103–17

Ottanta disegni di Francesco Borromini, dalle Collezioni dell'Albertina di Vienna (exh. cat. by H. Thelen, Rome, Villa Farnesina, 1958)

M. Johansen: 'La prospettiva di illusione del Borromini', *Anlct. Romana Inst. Dan.*, ii (1962), pp. 101–17

M. Tafuri: 'La poetica borrominiana: Mito, simbolo, ragione', *Palatino*, x/3–4 (1966), pp. 184–93

H. Thelen: *Francesco Borromini: Die Handzeichnungen*, i (Graz, 1967)

A. Bruschi: *Borromini, manierismo spaziale oltre il Barocco* (Bari, 1978)

R. Sinisgalli: *Borromini a quattro dimensioni* (Rome, 1981)

PETER STEIN

Borsippa [Barsippa, Barsip; now Birs Nimrud]. Ancient site in Iraq, *c.* 17 km south-west of Babylon. The city flourished in the 2nd and 1st millennia BC and was important for the cult of the Babylonian deity Nabu, god of writing and scribal knowledge. The most impressive feature of the site is the 47 m-high remnant of a ziggurat, part of the Temple of Nabu. In the 19th century the site was thought to be part of the ruins of Babylon and was investigated by Claudius James Rich, Henry Rawlinson and Hormuzd Rassam. In the 20th century it was investigated by Robert Koldewey and later by a team from Innsbruck University. The main collection of finds is in the British Museum, London. The ziggurat was built in the Old Babylonian period (first half of the 2nd millennium BC) and rebuilt in the Neo-Babylonian period (625–539 BC). Its upper portion is vitrified brick, probably burnt as a result of fires that were lit in trenches dug into the top of the ziggurat in the early Islamic period (*see also* ZIGGURAT). Numerous cuneiform tablets and smaller antiquities were found, such as a bronze door-sill from the cella of the temple (London, BM), as well as several *kudurrus* (boundary stones set up in temples to record land grants) and stelae of the Assyrian king Assurbanipal (*reg* 668–627 BC) and his brother Shamash-shuma-ukin, King of Babylon (*reg* 668–648 BC).

BIBLIOGRAPHY

RLA: 'Barsippa'

C. J. Rich: *Second Memoir on Babylon* (London, 1818)

J. E. Reade: 'Rassam's Excavations at Borsippa and Kutha, 1879–82', *Iraq*, xlviii (1986), pp. 105–16

MICHAEL ROAF

Borsos, József (i) (*b* Veszprém, 21 Dec 1821; *d* Budapest, 19 Aug 1883). Hungarian painter. He studied drawing under József Ágost Schoefft in Pest (now part of Budapest) from 1837 and often visited the studio of Miklós Barabás (1810–98). From 1840 he carried on his studies at the Akademie in Vienna under Leopold Kuppelwieser. Two years later he enrolled in Ferdinand Waldmüller's private Viennese school, which had a reputation for fostering free thinking. Borsos greatly influenced the work of his Austrian friend August Xaver Karl von Pettenkofer. Borsos exhibited regularly both in Pest and Vienna and lived for 21 years in Austria, where many of his works remain.

Borsos worked in all the major genres of the period, his subjects including portraits, genre scenes and still-lifes, as well as mythological, historical and biblical themes. In his still-lifes the influence of Flemish painting can be seen (e.g. *Still-life*, 1850; Pécs, Pannonius Mus.). His most significant works, however, are genre scenes and portraits. His early paintings are close to the peasant genre pictures of Waldmüller, as in *Grapes or a Kiss?* (1843; Budapest, N.G.). His later style is comparable to that of Friedrich von Amerling: in scenes such as *The Letter* (1852; Budapest, N.G.) the figures are surrounded by a rich, tapestried background. His outstanding picture *Girls After the Ball* (1850; Budapest, N.G.) is notable for its lively narrative element, its warm, rich atmosphere and its elegant presentation. The Biedermeier idyll long survived in his works, as in his 1861 version of *Pigeon Post*, originally painted in 1855 (priv. col., see 1981 exh. cat., no. 241). Borsos's portraits, some of which were commissioned by members of the Hungarian aristocracy in Vienna, relied on the decorative props and idealizing approach characteristic of the time, but they excelled in the delineation of character, as in the *Portrait of a Woman in a Velvet Jacket* (*c.* 1850) or the portrait of *Mátyás Zitterbarth* (1851; both Budapest, N.G.). The *Lebanese Emir* (1843; priv. col., see 1981 exh. cat., no. 239) shows Edmund Zichy in oriental costume.

In a lithograph produced with von Pettenkofer, Borsos immortalized a contemporary event: the first Hungarian constitutional National Assembly in 1848. With his painting the *National Guard* (Budapest, N.G.), he established the image of a new patriotic ideal. *The Widow* (1853; Budapest, N.G.) also draws on patriotic sentiment. In the second half of the 1850s, signs of exhaustion can be detected in Borsos's work. Returning to Hungary, in 1862 he set up a commercial photographic studio in Pest, in collaboration with the painter Albert Doctor, and thereafter abandoned all artistic activity.

BIBLIOGRAPHY

J. Kopp: *Borsos József* (Pécs, 1931)
Borsos József (exh. cat., Veszprém, Bakonyi Mus., 1971)
Művészet Magyarországon, 1830–1870 [Art in Hungary, 1830–1870] (exh. cat., Budapest, N.G., 1981), pp. 295–6, 350–51, 396–7, 460, 505–6

KATALIN GELLÉR

Borsos, József (ii) (*b* Hódmezővásárhely, 18 March 1875; *d* Debrecen, 23 Jan 1952). Hungarian architect and urban planner. He studied architecture at the Hungarian Palatine Joseph Technical University, Budapest, graduating in 1898, and later studied in Munich for a few months in 1898–9. He became known for his brickwork architecture, having studied the work of Fritz Höger in northern Germany and that of Ragnar Östberg in Scandinavia. Of his early works, the Reformed Church (1903–5), Tabán, Hódmezővásárhely, is built on a Greek-cross ground-plan in a mixture of Romanesque Revival and Gothic Revival styles reminiscent of Frigyes Schulek's Calvinist Church (1880–83), Szeged, while the Reformed Church (1909–10), Susán, Hódmezővásárhely, is marked by Art Nouveau detailing. From 1912 to 1935 Borsos held the post of Technical Councillor in Debrecen, where he produced an urban development plan (1928–30). His finest work, the Crematorium and Mortuary Building (1932), Debrecen, is symmetrically arranged around the arched main entrance of parabolic shape. Its brick surfaces are crenellated, and reinforced-concrete vaults overarch the interior areas. The picturesque high roofs, covered with blue-violet glazed tiles, show the influence of Hungarian National Romanticism and the Expressionism of northern Germany. Borsos also built vernacular-inspired schools and residential blocks in Debrecen. His final building, the Reformed Church (1941), Honvéd Square, Szeged, contrasts with his more ornate early work and is characterized by the compactness of its massive shapes and flat and arched homogeneous brick surfaces.

BIBLIOGRAPHY

Z. Rácz: 'Borsos József és az alföldi téglaépítészet' [József Borsos and the brick architecture of the Great Plains], *Magyar Építőművészet*, lxxvi/1 (1985), pp. 17–21

ÁKOS MORAVÁNSZKY,
KATALIN MORAVÁNSZKY-GYÖNGY

Borsos, Miklós [Nicolas] (*b* Nagyszeben [now Sibiu, Romania], 13 Aug 1906; *d* Budapest, 27 Jan 1990). Hungarian sculptor, medallist, draughtsman, engraver and painter. In 1922 he moved from Transylvania to Győr, Hungary, where, while preparing to become a painter, he learnt the craft of goldsmithing and engraving from his father. He studied at the Academy of Fine Arts, Budapest, in 1928–9. He also spent considerable time during these years in Italy and southern France. His taste was influenced mainly by Classical work. The drawings and paintings from this period can be regarded as preparation for his career as a sculptor, although it was not until the early 1930s that he took up full-time sculpting. At first he produced copper embossings. In 1938 a trip to Transylvania inspired him to create larger copper reliefs, such as *Women Hired to Mourn* (1939; Pécs, Pannonius Mus.). His first stone statue *Mother* (Győr, Xantus János Mus.) was sculpted in 1933. Partly because of the nature of the material, and also because of his deep knowledge of ancient Egyptian and Greek sculpture, his figure sculptures are built from basic, essential forms. His success as a sculptor enabled him in 1941 to give up engraving, which until then had provided his income.

In 1943 Borsos made a side altar of copper reliefs for the Catholic church in Győr-Nádorváros, depicting scenes from the life of Prince Emeric the Saint. From the same year his work became intimately linked to Tihany, a resort on Lake Balaton where he spent his summers. Beauty, harmony and contentment became characteristic features. In September 1945 he moved to Budapest, where he was a professor at the College of Applied Arts (1946–60), and at the Academy of Fine Arts (from 1981). The most significant works carved in the early 1940s are the heads, in which he tried to crystallize the forms, reducing them to essentials. Female heads of this period are not in general sculpted from a particular model; their expression is typified by an emerging smile, as in *Little Girl from Tihany* (basalt, 1943; Budapest, N.G.). Most of the male heads of the period are portraits and, although sculpted from memory, manage to convey the nuances of the subject's character, as in *Jenő Barcsay* (basalt, 1942; Budapest, priv. col., see László, 1979, pl. 13). Following a trip to Kraków in 1951 Borsos began using red marble and his style became more detailed and naturalistic (e.g. *József Egry*, 1951; Budapest, N.G.).

Despite the reduction to basic forms Borsos's more abstract sculptures are generally anthropomorphic, and their modelling recalls the shaping powers of natural elements, especially that of water-washed stone. These sculptures date mainly from the later 1940s (e.g. *Female Head*, white marble, 1948; Budapest, N.G.), and the 1960s (e.g. *Canticum canticorum*, marble, 1963; Vienna, Mus. 20. Jhts). *Black Torso* (basalt, 1957; Budapest, N.G.) represents the transition from the more realistic conception of the 1950s to the greater abstraction of his later period.

Borsos's activity as a medallist dates from 1947. Carved in negative relief, his medals are mostly portraits of artists on the obverse, with some aspect of their work on the reverse (e.g. *Vivaldi*, 1953; Budapest, N.G.). His drawings are generally rather laconic, using few lines and dots drawn with a pen or brush and representing Lake Balaton and mythical beings: sea gods, mermaids or steeds. He was also a prolific illustrator (see Babits, 1970, for an illustration (pen) of a Walt Whitman poem).

WRITINGS
Visszanéztem félutamból [Reflections at halfway] (Budapest, 1971) [memoirs]

BIBLIOGRAPHY
F. Gachot: 'Un sculpteur indépendant: Nicolas Borsos', *Nouv. Rev. Hongrie* (April 1941), pp. 336–7
I. Genthon: 'Miklós Borsos the Sculptor', *New Hung. Q.*, 10 (1963), pp. 63–9
G. László: *Borsos Miklós* (Budapest, 1965)
G. Perneczky: 'Reality and Myth: The New Sculpture of Miklós Borsos', *New Hung. Q.*, 20 (1965), pp. 99, 103
M. Babits: *Erato* (Budapest, 1970)
V. L. Kovásznai: 'Miklós Borsos at Seventy', *New Hung. Q.*, 64 (1976), pp. 52–6
G. László: *Borsos Miklós* (Budapest, 1979)
Borsos Miklós rajzai [Drawings by Miklós Borsos] (Budapest, 1985)
V. L. Kovásznai: *Borsos Miklós* (Budapest, 1989)

S. KONTHA

Borsseler [Borselaer; Borsselaer; Busler; Bustler], **Pieter** [Petrus] (*fl* 1664–87). Dutch painter, active in England. His earliest known dated work is a three-quarter-length portrait of a fellow Roman Catholic, *Dame Mary Yate* (1664; Amsterdam, Rijksmus.), but his key work is *Sir William Dugdale* (1665; Merevale Hall, Warwicks), which is imbued with the sombre melancholy in which he specialized. His portraits are often of high quality and painted in an individual style, totally Dutch in temper and quite independent of the school of Peter Lely. Also at Merevale Hall are portraits by him of *Lady Dugdale* and *Sir Orlando Bridgman*, the latter being a forceful likeness that was evidently well received as there are other versions. One of these is or was at Bisham Abbey, Bucks, where a large number of portraits by him, mostly of members of the Hoby family, survived. The most memorable is of an elderly sitter, *Mrs Peregrine Hoby*, a typical example of the painter's skill at portraying grim fortitude. The painting of her hand is characteristically careful, but in other works, notably the *Samuel Butler* (London, N.P.G.), almost certainly by him, the fingers appear spindly and exaggerated. The latter work, with its stylized drapery, provides an apt comparison with the same sitter's portrait by Gerard Soest (London, N.P.G.), the painter whose manner Borsseler most closely approaches.

'Petrus Busler. . . . Lymn' of St Peter-le-Poer, London, was indicted for recusancy in December 1673, and similar charges were laid against him when he lived in St Gregory's parish in 1678–9. He returned to the northern Netherlands to Middelburg, where he painted the group portrait, *Five Regents of the Tuchthuis* (house of correction; 1683; Amsterdam, Rijksmus.) in his usual style. He was commissioned to paint chimney-pieces (*in situ*) for the town hall in 1684 and 1687. Buckeridge mentioned a picture by 'Bustler' of 'three boors playing together, in different actions', with the landscape provided by Prosper Henry Lankrink and a dog by Abraham Hondius.

BIBLIOGRAPHY
B. Buckeridge: 'An Essay towards an English School of Painters', *The Art of Painting*, ed. R. de Piles (London, 3/?1750), p. 360
H. Walpole: *Anecdotes of Painting in England (1762–71)*, ed. R. W. Wornum (1849), ii, pp. 457–8
C. H. Collins Baker: 'Pieter Borsseler', *Connoisseur*, lxiv (1922), pp. 5–15 [repr. Merevale Hall and Hoby portraits]
H. Bowler, ed.: 'London Sessions Records', *Catholic Rec. Soc.*, xxxiv (1934), pp. 157, 213, 221, 238
A. Staring: 'Weinig bekende portrettisten, II', *Oud-Holland*, lxi (1946), pp. 33–42
M. Whinney and O. Millar: *English Art, 1625–1714* (Oxford, 1957), p. 184
The Age of Charles II (exh. cat., ed. H. Brooke; London, RA, 1960–61), pp. 73–4, 134–5, 138
P. J. J. van Thiel and others: *All the Paintings of the Rijksmuseum in Amsterdam* (Amsterdam, 1976), p. 133
E. K. Waterhouse: *Painting in Britain, 1530–1790*, Pelican Hist. A. (Harmondsworth, 1953, rev. 4/1978), pp. 110, 344

RICHARD JEFFREE

Borssom [Boresom; Borssum], **Anthonie van** (*b* Amsterdam, *bapt* 2 Jan 1631; *d* Amsterdam, *bur* 19 March 1677). Dutch painter and draughtsman. There are no surviving documents to support the common assumption that he was a pupil of Rembrandt, although some of his drawings show the influence of Rembrandt's landscape etchings of the 1640s (Bartsch: *Catalogue raisonné*, 1880, nos 222–8, 232). These compositions always followed a particular formula: water in the foreground, a farm, windmill or ramshackle barn among trees in the middle ground and, to one side, a distant view of buildings below a low skyline. Various landscapes with windmills bearing the signature *A V Borssom* have these characteristics (Amsterdam, Rijksmus.; Dresden, Kupferstichkab.; Frankfurt am Main, Städel. Kstinst.). Van Borssom's practice of applying pale watercolour washes to his drawings made them popular with collectors and imitators, especially in the 18th century. Although these drawings sometimes represent recognizable buildings, they are not intended to be topographical, unlike his drawings of churches, castles and city gates, which he must have made during a trip

Anthonie van Borssom: *Castle Toutenburg at Maartensdijk*, drawing, 222×342 mm, *c.* 1660 (New York, Pierpont Morgan Library)

through Utrecht, Gelderland and the Lower Rhine area, including views of Naarden, Maartensdijk (see fig.), Soest, Oosterbeek, Hoog-Elten and Cleves.

Van Borssom was far less productive as a painter. His paintings (mainly landscapes) are rather eclectic and have no personal, clearly recognizable character. They show no sign of Rembrandt's influence. Only five paintings are dated, making it difficult to establish a chronology or stylistic development. They include *Interior of a Church* (165(?)—the last number is illegible; The Hague, Rijksdienst Beeld. Kst; Sumowski, 1983, no. 210), which is painted in the manner of Gerrit Houckgeest and Hendrik van Vliet, and his earliest known dated work, a *Village Road* (1655; Hamburg, Ksthalle), which shows the influence of the early work of Jacob van Ruisdael. A *Panoramic Landscape with a View of the Schenkenschans and Hoog-Elten* (Düsseldorf, Kstsamml. Nordrhein-Westfalen) is dated 1666. This and a comparable undated panoramic landscape (Philadelphia, PA, Mus. A.), are reminiscent of the work of Philips Koninck, but the staffage of cattle is inspired by Paulus Potter, as are at least five painted cattle pieces, undated but signed *AVBorssom* (e.g. Bamberg, Neue Residenz, Staatsgal.; Cambridge, Fitzwilliam; The Hague, Mus. Bredius). The composition and some details of *Cows in a Meadow* (Copenhagen, Stat. Mus. Kst) are obvious borrowings from Paulus Potter's famous *Bull* (1647; The Hague, Mauritshuis). Van Borssom's most successful works are the *Dune Landscape* (Hamburg, Ksthalle), *River View with a Rider* (Budapest, N. Mus.) and several *Moonlit Landscapes* (e.g. Amsterdam, Rijksmus.) painted in the manner of Aert van der Neer. His last known dated painting, *Panoramic Landscape with a Rider* (1671; Copenhagen, Stat. Mus. Kst), is reminiscent of the landscapes of Hendrick Vroom.

BIBLIOGRAPHY
F. Robinson: *Netherlandish Artists* (1979), 5 [IV] of *The Illustrated Bartsch*, ed. W. Strauss (New York, 1987)
W. Sumowski: *Drawings of the Rembrandt School*, ii (New York, 1979), nos 287–367 [see also review by B. P. J. Broos in *Oud-Holland*, xcviii (1984), pp. 176–8]
——: *Gemälde der Rembrandtschüler*, i (Landau, 1983), pp. 426–56
B. P. J. BROOS

Bort, Jaime (*b* San Mateo, Castellón, ?early 18th century; *d* Madrid, 2 Feb 1754). Spanish sculptor and architect. In 1733 he was appointed city and diocesan architect for Cuenca, where he designed the town hall in 1734. He was subsequently summoned by the chapter of Murcia Cathedral in 1736 and appointed surveyor to the fabric and city architect. He directed works on the new façade of the cathedral (1736–49), which is really a retable in stone and decorative marbles, albeit on a monumental scale, and is scenographically designed to complement the townscape. Jacopo Vignola's two-storey scheme for the façade of Il Gesù, Rome (*see* ROME, §V, 16, and figs 49 and 50), is the ultimate model, but it was modified by Bort to form a complex rhythm of fluid curves and powerful columnar projections. The wealth of fine detail recalls French Rococo—in particular Juste-Aurèle Meissonier's design (1726) for St Sulpice, Paris—while exploiting the existing Renaissance elements of the building. The curved cresting of the façade, like an ornamental Spanish comb used to hold a mantilla in place, has a deep concave surface. Bort's pupils executed this work, which recalls the expedients in Andrea Pozzo's treatise on perspective, *Perspectiva Pictorum et Architectorum* (1693–1700). While at Murcia, Bort was involved in many other projects, for example the unrealized scheme for an oval plaza for the Alameda del Carmen (1742) and the design for the tabernacle of S Maria de Elche (1742), executed in Genoa by Pietro Antoni Geroni. In 1749 Bort was called to Madrid to direct engineering works, including the Puente Verde (1749–50; destr. 1909) over the River Manzaneres, which was decorated with sculptures by his brother Vicente Bort. Ferdinand VI paid for him to visit Paris and other European capitals, and as a result of these travels he wrote a treatise on urban administration, which has remained in manuscript form.

BIBLIOGRAPHY
A. Baquero: *Los profesores de las bellas artes murcianos* (Murcia, 1913)
E. Gómez Piñol: 'Jaime Bort y la fachada occidental de la Catedral de Murcia: Algunas consideraciones sobre la índole estilística de su diseño', *Actas del XXIII congresso internacional de historia del arte. España entre el Mediterraneo y el Atlantico: Granada, 1973*, ii, pp. 500–14
A. E. Pérez Sánchez: *Murcia: Arte* (Madrid, 1976)
A. Martínez Ripoll: 'Urbanismo utópico dieciochesco: La nueva Plaza de la Alameda del Carmen, en Murcia, por Jaime Bort', *An. U. Murcia*, xxxvi (1977–8), pp. 297–324
M. L. Tarraga: 'Los hermanos Jaime y Vicente Bort en la Corte: El Puente Verde y el de Trofa', *Imafronte*, 2 (1986), pp. 65–82
JOAQUÍN BÉRCHEZ

Bortnyik, Sándor (*b* Marosvásárhely [now Tîrgu Mureş, Romania], 3 July 1893; *d* Budapest, 3 Dec 1976). Hungarian painter, printmaker and poster designer. He was a leading figure in the avant-garde and a member of the group centred round the journal *MA* edited by Lajos Kassák. Bortnyik started his career as a poster designer; one of his first successes, the *Unicum* poster (1915; see 1986 exh. cat., p. 52), remained in print for decades. During 1918–19 his linocuts (e.g. *Red Star, Lenin and Liebknecht*) adorned the title page of *MA*. His paintings of that period, *Red Locomotive* (Budapest, N. Mus., Dept Mod. Hist.), *Red Factory* (Pécs, Pannonius Mus.) and *Yellow-green Landscape* (priv. col., see Borbély, 1971, illus. 10), show his attempts to achieve harmony and order through an increasingly abstract use of colour symbolism and form. Forced to emigrate when the Council Republic fell in 1919, he went to Vienna, then to Weimar; he also worked in Berlin and Kassa (now Košice, Slovakia). In 1921, at the same time as Kassák, he began to produce abstract architectonic Constructivist works. Characteristic of the six-page *Album* is the rhythmical distribution of three or four colours and various geometrical figures, along with the occasional individual letter. During this period he also produced radically different pictures, such as the Cubo-Futurist *Marchers*, the heroic, idealist *Smiths* and the *Lamplighter* (all Budapest, N.G.). The latter shows Bortnyik's move from colour symbolism to a concern with light, using the image of the worker as a Promethean bringer of light, the moon halo-like behind his head.

The satirical tone characteristic of Bortnyik's later work first appeared in *The Prophet* (1922; Budapest, N.G.), a portrait of Kassák in which the poet, dressed in a black gown, is depicted holding a book and towering over his awe-struck disciples. After separating from Kassák in 1922, Bortnyik went to Weimar. At the end of the year, at the Sturm-Galerie in Berlin, he held an exhibition of his Viennese paintings, which were bought by a Swedish art collector. Bortnyik did not wish to identify himself with the Bauhaus, despite remaining in touch with its main practitioners. He returned to architectonic Constructivism, although he was now concerned with the arrangement of real objects in a constructed space. In 1924 he began satirical depictions of human figures and rigid architectural forms, for example *Green Donkey, New Adam* and *New Eve* (all 1924; Budapest, N.G.). After his return to Hungary in 1925 Bortnyik painted a Neo-classical lyrical portrait of his wife *Clare* (priv. col.), but with *Machine Man* (begun 1927) and *Machine Knight* (1928; Budapest, N.G.) his satirical tone turned into a more general critique of the machine age.

In 1928 Bortnyik opened the Workshop, a private school for poster design; Victor Vasarely was one of his students there. Bortnyik's commercial posters engendered a school of followers. They are characterized by their formal purity, derived from Bauhaus ideals, and arresting wit. The *Modiano* posters show these features markedly (see Borbély, 1971, pp. 100–01). The school closed in 1938 for financial reasons. From the mid-1930s Bortnyik had returned to painting, influenced by the Group of Socialist Artists formed in Budapest in 1934. This influence is evident in his recurrent use of the motif of the reading man and in his use of the sturdy figure, as in the *Peasant Man with a Spade* (1935; priv. col., see 1977 exh. cat., pl. 30). After World War II Bortnyik began to design political posters, and between 1946 and 1949 he edited the journal *Szabad Müvészet*. In 1948–9 he taught at the School of Applied Arts and from 1949 to 1956 was Director of the School of Fine Arts in Budapest. His creative work was summed up in a series of 50 paintings entitled *Modernized Classics* (Budapest, N.G.), in which he parodied historical masterpieces by transposing them in the manner of 20th-century painters. His sole interest remained satire and caricature. *Hero of our Days* (1963; Budapest, N.G.) shows Rodin's *Thinker* hidden in the shade while opposite looms the enormously muscular figure of a football player with a diminutive head.

BIBLIOGRAPHY
A. Kemény: 'Bortnyik képei és grafikája' [Bortnyik's paintings and drawings], *MA* (15 June, 1919)
Bortnyik Sándor Albuma [The album of Sándor Bortnyik], intro. L. Kassák (Vienna, 1921)
L. Borbély: 'Bortnyik Sándor korai müvészete' [The early works of Sándor Bortnyik], *Müvészettörténeti Értesitő*, 1 (1969), pp. 46–72
L. Borbély: *Bortnyik Sándor* (Budapest, 1971)
É. Körner: *Bortnyik Sándor* (Budapest, 1975)
Bortnyik Sándor emlékkiállítása [Sándor Bortnyik commemorative exhibition] (exh. cat., ed. L. Borbély; Budapest, N.G., 1977)
100 + 1 éves a magyar plakát (exh. cat., Budapest, A. Hall, 1986)
NÓRA ARADI

Borzone, Luciano (*b* Genoa, 1590; *d* Genoa, 12 July 1645). Italian painter. He painted portraits, religious works and genre scenes and was one of the first Genoese painters to respond to the new art of Caravaggio. An unusually cultivated artist, educated and lively, he etched for pleasure, illustrated books and wrote poetry in the Genoese dialect. He moved in literary circles and knew the poet Gabrielle Chiabrera; he also knew aristocrats such as Gian Carlo

Doria, his first patron, and Giacomo Lomellini (1586–1660).

Borzone trained first with his uncle, Filippo Bartolotto, a modest portrait painter, and later in the workshop of Cesare Corte (1550–1613/14); he was also attracted to the art of Giovanni Battista Paggi and Bernardo Castello. It may have been through Corte, a collector and dealer in Venetian art, that Borzone studied the works of Titian, Veronese and the Bassani, who were to influence the quiet naturalism of his mature art. He acted as adviser to Doria over the purchase of paintings, and in this capacity travelled to Milan in the second half of 1614; it was a journey of crucial importance to his career and to the formation of his style. In Milan he was brilliantly successful as a portrait painter and was deeply impressed by the works of the Milanese artists Giulio Cesare Procaccini and, above all, Cerano.

He continued to paint portraits and portrait miniatures (Soprani) after his return to Genoa. Two paintings, both *Portrait of a Man* (Turin, Gal. Sabauda, see Manzitti, p. 649; priv. col., see Ghio Vallarino, no. 15), are now attributed to Borzone. The Venetian influence is strong in such early works as the *Baptism* (1620–21; Genoa, Pal. Bianco), which was inspired by Veronese and admired by Orazio Gentileschi during his stay in Genoa (1623), and the more broadly painted *Virgin and Child with St Bernard* (1629; Genoa, S Gerolamo di Quarto), Borzone's next dated work. Borzone's chronology remains uncertain, but the *St Francis in Ecstasy* (Turin, Accad. Albertina) and the *Stigmatization of St Francis* (Genoa, Conserv. Suore S Giuseppe), which are indebted both to Venetian art and to Cerano, are probably youthful works, while a date in the 1620s has been proposed (Pesenti) for a group of pictures that includes *Anchior Receiving the Head of Holofernes* (Genoa, priv. col., see Pesenti, pl. 48), *Susanna and the Elders* (Genoa, priv. col., see Pesenti, pl. 49), *Ecce homo* (Genoa, priv. col., see Pesenti, pl. 51), *Mary Magdalene at the Foot of the Cross* (Genoa, S Rocco), *St Frances of Rome* (Genoa, S Caterina) and *St Vincent Ferrer Preaching* (Genoa, S Maria di Castello).

In the 1630s Borzone was influenced by the art of Caravaggio. He had perhaps visited Rome and encountered the master's work there, but it is more likely that he had seen the works of Bartolomeo Manfredi and Valentin de Boulogne, who were followers of Caravaggio, in Genoese collections. In such mature works as the *Adoration of the Shepherds* (Savona, Pin. Civ.), which may be placed in the early 1630s, and in the dated *Ecce homo* (1637, priv. col., see Pesenti, pl. 52), Borzone abandoned the complex structure of late Mannerist painting and, inspired by Caravaggio, developed a new simplicity and clarity, conveying emotion with warmth and intensity.

There are two dated works from the 1640s, the *Martyrdom of St Barbara* (1643; Loano, Savona, parish church) and the *Adoration of the Shepherds* (1645; Genoa, SS Annunziata del Vastato), his most fully Caravaggesque work. The *Blind Belisarius* (Chatsworth, Derbys), distinguished by its powerful and warm realism, is close to the *St Barbara* and, with *Job Derided*, the *Denial of St Peter* (both Genoa, priv. col., see Pesenti, pls 56, 58) and the *Banquet of Rosamund* (priv. col., see Ghio Vallarino, no. 17), is likely to date from Borzone's maturity. While

painting the *Adoration of the Shepherds* Borzone fell from the scaffold and died, and his sons, Giovanni Battista and Carlo, were left to complete it.

BIBLIOGRAPHY

DBI [with bibliog. to 1971]
R. Soprani: *Vite* (1674), pp. 179–85; ed. C. G. Ratti (1768–9), i, pp. 104, 243–54, 256–7; ii, p. 75
L. Alfonso: 'Luciano Borzone', *La Berio*, ii (1975), pp. 38–51
F. R. Pesenti: *La pittura in Liguria: Artisti del primo seicento* (Genoa, 1986), pp. 67–76
P. Pagano and M. C. Galassi: *La pittura del '600 a Genova* (Milan, 1988), pls 97–108
C. Manzitti: *Borzone Luciano, la pittura in Italia: Il seicento*, 2 vols (Milan, 1989), pp. 648–9
L. Ghio Vallarino: *Luciano Borzone, Genova nell'età barocca* (Bologna, 1992), pp. 102–6
M. Newcome: *Luciano Borzone, Kunst in der Republik Genua, 1528–1815* (Frankfurt am Main, 1992), pp. 98, 602–3

MARIA CLELIA GALASSI

Bos, Balthasar [Balthazar] **van den** [Sylvius] (*b* 's Hertogenbosch, 1518; *d* Antwerp). Flemish engraver. He is thought to have worked in Rome in the workshop of Marcantonio Raimondi. In 1543 he moved to Antwerp, where he joined the painters' guild in 1551. He made reproductive engravings after such artists as Raphael, Giulio Romano, Frans Floris, Lambert Lombard, Hieronymus Bosch and Maarten van Cleve, as well as from his own designs. Bos's earliest dated prints comprise a series of the *Four Evangelists* (1551; Hollstein, nos 6–9). His work was published by Hieronymus Cock and Hans Liefrinck.

BIBLIOGRAPHY

Bénézit; Hollstein: *Dut. & Flem.*; Thieme–Becker
S. Schele: *Cornelis Bos: A Study of the Origins of the Netherland Grotesque* (Uppsala, 1965), pp. 25, 159, 207, 221

Bos [Bosch; Bus], **Cornelis** [Sylvius] (*b* 's Hertogenbosch, *c.* ?1510; *d* Groningen, before 22 April 1566). Flemish printmaker. In 1540 he was registered as a citizen of Antwerp and became a member of the city's Guild of St Luke, although it is possible he was in the city for some time before this date. His first known engraving is *Prudence and Justice* (1537; Hollstein, no. 71) after Maarten van Heemskerck. There are several engravings based on Classical statues (e.g. *Laokoon*, 1548; Hollstein, no. 60) and the work of Marcantonio Raimondi and Agostino Veneziano, suggesting that Bos may have gone to Rome some time before 1540. It is, however, possible that Bos copied the Italian originals from drawings or prints brought back from Italy by other artists. Between 1540 and 1544 Bos worked in Antwerp as an engraver. Many of his engravings served as illustrations for books, including two treatises on architecture by Vitruvius and Serlio, which were published by Pieter Coecke van Aelst. Bos also provided woodcut designs for a book on anatomy produced by the printer and publisher Antoine de Goys and for a book on Moorish arabesque ornament (*Livre de moresques*, Paris, 1546), the title-page of the latter playing a crucial role in the development of grotesque scrollwork in Holland. It is generally agreed that this type of ornament was first introduced by Cornelis Floris but that it was Bos who made important contributions to its development, providing a source of inspiration to subsequent generations of craftsmen. Apart from architectural, anatomical and decorative designs, Bos also produced prints of biblical, mythological and allegorical subjects.

In 1544 Bos fled from Antwerp because of the persecution of the Libertines, a religious sect to which he belonged. He renewed his collaboration with van Heemskerck, and the fact that he seems to have established contacts with Dirck Coornhert, Jan van Scorel and others suggests that he went to Haarlem.

BIBLIOGRAPHY
Bénézit; Hollstein: *Dut. & Flem.*; Thieme–Becker
S. Schele: *Cornelis Bos: A Study of the Origins of the Netherland Grotesque* (Uppsala, 1965); rev. by H. Mielke in *Z. Kstgesch.*, xxxi/4 (1968), pp. 340–45

Bos, Jacob(us) (*b* 's Hertogenbosch, *c.* 1520; *fl* Rome, *c.* 1549–80). Flemish engraver. He was active in Rome from 1549 onwards and probably learnt engraving from a pupil of Marcantonio Raimondi. Bos's engravings are confined almost exclusively to designs made by others, such as Raphael (e.g. the *Evangelist* series; Hollstein, nos 4–17) and Antonie Blocklandt (e.g. the *Dream of Jacob*; Hollstein, no. 1). Bos's prints include biblical subjects, Roman architecture and maps. He worked for such publishers as Antonio Lafréry, Romae Michael, Franciscus Tramezini, Antonio Salamanca and Jan de Cock (*fl* 1506–29).

BIBLIOGRAPHY
Bénézit; Hollstein: *Dut. & Flem.*; Thieme–Becker

JETTY E. VAN DER STERRE

Bōsai. *See* KAMEDA BŌSAI.

Bosarte, Isidoro de (*b* Baeza, 1747; *d* Madrid, 22 April 1807). Spanish writer. A defender of classicism, he dedicated himself to its study. He was both a member and the secretary of the Real Academia de Bellas Artes de S Fernando in Madrid. From 1778 to 1786 he accompanied Vicente Osorio y Moscoso, Conde de Aguilar (*d* 1786), on his embassies to the courts of Turin and Vienna. Bosarte's writings testify to his knowledge of Egyptian, Greek, Roman and early Christian art. His most important work, *Viaje artístico a varios pueblos de España* . . . (Madrid, 1804), emulating the famous journey of Antonio Ponz, was intended to be the first of several volumes; he did not continue the project, because of the poor reception it was given due to his radically classicist posture. The text describes a journey through the provinces of Segovia, Valladolid and Burgos, emphasizing their works of art, particularly the Gothic and medieval ones, and intolerantly rejecting Baroque works. Bosarte employed modern criteria for the classification of the arts, demonstrating his knowledge of the most advanced currents of thought in Europe.

WRITINGS
Disertación sobre los monumentos antiguos pertenecientes a las nobles artes de la pintura, escultura y arquitectura, que se hallan en la provincia de Barcelona (Madrid, 1786)
Observaciones sobre las bellas artes entre los antiguos hasta la conquista de Grecia por los romanos (Madrid, 1791)
Gabinete de lectura española o colección de muchos papeles curiosos de escritores antiguos y modernos de la nación (Madrid, [*c.* 1793])
Viaje artístico a varios pueblos de España, con el juicio de las obras de las tres nobles artes que en ellos existen, y épocas a que pertenecen . . . (Madrid, 1804); rev., with intro. by A. E. Pérez Sánchez (Madrid, 1978)

BIBLIOGRAPHY
F. Zamora Lucas and E. Ponce de León: *Bibliografía española de arquitectura, 1526–1850* (Madrid, 1947), p. 143
J. A. Gaya Nuño: *Historia de la crítica de arte en España* (Madrid, 1975)
A. Bonet Correa and others: *Bibliografía de arquitectura, ingeniería y urbanismo en España (1498–1880)* (Madrid, 1980)

JAVIER RIVERA

Bosboom, Johannes (*b* The Hague, 18 Feb 1817; *d* The Hague, 14 Sept 1891). Dutch painter. In 1831 he joined the studio of Bartholomeus J. van Hove, the Hague cityscape painter, who lived next door to his family. Initially Bosboom helped his teacher paint sets for the theatre and a number of cityscapes. Around the age of 20 he decided to concentrate on depicting church interiors. This decision determined his entire career, as his works in this genre were to establish his reputation. In his autobiography, Bosboom explained that his first successes with church interiors (at exhibitions in 1836 and 1838), together with his natural inclination to record the impressions that churches made on him, had led to his choice. Subsequently, he wrote, he was influenced by the Romantic movement, particularly by Wijnand Johannes Josephus Nuyen. Although Nuyen's influence is apparent in his early work, for example *View of the Parisian Quay at Rouen* (1839; priv. col., on loan to The Hague, Gemeentemus.), Bosboom gradually abandoned Romanticism for a more sober treatment of his subjects.

After training in The Hague, Bosboom travelled to Germany, Belgium and France between 1835 and 1839 with his fellow students Samuel Verveer and Cornelis Kruseman. In 1836 he moved into a studio in The Hague, where he surrounded himself with the 17th-century furniture and church ornaments that can be seen in a beautiful watercolour of the *Artist's Studio* (The Hague, Gemeentemus.). Bosboom used these objects to provide authentic detail in his meticulous paintings of church interiors, which are often both studies of architectural space and light and precise historical reconstructions, populated with figures in 17th-century costume; for example, *Communion Service in St Gertrude's Church, Utrecht* (1852; Amsterdam, Hist. Mus.; see fig.). In 1851 he married the historical novelist Anna Louisa Geertruida Toussaint, after which he spent a considerable amount of time in her birthplace, Alkmaar. He also found subjects for his paintings in the other towns in the province of Noord Holland.

Bosboom was a skilful and successful watercolour painter. He drew on the same subjects as for his oils—principally church interiors—but dispensed with detail to create a more atmospheric evocation of space and light through broad washes of colour, for example in *Interior of a Church in Delft* (n.d.; Montreal, Mus. F.A.). His watercolours were particularly popular with collectors, to whom he usually sold them direct. In 1855 he was elected an honorary member of the newly formed Société Belge des Aquarellistes.

Around 1850 Bosboom began to produce his first paintings of the synagogues of Amsterdam and The Hague. In his later representations of this subject, such as *Interior of the German Synagogue in The Hague* (late 1870s; Dordrecht, Dordrechts Mus.), there is a particularly strong use of chiaroscuro in the manner of Rembrandt. Monasteries also featured in Bosboom's paintings, for instance in

Johannes Bosboom: *Communion Service in St Gertrude's Church, Utrecht*, oil on canvas, 925×1150 mm, 1852 (Amsterdam, Historisch Museum)

Monks Playing the Organ (1850; Amsterdam, Hist. Mus.). During the summer of 1864 he stayed in Kleef (Cleves), where he painted the *Ambulatory of the Minoret Monastery in Kleef* (Rotterdam, Mus. Boymans–van Beuningen).

Following the death of his twin brother Nicolas in 1862, Bosboom suffered a period of mild depression. However, after a trip to Huy, Chaudfontaine, Koblenz and Trier in 1865, he completed four major works between 1867 and 1871, including *Interior of Trier Cathedral* (Toledo, OH, Mus. A.) and *Grote Kerk in Alkmaar* (Rotterdam, Mus. Boymans–van Beuningen). In 1876 he stayed in the rural provinces of Groningen and Drente where farming life, as well as the local churches, provided him with subject-matter. During the last ten years of his active life Bosboom worked almost entirely in watercolour. In 1890 he suffered a stroke, and he died the following year.

Bosboom exhibited widely and received numerous honours during his lifetime. He belongs to a long Dutch tradition of church-interior painting established by Gerrit Houckgeest and Emanuel van Witte, but on the strength particularly of his freer watercolours and his views of the fishing port of Scheveningen painted in the summer of 1873, he has been seen as an important influence on the younger generation of the Hague school.

WRITINGS
Een en ander betrekkelijk mijn loopbaan als schilder, beschreven door Johannes Bosboom [A few things concerning my career as a painter, described by Johannes Bosboom] (Rotterdam, 1891/R 1946) [with commentary by A. Glavimans]

BIBLIOGRAPHY
T. G. H. Marins and W. Martin: *Johannes Bosboom* (The Hague, 1917)
Johannes Bosboom (1817–1891) (exh. cat., Delft, Stedel. Mus. Prinsenhof, 1958–9)
The Hague School: Dutch Masters of the 19th Century (exh. cat., ed. R. de Leeuw, J. Sillevis and C. Dumas; Paris, Grand Pal.; London, RA; The Hague, Gemeentemus.; 1983), pp. 173–9, 325 [with bibliog.]
WIEPKE F. LOOS

Bosch, Esias (*b* Winburg, 11 July 1923). South African potter. He was educated at Heidelberg and Potchefstroom (both nr Johannesburg) and began a fine arts degree at the University of the Witwatersrand, which he left after two years to work for a four-year painting diploma at the Johannesburg School of Art. In 1949 he won a three-year scholarship to study ceramics in Britain. He spent one year at the Central School of Arts and Crafts, London, where he worked under Dora Billington (1890–1968) and acquired his interest in pottery. He spent another two years working in such studios as those of Raymond Finch (*b* 1914) in Winchcombe, Glos, and Michael Cardew in Cornwall. He returned to South Africa in 1952 and taught ceramics at the Technical College in Durban (1952–4) and at the Pretoria Art School (1954–6). At the same time he established his own earthenware studio, specializing in simple white and green wares. He later established a studio near White River and, after working again briefly for Cardew in Nigeria, made the transition to wood-fired stoneware. He also produced high-quality porcelain and enormous stoneware tiles with bird, animal and insect motifs, seen in such prominent buildings in Johannesburg as the International Departure Hall at Jan Smuts Airport (1972) and the Schlesinger Centre (1967; now the Wesbank Building). His work is dominated by an insistent concern for technical excellence.

BIBLIOGRAPHY

M. L. van Biljon: 'Esias Bosch, die Pottebakker', *Lantern*, ix (1960), pp. 262–9

F. G. E. Nilant: *Contemporary Pottery in South Africa* (Cape Town, 1963)

A. E. DUFFEY

Bosch, Frederik David Kan (*b* Potchefstroom, South Africa, 17 June 1887; *d* Noordwijk aan Zee, Netherlands, 20 July 1967). Dutch archaeologist. Educated in the Netherlands, he studied Dutch literature at Leiden University (1906) but then specialized in Sanskrit and Indian archaeology. He was appointed adjunct archaeologist of the Archaeological Survey in Batavia (now Jakarta) under N. J. Krom at the end of 1914, and in 1916 he became head of the Survey and of the Museum of the Batavia Society (now Museum Nasional, Jakarta). He concentrated on epigraphy and started to formulate his ideas on the origin of Hindu–Javanese art. Another topic was the relationship between written and visual sources, particularly with reference to the Borobudur relief series. He also organized restoration and reconstruction projects of various monuments. In 1936 Bosch returned to the Netherlands. He received an extraordinary professorship in archaeology and ancient history of the East Indies in May 1938 in Utrecht and became Krom's successor in Leiden (1946–57). In 1944 he became president of the archaeological Kern Institute in Leiden and was engaged on the *Annual Bibliography of Indian Archaeology*. He concentrated on the symbolism and religious background of ornamentation and developed a theory on the lotus bulb with creepers (the golden germ) as the basis of all forms.

WRITINGS

De Gouden Kiem [The golden germ] (Amsterdam, 1948; Eng. trans., The Hague, 1961)

BIBLIOGRAPHY

Hiranyagarbha: A Series of Articles on the Archaeological Work and Studies of F. D. K. Bosch (The Hague, 1961) [with a bibliography of Bosch's writings]

H. I. R. HINZLER

Bosch, Hieronymus [Hieronimus, Jérôme, Jheronimus; Aken, Jeroen van; El Bosco] (*b c.* 1450; *d* 's Hertogenbosch, *bur* 9 Aug 1516). Netherlandish painter and draughtsman. The most distinctive and idiosyncratic of 15th-century Netherlandish artists, he produced a body of work remarkable for its depiction of fantastic, often diabolic, creatures, generally moralizing representations of the consequences of sin and folly.

I. Life, commissions and patrons. II. Work and iconography. III. Style, technique and chronology. IV. Critical reception and posthumous reputation.

I. Life, commissions and patrons.

Bosch came from a family of painters originally from Aachen (hence the painter's real name of Jeroen van Aken). His great-grandfather, a painter called Thomas, migrated westward, like many other artists, and in 1404 became a citizen of Nijmegen. Thomas's brother Johan den Meler ('the painter') was also active there. Thomas's son Jan (*d* 1454) is recorded at 's Hertogenbosch in 1426. Four of Jan's five sons were painters, including Hieronymus's father, Antonius. Hieronymus's brother Goossen was also a painter.

Hieronymus Bosch is first documented in 1474 and first mentioned as a painter in 1480–81. In June 1481 he appears to have married the daughter of a well-to-do member of the local patriciate, Aleyt Goyarts van den Meervenne (*d* 1522–3), who was 25 years his senior; the marriage was apparently childless. In 1488 Bosch owned half a house with its grounds, inherited from his wife, in the Schildersstraetken, 's Hertogenbosch. During the period 1474–98 there are fourteen documents concerning financial transactions by Bosch and his wife, four of which relate to Bosch selling his wife's real estate for cash (not, however, including their principal property, the estate of Ten Roedeken), perhaps because art was not bringing him a sufficient income. Thus already by 1500—before he had achieved fame as an artist—Bosch did not have to paint for a living and was wealthy enough to paint whatever he chose. In fact, tax records for the years 1502–3 and 1511–12 show that Bosch was in the wealthiest top 10% of citizens of 's Hertogenbosch (see Blondé and Vlieghe, 1989).

Important to Bosch's social position in the town was his membership of the Brotherhood of Our Lady, from whom he received his first commissions. An ordinary member from 1486–7 onwards, at the new year of 1488 he was already a guest of honour at the annual 'swan banquet', and he became a sworn member in that year— an early indication of his high social status. Of *c.* 300 sworn members, more than half were priests or *magistri* (academics). Officially only *clerici* (those who had taken at least minor orders) could be sworn members, but exceptions were made for aristocrats, magistrates, large landowners and prosperous businessmen. Bosch was either a member of this latter category, perhaps through marriage, or a *clericus* with some previous education; or he may have qualified on both grounds. At this time he was only about 38, and the honour was unusual for a 'craftsman': he was the only artist to be a sworn member. For the Brotherhood, Bosch executed five minor works in 1493, 1503–4, 1508–9 and 1511–12.

According to J. B. Gramaye (1610), there were several altarpieces by Bosch in the St Janskerk in 's Hertogenbosch (now all untraced). They included an altarpiece for the Brotherhood's chapel, of which Bosch painted the inner wings, an altarpiece of the *Creation of the World* (*Hexameron mundi*) for the high altar (probably commissioned by the church), an altarpiece with four scenes from the *Story of Judith* and the *Story of Esther* for the chapel of St Michael

1. Hieronymus Bosch: triptych with *The Haywain*, oil on panel, 1.35×1.00 m (central panel), 1.35×0.45 m (wings), *c.* 1500 (Madrid, Museo del Prado)

(donor unknown) and, finally, an altarpiece with the *Adoration of the Magi*. Also in the church were paintings of *David and Abigail* and *Solomon and Bathsheba*, both of which are known from later copies (Switzerland, priv. col.).

Bosch also supplied works of a traditional religious kind for several wealthy members of the bourgeoisie, including the Bronckhorst–Bosschuysse family, for whom he painted an *Adoration of the Magi*, and other unidentified families (another version of the *Adoration of the Magi*, Madrid, Prado; the *Ecce homo*, Frankfurt am Main, Städel. Kstinst. & Städt. Gal.; the *Crucifixion*, Brussels, Mus. A. Anc.). A triptych with the *Martyrdom of St Ontcommer* (Venice, Doge's Pal.) was probably painted for an Italian patron, perhaps from northern Italy. The Brotherhood no doubt offered Bosch useful social contacts, among them several Spaniards in Brabant. Diego de Guevara, father of Felipe de Guevara, who was already a member of the Brotherhood in 1498–9, possessed six paintings by Bosch, including the tabletop with the *Seven Deadly Sins* and an original version of *The Haywain* (both Madrid, Prado; see fig. 1). Another member was Count Hendrick III of Nassau, who probably commissioned the '*Garden of Earthly Delights*' (Madrid, Prado; see fig. 3 below), which was kept at his court in Brussels. The Brotherhood generally afforded more contact with courtiers, patricians and the Dutch nobility than with the rulers of the Netherlands. It thus speaks highly for Bosch's status that the Burgundian ruler Philip the Fair ordered a large altarpiece with the *Last Judgement* from him in 1504 (to which the fragment in

Munich, Alte Pin., may belong)—the only commission for which there is documentary evidence. Philip may also have ordered a *Temptation of St Anthony* in 1505, and before that, according to inventories, Isabella the Catholic (*d* 1505) owned works signed by Bosch. A *Temptation of St Anthony* was also in the collection of Margaret of Austria, while Philip of Burgundy, Bishop of Utrecht (1465–1524), possessed at least one humorous scene by Bosch and also a *Stone Operation* (or '*Cure of Folly*'; version, Madrid, Prado, probably not the original; see fig. 7 below), although not stated as painted by Bosch. In these cases it is not known whether the works were acquired through intermediaries or commissioned direct from the artist.

The works ordered or bought by the ruling nobility all belong to a single category (the *Last Judgement* and scenes of hermits) and were apparently supplied after 1500, while the Dutch nobility owned one humorous scene and the '*Garden of Earthly Delights*'. There is no trace of Bosch's many secular moralizing compositions in aristocratic circles. Paintings of this kind in Spanish collections in the late 16th century seem to have been acquired a good while after Bosch's death. This was certainly the case with the large group of works systematically assembled by Philip II of Spain and possibly those owned by de Guevara. It is thus apparent that the aristocracy showed interest in Bosch at a very late stage, perhaps when he already had a certain reputation. Moreover, the ruling nobility was interested in a particular genre for which he became famous only in the 16th century, that of fantastic *diablerie*. Yet it is unclear to what extent they appreciated and understood his imagery. Antonio de Beatis's description (1517) of the 'Garden of Earthly Delights', for instance, shows a total failure to understand it. Bosch's work, in fact, may have been deliberately emptied of any specific content, so that it would find favour as a curiosity and allow private interpretations.

For most of the untraced works by Bosch, now known only from copies, replicas and inventories, there is no contemporary archival evidence. However, since they contain several basic elements of what may be called an early bourgeois ideology and their original function is obscure, it has been suggested that they were intended mainly for an upper middle-class urban public. Perhaps many of them were executed in the popular technique of watercolour on canvas: this was less expensive. Knowledge is greatly hindered by the rarity of upper middle-class inventories for the citizens of the south-eastern Netherlands in the period c. 1480–1520.

II. Work and iconography.

All the classifications of Bosch's work according to chronological phases and stylistic development so far proposed are self-contradictory and subjective (see §III below). The situation is further complicated by the fact that many of the works are now known only from documents and prints (e.g. the *Blind Leading the Blind*). They are thus best considered in terms of their iconography, which is extremely varied. The subjects can be roughly divided into two categories, though to some extent these overlap. Furthermore, many of the works are composed of dozens of small scenes that cannot be immediately related to any single theme, such as the main subject of the picture.

1. Religious. 2. Moralizing. 3. Sources.

1. RELIGIOUS. Besides those works (untraced) previously in the St Janskerk, 's Hertogenbosch, Bosch's religious pictures included the *Story of Jonah*, which was in Cardinal Grimani's collection in Venice in 1521 (untraced), and two panels (both Rotterdam, Mus. Boymans–van Beuningen) depicting *Noah's Ark on Mt Ararat* and *Monsters Populating the Earth* (?after the Fall of the Rebel Angels); their shape suggests that they were wings of a triptych, of which the central panel may have represented the *Flood* (untraced). Among his other (untraced) Old Testament scenes, to all of which a metaphorical meaning was attached in the 16th century, were: the *Tower of Babel* (the struggle against tyranny and discord), *Lot and his Daughters* (unchasteness and 'unequal love') and *Job* (*patientia* or long-suffering).

The hermits and saints painted so often by Bosch, for instance the altarpiece of the *Hermits* (Venice, Doge's

2. Hieronymus Bosch: triptych with the *Last Judgement*, oil on panel, 1.64×1.27 m (central panel), 1.64×0.60 m (wings) (Bruges, Groeningemuseum)

3. Hieronymus Bosch: triptych with the '*Garden of Earthly Delights*', oil on panel, 2.20×1.95 m (central panel), 2.20×0.97 m (wings), *c.* 1504 (Madrid, Museo del Prado)

Pal.), not only conveyed a narrative didactic religious message, illustrating the lives of the saints, but also often contained a moralizing message. They served as an admonition to self-control (especially over bodily passions), patience and constancy in the face of temptation, as in depictions of St Jerome (e.g. Ghent, Mus. S. Kst.; Venice, Doge's Pal.); the *Temptation of St Anthony* (e.g. Madrid, Prado; Venice, Doge's Pal.); *St Giles* (Venice, Doge's Pal.); and *St John the Baptist in the Wilderness* (Madrid, Mus. Lázaro Galdiano). The essential significance of the hermit saint's life, as seen by Bosch, is the rejection of society and the withdrawal from all earthly vices, a strong theme among the early humanists of the Upper Rhine (e.g. Sebastian Brant, Geiler von Kaisersberg, with whom Bosch had so much affinity. The hermit's trials, they believed, were much easier to bear than those of worldly people—a view hard to reconcile with the practical morality of the same early humanist groups and their bourgeois sympathizers. The hermit was thus apparently more of a rhetorical model, an epitome of the wise man, impervious and invulnerable. The humanists also admired the hermit's self-control and single-mindedness. Hermits were the only group of saints whom Bosch depicted independently, in their own right as a type and an exemplary ideal. The backgrounds of Bosch's representations of hermit saints are rarely directly connected with their relevant legend. They are the artist's invention, often implying a wholly independent ethical system. This is especially the case with the famous triptych with the *Temptation of St Anthony* (Lisbon, Mus. N. A. Ant.), in which Bosch used the hermit as a vehicle for his own convictions or rather those of the group for which it was intended.

Apart from the hermits, he made few paintings of saints: none, for instance, of the Virgin, St Anne and other devotional saints who were then so popular. He was certainly not working to meet the needs of the ordinary devotee, but for particular patrons for whom his own intellectual contribution was generally decisive. Other depictions include *St John on Patmos* (Berlin, Gemäldegal.) and several untraced works: *St Martin and the Beggar* (preserved in a print published by Hieronymus Cock), *St John the Evangelist* (formerly in the collection of Mencía de Mendoza, the third wife of Hendrick III of Nassau), the *Conversion of St Paul* (in the 17th century with the Antwerp art dealer Forchondt) and *St Dominic and the Heretics* (mentioned by Karel van Mander).

Bosch also used depictions of the Last Judgement (e.g. Bruges, Groeningemus.; see fig. 2) as a vehicle for his ethical views: he presented a fundamentally pessimistic concept of the world, in which all men were foolish and sinful and very few could expect salvation. Bosch did not represent the resurrection of the dead, and the division between sheep and goats is not very equal. Compared to the few blessed, there is always a legion of damned, already tormented by devils on earth.

Eschatological thinking was of lasting importance in Bosch's work. He saw mankind in the light of eternity, the eschatological schema serving as a final legitimization of his secular ethical views. In the tabletop with the *Seven Deadly Sins*, roundels in the corners depict the Four Last Things (*Death, Hell, Terrestrial or Earthly Paradise* and *Celestial Paradise*), with the all-seeing eye of Christ in the centre. Similar scenes—the *Blessed in the Terrestrial Paradise*, the *Ascent of the Blessed into the Celestial Paradise*, the *Fall of the Damned* and *Hell*—are represented in four other panels (all Venice, Doge's Pal.). *The Haywain* (see fig. 1 above) and the '*Garden of Earthly Delights*' (see fig. 3) both have a representation of Hell on the right-hand panel.

Hay was at that time a symbol for everything worthless and transient; Bosch applied it to all earthly possessions and pleasures that men blindly pursue, leading to eternal damnation (the wain is driven by devils towards hell). The haywain motif is not his own invention: a 16th-century print of the same title (Nuremberg, Ger. Nmus.) bears long inscriptions based, on the evidence of language, on a Utrecht source of *c.* 1500.

In the triptych with the '*Garden of Earthly Delights*', Bosch depicted the history of the world in terms of the *Creation of the World* by God the Father (on the outer wings), the earthly or *Terrestrial Paradise* (Garden of Eden) on the left inner wing and *Hell* on the right inner wing—all treated *sub specie sexualitatis et procreationis*. On the outer side the newly created world is already clothed in wonderful flora, symbols of nature and sexuality, which are also found in the central panel and in temptation scenes by the artist. The left wing shows the institution of marriage (Adam and Eve) and already hints at the sexual perversion of it (the owl in the fountain). The central panel shows the false paradise of love, probably as the *aetas aurea* from Adam to Noah, to be repeated at the end of the world *sub specie luxuriae* ('*sicut in diebus Noe . . .*'). This grail, as the *pseudo-paradisus amoris* was called in the 15th and 16th centuries, is situated between the earthly and the supernatural and contains both heavenly and diabolical elements: thus some interpreters see it as depicting a paradisiacal state, others a state of sin. The ambiguity is, in fact, intended and is fundamental to a proper understanding of the triptych. Its 'message' is approximately as follows: sexuality can become an end in itself, owing to an unchaste interpretation of the paradisiacal state of marriage instituted by God, with the command to increase and multiply. Thus men and women believe they are living in a lovers' paradise (the grail), but it is really false and pernicious. Bosch supported this view 'historically': sex and procreation were known from the beginning (the outside of the wings); in the 'golden age' they turned to *luxuria*; and at the end of the world (which may come at any time) they will again lead back to evil. The preaching of 'pure' marriage is not so much a matter of religious thinking as of the upper middle-class preoccupation with marriage, the family and the household (concerns that were strongly promoted *c.* 1500).

Besides Old Testament themes, saints and moralizing religious subjects, Bosch painted many scenes from the *Life of Christ*, centering on his childhood and the Passion. To the first category belong the *Nativity* (copy, Cologne, Wallraf-Richartz-Mus.), the *Adoration of the Magi* (Madrid, Prado, and copies after several lost prototypes); the *Flight into Egypt* (untraced; mentioned by van Mander) and *Christ among the Doctors* (copies in Paris, Louvre, and elsewhere). From Christ's ministry there is only the *Marriage at Cana* (possible copy, Rotterdam, Mus. Boymans–van Beuningen). The cycle of the *Passion* is introduced by *Christ Driving the Money-changers from the Temple* (copies, Glasgow, A.G. & Mus., and Copenhagen, Stat. Mus. Kst) and the *Entry into Jerusalem* (untraced; ex-G. de Haen priv. col., Cologne, 1581). Then come the *Betrayal of Christ* (untraced, ex-Philip II priv. col.; copies, San Diego, CA, Mus. A., and Amsterdam, Rijksmus.), *Christ before Pilate* (copies, Rotterdam, Mus. Boymans–

4. Hieronymus Bosch: *Crowning with Thorns*, oil on panel, 730×590 mm, *c.* 1490–1500 (London, National Gallery)

van Beuningen, and Princeton, NJ, U. A. Mus.), the *Ecce homo* (Frankfurt am Main, Städel. Kstinst. & Städt. Gal.), the *Crowning with Thorns* (London, N.G.; see fig. 4), the *Mocking of Christ* (Madrid, Escorial), the *Carrying of the Cross* (versions, Madrid, Escorial (ex-Philip II); Ghent, Mus. S. Kst.; Vienna, Ksthist. Mus.), the *Crucifixion* (Brussels, Mus. A. Anc.), the *Entombment* (drawing, London, BM), the *Lamentation* (two untraced prototypes) and the *Descent into Limbo* (untraced, ex-Archduke Ernest priv. col., 1593; variant versions survive). In the *Passion* scenes Bosch emphasized the suffering and patience of Christ and the bestiality of his tormentors, who represent the blind and sinful world *par excellence*. It has often been suggested that the way in which Christ looks directly at the spectator is intended to recall the *Imitatio Christi* in the *Devotio moderna*. This sorrowful glance is reminiscent of early humanist visions, such as those expressed in Thomas More's *De tristitia Christi*. The Christocentrism itself recalls the *Devotio moderna*. The sources of Bosch's religiosity have not yet been fully explored. The ordinary late medieval devotional literature explains many elements, but by no means all. Bosch's attitude to religion, as manifested in his works, may well have been determined by the taste of advanced bourgeois circles, whose religious outlook was itself an amalgam of 'typical late medieval' thought, early humanism and the *Devotio moderna*.

2. MORALIZING. Bosch's many secular moralizing works served as a vehicle for expressing his thoughts on norms and values. The most detailed explanations of these paintings—and those best founded historically—are those of Dirk Bax, who pointed out that nearly all the vices depicted by Bosch are regularly characterized as 'follies'

and are generally ascribed to a motley group of members of the lowest social class. The principal vices represented are unchastity, profligacy, quarrelsomeness, gluttony, drunkenness and self-inflicted poverty. Bosch's connection between 'vice' or 'evil behaviour' and 'folly' or 'stupidity'—a theme explored in such paintings as the *Stone Operation*, the *Blind Leading the Blind* and the *Ship of Fools* (see fig. 5)—was in tune with the intellectual outlook of the day. The equation of virtue and wisdom, and vice and folly, is found in the 15th-century 'literature of folly', such as Sebastian Brant's *Narrenschiff* ('Ship of fools'; 1494), the works of Thomas Murner and many other less-known or anonymous authors. Detachment, moderation, self-knowledge, control over passions, and, above all, reason were regarded as important values. This morality, which arose in bourgeois circles *c.* 1460–90, was aimed at defending the status quo, though it departed from the old order's ideology by virtue of its rationalism, ethicism and individualism. In Bosch's work the equation between folly, sin and (socially) reprehensible behaviour is not consciously expressed by a specific type representing folly; it is incidentally implied, as though Bosch regarded it as a self-evident basis for his moral precepts. It is not a question of his having been 'influenced' by the literature of folly: there was a common ideology that found expression in all the various media.

In line with contemporary attitudes towards 'social deviation', Bosch associated sin and folly with a large cross-section of society's lower classes: whores, jailbirds, topers and revellers, vagabonds, beggars and travelling mountebanks, procuresses, common soldiers and poor people of all sorts. Whereas earlier the poor had not been

frowned on, in the later Middle Ages they began to be strictly controlled and stigmatized as good-for-nothing parasites and idlers. This reached a climax *c.* 1525, when the regulations for poor-relief were extensively overhauled. From the 14th century onwards, and especially in the 15th and 16th centuries, a number of satirical texts contained long lists of 'depraved persons', who it was thought should be banished from society, as fools were in the relevant literary genre. Fools and social undesirables were thus condemned to suffer a similar fate in both literature and art. Bosch in his pictures provided countless deviants whom he placed in hell or in the company of demons. Vagrants are another common subject in his work, as in *The Vagabond* (Rotterdam, Mus. Boymans–van Beuningen; see fig. 6), *The Conjurer* (preserved only in copies and imitations), the foreground figures of the centre panel and the outer wings of *The Haywain* and several other lost works: *The Verdict*, *The Fosterer* and the *Blind Leading the Blind*.

The vices condemned by Bosch can be divided into four categories. In the first place, he disapproved of giving way to 'wild' bodily impulses: aggression, love of food and drink and, above all, sexuality. This accorded with contemporary ideas, which were expressed in the opposition of nature and culture, savagery and civilization, in both pictures and moral treatises. Bosch interpreted these ideas from a concrete social point of view, using everyday figure types. He also disapproved of popular festivities and amusements, seen as opportunities for carnality and ill-breeding, a love of pleasure and roisterous behaviour—vices constantly associated with the common people.

The third category is concerned with work and idleness, wealth and poverty, avarice and prodigality. Here Bosch's position was more moderate: he seems to have condemned the love of gain for its own sake but was even more opposed to extravagance. Self-inflicted poverty was often associated with those on the lowest rung of the social ladder and ascribed to vices from the first two categories: drunkenness, whoring and excessive merrymaking. In contrast, he praised the love of work and a moderate use of money and property. All this is reflected in *The Haywain*, the *Death of the Miser* (Washington, DC, N.G.A.) and the *Scenes of Idleness* (preserved only in 16th-century prints). The fourth and last category with which Bosch was concerned is rash and baseless aggression. He was an advocate of constant watchfulness, reticence, attentiveness, detachment, restraint and caution, as can be seen in the drawing of the *Owl in the Tree* ('The Field Sees, the Wood Listens'; Berlin, Kupferstichkab.) and the painting 'Keep a Weather Eye Open' (*c.* 1600; Heverlee, Arenberg col.).

The concept of threat plays a central part in Bosch's world view: the individual is attacked in his moral and spiritual integrity by his own impulses, rooted in sensuality, by the external world and by supernatural forces of evil. Fear, both of material ruin and of spiritual damage, was a basic element of bourgeois culture *c.* 1500. The self was regarded as an extremely weak entity, constantly obliged to resist and remain firm. Along with the sense of the individual's weakness goes an obsession with self-preservation as the ideal of utilitarian wisdom. Folly is self-destructive, leading to eternal damnation and the company

5. Hieronymus Bosch: *Ship of Fools*, oil on panel, 579×326 mm, *c.* 1490–1500 (Paris, Musée du Louvre)

of devils, a state Bosch saw embodied in the lowest ranks of human society.

Although Bosch himself belonged to the wealthiest and socially highest class in 's Hertogenbosch, the attitudes to work, money, possessions and their use, as expressed in his paintings, seem typical of the contemporary urban middle class (guilds, not commerce). The main emphasis is on moderation, avoiding unbridled acquisitiveness and also blind indifference. Then comes the defence of the work ethos and the loathing of extravagance, which leads to poverty and ruin. All this is related to *oeconomica* or domestic economy: a life of peace and contentment with the fruits of one's labour, eschewing the desire for gain and novelty. Bosch endorsed the ideology of an urban middle class of craftsmen and small producers, to whom economy was also a moral question. This is certainly not a capitalist vision, but the emphasis on work and thrift (expressed negatively by Bosch: the rejection of laziness and squandering) already helps to prepare the way for capitalist discourse.

3. SOURCES. Bosch made extensive use of lower-class 'folklore', such as popular songs, ballads, proverbs, sayings and metaphors—all of which was then pressed into the service of an élite, bourgeois system of morals and satirical method. For Bosch the language and proverbs of the lower classes (whether these were substandard or not) presented a certain sense of obscurity, which was still deliberately cultivated as the vehicle of an intellectual morality: 'the wise man speaks in riddles'. At the same time he used popular modes of expression and thought subconsciously to give form to his ideas. He also drew extensively on the inversive mode of expression in popular seasonal revels, for example Shrovetide. This may explain why he constantly represents wrong types of behaviour and never those he considered right. The principle of reversal is a widely recognized anthropological phenomenon: the central categories of a culture are dialectically defined by proclaiming their opposite, in a fictitious breach of the norm that, in fact, confirms it as well as providing amusement.

Folklore traditions also provided specific subjects to be represented in Bosch's work, as in the following paintings (all untraced): the *Mock Tournament on the Ice*, *The Elephant*, *Strife and Dance on Shrove Tuesday and in Lent*, the *Blind Men's Boar Hunt*, in all of which a burlesque contest is the central feature. This explicit content, however, is used metaphorically to convey a more fundamental message. *Strife and Dance on Shrove Tuesday* is a metaphor for the opposition between rival sets of values: in literature, from *c.* 1500 it is always Lent that wins, but in art, the outcome is uncertain, for Bosch attached too many negative connotations to carnival time. The other scenes are also metaphorical: by depicting opposites, they satirize foolish, aggressive and licentious popular amusements (e.g. the *Mock Tournament*), the ill-effects of error and rashness (e.g. the *Blind Men's Boar Hunt*) or unthinking hostility between social groups and classes (e.g. *The Elephant*). Other folklore themes in Bosch's work centre on the ritual celebration of folly. The *Stone Operation* or '*Cure of Folly*' (see fig. 7) is not inspired by real surgical procedures (in medieval times it was thought that cutting

6. Hieronymus Bosch: *The Vagabond*, oil on panel, 710×706 mm, *c.* 1510 (Rotterdam, Museum Boymans–van Beuningen)

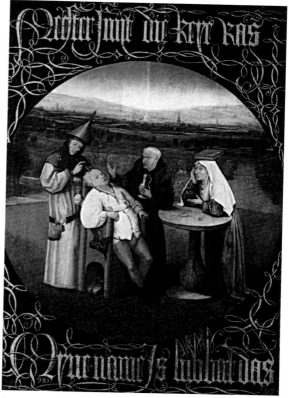

7. Hieronymus Bosch (?copy after): *Stone Operation* (or *Cure of Folly*), 480×350 mm, *c.* 1475–80 (Madrid, Museo del Prado)

a stone out of a madman's head would cure him) but by burlesque illustrations of the futility of trying to make fools wise. The *Shearing of the Fool* (drawing, London, BM) is based on similar organized spectacles, intended to hold up folly to public opprobrium but later forbidden by the authorities because of their 'licentious' character.

III. Style, technique and chronology.

Bosch's technique and style are not homogeneous, which has led to much confusion. For example he seems to have used several different techniques of underdrawing. Van Schoute (1967) examined with infra-red reflectography six panels accepted as authentic and identified what seemed to him three sketching techniques. His first category, to which he assigned the *Crowning with Thorns* (London, N.G.) and the *St John on Patmos* (Berlin, Gemäldegal.), consists of sketches drawn with a coarse brush and diluted paint, giving few details and merely indicating a general design. Individual strokes are short and of unequal length. Many changes of form were made at the painting stage. In his second category are the *Ship of Fools* (Paris, Louvre) and the *Allegory* (New Haven, CT, Yale U.A.G.), in which the underdrawing has areas of profuse hatching, giving an impression of great care and accuracy. Parallel oblique strokes, with a slightly mechanical effect, run from upper left to lower right. Changes of form are fairly minor. In his third and final category he placed the *Carrying of the Cross* (Ghent, Kon. Mus. S. Kst.) and the outer wings of the triptych with the *Temptation of St Anthony* (Lisbon, Mus. N. A. Ant.): these, he suggested, are characterized by a not very detailed sketch, in lines of moderate thickness that are often interrupted but firm and give only a summary indication of the different forms. Here again, an unusual number of changes of form and composition is evident in the final painting.

Filedt Kok (1972–3), by contrast, distinguished only two types of underdrawing in Bosch's work. The first group, in a 'sketchy' style, exemplified in the *St Christopher* (Rotterdam, Mus. Boymans–van Beuningen), is based on a broad, summary underdrawing, visible only under the garments, executed with a coarse brush in thin paint. Not much was changed in the painting, though the forms were further elaborated. Grouped around this work are other compositions showing a saint in a landscape, such as the *St John on Patmos*, in which the underdrawing consists of mostly straight lines of varying width, some simple, others repeated alongside or over one another. The hatched strokes are made up of short, rather irregular lines. To this group may be added the *St John the Baptist in the Wilderness* (Madrid, Mus. Lázaro Galdiano) and the *St Jerome* (Ghent, Mus. S. Kst.). All these works form a more or less coherent stylistic group.

To the second main group, described as in a 'careful' style, Filedt Kok assigned the *Carrying of the Cross* (Ghent, Mus. S. Kst.), featuring a confident, flexible line gracefully indicating forms and contours, with a little hatching here and there. This technique is also found in van Schoute's second group and in such works as the *Death of the Miser* and *The Vagabond* (both Washington, DC, N.G.A.). In this latter work, the profuse diagonal hatching is more

varied and three-dimensional in character. This very carefully modelled underdrawing was preceded by a preliminary sketch, some traces of which can still be discerned. The works in this group, including the inside of the wings of the Lisbon triptych with the *Temptation of St Anthony*, exhibit the same careful underdrawing and thinly applied paint, with many white highlights.

As Filedt Kok pointed out, these two different styles of underdrawing sometimes occur together, as in the Lisbon triptych, and thus afford no evidence as to chronology. Such differences in the amount of detail in underdrawings, for instance between foreground and background figures, also occur in the works of Bosch's contemporaries and are easily explained by the degree of attention given to the various elements. Filedt Kok further suggested that there may be a connection between the manner of drawing and the technique of the final painting, that it is the very thinly painted panels that have the most precise underdrawing. This second conclusion, while valid for certain groups, is contradicted by such works as the *Crowning with Thorns*, which is thinly painted over a schematic underdrawing (see fig. 4 above).

Just as Bosch's paintings exhibit many styles of underdrawing, ranging from very careful to extremely casual, they also reveal totally different pictorial styles—sometimes carefully painted, with thick impasto, sometimes rapidly applied in an apparently slapdash manner, with a thin layer of paint. There are also many intermediate stages. To the first extreme belong, for example, the left wing and central panel of the 'Garden of Earthly Delights', the outer side of the Bruges *Last Judgement*, the triptychs of the *Hermits* and the *Martyrdom of St Ontcommer* and *St John the Baptist in the Wilderness*. Examples of the second style are the central panel and right wing of *The Haywain*, the *Death of the Miser*, *The Vagabond* and others.

Despite the fact that Bosch's different styles of underdrawing and painting technique provide no help whatsoever in dating, it is possible to identify recurring patterns in individual groups of paintings. For instance a fundamental similarity of technical execution exists between three of Bosch's large triptychs: the 'Garden of Earthly Delights', *The Haywain* and the *Last Judgement*. In each case the left wing is thickly and carefully painted, while the underdrawing is entirely or nearly invisible. The right wing is executed more rapidly, with a thin, transparent layer of paint, with the underdrawing visible in many places. The central panel in each instance is intermediate between the other two styles. The underdrawing on the outer wings is invisible throughout, while the structure of the paint layer varies from moderate to very thick.

IV. Critical reception and posthumous reputation.

Besides Philip the Fair, Isabella the Catholic, Margaret of Austria and Philip of Burgundy, there were other collectors of Bosch's works in the first half of the 16th century. In 1521 and 1528 at least five paintings were in the possession of Domenico and Marino Grimani in Venice. The collection of paintings by Bosch assembled by Mencía de Mendoza, Marquesa de Cenete and third wife of Hendrick III of Nassau, suggests that Spanish interest in Bosch's work may have been linked to a local tendency towards eschatologism and prophetism, which verged on heresy: the heretical group of the Alumbrados (Enlightened Ones), associated with the Third Order of St Francis, presented features of Erasmianism and free thought, as well as apocalyptic claims, and their earliest centre, in 1519, was at the house of Mencía de Mendoza in Guadalajara.

Another Bosch collector, imprisoned on a charge of heresy, was the humanist Damião de Goes. Thus c. 1500 there seem to have been certain inherent ideological tendencies in Spanish aristocratic and court circles that, while not strictly heretical, prepared the way for an interest in one aspect of Bosch; by the first half of the 16th century some humanist circles, inclining to heterodoxy, had gone still further and actually saw Bosch as a kindred spirit. This would mean that in Spanish and Spanish–Burgundian circles Bosch was approached one-sidedly from the beginning and was very soon 'reinterpreted' or endowed with a spurious content, giving rise to the 'Bosch myth'. The myth was fundamentally twofold: an orthodox Bosch and a heretical one.

Other 16th-century collectors of Bosch were Cardinal Antoine Perrenot de Granvelle (1530–86), Fernando Alvárez de Toledo, Duque de Alba, and his illegitimate son Fernando de Toledo (d 1591), Archduke Ernst of Austria and his brother, Emperor Rudolf II of Prague. However, it was, above all, Philip II of Spain who systematically procured important works by Bosch, presenting them, from 1574, to the monastery of the Escorial. In the 17th century Spanish royal collections were enriched by dozens more examples of Bosch's works, most of which have been lost.

It was in Spain, too, that 'El Bosco' became a familiar name in art and literary writings until c. 1800. From Felipe de Guevara, Ambrosio de Morales and Fray José de Sigüenza in the 16th century and the early 17th to Antonio Ponz and J. A. Ceán Bermúdez in the late 18th, dozens of art theorists have kept alive Bosch's fame in Spain. Many literary works, for example entremeses (short comic interludes) by Felix Lope de Vega (1562–1635), used his name.

References to Bosch in Italian art treatises are briefer: he was mentioned by Guicciardini, Vasari and Lomazzo, always as the embodiment of the fantastic, absurd and grotesque. In the Netherlands it was, above all, Karel van Mander's *Schilderboeck* that provided an appreciation of Bosch and information concerning some of his lost works. Bosch then fell out of favour, except in Spain, and although he was mentioned in the art literature of the 17th and 18th centuries, it was without special enthusiasm. He was not rediscovered until the end of the 19th century, when his apocalyptic vision began to be appreciated for new reasons.

BIBLIOGRAPHY
Ceán Bermúdez; *EWA*; Thieme–Becker

EARLY SOURCES
G. Vasari: *Vite* (1550, rev. 2/1568); ed. G. Milanesi (1878–85)
F. de Guevara: *Comentarios de la pintura* (MS., c. 1560); ed. A. Ponz (Madrid, 1788), pp. 41–4
L. Guicciardini: *Descrittione di . . . tutti Paesi Bassi* (1567)
G. P. Lomazzo: *Trattato dell'arte de la pittura, scultura ed architettura* (MS., 1584); ed. (Rome, 1844), ii, pp. 201–2
K. van Mander: *Schilder-boeck* ([1603]–1604)
J. de Sigüenza: *Historia de la Orden de San Jerónimo* (1605/R Madrid, 1905), pp. 837ff

A. Ponz: *Viaje* (1772–94); ed. C. M. de Rivero (1947)
X. de Salas: *El Bosco en la literatura española* (Barcelona, 1943)
A. Salazar: 'El Bosco y Ambrosio de Morales', *Archv. Esp. A.*, xxviii (1955), pp. 117–38
X. de Salas: 'Más sobre El Bosco en España', *Homenaje a J. A. van Praag* (Amsterdam, 1956), pp. 108–13
M. Levisi: 'Hieronymus Bosch y los *Sueños* de Francisco de Quevedo', *Filología*, ix (1963), pp. 163–200
H. Heidenreich: 'Hieronymus Bosch in Some Literary Contexts', *J. Warb. & Court. Inst.*, xxxiii (1970), pp. 171–99

DOCUMENTARY SOURCES
C. Justi: 'Die Werke des Hieronymus Bosch in Spanien', *Jb. Preuss. Kstsamml.*, x (1889), pp. 141–4
J. Ebeling: 'Jheronimus van Aken', *Miscellanea Jan Gessler*, i (Antwerp, 1948), pp. 444–57
P. Gerlach: 'De bronnen voor het leven en het werk van Jeroen Bosch' [Sources for the life and work of Hieronymus Bosch], *Brabantia*, xvi (1967), pt 1, pp. 58–65, pt 2, pp. 95–104; Fr. trans. of pt 2, *Gaz. B.-A.*, 6th ser., lxxi (1968), pp. 109–16
——: 'Jheronimus van Aken alias Bosch en de Onze-Lieve-Vrouw-Broederschap', *Jheronimus Bosch: Bijdragen bij gelegenheid van de herdenkingstentoonstelling te 's Hertogenbosch 1967* [Essays on the occasion of the memorial exhibition at 's Hertogenbosch 1967], pp. 48–60
J. K. Steppe: 'Jheronimus Bosch: Bijdragen tot de historische en de ikonografische studie van zijn werk', *Jheronimus Bosch: Bijdragen bij gelegenheid van de herdenkingstentoonstelling te 's Hertogenbosch 1967*, pp. 5–41 [with ref. to edns of Spanish royal inventories and others]
P. Gerlach: 'Oirschot en de familie vanden Meervenne', *Campina*, ii (1973), pp. 183–93
F. Gorissen: *Das Stundenbuch der Katharina von Kleve: Analyse und Kommentar* (Berlin, 1973), pp. 1100–08, 1129–65 [the van Aken family in Nijmegen and 's Hertogenbosch, c. 1350–1516, with geneaological charts and transcriptions of the relevant docs]
P. Vandenbroeck: 'Rudolf II als verzamelaar van werk van en naar Jheronimus Bosch', *Jb.: Kon. Mus. S. Kst.* (1981), pp. 119–33
B. Blondé and H. Vlieghe: 'The Social Status of Hieronymus Bosch', *Burl. Mag.*, cxxxi/1039 (1989), pp. 699–700

BIBLIOGRAPHIES
W. Gibson: *Hieronymus Bosch: An Annotated Bibliography*, ed. C. Harbison (Boston, MA, 1983) [for the lit. to 1983]
P. Vandenbroeck: 'Über neuere Bosch-Literatur', *Krit. Ber.*, xiv (1986), p. 52 [suppl. to Gibson]

MONOGRAPHIC STUDIES
P. Lafond: *Hieronymus Bosch* (Brussels and Paris, 1914)
M. J. Friedländer: *Die altniederländische Malerei*, v (Berlin, 1927); Eng. trans. as *Early Netherlandish Painting* (Leiden, 1967–76)
Jeroen Bosch (exh. cat. by D. Hannema and J. G. van Gelder, Rotterdam, Mus. Boymans, 1936)
L. von Baldass: *Hieronymus Bosch* (Vienna, 1941, 2/1959)
C. de Tolnay: *Hieronymus Bosch*, 2 vols (Baden-Baden, 1965)
D. Buzzati and M. Cinotti: *L'opera completa di Hieronimus Bosch* (Milan, 1966)
Jheronimus Bosch (exh. cat., ed. K. G. Boon and others; 's Hertogenbosch, Noordbrabants Mus., 1967)
W. S. Gibson: *Hieronymus Bosch* (London, 1973)
J. Snyder: *Bosch in Perspective* (Englewood Cliffs, NJ, 1973)
S. Takashika: *The Complete Work of Jheronimus Bosch* (Tokyo, 1978) [best illus]
R. Marijnissen and P. Ruyffelaere: *Jheronimus Bosch* (Antwerp, 1987) [does not cover lost works, tapestries or graphic work; concentrates on the artist's religious work]
P. Vandenbroeck: *Jheronimus Bosch: Tussen volksleven en stadscultuur* [Hieronymus Bosch: between the life of the people and urban culture] (Berchem and Antwerp, 1987)

ICONOGRAPHY
D. Bax: *Ontcijfering van Jeroen Bosch* (The Hague, 1949); Eng. trans. as *Hieronymus Bosch: His Picture Writing Deciphered* (Rotterdam, 1979)
——: 'Beschrijving en poging tot verklaring van het *Tuin der Onkuisheid-drieluik* van Jeroen Bosch, gevolgd door kritiek op Fraenger', *Acad. Anlct.: Kl. S. Kst.*, lxiii (1956) [whole issue devoted to iconog. study of the '*Garden of Earthly Delights*']
J.-P. Jouffroy: '*Le Jardin des Délices*' de Jérôme Bosch: Grandeur nature (Paris, 1977) [good illustrations]
D. Bax: 'Hieronymus Bosch and Lucas Cranach: Two *Last Judgement* Triptychs. Description and Exposition', *Acad. Anlct.: Kl. S. Kst.*, cxvii (1982) [whole issue]

P. Vandenbroeck: 'Jheronimus Bosch' zogenaamde *Tuin der Lusten*: I' [Hieronymus Bosch's so-called Garden of Earthly Delights: I], *Jb.: Kon. Mus. S. Kst.* (1989), pp. 9–210

——: 'Jheronimus Bosch' zogenaamde *Tuin der Lusten*: II', *Jb.: Kon. Mus. S. Kst.* (1990), pp. 9–192

TECHNIQUE

R. van Schoute: 'Over de techniek van Jeroen Bosch', *Jheronimus Bosch: Bijdragen bij gelegenheid van de herdenkingstentoonstellingte 's Hertogenbosch 1967* [Essays on the occasion of the memorial exhibition at 's Hertogenbosch 1967], pp. 72–9

M. Sonkes: 'Le Dessin sous-jacent chez les primitifs flamands', *Bull. Inst. Royal Patrm. A.*, xii (1970), pp. 195–225

J. P. Filedt Kok: 'Underdrawing and Drawing in the Work of Hieronymus Bosch: A Provisional Survey in Connection with Paintings by him in Rotterdam', *Simiolus*, vi (1972–3), pp. 133–62

P. Vandenbroeck: 'Problèmes concernant l'oeuvre de Jheronimus Bosch: Le Dessin sous-jacent en relation avec l'authenticité et la chronologie', *Le Dessin sous-jacent dans la peinture, Colloque IV: Leuven, U. Catholique, 1981*, pp. 107–19

M. del Carmen Garrido and R. van Schoute: 'El tríptico de la *Adoración de los magos* de Hieronymus van Aeken Bosch: Estudio técnico', *Bol. Mus. Prado*, vi (1985), pp. 59–77

——: 'Les *Péchés capitaux* de Jérôme Bosch au Musée du Prado à Madrid: Etude téchnologique, premières considérations', *Le Dessin sous-jacent dans la peinture, Colloque VI: Leuven, U. Catholique, 1985*, pp. 103–6

PAUL VANDENBROECK

Bosch, Theo (*b* Amsterdam, 24 Feb 1940). Dutch architect and teacher. He studied at the Academy of Architecture and worked in various architects' offices in Amsterdam before joining Aldo van Eyck's office in 1965, becoming his partner in 1971. He worked independently after 1984. He was one of the few designers in the Netherlands to adopt a particular interest in the synthesis between urban-planning infill, spacious architectonic expression and optimal practicality. He considered people to be more important than philosophy, whether for houses or utilitarian buildings. His regard for the future occupants of his buildings extended to anticipating often unformulated living requirements from his own observations. His architecture is never obtrusive but joins seamlessly to existing structures as well as allowing for future ones. In the debates about Amsterdam's Nieuwmarkt district Bosch supported residential use for newly built urban formations. His design for the Faculty of Languages, University of Amsterdam, attracted much national and international approval; in it, late 20th-century construction replaces small-scale historical canal architecture. Other important buildings are his houses on the Sijzenlaan (1989), Deventer, and Elandstraat (1990) in The Hague; the Willemshuis Stadhouderskade office (1991), Amsterdam, and Filmwijk houses (1992) in Almere. In 1987 he was appointed chairman of the Welfare Commission in The Hague. He also taught architecture, at the University of Amsterdam and abroad.

BIBLIOGRAPHY

P. Buchanan: 'New Amsterdam School', *Archit. Rev.* [London], clxxvii/1055 (1985), pp. 14–38

H. van Dijk: 'Bosch Boogjes', *Archit. Rev.* [London], clxxviii/1064 (1985), pp. 26–31

RAINER BULLHORST

Boschetto. *See* BUSCHETTO.

Boschini, Marco (*b* Venice, 1605; *d* Venice, 1 Jan 1681). Italian art critic, dealer, engraver, restorer and painter. His place in history rests firmly on the hyperbolic 681-page poem *La carta del navegar pitoresco* (Venice, 1660), whose title and subtitle may be translated as 'The map of pictorial navigation. Dialogue between a dilettante Venetian senator and a professor of painting, under the names of Ecelenza and Compare; divided into eight winds which lead the Venetian boat across the high seas of painting as the dominant power of that sea to the confusion of him who does not understand compasses'. It is an intensely patriotic and polemical defence of Venetian painting written in Venetian dialect and directed against those Roman and Tuscan standards represented by Giorgio Vasari. As the full title suggests, Boschini is enamoured with Giambattista Marino's metaphoric language and frankly espouses a personal reading of art history from the perspective of an artist (he who 'understands compasses'). The apparently unstructured exposition rejects objective, comprehensive and logically organized theories of art in favour of an eccentric art criticism that attempts to capture the immediacy and pleasure of vision itself.

In his argument against Vasari, Boschini rejected more than Tuscan artistic ideals, notably the classicizing standards of *disegno* (linear delineation, ancient statues and ideal proportions). He looked at paintings more with the artist's eye for formal problems than the humanist's understanding of content. The ekphrastic tradition that emphasized narrative had little appeal for him; he revelled instead in the beauty of movement (only loosely attached to narrative) and in pure, sensuous form (what does the colouring taste like? what does the light sound like? what does the pigment feel like?). He also dismissed Vasari's interest in the biographical component of art criticism as irrelevant to the image itself.

The *Carta* dominated Venetian art criticism into the 18th century and, despite the obstacles presented by the Venetian dialect, also prompted considerable comment, often derisive, throughout Italy, notably in the work of Filippo Baldinucci, Giovanni Pietro Bellori, Luigi Pellegrino Scaramuccia and Francesco Scipione Maffei. Boschini wrote a more accessible version of the *Carta* as an introduction to the second edition of his guidebook *Le ricche minere della pittura veneziana* (Venice, 1674; originally published in 1664). Although the title is still metaphorical ('The rich mines of Venetian painting'), this book differs considerably in form and purpose from the *Carta*. It is much shorter, rendered into Tuscan, presumably for the tourist trade, and more clearly structured: a history of Venetian painting and a theoretical section divided into *disegno*, *colorito* and *invenzione*. The new audience also encouraged Boschini to adopt a different, less polemical theme: 'Brief instructions on how to understand the styles of Venetian painters' is the heading to the introduction, indicating that Boschini's primary interest was connoisseurship. Hence the 'Breve instruzione' may be situated in a tradition started by Giulio Mancini and Abraham Bosse. *Le ricche minere* may not have been the first guidebook to painting in Venice but it was the most complete to date and served as the foundation for the later guides by Fioravante Martinelli, Anton Maria Zanetti (ii) and Giambattista Albrizzi (1698–1777). It dealt only with paintings in public places; private galleries were to be covered in another book. Boschini wrote *I gioielli pittoreschi* ('the painterly jewels') in 1676; this was the first guidebook to Vicenza.

Boschini studied painting with Palma Giovane, but his activity as a painter can be identified in only one work (*Last Supper*, ex-S Gerolamo, Venice; untraced), apparently in the style of Tintoretto. However, he was friendly with many painters, mostly Venetian, including Pietro Liberi, Nicolas Régnier, Pietro della Vecchia and Dario Varotari the younger (*fl* 1660); he met Pietro da Cortona, Giuseppe Maria Stanzani Mitelli and Velázquez on their visits to Venice. He also studied engraving, with Odoardo Fialetti from Bologna, and engraved portraits, stage sets and maps (e.g. *Il regno tutto di Candia*, Venice, 1644; *L'arcipelago con tutte le isole*, Venice, 1658). His most original work, however, consists of 25 inventions of imaginary paintings by such 17th-century Venetian artists as Pietro Liberi and Pietro della Vecchia, each with a descriptive poem attached. As an art dealer, and in collaboration with della Vecchia and Paolo del Sera, Boschini encouraged the export of paintings, a practice that he had vigorously condemned in the 'Breve instruzione'. His clients included Cardinal Leopoldo de' Medici and Alfonso IV, Duke of Modena. The *Carta* was dedicated to the voracious collector Leopold Wilhelm, Archduke of Austria, presumably as a business promotion.

WRITINGS

La carta del navegar pitoresco (Venice, 1660); ed. A. Pallucchini (Venice and Rome, 1966) [indispensable guide through the maze of Ven. dialect with excellent intro.]
Le minere della pittura veneziana (Venice, 1664)
Le ricche minere della pittura veneziana (Venice, 1674)
I gioielli pittoreschi: Virtuoso ornamento della città di Vicenza (Vicenza, 1676)

DBI   BIBLIOGRAPHY

M. Pittaluga: 'Eugène Fromentin e le origini della moderna critica d'arte', *L'Arte*, xxi (1918), pp. 5–25 [the first, and still essential, consideration of Boschini as an art critic]
L. Lopresti: 'Marco Boschini scrittore d'arte', *L'Arte*, xxii (1919), pp. 13–33 [excellent elaboration of Pittaluga]
R. Maschio: 'La casa di Marco Boschini', *Atti Ist. Veneto Sci., Lett. & A.*, cxxxiv (1976), pp. 115–42
R. Grazia: 'Contributi boschiniani', *Stud. Seicent.*, xviii (1977), pp. 207–44 [important documentary discoveries]
J. Fletcher: 'Marco Boschini and Paolo del Sera: Collectors and Connoisseurs of Venice', *Apollo*, cx (1979), pp. 416–24
F. Bernabei: 'Il problema dell'identificazione stilistica in Marco Boschini', *A. Veneta*, xxxvii (1983), pp. 109–19
P. Sohm: *Pittoresco: Marco Boschini, his Critics and their Critiques of Painterly Brushwork in Seventeenth- and Eighteenth-century Italy* (Cambridge, 1992)

PHILIP SOHM

Boscry [Boucry], **Pierre** (*b* Paris, 1 June 1700; *d* Paris, 1 March 1781). French architect. He was the son of Charles Boscry, a building contractor and mason from Paris. The works of father and son, who frequently worked on the same schemes in Paris in the first third of the 18th century, are often difficult to distinguish. Charles Boscry built the Hôtel de Clermont (also known as the Hôtel de Saissac; 1714; altered) at 69, Rue de Varenne under the direction of Alexandre-Jean-Baptiste Le Blond, the Maison Bernard (1714) in the Rue de la Huchette and the Hôtel d'Avaray (1720–21; now the Dutch Embassy) at 85, Rue de Grenelle under the direction of JEAN-BAPTISTE LE ROUX. Pierre Boscry worked on the Hôpital des Incurables (1724) and designed the Maison Catherinet (1728) in the Rue Mazarine. He provided designs for the portals of the Marché de Bucy (1726) and the Hôtel de Montauban (destr.) in

the Rue de l'Université, which was engraved by Jean Mariette in *L'Architecture française* (Paris, 1727–38). Pierre Boscry was already known in the Faubourg Saint-Germain when he received his most important commissions from Paul de Grivel, Comte d'Orrouer, and his family, helped by his earlier collaboration with Le Roux on the Hôtel d'Avaray. The Comtesse du Prat, sister-in-law of the Comte d'Orrouer, became discontented with Le Roux and asked Boscry to enlarge the left wing of her town house, the Hôtel du Prat, 60, Rue de Varenne, in 1732. In the same year, Boscry was commissioned by the Comte d'Orrouer to design the Hôtel de Bauffremont (87, Rue de Grenelle), an important building decorated by Nicolas Pineau. On the garden elevation the central range is gently curved, with round-headed windows, and ornamented with a large balcony carried on stone brackets. The Marquise de Feuquières, sister of the Comte d'Orrouer, then commissioned Boscry to design two houses, the first in 1736 (58, Rue de Varenne) and the second in 1738 (62, Rue de Varenne; altered and rebuilt in 1785 by Jacques-Denis Antoine), which had a terraced garden giving on to the street. Boscry also provided the design for the chapel of the Collège des Lombards (1738; Rue des Carmes), the façade of which has an elliptical porch crowned by a pediment, as well as others for the château and garden at Neuilly-Plaisance.

BIBLIOGRAPHY

F. de Catheu: 'L'Architecte Pierre Boscry, les sculpteurs Nicolas et Dominique Pineau', *Bull. Soc. Hist. A. Fr.* (1950), pp. 20–93
M. Gallet: 'The Hôtel d'Orrouer', *Apollo*, 2 (1968), pp. 80–85
La Rue de Varenne (exh. cat., Paris, Mus. Rodin, 1981), pp. 37–8, 40–41, 48

BRUNO PONS

Bose, Nandalal (*b* Kharagpur, 3 Dec 1882; *d* Shantiniketan, 16 April 1966). Indian painter and teacher. The foremost student of Abanindranath Tagore and a close associate of Rabindranath Tagore (*see* TAGORE, (1) and (3)), he was a resourceful artist and teacher. His early paintings (e.g. *Sati*, watercolour, *c.* 1907; destr.; copy in Delhi, N.G. Mod. A.), revivalist in style and mythological and literary in content, were influenced by the cultural nationalism of Ernest Binfield Havell and of Sister Nivedita and by the early work of Abanindranath Tagore. These paintings brought him to public notice while he was still a student. His sensibility was modified by his study of the wall paintings of Ajanta and of East Asian art, which he was encouraged in first by the Japanese artist Arai Kempo (1878–1945) in 1916 and later by a visit in 1924 to China and Japan. These interests were supplemented by the ideas of Rabindranath Tagore, Ananda Kentish Coomaraswamy, Okakura Kakuzo and Mahatma Gandhi (*see also* INDIAN SUBCONTINENT, §V, 4(x)). In 1920 he went to Shantiniketan in Bengal to set up an art school as part of Rabindranath Tagore's comprehensive educational programme. Under his leadership this became the most vital centre of modern Indian art in the 1930s and 1940s.

At Shantiniketan Bose painted fewer mythological subjects, became more responsive to his environment and during the next 25 years painted his most enduring works (e.g. *Ashram*, tempera on paper, 1934; Delhi, N.G. Mod. A.). His commitment to art as an expression of life and to the role of education in society led him to incorporate collaborative public art projects into his teaching programme and to design murals, posters, stage sets and costumes and children's illustrated books, and to arrange fairs and festivals. Inspired by Gandhi, he worked with indigenous materials and collaborated with craftsmen, seeing arts and crafts as a continuum whose shared principles he elaborated in his theoretical writings.

For illustration of work *see* INDIAN SUBCONTINENT, fig. 315.

WRITINGS
Drishti O Shrishti [Vision and creation] (Calcutta, 1985) [collected writings]

BIBLIOGRAPHY
An Album of Nandalal Bose (Calcutta, 1956) [with biog. note]
K. G. Subramanyan: 'The Drawings of Nandalal Bose', *A. Her.*, ii (1979), pp. 55–71
Nandalal Bose: Centenary Exhibition (exh. cat., ed. L. P. Sihare; New Delhi, N.G. Mod. A., 1983)
R. L. Bartholomew, ed.: *Nandalal Bose: A Collection of Essays* (New Delhi, 1983)
                                    R. SIVA KUMAR

Boselli, Felice (*b* Piacenza, 20 April 1650; *d* Parma, 23 Aug 1732). Italian painter. He was an immensely successful and prolific still-life painter, whose naturalistic works, which are mainly kitchen and pantry scenes, show a variety of meats, fish, game and shellfish, occasionally accompanied by figures. From 1665 to 1669 he studied in Milan with either Panfilo or Michelangelo Nuvolone (it has not yet been determined which of them was his teacher) and absorbed the influence of Lombard painters, such as Evaristo Baschenis, and of Flemish still-life painters, such as Pieter Aertsen and Joachim Beuckelaer, whose influence was particularly evident in Boselli's early works. He may also have been inspired by Neapolitan still-life painting and particularly by the art of Giuseppe Recco, who had worked in Milan. In 1669 Boselli returned to Piacenza and in 1673 settled in Parma.

Boselli's first important commissions came from the Sanvitale family, for whose residence, the Rocca at Fontanellato, he created many still-life paintings; he also frescoed the theatre (destr.) and a frieze of vases of flowers and landscapes (1681–90) in the reception hall. Boselli admired Parmigianino's frescoes of *Diana and Actaeon* (1523) in the Rocca and made ten free copies of these works (Parma, G.N.). In his early career Boselli experimented with figure painting, but with little success. Among such works is the portrait of *Lieutenant Sopransi*, signed and dated 1685 (priv. col., see Biagi Maino, fig. 472), and a portrait series (Fontanellato, Mus. Rocca Sanvitale).

In 1699 Boselli began to work for the Meli Lupi family of Soragna, for whom he created two series of six ovals (priv. col., see Salerno, pp. 342, 344, 345), which have the rich surfaces and warm, earthy colours characteristic of his style. At the end of his long career Boselli changed his style of brushwork, using more rapid, nervous strokes and at times leaving small streaks and droplets of paint to sparkle on the surface. Among his late works are the *Still-life with Turkey* (Marano, Bologna, Molinari Pradelli priv. col., see Biagi Maino, fig. 484) and the *Still-life of Game* (1730; Modena, Gal. Cámpori). Much of his output survives in private collections in Parma and Piacenza.

BIBLIOGRAPHY
F. Arisi: *Felice Boselli, pittore di natura morta* (Rome and Piacenza, 1973)
L. Salerno: *La natura morta italiana, 1560–1805* (Rome, 1984)
D. Biagi Maino: 'Felice Boselli', *La natura morta in Italia*, ed. F. Porzio (Milan, 1989), i, pp. 398–9 [with full bibliog.]
                                    FIORENZA RANGONI

Boselli, Giacomo (*b* Savona, 1744; *d* ?1808). Italian ceramics painter. From an early age he was attracted to the traditions of Ligurian pottery and worked in both Liguria and Marseille, France. It was, however, chiefly in Savona that his products were most favourably received because of his ability to continue the traditions of the maiolica factories of the Chiodo and Levantino families. His workshop's production was influenced by the work of famous local artists; the variety of wares produced included maiolica, porcelain and cream-coloured earthenware decorated with both enamels and high-temperature colours. His wife Clara [Chiarina] Boselli was a skilled painter of flowers and small figures; after Boselli's death she continued to run the factory.

BIBLIOGRAPHY
F. Noberasco: *Artisti savonesi* (Savona, 1931)
G. Morazzoni: *La maiolica antica ligure* (Milan, 1951)
P. Torriti: *Giacomo Boselli e la ceramica savonese del suo tempo* (Genoa, 1965)
                            CARMEN RAVANELLI GUIDOTTI

Boshier, Derek (*b* Portsmouth, 19 June 1937). English painter, sculptor, photographer and printmaker. He studied painting and lithography at Yeovil School of Art in Somerset (1953–7), Guildford College of Art (1957–9) and the Royal College of Art, London (1959–62), where he was one of the students associated with Pop art. Like R. B. Kitaj and David Hockney, Boshier juxtaposed contrasting styles within his paintings, but he favoured topical subject-matter such as the space race, political events and the Americanization of Europe. The satirical edge of such paintings as *Identi-kit Man* (1962; London, Tate), which pictured the threat posed by advertising to individual identity, was prompted by his reading of Marshall McLuhan, Vance Packard and other commentators. In the autumn of 1962 Boshier went to India on a one-year scholarship, producing paintings based on Indian symbolism (accidentally destr.). Returning to England he adopted a hard-edged geometric style, often using shaped canvases, abandoning overt figuration but continuing to allude through form to architectural structures and to the grid plans of cities.

In 1966 Boshier turned briefly to sculpture, producing elemental shapes made of perspex and neon, in effect a jazzy version of nascent Minimalism. During the 1970s he experimented with different media, producing photographs, films, collages, constructions, books, posters and record covers. The diversity of this output was unified by his response to contemporary events, his insistence on the social context, his unmasking of the sinister aspects of advertising and his promotion of radical politics.

Boshier returned to painting in 1979, and in 1980 he took up a teaching post in Houston, Texas, where he began introducing poignant, sometimes comical, figures into his canvases. Often garishly coloured and rough in execution, these painted observations of human behaviour earned him a new and devoted following.

BIBLIOGRAPHY

Derek Boshier: Work 1971–4 (exh. cat. by D. Boshier, U. Manchester, Whitworth A.G., 1975)

Lives: An Exhibition of Artists whose Work Is Based on Other People's Lives, Selected by Derek Boshier (exh. cat., intro. D. Boshier; ACGB, 1979)

Derek Boshier: Texas Works (exh. cat. by D. Brauer and D. Boshier, London, ICA, 1982)

Derek Boshier: Selected Drawings 1960–1982 (exh. cat. by M. Livingstone and D. Boshier, Liverpool, Bluecoat Gal., 1983)

Derek Boshier (exh. cat., intro. M. Livingstone; Paris, Gal. du Centre, 1993)

For further bibliography see POP ART.

MARCO LIVINGSTONE

Bosio, Antonio (*b* La Vittoriosa, Malta, 1575; *d* Rome, 5 Sept 1629). Italian antiquary. He was the illegitimate son of Giovanni Ottone, vice-chancellor of the Hieronymite Order. Between 1587 and 1589 he studied law at the Collegio Romano in Rome. He soon began to investigate Early Christian history, enlarging upon the work of his mentor, Onofrio Panvinio (*d* 1569), whose *De ritu sepeliendi mortuos* (Rome, 1569) recorded for the first time a total of 43 Roman cemeteries. In 1593 Bosio and Pompeo Ugonio, his professor of letters at the Sapienza, undertook the first exploration of the Catacombs of Domitilla on the Via Ardeatina (*see* ROME, §V, 13). This was followed by other discoveries: the cemetery of Ciriaca on the Via Tiburtina (1593); the Catacombs of SS Pietro and Marcellino on the Via Labicana; the Catacombs of S Valentino on the Via Flaminia and the underground basilicas in the Catacombs of SS Trasone and Saturnino on the Via Salaria Nuova (1594); and the Catacombs of Lucina beneath the basilica of S Paolo fuori le Mura on the Via Ostiense (1595). Bosio returned to the cemetery of Ciriaca in 1597 and broke into the *cubiculum* of the Catacombs of S Callisto. Also in 1597 he completed the *Historia passionis SS Martyrum Caeciliae* (Rome, 1600), illustrated with engravings by Antonio Tempesta. During 1601 he broke into the Catacombs of St Agnese and the Jewish catacombs. That year he also met the French antiquary Nicolas-Claude Fabri de Peiresc with whom he maintained a long correspondence. In 1608 he discovered the Catacombs of St Ermete. At this time he and several assistants began to assemble the results of his researches, which are recorded in two autograph manuscripts: *Acta et vitae sanctorum* (Rome, Bib. Vallicelliana, Cod. 3–4). All that survives of Bosio's preliminary project for the *Roma sotterranea*, which was first composed in Latin, is a fragment pertaining to the Via Aureliana and Via Cornelia (Rome, Bib. Vallicelliana, Cod. G. 5). The publication of *Roma sotterranea* in Italian and with more than 200 illustrations by Francesco Fulcaro was postponed by Bosio's death. The edition that appeared posthumously between 1632 and 1634 was edited by Giovanni Severano, whose Latin translation followed within three years. In 1651 Paolo Arringhi published an amplified edition of Bosio's work as *Roma subterranea novissima*.

UNPUBLISHED SOURCES

Rome, Bib. Vallicelliana, Cod. 3–4 [*Acta et vitae sanctorum, antiqua monumenta sacra et prophana itemque adversaria variae eruditionis pro illustrando opere de sacris coemeteriis*]

WRITINGS

Historia passionis SS Martyrum Caeciliae Virginis, Valeriani, Tiburtii, et Maximi, nec non Urbani et Luccii pontificum et martyrum vitae (Rome, 1600)

G. Severano, ed.: *Roma sotterranea: Opera postuma . . . Nella quale si tratta de' sacri cimiterii di Roma* (Rome, 1632); 2nd ed. published as *Sculture e pitture sagre estratte dai cimiterij di Roma* (Rome, 1737)

P. Arringhi, ed.: *Roma subterranea novissima: In qua, post A. Bosium . . . Io Severanum . . . et celebres alios scriptores antiqua Christianorum et praecipue martyrum coemeteria*, 2 vols (Rome, 1651) [Lat. trans.]

DBI

BIBLIOGRAPHY

A. Valeri: *Cenni biografici di Antonio Bosio* (Rome, 1900)

K. Waetzoldt: *Die Kopien des 17. Jahrhunderts nach Mosaiken und Wandmalerei in Rom* (Vienna, 1964)

G. Bovini: *Gli studi di archeologia cristiana dalle origini alla metà del secolo XIX* (Bologna, 1968)

W. Wisachermann: 'Die Entstehung der christlichen Archäologie im Rom der Gegenreformation', *Z. Kirchgesch.*, lxxxix (1978), pp. 136–49

G. C. Wataghin: 'Roma sotterranea: Appunti sulle origini dell'archeologia cristiana', *Ric. Stor. A.*, x (1980), pp. 5–14

I. Herklotz: '*Historia sacra* und mittelalterliche Kunst während der zweiten Hälfte des 16. Jahrhunderts in Rom', *Baronio e l'arte. Atti del convegno internazionale di studi. Sora, 1984*, pp. 23–74

PHILIP J. JACKS

Bosio, François-Joseph [Giuseppe Francesco], Baron (*b* Monaco, 19 March 1768; *d* Paris, 29 July 1845). French sculptor of Monegasque birth. He trained in Paris in the studio of Augustin Pajou in the period 1785–8. He was an officer in the French army in Italy during the Revolutionary wars, but by 1802 he had resigned his commission. He stayed in Italy, presumably studying and practising as a sculptor until his return to Paris in 1807. Thanks to Lorenzo Bartolini he was employed to work on some of the stone bas-reliefs (1807–10; *in situ*) for the Colonne de la Grande Armée in the Place Vendôme, Paris. His first exhibit at the Salon was *Cupid Shooting his Arrows* (plaster; untraced) in 1808. A marble version (St Petersburg, Hermitage) was ordered by Empress Josephine. Reminiscent of Giambologna's *Mercury*, this Neo-classical work was completed in 1812.

Before 1815 the imperial family and court formed a large part of the subject-matter of Bosio's sculpture: at the 1810 Salon he exhibited marble busts of *Napoleon* (Versailles, Château), *Empress Marie-Louise* (Monte Carlo, Mus. N.) and *Queen Hortense* (Malmaison, Château N.) among others. Somewhat earlier he had carved a marble statue of *Empress Josephine* (destr. 1870) based on the antique *Venus Pudica* type, at the same time executing a ravishing portrait bust of her (numerous versions, e.g. plaster; Malmaison, Château N.). In 1812 he exhibited a statuette of the *King of Rome as a Child* (marble; Versailles, Chateau; see Hubert, 1964, pl. lv), as well as the plaster version (untraced) of his statue of *Aristeus, God of Gardens* (marble, exh. 1817 Salon; Paris, Louvre; see Barbarin, pl. 34/1) and the statue of the *King of Westphalia* (marble; Ajaccio, Mus. Fesch).

Bosio continued to receive important official commissions under the restored Bourbon monarchy (1814–30), having shown a marble bust of *Louis XVIII* (numerous versions, e.g. Marseille, Mus. B.-A.) at the 1814 Salon. These included a marble statue of *Louis-Antoine, Duc d'Enghien* (commissioned 1815; Versailles, Château); a bronze equestrian statue of *Louis XIV* (1816–22), still in the Place des Victoires, Paris; and a kneeling marble statue of *Louis XVI* (completed 1825) in the Chapelle Expia-toire, Paris. For all these commissions he returned to the traditions of 17th-century French sculpture. He also made a well-known costume piece, the life-size statue of *Henry of Navarre as a Boy* (plaster, 1822; untraced; marble, exh. 1824 Salon; Pau, Mus. B.-A.; silver, 1824; Paris, Louvre; see fig.), as well as the bronze *Quadriga Driven by the Personification of the Restoration* (1829) designed to replace the *Horses of San Marco* on top of the Arc de Triomphe du Carrousel, Paris (*in situ*).

Bosio became a member of the Institut de France in 1816 and a professor at the Ecole des Beaux-Arts the following year. He received numerous honours, becoming Premier Sculpteur du Roi in 1822 and eventually being created Baron Bosio in 1828. After 1830 his Neo-classical style was regarded as old-fashioned, but he still received commissions from the new government of Louis-Philippe (1830–48). These included a marble group of *History and the Arts Consecrating the Glory of France* (exh. 1844; Versailles, Château) for the new historical museum at

François-Joseph Bosio: *Henry of Navarre as a Boy*, silver, h. 1.25 m, 1824 (Paris, Musée du Louvre)

Versailles; a marble statue of *Queen Marie-Amélie* (com-missioned 1841; Versailles, Château); and a colossal bronze statue of *Napoleon I* (1840; taken down after 1945; rest. 1985; in store) for the Colonne de la Grande Armée at Boulogne-sur-Mer.

Bosio was both extremely gifted and productive. He was committed to Neo-classicism and drawn to youth and feminine charm, so that his statues of *Hyacinthus* (marble, exh. 1817 Salon; Paris, Louvre), *Flora* (plaster, 1840; Turin, Pal. Reale) and *Young Indian Girl* (marble, 1842–5; Avignon, Mus. Calvet) compare favourably with the colossal bronze group *Hercules Fighting Achelous in the Guise of a Snake* (1814–24; Paris, Louvre). One of his last portraits, the bust of his daughter the *Marquise de la Carte* (1836; priv. col.; see Hubert, 1964, pl. lvii), shows traces of a delicate talent inspired by Canova.

Bosio's brother, Jean-Baptiste-François Bosio (1764–1827), with whom he is sometimes confused, was a painter and draughtsman. Jean-Baptiste-François's son, Astyanax-Scévola Bosio (1793–1876) was a sculptor and pupil of his uncle.

BIBLIOGRAPHY
Lami
L. Barbarin: *Etude sur Bosio: Sa vie et son oeuvre* (Monaco, 1910)
G. Hubert: *Les Sculpteurs italiens en France sous la Révolution, l'Empire et la Restauration, 1790–1830* (Paris, 1964)
——: 'François-Joseph Bosio, sculpteur monégasque', *An. Monég.*, xi (1985), pp. 82–119
N. Hubert: 'Jean-Baptiste-François Bosio, peintre monégasque (1764–1827)', *An. Monég.*, x (1986), pp. 105–112
La Sculpture française au XIXe siècle (exh. cat., ed. A. Pingeot; Paris, Grand Pal., 1986)
G. Hubert: 'Astyanax-Scévola Bosio, sculpteur (1793–1876)', *An. Monég.*, xviii (1994), pp. 57–92

GÉRARD HUBERT

Bosnia and Herzegovina. Country in the Balkan Pen-insula, south-eastern Europe, formerly a republic in Yu-goslavia. It borders Serbia, Croatia and Montenegro and covers 51,564 sq. km (see fig. 1). Bosnia occupies the northern portion of the republic, Herzegovina the south-ern; they were united in the early Middle Ages. The capital is SARAJEVO. The population was *c.* 4.5 million in 1991, comprising Muslims, Serbs (mainly Orthodox Christian) and Croats (mainly Roman Catholic) as well as numerous minorities. Considerable areas are covered by forest and woodland, with only *c.* 8% of the region being less than 150 m above sea-level. Climatically the country is divided into a southern, Mediterranean zone and a northern, continental one.

Occupied from Palaeolithic times, the area was sporad-ically penetrated from AD 375 by the South Slavs and, according to Constantine VII (*reg* AD 912–59), was settled by the Croats in AD 626. It was ruled by the indigenous Bans (suzerains of the Hungarian/Croatian kings) from the 12th century. Bosnia became an independent kingdom in the 14th century but was conquered by the Ottoman Turks in 1463 and became part of the Ottoman empire. The country was placed under Austrian administration in 1878 and was annexed by Austria-Hungary in 1908. In 1918 it was incorporated into the Kingdom of Serbs, Croats and Slovenes (known from 1929 as the Kingdom of Yugoslavia). In 1941–5 it became part of the wartime state of Croatia but was constituted as a separate republic of the Communist People's Republic of Yugoslavia in

1. Map of Bosnia and Herzegovina; those sites with separate entries in this dictionary are distinguished by CROSS-REFERENCE TYPE

1945. Bosnia and Herzegovina's declaration of independence from Yugoslavia in 1992 was followed by a protracted war, during which many historical buildings and works of art were destroyed.

I. Architecture. II. Painting, graphic arts and sculpture. III. Decorative arts. IV. Collections and museums.

I. Architecture.

There is evidence of Early Christian basilicas at about 20 locations in Bosnia and Herzegovina. Dating to the 5th century AD, they were rustic buildings often erected on the foundations of earlier Roman buildings. Subsequent churches (all destr.) include the basilica in Zenica (5th–

6th centuries AD) and the proto-Romanesque basilicas in Zavala, Glamoč and Livno, as well as the Romanesque basilicas in Sarajevo (11th–12th centuries) and at Blažuj, with six apses. The Romanesque spire of St Luke's Roman Catholic Church in Jajce survived until 1992. From the 13th century, architecture in Bosnia reflected the religious division between the aristocracy, who by and large remained Roman Catholic, and the rest of the population, who were split between Roman Catholicism and Bosnian Christianity, a schism of the Roman church. The architecture of the aristocracy (castles and manors) was influenced by Western Europe: the 15th-century royal castle built for the Kotromanić-Tvrtković family in Jajce was late Venetian Gothic in style. Two Gothic Roman Catholic churches were built in Srebrenica and Bihać but were turned into mosques in the 16th century. Examples of traditional vernacular timber buildings are at Vranduk. *Stećaks* (tombstones of both religions), often on a monumental scale, display remarkable architectural qualities (see fig. 3 below).

In the centuries following the Turkish conquest of 1463, Islam spread gradually and had a profound influence on architecture. The Turks introduced new constructional elements: columns, pilasters, arches, pendentives and domes. The main buildings were mosques (see fig. 2), baths, mausoleums, caravanserais, inns and bridges, as at Mostar (1566; destr. 1993). Fortified manors (*kule*), multistorey cubical structures with massive walls, were also built. An outstanding example of Ottoman-influenced domestic architecture is the Svrzo House (16th century) in Sarajevo. Housing in the 15th and 16th centuries was of a high standard, with a communal water supply, built-in furniture, showers and lush gardens (*see* SARAJEVO). There were also numerous cafés, set in what the 17th-century Turkish writer Evliya Çelebi described as 'gardens of paradise'. The chief builders and architects of these projects were Croats from Dubrovnik, whose constructions included the Ferizbey Baths (1509) and the Gazi Husrefbey Mosque (1530; damaged 1992–4), both in Sarajevo. Thus the influence of Western architecture again penetrated Bosnia, although Islamic buildings were built to a standard code (e.g. the Vučjaković Mosque, Mostar, 1564).

The Austrian occupation of 1878 and later annexation restored Western influence. The development of an infrastructure, including the first railway system, the construction of public buildings and military barracks and the building regulations of 1893 followed. The Austrian failure to understand the subtlety of Bosnian architecture, however, led to incongruous developments in the Moorish style, such as the Town Hall in Sarajevo (1890–96; destr. 1992) by the Croatian architects Vanek and Ćiril Iveković (1864–1933). Public buildings in Sarajevo were built in a multitude of eclectic styles: the National Museum (1913; by Karlo Paržik (1857–1942); damaged 1992) is in Renaissance Revival style and consists of four well-proportioned pavilions around a garden square; it is one of the finest buildings in Sarajevo. Paržik also built the Palace of Justice, the Technical Faculty and the National Theatre. The Tuscan eclectic style is represented by the Railway Council Building by Panek and Knezarek, and the Presidency Building by Josip Vancas (1859–1932). Among residential buildings, the Officers' Pavilions by Tenies are outstanding. The most prominent example of the Secessionist style is the Slavija apartment building (1911) by Otto Wagner's pupil Jan Kotěra.

The creation of the Kingdom of Yugoslavia, dominated by Serbia, led Bosnian architecture to lose its refinement, and Sarajevo in particular became a dusty and unkempt city that leant heavily on its Turkish and Austrian heritage. It survived World War II without damage, but the Communist regime after 1945 favoured often dreary industrial building and housing. The only bright star in this architectural decline was the Croatian architect JURAJ NEIDHARDT, who had worked in Le Corbusier's studio and who moved to Sarajevo in 1937. He headed the newly established Architectural Faculty at the university there, and through his teaching and his own work he influenced a new and talented generation of architects. Neidhardt's greatest achievements include the Philosophy Faculty Building (1955–9; damaged 1990s), the Institute of Physics and Chemistry (1959–64) and the urban plan for the Marindvor Centre, all in Sarajevo. The emphasis on displaying the 'successes' of Socialism succumbed in the 1980s to rabid commercialism, and the architecture of Sarajevo suffered from the hastily built American-financed development for the Winter Olympic Games of 1984. Oversized skyscraper hotels and massive buildings (e.g. Holiday Inn; damaged 1990s) ruined what remained of urban harmony. Under the Communist regime the architecture of the Austrian period was also denigrated on ideological grounds. Subsequent reappraisal, however, and careful refurbishment, led to a new recognition of its inherent quality.

BIBLIOGRAPHY

D. Grabrijan and J. Neidhardt: *Arhitektura Bosne i put u savremeno* [The architecture of Bosnia and the path towards modernity] (Sarajevo, 1957) [private edn]

Enciklopedija likovnih umjetnosti [Encyclopedia of fine arts] (Zagreb, 1959), pp. 449–63

PAUL TVRTKOVIĆ

II. Painting, graphic arts and sculpture.

In the late 14th century and early 15th, important manuscript illuminations were executed in Bosnia, including the collection of texts copied by Hval (1404; Bologna, Bib.

2. Ali Pasjia mosque, Sarajevo, 1560–61; interior

U., No. 3575 B). The numerous miniatures in the collection show Gothic stylistic features in the rendering of human bodies and faces. *Stećaks*— tombstones created by the Bosnians in the 14th and 15th centuries (sometimes called Bogomil tombstones)—survive in their thousands. Their stylized relief decoration indicates a synthesis of Latin and Byzantine models, with traces of Illyrian, Classical and Slavonic traditions. They are ornamented with vine scrolls and figures engaged in feudal pursuits. Examples at Radimlja and Stolac show large standing figures with raised hands (see fig. 3).

Islamic influences were predominant in Bosnian art for 400 years after the Ottoman conquest (1463). Islamic painting and sculpture were strictly non-figurative and usually embellished items of applied art and architecture. Manuscript illumination was another important form, and the Koran was transcribed in Sarajevo in 1567 (Belgrade, Mus. Applied A.). The Orthodox Church was recognized by the Ottoman rulers, however, and Orthodox art was allowed to develop along traditional lines. Wall painting flourished especially between 1550 and 1620, when unknown painters worked in the monastery at Papraća, and when Longin (*fl* 1563–97) and Jovan and Georgije Mitrofanović (*fl* 1615/16–22) worked in Papraća and Lomnica Monastery (*see* POST-BYZANTINE ART, §III, 2(iii)). Longin also painted the iconostasis of 30 icons (1578; *in situ*) at Lomnica Monastery. His style is characterized by a bright palette and unusual gradations of tone. Bosnian Franciscans also collected works by foreign artists, as well as the

paintings of Stjepan Dragojlović (*b* ?1569) executed between 1579 and 1621.

Central European eclecticism (neo-Romanticism, the Renaissance Revival, the Vienna Secession and the Gothic Revival) was introduced with Austro-Hungarian administration (1878), while indigenous painting remained largely at the level of descriptive illustration and dilettantism. However, a group of painters who had studied in Vienna began work in the early 20th century. They all showed the influence of academicism at the start of their careers but became more individual in their approach as their careers progressed. Milenko Atanacković (1875–1955) became a naive artist, Atanasije Popović (1881–1948) chose *pleinairisme*, while Lazar Drljača (1881–1970) turned to Impressionism. Djoko Mazalić (1888–1975) dedicated himself to formal Expressionism, while Roman Petrović (1896–1947) developed an Expressionism that emphasized social themes. At the exhibition of Bosnian artists in Sarajevo in 1917 Karlo Mijić (1887–1964) exhibited his first engravings and Petar Šain (1885–1965) was represented by his wood-carvings.

The group SHS, established after World War I, arranged annual exhibitions in 1921–3; its function was taken over by the Cvijeta Zuzorić group in 1924. After World War I many Bosnian artists worked abroad, mostly in Belgrade and Zagreb or Paris and London, including Jovan Bijelić (1888–1964), Nedeljko Gvozdenović (*b* 1902), Kosta Hakman (1899–1961), Omer Mujadžić (*b* 1903), Radovan Kragulj (*b* 1934), Radenko Mišević (1920–95) and the conceptual artist BRACO DIMITRIJEVIĆ. The Association of Artists of Bosnia and Herzegovina and the State School of Painting were established in Sarajevo in 1945. Social themes had dominated in the inter-war period in the work of Danijel Ozmo (1912–42), Ismet Mujezinović (*b* 1907), Vojo Dimitrijević (1910–81) and Branko Šotra (1906–60), to be replaced after 1945 by themes of reconstruction as well as of war. Realism was the most popular style, but painters with a more modern sensibility also appeared, such as Rizah Štetić (1908–74), Behaudin Selmanović (1915–72) and Mica Todorović (1897–1981).

SOCIALIST REALISM was abandoned after Yugoslavia's ideological break with Stalin and the USSR (1948), and artists educated abroad who had a modern approach represented the mainstream; characteristic of this spirit was *Sarajevo in the Rain* (1949), by Vojo Dimitrijević (1910–81). Other notable painters were Ljubo Lah (*b* 1930), Ibrahim Ljubović (*b* 1938; influenced by neo-Romanticism and fantasy), Milorad Corović (*b* 1932), Ljubomir Perčinlić (*b* 1939) and later Edin Numankadić (*b* 1948; abstraction), Tomislav Dugonjić (*b* 1932; neo-Constructivism), Mario Mikulić (1924–91), Nada Pivac (*b* 1926; portraiture), Afan Ramić (*b* 1932; landscape), Kemal Sirbegović (*b* 1952; geometrization), Mehmed Zaimović (*b* 1938), Seid Hasanefendić (*b* 1935; language of signs and symbols) and Safet Zec (*b* 1943). In drawing and painting a Romantic expressionism was revealed particularly in the work of Ismar Mujezinović (*b* 1942) and Mersad Berber (*b* 1940), while a stylized approach dominated in graphic art (e.g. the work of Borivoje Aleksić, *b* 1936). Printmaking had a prominent place in Bosnian art. A highly developed technique and strict precision

3. Bosnian Christian tombstone (*stećak*), Stolac, 14th–15th centuries

characterized the work of such artists as Memnuna Vila-Bogdanović (*b* 1934), Dževad Hozo (*b* 1936), Halil Tikveša (*b* 1935), Emir Dragulj (*b* 1939) and Virgilije Nevjestić (*b* 1935).

Important sculptural monuments were produced, for example the partisan cemetery (1965) in Mostar by Bogdan Bogdanović (*b* 1922) and the *Memorial to the Revolution* (1970–72) on Mt Kozara by DUŠAN DŽAMONJA. Independent experimentation close to that in contemporary Western European art was evident in the work of Alija Kučukalić (1937–92), Boško Kućanski (*b* 1931) and Arfan Hozič (1928–90). After the opening of the Academy of Arts in Sarajevo in 1972, a generation of talented young artists appeared, including Nusret Pasić (*b* 1951) and Radoslav Tadić (*b* 1946) in painting, Mustafa Skopljak and Kemal Selaković (*b* 1939) in sculpture, Mustafa Ibrulj and Branko Bacanović in design, and Petar Waldegg in graphic art. The neo-Romantics Sead Musić (*b* 1943) and Salim Obralić (*b* 1943) belonged to the group that worked under the motto 'the revival of the picture'. Jusuf Hadžifejzović (*b* 1956) practised conceptual art, as did, to some extent, the group Zvono, which rarely exhibited at official shows. Besides Sarajevo, the cities of Mostar, Banja Luka and Tuzla became important artistic centres where many significant Bosnian painters worked, including Karlo Afan de Rivera (1885–1979), Mirko Kujačić (*b* 1901), Mustafa Peco (*b* 1927) and Muradif Cerimagić (*b* 1949). Original artists received support from such critics as Muhamed Karamehmedović, Azka Begić and Nermina Kurspahić (*b* 1956). There were also notable figures working in the area of photography, including Gojko Sikimić (*b* 1956), Branko Popovič (*b* 1943) and Kemal Hedžič (*b* 1949).

BIBLIOGRAPHY

I. Lovrenović: *Bosna i Hercegovina* (Sarajevo, 1980)
Likovna enciklopedija Jugoslavije [Encyclopedia of the fine arts in Yugoslavia], i (Zagreb, 1984)

PREDRAG FINCI

III. Decorative arts.

The decorative arts of Bosnia and Herzegovina mix three types of influence: archaic rural traditions, European and Ottoman Turkish. From Roman times to the 20th century flagstone-lined interiors, with a central hearth, were complemented by such iron utensils as a dome (*sadj*) heaped with coals for cooking bread. Stone seating was covered with pieces of felt and sheepskin, from the latter of which the Herzegovinian bonneted cloak (*bicalj*) was made. Coarse textiles woven from natural, undyed wool, textured, handwoven linen (*uzvod*) with simple, geometric embroidery, black unglazed pottery and such carved wooden objects as cups and distaffs were ubiquitous. With the arrival of the Slavs in the 6th–7th century, the local stockbreeding population moved into the more mountainous regions: the conservative fascination with the solar symbolism shown on carved wooden pieces from these regions, such as three-legged chairs (*stolovaca*s), chests and distaffs, is thus probably a pre-Slavic tradition. On the other hand, the shapes of some Bosno-Herzegovinian wooden vessels, particularly the ovoid cups with large wing handles, were probably introduced by the Slavs.

Bosnia adopted a European-related style in the early 14th century, when rich silver, copper and lead mines were opened and gave Bosnia the wealth to become an independent kingdom between 1377 and 1463. In the 14th and 15th centuries cast and repoussé silver vessels and jewellery were produced in an original Gothic style based on Neapolitan, French, Hungarian and Mamluk models. Hemispherical and oval drinking bowls were produced, decorated with scalloped edges, lobed walls, trefoil and palmette scrolls, arcading and separately cast and enamelled additions. Simple, European-style heraldry was used along with figurative, secular scenes, often of the hunt. The ornamental style current in the Bosnian Kingdom generally lost its figurative decoration in later centuries, although it survives to the present on repoussé metalwork, painted ceramics such as those from Visnjica and embroideries. The second major European style to affect decorative arts in Bosnia and Herzegovina was Art Nouveau. Although this style is seen principally in architectural design in those towns under Austro-Hungarian administration, most Bosnian domestic interiors displayed imported Art Nouveau textiles, silver objects and enamelled glass.

Since Turkish occupation in 1463 the wealthiest urban population was Muslim, and architecture, interior design and urban dress were strongly Oriental. Woven and embroidered textiles played an important role in decoration: floors and seats were covered with rugs, carpets and gold-embroidered velvet cushions, and embroidered textile panels were hung on walls. Wooden panels inset with mother-of-pearl acted as seatbacks; hexagonal coffee-tables with similar inlay supported round brass trays. Ceramics and metalwork were set on a high shelf encircling the room. A brass samovar in the centre of the room provided warmth and heated food. Vessels included a typical covered metal dish (*sahan*), decorated with engraving and a black material (*savat*) imitating niello. Bed-linen, clothes and silk dowry embroideries were kept in carved chests, the interior with a mirror surrounded by painted floral decoration, or in a large cupboard (*musandera*). Local manufacturing imitated prized imported goods (such as Chinese blue-and-white flasks and souvenirs from Mecca). Face towels and headscarves were home-woven; plainer, dark textiles were store-bought. Filigree work was fashionable in jewellery design, much of the inspiration coming from Ottoman Turkey. The change away from this traditional Orientalism was abrupt, arriving with the Communist regime after World War II.

BIBLIOGRAPHY

J. de Asboth: *An Official Tour through Bosnia and Herzegovina* (London, 1890)
M. A. Karamehmedovic: *Umjetnicka obrada metala* [The artistic working of metal] (Sarajevo, 1980)
C. Silic, ed.: *Guide to Collections of the Regional Museum of Bosnia and Herzegovina* (Sarajevo, 1984)

MARIAN WENZEL

IV. Collections and museums.

The earliest collections in Bosnia and Herzegovina are in the Franciscan monasteries in Jajce (damaged 1992–4), Fojnica, Kreševo, Sutjeska (damaged 1992) and Livno, dating to 1300. They include small collections of art objects that belonged to medieval Bosnian royalty and also religious treasures. The Austro-Hungarian administration from 1878 introduced widespread 'Europeanization'. In 1888 the National Museum was established in Sarajevo in order to collect, classify and exhibit the country's enormous riches. In four buildings (erected in 1913) with 12,000 sq. m of exhibition space, there are displays of archaeology, ethnography and natural history. This institution represented one of the leading research and scientific museological establishments in southern Europe, but buildings and contents were damaged in 1992–4. The first art gallery in Bosnia and Herzegovina was established in Sarajevo in 1930 and contained over 600 items. In 1959 it became an independent institution with 3000 works, mainly by indigenous artists. The Museum of the City of Sarajevo was established in 1949, and Mirko Komosar opened a private gallery in 1950; the latter contains 150 paintings, sculptures and graphic works by Bosnian and Croatian artists. The private collection of Ilija Buljovčić contains works by artists from Serbia and Hungary as well as Bosnia.

BIBLIOGRAPHY

Enciklopedija likovnih umjetnosti [Encyclopedia of fine arts], ii (Zagreb, 1962), p. 347, iii (Zagreb, 1964), pp. 516–17

PAUL TVRTKOVIĆ

Bosra [Arab. Buṣrā; anc. Bostra]. Town in southern Syria, 110 km south-east of Damascus. Originally an Arab settlement, it came under Nabataean rule after 144 BC. After being annexed by the emperor Trajan in AD 106 it became the capital city of the Roman province of Arabia; most of its ancient remains date from this period. Bosra was an important Christian city in the Late Byzantine period; it was captured by the Muslim Arabs in AD 635.

1. ANCIENT. Vestiges of the ancient city walls survive only in the north-west, the areas where pottery sherds from Middle Bronze II period (*c.* 2000–*c.* 1550 BC) constitute the oldest traces of settlement. Pottery also provides evidence of Nabataean habitation throughout the city; the eastern section may have been founded by the Nabataeans as there is no indication of an earlier phase of building there. The Roman *decumanus* (main road), which runs from east to west, is intersected by several north–south streets, mostly crossing it at an oblique angle and in a variety of alignments. It is lined by Roman buildings from the 2nd century AD, including gateways to the west and east, a tetrapylon, a monumental triumphal arch, baths in the south and the centre, a nymphaeum and a sanctuary known as the Kalybe. The monument known as the market can be identified as part of the central baths on the basis of its pools and hypocausts. The forum was probably to the west of this building, now a flat sunken area in the modern town; a cryptoporticus about 100 m long ran along the south side. The theatre, the best-preserved Roman monument in the town (see fig.), dates from the early 3rd century AD to judge from the style of its decoration. The warehouse building in the north, the hippodrome in the south outside the town and two well-preserved water reservoirs also date from the Roman period. The Nabataean and Roman shrines were presumably located in the eastern part of the town, but the only

Bosra, Roman theatre, 2nd century AD

record of them is on coins and inscriptions. The existence of modern buildings has prevented the discovery of any ancient houses.

BIBLIOGRAPHY

Enc. A. Ant.: 'Bostra'; Stillwell: 'Bostra'
R. E. Brünnow and A. von Domaszewski: *Die Provincia Arabia*, iii (Strasbourg, 1909), pp. 1–84
H. C. Butler: *Southern Syria* (1923), II/a of *Princeton Archeological Expeditions to Syria 1904–5 and 1909* (Leiden, 1914–30), pp. 215–95
E. Frézouls: 'Les Théâtres romains de Syrie', *An. Archéol. Syrie*, ii (1952), pp. 46–100
H. Seeden: 'Busra 1980: Reports of an Archeological and Ethnographic Campaign', *Damas. Mitt.*, i (1983), pp. 77–94
J. M. Dentzer: 'Les Sondages de l'arc nabatéen et l'urbanisme de Bosra', *Acad. Inscr. & B.-Lett.: C. R. Séances* (Jan–Mar 1986), pp. 62–87
K. Freyberger: 'Zur Datierung des Theaters in Bosra', *Damas. Mitt.*, iii (1988), pp. 17ff
——: 'Einige Beobachtungen zur städtebaulichen Entwicklung des römischen Bostra', *Damas. Mitt.*, iv (1989), pp. 45ff

K. FREYBERGER

2. EARLY CHRISTIAN AND ISLAMIC. Bosra became the seat of a bishopric and later an archbishopric, where important theological controversies took place. Despite efforts to keep the region Orthodox, Bosra came under the control of the Ghassanids, Monophysite Christian Arabs who dominated the region in the 6th century AD. Monuments from the Christian era include the ruins of a cathedral, erected by Archbishop Julianus in honour of the martyrs Sergius, Bacchus and Leontius (513; *see* EARLY CHRISTIAN AND BYZANTINE ART, fig. 19). The vast central space (40×40 m) was covered with a dome; the square was extended on the east with an apse, two sacristies and side chapels. Very little remains of the bishop's palace near by. A new cathedral was discovered, in the early 1990s, to the east of the ancient cathedral by the French archaeological mission. The convent, perhaps dedicated to St Sergius, preserves the walls and apse of its church, reputedly the place where Bahira, a Nestorian monk who lived in Bosra at the beginning of the 7th century, according to tradition predicted the prophetic vocation of the young Muhammad, who had accompanied his uncle on a caravan journey from Arabia to Syria.

Muhammad stopped again at Bosra when leading the caravan of Khadija, a rich widow from Mecca whom he later married. The little mosque known as al-Mabrak (Arab. 'place of kneeling') was built over the spot where the Prophet's camel would have knelt down and where the Prophet would have prayed. An inscription in the mihrab of the mosque from the time of the Umayyads (*reg* 661–750) evokes this event. Bosra was the first city in Syria conquered by the Arabs (635). It was attached administratively and militarily to Damascus, and the Umayyads built the mosque of 'Umar, comprising a prayer hall of two bays opening on to a court surrounded by two porticos. In 720–21 a structure was added on the roof for the call to prayer. A troubled period followed the accession of the Abbasids in 749, and Bosra was sacked several times. The city was brought back to prosperity under the Saljuq Turks (*reg* 1078–1117 in Syria) and their Burid governors. They made it a stronghold, to block the Crusaders at Jerusalem from gaining Damascus, and added the tower that stands to the south of the theatre. The governor of the city, Kumushtakin (Turk. Gümüshtekin), restored the mosque of 'Umar. An inscription gives the date AH 506 (AD 1136–7); a new portico and a square minaret were added to the old building, and a portico was extended along the length of the principal façade. Kumushtakin also built a small oratory (1133–4) dedicated to the legendary figure al-Khadir (Khidr) in the north-west of the city and a madrasa (1136) in the north-east. The al-Mabrak Madrasa encompassed the old mosque of that name and the adjacent prayer hall. Of cruciform plan, it is the oldest surviving MADRASA in Syria.

The Ayyubids (*reg* 1186–1260 in Syria) continued the work of their predecessors. They transformed the Roman theatre into a mighty citadel: the stage and the seats were covered with such new constructions as a cistern, magazine, mosque, bath and stables. A ring of towers was placed at regular intervals along the *chemin-de-ronde* to close and protect the fortification. This impressive ensemble, one of the chief monuments of medieval Islamic military architecture, succumbed to the Mongols, who ravaged the citadel in 1261. It was restored by Baybars I (*reg* 1260–77), the Mamluk sultan of Egypt, but Bosra was reduced to a small market town, occasionally visited by pillaging Bedouins. European travellers in the 19th century were struck by the beauty of its Roman ruins; many of the inscriptions and buildings were published by the Princeton Expedition (1904–5, 1909). The Syrian Department of Antiquities and the French and German institutes in Damascus restored some of the monuments, and the city is one of the most popular tourist centres in Syria.

BIBLIOGRAPHY

Enc. Islam/2: 'Boṣrā'
J. Sauvaget: 'Les Inscriptions arabes de la mosquée de Boṣra', *Syria*, xxii (1941), pp. 53–65
——: 'Notes sur quelques monuments musulmans de Syrie à propos d'une étude récente', *Syria*, xxiv/3–4 (1944–5), pp. 211–31
A. Abel: 'La Citadelle eyyubide de Bosra Eski Cham', *An. Archéol. Syrie*, vi (1956), pp. 95–138
S. Muqdad: *Bosra: Guide historique et archéologique*, pub. Dir. Gen. Ant. Mus. Répub. Arabe Syrienne (Damascus, 1974)
S. Moujdab and S. Ory: 'Bosra, cité islamique', *Archéologia*, cxlviii (1980), pp. 22–30
M. Meinecke: 'Der Hammam Manjak und die islamische Architectur von Busra', *Berytus*, xxxii (1984 (1986)), pp. 181–90
M. Sartre: 'Bostra, chrétienne et byzantine', *Bostra: Des origines à l'Islam* (Paris, 1985), pp. 99–139
J. M. Dentzer: 'Fouilles franco-syriennes à l'est de l'arc nabatéen (1985–87). Une nouvelle cathédrale?', *Corsi Cult. A. Ravenn. & Byz.*, xxxv (26–29 March 1988), pp. 13–34
F. A. Aalung, M. Meinecke and R. S. al-Muqdad: *Islamic Bosra: A Brief Guide*, Ger. Archaeol. Inst. (Damascus, 1990)
J. M. Dentzer and others: 'Nouvelles recherches franco-syriennes dans le quartier est de Bosra ach-Cham', *C.R.A.I.* (1993), pp. 117–47

SOLANGE ORY

Boss, roof. A roof boss (Fr. *bosse*: 'lump', 'knop') is the block, or keystone, at the intersection of ribs in a rib vault (*see* VAULT; for illustration *see* SECTION.). Particularly favoured in European medieval architecture, unnecessarily large blocks were used as a field for sculptural decoration, which both concealed the collision of the different ribs and their mouldings and provided additional dead-weight to assist in countering the thrusts engendered by the vaults themselves. Some Late Gothic English bosses are extremely large; those in the nave of Winchester Cathedral (*c.* 1440) and in King's College Chapel (1513–15), Cambridge, weigh several tonnes each.

The first bosses consisted simply of the junction of the converging ribs. The earliest use of a central keystone in a rib vault occurs in the transept aisles at Winchester Cathedral (after 1107). A single block forms the apex of both intersecting arches, with a shoulder to receive each rib. Earlier rib vaults (e.g. *c*. 1100; Durham Cathedral) were composed of one complete diagonal arch against which two arcs abutted, but this was unstable and unsightly. The use of a composite block at the junction of the ribs facilitated construction, especially in sexpartite vaults. Most early boss-stones have a hole drilled through the centre, presumably to hang lights.

Decorated bosses appeared in the mid-12th century in both France and England. The rib intersections at Saint-Denis Abbey (*c*. 1140), for example, have low-relief foliate designs at the centre, while larger foliate sculpture decorates the ambulatory bosses of St Germain-des-Prés, Paris (*c*. 1150). Outside Paris, at, for example, the west block of Saint-Leu-d'Esserent, St Martin, Etampes, and St Sulpice, Chars, more elaborate bosses appeared, which included figure sculpture, but in general the Early Gothic cathedrals of the period, such as Sens and Senlis, avoided superfluous decoration. In England, Canterbury Cathedral treasury and Bristol Cathedral chapter house (both *c*. 1155) have foliage and grotesque Romanesque bosses, and at Keynsham Abbey (Somerset), for example, bosses depict biblical scenes (see fig.). French cathedral workshops at Noyon, Laon and Notre-Dame, Paris, began to include circular foliate bosses from the early 1160s; but French bosses maintained a discreet presence until the 15th century, partly because, with such high vaults, they were difficult to see. While the bosses were sometimes surrounded by painted decoration on the vault-web, in the 13th century their generally muted role influenced all French-derived styles of architecture, except in England.

The English, beginning with the choir of Canterbury Cathedral (1174–84), adorned their relatively low vaults with a variety of large, colourful foliate bosses. With the development of tierceron and then lierne vaults, with their multiple rib junctions, bosses proliferated, mainly foliate until the last quarter of the 13th century, with such notable exceptions as Westminster Abbey and Hailes Abbey (ruined) and generally figurative after that (see GOTHIC, fig. 32), for example in the choir of Exeter Cathedral (see EXETER, §1(ii)). Complex iconographic cycles were illustrated down the entire length of a church or cloister vault, for example the *Apocalypse* sequence in Norwich Cathedral cloisters (1324–50). After *c*. 1380 heraldic devices were most common: Canterbury Cathedral cloister (*c*. 1390–1414) has nearly 850, and such bosses were always brightly painted. English Gothic began to influence northern Europe from *c*. 1300, but although Germany and Bohemia particularly enjoyed the elaborate English vault patterns, they did not adopt the profusion of sculptured bosses. False, wooden vaults in the Low Countries often have wooden figurative bosses set in bursts of gilded foliage, for example in the undercroft (1387) of Bruges Town Hall. Portugal and Spain almost rival England in their lavish, luxuriant display of late medieval bosses, as is shown at the Hieronymite monastery of Belém (vaulted after 1517) and the central lantern of Seville Cathedral (1513–19). Carved bosses also appear on the end of pendant drop vaults, for example in the Stephansdom (*c*. 1390), Vienna, and Henry VII's Chapel (*c*. 1512) at Westminster Abbey.

For a discussion of lifting bosses on ancient Greek buildings *see* GREECE, ANCIENT, §II, 1(ii).

BIBLIOGRAPHY

G. Street: *Some Account of Gothic Architecture in Spain* (London, 1865/R New York, 1980)
C. Cave: *Roof Bosses in Medieval Churches* (Cambridge, 1948)
L. Stone: *Sculpture in Britain: The Middle Ages*, Pelican Hist. A. (Harmondsworth, 1955)
G. Webb: *Architecture in Britain: The Middle Ages*, Pelican Hist. A. (Harmondsworth, 1956)
K. Clasen: *Deutsche Gewölbe der Spätgotik* (Berlin, 1958)
F. Cali: *L'Ordre Flamboyant et son temps* (Paris, 1967)
W. Swann: *Art and Architecture of the Late Middle Ages* (London, 1977)
J. Bony: *The English Decorated Style* (Oxford, 1979)

FRANCIS WOODMAN

Roof boss depicting *Samson and the Lion*, stone, 370×330 mm, from Keynsham Abbey, Somerset, *c*. 1170–80 (Bristol, Wansdyke District Council)

Bossan, Pierre (*b* Lyon, 23 July 1814; *d* Ciotat, 23 July 1888). French architect. His early life was typical of a minor 19th-century provincial practitioner. He was the son of a stonecutter and apprenticed to his father before his promise led him to study architecture, first at the Ecole des Beaux-Arts, Lyon, and then, about 1835, at the Ecole des Beaux-Arts, Paris, as a student of Henri Labrouste. Returning to Lyon in 1842, he was appointed diocesan architect in 1844, but abandoned this secure position to seek his fortune in Italy and Sicily. That adventure failed (costing his brother his life), and in 1850 Bossan returned, shattered, to Lyon. There, he became a disciple of the Catholic mystic Jean Vianney (*d* 1858), the Curé d'Ars, and he thenceforth devoted his life to a monastic existence, designing churches and teaching art. After 1850 he designed a series of ecclesiastical buildings that were among the most original, powerful and subtly nuanced to be built anywhere in France before 1920.

During the 1840s Bossan had been a Gothic Revivalist, and this is evident especially in the large church of St Georges (1844) and the nearby Maison Blanchon (1845), both in Lyon. Revivalism never satisfied him, according to his student Saint-Marie Perrin (1835–1917), and when Bossan re-established himself in the 1850s he worked to formulate a personal 'modern' style, reflecting locality and synthesizing the medieval and the classical. Consistency of historical style came to mean much less to Bossan than unity of composition. He elaborated classic monumental formulae, emphasizing scale and rhythm and de-emphasizing motif. Historical forms for him were timeless shapes and symbols, like the spreading arched façade of the pilgrimage church at La Louvesc or the towered, fortified configuration of the church at Fourvière (see below).

The problem of how to generate rationally a modern, French classicism from the facts of construction, society and climate had been posed by Labrouste in Paris during the 1830s. Bossan's solution was demonstrated in his parish church (1855) at Couzon-sur-Saône and the large church of the Immaculate Conception (begun 1856) in Lyon. In a position to review the developments of two decades, Bossan was able to create a personal response, the starting-point of which was the Mediterranean Byzantine style (especially in its orientalizing manifestations with which Bossan was familiar from Sicily). His churches were simply laid out and firmly vaulted with great structural lucidity. The pattern of articulation was carefully related to the construction and impressively broad and elastic. He achieved remarkable unity and force in his designs by envisioning each as the organic expression of a particular characteristic, such as simplicity, rusticity or splendour. He saw his churches as adapted to their character and environment, like different species of animals. In a robust physiognomy, Bossan believed, everything should participate in this quality, as in the Norman dray-horse or the Auvergnat bull, while in an elegant ensemble everything should be graceful, as with the gazelle or the Arabian horse. Most of his churches were in small towns in the Massif Central and thus were modest, compact designs, for example the parish churches at Bully (1855), Nandax (1859) and Neulise (1859). Some are almost brutal in their overscaling and ruggedness, as in the pilgrimage church at La Louvesc (1865) and the chapel Notre-Dame-de-la-Roche (1866). But in the Rhône plain Bossan could be rich and splendid, as in the pilgrimage church (1862) at Ars (Ain) and especially his last great work, the church of Notre-Dame de Fourvière (1872–96), richly clothed in sculpture, paintings and carved ornament, and which dominates Lyon on its western cliffs.

BIBLIOGRAPHY
G. M. Perrin: *Pierre Bossan, architecte* (Lyon, 1889)
F. Thiollier: *L'Oeuvre de Pierre Bossan* (Montbrison, 1891)
G.-M. Perrin: *La Basilique de Fourvière* (Lyon, 1896)

DAVID VAN ZANTEN

Bosschaert. Dutch family of painters of Flemish origin. (1) Ambrosius Bosschaert (i) was one of the first artists to specialize in FLOWER PAINTING in the northern Netherlands. Other members of what has become known as the Bosschaert dynasty of fruit and flower painters include his three sons (2) Ambrosius Bosschaert (ii), Johannes Bosschaert (*b* ?Arnemuiden, 1610–11; *d* 1628 or later) and Abraham Bosschaert (*b* Middelburg, *c.* 1612–13; *d* Utrecht, 1643), as well as his brother-in-law BALTHASAR VAN DER AST and the latter's lesser-known brother Johannes van der Ast. Johannes Bosschaert seems from an early age to have been a talented painter, whose few surviving works are mostly horizontal in format and strongly influenced by his uncle Balthasar van der Ast. By contrast, Abraham Bosschaert apparently favoured an oval format and was a much less skilled artist, to judge from the equally small number of known paintings by him. It was, in fact, the eldest son and namesake who most closely followed the tradition established by Ambrosius Bosschaert the elder, whose activities in Middelburg at the beginning of his career made it the centre of flower painting in the Netherlands. This switched to Utrecht after Ambrosius the elder's move there in 1616; all of his sons were active in Utrecht, as were van der Ast and other important exponents of the genre (e.g. Roelandt Savery).

(1) Ambrosius Bosschaert (i) (*b* Antwerp, *bapt* 18 Nov 1573; *d* The Hague, 1621). Painter and dealer. He left Antwerp with his parents *c.* 1587 because as Protestants they were vulnerable to religious persecution; the family moved to Middelburg, where in 1593 Ambrosius became a member of the Guild of St Luke, of which he served as Dean on several occasions (1597, 1598, 1603, 1604, 1612 and 1613). In 1604 he married Maria van der Ast, the sister of Balthasar van der Ast who later became his pupil and possible collaborator. Bosschaert bought a house in Middelburg in 1611. There are flower-pieces by Bosschaert that are signed (with a monogram) and dated between 1605 and 1621, though there were two periods of artistic inactivity, in 1611–13 and 1615–16, when he was probably more active as a dealer in the art of both Dutch and foreign artists (e.g. Veronese and Georg Flegel). He was recorded in Bergen-op-Zoom in 1615 and became a citizen of Utrecht in 1616, where his name appears in the register of the Utrecht Guild of St Luke for the same year. In 1619 he was involved in a court case in Breda, where he lived from that year. He died during a journey to The Hague.

With his flower paintings Bosschaert founded a genre that continued unchanged in Middelburg until the mid-17th century: a symmetrically composed bunch of flowers, generally consisting of cultivated species, painted precisely and with an almost scientific accuracy. The vertically constructed bouquet generally consists of tulips—still a novelty at that time—in the centre, roses at the lower edge of the container and an exotic species, such as lilies, rounding off the top (e.g. *Bouquet in a Stone Niche*, Wassenaar, S. J. van den Bergh priv. col., see Bol, pl. 22). The vase, of glass, metal or painted china, stands on a monochrome surface on which isolated accessories, often costly rarities, are placed: small animals, rare shells, in some cases just a few drops of water or flower petals (e.g. *Flower Piece*, Madrid, Mus. Thyssen-Bornemisza). A simple niche or an arched window with a view over a flat, 16th-century style landscape forms the background (e.g. *Vase of Flowers in a Window, c.* 1620; The Hague, Mauritshuis; see fig.). The *trompe-l'oeil* character of these pictures is particularly marked, although it is also emphasized by the volume of the flowers, which contrast with the flatly composed bouquets of Jan Breughel I.

Although Bosschaert's pictures combine flowers from different seasons, his floral compositions should be understood primarily as idealized depictions of flowers. Bol (1969) contended that they could not be interpreted symbolically, but subsequent research has inclined towards the view that, at least to some extent, the flower pictures of Bosschaert and his followers continue the 15th- and 16th-century Flemish tradition of using flowers as religious symbols. These pictures also served contemporary Dutch botanists and gardeners by providing an exact, true-to-life reproduction of foreign or hybrid species. This passion for exotic plants—which later culminated in what is known as the Dutch 'Tulip mania' (*c.* 1635–7)—was analogous to the interest in new and curious treasures (exotica, shells etc) which seafarers from Holland and Zeeland brought back from their travels in the Far East. Bosschaert may have painted his first flower-pieces as commissions for botanists and arrived at the deliberately composed floral bouquet by way of the individual studies required for such commissions.

Ambrosius Bosschaert (i): *Vase of Flowers in a Window,* oil on panel, 640×460 mm, *c.* 1620 (The Hague, Koninklijk Kabinet van Schilderijen 'Mauritshuis')

About 50 works by Bosschaert are now known; they were highly esteemed in his lifetime, but in the 18th and 19th centuries they were disregarded. The interest of collectors and scholars in his work was not reawakened until the 20th century, particularly in the work of Bol.

For further illustration *see* FLOWER PAINTING.

(2) Ambrosius Bosschaert (ii) (*b* Arnemuiden, Middelburg, 1609; *d* Utrecht, *bur* 19 May 1645). Son of (1) Ambrosius Bosschaert (i). He lived in Utrecht, where he married in 1634. His work has been recognized only since 1935 when Piet de Boer succeeded in differentiating it from pictures by his father and his brother Abraham. Ambrosius the younger's early pictures are signed *AB* in Gothic lettering, but after 1633 he used a more calligraphic, rounded abbreviation, almost Baroque in effect, or even his name in full. The first period of his creative output falls between 1626 and 1635. His flower-pieces from that time are viewed from above and have a low vanishing point; there are often exotic accessories and shells (e.g. *Bouquet with Frog and Lizard,* The Hague, S. Nystad Gal., see Bol, pl. 52b), while on one occasion later a live snake is introduced. In later work the high viewpoint and stiff composition of the pictures, especially of the still-lifes combining fruit and flowers, become noticeably less symmetrical and more spacious. These works also reveal the strong influence of his brother Abraham, evident both in the choice of format and in the preference for blue and yellow, as well as in a darker background and more compactly organized still-life arrangements (e.g. *Flowers in a Glass Vase,* 1635; Utrecht, Cent. Mus.; *Fruits and Parrots,* 1635; The Hague, Dienst Verspr. Rijkscol.). It is possible that many of the pictures ascribed to Ambrosius the younger for this period were begun by Abraham and finished after his death by Ambrosius the younger.

Ambrosius Bosschaert the younger's paintings are also marked by their strong religious message; his *Bowl of Fruit with a Siegburg Beaker* (Amsterdam, A. A. Bosschaert priv. col., see Bol, pl. 57) can be interpreted as alluding to the Fall of Man, the Crucifixion and the Redemption. Ambrosius the younger also painted *vanitas* still-lifes (e.g. ex-Schaap priv. col., Monte Carlo) and a unique *memento mori,* a macabre little picture showing a *Dead Frog* lying on its back surrounded by four black flies (Paris, Fond. Custodia, Inst. Néer.). The extremely limited colour range (grey and brown with white highlights) is reminiscent of monochrome still-lifes from Haarlem and Leiden.

BIBLIOGRAPHY
I. Bergström: *Dutch Still-life Painting in the 17th Century* (London and New York, 1956), pp. 54–68
L. J. Bol: *The Bosschaert Dynasty: Painters of Flowers and Fruit* (Leigh-on-Sea, 1960)
——: *Holländische Maler des 17. Jahrhunderts neben den grossen Meistern* (Brunswick, 1969)
P. Mitchell: *European Flower Painters* (London, 1973)
Stilleben in Europa (exh. cat., Münster, Westfäl. Landesmus., 1979), pp. 40–42, 57–9
I. Bergström: 'Composition in Flower Pieces of 1605–1609 by Ambrosius Bosschaert the Elder', *Tableau*, v (1982), pp. 175–6
Masters of Middelburg (exh. cat., Amsterdam, Waterman Gal., 1984)
M.-L. Hairs: *Les Peintres flamands de fleurs au XVII siècle* (Brussels, 1985), pp. 87–92, 196–9

IRENE HABERLAND

Bosse, Abraham (*b* Tours, 1602; *d* Paris, 1 Feb 1676). French printmaker and writer. He probably trained with Melchior Tavernier (1564–1641) in Paris, and his earliest datable works, a set of four landscapes after Matthäus Merian (i) (1622; Duplessis nos. 1040–43), were published by Tavernier. *Le Jardin de la noblesse française* (D 1301–18), the first of Bosse's important print series, was published in 1629. Its 18 plates after Jean de Saint-Igny show fashionably dressed ladies and gentlemen in a domestic environment. After several stays in his native Tours, Bosse settled in Paris in 1632, and from this date onwards his activities were indefatigable. Whatever their subjects, his prints almost invariably show the human figure in contemporary dress, so that such biblical subjects as the parables of the *Prodigal Son* (D 34–9), *Dives and Lazarus* (D 40–42) and the *Wise and Foolish Virgins* (D 43–9; *see* FRANCE, fig. 44) are direct commentaries on French society. Even such traditional themes as the *Five Senses* (D 1071–5, see fig.) or the *Four Seasons* (D 1082–5) are treated as genre subjects, with careful attention given to the costume and surroundings of the bourgeois participants, making them invaluable evidence for the social historian.

Bosse's interest in the theoretical aspects of his art grew out of his friendship with the geometer GÉRARD DESARGUES and the etcher and engraver Jacques Callot. Desargues's studies on perspective, which Bosse published in popular editions, enabled Bosse to develop his own

theories, and in 1648 the Académie Royale gave him permission to lecture on perspective. His influence was recognized three years later when he was made an honorary member of the Académie. From Callot, Bosse learnt the Italian manner of etching on a hard ground made from linseed oil and resin. This greatly facilitated the etching process and made for clarity and fineness of the etched line. For Bosse the aim of etching was to simulate engraving, and the practice of only finishing the plate with the engraver's burin was one that reproductive printmakers used thereafter. The theories on etching were published in 1645 as the *Traité des manières de graver en taille-douce*, Bosse's most influential treatise, which went through numerous editions in the next 150 years and was translated into several European languages. The very first manual for the printmaker, its interest lies as much in Bosse's illustrations as in his curiously written text (*see* ENGRAVING, §II, 4).

Bosse's rebellious spirit and unorthodox teachings led to vituperative arguments with the Académie, and he was expelled from it in 1661. His *Traité des pratiques géométrales et perspectives* was one of a number of polemical works devoted to promoting his own views in opposition to the Académie. He became increasingly bitter, and an attempt to set up a private school in opposition to the Académie

Abraham Bosse: *Touch*, from the series *Five Senses*, etching, 258×333 mm, *c.* 1635 (London, British Museum)

was condemned in 1662. In his later years he all but gave up creative work, producing a few religious prints and book illustrations as well as more polemical writings. The despotism of Charles Le Brun and the Académie Royale triumphed long before Bosse's death.

See also FAN, fig. 5; and PRINTS, figs 10 and 11.

WRITINGS
De la Manière de graver à l'eau-forte et au burin, et de la gravure en manière noire (Paris, 1645/*R* Bologna, 1937); rev. as *Traité des manières de graver en taille-douce*, ed. C. N. Cochin (Paris, 2/1758 [1769])
Manière universelle de M. Desargues pour pratiquer la perspective par petit-pied (Paris, 1648)
Sentimens sur la distinction des diverses manières de peinture, dessein et gravure (Paris, 1649); repr. with *Le Peintre converty*, intro. R.-A. Weigert (Paris, 1964)
Traité des pratiques géométrales et perspectives (Paris, 1665) [text of lessons given at the Académie Royale]
Le Peintre converty aux précises et universelles règles de son art (Paris, 1667); see also *Sentimens* above

BIBLIOGRAPHY
G. Duplessis: *Catalogue de l'oeuvre d'Abraham Bosse* (Paris, 1859) [D]
A. Blum: *Abraham Bosse et la société française au XVIIe siècle* (Paris, 1924)
——: *L'Oeuvre gravé d'Abraham Bosse* (Paris, 1924)
R.-A. Weigert: *Inventaire du fonds français: Graveurs du dix-septième siècle*, Paris, Bib. N., Cab. Est. cat., i (Paris, 1939), pp. 471–534 [catalogue follows Duplessis's numbering]
N. Villa: *Le XVIIe siècle vu par Abraham Bosse* (Paris, 1967) [useful plates]

COLIN HARRISON

Bosse, Harald Julius [Garal'd (Ernestovich)] (*b* nr Riga, 16 Sept 1812; *d* Dresden, 26 Feb 1894). German architect active in Russia. He began his education in Dresden, then underwent a four-year course at the court architectural school in Darmstadt, gaining practical experience in the construction of a theatre in Mainz. He received his major commissions during the 1840s and 1850s, building numerous aristocratic residences in various districts of St Petersburg, including Kochubey House on Konnogvardeysky (Horseguards') Boulevard (1853–5). On the façades he developed the Greek Revival style of Leo von Klenze; the interiors were in a variety of styles. For many years he worked for the imperial court, and in 1853–69 he rebuilt the house, constructed the servants' quarters and laid out the park (with E. Gan) at the Znamenka estate on the road to Peterhof, modernizing old Baroque decoration and transforming the French formal garden into an open English park. The full extent of Bosse's skill is evident in the Mikhaylovka country estate (1857–62; with Joseph Charlemagne). This major experiment in uniting nature and architectural structures removed the boundaries between park and buildings. The composition includes artificial waterfalls, numerous reservoirs, viewpoints, pergolas and conservatories. Bosse also worked in Riga, where he followed local traditions by building the Stock Exchange (1852–5) with the interior in Gothic Revival style and the façade in neo-Renaissance style. His design for the Reformed Church (1862) on the River Moyka in St Petersburg was in neo-Romanesque style (rebuilt 1930s by P. M. Grinberg and G. S. Rayts in Constructivist style as a cultural centre).

BIBLIOGRAPHY
V. I. Andreyeva: 'K voprosu ob izuchenii tvorchestva arkhitektora G. E. Bosse' [On the question of a study of the work of the architect G. E. Bosse], *Voprosy istorii, teorii i praktiki arkhitektury* [Questions regarding the history, theory and practice of architecture] (Leningrad, 1985), pp. 72–8
T. Ye. Tyzhnenko: 'Plastika fasadov, izyashchestvo inter'yerov' [The decoration of façades, the elegance of interiors], *Leningradskaya panorama* (1987), no. 9, pp. 31–2
——: 'Arkhitektor Garal'd Bosse (1812–1894): Problemy russkoy i zarubezhnoy arkhitektury' [The architect Harald Bosse (1812–1894): problems of Russian and foreign architecture], *Po uchebno-metodicheskim voprosam* [On study-methodology questions], ed. O. V. Vasilenko (Leningrad, 1988), pp. 48–56
——: 'Novatorstvo arkhitekturnogo tvorchestva G. E. Bosse' [Innovation in the architectural work of G. E. Bosse], *Pamyatniki kul'tury, novyye otkrytiya, yezhegodnik, 1989* [Cultural monuments, new discoveries, yearbook, 1989] (Moscow, 1990), pp. 432–46

SERGEY KUZNETSOV

Bosselt, Rudolf (*b* Perleberg-Brandenburg, 29 June 1871; *d* Berlin, 2 Jan 1938). German medallist, sculptor and writer. He trained in medal arts and sculpture at the Kunstgewerbeschule in Frankfurt am Main (1891–7) and in Paris (1897–9) at the Académie Julian. He dedicated himself to making medals and assimilated the naturalistic and Impressionist styles current in French art, as in his baptismal medal *Let the Child Come to Me* (1898–9; Frankfurt am Main, Mus. Ksthandwk). In 1899 Bosselt began to gain considerable public recognition in Germany for his medals, which after 1901 became more stylized and decorative. By 1905 he had produced a large body of work, including medals and several plaques of, mainly commissioned, portraits and exhibition notices. In addition, he promoted the revival of medal arts in Germany through his published writings. He was also widely known as a gifted *Jugendstil* craftsman as a result of his stay from 1899 to 1903 at the Künstler-Kolonie in Darmstadt, where he developed a close friendship with fellow worker Peter Behrens. Bosselt's output in Darmstadt consisted of jewellery and domestic items of decorative metalwork, which feature sculpted bronze figurines (e.g. table lamp, 1901; Darmstadt, Grand Duke von Hessen priv. col., see 1976 exh. cat., iv, p. 22). In 1907 he became a founder-member of the Deutscher Werkbund.

From 1903 to 1911 Bosselt taught sculpture at the Kunstgewerbeschule in Düsseldorf. By 1905 he was making free-standing, figurative sculpture and had begun to work in marble. From 1906 to 1909 his work was strongly influenced by the classicizing principles of Adolf von Hildebrand, and from 1909 he drew further inspiration from the ideas of Aristide Maillol, Auguste Rodin and George Minne. His sculptures express an inward state of heightened emotion through his use of gesture and sparse surface detail (e.g. *Quiver*, marble, 1909; Neuss, Clemens-Sels-Mus.). Until the early 1930s he also made portrait busts, reliefs, gravestones and several war memorials.

WRITINGS
Die Kunst der Medaille (Darmstadt, 1905)
Probleme plastischer Kunst und des Kunstunterrichts (Magdeburg, 1919)

BIBLIOGRAPHY
Ein Dokument deutscher Kunst—Darmstadt, 1901–1976: Die Künstler der Mathildenhöhe (exh. cat., ed. B. Rechburg; 5 vols, Darmstadt, Ausstellhallen Mathildenhöhe, 1976), iv, pp. 20–23
M. M. Moeller: *Der Sonderbund* (Cologne, 1984), pp. 99–105
U. Schmitt-Wischmann: *Mutter und Kind in der Plastik* (diss., Heidelberg, Ruprecht-Karls-U., 1987), pp. 179–83

ERICH G. RANFFT

Bossi, Benigno (*b* Arcisate di Como, 1727; *d* Parma, 4 Nov 1792). Italian stuccoist, printmaker, painter and collector. Before studying anything else he learned stucco decoration from his father Pietro Luigi (*d* 1754), who worked in Germany from 1743 until his death. Stucco work always remained Bossi's main activity, alongside that of printmaking, especially etching. His experiments in the latter field followed in the tradition of the great Venetian printmakers. He was encouraged by Charles-François Hutin, who was in Dresden from 1753 to 1757 and whom he followed to Milan and Parma. His first etching, based on a work by Bartolomeo Nazari (1693–1758), was done in Milan in 1758. From 1759 on he was in Parma, where he produced some plates for the *Iconologie tirée de divers auteurs* (1759) by Jean-Baptiste Boudard, and where he executed the stucco trophy decoration for the attic of S Pietro, the construction of which began in 1761. From this date Bossi also collaborated with the designer Ennemond-Alexandre Petitot, for whom he engraved the *Suite de vases tirée du cabinet de Monsieur du Tillot* (Milan, 1764). From 1 April 1766 Bossi was employed as a stucco artist at the Bourbon court in Parma, with an annual stipend of 5000 lire, and as a teacher at the Accademia di Belle Arti, where he won the prize for ornamentation. In 1767 reconstruction work began on the Palazzo del Giardino, where Bossi produced extensive stucco decoration notable for the elegance and lightness of the rocaille and Arcadian motifs interwoven in a way that just avoids symmetrical subdivisions of space. Among the few oil paintings securely attributed to Bossi are the altarpieces of the *Apparition of Soriano* (1781) and of the *Blessed Orsolina Veneri before Clement VII* (1786), the latter commissioned by Ferdinand I, King of Naples and Sicily (*reg* 1759–1825) for S Quintino in Parma. Bossi's prints merit separate consideration in terms of both quality and quantity. He preferred etching above all, especially for his original prints, such as the series of *Fisionomie possibili* (*c.* 1775–8) and the illustrations for such books as Gastone della Torre Rezzonico's *Discorsi accademici* (Parma, 1772). Bossi was also a passionate collector of prints, both for sale and as sources of new ideas for himself and the numerous pupils who were trained in his school. In his prints as well as through his draughtsmanship and stucco work, Bossi helped introduce to Parma the style of Central European Rococo.

BIBLIOGRAPHY

DBI; Thieme–Becker

M. Zanzucchi Castelli: 'Contributo allo studio su Benigno Bossi', *Parma per l'arte*, xi/3 (1960), pp. 149–85

E. Riccomini: *I fasti i lumi le grazie: Pittori del settecento parmense* (Parma, 1977), pp. 134–45

L. Fornari Schianchi: 'Il momento illuminista nell'arte parmense del '700 (Baldrighi–Ferrari–Bossi)', *L'arte del settecento emiliano: L'arte a Parma dai Farnese ai Borbone* (exh. cat., Parma, 1979), pp. 122–49

N. Moretti: 'Bossi, Benigno', *La pittura in Italia: Il settecento*, ii (Milan, 1989), pp. 636–7

L. FORNARI SCHIANCHI

Bossi, Dominik (*b* Monte, nr Balerna; *d* Prague, ?1628). Italian stuccoist, active in Prague. He settled in Prague in 1590 and was granted citizenship in Malá Strana in January 1591. One of his major commissions was the oval chapel of the Assumption (1590–1600), which was built for the Italian community in Karlova Ulice and was the first centralized Baroque building to be erected in Prague. In 1603 Bossi built the north part of the Augustinian monastery near the church of St Thomas in Malá Strana. In the following year he was involved with renovations to the same monastery. From 1602 he built the hospital for the Italian congregation opposite the site of the present Lobkowicz Palace (1703–69; now the German Embassy). This early Baroque building comprises four wings around an arcaded courtyard (later glassed over). The hospital church (1608–17), dedicated to S Carlo Borromeo and also built by Bossi, was one of the first domed Baroque buildings in Prague. In the construction of these buildings Bossi played an important role in the dissemination of Italian architectural concepts in Prague.

BIBLIOGRAPHY

DBI; Thieme–Becker

P. Preiss: *Italstí umelci v Praze* [Italian artists in Prague] (Prague, 1986)

CAROLA WENZEL

Bossi, Giuseppe (*b* Busto Arsizio, 11 Nov 1777; *d* Milan, 15 Dec 1815). Italian painter, collector and writer. He studied painting at the Accademia di Brera in Milan. Between 1785 and 1801 he lived in Rome, where he met such Neo-classical artists as Angelica Kauffman and Marianna Dionigi (1756–1826) as well as writers, scholars and archaeologists, notably Jean-Baptiste Séroux d'Agincourt, Giovanni Gherardo de Rossi (1754–1827) and Ennio Quirino Visconti. While in Rome he studied Antique and Renaissance works, making copies of the statues in the Museo Pio-Clementino and the frescoes by Raphael and Michelangelo in the Vatican, also furthering his studies of the nude in the Accademia di Domenico Conti and making anatomical drawings of corpses in the Ospedale della Consolazione. On his return to Milan in 1801 he became secretary to the Accademia di Brera, a post he held until 1807. During this period he devoted all his efforts to the restructuring of the Brera, providing it with new statutes and a major library and also founding the adjoining art gallery. He prevented numerous works from being smuggled abroad or dispersed and was responsible for their inclusion in the Pinacoteca di Brera. Among his most famous acquisitions were Raphael's *Marriage of the Virgin* (1504; *in situ*) and the *Virgin and Child* by Giovanni Bellini (*in situ*).

In 1802 Bossi travelled to Lyon, where he met such painters as Jacques-Louis David, Anne-Louis Girodet and François Gérard. This led to a socio-political slant in his painting, as in the *Italian Republic's Gratitude to Napoleon* (1802; Milan, Brera). He later diluted his youthful academicism with a more poetic and sensual style, as in his mythological frescoes *The Night and the Dawn* (1805–6; Erba, Como, Villa Amalia), which presage the development of his taste for Romanticism.

In Milan Bossi met such intellectuals as Giuseppe Parini, Pietro Verri and Alessandro Manzoni and people from the art world including Felice Giani, Vincenzo Camuccini, Conte Leopoldo Cicognara and, most significantly, Antonio Canova, who became a great friend and admirer of his work. In 1807 Prince Eugène de Beauharnais commissioned a copy of Leonardo da Vinci's *Last Supper* (*c.* 1495–7, Milan, S Maria delle Grazie), which gave Bossi an opportunity to carry out a detailed study of the work, both as an art historian and as a conservationist. The result was his most ambitious and learned publication, *Del Cenacolo di Leonardo da Vinci* (Milan, 1810).

Bossi was a passionate archaeologist, bibliophile and collector, constantly acquiring coins, paintings, sculpture, antiques and especially prints and drawings. His collection of prints served not so much to satisfy aesthetic needs as to provide documentary evidence to further his knowledge of art history. He was particularly interested in the Lombard school, collecting many drawings by Ambrogio Figino (then little known) and Leonardo, regarded as the founder of the school. He also owned a considerable body of drawings by Neo-classical artists, often given to him by such friends as Canova, Giuseppe Cades, Camuccini, Giuseppe Bernardino Bison (1762–1844), Andrea Appiani, Luigi Sabatelli and Giocondo Albertolli, as well as a collection of copies of Renaissance works by David Pierre Humbert de Superville that reveals an early interest in the Italian 'Primitives'. His collection of 3092 drawings, prints and engravings was auctioned in 1818; it was acquired in 1820 by the Venetian abbot Luigi Celotti and in 1822 by the Accademia di Belle Arti in Venice, where it remains in the Galleria dell'Accademia.

WRITINGS
R. P. Ciardi, ed.: *Giuseppe Bossi: Scritti sulle arti* (Florence, 1982)

DBI   BIBLIOGRAPHY
M. L. Gengaro: 'Della critica d'arte di G. Bossi', *Archv Stor. Lombardo*, lx (1933), pp. 528–38
C. Pedretti: 'I manoscritti Bossi all'Ambrosiana', *Rac. Vinc.*, xix (1962), pp. 294ff
Mostra dei disegni di Andrea Appiani e Giuseppe Bossi conservati nella Biblioteca dell'Accademia di Brera (exh. cat. by G. Ballo, Milan, Brera, 1966)
S. Samek Ludovici: *Dizionario biografico degli italiani*, xiii (Rome, 1971), pp. 314–19
A. Scotti: 'L'Accademia di G. Bossi e le trasformazioni del periodo napoleonico, Brera 1776–1815', *Brera, 1776–1815: Nascita e sviluppo di una istituzione culturale milanese* (Florence, 1979), pp. 49–67

SIMONETTA PROSPERI VALENTI RODINO

Bossuit, Frans van (*b* Brussels, ?1635; *d* Amsterdam, 22 Sept 1692). Flemish sculptor. Bossuit trained in Antwerp and Brussels before leaving for Italy *c.* 1655–60. From Florence, or perhaps Modena, where two of his earliest ivory reliefs have been found, he continued on to Rome, where he studied antique art and associated with the Schildersbent, a group of Flemish artists living in Rome. Bossuit returned to the Netherlands by 1685 and settled in Amsterdam, where he executed an ivory medallion portrait of the Stadholder *William III* (Amsterdam, Rijksmus.) in the following year.

Bossuit produced primarily small-scale reliefs. His work is classicizing in style, reflecting not only his experience of antique and contemporary Italian art but also perhaps the influence of the Baroque classicism of the sculptors active at Versailles, whom he may have encountered in France on his journey north. Nevertheless, the picturesque conception and dynamic exuberance of such works as *Venus and Adonis* (Amsterdam, Rijksmus.) are reminiscent of the Flemish sculptor Artus Quellinus (i), while his unusual combination of high-relief figures with low-relief backgrounds is derived from Verhulst. His early relief *Mercury, Io and Argus* (Wiesbaden, priv. col.), and its pendant the *Flaying of Marsyas* (Toronto, priv. col.; see Derveaux-Van Ussel, p. 207) were probably based on works by Balthasar

Permoser, and his *Rape of the Sabines* (Wiesbaden, priv. col.; see Derveaux-Van Ussel, p. 206) was modelled on Pietro da Cortona's painting of the same subject (Rome, Mus. Capitolino). His later reliefs, such as *Music* (Amsterdam, Rijksmus.), part of a series that included *Sculpture* and *Poetry*, are monumentally conceived and are marked by a new sobriety. Bossuit had no workshop and no pupils, but engravings of his work, published in the *Cabinet de l'art de sculpture par le fameux sculpteur Francis van Bossuit* (1727), provided models for artists well into the 18th century.

BIBLIOGRAPHY
Cabinet de l'art de sculpture par le fameux sculpteur Francis van Bossuit executé en yvoire ou ébauché en terre, gravées d'aprés les dessins de Barent Graat par Mathys Pool (Amsterdam, 1727)
M. Devigne: 'François Bossuit and Ignaz Elfhafen', *Burl. Mag.*, xlvii (1925), pp. 40, 45–6
G. van Bever: *Les 'Tailleurs d'yvoire' de la Renaissance au XIXme siècle* (1946), pp. 31–6
C. Theuerkauff: 'Zu Francis van Bossuit (1635–1692) "beeldsnyder in yvoir"', *Wallraf-Richartz-Jb.*, xxxvii (1975), pp. 119–82
G. Derveaux-Van Ussel: 'Frans van Bossuit', *Beeldhouwkunst in de eeuw van Rubens* [Sculpture in the century of Rubens] (Brussels, 1977), pp. 204–8

CYNTHIA LAWRENCE

Boston. American city, capital and financial and commercial centre of Massachusetts on the north-east coast of the USA. With an excellent natural harbour, it is the main port and largest city in New England. Originally built on the hilly Shawmut peninsula, where the Mystic and Charles rivers enter Massachusetts Bay, Boston was initially connected to the mainland only by Roxbury Neck, a low, narrow isthmus, now Washington Street, with the tidal flats, called the Back Bay, and Charles River to the north-west and a wide bay to the south. Rocks and earth from Copp's and Beacon hills have been used for extensive landfill to add to the city almost four times the area of the peninsula.

I. History and urban development. II. Art life and organization. III. Centre of production.

I. History and urban development.

In 1630 Puritans fleeing the control of the Church of England established a self-governing community in Boston, which was named after their home town and port in Lincolnshire, England. In the same year New Towne, a few kilometres to the west on the north bank of the Charles River, was chosen as the capital of the Bay Colony. In 1636 a theological college was established there; two years later New Towne's name was changed to Cambridge, after the English university town, and in 1638 the college was named after its first benefactor, John Harvard (1606–38). (Cambridge and Boston are now part of the same conurbation.) Boston was the site of crucial events—the Boston Massacre (1770) and the Boston Tea Party (1773)—leading up to the American Revolution (1775–83) against British rule.

The city has always been a major intellectual centre, where many architectural ideas have been successfully developed: there is a rich pre-Revolutionary architectural legacy; in the development of 19th-century American building and planning the city nurtured the talents of such innovators as Alexander Parris, H. H. Richardson and

Frederick Law Olmsted; and in the development of 20th-century architecture it provided a base for leading architects from Walter Gropius to I. M. Pei.

1. Before 1790. 2. 1790–c. 1875. 3. c. 1875–1918. 4. After 1918.

1. BEFORE 1790. During their first year of settlement the colonists lived in tents and wigwams. They soon built frame houses covered with weatherboard, much like those in parts of England, but they eliminated the hazardous thatched roofing and wooden chimneys. An early major municipal building was the Town House (destr.), erected in 1657 through a bequest from merchant Robert Keayne; a heavy timber structure with multiple gabled roofs, its open ground floor provided shelter for merchants, and an upper floor contained a library and court. Of the numerous frame houses of this period, only the Paul Revere House (c. 1680; rest. 1907–8) in the North End survives. Like other 17th-century residences, it has small diamond-paned windows, an upper storey overhanging the street and a massive brick end chimney.

By the end of the 17th century brick was more generally used. One unusually large commercial building, called the triangular warehouse (destr. 1824), had a strikingly tall pyramidal roof. Even grander was the large brick residence built by Peter Sargeant (1679; destr. 1864), later known as the Province House when it served as the residence of the governors of the colony. After 1686, when the original charter was declared null and void, Massachusetts became a royal colony. Accordingly, a house of worship for the Church of England, King's Chapel, Tremont Street, was built in 1688. With the arrival of merchant families the Puritan ethos of Boston began to change, and the character of domestic and public buildings followed that of England, with the late English Baroque and then the Georgian style.

Several buildings in the heart of Boston were rebuilt after a catastrophic fire in 1711. Nearly all were of brick. Although a new Town House was destroyed by fire in 1747, the surviving outer walls were incorporated into what is known today as the Old State House, State Street. Also built at this time were two surviving residences: the Pierce-Hichborn House (1711), next to the Revere House in the North End, and the Thomas Crease House (the Old Corner Book Store; 1711). The houses and churches of this period tended to be relatively simple in form and detail, for example the Episcopal Christ Church or Old North Church (1723; steeple 1740, by William Price), Causeway Street, built in the North End. Similar in external detail but planned for Congregational worship is Old South Meeting-house (1729), Washington and Milk streets. Their spires recall those devised by Christopher Wren for his City of London churches built during the last quarter of the 17th century.

Near the middle of the 18th century, the Georgian style in Boston became more elaborate and richly detailed, as in Faneuil Hall (1740–42), a gift to the city from the merchant Peter Faneuil (1700–43). Built of brick, with engaged Tuscan and Doric pilasters and a tall central cupola, it was designed by the painter John Smibert, but it was badly damaged by fire in 1761 and enlarged (1805–6) by Charles Bulfinch. Like the earlier Town House, it combined a large space below for merchants with room for public meetings on the upper floor, and it is still used today. Among the finest examples of fully developed Georgian architecture are the interiors of two Anglican churches by Peter Harrison of Newport: his new granite building for King's Chapel (1749–58), Tremont Street, Boston, and his Christ Church (1761–73), Zero Garden Street, Cambridge, built in wood. As in Harrison's other buildings, there is a clear debt to contemporary sources in London.

2. 1790–c. 1875. The greatest change in the character of architecture in Boston is often credited to CHARLES BULFINCH. His most important early work was the new Massachusetts State House (1795–7; extended; see fig. 1) inspired by William Chambers's Somerset House (from 1776), London. Even more important, as an urban plan, was Bulfinch's forward-looking project for a housing and public building complex called Franklin Place (or the Tontine Crescent; 1793–5), entirely demolished within 60 years (only the curve of Franklin Street survives). Among Bulfinch's other designs were two more ranges of town houses (destr.), Park Row (1803–5) and the Colonnade (1810–12), both of which faced towards the Common, an area in the south-west of the peninsula acquired by the town for pasturage in 1634 and now a public park.

Bulfinch left a lasting impression on the Mt Vernon area of Beacon Hill, which he laid out in 1795 with large lots and a central park square. The houses tended to be free-standing brick cubes set in gardens, for example the three that he designed for Harrison Gray Otis, Mayor of Boston. Bulfinch's second house for Otis, built 1800–02 on Mt Vernon and still free-standing in its own garden, is the best illustration of his hopes for the residential development of Beacon Hill. The lots were later filled by continuous row houses, but Louisburg Square, begun 1826 and largely built up by 1844, with bow-fronted town houses ranged around an oval open space, demonstrates Bulfinch's impact. His influence was also felt through the work of his assistant Asher Benjamin, architect of the Charles Street Meeting-house (1807); in the same tradition is the imposing Park Street Church (1809, by Peter Banner (fl 1796–1848)), which rises over the Common.

As Boston shipping grew in volume early in the 19th century, the commercial space along the waterfront was expanded by filling in the tidal flats with rock and soil from the hills. In the Mill Pond (formerly North Cove between Beacon and Copp's hills) Bulfinch laid out a grid of streets focused on a broad central avenue. On the former Town Cove to the south were built wharves and warehouses, particularly Bulfinch's huge brick-and-stone India Wharf (1803–7; destr.).

Granite was also used by a number of architects in early 19th-century Boston, for example Solomon Willard and ALEXANDER PARRIS, who designed the austere bow-fronted David Sears house (1816) on Beacon Hill. Bulfinch used it for such public buildings as Massachusetts General Hospital (1818–23; extended), the austere Doric portico of which reflected the growing interest in pure Greek forms, introduced by Parris. His most important enterprise was the Quincy Market (1825–6), east of Faneuil Hall, which consisted of three long granite buildings commissioned by Mayor Josiah Quincy (1722–1864); the long

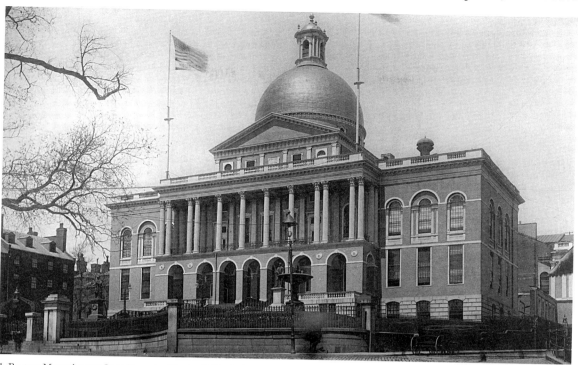

1. Boston, Massachusetts State House by Charles Bulfinch, 1795–7

central block ended in duplicate tetrastyle Ionic temple porticos, with a central block capped by a low hemispherical dome. Parris also used the Greek temple form in St Paul's Church (1819; now Cathedral), Tremont Street, but the most dramatic adaptation of Grecian forms was in Ammi B. Young's Boston Custom House (1837), State and India streets, a Greek Doric temple with additional hexastyle porticos providing side entrances. Originally the Custom House had a central rotunda capped by a dome, but in 1911–14 Peabody & Stearns placed an office tower on top of Young's base.

In the early 19th century the fascination with historical styles of architecture was manifest in Boston in some of the earliest examples of Egyptian, Gothic and Renaissance revivals. The Gothic Revival Bowdoin Street Congregational Church (1831–3), attributed to Solomon Willard, is an early example of the style, even if the details are not particularly archaeologically correct. The Egyptian Revival appeared in several cemetery gateways, including the gate (1832; rebuilt 1842) by Jacob Bigelow (1787–1879) for the Mt Auburn Cemetery, Cambridge, and Willard's gate (1840) for the Old Granary Burying Ground next to the Park Street Church, Boston. More imposing was Willard's 68 m granite obelisk (1825–43) in Charlestown (north of the Charles River) commemorating the Battle of Bunker Hill (1755). The more easily modulated Italian Renaissance style is well represented in the brownstone Boston Athenaeum (1849), Beacon Street, designed by Edward Clarke Cabot (1818–1901) and based on Palladio's Palazzo Iseppo da Porta (now Festa), Vicenza, Italy.

In the years before the Civil War (1861–5) there were significant additions to the urban plan. Mt Auburn Cemetery had been laid out in 1831 with drives winding through an idyllic pastoral landscape around copses and small lakes. The Public Garden on the south-west side of the Common was created in 1839 and improved after a landscaping plan by George F. Meacham in 1860. Perhaps the most important development of these years was the filling in of the Back Bay from 1857, gradually extending the new land south-west from Arlington Street and the Public Garden. Five broad streets led from the latter; the wide, central Commonwealth Avenue was divided by a landscaped parkway. At the approximate centre of the infill was set aside Copley Square, around which rose new public buildings and churches, making the Back Bay the cultural centre of the city. Prominent families moved from Beacon Hill to large new houses in this area, the predominance of mansard roofs giving it the character of the new Paris being built by Napoleon III.

The Hotel Pelham (1857, by ARTHUR DELEVAN GILMAN), a 'French flat' apartment building, was an early example in the Back Bay of this Second Empire style, which appealed to the French tastes of the Bostonians. More ornate is the Old City Hall (1865, by GRIDLEY J. F. BRYANT; now offices) in the old city centre. The Second Empire style was one of several architectural idioms that arose with the return of prosperity after the Civil War and avoided historical replication in favour of consciously modern although historically inspired forms. The principal alternative for public and government buildings was High Victorian Gothic Revival, an irregular, picturesque style that employed many varied building materials. A colourful version was employed for two buildings on Copley Square: Sturgis & Brigham's Museum of Fine Arts (1870–79; destr.; *see* STURGIS, JOHN HUB-BARD) and the Old South Church (1876) by CUMMINGS & SEARS. Perhaps the most vivid example is Ware & Van Brunt's Memorial Hall (1865–78; now missing its crock-eted tower) for Harvard University. The most significant event, however, was the decision by H. H. Richardson to set up his office in Brookline, MA, in 1874.

3. *c*. 1875–1918. With Richardson's arrival, the last quarter of the 19th century marked the emergence of Boston as a national centre of architectural innovation. He had been commissioned to build the Brattle Square Church (1870–72) in the Back Bay and Trinity Church (1872; *see* RICHARDSON, H. H., fig. 1), Copley Square. His massive round-arched style, adapted from Romanesque sources but increasingly abstracted into something highly personal, was used for a variety of works including such educational buildings in Cambridge, MA, as Sever Hall (1878–80) and Austin Hall (1881–4; see fig. 2) for Harvard University, and the large Ames Estate Store (1886–7; destr.) on Harrison Avenue, Boston. The Stoughton House (1882–3), Brattle Street, Cambridge, represents the Shingle style, Richardson's major contribution to residen-tial design.

The massive character of Richardson's work was con-tinued by his assistants SHEPLEY, RUTAN & COOLIDGE in the Grain and Flour Exchange (1891–3) and the 14-storey Ames Building (1889), an office block at 1 Court Street, Boston. This, like other Boston office blocks, was relatively low, owing to the reluctance of architects and clients to adopt the light metal frame then being exploited in Chicago. Within four years, however, tall office buildings were being hung on metal frames, beginning with the Winthrop Building of 1893–4 by Clarence H. Blackall (1857–1942).

The other style of national importance to emerge from Boston in the 1880s was a resurgent neo-classicism led by McKim, Mead & White. Their most influential building, the imposing Boston Public Library (1887–95; *see* MCKIM, MEAD & WHITE, fig. 2), drew on Italian Renaissance, Roman and contemporary French sources. Throughout the building sculpture and mural painting were incorpo-rated in rooms panelled with rare marbles, creating what the Library Trustees called a 'Place for the People' (*see* §II below). In 1883–6 the same firm built the John F. Andrew House in the Back Bay, an early evocation of Bulfinch's work, introducing a theme they perfected in their double bow-fronted Amory-Olney House (1890–92) further west on Commonwealth Avenue. Their bow-fronted granite George A. Nickerson House (1895–7) in the Back Bay referred to the work of Alexander Parris. Such houses were not so much a Georgian revival as a survival of Georgian forms that had never died out in Boston (Bunting, 1967). By the early 1890s countless variations on Georgian and Federal themes appeared in houses in the Back Bay as well as in the surrounding suburbs.

McKim, Mead & White made another significant con-tribution in Boston in their Neo-Georgian Boston Sym-phony Hall, Huntington Avenue, designed in 1892 but not built until 1900–01. During the hiatus they worked with Harvard physicist Wallace Clement Sabine (1868–1919) on the acoustics of the hall, which quickly set a new world standard for concert halls (*see* ACOUSTICS). Its exterior established a model followed in the Boston Opera House (1909), Washington Street, by Wheelright & Haven (*see* WHEELRIGHT, EDMUND M.). The neo-classical resur-gence was manifest in the Copley Plaza Hotel (1912) on Copley Square by Henry J. Hardenbergh with Clarence

2. H. H. Richardson: Austin Hall, Harvard University, Cambridge, Massachusetts, 1881–4

H. Blackall (1857–1942), which replaced the brick-and-terracotta Museum of Fine Arts. A new and larger Neo-classical Museum of Fine Arts was built (1907–15) on Huntington Avenue in the Back Bay from designs by Guy Lowell. Particularly grand was the large new domed church of Christ Scientist (1904–6), Huntington Avenue, by Charles Brigham (1841–1925) with Solon S. Beman.

Contemporary with McKim, Mead & White's introduction of a new vitality into neo-classical work in domestic and public buildings in Boston, Henry Vaughan (1846–1917) and RALPH ADAMS CRAM reinterpreted Gothic forms for church architecture. Vaughan's early chapel of St Margaret's Convent near Louisburg Square, Beacon Hill, was built in 1882.

Another innovation in Boston that spread nationwide was by landscape architect Frederick Law Olmsted, who, from 1878 until his retirement in 1895, devised an 'emerald necklace' (see OLMSTED, FREDERICK LAW, fig. 3) of connected parks and carriage parkways running from the Charles River around the Back Bay to the south of Boston all the way to the eastern shore on the estuary of the Neponset River. This linkage involved the reclamation of the Back Bay Fens and the making of Jamaica Pond and Franklin Park, connected to the Arnold Arboretum in Brookline. The system was further developed by Olmsted's former assistant CHARLES ELIOT, who by 1893 had got the Boston Metropolitan Park Commission set up. An important legacy of the work of Olmsted and Eliot was the first professional programme in landscape architecture set up at Harvard University in 1900.

4. AFTER 1918. In the years between the two world wars the development of architecture in Boston was steady. The Colonial Revival flourished, especially in the halls of residence or 'Houses' built by Harvard University along the Charles River in the late 1920s and early 1930s. Inspired by the colleges of Oxford and Cambridge in England, Coolidge, Shepley, Bulfinch & Abbott devised Georgian forms, set on irregular sites, and achieved a sensitive fusion of form, function and historical association. In several of the House quadrangles, 18th-century buildings were easily integrated among the new. Representative of the inter-war period were the great theatres and movie houses, for example the huge and lavish Metropolitan Theater (1925; now the Wang Center for the Performing Arts), Tremont Street, by Blackall, Clapp & Whittemore, with 4407 seats. Four large Art Deco office blocks were built during the 1920s. The most intriguing of these is the Boston Post Office and Federal Buildings complex (1929–31) designed by Ralph Adams Cram in conjunction with James A. Wetmore, which illustrates how Cram's use of stylistic references was keyed to functional purpose and psychological response. It also has diminishing setback blocks, which became characteristic of the Art Deco skyscraper and were mandated by the Boston building code in 1928.

The great change in Boston architecture, signalling a change nationwide, was occasioned by the arrival in 1937 of Walter Gropius to head the Harvard Graduate School of Design. Although a number of Boston architects were already developing their own version of the International Style, such as Eleanor Raymond (b 1887), whose achievements have tended to be overlooked, the presence of Gropius marked an abrupt shift to avant-garde Modernism in the north-east USA. After World War II Gropius set up The Architects' Collaborative (see TAC), an architectural firm dedicated to a collective approach to design. An early project was the new Harvard Graduate Center (1949) in the North Yard, whose pristine buff brick dormitory blocks were lifted up on slender columns. At the Massachusetts Institute of Technology, Cambridge, a different approach to Modernist design was demonstrated in the Baker House dormitory block design by Alvar Aalto. Instead of using abstract planar masses, Aalto bent the dormitory block (1947–9) into an S-curve to fit the site and to afford the most pleasing views across the Charles River. Two buildings of 1955 for MIT by Eero Saarinen, the Kresge Auditorium, housing a concrete shell formed of a triangular segment of a sphere, and the brick cylindrical Kresge Chapel show a typically contemporary individual approach. A more aggressive expressionism was developed in the 1960s in two government buildings in Boston: the State Health, Education and Welfare Service Center (1962–71; uncompleted), in the Government Center complex, whose overall design was by Paul Rudolph; and the celebrated Boston City Hall, won in competition by New York architects Kallman, McKinnell & Knowles in 1961 (see TOWN HALL). Finished in 1970, its rough-cast concrete recalled Le Corbusier's monastery of La Tourette in France. Le Corbusier's only building in North America was for Harvard University, the rough-cast concrete Carpenter Center for the Visual Arts (1961–4).

In the mid-1960s commercial development was vigorous at the southern edge of the Back Bay, most notably in the 52-storey Prudential Tower by Charles Luckman & Associates surrounded by lower apartment towers and a shopping centre. The most famous contribution to the skyline of the Back Bay was the new office tower designed

3. Boston, extension to the Boston Public Library by Philip Johnson, 1964–73; the tower for the John Hancock Insurance Company by Henry Nicholls Cobb, 1967, is in the background

in 1967 by I. M. Pei's associate Henry Nicholls Cobb (*b* 1926) for the John Hancock Insurance Company (see fig. 3 below). In the financial heart of the old city more glass towers rose in the late 1960s and 1970s. Despite the proliferation of high-rise office blocks Boston has preserved its Colonial and 19th-century legacy. The entire area of Beacon Hill was declared an historic district, and the disfigured Old Corner Book Store was restored to its 18th-century appearance. Reuse of Boston's old buildings was imaginative and effective, especially the transformation of the mansarded Old City Hall into offices and a restaurant and the refitting of the Quincy Market with a series of shops and restaurants.

Boston also figured prominently in the Post-modernist reaction to the non-referential, efficient sterility of Modernism, initially in the extension (1964–73) to the Boston Public Library by Philip Johnson (see fig. 3); it retains the general scale of the original, emulates its arches and uses an external sheathing of the same Quincy granite. References in new work to the architectural tradition of Boston increased markedly after 1970. One example that successfully draws on the entire range of Boston's neo-classical past is Rowe's Wharf (1982–8), a multi-use redevelopment on the waterfront. Designed by Adrian D. Smith of the Chicago office of Skidmore, Owings & Merrill, it incorporates office, residential, retail and hotel space in two polychrome wings connected by a great domed arch. Graham Gund demonstrated new and provocative ideas in his richly polychromatic and gilded office tower at 75 State Street (1987–9), which alludes to the 1920s in its setback towers. The past has often been a rich source for innovation in the architecture of Boston, especially so at the close of the 20th century.

BIBLIOGRAPHY

J. Winsor, ed.: *Memorial History of Boston*, 4 vols (Boston, 1881–3)
R. A. Cram: 'Architecture', *Fifty Years of Boston* (Boston, 1930)
W. Kilham: *Boston after Bulfinch* (Cambridge, MA, 1946)
H.-R. Hitchcock: *A Guide to Boston Architecture, 1637–1954* (New York, 1954)
S. B. Warner jr: *Streetcar Suburbs: The Process of Growth in Boston, 1870–1900* (Cambridge, MA, 1962)
J. E. Goody: *New Architecture in Boston* (Cambridge, MA, 1965)
B. Bunting: *Houses of Boston's Back Bay: An Architectural History, 1814–1917* (Cambridge, MA, 1967)
Back Bay Boston: The City as a Work of Art (Boston, 1969)
D. Freeman, ed.: *Boston Architecture* (Cambridge, MA, 1970)
W. M. Whitehill: 'The Making of an Architectural Masterpiece: the Boston Public Library', *Amer. A. J.*, xi (1970), pp. 13–35
R. B. Rettig, ed.: *The Architecture of H. H. Richardson and his Contemporaries in Boston and Vicinity* (Boston, 1972)
W. Holden: 'The Peabody Touch: Peabody & Stearns of Boston', *J. Soc. Archit. Historians*, xxxii (1973), pp. 114–31
W. M. Whitehill: *Boston: A Topological History* (Cambridge, MA, rev. 2/1975)
D. Shand-Tucci: *Built in Boston, City and Suburb, 1800–1950* (Boston, 1978/*R* Amherst, MA, 1988) [extensive cross-referenced bibliog.]
A. L. Cummings: *The Frame Houses of Massachusetts Bay, 1625–1725* (Cambridge, MA, 1979)
J. K. Holtz: *Lost Boston* (Boston, 1980)
D. Cole: *Eleanor Raymond, Architect* (Boston, 1981)
D. Lyndon: *The City Observed, Boston: A Guide to the Architecture of the Hub* (New York, 1982)
C. Zaitzevsky: *Frederick Law Olmsted and the Boston Park System* (Cambridge, MA, 1982)
W. Morgan: *The Almighty Wall: The Architecture of Henry Vaughan* (Cambridge, MA, 1983)
B. Bunting and M. H. Floyd: *Harvard: An Architectural History* (Cambridge, MA, 1985)
M. Southworth and S. Southworth: *The Boston Society of Architects A.I.A. Guide to Boston* (Chester, CT, 1987)

LELAND M. ROTH

II. *Art life and organization.*

The original Puritan English settlers in Boston created a strict theocracy that was essentially discouraging to artistic development. There was a proscription on religious painting; artisan-painters and itinerant limners concentrated on painting houses, heraldic devices and pictorial trade signs and producing engravings. Commissions from prominent local families made portraiture, or 'face-painting', dominant. Soon after 1660 there is evidence of a limner in Boston, who probably painted the portrait (*c.* 1665; priv. col.) of *John Endicott, Governor of Massachusetts* (*c.* 1588–1665). The earliest surviving works that can be positively dated were executed in 1670; the ministerial effigies of *John Davenport* (1670; New Haven, CT, Yale U. A.G.) and *John Wheelwright* (1677; Worcester, MA, A. Mus.) are attributed to the Boston-born John Foster, who also produced the first known colonial woodcut print, *Richard Mather* (*c.* 1670; see fig. 4). Thomas Child (*fl* 1678–1706) moved to Boston from London, and his activities decorating cannons, hatchments for funerals and in portraiture date from 1688. Early colonial portraits, modest in aesthetic character and technically crude, have their artistic origins in the Anglo-Dutch style, English provincial painting and Flemish Baroque taste.

By the early 18th century, as Boston showed increasing secularism, there was some early success in extending

4. John Foster: *Richard Mather*, woodcut, *c.* 1670 (Cambridge, MA, Harvard University, Houghton Library)

painting beyond portraiture. The flamboyant decorative landscape with figures appeared in America perhaps for the first time when William Clark (*fl* 1710–40) built a fine Palladian house (*c.* 1714), whose main parlour wall panels were decorated with landscapes. Anecdotal and landscape compositions also increased the range of painting. The settlers began to buy prints of colonial scenes, so that views of the city's harbour and prominent buildings were engraved with greater frequency. William Burgis (*fl* 1715–31) produced the first rudimentary cityscapes of Boston between 1722 and 1730. The acquisition of portraits on a more liberal scale by the emerging privileged class, whose tastes were derived directly from Georgian England, attracted professional British artists soon after 1725. These portrait painters began greatly to influence the Boston-born artisans and helped to make Boston the centre of colonial painting until the mid-18th century. The painter and engraver Peter Pelham, arriving from London in 1726, produced the first known colonial mezzotint engraving from his portrait of the clergyman Cotton Mather (1663–1728) in 1727. JOHN SMIBERT, who reached Boston in 1729, soon became one of the city's favourite portrait painters, introducing the latest fashionable formulae, sophisticated techniques and a style essentially derived from the Baroque. His extensive collection of engravings, paintings and prints of Old Masters was the only means through which many colonists could learn about European art.

Nathaniel Emmons (1703–40), Joseph Badger, Thomas Johnston (1708–67) and John Greenwood were Bostonian portrait painters practising under the combined influence of European examples and 'native' artisans, but their portraits tended towards generalization. The more gifted Robert Feke spent some time in the 1740s in Boston, painting his only known group there, *Isaac Royall and his Family* (1741; Cambridge, MA, Harvard U. Law Sch.). The English-born Joseph Blackburn also stayed temporarily, introducing the animation and frivolity of the Rococo style. JOHN SINGLETON COPLEY, born in Boston, was the first American to transform craftsmanship into artistry and to achieve international recognition. He attempted a range of subject-matter, although local conditions confined him mainly to portraiture: 'Was it not for preserving the resemblance of particular persons, painting would not be known [in Boston and the colonies],' he commented (Baigell).

The Revolutionary transition interrupted all the arts and crafts, but the pressures of political dissent encouraged print cartoons and caricatures. Paul Revere produced his famous, although technically awkward, print of the *Boston Massacre* (1770), and the blockade of Boston led to the series of watercolours (versions, 1768; Boston, MA, Hist. Soc.; Boston, MA, New England Hist. Geneal. Soc.; Salem, MA, Essex Inst.) depicting the event by Christian Remick (1726–?1784).

At the beginning of the 19th century Boston's artistic life was fragmentary, and tastes continued to remain close to those of London. The Boston Athenaeum was established as a library in 1807 and began to give annual exhibitions of painting, the first in New England, in 1826. Portraiture remained the dominant genre, and in 1805 Gilbert Stuart settled in Boston for the final, mature phase

of his career, having already received recognition by face-painting the famous in Philadelphia and Washington. Samuel F. B. Morse, however, given no commissions for his historical pictures, turned after 1815 to portraiture with considerably more reluctance. Washington Allston spent over 20 years in the area, his dark subjective Romanticism imbuing American art for the first time with a sense of mystery and solitude. By the mid-19th century the city had become an early centre for art collecting; as early as 1835 John Lowell (1799–1836) sent back to Boston from Luxor some pieces from the temple at Karnak, the first Egyptian monuments to come to America. In the 1840s an Art Union was established, patterned after the American Art Union of New York, an organization that bought, exhibited and sold original paintings and distributed prints each year to its members; but this was ended by a court decision citing it as a lottery.

During the last third of the 19th century encouragement of the arts became an important component of Boston civic identity. Copley Square was designated as the site of a cluster of institutions that set the tone for public art patronage: the first Museum of Fine Arts building (replaced on Huntington Avenue from 1907; *see* §I, 2 and 3 above); H. H. Richardson's Trinity Church with mural decorations and stained-glass windows by John La Farge; and the Boston Public Library with murals of 1895–6 (by Pierre Puvis de Chavannes) and 1894 (by EDWIN AUSTIN ABBEY and John Singer Sargent) and with bronze bas-relief doors by Daniel Chester French. The architects McKim, Mead & White collaborated in 1897 with Augustus Saint-Gaudens on the monument to Robert Gould Shaw (1837–63), the commander of the first African–American regiment to serve in the Civil War (*see* UNITED STATES OF AMERICA, fig. 21); facing the State House on Boston Common, this ensemble sought to knit together high-relief sculpture in an architectural framework with features of the natural landscape. Despite the lavishness of these commissions, the Puritan tradition occasionally reasserted itself: in 1893 the nude *Bacchante and Infant Faun* (New York, Met.) by the American sculptor Frederick William MacMonnies was offered as a gift for the courtyard of the library; it was refused after protest by the Watch and Ward Society, founded in 1884 as the New England Society for the Suppression of Vice.

Art education and the training and support of local artists were not neglected during this period. The School of the Museum of Fine Arts opened in 1877, in the same building as the museum. The Boston Art Club, organized informally by 20 artists in 1855, had over 800 members by 1881, and the Boston Art Students' Association (founded 1879), the Paint and Clay Club, the St Botolph Club and the Association of Boston Artists (all established in 1880) held regular exhibitions of the work of local and foreign artists. The appointment in 1873 by Harvard University of Charles Eliot Norton as the first Professor of Fine Arts in America laid the foundation for the academic study of art history; Norton's pupil Bernard Berenson assisted ISABELLA STEWART GARDNER in acquiring the Old Master paintings and decorative arts that enriched her Renaissance Revival palazzo, now Fenway Court, built by Willard T. Sears (*see* CUMMINGS & SEARS), which opened as a public museum in 1903.

As Bostonians became more cosmopolitan, tastes became less English in character. In 1883 the first exhibition in America of French Impressionist painting was held in Boston; it included Renoir's *Luncheon of the Boating Party* (1880–81; Washington, DC, Phillips Col.), as well as works by Monet, Camille Pissarro, Eugène Boudin and Alfred Sisley. Earlier in the century the painter and teacher William Morris Hunt had promoted the work of the Barbizon school, and many Boston artists supplemented their local training with experience in the workshops of Paris. As a result a large and important group of modern French painting began to accumulate in Boston in both private and public collections, at a time when the realistic Hudson River school tradition still prevailed in New York. French taste was also reflected in the work of artists connected with the Museum School: Edmund C. Tarbell, Thomas Wilmer Dewing, Willard Leroy Metcalf and especially Childe Hassam painted cityscapes and rural scenes, often with colonial associations, in a lively *plein-air* style that combined an Impressionist treatment of light and colour with a more conservative structural solidity (e.g. Childe Hassam: *Rainy Day in Boston*, 1885; Toledo, OH, Mus. A.; for illustration *see* HASSAM, CHILDE). This style reached its highest development in the first 30 years of the 20th century with the work of the Boston School; such painters as Frank W. Benson and William Paxton (1869–1941) fused Impressionist colour with academic technique to produce dignified portraits and genteel interiors (e.g. William Paxton: *New Necklace*, 1910; Boston, MA, Mus. F.A.). When a considerable part of the Armory Show was exhibited in Boston in 1913, however, the negative reaction highlighted the conflict between the local allegiance to the academic tradition and the progressive experiments of modernism. Such artists as Benson and Paxton moved in a contracting world of wealth and privilege that lent an increasingly conservative character to the city's art life. By the 1930s the American avant-garde had largely abandoned Boston for the larger and more diverse artistic community of New York, although in the 1940s Boston Expressionism briefly emerged in the work of such artists as Hyman Bloom.

BIBLIOGRAPHY
H. W. Cunningham: *Christian Remick, an Early Boston Artist* (Boston, 1904)
M. A. S. Shannon: *Boston Days of William Morris Hunt* (Boston, 1923)
G. F. Dow: *The Arts and Crafts in New England* (Topsfield, MA, 1927)
C. Lee: *Early American Portrait Painters* (New Haven, 1929)
T. C. Hall: *The Religious Background of American Culture* (Boston, 1930)
S. E. Morison: *Builders of the Bay Colony* (Boston, 1930)
A. Burroughs: *Limners and Likenesses: Three Centuries of American Painting* (Cambridge, MA, 1936)
D. Wecter: *The Saga of American Society: A Record of Social Aspiration, 1607–1937* (New York, 1937)
B. N. Parker and A. B. Wheeler: *John Singleton Copley: American Portraits* (Boston, 1938)
V. Barker: *American Painting: History and Interpretation* (New York, 1950)
C. Bridenbaugh: *Cities in Revolt: Urban Life in America, 1743–1776* (Oxford, 1955)
A. Eliot: *Three Hundred Years of American Painting* (New York, 1957)
O. T. Barck and H. T. Lefler: *Colonial America* (New York, 1958)
J. T. Flexner: *America's Old Masters* (New York, 1967)
M. Baigell: *A History of American Painting* (New York, 1974)
B. Novak: *American Painting of the 19th Century: Realism, Idealism and the American Experience* (New York, 1979)
P. J. Pierce: *Edmund C. Tarbell and the Boston School of Painting, 1889–1980* (Higham, MA, 1980)
The Bostonians: Painters of an Elegant Age, 1870–1930 (exh. cat., ed. T. J. Fairbrother; Boston, MA, Mus. F.A., 1986)

STEPHEN F. THORPE

III. Centre of production.

1. Furniture. 2. Metalwork. 3. Ceramics.

1. FURNITURE. In the 17th century the dominant furniture workshops in Boston were those of Ralph Mason (1599–1678/9) and Henry Messinger (*fl* 1641–81), both London-trained joiners who worked in the Anglo-Dutch Mannerist style using split turnings, bosses, triglyphs and dentils of exotic hardwoods reminiscent of Dutch furniture. The turner Thomas Edsall (1588–1676) arrived in Boston from London *c.* 1735; he made turnings and bosses for joined furniture and chairs with London-style ball-turned stretchers and stiles. By the late 17th century Mannerism in colonial furniture was superseded by the Baroque style with its sculptural forms and rich, unornamented surfaces (e.g. high chest-of-drawers, prob. Massachusetts, pine, walnut and maple, 1700–25; Boston, MA, Mus. F. A.). In Boston, this fashion manifested itself primarily in such pieces as the high chest-of-drawers with figured walnut veneer on a pine carcass that rests on a frame with turned legs.

In the early 18th century Boston craftsmen provided furnishings for a growing anglophile élite. This first generation of artisans was tightly interconnected through loyalty and an unofficial barter system that prevented many immigrants from establishing their own shops. Nevertheless, many new arrivals trained in London were employed by local cabinetmakers, who utilized their skills and knowledge of up-to-date fashions to produce furniture in the latest styles. Such journeymen were probably responsible for veneered chest-on-chests (e.g. chest-on-chest, Boston, MA, black walnut, burl walnut veneer and eastern white pine, 1715–25; Boston, MA, Mus. F. A.) in the Georgian style with canted corner pilasters and pull-out folding boards that were originally attributed to English makers. The typical forms of 18th-century case furniture were high chests, dressing-tables, chest-on-chests and bureau-bookcases. The pad foot was employed in New England, particularly Massachusetts, during the first half of the 18th century on chairs, small tables, case pieces and high chests. It extends from a slender cabriole leg and flares outward in a circular fashion before canting inwards to a smaller round base. Japanning was a Boston speciality, a result of the thriving trade with China and the corresponding popularity of chinoiserie decoration; an example is the high chest (*c.* 1736; Baltimore, U. MD Mus. A.) by the japanner Robert Davis (*fl* 1733–9). However, until the mid-18th century most examples were veneered, such as those produced by the Charlestown cabinetmaker Ebenezer Hartsherne or Hartshorn (1690–1781), while others were decorated with a block front, a contouring of the façade with three vertical panels of which the outer two were raised and the central one recessed—an innovation of Boston cabinetmakers that was popular from the 1730s until the 1780s. Other shaped case pieces are *bombé* in form, with the sides of the lower section swelling outwards in serpentine curves that are sometimes echoed by shaped drawers (e.g. desk, Salem, MA, mahogany and white pine,

1760–90; Boston, MA, Mus. F. A.). Although the form was derived from imported English bureau-bookcases, the complicated construction techniques were mastered only by such Boston craftsmen as Benjamin Frothingham sr of Charlestown, George Bright (1726–1805), John Cogswell (1738–1818) and a few others in nearby towns. In the 1770s many case pieces were modified with serpentine or oxbow fronts; some of the finest examples were embellished with carvings and figural sculpture by John (Simeon) Skillin (fl 1791). The demand for Neo-classical furniture was met by John Seymour (c. 1738–1818), who arrived from England c. 1784; he and his son Thomas Seymour (1771–1843) produced elegant tambour desks and semi-circular commodes with mahogany and satinwood veneers (see WOOD, colour pl. II, fig. 2).

Boston continued to be an important centre for furniture-making in the 19th century. In the early decades furniture in the bolder Empire style was produced by George Archibald and Thomas Emmons (fl 1813–24) as well as Isaac Vose and Joshua Coates (fl 1805–19). Closely related to French forms, their work incorporated broad expanses of figured mahogany veneer punctuated by cut brass inlay and ormolu. By 1850, the furniture industry produced Rococo and Renaissance Revival furniture for a burgeoning middle-class market. Among the well-known makers were George Croome (fl 1845–c. 1880) and George Ware (fl c. 1860). New forms ranged from pier tables and étagères to large sideboards and included a variety of specialized furniture, some with folding or mechanical parts for invalids, libraries or travel.

Despite the Great Fire of 1872 and the financial panic of the following year, Boston's furniture industry flourished until the end of the century. High productivity was due partly to the influx of unskilled Irish immigrants to man such new steam-powered factories as the A. H. Davenport Co. (1880–1906), which executed commissions for architects H. H. Richardson and McKim, Mead & White among others. In 1916 A. H. Davenport merged with Charles R. Irving & Robert Casson Co. (1893–c. 1970) and manufactured furniture primarily in the Gothic Revival style for Boston's commercial and ecclesiastical clients.

After World War II the studio crafts movement flourished in Boston. The Program in Artisanry at Boston University, instituted in 1975, became a dynamic centre for furniture-making under its founder, Dan Jackson (b 1938), and subsequently under Jere Osgood (b 1936) and Alphonse Mattia (b 1947). Although it ceased in 1985, it inspired many careers in furniture-making, some of which were featured in the exhibition *New American Furniture* in 1989 (Boston, MA, Mus. F.A.).

BIBLIOGRAPHY

R. H. Randall jr: *American Furniture in the Museum of Fine Arts, Boston* (Boston, 1965/R 1985)
W. M. Whitehill, B. Jobe and J. L. Fairbanks, eds: *Boston Furniture of the Eighteenth Century* (Boston, 1974)
J. Fairbanks and others: *Paul Revere's Boston, 1810–1835* (Boston, 1975)
P. Talbott: 'Boston Empire Furniture', *Antiques*, cvii (May 1975), pp. 878–86
A. Farnam: 'A. H. Davenport & Co., Boston Furniture Makers', *Antiques*, cix (May 1976)
P. Talbott: 'Boston Empire Furniture', *Antiques*, cix (May 1976), pp. 1004–13
A. Farnam: 'H. H. Richardson and A. H. Davenport: Architecture and Furniture as Big Business in America's Gilded Age', *Tools and Technologies, America's Wooden Age*, ed. P. B. Kebabian and W. C. Lipke (Burlington, VT, 1979), pp. 80–92
E. S. Cooke jr: 'The Boston Furniture Industry in 1880', *Old-time New England*, lxx/257 (1980), pp. 82–98
J. L. Fairbanks and E. Bidwell Bates: *American Furniture, 1620 to the Present* (New York, 1981)
J. Seidler: 'A Century in Transition: The Boston Furniture Industry, 1840–80', *Victorian Furniture*, ed. K. Ames (Philadelphia, 1983), pp. 65–83
New American Furniture, The Second Generation of Studio Furnituremakers (exh. cat. by E. S. Cooke jr, Boston, MA, Mus. F.A., 1989)
Collecting American Decorative Arts and Sculpture, 1971–1991 (exh. cat., intro. J. L. Fairbanks; Boston, MA, Mus. F.A., 1991)
P. Talbott: 'The Furniture Trade in Boston, 1810–1835', *Antiques*, cxli (May 1992), pp. 842–55

2. METALWORK.

(i) Silver. The craft of silversmithing began in Boston in 1652, when John Hull (1624–83) and Robert Sanderson (1608–93) became the first Masters of the Mint for the Massachusetts Bay Colony. Sanderson, who had trained in London, and Hull fashioned the first coins of the colony and much of its earliest plate and were well-respected members of the Puritan oligarchy. Their hollowware followed the latest fashions in silver imported from London and is characterized by a Mannerist style that features strong contrasts in shapes and textures (e.g. caudle cup, 1660–70; Boston, MA, Mus. F.A.). Hull's and Sanderson's dominance of the craft had faded by 1670, as had the authority of the Puritan founders, and a new group of merchants came to power whose religious, political and commercial interests were orientated towards England. These new arrivals, some of whom were officials of the provincial government, patronized Jeremiah Dummer (1645–1718), JOHN CONEY and Edward Winslow (1669–1753), the first Boston-born silversmiths. During this second period, vessel forms included monteiths, master salts and sugar-boxes in the Baroque style with elaborate repoussé chasing and cast ornament (see UNITED STATES OF AMERICA, fig. 48). The need for church plate also grew along with burgeoning congregations. Craftsmen derived their designs primarily from imported English wares, but they also utilized the skills of immigrant craftsmen who brought with them specialized skills, new techniques and the latest fashions. Their lack of family and religious connections prevented most immigrant craftsmen from establishing their own workshops; instead they performed specialized tasks or worked as anonymous journeymen in some of the larger Boston establishments.

Despite the talents of Boston's native-born and immigrant silversmith population, the economic slump of the 1730s resulted in the production of silver that was conservative in style, as seen in the work of Thomas Edwards (1701–55), Jacob Hurd (1703–58) and Samuel Edwards (1705–62). The craft as a whole concentrated less on evolving new forms than on creating finely raised and chased vessels, some engraved with coats of arms. Porringers, mugs and domed tankards changed little, while the apple-shaped teapot of the 1730s and 1740s gradually gave way to the more fashionable inverted pear form in the Rococo style by the 1760s (e.g. teapot by Paul Revere, 1760–65; Boston, MA, Mus. F.A.). With some exceptions, Boston silver from the 1760s to the end of the 18th century is conservative in contrast to the more elaborate

5. Three-handled loving-cup designed by H. Langford Warren, made by Arthur J. Stone and enamelled by Laurin Hovey Martin, silver gilt and enamel, h. 146 mm, w. 219 mm, 1906 (Cambridge, MA, Fogg Art Museum)

decoration found on the silver made in such rapidly growing cities as New York and Philadelphia. Boston patrons generally preferred heraldic engravings to the ciphers chosen by stylish New Yorkers, and they did not embrace the fashionable Rococo style as enthusiastically as did Philadelphians. The careers of PAUL REVERE and Benjamin Burt (1729–1805) spanned the latter half of the 18th century and the early decades of the 19th. Both produced a large quantity of silver for Boston patrons in the Rococo style, and towards the end of the 18th century both also made elliptical fluted vessels in the newly popular Neo-classical vein (e.g. teapot and stand by Benjamin Burt, 1790–1800; Boston, MA, Mus. F.A.). The following generation of silversmiths, which included Lewis Cary (1798–1834) and Obadiah Rich (*fl* 1830–50), produced more robust forms in the Empire style with mechanically produced naturalistic decoration.

During the second half of the 19th century such Boston firms as Shreve, Stanwood & Co. (1860–69), Crosby & Morse (1848–76) and Goodnow & Jenks (1893–*c.* 1905) created tea services and coffee services in the newly fashionable Renaissance Revival and Greek Revival styles. But by 1900 few workshops remained in Boston, for such larger concerns as Reed, Barton & Co. (founded 1886) of Taunton, MA, and the silverware firm of GORHAM (founded 1831) of Providence, RI, could produce their wares more competitively. One of the last apprentices to Goodnow & Jenks was George Christian Gebelein (1878–1945), a skilled practitioner of the Colonial Revival style, a dealer in antique American silver and a member of the

Society of Arts and Crafts, Boston. Founded in Boston in 1897, the Society was the first such group to be established in America. The metals department of the Society's Handicraft Shop offered classes in silversmithing in the Arts and Crafts and Colonial Revival styles, and fostered the development of silversmiths Mary Knight (*b* 1876) and Katherine Pratt (1891–1978). The most prominent and prolific silversmith in the Boston area was Arthur J. Stone (1847–1938). Born and trained in Sheffield, England, Stone moved to Gardner, MA, in 1896 and produced work on commission for many of Boston's prominent families (see fig. 5).

By the late 1920s, few silversmiths were working in Boston. Gebelein, Pratt and Karl Leinonen (1866–1957) continued to make some Colonial Revival pieces, but demand for locally made silver declined. Although metal-working classes were offered at the Museum School of the Museum of Fine Arts and at the Massachusetts College of Art, it was not until the establishment in 1975 of the Program in Artisanry at Boston University that a new group of metalsmiths developed. In 1989 the Program in Artisanry was relocated to the University of Massachusetts at Dartmouth, MA; all three schools maintain active metalsmithing programs. One of the most important 20th-century metalsmiths in Boston is Kansas-born Margret Craver (*b* 1907), who trained under Arthur Nevill Kirk in Detroit and *c.* 1930 with Baron Erik Fleming (1894–1954), silversmith to King Gustav VI Adolf of Sweden. Following her move to Boston in 1967, she revived the 16th-century enamelling technique of *en résille sur verre*, which she used in the production of hollowware and jewellery (e.g. necklace in gold, enamel and African black glass beads, *c.* 1981; Boston, MA, Mus. F.A.). After its closure in 1989 Craver's workshop was acquired by the Smithsonian Institution.

BIBLIOGRAPHY

L. I. Laughlin: *Pewter in America: Its Makers and their Marks*, 3 vols (i–ii, Boston, 1940/*R* Barre, 1969; iii, Barre, 1971; i–iii as 1 vol., 1969–71/*R* New York, 1981)
K. C. Buhler and G. Hood: *American Silver: Garvan and Other Collections in the Yale University Art Gallery*, 2 vols (New Haven, 1970)
M. G. Fales: *Early American Silver* (New York, 1970/*R* 1973)
G. Hood: *American Silver; A History of Style, 1650–1900* (New York, 1971/*R* 1989)
K. C. Buhler: *American Silver, 1665–1825, in the Museum of Fine Arts, Boston*, 2 vols (Boston, 1972)
B. M. Ward and G. W. R. Ward, eds: *Silver in American Life* (New York, 1979)
'The Art that is Life': The Arts and Crafts Movement in America, 1875–1920 (exh. cat. by W. Kaplan and others, Boston, MA, Mus. F.A., 1987)
E. C. Chickering: 'Arthur J. Stone: An Anglo-American Silversmith', *Apollo*, cxxx/330 (August 1989), pp. 95–101
P. Kane and others: *A Dictionary of Colonial Massachusetts Silversmiths Based on the Notes of Francis Hill Bigelow and John Marshall Phillips* (in preparation)

(ii) Pewter, copper, brass and other base metals. The presence of pewterers in Boston was recorded as early as 1635, when a Richard Graves arrived from London on the *Abigail.* By 1640 at least three other pewterers had settled in Boston: Samuel Grame (or Graemes) (*fl* 1639–45), Henry Shrimpton (*fl* 1639–66) and Thomas Bumstead (*fl* 1640–43). Perhaps the most celebrated of this early group are Edmund Dolbeare (1671–1706/11) and his son, John Dolbeare (1670–1740), whose large dishes reveal the 17th-century English method of hammering cast-pewter discs over wooden forms. Robert Bonynge (*fl* 1731–63) produced the first known examples of pewter beakers made in Boston (see Barquist, no. 205a). By 1800 the number of pewterers in the area had increased ninefold. The success of these craftsmen is remarkable since they were lacking tin, an essential metal in the making of pewter alloy. The British forbade the export of tin to the colonies to protect the British pewterers' guild, yet these entrepreneurs prospered by fashioning new pewter from inexpensive second-hand wares.

The number of pewterers remained stable during the early 18th century, while demand for this base metal and later for Britannia metal remained high. Roswell Gleason (1799–1887) of Dorchester was perhaps the most prominent local maker of pewter and other silverplated wares. South of Boston, in Taunton, MA, Reed & Barton (Henry G. Reed and Charles E. Barton) formed a partnership in 1840 and produced pewter and Britannia, later expanding to silver and silverplate production.

The Arts and Crafts Movement brought with it a revival of pewter as a means of romanticizing colonial life; Lester Howard Vaughn (1889–1961) of Taunton created pewter vessels and flatware in emulation of colonial forms before he changed to international modern designs in the style of the Danish silversmith Georg Jensen. During the colonial and post-Revolutionary era, some pewterers also styled themselves coppersmiths and braziers, because they handled metal through spinning and casting. The earliest of these craftworkers included Henry Shrimpton and Jonathan Jackson (1695–1736). An advertisement from the *Boston News-Letter* of 17 February 1737 indicates the variety of skills with base metals that were practised by these individuals (Dow, p. 126):

> William Coffin, at the Ostrich, near the Draw-Bridge, makes and sells Mill Brasses, Chambers for Pumps, Brass Cocks of all Sizes, Knockers for Doors, Brasses for Chaises and Sadlers, Brass Doggs of all sorts, Candlesticks, Shovels and Tongs, small Bells, and all sorts of Founders ware. Also, all sorts of Braziers and Pewterers ware, small Stills and worms, and all Sorts of Plumbers work; likewise Buys old copper, Brass, Pewter and Lead.

Despite the quantity of objects produced, information on makers for this period is scarce, and it is difficult to determine whether or when specialization in these materials began to occur. Rare, marked works in brass dating to the early 19th century by Boston makers William C. Hunneman and John Molineux suggest that these individuals worked more exclusively in brass than copper, yet it remains likely that brass was only one of the base metals in which they were proficient.

Perhaps the best-known colonial Boston coppersmith was Shem Drowne (1683–1776), deacon of First Baptist Church. Drowne's most distinctive works included the Indian archer weathervane (1716; Boston, MA Hist. Soc.) that once topped the Province House, and the famous grasshopper weathervane (1742; *in situ*) that he created for Faneuil Hall. Large-scale copper production in the USA was first successfully introduced by the silversmith Paul Revere, who in 1800 established a rolling mill in Canton that produced copper sheathing for sailing vessels. His son Joseph Warren Revere (1777–1868) inherited this business and reorganized it as the Revere Copper Company in an 1828 merger with James Davis of Boston, a maker of brass andirons.

Mid-18th-century copper ventures included the lively weathervane business of Leonard Wareham Cushing (1867–1933) and Stillman White established in Waltham, MA, in 1867, when the business was purchased at auction from the estate of Alvin L. Jewell, who had pioneered cast-iron and brass products in the area. Stillman White sold his interest in the company to Cushing in 1872, and Cushing's sons, Charles and Harry, joined their father to form L. W. Cushing & Sons. The family produced weathervanes until 1933, some of them taken from moulds that dated from the early days of Jewell's ownership.

By the end of the 20th century, copper's utilitarian uses were superseded by its new attraction for such contemporary artists as Yoshiko Yamamoto (*b* 1932) and Claire Sanford (*b* 1958), who explored electroforming and patination in this medium to add texture and colour to their work. Yamamoto has produced *Copper Vessel No. 16 (Big Pumpkin)* (1985) and Sanford *Growth Vessel* (early 1980s; both Boston, MA, Mus. F.A.).

BIBLIOGRAPHY

G. F. Dow: *Everyday Life in the Massachusetts Bay Colony* (Boston, 1935), p. 126
L. I. Laughlin: *Pewter in America, its Makers and their Marks*, 3 vols (i–ii, Boston, 1940/*R* Barre, 1969; iii, Barre, 1971; i–iii as 1 vol., 1969–71/*R* New York, 1981)
H. J. Kauffman: *American Copper & Brass* (Camden, NJ, 1968)
C. F. Montgomery: *A History of American Pewter* (New York, 1973)
M. Simpson: *All that Glisters: Brass in Early America* (New Haven, 1979)
J. A. Mulholland: *A History of Metals in Colonial America* (Tuscaloosa, 1981)

D. L. Barquist: *American and English Pewter at the Yale University Art Gallery* (New Haven, 1985)

P. M. Leehey and others: *Paul Revere—Artisan, Businessman, and Patriot, the Man behind the Myth* (Boston, 1988)

3. CERAMICS. The earliest mention of earthenware in New England appeared by 1644 in Essex County probate records. Although such documents cannot prove the presence of locally made goods at this early date, the few surviving examples of lead-glazed earthenware from this period have been attributed to Massachusetts or New England as early as 1675. A large supply of red clay along the Mystic River fostered the brickmaking and pottery industries in Boston's nearby towns of Charlestown and Medford and by the 18th century more than 40 potters were known to have worked in Charlestown; in 1750, approximately eight or nine shops were in simultaneous operation. The proliferation of potters in Charlestown explains why so few potters worked in Boston and why references are often found to what was called 'Charlestown ware'. Although attempts were made from the mid-18th century to make stoneware in Boston, domestic production was not stimulated until after the American Revolution, when charges levied on the weight of imported goods made stoneware an economically attractive commodity. After 1793 a Boston stoneware factory was established by Frederick Carpenter (1771–1827) and Jonathan Fenton (1766–1848). Their goods were made of clay shipped from Perth Amboy, NJ, an arrangement made possible by the financial backing of the Boston merchant William Little. Through Fenton's sons Richard Lucas Fenton (1797–1834) and Christopher Webber Fenton (1806–65) this enterprise eventually led to the establishment in 1849 of the United States Pottery Co. in Bennington, VT. The evidence for the production of such fine ceramics as tortoiseshellware is rather thin compared to that for redware and stoneware. However, at least one advertisement from the period suggests that tortoiseshellware was attempted as early as 1770.

By the mid-19th century one of the major potteries was the East Boston Crockery Manufactory. It was first established in Weston in 1765 by Abraham Hews (1741–1818); by the Civil War it had moved to North Cambridge, where porcelain, yellowware, Rockingham and Parian wares were produced in addition to an expanded line in ornamental ceramics.

HUGH CORNWALL ROBERTSON, who had worked as a manager of the East Boston Crockery Manufactory, established the Chelsea Keramic Art Works in Chelsea, MA (1872–89), and later the Dedham Pottery, Dedham, MA (1896–1943), which were prominent art potteries in the region. Other Arts and Crafts potteries included the Grueby Faience Co. (*see* GRUEBY, WILLIAM HENRY), the Marblehead Pottery, Marblehead, MA (1904–36; see fig. 6), and the Low Tiles, Chelsea, MA (1878–1907). The Paul Revere Pottery (1911–42) of Boston and Brighton was a reform-minded, subsidized pottery that employed young immigrant Italian and Jewish women. One of the few art potteries to flourish until the mid-20th century was the Dorchester Pottery, Dorchester, MA (1895–1979), which was best-known for its salt-glazed wares.

After the lull in nearly all craftsman-related industries in the second quarter of the 20th century, many university programmes devoted to ceramics were established. The subsequent proliferation of studio potters in the Boston area in the late 20th century was partly due to such professors as William Wyman (1922–80) at Massachusetts College of Art. Norman Arseneault (1912–84), who was particularly interested in glazes, taught in the ceramics department at the School of the Museum of Fine Arts,

6. Earthenware bowl with incised and glazed decoration, h. 98 mm, diam. 227 mm, from the Marblehead Pottery, *c.* 1910–15 (Boston, MA, Museum of Fine Arts)

Boston, for many years, and devoted his career to perfecting a tourmaline glaze. Richard Hirsch (*b* 1944) studied at the Rochester Institute of Technology School for American Craftsmen and during the 1970s taught at Boston University's short-lived but prestigious Program in Artisanry (1975–85).

BIBLIOGRAPHY
L. W. Watkins: *Early New England Potters and their Wares* (Cambridge, MA, 1950)

J. L. Fairbanks and others: *New England Begins: The Seventeenth Century*, ii (Boston, 1982), pp. 229–30, 303

S. H. Meyers: 'The Business of Potting, 1780–1840', *The Craftsman in Early America*, ed. I. M. G. Quimby (New York, 1984)

P. Evans: *Art Pottery of the United States: An Encyclopedia of Producers and their Marks* (New York, 1974, rev. 1987)

'*The Art that is Life': The Arts and Crafts Movement in America, 1875–1920* (exh. cat. by W. Kaplan and others, Boston, MA, Mus. F. A., 1987)

J. Skerry: 'Equal to any Imported from England: The Evidence for American Production of Tortoisewares', *36th Symposium of the American Ceramic Circle: Chicago, 1989*

JEANNINE FALINO

Boston & Sandwich Glass Co. American glass factory formed by Deming Jarves (1790–1869), who left the New England Glass Co. in 1825. He acquired a site and built a glasshouse in Sandwich, MA. In 1826 the Boston & Sandwich Glass Co. was incorporated, with Jarves gaining financial aid from several partners. In Sandwich Jarves was agent and general manager and during the following 22 years greatly increased the size and output of the company from 70 to over 500 employees and from £75,000 to £600,000 in value.

Table glass, lighting devices and ornamental wares were produced by using the fashionable techniques of each era. The firm's repertory included free-blown, mould-blown, cut, engraved, colourless and cased products, and various art wares, especially opaline, 'Peachblow' and satin glass. The company is best known for its lacy pressed glass (*see* UNITED STATES OF AMERICA, fig. 45), giving rise to the generic term 'Sandwich Glass' for any American examples of this type. The firm's products were of very good quality but, as with many other New England glasshouses, its fortunes declined after the Civil War (1861–5), and the works closed during the strike of 1888.

BIBLIOGRAPHY
R. W. Lee: *Sandwich Glass* (1939, rev. Northborough, MA, 7/1947)

K. M. Wilson: *New England Glass and Glassmaking* (New York, 1972)

ELLEN PAUL DENKER

Botanic [botanical] **garden.** A type of GARDEN developed by university medical schools in Europe from the mid-16th century for the collection and scientific study of plants; its origins lie in the monastic herbal gardens of the medieval period. The observation of plant specimens for educational purposes led to the establishment of numerous 'physic' gardens (*hortus medicus*): both Pisa and Padua had a botanic garden by 1544, and that at Florence was established in 1545; other early important examples include Leipzig (1580), Leiden (1587), Montpellier (1593), Oxford (1621), the Jardin des Plantes (1626), Paris, Uppsala (1665), Chelsea Physic Garden (1673), London, and Amsterdam (1682). The experimental method that was gradually beginning to dominate scientific study, together with the requirements imposed by the cultivation

of plants, soon began to overshadow the aesthetic qualities that had characterized the Renaissance and Baroque garden. Virtually all decorative elements, such as statues, grottoes, fountains or mazes, were excluded from the botanic garden, whose value resided in its collection of such rare and exotic plant species as the sunflower, the agave or the tomato, all from newly discovered parts of the world. Certain plants, including the tulip, fritillary, narcissus, iris and anemone, were particularly sought after in the 17th century because of their shape and colour.

The flowerbed forms the basic element of a garden layout, but those for botanic gardens were not based on the complicated polygonal shapes to be found in Baroque country-house and palace gardens. Designers of botanic gardens sought functional simplicity and tended to favour a square—or occasionally circular—plan divided by paths into four equal parts (see fig.), which represented the four quarters of the world. The paths were orientated to the cardinal points of the compass, and a well was often dug at the centre of the garden. The use of the square as a basic unit, sometimes made rectangular by laying out an adjacent pair, was the norm by the early 17th century. Flowerbeds were planted out in the light of current taxonomies, but since at this time occult natural magic played a significant role in scientific developments, their design was often influenced by astrological beliefs. The flowerbed functioned as a magical figure within which the magus–gardener practised natural magic, through which the plants would flourish in response to celestial influences. (The beds in the Giardino dei Semplici (1603) at Mantua, for example, took the plan of four equal squares within

Plan of the botanic garden, Padua; engraving from G. F. Tomasini: *Gymnasium Patavinum* (1654), i, p. 82

another, larger, square—the design used for contemporary horoscopes.)

From the outset some botanic gardens were attached to an eclectic natural-history museum. That at Pisa is an early instance; 17th-century examples include the Manfredo Settala Collection in Milan (now in Mus. Civ. Stor. Nat.) and the gallery built by John Tradescant and his son in their gardens (destr.) at Lambeth, London. Such museums, which developed from the Mannerist tradition of *Wunderkammern* and *Raritätenkammern*, often provided a laboratory for scientific inquiry and a studio for botanical artists. They not only contained libraries that included HERBALS and collections of plant illustrations, they also housed bones, minerals, shells, stuffed animals and various other exotic and curious objects, both natural and man-made. The world of garden plants in this way contributed to an overall encyclopedic presentation of the three kingdoms (animal, vegetable, mineral) of Nature—part of a true microcosm that reflected the complexity and variety of the universe. During the late 17th century and early 18th the scientific and didactic impetus found in the initial development of the botanic garden increased, while the beliefs and practices of natural magic, including astrology, began to disappear. Hitherto unknown plants were introduced into Europe from North America, South America, New Zealand and Australia, which not only fostered botanical research but yielded products of potential commercial value. Increasing attention was also paid to the problems of classification, which culminated in the work of the Swedish naturalist Carl Linnaeus (1707–78), head of the botanic garden at Uppsala and author of *Species plantarum* (1753) and other works, from whose classificatory system the present binomial nomenclature derives. The Linnaean revolution brought about a radical rethinking of the criteria used in planting out beds, while botany, finally recognized as a distinct scientific discipline, retained the botanic garden as its laboratory.

During the 19th century, when numerous tropical botanic gardens were established beyond Europe (e.g. Singapore, 1822), the educational example set by natural-history museums was taken up, and numerous botanic gardens were opened to the public. Modern visitors to those at Padua, Florence, Oxford and elsewhere are easily able to identify the original structure of these gardens of science and learning.

BIBLIOGRAPHY

H. Veendorp and L. G. M. Baas Becking: *1587–1937: Hortus academicus Lugduno Batavus: The Development of the Gardens of Leyden University* (Leiden, 1938)

'Il giardino dei semplici di Pisa', *Livorno e Pisa: Due città e un territorio nella politica dei Medici* (exh. cat., ed. L. Tongiorgi Tomasi; Pisa, Arsenale Galee, 1980)

J. Prest: *The Garden of Eden: The Botanic Garden and the Re-creation of Paradise* (New Haven and London, 1981)

L. Tongiorgi Tomasi: 'Projects for Botanical and other Gardens: A 16th-century Manual', *J. Gdn Hist.*, iii (1983), pp. 1–34

M. Azzi Visentini: *L'orto botanico di Padova* (Milan, 1984)

O. R. Impey and A. G. MacGregor, eds: *The Origins of Museums: The Cabinet of Curiosities in Sixteenth- and Seventeenth-century Europe* (Oxford, 1985)

G. Jellicoe and others, eds: *The Oxford Companion to Gardens* (Oxford, 1986)

LUCIA TONGIORGI TOMASI

Botelho, Carlos (António Teixeira Bastos Nunes) (*b* Lisbon, 18 Sept 1899; *d* Lisbon, 18 Aug 1982). Portuguese painter, printmaker and designer of tapestries and tile panels. Known primarily as a 'painter of Lisbon', he began his artistic career as an illustrator and cartoonist as well as writing a weekly satirical page (1928–50) in the newspaper *O sempre fixe*. He visited Paris in 1929, 1930–1 and again in 1937, when he was impressed by a retrospective exhibition of the work of van Gogh, whose influence is evident in Botelho's scenes of urban squalor of the late 1930s. He had begun to depict calm, unpopulated views of Lisbon in the early 1930s, for example *Side View of the Castle* (1935; Lisbon, Mus. Cidade), and from the early 1940s concentrated almost exclusively on this theme. The compositions became increasingly crisp and planar and the piling up of volumes and compression of space increasingly stylized, especially after he began to paint from memory in 1949. The tonalities of Botelho's paintings remained consistently pale, as in *Lisbon* (1969; Lisbon, Mus. Gulbenkian). For a number of years after the mid-1950s some of his works approached lyrical abstraction, without, however, abandoning the structure and rhythms of the cityscape.

BIBLIOGRAPHY

A. Quadros: *Carlos Botelho* (Lisbon, [1963])

J.-A. França: *A arte em Portugal no século XX* [Art in Portugal in the 20th century] (Lisbon, 1974, rev. 1985)

RUTH ROSENGARTEN

Botener, William. *See* WORCESTRE, WILLIAM.

Boterenbrood, Jan (*b* Nieuwe Amstel, 1886; *d* Amsterdam, 1932). Dutch architect. After attending technical school he worked in several architectural offices, including those of J. C. van Epen in Hilversum and Baanders Bros in Amsterdam. The latter were influential propagators of the principles of the Amsterdam school; Michel de Klerk had begun working there in 1911. Around 1920 a new group appeared, the 'second generation' of Amsterdam school architects, which included Jan Boterenbrood. They did not develop the original Expressionist style of the school further but simply interpreted the existing language of forms in a personal way. An important example of this style by Boterenbrood was the Huize Lydia (1925–7), Amsterdam, a refuge for Roman Catholic women and girls. The building is a work of fantasy, with elements indirectly adapted from the work of de Klerk, for example the tower and windows, which are in the shape of a parabola. More interesting and original was his competition design (1920) for a group of stepped buildings for the city of Sliedrecht. Although this particular project was not realized, he did build a number of other blocks in Amsterdam, for example the flats (1928–9) at the corner of Apollolaan and Bachstraat.

BIBLIOGRAPHY

G. Fanelli: *Architettura moderna* (1968)

Amsterdamse school, 1910–1930 (exh. cat. by A. Venema and others, Amsterdam, Stedel. Mus., 1975), pp. 60–61

HELEN BOTERENBROOD

Botero, Fernando (*b* Medellín, 19 April 1932). Colombian painter and sculptor. After attending a Jesuit school in Medellín he was sent to a school for matadors in 1944 for two years. He first exhibited in 1948 in Medellín with other artists from the region and provided illustrations for the Sunday supplement of the daily paper *El Colombiano* at this time. His discovery of the works of Diego Rivera, David Alfaro Siqueiros and José Clemente Orozco inspired paintings such as *Woman Crying* (1949; artist's priv. col., see 1979 exh. cat., p. 25). After studying at the San José high school in Marinilla, near Medellín, from 1949 to 1950 and then working as a set designer, he moved to Bogotá in 1951. A few months after his arrival he had his first one-man show there at the Galería Leo Matiz in 1951, at which time he was working under the influence of Gauguin and Picasso's work of the 'blue' and 'rose' periods. In 1952 Botero travelled with a group of artists to Barcelona, where he stayed briefly before moving to Madrid. From 1952 to 1953 he studied at the Academia de San Ferdinando in Madrid, although he was more interested in the paintings by Goya and Velázquez in the Prado. In 1953 he moved to Paris, where he lost his earlier fascination with the modern French masters and spent most of his time in the Louvre. He then travelled to Florence where he stayed from 1953 to 1954 studying the works of Renaissance masters such as Giotto, Uccello and Piero della Francesca.

Botero first visited the USA in 1957, buying a studio in New York in 1960. A number of works executed between 1959 and 1961, such as *Mona Lisa, Age Twelve* (1961; New York, MOMA), though figurative, showed the influence of Abstract Expressionism through the energetic handling of the paint. After a long period of development under the influence of various styles and artists, by about 1964 Botero had arrived at his mature style, characterized by the use of rotund figures and inflated forms, as in the *Presidential Family* (1967; New York, MOMA), in which he made allusion to the official portraits of Goya and Velázquez. Throughout his career Botero often made reference to past masters, sometimes to the point of caricature.

In 1973 Botero moved his studio from New York to Paris and began making sculptures. He concentrated exclusively on these between 1976 and 1977, extending his painting style and principles into three dimensions in works such as *Big Hand* (1976–7; Washington, DC, Hirshhorn), which was inspired by a detail of the *Victory of Samothrace* (Paris, Louvre). His paintings of the 1970s, such as the *House of Raquel Vega* (1975; Vienna, Mus. 20. Jhts), were a continuation of his mature style of the 1960s. In the 1980s he turned to subjects taken from bullfighting, for example in *Bull* (1987; priv. col., see 1987 exh. cat., pl. 13). One of his largest public sculptures in bronze, *Broadgate Venus* (London, Exchange Square), was unveiled in 1990.

BIBLIOGRAPHY
K. Gallwitz: *Fernando Botero* (London, 1976)
G. Arciniegas: *Fernando Botero* (New York, 1977)
Fernando Botero (exh. cat. by C. J. McCabe, Washington, DC, Hirshhorn, 1979)
C. Ratcliff: *Botero* (New York, 1980)
La Corrida: Fernando Botero (exh. cat. by M. Mafai, Milan, Castello Sforzesco, 1987)

Both. Dutch family of painters, draughtsmen and etchers, active also in Italy. The brothers (1) Andries Both and (2) Jan Both were the sons of Dirck Both (*d* 1664), a glass painter from Montfoort, who by 1603 had settled in Utrecht, where he apparently specialized in painting coats of arms on windows. Andries and Jan were in Italy between 1638 and 1641, when they shared a house on the Via Vittoria in the parish of S Lorenzo in Lucina. In 1641 they set off together for Holland, but on the way home Andries drowned in a canal in Venice, and Jan returned alone. The 17th-century biographer Joachim von Sandrart, followed by later writers, claimed that the brothers had collaborated on the greater part of the production. This view, however, has been largely revised by late 20th-century critics, and the two artists are better understood independently.

(1) Andries Both (*b* Utrecht, *c.* 1612; *d* Venice, 1641). After an apprenticeship in the workshop of Abraham Bloemart, where he is documented in 1624–5, Andries left Utrecht for Italy during the early 1630s. Among the works probably produced before his departure are a number of pen-and-ink landscape drawings such as the *Drawbridge near a Town Rampart* (Amsterdam, Rijksmus.). In 1633 he was at Rouen, as is confirmed by a signed, dated and inscribed drawing of *Four Peasants Eating and Drinking Outside* (Weimar, Schlossmus.). Towards the end of 1634 or early in 1635 he probably arrived in Rome, where he is documented from 1635 to 1641.

Andries is recorded in documents mainly as a collaborator painting the figures in the landscapes of his brother (2) Jan Both, but any collaboration between the two was probably limited to the exchange of drawings and suggestions. Andries in fact produced independent, low-life genre paintings, influenced by the tradition of Pieter Bruegel the elder, which was then undergoing a revival, most notably in the work of Adriaen Brouwer. Andries was indebted to Brouwer for the rustic peasant subjects of such early paintings as his *Interior of a Tavern* (Rome, Pal. Corsini), completed in Rouen, his signed and dated *Peasants in a Tavern* (1634; Utrecht, Cent. Mus.) and the *Card Players* (Amsterdam, Rijksmus.). The influence of northern subject-matter and figure styles persists in the *Quack Dentist* and the *Charlatan*, both dated 1634 (ex-Duke of Bedford priv. col., see Waddingham, figs 21–2). These two paintings were probably executed shortly after Andries's arrival in Rome, as is shown by their intensely luminous quality and their Italianate landscape backgrounds. There is a related preparatory drawing (Leiden, Rijksuniv., Prentenkab.) for the *Quack Dentist*; drawn with a broad-nib pen and brown ink and wash, it is typical of Andries's rather crude draughtsmanship. The composition was etched by Jan as representing *Feeling* in a series of the *Five Senses* (Hollstein, nos 11–15). Another significant element of Both's early development was the work of the artist known as the Pseudo-Van de Venne (or Van der Vinnen), who was probably active in the southern Netherlands in the 1620s. From him Both apparently derived a marked propensity for the caricature-like distortion of the faces and poses of his figures.

Andries's development as a genre painter, together with his close links in Rome from 1635 with Pieter van Laer (il Bamboccio), placed him in the group of artists known as the BAMBOCCIANTI and meant that he favoured the *bambocciata*, a variety of low-life painting then increasing in popularity through the late works of van Laer and the activities of other Bamboccianti such as Jan Miel and Michelangelo Cerquozzi. During the 1640s Andries helped define the thematic and formal repertory of the *bambocciata* tradition, which under his influence was enriched with subjects inspired by the lives of tramps and beggars. Both's interest in such subjects is evident in his drawing *Distribution of Soup to the Poor* (1636; Amsterdam, Rijksmus.) and in a painting of the same subject (Munich, Alte Pin.). In this painting, in its companion, *Strolling Musicians in a Courtyard* (Munich, Alte Pin.), and in two tavern scenes (both Feltre, Mus. Civ.) Both breathed new life into his thematic repertory as a northern artist by observing the often harsh reality of his Italian surroundings more objectively and toning down the element of caricature typical of his early works. These paintings and, more especially, his *Barber* (*c.* 1640; U. Göttingen Kstsamml.) are distinguished mainly by the accentuated and sober realism that characterizes the setting in which the scene unfolds. In this aspect Both followed the example set by van Laer in such works as his *Flagellants* (Munich, Alte Pin.) or his *Halt of the Hunters* (ex-G. Caretto priv. col., Turin; see Briganti, Trezzani and Laureati, fig. 1.17). Andries Both's interest in the urban landscape was undoubtedly encouraged through contact with his brother Jan, whose drawings from life executed in Rome show a similar desire to record his surroundings. In his turn, Andries probably provided drawings for the small figures in Jan's landscapes, perhaps even intervening directly in the series now in the Prado.

(2) Jan Both (*b* Utrecht, *c.* 1618; *d* Utrecht, Aug 1652). Brother of (1) Andries Both. He was one of the foremost painters among the second generation of DUTCH ITALIANATES. While working in Italy he specialized in genre scenes; however, on his return to the Netherlands he concentrated on wooded landscapes bathed in a golden light that illuminates the highly detailed foliage and trees. These realistic landscapes represent his most original contribution to Dutch painting and were much imitated by his contemporaries and by later artists.

1. LIFE AND WORK.

(i) Before 1641: early training and work in Rome. Jan trained in Utrecht between 1634 and 1637 with Gerrit van Honthorst, according to Sandrart; Burke has suggested that his early development as a landscape artist was inspired by the work of Carel de Hooch (*d* 1638), who was active in Utrecht during the 1630s and whose Italianate but realistically formulated landscapes presented an important alternative to the more traditional models of Cornelis van Poelenburch and Bartholomeus Breenbergh.

Sometime after 1637 Jan joined his brother Andries in Rome. Jan is documented there from 1638 to 1641, during which time he befriended Herman van Swanevelt and Claude Lorrain. He collaborated with Claude in 1638–9, and again in 1640–41, on two series of large landscapes (Madrid, Prado) commissioned for the Buen Retiro Palace in Madrid by Don Manuel de Moura, Marqués de Castel Rodrigo and ambassador of Philip IV. Both is credited with four canvases of vertical format from the series (2059,

2060, 2061 and 2066). Like Claude and van Swanevelt, Both arranged his landscapes along diagonal lines in order to achieve a greater feeling of depth. He unified the composition by means of a glowing, golden light, which was also inspired by Claude and was later to characterize his entire output. Both's canvases stand out from the others, however, by virtue of their greater attention to naturalistic details, which in Claude's paintings are depicted in a more abstract and idealized way. The figures of horsemen in the foreground of one work by Jan in the series, the *View of the Rotunda of the Villa Aldobrandini at Frascati* (2062), were probably painted by his brother Andries, a rare example of collaboration between the two brothers. Waddingham suggested that Jan and Andries also worked together on versions of the *Landscape near the Calcara with Morra Players* (Munich, Alte Pin.; Budapest, N. Mus.), both previously, and occasionally still, attributed to Pieter van Laer.

From his arrival in Rome, Jan Both was associated with the BAMBOCCIANTI, or followers of Pieter van Laer (il Bamboccio), who specialized in low-life scenes (*bambocciate*). Jan devoted himself to painting genre scenes with small figures, initially imitating his brother's style, as for example in *Festivity in front of the Spanish Embassy* (Stockholm U., Kstsaml.). This painting depicts a party organized by the Marqués de Castel Rodrigo in February 1637 and was probably executed shortly after that date, perhaps for the ambassador himself. Another work from the same period is the *Distribution of Soup to the Poor* (Arles, Mus. Réattu), which is closely linked, both in style and subject, to the *bambocciate* of Andries Both (to whom it was attributed by Burke). The pair of canvases *Market at Campo Vaccino* (Amsterdam, Rijksmus.) and *Morra Players beneath the Campidoglio* (Munich, Alte Pin.) are later in date but were still completed in Rome. In these works Jan's search for a strong sense of realism is expressed through his meticulous observation of light effects rather than in the small anecdotal scenes of Roman life. Another feature of these pendants, also inspired by Claude's example, is the juxtaposition of a scene in the cool light of morning with another bathed in the warm golden light of evening. Sandrart recorded that Both liked to portray different hours of the day. In addition to Both's paintings of *bambocciate*, he made drawings of similar subjects, such as *Beggars and a Roast-chestnut Vendor amid Roman Ruins* (Haarlem, Teylers Mus.), which can be dated to the early 1640s.

In another pair of pendants, the *View of the Ripa Grande* (Frankfurt am Main, Städel. Kstinst.) and the *View of the Calcara on the Tiber near the Ripa Grande* (London, N.G.; see fig. 1), both of which have a diagonal layout, the artist's interest in genre scenes yielded to his interest in the realistic representation of the urban landscape. These paintings are connected with drawings from life executed by Both during his stay in Rome, such as his *View of Ponte Rotto* (Frankfurt am Main, Städel. Kstinst.), a popular subject with the Dutch Italianates. By contrast, the location of his drawing *View of a Courtyard* (Leiden, Rijksuniv., Prentenkab.) cannot be precisely identified; its intensely realistic portrayal of the crumbling walls caught by a bright light herald the work of the later Dutch Italianate Thomas Wijck, who specialized in courtyard views.

1. Jan Both: *View of the Calcara on the Tiber near the Ripa Grande*, oil on panel, 421×550 mm, 1641–2 (London, National Gallery)

(ii) 1641 and after: the Netherlands. Jan probably returned to Utrecht in 1641, although the first record of his presence in the Netherlands is a drawing of a Dutch subject, *Wooded Landscape by a Stream* (Budapest, N. Mus.), dated 1643. He is documented with certainty in Utrecht in 1646 and 1649. After his return Jan Both completely abandoned low-life genre subjects and instead devoted himself to the realistic representation of Italianate landscapes. The lonely expanses of the Roman countryside and the paths that wind through the woods of the Apennines became the dominant themes of his work. None of Both's later paintings can be described as a view of an identifiable place, but all of them were based on studies and drawings brought back from Italy and convey an intense and convincing sense of realism, both in the clearly defined detail of the landscape and in the overall panoramic structure. The only dated work is *Landscape with Mercury and Argos* (1650; Schleissheim, Neues Schloss), completed in collaboration with Nicholas Knüpfer (*c.* 1603–?1660), who painted the figures. Burke has attempted to arrange Both's post-Italian works in chronological order on the basis of a comparison with the dated works by Herman Saftleven II that depend in part on Both's compositions; the latter can thus be dated as either contemporary or slightly earlier. Both's *Landscape with Travellers* (The Hague, Mauritshuis), which is still linked to the old Flemish landscape tradition of suggesting depth through the use of clearly defined layers of colour, dates from the early 1640s. So too does his *Wooded Landscape with River* (London, N.G.), in which, however, the different levels of the composition are linked together by a curving track, and the foreground is framed by trees. In *Landscape with Peasants on Muleback* (Montpellier, Mus. Fabre) the highly detailed vegetation in the foreground detracts from the overall coherence of the scene. A better integration between foreground and background was achieved by Both around the mid-1640s in two paintings of a *Rocky Landscape with Herdsman and Muleteers* (both London, N.G.; see fig. 2): in both works the composition is brought together by warm shades of green and brown and by the luminous atmosphere in which the individual details stand out against the light. Towards the end of his brief career the artist abandoned the sort of Italianate spatial structures that had often governed his compositions during the 1650s; in *Landscape with Travellers at a Ford* (Detroit, MI, Inst. A.), *Landscape with Riders* (Schwerin, Staatl. Mus.) and *Landscape with a Draughtsman* (Amsterdam, Rijksmus.) he composed broad sweeps of landscape that carry the eye in a variety of different directions. Both also practised etching and engraved a number of landscape compositions derived from his paintings, as well as the

2. Jan Both: *Rocky Landscape with Herdsman and Muleteers*, oil on canvas, 1.03×1.25 m, *c.* 1645 (London, National Gallery)

series of *Five Senses* based on drawings and paintings by his brother Andries.

2. COLLABORATION. On numerous occasions throughout his career Jan Both collaborated with other painters, the majority of whom specialized in figures and animals. Besides his brother Andries, Claude Lorrain and Nicholas Knüpfer, he worked with Cornelis van Poelenburch, Jan Baptist Weenix and Pieter Saenredam. With Knüpfer and Weenix he painted another *Landscape with Mercury and Argos* (*c.* 1650–51; Munich, Alte Pin.), the *Pursuit of Happiness* ('*Il contento*') (1651; Schwerin, Staatl. Mus.) and the *Seven Works of Mercy* (Kassel, Schloss Wilhelmshöhe); the figures that appear in these paintings are by Knüpfer, the animals by Weenix. Both's collaboration with van Poelenburch produced *Landscape with the Judgement of Paris* (London, N.G.). Unusually, however, Both provided the figures in Saenredam's *Interior of the Buurkerk in Utrecht* (1644; London, N.G.).

3. INFLUENCE AND POSTHUMOUS REPUTATION. The subject-matter and compositional formulae used by Jan Both in his landscapes were the main source of inspiration for the third generation of Dutch Italianates,

such as Willem de Heusch and Frederik de Moucheron, who during the second half of the 17th century repeated the Apennine scenes made popular by Both. His drawing style was closely copied by his pupil Jan Hackaert.

Like many other Italianate artists, Both was greatly admired by his contemporaries and by 18th-century writers and collectors but was completely neglected during the second half of the 19th century and the first half of the 20th, when native Dutch landscapes were preferred. The critical reassessment of Jan Both began with Waddingham's studies of the 1960s, which were followed by Burke's careful revision of the artist's pictorial oeuvre.

BIBLIOGRAPHY

Hollstein: *Dut. & Flem.*
C. de Bie: *Het gulden cabinet* (1661), pp. 156–8
J. von Sandrart: *Teutsche Academie* (1675–9); ed. A. R. Peltzer (1925), pp. 184–5
A. Houbraken: *De groote schouburgh* (1718–21), ii, p. 114
C. Hofstede de Groot: *Holländischen Maler* (1907–28), ix, pp. 418–517
L. de Bruyn: 'Het geboortjaar van Jan Both', *Oud-Holland*, lxvii (1952), pp. 110–12
M. R. Waddingham: 'Andries and Jan Both in France and Italy', *Paragone*, xv (1964), pp. 13–43
Nederlandse 17e eeuwse Italianiserende landschapschilders (exh. cat., ed. A. Blankert; Utrecht, Cent. Mus., 1965); rev. and trans. as *Dutch 17th-century Italianate Painters* (Soest, 1978), pp. 112–28

W. Stechow: *Dutch Landscape Painting of the Seventeenth Century* (London, 1966/*R* 1981), pp. 150–58

E. Haverkamp-Begemann: 'The Youthful Work of Andries Both: His Landscape Drawings', *Pr. Rev.*, v (1976), pp. 88–95

J. D. Burke: *Jan Both: Paintings, Drawings and Prints* (New York, 1976)

L. Salerno: *Pittori di paesaggio del seicento a Roma*, ii (Rome, 1979), pp. 424–37

L. Trezzani: 'Andries and Jan Both', *The Bambozzianti: Painters of Everyday Life in 17th-century Rome*, ed. G. Briganti, L. Trezzani and L. Laureati (Rome, 1983), pp. 194–221

A. C. Steland: 'Beobachtungen zu frühen Zeichnungen des Jan Both und zum Verhältnis zwischen Jan Both und Jan Asselijn in Rom vor 1641', *Niederdeutsche Beiträge zur Kunstgeschichte*, xxvii (1988), pp. 115–38, figs 1–26

LUDOVICA TREZZANI

Botkin. Russian family of collectors. The Botkin family was one of the most prominent in 19th-century Russia. Headed in Moscow by Pyotr Botkin (1781–1853), a tea merchant, the family included doctors, diplomats, scientists and artists. Of Pyotr's children, Vasily Botkin (1811–69) was a well-known literary and social critic, and Yekaterina Botkina was the mother of SERGEY SHCHUKIN, the famous collector of modern French art, while Dmitry Botkin (1829–89) and Mikhail Botkin (1839–1914) had a more direct influence on the development of Russian art. Dmitry, an admirer of Pierre Puvis de Chavannes, collected European paintings, assisted PAVEL TRET'YAKOV in his research into Russian art and donated many canvases to Tret'yakov's museum. In the 1870s and 1880s he served on the committee of the Moscow Arts Society and was president of the Moscow Society of Art Lovers (1877–88). Mikhail studied at the St Petersburg Academy of Art from 1856 and was awarded the title of 'history painter' in 1863; he was also an art historian, archaeologist and collector of Russian and European art. For many years he lived in Italy, eventually bringing back to St Petersburg many Renaissance works. In 1880 he published a biography of the Russian artist Aleksandr Ivanov, an artist whose work he collected and with whom he showed an affinity in his painting of New Testament themes. Although only a mediocre artist himself (he also painted portraits and genre scenes), as Director of the Museum of the Society for the Encouragement of the Arts and as a member of many committees he had a great influence in St Petersburg art institutions and societies (including the Academy and the Imperial Hermitage). Because of his conservative taste for classical form, towards the end of his life he came under increasing criticism in progressive circles.

WRITINGS

M. Botkin: *Aleksandr Andreyevich Ivanov: Yego zhizn' i perepiska, 1806–1858* [Aleksandr Andreyevich Ivanov: his life and correspondence, 1806–58] (St Petersburg, 1880)

A. Pyumin: 'Na ostrove vosnominaniy' [On an island of memories], *Nashe nasledie* (1991), no. 5, xxiii, pp. 146–54

JEREMY HOWARD

Botswana, Republic of [formerly Bechuanaland Protectorate]. Country in southern Africa bordered by Namibia to the west, Zimbabwe to the east and South Africa to the east and south. The capital is Gaborone. Part of the Kalahari Desert occupies two-thirds of the country. The Tswana peoples, who entered the area in the late 18th century and subjugated the indigenous San (Bushmen), make up 95% of the population. During the 19th century foreign influences included invasions by Zulus and Boers and contact with British Christian missionaries. The majority of the population (estimated at 1,300,000 in 1991) continues a pastoral way of life. The principal languages are Setswana and English. This entry covers the art produced in Botswana since colonial times. For art of the region in earlier periods, *see* AFRICA, §VII, 8; *see also* SAN.

Botswana's richest cultural heritage is San rock art, last produced in the first half of the 19th century at Tsodilo Hills (*see also* AFRICA, §VI, 15). In 1990 at D'Kar, between Ghanzi and Maun in the north-west, a group of Nharo San, including woman artist Cuinxae (Dada; *b* 1934), began painting on board and fabric using motifs that echo the art of their predecessors. Other traditional art forms that continue to be practised include pottery, particularly that produced by the Mbukushu in the northern Okavango region; basketwork of great variety made by the Yei of the same area; the wall decorations of the Tswana (especially the Kgatla sub-group) in the south and east; tapestry and other weavings produced by members of the Lentswe La Oodi Producers Cooperative Society, established at Oodi near Gaborone in 1973; wood-carvings produced by the Kalanga in the eastern region; and the ostrich eggshell decoration and beadwork of the San in the central and western Kalahari Desert.

In architecture, traditional styles of mud and thatch or reed housing are still built in the rural areas, while buildings in the urban centres follow contemporary international trends, using modern technology and materials. The visual arts in modern Botswana remain relatively undeveloped, primarily because the country has no national art school. Philip Segola (*b* 1948), perhaps one of the best known of late 20th-century Botswana painters, was one of the few to work in graphic media. His work synthesizes the mystique of ancient Botswana with the realities of modern life. Similarly, Mokwaledi Gontshwanetse (*b* 1965) depicted both traditional and modern Botswana life in his drawings and paintings. Bolaane Jack Mazebedi (*b* 1953) attempted to capture in the form and texture of his paintings the essence of Botswana's rock art, while Keeme Mosinyi (*b* 1953), working on canvas and paper, was influenced by traditional Botswana wall designs. While some Botswana artists, such as Neo Matome (*b* 1967), trained in Britain and the USA, many, such as Speedo Gaotlhalehwe (*b* 1952), were self-taught. Rantefe Mothebe (*b* 1940) began to paint after spending 21 years working in South African mines and drew much of his imagery from that experience. Even when Botswana artists, such as Victor Moremi (*b* 1941), were educated abroad, their imagery remained firmly rooted within Southern Africa. Thamae Setshogo (*b c.* 1970), who joined the Kuru Art Project in D'Kar in 1990, has also produced interesting work, mainly in acrylic or linocut (see fig.).

Apart from works made for sale to tourists, sculpture is not widely practised. Botswana has few well-known sculptors: David Manowe (*b* 1952) produced full-scale cement figures or animals, Masilonyane Radinoga (*b* 1956) worked primarily in wood and bone, while Moitshepi Modibela (*b* 1966) produced highly innovative wooden sculpture in a modern idiom.

By the early 1990s patronage came mostly from tourist and expatriate sources, although several corporations provided sponsorship or initiated collections of local art.

Thamae Setshogo: *Men Chasing Dogs*, linocut, 600×790 mm, 1991 (Gaborone, National Museum, Monuments and Art Gallery)

The Thapong International Artists' Workshop, whose founding chairperson was Veryan Edwards (*b* 1949), is held annually in Botswana, and has done much to promote the visual arts within the country and to encourage cultural interaction between local artists and those from neighbouring countries. In addition, exhibitions of contemporary art have been held at the National Museum, Monuments and Art Gallery (formerly National Museum and Art Gallery) since its opening in 1966 and at the new, purpose-built National Art Gallery (both Gaborone) since 1990. The National Museum, Monuments and Art Gallery also organizes a national art competition for schoolchildren and an annual *Artists in Botswana* exhibition. A national craft exhibition takes place each year. Exhibitions are also held at regional museums in Serowe, Mochudi, Molepolole and Francistown. Opening in 1985, the Molepolole College of Education began to play a leading role in establishing art education in Botswana.

BIBLIOGRAPHY
D. Lambrecht: 'Basketry in Ngamiland, Botswana', *Afr. A.*, i/3 (1968), pp. 28–30
M. L. Yoffe: 'Botswana Basketry', *Afr. A.*, xii/1 (1978), pp. 42–7
A. Larsson and V. Larsson: *Traditional Tswana Housing: A Study in Four Villages in Eastern Botswana* (Lund, 1984)
R. Levinsohn: *Art and Craft of Southern Africa* (Johannesburg, 1984)
T. Madondo: 'Reflections on Botswana's National Museum', *Botswana Rev.*, i/1 (1989), pp. 30–34, 37–9
A. Larsson: *Modern Houses for Modern Life: The Transformation of Housing in Botswana* (Lund, 1990)
E. Terry: 'Botswana Handicraft', *African Crafts*, ed. E. Melgin (Helsinki, 1990), pp. 44–8, 66–8
S. Williams: 'The Visual Arts of Botswana', *Art from the Frontline: Contemporary Art from Southern Africa* (exh. cat., Glasgow, A.G. & Mus.; Salford, Mus. & A.G.; Dublin, City Cent.; London, Commonwealth Inst.; 1990), pp. 36–43 [illustrates works by Speedo Gaotlhalehwe, Mokwaledi Gontshwanetse, Keeme Mosinyi and Philip Segola]
Art from the SADCC Region (exh. cat., Gaborone, N. Mus., Mnmts & A.G., 1990)
Artists in Botswana (exh. cats, Gaborone, N. Mus., Mnmts & A.G., 1990–)
Botswana Live (exh. cat., Gaborone, Botswana Soc., 1993)

S. R. P. WILLIAMS

Botta, Mario (*b* Mendrisio, Ticino, 1 April 1943). Swiss architect. He graduated in 1969 from the Istituto Universario di Architettura in Venice where his teachers included Carlo Scarpa and Ignazio Gardella. As early as 1965 he collaborated with Le Corbusier on the new Venice hospital project (unbuilt), and he gained practical experience in Le Corbusier's Paris office. In 1969 Botta met Louis I. Kahn and with him designed the exhibition on the Palazzo dei Congressi project in Venice. These experiences began his professional activity and left lasting impressions: he was able to assimilate the cultural influences in his first independent projects through a style permeated with confident quotations, yet not devoid of original touches.

The Casa Bianchi (1971–3), in Riva San Vitale, Ticino, is one of Botta's most eloquent works because of the complex relationship it established with its surroundings. The house, which is a tower, takes confident possession of the sloping terrain; the entrance is on the upper level, across a metal bridge, reversing the usual functional arrangement. It forms part of a series of one-family houses: in each, the primary volume is divided by an opening at the top corresponding to the axis of the stairs, making light the key instrument in the spatial organization of the houses' three habitable levels. This scheme governed the design of houses in Ticino at Pregassona (1979–80), Massagno (1980–81), Viganello (1980–81) and especially the Casa Rotonda (1981–2; see fig.) at Stabio, Ticino, a drum built of concrete blocks, with openings cut its entire height to admit light to the interior. This series constituted a form of experimentation with his own responses to the landscape, which developed the texture and colour of the materials, and which was most evident in the concave

Mario Botta: Casa Rotonda, Stabio, 1981–2

lower façade of the house (1983–4) at Morbio Superiore, Ticino.

The same approach was applied to larger buildings. The school (1972–7) at Morbio Inferiore, Ticino, represents a recapitulation of urban projects previously examined by the Ticinese school—Luigi Snozzi (*b* 1932), Tita Carloni (*b* 1931), Aurelio Galfetti (*b* 1936), Flora Ruchat (*b* 1937)—to which he belonged. The complex is differentiated from the indiscriminate urbanization surrounding it and is composed of a standard classroom repeated along a central arcade. Botta also used a variety of means to integrate visually a new building into a city. The composition of the Banque de l'Etat (1977–82) in Fribourg was resolved through the intersection of a central, cylindrical body by lateral wings aligned with surrounding buildings, picking up the rhythm of their traditional fenestration pattern. The Ransila I Building (1981–5), Lugano, however, reinforces the site's urban character by means of a deep hollowed volume and sophisticated treatment of the brick on its lateral façades. At the André Malraux Maison de la Culture (begun 1982) at Chambéry, Savoie, the articulation of the restored 19th-century barracks with Botta's new theatre block enabled the rotation of the barracks' original axis so as to re-align it with the road, creating an urban space that acknowledges the historic fabric of the city. In the Banca del Gottardo (1982–8), Lugano, materials are used to suggest the hierarchical organization of the façade: strips of pink stone and granite alternate on the four main blocks, which in turn alternate with the brise-soleil of the intervening courtyards. The cathedral of St Corbin at Evry near Paris, begun in 1991, is a brick cylindrical structure with a sloping transverse roof. Botta's design for the San Francisco Museum of Modern Art (1992–4), his first museum and the second-largest museum of modern art in the USA, incorporates a series of stepped spaces punctuated by a truncated section of a cylindrical skylight.

BIBLIOGRAPHY

E. Battisti and K. Frampton: *Mario Botta: Architetture e progetti negli anni settanta* (Milan, 1982)
P. Nicolin and F. Chaslin: *Mario Botta 1978–1982: Laboratoire d'architecture* (Milan, 1982)
R. Trevisiol, ed.: *Mario Botta: La Casa Rotonda* (Milan, 1982)
F. Dal Co, ed.: *Mario Botta: Architetture 1960–1985* (Milan, 1985)
Mario Botta (exh. cat. ed. S. Wrede; New York, MOMA, 1986)
'Mario Botta', *Archit. & Urb.*, ix (1986), pp. 100–07
R. Bevan: 'Focus on San Francisco', *A. Newspaper*, 44 (Jan 1995), p. 8

MERCEDES DAGUERRE

Bottalla, Giovanni Maria [il Raffaellino] (*b* Savona, 7 Feb 1613; *d* Milan, 1644). Italian painter. After receiving a literary education, he was sent by his father to Rome to study painting. There he copied the works of ancient and contemporary artists and came into contact with cardinals Francesco Barberini and Giulio Sacchetti. The latter, who nicknamed him Raffaellino, became his patron, thus allowing him the opportunity of studying with Pietro da Cortona. Bottalla, probably with Giovanni Francesco Romanelli, assisted Cortona with frescoes (1626–9) in the Villa Sacchetti (1625–9) at Castel Fusano, Rome. With the same artists he worked on the frescoed ceiling of the *salone* of the Palazzo Barberini in Rome, where he almost certainly painted the monochrome parts. His name appears on receipts in the Barberini archives between 1634 and 1639 (Lo Bianco). In 1641 and 1642 he painted two canvases for the Sacchetti family, the *Reconciliation of Jacob and Esau* and *Joseph Sold into Slavery by his Brothers* (both Rome, Pin. Capitolina). Another canvas, the *Banishment of Hagar and Ishmael* (Berlin, priv. col., see Migliorini, fig. 2), is perhaps from this Roman period (Migliorini). From Rome Bottalla went to Naples, where he produced oil paintings and frescoes (all untraced). Moving to Genoa, perhaps in the early 1640s, he painted a *Deucalion and Pyrrha* (Rio de Janeiro, Mus. N. B.A.), and possibly a *Martyrdom of St Sebastian* (Ravenna, Accad. B.A.), though Migliorini's attribution of this to Bottalla is not shared by Gavazza. In about 1643 Bottalla began to paint the monochrome frescoes with figures in the Palazzo Ayrolo Negrone, Genoa, but fatal illness prevented their completion, which was accomplished by Gioacchino Assereto in 1644.

BIBLIOGRAPHY

DBI [with bibliog.]
R. Soprani: *Vite* (1674); ed. C. G. Ratti (1768–9), pp. 300–303
M. Migliorini: 'Gio. Maria Bottalla: Un savonese alla scuola di Pietro da Cortona', *III Convegno storico savonese: arte a Savona nel seicento: Savona, 1978*, pp. 75–85
A. Lo Bianco: 'I disegni preparatori', *Il voltone di Pietro da Cortona in Palazzo Barberini*, ed. D. Bernini (Rome, 1983), pp. 53–90
E. Gavazza: 'Il momento della grande decorazione', *La pittura a Genova e in Liguria*, 2 vols (Genoa, 1971, rev. 1987), ii, pp. 185, 256
M. Newcome: 'La pittura in Liguria nel seicento', *La pittura in Italia: Il seicento* (Milan, 1989), pp. 16, 18, fig. 9

RITA DUGONI

Bottani, Giuseppe (*b* Cremona, 1717; *d* Mantua, 24 Dec 1784). Italian painter. He studied first in Florence under Antonio Puglieschi and Vincenzo Meucci (1694–1766). In 1735 he settled in Rome where, as a pupil of Agostino Masucci, he deepened his knowledge of the Antique and of the pictorial tradition of the 16th and 17th centuries. His paintings, executed in the classical Baroque style epitomized by Reni and Maratti, are characterized by their erudite composition, precise drawing and enamel-like colours. The large altarpiece of *St Paola Leaving for the Holy Land* (1745; Milan, Brera) reflects his study of the proto-Neo-classical style prevalent in Rome. He painted various religious works, mostly intended for churches in Pontremoli (Massa Carrara), from where his family derived. Among them are the *Madonna with Saints* (1756) and the *Assumption of the Virgin*, both in S Francesco, the *St Francis Xavier in Ecstasy* (signed and dated 1757) in S Niccolò and the *Ascension* (1764) in S Giacomo. The painting of the *Fair at Maccarese* (signed and dated 1755; Rome, Pal. Braschi) is typical of his landscape and genre scenes. In 1769 Bottani was appointed Director of the Accademia di Belle Arti in Mantua, where his activity provoked a classical trend in painting. During these years he executed a series of altarpieces for local churches, the designs for six high reliefs for a room in the Accademia and some paintings on secular themes. In his last period he painted *St Vincent Ferrer Preaching* (Mantua, Pal. Ducale) and the *Holy Family with SS Joseph, Zeno and Stephen* (1779; Mantua, S Apollonia), in both of which he demonstrates an extreme delicacy of execution.

BIBLIOGRAPHY

Bolaffi; *DBI*; Thieme–Becker
I. Faldi: 'Gli inizi del neoclassicismo in pittura nella prima metà del '700', *Nuove idee e nuova arte nel '700 italiano. Atti dei convegni lincei: Rome, 1977*, p. 507
S. Susinno: 'Gli scritti in memoria di Maria Cionini Visani ed un contributo a Giuseppe Bottani, pittore di storia', *Antol. B.A.*, ii (1978), pp. 308–12
Mantova nel settecento: Un ducato ai confini dell'impero (exh. cat., Mantua, Pal. Ragione, 1983), pp. 138–9, 165–73 [with full bibliog.]
S. Rudolph: *La pittura del '700 a Roma* (Milan, 1983), p. 753
A. M. Rybko: 'Bottani, Giuseppe', *La pittura in Italia: Il settecento*, ed. G. Briganti, ii (Milan, 1990), p. 637

ANA MARIA RYBKO

Bottari, Giovanni Gaetano (*b* Florence, 15 Jan 1689; *d* Rome, 4 June 1775). Italian historian, collector and writer. His special interests were the literature of Tuscany during the 14th and 15th centuries, medieval and contemporary art, sacred archaeology and ecclesiastical history. As a scholar of art he brought out (in 1730) a new edition of RAFFAELE BORGHINI's *Il riposo . . .* and wrote the *Dialoghi sopra le tre arti del disegno*, which was published some years later (Lucca, 1754). The artistic theories he expressed in these works owed something to L. A. Muratori and were influenced by a view of works of art as documents of their time. He exalted the classical traditions of Tuscan art in the early and high Renaissance, praised the classicism of the Carracci and bluntly opposed Mannerist and Baroque art. In the *Dialoghi* he demonstrated a practical interest, unusual for the period, in methods of restoring and conserving artefacts.

Bottari served the Corsini family from 1718, in Florence at first and then in Rome, where he was summoned in 1730 by Lorenzo Corsini, who had just been elected Pope as Clement XII. Bottari was given the chair of Ecclesiastical History at the Sapienza and the task of librarian to both the Pope and to his nephew, Cardinal Neri Corsini. The Palazzo Corsini, where Bottari lived, became a meeting-place for scholars and ecclesiastics, giving rise, in mid-century, to the famous group known as 'dell'Archetto', champions of Jansenism against the Jesuits.

For Clement XII Bottari built up one of the most celebrated private libraries of the time; it was particularly rich in historical, legal, ecclesiastical and artistic material and included a vast collection of prints and drawings (Rome, Bib. Accad. N. Lincei & Corsiniana and Ist. N. Graf.), which was cited in contemporary guidebooks as one of the best collections of graphic work in existence. He was especially interested in prints that reproduced works of art and thus provided a valuable study resource for artists and critics. He acquired the drawings mainly for Cardinal Corsini; he collected them together in volumes and marked the folios, neatly but not always reliably, with attributions. Bottari corresponded on books and the art market with learned Europeans, among them the collector Pierre-Jean Mariette in Paris, Giovan Pietro Zanotti and Luigi Crespi in Bologna and Francesco Maria Niccolò Gabburri and the archaeologist Antonio Francesco Gori in Florence. In Rome his artist friends, in particular the engravers Giuseppe Vasi, Giovanni Domenico Campiglia (*b* 1692) and Giovanni Battista Piranesi (of whose work he was especially fond), gave him the information and contacts that enabled him to advise Cardinal Corsini on the acquisition of a rich collection of pictures and antiques (Rome, Pal. Corsini).

In 1735 Bottari became Clement XII's private chaplain and the following year was given the task of editing a new edition of Antonio Bosio's *Roma sotterranea*, which came out in three volumes under the title *Sculture e pitture sagre estratte dai cimiteri di Roma* (Rome, 1737, 1747, 1754). His interest in ancient Christian monuments was informed by a nostalgia for the spiritual and moral purity of the early Christians. This concern for the documentary aspect of works of art inspired the compilation of the monumental four-volume *Il Museo Capitolino* (vols i and ii (1741) on sculpture; iii (1755) on portraits; and iv, published posthumously (1782) with a text by N. Foggini, on reliefs). This was the Capitolino's first catalogue, illustrated with engraved plates from drawings by Campiglia and complete with tabulated historical and iconographic commentary. In 1756 Bottari undertook his most significant work of art scholarship, the celebrated *Raccolta di lettere sulla pittura, scultura e architettura*, which came out in six volumes (Rome, 1757–68) and later included a seventh volume (1773), compiled by Luigi Crespi. It is a collection of letters on painting, sculpture and architecture from the 15th to the 18th century, culled from Roman archives, libraries and private collections, and was intended to provide useful material for art historians and artists' biographers. It also includes some highly informative letters from Bottari's contemporaries, and these provide a rich picture of cultural and artistic life in 18th-century Europe. Bottari's favourite themes are touched upon in the *Raccolta*: discussions on techniques of restoring, the opportunities for making such interventions, the problems of collecting, the keeping of records on picture sales, and theoretical disquisitions on topical issues. During these years Bottari also produced his edition in three volumes, with commentary, of Giorgio Vasari's *Vite* (Rome, 1759–60; see VASARI). This, the first modern edition, was prefaced by a lengthy introduction in which Bottari reaffirmed Florence's artistic primacy and urged respect for the proper identification and attribution of works of art.

WRITINGS

Dialoghi sopra le tre arti del disegno (Lucca, 1754)
Raccolta di lettere sulla pittura, scultura e architettura scritte da più celebri personaggi dei XV, XVI e XVII secoli (Rome, 1757–68); enlarged S. Ticozzi (Milan, 1822–5/*R* Olms, 1976) [contains 300 further letters written by contemp. figures]

BIBLIOGRAPHY

DBI [with bibliog.]
U. Procacci: 'Di uno scritto di G. Bottari sulla conservazione e il restauro delle opere d'arte', *Riv. A.*, xxx (1955), pp. 229–49
G. Previtali: 'Bottari, Maffei, Muratori e la riscoperta del medioevo artistico', *Paragone*, x/115 (1959), pp. 3–18
A. Silvagni: *Catalogo dei carteggi di G. G. Bottari e P. F. Foggini* (Rome, 1963)
S. Prosperi Valenti Rodinò: 'Le lettere del Mariette a G. G. Bottari nella Biblioteca Corsiniana', *Paragone*, xxix/339 (1978), pp. 35–62, 79–132
——: 'Il Fondo Corsini', *I grandi disegni italiani del Gabinetto nazionale delle stampe* (Milan, 1980), pp. 26–36
——: 'Le lettere di L. Crespi a G. G. Bottari nella Biblioteca Corsiniana', *Paragone*, xxxv/407 (1984), pp. 22–50

SIMONETTA PROSPERI VALENTI RODINÒ

Bottega [It.: 'shop']. Italian art or craft workshop or studio run by a master with assistants. The term is also applied by extension to the works of art produced by the assistants under the supervision of the master.

□

Böttger, Johann Friedrich (*b* Schleiz, 4 Feb 1682; *d* Dresden, 13 March 1719). German chemist and inventor. With the assistance of the scientist and mathematician Ehrenfried Walther von Tschirnhaus (1651–1708), he initiated experiments for the manufacture of gold from base metals (alchemy). This attempt attracted the attention of Frederick-Augustus I, Elector of Saxony, who obtained Böttger's services and kept him under virtual house arrest. The creation of gold did not succeed, but Böttger first developed a red stoneware called *Jaspis-porzellan* and then on 28 March 1709 discovered 'true' or hard-paste porcelain, which had until then only been produced in China and Japan. A factory was established in the Albrechtsburg in Meissen on 6 June 1710. There Böttger worked with David Köhler, Paul Wildenstein and Samuel Stöltzel to refine the new material and to create the necessary colours to decorate it. Initially the shapes were designed by the court goldsmith Johann Jacob Irminger (1635–1724), who in 1712 assumed the role of artistic director at the factory. Böttger's porcelain was creamy white and could be potted very thinly. Böttger did not see his invention reach its full potential, as very few satisfactory enamel colours had been created by the time of his death. His discovery, however, was to create a fashion for porcelain all over Germany for the next 60 years.

BIBLIOGRAPHY
E. Kramer: 'Ein Porträt J. F. Böttger', *Keramos*, xxx (1965), pp. 15–27
O. Walcha: *Meissener Porzellan* (Dresden, 1973; Eng. trans., London, 1981)

HUGO MORLEY-FLETCHER

Botti, Guglielmo (*b* Pisa, 9 Dec 1829; *d* Turin, ?after 1907). Italian restorer. He was a painter of stained-glass windows, completing those in Perugia Cathedral by 1868. Later he worked exclusively as a restorer, particularly of wall paintings. He achieved fame through his work, in 1856, on Benozzo Gozzoli's *Rape of Diana* in the Camposanto, Pisa, in which his aim was solely that of conservation. To this end he removed unsafe sections and simply replaced them securely on the wall, leaving repainted areas intentionally visible, in a conscious renunciation of the 'artistic' approach to restoration work. A trusted collaborator of Giovanni Battista Cavalcaselle, he worked on the frescoes in both the Upper Church of S Francesco, Assisi (1873), and also the Lower, particularly those by Ambrogio Lorenzetti (1874). He began restoration work in the Arena Chapel at Padua (1868–71) but was removed on the grounds of technical incompetence and replaced by Antonio Bertolli, who practised the same methods but was deemed to be more reliable. In 1873 Botti began a long career as curator of the Accademia in Venice and also as restorer of both pictures and frescoes, but his chaotic administration led to his dismissal in 1894. The new officials charged with guardianship of the city's artistic heritage (Adolfo Venturi, Giulio Cantalamessa) were more concerned with the appearance of works of art and exploited Botti's varnishing of Bartolomeo Vivarini's *St Augustine* (Venice, SS Giovanni e Paolo) to have him

transferred to Turin, where, as curator of the Museo Egizio, the last years of his life were spent in obscurity.

WRITINGS
Della conservazione delle pitture del Camposanto di Pisa (Pisa, 2/1864)

DBI

BIBLIOGRAPHY
A. Conti: *Storia del restauro e della conservazione delle opere d'arte* (Milan, 1973, 2/1988), pp. 250, 280–95, 353, 355–7
D. Levi: *Cavalcaselle: Il pioniere della conservazione dell'arte italiana* (Turin, 1988), pp. 337–9

ALESSANDRO CONTI

Botticelli, Sandro [Filipepi, Alessandro (di Mariano di Vanni)] (*b* Florence, 1444–5; *d* Florence, 17 May 1510). Italian painter and draughtsman. In his lifetime he was one of the most esteemed painters in Italy, enjoying the patronage of the leading families of Florence, in particular the Medici and their banking clients. He was summoned to take part in the decoration of the Sistine Chapel in Rome, was highly commended by diplomatic agents to Ludovico Sforza in Milan and Isabella d'Este in Mantua and also received enthusiastic praise from the famous mathematician Luca Pacioli and the humanist poet Ugolino Verino. By the time of his death, however, Botticelli's reputation was already waning. He was overshadowed first by the advent of what Vasari called the *maniera devota*, a new style by Perugino, Francesco Francia and the young Raphael, whose new and humanly affective sentiment, infused atmospheric effects and sweet colourism took Italy by storm; he was then eclipsed with the establishment immediately afterwards of the High Renaissance style, which Vasari called the 'modern manner', in the paintings of Michelangelo and the mature works of Raphael in the Vatican. From that time his name virtually disappeared until the reassessment of his reputation that gathered momentum in the 1890s (*see* §V below).

I. Life and work. II. Iconographical interpretation. III. Working methods and technique. IV. Character and personality. V. Posthumous reputation.

I. Life and work.

1. Training and early career, to *c.* 1478. 2. Years of maturity, *c.* 1478–90. 3. Late years, after 1490.

1. TRAINING AND EARLY CAREER, TO *c.* 1478. Botticelli (It.: 'a small wine cask'), a nickname taken from that of his elder brother, was the son of a tanner. He may briefly have trained as a goldsmith, but soon entered the studio in Florence of Fra Filippo Lippi, who taught him painting. He is mentioned as an independent master in 1470 (though he doubtless arrived at this status earlier). The same year he executed his first securely dated painting, the justly famous *Fortitude* (Florence, Uffizi; see fig. 1), completing the series of *Seven Virtues* commissioned from Piero Pollaiuolo for the Hall of the Mercanzia (the magistracy governing the Florentine guilds) in the Palazzo della Signoria, Florence. In his earliest works he was distinctly affected by Lippi's homespun view of visible creation, but already this was transformed into a more refined and abstracted vision of the world. In 1472 Botticelli joined the Compagnia di S Luca, the confraternity of Florentine painters, in the records of which Filippino Lippi, his late teacher's son, is named as his apprentice. On the feast of St Sebastian (20 January) in 1474 Botticelli's

1. Sandro Botticelli: *Fortitude*, tempera on panel, 1.67×0.87 m, 1470 (Florence, Galleria degli Uffizi)

St Sebastian (1473–4; Berlin, Gemäldegal.) was installed on a nave pillar in S Maria Maggiore, Florence. He was summoned to Pisa the same year to paint frescoes for the Camposanto, but instead worked for a time in the cathedral on a fresco of the *Assumption of the Virgin*, which he left incomplete. This no longer exists (destr. 1583), nor do the decorations that he made for the famous joust of Giuliano de' Medici (1453–78) in January 1475, including Giuliano's banner painted with an allegorical image of Minerva. Also lost is a fresco of the *Adoration of the Magi* painted in 1475 near the Porta della Catena of the Palazzo della Signoria, which was probably destroyed at the time of Vasari's 16th-century refurbishment. Three years later Botticelli painted over the Porta della Dogana a fresco of the Pazzi conspirators, who were hanged for the murder of Giuliano de' Medici, but this work was destroyed in 1494 when the Medici were expelled from Florence. Botticelli's portrait of *Giuliano de' Medici* (Washington, DC, N.G.A.) was apparently painted some time after the subject's murder.

2. YEARS OF MATURITY, *c.* 1478–90. More paintings are securely datable from the 1480s than from any other decade in Botticelli's career. In 1480 he painted a fresco of *St Augustine's Vision of the Death of St Jerome* for the church of the Ognissanti, Florence, as a pendant to Ghirlandaio's fresco of *St Jerome* of the same year (both *in situ*). The following year he painted a fresco of the *Annunciation* (Florence, Uffizi) for the Ospedale di S Martino alla Scala, Florence, and later in 1481 he was summoned to Rome by Pope Sixtus IV, together with Ghirlandaio and Cosimo Rosselli, to join Perugino in decorating the walls of the recently completed Sistine Chapel. Botticelli painted the *Temptations of Christ* on the right wall, devoted to scenes from the *Life of Christ*, and on the opposite wall, showing the *Life of Moses*, he painted *Moses and the Daughters of Jethro* and the *Punishment of Korah*; in addition he was responsible for a number of papal portraits in the register above. By the autumn of 1482 he was back in Florence: in October, with Perugino, Ghirlandaio and Pollaiuolo, he was commissioned to decorate a portion of the Sala dei Gigli in the Palazzo della Signoria, but only Ghirlandaio's *St Zenobius* was executed (*in situ*). In 1483 Botticelli and his studio painted four *spalliera* panels, depicting the *Story of Nastagio degli Onesti* (Madrid, Prado; London, Watney priv. col., see Lightbown, 1989, pl. 52) from Boccaccio's *Decameron* (v.8), commissioned on the occasion of the marriage that year of Giannozzo Pucci (1460–97) and Lucrezia di Piero Bini. The following year he painted frescoes in Lorenzo de' Medici's villa at Spedaletto, near Volterra, and in August 1485 he was paid for the altarpiece of the *Madonna with SS John the Baptist and John the Evangelist* (Berlin, Gemäldegal.) for the Bardi Chapel in S Spirito, Florence. In 1489 he was commissioned to paint an *Annunciation* (Florence, Uffizi) for the Guardi Chapel in the church of Cestello (later S Maria Maddalena dei Pazzi) in Florence, and between 1488 and 1490 he painted the *Coronation of the Virgin* for the goldsmiths' chapel, dedicated to St Eligius, in S Marco, Florence.

From about 1478 to 1490, the period of Botticelli's greatest activity and the time he painted his famous mythologies, his art increasingly combined the characteristic features of a courtly style (with antecedents ultimately deriving from Angevin Late Gothic art of the previous century) with qualities learnt from the study and analysis of Classical prototypes. The effect of this assimilation—a style simultaneously *nuovo* and *antico*—is first apparent in the *Primavera* (*c.* 1478; Florence, Uffizi; see fig. 2) and reached a highpoint in the *Birth of Venus* (*c.* 1484; Florence, Uffizi; see fig. 3). It is also evident in such religious works as the Bardi altarpiece, the *Lamentation* (Munich, Alte Pin.) and the great tondi (both Florence, Uffizi), known as the *Madonna of the Magnificat* (*Virgin and Child with Five Angels*) and the *Madonna of the Pomegranate* (*Virgin and Child with Six Angels*; see fig. 4). It appears in Botticelli's supple contours and the contrapposto poses, graceful proportions and balanced, natural movements of his figures, which respond to an invisible yet palpable rule of harmonic number. These figures are also very much of the Florentine present, for example the characters in the *Primavera* and *Pallas and the Centaur* (Florence, Uffizi), as well as those in the earlier *Adoration*

2. Sandro Botticelli: *Primavera*, tempera on panel, 2.03×3.14 m, *c.* 1478 (Florence, Galleria degli Uffizi)

3. Sandro Botticelli: *Birth of Venus*, tempera on canvas, 1.72×2.78 m, *c.* 1484 (Florence, Galleria degli Uffizi)

4. Sandro Botticelli: *Madonna of the Pomegranate*, tempera on panel, diam. 1.43 m, *c.* 1478–90 (Florence, Galleria degli Uffizi)

of the Magi (1475–6; Florence, Uffizi) painted for the Lama Chapel in S Maria Novella, Florence, all appearing in the elaborate contemporary courtly and festival costumes worn in the religious and civic celebrations attending the feasts of St John the Baptist (one of the patron saints of Florence) and the Epiphany, or the jousts and tournaments ordained to celebrate the signing of peace treaties. Botticelli's paintings of the Virgin similarly approximate to a quasi-courtly ideal of antique grace clothed in the garments of the Florentine present.

3. LATE YEARS, AFTER 1490. The frescoes from the Villa Lemmi, near Florence, showing a *Youth Presented to the Liberal Arts* and a *Young Lady with Venus and the Graces* (both Paris, Louvre), were almost certainly done in 1491, the date of the second marriage of Lorenzo Tornabuoni, who owned the villa. Otherwise, the only securely dated picture from the last two decades of Botticelli's life is the *Mystic Nativity* (London, N.G.; see fig. 5), which the artist signed 'at the end of the year 1500', that is, according to the Gregorian calendar, early in 1501. Botticelli's production doubtless declined markedly in the last 15 years of his life, perhaps partly owing (as Vasari suggested) to his undertaking the immensely ambitious project of illustrating Dante's *Divine Comedy* in a luxurious illuminated manuscript for Lorenzo the Magnificent's cousin and former ward, Lorenzo di Pierfrancesco de' Medici, which was never completed.

However, there is a deeper crisis of style and expression discernible in Botticelli's later works, beginning with the *Calumny of Apelles* (1490s; Florence, Uffizi (*see* HISTORY PAINTING, fig. 1)) and reaching a peak in such paintings as the *Mystic Nativity*, the *Mystic Crucifixion* (Cambridge, MA, Fogg), the *spalliera* panels with the *Story of Virginia*

(Bergamo, Gal. Accad. Carrara) and the *Story of Lucretia* (Boston, MA, Isabella Stewart Gardner Mus.) and the four panels of the *Life and Miracles of St Zenobius* (London, N.G.; New York, Met.; and Dresden, Gemäldegal. Alte Meister). In such works Botticelli increasingly rejected the courtly, ornamented style of his early maturity in favour of a retrospective appeal to the simplicity and affective directness of an earlier generation of painters, who had been masters of an apparently unforced moral and religious sentiment. (From the time of the Counter-Reformation to the 19th century this *maniera devota* was nostalgically understood as a characteristic of the 'Primitives', that is the painters working before Raphael who were untouched by the sophistication and aesthetic selfconsciousness that first arose with the dawn of the High Renaissance.) Botticelli's extraordinary mastery of drawing and elastic contour became progressively simplified and economized, occasionally producing even a crudeness of effect; his colours, notably his greens, yellows and reds, became brighter and purer in hue; and the action of his profoundly felt dramas was staged in an abstract and otherworldly environment that is the imaginative counterpart to the simple backdrops designed for a mystery play. There is no artistic ornament conceived for its own sake, and all is calculated to enhance a single narrative and emotional effect.

In the light of the rapid development that occurred in Florentine painting during the last two decades of Botticelli's life, the retrospection of his late works is the more astounding and poignant, especially given the critical role played by his own earlier work in helping to form the new style then reaching its first perfection in the art of Leonardo da Vinci and Michelangelo. Both knew the older master, and Michelangelo's methods and techniques of painting as exemplified in the Doni Tondo (*Holy Family*, *c.* 1503; Florence, Uffizi) are indeed unthinkable without the direct precedent of works such as Botticelli's *Coronation of the Virgin* for S Marco. Botticelli lived to see the achievement of Leonardo's unfinished *Adoration of the Magi* (1481; Florence, Uffizi) and Michelangelo's *David* (1504; Florence, Accad.), as well as the titanic competition of 1504 between the two in their battle-pieces for the Sala dei Cinquecento in the Palazzo della Signoria. By then his own art, by an effort of will, had abandoned a present he had helped to shape for the nostalgic values of an increasingly remote past—especially telling in this respect is the contrast of Leonardo's *Adoration of the Magi* with Botticelli's equally ambitious response in the preparation of a panel of the same subject (Florence, Uffizi), initiated some time after 1500 and also never completed. As Vasari said, Botticelli must have seemed a disappointed and sad relic of a bygone age.

II. Iconographical interpretation.

1. Mythological and allegorical works. 2. Religious works.

1. MYTHOLOGICAL AND ALLEGORICAL WORKS. In many respects Botticelli's art represents the maturation of the humanist conception of painting set forth in Alberti's *De pictura* (1436). (Alberti played a formative role in Lorenzo de' Medici's thinking about the arts, and his *De architectura* was first published, posthumously, in 1485

5. Sandro Botticelli: *Mystic Nativity*, tempera on canvas, 1085×749 mm, 1501 (London, National Gallery)

under Lorenzo's patronage, with a dedication by the humanist and poet Angelo Poliziano.) Botticelli, in such works as the *Primavera* and *Birth of Venus*, brought together the expressive content and forms of painting with those of the humanist poetic culture sponsored by Lorenzo, himself one of the most important vernacular poets of the century. Lorenzo's cultural programme was based on an attempt to raise contemporary forms of expression to the level of the legacy of the ancients, through both critical and historical study and the artistic emulation of ancient and Tuscan models; he also intended the arts to be seen and heard to speak a perfect Latin in the vernacular tongue, a perfect Tuscan in the Latin. Botticelli's paintings of ancient myth, called poetic fable in the Renaissance, were unprecedented in conception and hence, like Poliziano's *Stanze. . .per la giostra di Giuliano de' Medici* (begun 1476, uncompleted) and Lorenzo's *Comento* to his own sonnets, to which they have often been compared, are of prime importance in understanding Renaissance culture at one of its most fertile turning-points. They directly exemplify Alberti's concept of poetic *inventio* in painting, an activity of the painter Alberti defined as not analogous to but identical with poetic thinking. As examples of *inventio*, Alberti cited Lucian of Samosata's description of the Calumny of Apelles and Seneca's description of the Three Graces, the first of which was adapted by Botticelli for his own painting of the *Calumny of Apelles* and the second of which helped motivate the figures of the Graces in the *Primavera* (*see also* EKPHRASIS).

(i) The 'Primavera'. (ii) The 'Birth of Venus'. (iii) 'Mars and Venus'. (iv) The 'Calumny of Apelles'.

(i) The 'Primavera'. The *Primavera* is the most important of all Botticelli's poetic inventions, not only as a supreme work of art and the earliest and most ambitious of them, but also for historiographic reasons. The quality of writing devoted to it since Warburg's initial study (1893) has ensured it a fundamental role in developing conceptions of the Renaissance. Warburg understood it in the context of the humanist revival and imitation of ancient poetry and also drew attention to parallels in sensibility and detail between Botticelli's imagery and contemporary vernacular poetry of love, especially Poliziano's *Stanze*. Since this poem mythologizes a contemporary event, the joust won by Lorenzo's brother Giuliano in 1475, the painting has also been considered a manifestation of the quasi-chivalric civic rituals celebrated in such tournaments, which were held to celebrate the conclusion of peace treaties. With the revival of interest in the social context of Renaissance art, it has been suggested that the *Primavera* was painted at the time of a Medici wedding to decorate the house of the couple, a hypothesis conceived in reaction to the dominant interpretation of the previous scholarly generation, which held that Botticelli's imagery expresses the Neo-Platonic philosophy of love as expounded by Marsilio Ficino. Though different interpretations vary in detail and emphasis, they nevertheless have a great deal in common: that the theme of the painting is by definition Love, denoted by Venus; and that the *Primavera* is a prime manifestation of the culture sponsored by Lorenzo de' Medici, the patron of both Poliziano and Ficino. The primary dispute has been whether the *Primavera* expresses the values of high culture, Latinate and remote, or whether it responds to those of a more popular culture as expressed in the decoration of private houses, in the celebration of marriages and in civic festivals and tournaments.

On the one hand, there is no question of the unprecedented philological skill that contributed to Botticelli's invention for the *Primavera*, which does not illustrate an episode from ancient myth or story but in true Albertian style expresses a new poetic idea based on material gathered from several ancient witnesses, including Lucretius, Ovid, Horace, Seneca and Columella. Botticelli's genre is thus established as a form of *carmen rusticum* or farmer's song. His invention is of the unfolding of the first spring of the world, the archetype for all new springs to follow, beginning with the rough blowing of the West Wind over the bare earth, depicted as Zephyr's rape of the nymph Chloris, causing the earth to sprout forth, shown as the goddess Flora scattering the ground with flowers. The full ripeness of the season's regenerative fertility appears in Venus, the goddess of April, who stands in the centre attended by Cupid firing his flaming arrow, and spring draws to a close with the dance of the Three Graces and Mercury, the god of May, dispersing the last clouds in the sky with his caduceus. Mercury's identification with May is unique to the rustic calendar, organized according to the changing seasons of the farmer's year and followed before Julius Caesar's reform of the calendar based on calculation of the sun's movement. Mercury's appearance with the clothed and dancing Graces is also specifically archaic, as is the appearance of Venus, who is not nude and who assumes her primitive role as the *dea hortorum* (goddess of gardens). The invention is informed by genuine philological knowledge as well as a fine poetic instinct steeped in the study and imitation of ancient literary models, and this unique combination of qualities has led to the nearly universal consensus that it was devised by Poliziano.

On the other hand, despite the classically pure conception of the *Primavera*, Botticelli made no attempt to portray the gods in their ancient guises, showing them instead in contemporary vernacular costumes: Mercury wears a burnished sallet and carries an elaborately worked and jewelled parade falchion as his sword; the Graces are clad in buttoned chemises adorned with beautiful brooches, the one worn by the right-hand Grace suspended from a braided rope of false hair used as a decorative embellishment and to bind an elaborate coiffure set off by a spectacular hair ornament attached to a string of pearls; Venus is shown in a gown decorated with gold appliqué, over which she wears a distinctly old-fashioned cape, from the hem of which hangs a densely clustered row of pearls; and finally Flora appears wearing a painted dress with gold-embroidered sleeves, tied fashionably across the forearm. The ancient gods are shown, in other words, as contemporary Florentines and, moreover, are dressed in quasi-theatrical costumes designed for masquerades of the sort that Vasari wrote were invented by Lorenzo de' Medici for civic festivals and tournaments. Their vernacular character is also expressed in the normative conventions to which Botticelli turned in imagining the individual beauties of the several goddesses. These are not Classical but instead follow patterns specific to the vernacular convention, describing the beauty of the poet's lady from the top of her head to the tip of the toe, praising her golden hair, broad and serene brow, perfectly arched black eyebrows, serious eyes and smiling mouth set with pearl-like teeth, cheeks of privet flushed with rose, breasts set like apples on her slightly bowed chest and every limb perfectly articulated. Here again the *Primavera* finds its closest parallels in the work of Poliziano, whose *Stanze*, exquisitely Latinate in allusions and formal language, detail and imagery, had been written in the vernacular and within vernacular conventions at Lorenzo's behest.

Vernacular poetry is by definition poetry about the present and about love, the object of which—the poet's lady—represents a particular ideal, whether it is the erotic and sensual lady of the troubadours, the Christ-like beatitude of Dante's Beatrice, or the more purely poetic ideal celebrated in Laura by Petrarch. It is clear that the ideal portrayed in the *Primavera* is none of these, but is instead an idea of love invested in Venus, Venus in her fully recovered and understood Classical meaning as the animating spirit of regenerative life in nature and Venus, too, as the spirit animating the revival taking place in the Florentine present. As a concept of love, she finds her place in the great tradition of Italian love poetry. Yet as also a new concept defined by her very antiquity, a truly classic idea of love in the world completely assimilated within the vernacular tradition, Venus also redefines the present. While it is true that Ficino's Neo-Platonic concept of love is not the same as that invested in the poetic lady of the troubadours or in Petrarch's Laura, it is also true that in the Venus of the *Primavera*, as also for the lady described in Lorenzo de' Medici's *Comento*, the poetic and Petrarchan lady is for the first time conceived as a principle of natural, divine perfectibility attainable in this world. She may therefore be legitimately understood in the context of Ficino's Neo-Platonism, bringing philosophy within the embrace of art, though not as the unitary expression of a single culture, high or low. Rather, the *Primavera* in its fullness, like Poliziano's *Stanze*, embodies an art that is at its purest and most refined, while at the same time it draws from the wellspring of contemporary experience and the popular imagination as expressed in ballads and as enacted in the civic rituals of Florence.

(ii) The 'Birth of Venus'. As a new idea, the idea of love first given painted form in the *Primavera* naturally required a new style for its expression, the lineaments of which reached their full form in Botticelli's *Birth of Venus*. The subject is the same as in the *Primavera*, namely the springtime advent of Venus, with Zephyr carrying Chloris on the left, the roses generated by his warming breath falling to the earth, and Flora on the right, clad in her white dress painted with budding flowers and preparing to mantle the goddess with a fully flowered cloak. Here, however, Venus does not appear as the humble garden goddess she was for the primitive peoples but resplendently nude and in her Classical form, in fact so shown for the first time since antiquity. She is the fully conceived nature goddess of the Roman Empire, *Venus Genetrix* as hymned by Lucretius and as painted by Apelles in his famous *Venus Anadyomene* ('foam-born Venus'), which Ovid described as 'nuda Venus madidas exprimit imbre comas', and to which Botticelli alluded in the goddess's gesture of pressing her golden hair against her body. Though her individual features are still imagined in accordance with the normative Petrarchan conventions, namely dark and perfectly arched eyebrows, apple-like breasts and long golden tresses, these have been assimilated within a canon of beauty directly based on study of the ancient statue type of the *Venus pudica*, which gives a second meaning to Venus's gesture of modestly veiling her private parts. It is through such assimilation and refinement of the means of art, elevating the expressive potential of received traditions through the study and redeployment of ancient models, that Botticelli's art again finds its closest parallel with Poliziano's *Stanze*, at one and the same time *antico* and *nuovo*, perfectly Latin in a vernacular mode.

(iii) 'Mars and Venus'. Venus again makes her appearance, dressed as a Florentine nymph, in the *Mars and Venus* (*c.* 1485; London, N.G.; see fig. 6) but is here imagined in a darker guise. Though this painting too has been interpreted as possibly a marriage picture, or as a mildly erotic

6. Sandro Botticelli: *Mars and Venus*, egg tempera on panel, 692×1734 mm, *c.* 1485 (London, National Gallery)

picture of post-coital contentment, the image it presents has a more sinister character. The *satyriscus* (little satyr) blowing a conch is an image uniquely determined by two ancient scholia to Aratus's *Phaenomena*, published in Poliziano's *Miscellanea* (1489) and there interpreted as denoting panic terrors, empty phantasms inspiring fear (which is also the meaning of the *satyriscus* masking himself with Mars' helmet). *Phantasmata* are nightmare visions, and numerous ancient and Early Christian authorities, among them Augustine and Jerome, attested that satyrs and *satyrisci* were nightmare demons also known as *incubi*, which in their very nature especially provoked sexual terrors in the dreams of those bound in a state of sensual error and confusion. Mars in uneasy sleep is assailed by demons, who make lewd gestures towards Venus with their tongues and lift his jousting lance in order to poke a wasps' nest in the hollow of a tree against which his head rests and around which angry wasps are beginning to swarm. The idea of love here invested in Venus seems to be revealed, not in a positive celebration of the spirit animating natural life shown in the *Primavera* and *Birth of Venus* but as an empty sensual fantasy that disarms and torments the slumbering spirit of a once virile martial valour.

(iv) The 'Calumny of Apelles'. A similar pessimism can perhaps be discerned in Botticelli's *Calumny of Apelles*, a profoundly humanist work based on Lucian's rhetorical essay on Slander. The painting announces its theme of Slander by reference to a *koinos topos* (literary commonplace), Lucian's *ekphrasis* of an allegorical painting by Apelles in which Calumny, adorned by Treachery and Deceit, appears accusing Innocence before an ass-eared Judge whose heart is moved by her beauty and the blandishments of Ignorance and Suspicion, even as Repentance escorts Truth, too late, into the Judgement Hall. The genre of Botticelli's painting is determined by Lucian, whose essay is a virtuoso exercise in the rhetoric of display and whose subject is the power of rhetoric to make the heart love even that which is vile and putrid. The form given by Botticelli to the particular *topos* of Apelles' *Calumny* is calculated to provoke a further rhetorical response to the theme of Slander by setting the story in a Judgement Hall richly ornamented with sculptures that supply other *topoi* variously drawn from ancient history (the Justice of Trajan), biblical narrative (Judith and Holofernes), ancient myth (Apollo and Daphne) and vernacular story (Nastagio degli Onesti). Strictly speaking, there is no 'right' or 'wrong' iconographical reading of his painting in the narrow sense, save for its injunction to the viewer to blame the demon Calumny, tricked out in the seductive rhetorical colours of Treachery and Deceit, and to praise naked Truth who has no need of artful adornment. This may be done in general and in particular, with reference to legendary and historical examples on the one hand or to real people and current events on the other. Underlying the theme of Slander is a genuine preoccupation with the fictive powers of art to move the heart, not only to love of the truth, but also to love of falsity and evil.

2. RELIGIOUS WORKS. The same lineaments of poetic beauty that characterize the protagonists of the *Primavera* and the *Birth of Venus* are also evident in Botticelli's depictions of the Virgin, saints and angels in such religious works as the St Barnabas altarpiece, the Bardi altarpiece and the great tondi of the *Madonna of the Magnificat* and the *Madonna of the Pomegranate*. In all of them the Virgin appears blonde and with black eyebrows arched in a perfect bow, her flesh tones painted in the perfect ivory and vermilion colours of the Petrarchan lady. The paradise created by the presence of the lady, a convention of love poetry spectacularly made visible in the garden setting of the *Primavera*, finds its poignantly evocative counterpart in the Bardi altarpiece, which also embodies a new poetic invention on the religious theme of the Immaculate Conception, a subject then yet to be given its canonical formulation in the conventions of painting. The Virgin appears enthroned, with SS John the Baptist and John the Evangelist standing on either side, in a *hortus conclusus* (enclosed garden), a perfected earthly paradise ornamented with the plants that provide the biblical basis for her immaculacy: the rose of Jericho, the cedar of Lebanon, the olive and the lily. In such works too the Virgin is shown as a contemporary young Florentine woman, her chemise appearing in puffs at the sleeves, wearing luxurious transparent veils and her costume elaborately embroidered with gold at the hems.

The Dominican friar Girolamo Savonarola undoubtedly had such images in mind when he complained that the images in the churches of the Virgin, St Elizabeth and the Magdalene were painted like nymphs in the likenesses of the young women of Florence, thundering: 'You have made the Virgin appear dressed as a whore'. In his sermons he upbraided the young women of Florence for wearing such dress and castigated painters for representing them in sacred guise, urging everyone to burn their copies of the *Decameron* and all lascivious images. Savonarola's preaching in the 1490s had become highly apocalyptic in character, warning of the punishment to be visited on the city for its sins and of the impending end of the world, and his sermons increasingly adopted the eschatological methods of Joachim of Fiore who, in the 12th century, had been the first to interpret the book of the Apocalypse in the light of contemporary figures and events. Not long after executing the *Calumny of Apelles*, Botticelli painted the *Mystic Crucifixion*, in which a view of Florence appears sparkling in the sunlight, a kind of new Jerusalem cleansed after suffering God's wrath, the *flagellum Dei* (scourge of God) imagined as fiery torches raining through a dark storm cloud retreating from the city.

The imagery of the *Mystic Nativity* was motivated by the same interpretative schemata that Savonarola had revived. The painting bears a Greek inscription identifying its subject as the Second Coming of Christ as foretold in the Revelation of St John and announcing Christ's coming in the year 1500 during the tribulations then afflicting the Italian peninsula. The inscription reads:

> I, Alessandro, painted this picture at the end of the year 1500, in the troubles of Italy, in the half-time after the time, during the fulfilment of the 11th chapter of John, in the second woe of the Apocalypse, in the loosing of the devil for three and a half years. Afterward he shall be chained according to the

12th chapter and we shall see him [trodden down] as in this picture.

In the painting five devils are shown crushed in sliding crevasses opening up in the earth. In the foreground angels embrace three robed men crowned with the poet's bay, and two more angels bearing laurel branches stand to either side of the crib presenting five worshippers to the infant Christ, two of them clearly identifiable as shepherds and all of them similarly crowned with laurel. The three angels who kneel on the roof of the stable, dressed in red, white and green, are especially significant in the context of Joachimistic prophecy, as are the 12 angels bearing crowns and laurel branches, also dressed in red, white and green (the green a verdigris that has deteriorated to brown), who descend to earth in a golden circle of light. The colours are those traditionally assigned to Charity (red), Faith (white) and Hope (green), and it had been Joachim who identified the three realms, or stages, of the world with an Old Testament age of Hope, a New Testament age of Faith and a post-Apocalyptic age of Charity, or perfect Love, the future age initiated by the Second Coming of Christ. He named this as the age of the eternal Evangel (the book held by the central angel painted by Botticelli on the roof of the shed), when Hope and Faith would come together in perfect Charity, and he imagined that with the Second Coming of Christ and the expulsion of the devil from the world heaven would descend to earth and join with it, and men and angels would live together for a thousand years in a state of Christian love, until the end of the world in the day of the Last Judgement.

The Savonarolan image of the Second Coming painted in the *Mystic Nativity* is at the same time humanistically determined, as the wording of the inscription in Greek makes clear. The 12 angels bearing laurel branches and 12 crowns (an allusion to the 12-gated city of the Revelation of John, the new Jerusalem with a gate for each of the 12 tribes of Israel) strongly resemble the Florentine nymphs of Botticelli's mythological pictures, and the men embraced by angels appear as poets crowned with Laurentian no less than Petrarchan laurel. The concept of the painting, in other words, is as much indebted to the Medicean poets and humanists formerly supported by Lorenzo the Magnificent, many of whom had become followers of Savonarola known as the Laurentians, as it is of the apocalyptic visions of the friar himself. An idea of Love originally personified as Venus, expressing a yearning for a lost age of perfection once attained by the ancients, has changed into a new idea of Love figured in Charity, expressing a yearning for an as yet unattained age of perfection. That these two different ideas of Love find their common ground in art, in the perfection of humanity through poetry, is also consistent within the work of a painter whose last years were spent in reading and illustrating the poetic theology of Dante and who, in Vasari's view, wasted his time commenting on it. However that may be, the *Mystic Nativity* is Botticelli's most ambitious late painting, conceived on the basis of a Dantean assimilation of theology into poetry.

III. Working methods and technique.

Since the 1980s Botticelli's panel paintings have been the subject of considerable scientific examination, with the result that a great deal is known about his technique. Botticelli was highly skilled and employed the same methods consistently throughout his career, but though conservative in his approach, he was not unwilling to vary the usual procedures to adopt recent innovations. This is most notable in his use of *tempera grassa*, a medium that was new to Italy, in which the egg yolk (the usual binder for tempera) was modified by the addition of oil to make the paint more transparent.

In many respects, however, Botticelli followed the traditional methods that had been perfected in the previous century and were described by Cennino Cennini in his *Libro dell'arte* of the 1390s (*see* PANEL PAINTING, §§1 and 2, and TEMPERA, §1). Like most Italian panels of the period, the support was poplar coated with gesso. On this the contours of the figures were established by a careful underdrawing in charcoal, done freehand without a cartoon, and the architectural features were indicated by incised lines made with a stylus. He then laid in the foundation colours, which varied according to the area of the finished painting: white lead, or the unprimed gesso, provided a base for the flesh tones, carbon black or malachite for the trees and landscape. Then—and here he departed from Cennini—he made a second preparatory drawing in black ink and wash applied with a brush, resetting the contours and giving his figures body and weight through modelling the lights and shadows. Many pentiments occur at this stage, notably in the placement of the hands and feet, indicating the importance to Botticelli of gestural expressiveness and graceful movement. Though these underdrawings are clearly defined— indeed virtually complete monochromes—they do not extend to broad areas of sky and landscape background, a phenomenon that recalls Leonardo's criticism of Botticelli for being indifferent to such things (see M. Kemp and M. Walker, *Leonardo on Painting*, New Haven and London, 1989, pp. 201–2).

Botticelli's pigments were of the finest, including malachite, verdigris (copper green), ultramarine, cinnabar, red, white and yellow lead, red lake and carbon black. Generally they were applied in thin, opaque layers known as 'scumbles', but the reds and dark greens were frequently glazed. As the painting was built up, it gradually acquired a compact density, producing an exquisite, enamelled effect composed of infinite tonal gradations that create an extraordinary luminous subtlety, especially in areas representing reflected light. Unfortunately, many of his paintings have lost the fullness of their beauty with the passage of time, sometimes owing to abrasion or over-zealous restoration, sometimes to the tendency of colours to become more transparent or to change their nature over the years. Copper resinate, for example, which Botticelli employed extensively, turns from green to brown, resulting not only in an irreversible chromatic change but also in excessive contrast and loss of luministic gradation. An example appears in the green vestment worn by St Augustine in the S Marco *Coronation of the Virgin*, where the copper resinate glazed over malachite has permanently darkened, which flattens the voluminous effect of the garment. Another is in the *Primavera*, in which the bright white of the Graces' gowns is permanently out of balance with the darkened greenery behind.

Botticelli's technique is at its most refined in the rendering of the flesh tones, in which semi-transparent ochres, whites, cinnabars and red lakes are laid over one another in such minute brushstrokes as to render the gradations all but invisible. The faces of his women are exquisitely pale and porcelain-like, with the faintest pink blushes in the areas of the cheeks, nose and mouth, thus embodying the familiar Petrarchan metaphorical conventions. By contrast his infants and children are endowed with more intensely coloured, ruddier complexions made by cinnabar glazes and accents in red lake, while his men appear with darker flesh modelled from ochre applied over the black wash underdrawing, which sometimes remains visible and reinforces the more pronounced male bone structure and such features as the eye cavities. For gilding Botticelli often used finely powdered gold mixed with an adhesive and applied like any other colour. In the *Birth of Venus* and the *Madonna of the Magnificat*, for example, this gold paint, known as shell gold (*conchiglia*), was used to represent highlights in the hair, again rendering as literal the Petrarchan likening of the lady's tresses to spun gold. The decorative patterns of Venus's and Flora's costumes in the *Primavera* were also painted in shell gold, the gold being overpainted with red lake and black where the garments turn into the shadow. Similar effects appear throughout the whole of Botticelli's oeuvre. A further example of his illusionistic use of gold appears in the *Madonna of the Pomegranate*, in which the checked blanket beneath the infant Christ is rendered in malachite painted over gold leaf. Using a technique known as *sgraffito*, Botticelli then scratched through the green pigment to create the gold-checked pattern; in the areas of shadow the gold itself was scratched through to the underlying red bole.

As might be expected from the tensile line characterizing the figures in his paintings, Botticelli's drawings demonstrate that he was a superb draughtsman. Vasari indeed singled out Botticelli's drawings for the care and judgement the artist expended on them and said that because of their excellence they were greatly sought after by other artists. Undoubtedly many have perished because of frequent use by those artists, but exquisite examples survive (among them a famous study for a Pallas). These show Botticelli's refined skill with chalk, pen and bistre, and also tempera, and his pioneering use of paper tinted with roses, violets, yellows and greys, which establish a middle value for figures, modelled up with whites in the light and down with darker colours and washes into the shadows. The Dante illustrations are unique in being executed only in outline (as Botticelli intended to colour them). They comprise 92 parchment sheets (divided between Berlin and the Vatican) illustrated on one side and with the text of an entire canto written on the other by Niccolò Mangona, who worked as a scribe in Florence between 1482 and 1503. The drawings vary greatly in completion, and some were never begun. They were initially scratched into the parchment, then overdrawn with slate and ink preparatory to being filled in with coloured inks. Some of the ink tracing is done with the utmost care, some is less advanced (and in places scratched out with a pin), and execution of the colouring did not progress very far.

In common with other painters of the time, Botticelli worked with craftsmen in other media, for example providing designs for ecclesiastical vestments and furnishings (examples in Sibiu, Brukenthal Mus.; Milan, Mus. Poldi Pezzoli). He painted decorations for Florentine civic celebrations, the most famous of which was the banner (destr.) carried by Giuliano de' Medici in his famous joust of 1475, and Vasari reported that he devised a new, more permanent method using coloured strips of cloth for realizing such images. He also worked closely with masters in the new art of engraving, supplying drawings for Baccio Baldini in particular, but the precise nature of his participation in this popular form of image-making, though certainly extensive, has yet to be established. The problem is complicated by the fact that his engravers were able to reproduce his characteristic style only superficially, as seen, for example, in the engravings after Botticelli's designs for Cristoforo Landino's edition (1481) of Dante's *Divine Comedy*.

IV. Character and personality.

In the first edition of the *Vite* (1550), Vasari cast Botticelli's biography as a kind of morality play, describing him as a quick-witted, high-spirited and worldly youth who won success quickly, only to decline with the turn of Fortune's wheel into inactivity, poverty and religious despair in old age. Mentally hyperactive and impatient in school, he was withdrawn early and apprenticed, his talent immediately becoming apparent. He enjoyed patronage from the most important Florentine families, in particular the Vespucci and the Medici, and Vasari emphasized his closeness to Lorenzo the Magnificent. Botticelli never married, instead preferring the companionship of his family, friends and workshop, which was quite large. Vasari also stressed the artist's sharp wit, his love of clever sayings and practical jokes, describing him as a person of sophistication who greatly admired people knowledgeable about art, but who lost precious time commenting on Dante and drawing illustrations for the *Divine Comedy*. According to Vasari, in later years he fell victim to melancholy and became a follower of Savonarola. Vasari softened this portrait in the second edition of the *Vite* (1568), in which he deleted his moral judgement on Botticelli's decline and enriched his biography with additional factual and anecdotal detail, but the essential outline remains the same. Though his report of Botticelli's poverty and inactivity in the last 15 years of his life is to some degree exaggerated, the overall picture has not substantially altered.

Botticelli's links with the wider family of Lorenzo de' Medici were extensive, at least until Lorenzo's death in 1492 and the expulsion of the Medici two years later. There is reason to think that his first important commission, *Fortitude* (1470), was won through Lorenzo's influence, occasioning the breaking of the contract originally awarded to Pollaiuolo, and the *St Sebastian* (1473–4) may have been commissioned by Lorenzo himself. Botticelli is mentioned in Lorenzo's own comic poem *I beoni* ('The drinkers'; 1472–4). Poliziano, tutor to Lorenzo's son Piero, recorded three of Botticelli's jokes in his *Detti piacevoli* (1477–82). Two of them were repeated by the Anonimo Magliabecchiano (*c.* 1540), and the third is a quadruple play on words: 'Un bisticcio piacevole mi disse a questi dì Sandro di Botticello:—Questo vetro chi 'l votrà? Vo' tre, e io v'atrò!' ('The other day Sandro Botticelli told me a pleasing pun:—'Who'll empty this glass? You'll need three, and I'll help them!'). Poliziano has long been recognized as responsible for helping Botticelli with the inventions for some of his paintings of mythological subjects (*see* §III, 1 above). On a more extensive plane, the immersion in poetry that is implied by Vasari's statement that Botticelli 'commented on' Dante similarly finds expression in the inventions and interpretative decorum that inform his mythological paintings.

Botticelli's brother Simone is documented as a *piagnone*, or 'weeper', as Savonarola's followers were called, and Vasari was doubtless correct in reporting that Botticelli himself was 'extremely partisan to that sect'. The Greek inscription with which Botticelli signed and dated the *Mystic Nativity* clearly indicates a humanist point of departure and suggests that Botticelli, like the philosopher Giovanni Pico della Mirandola (1463–94) and many humanists formerly protected by Lorenzo de' Medici, had become moved by Savonarola's apocalyptic preaching after Lorenzo's death and in the face of the consequent turmoil that beset Florence and Italy.

V. Posthumous reputation.

Having been one of the most esteemed painters in Italy during his lifetime, Botticelli was soon eclipsed by the artists of the High Renaissance and long neglected thereafter. Despite occasional references to his art in such ultramontanist works as Alexis-François Rio's *De l'art chrétien* (1861–7), a fragmentary version of which was published in 1836, Botticelli's reputation did not enjoy a notable rise in critical esteem until the end of the 19th century; notwithstanding John Ruskin's moralistic—and ambiguous—treatment of him in the 1870s, it has been shown that, contrary to common supposition, neither the Nazarenes in Germany nor the Pre-Raphaelites in England were especially interested in him. Nevertheless, important paintings by Botticelli were gradually entering the great museums of Europe. The *St Sebastian* and the Bardi altarpiece, for example, went to Berlin in the 1820s and *Mars and Venus* to the National Gallery in London in the 1860s, the decade in which the *Primavera* and *Birth of Venus* were also given prominent public display for the first time in the Galleria dell'Accademia in Florence. The Villa Lemmi frescoes were acquired by the Louvre, Paris, in the 1870s and three of the four *Nastagio degli Onesti* panels by the Prado, Madrid, at the end of the century. Museum acquisition and display were slightly in advance of public and critical response and in an important way laid the foundations for it.

The true revival of interest in Botticelli was the product of gradually developing 19th-century interest in the literary and political culture in Florence at the time of Lorenzo the Magnificent, and the concomitant rise in appreciation for the arts contemporary with him. William Roscoe's *Life of Lorenzo de' Medici* (London, 1796, rev. Heidelberg, 2/1825–6), which published many of his poems and those of his humanist contemporaries, Giosué Carducci's preface to his edition (1863) of Poliziano's *Stanze*, and

numerous documentary and philological studies by Carducci's collaborator Isidoro del Lungo set high standards both of scholarship and sensibility. This sensibility found a response in Walter Pater's famous essay of 1873, and it was these works, and the literature to which they gave rise, that also set the tone for the earliest scholarly studies of Botticelli: in Germany with Warburg's dissertation (1893) on the *Primavera* and *Birth of Venus*, which inspired an entire school of art-historical research, and Ulmann's monograph (1893), the first devoted to him; and in the UK and USA with the Aesthetic Movement that stemmed from Pater and found its scholarly fruition in the work of Crowe (1886), Berenson (1896) and Horne (1908), whose monograph on Botticelli, dedicated to Pater, is perhaps the best that has ever been written on any Renaissance artist. The quality of Warburg's and Horne's work in particular ensured the centrality of Botticelli's achievement to subsequent evaluations of Renaissance art and culture. Investigation of the Neo-Platonic foundations to the Renaissance revival of antique forms, for example, especially as undertaken by Chastel, Wind and Panofsky, has in particular taken Botticelli's mythologies as a primary point of departure. Since the 1890s Botticelli's stature has been accorded the full critical and historical acknowledgement that is its due, and this will undoubtedly continue to be true in proportion as the stature of Renaissance culture in 15th-century Florence is itself acknowledged and valued.

BIBLIOGRAPHY

EARLY SOURCES

A. Poliziano: *Detti piacevoli* (MS., 1477–82); ed. T. Zanato (Rome, 1983)

A. Billi: *Il libro di Antonio Billi* (MS., *c.* 1481–1536; Florence, Bib. N.); ed. C. Frey (Berlin, 1892)

F. Albertini: *Memoriale di molte statue et picture sono nella inclyta ciptà di Florentia* (Florence, 1510); ed. O. Campa (Florence, 1932)

Il codice Magliabechiano (MS., *c.* 1540; Florence, Bib. N.); ed. C. Frey (Berlin, 1892)

G. Vasari: *Vite* (1550, rev. 2/1568); ed. G. Milanesi, iii (1878–85), pp. 309–331

V. Borghini: *Il riposo* (Florence, 1584)

F. Bocchi: *Le bellezze della città di Fiorenza* (Florence, 1591); rev. G. Cinelli (Florence, 1677)

GENERAL

J. A. Crowe and G. B. Cavalcaselle: *Storia della pittura italiana dal secolo II al secolo XVI* (Florence, 1894), vi, pp. 203–310

B. Berenson: *Florentine Painters of the Renaissance* (New York, 1896/R 1900, 1909)

R. van Marle: *Italian Schools*, xii (1931)

E. Wind: *Pagan Mysteries in the Renaissance* (London, 1958) [the most important and complete Neo-Platonic interpretation of Botticelli's mythological paintings]

A. Chastel: *Art et humanisme à Florence au temps de Laurent le Magnifique* (Paris, 1959, rev. 1982)

E. Panofsky: *Renaissance and Renascences in Western Art* (Stockholm, 1960/R New York, 1972)

L. D. Ettlinger: *The Sistine Chapel before Michelangelo: Religious Imagery and Papal Primacy* (Oxford, 1965)

R. Salvini and E. Camesasca: *La Cappella Sistina in Vaticano* (Milan, 1965)

M. Reeves: *The Influence of Prophecy in the Later Middle Ages: A Study in Joachimism* (Oxford, 1969)

D. Weinstein: *Savonarola and Florence: Prophecy and Patriotism in the Renaissance* (Princeton, 1970)

A. Garzelli: *Il ricamo nell'attività artistica di Pollaiuolo, Botticelli, e Bartolomeo di Giovanni* (Florence, 1973)

K. Langedijk: *The Portraits of the Medici, 15th–18th Centuries*, 3 vols (Florence, 1981–7)

S. Meltzoff: *Botticelli, Signorelli and Savonarola: Theologia, Poetica and Painting from Boccaccio to Poliziano* (Florence, 1987)

J.-M. Massing: *La Calomnie d'Apelle* (Strasbourg, 1990)

MONOGRAPHS

W. Pater: 'Sandro Botticelli', *Studies in the History of the Renaissance* (London, 1873); rev. as *The Renaissance: Studies in Art and Poetry* (London, 1877, rev. 4/1893); ed. D. L. Hill (Berkeley, 1980)

H. Ulmann: *Sandro Botticelli* (Munich, 1893)

A. Warburg: *Botticellis 'Geburt der Venus' und 'Frühling': Eine Untersuchung über die Vorstellungen von der Antike in der italienischen Frührenaissance* (Hamburg and Leipzig, 1893); repr. in *Gesammelte Schriften* (Leipzig and Berlin, 1932), pp. 1–60; It. trans. in *La rinascita del paganesimo antico* (Florence, 1966), pp. 1–58

H. P. Horne: *Alessandro Filipepi Commonly Called Sandro Botticelli, Painter of Florence* (London, 1908/R Princeton, 1980, rev. Florence, 1986) [still fundamental, with documents and original texts of early biographers; 1986 edn incorporates Horne's previously unpubd notes]

J. Mesnil: *Sandro Botticelli* (Paris, 1938)

R. Salvini: *Tutta la pittura del Botticelli* (Milan, 1958) [complete illus]

G. C. Argan: *Botticelli* (Geneva, 1967)

G. Mandel: *L'opera completa del Botticelli* (Milan, 1967) [complete illus]

R. Lightbown: *Sandro Botticelli*, 2 vols (London, 1978); rev. as *Sandro Botticelli: Life and Work* (London, 1989)

U. Baldini: *Botticelli* (Florence, 1988)

N. Pons: *Botticelli: Catalogo completo* (Milan, 1989) [complete illus]

C. Caneva: *Botticelli: Catalogo completo* (Florence, 1990) [complete illus]

SPECIALIST STUDIES

G. Poggi: 'La Giostra Medicea del 1475 e la "Pallade" del Botticelli', *L'Arte*, v (1902), pp. 71–7

J. Mesnil: 'Les Figures des Vertus de la Mercanzia: Piero del Pollaiuolo et Botticelli', *Misc. A.*, i (1903), pp. 43–6

——: 'Botticelli à Rome', *Riv. A.*, iii (1905), pp. 112–23

H. P. Horne: 'The *Last Communion of St Jerome* by Botticelli', *Bull. Met.*, x (1915), pp. 52–6, 72–5, 101–5

E. H. Gombrich: 'Botticelli's Mythologies: A Study in the Neoplatonic Symbolism of his Circle', *J. Warb. & Court. Inst.*, viii (1945), pp. 7–60; repr. in *Symbolic Images* (London, 1972), pp. 31–81

J. Pope-Hennessy: *Botticelli: The 'Nativity' in the National Gallery* (London, 1947)

P. Francastel: 'La Fête mythologique au Quattrocento: Expression littéraire et visualisation plastique', *Rev. Esthét.*, v (1952), pp. 376–410; repr. in *Oeuvres*, ii (Paris, 1965)

——: 'Un mito poetico y social del Quattrocento: La Primavera', *Torre*, v (1957), pp. 23–41; repr. in *Oeuvres*, ii (Paris, 1965)

M. Levey: 'Botticelli and Nineteenth-century England', *J. Warb. & Court. Inst.*, xxiii (1960), pp. 291–306

L. Donati: *Il Botticelli e le prime illustrazioni della Divina commedia* (Florence, 1962)

G. Walton: 'The Lucretia Panel in the Isabella Stewart Gardner Museum in Boston', *Essays in Honor of Walter Friedlaender* (New York, 1965), pp. 177–86

C. Dempsey: '*Mercurius Ver*: The Sources of Botticelli's *Primavera*', *J. Warb. & Court. Inst.*, xxxi (1968), pp. 251–73

W. Welliver: 'The Meaning and Purpose of Botticelli's *Court of Venus* and *Mars and Venus*', *A. Q.* [Detroit], xxxiii (1970), pp. 347–55

C. Dempsey: 'Botticelli's Three Graces', *J. Warb. & Court. Inst.*, xxxiv (1971), pp. 326–30

J. Shearman: 'The Collection of the Younger Branch of the Medici', *Burl. Mag.*, cxvii (1975), pp. 12–27

W. Smith: 'On the Original Location of the *Primavera*', *A. Bull.*, lvii (1975), pp. 31–40

K. Clark: *The Drawings by Botticelli for Dante's Divine Comedy, after the Originals in the Berlin Museums and the Vatican* (London, 1976)

R. Hatfield: *Botticelli's Uffizi 'Adoration': A Study in Pictorial Content* (Princeton, 1976)

M. Levi D'Ancona: *Botticelli's 'Primavera': A Botanical Interpretation Including Astrology, Alchemy and the Medici* (Florence, 1983)

U. Baldini and others: *La Primavera del Botticelli: Storia di un quadro e di un restauro* (Florence, 1984); Eng. trans. by M. Fitton as *Primavera: The Restoration of Botticelli's Masterpiece* (London, 1984)

E. Callmann: 'Botticelli's *Life of San Zenobius*', *A. Bull.*, lxvi (1984), pp. 492–5

P. Dreyer: 'Botticelli's Series of Engravings of "1481"', *Prt Q.*, i/2 (1984), pp. 111–15

——: *Dantes Divina Commedia mit den Illustrationen von Sandro Botticelli* (Zurich, 1986)

A. del Serra and others: '*La Nascita di Venere*' e '*l'Annunciazione*' del Botticelli restaurate, Florence, Uffizi, Studi e Ricerche, 4 (Florence, 1987)

R. Stapleford: 'Botticelli's *Portrait of a Young Man Holding a Trecento Medallion*', *Burl. Mag.*, cxxxix (1987), pp. 428–36

P. Dreyer: 'Raggio Sensale, Giuliano da Sangallo und Sandro Botticelli—Der Höllentrichter', *Jb. Berlin. Mus.*, xxix–xxx (1987–8), pp. 179–86

H. Bredekamp: *Botticelli 'Primavera': Florenz als Garten der Venus* (Frankfurt am Main, 1988)

S. Buske: *Sandro Botticelli, Weibliches Brustbildnis (Idealbildnis Simonetta Vespucci?)* (Frankfurt am Main, 1988)

'*L'Incoronazione della Vergine*' del Botticelli: Restauro e ricerche (exh. cat., ed. M. Ciatti; Florence, Uffizi, 1990)

C. Dempsey: *The Portrayal of Love: Botticelli's 'Primavera' and Florentine Humanist Culture at the Time of Lorenzo the Magnificent* (Princeton, 1992)

CHARLES DEMPSEY

Bötticher, Karl (Gottlieb Wilhelm) (*b* Nordhausen, 29 May 1806; *d* Berlin, 19 June 1889). German architect, theorist, teacher and writer. He entered the Berlin Bauakademie in 1827 and soon became a leading figure in the new Architekten-Verein zu Berlin (*see* BERLIN, §II, 3). Like many of his generation, he was much influenced by Karl Friedrich Schinkel and had a youthful fascination with the Gothic. His first book was a study of medieval timber architecture. He was particularly concerned with the relationship between style and construction and he soon began to apply this analysis to Greek architecture. The result was his monumental *Die Tektonik der Hellenen* (1843–51). The *Rundbogenstil* architect Heinrich Hübsch had already suggested that the forms of ancient Greek architecture were based on stone construction and not derived from timber antecedents. Bötticher expanded this insight into a vast system that explained all of Greek architecture in structural terms. For him, Greek architecture was rational building, its forms corresponding absolutely to the requirements of the stone used in its post and lintel construction. This constituted a major upheaval in the interpretation of Classical architecture, insisting that its elements were sanctioned neither by their historical pedigree nor by Platonic perfection of form, but rather by immutable physical and material laws. Bötticher briefly considered synthesizing Greek and Gothic structural principles to form a new style, but he quickly abandoned the idea, arguing that it would be superficial. In a prophetic 1846 address to the Berlin Architekten- und Ingenieur-Verein on the anniversary of Schinkel's birthday, he argued that both Greek and Gothic architecture had exhausted the tectonic possibilities of stone architecture. Instead, he argued that a new modern style required the application of new principles, and that these were already available with iron construction.

From 1839 Bötticher taught at the Bauakademie, where his strongly materialist view of architecture was particularly appropriate to the school's eclecticism. By looking at architecture according to abstract laws independent of specific styles, he made it possible to teach all styles with equanimity, rooting them in academic rules rather than artistic judgements. If the results were less poetic, they were nevertheless often more scholarly and historically faithful. Bötticher's theories were imbued with a deeply political conception of architecture and, like Schinkel, he was a devoted servant of the State, which viewed architecture as an instrument of Prussian policy. During the revolutions of 1848–9 he served loyally in the Prussian army and took part in the occupation of Baden. His loyalty was repaid with prestigious posts in the Prussian art establishment: in 1844 he was made a professor at the

Bauschule in Berlin and in 1868 was appointed director of the sculpture department of the city's Königliche Museen. In later years his interests turned more towards archaeology and in 1862 and 1877 he visited Greece. He retired in 1878 and spent the last decade of his life in scholarly research.

Bötticher himself built little, but he exerted a prodigious influence through numerous pupils, including such distinguished architects as Martin Gropius and Friedrich Adler. His principal achievement was to take Schinkel's synthetic classicism and to extend its life by anchoring it to a rigorous theory of constructive logic. Although his influence was initially limited to Prussia, he helped to ensure that the architecture of the Berlin Bauakademie, in terms of its political allegiance, its academic and materialistic character and its deeply archaeological nature, would contribute to the architectural style of imperial Germany.

WRITINGS

Die Holzarchitektur des Mittelalters (Berlin, 1835–42)
Die Tektonik der Hellenen (Potsdam, 1843–51, rev. 1881)
Das Prinzip der hellenischen und germanischen Bauweise hinsichtlich der Uebertragung in die Bauweise unserer Tage (Berlin, 1846)
Der Hypäthraltempel, auf Grund des Vitruvischen Zeugnisses gegen Prof. Dr L. Ross (Berlin, 1847)
Der Grab des Dionysus. An der Marmorbasis zu Dresden (Berlin, 1858)
Der Omphalos des Zeus zu Delphi (Berlin, 1859)
Bericht über die Untersuchungen auf der Akropolis im frühjahre 1862 (Berlin, 1863)
Dirke als Quelle und Heroine (Berlin, 1864)
Königliche Museen: Erklärendes Verzeichnis der Abgüsse antiker Werke (Berlin, 1871, 2/1872)
Der Zophorous am Parthenon hinsichtlich der Streitfrage über seinen Inhalt und dessen Beziehung auf dieses Gebäude (Berlin, 1875)
Die Thymele der Athena-Nike auf der Akropolis von Athen, in ihrem heutigen Zustande (Berlin, 1880)

BIBLIOGRAPHY

E. Jacobsthal: *Rückblicke auf die Baukünstlerischen Prinzipien Schinkels und Böttichers* (Berlin, 1890)
C. Lohde-Bötticher: *Aus dem Leben Karl Böttichers* (Gotha, 1890)
R. Streiter: *Karl Böttichers Tektonik der Hellenen: Als Aesthetische und Kunstgeschichtliche Theorie: Eine Kritik* (Hamburg, 1896)
E. Börsch-Supan: *Berliner Baukunst nach Schinkel* (Munich, 1977)
Berlin und die Antike (exh. cat., ed. W. Arenhövel; Berlin, Schloss Charlottenburg, 1979)

MICHAEL J. LEWIS

Botticini, Francesco [Francesco di Giovanni di Domenico] (*b* Florence, 1446–7; *d* Florence, 16 Jan 1498). Italian painter. His father, Giovanni di Domenico di Piero, was a painter of playing cards. On 22 October 1459 Botticini was appointed as a salaried assistant in Neri di Bicci's thriving workshop at the relatively late age of about 13. This arrangement meant that Botticini could complete his training while at the same time gaining experience of a higher level than that available to him in his father's more modest workshop. Although his contract was drawn up for one year, he left his master on 24 July 1460, after only nine months. The fact that he was the son of an artisan painter accounts for his being independent at so early an age and for his relatively brief apprenticeship. By 1469 he probably had his own workshop, since he is referred to in an arbitration document of that year as *dipintore*.

On 16 March 1471 Botticini joined the Compagnia dell'Arcangelo Raffaello, which at that time owed him for 'the painting of an angel Raphael'. This information provides concrete evidence for the attribution to Botticini of a panel with the *Three Archangels* (*c.* 1470; Florence, Uffizi; see fig.), which was painted for the company's altar in Santo Spirito. The frame was gilded by the painter Chimento di Piero on 13 March 1471.

The monumental *Tabernacle of the Sacrament* (Empoli, Mus. Dioc.) was commissioned for the high altar of the Collegiate church of Empoli in March 1484 by the Compagnia Sant'Andrea della Veste Bianca. The work was to have been completed on 15 August 1486, but the terms of the contract were not honoured and it was installed only in 1491, when a committee of artists including Domenico Ghirlandaio, Filippo di Giuliano, Neri di Bicci and Alesso Baldovinetti appraised it. However, even at this date, the altarpiece was not complete, and on 10 August 1504 Botticini's son Raffaello (1477–after 1520) was commissioned to finish the work according to the terms of the original project (Poggi, 1905; Paolucci, 1985). In the side compartments that frame the central compartment with ciborium (now empty) are St Andrew, patron saint of the church and the company, and St John the Baptist, who points to the space in the centre where the Eucharist was kept. The predella is divided into three compartments with the *Last Supper* in the centre and the stories of the *Martyrdom of St Andrew* and the *Martyrdom of St John the Baptist* on either side. A large and sumptuously decorated wooden frame, beautifully carved and gilded, unites the various painted compartments.

The *Tabernacle of the Sacrament* ably combines the most important pictorial innovations that were being made by the foremost Florentine painters of the time, among them Verrocchio, Filippino Lippi, Perugino and Botticelli, whose influence became increasingly apparent in Botticini's work. It also reveals an interest in the various currents of Flemish painting that were well represented in Florence, ranging from the intimate and luminous works of Hans Memling to the monumental qualities of Hugo van der Goes. Furthermore, the tabernacle shows close stylistic parallels with various works that Botticini painted for Empoli (Paolucci, 1985) and with other works that scholars, from Cavalcaselle and Milanesi onwards, have tentatively attributed to him. These include the *Tabernacle of St Sebastian* (*c.* 1475; Empoli, Mus. Dioc.), once in the Chapel of S Sebastiano in the Collegiate Church at Empoli, where it framed a statue of the saint by Antonio Rossellino, and the two altarpieces painted for Santo Spirito in Florence: the Uffizi *Three Archangels* and *St Monica and Augustinian Nuns* (*c.* 1470; *in situ*). These works are among Botticini's best; they show him to have been sensitive to works produced by the Pollaiuolo workshop as well as a discerning follower of Botticelli, whose elegant sophistication he translated into more literal and concrete terms.

The two panels of *St Monica* and *St Augustine* (both Florence, Accademia) are of a similar high quality, as is the *Virgin and Child with Saints* (1471; Paris, Jacquemart-André); the treatment of the figures in the last-mentioned, however, is more traditional and mechanical, contrasting greatly with the much freer handling of figures in the fervent *Virgin, St John the Baptist and Angels Adoring the Christ Child* (Modena, Gal. & Mus. Estense) and the *Crucifixion and Saints* (1475; ex-Berlin, Kaiser-Friedrich Mus.; destr.). He carried out various works for Matteo Palmieri, a government official, writer and discerning patron of the arts. These include the *Assumption of the*

Francesco Botticini: *Three Archangels*, tempera on panel, 1.35×1.54 m, *c.* 1470 (Florence, Galleria degli Uffizi)

Virgin (*c.* 1474–6; London, N.G.) with a portrait of Palmieri as donor and a panoramic view of Florence in the background, as well as some manuscript illuminations. Botticini also seems to have prepared embroidery designs (Garzelli, 1973).

The altarpiece of *St Jerome in Penitence, with Saints and Donors* (*c.* 1484–91; ex-Fiesole, S Girolamo, now London, N.G.) is of particular iconographical interest: the four saints and the kneeling donors are shown worshipping a picture of St Jerome, which is placed in the centre of the panel in a scalloped frame. In this picture within a picture St Jerome is on a larger scale than the donors and the musician angels. An imposing altarpiece of the *Virgin and Child Enthroned with Saints and Angels* (New York, Met.), already attributed to Botticini (Zeri, 1971), has been documented as his work (Roani Villani, 1988). It came from the altar of the Compagnia della Vergine in Fucecchio and dates from 1493. So far, no frescoes can be attributed to Botticini. He may have preferred to work on easel paintings and certainly won for himself a high degree of appreciation and success in that medium. His workshop

was one of the most important of its day in the production of decorative, artisan-style works.

BIBLIOGRAPHY

Colnaghi; *DBI*; Thieme–Becker

Neri di Bicci: *Le ricordanze, 1453–1475*, ed. B. Santi (Pisa, 1976), pp. 126–7, 333

G. Vasari: *Vite* (1550, rev. 2/1568), ed. G. Milanesi (1878–85), iv, pp. 245–7

G. B. Cavalcaselle and J. A. Crowe: *Storia della pittura in Italia dal secolo XII al secolo XVI*, 8 vols (Florence, 1875–98), vii, pp. 110–18

G. Milanesi: 'Documenti inediti', *Buonarroti*, xvii (1896), pp. 110, 137

G. Poggi: 'Della tavola di Francesco di Giovanni Botticini per la Compagnia di Sant'Andrea di Empoli', *Riv. A.*, iii (1905), pp. 258–64

P. Bacci: 'Una tavola sconosciuta con San Sebastiano di Francesco di Giovanni Botticini', *Boll. A.*, n.s. iv (1924–5), pp. 337–50

R. van Marle: *The Development of Italian Schools of Painting*, 19 vols (The Hague, 1931, 2/1970), xiii, pp. 390–427

M. Davies: *The Earlier Italian Schools*, London, N.G. cat. (London, 1951, 2/1961), pp. 118–27

B. Berenson: *Florentine School* (1963), p. 39

Arte in Valdelsa (exh. cat., ed. P. dal Poggetto; Certaldo, Pal. Pretorio, 1963), p. 60

L. Bellosi: 'Intorno ad Andrea del Castagno', *Paragone*, xviii/211 (1967), pp. 10–15

E. Fahy: 'Some Early Italian Pictures in the Gambier Parry Collection', *Burl. Mag.*, cix (1967), pp. 128–39

B. Berenson: *The Drawings of Florentine Painters*, 2 vols (Chicago, 1938, rev. 2/1969), i, p. 70; ii, p. 61

H. Friedman: 'Iconography of an Altarpiece by Botticini', *Bull. Met. Mus. A.*, xxviii (1969), pp. 1–17

F. Zeri and E. Gardner: *The Metropolitan Museum of Art, Italian Paintings: Florentine School* (New York, 1971), pp. 125–7

A. Garzelli: *Il ricamo nell'attività artistica di Pollaiuolo, Botticelli e Bartolomeo di Giovanni* (Florence, 1973), pp. 20–22

M. Boskovits: 'Una scheda e qualche suggerimento per un catalogo dei dipinti ai Tatti', *Ant. Viva*, xiv/2 (1975), pp. 9–21

M. Laclotte and E. Mognetti: *Avignon, Musée du Petit Palais: Peinture italienne* (Paris, 1976)

A. Padoa Rizzo: 'Per Francesco Botticini', *Ant. Viva*, xv/5 (1976), pp. 3–19

F. Petrucci: *Introduzione alla mostra fotografica di Antonio Rossellino* (Settignano, 1980), p. 40

A. Garzelli: *La miniatura fiorentina del quattrocento*, 2 vols (Florence, 1985), i, pp. 95–7

A. Paolucci: *Il Museo della Collegiata di Empoli* (Florence, 1985), pp. 114–24

A. Padoa Rizzo: 'Pittori e miniatori nella Firenze del quattrocento: In margine a un libro recente', *Ant. Viva*, xxv/5–6 (1986), pp. 5–15

R. Roani Villani: 'Relazione sulle pitture: Contributo alla conoscenza del patrimonio artistico della diocesi di S Miniato', *Erba d'Arno*, xxxii–xxxiii (1988), pp. 62–94

ANNA PADOA RIZZO

Bottini, George (Alfred) (*b* Paris, 1 Feb 1874; *d* Villejuif, nr Paris, 16 Dec 1907). French painter and printmaker. The son of an Italian hairdresser, Bottini always lived in the Montmartre area of Paris except for two years' military service (1895–7). He favoured the English fashions, bars and language (as in the titles of his pictures and the spelling of his first name). Apprenticed with Annibale Gatti (1828–1909) from 1889 to 1891, he studied at Fernand Cormon's studio and first showed at Edouard Kleinmann's gallery in 1894. From 1897 he showed large oil paintings at the Salon of the Société Nationale des Beaux-Arts. He collaborated on woodcuts with Harry van der Zee from 1896 in compositions influenced by Japanese prints, for example *Arrival at the Masked Ball* (1897; Paris, Bib. N., Cab. Est.). His woodcuts, lithographs and etchings sold quickly after publication by Edmond D. Sagot. Bottini illustrated for *Le Rire* in 1897, made several posters and from 1902 to 1904 did illustrations for books by Gustave Coquiot and Jean Lorrain. His short career ended in an asylum where he died from syphilis, which he had contracted at the age of 15.

His typical subject-matter was the female inhabitants of the Montmartre cafés, bars and brothels of the Belle Epoque. He had an elegant compositional style and a rich sense of colour. After a cloisonnist phase (1895–6), he developed a lighter touch and Art Nouveau manner in 1898. Between 1899 and 1904 he employed stronger colour and more strictly geometric forms. Linearism, strength of movement and clarity characterize his output until 1905. After 1906 his draughtsmanship became weaker and the subjects shifted from café life to odalisques and actresses. He painted with mixtures of gouache and watercolour, plus tea, iodine and coffee, and ironed his pictures to give them a shiny surface. *Woman with a Parrot* (oil, 1905; Paris, Mus. d'Orsay) shows Edouard Manet's influence, but the style and subject-matter of Bottini's work have more in common with Henri de Toulouse-Lautrec. Large collections of his work are in the Musée du Petit Palais, Geneva, and the Bibliothèque Nationale, Paris.

BIBLIOGRAPHY
George Bottini: Painter of Montmartre (exh. cat. by E. C. Southard, Oxford, OH, Miami U., A. Mus., 1984)

EDNA CARTER SOUTHARD

Bottschild, Samuel (*b* Sangerhausen, 30 July 1641; *d* Dresden, 29 May 1706). German painter, draughtsman, graphic artist and writer on art. He was a son and pupil of Andreas Bottschild II (*c.* 1590–1657), a painter and engraver, who decorated churches in Sangerhausen. Samuel had further training with his brother Johann Andreas Bottschild (*b* 1630; *d* after 1670), with whom he went to Saxony. In 1658–61 they worked jointly on gallery paintings of 19 scenes from the *Passion* (heavily restored 1852) in the Dorfkirche at Hohnstädt, near Leipzig. The decorations for the banqueting hall of Schloss Rötha, near Leipzig (*c.* 1668–70; destr.), were Bottschild's first complete programme of mythological themes. At Rötha he also completed two group portraits of the female and male lines of the Friesen family (Dresden, Inst. Dkmlpf.)

In 1673 Bottschild painted a *Presentation in the Temple* for Freiberg Cathedral. It was probably after this that he left for Italy with his cousin and pupil HEINRICH CHRISTOPH FEHLING. Primarily visiting Rome and Venice, he studied the Italian masters, copying from Titian, Veronese, the Carracci, Bernini, Pietro da Cortona and Simone Cantarini, among others, and drawing from works of antiquity and contemporary life. He returned to Dresden from Venice in 1676 and in 1677 was appointed chief court painter and personal servant to Elector John George II (*reg* 1656–80), whose portrait he painted in 1678 (Dresden, Hist. Mus.). Subsequently Bottschild produced imposing full-length portraits of *Elector John George III* (1682, 1685, 1693) and *Elector John George IV* (1692; Dresden, Hist. Mus.). He also painted the masters of the Leipzig guild of shopkeepers (1679–96; Leipzig, Mus. Bild. Kst.) and members of the Zinzendorf family (?after 1700; Herrnhut, Brüdergemeinde). In 1693 he donated an altarpiece of the *Raising of the Brazen Serpent* (destr.) to the Dreikönigskirche in Dresden, and in 1698 he supplied full-length paintings of *Christ and the Four Evangelists* (destr. 1943) for the redecoration of the Matthäikirche in Leipzig. Bottschild painted frescoes at the Starkisches Haus, Dresden (*c.* 1683; destr. 1760), and at Bobersen, near Riesa in Saxony (*c.* 1696; destr.). His three ceiling paintings (after 1693; destr. 1945) in the palace of the Grosser Garten in Dresden ranked among the outstanding works of High Baroque monumental painting in Saxony.

Bottschild's drawings (Berlin, Kupferstichkab.; Dresden, Kupferstichkab.; Leipzig, Graph. Samml. Mus. Bild. Kst; Weimar, Graph. Samml.; and Vienna, Albertina) include sketches for graphic works published as a series of 48 etchings, *Opera varia historia poetica* (1693) (Hollstein, nos 1–48), in collaboration with M. Bodenehr (1665–1748) and C. Heckel (*d* 1705). In his manuscript *Kurtzer Unterricht, Observationes und Reguln von der Mahlerey* (*c.* 1686; Copenhagen, Kon. Bib.) he set out the aesthetic ideals he upheld as director of the Malerakademie. In 1699 he was appointed inspector of the Elector's paintings and successfully increased and preserved the collection.

Bottschild's main achievement was in reinvigorating decorative wall painting in Saxony. Influenced by Italian traditions even before his Italian journey, he produced illusionistic paintings that seem to open up the ceiling space. His allegorical and mythological compositions are bordered by heavy stuccowork, the many figures often sharply isolated from each other and strongly animated, with a picturesque use of colour contrasts. However, the figures are not placed within an illusionistic architecture but float in an unstructured, cloudy space. In the works of his last decade, influences of French court art are apparent, and in his portraits the former solemnly decorative quality gave way to a muted, aristocratic aura, with a deepening of spiritual and emotive qualities. Despite this stylistic shift, he was increasingly eclipsed by French and Italian artists working at the Dresden court under Elector Frederick-Augustus I (*reg* 1694–1733).

BIBLIOGRAPHY

Hollstein: *Ger.*
E. Sigismund: 'Der Dresdener Oberhofmaler Samuel Bottschild', *Dresdn. Anz.*, xii, xiii (1903), pp. 61–3, 65–7
H. von Friesen-Rötha: 'Schloss Rötha und die Freiherren von Friesen', *Mitt. Landesver. Sächs. Heimatschutz*, xxx (1930), pp. 37–100
F. Löffler: 'Die Monumentalmalerei des Barock in Dresden', *Jb. Pfl. Kst.*, iv (1956), pp. 5–23
R. Josephson: *Ehrenstrahls målalära* [Ehrenstrahl's painting theory] (Stockholm, 1959), pp. 26–76
G. Adriani: *Deutsche Malerei im 17. Jahrhundert* (Cologne, 1977), pp. 94, 160, 178, 180
H. Prinz: 'Samuel Bottschild—das Taschenberg-Palais und das Starkische Haus', *Dresdn. Kstbl.* (1987), pp. 18–24

CHRISTIAN DITTRICH

Bouchard, Henri (*b* Dijon, 13 Dec 1875; *d* Paris, 30 Nov 1960). French sculptor. He studied at the Ecole des Beaux-Arts in Paris and in 1901 won the Prix de Rome. While working in Rome at the Académie Française from 1901 to 1905 he rejected the study of antiquity, preferring to choose his models from the countryside in order to demonstrate loyalty to his rural origins. On his return to Paris he continued to render the movements of people at work, as in *Grapepicker from Burgundy* (1909; Dijon, Mus. B.-A.), and he set himself the task of paying homage to important historical figures of his native region, such as *Claus Sluter* (1910; Dijon, Pal. Ducs), making use of his imagination if there was no surviving contemporary portrait to which he could refer.

Bouchard's early commissions for commemorative monuments included a memorial to a military airship disaster at Trévol, Ain, in 1910, in which he represented the dead heroes as sculpted figures stretched out on a sloping support, a compromise between the vertical figures of military monuments and the recumbent figures of tombs. About this time he did a commission for the city of Geneva of a monument in stone of Calvin and fellow reformers Beza and Farel. After World War I his career followed traditional lines: he exhibited regularly at the Société Nationale des Beaux-Arts, received the medal of honour in 1925 and became a professor at the Ecole des Beaux-Arts in Paris in 1929. He was named a member of the Institut de France in 1933 and Commandeur of the Légion d'honneur, produced portraits in the form both of sculptures and engraved medals, and from 1932 to 1934 carved the tympanum of the church of St Pierre de Chaillot, designed by Emile Bois. In 1937 Bouchard was a member of the jury at the Exposition Universelle in Paris

and produced for it a figure of *Apollo* that dominates the terrace of the Trocadéro. Bouchard was one of the leaders of the officially sanctioned figurative and commemorative sculpture prevalent in France in the early 20th century. Although virtually oblivious to modern life and art, it is perhaps because of its very traditionalism that Bouchard's work was later re-examined as bearing witness to the contradictions of the 1930s.

BIBLIOGRAPHY
Henri Bouchard, 1875–1960 (exh. cat., Paris, Assoc. Amis Henri Bouchard, 1965)

ELISABETH LEBOVICI

Boucharde [bush hammer]. Mallet studded with V-shaped indentations used in sculpture to wear down the surface of the stone or material.

□

Bouchardon. French family of artists. Jean-Baptiste Bouchardon (1667–1742) was an important craftsman in Burgundy and Champagne, working as a sculptor, architect and gilder. He was apparently assisted at times by his daughter Jacquette Bouchardon (1694–1756). His elder son (1) Edme Bouchardon was thought by contemporary connoisseurs to be the greatest sculptor and draughtsman in France, dedicated to an ideal of classical severity allied with increasing naturalism, though this opinion is now thought exaggerated. His most important work was an equestrian monument to *Louis XV* (destr. 1792) in Paris, which was not complete at his death. His brother (2) Jacques-Philippe Bouchardon spent the bulk of his career in Sweden, where he produced some attractive portraits and influenced the development of a Rococo style in the decorative arts.

BIBLIOGRAPHY
Lami; Thieme–Becker
A. Roserot: 'Jean-Baptiste Bouchardon, sculpteur et architecte à Chaumont-en-Bassigny (1667–1742)', *Réun. Soc. B.-A. Dépt.* (1894), pp. 223–82

(1) Edme Bouchardon (*b* Chaumont-en-Bassigny, Haute-Marne, 29 May 1698; *d* Paris, 27 July 1762). Sculptor and draughtsman. He was a pupil of his father, and his earliest work, the low relief of the *Martyrdom of St Stephen* (1719–20) for the tympanum above the main portal of the church of St Stephen at Dijon (now Dijon, St Benigne; *in situ*), was executed in collaboration with Jean-Baptiste. His training must have been solid, for his technique was so competent that only a year after arriving in Paris in 1721, ostensibly to study with Guillaume Coustou the elder, he won the Prix de Rome for sculpture, with *Gideon Choosing his Soldiers by Watching them Drinking* (untraced). He travelled to Rome in 1723 with the winner of that year's Prix de Rome, Lambert-Sigismond Adam, and the two became rivals.

While in Rome, Bouchardon made large numbers of drawings in red chalk after ancient sculptures and monuments, and after the paintings of Michelangelo, Raphael and Domenichino (three sketchbooks; New York, Pierpont Morgan Lib.). He also worked on the obligatory copy in marble after an antique sculpture for the French king, in his case a free interpretation (1726–30; Paris, Louvre) of the Barberini *Faun* (Munich, Glyp.). Its completion, however, was delayed for some years by the artist's standards of perfection and by his willingness to undertake private commissions, for he was already a fully formed artist when he arrived in Rome and quickly gained a reputation in papal circles and among the expatriates around the Villa Medici. Indeed, news of these works reached Paris, where the Duc d'Antin ruefully remarked that 'it is not to enrich foreign countries that the King spends so much on his Académie'. In addition to the restoration of ancient statues, notably the transformation of an antique torso into the *Goddess of Riches* (1731; Berlin) for Cardinal Melchior de Polignac, he took part in the competition for the Trevi Fountain, Rome, which was won by his rival Adam but executed (1732–1760s) by Nicola Salvi, and designed statues for S Giovanni Laterano, Rome, which were never worked up.

Despite the failure to carry through any large-scale monuments, Bouchardon's period in Rome was his most productive, notable for a series of portrait busts. Of these, the most revolutionary was that of the antiquary and spy *Philip, Baron von Stosch* (1727; Berlin, Skulpgal.), which is completely classical in conception. Stosch is depicted with uncompromising severity, his torso naked save for a token drapery over his left shoulder, still and calm, almost as a pastiche of a Roman emperor. The formula was repeated in the bust of *John, Lord Hervey* (1728–9; Melbury House, Lady Teresa Agnew, priv. col., see 1985–6 exh. cat., p. 312), which, however, lacks the monumental solidity of Stosch's head and wide chest. Bouchardon was much in demand within the circle around the Old Pretender, James Stuart (1688–1766), the claimant to the English throne, and made busts of the *Duchess of Buckingham, Lady Lechmere of Evesham* and an unidentified 'M. de Gordon' (all untraced). The circle at the Académie de France too held him in high esteem, and he made busts of *Marie-Thérèse Gosset*, wife of Nicolas Vleughels, Director of the Académie, and of *Cardinal de Rohan* (1731; destr.) and *Cardinal Melchior de Polignac* (1737 Salon; Meaux, Mus. Bossuet). His fame with connoisseurs was also responsible for his being commissioned to portray the new Pope, *Clement XII* (1730; Florence, Prince Tommaso Corsini priv. col., see Levey, p. 97), which, contrary to the extreme simplification of the bust of Stosch, is indebted to the Baroque masters Bernini and Algardi, with great care taken with the naturalism in the folds of skin in the old man's face, his weak eyesight and the richness of the vestments.

On his return to Paris in 1733, Bouchardon was offered several relatively unimportant commissions by the King, for a statue of Louis XIV to replace one in Notre Dame, which he never completed; subsidiary groups on the Bassin de Neptune (1735–40) at the château of Versailles; and a strikingly Baroque *Athlete Overcoming a Bear*, ordered by the King in 1735 as a gift for his Garde des Sceaux and placed in his park at Gros-Bois. For St Sulpice, Paris, he was commissioned to make 24 stone statues but completed only 10, very likely with considerable studio assistance (e.g. *Christ at the Column*, c. 1735; *in situ*). He was also accepted (*agréé*) at the Académie Royale and in 1736 appointed draughtsman to the Académie des Belles-Lettres et Inscriptions. This offered an annual income of 1000 livres, in return for which the artist was expected to provide designs for the medals and tokens for the royal mint. He fulfilled the task with great competence until his

1. Edme Bouchardon: *Design for a Token for the Trésor Royal*, red chalk, diam. 210 mm, 1748 (New York, Metropolitan Museum of Art)

death. The resulting drawings are always in red chalk, from which it was easy to take a counterproof in preparation for the die-cutting, and they were routinely mounted on blue paper to show to the King for approval. Each is drawn in low relief on a 210 mm circular format. Large numbers of these designs and sketches have survived (e.g. Paris, Hôtel de la Monnaie and Bib. N.; and New York, Met.; see fig. 1). Bouchardon proved equally adept at providing copies in red chalk (Paris, Louvre) of gems, which were engraved by the Comte de Caylus for Pierre-Jean Mariette's *Traité des pierres gravées* (1750). His versatility as a draughtsman can be seen in the suites of *Cris de Paris*, probably made at the instigation of Caylus and engraved by him between 1737 and 1746 (original drawings: London, BM). His drawings are generally made in a calm, easy style, with clearly defined contours and long strokes of regular shading, giving an impression of high relief but slightly monotonous regularity.

Much of the remainder of Bouchardon's career was taken up with a small number of important commissions, which he executed slowly and with difficulty. In 1736 he was commissioned to erect the tomb of the *Duchesse de Lauragais* (1736–8; destr.) in St Sulpice and a low relief for the chapel at Versailles (1737; maquette, exh. Salon, 1739). In 1739 he signed the contract with the city of Paris for his most important surviving work, the fountain in the Rue de Grenelle (*see* FRANCE, fig. 37). While the location was hardly of great importance—a narrow street sloping west towards the Invalides—the project attracted a great deal of attention. Indeed, the modesty of the situation presented Bouchardon with almost insuperable difficulties, and he spent long hours over the design. The solution can hardly have been the fountain he had dreamt of since his days in Rome: three brilliant white statues are placed high above the street on an architectural façade, the seated one representing the city of Paris, the two reclining figures that flank it representing the rivers Seine and Marne. Some way beneath are graceful representations of the Four Seasons, and beneath them low reliefs of putti playing. Whereas the individual elements, especially towards the base, are of great distinction, the ensemble was criticized by contemporaries as banal when it was completed in 1745, and the *raison d'être* of the fountain—the provision of water—was reduced to an almost invisible tap at its base. Mariette leapt to Bouchardon's defence with an anonymous pamphlet, but his argument that the fountain has great richness in its simplicity is unconvincing.

Bouchardon's most important commission from the crown was for a statue of *Cupid Cutting a Bow out of Hercules' Club* (Paris, Louvre; see fig. 2) for the Salon d'Hercule at Versailles, ordered by Philibert Orry de Vignory in 1740 but not completed until *c.* 1750. The pose of Cupid was probably inspired by Parmigianino's painting of the same subject (1530s; Vienna, Ksthist. Mus.), of which Bouchardon would no doubt have known a copy in the collection of Louis, Duc d'Orléans at the Palais-Royal. Despite this, the King and his court misunderstood the combination of realism in the figure with the mythological subject and complained that a street urchin had intruded into the royal palace. The sculpture was quickly relegated to the hunting lodge at Choisy, where, however, it was placed in a special temple of its own.

In 1743 Bouchardon was commissioned by Louis XV to design a monument to his chief minister, Cardinal Fleury, who had died that year. He won the commission in the face of competition from rivals Adam and Jean-Baptiste Lemoyne (ii), but for unexplained reasons he never completed it and the final monument (destr.) was made by Lemoyne, at the expense of Fleury's family. Bouchardon's surviving maquettes show a development in plasticity and a renunciation of 17th-century rhetoric, as in *Cardinal Fleury Dying in the Arms of Religion* (maquette, 1745; Paris, Louvre). In 1745 the sculptor was at last received (*reçu*) into the Académie Royale, on presentation of a small marble statue of the *Crucified Christ* (Paris, Louvre). In 1746 he was appointed assistant professor and became full professor in the following year. Having exhibited at the Salon in Paris since its opening in 1737, in 1749 and 1751, together with other prominent members of the Académie (François Boucher, Charles-Antoine Coypel and Charles-Joseph Natoire), he refused to submit work there as a protest against the increasing art criticism of such writers as Etienne La Font de Saint-Yenne.

Despite the reservations over the fountain in the Rue de Grenelle, the city of Paris offered Bouchardon one of the most prestigious commissions of the century in 1749: the equestrian statue of *Louis XV* (destr. 1792) for the newly arranged Place Louis XV (now Place de la Concorde) by Anges-Jacques Gabriel. Bouchardon worked with even more than his customary diligence at the project—there are 300 drawings connected with it in the Louvre alone—but failing health and his perfectionism caused it to remain unfinished at his death. Of the various equestrian statues of Louis XV—by Lemoyne at Bordeaux (destr. 1792), by Jacques-François-Joseph Saly at Valenciennes (destr. 1792) and by Jean-Baptiste Pigalle at Reims

2. Edme Bouchardon: *Cupid Cutting a Bow out of Hercules' Club*, marble, completed *c.* 1750 (Paris, Musée du Louvre)

(destr. 1790s)—Bouchardon's is the most successful and distinctive. The plaster maquette was finally ready in 1757, and the bronze was cast in the following year. Engravings and a reduction (Paris, Louvre) clearly show that it was the most original of the derivations from the antique statue of *Marcus Aurelius* (see ROME, ANCIENT, fig. 61), which Bouchardon had drawn in Rome: the horse is more naturalistic, and the King, dressed entirely in antique costume, sits comfortably but gracefully in the saddle. The base is remarkably innovative, with four idealized and graceful Virtues as supporters in place of the conventional slaves. Unfortunately, these were cast after Bouchardon's death, and the monument, finished by Pigalle, was not inaugurated until 1763, after the end of the Seven Years

War (1756–63). By the time of the French Revolution, it had become a symbol of despotism and was therefore destroyed in 1792 (*see also* EQUESTRIAN MONUMENT).

After Bouchardon's death, his champion Caylus read his obituary to the Académie, praising his diligence and devotion to the antique ideals of nobility and simplicity and recommending him as a model for young sculptors. Mariette too praised his love of the Antique, while Charles-Nicolas Cochin (ii) called him 'the greatest sculptor and draughtsman of the century'. Denis Diderot felt that his work was imbued with the 'spirit of nature and antiquity, that is to say simplicity, strength, grace and truth'. In spite of his fame during his lifetime, Bouchardon's stature has since been reduced to that of an important precursor of Neo-classicism, whose promise was greater than his achievement.

Mariette

BIBLIOGRAPHY
A.-C.-P. de Tubières, Comte de Caylus: *Vie d'Edme Bouchardon, sculpteur du roi* (Paris, 1762) [eulogy presented before the Académie]
M.-F. Dandré-Bardon: *Anecdotes sur la mort de Bouchardon* (Paris, 1764)
A. Roserot: 'Edme Bouchardon dessinateur', *Réun. Soc. B.-A. Dépt.* (1895), pp. 588–616
F. Mazerolle: *Les Dessins de médailles et de jetons attribués au sculpteur Edme Bouchardon* (Paris, 1898)
A. Roserot: *Les Grands Sculpteurs français du XVIIIe siècle: Edme Bouchardon* (Paris, 1910)
A. Blanchet: 'Les Jetons dessinés par le peintre Louis II Boulogne et le sculpteur Edme Bouchardon', *Rev. Numi.*, n.s. 3, xxvii (1924), pp. 55–105
K. T. Parker: 'Bouchardon's *Cries of Paris*', *Old Master Drgs*, v/19 (1930), pp. 45–8
J. Guiffrey and P. Marcel: *Inventaire général des dessins du Musée du Louvre et du Musée de Versailles: Ecole française*, i (Paris, 1933)
P. Metz and P. O. Rave: 'Eine neuervorbene Bildnisbüste des *Barons Philip von Stosch*', *Berlin. Mus.: Ber. Staatl. Mus. Preuss. Kulthes.*, n.s. vii/1 (1957), pp. 19–26
E. M. Vetter: 'Edme Bouchardon in Rom', *Heidelberg. Jb.*, vi (1962), pp. 51ff
Edme Bouchardon (exh. cat., ed. O. Colin; Chaumont, Mus. Mun., 1962)
G. Weber: 'Etudes et documents: Quelques dessins inédits d'Edme Bouchardon', *Bull. Soc. Hist. A. Fr.* (1968), pp. 191–200
——: 'Der Statuenzyklus von Edme Bouchardon in Saint-Sulpice', *Wien. Jb. Kstgesch.*, xxii (1969), pp. 120–47
W. Kalnein and M. Levey: *Art and Architecture of the 18th Century in France*, Pelican Hist. A. (Harmondsworth, 1972), pp. 55–63
L. Duclaux: *La Statue équestre de Louis XV: Dessins de Bouchardon. . .dans les collections du musée du Louvre* (Paris, 1973)
W. Ames: 'Bouchardon and Company', *Master Drgs*, xiii/4 (1975), pp. 379–400
P. Bjurström: 'A Collection of Drawings by Edme Bouchardon at the Royal Library, Stockholm', *Nmus. Bull.*, ii/3 (1978), pp. 113–20
De la Place Louis XV à la Place de la Concorde (exh. cat., ed. J.-M. Bruson and others; Paris, Mus. Carnavalet, 1982) [essay by P. Sorel on Bouchardon's *Louis XV*]
The Treasure Houses of Britain: Five Hundred Years of Private Patronage and Art Collecting (exh. cat., ed. G. Jackson-Stops; Washington, DC, N.G.A., 1985–6), p. 312
Französische Zeichnungen im Städelschen Kunstinstitut, 1550 bis 1800 (exh. cat. by M. Stuffmann, Frankfurt am Main, Städel. Kstinst. & Städt. Gal., 1986–7), pp. 118–22
M. Levey: *Painting and Sculpture in France, 1700–1789*, Pelican Hist. A. (New Haven and London, 1993), pp. 93–101

(2) Jacques-Philippe Bouchardon (*b* Chaumont-en-Bassigny, Haute-Marne, 1 May 1711; *d* Stockholm, 19 Dec 1753). Sculptor and draughtsman, brother of (1) Edme Bouchardon. He studied with his father but enlisted in the army in 1730 and was bought out only with the help of the Comte de Caylus. By 1735 he had entered his brother's studio in Paris and probably collaborated on his works for St Sulpice, the fountain in the Rue de Grenelle

and the Bassin de Neptune at Versailles. In 1740 the Swedish ambassador in Paris, Count Carl Gustav Tessin, arranged for Jacques-Philippe to travel to Stockholm to work on the decoration of the Royal Palace. His principal task was to carve reliefs on the ceiling of the chapel and over the windows (where he placed figures of the 12 Apostles) and to carve the pulpit, which has heavy Baroque drapery and a baldacchino (1749–51; *in situ*). He also worked on a relief of *Christ at Gethsemane* (destr.). Other work in the palace includes the eight groups of putti carrying lanterns on the main staircase (1752; cast in bronze, 1754–62), which quickly became a popular motif in Swedish decorative arts. Jacques-Philippe also received numerous commissions for sculpted portraits, which remain his most original products. Works such as the painted terracotta of *Gustav III as a Child* (*c.* 1750; Stockholm, Nmus.) show the technical skill of Edme Bouchardon with a distinctively personal grace and charm. The most popular of his portraits was the bust of *Charles XII*, originally designed in 1747 (Stockholm, Kun. Slottet), of which numerous replicas in bronze were issued. Jacques-Philippe's work on royal commissions was interrupted by a journey to Rome in 1751 and curtailed by his premature death two years later.

BIBLIOGRAPHY
A. Lindblom: *Jacques-Philippe Bouchardon och de franska bildhuggarna vid Stockholms slott under rokokotiden* [Jacques-Philippe Bouchardon and French sculpture at the Stockholm Castle during the Rococo] (Uppsala, 1924)
——: 'J.-P. Bouchardon', *Gaz. B.-A.*, n. s. 4, xi (1925), pp. 95–107, 145–55, 189–205
1700-tal: Tanke och form i rokokon [18th century: thought and form in the Rococo era] (exh. cat., ed. S. Lindroth; Stockholm, Nmus., 1980), nos 358, 374, 537, 682–5
P. Bjurström: *French Drawings: Eighteenth Century*, Stockholm, Nmus. cat. (Stockholm, 1982), nos 815–21

COLIN HARRISON

Boucher, François (*b* Paris, 29 Sept 1703; *d* Paris, 30 May 1770). French painter, draughtsman and etcher. Arguably it was he, more than any other artist, who set his stamp on both the fine arts and the decorative arts of the 18th century. Facilitated by the extraordinary proliferation of engravings, Boucher successfully fed the demand for imitable imagery at a time when most of Europe sought to follow what was done at the French court and in Paris. He did so both as a prolific painter and draughtsman (he claimed to have produced some 10,000 drawings during his career) and through engravings after his works, the commercial potential of which he seems to have been one of the first artists to exploit. He reinvented the genre of the pastoral, creating an imagery of shepherds and shepherdesses as sentimental lovers that was taken up in every medium, from porcelain to toile de Jouy, and that still survives in a debased form. At the same time, his manner of painting introduced the virtuosity and freedom of the sketch into the finished work, promoting painterliness as an end in itself. This approach dominated French painting until the emergence of Neo-classicism, when criticism was heaped on Boucher and his followers. His work never wholly escaped this condemnation, even after the taste for French 18th-century art started to revive in the second half of the 19th century. In his own day, the fact that he worked for both collectors and the market, while retaining the prestige of a history painter, had been both Boucher's strength and a cause of his decline.

I. Life and work. II. Working methods and technique. III. Critical reception and posthumous reputation.

I. Life and work.

1. Early years, before 1734. 2. Maturity, 1734–64. 3. Last years, 1765–70.

1. EARLY YEARS, BEFORE 1734. Boucher was born into a humble milieu: his father, Nicolas Bouché (*b* after 26 May 1672; *d* 1743), who was probably his first teacher, was a painter attached to the guild-like Académie de Saint-Luc, rather than to the Académie Royale de Peinture et de Sculpture. Boucher's first surviving paintings, *St Bartholomew* and *St Andrew* (priv. cols, see 1986–7 exh. cat., no. 1) from a set comprising *Christ*, the *Virgin* and the *Apostles* that was engraved in 1726 for Edme Jeaurat (1699–1789), were probably produced during this period. According to the *Galerie françoise*, he created a sensation at the age of 17 with a painting of the *Judgement of Susanna* (priv. col., see 1986–7 exh. cat., p. 47). He was noticed by François Lemoyne, who not only predicted a great future for him but also extended him the official protection that allowed him to compete for the Prix de Rome. Boucher won this in 1723, with a painting on the subject of *Evilmerodach Delivering Jehoiachin* (untraced). He should then have spent three years studying at the Académie de France in Rome, but the funds for this were allocated instead to favourites of the Duc d'Antin, Surintendant des Bâtiments du Roi. Boucher was thus forced to earn his living without the full academic training that would have enabled him to obtain prestigious commissions. Between *c.* 1723 and *c.* 1728 he worked for the engraver and publisher Jean-François Cars (1661–1730), supplying him with drawn reductions of his own earlier paintings and with compositions for thesis plates. During this period he was noticed by Jean de Julienne, who recruited him to make etchings after Watteau's drawings for *Figures des différents caractères* (1726–8), of which he executed the lion's share. The other significant product of these years was the set of 25 drawings that he made in 1727–8 (Paris, Louvre, Cab. Dessins) to illustrate the third edition of Père Daniel's *Histoire de France*.

Despite Boucher's assertion to Mariette that he owed nothing to Lemoyne, his known works from this period betray the strong influence of the older master, even

1. François Boucher: *Madame Boucher*, oil on canvas, 573×683 mm, 1743 (New York, Frick Collection)

though his pupillage was largely nominal; it can be seen, for example, in *Rebecca and Eliezer* (Strasbourg, Mus. B.-A.). However, it is equally clear that he rapidly forged a personal style; it was, indeed, the very idiosyncrasy of his style—such as can be seen in the drawings for the *Histoire de France* and in two paintings once owned by Jullienne, *Noah Entering the Ark* and *Noah's Sacrifice* (both priv. col., see 1986–7 exh. cat., nos 10–11)—that began to make his reputation. His pictures were already characterized by a great painterliness of technique, which has sometimes resulted in finished works being mistakenly called sketches; by brilliant, saturated colours; and by a wealth of picturesque detail, for which the inspiration seems to have been the work of Giovanni Benedetto Castiglione and Italianate Dutch pastoral landscapes.

Boucher's activities proved sufficiently lucrative to fund the vital journey to Italy in April–May 1728. In order to minimize the cost, he travelled in the company of three members of the van Loo family: Carle, Louis-Michel and François. Nicolas Vleughels, Director of the Académie de France in Rome, found Boucher lodgings in an outbuilding of the Académie. Boucher's precise activities in Italy remain slightly mysterious. Unlike the van Loos, he won no prizes; also, as suggested by his subsequent advice to his pupils Johann Christian von Mannlich and Jean-Honoré Fragonard, he was disinclined to pursue the usual academic path of making copies after Michelangelo and Raphael.

Instead, Boucher's drawings reveal that he studied above all the great masters of the Baroque. He made copies, among others, after Bernini's *Neptune* from the Moro Fountain in Piazza Navona, Rome (drawings ex-Gal. Pardo, Paris, see 1986–7 exh. cat., p. 63); after Giovanni Battista Gaulli's pendentives in S Agnese in Agone, Rome (drawings Paris, Louvre, Cab. Dessins); and after Luca Giordano's *Triumph of Judith* (drawings Vienna, Albertina). These and other drawings suggest that he must have travelled to Naples, Venice and Bologna. It is clear from the paintings he made after his return to Paris that he also deepened his knowledge of Castiglione (copiously represented in Venetian collections) and learnt to emulate both his subject-matter and his bravura technique. According to Papillon de La Ferté, Boucher supported himself in Rome by painting several works 'in the Flemish manner', none of which can be securely identified. Such works of his as *Hercules and Omphale* (Moscow, Pushkin Mus. F.A.) and *Return from the Market* (Springfield, MA, Mus. F.A.) should probably also be ascribed to the years in Rome.

Around 1731 Boucher returned to Paris and resumed his former activities as printmaker and book illustrator. Among others he illustrated *Les Métamorphoses d'Ovide* (Amsterdam, 1732; *see* BOOK ILLUSTRATION, fig. 4). He also made 12 etchings for the set of 30 *Diverses figures chinoises peintes par Watteau . . . au château de La Muette*, published by François Chéreau and Louis Surugue in November 1731. In the same month, he was approved (*agréé*) by the Académie Royale. He was now almost 30 and, after the false dawns of his *Susanna* and the Prix de Rome, still had his reputation to make. He set out to achieve this by painting a series of large, striking compositions, chiefly on mythological subjects, including *Venus*

Asking Vulcan for Arms for Aeneas (1732; Paris, Louvre), *Cephalus and Aurora* (1733; Nancy, Mus. B.-A.), *Mercury Confiding the Infant Bacchus to the Nymphs of Nysa* and the *Rape of Europa* (both London, Wallace). Among the religious paintings of this period is *Moses before the Burning Bush* (priv. col., see 1986–7 exh. cat., no. 14). A third type of composition—and one that he was to make so much his own that 'les enfants de Boucher' became a term of art—showed putti and cupids engaged in various activities (e.g. *Cupids Catching Birds*, Providence, RI Sch. Des. Mus. A.). All of these pictures were made for the lawyer François Derbais, an obscure collector and son of the marble mason and sculptor Jérôme Derbais; he appears, in return, to have allowed his house to become a kind of unofficial gallery for the display of Boucher's works. On 21 April 1733 Boucher married Marie-Jeanne Buseau (1716–after 1786), who is thought to have subsequently often served as his model. His portrait of her, *Madame Boucher* (1743; see fig. 1), is in the Frick Collection, New York. Their son, Juste-François Boucher (1736–82), became a furniture designer.

2. MATURITY, 1734–64. Boucher's efforts to achieve recognition rapidly proved effective. On 30 January 1734 he was received (*reçu*) at the Académie Royale, on presentation of *Rinaldo and Armida* (Paris, Louvre). More importantly, in 1735 he was offered his first royal commission, to paint four large pictures of putti emblematic of the *Virtues* for the Chambre de la Reine at Versailles (*in situ*), which would replace earlier paintings by Gilbert de Sève. In the following year he was invited to contribute the *Leopard Hunt* (Amiens, Mus. Picardie) to the series of exotic hunts painted by Jean-François de Troy, Charles Parrocel, Carle Vanloo and other artists for the dining-room of Louis XV's Petits Appartements at the château of Versailles. In 1738 Boucher was commissioned to paint an additional hunt, the *Crocodile Hunt* (1739; Amiens, Mus. Picardie).

(i) Cabinet pictures and other paintings for collectors. (ii) Tapestry designs. (iii) Pastoral paintings, porcelain designs and stage designs. (iv) Major paintings. (v) Work for Louis XV and the Marquise de Pompadour.

(i) Cabinet pictures and other paintings for collectors. Royal favour was matched by the enthusiasm of private collectors: after his return from Italy, he seems to have deliberately sought these, rather than the official commissions for ecclesiastical or public buildings that might have brought him greater fame but less financial reward for a much greater expenditure of time. To attract collectors, he painted cabinet-sized pictures in a variety of modes: in addition to the mythologies and putti-pictures at which he had already proved himself adept, he painted landscapes, pastorals and scenes of both low and high life in domestic interiors, the most celebrated of these last being *La Belle Cuisinière* (Paris, Mus. Cognacq-Jay), *La Belle Villageoise* (untraced; version, Pasadena, CA, Norton Simon Mus.) and *Family Taking Breakfast* (1739; Paris, Louvre; see fig. 2). Details of compositions such as these and the earlier *Rape of Europa* (London, Wallace) also showed Boucher's virtuosity in the painting of still-lifes. Nor did he neglect the promise implicit in the decorative paintings

2. François Boucher: *Family Taking Breakfast*, oil on canvas, 815×655 mm, 1739 (Paris, Musée du Louvre)

that he had made for Derbais: he executed a number of larger, showy canvases that easily took their place in schemes of Rococo decoration, although the motifs were now pastoral rather than mythological, as can be seen most notably in the set of four canvases conceived for an unknown location: the *Return from the Market* (Norfolk, VA, Chrysler Mus.), the *Happy Fisherman* (Pittsburgh, PA, Frick A. Mus.), *Village Happiness* and the *Halt at the Fountain* (both Munich, Bayer. Landesbank, on loan to Munich, Alte Pin.).

When Boucher painted these pictures the Salon, which since 1699 had largely been discontinued, had not yet been revived; so the numerous engravings after his works that began to appear were probably intended to make both them and himself more marketable, following the example set by Jullienne's manipulation of Watteau's artistic legacy. Boucher's compositions were reproduced by a wide variety of engravers, such as Etienne Fessard (1714–77), Edmé Jeaurat, Michel Aubert (1700–57), Bernard Lépicié and especially Pierre Aveline (ii); they were published by, among others, Louis Jacob (*b* 1712), Jeaurat, Jean-François Cars and François Chéreau. By 1736 his works were also being engraved for and published by one of the foremost promoters of the Rococo, Gabriel Huquier, and the prints were being publicized in the *Mercure de France*. Around the same date, the plates of one of the 18th century's most bizarrely ambitious projects of international artistic cooperation were published in Paris: Owen McSwiny's *Tombeaux des princes, des grands capitaines et autres hommes illustres*, eight of the eleven allegorical title-pages being after Boucher's designs.

(ii) Tapestry designs. In 1736 Boucher began another mainstay of his career, one that was to diffuse his imagery throughout Europe and even as far as China: tapestry cartoons. The invitation to make designs for the Beauvais factory must have come from Jean-Baptiste Oudry shortly after his appointment as director of the factory in March 1734; Boucher's first three designs for the *Fêtes de village à l'italienne* were ready by 1736. The *Fêtes italiennes* (as they are commonly known) eventually consisted of eight pieces, apparently designed in two sets of four: the first set, which had been woven by 1739, was more rustic in character but with the Italianate settings that gave the series the second part of its name; the second, woven from 1742 onwards, showed more refined figures celebrating and playing at pastoral love in the open air (*see* BEAUVAIS, fig. 5), justifying the first part of the title. Tapestries from the two sets were equally popular, but it was those from the second set that contributed most to the diffusion of Boucher's pastoral imagery throughout Europe. They were succeeded at Beauvais by the *Story of Psyche*; this was first discussed in 1737, but Boucher's first full-size painting for it, *Psyche Refusing Divine Honours* (untraced; grisaille sketch, Blois, Château), was not exhibited until the 1739 Salon. The five tapestries in the series were woven in 1741–2. It was followed by *La Tenture chinois*, for which Boucher made ten coloured oil sketches, eight of which were exhibited at the 1742 Salon (all Besançon, Mus. B.-A.). From these, Jean-Joseph Dumons de Tulle (1687–1779) worked up the cartoons. Boucher painted the first two cartoons of the next series, the *Loves of the Gods*, in 1747, but the first weaving did not come off the looms until 1749. The first two tapestries of the *Fragments of Opera* were woven in 1752; finally, in the same vein as the *Fêtes italiennes* but with a much greater element of artificiality, the first tapestries of the set known as *La Noble Pastorale* were woven in 1755.

Also in 1755, however, Boucher was appointed Inspecteur sur les Ouvrages at the Gobelins tapestry factory, replacing Oudry, who had recently died. The Gobelins, which had long been worried by the commercial success of Boucher's designs for the rival factory at Beauvais, insisted that he should cease to supply Beauvais with models. He had already worked for the Gobelins, but only by supplying paintings to be used as designs for unique weavings for the Marquise de Pompadour, the most notable examples being the *Rising of the Sun* and the *Setting of the Sun* (both 1753; London, Wallace; for the latter painting *see* FRANCE, fig. 24). After his appointment at the Gobelins, however, Boucher supplied as models small paintings rather than full-scale cartoons; none was as successful as his Beauvais designs. He did produce the full-scale design (1757; Paris, Louvre) for the tapestry of *Venus in the Forge of Vulcan* (London, Osterley Park House; *see* TAPESTRY, fig. 10) as one of a set of four in the series the *Loves of the Gods* commissioned by the King. Ironically, the only successful series, the so-called 'Tentures de Boucher', was designed by Maurice Jacques (*c.* 1712–84), and Boucher's part in it was confined to providing models for the figures. By this date, however, the use of tapestry to make up the complete décor of a room was no longer fashionable in France, and almost every set of the Tentures de Boucher was exported, mostly to England; the first (1764–71; New York, Met.) was sold to Croome Court, Hereford & Worcs.

(iii) Pastoral paintings, porcelain designs and stage designs. Boucher's activity as a designer of tapestries was only one of the ways in which his compositions—which could be reproduced in many different forms—helped to set his stamp on a whole area of Rococo imagery. His most original contribution in this respect was his revival of the painted pastoral, which took its character from contemporary developments on the stage, notably the comic operas produced for the Théâtre de la Foire by Boucher's friend Charles-Simon Favart (1710–92). These may have already partly inspired the *Fêtes italiennes* and almost certainly did inspire two of Boucher's earliest pastorals in the new mode, the *Gallant Shepherd* and the *Kind Shepherd*, painted *c.* 1738–9 as overdoors for a room hung with three of the *Fêtes italiennes* in the Hôtel de Soubise, Paris (now the Archives Nationales; overdoors *in situ*). The novelty Boucher introduced was to depict country folk clad in the half-naturalistic, half-embellished costume of the popular stage, acting out scenes of pastoral love imbued with the sentiment newly fashionable among their social superiors. The most celebrated of the plays by Favart from which Boucher drew his inspiration was *Les Vendanges de Tempé*, first performed in 1745 and restaged in 1752 as a more elaborate ballet-pantomime entitled *La Vallée de Montmorency*. From this piece, Boucher painted such scenes as *Pensent-ils au raisin?* (1747; versions, Chicago, IL, A. Inst.; Stockholm, Nmus.). From 1749 onwards he also used it as the basis for a series of figures drawn for the porcelain factories of Vincennes and Sèvres. The most notable of these are *Babet* (or *La Petite Fille à la cage*) and *Corydon* (or *Le Porteur d'oiseaux*; both 1753, see 1986–7 exh. cat., nos. 104–5).

Yet another activity of Boucher's mature years was that of stage designer. He worked for the Académie Royale de Musique (the Opéra) from 1737 to 1739 and again (or possibly without interruption) from 1744 to 1748. The oil sketch *Le Hameau d'Issé* (1741; Munich, Alte Pin.) may have been a stage design for the pastoral opera *Issé*, performed in 1742. He also provided costumes and stage designs for such productions of the Théâtre de la Foire as Favart's *L'Ambigu de la Folie* (1743).

(iv) Major paintings. Boucher was capable of working in an astonishing variety of idioms. The 1740s saw the apogee of his career as a painter, and 1742 was his *annus mirabilis*, for in that year, in addition to his work for Beauvais and his stage designs, he painted or exhibited some of his most celebrated compositions. These include *Diana after the Bath* (exh. Salon 1742; Paris, Louvre; see fig. 3), the *Lady*

3. François Boucher: *Diana after the Bath*, oil on canvas, 560×730 mm, 1742 (Paris, Musée du Louvre)

4. François Boucher: *Triumph of Venus*, oil on canvas, 1740 (Stockholm, Nationalmuseum)

Tying her Garter (or *La Toilette*, Madrid, Mus. Thyssen-Bornemisza), *Leda and the Swan* (exh. Salon 1742; Beverly Hills, CA, Stewart A. Resnick priv. col., see 1991–2 exh. cat., no. 49; copy, dated 1742, Stockholm, Nmus.) and *Landscape with Frère Luce* (exh. Salon 1742; Moscow, Pushkin Mus. F.A.). Two of the pictures, the *Lady Tying her Garter* and the copy of *Leda and the Swan*, were painted for one of Boucher's most important (and perhaps most sympathetic) patrons, Count Carl Gustav Tessin, who was coming to the end of his posting as Swedish Ambassador in Paris. He had already commissioned the *Triumph of Venus* (1740; Stockholm, Nmus.; see fig. 4), which may be seen as a summing up of Boucher's strengths as a painter. After his return to Stockholm in 1742, Tessin ordered from Boucher, on behalf of Crown Princess (later Queen) Lovisa Ulrica of Sweden, the *Four Times of Day*, a set of paintings showing a young woman's activities at various hours. This might have become Boucher's most varied achievement among his interior genre scenes, but ultimately he could only be persuaded to paint the exquisite *Marchande de modes (Le Matin)* (1746; Stockholm, Nmus.; signed and dated copy, London, Wallace). Apart from this, only the *Family Taking Breakfast*, mentioned above, which depicts the artist's own family, shows how successful Boucher might have been as a painter of upper-class genre

scenes. Instead, commissions for a very different kind of picture (and perhaps some growing weakness in his eyes) encouraged him in a quite different direction.

(v) Work for Louis XV and the Marquise de Pompadour. The reason that Boucher repeatedly gave for failing to complete his Swedish commissions was volume of work, above all for the Crown. Between 1741 and 1747 he painted four overdoors for the Cabinet des Médailles, around fifteen pictures for the château of Choisy, which Louis XV had bought from the estate of Marie-Anne de Bourbon, Princesse de Conti (1666–1739), in 1739, and two overdoors originally intended for the apartment of the prudish Dauphin at Versailles but instead taken by Louis XV for the château of Marly: *Venus Asking Vulcan for Arms for Aeneas* (1747; Paris, Louvre) and the *Apotheosis of Aeneas* (untraced; formerly Manila, Phil. A.G.). For an artist capable of working at Boucher's speed, this was not very much, and it is probable that it was well-paid printed commissions that really kept Boucher busy. From these years also dates one of his most celebrated images, repeated in a number of versions by the master and his studio for unknown clients: the *Dark-haired Odalisque* (untraced; copy dated 1745, Paris, Louvre). The subject of another famous work of Boucher's, the enticingly erotic

Reclining Nude (1752; Munich, Alte Pin.; *see* PORTRAITURE, fig. 4) has sometimes been identified with Louise O'Murphy, one of Louis XV's minor mistresses.

Between 1747 and her death in 1764 the Marquise de Pompadour, the King's *maîtresse en titre*, became Boucher's most enthusiastic admirer and patron. She cannot, perhaps, be blamed for innate weaknesses in the artist that had already manifested themselves before her appearance, but her patronage did encourage Boucher to persist in the stereotyped production of frivolous, garish mythologies and pictures of children mimicking adult activities. These include the *Arts and Sciences* (*c.* 1750–53; New York, Frick), a series of eight canvases that she commissioned to decorate one of her houses (the château of Crécy or of Bellevue), pictures that depict children carrying on such activities as astronomy, chemistry and hydraulics. Paradoxically, she also persuaded him to attempt religious subjects, completely against his inclination. Yet among the mythologies were such masterpieces as the *Rising of the Sun* and the *Setting of the Sun* (both 1753; London, Wallace), and among the religious paintings were such poetic transformations of the themes of maternity and domesticity as the *Light of the World* (1750; Lyon, Mus. B.-A.). The Marquise de Pompadour also commissioned from Boucher a number of portraits of herself, thereby eliciting a series of masterpieces in a field that he scarcely otherwise essayed. Two of these images show her seated in an interior (1756; Munich, Bayer. Hypo-Bank, on loan to Munich, Alte Pin.; *see* DRESS, fig. 45; 1758; priv. col., see Ananoff and Wildenstein, no. 504). It has been suggested that Boucher collaborated on the 1756 portrait with his friend Alexander Roslin. In one portrait (1758; London, V&A), the Marquise de Pompadour is seated in a garden, and in another (1759; London, Wallace) she stands in a garden. Moreover, Boucher provided for the dairy at Crécy designs for sculptures of children that were subsequently used as models for porcelain at Vincennes and Sèvres. He taught the Marquise de Pompadour to etch, and he designed a set of intaglios that were carved by Jacques Guay, after which she made etchings under his supervision. As well as designing tapestries to be woven uniquely for her (see above), he provided designs for her private theatrical productions at her house at Bellevue.

3. LAST YEARS, 1765–70. Boucher's official recognition did not end with the Marquise de Pompadour's death. In August 1765 he was appointed Premier Peintre du Roi and elected Director of the Académie Royale, succeeding Carle Vanloo. He was as active as ever, particularly as a draughtsman for such enthusiastic collectors of his drawings as Paul Randon de Boisset, Pierre-Jacques Bergeret de Grancourt and Jean-Claude Gaspard de Sireul. It was around this time that Gilles Demarteau and Louis-Marin Bonnet began to flood the market with reproductions of his drawings in the newly invented crayon manner. However, Boucher exhibited less at the Salon, in part probably because of the increasingly outspoken criticism of his by now old-fashioned style and imagery. Some of the most pleasing of his later paintings are small, deliberately artificial but supremely painterly landscapes, such as the *Landscape with a Young Fisherman and his Companions* (1768; Manchester, C.A.G.). Yet to the last he remained capable

of producing large decorative paintings, whether pastoral landscapes, such as the pair the *Shepherd's Idyll* and *The Washerwomen* (both 1768; New York, Met.), or Castiglionesque works, such as the *Rest on a Journey* (1765) and the *Return from the Market* painted for Bergeret de Grancourt (both Boston, MA, Mus. F.A.). He also painted mythologies, such as the set of six executed for the hôtel particulier of J.-F. Bergeret de Frouville (four, Fort Worth, TX, Kimbell A. Mus.; two, Malibu, CA, Getty Mus.). In addition he was offered more serious commissions, such as that for a *Continence of Scipio*, which Marie-Thérèse Geoffrin offered him in 1766 on behalf of Stanislav II Poniatowski of Poland, or for a painting of one of the *Generous Actions of Sovereigns* for the gallery at Choisy (1764); but he never executed them. He was, however, still supplying paintings for use by the Gobelins and was once again designing sets for the Opéra. It is therefore a little incongruous that his last recorded commission should have been to decorate the staircase of the archiepiscopal palace next to Notre-Dame, Paris, which was rebuilt in 1770 by Pierre Desmaisons (1733–91). Boucher progressed far enough to make a pair of drawings (untraced) for this project, representing *Religion* and *Hope*, but he died suddenly in May of that year.

II. *Working methods and technique.*

Even if Boucher's own estimates of his oeuvre as some 10,000 drawings and more than 1000 paintings are exaggerated, he was still among the most prolific artists in 18th-century France. He was, moreover, among the most versatile: he made etchings, drawings, paintings, tapestry cartoons and designs for the stage, for porcelain, book illustrations, thesis plates and fans. Indeed, the only medium in which he did not work—in common with all his contemporaries—was fresco.

1. ETCHING. Boucher began his career as an etcher, although he practised the medium only rarely in later life. He served his apprenticeship making etchings after Watteau's drawings for the *Figures des différents caractères*, and his prints are among the most successful in capturing the fugitive effects of light in Watteau's drawings. He manipulated the etcher's needle like a drawing implement, using short strokes for shading and texture, longer ones for the outline and dots for areas of highlights. Among the etchings from Boucher's maturity, one of the most notable is *The Laundress* (1756), in which a young woman is hanging out the washing in front of a thatched cottage, while a stream and a ramshackle shed add further picturesque detail. This large plate (296×215 mm), one of Boucher's most ambitious, was created from a variety of delicate lines, hatching and the repeated biting of the plate at several stages of its creation. The result is a print of great charm, with the effects of light, atmosphere and tonal variety subtly conveyed. The finished state shows a few areas reworked with the burin to strengthen details. By comparison with less practised contemporaries, Boucher's etching technique was regular and accomplished, the lines of shading evenly spaced and carefully matched in intensity. Boucher also collaborated with other artists in his prints: for the frontispiece to an edition of Pierre

Corneille's play *Rodogune* (1759), he seems to have made studies of the principal groups in red chalk (New York, Pierpont Morgan Lib.), a number of studies of single figures and a study of the whole composition in pen and ink (see 1973–4 exh. cat., nos 80–81). He then made the initial etching, concentrating on the complicated folds of the draperies and the expressions of the protagonists, with heavily accented mouths, nostrils and eyebrows. The second state of the print is signed by the Marquise de Pompadour, who may have contributed some of the fine detail to the figures; however, it was Charles-Nicolas Cochin (ii) who went over the entire plate with the burin, making the lines more solid and permanent.

2. DRAWING. Boucher's drawings are as varied in technique as in function. From his early years of working for Jean de Jullienne he acquired enormous facility in the use of red chalk, and he assimilated Watteau's particular technique of *trois crayons*, red, black and white chalks for the same drawing. It was only later that he added pen and ink to his repertory and the more demanding technique of brush and ink, with washes for the shadows. He even occasionally used pastel, not as a specialist like Maurice-Quentin de La Tour but to make finished studies for use in larger compositions. He drew on different papers, blue, brown or white, of differing qualities.

Boucher began a picture by making a rapid sketch in black chalk of the whole composition. He then made studies of individual figures, usually in red chalk, either from life in the academic manner or, in his later years, from memory. As Joshua Reynolds reported in his Discourse X, 'He said when he was young, studying his art, he found it necessary to use models, but he had left them off for many years.' Despite this claim and the common complaint of the critics that his paintings were 'unnatural', Boucher seems to have drawn directly from the model for most of his figures, both male and female. For the nudes, he used long, smooth strokes of chalk, with smoothly graduated shading and carefully reinforced outline. When using white heightening on the flesh, he applied it in a careful network of short strokes. Occasionally, as for example in a study of a *Boy Holding a Parsnip* (1738; Chicago, IL, A. Inst.), he used pastels, creating a finished work of art at the same time as a study for a painting, in this case the *Boy and the Cook* (?*c.* 1738; priv. col., see 1986–7 exh. cat., no. 28). This rare pastel and a great many of the drawings were highly regarded by collectors, and studies of single figures were engraved in the crayon manner by such practitioners as Gilles Demarteau and Louis-Marin Bonnet. Boucher's pen-and-ink drawings are much rarer; he seems to have adopted the technique towards the middle of his career, principally for compositional studies and for finished drawings for the engraver.

3. PAINTING. Boucher's early paintings show very strongly the influence of such 18th-century Venetian masters as Sebastiano Ricci and Giovanni Antonio Pellegrini: colours are strong and saturated and applied in short strokes of the brush. The most striking example of the influence of Castiglione's work on Boucher's technique is *Moses and the Burning Bush* (priv. col., see 1986–7 exh. cat., no. 14). It is painted in brutal, almost violent strokes

in primary colours, and everything in the picture is subordinated to the vigour and virtuosity of the handling.

From this youthful bravura, Boucher's manner of painting developed a calmer, more conventional finish, but he never aspired to the polished surface of his master Lemoyne. Even in his rare works on copper, such as the *Landscape with Frère Luce* (exh. Salon 1742), he retained his characteristically free style. He gradually came to abandon painting on panel in favour of canvas, even for tapestry cartoons, which were conventionally painted on paper. He experimented little with other supports, apart from the unique *Frère Philippe's Geese* (Besançon, Mus. B.-A. & Archéol.), painted in gouache on silk, perhaps as a fan. In preparing a major commission, Boucher often made not only large numbers of preparatory drawings, both of individual figures and of the whole composition, but also sketches in oils, either monochrome or in colours. Such sketches, intended to fix the general disposition of the composition, were made very rapidly. Occasionally, Boucher made sketches both in grisaille and in colours, as in the case of the late tapestry design *Venus in the Forge of Vulcan*, which was first studied as a small grisaille (Paris, Mus. A. Déc.). The larger coloured sketch (Williamstown, MA, Clark A. Inst.), which was probably made for the Marquis de Marigny, follows the first closely; the final painting (Paris, Louvre) was exhibited at the Salon of 1757.

Boucher also prepared grisaille sketches in oil for the engraver. The reasons for this are unknown, since the technique allowed the engraver much greater freedom. Thus he provided his friend Laurent Cars with the grisaille sketch of *France Bemoaning the Troubles that Divide her*, to serve as the model for the frontispiece of Poullain de Saint-Foix's *Catalogue des chevaliers, commandeurs et officiers de l'ordre du Saint-Esprit* (Paris, 1760).

III. Critical reception and posthumous reputation.

1. CRITICAL RECEPTION. Boucher's success with collectors and patrons was matched for most of his career by the adulation of the critics. Until the revival of the Salon in 1737 there was little criticism in the press, and after that date most judgements were conventionally favourable, with Boucher quickly apostrophized as 'le peintre des grâces' or the 'Anacréon de la peinture', considered especially good at painting women. For a few critics, Boucher was a legitimate target for attack. Thus in 1753 Estève complained that vigorous actions necessitated a forceful style, which Boucher did not possess. This brought a furious reply from Charles-Nicolas Cochin (ii), who effectively silenced Estève by maintaining that, knowing nothing of painting, he had no right to criticize.

Such exchanges probably did no great harm to Boucher's reputation. However, in 1747 Charles-François Le Normand de Tournehem, Directeur-Général des Bâtiments du Roi, revived the idea of a competition between the leading painters, such as had been held in 1727. No prize was eventually awarded; public opinion could not decide between Charles-Joseph Natoire's *Triumph of Bacchus* and Boucher's *Rape of Europa* (both Paris, Louvre). More importantly, Etienne La Font de Saint Yenne and others published articles on Boucher's painting that criticized his colour and choice of subject. For such writers, history painting remained the highest ideal in art, and pink boudoir paintings were generally considered unworthy.

Diderot's Salon reviews, which appeared in the *Correspondance littéraire et artistique* between 1759 and 1781, coincided with the years of Boucher's maturity and decline. Although Diderot never ceased to be seduced by the artist's extraordinary gifts, his remarks became increasingly less charitable as he became convinced that Boucher was wasting his talents on unworthy subject-matter. In 1761, for example, he was captivated by Boucher's charming fantasies but recognized that 'this man has everything, except the truth'. Truth, either to nature or to a noble antique ideal, was the essence of Diderot's aesthetic, and by 1763 he openly deplored the energy Boucher spent on frivolous subjects, suggesting, with some justification, that he had been corrupted by success and was, furthermore, exerting a harmful influence on younger painters, who sought to imitate his rosy babies and amorous peasants rather than to seek honour with history painting. In 1765 Diderot condemned Boucher outright. The immediate cause of this hostility was Boucher's appointment as Premier Peintre du Roi in succession to the history painter Carle Vanloo. Diderot castigated Boucher as depraved, both morally and artistically: 'The degradation of taste, of colour, of composition, of characters, of expression and of drawing followed step by step from the depravation of morals.' What use, argued Diderot, was an extraordinarily fertile imagination, if its only source of inspiration was prostitutes of the lowest order? Diderot concluded that Boucher had no taste and was 'a false good painter, as one is a false good spirit'.

2. POSTHUMOUS REPUTATION. Diderot's view of Boucher as the depraved painter of a depraved society persisted during the French Revolution. The pupils of Jacques-Louis David, who was the principal force in the artistic revolution against Boucher, derided him fanatically. As Neo-classicism became increasingly identified with the authoritarianism of the Académie, young Romantic artists and writers began to champion the unfashionable artist for his freedom and Frenchness: Théophile Gautier, Victor Hugo and Gérard de Nerval were all ardent partisans of the Rococo. Simultaneously, 18th-century French painting came to be identified with left-wing politics. However, sybaritic wealthy collectors such as Richard Seymour-Conway, 4th Marquess of Hertford, and wealthy banking families such as the Rothschilds began to pursue Boucher's works at auction; during the Second Empire, such leading painters as Alexandre Cabanel and William Bouguereau made pastiche Bouchers for pastiche 18th-century interiors. By the end of the 19th century American collectors had entered the field, and their public and private collections of Boucher's paintings and drawings are now the richest in the world. The scholarly study of Boucher's life and work began with the publication of the Goncourt brothers' monograph and catalogue in 1862. For them, Boucher was 'one of those men who signify the taste of a century, who express it, personify it and embody it'; 'prettiness' was 'the spirit of the age' and 'the genius of Boucher'. This view pervades all subsequent monographs,

and, although knowledge of particular works and particular periods increases, Boucher remains the painter of a frivolous aristocracy or an aspiring middle class.

For a further illustration *see* PAINTBOX.

BIBLIOGRAPHY

Mariette

Desboulmiers [J.-A. Jullien des Boulmiers]: 'Eloge de M. Boucher, premier peintre du roi & directeur de l'Académie royale de peinture & sculpture, mort le 30 mai 1770', *Mercure de France* (Sept 1770), pp. 181–9

J.-B. Restout, ed.: *Galerie françoise, ou portraits des hommes et des femmes célèbres qui ont paru en France* (Paris, 1771)

D.-P. Papillon de la Ferté: *Extrait des differens ouvrages publiés sur la vie des peintres*, ii (Paris, 1776), pp. 657–62

E. de Goncourt and J. de Goncourt: *Boucher* (Paris, 1862) [repr. in *L'Art du dix-huitième siècle* (Paris, 3/1880)]

A. Michel: *François Boucher* (Paris, 1889; rev. with cat. by L. Soullié and C. Masson [1906])

M. Fenaille: *Etat général des tapisseries de la manufacture des Gobelins*, 6 vols (Paris, 1903–23)

P. de Nolhac: *François Boucher: Premier peintre du roi* (Paris, 1907) [with cat. by G. Pannier; repr. without cat., 1927]

M. Fenaille: *François Boucher* (Paris, 1927)

H. Voss: 'François Boucher's Early Development', *Burl. Mag.*, xcv (1953), pp. 81–93; xcvi (1954), pp. 206–10

J. E. Ruch: 'An Album of Early Drawings by François Boucher', *Burl. Mag.*, cvi (1964), pp. 496–500

A. Ananoff: *L'Oeuvre dessiné de François Boucher (1703–1770): Catalogue raisonné*, i (Paris, 1966); review by R. S. Slatkin in *Master Drgs*, v (1967), pp. 54–66

R. S. Slatkin: 'Some Boucher Drawings and Related Prints', *Master Drgs*, x (1972), pp. 264–83

François Boucher in North American Collections: 100 Drawings (exh. cat. by R. S. Slatkin, Washington, DC, N.G.A.; Chicago, IL, A. Inst.; 1973–4)

A. Ananoff and D. Wildenstein: *François Boucher*, 2 vols (Lausanne and Paris, 1976) [cat. of paintings]; review by R. S. Slatkin in *Burl. Mag.*, cxxi (1979), pp. 80–88

J.-L. Bordeaux: 'The Epitome of the Pastoral Genre in Boucher's Oeuvre: *The Fountain of Love* and *The Bird Catcher* from *The Noble Pastoralè*, *Getty Mus. J.*, iii (1976), pp. 75–101

E. A. Standen: 'The Story of the Emperor of China: A Beauvais Tapestry Series', *Met. Mus. J.*, xi (1976), pp. 103–17

——: 'Fêtes Italiennes: Beauvais Tapestries after Boucher in the Metropolitan Museum of Art', *Met. Mus. J.*, xii (1977), pp. 107–30

P. Jean-Richard: *L'Oeuvre gravé de François Boucher dans la collection Edmond de Rothschild* (Paris, 1978)

R. Savill: 'François Boucher and the Porcelains of Vincennes and Sèvres', *Apollo*, cxv (1982), pp. 162–70

François Boucher: Paintings, Drawings and Prints from the Nationalmuseum, Stockholm (exh. cat., Manchester City A. Gals, 1984)

E. A. Standen: 'The *Amours des Dieux*: A Series of Beauvais Tapestries after Boucher', *Met. Mus. J.*, xix–xx (1984–5), pp. 63–84

B. S. Jacoby: *François Boucher's Early Development as a Draughtsman, 1720–1734* (New York and London, 1986)

G. Brunel: *François Boucher* (Paris, 1986; Eng. trans., 1986)

A. Laing: 'Boucher et la pastorale peinte', *Rev. A.* [Paris], lxxiii (1986), pp. 55–64

François Boucher (1703–1770) (exh. cat., ed. A. Laing; New York, Met.; Detroit, MI, Inst. A.; Paris, Grand Pal.; 1986–7) [includes paintings, tapestries and porcelain]

A. Laing: 'Trois lettres de François Boucher et de sa femme à l'auteur dramatique Favart', *Archus A. Fr.*, xxix (1988), pp. 19–22

The Loves of the Gods: Mythological Painting from Watteau to David (exh. cat. by C. Bailey, Paris, Grand Pal.; Philadelphia, PA, Mus. A.; Fort Worth, TX, Kimbell A. Mus.; 1991–2), pp. 371–427

ALASTAIR LAING

Boucher, Jean (*b* Bourges, *c.* 1575; *d* Bourges, 1633). French painter. He was in Rome in 1596 and again in 1600; surviving drawings from an album that has since been broken up (examples in Bourges, Mus. Berry; Paris, Ecole N. Sup. B.-A. and Louvre) show that he had seen both antique sculpture and the work of Raphael. He made two further journeys to Rome in 1621 and 1625, but these do not seem to have greatly affected his style. Apart from these periods abroad and a visit to Fontainebleau in 1602, Boucher remained in Bourges. In 1604 he painted a *Mary Magdalene in the Desert* (Bourges, Mus. Berry), the restrained style of which reflects the influence of Italian artists such as Girolamo Muziano and Scipione Pulzone. However, his first surviving important painting is the *Nativity* (formerly called *Adoration of the Shepherds*, 1610; Bourges Cathedral), signed, as are many of his paintings, *Ioannes Boucher Bitur* (i.e. of Bourges) *Invenit et Fecit 1610*. Boucher had by then established his style, which barely changed during the rest of his career. His realistic vision, expressed through light effects, simple, well-balanced compositions and solid figures, served to express his sincere religious convictions. These characteristics are apparent in *St Peter and St Paul Bidding Each Other Farewell before their Martyrdom* (1630; Bourges, St Bonnet), one of Boucher's last known works.

Boucher's busy studio produced mainly devotional works for the Church, including the *Presentation in the Temple* (1620; Dijon, Mus. Magnin); the *Adoration of the Magi* (1622; Bourges, Mus. Berry); and the *Lamentation* (1630; Bourges, Church of the Carmelites). In 1630 Boucher painted for the chapel he had endowed in St Bonnet a triptych depicting his patron saint, *St John the Baptist*, in the central panel (now Bourges Cathedral); the wings of the triptych (now Bourges, Mus. Berry) were realistic portraits of the artist and of his mother. Boucher seems to have been one of the first French artists to draw academy figures.

BIBLIOGRAPHY
P. de Chennevières-Pointel: *Recherches sur la vie et les ouvrages de quelques peintres provinciaux de l'ancienne France*, ii (Paris, 1850), pp. 87–120
J. Thuillier: 'Du "Maniérisme" romain à l'"atticisme" parisien: Louis Brandin, Jean Boucher, Pierre Brébiette, Laurent La Hyre', *Etud. Rev. Louvre*, i (Paris, 1980), pp. 23–31
Jean Boucher de Bourges, ca 1575–ca 1633 (exh. cat. by J. Thuillier, Bourges, Mus. Berry; Angers, Mus. B.-A.; 1988) [cat. rais.]
THIERRY BAJOU

Boucheron. Italian family of gold- and silversmiths. Andrea Boucheron (*b* Turin, *c.* 1692; *d* Turin, 1761) was apprenticed in Paris to Thomas Germain. He was called back to Turin by Victor-Amadeus II of Savoy (*reg* 1720–30), where he opened two workshops and became goldsmith to the court of Charles Emanuel III (*reg* 1730–73) in 1737. Almost all of his works have been lost; all that remains is the bronze and silver tabernacle of the Sacro Pilone in the church at Vicoforte near Mondovì, produced between 1750 and 1752 in collaboration with François Ladatte. Andrea's son Giovan Battista Boucheron (*b* Turin, 1742; *d* Turin, 1815), after being taught by his father, went to Rome in 1760. There he completed his training by studying sculpture in the Collini brothers' workshop. He was active in Paris and Rome and from 1763 succeeded his father as court goldsmith. In 1776 he became director of the royal goldsmiths' workshop. His drawings (Turin, Mus. Civ. A. Ant.) and his theoretical writings on his craft—for example *Osservazioni pratiche sopre l'eccellenza de' lavori d'oro, d'argento e di qualcunque altra sorte di metalli* (1978; Turin, Bib. Reale, Miscellanea patria, clv no. 19)—as well as his various pieces in gold and silver confirm his role as one of the main figures in the field of secular silverwork in the second half of the 18th century and the early 19th. His style was primarily classicist but with French and English elements (e.g. a silver-gilt pair of candlesticks, 1783; London, V&A; *see* ITALY, fig. 91).

BIBLIOGRAPHY
G. Claretta: 'La campagna ducale e la famiglia Boucheron', *Atti Soc. Archeol. & B. A. Prov. Torino*, i (1875–6), pp. 246, 250–52
A. Bargoni: 'Argenti', *Mostra del barocco piemontese*, ed. V. Viale (Turin, 1963), pp. 19–115
Schede Vesme, 2 vols (Turin, 1963–6), i, pp. 193–4, 199–201; ii, pp. 246–8, 597–8
A. Bargoni: *Maestri orafi e argentieri in Piemonte dal XVII al XIX secolo* (Turin, 1976)
ANGELA CATELLO

Bouchot, Henri (*b* Gouille, nr Beure, Doubs, 26 Sept 1849; *d* Paris, 10 Oct 1906). French art historian. He graduated from the Ecole des Chartes in Paris in 1878 and the following year began work at the Cabinet des Estampes, a department of the Bibliothèque Nationale, where he spent the rest of his career: he was sub-librarian (1885), librarian (1888), assistant curator (1898) and finally curator (1902), succeeding Georges Duplessis (1834–99). He became a member of the Institut in 1904. Under his leadership, the Cabinet des Estampes became accessible to a wide public. He compiled numerous catalogues of the collections and researched the works of contemporary artists in order to expand the collection. The great work of his career was the organization of the exhibition of early French painting (Les Primitifs français) in Paris in 1904. This was immensely successful, but in his desire to make people recognize the importance of French medieval art in relation to the Italian and south Netherlandish schools, Bouchot sometimes made questionable attributions in his catalogue. At the Bibliothèque Nationale in 1906 he organized an important exhibition of 18th-century miniatures and prints and undertook a book on the subject, which was interrupted by his sudden death. Married to the miniaturist Claire Chevalier, he had two children. His daughter Jacqueline (1893–1975), who married the sculptor Georges Saupique, worked at the Louvre and was curator, then chief curator, of the Cabinet des Dessins from 1945 to 1963. Henri Bouchot, an assiduous worker, was interested in a wide range of subjects. Apart from his numerous art historical publications, he wrote poems in the patois of his home province, the Franche-Comté.

WRITINGS
Les Portraits aux crayons des XVIe et XVIIe siècles conservés à la Bibliothèque nationale (1525–1646) (Paris, 1884)
Notice sur la vie et les travaux d'Etienne Martellange, architecte des Jésuites (1569–1641), suivi du catalogue de ses dessins (Nogent-le-Rotrou, 1886)
with G. Duplessis: *Dictionnaire des marques et monogrammes des graveurs* (Paris, 1886)
Inventaire des dessins et estampes relatifs au département de l'Aisne, Paris, Bib. N. cat. (Paris, 1887)
Jacques Callot, sa vie, son oeuvre et ses continuateurs (Paris, 1889)
Inventaire des dessins exécutés pour Roger de Gaignières et conservés aux Départements des Estampes et des Manuscrits, Paris, Bib. N. cat. (Paris, 1891)
Les Clouet et Corneille de Lyon (Paris, 1892)
Le Cabinet des Estampes de la Bibliothèque nationale, guide du lecteur, Paris, Bib. N. cat. (Paris, 1895)
Catalogue des dessins relatifs à l'histoire du théâtre conservés au Département des Estampes, Paris, Bib. N. cat. (Paris, 1896)
Les Deux Cents Incunables xylographiques du Département des Estampes, Paris, Bib. N. cat. (Paris, 1903)

Les Primitifs français (exh. cat., Paris, Bib. N. and Pav. Marsan, Exp. St Jean, 1904)

Les Primitifs français, 1292–1500 (Paris, 1904)

Exposition d'oeuvres d'art du XVIIIe siècle à la Bibliothèque nationale (exh. cat., Paris, Bib. N., 1906)

Regular contributions to periodicals including *Burl. Mag.*, *Gaz. B.-A.* and *Rev. A. Anc. & Mod.*

DBF

BIBLIOGRAPHY

G. Gazier: 'Henri Bouchot', *Mém. Soc. Emul. Doubs* (1906), pp. 35–49

E. Bourdin: *Henri Bouchot de l'Institut 1849–1906: L'Homme et l'oeuvre* (Besançon, 1907)

MADELEINE BARBIN

Boucle, Pierre [Boeckel, Bouck, Boucken, Pieter van; Vanboucle, Pieter] (*b* ?Antwerp, *c.* 1610; *d* Paris, 1673). Flemish painter, active in France. He may have studied still-life painting with Frans Snyders in Flanders, but by 1629 he was in Paris, where he settled in the community of Flemish painters in the Saint-Germain-des-Prés district, which lay outside the jurisdiction of the Painters' Guild (Maîtrise). For some time he worked with the still-life painter Lubin Baugin in the studio of Simon Vouet, where they produced cartoons for tapestries (untraced). He probably also had contacts with the still-life painters Jacques Linard and Louise Moillon, with whose style his work has affinities. Boucle's work had a broad appeal—his paintings appear in inventories of royal collections and shop keepers alike and are now mostly in private collections. Works such as *Fish and Shells* (Narbonne, Mus. A. & Hist.), depicting a cat leaping on to a rustic table heaped with fish, have an anecdotal quality that betrays the artist's Flemish origins. The subject is treated in a highly realistic way with great attention paid to the rendering of different textures. *Basket of Fruit* (1649; Toledo, OH, Mus. A.), in which a basket of grapes, pears and apples is depicted on a stone plinth set within a shallow space, comes closer to the French style; the crispness characteristic of Moillon, however, is replaced by Boucle's attempt to integrate the still-life elements with the background through a more naturalistic rendering of light.

BIBLIOGRAPHY

M. Faré: *La Nature morte en France* (Geneva, 1962)

——: *Le Grand Siècle de la nature morte en France* (Fribourg, 1974)

La Peinture française du XVIIe siècle dans les collections américaines (exh. cat. by P. Rosenberg, Paris, Grand Pal.; New York, Met.; Chicago, IL, A. Inst.; 1982)

LESLEY STEVENSON

Boucry, Pierre. *See* BOSCRY, PIERRE.

Boudard, Jean-Baptiste (*b* Paris, 1710; *d* Parma, 6 June 1768). French sculptor, active in Italy. He won the Prix de Rome in 1732 but left for the Académie de France in Rome at his own expense, arriving *c.* 1733. There he executed, among other works, a model in wax of the royal arms for the façade of the Palazzo Mancini, home of the Académie de France, and a marble copy of the *Spinario* (untraced). He also contributed to the sculptural decoration of S Giovanni in Laterano (Lateran Basilica). In 1741 he was in Naples and in Venice, where he may have modelled the powerful bust of *Father Lodolli* (terracotta, 1744; St Petersburg, Hermitage).

During a brief period in France, in 1746–8, Boudard produced statues of *Prayer* and *Contemplation* (both destr.) for the convent of St Pierre, Lyon, but by 1748 he was in Chambéry, in the service of Philip of Bourbon, who was shortly to become Duke of Parma; in 1749 Boudard followed him there, and he was documented as professor of sculpture at the Accademia di Belle Arti, Parma, in 1752. In 1759 he published his *Iconologie tirée de divers auteurs*, a handbook of symbols for the use of artists for which he drew the 630 illustrations. From 1753 until his death he devoted himself to his masterpiece, the sculptural decoration of the gardens of the Palazzo Ducale in Parma, working as the principal collaborator of Ennemond-Alexandre Petitot, the court architect. The principal statues (all marble; *in situ*) range in style from the classical *Venus with a Dolphin*, inspired by the Medici *Venus*, and the French Baroque of the most famous group of the ensemble, *Silenus Bound by Cromi, Mnasilo and Egle* (1765–9), to the group of allegorical statues, including those representing *Vertumno* and *Pomona* (both 1756–7), with their reminiscences of Tuscan Mannerist sculpture.

Boudard collaborated with Petitot on other projects, including the impressive stucco decoration (1755–6) of the Great Salon of the Palazzo Ducale at Colorno, near Parma, and the rebuilding of the main square in Parma, for which he modelled a terracotta group of the *Virgin and Child* (model in plaster, *c.* 1760, Parma, Pal. del Governatore; it was not executed in marble). He also executed a number of portrait busts, among which are the intimate and informal portrait of the abbot *Carlo Innocenzo Frugoni* (terracotta, 1764; Parma, Accad. B.A.) and the elaborate state portrait of his patron, *Philip of Bourbon-Parma* (marble, 1764, Parma, G.N.; version, marble, 1765, London, V&A).

Among Boudard's last works is the Neo-classical funeral monument for *Leopold of Hesse Darmstadt* (black and white marble, 1765; Fidenza, Church of the Capuchins). His career illustrates the wide and lively diffusion of French art through Europe in the 18th century by emigrant artists.

Lami

BIBLIOGRAPHY

E. Riccomini: *Vaghezza e furore, la scultura del settecento in Emilia e Romagna* (Bologna, 1977), pp. 93–8

Soufflot et son temps (exh. cat. by M. Gallet and others, Lyon, Mus. B.-A., 1980), p. 95

F. Barocelli: *Jean-Baptiste Boudard, 1710–1768* (Milan, 1990)

GUILHEM SCHERF

Boudewijns [Baudewyns; Bauduins; Boudewyns], **Adriaen Frans** [Adrien-François] (*bapt* Brussels, 3 Oct 1644; *d* Brussels, 1711). Flemish painter, draughtsman and engraver. He was the son of Nicolas Boudewijns and Françoise Jonquin. On 5 October 1664 he married Louise de Ceul, and on 22 November 1665 he became a master in the Brussels Guild of St Luke, after having been registered as a pupil of Ignatius van der Stock (*fl* 1660) in the same year. By 1669 he had fled to Paris, where he met fellow Flemings, Pieter Boel, Abraham Genoels, Adam Frans van der Meulen and Jan van Hughtenburgh (1647–1733), and where he was mainly active as an engraver. He engraved van der Meulen's *Battles of Louis XIV* and numerous works by Genoels, van Hughtenburgh and by himself. These prints combine bold execution with careful attention to detail. In 1669–70 he was sent to the southern Netherlands with Genoels and van Hughtenburgh to draw

Adriaen Frans Boudewijns: *Italianate River Landscape*, red chalk, 291×388 mm (Dresden, Kupferstichkabinett)

three views of the château of Mariemont as tapestry designs for the Gobelins. In the Gobelins accounts there is evidence that the three artists were also paid for a series of tapestry designs depicting the *Months of the Year*. On 12 January 1670 his second marriage took place, to Barbara van der Meulen, Frans's sister. After her death in 1674, he left Paris and returned to Brussels, where he is first mentioned in 1677. In 1682 he accepted Andries Meulebeeck and Mattijs Schoevaerdts as pupils, and in 1694 his cousin Adriaen Boudewijns (*b* 1673) was apprenticed to him.

All the surviving paintings by Adriaen Frans Boudewijns were probably produced after his return from Paris. They are all landscapes, meticulously painted (e.g. *Landscape with Animals*; Aalst, Gal. Pintelon) and often peopled with figures painted by Pieter Bout. Several feature brightly lit sand flats surrounded by trees and are related in style of composition and choice of motifs to the work of Jacques d'Arthois and Cornelis Huysmans. There are also a number of flat landscapes with Italianate architectural features and a row of hills as a backdrop (see fig.); a series of village and river landscapes in which the compositional structure and technical precision recall the style of Jan Breughel I.

Among the surviving drawings by Boudewijns are two signed examples (both Dresden, Kupferstichkab.), oval in shape and depicting an Italianate river landscape. Their high degree of finish suggests that they are preparatory studies for prints. The delicate yet confident handling that characterizes these drawings as well as Boudewijns's later painted work was imitated in a clumsy manner by his cousin.

BIBLIOGRAPHY

A. Michiels: *Histoire de la peinture flamande depuis ses débuts jusqu'en 1864*, 10 vols (Paris, 1865–76), pp. 335–42
Y. Thiéry: *Le Paysage flamand au XVIIe siècle* (Paris and Brussels, 1953), pp. 149–50
Y. Thiéry and M. Kervijn de Meerendré: *Les Peintres flamands de paysage au XVIIe siècle: Le Baroque anversois et l'école Bruxellois* (Brussels, 1986)

HANS DEVISSCHER

Boudin, (Louis-)Eugène (*b* Honfleur, 12 July 1824; *d* Deauville, 8 Aug 1898). French painter. The son of a mariner, he served as a cabin boy on his father's coastal vessel and thus became familiar with the moods and atmosphere of the sea, which, with the Normandy grazing lands, was his main subject-matter. After a year of schooling in Le Havre in 1835, Boudin worked with a local printer and then with a stationer and framer who displayed paintings by visiting artists; thus he became acquainted with Théodule Ribot, Thomas Couture and Jean-François Millet (ii), as well as Constant Troyon and Eugène Isabey, who were important influences. By 1844 he had set up his own stationery business from which he withdrew in 1846 after spending all his money on buying a conscription

Eugène Boudin: *Return of the Terre-Neuvier*, oil on canvas, 0.74×1.00 m, 1875 (Washington, DC, National Gallery of Art)

substitute. In 1847 he decided to become a professional painter and went to Paris, where he was stimulated by the landscapes, marines and still-lifes of the 17th-century Dutch school and contemporary Barbizon paintings. He copied Old Masters, some of which he did for Baron Isidore-Justin-Séverin Taylor, who subsidized Boudin's travel in northern France and Belgium in 1849. In 1851 Boudin was granted a three-year scholarship by Le Havre Municipal Council to work in Paris, Rouen and Caen, as well as locally. In 1854 he made wider contacts with the group of artists who frequented the Ferme Saint-Siméon, near Honfleur. His visit in 1855 to Quimper aroused an interest in local costume (e.g. *Breton Festival, c.* 1864; priv. col., see Jean-Aubry, 1968, p. 34); a second, extended Breton tour in 1857 enamoured him of the landscape and yielded an important sequence of monochrome drawings reflecting Barbizon influences. At an exhibition of the Société des Amis des Arts du Havre in 1858, Boudin met Claude Monet to whom he offered substantial encouragement, stressing particularly the primacy of working directly from nature. In 1859 Boudin's *Pardon of Ste-Anne-la-Palud* (1858; Le Havre, Mus. B.-A.) was accepted at the Paris Salon, where it was praised by Charles Baudelaire. In the same year Boudin befriended Gustave Courbet, the style of whose largely studio-painted sea and sky pictures he raised to a new pitch of naturalism.

In 1861 Boudin worked briefly with Troyon in Paris, squaring up larger subjects and occasionally painting the skies. He encountered Camille Corot and Charles-François Daubigny, whose works had already impressed him, the former appropriately designating him 'le roi des cieux'. From 1863 to 1897 he exhibited regularly at the Salon, usually a single work or pair of paintings; he was also represented in the First Impressionist Exhibition of 1874. In 1864 Boudin met Johan Barthold Jongkind, with whose art his has many affinities. In 1881 he signed a contract with the dealer Paul Durand-Ruel, with resulting American sales.

Boudin's life followed a consistent pattern of annual travel to his favoured sites in Normandy and Brittany, as well as Bordeaux, and in the 1890s the French Riviera. He inscribed his works with both location and date. During the Franco-Prussian War (1870–71) he visited Belgium and the Netherlands, and he extended his later tours to Brussels, Antwerp, Dordrecht, Rotterdam and Scheveningen. From 1892 to 1895 he regularly visited Venice and depicted traditional views with a cool, resonant luminosity, as in *Venice* (1895; Washington, DC, Phillips Col.).

Boudin's reputation was forged on his scenes of harbours, rivers, estuaries and coasts and their shipping (see fig.), but he also made some inland landscapes and a long series of still-lifes in the tradition of Jean-Siméon Chardin (e.g. *Still-life with Lobster on White Cloth, c.* 1862; Atlanta, GA, High Mus. A.); these culminated in the decorative panels of exotic birds, fruit and flowers painted in 1869 for the Château de Bourdainville. His figure subjects range from studies of peasants at their festivities or devotions to marketing scenes and washerwomen; however, his most famous sequence is his depictions of beach scenes (1860–94), prompted by Isabey, showing the bourgeoisie and aristocracy at recreation on the sands of Deauville and Trouville (e.g. *Beach Scene at Trouville*, 1880; Philadelphia, PA, Mus. A.).

Boudin prefigured Impressionism with his acute and subtle awareness of atmospheric luminosity, with particular emphasis on passing effects of wind-blown cloud and sea. His penchant for cool, silvery lighting and blond tonality is often enlivened with brilliant touches of colour in costumes, flags or bunting, while a richer intensity of hue is seen in his warmer, southern seascapes. Despite a generalization of forms, broken contours, an impasto of splintery brushstrokes of broadly suggestive immediacy and an overall instantaneity of vision, he never pushed as far as the Impressionists in the visual analysis and optical blend of colour divisions; nor did he attempt the mix of short or scrolling brushstrokes of his unofficial pupil, Monet. He did not paint the same subjects consecutively under varying atmospheric conditions but often returned at longer intervals to a favourite motif such as the Etretat cliffs or Trouville jetties. Although Boudin's stylistic development is neither extreme nor dramatic, his tendency to greater emptiness and animated effects became exaggerated in his last decade to a wild and broken handling and severe formal austerity.

Throughout his career Boudin made bright, lively and schematic pastels, and he filed for reference a vast oeuvre of watercolours revealing a sparse skeleton of chalk or graphite over which float broad, approximate washes of vibrant yet delicately transparent colour. At the end of his life he made one original lithograph and a brilliantly vital, if technically flawed, marine etching that indicate the ability if not the inclination to become an important printmaker.

BIBLIOGRAPHY

G. Cahen: *Eugène Boudin: Sa vie et son oeuvre* (Paris, 1900)
G. Jean-Aubry: *Eugène Boudin d'après des documents inédits: L'Homme et l'oeuvre* (Paris, 1922); rev. with R. Schmit as *La Vie et l'oeuvre d'après les lettres et les documents inédits d'Eugène Boudin* (Neuchâtel, 1968; Eng. trans., Greenwich, CT, 1968)
Boudin aquarelles et pastels (exh. cat., Paris, Louvre, 1968)
R. Schmit: *Eugène Boudin, 1824–1898*, 3 vols (Paris, 1973/*R* 1984) [cat. rais.]
V. Hamilton: *Boudin at Trouville* (London, 1993)

HARLEY PRESTON

Boudin, Léonard (*b c.* 1735; *d* Paris, 20 Nov 1807). French cabinetmaker and dealer. He owes his reputation more to his activities as a dealer than as a cabinetmaker. Before he became a *maître-ébéniste* (4 March 1761) in Paris, he worked for Pierre Migeon, Roger Vandercruse and Macret. His own work, essentially in the Louis XV style, is not particularly different from that of his colleagues either in form or in the use of lacquer (e.g. Versailles, Château) or japanning with European decoration (e.g. Stockholm, Kun. Husgerådskam.). He was, however, particularly talented as a marquetry craftsman, as seen on his secrétaires (e.g. Cleveland, OH, Mus. A.), including one (Paris, Petit Pal.) stamped R.V.L.C.. While managing his workshop, he dealt in both new and antique furniture. After 1770 he made this his main business and he added his own stamp to those of his subcontracted colleagues. His business was extremely successful and from 1791 he described himself as an interior decorator.

BIBLIOGRAPHY

F. de Salverte: *Les Ebénistes du XVIIIème siècle, leurs oeuvres et leurs marques* (Paris, 1923, rev. 5/1962)
J. Viaux: *Bibliographie du meuble (Mobilier civil français)*, 2 vols (Paris, 1966–88)

JEAN-DOMINIQUE AUGARDE,
JEAN NÉRÉE RONFORT

Boudin, Thomas (*b c.* 1570; *d* Paris, 21 March 1637). French sculptor. His father Guillaume Boudin (*fl* 1567–1614) specialized in carved panelling and furniture decorated in the antique taste. Thomas was apprenticed to Mathieu Jacquet in 1584 and remained with his workshop until 1595. Though he bore the title Sculpteur du Roi from 1606, his court works, including a chimney-piece (wood, 1606) for the Chambre du Roi at the Louvre, Paris, a bas-relief (bronze; destr.) for the pedestal of Pietro Tacca's equestrian statue of *Henry IV* erected on the Pont Neuf in 1635, and the chimney-pieces for the Throne Room of the Hôtel de Ville, Paris (1617; destr.), and for the château of Chilly (1632; destr.) are less significant than his religious oeuvre. This includes seven high-reliefs (stone, 1610–12; *in situ*) around the choir of Chartres Cathedral. Their traditional, vigorously frontal composition, with the figures modelled almost in the round so that they appear to be free-standing against a plain background, is combined with a late Mannerist complication of drapery and hairstyle. Other sculptural decorations, such as the high altar of St Germain-l'Auxerrois (1613–14), the choir (1625) of the abbey of St Victor, the monumental reliquary (1626–8) at Saint-Denis Abbey, the tabernacle (1634) of the high altar of St Nicolas-des-Champs and statues on the façade of St Gervais–St Protais, all in Paris, have been destroyed. The static quality, simplicity and technical probity of his art can be seen in the marble praying effigies of *Diane de France, Duchesse d'Angoulême* (1621; Paris, Bib. Hist.) and *Madeleine Marchand* (1625; Paris, Louvre) and in the wooden statuettes of *St Gervais* and *St Protais* (Paris, St Gervais–St Protais).

Thomas's brother Jacques Boudin (*b* 1586; *fl* until 1645) worked as a sculptor in Orléans from 1614, and his son, also named Thomas Boudin (*b* 1610; *fl* until 1660), executed several funerary monuments: only that to *Maximilien de Béthune, Duc de Sully and his Wife Rachel de Cochefilet* (marble, 1642; Nogent-le-Rotrou, Hôtel-Dieu) is known to survive.

BIBLIOGRAPHY

R. Vitry: 'Les Boudin et les Boudins, deux familles de sculpteurs de la première moitié du XVIIe siècle', *Gaz. B.-A.*, n.s. 6 (1937), pp. 38ff
G. Bresc-Bautier: 'Thomas Boudin (*c.* 1570–1637) sculpteur du roi: A propos d'une statue priante du Louvre', *Rev. Louvre*, xxix/2 (1979), pp. 90–99

GENEVIÈVE BRESC-BAUTIER

Boudolf, Jan [Baudolf, Jan; Bandol, Johannes; Bondol, Jean; Jean de Bruges; Jehan de Bondolf; Johannes de Brugis] (*b* Bruges; *fl* 1368–81). South Netherlandish painter and illuminator. By 1368 at the latest he was in France, in the service of Charles V as court painter and 'valet de chambre'; in this year the King gave him a house in Saint-Quentin, northern France, in gratitude for his services. Boudolf regularly drew a substantial salary and by 1374 employed an assistant. Apart from the royal commissions, which are always referred to as 'paintings', Boudolf undertook other tasks. In 1371–2 a 'Jehan le peintre de Bruges', living in Dijon and identified with Jan Boudolf, was paid by Philip the Bold, Duke of Burgundy. A *St Christopher* in the church at Semur-en-Auxois may be attributed to him. Between 1371 and 1373 he decorated, among other things, a sedan chair for Margaret of Brabant, Countess of Flanders (1310–82), and in 1377 was paid for tapestry designs (untraced) for Louis I, 1st Duke of Anjou (*see* ANJOU, (8), §II(1)), Charles V's brother. In 1378 a Juan de Brugas was in the service of Pedro IV, King of Aragon (*reg* 1336–87), and some scholars have identified this figure with Boudolf, although this remains hypothetical. In 1380 the French royal administration granted him a pension for life, but there is no further mention of his name after 1381.

As court painter, Boudolf was a dominant influence in the group of artists working at the French court from the mid-14th century who strongly influenced French art by their opposition to the conservative, rather mannered French style and their increased emphasis on realistic representation. Boudolf's one signed work is a dedicatory miniature in a *Bible historiale* (The Hague, Rijksmus. Meermanno–Westreenianum, MS. 10 B 23; see fig.). This was presented to Charles V on 28 March 1372 by Jean de Vaudetar, his adviser. The miniature, which is on a folding

Jan Boudolf: *Charles V Receiving the Manuscript from Jean de Vaudetar*, 292×215 mm; dedicatory miniature from a *Bible historiale*, 1371 (The Hague, Rijksmuseum Meermanno–Westreenianum, MS. 10 B 23, fol. 2*r*)

insert, has an inscription in gold letters of the name Boudolf and the date 1371. It is slightly damaged and shows the King in academic dress, receiving the manuscript from de Vaudetar's hands. The occasion is presented vividly, and Boudolf's role as an innovator is clear. An attempt has been made to place the figures in a three-dimensional setting, with the tiled floor drawn in perspective, the canopy over the king's throne and the trefoil cusped arch in the foreground. The figures have an individualized and realistic physiognomy and are executed in semi-grisaille, which adds to the three-dimensional effect. Certain French stylistic elements are recognizable, but at the time this miniature must have seemed progressive.

The attribution of the remaining miniatures in the Bible is uncertain. A poem at the back of the manuscript by the copyist Raoulet d'Orléans attributes the miniatures to a single hand, and some critics have recognized the work of Boudolf himself in a number of them. This seems unlikely, however, as the manifest differences in style with the rather solemn effect of the dedicatory miniature could then only be a consequence of the more narrative character of the text illustrations. It seems more likely that the illuminators of the circle of the Master of the Boqueteaux were responsible for them. This group illustrated a Bible, translated by Jean de Sy and commissioned by Charles V's father, John II (Paris, Bib. N., MS. fr. 15397), in two stages. In 1356 they painted a first series of miniatures in a somewhat old-fashioned, typically Parisian style; *c.* 1370 Charles V asked the group to paint the remaining miniatures, but the work was never completed. During this second period it is likely that the group worked in close collaboration or perhaps under the direction of Boudolf, as his influence is obvious. Among the many manuscripts decorated by this workshop is a copy of St Augustine's *City of God*, produced for Charles V (*c.* 1376; Paris, Bib. N., MSS fr. 22912–13).

In the light of the relationship between Boudolf and the circle of the Master of the Boqueteaux, Meiss questioned whether the best of their illuminations should not be attributed to Boudolf himself. If this assumption is correct, it implies that Boudolf might have started his career as early as *c.* 1355, working for John II. Whatever the case, the fact of his relationship with the artists around the Master of the Boqueteaux is clear, and their style is highly dependent on his.

At the end of January 1377 Boudolf received payment from Louis of Anjou for the designs for a series of six tapestries with scenes from the *Apocalypse* (Angers, Château, Col. Tap.; *see* ANGERS, §3). In 1379 and 1381 he was again paid by the Duke for designs, and although there is no explicit mention of the Apocalypse, it may safely be assumed that the same series was involved. The tapestries were woven by Robert Poinçon, through the intervention of the tapestry dealer Nicolas Bataille (payments to the latter date from 1377 and 1379). A note of 1380 in the inventory of the Louvre reveals that Boudolf used a 13th-century manuscript (Paris, Bib. N., MS. fr. 403) from Charles V's library as a model (Delisle). Comparison of the two, however, has shown that Boudolf did not literally copy the illustrations from this codex but also used other manuscripts as sources. The scenes in the tapestries are readily accessible to the viewer owing to their interchanging red and blue backgrounds, the figures, which stand out sharply as silhouettes, and the relative absence of depth to the images. There is, however, a suggestion of landscape, and an attempt has been made to render architectural features in perspective. As in the dedicatory miniature, there is a characteristic sense of realism and even naturalism in these images, especially in the vegetation, the faces and the gestures, and the way dramatic events are shown. As a whole the work seems to be more linear than the miniatures, which could be a consequence of translating the image from a painted model to the tapestry.

BIBLIOGRAPHY
Thieme–Becker
L.-V. Delisle: *Cabinet des manuscrits de la Bibliothèque Impériale* (Paris, 1868–81)
H. de Marez: 'Jan van Brugge', *Onze Kst*, ii (1903), pp. 153–63
A. W. Byvanck: *Les Principaux Manuscrits à peintures de la Bibliothèque Royale des Pays-Bas et du Musée Meermanno-Westreenianum à la Haye* (Paris, 1924), pp. 104–10
E. Panofsky: *Early Netherlandish Painting* (Cambridge, MA, 1953), pp. 35–40
L. M. J. Delaissé: 'Enluminure et peinture dans le Pays-Bas', *Scriptorium*, xi (1957), pp. 110–11
R. Planchenault: *L'Apocalypse d'Angers* (Paris, 1966)
M. Meiss: *French Painting in the Time of Jean de Berry: The Late Fourteenth Century and the Patronage of the Duke*, i (London and New York, 1967), pp. 21–2, 100, 113, 310–11
La Librairie de Charles V (exh. cat. by F. Avril and J. Lafaurie, Paris, Bib. N., 1968), pp. 72–3
C. R. Sherman: *The Portraits of Charles V of France (1338–1380)* (New York, 1969), pp. 26–8
G. Souchal: *Les Tapisseries de l'Apocalypse d'Angers* (Milan, 1969)
F. Avril: *Manuscript Painting at the Court of France: The Fourteenth Century (1310–1380)* (London, 1978), p. 110
Die Parler und der Schöne Stil, 1350–1400 (exh. cat., Cologne, Josef-Haubrich-Ksthalle, 1978), i, pp. 68–9, 202–3
Verluchte handschriften uit eigen bezit (exh. cat., The Hague, Rijksmus. Meermanno-Westreenianum, 1979), p. 13
Les Fastes du gothique (exh. cat., Paris, Grand Pal., 1981), pp. 331–2
W. Hansmann: *Die Apokalypse von Angers*, Du Mont Taschenbücher, 104 (Cologne, 1981)
P.-M. Auzas and others: *L'Apocalypse d'Angers: Chef-d'oeuvre de la tapisserie médiévale* (Fribourg, 1985)
G. Henderson: 'The Manuscript Model of the Angers Apocalypse Tapestries', *Burl. Mag.*, cxxvii (1985), pp. 209–18
J. Sterling: *La Peinture à Paris*, i (Paris, 1987), pp. 187–202
F. Joubert: 'Le Sainte Christophe de Semur-en-Auxois: Jean de Bruges en Bourgogne', *Bull. Mnmtl* (1992), pp. 165–77
M. Smeyrs and others: *Naer natueren ghelike: Vlaamse miniaturen voor Van Eyck* (Leuven, 1993), pp. 210–14

M. SMEYERS

Bouffioulx. Belgian centre of ceramics production, near Charleroi. Potters were working in Bouffioulx from the 13th to the 15th century. The first mention of a master potter at Bouffioulx was in 1528, brown and grey salt-glazed stoneware being made from *c.* 1530. During the first half of the 16th century wares produced included tankards with ovoid bodies (often decorated with a figure) and ovoid pitchers, sometimes with three handles and decorated with three faces. During the second half of the 16th century production also included *schnellen* (tall, tapering tankards). The influence of the Raeren workshops is evident especially in the decoration, which included armorial bearings, medallions, figures, flowers and foliage.

BIBLIOGRAPHY
D. A. Van Bastelaer and J. Kaisin: 'Les Grès-cérames ornés de l'ancienne Belgique ou des Pays-Bas improprement nommés grès flamands Châtelet et Bouffioulx', *Bull. Comm. Royales A. & Archéol.*, xix (1880), pp. 98–182
M. Mariën: 'Grès de Bouffioulx aux armes d'Oumal', *Le Parchemin*, ccxxxi (1984), pp. 188–208

CLAIRE DUMORTIER

Bough, Sam(uel) (*b* Carlisle, 8 Jan 1822; *d* Edinburgh, 19 Nov 1878). English painter, active in Scotland. Largely self-taught apart from a short period of instruction under the engraver Thomas Allom (1804–72), Bough worked as a theatrical scene-painter in Manchester, Glasgow and Edinburgh, where he settled in 1855. Initially influenced by Turner and David Cox, he sketched out of doors in his spare time, first exhibiting at the Royal Scottish Academy in 1844. Daniel Macnee encouraged him to devote himself to landscape. In Cadzow Forest near Glasgow he developed methods of working directly from nature, capturing transient effects of weather and atmosphere, as in the oil painting *Cadzow Forest* (1855; Glasgow, A.G. & Mus.). His views of the Clyde, Broomielaw and London ports of the 1850s and 1860s balance Realism with a feeling for the colour and drama of natural phenomena and of crowds in movement (e.g. *Port Glasgow Harbour*, oils, 1853; U. Glasgow, Hunterian A.G.).

Bough became an associate of the Royal Scottish Academy in 1856 and was elected a full member in 1875. He earned great popularity for his watercolours, becoming vice-president of the new Scottish Watercolour Society in 1878. In his later years he painted historical and contemporary scenes, especially of the Fife fishing communities. The Forth and East Lothian coasts remained favourite subjects, although he worked in the Scottish Highlands, in Norway, on the Rhine and frequently in the Netherlands. Bough also illustrated the works of Robert Burns and Sir Walter Scott. He had a bohemian lifestyle and enjoyed a wide circle of friends including writers, actors, clerics and musicians. He himself was a poet and talented violinist.

BIBLIOGRAPHY
Bénézit; *DNB*; Thieme–Becker
S. Gilpin: *Sam Bough R.S.A.: Some Account of his Life and Works* (London, 1905)
J. L. Caw: *Scottish Painting Past and Present, 1620–1908* (Edinburgh, 1908/R 1975), pp. 188–90
M. Hardie: *Watercolour Painting in Britain*, iii (London, 1968), pp. 183–6
D. Irwin and F. Irwin: *Scottish Painters at Home and Abroad, 1700–1900* (London, 1975), pp. 360–61
W. R. Hardie: *Scottish Painting, 1837–1939* (London, 1976, rev. 2/1990), pp. 22–3
J. Halsby: *Scottish Watercolours, 1740–1940* (Braintree, 1986), pp. 112–16
Town and Country: The Social Scene in Scotland, 1850–1920 (exh. cat., ed. C. A. P. Willsdon; U. Glasgow, Hunterian A.G., 1986)
D. Macmillan: *Scottish Art, 1460–1990* (Edinburgh, 1990), pp. 229–30

CLARE A. P. WILLSDON

Bouguereau, William(-Adolphe) (*b* La Rochelle, 30 Nov 1825; *d* La Rochelle, 19 Aug 1905). French painter. From 1838 to 1841 he took drawing lessons from Louis Sage, a pupil of Ingres, while attending the collège at Pons. In 1841 the family moved to Bordeaux where in 1842 his father allowed him to attend the Ecole Municipale de Dessin et de Peinture part-time, under Jean-Paul Alaux. In 1844 he won the first prize for figure painting, which confirmed his desire to become a painter. As there were insufficient family funds to send him straight to Paris he painted portraits of the local gentry from 1845 to 1846 to earn money. In 1846 he enrolled at the Ecole des Beaux-Arts, Paris, in the studio of François-Edouard Picot. This was the beginning of the standard academic training of which he became so ardent a defender later in life. Such early works as *Equality* (1848; priv. col., see 1984–5 exh. cat., p. 141) reveal the technical proficiency he had attained even while still training. In 1850 he was awarded one of the two Premier Grand Prix de Rome for *Zenobia Discovered by Shepherds on the Bank of the River Araxes* (1850; Paris, Ecole N. Sup. B.-A.). In December 1850 he left for Rome where he remained at the Villa Medici until 1854, working under Victor Schnetz and Jean Alaux (1786–1864). During this period he made an extensive study of Giotto's work at Assisi and Padua and was also impressed by the works of other Renaissance masters and by Classical art. On his return to France he exhibited the *Triumph of the Martyr* (1853; Lunéville, Mus. Lunéville; see fig. 1) at the Salon of 1854. It depicted St Cecilia's body being carried to the catacombs, and its high finish, restrained colour and classical poses were to be constant features of his painting thereafter. All his works were executed in several stages involving an initial oil sketch followed by

numerous pencil drawings taken from life. Though he generally restricted himself to classical, religious and genre subjects, he was commissioned by the state to paint *Napoleon III Visiting the Flood Victims of Tarascon in 1856* (1856; Tarascon, Hôtel de Ville), so applying his style to a contemporary historical scene. In 1859 he provided some of the decorations for the chapel of St Louis at Ste Clothilde church, Paris (*in situ*), where he worked under the supervision of Picot. The austere style of the scenes from the life of St Louis reflect Bouguereau's knowledge of early Italian Renaissance art.

Among Bouguereau's Salon entries of the 1860s was *Destitute Family* (1865; Birmingham, Mus. & A.G.), exhibited in 1865, which conformed to a declining though still prevalent fashion for moving contemporary subjects. It depicts a mother surrounded by her children, seated by the Madeleine church in Paris. Though the mournful mother and wretched children were intended to play upon the emotions of the public, the classically inspired architectural backdrop and carefully arranged poses tend to idealize and ennoble the subject so as to avoid offence by too honest a form of realism. In 1867 he executed the

1. William Bouguereau: *Triumph of the Martyr*, oil on canvas, 3.44×4.28 m, 1853 (Lunéville, Musée de Lunéville)

ceiling decorations for the chapels of St Pierre-Paul and St Jean-Baptiste at St Augustin church in Paris (*in situ*), where he was required to follow the rigid instructions of the commissioning body. In 1869 he painted decorations and the ceiling of the Salle des Concerts at the Grand Théâtre de Bordeaux (*in situ*). He remained in the capital during the siege of Paris (1870–71) in the Franco-Prussian War and in 1875 he began teaching at the Académie Julian in Paris. The sober, even melancholy, nature of several works of the 1860s gave way to lighter, playful paintings in the 1870s. Most notable of these is *Nymphs and Satyr* (1873; Williamstown, MA, Clark A. Inst.; see fig. 2), which depicts nymphs playing around a satyr in a woodland setting. Employing an elegant, dynamic composition, the work was much praised by critics as well as being favoured by Bouguereau himself. A similar spirit pervades *Donkey Ride* (1878; Jacksonville, FL, Cummer Gal. A.), which was based upon the traditional festival that accompanies the harvest. Bouguereau was always eager to include children in his works and he here altered the figure playing Bacchus from the traditional young man to a small child. This prevalent use and idealization of children is often responsible for the sentimentality that mars many of his works.

In 1881 Bouguereau was commissioned to provide decorations for the Chapelle de la Vierge of the St Vincent-de-Paul church in Paris (*in situ*). He executed eight large paintings depicting traditional scenes from the life of Christ, the last of which was finished in 1889. In 1884 he completed the huge painting of the *Youth of Bacchus* (1884, 3.31×6.1 m; priv. col., see 1984–5 exh. cat., pp. 24–5) showing the young god amidst a wild, dancing crowd at the coming of summer. As it was highly priced by Bouguereau, the work remained in his studio until his death. Many of the figures in the painting were inspired by those in contemporary and antique sculpture, an influence that was noticeable in other works also. In 1888 he was appointed a professor at the Ecole des Beaux-Arts in Paris. He continued painting and exhibiting until his death and among his later canvases is the characteristic work *Admiration* (1897; San Antonio, TX, Mus. A.), which shows how little his style had changed throughout his life. In addition to his better-known figure works, Bouguereau was also admired for his portraits, one of the most striking being *Aristide Boucicart* (1875; Paris, Bon Marché Col.), a stern three-quarter-length portrait of the founder of the famous Bon Marché store in Paris.

Although his work was widely collected by the English and more especially by the Americans in his lifetime, Bouguereau's reputation in France was more equivocal—indeed quite low—in his later years. While popular with the public and various critics, his work ignored the increasing demand for paintings of modern life which had been made by Charles Baudelaire and was to be fulfilled by the Impressionists. He remained a staunch supporter of the academic training system at a time when it was criticized for stifling originality and nurturing mediocrity. With the advent of modernism he was scorned as one of the most prominent representatives of everything the new movement opposed: high technical finish, narrative content, sentimentality and a reliance on tradition. This hostility was further heightened by the perceived association of academic painting with the bourgeois values that had resulted in world war. However, recent more objective assessments have reinstated Bouguereau as an important 19th-century painter.

BIBLIOGRAPHY

L. Baschet: *Catalogue illustré des oeuvres de W. Bouguereau* (Paris, 1885)
M. Vachon: *W. Bouguereau* (Paris, 1900)
Oeuvres italiennes de Bouguereau (exh. cat., ed. R. Jullian; Lyon, Mus. B.-A., 1948)
William-Adolphe Bouguereau (exh. cat., Paris, Gal. Breteau, 1966)
William-Adolphe Bouguereau (exh. cat. by R. Isaacson, New York, Cult. Cent., 1974–5)
The Other Nineteenth Century: Painting and Sculpture in the Collection of Mr and Mrs Joseph M. Tanenbaum (exh. cat., Ottawa, N.G., 1978), pp. 54–60
R. Lack: *Bouguereau's Legacy to the Student of Painting* (Minneapolis, 1982)
William Bouguereau (exh. cat. by L. d'Argencourt and others, Paris, Petit Pal.; Montreal, Mus. F.A.; Hartford, CT, Wadsworth Atheneum; 1984–5)

2. William Bouguereau: *Nymphs and Satyr*, oil on canvas, 2.6×1.8 m, 1873 (Williamstown, MA, Sterling and Francine Clark Art Institute)

Boulanger, Gustave(-Clarence-Rodolphe) (*b* Paris, 25 April 1824; *d* Paris, Oct 1888). French painter. Born of creole parents, Boulanger became an orphan at 14. His uncle and guardian sent him to the studio of Pierre-Jules Jollivet and then in 1840 to Paul Delaroche, whose prosaic Realism and dry, careful technique influenced Boulanger's style of painting. A first visit to Algeria in 1845 gave him an interest in North African subjects, which was taken up later by his friend Jean-Léon Gérôme. In 1849 he won the Prix de Rome with *Ulysses Recognized by his Nurse* (Paris, Ecole N. Sup. B.-A.), in which he combined academic figure drawing with Pompeian touches inspired by Ingres's *Antiochus and Stratonice* (1840; Chantilly, Mus. Condé). Boulanger's knowledge of the ruins at Pompeii, which he visited while studying at the Ecole de Rome, gave him ideas for many future pictures, including the *Rehearsal in the House of the Tragic Poet* (1855; St Petersburg, Hermitage), in which the influence of *Stratonice* is still obvious. This was later developed into the *Rehearsal of the 'Flute Player' and the 'Wife of Diomedes'* (1861; Versailles, Château), which recorded the preparations being made for a performance given before the imperial Court in Napoleon's mock-Pompeian Paris house. Boulanger specialized in painting studies of daily life from ancient Greece and Rome, as well as Arab subjects. He also painted a number of decorative schemes, at the theatre of the Casino in Monte Carlo (1879), at the Paris Opéra (1861–74) and other locations, opportunities gained through his friendship with CHARLES GARNIER, his fellow *pensionnaire* at the Ecole de Rome. He entered the Institut de France in 1882 and became an influential teacher, well known for his dislike of the Impressionists and their successors.

WRITINGS

A nos élèves (Paris, n.d. [early 1880s])

BIBLIOGRAPHY

M. Lavoix: 'G. Boulanger', *Grands peintres français*, vii (Paris, 1886)
L'Art en France sous le Second Empire (exh. cat., Paris, Grand Pal., 1979), pp. 313–14
J. Foucart and L. A. Prat: *Les Peintures de l'Opéra de Paris, de Baudry à Chagall* (Paris, 1980)

JON WHITELEY

Boulanger, Louis(-Candide) (*b* Vercelli, Piedmont, 11 March 1806; *d* Dijon, 5 March 1867). French painter, illustrator, set designer and poet. He studied at the Ecole des Beaux-Arts in Paris under Guillaume Lethière from 1821. The *Punishment of Mazeppa* (1827; Rouen, Mus. B.-A.), inspired by the scene from Byron's poem, in which Mazeppa is tied to the back of a wildly stampeding horse, is his most important early painting and one of the key images of the Romantic movement.

Early in his career Boulanger became friendly with Eugène and Achille Devéria. Through them he met Victor Hugo, who became his ardent supporter and the source of many of his most typical works. Among Boulanger's illustrations were those for Hugo's *Odes et ballades* (1829), *Les Orientales* (1829), *Les Fantômes* (1829) and *Notre-Dame de Paris* (1844). Boulanger interpreted the macabre and romantic quality of Hugo's texts with an imaginative power and freedom that anticipated Redon (e.g. '*She died at 15, beautiful, happy, adored . . .*' from *Les Fantômes*). He also designed scenery for Hugo's plays, *Hernani* (1830), *Marion de Lorme* (1831) and *Lucrèce Borgia* (1833). Boulanger was a capable portrait painter, who depicted many of the figures of the Romantic milieu, including Hugo himself (*c.* 1832; Paris, Mus. Victor Hugo). In 1828 Hugo dedicated a poem inspired by *Mazeppa* to the painter and for a brief time Boulanger's critical reputation and popular esteem rivalled that of Delacroix. However, like many other artists of the period, he found himself unable to develop his youthful energetic manner into an equally powerful mature style. By the 1840s he was working in an increasingly insipid and unconvincing academic manner (e.g. *Shepherds at the Time of Virgil*, exh. Salon 1845; Dijon,

Mus. B.-A.), although his pastels possess qualities that link him to the more spontaneous and intimate work of Paul Huet and Eugène Boudin. In 1847 he painted *St Denis Preaching* for the church of St Médard, and in 1850 *Souls in Purgatory* and *Souls Delivered* for St Roch (both in Paris). In 1860 Boulanger became the Director of the Ecole Imperiale des Beaux-Arts at Dijon where he encouraged an enlightened and progressive teaching programme.

BIBLIOGRAPHY

A. Marie: *Le Peintre poète Louis Boulanger* (Paris, 1925)
T. Gautier: *Histoire du Romantisme suivie de notices romantiques* (Paris, 1927)
Louis Boulanger, peintre-graveur de l'époque romantique, 1806–1867 (exh. cat., ed. M. Geiger; Rouen, Mus. B.-A., 1970)
M. Geiger: 'Louis Boulanger, ami et illustrateur d'Alexandre Dumas', *Mém. Acad. Sci., A. & Lett. Dijon*, cxxii (1973–5), pp. 319–28

MICHAEL HOWARD

Boularchos (*fl* late 8th century BC). Greek painter, none of whose work survives. Boularchos is known only from two references in Pliny (*Natural History* VII.126, XXXV.55). King Kandaules, also called Myrsilos, of Lydia (*d* late 8th century BC) bought a picture of the *Defeat of the Magnetes* by Boularchos, paying the picture's weight in gold. The date and circumstances of the battle are uncertain, but it is unusual that a Greek artist painted a Greek defeat. The early date assigned to Boularchos and the story of the Lydian gold cast doubt on the historicity of Pliny's account.

BIBLIOGRAPHY

K. Jex-Blake and E. Sellers: *The Elder Pliny's Chapters on the History of Art* (London, 1896/R Chicago, 1976)

C. HOBEY-HAMSHER

Boulenger, Hippolyte (*b* Tournai, 8 Oct 1837; *d* Brussels, 4 July 1874). Belgian painter. He spent a poverty-stricken youth in Paris and Brussels and was orphaned at an early age. He worked in Brussels with a contractor for decorative work named Colleye. He was enrolled at the Académie Royale in Brussels from 1854 to 1856 and from 1859 to 1861.

From 1863 Boulenger adopted nature as his main subject-matter. His meeting with Camille van Camp (1834–91) in 1864 had a decisive influence on his career. Van Camp, an amateur painter and a great admirer of the Barbizon school, was rich and able to support the impoverished Boulenger. At van Camp's suggestion, Boulenger went to live and work in Tervuren, an unspoilt region of fields and woods near Brussels. There he became the central figure of a painters' colony that included Alphonse Asselbergs (1839–1916), Edouard Huberti and Joseph Coosemans (1828–1904). In 1866 Boulenger exhibited four works at the triennial salon in Brussels. In the catalogue, he had 'école de Tervuren' printed after his name. He participated regularly in the salons and was the leader of the Romantic-Realist school of landscape painting in Belgium (see BELGIUM, §III, 4). He attracted attention with dramatic landscapes, rough in quality and with a realistic palette to which his contemporaries were unaccustomed, for example *Landscape with Sheep* (1869; priv. col., see 1980 exh. cat.).

Boulenger's periods of creativity were occasionally interrupted as a result of his irregular way of life and bouts of depression. However, in 1869 he married and went to live in Zaventem, near Brussels. He was by then under contract to the Brussels art dealers the Van der Donckt brothers, and his life achieved a degree of regularity. He returned to Tervuren from 1869 to 1873, but he now spent every summer in the Ardennes and the Meuse valley. His most productive year was 1871. In that year he also painted along the River Scheldt in Antwerp. His work ranges from realistic and balanced landscapes, dominated by skies, to expressionistic sketches and dramatic compositions, such as *Cloud Study* (1869; Brussels, Mus. Ixelles). Particularly in the 1870s he showed a preference for extreme atmospheric effects, which inspired him to a very free use of colour and a sketchy technique. In a span of less than ten years he created a homogeneous and extremely personal body of work that is a powerful expression of his tortured personality.

BIBLIOGRAPHY

De school van Tervuren (exh. cat., Tervuren, Kon. Mus. Midden-Afrika, 1967)
Les Yeux et les pinceaux—Hippolyte Boulenger 1837–1874 (exh. cat., Brussels, Musées Royaux B.-A., 1974)
Het landschap in de Belgische kunst 1830–1914 (exh. cat., Ghent, Mus. S. Kst., 1980)

ROBERT HOOZEE

Bouleuterion. Ancient Greek term for the meeting room of the *boule* ('assembly of citizens'), the main organ of a democratic city. Politics and architecture are closely linked in this building type, as with the PRYTANEION, which was sometimes near the bouleuterion, bordering the agora or a sanctuary (*see also* GREECE, ANCIENT, §II, 1(i)(b)).

Attempts to catalogue the bouleuteria are problematic: many of these buildings have been insufficiently investigated or may have been restored at some time; above all many are not definitely bouleuteria and may even represent building types that are sometimes wrongly thought of as bouleuteria. In addition, certain recently-discovered bouleuteria are of particular interest, though not yet well known. At Agrigento it is possible to discern successive phases of the bouleuterion; while the small isolated theatral structure at Kassope in Epirus is not a bouleuterion for certain. Thus any typology is random, the more so because

analysis shows that in reality there is not one specific architectural form of bouleuterion. Even when a city had a functional room conceived of as a bouleuterion, the *boule* could always meet elsewhere; for example in the theatre or the ekklesiasterion (people's assembly hall), as in Delos, or at the Acropolis, as in Athens. In any case, meetings in the *boule* were originally held in rooms not specifically designated for the purpose, such as the megaron.

It seems possible, however, to distinguish two main categories of bouleuterion. The first, encompassing the oldest, includes long buildings, generally with axial colonnades; the members of the *boule* no doubt met there on wooden benches. This type resembles the 'double' STOA with two aisles and includes the supposed bouleuteria of Delos and Delphi (early 6th century BC), and those of Orchomenos, Olynthos, Kalauria and Mantinea (4th–3rd centuries BC). The second category comprises buildings known from literary, epigraphic or archaeological indications to have been bouleuteria and adapted to this function. Their architecture is like that of an ODEION (small covered theatre), but without any stage (which may have led to confusion between the two uses). They occur in Athens (Old Bouleuterion, early 5th century BC; New Bouleuterion, late 5th century BC), Gortyn, Ephesos (3rd century BC, remodelled 1st century BC), Priene (2nd century BC) and Miletos (2nd century BC, remodelled 2nd century AD; see fig.). In the oldest examples the tiers of seats arranged on three sides were rectilinear. The view would sometimes have been obscured by vertical roof supports, placed near the centre of this square or rectangular room; indeed, the layout posed structural problems. Gradually, the pillars were built closer to the walls, and in sufficiently small rooms they were no longer even necessary (e.g. at Iasos, Nysa and Alabanda). At the same time, the seating tiers became curvilinear (see fig.), making true stepped rows of seating. This category, particularly well represented in Asia Minor, normally had one storey with windows; the room was sometimes preceded by a colonnaded vestibule (as in Ariassos) or at least a vestibule with many doors (at Miletos a monumental gateway and a colonnaded court form part of the complex; *see* GREECE, ANCIENT, fig. 11). Statues formed part of the decoration.

There should possibly be a third category, for buildings which *a priori* do not appear to fit either of the first two. At Olympia two oblong rooms completed by an apse took the place of the bouleuterion from the 6th century BC. At nearby Sikyon, from the end of the 4th century BC, a large square room enclosed with its many pillars a small auditorium with rectilinear steps surrounding two rows of curvilinear steps. The building at Olympia nevertheless stems from the long type of bouleuterion with an axial colonnade, the apse serving as a place for archives, like the north room of the Delos bouleuterion. That of Sikyon can be considered a primitive odeion. The bouleuterion at Glanum in France (*c.* 200 BC) linked an open-air rectangular auditorium to rectilinear steps around an altar and a vast stoa. The two main categories, therefore, clearly have some variations.

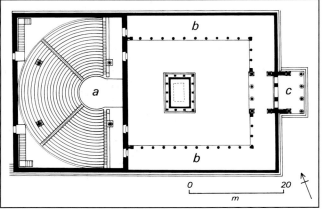

Bouleuterion at Miletos, plan of complex, remodelled *c.* 2nd century AD: (a) council chamber; (b) colonnades; (c) gateway

See also HALL, §II.

BIBLIOGRAPHY

D. Gneisz: *Das antike Rathaus: Das griechische Bouleuterion und die frührömische Curia* (Vienna, 1990)

'Bulletin d'architecture du monde grec', *Rev. Archéol.*, ii (1992), p. 287

MARIE-CHRISTINE HELLMANN

Boulle, André-Charles (*b* Paris, 11 Nov 1642; *d* Paris, 28 Feb 1732). French cabinetmaker. His family were originally from Guelderland in the Netherlands and went to Paris, where his father worked as a 'menuisier en ébène'. Boulle became a master before 1666, when he is recorded as a 'maître menuisier en ébène'; at this time he lived and worked in the rue de Reims near Saint-Etienne-du-Mont. He was granted the royal privilege of lodging in the Galeries du Louvre on 21 May 1672, having been recommended by Jean-Baptiste Colbert as the most adept among his profession in Paris. In the same year he received the title of Ébéniste, Ciseleur, Doreur et Sculpteur du Roi, the royal privilege allowing him to carry out the work of more than one profession; without such protection this would have been an infringement of the guilds' rules. In 1685 Boulle employed at least 15 workmen, and by 1720 the workshop had 20 work-benches and equipment for 6 bronzeworkers. Yet despite his success Boulle was dogged by financial difficulties, and his creditors sought permission to have him arrested in the Louvre in 1704. Boulle was an avid collector, and this had probably put a strain on his financial resources. The inventory of 1720 made after a fire in his workshops claims that before the fire his collection was composed of thousands of prints, drawings and paintings, including works by Mantegna, Raphael, Rubens, Le Brun and Stefano della Bella. In the *Abécédario* the print dealer and book publisher Pierre-Jean Mariette mentions that 'no sale of drawings or prints took place . . . at which he [Boulle] did not make frequent purchases without having the means to pay'. In 1715 Boulle drew up an act passing his business on to his sons; this lists creditors and stock, including pieces for specific clients (Samoyault). Boulle, however, remained involved in the business: as well as compiling the 1720 inventory of the workshops, which includes a section headed 'ordered works on which Boulle and his sons were working', the inventory after his death in 1732 shows that he was still in possession of seven work benches and models for mounts.

Boulle's clients are known from the inventories of the workshops and from those of individuals—mainly financiers, ministers or important officials—in which pieces are attributed to him. His work for the Crown was principally carried out for the Bâtiments du Roi, the state department in charge of the royal buildings (*see* MAISON DU ROI, §II). It consists mostly of marquetry and parquet floors and gilt-bronze decorative details, his masterpiece being the marquetry floors and wainscoting (destr.) in the Dauphin's apartments (completed 1683) at the château of Versailles.

Although the pieces from the Boulle workshops were not stamped, a considerable body of work has now been attributed to them, and Pradère gives a comprehensive

André-Charles Boulle: designs for furniture from his *Nouveaux Deisseins de meubles et ouvrages de bronze et de marquetrie, inventés et gravés par André-Charles Boulle* (Paris, 1707–30), pl. V

list, excluding clocks. As certain documentation exists for only a few pieces, the attributions remain tentative. Boulle's work is characterized by the use of fine, gilt-bronze mounts and magnificent marquetry of two main types: extraordinarily naturalistic floral marquetry in wood and that composed of metal (usually brass, pewter or copper) and tortoise-shell or ebony, which became known in the 18th century as boulle work or buhl work, whether produced by the Boulle workshops or not (*see* MARQUETRY, colour pl. VII). Documentary evidence, however, shows that furniture veneered with plain wood was also a large part of the workshop's production. The form of the furniture ranges from the late 17th-century cabinets supported by a pair of three-dimensional figures and veneered with floral marquetry (examples in London, Wallace; Malibu, CA, Getty Mus.; Duke of Buccleuch priv. col.) to the new forms, current in the 18th century, of the commode, bookcase, low armoire and *bureau plat*. The workshops also produced clockcases, which amounted to c. 30% of the stock in the 1720 inventory. His use of gilt-bronze mounts was innovative: he increased their scale and quantity and made them central rather than subordinate elements in the decorative design of the furniture.

Boulle designed furniture for the workshops. A number of designs are attributed to him (a checklist of which was published by Champeaux), and Jean Mariette published a folio of eight plates between 1707 and 1730 entitled *Nouveaux Deisseins de meubles. . .inventés et gravés par André-Charles Boulle* (see fig.). There is evidence that the workshop also used outside designers. Fuhring has identified a number of design drawings by Gilles-Marie Oppenord that relate to Boulle workshop furniture. Although the production of Boulle's workshops was aimed at the top end of the market, it was not composed of one-off pieces; rather, specific models were made repeatedly, often with minor variations. The pair of commodes (1708–09; Versailles, Château; *see* FRANCE, fig. 54) made by the Boulle workshops for Louis XIV's bedchamber in the Grand Trianon at Versailles were later reproduced by them: three were listed in the stock in the 1715 act of gift, and there are at least five surviving examples (New York, Met.; Petworth House, W. Sussex, NT; a pair at Vaux-le-Vicomte; and one ex-Jean Lombard col.). In the 1720s the *marchand-mercier* Thomas Joachim Hebert (*d* 1773) commissioned from the Boulle workshops replicas of successful models. The agreement dated 20 November 1723, for example, was for a replica of the commode mentioned above ('which commode must be the same as the King's at Trianon') and for a clock with the reclining figures of *Night* and *Day* after those in the Medici Chapel, Florence, by Michelangelo, a model that had also been in the possession of the King. Variations in the same model were produced through the use of marquetry panels and mounts of different designs. Among surviving examples of the six-legged side-table depicted in *Nouveaux Deisseins* (pl. V; see fig.) are those with the top veneered with a boulle-marquetry triumphal carriage drawn by oxen (ex-Duchess de Talleyrand col.; ex-Dennery col.; London, Wallace) and, alternatively, with a birdcage drawn by monkeys (London, Wallace). Boulle-marquetry furniture, particularly the productions of the Boulle workshops, remained in demand throughout most of the 18th century.

Models were still being copied in the 19th century: a pair of commodes (New York, Frick) made originally for the Grand Trianon are marked BLAKE OF LONDON, and three commodes (two Rouen, Mus. B.-A.; one Madrid, Pal. Real) were made by the Fordinois firm in Paris. Boulle's posthumous influence continued and his reputation was international.

BIBLIOGRAPHY

A. de Champeaux: 'Les Dessins d'André-Charles Boulle (1642–1732)', *Rev. A. Déc.*, vi (1885–6), pp. 51–5
G. Wilson: 'Boulle', *Furn. Hist.*, viii (1972), pp. 47–69
J.-P. Samoyault: *André-Charles Boulle et sa famille* (Geneva, 1979)
A. Pradère: *French Furniture-makers: The Art of the Ébéniste from Louis XIV to the Revolution* (London, 1990)
P. Fuhring: 'Designs for and after Boulle', *Burl. Mag.*, cxxxiv (1992), pp. 350–62
C. Sargentson: 'Markets for Boulle Furniture in Early Eighteenth-century Paris', *Burl. Mag.*, cxxxiv (1992), pp. 363–7

ELEANOR JOHN

Boullée, Etienne-Louis (*b* Paris, 12 Feb 1728; *d* 6 Feb 1799). French architect and writer. A gifted designer and admired teacher, Boullée became best known for the magnificent set of drawings he assembled for his treatise *Architecture, essai sur l'art* (Paris, Bib. N.). His father, Louis-Claude Boullée, was an architect, and his mother, Marie-Louise Boucher, may have been related to the painter François Boucher. Etienne-Louis studied painting with Jean-Baptiste-Marie Pierre until his father prevailed on him to pursue architectural studies with Jacques-François Blondel, a leading theorist of French classicism. Although he never went to Italy, Boullée was introduced by Jean-Laurent Legeay to the international Neo-classicism germinating in Rome during the 1740s. Legeay urged his students to complete their projects with a presentation drawing rendered in perspective that would be more intelligible to the client than the customary elevation. This encouraged pictorial effects of light and shadow and provided a link between the practice of architecture and the painting of architectural views. At the age of 19 Boullée began teaching at the Ecole des Ponts et Chaussées; he was admitted to second-class membership in the Académie Royale d'Architecture in 1762 and was promoted to first class in 1780. In 1795 he was a founder-member of the Institut de France.

In his early career Boullée concentrated on domestic architecture. Of his Parisian town houses, only the Hôtel Alexandre (1763–6) survives, much altered, at 16 Rue de Ville-l'Evêque. More famous at the time were the Grand Hôtel de Monville (1764–6) and the Hôtel de Brunoy (1774–9), where a statue of *Flora* presided over house and garden from a stepped podium above the temple-front portico; this statue both contributed to the pictorial effect when viewed from the adjacent Champs-Elysées and commented allegorically on the owner, Mme de Brunoy. Both buildings were more like villas than traditional mansions: only the Ionic portico and attic in the centre relieved the pronounced horizontality, achieved by keeping the low-pitched roofs invisible and by the reiteration of French doors or windows across the ground floor. This created the visual effect of one storey, an illusion strengthened by substituting historiated plaques for windows in the upper storey and attic and lighting these areas with skylights. Boullée's fondness for overhead lighting and blind façades was exploited more fully in his mature work.

Etienne-Louis Boullée: design for a cenotaph to Newton, pen-and-ink drawing with wash, 660×440 mm, 1784 (Paris, Bibliothèque Nationale)

In Boullée's view public architecture offered greater scope for the poetic, and after his appointment as Controller of Buildings at the Hôtel des Invalides in 1778 and at the Ecole Militaire in 1780 he no longer accepted private commissions. Although he was one of six architects asked by the Director of Buildings in 1780 to submit schemes for the remodelling and enlarging of the château of Versailles, his only work of that year was the conversion of the former Hôtel de la Force into a prison (destr.). In 1782 he resigned both controllerships to concentrate on his work as academician, theoretician and educator.

During the final decade of his life Boullée wrote *Architecture, essai sur l'art*, which he illustrated with the projects for public buildings designed between 1778 and 1788. These have contributed to his reputation as a visionary or even a megalomaniac, yet all were inspired either by actual projects or by officially defined programmes of the Revolutionary period, and several were produced in the hopes of receiving a particular commission. In addition to churches and palaces, there were buildings to house the various administrative and cultural functions then in the process of detaching themselves from the princely residence: courthouses, legislatures, theatres, libraries and museums. City gates, arches, bridges, lighthouses and other civil building types completed his proposed list of urban improvements. The cemetery designs corresponded to the Enlightenment cult of the monument as well as to contemporary recommendations to move burial-places from churchyards within the city to more hygienic locations outside the city walls.

The text of the *Essai* offers a commentary on the projects as well as the writer's aesthetic philosophy, though Boullée suggests 'that the reader consult my plans in place of all possible explanations, for I am convinced that what should be required of an artist is not that he explain well but that he execute well'. Refuting Claude Perrault's argument that architecture is pure invention or fantasy without basis in nature, Boullée discerned in both the human organism and the physical universe geometrical volumes that form the basis for beauty with their regularity, symmetry and variety. The sphere 'combines strict symmetry with the most perfect regularity and the greatest possible variety . . . the light effects that it produces are so beautiful that they could not possibly be softer, more agreeable or more varied'. Boullée was committed to expressive forms and to 'character' in architecture. His Palais de Justice rises above a basement prison, a metaphorical image of Vice overwhelmed by the weight of Justice. Especially appropriate to funerary architecture were his 'architecture of shadows' and his 'sunken architecture', whose monumental forms seem about to be swallowed by the earth.

The spherical form of his design for a cenotaph to Newton (1784; see fig.) envelops Newton with his discovery of the shape of the earth. The effect of the interior is of the heavens, the immortal resting-place. Related to Boullée's concern for symmetry was his concern for polarity, and he illustrated the interior of the cenotaph by day (when sunlight coming through apertures in the vault gives the effect of the starry firmament) and by night (when the interior would be artificially illuminated to suggest day).

The *Essai* remained unpublished until 1953, but the text and drawings offer evidence of the influence he exerted on his students, including Alexandre-Théodore

Brongniart, Jean-François-Thérèse Chalgrin and Jean-Nicolas-Louis Durand, and on the Académie's prize competitions, for which he helped to formulate the programmes and evaluate the entries. After Durand (even more influential as a teacher than his master) had deprived Boullée's geometry of its emotive force and symbolic content, reducing it to a design system based on the repetition of standardized units, it became an important source for the utilitarian tradition.

WRITINGS

Architecture, essai sur l'art (MS, *c.* 1788; Paris, Bib. N.); Eng. trans., ed. H. Rosenau as *Boullée's Treatise on Architecture* (London, 1953)

BIBLIOGRAPHY

E. Kaufmann: *Von Ledoux bis Le Corbusier* (Vienna, 1933)
——: *Three Revolutionary Architects* (Philadelphia, 1952)
R. Rosenblum: *Transformations in Late Eighteenth-century Art* (Princeton, 1967)
J.-M. Pérouse de Montclos, ed.: *Etienne-Louis Boullée: Architecture, essai sur l'art* (Paris, 1968)
A. M. Vogt: *Boullée's Newton-Denkmal: Sakralbau und Kugelidee* (Basle, 1969)
J.-M. Pérouse de Montclos: *Etienne-Louis Boullée, 1728–1799: Theoretician of Revolutionary Architecture* (New York, 1974)
H. Rosenau: *Boullée and his Visionary Architecture* (London, 1976)
A. Braham: *Architecture of the French Enlightenment* (London, 1980)
W. Szambien: 'Notes sur le recueil d'architecture privée de Boullée, 1792–1796', *Gaz. B.-A.*, xcvii (1981), pp. 111–24
R. A. Etlin: *The Architecture of Death: The Transformation of the Cemetery in 18th-century Paris* (Cambridge, MA, 1983)

RAND CARTER

Boullogne. French family of painters. They worked mainly in and around Paris for the King, private patrons and religious establishments from the mid-17th century into the early 18th. (1) Louis Boullogne was the first important member of the family, and he taught both his sons (2) Bon Boullogne and (3) Louis de Boullogne and his daughters Geneviève Boullogne (*b* Paris, 22 Aug 1645; *d* Aix-en-Provence, 5 Aug 1708) and Madeleine Boullogne (*b* Paris, 24 July 1646; *d* Paris, 30 Jan 1710). His daughters, who had been accepted (*reçu*) as members of the Académie Royale (7 Dec 1659) as still-life painters, were sometimes characterized as 'flower painters', and they, like their brothers, worked at the château at Versailles. Geneviève married the sculptor Clérion.

BIBLIOGRAPHY

Bellier de La Chavignerie–Auvray; Jal; Thieme–Becker
G. Brice: *Description historique de la ville de Paris* (Paris)
Piganiol de la Force: *Description historique de la ville de Paris et de ses environs* (Paris)
——: *Description de la chapelle du chasteau de Versailles* (Paris)
G. Brice: *Description nouvelle de ce qu'il y a de plus remarquable dans la ville de Paris*, 2 vols (Paris, 1684)
Florent Le Comte: *Cabinet des singularitez d'architecture, peinture, sculpture et graveure* (Paris, 1699, Brussels, 2/1702)
A.-N. Dézallier d'Argenville: *Abrégé de la vie des plus fameux peintres* (1745–52, 2/1762)
F. B. Lépicié: *Vie des premiers peintres du Roi depuis M. Le Brun, jusqu'à présent* (Paris, 1752)
Guillet de Saint-Georges: *Mémoires inédits sur la vie et les ouvrages des membres de l'Académie royale de peinture et de sculpture* (Paris, 1854)
Dubois de Saint-Gelais: *Histoire journalière de Paris* (Paris, 1885)
M. Fenaille: *Etat général des tapisseries de la manufacture des Gobelins depuis son origine jusqu'à nos jours, 1600–1900*, 4 vols (Paris, 1903–20)
Caix de Saint-Aymour: *Les Boullogne* (Paris, 1919)
G. Durand: *Saint-Riquier* (Paris, 1933)
A. Schnapper: *Tableaux pour le Trianon de marbre* (Paris and The Hague, 1967)
——: 'Le Grand Dauphin et les tableaux de Meudon', *Rev. A.* (1968)
L. Guilmard-Geddes: 'Esquisses des frères Boullogne pour l'église royale des Invalides', *Bull. Mus. Carnavalet* (1977)

(1) Louis Boullogne (*b* Paris, 1609; *d* Paris, 1674). After taking his first lessons from a mediocre painter in the Faubourg Saint-Germain, he became a pupil of Blanchard and started to become known. He probably owed his early patronage to his father, who worked at the Hôtel de Ville, Paris. Indeed, a crucifix that Louis painted for one of the rooms in the Hôtel de Ville pleased the municipal magistrates so much that they decided to grant him an allowance to enable him to continue his studies in Italy. Boullogne made the journey with the landscape painter Henri Mauperché. In Rome he met Sébastien Bourdon, with whom he formed a close and lasting friendship.

On his return to Paris, the city authorities continued to support him, employing him to produce the traditional group portrait that, since the Renaissance, the municipal magistrates commissioned to commemorate their election. Boullogne was soon in demand for both religious and secular works, and working for private and official patrons. In 1646 the Goldsmiths' Corporation commissioned him to paint the May of Notre-Dame (Arras, Mus. B.-A.), an altarpiece presented annually to the cathedral in Paris. He was commissioned two more times to paint the May, depicting the *Martyrdom of St Simon in Persia* (Arras, Mus. B.-A.) in 1648 and the *Beheading of St Paul* (Paris, Louvre) in 1657.

Boullogne's other religious works included a *Transfiguration* (1651) for the altar of a chapel in St Merri, Paris; six large works representing two episodes from the *Life of St Anthony*, two from the *Life of St Bernard*, the *Dream of St Joseph* and a *Visitation* for the Augustinian nuns of the Abbey (destr.) of the Faubourg Saint-Antoine, Paris; and a *Purification of the Virgin* for the Capuchin monks of the Marais. On the initiative of Anne of Austria, he painted the *Martyrdom of St Denis* for the abbey of Montmartre.

In 1648 Louis was among the founder-members of the Académie Royale de Peinture et de Sculpture, Paris. He was one of the first to donate to it one of his works, a *Roman Charity*, which he engraved himself; he may also have engraved his *Livre de portraicture* (1648), a type of anatomical study book. He became a professor of the Académie Royale in 1656, while also teaching his own pupils in his studio. Soon after the establishment of this institution he was asked by the collector Everard Jabach to make copies of works that he had acquired from the collection of Charles I, King of England and Scotland. Boulogne acquired a solid reputation in this field, and it is said that some connoisseurs were deceived, taking his copies for originals. This skill of adapting the styles of others was inherited by his sons, who, like many of their contemporaries, practised the art of pastiche.

As a decorator, Boullogne worked on vast projects in many private hôtels, including two ceiling paintings of *Diana* and *Apollo* for the residence that Bertrand de La Bazinière had had built on the Quai Malaquais and *Apollo and the Nine Muses* for Janin de Castille's hôtel in the Place Royale (now Place des Vosges). As Peintre du Roi,

Boullogne was commissioned to work at the royal palaces of Vincennes, the Louvre (where the payments for his restorations in the Grande Galerie after a fire, and for other work there are recorded between 1669 and 1671) and Versailles (where he was paid from 1671 until his death for paintings executed in the Appartement de l'Ordre Attique, which was destroyed soon afterwards during construction of the Grande Galerie). He was succeeded at Versailles by his children.

(2) Bon Boullogne (*b* Paris, *bapt* 22 Feb 1649; *d* Paris, 17 May 1717). Son of (1) Louis Boullogne. He was long regarded as the most gifted of the children. He took his first lessons from his father, whom he is thought to have assisted in the Grande Galerie of the Louvre. Through his father, who presented a half-length figure of *St John* by Bon to Jean-Baptiste Colbert, Contrôleur Général des Finances, he was sent to the Académie de France in Rome as a Pensionnaire du Roi. In this capacity, he made copies of famous works, in particular some frescoes by Raphael in the Vatican Loggie, intended for reproduction as Gobelins tapestries. The period he then spent in Lombardy helped to complete his training. He studied the work of Correggio and the Carracci, as well as Guido Reni,

Domenichino and Albani. Bon's painting, especially the mythological work, shows great affinities with the work of the Bolognese school, which was also to be found in the royal collections. Also of influence to Bon was Nordic art, as demonstrated in his female portraits framed by plant like motifs, a device taken up by his pupil Robert Tournières.

On his return to Paris, Bon was immediately employed at Versailles where his father was working (*see* (1) above). In 1677 he presented as his *morceau de réception* to the Académie the *Battle of Hercules with the Centaurs and the Lapiths* (Paris, Louvre; see fig.). The year after he was accepted (*reçu*) to the Académie, he painted the May offered by François de Villers and Laurent Pillard, which depicted the *Paralysed Man by the Pool* (1678; Arras, Mus. B.-A.). He continued to be in demand at Versailles, where he was probably involved in the decoration of the Escalier des Ambassadeurs under the direction of Le Brun. In 1679–80 he painted a ceiling with *Peace, Abundance and Victory* in the Appartement des Bains, where he also painted some overdoors. Also for Louis XIV, he painted *Art* (probably destr.), a pendant to *Nature* (Versailles, Grand Trianon) and *Venus at her Toilet with Mercury*,

Bon Boullogne: *Battle of Hercules with the Centaurs and the Lapiths*, oil on canvas, 1677 (Paris, Musée du Louvre)

commissioned for the Trianon (Grand Trianon). Bon also produced a painting for the palace chapel (then situated on the site of the future Salon d'Hercule), and he was commissioned to paint a *St Catherine* for the parish church of Versailles (financed by the Bâtiments du Roi) and a *St Louis* for the convent of St Cyr.

In the same period Boullogne painted a series of portraits, most of them now lost but recorded in engravings (e.g. the *Duc de la Meilleraye*, engraved by Gantrel in 1679; Paris, Bib. N.). His talent as a decorator found expression in the *Departure of the Tectosages for Italy* (Toulouse, Mus. Augustins) for the gallery of the Hôtel de Ville in Toulouse, which he painted with Jean Jouvenet and Antoine Coypel in 1684. For the ceiling of the Comédie Française in Paris he painted a vast composition of *Twilight Accompanied by Night, Apollo and the Nine Muses, along with Thetis and her Court*. He decorated the ceiling of the second Chambre des Requêtes with *Justice, Accompanied by Strength and Moderation, Ensures Peace and Watches Over the Arts*, in which his study of Italian *quadratura* is evident (modello, Paris, Carnavalet). The ceiling of the Escalier des Célestins, on which he painted the *Apotheosis of Pietro da Morone* (later Pope Celestine V), who founded the Order, was unfortunately destroyed by the construction of barracks (1895–1901).

In January 1684 Boullogne was appointed assistant professor at the Académie Royale, and he was elected to take the post of professor vacated when Jean Tuby resigned in December 1692. Works from the 1690s include *St Angilbert, Son-in-law of Charlemagne, Receiving the Habit of St Benoît from St Symphorian*, one of the paintings for a competition arranged by Abbé Charles d'Aligre (still *in situ* at Saint-Riquier, nr Abbeville) and the *Raising of Lazarus* (Paris, Louvre), painted for the Carthusian monks. The latter is an ambitious painting almost 8 m long with an architectural background in the style of Poussin, and reminiscent of the work of his brother (3) Louis de Boullogne. The Salon of 1699 was an opportunity for him to show the diversity of his subject-matter and of his talent. He exhibited portraits, genre paintings, mythological subjects and religious works.

The years 1700–10 were a period of intense activity for Boullogne. He painted many mythological subjects, including *Flora and Juno* for the Trianon at Versailles (Versailles, Grand Trianon); *Venus, Bacchus and Ceres* for Meudon (Paris, Louvre; oval replica, Troyes, Mus. B.-A.) and *Jupiter and Semele* (Le Mans, Mus. Tessé), exhibited at the Salon of 1704. During the same period he painted four overdoors for the Chambre du Roi at the château of Rambouillet, near Paris, paid for by Louis-Alexandre, Comte de Toulouse (1678–1737): *Acis and Galatea, Neptune and Amphitrite*, the *Rape of Proserpina* and *Io Changed into a Heifer, Writing her Name in the Sand* (all Tours, Mus. B.-A.). He also produced in this period the *Triumph of Amphitrite* (Dijon, Mus. Magnin), the *Birth of Venus* (Berlin, Gemäldegal.) the *Toilet of Venus* (Potsdam, Schloss Sanssouci), the last a development in a larger format of the group of *Venus at her Toilet* (*c.* 1700–10) painted for the Ménagerie at Versailles.

In the huge decorative project of the interiors of Les Invalides, Paris, Boullogne was primarily responsibile for the chapel of St Ambrose and then in 1703 for the chapel

of St Jerome, where he succeeded Charles-François Poërson (sketches Paris, Louvre, Carnavalet, and Mus. Armée). He also produced many religious paintings at this time, but most have disappeared. He worked at with his brother Louis at the chapel at the château of Versailles (vaults of the gallery on the north side and above the high altar), and in the chapel of the Holy Sacrament in the parish church of Versailles he painted a *Last Supper* (1711).

Usually Boullogne made preparatory drawings on grey paper, either in black chalk alone or heightened with white chalk, or in ink heightened with white. He sometimes produced engravings, such as the comic *Mercury Whipped by the Muses* (Paris, Bib. N.). A tireless worker, he was admired by his contemporaries for his grace and facility; his skill at pastiche, at which he excelled, deceived even Pierre Mignard I and Dézallier d'Argenville. He had many pupils, including Jean-Baptiste Santerre, Louis Sylvestre, Jean Raoux, Nicolas Bertin, Tournières and Pierre-Jacques Cazes. His reputation was such that he was asked by the King of Spain to become his principal painter.

BIBLIOGRAPHY
J. Wilhem: 'Une Esquisse de Bon Boulogne pour le plafond de la IIe Chambre des Requêtes du Parlement de Paris', *Archvs A. Fr.*, xxii (1959)
L. Guilmard-Geddes: '*La Justice assure la paix et protège les arts*: Une Esquisse de Bon Boullogne pour le Palais de Justice', *Bull. Mus. Carnavalet* (1975)
A. Schnapper: 'Plaidoyer pour un absent, Bon Boullogne', *Rev. A.* (1978)

(3) Louis de Boullogne (*b* Paris, 19 Nov 1654; *d* Paris, 21 Nov 1733). Brother of (2) Bon Boullogne. Like his brothers and sisters, he was taught by his father. In 1673 he won the Prix de Rome with *Crossing the Rhine*, which enabled him to travel to the Académie de France in Rome, apparently when his brother Bon returned from there. He, too, made copies of paintings for reproduction as tapestries by the Gobelins. In Rome he proved a diligent pupil, winning a prize at the Accademia di San Luca for a drawing of *Alexander Cutting the Gordian Knot* (Rome, Accad. N. S Luca).

After returning to France, Boullogne was employed at Versailles, like his brother. He produced several works for the Petits Appartements of the King and Queen of which *Erato and Melpomene* survives (Versailles, Grand Trianon). Soon after, he was accepted (*reçu*) by the Académie Royale (1 August 1681) with *Augustus Closing the Temple of Janus after the Battle of Actium* (Amiens, Mus. Picardie), an obvious allusion to the Peace of Nijmegen (1678–9) in which Louis XIV is identified with the Emperor Augustus.

After work for the chapel at Versailles (*see* (2) above), a *St Anthony* for the parish of St Cyr and a *Holy Family* for the chapel of the Maison de St Cyr, in 1686 was commissioned by Denis-Germain Godin and Pierre Anceau for his first May of Notre-Dame, *Christ and the Centurion* (Arras, Mus. B.-A.). In 1688 he painted a *Visitation* (Greenville, SC, Bob Jones U. Gal. Sacred A.), derived from a painting by Barotti in the Chiesa Nuova in Rome. With his brother Bon, he contributed to the decoration of the Trianon at Versailles, painting *Venus and Adonis* and *Venus, Hymen and Cupids* (both Versailles, Grand Trianon). The similarities of the brothers' styles makes it difficult sometimes to distinguish their work.

Louis de Boullogne: *Diana and her Companions Resting after the Hunt*, oil on canvas, 1.05×1.63 m, 1707 (Tours, Musée des Beaux-Arts)

In 1690 Louis took part, with Bon, in the competition arranged by Abbé Charles d'Aligre for the abbey in Saint-Riquier, presenting an *Annunciation* (lost). In the early 1690s he worked at the château of Chantilly for Henry-Jules, Prince de Condé (1643–1709). Although some of the works for the château have disappeared, several pictures remain in the church there, including the *Life of St Hubert* and the *Adoration of the Shepherds*, the latter derived from a work by Poussin (London, N.G.). Boullogne became an assistant professor at the Académie in 1690 and full professor in 1694. In 1695 he painted *Christ and the Woman with an Issue of Blood* (Rennes, Mus. B.-A. & Archéol.; sketch in Paris, Carnavalet) and a second May, commissioned by Adrien Poly and Louis du Mont depicting *Christ and the Woman of Samaria* (Wardour Castle, Wilts).

A period of intense activity working for private collectors and on official commissions began in 1697 with *Jupiter Caressed by Europa* and the *Abduction of Europa* for the staircase of the Trianon at Versailles. Boullogne exhibited 14 mythological, religious and portrait paintings at the Salon of 1699 and 18 at the Salon of 1704. In 1699 with Antoine Coypel, Charles de La Fosse and Jean Jouvenet he worked on the decoration of the Salon of the château of Marly with *Ceres: an Allegory of the Month of August* (Rouen, Mus. B.-A.). Also with these artists he worked on the Salon of the château of Meudon in 1700, painting *Cephalus and Procris* (Saint-Etienne, Mus. A. & Indust.), inspired by the Bolognese style. He participated in decorating the château of Fontainebleau with the harmonious *Minerva among the Sciences and Arts* and *Flora Crowned by Zephyr* (both Fontainebleau, Château) at Versailles for the Trianon he painted *Apollo and Hyacinthe* and *Apollo and the Daughter of Glaucus* (all Versailles, Grand Trianon), and the Ménagerie he produced *Venus Requesting Arms for Aeneas* (copy at Fontainebleau).

Around 1703, with La Fosse, Joseph Parocel and others, Boullogne worked on the cycle the *Life of St Augustine* in the refectory of the monastery of the Petits-Pères; Place des Victoires, Paris; the painted *The Baptism* (Bordeaux, Mus. Bordeaux), the *Ordination of the Saint* and other works. In 1707 he was employed, with Bon, by Louis-Alexandre, Comte de Toulouse, at the château of Rambouillet, where he painted two large overdoors for the Cabinet du Roi, *Diana and her Companions Hunting Wild Boar* and *Diana and her Attendants Resting after the Hunt* (see fig.; both Tours, Mus. B.-A.). This mythological inspiration, with an elegance inherited from early Italian models, is also found in *Mars and Venus* (1712; Berlin, Schloss Charlottenburg). Louis worked with Bon at the chapel at Versailles, where he painted the vaults on the south side and the chapel of the Virgin; in 1709 he painted an *Annunciation* for the altar of this chapel. He went on to produce other religious paintings for churches in Paris.

In 1716 Boullogne was commissioned to paint a work to adorn one of the fireplaces of the main hall in the Hôtel de Ville, Paris, that commemorated the enoblement by the King in 1715 of eight members of the town council (sketch, Paris, Carnavalet). Having achieved wealth and fame, he ceased painting almost completely when he was offered the *cursus honorum*, in which Antoine Coypel preceded him. After appointment as Rector of the Académie Royale in 1717, he became Director in 1722. Also in 1722 he was one of the first artists to be admitted into the Ordre de St-Michel, and he was commissioned to design the King's medals for the Académie des Inscriptions, of which he became a member. In November 1724 his 50 years of work decorating royal houses earned his ennoblement by Louis XV. In 1725 he became Premier Peintre du Roi, a position vacant since Coypel's death in 1722. He also painted for the Académie Royale the grisaille *Union of Painting and Sculpture* (priv. col.) engraved by Thomassin. Upon his death, his children inherited a considerable fortune. An important group of his studio drawings and preparatory studies is housed in the Musée du Louvre, Paris.

BIBLIOGRAPHY

A. Schnapper: 'Esquisses de Louis de Boullogne sur la vie de saint Augustin', *Rev. A.* (1970)

——: 'Louis de Boullogne à l'église de Chantilly', *Rev. A.* (1976)

H. Guicharnaud: 'Les *Quatre Eléments* de Louis de Boullogne: Etudes préparatoires', *Rev. Louvre* (1985)

A. Schnapper and H. Guicharnaud: *Louis de Boullogne, 1654–1733* (Paris, [1/1986])

H. Guicharnaud: 'Louis de Boullogne', *Dessins français du XVIIIe siècle, de Watteau à Lemoyne* (exh. cat., Paris, Louvre, 1987)

——: 'Les Dessins préparatoires de Louis de Boullogne pour les tableaux du choeur de Notre-Dame de Paris', *Gaz. B.-A.* (Oct 1989), pp. 127–42

——: 'Louis de Boullogne's Drawings for the Chapel of St Augustine in the Dome Church of the Invalides', *Master Drgs*, xxxii (1994), pp. 3–25

——: 'La Dynastie des Boullogne, peintres sous l'Ancien Régime', *L'Estampille—Objet d'Art* (June 1994), pp. 32–51

——: 'L'Oeuvre mythologique gravé de Louis de Boullogne', *Gaz. B.-A.* (Dec 1994), pp. 233–42

C. Constans: *Les Peintures du Musée National du château de Versailles et des Trianons* (1995)

H. Guicharnaud: 'Les *Minerve* de Louis de Boullogne (1654–1733)', *Rev. Louvre*, 2 (1995), pp. 44–51

HÉLÈNE GUICHARNAUD

Boulogne, Jean. *See* GIAMBOLOGNA.

Boulogne, Valentin de [Le Valentin] (*b* Coulommiers-en-Brie, Seine-et-Marne, *bapt* ?3 Jan 1591; *d* Rome, 18/19 Aug 1632). French painter, active in Italy. He spent most of his career in Rome, where he came under the influence of Caravaggio and Bartolomeo Manfredi. He continued to paint in a variant of their dramatic chiaroscuro style even after this had fallen out of fashion in Italy. Although he is best known for his low-life genre scenes of the kind popularized by Manfredi, these represent only one aspect of a more varied oeuvre that also includes devotional pictures, allegories and portraits. The poetic character of his style, at once violent and tender, makes him one of the most engaging French painters of the 17th century.

1. EARLY CAREER AND LIFE IN ROME. Valentin was the son of a painter and glassworker, also called Valentin de Boulogne, whose family had lived in Coulommiers since at least 1489. The surname appears to derive from Boulogne-sur-Mer, Pas-de Calais. One of his two brothers, Jean de Boulogne (*b* 8 June 1601), also became a painter. There is confusion about Valentin's date of birth, as his death certificate of 1632 says that he died aged 38, while Dauvergne transcribed the date on his now lost baptismal record as 3 January 1591. He presumably trained first in his father's studio and then perhaps in Paris or at Fontainebleau. At an unknown date he left for Italy. He may have

been the 'Valentino francese' mentioned in the Roman *Stati d'anime* for 1611 as living in the parish of S Nicola ai Prefetti with a Florentine painter named Polidoro. If he was in Rome at this date, it would confirm Sandrart's assertion that Valentin arrived in the city before Simon Vouet, that is before 1614. The first definite mention of his presence is in the *stati d'anime* for 1620, when he was living in the parish of S Maria del Popolo. He was described as 'Valentino Bologni, francese' and was living with Gérard Douffet, a painter from Liège, and David Lariche, a sculptor from Lorraine, with both of whom he was still living in 1622. In 1624–5 he shared his accommodation with 'David di Lorena scultore'. Also in 1624 Valentin, under the nickname 'Amador' or 'Inamorato', joined the group of mainly Dutch and Flemish painters called the Schildersbent. He nevertheless maintained contact with those of his fellow countrymen who were members of the Accademia di S Luca (of which Vouet was elected Principe in October 1624), and in September 1626 he was nominated, along with Nicolas Poussin, to take charge of the Accademia's festivities for the celebration of that year's feast of St Luke. From 1629 documents refer to the artist, who had servants, as 'Signor Valentino', and until 1632 Jean Lhomme, a little-known painter, is recorded as living with or near him.

The last years of Valentin's life are relatively well known. Like other French painters in Rome, he worked for the francophile Barberini family, and from 1627 Cardinal Francesco Barberini gave him regular commissions. A *David* (Fountain Valley, CA, priv. col., see 1982 exh. cat., no. 109) and a *Beheading of St John the Baptist* (ex-Gal. Sciarra, Rome, mid-19th century) date from these years. An *Allegory of Rome*—or *Allegory of Italy*—(Rome, Villa Lante) and a portrait of *Cardinal Barberini* (untraced) were paid for in 1628. A *Samson* (Cleveland, OH, Mus. A.) was paid for by Barberini at the end of 1630. The previous year Valentin had been commissioned to paint for the basilica of St Peter an altarpiece depicting the *Martyrdom of SS Processus and Martinian* (Rome, Pin. Vaticana), a mark of particular favour. Valentin also worked for other patrons in the Barberini circle, such as Cardinal Angelo Giori, private secretary to Urban VIII, for whom he painted a *St John the Baptist* and a *St Jerome* (both Camerino, Marches, S Marina in Via), and Cassiano dal Pozzo, of whom he made a portrait (untraced) that in 1689 was in the collection of Queen Christina of Sweden. He also painted a portrait of Urban VIII's jester *Raffaello Menicucci* (Indianapolis, IN, Mus. A.). One of Valentin's last commissions was the large painting *Gathering with a Fortune-teller* (priv. col., on loan to Toronto, A.G. Ont.), which he painted in the spring of 1631 for Fabrizio Valguarnera, a Sicilian nobleman who turned out to be dishonest. When Valguarnera was eventually brought to trial in Rome, Valentin was asked to describe his picture and the circumstances of the commission in a deposition dated July 1631. According to Baglione, Valentin died from a chill caught after bathing in a fountain following an evening of smoking and drinking. Baglione also stated that Cassiano dal Pozzo paid for the funeral.

2. WORKS AND STYLISTIC DEVELOPMENT. Valentin's surviving oeuvre is made up of around 75 paintings. A

further 10 pictures are known through copies. A few of the paintings from the last five years of Valentin's career, fortunately all masterpieces, are precisely datable; their characteristic execution and spirit make it possible to group around them a number of other pictures and thus to define Valentin's late style, which remained close to that of Caravaggio and Manfredi. Any other attempt to construct a chronology for his works must be conjectural.

The main question remains the date of the earliest extant works by Valentin. They were perhaps painted around 1615 or even a little earlier. A group of pictures that have a very different character to the late documented ones may be placed around this date. They depict relatively short figures with closed contours and a solid, sculptural quality, which emerge aggressively from a dark background. They are painted with a loaded brush and broken modelling and have a raw lateral lighting reminiscent of the work of the contemporary painter active in Rome known as Cecco del Caravaggio, who may have been French or from the north. The well-known *Cheats* (Dresden, Gemäldegal. Alte Meister) and the three-figure *Concert* (Chatsworth, Derbys) are good characteristic examples of this early style. Valentin's earliest religious works, the *Crowning with Thorns* (UK, priv. col.) and a *St Paul Writing* (sold Milan, Finarte, 1 Dec 1981), have very close links with northern artists such as Hendrick ter Brugghen. A *David* (Lugano, Col. Thyssen-Bornemisza) and two pendants, *Christ and the Woman of Samaria* and *Noli me*

tangere (both Perugia, G.N. Umbria), could be dated a little later.

Perhaps towards 1618 Valentin seems to have progressed to working on more monumental paintings. He became more skilful in his treatment of space and had clearly absorbed the influence of Caravaggio's *Calling of St Matthew* in S Luigi dei Francesi, Rome, as well as of certain paintings by Manfredi, such as the *Denial of St Peter* (Brunswick, Herzog Anton Ulrich-Mus.). Examples are Valentin's *Fortune-teller* (Toledo, OH, Mus. A.), the *Denial of St Peter* (Florence, Fond. Longhi) and *Soldiers Playing Cards and Dice* (France, priv. col.). *Christ Driving the Money-changers from the Temple* (Rome, Pal. Corsini), with its similar opposition of blues and resonant reds in a strong chiaroscuro, can be placed close in date to these pictures, perhaps around 1620. The paintings *Caesar's Pence*, the *Four Evangelists* (Versailles, Château), *Christ and the Woman Taken in Adultery* (Malibu, CA, Getty Mus.) and the *Innocence of Susanna* (Paris, Louvre) can probably all be dated around 1620–22, while the *Concert with a Classical Bas-relief* (Paris, Louvre) was probably executed a little later.

Towards the middle of the 1620s the modelling of the figures in Valentin's works appears to have become more complex, the psychological nuances more delicate and the colouring more refined, employing greys more readily, while the paint matter became fine, almost as if transparent. Pictures of this period are the *Crowning with Thorns* with

1. Valentin de Boulogne: *Four Ages of Man*, oil on canvas, 965×1340 mm, 1625–6 (London, National Gallery)

2. Valentin de Boulogne: *Judgement of Solomon*, oil on canvas, 1.76×2.10 m, *c*. 1625 (Paris, Musée du Louvre)

four figures (Munich, Alte Pin.), *Judith and Holofernes* (Valletta, N. Mus.), the *Four Ages of Man* (London, N.G.; see fig. 1), *Judith* (Toulouse, Mus. Augustins) and the *Judgement of Solomon* (Paris, Louvre; see fig. 2). The forceful and expressive portrait of *Raffaello Menicucci* can be placed around 1625.

The documented paintings from the last five years of Valentin's life allow an accurate definition of his style at a time when he was placing increasing importance on the psychological relationships between the figures in his works. The *Moses* in the Kunsthistorisches Museum, Vienna, can be compared to the Barberini *David* paid for in 1627. Alongside such masterpieces as the Caravaggesque *Allegory of Rome* (1628) and the *Martyrdom of SS Processus and Martinian* (1629), both painted with bold lyricism and a rare refinement, may be placed the melancholy and intense canvases of *Erminia and the Shepherds* (Munich, Alte Pin.), the *Fortune-teller* and the *Concert* with eight figures (both Paris, Louvre). Several vertical format figures of saints can be compared to the Barberini *Samson* (1631). These are the Giori *St Jerome* and *St John the Baptist* and another *St Jerome* (Wellesley Coll., MA, Mus.). The Valguarnera *Gathering with a Fortune-teller*, painted early in 1631, would appear to bring together for the last time Valentin's genre figures in a composition that is almost too overloaded. Among his last works may also be included another series of *Evangelists* (Switzerland, priv. col.), two standing figures of the adolescent *St John the Baptist* (Apiro, Collegiata S Urbano; Saint-Jean-de-Maurienne Cathedral) and a *Sacrifice of Abraham* (Montreal, Mus. F.A.).

BIBLIOGRAPHY

Thieme–Becker
G. Baglione: *Vite* (1642); ed. V. Mariani (1935), pp. 337–8
J. von Sandrart: *Teutsche Academie* (1675–9); ed. A. R. Peltzer (1925), p. 256
A. Dauvergne: 'Notes sur le Valentin', *Gaz. B.-A.*, i (1879), pp. 203–8
R. Longhi: 'A propos de Valentin', *Rev. des A.*, ii (1958), pp. 58–66
J. Thuillier: 'Un Peintre passionné', *L'Oeil*, xlvii (1958), pp. 27–33
M. Hoog: 'Attributions anciennes à Valentin', *Rev. des A.*, vi (1960), pp. 267–78
N. Ivanoff: *Valentin de Boulogne*, Maestri Colore, 171 (Milan, 1966)
I caravaggeschi francesi/Valentin et les caravagesques français (exh. cat. by A. Brejon de Lavergnée and J.-P. Cuzin, Rome, Acad. France; Paris, Grand Pal.; 1973–4)
J.-P. Cuzin: 'Pour Valentin', *Rev. A.* [Paris], xxviii (1975), pp. 53–61
La Peinture française du XVIIe siècle dans les collections américaines (exh. cat. by P. Rosenberg, Paris, Grand Pal.; New York, Met.; Chicago, A. Inst.; 1982)
M. Mojana: *Valentin de Boulogne* (Milan, 1989)

JEAN-PIERRE CUZIN

Boulton, Matthew (*b* Birmingham, 14 Sept 1728; *d* Birmingham, 17 Aug 1809). English manufacturer and engineer. At the age of 17 he entered his father's silver stamping and piercing business at Snow Hill, Birmingham, which he inherited in 1759. His marriage in 1756 brought a considerable dowry, providing capital for the establishment in 1762 of his factory in Soho, Birmingham, in partnership with John Fothergill (*d* 1782). Boulton progressed from the production of 'toys' in tortoiseshell, stone, glass, enamel and cut steel to that of tableware in SHEFFIELD PLATE, on which he obtained a monopoly, and later ormolu (e.g. two pairs of candelabra, *c*. 1770; Brit. Royal Col.; London, V&A) and silver, and enjoyed a reputation for fine craftsmanship. By 1770 his firm, known as Boulton & Fothergill, had nearly 800 employees and had mercantile contacts in virtually every town in Europe. His social, political and trade connections facilitated the establishment of assay offices in Birmingham and Sheffield in 1773, and in the former city Boulton's firm became one of the largest manufacturers of silver and Sheffield plate.

Boulton & Fothergill produced some of the best-designed plate and silver in the last quarter of the 18th century and fully exploited the technical advances of Joseph Hancock and R. A. F. de Réaumur. The thinner gauges of Sheffield plate available from the 1770s, and the precision of machine-produced, fly-punched parts that were cut, stamped and pierced in repeated patterns were suitable for regular, uniform Neo-classical designs, in which a clear distinction can be discerned between structure and decoration. As the items produced in silver, for example dinner services, tureens, coffee- and teapots and candelabra, were made increasingly for stock rather than to order, Boulton also adopted the manufacturing techniques of items in Sheffield plate for those in solid silver, especially for objects with simple forms requiring little chasing or hand-finishing. Notable among Boulton's products are a silver helmet-shaped ewer (1774; Birmingham, Mus. & A.G.), a similar silver-gilt ewer (1776; Boston, MA, Mus. F.A.), a pair of silver sauce tureens (1776; Birmingham, Assay Office), and a pair of Sheffield plate candelabra (1797; Birmingham, Mus. & A.G.). Many of his pattern books are in the Reference Library, Birmingham. Boulton trained his employees to his own processes rather than take on apprenticed silversmiths, and for silverware he used designs by the silversmiths Thomas Heming and Michelangelo Pergolesi (*fl* 1777–1801) and such architects as Robert Adam, who designed a set of eight sauceboats (1776–7; one London, V&A; *see* ENGLAND, fig. 79), James Adam, William Chambers, Robert Mylne, James Stuart and James Wyatt. Boulton's die-sinkers and medallists included the Frenchman JEAN-PIERRE DROZ and the German Conrad Heinrich Küchler (d 1821). Later distinguished silversmiths whom Boulton trained were Edward Thomason (1769–1849) and Benjamin Smith (1764–1823). Boulton also collaborated with his friend Josiah Wedgwood, who used similar design sources, production methods and marketing techniques and produced cut-steel frames for jasper cameos (examples in London, V&A).

Boulton was less a craftsman and designer than an industrial entrepreneur, organizing factory production of metalwork and managing designers both within and outside his extended workshop system, thereby revolutionizing the silver manufacturing trade and challenging the monopoly of silversmiths in London. He produced silver and Sheffield plate to the highest technical standard in the most fashionable styles and made such small wares as buckles and fittings available to a wider market. A large part of the production of silver, however, continued to consist of ornamental pieces that were expensive to produce. His production of ormolu, which ceased in the 1780s, was only partially successful, as he tried to compete with French manufacturers. As the processes involved in the manufacture of ormolu were not suited to mass-production, this part of his business failed to be profitable.

Towards the end of his life Boulton concentrated on his engineering enterprises. By 1787 his input of capital and the technical expertise of James Watt (1736–1819) enabled the widespread use of the steam engine, superseding water-power, for operating mechanical lathes and stamps, thereby increasing production up to tenfold. In Birmingham Boulton was co-founder of the Lunar Society and in London a fellow of the Royal Society. His scientific and intellectual friends included Sir Joseph Banks, Erasmus Darwin (1731–1802), Richard Lovell Edgeworth (1744–1817), Benjamin Franklin (1706–90), Samuel Galton, Sir William Hamilton (i), Sir William Herschel (1738–1822) and Joseph Priestley (1733–1804). The factory, known from 1781 as the Matthew Boulton Plate Co., continued after his death, producing such pieces as J. Widdowson's silver copy (1827; Birmingham, Assay Office) of the Warwick Vase (2nd to 4th century AD; Glasgow, Burrell Col.); it remained in operation until the 1840s and was sold in 1850.

DNB

BIBLIOGRAPHY

H. W. Dickinson: *Matthew Boulton* (Cambridge, 1936)
W. A. Seaby and R. J. Hetherington: 'The Matthew Boulton Pattern Books', *Apollo*, li (1950), pp. 48–50, 78–80
E. Robinson: 'Matthew Boulton: Patron of the Arts', *An. Sci.*, ix (1953), pp. 368–76
——: 'Eighteenth-century Commerce and Fashion: Matthew Boulton's Marketing Techniques', *Econ. Hist. Rev.*, n. s., xvi/1 (1963), pp. 39–60
R. Rowe: *Adam Silver* (London, 1965)
J. Cornforth: 'An Age of Optimism: The Lunar Society—I', *Country Life*, cxl (13 Oct 1966), pp. 906–8
The Lunar Society (exh. cat., Birmingham, Mus. & A.G., 1966)
E. Delieb and M. Roberts: *The Great Silver Manufactory* (London, 1971)
H. Honour: *Goldsmiths and Silversmiths* (London, 1971), pp. 216–21
Birmingham Gold and Silver, 1773–1973 (exh. cat., Birmingham, Mus. & A.G., 1973)
N. P. Goodison: *Ormolu: The Work of Matthew Boulton* (London, 1974)
N. McKendrick, J. Brewer and J. H. Plumb: *The Birth of a Consumer Society* (London, 1982/R 1983), pp. 69–77
Matthew Boulton and the Toymakers (exh. cat., London, Goldsmiths' Co., 1982)

RICHARD RIDDELL

Bouman [Bauman], **Elias** (*b* ?1636; *d* Amsterdam, *bur* 18 March 1686). Dutch architect. He trained as a bricklayer in his father's workshop, and after taking the qualifying examination (1659), was appointed Master Bricklayer. From 1681 until his death he was City Architect of Amsterdam. Bouman is known from several buildings he created in the Severe style—the last phase of Dutch classicism at the end of the 17th century—for the Portuguese-Jewish community in the city. Around 1651 he designed a distinguished house, which now serves as a public library among other functions, for the wealthy Isaak de Pinto. In the design, he incorporated parts of two existing buildings. The vertical articulation of the stone façade with pilasters is crowned by a projecting cornice and an attic. Bouman's most notable work is the imposing Portuguese Synagogue (1671), erected in what was then the Jewish district (*see* AMSTERDAM, §V, 3).

BIBLIOGRAPHY

A. M. Vaz Dias: 'Elias Bouman, de architect van de Portugese synagoge', *Amstelodamum*, xi (1934), pp. 87–91
F. A. J. Vermeulen: *Handboek tot de geschiedenis der Nederlandse bouwkunst* [History of Dutch architecture], iii (The Hague, 1941)
J. Rosenberg, S. Slive and E. H. ter Kulle: *Dutch Art and Architecture, 1600–1800*, Pelican Hist. A. (Harmondsworth, 1966)
J. F. van Agt: *Synagogen in Amsterdam* (The Hague, 1974)

PAUL H. REM

Boumann, Johann [Bouman, Jan] (*b* Amsterdam, 1706; *d* Berlin, 6 Sept 1776). Dutch architect and carpenter, active in Germany. One of many Dutch tradesmen invited to Prussia by Frederick William I, he arrived in 1732 in Potsdam, where he built the Dutch Quarter (1734–42) with its 134 red-brick and mostly Dutch-gabled houses. On the axis of the Quarter's Kreuzstrasse, he built a 'gloriette' pavilion (1739) on an island in the pond known as the Bassin. Later works in Potsdam included the execution of Georg Wenceslaus von Knobelsdorff's Französische Kirche (1752) on the Bassinplatz, modelled on the Pantheon, Rome, and the Berlin Gate (1752) in the new city wall, which was also influenced by Roman architecture. His design for the Rathaus (1753) in Potsdam was based on Palladio's unexecuted Palazzo Angarano, Vicenza. Crowning the composition is a domeless drum with colossal Corinthian columns and attic storey, topped by the gilt figure of Atlas bearing the globe.

Boumann was also active in Berlin, where he restored the Akademie building (1745) on Unter den Linden and executed Knobelsdorff's severely classical designs for the palace of Prince Heinrich (1748–64; after 1809 Friedrich-Wilhelm University; after 1949 Humboldt University). Frederick the Great's sketches determined the Baroque style of Boumann's Lutheran Cathedral (1747–50; remodelled by Schinkel 1816; destr. 1890s). In 1770–73 Boumann completed Jean-Laurent Legeay's Neo-classical St Hedwig's Roman Catholic Church (begun 1747), also on Unter den Linden. In the Royal Palace (1750–51; destr.) in Breslau (now Wrocław, Poland), Boumann repeated the sober classicism of the palace of Prince Heinrich but added elegant Rococo interiors. He was also responsible for numerous military buildings. Two of his sons became architects: Michael Daniel Philipp Boumann (*d* 1805), architect of Schloss Bellevue (1785), Berlin, and Georg Friedrich Boumann (1737–1812/18), who executed the plans of Georg Christian Unger (1743–1804/12) for the Royal Library (1774–80) in Berlin, as well as designs by Carl Gotthard Langhans for theatres in Charlottenburg (1788–9) and Potsdam (1795; destr.).

BIBLIOGRAPHY

H. L. Manger: *Baugeschichte von Potsdam, besonders unter Regierung König Friedrichs II* (Berlin, 1789–90)
C. Gurlitt: *Geschichte des Barockstiles und des Rococo in Deutschland* (Stuttgart, 1889)
M. Kania: *Potsdamer Baukunst* (Potsdam, 1915)
E. Hempel: *Baroque Art and Architecture in Central Europe*, Pelican Hist. A. (Harmondsworth, 1965)
H.-J. Giersberg and H. Knitter: *Potsdam* (Berlin, 1978)
F. Mielke: *Potsdamer Baukunst* (Berlin, 1981)

RAND CARTER

Bouqras. See BUQRAS.

Bouquel, Aníbal Alvarez. See ALVAREZ, (2).

Bourassa, Napoléon (*b* Acadie, Qué., 21 Oct 1827; *d* Lachenaie, Qué., 27 Aug 1916). Canadian architect, painter, sculptor, writer and teacher. He studied law in Montreal (1848–50), also attending classes under the Quebec painter Théophile Hamel until 1851. In 1852 Bourassa went to Italy, staying there for three years. Inspired by Victor Cousin's treatise *Du vrai, du beau, du bien* (Paris, 1826, rev. 2/1853), which popularized a philosophy of eclecticism, he sought to influence artistic trends in Canada not only through promoting art as a means of developing moral and intellectual values but through encouraging state patronage of the arts.

Among Bourassa's early paintings are portraits of his parents (1851; Quebec, Mus. Qué.) and of such leading churchmen as J.O. Archambault (St-Hyacinthe, Semin.). His first architectural work was the church of Notre-Dame-de-Lourdes, Montreal (begun 1872), for which he and a group of pupils also produced paintings and sculptures (*in situ*). Like several of Bourassa's projects, this was influenced by the work of Hippolyte Flandrin. In 1883 Bourassa failed to win the commission to decorate the new Legislative Assembly building in Quebec, but some preliminary drawings and paintings for a mural entitled *Apotheosis of Christopher Columbus* (Quebec, Mus. Qué.), influenced by Jean-Auguste-Dominique Ingres and Paul Delaroche, indicate his intentions. In 1889–92 he drew plans (Quebec, Mus. Qué.; Ottawa, N. Archv) for the decoration of Saint-Hyacinthe Cathedral, but the project was abandoned. Other churches to which Bourassa contributed are those at Montebello, Quebec, and St Anne at Fall River, MA, USA. He also produced sculptures of the politician Louis-Joseph Papineau (e.g. bust, Quebec, Mus. Qué.), whose daughter he married, and a few paintings on social themes (e.g. *Poverty*; Quebec, Mus. Qué.). Besides giving many lectures on art, he taught at the Ecole Normale Jacques-Cartier in Montreal and the Institut Canadien-Français des Arts et Métiers. He left more than 400 manuscript pages on art and some 1000 letters of social and political interest as well as of significance to 19th-century Canadian art history.

UNPUBLISHED SOURCES

Montreal, Oratory of St Joseph [misc. doc.]
Ottawa, N. Archv [drgs, photographs, MSS]
Quebec, Mus. Qué. [drgs, watercolours, ptgs]
Sainte-Foy, Archvs N. Qué. [letters]

BIBLIOGRAPHY

A. Bourassa: *Napoléon Bourassa (1827–1916): Un Artiste canadien-français* (Montreal, 1968)
R. Vézina: *Napoléon Bourassa (1827–1916): Introduction à l'étude de son art* (Montreal, 1976)
E. J. Sullivan: 'Napoléon Bourassa', *Can. Colr*, xiv (1979), pp. 32–7

RAYMOND VÉZINA

Bourbon [Borbón], House of. Dynasty of French and Spanish rulers, patrons and collectors. The French branch of the family (*see* §I below) ruled France from 1589 to 1792 and again from 1814 to 1830. The Spanish branch (*see* §II below) was established in 1700, when the grandson of the French king Louis XIV succeeded to the Spanish throne as Philip V.

I. French branch. II. Spanish branch.

I. French branch.

This line (see fig.) was descended from Robert Capet (1256–1317), Comte de Clermont-en-Beauvaisis, the sixth son of King Louis IX (*see* CAPET, (2)). (1) John II was a descendant in direct line of the first Duke of Bourbon, Louis I (*reg* 1327–41). John II's brother (2) Cardinal Charles renounced his title in favour of their younger brother, (3) Peter II. Suzanne (1491–1521) the sole heir of Peter II and his wife (4) Anne, died without issue. Louise of Savoy, the mother of Francis I of France, then claimed the duchy as granddaughter of Charles I (*reg* 1434–56), leading Suzanne's husband, Charles III of Montpensier (1490–1527), who was Constable of France, to defect to the service of Charles V of Spain (1523). The Bourbon name was thereupon vested in the cadet family branch, the Vendômes, and, through Anthony (*d* 1562), consort of Queen Joanna III of Navarre (*reg* 1555–72), niece of Francis I, it gained title to the throne of France: their son became the first Bourbon king of France, as (5) Henry IV, in 1589. From Henry IV and his wife, (6) Marie de' Medici, were descended all subsequent French kings: (7) Louis XIII, (8) Louis XIV, (10) Louis XV and (11) Louis XVI, the last of whom, with his wife, (12) Marie-Antoinette, was guillotined during the French Revolution. Louis XVI's brother (13) Louis XVIII reclaimed the throne in 1814; he was succeeded by another brother, (14) Charles X and by Louis-Philippe of the cadet Orléans branch of the Bourbon family (*see* ORLEANS, House of, (7)), who would be the last king of France.

BIBLIOGRAPHY

J. M. de La Mure: *Histoire des ducs de Bourbon et des comtes de Forez*, 4 vols (Paris, 1860–8)
P. Van Kerrebrouck: *La Maison de Bourbon, 1256–1987*, Nouvelle histoire généalogique de l'auguste Maison de France, iv (Villeneuve d'Ascq, 1987)

(1) John [Jean] **II**, Duke of Bourbon (*b* Moulins, 30 Aug 1426; *reg* 1456–88; *d* Moulins, 1 April 1488). He was the eldest son of Charles I (*reg* 1434–56) and Agnès of Burgundy (*d* 1476). He married Joanna of France (*d* 1482), the daughter of King Charles VII, in 1452, Catherine d'Armagnac (*d* 1487) in 1484 and Jeanne de Bourbon-Vendôme (*d* 1511) in 1487. From 1449 he was captain in Normandy and was royal lieutenant (1451) and governor of Guyenne (until 1454). He opposed King Louis XI's efforts to reduce feudalism and was a main adherent to

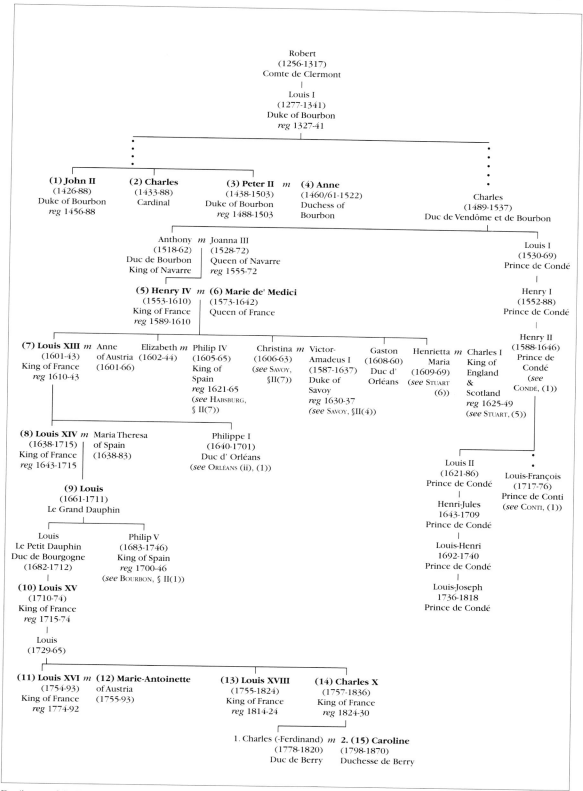

Family tree of the French branch of the Bourbon dynasty

the League of the Public Weal. Through political manoeuvres, he became Constable of France in 1483.

In Moulins, John II surrounded himself with artists and writers, including the musician Joachim Okeghem, the poets Henri Baude, Octavien de Saint-Gelais, François Villon and Georges Ravel, author of the *Livre des armes des pays de Bourbonnais et d'Auvergne*. A number of works were dedicated to the Duke, a noted bibliophile: Conrad Heingarter's *Commentaire sur le Quadripartitum de Ptolémée* (Paris, Bib. N., MS. lat. 11232); Guillaume Menard's translation of Ludolf the Carthusian's *Vita Christi*; and Toussaint de Villeneuve, Bishop of Cavaillon's *Petit médicinal* (Paris, Bib. N., MS. fr. 2445). The Duke ordered copies, many from the scribe and dealer Michel Gonneau, of various Classical texts, and he also owned a copy of Dante's *Divine Comedy*. The humanist Jean Robertet was his secretary and librarian.

John II's first wife, Joanna of France, owned over 12 manuscripts of her own, in which she placed her motto AU CHOIS T'E ELUE. Antoine de Lévis dedicated to her his *Défenseur de la conception immaculée de la sainte Vierge* (Paris, Bib. N., MS. fr. 989), in the frontispiece of which she is depicted by the Master of Jouvenel des Ursins, and Jean Henry of Paris his *La Gésine Notre Dame* (Paris, Bib. N., MS. fr. 1866). Joanna kneels before the Virgin of the Immaculate Conception in a diptych (Chantilly, Mus. Condé) by a follower of Rogier van der Weyden. In 1484, on the occasion of Catherine d'Armagnac's entry into Moulins, the sculptors Michel Colombe, Thévenin l'imagier and Jean de Rouen and the painters Claude Avisart, Pérot Sormeau and Piètre Claude were summoned. Catherine had a Book of Hours (ex-Frankfurt) illuminated *c.* 1486 by Jean Bourdichon. The painters Etienne Saulnier, Pierre Guizebert and Guillaume Mémorin were called on for the entry of Jeanne of Bourbon into Moulins in 1487.

John II initiated architectural and sculptural projects in Moulins and its outlying region. Construction of the collegiate church of Moulins (a cathedral since 1824) was begun in 1474. The portal of 1487–8 (destr.) included statues of *John II* and *Jeanne of Bourbon*. John II also ordered works at the castle of Moulins. More important was the construction of a SAINTE-CHAPELLE at Bourbon-l'Archambault (Allier). It included statues of the Twelve Apostles within and, on the portal, *St Louis* on the trumeau and *Adam* and *Eve* as well as standing figures of the Duke and Duchess on the embrasures. The only extant fragment of this sculptural campaign is a small sandstone kneeling figure (Baltimore, MD, Walters A.G.) depicting *John II* as peer of France with the collar of the Order of St Michael. Attributed to Michel Colombe, it was in the crypt at the foot of a votive Crucifixion with a figure of Joanna of France.

The *Annunciation* (Chicago, IL, A. Inst.) and *Meeting of Joachim and Anna at the Golden Gate with Charlemagne* (London, N.G.), two panels attributed to the MASTER OF MOULINS (*see* MASTERS, ANONYMOUS, & MONOGRAMMISTS, §I) were allegedly commissioned by John II. The Duke may have availed himself of the skills of the Florentine painter Benedetto Ghirlandaio, long active in France; around 1483 Ghirlandaio was at Bourbon-l'Archambault, where he executed an altarpiece of the *Nativity* (Aigueperse, Notre-Dame) for the Montpensier family.

BIBLIOGRAPHY
H. de Surirey de Saint-Rémy: *Jean II de Bourbon, duc de Bourbonnais et d'Auvergne, 1426–1488* (Paris, 1944)
M. Weinberger: 'A French Model of the Fifteenth Century', *J. Walters A.G.*, ix (1946), pp. 8–21
P. Pradel: *Michel Colombe* (Paris, 1953)

PATRICK M. DE WINTER

(2) Cardinal **Charles of Bourbon** (*b* Moulins, 1433; *d* Lyon, 13 Sept 1488). Brother of (1) John II. Powerful family influence ensured that at the age of 13 he was confirmed by the Pope as Archbishop of Lyon. Thereafter his close association with Louis XI as royal councillor and diplomat brought him many favours, including the rich revenues of several abbeys and priories, and in 1476 he was made Cardinal by Sixtus IV. After Louis XI's death in 1483 Charles retired from the court at Paris to Lyon, and, on his eventual succession to the dukedom in 1488, he renounced the title in favour of his younger brother, (3) Peter.

As early as 1469 Charles of Bourbon used the revenues of the abbey of St Vaast, near Arras, to purchase a large number of textiles in Bruges, including four silk hangings of the *Story of Geoffrey of Boulogne* and a tapestry with silk of the *Story of St Anne*. Most of the surviving works of art once owned by him, however, appear to have been acquired after 1476, since they bear his arms as cardinal. Among these are two tapestries of the *Coronation of the Virgin* and *Adoration of the Magi* (both Sens Cathedral) and two more of the *Story of Hercules* (Paris, Mobilier N.; Wellesley Coll., MA, Jewett A. Cent.), all of which were probably woven in the Low Countries. Charles also owned the Versailles Livy (Paris, Bib. N., MSS fr. 273–4), a copy of Pierre Bersuire's French translation of Livy with many illuminations in a style close to that of Jean Fouquet; an illuminated copy of the *Vie de Saint Louis* (Paris, Bib. N., MS. fr. 2829), which includes in its elaborate frontispiece two full-length portraits of the Cardinal; a Greek–Latin Gospels (Paris, Bib. N., MS. grec 55) illuminated by the Master of Jacques de Besançon; and a French illuminated Missal (Montbrison). Nearly all these works bear his personal device of the *épée flamboyante*, his motto *n'espoir ne peur* and the monogram CHB. Charles's emblems are also found in the late 15th-century stained glass at Moulins Cathedral and were once part of the lost wall paintings in the Bourbon family chapel in Lyon Cathedral, begun in 1486 but completed after his death by Peter II and Anne of Bourbon. (A Book of Hours also illuminated in the style of Fouquet (Copenhagen, Kon. Bib., MS. GKS 1610) has been falsely equipped with Charles's emblems and was never his.)

The finest representation of Charles is the small half-length panel portrait of him as cardinal (Munich, Alte Pin.) attributed to the Master of Moulins; this is often dated to after his return to the Bourbonnais in 1483, but it may be earlier (*see* MASTERS, ANONYMOUS, AND MONOGRAMMISTS, §I: MASTER OF MOULINS). In addition to an early copy of this panel (Chantilly, Mus. Condé) there are portraits of Charles on a bronze medal probably celebrating his entry into Lyon in December 1485 and in the stained-glass windows of the Bourbon chapel in Lyon Cathedral. A further portrait is preserved in early 16th-century stained glass at Moulins Cathedral, and a bust of

St Majolus from Le Veurdre (*c.* 1470; Moulins, Mus. Moulins) may be a disguised portrait.

Although Charles visited Rome in the 1480s and sponsored Paoli Emili, a Veronese humanist in Paris who dedicated his *Galliae antiquitates* to the Cardinal, the surviving works of art either owned by or made for him show no preferences for Italian art. In this respect Charles was very similar to most other contemporary French nobles and clerics, but unlike many of them he seems not to have been an enthusiastic collector of illuminated manuscripts. At least part of his goods were dispersed by sale at Moulins in 1490, when Charles VIII bought six tapestries of the *Destruction of Jerusalem* and seven of the *Story of Hercules*, remains of which may be the two pieces mentioned above.

BIBLIOGRAPHY

Y. Labande-Mailfert: 'L'Epée, dite "flamboyante", de Charles VIII', *Bull. Mnmtl*, cvii (1950), pp. 91–101

Anne de Beaujeu (exh. cat., ed. M. Meras; Lyon, Archvs Dépt. Rhône, 1986)

SCOT MCKENDRICK

(3) Peter [Pierre] **II**, Duke of Bourbon [Peter of Beaujeu] (*b* Moulins, 1 Dec 1438; *reg* 1488–1503; *d* Moulins, 10 Oct 1503). Brother of (1) John II. He was governor of Guyenne from 1472, and John II granted him the county of Clermont and lordship of Beaujolais in 1476; he became Comte de la Marche (1477), Comte de Gien and governor of Languedoc (1481). In 1489 Peter purchased the viscountships of Carlat and Murat. Trusted by Louis XI, he was awarded royal posts and in 1474 married the King's elder daughter, (4) Anne. In 1488 Peter became Duke of Bourbon after Anne negotiated, in Lyon, his brother Cardinal Charles's renunciation of the title. From 1491 the Duke and his wife resided in their duchy. They were the last princes to exercise patronage on a court scale in France, motivated by dynastic as well as aesthetic reasons.

During Peter II's reign, works were pursued at several sites in the duchy, where his arms and initials (and those of his wife) are prominently displayed. Among these are the stained-glass windows (completed *c.* 1498) in the apse of Moulins Cathedral, which depict the ducal family. Works were also carried out on the Duke's order in the lordship of Beaujeu. For the collegiale of Beaujeu (Rhône) the Lyon painter Claude Guinet (*fl* 1493; *d* 1512) produced a panel with predella depicting *St Barbara and her Martyrdom* (dated 1508; Lyon, Mus. B.-A.). Also due to a ducal commission is the portal of the church at Villefranche-sur-Saône, completed in 1520 at Anne's order. Peter and his wife ordered the continuation of works in the axial chapel of Lyon Cathedral, the burial place of Cardinal Charles. The marble revetment completed in 1508 includes the initials of Peter and Anne and their motto.

Peter II already had a substantial library when he inherited the family holdings. Among his manuscripts was a Bible moralisée containing illuminations by the Limbourg brothers (Paris, Bib. N., MS. fr. 167), which he ordered Jean and François Colombe to complete. In 1476 Peter appropriated part of Jacques d'Armagnac's library, including the first volume of the *Antiquités judaïques* (Paris, Bib. N., MS. fr. 247), with illuminations by Jean Fouquet. At Moulins his books were cared for by the humanist François Robertet, who left both his ex-libris and notes in these volumes (dispersed; some Paris, Bib. N. and London, BL). Peter II instigated the compilation of the *Coutumes juridiques du Bourbonnais*, completed at Anne's commission in 1520. The Duke protected scholars, rhetoricians and poets, among them Jean Lemaire de Belges and Jean Marot.

Peter II is depicted in three works by the MASTER OF MOULINS (see MASTERS, ANONYMOUS, AND MONOGRAMMISTS, §I): he is presented by St Peter in the left wing of a dismantled triptych of *c.* 1492–3 (Paris, Louvre); behind King Charles VIII in the frontispiece of the statutes of the Order of St Michael (Paris, Bib. N., MS. fr. 14363, fol. 3*r*), which was given to the young King in 1493; and, most formally, facing his wife and daughter in the triptych of *c.* 1500 in Moulins Cathedral. The last exalts the Bourbons (the dalmatic of St Peter, who is shown presenting the Duke, is embroidered with the ducal motto *Espérance*) and their Order of Notre-Dame.

BIBLIOGRAPHY

J. M. de La Mure: *Histoire des ducs de Bourbon et des comtes de Forez*, ii (Paris, 1868)

P. Durrieu: 'Un Chef-d'oeuvre de la miniature française sous Charles VIII', *Manuscrit*, i (1894), pp. 19–22

J. C. Varennes: *Quand les ducs de Bourbon étaient connétables de France* (Paris, 1980)

(4) Anne, Duchess of Bourbon [Anne of France; Anne of Beaujeu] (*b* Genappe, between Dec 1460 and Jan 1461; *d* Chantelle, 14 Nov 1522). Wife of (3) Peter II. She was the daughter of King Louis XI of France and Charlotte of Savoy. Anne's contemporaries praised her as 'Madame la grande' for her political skills. She was acting regent of France for her young brother Charles VIII from 1483 to 1491, negotiating his marriage to Anne of Brittany, which led to the annexation of that duchy to the kingdom. From 1491, when she and her husband retired to their estate, Anne's diplomatic activity was centred on Bourbon concerns. She arranged for the marriage of Suzanne (1491–1521), her sole heir, to her cousin Charles of Bourbon-Montpensier (the Constable of Bourbon) on 10 May 1505 in order to retain the duchy in the family, despite earlier pledges that it would revert to the Crown should there be no direct male heir. Respite was only temporary, however: Anne witnessed her daughter's death, and the latter left no surviving issue. Anne and Peter II were historically the most active patrons in Moulins and the Bourbonnais. Anne was instrumental in the development of the serene style that blended southern Netherlandish realism and Italian monumental harmony into traditional Gothic forms and that flourished in central France around 1500.

1. ARCHITECTURE, SCULPTURE AND GARDENS. Transformations and additions to Moulins Castle were begun soon after 1491. In 1496–7, Marceau Rosier (*fl* 1495–8), a royal master mason, began building the *bâtiment neuf*, including a chapel dedicated to St Louis. It is an early manifestation of Italian Renaissance styles. Of the complex, destroyed in 1755, there remains a gallery of six bays with arches resting on square capitals. At the centre is a square pavilion (now the Musée de Moulins). The sculptural decoration bears the initials P A knotted with acanthus leaves and swags. Woodwork for these

Jean de Chartres: *St Anne Teaching the Infant Virgin to Read*, limestone, h. 920 mm, from the Bourbon château at Chantelle, *c.* 1503 (Paris, Musée du Louvre)

(now the cathedral) and in 1507, again in Moulins, she founded the Hôpital St Gilles (destr.).

At Yzeure, outside Moulins, in 1495 Anne commissioned the construction of the château of Beaumanoir (partly destr.) from Gilbert Barrevau (*fl* 1495–8), Guillaume Esmelet (*fl* 1495–8) and Michelet (*fl* 1495–8), essentially for the purpose of raising her daughter. Here too were gardens, with unusual trees (*arbres estranges*), a bridge, fountain and an aviary. The Duke and Duchess ordered the rebuilding of the castle of Segance (partly destr.) and the completion of the Sainte-Chapelle at Bourbon-l'Archambault and the Minim convent (partly destr.) at Gien. At Gien, Anne also ordered the building (1494–1500) of the château, unusual for its red brick surfaces decorated with black bricks. Major building works were undertaken at the castle of Chantelle, their favoured residence, by 1496 (destr. 1633). Statues of the patron saints of the ducal family were unearthed in the late 19th century from the chapel site at Chantelle: *St Anne* coaching, with touching grace, the young Mary in her reading (see fig.), *St Peter*, dignified and worldly, and *St Suzanne*, coquettishly arrayed (all Paris, Louvre). They are by Jean (Guillaumet) de Chartres (*fl* 1493–1511), a pupil of Michel Colombe, mentioned by Colombe in December 1511 as *tailleur d'ymaiges de Madame de Bourbon*. The first record of a payment from the Duchess to the sculptor was in 1501, for an *Annunciation* for the portal of the Carmelite church, Moulins, a fragment of which (the head of the Virgin) survives (Moulins, Mus. Moulins). Sculptural fragments, including two bishop saints, a female saint and the head of a young warrior with laurel wreath (Moulins, Mus. Moulins), from the collegiate church suggest that much of Jean de Chartres's activity was probably concentrated here. A substantial group of sculpture in the Bourbonnais, especially at the châteaux of Jaligny and Yzeure, is related to the work of Jean de Chartres, and some is perhaps attributable to Anne's patronage.

2. PAINTING, METALWORK AND MANUSCRIPTS. The Duchess was instrumental in the activity of painters at Moulins, principally the MASTER OF MOULINS (*see* MASTERS, ANONYMOUS, AND MONOGRAMMISTS, §I), who has been plausibly identified as the Fleming Jean Hey. Among the works by this artist is the portrait of the infant *Dauphin Charles-Orland* (1494; Paris, Louvre) that Anne sent to her brother Charles VIII during his campaigns in Italy. In the Master's monumental triptych of *c.* 1500 in Moulins Cathedral, Anne is shown kneeling, followed by her daughter Suzanne and presented by her patron saint. Mother and daughter, introduced by St John the Evangelist, also appear in two fragments of the right wing (Paris, Louvre) of a triptych of *c.* 1492–3. The painter Jean Richer (*fl* 1502–11) of Orléans, who trained with Francesco Laurana in Avignon, was in Moulins by 1502. Pierre l'Italien (*fl* 1504–19), documented until 1519 as *enlumineur de madite dame*, was also active there. Etienne Saulnier (*fl* 1497; *d* 1503) worked at Beaumanoir as stained-glass maker in 1497; he seems to have been in Anne's service until he died in 1502–3.

Peter and Anne appear with saints on a miniature gold enamelled diptych (London, Wallace) based on the Moulins triptych, possibly a commemorative gift from Anne

structures was fashioned by Jehan Le Moyne (*fl* 1495–8), Rolet Corchin (*fl* 1495–8), Jehan de Reins (*fl* 1495–8) and Pierre Napolitain (*fl* 1495–1500). Adjacent gardens commissioned by the Duchess were tended by Jehan Le Vasseur, *gouverneur du jardin*, one of whose principal assistants, Domingo Genevoix (*fl* 1495–1501), was probably Italian. These gardens included an Italian marble fountain, which Anne compelled the city of Lyon to purchase for her from the Capponi family of bankers in 1493. The sculptor Jean de Rouen made fittings for it in 1496–7. Other sculptures at the castle were figures of *St Peter* and *St Anne* on the west gate. The Duchess also saw to the completion of the collegiate church in Moulins to her daughter. Jean Mangeot (*fl* 1497–1502), recorded as the Duchess's goldsmith from 1497 until at least 1502, was perhaps its maker. Other goldsmiths were Jean de Benhaud (*fl* 1500–05), Remonnet Guionnet (*fl* 1505–8), who provided headwear for Suzanne, and Arnould du Vivier (*d* 1505) of Tours, who supplied rings. Documentation recording the names of the artists who furnished reliquaries and other metalworks for ducal chapels, especially at Moulins and Chantelle, is lacking.

Anne gathered educational precepts emphasizing social relationships and the requirements of self-discipline in a volume dedicated to her daughter. Entitled *Le Parfait Amour: Enseignements d'Anne de France à sa fille Suzanne*, the manuscript (St Petersburg, Hermitage, Dubrowski MS. 5[2.42]) was completed shortly before 1505. It contains 19 illuminations, one depicting the Duchess and her daughter, attributable to the Master of Petrarch's Triumphs. The text was printed in Lyon by Le Prince before 1521.

The Bourbon library in Anne's time was one of the largest in France, comprising some 324 titles in Moulins and another 170 at the castle of Aigueperse, among them works by Virgil, Aesop, Terence, Cicero, Ovid, Aristotle and Pliny. Some authors dedicated works to Anne, for example Jean Lemaire de Belges, who wrote his *Temple d'honneur et de vertues* in memory of Peter II. The *Histoire de Louis de Bourbon* was also done for Anne. Her Book of Hours (New York, Pierpont Morgan Lib., MS. 677), produced before her marriage and with 107 full-page miniatures, is one of the most exacting productions of Jean Colombe's atelier. Anne inherited Louis de Laval's books in 1489, including his Book of Hours (Paris, Bib. N., MS. lat.920), Colombe's most significant work.

BIBLIOGRAPHY

A. M. Chazaud, ed.: *Les Enseignements d'Anne de France, duchesse de Bourbonnois et d'Auvergne, à sa fille Suzanne de Bourbon* (Moulins, 1878)

P. Pélicier: *Essai sur le gouvernement de la dame de Beaujeu, 1483–1491* (Chartres, 1882)

P. Dupieux: *Les Artistes à la cour ducale des Bourbons: Les Maîtres de Moulins* (Moulins, 1946)

P. Pradel: 'Le Sculpteur Jean de Chartres et son atelier', *Bull. Mnmtl*, civ (1946), pp. 47–61

N. Reynaud: 'Les Portraits des Bourbons au Louvre', *Rev. Louvre*, xiii (1963), pp. 159–66

P. Pradel: 'Le Premier Edifice de la Renaissance en France', *Mem. Soc. N. Antiqua. France*, iv (1969), pp. 243–58

J. C. Varennes: *Anne de Bourbon, roi de France* (Paris, 1987)

PATRICK M. DE WINTER

(5) Henry [Henri] **IV**, King of France [Henry, King of Navarre] (*b* Pau, 14 Dec 1553; *reg* 1589–1610; *d* Paris, 14 May 1610). He was King of Navarre from 1572 and became the first Bourbon king of France when his Valois predecessor, Henry III, died in 1589 without male heirs. The new king was a Protestant, and France, divided by the Wars of Religion, was not prepared to accept his rule peacefully. After four years of civil war, Henry converted to Roman Catholicism on 25 July 1593 and won the surrender of Paris, stronghold of resistance to him. He entered the city on 22 March 1594 and began to unify the realm (see fig.).

Henry IV re-established the court in Paris after its long exile in the Loire Valley and made it the site of his most important activity as a patron. His city planning (*see* PARIS, §II, 3) was related to his efforts to centralize the power of

Henry IV as the Gallic Hercules with Navarre and France, engraving after Jacob Bunel, *c.* 1594 (Paris, Bibliothèque Nationale)

the Crown and to establish Paris as the capital of a unified French state. Immediately after capturing Paris, he began to enlarge the royal palace, the Louvre (*see* PARIS, §V, 6(ii)). This shrewd political decision publicized his intention to reside in the city and projected an image of monarchical continuity. His first goal was to link the Louvre to the Palais des Tuileries outside the city wall. He built the Grande Galerie du Bord de l'Eau (1599–1608) along the Seine and added a connecting wing to the Tuileries and an upper storey to the Petite Galerie. A new design in 1603 called for the demolition of all buildings between the two palaces, the city wall included, so that the palaces would directly face one another. Contemporary memoirs indicate that around 1609 Henry decided to enclose the north side of the precinct by building another long gallery. The conception of this enormous courtyard formed by the two palaces and two connecting galleries was the distinguishing feature of Henry IV's design for the Louvre. Although he completed only the Grande Galerie, his scheme guided building at the Louvre until the 19th century.

The interest in design on an urban scale and in panoramic views demonstrated at the Louvre was further developed in new public buildings in Paris. Henry IV completed the Pont Neuf (1599–1604), the first bridge in Paris offering an unobstructed view of the Seine. It provided a prominent platform for the equestrian statue of *Henry IV* commissioned by his wife, (6) Marie de'

Medici, in 1604 and placed on the tip of the Ile de la Cité in 1614 (*see* (6) below). In 1605 the King announced the creation of the Place Royale (now Place des Vosges), with ground-floor shops and artisans' housing above. The silkworks on the north side of the square were replaced by a symmetrical range of pavilions in 1607–8, and thereafter the Place Royale became an aristocratic residential precinct. The King's commitment to commercial and artisanal activity was satisfied at the Place Dauphine, begun in 1607 (*see* PARIS, fig. 3). The land for the two squares was donated by the Crown, but construction was paid for by the individual plot owners, who were required to follow the royal façade design. In 1607 the King also began the first monumental plague hospital in Europe, the Hôpital St Louis, designed by Claude Vellefaux (1559–1619). Plans for a third royal square, the Place de France, and the Collège Royal were announced in 1609 but were abandoned after the King's assassination the following year. The architects of the royal projects are unnamed in the documents. The two completed squares and the Louvre were probably designed by the royal architects Louis Métezeau (*see* MÉTEZEAU, (1)) and Jacques Androuet Du Cerceau (ii) (*see* DU CERCEAU, (3)), both appointed in 1594, but their individual contributions cannot yet be defined with certainty.

At his favoured country retreat the King pursued less ambitious renovations and extensions. At the château of Fontainebleau he built the Cour des Offices and Porte Dauphine, modified the Cour Ovale and the gardens and sponsored various interior decorations (*see* FONTAINE-BLEAU, §1). At the château of SAINT-GERMAIN-EN-LAYE he continued construction of the Château-Neuf begun by Philibert de L'Orme and built a terraced garden along the steep slope towards the River Seine, most remarkable for the automata and grottoes designed by Thomas Francini. Henry rewarded Marie de' Medici for the birth of their son, the future Louis XIII, with the château of Montceaux-en-Brie (Seine-et-Marne; largely destr.), while giving Henriette d'Entragues, one of his mistresses, the château of Verneuil-sur-Oise (destr.). Salomon de Brosse completed both buildings, which were originally designed by his grandfather Jacques Androuet Du Cerceau (i).

Buildings constructed under Henry IV were typically of brick and stone and drew on the stylistic vocabulary of French architecture of the last third of the 16th century. While the architectural forms of his reign were conservative, his programme was innovative in its social goals and methods of development. His projects were intended to promote domestic manufactures and crafts. Even in the building of apartments for artists in the Grande Galerie of the Louvre, his primary aim was not to cultivate the magnificence of his court but to foster craft production throughout France. Painting and humanist culture did not interest the King, but he appreciated the value of the arts in regenerating the French economy. Although his aim of forging an alliance between court and commerce failed, Henry IV successfully launched the transformation of Paris into a modern capital. Otherwise, the restoration of peace and prosperity was Henry IV's chief contribution to French culture; its fruits were reaped later in the 17th century.

BIBLIOGRAPHY

J. Berger de Xivrey and J. Guadet: *Recueil des lettres missives de Henri IV*, 9 vols (Paris, 1843–76)
N. Valois: *Inventaire des arrêts du Conseil d'Etat de Henri IV*, 2 vols (Paris, 1886–93)
R. Mousnier: *L'Assassinat d'Henri IV* (Paris, 1964; Eng. trans., London, 1973)
C. Vivanti: 'Henri IV, the Gallic Hercules', *J. Warb. & Court. Inst.*, xxx (1967), pp. 176–97
J.-P. Babelon: 'Les Travaux de Henri IV au Louvre et aux Tuileries', *Mém. Soc. Hist. Paris & Ile-de-France*, xxix (1978), pp. 55–130
——: *Henri IV* (Paris, 1982)
D. Buisseret: *Henri IV* (London, 1984)
J. Garrisson: *Henri IV* (Paris, 1984)
M. Greengrass: *France in the Age of Henri IV: The Struggle for Stability* (London, 1984)
H. Ballon: *The Paris of Henri IV: Architecture and Urbanism* (Cambridge, MA, 1991)

(6) Marie de [Maria de'] **Medici**, Queen of France (*b* Florence, 26 April 1573; *d* Cologne, 3 July 1642). Wife of (5) Henry IV. She was the daughter of Francesco I, Grand Duke of Tuscany (*see* MEDICI, DE', (16)), and lived in Florence until her marriage in 1600. The Florentine court supplied her with several artists who settled in Paris, notably Thomas Francini, Alexandre Francini and Pietro Francavilla, and this influenced her first important commission, an equestrian statue of *Henry IV*. In 1604 she ordered the statue from Giambologna, and the finished work was placed on the tip of the Ile de la Cité, Paris, in 1614, halfway across the Pont Neuf: the horse by Giambologna, the rider (both destr.) by his assistant Pietro Tacca and the four slaves (Paris, Louvre) of the pedestal by Francavilla. Because of Medici traditions of patronage it is often assumed that the Queen inspired the early 17th-century royal building programme in Paris (*see* (5) above), but there is no evidence that she played any part in it. Her patronage was limited to two other projects during Henry IV's reign: the decoration of the chapel of the Trinité at the château of Fontainebleau by Martin Fréminet and the completion of the château of Monceaux en Brie (*c.* 1601–23; largely destr. 1793) by Salomon de Brosse. Marie also planned a tomb for her husband, which was begun in 1613 by one of the Métézeau brothers, Louis or Clément (successive Architects to the King), but never completed.

Marie emerged as an important patron during her regency (1610–17) for her son, (7) Louis XIII. In 1611 she decided to build a new residence in Paris modelled on her childhood home, the Palazzo Pitti, Florence, and sent Louis Métézeau there to make drawings. In 1612–13 de Brosse won the competition for what was to become the Palais du Luxembourg (*see* PARIS, §V, 8). He set a traditional French château plan in a suburban garden, acknowledging the Florentine model only in his elevations and use of rustication. The Jardins du Luxembourg, which followed the Boboli Gardens, Florence, in their general layout, were notable for their parterres, designed by Jacques Boyceau, and the architectural grotto, probably by the Francini brothers. To supply the palace with water the Queen had the Arcueil Aqueduct (1613–23) built, in which de Brosse and Thomas Francini were involved. Following a rift with her son in 1617, Marie was forced to spend two years in Blois, where she had de Brosse add a pavilion to the château (1617–18; destr. 1635).

In the 1620s Marie concentrated on the interior decoration of her palace. In 1622 she commissioned Peter Paul

Rubens to paint two cycles, the *Life of Marie de' Medici* and that of *Henry IV*. The *Marie de' Medici* cycle (Paris, Louvre; *see* HISTORY PAINTING, fig. 2) was installed in the west gallery in 1625; the *Henry IV* cycle was not executed. In the Cabinet des Muses she hung a series of paintings by Giovanni Baglione of *Apollo and the Nine Muses* (*c.* 1620–21; Arras, Mus. B.-A.), and the Cabinet Doré was decorated with a series of works by contemporary Florentine painters (Jacopo Ligozzi, Domenico Passignano, Giovanni Bilivert and others) on the history of the Medici family (Broomhall, Fife). After receiving an *Annunciation* (Paris, Louvre) from Guido Reni, Marie invited the artist to Paris in 1629 to paint the *Henry IV* cycle. Reni declined, but other foreigners attended her court: Frans Pourbus the younger (1609–15), the poet Giambattista Marino (1615–23) and Orazio Gentileschi (1624–6). Philippe de Champaigne (*see* CHAMPAIGNE, (1)) was appointed Peintre de la Reine in 1628. Among the French artists who enjoyed this contact with Italian culture was Nicolas Poussin, employed at the Palais du Luxembourg *c.* 1621–3. After losing a political struggle with Cardinal Richelieu in 1630, Marie left France and ended her life in exile. The collection she left behind had a lasting impact on French painting and art theory, not by advancing any one style but by introducing the work of Rubens and contemporary Italian painters to Paris.

BIBLIOGRAPHY

A. Hustin: *Le Palais du Luxembourg* (Paris, 1904)
C. Sterling: 'Une Nouvelle Oeuvre de Gentileschi peinte en France', *Rev. Louvre*, xiv (1954), pp. 212–20
—: 'Gentileschi in France', *Burl. Mag.*, c (1958), pp. 112–20
A. Blunt: 'A Series of Paintings Illustrating the History of the Medici Family Executed for Marie de Médicis', *Burl. Mag.*, cix (1967), pp. 492–8, 562–6
J. Thuillier and J. Foucart: *Rubens' Life of Marie de' Medici* (New York, 1969)
D. Marrow: *The Art Patronage of Maria de' Medici* (Ann Arbor, 1982)
S. Saward: *The Golden Age of Marie de' Medici* (Ann Arbor, 1982)
J. Thuillier: 'La Galerie de Marie de Médicis: Peinture, poétique et politique', *Actes du colloque Rubens: Florence, 1983*, pp. 249–66

HILARY BALLON

(7) Louis XIII, King of France (*b* Fontainebleau, 27 Sept 1601; *reg* 1610–43; *d* Saint-Germain-en-Laye, 14 May 1643). Son of (5) Henry IV and (6) Marie de' Medici. From an early age he showed an interest in the arts. After his father's assassination in 1610, his mother became Regent (1610–17) and conspired to keep him from power: their struggle led to war before Louis succeeded in 1623 in imposing his authority. Much of his reign was taken up with warfare, which included an internal war with the Huguenots (concluded in 1629 by the Peace of Alès), as well as several external conflicts. He did not greatly enjoy the social life of the court, and his religious sentiments did not allow him to make a display of wealth; his patronage was therefore relatively modest but nonetheless significant.

Louis XIII believed that a programme of major building works would enable him to assert royal power against his mother's Italian faction, but unstable finances restricted the work carried out. He built a small hunting-lodge (1623–4) at Versailles and gradually acquired the surrounding land. About this time Mavin Le Bourgeois made a flintlock hunting gun (St Petersburg, Hermitage; *see* ARMS AND ARMOUR, fig. 7) for the King, who had developed an early enthusiasm for firearms. Subsequently the hunting-lodge

was enlarged and modified (1631–4) to become the first château of Versailles; Louis himself supervised the architect, Philibert Le Roy. The gardens at Versailles were laid out by Jacques Boyceau and Jacques de Menours (1591–1637). Louis also attempted to modernize and complete the building programme begun by Henry IV at the Palais du Louvre, Paris, with Jacques Le Mercier as his architect; in 1624 he laid the foundation stone of the Pavillon de l'Horloge, while the west wing was added from 1624 to 1627. The King also initiated work on a château at Vincennes and carried out improvements in the decoration of the interiors and gardens at the royal residences of Saint-Germain-en-Laye and Fontainebleau. Louis gave land near the Place Royale (now Place des Vosges) in Paris for the church of St Louis (now St Paul–St Louis); it was built (1627–41) in a style that he favoured, a restrained version of the Baroque Jesuit style that had been used in building Il Gesù in Rome. Louis did not greatly engage in court ceremonial, but his triumphal entry into Paris in 1628, marking his victory at La Rochelle, was fully celebrated, 12 ceremonial arches (designs Paris, Bib. N.) being erected for the occasion.

Louis commissioned a portrait of himself aged 21 (1622; Pasadena, CA, Norton Simon Mus.) from Rubens, as well as some designs for tapestries, but soon moved away from Rubens's style. In 1627 he gave the post of Premier Peintre du Roi to SIMON VOUET, whose many works for the King included such allegorical paintings as *Charity* (1628; Paris, Louvre) for Saint-Germain-en-Laye and the *Vow of Louis XIII* (1638; Neuilly-Saint-Front, Aisne, parish church), commemorating the King's dedication of the French nation to the Virgin. Philippe de Champaigne (*see* CHAMPAIGNE, DE, (1)) became Peintre de la Reine to Marie de' Medici in 1628; the work he executed for Louis included a portrait of him (Madrid, Prado), *Louis XIII Crowned by Victory* (Paris, Louvre) and the *Vow of Louis XIII* (1637; Caen, Mus. B.-A.). NICOLAS POUSSIN, although resident in Rome during most of the reign, was prevailed on to accept the post of Premier Peintre between 1640 and 1642; a project to decorate the Grande Galerie of the Palais du Louvre with grisaille paintings proved abortive, but he produced a number of other works for the King, including the *Institution of the Eucharist* (1641; Paris, Louvre) for the royal chapel at Saint-Germain-en-Laye.

BIBLIOGRAPHY

L. Hautecoeur: *Architecture classique* (1943–57), i, pp. 525–31
P. Chevalier: *Louis XIII: Roi cornélien* (Paris, 1979)
A. Lloyd Moote: *Louis XIII, the Just* (Los Angeles and London, 1989)

GILES CLIFFORD

(8) Louis XIV, King of France (*b* Saint-Germain-en-Laye, 5 Sept 1638; *reg* 1643–1715; *d* Versailles, 1 Sept 1715). Son of (7) Louis XIII. He was less than five years old when his father died in 1643, and he was placed under the guardianship of his mother, Anne of Austria (1601–66), who was regent until he came of age in 1651, and of the Prime Minister, Cardinal Jules Mazarin, who ruled France until 1661, the beginning of Louis XIV's period of personal rule. The King's policy of French domination in Europe caused him to draw France into numerous wars, successful at first, but from 1689 a heavy burden on the kingdom. Louis's concern with his own glory inevitably inclined him towards the lavish and splendid, and he was a systematic and magnificent patron and collector. He was able to indulge these two activities to the full during the prosperous period of his personal reign but was later forced to curb them due to financial difficulties, nevertheless remaining an unforgettable and unequalled model for all the sovereigns of Europe.

Louis XIV's personal artistic taste is difficult to discern, concealed as it is by his deliberate exploitation of the arts for the purposes of his own prestige and by the actions of his ministers, particularly Jean-Baptiste Colbert (*see* COLBERT, (1)), in whom he entrusted considerable power. He acquired from his mother a taste for beautiful objects and was also influenced by the example of Cardinal Mazarin (*see* MAZARIN, (1)), a great and expert patron and collector, who at his death left the King an enormous collection, of which he accepted only five paintings and eighteen diamonds. In 1665 Louis admitted to Paul Fréart de Chantelou that 'if he had but applied himself betimes to the consideration of pictures, he would have been a connoisseur; but he had only given them regard for some four or five years'. Louis XIV was thus not a connoisseur, nor did he ever become one. His passion for buildings and gardens, on the other hand, led him to develop a sense of and taste for architecture; although uncultured, he had, according to the Duc de Saint-Simon's *Mémoires*, 'an accurate eye for soundness, proportion and symmetry'. His love of splendour led him to pay great attention to all the details of the decoration and furnishing of the royal houses, which led to a rapid development of the decorative arts in France (*see* LOUIS XIV STYLE).

Louis XIV as Protector of the Arts by Henri Testelin, oil on canvas, 3.90×2.90 m, 1667 (Versailles, Musée Nationale du Château de Versailles et de Trianon)

1. Administrative structures. 2. Architecture, interior decoration and gardens. 3. Sculpture, engraved gems, coins and medals. 4. Painting, graphic arts and manuscripts. 5. Decorative arts.

1. ADMINISTRATIVE STRUCTURES. Louis XIV's influence on the arts took the form of a state policy, carried out by means of appropriate official structures (*see* MAISON DU ROI). At the summit of the hierarchy of the artistic administration was the Surintendant des Bâtiments, Arts et Manufactures du Roi; he organized the financing and direction of all projects. This post was occupied first by administrators—Colbert (1664–83), the Marquis de LOUVOIS (1683–91), Edouard Colbert, Marquis de Villacerf (1691–9)—and then (1699–1708) by the architect Jules Hardouin Mansart (*see* MANSART, (2)). The next holder of the post, the Duc D'ANTIN, lost the power to authorize expenditure and was Directeur only. Creative work was dominated by two privileged artists, the Premier Peintre du Roi and the Premier Architecte du Roi. They received the major commissions and were entrusted with the artistic direction of all projects.

With regard to the decorative arts, specialized workshops under the authority of the Premier Peintre ensured production of the articles required for the royal palaces. The GOBELINS factory produced tapestries (from 1662) and furniture and other objects (from 1667), the Beauvais factory (*see* BEAUVAIS, §2) produced low-warp tapestries (from 1664), and the SAVONNERIE factory produced carpets. The department of Menus Plaisirs du Roi (*see* MAISON DU ROI, §III) organized the decorations for court festivities, following designs by the Dessinateur de la Chambre et du Cabinet du Roi, the most famous of whom was Jean Berain I.

The Surintendant was also in charge of organizing and adding to the royal collections, assisted by Gardes (keepers) for antiquities, paintings, manuscripts and furniture (for the last *see* MAISON DU ROI, §IV). The King showed his interest in his collections by establishing the Petite Galerie at Versailles, to which he could retire from the Grand Appartement, or state rooms, as well as several cabinets or studies set aside for his paintings, medals and *objets d'art*.

Art theory and teaching were entrusted to the academies; the Académie Royale de Peinture et de Sculpture, which was reformed in 1664, and the Académie Royale d'Architecture, which was founded in 1671 (*see* PARIS, §VI, 1 and 2). The young artists who were awarded prizes in academic competitions were sent to perfect their work at the Académie de France in Rome, which was founded in 1666.

With the power conferred by all these means of influence, Louis XIV effectively reigned over the arts (see fig.). His intention to use the arts as a medium of propaganda was clearly demonstrated by the publication, begun in 1667, of the *Cabinet du Roi*, a series of 956 engravings, bound in 23 folio volumes, devoted to the royal buildings and collections, which he intended to distribute as gifts to distinguished persons and foreign sovereigns.

2. ARCHITECTURE, INTERIOR DECORATION AND GARDENS. Such was the King's passion for building that

his life was spent in palaces that were almost permanently under construction or undergoing alterations. The works undertaken during his reign had a formidable influence and were without parallel in extent and quality. From 1661 his Premier Architecte, Louis Le Vau, produced designs for completing the Palais du Louvre (see PARIS, §V, 6(ii)). These, however, were rejected, and alternative plans were submitted by Gianlorenzo Bernini, who came to France in 1665 to put them into execution. The fact that his Italian Baroque design was eventually abandoned was as much a reflection of national vanity as of stylistic preference, but the building along the east front of the famous colonnade, whose design is attributed to Claude Perrault, marked the ascendancy of the French classical style in architecture. (For a discussion of the disputed authorship of the colonnade see LE VAU, (1), §4.) In 1668 Le Vau began to extend the château of VERSAILLES, but the King insisted that he preserve the original hunting-lodge built by Louis XIII. This constraint was to lie heavily on the building, from then on condemning it to face the world with principal façades in two different styles.

On Le Vau's death in 1670, Louis XIV kept the former's assistant, François d'Orbay, in his service; he did not, however, make him Premier Architecte. Instead, he commissioned Libéral Bruand to execute the Hôtel des Invalides (see PARIS, §V, 7) in 1671, and Antoine Le Pautre to execute the first château of Clagny, near Versailles, in 1674. Both were replaced on these sites in 1675 by Hardouin Mansart, who rapidly gained the King's confidence and was made Premier Architecte in 1681. Hardouin Mansart carried out an immense volume of work for Louis XIV, including the enormous, final version of the extensions to Versailles, the château of MARLY and the Grand Trianon (see VERSAILLES, §3), and in Paris the Dôme des Invalides and the Place Vendôme. Louis XIV's own taste was a determining factor in the choice made between various options for all these projects; it sometimes proved a constraint, as in the case of the peristyle of the Trianon, which was the King's personal idea imposed in the architect's absence. The overall style in these works was, nevertheless, Mansart's, except in the case of Marly, which was distinguished by a taste for the picturesque due to the King's own choice and the intervention of Le Brun.

The King's taste in interior decoration was initially marked by the solemn magnificence of the Grand Appartement and the Escalier des Ambassadeurs at Versailles in the 1660s and 1670s. As he grew older, however, he moved consciously towards a more light-hearted style: in 1698 he called for 'youth [to be] blended into what we will do' (see DRESS, fig. 41). The origin of this new style, exemplified by the interiors at the Trianon and Marly, is often mistakenly attributed to the period of the Regency of Philippe II, Duc d'Orléans, after the King's death in 1715.

Louis XIV also had a passion for gardens and employed ANDRÉ LE NÔTRE, who created a new style 'à la française' (see GARDEN, §VIII, 4(ii)). The King wanted the parks of Versailles and Marly to be filled with statues, fountains and flowers, and his demands were largely responsible for creating their sumptuous magnificence; indeed, he attached so much importance to this that he personally wrote a manuscript guide to the gardens at Versailles, *La*

Manière de montrer les jardins de Versailles (1702–4; Paris, Bib. N. Cab. Est., Ve 1318).

3. SCULPTURE, ENGRAVED GEMS, COINS AND MEDALS. In 1688 Louis XIV had a marble equestrian statue of himself by Bernini transformed into a *Marcus Curtius Throwing himself into the Flames* and relegated to a distant part of the gardens at Versailles. In so doing he seemed to be allying himself with the classicizing trend in French sculpture and rejecting the excesses of the Italian Baroque style. He seems, however, to have considered sculpture as no more than the natural complement to architecture and landscape gardening—hence the enormous quantity of works in gilt lead, marble, bronze and other materials ordered for the façades and gardens at Versailles and at Marly, most of the former still *in situ*. It was significant that he did not have a Premier Sculpteur, even though François Girardon effectively occupied this position from 1685; the designs for sculptures for royal projects were often executed by Le Brun, and sculpture itself came under the auspices of the same academy as painting. Like his contemporaries, the King appears to have been obsessed by antique statuary—although, also like them, he often reduced it to an ornamental role. Following the example of Francis I, Louis XIV had casts made of the most famous antique pieces and had them copied in marble or bronze. He also acquired originals in Rome and even in France, as in the case of the Arles *Venus* (Paris, Louvre) in 1684. While the gardens and façades of Versailles were lavishly decorated with sculpture by contemporary artists, including Girardon, Balthazar Marsy, Gaspard Marsy, Jean-Baptiste Tuby and, in the latter part of the reign, Antoine Coyzevox, the Grands Appartements held only two contemporary sculptures, busts of Louis by Jean Warin and by Bernini (both *in situ*), but contained 49 antique works (41 busts and 8 statues), many still at Versailles. The most striking works executed for Louis XIV were monuments to himself: equestrian and pedestrian statues by Girardon, Etienne Le Hongre and Martin Desjardins (all destr. 1790s).

Louis XIV's passion for ancient art also extended to cameos and engraved gems, as well as to coins and medals. He had entire collections of these items bought in order to swell the holdings of the Bibliothèque Royale in Paris or his own Cabinet des Médailles at Versailles. These form the nucleus of the present-day Cabinet des Médailles at the Bibliothèque Nationale, Paris. Both ancient and modern bronzes were sought after with equal zeal for the decoration of the royal residences. By 1684 the inventories of the Garde Meuble listed 168 such pieces; by 1713 they listed 309. Most of these were modern works, heavily dominated by the production of the Florentine workshops of Giambologna, Antonio Susini, Francesco Susini, Pietro Tacca and Ferdinando Tacca. The collection was largely dispersed in the aftermath of the French Revolution.

4. PAINTING, GRAPHIC ARTS AND MANUSCRIPTS. Not being a true connoisseur, Louis XIV saw painting chiefly as an obligatory decoration for the royal residences and as a means to celebrate his own glory. CHARLES LE BRUN's noble and learned style suited perfectly his ambitions. By giving Le Brun the post of Premier Peintre in

1664 and making him director of the Gobelins, Louis orientated all official art towards academicism. Most of the paintings at Versailles were of a purely decorative character with little value beyond that function. The exceptions were the great masterpieces of Le Brun: the walls and vault of the Escalier des Ambassadeurs (begun 1671; destr.) and the vault of the Galerie des Glaces (begun 1678). From 1683 Louvois supported Pierre Mignard I against Le Brun and obtained a commission for him to paint the Petite Galerie at Versailles. Eventually he had Mignard appointed Premier Peintre (1690). The death of Le Brun, the decoration of the Trianon (where a bucolic style and imagery replaced the heroic style of Versailles) and the general evolution of taste brought about the victory of the colourist party over the protagonists of the academic style (see RUBÉNISME); towards the end of the reign a freer style emerged, exemplified by the work of Charles de La Fosse and Jean Jouvenet at the Invalides and by that of Antoine Coypel in the chapel at Versailles.

Louis XIV's activities as a collector were of the greatest importance, despite the fact that he made his acquisitions guided by an academic taste that gave precedence to the great Italian painters of the Renaissance, to the Bolognese school of the late 16th century and the early 17th, to the Flemings Peter Paul Rubens and Anthony van Dyck and to such modern classicizing French masters as Nicolas Poussin and Le Brun. With the exception of Rembrandt, Louis regarded the works of Dutch painters, particularly of genre scenes, as trivial, on one occasion ordering 'take these apes from my sight'. Nevertheless, taking these predilections into account, he greatly augmented the royal collections by means of gifts, purchases from dealers and the absorption of complete collections. He acquired the famous collection of EVERARD JABACH in 1662 (100 paintings), that of the Duc de Richelieu (see RICHELIEU, (ii)(2)) in 1665 (25 paintings, including 13 by Poussin) and a second collection belonging to Jabach in 1671 (101 paintings and 5542 drawings). The acquisition of the Jabach drawings led to the establishment of the Cabinet des Dessins, the nucleus of the drawings collection of the Musée du Louvre. This was subsequently augmented by drawings from the studios of Le Brun, Adam Frans van der Meulen and Mignard.

By 1672 the paintings in the King's collection occupied seven rooms at the Louvre; in 1683 a large number of works were removed to Versailles to decorate various apartments and to form a small museum in the Petite Galerie and adjacent rooms. Among works acquired by Louis XIV that are today among the treasures of the Musée du Louvre are: Raphael's *St Michael, St George and the Dragon* and portrait of *Baldassare Castiglione* (Mazarin col., 1661); Titian's *Entombment* (Jabach col., 1662) and *Concert champêtre* (Jabach col., 1671); Jacopo Tintoretto's *Susanna and the Elders* (Marquis d'Hautrive col., 1684); Annibale Carracci's *Fishing* and *Hunting* (gift of Prince Camillo Pamphili, 1665) and the *Sacrifice of Abraham* (Jabach col., 1671); Guido Reni's *Hercules and the Hydra of Lerna* and *Nessus and Dejaneira* (Jabach col., 1662); Francesco Albani's *Actaeon Changed into a Stag* (gift of André Le Nôtre, 1693); Poussin's *Israelites Gathering Manna in the Desert* (Nicolas Fouquet col., 1661), *Four Seasons* and *Bacchanal with a Guitar Player* (Richelieu col.,

1665) and *Rape of the Sabines* (1685); Rembrandt's *Portrait of the Artist at his Easel* (1671); van Dyck's portrait of the *Princes Palatine Charles Louis and Robert* (Jabach col., 1671); and Rubens's *Kermesse* (1685). In addition, the Bibliothèque Royale was enriched with works now belonging to the Bibliothèque Nationale, including the manuscript collection of Philippe de Béthune (1561–1649), acquired in 1662, the 123,400 prints of the Abbé MICHEL DE MAROLLES, acquired in 1667, and the collection of documentary drawings relating to the history of France assembled by Roger de Gaignière, acquired in 1715.

5. DECORATIVE ARTS. An account of the influence of Louis XIV on the decorative arts in France is to a great extent the same as an account of the history of the first 50 years of the royal factories of the Gobelins, Beauvais and Savonnerie (mentioned in §1 above). The need for suitable furnishings for the royal residences meant that under Colbert's management and Le Brun's artistic direction the output of the factories reached unparalleled levels. At the Savonnerie were woven the magnificent carpets for the Galerie d'Apollon and the Grande Galerie at the Louvre, while at the Gobelins painters, cabinetmakers, dyers, weavers, goldsmiths, sculptors and engravers were employed. Among the most distinguished cabinetmakers working for the King were Domenico Cucci, Alexandre-Jean Oppenordt (1639–1715) and ANDRÉ-CHARLES BOULLE, the last of whom gave his name to the furniture inlaid with brass and tortoiseshell marquetry that is so much associated with the Louis XIV style. When at the height of his power, the King even had a suite of solid silver furniture made for the Salon d'Apollon at Versailles. Though this was melted down during the financial crisis of 1689, it is known from an engraving after Jean Berain I (e.g. Versailles, Château). In addition to items made at the royal factories the King collected porcelain, rock-crystal vases and *objets d'art* made from hardstones. This porcelain and the hardstone objects, imported from China, Italy and Germany, were often provided with silver or gold mounts by French craftsmen. Much of this furnishing was dispersed at the end of the 18th century.

WRITINGS

S. Hoog, ed.: *La Manière de montrer les jardins de Versailles* (Paris, 1982)

BIBLIOGRAPHY

J. Guiffrey, ed.: *Comptes des Bâtiments du Roi sous le règne de Louis XIV*, 5 vols (Paris, 1881–1901)

P. Fréart de Chantelou: *Journal du voyage du cavalier Bernin en France*, ed. L. Lalanne (Paris, 1885/R Aix-en-Provence, 1981; Eng. trans., Princeton, 1985)

J. Guiffrey, ed.: *Inventaire général des meubles de la Couronne sous le règne de Louis XIV*, 2 vols (Paris, 1886)

E. Engerand, ed.: *Inventaire des tableaux du Roi rédigé en 1709 et 1710 par N. Bailly* (Paris, 1889)

H. Jouin: *Charles Le Brun et les arts sous Louis XIV* (Paris, 1889)

L. Hautecoeur: *Architecture classique*, II/i and ii (1948)

C. Pinatel: *Les Statues antiques des jardins de Versailles* (Paris, 1963)

B. Jestaz: 'Le Trianon de marbre, ou Louis XIV architecte', *Gaz. B.-A.*, n. s. 5, lxxiv (1969), pp. 259–86

C. Constans: 'Les Tableaux du grand appartement du Roi', *Rev. Louvre*, xxvi/3 (1976), pp. 157–73

S. Hoog: 'Les Sculptures du grand appartement du Roi', *Rev. Louvre*, xxvi/3 (1976), pp. 147–56

Collections de Louis XIV: Dessins, albums, manuscrits (exh. cat., ed. R. Bacou; Paris, Mus. Orangerie, 1977)

F. Bluche: *Louis XIV* (Paris, 1986)

A. Brejon de Lavergnée: *L'Inventaire Le Brun de 1683: La Collection de tableaux de Louis XIV* (Paris, 1987)

M. Martin: *Les Monuments équestres de Louis XIV* (Paris, 1987)

BERTRAND JESTAZ

(9) Louis de Bourbon (*b* Fontainebleau, 1 Nov 1661; *d* Meudon, 14 April 1711). Son of (8) Louis XIV. Since he predeceased his father, he spent his entire life as heir to the French throne, becoming known as 'Le Grand Dauphin'; his son became Philip V of Spain. After a period of soldiering in his youth, Louis settled down to a life of leisure, the chief pleasures of which were hunting and collecting art and objects. For over a decade he lived in apartments at Versailles; Monicart listed much of their contents. It is not easy to assess which features of the decoration were the Dauphin's own choice. The elaborate floor by Pierre Gole in the Cabinet Doré was taken up in 1688, while Poussin's *Triumph of Flora* (Paris, Louvre) appears to have been removed in 1700, and this may show that they were not to his liking. The painter Pierre Mignard I and the sculptor Jean-Louis Lemoyne were employed on decorations. The cabinetmaker Domenico Cucci worked on the Cabinet Doré, and Andre-Charles Boulle was the central figure in the decoration of the Cabinet de Glaces (1682–6), at a cost of 94,000 livres. These rooms, which were hung with the works of such masters as Titian, Rubens, Veronese, Giorgione and Guercino, soon became the focus of visitors' admiration; such was their attraction that in the 1690s the Dauphin had a second set of rooms, known as his 'caveau', decorated for his private use.

In 1693 the Dauphin inherited the château of Choisy from the Duchesse de Montpensier. He had already ordered new furnishings when Louis XIV organized the acquisition of the château of MEUDON, above the Seine at Versailles, as the Dauphin's official residence, giving Choisy in part-exchange. At Meudon the Dauphin's patronage flourished. He first stayed there in 1695; he spent the late 1690s in altering and decorating the existing building, later known as the Vieux Château, in a style heavily influenced by Jean Berain I and executed by such artists as Claude Audran III. At the time of acquisition the Crown was in a financial crisis, and the use of gilding was restricted by edict. This may account for the decoration of at least one room in the varnished wood style known as *lambris des capuchines*, Cucci being one of the craftsmen. Elsewhere more conventional fashion reigned, shown in the King's Room by the use of 62 mirrors by Nicolas Briot. Mignard, now the Premier Peintre du Roi, was involved in the design of sculpture, and the royal architect Jules Hardouin Mansart was employed, together with André Le Nôtre, to work on the gardens. In spite of the financial problems, one million livres was spent on the Vieux Château. One of the most extraordinary and innovative works was the chimney-piece (1699) in the Chambre du Dauphin, on which 14 craftsmen worked; it used marble, bronze and tortoiseshell inlay and cost 8774 livres. A painting by an unknown artist of the *Grand Dauphin in his Room* (Versailles, Château) shows a similar piece in the background, but the setting is at Versailles (Walton).

The Dauphin also added to Meudon one major wing, called the Aile des Marronniers (1702), the chapel (1702) and, finally, a second château, the Château Neuf (1706–9), alongside the first. Hardouin Mansart was employed as architect on these projects. The Aile des Marronniers was a low building, originally intended to house guests; the Dauphin, however, took one room for his own use. The chapel was decorated with an *Annunciation* and a *Resurrection* by Antoine Coypel. The Château Neuf, Mansart's last major work, was innovative in using corridors to provide privacy for the apartments within; in this respect it was unlike other contemporary buildings and may thus be taken to reflect the client's taste. The Dauphin decorated Meudon with a collection, similar to the one he had established at Versailles, of new and old paintings and objects of crystal, agate, gold, silver and porcelain, a fair proportion of which was Asian, much of it from Thailand. He did not differ radically from his contemporaries in his tastes, but the delicate tone of the interiors at Meudon is a move away from the heavy display of the 17th century towards a lighter style. The Dauphin was not above using works originally ordered by his father, such as the *Labours of Hercules* (Paris, Louvre) by Noël Coypel. His liking for chinoiserie and his choice of Mansart as architect are also reflections of his father's later taste. That he cared for the works he possessed is perhaps reflected in the use at Versailles of satin roller-blinds to protect them from light.

Very little survives from the Grand Dauphin's patronage. His apartments at Versailles were redecorated after his death; the Vieux Château at Meudon was demolished by Napoleon I after an explosion, and only part of the Château Neuf survives. The collections were dispersed, though some pieces have found their way into the French national collections.

BIBLIOGRAPHY

J. B. de Monicart: *Versailles immortalisé* (Paris, 1720)

J. J. Guiffrey, ed.: *Inventaire général du mobilier du Palais de Versailles* (Paris, 1885–6)

P. Biver: *Histoire du château de Meudon* (Paris, 1923) [very detailed account, with illus. and inventories]

P. Verlet: *Versailles* (Paris, 1961)

N. Mitford: *The Sun King* (London, 1966), pp. 105–12

P. Thornton: *Seventeenth-century Interior Decoration in England, Holland and France* (New Haven, 1978)

I. Dunlop: *The Royal Palaces of France* (London, 1985)

G. Walton: *Louis XIV's Versailles* (Harmondsworth, 1986)

GILES CLIFFORD

(10) Louis XV, King of France (*b* Versailles, 15 Feb 1710; *reg* 1715–74; *d* Versailles, 10 May 1774). Great-grandson of (8) Louis XIV and grandson of (9) Louis de Bourbon. France was governed by Philippe II, Duc d'Orléans (*see* ORLÉANS, House of, (3)), until Louis came of age in 1723. Although he declared in 1744 that he would rule without a chief minister, his indolence and lack of self-confidence made him incapable of leadership. With factions of ministers and courtiers effectively taking over government, he secluded himself at court, hunted and enjoyed a succession of mistresses. This lifestyle undermined his early popularity and led to declining royal authority, but it had major implications for artistic and architectural patronage. While Louis XV lacked Louis XIV's interest in the propaganda value of art, he maintained his predecessor's administrative structures and helped shift emphasis from the 'majestic' to the 'charming' (*see* LOUIS XV STYLE). Most decisions were entrusted to the Directeur-Général des Bâtiments du Roi, though Louis

XV's architectural interests and influence are widely recorded. He studied architectural drawings and himself made drawings and altered details. His working relationship with the Premier Architecte, Anges-Jacques Gabriel (*see* GABRIEL, (3)), was close and long-lasting.

At Versailles, Louis XV desired a balance between the public, monumental *gloire* associated with Louis XIV and *commodité*, the more intimate, domestic comfort (*see* VERSAILLES, §1) typical of the Rococo. This was evident in the apartments laid out in 1730 for his wife, Maria Leszczyńska (1703–68), and in Gabriel's transformation (1738) of Louis XIV's private suite into smaller rooms (e.g. Cabinet de la Pendule, Cabinet Intérieur) and design for the King's new bedchamber. Royal taste was epitomized in the gilt wall carvings (*in situ*) by Jacques Verberckt, commodes by Antoine-Robert Gaudreaus and Jacques Caffieri and the Cabinet Intérieur desk (1760–69; *in situ*) by Jean-François Oeben and Jean-Henri Riesener. Although Gabriel's Pavillon français (1749), Petit Trianon (1760–64) and Opera House (1763–70) at Versailles show a classical restraint, Louis XV's personal tastes probably remained true to the Rococo, as indicated by his appointment of François Boucher as Premier Peintre in 1765 and his long employment of the cabinetmaker Gilles Joubert. The King also supervised additions and alterations to the châteaux of FONTAINEBLEAU, COMPIÈGNE, CHOISY-LE-ROI, Bellevue and Muette, commissioned Gabriel's Ecole Militaire (1751–68), Paris, and chose Gabriel as architect of the Place Louis XV (now Place de la Concorde; *see* PARIS, fig. 6), Paris, in 1750.

The sporadic documentation of Louis XV's acquisition of paintings and sculpture indicates that he was less interested in them than in architecture and the decorative arts. The long periods during which the post of Premier Peintre was vacant (1737–47, 1752–62) suggest royal apathy, as well as reflecting the Crown's precarious finances. Louis XV admired the *Apotheosis of Hercules* (1736; Versailles, Château) by François Lemoyne and appointed him Premier Peintre in 1736, but his lack of commitment to history painting was indicated by his removal of paintings by Nöel Hallé, Carle Vanloo and Joseph-Marie Vien commemorating the lives of Roman emperors (Amiens, Mus. Picardie; Marseille, Mus. B.-A.), commissioned for the château of Choisy in 1764. Louis's passion for the hunt was reflected in numerous commissions from the animal painters François Desportes and Jean-Baptiste Oudry, whose *Royal Hunts* series (1733–46) was translated into tapestries that hang in their original settings at Versailles, Fontainebleau and Compiègne. Jean-Baptiste Lemoyne (ii), a prolific court portrait painter, was the King's favourite sculptor.

Louis XV's interest in art has been traditionally overshadowed by that of his mistress, the Marquise de Pompadour (*see* POISSON, (1)), especially in their patronage of porcelain manufacture. However, his establishment of a factory at Vincennes (1745) predated her presentation at court; he presided at the factory's annual exhibitions, subsidized it and in 1759 bought it outright (*see* VINCENNES, §2).

BIBLIOGRAPHY

P. Hunter: 'A Royal Taste: Louis XV, 1738', *Met. Mus. J.*, vii (1973), pp. 89–113

A. Marie and J. Marie: *Versailles au temps de Louis XV, 1715–1745* (Paris, 1984)
M. Antoine: *Louis XV* (Paris, 1989)
Louis XV and Madame de Pompadour: A Love Affair with Style (exh. cat., ed. P. Hunter-Stiebel; Memphis, TN, Dixon Gal., 1990)

(11) Louis XVI, King of France (*b* Versailles, 23 Aug 1754; *reg* 1774–92; *d* Paris, 21 Jan 1793). Grandson of (10) Louis XV. His interests included locksmithing, metalwork, woodwork, stonemasonry and cartography. He delegated artistic patronage to the Comte d'Angiviller, Directeur-Général des Bâtiments du Roi, and shared his belief in encouraging art that stressed high-minded, patriotic sentiment. History painting commissions ensued from such artists as François-André Vincent, Jean-Simon Berthélemy and Jacques-Louis David. Sculpture was equally patriotic, reflected in d'Angiviller's statuary series (1776–87) commemorating the great men of France. Documentation of the King's own taste suggests that he preferred what were considered lesser genres. He told the portrait painter Elisabeth-Louise Vigée Le Brun, 'I have no knowledge of painting, but you make me fond of it'. He admired landscape painting and architecture by Hubert Robert, whom he appointed Keeper of the King's Pictures in 1784, still-lifes by Gerard van Spaendonck and military paintings by Louis-Nicolas van Blarenberghe. Dutch paintings of the 17th-century were also acquired for the royal collection during his reign. A keen huntsman, Louis XVI bought the studio contents of the animal painter François Desportes in 1784. At Versailles he commissioned the library (1774) and the redecoration of Queen Marie-Antoinette's private suite (1783) and his own dressing-room (1788). His principal architect, Richard Mique, adhered to the LOUIS XVI STYLE favoured by Ange-Jacques Gabriel. Louis XVI himself designed the Pavillon Triveau (1783; destr.), a hunting-lodge in this style for the château of Meudon. His most remarkable act of patronage was the commission for a 362-piece service of Sèvres porcelain (1783–92; Windsor Castle, Berks, Royal Col.) for his personal use at Versailles, left incomplete on his death; its reserves, which illustrate François de Salignac de la Mothe-Fénelon's *Les Aventures de Télémaque* (The Hague, 1699), are Neo-classical in style and moralizing in content, thus according closely with d'Angiviller's artistic ideology. Louis's inadequate handling of the deepening financial and administrative crises of the *ancien régime* hastened the outbreak of the Revolution. He was imprisoned, relieved of his powers with the proclamation of the First French Republic in September 1792, tried for treason and guillotined.

BIBLIOGRAPHY

E. Vigée Le Brun: *Souvenirs de Madame Vigée-Lebrun* (Paris, 1869; Eng. trans., London, 1989)
V. Cronin: *Louis and Antoinette* (London, 1974)
E. Lever: *Louis XVI* (Paris, 1982)
G. de Bellaigue: *Sèvres Porcelain in the Collection of Her Majesty the Queen: The Louis XVI Service* (Cambridge, 1986)
F. Cirio: 'Louis XVI, architecte: Le Pavillon Triveau à Meudon', *Rev. A.* [Paris], lxxxv (1989), pp. 84–5
J.-M. Perouse de Montclos and R. Polidori: *Versailles* (Paris, 1991; Eng. trans., New York, 1991)
M. Levey: *Painting and Sculpture in France, 1700–1789* (New Haven and London, 1993)

(12) Marie-Antoinette (-Josèphe-Jeanne), Queen of France (*b* Vienna, 2 Nov 1755; *d* Paris, 16 Oct 1793). Consort of (11) Louis XVI. She was the daughter of the Holy Roman Emperor Francis I (*reg* 1745–65) and Maria-Theresa, Queen of Hungary and Bohemia (*see* HABSBURG, §I (21)). In 1770 she married the future Louis XVI. She took greater interest in art than did her husband, especially in portraiture and the decorative arts. She commissioned numerous artists to portray her, including her Peintre de la Reine, Joseph Ducreux, Joseph-Siffred Duplessis, Adolf Ulric Wertmüller, Aleksander Kucharski and, most famously ELISABETH-LOUISE VIGÉE LE BRUN. The Vigée Le Brun portraits evolved from the full-length, white-satin *robe à paniers* version (1778; Vienna, Ksthist. Mus.) to the informal, half-length *Marie-Antoinette en gaulle* (1783; priv. col.), which depicts the Queen in a light dress and simple hat, holding a rose; the picture's naturalism was attacked as undignified at the Salon of 1783. Vigée Le Brun's best-known portrait, depicting the Queen with her children (1787; Versailles, Château), attempted a compromise between regal grandeur and loving motherhood. Although Vigée Le Brun's memoirs exaggerated her intimacy with Marie-Antoinette, the Queen secured the artist's election to the Académie Royale in 1783. Other painters admired by Marie-Antoinette included Joseph Vernet and Hubert Robert, and Louis-Jacques Durameau's historical paintings reflected her enthusiasm in the mid-1770s for revived archaic national dress.

Marie-Antoinette's Versailles apartments, notably the Cabinet Doré (1783) and the Méridienne (1785), were designed in an early Neo-classical style (sometimes called 'Marie-Antoinette') by Richard Mique and the brothers Jean-Simon Rousseau and Jean-Hugues Rousseau (*see* VERSAILLES, §1). The Queen retained Jean-Henri Riesener as her cabinetmaker, but her jewellery cabinet (1787; Versailles, Château) by Jean-Ferdinand-Joseph Schwerdfeger is more rigorously Neo-Classical than Riesener's furniture. She ordered the replacement of the botanical garden with an Anglo-Chinese garden (1774–7) by Mique and Robert (*see* VERSAILLES, §2). When in 1774 Louis XVI presented her with the Petit Trianon as a private retreat (*see* VERSAILLES, §4), she supervised its redecoration and commissioned Mique's theatre in its grounds (1779–80). Her tastes were epitomized in the 'Rustic hamlet', which included the Queen's house, a mill, dairy, fishery and cottages (1783–5) and which reflected her enthusiasm for Jean-Jacques Rousseau's cult of nature, sensibility and innocence, as did her dairy (1785–7) at RAMBOUILLET by Robert and Jacques-Jean Thévenin, with sculpture by Pierre Julien and Sèvres porcelain (*see* SÈVRES PORCELAIN FACTORY, fig. 2). Other works undertaken by Mique for Marie-Antoinette included interiors of the château of Fontainebleau and Saint-Cloud (*see* FONTAINE-BLEAU, §1, and SAINT-CLOUD, §1).

Although Marie-Antoinette's clothes, designed by Rose Bertin (1747–1813), reacted against formal court dress and aimed at Rousseauesque simplicity, their cost, with that of her jewellery, exceeded her wardrobe allowance. As perceived by aristocratic and popular opinion, Marie-Antoinette's extravagance and her alleged promiscuity undermined royal authority. War defeats and hatred of the Queen catalysed the overthrow of the monarchy, followed by her imprisonment, trial for treason and execution.

BIBLIOGRAPHY
E. Vigée Le Brun: *Souvenirs de Madame Vigée Lebrun* (Paris, 1869; Eng. trans., London, 1989)
M. Jallut: *Marie Antoinette et ses peintres* (Paris, 1955)
J. Baillio: 'Le Dossier d'une oeuvre d'actualité politique: *Marie Antoinette et ses enfants* par Mme. Vigée Le Brun', *L'Oeil*, cccviii (1981), pp. 34–41, 74–5; cccx (1981), pp. 53–60, 90–91
R. G. Carrott: 'The Hameau de Trianon: Mique, Rousseau and Marie-Antoinette', *Gaz. B.-A.*, n. s. 5, cxiii (1989), pp. 19–28
P. de la Ruffinière du Prey: 'The Queen's Dairy, Rambouillet', *Country Life*, clxxxiv (25 Jan 1990), pp. 88–91
I. Dunlop: *Marie Antoinette* (London, 1993)

MARK STOCKER

(13) Louis XVIII, King of France (*b* Versailles, 17 Nov 1755; *reg* 1814–24; *d* Paris, 16 Sept 1824). Brother of (11) Louis XVI. He was Comte de Provence and was known as Monsieur until, after the death of Louis XVII, he became king in exile in 1795; his reign began when he returned to France in 1814. At the age of 26 he owned 180 pictures and 3357 drawings, the great majority of them Dutch or Flemish. His premier architecte, Jean-François-Thérèse Chalgrin, enlarged the château of Brunoy, southeast of Paris, for him and designed a centrally heated pavilion (both destr.), whose biggest room was a library, in a park beside the château of Versailles. Between 1781 and 1786 alone Louis ordered 255 armchairs from Georges Jacob (ii); one of his desks (Paris, Pal.-Bourbon) is so advanced in conception that its legs are in the shape of republican fasces. During the Revolution and his exile Louis had little time for art, although François Huet-Villiers (1772–1813) painted him in England in 1812 (priv. col.). Louis appreciated the fashionable taste of the day and, when he returned to France in 1814, he liked the Empire style, saying that Napoleon had been a good concierge. Louis altered little in the royal palaces, although in 1821–2 the Throne Room of the Château des Tuileries, Paris, was redecorated in a more sumptuous and flowery manner than the Empire style, under the direction of Jean-Démosthène Dugourc, who had been his Dessinateur du Cabinet before 1791.

Louis XVIII was proud of the new Musée du Louvre in Paris and quarrelled with Arthur Wellesley, 1st Duke of Wellington, in September 1815, when the Allies removed some works of art seized under the Empire. The King's favourite artist was François Gérard, whom he created Premier Peintre du Roi as a reward for his *Entry of Henry IV into Paris* (1817; Paris, Louvre), which depicts reconciliation among Frenchmen, something that Louis tried to achieve in his life. Among numerous royal commissions Gérard painted *Louis XVIII* in his study in the Tuileries and the King's last attachment, *Mme du Cayla and her Children*; both pictures, and some of the King's furniture, are now in her descendants' Château d'Haroué, near Nancy. The King also commissioned for Mme du Cayla the simple and elegant château of Saint-Ouen (1821–3; now a museum), north of Paris, built by Jacques-Ignace Hittorff. The King regularly went to the Salon. Other painters he patronized were Lizinka de Mirbel (1796–1849), Peintre en Miniature de la Chambre; Mme Marie Victoire Jacquotot (1772–1855), his Peintre sur Porcelaine, whom he compared to Raphael; Antoine-Ignace Melling, his Peintre-paysagiste de la Chambre, who drew gouaches (1817; Paris, Louvre) of Gosfield and Hartwell, his English residences; Antoine-Jean Gros, from whom he ordered the *Departure of Louis XVIII from the Tuileries* (1816; Versailles, Château); and Pierre Guérin. The last two contributed to the remarkable series of portraits of royalist Vendéen leaders (Cholet, Mus. A.) that Louis XVIII had ordered for an antechamber at the château of Saint-Cloud (destr. 1870). A room in the Louvre is devoted to Louis's furniture and porcelain.

UNPUBLISHED SOURCES
Paris, Archvs N., R5, 03 [pap. of the household of Louis XVIII as Comte de Provence and King]

BIBLIOGRAPHY
R. Dubois-Corneau: *Le Comte de Provence à Brunoy* (Paris, 1909)
J. Robiquet: 'La Propriété de la Comtesse de Balbi et du Comte de Provence à Versailles', *Rev. Hist. Versailles* (Jan 1921), pp. 1–15
F. Boyer: 'Louis XVIII et la restitution des oeuvres d'art confisquées sous la Révolution et l'Empire', *Bull. Soc. Hist. A. Fr.* (1965), pp. 200–07
R. J. Charleston: 'French Porcelain for the Duke', *Apollo*, xcviii (Sept 1973), pp. 27–33
P. Mansel: *Louis XVIII* (London, 1981)

(14) Charles X, King of France (*b* Versailles, 9 Oct 1757; *reg* 1824–30; *d* Görz [now Gorizia, Italy], 6 Nov 1836). Brother of (13) Louis XVIII. He was the Comte d'Artois before succeeding to the throne. The most important artist in his household was François-Joseph Bélanger, Dessinateur de la Chambre, du Cabinet et de la Garde-Robe. With the help of Bélanger and Jean-Démosthène Dugourc, Charles redecorated and refurnished, in a lavish version of the Louis XVI style, his apartments in Versailles (where he installed a Cabinet Turc), his residence in Paris, the Hôtel du Temple (destr.), and the château of Maisons, outside Paris. Bélanger's masterpiece for Charles was the Pavillon de Bagatelle (1777; altered) in the Bois de Boulogne, Paris. Artois loved women: Bagatelle was adorned with statues (destr.) of *Cupid, Folly, Night* and *Pleasure*, all by Charles Lhuillier, while a medallion by Lhuillier, from a design by Bélanger, at Maisons (redecorated 1779–81) shows two women crowning Priapus with garlands. Hubert Robert painted six views of ruins (New York, Met.) for the bathroom at Bagatelle, and Jacques-Louis David's *Paris and Helen* (Paris, Louvre) was also commissioned by Artois. When he returned to France in 1814, after 25 years of exile, Charles reappointed Bélanger to his former position, but his patronage declined. The 'Charles X style' owes more to his daughter-in-law, (15) Caroline, Duchesse de Berry; the Musée Charles X, featuring Egyptian antiquities, in the Louvre, Paris, was an initiative of Pierre-Louis-Jean-Casimir de Blaces d'Aulps, the Duc de Blacas. Charles X was overthrown in the July Revolution of 1830 and was replaced on the throne by Louis-Philippe, King of the French (*see* ORLÉANS, House of, (7) (7)).

UNPUBLISHED SOURCES
Paris, Archvs N., Series R6, O3 [pap. of the household of Charles as Comte d'Artois and King]

BIBLIOGRAPHY
J. Robiquet: *L'Art et le goût sous la Restauration* (Paris, 1928)
F. Waquet: *Les Fêtes royales sous la Restauration* (Geneva, 1981)
J.-L. Gaillemin, ed.: *La Folie d'Artois* (Paris, 1988)

(15) (Marie-)Caroline, Duchesse de Berry [Berri] (*b* Naples, 5 Nov 1798; *d* Schloss Brunnsee, Austria, 16 April 1870). Daughter-in-law of (14) Charles X. Related to the Spanish branch of the Bourbon dynasty through her father, Francis II of Naples, in 1816 she married Charles-Ferdinand, Duc de Berry, younger son of the future Charles X. Berry was a keen collector, and the couple often visited artists' studios together. After his assassination in 1820, Marie-Caroline found the arts a consolation; she bought 22 pictures at the Salon of 1824 alone. Her favourite artists were such contemporary Frenchmen as Eugène Lami, Jean-François Garneray and Eugène Isabey. She liked unpretentious pictures of women of the Vendée or the crowd outside a Paris theatre, as well as royal portraits and scenes from the life of Henry IV (e.g. Pierre Révoil's *Henry IV Playing with his Children*, 1817; Pau, Château). She was painted by François Gérard (1820) and Thomas Lawrence (1825; both Versailles, Château) and, wearing a striking Gothic belt set with diamonds (1827; Amiens, Mus. Picardie), by Alexandre-Jean Dubois-Drahonet (1791–1834). In 1829 she commissioned two important works from Eugène Delacroix, *Quentin Durward and Le Balafré* (Paris, Louvre, on dep. Paris, Mobilier N.), which reflects her fashionable interest in the novels of Sir Walter Scott, and the *Battle of Poitiers* (Paris, Louvre). The Duchesse employed J. A. Froelicher in 1820–22 to add a strikingly simple hospice and chapel to her château at Rosny-sur-Seine, between Paris and Rouen, which was filled with the finest furniture of the age, some of it covered in embroideries made by the Duchesse and her ladies-in-waiting. Although few of her interior fittings remain at the château, there is some of the Neo-classical furniture that was supplied to her by François Jacob-Desmalter. Other remnants of the Duchesse's incomparable collections of pictures, jewellery, furniture and porcelain can be seen at Rosny and in the Musée des Arts Décoratifs in Bordeaux. The July Revolution of 1830 drove her into exile, and much of what she owned was dispersed in sales or among her Austrian and Italian descendants.

BIBLIOGRAPHY
Vicomte de Reiset: *La Duchesse de Berri* (Paris, 1906)
A. Castelot: *La Duchesse de Berri* (Paris, 1963)
B. Scott: 'The Duchesse de Berri as Patron of the Arts', *Apollo*, cxxiv (1986), pp. 345–53

PHILIP MANSEL

II. Spanish branch.

The last Habsburg monarch in Spain was Charles II (*see* HABSBURG, §II (10)). His half-sister Maria Theresa of Austria had married Louis XIV of France, and on 2 October 1700 their grandson Philip, Duc d'Anjou, was proclaimed King of Spain as (1) Philip V. This began a new dynasty (*see* fig.) of French origin and precipitated the War of the Spanish Succession (1701–14). Both Philip and his second wife, (2) Elizabeth Farnese, formed important collections. In 1746 (3) Ferdinand VI, Philip's son, became king. He was succeeded in 1759 by his half-brother (4) Charles III, who, aside from collecting, is noted for his promotion of decorative arts production in Spain. His brother the Infante (5) Don Luis Antonio was also a patron and amateur art connoisseur. Charles III was succeeded by his son (6) Charles IV, who ruled until 1808. During the Peninsula War (1808–14) and the reign of Napoleon I's brother, Joseph Bonaparte, many works of

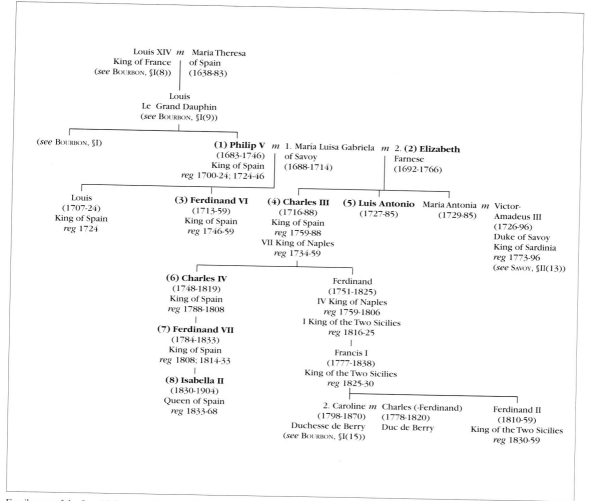

Family tree of the Spanish branch of the Bourbon dynasty

art from the Spanish royal collections were taken to France, including paintings, jewels and precious objects. The suppression of religious orders in Spain and the consequent requisitioning of their art treasures contributed to this loss. With the return of (7) Ferdinand VII to Spain in 1814 and the signing of the second Treaty of Paris in 1815, some works were brought back. During Ferdinand's reign the Museo del Prado, Madrid, was created to gather together the works of the royal collections that had been dispersed among the various palaces. Ferdinand VII was succeeded by his daughter (8) Isabella II.

BIBLIOGRAPHY

P. de Madrazo: *Viaje artístico de tres siglos por las colecciones de cuadros de los reyes de España* (Barcelona, 1884)

L'Art européen à la cour d'Espagne au XVIIIe siècle (exh. cat. by Y. Bottineau, J. Baticle and A. E. Pérez Sánchez, Bordeaux, Mus. B.-A.; Paris, Grand Pal.; Madrid, Prado; 1979–80)

PILAR BENITO

(1) Philip [Felipe] **V**, King of Spain (*b* Versailles, 19 Dec 1683; *reg* 1700–46; *d* Madrid, 9 July 1746). He was the son of Louis, Dauphin of France, and grandson of Louis XIV (*see* §I(8) and (9) above). His grandfather gave him the title of Duc d'Anjou. He was brought up at the French court, where his tutors included François de Salignac de la Mothe-Fénelon. He enjoyed open-air activities, but his character was apathetic and tended to melancholia, as depicted in a portrait of him painted in Paris in 1701 by Hyacinthe Rigaud (Versailles, Château). In 1700 he succeeded to the Spanish throne on the death without issue of Charles II, arriving in Madrid in April 1701. In the same year he married María Luisa Gabriela of Savoy, and on her death in 1714 he married (2) Elizabeth Farnese. In January 1724 Philip abdicated in favour of his son, Louis (*b* 1707), who died shortly after in August 1724, when Philip resumed the throne until his own death in 1746.

In contrast to the luxury and brilliance of the French court, the Spanish royal palaces were austere. Between 1719 and 1721 Philip began to plan and build near Segovia the palace of SAN ILDEFONSO, surrounded by gardens and fountains, and he brought in French workers for its construction. The palace was designed by Teodoro Ardemans; a recasing of the structure was begun in 1735 by FILIPPO JUVARRA and was completed in 1739 by GIOVANNI BATTISTA SACCHETTI. This became Philip's favourite residence, and he is buried in its chapel. Following the destruction by fire of the Alcázar in Madrid on Christmas Eve 1734, Philip built the new Palacio Real, in the Italian style, the principal architects of which were Juvarra and Sacchetti (see MADRID, §IV, 2). The new building had a marked effect on 18th-century Spanish architecture. Statues in stone and marble were commissioned for the fountains and gardens of San Ildefonso and to adorn the new palace in Madrid. Complex iconographical programmes were carried out by such French sculptors as René Carlier, Antoine (d 1761) and Hubert Dumandré (d 1781), Pierre Pitué, René Fremin (who produced the bust of *Philip V*, after 1721, and among a series of Virtues the bronze figures of *Justice* and *Strength*; all Madrid, Pal. Real) and Jean Thierry II (fountains of *Neptune* and *Apollo*, 1721–8; La Granja S Ildefonso, Pal.) and by the Italian Giovanni Domenico Olivieri.

The fire also destroyed more than 500 paintings in the royal collection. Philip and Elizabeth increased the acquisition of paintings considerably. Important collections were purchased and later displayed at San Ildefonso, including that of Carlo Maratti, which arrived from Italy in 1723; the magnificent collection of Classical sculpture that had belonged to Christina, Queen of Sweden, was acquired in 1724, and numerous lesser collections of Italian and Flemish paintings were also purchased. The King also inherited the so-called 'Trésor du Dauphin', which consisted of objects of daily use made of crystal and ornamented with precious gemstones.

Royal commissions were given to French and Italian painters who settled in Spain: Michel-Ange Houasse, who arrived in 1715 (*Louis I*, 1717; Madrid, Prado); Jean Ranc, who came in 1722 (*Family of Philip V*, 1722–3; Madrid, Prado); Andrea Procaccini, who arrived in 1720; Domenico Maria Sani (1690–1772); and Louis-Michel van Loo, who came in 1737 (*Family of Philip V*, 1743; Madrid, Prado; for illustration see BOURBON, §II(2)). These portraits in the French style, as well as large-scale tapestry cartoons designed by these artists, were important in setting the tone of the court of Philip V. After the Treaty of Utrecht in 1713 and the loss by Spain of her Flemish provinces with their tapestry works, Philip V brought in Flemish workers to found the Real Fábrica de Tapices de S Bárbara (after 1721; see SPAIN, §XI, 4). There was new interest in the 17th-century Sevillian school of painting, especially the work of Murillo, which became known to Philip and Elizabeth during the residence of the court in Seville between 1729 and 1733. During Philip's reign there were preparatory meetings of foreign and Spanish artists that culminated in the creation of the Real Academia de Bellas Artes de S Fernando in 1744, two years before the death of the King, who previously had founded the Academia de Medicina (1734) and the Academia de la Historia (1734–6), all in Madrid.

BIBLIOGRAPHY
Y. Bottineau: *El arte cortesano en la España de Felipe V, 1700–46* (Bordeaux, 1962, rev. Madrid, 1986)
F. J. Sánchez Cantón: *Escultura y pintura del siglo XVIII* (Madrid, 1965)
J. Urrea Fernández: *La pintura italiana del siglo XVIII en España* (Valladolid, 1977)

MERCEDES AGUEDA

(2) Elizabeth, Queen of Spain [Elizabeth Farnese] (*b* Parma, 25 Oct 1692; *d* Aranjuez, 11 July 1766). Wife of (1) Philip V. She was the daughter of Odoardo Farnese (*see* FARNESE, (5)). Her importance for the history of patronage derives both from her activities as queen-consort of Spain (1715–46), queen-dowager (1746–59, during the reign of her stepson Ferdinand VI; *see* (3) below) and queen-mother (from the accession in 1759 of her son Charles III; *see* (4) below), and from her role as the juridical means by which the important Farnese collections, both in Parma and Rome, were transmitted to the House of Bourbon.

Elizabeth herself was a highly accomplished draughtsman and amateur painter, as surviving work from her early years shows (e.g. the *Fainting of Esther*; Parma, Mus. Lombardi). Many of these early works were copies of paintings in the Farnese collections or from the immensely rich decorative schemes of the churches of Parma and thus attest to her first-hand knowledge of the artistic holdings of her family and to the visual tradition of her native duchy. Thus, although she was fully alert to the political benefits to be extracted from patronage to fulfil her own highly ambitious dynastic policies, her personal affinities for a range of artistic production and practical knowledge of certain techniques can be documented. Wedded to her palpable aesthetic and cultural affinities was an imperious temperament, a determination to govern and a will of iron. Although it would be mistaken to see Philip V as totally the pawn of his new wife, Elizabeth quickly established a massive dominance over her husband and secured her own position as by far the most influential voice at court, effectively displacing the King from the centre of power, a position caught uncannily in Louis-Michel van Loo's *Family of Philip V* (1743; Madrid, Prado; see fig.), in which the Queen is placed virtually at the centre of a complicated group portrait, closest to the crown. She also engineered the dramatic pruning of the French faction at the court of Madrid, which had significant implications for official patronage by rendering the flow of commissions to French artists less automatic and by softening the drive to an academization of the arts in Spain along Gallic lines. Philip's two sons from his first marriage had precedence in the Spanish succession, and any political prospects Elizabeth's sons might have had seemed bound up with her extraordinary clutch of dynastic claims on Italian sovereignties. The italianization of Spain's foreign policy, linked with Elizabeth's profound knowledge of her native culture, skewed royal patronage towards the Italian peninsula while diminishing the influence from Versailles.

The intimate and passionate nature of the relationship between Philip and Elizabeth meant that they were rarely apart. The Queen was consulted on virtually every question, and most of the major royal commissions in Spain between 1715 and 1746 must be seen as the result of decisions taken jointly by the King and Queen. It is, however, possible to define specific areas of interest for both partners, as inventories drawn up at the time of Philip V's death in 1746 give a clear picture of their respective

Family of Philip V by Louis-Michel van Loo, oil on canvas, 4.06×5.11 m, 1743 (Madrid, Museo del Prado)

personal collections of paintings. Works by significant 16th- and 17th-century artists were listed as belonging specifically to the Queen: Guido Reni's *St Sebastian* (Madrid, Prado), two compositions by Nicolas Poussin (both lost) and the *Virgin, Christ Child and St John the Baptist* (c. 1516; Madrid, Prado) by Correggio. An affinity with Flemish 17th-century art, an area in which the Spanish royal collections were already very rich, is supported by the presence of works by most of the celebrated painters from the southern Netherlands: Anthony van Dyck's *Sir Endymion Porter with van Dyck* (c. 1623), the *Portrait of the Artist's Wife, Maria Ruthven* and autograph versions of the pendant portraits of *Frederik Hendrik of Orange* and *Amalia of Solms-Nassau* (c. 1628; all Madrid, Prado); paintings then attributed to Peter Paul Rubens and Jacob Jordaens; and landscape, genre and still-life paintings by members of the Bruegel family, Paul Bril, Jan Fyt and David Teniers II. Although a significant patron of decorative pictorial cycles, Elizabeth also found room for cabinet pictures from the north, while nevertheless appearing to have used the series of *Five Senses* by Abraham Janssen (Segovia, Pal. Granja S Ildefonso), as she did the work of contemporary Italian artists, to organize an individual room around a single iconographic scheme.

Elizabeth broke fresh ground with her enthusiasm for 17th-century Spanish painting and the acquisitions she made during the prolonged installation of the court in Seville from 1729 to 1733, notably paintings by Bartolomé Murillo (e.g. *Vision of St Bernard, c.* 1660; Madrid, Prado), which opened up a new area for royal collecting. Just as the King did not share her enthusiasm for Murillo and the Andalusian artists of the 17th century, Elizabeth, in turn, preferred very few individual commissions to Jean Ranc, who was much favoured by the King for official court portraits, apart from a depiction of her favourite dog, *Lista* (Riofrío, Royal Pal.), an exception that made an important contribution to the evolution of canine portraiture as a developing field of court painting. Her gift of Diego Velázquez's *Self-portrait* (Valencia, Mus. B. A.) to the celebrated castrato Farinelli attests both to the high value she accorded music and to the presence in her personal collection of work by the leading 17th-century painter–courtier in Spain. Her acquisitions of paintings from earlier epochs was balanced, however, by a keen interest in contemporary art. The presence of Antoine Watteau's *Marriage Contract* and *Assembly in a Park* (both Madrid, Prado) points to her cosmopolitan outlook, albeit a cosmopolitanism with a strong Italian flavour. Her inclination to employ contemporary Italian artists appears most clearly in the commissions surrounding the royal couple's numerous architectural projects. The original designs for the palace of SAN ILDEFONSO, near Segovia, where work began in 1721, were provided by the architect TÉODORO ARDEMANS, but Elizabeth ensured the participation of a number of Italian painters, architects and decorators, among them ANDREA PROCACCINI, a pupil of Carlo Maratta, who played a major role in the elaboration and italianization of San Ildefonso, grouping around him a collection of Italian protégés from Parma, Bologna and Piacenza who were responsible for the interiors of many of the significant royal palace projects of the reign. He also played a major role in the acquisition by the Spanish crown of Maratta's collection (1723) and of the antique sculptures previously owned by Christina, Queen of Sweden, both of which Elizabeth eventually housed at San Ildefonso; Andrea Sacchi's portrait of *Francesco Albani*, along with Maratta's own portrait of *Andrea Sacchi* (*c.* 1665; both Madrid, Prado); and compositions then attributed to Giovanni Bellini and Guido Reni. Procaccini and the marchese Annibale, who assembled a notable personal collection of pictures and ceramics from which the Queen made a number of acquisitions following his death in 1752, acted as Elizabeth's artistic advisers and agents, strengthening the networks stretching back to the Italian courts. The Queen was also advised by the Spanish ambassador to Rome, Cardinal Trojano Acquaviva, who alerted her to sales of paintings in the papal capital and commissioned in 1745, as a gift for her, a canvas by Joseph Vernet depicting the cardinal and his suite at the Farnese palace of Caprarola (Philadelphia, PA, Mus. A.).

A significant phase in the italianization of San Ildefonso followed the arrival in Spain (1735) of FILIPPO JUVARRA, who initiated commissions for cycles of paintings for two of the palace's great state rooms: one for the throne room depicting episodes from the *Life of Alexander the Great*, in reference to the King and executed by a variety of predominantly Italian painters, including Sebastiano Conca (*Alexander Sacrificing in Solomon's Temple, c.* 1735; Segovia, Pal. Granja), Francesco Trevisani (*Family of Darius before Alexander*, 1735; Riofrío, Pal. Real), Francesco Solimena, Donato Creti (1671–1749), Agostino Masucci and Giambattista Pittoni (*Triumphal Entry of Alexander into Babylonia*, 1737; Madrid, Patrm. N.); the second, for the bedchamber, of biblical scenes executed exclusively by Giovanni Paolo Panini, from Piacenza, complemented by overdoors (1735; *in situ*) painted by Andrea Locatelli. The Italian preponderance never became suffocatingly exclusive, however; François Lemoyne's contribution to the throne-room cycle, passed, after his suicide, to Carle Vanloo (*Porus Defeated by Alexander*; Madrid, Escorial), a francophone artist who maintained strong links with the court of Turin. The garden of SAN ILDEFONSO clearly looked to French models, and its most significant sculptures were executed by RENÉ FRÉMIN.

San Ildefonso was not, however, the focus of Juvarra's activities in Spain. He had been summoned to Madrid to build the new royal palace after fire had gutted much of the old Alcázar in December 1734. The choice of Juvarra to build a new and imposing palace that would serve as a statement of the dynasty's renovating presence in Madrid, although widely viewed as another expression of Elizabeth's determination to employ Italian artists to work on the great crown projects of Spain, seems in fact to have been based on the royal couple's knowledge of his work in Lisbon. The architect's death in 1736 reopened the question of the design of the new palace, which had now assumed European significance as the most important architectural and decorative commission of the decade (*see* MADRID, §IV, 2). Here Elizabeth intervened by securing the services of Juvarra's pupil GIOVANNI BATTISTA SACCHETTI, who left the court of Turin in 1736 to begin realizing, albeit in a dramatically reduced version, the master plan (model; Madrid, Mus. Artilleria) of his teacher.

The King's death in 1746 totally altered Elizabeth's position. Her attempt to retain some control over state policy and to preserve a presence in Madrid spurred the new king, Ferdinand VI, to restrict her field of manoeuvre to San Ildefonso. A virtual exile from court, by the time the dowager queen retired to San Ildefonso it had been transformed into a residential palace renowned for its design and its collections. Here Elizabeth supported the entrepreneurial activities of Ventura Sit (*d* 1755) to establish a royal glassworks (*see* SPAIN, §VIII, 3). The emblematic importance of the palace was its choice as the site for the tombs of Philip and Elizabeth, thus breaking with the tradition of the Spanish Habsburg sovereigns and consorts, all of whom were buried in the vault at the Escorial. The elaboration of a pantheon for Philip and for herself was executed between 1756 and 1758, under the supervision of Semprionio Subisati, by two francophone sculptors, Hubert Dumandré (*d* 1781) and Pierre Pitué (*b* 1743–4). Elizabeth was determined not to retrench expenditure on artistic policies; her advisers were transferred from Madrid to San Ildefonso, and as a result, from 1746 until Ferdinand's death in 1759, there were two major centres of royal patronage: that of Ferdinand and María Bárbara at Madrid and that of Elizabeth at San Ildefonso. Indeed, the antipathy between the two queens generated artistic commissions. The demands of court protocol and the project to erect his father's tomb at San Ildefonso meant that Ferdinand had to visit his stepmother occasionally, and tradition has it that her desire to reduce contact with the new King and Queen to a bare minimum inspired Elizabeth to build a new palace (from 1752) nearby at Riofrío, designed by Virgilio Rabaglio, from the Ticino, to which she could easily retreat when her stepson and his wife chose to stay at San Ildefonso.

The death of María Bárbara in 1758 plunged Ferdinand VI into a depression from which he never recovered, and he died in 1759. Elizabeth assumed the government of Spain until the arrival of her son Charles III and his wife from Naples. The death of Queen María Amalia in 1760 restored her to the role of the first princess at the court of Madrid. Installed in the capital at the palace of Buenavista, she attempted to assert her control over her equally forceful son. Weakness of sight, however, blunted her activities both as a political force and as a patron of the arts. At her death in 1766, she bequeathed a rich cultural legacy to her children: on a practical level, much of her extensive personal collections were divided between her three sons, Charles III, King of Spain, the Duke of Parma and Don Luis, the value of the paintings being adjudicated by Anton Raphael Mengs; on another level, all three princes had been influenced by her example and, by the time of her death, had become notable patrons of the arts.

BIBLIOGRAPHY

E. Armstrong: *Elizabeth Farnese: The 'Termagant' of Spain* (London, 1892)

M. E. Bertoli: 'Il viaggio nuziale di Elisabetta Farnese da Sestri Levante a Marsiglia', *Riv. Ingauna & Intemelia*, n.s. 8 (1953), pp. 17–23

Y. Bottineau: 'El Panteón de Felipe V en la Granja', *Archv Esp. A.*, xxviii (1955), pp. 263–6

E. Battisti: 'Juvarra a San Ildefonso', *Commentari*, ix (1958), pp. 273–97

J. J. Luna Fernández: 'Jean Ranc', *Reales sitios: Rev. Patron. N.*, liv (1977), pp. 65–72

J. Urrea Fernández: *La pintura italiana del siglo XVIII en España* (Valladolid, 1977)

A. E. Pérez Sánchez: 'Peinture et peintres italiens à la cour d'Espagne au XVIIIe siècle', *L'Art européen à la cour d'Espagne au XVIIIe siècle* (exh. cat., ed. Y. Bottineau, J. Baticle and A. E. Pérez Sánchez; Bordeaux, Gal. B.-A.; Paris, Grand Pal.; Madrid, Prado; 1979–80), pp. 165–205

Y. Bottineau: *L'Art de cour dans l'Espagne des lumières, 1746–1808* (Paris, 1986)

El arte en las cortes europeas del siglo XVIII (Madrid, 1988), pp. 23–32, 137–46, 351–7, 443–50

Y. Bottineau: *L'Art de cour dans l'Espagne de Philippe V, 1700–1746* (Sceaux, 1993)

Du duc d'Anjou à Philippe V: Le Premier Bourbon d'Espagne (exh. cat., Sceaux, Château, Mus. Ile de France, 1993)

Filippo Juvarra, 1678–1736: De Messina al Palacio Real de Madrid (exh. cat., Madrid, Pal. Real, 1994), pp. 239–49, 251–75

ROBERT ORESKO

(3) Ferdinand [Fernando] **VI**, King of Spain (*b* Madrid, 23 Sept 1713; *reg* 1746–59; *d* Villaviciosa de Odón, 10 Aug 1759). Son of (1) Philip V. His mother was María Luisa Gabriela of Savoy. He became heir to the Spanish throne on the death of his elder brother, Louis, in 1724 and was crowned in 1746. In 1729 he had married María Bárbara of Braganza, daughter of John V of Portugal; her cultivated upbringing was a considerable influence on her husband. Ferdinand's patronage of foreign artists led to the development in Spain of the more cosmopolitan art current in Europe in the mid-18th century. French influence lessened slightly during his reign, and Italian art became more dominant at the Spanish court. This reflected Ferdinand's own taste, and the monarchs identified themselves completely with the new style and with the artistic scene. The Real Academia de Bellas Artes de S Fernando, Madrid, founded in 1744, was officially established in 1752, and under its auspices young artists were sent to study in Rome with a royal bursary.

Ferdinand's reign was marked by the influence of such architects as François-Antoine Carlier and Santiago Bonavía. The King commissioned Bonavía to rebuild the Palacio Real in Aranjuez after a fire in 1748 and to carry out extensive urban developments in the city. Spanish architects, such as Ventura Rodríguez, who worked at the Palacio Real in Madrid, assimilated the style of their French and Italian counterparts. One of the most important projects of the royal couple was the foundation of the church of S Bárbara and the convent of the Visitación, known as the Salesas Reales, in Madrid, built between 1750 and 1757 by Francisco Moradillo (*fl* 1745–69) from plans by Carlier. The church contains Ferdinand's tomb, by Francesco Sabbatini. Its sumptuous decoration and the rare materials employed reflect the character of the court of Ferdinand and Bárbara.

Ferdinand's policy of neutrality and the country's economic recovery made his reign a period of peace and prosperity, and this was reflected in court art and celebrations characterized by gaiety, refinement and pageantry. The manufacture of cloth of gold and silver and of fine textiles was encouraged, and no sumptuary laws were enacted, as they had been under Philip V; this contributed to making the arts more decorative and elaborate. The theatres of Aranjuez and Buen Retiro became the settings of operatic celebrations staged by Carlo Broschi Farinelli, the talented Italian singer and scenographer who held an important and influential place at the Spanish court. The entertainments he created, on which considerable sums were spent, included the construction in 1752 of the Escuadra del Tajo (the Tagus Squadron), a flotilla of 15 boats in which the royal family took pleasure trips on the river. The intimate yet lavish nature of such festivities was recorded by Francesco Battaglioli in *Ferdinand VI and Bárbara of Braganza with their Guests in the Gardens of Aranjuez for the Feast Day of St Ferdinand* (1756; Madrid, Prado).

Under Ferdinand several Italian artists came to Spain, some of whom, such as Giacomo Pavia (1699–1750) and Battaglioli, created stage sets for the opera under Farinelli's direction. In 1747 Jacopo Amigoni was summoned to work at the Spanish court, followed in 1753 by Corrado Giaquinto. Amigoni was commissioned to provide decorations for the palace in Aranjuez on the theme of the virtues pertaining to the monarchy. Amigoni was also involved in the decoration of the convent of the Visitación. Giaquinto was appointed Pintor de Cámara and Director of the Real Academia de Bellas Artes de S Fernando in 1753, and his influence was considerable. He prepared sketches for the fresco decoration of the church of the convent of La Visitación, carried out (1757–8) by Luis González Velázquez and Antonio González Velázquez. These included the *Birth of the Virgin* (Detroit, MI, Inst. A.). Giaquinto's sketches for the fresco paintings he carried out in the Salon de Colunnas in the Palacio Real, Madrid, include the *Birth of the Son* and the *Triumph of Bacchus* (both 1760; Madrid, Prado). Charles-Joseph Flipart came to Spain in 1748 and was appointed painter and engraver to the court in 1753. His royal commissions for the convent of La Visitación included the large altarpiece of the *Giving of Seville to St Ferdinand* (1756; *in situ*; sketch, Madrid, Prado).

BIBLIOGRAPHY

A. Danvila: *Fernando VI y Doña Bárbara de Braganza* (Madrid, 1905)

C. de Polentinos: 'El monasterio de la Visitación de Madrid (Santa Bárbara o las Salesas)', *Bol. Soc. Esp. Excurs.*, xxiv (1916), pp. 257–83

F. García Rives: *Fernando VI y Doña Bárbara de Braganza: Apuntes para su reinado* (Madrid, 1917)

F. J. Sánchez Cantón: 'Las bellas artes en el reinado de Fernando VI', *Academia: Bol. Real Acad. B.A. San Fernando*, ix (1959)

C. Farinelli: *Fiestas reales en el reinado de Fernando VI* (Madrid, 1972)

J. J. Martín González: 'Las ideas artísticas de Doña Bárbara de Braganza', *Bracara Augusta*, 37 (1973)

C. Bedat: *L'Académie des beaux-arts de Madrid, 1744–1808* (Toulouse, 1974)

J. Hernández Ferrero: 'Evolución arquitectónica y últimas obras del Palacio real de Aranjuez', *Reales Sitios: Rev. Patrm. N.*, xlii (1974), pp. 65–74

J. J. Luna: 'El retrato de Fernando VI y Bárbara de Braganza con su corte por Amiconi', *Archv Esp. A.*, 52 (1979), pp. 339–41

J. Urrea Fernandez: 'Introducción a la pintura rococó en España en la época de Fernando VI', *Catedra Feijóo* (Oviedo, 1981), pp. 315–36

FRANCISCO JAVIER PIZARRO GOMEZ

(4) Charles [Carlos] **III**, King of Spain [Charles VII, King of Naples] (*b* Madrid, 20 Jan 1716; *reg* 1734–59 [Naples], 1759–88 [Spain]; *d* Madrid, 14 Dec 1788). Son of (1) Philip V. He was brought up by his mother, (2) Elizabeth Farnese, at the court of San Ildefonso, and his portrait was painted at an early age by Jean Ranc (*Charles III as a Child*, c. 1725–30; Madrid, Prado). Through his mother's political activities, he inherited in 1731 the duchies of Parma, Piacenza and Tuscany. He ascended the throne of Naples in 1734, married Maria Amalia of Saxony on 19 June 1738 and succeeded to the Spanish throne on the death of his half-brother (3) Ferdinand VI in 1759. From his youth Charles showed great interest in mechanics, architecture, botany and zoology. Among his favourite hobbies were hunting and fishing, which he pursued all his life.

During the 25 years of Charles's reign over the kingdom of Naples there was a remarkable flowering of the arts, and to this period belong several major architectural schemes. The King established the habit of residing periodically in different palaces, such as at Capodimonte (begun 1738 by Giovanni Antonio Medrano, assisted by Antonio Canevari) and Portici, all of which were in attractive landscape settings and surrounded by formal gardens. Charles used local architects for some of his building projects, but in 1751 invited the renowned Ferdinando Fuga and Luigi Vanvitelli to Naples. From Vanvitelli the King commissioned the immense royal residence of Caserta (begun 1752), near Naples. Sculpture was an integral part of Vanvitelli's designs both for interior decoration and for the royal gardens, as at Caserta. Many of these schemes, completed by Charles's son Ferdinand IV, were carried out by local artists, such as Tommaso Solari (*d* 1779) and Andrea Violani, in a style that tended to be classical, most notably in the garden fountains, and that introduced the taste for displaying antique sculpture. In Naples, Charles was responsible for important public buildings, including the theatre of S Carlo (1737; destr. 1816) by Medrano, with the contribution of Fuga and Giovanni Maria Galli-Bibiena; the enormous Albergo de' Poveri, begun by Fuga in 1752; and the Foro Carolino (1757–65, now Piazza Dante) by Vanvitelli.

Charles did not appear to have such well-defined ideas in his choice of painting, nor was his taste so refined, which may explain his preference for such artists as Giovanni Maria delle Piane, called Molinaretto (1660–1745), and Clemente Ruta (1685–1767) rather than more gifted artists of the late Neapolitan Baroque, such as Francesco Solimena, Francesco de Mura or Giuseppe Bonito. Later, however, commissions were given to these artists as a result of the intervention of Maria Amalia: to Solimena for *Allegory of the Marriage of Charles VII and Maria Amalia* (fresco, 1738; Naples, Pal. Reale; destr.); to Mura for *Virtues of Charles VII and Maria Amalia* (fresco, 1738; Naples, Pal. Reale); and to Bonito for the *Turkish Ambassador at the Court of Charles VII of Naples* (1741; Madrid, Prado). She was also responsible for inviting Anton Raphael Mengs to Naples in 1759 to paint portraits of the royal family and to paint the *Presentation of the Virgin in the Temple* (1759) for the high altar of the chapel at Caserta. During Charles's reign in Naples the Capodimonte porcelain factory (1743) and a maiolica factory at Caserta (1753) were founded to meet the royal demand. The Real Laboratorio delle Pietre Dure was also established, as well as tapestry works using Florentine craftsmen (*see* NAPLES, §III). A significant event for European art was the discovery and excavation of Herculaneum in 1738 and Pompeii in 1748. Following the publication of *Antichità di Ercolano esposte* (Naples, 1757–96), which was dedicated to Charles VII, antique Roman compositions became part of the repertory of Neoclassical painting.

In 1759 Charles became king of Spain; his departure from Italy is shown in the pair of paintings *Embarkation of Charles III in Naples* (1759; Madrid, Prado) by Antonio Joli. In 1761 Maria Amalia died in Madrid. Charles III continued with the artistic projects already begun, one of the most important being the decoration of the new Palacio Real, Madrid, an undertaking that contributed greatly to the revival of the arts in Spain. The decoration of the ceilings had been started by Corrado Giaquinto, who left Spain in 1762, shortly after Mengs arrived in 1761 at the invitation of the King. Mengs was responsible for the *Apotheosis of Trajan* (1774) and the *Apotheosis of Hercules* (1761–9) for the King's apartments (Madrid, Pal. Real). Mengs's classicism, use of cool colours and types of composition became models for contemporary Spanish painters. He was appointed Primer Pintor del Rey in 1766 and had been made honorary Director of Painting at the Real Academia de Bellas Artes de S Fernando in 1763, where his work and writings were very influential. Mengs was in Spain until 1769 and again between 1774 and 1776, and among his many official portraits of the royal family is that of *Charles III* (c. 1761; Madrid, Prado). In 1762 Giambattista Tiepolo arrived in Madrid, summoned by Charles to paint the main rooms of the Palacio Real. His *Glorification of the Spanish Monarchy* in the Throne Room and *Triumph of Aeneas* (both 1762–6; Madrid, Pal. Real) display richness in colouring and a Venetian sensuality. Tiepolo's last major project before his death in Madrid in 1770 was the commission to paint a series of altarpieces for the new church of S Pascual Bailón, at Aranjuez, for which sketches were shown to and approved by Charles III at San Ildefonso; one of the completed paintings is the *Immaculate Conception* (1767; Madrid, Prado).

The King's preoccupation with public works resulted in major improvements in Madrid, including one of the main thoroughfares of the city, the Paseo del Prado (begun 1767), along which were the fountains of *Cibeles* (c. 1781) by Robert Michel and Francisco Gutiérrez, of *Apollo* (1777–1802) by Manuel Francisco Alvarez de la Peña and of *Neptune* (c. 1777–86) by Juan Pascual de Mena, the last after a design by Ventura Rodríguez. The Paseo is flanked by public facilities, including the Gabinete de Historia Natural (now the Museo del Prado), begun in 1785; the Jardín Botánico, founded in 1775; and the Observatorio Astronómico (1790), all by Juan de Villanueva; and the Hospital de S Carlos (1756–81) by Francesco Sabbatini (only part of the projected building was erected; now the Centro de la Reina Sofía). Sabbatini had been brought from Italy by the King in 1760 and made Arquitecto Mayor de las Obras Reales in the same year. Private buildings put up along this tree-lined avenue included the palaces of Villahermosa (1771–83) by Silvestre Pérez and

Manuel Martin Rodríguez and of Buenavista (1772; now Min. Ejército) by Pedro Arnal (*b* 1735). In the centre of the capital, service buildings were erected, such as the Casa de la Aduana (from 1760) by Sabbatini and the Casa de Correos (1768) by Jaime Marquet (*d* 1782). New city boundaries were set by the Puerta de Alcalá (1764–78), a magnificent triumphal arch erected in honour of Charles III, and by the Puerta de San Vicente (1775; destr.), both by Sabbatini. With the building activity went extensive work to pave and light the streets, and a proper sewage system was laid (from 1761, all from plans by Sabbatini). These improvements transformed Madrid into a modern city to compare with others in Enlightenment Europe.

The King's foreward-looking policies and essentially practical aims for improvement were not confined to Madrid. An extensive programme of modernization throughout Spain included bridge-building, digging canals, such as the Imperial in Aragon (1768–90), and the construction of roads between many of the principal cities. The Neo-classical architect Ventura Rodríguez, appointed chief of works of the city of Madrid in 1764, was also architectural adviser to the Council of Castile, and through this body he was able to influence the design and supervise the erection of such public buildings as schools, hospitals and town halls, as well as schemes for the development of towns.

Charles III made changes at the royal palaces: at the Escorial he adapted one wing for his private apartments and built for his sons the Casita del Príncipe and Casita de Arriba (begun 1773), designed by Villanueva. At the Pardo he doubled the palace in size (1772, by Sabbatini) and built the Casita del Príncipe (1784), also from designs by Villanueva. In the town of Aranjuez he carried out a scheme for urban development, enlarged the palace and made changes to its surrounding gardens (two wings dated 1772 and 1777, the chapel in 1780, and the theatre, all designed and directed by Sabbatini).

The façade of the Real Academia de Bellas Artes de S Fernando, in new premises in the Calle de Alcalá, then called the Palacio Goyenseche, was remodelled in the new reign by Villanueva and given a severe Neo-classical appearance (1773). The possibility of working at court and the Academia's emphasis on academic teaching attracted Spanish artists to Madrid. Two of the most gifted received royal commissions and worked at the Palacio Real: Francisco Bayeu (*Olympus* and the *Fall of the Giants*, 1764; Madrid, Pal. Real) and Mariano Salvador Maella, who painted the dignified portrait of *Charles III Wearing the Mantle of his Order* (1784; Madrid, Pal. Real; sketch, Agen, Mus. B.-A.). It is possible that Luís Meléndez also received royal patronage, as nearly half his known still-life paintings (*c.* 1772; Madrid, Prado) decorated the royal

Charles III Lunching before his Court, by Luis Paret, oil on panel, 500×640 mm, *c.* 1770–72 (Madrid, Museo del Prado)

residence at Aranjuez. Another gifted artist who enjoyed encouragement from the monarchy was the Rococo painter Luis Paret; his fascinating *Charles III Lunching before his Court* (*c*. 1770–72; Madrid, Prado; see fig.) depicts the protocol at the Spanish court, as well as capturing its atmosphere. The King also enlarged the royal painting collection through purchase, using Mengs as an agent.

The Real Fábrica de Tapices de S Bárbara was now stimulated by the appointment of Mengs as Director (1762–76), followed by Maella in 1776 and by Bayeu in 1777. Charles commissioned many decorative sets of tapestries, with hunting scenes and popular scenes of life in Madrid, for the royal residences of the Escorial and the Pardo. The cartoons were painted by such artists as José del Castillo (between 1773 and 1775), Guillermo Anglois (*fl* 1761–75) and Bayeu, among whose work was *Paseo de las delicias* (cartoon, 1785; Madrid, Prado) from a series woven for the Pardo.

The Buen Retiro porcelain factory was founded in 1760 with craftsmen from Naples. Their work, with Rococo and classical designs and intended for use by the royal family, is preserved in the Gabinete de la Porcelana (from 1763; Aranjuez, Pal. Real) and in the Sala de Porcelana (Madrid, Pal. Real). The Real Laboratorio de Piedras Duras, founded in 1764, was modelled on the similar establishment in Florence. Both factories were destroyed in the Peninsular War. The Real Fábrica de Vidrio y Cristal at San Ildefonso was enlarged, and foreign craftsmen were employed to introduce new techniques and to make the chandeliers and vast mirrors for the Palacio Real, Madrid. The King's policy was to create an entirely Spanish labour force that would eventually lead to a ban on the import of such luxury objects.

Sculpture was stimulated by the changes carried out during the reign of Charles III and by the demand for work for the royal residences. In 1784 the Real Academia de Bellas Artes de S Fernando prohibited the use of wood, the traditional material in Spain for religious images, and decreed that statues, fountains and altarpieces should be made in stone or marble. Almost all the court sculptors were students and teachers at the Academia, and their strong movement towards Neo-classicism was to be consolidated during the reign of Charles IV. Among their work is the finely detailed bust of *Charles III* (1762; Madrid, Real Acad. S Fernando) by Juan Pascual de Mena.

During Charles's reign academic studies developing in Madrid at the Real Academia de Bellas Artes de S Fernando were extended with the founding of the academies of S Carlos in Valencia in 1768 and in Mexico in 1784. Through these establishments aesthetic taste was guided towards classicism. They also promoted the freedom of the arts, which were still bound by the guild traditions, and laws were passed permitting architects and artists to practise throughout the peninsula. An extension of these developments was the installation by Charles III of the Real Calcografía (1789) in the Academia de S Fernando, which established and encouraged the teaching and dissemination of engravings.

In 1786 Francisco de Goya was appointed Pintor del Rey. He had previously worked at the Real Fábrica de Tapices (from 1774) and in 1788, the year of the King's death, he painted the portrait of *Charles III Dressed as a Hunter* (priv. col.). Goya's great success at court, however, was to come during the reign of Charles IV.

BIBLIOGRAPHY

A. Ferrer del Rio: *Historia del reinado de Carlos III en España* (Madrid, 1856)
A. Zanelli: *Don Carlos di Borbone a Firenze nel 1732* (Turin, 1887)
M. Danvila y Collado: *Reinado de Carlos III* (Madrid, 1891)
Conde de Fernan Nuñez: *Vida de Carlos III*, 2 vols (Madrid, 1898)
C. di Taranto: *L'infante di Spagna, Carlo di Borbone, in Italia prima della conquista del regno* (Naples, 1905)
Duque de Maura: *Vida y reinado de Carlos III* (Madrid, 1942)
G. Falzone: *Carlo III e la Sicilia* (Palermo, 1947)
C. Bedat: *L'Académie des beaux-arts de Madrid, 1744–1808* (Toulouse, 1974)
Civiltà del '700 a Napoli, 2 vols (exh. cat., Naples, Capodimonte, Pal. Reale, Mus. N. S Martino, 1979–80)
A. Hull: *Charles III and the Revival of Spain* (Washington, DC, 1980)
J. Urrea: 'Sobre la formación del gusto artístico de D. Carlos de Borbón', *Bol. Semin. Estud. A. & Arqueol.*, xlvii (1981), pp. 395–402
Y. Bottineau: *L'Art de cour dans l'Espagne des lumières, 1746–1808* (Paris, 1986)
C. Sambricio: *La arquitectura de la ilustración en España* (Madrid, 1986)
Painting in Spain during the Later 18th Century (exh. cat., ed. M. Helston; London, N.G., 1989)

(5) Infante Don **Luis Antonio de Borbón** (*b* Madrid, 25 July 1727; *d* Arenas de San Pedro, 7 Aug 1785). Son of (1) Philip V. His mother was (2) Elizabeth Farnese and his younger brother was (4) Charles III. Don Luis was destined for the Church, being appointed Archbishop of Toledo and Cardinal when he was only seven and Archbishop of Seville in 1741. He was never ordained as a priest, however, and in 1754 he renounced all his ecclesiastical titles. On 27 June 1776 he married María Teresa Vallabriga (1758–1820), an Aragonese noblewoman, by whom he had three sons. His marriage meant that he and his sons could not succeed to the throne, and he lived in exile in his palace at Arenas de San Pedro (Ávila), where he gathered a small court.

Don Luis received an upbringing devoted to the arts from his mother at the palace of San Ildefonso, and he represents clearly the cultivated tradition of the 18th century. A lover of hunting, he formed a collection devoted to natural history, a Gabinete de Historia Natural. He was himself a musician and employed the violinist Manfredi and the composer Luigi Boccherini, who, from 1770 onwards, dedicated many compositions to him. In 1763 he commissioned Ventura Rodríguez to design and make plans for the Palacio Boadilla del Monte (façade 1765), Madrid, and to renovate his palace at Arenas de San Pedro (1776–85); he also arranged for Goya to paint the architect's portrait (1784; Stockholm, Nmus.). In 1756 Don Luis appointed the Genoese Francesco Sasso (*d* 1774) as his Pintor de Cámara. In 1763 he granted an allowance to Luis Paret to enable him to study for three years in Rome; *Masked Ball* (*c*. 1767; Madrid, Prado) was painted for him by Paret. In 1768 he inherited four paintings (untraced) from his mother's private collection. Anton Raphael Mengs, when he left Spain in 1776, was charged with buying paintings for Don Luis in Italy, including *St John the Baptist* (school of Raphael; Florence, Uffizi). In 1783 Don Luis commissioned Goya to paint a series of portraits of his family. The *Family of Don Luis* (1783; Parma, Corte Mamiano Found.) is a rare example in Spanish painting of a conversation piece. The scene conveys the intimate atmosphere of the *soirées* at the court of Don Luis at Arenas de San Pedro, and Goya's presence seated before a large canvas recalls *Las Meninas* (Madrid, Prado) by Diego Velázquez, which may have inspired the composition. Other contemporary painters who worked for Don Luis were Gregorio Ferro, Joaquín Inza and Francisco Bayeu. His collection contained Flemish paintings by Paul de Vos, David Teniers, Jan Breughel, Jan van Kessel; Italian paintings by Esteban Jordán, Francesco Solimena, Gabriel Joli, Salvator Rosa and Andrea del Sarto; and among Spanish artists were works by Bartolomé Esteban Murillo, Velázquez and Juan de Arellano. On his death the collection was divided among his wife and three sons, and some paintings were auctioned as requested in his will. In the 19th century other paintings were sold by his heirs and entered the collections of José Madrazo y Agudo and José, Marques de Salamanca.

UNPUBLISHED SOURCES

Madrid, Archv Hist. Protocolos, Protocolo 20822 [*Testamentaría Infante Don Luis*, 1797; list of pict. in his col.]

BIBLIOGRAPHY

A. Ponz: *Viage* (1772–94); ed. C. M. de Rivero (1947), vi, pp. 145–52
P. Gassier: 'Les Portraits peints par Goya pour l'Infant Don Luis de Borbón à Arenas de San Pedro', *Rev. A.*, 43 (1979), pp. 9–22
N. Glendinning: 'Goya's Patrons', *Apollo*, lxiv (1981), pp. 236–47
J. M. Arnaiz and A. Montero: 'Goya y el Infante Don Luis', *Antiquaria*, 27 (1986), pp. 44–55
P. Gassier: '¿Un retrato de Boccherini por Goya?', *Goya: Nuevas visiones: Homenaje a Enrique Lafuente Ferrari* (Madrid, 1987)

(6) Charles [Carlos] **IV**, King of Spain (*b* Naples, 11 Nov 1748; *reg* 1788–1808; *d* Naples, 20 Jan 1819). Son of (4) Charles III. His mother was Maria Amalia of Saxony. He was brought up in Naples until 1759, when, on his father's succession to the Spanish throne, he moved to Madrid as heir, with the title of Prince of Asturias. In 1765 he married Maria Luisa of Parma (1751–1819). In 1808, as a result of Napoleon's political schemes, he was forced to abdicate in favour of his son (7) Ferdinand VII. Charles was detained in France during the Napoleonic invasion of Spain and then lived in Rome and Naples until his death. He was a weak character who took little interest in government, being dominated first by his wife and then by his favourite, Manuel Godoy, Prince de la Paz. Naturally inclined towards the fine arts, he practised painting and drawing and had a special liking for the decorative arts. He was an accomplished carpenter and formed a fine collection of clocks (Madrid, Pal. Real). Charles is distinguished among Spanish monarchs of the 18th century for his refined and exquisite taste; he encouraged the introduction of Neo-classicism at court and made a significant contribution to both the creation and acquisition of works of art for the royal residences.

Charles completed many of the architectural works begun by his father at the palace of the Pardo and at the Escorial (including the staircase, 1793, by Juan de Villanueva). He was principally concerned with the Palacio Real, Madrid, with the palace at Aranjuez (including the King's Oratory, 1790–91, and the Queen's Room or Salón de Espejos, 1791–5) and with completing and decorating the smaller adjacent houses built for the royal princes. For these the King employed Villanueva, who also supervised the interior decoration. Other architects engaged were the elderly Francesco Sabbatini and Isidro González Velázquez. The decorative style of Charles's reign is characterized by the use of imported French furniture, marble, porcelain, embroidery and silks, and Spanish and imported carpets and tapestries. All these elements were combined to create settings of great beauty in the Empire and Neoclassical styles. Examples of the latter are the fine interior of the Casita del Príncipe at the Pardo (built by Villanueva in 1784, the decoration continuing under his direction until 1796) and the Casita del Príncipe at the Escorial (begun *c.* 1771 and decorated under Charles IV from 1789, with ceiling ornament inspired by Etruscan and Pompeian art). In both of these buildings important contributions were made by such foreign artists as Giovanni Battista Ferroni and Jean-Démosthène Dugourc. His favourite among these intimate retreats was the Real Casa del Labrador (*c.* 1792–1800) by Villanueva at Aranjuez; the decoration here shows Charles's interest in classical art, and it contains the celebrated Gabinete de Platino (*see* SPAIN, fig. 30). Made in the Empire style in Paris in 1805 by Charles Percier and Pierre-François-Léonard Fontaine, this is hung with paintings, including the *Seasons* by Antoine-Louis Girodet. The surrounding gardens, the Jardín del Príncipe, were ornamented by Villanueva with fountains and a classical temple, and their design shows elements of an early taste for Romanticism. The interiors of Aranjuez and the Real Casa del Labrador were adorned with fine decorative sculpture in the Neo-classical style by José Ginés, and Juan Adán made fountains for the gardens, such as *Hercules and Antaeus* (1807–8; Aranjuez, Jard. Príncipe).

Charles's love of paintings began when he was young, and as heir to the throne he built up a magnificent collection in the Casita del Príncipe at the Escorial, including works by Veronese, Andrea del Sarto (*Sacrifice of Isaac*, *c.* 1529–30; Madrid, Prado), Guercino, Anton Raphael Mengs, who painted Charles's portrait as *Prince of Asturias* (*c.* 1765; Versailles, Château), and Alonso Cano (*Virgin and Child*, *c.* 1646–50; Madrid, Prado). The collection included flower pieces, still-lifes and genre paintings, mostly by Flemish artists, and also showed an early taste for Romantic landscapes by such artists as Claude-Joseph Vernet, Jean Pillement (e.g. in Madrid, Prado) and the Spaniard Mariano Sanchis. The collection was described and praised by many travellers, including Antonio Ponz (pubd 1772–94) and Jean-François Bourgoing (pubd 1788).

After his succession in 1788, Charles IV increased his purchases. In 1790 he acquired further paintings by Mengs, *Mary Magdalen* and *St Peter* (both Madrid, Prado), from the Armencio Pini collection; and in Seville in 1795 he purchased paintings by Bartolomé Esteban Murillo (*Virgin of the Rosary*, 1650–60; *Virgin and Child*, *c.* 1650–60; *Dolorosa*, *c.* 1668–70; *Vision of St Francis*, 1667–75; *Martyrdom of St Andrew*, 1675–82; all Madrid, Prado), as well as other examples of Andalusian Baroque painting. In Valencia in 1800 Charles bought the important altarpiece of *St Esteban* (1560–70; Madrid, Prado) by Juan de Juanes, and he subsequently added works by other Valencian painters such as (in 1802) Francisco Ribalta's *St Francis Comforted by Angel Musicians* (*c.* 1620; Madrid, Prado). The King made acquisitions from the estate of the

Duquesa de Alba in 1802, at the sale of the Chopinot collection in 1805 and from the estate of F. Bruna in 1807.

Charles retained agents throughout Europe; the dealer Abadía in Paris sent him Sèvres porcelain, clocks and books and six other landscapes by Vernet that had been especially commissioned by the King for the Casita at the Escorial (Madrid, Prado; London, Apsley House). Dugourc sent clocks and jewels from Paris for Queen Maria Luisa. Through Juan Cornejo the King acquired paintings from Italy, and paintings and objects of archaeological interest came from Antonio Moresqui in Naples. The Spanish Ambassador in Rome acted as agent, purchasing clocks, precision and musical instruments and passing on his own collection of antique Roman busts to the King (all Madrid, Pal. Real, and Aranjuez, Real Casa Labrador).

Mariano Salvador Maella was appointed Pintor de Cámara in 1789 and worked on royal projects, mainly on ceiling paintings in fresco (e.g. Casita del Príncipe, 1789; Madrid, Pal. Pardo). In 1790 Charles IV appointed Francisco de Goya, Primer Pintor, and among the portraits by Goya of the King and royal family is the *Family of Charles IV* (1800; Madrid, Prado; *see* GOYA, FRANCISCO DE, fig. 3). The King was patron of the Real Fábrica de Tapices de S Bárbara and commissioned tapestries on popular subjects for the Pardo and the Escorial, many after cartoons by Goya (*see* TAPESTRY, fig. 11); the Buen Retiro porcelain factory produced works in the Neo-classical style and imitated English Wedgwood pieces; and in 1795 the King founded the Real Fábrica de Marfiles at Aranjuez to produce works in ivory (destr. 1808 during the French invasion).

During his exile in Italy, Charles IV surrounded himself with *objets d'art* and formed a new collection of about 700 paintings, mainly by Italian Renaissance and Baroque artists. He also collected contemporary art, especially by Spanish Neo-classical painters, such as José de Madrazo y Agudo and Juan Antonio Ribera y Fernandez, and he commissioned works from Spanish sculptors who were resident or studying in Rome, such as Ramón Barba, to whom he awarded a bursary from 1801 and who made busts in marble of *Charles IV* and *Maria Luisa* (both 1817; Madrid, Pal. Real).

BIBLIOGRAPHY
A. Ponz: *Viaje* (1772–94); ed. C. M. de Rivero (1947)
J.-F. de Bourgoing: *Nouveau Voyage en Espagne* (1788)
J. Zarco Cuevas: *Cuadros reunidos por Carlos IV, príncipe, en su casa de campo de El Escorial* (El Escorial, 1934)
A. Perera: 'Carlos IV: Mecenas y coleccionista de obras de arte', *A. Esp.*, xxxi (1958), pp. 8–35
A. Muriel: *Historia de Carlos IV* (Madrid, 1959)
J. J. Junquera: *La decoración y el mobiliario de los palacios de Carlos IV* (Madrid, 1979)
I. Rose: *Manuel Godoy: Patron de las artes y coleccionista*, 2 vols (Madrid, 1983)
Y. Bottineau: *L'Art de cour dans l'Espagne des lumières, 1746–1808* (Paris, 1986), pp. 345–85

MERCEDES AGUEDA

(7) Ferdinand [Fernando] **VII**, King of Spain (*b* San Ildefonso, nr Segovia, 13 Oct 1784; *reg* 1808, 1814–33; *d* Madrid, 29 Sept 1833). Son of (6) Charles IV. His mother was Maria Luisa of Parma. He received his early education from Padre Scio (Felipe Scio de San Miguel, 1738–96) and Canon Juan Escóiquiz, the latter exercising the greater influence on Ferdinand's preparation for the throne. He

was sickly and timorous as a youth and had serious conflicts with Manuel Godoy, Prince de la Paz, the favourite of Charles IV. After the Mutiny of Aranjuez in March 1806, Godoy was dismissed, and in 1808 Charles abdicated in favour of his son. Ferdinand significantly contributed to the establishment of the Museo del Prado in Madrid. After the French occupation of Spain (1808–14) and his accession once more to the throne, he originated the idea of establishing a museum that would gather together the royal collections, which were scattered in various palaces and properties. The final choice for the location was the newly created Museo Nacional de Ciencias Naturales, housed in a structure built by Juan de Villanueva in 1785. Ferdinand personally underwrote the expenses involved in the repair and completion of the building, as well as financially supporting many of the later acquisitions. The museum was officially opened on 19 November 1819 as the Museo Real del Prado, with Alvaro de Bazan, Marqués de Santa Cruz, as its first Director. Paintings from the Spanish school were the first to be displayed in the new quarters, and such artists as Velázquez, Ribera, Zurbarán and Goya were represented. In addition to works from the royal collections, the museum received several others that had been purchased by Ferdinand himself (e.g. Ribera's *Trinity*, Velázquez's *Crucifixion* and Juan de Juanes's *Visitation by the Virgin*). He also donated paintings by Murillo, Ribera, Dürer, Titian and Rubens that he had previously deposited in the Real Academia de Bellas Artes de S Fernando. In 1832 he authorized the purchase of such important works as the *Triumph of St Hermengild* by Francisco de Herrera (ii) and two paintings by Ribera, the *Immaculate Conception* and *St Augustine at Prayer*. Since it was a royal foundation, the museum was always considered part of the royal heritage; on Ferdinand's death its contents were evaluated and inventoried, and their division was avoided through a financial contribution made by Ferdinand's daughter (8) Isabella II.

BIBLIOGRAPHY
P. de Madrazo: *Viaje artístico de tres siglos por las colecciones de cuadros de los reyes de España* (Barcelona, 1884)
P. Beroqui: *El Museo del Prado: Notas para su historia* (Madrid, 1933)
J. Arzadun: *Fernando VII y su tiempo* (Madrid, 1943)
A. Rumeu de Armas: *Origen y fundación del Museo del Prado* (Madrid, 1980)
S. Alcolea Blanch: *Museo del Prado* (Barcelona, 1991)

CONCHA VELA

(8) Isabella II, Queen of Spain (*b* Madrid, 10 Oct 1830; *reg* 1833–68; *d* Paris, 9 April 1904). Daughter of (7) Ferdinand VII. Her mother was the King's fourth wife, Maria Christina of Naples (1808–78). Isabella was three years of age when she succeeded to the throne; her mother acted as regent. Ferdinand VII's brother Charles had expected to succeed him, however, a situation that precipitated the first Carlist war (1833–40). Maria Christina was forced into exile and replaced as regent by the victorious General Baldemero Espartero; he was overthrown in 1843 by General Ramón Narváez, who declared Isabella II of age. Spain nevertheless continued to be ruled by generals. Following a popular revolt in 1854, Isabella II permitted limited reforms, but these were short-lived; on 29 September 1868 she was deposed and forced to flee to Paris, where she afterwards mainly resided. There was some improvement in the Spanish economy during Isabella's reign and in the so-called *renovación isabelina* new public buildings were opened in Madrid; these included the Teatro Real (opened 1850) by Martín López Aguado, the Congreso de los Diputados (1843–50) and the Universidad Central (1843–52) by Narciso Pascual y Colomer, and the Palacio de Bibliotecas y Museos (1866–92; now the Biblioteca Nacional y Museo Arqueológico Nacional) by Francisco Jareño y Alarcón. Urban reforms included the Puerta del Sol (1859), Madrid, by Lucio del Valle (1815–74) and the construction of the railway system. Although these works doubtless brought improvements, they were generally not of architectural distinction. Isabella supported the Museo del Prado, Madrid, financially, and during her reign some redecoration at the palace at Aranjuez was carried out (*see* SPAIN, fig. 31).

BIBLIOGRAPHY

J. A. Gaya Nuño: *Arte del siglo XIX*, A. Hisp., xix (Madrid, 1966)

J. M. Moreno Echevarría: *Isabel II: Biografía de una España en crisis* (Barcelona, 1973)

P. Navascués Palacio, C. Pérez Reyes and A. M. Arias de Cossío: *Del neoclasicismo al modernismo* (1980), v of *Historia del arte hispánico*, ed. J. Rogelio Buendía (Madrid, 1978–80)

☐

Bourbon del Monte, Francesco Maria (*b* Venice, 5 July 1549; *d* Rome, 17 Aug 1626). Italian cardinal and patron. He was the younger brother of Guidobaldo (1545–1607), the scientist, mathematician and patron of Galileo Galilei, who wrote a treatise on perspective (1600). Francesco was educated at the della Rovere court at Urbino, where he probably studied with the poet Agostino Gallo (1499–1570) and the mathematician Federico Commandino (1509–75); certainly he developed a passion for music and for art. It is traditionally believed that he left the della Rovere court while still very young to join that of Cardinal Alessandro Sforza (1534–81) in Rome. When Sforza died Francesco entered the service of Cardinal Ferdinando de' Medici, who, on his succession as Grand Duke of Tuscany, renounced his cardinalate and persuaded Pope Sixtus V to confer it on Francesco (1588).

Francesco was a man of wide culture and varied interests: he was a connoisseur of music and painting, he practised alchemy and had a great interest in science. Politically, he was always a partisan of the French, and the writers who described him as an uncultured libertine (for Dirck Amayden's biography see Spezzaferro) were adherents of the pro-Spanish party and intended to block his election to the papacy. His collection contained about 700 paintings, ancient statuary, the Portland Vase (London, BM) and various musical instruments. The paintings included works of Renaissance masters, but especially those of such contemporary artists as Caravaggio, Agostino Carracci, Annibale Carracci, Guido Reni, Giovanni Battista Caracciolo, Scipione Pulzone, Giovanni Baglione, Antiveduto Grammatica, Jusepe de Ribera, Guercino, Carlo Saraceni, Alessandro Turchi, Girolamo Muziano, the Cavaliere d'Arpino and Adam Elsheimer.

Francesco's patronage of the arts was based on his prominent position, both in the Congregazione delle Fabbrica of St Peter's and in the Accademia di S Luca, of which he was a patron from 1596, together with Cardinal Gabriele Paleotti. From 1621 he also patronized singers in the papal choir. Less well known, but no less important, was his patronage of the poet Torquato Tasso and the scientist Galileo Galilei. The latter obtained the chair of mathematics in Pisa through his good offices and those of his brother Guidobaldo with Grand Duke Ferdinand I of Tuscany.

Francesco is particularly famous as the first patron of Caravaggio, who was his guest in Palazzo Madama from 1596–7 to at least November 1600. Early sources record the following works as having been painted for him by Caravaggio: *The Concert of Youths* (New York, Met.), *the Lute-player* (New York, Wildenstein's, on loan to New York, Met.); *St Catherine of Alexandria* (Madrid, Mus. Thyssen–Bornemisza); a *Sacred Love Conquering Profane Love* and a *Vase of Flowers with the Transparencies of Water and Glass* (both untraced). According to the 1627 inventory of the collection, he also possessed the following works by Caravaggio: *The Cardsharps* (Fort Worth, TX, Kimbell A. Mus.); *The Fortune-teller* and *St John the Baptist* (both Rome, Mus. Capitolino); and an *Ecstasy of St Francis* (often identified with the picture in Hartford, CT, Wadsworth Atheneum). In 1608 the Cardinal presented the *Medusa* (Florence, Uffizi) to Grand Duke Ferdinand. After the recent restoration of a small room, the 'Camerino Ludovisi', in Francesco's villa near the Porta Pinciana (now the Casino Ludovisi), the ceiling painting in oils, *Jove, Neptune and Pluto*, is considered to be wholly autograph. In 1599 the Cardinal obtained for Caravaggio his first public commission: the two canvases of the *Calling of St Matthew* and the *Martyrdom of St Matthew* in S Luigi dei Francesi.

After 1620 the Cardinal had Andrea Sacchi under his protection. He undoubtedly fostered Sacchi's participation in the life of the Accademia di S Luca, whose patron he was. For the Cardinal Sacchi painted a cycle representing the seasons in the loggia (destr.) in the Ripetta garden. Francesco commissioned the Casa Pia delle Malmaritate at the church of S Chiara alla Ciambella, where Andrea Sacchi painted a *Virgin and Child* (untraced), and he also sponsored the restoration by Mario Arconio of the convent of the church of S Urbano ai Pantani, for which Sacchi painted *St Urban and Saints* (also untraced).

DBI   BIBLIOGRAPHY

G. Baglione: *Vite* (1642); ed. V. Mariani (1935), p. 136

G. P. Bellori: *Vite* (1672); ed. E. Borea (1976), pp. 216n, 217n, 219n, 222n, 231n, 233n, 537–9, 541, 543

G. B. Passeri: *Vite* (1679), ed. J. Hess (1934), pp. 311–12

G. Mancini: *Considerazioni sulla pittura*, ed. A. Marucchi and L. Salerno, 2 vols (Rome, 1956–7), i, pp. 225–6

F. Haskell: *Patrons and Painters* (London, 1962; rev. New Haven and London, 1980)

D. Heikamp: '*La Medusa* di Caravaggio e l'armatura dello Scià di Persia', *Paragone*, xvii/199 (1966), pp. 62–76

C. L. Frommel: 'Caravaggio Frühwerk und der Kardinal Francesco Maria del Monte', *Stor. A.*, 9–10 (1971), p. 31

L. Spezzaferro: 'La cultura del Cardinal del Monte e il primo tempo del Caravaggio', *Stor. A.*, 9–10 (1971), pp. 57–91

A. Sutherland Harris: *Andrea Sacchi* (Oxford, 1977)

F. T. Camiz: 'The Castrato Singer: From Informal to Formal Portraiture', *Artibus & Hist.*, xviii (1988), pp. 171–86

A Caravaggio Rediscovered: The Lute Player (exh. cat. by K. Christiansen, New York, Met., 1990)

M. G. Bernardini: 'Caravaggio's Jove, Neptune and Pluto: The Cosmos in One Room', *A. & Dossier*, 60 (1991), pp. 18–21
M. Cinotti: *Caravaggio: La vita e l'opera* (Bergamo, 1991)

PIETRO ROCCASECCA

Bourdaloue, Claude de (*b* Bourges; *d* Paris, 1715). French collector, patron and amateur draughtsman. A member of the Bourges family that included the great Jesuit preacher Father Louis de Bourdaloue, Claude de Bourdaloue built up a collection in Paris (mostly untraced), which Germain Brice, who gives no specific details, knew to include a hoard of paintings and drawings by famous masters, a large collection of rare prints and a considerable number of antique engraved gems. Bourdaloue also owned Rubens's manuscript *Pocketbook* on art, which he had purchased from Roger de Piles; after his death it was acquired by André-Charles Boulle, but was badly damaged in a fire in 1720 in Boulle's studio in the Louvre, Paris (fragments and partial transcripts survive). De Piles recorded that the *Pocketbook* included Rubens's observations on optics, chiaroscuro, proportion, anatomy and architecture as well as extracts from poetry concerning human passions, with illustrations copied from 'the best masters', principally Raphael. Bourdaloue is known to have commissioned drawings (untraced) from Raymond Lafage in the early 1680s, hiring him at one louis per day; Mariette recorded seeing pen and ink landscape drawings (untraced) made by Bourdaloue himself. Bourdaloue's portrait was painted by Nicolas de Largillière and engraved by Nicolas Pitau (ii).

BIBLIOGRAPHY
Mariette
R. de Piles: *Conversations sur la connaissance de la peinture et sur le jugement qu'on doit faire des tableaux* (Paris, 1677/*R* Geneva, 1970), pp. 219–20
G. Brice: *Description nouvelle de la ville de Paris* (Paris, 1713), i, p. 294
E. Bonnaffé: *Dictionnaire des amateurs français au XVIIe siècle* (Paris, 1884), pp. 38–9
M. Jaffé: *Van Dyck's Antwerp Sketchbook* (London, 1966), pp. 16–26, 32–42, 77–80, 89–91 [on Rubens's *Pocketbook* and transcripts]
Rubens: Paintings, Drawings, Prints in the Princes Gate Collection (exh. cat. by H. Braham, U. London, Courtauld Inst. Gals, 1988–9), pp. 50–53

ANNE THACKRAY

Bourdelle, Emile-Antoine (*b* Montauban, 30 Oct 1861; *d* Le Vésinet, nr Paris, 1 Oct 1929). French sculptor, painter and draughtsman. After working with his father, a cabinetmaker, in 1876 he entered the Ecole des Beaux-Arts in Toulouse. In 1884 he was admitted as a pupil of Alexandre Falguière to the Ecole des Beaux-Arts in Paris, but in rebellion against academic training left two years later. He then moved into a house (now the Musée Bourdelle) in the Impasse du Maine; Jules Dalou, for whom he had the greatest admiration, lived near by.

Bourdelle had begun exhibiting at the Salon of the Société des Artistes Français in 1884 and at the Société Nationale des Beaux-Arts from 1891. In 1893 he became an assistant in Auguste Rodin's studio, remaining there until 1908. This period was marked principally by his first major commission, the War Memorial (1895–1902) at Montauban, and by commencement of his *Beethoven* series, comprising 45 sculptures as well as pastels and drawings, work on which continued until 1929. In an act of identification with the composer, having modelled several works of a more traditional nature, Bourdelle executed the *Big*

Tragic Mask (1901; Paris, Mus. Bourdelle), the ravaged features of which, along with its wild and spontaneous execution, conveyed his notions of Beethoven's inner torment. The same dramatic lyricism characterizes the Montauban monument, which recalls François Rude's high relief '*La Marseillaise*' (stone, 1835–6) on the Arc de Triomphe de l'Etoile, Paris, and Rodin's *Call to Arms*; despite critical attacks Rodin defended Bourdelle's monument, admiring its heroic spirit and 'explosive rhythm'.

After 1900 Bourdelle's counterbalancing search for order and simplicity of line, mass and modelling led to a new monumentality in his work. Finding new inspiration in the rigorous art of ancient Greece, he executed a series of studies for his *Head of Apollo* (1900–09; versions, Paris, Mus. d'Orsay, Mus. Bourdelle), a work in which he saw himself as having at last broken free from the influence of Falguière, Dalou and Rodin. The *Apollo* was followed by *Penelope* (1905–7; version, Paris, Mus. Bourdelle), *Fruit* (1906; version, Paris, Mus. Bourdelle) and, finally, *Hercules the Archer* (1910; Paris, Mus. d'Orsay), in which this series of developments towards a daring synthesis of form reached its conclusion. Around the same time the combined influences of Rodin and medieval sculpture came together in Bourdelle's statue of *Jean-Baptiste Carpeaux* (1909–10; Lyon, Mus. B.-A.).

Bourdelle was highly productive during the period 1909–14. Through Gabriel Thomas (for whom he had executed the theatre decoration for the Musée Grévin, Paris, in 1900), he and Auguste Perret were commissioned to co-design the façade of the Théâtre des Champs-Elysées, Paris. The result, executed in 1911–13, was a

Emile-Antoine Bourdelle: *Dance*, plaster model for one of the metopes of the Théâtre des Champs-Elysées, Paris, h. 1.74 m, 1912 (Paris, Musée Bourdelle)

frieze (14 m in length) of the *Meditation of Apollo with the Muses* and five low reliefs, *Tragedy, Comedy, Music, Dance* (for plaster model see fig.) and *Les Arts plastiques* (architecture and sculpture; all *in situ*), the agitated figures for which were inspired by Bourdelle's own drawings of the dancer Isadora Duncan. Bourdelle executed a cycle of frescoes within the theatre. He also produced a number of portraits during this period, including a life-like sculpture of *Jean-Auguste-Dominique Ingres* (1908; version, Paris, Mus. Bourdelle) and a portrait of *Dr Koeberlé* (1914; version, Paris, Mus. d'Orsay), the latter of which has an extraordinary intensity of expression. Bourdelle worked slowly and thoroughly on these pieces, requiring numerous sittings from his subjects. He continued to make portraits into the 1920s, for example *Anatole France* (bronze, 1919) and *Auguste Perret* (1922; both Paris, Mus. d'Orsay), as well as a few mythological works, including the huge low relief of *Aphrodite* (1924) made for the opera house at Marseille. However, after World War I he concentrated on designing public monuments, including such memorials to the dead as those at Montceau-les-Mines (1919), Saône-et-Loire, and at Trôo (1923), Loir-et-Cher, and the *Virgin of the Offertory* (1919–22) at Niederbruck, Haut-Rhin. His major monuments are the statue of *France Saluting America* (1925; Paris, Mus. Bourdelle), the monument to *Adam Mickiewicz* (1908–29; Paris, Cours la Reine) and the large equestrian monument to the 19th-century hero *General Carlos Maria Alvear* (1912–25; Buenos Aires, Plaza de la Recoleta), the pedestal of which displays four monumental statues: *Force, Eloquence, Victory* and *Freedom*.

The Musée Bourdelle, founded by the artist's wife and daughter in his old home in Paris, contains a number of Bourdelle's original casts, from which works continue to be reproduced.

BIBLIOGRAPHY
G. Varenne: *Bourdelle par lui-même* (Paris, 1937)
I. Jianou and M. Dufet: *Bourdelle* (Paris, 1965, 3/1984) [with cat. rais.]
C. M. Lavrillier and M. Dufet: *Bourdelle et la critique de son temps* (Paris, 1979)
D. Basdevant: *Bourdelle et le Théâtre des Champs-Elysées* (Paris, 1982)
La Sculpture française au XIXe siècle (exh. cat. by A. Pingeot, A. Le Normand-Romain and I. Lemaistre, Paris, Grand Pal., 1986)
1913: Le Théâtre des Champs-Elysées (exh. cat. ed. J. M. Nectoux and A. Le Normand-Romain, Paris, Mus. d'Orsay, 1987–8)
Le Corps et morceaux (exh. cat. by M. Pingeot and A. Le Normand-Romain, Paris, Mus. d'Orsay, 1990)
Bourdelle: 'Herakles archer': Naissance d'une oeuvre (exh. cat. by A. Le Normand-Romain, Paris, Mus. Bourdelle, 1992)

ANTOINETTE LE NORMAND-ROMAIN

Bourdichon, Jean (*b* 1457; *d* Tours, 1521). French painter and illuminator. He worked in Tours towards the end of the 15th century and was an official painter to Louis XI, Charles VIII, Louis XII and Francis I. Despite the absence of Bourdichon's name from contemporary historical writings, he enjoyed the highest reputation in his own day. This is clear not only from the rank of those who commissioned work from him and from the sumptuous quality of his surviving works but also from the sheer quantity of works he produced, which implies that he had assistants to help him keep up with demand. Having already worked for Louis XI for two years, Bourdichon succeeded Jean Fouquet as Peintre du Roi in 1481. He was in favour at court and well regarded by

Charles VIII, who had a workshop set up for him in the castle at Plessis-lès-Tours and provided generous dowries for his daughters; the painter enjoyed a long official career and lived in considerable comfort as a landowner. Bourdichon received a regular wage as 'painter and valet de chambre in ordinary' and was mentioned in the royal accounts, mainly with reference to the numerous functional decorations and temporary creations for which he was responsible. His name also appears in connection with designs for coins, stained-glass windows and silver or gold plate. He received a considerable number of commissions for paintings on wood, particularly of the Virgin in glory, and for various portraits. Only one of Bourdichon's panel paintings is known to survive (*see* §1 below), but far more of his work as an illuminator is extant. As his success brought him both imitators and subcontractors, it seems appropriate to reduce his corpus to those manuscripts that are most similar to his only documented work, the Grandes Heures of Anne of Brittany. His activities as an illuminator are otherwise poorly documented; the only works mentioned are the *Papaliste* (1480) for Louis XI, four 'histories' (1483) for Queen Charlotte of Savoy, a miniature (*c.* 1485) for Charles of Angoulême and 'several histories' (1492) for Queen Anne of Brittany.

1. Works, *c.* 1480–*c.* 1504. 2. The Grandes Heures of Anne of Brittany and later works.

1. WORKS, *c.* 1480–*c.* 1504. Contrary to scholarly opinion since Mâle, the Bourbon–Vendôme Hours (*c.* 1480; Paris, Bib. Arsenal, MS. 417) should certainly be removed from Bourdichon's oeuvre, and his earliest work traced instead to a Book of Hours of the Use of Rome (*c.* 1480–85; Malibu, CA, Getty Mus., MS. 6). The miniatures are extremely fresh and of excellent quality, using a classical iconography drawn from the tradition of the small Books of Hours ascribed to Fouquet's workshop, but the approach reveals a certain independence from these models. Bourdichon's work can generally be distinguished from that of Fouquet's direct followers by a taste for clear colours and goldwork, as well as by the use of fairly large figures pushed into the foreground and an early predilection for night scenes with artificial lighting. In the Getty Hours, however, Bourdichon's iconographical solutions were not yet firmly established in the form they were later to adopt. The figures here are well constructed and well balanced but have no real volume, although they do already have the coldness of expression and the fixed attitudes of the later works. The landscapes are agreeable but have little character, while the architectural structures with shell-shaped niches—a brilliant reference to the Italian Renaissance—are tacked on behind the figures without any true expression of space. The manuscript has a calendar intended for Le Mans. Another Book of Hours (Frankfurt am Main, Mus. Ksthandwk., L.M.48), also with a Le Mans calendar, appears to be exactly contemporary and is closely linked in its marginal decoration and iconography.

Only dispersed fragments survive of the so-called Hours of Henry VII of England (*c.* 1500), but eight full-page miniatures surrounded by simple flat gold frames have been grouped together (Backhouse, 1973, 1983): *Pentecost, Job*, the *Virgin Annunciate* (London, BL, Add. MS. 33254,

T, U and V, respectively), *St Luke* (Edinburgh, N. Lib., MS. 8999), the *Adoration of the Magi, Presentation in the Temple, Flight into Egypt* and *David and Bathsheba* (New York, B. H. Breslauer priv. col.). The whereabouts of a further leaf, the *Nativity* (taken to the British Museum, London, for examination in 1952) are unknown. In these Bourdichon most effectively introduced the new pictorial idea of the dramatic close-up by cutting out a fragment of the scene as if frozen; his method here was to place large figures very close to the foreground, filling the page, while eliminating detail and thus emphasizing the direct presence of the characters. The strong Fouquet-style folds of the drapery, rather arbitrarily arranged, are highlighted with systematic gold hatching. In spite of these gold highlights, however, the strongly coloured drapery gives no feeling of ambient lighting, and the figures stand out from the background almost as if in silhouette.

The manuscript must have been broken up in England during the 17th century. Traditionally thought to have belonged to Henry VII, it has been convincingly suggested that it was intended for Louis XII (Backhouse, 1973, 1983), although this has not been verified. Some 50 leaves of text have been preserved, most of which (London, BL, Royal MS. 2.D.XL) retain superb lateral borders that are unique in Bourdichon's oeuvre. They consist of panels, the same height as the text, and display an exceptional combination of large naturalistic flowers and imaginary acanthus in white, bright blue and magenta, accompanied by insects, depicted in sharp relief and casting their shadows on the gold background. This mixture of realistic plants with decorative elements was inspired by the style of Ghent and Bruges manuscripts, although here Bourdichon (working with assistants) depicted the whole plant with flowers reaching to the top of the border rather than the cut flowers to be seen in contemporary manuscripts of the GHENT-BRUGES SCHOOL. Bourdichon also grafted his acanthus straight on to the stems of his plants—a unique feature that has made it possible to identify with certainty two further leaves, the *Visitation* (Bristol, Mus. & A.G.) and the *Arrest of Christ* (Paris, Mus. Marmottan, MS. Wildenstein 152).

Shields and prayers in the luxurious Hours of Frederick III of Aragon (1501–4; Paris, Bib. N., MS. lat. 10532) identify the manuscript with this ruler. It contains miniatures that are clearly Bourdichon's work with borders executed by a Neapolitan artist in a completely different style; the miniatures were painted on small rectangles (120×70 mm) of extremely fine parchment that were then glued to spaces left blank in the middle of the rich Italianate frames. Avril (1984 exh. cat.) pointed out that some of the figures executed by the artist who painted the frames overlap on to the edge of Bourdichon's work. As Avril attributed these frames to Giovanni Todeschino (*fl* Naples, 1487–1500), illuminator to the king in Naples, he concluded that the manuscript was entirely executed in Naples before Frederick's exile in 1501. There is documentary evidence, however, for Bourdichon's presence in Tours between 1498 and 1500, as well as other historical reasons for thinking that he could not have undertaken this lengthy task in Naples. It is more likely that Frederick, defeated by the French in 1501 and consigned to a gilded exile in Tours, should have taken his official illuminator

Todeschino—last mentioned in Naples in 1500—with him; and that it was thus in Tours that the two artists worked in close collaboration. Another example of collaboration between these two artists has been recognized in a collection of prayers of Leonardo Corvino, *Officia Octo* (London, BL, Add. MS. 21591). Although other works establish a link between Bourdichon and Naples, they could also have been commissioned in Tours during this same period by some member of Frederick's household circle who returned to Naples after his death: the format of Bourdichon's triptych with the *Virgin with SS John the Baptist and John the Evangelist* (Naples, Capodimonte) would have made it easy to transport, while the fact that it was painted on oak makes it unlikely that it would have been executed in Italy.

Bourdichon does not in fact appear to have been in Italy: Vitry and Mâle (1946) had already pointed out that his Italian characteristics were acquired second-hand and that the conventions observed in the execution of his antique settings made it unlikely that he had travelled to Italy, and they also observed that the softening of his style was independent of any contact with Italian art. The Hours of Aragon contain what are undoubtedly Bourdichon's finest miniatures. This is possibly due to their small format, which must have suited his particular talent better; their smooth, soft touch rivals that of the frames, although Bourdichon did not seek to imitate the latter's colouring. The artist rendered the conventional compositions in his repertory more convincing by trying to give relief to the forms and by using chiaroscuro, and he limited his use of finely hatched gold highlights. The miniatures are surrounded with simple flat gilded frames, which the Italian illuminator set within lightly constructed shrines. The whole forms a particularly accomplished work of art.

2. THE GRANDES HEURES OF ANNE OF BRITTANY AND LATER WORKS. There is documentary evidence for large payments, initiated by Anne of Brittany in March 1508, that were to be made to Bourdichon for 'richly and sumptuously historiating and illuminating a large Book of Hours for her use'. The Grandes Heures of Anne of Brittany (*c.* 1503–8; Paris, Bib. N., MS. lat. 9474) is clearly an exceptional book fit for a queen, given the number and size of its paintings (originally *c.* 51, of which 49 survive) executed on the *verso* of separate leaves, the *rectos* of which were left blank and faced the incipits of the services and the prayers. The paintings are all full-page miniatures, mostly showing scenes with half-length figures, beginning with a double-page frontispiece showing Anne accompanied by her patron saints praying before a *Pietà* (see fig. 1). The figures are generally shown less close-up than in the Hours of Henry VII because of the format of the leaves; the fact that these are taller obliged the artist to take a viewpoint further back from the subject and to elongate the figures in order to fill the space. As in the case of the London leaves, these miniatures are meant to rival paintings in their exceptional size and discreet gilded frames.

The illustrations must have been executed over a significant period of time because the manner of their execution is not consistent: the *Annunciation* (fol. 26*v*) and the *Visitation* (fol. 35*v*) are remarkably light, flat and pink and are strongly highlighted with long, very firm gold

1. Jean Bourdichon: *Anne of Brittany with Saints*, 300×195 mm; miniature from the Grandes Heures of Anne of Brittany, *c.* 1503–8 (Paris, Bibliothèque Nationale, MS. lat. 9474, fol. 3*v*)

also adapt them while working. On folio 159*v*, for example, the drawing of the Virgin's sleeves and the position of the Child were considerably reworked on the parchment itself, which proves that these pages were his own work.

This manuscript is particularly renowned for its incomparable herbarium, populated with insects, which decorates all the margins of the text; its singularity was emphasized in the final payment made by Francis I in 1515, which praises the 'rich flowers, trees and vignettes all different and close to life'. The borders show complete plants against a gold background, as minutely observed as in a botanical treatise; indeed, each plant is accompanied by its scholarly name in Latin at the top and its common name in French at the bottom. The calendar that accompanies the Hours is also innovative, as the text is set on *trompe l'oeil* panels that are placed in front of the landscape, with people working on the Labours of the Month depicted at the foot of the page. A contemporary book with iconographically similar miniatures by Bourdichon is the Missal of Jacques de Beaune (1506/9–11; Paris, Bib. N., MS. lat. 886). Three later Books of Hours adapt the compositions with half-length figures previously used in the Grandes Heures of Anne of Brittany, inserted in heavy architectural frames like self-supporting altarpieces (New York, Pierpoint Morgan Lib., MS.M. 732; Waddesdon Manor, Bucks, NT and Boston, MA, Isabella Stewart Gardner Mus., MS. 8).

The exact date of the secular manuscript *Quatre états de la société* (*c.* 1505–10; Paris, Ecole B.-A., M. 90–93) is not known, but judging by its style and the figures' costumes it must have been executed at roughly the same time as two other secular manuscripts by Bourdichon (see below). The original location of these four leaves, irregularly cut out around the gilded frames of the miniatures, remains unknown, but they may have formed part of a book, possibly a collection of moralizing poems. The miniatures are clearly by Bourdichon's hand: they have his characteristic figures, drapery, gold tooling, colours, effects suggesting sunset or night and his descriptive taste for interiors and furnishings. They were surrounded by the usual graded violet-hued background imitating the shadow cast by their flat gilded frames.

Around 1508 Bourdichon illustrated *Le Voyage de Gênes* (Paris, Bib. N., MS. fr. 5091), one of the accounts of Louis XII's victorious siege of Genoa in April 1507. It was written in verse by the King's official poet, Jean Marot, and illustrated with 11 full-page miniatures for Anne of Brittany, who is shown on folio 1 receiving her book from Marot in the presence of her ladies-in-waiting and the lords of the court. The scenes depicting the different episodes of the campaign alternate with complicated allegorical scenes in which Genoa is personified as a young Italian woman debating with Merchandise and the People (fol. 6*v*), weeping with Despair, Sorrow and Anger (fol. 34*v*) and witnessing at last the apparition of Reason, naively depicted as a Queen of Heaven (fol. 37*v*). The narrative scenes were more inspired, and the artist plays felicitously on the decorative qualities of his subjects' attire. Louis XII is shown with several different sets of paraphernalia and with various different emblems (see fig. 2). Overall, the work is more highly coloured and the brushwork more vigorous than in the *Quatre états*.

hatching and without any atmospheric effects; the softened blue of the distance in these pictures differs from the raw ultramarine used for the distance in the frontispiece and some of the last images. In the *Nativity* (fol. 51*v*), on the other hand, which is undoubtedly the most apposite of the miniatures, the clothing has no gold highlights in spite of the effect of artificial lighting that Joseph's lantern gives this night scene; the execution of the Virgin's blue cloak is soft and matt, and the effect of depth is sensitively rendered. In the majority of the miniatures, however, the figures are heavily highlighted with complex gold hatching and stand out as if detached from artificial landscapes that abruptly turn blue in the distance. Some pages are marred by excessive decoration, as in the case of the *Repentance of David* (fol. 91*v*), which is a showy accumulation of colours and tooled gilding. The underdrawings in brown ink can be seen quite clearly on the blank *recto* sides of the miniatures, and it is possible to make out that they were energetic, rapidly executed and expressive. The images were visibly reworked during the process of execution, showing that although the artist had a stock of iconographical models that he constantly used and reused, he could

2. Jean Bourdichon: *Louis XII Leaving Alexandria*, 307×210 mm; miniature from Jean Marot: *Le Voyage de Gênes*, *c*. 1508 (Paris, Bibliothèque Nationale, MS. fr. 5091, fol. 15*v*)

The *Epîtres des poètes royaux* (*c*. 1510; St Petersburg, Saltykov-Shchedrin Pub. Lib., MS. fr. F.v. XIV, 8) is a curious collection of 11 poems or epistles with political connotations, presented as if it were the tender correspondence between Anne of Brittany and King Louis XII, who was then fighting the Venetians after the victory in Aguadel (1509). It was illustrated with 11 full-page paintings on the *verso* of folios facing the beginning of each text, with alternating narrative and allegorical scenes. As in *Le Voyage de Gênes*, the descriptive and contemporary scenes are much more interesting than the allegorical or mythological ones. Bourdichon's vein as an interpreter of allegories or ancient myths reveals a taste as mediocre as that of the rhetoricians whose words he illustrated, but he always depicted everyday scenes, in this case mainly interiors, with appropriate dignity; the images also offer valuable documentary information about contemporary costumes, armour, furnishings and everyday objects. These miniatures must have been executed very close in time to those of the *Voyage de Gênes*, particularly if the scene in which Jean Marot hands over his book is compared with various scenes in the *Epîtres*, which show Anne attended by her ladies-in-waiting. The emblems of the two sovereigns appear everywhere, particularly in the stained-glass windows, which depict their coats of arms or their initials, and in the hangings covered with fleurs-de-lis, with cords or with porcupines, or in the red and gold canopies in the

King's colours. These are among Bourdichon's most carefully executed large format miniatures, and they are especially luxurious, with a regal use of gold in the clothing and hangings echoing the gold of the artist's favourite frames, with their cast shadows. His large figures fill each picture, and the effects suggesting the texture of the cloth are attentively rendered. There are no marginal decorations accompanying the text, which is written in a round Italian-style script.

BIBLIOGRAPHY

E. Mâle: 'Trois oeuvres nouvelles de Jean Boudichon', *Gaz. B.-A.*, i (1902), pp. 185–203
P. Vitry: 'De quelques travaux récents relatifs à la peinture française du XV siècle', *Bull. Soc. Archéol. Touraine*, xiv (1903), pp. 33–73
D. MacGibbon: *Jean Bourdichon* (Glasgow, 1933)
A. de Laborde: *Les Principaux Manuscrits à peintures conservés dans l'ancienne bibliothèque impériale publique de Saint-Petersbourg*, 2 vols (Paris, 1936–8)
E. Mâle: *Jean Bourdichon: Les Heures d'Anne de Bretagne* (Paris, 1946)
P. Wescher: *Jean Fouquet et son temps* (Basle, 1947)
R. Limousin: *Jean Bourdichon* (Lyon, 1954)
J. Backhouse: 'Bourdichon's *Hours of Henry VII*', *BM Q.*, xxxvii (1973), pp. 95–102
J. P. Harthan: *Books of Hours and their Owners* (London, 1977)
J. Backhouse: 'French Manuscript Illumination, 1450–1530', *Renaissance Painting in Manuscripts: Treasures from the British Library* (exh. cat., ed. T. Kren; Malibu, CA, Getty Mus.; New York, Pierpont Morgan Lib.; London, BL; 1983), pp. 163–8
Dix siècles d'enluminure italienne, VI–XVI siècles (exh. cat. by F. Avril, Paris, Bib. N., 1984)
W. Voelke and R. Wieck: *The Bernard H. Breslauer Collection of Manuscript Illuminations* (New York, 1992)
Les Manuscrits à peintures en France, 1440–1520 (exh. cat. by F. Avril and N. Reynaud, Paris, Bib. N., 1993), pp. 293–305

NICOLE REYNAUD

Bourdin, Michel (*b* ?Orléans, *c*. 1580; *d* Paris, Nov 1650). French sculptor. He was established in Paris by 1609 and was described in this period as a 'sculptor in wax': he modelled a head in wax of *Henry IV* after his assassination in 1610 (perhaps the head of the King in Mus. Carnavalet, Paris). He is best known, however, as a sculptor of tombs and altar decorations, though little of his work survives intact. From 1618–21 he worked on the high altar at Saint-Sulpice, Paris, providing four black marble columns, four statues of *Angels Holding the Instruments of the Passion* (wood painted to imitate bronze parcel gilt) and two large polychromed wood statues of *St Sulpice* and *St Peter* (all untraced). At this time he also constructed the high altar (untraced) of the abbey of Saint-Sulpice-les-Bourges, paid for by Henry II of Bourbon, Prince de Condé; a terracotta *Pietà* (Salbris, Loir-et-Cher, parish church) may be a fragment from this. From 1622 onwards he was intermittently involved with works at Orléans Cathedral: he supplied drawings and models for the screening of the choir (destr.) and sculpture and decorative panelling in black and white marble for the apsidal chapel commissioned by Anne de Caumont, Comtesse de Saint-Pol. At the time of his death Bourdin seems only to have roughed out the marble figures of *Faith*, *Hope* and *Charity* for the latter project, and it was probably finished on a less ambitious scale than planned by his son, also named Michel (1609–78), with a central figure of the *Virgin of Sorrows* inspired by Germain Pilon.

Among Bourdin's many tomb sculptures were the black marble wall tablet for the *Maréchal de Villars* in Saint-Sulpice (1615; untraced) and a new mausoleum for Louis XI at Notre-Dame de Cléry (Cléry-St-André, Loiret), on which he worked from 1617. Only the kneeling marble figure of *King Louis* (1622) survives, and its powerful modelling and simple volumes are typical of Bourdin. Other surviving funerary sculptures include the calm, powerful, black and white marble effigy of Jean Bardeau (1634; Nogent-sur-Oise, parish church). The black and white marble and gilded bronze tomb of *Pierre Dauvet* at Saint-Vallerian, Yonne (after 1643), differs from his other works in having a statue of *St John the Baptist Preaching* in a niche above the sarcophagus. It seems likely that the recumbent effigy, in the same materials, of *Jacques Douglas* in St Germain-des-Prés, Paris, commissioned in 1646 but uncompleted at the sculptor's death, is largely the work of his son Michel.

Because of Bourdin's prolific output, many unsigned tomb sculptures of the period that only resemble his style in the most general way have been attributed to him. These include the praying figure of *Diane de Poitiers* (black and white marble; Château d'Anet, chapel) and those in white marble of the Rostaing family (St Germain-l'Auxerrois, Paris) and Philippe de Castille (Meaux Cathedral).

BIBLIOGRAPHY

F. Dupuis: 'Michel Bourdin, statuaire orléanais', *Bull. Soc. Archéol. Orléan.* (1863), pp. 61–5
P. Vitry: 'Les Boudin et les Bourdin, deux familles de sculpteurs de la première moitié du XVIIe siècle', *Gaz. B.-A.*, xvii (1897), pp. 149–58
J. Ciprut, ed.: 'Documents sur le sculpteur Michel Bourdin l'Aîné', *Bull. Soc. Hist. A. Fr.* (1959), pp. 145–71
J. Coural: 'Notes sur Michel II Bourdin', *Gaz. B.-A.*, liv (1959), pp. 279–86
P. Chaleix: 'De la sculpture funéraire sous Henri IV et Louis XIII', *Gaz. B.-A.*, xc (1977), p. 93
M. T. Glass-Forest: 'Les Sculptures de Michel Bourdin au maître-autel de l'église Saint-Sulpice de Paris', *Archvs A. Fr.*, xxvii (1985), pp. 135–7

GENEVIÈVE BRESC-BAUTIER

Bourdon, Francisque. *See* BORDONI, FRANCESCO DI BARTOLOMEO.

Bourdon, Sébastien (*b* Montpellier, 2 Feb 1616; *d* Paris, 8 May 1671). French painter, draughtsman and engraver. Although he was one of the most successful painters of the mid-17th century in France and highly praised by the writer André Félibien, he was also widely criticized for never achieving a fixed style of his own. He began his career as an imitator of the Bamboccianti and of Giovanni Benedetto Castiglione. He later produced altarpieces in a vigorous Baroque style and portraits in the manner of Anthony van Dyck before coming under the classicizing influence of Nicolas Poussin. Towards the end of his career, in a lecture to the Académie Royale, he recommended that young artists reject uniformity of inspiration. Remarkably, he was able to give a personal flavour to his work in any style and genre.

1. TRAINING AND YEARS IN ROME, TO 1637. He was born into a Protestant family, the son of Marin Bourdon, a master painter and glass painter, and Jeanne Gaultière, the daughter of a master goldsmith. He probably left Montpellier for Paris when the city was besieged by Louis XIII in 1622. After seven years of apprenticeship in the workshop of a certain Barthélemy (perhaps the painter-enameller Jean Barthélemy, active at Fontainebleau), he went *c.* 1630 to Bordeaux, where he is said to have executed a frescoed vault in a nearby château. Guillet de Saint-Georges records that he was subsequently in Toulouse, enlisted in the army, but that an officer, taken with his talent, discharged him from his enlistment. Bourdon then went to Rome, where he is mentioned in 1634. There he worked for a picture dealer called Escarpinelli, for whom he made copies and pastiches of works by such diverse artists as Claude Lorrain, Andrea Sacchi, Michelangelo Cerquozzi and Castiglione. This experience, which must have developed his stylistic versatility, also prevented him from receiving a serious and consistent training, a shortcoming his contemporaries always deplored. Moreover, with the exception of Sacchi, he does not appear to have had close personal contact with prominent Roman artists. Nevertheless, some of the pictures painted after his return to Paris, notably the *Flight into Egypt* (Paris, Louvre), indicate that he must have looked at paintings by such artists as Cortona, Domenichino and Giovanni Lanfranco.

In fact, Bourdon's closest associates in Rome were the painters of *bambocciate*—Pieter van Laer and Jan Miel—with whose work his own fluently painted genre scenes (e.g. *The Encampment*, Oberlin Col., OH, Allen Mem. A. Mus.) have sometimes been confused. His canvases, with their characteristic slightly metallic greys, possess a restraint and a poetic quality, as well as a sophistication of composition, that the northern artists rarely equalled. *The Limekiln* (Munich, Alte Pin.) is one of Bourdon's most accomplished paintings of this type. Compared with genre scenes such as the *Fortune-teller* (Valenciennes, Mus. B.-A.), which appear to have constituted the staple of his production in this period, a small, circular painting on copper of *Venus and Adonis* (Prague, N.G., Šternberk Pal.) suggests a more diverse inspiration. Bourdon seems to have attracted several discerning patrons in Rome, including Louis Hesselin, Maître de la Chambre aux Deniers, who helped him in his hurried departure from the city in 1637, possibly in fear that he would be denounced for his religion. On his return journey to France, Bourdon stopped in Venice: the *Adoration of the Magi* (Potsdam, Schloss Sanssouci) and the *Death of Dido* (St Petersburg, Hermitage), painted shortly after his return to Paris, show a Venetian-inspired sense of colour new to Bourdon's work.

2. PARIS, STOCKHOLM AND MONTPELLIER, FROM 1637. The chronology of Bourdon's Parisian period, from his return from Rome in 1637 until his departure for Sweden in 1652, is not easy to establish; his work moved in the most diverse, even contradictory directions. Nevertheless, it was at this time that he established himself as a distinctive artist. Some works, probably painted before 1640 and representing principally Old Testament themes, including *Jacob Sold by his Brothers* (Petworth House, W. Sussex, NT) and the *Departure of Jacob* (Houston, TX, Mus. F.A.), are treated in the manner of Castiglione. Bourdon also continued to paint *bambocciate*, such as *Encampment by Ruins* (Caen, Mus. B.-A.), *The Beggars* (Paris, Louvre), the *Gypsies' Halt* (Montpellier, Mus.

Sébastien Bourdon: *Meeting of Antony and Cleopatra*, oil on canvas, 1.46×1.97m, *c.* 1645 (Paris, Musée du Louvre)

Fabre) and *The Smoker* (Hartford, CT, Wadsworth Atheneum), which differ from their northern models in their sense of light, their studied colour harmonies and compositions in which the spectator seems to surprise the figures in their activities, as in *Peasants Playing Cards in the Open-air* (1643; Kassel, Schloss Wilhelmshöhe). They belong to the naturalist current of work in France in the early 1640s, represented by such artists as the Le Nain brothers and Jean Tassel. But Bourdon began to make his mark with grander, more dynamic Baroque works, most often composed along a vigorous diagonal, as in *Solomon Sacrificing to the Idols* and *Augustus before the Tomb of Alexander* (both Paris, Louvre), as well as the *Sacrifice of Iphigenia* (Orléans, Mus. B.-A.) and *Scene of Sacrifice* (Lyon, Mus. B.-A.).

Bourdon was quickly recognized as one of the major artistic personalities in Paris and was granted lodgings in the Louvre before 1641. He worked *c.* 1642 with Charles Le Brun on a ceiling painting for Hesselin's château of Chantemesle (destr.) and in 1643 was commissioned to execute the MAY OF NOTRE-DAME DE PARIS *Martyrdom of St Peter* (Paris, Notre-Dame). This important work welds his influences into an original and powerful synthesis. A similar diversity of inspiration, drawing from the Bolognese and the Venetian schools as well as from the followers of Caravaggio, is also found in the superb *Meeting of Antony and Cleopatra* (Paris, Louvre, see fig.). These works stand in contrast to the contemporary classicism, influenced by Poussin's visit to Paris in 1641–2, of artists such as Eustache Le Sueur. However, Bourdon was not insensible to this current, as can be seen in the *Continence of Scipio* (Grenoble, Mus. Peint. & Sculp.), painted for the Hôtel de Bretonvilliers, Paris, the *Presentation in the Temple* (Paris, Louvre) and the *Holy Family* (Salzburg, Residenzgal.), which are characterized by more static compositions built up in planes parallel with the picture surface. Poussin's influence is even clearer in *Christ and the Children* (Chicago, IL, A. Inst.) and the *Massacre of the Innocents* (St Petersburg, Hermitage), which belong with the vein of Parisian classicism current at the end of the 1640s and exemplified in the work of Charles Le Brun, among others. With Le Brun, Bourdon was one of the small group of like-minded artists who created the Académie Royale de Peinture et de Sculpture in 1648 (*see* PARIS, §VI, 1).

Bourdon's Parisian successes and, no doubt, his friendship with the influential Félibien were responsible for the commission for an altarpiece, the *Martyrdom of St Andrew* (Toulouse, Mus. Augustins; upper part, *God the Father Surrounded by Angels*, Lille, Mus. B.-A.), for the high altar of St André, Chartres. They also resulted in an invitation to Stockholm from Queen Christina in 1652. The unsettled state of Paris during the disturbances of the Fronde prompted Bourdon to accept the post she offered of court painter. He was commissioned to design, in a classicizing style, the mausoleum of Gustav II Adolf, the Queen's father. The project did not materialize, however, because of her abdication in 1654. In Stockholm, Bourdon for the most part painted portraits (nothing is known of any he may have done previously). He represented Christina on several occasions: on horseback for a portrait intended for Philip IV of Spain (Madrid, Prado), seated (oil sketch; Béziers, Mus. B.-A.) and in half-length (Stockholm, Nmus.). Portraits of his principal sitters also include *Gustav Gustavson of Wasaborg* (Uppsala, Uppsala U.) and his children, the Counts Palatine, *Karl Gustav* (?replica; Stockholm, Nmus.), *Johann Adolf* (Montpellier, Mus. Fabre) and those of many other court personalities, such as *Countess Ebba Sparre* (Washington, DC, N.G.A.). Bourdon's portrait style was much influenced by that of Anthony van Dyck, and he laid the emphasis less on psychology than on the hands and the drapery, in which the folds and play of light are often painted with great bravura.

Bourdon returned to Paris in 1654 and was named Recteur of the Académie in 1655. In that year he was commissioned to complete the series of six tapestry cartoons illustrating the lives of St Gervase and St Protase for the church of St Gervais-St Protais, Paris, left incomplete at the death of Le Sueur; but he only carried out the *Beheading of St Protais* (Arras, Mus. B.-A.). In 1657 he went to Montpellier, where he executed the *Fall of Simon Magus* for the high altar of the cathedral (*in situ*), as well as numerous portraits, probably including the *Portrait of an Unknown Man* (Chicago, IL., A. Inst.) and that of a *Man with Black Ribbons* (Montpellier, Mus. Fabre). He also executed a series of seven canvases of the *Acts of Mercy* (Sarasota, FL, Ringling Mus. A.), which became widely known through his own engravings (e.g. Paris, Bib. N., Cab. Est.). He was back in Paris in 1658.

Under the influence of Poussin's works, which were to be seen in many Parisian collections, landscape took a growing place in Bourdon's art, and he began to use saturated, even strident, colours to lift his chromatic harmonies, though never entirely to disrupt them. His landscapes are animated with figures and punctuated with antique buildings, as in the *Finding of Moses* (Washington, DC, N.G.A.) and the *Holy Family with Washerwomen* (Brest, Mus. Mun.). In other cases the landscape becomes the dominant element, with the figures reduced to staffage, as in the *Landscape with Figures* (New York, Met.). Nature is always recomposed in an ideal rather than natural vision, as in *Landscape with a Mill* (Providence, RI, Sch. Des., Mus. A.) and *Landscape with the Return of the Ark* (London, N.G.).

In 1663 Bourdon was commissioned to decorate the gallery of the Hôtel de Bretonvilliers, Paris, with scenes from the *Story of Phaethon*. The resulting scheme was immediately considered a masterpiece. Now destroyed, it is known through the engravings of Bourdon's pupil, Jacques Friquet de Vauroze (1638–1716), through copies drawn by Michel Corneille (ii) (Montpellier, Mus. Atger), through a number of preparatory drawings by Bourdon himself (e.g. Paris, Louvre and Ecole N. Sup. B.-A.) and through an oil sketch (Avignon, Mus. Calvet). It would

appear also to have been in the manner of Poussin. Bourdon delivered four lectures at the Académie Royale: the *Commentaire des 'Aveugles de Jéricho' de Poussin* in 1667, the *Commentaire du 'Martyre de Saint Etienne' de Carrache* in 1668, *Sur la lumière selon les différentes heures du jour* in 1669 and *Sur les proportions de la figure humaine expliquées sur l'Antique* in 1670. Death prevented him from carrying out what, in spite of his success, was his only royal commission: three compartments on the theme of Hercules for the ceiling of the Chambre du Roi in the Tuileries, Paris.

BIBLIOGRAPHY
A. Félibien: *Entretiens sur les vies et les ouvrages des plus excellens peintres anciens et modernes* (Paris, 1666–88, Trévoux, 1725/*R* London, 1967)
Guillet de Saint-Georges: 'Mémoire historique des principaux ouvrages de M. Bourdon lu à l'Académie le samedi 7 Juin 1692', *Mémoires inédits sur la vie et les ouvrages des membres de l'Académie Royale*, ed. L. Dussieux, E. Soulier, P. de Chennevières, P. Mantz and A. de Montaiglon, i (Paris, 1854), pp. 87–103
C. Ponsonnailhe: *Sébastien Bourdon, sa vie et son oeuvre* (Paris, 1886)
G. E. Fowle: *The Biblical Paintings of Sébastien Bourdon* (diss., U. Michigan, 1970; microfilm, Ann Arbor, 1981)
Le Peinture française du XVIIe siècle dans les collections américaines (exh. cat. by P. Rosenberg, Paris, Grand Pal; New York, Met.; Chicago, IL, A. Inst.; 1982)
THIERRY BAJOU

Bouret, Etienne-Michel (*b* 1710; *d* Paris, 1777). French administrator, property developer and patron. He was related to the financiers and speculators Bouret de Villaumont and Bouret de Vézelay, and he amassed a vast income from offices that included Paymaster-General to the Royal Household (1738), tax collector (1747) and Postmaster-General (1752). Bouret used his fortune to speculate in property and built several residences where he lived in ostentatious luxury. In 1742 Bouret commissioned the Château de Croix-Fontaine to be built in Sénart forest, south-east of Paris, along with a hunting lodge where he intended to entertain Louis XV. He also built a sumptuous pavilion at Gonesse and a hôtel in the Rue de la Grange-Batelière, Paris. From 1767 to 1770, Bouret purchased five plots along the Rue du Faubourg Saint-Honoré in the Champs-Elysées district that was then in a boom period. He redivided the plots into six properties, planning to build mansions and sell them at a large profit. The buildings proposed were the Hôtel Bouret (or Andlau), the Hôtel Sabran, two hôtels belonging to Bouret's son-in-law Legendre de Villemorin (also known as the Hôtels Bérenger), the Hôtel Vergès (or Sébastiani), which was built by Boursier, and the Hôtel Brunoy, for which Etienne-Louis Boullée produced a plan. The scheme ruined Bouret, who was forced to sell the properties singly from 1773, leaving most of the hôtels uncompleted or still at the planning stage; none have survived.

BIBLIOGRAPHY
P. Clement and A. Lemoine: *M. de Silhouette Bouret: Les Derniers Fermiers-généraux: Etudes sur les financiers du XVIIIe siècle* (Paris, 1872)
R. Dupuis: 'Bouret le bâtisseur et ses hôtels du Faubourg Saint-Honoré', *Bull. Soc. Hist. VIIIe & XVIIe Arrond. Paris* (1934–5), pp. 248–90
VALÉRIE-NOËLLE JOUFFRE

Bourgeau, Victor (*b* Lavaltrie, Qué. 1809; *d* 1888). Canadian architect. His early career was spent as a member of an itinerant team of wood sculptors working on the interior decoration of churches in the Montreal area. In

1839 he settled in Montreal, which was then rapidly expanding, with opportunities for building in the new parishes of the neighbouring seigneuries. Ignace Bourget, who became the second bishop of Montreal in 1840, was looking for an architect capable of building sturdy religious and institutional buildings within a fixed budget and chose Victor Bourgeau.

Using examples from newspapers and architectural pattern books, Bourgeau provided plans for the new parish buildings. He also received commissions outside the diocese of Montreal, and almost two hundred churches are attributed to him, most of which survive. Notable examples in Montreal include St Pierre-Apôtre, Dorchester Boulevard and Visitation Street (1851–3), the Hôtel-Dieu or General Hospital (1860), the convent of the Soeurs de la Charité, known as the Grey Sisters (1869), the cathedral of St Jacques-le-Majeur, Dorchester Boulevard and Dominion Square (1875–85), and numerous churches on the outskirts of Montreal. In the 1870s he was responsible for alterations to the interior of the church of Notre-Dame. Although he mainly used a grey local stone for his buildings in Montreal, he also used brick for more modest commissions. He followed carefully developments in ecclesiastical architecture in the United States and was influenced by the work of Richard Upjohn, Minard Lafever, Samuel Sloan and James Renwick, which he adapted to the needs of the Catholic liturgy. However, his conventual buildings, mostly still in use, follow the plans and elevations that had been standard since the late 18th century, with only a few ornamental motifs typical of the mid-19th century.

BIBLIOGRAPHY

A. Gowans: *Building Canada: An Architectural History of Canadian Life* (Toronto, 1966)
J.-C. Marsan: *Montréal en évolution: Historique du développement de l'architecture et de l'environnement montréalais* (Montreal, 1974)
P. Lambert and R. Lemire: *Inventaire des bâtiments du vieux Montréal* (Montreal, 1977)

RAYMONDE GAUTHIER

Bourg-en-Bresse. *See* BROU, PRIORY CHURCH.

Bourgeois, Louise (*b* Paris, 25 Dec 1911). American sculptor, painter and printmaker of French birth. Her parents ran a workshop in Paris restoring tapestries, for which Bourgeois filled in the designs where they had become worn. She studied mathematics at the Sorbonne before turning to studio arts. In 1938, after marrying Robert Goldwater, an American art historian, critic and curator, she went to New York, where she enrolled in the Art Students League and studied painting for two years with Václav Vytlačil (*b* 1892). Bourgeois's work was shown at the Brooklyn Museum Print Exhibition in 1939. During World War II she worked with Joan Miró, André Masson and other European expatriates.

Although Bourgeois exhibited with the Abstract Expressionists—and, like them, drew from the unconscious—she never became an abstract artist. Instead, she created symbolic objects and drawings expressing themes of loneliness and conflict, frustration and vulnerability, as reflected in her suite of engravings and parables, *He Disappeared into Complete Silence* (1947).

In 1949 Bourgeois had her first sculpture exhibition, including *Woman in the Shape of a Shuttle* (1947–9; New York, Xavier Fourcade), at the Peridot Gallery; this work proved typical of her wooden sculpture and foreshadowed her preoccupations of the following years. Her first sculptures were narrow wooden pieces, such as *Sleeping Figure* (1950; New York, MOMA), a 'stick' figure articulated into four parts with two supporting poles. Bourgeois soon began using non-traditional media, with rough works in latex and plaster contrasting with her elegantly worked pieces in wood, bronze and marble. In the 1960s and 1970s her work became more sexually explicit, as in the *Femme Couteau* group (1969–70; King's Point, NY, J. and E. Spiegel priv. col.) and *Cumul I* (1969; Paris, Pompidou). The psychological origins of her work are particularly evident in *Destruction of the Father* (1974; New York, Xavier Fourcade). Bourgeois's work was appreciated by a wider public in the 1970s as a result of the change in attitudes wrought by feminism and Post-modernism.

BIBLIOGRAPHY

W. Anderson: 'American Sculpture: The Situation in the Fifties', *Artforum*, v (1967), pp. 60–67
L. R. Lippard: 'Louise Bourgeois: From the Inside Out', *From the Center: Feminist Essays on Art* (New York, 1976)
Louise Bourgeois (exh. cat. by D. Wye, New York, MOMA, 1982) [with many pls, chronology and bibliog.]

RINA YOUNGNER

Bourgeois, Sir Peter Francis (*b* London, 1756; *d* London, 7 Jan 1811). English painter and art collector of Swiss descent. Born to a family of Swiss watchmakers in London, Bourgeois was apprenticed as a boy to P. J. de Loutherbourg. The latter heavily influenced his art, which was to elevate him to membership of the Royal Academy in 1793. Bourgeois specialized in landscape and genre scenes and achieved recognition in his own day with works such as *Tiger Hunt* and *William Tell* (both *c*. 1790; London, Dulwich Pict. Gal.), but his works are no longer regarded as of any note.

Bourgeois was linked from an early age with Noël Desenfans, who in effect adopted him when his father left London for Switzerland. Desenfans promoted Bourgeois's reputation as an artist and involved him in his own activities as a picture dealer. Bourgeois became passionately interested in buying paintings, and in the last 15 years of his life bought considerable numbers, sometimes creating financial problems for the partnership. His taste was characteristic of the traditional Grand Manner of his time, concentrating on the great names of the 16th and 17th centuries, particularly academic works and paintings of the Netherlandish schools.

It was Bourgeois who persuaded Desenfans to retain their collection as an entity, and to leave it to a suitable institution. Desenfans, on his death in 1807, left his pictures for life jointly to his wife and to Bourgeois. The latter, charged with the commission of finding an institution that would preserve the collection as a group, settled on Dulwich College, then a small educational foundation with its own picture gallery. On Bourgeois's death a new gallery was built at Dulwich, financed by Mrs Desenfans, the College and his own bequest; it was designed by his friend Sir John Soane and contained accommodation for the paintings and a mausoleum for Bourgeois and Desenfans.

Bourgeois was described by contemporaries as vulgar and socially ambitious, but good-hearted. He played a prominent part in the internal battles at the Royal Academy in 1805–6, supporting James Wyatt, with Sir John Soane.

BIBLIOGRAPHY
E. T. Cook: *Dulwich College Picture Gallery*, Dulwich Pict. Gal. cat. (London, 1918)
P. Murray: *The Dulwich Picture Gallery*, Dulwich Pict. Gal. cat. (London, 1980)
G. Waterfield: *Collection for a King* (London, 1985)

GILES WATERFIELD

Bourgeois, Victor (*b* Charleroi, 29 Aug 1897; *d* Brussels, 24 July 1962). Belgian architect, theorist and urban planner. He grew up in the Pays Noir, the most heavily industrialized region of Belgium, an experience that led to his early and intense interest in social issues. He studied at the Académie Royale des Beaux-Arts et Ecole des Arts Décoratifs in Brussels (1914–18) and began practising architecture immediately. In 1919–20 he was part of the technical department of the Société Nationale des Habitations à Bon Marché, which was created to find rapid solutions to the problem of workers' housing. Upon his return from several trips to the Netherlands, he built his first major work, a small housing group (1922) in the Rue du Cubisme in the Koekelberg district of Brussels. It had an expressively modelled elevation and composition of separate volumes somewhat suggestive of similar developments of the time in the Netherlands, but its sober use of materials in their natural state also clearly showed its origins in the work of H. P. Berlage, for whom Bourgeois had great admiration.

During the same period, being aware of the importance of the logistic support provided by the mass media, Bourgeois founded several journals devoted to the expression of new ideas: *Au Volant* (1919), *Le Geste* (1920) and, most importantly, *7 Arts* (1922–8), a weekly magazine of information and artistic debate through which he made close contact with a number of members of the international avant-garde. By the end of 1922 he had begun work on his best-known commission, the Cité Moderne, completed in 1925. This complex of 300 dwellings in the Berchem-Saint Agathe district of Brussels may fairly be described as the first large housing scheme in the International style; indeed, in the forms of the flat overhanging roofs and the lively zigzag façades of the unit rows, it looks forward to even later styles such as the work of Groep 32 and Hans Scharoun. Like similar Netherlands complexes of the 1920s, but unlike the *Siedlungen* built in Germany in the same decade, the Cité Moderne disposes its Modernist forms in a relatively low-density garden-suburb plan around a village green and community-facilities building. The project was widely published, and Bourgeois was invited to design a house at the Weissenhof model village (1927) in Stuttgart.

In 1928 Bourgeois chaired the opening meetings of CIAM at La Sarraz (*see* CIAM and fig. 2), organizing its congresses in Frankfurt am Main (1929) and Brussels (1930). His contributions were founded on his own professional experimentation and included the organization of a Belgian section of CIAM and the gathering of

information on economic, trade-union and political matters. From this time his preoccupations turned increasingly towards urban planning. He drew up several solutions for the restructuring of Brussels (1930–33), with the aim of stimulating discussion, and published the results in his new journal on urban management entitled *Bruxelles* (1933–5). With sociologist Paul Otlet (1868–1944) he proposed a design for a Cité Mondiale (1932) to be erected in the green belt around Brussels. He began teaching at the Institut Supérieur des Arts Décoratifs in Brussels in 1927, offering courses in 'pure form' (1927–38) and architecture (1939–62).

For the remainder of Bourgeois's life his architectural practice was concerned with social issues, and many of his commissions were generated by the programmes and policies of the democratic socialist movement. The Ecole du Centre (1937) in Hornu is the best-known of several schools that he built in connection with the relatively late arrival of compulsory public education in Belgium. He worked on group-holiday facilities for workers, on day nurseries such as Le Berceau (1955) in Marcinelle and on health-care facilities such as his last major work, the Rayon de Soleil hospital complex (1962) in Charleroi. The latter, like many of his post-war buildings, is in a fairly conventional late modern style, but his interest in urban design and its social effects continued undiminished. At his death he was working on a development plan for the centre of Ixelles in Brussels.

WRITINGS
with C. van Eesteren and S. Giedion: *Rationnelle Bebauungsweisen* (Frankfurt am Main, 1931)
with R. De Cooman: *De l'Architecture au temps d'Erasme à l'humanisme social de notre temps* (Brussels and Paris, 1949)
L'Architecte et son espace (Brussels, 1955)

BIBLIOGRAPHY
P. L. Flouquet: *Victor Bourgeois: Architectures, 1922–52* (Brussels, 1952)
G. Linze: *Victor Bourgeois* (Brussels, 1960)
Victor Bourgeois, 1897–1962 (exh. cat. by R. Delevoy and others, Brussels, Ecole N. Sup. Archit. A. Visuels, 1971)
S. Goyens de Heusch: *7 Arts: Un Front de jeunesse pour la révolution artistique* (Brussels, 1976)

HERVÉ PAINDAVEINE

Bourges [Lat. Avaricum]. French city, capital of Berry. It is situated on a limestone spur surrounded by marshlands at the confluence of the rivers Yèvre and Auron.

I. History and urban development. II. Buildings.

I. History and urban development.

Avaricum was an important urban centre from *c.* 500 BC, the *civitas* capital of the Bituriges and, under Roman occupation, the capital of the province of Aquitaine. Fortifications erected in the last quarter of the 3rd century AD, in response to the invasions of AD 256–7, confined Avaricum within its walls for several centuries. From the 5th century AD the religious function of the city developed. Bourges was the seat of a huge diocese, with the cathedral of St Etienne inside the walls and, from the 7th century, monastic settlements round about. The city was radically transformed when the Viscounty of Bourges became royal property in 1101 and by rapid economic development in the 12th century. In November 1172 Bourges was the target of a military demonstration by Henry II, King of England, who claimed it as part of the inheritance of his wife, Eleanor of Aquitaine (1122–1204). A new defensive wall was built outside the old city limits, reinforced by a donjon, the symbol of Capetian power in Berry. These were complete by 1183, when King Philip II Augustus (*reg* 1180–1223) authorized buildings to extend beyond the old wall. The rebuilding of the cathedral (*see* §II, 1 below), begun after this date, was completed in 1255.

In the 14th century Bourges again became an important artistic centre under the patronage of Jean, Duc de Berry, who employed artists from Flanders, Paris and the Loire Valley on his works in the city from 1361: Guy de Dammartin and Drouet de Dammartin built the ducal palace between 1367 and 1398 (*see* DAMMARTIN, DE, (1) and (2)); André Beauneveu and Jean de Cambrai decorated the Sainte-Chapelle (*see* §II, 2 below). In 1422, while Paris was occupied by the English, the Dauphin, the future Charles VII, gave Bourges the status of a royal capital and set up his administration there. A wealthy middle class developed, led by Jacques Coeur, the King's Treasurer. The palace (*see* §II, 4 below) that he had built between 1443 and 1451 is one of the best surviving examples of urban civic residences at the end of the Middle Ages.

In the early 16th century, after the fire that burnt much of the town in 1487, stone houses were built, such as the Hôtel Lallemant, a masterpiece of the early Renaissance, with timber-frame houses in the commercial suburbs. The town lost its drive at the end of the century, however, owing to the cessation of the fairs instituted by Charles VII and the violence brought by the Wars of Religion. In the 17th century there was a noticeable increase in building, which centred around Jean Lejuge (*fl* 1622–48), architect to Henri II, Prince de Condé. Neo-classical houses were built at the heart of the town, the Jesuit college was built to plans by Etienne Martellange, and at the end of the century the archbishop's house was rebuilt from plans by Jean-Baptiste Bullet de Chamblain.

The town continued to decline until the mid-19th century, when metallurgical industries developed in Berry, and armaments works and the Mazières iron foundries were set up in Bourges. Residential areas for the workers grew up, a new network of roads was created, and important public buildings were erected. The crisis in the metallurgical industry at the end of the century brought a near-fatal blow to the town. Manufacturing industries revived after World War II, and Bourges now has a population of *c.* 80,000. It has retained its role as the capital of Berry and has been able to preserve its artistic inheritance.

BIBLIOGRAPHY

A. Buhot de Kersers: *Histoire et statistique monumentale du département du Cher* (Bourges, 1875–98), ii
P. Gauchery and A. de Grossouvre: *Notre vieux Bourges* (Bourges, 1912/R 1980)
C. Gauchery-Grodecki: 'L'Architecture en Berry sous le règne de Henri IV et au début du XVIIe siècle', *Mem. Un. Soc. Sav. Bourges*, iii (1951–2), pp. 77–131
G. Devailly and others: *Histoire du Berry* (Toulouse, 1980)
E. Meslé: *Histoire de Bourges* (Roanne/Le Coteau, 1983)

ANNIE CHAZELLE

II. Buildings.

1. Cathedral. 2. Sainte-Chapelle. 3. St Ursin. 4. Hôtel Jacques-Coeur.

1. CATHEDRAL. The circumstances in which the first metropolitan church was established were described by Gregory of Tours (*History of the Franks* I.31). The first building for which evidence survives dates from the mid-11th century, when the cathedral stood on its present site at the top of the town, up against the wall of the Gallo-Roman city, with its apse probably built into one of the towers. The nave was about the same width (*c.* 13 m) as the existing central vessel. It may have been an aisleless building, like many Romanesque churches in Aquitaine.

A number of additions were made to or planned for this church during the second half of the 12th century. The two that survive are the sculptured portals now attached to the north and south aisles of the Gothic cathedral. It has been argued that they were assembled from fragments of a west front supposed to have been built during the 1170s, as a lease issued in 1172 implies that there were thoughts of a new west front at that time. The style of the sculpture, however, suggests an earlier date, and most scholars prefer the 1160s (*see* §(ii) below). Presumably at the same time or not long after, lateral extensions were made to the choir. Here the evidence exists only in the form of excavated foundations, which are fragmentary and open to a range of interpretations. The suggestion that they formed a transept is misleading because the floor levels on either side must have been different. Another assumption—that these works, like the 11th-century church, were contained within the Gallo-Roman wall—is also open to question. The masonry of the chapel of Ste Solange, which lies beyond the wall on the south side of the Gothic choir, was evidently connected with one of the extensions, and this implies that a whole new east end was projected. In conjunction with the

1. Bourges Cathedral, choir, view towards the east, begun ?1180s

document of 1172 that anticipated a new west front, the evidence suggests the intention to remodel the building as at Saint-Denis Abbey, the cathedrals of Chartres and Reims and at Saint-Gilles-du-Gard in Provence.

Work on the east end was interrupted, however, perhaps as a result of the disturbances of November 1172, and resumed only after 1183, this time as a total rebuilding in a purely Gothic idiom. The starting date normally given is 1195. This comes from a document assigning funds for the *reparatio* of the church, but it proves only that work was in hand at the time. There is a strong possibility that Bourges Cathedral was started before either Chartres or Soissons, so that it has a claim to be considered the first of the High Gothic cathedrals.

(i) Architecture. (ii) Sculpture. (iii) Stained glass.

(i) Architecture. Historically, the Gothic cathedral can be regarded as one of the long-term consequences of the acquisition of Bourges by Philip I (*reg* 1060–1105), which brought the city within range of the stylistic developments that were to shape its architectural character. The plan of the building is extremely simple and homogeneous. There is no transept. The nave and choir together comprise six double bays plus a single bay that is incorporated into the vaulting system of the apse. There are two aisles, one higher than the other, both of which go right round the building. There are five small chapels on the apse and five portals in the west front. The elevation (see fig. 1) can be described as three- or five-storey, according to the point of view adopted. The high vaults are sexpartite (*see* GOTHIC, fig. 5), the rest quadripartite, except in the outer ambulatories of both crypt and choir, where there are some additional ribs. Work began with the choir, which was in use by 1214. The nave was substantially complete by 1255, but consecration did not take place until 1324.

It has generally been presumed that the only alteration made to the design during the building campaign was to add the chapels. These are unusual in being corbelled out of buttresses like the turrets or bartizans of castles; but although there are disturbances in the vicinity of the axial chapel suggesting that they were afterthoughts, the chapels were intended from the start. On the other hand, there seem to have been some rather significant second thoughts about the main arcade. In the crypt is an enormous wall, nearly 3 m thick, built to support the main arcade in the church above, though in the event it was hardly used. This crypt wall was probably designed to carry a paired-column arcade of the type found at Sens Cathedral or in the progeny of Bourges at the cathedrals of Le Mans and Coutances. Differences in the vault pattern between crypt and choir confirm the inference that the design was changed, and the distribution of two types of abacus moulding (that used in the crypt appearing in the upper choir only on the outer wall) falls neatly into place. Otherwise, changes show the masons of Bourges keeping abreast of technical improvements and stylistic fashions during the years the cathedral was being built. In the windows simple lancets give way to plate tracery, and plate tracery to bar tracery. The pitch of the flying buttresses was also altered, although apparently at the expense of structural efficiency.

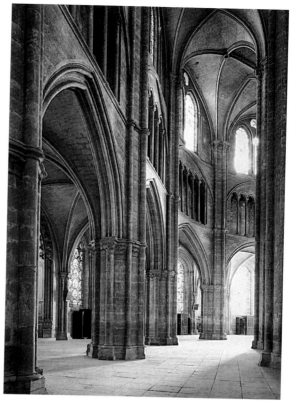

2. Bourges Cathedral, north choir aisles, begun ?1180s

The west front took a long time to complete and was the source of recurrent problems, which had their origin in the nature of the site. The cathedral is poised on the top of a hill and had to be underpinned at either end. At the east this task was performed by the crypt, at the west by a ramp, represented by the steps leading up to the façade. The ground beneath the ramp is honeycombed by caves and fissures that ruled out tall towers, and the west front was conceived on an unusually modest scale. Even so, the south tower showed signs of keeling over soon after it was completed in the mid-14th century and had to be shored up by an enormous buttress. The north tower took even longer to build, and it collapsed almost at once (1506). It was replaced by the early 16th-century tower, which is now the most conspicuous feature of the exterior.

Despite these adventitious circumstances the architectural character of the building, once established, remained unimpaired. The cathedral makes its effect almost entirely as an organization of interior space. This is handled with immense confidence and sophistication in a succession of calculated contrasts and repetitions. The controlling idea is the section, which is defined by an equilateral triangle and actually looks triangular, the aisles and nave forming an ascending hierarchy. The outer aisles are broad and squat to a degree that would be absurd in any other combination, while the inner aisles (see fig. 2) are immensely tall and therefore look narrower than they really are. The nave itself is higher still (37.15 m) but also broad.

These spatial modulations were carefully contrived. A sense of spatial continuity across the building is conveyed in a novel way by duplicating certain features of the main elevation in the secondary elevation of the inner aisles. Each is three-storey, and in the choir at least the middle sections are virtually identical. Moreover, the tall columns of the main arcades (h. 16 m) are, as it were, repeated on the other side of the aisles, where they appear as bulges in the wall. In this they echo the design of the main elevation above the arcades, where the columns seem to push through the wall right up to the vault springers. The impression is thus created of a building in which the primary elements are two rows of vertical members that no longer support walls from below in the traditional manner but are linked together by three series of arches, one forming the arcades, the second the triforium and the third the wall ribs of the vaults. This completely reverses the normal relation between supports and what is supported. The treatment of the column capitals is in line with this reading of the structure: they are highly attenuated and were conceived not as terminal members crowning ordinary columns but rather as friezes.

There were no precedents for such a building, but the separate ingredients can be traced back to many sources. The plan belongs to a group that includes Sens Cathedral, Notre-Dame at Paris and Notre-Dame at Mantes, the transept being optional. Similar curious chapels were used in Sainte-Croix (destr.), Etampes, and were also in a sense the diminutive alternative to a type of chapel that originated at Pontigny Abbey and St Remi at Reims, represented in Bourges at the later church of St Pierre-le-Guillard. St Remi also supplied the idea for certain features of the exterior. The design of the triforium probably owed something to Fontgombault Abbey, Indre. The staggered section was reminiscent of Cluny III and even Old St Peter's in Rome. Nearer at hand were St Martin at Tours and La Charité-sur-Loire. The two most telling items among the forerunners of Bourges were the false tribune gallery and the giant order. Both occurred sporadically in a wide range of Romanesque buildings, but they seem to have come together in an Early Gothic version at Notre-Dame (destr.) at Valenciennes. It was perhaps from that region that the architect of Bourges came, and his distinctive contribution was to eliminate the last vestiges of the gallery in favour of emphatic vertical accents.

The influence of Bourges can be detected at several levels. The number of close copies was not large, and none of them attempted to reproduce the same elevation in successive planes. In France the two obvious cases are the choirs of the cathedrals of Le Mans and Coutances, which took up the theme of the staggered section but put it to very different uses. In Spain there are many allusions to Bourges at the cathedrals of Toledo and Burgos, but the architectural effects achieved owe nothing to the French cathedral. If there was any part of medieval Europe where Bourges provided a real stimulus to the imagination of architects, it was probably in Catalonia, where during the first half of the 14th century a succession of gigantic churches was started, all of which in varying degrees can be said to have taken the spatial arrangements at Bourges as their point of departure: the cathedrals of Girona, Barcelona and Palma de Mallorca, and S Maria del Mar at Barcelona. If the theme of high aisles and relatively small clerestories can be regarded as stemming from Bourges, its influence in Spain persisted right to the end of the Middle Ages, for example in the 16th-century Castilian cathedrals of Segovia and Salamanca. Its most outstanding progeny were undoubtedly in Italy, at Milan Cathedral and S Petronio, Bologna, but its ghost can still be recognized in the 16th-century Renaissance church of St Eustache in Paris.

It was not really feasible to attempt a church of the Bourges type unless there were enough resources to do it on a grand scale. There are no small versions of Bourges. However, the idea of building a church around rows of vertical supports could be generalized, and it was taken up and developed in a number of interesting ways. In France, Germany and Italy it merged with spatial formations that had already been evolving in Romanesque times. In the German *Staffelkirchen* the staggered section was retained, but the clerestory was abandoned, an arrangement that led imperceptibly to the notion of a hall church. In the secular sphere the same sort of architectural thinking can even be recognized in some of the great medieval timber-framed barns.

BIBLIOGRAPHY

A. Martin and C. Cahier: *Monographie de la cathédrale de Bourges*, 2 vols (Paris, 1841–4)
R. Branner: *La Cathédrale de Bourges et sa place dans l'architecture gothique* (Paris, 1962); rev. and Eng. trans. by S. Prager Branner (New York, 1989) [full bibliog.]
J. Bony: *French Gothic Architecture of the 12th and 13th Centuries* (Berkeley, 1983)

PETER KIDSON

(ii) Sculpture.

(a) Lateral portals. Around 1225 two portals composed of 12th-century sculpture were installed in the fifth bays of the aisles, corresponding exactly to the western limit of the liturgical choir. It has been argued that they were carved for a new west front apparently proposed in 1172 (Branner), but the style of the sculptures suggests a date in the 1160s; it was later proposed that they were always intended for lateral entrances (New-Smith). The present arrangement, however, reveals a lack of homogeneity in both iconography and style, and some of the elements fit awkwardly into their 13th-century frame.

The tympanum of the north portal bears the *Virgin and Child* enthroned flanked by angels, the *Adoration of the Magi*, a figure perhaps representing *St Joseph*, the *Annunciation* and the *Visitation*. An *Annunciation to the Shepherds*, with much smaller-scale figures, was carved in the 13th century to complete the Infancy cycle. Angels and prophets appear on the archivolts, but the two column statues, representing female figures, have not been identified. On the south portal *Christ in Majesty* on the tympanum is surrounded by the Evangelist symbols, with the *Twelve Apostles* enthroned on the lintel (see fig. 3). Of the six Old Testament figures on the embrasures, only *Moses*, who carries the Tablets of the Law, can be identified. The historiated capitals above carry an Old Testament programme that bears little relation to the *Christ in Majesty* on the tympanum: the *Expulsion from Paradise*, the *Fall of Adam and Eve*, *David*, *Noah*, the *Sacrifice of Isaac* and *Samson and the Lion*. The portals are also distinctive for

3. Bourges Cathedral, south portal, 1160s

the wealth of ornamental carving that covers the jambs and archivolts, particularly on the north portal, and for the diversity of their stylistic sources. Two styles can be detected. One is relatively archaic, with solid and rather dull forms, while the other is more original: some of the sculpture, for example, shows close similarities to the Royal Portal at Chartres Cathedral (e.g. *Moses* on the south portal), but the forms are lively and full of fantasy, distinguishing them from their model.

(b) West portals. The west façade is enriched by five portals opening into the nave and aisles, a design that was unique for its time in France. They bear a coherent programme: the *Last Judgement* of the central portal is flanked by a portal dedicated to the Virgin on the north and to St Stephen, the patron saint of the cathedral, on the south. The outer portals are dedicated to canonized archbishops of Bourges: St William (1205–9; *can* 1218) and St Ursinus (*fl* 3rd century), the first bishop and founder of the diocese.

The portals have been much altered. Those dedicated to St William and the Virgin were rebuilt between 1511 and 1515 after the north tower collapsed, although the original 13th-century *Assumption* and *Coronation of the Virgin* were preserved on the latter. The St William portal is more homogeneous, but its Late Gothic style already shows some Renaissance influence. Further damage was caused by the Huguenots in 1562, when the embrasure statues were destroyed, and during the French Revolution. Restorations were carried out between 1829 and 1846, but sections of the tympana and archivolts are completely disfigured. The provenance of the stylistically diverse column statues now installed on the central portal is

unknown, although at least one may come from the Sainte-Chapelle, Bourges (*see* §2 below).

The central portal was largely inspired by the iconography of the *Last Judgement* portal on the west front of Notre-Dame, Paris, although there are variations in detail. The *Christ-Judge* on the tympanum is surrounded by four angels bearing the instruments of the Passion and flanked by the *Virgin* and *St John* in intercession. Below, the *Separation of the Blessed and the Damned* is arranged on either side of *St Michael Weighing Souls*, with the *Resurrection of the Dead* on the lintel. The archivolts complete the programme with seraphim, angels, enthroned male figures in prayer and confessors. The martyrs and prophets on the two outer archivolts are modern, as is the trumeau figure of *Christ*. On the gable of the central portal the *Intercessors* again appear, and in the spandrels of the rose are the *Wise and Foolish Virgins*.

The adjacent portal on the south represents events from the *Life of St Stephen*. His ordination as deacon and his arrest are shown on the lintel, and above is his martyrdom, with the figure of Christ standing at the apex of the tympanum. The trumeau figure of the saint is modern. The outer portal on the south bears rich narrative reliefs of the *Life of St Ursinus*, reflecting contemporary interest in the cult of local saints. The cycle begins on the lintel, where St Peter sends SS Ursinus and Justus on their mission to Gaul, and ends at the apex of the tympanum with the baptism of the Roman senator Leocadius and his son. The socle zone of the portals has blind arcading, as at Notre-Dame, Paris, with narrative reliefs in the spandrels; the reliefs of the two left portals have been destroyed, and the cycle now starts on the left jamb of the central portal with the *Creation of Angels* and continues to the far right buttress, ending with the *Drunkenness of Noah*.

The three surviving portals and the socle reliefs show numerous features characteristic of sculpture in the Ile-de-France of the second quarter of the 13th century. The sculptures of the St Ursinus and St Stephen portals appear to be derived from Amiens Cathedral, but they seem somewhat stiff and provincial compared to the central portal, which shows the influence of Parisian art of the 1240s. The picturesque flavour of the latter and its graceful, expressive figures are reminiscent, however, of work on the west portals at Reims Cathedral.

(c) Choir-screen. The 13th-century choir-screen was damaged by the Huguenots in the 16th century, restored in the 17th century but destroyed in the 18th; numerous fragments (Bourges, Mus. Berry; Bourges Cathedral, crypt; Paris, Louvre) testify, however, to its importance. It carried a *Passion* cycle on three sides of the parapet, running above the arcading. The cycle began on the north face with *Judas and the 30 Pieces of Silver*. On the front were depicted the *Crucifixion* (over the central arch), the *Deposition, Entombment, Soldiers Guarding the Tomb* and the *Three Marys at the Tomb*. The cycle ended on the south side with the *Harrowing of Hell*. Standing figures of *Apostles* were set in the spandrels of the arcade. The backgrounds of the reliefs were originally inlaid with glass. The figures are executed in a vigorous style that belongs to the

monumental, classicizing traditions in sculpture of mid-13th-century Paris, which culminated in the *Apostles* of the Sainte-Chapelle.

BIBLIOGRAPHY

A. Boinet: *Les Sculptures de la cathédrale de Bourges* (Paris, 1912)

R. Branner: 'Les Portails latéraux de la cathédrale de Bourges', *Bull. Mnmtl*, cxv (1957), pp. 263–70

C. Gnudi: 'Le Jubé de Bourges et l'apogée du "classicisme" dans la sculpture de l'Ile-de-France au milieu du XIIIe siècle', *Rev. A.* [Paris], iii (1969), pp. 18–36

W. Sauerländer: *Gotische Skulptur in Frankreich, 1140–1270* (Munich, 1970; Eng. trans., London, 1972)

F. Joubert: 'Les Voussures déposées du portail central de la cathédrale de Bourges', *Bull. Mnmtl*, cxxxii (1974), pp. 273–86

A. New-Smith: *Twelfth-century Sculpture at the Cathedral of Bourges* (diss., U. Boston, MA, 1975)

T. Bayard: *Bourges Cathedral: The West Portals*, Garland Lib. Hist. A. (New York, 1976)

F. Joubert: *Le Jubé de la cathédrale de Bourges* (diss., Paris U. IV, 1976)

——: 'Le Jubé de Bourges: Remarques sur le style', *Bull. Mnmtl*, cxxxvii (1979), pp. 341–69

——: *Le Jubé de Bourges, Doss. Mus. Louvre, Exp.—Doss. Dépt. Sculp.* (Paris, 1994)

FABIENNE JOUBERT

(iii) Stained glass. The choir of Bourges Cathedral has one of the most vivid and sophisticated iconographic programmes of the early 13th century. In the ambulatory are ten medallion windows (1200–14) with varied and complex armature framework. On either side of the axial chapel are the windows of the *New Alliance* and the *Last Judgement*, followed on the north by the *Prodigal Son*, the *Good Samaritan*, the *Relics of St Stephen* and the parable of *Dives and Lazarus*, and on the south by the *Passion*, *Apocalypse*, *Life of St Thomas* and *Life of Joseph*. The 13th-century glazing of the axial chapel has disappeared, but textual sources confirm that the themes depicted were the *Life of the Virgin*, the *Infancy of Christ* and a *Tree of Jesse*. In the

remaining chapels are scenes from saints' lives organized in thematic groups, comprising, in the first chapel to the north, the preachers and missionaries *Denis*, *Peter and Paul* and *Martin*, followed by the great eastern saints *Mary Magdalene*, *Nicholas* and *Mary of Egypt*. In the first chapel to the south are depicted the deacon martyr saints *Lawrence*, *Stephen* and *Vincent* and in the final chapel *James the Great*, *John the Baptist* and *John the Evangelist*. The clerestory windows date from slightly later in the campaign and show large hieratic images of prophets and Apostles in typological correspondence.

Stylistically, the ambulatory windows fall into three separate groups. The Good Samaritan workshop was responsible for the windows of the *Good Samaritan* (see fig. 4), *Passion*, *Apocalypse* and *Life of St Mary Magdalene*, which have highly energetic figures, expressive profiles and sharply nested V-shaped drapery folds, features that can be associated with trends in western France, notably at Poitiers Cathedral. In the windows of the *Relics of St Stephen*, *Dives and Lazarus* and the *Life of St Stephen*, the work of the Relics Master appears equally calligraphic, but with rounded heads and simpler drapery patterns. The Classical Master was responsible for the window of the *New Alliance* and *Last Judgement*, which have the rich modelling, classicizing drapery folds and elegant figural types associated with northern France and the *St Eustache* window at Chartres Cathedral. The choir aisles and nave of Bourges Cathedral house glass of the 15th century (see GOTHIC, fig. 103), remarkable for its spatial experimentation and elegant figure style. The glass was restored in the 19th century by Nicolas Coffetier (1821–84).

BIBLIOGRAPHY

L. Grodecki: 'Le "Maître du bon Samaritain" de la cathédrale de Bourges', *The Year 1200: A Symposium*, ed. J. Hoffeld, iii (New York, 1975), pp. 339–59

L. Grodecki and F. Perrot: *Les Vitraux du centre et des pays de la Loire*, Corp. Vitrearum Med. Aevi, ii (Paris, 1981), pp. 168–85

VIRGINIA CHIEFFO RAGUIN

2. SAINTE-CHAPELLE. Although the reconstruction of the old royal palace in Bourges, under the direction of Guy de Dammartin, was begun by Jean, Duc de Berry, sometime in the early 1370s, the addition of a palace chapel appears not to have been decided until the early 1390s. Based on the design of the Sainte-Chapelle in Paris, it was dedicated on 18 April 1405 under the name Chapelle Ste Sauveur. The master of painting and sculpture was André Beauneveu, who was probably succeeded in this position by Jean de Cambrai. Several important monuments were housed in the chapel, including the tomb of *Jean, Duc de Berry* (*c.* 1410–16) by Jean de Cambrai, the only documented work of sculpture connected with the chapel, the marble group known as Notre-Dame-la-Blanche (both now in Bourges Cathedral) and perhaps three stone statues of the *Virgin and Child*, *St John the Baptist* and a courtier, all now located in the village church of Morogues (Cher).

In 1693 fire destroyed the roof and weakened portions of the upper stonework, which toppled into the chapel during a violent storm on 18 February 1756. Soon afterwards the entire structure was demolished. The chapter's

4. Bourges Cathedral: *Traveller Attacked by Thieves* (detail) by the Good Samaritan Master, stained-glass window on north side of ambulatory, *c.* 1210

movable possessions, the interior furnishings, monuments and stained glass were then removed to the cathedral, where an inventory was made, but none of the documents connected with these events mentions the sculpture that adorned the building. The visual evidence, however, in the form of manuscript illuminations that may represent the chapel, 17th- and 18th-century paintings and drawings and a wooden model of 1766 (Bourges, Hôtel Jacques Coeur), does show that there was a variety of sculpture on both the exterior and interior. Although disagreeing on details, the sources all agree that a series of life-size statues of the 12 Apostles was attached to the main piers of the building's interior.

There is only the most precarious circumstantial evidence, however, to indicate that the sculptural fragments that have subsequently been identified with the building were originally part of its fabric. These comprise the head of an angel (ex-Hervet priv. col., Bourges), five small statues of prophets and the head of a sixth, two other heads (h. *c.* 340–360 mm; all now Bourges, Mus. Berry) and one or two of six statues now on the right jamb of the central portal of the cathedral's west façade. One of the six prophet figures in particular (see fig. 5) is almost certainly by Beauneveu, because its style closely resembles that of the first 24 miniatures representing seated prophets and Apostles in a Psalter of the Duc de Berry (Paris, Bib. N., MS. fr. 13091) documented to Beauneveu in the Duke's inventories. With this figure may be grouped some of the other prophet statues. Any remaining attributions must be tentative, although two of the prophets have some of the characteristics of Jean de Cambrai's style. If these prophet statues did indeed come from the chapel, they would have been placed either in the central portal or included as part of the exterior decoration on the windows of the oratories erected for the Duc and Duchesse.

See also SAINTE-CHAPELLE.

BIBLIOGRAPHY
A. de Champeaux and P. Gauchery: *Les Travaux d'art exécutés pour Jean de France, duc de Berry, avec une étude biographique sur les artistes employés par ce prince* (Paris, 1894)
P. Gauchery: 'Mémoire historique et descriptif du palais construit à Bourges pour Jean de France, duc de Berry', *Mém. Soc. Antiqua. Cent.*, xxi (1895–6), pp. 75–101
——: 'Le Palais du duc Jean et la Sainte-Chapelle de Bourges', *Mém. Soc. Antiqua. Cent.*, xxxix (1919–20), pp. 37–77
——: 'Renseignements complémentaires sur la vie et les travaux de Jean de France, duc de Berry, d'après les documents nouveaux', *Mém. Soc. Antiqua. Cent.*, xl (1921), pp. 195–211
G. Troescher: *Die burgundische Plastik des ausgehenden Mittelalters und ihre Wirkungen auf die europäische Kunst*, 2 vols (Frankfurt am Main, 1940)
——: 'Drei Apostelköpfe aus der Sainte-Chapelle in Bourges', *Jb. Preuss. Kstsamml.*, lxiii (1942), pp. 79–89
S. Scher: 'André Beauneveu and Claus Sluter', *Gesta*, vii (1968), pp. 3–14
M. Meiss: *French Painting in the Time of Jean de Berry: The Late Fourteenth Century and the Patronage of the Duke*, 2 vols (London, 1969)
S. Scher: 'Un Problème de la sculpture en Berry: Les Statues de Morogues', *Rev. A.* [Paris], xiii (1971), pp. 11–24
——: 'Note sur les vitraux de la Sainte-Chapelle de Bourges', *Cah. Archéol. & Hist. Berry*, xxxv (1973), pp. 23–44
A. Erlande-Brandenburg: 'Jean de Cambrai, sculpteur de Jean de France, duc de Berry', *Mnmts Piot*, lxiii (1980), pp. 143–86
J.-Y. Ribault: 'André Beauneveu et la construction de la Sainte-Chapelle de Bourges: Précisions chronologiques', *Actes des journées internationales Claus Sluter: Dijon, 1992*, pp. 239–47

5. Statue of a prophet, attributed to André Beauneveu, limestone, h. 1.35 m, possibly from Sainte-Chapelle, Bourges, *c.* 1390–1405 (Bourges, Musée du Berry)

S. Scher: 'Bourges et Dijon: Observations sur les relations entre André Beauneveu, Jean de Cambrai et Claus Sluter', *Actes des journées internationales Claus Sluter: Dijon, 1992*, pp. 277–93

STEPHEN K. SCHER

3. ST URSIN. The collegiate church of St Ursin, founded in the 6th century and rebuilt in the 11th, was demolished in 1781. According to Nicolas Catherinot, a large cross with a central medallion containing the Lamb of God adorned the gable of the façade. This was a regional device: examples dating from the mid-12th century survive

at Avord, St Michel, Chârost, Jussy-Champagne, Vornay and the collegiate church of Notre-Dame, Mehun-sur-Yèvre, all within 25 km of Bourges.

The only substantial surviving fragment of St Ursin is the Romanesque portal, which was transferred to the gardens of the Prefecture in 1810. The architectural design is similar to that of the comparatively plain west doorway of St Blaise, La Celle-Bruère. The inner order of the portal is framed by a simple archivolt carried by coursed columns with squat acanthus capitals. The shafts are carved in shallow relief with quadrupeds entangled in undulating vine stems that produce rounded, polylobe leaves and bunches of grapes. The outer faces of the doorposts are carved with similar foliage: trilobe leaves curl into medallions, some of which contain beasts. The upper courses of the doorposts, which slope forwards to compensate for the discrepancy with the plane of the tympanum, are also carved with quadrupeds. On the inner faces of the doorposts are plain engaged half-columns carrying squat foliate capitals. The lintel, composed of nine blocks of stone, is carved with a thick-stemmed *rinceau* sprouting trilobe leaves and dotted with spheres. A very similar *rinceau* decorates a capital in the nave of the church at Saint-Genou, west of Bourges. The tympanum, surrounded by a flat band of voussoirs and a band of *rinceaux*, is divided into three coursed registers. The secular subject-matter is extremely unusual. At the top are scenes from the beast epic *Le Renard*: on the left a donkey (or perhaps Ysengrin the wolf) sits on his hindquarters and addresses two smaller beasts; in the centre a crane plunges its beak into Renard's throat to extract a bone, and on the right is the funeral of Renard. In this last scene Renard, playing dead, is ready to pounce on the cock Chantecler and his wife, who are drawing the hearse. Leading the procession is Brun the bear. In the middle register is a boar and deer hunt clearly inspired by antique sarcophagus reliefs. It has been suggested that a hunt depicted on a sarcophagus in St Etienne, Déols, provided the model. On the lower register, under an arcade and identified by inscriptions, are the *Labours of the Months*, beginning with February (warming) and ending with January (feasting). Overlapping the lower border of the tympanum and the keystone of the lintel is a stone bearing the inscription GIRAVLDVS FECIT ISTAS PORTAS; this is probably the signature of the sculptor. Giraldus's flat technique, in which the carving is largely restricted to two planes, may have been influenced by ivories. Although the portal is usually dated to the late 11th century on stylistic grounds, it was probably carved in the second quarter of the 12th century.

BIBLIOGRAPHY

N. Catherinot: *Annales typographiques de Bourges* (Bourges, 1683/*R* Chicago, 1942)
R. Crozet: *L'Art roman en Berry* (Paris, 1932), pp. 297–301
J. Favière: *Berry roman*, Nuit Temps (La Pierre-qui-Vire, 1970), pp. 213–14

KATHRYN MORRISON

4. HÔTEL JACQUES COEUR. The 'grant maison' built in his native city from 1443 to 1451 by the banker JACQUES COEUR is a rare example of a late medieval urban residence. It is well preserved, its size and the richness of its decoration are exceptional, and it is a closely dated building, erected in a single campaign. In conception it looks back to the castles (destr.) built for Jean, Duc de Berry, by Guy and Drouet de Dammartin and forward to developments in the 16th century. The house was only just finished at the time of Jacques Coeur's arrest in 1451; it was mutilated and altered when it was used as the city hall (1682–1858) and later as the court-house (1858–1920). Major restorations were executed in 1858–70 and 1927–38; the last returned the building to its original state.

It lies between the Gallo-Roman city wall to the west and a street to the east and is an irregular quadrangle in plan (60×40 m). The buildings are arranged around a courtyard, with the principal range of apartments built on the former city wall, following its irregular course and connected to it by two of the towers. The west façade (see fig. 6), dominated on the north by the tower-donjon and its hexagonal upper storey, resembles a feudal castle and brings to mind the nearby castle of Mehun-sur-Yèvre (Cher; ruined), built by the Duc at the end of the 14th century, the appearance of which is known from the Très Riches Heures (Chantilly, Mus. Condé, MS. 65, fol. 161*v*). The contrast with the side of the house facing the city is great. The square entrance pavilion, with a chapel in the upper storey, rises above the long plain façade (40 m) that follows the curve of the street. The double passageway is surmounted by a large niche under a canopy, which sheltered an equestrian statue of *Charles VII* (destr.), and a window into the chapel, the tracery of which has a pattern of a large fleur-de-lis and two hearts. These marks of allegiance to the sovereign are accompanied by the personal emblems of the banker (hearts and scallop shells; canting arms) and his motto set on the sills below the

6. Bourges, west range of the Hôtel Jacques-Coeur, 1443–51

windows and on the parapets (rest.). The carved figures of a man and a woman, leaning out of false windows and observing the street from the first floor of the pavilion, belong to a more picturesque genre. The refined decoration of the upper stages of an elegant stair turret at roof-level recalls the tops of the towers of the castle at Mehun-sur-Yèvre.

The arrangement of the courtyard, even though irregular, heralded that of the later town house: private apartments at the back and low wings adjoining the entrance pavilion on the other three sides. The façade of the main apartments, with three projecting stair-turrets, has an abundant variety of still completely medieval decoration on the window sills of the large spiral stair (in the centre), the bas-reliefs of which illustrate the origins of Jacques Coeur's fortune (e.g. exotic trees, spinners, fullers of cloth), and especially on the high parts of the turrets, where the decoration (polylobed arches, finely arcaded blind cornices, pierced balustrades) was also inspired by the towers of Mehun. By contrast, the three front wings that shelter the galleries are distinguished by regular bays (depressed arches and casement windows with lozenged sills) and sober decoration. Later developments are anticipated in the latticework effect achieved by crossing horizontal and vertical elements and in the new role of the galleries, which are no longer simple passages but wide (5 m) areas of circulation, independent of the other parts of the building.

The interior plan is arranged around the two state rooms at the centre, which are based on those at the Duc de Berry's palace near by (destr.). The decoration (mostly rest.) of the great banqueting-hall on the ground floor is another form of homage to the King, whose emblems (rose trees, iris, fleurs-de-lis and winged deer) are found on the frieze of the monumental fireplace (in the form of a fortified castle, like those of the ducal palace) and on the adjacent door (de Mérindol). The arrangement of the apartments on either side of the two halls shows great concern for privacy, with garderobes and access to individual rooms by passages and spiral staircases in the thickness of the rear wall.

The high galleries, covered by four-centred wooden vaults and provided with fireplaces, connect the apartments with the chapel, which is 5 m square, with two small vaulted oratories in the thickness of the side walls (as in the Duc's two Saintes-chapelles at Bourges and Riom). The patterned vault (as at Riom), in two bays, is entirely painted with a flight of angels (rest. 1869), which Grodecki attributed to the author of the cartoons for the stained glass of the Jacques Coeur Chapel in Bourges Cathedral, a painter who was possibly trained in the circle of Jan van Eyck.

BIBLIOGRAPHY

Hazé: *Notices pittoresques sur les antiquités et les monuments du Berri* (Bourges, 1834), pp. 20–48, pls 10–37
P. Gauchery: 'L'Hôtel Jacques Coeur de Bourges: Nouveaux documents sur son état primitif, ses restaurations, ses mutilations', *Mém. Soc. Antiqua. Cent.*, xxxviii (1917–18), pp. 155–88
M. Aubert and G. Duhem: 'Deux Etuves du moyen âge conservées en France', *Bull. Mnmtl*, lxxxviii (1929), pp. 479–82
A. Gandilhon: 'Un Etat des lieux de l'hôtel Jacques-Coeur à Bourges dressé en 1636', *Bull. Philol. & Hist.* (1930–31), pp. 159–71
A. Gandilhon and R. Gauchery: 'L'Hôtel Jacques Coeur', *Congr. Archéol. France*, xciv (1931), pp. 56–104

P. Chenu: 'Une Vue inédite de la façade ouest de l'hôtel Jacques Coeur', *Mém. Soc. Hist. Cher*, n.s. 3, iv (1936), pp. 119–23
H. Huignard: 'La Restauration de l'hôtel Jacques Coeur à Bourges', *Mnmts Hist. France*, iii (1938), pp. 151–68
S. Pajot: 'La Sculpture en Berry à la fin du moyen âge et au début de la Renaissance', *Mém. Soc. Antiqua. Cent.*, xlviii (1938–41), pp. 89–106
M. Mollat: *Les Affaires de Jacques Coeur: Journal du procureur Dauvet*, 2 vols (Paris, 1952–3)
J. Y. Ribault: 'Chantiers et maîtres d'oeuvre à Bourges durant la première moitié du XVe siècle: De la Sainte-Chapelle au Palais Jacques Coeur', *93e Congrès national des sociétés savantes: Section d'archéologie: Tours, 1968*, pp. 387–410
C. Schaefer: 'Le Livre d'heures dit de Jacques Coeur, de la Bibliothèque de Munich', *Bull. Soc. N. Antiqua. France* (1971), pp. 143–56
B. Callède: 'Etudes des peintures murales dans la chapelle de l'hôtel Jacques Coeur à Bourges', *Stud. Conserv.*, xx (1975), pp. 195–200
L. Grodecki: 'Le Maître des vitraux de Jacques Coeur', *Études d'art français offertes à Charles Sterling* (Paris, 1975), pp. 105–25
C. de Mérindol: 'L'Emblématique des demeures et chapelles de Jacques Coeur: Une Nouvelle Lecture: La Grande Loge de Montpellier et les monuments de Bourges', *110e Congrès national des sociétés savantes: Section d'histoire médiévale: Montpellier, 1985*, ii, pp. 153–78
W. Prinz, R. G. Kecks and U. Albrecht: *Das französische Schloss der Renaissance: Form und Bedeutung der Architektur* (Berlin, 1985), pp. 52–6
J. Y. Ribault: 'L'hôtel Jacques Coeur', *Architecture en région centre*, ed. J. M. Pérouse de Montclos (Paris, 1988), pp. 213–20
C. de Mérindol: 'Nouvelles observations sur l'hôtel Jacques Coeur à Bourges: l'hommage au roi', *Bull. Soc. N. Antiqua. France* (1989), pp. 189–210
J. Favière: *L'Hôtel de Jacques Coeur à Bourges* (Paris, 1992)

CATHERINE GRODECKI

Bourgevin de Vialart, Charles Paul Jean-Baptiste, Comte de Saint-Morys. *See* SAINT-MORYS, CHARLES PAUL JEAN-BAPTISTE DE BOURGEVIN VIALART DE.

Bourguignon, Hubert-François. *See* GRAVELOT.

Bourke, Brian (*b* Dublin, 27 Nov 1936). Irish painter, sculptor and printmaker. He studied at the National College of Art in Dublin and St Martin's School of Art and Goldsmith's College in London. His early paintings, which included landscapes such as *Winter* (*c.* 1966; Dublin, Allied Irish Bank) and life-size nude self-portraits, were indebted to German Expressionism and to the work of Alberto Giacometti in their warm-toned colours and loose application of paint or pastel. These were followed by painted and sculpted portraits of his wife and friends in bronze or fibreglass, such as *Head of L.T.* (1971; Dublin, Dawson Gal.). From 1971 he concentrated on a recurring image of a small, primitive sculpture as a sign for himself, reduced in mocking fashion to a formalized bust or head. He related this fascination with identity to the character of Don Quixote, for example in the painted wood sculpture *Don Quixote* (1980–81; Dublin, Allied Irish Bank); sometimes he conceived of this image as two selves, as in the etching *Knight and Squire* (1979), in which the emaciated Don is contrasted with his sanguine servant. Similar moods were conveyed in his later ink drawings, *Out of the Head* (see 1985 exh. cat.), in which he imitated Renaissance profiles in their exactitude of line and emphasis on perspective.

BIBLIOGRAPHY

The Delighted Eye: Irish Painting and Sculpture of the Seventies (exh. cat. by F. Ruane, Dublin, A. C. Ireland, 1980)
J. White: *Brian Bourke* (Dublin, 1981)
Brian Bourke—Out of the Head: Artist's Response—6 (exh. cat., Dublin, A. C. Ireland, 1985)

HILARY PYLE

Bourke-White [née White], **Margaret** (*b* New York, 14 June 1904; *d* Darien, CT, 27 Aug 1971). American photographer. She studied at Columbia University, New York (1921–22), where she was influenced by Clarence H. White's photography course. After attending a number of colleges she decided in 1927 to pursue a career in photography and moved to Cleveland, OH, where she set up a photographic studio. Her industrial images caught the attention of Henry Luce (1898–1967), the founder of *Time* and *Fortune* magazines, and he invited her to become the first staff photographer for *Fortune* in 1929.

In 1930 *Fortune* paid for Bourke-White to photograph German industry, for example *Workmen in the AEG Plant* (1930; see Silverman, p. 39). Although the editors were interested in a project on the USSR, they doubted that the Soviet authorities would grant the permission to photograph industry there. Bourke-White decided to pursue the matter and photographed subjects such as *Dam at Dnieperstroi* (1930; see Silverman, p. 42). Her experience was recorded in *Eyes on Russia* (New York, 1931). In 1930 she established a photographic studio in the Chrysler building in New York. She visited Russia again in 1931 and in 1932 and then in 1941.

Although both Paul Strand and Charles Sheeler had created classic machine-age compositions, Bourke-White brought new drama and action to her industrial work for *Fortune*. In 1934, however, the magazine commissioned her to photograph the area of the American Midwest known as the Dust Bowl. It was this story documenting the great drought and rural exodus that changed her attitude towards the role of the photographic essay, which she pioneered as a medium to examine social issues from a humanitarian perspective.

When Luce launched *Life* magazine in 1936 Bourke-White joined the staff, and her *Fort Peck Dam, Montana* (Chicago, IL, A. Inst.) appeared on the first cover. Also in the late 1930s she collaborated with the writer Erskine Caldwell (*b* 1903), her husband from 1939 to 1942, on four projects: *You Have Seen their Faces* (New York, 1937), which included such photographs as *Maiden Lane, Georgia* (1936; see Callahan, p. 93), *North of the Danube* (New York, 1939), a photographic study of the conflict in the Sudetenland, *Say, is this the USA* (New York, 1941) and *Russia at War* (London, n.d.).

From 1942 to 1945 Bourke-White was a war correspondent, accredited first to the US Army Air Force. On assignment for *Life*, she worked in Britain, Germany, North Africa and Italy. She photographed images such as *Harbour of Naples* (1944; see Silverman, p. 143) and in 1945 the concentration camps of *Erla* (see Silverman, pp. 164–5) and *Buchenwald* (see Silverman, p. 166). Visits to India (1946 and 1947–8) and South Africa (1949–50) produced two of her most penetrating and renowned images: *Mahatma Gandhi Spinning* (1946; Chicago, IL, A. Inst., see 1985 exh. cat., no. 8), and *A Mile Underground* (1950; see 1985 exh. cat., no. 9), from a series on the Kimberley Diamond Mine, South Africa. In 1969 Parkinson's disease forced her to retire.

For illustration of work *see* PHOTOGRAPHY, fig. 25.

WRITINGS
Portrait of Myself (New York, 1963)

BIBLIOGRAPHY
S. Callahan, ed.: *The Photographs of Margaret Bourke-White* (New York, 1972)
J. Silverman: *For the World to See: The Life of Margaret Bourke-White*, preface A. Eisenstaedt (London and New York, 1983)
A Collective Vision: Clarence H. White and his Students (exh. cat., ed. L. Barnes, C. Glenn and J. Bledsoe; Long Beach, CA State U., A. Mus., 1985)
V. Goldberg: *Margaret Bourke-White: A Biography* (New York, 1986)
CONSTANCE W. GLENN

Bourla, Pierre (Bruno) (*b* Paris, 19 Dec 1783; *d* Antwerp, 31 Dec 1866). Belgian architect. He completed his architectural training in Paris under Charles Percier-Bassant, settled in Belgium in 1816 and soon distinguished himself by winning competitions in Ghent (1817, 1818) and Antwerp (1819). In 1819 he was appointed municipal architect to the City of Antwerp and professor at the local Academie voor Schone Kunsten (for which he designed a museum and gateway in 1841). As the most important architect in Antwerp of his generation, he was responsible for a wide variety of works in the city, ranging from an extensive remodelling (from 1824) of the 16th-century Stadhuis and the restoration (1827) of the Gothic Cathedral to the improvement of the wharves, docks and residential streets (1829–51); he also designed schools (1828–9, 1845) and several prominent public buildings. Bourla's masterpiece is the Koninklijke Nederlandsche Schouwburg (Royal Dutch Theatre; 1827–34), Komedieplaats, Antwerp. With a plan based on Parisian models and a polychromatic exterior, reflecting the far-reaching influence of Percier and Pierre-François Fontaine, it is a salient example of the transition from austere Neoclassicism to the more plastic, romantic or eclectic classical style in European architecture.

BIBLIOGRAPHY
E. Beausacq: 'Levensschets van Pieter Bourla', *Vl. Sch.*, xiv (1868), pp. 2–4
Een eeuw openbare werken te Antwerpen (exh. cat., Antwerp, Stedel. Festzaal, 1964), i, pp. 31–3
ALFRED WILLIS

Bourne, John Cooke (*b* London, 1814; *d* Feb 1896). English painter and lithographer. He was a pupil of John Pye, the landscape engraver, and was influenced by the watercolours of Thomas Girtin and John Sell Cotman. Bourne became a fine draughtsman, with an individual vision and understanding of the changing landscapes created by the expansion of the railways. He was encouraged by the antiquarian John Britton to translate his colour-wash drawings into lithographs, for Britton's *Drawings of the London and Birmingham Railway* (1839). The drawings contain a wealth of technical and social detail of the engineering work in progress. Bourne also illustrated Britton's *The History and Description of the Great Western Railway* (1846) with lithographs of Isambard Kingdom Brunel's completed railway, showing accurate technical information on rolling-stock and civil engineering works (for illustration *see* VIADUCT). Robert Hay's *Illustrations of Cairo* (1840) also had lithographs by Bourne.

In 1847 Bourne accompanied the engineer Charles Vignoles to Russia where, for 12 years, he was resident artist on civil engineering projects, and where he took some photographs of the projects that were exhibited at the Royal Photographic Society exhibition in London in 1854. After his return to England he achieved a modest reputation as a landscape watercolourist. When he died, his early railway prints were forgotten, but they remain his most original work.

BIBLIOGRAPHY
F. D. Klingender: *Art and the Industrial Revolution* (St Albans, 1972/R 1975), pp. 133–42
The Navvies Build: J. C. Bourne's Railway Drawings (exh. cat., Telford, Ironbridge Gorge Mus., 1980) [Elton col.]

JOHN FORD

Bourne, Samuel (*b* Mucklestone, Staffs, 1834; *d* Nottingham, 24 April 1912). English photographer. He photographed extensively in India between 1863 and 1869 and is known for the elegant compositional structure of his images and for the rugged conditions under which he worked. He began photographing in 1853 in the Midlands. A decade later he moved to India and established a photographic firm in Simla with Charles Shepherd. His legendary Himalayan expeditions in 1863, 1864 and 1866 produced hundreds of dramatic views (London, V&A). His architectural studies were widely sold; his mountain landscapes and ethnographic studies, few of which survive, sold less well. On returning to England in 1870 he left the partnership of Bourne and Shepherd and became a successful manufacturer, although continuing to work as a photographer and watercolour painter until his death.

BIBLIOGRAPHY
C. Worswick and A. Embree: *The Last Empire: Photography in British India, 1855–1911* (New York, 1977)
Samuel Bourne: Photographic Views in India (1834–1912) (exh. cat. by R. Taylor, Sheffield City Polytechnic, 1980)
Samuel Bourne, in Search of the Picturesque (exh. cat. by S. I. Williams, Williamstown, Clark A. Inst., 1981)
P. F. Heathcote: 'Samuel Bourne of Nottingham', *Hist. Phot.*, vi/2 (1982), pp 99–112
A. Ollman: *Samuel Bourne, Images of India* (Carmel, 1983)

ARTHUR OLLMAN

Boursse, Esaias (*b* Amsterdam, 3 March 1631; *d* at sea, 16 Nov 1672). Dutch painter and draughtsman. Boursse was the son of Walloon parents, Jacques Boursse and Anne de Forest. A testimony of 23 July 1658 states that Esaias's brother Jan provided for his artistic training. There is nothing to confirm a view of the early 20th-century scholars Bode, Bredius and Valentiner that Boursse was a pupil of Rembrandt, although the two artists may have had some contact, since Rembrandt lived near Jan in Amsterdam. According to an inventory of 24 November 1671, Jan collected a number of paintings, drawings and etchings by Rembrandt.

Esaias entered the Amsterdam Guild of St Luke about 1651 and shortly thereafter travelled to Italy; he returned to Amsterdam about 1653. His paintings usually depict women quietly performing household tasks in intimate middle-class interiors. He also illustrated outdoor activities with figures in small courtyards and alleyways. His subject-matter and composition, well-appointed domestic space and backlighting by means of a window or door, recall the late 1650s style of Pieter de Hooch, who possibly influenced him. However, most of his domestic interiors are not as orderly as de Hooch's, his figures are more solemn, and his painting technique has a rougher surface texture

and darker tonality. Most of Boursse's paintings appear to have been produced in the late 1650s. Three are dated: *Woman Cooking beside an Unmade Bed* (1656; London, Wallace), *Woman Scraping Radishes* (1658; sold R. H. Ward, Amsterdam, 19 May 1934) and *Interior with Woman at a Spinning Wheel* (1661; Amsterdam, Rijksmus.).

Esaias drew up a will in 1661 before embarking as a midshipman in the service of the Dutch East India Company. During this voyage he made drawings of the inhabitants of Ceylon (Sri Lanka) as well as a view of the Cape of Good Hope; these works are listed in Jan's inventory of 1671. Esaias returned to Amsterdam on 18 July 1663. On 24 October 1672 he went on a second trip for the East India Company. He died aboard ship.

BIBLIOGRAPHY
NKL; Thieme-Becker
W. von Bode and A. Bredius: 'Esaias Boursse, ein Schüler Rembrandts', *Jb. Kön.-Preuss. Kstsamml.*, xxvi (1905), pp. 205–14
W. R. Valentiner: 'Esaias Boursse', *A. America*, i (1913), pp. 30–39
A. Bredius: *Künstler-Inventare: Urkunden zur Geschichte der holländischen Kunst des XVIten, XVIIten, und XVIIIten Jahrhunderts*, i (The Hague, 1915), pp. 120–26
W. R. Valentiner: 'Dutch Painters of the School of Pieter de Hooch (Part I: Esaias Boursse)', *A. America*, xvi (1928), pp. 168–80
F. G. Waller: 'De familie van de schilders Boursse en de Nise', *Mdbl. Ned. Leeuw*, l (1932), col. 237–43
Tot lering en vermaak: Betekenissen van Hollandse genrevoorstellingen uit de 17de eeuw [For instruction and pleasure: meanings of Dutch genre paintings of the 17th century] (exh. cat. by E. de Jongh and others, Amsterdam, Rijksmus., 1976), pp. 44–9
Masters of 17th-Century Dutch Genre Painting (exh. cat. by P. Sutton and others, Philadelphia, PA, Mus. A.; W. Berlin, Gemäldegal.; London, RA; 1984), pp. 155-6

C. VON BOGENDORF RUPPRATH

Bousseau, Jacques (*b* La Crépelière, Chavagnes-en-Paillers, 17 March 1681; *d* Valsaín, Spain, 13 Feb 1740). French sculptor. He studied with Nicolas Coustou and won the Prix de Rome in 1705 with a low relief of *Judith before Holofernes* (untraced). He was in Rome from 1709 to 1712 and at the Villa Borghese made a marble copy of the Antique group of the *Centaur with Cupid* (completed 1712; untraced since 1858), which was installed in the park at Marly in 1715.

On his return to Paris, Bousseau was accepted (*agrée*) by the Académie Royale in 1713 and received (*reçu*) as a full member in 1715 on presentation of a marble statue of a *Soldier Bending his Bow* (Paris, Louvre). This well-received work, of which the noted collector Lalive de Jully owned a terracotta version, has a dynamic, Rococo quality in the treatment of the swirling drapery, and in the multiplicity of planes of which it is composed, that owes much to Coustou (e.g. *Meleager Slaying the Stag*, marble; Marly-le-Roi, Parc). From 1715 to 1720 he worked with Antoine Coyzevox.

In 1726 Bousseau completed the marble group *Zephyr and Flora* (Paris, priv. col., see Souchal, i, p. 59) left unfinished by René Frémin and Philippe Bertrand. At the same period he worked for the Cardinal de Noailles on the decoration of the family chapel in Notre-Dame, Paris (dismantled; marble statues of St Maurice and St Louis, both 1729, Choisy-le-Roi, church), and soon afterwards received commissions for two monumental marble statues of *Magnanimity* (1726–30) and *Religion* (1731–6) for the vestibule of the chapel at Versailles (the former *in situ*; the latter now Paris, Dôme des Invalides).

Also dating from the 1720s and sharing the same stylistic characteristics derived from Coustou is the marble *Angel* (Paris, Saint-Denis) that is the only surviving fragment of the monument for the heart of Count René d'Argenson (*d* 1721) once in the church of the convent of les Filles de la Madeleine (du Trainel) in Paris.

In 1736, at the suggestion of Frémin, who had been working for Philip V of Spain since 1721, Bousseau was invited to complete the sculptural decoration of the gardens at the palace of La Granja de San Ildefonso near Madrid begun by Frémin and Thierry. In April 1738 Bousseau was made Premier Sculpteur du Roi and worked at both La Granja and Aranjuez (where he executed two groups of *Nymphs Playing with Dragons* in lead). At La Granja he completed works designed or left unfinished by his predecessors as well as creating a number of new statues, which were themselves in some cases finished after his death by his successors Hubert Dumandré and Pierre Pitué. Outstanding among the works attributable to Bousseau at La Granja are the fourteen marble statues, at L'Allée Longue, especially the four graceful *Nymphes*, and the pretty, Rococo lead statues of the nymphs of the *Baths of Diana*.

Lami

BIBLIOGRAPHY

M. Digard and J. Digard: 'Les Travaux du sculpteur Jacques Bousseau dans les jardins royaux d'Espagne', *Gaz. B.-A.*, 6th ser., lxxix (1937), pp. 315–28
R. Crozet: 'Le Sculpteur Jacques Bousseau, 1681–1740', *Rev. Bas-Poitou*, (Jan 1944), pp. 3–12
Y. Bottineau: *L'Art de cour L'Espagne de Philippe V 1700–1746* (Bordeaux, [1960], Paris 2/1992), pp. 559–63
F. Souchal: 'A propos de Jacques Bousseau . . .', *Philippe V d'Espagne et l'art de son temps* (Sceaux, 1995), pp. 221–32

GUILHEM SCHERF

Boussingault, Jean-Louis (*b* Paris, 9 March 1883; *d* Paris, 17 May 1943). French painter and illustrator. He was trained in Paris at the Ecole des Arts Décoratifs and then at the Académie Julian. In 1901 he studied lithography and from 1902 to 1903 did his military service, through which he met André Dunoyer de Segonzac. In 1904 he studied under Luc Olivier Merson and Jean-Paul Laurens at the Académie Julian with Dunoyer de Segonzac and there met Luc-Albert Moreau. These three artists became close friends and adopted a similar naturalist style that was maintained through the rise of Cubism. From 1906 to 1908 Boussingault shared a studio with Dunoyer de Segonzac, and in the summer of 1908 all three went on a painting trip to St Tropez.

Boussingault was rarely satisfied with his work and destroyed many of his paintings. He first exhibited at the Salon des Indépendants in 1909 and later at the Salon d'Automne and regularly at the Galerie Marseilles in Paris. From 1911 to 1913 he worked on a vast decorative panel, *Promenade* (see Huyghe and Bazin, p. 287), commissioned by the couturier Paul Poiret, which was exhibited at the Salon d'Automne in 1913. He frequented the fashionable bars and race-tracks of Paris, becoming a chronicler of Parisian life through his paintings and contributions to the journals *Le Témoin*, *Panurge*, and *Schekerezade*. He also painted still-lifes, flower pictures and portraits. As a book illustrator Boussingault provided lithographs and engravings for J.-L. Duplan's *Tableau de la vénerie* in 1923, for Léon-Paul Fargue's *D'après Paris* in 1931 (see Lake and Maillard, p. 40) and for Charles Baudelaire's *Le Spleen de Paris* in 1932; he also helped found the Société des Peintres-graveurs Indépendants. He was represented at the exhibition *L'Art indépendant: Maîtres d'aujourd'hui* in the Petit Palais in Paris on the occasion of the *Exposition internationale des arts et techniques dans la vie moderne* (1937) and at that time he designed a mural decoration for the Palais de Chaillot, Paris.

Bénézit; *DBF*

BIBLIOGRAPHY

R. Huyghe and G. Bazin: *Histoire de l'art contemporain* (Paris, 1935/*R* New York, 1968) pp. 285–6
C. Lake and R. Maillard: *A Dictionary of Modern Painting* (London, 1964)

□

Boussod, Valadon & Cie. French firm of dealers. In 1856 Léon Boussod (*b* Paris, 6 June 1826; *d* Paris, 1896) entered into partnership with Adolphe Goupil, and in 1861 they formed a company with Vincent van Gogh (1820–88), uncle of the painter Vincent van Gogh. René Valadon (1848–1921) married Boussod's daughter in 1875 and became an associate of the firm of Goupil in 1878. Boussod, Valadon & Cie was founded in 1884 by Boussod and Valadon, with Goupil and his son Albert Goupil (1806–84) as backers. The firm was a successor to that of Goupil, and after Adolphe Goupil's retirement in 1886 it continued to be known familiarly by that name. In 1886 Boussod brought his son Etienne Boussod (1857–1918) into the business. Another son, Jean Boussod (1860–1907) entered this tightly knit family business in 1887, followed by a son-in-law, Léon Avril (1856–1942). After Adolphe Goupil's death in 1893 the head office was established at 24, Boulevard des Capucines, and when Léon Boussod died in 1896, Valadon became Director. In 1898 Valadon formed a new company with Etienne Boussod and Auguste Avril; this lasted until 1919.

During the existence of their firm, Léon Boussod and Valadon continued the practices established by their predecessor Goupil. They dealt in the sale of prints, chiefly after artists popular in the Salons. They carried a stock of paintings chosen to please a particular clientele, both in Paris and abroad. They also specialized in aquatints. In 1886 Boussod set up the firm's photographic studio and its printing press at Asnières. He received the medal of the Légion d'honneur for his work on the techniques of photogravure and photoglypy, thus providing a link between the earlier 19th-century revival of printmaking and the mass reproduction of works of art characteristic of the late 19th century. The association with the dealer Vincent van Gogh helps to account for the number of works by artists of the Hague school bought and sold by the firm: Anton Mauve, a nephew of Boussod's by marriage, was one favourite; Jacob Maris was another. This taste was also encouraged by the presence of a young trainee manager, Elbert van Wisselingh, son of a prominent Dutch dealer. The contact with the Netherlands brought customers, as well as painters, into business relations with the firm: H. W. Mesdag, a painter and collector who was one of its most enthusiastic customers, bought a large part of his collection from the firm, now at the Rijksmuseum

Hendrik Willem Mesdag in The Hague. Mesdag's purchases were predominantly of pictures by artists of the Hague school (e.g. Jacob Maris, *Stone Mills*, *c*. 1870s; The Hague, Rijksms. Mesdag) and by contemporary French landscape painters (e.g. Corot, *In the Dunes*, *c*. 1855–65; The Hague, Rijksms. Mesdag), some of whom, notably Jean-François Millet, had been a formative influence on the Dutch.

The firm also had a branch in London, known as the Goupil Gallery, located at 116–117 New Bond Street. From 1878 to 1896 its director was David Croal Thomson (1855–1930), who had an interest in Dutch art, the work of the New English Art Club, and Whistler. In 1891 he was instrumental in the sale of Whistler's *Arrangement in Grey and Black. No. 1: Portrait of the Artist's Mother* (1872; Paris, Mus. d'Orsay) to the Musée du Luxembourg. In March 1892 the Goupil Gallery held a show of Whistler's 'Nocturnes, Marines & Chevalet Pieces', which was a great critical success. He also admired the work of the Barbizon school and published a book on the subject, *The Barbizon School of Painters* (London, 1890). The popularity of French and Dutch landscape painting among Scottish collectors may be accounted for by Thomson's interest, which he shared with Alexander Reid, a young dealer from Scotland who had also spent time at Boussod, Valadon & Cie in Paris. However, Thomson's attempts to promote Impressionism in Britain were not successful: in 1889 an exhibition of works by Monet attracted few visitors.

In Paris, Boussod, Valadon & Cie also dealt in the works of the Impressionists. This came about through the interests of Theo van Gogh (1854–91), who in 1878 had taken up a post at the Paris branch of Goupil. In 1884 he began to acquire works by Camille Pissarro and Alfred Sisley. Valadon began to take an interest in Monet, particularly after his reputation had been established towards the end of the 1880s, and in 1888, through Theo van Gogh, ten of Monet's recent landscapes of Antibes were bought for the firm and exhibited at their premises. Degas's works were also purchased, among them *Woman with Chrysanthemums* (1865; New York, Met.) in 1887. After Theo van Gogh's premature death in 1891, Maurice Joyant (1864–1930) took his place as buyer for the firm, and, although he sold off a number of Impressionist pictures, he continued to buy from Monet. In May and June 1892, the firm held an exhibition of works of Berthe Morisot. After Joyant left the firm in 1893 (*see* MANZI-JOYANT), it followed a policy of buying works of the Barbizon school and its followers, including those of Etienne Moreau-Nelaton, Alexander Young (*fl* 1889–93) and John Day. Important paintings by Corot, Jules Dupré and Charles-François Daubigny and by the Impressionists were part of the stock sold off at Boussod, Valadon & Cie's closing sale, held at the Galerie Georges Petit on 3 March 1919.

BIBLIOGRAPHY

D. Croal Thomson: *The Barbizon School of Painters* (London, 1890)

J. Rewald: 'Theo van Gogh, Goupil and the Impressionists', *Gaz. B.-A.*, n. s. 5, lxxxi (1973), pp. 1–108

S. Houfe: 'David Croal Thomson, Whistler's Aide-de-camp', *Apollo*, cxix (1984), pp. 112–19

'*Les Marchands de van Gogh*': *Van Gogh à Paris* (exh. cat. by M. Nonne, Paris, Mus. d'Orsay, 1988), pp. 330–45

LINDA WHITELEY

Bout, Pieter [Peeter] (*bapt* Brussels, 5 Dec 1658; *d* Brussels, 28 Jan 1719). Flemish painter, draughtsman and etcher. He enrolled at the Brussels guild of painters in 1671; his teacher is not known. From *c*. 1675 he spent several years in Paris, where he frequently collaborated with Adriaen Frans Boudewijns, a fellow countryman, as in the *Village Fair* (1686; Antwerp, Kon. Mus. S. Kst.), for which he painted the figures. He was then active in Brussels, where he married in 1695. He probably visited Italy.

Almost all Bout's dated works were made before 1700. He painted views of towns, villages, ports and beaches in the tradition of Jan Breughel I. They are similar to the paintings of Boudewijns and Jacques d'Arthois, for whom he also often painted staffage. He also painted Italianate landscapes in the manner of Nicolaes Berchem, such as the *Resting Place* (*c*. 1680; Amsterdam, Rijksms.). His paintings have an easy and lively character, and he used the brush with precision, as in the *Return of the Fishermen* (1677; Frankfurt am Main, Städel. Kstinst. & Städt. Gal.).

Thematically as well as compositionally, Bout's drawings and etchings are similar to the paintings; the drawings are usually in pen and wash, executed with close attention to detail, for example the *Beach Scene with Fish Merchants* (Rotterdam, Boymans–van Beuningen). There are five of his own etchings and three executed by A. F. Bargas (possibly his pupil) after his designs, characterized by fine, sketchy lines, in some places retouched with the burin. Also typical are the heavy, rather unsophisticated shadows.

BIBLIOGRAPHY

Hollstein: *Dut. & Flem.*; Thieme–Becker

R. van Eynden and A. van der Willigen: *De geschiedenis der vaderlandsche schilderkunst, sedert de helft der XVIIIde eeuw* (Haarlem, 1816–40), i, p. 128; iv, pp. 103–4

MANFRED SELLINK

Boutet de Monvel, (Louis-)Maurice (*b* Orléans, 18 Oct 1851; *d* Nemours, Seine-et-Marne, 16 March 1913). French painter and illustrator. From 1869 he took a course at the De Rudder school of art and in the following year was admitted to the Ecole des Beaux-Arts in Paris, where he worked in the atelier of Alexandre Cabanel. He took part in the Franco-Prussian War (1870–71) and afterwards studied under Jules Lefebvre, Gustave Boulanger and Carolus-Duran. From Carolus-Duran he acquired a liking for portraiture (e.g. *Rachel Boyer as Diana*, 1886; Paris, Louvre) and for the works of Ribera, which he admired particularly for their dark and resinous tones. From 1873 he exhibited at the Salon and in 1885 he created a stir with his *Apotheosis of a Scoundrel* (or *Apotheosis of Robert Macaire*; Orléans, Mus. B.-A.), a work imbued with a violently anti-republican spirit. As well as painting, he illustrated children's literature, beginning with the successful *La France en zig-zags* (1881). Other collections followed: *Vieilles chansons pour les petits enfants* and *Chansons de France pour les petits français* (both Paris, 1883), two books of songs for which he provided illustrations, and Anatole France's *Nos enfants: Scènes de la ville et des champs* (Paris, 1887). In these works, Boutet de Monvel's delicate and refined draughtsmanship enhanced the authors' delight in the world of children. He managed to retain the individuality of his subjects, using a modern style that was influenced by Japanese aesthetics. His fame spread quickly: numerous exhibitions were organized in Europe as well as in the USA, and many foreign editions of his works were published. His finest work is *La Vie de Jeanne d'Arc* (Paris, 1896), for which he provided both text and illustrations (drawings; Washington, DC, Corcoran Gal. A.).

BIBLIOGRAPHY

A. Nourrit: 'Artistes contemporains: Maurice Boutet de Monvel', *Rev. A. Anc. & Mod.*, xxxiv/2 (1913), pp. 133–48

Catalogue of a Collection of Drawings and Sketches by Louis Maurice Boutet de Monvel (exh. cat., Buffalo, Albright A.G., 1920)

D. Autie: 'Livres pour enfants: Maurice Boutet de Monvel et les petits enfants de la IIIe République', *Impact*, 13 (1977), pp. 36–8

F. C. Heller: 'Maurice Boutet de Monvel: Illustrateur de livres d'enfants', *Rev. Bib. N.* (Spring 1988), pp. 14–25

THALIE GOETZ

Bouthroton. *See* BUTRINT.

Bouts. Netherlandish family of painters. (1) Dieric Bouts the elder presumably trained in his native Haarlem. About 1447–8 he married Katharina van der Bruggen (*d* 1472), alias Metten Ghelde ('with the money'), the daughter of a wealthy citizen of Leuven in Brabant, where by 1457 he had settled and established a sizeable workshop. They had four children: Dieric Bouts II (*b c.* 1448–9; *d* 1491), (2) Albrecht Bouts, Katharina and Gertrud. After the death of his first wife, Dieric Bouts I married Elizabeth van Voshem, daughter of a former mayor of Leuven. They had no children. The sons of the first marriage were both trained as painters, and Dieric Bouts the younger apparently inherited his father's shop in 1475, while Albrecht established his own workshop, also in Leuven. Although Dieric II is mentioned in the archives of Leuven, no paintings can be assigned to him with certainty, whereas a number can be ascribed to Albrecht. At least one of Dieric II's sons, Jan Bouts (*b c.* 1478; *d c.* 1530), became a painter.

BIBLIOGRAPHY

E. van Even: *L'Ancienne Ecole de peinture de Louvain* (Brussels and Leuven, 1870) [documentation relating to whole family; also pubd in sections in *Messager Sci. Hist. Belgique* (1866), pp. 1–55, 241–338; (1867), pp. 261–315, 439–97; (1868), pp. 454–86; (1869), pp. 44–86, 147–95, 277–341]

W. Schöne: *Dieric Bouts und seine Schule* (Berlin and Leipzig, 1938) [also incl. many doc.]

(1) Dieric [Dierick; Dirk; Thierry; Theodoricus] **Bouts I** (*b* Haarlem, *c.* 1415; *d* 1475). He is mentioned several times in the archives of Leuven between 1457 and his death, although his name is sometimes confused with that of Hubrecht Steurbout, another painter in Leuven. In 1468 Bouts was named official painter to the city. A century later the chronicler in Leuven, Joannes Molanus, remarked that he 'excelled as an innovator in depicting the countryside'. Bouts was also described, by van Mander ([1603]–1604), as a founder of the Haarlem school of painting along with Albert van Ouwater and Geertgen tot Sint Jans. However, it is his representation of landscape that is still recognized as his principal contribution to 15th-century Netherlandish painting.

1. Life and work. 2. Working methods and technique. 3. Posthumous reputation.

1. LIFE AND WORK.

(i) Early works, before *c.* 1460. (ii) Mature works, after *c.* 1460.

(i) Early works, before c. *1460.* The date of Dieric's departure from Haarlem is not known. He may have visited Leuven as early as 1444 but probably did not establish citizenship there until the mid-1450s. Several secondary sources refer to his close association with Haarlem. Among the famed Netherlandish artists named by Guicciardini (1567) is a 'Dirick da Lovano' and a 'Dirick d'Harlem', a confusion repeated by Vasari (1568). In the French edition of Guicciardini (Arnhem, 1613), Pierre du Mont added a note referring to a painting by Bouts that he had seen with episodes of the *Life of St Bavo* (untraced), which included the 'fair countryside around the town of Haarlem'. In the third edition of a book of portraits of famous Netherlandish artists (Dominicus Lampsonius' *Pictorum aliquot celebrium Germaniae inferioris effigies*, Antwerp, 1572) an inscription added beneath the engraved portrait of Bouts stated: *Floruit Harlemi et Lovanii an. 1462.* Van Mander, who called him 'Dirck van Haerlem', mentioned his famous house in Haarlem with its antique façade, and he further described a triptych by Bouts he had seen in Leyden, which was dated 1462 and signed 'Dirick, who was born in Haarlem, made me in Leuven'.

The attributions of works presumed to have been painted by Bouts in Haarlem in the 1440s are controversial. None is documented, and some have been attributed to Ouwater and Petrus Christus (another Netherlandish artist often linked to Haarlem), painters with whom Bouts shares many stylistic traits. The altarpiece of the *Virgin* (Madrid, Prado) is a triptych with scenes of the *Annunciation*, *Visitation*, *Nativity* and *Adoration of the Magi* (two on the central panel). The influence of Rogier van der Weyden is apparent in the simulated architectural frames with sculpted voussoirs and in the composition of the *Visitation*. The affinities with the art of Ouwater, however, are more revealing. Like him, Bouts painted stocky figures with large heads and fleshy hands, and a strong side light models the faces vividly. Resembling puppets, they move mechanically, with minimal gestures. Also like Ouwater, Bouts placed the figures back from the foreground in a deep space. Highly detailed landscapes form the backgrounds. A half-length *Virgin and Child* (Florence, Bargello; replica, New York, Met.) displays a similar peasant-like head type for Mary and the same stumpy fingers as in the Prado altarpiece. These features also appear in a copy of another *Virgin and Child* (New York, Met.), set in a chamber with a landscape view from a window.

The influence of Rogier van der Weyden is much stronger in the 1450s, perhaps indicating Dieric's closer contacts with Brabant and Leuven. The huge altarpiece of the *Deposition*, with the *Crucifixion* and *Resurrection* on the wings (Granada, Capilla Real; small replica, Valencia, Colegio del Patriarca), repeats the simulated architectural framework of Rogier, and several figures, including the group of John the Evangelist, the Virgin and the twisting Mary Magdalene under the Cross, are also quotations from works by van der Weyden. In the *Crucifixion* on the left wing, the swooning pose of Mary in the lower left corner repeats that of the fainting Virgin in Rogier's *Deposition* (Madrid, Prado), an influential work that was in Leuven in the mid-15th century. The distinctive features of the early Haarlem school persist, however, in the diagonal placement of the figures, the coarser and strongly modelled facial types and the detailed landscape background that extends continuously across the three panels. That both the Prado altarpiece and the Granada *Deposition* triptych were in Spanish collections by the late 16th century suggests that they may have been taken from Haarlem during the Spanish occupation of 1573.

Identical head types are found in the *Entombment* (London, N.G.), executed in tempera on linen. This was probably part of an ensemble (perhaps a triptych with side wings in two tiers) with a central *Crucifixion*. Two other works on canvas of nearly identical size, an *Annunciation* (Malibu, CA, Getty Mus.) and a *Resurrection* (Pasadena, CA, Norton Simon Mus.), have been considered by some scholars to be part of the same triptych. Another of Bouts's early works is a *Lamentation* (untraced, but known from many versions, e.g. Paris, Louvre), in which the mourners are stretched out and arranged in an inverted triangular plan that leads the eye back to the colourful landscape. The mechanical distribution of rigidly posed figures in space culminates in the triptych of the *Martyrdom of St Erasmus* (Leuven, collegiate church of St Peter). The frame carries an unverified (?early 20th century) inscription: *Opus Theodorici Bouts. Anno MCCCC4VIII* (?1448 or 1458), and the work very likely is one of Dieric's earliest commissions after establishing residence in Leuven. The theatrical aspects of the gruesome martyrdom are greatly tempered by the artificial detachment of the witnesses, who appear as actors symmetrically arranged in a tableau around the winch, parallel to the surface in the foreground, on which Erasmus lies. SS Jerome and Bernard stand calmly before landscapes in the wings.

(ii) Mature works, after c. 1460. The art of Dieric Bouts reached a synthesis in the 1460s. His masterpiece is the well-documented altarpiece of the *Holy Sacrament* (1464–8; Leuven, collegiate church of St Peter). Four members of the brotherhood of the Holy Sacrament in Leuven commissioned the triptych with instructions that the wings were to have Old Testament scenes serving as antetypes for the main panel, the *Last Supper* (see fig. 1). Bouts was advised by two professors of theology. Three of the Old Testament scenes were taken from the *Speculum humanae salvationis*—the *Gathering of Manna*, the *Meeting of Abraham and Melchizedek* and the *Feast of the Passover*—to which was added a fourth, *Elijah in the Desert*. The paintings on the outer sides of the wings, constituting a memorial of Old Testament oblations to the Lord, do not survive.

The Last Supper was a rare theme in Netherlandish art. In keeping with the brotherhood who commissioned it, Bouts concentrated on the institution of the sacrament of the Eucharist and was not concerned with the drama of Christ's announcement of the betrayals of Peter and Judas (Judas is hardly identifiable among the Apostles at the table) or with the emotional leavetaking of Christ from his disciples. Bouts carefully organized the composition to underscore the timeless qualities of the event. The Apostles

1. Dieric Bouts I: *Last Supper*, central panel from the altarpiece of the *Holy Sacrament*, oil on oak panel, 1.80×1.51 m, 1464–8 (Leuven, collegiate church of St Peter)

are lean, rigidly posed figures symmetrically placed about three sides of the square table placed in the centre of the room; their movements are frozen, with only the hands repeating stereotyped gestures of adoration. The heads are all of a similar type, with Christ slightly larger in scale and placed on the central axis before a cross formed by the decoration of the firescreen. Like a priest, he lifts the Host above the chalice with the wine to bless it. The scene is viewed from a high vantage-point, allowing the artist to mark out the deep perspective projection with the lines of the floor, walls and ceiling converging at a point on the mantel of the fireplace. Open windows and doors and a vestibule lend an airiness to the harsh confines of the room, and a bright light, flooding the interior from the left, models the space with highlights and shadows. Colours are bright and clear, details are sharp and precise. The unbearded servant directly to the right of Christ has been identified as the elder of the brotherhood, Rase van Baussele. The lone figure standing against the wall on the right has usually been identified as Bouts himself, while the two younger observers looking in from the kitchen window have been seen as his two sons. Appealing though these identifications may be, the three figures beyond the table are probably the other three *meesters* of the brotherhood who signed the contract. Two of them, Reyner Stoep and Stas Roelofs, were bakers, and they appropriately appear in the kitchen window.

The four side panels are truly original compositions in which Bouts transformed the simple groups of figures in the woodcut illustrations of the *Speculum humanae salvationis* into more complex studies of figures in landscapes and a domestic interior. The *Feast of the Passover* repeats on a smaller scale the setting for the *Last Supper*, with six puppet-like attendants placed discreetly on three sides of the square table. All elements of the Passover feast are presented, including the paschal lamb, the wild lettuce and the staves held by the participants. Their colourful costumes evoke the sense of some remote and exotic historical ritual. The other stories take place in deep landscapes, and they give some idea of why Bouts was praised as the inventor of landscape painting. Although he did not paint pure landscapes in the modern sense, his compositions can often be described as landscapes with figures rather than figures with landscapes. Jan van Eyck excelled in transforming the backgrounds of his paintings into vivid, far-distant landscapes seen through loggias or windows behind the large foreground figures. Bouts seems to have worked in reverse, mapping out a continuous landscape, with clearly marked stage wings or coulisses staggered in parallel planes along an undulating road that leads the eye into depth; the spaces between the coulisses create open cells in which he then placed the figures. The *Gathering of Manna* is a good example: the four foreground figures are not composed symmetrically or in a single plane but are

2. Dieric Bouts I: *Ordeal by Fire*, right panel of the *Justice of Emperor Otto III*, oil on oak panel, 3.24×1.82 m, 1471–3 (Brussels, Musée d'Art Ancien)

placed along diagonal axes. Behind the shallow mound that marks off the foreground, the other figures, gradually reduced in scale, are staggered throughout the expanse of landscape, creating a step-by-step projection from the foreground to the far distance. This was new. Furthermore, Bouts was aware of the dramatic moods evoked by the chromatic qualities of the sky, especially those of daybreak in the *Gathering of Manna* and early morning in *Elijah in the Desert*.

In 1468 Bouts received an important commission from the town council of Leuven. Three sets of panels were ordered, perhaps meant to rival the judgement panels painted by Rogier van der Weyden for the town hall in Brussels. Two pairs were to commemorate examples of justice administered in secular history, and the third was a triptych dedicated to the ultimate example of Christian justice, the *Last Judgement* (central panel, untraced; wings, perhaps those on dep. at Lille, Mus. B.-A. from Paris, Louvre; *see* BELGIUM, fig. 12). Documents record that Bouts completed the *Last Judgement* in 1470 and that at his death he was still working on the first pair on a secular theme, depicting the *Justice of Emperor Otto III* (both Brussels, Mus. A. Anc.). One panel of this, the *Ordeal by Fire*, was finished and installed in the town hall in 1473; the other, the *Execution of the Innocent Count*, was completed by assistants in 1481. Apparently the second set of secular histories was never begun.

An Augustinian doctor of theology in Leuven, Jan van Haeght, was appointed Dieric's adviser for the story of the Holy Roman Emperor Otto III. The legend, found in a chronicle by Godfrey of Viterbo (*d* 1191), relates the story of the false accusation made by the Holy Roman Empress against a count who had rejected her advances, for which he was then beheaded (first panel). The victim's widow went before the Emperor, and to establish the truth and to prove her husband's innocence she took the ordeal by fire, a medieval practice that involved holding a red-hot iron; Otto III, convinced of the miscarriage of justice, had his slanderous wife burnt at the stake (second panel). The *Ordeal by Fire* (see fig. 2) is set in a deep throne room rendered in single-point perspective. Three pairs of courtiers stand about the enthroned Otto III, while the countess, holding the red-hot iron in one hand, her husband's head in the other, kneels before him. Because of the painting's large format, Bouts had to design life-size figures in a narrow space, and the results were not wholly successful. The witnesses appear as long-limbed mannequins barely responding to the miraculous demonstration. One figure in each of the three groups appears to be a portrait of a town council member. In the distant landscape the Empress is burned at the stake. The *Execution of the Innocent Count* takes place outside the imperial palace. Behind the dwarfish walls stands the Empress, who utters the calumny to Otto III. To the left the count and his wife are led by a tonsured monk (identified as Dieric's adviser, Jan van Haeght) to the place of execution. The execution occurs in the foreground, and behind the countess, who receives the severed head from the executioner, stand six witnesses, clearly portraits of other council members. This is one of the earliest examples of the secular group portrait in Netherlandish art. The figures

3. Dieric Bouts I: *Virgin Nursing the Child*, oil on oak panel, 370×275 mm, 1460–65 (London, National Gallery)

of the infants in Rogier's versions of the subject. Her face, however, has a firmer bone structure than Rogier's Virgins: the forehead is wide and high, the eyes downcast with heavy lids and sockets. The figures' fingers retain a more fleshy appearance, reminiscent of Dieric's earlier works, and as if to compensate for the overly monumental characterization of the Virgin, Bouts rejected Rogier's abstract background and placed her in an open chamber with a brocaded wall hanging and an open window through which a poetic townscape is seen. Bouts sometimes placed Mary against a dark background (e.g. *Virgin and Child*, Washington, DC, N.G.A.), and the child often sprawls backward in a rather ungainly position (e.g. Cambridge, MA, Fogg) or plays with rosary beads (e.g. Copenhagen, Stat. Mus. Kst). The popularity of these standardized compositions might suggest that Bouts, like Rogier van der Weyden, combined a half-length Virgin with a half-length donor portrait in diptych form, but there is little evidence of this.

Of the few known portraits by Bouts, most are fragments from larger compositions, for example two male portraits (New York, Met.). In both, the heads face right, contrary to the established convention for devotional diptychs, in which the Virgin always appears on the left in keeping with hieratic order. The *Portrait of a Man* (1462;

are posed stiffly, next to one another, their heads portrayed in three-quarter view, creating an artificial and detached ensemble simply inserted into the narrative. The inept painting of the tall figure standing in the left foreground and the executioner in the centre is evidence that workshop assistants completed the panel. In 1480 Hugo van der Goes was called in to assess the completed panels for the council and the heirs of Dieric's workshop.

The two paintings tentatively identified as the wings of the *Last Judgement* depict the *Ascent of the Blessed into Paradise* (*see* BELGIUM, fig. 12) and the *Fall of the Damned*. The paradise of the left wing features one of Dieric's more idyllic landscapes, with an angel in rich brocades guiding a company of the blessed into a deep landscape with a Fountain of Life and a high mound from which other naked souls, tiny in scale, are escorted into the heavens to be received in an aureole of bright light. In the right panel, the damned, screaming and fighting, plunge headlong into an abyss of darkness. The appearance of the missing central panel is known from a crude copy of the whole triptych (Munich, Alte Pin.).

A speciality of Bouts and his workshop was the half-length Virgin and Child, a favourite Netherlandish theme. A distinct similarity to the work of Rogier van der Weyden characterizes the *Virgin Nursing the Child* (1460–65; London, N.G.; see fig. 3): Mary is no longer the plain, peasant-like woman of Dieric's earlier works but has the refined and elegant countenance of van der Weyden's Virgins, and the nude child's posture is as sprightly as that

4. Dieric Bouts I: *Portrait of a Man*, oil on panel, 318×203 mm, 1462 (London, National Gallery)

London, N.G.; see fig. 4) is certainly by Dieric's own hand and could have formed the right wing of a diptych. The softly modulated shadows describing the contours of the cheek and jaw, the fleshy hands and the upward gaze of the heavy-lidded eyes are familiar features in his paintings. The saintly man, however, inhabits the 'real' world: Bouts placed him in the corner of a room with an open window and a distant landscape. Unlike the portraits of Jan van Eyck or van der Weyden, in Dieric's the natural world encroaches on the character of man (as it does in fig. 2). This earthier approach to man and his religious experience reflects the homely character of the Dutch tradition to which Bouts belonged throughout his career.

2. WORKING METHODS AND TECHNIQUE. While many of Bouts's compositional devices owe much to van der Weyden, his technique is much more indebted to that of Jan van Eyck. Bouts's underdrawings are highly detailed, tight and controlled rather than fluid and lyrical, as are those of Rogier. And rather than applying the paint in broad blocks of colour controlled by elegant lines, Bouts, like van Eyck, gave depth and translucency to the surface by building up pigments in enamel-like layers. He was chiefly a colourist, a local colourist, in that his pigments are pure and saturated primary and secondary hues. His reds are bright scarlet or madder lake; his yellows are luminous and rich; his greens are deep and dark. The paint is put down with meticulous strokes that create a continuous flow of colour nuances similar to those of van Eyck. Through these subtle gradations Bouts captured the richness of different textures. His rendering of precious stones is crisp, yet they seem to glow within their polished surfaces. His skies are particularly appealing, with their soft atmospheric tonalities of specific times of the day. With softly graduated hues of red and orange, Bouts

achieved romantic early morning scenes; a deep blue hovering over a milky haze on the horizon enlivens his daytime settings.

It is perhaps Bouts's masterly control of warm local colours that distinguishes his works from those of his apprentices and followers. Surviving documents indicate that he ran a large workshop in Leuven. His sons apparently headed the list of apprentices, and their collaboration in some of the later works can be discerned. Among other noted apprentices trained by Bouts was the MASTER OF THE TIBURTINE SIBYL (*see* MASTERS, ANONYMOUS, AND MONOGRAMMISTS, §I), who established a shop in Haarlem following Bouts's death.

3. POSTHUMOUS REPUTATION. The influence of Bouts was more pervasive than that of Rogier van der Weyden, dominating northern painting until the end of the 15th century. It was particularly strong in Germany (e.g. *see* MASTERS, ANONYMOUS, AND MONOGRAMMISTS, §I: MASTER OF THE EHNINGEN ALTAR). The countless panels produced in Bouts's style have complicated the study of his oeuvre. In 1925 Friedländer attributed 33 works to Bouts himself, to which he added three more in a supplementary volume that appeared in 1937. The following year Schöne, in his comprehensive monograph, drastically reduced this number to 14. Some of the rest he attributed to the MASTER OF THE PEARL OF BRABANT (*see* MASTERS, ANONYMOUS, AND MONOGRAMMISTS, §I), whom he tentatively identified as Dieric's eldest son. Others were given to the MASTER OF THE MUNICH ARREST OF CHRIST (*see* MASTERS, ANONYMOUS, AND MONOGRAMMISTS, §I), to the Master of the Rotterdam St John on Patmos (named for the painting in the Museum Boymans–van Beuningen) and, more convincingly, to Bouts's younger son, (2) Albrecht. While Friedländer's list may be

5. Dieric Bouts I: 'Pearl of Brabant', triptych, oil on panel, 626×1176 mm (Munich, Alte Pinakothek)

generous, Schöne's proposition seems extreme, particularly in regard to the paintings grouped around the 'Pearl of Brabant' (Munich, Alte Pin.), one of the most important triptychs generally ascribed to Dieric Bouts the elder (see fig. 5). This work, with the *Adoration of the Magi* on the central panel and *St John the Baptist in the Wilderness* and *St Christopher Crossing a River* on the wings, embodies all the finer qualities of the master's style. Other paintings generally attributed to Dieric Bouts the elder, but given to the son by Schöne, include the *Virgin and Child Enthroned between SS Peter and Paul* (London, N.G.), the *Virgin and Child Enthroned between Angels* (Granada, Capilla Real), *Moses before the Burning Bush* (Philadelphia, PA, Mus. A.) and *Christ in the House of Simon* (Berlin, Gemäldegal.). The paintings grouped by Schöne with the *Arrest of Christ* and the *Resurrection* in Munich (both Alte Pin.) include the altarpiece of *St Hippolytus* (Bruges, St Sauveur), a triptych that admittedly seems weak in design and awkward in the articulation of the horsemen. It was left unfinished in Dieric's studio, and the left wing and the grisaille figures on the reverse of the shutters were painted by Hugo van der Goes. The Master of the Rotterdam St John on Patmos, clearly a follower of Bouts, was credited by Schöne with the *St Luke Drawing the Virgin* (Penrhyn Castle, Gwynedd, NT) and a *St Jerome in the Wilderness* (formerly Leipzig, R. Brockhaus priv. col.).

NBW

BIBLIOGRAPHY

P. Heiland: *Dierick Bouts und die Hauptwerke seiner Schule* (Potsdam, 1902)

M. J. Friedländer: *Die altniederländische Malerei*, iii (Berlin, 1925); Eng. trans. as *Early Netherlandish*, iii (1968)

L. Baldass: 'Die Entwicklung des Dirk Bouts', *Jb. Ksthist. Samml. Wien*, n. s., vi (1932), pp. 77–114

G. J. Hoogewerff: *De Noord-Nederlandsche schilderkunst*, ii (The Hague, 1937), pp. 71–6

W. Schöne: *Dieric Bouts und seine Schule* (Berlin and Leipzig, 1938)

A. M. Hammacher: *Dieric Bouts: De 'Avondmaeltyt' in der kerke Sint Peter te Leuven* (Amsterdam and Antwerp, 1939)

M. J. Schretlen: *Dirck Bouts* (Amsterdam, 1946)

J. G. van Gelder: 'Het zogenaamde portret van Dieric Bouts op "Het Werc van den Heiliche Sacrament"', *Oud-Holland*, lxvi (1951), pp. 51–2

P. Coremans, R. J. Gettens and J. Thissen: 'La Technique des "primitifs flamands": Etude scientifique des matériaux, de la structure et de la technique picturale, ii: Th. Bouts: Le Retable du Saint-Sacrement', *Stud. Conserv.*, i (1952), pp. 3–29

E. Michel: *Musée national du Louvre: Catalogue raisonné des peintures flamandes du XVe et du XVIe siècle* (Paris, 1953), pp. 24–6

E. Panofsky: *Early Netherlandish Painting* (Cambridge, MA, 1953), i, pp. 313–19

M. Davies: *The National Gallery, London*, 2 vols (1953–4), iii of *Les Primitifs flamands, I: Corpus* (Antwerp, 1951–)

——: *Early Netherlandish School*, London, N.G. cat. (London, 2/1955)

V. Denis: *Dieric Bouts* (Brussels and Amsterdam, 1957)

P. Philippot: 'A propos de la *Justice d'Othon* de Thierry Bouts', *Mus. Royaux B.-A. Belgique; Bull.*, n. s., vi (1957), pp. 55–80

Dieric Bouts (exh. cat. by F. Baudouin and K. G. Beets, Brussels, Pal. B.-A.; Delft, Stedel. Mus. Prinsenhof; 1957–8)

F. Van Molle and others: 'La *Justice d'Othon* de Thierry Bouts', *Bull. Inst. Royal Patrm. A.*, i (1958), pp. 7–69

H. Adhémar: *Le Musée National du Louvre, Paris* (1962), v of *Les Primitifs flamands, I: Corpus* (Antwerp, 1951–), pp. 33–65

R. van Schoute: *La Chapelle Royale de Grenade* (1963), vi of *Les Primitifs flamands, I: Corpus* (Antwerp, 1951–), pp. 29–57

A. Châtelet: 'Sur un *Jugement dernier* de Dieric Bouts', *Ned. Ksthist. Jb.*, xvi (1965), pp. 17–42

J. Białostocki: *Les Musées de Pologne* (1966), ix of *Les Primitifs flamands, I: Corpus* (Antwerp, 1951–), pp. 21–35

Tentoonstelling—Dirk Bouts en zijn tijd (exh. cat., Leuven, Mus. Vander Kelen-Mertens, 1975)

Albrecht Bouts: *Christ in the House of Simon*, oak panel, 410×610 mm (Brussels, Musée d'Art Ancien)

A. Châtelet: *Les Primitifs hollandais* (Paris, 1980); Eng. trans. as *Early Dutch Painting* (Oxford, 1981), pp. 75–84

J. L. Bordeaux: 'Authentiqué sans réserves', *Conn. A.* (1986), pp. 36–41 [on ptgs in the Norton Simon and the Getty Mus.]

R. Koch: 'The Getty *Annunciation* by Dieric Bouts', *Burl. Mag.*, cxxx (1988), pp. 509–22

H. Mergler: *Dirk Bouts and his Workshop* (diss., Cleveland, OH, Case W. Reserve U., in preparation)

(2) Albrecht [Aelbrecht; Albert] **Bouts** (*b* Leuven, *c.* 1452–5; *d* 1549). Son of (1) Dieric Bouts I. Three works carry his monogram. The major piece is a triptych with the *Assumption of the Virgin* (Brussels, Mus. A. Anc.), a work mentioned by the chronicler Molanus in his unfinished history of Leuven (*c.* 1575) as in a chapel of the Virgin in St Peter's, Leuven. A man and woman kneeling in the right wing have been considered portraits of Albrecht Bouts and his second wife, Lisabeth Nausnyders, since an angel hovering above them holds a coat of arms with the insignia of the painters' guild, two crossed arrows and the letter A (?Albrecht). Two panels depicting the *Annunciation* (Munich, Alte Pin.; replica, Stockholm, Nmus.) have similar armorials.

A number of paintings of uneven quality, which are difficult to date, have been attributed to Albrecht and his workshop. He specialized in small devotional works that found a ready market in Antwerp. Especially popular was an archaic type of icon in the form of a diptych with a bust of Christ as the Man of Sorrows, juxtaposed with a bust of the praying Virgin (e.g. Aachen, Suermondt-Ludwig-Mus.). Albrecht also perpetuated compositions invented by his father. His *Last Supper* (Brussels, Mus. A. Anc.) is a variant of the central panel of the *Holy Sacrament* altarpiece in St Peter's, Leuven, and the *Christ in the House of Simon* (Brussels, Mus. A. Anc.; see fig.) is a reversed copy of his father's painting (Berlin, Gemäldegal.).

Compared with his father's style, Albrecht's figures are wrapped in fussy draperies with intricate pockets of folds concealing the form of the body. His brushwork is thicker, his colours darker and muddier. Although he frequently followed the compositions of his father and those of Rogier van der Weyden and Hugo van der Goes, his designs tend to be overcrowded, and in his landscape backgrounds the clarity in spatial projection is obscured by the repetition of landscape motifs. In these respects, Albrecht's paintings reflect the transition between the 15th-century style of his father and the eclectic style of Antwerp Mannerism prevalent in the early decades of the 16th. The practice of mass production then current in Antwerp is evidenced by the numerous replicas that issued from his shop.

BIBLIOGRAPHY

M. J. Friedländer: *Die altniederländische Malerei*, iii (Berlin, 1925); Eng. trans. as *Early Netherlandish*, iii (1968), pp. 38–42

W. Schöne: *Dieric Bouts und seine Schule* (Berlin and Leipzig, 1938), pp. 190–207

W. M. Staring: 'De *Maria-Hemelvaart* van Albert Bouts', *Oud-Holland*, lxii (1947), pp. 182–8

M. Wera: 'Contribution à l'étude d'Albert Bouts', *Rev. Belge Archéol. & Hist. A.*, xx (1951), pp. 139–44

D. Hollanders and others: 'Scènes de la *Passion du Christ* attribuées à Albert Bouts', *Area Louvan.*, iv (1975), pp. 83–135

C. Dechamps: 'Albert Bouts, alias le Maître de l'Assomption de la Vierge', *Rev. Archéologues & Historiens A. Louvain*, x (1977), pp. 304–6

JAMES SNYDER

Bouvard, (Joseph-)Antoine (*b* Saint Jean de Bournay, Isère, 20 Feb 1840; *d* Marly-le-Roi, Yvelines, 5 Nov 1920). French architect. After employment on council building projects in the Isère département, he studied at the Ecole des Beaux-Arts under Constant Dufeux (1864–8), simultaneously working for the administration of the city of Paris, which in 1871 he joined as a civil servant, eventually becoming in 1897 Directeur administratif des services d'architecture, des promenades et des plantations.

In 1882 he proposed the use of timber-framing as a means of construction for temporary schools and he pursued this idea in 1883 by using a metal framework for the barracks of the Republican Guard at 4 Rue Schomberg, Paris. On the flat façade the geometry of the structure stands out, framing panels of coloured bricks. A similarly modern austerity appears in the architecture of his school complex at Rue Saint Lambert, Paris (1890–93).

Bouvard was one of the architects of the Bourse du travail at 3 Rue du Château d'Eau, Paris (1888–92), and of the railway station of Château-Creux, St Etienne (1887), built by the Compagnie du Paris-Lyon-Marseille, to which he was architectural adviser. He was awarded several medals for his collaboration in the 1878 and 1889 Expositions Universelles. He retired in 1911 and went to Brazil, at the request of the municipal council of Saõ Paulo, for whom he designed the Don Pedro II park and a public square.

BIBLIOGRAPHY

J. Lacroux: *La Brique ordinaire au point de vue décoratif* (Paris, 1878)

L'Architecture, vi (1893), pp. 124–5 [contains illustrations of Bouvard's designs]

A. M. CHATELET

Bouverie, John (*b c.* 1723; *d* Guzel Hisar, Turkey, 19 Sept 1750). English collector and antiquarian. He was educated at New College, Oxford. After inheriting a large fortune, he went on the GRAND TOUR to Italy (1740–42). He travelled extensively throughout his short life and went to Italy several times, acquiring antiquities, paintings, engravings, medals, cameos and, above all, drawings. His collection of Old Master drawings was one of the most important assembled in England in the first half of the 18th century. It included examples by Leonardo, Michelangelo, Raphael, Rembrandt and particularly Guercino. Many of these are still identifiable by their beautiful mounts, which have a distinctive ruled and patterned border (*see* DISPLAY OF ART, §IV).

The provenance of the Bouverie drawings was lost sight of until the early 1990s, and until then these mounts were rather misleadingly known as 'Casa Gennari' mounts (from the family name of Guercino's descendants). The greater part of the Bouverie collection was inherited in the first half of the 19th century by the 1st Earl of Gainsborough, in whose family it descended. Large sections were sold at Christie's, London, in 1859, when it is thought the drawings were stamped with the collector's mark 'B' (*see* Lugt), and again in 1922. The drawings are now widely scattered, but many are still in British collections. As an antiquarian, Bouverie is best known for an expedition from Naples to Asia Minor that he helped to organize and finance, which began in 1750. He travelled with the archaeologists JAMES DAWKINS, ROBERT WOOD and the topographical artist GIOVANNI BATTISTA BORRA. Bouverie kept a diary in which he recorded the monuments seen. He died during the journey, and Dawkins and Wood later included a short obituary of him in their *Ruins of Palmyra* (London, 1753).

BIBLIOGRAPHY
F. Lugt: *Marques*, suppl. (1956), p. 407, no. 2858c [incorrectly as the mark of the Hon. Edward Bouverie (1738–1810)]
D. Mahon: 'Drawings by Guercino in the Casa Gennari', *Apollo*, lxxxvii (1968), pp. 350–51
M. Laskin and M. Pantazzi: *European and American Painting, Sculpture and Decorative Arts, 1300–1800*, Ottawa, N.G. cat. (Ottawa, 1987), pp. 288–9
Drawings by Guercino from British Collections (exh. cat. by N. Turner and C. Plazzota, London, BM, 1991) [re-establishes correct Bouverie proven. for the col. of drgs]
N. Turner: 'John Bouverie as a Collector of Drawings', *Burl. Mag.*, cxxxvi/1091 (1994), pp. 90–99

S. J. TURNER

Bouwens van der Boijen, William (Oscar) (*b* The Hague, 1834; *d* Jouy-en-Josas, 13 Sept 1907). French architect of Dutch birth. He moved to France about 1840, when his mother, who was divorced, married the French architect Léon Vaudoyer, who, like her, was a Protestant. In 1868 he adopted French nationality. Bouwens studied architecture (1853–7) at the Ecole des Beaux-Arts in the ateliers of Henri Labrouste and Vaudoyer. Thanks to the influence of his stepfather he then joined the administration of the City of Paris, first as deputy inspector to his stepfather at the Conservatoire des Arts et Métiers and from 1860 as chief architect for the 16e arrondissement. Through his involvement in the development of Auteuil he gained the confidence of its backer, Baron Erlanger, a businessman of German origin who had made his fortune in France under the Second Empire, and this led to some private commissions. In 1861 Bouwens also married into a German family with connections in international finance. The resulting network of family connections and private patronage enabled him to give up his administrative posts and devote himself entirely to a wealthy and cosmopolitan clientele, many of whose members were Jewish or Protestant, for which he produced work in an eclectic and refined style that was rooted in the Second Empire. This clientele expanded from the financial world to include collectors, authors and foreign aristocrats.

Bouwens worked almost exclusively in the north-west part of Paris, the banking quarter around the Chaussée d'Antin, the Grands Boulevards, Faubourg Saint-Honoré and the Parc Monceau. There he specialized in sumptuous apartment buildings and private town houses, mostly in a soberly elegant style drawn from French Renaissance and other classical vocabularies and with luxurious yet re-strained interiors often organized around vast, top-lit galleried stair halls. Examples of this work include 47 Rue de Monceau (1865) for the financier Eugène Péreire, and the Hôtel Cernuschi (*c.* 1880; now the Musée Cernuschi), 7 Avenue Velazquez, for the collector Henri Cernuschi. For all the fundamentally Parisian quality of his architec-ture, Bouwens also received some commissions from the

French provinces and from abroad—among them 69–71 Brook Street (1891), London, built in an opulent Louis XV manner for the American banker W. H. Burns. He also built tombs, including that for *Alexandre Dumas fils* (1895) in Montmartre Cemetery and for *Henri Cernuschi* (1897) in Père Lachaise, both in Paris, as well as mausolea for the *Bates Family* (1875) in New York and *Julius Beer* (1876) in Highgate Cemetery, London. The latter, based on the Mausoleum of Halikarnassos, is generally credited to John Oldrid Scott, but Scott appears to have acted only as supervising architect.

Bouwens's most important work, however, was the head office of the Crédit Lyonnais, Paris, for which he worked on a series of schemes from 1876 to 1905. The bank's founder, Henri Germain, bought the Hôtel de Boufflers at the corner of the Boulevard des Italiens and the Rue de Choiseul with the intention of constructing a Parisian headquarters there. By 1913 the building had been extended to cover the entire block, though after 1905, the project was directed by Victor Laloux and André Narjoux (1867–1934). Bouwens's skill in blending luxury, classicism and rationalism is clearly demonstrated in this building, seen in his pioneering use of glass-block floors that, combined with slender and widely spaced supports, pro-vided natural lighting for the two- and four-storey strong-rooms. The façade on the Boulevard des Italiens, its central pavilion directly inspired by the Pavillon de l'Hor-loge at the Louvre, provides an imposing contrast to the functional lateral façades. The most dramatic element of the building is the magnificent double-spiral iron and stone staircase, modelled on the one in the château of Chambord, which acts as the hub of activity in the bank.

Bouwens was assisted in his work by his son Richard Bouwens van der Boijen (*b* Paris, 1863; *d* Paris, 1939). Like his father, he married into a banking family and established a clientele of financiers. His work was charac-terized by an attempt to combine a rational approach with high-quality detailing. One of his most important works was his own house (1898–1900) at 8 Rue de Lota, Paris, which won a prize in the Ville de Paris façade competition of 1901. It has a simple flat façade in Florentine palazzo style, decorated with coloured tiles. He also built two adjoining blocks of flats (1905–6) in the Quai Anatole France, in reinforced concrete and stone, which show a striving for originality and an effort to create a new and luxurious style for a wealthy clientele; one of them pioneered the use of split levels in Parisian blocks. During the 1920s and 1930s Richard Bouwens designed interiors for the ocean liners *Paris* (1921), *Ile de France* (1927) and *SS Normandie* (1935), the last in association with Roger-Henri Expert. These luxurious yet restrained interiors are characterized by the Art Deco style.

BIBLIOGRAPHY
E. Viollet-le-Duc and F. Narjoux: *Habitations modernes* (Paris, 1873–5), ii, pp. 17–19, pl. 178–80, 184–7
A. Raguenet: *Monographies de bâtiments modernes* (Paris, [*c.* 1900]), p. 156, pl. 188–91 [on 8 Rue de Lota, Paris]
Obituary, *Le Figaro* (15 Sept 1907), p. 2
L. Hautecoeur: *Histoire de l'architecture classique en France*, vii (Paris, 1957), pp. 164–5, 326
J. L. Bauduin: *William et Richard Bouwens van der Boijen* (diss., U. Paris, 1984)

——: 'Richard Bouwens van der Boijen ou les fastes intérieurs des transatlantiques', *Colóq. A.*, xlv (1985), pp. 50–57

MARIE-LAURE CROSNIER LECONTE

Bouzianis, Giorgos (*b* Athens, 23 Oct 1885; *d* Athens, 23 Oct 1959). Greek painter. In 1906 he graduated from the Higher School of Fine Arts in Athens. The following year he went to Munich on a privately sponsored grant, where he studied with the German painter Walter Thor (1870–1929). In 1908 he studied at the Akademie der bildenden Künste in Munich under the German painters Otto Seitz (1842–1912) and Georg Schildknecht (*b* 1850). In 1909 he went to Berlin and worked for a year at the studio of Max Liebermann. On his return to Munich in 1910 he struck up a friendship with de Chirico. His output of this period consisted mainly of portraits, which he exhibited in Munich at the Kunstverein and the Künstler Genossenschaft, of which he soon became a member. Between 1917 and 1921 he exhibited at the Galerie Anton Rithhaler, showing works such as *Portrait of a Man* (1917; Athens, N.G.), in his new Expressionist style. From 1920 to 1932 he was supported by the Galerie Berchfeld of Leipzig, who built a studio for him in Eichenau. In 1927 he had his first one-man show at the Kunsthutte in Chemnitz. That same year he became a member of the Munich Secession and in 1928 he participated in their exhibition at the Glaspalast in Munich. The critics gave him enthusiastic notices and he sold most of his works. It was at the expense of the Galerie Berchfeld that he lived in Paris between 1929 and 1932, producing a series of remarkably loose watercolours, such as *Landscape in Dieppe* (1931; priv. col., see Papastamos, p. 191). On his return to Munich he found that his painting was discouraged by the Nazis. In 1935 he returned to Athens, urged by the Greek government who promised him a professorship at the Higher School of Fine Arts. That promise was never kept and Bouzianis, having sold his studio in Germany, was faced with privation. He continued to produce brooding and psychologically penetrating portraits, such as *Portrait of Polyxeni Kokali* (1937; priv. col., see Papastamos, p. 193), while living in isolation and teaching private students. His sole one-man show in Greece took place at the Parnassos Gallery in Athens (1949) and inaugurated his reception in Greek artistic life. He was a founder-member of the group Stathmi in 1949. From then on he participated in many Greek and international exhibitions. Although he adopted an Expressionist style, he did not share its ideology or social concern. His subject-matter was restricted mainly to the human face and body. His intense distortions and violent colours attempted to express the artist's preoccupation with the sense of the tragic in life.

BIBLIOGRAPHY
D. Papastamos: *Painting 1930–40: The Artistic and Aesthetic Vision of the Decade* (Athens, 1986), pp. 185–97

FANI-MARIA TSIGAKOU

Bove, Osip (Ivanovich) (*b* St Petersburg, 4 Nov 1784; *d* Moscow, 28 June 1834). Russian architect and urban planner. He was the son of the painter Vincenzo Giovanni Bova (1754–1815), an emigré from Naples, and he later changed his name to Bove. He obtained his first knowledge of architecture from the architect Francesco Camporesi (1747–1831) before becoming a pupil and later architectural assistant (1802–12) at the Architecture School of the Kremlin Construction Department in Moscow. His first practical works were in Tver' and Moscow with the architects Karl Rossi and Matvey Kazakov, who had a great influence on his work. His subsequent activities were associated with his work on the Committee for Construction in Moscow, which was in charge of the restoration of the city following its destruction (1812) during Napoleon's invasion. As chief architect in the committee's 'façade section', Bove had great influence on the character of building in Moscow after the fire, distinguished by stylistic unity and high artistic standards. He was involved in a wide range of creative activity: he was an outstanding architect, a fine artist, a construction expert and an organizer of construction projects. In 1816 the Academy of Arts in St Petersburg granted Bove the title of architect, and in 1819 he was appointed head of the III order of the Master [architect] Party for Civic Architecture, placing in his control the organization of civic construction in the entire city.

Bove's talent as an urban planner was revealed most fully in his work in developing the centre of Moscow, a homogeneous system of squares that connected with the historic centre, the Kremlin, which retained its predominant importance. By rebuilding the Trading Rows (1814–15; destr. 1895) in Red Square, Bove brilliantly solved the problem of including this classical building in the historically evolved ensemble of the ancient square bordered by the fortified walls of the Kremlin. Bove had a leading role in the creation of Moscow's first regular ensemble, Theatre Square, built to a single overall plan. The main building in the square, the Bol'shoy Theatre, was built (1821–4) by Bove reworking a design by Andrey Mikhailov (rebuilt 1856, after a fire, by Al'bet Kavos). The celebrated Maly Theatre was established in one of the buildings Bove had designed in the square in 1823 (rebuilt 1837–43 by Konstantin Ton).

Bove was a master of minor forms, evident in his designs for the Aleksandrovsky sad (Alexander Garden)

Osip Bove: triumphal arch at the Tver' Gate, Moscow, 1827–34 (since repositioned in Victory Square, Moscow); from a 19th-century lithograph

situated by the Kremlin wall as part of the carefully planned centre of Moscow. He also played a large part in the development of a new type of residential house in Moscow after the fire, a detached town house combining the traditions of a town estate for gentry with features of a house as part of a street, and the intimacy of a small residential house with the magnificence of a building overlooking a main road in the city. The best of these was Prince N. S. Gagarin's house on Novinsky Boulevard (1817; destr. 1941). The most famous of Bove's public buildings is the First Moscow City Hospital (1827–33) on Bol'shaya Kaluzhskaya Street (later Lenin Prospect), which developed the design of the detached town house and was treated by the architect as an important addition to the city. Near the Catherine Hospital he rebuilt (1825–8) the monumental house of S. S. Gagarin at the Peter (Petrovskiye) Gates. Among Bove's religious buildings, the most accomplished is the rotunda of the church of the Virgin of All Sorrows (1832–6) on Bol'shaya Ordynka, with a splendidly designed interior, distinguished by its refined decoration. Bove was also responsible for the plan of the cathedral of the Trinity in the Danilov monastery, executed in Neo-classical style (1833–c. 1838; now the administrative centre of the Moscow patriarchate).

The patriotic theme of Russia's military prowess and glory, which runs through all Bove's creative work, was given the most brilliant tangible form in the triumphal arch at Tver' Gate (1827–34; see fig.), the main entrance into Moscow from St Petersburg, which became the figurative embodiment of Russia's victory in the Patriotic War (1812–14) against Napoleon. It is distinguished by the solemnity of the forms of the order and their organic synthesis with the sculpture (by Ivan Timofeyev (*d* 1830) and Ivan Vitali). It has now been moved to Victory Square.

BIBLIOGRAPHY
Z. K. Pokrovskaya: *O. I. Bove* (Moscow, 1964)

Z. K. POKROVSKAYA

Bowcher, Frank (*b* London, 1864; *d* London, 6 Dec 1938). British medallist and sculptor. He studied in London at the National Art Training School, under Edward Onslow Ford; and in Paris, where he was influenced by the work of Jules-Clément Chaplain and Oscar Roty. In 1886 he produced a medallic portrait of the *Khedive of Egypt* and in the following year was commissioned by the Royal Mint to produce designs for the Egyptian coinage. The 1890s saw an increasing number of commissions for medals: from the City of London for the *Visit of the King and Queen of Denmark*, the *Opening of Tower Bridge* and the *Diamond Jubilee*; from the Geological Society for the *Joseph Prestwich* medal; and from the Royal College of Science for the *Thomas Huxley* memorial medal (all London, B.M.). In 1903, following the death of George William de Saulles, Bowcher stepped in to finish the great seal of Edward VII. He was a founder-member of the Royal Society of British Sculptors and until the 1930s exhibited regularly at the Royal Academy. In the early 1920s he produced, under the direction of M. H. Spielmann (1858–1948), a series of plaquettes of the rulers of Baroda.

BIBLIOGRAPHY
Forrer
B. Dolman: *A Dictionary of Contemporary British Artists, 1929* (London, 1929)

E. J. Pyke: *A Biographical Dictionary of Wax Modellers* (Oxford, 1973)

MARK JONES

Bowdoin, James, III (*b* Boston, MA, 22 Sept 1752; *d* Buzzard's Bay, MA, 11 Oct 1811). American diplomat and collector. He was born into a prominent New England mercantile family of broad political and intellectual interests. Using the fortune garnered by his grandfather, a sea captain and merchant, he built on the collection, one of the first in the United States, begun by his father James Bowdoin II (1726–90), eventually bequeathing it to Bowdoin College, Maine, which was named after his father. The collection includes 70 paintings—mainly copies after Old Masters, the first Old Master drawings to arrive in America, and several prints, the latter probably collected by James II. It is likely that James III purchased at least 34 of the paintings in Europe, where he studied, later travelled, and was Minister Plenipotentiary to Spain under President Thomas Jefferson between 1805 and 1808. From the Scottish-born portrait painter John Smibert he probably acquired additional copies but also, more significantly, two portfolios totalling 141 drawings. Most notable among them are a landscape traditionally attributed to Pieter Bruegel I and a Beccafumi fresco study. The painting collection is distinguished by portraits of *Thomas Jefferson* and *James Madison* by Gilbert Stuart, as well as by family portraits by Joseph Blackburn, Smibert and Robert Feke, which James III's widow Sarah Bowdoin (1761–1826) added to the bequest. According to Wegner, James III may have been influenced in his collecting intentions both by the display of masterpieces he saw in Napoleon's Paris and by Jefferson's own accumulation of portraits of ancient and modern worthies who represented an ethical and cultivated life.

BIBLIOGRAPHY
M. S. Sadik: *Colonial and Federal Portraits at Bowdoin College* (Brunswick, 1966)
Governor Bowdoin and his Family (exh. cat. by R. L. Voltz, Brunswick, ME, Bowdoin Coll. Mus. A., 1969)
D. P. Becker: *Old Master Drawings at Bowdoin College* (Brunswick, 1985)
S. E. Wegner: 'The Collection of James Bowdoin III (1752–1811)', *College Art Association Sessions* [abstracts] (New York, 1991), pp. 192–3

DIANE TEPFER

Bowdoin Painter. *See* VASE PAINTERS, §II.

Bower [Bowers], **Edward** (*d* London, between 27 Dec 1666 and 8 Jan 1667). English painter. He worked principally in London (often inscribing his canvases as painted at Temple Bar) and was an active member of the Painter-Stainers' Company, of which he was Master in 1661–2. His provincial, even archaic, style is akin to that of Gilbert Jackson in being only superficially affected by the work of Anthony van Dyck or Peter Lely. Although Bower's use of paint is always rather dry and his draughtsmanship uncertain, his characterization is sympathetic, sometimes idiosyncratic, and his compositions are unconventional. His earliest extant portrait (1636; priv. col.) reveals the decorative quality, the arresting use of accessories, the gauche charm and the interest in elaborate costume that are so marked in his most important work, the full-length *Portrait of a Man* (1638; Dunster Castle, Somerset, NT). This is painted in a vernacular Baroque style, later to be used in a more sophisticated manner by William Dobson.

During the Civil War, Bower was patronized, not necessarily exclusively, by parliamentarians such as John

Pym, of whom Bower made a portrait. His portrait of *Ferdinando Fairfax, 2nd Baron Fairfax of Cameron* (1646; York, C.A.G.) was probably painted in Bath. The sitter described Bower as 'servant to Vandike'. Bower's portrait of *Lady Drake* (1646; York, C.A.G.) shows him attempting to emulate the sense of movement found in van Dyck's work. In contrast, the ambitiously designed equestrian portrait of *Thomas Fairfax, 3rd Baron Fairfax of Cameron*, engraved by William Marshall for publication in 1647, belongs to an older tradition. Bower's best-known work is his seated portrait of *Charles I at His Trial*, probably based on sketches made from life, of which a number of signed versions are known (all 1648–9; e.g. Brit. Royal Col.; Antony House, Cornwall, NT; Belvoir Castle, Leics).

UNPUBLISHED SOURCES
London, Guildhall Lib. [*The Booke of Orders and Constitutions*, Painter-Stainers' Company]

BIBLIOGRAPHY
Waterhouse: *16th & 17th C.*
M. Whinney and O. Millar: *English Art, 1625–1714*, Oxford Hist. Eng. A. (Oxford, 1957), pp. 79–80
O. Millar: *The Tudor, Stuart and Early Georgian Pictures in the Collection of Her Majesty the Queen* (London, 1963), i, p. 114

OLIVER MILLAR

Bowes, John (*b* London, 19 June 1811; *d* Streatlam, Co. Durham, 9 Oct 1885). English landowner, industrialist, collector and museum founder. He was the illegitimate son of John Bowes, 10th Earl of Strathmore; brought up as an earl's son, he inherited the Bowes family estates but not the earldom. He developed the family coal mines and ventured into shipping, and was MP for South Durham (1832–47). His wealth and public service did not make him wholly acceptable in English society and he therefore made Paris his principal home from 1847. There he purchased the Théâtre des Variétés, and married the actress and painter Josephine Coffin-Chevallier (1825–74), for whom he bought the Château du Barry, Louveciennes.

About 1860 the couple decided to found a museum in Barnard Castle, Co. Durham. They commissioned Jules Pellechet (1829–1903) to design a French Renaissance-style building (1869–71) to house their Second Empire furniture and paintings and their large collections of porcelain, faience, tapestries, embroideries, furniture, clocks and *objets d'art*. The paintings included El Greco's *Tears of St Peter* (late 1580s), which Bowes purchased in 1869 for eight pounds. The Bowes also bought works (e.g. Courbet's *View near Ornans*) from contemporary French painters, with whom Josephine had exhibited at the Salons of 1867 to 1870.

BIBLIOGRAPHY
C. E. Hardy: *John Bowes and the Bowes Museum* (Newcastle upon Tyne, 1970, rev. 3/1982)
E. Young: *The Bowes Museum, Barnard Castle, County Durham: Catalogue of Spanish and Italian Paintings* (Durham, 1970, rev. 2/1988)
E. Conran, ed.: *The Bowes Museum* (London, 1992)

ELIZABETH CONRAN

Bowler, Henry Alexander (*b* London, 30 Nov 1824; *d* London, 6 Aug 1903). English painter and teacher. He studied at J. M. Leigh's school and the Government School of Design, Somerset House, London. He specialized in landscape and genre subjects, exhibiting at the Royal Academy intermittently between 1847 and 1871. In 1855 he exhibited what is now his best-known painting, *The Doubt: Can These Dry Bones Live?* (London, Tate), which shows a woman leaning on the headstone of a grave. The subject-matter of the painting, with its clean-cut forms and bright, translucent colours, strongly suggests the influence of the Pre-Raphaelites, although Bowler did not know any of them personally. Many of his 16 exhibited works in oil and watercolour were landscapes. *Luccombe Chine, Isle of Wight* (1860; London, V&A) is a watercolour that harks back to the sharply focused, botanical approach to landscape painting favoured by the Pre-Raphaelites during the late 1840s and early 1850s.

Bowler was also an art teacher. He was appointed Headmaster of Stourbridge School of Art in 1851 and soon after this was transferred to Somerset House, London. In 1855 he became an inspector in the Department of Science and Art at South Kensington; he was closely involved in the organization of the International Exhibition there in 1862 and in subsequent international exhibitions. In 1876 he was appointed Assistant Director of Art at the South Kensington Museum. He retired from this post in 1891 but meanwhile taught perspective at the Royal Academy from 1861 to 1899.

BIBLIOGRAPHY
E.C. Clifford: 'Nature Study', *A. J.* [London] (1908), p. 108
Catalogue of Water-colour Paintings by British Artists and Foreigners Working in Great Britain, V&A (London, 1908, rev. 2/1927), pp. 42–3

JENNY ELKAN

Bow Porcelain Factory. English ceramic manufactory. The first Bow patent for 'a certain material whereby a ware might be made ... equal to ... China or Porcelain ware imported from abroad' was taken out in east London in December 1744 by the Irish artist Thomas Frye (*c.* 1710–62) and by Edward Heylyn (1695–1765). The early undertaking, significantly named 'New Canton', was founded to undercut Chinese imports and was probably financed by Alderman George Arnold (1691–1751). John Weatherby (*d* 1762) and John Crowther (*d* 1790), who had been partners in pottery and glassmaking ventures since 1725, completed the board of proprietors. An important ingredient in the original paste and mentioned in the 1744 patent was 'Unaker', possibly a china clay imported from Carolina. The soft paste used at Bow was unique in being the first to incorporate calcined bone-ash (mentioned as 'Virgin earth' in the second Bow patent of 1749–50) to increase strength and whiteness. Bow had a seminal influence on the course of English porcelain-making through its pioneer use of bone-ash, which continued to be an important ingredient in later bone china.

Bow's early wares were simply shaped, utilitarian pieces decorated in Chinese style in underglaze blue, the earliest shade being a distinctive royal blue. White wares decorated in relief with applied sprigs of prunus blossom, imitating Chinese Dehua wares made in Fujian Province (*see* CHINA, §VII, 3(vi)(c)) were also produced. From about 1750 both Chinese and Japanese overglaze enamelled designs were used, especially those in 'Kakiemon style' (*see* KAKIEMON WARE), and the forms of wares derived from both Europe and East Asia. Figures made during the early period were often inspired by French prints and by engravings of contemporary stage characters, such as Kitty Clive as the 'Fine Lady' in Garrick's *Lethe* (1750; London, BM), engraved by Charles Mosley (*d*?1770) and copied from Thomas Worlidge's watercolour (untraced). Few names of individual workers or modellers have survived, but the anonymous 'Muses' Modeller', whose subjects included Classical gods and the Muses, produced an unmistakable personal style through the use of disproportionately small heads, with heavy-lidded eyes, wide brows and receding chins, on long-armed bodies dressed in heavily folded draperies.

Bow's trading was widespread at home and overseas, especially in the American colonies, and it was during the 1750s that the factory was most prosperous. About 1756 overglaze transfer-printing in brick-red, purple, lilac or black was introduced at Bow, with many of the prints originating from French engravings. After 1756 the oriental influence gradually lessened. Underglaze blue was much less bright than at first, and, though some wares continued to be decorated in Chinese style, and a powder-blue ground was popular, European styles became dominant by 1760. Figures were often straight copies of Meissen originals. There was no regular factory mark.

By 1762, after the death or bankruptcy of most of the original partners, John Crowther remained the sole proprietor of the company. His firm made great efforts to produce the more florid Rococo wares typified by the Chelsea factory's 'Gold Anchor' pieces (1758–70; *see* CHELSEA PORCELAIN FACTORY) but was hindered by underfiring of the heavy bone-ash paste and sometimes by inexpert workmanship. Although some of the later figures are noteworthy, standards generally declined. Bow had first opened a retail City Warehouse on Cornhill in 1753. This moved to the Poultry and then to St Paul's Churchyard, where it closed finally in 1773. The factory itself was closed by March 1774, and then let to a china maker, William Brown, in 1774–6. By 1780 it had become a tar and turpentine factory. The equipment and stock were reputedly sold to William Duesbury (1725–86) and moved to his Derby porcelain factory.

BIBLIOGRAPHY
W. Chaffers: *Marks and Monograms* (London, 1843, rev. 15/65), ii
F. Hurlbutt: *Bow Porcelain* (London, 1926)
H. Tait: 'The Bow Factory under Alderman Arnold and Thomas Frye, 1745–59', *Trans. Eng. Cer. Circ.*, v/pt 4 (1963), pp. 195–216 [inc. 8 pp. of pls]
E. Adams: 'The Bow Insurances and Related Matters', *Trans. Eng. Cer. Circ.*, ix/pt 1 (1973), pp. 267–75 [inc. 15 pp. of pls]
——: 'Ceramic Insurances in the Sun Company Archives, 1766–74', *Trans. Eng. Cer. Circ.*, x/pt 1 (1976), pp. 1–38 [inc. 9 pp. of pls]
E. Adams and D. Redstone: *Bow Porcelain* (London, 1981, rev. 1991)
A. Gabszewicz and G. Freeman: *Bow Porcelain: The Collection Formed by Geoffrey Freeman* (London, 1982)
J. Howell: 'The Bow China Warehouse, Cornhill: Notes about the Premises', *Trans. Eng. Cer. Circ.*, xii/pt 1 (1984), pp. 38–40 [inc. contemp. notices and adverts]

ELIZABETH ADAMS

Bowyer, Robert (*b* London, *c.* 1758; *d* Byfleet, Surrey, 4 June 1834). Miniature painter and publisher. He was originally self-taught and then a pupil of John Smart (1741–1811), whose work he copied and whose style he imitated: between 1783 and 1828 he was an occasional exhibitor at the Royal Academy, being appointed in 1789 painter in watercolours to George III and miniature painter to Queen Charlotte (1744–1818). He was a keen promoter of history painting and in 1792 launched a prospectus for

an edition of David Hume's *History of England*, to be 'superbly embellished' with illustrations engraved after historical paintings by leading artists, including Benjamin West, Robert Smirke, Francis Wheatley and Philippe-Jacques de Loutherbourg. Bowyer also published the *Historic Gallery*, which, until its failure, with great financial loss, in 1806, provided substantial patronage to history painters and fostered a taste for national history paintings, especially of medieval subjects. The five folios that appeared contained, in addition to engravings of historical paintings, engraved portraits, manuscripts and antiquarian material. Bowyer also published *An Imperial Narrative of Events from 1816 to 1822* (London, 1823) and *Facsimiles of Water Colour Drawing* (London, 1825).

DNB   BIBLIOGRAPHY
T. S. R. Boase: 'Macklin and Bowyer', *J. Warb. & Court. Inst.*, xxvi (1963), pp. 148–77
D. Foskett: *A Dictionary of British Miniature Painters* (1972), i, p. 176; ii, pl. 25

DAVID BLAYNEY BROWN

Box, gold. Box made to contain snuff, powder etc, to be displayed or carried on the person. A history of gold boxes should properly begin with a reference to pomanders, scentballs, muskballs or *boîtes-de-senteurs*, as they were variously described. By the 17th century these objects were extremely fashionable and were to be found on nearly every dressing-table and in every pocket. They took the form of globular receptacles used to contain perfume or aromatic disinfectants and were often divided into hinged cells or *loculi*. They were an essential item for public appearances at a time of less than sanitary conditions and poor personal hygiene.

By the 18th century boxes were designed to hold a variety of contents. The first snuff-boxes as such seem to

Gold boxes (clockwise from top left): snuff-box by Jean Frémin, red gold with enamelled polychrome flowers and translucent green leaves, 87×40×68 mm, Paris, 1756–7; box set with a mosaic of carved mother-of-pearl on gold, 76×35×59 mm, Paris, 1744–5; box with alternating orange and olive-green enamelled bands relieved by gold sprays of flowers and leaves, 72×35×54 mm, Paris, 1750–52; snuff-box by Michel-Robert Hallé, engraved with laurel sprays relieved by royal blue foliage *basse taille* enamel, 72×34×53 mm, Paris, 1749–50 (New York, Metropolitan Museum of Art)

have taken the form of a pear and were known as *poires-à-poudre*, with an opening in the top to allow a small amount of the fine powder to be poured on to the back of the hand before being inhaled in each nostril. Later examples are usually rectangular or oval in form (*see also* CHINA, XIII, §23). Many boxes intended for the pocket were known as *drageoirs*, sweetmeat- or comfit-boxes. Patch-boxes, *boîtes-à-mouches*, were generally rectangular or sometimes oval in form and smaller and flatter than snuff-boxes. Sponge-boxes, *boîtes-à-éponge*, were often spherical in form. Small boxes made to contain minute tablets of soap, *boîtes-à-savonette*, were also produced. A popular form of box contained both patches and rouge and was known as a *boîte-à-rouge et à-mouches*, usually small and rectangular in form; its lid, lined with a piece of mirror-glass, opened to reveal the cover or covers of either one or two inner compartments and a space running the length of the box, intended to hold a small, gold-handled brush.

Boxes were often intended as luxurious gifts, either personal or diplomatic, and as such were given elaborate and elegant decoration (see fig.), for example with enamelling or engraving. In the 18th century Paris was undeniably the most sophisticated centre of production and strongly influenced the design and making of boxes in other European countries.

For further information and bibliography *see* AUSTRIA, §X; FRANCE, §X, 2; GERMANY, §X, 3; THE NETHERLANDS, §X, 3; SWEDEN, §X, 1; and ENGLAND, §X, 3.

A. KENNETH SNOWMAN

Boxall, Sir **William** (*b* Oxford, 29 June 1800; *d* London, 6 Dec 1879). English painter and museum director. The son of an Oxford taxation official, he entered the Royal Academy Schools, London, in 1819. He worked in London between 1823 and 1833, chiefly as a portrait painter but occasionally exhibiting history and subject pictures in an endeavour to gain recognition; among the subjects he painted were mythological scenes and literary themes from Milton and Shakespeare. However, Boxall's success lay in portraiture, and between the mid-1830s and the 1860s he enjoyed some reputation as a society painter and also for his likenesses of leading literary, artistic and intellectual figures of the day, for example *John Gibson* (1864; London, RA). To further his ambition to succeed as a history painter he travelled and studied in Italy (1833–6), but portraiture remained his principal employment, accounting for most of his exhibited works (London, RA, 1818, 1823–66, 1880; London, British Institution, 1826–44). He was elected ARA in 1851 and RA in 1863.

In 1865 Boxall succeeded Sir Charles Eastlake as Director of the National Gallery, London, an office he held with distinction until 1874. He negotiated the purchase of Sir Robert Peel's collection for the National Gallery and made a number of discerning acquisitions (including Piero della Francesca's *St Michael*, the Michelangelo *Entombment* and *Madonna and Child with St John and Angels*, the Demidoff Altarpiece by Carlo Crivelli and Pieter de Hooch's *Woman and her Maid in a Courtyard*, the first picture by that artist to enter the collection). He was knighted in 1871. The contents of his studio were auctioned at Christie's on 8 June 1880.

UNPUBLISHED SOURCES
London, N.G. [Boxall MSS]
BIBLIOGRAPHY
DNB
M. J. H. Liversidge: 'John Ruskin and William Boxall', *Apollo*, lxxxv (1967), pp. 39–44
M. Levey: 'A Little-known Director: Sir William Boxall', *Apollo*, ci (1975), pp. 354–9

M. J. H. LIVERSIDGE

Boxer, David (*b* St Andrew, Jamaica, 17 March 1946). Jamaican artist and art historian. He studied at Cornell University and at Johns Hopkins University where he was awarded a PhD in 1975. He studied briefly under the American painter Fred Mitchell (*b* 1903) while at Cornell, although he was essentially self-taught as an artist. He developed a coherent but continuously evolving iconography consisting of complex and often highly personal metaphors that commented on the human condition and the anguish of modern existence. Although he also produced non-figurative works, he usually concentrated on the human figure (e.g. *Pietà in Memory of Philip Hart* 1986; Kingston, N.G.). He often worked with 'appropriated images', borrowed from myths, religion, music, history, archaeology and art history. These images, often mechanical reproductions of his sources, were transformed, cruelly assaulted sometimes, through a surrealist method of association.

The major multi-media installation *Headpiece. The Riefenstahl Requiem* (1986; Kingston, N.G.) summarized some of Boxer's major thematic concerns, namely the self-destructive forces in the individual as well as in society, through references to war, genocide and natural catastrophe; the juxtaposition of Classical Apollonian and Dionysiac motives; and mythological figures such as Icarus, Narcissus and the Three Graces. Boxer worked in a wide variety of media, ranging from experimental painting techniques to collage and assemblage, photography and video. In 1975 he became Director/Curator of the National Gallery of Jamaica in Kingston. He resigned from the post of director in 1991 to become Director Emeritus/Chief Curator of the Gallery.

BIBLIOGRAPHY
In Situ II: Some Persistent Themes (exh. cat. by V. Poupeye-Rammelaere, artist's studio, Kingston, 1988)
P. Archer Straw and K. Robinson: *Jamaican Art* (Kingston, 1990), pp. 96–7, 113–16, 159–60

VEERLE POUPEYE

Boy [Boyen; Boyens], **Willem** [Guillaume; Villem] (*b* Mechelen, *c.* 1520; *d* Stockholm, 16 April 1592). Flemish sculptor and architect, active in Sweden. He is first recorded at the court of Gustav I Vasa (*reg* 1523–60) in 1557–8. Boy executed a gilded wood relief portrait of the King (Mariefred, Gripsholm Slott, Stat. Porträttsaml.), as well as his tomb (1562–83; Uppsala Cathedral; *see* SWEDEN, fig. 12). The latter, in red and white alabaster, is the earliest large-scale example of such a work in the Renaissance style in Sweden and is influenced by Dutch examples, with recumbent figures of the King and his two queens and an obelisk at each corner.

Boy's work as an architect included alterations to the Royal Palace, Stockholm, from 1577 to 1592 (destr. 1697) and the castle at Svartsjö, near Stockholm (1570–90; destr. 1687; replaced 1730s). At Stockholm, the medieval building was given columned arcading, decorative gables and richly decorated roofs for the towers. Svartsjö was reshaped into a three-storey building with a Renaissance cupola; the circular courtyard in front of the castle was surrounded by curved arcades of two storeys, and the castle was completed by seven symmetrically grouped towers with elegant roofs. The whole building was a blend of traditional Scandinavian and Renaissance architecture. The churches of St Klara and St Jakob in Stockholm, inspired by Gothic architecture, were also the work of Boy; he may also have been involved in the redesigning of Uppsala Castle (1580s) for John III (reg 1568–92), although not to any great extent; it is unclear how much Boy's designs for John III owe to the King's antiquarian interests.

See also SWEDEN, §II, 2.

BIBLIOGRAPHY

SVKL; Thieme–Becker
A. Hahr: Studier i Johan III's renässans, II. Villem Boy: Bildhuggaren och byggmästeren [Studies in Johan III's Renaissance, II. Villem Boy: sculptor and master builder] (Uppsala and Leipzig, 1910) [with Ger. summary]
E. Lundberg: Byggnadskonsten i Sverige: Sengotik och renässans [Architecture in Sweden: Late Gothic and Renaissance] (Stockholm, 1948)
N. Sundquist: Willem Boy i Uppsala (Uppsala, 1971)

TORBJÖRN FULTON

Boyadjiev, Zlatyu (b Brezovo, nr Plovdiv, 22 Oct 1903; d Plovdiv, 2 Feb 1976). Bulgarian painter. In 1932 he graduated from the Academy of Art, Sofia, having studied under Tzeno Todorov (1877–1953). In 1939 he went to Italy, where he studied painting. On his return to Bulgaria, he was a founder of the 'Baratzite' group, along with his fellow artists Vasil Barakov (b 1902) and David Peretz (1906–82). Mainly a painter of figure compositions, portraits and landscapes, Boyadjiev experimented with different styles and techniques, ranging from a type of Impressionism to a treatment of the form in a synthesized and monumental manner (e.g. Autumn, 1921; Sofia, N.A.G.; see BULGARIA, fig. 8; and Slaughtering a Pig, Christmas, 1943; Plovdiv A.G.). In 1951, due to a serious illness, his right hand and part of his body became paralysed. After two years he began to paint again, this time using his left hand. As a result, his style changed drastically. His paintings became expressive and dramatic and he paid special attention to folkloric and mythical motifs. Some of his works involve the observer in their intricate plots, while others are mystical and filled with symbolism, as in the Village of Brezovo (1959; Sofia, N.A.G.), On the Way to the Slaughterhouse (1960; Plovdiv A.G.) and Two Weddings (1972; Sofia, N.A.G.). A permanent exhibition of his work is located in his home town of Brezovo.

BIBLIOGRAPHY

T. Lavrenov: Zlatyu Boyadjiev (Sofia, 1958)
Zlatyu Boyadjiev (exh. cat., Sofia, 1974)

MARIANA KATZAROVA

Boyana. Village 8 km south of Sofia in Bulgaria, famous for its two Byzantine churches. The earlier of the pair, which stand side by side, is dedicated to the Virgin; various building dates have been proposed, including the 10th century, the 11th and the early 12th. It is a small cruciform structure with a dome over a high drum and an apse pierced with arched windows. Several badly damaged frescoes survive inside, depicting the Fathers of the Church Officiating at a Service, the Dormition of the Virgin and the Crucifixion.

The second church is dedicated to SS Nicholas and Panteleimon, and according to an inscription its construction and decoration were funded by Sebastokrator Kaloyan in 1259. It has two storeys: the ground floor was used for burials and the upper floor as a chapel. Its cruciform plan is surmounted by a dome supported by pendentives. The wall paintings (see BULGARIA, fig. 5) were executed in tempera and are often thought to derive from the Komnenian style of painting found in several churches at VELIKO TĂRNOVO; their high quality also suggests some Western influence. The dome shows Christ Pantokrator, with eight angels on the drum and four evangelists on the pendentives; a large Virgin with a row of saints below fills the apse. The vaults and lunettes are covered with such scenes as the Ascension, the Transfiguration, the Pentecost, the Annunciation, the Visitation of the Virgin, the Nativity, the Purification of the Virgin, the Baptism, the Raising of Lazarus, the Entry into Jerusalem, the Last Supper, the Way of the Cross, the Crucifixion, the Descent into Limbo and the Three Marys at the Tomb. The Virgin and Child are depicted over the entrance of the church, with the Hand of God shown higher up and St Joachim and St Anne bowing their heads on either side. The upper registers of the north and south walls depict scenes from the Life of Christ and the Passion respectively, while the lower registers and pillars of the church show full-length warrior saints with highly individualized faces. Among the most noteworthy figures shown are Sebastokrator Kaloyan and Desislava, his consort, who is given a particularly elegant portrayal. They are paired with portraits of the reigning Bulgarian King Constantine Tich Asen (reg 1257–77) and Queen Irene.

BIBLIOGRAPHY

A. Grabar: L'Eglise de Boïana (Sofia, 1924)
——: La Peinture religieuse en Bulgarie (Paris, 1928), pp. 88, 117–74
K. Mijatev: Peintures murales de Bojana (Sofia and Dresden, 1961)

TANIA VELMANS

Boyar Pisanitsy. Site of petroglyphs dating to the end of the first millennium BC, in the Boyar Mountains near the village of Abakan-Perevoz in the Middle Yenisey Basin in Siberian Russia. Discovered by Alexander V. Adrianov in 1904, the petroglyphs were engraved using pecking technique; most of the images are in silhouette but some are in low relief. Anthropomorphic figures are rendered frontally while animals are shown in profile. At Bol'shaya (Greater) Boyar Pisanitsy there is a frieze with a panorama of a village with log cabins and yurts, herds of animals, with running sheep portrayed in the Scythian–Siberian Animal Style, small schematic human figures and outline images of cauldrons of Scythian type. The images at Malaya (Lesser) Boyar Pisanitsy are executed in similar style, but the composition is more schematic. There are, however, precise depictions of the construction of timber houses with gable roofs.

BIBLIOGRAPHY

M. A. Devlet: *Bol'shaya boyarskaya pisanitsa / Rock Engravings in the Middle Yenisei Basin* (Moscow, 1976) [bilingual text]

V. YA. PETRUKHIN

Boyce, George Price (*b* Bloomsbury, London, 24 Sept 1826; *d* Chelsea, London, 9 Feb 1897). English painter. He was the son of a prosperous wine merchant and pawnbroker. His childhood was spent in London, and in 1846 he was apprenticed to the firm of architects Wyatt & Brandon, where he remained for three years. He was always fascinated by ancient buildings but gradually lost interest in architecture as a career. In 1849, perhaps as a result of meeting David Cox at Betws-y-Coed (Gwynedd, Wales), he decided to become a painter. In the early 1850s Boyce drew landscape and architectural subjects with a fluent watercolour technique derived from Cox. In 1854 Boyce made an extended journey to Italy; he painted views of buildings in Venice and Verona, which were commended by Ruskin, and semi-abstract twilight studies, which anticipate Whistler's nocturnes.

Towards the end of the 1850s Boyce adopted a technique of minute detail and bright colour; various watercolours of this period, such as the *Mill on the Thames at Mapledurham* (1860; Cambridge, Fitzwilliam), are among the most intense and objective of all Pre-Raphaelite landscapes. Boyce abhorred conventional compositions and picturesque detail; he sought viewpoints from which the landscape and buildings might be seen in intriguing conjunction. He was fond of painting trees in full foliage and often used these to screen time-worn buildings; the greens of grass and leaves and the reds of brick and tiles are colours that frequently recur in his watercolours at this stage. Boyce ranged England in search of subjects; his favourite area for painting was the Thames Valley between Reading and Oxford. In the course of a peripatetic career he frequently visited France and Italy, and in 1861–2 he travelled to Egypt.

Boyce was a gregarious man, and many of his friends were painters. His sister Joanna was a talented painter who married the artist Henry Tanworth Wells (1828–1903). Around 1849 Boyce met D. G. Rossetti; the two became close friends and frequent companions during the following 25 years. From 1863 Boyce lived in the rooms in Chatham Place, Blackfriars (London), that Rossetti vacated after the death of his wife. In 1868 Boyce commissioned Philip Webb to build a house in Chelsea: West House was completed in 1870, and Boyce lived there until the end of his life. He filled the house with an important collection of paintings; he owned many works by Rossetti, including *Bocca Baciata* (1859), which he had commissioned. Boyce kept a diary from 1851 to 1875, and, although it survives only in a censored and incomplete form, it provides an invaluable record of, and insight into, the convivial circle of painters to which he belonged.

As he was of independent means Boyce followed his artistic inclinations without being concerned whether his works would find a ready market. Even if his professional status was uncertain, he was committed to painting and exhibited regularly: at the Royal Academy (1853–61) and in 1857 at the exhibition of Pre-Raphaelite pictures held at Russell Place, London. In 1858 he was a founder-member of the Hogarth Club. In 1864 he was elected an associate of the Old Water-Colour Society, where he exhibited most summers until 1890 and often showed sketches in the winter exhibitions. Boyce was hurt that he had to wait until 1878 to become a full member of the Society. The contents of Boyce's studio were auctioned at Christie's on 1 July 1897.

BIBLIOGRAPHY

A. E. Street: 'George Price Boyce, RWS', *Archit. Rev.* [London], v (1899), pp. 151–60
R. Davies, ed.: 'Extracts from Boyce's Diaries, 1851–75', *Old Wtrcol. Soc. Club*, xix (1941), pp. 1–71
V. Surtees, ed.: *The Diaries of George Price Boyce* (Norwich, 1980) [annotated rev. of the diaries with a biog. intro.]
P. Gerrish Nunn: 'Case Histories: Joanna Mary Boyce', *Victorian Women Artists* (London, 1987), pp. 146–58
George Price Boyce (exh. cat. by C. Newall and J. Egerton, London, Tate, 1987)

CHRISTOPHER NEWALL

Boyce, Joanna Mary. *See* WELLS, JOANNA MARY.

Boyce, Sonia (*b* London, 1962). English painter, draughtswoman and multi-media artist. She studied art at East Ham College and Stourbridge College of Art until 1983. Boyce's early works were large chalk-and-pastel drawings that show her interest in depicting friends, family and childhood experiences. In them she often included depictions of wallpaper patterns and bright colours associated with the Caribbean and experienced through her own particular background. Through them she also examined her position as a black woman in Britain and the historical events in which that experience was rooted (e.g. *Lay Back, Keep Quiet and Think of What Made Britain so Great*, charcoal, pastel and watercolour on paper, 4 parts, 15.25×6.50 m each, 1986; AC Eng). Making these experiences visible was her main concern in what could be seen as a form of social realism. In her later works she used such diverse media as digital photographs, laser photographs and pastel to produce composite images depicting contemporary black life (e. g. *From Someone Else's Fear Fantasy (a Case of Mistaken Identity, this Is No Bed of Roses) to Metamorphosis*, mixed media on photographic paper, 1372×914 mm, 1987; artist's col.) In them she shifted her emphasis from what could be seen as a culturally separatist approach, a truth to a specific ethnic experience to focus instead on the communicative abilities and power of the work itself. Her themes, however, continued to be the experiences of a black woman living in a white society, and how religion, politics and sexual politics made up that experience.

BIBLIOGRAPHY

Sonia Boyce (exh. cat., intro P. Ntuli; London, Air Gal., 1987) [texts by Boyce]
The Impossible Self (exh. cat. by B. Ferguson, S. Nairne, S. Boyce and others, Winnipeg, A.G., 1988)
M. Corris: 'Sonia Boyce at Vanessa Devereux Gallery', *Artforum*, xxx (1992), p. 124   □

Boyceau (de la Barauderie), Jacques (*b* Saint-Jean-d'Angely, Charente-Maritime, *c.* 1562; *d* Paris, *c.* 1634). French garden designer and theorist. Of Huguenot origin, he seems early to have enjoyed the favour of Henry of Navarre, later Henry IV. A respected member of the royal entourage, Boyceau was appointed Surintendant des Jardins du Roi in the succeeding reign of Louis XIII. Consequently, he was in a position to exert substantial influence in determining the nature of garden design at that time. In his *Traité du jardinage*, published in 1638, Boyceau succinctly summarized the history of French gardening and codified the rules that would govern the 17th-century formal garden. For the first time a French designer adopted an aesthetic point of view, thereby promoting the intellectual climate that was to establish gardening as a fine art. He introduced a new feeling for monumental scale to the French garden, insisting that it should reflect a strong sense of organic unity in which order, symmetry, and visual harmony would be all-pervasive.

Boyceau appears to have been largely responsible for the gardens of the Luxembourg Palace, Paris (*c.* 1611–29), and, in collaboration with his nephew Jacques de Menours (1591–1637), those of the first Versailles (*c.* 1631–6). Among other gardens, he may be credited with parterre designs for Fontainebleau, Saint-Germain-en-Laye, and the Louvre and the Tuileries in Paris.

WRITINGS

Traité du jardinage: Selon les raisons de la nature et de l'art (Paris, 1638)

BIBLIOGRAPHY

F. H. Hazlehurst: *Jacques Boyceau and the French Formal Garden* (Athens, GA, 1966)

F. HAMILTON HAZLEHURST

Boychuk [Boitchuk], **Mykhaylo** [Mikhail] (*b* Romanivka, nr Ternopil, 30 Oct 1882; *d* 1939). Ukrainian painter, teacher, theorist and restorer. From 1899 to 1905 he studied as the Matejka Academy of Art in Kraków and from 1905 at the Akademien der Bildenden Künste in Munich and Vienna. He lived and worked in Paris from 1908 to 1911 and visited Italy in 1910–11. He then moved to Lemberg (now L'viv), where he restored medieval paintings, and from 1917 settled in Kiev. After the Russian Revolution he emerged as one of the major artists who called for the revival of the Ukrainian national artistic tradition, regarding monumental painting as the most appropriate form. His paintings combine such timeless motifs as labour, motherhood, and man's relationship to the soil with an acute sense of the great dramas of his time and are produced in a highly distinctive continuation of the Ukrainian Art Nouveau style. He drew on the traditions of Byzantine mural painting, Italian early Renaissance art and the medieval art of Ukraine, as well as on the stylistic features of folk art. He was an outstanding teacher and theorist who defended his ideas vigorously and skilfully in public appearances, uniting around him a set of like-minded young artists and creating a tendency that became known as 'Boychukism'. From 1927 the positions taken by Boychuk and his circle, which included Sofiya A. Nalepins'ka-Boychuk (1884–1929), Ivan I. Padalka (1897–1938) and Vasyl' F. Sedlyar (1899–1938), predetermined the activities of the ASSOCIATION OF REVOLUTIONARY ART OF UKRAINE (ARMU). Boychuk and his followers executed monumental frescoes in the Luts'k Barracks (1919) and the Cooperative Institute (1922–3), both in Kiev, at a sanatorium (1927–9) on the Khadzhibey Lagoon at Odessa and in the foyer of the Krasnovods'ky Theatre

(1933–5) in Kharkiv. Accused of 'bourgeois nationalism', he and several of those in his circle fell victim to Stalin's 'Great Terror' (1934–9), and all his wall paintings were destroyed. Boychuk's legacy, which can be judged from photographic reproductions and some surviving easel paintings, is a major influence on Ukrainian painting of the late 20th century.

BIBLIOGRAPHY

K. Slipko-Moskal'tsev: 'M. Boychuk', *Ukraïns'ke malyarstvo* [Ukrainian painting] (Kharkiv, 1930), pp. 7–51

E. Kholostenko: *Monumental'ne malyarstvo Radyans'koï Ukraïny* [Monumental painting of the Soviet Ukraine] (Kiev, 1932)

V. P. TSEL'TNER

Boyd. Australian family of artists and writers founded by the landscape painters Arthur Merric Boyd (1862–1940) and his wife Emma Minnie Boyd (1858–1936). Their children included (William) Merric Boyd (1888–1959), who founded Australia's first significant studio pottery at Murrumbeena with his wife, the ceramicist Doris Lucy Eleanor Boyd (*c.* 1883–1960); and (Theodore) Penleigh Boyd (1890–1923), who was a noted landscape painter and etcher. Penleigh's son (1) Robin Boyd became a well-known architect and writer, who helped to develop a more critical approach to Australian architecture and culture. Merric and Doris had five children, all of whom became artists and were at some stage involved with ceramic art. Among them were Lucy Boyd (*b* 1915); Guy Boyd (1923–88), who was also a sculptor; David Boyd (*b* 1925); and Mary Boyd (*b* 1926), who married John Perceval (1944) and then Sydney Nolan (1978). The most noted, however, was (2) Arthur Boyd, the celebrated Expressionist painter.

(1) Robin (Gerard Penleigh) Boyd (*b* Melbourne, 3 Jan 1919; *d* Melbourne, 16 Oct 1971). Architect and writer. He was articled to Kingsley Henderson (1882–1942) from 1936 to 1940 and also worked for ROY GROUNDS while studying part-time at the Royal Melbourne Technical College and the University of Melbourne. After service in World War II he set up his own office (1946–53), then practised in partnership with Grounds and FREDERICK ROMBERG from 1953 to 1962 and with Frederick Romberg alone after 1962. From the beginning of his career Boyd was a tireless promoter of architecture, particularly Australian. He contributed regularly to newspapers and professional journals as well as working for radio and television, and he wrote many books on Australian architecture and society, several of which became classics. He was also instrumental in introducing developments in modern Japanese architecture to the West through his books on the subject. He was a fine, witty and satirical writer who particularly wished to stimulate open public debate on the built environment at a time when the prevailing context in Australia inclined towards provincialism. Alongside these activities Boyd maintained a substantial practice as an architect, which he considered his principal role. He was influenced by Grounds and Harry Seidler in his early domestic work but rapidly developed his own highly experimental and inventive direction, and the varied generating themes of his house projects were as provocative as his writings. His work was much affected by the enthusiasm in the 1950s for dramatic structural forms and unconventional plan geometries as the basis for architectural expression, but it was always responsive to particular sites and clients. Examples of this approach, all in Melbourne, include the sprayed concrete 'Ctesiphon arch' paraboloid construction used in Ctesiphon House and shop (1952), Jordansville; the staggered plan of Troedel House (1954–5), Wheeler's Hill, cleverly reinterpreting the colonial verandah; his own courtyard house (1957–8), South Yarra, with a roof carried on suspended steel cables; and Featherstone House (1967–9), Ivanhoe, with its series of stepped living platforms cantilevered over an internal garden and lit through a translucent insulated roof. He also carried out a number of more substantial buildings, notably the elegant, multistorey Domain Park Flats (1960–62), South Yarra, and the Brutalist-inspired Menzies College (1965–70) at La Trobe University, both in Melbourne.

WRITINGS

Victorian Modern (Melbourne, 1947)
Australia's Home (Melbourne, 1952, rev. 3/1987)
The Australian Ugliness (Melbourne, 1960, rev. 1968)
Kenzo Tange (New York, 1962)
The Puzzle of Architecture (Melbourne, 1965)
New Directions in Japanese Architecture (London and New York, 1968)
with M. Strizic: *Living In Australia* (Sydney, 1970) [illus. with his own archit.]
The Great, Great Australian Dream (Sydney, 1972)

BIBLIOGRAPHY

Sir Z. Cowan, ed.: 'Homage to Robin Boyd', *Archit. Australia*, lxii/2 (1973), pp. 51–91
C. Hamann: 'Roy Grounds, Frederick Romberg and Robin Boyd', *Architects of Australia*, ed. H. Tanner (South Melbourne and Artarmon, NSW, 1981), pp. 129–39
——: 'Against the Dying of the Light: Robin Boyd and Australian Architecture', *Transition*, 29 (1989), pp. 9–26
Robin Boyd: The Architect as Critic (exh. cat., ed. K. Burns and H. Edquist; Melbourne, State Lib., La Trobe Col., 1989)
H. Edquist and H. Stuckey, eds: 'Special Issue: Robin Boyd', *Transition*, 38 (1992) [contains list of works]

RORY SPENCE

Arthur Boyd: *Nude with Beast III*, oil and tempera on board, 1.60×1.83 m, 1962 (Melbourne, National Gallery of Victoria)

(2) Arthur (Merric Bloomfield) Boyd (*b* Murrumbeena, nr Melbourne, 24 July 1920). Painter, potter, etcher, lithographer and draughtsman, active also in England; cousin of (1) Robin Boyd. He was taught by his parents and by his grandfather and briefly attended evening classes at the National Gallery School in Melbourne. From 1941 to 1944 he served in the army in World War II and moved in the circles of artists associated with the Australian Contemporary Art Society. He met John Reed (*b* 1901) and formed friendships with Sidney Nolan, John Perceval (*b* 1923), Peter Herbst (*b* 1919) and Noel Counihan; he also met the European Expressionist painters Josl Bergner and Danila Vassilieff, who had migrated to Australia. During this period Boyd developed a figurative idiom drawn from Surrealism, Social Realism and Expressionism, and he acquired the immediacy and spontaneity of handling that was to be characteristic of much of his later work.

After leaving the army, Boyd joined with Perceval and Herbst to set up the Arthur Merric Boyd Pottery Workshop at Murrumbeena. Realizing that his despairing wartime paintings might no longer find favour, Boyd turned in the 1950s to the religious mysticism traditional in his family. He was inspired by the work of Pieter Bruegel the elder and Rembrandt, and he created a number of biblical paintings, such as *Susanna and the Elders* (1945–6; Canberra, N.G.), in which humour and piety, the material and the spiritual blend in a manner that was to remain typical of his oeuvre. In 1958 he had a major success with his *Bride* series, sometimes called his *Allegorical Paintings* (see 1962 exh. cat.), a series of compositions of large figures, dealing with the life and death of a half-caste man and his bride.

From 1959 to 1971 Boyd lived in England, at first in London, where he formed a lasting friendship with the Australian poet Peter Porter, and later in Suffolk. The writer and gallery director Bryan Robertson arranged a retrospective exhibition of his work at the Whitechapel Gallery, London, in 1962. During the 1960s Boyd painted series such as *Nude with Beast* (see fig.) and *Nebuchadnezzar*, placing legendary and historical figures in Antipodean settings. In 1971 Boyd returned to Australia on a Fellowship to the Australian National University in Canberra. Subsequently he acquired properties on the Shoalhaven River, NSW, and began to divide his time between Suffolk and Australia. Landscape painting, which had formed a large part of his youthful work, once more became a major preoccupation. Unlike his earlier bush settings, the landscapes of the 1970s and 1980s are of identifiable scenery, such as the Pulpit Rock range and the winding Shoalhaven River, with its boating and bathing. There are 16 large Shoalhaven riverbank scenes (1974 onwards) on display in the National Gallery of Victoria, Melbourne. After giving an Australian sense of place to Classical and traditional themes such as *Narcissus*, *Lysistrata* or the *Return of the Prodigal Son*, Boyd turned to contemporary subjects in the *Bather* sequence (1984 and 1985). Major commissions of the 1980s included the maquette for the mammoth tapestry destined for the reception area of the new Parliament House in Canberra.

Boyd also designed stage sets, including one for Robert Helpman's ballet *Electra* (first produced in March 1963). Throughout his career he produced both sculpture and paintings in the ceramic medium, published sets of etchings and lithographs and executed a large number of drawings.

BIBLIOGRAPHY

Arthur Boyd (exh. cat. by B. Robertson, London, Whitechapel A.G., 1962)
F. Philipp: *Arthur Boyd* (London, 1967)
Arthur Boyd Retrospective (exh. cat. by T. G. Rosenthal and C. Oliver, Edinburgh, Richard Demarco Gal., 1969)
I. von Maltzahn: *Arthur Boyd: Etchings and Lithographs* (London, 1971)
G. Gunn: *Arthur Boyd: Seven Persistent Images* (Canberra, 1985)
U. Hoff: *The Art of Arthur Boyd* (London, 1986)
P. Dobrez and P. Herbst: *The Art of the Boyds: Generations of Artistic Achievement* (Sydney and London, 1990)
Arthur Boyd Retrospective (exh. cat. by B. Pearce, Sydney, A.G. NSW, 1994)

URSULA HOFF

Boyd, Harriet (Ann) (*b* Boston, MA, 11 Oct 1871; *d* Washington, DC, 31 March 1945). American archaeologist. She was a pioneer of the archaeological excavation of Minoan Crete, first travelling in the island in 1900 as a fellow of the American School of Classical Studies in Athens. Adventurous and intrepid, she explored the area of east Crete around the Isthmus of Hierapetra, covering the rough terrain on mule-back. At the suggestion of Sir ARTHUR EVANS, then beginning his investigation of Knossos, she excavated at Kavousi on the eastern side of the Gulf of Mirabello, revealing remains of an early Iron Age site. On her return to Crete in 1901 information from a local peasant led to her most remarkable discovery, the prosperous Minoan town of GOURNIA, where she directed excavations in 1901, 1903 and 1904, often employing a workforce of more than a hundred. She succeeded in unearthing virtually the whole town, and the evidence, which she published with exemplary speed, provided useful comparisons with that from the grander palace sites at Knossos and Phaistos. She married the English anthropologist Charles Henry Hawes in 1906 and, after doing relief work during World War I and raising a family, became a lecturer in pre-Christian art at Wellesley College, MA, from 1920 to 1936.

WRITINGS
Gournia, Vasiliki and Other Prehistoric Sites on the Isthmus of Hierapetra, Crete (Philadelphia, 1908)

BIBLIOGRAPHY
Obituary, *Amer. J. Archaeol.*, xlix (1945), p. 359
R. Higgins: *The Archaeology of Minoan Crete* (London, 1973)
M. Allsebrook: *Born to Rebel: Life of Harriet Boyd Hawes* (Oxford, 1992)

J. LESLEY FITTON

Boydell, John (*b* Dorrington, Salop, 19 Jan 1719; *d* London, 12 Dec 1804). English engraver and print-seller. The son of a land surveyor, Boydell at first pursued his father's occupation. In 1731 the family moved to Hawarden in Flintshire (now Clwyd), Wales, where he began making copies of book illustrations. He saw an engraving of *Hawarden Castle* (*c.* 1740) by William Henry Toms (*c.* 1700–*c.* 1750) that induced him to go to London in 1740 to become Toms's apprentice. He also enrolled in the St Martin's Lane Academy. In 1746 he established himself as an independent engraver with a shop on the Strand, where he produced inexpensive topographical prints and published his first collection of engravings, *The Bridge Book* (*c.* 1747). In 1751 he moved to a larger shop in Cheapside, where he began to import landscape prints after Claude Lorrain and Salvator Rosa. Boydell paid unprecedented sums to William Woollett to engrave Claude's *Temple of Apollo* (*c.* 1760; painting 1663; Anglesey Abbey, Cambs, NT) and Richard Wilson's *Destruction of the Children of Niobe* (1761; painting *c.* 1759–60; New Haven, CT, Yale Cent. Brit. A.), both of which were commercially successful. His low-cost publication, *A Collection of One Hundred and Two Views, &c, in England and Wales* (1755), likewise sold a large number of copies.

Never more than a mediocre engraver himself, Boydell virtually stopped engraving in order to capitalize on the growing print market in England. He increased his fortune through sales of Woollett's line-engraving after Benjamin West's popular and controversial *Death of General Wolfe* (1776; painting 1770; Ottawa, N.G.). Boydell's discovery of the European market for English prints and his subsequent dealings in print exports established his reputation internationally. His growing respectability resulted in his appointment as Alderman for Cheapside (1785), Sheriff of London (1785) and Lord Mayor of London (1790–91).

Boydell's success encouraged him to embark on his most ambitious project, the 'Shakespeare Gallery'. This idea was first proposed, possibly by George Romney, at a dinner party in November 1786 as a means of creating patronage for history painting in England. It consisted of three elements: a series of oil paintings representing scenes from Shakespeare's plays; a folio collection of engravings after the paintings; and a new edition of Shakespeare's plays (published 1802), edited by George Steevens (1736–1800), also with accompanying engravings. Boydell risked an enormous sum on this venture, relying on the popularity of Shakespeare's plays and the stability of the European market. The Gallery opened at 52 Pall Mall on 4 May 1789 with 34 paintings by Sir Joshua Reynolds, Benjamin West, Henry Fuseli, Joseph Wright of Derby, James Northcote and others. Although some works were praised, critics attacked the artists' inaccurate interpretations of the plays and impugned Boydell's motives. Among the most savage attacks was James Gillray's print *Shakespeare Sacrificed: Or the Offering to Avarice* (20 June 1789). Subscribers to the prints became disgruntled at the long delays, and Boydell's employment of a quick, but sometimes sloppy, stipple technique in order to speed up production caused further criticism. The outbreak of war with France in 1793 destroyed his hopes for expanding his export market.

During the 1790s Boydell financed other ventures. He paid James Heath 2000 guineas for a line-engraving after John Singleton Copley's *Death of Major Pierson* (1796; painting 1783; London, Tate), but the years Heath took to make the engraving diminished public interest in the once-topical subject. Boydell also commissioned and donated portraits and paintings of episodes from English history, such as Northcote's *Death of Wat Tyler* (1786–7; destr. 1940), to the Common Council Chamber at the Guildhall, London. He began to publish William Combe's *An History of the River Thames* (1794–6) with topographical engravings by Joseph Farington, but adverse critical reaction halted the project. Boydell's various failures forced him to sell off his stock by a lottery, which was held a month after his death, on 28 January 1805. The subsequent sale of the Shakespeare Gallery pictures at Christie's fetched only £6182 for the lottery winner. Despite the eventual failure of his attempt to revive history painting in England, Boydell was a central figure in the growth of 18th-century English engraving.

WRITINGS

A Catalogue of Pictures in the Shakespeare Gallery, Pall Mall (London, 1789, 2/1802)

PRINTS

The Bridge Book ([London], *c.* 1747)

BIBLIOGRAPHY

A. Graves: 'A New Light on Alderman Boydell', *Mag. A.*, xxi (1897) [complete issue]
L. Thompson: 'The Boydell Shakespeare: An English Monument to Graphic Arts', *Princeton U. Lib. Chron.*, vii (1944), pp. 20–33
T. Balston: 'John Boydell, Publisher: "The Commercial Maecenas"', *Signature*, n.s., viii (1949), pp. 3–22
W. Friedman: *Boydell's Shakespeare Gallery* (New York, 1976)
A. Griffiths: 'A Checklist of Catalogues of British Print Publishers *c.* 1650–1830', *Prt Q.*, i/1 (1984), pp. 14–15 [lists Boydell's catalogues]
S. Bruntjen: *John Boydell, 1719–1804: A Study of Art Patronage and Publishing in Georgian London* (New York, 1985)

SHEARER WEST

Boye, Pierre (*fl* 1313/14–51). French sculptor. He has sometimes been identified with Pierron Boi, a stone-carver mentioned in 1286 and 1311 in the town rolls of Ypres, but Baron's attribution to Boye of the tomb of *Clement VI* hardly allows for such an early beginning to his career. He was in Paris in 1313–14, where he participated with Jean Pépin de Huy and others in the execution of the tomb of *Otto IV, Count of Burgundy* (mostly destr.) commissioned by his widow, Mahaut, Countess of Artois. In 1317 she ordered an alabaster *Virgin and Child* (destr.) from the sculptor, which was destined as a gift for her niece, Alix de Vienne, mother superior of the Franciscan nuns at Lons-le-Saunier (Jura).

Boye's style is known from the remains of the tomb of *Clement VI* (Haute-Loire, La Chaise-Dieu, abbey church; Le Puy, Mus. Crozatier). Materials were acquired for the tomb in 1342, and the work was completed between 1349 and 1351, probably at the papal court in Avignon, by a team of artists directed by Boye. After Clement's death in 1352 his tomb was installed in the church of La Chaise-Dieu Abbey (Haute-Loire), where the Pope had been a monk. The monument was attacked and partially destroyed by Protestants in 1562. The restored *gisant* remains in the church. It originally rested on a black marble sarcophagus decorated with white marble reliefs representing a cortège of family members, a procession of 44 mourners that included male and female figures in both lay and clerical dress. The delicate but bland faces and refined drapery of the figures reveal a close affinity to court works, especially the tombs executed for the first Valois kings at Saint-Denis Abbey.

BIBLIOGRAPHY

Lami; Thieme–Becker
F. Baron: 'Pierre Boye', *Bull. Soc. Hist. A. Fr.* (1959), pp. 101–3
Les Fastes du gothique: Le Siècle de Charles V (exh. cat., Paris, Grand Pal., 1981–2), no. 47, p. 434
M. Beaulieu and V. Beyer: *Dictionnaire des sculpteurs français du moyen âge* (Paris, 1992), p. 60
J. Gardner: *The Tomb and the Tiara: Curial Tomb Sculpture in Rome and Avignon in the Later Middle Ages* (Oxford, 1992)

DOROTHY GILLERMAN

Boyle, Mark (*b* Glasgow, 11 May 1934). Scottish sculptor, performance artist and painter. He studied law at the University of Glasgow (1955–6) but received no formal art training. He had a number of jobs until devoting himself entirely to art in 1958, when he met the artist Joan Hills (*b* Edinburgh, 1936) and began living and working with her. His earliest works were paintings, which were featured in his first one-man show in 1963. From 1964 he organized a series of events presented in front of an audience, beginning with *Suddenly Last Supper* (1964) at a flat in London. This consisted of films projected on to a variety of surfaces, including a reproduction of Botticelli's *Birth of Venus* (original Florence, Uffizi) projected on to a nude woman in the same pose; the films were destroyed by fire or acid while still running, and during the performance the entire contents of the flat were removed, leaving the audience alone. Another event staged in London in 1964 was *The Street*, in which a group of people was led unknowingly into the back of a shop; once they were in place a screen was pulled back to reveal the street outside, with the variety of its activity presented as a 'found' performance.

After 1967 Boyle moved away from events and from the light shows he created for live performances by such rock musicians as the Soft Machine and Jimi Hendrix. Between August 1968 and July 1969 he invited members of the public to his studio, where they were blindfolded and asked to throw darts (1000 in all) at a map of the world. These randomly selected locations formed the start of the project *Journey to the Surface of the Earth*. Boyle and Hills planned to visit each of the locations and make an exact relief reproduction of an area of the surface there, as in *Hague Study* (1970; The Hague, Gemeentemus.), using a process of casting in fibreglass and other materials first employed by him in the mid-1960s (for illustration *see* FIBREGLASS). The project was intended as a means of revealing the beauty and interest of traditionally banal materials, such as rock, earth and sand, and of making the viewer more perceptually aware. It became his life's work, extended to include other places the artists happened to visit. From the 1980s, working as the Boyle Family, they were helped by their children, Georgia Boyle (*b* 1962) and Sebastian Boyle (*b* 1964).

BIBLIOGRAPHY

Journey to the Surface of the Earth: Mark Boyle's Atlas and Manual (exh. cat., The Hague, Gemeentemus., 1970)
Beyond Image: Boyle Family (exh. cat. by Boyle Family and D. Thompson, London, Hayward Gal., 1986)   □

Boyle. English family of patrons and collectors. (2) Richard Boyle was also architect.

(1) Richard Boyle, 1st Earl of Cork (*b* Canterbury, 13 Oct 1566; *d* Youghal, Cork, 15 Sept 1643). Patron and collector. He was a man of great energy and ability; coming to Ireland in 1588 as an adventurer, he became indispensable to the English government there, although he was criticized for irregular financial practices. The wealth he acquired through his first marriage enabled him to purchase Sir Walter Raleigh's 12,000-acre portion of the lands confiscated after the Desmond Rebellion (1570). Boyle was committed to the development of manufacture and trade: he developed ironworks, built bridges and harbours and founded towns. In 1620 he was created Earl of Cork. He was interested in the arts insofar as they were reflections of his and his family's rising social status. During his lifetime he had two tombs made for himself: one (1620) in St Mary's, Youghal, by Alexander Hills of Holborn, and a second vast, multi-tiered construction (1631) in St Patrick's Cathedral, Dublin, carved by Edmond Tingham (*fl c.* 1630), a sculptor in Dublin. Boyle also erected a monument to his eldest son, Roger Boyle (*d* 1615), in the parish church at Deptford and a monument to his parents in the parish church at Preston, Kent. He was very interested in building; his principal houses were at Lismore, Waterford (1604), and at Youghal (1615). At Maynooth, Kildare, he built a house for his son-in-law, Lord Kildare. He also built houses in Ireland at Broghill, Gill Abbey, Castlelyons, Cork and Askeaton, Limerick, and he significantly altered Stalbridge, Dorset (1638–9): all of these houses have disappeared. The interiors of Boyle's houses were luxurious: his accounts record that from 1613 he was buying tapestries, furniture, upholstery, silver and jewellery, both in London and in Dublin. He is particularly important for having been one of the earliest patrons of painting in Ireland. In 1621 he commissioned portraits of himself and five members of his family from a French artist. In 1617 he bought pictures from a Dutch merchant, and in 1624 he commissioned another portrait of himself; the National Portrait Gallery, London, has a miniature of him by Isaac Oliver. Boyle's is the only surviving inventory of paintings before 1660.

DNB

BIBLIOGRAPHY

R. E. W. Maddison: *The Life of the Honourable Robert Boyle FRS* (London, 1969), pls II–V, XI–XII

A. Crookshank: 'Lord Cork and his Monuments', *Country Life*, cxlix (27 May 1971), pp. 1288–90

JOHN TURPIN

(2) Richard Boyle, 3rd Earl of Burlington and 4th Earl of Cork (*b* London, 25 April 1694; *d* London, 4 Dec 1753). Patron, collector and architect, great-grandson of (1) Richard Boyle. He was born into a privileged class, in which he was heir to huge estates in Yorkshire and Ireland. Burlington also owned expensive properties in and around London. Referred to by Horace Walpole as the 'Apollo of the Arts', he is famous for his association with the British Palladian Revival (*see* PALLADIANISM), of which he was not only a strong supporter but also one of the strictest exponents. When in 1717 he received permission to grant leases on land behind Burlington House, Piccadilly, many Palladian architects designed buildings in Burlington Street, Savile Row and Sackville Street, London. An avid collector of drawings by Palladio and by Inigo Jones, he disseminated Palladian style through books of engravings and an accurate translation of Palladio's treatise. Burlington's own important buildings include Chiswick House (1725–9), near London, and the Assembly Rooms (1731–6), York. Burlington's interest covered all the fine arts, however, including music and literature. The patronage he practised was considerably different from that of other 17th- and 18th-century aristocrats in that it was much more than a mere economic relationship through which he could assert his social status and power; for Burlington patronage was the expression of a philosophical notion, the means by which to achieve a programme for modernity.

1. Early years and first Grand Tour, to 1715. 2. Development of connoisseurship and second Grand Tour, 1715–19. 3. Architectural practice, after 1719. 4. Theory and influence.

1. EARLY YEARS AND FIRST GRAND TOUR, TO 1715. Unlike other aristocrats, Burlington did not matriculate at either Cambridge or Oxford University. He must therefore have been educated privately at home, under the careful supervision of his mother and such eminent guardians as the enlightened John Lord Somers. They ensured that he was versed in music and literature and seem generally to have fostered in him an interest and curiosity for the visual arts, possibly helped by Richard Graham, a trusted administrator of the family's fortune, who had also supplied the list of 'painters, both ancient and modern' attached to John Dryden's translation of Du Fresnoys's *De arte graphica*. It was at the sale of Graham's collection of paintings, on 6 March 1711/12, that acquisitions by Burlington were first recorded. He bought a landscape with figures hawking by Philips Wouwerman, a landscape with S Giovanni in Laterano in the distance by Gaspard Dughet, a landscape with fishermen drawing their nets by Filippo Laura (all of which subsequently hung at Chiswick House in the Blue Velvet Room); and a round landscape with shepherds by Philipp Peter Roos [Rosa da Tivoli].

Burlington's education reflected the new Whig ideology of virtue and politeness, as formulated by Anthony Ashley Cooper, 3rd Earl of Shaftesbury. He totally identified with the ideas expressed by Shaftesbury in the *Letter Concerning Design* (1712), and saw his role as that of establishing and fostering the much advocated 'National Taste'. Until at least 1714 Burlington was a connoisseur and virtuoso in Shaftesbury's mould: one who limited involvement with the arts to pure aesthetic appreciation and committed patronage. Around 1711–12 he began to arrange weekly concerts at Burlington House, Piccadilly, London. From 1712 to 1715 Burlington House was the home of the German composer George Frideric Handel. In winter 1711–12 Giovanni Antonio Pellegrini painted two large canvases for the hall at Burlington House, and between 1713 and 1715 Sebastiano Ricci executed a series of canvases covering the upper walls and ceiling of a newly constructed staircase there.

Burlington's Grand Tour (May 1714–May 1715) marked the end of his adolescence. It was planned to bring him back to England in time for his coming of age, thus also with his coming into his hereditary fortune as well as political duties. During his Grand Tour his taste began to take a more definite and personal shape. He was accompanied by a tutor, servants and an artistic adviser, the French painter Louis Goupy, who advised Burlington in his acquisition of paintings. Burlington's travelling account-book (now at Chatsworth House, Derbys) records payments for paintings from as early as June 1714. At this date he was in Brussels acquiring 'small pictures', mostly wooden panels of genre scenes by 17th-century Flemish and Dutch painters. Quite predictably, however, the heaviest and most lavish expenses for paintings were incurred in Italy, and particularly in Rome, where the party arrived in September 1714, leaving five months later.

Burlington's acquisitions hint of a taste less alert to the most recent trends of Roman painting than other English travellers, such as, his friends Thomas Coke and Sir Andrew Fountaine; yet they reveal a consistent interest in Italian seicento classicism, including as they did paintings by Annibale Carracci (the *Temptation of St Anthony*), Domenichino (the *Madonna della Rosa*), Pietro da Cortona, Giacinto Brandi and Carlo Maratti. At this time Burlington's only concessions to contemporary painting were some views of Rome and Florence by Gaspar van Wittel and, in Venice, 12 pastels by Rosalba Carriera. The second longest stay in the course of the Grand Tour was in Paris where the Earl and his retinue remained from 27 March 1714/15 to 2 May. Here too he engaged in buying paintings, notably van Dyck's *Belisarius* from the Duke of Melfort's collection, and two works by Sébastien Bourdon (the *Crucifixion of St Peter* and a *Holy Family*).

While abroad Burlington visited private and public collections, gardens and palaces, but his preferred pastime was going to the opera and attending concerts. In Rome he regularly attended performances at the Teatro Capranica and at Cardinal Pietro Ottoboni's private theatre in the Palazzo della Cancelleria. Ottoboni became Burlington's idea of a model patron and connoisseur. It was probably in the environment of the Ottoboni palace that Burlington first met WILLIAM KENT and Filippo Juvarra. Kent was subsequently persuaded by Burlington to return to London, where he undertook works for him. The subsequent cultural life of Burlington House and Chiswick was modelled on that of the Palazzo della Cancelleria.

2. DEVELOPMENT OF CONNOISSEURSHIP AND SECOND GRAND TOUR, 1715–19. Back in England, and by now the master of his own fortunes, Burlington began to diversify his interests and to support the arts on a lavish scale. In 1715 there was a turning-point when he not only started patronizing poets, such as John Gay (who resided at Burlington House) and Alexander Pope, but he also turned his attention to two major contemporary publications, namely Colen Campbell's *Vitruvius Britannicus* and James Leoni's translation of Palladio's *Quattro libri dell'architettura.* Campbell's call for a return in architecture to the decorum and correctness of the Ancients, of which Andrea Palladio and Inigo Jones were the most respected representatives, had an unresistible appeal for Burlington, who must have recognized its fundamental similarities with Ottoboni's and the Arcadia's programme of Renaissance-inspired classical revival of all branches of the arts. These ideas were further strengthened by renewed contact with John Talman, the architect and antiquary whom the Earl had first met in Rome, and who returned to London in 1716. Between *c.* 1717 and 1720 COLEN CAMPBELL remodelled and refaced Burlington House into a model Palladian town house, to designs derived from the Palazzo Porto at Vicenza (see fig. 1). Kent worked on the interior decoration.

Burlington's attitude towards connoisseurship also appears to have been affected by the events of 1715. From this time he did not just limit himself to collecting works of art and supporting artists, but he became an amateur artist himself, first dabbling as a garden designer in the grounds of his estate at Chiswick, and then turning into a

1. Burlington House, Piccadilly, London; remodelled by Colen Campbell *c.* 1717–20

fully fledged architect. For Shaftesbury, and for 18th-century society at large, artistic practice by an aristocrat was seen as a virtual threat to the social edifice, and Burlington's activity inevitably attracted much waspish criticism from his contemporaries. On the other hand, it was precisely this new, direct involvement in art that made Burlington's patronage after 1715 so unique and effective. More than anybody else, Burlington contributed to transformation of the social status of the British artist: he bridged the social gap between patron and artist by sharing with the latter the experience of creation. For Burlington his practice of architecture represented the ultimate expression of social virtue; designing buildings was neither a diminishing and debasing activity, nor did it entail any risk of social upset. On the contrary, for him architecture was one of the aristocracy's most refined means of exercising the function of government, since architecture shapes man's environment and organizes, through its rational control of space, the public and private activities of different and conflicting social classes. This was particularly relevant at a time when London was expanding at an unprecedented pace (*see* LONDON, §II, 3), and the rising entrepreneurial classes were perceived as a potential threat to the ordered development of the urban environment.

By 1717 Burlington had designed his first building, the so-called New Bagnio, in the grounds of his Chiswick estate, shown in the background of Jonathan Richardson's portrait of the Earl of *c.* 1717–19 (London, N.P.G.; see fig. 2). Indeed it was at Chiswick that he made his first experiments as an architect and where he developed his ideas on garden design (*see* CHISWICK HOUSE, §2). These were revolutionary for England since they were predicated on Italian precedents that he had studied in the course of his travels and also incorporated many elements borrowed from the practice of stage design. Burlington's style in gardening was not static; it evolved and reflected the sharing of ideas that took place between himself and Alexander Pope, who was equally preoccupied with gardening issues. Gradually Burlington developed a broad naturalistic style, grounded in the concept of *imitatio ruris*, for which he drew inspiration both from Roman Classical precedents, as described by Pliny, Varro and Columella, and from the imperial gardens of China. The latter were publicized in 1724 by the Jesuit father Matteo Ripa in a book of engravings.

As Burlington's interest and understanding of architecture increased, he became aware that a second trip to Italy was necessary, the ultimate goal being the study of the masterpieces of Renaissance architecture in the Veneto as well as in Rome. His second trip took place in 1719, but only very few scanty references to it survive. Burlington left England sometime between July and August 1719, accompanied by several servants, including Samuel Saville, an architectural draughtsman. The group remained in Paris until September 1719, then headed south, towards Florence and Rome, where they must have stopped for some time and engaged in the study of buildings. In his capacity as Director of the newly established Royal Academy of Music (founded July 1719) in Rome Burlington secured the services of several leading singers for the forthcoming season. Inevitably this brought him back into the lively Ottoboni circle, renewing contacts and making new ones. He met again with Kent and, possibly thanks to him, developed a new interest in Roman painting, commissioning paintings from Giuseppe Chiari (the *Presentation at the Temple*), Imperiali (*Woman with Cattle*), Giovanni Paolo Panini (the *Arch of Constantine*) and Giovanni Gioseffo dal Sole (*Hagar and the Angel*). Sometime in October 1719 Burlington moved north, directed towards the Veneto. According to Kent, who was then himself travelling back to England, 'he was agoing towards Vicenza and Venice to get Archetecs to draw all ye fine buildings of Palladio'. He was in fact in Vicenza by 3 November, the date which he inscribed on an edition of 1601 of Palladio's *Quattro libri dell'architettura*; he had this copy interleaved with blank pages, in which he annotated his observations on the actual buildings. At this time Burlington must have met Francesco Muttoni, a Palladian architect active in Vicenza for some years. Muttoni appears to have been one of the architects engaged by Burlington to produce a survey of Palladio's buildings. Twelve drawings by him survive at Chatsworth illustrating five buildings by Palladio or attributed to him by Muttoni, as well as four works by Muttoni himself. All the drawings were provided with double scales in English and Vicentine feet for the purpose of study. The other architect to whom Burlington turned for accurate survey drawings of Palladio's architecture was Antonio Visentini, who ran in Venice a thriving business in architectural views of the Grand Canal. It was presumably in autumn 1719 that Burlington commissioned from him 84 drawings (London, RIBA), of which 24 are illustrations of buildings by Palladio. Burlington's aim was to assemble a wide record of Palladio's built works, which could then be usefully compared with his theoretical writings. This attitude soon stretched to include the pursuit of Palladio's original drawings together with those by Inigo Jones, the other great 'authority' on whom Burlington, and the Neo-Palladians at large, relied so heavily (*see* §4 below).

Burlington returned to England at the beginning of December 1719, having managed to secure the services of Kent, who became a resident of Burlington House and the Earl's closest collaborator. Although architecture had become Burlington's principal interest, he maintained an active interest in painting, sculpture, music and literature. He patronized the sculptors Michael Rysbrack, Peter Scheemakers and Giovanni Battista Guelfi; the painters Pieter Andreas Rysbrack, Jacques Rigaud, George Lambert, Jean-Baptiste van Loo, Jonathan Richardson sr, William Aikman and Charles Jervas. In the fine and decorative arts, as in architecture, Burlington favoured a form of restrained classicism, and was not easily swayed by new fashions. His painting collection generally remained representative of 16th- and 17th-century Italian and French masters. In court circles, his influence in matters of taste was great but effectively limited to architecture and music.

2. *Earl of Burlington* by Jonathan Richardson, oil on canvas, 1.46×1.17m, *c.* 1717–19 (London, National Portrait Gallery)

3. ARCHITECTURAL PRACTICE, AFTER 1719. During the 1720s Burlington was engaged on several private commissions, designing houses for aristocatic friends or relatives. His chief preoccupation of the decade was the building of his own villa at CHISWICK HOUSE (see fig. 3). Begun in 1725, it was modelled on Palladio's Villa Capra (or Rotonda) at Vicenza, with additional elements taken from Palladio's Villa Foscari at Malcontenta di Mira, near Venice, and from Scamozzi's Rocca Pisana (1575–8) at Lonigo. In May 1730 Burlington was approached by the directors of the Assembly Rooms at York with a request that he design a new building for 'dancing, cards, refreshments, and perhaps underground, a place with a chimney for footmen'. The only comparable building was Jones's Banqueting House (1619), Whitehall, London, originally used for court masques and receptions. This Burlington revised in the light of the pseudo-classical prototype

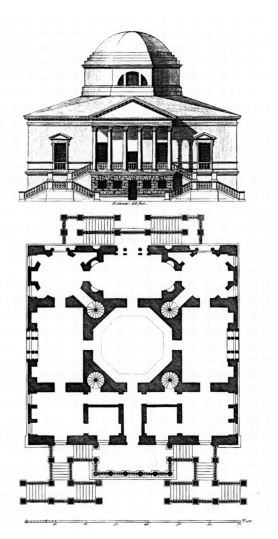

3. Richard Boyle: Chiswick House, begun 1725; illustration from William Kent: *Designs of Inigo Jones* (1727)

provided by Palladio's interpretation of Vitruvius's Egyptian Hall, the free-standing Corinthian colonnade of which enabled Burlington to solve the problem of the corner by introducing one column in each right angle of the colonnade. The clerestory was treated with pilasters instead of columns to outline the strengthened elements of the building's skeleton. This entailed using either a folded pilaster or corner pier, and Burlington chose the latter solution. The elevation of the Assembly Rooms (see fig. 4; replaced in 1828 by a Neo-classical front) was as uncompromising as its interior: a convex portico modelled on standard reconstructions of the Temple of Bacchus. The three arches of the Roman temple's portico were altered for the Assembly Rooms by introducing Corinthian columns that support entablatures; mullions above them in the upper part of the archway were to be read as a Diocletian window. This motif, filled in, was repeated in the low side wings that carried open pediments. The elevation thus used elements both from the Temple of Bacchus and from the Roman baths; the way in which volumes related to one another was, however, entirely novel. The building (completed 1732) was conceived as a number of pure solids intersecting each other, in which the clarity and purity of the geometric shapes replace traditional decoration (for illustration of the ground-plan *see* ASSEMBLY ROOMS). The Assembly Rooms were Burlington's last work, and it is not clear why he abandoned so abruptly architectural design and retreated to the more normal role of architectural adviser. An increasingly scholarly involvement with architecture is suggested by his acquisition of the greater part of his architectural books over the period 1735–41.

4. THEORY AND INFLUENCE. It is generally accepted by scholars that Burlington promoted a number of initiatives without which Palladianism would not have turned out to be as successful as it was. He appears to have understood the need to operate on two levels: a theoretical and didactic one, purely addressed to the architects; and a political one aimed at ensuring the diffusion of the new architectural taste through the control of the key architectural jobs in the Royal Office of Works. The first aim was achieved by providing a hand-picked group of budding architects with a wealth of sources, published and unpublished, which had not previously been available in England. He extensively acquired architectural drawings, especially in 1721–3, by Palladio, Jones and Scamozzi, and also gathered Renaissance sketchbooks after the Antique, drawings of interiors and stage designs. He had detailed surveys made of Inigo Jones's buildings, and was constantly in search of lost or unattributed works, for example the Earl of Strafford's ruined house at Naas, near Dublin, which he had investigated by Sir Edward Lovett Pearce. Study of actual buildings and of projects related to them was inseparable from that of the general theory of architecture, and here Burlington encouraged the publication of a new, accurate English translation of Palladio's *Quattro libri*; this English edition was crucially important for the diffusion of Palladian style among British architects. The project was first started by Campbell, who only succeeded in bringing out in 1728 a translation of the first book, and was eventually brought to fruition by Isaac Ware in 1738.

4. Richard Boyle: elevation of the Assembly Rooms, York, 1731–2; engraving from the expanded edition of *Fabbriche antiche disegnate da Andrea Palladio* (1730)

The publishing ventures with which Burlington was personally involved had much less impact. Both *The Designs of Inigo Jones and Others* (1725–7) and the *Fabbriche antiche disegnate da Andrea Palladio* (1730) lacked any exhaustive explanatory text and made no effort to appeal to the wide public of artisans and builders.

If there is any academicism in Burlington's work, it stems from his accurate reading of Italian Renaissance treatises (compounded by his own first-hand observations of buildings) and from the development of an architectural system that accepts in an uncompromising way the distinction (originally from Leon Battista Alberti) between the working of column and pier. This system accepted the column only as a loadbearing element, so reducing to a minimum the ornamental function of the orders. In comparison with the work of contemporaries, Burlington's architecture appears frigid, because his was a proper archaeological reconstruction; he refused to operate within a system that mixed Greek with Roman traditions.

Despite his choice of Palladio and Jones as authoritative guides, Burlington was in fact a highly original architect, working in an idiom that can unhesitantly be described as being ahead of his time. The striking and often jarring quality of his architecture is achieved by producing large surfaces of bare, smooth astylar wall, interrupted only by neatly cut out fenestration, by juxtaposing pure volumes, untrammelled by decoration to achieve the typical staccato quality (first noticed by Rudolph Wittkower), and finally, by constantly avoiding any chiaroscural treatment of the façade. These features were characteristic of his work from very early in his career until his later essays; they are perfectly illustrated by, for example, the Westminster Dormitory (1721), London, the Almshouses at Sevenoaks

(1726), the new villa at Chiswick, the Chichester Council House (1730) and the Assembly Rooms at York. The result was an architecture of a logical clarity unparalleled until the surge of Neo-classicism in the latter part of the century.

UNPUBLISHED SOURCES

Chatsworth House, Derbys [corr. from Lord Burlington to Lady Burlington]
Norfolk, Narford Hall, Andrew Fountaine Col. [corr. from Lord Burlington to Sir Andrew Fountaine]

BIBLIOGRAPHY

F. Kimball: 'Burlington Architectus: Part I', *RIBA J.*, xxxiv (1927), pp. 675–93
—: 'Burlington Architectus: Part II', *RIBA J.*, xxxv (1927), 125–9
H. F. Clark: 'Lord Burlington's Bijou Villa', *Archit. Rev.* [London], xcvii (May 1944), pp. 125–9
J. Lees Milne: *Earls of Creation: Five Great Patrons of Architecture* (London, 1962, rev. 2/New York, 1963)
I. H. Goodhall: 'Lord Burlington's York Piazza', *York Georgian Soc. Annual Report* (1970)
J. Wilton Ely, ed.: *Apollo of the Arts: Lord Burlington and his Circle* (Nottingham, 1973)
R. Wittkower: 'Lord Burlington and William Kent', *Palladio and English Palladianism* (London and New York, 1974)
—: 'Lord Burlington's Work at York', *Palladio and English Palladianism* (London and New York, 1974), pp. 137–8
K. Downes: 'Chiswick Villa', *Archit. Rev.* [London], clxiv/980 (1978), pp. 225–36
J. Harris: *The Palladians* (London, 1981), pp. 71–80
C. M. Sicca: 'Lord Burlington at Chiswick: Architecture and Landscape', *Gdn Hist.*, x/1 (1982), pp. 36–9
R. White, ed.: *Lord Burlington and his Circle* (London, 1982)
J. Wilton Ely: 'Lord Burlington and the Virtuoso Portrait', *Archit. Hist.*, xxvii (1984), pp. 376–81
G. Knox: 'Sebastiano Ricci at Burlington House: A Venetian Decoration *alla romana*', *Burl. Mag.*, cxxvii (Sept 1985), pp. 601–9
T. Rosoman: 'The Interior Decoration and Use of the State Apartments of Chiswick House, 1727–70', *Burl. Mag.*, cxxvii (Oct 1985), pp. 663–77

P. Leach: 'Lord Burlington in Wharfedale', *Archit. Hist.*, xxxii (1989), pp. 68–85
C. M. Sicca: 'The Architecture of the Wall: Astylism in the Architecture of Lord Burlington', *Archit. Hist.*, xxxiii (1990), pp. 83–101

CINZIA MARIA SICCA

Boymans [Boijmans]**, F(rans) J(acob) O(tto)** (*bapt* Maastricht, 1 Nov 1767; *d* Utrecht, 19 June 1847). Dutch lawyer and collector. His father, Johannes Andreas Boijmans, was a doctor in Maastricht; his mother was Theodora Barbara Berg. He took his doctoral degree at the Hogeschool in Utrecht. In 1787 he married Jonkvrouw Arnoudina Elisabeth van Westreenen, who died only two years later; their son Jan André Boymans was born in 1788. Boymans travelled a great deal in Europe, visiting Paris, Brussels and Rome several times, and bought paintings, drawings and other works of art. When his son came of age, he decided to sell the collection to realize Jan André's maternal inheritance. But Cornelis Apostool, then Director of the Koninklijk Museum in Amsterdam, declined to buy the whole collection for the State. Boymans even wrote personally to the king but this, too, was to no avail and he finally decided to sell his collection by auction in Amsterdam. The sale catalogue of 31 August 1811 lists 431 paintings and *c.* 4000 drawings. However, as no suitably high bids were received, the sale was cancelled.

In 1818 Boymans was made a judge, and from 1821 to 1839 he worked in Utrecht. He had considered donating his collection to the town of Utrecht, but the burgomaster apparently took a personal dislike to him and had a low opinion of the collection. Boymans then turned to Rotterdam, where he was on good terms with the burgomaster M. C. Bichon van Ijsselmonde, and in 1841 suggested that if the Rotterdam authorities were to purchase the Schielandhuis (1662–5; designed by Pieter Post, completed by Jacob Lois), his collection could be housed there. The purchase was made the same year and shortly thereafter Boymans sent some paintings to Rotterdam to be measured and fitted into the Schielandhuis. In 1842 Rotterdam's town council accepted Boymans's plan to establish a 'Museum Boymannianum'. The final decision was, however, postponed many times. Boymans made his will just before he died, leaving all his possessions to Rotterdam on condition that a museum was founded. An inventory of the collection was made by Arnoldus Lamme and his son, the painter and art dealer Arie Johannes Lamme; they listed 1193 paintings, 116 portfolios of drawings, 37 portfolios of prints and a collection of porcelain.

On 28 October 1847 the Rotterdam city council accepted the legacy, and on 9 December the collection arrived at the Schielandhuis; the museum was installed on the upper floor, while the rooms downstairs were reserved for an 'academy of arts'. The Boymans Museum opened on 3 July 1849; Arie Johannes Lamme was appointed its first director in 1852. Only 406 of the paintings were exhibited. A large part of the collection was auctioned in 1853, 1854 and 1855 in order to finance new acquisitions. The remaining collection still contained a selection of minor masters until the building caught fire on the night of 15–16 February 1864 and 300 paintings, 13 portfolios of drawings and most of the prints and ceramics were destroyed; the losses included works by Hendrick Goltzius, Frans Hals, Pieter de Hooch, Pieter Lastman, Paulus Potter, Jacob van Ruisdael, Jan van Scorel and Gerard ter Borch (ii). The present museum, housed in its own building (1935; by A. van der Steur and D. Hannema), nevertheless still possesses a number of masterpieces from the original Boymans collection, such as Philips Koninck's *Panorama*, Carel Fabritius's *Portrait of a Man*, Adriaen van Ostade's *Lawyer* (1637), Ruisdael's *Cornfield* and Jan Steen's *Feast of St Nicholas*.

BIBLIOGRAPHY
Catalogue d'un magnifique cabinet de tableaux . . . par Monsieur F. J. D. Boymans (Amsterdam, 1811) [copy with notes in Rotterdam, Boymans–van Beuningen]
C. Kramm: *De levens en werken der Hollandsche en Vlaamsche kunstschilders, beeldhouwers, graveurs en bouwmeesters*, i (Amsterdam, 1857), p. 144
P. Haverkorn van Rijsewijk: *Het Museum Boijmans te Rotterdam* (The Hague and Amsterdam, 1909)
E. W. Moes and E. Biema: *De Nationale Konst-Gallery en het Koninklijk Museum* (Amsterdam, 1909), pp. 143–4, 185

J. GILTAIJ

Boys, Thomas Shotter (*b* Pentonville, London, 2 Jan 1803; *d* London, 10 Oct 1874). English painter and printmaker. He was apprenticed on 4 February 1817 to George Cooke. His early training in engraving influenced his future career; his ability to draw a fine line, lay aquatint washes and hand-colour prints was an important factor in the creation of his particularly lucid style of watercolour landscapes and townscapes. At this time Cooke was engraving picturesque views by Turner and James Hakewell (1778–1843) as well as his own view of the Thames (1822); Boys went on to establish a reputation for his own lithographed volumes of picturesque tours.

By 1824 Boys was in Paris where he met Richard Parkes Bonington, the Fielding brothers and William Callow, with whom he later shared a studio. British engravers had been in demand in Paris since the 18th century and in the early 1820s many were working on Baron Isidore-Justin-Severin Taylor's *Voyages pittoresques et romantiques dans l'ancienne France* (Paris, 1820–75). Lithography became popular when Godefroy Engelmann opened his Imprimerie Lithographique in 1816, and from here, or from one of his English acquaintances employed by J. F. d'Ostervald (Taylor's editor), Boys acquired skills in the medium in which his best-known work is executed. His *Picturesque Architecture in Paris, Ghent, Antwerp, Rouen &c* (see LITHOGRAPHY, fig. 2), published by Charles Hullmandel in 1839, was by no means the first of its genre; but Boys's volume and its successor, *Original Views of London as it Is* (1842), are among the most splendid of such albums. Large in format, bearing elaborate title-pages and comprising a sequence of townscapes, which are startling for their combination of the familiar with provocative vistas, these two volumes display a preoccupation with design and abstract form that belies the artist's professed intention to surpass all previous endeavours (which he described as 'damndest, lying, ill-got-up, money-getting clap-traps') and to do 'Paris *as it is*'.

Boys's work was well received but the craze for picturesque tour books was waning by 1842, and he travelled between Paris and London in search of markets. His highly refined watercolours exhibited at the New Water-Colour

Thomas Shotter Boys: *Quai de La Grève, Paris*, watercolour, 2.88×4.02 m, 1837 (London, Victoria and Albert Museum)

Society often sold for low prices. He was an associate there from 1840 and a full member from 1841. In 1846 he had to look for work as a drawing-master in Cheltenham and five years later was advertising his services as a tinter of architectural drawings. The failure in business and subsequent retirement of his cousin, the publisher Thomas Boys, in 1859 destroyed his hope of publishing a further album, *Remains of Old England*, which would presumably have been modelled on Baron Taylor's *Voyages*.

Boys's work in watercolour is often confused with that of his friend Bonington. They owned examples of each other's work and painted together: Bonington's *Les Salinières, Trouville* (1826; priv. col., see Roundell, p. 68) is painted from the same spot as Boys's rendering of the same subject (priv. col., see Roundell, p. 68) and is inscribed, apparently in Boys's hand: 'Drawn for me by R. P. Bonington'. Virtually all the celebrated views of Paris by Bonington were also rendered by Boys (see fig.) for example the Institut, the Pont Neuf and the Pont Royal. Boys invariably had a crisper touch and a more rigorous attention to architectural mass and proportion than Bonington. His view of the Institut (1830; New Haven, CT, Yale Cent. Brit. A.) is altogether more conventional and stable than Bonington's. His later watercolour views of European capitals (e.g. *Dresden*; 1843; Birmingham, Mus. & A.G.) make use of the camera obscura and are somewhat static, with elaborate surface detail. However, Boys was one of the most sophisticated and design-conscious artists of the Anglo-French picturesque movement.

BIBLIOGRAPHY
H. Stokes: 'Thomas Shotter Boys', *Walker's Q.*, xviii (1926), pp. 1–47
G. von Groschwitz: 'The Prints of Thomas Shotter Boys', *Prints*, ed. C. Zigrosser (New York and London, 1962)
J. Roundell: *Thomas Shotter Boys, 1803–1874* (London, 1974) [fully illus. monograph]
M. Pointon: *The Bonington Circle: English Watercolour and Anglo-French Landscape, 1790–1855* (Brighton, 1985)

MARCIA POINTON

Boytac, Diogo. *See* BOITAC, DIOGO.

Boyvin, René (*b* Angers, *c.* 1525; *d* ?Angers, *c.* 1625). French engraver, etcher and designer. Vasari, in his *Vita* of Marcantonio Raimondi, mentions that 'after the death of Rosso [Fiorentino], we saw the arrival from France of all the engravings of his works'. He attributed this upsurge of engraved reproductions 'to the copperplate engraver René', that is René Boyvin. He came to Paris *c.* 1545 from Angers, where he was an associate of the mint. In Paris he may have been in contact with Antonio Fantuzzi, and he is known to have renewed a contract of service with the engraver Pierre Milan in 1549 (Parent). In 1553 he completed two plates that Milan had failed to finish for the music publisher Guillaume Morlaye (*c.* 1510–after 1558); one of these was the *Nymph of Fontainebleau* (Levron, 169; *see* FONTAINEBLEAU SCHOOL, fig. 1). He later opened his own workshop, and it is known that Lorenzo Penni, the son of Luca, was working for him in October 1557. Boyvin survived for many years despite the Calvinist beliefs for which he was imprisoned in January 1569. He seems to have published nothing under his own name between 1569 and 1574. His last dated work is from 1580, but it appears that he was still alive well into the 17th century.

An elegant, precise engraver, if sometimes a little dry, Boyvin contributed through his productivity to the spread of the style and themes of the FONTAINEBLEAU SCHOOL. Robert-Dumesnil attributed 226 plates to him and Levron 295. Confusion still exists, however, between his work and that of Milan. In his most famous work, *Le Livre de la conqueste de la toison d'or par le Prince Iason de Tessalie* (1563; L 16–41), which reproduced the drawings of Léonard Thiry in 26 plates, Boyvin displayed a particular aptitude for chiaroscuro effects. Although he was primarily a reproductive engraver, Boyvin also designed and executed numerous refined decorative prints that served as models for goldsmiths and jewellers (e.g. the *Panneaux d'ornements* and the *Livre de bijouterie*).

BIBLIOGRAPHY

G. Vasari: *Vite* (1550, rev. 2/1568); ed. G. Milanesi (1878–85), v, p. 433

A. P. F. Robert-Dumesnil: *Le Peintre-graveur français*, viii (Paris, 1850), pp. 11–88

A. Linzeler: *Inventaire du fonds français: Graveurs du XVIe siècle*, Paris, Bib. N., Dépt Est. cat., i (Paris, 1932), pp. 166–207

J. Levron: *René Boyvin, graveur angevin du XVIe siècle* (Angers, 1941) [L]

L'Ecole de Fontainebleau (exh. cat., Paris, Grand Pal., 1972), pp. 28, 248–9

A. Parent: *Les Métiers du livre à Paris au XVIe siècle (1535–1560)* (Geneva, 1974), p. 67

Ronsard, la trompette et la lyre (exh. cat., ed. J. Céard and D. Ménager; Paris, Bib. N., 1985)

The French Renaissance in Prints from the Bibliothèque Nationale de France (exh. cat., New York, Met., 1995)

MARIANNE GRIVEL

Boze, Joseph, Comte de (*b* Martinques, Bouches du Rhône, 6 Feb 1745; *d* Paris, 17 Jan 1826). French painter and inventor. He was the son of a sailor and studied painting at Marseille before settling in Arles. In 1778 he moved to Paris, where he studied with the pastellist Maurice-Quentin de La Tour. He attempted some technical improvements in the fixing of pastel and established a reputation for himself as an engineer and mechanic, his system for bridling and instantaneously unbridling four-horse wagons receiving the approval of the Académie des Sciences when tested at Versailles. Boze was presented to Louis XVI by the Abbé de Vermont, confessor to the Comte de Brienne and Queen Marie-Antoinette. Thereafter, he had a fairly successful semi-official career executing miniatures and portraits of the royal family and the court, most notably his *Louis XVI* of 1784 (France, priv. col.) and the ravishing *Jeanne-Louise Genet, Mme Campan*, Marie-Antoinette's Première Dame de la Chambre (1786; Versailles, Château). He also, from 1782, exhibited pastels and miniatures at the Salon de la Correspondance, Paris. These are mostly in an oval format and are of varying quality—some spirited and lively, others stiff and wooden.

During the French Revolution, Boze depicted numerous important figures—*Honoré-Gabriel Mirabeau* (pastel, 1789, Versailles, Château; full-length oil, 1789–90, Aix-en-Provence, Mus. Granet), *Maximilien de Robespierre* (1791; Paris, Carnavalet; Versailles, Château) and *Jean-Paul Marat* (1792; Paris, Carnavalet). Boze's prolific output during the early years of the Revolution has led to the dubious attribution to him of many pastels and drawings of court and political figures. He was not an academician, and so his first Salon exhibit did not come until the open Salon of 1791. There his work was severely criticized, his weaknesses in draughtsmanship betraying his lack of formal training, and he gave up exhibiting. Later his pre-Revolutionary connections worked against him, and in 1793 he was arrested and imprisoned for refusing to testify against Marie-Antoinette. He was freed after the fall of Robespierre in August 1794, but lack of work forced him to move to the Low Countries and later England, where he was given a pension by the Comte de Provence, the future Louis XVIII. On the rise of Napoleon, Boze returned to France. In 1801 his work for Napoleon led to an acrimonious exchange with his fellow artist Robert Lefèvre. Boze exhibited a canvas depicting the *First Consul and General Berthier at the Battle of Marengo* (untraced; coloured stipple engraving by Antoine Cardon), painted mostly by Lefèvre with background by Carle Vernet. He charged an admission fee and showed the work in London and Amsterdam under his own name. Lefèvre accused Boze of this deception in the *Journal des Arts* and the *Moniteur Universel*, saying that Boze was incapable of painting a full-length figure in oils and in his turn claiming that he had painted other, earlier works presented by Boze as his own, such as the portrait of *Mirabeau*. There is some evidence that this was more than a retaliatory blow, differences in execution indicating that Boze painted only the head of Mirabeau.

After the restoration of the monarchy in 1814, Boze's previous loyalty was rewarded with the title of Comte in 1816. His last years were not very productive, his best-known late work being his *Maréchal Charles, Marquis de Castries* (Versailles, Château).

BIBLIOGRAPHY

J. A. Volcy-Boze: *Le Comte Joseph de Boze, peintre de Louis XVI* (Marseille, 1873)

N. Herbin-Devedjian: 'Un Artiste sous la Révolution: Le Peintre Joseph Boze', *Bull. Soc. Hist. A. Fr.* (1981), pp. 155–64

SIMON LEE

Bozen. *See* BOLZANO.

Boznańska, Olga (*b* Kraków, 15 April 1865; *d* Paris, 26 Oct 1940). Polish painter. She took drawing lessons at home from the age of nine and began regular studies in 1883 under the portrait painter Kazimierz Pochwalski (1855–1940). She continued her training in 1884–5 at the Adam Baraniecki School of Art, the only school in Kraków accessible to women at that time. She went to Munich for further study, working in the studio of Carl Kricheldorf (*b* 1863) in 1886–7, and in that of Wilhelm Dürr (1857–1900) in 1888. In 1889 she participated in the Internationale Kunstausstellung in Munich and opened her own studio, which over the next decade became a meeting-place for students. In 1895 she ran a private school of painting founded by Professor Theodor Humml (1864–

1939). However, she declined the headship of a department for young women at the School of Fine Arts in Kraków. In 1898 she settled in Paris.

Boznańska's art of this period was characterized by the flattened sense of space in the compositions. Critics put this down to the influence of French art, and Boznańska herself claimed that she owed no more than her studio-technique skills to her Munich tutors. She admired the portraiture of Wilhelm Leibl, but she was inspired more by the compositional arrangements and palette of Velázquez, as well as by Manet's paintings and by Japanese woodcuts. She gradually broadened her palette through her studies in black and ochre tones and olive and emerald greens, which she introduced to her predominantly greying tones. Abandoning traditional perspective, she based her tonalities of receding planes on the contrast or harmony obtained from several closely related colours. An early example of this was *Flower Sellers* (1889; Kraków, N. Mus.), an intimate scene of three girls in an interior that recedes into the landscape beyond the window.

One of Boznańska's favourite subjects was portraiture. The Munich painter Paul Nauen (*b* 1859) was the subject of a portrait (1893; Kraków, N. Mus.) for which she won a gold medal in Vienna for its skilful composition with dark tones played against a lighter background. A characteristic of her work was the domination of colour over form; she consistently broke it up into tones and half-tones. In her portraiture she eliminated any form of narrative by presenting reality as an external phenomenon. She characterized her models by seizing upon the appropriate colour key for them.

In 1898, the year she settled in Paris, Boznańska also became a member of the Sztuka Polish Artists' Society and was elected its chairwoman in 1913. From 1904 Boznańska was a member of the Société Nationale des Beaux-Arts, in which she exhibited from 1896; from 1906 she was a member of the International Society of Sculptors, Gravers and Painters; and from 1911 she was a founder-member of the Society of Polish Artists in Paris. Boznańska took part in many international exhibitions—in Vienna, Munich, Berlin, London, Amsterdam, Rome and Pittsburgh, often as a representative of the French contingent, side by side with Claude Monet, Maurice Denis or Pierre Bonnard, and winning various medals and distinctions.

Throughout her life Boznańska painted a number of self-portraits, often introspective and self-critical, for example *Self-portrait in a Hat with a White Ribbon* (oil on cardboard, *c.* 1906; Kraków, N. Mus.; see fig.). In general, her portraits contain a significant level of symbolism, with a highly defined figure–background relation. She contrasted the expression of the sitter with the rest of the composition, which dissolved in the undefined and rather sultry surrounding climate. Her paintings could be compared to faded frescoes. At the end of the 1890s she developed a painting technique using dry areas of oil paint on ungrounded cardboard, without using any varnish during the final stages. Its matt tone deprived its colour of any intensity. She also painted still-lifes, flowers and interiors. In 1910 she was awarded the Légion d'honneur for her artistic activities, and in 1938 she received the Polish order, Polonia Restituta.

Olga Boznańska: *Self-portrait in a Hat with a White Ribbon*, oil on cardboard, 710×510 mm, *c.* 1906 (Kraków, National Museum)

BIBLIOGRAPHY
SAP; Thieme–Becker
W. Ritter: 'Correspondance de Vienne', *Gaz. B.-A.*, xxxviii (1896), pp. 355–60
Olga Boznańska (exh. cat., Kraków, N. Mus., 1960)
H. Blum: *Olga Boznańska* (Warsaw, 1974) [bibliog. and excellent pls]
W. Juszczak: *Modernizm: Malarstwo Polskie* [Modernism: Polish painting] (Warsaw, 1977), pp. 332–3
La Peinture polonaise du XVIe au début du XXe siècle, Warsaw, N. Mus. cat. (Warsaw, 1977), pp. 107–16
Polnische Malerei von 1830 bis 1914 (exh. cat., Kiel, Ksthalle; Stuttgart, Württemberg. Kstver.; Wuppertal, von der Heydt-Mus.; 1978)
Münchner Maler im 19. Jahrhundert (Munich, 1981–3), i, pp. 121–2
Symbolism in Polish Painting, 1890–1914 (exh. cat., Detroit, MI, Inst. A., 1984), pp. 35–41
Voices of Freedom: Polish Women Artists and the Avant-Garde, 1880–1990 (exh. cat. by A. Morawinska, Washington, DC, N. Mus. Women A., 1991), pp. 13, 21–9, 40–41

ELŻBIETA CHARAZIŃSKA

Bozo, Dominique (*b* Alençon, 28 Jan 1935; *d* Paris, 28 April 1993). French museum curator. He began his career as a teacher. After studying at the Ecole du Louvre, in 1966 he joined the Ministry for Cultural Affairs, with a subsequent appointment to the Musée National d'Art Moderne, then housed at the Palais de Tokyo. When the museum transferred to the Centre Georges Pompidou, Bozo undertook the difficult task of transferring the collection. As director of the museum he established an international reputation for the balance he achieved of a historical and contemporary collection. For several years he was also involved with the complex task of establishing the collection that formed the Musée Picasso in the 17th-century Hôtel Salé, Paris, through negotiations with the artist's widow, Jacqueline Picasso. Bozo's achievement was a comprehensive and impressive collection. From 1986 to 1990 he was head of the department of plastic arts at the Ministry for Cultural Affairs. During this period Bozo was also responsible for moving the Impressionist collection to the Musée d'Orsay from the Jeu de Paume, which became an exhibition space for comtemporary art. In 1990 Bozo was reappointed director of the Musée National d'Art Moderne and in the following year he became President of the Pompidou complex.

BIBLIOGRAPHY
Obituary, *The Times* (30 April 1993)

☐

Bozzato. *See* PONCHINO, GIAMBATTISTA.

Bozzetto [*Abbozzo*; It.: 'sketch']. Rough, preliminary version of a composition. The term *bozzetto* is used for the initial outline, drawing or underpainting of a picture and for the roughly shaped piece of material approximating the finished form of a sculpture.

See also OIL SKETCH and MODELLO.

RUPERT FEATHERSTONE

Bra, Théophile-François-Marcel (*b* Douai, 23 June 1797; *d* Douai, 2 May 1863). French sculptor. He was the son of the sculptor Eustache-Marie-Joseph Bra (1772–1840) and studied in Paris under Pierre-Charles Bridan and Jean-Baptiste Stouf. He competed unsuccessfully for the Prix de Rome in 1816 and 1817, winning second prize in 1818 with his relief *Chélonis Pleading for her Husband Cléombotte* (Douai, Mus. Mun.). However, he enjoyed early success at the Salon; after the plaster of his *Aristo-demus at his Daughter's Tomb* had been shown in 1819, a marble version (Douai, Mus. Mun.) was commissioned by the State: it was exhibited at the 1822 Salon. Similarly, Bra showed a plaster of his *Ulysses on Calypso's Isle* at the Salon of 1822, which resulted in a commission for a marble version of the same subject (1831 Salon; Compiègne, Château). In this colossal figure, Bra eschews outward drama in favour of a calm, meditative attitude. The commissions that he received from the State under the Bourbon Restoration and during the July Monarchy in-cluded statues of a *Guardian Angel* (1833–5) and of *St Amelia* (1835–8) for La Madeleine, Paris; spandrel reliefs of a *Grenadier* and a *Chasseur* (1833–5) for the Arc de Triomphe de l'Etoile, Paris; and work for the Colonne de la Grande Armée at Boulogne. Bra was associated with Saint Simonian, Christian Socialist and Somnambulist groups, and prophesied an exalted role for the arist in a perfected society. Copious literary jottings, accompanied by eccentric, visonary pen and ink drawings, are preserved at the Bibliothèque Municipale, Douai. After 1847 he worked in Lille, notably on the pediment of the Hôtel de Ville (1849–50), but his final years were spent in Douai.

Lami

BIBLIOGRAPHY
J. de Caso: *David d'Angers: L'Avenir de la mémoire* (Paris, 1988)

N. McWilliam: *Dreams of Happiness: Social Art and the French Left, 1830–1850* (Princeton, 1993)

PHILIP WARD-JACKSON

Braamcamp, Gerrit (*bapt* 18 Oct 1699; *d* 17 June 1771). Dutch collector and patron. He was the eldest son of Jan Braamcamp (*c.* 1671–1713) from the province of Over-ijssel, who settled in Amsterdam and became a successful wine merchant. Gerrit joined the family business and after the death of his parents expanded the range of the business. He shipped wood, rope, cheese and textiles to Lisbon, where his brothers Dirck (1701–after 1771) and Herman (1709–after 1771) had settled. From 1736 Braamcamp operated a profitable timber company, which made him a large fortune. His wealth enabled him, a childless widower from 1742, to collect art. From *c.* 1743 he collected paintings, prints and drawings, sculpture, gold, silver and glass, porcelain and lacquerwork. By 1751 his collection amounted to *c.* 170 paintings, growing to *c.* 380 works 15 years later. Between 1750 and 1760 he lived in part of the Trippenhuis in Amsterdam, later moving to a large house on the Herengracht. His collection was internationally renowned and was visited by many.

Braamcamp's main interest was paintings and drawings by Dutch artists of the 17th century. He owned fine work by Gerrit Dou (including the triptych *The Nursery*, lost in 1771 and known only through the copy by Willem Joseph Laquy (1738–98), Amsterdam, Rijksmus.), Paulus Potter, Jan Steen and Rembrandt (including his *Christ in the Storm on the Lake of Gennesareth*, Boston, MA, Isabella Stewart Gardner Mus.), many works by Gabriel Metsu (e.g. *Old Woman with a Book by a Window*, London, N.G.), Adriaen van Ostade, Philips Wouwerman and Jan van der Heyden. Braamcamp also bought works by Flemish masters, and he was very interested in Italian art, although many works listed as such in the sale catalogue were probably incor-rectly attributed. He also patronized contemporary artists; for example Jacob de Wit and Jacob Xavery IV (1736–after 1779) executed commissions for him, and the latter, at one time Braamcamp's protégé, painted his portrait (untraced).

In 1766 Braamcamp sold a number of lesser paintings, and six years later sold his drawings, most of which were Italian and Dutch. At the end of his life he decided to sell his entire collection but died shortly before the auction. After his death the collection was exhibited to the public for three weeks, before the sale on 31 July 1771. Catherine II of Russia purchased a number of his paintings, but all were lost at sea on the way to St Petersburg.

BIBLIOGRAPHY
C. Bille: *De tempel der kunst of het kabinet van den Heer Braamcamp*, 2 vols (Amsterdam, 1961)

J. A. VAN DER VEEN

Brabant Fauvism. Term first used in 1941 by the Belgian critic Paul Fierens to describe the style of painting of an informal group of artists active in and around Brussels (Brabant province), *c.* 1910–23. Its founder-members in-cluded Fernand Schirren, Louis Thévenet, Willem Paerels (1878–1962), Charles Dehoy and Auguste Oleffe, who had already been grouped together in Le Labeur art society, founded in 1898. When, in 1906, Oleffe moved to

Auderghem, his house became an established meeting-place, and Edgard Tytgat, Jean Brusselmans, Anne-Pierre de Kat (1881–1968) and the most prominent member of the group Rik Wouters became associated. The first exhibition of the work of those who were later called the Brabant Fauvists was held at the Galerie Giroux in Brussels in 1912. Inspired by a variety of directions within Impressionism, the group rejected Symbolism and was heavily influenced by James Ensor. They sought to express themselves through a clear visual language, with pure glowing colours and precise composition. They chose simple subjects, such as still-lifes, harmonious landscapes and scenes from everyday life executed in a painterly manner with spontaneous, expressive brushstrokes, for example Wouters's *Woman Ironing* (1912; Antwerp, Kon. Mus. S. Kst.) and Schirren's *Woman at the Piano* (1915–17; Brussels, Mus. A. Mod.).

BIBLIOGRAPHY
P. Fierns: 'A.-P. de Kat', *Rev. Apollo*, 6 (Nov 1941)
Le Fauvisme brabançon (exh. cat. by S. G. de Heusch, Brussels, Crédit Com. Belg., 1979)
S. G. de Heusch: *L'Impressionnisme et le fauvisme en Belgique* (Antwerp, 1988)

ELS MARÉCHAL

Brabazon, Hercules Brabazon (*b* Paris, 21 Nov 1821; *d* 14 May 1906). English watercolourist. Baptized Hercules Brabazon Sharpe, the son of landed gentry, he inherited the family estates in 1847 and 1858, which occasioned a legal change in his surname. From that date Brabazon dedicated himself to watercolour, living in Sussex during part of the year and travelling annually on the Continent, especially to the Alps and the Mediterranean. He also visited Africa, India and the Middle East in the 1860s and 1870s and produced thousands of landscapes during his career, for example *Street in Cairo* (London, V&A). Brabazon studied briefly with James D'Egville (*d* 1880) and Alfred Downing Fripp (1822–95), but he was largely a self-taught amateur, learning from his contemporaries and from the Old Masters, particularly Velázquez, whose works he copied. His broad style is closest to early 19th-century *plein-air* painters, including David Cox, Peter de Wint, William James Müller and J. M. W. Turner. Ruskin and D. S. MacColl praised Brabazon as Turner's rival as a colourist. Brabazon's watercolours link the impressionistic fluid technique of early 19th-century painters to the work of progressive English artists of the *fin-de-siècle*, influenced by Whistler and the French.

Brabazon was little known publicly until his first exhibition with the New English Art Club in 1891. His young admirers, J. S. Sargent, Philip Wilson Steer and D. S. MacColl championed his one-man exhibition at the Goupil Gallery in 1892. He had several more one-man shows there and was a member of the New English Art Club and the Pastel Society. The contents of his studio were auctioned in London at Christie's (18–19 March 1926 and 18, 21 March 1927) and Sotheby's (19–20 June 1928).

BIBLIOGRAPHY
D. S. M. [D. S. MacColl]: 'Art: Mr Brabazon's Water-colours', *The Spectator*, lxix (1892), pp. 851–2
F. Wedmore: *Hercules Brabazon Brabazon* (Battle, 1906)
C. L. Hind: *Hercules Brabazon Brabazon, 1821–1906: His Art and Life* (London, 1912)
An Exhibition of Watercolours and Drawings by Hercules Brabazon Brabazon, 1821–1906 (exh. cat. by A. Weil, London, Leighton House A.G. & Mus., 1971)
Hercules Brabazon Brabazon, 1821–1906 (exh. cat., ed. A. Weil; London, F.A. Soc., 1974)

HILARIE FABERMAN

Bracamonte y Guzmán, Gaspar de, 3rd Conde de Peñaranda (*b* Peñaranda de Bracamonte, nr Salamanca, 1596; *d* Madrid, 14 Dec 1676). Spanish statesman and patron. Though destined for legal and literary studies, on inheriting the title he became a diplomat in the service of Philip IV and was the King's plenipotentiary in the discussions with the Dutch Republic at the Peace of Westphalia (1645–8). During these negotiations in Münster he commissioned a portrait miniature from Gerard ter Borch (ii) (1646; Rotterdam, Boymans–van Beuningen). He was President of the Consejo de Ordenes (1651), of the Consejo de las Indias (1653), Viceroy of Naples (1658–64) and President of the Consejo de Italia (1664). Philip IV appointed him to the Junta de Gobierno to advise the Queen Regent during the minority of Charles II (*reg* 1665–1700). While in Naples, Bracamonte y Guzmán lived for a time in the palace of Gaspar Roomer en Barra from Antwerp, a merchant and collector of paintings. During the six years of his viceroyalty of Naples, he initiated various building works in the city, in the churches of S Domenico Soriano, S Maria del Pianto, S Nicolà del Molo, that of the Carmelites in Chiaia and the Romitaggio della Madre Suor Orsola. He commissioned Andrea Vaccaro and Luca Giordano to paint canvases for S Maria del Pianto (1660–62) and for the church of the Spanish convent of Discalced Carmelites which he founded in Peñoranda de Bracamonte in 1669, also the site of his burial. On his return to Spain in 1664 he took with him the 18 paintings he had purchased for Philip IV that year at the auction of the property of GIOVAN FRANCESCO SERRA, Marqués di Cassano. He had his own gallery, but its contents are not known. It probably contained works acquired in Germany, France and Italy.

BIBLIOGRAPHY
D. A. Parrino: *Teatro eroico, e politico de' Governi de' Viceré del Regno di Napoli* (Naples, 1692–4)
A. E. Pérez Sánchez: *Pintura italiana del siglo XVII en España* (Madrid, 1965)
H. Wethey: 'The Spanish Viceroy, Luca Giordano and Andrea Vaccaro', *Burl. Mag.*, cix (1967), pp. 678–86
E. Nappi: 'I Viceré e l'arte a Napoli', *Napoli Nob.*, n. s. 2, xxii/1–2 (1983), pp. 41–57
Pintura napolitana del Caravaggio a Giordano (exh. cat., ed. A. E. Pérez Sánchez; Madrid, Prado, 1985)
A. Vannugli: *La collezione Serra di Cassano* (Salerno, 1989)

NATIVIDAD SÁNCHEZ ESTEBAN

Bracceschi, Giovanni Battista. *See* BERTUCCI, (1).

Braccesco, Carlo [Carlo da Milano] (*fl* Liguria, 1478–1501). Italian painter. He is first documented in 1478, when he executed the polyptych at Montegrazie, near Imperia; signed *Carolus Mediolanensis*, this large, three-tiered structure appears to be his only signed painting. An essentially Late Gothic, Lombard basis is agreed for this work, the complex sources of which also include Catalan and Venetian influences, the latter suggesting an affinity with such artists as Carlo Crivelli. Braccesco is also

Carlo Braccesco (attrib.): tritych of the *Annunciation with Saints*, central panel, 1.58×1.07 m, wings with *SS Benedict and Augustine* (left) and *SS Stephen and Angelus* (right), 1.05×0.52 m, *c*. 1494 (Paris, Musée du Louvre)

recorded (as Carlo da Milano) between 1481 and 1501 in a series of documents, mostly Genoese, relating to important commissions (all untraced). In 1481–2 he decorated the façade of the Palazzo delle Compere, Genoa, with a St George on Horseback. Between 1482 and 1484 he and Ambrogio de' Fiori produced four stained-glass windows for the chapel of S Sebastiano in Genoa Cathedral, then frescoed the walls, apse and exterior arch of the same chapel. In 1484 he undertook to paint a polyptych depicting the Assumption of the Virgin for the Carmelites of S Maria degli Angeli. By 1492 he had probably executed a polyptych depicting the Virgin and Child for the unidentified locality of Belgandura. By 1494 he had completed a *Maestà* for the Commune of Levanto, and in that year or immediately afterwards he frescoed the chapel of the Nativity in the church of Nostra Signora del Monte, Genoa. In 1497 Cristoforo della Torre, who had been commissioned to paint the organ case of Genoa Cathedral, arranged for Braccesco to paint six Saints on the shutters and a monochrome Annunciation on the outer face. In 1500 Braccesco may have participated in the decoration of the *caminata* (large hall) in the palazzo of Antonio Lomellini: Giacomo di Bartolomeo Serfolio and Leonoro dell' Aquila arranged for twelve medallions and four heraldic emblems to be painted on the frieze, either by Braccesco or by Stradioto. The document of 1501 refers to a commission to paint a polyptych of the Assumption

of the Virgin, to be modelled on the one made by Giovanni Mazone for Baldassare Lomellini in S Teodoro, Genoa.

Braccesco's activity apart from his signed and documented works has been reconstructed on the basis of Longhi's attribution to him of an *Annunciation with Saints* (Paris, Louvre; see fig.), which is datable to shortly before 1495. It is a work of extraordinary quality, characterized by the successful grafting of Netherlandish and Mediterranean elements on to the most recent developments in Lombard painting. It seems, in turn, stylistically and chronologically related to *SS Erasmus and Jerome* and the *Holy Bishop and St Pantaleon* (both Levanto, S Andrea), fragments of painted cloth from a standard or altar curtain, in which the figures are set in a sunlit landscape reminiscent of the work of Nicolò Corso. If Longhi's attribution is accepted, the Louvre *Annunciation* would follow a now dispersed polyptych depicting *St Andrew*, painted by 1494, probably for the Commune of Levanto (main sections, untraced: ex-Herconway priv. col., London; ex-priv. col., Milan; predella panels: New York, Kress Found.; Venice, Ca' d'Oro; Avignon, Mus. Petit Pal.). A *Virgin and Child with Angels* (ex-Roerlich priv. col., New York) may also belong to the same polyptych, whose range of styles suggests an execution spread probably over several years. If the predella seems close to the works in Paris and Levanto, the principal elements, more clearly related to Vincenzo Foppa, seem still to be close to the central section of a polyptych at Borzone dated 1484. The stages following the Montegrazie Polyptych of 1478 are represented by a panel of unknown origin depicting *SS Vincent Ferrer and Peter Martyr* (untraced; see Boskovits, 1982) and by a *Virgin and Child with Angels* (Genoa, priv. col.). A Netherlandish influence is clearly seen in the detached fresco of the *Vision of St Dominic* (Genoa, S Maria di Castello), which is even more problematic in that it has been variously dated to *c.* 1470 (Boskovits) and after 1478 (most others).

The foregoing suggested chronology is not universally accepted, some scholars preferring a traditional attribution of the later paintings to the anonymous Master of the Louvre Annunciation. Arslan assigned to this artist the *St Andrew* polyptych and the Levanto fragments as well as the Louvre painting. Birolli and the *DBI* largely concur but restore the Levanto works to Braccesco.

DBI   BIBLIOGRAPHY
R. Longhi: *Carlo Braccesco* (Milan, 1942); also in *Lavori in Valpadana* (Florence, 1973), pp. 267–87
F. Zeri: 'Two Contributions to Lombard quattrocento Painting', *Burl. Mag.*, xcvii (1955), pp. 74–7; also in F. Zeri: *Giorno per giorno nella pittura* (Turin, 1988), pp. 329–31
E. Arslan: 'Il "Maestro dell'Annunciazione del Louvre" e Carlo Braccesco', *Scritti di storia dell'arte in onore di Mario Salmi*, ii (Rome, 1962), pp. 439–50
Z. Birolli: 'Il formarsi di un dialetto pittorico nella regione ligure-piemontese', *Boll. Soc. Piemont. Archeol. & B.A.*, xx (1966), pp. 115–25
G. V. Castelnovi: 'Il Quattro e il primo cinquecento', *La pittura a Genova e in Liguria dagli inizi al cinquecento*, ed. C. Bozzo Dufour, i (Genoa, 1970, rev. 1987), pp. 97–105, 145–7
M. Boskovits: 'Un Tableau inédit de Carlo Braccesco', *Rev. A.*, lvii (1982), pp. 77–8 [on *SS Vincent Ferrer and Peter Martyr*]
——: 'Nicolò Corso e gli altri: Spigolature di pittura lombardo-ligure di secondo quattrocento', *A. Crist.*, lxxv (1987), pp. 351–86 (368–79, 383–4)
P. Donati: 'Carlo Braccesco a Levanto', *A. Lombarda*, lxxxiii (1987), pp. 20–26
M. Natale: 'Pittura in Liguria nel quattrocento', *La pittura in Italia: Il quattrocento*, ed. F. Zeri (Milan, 1987), pp. 15–30 (21–4)
                    VITTORIO NATALE

Bracci, Pietro (*b* Rome, 16 June 1700; *d* Rome, 13 Feb 1773). Italian sculptor. He studied under Giuseppe Bartolomeo Chiari and from 1725 kept a diary in which he recorded the details of his commissions. The first one he mentioned was for the marble portrait busts of *Cardinal Fabrizio Paolucci* and *Innocent XII* (both Rome, SS Giovanni e Paolo), commissioned in 1725; these early busts show Bracci's particular ability for carving individualized portraits. In 1726 he was commissioned to carve the wall memorial to *Cardinal Fabrizio Paolucci* (Rome, S Marcello al Corso). It shows a winged figure of Fame superimposed on a pyramid in relief; Fame holds a trumpet and supports a portrait medallion of the Cardinal. Bracci frequently repeated this design during his career. With the exception of that to *Benedict XIV* (completed after 1769; Rome, St Peter's), he was responsible only for the sculpture of funerary monuments, the overall designs being entrusted to architects or painters. The figures were usually carved in white marble and the pyramids and bases in coloured marble. In 1730 he carved two life-size statues for the basilica of Mafra, Portugal: *St Peter Nolasco* and *St Felix of Valois*. In the execution of the drapery, these display not only his characteristic use of sharp-edged folds but

also an exaggerated, windswept style, which became more controlled in his later works.

In 1732 Bracci carved a classicizing relief of *St Andrew Corsini Washing the Feet of the Poor* for the Capella Corsini, S Giovanni in Laterano in Rome. Reflecting the contemporary interest in antique Roman reliefs, the Corsini relief is probably the finest of the four executed by Bracci: the others decorate the porticos of S Giovanni in Laterano (*St John the Baptist Reproves Herod*, 1734) and S Maria Maggiore (*St Flavius in the Council of 465*, 1742) and the façade of S Giovanni dei Fiorentini (*Baptism of Christ*, 1734–5). Confirming this interest in Classical sculpture, Bracci was also involved in restoration: in 1732 he worked extensively on some of the figures on the Arch of Constantine in Rome for Clement XII. He also restored statues for Cardinal Alessandro Albani's private collection in the Villa Albani, Rome (e.g. the figure of *Antinous*, rest. before 1733; Rome, Mus. Capitolini).

In 1734 Bracci executed the tomb of *Benedict XIII* in S Maria sopra Minerva in Rome (see fig.). The Pope is depicted genuflecting towards the high altar, his face expressing rapt devotion. On the left of the sarcophagus Bracci carved a figure of Religion with an incense burner, while the figure of Humility on the right is by Bartolommeo Pincellotti (*d* 1740). The sensitive portrayal of the pontiff was an innovation in papal tomb design, contrasting with the more impersonal depictions of earlier popes. For the tomb (1739–42) of *Maria Clementina Sobieska Stuart*, the wife of James Stuart, the Old Pretender, in St Peter's in

Pietro Bracci: tomb of *Benedict XIII*, marble, 1734 (Rome, S Maria sopra Minerva)

Rome, Bracci carved a female figure, accompanied by putti, who sits on the sarcophagus, holding a gilded flame and supporting the portrait medallion. The composition is united by cascading drapery in pink marble. The tomb of *Cardinal Renato Imperiale* (1741; Rome, S Agostino) combines motifs from Bracci's wall memorials, with a figure of Fame holding a portrait medallion against the pyramid relief. The triangular composition is emphasized by the figures of Charity and Fortitude, who sit on either side of the sarcophagus.

Bracci's monument to *Carlo Leopoldo Calcagnini* (1748; Rome, S Andrea delle Fratte) follows the format and scale of his monument to *Cardinal Fabrizio Paolucci*, the figures being placed against a pyramid in relief. The figure of Fame kneels on the base while copying with a quill pen an inscription from a book on to the pyramid, which is supported by a lion steadying a bronze ball with his left paw. The portrait medallion is fixed to the pyramid and surmounted by a marble swan. The act of writing is reminiscent of Bernini's monument to *Urban VIII* in St Peter's, though both of these tombs by Bracci have a precedent in Bernardino Cametti's monument to *Gabriele Filippucci* (*c.* 1706; S Giovanni in Laterano). In St Peter's Bracci also contributed to the series of marble statues depicting the founders of religious orders, carving *St Vincent de Paul* (1754), the *Blessed Girolamo Emiliani* (1756) and *St Norbert* (1758). The figures show his love of the serpentine curve and further demonstrate his skill at characterization. One of Bracci's best-known works is the central group for the Trevi Fountain in Rome, which was originally commissioned from Giovanni Battista Maini but completed by Bracci, whose work was in place in 1762. The marble figure of the bearded *Oceanus* (h. 5.80 m), more elegant and serpentine than Maini's original model, stands on a huge shell drawn by winged horses and controlled by tritons. His left arm projects dramatically from the central niche and directs the viewer to the scene below.

In his second monument for St Peter's, that to *Benedict XIV* (completed after 1769), Bracci was responsible for the whole concept, and the resulting work reveals his debt to Bernini's monument to *Alexander VII*, also in St Peter's. Bracci broke with tradition by carving the Pope standing triumphant, his right arm outstretched, while the left grasps the beautiful cherub-head arm terminal on his throne. On the left is a figure of Sacred Knowledge, carved by Bracci, while the rarely depicted figure of Disinterestedness on the right was executed by Gaspare Sibilla (*d* 1782) from Bracci's design. Bracci's work represents the last phase of Roman Baroque sculpture. His clearcut flowing drapery for male figures is often reminiscent of Pierre Legros (ii), and the drapery on his female figures is marked by its light and delicate folds. However, the robustness of most of his figures and his sense of design are inspired chiefly by Camillo Rusconi and Bernini.

UNPUBLISHED SOURCES
Florence, Bib. N. Cent., MS. Codex Palatino E.B.9.5.: F.M. fol. 2136 [F. M. N. Gabburri: *Vitae* (1739)]

BIBLIOGRAPHY
C. Gradara: *Pietro Bracci, scultore romano, 1700–1773* (Milan, 1921) [with transcript of Bracci's diary]
A. de Carvalho: *A escultura em Mafra* (Lisbon, 1950, rev. Mafra, 2/1956)
J. A. Pinto: *The Trevi Fountain* (New Haven, 1986)

FLAVIA ORMOND

Bracciano, Duca di. *See* ODESCALCHI, (2).

Bracciano, Paolo Giordano II Orsini, Duca di. *See* ORSINI, (2).

Bracciolini, (Gian Francesco) Poggio (*b* Terranova, Tuscany, 11 February 1380; *d* Florence, 30 October 1459). Italian scholar, collector and writer. After notarial training in Florence, during which he came under the influence of the humanist Chancellor Coluccio Salutati (1331–1406), Poggio worked as a papal bureaucrat from 1404 to 1453, with intermissions including a period in England (1418–23); he then became Florentine Chancellor himself (1453–6). The earlier part of his life was marked by discoveries of Latin texts hitherto unknown, including works of Lucretius, speeches of Cicero, Vitruvius' *On Architecture* and the complete works of Quintilian. He later issued histories and treatises on moral, social and scholarly questions.

In the opening years of the 15th century, Poggio was responsible, under the influence of Salutati and Niccolò Niccoli, for the first examples of a new, humanistic script based on Carolingian script and Roman inscriptions, the clarity and beauty of which led to it gradually replacing Gothic lettering in manuscripts and print. A collector of ancient inscriptions from his earliest days in Rome, Poggio was equally interested in the monuments of the city. Aided by texts he himself had found, as well as by inscriptions and close personal observation, he gave a nostalgic but precise account of urban topography in Book I of his *De varietate Fortunae* (1448; *see* ROME, §VII, 3), which overturned many traditional identifications. At his villa, in Fiesole, he installed antique statuary, inscriptions and coins collected for him from as far away as Greece (*see* ACADEMY); a passing comment in a letter to Niccoli shows Donatello approving one of his pieces. A silver reliquary bust commissioned by Poggio is now in New York (Met.).

WRITINGS
Opera (Strasbourg, 1511); ed. R. Fubini as *Opera Omnia*, 4 vols (Turin, 1964–9) [incl. *De varietate fortunae*]

BIBLIOGRAPHY
E. Walser: *Poggius Florentinus* (Berlin, 1914)
J. J. Rorimer: 'A Reliquary Bust Made for Poggio Bracciolini', *Bull. Met.*, xiv (1955–6), pp. 246–51
R. Weiss: *The Renaissance Discovery of Classical Antiquity* (Oxford, 1969, rev. 1988), pp. 59–60, 63–6, 147–9, 205

M. C. DAVIES

Bracelli, Giovanni Battista (*fl* 1616–50). Italian painter and printmaker. Baldinucci mentioned several artists of this name: a Bracelli born in Genoa who died aged 25, a Bracelli from Florence who was a pupil of Giulio Parigi, a painter called Bracelli nicknamed il Bigio and a Bracelli who was a follower of Jacopo da Empoli and who among other works published, in Livorno in 1624, some interesting etchings referred to as *Oddities*. While the Genoese and the Florentine Bracelli are clearly distinct personalities, the other references may possibly concern the same individual. The name Bracelli appears after 1624 in a series of engravings printed in Rome. In 1632 an extremely rare and bizarre *Illustrated Alphabet* was printed in Naples and appears closely related to the fantastic vein of the *Oddities*.

BIBLIOGRAPHY

Thieme–Becker

F. Baldinucci: *Notizie* (1681–1728); ed. F. Ranalli (1845–7)

A. Mariani: 'Giovanni Battista Bracelli', *Il seicento fiorentino: Biografie* (exh. cat., Florence, Pal. Strozzi, 1986), pp. 42–4

——: 'Bracelli o Brozzé, detto il Bigio, Giovanni Battista', *La pittura in Italia: Il seicento*, ii (Milan, 2/1989), pp. 651–2

ANNAMARIA NEGRO SPINA

Brack, John (*b* Melbourne, 10 May 1920). Australian painter, teacher and lecturer. After studying at the National Gallery of Victoria School in Melbourne under William Darby (1946–9), Brack worked in the Gallery's print room until 1957. He later worked as a teacher and from 1963 was head of the School. The purchase by the National Gallery of *The Barber's Shop* and *Collins Street 5pm* in the early 1950s helped to launch Brack's career. The influence of Seurat and Manet can be noted in the construction and composition of early works such as *The Bar* (1954), based on Manet's *A Bar at the Folies-Bergère*. Although many of his contemporaries and forerunners painted Australian mythical and historical scenes, Brack always depicted his own times, and especially the people, suburbia and consumerism of urban Melbourne. He employed an unemotional style in works such as his studio nudes (e.g. *Nude on a Small Chair*, 1975; Melbourne, Joseph Brown Gal.), but frequently included simple satire and comedy.

BIBLIOGRAPHY

R. Millar: *John Brack* (Melbourne, 1971)

John Brack: A Retrospective Exhibition (exh. cat. by R. Lindsay, Melbourne, N.G. Victoria, 1987)

CHRISTINE CLARK

Bracket system. Roof support system composed of bearing blocks and bracket arms, and particularly associated with East Asia. The underlying structural principle—that bearing blocks may support more bearing blocks—can result in systems of great complexity.

1. CHINA. The Chinese bracket system is a complex of timber bearing blocks (*dou*) and arms (*gong*), arranged in distinct sets and placed either on top of a column or on a beam joining the tops of columns. The bracket system helps to transfer the weight of the roof frame to the network of columns. The two basic elements of the system, *dou* and *gong*, were used as early as the first millennium BC in elementary forms of bracketing to bear the weight of the eaves, beams and rafters. By the Tang period (AD 618–907) these elements were combined with the CANTILEVER (Chin. *ang*), which made possible wide, overhanging eaves to protect the woodwork and rammed-earth (*hangtu*) walls of the building without the use of extra brackets that would add to the overall height of the building. An important extant example from this period is the main hall of Foguang Temple in Wutai, Shanxi Province (AD 857; *see* CHINA, §II, 2 and fig. 20), which has two cantilevers for each bracket set on the external columns and an eaves overhang of more than 4 m.

The bracket system was first codified in the 12th-century architectural manual *Yingzao fashi* ('Building standards'; 1103; *see* CHINA, §II, 2), which details the names, standard measurements and relationships between the various components of the system. The dimensions of each component were related to a standard module system that governed the sizes of all timber members of a building. From the 15th century onwards, the bracket system changed in a number of ways: the size of the bracket set became smaller in relation to the height of the columns, intercolumnar bracket sets increased in number, and the *ang* lost its shape and original structural function as a lever to support the eaves. However, mortice-and-tenon joints remained the chief means of connecting the members of the bracket set, and the members continued to be painted according to particular colour schemes. Although the bracket system has often been regarded as a distinguishing feature of Chinese architecture, its use was largely limited to the design of palaces, temples, mansions of the wealthy and other important structures.

See also CHINA, §II, 1(i).

BIBLIOGRAPHY

Liang Ssu-ch'eng: *A Pictorial History of Chinese Architecture: A Study of the Development of its Structural System and the Evolution of its Types*, ed. W. Fairbank (Cambridge, MA, 1984)

N. Shatzman Steinhardt: *Chinese Traditional Architecture* (New York, 1984)

Zhongguo gudai jianzhu jishu shi [History of ancient Chinese architectural technology] (Beijing, 1985), pp. 57–150

STANISLAUS FUNG

2. KOREA. The bracket (Kor. *kongp'o*) in traditional Korean wooden architecture is composed of a capital, bracket arms and small blocks supporting the bracket members. It is placed between the vertical columns and the horizontal beams and girders to serve the twofold purpose of decoration and structural strengthening. Brackets have been adopted in the construction of palaces, temples and other monumental buildings. The depiction of buildings with bracket structures in wall paintings of the Koguryŏ period (37 BC–AD 668) suggests that a fairly developed system was in use as early as the 4th century AD.

The four main types of Korean bracket are: column-head brackets (*chusimp'o*), the oldest type of structure, resting on column heads alone; multi-cluster brackets (*tapo*), which lie not only on the columns but also on outer tie-beams; wing-type brackets (*ikkong*), the simplest and sturdiest of Korean bracket structures; and slanted bracket arms (*ha'ang*), extending both inwards and outwards, supplying leverage to the deep eaves. These bracket structures were much influenced by the Chinese system of brackets (*dougong*; *see* §1 above).

BIBLIOGRAPHY

Sin Yong-hun and Kim Tong-hyŏn: *Hanguk ko kŏnch'uk tanjang* [A brief review of the old architecture of Korea], 2 vols (Seoul, 1975–7)

Chŏng In-guk: *Hanguk kŏnch'uk yangsik non* [A stylistic theory of Korean architecture] (Seoul, 1988)

——: 'Koryŏ–Chosŏn mokcho kŏnch'uk' [The wooden architecture of Koryŏ and Chosŏn periods], *Hankuk misulsa hyŏnhwang* [A review of Korean art history] (Seoul, 1992)

CHANG KYUNG-HO

3. JAPAN. In Japanese architecture, the simplest support for a purlin (*keta*) is a boat-shaped bracket arm (*funa-hijiki*; see fig. (a)) placed directly on the top of a pillar. The most elementary bracket complex consists of one large bearing block (*daito*) supporting one bracket arm (*hijiki*), the combination being called a pair (b). Three

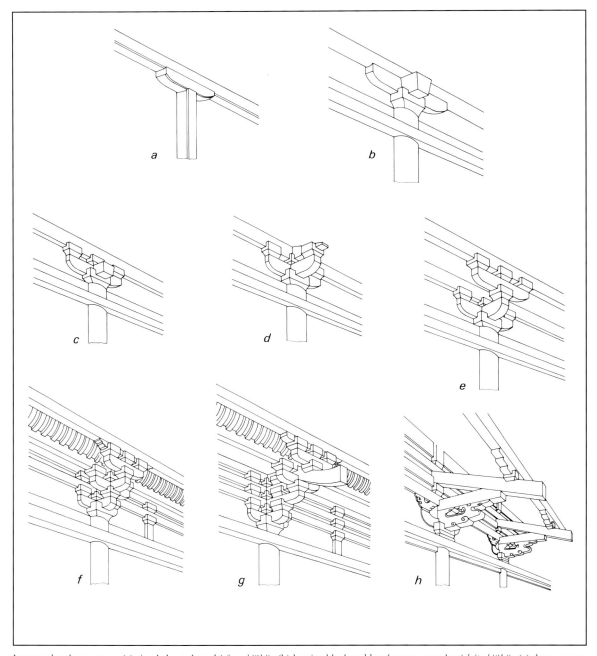

Japanese bracket systems: (a) simple boat-shaped (*funa-hijiki*); (b) bearing block and bracket arm complex (*daito-hijiki*); (c) three-on-one complex (*mitsudo-tokyō*); (d) three-on-one right-angle complex (*demitsudo*); (e) one-stepped complex (*degumi*); (f) two-stepped complex (*futatesaki-tokyō*); (g) three-stepped complex (*mitesaki-tokyō*); (h) cloud-patterned complex (*kumo-tokyō*)

smaller bearing blocks placed across the top of this bracket arm, all parallel to the wall plane, creates a three-on-one non-projecting bracket complex (*mitsudo-tokyō*; (c)). If another bracket arm is attached at right angles to the same large bearing block, and a small bearing block is added on its outer end, a three-on-one right-angle complex (*demitsudo*; (d)) is formed. When another bracket arm is inserted

into the bearing block, projecting at right angles from the centre of the basic bracket arm, and three bearings are arranged upon it, one 'step' forward has been created, so that the system exists on two vertical planes; this is called a one-stepped bracket complex (*degumi*; (e)). A two-stepped bracket complex (*futatesaki-tokyō*; (f)) is made by adding a right-angled bracket arm with bearing block that extends from the bracket complex of the first projecting pair. To support the eaves and to counteract the downward pressure of the roof structure, a tail rafter (*odaruki*) is often added, passing through the bracket arm that formed the first stepped complex. A large bearing block is placed on the end of the tail rafter to support the second stepped complex. Repeating the procedure produces a three-stepped bracket complex (*mitesaki-tokyō*; (g)), the most widely used bracket system in Japan. The best-known examples are from the 8th century AD in the *kondō* (main image hall) at the temple Tōshōdaiji, Nara (*see* NARA, §II, 9). Four-stepped bracket complexes are more usual under the roofs of two-storey pagodas (*tahōtō*).

Bracket complexes constructed after the end of the Heian period (794–1185) show Chinese influence and are divided into three styles: Wayō, Zen and Daibutsu. In its pure form, the Wayō or Japanese style follows the ancient arrangement of the bracket system. The Zen style is markedly more exuberant and ornate than the conservative Wayō style: the bracket arms are longer and carry more bearing blocks. Unsupported bracket complexes fill the interstices between those set on pillars. There are examples of bracket arms and bearing blocks that were carved in a single unit. In both the Wayō and the Zen styles, bracket complexes are usually set on top of pillars. In the Daibutsu style, bracket arms are inserted into the pillars and the complexes built up accordingly, as in the Great South Gate (Nandaimon) at the temple Tōdaiji, Nara (*see* NARA, §III, 4).

Cloud-patterned bracket complexes (*kumo-tokyō*; (h)), in which the bearing block (*kumo-to*) and bracket arm (or corbel; *kumo-hijiki*) are both carved into cut-out cloud patterns, were used only in three temples (late 7th century–early 8th) in the Ikaruga district of Nara: the *kondō*, the five-storey pagoda and the Middle Gate (Chūmon) at Hōryūji; the three-storey pagoda at Hōkiji; and the reconstructed three-storeyed pagoda (originally built 7th–8th century; destr. 1944) at Hōrinji.

BIBLIOGRAPHY
M. Ōoka and O. Mori: *Architecture and Gardens*, vi of *Pageant of Japanese Art* (Tokyo, 1957–)
K. Suzuki: *Early Buddhist Architecture in Japan* (New York and San Francisco, 1980)
M. N. Parent: *The Roof in Japanese Buddhist Architecture* (Tokyo and New York, 1983/R 1985)

MARY NEIGHBOUR PARENT

Bracquemond. French family of artists.

(1) Félix(-Auguste-Joseph) Bracquemond (*b* Paris, ?28 May 1833; *d* Sèvres, nr Paris, 27 Oct 1914). Printmaker, designer, painter and writer. From a humble background, he set out on an artistic career after meeting the painter Joseph Guichard, a pupil of Ingres and Delacroix, who was to be his only teacher. He was brought up by a philanthropist friend of Auguste Comte, Dr Horace de Montègre, whose portrait he drew in pastel in 1860 (Paris, Mus. d'Orsay). Comte's positivist philosophy was a considerable influence on Bracquemond's aesthetic ideas. From 1852 he exhibited at the Salon both drawn and painted portraits in the style of Ingres, for example *Mme Paul Meurice* (Compiègne, Château), but he gave up painting after 1869.

Bracquemond is better known as a printmaker and designer. He taught himself etching and began working in the medium as early as 1849, supporting himself with difficulty by means of commercial lithographic work. He was one of the last friends of Charles Meryon and with him was the principal inspiration of the etching revival in France (*see* ETCHING, §V). In 1862 he founded the Société des Aquafortistes, which included a large proportion of the etchers of the period. His masterpiece and best-known etching is *Le Haut d'un battant de porte* ('The top of a door', 1852; see fig.), a startling combination of the prosaically macabre and decorative *trompe l'oeil*. Bracquemond produced almost 900 plates, divided about equally between original and reproductive prints. He etched portraits (e.g. *Meryon*, 1853; *Edmond de Goncourt*, 1882) and some 80 landscapes, many in the spirit of Corot (e.g. *Willow Trees in Mottiaux*, 1868), but specialized in depicting animals, particularly ducks (e.g. *Teal*, 1853). His reproductive prints convey with astonishing faithfulness the different styles of such painters as Ingres, Delacroix (*Boissy d'Anglas*, 1881), Corot, Millet, Ernest Meissonier (*The Brawl*, 1885) and Gustave Moreau (*King David*, 1884).

Admired by Théophile Gautier and Edmond About at the Exposition Universelle in 1855, Bracquemond rapidly became a central figure in the Parisian artistic and literary avant-garde. Among his numerous friends were Théodore de Banville, Baudelaire, Jules Champfleury, Paul Gavarni and the Goncourt brothers, whom he came to know largely through the publisher Poulet-Malassis, for whom he worked from the end of the 1850s. From the early 1860s he belonged to Manet's circle. He encouraged Manet to etch and took part with him in the Salon des Refusés in 1863 and then in the gatherings at the Café Guerbois. Bracquemond exhibited at the Impressionist exhibitions of 1874, 1879 and 1880.

Bracquemond was one of the first to discover and popularize Japanese prints, having reputedly come upon Hokusai's *Manga* in Auguste Delâtre's printshop. He adopted their asymmetrical compositions and specific naturalistic motifs in his etchings and ceramics, which he began designing in the 1860s. He worked for a while in the studio of Joseph-Théodore Deck (1823–91), where he learnt the technique of enamel painting. In 1866 he was commissioned by Eugène Rousseau (1827–91) to design a large faience service. The 'Rousseau service' incorporates motifs from his animal etchings: for example, *The Duck*, published in *L'Artiste* (1856), was reused on one of the plates (Nevers, Mus. Mun.), as were some motifs from the etching *Teal* (1853; dinner plate, Paris, priv. col.), which shows his continued interest in Japanese aesthetics combined with a more delicate and refined sense of composition and colour. The more abstract style of his 'Flower and ribbon service' of 1879 anticipates the designs of the Art Nouveau movement. From 1873 to 1880 he was head of the Auteuil studio (near Paris) of the Haviland Limoges factory, where he personally designed individual pieces and several important porcelain services including the 'Parisian service' of 1876. While director of the Haviland factory he continued to exhibit his etchings at the Salon. His greatest success as a printmaker was in 1900, when his etchings won first prize at the Exposition

Félix Bracquemond: *Le Haut d'un battant de porte* ('The top of a door'), etching, 279×381 mm, 1852 (Paris, Bibliothèque Nationale)

Universelle in Paris. He designed furniture, gold and silver jewellery and tableware, bookbindings and tapestry in collaboration chiefly with Rodin and Jules Chéret. His furniture designs for Baron Joseph Vitta's Villa La Sapinière at Evian were shown at the Salon of 1902. At the end of his life he produced designs for decorative art for his friend and devoted admirer, the writer and critic Gustave Geffroy, who was then director of the Gobelins.

Bracquemond published theoretical writings, particularly from 1878 onwards. His very personal theory of the art of relief and the place of colour in design is summarized in *Du dessin et de la couleur* (1885). He was a founder-member of the Société des Artistes Français and later belonged to the Société Nationale des Beaux-Arts. In 1890 he founded the Société des Peintres-Graveurs Français to preserve the art of original engraving against the rapid development of photographic techniques.

WRITINGS
Du dessin et de la couleur (Paris, 1885)

(2) Marie Bracquemond [née Quivoron-Pasquiou] (*b* Argenton, nr Quimper, 1 Dec 1840; *d* Sèvres, nr Paris, 17 Jan 1916). Painter, draughtsman, printmaker and designer, wife of (1) Félix Bracquemond. After a difficult start in life, she began to study drawing at Etampes, near Paris. She took advice from Ingres but never received any formal teaching. Admitted to the Salon from 1857, she was commissioned by the State to copy pictures in the Louvre.

There she met Félix Bracquemond in about 1867 and married him on 5 August 1869. She was involved in her husband's work for the Haviland Limoges factory and produced in particular several dishes and a wide panel of ceramic tiles entitled the *Muses*, shown at the Exposition Universelle in Paris in 1878; the sketch for this was shown at the Impressionist Exhibition of 1879 and was greatly admired by Degas. Originally very much influenced by Ingres and then by Alfred (Emile-Léopold) Stevens, her style of painting changed completely *c.* 1880 as a consequence of her admiration for Renoir and Monet and subsequently because of advice from Gauguin. The few pictures surviving from this period illustrate her conversion to a clearly Impressionist style, comparable to that of Berthe Morisot and Mary Cassatt. Examples include *The Lady in White* (1880; Cambrai, Mus. Mun.), *On the Terrace at Sèvres* (*c.* 1880; Geneva, Petit Pal.) and *Afternoon Tea* (*c.* 1880; Paris, Petit Pal.). After exhibiting at the Salon in 1874 and 1875, she took part in the Impressionist exhibitions of 1879, 1880 and 1886. In spite of the support of friends such as Gustave Geffroy, her husband was against any broadening of her career, and confined to Sèvres she produced only a limited amount of work. The retrospective exhibition of 1919 at the Galerie Bernheim-Jeune, Paris, included 90 paintings (to a large extent small sketches), 34 watercolours and 9 engravings. She also produced ceramics and several drawings for *La Vie moderne* (1879–80).

Félix and Marie's son Pierre Bracquemond (*b* Paris, 26 June 1870; *d* Paris, 29 Jan 1926) was a pupil of his father and as such was involved in works for the Gobelins. He pursued a career as an interior decorator (carpets, tapestries) and painter (nudes, seascapes), chiefly employing the technique of encaustic painting. He left several critical articles and important unpublished manuscripts on the life of his parents and the aesthetic ideas of his father.

BIBLIOGRAPHY

H. Beraldi: *Les Graveurs du XIXème siècle*, iii (Paris, 1885/*R* 1980)
Félix et Marie Bracquemond (exh. cat., ed. J.-P. Bouillon; Mortagne-au-Perche, Maison Comtes du Perche, 1972)
Céramique impressionniste (exh. cat., ed. J.-P. Bouillon, J. d'Albis and L. d'Albis; Paris, Bib. Forney, 1974)
Hommage à Félix Bracquemond (exh. cat. by J.-P. Bouillon, Paris, Bib. N., 1974)
J.-P. Bouillon: *Félix Bracquemond: Les Années d'apprentissage, 1849–1859* (diss., U. Paris I, 1979)
The Crisis of Impressionism, 1878–1882 (exh. cat., ed. J. Isaacson; Ann Arbor, U. MI, Mus. A., 1979)
J.-P. Bouillon and E. Kane: 'Marie Bracquemond', *Woman's A. J.*, v/2 (1984), pp. 21–7
T. Garb: *Women Impressionists* (Oxford, 1986)
J.-P. Bouillon: *Félix Bracquemond, le réalisme absolu: Oeuvre gravé, 1849–1859, catalogue raisonné* (Geneva, 1987) [with complete bibliog.]
Le Service 'Rousseau' (exh. cat. by J.-P. Bouillon, C. Shimizu and P. Thiébaut, Paris, Mus. d'Orsay, 1988)
Félix Bracquemond (exh. cat. by C. van Rappard-Boon, Amsterdam, Rijksmus. van Gogh, 1993)

JEAN-PAUL BOUILLON

Bractwo Świetego Łukasza. *See* FELLOWSHIP OF ST LUKE.

Bradford, William (*b* Fairhaven, MA, 30 April 1823; *d* New York, 25 April 1892). American painter and photographer. He became a full-time artist about 1853 after spending a few years in the wholesale clothing business. In 1855 he set up a studio in Fairhaven, MA, and made a living by painting ship portraits. At the same time he studied with the slightly more experienced marine painter Albert van Beest (1820–60), and they collaborated on several works. By 1860 Bradford had moved to New York and was starting to gain a reputation for such paintings of the coast of Labrador as *Ice Dwellers Watching the Invaders* (*c.* 1870; New Bedford, MA, Whaling Mus.), which were based on his own photographs and drawings. From 1872 to 1874 he was in London, lecturing on the Arctic and publishing his book *The Arctic Regions* (1873). Queen Victoria commissioned him to paint an Arctic scene that was shown at the Royal Academy in 1875. On his return to the USA, Bradford was elected an associate member of the National Academy of Design. In later years his tight, realistic style went out of favour as French Impressionism became increasingly popular.

WRITINGS
The Arctic Regions (London, 1873)

BIBLIOGRAPHY
William Bradford, 1823–1892 (exh. cat., ed. J. Wilmerding; Lincoln, MA, DeCordova & Dana Mus., 1969)
F. Horch: 'Photographs and Paintings by William Bradford', *Amer. A. J.*, v (1973), pp. 61–70

MARK W. SULLIVAN

Brady, Mathew B. (*b* Warren County, NY, 1823; *d* New York, 15 Jan 1896). American photographer. At the age of 16 he left his home town and moved to nearby Saratoga.

There he learnt how to manufacture jewellery cases and met William Page, who taught him the techniques of painting. Impressed by his ability, Page took Brady to New York in 1841 to study with Samuel F. B. Morse at the Academy of Design, and to attend Morse's school of daguerreotypy; there Brady learnt the details of photographic technique. After experimenting with the medium from 1841 to 1843, Brady set up his Daguerrean Miniature Gallery in New York (1844), where he both took and exhibited daguerreotypes. Very soon he established a considerable reputation and in 1845 won first prize in two classes of the daguerreotype competition run by the American Institute. He concentrated on photographic portraits, especially of famous contemporary Americans, such as the statesman *Henry Clay* (1849; Washington, DC, Lib. Congr.). In 1847, with his business flourishing, he opened a second studio, in Washington, and in 1850 published his *Gallery of Illustrious Americans* (New York). These were lithographic portraits of eminent Americans, such as General Winfield Scott and Millard Fillmore, taken from Brady's original daguerreotypes.

In 1851 Brady contributed a number of daguerreotypes to the Great Exhibition in London, which included the largest photographic display so far held. The Americans took all the top awards, Brady himself winning first prize. While in London he also learnt of the new wet collodion or 'wet plate' process and met one of its leading practitioners, Alexander Gardner. Soon after his return to New York in 1852 the ambrotype (a collodion glass positive with black backing) became his dominant medium. In 1853 he opened a larger gallery in New York and in 1858 added a gallery to his studio in Washington. In 1856, persuaded by Brady, Gardner came to New York where he was put in charge of the new gallery. He brought with him the details of a process enabling the production of enlargements from wet plate negatives, which allowed Brady to make large 'Imperial' size portraits. In 1860 Brady opened the largest of his galleries in New York, called the National Portrait Gallery, and that year he took his famous photograph of *Abraham Lincoln* (1860; Washington, DC, Lib. Congr.), the first of many, on the occasion of Lincoln's speech to the Cooper Union. Lincoln, who was elected president the following year, attributed his success to a Brady *carte-de-visite* (*see* PHOTOGRAPHY, §I, 2).

In 1861, at the outbreak of the American Civil War, Brady gave up his lucrative career as a portrait photographer and decided to devote himself to documenting the events of the war. During the first few months of the following year he organized and equipped at his own expense several teams of cameramen to send to the numerous sites of conflict. Among the photographers he employed, apart from himself and Gardner, were Timothy O'Sullivan, William R. Pyell, J. B. Gibson, George Cook, David Knox, D. B. Woodbury, J. Reekie and Stanley Morrow. Though working in extremely difficult conditions, Brady and his team were able to cover virtually all the battles and events of the war. Those photographs taken by Brady himself included portraits of the protagonists, such as *Robert E. Lee* (1865; Washington, DC, Lib. Congr.), taken after his defeat, and numerous images of its horrors, such as *On the Antietam Battlefield* (1862; Washington, DC, Lib. Congr.). Some of his photographs, such as *Dead Confederate Soldier with Gun* (1863; Washington, DC, Lib. Congr.), were stereoscopic views.

Brady had embarked on this vast enterprise in the belief that both private individuals and, more importantly, the state would be interested in purchasing the photographs after the war. In fact, the trauma and destruction it caused led to a general desire to forget. Burdened by huge debts, he tried to persuade the government to buy his collection for the archives. It was not until 1875 that it finally did so, after a vote in Congress. The purchase came too late, however: Brady had been forced to sell all his properties except for the one in Washington, which was run by his nephew Levin Handy. Though reduced to poverty, he produced a few further portrait photographs, such as *Chiefs of the Sioux Indian Nations* (1877; Washington, DC, Lib. Congr.). He sold the last of his galleries in 1895.

BIBLIOGRAPHY

R. Meredith: *Mr Lincoln's Cameraman* (New York, 1946)
J. D. Horan: *Mathew Brady: Historian with a Camera* (New York, 1955)
P. Pollack: *The Picture History of Photography* (New York, 1977), pp. 56–9
G. Hobart: *Mathew Brady* (London, 1984)

Braem, René [Renaat] (*b* Antwerp, 21 Aug 1910). Belgian architect and writer. He studied architecture in Antwerp, first at the Koninklijke Academie voor Schone Kunsten (1926–31) and then at the National Hoger Instituut voor Schone Kunsten until 1935. He was influenced by Soviet Constructivism, and while studying he designed a project for a linear city between Antwerp and Liège for which he produced several dozen drawings using gouache and collage. From 1936 to 1937 he worked in Paris with Le Corbusier, and he became a member of the Belgian section of CIAM from 1939. His early, modernist architectural theories were similar to those of Le Corbusier and were expressed in the construction of the Kiel district (1949–58) and the tower of the Administrative Centre (1951), both in Antwerp, as well as the Sint Martensdal district of Leuven. He later evolved a 'biomorphic' lyricism, which is most evident in the flowing lines of the low-cost housing (1965–70) he built at Boom, the Cité Arena (1960–61) at Deurne and the building (1971–8) for the rectorate of the Vrije Universiteit of Brussels, constructed on an oval plan. He also continued to design private houses. Braem was a tireless polemicist and very talented draughtsman. He edited the journals *Bouwen en wonen* (1952–62) and *Plan* (1963–5) and stimulated architectural debate in Belgium throughout his career by the adoption of extreme positions and the design of utopian cities.

WRITINGS

Het lelijkste land ter wereld [The ugliest country in the world] (Leuven, 1968)

BIBLIOGRAPHY

F. Strauven: *René Braem: Architecture* (Brussels, 1985)

ANNE VAN LOO

Braga. Capital city of the Portuguese province of Minho, seat of the primate of Portugal. It has a population of *c.* 64,000. The city's name is derived from that of the Bracari, an Iron Age tribe that settled between the Minho and Douro rivers. Under the Romans the settlement received the name of Bracara Augusta and grew in importance to become one of the main seats of administration in the Roman province of Tarraconensis. In the 3rd century AD the fall of the Roman Empire and the Barbarian invasion forced the construction of fortified walls and it became the capital of a new province, Gallaecia, which extended between the Douro and the Bay of Biscay. Christianity spread rapidly in the city from the 4th century. Little survives from the Roman period other than some mosaics and other archaeological remains, which provide some evidence of ceramic and glass production, and an antique stone statue of a deity protecting a fountain, the so-called *Fonte do idolo* (Rua do Raio, near the Palácio do Raio). After the invasion of the peninsula by Germanic tribes at the beginning of the 5th century, Braga became the Suevi capital. The nearby funerary chapel of S Frutuoso de Montélios was built under the Visigoths in the 7th century. The city was captured in 716, burnt by the Moors and almost abandoned after the 8th century. In the 11th century it passed to León, the successor to the Visigothic kingdom. The bishops of Braga, who used the title Primate of All Spain, returned from the north, and the Romanesque cathedral was built, probably in 1090, at the same time as the first cathedral school. Reconstruction of the city was carried out slowly. From then on Braga was involved in European expansion from the Reconquest and the arrival in the peninsula of Henry of Burgundy, Count of Portugal (*reg* 1095–1112), and in the seigneurial movement for separation from León.

Count Henry and his wife Teresa (*d* 1130) are buried in the cathedral. Because the conquests of their son, Alfonso I (*reg* 1112–85), were to the south, the area's financial and political centre also moved, and Braga lost much of its importance. During the 14th century, as a result of the plague and the war between the pretenders to the throne following the death of King Ferdinand (*reg* 1367–83), the city walls were restored, and a precentor of Braga Cathedral negotiated the first Portuguese–English alliance (1373). John I (*reg* 1385–1433), the husband of Philippa of Lancaster, held his first *cortes* (Port.: 'parliament') in Braga. Their son, Infante Alfonso (*d* 1400), is buried in the cathedral in a copper tomb sent from Flanders by Isabel of Portugal. Another fine Gothic tomb is that of *Archbishop Gonçalo Pereira* (*d* 1348). At the beginning of the 16th century Archbishop Diogo de Sousa (*reg* 1505–32) brought the Renaissance to Braga with the construction of new buildings and the laying out of large, open spaces, which changed the look of the medieval city. An engraving (1594) of the city by Georg Braun (1542–1622) of Cologne is included in the *Civitates orbis terrarum* (Cologne, 1672).

In the 17th century many people emigrated from the Braga region to Brazil; some returned with fortunes. Maize was introduced, and agriculture prospered. Part of the resulting wealth was spent on social events and the building of churches (e.g. Santa Cruz), mansions and convents in the city. Whereas in the 15th and 16th centuries southern Portugal, especially Lisbon, had greater aesthetic and economic influence, the north-east was more influential in the 17th and 18th centuries, with Baroque and Rococo styles dominating both new projects and the transformation of existing buildings. For example, at the monastery of Tibães (?11th century; mostly destr.) near Braga, the mother house of the Spanish and Portuguese Benedictines,

André Ribeiro Soares da Silva redecorated the interior of the church (1760); he also designed a number of buildings in the city (*see* SOARES DA SILVA, ANDRÉ RIBEIRO and fig. 2). The new sacristy of Braga Cathedral was designed by João Antunes at the end of the 16th century.

The spectacular sanctuary of Bom Jesus do Monte (1784–1811; see fig.) on a hill near Braga was commissioned by Archbishop Rodrigo de Moura Teles and designed principally by CARLOS LUIS FERREIRA AMARANTE. It consists of a series of garden terraces with stairways, fountains, chapels and statues laid out with Baroque theatricality. During the 18th century two Braganza princes were Archbishop–primate of Braga: José de Braganza (*reg* 1741–56), who enlarged the Archbishop's Palace (second half of the 18th century; now Bib. Pub.), giving it a rocaille façade, and Gaspar de Braganza (*reg* 1758–89). Braga had an important tradition of craftsmanship in *talha* ('carved and gilded wood'), painting, bronze gilding, silverwork and silk- and linen-weaving which flourished in the 18th century. In the mid-18th century MARCELIANO DE ARAÚJO executed a number of sculptures that remain in the city, and the interesting *Mapa das ruas de Braga* (1750; Braga, Bib. Pub.) was produced, which shows the city's streets with the elevations of the houses.

In the 19th century, Braga's growth was stimulated by wealth from Brazil, new industries and the strengthening of the commercial middle classes. The city was modernized, and some of the old open spaces were made into avenues. Development continued in the 20th century, with the destruction of some medieval and Baroque buildings. In the 1960s, which brought war with the Portuguese colonies and a new period of emigration, great structural changes occurred; urban planning included new streets and an avenue ring-road. A statue was erected to the philosopher *Francisco Sanches* (Largo São João do Souto) by João Rafael de Basto d'Eça Barata Feyo (*b* 1938). Growth during the 1970s and 1980s made Braga the third most populous city in the country. Sculpture of this period is represented by a statue (1989) paying homage to the visit to Braga of Pope Paul VI by Zulmiro de Neves Carvalho (*b* 1940) and a group (1993) by José Rodrigues (*b* 1936) on the university campus, opposite Bom Jesus Hill.

BIBLIOGRAPHY
R. Smith: *The Art of Portugal* (London, 1968)
A. J. Costa, S. Pinto and J. Vasconcelos, eds: *Dicionário de história de Portugal: Verbo enciclopedia luso-brasileira de cultura*, 4 vols (Lisbon, 1971)
A. H. de Oliveira Marques: *História de Portugal*, 3 vols (Lisbon, New York and London, 1972–6)
P. Oliveira, S. Moura and J. Mesquita: *Braga: Evolução estrutura urbana* (Braga, 1982)
M. Martins, M. Delgado and S. Lemos: 'Roteiro arqueológico', *Bracara Augusta* (1989)

CESAR VALENCA

Braga, Leandro (*b* Braga, 1839; *d* Lisbon, 1897). Portuguese wood-carver and cabinetmaker. At the age of 14 he was sent by his father to Lisbon to the workshop of Inácio Caetano, a master cabinetmaker and wood-carver who was working for the royal household at the Palácio das Necessidades. In 1862 Braga moved to the workshop of Célestin-Anatole Calmels (1822–1908), a French sculptor

Braga, sanctuary of Bom Jesus do Monte, principally by Carlos Luis Ferreira Amarante, 1784–1811

who had settled in Portugal, with whom he collaborated on commissions for sculpture and decorative work. In 1865 he passed the qualifying examination as a master craftsman and then designed and decorated the royal box in the Teatro São Carlos in Lisbon. In the same year he opened a workshop in the Calçada do Combro in Lisbon. One of his apprentices was JOSÉ MALHOA, a naturalist painter active in the late 19th century and early 20th. Braga continued to collaborate with Calmels, and in 1867 Braga carved the two winged figures, the draperies and the crowned finial of the canopy (*in situ*) that framed the portrait of *King Luis I* in the Câmara dos Dignos Pares do Reino (Assembly Hall of the House of Peers; later Assembly of the Republic). Braga later designed and executed the president's throne in the same chamber. His fame as a cabinetmaker reached Ferdinand II, King of Portugal, who visited his workshop and gave him commissions for the Palácio da Ajuda and the Palácio de Belém. In the former Braga decorated Queen Maria II's boudoir, a room dominated by a huge mirror surmounted by a carved entablature inspired by the Joanine style. He also carved the dark oak cupboards that are covered in an exuberant design similar to that of 18th-century altars. In the Palácio de Belém his most important piece was the imperial bed built for the marriage of Prince Charles (later King of Portugal, *reg* 1889–1908) to Amélia of Orléans (1865–1951). In 1875 Braga undertook the decoration of the 'chalet' of Maria Luisa de Sousa Holstein, Duquesa de Palmela, in Cascais; many pieces of furniture and interior decoration were also commissioned from him for summer mansions both in Cascais and in Sintra, including the Palácio de Biester. Braga's style as wood-carver, cabinetmaker and decorator includes revivals of late Renaissance, Baroque and late 18th-century and early 19th-century Portuguese styles interspersed with French designs: Régence, Louis XV and, more rarely, Louis XVI. Examples of his furniture in the French Louis XV style include the secrétaire he made for Queen Amélia. For the palace of the Marquês da Foz in Lisbon, remodelled in 1889, he created some of his finest revivalist furniture, including the splendid Meissonnier-inspired panelling of the ball-room and the window-frame conceived as a piece of Louis XV style furniture. He executed ornamental carvings as well as furniture, for example the decoration of the Chariot of the Arts for the civic procession to celebrate the tercentenary of the death of the national poet Luis de Camões in 1880. Braga died when work commissioned by the Duques de Palmela was being executed in his work-shops in Rua do Salitre and Rua da Rosa, Lisbon. An exhibition of his work was organized in 1897 in the palace of the Marquês da Foz in Avenida da Liberdade, which included 70 of Braga's pieces accompanied by drawings, photographs and the iron stamp *L. Braga, Lisboa* with which he marked his work. The concise catalogue pub-lished at the time is the best record of his work.

BIBLIOGRAPHY
'Sala das sessões da Câmara dos Pares', *Occidente*, 1 (1873)
C. A.: 'Leandro Braga', *Occidente*, 659 (1897)
Trabalhos de Leandro Braga (exh. cat., Lisbon, Pal. Foz, 1897)
R. Artur: *Arte e artistas contemporâneos* (Lisbon, 1898)
Objectos d'arte e mobiliário antigo (sale cat., Lisbon, Pal. Foz, 1901)
A. Guimarães: 'O grande artista Leandro Braga', *Rev. Guimarães*, xxxii (1922)
L. de Barros: *Duas visitas a Versailles, 1938–1951* (Lisbon, 1981)
A. Pimentel: 'O cortejo cívico das comemorações camoneanas de 1880', *Actas do 1° Congresso de Sintra sobre o Romantismo: Sintra, 1988*
MARIA HELENA MENDES PINTO

Bragaglia. Italian family of photographers. Anton Giulio Bragaglia(*b* nr Rome, 11 Feb 1890; *d* Rome, 15 July 1960) first became interested in photography when he and his brother Arturo Bragaglia (*b* nr Rome, 7 Feb 1893; *d* Rome, 1962) were studying cinematography in Rome at Cines, the film production company of which their father had been director since 1906. Partly in response to the *Manifeste de fondation du Futurisme* by Marinetti (1909) and to the *Manifesto della pittura futurista* (1910) by Marinetti, Boc-cioni, Bonzagni, Carrà and Russolo, Anton Giulio Braga-glia began to formulate his theory of *fotodinamismo*. The essays of Henri Bergson, which had recently been trans-lated into Italian, were further inspiration, and they pro-posed a novel concept of time. Aided in his experiments by his brothers Arturo and Carlo Ludovico (*b* 1894), he attempted to produce a visual representation of this new concept.

For Anton Giulio Bragaglia, *fotodinamismo* was 'the synthesis of the trajectory' of a gesture; he achieved this by fixing the image of the body's transition from one position to another in such a way that it was dematerialized by its own dynamism in space and not, as in the chrono-photography devised by Marey and the photo-sequences of Muybridge, through the successive instants of motion. In 1911 the results of the Bragaglia brothers' experiments were exhibited as the first *fotodinamiche* in the Mantegazza bookshop in Rome. In 1912 Anton Giulio Bragaglia published *Fotodinamismo futurista*, explaining his theory. The book attracted attention not least for the novelty of its ideas. In 1913 two new editions were published with the addition of illustrations, for example *Greetings!* and *The Futurist Painter Giacomo Balla*, some of which form

the only existing documentation of photographs that have since been lost.

Boccioni and other Futurist painters challenged the seriousness of Anton Giulio Bragaglia's work, and in 1913 they published a 'Notizia' in the magazine *Lacerba* (1 Oct), in which they denied that the Bragaglias' work had any aesthetic value whatsoever, declaring it to be merely innovation in the field of photographic technique. Anton Giulio Bragaglia's work was instead one of the first conceptual analyses of the language of photography that was neither dependent on the picturesque nor on the documentary form. In 1914 Anton Giulio Bragaglia aban-doned photography to work with film and theatre, and for the next two years he worked with Enrico Prampolini producing avant-garde films, including *Thais* (1916) and *Perfido incanto* (1916). Arturo Bragaglia opened a photo-graphic portrait studio in Rome (1914), and his portraits were particularly popular among actors and artists.

In 1918 the Bragaglia brothers opened the Casa d'arte Bragaglia in Rome, a venue for exhibitions and cultural debates. In 1922 they founded the Teatro degli Indepen-denti, which brought the new European theatre to Italy for the first time and presented avant-garde works by authors such as Brecht, Apollinaire and Laforgue. There-after Anton Giulio Bragaglia's involvement with photog-raphy was only occasional, and his essays on the subject alternated with a much larger body of work dedicated mostly to theatre; his photodynamic research re-emerged in 1930, however, with the publication by Marinetti and Tato (Guglielmo Sansoni; 1896–1974) of the *Manifesto della fotografia futurista*, although this described a different technical and ideological application nearer, for example, to the methodology of László Moholy-Nagy. In 1922 Arturo Bragaglia formed a partnership with Riccardo Bettini, a member of a dynasty of photographers from Livorno, dividing his time between photography and working as a character actor in films such as *Miracolo a Milano*.

WRITINGS
Fotodinamismo futurista (Rome, 1912, rev. Turin, 1970) [Anton Giulio Bragaglia]
BIBLIOGRAPHY
G. Lista: *Futurismo e fotografia* (Milan, 1979)
Photographie futuriste italienne (exh. cat. by G. Lista, Paris, Mus. A. Mod. Ville Paris, 1981)
I. Zannier: 'Fotodinamismo', *Il fotografo a Milano* (1982)
Futurismo e futurismi (exh. cat., Milan, 1986)
G. Scimé, ed.: *Il laboratorio dei Bragaglia: 1911–1932* (Ravenna, 1987)
I. Zannier: *L'occhio della fotografia* (Rome, 1989)
ITALO ZANNIER

Braganza, House of. Portuguese family of rulers, collec-tors and patrons. Alfonso, 1st Duque de Braganza (1370–1461), was the illegitimate son of John I, King of Portugal (*see* AVIZ, (1)). His great-grandson (1) Jaime, 4th Duque de Braganza, was known primarily as a patron of architec-ture—military and ecclesiastic—and for the restoration and building of family palaces, notably at Vila Viçosa where he created a literary and humanist court. Jaime's son (2) Teotónio also founded several religious convents and built up a distinguished library of rare manuscripts and books. Subsequent generations (see fig.) were known for their humanist courts at the family seat of Vila Viçosa, which, from 1560 when Portugal was under Spanish rule, offered

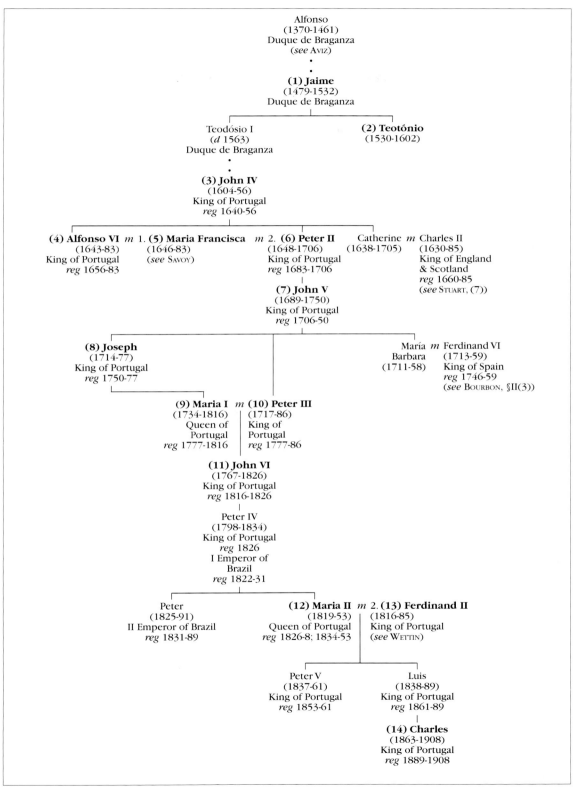

Family tree of the Braganza dynasty

an alternative to the court at Lisbon and contributed to the restoration of the Portuguese crown in 1640 under (3) John IV. John's son (4) Alfonso VI was physically and mentally handicapped; his brief marriage to (5) Maria Francisca was annulled and he was deposed by his brother (6) Peter II, who subsequently married Maria Francisca. The reign of his son (7) John V was a golden age of patronage due to political stability and the vast revenues from the discovery of gold in the Portuguese colony of Brazil. He acquired and commissioned an important international collection of paintings and sculpture, invited foreign artists to the court and commissioned major architectural projects. The courtly stately JOANINE style named after him showed the influence of the Italian Baroque and the grandeur of Louis XIV. The great earthquake in 1755 in the reign of (8) Joseph resulted in the virtual replanning of Lisbon. Joseph's daughter (9) Maria I combined progressive economic policies and industrial development with political conservatism; her husband and uncle (10) Peter III is known primarily for the development of the Queluz Palace. The reign of their son (11) John VI, however, was another age of distinguished patronage. As a result of the Napoleonic invasions he went into exile with the court to Brazil, where, as Prince Regent, he had a profound influence on artistic life, establishing art educational institutions and, through the French artistic commission to Rio de Janeiro that he organized in 1816, helping to introduce Neo-classicism to the country. His son became Peter I, Emperor of Brazil (*reg* 1822–31), and later Peter IV, King of Portugal (*reg* 1826). Peter abdicated as Emperor of Brazil in favour of his son, who ruled as Peter II, Emperor of Brazil, from 1831 until Brazil became a republic in 1889. He designated his daughter (12) Maria II as Queen of Portugal, but because of the civil war she was not secured on the throne until 1834. In 1836 she married (13) Ferdinand II, and in the same year they jointly founded the Academias das Belas Artes in Lisbon and Oporto in 1836; after her death, Ferdinand established other art institutions and purchased numerous works of art both for himself and for a national collection. The descendants of Maria and Ferdinand, including their grandson, (14) Charles, ruled until 1910, when the monarchy was abolished; these members were Wettins in the male line (*see* WETTIN).

See also PORTUGAL, §XII and BRAZIL, §I.

BIBLIOGRAPHY
R. C. Smith: *The Art of Portugal: 1500–1800* (London, 1968)

☐

(1) Jaime, 4th Duque de (*b* Vila Viçosa, 1479; *d* Vila Viçosa, 20 Sept 1532). His father, Dom Fernando II, 3rd Duque de Braganza, was executed in 1483 in Évora as a result of disputes between John II and the nobility. Dom Jaime and his brothers went into exile at the Spanish court, where his education was supervised by his uncle, Dom Álvaro, who accompanied him. He was taught by the Italian humanist Pietro di Anghiera (1457–1526) and by Diogo de Sigi (Sigeu), who dedicated an essay to him (*Epistolarum familiarium*, 1514). On the accession of Manuel I to the throne in 1496 Dom Jaime was conceded the lordship and property of the House of Braganza, which was now restored to its previous splendour, with a charter allowing him to use the royal coat of arms and to hold a princely court. The following year he was appointed heir presumptive to the throne in the absence in Castile of King Manuel. His first wife was beheaded in 1512, accused of adultery with a court page, and the conquest of the Moroccan city of Azamor (now Azemmar; 1513), which was successfully led by Dom Jaime, is traditionally said to have been undertaken in order to distract him from his sufferings over the circumstances of his wife's death and to allow him to perform heroically before the King.

The Duque's patronage was primarily in the field of architecture. He was interested in military architecture and fortified the stronghold of Azamor, converted the Alcaçova *solar*, or country house, at Vila Viçosa, the original seat of the Braganza family, into a fortified castle along the lines of contemporary Italian models (1529), and he also constructed the castle of Évora-Monte (near Estremoz). Non-military architectural commissions included the construction (begun 1501) of the new Ducal Palace outside the city walls of VILA VIÇOSA with a chapel and cloister in the *Mudéjar* style, which was widely employed in Alentejo province. The present palace dates mainly from the 17th century, and its façade was faced with marble in 1601; it now houses the Braganza archives and collection. The restoration of the palaces of Lisbon (Maítires) and Évora (Portas da Moura) was initiated by Dom Jaime, as well as the ducal country house and the Tapada, a walled deer-park, both at Vila Viçosa. His profound religious belief led him to promote the founding in Portugal in 1500 of the Order of Capuchin monks, for whom he built in Vila Viçosa the hermitage of Nossa Senhora da Piedade, which he often visited and indeed considered entering, but he was forbidden to do so by the King. He funded the construction of the Convento do Bosque, Borba, and also restored the church and convent of the Augustines, being made patron of the Order by papal concession. The church was rebuilt in 1634 as a ducal pantheon. In 1529 he founded and paid for the Convento de Chagas de Cristo on lands adjacent to the palace, and the church was used as a pantheon by successive duchesses of Braganza. He financed the foundation of the Misericórdia of Vila Viçosa, as well as linking this institution with the Hospital of Espirito Santo. He also took a close interest in contemporary European politics and culture and supported a school of astronomy (established 1526) in the palace under the directorship of the Spanish physician Antonio de Oliveros; he appointed distinguished foreign teachers to educate his children and promoted the humanist and literary character of his Renaissance court.

BIBLIOGRAPHY
A. C. de Sousa: *História genealógica da casa real portuguesa*, iii (Lisbon, 1738; Coimbra, 2/1947)
D. F. Manuel de Mello: *D. Teodósio, 2° duque de Bragança* (Lisbon, 1944)
D. Peres: *Conquista da Azamor pelo Duque de Bragança, D. Jaime* (Lisbon, 1951)
J. Teixeira: *O paço ducal de Vila Viçosa* (Lisbon, 1983)

(2) Teotónio [Theotónio] **of Braganza** (*b* Coimbra, 2 Aug 1530; *d* Valladolid, 28 Aug 1602). Son of (1) Dom Jaime, 4th Duque de Braganza. Educated in the Ducal Palace of VILA VIÇOSA, he was taught by Cataldo Sículo, an Italian humanist who came to the Portuguese court in

1486 from the university of Bologna, and by Diogo de Sigi (Sigeu) and Juan Fernandez from the university of Alcalá de Henares. He then studied at the College of Humanities of the university of Coimbra, and the Jesuit College in the monastery of Santa Cruz, Coimbra. He wanted to become a member of the Society of Jesus. Ignatius Loyola invited him to Rome and gave him dispensation from his vows so that as a layman he might render greater services to God.

At an early age Dom Teotónio travelled in Spain, Italy, France, Germany and England. On his return to Portugal he accepted the post of chief treasurer of the Guimarães Collegiate and of a humble church in the province of Trás-os-Montes. In Salamanca he made the acquaintance of St Teresa of Ávila (1515–82), who sought his influential support, and at her request he began to promote the foundation of Carmelite convents in Spain at Zamora, Torrijos, Segovia and Madrid. He published a work of importance to the Order, *La vida y milagros de el glorioso Padre San Alberto* (Évora, 1582), and dedicated it to St Teresa; he also funded the first published work of St Teresa, the *Camino de perfección* (1583), in homage to her and to make her mystical writings more widely known.

In 1578 Dom Teotónio was appointed Bishop of Fez and assistant (*coadjutor*) to the Cardinal Infante Dom Henrique, Archbishop of Évora, succeeding him as archbishop in December 1578 when Dom Henrique became king (*see* AVIZ, (11)). In Fez he was active as a prelate and humanist, and he founded monasteries and charitable institutions including the Hospital da Piedade for contagious diseases and the Recolhimento da Piedade (1581) for homeless young noblewomen. In Portugal he founded the convent of Nossa Senhora da Graça, Torrão, near Évora, and those of S Salvador (1590) and Remédios (1594), as well as the Charterhouse of Scala Scoeli (1578–94), all in Évora. The Charterhouse is an important building in the Mannerist style designed by Giovanni Vicenzo Casale (*c.* 1540–93); Dom Teotónio endowed the foundation, donated silver, vestments and statues and bequeathed to it his important collection, comprising rare books and manuscripts in Greek, Arabic, Syrian and other oriental languages, the works of Aristotle and a large number of works by Portuguese authors.

WRITINGS
La vida y milagros de el glorioso Padre San Alberto (Évora, 1582)
Epistola ad Gregorium XIII (Évora, 1583)
Regimento do auditório ecclesiastico do Arcebispado de Évora e a sua relaçam (Évora, 1598)

BIBLIOGRAPHY
N. Agostinho: *Relaçam summaria da vida do illustrissimo . . . Dom Theotónio* [Brief account of the life of the most illustrious D. Theotónio] (Évora, 1614)
B. Teles: *Cronica da Companhia de Jesus*, i (Lisbon, 1645)
A. F. Barata: *Esboços cronologicos-biograficos do Arcebispo da Igreja de Évora* [Chronological and biographical notes on the archbishop of the church of Évora] (Coimbra, 1874)
P. Gomes: *O Arcebispo de Évora D. Teotónio de Brança* (Braga, 1984)

JOSÉ TEIXEIRA [JOÃO]

(3) John [João] **IV**, King of Portugal (*b* Vila Viçosa, 1604; *reg* 1640–56; *d* Lisbon, 1656). Great-great-grandson of (1) Jaime, 4th Duque de Braganza. As 8th Duque de Braganza, he inherited a large fortune and the Ducal Palace of VILA VIÇOSA, Alto Alentejo, where a Renaissance court

had been established by Teodósio I, 5th Duque de Braganza (*d* 1563), and João I, 6th Duque de Braganza (1543–85). Education and music were important areas of the family's patronage, and John IV was a considerable musician and musicologist himself.

Due to the constant threat of invasion from Spain after the restoration of the Portuguese crown in 1640, John IV's activities as a patron of art centred on building programmes that related to the defence of the country. In 1647 he founded the Aula de Fortificação e Arquitectura Militar in Lisbon, of which the director was Luis Serrão Pimentel (1613–78). Many foreign architects and engineers came to Portugal during his reign, including Michel Lescole (*fl c.* 1653–*c.* 1700), who was active in the north, Jean Gilot (*fl* 1646–57) and the Dutch Jesuit Johan Cosmander (Sciemans) (*fl c.* 1643), who designed the forts of Sesimbra and Olivença, the latter carried out by Gilot, and probably those of Oeiras and Paço de Arcos.

The presence of foreign technicians and architects brought about some modifications to the style of architecture and the introduction of elements of Baroque ornament, most evident in the gateways of military establishments; however, this represented only a mild superimposition on the traditional features of Portuguese architecture, which at this period was characterized by a tendency to austerity, the adoption of a geometric solidity in overall design, the absence of decoration and an accentuated horizontality; this was combined with the local interpretation of the treatises of Palladio and Serlio. These characteristics are to be found in the convent (founded 1267, rebuilt 1634) and church (begun 1653, conceacrated 1677) of S Agostinhos at Vila Viçosa, the pantheon of the Braganzas. The church of the Beatas Capuchas (begun 1652) in Braga, also built through John IV's patronage, shows greater acceptance of the Baroque, being one of the first attempts in this style in northern Portugal. The façade features curved pediments enclosing scrolled cartouches, and the ground-plan and the other elevations are of a typical box church. The interior is decorated with *azulejos* and carved and gilded wood (*talha*).

Painting under John IV's patronage was dominated by the figure of José de Avelar Rebelo, who painted the King's portrait (1649; Vila Viçosa, Ducal Pal.), and Domingos Vieira. Both artists were responsible for introducing the Baroque style into Portuguese painting.

BIBLIOGRAPHY
A. C. de Sousa: *História genealógica da casa real portuguesa*, iii (Lisbon, 1738; Coimbra, 2/1947)
G. Kubler: *Portuguese Plain Architecture: Between Spices and Diamonds, 1521–1706* (Middletown, CT, 1972)
V. M. Godinho: 'Restauração', *Dicionário de história de Portugal* (Oporto, 1985)
P. D. Pereira: 'João, IV, D.', *Dicionário da arte barroca em Portugal*, ed. J. F. Pereira (Lisbon, 1989)

(4) Alfonso [Afonso] **VI**, King of Portugal (*b* Lisbon, 12 Aug 1643; *reg* 1656–83; *d* Sintra, 12 Sept 1683). Son of (3) John IV, King of Portugal. Physically and mentally weak, he left the government of his country to Dom Luis de Vasconcelos e Sousa, 3rd Conde de Castelo Melhor (1635–1724), who opted for a policy of centralization and the withdrawal of power from the nobility. In 1666 the King married Marie Françoise of Nemours (Queen Maria

Francisca; *see* (5) below) with elaborate celebrations including a ceremonial entry into Lisbon. The temporary triumphal arches and columns erected for the occasion by Portuguese, French, German, English, Italian and Flemish merchants and representatives of the various crafts are recorded in a series of drawings and designs (Vila Viçosa, Ducal Pal., MS. XCVII). The War of Restoration continued and a heavy defeat was inflicted on the invading Spaniards at Ameixial in 1663. To commemorate the battle the King commissioned the Piedade Church, Santarém, designed by Jácome Mendes in 1664; although it is in traditional style, it represents a period of transition in Portuguese architecture, the innovative feature being the centralized plan, one of the earliest examples of its kind in Portugal. In 1668 the King's brother, Dom Pedro, drove out the Conde de Castelo Melhor, deposed Alfonso and had his marriage annulled, taking power himself in a palace *coup d'état* that was encouraged by the Queen and the nobles who were seeking more power; he succeeded to the throne in 1683 as Peter II (*see* (6) below). His action was based on the King's incapacity to deal with either the economic crisis arising from the war against Spain or the protection of his colonies and their trade, then threatened by the naval supremacy of the English and the Dutch.

BIBLIOGRAPHY
A. M. Alves: *As entradas régias portuguesas* [The Portuguese royal entries] (Lisbon, n.d.)
P. D. Pereira: 'Afonso VI', *Dicionário da arte barroca em Portugal*, ed. J. F. Pereira (Lisbon, 1989)

FILMS
J. M. Grilo: *O processo do rei* [The king's trial] (Lisbon and Paris, 1989) [film, 35 mm, colour, 90 minutes; videotape, 1990; the deposition of Alfonso VI]

LUISA ARRUDA

(5) Maria Francisca (Isabel) [Marie-Françoise-Elisabeth], Queen of Portugal (*b* Paris, 21 June 1646; *d* Lisbon, 27 Dec 1683). Wife of (4) Alfonso VI, King of Portugal and (6) Peter II, King of Portugal. She was the daughter of Charles Amadeus, 6th Duke of Nemours (*d* 1652; *see* SAVOY and fig.), and Isabelle de Vendôme. Her marriage to Alfonso VI was part of Louis XIV's policy to bring Portugal into close alliance with France, and followed the failure to arrange other dynastic marriages between the two countries. The marriage contract was signed in Paris in February 1666, the proxy wedding took place at La Rochelle, and the Queen made her entry into Lisbon on 29 August of that year. The King was physically and mentally handicapped, and in 1667 the Queen left the royal palace to live in the Convento da Esperança, Lisbon. The marriage was annulled on 23 March 1668 and on 27 April she married her former brother-in-law (from 1683 Peter II; *see* (6) below), who was regent, having deposed Alfonso. In 1667 the Queen founded in Lisbon the Convento da Santa Cruz (later known as Santo Crucifixo), under the direction of four French Capuchin nuns; she also patronized the foundation of the Recolhimento do Anjo in Oporto. Her presence led to the marked influence of French culture in Portugal especially among the aristocracy.

BIBLIOGRAPHY
A. A. Dória: *A rainha D. Maria Francisca de Sabóia* (Oporto, 1944)
Nobreza de Portugal e do Brasil, i (Lisbon, 1960), pp. 533–68
A. A. Dória: 'Alfonso VI', *Dicionário de história de Portugal*, i (1975), pp. 44–6

——: 'Maria Francisca Isabel de Sabóia', *Dicionário de história de Portugal*, iv (1975), pp. 183–5

JOAQUIM JAIME B. FERREIRA-ALVES

(6) Peter [Pedro] **II**, King of Portugal (*b* Lisbon, 6 April, 1648; *reg* 1683–1706; *d* Alcântara, 9 Dec 1706). Son of (3) John IV, King of Portugal, brother of (4) Alfonso VI, King of Portugal and husband of (5) Maria Francisca. He deposed Alfonso VI after a *coup d'état* in 1668 and was proclaimed regent. The wars against Spain following the establishment of an independent Portugal in 1640 continued during his regency and reign, accompanied by a critical economic situation. The politics of art patronage during his short reign are not clear, with research in this area yet to be done. Essentially it was the nobility and the religious orders who were the principal patrons. In the arts it was a period of affirmation of the values of Portuguese culture, expressed in an original form of the Baroque. The King's second marriage to Maria Sophia, daughter of Philip William of Neuburg, was celebrated with a ceremonial entry into Lisbon in 1687, when the city, in spite of its medieval appearance, was transformed into a Baroque stage for the reception. Naval battles on the River Tagus, a great colonnade and bridge joining the river to the royal palace, statues, triumphal arches and buildings erected for bullfights and fireworks were among the temporary edifices designed by Mateus do Couto (*fl* 1617–69) and João Nunes Tinoco.

Foreign artists contributed to the spread of the Italian Baroque style in Portugal, among them Guarino Guarini, who designed the church of the Divina Providência in Lisbon, a project that was never carried out, and Giacomo Filippo Parodi (1630–1702), who provided sculptures for the Loreto Church in Lisbon (destr. 1755). The Plain Style (*see* PORTUGAL, §II, 2) continued to predominate in architecture in spite of such examples of the Italian Baroque style as the church of S Engrácia, Lisbon, designed by João Antunes, who was appointed court architect in 1699. The royal arms on the tympanum of the church indicate royal patronage, as Peter II was the head of the brotherhood of noblemen who ordered the building of the church. The exteriors of buildings of this period are characterized by a horizontality and sobriety that are in great contrast with the exuberant decoration of the interiors, which have inlaid, painted ceilings exhibiting Flemish influence, paintings, sculptures including gilded carvings and revetments of blue-and-white glazed tiles (*azulejos*), often covering the entire surface of the walls.

Sculpture was produced in provincial centres, often depending for important commissions on religious houses, where schools of craftsmen would be established, as at Alcobaça Abbey, which was a centre of production specializing in work in painted terracotta (e.g. sanctuary statues of 1669–72). Noted sculptors of the period were Manuel Pereira, who executed the *Virgin of the Rosary* and the *Crucifixion* in the church of S Domingos, Bemfica, and Frei Cipriano da Cruz, whose most important works are the *Pietà* (*c.* 1685), the *Archangel Michael* (Coimbra, Mus. N. Machado de Castro) and *St Lutgard with the Crucified Christ* (1692–5; Tibães, S Martino).

Painting followed the general development of art in Spain. Domingos Vieira, who painted portraits of Portuguese society in the Spanish style (examples in Lisbon,

Mus. N. A. Ant.), was appointed court painter, and in 1678 he was succeeded in the position by Bento Coelho da Silveira; there are important works by Coelho da Silveira in the convent of Madre de Deus (scenes from the *Life of St Francis*) and the convent of Encomendadeiras da Encarnação (scenes from the *Life of the Virgin* and the *Life of St Benedict*), both in Lisbon. Other artists of repute were Félix da Costa Meesen, author of *A antiguidade da arte da pintura* (1699) and Josefa de Ayala. In the decorative arts a national style of carved and gilded wood, *talha*, developed for altars or other parts of the church, as in the Marvila Church, the church of Conceição dos Cardeis and the church of Madre de Deus, all in Lisbon. *Azulejos* were combined with *talha*, spreading into large figurative panels of cobalt blue and white, which, together with the gold of the *talha*, resulted in a form of interior decoration peculiar to Portuguese Baroque.

BIBLIOGRAPHY

N. Correia Borges: *A arte nas festas do casamento de D. Pedro II* (Coimbra, n.d.)

G. Kubler and M. Soria: *Art and Architecture in Spain and Portugal and their American Dominions* (Harmondsworth, 1959)

P. D. Pereira: 'Pedro II, D.', *Dicionário da arte barroca em Portugal*, ed. J. F. Pereira (Lisbon, 1989)

LUISA ARRUDA

(7) John [João] **V**, King of Portugal (*b* Lisbon, 22 Oct 1689; *reg* 1706–50; *d* Lisbon, 31 July 1750). Son of (6) Peter II, King of Portugal. John V was the last absolute monarch of Portugal; his long reign was a period of peace and great prosperity because of the discovery in Brazil of gold and diamonds. The royal revenue of a fifth of their value enabled the King to undertake an extensive building programme, the massive endowment of churches and religious foundations and the lavish commissioning of works of art in France and Italy. This was intended to bring Portugal in line with current European artistic and cultural movements and also to raise the prestige of both the country and the Braganza dynasty. The best foreign artists obtainable were called to Portugal, and although John V drew from a variety of sources, from the beginning his main inspiration was the art of Baroque Rome. This predilection is particularly marked in architecture and is exemplified by the Menino de Deus Church (begun 1711), Lisbon, designed with an octagonal nave and a ceiling with illusionistic architectural decoration.

This cultural affinity was paralleled on a political level and culminated in 1748, when the deeply religious King (and his successors) were given the title of *rex fidelissimus* in recognition of his devotion to the Church. Political links with Rome were sustained throughout the reign and were marked by a succession of lavish and successful embassies, including that of the cultivated Rodrigo Aires de Sá e Meneses, Marquês de Fontes e Abrantes (*see* FONTES E ABRANTES), to the Holy See in 1712; by the participation of a Portuguese armada at the Battle of Matapan against the Turks (1717); and by Clement XI's grant of the status of Patriarch (1717) and Cardinal (1737) to the Archbishop of Lisbon.

The major project of John V's reign was the palace-convent of MAFRA (1717–35; for illustration *see* MAFRA and LUDOVICE, JOÃO FREDERICO), which contains many references to Baroque buildings in Rome, particularly to

St Peter's and S Agnese in Agone by Francesco Borromini. The architect generally associated with Mafra, JOÃO FREDERICO LUDOVICE, was also responsible for the royal programme in the new apse (1718–46) of Évora Cathedral (*see* ÉVORA); the improvement to the Paço da Ribeiro, Lisbon; the enlargement of the Royal Chapel (all destr. 1755); and the renovation of the interior of St Dominic, Lisbon. Filippo Juvarra was summoned from Turin to Lisbon in 1719 and spent six months designing a large church and palace for the newly created Patriarchate in Lisbon, a project that was not realized. The Italian architect Antonio Canevari was in Portugal from 1727 to 1732, and his work there included a clock-tower for the royal palace, Lisbon (destr. 1755). In Rome he had designed the new seat for the Accademia degli Arcadia, called the Bosco Parrasio, on the Gianicolo, funded by John V and inaugurated in 1726. During the last decade of his reign the King also commissioned two important constructions of Italian design for Lisbon, the palace-convent of Nossa Senhora des Necessidades for the Oratorians, and the magnificent chapel of St John the Baptist in the Jesuit Church of S Roque, designed and constructed by Nicola Salvi and Luigi Vanvitelli in Rome and then shipped to Lisbon, where it was installed in 1747.

For Mafra the King commissioned an important series of marble statues from leading Italian sculptors including Carlo Monaldi, Giovanni Battista Maini, Filippo della Valle and Pietro Bracci. The Italian sculptor Antonio Bellini was responsible for the statues in the choir at Évora Cathedral. This importation of works and artists was intended to supplement the mediocre work of Portuguese sculptors, of whom only José de Almeida showed any great ability; he was sent by the King to Rome *c.* 1720, where he trained at the Academia de Portugal. The Academia was active from the 1720s and during the JOANINE period, when many Portuguese artists, especially painters, were taught by Italian painters such as Benedetto Luti, Francesco Trevisani and Paolo de Matteis (1662–1728). The results were disappointing, the most successful being achieved by Francisco (Lusitano) Vieira de Matos, who arrived in Rome in 1712. The King therefore invited Italian painters to work in Portugal, among them Guilio Cesare Termine (*d* 1734) and Domenico Duprá; the latter is said to have painted the portrait of the King (*c.* 1720) displayed in the library (1716–28; see fig.), which John V donated to the university of Coimbra. French artists, such as Pierre-Antoine Quillard and Jean Ranc, who both arrived in 1726, brought the Rococo style to the court.

The continuous programme of renovation, the *luzes joaninas* or Joanine enlightenment, was an aristocratic and Catholic movement that was intended to modernize Portugal. The King's artistic relations with France can be connected with his desire to emulate the grandiose style of Louis XIV in order to add lustre to his reign, and he gave important commissions to French artists. He ordered magnificent silver tableware from Thomas Germain and François-Thomas Germain (*see* GERMAIN; *see also* PORTUGAL, §IX), and through Pierre-Jean Mariette he commissioned an extensive collection of engravings by leading European artists, which were destined for the library of the royal palace in Lisbon. Mariette also assembled the royal collection of paintings, and 70 pictures

John V, attributed to Domenico Duprá, oil on canvas, *c.* 1720, displayed in the library (1716–28) donated by the King to the University of Coimbra

arrived in Lisbon in 1727 (all destr. 1755); these were mainly by 17th-century North European artists such as Peter Paul Rubens, Rembrandt, Anthony van Dyck and French artists such as Claude Lorrain and the Le Nain family.

The cultural links with central Europe during the reign came through the King's marriage in 1708 to Maria Anna of Austria (1683–1754), the daughter of Emperor Leopold I (*see* HABSBURG, §I, (19)). The German circles around the Queen were dominated by clerics, including her Jesuit confessor Anton Stieff, the author of the festive illuminations of the house of the Resident, Josef Zignony, to celebrate the birth of the Archduke Charles. Although they had little direct influence on Portuguese art, these German circles are traditionally held responsible for the ascendancy and influence of Ludovice.

The King's long career as a patron of art is commemorated in the marble bust of *John V* (*c.* 1745; Lisbon, Pal. N. Ajuda) by ALESSANDRO GIUSTI, which shows a majestic monarch in court armour, crowned by a laurel wreath and accompanied by symbols of the Arts and Sciences.

BIBLIOGRAPHY

F. X. da Silva: *Elogio fúnebre e histórico de D. João V* (Lisbon, 1750)
Ayres de Carvalho: *D. João V e a arte do seu tempo* (Lisbon, 1962)
Y. Bottineau: 'Le Goût de Jean V: Art et gouvernement', *Bracara Augusta* [Braga] xxvi/64 (1973), pp. 341–53
M. T. Mandroux França: 'Les Mariette et le Portugal', *Archvs Cent. Cult. Port.* (Paris, 1983)
Roma lusitana, Lisbona romana (exh. cat., ed. G. Borghini; Rome, S Michele a Ripa, 1990–91)

JOSÉ FERNANDES PEREIRA

(8) Joseph [José], King of Portugal (*b* Lisbon, 1714; *reg* 1750–77; *d* Lisbon, 1777). Son of (7) John V, King of Portugal. In his reign, town planning and architecture in Portugal developed rapidly owing to the activity of his Prime Minister, Sebastião José de Carvalho e Melo, from 1769 Marquês de POMBAL, who acted with the approval and sanction of the King but whose patronage of the arts was due more to his own personality as an enlightened despot than to the monarch himself. The King also acted on his own initiative, however, and commissioned works of interest both before the earthquake of November 1755 and during Pombal's subsequent replanning of the city (*see* LISBON, §1 and fig. 2). Most significant in this respect was the King's love of Italian opera, the lyric drama cultivated in leading European courts of the 18th century. He invited the gifted Italian architect and theatre designer Giovanni Carlo Galli-Bibiena (*see* GALLI-BIBIENA) to come to Portugal early in 1752 and design an opera house beside the Paço da Ribeira, which came to be known as the 'Opera do Tejo' from its position facing the river Tagus. Set into the west front of the palace, with which it communicated, the theatre was orientated longitudinally east–west, the stage and dressing-rooms being at the east, the auditorium, which seated 600, at the west, and the two main façades overlooked the Tagus to the south and the city to the north, where the chief entrances were sited. The building was totally destroyed in the earthquake in 1755, only seven months after its inauguration. Its appearance is known through an engraving by Jacques-Philippe Lebas in *Des plus belles ruines de Lisbonne* (Paris, 1757) and a ground-plan and elevation, which have allowed the architect Sérgio Infante to recreate the original layout (see 1987 exh. cat., pp. 39–43). The interior was lined with wood sumptuously decorated in gold and white.

Other royal commissions for Bibiena were the little Teatro de Salvaterra (inaugurated 21 January 1753; destr.); the Paço de Salvaterra, a royal palace used in winter for hunting; and another palace (destr.) adjacent to the temporary wooden palace at Ajuda, used by the royal family following the earthquake in 1755. In 1760 Bibiena was also commissioned by the King to design the circular-plan church of Nossa Senhora do Livramento (known as the Igreja da Memória) at Ajuda; following the death of Bibiena in October 1760 the building was completed by Mateus Vicente de Oliveira, although not according to the original design. The strong tradition of Portuguese craftsmanship continued throughout Joseph's reign, at the end of which Portuguese furniture underwent a change in style from Rococo to that known as 'Dom José', in which straight lines replaced the curves of the earlier period (*see* PORTUGAL, §VI, 3). The King also patronized French craftsmen, among them the silversmith François-Thomas Germain, from whom he commissioned a silver tureen and platter (for illustration and discussion *see* GERMAIN, (2)).

BIBLIOGRAPHY

J.-A. França: *Lisboa pombalina e o iluminismo* (Lisbon, 1965, *R* 1988)
Desenhos dos Galli-Bibiena: Arquitectura e cenografia (exh. cat. by M. A. Beaumont, M. Carlos de Brito and S. Infante, Lisbon, Mus. N. A. Ant., 1987)

JOSÉ EDUARDO HORTA CORREIA

(9) Maria I, Queen of Portugal (*b* Lisbon, 17 Dec 1734; *reg* 1777–1816; *d* Rio de Janeiro, 20 March 1816). Daughter of (8) Joseph, King of Portugal. She was brought up in the court of her grandfather, John V (*see* (7) above), and was taught Latin, studied music and showed an interest in painting, taking lessons with Domingos António de Sequeira. In 1760 she married her paternal uncle, the Infante Dom Pedro, who became Peter III (*see* (10) below), and they lived at the QUELUZ PALACE (begun 1746), which the latter had built; here she gradually withdrew from court affairs. During her reign, material progress was united with political conservatism. The Marquês de POMBAL was dismissed and confined to his estates. The Queen managed economic policies and industrial development, modernizing the Real Fábrica das Sedas (est. 1757) and encouraging the manufacture of other goods, abolishing the fiscal rates on raw materials imported at the royal workshops; the Escola de Fiação of Trás-os-Montes was inaugurated in 1778. She provided a stimulus for cultural and artistic life by founding and becoming patron in 1779 of the Real Academia das Ciências, a literary and scientific institution that sent scholars to study in Europe and to explore the colonies and collect botanical specimens. She founded the Real Biblioteca Pública da Corte in 1796; other institutions founded in her reign included the Aula Pública de Debuxo e Desenho in Oporto (1779), and in Lisbon the Aula Régia de Desenho (1781) and the Academia do Nu (1780), where Domingos Francisco Vieira Portuense was the professor. The Academia Real de Fortificação Artilharia e Desenho (founded 1790), the Seminário Cernache (1791), the Academia Real de Guardas Marinhas (1769) and the Observatório Real de Marinha (1798) were among the establishments that were aimed at bringing the standard of Portuguese technical and cultural life closer to that of the rest of Europe. She also founded (1782) the Real Casa Pia de Lisboa, a charitable institution that among other functions served as a training school for various trades and a centre for the study of the fine arts, sciences and humanities. Her architectural patronage included the Basilica da Estrêla (1779–90), Lisbon, commissioned to fulfil a vow taken regarding the birth of an heir. It was built according to a late-Baroque design, deriving from the palace-convent of MAFRA, by MATEUS VICENTE DE OLIVEIRA and completed by Reinaldo Manuel dos Santos. The Teatro S Carlos (1792–3), Lisbon, designed in Neoclassical style by JOSÉ DA COSTA E SILVA, brought Portuguese architecture closer to contemporary European developments.

BIBLIOGRAPHY
F. Benevides: *Rainhas de Portugal* (Lisbon, 1878–9)
H. C. Ferreira Lima: *Princesas artists: As filhas de Dom José I* (Coimbra, 1925)
C. Beirão: *Dona Maria I* (Lisbon, 1934)
J.-A. França: *A arte em Portugal no século XIX* (Lisbon, 1966)
JOSÉ TEIXEIRA

(10) Peter [Pedro] **III**, King of Portugal (*b* Lisbon, 5 July 1717; *reg* 1777–86; *d* 5 March 1786). Son of (7) John V, and brother of (8) Joseph. He married his niece, later Maria I (*see* (9) above), in 1760; she succeeded Joseph in 1777 and Peter, as her consort, received the honorary title of Peter III. Politically incapable, he dedicated himself to the life of the court. His main interest was his hunting lodge at Queluz, near Lisbon, which he inherited in 1742 and from 1746 expanded to become a royal palace in anticipation of his marriage (*see* QUELUZ PALACE). The architecture by MATEUS VICENTE DE OLIVEIRA and JEAN-BAPTISTE ROBILLON, gardens, also by Robillon, paintings, notably by Pedro Alexandrino de Carvalho, and interior decorations by SILVESTRE DE FARIA LOBO and Antoine Collin, are all French Rococo in inspiration. Queluz is often compared to the château of Versailles in France, where Maria had been brought up, but the scale is more that of a *maison de plaisance* in the manner of Schloss Sanssouci (1745–7) in Potsdam. Life in the palace, characterized by a curious mixture of European, Oriental and Brazilian customs, was described by William Beckford.

BIBLIOGRAPHY
G. Chapman, ed.: *The Travel-diaries of William Beckford of Fonthill* (Cambridge, 1928), ii, pp. 357–71
J.-A. França: *Lisboa pombalina e o illuminismo* (Lisbon, 1965/*R* 1988)
R. C. Smith: *The Art of Portugal: 1500–1800* (London, 1968)

(11) John [João] **VI**, King of Portugal (*b* Lisbon, 13 May 1767; *reg* 1816–26; *d* Lisbon, 10 March 1826). Son of (9) Maria I and (10) Peter III. He received the protection of, and was educated under the supervision of, the Marquês de POMBAL, who wanted him to replace Maria on the throne. He was taught the humanities and sciences and acquired a refined taste, which was reflected in the music of the Royal Chapel Choir whose singing achieved excellence. He became Prince Regent in 1792. His reign was marked by problems because of political events, his mother's mental illness, the exile of the court to Rio de Janeiro during the Napoleonic invasions (1808–21) and the first insurrections of the Liberal movement culminating in the 1820 Revolution. He planned to establish a Luso-Brazilian empire under the Braganza dynasty and skilfully laid the foundations for the future kingdom of Brazil (1822) by means of a judicious legislative policy. He founded various institutions: in Brazil these included the Impressão Régio, Jardim Botânico, Teatro Real de S João (1813), the Biblioteca Pública, the Academia de Belas-Artes and Escola Real de Artes e Ofícios (1816). The last two institutions testify to his interest in the arts, which culminated in his organization of the French artistic commission to Rio de Janeiro (1816), directed by the architect AUGUSTE-HENRI GRANDJEAN DE MONTIGNY, which had a profound influence in Brazil. In Lisbon he established the Colégio da Educçacao Militar de Artilharia da Corte (1803) and the Ordem Militar de Nossa Senhora da Conceição (Military Order of Our Lady of Conception, 1816). The Ajuda Palace (begun 1802; also called Nossa Senhora da Ajuda), in Lisbon, built during his reign, was intended to replace the palace destroyed in the earthquake of 1755. Designed by JOSÉ DA COSTA E SILVA in collaboration with Francisco Saverio Fabri, it was never completed. During his regency the Neo-classical style became evident in metalwork and, later, the Empire style, one of the finest examples being the 'Wellington Plate' (London, Apsley House; *see* PORTUGAL, §IX and fig. 18) that he commissioned as a gift for Arthur Wellesley, 1st Duke of Wellington.

See also BRAZIL, §X.

BIBLIOGRAPHY
O. Lima: *D. João VI no Brasil* (Rio de Janeiro, 1908)
P. Calmon: *O rei do Brasil: Vida de D. João VI* (Rio de Janeiro, 1935)
A. de Turnay: *A missão artística de 1816* (Rio de Janeiro, 1956)
L. Martins Costa and others: *Memória da independência, 1808–25* (Rio de Janeiro, 1972)
J. Veríssimo Serrão: *História de Portugal*, vi (Lisbon, 1984), pp. 13–336

(12) Maria II, Queen of Portugal (*b* Rio de Janeiro, 4 April 1819; *reg* 1826–8; 1834–53; *d* Lisbon, 15 Nov 1853). Granddaughter of (11) John VI, King of Portugal. At the age of nine she left Brazil to live in Vienna at the court of her maternal grandfather, Francis II, Holy Roman Emperor (*reg* 1804–35), later moving to London, where she attended the English court. Her uncle, Dom Miguel (1802–66), led a *coup d'état* in Portugal, proclaiming himself absolute monarch (1828–34) and so preventing the arranged marriage between himself and Maria after the conditional abdication of her father, Peter IV, King of Portugal (*reg* 1826) and Emperor of Brazil (*reg* 1822–34) in her favour and following the granting of a liberal constitutional charter to the kingdom (1826). Maria then lived in France, returning to Portugal at the end of the civil war between the Miguelists and the Liberals in 1834. In 1836 she married Ferdinand Saxe-Coburg-Gotha, later King of Portugal (*see* (13) below), by whom she had many children.

Political instability and constant revolutions meant that only in the last years of her reign, during the period around 1851 known as the *Regeneração*, did the country enjoy a measure of material progress. The first Portuguese industrial exhibition was held in 1838 and during her reign the Ministry of Public Works was created. In this period Romantic literature flourished: both Alexandre Herculano (1810–78) and Almeida Garrett (1799–1854) were at the peak of their careers; the latter became director of the Conservatório de Música e do Teatro, establishing the foundations of the Teatro Nacional. An important school of painters who had been trained abroad emerged; it included Francisco Metrass, Visconde de Meneses, Miguel Angelo Lupi and António Manuel de Fonseca among others. After the foundation of the Academia de Belas-Artes in 1836 under the patronage of Maria and Ferdinand, the first exhibitions of the visual arts in Portugal were held. The Queen commissioned the Teatro Nacional Dona Maria II (1842–6), Praça do Rossio, Lisbon, designed by FORTUNATO LODI. In 1834 the São Bento Palace, Lisbon, was restored and adapted as the Parliament building.

BIBLIOGRAPHY
Marquês de Fronteira: *Memórias do Marquês de Fronteira e Alorna* (Coimbra, 1927)
E. de Lemos: *Dona Maria II, rainha e mulher* [Queen Maria II, the queen and the woman] (Lisbon, 1954)
J.-A. França: *O Romantismo*, 5 vols (Lisbon, 1974–5)

(13) Ferdinand [Fernando] **II**, King of Portugal (*b* Vienna, 29 Oct 1816; *d* Lisbon, 12 Dec 1885). Husband of (12) Maria II, Queen of Portugal. He was the eldest son of Duke Ferdinand George Saxe-Coburg-Gotha and Marie Antoinette Kohary and a cousin of Prince Albert of Saxe-Coburg (consort of Queen Victoria), whom in many ways he resembled. He received a modern education based on a German curriculum emphasizing the natural sciences, history and mathematics and classical and modern languages, for which he showed a great facility, being fluent in English, French, Italian, Spanish, Greek and Latin, as well as German and Hungarian and, later, Portuguese. His knowledge of music came from his youth in the atmosphere of post-Congress Vienna. In 1836 he married Maria II, Queen of Portugal (*see* (12) above), and he supervised the refined and progressive education of their many children. He played a conciliatory and pacifying political role during a period of constant rebellion when the throne was often threatened. He was a reliable counsellor to the Queen, maintaining and reinforcing constitutional law, and when he was offered the thrones of Greece (1862), Mexico (1863) and Spain (1869) he safeguarded the interests of Portugal, his adopted country.

Ferdinand's preferred role as minister of the arts was ahead of its time; he and Maria founded the Academia de Belas-Artes (1836), which led to a flourishing school of Portuguese painters, whom Ferdinand encouraged and whose exhibitions he attended. He acquired works by as yet unknown artists, serving both as critic and patron when the painters became better known, and the market, because it was restricted, followed his lead and taste. The generation of painters of the Romantic and Naturalist schools gained prestige from this recognition, and the most gifted of them received grants to study in Rome and Paris; they included António Manuel da Fonseca, Visconde de Meneses, Cristino da Silva, Tomás José da Anunciação and Columbano Bordalo Pinheiro. Their most important works were purchased direct by the King and many formed the basis of the present Museu Nacional de Arte Contemporânea, Lisbon. He donated large sums for the foundation of a National Gallery for Paintings in Lisbon (today the Museu Nacional de Arte Antiga); the first catalogue was published in 1868, and the paintings, many from suppressed convents, were exhibited at the Monastery of S Francisco. Among the works acquired for the collection were Hans Holbein I's *Virgin and Child*, Jan Breughel I's *Acts of Mercy*, from the Palavicini Collection in Rome, and Raphael's *Prophet Eusebius*. The paintings already in the royal collection, which he had restored in Germany, were housed in the Palacio das Necessidades (*see* LISBON, §3) and included Hieronymus Bosch's triptych the *Temptation of St Anthony* and Hans Holbein I's *Font of Life* (1519; both now Lisbon, Mus. N. A. Ant.). He initiated the major retrospective exhibition of Portuguese and Spanish decorative art (1882), held in the Alvor Palace, Lisbon, which had an enormous public impact and stimulated an interest in the national artistic heritage. He promoted and gave money for the conservation of Portuguese historic monuments, and in order to safeguard their preservation a director of restoration was appointed at the Batalha Abbey, an important example of Portuguese Gothic architecture (*see* BATALHA and fig.). He also financed restoration at the Hieronymite Monastery, Lisbon, the Convento de Cristo, Tomar, the Belém Tower, Lisbon, and the Palace of the Duques de Braganza, Barcelos.

Ferdinand had an excellent baritone voice, and he held a special affection for the opera house, the Teatro Real of

Ferdinand II, King of Portugal, wearing North African costume, photograph, *c.* 1857 (Vila Viçosa, Ducal Palace)

S Carlos. He gave grants to numerous musicians and had music dedicated to him by Gioacchino Antonio Rossini (*Mass*, 1865) and Franz Liszt, who played in Lisbon in 1845 and who dedicated a *Heroic March* to him. In 1869 he contracted a morganatic marriage with an opera singer, the Condessa d'Edla.

Ferdinand's architectural commissions included, from WILHELM LUDWIG ESCHWEGE, the Castelo da Pena (1840) at Sintra, where traditionally the Portuguese court spent the summer. The baronial castle is enhanced by a land-scaped garden and a majestic setting, immortalized by Byron. The initial project had a more international Gothic Revival flavour, but Ferdinand's stylistic choices were eclectic and this style is combined with neo-Manueline influences; a result of this building was the initiation of a movement to revive national values.

He built up a ceramics collection noted for its Italian maiolica and Meissen porcelain, and his collection of gold- and silverware included fine examples of Portuguese and German pieces. His important collection of engravings included some by Rembrandt; Ferdinand himself was an able etcher, depicting aspects of everyday life, animal themes or scenes revealing a surrealist imagination, some-times bordering on the grotesque, which is one aspect of his romantic personality, as epitomized in a photograph of *c.* 1857 (see fig.).

BIBLIOGRAPHY
F. C. Pinto Coelho: *Contemporâneos ilustres: Dom Ferdinand II* (Lisbon, 1878)
E. Soares: *El rei Dom Fernando II* (Lisbon, 1946)
J. Teixeira: *Dom Fernando II: Rei-artista, artista-rei* (Lisbon, 1987)
JOSÉ TEIXEIRA

(14) Charles [Carlos], King of Portugal (*b* Lisbon, 28 Sep 1863; *reg* 1889–1908; *d* Lisbon, 1 Feb 1908). Ruler and painter, grandson of (12) Maria II and (13) Ferdinand II. His reign was difficult, largely owing to the Republican movement that grew in strength from 1891. He showed very early ability as an artist, but the fact that he painted and submitted works in competition for exhibition was often criticized by political opponents. He was taught drawing by António Manuel da Fonseca and Miguel Angelo Lupi and later had lessons from the Spanish watercolourist Henrique Casanova (1850–1913). In 1888 he exhibited at the Exposição Industrial Portuguesa and from 1891 to 1899 at the Salons of the Grémio Artístico (Guild of Artists), specializing in watercolour and pastels, and from whom in 1897 he received a medal of honour. He was a sensitive painter of seascapes, but it was in his depiction of the flat lands of the Alentejo, the ancestral domain of the house of Braganza, that he converted the naturalism of the Barbizon school to an essentially Por-tuguese idiom in his use of structure and colour. The quality of his work is seen in *Alentejo Countryside* (1898; Lisbon, Mus. N. A. Contemp.), which he exhibited in the 8th Grémio Artístico exhibition. The scene consists of a vast plain illuminated by delicate, filtered light. Nothing breaks or distracts the eye from this deserted place, which stretches to the horizon and which a band of misty light extends to infinity. The composition, in its two clearly defined zones of sky and earth and its wide format, reflects the extent of the plain and its dramatic solitude.

Charles received a silver medal at the Paris Exhibition of 1900 with *Raising the Nets on a Tunny-fishing Boat* (untraced), which once belonged to the collection of William II, King of Prussia and Emperor of Germany. From 1901 to 1906 Charles exhibited at the Sociedad Nacional de Belas Artes. Here he showed *The Cork Oak* (pastel, 1905; Vila Viçosa, Ducal Pal.), in which he captured the essence of the countryside and showed the feel for nature that characterized his work. Set in a remote Alentejo hillside, the foreground is dominated by a bare, textured cork tree, its roots emerging starkly from the sun-baked earth and its vigour contrasting strongly with the serenity of the surrounding plain.

BIBLIOGRAPHY
Sua Magestade El-Rei D. Carlos I e a sua obra artística e científica (Lisbon, 1908)
A. de Lucena: *D. Carlos de Bragança na arte portuguesa* (Lisbon, 1946)
J.-A. França: *A Arte em Portugal no século XIX*, i (Lisbon, 1966), pp. 241–2
LUCÍLIA VERDELHO DA COSTA

Braghieri, Gianni. *See under* ROSSI, ALDO.

Brahe, Tycho (*b* Knudstorp Manor, Scania, 14 Dec 1546; *d* Prague, 24 Oct 1601). Danish astronomer and patron, active in Bohemia. He came from an old noble family and became known throughout Europe for his book *De nova stella* (1573), which overturned traditional theories on astronomy and cosmology. In order to secure Brahe's services, in 1576 Frederick II, King of Denmark and Norway, granted him for life the island of Hven, in the sound between Denmark and Sweden, and funds to erect a dwelling there; on 8 August 1576 the foundations of Uraniborg were laid. In addition to housing Brahe and his family, guests and assistants, it served as an observatory, chemical laboratory and museum. Just south of the site a new semi-underground observatory, Stjerneborg, was built *c.* 1584. For 20 years Brahe led a research institute that was not only visited by other scholars but also by such dignitaries as James VI, King of Scotland (later James I, King of England), in 1590. In 1597, however, Brahe quarrelled with Christian IV, King of Denmark and Norway, and as a result accepted Emperor Rudolf II's invitation to Prague. The complex on Hven, however, was demolished soon after Brahe's departure. Knowledge of the buildings is, therefore, based primarily on Brahe's descriptions, various contemporary depictions and 20th-century excavations. These reveal that Uraniborg was a relatively small, domed building; its internal cruciform plan, the central part of which measured *c.* 14×14 m, corresponded to the observatory towers and entrance projections of the façades. It was surrounded by a garden, and the whole complex was bounded by a high garden wall, with gate-houses in the east and west corners, servants' quarters to the north, and a printing press to the south. Symmetry and order dominated the plan: paths from the four corner buildings led to the house, inside which corridors intersected under the central dome. Brahe, who described Uraniborg as his 'philosophical house', must be credited with the general architectural conception, which was inspired by such contemporary Italian villas as Palladio's Villa Rotunda, Vicenza. The only architect known with certainty to have worked on Hven, Hans van Steenwinckel I (*see* STEENWINCKEL, VAN, (1)), arrived in Denmark a year after construction began. Other architects in the service of the King of Denmark have been suggested in this connection, most recently the Italian-trained Dutch sculptor Johan Gregor van der Schardt, who worked for Frederick II from 1577 to 1579. Schardt's architectural expertise is, however, described in only one letter, and his involvement in the planning of Uraniborg and the execution of the allegorical sculpture there remains only an interesting hypothesis.

For an illustration of a zodiacal armillary sphere made by Brahe *see* SCIENTIFIC INSTRUMENTS, fig. 1.

DBL

BIBLIOGRAPHY

F. Beckett and C. Christensen: *Uraniborg og Stjørneborg* [Uraniborg and Stjerneborg] (Copenhagen and London, 1921) [with Eng. summary]
C. H. Jern: *Uraniborg: Herresätte och Himlaborg* [Uraniborg: manor house and heavenly city] (Lund, 1976) [with Eng. summary]
H. Honnens de Lichtenberg: 'Johan Gregor van der Schardt: Sculptor and Architect', *Hafnia: Copenhagen Papers in the History of Art*, x (1985), pp. 147–64
V. E. Thoren: *The Lord of Uraniborg: A Biography of Tycho Brahe* (Cambridge, 1990)
H. Honnens de Lichtenberg: *Johan Gregor van der Schardt: Bildhauer bei Kaiser Maximilian II am dänischen Hof und bei Tycho Brahe* (Copenhagen, 1991)

HUGO JOHANNSEN

Brahmaur [Bharmaur; anc. Brahmāpura]. Capital of the Varman dynasty, 75 km east of Chamba in Himachal Pradesh, India, notable for its wooden temples. Numerous shrines were built at Brahmaur, deodar trees (*Cedrus deodara*) supplying the material as elsewhere in the Himalayas. Heavy snow and earthquakes have necessitated renovations, but some 9th-century AD portions of the Lakshanadevi Temple have survived. These include a façade, hall pillars, a ceiling and the inner sanctum doorway. Influence from Kashmir is evident in the trefoil pediment over the doorway and in the figure of Vishnu contained within. The temple, dedicated to Durga Mahishasuramardini (She who Slays the Buffalo Demon), enshrines a metal image of the goddess (h. 1.25 m) bearing an inscription of King Meruvarman of the Varman dynasty. Figures of the god Ganesha and of Shiva's bull, Nandi, at Brahmaur also carry inscriptions of Meruvarman; all were cast by the artist Gugga in the 8th century AD (*see* INDIAN SUBCONTINENT, §V, 7(ii)). The Nandi (half life-size) is in a pavilion before the Manimahesvara Temple, a stone structure with a curvilinear spire capped with a wooden roof. The temple's niches are mostly empty, and there is little ornament. The Narasimha Temple on the north edge of the complex is a similar structure. Both buildings date to the 10th century.

See also INDIAN SUBCONTINENT, §III, 5(i)(b).

BIBLIOGRAPHY

J. P. Vogel: *Antiquities of Chamba*, i (Calcutta, 1913)
H. Goetz: 'The "Basholi" Reliefs of the Brahmor Kothi, *c.* AD 1670', *Roopa-Lekha*, xxv (1954), pp. 1–12
——: *The Early Wooden Temples of Chamba* (Leiden, 1955)
M. Postel, A. Neven and K. Mankodi: *Antiquities of Himachal* (Bombay, 1985), pp. 42–6

KIRIT MANKODI

Brailes, William de. *See* WILLIAM DE BRAILES.

Brak, Tell. Site in eastern Syria near the River Jaghjagh, which runs through the fertile Khabur Plain. It flourished *c.* 3500–1280 BC. Major ancient trade routes crossed near Tell Brak, and throughout its history it was open to foreign influences. It was excavated by Max Mallowan in 1937–8 and by David and Joan Oates from 1976. Most of the objects are now in the National Museum, Aleppo, the Dayr al-Zawr Museum, the British Museum, London, and the Ashmolean Museum, Oxford. The tell is one of the largest mounds in northern Mesopotamia. Fine polychrome Halaf pottery shows that it was an important site already in the 6th millennium BC, and a few sherds indicate that it was founded even earlier. The excavations have not, however, penetrated deeper than the end of the Ubaid period, *c.* 4000 BC. The main discoveries date to the Uruk, Early Dynastic, Akkadian and Mitannian periods (*see* MESOPOTAMIA, §I, 2), and the site was abandoned *c.* 1280 BC.

1. ARCHITECTURE AND GENERAL DEVELOPMENT. The earliest important structure is the Eye Temple, a building with stone buttresses that stands on a massive brick platform probably built up over a long period. Among the bricks were small, valuable votive deposits: beads, stamp seals and amulets. A frieze of white and grey stone with a gold surround fixed with silver nails adorned the altar. Details of the construction and decoration of the temple have parallels with structures of the Uruk period in southern Mesopotamia, but the site continued in use into the 3rd millennium BC.

The distribution of the pottery shows that Brak had covered its full area and accumulated most of its height by *c.* 3000 BC. The excavations have not found major structures of the early 3rd millennium BC, but by the mid-3rd millennium BC, Brak was one of several important cities in the Khabur region. Although no tablets have been found at Brak, recent discoveries at nearby Tell Beidar show that this civilization was literate. Its golden age was during the Akkadian period, c. 2350–2200 BC. Three major buildings have been excavated; two have similar plans, though they are at opposite ends of the tell. A small shrine block faces a courtyard on the east side, while a larger court to the south is surrounded by rooms with wide entrances. Elaborate niched decoration is applied inside and out. Sealed bullae show that both buildings were used for administration among other things, but it is not clear whether they were temples or palaces. These two buildings were ritually closed in an extraordinary way. First, special deposits including copper objects, seals, silver treasure and large beads made of semi-precious stones were placed on the floors. One building also contained a human-headed bull statue, while the bodies of several donkeys were placed on the floor of the other. Then the buildings were filled with earth to a height of at least 2 m, and further ritual deposits of pottery were placed upside down on top.

The third major building was the 'Palace of Naram-Sin'. This is the only building in 3rd-millennium BC, Syria that is datable by the name of its founder stamped on the bricks, and it proves that Brak was an administrative centre in the Akkadian empire. The building is massive, with walls up to 10 m thick. The plan shows many long magazines arranged around several courtyards, and it may have been used partly as a fortress and grain store.

Brak continued to be a large city until the end of the 3rd millennium BC, but probably under native rule. A seal impression in the best Late Akkadian style, of Talpush-atili (?after 2200–before 2100 BC), the Hurrian ruler of the city of Nagar, may give us its ancient name. The size of the city later contracted drastically. Material of the Old Babylonian period exists but has not yet been excavated. On top of it the Mitannian town clustered near a simple temple and a palace of the Mitannian kings, though the settlement was too small for this to have been their capital. This palace stands on the top of the mound, high above the plain. The brickwork includes engaged half-columns. Large rooms surround a central courtyard. Fragments of gold and glass, tablets recording royal decisions and beautiful examples of the painted Nuzi ware were found. The settlement was destroyed in the early 13th century BC during the expansion of the Middle Assyrian kingdom.

2. ARTEFACTS. Tell Brak is one of the most important sources of Near Eastern stamp seals and amulets. Hundreds came from the Eye Temple and elsewhere, mostly dating to the 4th millennium BC. The most famous objects are the 'Eye Idols' (e.g. London, BM, WA 126475; see fig.), primitive white stone figurines, each with two enormous eyes on top; they have not been found elsewhere. A great variety of small stone amulets includes beautiful stone animals with a simple drilled stamp seal design on the back. Other stamp seals are round, square and kidney-shaped. A cylinder seal found in a level dated to c. 3500 BC is the earliest cylinder seal ever discovered. It has a crude design with a bear and rows of animals. An impression of another early cylinder seal shows an exquisite scene of a

Tell Brak, stone 'Eye Idol', h. 540 mm, from the Eye Temple, probably 4th millennium BC (London, British Museum)

lion attacking a gazelle with a vulture looking on (both Dayr al-Zawr Mus.). Four white stone sculptured heads from the Eye Temple (Aleppo, N. Mus.; London, BM) represent a mode of simplification and stylization of the human form unknown elsewhere in the Ancient Near East.

In the Early Dynastic period the art of Brak was restricted to unremarkable cylinder seals; a few demonstrate links with far distant places. The 'Brak style' must have originated at this time as a derivative of Early Dynastic glyptic art; the range of subjects is the same, but there are also special features, such as detached lion and bull heads and geometric bands. This style occurs occasionally at other Syrian sites, but Brak is the only place where it is common. It continued into the Early Akkadian period, when the Akkadian style was also used. Akkadian seals from Brak show no sign of local influence, but they are equal in quality to the best pieces from elsewhere. A splendid statue of a human-headed bull with inlaid eyes, found in one of the Akkadian buildings, must belong to the early Akkadian or late Early Dynastic period (Dayr al-Zawr Mus.). The general conception resembles sculptures from Sumer and Ebla, but the stylization is original and charming.

The material from the Mitanni level (mostly Dayr al-Zawr Mus.) shows a normal range of Mitannian seals, including two impressions of the well-known seal of King Saushtatar (?c. 1450–c. 1400 BC; for illustration see MITANNIAN) on tablets sealed by his successors. Brak is probably much closer to the place of manufacture of this seal, with its mixture of Syrian motives, than NUZI in eastern Iraq, where an impression of it was first found. A crude seated statue found in the palace does not support claims for the existence of an important lost Mitannian school of sculpture.

BIBLIOGRAPHY

M. E. L. Mallowan: 'Excavations at Brak and Chagar Bazar', *Iraq*, ix (1947)
B. Buchanan: *Cylinder Seals*, i of *Catalogue of the Ancient Near Eastern Seals in the Ashmolean Museum* (Oxford, 1966)
B. Buchanan and P. R. S. Moorey: *The Prehistoric Stamp Seals*, ii of *Catalogue of the Ancient Near Eastern Seals in the Ashmolean Museum* (Oxford, 1984)
D. Oates: 'Excavations at Tell Brak, 1983–84', *Iraq*, xlvii (1985), pp. 159–74
D. Oates and J. Oates: 'Akkadian Buildings at Tell Brak', *Iraq*, li (1989), pp. 193–212
——: 'A Human-headed Bull-statue from Tell Brak', *Cambridge Archaeol. J.*, 1 (1991), pp. 131–9
——: 'Excavations at Tell Brak 1990–91', *Iraq*, liii (1991), pp. 127–46
D. Matthews and J. Eidem: 'Tell Brak and Nagar', *Iraq*, lv (1993), pp. 201–7
D. Oates and J. Oates: 'Excavations at Tell Brak 1992–93', *Iraq*, lv (1993), pp. 155–99

D. M. MATTHEWS

Brake, Brian (*b* Wellington, 27 June 1927). New Zealand photographer and film maker. He came to photography through membership of the Christchurch Camera Club. Moving to Wellington in 1945 he became an assistant to Spencer Digby, one of the country's leading portrait photographers. After five years he moved as a cameraman and director to the government-sponsored National Film Unit, where one of his notable achievements was the *Snows of Aorangi*, on which he collaborated with John Drawbridge and the composer Douglas Lilburn. Although this film proved popular at the time, its worth was not properly recognized by the controllers of the Film Unit, and Brake therefore moved to London where he freelanced as a photojournalist. From 1955 to 1966 he worked for the international agency Magnum in Paris and New York. He also worked for the Rapho agency, undertaking assignments for *Life Magazine*, *National Geographic*, *Horizon* and *Paris-Match*. Independent of the agencies, he collaborated with the New Zealand author Maurice Shadbolt. From 1962 to 1976 he was based in Hong Kong where he worked on special *Time-Life* assignments. In 1970 he formed Zodiak Films, a documentary film company producing films for an Indonesian oil company. In 1976 he returned to New Zealand where he established a New Zealand Centre of Photography.

PHOTOGRAPHIC PUBLICATIONS

New Zealand: Gift of the Sea, text by M. Shadbolt (Christchurch, 1963)
Sydney (London, 1980)

Contemp. Phots

BIBLIOGRAPHY

WILLIAM MAIN

Bramante, Donato (*b* Monte Asdrualdo [now Fermignano, Marches], ?1443–4; *d* Rome, 11 April 1514). Italian architect, painter and engineer. His esteemed reputation as the father of High Renaissance architecture rests on a series of projects initiated towards the end of his life in Rome, including the enormous extension to the Vatican Palace and the new plans for the rebuilding of St Peter's. Although few of these buildings, even his masterpiece, the Tempietto, exist in the form in which they were conceived, it is still clear that they constituted a decisive departure from the traditions of the recent past. Due to his patron Pope Julius II taking full advantage of the opportunities presented, and through a profound re-evaluation of the heritage of Classical antiquity, Bramante achieved in these buildings a dignity and majesty quite new to Renaissance architecture. Already recognized by his contemporaries as a great innovator, Bramante had by far the most enduring and pervasive influence on the course of architecture throughout the 16th century.

I. Life and work. II. Critical reception and posthumous reputation.

I. Life and work.

1. Early life and training, to late 1470s. 2. Milan and Lombardy, late 1470s–1499. 3. Rome, 1500–14.

1. EARLY LIFE AND TRAINING, TO LATE 1470s. Bramante's place of birth—the small town of Monte Asdrualdo in the papal state of Urbino, where his father was a farmer—is certain, but his birth date can only be inferred from Vasari's assertion that Bramante was 70 when he died. According to Vasari, Bramante's father directed him to turn to painting once he had learnt to read, write and use the abacus; having abandoned his family's way of life, however, he was later excluded from his modest family inheritance. Possible clues about his artistic education can be gleaned from early sources: that he enjoyed most the works of the local painter Fra Carnevale and delighted in perspective and architecture (Vasari) or that he was a follower of Mantegna and Piero della Francesca (Saba da Castiglione). Whatever his actual training, he almost certainly acquired his early expertise as a painter and designer in Urbino, and this experience was partly to determine the course of his artistic career. At Urbino he would have become familiar with the splendid court and flourishing artistic community centred around Count (later Duke) Federigo da Montefeltro, which attracted such eminent figures as Leon Battista Alberti and Piero della Francesca. He would have witnessed at first hand the continuing construction of the ducal palace under Luciano Laurana and perhaps later under Francesco di Giorgio Martini, whose presence in Urbino is recorded in 1476. In addition, he would no doubt have come into contact with many of the artists and craftsmen who came to work on the palace decorations, not only from Florence and central Italy but also from northern Italy and beyond.

Bramante's future career as a painter and master of perspective must have been greatly stimulated by the work of Piero della Francesca and other artists and designers who worked at the palace. A specific example mentioned by Vasari is Fra Carnevale's altarpiece for S Maria della Bella, Urbino. This has sometimes been identified with the Barberini Panels (*c.* 1465–70; *Birth of the Virgin*, New York, Met.; *Presentation of the Virgin*, Boston, MA, Mus. F.A.), with their highly elaborate architectural backdrops of *all'antica* buildings painstakingly rendered in linear perspective (but *see* MASTERS, ANONYMOUS, AND MONOGRAMMISTS, §I: MASTER OF THE BARBERINI PANELS). More immediately comparable to Bramante's paintings, however, are the mural decorations at Loreto of his slightly older contemporary, Melozzo da Forlì, which, with their fictive architectural frameworks and bold foreshortenings, achieve startling and daring *trompe l'oeil* effects.

In Urbino, Bramante would also have had early exposure to avant-garde architectural taste under the motivating influences of Alberti and Laurana. The ducal palace itself, which so eloquently reveals the possibilities of architecture as a vehicle of aristocratic patronage, would have demonstrated to him how the new Renaissance style could be adapted, with a sufficiently well-organized workforce, to projects of colossal scale. There is no reason, however, to suppose that Bramante was involved in designs for the palace, although a number of late additions, notably the Temple of the Muses and the elaborately decorated Cappella del Perdono (1470s), both presumably built under Francesco di Giorgio, with their rich mouldings and elaborate terracotta barrel vaults are very close in spirit to some of Bramante's future Milanese projects.

Bramante probably left Urbino in 1472. He eventually moved north to Lombardy, where he undertook minor commissions 'in one city after the other' (Vasari). He finally settled in Milan, probably during the late 1470s, and the ascendancy of the brilliant court of Ludovico Sforza, Duke of Milan, who was a nephew of Federigo da Montefeltro's wife, Battista Sforza (d 1472), encouraged him to remain there for more than 20 years (see SFORZA, (5)).

2. MILAN AND LOMBARDY, LATE 1470s–1499.

(i) Painting. (ii) Architecture.

(i) Painting. The earliest work assigned to Bramante by Marcantonio Michiel was the fresco decoration commissioned in 1477 for the façade of the Palazzo del Podestà in Bergamo (detached fragments in Bergamo, Pal. Ragione). The design, executed with collaborators, consists of a band at the level of the *piano nobile* with pilasters separating the actual windows from fictive compartments housing seated figures of philosophers, the robustness and vitality of which recall the style of Melozzo. Later, in Milan, Bramante depicted 'the poet Ausonius . . . together with other coloured figures' (Lomazzo, IV.xiv) on a façade in the Piazza de' Mercanti. The one surviving painted façade design in Milan attributable to him is that of the Casa Fontana-Silvestri (date uncertain), a two-storey arrangement of columns and pilasters carrying entablatures with elaborately sculpted friezes, the lower providing the platform for four *trompe l'oeil* bronze statues of allegorical figures. More ambitious is the design attributed to him for the room decorations for the Casa Panigarola-Prinetti (1480s; substantial fragments in Milan, Brera). This consists of a series of niches that hold standing figures bearing arms, and a panel, formerly above the portal, depicting the philosophers Heraclitus (in tears) and Democritus (laughing). The figure style, especially the linear quality of the drapery, is reminiscent of Mantegna, as is the fanciful antiquarianism of the architectural design, for example the figurative frieze showing ancient rituals behind the two philosophers and the alternating sequence of paterae and striations, presumably inspired by a Doric frieze, that runs around the backs of the niches. The most ambitious of Bramante's wall paintings is the so-called *Argus* (c. 1490–93) in the Cortile della Rocchetta of the Castello Sforzesco, Milan, which was painted for the Duke of Milan. The elegantly posed, semi-nude hero stands at the foot of a

tunnel-like flight of steps upon a kind of balcony of striking illusionism, consisting of a pair of superimposed pedestals supported upon corbels, framing a recessed tondo of fictive bronze. The one panel painting usually thought to be by Bramante, on the authority of Lomazzo, is the distinguished half-length *Christ at the Column* (c. 1490; Milan, Brera), which reveals some familiarity with Venetian art in the clarity and colouristic variation of the skin tones and perhaps also with Ferrarese art in the sinuosity of the contours.

(ii) Architecture. In Milan, Bramante turned increasingly to architecture. According to Vasari, he resolved to do so when he first saw Milan's enormous cathedral. He may have already become involved in architectural projects during the early 1470s, perhaps playing some part in the designs for the remodelling of the Palazzo del Podestà in Bologna (attributed to Aristotele Fioravanti) and of the Loggia in Brescia (sometimes attributed to Tommaso Formenton), both of which are close to his Milanese works in style and architectural vocabulary. He may have hoped to displace his rivals in Milan and establish himself as ducal architect-in-chief, but this was not to be; as an outsider like his friend and contemporary Leonardo da Vinci, who lived there from c. 1483 to 1499, he received only a limited number of commissions from the Duke. He was also unable to circumvent the guild system that so effectively controlled the building trade in Milan, and most of his works were taken on as collaborations with local sculptor-architects, notably Giovanni Antonio Amadeo. Bramante certainly guided some of the most far-reaching projects of the period, however, and his expert opinion was sought in 1487–90 in connection with the crossing of Milan Cathedral (for which he proposed a Gothic design). He no doubt cultivated and maintained contact, both in Milan and on the lengthy trips he made to Florence and Rome in the 1490s, with other leading architects of the period, including Francesco di Giorgio, who inspected the cathedral in 1490, and Giuliano da Sangallo, who came to Milan in 1492.

(a) Early designs, S Maria presso S Satiro and Pavia Cathedral. (b) S Maria delle Grazie, S Ambrogio and Vigevano.

(a) Early designs, S Maria presso S Satiro and Pavia Cathedral. Bramante's increasing zest for architecture is apparent in his earliest documented work, the Prevedari engraving (signed; 1481; two surviving impressions in London, BM, and Milan, Perego priv. col.), commissioned by the painter Matteo Fedeli (d 1505) and engraved by Bernardo Prevedari, from whom its name is taken. The image lacks a conventional subject and depicts a monk who, unheeded by groups of bystanders, kneels before a candelabrum-column supporting a crucifix. The architectural setting, a large building meticulously delineated in oblique one-point perspective, is given unusual prominence and becomes in effect the main subject. The building is identifiable as pagan by its ruined condition and its elaborate *all'antica* ornament, including ritualistic friezes, centaurs and heads in roundels, the most conspicuous of which is turned to face away from the crucifix. The plan of the building is depicted as a domed Greek cross with groin-vaulted arms inscribed within a square. This derives

1. Donato Bramante: crossing of S Maria presso S Satiro, Milan, showing 'choir' painted in *trompe l'oeil* perspective, *c.* 1482

house a miracle-working image of the Virgin was begun as early as 1478, Bramante's involvement is not documented until 1482, about when the chapel, parts of which can still be seen at the crossing when viewed from the Via del Falcone, was transformed into the present structure. Despite the building's unusual shape, the design was probably conceived as a whole. The church, attached to the small, round, 9th-century church of S Satiro (the exterior of which was refaced), is planned as a conventional Latin cross with aisled nave, domed crossing and three-bay transepts. However, the chancel arm was omitted because of the proximity of the Via del Falcone; instead there is a shallow niche, which, through the *trompe l'oeil* perspective design of its terracotta surface, achieves the striking illusion that it too is three full bays in extent (see fig. 1). The niche houses the image of the Virgin at the perspective focus above the altar, an arrangement resembling, albeit on a much larger scale, such objects as Desiderio da Settignano's Altar of the Sacrament (*c.* 1461; Florence, S Lorenzo). Two doors lead into the transepts from Via del Falcone to regulate the throngs of pilgrims.

Although the regularity of the plan of S Maria, especially the way in which the aisles continue into the transepts, has been likened to Brunelleschi's S Spirito in Florence, these features are also notable characteristics of Milan Cathedral. The style and decoration of the architecture, however, are profoundly classical and quite without precedent in Milan. The closest parallel is Alberti's S Andrea (1470) in Mantua, which probably inspired the use of monumental barrel vaults and arches on piers faced with two sizes of pilaster: the smaller supporting the side arches and the larger rising to the springing of the vault. The influence of Alberti may even extend to the darkness of the interior, which reflects an aesthetic for church design promoted in Alberti's *De re aedificatoria* (VII.xii). On the other hand, the elaborate coffering in the dome and barrel vaults as well as the elaborate detailing of the capitals and friezes, all richly crafted from gilded terracotta, are in keeping with the traditional Milanese fondness for ornamentation.

The façade of S Maria (covered over in the late 19th century) was never completed, but there is a long rear elevation on Via del Falcone, executed in exposed brick and terracotta. The Corinthian pilasters, paired at the corners, are here raised up on stacked pedestals and are taller than those inside, and the entablature, which has a very high and uncanonical panelled frieze, is interrupted by an even taller pilaster order that marks the crossing. At the intersection of the right transept and the nave is Bramante's remarkable octagonal sacristy. Apart from the octagonal sacristies at Loreto (see below), its most immediate model is local: the chapel of S Aquilino attached to the Early Christian church of S Lorenzo, Milan, both of which were then believed to be antique. The lower storey of the interior of Bramante's sacristy has eight large niches that are alternately curved and rectangular, folded ornamental pilasters in the corners with exquisitely wrought stone Corinthian capitals, and an entablature with *all'antica* heads and reliefs in the tall frieze executed by Agostino Fonduli. A second storey is encircled by a gallery with two arched openings on each side; the lighting is from the

ultimately from Byzantine models, such as S Marco in Venice, rather than from ancient Roman ones, although it conforms to a local Milanese tradition instituted by Antonio Filarete that was doubtless considered essentially antique. In elevation, the corner spaces are spanned by small arches supporting an entablature, which becomes the impost of larger arches of the arms; immediately above, another entablature provides the impost for the springing of the crossing vault. This system of interlocking arches suggests that Bramante was familiar with Brunelleschi's churches, but his design eschewed the latter's columns in favour of piers and pilasters, as in works by Alberti and Francesco di Giorgio, considerably enhancing its grandeur. Two sizes of pilasters are used, taller ones with elaborate Corinthian capitals for the arms of the cross and smaller pilaster-strips without capitals—a favourite motif of Francesco di Giorgio—for the subsidiary corner spaces.

The first major work built by Bramante, the pilgrimage church of S Maria presso S Satiro, Milan, is contemporary with the Prevedari engraving. Although a small chapel to vault above, a feature anticipated in the Prevedari engraving.

In 1488 Bramante became involved in the design of his most ambitious project in Lombardy, the rebuilding of Pavia Cathedral, where the Duke of Milan's brother, Cardinal Ascanio Sforza, was bishop. Although work had begun two years previously under Giovanni Antonio Amadeo, Bramante prepared a new design. Progress remained slow, and in 1497, by which time he took no further part, a revised project was prepared by Amadeo and Giovanni Giacomo Dolcebuono, and a model was commissioned (Pavia, Pin. Malaspina). The building, however, seems to be reasonably faithful to Bramante's design up to the height of the side chapels, since part of the exterior, including one of the eastern chapels, and most of the crypt had been completed by 1497. The layout is based on a Greek cross with an enormous octagonal crossing and aisles running along all four arms. He seems to have intended the entrance arm to be just four bays in length (of which three were eventually completed) so as to reach the Piazza del Duomo, although in Amadeo and Dolcebuono's model it is extended to eight bays, and the layout is thus changed to a Latin cross. Bramante may have also envisaged the octagonal sacristies positioned in the angles of the cross, the eastern pair of which were realized.

Precedents for the regularly organized plan at Pavia, which has close parallels in the contemporary drawings of Leonardo da Vinci, again include Milan Cathedral and S Lorenzo, Milan, which has an octagonal crossing similarly inscribed in a square and a dome supported on eight piers. By far the closest model for the plan, however, is the sanctuary church (1470) designed by Giuliano da Maiano at Loreto, which has an octagonal dome, aisled arms and octagonal sacristies in the corners (*see* LORETO, §II, 1(i)(a)). Bramante's responsibility for the awesome, stone-faced interior of Pavia Cathedral probably only extends as far as the order of Corinthian pilasters from which the aisle vaulting springs. Above this the design lacks the consistency and coherence of Bramante's other Milanese works. At one point an arcade is curiously sandwiched between an architrave and a cornice as though it were a giant frieze. Such oddities may be attributed to Amadeo and Dolcebuono, who may have effected substantial changes to the upper levels of the design. Bramante's low and austere crypt, with its arches and flattened vaults supported on pedestals, is the most uncompromising part of the building. The segmental vaults of the crypt's main apses, with radial ribs between arches, recall Brunelleschi's umbrella domes in Florence in the Old Sacristy (from 1419) of S Lorenzo and the Pazzi Chapel (1429) in Santa Croce, but they may have been derived from the Roman pumpkin domes visible at Hadrian's Villa (*c*. AD 125) at Tivoli.

(b) S Maria delle Grazie, S Ambrogio and Vigevano. The prestigious project for a new eastern end (*tribuna*) to the church of S Maria delle Grazie, Milan, was commissioned by the Duke as a mausoleum; work began on 29 March 1492 (*see* MILAN, fig. 3). The basic design, attached to Guiniforte Solari's Late Gothic nave (1463), seems to have been Bramante's, although this has not been proved conclusively; if so, he must again have been working in

2. Donato Bramante: S Maria delle Grazie, Milan, begun 1492; interior looking east

conjunction with Amadeo and Dolcebuono, who are documented. The layout consists of an enormous square crossing crowned with a hemispherical dome, vast apses to left and right and a square chancel covered by a remarkable umbrella vault and with a further apse beyond (see fig. 2). Bramante's fascination with apsidal design, which characterizes virtually all his church designs from Pavia Cathedral on, may here have had specific funerary associations. The planning has similarities with the earlier ducal funerary church, the Certosa di Pavia (begun 1396), which has a crossing with three trilobed arms, but it is more closely related to Francesco di Giorgio's S Bernardino degli Zoccolanti (1482–90) at Urbino, the trilobed funerary church designed for Federigo da Montefeltro, and ultimately to Brunelleschi's Old Sacristy, which served as a Medici mausoleum. This last debt is also evident in the articulation of the crossing, with Corinthian pilasters folded around the corners, and the concentric archivolts, which have a memorable sequence of wheel-like tondi between them. Similarly conceived buildings, however, had already appeared in and around Milan, most notably the Portinari Chapel (before 1468) attached to S Eustorgio. At S Maria delle Grazie the design was adapted to truly monumental proportions. The overall coherence of the interior, which was executed largely in terracotta and stucco, nevertheless points to Bramante as the designer, as does the handling of such details as the raising of the pilasters on to pedestals and the placing of panels in the frieze, both of which recall the rear façade of S Maria presso S Satiro. The less coherent and more ornamental exterior, which was conceived as a series of superimposed storeys, seems much less characteristic of Bramante, and he may have played little part in its design.

Around 1492 the Duke of Milan commissioned Bramante to design the courtyard known as the Canonica at the Romanesque abbey church of S Ambrogio, Milan. The courtyard, of which only two incomplete sides were ever built, abuts the north wall of the church; its main axis is marked by a doorway into the building. On each side there are 11 arches, which, except at the centre, are supported on columns with Corinthian capitals. The central arch, twice as wide and almost twice as tall as the others, is supported on slender piers, each faced with a pilaster and raised on a tall pedestal. The columns next to the piers and those at the angles were made to resemble tree trunks. This motif, apart from being an emblem of the Duke, provides a learned antiquarian reference to the historical ancestry of the column as described by Vitruvius and illustrated by both Filarete and Francesco di Giorgio in their treatises. In 1497 Cardinal Ascanio Sforza commissioned Bramante to design a new monastic complex at S Ambrogio (executed mostly during the later 16th century). It is organized around a neighbouring pair of suitably restrained courtyards, descriptively known as the Doric and Ionic Cloisters. These are almost identical, with widely spaced columns carrying arches via entablature blocks and with tapering square-sectioned pillars at the angles, a type of support known to Francesco di Giorgio as a *colonna piramidale*. The corner pillars have Doric capitals even in the Ionic Cloister: the same combination also occurs in Giuliano da Sangallo's atrium (1491) at S Maria Maddalena dei Pazzi in Florence. The upper storeys in both cloisters have blind arches and a doubled rhythm of much shorter pilasters. Although typical of Lombard courtyard design, this arrangement closely resembles a drawing by Giuliano da Sangallo of the ruined Portico of Pompey in Rome and may well reflect an outlook of renewed antiquarianism (Rome, Vatican, Bib. Apostolica, MS lat. 4424).

In 1492–4, on the Duke's initiative, a new square was laid out in Vigevano, 12 km south-west of Milan. The work, which was carried out almost certainly to outline designs by Bramante, who was recorded there in 1492–6, involved the wholesale demolition of much of the old centre to create an open space extending more than 130 m from the façade of the cathedral—a size unprecedented in Lombardy—and the construction of new façades around three of the sides interrupted only at the dominant, towered entrance to the ducal castle towards the western end. Models for the scheme include the Piazza S Marco in Venice and the Renaissance Piazza della Loggia (*c.* 1485) in Brescia, as well as the ancient Forum Romanum as described by Vitruvius and Alberti, whose writings are echoed in an inscription on the castle tower. The façades, which have painted decorations (rest. 19th century), are of uniform design, with ground-level columned porticos (as recommended by Vitruvius), an upper floor with arched windows and an attic. The bay sequence is broken, however, by two painted triumphal arches (only partly rest.), which mark the position of roadways and were

almost certainly designed by Bramante. One, positioned near the centre of the short western end, is a single-arch design similar to the central arches of the S Ambrogio Canonica; in combination with framing pilasters at the upper level, the arrangement closely resembles a slightly earlier archway in the piazza at Brescia. The other arch, in the angle facing the castle tower, is a triple-arch design similar to the façade of Alberti's S Andrea (1472) in Mantua. As also in the Prevedari engraving, the capitals have bands of lattice decoration at their necks, no doubt to allude to the basket mentioned by Vitruvius in his account of the legendary origins of the Corinthian order (IV.i.g).

Bramante may have designed the Palazzo delle Dame in the castle complex at Vigevano, which has a colonnaded loggia above a massive arcaded basement, with recessed rims around the piers and arches similar to the arcades in Francesco di Giorgio's Urbino Cathedral (begun before 1482; altered 1789). He may also have been responsible for the façade of S Maria Nascente at nearby Abbiategrasso. This has a monumental arch set on two storeys of coupled columns and the whole inserted into one side of a pre-existing forecourt; it carries an inscription of 1497 but was completed only in the 17th century.

3. ROME, 1500–14.

(i) Early works and the Tempietto. (ii) Commissions for Pope Julius II. (iii) Non-papal late works.

(i) Early works and the Tempietto. In September 1499 Milan fell to the French, and the Duke was driven from power. Bramante left Lombardy and headed for Rome, arriving there, according to Vasari, just before the Holy Year of 1500. He soon received commissions from Pope Alexander VI to paint the papal arms over the main portal of S Giovanni in Laterano and to design two fountains, one in Trastevere (destr.), the other in the forecourt of St Peter's, fragments of which were reused by Carlo Maderno in 1614 for the fountain that now stands on the piazza's right-hand side. Vasari also claimed that Bramante was consulted in connection with a number of major buildings of the period, including the palace of Cardinal Raffaello Riario (now the Palazzo della Cancelleria; begun *c.* 1485; see ROME, §V, 23(i)), and that he actually made plans for the Palazzo Corneto (now Palazzo Giraud-Torlonia), a building of compact layout and restrained design but nonetheless a plausible attribution. Principally, however, he is described as devoting his time to the study and measurement of ancient buildings in Rome, Tivoli and further afield around Naples. This may indeed be true to judge from the remarkable increase in scale and monumentality and growing awareness of classical norms apparent in his architecture at this time.

Bramante fostered connections with those members of the papal circle with Spanish affiliations, such as Cardinal Oliviero Carafa, who supplied him with his first major Roman commission in 1500, the cloister at S Maria della Pace (completed 1504; see fig. 3). In some respects the design still relies on the formal vocabulary of his previous works: the pilasters on the courtyard side articulating the piers of the lower storey are raised upon pedestals, the subordinate pilaster-strips under the groin-vaulted arcades lack capitals, and the trabeated upper storey, which is not particularly

3. Donato Bramante: cloister of S Maria della Pace, Rome, completed 1504

tall, has a doubled rhythm. The design may also have taken into account recent architectural developments in Rome: the pier-arcade with attached order, although still most unexpected in a monastic cloister, appears earlier in the courtyard of the Palazzo Venezia (1464). Compared with contemporary Roman architecture, however, the cloister is much more rigorous in its geometry and the application of the orders. The square plan with four bays to each side is based on the module of a single bay measured from the centres of the pilasters, so that the pilasters in the corners appear only as thin fillets, as in Brunelleschi's Old Sacristy at S Lorenzo, Florence. The pilasters of the lower storey have Ionic capitals, the conventional choice for a cloister, and those above have Composite capitals, which complement the Ionic ones with their volutes; the additional supports between the piers at this level are slender columns with less ornamental Corinthian capitals. The corbels in the frieze above, which derive from the top storey of the Colosseum, add suitable weight to the terminal entablature.

It was probably about this time that Bramante received the commission for his epoch-making Tempietto, even though its style suggests that the design, which is undocumented, was substantially redrafted several years later. The date 1502 appears in an inscription in the crypt and refers either to the commission—transmitted by Cardinal Carvajal from Ferdinand II, King of Sicily and Aragón, and Isabella, Queen of Castile and León—or to the actual beginning of work. The circular building, which stands in a courtyard next to S Pietro in Montorio (see fig. 4), serves as a shrine marking the supposed site of St Peter's crucifixion; at its very centre is the hole reputedly for the cross, exposed in the crypt and also visible through an opening in the paved floor above. Despite its tiny size, the Tempietto is majestically conceived. The shrine is encircled by a ring of sixteen Doric columns raised on three steps, with an entablature and balustrade above; the upper level has a drum and a dome with a crowning finial (altered in 1605). Under the colonnade, respondent pilasters frame windows alternating with niches and three portals (only one of which is original); panelled pilaster-strips around the drum frame a similar arrangement of openings. The interior also has Doric pilasters but with alternating narrow and wide bays, the ample niches in the wide bays for the portals (originally only one) and the altar.

In its basic design and function, Bramante's Tempietto can be related to structures built to house precious relics, such as Matteo Civitali's tempietto for the Volto Santo (1484) in S Martino, Lucca. Yet despite the externally

4. Donato Bramante: Tempietto, Rome, after 1502

expressed drum, with its arguably Christian associations, the design is conceived much more on the model of an ancient round peripteral temple. Temples of similar composition, with colonnades, attics and domes, appear in drawings by Francesco di Giorgio (Turin, Bib. Reale, Cod. Sal. fol. 84); Bramante's Tempietto, however, relies on a much more archaeologically informed knowledge of ancient prototypes, such as the Temple of Vesta (late 2nd century BC) by the Tiber and the so-called Temple of Portumnus near Ostia, which has an interior with niches and a crypt below.

The Tempietto also depends to an unprecedented degree upon a new understanding of the rules set out by Vitruvius for temple design in general and for the Doric order in particular (III and IV). With exemplary dimensional rigour, the diameters of the interior and the colonnade, and the main elevational heights, are all based on the modular diameter of the columns. Moreover, the Tempietto's Doric order is not only the first Renaissance example to incorporate a proper Doric frieze with triglyphs and metopes, here carved with the instruments of the Christian liturgy, but also the earliest to conform in its proportions and the precise sequence of its constituent members to the Vitruvian canon. The Doric order itself was presumably selected according to Vitruvian rules of decorum (see ORDERS, ARCHITECTURAL, §I, 2(i)(c)) for its suitable associations with the building's dedicatee, the strong and heroic St Peter. The adoption of respondent pilasters under the colonnade constitutes a departure from both Vitruvius and circular temple prototypes but helps emphasize the radial component to the design, which directs attention towards the hallowed site at the building's

heart. An unexecuted scheme recorded in Serlio's treatise (Book III) to remodel the courtyard and enclose the building within a tall, circular cloister would have made this central focusing even more emphatic.

(ii) Commissions for Pope Julius II. Bramante's architectural ambitions were to be matched by those of Julius II, elected Pope on 31 October 1503 (see ROVERE, DELLA (i), (2)). Bramante had already been in contact with Julius's cousin Cardinal Raffaelle Riario, but he may have been recommended by Cardinal Ascanio Sforza, Julius's confidant and Bramante's former patron. Julius was quick to dispense with the services of his former architect, Giuliano da Sangallo, as he began to plan a number of magnificent projects in and around St Peter's and the Vatican, for which he assembled many of the leading artists of the period, including Michelangelo and Bramante, who was then aged about 60. It is even possible that Bramante assisted Michelangelo in the perspective and architectural framework of the Sistine Chapel ceiling (1508–12), which has some considerable similarities with the *Argus* in the Castello Sforzesco (see §2(i) above). Now established as, in effect, the official papal architect, Bramante embarked on a series of far-reaching projects that would rival even those of Roman emperors; for these he was well rewarded financially by Julius, who appointed him to the honorary office of *Piombo*.

(a)Vatican Palace. (b) St Peter's. (c) S Maria del Popolo and other work.

(a) Vatican Palace. The main adjunct to the Vatican Palace designed by Bramante is the colossal extension known as the Cortile del Belvedere, on which work began in the spring of 1505 (see ROME, §V, 14(iii)(a), and fig. 35). Although the design was modified by Pirro Ligorio before its completion (c. 1565) and altered by Domenico Fontana (1587–8), Bramante's scheme is faithfully recorded, most notably by Bernardino della Volpaia in the Codex Coner (London, Soane Mus.). The courtyard was intended to link the palace of Nicholas V to the Belvedere of Innocent VIII with its new sculpture court (completed 1506; remodelled 1773), situated more than 300 m to the north. The Cortile, arranged in three vast, ascending terraces, was designed to form a carefully considered composition, especially when viewed from the Pope's third-storey private apartment at the southern end. The long flanks of the Cortile house corridors and rise to roughly the same height, with three storeys for the lowest terrace and one storey for the top. A straight flight of steps once linked the lowest terrace, designed for use as a theatre, with the intermediate one, and a pair of transverse zigzag ramps to either side of a nymphaeum connected this level with the upper terrace. At the centre of the short northern end of the upper terrace, a broad single-storey semicircular exedra provided a fitting climax to the vista and gave access to the sculpture court. It was approached by a remarkable flight of concentric convex and concave steps, which thus combined the forwards and sideways movement of the steps and ramps below.

The Cortile's monumental conception depends, at least in part, on an archaeological awareness of ancient complexes in the vicinity of Rome. The terracing was probably inspired by the enormous Temple of Fortuna Primigenia complex at Palestrina (*see* PRAENESTE, fig. 1), which also incorporates ramps and semicircular flights of steps; the exedra resembles that of one of the ancient bath complexes, and the covered corridors may have been based on such *cryptoportici* as those at Hadrian's Villa at Tivoli. The inventive elevations, however, are less immediately dependent on ancient precedent, although the Doric–Ionic–Corinthian sequence for the three-storey lower terrace, the first such occurrence in Renaissance architecture, derives ultimately from the Colosseum. This elevation has an arcaded lower storey with piers and attached Doric pilasters, a second storey with Ionic pilasters overlaid on half-pilasters and with pedimented windows flanked by niches, and an open top storey with Corinthian pilasters and smaller Doric columns between them supporting an unusual panel similar to those at S Maria presso S Satiro; the single-storey elevation for the upper terrace also has Corinthian pilasters but with a triumphal-arch system of alternating wide and narrow bays.

Bramante also designed the spiral staircase-ramp, embellished with central supporting columns, in a tower near the sculpture court. Although the columns share a common spiral architrave, their capitals and proportions follow a sequence similar to that of the courtyard, which begins with a Tuscan order and is followed by a less robust Doric order, then progressively by more slender Ionic and Composite ones (see fig. 5). Vasari recognized a medieval precedent for the staircase in the 13th-century campanile of S Nicola at Pisa, but Palladio identified an internal staircase in the Porticus of Pompey as Bramante's model (I.xxviii). Bramante was also responsible for the Porta Julia, the external portal surrounded by massive blocks of rustication that leads into the Cortile's lower terrace, and for a wooden dome with an arcaded drum (1509; destr. 1523) on top of the nearby Borgia tower. Other designs by Bramante connected with the palace include the loggias of the neighbouring Cortile di S Damaso (begun by 1509; completed under Raphael), which has two storeys of arches with applied pilasters at first- and second-floor levels and a colonnaded storey at the top.

(b) *St Peter's.* On 18 April 1506 the foundation stone was laid for the first of the four enormous crossing piers of the new St Peter's (*see* ROME, V, 14(ii)(a)). Although little of Bramante's project for the church was actually realized, his plans formed the basis of all subsequent designs, including Michelangelo's. The impetus for the rebuilding of the venerated but dilapidated Early Christian basilica may have been provided by Julius's desire to find a suitable setting for the monumental tomb he commissioned from Michelangelo in 1505. Bramante's design, which was preferred to proposals submitted by Giuliano da Sangallo and Fra Giocondo, is represented on Caradosso's foundation medal (1506; e.g. London, BM), and the same design, apart from some minor deviations of detail, is recorded in a half-plan drawing known as the Parchment Plan (Florence, Uffizi, 1A; *see* ROME, fig. 35). The layout seems to have grown out of the ideas he had considered at Pavia Cathedral and S Maria delle Grazie, namely a domed Greek cross inscribed within a square and with apses on the main axes. It is here further elaborated with four subsidiary domes on the diagonals, where the Greek-cross arrangement is repeated on a smaller scale, and with four corner towers. The centre of the design corresponds fittingly with the revered tomb of St Peter, and the multi-domed layout recalls that of earlier sepulchral churches, such as S Marco, Venice; in other respects, the design can be related to the Early Christian S Lorenzo (*c.* AD 370), Milan, which has half-domes and corner towers. The arrangement of the crossing, however, although not so different from that in Pavia Cathedral, is a major innovation in church design, with diagonal chamfers to the massive crossing piers giving the dome a much greater diameter than the width of the arms.

In its enormous scale Bramante's design for St Peter's was quite without precedent for a post-medieval church and relied heavily on ancient Roman bath complexes, which seem to have inspired a wholly new approach to spatial planning. Whereas during the 15th century internal spaces were conceived as a product of designing walls, in St Peter's the walls were a product of designing spaces. Through this new approach, greatly aided by Bramante's revival of Roman brick-and-concrete construction, the massive vault-bearing walls took up the residual areas between neighbouring spaces and were hollowed out in a multitude of alcoves, arches and niches. Bramante's design for the dome, with its colonnaded drum resembling a circular temple and its crowning lantern, is known also

5. Donato Bramante: spiral staircase-ramp, Cortile del Belvedere, Rome, *c.* 1505

from a plate in Serlio (Book III). In shape (hemispherical on the inside, stepped and dishlike on the outside) as well as in size (diam. 40.5 m when eventually realized), the design abandoned contemporary practice and was closely modelled instead on the Pantheon (diam. *c.* 43 m; *see* ROME, §V, 8). The much greater overall size of St Peter's, however, compared with the Pantheon, was no doubt regarded as emblematic of the triumph of Christianity over ancient paganism and of the authority of papal rule.

The Parchment Plan design was, nevertheless, just one of many alternatives considered even as construction progressed. Other proposals included retaining the choir begun in 1452 under Nicholas V by Bernardo Rossellino, which Bramante completed, and adding ambulatories to the arms; there were even designs for a surrounding precinct. Bramante may also have been responsible for a Latin-cross scheme (Florence, Uffizi, 20A) intended to cover fully the hallowed site of the earlier basilica, which would have offered liturgical and ceremonial advantages and would have provided the building with a dominant façade lacking in the Parchment Plan design. No decision seems to have been made by Bramante's death, however, even though the crossing had been substantially completed up to the height of the drum, with piers and attached Corinthian pilasters using capitals copied from those inside the Pantheon. According to Vasari, Bramante intended the exterior to be Doric, and he certainly used this order for the outside of the 15th-century choir and the temporary stone shelter (1513; destr. 1592) over the site of St Peter's tomb. The latter's design, three bays with a paired order at either end, was similar to that of the Basilica Aemilia (179 BC) in the Forum Romanum.

(c) S Maria del Popolo and other work. Another church project in Rome commissioned from Bramante by Julius II was the extended choir for S Maria del Popolo (completed 1509), built to house the tombs of *Cardinal Ascanio Sforza* and *Cardinal Girolamo Basso della Rovere* (*d* 1507). The tombs are set below innovative Serlian windows either side of a square space covered by a saucer dome, approached from the pre-existing crossing through a barrel-vaulted bay, with another barrel-vaulted bay and apse beyond. The second barrel vault has coffering modelled on the entrance into the Pantheon, and the lowest coffer on the southern side is left open to make a window, an arrangement sometimes found in ancient *cryptoportici.* Apart from the saucer dome, frescoed by BERNARDINO PINTURICCHIO (*c.* 1510), the interior is remarkably stark, only articulated by plain pilaster-strips. It typifies the conception of true *all'antica* architecture that Bramante arrived at late in his career. The Pope then commissioned Bramante to rebuild the church of SS Celso e Giuliano in Banchi (begun 1509; abandoned *c.* 1513; rebuilt after 1733); like a reduced version of St Peter's, this was planned as a domed Greek cross with four subsidiary domes and chamfered piers at the crossing. The interior was again very severe, simply articulated by plain pilaster-strips and corresponding ribs across the barrel-vaulted arms.

The Via Giulia, which runs close to the Tiber in a straight line towards the Vatican, was laid out by Bramante in 1507 as an important element in Julius's policy of renewing the fabric of the ancient city. In the following year Bramante started work on the enormous Palazzo dei Tribunali (abandoned 1511; most destr.), which was intended to bring together all the city's civil and ecclesiastical courts and to provide accommodation for the judges. The complex was to be arranged around a square courtyard with corner towers and a church, S Biagio della Pagnotta, projecting at the rear towards the Tiber. The layout is known principally from a drawing (Florence, Uffizi, 136A), which shows considerable similarities with the plans of the Cancelleria and other palaces for cardinals; the courtyard, with applied half-columns, recalls especially that of the Palazzo Venezia (begun 1455). Above all, it resembles Giuliano da Sangallo's scheme in the Codex Barberini (1488; Rome, Vatican, Bib. Apostolica, MS. lat. 4424) for a palace for the King of Naples. The four-storey main façade is known principally from the foundation medal of 1508 (e.g. Rome, Vatican, Medagliere), which shows a third tower at the centre rising in three battlemented stages to give a castle-like exterior resembling that of the Castello Sforzesco, Milan, and having similarities also with the mid-15th-century Palazzo dei Senatori, Rome. The lower level, a fragment of which survives, was rusticated with massive stone blocks and would have had openings for shops. The east end of S Biagio would, once again, have resembled the crossing of St Peter's combined with a two-bay nave as in the 15th-century church of S Maria della Pace.

Bramante designed several other works for Julius outside Rome. In 1508 he prepared designs to encase the Santa Casa, the house inside the sanctuary church at Loreto believed to be the Virgin's, in a lavish marble exterior (*see* LORETO, §II, 1(ii)(a) and fig. 3). The three-by-five-bay structure has Corinthian half-columns, associated by Vitruvius with maidenhood, arranged like a triumphal arch in narrow and wide bays. The half-columns are fluted, and all other available surfaces are decorated, incorporating a profusion of relief sculpture and statuary by Andrea Sansovino and others. Bramante also designed a very restrained, towered façade (unexecuted) for the church itself, recorded in a foundation medal of 1509 (e.g. Rome, Vatican, Medagliere), and a papal palace complex in the form of a monumental rectangular forecourt (1510; *see* LORETO, §II, 2 and fig. 1) that was realized in part, though with changes, under Sansovino and Antonio da Sangallo (ii). It has two-storey arcades with Doric and Ionic pilasters and defensive towers on the external angles. Elsewhere, it was almost certainly Bramante who designed the courtyard of the Rocca at Viterbo, with side-loggias of columns above piers (1506; later modified), and the fortress at Civitavecchia (1508), which has low bastions at the four corners and a large internal courtyard with chamfered angles, similar to those in the earlier Belvedere statue court at the Vatican.

(iii) Non-papal late works. Bramante's Palazzo Caprini (*c.* 1510; also known as the House of Raphael, who bought it in 1517) was built in Rome for the apostolic protonotary, Adriano de Caprinis. The building (subsequently remodelled) occupied a shallow site on the approaches to St Peter's; as was the custom in Rome, it had a row of shops at street level and living accommodation above. The design

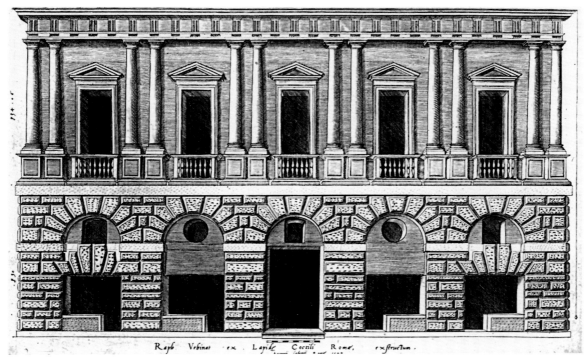

6. Donato Bramante: facade of the Palazzo Caprini, *c.* 1510; from an engraving by Antoine Lafréry, 1549

of the façade, best known from Antoine Lafréry's engraving (1549; see fig. 6), marked a watershed in palace design through the contrasting treatment of its two storeys, which accorded with their respective uses. The massive and ruggedly rusticated lower storey was treated as a five-bay arcade with openings for the main entrance and the four shops and with mezzanines for the shopkeepers' accommodation. The refined and elegant *piano nobile* above had pairs of Doric three-quarter columns, which stood on pedestals aligned with the piers below, supported a full Doric entablature and framed five pedimented windows with balustraded balconies. The design departed from previous façade arrangements in Rome, which were usually three storeys tall and had either plain stuccoed brickwork pierced by distinctive transom and mullion windows (e.g. Palace of Nicholas V in the Vatican and Palazzo Venezia) or orders of pilasters overlaid on rustication (e.g. Cancellaria or Palazzo Corneto), although, like the Palazzo Caprini, the order was usually omitted from the basement. It differed above all in its monumentality, having three-quarter columns rather than pilasters and a more pronounced rustication. The Palazzo Caprini façade may have been inspired to some extent by ancient temples or tombs with tall and massive substructures, although the direct influence of ancient prototypes is slight, being limited to the patterning of the stuccoed brick rustication and, in particular, to the design of the outer arches, which, with their inserted flat arches, closely resemble an ancient portal that formed part of the Temple of Romulus (now SS Cosma e Damiano) in the Forum Romanum. On the other hand, the underlying principles of Classical propriety, together with such Vitruvian details as placing the triglyphs at the extremities of the entablature, gave the façade a Classical spirit and authority that was new to Renaissance palaces.

The ruinous Nymphaeum outside Genazzano, attributed to Bramante by Frommel, was arguably designed for Cardinal Pompeo Colonna *c.* 1508–11, although the dating is far from certain. It was a recreational pavilion shelved into a hillside and used for viewing spectacles staged in and around a lake formed by damming a stream in the valley below. It had a three-bay, vaulted *loggia* at the front with apsed ends (an arrangement similar to that of Raphael's Villa Madama, begun *c.* 1516); behind, on a slightly higher level, was a further three-bay area with a central apse, close to which was a domed octagonal bathhouse. The antiquarianism of the scheme, together with such motifs as the Serlian openings with roundels between concentric arches, seen also in S Maria delle Grazie, Milan (see fig. 2 above), support the attribution to Bramante. Other details, however, such as the non-standard proportions of the Doric order, used throughout, seem inconsistent with his mature style.

II. Critical reception and posthumous reputation.

When Bramante died, a year after Julius, he received a magnificent funeral in St Peter's, where his body was brought for burial. His contribution to architecture was quite apparent to his immediate followers, and it was they who established his enduring fame. An early and rather humorous portrait of the architect was presented by A. Guarna in his *Simia* (1516), but Bramante was also seen early on as having brought the art of architecture back to the standards of Classical antiquity, a view cogently expressed in Raphael's letter about the state of the arts addressed to Pope Leo X (*c.* 1516–18; Munich, Bayer. Staatsbib., cod. it. 37b), where architecture's recent advancement 'may be seen in the many beautiful buildings by Bramante'. Serlio, in book III of his treatise, made a much more forthright claim when he specifically singled out Bramante as having 'revived the good architecture which had been buried until his time'. In so doing Serlio consigned Bramante's contemporaries, including Giuliano da Sangallo and Fra Giocondo, to a lower league, and his legendary fame was thus crystallized. A similar estimation eventually formed the basis for a considerable elaboration by Vasari, who presented Bramante as the pioneering force in architecture for the third and final phase in the revival of the arts, and this view of Bramante as the father-figure of High Renaissance architecture has coloured all subsequent accounts of his career.

Many of Bramante's buildings and projects were recorded early, some even during the initial stages of construction as in the case of Bernardino della Volpaia's drawings in the Codex Coner. Although widely circulated through both drawings and foundation medals, Bramante's designs were transmitted most effectively by Serlio's treatise, which provides detailed descriptions and illustrations of most of his major Roman projects, including them in the book (III) that deals primarily with antiquities. Subsequently, in Palladio's *I quattro libri*, Bramante was to receive the unqualified accolade of being the only contemporary architect (apart from Palladio himself) to be illustrated, his Tempietto appearing as the only contemporary example in the final book on temples (IV. xvii).

The weighty and decorous style of classical architecture that Bramante was largely instrumental in establishing was enormously influential. Few subsequent architects remained untouched, for example, by the new approach to spatial planning that Bramante had introduced. The style enjoyed a continuing popularity in Rome and was brought to northern Italy during the 1520s by his followers Giulio Romano, Michele Sanmicheli and Jacopo Sansovino, whence it was eventually disseminated throughout Europe. The fact that the style was by no means one of slavish revivalism in great part explains its success. Bramante was certainly attracted by Vitruvian orthodoxy, and this was an overriding concern in such buildings as the Tempietto, which became a modern classic. Yet he was also, as Vasari noted, attracted by the possibilities of invention: the Cortile del Belvedere, for example, was a most ingenious, evocative, but essentially modern reinterpretation of Classical themes, which fired the imagination of successors such as Raphael or Jacopo Vignola in the design of similar projects. Bramante's plans for St Peter's were to exert a profound influence on later church design. Michelangelo explicitly voiced a desire to return to Bramante's Greek-cross arrangement for St Peter's, and all the intervening redraftings of the plans were indebted to Bramante. Numerous other churches built in Italy during the 16th century were also inspired by his designs, and ultimately the idea of a great domed classical church became a standard throughout Europe. Similarly, the Palazzo Caprini became a source for subsequent palace designs, to the extent that many of the major palace façades of 16th-century Italy depend on it in some way; several, especially those of Sanmicheli, Sansovino and Palladio, are in effect creative variations. It is Bramante's influence on his immediate followers, and from them on posterity, rather than his own changed and disfigured buildings that finally holds the key to his deservedly great reputation.

BIBLIOGRAPHY

EARLY SOURCES

A. Guarna: *Simia* (MS., 1516; Milan, Bib. Trivulziana); ed. G. Nicodemi (Milan, 1943)

M. Michiel: *Notìzia d'opere di disegno nella prima metà del secolo XVI* (MS.; 1521–43); ed. J. Morelli (Bassano, 1800; rev. Bologna, 1884)

S. Serlio: *Delle antichità* (Venice, 1540) [Book III of his treatise, fol. 64v of the 1619 edn]

G. Vasari: *Vite* (1550, rev. 2/1568); ed. G. Milanesi (1878–85), iv

Saba da Castiglione: *Ricordi* (Venice, 1554), iii, p. 138

A. Palladio: *I quattro libri dell'architettura* (Venice, 1570)

G. P. Lomazzo: *Trattato dell' arte della pittura* (Milan, 1584); ed. R. P. Ciardi in *Lomazzo: Scritti sull'arte*, 2 vols (Florence, 1973–4)

MONOGRAPHS

C. Baroni: *Bramante* (Bergamo, 1944)

G. Chierici: *Bramante* (Milan, 1954)

O. H. Förster: *Bramante* (Vienna and Munich, 1956)

G. Chierici: *Donato Bramante* (New York, 1960)

A. Bruschi: *Bramante architetto* (Bari, 1969)

Studi bramanteschi: Atti del congresso internazionale: Milano, Urbino, Roma, 1970

A. Bruschi: *Bramante* (Bari, 1973; Eng. trans., London, 1977)

URBINO AND MILAN

F. Malaguzzi-Valeri: *Bramante e Leonardo* (1915), ii of *La corte di Ludovico il Moro* (Milan, 1913–23)

A. Pica and P. Portaluppi: *Il gruppo monumentale di S. Maria delle Grazie* (Rome, 1938)

C. Baroni: *Documenti per la storia dell'architettura a Milano nel rinascimento e nel barocco*, i (Florence, 1940); ii (Rome, 1968)

P. Rotondi: *Il palazzo ducale di Urbino*, 2 vols (Urbino, 1950–51; Eng. trans., London, 1969)

W. Suida: *Bramante pittore e il Bramantino* (Milan, 1953)

F. Graf Wolff Metternich: 'Der Kupferstich Bernardos de Prevadari', *Röm. Jb. Kstgesch.*, xi (1967–8), pp. 9–97

A. Palestra: 'Cronologia e documentazione riguardante la costruzione della chiesa di S. Maria presso S. Satiro', *A. Lombarda*, 14 (1969), pp. 154–60

R. V. Schofield: 'A Drawing for S. Maria presso S. Satiro', *J. Warb. & Court. Inst.*, xxxix (1976), pp. 246–53

G. A. Dell'Acqua and G. Mulazzani: *Bramantino e Bramante pittore* (Milan, 1978)

La scultura decorativa del primo rinascimento: Atti del I convegno internazionale di studi: Pavia, 1980 [several interesting articles]

R. V. Schofield: 'Ludovico il Moro and Vigevano', *A. Lombarda*, 62 (1982), pp. 93–140

A. Palestra: *La Madonna miracolosa di S. Satiro, 1200 –c. 1983* (Milan, 1983)

L. Patetta: 'Bramante e la trasformazione della basilica di Sant' Ambrogio a Milano', *Boll. A.*, lxviii/21 (1983), pp. 49–74

S. Maria delle Grazie (Milan, 1983)

Bramante a Milano: Atti del congresso internazionale: Milano, 1986

R. V. Schofield: 'Florentine and Roman Elements in Bramante's Milanese Architecture', *Florence and Milan: Comparisons and Relationships*, i (Florence, 1989), pp. 201–22

C. D. Nesselrath: *Die Säulenordnungen bei Bramante* (Worms, 1990)

A. E. Werdehausen: *Bramante und das Kloster S. Ambroggio in Mailand* (Worms, 1990)

ROME

H. von Geymüller: *Les Projets primitifs pour Saint-Pierre* (Paris, 1875–80; German ed. Vienna, 1875–80)

K. Frey: 'Zur Baugeschichte des St. Peter', *Jb. Kön.-Preuss. Kstsamml.*, xxxi (1910), pp. 1–95; xxxiii (1913), pp. 1–153; xxxvii (1916), pp. 22–136 [CH]

D. Frey: *Bramante-Studien* (Vienna, 1915)

J. S. Ackerman: *The Cortile del Belvedere* (Rome, 1954)

F. Graf Wolff Metternich: 'Le Premier Projet pour St Pierre', *Studies in Western Art: Acts of the Twentieth International Congress of the History of Art: New York, 1961*, ii, pp. 70–81

——: 'Bramante's Chor der Peterskirche zu Rom', *Röm. Qschr.*, lviii (1963), pp. 271–91

G. De Angelis d'Ossat: 'Preludo romano del Bramante', *Palladio*, xvi (1966), pp. 92–124

S. Segui, C. Thoenes and L. Mortari: *SS Celso e Giuliano*, Le Chiese di Roma Illustrate (Rome, 1966)

L. H. Heydenreich: 'Bramante's "Ultima Maniera"', *Essays in the History of Architecture Presented to R. Wittkower* (London, 1967), pp. 60–63

C. L. Frommel: 'Bramante's "Ninfeo" in Genazzano', *Röm. Jb. Kstgesch.*, xii (1969), pp. 137–60

——: *Der römische Palastbau der Hochrenaissance* (Tübingen, 1971)

E. Bentivoglio and S. Valtieri: *S. Maria del Popolo a Roma* (Rome, 1976)

R. Tuttle: 'Julius II and Bramante in Bologna', *Le arti a Bologna e in Emilia dal XVI al XVIII secolo: Atti del XXIV Congresso internazionale di storia dell'arte: Bologna, 1979*, pp. 3–8

C. Robertson: 'Bramante, Michelangelo and the Sistine Ceiling', *J. Warb. & Court. Inst.*, xlix (1986), pp. 91–105

T. Carunchio: 'Il chiostro di S. Maria della Pace: Note e considerazioni', *Quad. Ist. Stor. Archit.*, 1–10 (1987), pp. 293–300

F. Graf Wolff Metternich and C. Thoenes: *Die frühen St.-Peter-Entwürfe, 1505–1514* (Tübingen, 1987)

F. Fagliari Zeni Buchicchio: 'La rocca del Bramante a Civitavecchia: Il cantiere e le maestranze da Giulio II a Paolo III', *Röm. Jb. Kstgesch.*, xxiii–xxiv (1988), pp. 275–383

M. Wilson Jones: 'The Tempietto and the Roots of Coincidence', *Archit. Hist.*, xxxiii (1990), pp. 1–28

PAUL DAVIES, DAVID HEMSOLL

Bramantino [Suardi, Bartolomeo] (*b* ?Milan, *c.* 1465; *d* Milan, 1530). Italian painter and architect. He was one of the leading artists in Milan in the early 16th century. His early training as a goldsmith may indicate a relatively late start to his activity as a painter, and none of his work may be dated before 1490. The style of his early work parallels that of such followers of Vincenzo Foppa as Bernardino Butinone, Bernardo Zenale and Giovanni Donato da Montorfano. He assumed the name Bramantino very early in his career, indicating that he was in close contact with Donato Bramante, whose influence is uppermost in his early work. Probably his earliest surviving painting is the *Virgin and Child* (Boston, MA, Mus. F.A.). It is an adaptation of a type of half-length Virgin with standing Christ Child well known in Milan. The linear emphasis and the dramatic treatment of light are aspects derived from Bramante's work. Bramantino stressed graphic quality in this picture, and throughout his early work he was considerably influenced by Andrea Mantegna and by the visual aspects of prints. His *Risen Christ* (Madrid, Mus. Thyssen–Bornemisza) derives from Bramante's *Christ at the Column* (*c.* 1490; Milan, Brera) but has a more precise musculature and a much harder use of line. The conception of the figure set against a rocky background, derived from Leonardo da Vinci's *Virgin of the Rocks* (versions, London, N.G.; Paris, Louvre; *see* LEONARDO DA VINCI, fig. 2), also indicates Bramantino's persistently eclectic nature.

Bramantino's interest in perspective and illusionism, also derived from Bramante, is evident in the *Pietà* fresco lunette from S Sepolcro, Milan, and in the *Adoration of the Shepherds* (both Milan, Bib. Ambrosiana). A feature of all his earlier paintings is that they are idiosyncratic in their iconography. This is particularly apparent in *Philomen and Baucis* (Cologne, Wallraf-Richartz-Mus.), where he chose an unusual subject from Ovid's *Metamorphoses*, for which he had no prototype, and developed it by reference to the iconography of the Supper at Emmaus, exploring the

Bramantino: *Adoration of the Magi*, oil on panel, 570×550 mm, *c.* 1500 (London, National Gallery)

Christian notion of the Eucharist in a Classical context. Similarly, in the *Adoration of the Magi* (*c.* 1500; London, N.G.; see fig.) he explored the significance of the Epiphany with references beyond the simple narrative. Here, typically, he controlled the broad iconographic reference with a masterful use of perspective and composition that gives the painting, despite its small scale, the aspect of a monumental altarpiece. The early work culminates in the series of 12 large tapestries of *The Months* (Milan, Castello Sforzesco), commissioned by Gian Giacomo Trivulzio and designed between 1501 and 1508. The scale of these works gave ample scope for the innovative treatment of subject and form. In particular, he added to traditional images of the months many references to antique works of art with which he seems to have been directly familiar. The style of the figures in the tapestries is more rounded and heavy and the composition more static; its counterpart is found in the *Virgin and Child with SS Ambrose and Michael* (Milan, Bib. Ambrosiana), which also may be dated to this period. This painting shows a greater competence in the use of oil and a softer treatment of form than in his earlier works.

Throughout much of 1508 Bramantino was in Rome, where he did work (destr.) in the papal apartments in the Vatican for Julius II. After his return to Milan, *c.* 1509, his prominence led to the receipt of a number of commissions. In 1519 he was a member of a committee advising on the construction of Milan Cathedral, and he was praised by Cesare di Lorenzo Cesariano in his edition of Vitruvius (Como, 1521). As a loyalist to the Sforza, in 1525 he was banished from Milan, though the same year he was appointed official architect and painter by Francesco Maria, the last Sforza Duke of Milan.

Bramantino's later work is principally religious, and its uniformity of style makes any precise chronology very difficult. In his largest picture, the *Crucifixion* (Milan, Brera), the subject is treated with great stillness, the paint is applied softly and the figures are constructed almost as patterns of flowing drapery. This picture is modelled on a characteristic Lombard formula, which was developed in quite a personal way by the inclusion of mysterious Classical architecture. The interest in the antique is a constant theme in his later work; in his altarpiece *Virgin and Child with Saints* (Florence, Pitti) the figures are statically arranged with an architectural background, recalling the reliefs from the period of Marcus Aurelius on the attic storey of the Arch of Constantine in Rome. Another late work, the *Flight into Egypt*, painted for the sanctuary of the Madonna del Sasso, Locarno (*in situ*), shows, less typically, his ability to depict landscape in an evocative and romantic way, indicating how at this stage he was affected by the example of Leonardo da Vinci.

Bramantino was also responsible for one architectural work, the funerary chapel of Gian Giacomo Trivulzio at S Nazaro Maggiore, Milan, designed in 1512. The chapel, which acts as a façade and vestibule to the church, combines various elements. It was developed from the pattern of such 15th-century chapels as the Portinari Chapel at S Eustorgio, Milan, and the Colleoni Chapel at Bergamo Cathedral, but the site gives it much greater prominence. The octagonal plan and extensive crypt are directly derived from antique examples, as was the projected portico, one of the first revivals of the temple front since antiquity. The plain style of the architecture, with its massive Tuscan order, is a departure from the highly ornamental style of Bramante and his contemporaries in Milan.

To an unusual degree, Bramantino's work encompasses the change in north Italian art from the graphic style of the 15th century to the more rounded, softer style of the 16th century. While he was a major figure in his lifetime, his work was relatively uninfluential. Much of his work is the product of his own rather tortuous design processes and theoretical interests. Throughout his career he demonstrated a considerable interest in architectural theory, the revival of the Antique and perspective, on which he wrote a treatise (parts preserved by Giovanni Paolo Lomazzo; see Suida).

BIBLIOGRAPHY

G. Fiocco: 'Il periodo romano di Bartolomeo Suardi detto il Bramantino', *L'Arte*, xvii (1914), pp. 24–40
C. Baroni: 'Leonardo, Bramantino ed il mausoleo di G. Giacomo Trivulzio', *Rac. Vinc.*, xv–xvi (1934–9), pp. 201–70
G. Hoogewerff: 'Documenti in parte inediti che riguardano Raffaello ed altri artisti contemporanei', *Rendi. Pont. Accad. Romana Archeol.*, 3rd ser., xxi (1945–6), pp. 253–68
W. Suida: *Bramante pittore e il Bramantino* (Milan, 1953)
M. Valsecchi: *Gli arazzi dei 'Mesi' del Bramantino* (Milan, 1968)
G. Mulazzani and G. A. dell'Acqua: *Bramantino e Bramante pittore: Opera completa* (Milan, 1978)
N. Forti Grazzini: *Gli arazzi dei 'Mesi' Trivulzio: Il committente, l'iconografia* (Milan, 1982)
C. Perogalli and G. B. Sannazzaro: 'Le architetture fortificate negli arazzi Trivulzio e nei dipinti del Bramantino', *Rass. Stud. & Not.*, x (1982), pp. 305–57
L. Cogliati Arano and G. Sironi: 'A proposito del Bramantino', *A. Lombarda*, 86–7 (1988), pp. 36–42

CHARLES ROBERTSON

Brambilla, Ambrogio (*fl* Rome, 1579–99). Italian print-maker and cartographer. Of Milanese origin, he is recorded first in Rome in 1579 as a member of the Congregazione dei Virtuosi al Pantheon, and he remained there at least until 1599, the date of his last work. In 1582 Brambilla produced a series of 135 small engravings of emperors from Julius Caesar to Rudolf II and in 1585 another series, of the popes to Sixtus V. His most successful works, however, were prints of scenographic reconstructions of antiquity such as the *Sepulchre of Lucius Septimius* (1582) and contemporary views of ancient and modern Rome, for example the *Belvedere del Vaticano* (1579) and the *Fireworks Display at Castel Sant'Angelo* (1579). Many of his prints depicting ancient monuments, produced after 1577, were included in the *Speculum Romanae magnificentiae* (see Hülsen). He also produced prints depicting popular games and street scenes (e.g. Rome, Calcografia N., no. 1179). In 1589 he engraved the *Last Judgement* after a relief sculpture in wax on slate by Giacomo Vivio based on Michelangelo's painting in the Sistine Chapel, Rome. Two unpublished engravings depict a *Perspective Map of Ancona* (1585) and a *View of the Catafalque for the Funeral of Cardinal Alessandro Farnese* (1589; both Milan, Castello Sforzesco). Later sources record Brambilla's activity as a poet, sculptor in bronze, painter and architect.

BIBLIOGRAPHY

DBI; Thieme–Becker
F. Ehrle: *Roma prima di Sisto V: La pianta di Roma di Pérac-Lafréry del 1577* (Rome, 1908)
C. Hülsen: 'Das *Speculum Romanae magnificentiae* des Antonio Lafréry', *Collectanea variae doctrinae Leoni S. Olschki bibliopolae Florentino sexagenario* (Munich, 1921), pp. 121–70
P. Arrigoni and A. Bertarelli: *Piante e vedute di Roma e del Lazio conservate nella raccolta delle stampe e dei disegni* (Milan, 1939)
O. A. P. Frutaz: *Le piante di Roma* (Roma, 1962)
L. Benevolo: *La città italiana nel rinascimento* (Milan, 1969), pp. 104–5
I ponti di Roma dalle collezioni del Gabinetto nazionale delle stampe (exh. cat., ed. M. Catelli Isola and E. Beltrane Quattrocchi; Rome, Villa Farnesina, 1975), pp. 33–5
F. Borroni: *Carte, piante e stampe storiche delle raccolte lafreriane della Biblioteca nazionale di Firenze* (Rome, 1980)

STEFANIA MASSARI

Brambilla, Francesco (i) (*fl* Milan, 1560; *d* 22 May 1570). Italian sculptor. He was first documented at Milan Cathedral on 3 August 1560, when he was commissioned to prepare ornamental work for the old organ and to finish it in collaboration with Martino da Vimercate (*fl* 1559–82). In 1565 Brambilla was commissioned to carve the eastern doorway of Milan Cathedral's transept; the doorway was not finished, but some reliefs from it survive in the chapel of the Madonna dell'Albero. On 7 August 1566 Brambilla was paid for the pedestal (*in situ*) for a statue of *Pope Pius IV* by Angelo Siciliano in the cathedral; it is a highly ornate work that demonstrates his love of vigorous plasticity and exuberant decorative sense. These qualities impressed even Giorgio Vasari on his visit to Milan in 1566: he described this work as being 'pierced with holes all over with a group of putti and stupendous foliage' and wrote that its creator was 'a very studious young man'. Such a description, referring to an artist who would be dead in four years, raises doubts about Vasari's judgement and poses the problem of whether the pedestal should not instead be attributed to FRANCESCO BRAMBILLA (ii), who was presumably younger, given that he died in 1599. (The same problem arises with a document of 16 May 1569 allowing Brambilla to work under the guidance of the Lombard sculptor Giovan Battista Rainoldi (*fl* mid-16th century), something that would make little sense if it referred to a mature artist.) It has been proposed (Bossaglia) that the two sculptors were one man, in which case the death of Francesco Brambilla in May 1570 refers to yet another unidentified person. In the face of such uncertainty, which may be resolved by the discovery of new documents, it may be prudent to work with the hypothesis of two sculptors with the same name.

BIBLIOGRAPHY
DBI; Thieme–Becker
G. Vasari: *Vite* (1550, rev. 2/1568); ed. G. Milanesi, vi (1881), pp. 480, 517
A. Venturi: *Storia*, x (1935), p. 702
R. Bossaglia: 'Scultura', *Il duomo di Milano*, ii (Milan, 1973)
M. T. Fiorio and A. P. Valerio: 'La scultura a Milano tra il 1535 e il 1565: Alcuni problemi', *Omaggio a Tiziano: La cultura artistica milanese nell'età di Carlo V* (Milan, 1977), pp. 130–31

Brambilla, Francesco (ii) (*fl* Milan, from 1570; *d* Milan, 1599). Italian sculptor. From documentary evidence chronicling his activity at Milan Cathedral from 1570 to 1599 it is possible to reconstruct his career, identify a phase (1572–86) of close collaboration with Pellegrino Tibaldi and conclude that Brambilla assumed the role of first sculptor of the cathedral. However, there is a possibility that he was the same person as FRANCESCO BRAMBILLA (i). From 1570 Francesco Brambilla (ii) participated in the programme of remodelling the interior of the cathedral instigated by Carlo Borromeo II, Archbishop of Milan. Collaborating with Tibaldi, who provided the designs, Brambilla prepared terracotta models for the wooden choir (*in situ*) of scenes from the *Life of St Ambrose* (one model, Milan, Mus. Duomo), for the statues (*in situ*) for the minor altars and for the marble enclosure (*in situ*) around the choir. In 1584 he delivered clay models for the reliquary bust of *St Tecla* (Milan Cathedral, chapterhouse sacristy). All these works are in a classicizing style, evidently influenced by Michelangelo, characterized by the severe monumentality in which Tibaldi's influence can be discerned. After Borromeo's death (1584) and Tibaldi's departure for Spain (1586), Brambilla continued his activity in Milan Cathedral and virtually assumed the role of overseer for the cathedral sculpture. His most engaging works belong to this phase of his career: the four energetic figures of the *Doctors of the Church* on the southern pulpit (*in situ*), the models (1589; Milan Cathedral) for which were cast in bronze by Giovanni Battista Busca in 1599. Brambilla's involvement in this work is documented by the inscription on the base of *St Augustine*: *Franciscus Brambilla formavit/Io. Baptista Busca fundit MDIC* ('Francisco Brambilla modelled/Giovanni Battista Busca cast 1599'); the attribution of the *Evangelists* on the north pulpit is based on documentation. Early sources also mention Brambilla working for the Certosa, Pavia, and for the churches of S Maria presso S Celso and S Sebastiano, Milan, but no further details are documented.

BIBLIOGRAPHY
G. Vasari: *Vite* (1550, rev. 2/1568); ed. G. Milanesi, vi (1881), pp. 480–517
R. Bossaglia: 'Scultura', *Il duomo di Milano*, ii (Milan, 1973)

M. Cinotti: 'Tesoro e arti minori', *Il duomo di Milano*, ii (Milan, 1973), pp. 265, 275–7, 280–81
R. Bossaglia and M. Cinotti: *Tesoro e Museo del duomo*, ii (Milan, 1978), pp. 11–13, 26
E. Brivio: *La scultura del duomo di Milano* (Milan, 1982), pp. 33–8
G. Anedi: 'Brambilla, Francesco jr.', *Il duomo di Milano: Dizionario storico, artistico e religioso* (Milan, 1986), pp. 106–8

MARIA TERESA FIORIO

Brame, Hector(-Henri-Clément) (*b* Lille, 1831; *d* Paris, 1899). French dealer. The course of his career was entirely shaped by Achille Ricourt (1797–1879), who with funds from the Brame family founded the periodical *L'Artiste*, which he directed from 1831 to 1838, and in which he did much to encourage an interest in modern painting, particularly landscape. After financial failure at *L'Artiste*, Ricourt turned to theatrical management. It was at this point that the young Hector Brame arrived in Paris as Ricourt's protégé and was at once drawn into his theatrical and artistic circles. Following Ricourt's advice, he enrolled at the Conservatoire to train as an actor. At the same time, he haunted sales, visited artists' studios and finally, though already engaged at the Odéon theatre, decided on a change of career and set up as a picture dealer in the Rue Taitbout. The enthusiasm he had acquired from his friend for Eugène Delacroix (Ricourt had owned a number of works by him, including the portrait of *Nicolò Paganini* (Washington, DC, Phillips Col.)) and for the school of 1830 drew him *c.* 1862 to the young Paul Durand-Ruel (see DURAND-RUEL, (2)) whose father had known Ricourt well during the latter's days at *L'Artiste*. Durand-Ruel in his memoirs described the young Brame as 'très actif, ardent et excellent vendeur, mais ses ressources étaient malheureusement fort limitées'. Thus, in the joint purchases on which they were soon to embark, Durand-Ruel frequently bought back Brame's share. Many of these pictures were works by landscape artists whose studios they visited together. Their most important transaction was the acquisition in 1866 of 70 works by Théodore Rousseau, following which they held a special exhibition at the Cercle Artistique in the Rue de Choiseul. Among the many collectors whom they supplied with pictures during the 1860s were a number connected with music and the theatre: the pianist Antoine-François Marmontel (1816–98), for instance, and the singers Léon Carvalho (1825–97) and Jean-Baptiste Faure.

Artists who sold regularly to the two dealers included Eugène Fromentin, Camille Corot, Jules Dupré and Narcisse Diaz, who also sold Brame his Paris house. Brame installed Fromentin in it, and later Ferdinand Roybet, who was to fill it with a spectacular collection of Renaissance *objets d'art*. Jean-François Millet's biographer Alfred Sensier attributed that artist's financial success after 1866 in part to Brame. Emile Zola, who drew largely on the character of Brame for the dealer Naudet in his novel *L'Oeuvre* (1886), stressed his worldly elegance, 'voiture à la porte, fauteuil à l'Opéra', and commented on Brame's methods of improving the social standing of the artists he supported as well as his calculated campaign to boost the prices of their work. This, with some artistic licence, was based particularly on Brame's collaboration with Roybet, who painted Brame's portrait in 1872 (Lyon, Mus. B.-A.).

In 1865 Brame had married the sister of Gustave Tempelaere, a fellow-dealer with a particular interest in Henri Fantin-Latour. Brame's own taste seems to have been for rich, dark, painterly works. He was on close terms with Diaz, bought regularly from Henri Regnault, commissioned Carolus-Duran to paint his young son and chiefly admired, among the Impressionists, Edgar Degas. During the Franco-Prussian War and the Commune (1870–71) Brame worked from Brussels, where Diaz too was in exile. He continued to make joint purchases with Durand-Ruel and maintained a regular correspondence with him during these years, but combined operations virtually ceased after 1872. His son Hector-Gustave Brame took over from his father at the gallery, which was by then in the Rue Laffitte, in about 1892. He continued the policies of his father and maintained the connection with Degas. His son Paul-Louis Brame continued the business and when he died in 1971 was succeeded by Philippe Brame.

BIBLIOGRAPHY

A. Sensier and P. Mantz: *La Vie et l'oeuvre de Jean-François Millet* (Paris, 1881)
E. Zola: *L'Oeuvre* (Paris, 1886)
P. Brady: *'L'Oeuvre' de Emile Zola: Roman sur les arts, manifeste, autobiographie, roman à clef* (Geneva, 1967)
S. Monneret: *L'Impressionnisme et son époque: Dictionnaire international*, 4 vols (Paris, 1978–81)
A. Distel: *Les Collectionneurs des impressionnistes: Amateurs et marchands* (Düdingen, 1989)

LINDA WHITELEY

Bramer, Leonard [Leonaert; Leonardo delle Notti] (*b* Delft, 24 Dec 1596; *d* Delft, *bur* 10 Feb 1674). Dutch painter and draughtsman. The first record of Bramer's career concerns his journey through France and Italy, which he began in 1614. In France he visited Arras, Amiens, Paris, Aix-en-Provence and Marseille. While in Aix he contributed a drawing and a dedicatory poem dated 15 Feb 1616 to the *Album Amicorum* (Leeuwarden, Prov. Bib. Friesland) of his compatriot Wybrand de Geest. This drawing, his earliest known work, depicts three figures in a landscape and shows similarities with the work of Adriaen van de Venne, his reputed teacher (an improbable hypothesis, since van de Venne worked outside Delft and was only 25 when Bramer left Holland). Bramer has also been erroneously described as a follower of Rembrandt.

In Italy, Bramer visited Genoa and Livorno before arriving in Rome, where he lived from 1619 to 1625. De Bie stated that he also visited Venice, Florence, Mantua, Siena, Bologna, Naples and Padua before returning to Delft in 1628 following trouble with the Italian police after a brawl. It is unlikely that Bramer stayed (in Parma) under the patronage of Mario Farnese (Wichmann), because Mario (*d* 1619), a member of a collateral branch of the Farnese family, the dukes of Latera, lived in Rome as general of the pontifical artillery. Another Roman patron of Bramer was the Dominican Cardinal Desiderio Scaglia, an influential member of the papal court under Gregory XV and Urban VIII.

In Rome, Bramer was influenced by the Caravaggesque painters, particularly Adam Elsheimer. His predilection for nightpieces with dramatic chiaroscuro earned him the nickname 'Leonardo delle Notti'. There are no dated paintings from this Italian period—his earliest is dated 1630—but the style of these works probably resembled his later datable works, as Bramer's style did not evolve greatly.

Most of Bramer's paintings feature many small figures set among antique buildings, ruins or thick, dark woods, dramatically lit from one side or from behind, for example *Hecuba* (1630; Madrid, Prado; see fig.). Bramer never concerned himself with details, which are often only sketched in, especially faces and architecture, but concentrated more on composition and preferred expressiveness to formal perfection. This caused later critics to consider him a good psychologist but a poor draughtsman; this, however, was due to Bramer's preoccupation with Italian Baroque art theory, with its emphasis on *Inventio* as the highest artistic quality and the *Concetto* as the basis of creation, ideas stronger in Italy than in the Netherlands.

Bramer's choice of subjects also reflects his preoccupations with Italian rather than Dutch art practice. His paintings generally depict mythological, allegorical, historical or biblical scenes (e.g. the *Denial of St Peter*, Amsterdam, Rijksmus.), rather than popular Dutch subjects such as landscapes, still-lifes, portraits and genre pieces. Even the Italianate pastoral scenes favoured by compatriots such as the Utrecht Caravaggisti are rare in his work. This was probably due to the influence of his patrons, first in Rome and later in the Netherlands, rather than to a lack of contact with other Dutch painters. Bramer was among the earliest members of the Bentvueghels or SCHILDERSBENT, the company of Dutch artists formed in Rome in the early 1620s; he was known under the *Bent*-name of Nestelghat.

Bramer became a member of the Guild of St Luke in Delft in 1629. His prominent position is shown by the commissions given to him before 1647 by Stadholder Frederick Henry and his nephew Prince John Maurice of Nassau-Siegen for their palaces at The Hague (now the Mauritshuis), Rijswijk and Honselaarsdijk (both destr.). Bramer also worked for public institutions in Delft and the surrounding cities from 1630 to 1670. He even tried to use the Italian fresco technique for some murals in the Gemeenlandshuis van Delfland, the Nieuwe Doelen and the corridor of the house of his neighbour Anthonie van Bronchorst in Delft; these did not survive the unsuitable Dutch climate despite Bramer's frequent restorations. In 1668 the artist painted an *Ascension* on the ceiling of the main hall of the Prinsenhof in Delft (*in situ*; now Delft, Stedel. Mus. Prinsenhof).

After 1635 Bramer produced many drawings. Only rarely are the drawings related to his paintings; most are independent works of art, often representing literary or historical scenes. Many form large cycles illustrating a particular book, for example the Bible (Amsterdam, Rijksmus.), Quevedo's *Sueños* and the picaresque novel *Lazarillo de Tormes* (both Munich, Staatl. Graph. Samml.), Ovid and Virgil, some containing up to 100 drawings. Most of these cycles are executed in ink or pencil, but some are watercolours painted in an original style showing the influence of Italian Mannerism. The illustrations always follow the text closely enough to show that Bramer was a discriminating reader and did not always follow pictorial conventions.

Leonard Bramer: *Hecuba*, oil on copper, 450×590 mm, 1630 (Madrid, Museo del Prado)

An album attributed to Bramer (Amsterdam, Rijksmus.) contains 56 drawings rapidly sketched in black chalk, which are copies of paintings by contemporary artists, most of whom are named on the bottom of each drawing. The owners of the works were mostly wealthy Delft burghers, artists and art dealers, as can be seen from an inscription on the back of one drawing. The artists whose works are represented include Jan Asselijn, Gerard ter Borch (ii), Adriaen Brouwer, Karel Dujardin, Gerrit van Honthorst, Roelandt Savery, Hercules Segers and Bramer himself. The album originally consisted of many more drawings, but it nevertheless gives a useful insight into the quality of mid-17th-century Delft art collections. The function of the album is uncertain, but it was probably intended as an illustrated catalogue of paintings to be sold by the named owners. No other album of its kind exists.

Bramer lived with his sister in a smart house in the centre of Delft. He is not known to have had any pupils. Adriaen Verdoel (*c.* 1620–*c.* 1690) and even Johannes Vermeer have been suggested, but there is no conclusive evidence, although Bramer and Vermeer's parents are known to have been friends. After his death, Bramer's fame declined quickly and steadily until the late 19th century.

BIBLIOGRAPHY

Thieme–Becker
C. de Bie: *Het gulden cabinet* (Antwerp, 1661), pp. 252–3

H. Wichmann: *Leonaert Bramer, sein Leben und seine Kunst* (Leipzig, 1923) [Only extant monograph on Bramer, but partially outdated and incomplete]
G. J. Hoogewerff: *De Bentvueghels* (The Hague, 1952)
J. M. Montias: *Artists and Artisans in Delft: A Socio-economic Analysis of the Seventeenth Century* (Princeton, 1982)
J. ten Brink Goldsmith: 'From Prose to Pictures: Leonaert Bramer's Illustrations for the Aeneid and Vondel's Translation of Virgil', *A. Hist.*, vii/1 (March, 1984), pp. 21–37
M. Plomp: ' "Een merkwaardige verzameling teekeningen" door Leonaert Bramer' ['A remarkable collection of drawings' by Leonaert Bramer], *Oud-Holland*, c/2 (1986), pp. 81–153

J. W. NOLDUS

Bramley, Frank (*b* Sibsey, Lincs, 6 May 1857; *d* Chalford, Glos, 10 Aug 1915). English painter. He attended Lincoln School of Art from 1873 to 1878. He studied from 1879 to 1882 with Charles Verlat at the Koninklijke Academie voor Schone Kunsten in Antwerp, as did other future Newlyn school painters such as Fred Hall (1860–1948), Thomas Cooper Gotch and Norman Garstin. After a period in Venice (1882–4) Bramley joined the artists' colony in Newlyn, Cornwall, where he stayed until 1895. The NEWLYN SCHOOL became known for its Cornish genre scenes and *plein-air* approach, but *Domino* (1886; Cork, Crawford Mun. A.G.) typifies Bramley's initial interest in interiors with varied natural and artificial light effects, as well as his involvement with tonal harmonies and the surface qualities of the square brush.

Like Garstin and Hall, Bramley tried to balance his own aesthetic concerns with an emotional and narrative content that would appeal to the general public. *A Hopeless Dawn* (1888; London, Tate; *see* ENGLAND, fig. 21) successfully combined formal strengths with the dramatic and emotional power that *Domino* lacked. It was purchased by the Chantrey Bequest trustees and established Bramley's reputation. In the early 1890s his paint became brighter, thicker and looser. His subject-range narrowed to portraits, rural genre paintings—often symbolic—and quiet scenes of the elderly reflecting on their past. Bramley regularly exhibited at the Royal Academy from 1884 to 1912. He was made an ARA in 1894 and an RA in 1911. He settled in Grasmere, Westmorland (now Cumbria), in 1900.

BIBLIOGRAPHY
C. Hiatt: 'Mr Frank Bramley, ARA, and his Work', *Mag. A.* (1903), pp. 54–9
Artists of the Newlyn School, 1880–1900 (exh. cat. by C. Fox and F. Greenacre, Newlyn, Orion Gals, 1979), pp. 162–71
Painting in Newlyn, 1880–1930 (exh. cat. by C. Fox and F. Greenacre, London, Barbican A.G., 1985)
B. Cogger Rezelman: 'Frank Bramley's *Primrose Day*: A Disraeli Tribute and Artistic Gamble', *Vict. Rev.*, xvii/1 (1991), pp. 51–77
BETSY COGGER REZELMAN

Brancacci, Felice (di Michele) (*b* Florence, 1382; *d* Siena, 1449–55). Italian patron and diplomat. He was a member of a Florentine patrician family with interests in shipping. Between 1412 and 1433 he held various public offices and served the Florentine republic on diplomatic missions involving the supervision of military campaigns. In 1422–3 he was sent as ambassador to Cairo to secure commercial concessions for Florentine merchants. He favoured a close relationship between Florence and the papacy and in 1433 went to Rome on a diplomatic mission to offer the protection of Florence to Pope Eugene IV. Felice's importance for the history of art rests on the presumption that he commissioned the frescoes (*c.* 1425–8) painted by MASOLINO and MASACCIO in the Brancacci Chapel in S Maria del Carmine, Florence. Although Felice was legal owner of the chapel from 1422 to 1434, no evidence links him directly to the two artists. The chapel was founded by his uncle, Pietro Brancacci (*d* 1366–7), whose son Antonio Brancacci made a bequest concerning it in his will dated 16 August 1383. The frescoes in the chapel remained unfinished when Masolino and Masaccio went to Rome, presumably at the beginning of 1428. Felice's second will of 5 September 1432 contains a provision that his heirs and executors were to undertake the completion of the decorations should they be unfinished at the time of his death. The frecoes, however, remained incomplete until they were finished by Filippino Lippi in the late 1480s. In 1434, when Cosimo de' Medici returned to Florence after a year's exile, Felice himself went into exile to Siena, compromised by suspicions of having plotted against the Medici.

BIBLIOGRAPHY
DBI
H. Brockhaus: 'Die Brancacci-Kapelle in Florenz', *Mitt. Ksthist. Inst. Florenz*, iii (1929–32), pp. 160–82
U. Procacci: 'Sulla cronologia delle opere di Masaccio e di Masolino tra il 1425 e il 1428', *Riv. A.*, xxviii (1953), pp. 16–31
P. Meller: 'La cappella Brancacci', *Acropoli*, 3 (1960–61), pp. 186–277
A. Molho: 'The Brancacci Chapel: Studies in its Iconography and History', *J. Warb. & Court. Inst.*, xl (1977), pp. 70–71, 74–81, 86–96
J. Beck: *Masaccio, the Documents* (Locust Valley, 1978), pp. 55–60
HELLMUT WOHL

Branchidai. *See* DIDYMA.

Branco, Cassiano (*b* Lisbon, 15 Aug 1897; *d* Lisbon, 24 April 1970). Portuguese architect. He graduated in architecture (1926) from the Escola de Belas Artes, Lisbon, and early in his career produced one of the most impressive Art Deco buildings in Lisbon, the Eden cinema (1930–31; with Carlos Dias; later altered), Praça dos Restauradores. This building incorporated suggestions of Futurism, notably in the dynamic spatial design and definition of the main entrance and staircase system as well as the volumetric glass façade. He also designed one of the city's most imaginative Rationalist buildings, the Hotel Vitória (1934; *see* PORTUGAL, fig. 5), Avenida da Liberdade. He later worked on the Coliseum (1939; with Júlio de Brito and Mário de Abreu) in Rua Passos Manuel, Oporto, another important Modernist building. One of the most talented architects of the early Modern Movement in Portugal, Branco was an unusual figure and a combative personality; his early involvement in left-wing political activity resulted in his increasing professional isolation in the context of the reactionary government (1932–68) of António de Oliveira Salazar. Receiving almost no official commissions during the 1930s, he worked for private builders in Lisbon on various developments whose ground-plans were as conventional as their façades were inventive; examples include 179A Rua do Salitre (1934); 44–48 Avenida Álvares Cabral (1936); 3–9A Rua Nova de São Mamede (1937); and 27 Avenida Defensores de Chaves (1937). He also designed town houses with a lively Purist treatment of mass, including several in Avenida A. José de Almeida (1933) and 87 Avenida C. Bordalo Pinheiro (1937; destr.), as well as the mirror-decorated Café Cristal (1940–42; destr.), 131 Avenida da Liberdade, all in Lisbon. He later made surprising and ironical use of the historicist vocabulary of the officially approved style, for example Parque Portugal dos Pequenitos (1937–44) in Coimbra and Hotel do Luso (1938; altered), near Coimbra, and the Império cinema (1948; altered), Alameda Afonso Henriques, and residential block (1951), Praça de Londres, both in Lisbon. He also worked on plans for bridges and dams, and a railway station for Benguela in Angola.

BIBLIOGRAPHY
J.-A. França: *A arte em Portugal no século XX* (Lisbon, 1974), pp. 229–31
Cassiano Branco (exh. cat. by R. Hestnes Ferreira and F. Gomes da Silva, Lisbon, Assoc. Arquit., 1981 and 1986)
Cassiano Branco—Uma obra para o futuro, Câmara Municipal, ed.; coordination by M. do Rosário Bonneville and others (Lisbon, 1991)
JOSÉ MANUEL FERNANDES

Brancusi, Constantin (*b* Hobitza, Gorj, 19 Feb 1876; *d* Paris, 16 March 1957). French sculptor, draughtsman, painter and photographer of Romanian birth. He was one of the most influential 20th-century sculptors, but he left a relatively small body of work centred on 215 sculptures, of which about 50 are thought to have been lost or destroyed.

1. Early years, to *c.* 1907. 2. Years of maturity, *c.* 1907–34. 3. Final projects, 1935 and after.

1. EARLY YEARS, TO *c.* 1907. The fifth of seven children of a family of peasants, he left his tiny village *c.* 1887 for Slatina, after which he made his way to Craiova, the provincial capital of Oltenia. There he became a student at the School of Arts and Crafts in 1894. Mechanical technology, industrial design, mathematics and physics figured prominently on his syllabus with some theoretical studies. He did not, therefore, receive a traditional academic training in sculpture; in fact he began studying at the newly founded Academy of Fine Arts in Bucharest, but even there instruction was still at an experimental stage, particularly in sculpture.

Brancusi is thought to have been prolific in his student years in Craiova. Various objects subsequently discovered on the premises of his old school have been attributed to him, some of them perhaps as collaborations with other fellow students, including a walnut casket (Craiova, Maria C. S. Nicolăescu-Plopșor priv. col., see Brezianu, 1976, p. 203), two elaborately carved limewood frames (Craiova, Mus. Sch. A. & Crafts), a loom (see Brezianu, 1976, p. 199) and a rather peculiar oak corner chair (see Brezianu, 1976, p. 204). His first documented sculpture also dates from this period: a clay bust, based on a photograph, of *Gheorghe Chitu* (exh. 1898; lost; see Brezianu, 1976, p. 206), a hero of the Revolution of 1848 and founder of the School of Arts and Crafts in Craiova. Brancusi studied sculpture from 1898 to 1902 at the Academy of Fine Arts in Bucharest. Among the few surviving sculptures of this period are a portrait of one of his friends from Craiova, *Ion Georgescu-Gorjan* (1902; Bucharest, Stefan Georgescu-Gorjan priv. col., see Brezianu, 1976, p. 64), and a plaster bust of the Roman *Emperor Vitellius* (1898; Craiova, Mus. A.).

In 1903 Brancusi left Romania for Paris, according to his own romanticized account (Jianou, p. 30) taking nearly two years to arrive there by foot but reaching the city in the summer of 1904. Supporting himself by washing dishes in a restaurant, from April 1905 to 1907 he studied at the Académie des Beaux-Arts under Antonin Mercié. Only one sculpture from 1905 survives, *Pride* (Craiova, Mus. A.), the head of a young girl cast in bronze from plaster. This was one of three works exhibited at the Salon d'Automne in 1906. It was succeeded by representations of children, such as *Head of Child* (exh. 1907, Paris, Salon), in which he revealed his incipient interest in the partial figure, and *Torment* (versions in plaster and bronze; all priv. cols, see Brezianu, 1976, pp. 88, 90, 92–3), for which he used the same boy as a model, and in which the influence of Medardo Rosso and especially of Auguste Rodin is apparent. A marble version of *Torment*, known only from a photograph (see Geist, 1975, p. 174), may have been Brancusi's earliest attempt at direct carving. Two other projects were executed by Brancusi in 1906: a portrait of the painter *Nicolae Darascu* (Bucharest, Mus. A.), in which he continued to experiment with the partial figure by eliminating the right arm almost at shoulder level, and a beautiful marble head entitled *Sleep* (see Brezianu, 1976, p. 95).

In 1907 Brancusi received a commission from a rich Romanian widow for a funerary monument in memory of her recently deceased husband. The contract stipulated a stone pedestal and two sculptures in bronze: an allegorical figure of a weeping woman and a portrait bust to be executed after a photograph. Initially Brancusi intended to comply with this plan, but he destroyed his first model as unimaginative and instead made the bold decision to represent a nude figure kneeling in prayer. The *Prayer* and the portrait of *Petre Stănescu* (Buzău, Dumbrava Cemetery) bring to a close Brancusi's formative years.

2. YEARS OF MATURITY, *c.* 1907–34.
(i) Direct carvings and bronzes. Later in 1907 Brancusi produced the first version of *The Kiss*, a subject to which he returned as late as 1945, one of his first direct carvings and one which marked a dramatic change in his aesthetic in favour of a powerful reduction to simplified block-like form, the two figures seeming to merge into one entity. The earliest example of the series is generally thought to be a bust-length version (stone; Craiova, Mus. A.) but may have been a full-length version (Paris, Montparnasse Cemetery). There were at least six other versions (e.g. Philadelphia, PA, Mus. A.; and four undocumented versions that were never exhibited or sold, e.g. Paris, Pompidou). Also dating from 1906–8 are the *Wisdom of the Earth* (limestone; Bucharest, Mus. A.), a strange and disturbing representation of a seated woman, and the closely related *Ancient Figure* (Chicago, IL, A. Inst.), which Brancusi appears to have later repudiated but which is usually considered to be by his hand.

Like many 20th-century artists Brancusi looked for inspiration to non-European cultures as a source of 'primitive' vitality (*see* PRIMITIVISM, §2) and under their impact abandoned modelling in favour of carving. Although he did not make reference to African sculpture, a major influence on avant-garde artists of the period, in 1907–8 he carved several mask-like faces in stone (untraced; see Tabart and Monod-Fontaine, fig. 5; e.g. *Head of a Young Girl*, see Geist, 1975, p. 176), that bear comparison with African-influenced works of similar date by Pablo Picasso and André Derain. Brancusi's complete break with formulas associated with Rodin's work cannot be convincingly explained by reference to African models, but he may have turned to the exotic repertory of Romanian masks, such as those representing animal or comic characters, traceable through ancient and Byzantine mimes to Dionysian rites and still used in Romania in performances at the close of New Year celebrations. In this dependence on forms of folk art, another aspect of his primitivist impulse, Brancusi again demonstrated his alliance with the concerns of other avant-garde artists of the late 19th century and early 20th, including Gauguin, Derain, Picasso and Matisse.

In 1909 Brancusi turned to subjects such as the *Sleeping Child* and the *Sleeping Muse* (e.g. *Sleeping Muse*, 1910; Paris, Pompidou), in which he boldly introduced ovoids as virtually self-sufficient objects, remaining on the threshold of abstraction through the identification of the forms with the human body. In the most extreme works of this type, such as *Sculpture for the Blind* (1916; Philadelphia, PA, Mus. A.; see fig. 1) and the *Beginning of the World* (1920;

1. Constantin Brancusi: *Sculpture for the Blind*, marble, h. 153 mm, 1916 (Philadelphia, PA, Museum of Art)

Pasadena, CA, Norton Simon Mus.), the near perfection of the ovoids and the smoothing out of the protuberances have erased the facial features to such an extent that the human subject is almost unrecognizable.

The reductionist tendencies and organic softening of Brancusi's sculpture at this time can be attributed in part to his friendship from 1909 with Amedeo Modigliani, who had sought him out because of his interest in carving, and to the far-reaching influence on him of the work of Elie Nadelman, whose sculpture and drawings were exhibited with great success at the Galerie Druet in the same year. Nadelman's work appears to have prompted the ideas developed by Brancusi in such bronzes as the *Sleeping Muse*, *The Muse* (ex-Guggenheim, New York; see Geist, 1975, p. 83) and *The Danaïde* (1911; London, Tate). *Mlle Pogany* (plaster, 1912; Paris, Pompidou), exhibited in 1913 at the Armory Show in New York, was followed by later bronze versions (1913; Bucharest, Mus. A.; see fig. 2; 1919; Winnetka, IL, Mr and Mrs James Alsdorf priv. col., see Geist, 1975, p. 92; 1931; Philadelphia, PA, Mus. A.) that vividly demonstrate Brancusi's method of progressive reduction and simplification of form.

A similar process of abstraction was applied by Brancusi to a series of sculptures of birds, inaugurated in 1910 with the mythical *Maiastra* (bronze; London, Tate), further developed in the *Golden Bird* (1919; Chicago, IL, A. Club) and culminating in the *Bird in Space* series, of which the

first version was made in 1923 (New York, Mrs Wolfgang Schoenborn priv. col., see Geist, 1975, p. 113). Brancusi was rare among 20th-century sculptors in his interest in portraying animals with tenderness, originality and affection, often with a touch of mischievous humour. Among such subjects were *The Penguins*, represented in groups of two or three (1912–14; e.g. Philadelphia, PA, Mus. A.), *The Fish* (Winnetka, IL, Mr and Mrs James Alsdorf priv. col., see Geist, 1975, p. 114), *The Cock* (New York, MOMA), the *Little Bird* (1925; New York, Marlborough Gal.), *The Seal* (1924–36; New York, Guggenheim) and flying and earthbound *Turtles* (e.g. Paris, Pompidou). The *Nocturnal Beast* (*c.* 1930; Paris, Pompidou; see fig. 3), carved in wood, depicts a solitary creature, perhaps a hedgehog, scurrying silently in search of nourishment; the entire mystery of its nocturnal existence is evoked in the simple, humped shape.

(ii) Works in wood. Brancusi's interest in wood extended beyond sculpture to more purely practical applications, for example as furniture for his studio or as bases or plinths for his sculptures. The earliest documented wooden sculpture, the *First Step* (1913; see Geist, 1975, p. 180), was exhibited in 1914 at Alfred Stieglitz's gallery, 291, in New York; although he later destroyed this work, preserving only the head by casting it in bronze as the *First Cry* (Lady Nika Hulton, on loan to Humlebaek,

2. Constantin Brancusi: *Mlle Pogany*, polished bronze with black patina, 440×245×305 mm, 1913 (Bucharest, Museum of Art)

Louisiana Mus.), he soon began to produce roughly carved wooden bases for other works and to present those virtually as sculptures in their own right, perhaps prompted by the ready-mades of his friend Marcel Duchamp. In 1915 Brancusi made his first functional objects, the arch and the bench, followed by an entire array of furniture for his studio; these objects, too, suggest his awareness of the Dada movement in Paris, with which he became closely involved, especially through his friendship with another native Romanian, the poet Tristan Tzara.

The prototypes of Brancusi's wooden columns, cups, arches and in some cases his wooden sculptures can be traced to Romanian folk art and in particular to wood carvings. Each of the constituent sections of the *King of Kings* (New York, Guggenheim), for example, made in the early 1930s, bears a strong formal resemblance to such objects of everyday use as chairbacks, mill screws, porch pillars and mugs; the very title of this work may have been inspired by traditional Romanian Christmas carols, in which each new verse begins with the phrase in question.

(iii) Photography. Brancusi had taken photographs while a student, but it was not until 1921, when he met Man Ray, that the form took on a particular significance. Partly due to dissatisfaction with other people's photographs of his sculpture, he installed a darkroom in his studio and asked Man Ray's assistance in improving his photographic technique. Brancusi's photographs are not simply records of his sculpture; they show a concern with light and environment inherent in his sculptural works and often document the evolution of a sculpture. They fall into two categories: pictures of single sculptures isolated from their studio background, for example of the marble sculpture of 1912, *Mlle Pogany, Full Face* (see 1978 exh. cat., no. 16), and photographs of the studio environment, such as *General View of the Studio, 8, Impasse Ronsin, Paris 15e* (*c.* 1925; see 1978 exh. cat., no. 11). An archive of Brancusi's photographic work is housed in the Musée National d'Art Moderne in Paris and contains about 1250 photographic prints and 560 original negatives, mostly glass.

3. Constantin Brancusi: *Nocturnal Beast*, wood, 247×693×178 mm, *c.* 1930 (Paris, Pompidou, Musée National d'Art Moderne)

3. FINAL PROJECTS, 1935 AND AFTER. In 1935 Brancusi was commissioned by the maharajah Jaswant Rao Holkar II of Indore to build a Temple of Deliverance in the grounds of his palace in India as a place of meditation; after the death of the maharajah's young wife in 1936 it was also to be a mausoleum. Brancusi, who had wished to build a Temple of Love as early as 1930, discussed his plans with the Romanian engineer Stefan Georgescu-Gorjan in Paris in 1936 and visited India from December 1937 to January 1938. For political and other reasons the temple was never built.

Brancusi's only completed monumental complex, considered by some his greatest work, synthesizing the elements of his previous art, was the Tirgu-Jiu Complex in Romania, inaugurated on 27 October 1938. It consists of the *Endless Column* (see fig. 4), intended as a votive and funerary monument in memory of the soldiers who fell during World War I, the *Table of Silence* (a circular table surrounded by twelve circular hour-glass-shaped stools), the *Gate of the Kiss* (flanked by stone benches placed on each of the short sides) and thirty square hour-glass stools arranged in groups of three stools arranged in five recessed niches on each side of the alley uniting the table and portal. He had made four other *Endless Columns*, one of which was carved from an oak tree in the garden of Edward J. Steichen (*c.* 1920; ex-Voulangis, see 1969 exh. cat., p. 91). After completion of the ensemble, Brancusi concentrated

his attention largely on refining and simplifying his favourite motifs, such as *The Kiss* and the *Bird in Space*, to which he remained faithful to the end of his life.

BIBLIOGRAPHY

V. Huszár: 'Constantin Brancusi', *De Stijl* (1917–18)
D. V. Baker, ed.: 'Brancusi', *Little Rev.* (Autumn 1921; *R* in *The Little Review Anthology*, New York, 1953) [whole issue; illus. with photographs by Brancusi]
W. Zorach: 'The Sculpture of Constantin Brancusi', *The Arts* [New York], ix/3 (1926), pp. 145–50
T. van Doesburg: 'Constantin Brancusi', *De Stijl*, 79–84 (1927), pp. 81–6
C. Gieldion-Welcker: 'Constantin Brancusi', *Horizon*, 11 (1949), pp. 193–202
C. Zervos: 'Brancusi', *Cah. A.*, xxx (1955), pp. 153–243; as book *Brancusi: Sculpture, peintures, fresques, dessins* (Paris, 1957)
D. Lewis: *Brancusi* (London, 1957)
H.-P. Roche: 'Souvenirs sur Brancusi', *L'Oeil*, 29 (1957), pp. 12–17
C. Gieldion-Welcker: *Constantin Brancusi* (Neuchâtel, 1959)
I. Jianou: *Brancusi* (Paris, 1963)
B. Brezianu: 'Les Débuts de Brancusi', *Rev. Roum. Hist. A.*, i/1 (1964), pp. 85–100; Eng. trans. in *A. J.* [New York], xxv/1 (1965), pp. 15–25
——: 'Pages inédites de la correspondance de Brancusi', *Rev. Roum. Hist. A.*, i/2 (1964), pp. 385–400
P. Neagoe: *The Saint of Montparnasse* (Philadelphia and New York, 1965)
P. Comarnesco, M. Eliade and I. Jianou: *Témoignages sur Brancusi* (Paris, 1967)
V. G. Paleolog: *Tinereţea lui Brâncusi* (Bucharest, 1967)
P. Pandrea: *Amintiri si exegeze* (Bucharest, 1967)
S. Geist: *Brancusi: A Study of the Sculpture* (New York, 1968)
B. Brezianu: 'Brancusi l'artisan', *Rev. Roum. Hist. A.*, vi (1969), pp. 19–30
A. T. Spear: *Brancusi's Birds* (New York, 1969)
Constantin Brancusi (exh. cat. by S. Geist, New York, Guggenheim, 1969)
E. Balas: 'The Sculpture of Brancusi in the Light of his Romanian Heritage', *A. J.* [New York], xxxv/2 (1975)
S. Geist: *Brancusi: The Sculpture and the Drawings* (New York, 1975)
B. Brezianu: *Brancusi in Romania* (Bucharest, 1976)
V. G. Paleolog: *Brancusi, Brancusi* (Craiova, 1976)
Constantin Brancusi (exh. cat., Duisburg, Lehmbruck-Mus., 1976)
E. Balas: 'The Myth of African Negro Art in Brancusi's Sculpture', *Rev. Roum. Hist. A.*, xiv (1977), pp. 107–24
S. Geist: *The Kiss* (New York, 1978)
Constantin Brancusi: Photographies (exh. cat., essays by Y. Nakahara, E. Hosoe and K. Monon; Tokyo, Gal. Tokoro, 1978) [Jap. and Fr. text]
Brancusi photographe (exh. cat. by M. Tabart and I. Monod-Fontaine, Paris, Pompidou, 1979)
D. Grigorescu: *Brancusi* (Bucharest, 1980)
A. Istrati and N. Dumitresco: *Brancusi* (Paris, 1986)
R. Varia: *Brancusi* (New York, 1986)

SANDA MILLER

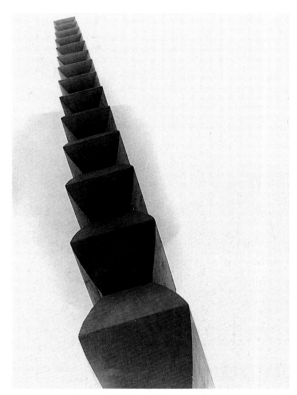

4. Constantin Brancusi: *Endless Column*, iron beads on a steel core, h. 29.33 m, 1938; part of the Tirgu-Jiu Complex, Tirgu-Jiu, Romania

Brand. Austrian family of painters.

(1) Christian Hilfgott [Hülfgott] **Brand** (*b* Frankfurt an der Oder, 16 March 1694; *d* Vienna, 22 July 1756). He attended school in Hamburg but later lived in Regensburg, where his acquaintance with Christoph Ludwig Agricola led him to take up landscape painting. About 1720 he went to Vienna. From 1726 to 1728 Brand studied at the Akademie der Bildenden Künste in Vienna, was elected as one of its first honorary members in 1751 and became an academic advisor in 1754. In 1738 Brand is mentioned as an imperial court painter, a position he held for the rest of his life.

Brand belongs to a group of minor Austrian painters of cabinet pictures that included Karl Aigen (1684–1762), Josef Orient (1677–1747), Franz de Paula Ferg, Franz Christoph Janneck and his son (2)Johann Christian Brand, and his work is not always easily distinguishable from theirs. Brand's earliest works, such as *Landscape with Trees*, *a Village and Peasants* (Prague, N.G., Šternberk Pal.), have dark tonalities, which later become brighter, reflecting the influence of the Rococo, as in *Ruin with Shepherds* (Prague, N.G., Šternberk Pal.). All his works show a close study of 17th-century Dutch and Flemish art. His paintings carried out in the Dutch manner especially pleased contemporary collectors.

ELISABETH HERRMANN-FICHTENAU

(2) Johann Christian Brand (*b* Vienna, 6 March 1722; *d* Vienna, 12 June 1795). Son of (1) Christian Hilfgott Brand, from whom he received his first instruction in landscape painting. In 1736 he became a pupil at the Akademie der Bildenden Künste, Vienna. In 1751–6 he was in the service of Nikolaus VIII, Graf Palffy, on his estates in Hungary and at his residence in Bratislava (now Slovakia). During this period he painted his earliest-known *veduta*, *Landscape near Devin Castle, at the Confluence of the Morava and the Danube* (Prague, N.G., Šternberk Pal.). After returning to Vienna, Brand was commissioned in 1758 by the imperial family to paint a series of four scenes of a *Heron Hunt in the Region of Laxenburg* (Vienna, Belvedere, Österreich. Barockmus.). These were the first great studies from nature of the area around Vienna, recognizable in its topographical features and characteristic atmosphere. They are bird's-eye views, whereas in the two large *vedute Lake of Neusiedl* (1764) and *Bruck Castle* (1765; both Austria, priv. col.), the observer's standpoint is a hill with a view of the wide plain, so that the horizon is lowered.

However, idealized landscape also accounts for a large part of Brand's output, derived in particular from 17th-century Dutch and Italian painting. The 20 monochrome pastels in the Dutch manner (1765; Vienna, Hist. Mus.)

ordered by Empress Maria-Theresa for the decoration of the Rotes Pastellzimmer in the Blauer Hof at Laxenburg were in deliberate contrast to the blue pastels executed two years earlier in the French Rococo style by Jean Pillement. In 1766 Brand was appointed court painter, a position that provided him with a regular income and further imperial commissions, such as that for his celebrated *Battle of Hochkirch* (after 1769; Vienna, Belvedere, Österreich. Barockmus.).

On 11 March 1769 Brand was appointed a member of the Vienna Akademie; his reception piece was *Landscape with Workers in the Vineyard* (1769; Vienna, Akad. Bild. Kst.); on 5 May of the same year he was appointed to the academic board and made Professor of Landscape Drawing. However, Brand was only able to teach there after the death in 1771 of Franz Edmund Weirotter, who had been the first teacher of landscape drawing at the Akademie. From 1759 Brand corresponded with Jean-Georges Wille in Paris and exchanged numerous paintings and drawings with him. Brand shared Wille's view on the importance of drawing from nature for specific details, taught at the Académie Royale de Peinture et de Sculpture in Paris and expressed in many contemporary aesthetic writings. Brand went further, however, instructing his pupils to make landscape studies entirely from nature also for general effects. The sensitive management of form in Brand's drawings and watercolours reveals French influence, but his intellectual grasp of reality makes clear an individual approach to the scene where the human being is harmoniously integrated into the landscape and shown engaged in appropriate activities, as in his many drawings of the Prater and the regions around Vienna (e.g. Vienna, Albertina, Akad. Bild. Kst. and Hist. Mus.). The peak of Brand's progressive view of the painted *veduta* is seen in the *Great*

Johann Christian Brand: *Great Sand-pit*, oil on canvas, 0.64×1.15 m, 1774 (Nuremberg, Germanisches Nationalmuseum)

Sand-pit (1774; Nuremberg, Ger. Nmus.; see fig.), where nature is the main subject: the large Schlosshof is less significant than the wild rocky terrain of the mountain crest at Devin, illuminated by harsh sunlight. For such paintings Brand made sketches from nature in black or red chalk (e.g. study for the *Great Sand-pit*, Vienna, Akad. Bild. Kst.), and the finished oil painting was executed in the studio.

In 1773 Brand started to draw sketches for a series of prints, after the example of Edme Bouchardon's *Cries of Paris* (1737–46). 'Street cries' were a type of print widely sold at that time in many European cities. The first edition of Brand's *Drawings of Ordinary People and especially Cries of Vienna* appeared in 1775–6, engraved by pupils of the Kupferstecher Akademie, which was founded in 1766 (original drawings of *The Ribbon Seller* and *The Straw Cutter* in Vienna, Albertina). The six drawings *Views of the Town of Klosterneuburg* (c. 1779; Vienna, Akad. Bild. Kst.) were also models for copperplate engravings that were never executed; this set of small detailed pictures of a medieval town anticipates the subject-matter and style of series produced by Romantic artists. With the appointment of Heinrich Füger as deputy director at the Vienna Akademie in 1783, Neo-classical currents began to appear in Brand's work. Mythological, historical and religious themes were adopted, and landscape was treated as a mere stage (e.g. the scene from an idyll by the poet Salomon Gessner, *Here Lie the Ashes of Mycon*, 1787; priv. col.). Characteristic features in the ideal landscapes of this phase were ancient ruins, temples and funerary monuments.

At heart, however, Brand remained devoted to observed nature. In his late work *View of Klosterneuburg from the Bisamberg* (1792; Klosterneuburg, Augustin.-Chorherrenstift), the Danube plain is seen almost as a panorama in a view notable for a new sense of atmospheric depth. The small, hastily painted oil sketch *Danube Landscape with Vienna, Viewed from the Bisamberg* (Vienna, Belvedere, Österreich. Barockmus.) marks a final phase in Brand's development. It appears to have been painted in nature, and it thus constitutes a move towards the *plein-air* painting of the 19th century. In his technique and handling of colour and light, Brand remained subject to the decorative principles of the Rococo. His importance lies both in the new perception of nature in his drawn studies and in a new realism in his landscape *vedute*.

BIBLIOGRAPHY

Thieme–Becker

K. Garzarolli-Thurnlackh: *Die barocke Handzeichnung in Österreich* (Zurich, 1928)
H. Aurenhammer: 'J. C. Brand und die Entdeckung der Wiener Landschaft', *Mitt. Österreich. Gal.*, xxxiv–xxxvi (1959), pp. 12–23
F. Novotny: *Painting and Sculpture in Europe, 1780–1880*, Pelican Hist. A. (Harmondsworth, 1960), pp. 38, 46
P. Pötschner: *Genesis der Wiener Biedermeierlandschaft*, Wiener Schriften, 19 (Vienna, 1964)
H. Kaut: *Kaufrufe aus Wien* (Vienna and Munich, 1970)
R. Feuchtmüller: *Kunst in Österreich*, ii (Vienna, Munich and Basle, 1973)
S. Hofstätter: *Johann Christian Brand, 1722–95* (diss., U. Vienna, 1973)
Österreichische Barockmaler aus der National-Galerie in Prag (exh. cat., ed. P. Preiss; Vienna, Belvedere, 1977–8)
P. Pötschner: *Wien und die Wiener Landschaft* (Salzburg, 1978)
E. Baum: *Katalog des Österreichischen Barockmuseum in Unteren Belvedere in Wien* (Vienna and Munich, 1980), pp. 62–88

S. SCHUSTER-HOFSTÄTTER

Brandani, Federico (*b* Urbino, *c.* 1524–5; *d* Urbino, 20 Sept 1575). Italian stuccoist and sculptor. He enjoyed extensive patronage from the court of Guidobaldo II della Rovere, Duke of Urbino, for whom he modelled fireplaces and entire ceilings representing allegories of princely prerogative and aristocratic supremacy. This practice, unusual in Italy (where stucco was generally a decorative adjunct to fresco), may be partly explained by the fact that Guidobaldo did not retain a permanent court painter.

Between 1538 and 1541 Brandani was apprenticed in Urbino to Giovanni Maria di Casteldurante, a maiolica artist, but his earliest known work (*c.* 1551) is the luxuriant and overcrowded stucco ceiling, modelled with five relief scenes from the *Life of St Peter*, in the chapel of the Palazzo Corte Rossa, Fossombrone, near Urbino, for Cardinal Giulio della Rovere (1533–78). In 1552–3 Brandani made contributions to the stucco decoration at the Villa Giulia, Rome, modelling friezes, small roundels and grotesques in the rooms left and right of the entrance.

Brandani's first independent commission (*c.* 1559) was a ceiling at the Palazzo Ronca at Fabriano; this has boldly inventive strapwork, using elements from engravings by Enea Vico and from Book IV of Sebastiano Serlio's treatise on architecture. This ceiling is surpassed in intricacy only by the one he made (*c.* 1559) at Palazzo Tiranni, Cagli, near Urbino, which betrays an acquaintance with Lelio Orsi's decorative designs. In the Palazzetto Baviera, Senigallia (begun 1560), the reliefs of the Salone di Ercole and Salone di Troia are copied from drawings for maiolica by Battista Franco but those of the Salone della Repubblica Romana are of his own design, competently adapting elements from Polidoro da Caravaggio and Taddeo Zuccaro. Of Brandani's work at Castello di Montebello, near Urbino, four putti are particularly remarkable for their Mannerist sophistication.

Between 1567 and 1575 Brandani increasingly undertook religious commissions: in the relief of the *Beheading of St Catherine* (*c.* 1568) for the altar of S Caterina, Urbino, and again in his reliefs for S Maria Novella, Orciano (*c.* 1569), and the chapel of Guidobaldo II in the Palazzo Ducale, Urbino (*c.* 1570), he employed a forced expressiveness. From this he subsequently retreated under the influence of the *Decreta Concilii Urbini* of 1570, which required sacred imagery to excite feelings of piety in the onlooker.

Count Antonio II Brancaleone (*fl* 1556–98) of Piobbico, who had been enriched in 1570 by Turkish plunder, commissioned Brandani to rebuild the family church of S Stefano, Finocchetto. Brandani's life-size statues of the *Apostles* and *Prophets* (1570–*c.* 1573) survived the destruction by earthquake of the building in 1781. They include *David* gazing upwards in ecstatic vision. In the slightly more than life-size relief of the *Crucifixion* (*c.* 1572–3) for the altar in the Bonamini Chapel, S Agostino, Pesaro, the emaciated Christ and the sorrowful Mary Magdalene are devised to induce a strong sense of repentance in the viewer. Brandani's *Adoration of the Shepherds* (1574) in the confraternity of S Giuseppe, Urbino, is a masterpiece of naturalism in which life-size figures in contemporary dress concentrate on the Child with individualized responses of delight.

BIBLIOGRAPHY

L. Pungileoni: 'Notizie istoriche di Federico Brandano', *G. Arcad. Roma*, xxxi (1826), pp. 361–79

L. Serra: *L'arte delle Marche: Il periodo del rinascimento* (Rome, 1934), ii, pp. 196–218

P. Hoffmann: 'Scultori e stuccatori a Villa Giulia', *Commentari*, no. 1 (1967), pp. 48–66

A. Antonelli: 'Contributi a Federico Brandani', *Not. Pal. Albani*, ii/1 (1973), pp. 43–9

L. Fontebuoni: 'Gli stucchi di Brandani', *I Brancaleoni e Piobbico* (Urbania, 1985), pp. 235–84

D. Sikorski: 'Il palazzo ducale di Urbino sotto Guidobaldo II (1538–74): Bartolomeo Genga, Filippo Terzi e Federico Brandani', *Il palazzo di Federico da Montefeltro: Restauri e ricerche*, ed. M. L. Polichetti (Urbino, 1985), pp. 67–90

——: *Brandani and his Patrons* (diss., U. London, Courtauld Inst., 1988)

——: 'Guidobaldo II e il palazzo di Pesaro', *Ric. Stor. Pesaro*, iii (1989)

DARIUS SIKORSKI

Brandenburg. Cathedral city in Germany, in the region of Potsdam an der Havel, between the Beetzsee and the Plauer See. It is an administrative centre and industrial town with a population of *c.* 94,000. A member of the Hanseatic League until 1470, Brandenburg is notable for its medieval brick buildings. It was a centre of glass production from the 17th century.

The Dominsel was the site of a fortified settlement belonging to the Slav Hevellers; it was conquered in 928 by King Henry the Fowler (*reg* 919–36), who built a Saxon castle there. Emperor Otto I (*reg* 936–73) made it an episcopal see in 948. After the Wend uprising in 983 Brandenburg reverted to Wend ownership. In 1157 it was inherited by Markgraf Albert the Bear (*reg* 1134–70), and the bishopric was reinstated in 1161. The cathedral district, with two wards that were Slav settlements, retained its independence until 1930.

Until 1715 Brandenburg consisted of two towns. The suburb of Parduin to the west was a settlement of smallholders. Its parish church, assigned to Premonstratensians in 1147, served as the cathedral chapter in 1161–5. The town came under the authority of Magdeburg in 1170 and was alluded to in 1216 and 1241 as the 'vetus' or 'antiqua civitas' (old town). Luckeberg, a Netherlandish trading settlement, with the Nikolaikirche (1170–*c.* 1230) was incorporated into it in 1248. The market area to the south-east was referred to in 1196 as the 'nova civitas'. Until 1360 the two towns shared a town hall located on the Lange Brücke. There is evidence of a court of justice in Brandenburg from 1315, and in 1431 it entered the league of towns of the Brandenburg March. The Reformation was introduced in 1546 and the bishopric abolished in 1598.

Surviving churches include many fine examples of *Backsteingotik*. The cathedral chapter moved to the Dominsel in 1165. The Cathedral of SS Peter and Paul is a cruciform, columnar basilica, 57.7 m long internally, with a two-tower façade and a crypt below the choir and crossing. The two-storey 'Bunte Kapelle' in the north transept was consecrated in 1235. After 1377 a choir with a five-sided apse was added, and the cathedral was vaulted. Stained glass, wall paintings and rich furnishings have been preserved. The east and north ranges of the cloister date from the 13th and 14th centuries. From 1507 the canons abandoned communal life and built their own premises; between 1706 and 1937 the cloister was used by the

Ritterakademie (school for young noblemen). The Petri-kapelle, an Early Gothic building with Late Gothic vaulting south of the cathedral, has been the church of the cathedral parish since 1320.

The granite westwork of the Gotthardtkirche, which became the parish church of the Old Town in 1166, dates from the original building. In 1456 Henrik Reinstorp (*fl* 1435–after 1456) started to convert it to a brick hall church of three aisles and seven bays, with a hall choir and ambulatory, which was completed in 1475. The interior is dominated by its Baroque fittings. The town hall of the Old Town at the south side of the market is a two-storey brick building with decorative gables dating from 1470–80. In front of the side facing the market is a monumental sandstone figure of *Roland* (1474; h. more than 5 m), and the Late Gothic Ordonnanzhaus (barracks) stands near by. In 1237 a Franciscan monastery was founded near the town wall in the southern part of the Old Town; its former church of St Johannes is a brick hall building. The Early Gothic Nikolaikirche, a three-aisled basilica to the west, has a two-bay choir and apses terminating the aisles.

St Katharinen, the parish church of the New Town and mentioned in 1217, was demolished in 1395. An indulgence was granted in 1381 giving permission for the new building, which was designed and supervised by HINRICH BRUNSBERG from 1401. This brick hall church, Brunsberg's masterpiece, is a superb example of late *Backstein-gotik*, and the filigree decoration made from glazed, shaped

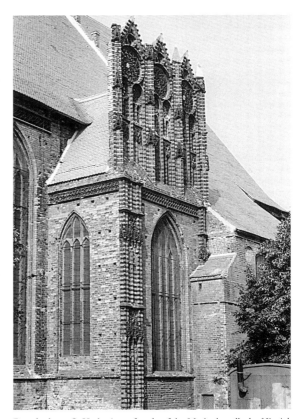

Brandenburg, St Katharinen, façade of the Marienkapelle, by Hinrich Brunsberg, *c.* 1401–34

bricks of varying colours on the imposing façades of the Schöppenkapelle and the Fronleichnamskapelle (now the Marienkapelle; see fig.) is particularly splendid. The town hall of the New Town and other buildings near the market were destroyed in 1945. The former Dominican friary of St Paul (ruined) in the south part of the New Town was endowed with land in 1286 and 1311. Of the chapels outside the New Town the Jakobskapelle, built in 1349, has survived. The central structure of the Marienkirche, founded in 1136 on Harlunger Berg, was demolished in 1722.

In spite of severe damage during World War II some old houses, schools and granaries have survived. As well as fragments of the wall, the remaining sections of the town's brick fortifications include the Rathenower and Plauer gate-towers in the Old Town, and in the New Town the Steintorturm (c. 1400) and the Mühlentorturm; the latter was built by Nikolaus Kraft in 1411.

BIBLIOGRAPHY
P. Eichholz, ed.: *Stadt und Dom Brandenburg* (1912), ii/3 of *Inventar der Bau- und Kunstdenkmäler in der Provinz Brandenburg* (Berlin, 1912)
H. Hootz, ed.: *Mark Brandenburg und Berlin*, Deutsche Kunstdenkmäler: Ein Bildhandbuch (Leipzig and Darmstadt, 1971)
H. Drescher and others: *Die Bau- und Kunstdenkmäler in der DDR: Bezirk Potsdam* (Berlin, 1978)
E. Lehmann, ed.: *Bezirke Berlin/DDR und Potsdam*, Dehio-Handbuch (Berlin, 1983)
ERNST ULLMANN

Brandenburg glassworks. Glass manufactory in Brandenburg. The first Brandenburg glassworks was established in 1602 by Joachim Frederick, Elector of Brandenburg (*reg* 1598–1608), and was run by Bohemian glassmakers. The earliest products included coloured and marbled glass. In 1607 the factory was transferred to Marienwalde, near Küstrin (now Kostrzyn, Poland), and another factory was built in Grimnitz in 1653. Both factories produced window glass and simple drinking vessels based on Bohemian models and painted with enamels or, from the mid-17th century, engraved. In 1674 Frederick William, Elector of Brandenburg, built another factory at Drewitz near Potsdam for the production of glass crystal. The glass-engraver Georg Gondelach came from Dessau to work there from 1677, accompanied by the engraver Christoph Tille (*fl* 1685) and the enamel-painter Ruel. After the arrival of the glassmaker Johann Kunckel (1630–1703), the great period of Brandenburg glass began. Kunckel operated the glassworks in Drewitz from 1679 to 1682, while the Elector built a new glassworks in Potsdam. In 1679 Kunckel published his *Ars vitraria experimentalis*, which was the most important account of glassmaking during this period. In a secret laboratory that the Elector had given him on the Pfaueninsel in the Wannsee, Kunckel carried out various experiments, reducing crizzling by adding chalk to the batch and creating the process for making gold-ruby glass. In 1680 the Elector hired Martin Winter (*d* 1702) and in 1683 his nephew Gottfried Spiller (1663–1728) as glass-engravers. In 1688 Winter introduced relief-cutting and built a water-powered engraving workshop. Spiller produced the most outstanding figurative engravings on Brandenburg glass; in addition to his work in *tiefschnitt* (intaglio) and *hochschnitt* (relief; e.g. covered

goblet, c. 1700; London, V&A), he also worked in gold-ruby glass. Spiller was succeeded by the engraver Elias Rosbach (1700–65), who had worked in Berlin from 1727. Around 1742 Rosbach went to Zechlin, to which the glassworks at Potsdam had been relocated (1736). In addition to the engraving and cutting, high-quality gilding is a mark of Potsdam and Zechlin glass. During the first half of the 19th century Zechlin produced cut glass in the Empire and Biedermeier styles, including pieces with cameo incrustations. From c. 1840 primarily simple, utilitarian wares were produced.

BIBLIOGRAPHY
R. Schmidt: *Brandenburgische Gläser* (Berlin, 1914)
R. J. Charleston: *Masterpieces of Glass* (New York, 1980), pp. 138–41
WALTER SPIEGL

Brandes, Jan Laurens Andries (*b* Rotterdam, 13 Jan 1857; *d* Weltevreden [now Jakarta], 26 June 1905). Dutch archaeologist. The son of a theologian, he was supposed to study theology but felt more attracted to Asiatic languages and studied Sanskrit, Malay and Old Javanese at Leiden University from 1879 to 1883. In 1884 he completed a thesis on linguistics. In 1884 Brandes was appointed civil servant in Indonesian languages in Batavia (now Jakarta). Between 1884 and 1898 he concentrated on Old Javanese inscriptions, manuscripts and literature. A visit to H. N. van der Tuuk in 1885 gave him much inspiration. Through the inscriptions Brandes discovered the ancient monuments, and he started to specialize in the role of ornamentation. In 1900 he was appointed head of the Borobudur Restoration committee, and in 1901 he became head of the Commission for Archaeological Survey in the Dutch East Indies (now Indonesia). During a visit to Hanoi in 1902, he became aware of the Chinese influences in East Javanese art. He wrote important articles on the foreign origin of ornamentation in Javanese art and compiled monographs on two 13th-century East Javanese temples, Candi Jago (pubd 1904) and Candi Singasar (pubd 1909).

WRITINGS
Beschrijving van de ruïne bij de desa Toempang, genaamd Tjandi Djago, Archaeologisch Onderzoek op Java en Madoera, i (Jakarta, 1904)
Beschrijving van Tjandi Singasari en de wolkentooneelen van Panataran, Archaeologisch Onderzoek op Java en Madoera, ii (Jakarta, 1909)
For a bibliography of Brandes' works, see *Maatsch. Lettknd. Bijdr. Hand.* (1905–6), pp. 46–51
H. I. R. HINZLER

Brandi, Giacinto (*b* Gaeta or Poli, 1621; *d* Rome, 19 Jan 1691). Italian painter. His early training was in Rome, in the workshop of the sculptor Alessandro Algardi, who encouraged his inclination towards *disegno* (Baldinucci). He then worked under the Bolognese Giovanni Giacomo Sementi, an uninspired imitator of Guido Reni. Sementi died in 1636, and in 1638 Brandi visited Naples. In 1646–7 he was again in Rome, employed in the workshop of Giovanni Lanfranco, who had recently returned from Naples. This is confirmed by Brandi's *Joseph's Dream* (Rome, Gal. Corsini), which is based on one of Lanfranco's works. In 1647 Brandi joined the Accademia dei Virtuosi al Pantheon in Rome and from 1651 was present at the meetings of the Accademia di S Luca.

Shortly after 1650 Brandi executed canvases with scenes from the *Life of the Virgin* for the ceiling of S Maria in Via Lata, Rome, which were much admired (Titi). Only one, the *Coronation of the Virgin*, survives (*in situ*). In 1653 he completed frescoes of mythological scenes in the Palazzo Pamphili in Piazza Navona, Rome. By 1657 he was considered one of the most promising painters in the city (Scannelli). Between 1655 and 1660 Brandi came under the influence of Mattia Preti, and his *Lot and his Daughters* (Rome, Gal. Corsini), for example, is a fusion of Preti's naturalism and Guercino's eloquent light effect. During these years Brandi also decorated the chapel of S Giuseppe in the church of Gesù e Maria, Rome; his central canvas of *St Joseph in Glory* dramatically contrasts the sweeping draperies derived from Lanfranco with the saint's head depicted against the light. This work was followed by the *Forty Martyrs* (Rome, Stimmate di S Francesco), in which the modelling of the nudes is softened by a dense atmospheric chiaroscuro.

Probably in 1661 Brandi went to Gaeta, where he executed decorative frescoes and a canvas of the *Martyrdom of St Erasmus* in the crypt of the cathedral (1666; *in situ*). In these works his personal style emerged in thick and substantial brushwork, reinforced with a lively play of light that gave the forms an almost sculptural quality. His *St Roch* (early 1660s; Rome, S Rocco), commissioned by Cardinal Francesco Barberini, also shows that he had been influenced by the broad and fluent handling of Guercino's early work. This manner so impressed Preti that in 1665, writing to the Sicilian collector Antonio Ruffo, he praised Brandi over Pier Francesco Mola, Ciro Ferri and Carlo Maratti. Brandi's *St Sebastian* (Florence, Fond. Longhi) and a *St Gregory in Ecstasy* (Monte Porzio Catone, S Gregorio Magno) were painted *c.* 1666. In 1668, following the resignation of Pietro da Cortona, Brandi was nominated Principe of the Accademia di S Luca. The following year he completed the *St Carlo Borromeo Administering the Sacrament to the Plague-stricken* (Milan, S Maria della Vittoria). Between 1666 and 1671 he sent canvases, mainly of saints, to the church of the Ospedale di S Maria delle Grazie at Saragossa and to the church of the convent of the Capuchins at Toledo and painted an altarpiece of the *Annunciation* (Rome, S Maria Annunziata).

In 1671 he was commissioned by Cardinal Luigi Omodei (*b* 1608) to fresco the dome and lantern of S Carlo al Corso, Rome. Subsequently he added the *Prophets* on the pendentives of the dome, in a style clearly influenced by Maratti, and frescoes, glorifying St Carlo Borromeo, on the vaults of the transept, presbytery and semi-dome of the apse, completed in 1677. In the same year Omodei commissioned him to fresco the central vault of the nave with the *Fall of the Rebel Angels*. This vast programme of decoration showed a marked stylistic change, with a renewed interest in linear effects. Brandi's canvases of the same period, such as the *Martyrdom of St Blaise* (Rome, S Carlo ai Catinari), indicate a parallel development from his earlier dramatically lit and highly coloured work to a tightly controlled classicizing manner. For Monsignore Giorgio Bolognetti (1595–1686), Brandi painted an altarpiece of the *Guardian Angel* (Rome, SS Angeli Custodi), as well as fresco decorations and an altarpiece of the *Coronation of the Virgin* (1678–80; Rome, Gesù e Maria). On Maratti's

recommendation Brandi was invited in 1680 to paint ceiling frescoes (completed 1686) in S Silvestro in Capite, Rome. There he depicted the *Assumption of the Virgin with St Sylvester*, returning to Lanfranco's monumental and dramatic manner in order to compete with Giovanni Battista Gaulli's brilliantly dynamic frescoes (1672–9) in the Gesù. In Brandi's late work, such as the *Martyrdom of St Andrew* (1685; Rome, S Maria in Via Lata) and the *Holy Trinity* (Rome, S Francesca Romana), the rigour of the design beneath the dynamic contrast of light and shade became more pronounced and even more controlled.

BIBLIOGRAPHY

F. Scannelli: *Il microcosmo* (Cesena, 1657/*R* Milan, 1966), p. 208

F. Titi: *Studio di pittura, scoltora et architettura nelle chiese di Roma* (Rome, 1674), p. 350

F. Baldinucci: *Notizie* (1681–1728); ed. F. Ranalli (1845–7)

B. de Dominici: *Vite* (1742–5), iii, pp. 274–6

V. Ruffo: 'La Galleria Ruffo nel secolo XVII in Messina', *Bol. A.*, x (1916), p. 256

A. Pampaloni: 'Per Giacinto Brandi', *Bol. A.*, n. s. 5, lviii (1973), pp. 123–66

F. Navarro: 'Brandi, G.', *La pittura in Italia: Il seicento*, ii (Milan, 1989), pp. 652–3

CONCETTA RESTAINO

Brandin, Philipp (*b* Utrecht, *c.* 1550; *d* Nyköping, 1594). Dutch architect and sculptor, active in Germany. He worked from 1563 to 1574 for Johann Albrecht I, Herzog von Mecklenburg, and from 1569 to 1571 built a house (now the Stadtgeschichtliches Museum) in Wismar for Bürgermeister Schabbelt; its Dutch structural and ornamental forms were a strong influence on subsequent architecture in Mecklenburg. His fountain in Wismar market-place, comprising a 12-sided pavilion with ornamental herm-pilasters, was completed in 1602 by his pupils. From 1574 Brandin executed various works for Ulrich III, Herzog von Mecklenburg–Güstrow, including the Schloss at Güstrow, where, having been appointed court builder in 1583, he erected the north wing following a fire; the work was completed by his pupil Claus Midow (*d* 1602). In Güstrow Cathedral, in accordance with Ulrich's plan to convert the building into a court church where the ducal tombs would be housed in the choir, Brandin started work in 1575 on the memorial to Borwin II, the cathedral's founder. An austere classical aedicula with Dutch Renaissance ornament frames the Mecklenburg family tree, with an over life-size recumbent figure of the reigning duke in armour at its base. Brandin's wall-tomb of the Herzogin Dorothea, Ulrich III's sister, a recumbent figure in white marble, dates from the same year. Brandin's greatest work was the tomb (from 1585; completed by Brandin's pupils) in Güstrow Cathedral of Ulrich III and his two wives, Elizabeth of Denmark and Anna of Pomerania, on which the artist worked during the lifetime of each subject. The three life-size white marble figures, kneeling at prie-dieus and turned towards the altar, are portrayed with lifelike accuracy and in the costume of the period. A black marble rear wall, divided into three by pilasters, bears the family tree of each of the figures. The tomb is framed in an aedicula that, in contrast to the tomb executed by Brandin ten years earlier, displays freer, Mannerist features; two caryatids support an entablature with a continuous cornice, above which rise richly decorated family crests. On the bases of the aedicula are relief scenes from the *Life* and

Passion of Christ. These tombs made Brandin the foremost master of the 16th century in Mecklenburg and helped to propagate the Dutch Renaissance in the face of the former dominance of the Italian.

BIBLIOGRAPHY

Die Kunst und Geschichtsdenkmäler des Grossherzogtums Mecklenburg-Schwerin, iv (Schwerin, 1901)
G. Baier: 'Stuckdekor und Stukkateure des 16. und 17. Jahrhunderts im Güstrower Schloss', *Mitt. Inst. Dkmlpf. Schwerin* (1970), pp. 105–20
Deutsche Kunstdenkmäler: Ein Bildhandbuch (Munich and Berlin, 1971)
G. Baier and J. Voss: 'Zur wiederentdeckten Ausmalung eines Turmkabinetts im Güstrower Schloss', *Mitt. Inst. Dkmlpf. Schwerin* (1973), pp. 212–42
G. Bosinski: *Güstrow und seine Kirchen* (Berlin, 1980)

CAROLA WENZEL

Brandini, Bartolomeo. *See* BANDINELLI, BACCIO.

Brandl [Brandel; Prandl], **Petr** (*b* Prague, 24 Oct 1660; *d* Kutná Hora, 24 Sept 1735). Bohemian painter. He was born into a craftsman's family and apprenticed *c.* 1683–8 to Kristián Schröder (1655–1702), curator of the gallery of Prague Castle, where he met Italian and Dutch artists. Painters based in Prague who influenced him were the Swiss Johann Rudolf Bys, the Flemish Abraham Godyn (*fl* 1679–93) and in particular the Austrian Michael Wenzel Halbax. From Halbax, Brandl derived a style employing chiaroscuro and remarkably substantial figures; from Michael Willmann and Jan Liška (*c.* 1650–1712) he adopted a freehand dynamic manner. His early works include *St Mary Magdalene* (1693; Mníšek pod Brdy, St Wenceslas) and the *Annunciation* (1697; Prague, N.G., Convent of St George); the influence of Halbax is particularly apparent *c.* 1700, in works such as the *Beheading of St Barbara* (1699; Manětín, St Barbara), but Brandl gradually advanced towards far more plastic portrayals in vividly contrasting colours, e.g. the *Birth of the Virgin* (1703; Doksany, abbey church).

The development of Brandl's art can be divided roughly into decades. In the first decade of the 1700s he combined massive sculptural figures with the use of light to create dramatic effects. At first he conceived his compositions around a central axis and diagonals; gradually, however, just as in radical Baroque architecture, he introduced convex–concave curves. Around 1710 Brandl collaborated with the sculptor Matyáš Braun, drawing sketches for his statues such as *St Lutgard* on the Charles Bridge in Prague. Braun's conception of light penetrating the material dynamics of the figure made a marked impression on Brandl. In works of the 1710s, such as the *Baptism* (1715–16; Manětín, St John the Baptist), this conception of images becomes all important. *SS Joachim and Anna* (1716; Prague, Our Lady of Victory), the *Death of St Vintíř*

Petr Brandl: *Elijah with the Angel*, oil on canvas, 1.87×2.48 m, 1724 (Prague, Our Lady of Victory)

(1718) and the *Death of St Benedict* (1719; both Prague, St Margaret) elaborate further striking light effects.

It was not until 1720 that a certain balance was struck between the static and the dynamic light effects, as in the large *History of Joseph of Egypt* (?1721; Jindřichův Hradec, Castle). In the ensuing decade Brandl increased his dramatic power in *St John Nepomuk* (1721; Hradec Králové, Assumption) and *Elijah with the Angel* (1724; Prague, Our Lady of Victory; see fig.), but it was probably after 1725 that he produced his greatest work. In paintings such as the *Adoration of the Magi* (1727; Smířice, church of the Revelation of the Lord), enduringly powerful, animated figures convey a lyrical sentiment; the scenes, with all their pathos, communicate directly. At this period Brandl again worked with Matyáš Braun, on Count Franz Anton von Sporck's estate at Kuks, where he painted a *Flight into Egypt* (c. 1726–31; damaged) for a chapel in Bethlehem Wood. Following the compelling *Assumption of the Virgin* (1728; Vysoké Mýto, St Lawrence) and *St Lutgard* and *St Julian* (1729; both Sedlec, Virgin), the pictures from 1730, such as the *Glorification of St Ignatius* (1730; Hradec Králové, Assumption), show a marked decline.

Besides large altar paintings Brandl painted several small portraits. The early ones show the influence of Jan Kupecký, but gradually Brandl introduces a histrionic manner. There are a number of self-portraits from between c. 1698 and 1725 (e.g. Prague, N.G., Convent of St George; Prague, N. Mus.), showing the artist's justified self-assurance. He specialized in half-length figures and heads of saints, particularly apostles. His genre scenes, such as *Three Women and a Hunter* (c. 1720; Prague, N.G., Šternberk Pal.), make a festive, almost theatrical impression.

Brandl was the greatest Bohemian painter of the Baroque period, endowing all his work with an optimistic exuberance. From his youth he defied the discipline of the guild and lived a boisterous life, favoured both in his gifts and by the aristocracy.

BIBLIOGRAPHY

Petr Brandl (exh. cat. by J. Neumann, Prague, N.G., 1968)

P. Preiss: 'Malířství vrcholného baroka v Čechách' [Paintings at the height of the Baroque in the Czech lands], *Dějiny českého výtvarného umění* [History of Czech fine arts] (Prague, 1989), pp. 574–89

IVO KOŘÁN

Brandon, 7th Duke of. *See* HAMILTON, ALEXANDER.

Brands, Eugène [Eugenius] (*b* Amsterdam, 15 Jan 1913). Dutch painter and draughtsman. He studied at the Handelsschool (1927–31) and at the Kunstnijverheidsschool (1931–4), both in Amsterdam. During World War II he created Surreal assemblages and abstract drawings, and his work was shown for the first time in 1946 in the *Jonge schilders* exhibition in the Stedelijk Museum, Amsterdam. In August 1948 he joined the Dutch Experimentele Groep, which later became part of Cobra. Compared to the work produced by members of Cobra such as Constant or Karel Appel, his work is dreamy and poetic. His starting-point was the world of the child and humanity in its natural state, where magic, eroticism and cosmos are central notions, for example *Walking House* (1951; Copenhagen, Paul and Djula Lernø priv. col.). He collected ritual objects and music from primitive peoples.

Until 1960 Brands produced small-scale paintings on canvas and paper, depicting a world full of symbols such as arrows, lock and key and parts of the body. He also created such relief assemblages as *Milky Way 10* (1966–7; see 1969 exh. cat.). The Surreal element continued to have a dominant presence in his work. After 1960 his canvases became larger, with strong, individual characteristics. They comprise fields of vaguely outlined colours, mainly orange, white, yellow, bright green and pale blue. Later works show no substantial change in style.

BIBLIOGRAPHY

Eugène Brands: Schilderijen, assemblages, en gouaches (exh. cat., intro. E. Brands; Amsterdam, Stedel. Mus., 1969)

Eugène Brands (exh. cat., The Hague, Nouv. Images, 1977)

JOHN STEEN

Brandt, Bill (*b* Hamburg, 3 May 1904; *d* London, 20 Dec 1983). English photographer of German birth. The son of a British father and a German mother, he suffered the traumas of World War I, followed by a long period of illness with tuberculosis. This affliction caused Brandt to spend much of his early youth in a sanitarium in Davos, Switzerland. Between the ages of 16 and 22 Brandt derived a lot of his knowledge of the world from illustrated books and magazines. His mother was an enthusiast for poster art and took *Das Plakat*, an up-to-date journal of graphic art that featured work of such contemporaries as Lucian Bernhard (1883–1972). As a boy Brandt became proficient in drawing and painting in watercolours.

Brandt travelled to Vienna in 1927 to see a lung specialist and was cured. He decided to work in a photographic studio in the city. He took his first major portrait, of the poet *Ezra Pound*, in Vienna in 1928 (see Mellor, p. 40). Pound suggested that Brandt contact Man Ray in Paris, offering an introduction. Brandt took the advice and assisted Man Ray for three months (1929–30). In Paris he discovered Surrealist art in its heyday: the books, new magazines, films by Luis Buñuel (1900–83) and Dalí and the role of photography in the movement. Brandt's early photography showed the influence of André Kertész and Eugène Atget. He tried to document city types, such as *Racegoers, Paris* (1930; see Mellor, p. 7), and Parisian life, as in *Fleamarket, Paris* (1929; see Mellor, p. 9).

By the time he came to London in 1931 he was a well-informed young photographer. In 1932 he married and settled in Belsize Park, London. From this vantage point, among his English uncles and cousins and their households, he made the photographs that were published as his first book, *The English at Home*. This book contains some of Brandt's most compelling reportage. Through the camera he discovered the country, invested with enormous significance from his childhood. He explored high life—cocktails on a Surrey lawn, backgammon after dinner in Mayfair—and life belowstairs, in the bars of the East End and, inevitably, at the race-track. A similar intimate scrutiny of English ways, and a use of critical description, is characteristic of passages in Rosamond Lehmann's novel *The Weather in the Streets* (London, 1936), which Brandt greatly admired.

Brandt's second book, *A Night in London*, published in the same series as Brassaï's *Paris de nuit* (London, 1933), encompassed social events and strata, with staged scenes where necessary. Brandt's familiarity with the problems of night photography was to be turned to exceptionally vital account during the period of the Blitz (1939–40). Brandt met Tom Hopkinson, editor of *Picture Post*, in 1936 and contributed both to that magazine from 1938 to 1949 and, during the 1940s, to the smaller and more literary *Lilliput*. He also worked for *Weekly Illustrated* in the late 1930s and had work published in *Verve*. He photographed London during the blackout and, for the Ministry of Information, under bombardment—a set of photographs intended to bring home to the Americans the realities of the Blitz (see Mellor, pp. 33–7). Brandt's eye for narrative detail and his relish for the effects of moonlight ally him to the prose writer Elizabeth Bowen (1899–1973), whom he knew and much admired at this period.

Brandt undertook his sharpest social reporting on his first visit to the north of England in 1937. His photographs of northern cities and of unemployed miners searching for coal were not published until the 1940s but were then used with great skill by Hopkinson as emblems of industrial hardship in a 'Special Austerity Issue' in spring 1947. During the 1940s Brandt worked for a prolonged period as a portraitist and also as a landscape photographer, publishing the images as *Literary Britain*.

From 1945 Brandt began to concentrate his creative powers on an investigation of the female form, eventually published as *Perspective of Nudes* (see fig.). Brandt had always used a Rolleiflex camera, but for this series he turned, in the spirit of Surrealist automatism, to a camera whose tiny aperture hardly allowed him to see the subject: a brass and mahogany camera with an extremely wide-angle lens. This gave Brandt precisely the imaginative

distortions he wished to explore. The wide-angle camera-work used in Orson Welles's film *Citizen Kane* (1941) confirmed Brandt's desire to experiment. The six sections of *Perspective of Nudes* offer one of the most profound celebrations of the nude in 20th-century art. From 1945 he worked as a freelance photographer in London. A number of his works were published as *Shadow of Light*.

PHOTOGRAPHIC PUBLICATIONS

The English at Home (London, 1936)
A Night in London (London, 1938)
Literary Britain (London, 1951)
Perspective of Nudes (London, 1961)
Shadow of Light (London, 1966, rev. 1977)

BIBLIOGRAPHY

R. B. Kitaj: 'R. B. Kitaj and Two Faces of Ezra Pound', *Creative Cam.*, 210 (1982), pp. 536–7
M. Haworth-Booth: 'Remembering Bill Brandt', *V&A Mus. Album*, iii (London, 1984), pp. 40–45
Literary Britain—Photographed by Bill Brandt (exh. cat., ed. M. Haworth-Booth; London, V&A, 1984)
D. Mellor: *Bill Brandt: Behind the Camera—Photographs 1928–1983*, intro. M. Haworth-Booth (Oxford and New York, 1985)
I. Jeffrey: *Bill Brandt Photographs, 1929–1983* (London, 1993)
N. Warburton, ed.: *Bill Brandt: Selected Texts and Bibliography* (Oxford, 1993)

MARK HAWORTH-BOOTH

Brandt, Federico (*b* Caracas, 17 May 1878; *d* Caracas, 25 July 1932). Venezuelan painter. In 1896 he began studying at the Academia de Bellas Artes, Caracas, under Emilio Mauri (1855–1908) and Antonio Herrera Toro. In 1902 Brandt travelled to Paris, where he attended the Académie Colarossi and the Académie de la Grande Chaumière, as well as the studios of the painters Jean-Paul Laurens and Antonio de La Gandara. He then moved to the Netherlands to study Dutch painting, which had a permanent influence on his work, although his output at this stage was still sporadic. At the end of 1903 he returned to Venezuela. Between 1904 and 1907 Brandt regularly attended the workshops at the Academia de Bellas Artes, Caracas. From 1912, coinciding with the creation of the anti-academic Círculo de Bellas Artes in Caracas, he painted with greater regularity and enthusiasm, motivated in part by the innovations of the painters Samys Mützner, Nicolas Ferdinandov and Emilio Boggio; Mützner was particularly influential to him. His liking of Dutch painting, of antique objects and architectural space led him to produce intimate still-lifes, interiors, landscapes and portraits (e.g. *Interior with Dolls*, 1927; Caracas, Gal. A. N.).

BIBLIOGRAPHY

A. Boulton: *Historia de la pintura en Venezuela*, 3 vols (Caracas, 1968, rev. 1973)
J. Calzadilla: *Federico Brandt* (Caracas, 1972)

YASMINY PÉREZ SILVA

Brandt, Józef (*b* Szczebrzeszyn, nr Lublin, 1 Feb 1841; *d* Radom, 12 June 1915). Polish painter. From 1858 he was in Paris, registered as a student of engineering at the Ecole des Ponts et Chaussées, but from 1859 he studied painting under the guidance of the Polish artist Juliusz Fortunat Kossak and also took instruction from Henryk Rodakowski and worked briefly with Léon Cogniet. In 1860 Brandt returned to Poland with Kossak, and the two artists travelled to the Ukraine and Podole: the beauty of the eastern borderlands made a lasting impression on Brandt,

Bill Brandt: *Nude*, photograph, 1953; from B. Brandt: *Perspective of Nudes* (London, 1961), pl. 38 (London, Victoria and Albert Museum)

and this region became the chief setting for his paintings. Until 1862 Brandt remained largely under Kossak's influence, both in his subject-matter (drawn largely from the 17th-century military and hunting life of the borderlands) and in his colouring and technique, especially in his watercolours. In 1861 Brandt exhibited a series of drawings and watercolour sketches in Warsaw at the Society for the Promotion of the Fine Arts, drawing his subjects from patriotic literature, and his work was well-received by the public.

In 1862 Brandt travelled to Munich and studied there under Franz Adam (1815–86), a then-celebrated painter of horses and armies, Theodor Horscheldt and Karl Theodor von Piloty, developing an interest in Dutch painting, particularly the 'minor Dutch masters' of the 17th century, whose meticulous finish and pale gold colouring he emulated. In 1867 he opened his own studio in Munich and became the leading figure among the many Polish painters based in the city. His large *Battle near Chocim* (1867; Warsaw, N. Mus.), showing the victory of the Polish army over the Turks in 1621, was exhibited at the Exposition Universelle in Paris in 1867 and attracted great public interest and acclaim. Further success came in 1870 with *Czarniecki at Koldynga* (Warsaw, N. Mus.), showing an episode from the Polish–Swedish wars, and several other compositions glorifying the traditional Polish ideals of knightly heroism and the love of the countryside and hunting.

Around 1880 Brandt adopted lighter, cooler tones, as seen in *Meeting on a Bridge* (1884; Kraków, N. Mus.), where attention is evenly spread over the figures and the landscape setting of the muddy road, the fences, and the fields and water beyond. Brandt, however, retained his vision of Polish history as a legendary, exotic world rich in elaborate armour, colourful uniforms and Eastern costumes, as seen in the *Departure from Wilanów* (1897; two versions, Warsaw, N. Mus. and Kielce, N. Mus.), which shows the stately departure of the Polish King John Sobieski and his Queen, Mary, from their royal residence near Warsaw. Brandt continued to produce works of this kind during the following 15 years, although in general he became rather more mannered and less inventive in the treatment of his subjects.

BIBLIOGRAPHY

PSB; *SAP*; Thieme–Becker

W. Husarski: *Józef Brandt* (Warsaw, 1929)

J. Derwojed: *Józef Brandt* (Warsaw, 1969)

Polnische Malerei von 1830 bis 1914 (exh. cat., Kiel, Christian Albrechts-U., Ksthalle; Stuttgart, Württemberg. Kstver.; Wuppertal, Von-der-Heydt-Mus.; 1978–9)

La Peinture polonaise du XVIe au début du XXe siècle (exh. cat., Warsaw, N. Mus., 1979)

Münchner Maler im 19ten Jahrhundert (1982), ii of *Bruckmanns Lexikon der Münchner Kunst* (Munich, 1981–3), p. 27

W kręgu Brandta w 70 rocznicę śmierci malarza [Brandt circle, on the occasion of the 70th anniversary of the artist's death] (exh. cat., Radom, Dis. Mus., 1985)

WANDA MAŁASZEWSKA

Brandt [née Liebe], **Marianne** (*b* Chemnitz, 1 Oct 1893; *d* Kirchberg, 18 June 1983). German metalworker and designer. One of the best-known of the BAUHAUS metalworkers, she studied painting and sculpture at the Kunstakademie in Weimar (1911–14). Around 1923 she went to study at the Bauhaus in Weimar and on the advice of László Moholy-Nagy joined the metal workshop there. The development of her work parallels the philosophical developments at the Bauhaus, from the craft orientation of the Weimar period (1919–25) to the interest in technology and industrial design of the Dessau period (1925–33). Her early designs, for example the hand-crafted nickel-silver teapot (1924; New York, MOMA) and brass and ebony tea-essence pot (1924; Berlin, Bauhaus-Archv), are based on pure geometrical forms—cylinders, spheres and hemispheres. Functional considerations are secondary to aesthetic concerns. Her later designs, particularly those for lighting fixtures, reflect the influence of Moholy-Nagy. Under his direction the metal workshop concentrated on producing prototypes for mass production. Notable among Brandt's lamp designs are a ceiling fixture (1925), equipped with chains so the globe could be lowered to change the bulb, an adjustable ceiling light (with Hans Przyrembel; 1926; e.g. at Berlin, Bauhaus-Archv) and the 'Kandem' bedside table lamp on a flexible stem (1927). The last was one of several lamps by Brandt that were commercially manufactured by Körting & Mathiesson, Leipzig, from 1928. Brandt was the head of the metal workshop at the Bauhaus from 1928 to 1929. She worked as an independent designer from 1933 and was an instructor at the Hochschule für Bildende Künste, Dresden (1949–51), and the Institut für Angewandte Kunst, Berlin (1951–4). For an illustration of a brass ashtray *see* BAUHAUS, fig. 2.

BIBLIOGRAPHY

W. Scheidig: *Crafts of the Weimar Bauhaus, 1919–1924: An Early Experiment in Industrial Design* (London, 1967)

50 Jahre Bauhaus (exh. cat., Stuttgart, Württemberg. Kstver., 1968)

E. Neumann, ed.: *Bauhaus and Bauhaus People* (New York, 1970)

DONNA CORBIN

Brandt, Reynier [Reinier; Reijnier] (*b* Wesel, Gelderland, 1702; *d* Amsterdam, 1788). Dutch silversmith. In his youth he moved to Amsterdam, where he was active from *c*. 1734; a silversmith with the initials R.B. received the citizenship of Amsterdam that year. He specialized in delicate bread- and cake-baskets in the Rococo style, all of which have the same basic form: a graceful ogee-shape with an openwork body and curving sides tapering into handles at either end. They are decorated with openwork patterns of trellis or foliage. The rims and bases are trimmed with linked volutes or fillets and groups of flowers and fruits, and Rococo scrolls form the feet (e.g. basket, 1770; Amsterdam, Rijksmus.). In the later 18th century, with increasing mechanization, some components of his baskets were machine-made. Though chiefly known for these elaborately decorated objects Brandt also produced relatively plain ones, for example an inkstand of 1735 (Amsterdam, Rijksmus.), which is undecorated except for a small pierced lid, and a large tureen and salver (1765; Amsterdam, Hist. Mus.), whose only decoration is the figure of a cow that forms the handle of the tureen cover, and rocaille motifs on the feet and handles of the tureen itself.

BIBLIOGRAPHY

M. H. Gans and T. M. D. de Wit-Klinkhamer: *Dutch Silver* (London, 1961)

Meesterwerken in zilver/Amsterdam zilver, 1520–1820 (exh. cat. by K. A. Citroen, Amsterdam, Mus. Willet-Holthuysen, 1984)

□

Brandtner, Fritz [Friedrich] **(Wilhelm)** (*b* Danzig, Germany [now Gdańsk, Poland], 28 July 1896; *d* Montreal, 7 Nov 1969). Canadian painter of German birth. He was self-taught as an artist while in Danzig during the 1920s. He was attracted by Expressionist ideas and studied the work of contemporary artists in Germany through exhibitions and in books. Equally important was his experience of nature in the Baltic coastal region. A small, vivid painting, *Bather, Baltic Sea* (1925; Montreal, priv. col., see 1982 exh. cat., no. 1), which he took with him to Canada in 1928, echoes these experiences with stylistic influences from Max Pechstein and Paul Gauguin.

In Winnipeg, Brandtner found work as a designer for a mail-order catalogue. There he also formed a warm friendship with LeMoine FitzGerald. However, his highly coloured, emotionally aggressive drawings and paintings found few positive responses in Winnipeg, which had as yet little exposure to modern European art. In 1934, on FitzGerald's advice, Brandtner moved to Montreal, where he devoted himself to painting and to teaching art to underprivileged children. He was commissioned to design a number of murals, including several for the Canadian National Railway for various parts of the country. In these he pioneered the use of carved and painted linoleum. His mural for the ballroom of the Newfoundland Hotel, St John's, is a colourful, stylized rendering of musicians in carnival costume, the surface animated by textural variety. Other murals involved working in cast cement, stone, engraved steel and glass, as well as painting on canvas. He was among the first in Canada to experiment with abstract, Cubist and Constructivist styles, and his strength lay in his ability to assimilate influences into an intense personal statement. His lifelong concern for social issues, especially during the years of depression and war, is reflected in such works as the *Age of Anxiety* (see 1982 exh. cat., p. 47). Reminiscent of the work of Otto Dix, this work makes heavy use of black, depicting an urban crowd as if emerging from a station, with taut, harassed faces, uncertain of the future. Brandtner's defence of the artist's creative freedom of expression, recorded eloquently in his personal journals, permeates his art.

BIBLIOGRAPHY
Canadian Painting in the Thirties (exh. cat. by C. C. Hill, Ottawa, N.G., 1975)
The Brave New World of Fritz Brandtner (exh. cat. by H. Duffy and F. K. Smith, Kingston, Ont., Queen's U., Agnes Etherington A. Cent., 1982)

FRANCES K. SMITH

Brangwyn, Sir **Frank** (*b* Bruges, 12 May 1867; *d* Ditchling, Sussex, 11 June 1956). English painter and graphic artist. Largely self-taught, he helped his father, William Brangwyn, who was an ecclesiastical architect and textile designer in Bruges. After his family moved to England in 1875 Brangwyn entered the South Kensington Art Schools and from 1882 to 1884 worked for William Morris. Harold Rathbone and Arthur Mackmurdo encouraged him to copy Raphael and Donatello in the Victoria and Albert Museum, complementing his already broad knowledge of Dutch and Flemish art.

Brangwyn's *plein-air* work in Cornwall from 1884 to 1888 resulted in a series of oils, exhibited at the Royal Academy and the Royal Society of British Artists, London, in which the subdued tones indicate the influences of Whistler and the Newlyn school. Journeys to the Near East, South Africa and Europe in the early 1890s, and contact with Arthur Melville, encouraged the use of a brighter palette in exotic subjects such as the *Slave Market* (1892; Southport, Atkinson A.G.). He held his first one-man exhibition in 1891, and the success of his *Buccaneers* (St Louis, MO, George Washington U. Gal. A.) at the Paris Salon in 1893 was the beginning of an international reputation that continued throughout his career, particularly in Europe and the USA. He visited Venice in 1896 and was greatly excited by its pageantry and by the art of Titian and Veronese. These were the sources, with Delacroix, the European Symbolists, Dutch and French Realists, William Morris and the Pre-Raphaelites, that shaped his mature style in oils and murals.

In 1895, at the same time as he was establishing his reputation as an illustrator, Brangwyn received his first decorative commission, for Siegfried Bing's Maison de l'Art Nouveau in Paris. His first major British mural commission was the series of historical panels (1901–9; *in situ*) for Skinners' Hall in London . These synthesize keen observation from nature with inspiration from past and present art in a highly integrated symbolic and decorative ensemble, expressing his philosophy of art as the means to unite Man, God and Creation. The first panel, *Departure of Sir James Lancaster for the East Indies*, won his election as ARA in 1904 and, with his *Modern Commerce* panel (1900–06) at the Royal Exchange, London, led to many subsequent mural commissions in Britain and abroad. These included the scenes of contemporary industry and life for the Venice Biennales of 1905 and 1907 (1905 panels now in Leeds, C.A.G.) and for Lloyd's Register of Shipping (1908–14; destr.), London; historical murals for the Cuyahoga County Court House (1912), Cleveland, OH, and the State Capitol (1915), Jefferson City, MO; and work at Christ's Hospital (1912–23), Horsham, and St Aidan's Church (1909–16), Leeds.

The earthquake of 1910 in Messina, Sicily, inspired a notable series of watercolours, while in etching, which he had begun in 1904, he evolved a monumental style using strong chiaroscuro. Industry, shipping and contemporary London and Venice were favourite themes, as in *S Maria della Salute* (1908; see Gaunt, pl. 118). Work in other media included still-lifes and paintings in oil, such as the *Rajah's Birthday* (1908; Leeds, C.A.G.) and *The Swans* (*c.* 1924; London, William Morris Gal.), lithographs, war posters, and pageant, scenery and architectural designs.

From 1924 Brangwyn was occupied with what he regarded as the culmination of his life's work, the commission from Edward Guinness, 1st Earl of Iveagh, for panels for the Royal Gallery in the House of Lords, Houses of Parliament, London, to form part of the Peers' War Memorial. These illustrated British Empire themes but were rejected by the Lords as being too flamboyant for their setting. On completion in 1933 they were purchased for the Guildhall, Swansea: they are still *in situ*.

Brangwyn was elected RA in 1919 and became President of the Society of Graphic Artists in 1921, having served as President of the Royal Society of British Artists (1913–18). After his murals of 1930–34 for the Rockefeller Center, New York, he devoted himself to religious art (e.g. the *Stations of the Cross*; from 1935; lithographs made for locations including Campion Hall, Oxford, where examples remain, and the monastery of St André (Zevenkerken), near Bruges), some furniture and ceramic designs, the creation of a museum for his work at Bruges and the donation of collections of his work to museums at Walthamstow, near London, and Orange, France, among others. He was knighted in 1941. Brangwyn paid little regard to contemporary developments in art and in his later years lived virtually as a recluse at Ditchling, where he had settled in 1918.

BIBLIOGRAPHY

DNB; Thieme–Becker

W. S. Sparrow: *Frank Brangwyn and his Work* (London, 1910)

——: *Prints and Drawings by Frank Brangwyn* (London, 1919)

H. Furst: *The Decorative Art of Frank Brangwyn* (London, 1924)

Exhibition of Paintings, Drawings and Etchings by Frank Brangwyn, RA (exh. cat., London, 184 Queen's Gate, 1924) [exh. organized by Barbizon House]

M. S. Salaman: *Modern Masters of Etching, No. 1: Frank Brangwyn, RA* (London, 1925)

W. Gaunt: *The Etchings of Frank Brangwyn, RA* (London, 1926)

M. S. Salaman: *Modern Masters of Etching, No. 30: Frank Brangwyn, RA* (London, 1932)

F. Rutter: *The British Empire Panels by Frank Brangwyn, RA* (Leigh-on-Sea, 1937)

Works by Sir Frank Brangwyn (exh. cat., London, RA, 1952)

C. Bunt: *The Watercolours of Sir Frank Brangwyn, RA* (Leigh-on-Sea, 1958)

V. Galloway: *The Oils and Murals of Sir Frank Brangwyn, RA* (Leigh-on-Sea, 1962)

J. Boyd: *The Drawings of Sir Frank Brangwyn, RA* (Leigh-on-Sea, 1967)

Frank Brangwyn Centenary (exh. cat., Cardiff, Welsh A. C., 1967)

Catalogue of the Works of Sir Frank Brangwyn, RA, 1867–1956, London, William Morris Gal. cat. (Walthamstow, 1974)

R. Brangwyn: *Brangwyn* (London, 1978)

The Art of Frank Brangwyn (exh. cat. by J. Freeman, Brighton Poly.; London, F.A. Soc.; 1980)

D. Marechal: *Collectie Frank Brangwyn*, Bruges, Brangwynmus. cat. (Bruges, 1987)

C. A. P. Willsdon: *Mural Painting in Britain, 1840–1940* (Oxford, in preparation)

CLARE A. P. WILLSDON

Brankston, A(rchibald) D(ooley) (*b* Shanghai, 18 Dec 1909; *d* Hong Kong, Jan 1941). English art historian. Fluent in Chinese, he was employed as a civil engineer in China from 1933 to 1934. He then helped with cataloguing, photographing and arranging the exhibits for the International Exhibition of Chinese Art at the Royal Academy in London (1935–6; *see* CHINA, §XX). This was followed during the next 18 months by visits to Beijing and Jingdezhen as a Universities China Committee Scholar to study Chinese ceramics. He returned to London in 1938 and became assistant keeper in the Department of Oriental Antiquities in the British Museum. In July 1940 he moved to Hong Kong to enter government service, where he died in 1941. He is best remembered for his pioneering work on Ming ceramics, *Early Ming Wares of Ching-tê-chên*.

WRITINGS

Early Ming Wares of Ching-tê-chên (Beijing, 1938/*R* Hong Kong, 1970)

'Yüeh Ware of the "Nine Rocks" Kiln', *Burl. Mag.*, lxxiii (1938), pp. 257–62

'Descriptions of Specimens', *Trans. Orient. Cer. Soc.*, xvi (1938–9), pp. 56–61

'Chinese Bronze Mirrors from the District of Yüeh', *Trans. Orient. Cer. Soc.*, xvii (1939–40), pp. 56–64

BIBLIOGRAPHY

'Mr A. D. Brankston', *Trans. Orient. Cer. Soc.*, xviii (1940–41), pp. 17–18

MARGARET MEDLEY

Braque, Georges (*b* Argenteuil-sur-Seine, Seine-et-Oise, 13 May 1882; *d* Paris, 31 Aug 1963). French painter, collagist, draughtsman, printmaker and sculptor. His most important contribution to the history of art was his role in the development of what became known as CUBISM. In this Braque's work is intertwined with that of his collaborator PABLO PICASSO, especially from 1908 to 1912. For a long time it was impossible to distinguish their respective contributions to Cubism, for example in the development of COLLAGE, while Picasso's fame and notoriety overshadowed the quiet life of Braque.

1. Life and work. 2. Working methods and technique.

1. LIFE AND WORK.

(i) Early work and Cubism, before 1918. (ii) Work between the wars, 1918–39. (iii) Late work, from 1940.

(i) Early work and Cubism, before 1918. His family moved in 1890 to Le Havre, where his father had a painting and decorating business. In 1897 Braque entered the municipal art school, where he met and became friendly with Othon Friesz and Raoul Dufy. He joined them in Paris at the turn of the century and, after a year of army service, settled in Montmartre in 1902. He began to visit the Musée du Louvre, where he encountered van Gogh's work, and that October he began to study at the Académie Humbert, where his fellow students included Francis Picabia and Marie Laurencin. The following year he studied briefly with Friesz and Dufy again at Léon Bonnat's studio at the Ecole des Beaux-Arts, but academic training held little interest for him and was short-lived. In 1905 he saw the work of Derain and Matisse at the Salon d'Automne, and in the same year he became friendly with the sculptor Manolo and the writer Maurice Raynal, spending the summer with them on the Normandy coast. These two events were both important in his association with Fauvism; Raynal and Manolo were both fellow members of the Cercle de l'Art Moderne, founded in Le Havre in the spring of 1906. In March of that year Braque exhibited his works for the first time at the Salon des Indépendants. In the summer he painted in Antwerp with Friesz, producing such Fauvist works as *Landscape near Antwerp* (priv. col., see Russell, pl. 3), and he spent the following winter at L'Estaque, near Marseille. The German collector Wilhelm Uhde bought five of his paintings from the Salon des Indépendants of spring 1907. Around this time he first met Daniel-Henry Kahnweiler and was introduced by Guillaume Apollinaire to Picasso.

In the autumn of 1907, first at L'Estaque and then back in Paris, Braque began his transition away from bright, Fauvist hues to a more subdued style, possibly as a result of the memorial exhibition of Cézanne's work at the Salon d'Automne of 1907. This transition was given additional impetus by Braque's visit, accompanied by Apollinaire, to Picasso's studio in late 1907, where he saw the *Demoiselles d'Avignon* (1907; New York, MOMA). While startling in its rawness in comparison to Matisse's contemporary large figure compositions, Braque's response was his *Large Nude* (1908; priv. col., see Mangin [Worms de Romilly], i, no. 5). In this important work Braque accepted the schematized structure, shallow space and subdued colour of Picasso's work. Another trip to L'Estaque in the summer of 1908 led to his first fully developed Cubist paintings, a group of landscapes with buildings, one of the best known being *Houses at L'Estaque* (Berne, Kstmus.). These were exhibited at the Galerie Kahnweiler in November, having been rejected by the Salon d'Automne. Their exhibition gave rise to the first reference in print to Braque as a painter of 'cubes', which came in a review by Louis Vauxcelles in *Gil Blas*, apparently echoing a remark made by Matisse. However, the term 'Cubism' as a critical label has a misleadingly geometric implication and was not proposed by either Braque or Picasso.

Later in 1908 Braque took the traditional theme of *Musical Instruments* (e.g. Mangin [Worms de Romilly], i, no. 7) and treated it with the Cubist stylization. At La Roche-Guyon during June and August 1909 Braque painted five views of the castle (e.g. *La Roche-Guyon: The Castle*, 1909; Eindhoven, Stedel. Van Abbemus.). These consolidated the flat treatment of landscape space introduced at L'Estaque, with thinner, more liquid paints. The still-lifes executed in Paris the following winter, including *Piano and Guitar, Violin and Palette* (both 1909–10; New York, Guggenheim) and the volumetric *Violin and Pitcher* (1910; Basle, Kstmus.) are less diaphanous, and the latter is arguably Braque's greatest Analytical Cubist dissection of form. The two violin images include *trompe l'oeil* representations of a nail with its shadow, which have been widely discussed in Cubist literature and which have been referred to as reminders of naturalistic illusionism in contrast to the new Cubist vision. In the winter of 1909–10 Braque and Picasso both had studios in Montmartre and saw each other daily.

Analytical Cubism reached its apogee in 1910–11 in increasingly painterly, nearly monochrome, brown canvases of still-lifes and, to a lesser extent, figures. One of the most important works of the period is the *Portuguese Man* (Basle, Kstmus.), begun in Céret in the French Pyrenees *c.* September 1911 but probably not finished until Braque returned to Paris in January 1912. In it he introduced stencilled letters and numbers in the upper part of the canvas, suggesting the backdrop of the café where the guitarist plays, yet pictorially these clean-edged letters sit on the surface. Braque's interest in the human figure remained primarily formal, and he showed little concern or flair for portraiture.

In 1911 Kahnweiler commissioned *The Fox* (New York, MOMA), one of Braque's first engravings, and about this time Braque began experimenting more significantly with other media and techniques and with new shapes, such as the circular canvas of *Soda* (1911; New York, MOMA). He also began to experiment with the application of paint, mixing it with sand (as in *Still-life with Grapes*, 1912; Paris, Gal. Louise Leiris), just as Picasso was introducing the use of Ripolin enamel. From 1912 Braque also began using a house-painter's comb to introduce areas of imitation wood-grain into his paintings. In 1912, the year of Braque's

marriage to Marcelle Lapre, he and Picasso stayed at Sorgues, near Avignon, and began using pre-existing objects and materials in their paintings (as in Picasso's *Still-life with Chair-caning*, 1912; Paris, Mus. Picasso; *see* CUBISM, fig. 1), partly to preserve a connection with reality in their works and partly out of an apprehension that their works were becoming, or were being seen as, too abstract. There was also a desire to reintroduce colour into their increasingly monochrome canvases. In the same year, according to Rubin (1989–90), Braque produced the first Cubist paper sculptures, probably using them in relation to painting as part of an enthusiasm for popular culture. This led him to the technique of papier collé, first explored in *Fruit Dish and Glass* (1912; priv. col., see Mangin [Worms de Romilly], i, no. 150). The artificial wood-grain paper (*faux bois*) that he stuck to paper on which he drew preserved the brown tonality of Analytical Cubism and acted as an integral part of the structure of the drawing, whereas Picasso's experiments with collage at the same time played on the deliberate disjuncture of material and means of expression between the inserted material and the rest of the work. Braque experimented for more than a year with wood-grain effects, for example using them with oil paint, as in *Fruit Dish and Ace of Clubs* (1913; Paris, Pompidou), and employing such paintings as points of reference for papiers collés such as *The Clarinet* (1913; New York, MOMA; see fig. 1). He began to experiment with newspaper cut into shapes, for example that of a guitar in *Collage with Newspaper* (1912; priv. col., see 1982 exh. cat., *Braque: Les Papiers collés*, p. 133), but it was not until the end of 1913 that he began using differently coloured paper to break away from the characteristic Cubist brown, for example in *Pipe, Glass and Die* (1914; Hannover, Sprengel Mus.), although even here he seems to have been more interested in quietly activating the white ground as a positive shape. Even at this stage, however, Braque showed comparatively little interest in introducing other pre-existing elements into his collages and preferred to draw the playing cards or pages of music that were often central to the composition. The austerity of Braque's work, in particular, at this time and the relentless formal interest in the narrow range of recurrent subject-matter (*see* STILL-LIFE, fig. 8), together with his interest in the actual means of picture-making rather than in extra-pictorial associations, established his reputation as the most rigorous exponent of Cubism. The same formal interest in the work not only of Braque but also of Picasso contributed perhaps to the act that their enterprise somehow managed to appear more abstract than it was in their own minds. Thus there followed a whole generation of international artists, including Kazimir Malevich and Piet Mondrian, who observed Cubism at a certain remove and then explored pure abstraction. Perhaps Cubism's greatest achievement, however, was its enshrinement of pictorial ambiguity through snatches of objects, word fragments and double meanings, and private and fanciful associations.

One of the important impulses of Cubism immediately before the outbreak of World War I was its focus on the boundaries of the conventional pictorial field. In early 1914 both Braque and Picasso included painted name labels within their compositions (e.g. Braque's *Music*, 1914; priv. col., see 1949 exh. cat., p. 71). Their idea brilliantly

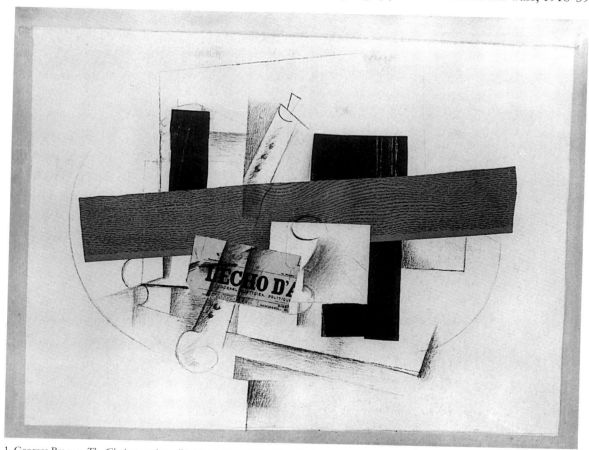

1. Georges Braque: *The Clarinet*, papier collé, 0.95×1.20 m, 1913 (New York, Museum of Modern Art)

encapsulated paradoxical characteristics: both the *tableau objet* concept and the relativity and limits of illusionism. While Picasso developed the witty device of the pasted paper 'frame', which mocked exhibition culture, Braque continued to experiment with variations on the rectilinear pictorial format, for example in his *Still-life with Pipe* (1914; Paris, Pompidou).

Braque was called up for military service in August 1914, and he was wounded in the head and temporarily blinded on 11 May 1915 at Carency. He resumed painting in late 1916, with only three works dated to that year. The following year he produced an impressive horizontal *Still-life* with a 'false' painted nameplate (priv. col., see Mangin [Worms de Romilly], ii, no. 8) and resumed the theme of the shaped canvas. Among a number of lozenge formats is the *Glass and Ace of Clubs* (1917; New York, Krugier Gal.), which is especially interesting because of the reappearance of the false nameplate, now used to set off an incised lozenge on top of an imitation stone rectangle possibly related, according to Jean Leymarie (see 1973 exh. cat.), to low reliefs by Henri Laurens. The unusual octagonal works of 1918, including the collage *Guitar* (Columbus, OH, Mus. A.) and *The Goblet* (Philadelphia, PA, Mus. A.), are also interesting, but more important, as a statement of Braque's intention to resume the issues

interrupted by the war, was the fine papier collé *Clarinet* (1918; Philadelphia, PA, Mus. A.), which uses the stable, coloured, interlocking planes of pre-war Synthetic Cubism.

(ii) Work between the wars, 1918–39. In the winter of 1918–19 Braque began work on large-scale still-life compositions that continued to show an interest in the geometric austerities of Cubism but in which he also began to use richer, vivid surfaces. The impressive *Café-bar* (Basle, Kstmus.; see fig. 2) was one of the first in a series of paintings of still-life subjects placed on the *guéridon*, the round-topped pedestal table in his studio that reappeared in his paintings for the next decade and that gave its name to this series. It was soon followed by *Guitar and Glass: Socrates* (1921; Paris, Pompidou), one of the early *Fireplace* series, in which the still-life is seen against a mirror on an elaborate mantelpiece. In both series the compressed objects are given complex patterning and outlines, and in both series Braque adopted an unusual vertical format (e.g. *The Table*, 0.73×1.8 m, 1928; New York, MOMA). In 1921 he executed a series of engravings for Erik Satie's play with music *Le Piège de Méduse*.

The shift from the imitation of humble wood *c.* 1912 to the imitation of marble in the *Fireplace* series (e.g. the *Marble Table*, 1925; Paris, Pompidou) shows a change of

2. Georges Braque: *Café-bar*, oil on canvas, 1.63×0.83 m, 1919 (Basle, Kunstmuseum)

Braque from reassessing the possibilities of Cubism in such works as *The Guéridon* (1928–9; Washington, DC, Phillips Col.).

In 1929 Braque visited Dieppe and the Normandy coast of his youth, deciding to build a studio, designed by Paul Nelson, near by at Varengeville-sur-Mer, where he spent many summers. He began to paint small-scale landscapes again (e.g. *Dieppe Beach*, 1929; Stockholm, Mod. Mus.), and the already evident new interest in colour, decoration and ornament increased in such still-lifes as the *Blue Mandolin* (1930; St Louis, MO, A. Mus.). In some cases rhythmical patterns of lines served as an ornamental background to strongly curved outlines of shapes, as in the *Clay Pipe* (1931; New York, MOMA). This new concern for linear elements led Braque to study Greek vase paintings in the Musée du Louvre, which stimulated his interest in Classical subject-matter, and to a period of graphic work culminating in a commission from Ambroise Vollard to illustrate Hesiod's *Theogony* with 16 etchings (1932; see fig. 3). In his paintings, however, he continued to concentrate on texture and ornament, enriched with such new colours as the dominant pink of the *Pink Tablecloth* (1931–3; Provincetown, MA, Chrysler A. Mus.).

Around 1936 the focus of Braque's paintings began to shift from the still-life to wider interior views. Into ornately decorated rooms he introduced impersonal, flattened figures, as in *Woman with Mandolin* (1937; New York, MOMA) or *The Duet* (1937; Paris, Pompidou). The new mood suggested by his use of brighter colours was offset, however, by a series of macabre *vanitas* still-lifes, linked

mood underlying Braque's work in the 1920s and a new taste for luxuriant and decorative material. He also reintroduced the figure into his work about this time in the form of a series of paintings of semi-draped *Canéphores* or ceremonial basket-bearers, which he began in 1922 (e.g. *Nude Woman with a Basket of Fruit*, 1926; Washington, DC, N.G.A.). These represented in part a response to Picasso's new classicism, but they were in no way imitative of Picasso and were partly intended as tributes to Ingres, Corot and Renoir, reflecting Braque's response to the 'return to order', which sought to re-establish values lost in the chaos of the war. In 1924 he designed the décor for the Ballets Russes production of *Les Fâcheux* and in the same year he signed a contract with Paul Rosenberg's Galerie de l'Effort Moderne, Paris, the major promoter of Cubism in the 1920s, after having been represented by Kahnweiler in the pre-war period. The new-found sensuous lyricism of this period did not, however, prevent

3. Georges Braque: etching, illustration to Hesiod's *Theogony*, 301×222 mm, 1932 (New York, Museum of Modern Art); published by Maeght Editeur (Paris, 1955), pl. 29

4. Georges Braque: *Studio II*, oil on canvas, 1.31×1.62 m, 1949 (Düsseldorf, Kunstsammlung Nordrhein–Westfalen)

to the theme of the artist's studio, that he began in 1938 (e.g. *Vanitas*, 1939; Paris, Pompidou), possibly in despair at the approach of World War II. He also built a sculpture studio near his house at Varengeville and began experimenting with sculpture about this time, producing simple and playful, if rather two-dimensional works such as *Horse and Cart* (bronze, 1939–40; Paris, Pompidou).

(iii) Late work, from 1940. Following the German occupation of Paris in June 1940, Braque went to Limoges and then the Pyrenees, but in the autumn he returned to Paris, where he remained for most of the war. After a year of artistic inactivity, in 1941 he began painting again. His work during the occupation was characterized by a series of stark interiors, such as *Washstand at the Window*, and still-lifes dominated by sombre colours, such as the *Black Fish* (both 1942; Paris, Pompidou). He still persevered, however, with earlier innovations, such as the false frame and title plaque of *My Bicycle* (1941–60; priv. col., see Descargues, Malraux and Ponge, p. 191). In 1944 he returned to Varengeville and embarked on a new series of spatially complex interiors (e.g. the *Billiard Table*, 1945; Paris, Pompidou). Seven paintings in this series were completed by 1949. Soon after the end of the war Braque began to explore colour lithography, beginning a close

association with the master printer Fernand Mourlot and his new dealer, Aimé Maeght. In 1949 he also finished five of a new series of *Studio* paintings (e.g. *Studio II*; Düsseldorf, Kstsamml. Nordrhein–Westfalen, see fig. 4), a series that he extended to nine by 1956. All but one of this series are large in scale, the exception being the first, *Studio I* (1949; Paris, Guerlain priv. col.), which is in some ways the finest: it centres on the elemental figure–ground relationship of a white vase on a black ground, complicated by the fact that the vase seems to rest on a second picture-within-the-picture of a black jug and fruit bowl. In 1953 he was commissioned by Georges Salles to decorate the ceiling of the Henry II (or Etruscan) room in the Palais du Louvre with the bird motif that had already appeared in the *Studio* series. The next year he finished a design for stained-glass windows for the church in Varengeville (*in situ*). His output of graphic work continued, including colour lithographs such as *Leaves, Colour, Light* (1953–4) and colour etchings such as *Amaryllis* (1958), one of his most lyrical works. The earlier bird motif was now transformed into a number of images of flight in such paintings as *Bird Returning to its Nest* (1955) and *On the Wing* (1956–61; both Paris, Pompidou). There was also a series of narrow horizontal landscapes (1955–8) with wide painted frames (e.g. *Field at Colza*, 1956–7; Paris, M. & Mme Claude Laurens priv. col.). By the end of the 1950s the densely worked and textured surface that had become characteristic of Braque's style had begun to influence younger artists such as Nicolas de Staël. Braque became chronically ill in 1959 and left unfinished his last canvas, the *Weeding Machine* (1961–3; Paris, Pompidou).

2. WORKING METHODS AND TECHNIQUE. Braque was responsible with Picasso for many of the innovations and experiments associated with Cubism. The exact significance of Braque's contribution was emphasized by William Rubin in his close study of the chronology of the development of Cubism (see 1989–90 exh. cat.). Rubin stressed Braque's experiments in paper sculpture, mentioned in a letter of August 1912, as well as attributing to Braque the introduction of many techniques associated with collage, such as stencilling and combed false wood-grain effects. Braque's role in the development of collage was more enduring and consolidating than that of Picasso, who experimented immediately with a wide variety of papers, including daily newspapers and other aspects of popular culture, while Braque at first worked more slowly through the spatial and tactile associations of wood-grain paper (for further discussion *see* §1(i) above).

Throughout his career Braque painted slowly and directly, without preparatory drawings. During the Cubist period in particular he drew upon painter–decorator techniques he had learnt in his youth, such as the use of the metal comb to imitate wood-grain, and he continued to use sand in his paint throughout his career. After World War I, until about the end of the following decade, Braque prepared canvases with a black ground, which allowed him to leave a dark outline around the forms and also had the effect of enriching the luminosity of the overlaid colours. From the 1920s he started to work concurrently on several paintings, sometimes on different themes, and he began what became an enduring practice of having many half-finished canvases in his studio at any one time, occasionally as many as 30. In the 1930s he experimented with drawing finely scratched lines on plaster panels, which he first covered with a dark paint. The idea for these *plâtres gravés* was partly derived from pre-Classical Greek intaglios that he had seen in the Musée du Louvre, heralding his interest in Classical subjects in the 1930s and his subsequent interest in graphic work.

WRITINGS
S. Appelbaum, ed.: *Illustrated Notebooks, 1917–1955* (New York, 1971)

BIBLIOGRAPHY
R. Bissière: *Georges Braque* (Paris, 1920)
D. Cooper: *Braque: Paintings, 1909–1947* (London, 1948)
Georges Braque (exh. cat. by H. R. Hope, New York, MOMA, 1949)
S. Fumet: *Sculptures de Georges Braque* (Paris, 1951)
D. Vallier: 'Braque, la peinture et nous', *Cah. A.*, xxix (1954), pp. 13–24
J. Russell: *Georges Braque* (London, 1959)
N. Mangin [Worms de Romilly]: *Catalogue de l'oeuvre peint de Georges Braque*, 7 vols (Paris, 1959–82)
J. Richardson: *Georges Braque* (New York, 1961)
F. Mourlot: *Braque lithographe* (Monaco, 1963; Eng. trans., 1963)
S. Fumet: *Georges Braque* (Paris, 1965)
E. Mullins: *Braque*, World A. (London, 1968)
P. Descargues, A. Malraux and F. Ponge: *Georges Braque* (Paris, 1971)
Braque: The Great Years (exh. cat. by D. Cooper, Chicago, IL, A. Inst., 1972)
Georges Braque (exh. cat., ed. J. Leymarie; Paris, Mus. Orangerie, 1973)
W. Rubin: 'Cézannism and the Beginnings of Cubism', *Cézanne: The Late Work* (exh. cat., ed. W. Rubin; New York, MOMA, 1977), pp. 151–202
A. Martin: *Georges Braque: Formation and Transition, 1900–1909* (diss., Cambridge, MA, Harvard U., 1979)
P. Pouillon and I. Monod-Fontaine: *Oeuvres de Georges Braque, 1882–1963* (Paris, 1982)
D. Vallier: *Braque: L'Oeuvre gravé* (Paris, 1982)
Braque: Les Papiers collés (exh. cat. by E. A. Carmean jr and I. Monod-Fontaine, Washington, DC, N.G.A.; Paris, Pompidou; 1982)
Georges Braque en Europe: Centenaire de la naissance (exh. cat., ed. G. Martin-Méry; Bordeaux, Gal. B.-A.; Strasbourg, Mus. A. Mod.; 1982)
Georges Braque: The Late Paintings, 1940–63 (exh. cat. by H. B. Chipp, Washington, DC, Phillips Col.; San Francisco, CA, F.A. Museums; Minneapolis, MN, Walker A. Cent.; Houston, TX Mus. F.A.; 1982–3)
Georges Braque, 1882–1963 (exh. cat. by P. Daix, I. Monod-Fontaine and M. T. Ocaña, Barcelona, Mus. Picasso, 1986)
S. Fauchereau: *Braque* (Paris, 1987)
B. Zurcher: *Georges Braque: Life and Work* (New York, 1988)
Picasso and Braque Pioneering Cubism (exh. cat. by W. Rubin, New York, MOMA, 1989–90)
K. Wilkin: *Georges Braque* (New York, 1991)
C. Poggi: *In Defiance of Painting: Cubism, Futurism and the Invention of Collage* (New Haven, CI, 1993)

For further bibliography *see* CUBISM.

LEWIS KACHUR

Brascassat, Jacques-Raymond (*b* Bordeaux, 30 Aug 1804; *d* Paris, 28 Feb 1867). French painter. He began his artistic career in Bordeaux at the age of 14 with the landscape painter Théodore Richard (1782–1859) and showed an early interest in drawing animals. By 1825 he was studying under Louis Hersent at the Ecole des Beaux-Arts in Paris and was sent to Italy the following year, despite coming only second in the Prix de Rome with *Hunt of Meleager* (Bordeaux, Mus. B.-A.). In Rome Brascassat met Théodore-Caruelle d'Aligny, with whom he spent most of his first year sketching in the surrounding countryside, producing such masterly works as *View of Marino, Morning* (Orléans, Mus. B.-A.). The history paintings he sent back to Paris, however, met with little success. Returning to Paris in 1830, he rejoined d'Aligny at Barbizon in 1831 and exhibited six landscapes of the area at the Paris Salon.

At the Salon of 1831 Brascassat received a first prize for his landscapes, while a special mention was made of his animal pieces, a genre that he subsequently made his own, abandoning history painting completely. By 1837 when he exhibited *Bulls Fighting* (Nantes, Mus. B.-A.) at the Salon his reputation as an animal painter was firmly established. The massive popularity of his works provoked the scorn of the critics, whose cutting comments on his entries at the Salon of 1845, coupled with the artist's failing health, prompted him to stop exhibiting at the Salon, despite his reception as an Academician the following year. Brascassat continued to produce landscapes from nature, drawing when he was no longer able to paint, and such works as a *Study of Oak and Elm Trees at Magny* (1865; Reims, Mus. St-Denis) show his continuing sensitivity as a landscape painter.

BIBLIOGRAPHY
P. Miquel: *Le Paysage français au XIXe siècle, 1824–1874: L'Ecole de la nature*, ii (Maurs-la-Jolie, 1975), pp. 248–67
Barbizon au temps de J.-F. Millet, 1849–1875 (exh. cat., ed. G. Bazin; Barbizon, Salle Fêtes, 1975), pp. 126–9

Théodore Caruelle d'Aligny et ses compagnons (exh. cat., ed. M. M. Aubrun; Rennes, Mus. B.-A. & Archéol., 1975)

LORRAINE PEAKE

Braschi, Giovanni Angelo. *See* PIUS VI.

Brasília. Capital city of Brazil. Founded on the central plateau *c.* 1000 km from the Atlantic coast, within a federal district in Goiás state, the city (population *c.* 400,000) was inaugurated in 1960. The establishment of a new federal capital was part of a series of modernization measures drawn up by Juscelino Kubitschek when he became President of Brazil in 1956; the city was intended to be the urban and architectural expression of those measures, symbolizing the national reconstruction of Brazil. A national competition for the master-plan (*plano piloto*) was held in 1957 and won by Lúcio Costa. His proposal (for illustration *see* COSTA, LÚCIO) was inspired by the urban planning principles of CIAM and its Athens Charter (1933), which included functional zoning and the use of isolated, single-function buildings; these principles were realized for the first and only time at Brasília.

In his manifesto Costa explained the guiding principle behind his aeroplane-shaped plan, partly enclosed by an artificial lake, as the gesture of possession: two axes that form a cross. It also incorporated advanced principles of highway technology, fulfilling Kubitschek's explicit intention of building a city for the motor car. Thus the curved north–south axis (the 'wings' of the aeroplane) was designed as a linear traffic artery, with the main residential sectors, framed by a dense belt of trees, spread along it in superblocks: areas 350 m square in which six-storey blocks of flats built on pilotis were placed. The superblocks are grouped in neighbourhood units together with local businesses and schools. At the junction of the two axes are the commercial and entertainment sectors, with the campus of the University of Brasília in open ground beyond. The monumental east–west axis contains the cultural sector, with the Museum of Brasília, library, theatre and cathedral, and the administrative sector. Here the Esplanada dos Ministérios, lined with identical government blocks, terminates at the triangular Praça dos 3 Poderes, where the buildings for the three branches of government are placed: the Palácio de Alvorado (presidential palace), the Supreme Court and the Congresso Nacional complex at the apex. Oscar Niemeyer, who was Chief Architect at Brasília for the first five years of construction, achieved a logistic miracle in completing most of the main public buildings in time for inauguration in 1960, and his elegant and original designs provide an appropriate architectural expression of Costa's lucid and integrated plan (for further discussion and illustration *see* NIEMEYER, OSCAR; *see also* GLASS, fig. 8). Much of the landscaping was carried out by ROBERTO BURLE MARX.

In practice, however, the plan for Brasília created several problems, the most crucial being the lack of provision for low-cost housing, which developed instead in unplanned satellite settlements between 13 and 43 km from the centre. The census of 1985 recorded only 25% of the total population of the Federal District of Brasília as living in the city inscribed by the pilot plan. In 1987 Costa produced a plan for the extension of Brasília with new wings for low-cost housing, which was faithful to the intent of the original. This proposal was widely criticized, however, a reflection of changing views on urban planning.

BIBLIOGRAPHY

L. Costa: 'Relatório sobre o plano piloto de Brasília', *Leituras de planejamento e urbanismo*, IBAM (Rio de Janeiro, 1965)
——: 'O urbanista defende a sua capital', *Acrópole*, xxxii/375–6 (1970), pp. 7–8
M. Gorowitz: *Brasília: Uma questão de escala* (São Paulo, 1985)
A. Paviani, ed.: *Brasília: Espaço urbano em questão* (São Paulo, 1985)

REGINA MARIA PROSPERI MEYER

Brașov. Romanian town in Transylvania. Situated near a commercial route between Central Europe and the Balkans, it developed, according to tradition, first around the church of St Bartholomew under the Sprenghi Hill; further development took place under the Tîmpa Hill. It was colonized by the Teutonic Knights in 1211, and in 1223 an archdeacon's seat was established under papal authority. The Evangelical church of St Bartholomew, the oldest ecclesiastical building in the town, appears to date from the second half of the 13th century but is sometimes identified with a Premonstratensian nunnery, recorded in 1235. One of the most characteristic monuments of Transylvanian Early Gothic architecture, the basilica has a choir with two bays (one polygonal, the other square) and two pairs of lateral chapels, a transept, three aisles and two massive west towers. It was influenced by the Cistercian monastery of Cîrta and the Romanesque Benedictine style of Hungary. Protective walls surrounded the church and a fortress stood guard on the Sprenghi Hill above. The town's fortifications were developed in response to an increasing Ottoman threat, and by the 16th century they were the most powerful in Transylvania. Brașov had three gates from a very early date; the present Ecaterina Gate is the external tower of one of them. Maintenance of the bastions was entrusted to the guilds. The best preserved is the hexagonal Weavers' Bastion (now a museum), reconstructed in 1750.

Some sources relate that the Brașovia fortress, situated on top of the Tîmpa Hill, was built as a royal castle after the expulsion of the Teutons (1225) but was destroyed in 1445. It contained a chapel to St Leonard, the demolition of which was approved in 1458 on the condition that an altar was built to this saint in the parish church. The chapel may have been part of a monastic establishment (not later than the second half of the 13th century). According to references from 1395 and 1411, there was a chapel on St Martin's Hill, although the oldest parts of the present building date to after 1447.

In the 15th century Brașov became the largest town in Transylvania. The reconstruction of the Romanesque parish church of St Mary, which probably began in the late 14th century and ended by the mid-15th, was largely patronized by a parishioner called Toma. Restoration of the interior took place after a fire in 1689, and after the Reformation it became an Evangelical church. Named the Black Church after 1789, this Gothic hall structure is the largest medieval church in Transylvania. The choir has three aisles with octagonal pillars, a polygonal apse and a vestry on the north side. The main body of the church also has three aisles with octagonal pillars, though not in line with those in the choir, and two west towers, the south-west one being the best preserved. The exterior of the choir has simple, stepped buttresses ending in finials, each with a statue under a canopy and on the walls a gallery with a stone parapet. The iconographic programme and location of the statues are reminiscent of the decoration of the church of Sebeș Alba. Of the five portals, the north-east 'Golden Gate' and the principal west portals have particularly rich decoration and are evidence of the presence of the itinerant workshop of the church of St Elizabeth of Košice.

In the late 14th century the Orthodox church of St Nicholas was built at Scheia Brașovului outside the town. The first wooden structure was followed by two in stone (in the mid-15th century and early 16th respectively). The third building was enlarged to the west at the end of the 16th century by means of a narthex with three aisles. Around 1740 the apse was replaced by a trifoil plan. The town hall (now the Museum of History) was built in the main square and developed on the site of a 14th-century watch-tower. Reconstruction of the 16th-century building took place in 1770–74. A fire in 1689 damaged a number of medieval structures in the town, but surviving buildings include a patrician home in the town square, which houses 16th-century wall paintings; the Roman Catholic church (1776–82) was built by Iosef Carol Lamasch on the site of the 14th-century Dominican monastery of SS Peter and Paul and is a fine example of the town's Baroque architecture.

BIBLIOGRAPHY

E. Jekelius, ed.: *Das Burzenland: Kronstadt*, iii (Brașov, 1928)

G. Treiber: 'Ausgrabungen der Bergkirche der Brașoviaburg auf der Zinne', *Siebenbürg. Vjschr.*, liv (1934)

A. Ferenczi: 'Die Bauperioden der Burgkirche der Brașoviaburg, *Siebenbürg. Vjschr.*, lviii (1935)

V. Vătășianu: *Istoria artei feudale in Țările române* [The history of feudal art in the Romanian countries], i (Bucharest, 1959), pp. 12–13, 285

M. Nistor: 'Cetatea Brașovului' [The Brașov fortress], *Cumidava*, i (1967)

L. Munteanu and M. Beldie Dumitrache: 'Rezultatele cercetărilor arheologice la Biserica Sf. Nicolae din Scheii Brașovului, etapa 1975' [The result of the archaeological researches at the church of St Nicholas in Scheia Brașovului, 1975 phase], *Rev. Muz. & Mnmt.: Ser. Mnmt. Ist. & A.*, 1 (1976)

D. N. Busuioc: 'Arhitectura gotică timpurie din Țara Bîrsei in lumina unor noi cercetări' [The Early Gothic architecture in Barsei Country in the light of new researches], *Stud. Cerc. Istor. A.*, xxv (1978), pp. 8–13

P. Niedermaier: *Siebenbürgische Städte* (Bucharest, 1979), pp. 123–7

SUZANA MORE HEITEL

Brașovan, Dragiša (*b* Vršac, 25 May 1887; *d* Belgrade, 10 June 1965). Serbian architect. He studied (1907) at the Technical University in Budapest and received a diploma (1912) from the University of Belgrade. From 1912 to 1918 he worked in Budapest, on the design of theatres, public buildings and private villas, exhibiting his projects with the progressive group Oblik (Form). After World War I he opened his own practice in Belgrade. Up to 1930 he followed the middle course of Central European eclecticism, thereafter developing an interest in a decorative form of Modernism, a kind of formalism where perfectly functional elements are articulated for purely decorative reasons. This produced modern architectural massing, decorated with plain cornices, window frames and facings concealing structural members. He received the International Grand Prix for Architecture for his Yugoslav Pavilion at the Exposició Internacional, Barcelona (1929). His main works are the Chamber of Commerce Headquarters (1930), Belgrade; the Air Force Headquarters (1935), Zemun; the State Printing Works Building (1938), Senjak; and many blocks of flats. Other buildings include the Workers' Chamber (1933) and the Government Building (1939), both in Novi Sad. After World War II he designed many new workers' housing settlements in Serbia and the Hotel Metropol (1955), Belgrade. The Officers' Headquarters at Dedinje, Belgrade, shows signs of regression into Serbian folk eclecticism.

BIBLIOGRAPHY

Enciklopedija likovnih umjetnosti, i (Zagreb, 1959), p. 489

PAUL TVRTKOVIĆ

Brass. The alloy of copper and zinc. The alloy of copper and tin is bronze, while alloys with both zinc and tin are known as gunmetals. Many of the alloys that are described as bronze are in fact brass; for a discussion of the origins and usage of these terms *see* BRONZE.

BIBLIOGRAPHY

E. R. Caley: *Orichalcum and Related Ancient Alloys*, American Numismatic Society Publication, no. 151 (New York, 1964)

P. T. Craddock, ed.: *2000 Years of Zinc and Brass*, BM Occas. Pap., no. 50 (London, 1990)

I. Properties. II. Production. III. Uses.

I. Properties.

These depend very much on the zinc content, which gives a wide range of alloys. The properties of certain alloys will be considered here in order of ascending zinc content. For further technical information the reader should consult the publications of the Copper Development Association in Britain or of the corresponding group elsewhere.

Many copper alloys, including bronzes, have a small percentage of zinc as a deoxidizer. It scours out any dissolved oxygen in the metal and reduces gas porosity in the subsequent casting. For example, the alloy commonly used for sculpture in North American foundries contains 5% zinc with 90–95% copper, 3–4% silicon and 1% manganese; it is extremely malleable and pours very smoothly since it oxidizes less than traditional alloys. Brasses with *c.* 10–15% zinc are known as gilding metal, not so much because they are suitable for gilding but because they resemble gold in colour. These alloys have always been popular for costume jewellery and decorative metalwork, from the time of the Romans to the 18th century, when a variety known as pinchbeck was used, and right up to the present day. They are very ductile, and as the zinc content increases they become stronger but more brittle, hence the cracks seen on many thin-walled brass vessels.

The alloy with *c.* 25–35% zinc, known as red or common brass, is perhaps the most common. It has excellent all-round properties, being easy to cast, machine and work. It is especially suited to such industrial processes as spinning and extrusion. The bright golden-yellow colour is attractive, and this, coupled with the relative cheapness of the alloy, has ensured its usage for a wide range of objects and fittings.

Brass with *c.* 40% zinc, known as yellow or Muntz metal, is widely used for castings and sometimes for hot working. Alloys with more zinc than this tend to be brittle and impossible to work, but some 19th-century castings have up to 50% zinc. This made a cheaper alloy, because the zinc was so much less expensive than the copper, but the metal is rather grey and unattractive as well as brittle. For bidri, an alloy containing *c.* 90–98% zinc, *see* §II below.

All brasses tend to lose zinc as they weather, a process known as dezincification. This can often be seen on old brass, where the use of household cleaners over many years has selectively removed the zinc, leaving pinkish areas of almost pure copper on the surface.

Both brass and gunmetal may contain some lead, in which case they should be termed leaded brass or gunmetal. The lead improves their casting properties by lowering the melting temperature and rendering the molten alloy more fluid.

P. T. CRADDOCK,
with additional information by FRANCESCA BEWER

II. Production.

Brass is by far the most common copper alloy, but in comparison with bronze its history is relatively short. Bronze was first used in the late 4th millennium BC (*see* BRONZE, §II, 1), while brass only rose to prominence in the late 1st millennium BC; indeed, it was probably the last major alloy to be discovered before the Industrial Revolution. The reason for the late arrival of brass is the great volatility of zinc. At the temperature necessary to smelt zinc from its ores, zinc is a gas. In simple shaft furnaces other metals will collect in the bottom as dense, molten droplets to form an ingot, but zinc simply vaporises and goes up the flue, to be lost as smoke. Thus, metallic zinc was not produced until the development of special furnaces incorporating distillation apparatus to condense the metal away from contact with air. Such furnaces were first developed in India *c.* AD 1000 (*see* §3 below). Brass was in use, however, long before zinc itself was known. This apparent anomaly arose because early brass was made directly from copper metal and zinc ore. Comments by Pliny the elder suggest that some early brasses were produced simply by smelting a mixed copper–zinc ore, but his text is unclear; this account of brass will start with an assessment of the possibilities of a 'natural brass'.

1. 'Natural brass' and early production methods. 2. The cementation process. 3. Speltering.

1. 'NATURAL BRASS' AND EARLY PRODUCTION METHODS. Pliny implied that brass (*aurichalcum*) had once been produced naturally from a special ore found on Cyprus but that the source had been exhausted, and an artificial *aurichalcum* had to be made by mixing copper with zinc ore. By the time that Pliny was writing, in the 1st century AD, brass had been made by the latter process for some time, so the natural *aurichalcum* could well be hearsay. However, 'natural brasses' are certainly possible: some Pre-Columbian copper-alloy artefacts from Argentina have been shown to contain several percent zinc, and experiments in China have demonstrated that alloys of copper and zinc can be produced by a primitive smelting process using a mixture of copper and zinc ores. More significantly, a few copper alloys containing some zinc

have been excavated from sites in the Near and Middle East dating from the end of the 2nd millennium BC and beginning of the 1st. Assyrian records from this period mention, in addition to ordinary copper, a special 'copper of the mountain' that was highly prized. This could be synonymous with the contemporary Greek material *oreikhalkos*, which also meant 'copper of the mountain' and later came to refer to brass. Possibly 'copper of the mountain' was a natural brass produced from a zinc-rich copper ore, a contention that is supported by some of the

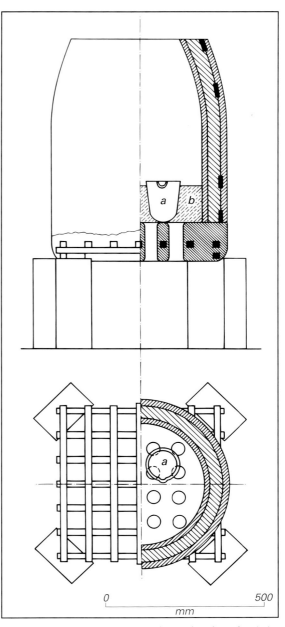

1. Section through a brass cementation furnace, based on a description given in the 12th century by Theophilus

bronze bowls discovered at the ancient Assyrian palace of Nimrud, which have been found to contain several percent zinc.

There are numerous Greek references to *oreikhalkos* from the 7th century BC, and they all speak of the metal as an exotic and highly prized material. Indeed, Plato in the *Critias* placed the value of *oreikhalkos* between that of gold and silver. Initially, *oreikhalkos* may have been produced as a natural alloy by co-smelting mixed ores, but there is one extraordinarily early reference to the production of brass from copper and zinc metals. This was made by the geographer Theopompos in the 4th century BC and recorded by Strabo in his *Geography*: 'There is a stone near Andeira which yields iron when burnt. After being treated in a furnace with a certain earth it yields drops of false silver. This, added to copper, forms the so-called mixture which some call *oreikhalkos*.' (Caley, p. 18)

The place in question is almost certainly the mine of Balia Maden, which lies near the site of ancient Andeira in north-west Turkey. The mine has a long history, producing silver from a mixed lead–zinc–iron-pyrites ore that was rich in such other metals as arsenic and antimony, as well

2. Part of a medieval zinc-smelting furnace excavated at Zawar, Rajasthan

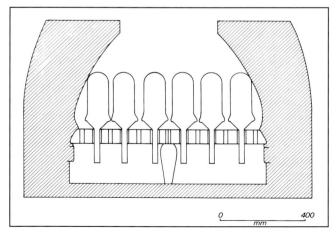

3. Simplified section through one of the zinc-smelting furnaces at Zawar, Rajasthan

as silver. These ores are quite common, but they are difficult to smelt with only simple technology. The Greeks may have used a method similar to that recorded by Agricola in his description of the German mines at Rammelsberg in the 16th century AD. According to Agricola, drops of metallic zinc condensed on the flue walls during the smelting, though most of the zinc would have been lost up the flue. The German miners called this metallic zinc 'false silver' and used it to produce a superior brass. They also scraped off the zinc oxide that formed in considerable quantities on the walls of the furnace and mixed it with charcoal and finely divided copper to make brass, heating it in a closed crucible to a temperature of about 1000° C. The charcoal reduced the zinc oxide to zinc vapour, which could not escape from the closed crucible but instead was absorbed into the exposed surfaces of the copper to form brass directly.

It is almost certain that a process similar to this first took place at Balia Maden or at some other mine near by, because this is the region in which brass first became common, and by the beginning of the 1st century BC local coins of low denomination were regularly being produced in brass (*see* §III, 1 below). It would have been obvious that *oreikhalkos* could be made from the zinc oxide as well as from the drops of 'false silver', and from there it would have been a short step to use zinc ores by themselves. Thus, the direct method of producing brass from copper and zinc ore in a crucible, known as the cementation process, was born. The process survived with only minor changes until the mid-19th century.

2. THE CEMENTATION PROCESS. Most of the zinc ores in the Middle East are sulphidic, so before they could be used in the cementation process they had to be converted to the oxide. This operation, which was first described by Dioscorides in the 1st century BC, was one of sublimation and gave a very pure product, which can be seen in the composition of brasses from the Middle East. It remained in use through the medieval period and was described in the 13th century by Marco Polo, who saw it in operation in Kirman: 'They take a vein of earth that is suited for the purpose and heap it in a furnace with a blazing fire above which is an iron grid. The fumes and vapour given off by this earth and trapped by the grid constitute *tutty* [zinc oxide].' (Latham, p. 39)

In Europe the zinc ore calamine (Amer.: smithsonite) was much more common. This is the carbonate, and it could be used without the elaborate pretreatment necessary for the sulphidic ores. An excellent and very detailed description of brass production in 12th-century Europe (see fig. 1) was given by Theophilus (Dodwell, pp. 123–4):

> Put in the furnace three, or four, or five [crucibles]—as many as the furnace can take—and surround them with coals [charcoal]. When they are hot, take the calamine. . .which has been finely ground with coal, put some in each crucible— about a sixth full—top it up with copper and cover with coals. . . . When the copper has completely melted, take a thin iron rod. . .and carefully stir so that the calamine is mixed with the copper. Then. . .put calamine in all of them as before, fill up with copper and cover with coals. When it has been completely melted again, stir it again with great care, and,

taking one crucible off with the tongs, pour it all out in the trenches dug in the ground and return the crucible to its place.

Subsequent accounts of the process include such texts as the *Pirotechnia* of Vannuccio Biringucci, the *Beschreibung allerfürnemsten mineralischen Ertzt Berckwercksarten…* (1580) of Lazarus Ercker, *L'Art de convertir le cuivre rouge en cuivre jaune* (1766) by Col. Galon and H. L. Duhamel du Monceau, and Diderot's *Encyclopédie*. The last contemporary description of the cementation process was given by J. Percy in his *Metallurgy* of 1860, in which he described the old process as practised in Wales in the 1790s and said that it had been carried on in Birmingham until recently and that some cementation furnaces might still be operating.

The reason for the decline of the cementation process in Europe through the first half of the 19th century was the growing prevalence of speltering. Although the cementation process was in some ways more efficient, since the brass was made directly from the zinc ore instead of from the metal, it was very difficult to control the amount of zinc in the alloy and impossible to make high-zinc brasses containing more than *c.* 30% zinc. Another disadvantage with European cementation brass was that it

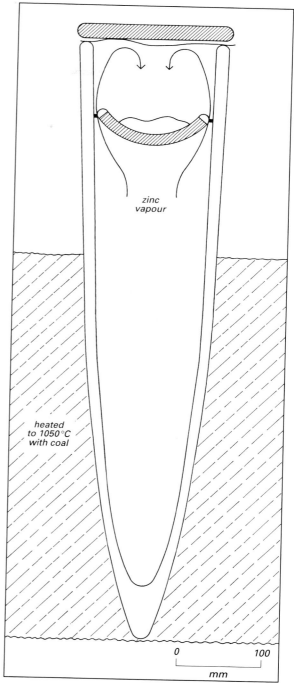

5. Simplified section through a Chinese zinc-smelting retort

4. Zinc smelting in China in the 17th century; woodcut from Song Yingxing: *Tian gong kai wu* ['The workings of heaven revealed'], 1637

usually contained undesirable impurities derived from the ore, particularly lead and iron.

3. SPELTERING. In this process superior brass is made by mixing copper and metallic zinc together. Speltering seems to have developed in the Indian Subcontinent,

6. Zinc smelting by the traditional method in China in the 1980s

where brass has a long history, certainly going back to the late 1st millennium BC. At first Indian brasses were made by the cementation process, and some of the early literature seems to refer to this, describing, for example, how zinc ore added to copper in a crucible will turn it golden. However, various Indian scientific and alchemic writings suggest that metallic zinc was known over 2000 years ago, and quite detailed descriptions of the speltering process survive from *c.* AD 1000.

Recent excavations at Zawar, near Udaipur in Rajasthan, where zinc production on an industrial scale was in full swing by the 12th century, have uncovered the intact remains of medieval furnaces and retorts (see fig. 2). The zinc ore was sphalerite, which was first roasted to remove the sulphur and then powdered and made into small balls, with charcoal and sticky organic materials as a binder. Contemporary scientific treatises, for example the *Rasaratnasamuccaya*, give lists of the ingredients to be added: 'Zinc ore is to be powdered with lac, treacle, white mustard, the myrobalans, natron and borax, and the mixture boiled with milk and ghee and made into balls. These are to be enclosed in a retort and heated strongly.' (Ray, p. 171)

The ingredients sound a little fanciful, perhaps more appropriate to the laboratory than to the commercial enterprise that flourished at Zawar, but the principle is sound enough, and examination of the retort contents has confirmed that it was made of a network of small balls fused together. It is impossible to say what material was used as the binding agent, as it would have burnt out, but

in the 19th century cow dung was used in copper smelting. The *Rasaratnasamuccaya* says that when the balls had been loaded into the retorts (described as being shaped like an aubergine), a condenser was sealed in place, terminating in a long, thin clay tube (see fig. 3). This is exactly what has been found at Zawar, where in addition a stick was pushed through the contents. When the retort was heated the organics burnt off, but the rest of the charge began to fuse, thus preserving the open structure. This was essential if the reducing gases were to circulate freely and the forming zinc vapour escape to the central channel left by the now-charred stick. The text describes the process whereby the inverted crucibles or retorts were placed in the hot upper chamber and the zinc collected in a cool chamber beneath: 'A vessel filled with water is to be placed inside a *koṣṭhī* apparatus [furnace] and a perforated plate placed over it; a crucible charged as described above is to be fixed in an inverted position over the plate and strongly heated by means of jujube wood charcoal.' (Ray, p. 172)

The site at Zawar is made up of huge mounds containing millions of spent retorts, and in some places the ancient *koṣṭhī* lie buried. One example, dating from the 14th century, has been excavated with the retorts still in place from the last firing. Thirty-six retorts had been placed in a 6×6 arrangement in each furnace. The excavated block was made up of a row of 7 furnaces shaped like truncated pyramids, each with 36 retorts, and thus a total of no less than 252 retorts were fired simultaneously. The zinc would condense in the necks of the clay condensers and drip into receiving vessels below. A furnace block such as this would probably have been capable of producing 25–50 kg per day, and it is assumed that many such blocks would have been operational. It is estimated that somewhere in the region of about 50,000–100,000 tonnes of zinc were produced at the site during its operational life, which lasted until the early 19th century, and that most of this would have been used for brass production.

The early history of brass in China is not well researched. The first references to zinc date from the late 15th century and the early 16th, when it was described as 'superior tin' or 'poor lead'. Despite the latter name, it was much valued because it could be mixed with copper to produce brass superior to that produced by the old cementation process. The process of zinc-making is illustrated in the *Tian gong kai wu* ('The workings of heaven revealed'; 1637) by Song Yingxing (see fig. 4) and seems very similar to that practised in south-west China in the late 20th century. It is based on the principle of the Mongolian still, with an internal condenser in the form of a saucer (see fig. 5). The charge of zinc ore and powdered coal is placed in the retort, and about 36 retorts are stacked together in trough-shaped furnaces (see fig. 6). The retorts are fired open for several hours to calcine the ore, and then the collecting saucers are added and loose fitting lids put on the retort tops. The zinc vapour begins to condense on the underside of the lids and drips back down into the saucers. As in India, most of the zinc was used to make brass. Zinc and brass production grew rapidly into a large-scale industry, and by the beginning of the 17th century China was exporting considerable quantities of zinc to Europe.

7. Horizontal retort zinc-smelting furnaces, Liège, early 19th century

In Europe some quality brass had been made from the 17th century, using the metallic zinc imported from the East or that collected from the flues of such smelters as those at Rammelsberg. It was used for making scientific instruments and costume jewellery. A number of special alloys were developed, among them pinchbeck (*see* §I above), the success of which lay in the use of zinc metal. Industrial production of zinc began in Bristol in the 1740s, when William Champion, a prominent local brass-maker, developed a process of zinc smelting by downward distillation. The principle was identical to that used in the Indian process, but on a much larger scale. The charge of zinc ore and charcoal was placed in six very large retorts in a furnace, the iron necks of the retorts protruding down through the furnace floor into the cool chamber, where the zinc was collected in vessels of water. The furnace itself was an adaptation of those used by the local Nailsea glass-makers, a good and quite typical example of technical cross-fertilization. Champion's ambitious spirit was perhaps better suited to technical innovation than to business: his industrial empire outran his resources, and he was declared bankrupt. However, the brasses produced by his process were highly satisfactory. It was said of James Emerson, a former employee of Champion who set up his own business: 'His brass is. . .more malleable, more beautiful, and of a colour more resembling gold than ordinary brass is. It is quite free from knots or hard places, arising from iron, to which other brass is subject, and this quality, as it respects the magnetic needle, renders it of great importance in making compasses.' (R. Watson,

Chemical Essays, London, 1784, pp. 47–8, reported in Day, 1973, p. 124)

The downward distillation process, or the 'English process' as it came to be known, was taken up by a few local brass-makers but without great success, since it was too expensive for utilitarian goods. It was rapidly superseded by other developments in Europe, particularly in Silesia and Belgium. In the Belgian (or Dony) process, developed by Jean-Jacques Daniel Dony in the early 19th century (Ladeuze, De Jonghe and Pauquet, 1991, pp. 15–34), some hundreds of retorts were fired together in double horizontal banks (see fig. 7). This method became one of the standard means of zinc production around the world, but from the beginning of the 20th century zinc began to be made electrolytically, and this now accounts for the majority of the world's production.

BIBLIOGRAPHY

Pliny: *Natural History*, XXXIV, ii
Dioscorides: *Materia medica* (AD 512); Eng. trans. by J. Goodyer (1655), ed. R. T. Gunter (Oxford, 1934), p. 234
Theophilus [Rugerus]: *De diversis artibus* (?1110–40); Eng. trans. by C. R. Dodwell as *The Diverse Arts* (London, 1961), pp. 123–4
V. Biringucci: *De la pirotechnia . . .* (Venice, 1540); Eng. trans. by C. S. Smith and M. T. Gnudi as *The Pirotechnia of Vannuccio Biringucci* (New York, 1942), pp. 70–76
G. Agricola: *De re metallica* (Basel, 1556; Eng. trans., London, 1912), p. 234
L. Ercker: *Beschreibung allerfürnemsten mineralischen Ertzt Berckwercksarten . . .* (Frankfurt am Main, 1580); Eng. trans. by A. G. Sisco and C. S. Smith as *Lazarus Ercker's Treatise on Ores and Assaying* (Chicago, 1951), pp. 254–8
Col. Galon and H. L. Duhamel du Monceau: *L'Art de convertir le cuivre rouge en cuivre jaune* (Paris, 1766); Eng. trans. by A. P. Woolrich and

A. den Ouden as *Galon and Duhamel du Monceau: The Art of Converting Red, or Rosette, Copper into Brass* (Eindhoven, n.d.)

D. Diderot and J. D'Alembert: *Métallurgie, Calamine*, vi of *Encyclopédie* (Paris, 1768)

J. Percy: *Metallurgy: Fuels, Fireclays, Copper, Zinc and Brass* (London, 1861)

P. Ray: *History of Chemistry in Ancient and Medieval India* (Calcutta, 1956)

R. E. Latham: *The Travels of Marco Polo* (London, 1958)

E-tu Zen Sun and Shiuo-chuan Sun: *T'ien-kung k'ai-wu: Chinese Technology in the 17th Century* (Philadelphia, 1966)

J. Day: *Bristol Brass* (Newton Abbot, 1973)

R. Halleux: 'L'Orichalque antique', *Ant. Class.*, xlii (1973), pp. 64–81

J. Needham: *Science and Civilisation in China*, v/ii (Cambridge, 1974)

A. R. Gonzalez: 'Pre-Columbian Metallurgy of Northwest Argentina', *Pre-Columbian Metallurgy of South America*, ed. E. P. Benson (Washington, DC, 1979), pp. 132–202

P. T. Craddock, A. M. Burnett and K. Preston: 'Hellenistic Copper-base Coinage and the Origins of Brass', *Scientific Studies in Numismatics*, ed. W. A. Oddy, BM Occas. Pap., no. 18 (London, 1980), pp. 53–64

P. T. Craddock: 'Report on the Composition of Metal Tools and Weapons from Ayia Paraskevi, Vounous, and Evereti, Cyprus', appendix to E. Peltenberg: *Cypriot Antiquities in the Birmingham Museum and Art Gallery* (Birmingham, 1981), pp. 77–8

Sun Shuyun and Han Rubin: 'Zhongguo zaoqi tongqi de chubu yanjiu' [A preliminary study of early Chinese copper and bronze artefacts], *Kaogu xuebao*, iii (1981), pp. 287–302 [Eng. abstract p. 302]

C. F. A. Schaeffer-Forrer, U. Zwicker and K. Nigge: 'Untersuchungen an metallischen Werkstoffen und Schlacken aus dem Berich von Urgarit', *Mikrochimica Acta*, i (Vienna, 1982), pp. 35–61

P. T. Craddock: 'The Early History of Zinc', *Endeavour*, xi (1987), pp. 183–91

M. J. Hughes and others: 'The Evidence of Scientific Analysis: A Case Study of the Nimrud Bowls', *Bronzeworking Centres of Western Asia*, ed. J. Curtis (London, 1988), pp. 311–16

F. Ladeuze, L. De Jonghe and F. Pauquet: 'Vielle-Montaigne, l'exploitation minière et la métallurgie du zinc dans l'ancien duché de Limbourg', *Bull. Trimest. Crédit Com. Belgique*, 178 (1991), pp. 15–34

III. Uses.

1. Ancient world. 2. Indian subcontinent. 3. Islamic lands. 4. China. 5. Europe.

1. ANCIENT WORLD. The production of brass on an industrial scale began in the late 1st millennium BC, almost certainly somewhere between Greece and India, using the cementation process of reacting zinc ore with copper metal (*see* §II, 1 above). It is likely that the first brasses came from this region, but unfortunately little analytical work has yet been done on copper alloys of such relevant civilizations as the Achaemenid Persians (7th–4th centuries BC) or the Mauryans of north India (4th–2nd centuries BC) or of the Hellenistic states that sprang up in the wake of Alexander the Great's short-lived empire of the 4th century BC. Some isolated examples have been found, and there is a little documentary evidence in the *Inscriptiones graecae* in the form of lists of offerings made at Greek temples. From the 4th century BC these differentiate between objects made of brass (*oreikhalkos*) and those of bronze or copper (*khalkos*).

The first regular series of surviving brasses that have so far been identified are some of the coins of Mithridates VI, who ruled much of Asia Minor between 121 BC and 63 BC. The brass coins all contain *c.* 20% zinc, made by the cementation process, and they commence *c.* 100 BC. The coins were minted in north-western Asia Minor, at Bithynia and Phrygia, whence there is other evidence of an early interest in brass and even in zinc. The copper-base coins in this series include both bronze and brass

8. Early brass coins from Asia Minor: (a) and (b) Pergamon, mid-1st century BC; (c) SC coin of the reform of the Eastern coinage, 27 BC; (d) *dupondius* and (e) *sestertius* of the general reform of 23 BC

(see fig. 8a–b), and there was a conscious selection of alloy for particular types. This practice continued in the region for the next half-century or so, down to the reform of the Eastern coinage undertaken by Augustus when he became emperor in 27 BC (8c). The *C4* coins were then made of brass and the *aes* of copper. This process seems to have been a trial run for the great central coin reform of 23 BC, when large numbers of copper-base coins were minted in Rome, including the *dupondii* and *sestertii* of brass (8d–e) and the *aes* of copper, clearly based on the preceding *C4* coinage. Thus, the coins of Mithridates VI seem to be directly ancestral to the reformed coins of the Roman Empire itself. The *dupondii* and *sestertii* were minted in enormous numbers and, from the 18th century, were known by numismatists as the 'first brass' series; they probably represent the first large-scale use of brass anywhere.

The coins made over the first 50 years of the Roman Empire usually contain *c.* 20–28% zinc with very little tin or lead; they were almost certainly made of cementation brass. However, after the mid-1st century AD the zinc content declines, and there is a corresponding rise in the lead and tin content, which suggests that scrap metal was being added to the brass. The decline in zinc content continued until, by the end of the 2nd century, none of the coins of the central mints could be described as being of brass at all. This led Caley to claim that the secret of brass-making had been lost, but in fact the situation was more complex. It seems that during the last years of the Republic and the early years of the Empire the use of brass was concentrated in coinage, military fittings and such decorative metalwork as brooches and fibulae, but otherwise bronze was still prevalent. Indeed, it is no exaggeration to state that most military fittings were of brass and, what is more, of undiluted, high-zinc brass straight from the cementation crucible. The contemporary civilian decorative metalwork tended to be made from a diluted brass with rather less zinc but some tin and lead. This suggests that in the early Imperial period, at least, there could have been an Imperial monopoly on the production of brass. In general, during the Roman Empire *c.* 20–30% of copper alloys contained significant amounts of zinc, with no sign of the fall off suggested by Caley. However, bronze remained the prevalent alloy and was used almost exclusively for some types of art metalwork, for example statues and mirrors.

2. INDIAN SUBCONTINENT. Brasses have been found among the metalwork excavated at Taxila, in Pakistan, a city that rose to prominence as a trading centre in the last centuries of the 1st millennium BC, after Alexander's campaigns had opened up contact and commerce between the Mediterranean and the East. Many of the metal vessels found at Taxila are local brass copies of Greek types, whereas the originals would have been of bronze. Unfortunately, metalwork from other major urban sites of the same period has not been analyzed. From the Gupta period (4th–5th century AD) copper-alloy statuettes of deities etc. were produced in quantity in north India, and analysis has shown that these are almost all of brass. This tradition of image-making in brass continued all over north India and Tibet until the mid-20th century; it still

flourished in Nepal in the late 20th century (*see* NEPAL, §VI, 4 and TIBET, §§III and V, 6). In south India, where trade contacts with the rich tin sources of South-east Asia were much stronger, statuettes continued to be made exclusively of bronze up to about the 15th century.

Not only did India have a precocious use of brass, but the technology was very advanced, and zinc metal was being produced on an industrial scale from *c.* AD 1000 (*see* §II, 3 above), enabling superior brass to be made by speltering copper and zinc metals. Enormous quantities of metal must have been used on vessels alone, since they have always been of brass in India.

A distinctive and uniquely Indian material is bidri (*see* INDIAN SUBCONTINENT, §VIII, 15(v)). This is an alloy containing *c.* 90% zinc and 5% copper. Vessels and a whole range of decorative metalwork are cast from the dull grey metal, then inlaid in silver with intricate floral patterns and arabesques before being dipped in a hot solution of salt, nitre and ammonium chloride, which gives the base metal an attractive matt black patination. Bidri has been made in Muslim areas throughout the Subcontinent, including the town of Bidar in the Deccan, from which it takes its name and whence it is supposed to have originated in the 15th century.

See also INDIAN SUBCONTINENT, §VII, 15(iii).

3. ISLAMIC LANDS. Islamic writers, for example Abu'l-Qasim Kashani, writing *c.* 1300, listed all tin sources as being well outside the Islamic world. The unavailability of

9. Brass-smith beating out a bucket, Fez, Morocco, 1980

tin in the Islamic world is reflected in the copper alloys, which are almost exclusively of brass (though they are often described as bronze), with the exceptions of mirrors and certain special high-tin bronzes (*see* BRONZE, §II, 6). On technical grounds Islamic metalwork can be divided into two groups: the cast metalwork that tends to be of brass, with *c.* 10% zinc and similar amounts of lead and a little tin, and the thinner pieces made from sheet brass that tend to have *c.* 20% zinc and only traces of other metals. The sheet metalwork was generally shaped by hammering (see fig. 9), but by the 13th century some vessels were formed by spinning. Islamic brassware was often richly decorated by chasing, emphasized by bitumen, and inlaid with silver or, more rarely, with gold. From the 16th century brass became less popular for everyday use and was replaced by tinned copper.

See also ISLAMIC ART, §IV, 1(i)–(iii) and 2(i).

4. CHINA. The evidence for the history of brass in China is rather sparse, but it seems that the alloy sprang to prominence very quickly *c.* 1500. This assumption is based on analyses of the coinage, which was of bronze until the late 15th century, when there was a change to brass; contemporary records speak of making the coinage from copper and a 'new' tin, almost certainly metallic zinc. Caution should be exercised here: a similar study of British coinage would suggest that the use of brass did not start until the 1930s with the minting of the brass threepenny bit. However, analyses of copper alloys of the Song (960–1279) and Ming (1368–1644) periods suggest that bronze remained the usual alloy, at least for art metalwork. From the 16th century brass replaced bronze almost completely. The technology and indeed the basic design of the ritual vessels and statuettes remained much the same, and the difference between the colour of the earlier, heavily leaded bronzes and the golden, high-zinc brass would have been nullified by the dark varnish or patination that almost invariably covers the later metalwork.

5. EUROPE. In the West the watershed between the general use of bronze and that of brass seems to have come with the fall of the Western Empire in the 5th century AD. Virtually all the sources of tin on which the Middle East and the Mediterranean relied were in the north-west of the Empire, so the loss of the tin-producing provinces of Britannia, Hispania and Pannonia must have severely curtailed production and supply. Analyses of Coptic metalwork, for example, show that by the 6th and 7th centuries AD brass had already largely replaced bronze; by the time industry had recovered in medieval Europe, brass was the prevalent copper alloy. Zinc ores are quite abundant over much of the earth's surface, including the Middle East, whereas tin is rare. The account by Stephanos of Alexandria in the 7th century AD of tin being brought to Egypt from Cornwall after miraculous voyages only serves to emphasize its rarity.

When Europe emerged from the Dark Ages brass was already prevalent. Analyses of some specific issues of base silver coins from Saxon England have shown that they were debased with brass of regular composition, and it is calculated that the smiths would have needed about ten

tonnes of brass, which suggests they had access to freshly smelted metal. The chief areas of production lay in northern Italy, southern Germany and Flanders, and it is believed that the 12th-century writer Theophilus, whose work *De diversis artibus* contains a detailed description of brass-making and working (*see* §II, 2 above), was a German. There is increasing evidence that the calamine zinc deposits at Stolberg, near Aachen, were exploited in Roman times, and it seems probable that this industry survived the barbarian onslaught of the 4th and 5th centuries, joined later by La Calamine (Kelmis, now in Belgium).

By the time of Charlemagne (*reg* 742–814) the brass industry was capable of producing major items of considerable artistic and technical sophistication, for example the doors of the Palatine Chapel, Aachen, and of the cathedrals of Hildesheim (*see* DOOR, fig. 3) and Mainz, together with crosses, fonts and other major ecclesiastical fittings. In the medieval period the industry was centred in such small towns as Dinant (hence the term dinanderie to describe medieval decorative brasswares) and Huy on the river Meuse, and in other centres throughout the Meuse Valley. The workshops in these towns produced a wide range of cast and hammered domestic vessels but are especially renowned for the church fittings, for example memorial brasses and lecterns, which once adorned the churches of all Christendom but, after centuries of strife and neglect, survive chiefly in England. Another centre developed in the late medieval period at Nuremberg (*see* NUREMBERG, §III, 2(ii)), utilizing the metal deposits at Rammelsberg and other mines in the Harz Mountains. This seems to have produced smaller, more domestic wares but on a very large scale. Documents from the early 16th century list enormous quantities of brassware shipped out to West Africa, with thousands of brass vessels being sent to individual trading stations. This trade demonstrates that brass production was now a major and increasingly international industry. The rise of the British brass industry dates from the end of the 17th century. Bristol was the first substantial centre and always specialized in sheet metalwork, including all manner of pots and pans. Much of the trade was for export.

The earlier centres, for example Bristol and Stolberg, favoured traditional water-powered hammers (see fig. 10) to fashion their wares, but as the Industrial Revolution gathered momentum such innovations as the fly press, for mass production of simple pressed metalwork such as brass buttons, and steam-powered lathe were introduced elsewhere, for example at Birmingham, which already specialized in cast brass.

In the past 500 years to the end of the 20th century brass was the predominant copper alloy owing to its attractive appearance, relative cheapness and ease of working. Although for utilitarian purposes it came to be largely replaced by enamelled iron or aluminium, it continued to be used for sculpture and decorative items.

BIBLIOGRAPHY
J. Tavenor-Perry: *Dinanderie: A History and Description of Medieval Art Work in Copper, Brass and Bronze* (London, 1910)
F. S. Taylor: 'The Alchemical Works of Stephanos of Alexandria', *Ambix*, i (1938), pp. 116–39
J. Marshall: *Taxila* (Cambridge, 1951)

10. Brass vessels being beaten out by water-powered hammers, Stolberg, Germany, late 19th century

O. Werner: *Spektraanalytische und metallurgische Untersuchungen an indischen Bronzen* (Leiden, 1972)

J. W. Allan: *Persian Metal Technology, 700–1300 AD* (London, 1979)

A. M. Burnett, P. T. Craddock and K. Preston: 'New Light on the Origin of *Orichalcum*', *Proceedings of the 9th International Congress of Numismatics: Berne, 1979*, vi, pp. 263–8

P. T. Craddock: 'The Copper Alloys of the Medieval Islamic World', *World Archaeol.*, xi (1979), pp. 68–79

H. Dannheimer: 'Zur Herkunft der 'koptischen' Bronzegefässe der Merowingerzeit', *Bayer. Vorgeschbl.*, xliv (1979), pp. 123–47

G. R. Gilmore and D. M. Metcalf: 'The Alloy of the Northumbrian Coinage of the Mid-ninth Century', *Metallurgy in Numismatics*, ed. D. M. Metcalf and W. A. Oddy (London, 1980), pp. 88–93

W. A.Oddy and W. Zwalf, eds: *Aspects of Tibetan Metallurgy* (London, 1981)

U. von Schroeder: *Indo-Tibetan Bronzes* (Hong Kong, 1981)

E. W. Herbert: *The Red Gold of Africa* (Whitewater, WI, 1984)

P. T. Craddock: 'Three Thousand Years of Copper Alloys', *Application of Science in the Examination of Works of Art*, ed. P. England and B. van Zelst, v (Boston, 1985), pp. 59–67

P. T. Craddock and J. Lambert: 'The Composition of the Trappings', appendix to I. Jenkins: 'A Group of Silvered-bronze Horse-trappings from Xanten (Castra Vetera)', *Britannia*, xvi (1985), pp. 141–64

M. de Ruette: 'Etude technologique de la fonderie de laiton au moyen âge dans les Pays-Bas méridionaux et la principauté de Liège', *Rev. Archéologues & Historiens A. Louvain*, xix (1986), pp. 338–60

S. G. Bowman, M. R. Cowell and J. Cribb: '2000 Years of Coinage in China', *J. Hist. Metal. Soc.*, xxiii (1989), pp. 25–30

P. T. CRADDOCK

Brassaï [Halász, Gyula] (*b* Brasso, Transylvania, Hungary [now Romania], 9 Sept 1899; *d* Nice, 8 July 1984). French photographer, draughtsman, sculptor and writer of Hungarian birth. The son of a Hungarian professor of French literature, he lived in Paris in 1903–4 while his father was on sabbatical there, and this early experience of the city greatly impressed him. In 1917 he met the composer Béla Bartók, and from 1918 to 1919 he studied at the Academy of Fine Arts in Budapest. Due to the hostility between Hungary and France in World War I he was unable to study in France and so moved to Berlin in late 1920. There he became acquainted with László Moholy-Nagy, Kandinsky and Kokoschka and in 1921–2 attended the Akademische Hochschule in Charlottenburg, Berlin. He was a keen draughtsman and while there produced a series of characteristic drawings of nudes executed in an angular, emphatic style. In 1924 he moved to Paris, where he quickly became involved with the artists and poets of the Montmartre and Montparnasse districts while supporting himself as a journalist. In 1925 he adopted the name Brassaï, derived from that of his native town, and throughout that year he continued drawing as well as making sculptures. In 1926 he met André Kertész, who introduced him to photography. In 1930 Brassaï began taking photographs of Paris at night, concentrating on its architecture and the nocturnal activities of its inhabitants. These were collected and published as *Paris de nuit* in 1933 and showed the night workers, cafés, brothels, theatres, streets and buildings of the capital. The artificial lighting created strong tonal contrasts, lending the images a strikingly evocative beauty. Some of his photographs were included in the exhibition *Modern European Photographers* at the Julien Levy Gallery in New York in 1932, and the following year at the Arts et Métiers Graphiques in Paris he had a one-man show of his photographs of Paris, which travelled to the Batsford Gallery in London the same year.

Brassaï: *Picasso in his Studio, Rue des Grands Augustins, Paris*, gelatin silver print, 491×371 mm, 1939 (Rochester, NY, International Museum of Photography at George Eastman House)

In 1932 Brassaï was asked by Tériade to photograph some of Picasso's sculptures for the first issue of *Minotaure*, which appeared in 1933. This commission opened up a lifetime's friendship between Brassaï and Picasso. Through his association with *Minotaure*, Brassaï also came to know the Surrealists. For subsequent issues of *Minotaure*, until its collapse in 1939, he provided photographs of the studios of such artists as Alberto Giacometti, Jacques Lipchitz and Henri Laurens. During the 1930s he continued photographing Paris at night, producing such images as *Pont-des-Arts, Paris* (1934; Paris, Bib. N.), in which the atmosphere is enhanced by the presence of fog. He also took daylight shots, such as *Montmartre, Paris* (1936; see Grenier, pl. 5). In these photographs, as in all his work, he used no manipulative methods or trick techniques. Employing black-and-white film only, he worked slowly and waited to capture the right image rather than selecting from several.

In addition to contributing to *Verve*, *Labyrinthe*, *Liliput*, *Coronet*, *Life* and others in the 1930s and 1940s, in 1937 Brassaï began work for *Harper's Bazaar*, in close collaboration with its editor, Carmel Snow. After the German occupation of Paris in 1940 Brassaï refused to ask permission to photograph and was consequently unable to publish any work. In late 1943 he began taking more photographs of Picasso's sculptures, covering the entire range of the artist's production in this medium, from bronzes to fragile assemblages and even torn and 'sculpted' scraps of paper. The project took until 1946 to finish and resulted in *Les Sculptures de Picasso* (1948). In 1944 Brassaï took up drawing again and had his first exhibition of drawings at Renou et Colle in Paris in 1945, followed by the publication of *Trente dessins* (Paris, 1946), with poems by Jacques Prévert. Brassaï also created set designs for Prévert's ballet *Le Rendezvous* using huge photographic images; it was performed at the Théâtre Sarah-Bernhardt in Paris in 1945.

After World War II Brassaï resumed his work for *Harper's Bazaar*, which was to continue until the late 1960s. He was commissioned to photograph various painters and their studios, including Braque (1946; Paris, Bib. N.), Bonnard, Giacometti and Le Corbusier. For the same magazine Brassaï was also sent abroad to Greece, Turkey, Morocco, Italy, Britain, the USA and elsewhere. These foreign travels led to such photographs as that of a grotesque sculpture at the Villa Orsini in Bomarzo, Italy (1952; see Grenier, pl. 48). In 1949 he published the extended Surrealist poem *Histoire de Marie*, which was based on his concierge, with a foreword by Henry Miller. Brassaï continued to produce sculpture on occasion, and in 1951 he executed a series of highly simplified female forms cut from stone (see *Brassaï*, 1952). In 1956 he made a short film entitled *Tant qu'il y a aura des bêtes* using a 16 mm camera and filming at the zoo at Vincennes in Paris. From the early 1930s, while roaming Paris, he had begun to take photographs of the graffiti he found carved in the walls. He continued to photograph these curious, 'primitive' scratchings and in 1961 published a collection of them in *Graffiti de Brassaï*, with a text by Picasso. Brassaï's book *Conversations avec Picasso* (1964) was the fruit of his friendship with the great artist and included conversations and other memoirs together with 57 photographs of Picasso, his work and his friends (see fig.).

After the 1960s Brassaï concentrated on organizing and making prints of photographs he had made earlier. From this later period came *Le Paris secret des années 30* (1976), which included more images of Paris in the 1930s, with written descriptions of his experiences of the city at that time, and *Les Artistes de ma vie* (1982), which brought together photographs, mainly from the 1940s, that he had taken for *Harper's Bazaar* and other magazines, together with brief texts about the artists. In 1978 Brassaï was awarded the first Grand Prix National de la Photographie in Paris.

WRITINGS

Histoire de Marie, foreword H. Miller (Paris, 1949)
Conversations avec Picasso (Paris, 1964); Eng. trans. as *Picasso and Co.* (London, 1967)
Henry Miller: Grandeur nature (Paris, 1975)

PHOTOGRAPHIC PUBLICATIONS

Paris de nuit, text by P. Morand (Paris and London, 1933); Eng. trans. as *Paris after Dark* (London, 1987)
Les Sculptures de Picasso, text by D.-H. Kahnweiler (Paris, 1948; Eng. trans., London, 1949)
Brassaï, text by H. Miller (Paris, 1952)
Graffiti de Brassaï, text by P. Picasso (Paris and Stuttgart, 1961)
Le Paris secret des années 30 (Paris, 1976; Eng. trans., London and New York, 1976)
Les Artistes de ma vie (Paris, 1982; Eng. trans., London and New York, 1982)

BIBLIOGRAPHY

Brassaï (exh. cat. by L. Durrell and J. Szarkowski, New York, MOMA; St Louis, A. Mus.; 1968–9)
R. Grenier: *Brassaï* (Paris, 1987; Eng. trans., London, 1989)
Picasso vu par Brassaï (exh. cat. by M.-L. Bernadec and J.-F. Chevrier, Paris, Mus. Picasso, 1987)

PHILIP COOPER

Brasses, monumental. A term used to describe any inscription, figure, shield of arms or other device engraved for a commemorative purpose in flat sheet brass. It is found as early as 1486 in the will of William Norreys of Ash-Next-Sandwich, Kent. Such memorials became established in 13th-century Europe as a very satisfactory form of inlay for a grave slab. They recorded the death and status of the deceased and, particularly important, attracted prayers for the soul in Purgatory. Monumental brasses are therefore usually found in churches.

Brasses were manufactured almost exclusively in north-western and central Europe, although they were exported as far south as Madeira. This form of monument was, as with tomb effigies, initially patronized by the higher clergy, although very occasionally royalty chose to be so represented. Examples are the brasses of *Philip* and *John* (destr.), sons of Louis VIII of France, formerly at Notre-Dame, Poissy, of *Queen Margaret* (1295; destr.), wife of Louis IX, formerly at Saint-Denis Abbey, and the surviving brass of *King Eric VI of Denmark and Queen Ingeborg* (1319) at Ringsted Cathedral. By the 14th century production was prolific, catering for all persons of high status and extending to merchants, minor officials, tradesmen and ultimately any person of means, leading in England and Flanders to the laying of numerous small memorials. The popularity of such commemoration, which was neither expensive nor obtrusive, was greatly reduced by the destruction and iconoclasm caused in the religious strife of the 16th century, although it remained high in England until the 1630s.

Brasses were made from latten plate, a form of brass produced by the permeation of copper and zinc oxide derived from heating calamine ore. A typical 15th-century consistency for such plate was 78% copper, 18% zinc and 4% iron and lead. The plate was engraved with graving tools, the hand-controlled burin and chisels hardened and shaped for the purpose. The plate was set into a slab in which a recess was carved to allow the metal to lie flush with the surface, the resulting indent or matrix frequently surviving when brasses were destroyed. In the 13th and early 14th centuries the plates were set in place by bitumen and reinforcing bars, but after *c.* 1340 rivets were usually inserted, embedded in lead. The engraved lines were inlaid with colour, usually black, the heraldry being appropriately tinctured. Gilding was occasionally applied, more particularly to brasses set on high tombs or on walls, and in rare cases enamelled copper trays were inserted for heraldic features.

The main centres of production were evidently Paris, Tournai, Ghent and London, with Cologne, Nuremberg and Breslau (now Wrocław, Poland) important for short periods. There was, moreover, much provincial work, evidence in Britain indicating the importance of Bury St Edmunds, Coventry, Norwich, York and probably Boston (Lincs). Immediate access to all raw materials was not necessary, most if not all the plate used in England being imported. Access to stone and to waterways facilitating transport was more important than access to metal.

The craftsmen primarily responsible for monumental brass-engraving were the marblers, workers in flat stone (responsible for the making of tomb-boxes), but they were not responsible for the sculpture. In London, Adam of Corfe and Henry Lakenham were probably important in the early and late 14th century respectively, and in the 15th century William West, John Essex, Thomas Stevyns, James Reames, John Lorymer and Henry Lorymer are documented, with workshops in the immediate vicinity of St Paul's Cathedral or Blackfriars. Contracts show that among masters in Tournai were the d'Escamaing and Hanette families in the 14th century and Alardin Genois in the 15th. In Ghent the families of van Meyere and Dedeline and Hugo Goethals were similarly reputable. In Germany, bronze-founders engraved brasses, notably the Vischer family in Nuremberg and, in the 16th and 17th centuries, the Hilligers of Freiberg and Dresden. Goldsmiths, bell-founders and other craftsmen made brasses in small numbers; more significant is the involvement of certain glaziers, whose designs had direct application in the representation of kneeling figures and architectural ornament. William Heyward, an important Norwich glazier, is shown by a will of 1504 to have made a brass at West Harling, Norfolk. Following the decline of the marblers in Europe in the 16th century, their role was assumed by sculptors in England and specialist metalworkers in Flanders.

The nature of the brass-engraver's business is recorded in wills and contracts, which register the detailed specifications laid down for important commissions, with verses and patterns provided, dates of completion specified with penalty clauses and bonuses, and precise requirements relating to arms and the overall presentation of the effigies, frequently referring to existing memorials. The relationship of the client and craftsman in late 16th-century England is revealed in the cartoons for the Gage monuments at St Peter, West Firle (Sussex), prepared by Garat Johnson (*see* JOHNSON, (1)) of Southwark, with critical comments by John Gage himself.

The design of most brasses followed workshop patterns, and most can be studied as examples of series rather than individual works of art. The basis of the design was a representation of the deceased, but in its simplest form a brass consisted of an inscription, which was frequently complemented by a shield of arms or merchant mark or occasionally a rebus. Representations of full- or half-length figures were common, and in more elaborate examples the figures were framed by a canopy of honour, the whole bordered by an inscription. Evangelist symbols were commonly placed at the corners of the inscription, having a protective symbolism. In many large Flemish compositions and a few English ones, angels supported cushions behind the heads. Footrests took many forms, mainly lions and dogs, but heraldic or canting devices were frequently preferred. Flemish 14th-century canopies derived inspiration from the miniature architecture of metalworkers, with massed tabernacles and representations of saints, prophets and angels, while in Germany in the late 15th and early 16th centuries canopies took the form of entwined branches. Following the designs of incised and relief slabs, in 14th-century England cross compositions were adopted, showing a half- or full-length figure of the deceased in the expanded centre of a cross, latterly of octofoil form, the stem decorated with leaves and resting on a stepped base.

Bracket brasses, in which the figure was depicted within a canopy, supported below by the shafted bracket, were apparently derived from wall tabernacles. Backgrounds on English brasses were usually provided by the stone, with inlays of shields, scrolls and devices on more elaborate examples. On many continental examples the entire background was engraved, on 14th-century Flemish work with quadrilobe medallions and grotesques and on 15th-century German brasses with curtains on runners.

Not surprisingly, there is a strong relationship between brasses and sculpted effigies, especially in England, both showing a certain inconsistency in the representation of figures as horizontal yet living, but differing in design to accommodate vertical features, such as canopies and tomb-chests with weepers, within a flat composition. This is admirably illustrated by the brass of *Sir Hugh Hastings* (1347) at St Mary the Virgin, Elsing, Norfolk, which is closely related in its canopy, its equestrian figure in the canopy oculus and its tabernacles supported by brackets to the tomb of *Aymer de Valence, Earl of Pembroke* (*d* 1324), in Westminster Abbey, both influenced by that of *Edmund Crouchback, Earl of Lancaster* (*d* 1296), to whom Sir Hugh was related.

There is some association with identified artists. A painting (untraced) attributed to Rogier van der Weyden formed the basis of the design of the brasses laid *c.* 1450 to commemorate the Cistercian foundations of Isabel of Portugal, Duchess of Burgundy, one of which survives at Basle (Hist. Mus.). Bernt Notke of Lübeck was evidently the designer of the Hutterock brass (1505) in the Marienkirche there. Albrecht Dürer is associated with the design of brasses at Meissen Cathedral made by Hermann Vischer the younger, notably that of *Duchess Zedena* (1510), and the painting of *Duke Henry the Pious of Saxony* by Lucas Cranach (i) was undoubtedly the model for the *Duke Henry the Pious* brass (1541) at Freiberg Cathedral.

While the oldest surviving brasses are in Germany, at Augsburg (SS Ulrich und Afra; 1187), Verden (St Andreas; 1231) and Hildesheim Cathedral (1279), in the 13th century the French workshops seem to have been the most productive, although the brasses are recorded only in drawings. During the 14th century the most internationally sought-after brasses were the rectangular plate and separate inlay compositions of the Franco-Flemish school, of which Tournai was the main centre. The very stylized treatment and elaboration of canopy and background design are well illustrated on the brass of *Bishops Serken and Mul* in Lübeck Cathedral (1350; see fig.). Yet the best London work was of very good quality, as shown by the *Camoys* and *Seymour* series, named after brasses of these families at St George, Trotton, W. Sussex (*c.* 1310) and St Mary, Higham Ferrers, Northants (1337), and standards remained high until the mid-15th century. During the 15th century brasses were produced in many European centres, but the design of much London work declined in quality, and Flemish brasses, although of the highest technical

excellence, were over-complex. In contrast, in the best German brasses the boldness and emphasis on the main figure could withstand the shading lines that were increasingly applied. The same tendencies became more marked in the 16th century, when English brasses were trivialized by repetitious production and debased design.

Widespread destruction in the mid-16th century had a marked effect on production in the European mainland and on the English provincial workshops; an interesting consequence was the common reuse of brasses by engraving on the reverse. The revival in Britain owed much to émigrés such as the Cure and Janssen families, and brass design complied with the new demands for realism and classical settings, the memorials becoming essentially secular in purpose. With such notable exceptions as the works of Edward Marshall at SS Peter and Paul, East Sutton, Kent (1629), and St Mary, Chigwell, Essex (1631), the quality of English brasses was deteriorating significantly at the time when renewed iconoclasm discouraged all but the very occasional production of memorial effigies. In continental Europe the decline was even more marked, and there are very few 17th-century brasses, some of which, as that of *Pedro de Valencia* at St Jacobskerk, Bruges, are engraved on the reverse of earlier memorials. The revival of brasses in Britain in the 19th century was inspired by the return to favour of Gothic art.

BIBLIOGRAPHY

M. Stephenson: *A List of Monumental Brasses in the British Isles* (London, 1926, rev. 1938/*R* Ashford, 1964)
W. Paatz: *Bernt Notke und sein Kreis* (Berlin, 1939)
H. K. Cameron: *A List of Monumental Brasses on the Continent of Europe* (London, 1970, rev. 1973)
S. Badham: *Brasses from the North-east* (London, 1976)
R. Emmerson: 'Monumental Brasses: London Design, *c.* 1420–85', *J. Brit. Archaeol. Assoc.*, cxxxi (1978), pp. 50–78
M. W. Norris: *Monumental Brasses: The Craft* (London, 1978)
——: *Monumental Brasses: The Memorials*, 2 vols (London, 1978)
J. Blair: 'Henry Lakenham, Marbler of London and a Tomb Contract of 1376', *Antiqua. J.*, lx (1980), pp. 66–74
J. Page-Phillips: *Palimpsests: The Backs of Monumental Brasses*, 2 vols (London, 1980)
J. Coales, ed.: *The Earliest English Brasses: Patronage, Style and Workshops, 1270–1370* (London, 1987)
Monumental Brasses: The Portfolio Plates of the Monumental Brass Society, 1894–1984 (Woodbridge, 1988)

MALCOLM W. NORRIS

Bratby, John (Randall) (*b* London, 19 July 1928; *d* Hastings, E. Sussex, 20 July 1992). English painter, writer and teacher. He studied at the Kingston College of Art (1948–50) and later at the Royal College of Art (1951–4), where he was awarded a bursary to travel in Italy. However, he was not very stimulated by the art he saw there and subsequently preferred not to travel; his taste for domestic life in England is reflected in his painting (e.g. *Window, Self-portrait, Jean and Hands*, 1957; London, Tate). He worked in a harsh realist style, applying the paint thickly in vibrant colours, and portraying sometimes ugly and desperate faces. He primarily chose his family as subjects and incorporated all the clutter of urban domestic life in his paintings (e.g. *Still-Life with Chipfryer*, 1954; London, Tate). It was this concern with social realism that brought Bratby into contact with Jack Smith, Edward Middleditch (*b* 1923) and Derrick Greaves (*b* 1927), and these artists became the main exponents of the KITCHEN SINK

Monumental brass of *Bishops Serken and Mul* (detail), Flemish, 1350 (Lübeck Cathedral)

SCHOOL. However, while the Kitchen Sink artists shared a desire to depict the banality of a working-class domestic environment, Bratby's use of colours and his more middle-class surroundings distinguished his style from that of his peers. Bratby taught for two brief periods, first at Carlisle College of Art (1956) and then at the Royal College of Art in London (1957–8). In the late 1960s he started a series of portraits of celebrities, including the actress *Billie Whitelaw* (1967; priv. col., see N.P.G. exh. cat., p. 33); the series developed into a *Hall of Fame* during the 1970s. He painted cityscapes on trips abroad in the 1980s but concentrated on self-portraits and portraits of his second wife, in intimate poses and with bright colours and an economy of line. Bratby was also a successful novelist.

BIBLIOGRAPHY
A. Clutton–Brock: *John Bratby, A.R.A.*, Painters of Today (London, 1961)
John Bratby: Venice, the Hemingway Suite (exh. cat. by A. Lambirth, London, Albemarle Gal., 1991)
John Bratby: Portraits (exh. cat. by R. Gibson, London, N.P.G., 1991)

Bratislava [formerly Ger. Pressburg; Hung. Pozsony]. Former capital of the kingdom of Hungary (1536–1853), capital city of the autonomous republic of Slovakia in the Czechoslovak Republic (1919–38 and 1945–92), capital of the 'autonomous' Slovak Republic (1938–45) and capital of independent Slovakia (from 1993). It lies in the extreme southern part of the republic close to the borders of Austria and Hungary and is on the left bank of the Danube, to the east of the mouth of the River Morava.

1. History. 2. Urban development. 3. Museums and collections.

1. HISTORY. Remnants of prehistoric and Celtic settlements have been found in the city and its environs, as well as ruins of a Roman fort called 'Gerulata', which was part of the outer territories of the Roman Empire from the end of the 1st century AD to the 4th. Avar finds from the 6th century AD have also been unearthed, while ruins of a Slavonic settlement have been found dating from the 9th century AD. The first recorded mention of the city under the name 'Braslavespurch' occurred in the *Annales juvavenses antiqui* (AD 907) and probably derives from a personal name. From the 10th century it was an important fort on the western borders of Hungary overseeing the main route along the Danube to Vienna. Under Stephen I (*reg* 1001–38) it became the seat of a county. The St Salvator Deanery was within the walls of the castle and a merchant settlement, noted as significant by the 12th-century Arab traveller al-Idrisi, lay at the foot of the castle. Between 1246 and 1273 the city changed rulers several times when Austrian princes, Hungarian kings and Ottokar II, King of Bohemia, fought for its control. From 1287 to 1291 the city was in Austrian hands. It was invested with a Charter of Royal Privileges in 1291 by Andrew III, King of Hungary (*reg* 1290–1301), and in 1405 a decree by King Sigismund of Hungary and Bohemia (later Holy Roman Emperor) recognized its importance as a major commercial centre lying on the route to the west by confirming its status as a Free Royal City. Following devastating raids in the region by Jan Žižka's Bohemian Hussites, the city was fortified from 1423. A new residence was built in the

castle enceinte for the emperor Sigismund, who in 1436 issued the city with its coat of arms. In 1465 King Matthias Corvinus founded the first university in Slovak territory, the Academia Istropolitana (now the drama department of the Academy of Fine Arts), which existed until 1490. Following its acquisition by Ferdinand (later Ferdinand I of Germany and Holy Roman Emperor) in 1526, the city was proclaimed capital of the Habsburg-dominated part of Hungary in 1536; it became the administrative centre, seat of the Hungarian parliament and place of coronation of the Hungarian kings. By the second half of the 18th century it was the largest city in Hungary. The last session of the Hungarian parliament held in the city was also the first ministry to be accountable to the new parliament transferred in 1848 to Pest (now part of Budapest). Following the collapse of Austria–Hungary, Bratislava was occupied in January 1919 by troops of the Czechoslovak Republic, of which it was immediately declared a part. In 1938, at the partitioning of Czechoslovakia, it became the capital of the 'autonomous' Slovak Republic. During World War II it was occupied by the Germans and in 1945 was liberated by the Soviet Army. After the war, Bratislava again became part of a unified Czechoslovakia, and in 1993 it became capital of an independent Slovakia.

2. URBAN DEVELOPMENT. In 1221 the chapter of the castle was transferred to the merchant settlement at the foot of the castle walls, while within the castle a stone tower was erected in 1245. In the 13th century the town developed around a rectangular market-square, and by the beginning of the 14th century it was fortified. By the early 15th century the outlying areas of the town were also fortified; however, at the end of the 18th century most of the walls were dismantled, and today only St Michael's Gate to the north, with its 18th-century superstructure and tower, remains.

The Gothic Franciscan church (consecrated 1297) was extensively renovated between 1613 and 1616 after an earthquake; of the original building, only parts of the west front and the vaulted chancel remain. The church was restored in 1897, and its original medieval tower is in the Janko Král Park in the suburb of Petržalka. The former convent church of the Poor Clares (now a hall for chamber concerts and exhibition space for the Municipal Gallery) was begun at the end of the 13th century, and its chancel, built in the early 14th century, was extended in the last third of that century. St Catherine's Chapel, in the Cistercian monastery near St Michael's Gate, was built in Gothic style between 1311 and 1325; the monastery itself was rebuilt in the 18th century. The Old Town Hall (now the Municipal Museum) was formed from a palace and tower of c. 1387, later to be augmented by the nearby Pawer House (c. 1422). The entire complex was rebuilt c. 1440 in Late Gothic style and again in 1496–7; the Renaissance arches of its arcaded courtyard, however, date from 1581. Bratislava is dominated by several 14th-century Gothic buildings, among them St Martin's Cathedral, a hall church that was the coronation church of the kings of Hungary from 1563 to 1830. The cathedral's general features reflect the characteristic style of the guild of master-builders who had worked on the Stephansdom in Vienna. For example, the design for the vaulting (completed 1452; Vienna,

Akad. Bild. Kst., Inv. 16925) of the cathedral was drawn up by the Viennese master Hans Puchsbaum. The influence of the Austrian builders is also apparent in the spires of the Franciscan church, the church of the Poor Clares and the chapel of St John the Evangelist.

The Late Gothic buildings of the castle (see fig. 1) were begun around 1425 on the order of Sigismund. According to surviving accounts for 1434, the castle, with a rectangular ground-plan, was nearing completion under the supervision of the masterbuilder Konrad von Erling. Its architectural style suggests that the masons who worked on it belonged to the same guild as did those who were employed by Sigismund on buildings in Buda. The castle was further fortified between 1552 and 1562 after plans by Pietro Ferabosco. Decorations were executed in a Mannerist style, the most significant surviving example of which is the ornamentation of the balcony designed by Giulio Licinio.

The Counter-Reformation played an important role in the establishment of Baroque architecture in Bratislava. As the seat of the archbishopric of Esztergom, the city became a significant centre for the style. For example, Archbishop Péter Pázmány (*reg* 1616–73) commissioned from Jacopo Rava the Jesuit college (1628–35; now a Roman Catholic seminary). The general appearance of the city was determined by 18th-century buildings erected primarily by Baroque architects from Austria. The centrally planned Trinity Church (1717–27), with its elliptical ground-plan, was erected in the style of Johann Lukas von Hildebrandt, and its cupola (1736–40) was painted by Antonio Galli-Bibiena. The church of the Sisters of St Elizabeth of Hungary (1739–42) was built to the plans of Franz Anton Pilgram, while its ceiling frescoes (1742) were painted by Paul Troger. From 1729 Georg Raphael Donner (*see* DONNER, (1)) worked in Bratislava in the service of Prince-Archbishop Emmerich, Graf Esterházy-Galantha, Primate of Hungary, designing the Elemosynarius Chapel (1730–2) in the cathedral. Donner also executed sculpture (1733–4) for the cathedral's former high altar: *St Martin and the Beggar* (*in situ*; *see* SLOVAKIA, fig. 7) and two kneeling angels (Budapest, N.G.). His studio was an important centre for discussions about the theory of Classical art. Among his pupils were Adam Friedrich Oeser and the sculptor Ludwig Gode; the latter's workshop was important not only in the city but also in the whole of western Hungary. Such Viennese court architects as Jean Nicolas Jadot, Nikolaus Pacassi and Giovanni Battista Martinelli (1701–54) worked on the reconstruction of the castle at various times from 1751 to 1766, during the reign of Maria-Theresa. Between 1753 and 1756 the Royal Chamber (later the Palace of the Hungarian Parliament and now containing the University Library) was built to the plans of Martinelli and from 1772 altered by Franz Anton Hillebrandt. These Viennese architects and their local followers also built palaces for the aristocracy and town houses for the citizens. The Grassalkovich Palace, surrounded by a garden in the French style, was built outside the city after 1760 by Andreas Mayerhofer. The classicizing late Baroque Palace of the Primate was built between 1777 and 1781 to the design of Melchior Hefele (see fig. 2). The wall paintings (1781) in its chapel are by Franz Anton Maulbertsch and its statues by Franz Xaver Messerschmidt, the city's most significant late Baroque sculptor. Fewer buildings of note were constructed in the first half of the 19th century; Neo-classical buildings are mostly the work of local masters.

After railway links with Austria and Hungary were established, Bratislava enjoyed an economic upsurge in

1. Bratislava Castle, *c.* 1425–*c.* 1434

2. Bratislava, main façade of the Palace of the Primate by Melchior Hefele, 1777–81

the last third of the 19th century, especially from the late 1860s and early 1870s, when the city established its industrial base. The area surrounding the historic city centre was principally affected by the large-scale programme of building in historicizing style undertaken in 1872, when regulations for urban planning were introduced. Ödön Lechner built St Elizabeth's Church (1906–13) and the grammar school (1908) in Hungarian Secession style. During the period of the Czechoslovak Republic, extensive building projects were undertaken. In 1929, for example, there was an international competition for proposed urban development. As a result, many hotels, banks, office buildings, department stores and low-cost family dwellings were constructed during the late 1920s and the 1930s, reflecting the various architectural styles popular at the time and greatly contributing to the general modern appearance of the city. After World War II Bratislava was further expanded by the incorporation of its suburbs. Under a massive new building programme, areas were modernized, extensive housing estates were built and other urban development projects were carried out.

3. MUSEUMS AND COLLECTIONS. Bratislava has several important archives, museums and art galleries. The Municipal Museum (Městské Múzeum) was founded in 1868 to hold the city's collection of antiquities. Its medieval section is housed in the Old Town Hall and in such other historical buildings as St Michael's Tower and the Hummel House. The Municipal Gallery (Městské Galéria), founded in 1959, maintains a separate fine arts collection, with most of its holdings in the Baroque Mirbach Palace and Pálffy Palace. Its medieval collection is housed in the former convent church of the Poor Clares. The Slovak National Museum (Slovenské Národné Múzeum), founded in 1961, has a small national collection and

maintains the castle and its museum, while the Slovak National Gallery (Slovenská Národná Galéria) is the principal fine arts museum of Slovakia, housing an outstanding collection of medieval painting and sculpture and modern art. The Archive of the City of Bratislava, effectively its Records Office, contains documents from the 13th century. It also has an almost complete collection of the written records of the city from 1402. The Central Archive of Slovakia also holds important documents.

BIBLIOGRAPHY

G. Weyde: *Pressburger Baumeister der zweiten Hälfte des XVIII. Jahrhunderts* (Bratislava)
T. Ortvay: *Geschichte der Stadt Pressburg*, 6 vols (Pressburg, 1893–1903)
V. D. Mencl: *Bratislava: Stavební obraz mesta a hradu* [Bratislava: an architectural picture of the city and the castle] (Prague, 1936)
E. Hoffmann: 'Pressburg im Mittelalter: Vergessene Künstler, verlorene Denkmäler', *Sostdt. Forsch.*, ii (1938), pp. 280–334
M. Váross, ed.: *Bratislava: Stavebný vývina pamiatky mesta* [Architectural development and monuments of the city] (Bratislava, 1961)
V. Horváth, D. Lehotská and J. Pleva: *Dějiny Bratislavy* [The history of Bratislava] (Bratislava, 1978)

ERNŐ MAROSÍ

Bratke, Oswaldo Arthur [Carlos] (*b* Botucatú, São Paulo, 24 Aug 1907). Brazilian architect. He graduated as an engineer–architect from the Mackenzie School of Engineering, São Paulo, in 1931 when he also won first prize in an open competition for the Boa Vista viaduct, São Paulo, with an Art Deco design. About 1934 he set up a design and construction firm with Carlos Botti (1906–42), building mainly private houses in original versions of styles such as neo-colonial, California mission and Spanish Renaissance. After Botti's death, Bratke concentrated on architectural projects and made a transition to modernism by fitting the traditional features of neo-colonial buildings, such as tiled roofs, overhanging eaves and verandahs, into the modern vocabulary. He was a highly practical architect with an interest in technical solutions, for example waterproofing and insulating flat roofs, and the design of construction components such as windows, doors and prefabricated kitchens and bathrooms, and was one of the few people in his generation not to be influenced directly by Le Corbusier, preferring the work of Mies van der Rohe and Richard Neutra. Bratke designed some of the most beautiful houses in São Paulo, one of the best being his own house (1953) with a simple, Miesian rectangular plan and with all interior spaces opening on to the garden through a covered walkway built along the sunny, north-facing façade. In the adjoining guest pavilion, a timber deck and sliding timber wall panels were reminiscent of traditional Japanese houses. As well as several hundred private houses, Bratke's most important works include the ABC office buildings (1952), Morumbi children's hospital (1953), the Bom-Bril factory (1958) and the Matarazzo Metallurgical Industries building (1960), all in São Paulo. He also produced urban plans for the Morumbi district of São Paulo (1950) and Ilha Porchat (1964) in São Vicente, S.P. In 1966 he prepared a master plan for housing at the Icomi manganese mines in the Território do Amapá; using local materials, he designed buildings to function in the hot, humid jungle climate, with overhanging eaves, double roofs and movable and fixed louvres. He retired from professional activity in 1967 when his son, Carlos Bratke (*b* 1942), graduated as an architect. As a formalist working in a Brutalist idiom, Carlos Bratke produced buildings that differed profoundly from his father's. The most important example of his work is the group of 36 office buildings (1976–84) carried out for his family's construction company in the southern part of São Paulo; while each retains individual characteristics, all of these conform to a single overall formal approach.

WRITINGS
'Núcleos habitacionais no Amapá', *Acrópole*, 326 (1966), pp. 17–38

BIBLIOGRAPHY
H. E. Mindlin: *Modern Architecture in Brazil* (Amsterdam and Rio de Janeiro, 1956)
S. Ficher and M. M. Acayaba: *Arquitetura moderna brasileira* (São Paulo, 1982)

SYLVIA FICHER

Brauer, Arik [Erich] (*b* Vienna, 4 Jan 1929). Austrian painter, printmaker, stage designer and singer. He studied from 1945 to 1951 with Albert Paris Gütersloh at the Akademie der Bildenden Künste in Vienna, where his colleagues included Ernst Fuchs, Wolfgang Hutter (*b* 1928) and Anton Lehmden (*b* 1929), with whom he helped develop the style known as PHANTASTISCHER REALISMUS. He first exhibited his works with the Art-Club at the Zedlitzhalle. In 1950 he cycled from Vienna to Paris, also travelling to Spain, North Africa, Israel and Yemen. During this period he struggled to earn a living as a folk singer. From 1958 he lived and worked as an artist in Paris, but from 1964 he divided his time between Vienna and the house he had decorated himself in Ein Hod, an artists' village in Israel.

Brauer's early paintings were strongly influenced at first by the peasant paintings of Pieter Bruegel I in the Kunsthistorisches Museum, Vienna, and then by the work of Hieronymus Bosch; Brauer developed an anecdotal style, mainly depicting rustic landscape genre scenes. After 1955, following a visit to Israel, he became interested in Persian and Indian miniatures; their influence introduced orientalizing elements and brilliant colours into his work, seen for example in *Jericho* (1956–7; Basle, Germaine Liechti priv. col., see Brauer, 1984, i, pp. 76–7) and in the *Rainmaker of Carmel* (1964; Hamburg, Rolf Gillhausen priv. col., see Brauer, 1984, i, pp. 250–51).

Brauer often used Jewish and Old Testament traditions as the basis of his works, which show a fairy-tale world, as is true of his portfolios of colour aquatints. He also designed stage sets, for example for the *Magic Flute* (1977; Paris, Théâtre National de l'Opéra), and was successful as a singer.

WRITINGS
Arik Brauer: Das Runde fliegt: Texte, Lieder, Bilder (Munich, 1983)
Arik Brauer: Werkverzeichnis, 3 vols (Dortmund, 1984)

PRINTS
Les Travaux des champs (Paris, 1967)
Aus den Sprüchen Salomos (Vienna, 1970–71)
Chass. Erzählungen (Paris, 1973)

BIBLIOGRAPHY
Die Wiener Schule des Phantastischen Realismus (exh. cat., Hannover, Kestner-Ges., 1965)
W. Schmied: *Brauer* (Vienna, 1972)
W. Koschatzky: *Brauer Graphik (das graphische Werk, 1971–1974)* (Glarus, 1974)

INGEBORG KUHN-RÉGNIER

Braun, Adolphe (*b* Besançon, 1812; *d* Dornach, 1877). French photographer. He worked in Paris as a textile designer, discovering his interest in photography in 1853, when he photographed a collection of 300 studies of flowers intended to serve as models for painters and fabric designers. He set up a studio in Paris in 1868. His subjects were very diverse—reproductions of works of art, architecture (e.g. the *Peristyle of the New Opéra*, *c.* 1874; see *Regards sur la photographie en France au XIXe siècle*, pl. 30), portraits, landscapes, still-lifes and unposed, spontaneous photographs of city life. He travelled widely in Europe and also in Egypt, producing panoramic landscape photographs. He published an album of his photographs of the landscapes of Alsace in 1858. From 1859 onwards he collaborated with many other French photographers, and from 1858 to 1862 he photographed landscapes in Switzerland, Germany and France. He was a member of the Société Française de Photographie from 1867, and he became official photographer to Pope Pius IX the same year. In 1868–70 he photographed in the Vatican, working on photographs of the Sistine Chapel and the sculpture collections. He produced a large collection of reproductions of works of art, including drawings and paintings in many of the great museums of Europe. He exhibited widely, including in Paris (1859), Manchester (1865), at the Exposition Universelle, Paris (1867), and in Vienna (1873).

PHOTOGRAPHIC PUBLICATIONS
Album de fleurs (Paris, 1854)
Catalogue général de photographies (Paris, 1887)

BIBLIOGRAPHY
R. Lecuyer: *Histoire de la photographie* (Paris, 1945), pp. 115–18
——: *Regards sur la photographie en France au XIXe siècle*, Berger Levrault (Paris, 1980)

PATRICIA STRATHERN

Braun [née Pfründt], **Anna Maria** (*b* Lyon, 1642; *d* Frankfurt am Main, 13 Aug 1713). German medallist and wax-modeller. She was the daughter of Georg Pfründt, wax-modeller, medallist and engraver. In 1659 she married the medallist Johann Bartholomäus Braun (*fl* 1636–74; *d* 1684); thus before 1659 her works are signed A.M.P., and after that year, A.M.B. Braun first worked in Nuremberg, and later in Frankfurt am Main, becoming particularly recognized as a portraitist. In the style of Alessandro Abondio she produced wax portrait reliefs of numerous members of the princely houses of the Netherlands, Germany and other countries; on two occasions she was summoned to the Viennese court. An example of her work is a portrait of Ludwig William, Margrave of Baden (Brunswick, Herzog Anton Ulrich-Mus.). Braun also modelled free-standing wax figures, such as the signed statuette of *Count Karl* in armour (Kassel, Hess. Landesmus.). She did not, however, limit herself to portraits, but also executed mythological scenes, such as the signed sculpture of the *Toilet of Venus* (Österreich. Mus. Angewandte Kst.). Braun's figure sculptures were based on her anatomical studies in wax; the figures were either modelled in coloured wax, or painted, partly clothed in wool and silk and adorned with beads and gems.

BIBLIOGRAPHY
Thieme–Becker
R. Büll: *Das grosse Buch vom Wachs*, 2 vols (Munich, 1977)

ELISABETH GUROCK

Braun, Matyáš Bernard [Mathias Bernhard] (*b* Sautens, 24 Feb 1684; *d* Prague, 15 Feb 1738). Bohemian sculptor of Tyrolean birth. With Ferdinand Maximilián Brokof he was the foremost Baroque sculptor in what is now the Czech Republic and a leading practitioner in central Europe of the dynamic style of Gianlorenzo Bernini.

1. CAREER TO *c*. 1720. Braun probably made a study journey to Italy, travelling to Venice, Florence and Rome, where he would have encountered the sculpture of Bernini and his followers. He is said to have met his future patron FRANZ ANTON VON SPORCK, for whom he later worked in Bohemia, at Bolzano in 1704. His first known work, commissioned by the Cistercian nuns of Plasy, is a sandstone group of the *Vision of St Lutgard* (1710) on the Charles Bridge in Prague. In this dynamic work, which, in contrast to earlier statues on the bridge, is designed to be seen from a multiplicity of viewpoints, St Lutgard with outspread arms is embraced by Christ's right arm, disengaged from the Cross. The group already has all of the characteristic qualities of Braun's sculpture: the stone has the appearance of solidified lava or frozen water, the composition is dramatic and non-axial, while light, seen through openings in the group, is used as a component in the creation of constantly changing visual effects. A second stone group on the bridge, representing *St Ivo* (1711), patron saint of lawyers, sheltering a widow and orphans, makes its effect through the graceful articulation of its mass.

From 1712 to 1720 Braun was at work on Graf von Sporck's estate of KUKS at Gradlič. As a visual embodiment of Sporck's ideas about the moral amelioration of humanity he produced eight statues of the *Beatitudes* (for illustration *see* KUKS) surrounding one of *True Faith* and two series of allegorical statues of *Virtues* and *Vices* with the *Angel of Blissful Death* and the *Angel of Woeful Death*. In addition he supplied 40 grotesque statues of dwarfs for the racecourse. For this huge commission and numerous others that he carried out for Sporck both at Kuks and at his estate at Lysá nad Labem, Braun probably made only the models himself, the carving of the stone being carried out by his extensive workshop.

In the period 1714–16 Braun decorated the Clam-Gallas Palace in Prague, designed by Johann Bernhard Fischer von Erlach (*see* PRAGUE, fig. 9). Most remarkable of the sculptures that he supplied are the two massively plastic stone entrance portals on the street façade. Each has two pairs of statues of *Hercules* acting as atlantids; the plinths incorporate reliefs of the *Labours of Hercules*. He also provided a fountain statue of *Triton* and thirteen statues of Olympian deities (seven now Prague, N.G., Convent of St George) for the pediment and attic balustrade of the façade. The particular decorative function of the latter is reflected in their relatively restrained and classicizing design.

The decoration of the Jesuit church of St Clement from 1715 to 1721 was the culmination of the first phase of Braun's activity in Prague. He provided stone statues of the *Evangelists* and the *Church Fathers* as well as woodcarvings for side altars, the pulpit and confessionals. The most famous and perhaps the earliest of the life-size stone statues is that of *St Jude* (Prague, N.G., Convent of St

George; see fig.), which carries dynamism to the point of ecstasy. The figural types designed for St Clement became part of the standard repertory of Braun's workshop and were repeated elsewhere, including at the church of Lysá nad Labem. The side altars at St Clement are decorated with flanking statues and above all with richly composed groups of saints and cherubs at their apex. Above the altar of *St Francis Xavier* (1716), for instance, St Carlo Borromeo gives thanks to the Crucified Christ for the ending of the Prague plague of 1714, while celebrating cherubs bind up the bones of the skeleton of Death. The altars of the *Purification of the Virgin* and of *St Leonard* (*c*. 1717–18), with similar groups, were also carved by Braun himself. Those of *St Heraclius* and of *St Joseph* (1720–21) are weaker and clearly workshop productions. Some of the statues on the confessionals, including, notably, a lyrical representation of the *Prodigal Son*, are by Braun; for others

Matyáš Bernard Braun: *St Jude*, stone, life-size, *c*. 1715 (Prague, National Gallery, Convent of St George)

he probably supplied the models only. The high altar of the pilgrimage church at Stará Boleslav, characterized by the dynamic asymmetry of its statues, dates from 1712–21, while Braun's largest work, the 20-m high Holy Trinity column in the square at Teplice, was built in 1718–19. It is decorated with statues and reliefs and culminates in a pylon surrounded by hovering cherubs.

2. CAREER AFTER *c.* 1720. During the 1720s Braun relied increasingly on his workshop (he had six apprentices by 1725), and the quality of his finished work suffered as a consequence. This is apparent in such works as the sculptural decoration of the church of St Cross in Litomyšl, the funerary monument of *Graf L. Schlick* (*d* 1723) in Prague Cathedral and the monument to *Emperor Charles VI* in Hlavenec, the latter commissioned at the suggestion of Sporck in 1725. The *Virgin* column at Jaroměř (1722–7) was also the result of collaboration with assistants. The tomb of Braun's mother-in-law, *Anna Miseliusova* (*d* 1721), also at Jaroměř, is, however, a work exceptional in both form and sentiment.

It was principally during a second phase of activity at Kuks, lasting from the mid-1720s into the early 1730s, that Braun supplied works of outstanding quality. Foremost among these are the extraordinary religious sculptures carved out of the living rock in the forest. They include statues of *Mary Magdalene, St John the Baptist* and the hermit saints *Onuphrius* and *Guarinus*, as well as a relief of *St Hubert.* Further works of the 1720s are a Crucifix and an *Annunciation* group (both Plzeň, A.G. W. Bohemia) for the convent at Plasy, which are from Braun's hand, and statuary for the Vrtbovsky Palace and the Kolovrat Palace in Prague, for which he provided the models only.

During the 1730s Braun suffered from tuberculosis, which further inhibited his input into the production of the workshop, while the oppressive political conditions of the reign of Emperor Charles VI seem to have reduced Braun's creative vitality to a mannered formula. He provided only sketch models for the stone groups of *Night* and *Day* (1734) in the Royal Garden, Prague, and for the decoration of the church at Horky (1735); work on sculpture for the façade of St Nicholas in Prague Old Town was delegated to his nephew Anthonín Braun (1709–42). Through the work of such followers as Jan František Pacák (1680–1756), Gregor Theny (1695–1759) and Severin Tischler (1705–*c.* 1752) Braun's style was carried on in hundreds of sculptures in eastern Bohemia.

BIBLIOGRAPHY

G. Pazaurek: *Franz Anton Reichsgraf von Sporck, ein Mäzen der Barockzeit, und seine Lieblingsschöpfung Kukus* (Leipzig, 1901)

O. J. Blažíček: *Sochařství baroku v Čechách* [Baroque sculpture in Bohemia] (Prague, 1958) [with Fr. and Ger. summary]

E. Hempel: *Baroque Art and Architecture in Central Europe*, Pelican Hist. A. (Harmondsworth, 1965), pp. 133–6

E. Poche: *Matyáš Bernard Braun* (Prague, 1986)

Matyáš Bernard Braun, Studie a materiály Národní galerie 4 [Studies and materials of the National Gallery 4] (Prague, 1988)

IVO KOŘÁN

Brauner, Victor (*b* Piatra Neamt, Moldavia, 15 June 1903; *d* Paris, 12 March 1966). Romanian painter, sculptor and draughtsman, active in France. As a child, he shared his father's passionate interest in spiritualism, heralding a lasting preoccupation with the occult. In 1912 he accompanied his family to Vienna, and from 1916 to 1918 attended the evangelical school at Brăila, near Galaţi, studying zoology with great enthusiasm; he also started to paint. In 1921 he spent a brief period at the School of Fine Arts in Bucharest, where his first exhibition was held in 1924 at the Galerie Mozart. The same year, Brauner and the poet Ilarie Voronca founded the review *75HP*, in which he published his manifesto of 'Pictopoésie' and an article on 'Le Surrationalisme'. From 1928 until 1931 he worked with the Dada and Surrealist review *UNU*, which reproduced his drawings and paintings. Settling in Paris in 1930, he met Constantin Brancusi, who introduced him to photography, and Yves Tanguy, through whom he met the major Surrealists. He lived in the same building as Tanguy and Alberto Giacometti. His premonitory *Self-portrait with Enucleated Eye* (1931; Paris, priv. col., see 1972 exh. cat., no. 7) became a *cause célèbre* for the Surrealists, whom he joined officially in 1932. André Breton wrote the introduction for his first one-man show at the Galerie Pierre in 1934, the year of *Monsieur K's Power of Concentration* (Paris, priv. col., see 1972 exh. cat., no. 20) and the *Strange Case of Monsieur K* (priv. col., see 1972 exh. cat., no. 19), departures from Brauner's earlier work and reminiscent of Alfred Jarry's *Père Ubu.* Returning to Bucharest briefly in 1935, he joined the clandestine Romanian Communist Party but left in 1936 at the beginning of the Soviet show trials.

In Paris in 1938 Brauner lost his left eye in a brawl in Oscar Domínguez's studio. He later wrote that it was 'the most painful and important fact of my life'. A period of somnambulatory, erotic paintings, full of lycanthropic, chimeric and alchemical imagery, such as *Chimera* (1941; Monte Carlo, Gal. Point), came to a halt during World War II. Brauner fled to Perpignan and then to the Pyrenees, maintaining contact with the exiled Surrealist group in Marseille. Brauner settled in the Hautes-Alpes in 1942. With no painting materials to hand, he began his 'candle drawings', inspired by stone textures and painted with coffee or walnut stain on relief drawings executed in wax, as in *Pantacular Portrait of Novalis* (1945; Paris, Pompidou). In 1943 he painted in oils on canvas primed with melted wax (*Blood Flower*; 1943; Houston, TX, Menil Col.). Paper collage was introduced in the *Ideal Man* (1943; Paris, Pompidou), the portrait of *Novalis* (1943; Paris, priv. col., see 1972 exh. cat., no. 246) and the ithyphallic sculpture *Number* (1943; Paris, priv. col., see 1972 exh. cat., no. 250). Alchemy, magic and the tarot inspired hermetic theories that were demonstrated in the 'multiple realities' of the many-limbed *Conglomeros* series (1941–5; plaster version, Paris, priv. col., see 1972 exh. cat., no. 251).

Returning to Paris in 1945, Brauner painted *Lion, Light, Liberty*, seven canvases conceived as a single work exhibited at the Galerie Cahiers d'Art in 1947 (e.g. Monte Carlo, priv. col., see 1985 exh. cat., p. 35). A one-man show at the Galerie Pierre Loeb in 1946 preceded his participation in the Exposition Internationale du Surréalisme at the Galerie Maeght in 1947, where his catalogue texts, one ostensibly by the 'Emperor of the kingdom of personal myth, signed Rotciv Renuarb', marked a highpoint in his megalomania. After convalescing from a serious illness in

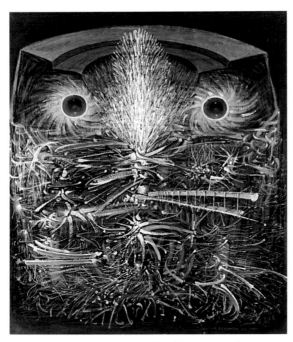

Victor Brauner: *'Endotête', Psychological Penetrations*, oil on canvas, 730×600 mm, 1951 (Paris, Pompidou, Musée d'Art Moderne)

Switzerland he returned to Paris for his first major exhibition at the Galerie René Drouin in 1948. He was officially excluded from the Surrealist group the same year for refusing to denounce his close friend, Roberto Matta, whose influence was becoming increasingly apparent in Brauner's own painting, for example the aggression and the lines of force in *'Endotête', Psychological Penetrations* (1951; Paris, Pompidou; see fig.). The autobiographical series of *Victors* or *Onomatamania* began in 1949. Many of these are static, two-dimensional works marked by bilateral symmetry and containing references to hieroglyphs and Aztec codices. In 1953 Brauner went to work in the potter Georges Ramié's studio in Vallauris, near Cannes, where he became involved with ceramics (e.g. *Cat*; 1957; Paris, L. Fini priv. col., see 1985 exh. cat., p. 90). From 1961 he worked in Varengeville, near Dieppe, and was chosen to represent France with a complete room of his works at the Venice Biennale in 1966, the year of his death. Many important works and the Victor Brauner archive were donated to the Musée National d'Art Moderne (now Centre Georges Pompidou) in Paris after his death.

BIBLIOGRAPHY

S. Alexandrian: *Victor Brauner, l'illuminateur* (Paris, 1954)
A. Jouffroy: *Victor Brauner*, Musée de Poche (Paris, 1959)
Victor Brauner: Paintings from 1932–1958 (exh. cat., text V. Brauner; Chicago, Richard L. Feigen and Co., 1959)
S. Alexandrian: *Les Dessins magiques de Victor Brauner* (Paris, 1965)
Victor Brauner (exh. cat. by D. Bozo and J. Leymarie, Paris, Mus. N. A. Mod., 1972)
Les Dessins de Victor Brauner au Musée National d'Art Moderne (exh. cat. by P. Georgel and D. Bozo, Paris, Pompidou, 1975)
Victor Brauner: Miti, presagi, simboli (exh. cat. by W. Schöneberger and S. Alexandrian, Lugano, Villa Malpersata, 1985) [It./Fr. parallel text]

SARAH WILSON

Braunerová [née Braun], **Zdenka** (*b* Prague, 9 April 1858; *d* Prague, 23 May 1934). Bohemian etcher, illustrator, painter and writer. As the daughter of František Augustín Braun, a prominent Bohemian politician, she was able to play a significant role in Bohemia's cultural life at the end of the 19th century and the beginning of the 20th, especially in the area of Czech–French cultural relations. She was a frequent visitor to Paris, where her elder sister, who was married to the writer Elémir Bourges, lived. She was instrumental in familiarizing Bohemian artists with French culture and introduced them to such prominent artists as Rodin, Redon and others. In Bohemia she was much to the fore in bringing writers and artists together and in discovering such artists as František Bílek. She painted landscapes and together with her teacher Antonín Chittussi established contacts in France with members of the Barbizon school. She was, however, primarily an etcher and illustrator and she specialized in etchings of Old Prague, for example *Maltézský plácek* (1905, e.g. Prague, N.G., Staré Město Old Town Hall). She made a significant contribution to the development of Bohemian book illustration with her design for Vilém Mrštík's *Pohádka máje* ('May legend'; 1897) and journal illustration in association with the *Revue moderne* and its publications (e.g. by Miloš Marten). She was interested in Japanese prints, Symbolism and the decorative reform movement, and she produced a set of hand-painted glass.

BIBLIOGRAPHY

M. Nováková: *Zdenka Braunerová* (Roztoky, n.d.)
P. H. Toman: *Zdenka Braunerová* (Prague, 1963)

PETR WITTLICH

Braunschweig. *See* BRUNSWICK.

Brauron. Site of an ancient sanctuary of Artemis on the east coast of Attica, 6 km north-east of Markopoulon, established by the 8th century BC. A special feature of the cult at Brauron was that the priestesses, known as Artemis' Bears (*arktoi*), were girls aged between five and ten, who resided within the sanctuary. A similar cult was subsequently introduced on the Athenian Acropolis, probably owing to the growing importance of aristocratic families with estates near Brauron. The site was excavated in 1946–52 and 1956–63 by J. Papadimitriou.

The Temple of Artemis (6th century BC) is a small, Doric, non-peripteral building of which only the foundations remain. Beyond it was a copious spring, liable to flood. A small, nondescript building some 10 m southeast of the temple was perhaps the residence of the Bears. The most important architectural remains are those of a Doric stoa (end of 5th century BC) to the north of the temple. It was intended to have three wings around a courtyard, of which the temple and other buildings formed the south side; only the north side and the initial sections of the west and east wings were built, however. Behind the north and (intended) west colonnades was a series of square rooms (6.3×6.3 m) with off-centre doors. In each room was a plinth with bronze-lined sockets to hold the feet of 11 full-size dining couches. In front of the couches were tables made from local limestone with marble tops. These rooms were probably provided not for the Bears but for adult worshippers, who may have approached the stoa over a stone bridge that crosses the river running along the western edge of the sanctuary from the sacred spring. Behind the stoa was a long hall where the women whom Artemis helped during childbirth deposited their offerings.

BIBLIOGRAPHY
B. Stais: 'Proistorikoi synoikismoi' [Prehistoric settlements], *Archaiol. Ephimeris* (1895), pp. 196–9
Praktika (1945–59) [excav. rep. from Brauron by J. Papadimitriou]
Ergon Archaiol. Etaireias (1961–2) [excav. rep. from Brauron by J. Papadimitriou]
K. Bouras: *I anastelosis tis stoas tis Brauronas* [Reconstruction of the stoa at Brauron] (Athens, 1967)
J. J. Coulton: *The Architectural Development of the Greek Stoa* (Oxford, 1976)

R. A. TOMLINSON

Bravo, Claudio (*b* Valparaíso, 8 Nov 1936). Chilean painter and draughtsman. He studied painting in Santiago in 1947–8 with the Chilean painter Miguel Venegas but lived in Spain from 1961 to 1972, and then in Tangiers. His entire artistic career was thus conducted outside his native country.

Bravo initially worked as a portrait painter, supporting himself in Spain through commissions, which also introduced him into Spanish high society. His sitters included General Franco and his family. Later, while still in Spain, he began painting packages and wrapped objects in a polished, highly detailed realist style bordering on Photorealism but consciously related to the Spanish still-life tradition represented by Zurbarán and Velázquez, whose work he greatly admired. He remarked that he hoped to be regarded as one of the few 20th-century painters to have respected the work of the Old Masters and learnt from it.

Working with both oil paints and pastels, after moving to Morocco, Bravo combined objects with human figures in interior spaces, displaying perfect control of the luminosity of the atmosphere and the strict perspective. While his technical facility was undeniable, the ambiguity of his subject-matter, and the mysteriousness of his settings, tempering the clarity of the figures and objects, led him beyond the mere reproduction of appearances. Unlike the Photorealists, who tended to present their images as straightforward visual evidence, Bravo used his motifs as a way of dealing with obsessions such as narcissism or the random meeting of figures unconnected in time. An illusory and confusing interplay between reality and representation is central to Bravo's work, leaving the spectator unsure whether what he is seeing lies inside or outside the painting.

BIBLIOGRAPHY
Claudio Bravo (exh. cat., Madrid, Gal. Vandrés, 1974)
M. Ivelić and G. Galaz: *La pintura en Chile desde la colonia hasta 1981* (Santiago, 1981)
Claudio Bravo (exh. cat., Hamburg, Gal. Levy, 1981)

MILAN IVELIĆ

Bray [Braij], de. Dutch family of artists. (1) Salomon de Bray was the son of Simon de Bray, who moved to Holland from Aelst in the Catholic southern Netherlands. Salomon was a man of versatile talents, with interests ranging from painting to poetry and urban planning. He married in 1625 and three of his sons became artists: (2) Jan de Bray, Dirck de Bray (*fl* 1651–78), an engraver and painter, and

Joseph de Bray (*d* 1664), a painter of still-lifes. Jan de Bray's *Banquet of Anthony and Cleopatra* (1669; Manchester, NH, Currier Gal. A.) is generally thought to depict his parents as Anthony and Cleopatra and himself and his siblings as their attendants. During the plague epidemic in Haarlem in 1664, Salomon de Bray, two of his sons and two daughters died.

BIBLIOGRAPHY
W. Bernt: *Die niederländischen Maler des 17. Jahrhunderts*, 4 vols (Munich, 1948–62); Eng. trans. by P. S. Falla (New York and London, 1970, 3 vols), i, pp. 18–19, 179–82
S. Slive: *Frans Hals* (London, 1974), p. 61
B. Haak: *The Golden Age: Dutch Painters of the 17th Century* (New York and Amsterdam, 1984), pp. 254–5, 379–80, 392
Frans Hals (exh. cat. by S. Slive, Washington, DC, N.G.A.; London, RA; Haarlem, Frans Halsmus.; 1989–90)

(1) Salomon de Bray (*b* Amsterdam, 1597; *d* Haarlem, 11 May 1664). Painter, draughtsman and designer, architect, urban planner and poet. From 1617 he was a member of the civic guard company of St Adriaen in Haarlem, where he is thought to have trained with Hendrick Goltzius and Cornelis Cornelisz. van Haarlem (though there is no evidence for this). He remained in Haarlem until his death. He was a sensitive and intelligent man who played an important role in various cultural projects and institutions in the city. In 1627 he was paid for sketches of the Zeylpoort in Haarlem; he co-founded the Haarlem Guild of St Hubert, for which he designed a drinking horn (drawing, 1630; Konstanz, Städt. Wessenberg-Gemäldegal.); in 1631 he helped reform the Haarlem Guild of St Luke, serving on its executive committee from 1633 to 1640; the same year he published a collection of engravings, with commentary, of the most important buildings by Hendrik de Keyser under the title *Architectura moderna*; in 1634 he supervised the repairs to an organ in a Haarlem church; and he took an interest in many architectural projects for the city, contributing, among other things, a plan for the enlargement of the city and models and drawings for the Nieuwe Kerk. In 1644–5 he was summoned to Nijmegen as a consultant architect to supervise the alterations to an orphanage and an old people's home, and in 1649–50 he contributed to the painted decoration of the Huis ten Bosch outside the Hague (*see* THE HAGUE, §IV, 3).

1. DRAWINGS AND DESIGNS. Salomon was active as a draughtsman throughout his career, beginning with a landscape drawing executed when he was 19 (Leipzig, Mus. Bild. Kst.), which foreshadows the work of Rembrandt. There are numerous drawings of religious subjects, of which one group of precise and carefully drawn sheets stands out; despite their high degree of finish, some were used as preliminary studies for paintings, such as *Judith and Holofernes* (1636; Konstanz, Städt. Wesenberg-Gemäldegal.) for the painting of the same subject (Madrid, Prado); a drawing of the *Annunciation* (1641; Carcassone, Mus. B.-A.) for a picture formerly on the Dutch art market; and *Rebecca and Eliezer* (1660; Hamburg, Ksthalle), which served as a basis for the painting (Douai, Mus. Mun.). De Bray also left behind numerous architectural drawings, such as that for the rebuilding of the Haarlem Stadhuis (1629; see fig.).

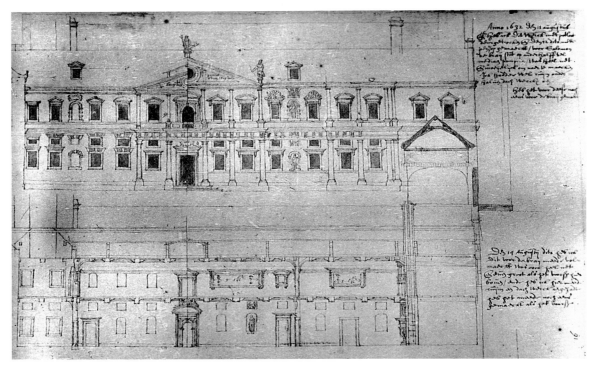

Salomon de Bray: sketch for the rebuilding of the Stadhuis, Haarlem, pen and ink with grey and yellow washes, 250×310 mm, 1629 (Haarlem, Gemeentearchief)

2. PAINTINGS. Salomon's painted oeuvre includes landscapes (e.g. Berlin, Gemäldegal.) and numerous religious and mythological scenes, for example *Jael, Deborah and Barak* (1633; Utrecht, Catharijneconvent), a forceful rendering of the biblical text, in which Jael is seen resolutely preparing to kill Sisera with the hammer and nail in her hand. This painting is typical of de Bray's manner of composing a scene of three figures, and in its powerful colour and treatment of light it reveals similarities with the work of Caravaggio. In the two large paintings that de Bray contributed to the Oranjezaal at the Huis ten Bosch, he adopted, perhaps unconsciously, the fashionable Flemish style and colouring of the other painted decorations in the programme.

Salomon was also active as a portrait painter, the earliest known example being the *Portrait of a Nun* (1622; Berlin, Gemäldegal.). From the middle of his career is the small, but superbly painted *Portrait of a Woman in Profile* (1636; ex-Althorp House, Northants, see von Moltke, no. 82). An unusually harmonious example is the *Portrait of a Woman* (1652; ex-art market, London, see von Moltke, no. 87). In his capacity as a portrait painter, de Bray may have known Frans Hals, for he signed and dated (1628) the portrait of a small girl who appears in the left foreground of Hals's *Portrait of a Family in a Landscape* (*c.* 1620; Viscount Boyne, on loan to Cardiff, N. Mus., see 1989–90 exh. cat., no. 10); this child's portrait could, however, have been a later addition.

Salomon de Bray's skills at observation are also evident in his genre pieces, such as the *Shepherdess with a Straw Hat* and its pendant *Shepherd* (both 1635; Dresden,

Gemäldegal. Alte Meister). Such subjects were interpreted by de Bray with freshness and great liveliness, qualities also apparent in *The Flute-player* (Brussels, priv. col., see von Moltke, no. 98) and the *Girl Combing her Hair* (Paris, Schloss priv. col., see von Moltke, no. 104), the latter perhaps inspired by a composition by Caesar van Everdingen. Salomon's painting of a *View in a Temple* (*c.* 1630–35; ex-art market, Berlin, see von Moltke, no. 116) is the only known example of an architectural subject in his oeuvre.

WRITINGS

Architectura moderna ofte bouwinga van osten tyt [Modern architecture in buildings of today] (Haarlem, 1631); ed. E. Taverne (Soest, 1971)

BIBLIOGRAPHY

J. W. von Moltke: 'Salomon de Bray', *Marburg. Jb. Kstwiss.*, xi–xii (1938–9), pp. 202–420

E. Taverne: Salomon de Bray's ontwerp voor de drinkhoorn van Het Loffelijke Gilde van St Hubert te Haarlem' [Salomon de Bray's design for the drinking horn of the Haarlem Guild of St Hubert], *Ned. Ksthist. Jb.*, xxiii (1972), pp. 261–71

——: 'Salomon de Bray and the reorganisation of the Haarlem Guild of St Luke: 1631', *Simiolus*, vi (1972–3), pp. 56–69

(2) Jan de Bray (*b* Haarlem, *c.* 1627; *bur* Haarlem, 4 Dec 1697). Painter, draughtsman and etcher, son of (1) Salomon de Bray. He spent virtually the whole of his career in Haarlem, except for the period 1686–8, when he lived in Amsterdam. After training with his father, Jan began working as a portrait painter in Haarlem in 1650, an activity he continued for the next 40 years. Between 1667 and 1684 he served on the committee for the Haarlem Guild of St Luke, whose leading members he portrayed in a picture dated 1675 (Amsterdam, Rijksmus.) that includes a self-portrait (Jan is seen standing and drawing on the left). He married three times, in 1668, 1670 and 1672. His first two wives died a year after their marriage, his third two years afterwards, and in each case the death was followed by disputes over the inheritance. Jan's bankruptcy of 1689 may have been a result of one of the lawsuits. He was 62 at the time, and from then onwards he seems to have lost his artistic drive, crushed by the financial blow and the consequent loss of social position.

1. PORTRAITS. More than half of Jan's painted output consists of individual portraits; besides these, there are double portraits and five large, extremely important group portraits (1663–75) relating to the regent and the local militia company. Jan's earliest dated painting, a *Portrait of a Girl* (1650; Prague, N.G., Šternberk Pal.), is tentative and subdued in style. Better and more typical is the *Portrait of a Man* (1658; Paris, Louvre), for which a preparatory study also survives (London, BM). The picture shows a man in his prime, with an imposing physical presence, facing towards the right; he is wearing severe, black garments, with a white collar. The sitter's lively facial expression—especially his attentive gaze towards the viewer—adds to the sense of immediacy conveyed by the portrait. Thus, although it was still relatively early in Jan's career as a portrait painter (he was just over 30 when he painted it), he had clearly already acquired considerable skill. Over the years he developed this sureness of touch to great perfection, though at the same time his portraits began to suffer from a certain impersonal superficiality that detracted from their content.

Jan can be seen at his best in the portrait of *Andries van der Horne* (1662; Lisbon, priv. col., see von Moltke, no. 47, wrongly identified as *Jean de Chambre*), a much more elegant half-length depiction of a middle-aged man, who looks out at the viewer confidently and somewhat critically. He holds a document in his right hand, his gloves in his left. Secure in the knowledge of his position in Amsterdam society, van der Horne observes life around him in with a cool, measuring eye. De Bray has conveyed a face full of character and endowed the sober black dress worn at the time with a festive brilliancy.

The group portrait of the *Leading Members of the Haarlem Guild of St Luke* (1675; Amsterdam, Rijksmus.) is remarkable for its sense of realism: the guild members seem to be discussing and debating some contentious point of the agenda. The intrinsically dry subject of a group of men all dressed in black was enlivened by the artist's ability to break down the conventional framework. One of his last-known works is the portrait of the Catholic priest *Johannes Groot* (1692; Haarlem, Bisschopp. Mus.), painted three years after his bankruptcy.

2. HISTORY SUBJECTS. Jan de Bray's painting of *Penelope and Odysseus* (1668; Louisville, KY, Speed A. Mus.; see fig.), a double portrait of a married couple dressed up in Classical guise, is a cross between history painting and pure portraiture. Penelope is shown holding a loom on which she had been working for years, hoping that Odysseus would return to her from the Trojan War. The dog, Argus, has recognized his master, even though Odysseus is disguised as a beggar. Happily reunited at last,

Jan de Bray: *Penelope and Odysseus*, oil on canvas, 1.10×1.65 m, 1668 (Louisville, Kentucky, J. B. Speed Art Museum)

the couple lean towards each other with great reserve, for the estrangement resulting from their long separation has to be overcome. Although scenes from Homer's *Odyssey* were relatively rare as subjects for paintings in the northern Netherlands before the end of the 17th century, both Salomon and Jan found the story an important source of inspiration. Jan depicted the scene of the return of Odysseus with great delicacy and psychological insight, in a beautifully unified composition.

As the years went by, Jan adopted an increasingly academic style in his paintings: it was streamlined but correspondingly less spontaneous. His picture of *David with the Harp* (1674; Brunswick, Herzog Anton Ulrich-Mus.) is an example of the rigidity that gradually overtook his work. The composition, depicting the solemn procession of King David bearing the Ark of the Covenant to Jerusalem, is carefully worked out; each figure is placed according to his importance. From a formal point of view, the representation is achieved with great success, yet it is missing the sense of immediacy that would otherwise have endowed the picture with real life. From the mid-1670s until his death, the contemporary preference for a more classicizing concept of art dominated his work, and as a result his originality gradually waned. This development may also help to explain why he gave up painting creatively towards the end of his life. Only two works are known from the period after his bankruptcy: besides the portrait of *Johannes Groot*, he painted the *Four Apostles* for a clandestine church in Amersfoort (1696; now Udenhout, parish church).

BIBLIOGRAPHY

W. Martin: *De Hollandsche schilderkunst in die zeventiende eeuw* (Amsterdam, 1935), i, pp. 27, 49, 117–19
J. W. von Moltke: 'Jan de Bray', *Marburg. Jb. Kstwiss.*, xi–xii (1938–9), pp. 421–523
J. Rosenberg, S. Slive and E. H. ter Kuile: *Dutch Art and Architecture, 1600–1800*, Pelican Hist. A. (Harmondsworth, 1966/R 1982), p. 321
Gods, Saints and Heroes: Dutch Painting in the Age of Rembrandt (exh. cat., ed. A. Blankert; Washington, DC, N.G.A.; Detroit, MI, Inst. A.; Amsterdam, Rijksmus.; 1980–81), pp. 224–9

J. W. VON MOLTKE

Brayer. Hand roller of rubber or gelatine used for applying ink to relief printing blocks (*see* PRINTS, §III, 1) or occasionally for the direct application of paint or ink to a surface.

RUPERT FEATHERSTONE

Brazil [Brasil], Federal Republic of. South American country. It is in the centre of the eastern side of the continent, bounded by all other South American countries except Chile and Ecuador. Geographic regions of Brazil include the equatorial north, containing the Amazon basin, extensive and scantily populated; the north-east, with a semi-arid interior reaching to the coast and a relatively dense but poor population; the south-east, populous and highly developed, with the main cities of São Paulo and Rio de Janeiro; the southern plateaux, occupied mainly by landowners of European origin; and the central plateaux, the western part of which contains the swampy depression of the Mato Grosso irrigated by the basin of the River Paraguay. The vegetation is essentially tropical, with rainforests in the north, pine forests in the south, *caatinga* (brushwood) in the arid north-east interior and savanna grasslands in the centre and south. Although its area of *c.* 8,512,000 sq. km takes up almost half the continent (see fig. 1), about 75% of the population live in urban centres, mostly in eastern Brazil along the coastline or on the major rivers. São Paulo, the largest centre of production in Latin America, is Brazil's financial capital and Rio de Janeiro its cultural capital. Brazil was colonized by Portugal after 1500, but the culture of the indigenous peoples survived (*see* §II below). Brazil became a kingdom in 1815, an independent constitutional empire in 1822 and a republic in 1889. Its federal capital, Brasília, was inaugurated in 1960.

For the history and art of Brazil before 1500, *see* SOUTH AMERICA, PRE-COLUMBIAN, especially §§I, V, VI and VIII.

I. Introduction. II. Indigenous culture. III. Afro-American culture. IV. Architecture. V. Painting, graphic arts and sculpture. VI. Furniture. VII. Ceramics and glass. VIII. Gold, silver and jewellery. IX. Textiles. X. Patronage, collecting and dealing. XI. Museums. XII. Art education. XIII. Art libraries and photographic collections.

I. Introduction.

The territory that became Brazil was discovered by Europeans at the end of the 15th century, and under the Treaty of Tordesillas, which divided the lands in the New World between Spain and Portugal, it was claimed for Portugal by Pedro Alvarez Cabral (1467–1520) after he landed there in 1500. However, it was only after the institution in 1534 of hereditary captains, each granted an area of coast and nominal hinterland together with political and economic privileges, that Brazil began to be populated by Europeans. In 1549 the first governor-general, Tomé de Souza, arrived to organize the administration of the colony, prompting more substantial development particularly in SALVADOR in the state of Bahia, which became the first capital. Jesuit, Benedictine and Franciscan missionaries also arrived to undertake the conversion of the indigenous population, and they provided the main stimulus for the arts in the 16th and 17th centuries, based on European styles, notably Portuguese and Spanish Baroque and Rococo.

Sugar production in the north-east dominated the first stage of Brazil's economy, becoming increasingly dependent on imported slave labour from Africa after 1560, which introduced another distinct ethnic contribution to Brazilian culture (*see* §III below). The wealth generated by sugar production led to a short-lived Dutch invasion and occupation (1630–54) of RECIFE in the state of Pernambuco and part of the north-east coast, where Johan Maurits, Count of Nassau-Siegen, was governor-general in 1637–43 (*see* NASSAU, (1)). The Dutch introduced new urban planning techniques, brought scientists and artists to document their conquest and produced the first examples of secular art in Brazil.

This trend was reinforced after the end of the 17th century by the second phase of economic development, the mining of gold, which was centred on Minas Gerais. Although most of the gold was exported to Portugal, considerable wealth went to the mining towns, notably OURO PRÊTO (formerly Vila Rica), providing funds for building and the arts and stimulating the development of

1. Map of Brazil; those sites with separate entries in this dictionary are distinguished by CROSS-REFERENCE TYPE

the Rococo style, which spread to Salvador, Recife and OLINDA. RIO DE JANEIRO, the port from which the gold was exported, came into prominence in 1763 when the capital was transferred there from Salvador, and again in 1808 when the Portuguese court moved from Lisbon to Rio as a result of the Napoleonic Wars. The city became the capital of the entire kingdom, and Dom João, the Prince Regent (later John VI, King of Portugal), set about improving its physical and cultural environment to suit its new status. Particular impetus to the arts was provided by the organization of a French artistic mission to Brazil (1816), whose purpose was the encouragement of the fine arts and architecture through practice and formal training and the foundation of such institutions as the Academia Imperial das Belas Artes, through which the academic European Neo-classical style was brought to the country.

At the same time, the development of coffee production opened up a new economic phase, accelerating the process of Brazilian emancipation. After the King returned to Portugal, his son declared independence (1822) and became Emperor, ruling as Peter I (reg 1822–31). The long reign of Peter II (reg 1831–89), a cultivated patron of the arts and sciences, generated considerable economic development marked by the expansion of the coffee trade, the arrival of many immigrants from Europe, the abolition of slavery and the building of railways and other technological innovations. However, the war with Paraguay (1865–70) brought about a serious financial and economic crisis, which led to the proclamation of the republic in 1889, and new social and political divisions involving military and civil factions emerged from the break-up of the centralized imperial system.

Between 1889 and 1930 SÃO PAULO increasingly replaced Rio de Janeiro as the economic and political centre of Brazil. Enormous urban growth was experienced after World War I, and a wave of modernization swept the country, accompanied by a preoccupation with the roots of national identity. The collision of progressive and conservative ideas culminated in the revolution of 1930 and the new government of Getúlio Vargas, which was followed by official acceptance and consolidation of the Modern Movement in the arts and the development of Brazil's highly original, lyrical version of the International Style, particularly in architecture. Repression and censorship during the dictatorship of Vargas (1937–45) were offset by the encouragement of industrial progress. Confidence increased with the presidency (1956–61) of Juscelino Kubitschek, who produced a major plan for the development of infrastructure and industry and initiated the construction of a new federal capital, BRASÍLIA, in the central highlands, stimulating avant-garde movements in the arts. The military coup of 1964 and the authoritarian governments that followed produced an economic boom but also a profound crisis due to external debts and inflation. Democracy was restored with the election by direct vote of President Fernando Collor de Mello (1989).

GENERAL BIBLIOGRAPHY

P. Calmon: *História do Brasil*, 7 vols (Rio de Janeiro, 1959)
S. Buarque de Hollanda, ed.: *História geral da civilização brasileira, 1500–1889*, 7 vols (Rio de Janeiro, 1960–72)
L. Castedo: *A History of Latin American Art and Architecture* (London, 1969), pp. 181–200, 266–92
P. M. Bardi: *História da arte brasileira: Pintura, escultura, arquitetura, outras artes* (São Paulo, 1975)
C. A. C. Lemos: *The Art of Brazil*, intro. P. M. Bardi (New York, 1983)
W. Zanini, ed.: *História geral da arte no Brasil*, 2 vols (São Paulo, 1983)
D. Ribeiro: *Aos trancos e barrancos: Como o Brasil deu no que deu* (Rio de Janeiro, 1985)

II. Indigenous culture.

Before the arrival of the Portuguese in 1500, the population of indigenous Amerindian peoples living in the territory that became Brazil totalled about three million. Their culture was still based on stone-tool technology, a factor partly explaining the difference in the process of colonization in Brazil compared to that of other Latin American countries where more sophisticated Pre-Columbian civilizations made a greater contribution to the new national identity: in all cases, however, the destruction of the indigenous culture was the norm—only about 200,000 Indians remained in Brazil at the end of the 20th century. Although the culture of the indigenous peoples of Brazil survived colonization, European and colonial interest in its art forms long remained marginal as remaining exotic traits were never really integrated into the mainstream of local artistic development. Between the 16th century and the 19th more or less fanciful descriptions of indigenous art were given in verbal or visual accounts by foreign and Brazilian travellers and artists, for example Pero Vaz de Caminha, Jean de Léry, Hans Staden, André Thevet, ALBERT ECKHOUT, JEAN-BAPTISTE DEBRET, Alexandre Rodrigues Ferreira and Johann Moritz Rugendas (*see* RUGENDAS, (2)). Scientific expeditions, which began to study Brazil in 1870, acquired a vast quantity of examples—almost always the best—of indigenous art, especially pottery from the island of Marajó, and this heritage forms part of the collections of the Museu Nacional and the Museu do Índio in Rio de Janeiro, the Museu Paulista at the Universidade de São Paulo and the Museu Paraense Emílio Goeldi in Belém.

The artistic activity of Brazilian Indians must be considered in the context of their culture and daily life. All works are intended for immediate practical purposes and are derived from a homogeneous culture, in which each element is a component in harmony with all others. The desire to perfect each work in accordance with tradition produces a formal severity and beauty, in which care is the basis of the aesthetic. Traditional indigenous art was based on three important types of production: weaving, pottery and body arts; all three continued to be produced after colonization. The abundance of plant materials resulted in the predominance of weaving and plaiting as art forms among Brazilian tribes, both in the past and present: leaves, palm fronds, lianas and a variety of fibres are used for baskets, sieves, fans, mats, belts, sleeping-nets, ceremonial masks and vestments, all decorated with ingenious and strictly geometric patterns. Outstanding examples are found in the work of the Timbira, Kayabi, Xavante, Desana, Tukuna and Paresi peoples, although the last three no longer produce ceremonial vestments and masks.

Pottery, more easily made and preserved, flourished in the Pre-Columbian period in four principal areas: MARAJÓ, Cunani, Maracá and SANTARÉM, all in the north of Brazil, and production continued after the European discovery and conquest of the territory. Traditional funerary urns from the island of Marajó, painted in two or three colours, reveal stylized geometric and non-figurative decorative designs that are extraordinarily well executed. Vases and *caretas* (modelled decoration) produced by the Tapajós from Santarém constitute an exception to the general rule of indifference to naturalistic human representation among the indigenous Brazilian peoples: for decoration they used zoomorphic and anthropomorphic elements that are often carefully realistic and concerned with individuality—unlike the peoples of the Andes, they did not have moulds. Other fine work includes the pottery of the Kadiwéu, decorated with incised designs, the zoomorphic panels of the Waurá and, above all, the *licocós* of the Karajá—small figures, single or in groups, and scenes portraying human beings and their immediate environment. These continued to be produced in the 20th century, although profoundly altered as a result of tourism, which created a new market.

In spite of the repressive effects of religious indoctrination, the body arts of indigenous Brazilians also continued to be practised in the 20th century as body painting, the wearing of feather ornaments and dramatic masked dances. The tribes of the Xingu, for example, use pigments from natural sources, such as vermilion from the urucu plant, black from the genipap tree and white from clay, to cover their bodies—at all ages—with a careful sense of fantasy. Equally splendid are the abstract patterns common among the Kadiwéu, who use them not on their bodies but on skins and woven fibre cloth. The body is also used for other aesthetic devices, especially on the face where such devices are intended to give a special shape: examples include the perforated earlobes of the Kaapor, Xavante and Timbira peoples, and lips perforated for the insertion of such decorative elements as rings, discs and pierced stone, sometimes of impressive size. The nose ornaments of the Yanomani and the parrot-tail feathers linking the nasal septum to the earlobe among the Tiriyo peoples are other examples of body arts that exploit the face. Necklaces made from feathers, teeth, claws, seeds, circles of mother-of-pearl and a range of other materials are frequently worn; outstanding examples include those made from feathers by the Kaapor and the rows of black zoomorphic figures incised in tucum palm-nut shells by the Tukuna. The male and female genitals are also given aesthetic treatment, for enhancement in the case of the men and for protection in that of the women. For all the body arts, each tribe had a particular decorative model that governed the items worn, which were also controlled by a sense of harmony of line and colour.

The use of feathers, in which the Kaapor peoples in particular but also the Mundurucú and Bororo excelled, is one of the most refined indigenous art forms in Brazil (see fig. 2). It is characterized by the purely decorative nature of each piece, involving a search for beauty through the extraordinary range of multicoloured tropical feathers used to create crests, diadems, coifs, garlands, belts, bracelets, armbands, anklets and *cache-sexes*. Many of these items, especially the fantastic masks used by men among the Tukano, Karajá, Bororo and Timbira peoples, remained an integral part of the tribal ceremonies that were essential to the preservation of their culture. An outstanding example, in the continuation of which the various forms of indigenous arts are powerfully integrated, is the Kuarup ritual in the Xingu region.

BIBLIOGRAPHY
K. von den Steinen: *Unter den Naturvölkern Zentral-Brasiliens* (Berlin, 1894)
C. M. Rondon: *Índios do Brasil*, 3 vols (Rio de Janeiro, 1946–58)
C. Lévi-Strauss: *Tristes tropiques* (Paris, 1955), pp. 95–105
D. Ribeiro and B. Ribeiro: *A arte plumária dos índios Kaapor* (Rio de Janeiro, 1957)
J. H. Steward, ed.: *Handbook of South American Indians*, i and iii (New York, 1963)
A. R. Ferreira: *Viagem filosófica pelas capitanias do Grão-Pará, Rio Negro, Mato Grosso e Cuiabá, 1783–1792* (Rio de Janeiro, 1971)
C. Andujar and D. Ribeiro: *Yanomani* (São Paulo, 1978)
M. Bisilliat: *Xingu* (São Paulo, 1978)
A. Bento de Araújo Lima: *Abstração na arte dos índios brasileiros* (Rio de Janeiro, 1979)
Arte plumaria del Brasil (exh. cat. by S. F. Dorta and L. H. Velthem, Mexico City, Mus. N. Antropol., 1982)
D. Ribeiro: 'Arte índia', *História geral da arte no Brasil*, ed. W. Zanini (São Paulo, 1983), i, pp. 46–87
R. E. Reina and K. M. Kensinger: *The Gift of Birds: Featherwork of Native South American Peoples* (Philadelphia, 1991)

III. Afro-American culture.

The traffic in slaves between 1560 and 1850 brought Africans to Brazil in numbers that must have totalled between four and six million. Most were put to work in the sugar mills of the north-east, the gold mines of Minas Gerais and the coffee plantations of Rio de Janeiro and the southern provinces. Many were subsequently employed by religious orders: by the second half of the 16th century both Africans and mulattos were engaged in carving and gilding work for the churches being constructed throughout the country. The Africans brought to Brazil came from an area between the Gulf of Guinea and the Congo basin and thus, in general, from technically sophisticated cultures, skilled in metallurgy and accustomed to sculpture. To some extent, therefore, they were more willing to undertake work for the churches because it had parallels in their native community art. Contact with the dominant Catholic religion also led to a process of eclecticism in their own art, but while they were obliged to change the outward appearance of their religions, artefacts and ceremonies, they could preserve their inner essence. Thus ritual Afro-Brazilian statuary developed basically from such West African plastic traditions as those of the Nago, YORUBA and other peoples, good examples being the Oxum (river goddess) figures of the Xangó religion of Pernambuco and the iron or wooden *exus* ('devil') figures and Gueledé masks of the Candomblé religion in Bahia.

The high point of the African contribution to mainstream Brazilian art was between the end of the 17th century and the beginning of the 19th, when the building activity of the religious institutions was increasingly enriched by gold-generated wealth (*see* §IV, 1(i) below). The African slaves could not express themselves in accordance with their original cultural heritage but were expected to reproduce in local terms the patterns of European Baroque that were adopted in Brazil. This process, however,

2. Featherwork of Bororo headman, Brazil; photograph by Karl von den Steinen, 1887–8

produced an interesting phenomenon: in the painted or carved figures required by the Catholic liturgy, the African physical type appeared with increasing frequency. Some of the greatest artists of the period were Africans or mulattos, including Antônio Francisco Lisboa (O Aleijadinho; *see* LISBOA, (2)), an architect–sculptor who worked in Minas Gerais; VALENTIM DA FONSECA E SILVA and Francisco das Chagas, sculptors working in Rio de Janeiro and Bahia; and José Teófilo de Jesus, a painter who worked between Bahia and Sergipe. MANOEL DA COSTA ATAÍDE is also thought to be of African descent. European models predominated in these artists' works (*see also* §§IV, 1(i)–(ii) and V, 1 below), but the traces of their African background cannot be ignored.

As Neo-classicism became established in the 19th century, however, the role of Africans in the development of the visual arts in Brazil diminished sharply and was transferred to music, dance and sport—activities in which the hereditary community spirit was more apparent. There were several reasons for this. The Neo-classical concept of beauty was based on the Greco-Roman model and rejected negroid or mulatto features: even at the end of the century Oscar Pereira da Silva (1867–1939) portrayed the theme of slavery using an anachronistic white Roman slave rather than a black African. The absence of Africans from the visual arts was reinforced by the changing role of the artist, increasingly less often a craftsman working under the aegis of the Church than a trained professional dependent on state patronage, and by the social and economic conditions of Africans in Brazil at this time that constituted a radical hindrance to their admission to the official practice of art. Between 1840 and 1889 there was also a renewed policy of persecution of the 'barbaric fetishism' of African cults in Brazil: their ceremonial centres were closed, their statues and cult objects destroyed, and the free expression of their creativity curtailed. Almost the sole appearance of the African in Brazilian art in the 19th century was as a lay figure in the vast series of documentary and pictorial records made by foreign artists visiting Brazil, notably JEAN-BAPTISTE DEBRET and Johann Moritz Rugendas (*see* RUGENDAS, (2); *see also* §V, 2(i) below).

In the last three decades of the century, however, the activities leading to the abolition of slavery resulted in a new awareness of African values, although at first only as the object of study. The first Afro-Brazilian collections were started at this time, beginning with that made by the ethnographer Nina Rodrigues between 1890 and 1904, part of which is now in the Museu Artur Ramos in Fortaleza. Other institutions continued the discovery and preservation of material that earlier had invariably been despised, for example carvings, utensils, jewellery, ceramics, basketry and clothing; collections are found in the Museu da Fundação Carlos Costa Pinto, Salvador; Museu da Polícia, Maceió; Museu Folclórico da Divisão de Discoteca, São Paulo; Museu de Arqueologia e Etnologia, Universidade de São Paulo; and the Museu Paraense Emílio Goeldi in Belém. However, the systematic rehabilitation of the African contribution to Brazilian culture dates only from the 1920s. It was a principal interest of the modernist revolution in Brazilian art, which broke with

3. Agnaldo Manoel dos Santos: *Totem*, wood, h. 1 m, *c.* 1950 (São Paulo, João Marinho private collection)

academicism, sought a return to national roots and affirmed the regenerating power of the archaic, and one of the first truly modern works in Brazilian art was *The Negress* (1923; U. São Paulo, Mus. A. Contemp.) by Tarsila do Amaral. The work of the sociologist Gilberto Freyre (1900–89) was of considerable importance in evaluating the role of Africans in the formation of the Brazilian family of races and culture, and he also organized the first Afro-Brazilian Congress (1934) in Recife.

Although artists of African origin whose work was orientated towards African sources contributed to the development of Brazilian art in the 20th century, their numbers bore no relation to the size of their racial element in Brazilian society. Many of the principal artists came from Bahia, the state in which African roots were strongest and continued to flourish. Of these, Deoscóredes Maximiliano dos Santos (Mestre Didi; b 1917) remained closest to his ancestral culture, of which he was also a practising high priest. His para-ritual objects—sculptures of leather, shells and vegetable fibres, such as palm-ribs—relate to the forces of nature and the divinities that represent them in the Afro-Brazilian pantheon of Yoruba origin. Agnaldo Manoel dos Santos (1926–62), part-African and part-Indian, produced hieratic and archaic wooden carvings combining archetypes from African tribal culture and medieval Catholic iconography (see fig. 3). Another fusion of cultures is seen in the totemic–emblematic painting of Rubem Valentim (b 1922): the figurative geometry of the 'implements' identifying each divinity of the cult (the *orixás do candomblé* or voodoo idols) are combined with the strict non-referential discipline of European Constructivism. Geometry also underlies the work of Emanoel Araújo (b 1940) in engravings, reliefs and sculptures reflecting the multiple totemic expression that suffuses the art of black Africa.

For further information on the diaspora of African culture *see* AFRICA, §VIII.

BIBLIOGRAPHY
G. Freyre: *Casa-Grande e Senzala: Formação da família brasileira sob o regime da economia patriarcal* (Rio de Janeiro, 1933)
A. Ramos: 'Arte negra no Brasil', *Cultura*, i/2 (1949), pp. 188–212
M. Barata: 'The Negro in the Plastic Arts of Brazil', *The African Contribution to Brazil* (Rio de Janeiro, 1966)
C. P. Valladares: 'O negro brasileiro nas artes plásticas', *Cad. Brasil.*, 47 (1968), pp. 97–109
N. Rodrigues: *Os africanos no Brasil* (São Paulo, 1976)
C. P. Valladares: *The Impact of African Culture in Brazil* (Rio de Janeiro, 1977)
M. Carneiro da Cunha: 'Arte afro-brasileira', *História geral da arte no Brasil*, ed. W. Zanini (São Paulo, 1983), ii, pp. 973–1033
M. S. Omari: *From the Inside to the Outside: The Art and Ritual of Bahian Candomblé*, Los Angeles, UCLA, Mus. Cult. Hist., Monograph 24 (Los Angeles, 1984)
——: 'The Role of the Gods in Afro-Brazilian Ancestral Ritual', *Afr. A.*, xxiii/1 (1989), pp. 54–61, 103–4

IV. Architecture.

1. Before c. 1850. 2. After c. 1850

1. BEFORE c. 1850.

(i) Early colonial, Baroque and Rococo, c. 1500–c. 1760. (ii) Neo-classicism, c. 1760–c. 1850.

(i) Early colonial, Baroque and Rococo, c. *1500–*c. *1760.* In the years immediately following its possession of Brazil and the introduction of hereditary captains (*see* §I above), Portugal was primarily concerned with the defence of the long coastline, and architectural activity was limited to uncomplicated fortifications and dwellings built with the techniques and materials at hand. Only with the arrival in 1549 of the first governor-general, Tomé de Souza, and with him the mason Luís Dias were more substantial

buildings constructed. In Salvador, the capital until 1763, Dias was responsible for the customs buildings and the first council chamber and jail, in addition to the defensive system. Other fortifications were built along the coast by the Portuguese engineer Francisco de Frias da Mesquita (*see* FRIAS, (2)), who worked in Brazil from 1603 to 1635; these included the forts of Lage (1606), Recife, Reis Magos (begun 1614), Natal, and S Marcelo (enlarged and completed in 1728 by the French brigadier Jean-Baptiste Massé), Salvador, in the north-east and S Mateus (begun 1617) at Cabo Frio in the south. The Casa da Torre at Garcia d'Ávila, north of Salvador, is the only surviving example of the civil buildings of a pioneer settlement of this period.

The most important stimulus to colonial architecture in Brazil, however, was provided by the religious orders. Members of the JESUIT ORDER, who also came with de Souza in 1549, brought architects, masons, building materials and even complete sets of components for churches to replace the primitive mud and thatch chapels built by the pioneers. Francisco Dias (1538–1623), who arrived in 1577 and was involved in the development of the early 'Missionary style' in Brazil, designed and built solid, rather grandiose Jesuit colleges and churches at OLINDA (1584) and Rio de Janeiro (1585). He also began the great collegiate church (completed 1672; now the cathedral) at SALVADOR, which is typical of the early churches designed on Portuguese models. Baroque characteristics became more evident in later works of the Jesuits, which spread as far north as Belém, Pará, on the delta of the Amazon, where important examples include the college of S Alexandre (begun 1670) and the adjacent church of S Francisco Xavier (1719/20). Although indigenous building skills were not available in Brazil to the extent that they were in other areas of Latin America with a more complex pre-Hispanic culture, in both of these buildings local Indians participated in the construction and interior decoration.

The Benedictine Order was also active in Brazil, particularly in the 17th century, and it commissioned work from three outstanding architects: Frei Macário de São João (d 1676) from Spain, who designed the ground-plans and original façades of the church of the Misericórdia (1659), the monastery of S Bento and the convent and church of S Teresa, Salvador; Gregório de Magalhães (1603–67), who planned the monastery (1649) at Santos; and Frei Bernardo de São Bento (1624–93) from Portugal, who modified and carried out (1670–80) Frias da Mesquita's original design for the Benedictine church in Rio de Janeiro. Although the Baroque architecture of the last is sober, echoing the Portuguese tradition, it has exuberant interior decoration incorporating gilded carvings (*talhas*), polychrome statues, silver candlesticks and paintings.

The contribution of the FRANCISCAN ORDER reached its high point in the convent of S Antonio (begun early 18th century, completed 1783) at João Pessoa, north of Recife, which has a tower coping faced with *azulejos* (glazed tiles). Other notable Franciscan buildings include the church of S Francisco da Penitência, Rio de Janeiro, built during the 17th and 18th centuries with a unity of conception and style not found again until the late 18th-century churches of Minas Gerais, at the end of the Baroque period; the church of the Third Order of S Francisco da Penitência (begun 1702), Salvador, planned by Gabriel Ribeiro (*d* 1719), which has a richly carved stone façade rare among Brazilian colonial churches that usually conceal behind somewhat solemn façades their exuberant interiors; and the adjoining convent and church of S Francisco, the church (begun 1708) being one of the most richly decorated in Brazil, with gilded carvings, sculpture and *azulejos*.

Remarkable developments also took place in civic and domestic architecture during the 17th century, particularly in the area between Salvador and, to the north-east, Recife and Olinda, where sugar production expanded. The Dutch occupation (1630–54; *see* §I above) in the north-east introduced the first attempts at urban planning, with RECIFE being planned on the basis of the new European rationalist models. New buildings in Salvador included the Casa de Câmara and prison building (begun 1660), designed in a Renaissance style, with Tuscan columns and an elegant staircase to a central courtyard. Large town houses built for wealthy landowners, though simple in design, were often complemented by elaborate portals, as in those built for the Saldanha, the Unhão, the Sete Candeeiros and the Conde dos Arcos, all in Salvador.

Other important examples of the monumental Baroque style (*c.* 1655–1760) in religious architecture include the basilica of Nossa Senhora da Conceição da Praia, Salvador, designed in 1736 by the military engineer Manuel Cardoso de Saldanha, which took over a century to complete, using stone imported from Lisbon. It is considered one of the best examples of Brazilian colonial architecture and is a reproduction of Italianate Portuguese Baroque. The church of Nossa Senhora da Glória do Outeiro (1717–39; see fig. 4), Rio de Janeiro, was the first religious building in Brazil with a polygonal plan, a form rarely used in Portugal but later adopted enthusiastically in Minas Gerais. Further north, the 'Pernambuco school', which began to flourish in Recife before the end of the 17th century, produced several notable buildings, including the convent of S Antonio (1697) by Fernandes de Matos; the magnificent Golden Chapel in the church of the Third Order of S Francisco da Penitência (dedicated 1703); and the church of S Pedro dos Clérigos (1731–82) by Manuel Ferreira Jácome, which took up the polygonal theme, with a dodecagonal interior set in a rectangular external form, and which has twin square towers topped by octagonal ogee cupolas above a three-storey façade.

The discovery of gold in Minas Gerais at the end of the 17th century enabled the Baroque spirit to reach its apogee in Brazil. Religious orders flourished in the gold-mining centres, and much wealth went into church building. The golden age of 'arquitetura mineira' began with the chapel of Nossa Senhora do Ó (begun 1719), Sabará, and the three-nave church of Nossa Senhora da Ascensão (now the cathedral), Mariana. In OURO PRÊTO (formerly Vila Rica), which became the administrative centre of the region, the church of Nossa Senhora do Pilar was built in only two years (1731–3), with a polygonal nave within the rectangular plan designed by the military engineer Pedro Gomes Chaves. Other churches in Ouro Prêto include Nossa Senhora do Rosário dos Pretos (1725–85), completed by José Pereira Arouca but said to have been designed by Manuel Francisco de Araújo; it has a unique double-oval plan with a flowing, convex façade topped by

4. Nossa Senhora da Glória do Outeiro, Rio de Janeiro, 1717–39

an ornate coronet pediment accentuated by circular towers. This church is seen variously as the culmination of Baroque three-dimensional movement and as one of the finest expressions of Rococo in Brazil. The pilgrimage church of Bom Jesus de Matozinhos (begun 1757), on a hilltop overlooking Congonhas do Campo, represents the dramatic fantasy of the final flowering of Brazilian Baroque. It was designed by the craftsmen Antonio Gonçalves de Rosa and Antonio Rodrigues Falcate and dominates an atrium in which stand 12 great figures of biblical prophets carved in soapstone (1800–05) by Antônio Francisco Lisboa (O Aleijadinho; for illustration *see* LISBOA, (2); *see also* §V, 1 below), an architect and sculptor who was one of the most remarkable figures of the colonial period.

(ii) Neo-classicism, c. 1760–c. 1850. The wealth produced by gold stimulated the construction of impressive secular buildings, although Portuguese models were necessarily simplified by the limitations of local technical resources. The most important residential building of the period in Ouro Prêto is the Casa dos Contos (1787) built for João Rodrigues de Macedo, the collector of taxes. Important civic buildings in the city include the Casa de Câmara and prison (now the Museu da Inconfidência), designed in 1745 by the military engineer José Fernandes Pinto Alpoim (1700–70) but not built until 1784 after modifications by the provincial governor of Minas Gerais, Luiz da Cunha Menezes; its symmetrical façade heralds Neo-classicism.

RIO DE JANEIRO was the centre of architectural development after 1763 when it became the capital. A single-storey residence for the governor, designed by Alpoim and completed in 1743, was raised to two storeys (1778–90) by the viceroy Luiz de Vasconcelos e Souza, who also redesigned its surroundings (now the Largo do Paço or Praça XV de Novembro) and installed a magnificent stone fountain attributed to the sculptor VALENTIM DA FONSECA E SILVA. The latter is also associated with the formation on reclaimed land of the Passeio Público (1779–83), with paths traversing gardens in the French manner, complete with fountains and statuary.

Just as the Baroque and Rococo reached their peak in Minas Gerais, the Italian architect ANTONIO GIUSEPPE LANDI was introducing the first signs of Neo-classicism to Brazil. Landi lived and worked in Belém after 1759, employing a style halfway between Baroque theatricality and Neo-classical restraint (see BELÉM (ii)). As well as working extensively on church interiors, he designed the octagonal chapel of S João Batista and the elegant Nossa Senhora das Mercês; more significantly, perhaps, he also designed the headquarters of the Companhia do Grão-Pará and the governors' palace (1771), Belém, which, despite its sober air—perhaps reflecting the influence of the POMBALINE STYLE in Lisbon—is among the finest buildings of the colonial period. The acceptance of Neo-classicism was assured when the Portuguese court moved to Brazil in 1808. The French artistic commission that arrived in Rio in 1816 to develop the fine arts and architecture (see §I above) included the architect Auguste-Henri-Victor Grandjean de Montigny, who had studied and worked in Paris and Rome and who became the first professor of architecture at the new Academia Imperial das Belas Artes.

By the time of independence in 1822, Brazilian architecture was already under the foreign influences that dominated it for most of the 19th century. The Neo-classicism that prevailed, particularly in Rio de Janeiro, was strongly influenced by the work of Grandjean de Montigny. Educated in the cultured, rational, urban classicism of Charles Percier and Pierre-François-Léonard Fontaine, he developed a style characterized by the sobriety of the Tuscan order, which transposed well into the Brazilian context and the austerity of the Pombaline stylistic tradition inherited from Lisbon. His first design in Rio was the building (1826; destr. 1939; façade re-erected in the Botanical Gardens) for the new Academia Imperial das Belas Artes. He also designed the Bolsa de Comércio (now the Casa França-Brasil) and customs house (both c. 1830) and some houses in Rio, including his own (now administrative offices on the campus of the Pontifícia Universidade Católica; for illustration see GRANDJEAN DE MONTIGNY, AUGUSTE-HENRI-VICTOR). His influence and that of his pupils at the Academia on the architecture and urban planning of Rio combined to give the city a more elegant and modern appearance.

Other European architects who moved to Brazil also contributed to the development of the academic Neo-classical style. PIERRE JOSEPH PEZERAT arrived in Rio in 1825 soon after graduating in Paris and worked as private architect to Peter I until the Emperor's abdication in 1831. Pezerat completed the Palácio da Quinta da Boa Vista (1827 and after; now the Museu Nacional), the Academia

Militar (later the Escola de Engenharia) and several houses, including that of the Marquesa de Santos, all in Rio. Another Frenchman, Louis Vauthier (1815–1901), was active in Recife from 1840 to 1846, where he designed the Teatro S Isabel (c. 1845), the Hospital Dom Pedro II (begun 1847), the Ginásio Pernambucano (1855) and the Assembléia Provincial (1876). Julius Friedrich Köller (1804–47), a military officer from Germany who came to Brazil in 1828 to build roads, also designed a number of buildings, including the Casa de Câmara in Itaboraí and in the nearby town of Maricá (both 1835), as well as the white church of the Glória (1842; with Philippe Garçon Rivière), a landmark in Rio, with neo-Gothic elements. Köller organized a colony of immigrants and founded the city of PETRÓPOLIS, where he designed the Palácio Rio Negro, the Emperor's summer residence (now the Museu Imperial), completed after Köller's death by one of Grandjean de Montigny's Portuguese students, José Maria Jacinto Rebelo (1821–71). Rebelo also designed the Hospital Dom Pedro II (completed 1852) at Petrópolis and the Palácio do Itamarati (1851–4; restored 1928–30), Rio, which became the seat of government for a period after 1889 and later the Ministry of Foreign Affairs.

BIBLIOGRAPHY
E. C. Falcão: *Relíquias da Bahia* (São Paulo, 1940)
A. Morales de los Ríos: *Grandjean de Montigny e a evolução da arte brasileira* (Rio de Janeiro, 1941)
C. M. da Silva-Nigra: *Construtores e artistas do mosteiro de São Bento do Rio de Janeiro* (Salvador, 1950)
P. Kelemen: *Baroque and Rococo in Latin America*, 2 vols (New York, 1951)
P. F. Santos: *O barroco e o jesuítico na arquitetura do Brasil* (Rio de Janeiro, 1951)
R. C. Smith: *Arquitetura colonial* (Salvador, 1955)
G. Bazin: *L'Architecture religieuse baroque au Brésil* (Paris, 1956; Port. trans., Rio de Janeiro, 1983)
L. Saia: *Arquitetura paulista* (São Paulo, 1960)
L. Castedo: *The Baroque Prevalence in Brazilian Art* (New York, 1964)
L. G. Machado: *Barroco mineiro* (São Paulo, 1969)
C. P. Valladares: *Análise iconográfica do barroco e neoclássico remanescentes no Rio de Janeiro*, 2 vols (Rio de Janeiro, 1978)
J. W. Rodrigues: *Documentário arquitetônico relativo à antiga construção civil no Brasil* (São Paulo, 1979)
C. P. Valladares: *Aspectos da arte religiosa no Brasil* (Rio de Janeiro, 1981)
D. Bayón and M. Marx: *L'Art colonial sud-américain* (Paris, 1990), pp. 293–343, 407–20
J. Bury: *Arquitetura e arte no Brasil colonial* (São Paulo, 1991)

2. AFTER c. 1850.

(i) Eclecticism, Art Nouveau and Neo-colonial, c. 1850–1920. (ii) Modernism, 1920–60. (iii) After 1960.

(i) Eclecticism, Art Nouveau and Neo-colonial, c. *1850–1920.* As in Europe, by the middle of the 19th century French academic Neo-classicism in Brazil had begun to give way to more eclectic attitudes and the use of various foreign styles, including Gothic Revival and Moorish; a prime example of this tendency is the Palácio do Catete (1858–67; now the Museu da República), Rio de Janeiro, built by the German Gustav Wähneldt in Venetian Renaissance style as a residence and later used as the seat of central government in Brazil until the inauguration of Brasília. There was also a return to colonial models, including the late 18th- and early 19th-century *fazendas* (ranches) of the coffee and cattle estates. This was encouraged by the painter Manuel de Araújo Pôrto Alegre (1806–79), Director of the Academia Imperial das Belas

Artes (1854–7), who questioned whether recent urban buildings were suited to the Brazilian climate and way of life and recommended the use of local motifs rather than classical ones for their decoration. Examples of this approach include *solars* (summer residences), enhanced with such local elements as *azulejos* (glazed tiles), and Neo-colonial *fazendas* such as that at Vassouras (1870s) in the state of Rio de Janeiro, where a simple appearance is belied by a florid Second Empire interior. Another influence was the iron and glass architecture of such designers as Joseph Paxton in England and Gustave Eiffel and Victor Baltard in France, made possible by industrial developments there. The pioneering building of this type in Brazil is the San José market, Recife, imported from France in 1873.

Towards the end of the 19th century, far-reaching urban developments began in São Paulo and Rio de Janeiro. In SÃO PAULO the Avenida Paulista was opened up and garden districts initiated, and in central Rio the creation of Avenida Rio Branco (1903–6) was followed by intensive building activity there: the Escola (now Museu) Nacional de Belas Artes (1908), with a façade inspired by the Louvre in Paris, was designed by the Spanish-born architect ADOLFO MORALES DE LOS RÍOS, the outstanding figure of the period, who also designed the Moorish-style Instituto de Pesquisas Oswaldo Cruz on the outskirts of Rio; the Teatro Municipal (1909), inspired by the Paris Opéra, was designed by the engineer Francisco de Oliveira Passos; and the Biblioteca Nacional (1910) was designed by Francisco Marcelino de Souza Aguiar (1855–1935).

Art Nouveau also flourished for a time in the work of the Swedish architect Carl Eckman (1866–1940), for example the Vila Penteado (1902), São Paulo, and the French architect VICTOR DUBUGRAS, for example the

Mairinque Railway Station (1907), São Paulo. However, Dubugras soon began to follow the Neo-colonial tenets expressed in 1914 by Ricardo Severo (1869–1940), a partner of the important eclectic architect FRANCISCO DE PAULA RAMOS DE AZEVEDO; in his search for national roots Severo turned again to the robust buildings of the colonial *fazendas*. Others, including José Mariano Filho (1875–1946), who designed his own house, the Solar do Monjope (destr. 1974), Rio de Janeiro, as an essay in early 19th-century Portuguese colonial domestic style, were adopting formal simplifications that heralded ready acceptance of the European Modern Movement.

(ii) Modernism, 1920–60. After World War I the enormous urban expansion in Brazil, particularly in São Paulo and Rio de Janeiro, made necessary the adoption of new building techniques for the construction of public buildings, offices and flats. The groundswell against the plethora of eccentric styles and crumbling academicism in favour of Modernism was first felt in the plastic arts, literature and music, exemplified in the SEMANA DE ARTE MODERNA in São Paulo (1922). Two architects, Antonio García Moya (1891–1956) of Spanish origin and Georg Przyrembel (1885–1956) from Poland, took part but neither was involved with real innovation, and Brazil's earliest Modernist buildings were built later in the pioneering work of GREGORI WARCHAVCHIK, who moved to São Paulo in 1923 after studying in his native Odessa and in Rome. In 1925 he published his manifesto, *Acerca de arquitetura moderna*, in São Paulo and Rio de Janeiro, in which he quoted from Le Corbusier's writings, and he built the first Modernist houses in Brazil, both in São Paulo: his own house (1927–8; altered 1935) and the Modernistic House (1927–30), Rua Itápolis, Pacaembú, which was exhibited to the public on its completion together with a collection of paintings, drawings and sculptures by rising modern artists. These and his other early houses were all typical rationalist designs in concrete reminiscent of early work by Le Corbusier.

The move towards Modernism, stimulated by Le Corbusier's lectures in São Paulo and Rio de Janeiro in 1929, culminated in the appointment of Lúcio Costa as Director of the Escola Nacional de Belas Artes in Rio de Janeiro following the revolution of 1930. Costa introduced Modernist teachers, including Warchavchik, and established a radical new curriculum, which the students continued to support even after he was forced to resign in 1931. A brief partnership between Costa and Warchavchik (1931–3) produced some more Modernist houses, including the Alfredo Schwarz House (1932), Rio, which gave ROBERTO BURLE MARX his first landscape commission. Frank Lloyd Wright gave further encouragement to the new generation of Brazilian architects at the first Salão de Arquitetura Tropical (1933) in Rio, where he was the president of honour.

In 1935 a series of large architectural competitions was held, including one for a new building to house the Ministry of Education and Health in Rio de Janeiro. This was won by a traditionalist design, but on the advice of a number of art critics and architects the Minister awarded the commission to LÚCIO COSTA, who assembled a team of young Modernists, including AFFONSO EDUARDO REIDY, Carlos Azevedo Leão and JORGE MOREIRA, joined

5. Lúcio Costa, Oscar Niemeyer and others (with Le Corbusier as adviser): Ministry of Education and Health, Rio de Janeiro, 1937–43; now the Palácio da Cultura

6. Lúcio Costa and Oscar Niemeyer (with Paul Lester Wiener): Brazilian Pavilion, New York World's Fair, 1939 (destr.)

later by Hernani Mendes de Vasconcelos and also OSCAR NIEMEYER (who assumed its leadership in 1939). At Costa's suggestion, Le Corbusier was invited back to Rio as adviser to the project; he stayed for a month in 1936, working with the team and leaving an outline plan. Le Corbusier's basic ideas were modified to suit local conditions, and the Ministry Building (1937–43; now the Palácio da Cultura; see fig. 5) became the prototype of modern architecture in Brazil, characterized by slender pilotis, glazed walls with *brises-soleil* in the form of horizontal louvres on the exposed façade and sculptural rooftop elements. The building brought together paintings by CÂNDIDO PORTINARI, sculpture by BRUNO GIORGI and gardens by Burle Marx, who all later collaborated on several other important buildings.

Another competition, for the Associação Brasileira de Imprensa (ABI) Building (1936), Rio, was won by the brothers Marcelo and Mílton Roberto; this building was among the earliest to have the design of façades wholly determined by fixed louvres, here arranged vertically (for illustration see ROBERTO, M. M. M.). Niemeyer's first independent work, the simple, white, rectilinear Obra do Berço day nursery (1937), Rio, also used vertical louvres on the exposed façade, but they were adjustable. In São Paulo the early work of Rino Levi, who studied in Rome, had a hint of Expressionism, for example in the residential Columbus Building (1932) and the entrance of the UFA Palácio cinema (1936). Other notable buildings of this period include the residential Esther Building (1938), São Paulo, by ALVARO VITAL BRASIL, the Santos Dumont Airport buildings (1937–44), Rio, by the Roberto brothers and the seaplane station (1938), also Rio, by ATTILIO CORRÊA LIMA. The new architecture of Brazil was brought to worldwide attention by the Brazilian Pavilion (1939; destr.; see fig. 6) at the World's Fair in New York, a commission won in competition by Lúcio Costa, who invited Niemeyer to participate in the design (with Paul

Lester Wiener in New York); this was followed by the exhibition *Brazil Builds* (1942) at MOMA, New York.

The Modern Movement became fully established in Brazil in the 1940s and 1950s. Reidy, who was chief municipal architect and planner for Rio de Janeiro, prepared a master-plan for the development on the Santo Antonio hill and also designed the elegant, serpentine seven-storey residential block in Pedregulho (1947–52; for illustration see REIDY, AFFONSO EDUARDO), as well as the technically sophisticated Museu de Arte Moderna (1952–60), which was destroyed in a fire in 1978. It was rebuilt in 1980 by Mindlin Associates, whose founder, HENRIQUE E. MINDLIN, specialized in the construction of large industrial and commercial complexes in the 1950s and 1960s. Mindlin's book (1956) became an important record of much of the 'heroic' period of modern architecture in Brazil. Later work by the pioneers included the Instituto Central do Cancer (1949–54) by RINO LEVI, the Roberto brothers' Marquês do Herval Building (1955) in Rio, its façade enlivened with patterns of *brises-soleil,* and the purist buildings of Jorge Moreira, for example at the Cidade Universitária (1949–62; with Aldary Henriques Toledo), Rio de Janeiro, for which he also produced the master-plan.

Early in the 1950s a different approach was developed by SÉRGIO BERNARDES, based on the direct expression of structure and materials; examples include the Macedo Soares House (1953) at the Samambáia estate, Rio, and the brilliant exhibition building (1953) for the Companhia Siderúrgica in Ibirapuera Park, São Paulo, an early tension structure. JOÃO B. VILANOVA ARTIGAS, who built the residential Louveira Building (1948) in São Paulo, an often-quoted example of the influence of Le Corbusier in Brazil, later became an influential teacher at the Universidade de São Paulo. OSWALDO ARTHUR BRATKE was also active in São Paulo in the 1940s and 1950s, as were FRANZ HEEP, Icaro de Castro Mello (*b* 1913), Helio Queiroz

Duarte (1906–74), Xenon Lotufo (b 1911) and Flaminio Saldanha (b 1905).

The outstanding figure of the period, however, was undoubtedly Niemeyer, whose lyrical work, mostly in reinforced concrete, developed a refined aesthetic formalism that seems to distil the essence of Brazilian art and culture and provides many of the popular images of Latin American architecture, for example the group of four minor masterpieces around the lake at Pampulha (1942–7), near Belo Horizonte (see NIEMEYER, OSCAR, fig. 1). When Costa won the competition in 1957 for the masterplan for a new capital city, BRASÍLIA (for illustration see COSTA, LÚCIO), it was Niemeyer as Chief Architect who made possible the artistic realization of a logistic miracle: the major public buildings, including the sculptural Congresso Nacional complex (see NIEMEYER, OSCAR, fig. 2), were all ready for the inauguration ceremonies in 1960. Despite its many shortcomings, it was at Brasília that images of Corbusian urbanism of the 1930s became reality, presenting one of the most memorable visions of 20th-century architecture.

(iii) After 1960. Niemeyer continued to work in Brasília after 1960, a well-known later building being that for the Ministry of Foreign Affairs, the elegant Palácio dos Arcos (1965), with landscaping by Burle Marx (for illustration see BURLE MARX, ROBERTO) and sculpture by Giorgi (see fig. 10 below). Other architects began to investigate different approaches. Some developed a Brutalist style in the mid-1960s and 1970s, although in a more refined form than in Europe. The São Paulo 'school' led by Vilanova Artigas, who designed the Faculty of Architecture Building

(1961; for illustration see ARTIGAS, JOÃO B. VILANOVA) at the university there, developed an architecture of powerful forms, extensive use of raw concrete and simple, often monumental envelopes covering lighter-weight structures housing the building functions; the work of Ruy Ohtake (b 1939) is another good example. PAULO MENDES DA ROCHA's work was also influenced by Vilanova Artigas; he built the Museu de Arte Contemporânea (1975; with Jorge Wilheim) at the Universidade de São Paulo. Bernardes, who worked extensively in urban planning and prepared a master-plan (1964) for the development of Rio de Janeiro, made the study of industrialized building an integral part of his commission and set up a research centre to carry out economic and technical studies, the results of which are seen in much of his later work. João Toscano (b 1933) in his Araraquara University (1974) and MARCELO FRAGELLI in his Piraquê Industry Building (1977), Rio de Janeiro, also adopted the constructionalist ethic, initiated by Bernardes in the 1950s, and JOÃO FILGUEIRAS LIMA's clarity of structural expression, as in the ascending helicoidal design of the Central Administration of Bahia (CAB) Chapel (1974; see fig. 7), Salvador, is reminiscent of this approach.

As Modernism lost ground, other names came to the fore with a variety of different approaches. For example, José Zanine Caldas (b 1918), a brilliant model-maker and self-taught architect, developed an original craft-based neo-vernacular style of building in and around Rio de Janeiro, which is reminiscent of early 19th-century colonial fazendas. SEVERIANO PORTO, who worked in the Amazon region, was concerned with regional, environmentally

7. João Filgueiras Lima: Central Administration of Bahia (CAB) Chapel, Salvador, Brazil, 1974

appropriate design and construction techniques. Joaquim Guedes, whose individual constructionalism was developed in a series of private houses in São Paulo in the 1960s and 1970s (for illustration see GUEDES, JOAQUIM), designed the new town of Caraíba (1976–80), where he based his plans on traditional village patterns and built simple, economic houses in environmentally appropriate forms and materials.

Many of the younger architects received their education in the provinces, and more diverse groups began to form in the 1980s. Well-known examples include Luiz Forte Netto (b 1935), a graduate of the Universidade Mackenzie, São Paulo, who worked with a group of younger architects: Vicente Ferreira de Castro Neto (b 1943), Orlando Busarello (b 1947), Silva Cândida Busarello (b 1947) and Adolfo Sakaguti (b 1954), all graduates of the Universidade Federal do Paraná, producing a number of commercial buildings in the fast-developing city of Curitiba, the state capital of Paraná; and Joel Ramalho Júnior (b 1934), another graduate of Mackenzie, who worked with Leonardo Toshiaki Oba (b 1950) and Guilhermo Zamoner Neto (b 1950), both graduates of Paraná, and designed the Expo Centre (1980), Recife, and the confidently Post-modern Legislative Assembly building (1982), Curitiba. Another Post-modern building, the Citibank Building (1983–6), São Paulo, by the partnership of CROCE, AFLALO AND GASPERINI, resulted from an internationalist approach, their later style reflecting contemporary overseas aesthetic developments.

BIBLIOGRAPHY

G. Warchavchik: 'Acerca de arquitetura moderna', Il Piccolo (15 June 1925)
P. L. Goodwin and G. E. Kidder Smith: Brazil Builds: Architecture New and Old, 1652–1942 (New York, 1943)
Archit. Forum, lxxxvii/5 (1947) [whole issue on Brazil]
Archit. Aujourd'hui, xxiii (1952) [whole issue on Brazil]
H.-R. Hitchcock: Latin American Architecture since 1945 (New York, 1955)
H. E. Mindlin: Modern Architecture in Brazil (Rio de Janeiro, 1956)
'Rapporto Brasile', Zodiac, 6 (1960) [special feature], pp. 56–139
O. Niemeyer: Minha experiência em Brasília (Rio de Janeiro, 1961)
G. Ferraz: Warchavchik e a introdução da nova arquitetura no Brasil, 1925–1940 (São Paulo, 1965)
F. Bullrich: New Directions in Latin American Architecture (London, 1969), pp. 22–7, 96–105
Y. Bruand: L'Architecture contemporaine au Brésil (Lille, 1973; Port. trans., São Paulo, 1981)
D. Bayón and P. Gasparini: Panorámica de la arquitectura latino-americana (Barcelona, 1977; Eng. trans., New York, 1979), pp. 39–61, 237–40
A. Amaral, ed.: Arte y arquitectura del modernismo brasileño, 1917–1930 (Caracas, 1978)
C. A. C. Lemos: Arquitetura brasileira (São Paulo, 1979)
'Modern Brazilian Architecture', Process: Archit., 17 (1980) [whole issue]
G. Ferrez and P. F. Santos: Marc Ferrez: Album fotográfico da construção da Avenida Rio Branco, 1903–1906 (Rio de Janeiro, 1982)
S. Ficher and M. M. Acayaba: Arquitetura moderna brasileira (São Paulo, 1982)
G. Rosso del Brenna: O Rio de Janeiro de Pereira Passos (Rio de Janeiro, 1985)

V. Painting, graphic arts and sculpture.

1. Before c. 1822. 2. After c. 1822.

1. BEFORE c. 1822. Artistic activity in colonial Brazil was almost exclusively linked to the work of religious orders throughout the country for the first century after Portuguese settlement. The Jesuits were the most active

in building, particularly colleges and churches, and this led to a need for wood-carvers and sculptors capable of supplying the demand for statues, crucifixes and retables. The first of these artists came from outside Brazil; in the first half of the 17th century, for example, the Portuguese João Correia worked in the states of Rio de Janeiro and Bahia, and Johann Xavier Traer (1668–1737), a carver and painter from the Tyrol, worked in the states of Maranhão and Pará. Traer, together with indigenous assistants, was responsible for the pulpits in the collegiate church of S Alexandre, Belém, the canopies of which are reminiscent of Central European Baroque design. The main Jesuit contribution to painting dates from the arrival in 1587 of Belchior Paulo, a Portuguese member of the order who worked until 1619 in the Jesuit colleges of Olinda, Salvador, Vitória, Rio de Janeiro and São Paulo. He was followed by several other Jesuit painters, chiefly from Portugal, France and the Netherlands, including Fernão Cardim, active in Olinda; João de Almeida (c. 1635–79), who was responsible for the decoration of the side altars (1668) in the church of S Francisco Xavier, Belém; and Francisco Coelho, who executed 16 paintings (1740) for the refectory of the college in Salvador. Jesuit carvers and painters also produced the magnificent gilded carvings (1665–70) that cover the classical-style altar of the collegiate church (now the cathedral) in Salvador.

The Benedictines produced works in Salvador, Olinda and São Paulo, but their finest artistic production was concentrated on the monastery of S Bento in Rio de Janeiro. In the 17th century, for example, this work included sculpture by the Brazilian-born Frei Agostinho de Jesus (b c. 1600), who was also a painter and potter, and by the Portuguese Frei Domingos de Conceião (c. 1643–1718), who produced carvings for the monastery church, including the two portals and most of the high altar retable (1693–4). Frei Ricardo do Pilar (d 1700), who arrived in Brazil from Germany in 1660, was perhaps the most significant artist working at the monastery; his surviving works include ten panels painted for the chancel of the church and the large canvas of Our Lord of the Martyrs, painted in 1690 for the sacristy.

The Dutch occupation in north-east Brazil (1630–54; see §I above) produced important changes in artistic production, in particular by introducing secular subjects. When Johan Maurits, Count of Nassau-Siegen (see NASSAU, (1)), came to Brazil in 1637 as governor-general, he brought with him several scientists, architects and artists, including the painters Frans Post and ALBERT ECKHOUT and the draughtsman Zacharias Wagener II (1614–68); they produced important records of landscapes, genre scenes, costumes, fauna and flora (see also §§II above and X below). The exoticism of the surroundings helped to develop the sensitivity of Post's landscapes, in particular the intensity of detail characteristic of tropical colours (e.g. a painting of the Island of Itamaracá, 29 km north-east of Recife, 1637; Amsterdam, Rijksmus., on loan to The Hague, Mauritshuis; for illustration see POST, (2)). Although less vigorous than Post's, Eckhout's work—mainly still-lifes and representations of local scenes and customs—also showed a skill that raised it above mere documentation. Wagener, who was a soldier and Nassau's steward, made drawings in his free time that are early examples of simple observation of the reality of Brazil. He also produced a manuscript, *Thierbuch Zoobiblion* (Dresden, Kupferstichkab.), consisting of drawings and picturesque descriptions of native animals.

During the second half of the 18th century the best colonial art in Brazil was produced by artists in the three centres of Rio de Janeiro, Bahia and Minas Gerais and by the more isolated painters Padre Jesuíno do Monte Carmelo (1764–1819) in São Paulo and João de Deus Sepúlveda in Pernambuco. The Baroque style began to appear at the beginning of the 18th century with the adoption of the illusionist perspective introduced by Andrea Pozzo in Rome. Between 1733 and 1743 Caetano de Costa Coelho painted an illusionistic architectural composition in the church of S Francisco da Penitência, Rio de Janeiro. Bahia was dominated by the work of José Joaquim da Rocha (1737–1807), a Brazilian trained in Europe who introduced Italian influences and whose religious works included the painting (1772–3) of the nave vault of the church of the Conceição da Praia and two panels (1777–92) for the church of the Misericórdia, both in Salvador.

In the state of Minas Gerais, the wealth produced by gold-mining in the 18th century was reflected in the exuberance of the painting, wood-carving and sculpture there. The Portuguese Antônio Rodrigues Belo (*b* 1702) introduced new techniques of ceiling painting, executing the chancel vault in the parish church of Cachoeira do Campo in 1755. Two of the most significant Brazilian artists during the transition from the Baroque to the Rococo style worked in Minas Gerais: MANOEL DA COSTA ATAÍDE, who executed one of the most important paintings of the colonial period in Brazil, the ceiling (1801–10; see fig. 8) of S Francisco de Assis da Penitência in Ouro Prêto; and the sculptor and architect Antônio Francisco Lisboa (O Aleijadinho), who worked there for more than 50 years after 1760. At a time when the colony was beginning to assert its own identity, Lisboa's prolific, varied work (for example *see* RETABLE, fig. 5) fused conventional religious imagery with elements of Brazilian experience, including the use of local materials such as soapstone. His statues of *Prophets* (1800–05; for illustration *see* LISBOA, (2)), carved for the pilgrimage sanctuary of Bom Jesus at Matozinhos, near Congonhas do Campo, together with 64 painted wood figures of the Via Crucis in chapels along the hillside path leading to the sanctuary, provided a formal model for Brazilian sculpture (*see also* §IV, 1(i) above).

In Rio de Janeiro, which became the capital in 1763, important work was done by VALENTIM DA FONSECA E SILVA, a sculptor and carver who was also responsible for the design and landscaping of the Passeio Público (1779–83), Rio, including pine-cone ornaments, obelisks, statues, a fountain and pavilions decorated by the painter Leandro Joaquim (1738–98). The move to Rio of the Portuguese royal court in 1808 (*see* §I above), however, resulted in a transformation of the visual arts in Brazil. The French artistic commission organized by the Prince Regent (later John VI, King of Portugal) was led by Joachin Lebreton (1760–1819) and included the painters NICOLAS-ANTOINE TAUNAY (for illustration *see* RIO DE JANEIRO) and JEAN-BAPTISTE DEBRET, the sculptor Auguste-Marie Taunay (1768–1824) and the engraver Charles-Simon Pradier

8. Manoel da Costa Ataíde: *Glorification of the Virgin*, painted ceiling (1801–10) of S Francisco de Assis da Penitência, Ouro Prêto

(1783–1847); they were joined in 1817 by the sculptors Marc Ferrez (1788–1850) and Zéphirin Ferrez (1797–1851). One of its main achievements was the founding of the Academia Imperial das Belas Artes in Rio de Janeiro (1826), from which the academic ideas of Neo-classicism began to spread throughout Brazil (*see* §2(i) below).

BIBLIOGRAPHY

T. Thomsen: *Albert Eckhout: Ein niederlaendischer Maler und sein Goenne Moritz der Brasilianer* (Copenhagen, 1938)
C. M. da Silva-Nigra: *Construtores e artistas do mosteiro de São Bento do Rio de Janeiro* (Salvador, 1950)
S. Leite: *Artes e ofícios dos Jesuítas no Brasil* (Rio de Janeiro, 1953)
L. Castedo: *The Baroque Prevalence in Brazilian Art* (New York, 1954)
A. Taunay: *A missão artística de 1816* (Rio de Janeiro, 1956)
E. Larsen: *Frans Post: Interprète du Brésil* (Amsterdam, 1962)
G. Bazin: *Aleijadinho et la sculpture baroque au Brésil* (Paris, 1963)
Z. Wagener: *Zoobiblion: Livro de animais do Brasil* (São Paulo, 1964)
J. R. Teixeira Leite: *A pintura no Brasil holandês* (Rio de Janeiro, 1967)
L. G. Machado: *Barroco mineiro* (São Paulo, 1973)
C. P. Valladares: *Rio barroco* (Rio de Janeiro, 1978)
——: *Aspectos da arte religiosa no Brasil* (Rio de Janeiro, 1981)

2. AFTER *c.* 1822.

(i) Neo-classicism to Romanticism, *c.* 1822–88. (ii) Early modernism, 1889–1930. (iii) Developments in modernism, 1931–60. (iv) After 1960.

(i) Neo-classicism to Romanticism, c. *1822–88.* For many years after independence from Portugal in 1822, artistic activity in Brazil was dominated by France, due largely to the influence of the Academia Imperial das Belas Artes

(founded 1826; *see* §§1 above and XII below). The Baroque and Rococo models that had been handed on by the system of apprenticeship were replaced by Neo-classicism, an understanding of which could only be acquired by academic training. At the same time, the domination of art patronage passed from the Church to the State, and secular subjects replaced religious ones (*see* §X below). The many aspects of Brazilian life in the 19th century were best documented by foreign travellers, both professional artists and amateurs, who recorded the flora, fauna, landscape and people of the country. Particularly important was a series of paintings executed between 1816 and 1831 by JEAN-BAPTISTE DEBRET, who was Professor of History Painting at the Academia, and the work of Johan Moritz Rugendas (*see* RUGENDAS, (2)), who visited Brazil in 1821 as draughtsman to the scientific expedition of the Russian diplomat Baron de Langsdorff. Other artist–travellers of the time, some of whom settled permanently in Brazil, included Emeric Essex Vidal, Louis Buvelot and Thomas Ender. Few Brazilian artists recorded the actual appearance of their country until later in the century, although Manuel de Araújo Pôrto Alegre (1806–79), Director of the Academia from 1854 to 1857, encouraged interest in the local environment and himself produced Romantic landscapes (e.g. *Brazilian Forest*, 1853; Rio de Janeiro, Mus. N. B.A.). Graphic artists also depicted Brazilian subjects. The first important lithographer in Brazil was the Swiss Johann Steinmann (1800–44), who worked in Rio (1825–33) and produced maps and popular prints. In 1839 Frederico Guilherme Briggs printed the first caricatures, a series of political attacks attributed to Pôrto Alegre. The first wood-engraving workshop was opened in Rio in 1870 by the Portuguese Alfredo Pinheiro; the technique was practised particularly expressively by Modesto Brocos y Gomez (1852–1936), who was also a painter.

Academic influences continued to prevail, however, and Brazilian painting and sculpture continued to be dominated by Neo-classicism throughout most of the 19th century. This can be seen in the paintings of VICTOR MEIRELLES DE LIMA and PEDRO AMÉRICO DE MELO (e.g. the *Battle of Avaí*, 5×10 m, 1872–7; Rio de Janeiro, Mus. N. B.A.) and the sculpture of Francisco Manuel Chaves Pinheiro (1822–84), for example the *Goddess Ceres* (Rio de Janeiro, Mus. N. B.A.), which was predominantly historical, religious and allegorical. Only in the last quarter of the century did Romantic, natural and nationalistic subjects become more popular. Under the influence of GEORG GRIMM, who arrived in Brazil from Germany in 1874 as professor at the Academia, many artists began to take up *plein-air* painting, for example JOÃO BATISTA CASTAGNETO and ANTONIO PARREIRAS. Brazilian themes that had occasionally appeared in rhetorical history scenes or idealizations of national types, such as those by Meirelles de Lima, Américo de Melo, Rodolfo Amoedo (1857–1941) and Henrique Bernardelli (1857–1936), also became more common during the period of economic growth in the last two decades of the 19th century; JOSÉ FERRAZ DE ALMEIDA JÚNIOR, in particular, introduced popular types and costumes of the interior of the state of São Paulo into his increasingly Realist paintings (e.g. *Brazilian Woodchopper*, 1879; Rio de Janeiro, Mus. N. B.A.).

(ii) Early modernism, 1889–1930. The proclamation of the republic in 1889, rapid industrialization and increasing popular interest in the visual arts in Brazil brought a desire for change, challenging conventional approaches. Teaching at the Academia, renamed Escola Nacional de Belas Artes, was partially reformed (*see* §XII below), and innovative young artists were encouraged by those who had undergone an academic training but had later become acquainted with the most recent European movements. The new approach was exemplified by the opening of the Atelier Livre in Rio de Janeiro, which was modelled on the Académie Julian in Paris at the instigation of Rodolfo Amoedo, Henrique and RODOLFO BERNARDELLI and ELISEU VISCONTI. Visconti in particular overcame a narrow academic training through his work with Eugène-Samuel Grasset in Paris. He returned to Brazil imbued with a mixture of Impressionism and Art Nouveau that informed his work for nearly 60 years (e.g. decorations for the Teatro Municipal in Rio de Janeiro, 1906–7; *in situ*). Contemporary styles and subject-matter were also reflected in the illustrations and caricatures of such draughtsmen as BELMIRO DE ALMEIDA.

Brazilian art as a whole, however, was marked by a persistent conservatism. The poet Oswald de Andrade from São Paulo, who had first-hand experience of Futurism in Europe, returned to Brazil in 1912 and worked hard for a radical reformulation of Brazilian culture. In particular he attacked Brazilian artists for their lack of interest in the landscape and people of their country. During this period São Paulo began to replace Rio as the centre of artistic activity in Brazil: the wealth generated by coffee production in the state enriched an élite who travelled regularly to Europe, bringing back avant-garde works and ideas. The Lithuanian-born LASAR SEGALL, trained in German Expressionism, first exhibited modern art in Rio de Janeiro and São Paulo in 1913, although this had little immediate impact. The real break came four years later with the work of Anita Malfatti (1896–1964) in São Paulo (e.g. *The Fool*, 1917; U. São Paulo, Mus. A. Contemp.). She had studied in Berlin and New York (1914–16), and her experience of Cubism and Expressionism made her exhibition of 1917 crucial for the development of Brazilian Modernism. This took firm hold after the SEMANA DE ARTE MODERNA in São Paulo (1922), which included an exhibition championed by leading writers, with paintings by Malfatti and EMILIANO DI CAVALCANTI, VICENTE DO REGO MONTEIRO and John Graz (1895–1980), drawings by OSWALDO GOELDI and sculptures by VICTOR BRECHERET (e.g. *Guitar-player*, 1923; São Paulo, Pin. Estado). Their approach to modernism drew on both international developments and Brazilian experience. Their enthusiasm was particularly stimulated by encounters in Europe with Futurism, Cubism, *L'Esprit nouveau* and Surrealism.

Tarsila, a pupil of Fernand Léger and André Lhote in Paris from 1920 to 1923, became the principal figure in Brazilian modernism on her return to São Paulo; her work effectively combined elements of geometric stylization, primitivism and Surrealism to convey a deep native lyricism (for illustration *see* TARSILA). This style of painting inspired Oswald de Andrade to issue the *Manifesto antropófago* (1928) in São Paulo, aiming at the reconciliation of external influences with local traditions. Surrealism also influenced two other painters: ISMAEL NERY of Pará, who met Marc Chagall in Paris in 1927, and CÍCERO DIAS from Pernambuco, whose watercolours recaptured in dreamlike scenes his childhood experiences in the sugar mills. Pernambuco also succeeded in establishing itself as an important centre through a regionalist movement led by the sociologist Gilberto Freyre after 1926. The heroic phase of modernism ended in 1930, when an exhibition of the work of artists of the Ecole de Paris was brought to Recife, Rio de Janeiro and São Paulo by Rego Monteiro, who had lived in France. It was the first time that the Brazilian public was able to see at first hand a collection of works by some of the great modern artists of Europe.

(iii) Developments in modernism, 1931–60. Conditions for the modernization of Brazil changed at the beginning of the 1930s. The repercussions of the international financial crisis of 1929 and the Brazilian revolution of 1930 and subsequent rise to power of Getúlio Vargas ended the ideological turbulence of the preceding decade and began a long period of state intervention and patronage of the arts. Modernism was officially accepted and was marked by two new concerns: social issues and professionalism. The determined audacity typical of early modernism was replaced by a more sober approach, which is clearly seen in the work of Tarsila, Cavalcanti and Segall, who moved to São Paulo in 1923, and also in the work of CÂNDIDO PORTINARI a little later. In the 1930s Portinari began a series of murals and large easel paintings, many commissioned by the State, on historical and social themes, in which he was influenced by Mexican Social Realism (e.g. *Coffee*, see fig. 9; for further illustrations of his work *see* PORTINARI, CÂNDIDO and NIEMEYER, OSCAR, fig. 1).

In parallel with this ideological approach, other groups of artists between 1931 and 1945 were concerned with improving the status of their profession, for example the Núcleo Bernardelli, formed in Rio in 1931, from whose ranks emerged at least two important painters: MÍLTON DACOSTA and JOSÉ GIANINI PANCETTI. In São Paulo, groups such as the Sociedade Pró-Arte Moderna, the Clube dos Artistas Modernos, the Salão de Maio and the Família Artística Paulista were formed in the 1930s, in which the first generation of modernists were joined by such rising artists as FLÁVIO DE CARVALHO, ALBERTO DA VEIGA GUIGNARD, ALFREDO VOLPI and CARLOS SCLIAR. Of these, it was Flávio de Carvalho who did most to promote the adventurous spirit of Brazilian modernism through this cautious period. His work (e.g. the *Final Ascension of Christ*, 1932; São Paulo, Pin. Estado) was enigmatic and violent and, although rooted in Viennese Expressionism, was responsible for the pioneering debate between Surrealism and abstract art in Brazil. Sculpture of this period included the Surrealist work of Maria Martins (1900–73), for example the *Great Serpent* (1942; Rio de Janeiro, Dalal Achcar priv. col., see 1987 exh. cat., p. 205), and the eclecticism of BRUNO GIORGI and Ernesto de Fiori (1884–1945), some of it commissioned in conjunction with the new architecture that was beginning to emerge in Brazil (*see* §IV, 2(ii) above). The work of the landscape architect and painter ROBERTO BURLE MARX was also important in this context.

9. Cândido Portinari: *Coffee*, oil on canvas, 1.31×1.97 m, 1935 (Rio de Janeiro, Museu Nacional de Belas Artes)

Only in the middle of the 1940s did modernist art extend outside São Paulo and Rio de Janeiro, and this was followed by new developments after the end of World War II. The art world in Brazil underwent a structural change with the appearance of the first museums of modern art between 1947 and 1949 (see §XI below) and the establishment of an art market, in which the first São Paulo Biennale (1951) was a vital factor. Subsequent exhibitions increased the availability of information about international movements to the art world and the general public, as did the arrival in Brazil of such foreign artists as MARIA ELENA VIEIRA DA SILVA, Arpad Szenes (1897–1984), Samson Flexor (1907–71), Heinrich Boese (1897–1982), Laszlo Meitner (1900–68) and Emeric Marcier (b 1916). The chief result of this process of fertilization was the development of abstract art in Brazil. Cícero Dias, who had lived in Paris since 1937, and ANTONIO BANDEIRA, who had moved there in 1946, were the pioneers, the former producing geometric abstraction (e.g. a mural in the Ministry of Finance in Recife, 1948) and the latter Art informel (e.g. Big City Illuminated, 1953; Rio de Janeiro, Mus. N. B.A.). Many artists gradually became associated with Art informel, including such Japanese–Brazilians as MANABU MABE and Tomie Ohtake (b 1913), together with IBERÊ CAMARGO, Yolanda Mohalyi (1909–78) and FRANS KRAJCBERG, who later dedicated himself to engraving, photography and sculpture with natural materials. However, it was geometric abstraction that became dominant during the 1950s. At the head of this movement were Abraham Palatnik (b 1928), Almir Mavignier (b 1925), Vieira da Silva and IVAN SERPA in Rio de Janeiro and Samson Flexor, Waldemar Cordeiro (1925–73) and Geraldo de Barros (b 1923) in São Paulo. They were encouraged by Max Bill's visit to Brazil in 1941, the first two São Paulo Biennales and the support of the critic Mário Pedrosa (1900–81).

In the second half of the 1950s, in the optimistic climate of the government of Juscelino Kubitschek, Concrete art became the spearhead of abstract art. This movement, in which poets and artists were again united, was centred on São Paulo, and the best-known artists were Cordeiro, Luís Sacilotto (b 1924), Lothar Charoux (1912–87) and Hermelindo Fiaminghi (b 1920). The Neo-Concrete group was formed in reaction to the mathematic certainty of Concrete art. It consisted mainly of artists working in Rio de Janeiro, who introduced subjective, symbolic and organic dimensions to their work. In the work of LYGIA CLARK (e.g. Rubber Grubs, 1964, remade by artist, 1986; Rio de Janeiro, Mus. A. Mod.), HÉLIO OITICICA, Aluísio Carvão (b 1918), Willys de Castro (1926–88), Lygia Pape (b 1929), Franz Weissman (b 1914) and AMÍLCAR DE CASTRO, the group's chief members, Constructivism and Dadaism were often combined; their ideas were supported by the writings of the poet and critic Ferreira Gullar (b 1930). There were many artists of this time who, without associating themselves with the Concrete or Neo-Concrete groups, submitted in varying degrees to the rigours of geometric abstraction, including such painters as Volpi (e.g. Night Façade, 1955; U. São Paulo, Mus. A. Contemp.; for illustration see VOLPI, ALFREDO), Mílton Dacosta (e.g. On a Brown Background, 1955; U. São Paulo, Mus. A. Contemp.), Rubem Valentim (b 1922), Dionísio del Santo

(b 1925) and Mira Schendel (1919–88) and the sculptor SÉRGIO DE CAMARGO.

However, the dominance of geometric abstraction met some intransigent opposition, even in the 1950s, for example from older artists such as Emiliano di Cavalcanti. Groups of graphic artists interested in Realism and Expressionism also formed in the 1950s, impelled by the Cold War and by the examples of Oswaldo Goeldi and LÍVIO ABRAMO; the most consistent of these was the Clube de Gravura in Pôrto Alegre (1950–56) led by Carlos Scliar, but other artists included the Magic Realist Marcello Grassman (b 1925) of São Paulo and the group of engravers centred on the studio of the Museu de Arte Moderna do Rio de Janeiro, which remained on the fringe of Art informel.

(iv) After 1960. All these initiatives were stifled by the political disturbances in Brazil in 1961 and after, and by the wave of figurative art that directly confronted social realities and was combined with the influence of Pop art. This new phase was exemplified by the popcret assemblages of Waldemar Cordeiro; the Negress and Animals series of Ivan Serpa (e.g. Head, 1964; U. São Paulo, Mus. A. Contemp.); the 'happenings' of WESLEY DUKE LEE and Nelson Leirner (b 1932); and the painting and graphic art of such artists as GLAUCO RODRIGUES, ANTÓNIO HENRIQUE AMARAL and ANTÓNIO DIAS. These developments were publicized by exhibitions, for example Opinião-65 and Nova objetividade brasileira (1967), both at the Museu de Arte Moderna do Rio de Janeiro. The latter was particularly important because it was simultaneously a résumé of the avant-garde movements of São Paulo and Rio de Janeiro and also marked a new battle between the geometric abstraction prevalent in the 1950s, especially Neo-Concrete art, and the new trends. The gap between them was bridged by Hélio Oiticica, whose work showed a new neo-Dadaist dimension. Notable sculpture was produced in this period by Bruno Giorgi (see fig. 10) for the new federal capital of Brasília.

This activity took place under the repressive military regime installed in 1964; however, the anti-cultural spirit that prevailed made avant-garde manifestations possible. Many of these went beyond traditional limits, for example the series of Domingos da Criação (1971) in Rio de Janeiro—events that called on everyone, artist or not, to participate in creative action. There was also a decentralization of art, with the appearance of museums and contemporary exhibitions throughout the country. Pernambuco was one of the most active centres at this time, with the work of the potter and painter FRANCISCO BRENNAND, the painter and engraver João Câmara Filho (b 1944) and the wood-engraver Gilvan Samico (b 1928), for example, drawing inspiration from popular art of the region. The interest in popular art also stimulated such artists as the sculptor Agnaldo Manoel dos Santos (for illustration of his earlier work see fig. 3 above) and the painters José Antônio da Silva (b 1909), DJANIRA, Raimundo de Oliveira (1930–66) and ANTÔNIO MAIA.

In the 1970s an ideology was imposed on Brazilian art by the dictatorship in power. However, individual artists could provide lively opposition to the official approach, as shown by events organized at the time by the Museu

10. Bruno Giorgi: *Meteor*, marble, h. 4 m, 1965, outside the Palácio dos Arcos (Ministry of Foreign Affairs), Brasília

de Arte Contemporânea of the Universidade de São Paulo and the Museu de Arte Moderna do Rio de Janeiro. Conceptual art, in particular, was adopted by the avant-garde. The most interesting artists of the period included Cildo Meireles (*b* 1948), Artur Alípio Barrio (*b* 1945), Antônio Manuel de Oliveira (*b* 1947), Carlos Zílio (*b* 1944), Waltércio Caldas Júnior (*b* 1946) and José Resende (*b* 1945). However, with the process of democratization that began in 1978, the Conceptual movement was soon completely extinguished. A new generation, concerned with a more humorous depiction of the reality of their country, was inspired by the expressive possibilities of such new international movements as the Italian *Transavanguardia* and German Neo-Expressionism. Its vitality was made evident in the exhibition *Como vai você, geração 80?* in the Escola de Artes Visuais, Rio de Janeiro, in 1984.

BIBLIOGRAPHY

J.-B. Debret: *Voyage pittoresque et historique au Brésil* (Paris, 1834–9)
J. M. dos Reis Júnior: *História da pintura no Brasil* (Rio de Janeiro, 1944)
G. Ferrez: *A mui leal e heróica cidade de São Sebastião do Rio de Janeiro* (Rio de Janeiro, 1965)
J. R. Teixeira Leite: *A gravura brasileira contemporânea* (Rio de Janeiro, 1966)
Art in Latin America since Independence (exh. cat. by S. L. Catlin and T. Grieder, New Haven, CT, Yale U. A.G.; San Francisco, CA, Mus. A.; New Orleans, LA, Mus. A.; and elsewhere; 1966)
R. Pontual: *Dicionário das artes plásticas no Brasil* (Rio de Janeiro, 1969)
A. Amaral: *Artes plásticas na semana de 22* (São Paulo, 1970)
P. M. Bardi: *Profile of the New Brazilian Art* (Rio de Janeiro, 1970)
——: *História da arte brasileira* (São Paulo, 1975)
A. Amaral, ed.: *Arte y arquitectura del modernismo brasileño, 1917–1930* (Caracas, 1978)
J. R. Teixeira Leite: *Pintura moderna brasileira* (Rio de Janeiro, 1978)
C. P. Valladares: *Rio neoclássico* (Rio de Janeiro, 1978)
N. Carneiro: *Rugendas no Brasil* (Rio de Janeiro, 1979)
J. Fekete: *Dicionário universal de artistas plásticos* (Rio de Janeiro, 1979)
R. Brito and P. V. Filho: *O moderno e o contemporâneo: O novo e o outro novo* (Rio de Janeiro, 1980)
M. J. Harrison and S. de Sá Rego: *Modern Brazilian Painting* (Albuquerque, 1980)
Grabadores brasileños contemporáneos (exh. cat. by E. von Lauenstein Massarani, Mexico City, Mus. A. Carrillo Gil, 1980)
J. Feinstein: *Feitura das artes* (São Paulo, 1981)
F. Morais: *Núcleo Bernardelli: Arte brasileira nos anos 30 e 40* (Rio de Janeiro, 1982)
Do modernismo à Bienal (exh. cat. by R. Abramo, F. Magalhães and M. B. Rosseti, São Paulo, Mus. A. Mod., 1982)
Q. Campofiorito: *História da pintura brasileira no século XIX* (Rio de Janeiro, 1983)
A. Trevisan: *Escultores contemporâneos do Rio Grande do Sul* (Pôrto Alegre, 1983)
'Arte contemporânea', *História geral da arte no Brasil*, ed. W. Zanini (São Paulo, 1983), ii, pp. 499–820
J. Marino, ed.: *Tradição e ruptura: Síntese de arte e cultura brasileiras* (São Paulo, 1984)
R. Brito: *Neoconcretismo: Vértice e ruptura do projeto construtivo brasileiro* (Rio de Janeiro, 1985)
R. Pontual: *Entre dois séculos: Arte brasileira do século XX na coleção Gilberto Châteaubriand* (Rio de Janeiro, 1987)
Modernidade: Art brésilien du 20e siècle (exh. cat. by A. Amaral and others, Paris, Mus. A. Mod. Ville Paris, 1987)
Art in Latin America: The Modern Era, 1820–1980 (exh. cat. by D. Ades, London, Hayward Gal., 1989)

VI. Furniture.

Furniture used in Brazil during the colonial period (from *c.* 1535) was basically Portuguese in origin. It reflected the various European influences—Spanish, Dutch, French and English—that had entered Portugal in the 15th century at the start of the Portuguese success in navigation, discovery and conquest (*see* PORTUGAL, §VI). At the beginning of this period the import of furniture followed the settlement of the religious orders, which established themselves in Brazil at an early stage, and the expansion of sugar production, which was then the principal source of wealth (for further discussion *see* §I above). Furniture destined for churches, administrative buildings and houses was almost all imported from Europe (except for rare and ephemeral pieces produced at village level) and was characterized by simplicity and robustness, with straight lines and little decoration. From the second half of the 17th century and especially throughout the 18th, gold production was at its height. During this period furniture became more complex and exuberant, with Baroque ornamentation and generous curved lines; examples can be seen in the monumental chests, altar credences, sacristy benches and cupboards and carved chairs that still exist in innumerable Brazilian churches and in the collections of the Museu de Arte Sacra de Universidade Federal Bahia, Salvador, and the Museu de Arte Sacra, São Paulo. The wood used most frequently was jacaranda. It was elegantly carved with a profusion of detail into a kind of lacework, which, by the end of the period, used as motifs the flora and fauna of the country.

The transfer of the Portuguese court to Brazil in 1808 changed the way of life in the isolated colony. Helped by a new economic cycle based on coffee production, the primitive living conditions and the basic accessories of daily life began to improve. In 1822 Brazil became independent, and the establishment of modern infrastructures accelerated urban development and created new standards of comfort. From this time a strong French influence could be seen in a succession of refined styles—

LOUIS XVI STYLE, EMPIRE STYLE and Restoration (*see* FRANCE, §VI, 4)—in materials and decoration. It was only at the turn of the century, under the auspices of Art Nouveau, that the idea of truly Brazilian furniture began to be accepted. Furniture was mass-produced for the first time, a reflection of the new impetus in industry. A further stimulus to furniture production were the Liceus de Artes e Oficios (Crafts and Trades Schools), especially those of Rio de Janeiro and São Paulo, which had been founded in the middle of the 19th century and were places both of learning and of production. The established middle class, which had become richer as a result of the coffee industry, still preferred to import furniture, for example the European Art Nouveau furniture for Villa Penteado (1920), one of the finest houses of the period in São Paulo. The emerging middle class, however, was ready to absorb nascent local production. The industrialist Alvaro Auler designed and made his own furniture and also designed the interior fittings of the Confeitaria Colombo, Rio de Janeiro.

Constructivist models from the Bauhaus dominated in the wave of modernization that swept the country from the beginning of the 1920s. The first Brazilian example is the wooden furniture and glass light-fittings in a pure and functional style created by Gregori Warchavchik for his Modernistic House (1930) in São Paulo. The influence of the more sensual Art Deco style can be seen in the furniture in Brazilian woods made in the 1930s by the

factory of Federico Opfido in São Paulo. The overtly Modernist architecture from the 1930s, influenced by Le Corbusier and Mies van der Rohe, and the interest in the synthesis of the arts meant that contemporary Brazilian architects were concerned to create furniture that suited the pure and functional lines of their buildings. An example is the pioneering series of pieces in wood, leather and metal designed by the team led by Lúcio Costa and Oscar Niemeyer for the Ministry of Education and Health in Rio de Janeiro (*see* §IV, 2(ii) above). At the same time, the Modernist involvement in the preservation of the national art heritage led to a rediscovery and reappraisal of vernacular furniture of the colonial period, in particular the rural furniture produced in Minas Gerais. This comprised chests, strongboxes for valuables or alms, tables, commodes, chairs, benches and cupboards (often painted inside with cheerful naïve floral patterns), which were made of such rare woods as jacaranda, cedar, mulberry and Brazilian mahogany. LINA BARDI BO, who designed the Museu de Arte Popular do União, Salvador, in the 1960s and the interior and fittings for the Museu de Arte de São Paulo (from 1947), also set up the Studio d'Arte Palma to make modern furniture and designed a chair inspired by the native sleeping-net (1948; see fig. 11). Joaquim Tenreiro (*b* 1906) settled in Rio de Janeiro in 1928. After working with such furniture firms as Laubisch and Hirth and Leandro Martins, in 1942 he began to design and produce his own furniture, opening a shop for

11. Lina Bardi Bo: chairs inspired by the native sleeping-net, wood and canvas, 1948 (São Paulo, Museu de Arte de São Paulo)

interior furnishings in Rio de Janeiro in 1947 and another in São Paulo in 1953. In 1967 he created the furniture for the Banqueting Room in the Palácio dos Arcos (Ministry of Foreign Affairs) in Brasília. His pieces are usually of jacaranda-wood and are characterized by the use of traditional seats and backs in plaited straw. Sérgio Rodrigues (*b* 1927) enjoyed international success with his design 'Poltrona Mole' (1961), an armchair in wood and leather. José Zanine Caldas (*b* 1919) designed Z-line furniture in wood veneers that were mass-produced in the 1950s. He also designed strong, bold wooden furniture using traditional techniques for the interiors of the houses he had designed for wealthy clients throughout the country (e.g. for Roberto Pontual in Buzios, near Rio de Janeiro, 1971–3; altered).

BIBLIOGRAPHY

T. Canti: *O móvel no Brasil: Origens, evolução e características* (Rio de Janeiro, 1980)
J. Marino: *Coleção de arte brasileira* (São Paulo, 1983)
J. R. Katinsky: 'Desenho industrial', *História geral da arte no Brasil*, ed. W. Zanini (São Paulo, 1983), ii, pp. 915–51
J. Marino, ed.: *Tradição e ruptura: Síntese de arte e cultura brasileiras* (São Paulo, 1984)
A. M. M. Monteiro and R. R. Macedo: *Joaquim Tenreiro: Madeira, arte e design* (Rio de Janeiro, 1985)
S. F. da Silva: *Zanine, sentir e fazer* (Rio de Janeiro, 1988)

VII. Ceramics and glass.

Before the arrival of the Portuguese in Brazil in the 16th century, there were four areas of ceramic production: Marajó, Cunani, Maracá and Santarém, all in the north of Brazil (for further discussion *see* §II above). Vernacular pottery developed throughout Brazilian territory, and production included such utilitarian objects as pitchers, cooling-jars, teapots, bowls, dishes, pots, skillets and plates, which were usually made by women. The chief centres of production were the Jequitinhonha Valley in Minas Gerais and the area of Vitória in the state of Espírito Santo; in the latter, wares were characterized by an intense, black colour. Figurative pottery was a family activity, which was particularly prevalent during the periods between harvests. The main production centres were in the north-east, in the interior of Bahia, the Paraíba Valley in São Paulo and São José in Santa Catarina. A wide variety of decorated wares were made from plain clay or were glazed with red lead.

The religious orders working in Brazil after the conquest often made ceramic figures for religious purposes. Two outstanding Benedictine potters during the colonial period were the Portuguese Frei Agostinho da Piedade (*d* 1661) and the Brazilian Frei Agostinho de Jesus (1600/10–1661). Although the former produced prolifically in the monastery of S Bento in Salvador, less than 50 pieces have been definitely attributed to him. There are three signed pieces, including the *Nossa Senhora de Montesserrate* (1636; Salvador, Inst. Geog. & Hist.), which shows a synthesis of Gothic, Renaissance and East Asian influences; *St Peter Weeping* (Salvador, Nossa Senhora de Monteserrate) and *St Amaro* (São Paulo, Mus. A. Sacra) are executed in a similar style. Frei Agostinho de Jesus visited Portugal in 1628 and acquired a taste for the Baroque, which is evident in the exuberant form and colour of such pieces as *Nossa Senhora do Rosário* (São Paulo, Basilica de S Bento) and *Nossa Senhora dos Prazeres* (São Paulo, Mus. A. Sacra). Another type of ceramic production during the colonial period was the tin-glazed *azulejo* (tile). These were decorated with blue and sometimes yellow designs and were used on the exteriors of religious, civic and residential buildings.

The most interesting potter working at the beginning of the 20th century was the painter ELISEU VISCONTI. From 1893 he spent some time in Paris as a pupil of Eugène-Samuel Grasset and became interested in the decorative arts through the influence of the Pont-Aven group and the Nabis. He created stained-glass windows, glass and ceramic vases, and he was concerned with the application of industry to art. Inspired by Art Nouveau he focused his designs on flowers, including the tropical *maracujá* (passion-flower) and the female figure. The painter Teodoro Braga (1872–1953) also experimented with the decorative arts, producing *c.* 1930 Art Deco ceramics that were inspired by the geometric Marajó patterns. These designs were also influential in stained-glass windows, which were frequently made for middle-class houses in São Paulo and Rio de Janeiro during the 1930s. In 1929 there was an exhibition of German decorative arts at the Escola Nacional de Belas Artes in Rio de Janeiro; it included pieces from the Deutscher Werkbund and led to a surge of interest in decorative arts. Shortly afterwards, the painter Paulo Rossi Osir (1890–1959) and other artists founded Osirarte for the industrial production of art pottery. Among Osir's products were tiles with designs by the painter Cândido Portinari for the Ministry of Education and Health in Rio de Janeiro and for Niemeyer's church in the suburb of Pampulha, Belo Horizonte (*see* NIEMEYER, OSCAR, fig. 1). In the late 20th century the most important potter was FRANCISCO BRENNAND. He set up a museum-workshop near Recife in an old ceramics factory that belonged to his family. Here he produced and exhibited small and monumental works, which included fantastic flowers and animals. He also created the ceramic murals for Guarapes Airport in Recife. Important non-figurative potters included Celeide Tostes (*b* 1935) in Rio de Janeiro and Megumi Yuasa (*b* 1937) in São Paulo.

Urban development and improved forms of communication after 1940 enabled a number of producers in rural areas to sell their work throughout the country. Vitalino Pereira dos Santos (1909–63), known as 'O Mestre Vitalino', was an active potter in Caruaru in Pernambuco and produced figures of bandits, soldiers, students and politicians. Largely due to his fame, Caruaru became the main centre for this type of figurative pottery; innumerable *bonequeiros* (dollmakers) began working full-time and supplied a predominantly tourist market.

BIBLIOGRAPHY

G. Cruls: 'Arte indígena', *As artes plásticas no Brasil*, ed. R. M. F. de Andrade (Rio de Janeiro, 1952), i, pp. 75–110
H. Borba Filho and A. Rodrigues: *Cerâmica popular do nordeste* (Rio de Janeiro, 1969)
C. P. Valladares and V. J. Salles: *Artesanato brasileiro* (Rio de Janeiro, 1978)
A. Bento de Araújo Lima: *Abstração na arte dos índios brasileiros* (Rio de Janeiro, 1979)

ROBERTO PONTUAL

VIII. Gold, silver and jewellery.

According to Antonio Blasquez, a contemporary chronicler, the first Portuguese goldsmith arrived in Brazil in 1561. Unlike their counterparts in Peru (*see* PERU, §V) and Mexico (*see* MEXICO, §VII), however, the earliest gold-and silversmiths in colonial Brazil relied on imported silver (usually from Peru) in exchange for slaves. The gold-mines in Minas Gerais, Goias, Mato Grosso, Bahia and São Paulo subsequently provided craftsmen with plentiful raw material for the production of gold jewellery and domestic objects. Most of the surviving silver from the 16th and 17th centuries is ecclesiastical. In addition to antependia, candlesticks, lamps and liturgical vessels, chased incense boats in the form of ships were popular (examples in Rio de Janeiro, Cathedral; Salvador, Mus. A. Sacra U. Fed. Bahia; São Paulo, Mus. A. Assis Chateaubriand; see fig. 12). One distinctly Brazilian form is the large, goblet-shaped holy water stoup.

In the 17th century the main centres of production of silver and jewellery were Salvador and Olinda, and the number of silversmiths in Salvador rose from 25 at the end of the 17th century to 150 in 1750. The craft was not necessarily restricted to workers of European origin: Jews, Africans, native Americans and mulattos made and sold gold- and silverware, although a series of decrees issued from 1621 sought to prevent these groups of craftsmen from working. One of the earliest known extant Brazilian pieces is the reliquary bust of *St Lucia*, made about 1630 by Frei Agostinho da Piedade (*d* 1661) for the monastery of S Bento in Salvador. It is often difficult to differentiate between Brazilian and Portuguese silverwork, although certain characteristics, largely derived from African and native American art, can be detected in many Brazilian pieces. A lantern in the treasury of Rio de Janeiro Cathedral, dating from the second half of the 17th century, is a typical Brazilian combination of exotic figures and native vegetal motifs combined with European elements. In contrast, a gold ciborium made for the church of S Teresa in São Paulo during the same period shows no Brazilian features and is obviously the work of a Portuguese-trained goldsmith with a full knowledge of the most fashionable European Baroque ornament. During this period considerable quantities of silverware were imported from Portugal, and periodic attempts were made by the guilds of Lisbon and Oporto to limit the activities of Brazilian craftsmen; a decree of 1678, reissued in 1703, for example, limited the number of goldsmiths working in Rio to three.

Extravagant Baroque forms were used throughout the 18th century, although certain elements of the Rococo style, for example rocaille motifs, were adopted. One of the most accomplished exponents of the Baroque style was Lourenco Ribeiro da Rocha, who was appointed assaymaster in Salvador in 1725. During the first half of the 18th century, native American craftsmen working under Jesuit supervision in the missions of Paraguay produced liturgical silver of astonishing richness. In 1766, however, a decree was issued, in force until 1815, prohibiting the manufacture of all gold and silver articles in Brazil. Its purpose, ostensibly to protect the interests of Portuguese craftsmen, was effectively to curtail the trade

12. Silver incense boat, h. 85 mm, l. 170 mm, from São Paulo, second half of the 17th century (São Paulo, Museu de Arte de São Paulo)

in contraband wares, on which the *quinto* or 'King's fifth' had not been paid. Many workers moved to Buenos Aires in Argentina, and the trade in silverware with that city, as well as with those in Peru, continued unchecked in Brazil. Yet this law appears to have been generally ignored; many craftsmen continued to work clandestinely in Brazil and struck their works with imitation Portuguese hallmarks. Most surviving 18th-century domestic silver pieces are either ewers, basins or salvers, although some *farinheiras* (bowls for manioc flour) are extant, sometimes made of gold and elaborately chased with Baroque ornament.

Neo-classical motifs appeared at the end of the 18th century and are often combined with other styles in the same piece. Good examples of this combination of styles include the antependium and tabernacle from the chapel of the Blessed Sacrament of Salvador Cathedral by Joao da Costa Campos (1791–8; Salvador, Mus. A. Sacra U. Fed. Bahia). Swags of husks, beading and other classical motifs are combined with a background of horizontal bands, but the overall effect is Baroque in style.

Towards the end of the 18th century Rio de Janeiro became an important centre of production where, in the 19th century, immigrant Italian, French and German craftsmen brought new techniques and to a certain extent developed the mechanized production of silverware. In the 19th century large quantities of candlesticks, snuffers and inkstands, often decorated with exotic foliage, were produced in Rio de Janeiro, together with *paliteiros* (toothpick holders) in the form of animals, mythological figures or plants. Large sums of money were spent on silver, as well as gold, horse trappings. Typical silver items from southern Brazil include a type of silver beaker with a swing handle and chain, known as a *guampa*, that was hung from the saddle and used to collect water without dismounting. In Rio Grande do Sul, where the herbal infusion *mate* was especially popular, a distinctive form of *chimarrao* (mate cup) and accompanying *bombilha* (sucking tube) was produced.

In the 20th century workers in Bahia continued to produce jewellery incorporating African and Vodoun motifs, the most popular being the *balanganda*, a pendant comprising numerous amulets that was worn on the belt by slaves and made of silver and occasionally of gold, depending on the wealth of their owner. African elements are also found in the *joias de coco* (gold-mounted coconut jewellery) produced in Minas Gerais.

Only a small proportion of surviving Brazilian gold- and silverwork is hallmarked, although a system of assaying had been established in Bahia as early as 1689. Some surviving 18th-century pieces are marked with a crowned B for Bahia, sometimes found in conjunction with a maker's mark. The marks of a crowned M, for Minas, and a crowned R, for Rio, were also used; 19th-century silver made in Rio is marked with a 10 (denoting the silver standard of 10 dineiros) and a maker's mark. The conjoined letters SP appear on a small group of mid-19th-century silver and probably denote that the piece was made in São Paulo.

BIBLIOGRAPHY

J. Valladares and G. Valladares: 'A ourivesaria no Brasil', *As artes plasticas no Brasil*, ed. R. M. F. de Andrade (Rio de Janeiro, 1952), i, pp. 203–63
P. A. Carvalho Machado: *Ourivesaria Baiana* (Rio de Janeiro, 1973)
M. Rosa: *A prata da casa* (Salvador, 1980)
H. M. Franceschi: *O oficio da prata no Brasil: Rio de Janeiro* (Rio de Janeiro, 1988)
R. Lody: *Pencas balangandas da Bahia* (Rio de Janeiro, 1988)

CHRISTOPHER HARTOP

IX. Textiles.

The indigenous peoples of Brazil had developed an established and productive tradition of weaving and plaiting with leaves, palm fronds and other vegetable fibres well before the arrival of the Portuguese in 1500. They created objects for domestic and ceremonial use, among the most striking of which are the robes and painted masks used by the Tukuna for ritual purposes, the sleeping-nets from the Rio Negro made from palm fibre and the cotton garments of the Paresi, which have elaborately woven geometrical patterns in yellow, red and black (*see also* §II above). Although increasing contact with white civilization resulted in the decline of this activity, some continuity was guaranteed by the transmission of these techniques and forms to village weaving and cloth production. The indigenous Indians in religious missions or in rural enterprises came into contact with European spinning and weaving equipment—the spindle, the cotton gin and the shaft loom—and incorporated them in their own tradition. The Brazilian textile tradition is the result of these three traditions. The principal fibre used is cotton, which is widely available, and also wool and various vegetable fibres.

Spinning and the related tasks of producing and dyeing thread are traditionally associated with women, who learn them in early childhood. For dyeing they use aniline extracted from some other textile, or natural ingredients from such plants as anil (indigo), *urucu* (annatto) and *quaresmeira* (Brazilian spider-flower), which, by maceration, fermentation and boiling, produce respectively a basic blue, red and yellow, from which a wide range of other colours can be obtained. The cloth is woven on two types of handloom: vertical (of disputed origin), which is widely used by the Amazonian Indians to make their sleeping-nets; and horizontal (of Portuguese origin), used in most other regions. Geometrical patterns predominate, based on straight lines. Figurative subjects are rare, although they do appear in the 'coast cloth', which the Negro *tercelões* of Bahia continued to produce in the

African tradition. Blankets, bedcovers and towels are produced, as well as vividly coloured sleeping-nets, which are very common in Ceará and are also found in Maranhão and Mato Grosso. The bobbin-lace work, produced from native cotton thread, usually by women and especially in the north-east of Brazil, is used to decorate trousseaus, babies' layettes, towels, pillow-cases and sheets and sacristy towels or altar cloths.

Weaving as an art form developed in Brazil only at the beginning of the 20th century. The pioneer figure was the painter ELISEU VISCONTI, who, after studying in Paris with Eugène-Samuel Grasset, returned to Brazil with a profound interest in applied arts. His designs for silk textiles exhibited in Rio de Janeiro in 1901 have foliage motifs inspired by Art Nouveau. The influence of modernism is apparent in the work of Regina Gomide Graz (1897–1973), who trained from 1913 to 1920 at the Ecole des Beaux-Arts et des Arts Décoratifs in Geneva and produced designs for cushions, blankets and tapestries with geometrical patterns influenced by Cubism and Art Deco. Some of her pieces featured in the inaugural exhibition of the Modernistic House of GREGORI WARCHAVCHIK in São Paulo in 1930. After this period, the development of tapestry as *obra teçida* ('woven work') was rapid and widespread in Brazil. The principal practitioners were Madeleine Colaço (*b* 1907) in Rio de Janeiro, who used motifs from national folklore; Genaro de Carvalho (1926–71) in Salvador, whose designs reflect the exuberance of tropical vegetation; and Jacques Douchez (*b* 1921) and Norberto Nicola (*b* 1930) in São Paulo, both of whom used abstract forms.

BIBLIOGRAPHY

A. Ramos and L. Ramos: *A renda de bilros e sua aculturação no Brasil* (Rio de Janeiro, 1948)
G. E. de Andrade: *Aspectos da tapeçaria brasileira* (Rio de Janeiro, 1977)
C. P. Valladares and V. J. Salles: *Artesanato brasileiro* (Rio de Janeiro, 1978)
P. M. Bardi: *O modernismo no Brasil* (São Paulo, 1982)
D. Ribeiro: 'Arte india', *História geral da arte no Brasil* (São Paulo, 1983), i, pp. 46–87
E. Kac and A. F. Fagundes: *Madeleine Colaço* (Rio de Janeiro, 1988)

X. Patronage, collecting and dealing.

For almost three centuries after colonization until the transfer of the Portuguese court to Rio de Janeiro (1808), artistic activity in Brazil depended primarily on the missions and religious orders that established themselves in the country. The undisputed strength of the Church came to a large extent from the administrative role it exercised in the colony, including responsibility for education. Countless sculptors, carvers and painters were employed by the Jesuits, Benedictines and Franciscans to work on their churches and colleges (*see* §V, 1 above). Much of this production and an important part of the vast cultural wealth of Baroque and Rococo paintings, *azulejos* (glazed tiles), gold- and silverwork, furniture and carvings owned by the religious orders, some of it imported from Europe, is still to be found in churches, convents and religious colleges throughout Brazil. During this period, apart from the work produced by foreign travellers and artists, the only secular element in Brazilian art was the documentary work of artists who came to Brazil with Johan Maurits, Count of Nassau-Siegen, in 1637. The Brazilian work of such artists as Frans Post, Albert Eckhout and Zacharias

Wagener II was taken back to the Netherlands in 1644, but in the 20th century some of it was returned to Brazilian collections; for example the Museu Nacional de Belas Artes in Rio de Janeiro acquired eight paintings by Post.

After the second half of the 18th century, when the mining of gold and diamonds led to the concentration of wealth and urbanization, especially in Minas Gerais, State intervention in culture and the arts increased considerably. Expansion of the religious orders in the gold-producing region was under the control of royal authority, which encouraged the construction of public buildings and the employment of artists to carry out their ornamentation. This climate promoted the development of a number of major artists, including the sculptor Antônio Francisco Lisboa (O Aleijadinho) and the painter Manoel da Costa Ataíde, although most of their work was still the result of ecclesiastical commissions. The secularization of art was stimulated by the introduction of art education in 1800 with the opening of the Aula Pública de Desenho e Figura in Rio de Janeiro but more particularly by the steps taken by the Prince Regent (later John VI, King of Portugal) after his arrival in 1808, in an attempt to develop the cultural life of the colony; this led to the encouragement of artistic creation passing more directly to the State and away from the Church. His initiatives, particularly the organization of a French artistic commission (1816; see §§I, IV, 1(ii) and V, 1 above), resulted in the foundation of some of Brazil's most important institutions, including the Academia Imperial das Belas Artes, Rio de Janeiro, as well as the first import of secular works of art from Europe: for teaching purposes, the commission brought with them 50 paintings, originals or copies, by European artists, including Eustache Le Sueur, Charles Le Brun, Poussin, Canaletto and Guercino. Several of these later disappeared, but the remainder ultimately formed the basis of the collection of foreign paintings in the Museu Nacional de Belas Artes in Rio de Janeiro. This museum, together with the Museu Imperial in Petrópolis, also received the collections of the emperor Peter II (reg 1831–89), who was a decisive influence in the development of the arts, constantly involved both officially and personally in encouraging their production and dissemination. The seeds of collecting, of an art market and of art criticism were planted during his reign, although restricted to a narrow circle centred on the court in Rio. Even after the proclamation of the republic (1889), the absolute hegemony of the capital as the artistic centre persisted until the first decades of the 20th century. Regular annual exhibitions were organized by the Academia Imperial das Belas Artes, official commissions for portraits and decorative or commemorative paintings increased, and private premises were opened to exhibit the work of individual artists then in vogue. The most systematic collections were begun at this time, such as that of Jonathas Abbot (d 1868) in Salvador, which was purchased by the provincial government in 1871 and later formed the basis of the Museu de Arte da Bahia. Outstanding collectors at the end of the 19th century included the Viscondessa de Cavalcanti and the Barão de São Joaquim; the Viscondessa was the first collector to bring back to Brazil a painting by Post, which is now in the Instituto Histórico e Geográfico Brasileiro, Rio de Janeiro, and the Barão acquired several works by Eugène Boudin that later passed to the Museu Nacional de Belas Artes.

Rapid industrialization and economic development after the end of the 19th century brought another change to the art world as private patrons began to appear, especially in São Paulo, which gradually succeeded Rio as the largest urban centre. The Semana de Arte Moderna (1922), which established modernism in Brazil (see §V, 2(ii) above), was the result of patronage by some of the most important individuals in economic and political circles of São Paulo. Private art collecting also began in earnest in the 20th century, beginning with such pioneers as Domingos de Góes and Gastão Penalva in Rio de Janeiro, and Carlos Costa Pinto and Francisco Góes Calmon in Salvador. They made a point of collecting paintings that were both old and Brazilian at a time when such works were being dispersed because of a general preference then for 19th-century French art. Other important collections of the colonial and imperial periods were made by José Mariano Filho, a historian and critic; Raymundo Ottoni de Castro Maya (1894–1968), an industrialist; the diplomat Joaquim de Souza Leão; and the antiquarian Francisco Marques dos Santos, all in Rio; and the entrepreneur João Marino (b 1929) in São Paulo. The collection of religious and folk art made by Abelardo Rodrigues of Pernambuco was acquired by the provincial government of Bahia and housed in the Solar do Ferrão in Salvador, while the collection of Brazilian and foreign modernist paintings and drawings of writer and critic Mário de Andrade (1893–1945) was absorbed into the collection of the Instituto de Estudos Brasileiros of the Universidade de São Paulo. State involvement in the arts continued, particularly in the direction of institutions such as schools, museums and foundations; for example the Vargas government initiated the modernization of teaching at the Escola Nacional de Belas Artes in 1930 (see §IV, 2(ii) above). Government patronage was also extended to individual artists, including Cândido Portinari in the 1930s and 1940s, and to many other artists with the construction of the new capital of Brasília in the 1950s and 1960s.

After 1945, with the establishment of the first museums devoted to modern art, the succession of international Biennales in São Paulo and the more consistent functioning of the art market, collectors in Brazil began to concentrate more on contemporary art. The largest of these collections, covering developments from the beginning of modernism in the 1910s to the late 20th century, was that of the former diplomat Gilberto Châteaubriand (b 1925) in Rio de Janeiro. Other collections of modern and contemporary art were formed by João Sattamini (b 1940) and Sérgio Sahione Fadel (who also collected a significant group of 19th-century works) in Rio; and by Adolphe Leirner, Ladi Biezus (b 1932), Ernesto Wolf and Rodolpho Ortenblad Filho in São Paulo. Some dealers, for example Jean Boghici (b 1930) and Max Perlingeiro (b 1945) in Rio, also collected on a considerable scale. For the most part these collections consisted almost entirely of Brazilian works, largely because of the strength of the internal market, which over-valued Brazilian artists, while protective legislation by import duties and the lack of international opportunities ensured that foreign works appeared on the market only rarely.

Many important collections later contributed to the foundation of new museums: the private collection of the industrialist Francisco Matarazzo Sobrinho (1898–1977), who was also the creator of the São Paulo International Biennale in 1951, was the basis of the Museu de Arte Moderna in São Paulo in 1948, and the collection of Assis Châteaubriand (1891–1968), the senator and journalist, founded the Museu de Arte de São Paulo in 1947. The industrialist Raymundo Ottoni de Castro Maya, who helped found the Museu de Arte Moderna do Rio de Janeiro in 1949, also opened two museums in the Santa Teresa and Alto da Boa Vista districts of Rio to house his collections of Brazilian art; and the Fundação Roberto Marinho created in 1983 includes the Marinho collection of contemporary art.

Private patronage and other private initiatives continued to expand in the latter part of the 20th century, for example through sponsorship of competitions, exhibitions, prizes and publications. Important newspapers such as the *Jornal do Brasil*, *Rede Globo* and *Manchete*—which set up the Museu Manchete in Rio based on the 20th-century Brazilian art collection of its president, Adolpho Bloch (*b* 1908)—stood out among firms supporting artistic activities in Brazil.

See also §§XI, XII and XIII below.

BIBLIOGRAPHY
C. M. da Silva Nigra: *Construtores e artistas do mosteiro de S Bento do Rio de Janeiro* (Salvador, 1950)
S. Leite: *Artes e ofícios dos jesuítas no Brasil* (Rio de Janeiro, 1953)
A. Amaral: *Artes plásticas na Semana de 22* (São Paulo, 1970)
A. C. da Silva Telles: *Atlas dos monumentos históricos e artísticos do Brasil* (Rio de Janeiro, 1975)
C. P. Valladares: *Aspectos da arte religiosa no Brasil* (Rio de Janeiro, 1981)
Q. Campofiorito: *História da pintura brasileira no século XIX* (Rio de Janeiro, 1983)
J. Marino: *Coleção de arte brasileira* (São Paulo, 1983)
M. R. Batista and Y. S. de Lima: *Coleção Mário de Andrade* (São Paulo, 1984)
J. R. Teixeira Leite and others: *Seis décadas de arte moderna na coleção Roberto Marinho* (Rio de Janeiro, 1985)
R. Pontual: *Entre dois séculos: Arte brasileira do século XX na coleção Gilberto Châteaubriand* (Rio de Janeiro, 1987)
F. Gullar and others: *150 anos de arte brasileira: Coleção Sérgio Sahione Fadel* (Rio de Janeiro, 1989)

XI. Museums.

The first museums in Brazil, including the Museu Nacional, Rio de Janeiro (founded 1818), the Museu Paraense Emílio Goeldi, Belém (1866), and the Museu Paulista da Universidade de São Paulo (1892), were all concerned with archaeology, history, anthropology and ethnography; not until the 20th century were museums established for the collection, conservation and exhibition of works of art. The first of these was the Pinacoteca do Estado in São Paulo, initially housed in the Liceu de Artes e Ofícios in 1905. Its foundation was due largely to José de Freitas Valle, a poet, patron and senator, who did much to introduce modernism into Brazil in the 1910s. By the late 20th century it contained a very large collection of 19th-century Brazilian paintings, especially works by José Ferraz de Almeida Júnior, Pedro Alexandrino Borges (1864–1942) and Henrique Bernardelli (1857–1936). After 1969 its collections of contemporary art were enriched by automatic annual acquisitions from the Salão de Arte

Contemporânea in São Paulo. The second art museum was founded in 1918: the Museu de Arte da Bahia, Salvador, originated in a purchase by the State in 1871 of paintings by local artists collected by Jonathas Abbot (*d* 1868). The collection, rich in porcelain, colonial art from Bahia and Luso-Brazilian furniture, was moved in 1982 to the Palácio da Vitória, built in 1924 with traditional architectural features.

Brazil's principal gallery for painting and sculpture, with works dating from the 13th century, is the Museu Nacional de Belas Artes, founded in Rio de Janeiro in 1937 and located in the building designed by Adolfo Morales de los Ríos for the Escola Nacional de Belas Artes, which operated there from 1908 to 1976. The basis of its collections came from the Escola Real das Ciências, Artes e Ofícios, instituted in 1816 on the arrival of the French artistic commission organized by the Prince Regent (*see* §X above), which brought paintings and prints from Europe for teaching purposes. Later acquisitions came from the royal collections, particularly of Emperor Peter II (*reg* 1831–89). Among its most important European paintings are works by Jacopo Bassano, Giambattista Tiepolo, Francesco Guardi, Frans Post and Eugène Boudin, but its great strength lay in its collection of Brazilian painting and sculpture from the mid-19th century to the early 20th, especially its patriotic scenes by Victor Meirelles de Lima and Pedro Américo de Melo and a comprehensive collection of works by Eliseu Visconti.

Museums concerned primarily with modern art were founded after World War II, when modernism had become well entrenched throughout Brazil. The first of these, the Museu de Arte de São Paulo, was established through the efforts of the senator and journalist Assis Châteaubriand (1891–1968) and the technical guidance of Pietro Maria Bardi (*b* 1900), its director. Its first assets included works by Mantegna, Giovanni Bellini, Tintoretto, Memling, Bosch, Frans Hals, El Greco, Goya, van Gogh, Gauguin, Degas and Picasso, but the museum at once turned towards new movements in art, especially through the educational activity of its Instituto de Arte Contemporânea. After 1967 it occupied a new building designed by Lina Bardi Bo. The second such museum was the Museu de Arte Moderna (1948), also in São Paulo, the original holdings of which consisted of works by European artists presented by the industrialist Francisco Matarazzo Sobrinho (1898–1977). The first São Paulo International Biennale was held there in 1951, but subsequent Biennales were moved to one of the pavilions designed by Oscar Niemeyer in the Parque Ibirapuera. In addition to retrospective exhibitions devoted to Brazilian artists, annual surveys of painting, drawing, engraving and sculpture were also held there, substantially enriching the museum's collection.

In 1949 the Museu de Arte Moderna do Rio de Janeiro was founded, modelled on MOMA in New York. Although it had no foundation collection and no building of its own until Affonso Eduardo Reidy's two-stage design was completed (1957 and 1967), its director during the 1950s and 1960s, Niomar Muniz Sodré (*b* 1922), acquired important donations from international and national sources, especially of abstract works. The museum was well known for its exhibitions of avant-garde movements (*see* §V, 2(iv) above) and for its introductory courses for children and adults run by the painter Ivan Serpa. In 1978 a fire destroyed more than 80% of the collections, and although the building was reconstructed in 1980, the museum's work was interrupted for many years.

For the wealth of its holdings, however, the Museu de Arte Contemporânea of the Universidade de São Paulo, founded in 1963 and occupying buildings in the Parque Ibirapuera and the university campus, outshines its fellow institutions. Its collections were based on a gift to the university of the holdings of the Museu de Arte Moderna de São Paulo, which was then passing through a crisis, together with the private collections of Matarazzo Sobrinho and Yolanda Penteado. These were rapidly increased by acquisitions made at each São Paulo Biennale, so that the museum holds perhaps the most important collection of international contemporary art in Latin America, from Cubism onwards. It is also rich in 20th-century Brazilian art, including, for example, a donation by Emiliano di Cavalcanti of 564 drawings made by him between the 1920s and 1950s. From its inception the museum favoured experimental art and exhibitions of the work of young artists, which then travelled to other provincial capitals.

Brazilian modernist works are also found in the Instituto de Estudos Brasileiros of the Universidade de São Paulo, which created a special section in 1968 to house works donated by Mário de Andrade (1893–1945), a writer and critic who was a pioneer supporter of modernism and throughout his life collected works by the principal modernists of Brazil as well as some foreign artists. Galleries devoted to the work of single artists are rare in Brazil. Exceptions include the Museu Lasar Segall, created in 1970 in the house in São Paulo where the artist lived and worked and containing a large part of his work and related documents; the Museu Antônio Parreiras in Niterói; and the Casa-Museu Portinari at Brodósqui. Museums of 20th-century art in other cities include the Museu de Arte do Rio Grande do Sul, Pôrto Alegre; the Museu de Arte Contemporânea, Curitiba; the Museu de Arte Moderna, Belo Horizonte; the Museu de Arte Moderna da Bahia, Salvador; and the Museu de Arte Contemporânea de Pernambuco, Olinda.

Two museums were founded in Rio by the industrialist and patron Raymundo Ottoni de Castro Maya (1894–1968): the Museu de Tijuca (1964), which houses a fine collection from the colonial and imperial periods in Brazil, including work by foreign artists who visited the country, with a particularly good group of watercolours by Jean-Baptiste Debret; and the Museu Chácara do Céu (1972), which houses his collections of 20th-century Brazilian art and French Realism, Impressionism and Fauvism. In Salvador the Museu da Fundação Carlos Costa Pinto, inaugurated in 1969, specialized in Portuguese and Brazilian furniture and silverware, including the finest existing collection of sets of jewellery from Bahia, as well as Chinese and European porcelain of the 17th, 18th and 19th centuries.

Three museums have outstanding collections of religious art, including wooden and terracotta statues and gold and silver liturgical objects: the Museu de Arte Sacra da Bahia in the Benedictine convent of S Teresa, Salvador (founded 1959); the Museu Arquidiocesano in Mariana (1961); and the Museu de Arte Sacra in the Franciscan monastery of Luz (1970), São Paulo. Other important museums include the Museu da Inconfidência, Ouro Prêto (1938), which contains relics of the miners' rebellion as well as sculptures by Antônio Francisco Lisboa and paintings by Manoel da Costa Ataíde; the Museu Imperial, Petrópolis (founded 1945), which received part of the collections of Emperor Peter II and has the fullest archive of historical and artistic documents of the Brazilian monarchy, together with an excellent gallery of 19th-century art; the Museu de Arte Técnica Popular e Folclore in São Paulo (founded 1947); the Museu da Coleção Abelardo Rodrigues, Salvador (1984); and the Museu do Pontal (Coleção Jacques van de Beuque), established in Rio in 1984.

For information on museum architecture in Brazil, *see* §IV, 1(ii) and 2(i) above.

BIBLIOGRAPHY

A. Sodré: *Museu imperial* (Rio de Janeiro, 1950)

P. M. Bardi: *The Arts in Brazil: A New Museum at São Paulo* (Milan, 1956)

F. de Camargo e Almeida: *Guia dos museus no Brasil* (Rio de Janeiro, 1972)

M. Pedrosa, ed.: *Museu de imagens do inconsciente* (Rio de Janeiro, 1980)

A. Amaral: *Pinacoteca do estado de São Paulo* (Rio de Janeiro, 1982)

A. de Oliveira Godinho, ed.: *O Museu de arte sacra de São Paulo* (São Paulo, 1983)

M. R. Batista and Y. S. de Lima: *Coleção Mário de Andrade* (São Paulo, 1984)

O. Marques de Paiva: *O Museu paulista da Universidade de São Paulo* (São Paulo, 1984)

A. Amaral: *Desenhos de di Cavalcanti na coleção do MAC* (São Paulo, 1985)

A. Mafra de Souza, ed.: *O Museu nacional de belas artes* (Rio de Janeiro, 1985)

XII. *Art education.*

Three centuries of colonial rule passed before formal institutions of art education were established in Brazil. From 1500 to 1800 artistic knowledge was transmitted by personal contact between masters and their apprentices. Even at the height of artistic production in the Baroque and Rococo periods, the teaching of art in Brazil continued to lack organization; moreover very few Brazilian artists were able to study in European academies. This situation began to change in 1800 with the foundation by Portuguese royal decree of the Aula Pública de Desenho e Figura in Rio de Janeiro, which established regular teaching under the command of a master painter, Manuel Dias de Oliveira (1764–1837), an exception among local artists in that he trained in Lisbon and with Pompeo Batoni in the Accademia di S Luca in Rome. His most important innovation in art education was to replace the copying of imported prints with life drawing.

The French art commission organized by the Prince Regent that arrived in Rio in 1816 led to the establishment of the Academia Imperial das Belas Artes (1826) and the provision of an academic art education based on the canons of Neo-classicism. The Academia was dominated initially by the Professor of History Painting, Jean-Baptiste Debret, who organized the first art exhibitions in Brazil (1829 and 1830), and by the French Neo-classical painter Félix-Emile Taunay (1795–1881), who became director in 1834. Exhibitions modelled on the salons in Paris were begun in 1840, and many future teachers studied in Europe, either through travel grants established in 1845 or the personal patronage of the emperor Peter II. Under the directorship of Manuel de Araújo Pôrto Alegre (1806–79) from 1854 to 1857, the Academia, although still élitist, became more receptive to national and contemporary trends: a pupil of French masters, Pôrto Alegre encouraged a Romantic depiction of the reality of life in Brazil and a reform in teaching towards the integration of art and industry.

The creation of the Liceu de Artes e Ofícios in Rio de Janeiro in 1856 marked the first effective move towards the democratization of art training, and during the imperial period (1822–89), perhaps in imitation of the education of the royal family, the rudiments of art were taught in both boys' and girls' schools in Brazil. Art education in schools increased most dramatically with the wave of liberalism that accompanied the industrial expansion of the country after 1870. The ideas of Walter Smith, a British educator working in Massachusetts, in particular his emphasis on the importance of drawing in the classroom, were highly influential on the reform of primary and secondary education proposed by the legal expert Rui Barbosa in 1882 and 1883.

In 1889 the Academia Imperial das Belas Artes, renamed as the Escola Nacional de Belas Artes, was partially reformed, although it continued to promote historical models. In 1930, however, under the aegis of the Vargas government, Lúcio Costa's short but influential directorship revolutionized its teaching and introduced European avant-garde ideas. Other educational reforms beginning in 1929 were based on the ideas of John Dewey, which stimulated the natural impulse of children to draw; in the following decades the first children's schools specializing in art were established, in particular the Escolinha de Arte do Brasil (1948), founded in Rio by the painter Augusto Rodrigues (b 1913), and rapidly expanded to other cities.

The educational function of museums and art galleries began to be exploited in Brazil at the end of the 1940s, especially at the Instituto de Arte Contemporânea of the Museu de Arte de São Paulo and the Setor de Cursos of the Museu de Arte Moderna in Rio de Janeiro. The latter was renowned for the teaching of art to infants and juniors in the years 1950–60 by Ivan Serpa and also for the engraving workshop founded there in 1959 by Johnny Friedlaender. Other influential schools in Brazil include the Escola Brasil, set up in São Paulo (1970) under the direction of four young local artists, all disciples of Wesley Duke Lee: Luís Paulo Baravelli (b 1942), José Resende (b 1945), Carlos Fajardo (b 1941) and Frederico Nasser (b 1945). At the end of the 20th century most states in Brazil had official art schools, generally administered by universities. The most important remained the Escola de Belas Artes of the Universidade Federal do Rio de Janeiro, the former Escola Nacional de Belas Artes. Important work was also done by the official but progressive Escola de Artes Visuais do Parque Lage in Rio, which organized important avant-garde events in the 1980s.

BIBLIOGRAPHY

A. Morales de los Ríos: *O ensigno artístico: Subsídio para a sua história* (Rio de Janeiro, 1942)

A. Galvão: *Subsídios para a história da academia imperial e da escola nacional de belas artes* (Rio de Janeiro, 1954)

M. Pedrosa: *Crescimento e criação* (Rio de Janeiro, 1954)

A. F. Taunay: *A missão artística de 1816* (Rio de Janeiro, 1956)

A. Mafra de Souza: *Artes plásticas na escola* (Rio de Janeiro, 1968)

A. M. Barbosa: *Teoria e prática da educação artística* (São Paulo, 1975)

——: *Arte-educação no Brasil: Das origens ao modernismo* (São Paulo, 1978)

F. Ostrower: *Criatividade e processo de criação* (Rio de Janeiro, 1986)

XIII. Art libraries and photographic collections.

Very few libraries existed in Brazil before the beginning of the 19th century; as a result there was no tradition of conserving either written or visual records of the nation's heritage during the first 300 years of Portuguese colonization. The only exceptions were the Jesuit, Benedictine and Franciscan convents founded in the 16th century. The libraries of the Benedictine monasteries of S Bento in Rio de Janeiro and Salvador kept valuable artistic records, including documents relating to the construction and decoration of their respective churches. Religious art in Brazil from the 16th century to the 18th still forms an important part of the conservation work begun in museums of sacred art, particularly the convent of S Teresa, Salvador, and the Franciscan monastery of Luz, São Paulo.

When the Portuguese court moved to Brazil in 1808, it brought equipment for the first printing plant in the country and in 1810 founded the Biblioteca Real in Rio de Janeiro, which became the Biblioteca Nacional in 1878. Gradually this library assembled the most complete collection in Brazil of documents relating to artistic production (including many foreign works) and of rare books, drawings and engravings. These collections were the subject of a series of studies and exhibitions in the 1950s held under the direction of Lygia da Fonseca Fernandes da Cunha (b 1922). Historical documents, books, drawings and engravings relating to Brazilian art of the colonial and imperial periods (from the 16th to the 19th century) were also collected by many of Brazil's principal museums, including the Museu Paulista, Universidade de São Paulo; Museu Imperial, Petrópolis; Museu da Inconfidência, Ouro Prêto; Museu Paraense Emílio Goeldi, Belém; and Museu da Imagem e do Som, São Paulo. Important collections are also held in such institutions as the Escola de Belas Artes of the Universidade Federal do Rio de Janeiro (formerly the Academia Imperial Escola Nacional); the Secretaria do Patrimônio Histórico e Artístico Nacional (SPHAN) in Rio; the Fundação Pró-Memória in Brasília; and the Instituto Histórico e Geográfico Brasileiro, based in Rio. The Fundação Raymundo Ottoni de Castro Maya in Rio is particularly rich in collections of the work of foreign travellers in Brazil during the first half of the 19th century. Some private libraries and collections, such as those of Gilberto Ferrez (b 1908) in Rio de Janeiro, were also created. In spite of the wealth and importance of these collections, however, economic constraints and the difficulty of training specialist personnel created problems in developing new, technological methods of conservation and presentation.

Documents relating to the republican period (after 1889) are found in the Instituto de Estudos Brasileiros of the Universidade de São Paulo, which was based on the library, archives and collections of photographs, paintings, drawings and engravings of the modernist writer and critic

Mário de Andrade (1893–1945). Donations of archives and libraries of other artists and art critics are found in the Sector de Documentação of the Fundação Nacional de Arte in Rio. In addition to museum archives, several other libraries in São Paulo also specialize in this period, including the Departamento de Documentação e Informação Artística of the Secretaria Municipal de Cultura; the Departamento de Pesquisa e Documentação de Arte Brasileira of the Fundação Armando Alvares Penteado; the architecture faculty of the Universidade de São Paulo; and the Arquivos Históricos Wanda Svevo of the Fundação Bienal. Another important library, in the Museu de Arte Moderna, Rio, was seriously damaged by fire in 1978.

Fewer photographic collections developed in Brazil, largely due to the difficulties of conservation in the humid, tropical climate. Growing interest in the cultural heritage of Brazil in the last decades of the 20th century, however, led to improvements in the storage and restoration of local photographic collections. Outstanding photographic archives include those of SPHAN in Rio, which pioneered the photographic documentation of Brazilian art and architecture; the Fundação Joaquim Nabuco de Pesquisas Sociais in Recife; the Seção de Iconografia of the Divisão de Documentação Social e Estatística, São Paulo; and the Instituto Nacional da Fotografia of the Fundação Nacional de Arte in Rio. The art historian and critic Clarival do Prado Valladares (1918–83) also created a valuable private photographic archive in Rio de Janeiro that covered the whole history of Brazilian art and architecture of all kinds, including popular art, which he used in his publications, such as *Arte e sociedade nos cemitérios brasileiros* (1972), *Análise iconográfica do barroco e neoclássico remanescentes no Rio de Janeiro* (1978) and *Nordeste histórico e monumental* (1983).

BIBLIOGRAPHY
L. F. F. da Cunha: 'A seção de iconografia da biblioteca nacional', *J. Comérc.* (22 May 1966)
Guia das bibliotecas brasileiras (Rio de Janeiro, 1969)
B. Kossoy: 'Fotografia', *História geral da arte no Brasil*, ed. W. Zanini (São Paulo, 1983), ii, pp. 867–913
G. Ferrez: *A fotografia no Brasil, 1840–1900* (Rio de Janeiro, 1985)
ROBERTO PONTUAL

Brazzacco. *See* PONCHINO, GIAMBATTISTA.

Brazzi. *See under* RUSTICI.

Bréa [Brea], Louis [Lodovico; Ludovico] (*fl* 1475–1522/3). French painter, also active in Italy. His first known work, a signed and dated triptych of the *Pietà* (1475) in the parish church at Cimiez, in his home town of Nice, is thoroughly Provençal in derivation, with its references to Enguerrand Quarton (in particular to the *Pietà* of Villeneuve-lès-Avignon; Paris, Louvre) and, in the lateral figures, to Jacques Durandi.

In 1483 Bréa was active in Genoa and Taggia while continuing to work on commissions for the Nice area. In the same year he painted an *Ascension* for S Maria della Consolazione, Genoa (Genoa, priv. col., see Algeri and De Floriani, fig. 279), and with Francesco da Pavia he was commissioned to produce a polyptych of the *Madonna of Mercy* (Taggia, Dominican Convent). In this latter work the Provençal elements are tempered with a greater

naturalism, probably learnt through the artist's acquaintance with south Netherlandish and Lombard paintings in Liguria.

In the following years Bréa is documented in Taggia several times. He worked there on the triptych of *St Catherine of Siena* (Taggia, Dominican Convent) in 1488 and on another triptych depicting the *Annunciation* for the same church (*in situ*). The date of the latter is disputed, but it still shows vivid signs of Provençal influence, with a use of perspective that is clearly of Lombard derivation, reminiscent of the work of Giovanni Mazone or Cristoforo de' Mottis (*fl* 1460–86). A collaboration with a Lombard painter may have been noted in an accompanying inscription, which is now destroyed and was only fragmentary and poorly decipherable when still visible.

In 1490 Bréa completed the three left-hand sections of a polyptych begun by Vincenzo Foppa some years before for the high altar of Savona Cathedral (Savona, oratory of S Maria di Castello). Bréa apparently had some difficulty in matching the monumentality of Foppa's figures and his vision of the landscape. Foppa's influence can be seen again in Bréa's later works, such as a *Virgin and Child Enthroned with Musicmaking Angels* (see B. Berenson, *Central and North Italian Schools* (London, 1968), fig. 204). Inspired no doubt by Foppa, in the following period he began to pay more attention to Lombard art. The signed triptych of the *Assumption of the Virgin* (1495; Savona, Mus. Cattedrale) shows affinities not only with south Netherlandish painting but also with Luca Baudo and such iconographic sources as the engraving of Bramante's *prospettiva fantastica* by Bernardo Prevedari (1481). A greater breadth and sense of volume in the figures can also be seen in the polyptych of the *Baptism of Christ* (Taggia, Dominican Convent) of the same year, although the wooden framework is constructed in an old-fashioned style typical of Liguria and Nice. The same architectural structure was repeated in later polyptychs, especially those made for clients in Nice, for example an *Annunciation* (1499; Lieuche, parish church), a *St Nicholas* (1500; Monaco Cathedral) and a *Virgin and Child Enthroned* (1501; Les Arcs, parish church). Two dismembered polyptychs must also date from the period after 1495; the one from S Bartolomeo degli Armeni, Genoa, had a central section depicting the *Crucifixion with the Virgin, SS John and Mary Magdalene* (Genoa, Gal. Pal. Bianco; see fig.), where the open landscape, poised between south Netherlandish and Lombard influences, anticipates the Ligurian paintings of Pier Francesco Sacchi (*c.* 1485–1528). The remaining panels are, probably, *St Nicholas of Tolentino* and *St Vincent Ferrer* (both Prague, N. G.) and *St Peter* (Genoa, Gal. Pal. Bianco). The other polyptych datable after 1495 depicts the *Assumption of the Virgin*, and its side panel, with the *Presentation of Christ* (both Avignon, Mus. Petit Pal.), presents a pleasing perspective view of Lombard derivation.

In 1502–3 Bréa collaborated in Genoa with Lorenzo Fasolo and Giovanni Barbagelata on some fresco and panel paintings (untraced) for the cathedral and S Maria del Carmine. In the following two years he was documented in Savona with Marco d'Oggiono. The first work in which he abandoned the polyptych structure in favour

Louis Bréa: *Crucifixion with the Virgin, SS John and Mary Magdalene*, oil on canvas, 770×420 mm, after 1495 (Genoa, Galleria di Palazzo Bianco)

of the large single altarpiece was the *Calvary with Saints* (1512; Cimiez, Nice, parish church). A similar approach can be seen in the signed and dated *Coronation of the Virgin* (1513; Genoa, S Maria di Castello) and the *Virgin of the Rosary* (1512–13; Taggia, Dominican Convent). In his last works, beginning with the *Conversion of St Paul* (after 1514; Genoa, S Maria di Castello), Bréa returned to the polyptych format. Extensive interventions by assistants are evident in the polyptych of the *St Devota* (after 1515; Dolceacqua, parish church), and in that of *St George* (1516; Montalto Ligure, parish church).

BIBLIOGRAPHY

DBI
L.-H. Labande: *Les Bréa: Peintres niçois des XVe et XVIe siècles en Provence et en Ligurie* (Nice, 1937)
A. Naldini: 'Contributo allo studio di Ludovico Brea', *A. Ant. & Mod.*, xxxi–xxxii (1965), pp. 302–10
Z. Birolli: 'Precisazioni sull'attività di Lodovico Brea', *Boll. A.*, n. s. 4, liii/1 (1968), pp. 27–31
G. V. Castelnovi: 'Il quattro e il primo cinquecento', *La pittura a Genova e in Liguria dagli inizi al cinquecento*, ed. C. Bozzo Dufour, i (Genoa, 1970, rev. 1987), pp. 147–8
A. De Floriani: 'Un dipinto inedito di Ludovico Brea', *Stud. Genuensi*, ix (1972), pp. 94–101
C. Varaldo: 'Ricerche per un'opera inedita a Minorca: Il polittico di Ludovico Brea ed Anselmo De Fornari', *Riv. Ingauna & Intemelia* (1973–5), pp. 46–52
M. Laclotte and E. Mognetti: *Peinture italienne*, Avignon, Mus. Petit Pal. cat. (Paris, 1977) [entries 45 and 46]
A. De Floriani: entry in *Interv. Rest. G.N. Pal. Spinola* (1983), pp. 12–17
M. Natale: 'Pittura in Liguria nel quattrocento', *La pittura in Italia: Il quattrocento*, ed. F. Zeri, 2 vols (Milan, 1987), pp. 15–30
G. Algeri and A. De Floriani: *La pittura in Liguria: Il quattrocento* (Genoa, 1991), pp. 313–18, 409–17

VITTORIO NATALE

Brébiette, Pierre (*b* Mantes-la-Jolie, nr Paris, *c.* 1598; *d* Paris, *c.* 1650). French engraver, draughtsman and painter. By 1617 he was in Rome, where he remained until 1625; he married in Paris in 1626. Although a painter of some renown, he was chiefly known for his work as an engraver. His inventive prints (examples Paris, Louvre; Rouen, Mus. B.-A.), often prepared from drawings in pen and ink, black chalk or red chalk, reveal his artistic and cutural development during the 1610s in Paris, where he modelled himself on the example of Ambroise Dubois, Martin Fréminet or Georges Lallemand; his work also shows affinities with that of Claude Vignon. Brébiette was also sensitive to the qualities of ancient reliefs and to the work of the painters of Bologna, as well as that of such northern European artists as Abraham Bloemaert. Mariette spoke of Brébiette's 'libertine verve', an appraisal that sits oddly with the precious, Venetian manner revealed by the only paintings of his that have so far been identified: the signed *Rape of Proserpina* (Châlons-sur-Marne, Mus. Mun.) and the *Holy Family* (ex-art market, Paris), originally attributed to Sebastiano Mazzoni (for example, 1922 gal. cat., Jean-Claude Serre & Jacques Legenhock, Paris, in association with the Annberg Gallery, Brussels, no. 13) but since identified with Brébiette by E. Jacques Thuillier from an engraving.

BIBLIOGRAPHY
Mariette
L. Rosenthal: 'Pierre Brébiette: Graveur français', *Gaz. B.-A.*, n. s. 3, v (1911), pp. 37–52
R.-A. Weigert: *Inventaire du fonds français: Graveurs du dix-septième siècle*, Paris, Bib. N., Cab. Est. cat., ii (Paris, 1951), pp. 106–43
J. Thuillier: 'Brébiette', *L'Oeil*, 77 (1961), pp. 48–56
——: 'Du *maniérisme* romain à l'*atticisme* parisien: Louis Brandin, Jean Boucher, Pierre Brébiette, Laurent de La Hyre', *La Donation Suzanne et Henri Baderou au Musée de Rouen: Peintures et dessins de l'école française*, i (Paris, 1980), pp. 23–31
P. Pacht-Bassani: *Claude Vignon* (Paris, 1993)

SYLVAIN KERSPERN

Brecheret, Victor (*b* São Paulo, 22 Feb 1894; *d* São Paulo, 18 Dec 1955). Brazilian sculptor. He first studied at the São Paulo Liceu de Artes e Ofícios and in 1913 he left for Rome, where he stayed for six years and completed his studies with Arturo Dazzi (1881–1966). During this period he fell under the influence of Emile-Antoine Bourdelle and especially of the Symbolist sculpture of Ivan Meštrović. On his return to São Paulo in 1919 the innovative force of his work immediately caught the interest of the young intellectuals and artists who shortly afterwards brought Modernism into being in Brazil with the SEMANA DE ARTE MODERNA in 1922 in São Paulo. Although he returned to Europe in 1921, before this took place, he contributed several works to this event, including some on a religious theme such as *Head of Christ* (bronze, 1920; U. São Paulo, Inst. Estud. Bras.), characterized by an extreme simplification of the figure and by a geometric stylization that prefigured Art Deco. In 1920 he created the commemorative medal for the centenary of Brazil's independence and was commissioned by the government of São Paulo to create a vast monument to the *Pioneers* for the Parque Ibirapuera in São Paulo; Brecheret finally executed the granite monument between 1936 and 1953.

When Brecheret returned to Paris he discovered the work of Constantin Brancusi and won a prize in the Autumn Salon of 1921 with his sculpture *Temple of My Race* (untraced). After some time in Rome he returned to São Paulo, where during the 1930s in particular he was active in modernist events. In the latter part of his life he temporarily abandoned his preferred medium, marble, to carry out a series of works in bronze or in other types of stone, in which he tried to transmute indigenous Brazilian folklore into a deeply telluric, organic abstraction. The bronze *Indian and Suaçuapara* (1951; U. São Paulo, Mus. A. Contemp.) is one of the most important pieces in the series. At the first São Paulo biennale in 1951 he was awarded first prize for sculpture in the national section.

BIBLIOGRAPHY
S. Milliet: *Pintores e pinturas* (São Paulo, 1940)
M. da Silva Brito: *História do modernismo brasileiro* (Rio de Janeiro, 1958)
P. M. de Almeida: *De Anita ao Museu* (São Paulo, 1961)
R. Pontual: *Arte brasileira contemporânea* (Rio de Janeiro, 1976)
W. Zanini, ed.: *História geral da arte no Brasil*, ii (São Paulo, 1983)

ROBERTO PONTUAL

Brecht, George (*b* New York, 7 March 1926). American sculptor, performance artist and writer. He studied at the Philadelphia College of Pharmacy and Science from 1946 to 1950 and in 1958–9 attended the class in Experimental Composition given by John Cage at the New School for Social Research in New York. Like fellow students soon associated with the PERFORMANCE ART events known as Happenings and with the emergence of the FLUXUS movement, Brecht was influenced by Cage's dissolution of boundaries between art, poetry, music, literature and theatre and by the role of chance and play in the creative act. After composing music with built-in chance durations or creating scores from game elements such as playing cards, he found music on its own too limiting and conceived of the 'event' as the determining structure for his work. He called his first one-man exhibition (New York, Reuben Gal., 1959) *Towards Events* as an indication of the total, multi-sensory experience he now sought to create, sometimes simply in the form of written instructions.

The sculptural assemblages created by Brecht from the late 1950s, such as *Repository* (1961; New York, MOMA), were sometimes reminiscent of the Surrealist box constructions of Joseph Cornell, but in such works *objets trouvés* are often displayed as open invitations to the spectator to engage with the work of art as if playing a game. In this sense Brecht's work as an object-matter remained closely attuned to the aesthetic of his events, while sometimes also encouraging comparisons with Pop art (for example, in the references to toys and other common artefacts) and anticipating the transcendence of idea over material fact of conceptual art.

In 1965 Brecht and Robert Filliou founded La Cédille Qui Sourit in Villefranche-sur-Mer, a shop and studio that Brecht described as 'a centre of ideas, a search, a cooperative attempt among artists or anyone else with an idea to work out' (see *Games at the Cedilla . . .*) and that he saw as a way of conveying his ideas to a larger audience. Later he created a number of inventions, some of them patented under the name of Brecht and McDiarmid Research Associates, that were often still imbued with the playful spirit of his art. In *Land Translocation Project* (*c.* 1967–72), for instance, he proposed to move the Isle of Wight to the Azores. From 1972 he lived and worked in Cologne.

WRITINGS
Chance Imagery (New York, 1966) [written 1957]
with R. Filliou: *Games at the Cedilla, or the Cedilla Takes Off* (New York, 1967)
with Patrick Hughes: *Vicious Circles and Infinity: An Anthology of Paradoxes* (New York, 1975)

BIBLIOGRAPHY
A. Hansen: *A Primer of Happenings and Time/Space Art* (New York, 1965), pp. 70, 71, 83, 94, 98, 99, 100, 115, 139
H. Martin: *An Introduction to George Brecht's Book of the Tumbler on Fire* (Milan, 1978) [with interviews and an anthology of texts by Brecht]
For further bibliography *see* FLUXUS.

ANDREW WILSON

Brecquessent, Jean de. *See* JEAN DE BRECQUESSENT.

Breda, Carl Fredrik von (*b* Stockholm, 16 Aug 1759; *d* Stockholm, 1 Dec 1818). Swedish painter, also active in England. He studied at the Kungliga Akademi för de Fria Konsterna in Stockholm from the late 1770s until 1787, when he painted *King Gustav III* in the prevailing Rococo style. Later that year he visited England, France and Italy, discovering the emergent Neo-classical style as well as the masterpieces of the Italian Renaissance. He then settled in London, working briefly in the studio of Joshua Reynolds, whose portrait he painted (1791; Stockholm, Ksthögsko-lan). Breda specialized in portrait painting and from 1788 exhibited annually at the Royal Academy in London. His style was eclectic, displaying the influence of such contemporaries as Reynolds and Gainsborough, as well as the Italian and Dutch Baroque masters, particularly Rembrandt.

Breda visited Birmingham during the early 1790s, painting portraits of several members of the Lunar Society, including *James Watt* (1792; London, N.P.G.). In 1795 he visited Paris; on his return to Stockholm the following year he immediately became a sought-after portrait painter and was made a professor at the academy that same year. The nascent Romanticism that can be seen in some of his London portraits developed steadily in the works painted during his later career in Stockholm. He was knighted in 1812 and was commissioned to paint the coronation portraits of King Gustav IV Adolf and King Karl XIII, neither of which he completed.

BIBLIOGRAPHY

E. Hultmark: *Carl Fredrik von Breda* (Stockholm, 1915)

A. Hahr: 'Ett till Sverige terbrdat [*sic*] Bredaporträtt', *Ksthist. Tidskr.* (1936)

MICHELLE FACOS

Breda Castle. Castle in Breda, north Brabant, Netherlands. It is one of the first examples of monumental Renaissance architecture in the Netherlands, constructed at a time (1530s) when large buildings there were still dominated by the Late Gothic style from Brabant. A fortress had stood on the site since the 13th century. In 1515–21 Count Henry III of Nassau (1483–1538) commissioned a gallery on the curtain wall and a portal, both with ornate pediments (destr.), which was the first known piece of Renaissance architecture in the Netherlands. In 1536 Henry initiated more thoroughgoing alterations, with the intention of replacing the Gothic castle with a modern palace. The design comprised a rectangular layout around a large courtyard overlooked by an arcade. From the courtyard a stately, covered double staircase led to the double-height great hall on the first floor, which occupied the entire west wing. The ground floor below this hall was originally an open hall of columns. This design was finally completed in 1686, when the medieval wing to the south was replaced.

Count Henry consulted the Italian artist Tommaso Vincidor on the design. Vincidor had been working in Antwerp since 1520, supervising the manufacture of tapestries to designs by Raphael, and he is recorded at Breda in 1534. This may account for the fact that the overall impression of the inner court is Italian or Spanish, with the classical superimposition of the Doric, Ionic and Corinthian orders. There were, however, various clumsy details in the use of classical features. The ground-floor arcade displayed classical tondi in the spandrels. The frieze and triglyphs, however, were positioned with unclassical proportions. The first floor has a series of Ionic pilasters, which have brackets placed between the capitals and the entablature, a device taken from timber construction, which seems unnecessary here. The second floor had, until extensive restoration work was carried out in 1826, Corinthian half-columns, again with brackets above the capitals. Over all the windows of this top floor were ornamental gables with spiral scrolls and angels' heads. This linked series of gables seems French rather than Italian in inspiration.

BIBLIOGRAPHY

T. M. Roest van Limburg: *Het kasteel van Breda* (Schiedam, 1903)

M. D. Ozinga: 'De strenge Renaissance-stijl in de Nederlanden naar de stand van onze tegenwoordige kennis' [The classical Renaissance style in the Netherlands from the standpoint of our present knowledge], *Bull. Kon. Ned. Oudhdknd. Bond*, xv (1962), pp. 9–34

R. van Luttervelt: 'Renaissance kunst in Breda: Vijf studies. IV, Tomaso Vincidor en het kasteel van Breda', *Ned. Ksthist. Jb.*, xiv (1963), pp. 31–60

K. A. OTTENHEYM

Bredius, Abraham (*b* Amsterdam, 18 April 1855; *d* Monte Carlo, 13 March 1946). Dutch art historian and museum director. He acquired his expertise in the field of Dutch 17th-century painting primarily through his travels. From 1889 to 1909 he was the Director of the Mauritshuis in The Hague, a position in which he reorganized the museum, acquired new works and enriched the collection with loans from his own private collection, thereby not only greatly improving the quality of the museum's collection but also increasing its popularity with the public. He published the first scholarly *Catalogue raisonné des tableaux et des sculptures du Musée Royal* (The Hague, 1895), which included many new attributions and archival facts. On his emigration to Monaco (1922), Bredius loaned his private collection to the municipality of The Hague, and it became the Bredius Museum. In 1937 Bredius attributed a painting of the *Supper at Emmaeus* to Vermeer; ten years later it was exposed as a fake painted by HAN VAN MEEGEREN (*c.* 1936; Rotterdam, Boymans–van Beuningen). Bredius was among the first art historians in the Netherlands to combine the stylistic analysis of Rembrandt, his favourite artist (on whom he compiled an important corpus of paintings), as well as of numerous smaller masters with a systematic examination of archival material. On his death he bequeathed 25 paintings to the Mauritshuis.

UNPUBLISHED SOURCES

The Hague, Rijksbureau Ksthist. Doc. [Bredius's notes]

WRITINGS

Bredius published most of his archival finds in *Oud-Holland*

Künstler-Inventare, 8 vols (The Hague, 1915–22)

Rembrandt (Utrecht and Vienna, 1935, rev. H. Gerson, London and New York, 3/1967)

BIBLIOGRAPHY

Feestbundel Dr Abraham Bredius, 2 vols (Amsterdam, 1915) [with bibliog.]

Dr Abraham Bredius, 1855–1925 (Amsterdam, 1925) [with bibliog.]

W. Martin: 'Abraham Bredius', *Jb. Maatschappij Ned. Letterknd. Leiden 1946–7*, pp. 29–41

A. Blankert: *Museum Bredius* (The Hague, 1978), pp. 8–19 [biog. essay by L. Barnouw de Ranitz]

M. de Boer and J. Leistra: *Bredius, Rembrandt en het Mauritshuis!!!: Een eigenzinnig directeur verzamelt* (Zwolle, 1991) [with bibliog.]

J. E. P. LEISTRA

Bredow, Rudolf (*b* Berlin, 2 Nov 1909; *d* Bremen, 17 Nov 1973). German painter. He studied under the woodengraver Hans Orlowski and the stage designer Harold Bengen at the Kunstgewerbeschule, Berlin (1930–34). Bredow was inspired by Erich Heckel, Karl Schmidt-Rottluff and, above all, Max Kaus. His depictions of picturesque towns and harbours, coastal and mountain landscapes, fruit and flowers and, less often, of people were shaped by his quest for motifs that characterized the region. They show tensions between glowing, sometimes even incandescent colours and sparsely outlined forms, especially in the watercolours, for example *Village Church in Greetsiel* (1957; Chemnitz, Städt. Kstsamml.) or *Hofwinkel mit Räucherhäuschen* (1957; Halle, Staatl. Gal. Moritzburg). In some of his chalk drawings and oil paintings Bredow sought to portray the objective in an abstraction, reminiscent of the geometric idiom of Werner Gilles or the abstract expressionism of Ernst Wilhelm Nay.

BIBLIOGRAPHY

G. Meissner: 'Rudolf Bredow', *Allgemeines Künstlerlexikon*, xiii (Munich and Leipzig, 1995)

G. Meissner and L. Tavernier: *Rudolf Bredow (1909–1973): Expressionist aus Überzeugung. Mit einem Verzeichnis der Ölgemälde, Aquarelle, Farbkreiden und farbigen Figurinen* (Munich, 1995)

LUDWIG TAVERNIER

Brée, van. *See* VAN BRÉE.

Breenbergh, Bartholomeus (*bapt* Deventer, 13 Nov 1598; *d* Amsterdam, *bur* 5 Oct 1657). Dutch painter, draughtsman and etcher. He was one of at least eight children of a wealthy Protestant family in Deventer, where his father was the town pharmacist. After his father's death in 1607, the family left Deventer, probably moving to Hoorn. No artist then living in Hoorn could plausibly have been Breenbergh's teacher, and given the fact that his earliest works reveal the stylistic influence of the Pre-Rembrandtists, it is more probable that he was apprenticed in Amsterdam. In 1619 he was called upon to give testimony in Amsterdam: on this occasion his profession was listed as 'painter'. His oeuvre can be divided stylistically and iconographically into two distinct groups. He belonged to the first generation of DUTCH ITALIANATES, northern artists who travelled to Italy in the 1620s and were inspired by the light and poetry of the southern landscape. The work of this period consists of numerous Italianate landscape drawings and paintings. On his return to the northern Netherlands he settled in Amsterdam, where he painted more severe and monumental landscapes, often with historical subjects, which were strongly influenced by the PRE-REMBRANDTISTS.

1. Life and work. 2. Critical reception and posthumous reputation.

1. LIFE AND WORK.

(i) Italian period, c. 1619–c. 1629. Late in 1619 Breenbergh arrived in Rome, where he remained for longer than was usual for northern artists. He made contact with Paul Bril, the 65-year-old painter from Antwerp, who had been working in Rome since *c.* 1580. According to Breenbergh's own testimony in 1653, he 'spent seven years with Bril' and copied a number of his paintings. Breenbergh was one of the founder-members of the SCHILDERSBENT, the association of northern artists active in Rome. He is portrayed in drawings of 1623 ascribed to Jan van Bijlert (Rotterdam, Boymans–van Beuningen), which represent the society's merry-making members, known as *Bentvueghels* ('birds of a feather'). His nickname within the fellowship was 'het fret' (Dut.: 'the weasel'). During his stay in Italy Breenbergh made many drawings in Rome and its environs, motifs that he later assimilated repeatedly into his paintings. His drawing style was influenced by Bril and CORNELIS VAN POELENBURCH, while his painting style owes much to the Pre-Rembrandtists, but also to van Poelenburch. Like them, Breenbergh painted landscapes in the new style introduced by Adam Elsheimer during the first decade of the 17th century and elaborated upon by Filippo Napoletano and Goffredo Wals. Their landscapes were directly inspired by nature, and they concentrated on the representation of light and space. Breenbergh's earliest paintings, dating from 1622, are busy, overcrowded landscapes containing awkward, wooden figures (e.g. *Landscape with the Finding of Moses*, 1622; Stockholm, Hallwylska Mus.), clearly the work of an inexperienced artist. The early work of Breenbergh has long been confused with the early work of van Poelenburch. This confusion originated in France in the 18th century, when a number of van Poelenburch's paintings were attributed to Breenbergh. In Napoleon's inventory of 1813, several paintings, which since the 17th century

had been considered to be by van Poelenburch, appeared under Breenbergh's name. Many related pieces have also been ascribed to him since then. It is only since 1969 that scholars have attempted to differentiate the two hands. Although it is now clear that the differences are usually greater than the similarities, the problem has yet to be definitively solved.

Between 1625 and 1630 Breenbergh painted landscapes with gently sloping hills and Roman ruins (e.g. roundel of *Landscape with Ruins*; Cambridge, Fitzwilliam), which greatly resemble van Poelenburch's production during the early 1620s. The scale of the architecture in Breenbergh's works, however, is usually larger and the figures smaller and less numerous than in Poelenburch's. Breenbergh frequently placed a tall architectural element (often seen from the narrowest side) in or near the centre of the composition or, alternatively, completely to one side, while van Poelenburch's compositions, with accents on both sides, are calmer and more balanced. The subtle green and grey tints in the soft slopes of the landscape, the meticulous detail and the manner of execution in which the individual brushstrokes are barely perceptible are strikingly similar for both painters. After 1630 Breenbergh developed his style in other directions, ending the possibility of confusion between the two artists.

While only a small portion of Breenbergh's painted oeuvre was made in Italy, the majority of his drawings date from this period. Of the *c.* 200 drawings known, only about 35 were made after his return to the Netherlands; the rest date to the period 1624–9. The earliest, from 1624, are much more accomplished than the paintings from the same period. Breenbergh's drawings are not sketches or preliminary studies for paintings, but autonomous works of art, most of which are signed and/or dated. The drawings are almost exclusively executed in a delicate technique of pen and brown ink with a brown, or in a few cases grey, wash. The execution of line is lively; the artist rarely employed continuous contour lines, but rather series of dots, curlicues and small dashes. The wash adds a note of calmness or stability, although never to such an extent that the drawings might be termed 'classical'. The combination of spontaneity and detail bespeaks technical prowess.

Many drawings were made on the spot, others (the most complete compositions) were carried out in the studio. He often depicted the ruins of Rome and the Campagna, usually set in a landscape, as in the large and impressive *Temple of the Sibyl at Tivoli* (New York, Pierpont Morgan Lib.) and *Ruins near Porta Metronia, Rome* (Oxford, Christ Church; see fig. 1). He also made pure landscape drawings (e.g. Budapest, Mus. F.A., see Roethlisberger, 1969, fig. 66). In contrast to his paintings, his drawings rarely include figures. The way in which Breenbergh represented ruins and rock formations is often reminiscent of Bril's draughtsmanship. Breenbergh's compositions, however, are more naturalistic. Whereas Bril continued to make clear distinctions between foreground, middle ground and background, Breenbergh adopted more subtle perspectival conventions, often using an oblique viewpoint or a pronounced diagonal. It is probable that Conte Orsini of Bracciano commissioned some of Breenbergh's drawings, including the series of views near

1. Bartholomeus Breenbergh: *Ruins near Porta Metronia, Rome*, brush and brown wash, 230×262 mm, *c.* 1625–7 (Oxford, Christ Church)

Bomarzo and Bracciano (ex-Bracciano priv. col., now scattered, e.g. Amsterdam, Rijksmus.; Paris, Louvre; London, BM), which are among the best examples within his drawn oeuvre.

(ii) Dutch period, c. *1629–57.* Breenbergh probably left Italy in 1629. He settled in Amsterdam by 1633, the year he married Rebecca Schellingwou, and remained there until his death. The early 1630s were the most productive period of Breenbergh's career and the period during which drastic changes took place in his style and choice of subject-matter. Undoubtedly under the influence of his renewed acquaintance with the work of the Pre-Rembrandtists, Breenbergh began to introduce biblical and mythological figures into his landscapes. The paintings are larger, the compositions more ambitious and the figures more emotive. His expressive figural types reveal affinities with those of the important Pre-Rembrandtist Pieter Lastman.

Breenbergh's choice of subject-matter, especially the interest in Old Testament themes, also seems to have been influenced by the Pre-Rembrandtists. In Breenbergh's representations (e.g. *Landscape with Tobias and the Angel,* 1630; St Petersburg, Hermitage), however, the biblical scenes are often placed further in the background, literally and figuratively assuming a smaller place within the composition. For this reason Breenbergh's paintings are difficult to categorize: most are not, strictly speaking, history pieces, but to term them 'landscapes with historical scenes' is to underrate the importance of the historical scenes within the compositions. The question is important in determining Breenbergh's position within 17th-century Dutch art in general and with respect to the Dutch Italianates in particular. Through the prominence of the historical scenes in the landscapes, Breenbergh and, to a lesser extent, van Poelenburch distinguish themselves from such later Dutch Italianates as Jan Both and Nicolaas

Berchem, whose staffage consisted of non-narrative figures. Although such incidental figures are also found in works by Breenbergh and van Poelenburch, they occur almost exclusively in earlier landscapes, painted during their stay in Italy.

A good example of Breenbergh's mature style is the *Landscape with Christ and the Woman of Samaria* (1636; Rome, Pal. Corsini; see fig. 2). He represented the themes several times, with a different approach each time. Landscape, architecture and figures form a far more harmonious whole in this picture than was usual in his early work, and the composition is lucid and balanced. Characteristic is the dark foreground with on one side a low coulisse and a view into the distance, and on the other side monumental Classical architecture. The palette reveals a tendency towards the monochrome that was typical of the latter half of the 1630s and for Breenbergh was perhaps related to his contact with Nicolaus Knüpfer (?1603–55), who was then working in Amsterdam. The lighting in the painting is somewhat agitated, with several scattered illuminated areas; Breenbergh never employed the warm, all-encompassing southern light that characterized some of the work of van Poelenburch and the following generation of Dutch Italianates. With only a few exceptions, Breenbergh always remained closer to the Pre-Rembrandtists in his treatment of light and landscape, and he was more manneristic in his approach than van Poelenburch, whom he nevertheless surpassed in monumentality.

During the late 1630s and the 1640s Breenbergh also made some 50 prints after his own drawings, mostly of ruins in or near Rome (Hollstein, nos 1–52). His productivity diminished significantly during his last 15 years, probably partly due to his having taken on other obligations. In 1652 and 1655 he was named as a merchant. However, the quality of the approximately 25 paintings from this period reached even greater heights. The pictures varied in type and format, ranging from landscapes with only a few large figures to architectural pieces containing crowded scenes (e.g. *Martyrdom of St Lawrence,* 1647; Frankfurt am Main, Städel. Kstinst.). The compositions became more monumental and the figures more emotive, even to the point of caricature. He also painted several pastoral landscapes with bathing figures (e.g. Rome, priv. col., see Roethlisberger, 1981, fig. 209) or with the famous scene from *Cimon and Iphigenia,* a theme from Boccaccio's *Decameron* that enjoyed remarkable popularity in the northern Netherlands between 1630 and 1650. Seven paintings by Breenbergh representing this subject are known.

During these years Breenbergh also painted a number of portraits (e.g. *Portrait of a Man,* 1641; GB, priv. col., see Roethlisberger, 1981, fig. 202a) of high artistic value. After 1647 there are no more dated or datable paintings or drawings until 1654, the date of his *Jacob Selling Corn to the People* (Dumfries House, Strathclyde). This is the only painting in his entire oeuvre of which he (a year later) made a replica (U. Birmingham, Barber Inst.); he was probably commissioned to do so. These two large canvases form the apex of his late monumental style, so different from the charming landscapes of his Italian period.

2. Bartholomeus Breenbergh: *Landscape with Christ and the Woman of Samaria*, oil on panel, 660×850 mm, 1636 (Rome, Palazzo Corsini)

2. CRITICAL RECEPTION AND POSTHUMOUS REPUTATION. It is curious that Breenbergh, whose production was considerable—there are more than 100 extant paintings—was so quickly forgotten in his own day. None of the contemporary artists' biographies mention him, and even Houbraken knew nothing more about this painter than his name and requested information from his readers. Few of his works appear in 17th-century Dutch inventories and auction catalogues; during the 18th century his name is encountered slightly more often. One of the reasons for this apparent neglect is the fact that, unlike van Poelenburch, he does not seem to have had any workshop or pupils, so that his style and subject-matter were not widely disseminated.

It is also quite possible that many of Breenbergh's paintings were sold abroad. Unfortunately nothing is known of his buyers and patrons, but in France he became famous. Not only are many of his works found in important 18th-century collections there, but he was also highly celebrated by French artists' biographers. His technique and choice of subject-matter influenced the drawing style of his near contemporary Claude Lorrain.

Like many Dutch Italianate painters, during the second half of the 19th century Breenbergh's paintings went out of fashion. However, by the end of the 1950s, when art historians ceased to concentrate all their attention on the so-called realist landscape painters of the Dutch golden age, his reputation began to recover.

BIBLIOGRAPHY
Hollstein: *Dut. & Flem.*
W. Stechow: 'Bartholomeus Breenbergh, Landschafts- und Historienmaler', *Jb. Preuss. Kstsamml.*, li (1930), pp. 133–40
M. Roethlisberger: *Bartholomaus Breenbergh: Handzeichnungen* (Berlin, 1969)
——: *Bartholomeus Breenbergh: The Paintings* (Berlin and New York, 1981)
NICOLETTE C. SLUIJTER-SEIJFFERT

Bregno. Italian family of sculptors and architects. They were active in the 15th century and the early 16th. One of the most important and extensive family dynasties in Italian Renaissance sculpture, the Bregni came from the village of Righeggia, near Osteno on Lake Lugano. Active primarily in northern Italy (Lombardy, Emilia, and the Veneto), a few Bregni also worked in central Italy. Several Bregno artists are documented, although the precise familial relationship between most of them is still unclear. The most important artists in the family were (1) Antonio Bregno I and his brother Paolo Bregno (*fl* Venice, *c.* 1425–*c.* 1460), (2) Andrea Bregno, (3) Giovanni Battista Bregno and (4) Lorenzo Bregno. Associated with Andrea Bregno were two of his brothers: Ambrogio Bregno (*d* before 1504) and Girolamo Bregno (*d* after 1504); a son Marcantonio Bregno; one Antonio Bregno II; and Domenico

Bregno [il Brieno]. The last three assisted with various architectural projects during the 1470s and 1480s, although their roles are not specified. Other Bregni briefly mentioned in documents, and about whom little is known, include Antonio di Pietro Bregno, active for a while with Giovanni Battista Bregno in Venice in 1509, and Cristoforo di Ambrogio Bregno [Brignono], who is documented with his brother Giovanni Antonio Bregno in Ferrara in 1502.

DBI   BIBLIOGRAPHY
B. Cetti: 'Scultori comacini: I Bregno', *A. Crist.*, xx (1982), pp. 31–44

STEVEN BULE

(1) Antonio (di Giovanni) Bregno I (*fl* Venice, ?1425; *d* 1457). He is first mentioned with his brother Paolo Bregno in 1777, the date of an engraving by Sebastiano Giammpiccoli of the tomb of *Doge Francesco Foscari* (*d* Nov 1457; see fig.) in S Maria dei Frari, Venice. The engraving carries the information that the tomb was 'designed and executed by the architect Paolo and the sculptor Antonio, the brothers Bregno of Como'. It would seem probable that this information was taken from a document then in the Foscari archive. The brothers presumably signed the document jointly. The designation of their professions as architect and sculptor respectively is likely to be an 18th-century anachronism; in the mid-15th century masons were not as specialized.

The Bregno brothers cannot positively be linked to any other commission, but they may have been active as masons at the Ca' d'Oro, Venice, in 1425, when an Antonio de Rigezzo da Como was working there with Matteo Raverti, and a Paolo was paid with him. In 1460 a mason named Paulo was a *proto* (overseer) at the Doge's Palace. It is tempting to identify him with Paolo Bregno and attribute to him the design of the second phase of the Foscari Arch in the courtyard of the Doge's Palace, which is stylistically very close to the Foscari Tomb. Markham

Antonio Bregno I and Paolo Bregno (attrib.): tomb of *Doge Francesco Foscari* (central part), marble, *c.* 1457 (Venice, S Maria dei Frari)

Schulz (1978) has made the strongest case against the Foscari Tomb being the work of the Bregni and has attributed it, and a number of other sculptural works in Venice and Dalmatia, to NICCOLÒ FIORENTINO, a sculptor who is known to have worked in Trogir, Dalmatia, after 1467. The stylistic similarities between his documented works and the Foscari Tomb, however, would not appear to be sufficient to justify the attribution of the Foscari Tomb to Niccolò, nor should the 18th-century attribution be discounted.

The Foscari monument is a wall tomb surmounted by a gable with Christ blessing on the pinnacle, flanked by the figures of the Annunciation. Two pages stand on high half-columns and hold back the awning to display the recumbent figure of the Doge on his sarcophagus surrounded by personifications of virtues. The figure style of the tomb shows the influence of contemporary painting, particularly of the Paduan work of Andrea Mantegna, and of Andrea del Castagno, who worked in Venice in the 1450s.

A group of sculptures in Venice, probably wrongly attributed to Antonio Rizzo at the start of his career, are stylistically close to the Foscari Tomb. They include the figures above the doorway of S Elena in Isola, the monument to *Orsato Giustiniani* (ex-S Andrea della Certosa, Venice; dispersed) and the figures above the doorway of S Maria dell'Orto. Of this group, the figure of *Fortitude* (*c.* 1442) on the Porta della Carta in the Doge's Palace seems to have much to recommend it as a product of the Bregno workshop (Planiscig). The *Annunciation* (London, V&A), which has also been attributed to the Bregno workshop, seems to be the work of the anonymous associate of Bartolomeo Buon, who in 1442–4 executed the portal of S Maria della Carità (now in the sacristy of S Maria della Salute, Venice).

BIBLIOGRAPHY
L. Planiscig: *Venezianische Bildhauer der Renaissance* (Vienna, 1921), pp. 30–37
G. Mariacher: 'Profilo di Antonio Rizzo', *A. Ven.*, ii (1948), pp. 67–84
——: 'New Light on Antonio Bregno', *Burl. Mag.*, xcii (1950), pp. 123–8
J. Pope-Hennessy: *Italian Renaissance Sculpture* (London, 1963, rev. Oxford, 3/1985), pp. 88, 331, 336–7
——: *Catalogue of Italian Sculpture in the Victoria and Albert Museum*, i (London, 1964), pp. 346–7
W. Wolters: *La scultura veneziana gotica, 1300–1460*, i (Milan, 1976), pp. 131–3, 292–4
A. Markham Schulz: *Niccolò di Giovanni Fiorentino and Venetian Sculpture of the Early Renaissance* (New York, 1978)
——: *Antonio Rizzo, Sculptor and Architect* (Princeton, 1983)

WOLFGANG WOLTERS

(2) Andrea (di Cristoforo) Bregno (*b* Osteno, nr Lugano, 1418; *d* Rome, Sept 1503). Nothing is known of Bregno's activity until his arrival in Rome in the 1460s, although his early works betray a Lombard training. During the pontificate of Sixtus IV he became the most popular and prolific sculptor of his day, with a large and well-organized bottega. He worked mainly on the decoration of tombs of prelates and dignitaries of the papal court. Bregno became famous in his lifetime and was mentioned, together with Verrocchio, by Giovanni Santi in *La vita e le geste di Federico di Montefeltro duca d'Urbino*, written between 1484 and 1487. The writer of a funeral epitaph actually compared him with Polykleitos. Bregno's work is characterized by great refinement and technical skill.

Although he was often not particularly inventive, he was certainly a fine sculptor of grotesques and other forms of ornamentation. He soon fell under the influence of Tuscan models, probably as a result of his contact with Mino da Fiesole, with whom he worked in Rome. There his style became more classical and its design more compact, with precise references to antique sculpture: documents show that he possessed a collection of antique objects recovered from excavations. He was also a friend of Platina, who held him in high esteem, as he wrote in a letter to Lorenzo the Magnificent.

The earliest example of Bregno's Roman production is the relief of *Cardinal de Cusa* (*d* 1464) depicted with St Peter and an Angel, a fragment of a tomb (destr.) in S Pietro in Vincoli, in which one can see an affinity with the trend towards adopting medieval forms apparent in Roman sculpture of *c.* 1460. The funerary monument of *Cardinal L. d'Albret* (*d* 1465) in S Maria d'Aracoeli already shows classicist sympathies. Almost contemporary are fragments of a ciborium for S Gregorio al Celio, which was mostly the work of Bregno's bottega. In 1466, with Giovanni Dalmata, he carved the tomb of *Cardinal Giacomo Tebaldi* in S Maria sopra Minerva, where the statue of *St Augustine* is undoubtedly his work. In 1473 Alessandro Borgia, later Pope Alexander VI, commissioned from Bregno a marble tabernacle, known as the Borgia Altar, located on the main altar of S Maria del Popolo until it was moved to the sacristy in the 17th century. In 1476–7, again with Dalmata, Andrea carved the tomb of *Cardinal Bartolomeo Roverella* in S Clemente, and in 1477 he also finished the tomb of *Cardinal Pietro Riario* (now Rome, SS Apostoli, Crypt). The design of this monument has also been attributed to Mino da Fiesole and Dalmata, but it appears to be the work of Bregno, since some of its architectural and decorative elements return later in such securely attributed works as the *Savelli* monument (1495–8) in S Maria d'Aracoeli. In the same years Bregno produced the tomb of *Cardinal Diego de Coca* (*d* 1477; see fig.) in S Maria sopra Minerva. In this reclining figure, which shows a fine plastic sense, Bregno revealed himself to be an exquisite decorative sculptor.

Other dated works by the artist are the monument to *Cardinal Cristoforo della Rovere and Cardinal Domenico della Rovere* (*d* 1479 and 1501 respectively) in S Maria del Popolo, on which Mino da Fiesole also worked, and the ciborium of S Martino al Cimino (1478), also in Rome. At the end of the 1470s Bregno worked with Dalmata and Mino da Fiesole on the internal transenna and the *cantoria* in the Sistine Chapel. After the departure from Rome of Dalmata and Mino da Fiesole, the supremacy in Rome of Bregno and his bottega was uncontested, while his fame as a sculptor spread all over Italy. Thus between 1481 and 1485, together with his assistants, he composed the Piccolomini Altar (signed and dated 1485) in Siena Cathedral, which was later embellished with sculptures (1501–4) by Michelangelo. Pursuing his intense interest in archaeology, in 1484 Bregno was already assisting in some excavations in Rome. In 1486 he worked on the monument to *Giovanni di Fuensalinda* (ex-S Giacomo degli Spagnoli, Rome; Rome, S Maria di Monserrato). Bregno also carved a shrine in the form of a tabernacle for the main altar of S Maria della Quercia in Viterbo. Between 1490 and 1495

Andrea Bregno: tomb of *Cardinal Diego de Coca, c.* 1477 (Rome, S Maria sopra Minerva)

he created a now dismembered altar (church of Boville Ernica; ex-Stroganoff col.; New York, Met.) for the Auditor of the Rota, Cardinal Guillermo de Pereirs, for whom he had also produced other works. His last documented works are the tabernacle of *Vannozza Cattanei* (1500–01) in S Maria del Popolo, and the tomb of *Pius II* (ex-St Peter's, Rome; Rome, S Pietro in Vincoli), which was mainly the work of the bottega. He probably also practised architecture, and some scholars attribute to him the façade of S Maria del Popolo, as well as a few elements in the Sistine Chapel.

BIBLIOGRAPHY

E. Muntz: *Les Arts à la cour des papes pendant les XVe et XVIe siècles*, i (Paris, 1878), pp. 89, 146, 200

A. Schmarsow: 'Maister Andrea', *Jb. Preuss. Kstsamml.*, iv (1883), pp. 18–31

E. Steinmann: 'Andrea Bregno Tätigkeith in Rom', *Jb. Preuss. Kstsamml.*, xx (1899), pp. 216–32

E. Lavagnino: 'Andrea Bregno e la sua bottega', *L'Arte*, xxvii (1924), pp. 247–63

H. Egger: 'Beiträge zur Andrea Bregno—Forschung', *Festschrift für J. van Schlosser* (Zurich, Leipzig and Vienna, 1927), pp. 122–36

E. Battisti: 'I comaschi a Roma', *Arte e artisti dei laghi lombardi*, i (Como, 1959), pp. 9, 20–29

G. S. Sciolla: 'Profilo di Andrea Bregno', *A. Lombarda*, 15 (1970), pp. 52–8

G. Santi: *La vita e le geste di Federico di Montefeltro duca d'Urbino* (Codice Vat. Ottob. Lat. 1305); ed. L. Michelini Tocci (Vatican City, 1985)

P. P. Bober and R. Rubinstein: *Renaissance Artists and Antique Sculpture: A Handbook of Sources* (New York, 1986)

GIOVANNA CASSESE

(3) Giovanni Battista [Giambattista] **(di Alberto** [di Roberto]) **Bregno** [Bregnon; de' Briani] (*b* 1467–77; *d* after 1518). Together with his brother (4) Lorenzo Bregno, he had a large workshop in Venice during the first years of the 16th century. Modern scholarship has elevated his status from that of a forgotten figure to that of one of the foremost Venetian sculptors of his generation. Nothing is known of his career before 1499, although many scholars consider it probable that he was trained in the workshop of Tullio Lombardo during the 1490s. His first documented commission was for the Beltiguoli Altar (1499–1503) in S Nicolò, Treviso. In 1502 Bregno received the commission to execute a low relief for the chapel of St Anthony in the basilica of Il Santo, Padua. While he did not execute the work, receipt of this commission suggests that he must already have achieved some degree of notoriety and maturity as a sculptor. A major obstacle to understanding Bregno's art is the problem of attribution— involving a small corpus of works—to Giovanni Battista or to Lorenzo, although this situation has been simplified by the efforts of scholars. The most important commission in Bregno's brief career was the decoration of the chapel of the Holy Sacrament in Treviso Cathedral. In addition to executing the pavement and steps leading to the chapel (1504–8), Bregno was also commissioned to carve a *Risen Christ* (1506–8; see fig.), two *Adoring Angels* and a figure of *St Peter* (all completed by Dec 1509). Additional work for the chapel commissioned from Giovanni Battista was apparently completed by Lorenzo. Bregno's figures for Treviso demonstrate a lightness and delicate movement that recall the sculpture of the Lombardo family. The use of contrapposto in the *St Peter*, as well as the harmonious drapery patterns that successfully reveal underlying anatomy, indicate Bregno's interest in contemporary classicizing forms. The slightly slender figure of the *Risen Christ* is quite elegant and highly refined, and characteristically combines a classical contrapposto with a slight axial twist, attesting to Bregno's great technical skill as a marble carver and to his indebtedness to the Lombardo family and to Antonio Rizzo.

Two extant low reliefs by Bregno are an attributed *Visitation* (Treviso Cathedral) and a documented *St George Killing the Dragon* (Venice, Monastery of S Giorgio Maggiore, dormitory façade), both of *c*. 1500. The *Visitation* is carved in a crisp style, somewhat akin to works by the Lombardi. The work is rich in surface-pattern, with subtle low-relief background details. The *St George* is quite different in approach and does not include the atmospheric qualities present in the *Visitation*. Both reliefs demonstrate a sense of movement, and the princess in the *St George* relief is remarkably expressive. Surface nuances in these works are achieved by a skilled use of the drill. Two elegant *Adoring Angels* (Venice, SS Giovanni e Paolo, and Berlin, Staatliche Museen Preussischer Kulturbesitz) are also attributed to Bregno and are indebted to earlier works by Tullio Lombardo, although Bregno was never overwhelmed by Lombardo's art to the point of losing his own artistic identity. The intricate articulation of the drapery is

Giovanni Battista Bregno: the *Risen Christ*, marble, h. 1.18 m, 1506–8 (Treviso Cathedral, Chapel of the Holy Sacrament)

reminiscent of the inclination for animated surfaces and technical virtuosity commonly found in the art of Lombard sculptors. Bregno was neither highly innovative nor entirely up to date with the new styles of his contemporaries; his frequent reliance on the art of Pietro Lombardo and sculpture of the 1490s, rather than on the later—and more popular—softened, classicizing style of Tullio Lombardo, appears to have been unique for his period. As has been observed by Schulz, however, Bregno's achievement rests in being one of the last and finest technicians in marble of a 15th-century Venetian sculpture tradition.

BIBLIOGRAPHY

DBI

P. Paoletti: *L'Architettura e la scultura del rinascimento in Venezia* (Venice, 1893)

W. Steadman Sheard: *The Tomb of Doge Andrea Vendramin in Venice by Tullio Lombardo* (diss., New Haven, CT, Yale U., 1971)

A. M. Schulz: 'Giambattista Bregno', *Jb. Berlin. Mus.*, xxii (1980), pp. 173–202

STEVEN BULE

(4) Lorenzo (di Alberto) [di Roberto] **Bregno** (*b* Verona, 1475–85; *d* Venice, 4 Jan 1525). Brother of (3) Giovanni Battista Bregno. His career began in Treviso, in the workshop of Giovanni Battista. The first documentary information about him dates from 1506, when he was paid for an unidentified work for the chapel of the Holy Sacrament in Treviso Cathedral, where his brother had been working since 1504. Work began in 1507 on the urn of *SS Theonestus, Tabra and Tabrata* on the high altar of Treviso Cathedral. This sculpture had been commissioned in 1485 from Pietro Lombardo, but according to research it may be the earliest surviving work by Bregno. There is documentation, however, for Bregno's authorship of the *Four Evangelists* (1511–12) and the *St Paul* (1513) in the chapel of the Holy Sacrament. In these works, as indeed in the urn, there are clear references to the sculpture of Antonio Lombardo and Pietro Lombardo (especially *The Evangelists* in the Giustiniani Chapel in S Francesco della Vigna, Venice). Other works of the period include the damaged altar of the *Holy Sepulchre* (not later than 1511) in the church of S Martino in Venice. In 1512 the artist produced three statues for an altar, later dismantled, in the Venetian church of S Marina; in the 19th century the *Magdalene* and the *St Catherine* were placed on the monument of *Doge Andrea Vendramin* in SS Giovanni e Paolo, while the statue of *St Marina* is at the Seminario Patriarcale. In 1515 Bregno executed sculptures for the altar of *St Sebastian* in the church of S Margherita in Treviso. These consist of a statue of the saint (now Treviso Cathedral) and a relief (now Budapest, Mus. F.A.), probably by an assistant.

During this period Bregno also produced the statues for various funerary monuments in Venice, including that of *Benedetto Pesaro* (S Maria dei Frari; the figure of *Mars* is by the Tuscan artist Baccio da Montelupo), as well as those of *Bartolomeo Bragadin* (SS Giovanni e Paolo) and *Lorenzo Gabriel*, Bishop of Bergamo (Vienna, Österreich. Mus. Angewandte Kst). This last work was dismantled after the suppression of the oratory (1810), and the life-size statue of the bishop is now in Vienna. In 1514 Bregno obtained the commission for three statues (*St Leonard, St Eustace* and *St Christopher*) to decorate the altar of the chapel of S Leonardo in Cesena Cathedral; these were installed in February 1517. Like the preceding works, they appear stylistically related to the Lombardi. In fact there were continuing contacts between Bregno and the Lombardo workshop: in 1516 Bregno provided Tullio Lombardo with the marbles necessary for the work in the Zen Chapel of the basilica of S Marco in Venice. Two years later Bregno himself was called to S Marco to construct the altar of *The Cross* in the main apse behind the presbytery. He decorated this with small statues of *St Francis* and *St Anthony of Padua*, and with reliefs, although the bronze door is by Sansovino. The high altar at the church of S Maria dei Frari, the attribution of which is disputed by critics, dates from the same period, as does the funerary monument to *Bartolino da Terni* (signed) in the church of the Santa Trinità in Crema. The statues in the Scuola di S Rocco, recently attributed to Bregno, and one of *St John the Evangelist* (Berlin, Staatl. Museen, inv. 2928), can also be assigned to this period. In 1522 Bregno worked on the funerary monument to *Bertucci Lamberti*

Lorenzo Bregno: *St Andrew*, 1524 (Venice, S Maria Mater Domini)

in Treviso Cathedral. He was active in the Venetian church of S Maria Mater Domini in 1524, producing the statues of *St Andrew* (see fig.) *St Peter* and *St Paul*, perhaps his best works, as they are least influenced by the academicism of the Lombardi. The other works in the church that are attributed to him were executed by his workshop after his death, with the help of the Paduan sculptor Antonio Minello.

DBI

BIBLIOGRAPHY

C. Grigioni: 'Un'opera ignota di Lorenzo Bregno', *L'Arte*, xiii (1910), pp. 42–8

G. Mariacher: 'Problemi di scultura veneziana', *A. Ven.*, iii (1949), pp. 95–9

A. M. Schulz: 'Lorenzo Bregno', *Jb. Berlin. Mus.* (1984), pp. 143–79

FILIPPO PEDROCCO

Brehme, Hugo (*b* Eisenach, Germany, 1882; *d* Mexico City, 1954). German photographer, active in Mexico. As a young man he travelled through Africa, taking photographs. An archive of some of these glass plates survives. He reached Mexico by way of Panama, Costa Rica, El Salvador and Guatemala, and took his first photographs in the Yucatán peninsula. He then opened a studio in Mexico City and settled in Mexico permanently. Together with Augustín Victor Casasola, he was among the most important photographers of the Revolution (1910–17). What he loved, however, were the beauties of the Mexican landscape. His book *Malerisches Mexico* was published by Ernst Wachsmuth in Germany in 1923, the same year in which he collaborated with Manuel Alvarez Bravo, later to become Mexico's leading photographer. Brehme's photography was not merely reportage. He sought to capture the spirit of the country rather than isolated events as, for example, in his photograph of Pancho Villa's horsemen, each in direct eye-contact with the photographer. In this he was like José Guadalupe Posada, who, in his woodcuts, was one of the first artists to capture the Mexican temperament. Occasionally, indeed, Posada worked from photographs by Brehme and also by Casasola. More than most foreigners, Brehme was able to feel real empathy with the country. He became an impressive interpreter not only of its customs and traditions, but also of its historical monuments and festivals.

BIBLIOGRAPHY
Fotografie Lateinamerika (Zurich and Berne, 1981)
H. Brehme: *Mexico pintoresco* (Mexico City, 1990)
E. Billeter: *Canto a la realidad fotografie Lateinamerika* (Barcelona, 1993)
ERIKA BILLETER

Breit, Johannes. *See* BRITTO, GIOVANNI.

Breitner, George Hendrik (*b* Rotterdam, 12 Sept 1857; *d* Amsterdam, 5 June 1923). Dutch painter and photographer. He trained as a painter and draughtsman at the academy in The Hague. Although the Dutch painter Charles Rochussen taught the students history and landscape painting, Breitner's interests did not lie in this area. In 1880 he worked for a year in the studio of Willem Maris after his academy training. Maris belonged to the Hague school of painters, who worked in the *plein-air* tradition of the French Barbizon school. Breitner painted outdoor life with them, although it was not the picturesqueness of the landscape or the Dutch skies that appealed to him. With Van Gogh he roamed the working-class districts of The Hague and through the dockyards of Rotterdam. Both artists recorded the vitality of city life in their sketchbooks. Breitner consciously chose these themes and motifs: he wanted to paint people going about their daily lives, and on his trips through the towns and docks he was constantly in search of motifs and impressions that he could use in his paintings.

In 1884 Breitner worked in Paris for six months, where his paintings included *Demolition in Montmartre* (see Hefting, 1968, pl. II). In 1886 he moved to Amsterdam, where he found plenty of subjects for his paintings: the building activities for the extension of the city and the life of the working-class areas such as Jordaan. In addition he made a series of paintings in his studio of his model Geesje Kwak, nude or wrapped in a kimono, for example *Girl in a Red Kimono* (*c.* 1893; Amsterdam, Stedel. Mus.). The

social life in the capital city also appealed to Breitner. He had contacts with poets and painters belonging to the Tachtigers and became friendly with Willem Witsen, a painter and photographer.

Breitner was also a photographer and used his photographs for creating paintings. It would seem that he had his camera constantly with him on his treks through different cities in order to capture the life around him. A number of his paintings seem to be closely based on photographs, for example those of Geesje Kwak and the painting *Three Girls in the Street* (1887; Amsterdam, Stedel. Mus.). He photographed life not only in Amsterdam but also in Paris, London and Berlin; on his trip to Berlin alone he took 200 photographs. In 1961, 2000 of his negatives were found to be part of his legacy (The Hague, Rijksbureau Ksthist. Doc.) and original prints are in the collections of the Rijksmuseum, Amsterdam, and the Prentenkabinet der Rijksuniversiteit, Leiden. His photographs were exhibited for the first time in 1962 at the Gemeentemuseum in The Hague. It was only when his photographs were seen next to his paintings, for example the photograph of *The Dam* (see 1977 exh. cat., pl. 42) and the painting the *Dam Square in Amsterdam* (1893–7; Amsterdam, Stedel. Mus.), that the influence of photography on his method of painting became clear: cut-off subjects, diagonal compositions, strong contrasts between light and dark and movement. Just like his photographs, his paintings have a snapshot quality. His wish to capture dynamism and movement in daily life is also clear from his sketches and paintings made before he began photographing in 1892. Both media served to record the interest in reality, impressions and atmosphere that was so typical of the character of the visual arts at the end of the 19th century.

See also NETHERLANDS, THE, fig. 23.

BIBLIOGRAPHY
P. H. Hefting and C. C. G. Quarles van Ufford: *Breitner als fotograaf* (Rotterdam, 1966)
P. H. Hefting: *G. H. Breitner* (Amsterdam, 1968)
George Hendrik Breitner: Gemälde, Zeichnungen, Fotografien (exh. cat., eds P. H. Hefting and H. L. C. Jaffé; Bonn, Rhein. Landesmus., 1977)
'Breitner', *Geschiedenis van de Nederlandse fotografie* [History of Dutch photography], ed. I. Th. Leijerzapf (Alphen aan den Rijn, 1984)
P. Hefting: *De foto's van Breitner* (The Hague, 1989)
M. Boom, ed.: *Fotokunst 19de eeuw* [19th century photographic art] (The Hague, 1989), pp. 193–4, pls 105–7
The Age of Van Gogh: Dutch Painting 1880–1895 (exh. cat., Glasgow, Burrell Col., 1990–91; Amsterdam, Rijksmus. van Gogh; 1991)
T. de Ruiter: 'Foto's als schetsbook en geheugensteun', *George Hendrik Breitner 1857–1923: Schilderijen, Tekeningen en foto's* (exh. cat., ed. R. Bergsma and P. Hefting, Amsterdam, Stedel. Mus., 1994)
MATTIE BOOM

Brekelenkam, Quiringh [Quirijn] **(Gerritsz.) van** (*b* ?Zwammerdam, nr Leiden, after 1622; *d* Leiden, ?1669 or after). Dutch painter. He probably trained in Leiden, possibly under Gerrit Dou. In 1648, with several other painters, he founded the Guild of St Luke in Leiden. He married for the first time in 1648 and again in 1656, a year after his first wife's death. In 1649 his sister Aeltge married the painter Johannes Oudenrogge (1622–53), and the couple soon moved to Haarlem while the Brekelenkam family remained in Leiden. About 1656 Brekelenkam apparently acquired a licence to sell beer and brandy, perhaps because his income as a painter was insufficient to support his large family (six children from his first marriage and three from his second). He continued to be active as an artist and paid his guild dues fairly regularly. The last dues were paid in 1667, and his last dated painting, the *Portrait of a Man Aged 33*, is from 1669.

Like many painters of his time, Brekelenkam was prolific, producing several hundred paintings of greatly varying quality. Most of these are genre scenes, although there are also individual and family portraits and some still-lifes. Other paintings show hermits praying (e.g. 1660; St Petersburg, Hermitage) or reading, a popular subject in Leiden. The genre paintings include inn scenes and numerous images of market stalls, but the majority of them depict either domestic scenes (e.g. *Old Woman Combing a Child's Hair*, 1648; Leiden, Stedel. Mus. Lakenhal) or workshop scenes, which were his speciality. In his *Tailor's Workshop* (1653; Worcester, MA, A. Mus.), the craftsman and his apprentices sit atop a table on the left side of the picture, where a combination of strong light from the window and the off-centre vanishing-point activates the space. On the right, in a dark vertical area, a woman sits calmly preparing a meal by a fireplace.

Brekelenkam's early genre works, from the 1640s and 1650s, are related in subject-matter to the Leiden 'fine' painters, a group of artists centred around Dou. But Brekelenkam seldom employed the minutely finished technique for which the 'fine' painters were famed, preferring a looser manner of handling, which has been compared to that of Gabriel Metsu; he also avoided prettifying his scenes of 'simple folk'. In his works, meaning is usually conveyed by form and composition rather than by emblematic or literary reference.

In the 1660s Brekelenkam followed the current fashion in painting high-life genre scenes: elegant conversations and ladies receiving letters or at their toilets. His manner often approaches that of Gerard ter Borch (ii), whose influence he clearly acknowledged in his *Woman at her Toilet* (1662; Lübeck, priv. col.), which borrows motifs from two works by that master. In Brekelenkam's *Interior* (1663; Zurich, Ksthaus), the humble kitchens of his earlier works have given way to a finely appointed home where a maid waits, market pail on her arm, for the money her elegant mistress is about to give her for the shopping. Hanging on the wall is a portrait of a man, perhaps the provider of the wealth that supports such refined domestic economy.

BIBLIOGRAPHY

H. Havard: *L'Art et les artistes hollandais*, iv (Paris, 1881), pp. 91–146

E. Plietzsch: *Holländische und flämische Maler des XVII. Jahrhunderts* (Leipzig, 1960), pp. 42–4

W. Stechow: 'A Genre Painting by Brekelenkam', *Allen Mem. A. Mus. Bull.*, xxx/2 (1973), pp. 74–84

Masters of Seventeenth-century Dutch Genre Painting (exh. cat., ed. P. C. Sutton; Philadelphia, PA, Mus. A., 1984), pp. 157–61 [with further bibliog.]

A. Lasius: *Quiringh Gerritsz. Brekelenkam* (diss., U. Göttingen, 1987)

ELIZABETH ALICE HONIG

Breker, Arno (*b* Elberfeld, 19 July 1900; *d* Düsseldorf, 13 Feb 1991). German sculptor and printmaker. After his first experiences of sculpture in his father's stonemason's workshop, he attended the Kunstgewerbeschule in Elberfeld (1916–20). Under the guidance of Wilhelm Kreis and Hubert Netzer he continued his studies at the Staatliche Kunstakademie, Düsseldorf (1920–25). Starting with abstract sculptures, bowl-like forms combined with metal constructions, he soon turned to figurative sculpture. The human form, whether as an individual portrait or a typical full-figure representation, was central to his work from then on.

In 1924 Breker travelled to Paris for the first time and subsequently lived there between 1927 and 1933. The loose and painterly surface treatment that had predominated in the works up until this time, modelled in clay and then cast in bronze, was replaced by smooth and polished surfaces, first with the *Torso with Bent Arms* (see Probst 1981, p. 5). This finish remained a characteristic feature and can be seen in connection with the artist's long friendship with Aristide Maillol, whom he had met at the beginning of his stay in Paris.

In 1933 Breker spent a year at the Villa Massimo in Rome. Ancient sculpture, with which he was chiefly occupied, became the model for his own work. In 1934 he moved to Berlin at the insistence of his friend Max Liebermann. The silver medal, which he won in 1936 after participating in a competition to design the ground for the Olympic Stadium in Berlin, became the starting-point for his many state commissions from 1938. Professor at the Hochschule für Bildende Kunst in Berlin, from 1937, he worked for public projects in several German cities. Among these the production of Albert Speer's architectonic design for the planned new Reichskanzlei, the triumphal arch and the large fountain in the centre of Berlin are particularly outstanding. The poses and formal arrangement of these sculptures and reliefs, taking the trained bodies of athletes as their models, were derived from ancient sculptures. The expressions and gestures of the male figures, however, were often made heroic and expressively emphatic (e.g. *Comrades*, 1940; see Probst 1987, p. 77–82). The themes of works such as *Readiness* (1939) and *Kneeling Woman* (1942; for both see Probst 1987, pp. 64–6, 106) were primarily virtues corresponding to Nazi race-related ideas. In 1945, 90% of his work, which was read as symbolizing National Socialism, was destroyed by the Allies.

Breker did not return to sculpture until the 1960s, after his return to Düsseldorf. He also concentrated increasingly on printmaking. He made portraits of personalities from various areas of public life, such as that of *Jean Cocteau* (h. 425 mm, 1963; Figueres, Teat.–Mus. Dalí). The full-length works, for example those for an *Olympia* cycle, which he began in 1976, continue the themes of form and content from the preceding decades.

WRITINGS

Paris, Hitler et moi (Paris, 1970)

V. G. Probst, ed.: *Schriften*, foreword F. J. Hall (Bonn, Paris, New York, 1983)

BIBLIOGRAPHY

Arno Breker: Skulpturen, Aquarelle, Lithographien, Radierungen (exh. cat., Bonn, Gal. Mario, 1974)

H. Lohausen, ed.: *Arno Breker: Der Portraitist* (Düsseldorf, 1980)

V. G. Probst, ed.: *Arno Breker: 60 ans de sculpture* (Paris, 1987)

BEATRICE V. BISMARCK

Bremen, the Schütting, north façade, 1594

Bremen. Capital city of the German state of the same name and the country's oldest port, situated on the banks of the River Weser *c.* 50 km south of the estuary. It was first mentioned in AD 782 and became a bishopric in 787 during the reign of Charlemagne (*reg* 768–814). The first and second cathedrals, both probably timber buildings, were constructed in 789 and 805 respectively. In 848, after the destruction of Hamburg by the Vikings, the two sees were united, and Bremen replaced Hamburg as the archbishopric, becoming the new missionary centre for the north. At this time the cathedral was fortified by a double ring-wall; in 1013 and 1043 the precincts of the cathedral were enclosed by a further stone wall, the line of which helped to determine the plan of the modern city. This part, including the deanery and the provost's house, is characterized by rounded blocks of buildings, the form usually associated with Frankish settlements, while the civic area along Langenstrasse and Obernstrasse had a regularly laid-out grid of *insulae*. In the 12th century Bremen achieved increasing political independence, and by the 14th century it had gained both economic and political influence, achieving city status in 1303. Bremen was accepted into the Hanseatic League in 1358. As its economy flourished, the city expanded. In 1308 the Stephani district was brought inside the city walls, and in 1623 the Neustadt was established on the opposite bank of the Weser. In 1802 the fortifications, originally built *c.* 1200 and later extended, were dismantled and the area converted to gardens.

The ecclesiastical and economic importance of Bremen led to the development of a rich and varied architecture from an early period. The earliest parish church, St Veith (1012–29; now the Unsere Lieben Frauenkirche), was built at the north end of the Marktplatz. Beneath the north aisle

of the church are the oldest surviving architectural remains in Bremen, the 11th-century vaulted crypt of the original building. The earliest surviving parts of the cathedral also date from the mid-11th century and suggest the previous existence of a flat-roofed, three-aisled basilica with nine bays, single-aisled transepts and an east and west choir, each with its own crypt. The stone relief of *Christ in Judgement*, located in the west crypt, also dates from this period.

Bremen underwent its biggest increase in building activity under Archbishop Gerhard II (*reg* 1219–58). Following the Westphalian model, seen for example in St Marien in Lippstadt, the cathedral was vaulted as a basilica and the Unsere Lieben Frauenkirche was converted into a three-aisled hall church. There is a striking similarity in both buildings in the use of octopartite vaulting with ring-shaped bosses, suggesting the involvement of the same masons' workshop. In 1229 Archbishop Gerhard II divided the town into four parishes: in addition to Unsere Lieben Frauenkirche, the churches included the Stephanikirche, developed from an 11th-century provost's house; the Ansgariikirche, developed from a canonical foundation established in 1187; and the merchants' church of St Martin. They were all converted into brick hall churches in the second half of the 14th century; all were seriously damaged by bombing in 1942–4, and the Ansgariikirche was destroyed. In the 13th century several monasteries were established in Bremen, although little of these buildings survives: in 1226 the Dominicans founded the Katharinen-Kloster, the Teutonic Order built the Heilig Geist-Spital (*c.* 1230) and the Franciscans built the Johannis-Kloster (*c.* 1240).

During the Middle Ages secular architecture became increasingly important. The appearance of the town was determined initially by gabled wooden houses, while stone was later first used for two-storey buildings. From the 13th century there was an increasing use of brick for houses, and from the 15th century it was also used in combination with ashlar. In the 15th century the Marktplatz, the civic focus of the town, was completely surrounded by buidings. To the north, between the market and Unsere Lieben Frauenkirche, the Late Gothic town hall (1405–10) was added. The two-storey brick building has a three-aisled, flat-roofed hall above a vaulted Ratskeller (town hall cellar), and on the first floor there is a flat-roofed chamber. The façade is decorated with life-size sandstone statues of the emperor with the seven electors and Prophets. The stone figure of *Roland* (1404) on the Marktplatz is part of the same iconographic scheme. When the town hall was altered (1608–15), the façade in particular was enhanced by the addition of a large number of sandstone reliefs that together provide an allegorical picture of the world. Shortly afterwards, the Güldenkammer, decorated with carvings and oil paintings, was created on the first floor as a new council chamber (*see* GERMANY, §V, 1). To the south, the Marktplatz is closed off by the Schütting (see fig.), the premises of the merchants' guild. The present sandstone building (1537–9), by the Antwerp architect Johann de Buschener (*fl* 1536–9), replaces one dating from 1425; in 1565 a new east gable was added, and in 1594 a new façade was built (*see* BENTHEIM, LÜDER VON), both the work of local masons. The building was severely damaged in 1944 and was restored in 1952. Of the many other buildings constructed in Bremen in the 16th and 17th centuries, only two survived World War II: the Stadtwaage (weigh-house; 1587) by Lüder von Bentheim and the Gewerbehaus (trade hall; 1618), originally built as a ballroom for tailors.

Bremen expanded beyond the city walls in the 18th and 19th centuries, then from 1852 according to a specific urban plan; a typical suburban dwelling of this period was a narrow, usually three-storey, terraced house modelled on the English pattern. Among the finest achievements of 20th-century architecture in Bremen is the Böttcherstrasse, which joins the southern side of the Marktplatz. In 1924–6 the west side of this old street was rebuilt by the architects Eduard Scotland (1885–1945) and Alfred Runge (1881–1946) in the vernacular style, with stepped gables and brick arcades. In 1925–31 the sculptor Bernhard Hoetger (1874–1949) added the Paula–Modersohn–Becker–Haus and Haus Atlantis on the east side, using expressionistic sculptural forms. The unusual Himmelsaal, with parabolic roof trusses and coloured glass bricks, is of interest because of its special light effects.

BIBLIOGRAPHY
R. Stein: *Romanische, Gotische und Renaissance: Baukunst in Bremen* (Bremen, 1962)
W. Dietsch: *Der Dom St Petri zu Bremen. Geschichte und Kunst* (Bremen, 1978)
S. Albrecht: *Das Bremer Rathaus im Zeichen städtischer Selbstdarstellung* (Marburg, 1993)

STEPHAN ALBRECHT

Bremmer, H(endricus) P(etrus) (*b* Leiden, 17 May 1871; *d* The Hague, 16 Jan 1956). Dutch collector and critic. He began his career as an artist, painting pointillist works such as *Landscape with a Windmill* (1894; Leiden, Stedel. Mus. Lakenhal), but soon turned to theory rather than practice. From 1895 he was an ardent defender of the anti-naturalist view, considering the role of art to be the representation of the inner life of the artist rather than the imitation of the visible world. He wrote widely on this and related topics in the periodicals *Modern Kunstwerke* (1903–10) and *Beeldende Kunst* (1913–38), which he edited: he also lectured extensively, and encouraged and supported young artists. Bremmer was extremely influential in the collecting of art in the Netherlands in the first years of this century, most spectacularly in the building up of the Kröller-Muller museum at Otterlo. He met Hélène Kröller-Muller in 1906 and inspired her to transfer her allegiance from Delft china to modern art: over the 30 years during which he guided her buying she acquired notable groups of works by Vincent van Gogh and Bart van der Leck, together with Piet Mondrian, one of the contemporary artists most closely associated with Bremmer and his anti-naturalist aesthetic theories. Bremmer's position of eminence in the Dutch art world was recognized by the award of an honorary degree from the University of Groningen in 1951.

BIBLIOGRAPHY
Herdenking dr. H. P. Bremmer (Rotterdam, 1956)
H. J. Vink: 'H. P. Bremmer: Kunstpedagoog en ondersteuner van kunstenaars', *Jb. Die Haghe* (1984), pp. 74–107
R. J. Willink: 'Bremmer en het blijvende in de kunst', *Jong Holland*, iii (Sept 1985), pp. 50–57

H. J. Vink: 'Bremmer, Spinoza en de abstracte kunst', *Jong Holland*, ii (May 1987), pp. 40–48
The Age of Van Gogh: Dutch Painting 1880–1895 (exh. cat., ed. R. Bionda and C. Blotkamp; Glasgow, Burrell Col., 1990)

JOOST WILLINK

Brendekilde, H(ans) A(ndersen) [Andersen, Hans] (*b* Brændekilde, Fyn, 7 April 1857; *d* Jyllinge, 30 March 1942). Danish painter, glass designer and ceramicist. He trained as a stonemason and then studied sculpture in Copenhagen at the Kongelige Danske Kunstakademi (1877–81), where he decided to become a painter. In 1884 he changed his name from Andersen to Brendekilde after his place of birth, as he was constantly being confused with his friend Laurits Andersen Ring, who moreover also took the name of his birthplace. In the 1880s Brendekilde and Ring painted together on Fyn and influenced each other's work. Brendekilde's art had its origin in the lives of people of humble means and in the country environment of previous centuries. He painted landscapes and genre pictures. He himself was the son of a woodman, and his paintings often contain social comment, as in *Worn Out* (1889; Odense, Fyn. Kstmus.), which shows the influence of both Jean-François Millet and Jules Bastien-Lepage. Brendekilde was a sensitive colourist, influenced by Impressionism, for example in *Harvesters, Raagelund* (1883; Odense, Fyn. Kstmus.). Sometimes his works were provided with distinctive carved frames, which themselves expand and complement the narrative of the picture. Around 1905 he began to depict the idyllic, though keeping the same range of motifs, depicting farm environments with hollyhocks and kindly old women and infants against white walls, without the earlier refined treatment of colour. He also painted landscapes on his journeys to Italy, Egypt and Syria. In his later years he painted large pictures with religious motifs. He also made ceramics with fairytale motifs at the Kahler factory in Næstved, and he was Denmark's first glass designer, working briefly at the Fyns Glasværker.

BIBLIOGRAPHY
H. Madsen: *Fynsk malerkunst* (Odense, 1949–64), i, pp. 56–65

CLAUDINE STENSGAARD NIELSEN

Brenet, Nicolas-Guy (*b* Paris, 30 June 1728; *d* Paris, 22 Feb 1792). French painter. He was the son of the medal-engraver Guy Brenet (*fl* 1716–42). In 1754, after an apprenticeship with François Boucher, he entered the Ecole Royale des Elèves Protégés, then directed by Carle Vanloo. In 1756 he went to the Académie de France in Rome, becoming the first student there to copy a work by Caravaggio (*The Entombment*, Rome, Pin. Vaticana). Returning to France in 1759 he stopped at Lyon, where he received important commissions from churches, including *Laban Seeking his Images* (Lyon, Hôtel-Dieu) and the *Miracle of the Building of the Church* (Lyon, St Bruno). These early works are characteristic of Brenet in their monumental compositions, balanced masses, solid forms and light, pearly colouring. He also painted a complete cycle of the *Life of Christ* (1762–9; *in situ*) for the church of Pont-de-Vaux, Ain, and throughout his career he maintained a connection with the Lyon area, painting *Healing of the Lame Man* and the *Martyrdom of St Peter* for the church of Saint-Chamond in 1788 (*in situ*).

In Paris, Brenet was approved (*agréé*) by the Académie Royale in 1762. He exhibited regularly at the Salon for the next 30 years, causing a stir in 1763 with *St Denis Praying for the Establishment of the Faith* (Argenteuil, St Denis). Until 1773 he supported himself chiefly by producing clear, elegant devotional works strongly influenced by van Loo and Jean Restout II. Despite a certain skill, conceded by Diderot in his *Salons*, they lack the imaginative power of the generation's most notable religious painter, Jean-Baptiste Deshays. Brenet was received (*reçu*) by the Académie in 1769, aged 40, with *Theseus Finding his Father's Sword* (Paris, Ecole N. Sup. B.-A.); he approached this ambitious subject, attempted in the previous century by Poussin and Eustache Le Sueur, with a sober conception and generous brushwork. Also shown at the 1769 Salon were his allegorical figures *Truth* and *Study*, which, together with *Faith*, *Prudence*, *Temperance* and *Strength*, form a great decorative cycle in the Parlement of Flanders (now Palais de Justice) in Douai.

The painting in 1773 of *St Louis Receiving the Tartar Ambassadors* for the Ecole Militaire in Paris (*in situ*) was a turning-point in Brenet's career. Here he combined religious painting with the new taste for subjects from national history, a tendency that was to receive official encouragement from the Comte d'Angiviller when he was appointed Directeur of the Bâtiments du Roi the following year. Brenet's real originality revealed itself at the Salon of 1777; with the *Death of Duguesclin* (Versailles, Château; see fig.), without doubt his masterpiece. In this heroic, medievalizing scene from French history he invented a new pictorial language, at once descriptive and emotional, on which 19th-century history painting came to depend. It rehabilitated the theme of the exemplary death—treated by Poussin in the *Death of Germanicus* (1628; Minneapolis, MN, Inst. A.) and Charles Le Brun in the *Death of Meleager* (1658; Paris, Louvre)—through a new interest in the historical reconstruction of post-Classical settings and costumes, a novelty that forcibly struck Brenet's contemporaries; at the same time it had an animated colouring and richness in its modelling and in the effects of light on faded draperies that recalled the work of Boucher and Jean-Baptiste-Marie Pierre. Brenet again exalted national heroes in *St Louis Dispensing Justice* (1785; Compiègne, Hotel-Dieu) and *Henry II Decorating the Vicomte de Taravannes* (1789; Versailles, Château). The latter, however, is deprived of vigour by a desire to freeze the scene and remove any lingering Rococo elements.

This stylistic direction had developed in a long series of paintings of antique subjects, starting with *Caius Furius Cressinus Accused of Sorcery* (exh. Salon 1775; Toulouse, Mus. Augustins) and including *Metellius Saved by his Son* (exh. Salon 1779; Nîmes, Mus. B.-A.) and *Virginius Stabbing his Daughter in Order to Tear her away from the Decemvir* (exh. Salon 1783; Nantes, Mus. B.-A.). In these Brenet, following the example of François-Guillaume Ménageot and Nicolas-Bernard Lépicié, laid the foundations of a 'virtuous' Neo-classical style, in which compositions, still following the rules of van Loo and Jean-Francois de Troy, are organized legibly within a firm architectural framework. The *Battle between the Greeks and the Trojans over the Body of Patroclus* (exh. Salon 1781; Nîmes, Mus. B.-A.) is exceptional in Brenet's work for

Nicolas-Guy Brenet: *Death of Duguesclin*, oil on canvas, 3.83×2.64 m, 1777 (Versailles, Musée National du Château de Versailles et de Trianon)

treating an epic theme, full of horror and tumult. Following the *Roman Women Giving up their Jewels for the Fatherland* (exh. Salon 1785; Fontainebleau, Château), the last of the series, *Scipio's Young Son Given by his Father to Antiochus* (exh. Salon 1787; Nantes, Mus. B.-A.), shows Brenet's adherence to the new artistic canons of the age of David, aligning a small cast of characters in friezelike fashion before a shallow space. The painting retains a beauty in its solid forms and a brightness of colouring that make Brenet an important figure in the movement for the restoration of history painting in France in the later 18th century.

BIBLIOGRAPHY
D. Diderot: *Salons* (1759–81); ed. J. Sezner and J. Adhémar (Oxford, 1957–67/*R* 1983)
M. F. Perez: 'Tableaux de Nicolas-Guy Brenet (1728–1792) conservés dans la région lyonnaise', *Bull. Soc. Hist. A. Fr.* (1973), pp. 199–212
——: 'Tableaux commandés à Nicolas-Guy Brenet pour l'église de Saint-Chamond (1785–1788)', *Bull. Soc. Hist. A. Fr.* (1978), pp. 173–89
M. Sandoz: *Nicolas-Guy Brenet (1728–1792)* (Paris, 1979)
Diderot et l'art de Boucher à David, les Salons: 1759–1781 (exh. cat., Paris, Hôtel de la Monnaie, 1984–5)

NATHALIE VOLLE

Brenna, Vincenzo (*b* Florence, 1745; *d* Dresden, 17 May 1820). Italian architect, interior designer and decorative painter. He studied in Rome under Stefano Pozzi from 1766 to 1768 and then in Paris. On his return to Italy he studied antiquities, copying frescoes (with Franciszek Smuglewicz) and measuring and sketching the Baths of

Titus (1774) and the villa of Pliny the younger at Lauren-tinum. He occasionally worked in Poland, where he showed his skill as an interior decorator. A designer of painted arabesque decoration, he combined classical ar-chitectural and landscape compositions with Baroque decorative effects. Notable examples include works at the palace of Izabella Poniatowska-Branicka and the royal palace in Warsaw, the Czartoryski Palace (the Pheasantry) at Natolin, and other great houses in Poland.

In late 1783 or early 1784 he was invited to St Petersburg by the heir to the Russian throne, Paul Petrovich (later Tsar Paul I, *reg* 1796–1801) for the building of his country residence at PAVLOVSK. Initially he was an assistant to CHARLES CAMERON, assuming chief responsibility in 1786. Almost all the principal apartments of the Great Palace were decorated to Brenna's designs. The low reliefs, ceilings and the decoration of the grand staircase and Upper Vestibule (1784–8) presented allegories of the Russian army's victories over Turkey. The central, Italian Hall, for which Cameron had previously prepared designs, was crowned by a dome with a lantern, and its decoration was conceived in the spirit of Italian Baroque. By 1794 the Halls of War and Peace, the Tapestry Room, the Library and the State Bedchamber were also completed.

With the accession of Paul I, Brenna, as chief court architect, took charge of many building projects in St Petersburg and at the Tsar's country residences. He extended the palace at Pavlovsk, adding side colonnades and wings, which somewhat overwhelm Cameron's core building, and decorated the new rooms (1797–1801). In the 1790s he worked on the decoration of the interiors at the Konstantinovskiy Palace (transferred to Pavlovsk from Tsarskoye Selo; destr. World War II) and the Gatchina Palace. The especially magnificent interiors of Paul I's palace at Gatchina are among the finest works of Russian architectural decorative art: they include Mariya Fyodo-rovna's State Bedchamber, executed in shades of white and light blue with gilding, and finished in Lyon silk with a subtle pattern in silver, and with a painted ceiling by Gabriel-François Doyen; the Oval Room, with painted decoration by Giovanni Scotti; and the Grecian Gallery, which contained four pictures by Hubert Robert. Brenna also played a major role in laying out the parks at Gatchina and Pavlovsk (1790s), which were a blend of formal and landscape compositions (for illustration of Pavlovsk *see* GARDEN, fig. 55). The varied style of Brenna's garden buildings echoed the mood of the two parks. These are the classical Round Hall or Music Room (1799–1800; inspired by a design by Cameron), the Amphitheatre (1792–3), the staircase and trellis by the Mariental Pond (1795–6), all at Pavlovsk; and at GATCHINA, the Venus Pavilion (1792) and Eagle Pavilion (late 18th century or early 19th) on the islands in the White Lake, the main entrance (the Admiralty Gates) and the Mask Pavilion (both 1794–6).

Also in the late 1790s Brenna was busy in St Petersburg, where he took part in the decoration of the Winter and Kamenny Ostrov palaces (late 1790s; *see* ST PETERSBURG, §IV, 1) and erected the Kazasi Theatre (1801; destr.), near the Nevsky Prospekt, and the Rumyantsev Obelisk (1798–9; moved in 1818 to the square between the Academy of Arts and the First Cadet Corps) on the Marsovo Pole

(Field of Mars). The culmination of his work, however, was Mikhaylovsky Castle (1796–1800; later Engineers' Castle; Inzhenerny Zamok). Built on a square plan with an octagonal internal courtyard, it was surrounded by the Moyka and Fontanka canals at their point of confluence, and it had the look of an impregnable fortress. The architecture of the palace was intended by Paul I to personify the majesty and strength of imperial authority. The classical stateliness of the colonnades, the heavy rustication of the walls, the great portico with obelisks and figures of knights, conspired with the capricious silhouettes of the chapel towers and the Oval Hall and the play of the projections and recessions to create a romanticized picture of a castle palace standing aloof from the city. The interiors were rich and solemn in appearance, lavishly adorned with painted decoration, sculpture, wall coverings, paintings and furniture by the finest craftsmen. Brenna's last work in Russia was the completion, to his own design, of Antonio Rinaldi's cathedral of St Isaac (1798–1801; rebuilt 19th century). In 1802 he left Russia for Germany, then went to France for several years before returning to Germany. Brenna founded no school as such in Russia; his sole pupil was Karl Rossi.

BIBLIOGRAPHY
N. Wrangel: 'Vintsent Frantsevich Brenna', *Staryye gody* [Yesteryear] (March 1908), pp. 169–73
E. L. Gatto: *Gli artisti in Russia*, vol. 2 (Rome, 1935)
V. K. Shuysky: *Vinchentso Brenna* (Leningrad, 1986)

N. A. YEVSINA

Brennand, Francisco (*b* Recife, 11 June 1927). Brazilian painter and ceramicist. He made an extended visit to Europe from 1949 to 1952, living mainly in Paris, where he studied with André Lhote and Fernand Léger, whose tumescent forms had a lasting influence on his work. On his return to Recife, where his family had long been responsible for a vast output of industrial ceramics, he dedicated himself increasingly to his work with pottery. He carried out ceramic murals in several Brazilian cities and abroad, the most outstanding being the *Battle of the Guararapes* (completed 1962; Recife, façade of the Banco Bandeirantes do Comércio), commemorating the war between the Portuguese and the Dutch in Brazil in the 17th century. For both his ceramics and his painting he drew inspiration mainly from popular art, blurring the distinction between the real and the imaginary, seeking an epic quality in simple acts of heroism and reinventing nature in fantastic flora and fauna. In later years he created monumental ceramic works in which eroticism is linked to powerful primitive forces. He transformed his studio–factory in Recife into a museum of his work but still used it as a studio.

BIBLIOGRAPHY
F. Morais: *Francisco Brennand* (exh. cat., Rio de Janeiro, Petite Gal., 1969)
R. Pontual: *Arte brasileira contemporânea* (Rio de Janeiro, 1976)
C. Leal: 'Francisco Brennand', *Visão da terra* (exh. cat., Rio de Janeiro, Mus. A. Mod., 1977), pp. 46–57
Expressionismo no Brasil: Heranças e afinidades [Expressionism in Brazil: legacies and affinities] (exh. cat. by S. T. Barros and I. Mesquita, São Paulo Bienal, 1985), pp. 51, 100, 116

ROBERTO PONTUAL

Brenner, Victor D(avid) (*b* Schavli, Kovno [now Kau-nas], 12 June 1871; *d* New York, 5 April 1924). American medallist of Lithuanian origin. He trained as a seal-engraver under his father and worked as a jewellery engraver and type cutter. In 1890 he went to New York, where he worked as a die engraver of badges, and in 1898 to Paris to study at the Académie Julian and later with Oscar Roty. He first exhibited medals in the early years of the 20th century. The influence of Roty is apparent in the low relief and soft-edged naturalism and also in the inclusion of flat expanses of metal in his designs. He occasionally ventured into sculpture, as in the Schenley Memorial Fountain (bronze; Pittsburgh, PA, Schenley Park), but he was best known for his medals and plaquettes, both struck and cast, and his sensitive portraits assured his popularity. The powerful head of President Roosevelt on the Panama Canal medal (bronze, 1908) and the tender *Shepherdess* plaquette (electrotype, 1907) demonstrate his range. He executed coins for the Republic of San Domingo and designed the American cent coin with the head of Abraham Lincoln first used in 1909.

BIBLIOGRAPHY

DAB; Thieme–Becker

L. Forrer: *Biographical Dictionary of Medallists* (London, 1902–30), i, pp. 277–9; vii, pp. 117–22; viii, p. 320

International Exhibition of Contemporary Medals, 1910 (exh. cat., intro. A. Baldwin; New York, Amer. Numi. Soc., 1911), pp. 26–34

Exhibition of American Sculpture (exh. cat., preface H. A. MacNeil; New York, N. Sculp. Soc., 1923), p. 30

D. Taxay: *The US Mint and Coinage* (New York, 1966), pp. 330–39

The Beaux-Arts Medal in America (exh. cat. by B. A. Baxter, New York, Amer. Numi. Soc., 1988)

PHILIP ATTWOOD

Brentano, Giuseppe (*b* Milan, 14 April 1862; *d* Milan, 31 Dec 1889). Italian architect. He enrolled in 1883 at the Politecnico, Milan, where he studied under Camillo Boito and Luca Beltrami. While a student, Brentano won a scholarship competition (1885) with designs for an exhibition building in the Greek style and a Gothic Revival church. In 1886 he entered the international competition for a new façade for Milan Cathedral, one of his rivals being Beltrami. The style of the new façade was already the subject of heated dispute between those who believed that the building was basically inspired by north European Gothic and those who believed it was entirely of the Lombard school of architecture. In an earlier competition (1881) organized by the Accademia di Brera, projects representing each viewpoint (by Carlo Ferrario (1833–1907) and Beltrami) had shared first prize, but they had aroused such controversy that the judgement had actually been overturned and the project by Beltrami, advocating the Lombard thesis and proposing a façade with a sloping roof and three portals, had been disallowed. For the second competition Brentano presented two alternatives: one with side towers, clearly of northern Gothic inspiration, and another, less elaborate and close to Beltrami's scheme but with five entrances. Invited to take part in the competition's second stage (1887), he embarked on a European research tour: in Vienna he had access to the office of Carl Hasenauer and other architects, before going on to Cologne, Rouen, Amiens and Paris. In 1888 he won the competition with a project that combined the Lombard Gothic features of Beltrami's scheme with detailing influenced by north European Gothic and the Viennese Gothic Revival. His premature death prevented his competition sketches from being translated into detailed designs, however, and the existing façade was not rebuilt.

BIBLIOGRAPHY

DBI; Thieme–Becker

A. Melani: 'La facciata del Duomo', *A. & Stor.*, vii (1888), ix (1890)

C. Boito: *Il Duomo di Milano e i disegni per la sua facciata* (Milan, 1889)

C. Bianchi: 'Commemorazione di Giuseppe Brentano', *Atti Coll. Ingeg. & Architteti Milano*, xiii (Milan, 1890)

L. Beltrami: *Giuseppe Brentano nel x anniversario di sua morte* (Milan, 1899)

M. G. Borghi: 'L'architetto Giuseppe Brentano e le sue lettere ai famigliari', *Rendi. Reale Ist. Lombardo Sci. & Lett.*, lxxv (Milan, 1942)

C. L. V. Meeks: *Italian Architecture, 1750–1914* (New Haven and London, 1966), pp. 230–37

GILDA GRIGIONI

Brentel [Brändel; Brendel], **Friedrich, I** (*b* Lauingen, nr Ulm, 9 July 1580; *d* Strasbourg, 17 May 1651). German engraver, painter, calligrapher and designer. He probably trained with his father, Georg Brentel (*c.* 1525/30–1610), who painted mainly heraldic miniatures. Friedrich's earliest signed work, a pen-and-wash copy of a Netherlandish Mannerist print, is dated 1596 (among 530 drawings by Brentel in Karlsruhe, Staatl. Ksthalle). Other early works show the influence of Tobias Stimmer and Wendel Dietterlin, as well as the detailed engraving skills of Etienne Delaune.

In 1601 Brentel became a citizen of Strasbourg and married. For his masterpiece he painted an untraced *Crucifixion* in opaque colours on parchment. Until 1620 he devoted himself mainly to printed graphic work and designs for cabinet panes. His first etching was produced in 1601 (see Wegner, no. 1). In 1610 he received an important commission: to depict the ceremonies in Nancy for the funeral of Duke Charles III and the oath of allegiance to Duke Henry II of Lorraine in large-format etchings. The sketched notes for these (Karlsruhe, Staatl. Ksthalle) are noteworthy, like other sketches for etchings by Brentel, for not being reverse images of the prints. The resulting five-part *Pompe funèbre de Charles 3e...* (w 4), completed with the cooperation of Matthäus Merian (i) by July 1611, shows Brentel's skill at clear spatial disposition, clearly visible distribution of crowds and exactitude of detail. In 1617–19 he etched several commissions for the court of the Dukes of Württemberg at Stuttgart, notably the court festivities of July 1617, again done with the cooperation of Merian (w 11). Brentel's ability to capture a building in perspective and enliven it with imaginatively distributed staffage is shown by the large-format etching (1619; w 20) of the interior of the Great Hall of the Stuttgart Lusthaus. These major printed graphic commissions ended with the copper engravings for the *Sylloge numismatum* of Johann Jacob Luck and the great etched genealogical tree of Eberhard von Rappoltstein (both 1620; w 20 and 21). After this, Brentel produced hardly any etchings, though he did several preliminary drawings for Léonard Gaultier and Claude Mellan's etchings illustrating the French edition of John Barclay's *Argenis* (Paris, 1623).

The onset of the Thirty Years War (1618–48) forced Brentel to alter his production methods at the beginning of the 1620s. From now on he worked almost exclusively as a miniaturist. Here he based himself, as his drawings also show, extensively on foreign (mostly printed graphic) models: firstly the Netherlandish Mannerists, later also

Rubens engravings and work by Jan van de Velde (from *c.* 1620), Jacques Callot and Matthäus Merian (from *c.* 1630), and Abraham Bosse (*c.* 1635). His thematic repertory was very broad: biblical subjects, lives of the saints, Classical history and poetry (particularly Ovid), allegory, landscape and contemporary events. His miniature portraits of the members of Upper Rhenish noble families are particularly charming: regular portraits in full or half figure with interior or landscape backgrounds, but in a miniature format (h. *c.* 100 mm); also portraits of the deceased or their widows (22 pieces from 1629–45, Karlsruhe, Staatl. Ksthalle; some probably workshop pieces). Brentel's miniatures are very finely worked and delicately coloured, more shaded than brightly colourful; the landscapes dissolve into a bluish distance. He described his technique for painting miniatures in gum pigments on parchment in 1642 in *Mahler und Illuminir Büchlein* (Göttingen, Ubib., Cod. MS. Uffenbach 49). His last great work, the richly illustrated *Stundenbuch* of Margrave William VII of Baden-Baden (1647; Paris, Bib. N., MSS. lat. 10567 & 10568), also demonstrates his skill as a calligrapher. The pretty illuminations of *Months of the Year* are mostly his own creation, though the other miniatures are again based on previous models.

Although only a minor master, Brentel was the leading painter in Strasbourg after the deaths of Stimmer and Dietterlin. His pupils included Johann Wilhelm Baur, his children Hans Friedrich Brentel and Anna Maria Brentel, his brother-in-law Hans Bühler, the miniaturists Johann Jakob Besserer and Johann Walther, the goldsmith Tobias Franckenberger and probably the still-life painter Sebastien Stoskopff.

BIBLIOGRAPHY

NDB; Thieme–Becker

J. von Sandrart: *Teutsche Academie* (1675–9); ed. A. R. Peltzer (1925), pp. 176, 181, 245

P. de Chennevières and A. de Montaiglon, eds: *Abécédario de P.-J. Mariette et autres notes inédites de cet amateur sur l'art et les artistes*, i (Paris, 1851–60/*R* 1966), i, pp. 187–8

A. Andresen: *Der deutsche Peintre-graveur*, iv (Leipzig, 1874), pp. 185–215

H. Rott: 'Strassburger Kunstkammern im 17. und 18. Jahrhundert', *Z. Gesch. Oberrheins*, xxxiii (1931), pp. 1–46

K. Obser: 'Oberrheinische Miniaturbildnisse Friedrich Brentels und seiner Schule', *Z. Gesch. Oberrheins*, lxxxvii (1935), pp. 1–35

W. Wegner: 'Untersuchungen zu Friedrich Brentel', *Jb. Staatl. Kstsamml. Baden-Württemberg*, iii (1966), pp. 107–96 [fundamental, with complete cat. of etchings] [w]

V. Beyer: 'Un *Castrum doloris* de Frédéric Brentel', *Rev. Louvre*, xxii (1972), pp. 315f

Zeichnung in Deutschland: Deutsche Zeichner, 1540–1640 (exh. cat. by H. Geissler; Stuttgart, Staatsgal., 1979–80), ii, pp. 37–9, 62

Die Renaissance im deutschen Südwesten (exh. cat., ed. H. Geissler; Heidelberg, Schloss, 1986), i, pp. 164, 221f, 368f, 407f; ii, p. 929

J. E. VON BORRIES

Brentel, Georg. *See under* MASTERS, ANONYMOUS, AND MONOGRAMMISTS, §III: MASTER B. G.

Brescia [Lat. Brixia]. Italian city at the foot of the Alps in Lombardy, with a population of *c.* 210,000. It was a notable Roman colony, an early centre of Christianity and a very prosperous city, as well as the focus of much artistic activity from the medieval period to modern times. The site was probably occupied by the Ligurians until the 4th century BC, and then by the Cenomani who were allied with Rome in 225 BC in the wars against other Celtic tribes.

In 89 BC Brixia was granted Latin citizenship and in 49 BC Roman citizenship also. It soon converted to Christianity and in the 4th century AD became a bishopric. Although there are few traces of the early urban development, architectural continuity between Roman and medieval Brescia is demonstrated by the remains of the forum and the citadel on the hill of Cidnéo, north of the forum. The most important fragments are preserved in the Lipsanoteca at the Museo Civico Cristiano, located in the former church of S Giulia.

The city was ransacked in 452 by Attila and occupied in 562 by the Lombards, who made it the seat of a duchy. The first important new building was S Maria Maggiore (6th–7th centuries; destr.). Under the rule of Desiderius (*reg* 756–74) and his consort Ansa, Brescia enjoyed a period of particular splendour and lively building activity. The most grandiose of the royal projects was the monastic complex of S Salvatore, which traditionally was founded in 753 by Ansa. Excavations in 1956–61 revealed the magnificent basilican plan of the church, probably superimposed on an original hall plan before the monastery came under imperial patronage (*c.* 816). The nave, articulated with arches supported on salvaged columns and lit by extensive fenestration similar to that of the Early Christian churches of Milan, is still partially decorated with foliate stuccowork and classicizing frescoes (*see* CAROLINGIAN, §IV, 1). In terms of quality the former can be compared with work at S Maria in Valle, Cividale del Friuli, while the latter are comparable to paintings at S Maria Foris Portas, CASTELSEPRIO. The principal Romanesque building is the Duomo Vecchio, known as the Rotonda owing to its circular plan (see fig.). It was erected in the 11th century on the site of S Maria Maggiore. Another centralized plan of Early Christian inspiration is found at S Maria in Solario (*c.* 1120) near S Salvatore; the chapel has an octagonal lantern that rests on a square base.

The city became a free commune at the beginning of the 12th century. It was captured by Emperor Frederick I in 1158 and became a member of the Lombard League in 1167. Later, torn apart by civil strife, it fell under the power of various rival factions: Ezzelino da Romano (1258), the Pallavicini, the Torriani, the Scaligeri (1316), the Angevins (1319), the Visconti and the Malatesta. The Visconti returned to power in 1421, but Brescia was finally ceded to Venice after the Battle of Maclodio in 1428. This was followed by a long period of peace and prosperity.

A surge of building activity in the early 13th century, including the completion of the town hall, or Broletto (begun 1187), a good example of the transitional phase from Romanesque to Gothic, culminated in 1237 with a new city plan. Between 1414 and 1419 Gentile da Fabriano worked on a fresco cycle (destr.) in the chapel of the Broletto, to a commission by Pandolfo III Malatesta (1370–1427). The artist's stay in Brescia may have played a part in the subsequent flowering of painting. Fabriano's idiom was partly continued by Andrea Bembo, who worked in a Late Gothic court style characteristic of Lombardy. These and other artists were followed by Vincenzo Foppa, the first famous Brescian painter of the Renaissance and a dominant figure in the city's artistic life.

The architectural influences that followed the annexation by the Venetian Republic drastically altered Brescia's

Brescia, Duomo Vecchio (the Rotonda), west elevation, 11th century

appearance. A new nucleus began to grow around the Loggia (1492–1575), a city palace constructed with the assistance of Jacopo Sansovino, Galeazzo Alessi and Andrea Palladio. The new religious buildings of the period include S Maria dei Miracoli (1487–1581), the original simple chapel that was extended to form a complex structure with refined decoration according to well-established Lombard formulae.

Another important project that continued throughout the second half of the 16th century was the reconstruction of the Castello, the major fortress on the hill of Cidnéo. The construction of the Duomo Nuovo (1604–1836) involved the most influential local architects. Giovan Battista Marchetti (1686–1758) was responsible for the design of the façade and Rodolfo Vantini (1791–1865) for the steep dome.

During the first half of the 16th century sculpture in Brescia, dominated by Maffeo Olivieri, was much less developed than painting, which reached the peak of its development; this period is well represented in the Pinacoteca Civica Tosio-Martinengo. The legacy of Foppa's luminosity and the innovative Venetian tonality represented in the city by Titian's polyptych of the *Resurrection* (1522) in SS Nazaro e Celso can be traced in works by the three principal painters, Giovanni Girolamo Savoldo, Gerolamo Romanino and Moretto, the last being the most highly regarded by the local patrons. The realism of the city's painters was taken up and continued by Giovanni

Battista Moroni, and it constituted a prelude to the artistic revolution brought about by Caravaggio. Brescian painting later became excessively decorative and highly successful. Its last great representative was GIACOMO CERUTI, who was active in Brescia from 1721 and faithfully depicted the poorest ranks of society.

Overall, artistic life in Brescia waned in the 18th century. The city was incorporated into the Cisalpine Republic in 1797 and was part of the Kingdom of Italy from 1805 to 1814. It was then under Austrian rule until 1859, despite a courageous uprising in 1849. The city walls began to be demolished from 1875. Brescia was badly bombed in 1944–5, and many buildings were demolished after World War II. This was followed by an extensive programme of redevelopment that included both the city centre and surrounding areas.

BIBLIOGRAPHY

G. Treccani degli Alfieri, ed.: *Storia di Brescia*, 4 vols (Milan, 1963)
G. Panazza: *La diocesi di Brescia: Corpus della scultura medievale*, 3 vols (Spoleto, 1966)
——: *La Pinacoteca e i musei di Brescia* (Bergamo, 1968)
San Salvatore di Brescia: Materiali per un museo, i (exh. cat., ed. R. Bettinelli and I. Vettori; Brescia, S Salvatore, 1978)
L. Anelli and A. Fappani: *Santa Maria dei Miracoli* (Brescia, 1980)
E. Guidoni: *Un monumento della tecnica urbanistica duecentesca: L'espansione di Brescia del 1237*, Lombardia: Il territorio, l'ambiente, il paesaggio (Milan, 1980)
R. Pallucchini: 'La pittura a Brescia nel settecento', *A. Ven.*, xxxv (1981–2), pp. 303–9
M. Gregori and others, eds: *Pittura del cinquecento a Brescia* (Milan, 1986)

V. Guazzoni: 'La pittura del seicento nei territori di Bergamo e Brescia', *La pittura in Italia: Il seicento*, ed. C. Pirovano, i (Milan, 1988), pp. 104–22

V. Frati and others: *Brescia, Le città nella storia d'Italia* (Bari, 1989)

GIUSEPPE PINNA

Brescia, Giovanni Antonio da. *See* GIOVANNI ANTONIO DA BRESCIA.

Brescia, Fra Raffaello da. *See* RAFFAELLO DA BRESCIA, Fra.

Brescianino [Piccinelli, Andrea] (*b* Siena, *c.* 1487; *d* after 1525). Italian painter. He may have trained with Girolamo del Pacchia (1477–?1533), but is first documented at Siena working with Battista di Fruosino (*fl* 1457–?1507) in the Compagnia di San Gerolamo in 1507. Immediately after, in Florence, he came under the influence of Raphael, Fra Bartolommeo and Leonardo da Vinci. His *Virgin and Child with Two Saints* (*c.* 1510; Buonconvento, Mus. A. Sacra Val d'Arbia) shows this early influence from Florence both in colouring and close figure grouping. Apart from a short visit to Rome (*c.* 1516) to assist Baldassare Peruzzi with the decoration of the Villa Farnesina, most of his time was spent in Siena. Frequent contact with Florence is suggested by his style of painting after 1510 and he probably had a workshop there run by his brother Raffaello Piccinelli (*fl* 1506–45). Works of slightly later date, such as the *Three Virtues* (*c.* 1517–18; Siena, Pin. N.), demonstrate that Andrea del Sarto became a dominant influence. In the *Coronation of the Virgin* (*c.* 1520; Siena, SS Pietro e Paolo) colours and compositional ideas from Sarto are combined with the local styles of Domenico Beccafumi and Girolamo del Pacchia. This altarpiece, with five predella panels depicting scenes from the *Life of Christ*, is one of his most substantial surviving works. He is last documented in 1525, in the confraternity of Florentine painters.

BIBLIOGRAPHY

A. Venturi: *Storia* (1901–40), ix/5, pp. 357–73

A. Salmi: *Il palazzo e la Collezione Chigi-Saracini* (Milan, 1967), pp. 107–15

N. Dacos: 'Peruzzi dalla Farnesina alla Cancelleria: Qualche proposta sulla bottega del pittore', *Baldassare Peruzzi, pittura, scena, architettura nel cinquecento* (Rome, 1987), pp. 469–90

Domenico Beccafumi e il suo tempo (exh. cat., ed. A. Bagnoli, R. Bartalini and M. Maccherini; Siena, Pin. N. and Pal. Pub. and elsewhere; 1990)

Bresciano, il. *See* ANTICHI, PROSPERO.

Bresdin, Rodolphe (*b* Le Fresne, 13 Aug 1822; *d* Sèvres, 11 Jan 1885). French printmaker and draughtsman. He grew up in Paris, leaving his working-class family as a teenager to take up a Bohemian lifestyle. Apparently self-taught, he executed his first crudely drawn etchings in 1839. He knew several writers, including Baudelaire and Jules Champfleury, and was himself the model for the latter's first novel, *Chien-Caillou* (1845), a romantic portrait of an eccentric, poverty-stricken artist. The title was Bresdin's nickname, actually a fractured version of Chingachgook, the hero of James Fenimore Cooper's novel *The Last of the Mohicans* (1826).

After 1848 Bresdin lived in isolation for over a year near Tulle, moving on to Bordeaux; by 1852 he was in Toulouse, where he spent nine years. He executed his first lithographs in 1854, including the *Comedy of Death* (see van Gelder, no. 84) and the *Flight into Egypt* (VG 85). In 1860 Bresdin began his lithographic masterpiece, the *Good Samaritan* (e.g. London, BM, VG 100; see fig.), which was originally entitled *Abd-el-Kader Aiding a Christian*; Bresdin moved back to Paris in 1861 to have it printed and shown in the Salon of that year. This very large lithograph (564×444 mm) was highly praised and was reprinted several times, providing Bresdin with an important source of income. Baudelaire subsequently secured him a commission to illustrate the new journal *Revue Fantaisiste* with 13 etchings.

Leaving Paris again in 1862, Bresdin had settled in Bordeaux by 1864, becoming a member of the Société des Amis des Arts there. Odilon Redon, who became a close friend to Bresdin, was one of his students at this time. Bresdin lived for short periods in Libourne, Paris and Biarritz before returning to Paris by 1869. He had received a commission in 1868 to illustrate a book of fables by Hippolyte Thierry, Comte de Faletans, and took up lithography again after a break of several years to produce the prints. Faletans refused many of Bresdin's early proofs, and publication was delayed until 1871, when Bresdin also finished major etchings of the *Enchanted House* (VG 135) and the *Holy Family* (VG 137–8).

Bresdin and his family left for Canada in 1873, realizing a lifelong dream to emigrate to a less industrialized country. He taught at an art school in Montreal, but in 1877 he returned disillusioned to France, his fare paid by writer friends including Victor Hugo. He etched a series of complex forest landscapes in 1880 (VG 142–7) and in 1883 executed two visionary scenes, an etching entitled *My Dream* (VG 150) and a lithograph of the *Miraculous Draught of Fishes* (VG 151). His fitful employment and chronic poor health caused him to become increasingly destitute. After working for a time as a street labourer in Paris, he eventually left his family in 1881, moving to Sèvres.

Over 150 prints by Bresdin are known, of which *c.* 130 are etchings. The remainder (excepting two experimental gelatin drypoints, VG 94–5) are lithographs. In several instances he transferred his etched designs to lithographic stones, and some images exist in both media (e.g. VG 86, 135). His drawings comprise both preliminary studies and finished works for presentation or sale. The former, for example *Sketch for a Battle in the Mountains* (1865; London, BM), are usually worked in India ink on a transparent tracing paper, often traced from other sources and then transferred to other sheets or printing plates. Most of Bresdin's finished drawings, such as *Peasant Interior* (1860; The Hague, Gemeentemus.), are pen and black ink and wash on white cardboard. The majority of his drawings and prints are on a small scale. His mature works are marked by an obsessive profusion of detail and a personal imagery fired by a romantic, pantheistic imagination rather than direct observation of nature. However, some of his characteristic images (landscapes, exotic horsemen, peasant genre scenes and macabre allegories) are derived from 17th-century Dutch art and from contemporary etchings or wood-engravings by artists such as Adolphe Hervier, Alexandre Decamps, Auguste Raffet and Gustave Doré. The prints are skilfully enriched by a welter of elaborate

Rodolphe Bresdin: *Good Samaritan*, lithograph, 564×444 mm, 1860–61 (London, British Museum)

textural effects, and the central figures, for instance in *Rest on the Flight into Egypt*, are often depicted within a dense mass of foliage.

Bresdin never achieved popular or critical success during his lifetime and was known only by a small circle of writers, artists and connoisseurs. He exhibited in the official Salon only six times between 1848 and 1879. His posthumous reputation was largely kept alive by Redon and a few print collectors in Europe and America until the revival of interest in 19th-century French printmaking during the second half of the 20th century. The facts of his life were surrounded by romantic legend until the publication of van Gelder's biography in 1976. The major public collections of Bresdin's works are in the Louvre and the Bibliothèque Nationale, Paris, the Gemeentemuseum, The Hague, the Rijksprentenkabinet, Amsterdam, the Metropolitan Museum of Art, New York, and the Art Institute of Chicago.

BIBLIOGRAPHY
H. A. Peters: *Die schwarze Sonne des Traums: Radierungen, Lithographien und Zeichnungen von Rodolphe Bresdin* (Cologne and Frankfurt, 1972)
R. de Montesquiou: *L'Inextricable Graveur* (Paris, 1913; Ger. trans., intro. P. Hahlbrock, Berlin, 1977)
D. van Gelder: *Rodolphe Bresdin*, 2 vols (The Hague, 1976) [VG; the fullest biography and the cat. rais. of the prints]
Rodolphe Bresdin, 1822–1885 (exh. cat., ed. D. van Gelder and J. Sillevis; The Hague, Gemeentemus., 1978)
R. Bacou: 'Rodolphe Bresdin et Odilon Redon', *Rev. Louvre*, xxix (1979), pp. 50–59
J. Baas Slee: 'A Literary Source for Rodolphe Bresdin's *La Comédie de la mort*', *A. Mag.*, liv/6 (1980), pp. 70–75
M. Parke-Taylor: 'A Canadian Allegory by Rodolphe Bresdin: *L'Apothéose de Cartier*', *Rev. A. Can.*, ix (1982), pp. 64–8
D. P. Becker: *The Drawings of Rodolphe Bresdin: Development and Sources with a Provisional Catalogue* (MA thesis, New York U., Inst. F.A., 1983)
——: 'Rodolphe Bresdin's *Le Bon Samaritain*', *Nouv. Est.*, 70–71 (1983), pp. 6–14

DAVID P. BECKER

Breslau. *See* WROCŁAW.

Breslau, Louise C(atherine) (*b* Munich, 6 Dec 1856; *d* Neuilly-sur-Seine, 12 May 1927). Swiss painter. She left Zurich at 19 to enter the Académie Julian in Paris. Her early career may be traced through entries in Marie Bashkirtseff's diaries, which express envy for Breslau's art, life and friends. These included Degas, Breton and Forain; a lifelong friendship with Sarah H. Purser left much informative correspondence (Dublin, N. Lib., Purser MSS). Breslau exhibited at the Salon from 1879; her first success was the *Portrait of Friends* (Geneva, Mus. A. & Hist.), which earned an honourable mention in 1881. The owner of *Le Figaro*, Fernand de Rodays, commissioned the portrait of his young daughter *Isabelle de Rodays* (Paris, Mus. A. Déc.), which was well received at the Salon of 1883, as was the genre scene entitled *Five o'Clock Tea* (Berne, Kstmus.). Originality and sober realism mark these works. *Under the Apple Trees* (1885; Lausanne, Pal. Rumine) exemplifies her ability as a *plein-air* artist, while *At Home* (1886; Paris, Mus. d'Orsay), an interior scene, breathes what she called the 'poésie de la monotonie'. She built up a wide portrait practice; her skill and empathy are evident in *Bergliot Björnson* (1889; Dublin, N.G.). She won a gold medal at the Exposition Universelle (Paris, 1889), the first foreign woman to be so honoured, and was a founder-member of the Société Nationale des Beaux-Arts

(1891). The French and Swiss governments began to buy her works, for example *Girls* (1893; Carpentras, Mus. Duplessis) and *Pensive Life* (1908; Lausanne, Pal. Rumine). Another gold medal in 1900 led to the Légion d'honneur, and official recognition of Breslau's merit culminated in a posthumous exhibition at the Ecole des Beaux-Arts in 1928.

BIBLIOGRAPHY
M. Bashkirtseff: *Journal* (Paris, 1887)
A. Alexandre: *Louise C. Breslau* (Paris, 1928)
M. Zillhardt: *Louise-Catherine Breslau et ses amis* (Paris, 1932)
E. von Bressendorf: 'Eine europäische Malerin aus München', *Die Weltkunst*, xlvii (1977), p. 1380

JOHN O'GRADY

Bretherton, James (*fl* London, 1770–90). English etcher. He exhibited three etchings at the Society of Artists in 1771, two after portraits of *Oliver Cromwell* and *Prince Rupert of the Rhine* by Samuel Cooper, the miniature painter, and one after an unattributed portrait of a lady. The following year he exhibited an etching 'from a drawing by Mr. Bunbury' there and thus found his true métier as an etcher of robust satirical prints. He produced over 60 plates after Henry William Bunbury, in etching and aquatint, between 1772 and 1783, including *Snip Français* and *Snip Anglais* (both 1773), *Hyde Park* (1781) and *Symptoms of Rearing* (1783; all London, BM). His original works include *Pot Fair* (1777) and *Trip to Scarborough* (1783; both London, BM), which satirizes contemporary fashions.

BIBLIOGRAPHY
F. G. Stephens and M. D. George: *Catalogue of Political and Personal Satires*, London, BM cat., v (London, 1935/*R* 1978)
M. H. Grant: *A Dictionary of British Etchers* (London, 1952)

Brethren of the Common Life. Religious group and important exponents of the movement known as the *Devotio moderna*, which flourished in northern Europe, particularly in the Netherlands, from the late 14th century to the early 16th. The movement stressed the importance of the inner life of the individual, with great emphasis on meditation. The Brethren (and the female equivalent, the Sisters) were groups of pious lay people and clerics who lived a devout and useful communal life dedicated to God. Associated with the Brethren but more formally constituted were the Augustinian Canons Regular of Windesheim near Zwolle, founded in 1387, which became the centre of a flourishing congregation of similar foundations upholding the ideals of the *Devotio moderna*. The Brethren were first established in Deventer and spread into both the southern Netherlands and neighbouring German regions.

The movement was developed by Gerard Groote (1340–84) and Florent Radewijns (1350–1400). Groote, a canon lawyer, lived as a Carthusian between 1374 and 1379, then left monastic life to preach moral reform throughout the diocese of Utrecht until his death of the plague. He particularly emphasized Apostolic poverty, the communal life and education; to him religion and learning were inseparable. At first he promoted communal living by groups of devout women, composing in 1379 a constitution for such a sisterhood, to whom he had given his own house in Deventer in 1374. The women were free to leave the community if they wished, but male communities were more formally constituted. Radewijns, vicar of the altar of St Paul in St Lebuinus, Deventer, and a close friend of Groote, gathered in his vicarage a group of men, admirers of Groote and his teachings. They formed the first free community of Brethren, living in 'the house of Florent', which was built in 1391. This, with the house built for the Zwolle community in the early 1390s, was the original house of the Brethren. In the 15th century numerous small communities were founded, with perhaps half a dozen Brethren in each, including Amersfoort (1395), Hulsbergen (1407), Brussels (1422), 's Hertogenbosch (1424), Gouda (1446), Nijmegen (1470), Utrecht (1475) and Berlicum (1482). In Germany the main houses included Munich (1401), Osnabrück (1410), Osterburg (1410), Cologne (1417), Herford (1426) and Hildesheim (1440).

Following the example of the primitive Church, the Brethren lived methodical and frugal lives, supported primarily by their own work (many were copyists). They were devout churchgoers, wore simple clothing and practised religious and spiritual exercises. Their twofold aim was to serve God and to induce others, by their example, to seek salvation. Their spiritual exercises emphasized meditation on sin, death, judgement and Hell as well as on the more comforting ideas of the Kingdom of Heaven and the blessings of God. The Brethren also maintained dormitories or hostels for poor pupils attending local schools, the first of which was the *Domus pauperum* at Deventer *c.* 1395–1403. In the 15th century some of these became schools, the first real one being that at 's Hertogenbosch, where Erasmus was educated between 1484 and 1487.

By the early 16th century the Brethren had begun to decline. Their lack of theological training meant that they did not become embroiled in the religious controversies of the period, but with the Reformation the small communities lost both their driving force and their desire for expansion. Both urban and ecclesiastical authorities discouraged such voluntary religious groups, and some houses either closed or became attached to collegiate houses. The Sisters had already more or less died out; from as early as 1400 groups of Sisters began to attach themselves to the Third Order of St Francis.

The ideas of the *Devotio moderna* movement are encapsulated in the writings of such men as Thomas à Kempis, whose *De imitatione Christi* (1418) was one of the most widely distributed books of the late Middle Ages. Emphasis was on the details of the Gospel concerning the life of Christ and the personal relationship between the individual and God. The Brethren were encouraged to perform spiritual exercises that were within the capacity of all, including meditation before a devotional image or after reading a text. Nicholas of Cusa (1401–64), a supporter of the Brethren, summed up in a sermon in 1451 what must have been the attitude of many of the Brethren towards art: 'All images are worthwhile; they are venerable insofar as they call to mind the saints and symbolize their lives.' Owing to the number of pupils in the Brethren's care, these ideas were pervasive and must have spread throughout the artistic community: the apparent crudeness and realistic exactness and the emphasis on expressiveness to

be found in much 15th-century northern Netherlandish art owes something to the ideas of the *Devotio moderna*. It is most clearly seen in the work of Dieric Bouts (i) and Geertgen tot Sint Jans, whose *St John the Baptist in the Wilderness* (Berlin, Gemäldegal.), for example, depicts the saint in solitary, agonized meditation.

The commissioning of lavish works of art and architecture was not, however, in the main tradition of the Brethren of the Common Life. Groote's pamphlet *Contra turrim traiectensem* (c. 1380), which opposed the building of the tower of Utrecht Cathedral, sums up their attitude. He objected both to the financial burden of such a project and to the fact that it was motivated by pride and vanity. The Augustinian houses of the Windesheim congregations were more lavish patrons of painting than the Brethren themselves. Both Geertgen tot Sint Jans and Dieric Bouts (i) painted works for the Haarlem house of Windesheim canons. Geertgen's *Lamentation* (Vienna, Ksthist. Mus.; see GEERTGEN TOT SINT JANS, fig. 1) is typical of *Devotio moderna* ideas relating to the importance of meditation on the Passion of Christ.

Despite their lack of interest in great art, the Brethren were foremost in promoting the transmission of texts. The circle that grew up around Florent Radewijns was one of copyists. Much of the output consisted of plain texts to be used for teaching and study, but fine editions could be produced to order. When printing became widespread in the last quarter of the 15th century, the brotherhoods in Brussels, Gouda and 's Hertogenbosch in the Netherlands and Marienthal and Rostock in Germany set up presses, particularly to produce pious works. Many block books produced in the Netherlands in this period, such as the *Ars moriendi* and *Canticum canticorum* (both 1466), were products of the spirit of the *Devotio moderna*. The *Ars moriendi*, with its advice on the best way to face the approach of death, is particularly typical.

BIBLIOGRAPHY

T. à Kempis: *De imitatione Christi* [1418]; ed. M. J. Pohl, *Opera omnia*, 7 vols (Freiburg, 1902–22)
M. J. Heimbucher: *Die Orden und Kongregationen der katholischen Kirche*, 2 vols (Paderborn, 1896–7, rev. 3/1933–4), pp. 424–8
A. Hyma: *The Christian Renaissance* (Hamden, CT, 1925, 2/1965)
E. F. Jacob: *Essays in the Conciliar Epoch* (Manchester, 1943, rev. 3/1963), pp. 121–53
T. Van Zijl: *Gerard Groote: Ascetic and Reformer, 1340–84* (Washington, DC, 1963)
R. R. Post: *The Modern Devotion*, Studies in Medieval and Reformation Thought, iii (Leiden, 1968)
A. Chatelet: *Early Dutch Painting in the Northern Netherlands in the Fifteenth Century* (New York, 1981)

VIRGINIA DAVIS

Breton, André (*b* Tinchebray, 19 Feb 1896; *d* Paris, 28 Sept 1966). French writer. While still an adolescent he came under the influence of Paul Valéry and Gustave Moreau, who for a long period were to influence his perception of beauty. From that time on, his poetic creation interrelated with his reflections on art, which like Gide's were conditioned by a moral code. He considered that it is not possible to write for a living, but only from interior necessity; in the same way, painting must always derive from an irrepressible need for self-expression. These criteria guided Breton both in his dealings with the Surrealist group (of which he was the uncontested leader) and in his articles on painting, collected in editions of *Le Surréalisme et la peinture* (first published in 1928).

Breton's family were of modest means. He was educated in the modern section of a lycée, without any Latin or Greek, and had embarked on a study of medicine when he was called up to serve in World War I. During this period he was drawn to poetry by his fascination with Arthur Rimbaud. His meeting with the aesthete Jacques Vaché temporarily dulled his interest in Rimbaud, and instead he turned to Guillaume Apollinaire, whose advice and friendship were a significant influence on him. Through Apollinaire he came into contact with Marie Laurencin, Derain, De Chirico and Picasso, and became friendly with the French poet and novelist Philippe Soupault. The review *Littérature* (1919–24), which he edited with Soupault and Louis Aragon, welcomed the newest talent. It then became a convert to Dada, contributing to the success of Duchamp, Picabia, Max Ernst, Arp and Man Ray. In an attempt to overcome the purely negative phase of Dada, Breton tried to organize a vast congress in Paris in 1921. Considering that Paul Valéry and Apollinaire had both in turn failed in their own missions, Breton wanted to define the constants of the modern spirit. The opposition of Tristan Tzara caused the initiative to fail. As a result Breton abandoned Dada, intending to concentrate on the writing of poetry.

By this time Breton's interest in SURREALISM had led him to investigate automatic writing and the importance accorded to the subconscious by Freud; he had already collaborated with Soupault on *Les Champs magnétiques* which appeared in *Littérature* in 1919. The dominance of Freud was seen in the *Manifeste du surréalisme—Poisson soluble*, which followed in 1924 and dealt with the psychic origins of the poetic image rather than with painting. However, the review *La Révolution surréaliste* (1924–9) opened the debate on this subject with an article by Max Morise, 'Les Yeux enchantés', which called for a plastic form for Surrealism, and which prompted a reply from Breton extending over several issues of *Le Surréalisme et la peinture* in *La Révolution surréaliste*. His first axiom in this was that 'The eye exists in a primitive stage'. The second, that a painting must open on to something else, beyond its appearance. Third, painting is a transcription of an 'interior model'. With these premises, he examined the activity of certain painters, including Picasso, De Chirico, Ernst, Man Ray, André Masson, Miró, Yves Tanguy and Arp, who were also represented in the first Surrealist group exhibition, *La Peinture surréaliste*, organized by Breton in 1925. He joined the French Communist Party in 1927.

In *Le Second Manifeste du surréalisme* (1929), Breton designated each creative individual to search for the 'state of mind in which life and death, reality and the imaginary, past and future, the communicable and incommunicable, the heights and depths, cease to be perceived as contradictory'. It condemned any deviation from this collectively adopted line of adhesion to historic materialism, while preserving the autonomy of art, and sharply criticized some early members of the movement for failing to maintain expected standards. Automatism was no longer the sole criterion of Surrealism. With *Nadja* (1928), he invented a new type of narrative, relating the strangest

encounters, the inexplicable coincidences of his life. As a guarantee of its authenticity, he provided photographic illustrations, thus inaugurating a new genre which he continued with *Les Vases communicants* (1932), *L'Amour fou* (1937) and *Arcane 17* (1945). Each work explores a particular aspect of the relationship between the conscious state and dreams, highlighting the objects and discoveries that create a capillary network connecting the two states.

Breton's aesthetic philosophy, developed along with his discoveries of Dalí, Victor Brauner, Oscar Domínguez and Roberto Matta, rested on several intangible convictions. Aesthetic feeling is manifested by 'a puff of wind on the temples'. It is linked to eroticism. 'First one must love', he said. 'There will always be time afterwards to analyse the reasons.' He proclaimed that 'convulsive beauty' was suspended in this movement, the role of the spectator being to disguise and to reveal it in turn. His interest in art and cult objects from the Pacific Islands and America helped him develop a practised eye, to recognize their considerable artistic worth, and in turn to contribute to their re-evaluation in the context of the Western world. In the same way he became enthusiastic about the work of self-taught artists and that of the mentally ill, whom he considered paradoxically as a reservoir of mental health, providing a key to freedom.

Breton left Europe in 1941, travelling first to the West Indies and then to the USA; he lived in New York and shared his Surrealist principles with David Hare, Gorky, Enrico Donati, Wifredo Lam, and the British painter Gordon Onslow-Ford (*b* 1912). He returned to Paris in 1946 and occupied himself for a long period on the completion of *L'Art magique* (1957, with Gérard Legrand), in which he discussed his long-held view of art as the vehicle of magic in archaic societies, and the crisis of magic transmitted in a more or less occult fashion by Leonardo Bosch, Dürer and Grünewald, up to the visionary world of Goya, Fuseli, Blake, Charles Méryon and Victor Hugo, to culminate in the works of Moreau and Gauguin; and finally the rediscovery of magic in Surrealism. In 1959, Breton's 22 parallel prose pieces, *Constellations*, were published with gouaches by Miró. The last edition of *Le Surréalisme et la peinture* appeared in 1965, and contained all his ideas on the artists participating in the Surrealist spirit, such as the French painters Pierre Molinier (1900–76), Jacques Herold (*b* 1910) and Toyen, and the Swedish painter Max Walter Svanberg.

WRITINGS

with P. Soupault: *Les Champs magnétiques* (Paris, 1919; Eng. trans., London, 1985)
Manifeste du surréalisme—Poisson soluble (Paris, 1924)
Nadja (Paris, 1928, 2/1964; Eng. trans., New York, 1960)
Le Surréalisme et la peinture (Paris, 1928, rev. 3/1965; Eng. trans., London and New York, 1972)
'Le Second Manifeste du surréalisme', *La Révolution surréaliste*, 12 (1929), pp. 1–17; repr. as book (Paris, 1930)
Les Vases communicants (Paris, 1932)
L'Amour fou (Paris, 1937; Eng. trans., Lincoln, NE, and London, 1987)
Arcane 17 (New York, 1945)
with G. Legrand: *L'Art magique* (Paris, 1957/R 1991)
Constellations (New York, 1959)
J.-M. Goutier, ed.: *Je vois, j'imagine* (Paris, 1991)

BIBLIOGRAPHY
M. Bonnet: *André Breton: Naissance de l'aventure surréaliste* (Paris, 1975)
J. Pierre: *André Breton et la peinture* (Lausanne, 1987)

André Breton: La Beauté convulsive (exh. cat., ed. A. Angliviel de la Beaumelle, I. Monod-Fontaine and C. Schweisguth; Paris, Pompidou, 1991)

H. Béhar: *André Breton, le grand indésirable* (Paris, 1990)

HENRI BÉHAR

Breton, Jules (*b* Courrières, Pas-de-Calais, 1 May 1827; *d* Paris, 5 July 1906). French painter and writer. After the death of his mother he was brought up in the village of Courrières by his father, grandmother and uncle. The last instilled in him respect for tradition and a commitment to the philosophical ideas of the 18th century. Breton's father, as supervisor of the lands of the Duc de Duras, encouraged him to develop a deep knowledge of and affection for his native region and its heritage, which remained central to his art.

Breton received his earliest drawing lessons at the College St Bertin (nr St Omer). In 1842 he met Félix de Vigne (1806–62), and from 1843 he studied with him and Hendrik Van der Haert (1790–1846) at the Academy of Fine Arts in Ghent. Breton's training was academic though he was aware of traditions of genre painting. During the spring of 1846 he worked at the Antwerp Art Academy under Baron Gustaf Wappers but spent most of his time at the museum studying the Flemish masters, including Hans Memling, Jan van Eyck and Rubens.

Breton went to Paris in 1847 to complete his education in the atelier of Michel-Martin Drolling, and he became friendly with the Realist painters François Bonvin and Gustave Brion. His painting (1849; priv. col., see 1980 exh. cat., p. 158) of the studio he shared with Ernest Delalleau (1826–64) illustrates his early Realist style.

During the Revolution of 1848 Breton sided with the liberals. *Misery and Despair* (1848; exh. Salon 1849; destr.) and *The Hunger* (1850; exh. Salon 1850–51; destr.) mirrored his preoccupation with social causes and his own intense struggle to make ends meet. The successful exhibition of *The Hunger* in Brussels and Ghent encouraged Breton to move to Belgium, where Félix de Vigne's daughter, Elodie, became his model and in 1858 his wife.

In 1852 Breton returned to France and made trips to the outskirts of Paris, garnering ideas for new canvases. The *Return of the Reapers* (exh. Salon 1853; priv. col.) is the first in a series of rural peasant scenes that Breton based on an awareness of contemporary themes and of similar subjects painted by Léopold Robert. Breton's interest in peasant imagery continued and in 1854 he settled in Courrières, where he began *The Gleaners* (Dublin, N.G.), a work inspired by seasonal field labour. The third-class medal it received at the Salon drew Breton to the attention of other artists including Jean-François Millet, and his career developed rapidly during the Second Empire. The *Blessing of the Wheat, Artois* (1857; Arras, Mus. B.-A.) was awarded a medal at the Salon of 1857 and due to the fervent support of Count Emilien de Nieuwerkerke his work was bought by the State.

Other major paintings of the 1850s present a serene view of field work; for example, the *Recall of the Gleaners* (1859; Paris, Mus. d'Orsay; see fig.) and *Dedication of a Calvary* (Lille, Mus. B.-A.), both shown at the Salon of 1859. In these canvases Breton's realistic themes were modified by an idealized treatment of physiognomy and anatomy that recalls works of the Italian High Renaissance, most notably those by Raphael. In 1861 Breton received the Légion d'honneur for works such as *The Colza* (1860; Washington, DC, Corcoran Gal. A.).

Breton travelled in 1862 and 1863 to the south of France where he did studies for the *Grape Harvest* (exh. Salon 1864; Omaha, NE, Joslyn A. Mus.), which marks the apex of his more classical style. By 1867 Breton's fame was further assured when he exhibited ten paintings at the

Jules Breton: *Recall of the Gleaners*, oil on canvas, 0.90×1.76 mm, 1859 (Paris, Musée d'Orsay)

Exposition Universelle in Paris and was awarded a first-place medal. His interest in provincial life, especially views and religious rites of Brittany (e.g. a *Great Breton Pilgrimage*, 1867; Havana, Mus. N. B. A.), continued throughout the 1870s and guaranteed his importance during the Third Republic.

In such later paintings as *St John* (1875; Norfolk, VA, Chrysler Mus.) Breton modified his Realist inclinations to create images with a pronounced Symbolist inflection. This shift is most notable in late poetic canvases such as the extremely popular *Song of the Lark* (1884; Chicago, IL, A. Inst.), where a solitary field worker is contrasted against a dimming light to create a highly subjective mood. Such paintings became increasingly sought after by American collectors, such as W. P. Wilstach, in the last years of the 19th century. Popular demand often led Breton to repeat motifs and to produce canvases that are feeble reflections of his more thoughtful works. The wide availability of his work through engravings enhanced his real talent and made him one of the best-known artists of the period.

Breton was also a productive writer. In 1875 he published a volume of poems, *Les Champs et la mer*, with considerable success, followed in 1880 by the long poem *Jeanne*. Such works as *La Vie d'un artiste: Art et nature* (1890), *Un Peintre paysan* (1896) and *Nos peintres du siècle* (1899) added to Breton's esteem in artistic, literary and official circles. He was appointed to the Institut de France in 1886. Breton's brother Emile (1831–1902) and daughter Virginie (1859–1935) were also painters.

WRITINGS

La Vie d'un artiste: Art et nature (Paris, 1890)
Un Peintre paysan (Paris, 1896)
Nos peintres du siècle (Paris, 1899)
La Peinture (Paris, 1904)

BIBLIOGRAPHY

M. Vachon: *Jules Breton* (Paris, 1899)
M. Fiddell Beaufort: '*Fire in a Haystack* by Jules Breton', *Bull. Detroit Inst. A.*, lvii/2 (1979), pp. 55–63
The Realist Tradition: French Painting and Drawing, 1830–1900 (exh. cat., ed. G. P. Weisberg; Cleveland, OH, Mus. A., 1980)
G. P. Weisberg and A. Bourrut Lacouture: 'Jules Breton's *The Grape Harvest at Château-Lagrange*', *A. Mag.*, lv (Jan 1981), pp. 98–103
Jules Breton and the French Rural Tradition (exh. cat., ed. H. Sturges; Omaha, NE, Joslyn A. Mus., 1982)
A. Bourrut Lacouture: '*Les Communiantes* (1884) de Jules Breton et le thème de la procession: Genèse d'une oeuvre d'après des documents inédits', *Bull. Soc. Hist. A. Fr.* (1985), pp. 175–200
A. Bourrut Lacouture and G. P. Weisberg: 'Delphine Bernard au Louvre en 1847 ou la rencontre du sacré et du profane dans l'oeuvre de Jules Breton (1827–1906)', *Gaz. B.-A.*, cviii (1986), pp. 31–7
A. Bourrut Lacouture: 'Jules Breton. *Une Source au bord de la mer*', *Arts de l'Ouest*, ed. D. Delouche, ii (Rennes, 1987), pp. 105–27

ANNETTE BOURRUT LACOUTURE,
GABRIEL P. WEISBERG

Breton, Luc-François (*b* Besançon, 6 Oct 1731; *d* Besançon, 23 Feb 1800). French sculptor. He was first apprenticed to a joiner and then (1743–9) to a woodcarver, Julien Chambert (*c.* 1690–before 1772). After working with Claude-François Attiret, Breton travelled in 1754 to Italy. In 1758 he won the first prize for sculpture at the Accademia di S Luca in Rome, with a bas-relief of *Metullus Saving the Image of Pallas* (terracotta; Rome,

Accad. N. S Luca). This helped him to obtain the commission for a bas-relief commemorating *General James Wolfe of Quebec*; of this work only Wolfe's head survives (terracotta; Besançon, Mus. B.-A. & Archéol.). In 1762 Breton was allocated a room at the Académie de France, thanks to Charles-Joseph Natoire's patronage. To this period belong his copies, made for purposes of study, of Gianlorenzo Bernini's *Blessed Ludovica Albertoni* and of the *Apotheosis of St Louis Gonzaga* after Pierre Legros (ii); he also translated into bas-relief Poussin's *Testament of Eudamidas* (all terracotta; Besançon, Mus. B.-A. & Archéol.).

After a journey to Naples with his friend Johann Melchior Wyrsch, Breton returned to Besançon in 1765, passing through Florence and Genoa, where he copied Puget's statue of *St Sebastian* in S Maria di Carignano. In 1769 a commission for two white marble angels for the altar of St Maurice, Besançon (now Besançon, Cathedral), led to a second visit to Rome. In 1772 Breton founded with Wyrsch the Ecole Gratuite de Peinture et Sculpture, in imitation of the academies of Lyon and Dijon. Breton combined teaching with the execution of numerous portrait busts, such as that of *Wyrsch*, portrayed without a wig, in the antique style of an Etruscan bust (terracotta; Besançon, Mus. B.-A. & Archéol.); of *Louis de Bauffremont* (marble; Paris, Louvre); of *Charles Roger de Bauffremont* (terracotta; Toledo, OH, Mus. A.); and of *Marguerite de Jouffroy d'Uzelles* (terracotta; Besançon, Mus. B.-A. & Archéol.). All these show Breton's talent for expressing in portraiture the sitter's character, whether graceful or majestic.

Breton was much in demand by the local nobility for improving their houses. In particular he executed the Fontaine des Dames behind the Hôtel de l'Intendance, Besançon, placing in it a bronze mermaid by Claude Lulier (*fl* 1545–78). The only funerary monument Breton ever made, commemorating *Charles-Ferdinand de la Baume, Marquis de Montrevel* in the church at Pesmes, was destroyed during the French Revolution; there survive only three studies in terracotta, representing a half-open tomb surmounted by a pyramid and the allegorical figures of *History* and *Time* (Besançon, Mus. B.-A. & Archéol.). This elegant composition, monumental without being ponderous, demonstrates that Breton was capable of holding his own with the sculptors of his time. His *Gypsy Girl* (marble; Scay-sur-Saône, Château) shows his skill in producing pastiche of the antique sculpture that he admired. The Musée des Beaux-Arts et d'Archéologie, Besançon, owns the most important collection of his works.

BIBLIOGRAPHY

Lami; Thieme–Becker
M.-L. Cornillot: *Luc Breton* (diss., Besançon, U. Franche-Comté, 1940)

CATHERINE LEGRAND

Bretonvilliers, Claud Le Ragois de (*b* 1582; *d* Paris, 1645). French patron. As a financier, he made a huge fortune as a collector of royal taxes from farms and was subsequently appointed Secrétaire de l'Etat. In 1637 he commissioned Jean Androuet du Cerceau to build him a luxurious *hôtel particulier* in Paris on the tip of the Ile Notre-Dame, part of the Ile St-Louis. Du Cerceau completed only the left wing of the court; by a second contract in 1638 the house was completed in 1643 by an unnamed architect—probably Louis Le Vau. The Hôtel Bretonvilliers enjoyed the finest situation in Paris by virtue of the view it commanded of the river. After the death of Bretonvilliers extensions and improvements to it were undertaken by his widow and subsequently by his son Bénigne de Bretonvilliers (d 1700). It was demolished in 1874–5 when the Pont Sully was built; its appearance is recorded in engravings by Caspar Merian (1660), Israël Silvestre and Jean Marot. The interior of the house was as magnificent as the exterior, with sumptuous furnishings and excellent paintings. On the first floor Sébastien Bourdon, inspired by Charles Le Brun's decoration in the nearby Hôtel Lambert, created in 1663 one of the most admired decorative ensembles of the 17th century. It consisted of nine paintings, depicting in the vault the *Legend of Phaëthon*, and wall panels representing the *Seven Liberal Arts* and the *Seven Moral and Heroic Virtues*, painted by Bourdon's pupils Jean-Baptiste Monnoyer and Jacques Friquet (1638–1716) to their master's designs. Another room was decorated by Simon Vouet with a wooden ceiling (destr.) depicting the *Triumph of Venus* and over the chimney-piece a painting of *Saturn Vanquished by Love, Venus and Hope* (c. 1645–6; Bourges, Mus. Berry); this was engraved by Michel Dorigny in 1646. A *Deposition* (untraced) by Daniele da Volterra was acquired by the Regent, Philippe d'Orléans, in 1719, when the house was converted into the Bureau des Aydes (a tax office). Bretonvilliers also owned four paintings (untraced) by Poussin, and the family possessed a collection of manuscripts, which was later acquired by the Bibliothèque Royale, Paris.

BIBLIOGRAPHY

G. Brice: *Description de la ville de Paris et de tout ce qu'elle contient de plus remarquable*, ii (Paris, 1684, rev. 9/1752), pp. 336–40
A.-N. Dézallier d'Argenville: *Voyage pittoresque de Paris ou indication de tout ce qu'il y a de plus beau dans cette grande ville en peinture, sculpture et architecture* (Paris, 1749, rev. 1765), p. 229
L. Dussieux and others, eds: *Mémoires inédits . . . des membres de l'Académie Royale* (Paris, 1854), i, p. 95
E. Bonaffé: *Dictionnaire des amateurs français au 17ème siècle* (Paris, 1884), pp. 143–4
G. Tallemant des Réaux: *Historiettes*, vi (Paris, 1934), pp. 364–7
L. Hautecoeur: *Architecture Classique*, i (Paris, 1943), pp. 27, 181, 182
J. Wilhelm: 'La Galerie de l'Hôtel de Bretonvilliers', *Bull. Soc. Hist. A. Fr.* (1956), pp. 137–50
C. Tooth: 'The Early Private Houses of Louis Le Vau', *Burl. Mag.*, cix (1967), pp. 510–18
Vouet (exh. cat. by J. Thuillier, B. Brejon de Lavergnée and D. Lavalle, Paris, Grand Pal., 1990–91), pp. 344–7

PIERRE CHALEIX

Bretschneider, Andreas, III (b Dresden, 1578; d Leipzig, ?1640). German etcher and wood-engraver. He settled in Leipzig in 1611, acquired the freedom of the city in 1615 and was last documented there in 1631. His engravings are almost always signed with a monogram or in Latin. Although he called himself a painter on his engravings, no significant paintings are known. Chiefly, he produced book illustrations and series of ornamental engravings, almost exclusively for the Leipzig publisher Henning Gross (1553–1621).

In Bretschneider's work the transition from the severe forms of scrollwork (*Rollwerk*) to the soft lines of 'gnarled' Baroque ornamentation (*Knorpelstil*) can be traced, revealing the influence of Lucas Kilian. His graphic works show a sure mastery of technique and a fertile imagination in the invention of ornament. He became known through a book of embroidery patterns, *Neu Modelbuch, darinnen allerlei künstliche Visierung und Muster* (Leipzig, 1619/R Wasmuth, 1892), in which the patterns, reproduced in outline, show proliferating vine scroll decoration combined with flowers, animals and human figures. He executed ornamental designs for several books, including Augustinus de Ramellis de Masanzana's *Schatzkammer mechanischer Künste* (Leipzig, 1620). His *Neuws Compertament Buchlein* (Brunswick, 1621; complete copy, Berlin, Kstbib. & Mus.) contains designs for consoles, marginal ornamentation, cartouches etc, in which he used the 'open shell' (*Ohrmuschelstil*) variation of the *Knorpelstil*.

BIBLIOGRAPHY
Thieme–Becker
A. Lotz: 'Das Ornamentwerk des Radierers A. Bretschneider', *Graph. Kst*, n. s. 1, i (1936), pp. 20–71
R. Zöllner: *Deutsche Säulen—Zieraten—und Schildbücher, 1610–1680: Ein Beitrag zur Entwicklungsgeschichte des Knorpelstils* (diss., Kiel, Christian-Albrechts U., 1959)
G. Spiess: *Neuws Compertament Buchlein*, vi of *Städt. Museum Braunschweig. Miszellen* (Brunswick, 1971)

S. TRÄGER

Brett, John (b Bletchingley, Surrey, 8 Dec 1831; d London, 7 Jan 1902). English painter. His father was an army veterinary surgeon attached to the 12th Lancers; for the first 15 years of Brett's life, his family followed the regiment, and when his father was permanently stationed at Maidstone they settled in the nearby village of Detling. During these early years Brett showed an equal enthusiasm for astronomy and painting, but in 1851 he received some drawing lessons from J. D. Harding and noted in his diary, 'From this circumstance I may date the commencement of my real education in art'.

Harding introduced Brett to Richard Redgrave, who set him to draw casts in the British Museum, and in 1853 he became a student in the Royal Academy Schools. However, it is clear from Brett's diary that John Ruskin and the Pre-Raphaelites had a more profound effect on his art than did the instruction in the Schools. He read Ruskin's pamphlet on Pre-Raphaelitism in 1852 and thought it 'gloriously written and containing much earnest, sound, healthy truth'. Around this time he was introduced to the poet Coventry Patmore, whose house was a meeting-place for writers and artists. Here in 1853 Brett met Holman Hunt, an artist he admired and was determined to emulate.

Brett read Ruskin's works avidly. The fourth volume of *Modern Painters (Of Mountain Beauty)* was published in 1856 and inspired him to set off for Switzerland where he met J. W. Inchbold, who was also there to paint mountain scenery. Inchbold's methods caused Brett to refine his own technique. The result was the *Glacier of Rosenlaui* (1856, exh. RA 1857; London, Tate), a small, glittering picture of Alpine rocks which was much admired by Holman Hunt and Dante Gabriel Rossetti. Greatly encouraged, Brett at once started work on his masterpiece, *The Stonebreaker* (1857–8; Liverpool, Walker A.G.), which depicts a young labourer beside a pile of flint stones in a summer landscape. Brett's writings confirm that the picture is an allegory of time (see Pointon, 1978), while his preliminary sketches make it clear that the thorns, thistles and other foreground details have a biblical significance. When shown at the Royal Academy in 1858 the picture provoked extravagant praise from Ruskin: 'in some points of precision it goes beyond anything the Pre-Raphaelites have done yet'. Ruskin's review concluded by urging the artist to paint the chestnut groves of the Val d'Aosta. This prompted Brett to return to Switzerland in June 1858. The resulting work, *Val d'Aosta* (1858; priv. col., see 1984 exh. cat., p. 174), was a painstaking depiction of the Alpine valley, which inspired a lengthy tribute from Ruskin when exhibited in 1859 but was generally regarded as a failure by other critics. His next painting was *The Hedger* (1860; priv. col., see 1984 exh. cat., p. 183), which depicts a countryman at work in a Kentish wood in spring. The picture illustrates a poem by Patmore and was bought by the collector B. G. Windus for £300.

Brett spent the winter of 1861–2 in Florence, where he painted a highly finished watercolour of the Ponte Vecchio and a panoramic view of the city, *Florence from Bellosguardo* (1862–3; London, Tate). The latter was rejected by the Royal Academy Hanging Committee. Criticism of his work, together with a cooling in Ruskin's enthusiasm, may have been responsible for his decision to abandon landscape subjects for marine painting. In 1863 he sailed aboard the steamship *Scotia* from Dover to Naples and spent the winter in Capri. In 1865 he was sketching in the Isle of Wight, where he painted the finest of all his watercolours, *February in the Isle of Wight* (Birmingham, Mus. & A.G.; see fig.). Around 1870 he met Mary Ann Howcroft, who became his wife and bore him seven children. Henceforth he spent each summer with his family on the coast, filling sketchbooks with annotated drawings and painting small oil sketches. The rest of the year was spent in London working on his large seascapes for submission to the Royal Academy.

Brett's most successful pictures were panoramic views of the sea, such as the early *British Channel Seen from the Dorsetshire Cliffs* (1871; London, Tate) and the later *Britannia's Realm* (1880; London, Tate), which is a spectacular aerial view of calm sea and sailing boats on a summer's day. His beach scenes with meticulously rendered boulders and rock formations tend to be laboured and repetitive.

Brett designed two houses in London for his family. The first, at Keswick Road, Putney, was an open-plan building with central heating and electric burglar alarms. The second, Daisyfield (1887), on Putney Heath Lane, was dominated by a tower which contained a large telescope for Brett's astronomical observations. The cost of these houses, together with the purchase of the 210-ton schooner *Viking* in 1883 and a steady decline in his picture sales, brought financial worries to his later years. Apart from an obituary in *The Times*, his death passed almost unnoticed, although William Michael Rossetti pointed out that 'there is no one to succeed to the precise place which he occupied with distinction'.

Brett's elder sister Rosa (1829–81) was a talented landscape painter who exhibited nine works at the Royal Academy between 1858 and 1881, three of them under the pseudonym 'Rosarius'. Her pictures are small in scale but are lovingly detailed and often reveal an unusual intensity of vision.

John Brett: *February in the Isle of Wight*, watercolour, bodycolour and gum with scratching out on paper, 460×354 mm, 1866 (Birmingham, City of Birmingham Museum and Art Gallery)

BIBLIOGRAPHY

A. Staley: *The Pre-Raphaelite Landscape* (Oxford, 1973)
M. Pointon: 'Geology and Landscape Painting in 19th-century England', *Images of the Earth* (Chalfont St Giles, 1978)
D. Cordingly: *John Brett 1831–1902* (diss., Brighton, U. Sussex, 1983)
P. Nunn: 'Rosa Brett: Pre-Raphaelite', *Burl. Mag.*, cxxvi (1984), p. 630 [with a checklist of known works]
The Pre-Raphaelites (exh. cat., London, Tate, 1984)
P. Nunn: 'Case Histories: Rosa Brett', *Victorian Women Artists* (London, 1987), pp. 187–200

DAVID CORDINGLY

Brettingham. English family of architects. (1) Matthew Brettingham (i) is perhaps best known for his work on Holkham Hall, Norfolk, which he considered, according to his son (2) Matthew Brettingham (ii), 'the great work of his life'.

(1) Matthew Brettingham (i) (*b* Norwich, 1699; *d* Norwich, 19 Aug 1769). Originally a bricklayer, he established a large business as a building contractor in his native Norfolk. In 1734 he was employed by Thomas Coke, 1st Earl of Leicester, to supervise the construction of Holkham Hall in Norfolk. The evolution of this great Palladian house is a complex matter, but it was essentially the product of a 'committee of taste' that comprised Thomas Coke, 1st Earl of Leicester, Richard Boyle, 3rd Earl of Burlington, and WILLIAM KENT. Several drawings by Kent survive for the elevations, chimney-pieces, the Marble Hall and the Triumphal Arch, but they are of a sketchy nature, and the completed work differs from them in some respects. The supervision of the work on the ground was entirely due to Brettingham, who in 1761 published *The Plans and Elevations of the Late Earl of Leicester's House at Holkham*, describing himself as 'architect' on the plates. His friendship with his client Lord Leicester fostered his taste as a Palladian architect and introduced him to a circle of aristocratic clients who appreciated his dignified and restrained architecture. In 1748 he was commissioned to design Norfolk House (1748–52; destr. 1938) in St James's Square, London, for Edward Howard, 9th Duke of Norfolk. Brettingham was responsible for the undemonstrative brick elevation towards the square, with its long row of well-proportioned pedimented windows, and for the plan, which ingeniously adapted that of the 'Family Wing' at Holkham to suit the constricted site of a London house; the magnificent Rococo interior decoration, however, was by an Italian, Giovanni Battista Borra. On the strength of Norfolk House, Brettingham was commissioned to design other London houses, including 5 St James's Square (1748–9), York House (1761–3; destr. 1908), Pall Mall, for Edward Augustus, Duke of York, and Egremont House (1756), Piccadilly, for Charles Wyndham, 2nd Earl of Egremont. Brettingham also worked for Lord Egremont at Petworth, W. Sussex, in 1754–6, carrying out internal alterations and designing lodges for the park that recall the demolished lodges at Holkham. His many country houses include Gunton Hall (1742), Norfolk, for Sir William Harbord, Euston Hall (1750–56), Suffolk, for Charles Fitzroy, 2nd Duke of Grafton, and the original design for Kedleston Hall (1758), Derbys, for Nathaniel Curzon, 1st Baron Scarsdale, where, however, he was superseded by James Paine and Robert Adam.

BIBLIOGRAPHY
Colvin
'Matthew Brettingham, the Architect of Holkham', *E. Anglian*, ii (1864), pp. 131–4
D. E. Howell James: 'Matthew Brettingham and the County of Norfolk', *Norfolk Archaeol.*, xxxiii (1962–5), pp. 345–50
St James's (1963), xxxix of *Survey of London* (London, 1900–), pp. 100–02, 136, 192–202, 364–7
D. E. Howell James: 'Matthew Brettingham's Account Book', *Norfolk Archaeol.*, xxxv (1971), pp. 170–82

JOHN MARTIN ROBINSON

(2) Matthew Brettingham (ii) (*b* 1725; *d* Norwich, 18 March 1803). Architect and dealer, son of (1) Matthew Brettingham (i). In 1747 he travelled to Rome in order to study architecture, remaining there for seven years. Thomas Coke, 1st Earl of Leicester, contributed to his expenses and instructed him to buy works of art, principally antique statues and busts for Holkham Hall. Brettingham's Rome Account Book (Holkham Hall, Norfolk, MS. 744) lists purchases and includes details of restoration and porterage. He also purchased objects for himself and his father or for subsequent trading. Although younger than Gavin Hamilton and Thomas Jenkins, Brettingham seems to have begun dealing in works of art in Rome before either of them, and, having adequate funds, he became well known there as a dealer. Besides sculpture, paintings, books and sundry objects he bought plaster casts and ordered moulds for casting some 12 statues and 120 busts after the Antique. His first idea (based on the example of Filippo Farsetti) had been to establish an Academy of Design in England. This received no support, so he proposed selling sets of plaster casts for gentlemen's houses. His clients included some of his father's patrons—Thomas Coke, Nathaniel Curzon, Charles Wyndham and Charles Lennox, 3rd Duke of Richmond and Lennox—but the enterprise was not really successful. After 1760 his moulds seem to have passed to John Cheere, and Brettingham's statues formed a basic repertory for house or garden decoration during the Adam period. The few architectural works he designed, such as additions at Charlton House (1772–6), Wilts, for the 12th Earl of Suffolk, lack the incisive character of works by his Neoclassical contemporaries.

BIBLIOGRAPHY
Colvin
J. Kenworthy-Browne: 'Matthew Brettingham's Rome Account Book, 1747–1754', *Walpole Soc.*, xlix (1983), pp. 37–132
——: 'Designing round the Statues: M. Brettingham's Casts at Kedleston', *Apollo*, cxxxviii (April 1993), pp. 248–52

JOHN KENWORTHY-BROWNE

Breu. German family of painters, draughtsmen and illuminators.

(1) Jörg Breu (i) [the elder] (*b* Augsburg, *c.* 1475–80; *d* Augsburg, May–Oct 1537). Of the trio of great Augsburg painters active *c.* 1500, Breu, compared with Hans Holbein the elder and Hans Burgkmair I, was the most versatile: as well as altarpieces he produced history paintings, portraits and frescoes and made designs for wood-engravers and glass painters. He was also, perhaps because of his humble origins as the son of the weaver Georg Breu, the most traditional of the three—an evaluation shared by his contemporaries. His background is vividly described in his *Chronik des Augsburger Malers Jörg Breu d. Ä., 1512–37* (*Die Chroniken der deutschen Städte*, xxix, ed. F. Roth, Leipzig, 1906), a commentary on day-to-day events in which he expressed support for the Reformation and the poor in vehement and sometimes radical terms.

1. EARLY WORKS IN AUSTRIA, TO 1502. Breu was apprenticed to Ulrich Apt the elder (*fl c.* 1486–1532) in Augsburg from 1493. He painted three large altarpieces during his journeyman years in Lower Austria, before establishing himself as a master craftsman in Augsburg in 1502. The altarpieces are each, in different ways, masterpieces, which rank among the best of the times. The eight panels of the altarpiece for the Stiftskirche, Zwettl (1500; *in situ*), depict the *Life of St Bernard* with freshness, realism and attractive natural subject-matter. This is particularly true of *St Bernard at the Corn Harvest*, where the monks are shown harvesting a field of undulating corn, and *St Bernard Healing a Possessed Woman*, where the dramatic event takes place under massed clouds in a realistically observed landscape of sea, mountains and rocks. Here, as in his later, realistic depictions of children and herds of animals, Breu made a significant contribution to the art of the DANUBE SCHOOL.

Breu's next commission was for 12 panels of an altarpiece of the *Passion* for the Carthusian monastery at Aggsbach (1501; two: untraced; two: Nuremberg, Ger. Nmus.; eight: Herzogenburg, Kstausstell. Stift). This altarpiece too derives its force from realistic representation,

Jörg Breu (i): *Crowning with Thorns*, oil on panel, 1.54×0.95 m, 1502 (Melk Abbey, SS Peter und Paul)

though the landscape backgrounds are mostly less dominant. In the vigorous scenes Breu's stylized figures and precisely characterized faces mark a departure from Late Gothic style. The influence of Jan Polack is perceptible in some of the panels, while certain figures are taken from engravings by Martin Schongauer and Albrecht Dürer. Nonetheless each composition is clear and fully thought out, and the figures give an impression of statuesque calm, even those making extreme gestures, as in the *Crowning with Thorns* and *Flagellation*.

Breu's use of external models, often also evident in later works, is pronounced in the altarpiece for the high altar of the abbey church at Melk (1502; *in situ*). In its 16 large vertical panels, some of which seem to have been completed by assistants, the borrowed elements are notably from Dürer. They reveal new compositional features that progress beyond Late Gothic style: the space and the figures are more clearly differentiated, the groups are more dynamically interrelated, as in the impressive *Crowning with Thorns* (see fig.), which shows five strongly posed tormentors arranged as if rotating around Christ. A magnificent related drawing (Munich, Staatl. Graph. Samml.) reveals Breu's careful preparatory work, based on intensive study, and his talented draughtsmanship. Other drawings can be connected with these altarpieces, but no independent drawings survive.

2. AUGSBURG, 1502 AND AFTER. Breu was established as a master in Augsburg by October 1502, when his brother Klaus Breu became an apprentice. Jörg's style relinquished its earlier expressiveness in favour of the prevailing influence of Burgkmair and Holbein. He painted the Canon leaf of the Frisingen Missal and designed two woodcuts for the Konstanz Missal (1504; cut by Erhard Ratdolt (1447–1528), with whom Breu collaborated again). Two panels, an *Adoration of the Magi* and an *Annunciation* (both 1509; Bavaria, priv. col.), survive from an altarpiece, while documented fresco commissions for the Augsburg churches of St Moritz (1505) and the Heilige Kreuz (1509) have been destroyed.

The years after 1510 were rich in works and prestigious commissions. Breu made several unadorned, natural versions of the *Virgin and Child*, showing Christ as ungainly as any ordinary baby (e.g. Aufhausen, after a Dürer drawing of 1509: 1512; Basle, Kstmus.; 1512, ex-Kaiser-Friedrich-Mus., Berlin, destr.; 1521, ex-Kaufmann priv. col.; 1523, Vienna, Ksthist. Mus.). A drawing of a *Young Woman* (1519; Berlin, Kupferstichkab.), halfway between a sketch from life and a study for the Virgin, illustrates the connection with a contemporary ideal of female beauty. The destroyed version of 1512 formed the highpoint of these images in its synthesis of realistic, lyrical landscape with a popular devotional image and theological meaning. The figure of God the Father giving his blessing, in the sky above the landscape, which recurs in the *Departure of the Apostles* (1514; Augsburg, Schaezlerpal. L; drawing, Berlin, Kupferstichkab.) and in other pictures (including profane subjects), seems to have been a personal iconographic feature.

Breu's largest commissions came from the Augsburg authorities and from the Fugger family. In 1516, with Apt and others, he decorated the Augsburg Rathaus with frescoes (destr.). The organ wings (*in situ*) in the Fugger Chapel (built 1512–21) of St Anna, Augsburg, were produced around the same time. The enormous wings (*c.* 6×3 m), showing the *Ascension* (left) and the *Assumption of the Virgin* (right), may have been painted before the small wings, which show four allegories on the *Invention of Music*. The large wings are in many details so reminiscent of Italian models—a Botticelli engraving and the fresco by Filippino Lippi in the Carafa Chapel of S Maria sopra Minerva in Rome—that a journey to Italy before their execution must probably be assumed. The over life-size Apostles in the foreground and, to the left, a group of contemporary portraits (including members of the Fugger family and perhaps a self-portrait) are set in a wide, bright landscape. The violent gestures, turbulent folds of clothing and strong colours are Mannerist features that predominated in Breu's work at that time. There are two copies of drawings for the *Invention of Music I* (1517, Florence, Uffizi; 1522, Berlin, Kupferstichkab.), while one authentic, undated preparatory drawing survives (Augsburg, Schaezlerpal.).

Breu contributed to the marginal drawings in the *Prayerbook of Maximilian I* (1513; Munich, Bayer. Staatsbib.). He also made drawings and designs for various stained-glass windows: *c.* 1515 he produced 14 sketches (Munich, Staatl. Graph. Samml.) towards a probable 20 panels of hunting and battle scenes with Maximilian I, painted by Hans Knoder in 1516. In the early 1520s he produced 12 drawings and designs (some survive through copies, Basle, Kstmus.; Berlin, Altes Mus.; Göttingen, Kstsamml. U.) for windows of the *Months*, for the

Hoechstetter family; only one of the original windows survives (Augsburg, Maximilianmus.), but the many copies and adaptations testify to the popularity of these designs. He also depicted six *Trades* (ex-Dresden, Hist. Mus.) and the *Story of Joseph* (Munich, Bayer. Nmus.), which again reveal his ability to depict everyday places, characters and situations precisely and realistically. Though Breu sided with the Reformation and wrote some anticlerical pamphlets, he also designed woodcuts devoted to the personality and policies of Charles V, including the ten-sheet series on his entry into Augsburg in 1530 and the tremendous sheet of the *Battle of Pavia*. Breu's sympathy for iconoclasm had not prevented him from producing altar paintings in the 1520s, but his final religious works are in the Protestant church of St Anna, Augsburg: a *Resurrection* and *Christ in Purgatory* (the 'Meiting Epitaph'; early 1530s) with glassy colours and rigid Mannerist figures.

The most important commissions Breu received towards the end of his life were from Anton Fugger and Duke William IV of Bavaria. The former commissioned Breu to paint the Hinterhaus or rear of the Fuggerhaus at Maximilianstrasse 36–8, Augsburg (1532–6; fresco fragments in the courtyard arcade). For William IV Breu painted the *Story of Lucretia* (1528; drawing, Budapest, N.G.) for a history cycle and the *Battle of Zama* for a battle cycle (1529; both Munich, Alte Pin.). These represent opposite extremes: the first reflects the architecture and artistic outlook of the Italian Renaissance; the second is set in a typically unrestrained northern naturalistic landscape.

No authenticated portrait paintings are known, although Breu's drawn *Self-portrait* (Szczecin, N. Mus.) survives. Buchner and Löcher have made other attributions, which merit fuller investigation. These include the early double portrait tentatively identified as *Coloman Helmschid and Agnes Breu* (the latter being Breu's sister; Madrid, Mus. Thyssen-Bornemisza), the *Portrait of a Husband and Wife* (1521; Innsbruck, Tirol. Landesmus.) and the *Portrait of a Young Man* (Hannover, Kestner-Ges.).

BIBLIOGRAPHY
Thieme-Becker
E. Buchner: 'Der ältere Breu als Maler', *Beitr. Gesch. Dt. Kst*, ii (1928), pp. 388–9
W. Wegner: 'Die Scheibenrisse für die Familie Hoechstetter von Jörg Breu', *Z. Kstgesch.* (1959), pp. 17–18
K. Löcher: 'Altdeutsche Bildnisse im Tiroler Landesmuseum Ferdinandeum in Innsbruck', *Alt. & Mod. Kst*, lxxxiv (1966), pp. 15–16
C. Menz: *Das Frühwerk Jörg Breu des Älteren* (Augsburg, 1982)

(2) Jörg Breu (ii) [the younger] (*b* Augsburg, *c*. 1510; *d* Augsburg, 1547). Son of (1) Jörg Breu (i). He was a pupil and assistant of his father, from whom he assumed the mastership and workshop sign in 1534. An earlier visit to Venice can be assumed on stylistic grounds. Few of Jörg the younger's paintings survive. The attribution of the *Capture of Rhodes by Artemisia* (1535; Munich, Alte Pin.), part of a battle cycle for William IV to which his father contributed, is uncertain. The four large panels of the *Seasons* (Berlin, Dt. Hist. Mus.) after his father's Hoechstetter designs were probably produced by the workshop. Jörg (ii) decorated a fireplace with frescoes in the house at Annastrasse 2, Augsburg (destr. World War II; see Hämmerle), and provided frescoes in Schloss Grünau near Neuburg an der Donau (1536–7; *in situ*) for

the Count Palatine. According to an inscription, he restored the ceiling (Munich, Bayer. Nmus.) originally painted by Peter Kaltenhofer (*d* 1490) in 1457 in the Weberhaus (Weaver's Hall) in Augsburg. No drawings by Breu for stained-glass panels survive, although he designed those depicting the *Story of Jason* (Munich, Bayer. Nmus.), the *Sacrifice of Isaac* and *Three Men in the Fiery Furnace* (both Neuburg, Schlossmus.). He made many designs for woodcuts (e.g. the *Rich Man and the Poor Lazarus*, 1545, comprising two blocks, 678×990 mm; see Hollstein: *Ger.*, pp. 398–9) to illustrate books and for single sheets, which include some of the best German examples of the 16th century (see Röttinger). His qualities as a draughtsman can be seen from the presentation sheet *Horseman Attacking a Fallen Warrior* (1543; New York, Pierpont Morgan Lib.; see fig.).

Breu and his workshop achieved their greatest successes illustrating high-quality manuscripts. The *Fechtbuch* ('Book of fencing', 1543; Dresden, Zent. Kstbib.), written for the Augsburg beadle Hector Mair, was followed by the *Ehrenbuch des herwartischen Geschlechts* (1545; Augsburg Stadtarchv), the *Ehrenbuch der Stadt Augsburg* (1545; Munich, Bayer. Nmus.) and the *Ehrenbuch des zünftigen Regimentes der Stadt Augsburg* (1545; Augsburg, Staats- & Stadtbib.). Breu also worked for the Fugger family (*Ehrenbuch des Fuggerschen Geschlechts*; Babenhausen, Fugger-Mus.) and for the Habsburgs (Vienna, Albertina; Vienna Staatsarchv). The magnificent illustrated manuscripts given by Jacob Herbrot of Augsburg to Henry VIII of England (*c*. 1540–41; Eton, Berks, Coll. Lib.) include a wealth

Jörg Breu (ii): *Horseman Attacking a Fallen Warrior*, pen and brush and black ink, heightened with white, on grey prepared paper, 222×171 mm, 1543 (New York, Pierpont Morgan Library)

of allegorical, historical and genre scenes in settings of pure Renaissance architecture, with clearly defined spaces, sumptuously executed with gold and silver illumination.

BIBLIOGRAPHY

Hollstein: *Ger.*; Thieme–Becker
H. Röttinger: 'Das Holzschnittwerk Jörg Breu des Jüngeren', *Graph. Kst*, i (1909) [supplement]
C. Dodgson: 'Ein Miniaturwerk Jörg Breus d. J.', *Münchn. Jb. Bild. Kst*, ii (1934–5), pp. 191–210
A. Hämmerle: 'Ein Augsburger Kaminfresko des jüngeren Jörg Breu', *Vjhft. Kst & Gesch. Augsburgs*, i (1936), p. 195ff
Zeichnung in Deutschland: Deutsche Zeichner, 1540–1640, 2 vols (exh. cat. by H. Geissler, Stuttgart, Staatsgal., 1979–80), i, pp. 10–11
Welt im Umbruch: Augsburg zwischen Renaissance und Barock, 2 vols (exh. cat., ed. B. Bushart; Augsburg, Städt. Kstsamml., 1980)
Drawings from the Holy Roman Empire, 1540–1680 (exh. cat. by T. DaCosta Kaufmann; Princeton U., A. Mus.; Washington, DC, N.G.A.; and Pittsburgh, Carnegie Inst., Mus. A.; 1982–3), pp. 38–9

GODE KRÄMER

Breuer, Marcel (Lajos) (*b* Pécs, 21 May 1902; *d* New York, 1 July 1981). American furniture designer and architect of Hungarian birth. In 1920 he took up a scholarship at the Akademie der Bildenden Künste, Vienna, but he left almost immediately to find a job in an architect's office. A few weeks later he enrolled at the Bauhaus at Weimar on the recommendation of the Hungarian architect Fred Forbat (1897–1972). Breuer soon became an outstanding student in the carpentry workshop, which he led in its endeavours to find radically innovative forms for modern furniture. In practice, this meant rejecting traditional forms, which were considered symbolic of bourgeois life. The results of these experiments were initially as idiosyncratic as those of other workshops at Weimar, including the adoption of non-Western forms, for example the African chair (1921; see Rowland, 1990, p. 66) and an aggressively castellated style inspired by Constructivism.

Breuer was impressed by De Stijl, whose founder Theo van Doesburg made his presence felt in Weimar in 1921–2. Breuer interpreted the De Stijl aesthetic in his designs, which were characterized by asymmetry, discrete elements and a tendency to view the design of a chair, for example, as an architectural experiment. Gerrit Rietveld's Red–Blue chair (1917; New York, MOMA) taught Breuer to distinguish between the frame of a chair and the supports for the sitter. Encouraged by Walter Gropius to think in terms of standardization, he used elements of the same width to facilitate manufacture. From 1923 he also turned to less expensive woods such as plywood, particularly in his children's furniture. After a brief period working as an architect in Paris (1924), Breuer rejoined the Bauhaus in Dessau as leader of the carpentry workshop. By 1925 he insisted on the complete rejection of formalism: if an object was designed in such a way that it fulfilled its function clearly, it was finished. Suitability for a particular function was not, however, enough in itself; there was also the quality factor. Ornamentation was not necessary to form a coherent set of furniture: a good chair would go with a good table.

In spring 1925 Breuer began to experiment with tubular steel, beginning with his Wassily chair (*see* GERMANY, fig. 51), which was allegedly inspired by the lightness and strength of his new Adler bicycle. Next he developed a

side chair with sled-like runners instead of legs. The following crucial stage was the cantilevered side chair, first developed by Mart Stam, although Breuer claimed that he had conceived the idea on turning one of his nesting stools on its side and subsequently confided it to Stam. Breuer's best-known side chair is the B32 (1928; New York, MOMA; see fig.) in chrome-plated steel, wood and cane, which is still mass-produced. He also produced tables, for example in steel tube and wood (*see* TABLE, fig. 2). Breuer negotiated privately to secure marketing by Standard-Möbel, which in April 1929 was bought up by the manufacturer Thonet. These chairs and the glass-topped tables that accompanied them were intended to be light, transparent and non-specific in function. Thus, for example, his small stacking stools could also be used as occasional tables. He also developed a range of modular furniture (cabinets, desktops, shelving) that could be assembled according to need (examples in New York, MOMA). The interiors that he designed in conjunction with Gropius's architectural office, such as the theatre director and producer Erwin Piscator's flat, have a beauty that Breuer liked to consider impersonal, arising not from ornament but from what he called the tools of living themselves and from the contrast of textures and surfaces.

Breuer was too much of an individualist to remain at the Bauhaus under Hannes Meyer; from 1928 to 1931 he worked for Gropius's office in Berlin and became increasingly involved in architectural projects. These were initially informed by an enthusiastically American style: his multi-level traffic scheme for the Potsdamer Platz of 1928, for example, was based on the flow diagrams of an American

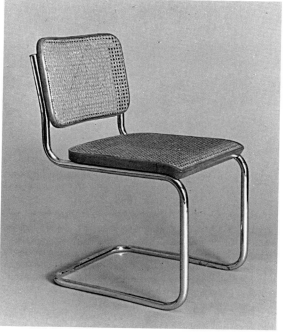

Marcel Breuer: B32 side chair, chrome-plated tubular steel, wood and cane, 800×445×476 mm, 1928 (New York, Museum of Modern Art)

assembly line. A constructivist phase followed, for example the Khar'kov Theatre project (1931). Finally he arrived at a Corbusian purism, exemplified in the Harnismacher house (1932), Wiesbaden, a piece of humanly made perfection in white stucco set against the natural landscape. From 1932 to 1935 Breuer led a nomadic existence, travelling around the Mediterranean and in North Africa and admiring what he saw as the impersonality and rationality of the vernacular architecture. In 1933 he won the International Aluminium Competition in Paris for aluminium furniture by exploiting the material's lightness and flexibility. In October 1935 he followed Gropius to England and on his suggestion designed a plywood version of his aluminium lounge chair for Jack Pritchard's Isokon Company. The Isokon long chair (1935; New York, MOMA), an early example of biomorphic design, was followed by plywood nesting tables and stacking chairs. With his partner and architect Francis Reginald Stevens Yorke (1906–62) he designed a pavilion for the Royal Show at Bristol in 1936, using stone and wood in the slab and panel forms favoured by the modern movement. The ambitious design for a Civic Centre of the Future for the British Cement Industries (1936) contains elements of all their favourite projects such as Y-shaped blocks of flats, which Breuer was later to implement.

In 1937 Breuer joined Gropius as a professor at Harvard University, Cambridge, MA, and together they created the Harvard school of third generation Modernists. Ironically, when Breuer finally arrived in the USA he was impressed not by large-scale American industry but by New England vernacular architecture. In their domestic architecture he and Gropius, who were partners (1937–41), successfully assimilated its use of wood and mortared rubble to the demands of the new architecture, and they delighted in the contrast between rough stonework and smooth white surfaces. In 1946 he formed his own partnership in New York. Although he experimented with wooden prefabricated housing and with the idea of the H-shaped house, he largely worked on ambitious projects for substantial industrial concerns and institutions in North and South America. In Europe he also designed resort buildings and housing, although his best-known building there is the Y-shaped UNESCO headquarters (1953–8) in Paris.

In 1963–6 he designed the Whitney Museum of American Art, New York, a massive, granite-faced building on Madison Avenue, designed to stand out from the surrounding office buildings. The façade is punctuated by obliquely angled windows, intended to prevent direct sunlight reaching the works of art housed inside. Breuer maintained his interest in textural contrast and his fondness for Corbusian pilotis; however, after World War II he suffered a loss of direction, and his work was at times overblown and unconvincing. His religious buildings, such as the St Francis de Sales church (1961–7), Muskegon, MI, are often strenuously modern, relying on feats of engineering to create excitement. His designs for private houses, and in particular his interiors, were generally much more successful. His great achievement lay in devising furnishings, appropriate for the modern interior, which retained their refreshingly clear and modern appearance over time. Among the most renowned of Breuer's pupils are I. M. Pei, Philip Johnson and Paul Rudolph.

WRITINGS

'Form Funktion', *Junge Menschen*, v/8 (1924) [issue devoted to the Bauhaus]
Architektur, Möbel, Design (Berlin, 1975)

BIBLIOGRAPHY

P. Blake: *Marcel Breuer: Architect and Designer* (New York, 1949)
P. Blake, ed.: *Marcel Breuer: Sun and Shadow* (New York, 1955)
C. Jones, ed.: *Marcel Breuer: Buildings and Projects, 1921–61* (London and Stuttgart, 1962; 2/New York, 1963)
H. M. Wingler: *Das Bauhaus* (Bramasche and Cologne, 1969; Eng. trans., Cambridge, MA, and London, 1969, rev. 1976)
D. Sharp, T. Benton and B. Campbell-Cole: *Pel and Tubular Steel Furniture of the Thirties* (London, 1977)
C. Wilk: *Marcel Breuer: Furniture and Interiors* (London, 1981)
A. Rowland: *The Bauhaus Source Book* (Oxford, 1990)

ANNA ROWLAND

Breuer, Peter (Christian) (*b* Cologne, 19 May 1856; *d* Berlin, 1 May 1930). German sculptor. He was apprenticed as a mason in Cologne and in 1874 attended sculpture classes at the Akademie der Bildenden Künste in Munich. In 1878–9 he completed his studies at the Berlin Staatliche Hochschule für Bildende Künste under Fritz Schaper. From 1879 he exhibited regularly at the Akademie der Künste, receiving his first small commissions for sculpted decoration at this time. He achieved recognition with *Spring* (marble, 1889; Essen, priv. col.; for illustration see 1984–5 exh. cat., p. 75) and assisted Reinhold Begas with his monument to *Emperor William I* in Berlin (bronze, 1892–7; destr. 1950). In 1898 he was admitted to the Akademie, after having received medals for *Adam and Eve* (original plaster cast, 1894, Munich, priv. col.; bronze copy, 1912, Karlsruhe, priv. col.; for illustration see Bloch, Einholz and Simson, 1990) and *'Suffer the little children to come unto me'* (marble, 1897). Sculptures such as these were popular and were frequently rendered in multiples in marble and bronze. He became a much sought-after sculptor of monuments who moved beyond an initial neo-Baroque phase to an appreciation of the classically inspired works of Adolf von Hildebrand. This development can be traced through several of his works: the series of monuments to *Johann Sigismund* (marble, 1898–1901; destr. 1954), formerly in the Siegesallee, Berlin, the statue of *Otto von Bismarck* (bronze, 1900) for Breslau [now Wrocław, Poland], the monument to *Emperor William I* (bronze, 1901) in Halle and the National Monument (1906–7) for Memel [now Klaipéda, Lithuania]. He achieved his artistic zenith in 1910 with the first version of the seated statue of *Ludwig van Beethoven*. A second version followed in 1916, and it was finally cast in bronze in Bonn in 1938, eight years after his death. The monument to *Otto Lilienthal* (bronze, 1912–14; Berlin, Bäke Park) is his last work based on the human image. From 1892 he was a teacher at the Staatliche Hochschule in Berlin and was Königlicher Preussischer Professor in 1896 and Academic Professor and Senator at the Akademie from 1905 to 1927. One of his most important students was Rudolf Belling.

BIBLIOGRAPHY

P. Bloch: *Skulpturen des 19. Jahrhunderts im Rheinland* (Düsseldorf, 1975), p. 46
P. Bloch and W. Grzimek: *Das klassische Berlin* (Berlin, 1978)
S. Einholz: *Peter Breuer: Ein Plastiker zwischen Tradition und Moderne* (diss., U. Berlin, 1984)

Rheinland-Westfalen und die Berliner Bildhauerschule des 19. Jahrhunderts (exh. cat. by B. Hüfler, Bottrop, Mod. Gal.; Cappenberg-Salm, Schloss Cappenberg; 1984–5), pp. 73–82

P. Bloch, S. Einholz and J. V. Simson: *Ethos und Pathos: Die Berliner Bildhauerschule, 1786–1914*, 2 vols (Berlin, 1990), i, pp. 54ff; ii, p. 425

SIBYLLE EINHOLZ

Breughel. *See* BRUEGEL.

Breuil, Abbé **Henri** (*b* Mortain, 28 Feb 1877; *d* L'Isle-Adam, 14 Aug 1961). French prehistorian. He was a professor at the Institut de Paléontologie Humaine and at the Collège de France, Paris; he first worked in northern and south-western France but later studied cave and rock art throughout the world. Breuil was one of the founders of the modern study of prehistory, and he created the chrono-stratigraphic approach, which permits classification of stone tool industries according to their geological location in river and marine terraces or their position in the sequence of layers of deposits in caves. In 1911 he established the chronological sequence of the Upper Palaeolithic period, proving that the Aurignacian stone tool tradition was earlier than the Solutrean (*see also* PREHISTORIC EUROPE, §§I and II). He created the first comprehensive classification of Early Palaeolithic stone tool industries, and in the 1930s he identified six phases in the Magdalenian culture. For 40 years Breuil dominated the field of Palaeolithic art studies, playing a key role in demonstrating the existence of Palaeolithic art and its symbolic value. He established the first chronology of cave art based upon stylistic features and interpreted Palaeolithic art as a whole as the expression of a religion oriented towards magic associated with hunting (*see* PREHISTORIC EUROPE, §II, 2(v)). He published papers and monographs on such major painted caves as LES COMBARELLES and FONT DE GAUME and was acknowledged as an expert on the world's rock art through his studies of sites in France, Spain, South Africa and the Sahara.

WRITINGS
'Les Subdivisions du Paléolithique supérieur et leur signification', *Congrès international d'anthropologie et d'archéologie préhistorique: Geneva, 1912*

Cinquante ans d'art pariétal (Montignac, 1952)

Quatre cents siècles d'art pariétal (Montignac, 1952); Eng. trans. by M. E. Boyle as *Four Hundred Centuries of Cave Art* (Montignac, 1952)

The Rock Paintings of Southern Africa, 4 vols (Clairvaux, 1958–60)

FRANÇOISE AUDOUZE

Breviary. Liturgical book containing the psalms, readings from the scriptures, the Church Fathers or the lives of the saints, antiphons and prayers that constitute the Divine Office for each day of the Christian Church year (*see* SERVICE BOOK). The Divine Office comprises the daily devotions observed at the eight canonical hours of the day (Matins, Lauds, Prime, Terce, Sext, None, Vespers and Compline), arranged around the psalms, so that all 150 psalms are read each week. Its text covers two distinct sections: the Temporal (or Proper of Time), containing the offices for Sundays and festivals commemorating the life of Christ and the weekdays of the year; and the Sanctoral (or Proper of Saints), with offices for the feast days of saints. Supplementary offices for certain occasions, for instance the Office of the Dead and Little Office of the Virgin, were sometimes added to the daily office, and a full version of the Breviary usually includes the whole Psalter with its calendar and litany.

The Breviary came into being in the 11th century as a compilation of various texts; previously its constituent parts were often divided into separate books. Although primarily a book for the use of priests and members of religious orders, it was to some degree, particularly in the later Middle Ages, used by the laity, probably for occasional rather than consistent use. For the clergy, the reading of the Breviary became increasingly obligatory, unless dispensation was officially sanctioned.

Breviaries produced for monks and nuns (monastic Breviary) had more lessons in the office of Matins on Sundays and feast days than those made for priests and the laity (secular Breviary). Sometimes the quantity of material contained in them was so great that they were divided in two, a winter (Advent to Easter) volume and a summer (Easter to Advent) volume, with a repeat of the calendar and the Psalter in each. Very few examples survive from before the 13th century, but there are some illustrated monastic Breviaries of the 11th and 12th centuries, most notably the Breviary of Oderisius from Montecassino (1099–1105; Paris, Bib. Mazarine, MS. 364). This contains figurative illustrations for some of the main feasts of the Church year. Most of the early examples before the end of the 13th century, however, have sparse decoration, usually limited to historiated initials for a few main feasts in the Temporal and the Sanctoral and for the psalms beginning daily Matins and Sunday Vespers. A

Breviary of Jean sans Peur, with miniature of the *Ascension, c.* 1413–19 (London, British Library, Harley MS. 2897, fol. 188v)

fairly extensively illustrated copy (late 13th century; Paris, Bib. N., MS. lat. 1023) was probably made for Philip IV, King of France, and is attributed to the Parisian illuminator Master Honoré.

In the period c. 1300–1550 several very elaborately illustrated Breviaries were produced, containing numerous full-page miniatures, framed pictures set into the text and historiated initials for both major and minor feasts, combined with complex decorative borders. Undoubtedly, the increasingly popular Books of Hours stimulated the production of these luxury Breviaries. Notable examples are the Breviary of Jeanne d'Evreux (c. 1334; Chantilly, Mus. Condé, MS. 51) and the BELLEVILLE BREVIARY (1323–6; Paris, Bib. N., MSS lat. 10483–4) by Jean Pucelle and his workshop; the Breviary of Charles V (before 1380; Paris, Bib. N., MS. lat. 1052; for illustration see VALOIS, (2)); the Breviary of Martin of Aragon (c. 1400; Paris, Bib. N., MS. Rothschild 2529); the Breviary of Jean sans Peur (c. 1413–19; London, BL, Add. MS. 35311 and Harley MS. 2897; see fig.); the Bedford Breviary (Salisbury Breviary) for John, Duke of Bedford (Paris, Bib. N., MS. lat. 17294); the Breviary of Philip the Good (1430–40; Brussels, Bib. Royale Albert 1er, MSS 9026 and 9511); the Breviary of Matthias Corvinus (Rome, Vatican, Bib. Apostolica, MS. Urb. lat. 112); and the GRIMANI BREVIARY (c. 1510–20; Venice, Bib. Marciana, MS. lat. I. 99). Significantly, all but the last of these were made for aristocratic lay patrons.

See also GOTHIC, fig. 74.

BIBLIOGRAPHY
Dict. Middle Ages; *LM*; *RDK*
J. van den Gheyn: *Le Bréviaire de Philippe le Bon* (Brussels, 1909)
V. Leroquais: *Les Bréviaires manuscrits des bibliothèques publiques de France*, 5 vols (Paris, 1927–43)
——: *Le Bréviaire de Philippe le Bon* (Paris, 1929)
C. Gaspar: *Le Bréviaire du Musée Mayer van den Bergh* (Brussels, 1932)
J. Porcher: *Le Bréviaire de Martin d'Aragon* (Paris, 1952)
M. Meiss: *The Master of the Breviary of Jean sans Peur and the Limbourgs: Lecture on Aspects of Art* (London, 1971)
H. Toubert: 'Le Bréviaire d'Oderisius', *Mél. Ecole Fr. Rome: Moyen Age, Temps Mod.*, lxxxiii (1971), pp. 187–261
L. Donati: *Bibliografia della miniatura* (Florence, 1972), pp. 449–59
M. Salmi and G. L. Mellini: *The Grimani Breviary* (London, 1972)
R. G. Calkins: *Illuminated Books of the Middle Ages* (Ithaca, NY, and London, 1983), pp. 226–34, 302–4

NIGEL J. MORGAN

Breviary of King Martin. Illuminated manuscript (Paris, Bib. N., MS. Rothschild 2529), perhaps the best example of the style practised by Catalan illuminators at the end of the 14th century and the beginning of the 15th. It was originally commissioned by King Martin of Aragon (*reg* 1395–1410) from the scribes and illuminators of the Cistercian abbey of Poblet, the burial place of the kings of Aragon. The manuscript was begun by 1398, when King Martin wrote to the Abbot of Poblet concerning the text of some prayers that were to be incorporated in it.

The illumination of the Breviary was a collaborative enterprise and the product of two decorative campaigns. The first, which continued until 1410, was for King Martin and must have been under way by 1403, when an illuminator was requested from the nearby abbey of Sant Cugat del Vallès to aid the advancement of the work. The second, from 1420 to 1430, was under the patronage of King Alfonso I. The style of the earlier illuminations is derived

from that of the workshop of the DESTORRENTS family of Barcelona. It is a mixture of French and Italian elements, characterized by bright, vivid colours and a profuse use of burnished gold-leaf. That of the later illuminations corresponds to the style of the Valencian workshop of the CRESPI (i) family. It appears to have been influenced by south Netherlandish painting and is reminiscent of the style of Jan van Eyck. The Breviary also includes a Calendar that shows some familiarity with the Belleville Breviary (Paris, Bib. N., MSS lat. 10483–4).

BIBLIOGRAPHY
A. Rubio y Lluch: *Documents per l'historia de la cultura catalana medieval* (Barcelona, 1908)
M. Meiss: 'Italian Style in Catalonia', *J. Walters A.G.*, iv (1941), pp. 45–87
J. Porcher: *La Bibliothèque Henri de Rothschild* (Paris, 1949)
——: *Le Bréviaire de Martin d'Aragon* (Paris, 1953)
P. Bohigas: *La ilustración y la decoración del libro manuscrito en Catalunya* (Barcelona, 1960–67), ii, pp. 233–41; iii, pp. 40–41, 163
Catalogue des manuscrits à peinture de la Péninsule Ibérique, Paris, Bib. N. Cat. (Paris, 1982), pp. 107–111

LYNETTE BOSCH

Brewer, Cecil Claude. *See under* SMITH & BREWER.

Brewster, John, jr (*b* Hampton, CT, 30 or 31 May 1766; *d* Buxton, ME, 13 Aug 1854). American painter. He was the son of Dr John Brewster, a prominent physician in Hampton, CT, and his first wife Mary Durkee. Born a deaf-mute, Brewster was taught at an early age to communicate through signs and writing. In addition he received instruction in painting from Rev. Joseph Steward (1753–1822), a successful local portrait painter. Essentially self-taught, Steward painted portraits in the manner of Ralph Earl, who inspired a regional portrait style in Connecticut in the 1790s. Brewster began painting full-length likenesses of his family and friends in the mid-1790s, such as the double portrait of his parents (Sturbridge, MA, Old Sturbridge Village), which includes a regional landscape view in the background, a characteristic of Connecticut portraiture of the period.

Brewster began a successful career as an itinerant artist in 1796, when he followed his brother Royal to Buxton, ME. Buxton became Brewster's permanent home between his extensive trips, throughout the north-eastern states, on which he painted portraits and miniatures. His portraits are executed in a flat, decorative style, with realistic likenesses of his subjects, elements related to folk art. Brewster's strong characterizations of his subjects are portrayed with great sensitivity. His finest works are the double portraits of 1799, *Comfort Starr Mygatt and his Daughter Lucy* (priv. col.) and *Lucy Knapp Mygatt and her Son George* (University Park, PA State U., Palmer Mus. A.). After 1805 he often signed and dated his work on the stretcher in pencil.

In 1817, at the age of 51, Brewster enrolled in the first class of the Connecticut Asylum for the Deaf and Dumb in Hartford, where he studied for three years. He returned to Buxton in 1820 and continued painting until his death.

BIBLIOGRAPHY
N. F. Little: 'John Brewster Jr, 1766–1854', *CT Hist. Soc. Bull.*, xxv/4 (1960), pp. 97–129
——: 'John Brewster Jr', *American Folk Painters of Three Centuries*, ed. J. Lipman and T. Armstrong (New York, 1980), pp. 18–26
B. T. Rumford, ed.: *American Folk Portraits* (Boston, 1981), pp. 65–7

J. Hill: 'Miniatures by John Brewster Jr', *The Clarion* (Spring–Summer 1983), pp. 49–50
Ralph Earl: The Face of the Young Republic (exh. cat. by E. M. Kornhauser and others, Hartford, CT, Wadsworth Atheneum, 1991), pp. 242–5

ELIZABETH MANKIN KORNHAUSER

Brey, Dietrich. *See* BRY, (1).

Brian. French family of sculptors.

(1) Joseph Brian (*b* Avignon, 25 Jan 1801; *d* Paris, 1 May 1861). He was introduced to drawing and sculpture in the small private art school opened in Avignon by his father (who ran a barber's shop next door); he also attended the local Ecole de Dessin. In 1815 he won a prize from the Musée Calvet, Avignon, which enabled him to go to Paris *c.* 1827; he became a pupil of François-Joseph Bosio and in 1829 won second place in the Prix de Rome competition with the group the *Death of Hyacinthus* (plaster; Avignon, Mus. Calvet). He spent two years at the Académie de France in Rome, where he was joined by his brother (2) Jean-Louis Brian; thereafter their work is often indistinguishable. They worked on several projects together, mostly in a Neo-classical style, among them the bronze statue of *Jean Althen* (1847; Avignon, Jardin du Rocher des Doms), which is signed *Brian frères*. In their partnership Joseph's role was principally that of entrepreneur.

(2) Jean-Louis Brian (*b* Avignon, 20 Nov 1805; *d* Paris, 15 Jan 1864). Brother of (1) Joseph Brian. Like his brother, he received his early training in Avignon, winning a Musée Calvet prize (1827) that enabled him to study in Paris in the studio of David d'Angers. In 1832 he won the Prix de Rome and joined his brother, at the Académie de France in Rome, where among other works he executed a marble statue of a *Young Faun* (Avignon, Mus. Calvet), which was much admired by Jean-Auguste-Dominique Ingres but which had only moderate success in the Salon of 1840. He collaborated with his brother on several works. Among his official commissions were some busts for Versailles and the Palais du Luxembourg, statues for the churches of St Vincent de Paul and St Augustin in Paris, a series of *Fames* (destr.) for the Hôtel de Ville, Paris, and a statue of *Nicolas Poussin* (bronze, 1847; Les Andelys, Place du Marché, destr.). His marble statue of *Jeanne d'Albret* (1843–8; Paris, Luxembourg Gardens), a particular success, is part of a series of famous women. During the Second Empire (1852–70) he worked on a number of decorative architectural projects, including some caryatids for the Denon and Daru pavilions of the Louvre and the clock ornament of the Gare de l'Est, Paris. His classicizing style changed little during his career, and despite his training with David d'Angers there is no trace of Romanticism in his sculpture.

Lami

BIBLIOGRAPHY
A. Le Normand: *La Tradition classique et l'esprit romantique* (Rome, 1981), pp. 243–56

ISABELLE LEMAISTRE

Brianchon, Maurice (*b* Fresnaye-sur-Sarthe, nr Alençon, 11 July 1899; *d* Paris, 1 March 1979). French painter, illustrator and stage designer. He studied briefly at the Ecole des Beaux-Arts in Bordeaux and from 1917 at the Ecole des Arts Décoratifs in Paris under Eugène Morand (*b* 1885), whose innovative teaching influenced his later work.

Brianchon was an eclectic artist, and there are traces in his work of many of the styles that succeeded each other in Paris during the period in which he worked. Taking landscapes, cityscapes and images of women as his main subject-matter, he nevertheless managed to maintain a distinctive approach based on a harmonious colour sense and a concern with calm, silent or moonlit atmospheres. *The Courtesans* (1932; Paris, Mus. A. Mod. Ville Paris) and *Rue La Fontaine* (1946; Geneva, Petit Pal.) are typical of his work as a painter. He also produced murals (e.g. *Symphony*, 1936; Paris, Pal. Chaillot), book illustrations (e.g. lithographs for André Gide's *Le Théâtre complet*, 8 vols, Neuchâtel and Paris, 1947–9), stage designs and designs for tapestries.

BIBLIOGRAPHY
L.-P. Fargue: *Maurice Brianchon* (Lausanne, 1943)
R. Rey: *Maurice Brianchon* (Paris, 1943)
R. Heyd: *Brianchon* (Neuchâtel, 1954)
C. Roger-Marx: *Eloge de Maurice Brianchon* (Paris, 1955)
Maurice Brianchon (exh. cat., ed. F. Daulte; Lausanne, Fond. Hermitage, 1989–90)

ALBERTO CERNUSCHI

Briani, Giovanni Battista (di Alberto) de'. *See* BREGNO, (3).

Bricci, Plautilla (*b* Rome, 13 Aug 1616; *d* after 1690). Italian architect and painter. She was the first woman to practise architecture whose reputation has survived to the present day. Her father, Giovanni Bricci (1579–1645), was a painter and musician, and her brother Basilio Bricci (1621–92) was himself an architect and painter. The full extent of her activities remains to be explored, but two commissions in Rome stand out. The first of these, the Villa Benedetti (destr. 1849), near the Porta S Pancrazio on the Janiculum Hill, was begun in 1663 for ELPIDIO BENEDETTI, agent to Cardinal Jules Mazarin in Rome. The structure if not all of the decoration was completed by 1665. Benedetti was so pleased with the result that in 1677 he published a guidebook to the villa (under an assumed name) giving detailed descriptions and views of the building along with an account of the roles played by Plautilla and her brother, with whom it is said she collaborated. According to Benedetti, Basilio was responsible for most of the architecture of the villa, while Plautilla embellished the interior with numerous allegorical and religious paintings. However, the building contracts and several preparatory drawings (all Rome, Archv Stato) make it clear that it was, in fact, Plautilla who designed the building with little if any creative input from Basilio. Possibly Benedetti was embarrassed to admit that his villa had been designed by a woman. The architecture of the Villa Benedetti, as recorded in views made before 1849, was highly unusual. With its varied elevations of open loggias, shifting, sometimes curved wall planes, and elaborate stuccowork, its character was robustly Baroque at a time when more classicizing styles were coming into vogue in Rome. The fantastic elements of the villa—it was called 'Il Vascello' because its front resembled the prow of a ship—may reflect Benedetti's own involvement in the design. Several temporary set pieces that he designed for various French ceremonies in Rome were of similar character.

Benedetti next commissioned Bricci to design the chapel of St Louis (1672–80), S Luigi dei Francesi, Rome. The flamboyant décor of the chapel reaffirms her affinity for the lively and now even more outdated forms of the Roman High Baroque. The arched entry to the chapel is wrapped with illusionistic drapery and stucco figures that recall Bernini's decorations in the Sala Regia (1656–7) of the Vatican Palace, Rome. An oval cupola overlaid with stucco relief spans the chapel itself; and the altarpiece is framed by concave polychromed marble wings. Plautilla's architectural achievement in the chapel is unfortunately somewhat compromised by her painting of *St Louis* over the altar. In this static composition—her only surviving canvas—there is none of the verve and animation of her architecture. In 1677 Benedetti gave her the lifetime use of a house he owned in the Trastevere quarter of Rome.

No further works by Bricci are known. The attribution to her of the Palazzo Testa-Piccolomini, Rome, has been overturned by recently published documents showing it to be by another architect, Filippo Barigioni. Nothing remains of her only other documented work, two painted door hangings executed after designs by Pietro da Cortona for the Palazzo Ghibbesio, Rome. D'Armailhacq and other 19th-century authors provided no support for their claim that she spent the last years of her life in a convent.

BIBLIOGRAPHY

DBI

M. Mayer [E. Benedetti]: *Villa Benedetti* (Rome, 1677); ed. with additions by G. P. Erico (Augusta, 1695)
A. D'Armailhacq: *L'Eglise de St Louis des Français* (Rome, 1894)
J. Varriano: 'Plautilla Bricci, *Architettrice*', An Architectural Progress in the Renaissance and Baroque: Sojourns in and out of Italy, Papers in Art History from the Pennsylvania State University, viii/1 (1992), pp. 266–79

JOHN VARRIANO

Brice, Germain (*b* Paris, 1652; *d* Paris, 18 Nov 1727). French writer. He was the first to think of giving to a description of Paris the form of a guided tour following an itinerary, with explanations of the artistic interest of the principal sites along the route. A polyglot and highly educated teacher of French, Brice enhanced the instruction of his foreign pupils by showing them around the city. He decided to publish this guided tour: the first edition of the *Description nouvelle de ce qu'il y a de plus remarquable dans la ville de Paris* appeared in 1684. Brice's main concern in its 564 pages was to provide information of an artistic nature on the public monuments of Paris, on the private collections of art lovers and connoisseurs and on artists' studios. Seven more editions were published during Brice's lifetime, as well as reprints in The Hague (1685) and Amsterdam (1718). In each successive edition Brice took note of the growth of the city and its new buildings, provided more precise details and corrected earlier errors, reflecting this in modifications to the title. From 1698 he included a map of Paris and in 1706 added engravings, whose quantity and quality he constantly improved. Being both conscientious and enthusiastic, he furthered his own education by studying the Old Masters and by visiting Italy. In the year of his death he was preparing a ninth edition, the first three volumes of which were completed

by Pierre-Jean Mariette and the fourth by the Abbé Gabriel-Louis Calabre Pérau (1700–67). Published in 1752 with 1915 pages, this preserves in the main Brice's text, with corrections and additions. The many editions of Brice's book, generally known as the *Description de la ville de Paris*, and their constant updating make it possible to follow the evolution and development of Paris, its increasing number of buildings and monuments and its artistic life over a period of 68 years.

WRITINGS
Description nouvelle de ce qu'il y a de plus remarquable dans la ville de Paris (Paris, 1684, rev. 1687, 1698, 1701, 1706, 1713, 1717, 1725, 1752/*R* 1971 with biog. study and table of edns by P. Codet)

BIBLIOGRAPHY
A. Bonnardot: *Gilles Corrozet et Germain Brice: Etudes bibliographiques* (Paris, 1881)
J.-J. Guiffrey: 'Testament, scellés et inventaire après décès de Germain Brice', *Bull. Soc. Hist. Paris & Ile-de-France* (1883), pp. 98–119

FRANÇOISE DE LA MOUREYRE

Briceño, Trixie [Beatrix; Beatriz] (*b* London, 16 Sept, 1911; *d* Sun City, AZ, 4 Nov 1985). Panamanian painter of English birth. She was one of the first women to make an important contribution to art in Panama, where she arrived in the 1950s. She began her studies in Panama under Juan Manuel Cedeño and continued in Brazil from 1958 to 1960. Her naive style, characterized by a strong sense of geometry and flat, bright colours, was unique in Panamanian art. Giving free rein to her imagination, she painted magical and humorous compositions that bordered on Surrealism, such as *Adam's Fruit Shop* (1977; Panama City, Mus. A. Contemp.), at times showing the influence of European artists such as Paul Klee, Joan Miró and René Magritte.

BIBLIOGRAPHY
Beatriz Briceño of Panama (exh. cat. by J. Gómez Sicre, Washington, DC, Pan Amer. Un., 1969)
Homenaje a Trixie Briceño (exh. cat. by A. Dutary, Panama City, Mus. A. Contemp., 1982)
E. Wolfschoon: *Las manifestaciones artísticas en Panamá* (Panama City, 1983), pp. 87, 322–33, 481–4

MONICA E. KUPFER

Bricher, Alfred Thompson (*b* Portsmouth, NH, 10 April 1837; *d* New Dorp, Staten Island, NY, 30 Sept 1908). American painter. A landscape painter who primarily painted seascapes, he was the son of an Englishman who had emigrated to the USA in 1820. While working in business, Bricher took art lessons at the Lowell Institute in Boston, MA, and by 1859 was able to set himself up as a painter in Newburyport, MA. His subject-matter derived from sketches made during his summer travels along the Maine and Massachusetts coasts and to the Bay of Fundy; during the winter he worked these into finished paintings. In 1869 Bricher moved to New York, where a lucrative arrangement with the chromolithography firm of Louis Prang & Co. gave his work wide exposure through commercial reproduction.

Bricher exhibited annually at the National Academy of Design in New York. A fine watercolour painter, he was also an active member of the American Society of Painters in Water-Colors. His watercolour *In a Tide Harbour* (untraced) was shown at the Exposition Universelle in Paris in 1878. A steady stream of buyers brought him financial and popular success, enabling him to own homes in Staten Island and Southampton, NY. Bricher's work reflected the Luminist aesthetic of sharply defined panoramic views suffused with crisp, clear light. He was particularly partial to low tide scenes (e.g. *Fog Clearing, Grand Manan, c.* 1898; Hartford, CT, Wadsworth Atheneum). His work lacked variety, though it was invariably painted with a high degree of finish.

BIBLIOGRAPHY

J. D. Preston: 'Alfred T. Bricher, 1837–1908', *A. Q.*, xxv (1962), pp. 149–57

Alfred Thompson Bricher, 1837–1908 (exh. cat. by J. R. Brown, Indianapolis, IN, Mus. A., 1973)

LEE M. EDWARDS

Brick. Small, regular-sized unit, usually of clay but also of calcium silicate (sand and lime) or concrete, used as a building material.

I. Materials and techniques. II. History and uses. III. Conservation.

I. Materials and techniques.

Raw materials for bricks are widespread; the method of manufacture is determined by the physical and chemical properties of the clay and by economic circumstances. Calcium silicate bricks are made of a damp mixture of sand with 10% hydrated lime, formed in a powerful press and steamed in an autoclave for several hours. Concrete bricks (*see* CONCRETE, §II, 1) are made from a Portland cement and sand mixture cast in moulds. In the most common format the length is approximately twice the width and three or four times the depth. The size and weight of a brick are such that the bricklayer can pick it up in one hand, although sizes have varied over the centuries. Square blocks and thin, tile-like bricks have also been used. Bricks are used either in massive load-bearing structures or as a thin cladding to other materials in a structural frame (*see* MASONRY, §§II and III, 3). The earliest use of brick was in areas where timber and stone were not readily available, and walls, arches, vaults and domes were all developed in brick. The ancient Romans sometimes used brick as a permanent formwork for concrete structures. Brickwork reinforced with iron bars or strips first appeared in the early 19th century. The structural strength of brickwork is achieved by laying in mortar and bonding so that all the vertical joints are staggered (*see* §3(i) below). Brick is especially desirable as a facing material, and an acceptable product can be made by methods as primitive or sophisticated as the market demands.

1. Manufacture. 2. Finishing. 3. Bricklaying.

1. MANUFACTURE.

(i) Adobe. Adobe bricks are always handmade under primitive conditions: there are no adobe brick factories. The clay is mixed with chopped straw and water, trodden and then worked with a hoe to form a paste suitable for moulding. It is left for at least a day before use to improve workability. An open-bottomed wooden mould is first wetted to stop the clay sticking, placed on flat ground covered with sand or straw and filled with clay. This is struck off level, the mould lifted off, wetted and placed alongside for moulding the next brick. The process of drying the rows of bricks is speeded up by setting them on edge when stiff enough to handle. Broken bricks can be soaked down and reused. The dimensions of adobe bricks are often twice those of fired clay ones.

(ii) Fired. Fired bricks can be made by hand or machine. The amount of mechanization in the manufacturing processes of clay winning, preparation, moulding, drying and firing can vary considerably; clays that are unsuitable for hand processing may often be used for mechanized manufacture. Clay winning and preparation by hand have been virtually superseded in industrialized countries. The clay is dug by mechanical excavators, including the shale-planer for hard clays, and may be stored in stockpiles to allow different seams of clay to be mixed and for winter frosts to break down hard lumps.

During preparation such undesirable materials as flints and limestone, which calcine on firing and slake on exposure to moisture, damaging the brick, are eliminated and other materials added to give the required characteristics. The latter may include sand to reduce plasticity and shrinkage, barium carbonate to stop efflorescence and metallic oxides for colouring (e.g. manganese dioxide for browns and greys). The materials are ground in a pan-mill and mixed with sufficient water for moulding. Soft and plastic clays are finally kneaded in a pug-mill (an arrangement of knives in a cylindrical tub, which may be positioned vertically or horizontally, depending on the type of machine) before moulding. Traditionally the clay for the yellow 'London Stocks' was reduced to a slurry in a wash-mill and mixed with chalk slurry before drying out in settling ponds. It was mixed with fuel and water in a pug-mill before use.

Bricks were originally moulded as for adobe, but in the late 12th century two other methods—pallet-moulding and slop-moulding—both done on a bench, were introduced, using sand and water respectively to release the brick from the mould; both methods continue to be used worldwide in non-mechanized brickyards. In the former process the mould, dusted with sand, fits over a stock board, shaped to form the 'frog' (indent) in the brick and nailed to the bench. More sand is sprinkled on the bench, and sufficient clay is rolled in it to form a rectangular clot, which is thrown hard into the mould, filling every corner (see fig. 1). The excess is cut away with a wire and the top smoothed with a stick dipped in water. The full mould is lifted off the stock, and the wet brick is turned out on to a pallet board to be removed for drying on a special flat-topped barrow. In slop-moulding the mould is dipped in water and placed directly on the bench. The clot is rolled in sand. The moulded brick, being softer, is laid on a 'flat' (carefully levelled and sanded surface) to stiffen for at least a day before being set on the drying hack. The soft-mud process is a mechanized form of pallet-moulding, in which a pug-mill forces clay of hand-moulding consistency into sanded multiple moulds, and the bricks are turned out on to boards for drying.

In the early 19th century large quantities of cheaply produced bricks, formed by extrusion (wirecut) or pressing, were needed to meet the demand from engineering work and the growing cities. In the wirecut process a

1. Fired brick manufacture, throwing a clot of prepared clay into the mould

on ledges on the walls, while in tunnel dryers they are stacked on slow-moving trucks. Drying begins with cool humid air to avoid cracking the bricks and ends with hot dry air.

To produce a solid building material bricks must be fired at a bright red heat (950–1150°C). From the earliest times clamps with channels in the base, in which the fuel was burnt, or updraught kilns, similar to contemporary pottery kilns, were used. Horizontal-draught and down-draught kilns have been used in the Western world from the early 19th century but for much longer in East Asia (see §II, 7 below). Continuous kilns, of which the Hoffmann kiln is the best-known of the many variations on that principle, were introduced from the 1860s. Tunnel kilns rapidly became more numerous in brickworks from the mid-20th century, as technical difficulties that had previously outweighed their advantages of fuel economy and better working conditions were overcome. In the firing process the bricks are stacked on edge, slightly apart to allow even heating from the fuel (wood, coal, oil or gas) burnt among and around them. For 'close-clamping', as practised in south-east England, 'town ash' from old refuse heaps or coke and anthracite dust is mixed with the clay, and the bricks themselves burn, packed tightly together and ignited by coke breeze or gas jets at the base of the clamp.

BIBLIOGRAPHY

E. Dobson: *A Rudimentary Treatise on the Manufacture of Bricks and Tiles*, 2 vols (London, 1850/*R* ed. F. Celoria, Stoke-on-Trent, 1971; rev. London, 14/1936)
H. Ward: 'Brickmaking', *Proc. Inst. Civ. Engin.*, lxxxvi/4 (1886), pp. 1–38, pls 7–8
C. E. Bourry: *Traité des industries céramiques* (Paris, 1897; Eng. trans., London, 1901, rev. 4/1926)
A. B. Searle: *Modern Brickmaking* (London, 1911, rev. 4/1956)
N. Lloyd: *A History of English Brickwork* (London, 1925/*R* Woodbridge, 1983)
F. H. Clews: *Heavy Clay Technology* (Stoke-on-Trent, 1955)
N. Davey: *A History of Building Materials* (London, 1961)
A. Clifton-Taylor: *The Pattern of English Building* (London, 1962)
F. J. Goodson: *Clay Preparation and Shaping* (London, 1962)
E. Rowden: *The Firing of Bricks* (London, 1964)
C. R. Atkinson: *Clay Winning and Haulage* (London, 1967)
K. C. Leslie: 'The Ashburnham Estate Brickworks, 1840–1968', *Sussex Indust. Hist.*, i (1971), pp. 2–21
K. Hudson: *Building Materials* (London, 1972)
J. Wight: *Brick Building in England from the Middle Ages to 1550* (London, 1972)
L. S. Harley: 'A Typology of Brick', *J. Brit. Archaeol. Assoc.*, 3rd ser., xxxvii (1974), pp. 63–87
J. Woodforde: *Bricks to Build a House* (London, 1976)
R. Brunskill and A. Clifton-Taylor: *English Brickwork* (London, 1977)
M. D. P. Hammond: 'Brick Kilns: An Illustrated Survey', *Indust. Archaeol. Rev.*, i (1977), pp. 171–92
P. J. B. L. Penfold: *Modern Brickmaking* (Ripley, Derbys, 1978)
J. P. M. Parry: *Brickmaking in Developing Countries* (Watford, 1979)
M. Hammond: *Bricks and Brickmaking* (Princes Risborough, 1981, rev. 1990)
R. Hillier: *Clay that Burns* (London, 1981)
R. W. Brunskill: *Brick Building in Britain* (London, 1990)

MARTIN D. P. HAMMOND

column of pugged clay, the length and width of a brick in section, is extruded and pushed sideways against wires, which slice it into bricks. Early wirecut bricks were pressed to give squarer edges for facing work. Around 1900 de-airing was introduced for a denser, more plastic clay. Wirecut bricks are frequently perforated to reduce weight and for easier drying and firing.

The stiff-plastic process suits harder clays, which are ground, screened, dampened and pugged. An initial pressing forms a rough clot, which a second pressing forms into a smooth-faced brick with a 'frog' top and bottom. This process has been replaced in the late 20th century by stiff-extrusion, forming wirecut bricks using a stiff-plastic clay. Semi-dry pressed bricks are made of hard shale ground to a coarse powder and screened. No water is added. The powder is passed through hoppers and powerfully pressed two to four times. Trapped air is released after the first pressing, and further pressings consolidate the bricks. This method is used to produce the Fletton bricks of Peterborough and Bedford in England from Lower Oxford Shale. In all these processes moulds are sized to allow for shrinkage in drying and firing. Textured facing bricks are made by sandblasting or scraping the surfaces of machine-made bricks.

Bricks should be thoroughly dried before firing. In pallet-moulding the bricks are lifted off the barrow between two pallet boards and set on the hack on edge, one course at a time. When stiffened they are 'skintled', set diagonally and further apart to speed up drying, which takes three to six weeks. From the early 19th century hot-floor dryers, heated by a furnace or by steam, allowed year-round brickmaking. The tunnel dryers and corridor dryers used in modern works are groups of long chambers heated by steam pipes, air-heaters or waste heat from the kilns. In corridor dryers the bricks dry on boards resting

(iii) Terracotta. The manufacture of structural terracotta (*see* TERRACOTTA, §I and CERAMICS, §I) involves a critical process of mixing clay, drying and firing. Clays selected for purity, heavy silicate content and good colour are fired at a high temperature to produce a fine-grained body resembling stoneware. The chemical recipes for terracotta and its 18th-century derivatives, Lithadipra and Coade

stone, were guarded secrets, but common additives included feldspar, ground glass, sand, china stone and ground-up old ware (grog) to control shrinkage. Terracotta can be hand-sculpted, moulded, cast or extruded and requires a rigorous, labour-intensive production process that is often dependent on timing and the placement of each piece in the kiln. Specifications for three-dimensional blocks, including the choice of webbing for a metal anchoring system in each hollow block, are produced by the architect and redrawn by the manufacturer at a scale of 13:12 to allow for shrinkage during firing. The precise specifications are then reproduced by modellers, since cutting or altering the blocks breaks the surface glaze, allowing water to penetrate the masonry.

Encaustic tiles are the most complex form of terracotta. Medieval examples have raised ridges to separate the areas for the secondary clay colours, which were added before firing. The process was lost in western Europe after the 16th century. A dust-pressed encaustic tile that combined different colours of clay in powder form under pressure before firing was developed by Prosser, Blashfield and Minton in the early 1840s and soon became the standard manufacturing method.

MARGARET HENDERSON FLOYD

2. FINISHING. Bricks produced from moulds of different shapes are used where large numbers of similar, non-standard forms are required to reproduce architectural details normally executed in stone. Segmental and circular bricks were used in ancient Rome for columns (see ROME, ANCIENT, §II, 1(ii)(b)) and elsewhere in the Roman Empire. Tracery and mouldings in brick occur in medieval buildings, and in the 16th century great skill was shown in the manufacture of bricks for ornamental chimney-shafts using collapsible moulds, for example at Hampton Court Palace, London (c. 1520). Large Staffordshire blue coping bricks were made in the 19th century for railway engineering work. From about 1850 a wide range of shaped bricks evolved in Britain; ranges in other countries are less extensive.

Bricks were also carved for decorative features or to produce different shapes. They were cut with a chisel and finished by rubbing with an abrasive stone. Simple carving was done from the Middle Ages by chamfering the corners off standard bricks to form 'squints' for turning 45° angles or 'cants' as part of a moulding. By the 17th and 18th centuries this technique had evolved into rubbed and gauged work for arches, niches and pilasters set into and contrasting in colour with the main brickwork face. 'Rubber' bricks of a sandy clay, carefully prepared to exclude stones and burnt to an even colour throughout, were made oversize for cutting, rubbing and carving to the precise shape required and laid in lime putty with thin joints (see §II, 3(ii)(b) below).

Glazed bricks are known from the 12th century BC in the Ancient Near East, where they were produced by methods similar to those of pottery (see ANCIENT NEAR EAST, §II, 5(ii)(b)) and glass. Lead- or soda-based glazes were applied to individual bricks, forming pictorial and geometrical bas-relief panels. Blues and yellows predominated. The Ishtar Gate (reconstructed in Berlin, Pergamonmus.) at Babylon, built for Nebuchadnezzar II

(reg 604–562 BC), was executed in this technique. Modern glazed bricks are made from fireclays and dipped in ceramic glazes before firing. Brown, salt-glazed bricks are produced by vapourized salt thrown in the kilns at the height of firing. Wood firing at a high temperature also forms a glaze on the exposed surface of the bricks, usually the end, header, face. These 'flared headers', varying in colour from light grey to almost black, were used in England in the diaper patterns of Tudor brickwork (see §3(iii) below).

Such effects are imitated in polychrome brickwork. Clays may be blended and stained to produce a wide range of colours; in the 19th century improved transport allowed bricks different in colour from locally made examples to be imported. Staffordshire blue bricks were used with red and white bricks and yellow 'London Stocks'. A notable exponent of this style, which has lately been revived, was William Butterfield, for example at Keble College (1867–83), Oxford (see also POLYCHROMY, §1). Brickwork may be painted to protect poor-quality bricks from weathering or to improve the colour of facing brickwork. Limewash, sometimes tinted, is traditional but has been replaced by special masonry paints. A red ochre wash was sometimes applied to brickwork that was too pale or uneven in colour.

For bibliography see §1(ii) above.

MARTIN D. P. HAMMOND

3. BRICKLAYING.

(i) Bonds. Bonding is the arrangement of bricks in a wall. Bricks are normally laid on their widest surface but may also be laid on edge (Rat-trap bond; see fig. 2g) or, for decorative use, on end (tack bond). The long face of the brick is known as a stretcher, the short end a header.

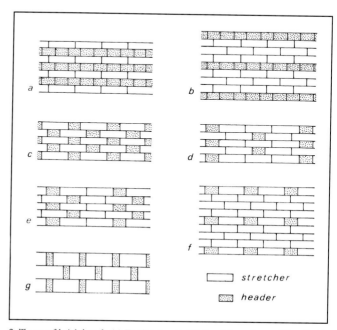

2. Types of brick bond: (a) English bond; (b) English garden-wall bond; (c) Flemish bond; (d) Sussex bond; (e) Monk bond; (f) Flemish stretcher bond; (g) Rat-trap bond

Different bonds show in the face of a wall as different patterns of headers and stretchers. The bonding of all except the earliest walls falls into three main classes. In English-type bonds each course comprises either headers or stretchers: in English bond itself (2a) single courses of headers and stretchers alternate, while in English garden-wall bond (2b; known as Colonial bond in Australia) single courses of headers are separated by three, five or seven courses of stretchers. Flemish-type bonds have headers and stretchers in every course: in Flemish bond itself (2c) single headers and stretchers alternate, but in Sussex bond (2d) there are three stretchers to each header and in Monk bond (2e) two. The third category, hybrid bonds, has courses of Flemish, Monk or Sussex bond separated by varying numbers of stretcher courses. These are named Flemish stretcher (2f), Monk stretcher and Sussex stretcher bonds respectively. In addition, walls of pure header or pure stretcher bond are also found. In Britain the use of these bonds has varied in different periods and in different areas. Modern cavity walls are normally laid in stretcher bond, but by the use of half-bricks the appearance of any of the traditional bonds can be imitated.

BIBLIOGRAPHY

R. Brunskill and A. Clifton-Taylor: *English Brickwork* (London, 1977)
A. D. Brian: 'The Distribution of Brick Bonds in England up to 1800', *Vern. Archit.*, xi (1980), pp. 3–11

ANTHEA BRIAN

(ii) Nogging. The 'brickefillyng' of timber-framing was practised by the mid-15th century, for example at Ewelme Almshouses (founded 1437) and Stonor Park (see fig. 3), both Oxon, and Hertford Castle gate-house (1462–5). The panels form simple patterns with bricks laid diagonally, horizontally and in a herringbone fashion (*see also* NORWICH, fig. 1). Standard bricks were normally used, and 15th-century framing commonly had hollowed sides to key the mortar. This decorative style continued into the 17th century, becoming simpler and widespread across central and southern England. In York, however, special bricks only *c.* 40 mm thick were laid on edge, in plain panels. Plain brick-nogged framing continued in use for vernacular architecture in the 18th century, and original wattle and daub was often replaced by brick nogging in the 18th and 19th centuries.

BIBLIOGRAPHY

An Inventory of Historical Monuments in the City of York, Royal Comm. Anc. & Hist. Mnmts & Constr. England, iii (London, 1972)
J. McCann: 'Brick Nogging in the Fifteenth and Sixteenth Centuries, with Examples Drawn Mainly from Essex', *Trans. Anc. Mnmt Soc.*, xxxi (1987), pp. 106–33

(iii) Diapering. The patterning of red brickwork with different coloured bricks, generally dark or glazed, is known as diapering. Although employed in Byzantine architecture, it was most popular in England in the early 15th century. Eton College (1440s), Bucks, introduced several influential, highly developed patterns, including tall crosses on stepped bases and abstract designs that are linked with examples in the Low Countries and Belgium (see §II, 3(i)(d) below). The most inventive period was in the 1470s and 1480s, for example at Buckden Palace, Cambs, Bishop Waynflete's Tower (*c.* 1475–80; rest. *c.* 1733) at Esher Place, Surrey (see fig. 4), and Kirby

3. Brick nogging at Stonor Park, Oxon, early 15th century

4. Diapering on Bishop Waynflete's Tower, Esher Place, Surrey, *c.* 1475–80; restored by William Kent, *c.* 1733

Muxloe Castle (1480), Leics, which included heraldic and other pictorial designs. The imaginative phase continued until the 1520s, for example in the gate-houses at Hadleigh Deanery (begun 1497), Suffolk, and Layer Marney Hall (c. 1520), Essex, but diapering later declined into predominantly trellis patterns on East Anglian buildings and was used less after 1600.

BIBLIOGRAPHY

N. Lloyd: *A History of English Brickwork* (London, 1925/R Woodbridge, 1983)
N. J. Moore: 'Brick', *English Medieval Industries*, ed. J. Blair and N. Ramsay (London, 1991)

NICHOLAS J. MOORE

II. History and uses.

1. Ancient world. 2. Byzantine world. 3. Post-Classical Western world. 4. Islamic lands. 5. Africa. 6. Indian subcontinent. 7. Central and East Asia. 8. South-east Asia. 9. Pre-Columbian Americas.

1. ANCIENT WORLD. Bricks developed from the use of roughly shaped lumps of clay (pisé), often laid on stone foundations. This primitive form of construction is first attested in Syria and Palestine in the Neolithic period from the late 9th millennium BC and continues to be used. The invention of the brick proper also dates from the Neolithic period, and the earliest attested examples were made in the Ancient Near East during the 8th millennium BC (e.g. at JERICO); at this time only unbaked (i.e. sun-dried) bricks were known. These were hand-modelled into elongated shapes with a rounded top ('hog-backed' bricks), often with finger impressions for keying mortar, and are the first evidence of prefabricated elements intended for architectural use. They were made of clay mixed with straw and were dried for several days or even weeks before being used.

The earliest known moulded bricks are the large examples (800×350×100 mm) excavated in Turkey at the site of Cafer (7th millennium BC). During the 6th millennium BC brickmaking technology developed considerably, and moulded bricks were mass-produced; they are easily distinguishable by their elongated shape but with their long sides pressed between planks. The top was still sometimes marked with fingerprints in order to improve the adhesion of the mortar (see fig. 5a). Handmade bricks, however, continued to be produced; round bricks (diam. 300 mm) dating from as late as the mid-5th millennium BC have been found in Palestine.

Unbaked bricks, moulded in a wooden frame as truly standardized construction elements, became widespread in Mesopotamia at the end of the 5th millennium BC and in Egypt at roughly the same time, corresponding to the emergence of complex architecture. Moulded bricks are generally rectangular and flat, with widely varying formats according to region, local tradition and period; bricks of different sizes, however, are sometimes found on the same site. Bricks of the second half of the 4th millennium BC (e.g. those used in the White Temple at Uruk) are known by the term *Riemchen*; they were the most widespread because of their size (c. 200×80×80 mm), weight and construction potential. The giant bricks also found at Uruk, known as *Patzen*, weighed many kilograms and were up to 800 mm long; they must, however, have been more

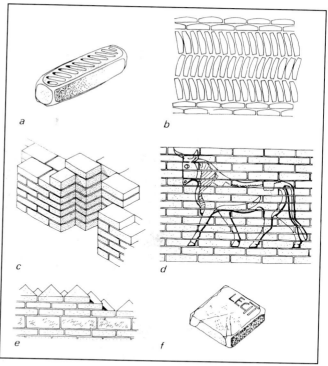

5. Brick types and uses in the ancient world: (a) clay brick marked with fingerprints, from Tell el-'Oueili, Iraq, late 6th millennium BC; (b) plano-convex bricks arranged in alternate horizontal and herringbone courses, from the Diyala region, Iraq, early 3rd millennium BC; (c) double niche façade decoration using square bricks and half-bricks, from Larsa, Iraq, 18th century BC; (d) baked bricks with glazed relief decoration, from Babylon, 6th century BC; (e) dressing of triangular and rectangular bricks, Roman, 2nd century AD; (f) brick stamped with name of Roman 2nd Legion, first half of 1st century AD

difficult to manipulate. Both types are found on other contemporary sites.

During most of the 3rd millennium BC, the Sumerian age, the plano-convex unbaked brick (i.e. with one surface very rounded) was commonly used in Mesopotamia. Bricks of this type were laid in horizontal courses or arranged in a herringbone pattern (5b). From the late 3rd millennium BC rectangular or square moulded bricks became the norm (5c). Oven-baked (fired) bricks, the same shape as the unbaked variety, began to be fairly widely used at about the same time, but oven-baking was an expensive operation as fuel was rare in the regions concerned. Baked bricks were, therefore, reserved for paving courtyards, for drains, water channels and for lining the walls of important administrative or religious buildings. Baked bricks were frequently stamped with an inscription commemorating the building or restoration of a public monument or temple. This was still common practice in Mesopotamia in the mid–1st millennium BC. Baked brick was also used to decorate façades or rooms with designs painted or moulded in relief and glazed. The most famous examples of this kind were the monuments of Babylon (Berlin, Pergamonmus.; 5d; *see* BABYLON, figs 1 and 2) and Susa (Paris, Louvre).

6. Fired brick temple of Gareus, Uruk (now Warka, Iraq), Parthian, before AD 110

Nevertheless, moulded unbaked brick continued to be the most widely used building material during the 2nd millennium BC, not only in Mesopotamia and Egypt but as far east as the Indus region and westwards to Mycenaean Greece and Crete. It was often found in conjunction with stone wall footings, at, for example, Ugarit in Syria (13th century BC). Unbaked brick was also used in association with timber-framing, as at ACEMHÖYÜK, possibly to give additional elasticity to buildings in regions prone to earthquake. A number of Mesopotamian sites of the early 2nd millennium BC, such as TELL EL-RIMAH, have elaborately decorated façades with details produced by specially moulded bricks (for illustration see TELL LEILAN). Unbaked brick was also used throughout the 1st millennium BC.

The Greeks, like the peoples of the Ancient Near East and the Egyptians, made extensive use of mud-brick ramparts, which were much more resistant and harder to dismantle than a fortification in baked brick or stone. Vitruvius recommended the use of unbaked brick for walls of all kinds (II, iii). From the Hellenistic age and during the period of the Roman Republic (323–c. 30 BC; see ROME, ANCIENT, §II, 1(ii)(b)), baked brick was used to bond walls, but it was not until the Imperial period that almost all constructions were of brick, with stone often retained only for architectural decoration. Brick and rubble courses were sometimes alternated. The size and appearance of Roman bricks varied considerably; they could be rectangular or triangular (5e) and fairly thin, more or less pyramidal (particularly when used with *opus reticulatum*; see MASONRY, §II) or circular or segmental when used for columns. They were sometimes stamped before baking and bore the name of a factory, a legion or some other symbolic mark (5f). At the same time in Mesopotamia, elaborate architecture of baked brick was commonly used for sacred and public buildings (see fig. 6).

Although brick was the cheapest and most functional of all architectural materials, adaptable even to such advanced architectural features as vaults, domes and arches, problems arose over preservation, particularly of unbaked brick. Without constant upkeep it soon began to suffer from erosion, particularly at the base of walls, and the surface coating (of gypsum or mud plaster) had to be replaced regularly. Although baked brick did not have to be coated, its surface and even its texture could nevertheless deteriorate; but, like stone, it could also be reused: the baked bricks of ancient Babylon, for example, were extensively pillaged to build the modern town of Hillah.

For further discussion of ancient Egyptian bricks see §5 below.

BIBLIOGRAPHY
M. J. Steve: 'Brique', *Dictionnaire archéologique des techniques*, 2 vols (Paris, 1963–4), pp. 167–71
A. Salonen: *Die Ziegeleien im alten Mesopotamien* (Helsinki, 1972)
M. Frizot: 'Comment construisaient les Grecs et les Romains?', *Doss. Archéol.*, xxv (1977), pp. 57–9
O. Aurenche: *Dictionnaire illustré multilingue de l'architecture du Proche Orient ancien* (Lyon, 1977)
——: *La Maison orientale: L'Architecture du Proche Orient ancien des origines au milieu du quatrième millénnaire* (Paris, 1981)
J. Margueron: 'Notes d'archéologie et d'architecture orientales, 4: Le Sillon destructeur (étude de cas)', *Syria*, lxii (1985), pp. 1–20
O. Aurenche and S. Calley: 'L'Architecture de l'Anatolie du sud-est au néolithique céramique', *Anatolica*, xv (1988), pp. 1–24

YVES CALVET

2. BYZANTINE WORLD. Baked brick continued to be used in wall construction by Byzantine builders, either on its own or in conjunction with cut stone or rubble. It was also the most common material for vaults and arches. Byzantine bricks were normally smaller and more irregular than Roman examples, measuring 320–380 mm square and 30–45 mm thick. Even within the same batch there is great variation, and the bricks are carelessly shaped in even some of the most extravagant building projects, such as the Great Palace in Constantinople. It became increasingly common to use spolia, as can be seen in the reconstruction (1042–8) of the church of the Holy Sepulchre at Jerusalem, where all the bricks were reused. When Byzantine masons worked in the provinces, bricks were occasionally imported, for example at Dereağzı (9th century) in southwest Turkey, where they were brought from the area of the Sea of Marmara. Moulds found at Qasr Ibn Wardan (c. AD 564) in eastern Syria, however, indicate that bricks were produced on the site. To compensate for the rough brick, lavish use was made of lime mortar in minimizing or covering irregularities. Mortar beds are usually as thick as the alternating brick courses, and their surfaces are planed and etched or trowelled downward.

Bricks were laid in horizontal courses, either extending through the thickness of the wall or as a facing on a rubble core. In the early 5th-century Land Wall of Constantinople (*see* EARLY CHRISTIAN AND BYZANTINE ART, §II, 3(i)(a)) the brick forms levelling courses that bind the wall together, alternating with courses of stone facing on a rubble core. This method was standard in Constantinople and was used, for example, in the much later Monastery of St Saviour in Chora. In areas where brick was not so readily available this *opus mixtum* (*see* MASONRY, §II) was often imitated with a small amount of brick used as facing material, as at Çanlı Kilise (11th century) in Cappadocia. The Byzantines also developed several distinctive methods of wall construction. In the recessed brick (or concealed course) technique, alternating bands of brick were set back from the wall surface and covered by mortar, making the mortar beds appear two or three times as thick as the brick courses and creating a striped surface. This technique was popular after the late 10th century and was often employed with reused materials. The *cloisonné* technique, in which the stones, laid in single courses, are individually framed by brick, was used in Greece from c. 900 and later in Serbia and western Turkey.

Brick decoration became increasingly common during the middle and late Byzantine periods, with the appearance of chevron, herringbone, meander, diaper, reticulate, roundel and other patterns in the niches and spandrels and on apse and flat wall surfaces. From the 10th to the 12th centuries, especially in Attica, Boeotia and the Argolid, the façades of many Greek churches were decorated with bricks to form pseudo-kufic designs, for example at the

7. Brick decoration and inscription, with alternate brick and stone construction and banded voussoirs, on the south façade of the church of the Pammakaristos, Istanbul, c. 1310

Theotokos church at Hosios Loukas. By the 13th century in north-west Greece bricks were cut to form geometric designs for wall decoration. They were also used to create the letters for monograms and inscriptions, as in Constantinople (now Istanbul) on the 14th-century church of St Saviour in Chora and the Pammakaristos (see fig. 7; *see also* CHURCH, fig. 12). Numerous brick inscriptions also appear on the walls of Constantinople and Thessaloniki.

In arch construction bricks were placed radially as voussoirs and occasionally alternated with stone voussoirs, while in vault construction they replaced Roman concrete as the standard building material. The use of brick made possible the development of various thin-shelled domes and vaults, often reinforced on the interior by brick ribbing. The largest and most famous of Byzantine brick domes, that of Hagia Sophia in Constantinople, set the standard for later Byzantine thin-shelled brick vaulting.

BIBLIOGRAPHY
G. C. Mars, ed.: *Brickwork in Italy* (Chicago, 1925)
J. B. Ward-Perkins: 'Notes on the Structure and Building Methods of Early Byzantine Architecture', *The Great Palace of the Byzantine Emperors: Second Report*, ed. D. Talbot Rice (Edinburgh, 1958), pp. 58–104
E. Reusche: *Polychromes Sichtmauerwerk byzantinischer und von Byzanz beeinflusster Bauten Südosteuropas* (diss., U. Cologne, 1971)
A. Pasadaios: *Ho keramoplastikos diakosmos tōn byzantinōn ktēriōn tēs Kōnstantinoupoleōs* [Ceramic decoration of the Byzantine buildings of Constantinople] (Athens, 1973)
P. L. Vocotopoulos: 'The Concealed Course Technique: Further Examples and a Few Remarks', *Jb. Österreich. Byz.*, xxviii (1979), pp. 247–60
G. Velenis: *Hermēneia tou exōterikou diakosmou stē byzantinē architektonikē* [The interpretation of exterior decoration in Byzantine architecture] (Thessaloniki, 1984)
R. Ousterhout: 'Observations on the "Recessed Brick" Technique during the Palaeologan Period', *Archaiol. Deltion*, xxxix (1990), pp. 163–70

ROBERT OUSTERHOUT

3. POST-CLASSICAL WESTERN WORLD.

(i) Before 1600. (ii) 1600 and after.

(i) Before 1600.

(a) Italy. (b) Germany, Austria and Switzerland. (c) The Low Countries. (d) British Isles. (e) France. (f) Scandinavia. (g) Eastern Europe and Russia. (h) Spain and Portugal.

(a) Italy. Following late Roman building traditions, brick remained a major building material in medieval Italy. Brick kilns were established under strict regulations outside such cities as Florence and Siena or even within their walls. The buildings are usually of red brick, as at the Arena chapel (1303), Padua, and S Maria delle Grazie (1466–90), Milan, but other colours are known: Il Santo (begun *c.* 1230s), Padua (*see* PADUA, §4(i) and fig. 3), for example, is in yellow brick. Buff bricks commonly appear in Venice, but some 15th-century buildings, for example S Maria della Carità (now part of the Galleria dell'Accademia), are in brown brick. The polychrome brickwork of the Doge's Palace (14th–15th centuries) incorporates white, red, green and yellow bricks. Some churches in Verona have single layers of the local red marble alternating with courses of red brick: at S Zeno Maggiore (rebuilt *c.* 1120) bricks are laid in groups of up to five courses.

Ecclesiastical. In the basilican churches of Rome, for example S Maria Maggiore (?*c.* AD 435), brick was used both as the structural material and as a field for rich decoration in the interior in another medium, initially mosaics or wall paintings. Both functions continued during the Middle Ages, and the use of brick as a decorative field was extended to the exterior, for example from the second quarter of the 13th century at S Marco, Venice. Little decorative use was made of the brickwork itself in 5th-century Rome or at S Apollinare Nuovo (493–525; rebuilt after 526) and S Apollinare in Classe (534–49) in Ravenna, which have exceptionally plain brickwork, using thin bricks with wide mortar joints; not even the windows are emphasized externally. Other buildings in Ravenna of this period, however, indicate some experiment. The upper part of the outer walls of the octagonal Orthodox baptistery, added *c.* 450, has two recessed panels on each face, and the cruciform Mausoleum of Gallia Placidia (*c.* 425–50) has blind arcades in the brickwork. The octagonal S Vitale (526–47) has brick pilasters on all three stages, while the windows of the raised centre are set within recesses. This treatment of the fenestration is found much later in the east end of S Fosca (probably 11th century), Torcello, and the visible windows of the brick structure of S Marco (begun 1042) in Venice. Byzantine influence was strong in the north Adriatic region from the 6th century.

Some brick buildings in Italy, especially the west front of churches, are faced with marble. Sometimes such a façade was intended but not completed, for example at S Petronio (begun 1390), Bologna (*see* BOLOGNA, §IV, 2), which has a few courses of marble laid at the base of the broad, rough brick façade. A similar scheme was intended for the great extension of Siena Cathedral, which was begun in 1339 but abandoned in 1348. When complete, however, a marble façade is integral to the design: S Miniato al Monte (11th century), Florence, is of red brick with a west front in white and dark green marble. Similarly, Palladio's original design of 1565 for S Giorgio Maggiore, Venice (1599–1610; *see* VENICE, §IV, 2(i)), included the white marble west front, although it was the last structure to be built and may not be completely truthful to his design. Substantial brick transepts extend beyond the line of the west front. At Milan Cathedral (begun 1385), however, much of the marble that covers the brick structure was added as late as 1805–13.

The usual intention for brickwork to be a visible part of the townscape is particularly evident in the churches of Venice and its islands. The main cruciform structure, including the window recesses, of SS Maria e Donato (completed 1140), Murano, is buff brick, but colour is introduced on the eastern apse. The lower blind arcade is mainly in red brick, and there is a bold string course beneath the upper, galleried storey. A double line of chevrons, beneath which is set coloured and white marble, is formed by recessing the brickwork. The gallery pillars and balustrade are white marble; the arcade has larger yellow bricks marked off by thin lines of red bricks. The central east apse of S Fosca, Torcello, has a band of chevron ornament marked by red brick indentations. The 14th-century mendicant churches of Venice, including the Dominican SS Giovanni e Paolo (1333–1430; *see* VENICE, fig. 22) and the Franciscan S Maria Gloriosa dei Frari (begun 1340; *see* VENICE, §IV, 4), have plain walls with corbel-tables below the eaves.

8. Palazzo del Comune ('Gotico'), Piacenza, begun 1280

The earliest surviving brickwork in Lombardy and Emilia Romagna is plain, such as the panels of brickwork in the main walls and apses of Parma Cathedral (consecrated 1106; see PARMA, fig. 1) and the early work at Cremona Cathedral (begun 1107; consecrated 1190). At Padua pilaster strips adorn the apses of Il Santo (begun c. 1230s) and the Arena chapel (1303). Later churches in Lombardy were given elaborate decoration. The openings on the north transept façade (1288) of Cremona Cathedral, which is divided into three by unornamented pilasters, are for display not illumination. The central section has a four-light window above the string course, with three-light windows in the flanking sections. The tympanum above each window is filled by a mass of brickwork. A terracotta plaque is inserted in the brick underneath the cusping of the western light. An upper row of three circular windows has elaborate mouldings. A heavy open arcade runs up the gables beneath the cornice, and the façade is topped by three arcaded pinnacles, each with a conical cap. The west front of S Maria del Carmine (1375–90), Pavia, is divided into five by giant pilasters, a string course of moulded brick arching over the windows of the three central divisions and elaborate mouldings around the central rose window. The outer pilasters of the west front of S Francesco (1230–98), Pavia, and the pinnacles above are arcaded. Work begun in 1390 on S Petronio, Bologna, continued until the brick vault of the nave was completed in 1659: the interior has retained its bare brick surfaces, including the ten compound brick piers (see BOLOGNA, fig. 5).

Detached brick campaniles are characteristic of medieval Italian churches. The campanile (1284) of Pavia Cathedral has corner pilasters faced in stone, while the 14th-century campanile of S Maria della Carità, Venice, has brick corner and centre pilasters. The bell-tower (1416) of S Andrea, Mantua, has brick pilasters with increasingly elaborate string courses between the first and second stages, between the third and belfry stages and below the top. The fenestration is plate tracery; cusped circular openings pierce the brickwork below the pointed arch in the belfry stage. (The present campanile (1903–12) of S Marco, Venice, is a reconstruction of that built in the second half of the 12th century and remodelled (1511–14) by Pietro Buon (ii).)

Secular. The use of brick in secular architecture was well established by the early 12th century, notably for the towers that became symbols of family prestige in the cities. In Bologna only two remain of more than 170: the Torre degli Asinelli (h. 97.5 m; 1109–10) and the Torre Garisenda (begun 1110), which was reduced in height in the 1350s owing to soil subsidence, when the two towers were linked. Of comparable height to the former are the Torre di S Dalmazzo and Torre dei Belcredi, Pavia, where there were some 100 in the late 12th century. Other surviving examples include the Torre di Ponte Molin (12th century) and Torre di Ezzelino (13th century), Padua, and the Torre del Moro (h. 42 m), Orvieto; all those in Florence have been demolished. The tradition was continued at Verona in the Torre del Gardello (1370), with balconied windows in the upper section, built by Cansignorio della Scala (*reg* 1359–75) as part of the brick Casa Mazzanti.

More substantial towers adorn major castles, for example the Castello di S Giorgio (1390–1406), Mantua, where deep machicolations take the battlements far beyond the vertical line of the structure. This feature is also found in the Porta Castello (1343), Vicenza, and on one of the corner towers of Malpaga Castle (14th century), south of Bergamo. Many buildings have so-called Ghibelline battlements with a swallowtail profile, including those added to the Arch of Augustus (27 BC; *see* ROME, ANCIENT, fig. 25) at Rimini, on the Castello Visconteo (1360–65), Pavia, and the Ponte Scaligero (1354–76; destr. 1945; rebuilt), Verona.

Several important civic buildings have brick above a stone ground-floor, for example the Palazzo Pubblico (1297/8–1310), Siena (*see* SIENA, fig. 9); the top storey of the wings was added in the same style in 1680. The Torre del Mangia, which was added (1339–48) to the design of Minuccio and Francesco di Rinaldi of Perugia, is an adaptation to civic use of the tall brick campanile (see above). The Palazzo del Comune ('Gotico'; begun 1280; see fig. 8), Piacenza, has a five-bay, open ground-floor faced with white marble, and a six-bay room on the first storey; the building is brick above the sills of the latter's three-light windows, which are set in elaborate arcading. Both the gable and the sides have a corbel-table inserted below brick Ghibelline battlements. Similarly, the upper two storeys of patterned brick on the portico and loggia of the Doge's Palace, Venice, are built on stone lower storeys.

Such private palaces in Florence as the Palazzo Strozzi (1489), are built of brick but have stone façades. The top storey of the central courtyard of the Palazzo della Cancelleria (*c.* 1483–1514), Rome (*see* ROME, §V, 23(i)), is also of brick. The tradition of stone façades has endured in Italy. The Fondaco dei Turchi in Venice, for example, was originally built in the 12th and 13th centuries; the present structure, rebuilt by Federico Berchet in 1858, has brick sides but retains a reproduction of the stone façade to the Grand Canal. An alternative covering, particularly in Venice and the Veneto, was stucco. At Vicenza, for example, Palladio used plasterwork resembling English pargetting on the Loggia del Capitaniato (1571), although previously he had used a thin plaster wash on the columns

on the east side of the courtyard of the Palazzo Thiene (*c.* 1545–50).

BIBLIOGRAPHY

G. E. Street: *Brick and Marble in the Middle Ages: Notes of a Tour in the North of Italy* (London, 1855, rev. 2/1874/*R* 1986)
F. Malaguzzi-Valeri: *L'architettura a Bologna nel Rinascimento* (Rocca San Casciano, 1899)
C. Roccatelli and E. Verdozzi: *Brickwork in Italy: A Brief Review from Ancient to Modern Times* (Chicago, 1925)
J. S. Ackerman: *Palladio* (Harmondsworth, 1966)
J. White: *Art and Architecture in Italy, 1250–1400*, Pelican Hist. A. (Harmondsworth, 1966/*R* New Haven, 1992)
D. Waley: *The Italian City-republics* (London, 1969, rev. Harlow, 3/1988)
R. A. Goldthwaite: 'The Building of the Strozzi Palace: The Construction Industry in Renaissance Florence', *Stud. Med. & Ren. Hist.*, x (1973), pp. 112–73
L. H. Heydenreich and W. Lotz: *Art and Architecture in Italy, 1400–1600*, Pelican Hist. A. (Harmondsworth, 1974)
R. A. Goldthwaite: *The Building of Renaissance Florence: An Economic and Social History* (Baltimore, 1980/*R* 1990)

DAVID H. KENNETT

(b) Germany, Austria and Switzerland. Although some examples of Roman brick remained, for example the early 4th-century basilica at Trier (*see* TRIER, fig. 1), until *c.* 1150 brick was rarely used in Germany; an early exception is the basilica (consecrated 827) that Einhard built at Steinbach, near Michelstadt, using bricks only 35–40 mm thick. This was partly owing to the prevailing view that churches, as partaking of the 'rock of Christ', should be built in solid ashlar, not soft, manmade materials. In regions lacking local stone, however, and in the coastal regions with suitable clay, especially in the north German lowlands, brick was used to replace earlier buildings or for new, larger ecclesiastical and secular buildings. The Premonstratensian church (1148) at JERICHOW ABBEY, near Tangermünde, has basalt foundations with brick used from the socle up, apart from the sandstone imposts. In plan and elevation the basilicas of St Blasius (1173–95), Brunswick, Ratzeburg Cathedral (begun 1170), the Marienkirche, Bad Segeberg (*c.* 1140–99) and Meldorf church (1250–1300), which have nave walls built of bricks *c.* 70–80 mm thick and supported by either piers or columns, do not belong to the Lombard tradition but are in the German Salian style.

The monastic orders, especially the Cistercians, were highly influential in the sudden expansion of brick-built architecture from the 13th century on the north German plain. In the remote heathlands of East Friesland, for example, locally produced brick was used for important monastic buildings of no lesser scale than contemporary ashlar buildings. The surviving details at Ihlow Abbey (founded 1220), near Aurich, show that natural stone was shaped for window and portal jambs, socle friezes, responds and vault ribbing. Numerous village churches were built under the influence of the monastic buildings: by 1550 there were no fewer than 200 brick churches on the east Friesian peninsula. There, and even more strikingly in Mecklenburg, red brick façades were attractively enlivened by elaborate decorative features, and brick came to surpass the traditional ashlar in decorative richness. This style, known as *Backsteingotik* (*see* GOTHIC, §II, 2(iii)(a)), is shown most strikingly in the cathedrals and city churches of north Germany, which demonstrate that brick was no longer considered an inferior substitute for stone. The standard was set by the Marienkirche (begun *c.* 1200; rebuilt from 1260), Lübeck (for illustration *see* LÜBECK), which is 80 m long and has a vault 38 m high. Other notable examples include St Nikolai (1270–*c.* 1350), Stralsund, the Marienkirche (*c.* 1295), Rostock, the nearby abbey church (1291–1336) at Doberan and St Marien (tower 1339–53; church destr. World War II), Wismar.

In south Germany a few Romanesque churches were built in brick, for example St Peter am Perlach (*c.* 1182), Augsburg, and the Martinskirche (late 12th century; destr. 1959–60), Freising. These were succeeded by Late Gothic brick buildings of great importance, for example St Martin (*c.* 1385–1505), Landshut (for illustration *see* LANDSHUT), which was largely built by Hans von Burghausen. Its fan vault (w. 12.2 m, h. 30 m) is carried on octagonal piers only 1 m thick, and the west spire (h. 130.6 m) is only *c.* 10 m lower than the stone spire of Strasbourg Cathedral. The Liebfrauenmünster (begun 1425) at Ingolstadt is a columnar basilica: its two west towers (late 15th century) are placed diagonally to the massive roof in a display of late medieval structural freedom. The massive Frauenkirche (1468–94), Munich (*see* MUNICH, §IV, 1), is in Bavarian block-built style with unadorned brick walls; in 1524–5 its two west towers were crowned by bulbous cupolas.

Although brickmaking techniques were soon introduced into the region that is now Austria by settlers from Bavaria, there are no notable examples of medieval ecclesiastical brick architecture, apart from the choir (1408) of the Franciscan church in Salzburg, which was built by Hans von Burghausen using locally produced bricks. As brick walls in Austria were usually rendered, decorative features specific to brick did not develop. Similarly, brick was not used for major buildings in Switzerland, although the brickmaking workshop at the Cistercian abbey of St Urban was well known in the second half of the 13th century. Some of the bricks and floor tiles manufactured there to renovate the abbey and to supply to local towns, castles and churches have decorative features almost without parallel elsewhere in Europe.

There are many important examples in Germany of secular brick architecture dating from before 1600, including city halls, gate-houses and town houses. From the 13th century assembly and municipal buildings were erected in the wealthy, independent Hanseatic towns of north Germany, often with lavish brick façades and richly ornamented stepped gables facing the market-place, for example at Münster and Königsberg (now Kaliningrad). In 1226, for example, the Lübeck town council built three houses parallel to each other; these were later linked after 1251 by a single façade, decorated with profuse blind tracery. Lavish façades with blind ornament and rows of windows also enlivened many gates and houses in the towns, especially in the 14th century. Notable examples of gate-houses include the Holstentor (1467–78; see fig. 9) and Burgtor (rebuilt 1444), both in Lübeck, the Treptower Tor (1400), Neubrandenburg, and the Ünglinger Tor (1380; rest. 1834), Stralsund.

9. Holstentor, Lübeck, 1467–78

BIBLIOGRAPHY

RDK: 'Backsteinbau'
R. Schnyder: *Die Baukeramik und der mittelalterliche Backsteinbau des Zisterzienserklosters St. Urban* (Berne, 1958)
A. Kamphausen: *Backsteingotik* (Munich, 1978)
G. Weiss and others: *Bremen, Niedersachsen*, Dehio-Handbuch, 11 (Munich and Berlin, 1992)

ROBERT NOAH

(c) The Low Countries. There is hardly any usable natural building stone in the Low Countries near the North Sea. Only central, southern and eastern Belgium and, within the modern Netherlands, the southern part of the province of Limburg, had a long tradition of quarrying building stone. The art of brickmaking was, therefore, a discovery of primary importance. After the Romans left the Low Countries, the technique was lost until the 12th century. Brick from the region is generally red, although sea clay also yielded a yellow product. Clay rich in lime has been dug from the 15th century from the River IJssel (near Gouda), these yellow bricks being known as IJssel stone.

The earliest reliably datable brick (*c.* 1130; 330×160×90–110 mm) was found in 1980 in the masonry grave of a countess of Holland at the former abbey church of Egmond. Brick construction, however, began in the northern provinces of Friesland and Groningen, probably encouraged by Cistercian and Premonstratensian foundations. The first building built wholly of brick may have been the Cistercian abbey of Klaarkamp at Rinsumageest (Friesland), founded before 1163 (destr. 1580; excavated 1939–41) and followed by the first church of its daughter house at Aduard (Groningen), founded 1192 (excavated 1939–41; 1953). Various Friesian and Groningen brick churches have been dated to the second half of the 12th century on stylistic grounds, but the earliest documentary evidence of brick building is a chronicle that states that from 1235 brick was used for the Premonstratensian house of Bloemhof at Wittewierum (Groningen; destr. after the Reformation). By this time, however, brick was in use as far away as Flanders and central Limburg. Datable buildings, either extant or excavated, include the Cistercian abbey church of Ter Duinen (West Flanders), begun 1214 (destr. 1566); the former Cistercian nunnery church at Loosduinen, near The Hague (see fig. 10), founded 1230; and the castle of Horn (nr Roermond), named in sources dated 1243. Until the mid-14th century brick buildings in Groningen had their own distinctive style.

Tufa and brick were initially used in combination, thus the oldest brick was approximately as thick as a tufa block (80–110 mm) but usually somewhat shorter (320–380 mm). In the north of the region, brick was used initially in the same way as tufa (i.e. as *Kistwerk*: 'rubble-work'). This produced a pattern of between three and eleven stretchers, alternating with one header. In the 13th century the number of stretchers was reduced to an average of two. In more southern areas rubble-work is rare, and pure Flemish bond (see fig. 2c above) is the rule, but there is also irregular bond. Masonry in layers of headers and stretchers became popular around 1325, first as English bond and later (*c.* 1500) as English cross bond; but the older bonding remained in use for a long time.

In the 13th century brick size was approximately 270–330×130–160×60–90 mm. The brick was baked in field kilns not far from the building site, where there was a supply of suitable clay and fuel. Some cities had their own brick kilns from the 14th century. Brick was also traded: Flemish brick was exported to England from the 13th century and later to Holland. This was a contributing factor to the reduction in brick size. Smaller bricks were in addition more economical to manufacture, easier to use and of better quality. The increasing use of brick instead of wood in town houses, built on marshy ground, also required smaller bricks. Taxes and penalties for given quantities of brick also forced a reduction in size. To keep matters under control, several cities imposed a standard size, the moulds for which were hung in front of or inside the town hall or church, as for example in Ghent (1371), Utrecht (1388), Delft (1420), Kampen (second half of the 15th century), 's-Hertogenbosch (1486) and Leiden (1527). Two standard sizes were often specified; in Kampen there were three. From the 14th century brick sizes decreased at varying speeds in different regions. This occurred most quickly in Holland, parts of Zeeland and Flanders, along the southern shore of the IJsselmeer and the River Vecht (Utrecht) and in western and central North Brabant. The IJssel stone decreased the most, to about 160×80×40 mm in the 16th century.

BIBLIOGRAPHY

W. J. A. Arntz: 'Tijdstip en plaats van ontstaan van onze middeleeuwse baksteen' [Time and place of origin of our medieval brick], *Bull. Kon. Ned. Oudhdkd. Bond*, n.s. 6, vii (1954), pp. 23–38

L. Devliegher: 'De vroegste gebouwen van baksteen in Vlaanderen' [The earliest brick buildings in Flanders], *Bull. Kon. Ned. Oudhdkd. Bond*, n.s. 6, x (1957), pp. 245–50

C. J. van Mansum: *Elseviers Dictionary of Building Construction* (Amsterdam and New York, 1959), p. 87 [in four languages]

J. Hollestelle: *De steenbakkerij in de Nederlanden tot omstreeks 1560* [Brickmaking in the Netherlands to *c.* 1560] (Assen, 1961)

W. J. A. Arntz: 'De middeleeuwse baksteen' [Medieval brick], *Bull. Kon. Ned. Oudhdkd. Bond*, lxx (1971), pp. 98–103

G. Berends: 'Baksteen in Nederland in de Middeleeuwen' [Brick in the Netherlands in the Middle Ages], *Restauratievademecum*, ed. W. F. Denslagen and others ('s-Gravenhage, 1989), *RVblad: Baksteen* [RV folios: brick], 2, pp. 1–19

H. P. H. Jansen and A. Janse: *Kroniek van het klooster Bloemhof te Wittewierum* (Hilversum, 1991), pp. 334–5

G. BERENDS

(d) British Isles. Brickmaking in the British Isles was revived in the mid-12th century, and the oldest surviving buildings belong to the Cistercian phases of Coggeshall Abbey (Essex). Its use developed in the 14th century, and by 1400 brick was commonly available in the eastern counties, from the East Riding of Yorkshire to Kent and in the region around London. Early brickwork was utilitarian. It was used sparingly as a substitute for stone in the dressing of rubble buildings, often rendered externally, and for window jambs, doorways, quoins, copings and staircases. It was valued as a fireproof material for lining fireplaces and chimneys and was often employed for the ribs and/or webs of vaulting for undercrofts, towers and, occasionally, high vaults. By 1400 brick had been incorporated in extensive municipal walls at Norwich (completed by 1343; partly surviving) and Hull (from 1321; destr. mid-18th century), the gates of cathedral closes,

10. Brick-built former Cistercian nunnery church, Loosduinen, near The Hague, founded 1230; left side belongs to the original church, right side built at the beginning of the 14th century

churches and monasteries, guildhalls and colleges at Cambridge University; it also appeared in castles, bishops' palaces, private houses and shops, a fountain at Hull and a tile-kiln at Boston (Lincs).

Brick first appeared as a facing material during the 14th century, for example in the Cow Tower (1398–9), Norwich, which was built for defensive artillery. Decorative brickwork was also employed at the mid-14th century church of St Mary, Lawford, Essex, where yellow brick is banded and chequered with flint and stone, and at the gate-house (c. 1381) of Thornton Abbey, Humberside, where a deep red facing sets off much elaborately carved stonework. The town walls at Hull were a rare example of its use for solid construction.

This essentially second-class brickwork was overtaken between 1410 and 1450 by buildings of well-made brick of good colour, expertly laid in English bond (see fig. 2a above), often accompanied by diapering (see §I, 3(iii) above), fine vaulting and elaborate corbel-tables and other decoration normally using carved rather than purpose-moulded bricks. During this period brick was established as a prestigious material, eagerly adopted by the wealthy and ambitious for important projects, even in areas of good building stone. This development was possibly initiated by Henry V, who rebuilt Sheen Palace, Richmond, in 1414 and founded three monasteries that were built at least partly in brick (all destr.).

Many of the surviving brick buildings of this period, such as Faulkbourne Hall (from 1439), Essex, Rye House (c. 1443), near Hoddesdon, Herts, Tattershall Castle (see TATTERSHALL) and Prior Overton's Tower (after 1437), Repton, Derbys, are of overwhelmingly foreign appearance, although a few, notably Eton College (1440s), Bucks, and Herstmonceux Castle (after 1440; dismantled 1777; rebuilt 1913), E. Sussex, form part of the English tradition. It is evident from the remaining buildings and documentary evidence that foreign brickmakers and layers were often dominant in their design and erection. The brickmasons who have been identified and the influences they introduced came from countries extending from north-east France to Germany. Innovations included the articulation of whole elevations by blind arcading, sometimes with cusped arches, and the use of decorative corbelling. Several designs were employed for the latter, including pointed and rounded archlets and trefoiled and cinque-foiled friezes. New methods of constructing brick vaulting were also introduced. Sometimes the seating of the shaft on the chimney-breast was masked by a stepped gablet on corbelled-out kneelers. Multiple layers of bricks might be carved together to form coving, for example under oriel windows. Other surviving examples influenced by foreign brick construction and decoration include Caister Castle (1432–5), Drayton Lodge and Middleton Tower, all Norfolk, the tower (1416–17) of the Holy Trinity chapel at Stonor Park, Oxon, the almshouse porch and the school at Ewelme, Oxon, Rochford Tower (c. 1450–60) at Skirbeck, Lincs, and part of the Church of All Saints, East Horndon, Essex.

The continued employment of foreign brickmasons on the most distinguished projects, such as Fox's Tower (1470–75) at Farnham Castle, Surrey (see fig. 11) and Kirby Muxloe Castle, Leics, is documented into the 1470s

11. Fox's Tower, Farnham Castle, Surrey, 1470–75

and early 1480s. In the second half of the 15th century, however, the growing number of brick buildings included many 'foreign' features drawn from the earlier period but developed into an experimental and inventive native style. Diapering was elaborated into one of the style's most characteristic features. The spiral brick chimney, first used at Rye House and Eton in the 1440s, was also much admired; by the 1480s there was a wide range of designs, on such impressive buildings as the tower (1482–3; destr.) at Tendring Hall, near Stoke-by-Nayland, Suffolk, which had many more chimneys than fireplaces. Staircases with continuous vaults, and trefoil-corbelled friezes, both present at Rye House, recur on several of the highest quality buildings up to the 1480s, for example at Oxborough Hall (begun c. 1481), Oxborough, Norfolk.

This style continued to evolve from about 1480 to after 1520, mainly in the eastern counties, especially for the country seats of bishops and gentry and for church towers and porches. Its characteristics were fine-quality brickwork, diapering and stone dressings, extravagant chimneys, trefoiled corbelling, perhaps above sunken panels, and fine mouldings or other carved work. From about 1520 until after 1540, there was a brief experiment with architectural terracotta (see §I, 1(iii) above), for example at Sutton Place, Surrey, in the mid-1520s, and its imitation in outsize bricks. This was also of foreign inspiration and was widely spread but limited in use.

For the rest of the 16th century brick architecture was less fashionable, although it became steadily more common in counties further west, especially for the chimneys and hearths of timber-framed or rubble buildings; in Herefordshire, Worcestershire and Cheshire, for example, the first brick houses were built for the gentry. Regional styles developed in some areas where brick was already well-established, such as Norfolk, where many country houses were built with octagonal angle-shafts, stepped gables, moulded pediments and simple diapering, set off by rendering to simulate stone dressings. The display of brick was rare in the south-west and north, where there was good quality stone. In Wales, brick was introduced for a few prestigious gentry houses after the construction of Bach-y-graig (begun 1567), near Tremeirchion, Clwyd.

BIBLIOGRAPHY

N. Lloyd: *A History of English Brickwork* (London, 1925)
N. J. Moore: *Brick Building in Mediaeval England* (diss., Norwich, U. E. Anglia, 1969)
J. A. Wight: *Brick Building in England from the Middle Ages to 1550* (London, 1972)
T. P. Smith: *The Medieval Brickmaking Industry in England, 1400–1450* (London, 1988)
N. J. Moore: 'Brick', *English Medieval Industries*, ed. J. Blair and N. Ramsey (London, 1991)

NICHOLAS J. MOORE

(e) France. Brick was rarely used in France, other than in the south-west. In the north-east it had been important under Roman rule but was not generally employed after the 5th century AD. St Pierre-aux-Nonnains at Metz, which belonged to a monastery founded in the 7th century, was, however, rebuilt in brick in the 10th century. The church of the Basse-Oeuvre (begun 997) at Beauvais is built of *petit appareil* with inserted bricks. Later medieval churches in northern France rarely use brick, and its use in secular architecture in this region was restricted before the 16th century to castles in Champagne, Picardy and Artois. Rambures (15th century) has four circular towers joined by walls 2.7 m thick. A wall-walk set on corbelling above the *chemin-de-ronde* is both ornamental and an additional form of defence.

Most of the finest brick buildings in the south-west are in and around Toulouse. St Sernin (consecrated 1096; *see* TOULOUSE, §2(i)(a)) is the largest surviving Romanesque church in France. The Dominican chapel (1230–98; now the Jacobin church; *see* TOULOUSE, fig. 1) has two aisles divided by a central row of brick columns. The popular name for Toulouse ('La Ville rose') indicates the city's extensive brick architecture, which included the tower (14th century; most destr. 1550) of the former Augustinian convent (now the Musée des Augustins) and the tower (1503–42) of the church of La Dalbade. Fourteenth-century brick parish churches south-west of Toulouse include that at L'Isle-en-Dodon, with a fortified apse, the completely fortified church (1304) at Simorre and the former cathedral at Lombez, which has an octagonal tower. The church at Gimont and the former cathedral at Saint-Lizier also have octagonal bell-towers. East of Toulouse there are 14th-century brick churches at Villefranche-de-Lauragais, with a fortified bell-tower, St Alain, Lavaur, and Notre-Dame-du-Bourg, Rabastens. The exterior of Albi Cathedral (begun *c.* 1277; *see* ALBI, §1 and fig.) resembles a fortress; the design of its tower may have been inspired by that at Rabastens.

Both Rabastens and the bastide at Villeneuve-sur-Lot are brick-built towns. The two surviving gates at the latter,

the Porte Monflanquin (after 1323) and the Porte de Pujols, are built of stone and brick, while the church of Ste Catherine is wholly brick; the houses, when timber-framed, have brick infilling. Houses at such other bastides as Granges-sur-Lot, Le Temple de Breuil (both Lot-et-Garonne) and Fleurance (Gers), are of flat Toulousian brick. Other gate-houses include those in brick at Lalinde (Dordogne) and of brick and stone at Labastide d'Armagnac.

The tradition of fortified brick buildings is strong in south-west France. The episcopal palace of La Berbie (begun *c.* 1228), Albi, contains a massive, square donjon of red brick. The Castillet at Perpignan, built as a gate-house in 1367, was enlarged to serve as a fort in 1483. The brick castle (1374–80) at Montaner has a donjon 36 m high. Houses in such major towns as Albi, Caussade and Montauban are brick-built. Examples in Toulouse include the Hôtel du Vieux-Raisin (now Béringuier-Maynier; 1573) and the conventual buildings of the former college of St Raymond.

During the 15th century, and later in north-east France, brick was used for the infilling of the larger timber-framed houses in both town and country. By the end of the 15th century brick was used in the large towns of the Loire Valley, such as Tours, where the Hôtel Tristan is built of brick above a stone semi-basement. The newel, arches and risers of an internal newel stair might be of brick, following contemporary practice in England. The north-east wing (1498–1508) of the château of Blois, built for Louis XII, has a fine red brick façade with a lozenge pattern in black brick. Royal patronage was also responsible for the use of brick in combination with stone at the château of Fontainebleau (from 1528), for Francis I, for the Vieux Château (after 1539) at Saint-Germain-en-Laye and the château of Anet (1547–55; much destr.), which was designed by Philibert de L'Orme and commissioned by Henry II for Diane de Poitiers. In Paris brick was not employed until the 16th century, for example for the Château de Madrid (1528; destr. 1793–1847), which was built by Francis I near the former south gate.

BIBLIOGRAPHY

L. Lefèvre: *La Céramique du bâtiment* (Paris, 1897; Eng. trans., London, 1900)
P. Lavedan: *Ou'est-ce que l'urbanisme: Introduction à l'histoire de l'urbanisme* (Paris, 1926)
——: *L'Architecture française* (Paris, 1944; Eng. trans., Harmondsworth, 1956)
A. Blunt: *Art and Architecture in France, 1500–1700*, Pelican Hist. A. (Harmondsworth, 1953, rev. 4/1980)
M. W. Beresford: *New Towns of the Middle Ages: Town Plantation in England, Wales and Gascony* (London, 1967/*R* Gloucester, 1988)
M. W. Thompson: *The Decline of the Castle* (Cambridge, 1987)

DAVID H. KENNETT

(f) Scandinavia. Valdemar I, King of Denmark (*reg* 1157–82), introduced brick to Scandinavia *c.* 1160, when he strengthened a section (l. 3.5 km) of the defensive Danework along the southern border. More important are the brick churches at Sorø Abbey (founded 1162) and St Bendt (rebuilt *c.* 1160), Ringsted, which have decorative corbel-tables; the larger openings and capitals are moulded brick. The probable importance of monasteries in the spread of brick is suggested by the Danish vernacular *munkesten* ('monkstone'). Influence from Lombardy is

generally supposed (*see* §(a) above). A more striking early example is the Vor Frue (*c.* 1170), Kalundborg (*see* RO-MANESQUE, fig. 21), with a central square tower rising slightly above the four octagonal towers set on the arms of the Greek-cross plan. Windows are simple and deco-ration minimal, for the church was also intended as a fortress. Plain brick is also used for the upper part of the round church (*c.* 1160–80) at Bjernede. The first use of brick in Skåne was at Gumlösa church (1191); it later spread through eastern Sweden and across to Finland.

Many Scandinavian cathedrals are partly or wholly in brick: in Denmark at Århus (begun 1190s), Odense (late 13th century), Ribe (Citizens' Tower, after 1283), Roskilde (begun *c.* 1175; *see* ROSKILDE, §1 and fig.) and Ålborg (1430); in Sweden at Strängnäs (begun 1270), Uppsala (*c.* 1280; *see* UPPSALA, §2 and fig.) and Västerås (second half of the 13th century); and in Finland at Porvoo (1418) and Turku (*see* TURKU, §3 and fig.). In the 13th century brick was widely employed at monasteries, for example at Løgum Abbey (*c.* 1200), which has both round and pointed arches, and for town and village churches. In Norway, however, wood and stone were the main building materi-als: brick, when used at all, was combined with stone, for example for the vaults and openings at St Olav's Priory (13th century), Oslo.

The dominant style is that of the Hanseatic lands (*see* §(b) above), although without the elaborate tracery some-times found there. Shield shapes and other prominent details were occasionally used, for example at Oppe-Sundby (nr Frederikssund) and on the churchyard gate-house at Vendel, although rich effects were sometimes achieved by simpler means, for example at Hollola (Fin-land), Karise (from 1261), Ønslev and at St Marien (1240), Sigtuna. The main features include moulded corbel-tables, blind lancet niches, lancet arches on brick corbels, recessed roundels, crosses and other shapes (often whitewashed), saw-tooth courses and herringbone brickwork. Poly-chromy was sometimes introduced by banding with stone or the decorative placing of black bricks; diapering was unusual, although present at Oppe-Sundby and, minimally, at Roskilde. St Peter's (begun *c.* 1300) at Malmö (*see* MALMÖ, §1) is a fully developed example of *Backsteingotik*.

Panelling was often restricted to gables, with lancets rising in series and the gables terminating in crow-steps. In Finland brick gables commonly adorned stone churches: Hattula is a rare example of a church mostly in brick. Such gables are especially striking when crowning stark brick towers, for example at St Peter (1400), Naestved. Monk bond (see fig. 2e above) was commonly used. Interiors are sometimes plain with simple piers (square at Turku, cylindrical at Strängnäs), although moulded-brick piers are found at Odense, Roskilde, the Storkyrkan (St Nikolai; begun 1279), Stockholm, and Vitskøl Abbey (ruined). The relatively light brick vaults enabled the use of moulded-brick ribs.

Secular brick architecture is mainly represented by late castles, although at Naestved there is a brick town hall (1450; rebuilt 1520) and 15th-century brick houses; there and elsewhere timber-framed houses have brick infilling. The castle at Hämeenlinna (Finland) is a rare 13th-century example (enlarged 15th century) of secular brick architec-ture, with a donjon in the manner of the Teutonic Knights

(*see* TEUTONIC ORDER, §2). In the mid-14th century Valdemar IV Atterdag, King of Denmark (*reg* 1340–75), added four brick towers to Vordingborg Castle, including the striking, circular Goose Tower, and probably built the similar Core (after 1360) at Helsingborg (*see* HELSING-BORG, §1 and fig.). Bricks from Kalø Castle (first half of the 14th century; ruined) were later used for Charlotten-burg Palace (1672–83), Copenhagen. Rygård (*c.* 1530) more closely resembles a manor house than a castle, but the high, almost windowless walls of Spøttrup (rebuilt 1570s) are of extreme severity. At Egeskov Castle (1554) the windows are regularly disposed, although otherwise it follows the *Backsteingotik* tradition, as do GRIPSHOLM CASTLE (rebuilt 1573) and Nyborg Castle (mid-16th century). The Renaissance windows and heavy Gothic corbelling on the manor house at Borreby (1556) combine to give an almost romantic appearance.

Hesselagergård (1538), near Gudme, which has Italian-ate curved gables, was probably designed by Martin Bussaert. Dutch influence was strong in the late 16th century, for example in the work of Hans van Paeschen (*fl* 1561–82) at Kronborg Castle, Helsingør (1570; *see* HELSINGØR, §2 and fig.) and at 76 Stengade (1579), Helsingør, a town house attributed to Antonis van Ob-berghen. Decorative gables with stone trim were common, and the bricks were sometimes laid in Flemish bond (see fig. 2c above), giving a mesh-like effect, for example at Berritsgård (1586), near Sakskøbing, Orbœklunde (1560–93), Rugård (late 16th century), near Hyllested, and Visborggård (1575–6). Dutch influence is also apparent on some churches, such as that at Slangerup (1576–88), built by Hans van Steenwinckel (i), and in the rich classical detailing on the east gable added to Valløby church in 1590. Finland was not influenced by Renaissance ideas until after 1600.

BIBLIOGRAPHY
J. Roosval: *Den Baltiska Nordens kyrkor* [The churches of Baltic Scandi-navia] (Uppsala, 1924)
A. Hahr: *Architecture in Sweden: A Survey* (Stockholm, 1938)
M. Mackeprang: *Vore Landsbykyrken: En Oversigt* [Our village churches: a survey] (Copenhagen, 1944)
T. Paulsson: *Scandinavian Architecture* (London, 1958)
J. M. Richards: *800 Years of Finnish Architecture* (Newton Abbot, 1978)
M. C. Donnelly: *Architecture in the Scandinavian Countries* (Cambridge, MA, 1992)

TERENCE PAUL SMITH

(g) *Eastern Europe and Russia.* Between the 10th and 13th centuries various Byzantine brick techniques (*see* §2 above) were used for churches in Kievan Rus'. The cathedral of St Sophia (1037), Kiev, for example, has a thin brick facing on stone walls; mortar conceals alternate layers of bricks, and part of the stonework is visible on the wall surface. The recessed brick technique was em-ployed in the Grand Duchy of Kiev and in Chernihiv, while buildings in SMOLENSK and Polotsk (mid-12th century) have alternating layers of brick and stone, some-times set with acoustic jars (also found in Kiev). The bricks varied in size (400×300×29–37 mm or 290–370×175–270×38–53 mm). Exterior decoration included regular niches and geometric, arcaded friezes under the eaves and glazed tiles and rhomboid plates in bright yellow, red, rusty violet and green, for example at SS Boris and Gleb (mid-12th century), Kolozh, now Grodno.

In Poland smaller bricks (225–270×100–120×40–46 mm) were used in the mid-12th century by craftsmen from western Europe to build arches and to decorate stone walls. This was most common in Mazovia (e.g. Czerwińsk, church of the canons regular), and also occurred in Silesia (e.g. Wrocław-Ołbin Benedictine Church; from 1138; destr. 1529). The use of thick Early Gothic brick spread east during the 13th century to the River Vistula; brick being introduced to the maritime provinces and the Teutonic kingdom by way of the Margraviate of Brandenburg and to Silesia and Lesser Poland from Saxony, France and Italy, mainly by the religious orders and workshops in cities. It was occasionally used in castles beyond the Vistula (e.g. Stołpie), in western Rus' (e.g. Kamenets, Belarus') and in Lithuania.

Brick was employed from early Gothic buildings either as *opus* (*see* MASONRY, §II) or alone, for example at the Prince's Chapel (before 1240), Legnica; sometimes there are herringbone sections (*opus spicatum*), as at Kamień Pomorski Cathedral (late 12th century–13th). The Wend bond was the earliest to be used, but it was gradually replaced by the Gothic (or Polish) bond. The size of bricks was related to standard units of measurement and changed from the first half of the 13th century (240–260×120–130×75–90 mm) to the second half (270–290×120–135×95–110 mm), later decreasing gradually. Decorative techniques varied; in Silesia and Lesser Poland, in Cistercian churches (e.g. Trzebnica, 1203–40, and Henryków, 1241–60), stone architectural details contrast with brick walls and piers (and occasionally vaults). Sometimes interiors have bands of brick and stone, for example at Mogiła and the Franciscan church (mid-13th century) at Zawichost. Bricks might also be moulded, decorated with glazed reliefs in bronze, yellow and green, have arcaded and geometric friezes below the eaves or be scored to resemble stone blocks, for example at the Cistercian churches of Kołbacz (1210–30) and Mogiła (after 1266) and the castle of the Teutonic Knights (rebuilt late 13th century) at TORUŃ. The decoration and portal at the Dominican church of St James (begun 1226) at SANDOMIERZ are particularly notable. Brick was occasionally used in Greater Poland, for example at the Premonstratensian convent (consecrated 1216) at Strzelno, but it did not appear as a homogeneous building material in Dominican architecture until the mid-13th century, influenced by techniques from Silesia and Lesser Poland (e.g. Poznań and Sieradz).

Brick was introduced to Bohemia and Moravia by the religious orders in the second quarter of the 13th century. At the convent of St Agnes (before 1234), Prague, brick walls and vaults are combined with stone. Such Cistercian churches as Velehrad Abbey (after 1228) and Sezemice (third quarter of the 13th century) have brick facings that also served as a field for architectural details. The parish church (*c.* 1290) at Nymburk is a rare example of the exclusive use of brick. A number of brick village churches (second quarter of the 13th century) in south-west Slovakia display details drawn from Lombard stone-carving (e.g. Diakovce) or brickwork from Saxony and Austria (e.g. Kolárovo and Šamorin).

The greatest development of brick architecture in central-eastern Europe took place in the 14th and 15th centuries and was concentrated in cities. The techniques used, in particular the Gothic bond (often with the inclusion of overburnt brick), as well as brick sizes and the forms of moulds, were no different to those in western Europe. Differences increased, however, between the brick and masonry architecture of southern Europe and the brick architecture (*Backsteingotik*) of the north. The block bond was used from the mid-16th century.

In Silesia the most notable 14th-century brick churches are those in Wrocław, usually with two towers and either of the hall type (e.g. the Augustinian church, 1334–75) or of the basilica type (e.g. SS Mary and Magdalene, late 13th century to 1358/71). The contrast between the stone detailing and the brick walls of the interiors was usually emphasized by paint; in some cases alternating bands of stone and brick were introduced (e.g. Nysa, St James, 1401–50). In Lesser Poland in the 14th century brick was initially used as a filler for the core of stone constructions (e.g. Kraków Cathedral, after 1320). Later it became the principal construction material (e.g. Kraków, St Mary, 1355/65–97; see fig. 12) although architectural details continued to be built of stone. In some cases brick walls were concealed by stone facing (e.g. the tower of Kraków Town Hall, late 14th century). Brick was the principal material used in civic architecture, including town houses and town halls (e.g. Wrocław Town Hall, 1471–1504; for illustration *see* WROCŁAW), and in military constructions, especially defensive walls, towers and castles (e.g. at

12. St Mary, Kraków, 1355/65–97

Sandomierz, 14th century, and Wojnowice, 1413–30). The northern practice of diapering with overburnt brick reached the south in the 15th century. In the 14th century brick techniques were introduced to Bohemia and Moravia via Silesia (e.g. Hradec Kralove Cathedral, before 1339). From the late 14th century Gothic brick was introduced in the eastern territories of the Polish kingdom, but its use was not widespread until the 16th century. Geometric decoration, using brick, of Russo-Byzantine derivation, was also used in Podolia (e.g. Chocim Castle, before 1480, and 1540–44).

In the 13th to 14th centuries the limit of western European brick construction in south-eastern Europe was marked by the churches (c. 1280) in the Cirşana Valley, Transylvania, although Byzantine techniques and the decoration of wall facings continued to be used in Orthodox churches in Wallachia, such as at St Nicholas (1364–77) in Curtea de Argeş (see ROMANIA, §II, 1 and fig. 2). In the 15th and 16th centuries Russo-Byzantine techniques featuring triangular and square designs were popular in Moldavia, where they were used at Khotin Castle (before 1480) and in a significant group of Orthodox churches (e.g. Neamţ, 1497–8; Snagov, 1512–21) that are also decorated with blind arcades, glazed plates and bands of brick and stone.

The most splendid examples of 14th- and 15th-century brick architecture are those built near the Baltic coast and connected with the architecture of north-western Europe. The churches are often monumental, with a single tower: some are basilican in plan, such as that at PELPLIN ABBEY (after 1276) and that of St James, Toruń (1309–50), but most often the brick churches built in towns are hall churches and churches of the mendicant orders as, for example, the church of St John (late 13th century-15th) in Toruń, the Franciscan church of St Mary (1350–70), Toruń, and the cathedral (1309–80) in Frombork. Secular buildings include the castles of the Teutonic Order at Malbork (for illustration see MALBORK CASTLE), episcopal palaces (e.g. Kwidzyń, 14th century), public buildings, including the town halls at Toruń (1259–74; rebuilt 1385–99; for illustration see TORUŃ) and Gdańsk (1379–89), residential houses and fortifications. The walls are decorated with overburnt bricks, geometrical friezes and moulded decorations for the windows. The gables have similar decoration, with blind strip windows, fluting and pinnacles. The brick vaults are ribbed. From the late 14th century a distinctive style of Late Gothic architecture emerged in western Pomerania and in Greater Poland. It was developed in particular by Hinrich Brunsberg, who devised richly carved decoration for the walls, pilaster strips and gables, using canopies, pinnacles, blind tracery and glazing. This is best illustrated by St Mary, Stargard Szczeciński (completed 1388; for illustration see BRUNSBERG, HINRICH), St Mary (c. 1399–1407), Chojna and the collegiate church of St Mary (workshop; 1442–8), Poznań. A distinctive style was used in Gdańsk from the mid-15th century, for example in the crystalline net vaults (c. 1500; derived from Saxony), gabled façades and smooth, flat walls of St Mary (1447–1502) and the symmetrical, framed wall sections and pointed arcading of the town buildings, such as that of the Confraternity of St George (1487–94).

Local variations developed under the influence of the main northern centres throughout Poland, especially in Ermeland and Mazovia (e.g. Warsaw, Royal Castle, 14th–15th centuries), Lithuania (e.g. Vilnius Cathedral, after 1387) and Belarus' (e.g. Mir Castle, mid-16th century). During the 15th and 16th centuries in the Grand Duchy of Lithuania such Russo-Byzantine elements as linear gable decoration were combined with the ribbed vaults and *Backsteingotik* structure of north German hall churches (see LITHUANIA) and defensive Orthodox churches. A Bernardine workshop in the first half of the 16th century was responsible for the outstanding Late Gothic façades of St Anne (completed 1581), Vilnius, and the house of Perkūnas, Kaunas.

Brick from eastern Europe was introduced to Muscovy in the second half of the 15th century by craftsmen from Lombardy in a combination of Italian forms and traditional Russian architectural styles, notably at the Kremlin in Moscow. Brick was used both in *opus incertum* fortifications (1485–95) and for the walls of the cathedral of the Dormition (1474–9), Uspenski, and was frequently combined with white stone. The traditional thin brick was also used in the 15th century. The new material influenced the form of friezes and decorative arcades on Orthodox churches and of the *kokoshniki* that decorate the cathedral of the Annunciation (1482–90), Blagoslovenny. The techniques used in the Kremlin became prevalent in princely castles (e.g. Uglich, c. 1492) and in Orthodox churches around Moscow, such as the 'tower' or 'turret' church of the Annunciation (1532) at KOLOMENSKOYE. The most outstanding example is St Basil's Cathedral (1555–61), Moscow (see MOSCOW, §IV, 2), in which red and polychrome glazed brick contrasts with geometrical and abstract decoration.

BIBLIOGRAPHY

V. Mencl: *Stredoveká architektúra na Slovensku* [Medieval architecture in Slovakia] (Prague and Prešov, 1937), pp. 301–50

D. Libal: *Gotická architektura v Čechách a na Moravě* [Gothic architecture in Bohemia and Moravia] (Prague, 1948), pp. 77–95, 146, 162

S. H. Cross: *Mediaeval Russian Churches* (Cambridge, MA, 1949), pp. 40–43, 64–7

V. Kotrba: *Česká středověká architektura cihlová* [Medieval brick architecture in Bohemia] (diss., Prague, Charles U., 1951)

T. Rudkowski: *Badania nad rozmiarami cegły średniowiecznego Wrocławia* [Research on the proportions of medieval bricks in Wrocław], Sprawozdania Wrocławskiego Towarzystwa Naukowego [Transactions of the Learned Society of Wrocław] 1952, vii (Wrocław, 1955)

Z. Tomaszewski: *Badania cegły jako metoda pomocnicza przy datowaniu obiektów architektonicznych* [The study of brick as an aid to dating architecture], Zeszyty Naukowe Poli. Warszaw., xi/4 (1955), pp. 31–52

A. V. Konorov: *K istorii kirpicha v Rossii v XI–XX st* [The history of brick in Russia in the 11th–20th centuries], Trudy Instituta Istorii Yestestvoznaniya i tekniki [Transactions of the Institute for Science and Technology], vii (Moscow, 1956)

Istoriya russkoy arkhitektury [History of Russian architecture] (Moscow, 1956), pp. 18–21, 35–7, 105, 122, 144–63

Z. Świechowski: 'Wczesne budownictwo ceglane w Polsce' [Early brick architecture in Poland], *Stud. z Dziejów Rzemiosła & Przemysłu* [Studies of the history of craft and industry], i (Wrocław, Warsaw and Kraków, 1961), pp. 84–117

——: *Budownictwo romańskie w Polsce: Katalog zabytków* [Romanesque architecture in Poland: a catalogue of monuments] (1963)

E. Małachowicz: 'Problemy konserwacji średniowiecznej faktury i polichromii architektury we Wrocławiu' [Problems of preserving the medieval fabric and architectural polychromy in Wrocław], *Ochrona Zabytków*, iv (1965), pp. 17–34

M. Brykowska: 'Sklepienia Krysztalowe: niektóre problemy' [Crystalline (net) vaults: some problems], *Późny Gotyk: Materiały sesji SHS* [Late

Gothic period: materials from SHS Symposium]: *Warszawa, 1965*, pp. 243–59

M. Arszyński: *Technika i organizacja budownictwa ceglanego w Prusach w końcu XIV i w pierwszej polowie XV wieku* [Techniques and organization of brick architecture in Prussia in the late 14th century and first half of the 15th], Studia z dziejów rzemiosła i przemysłu [Studies of the history of craft and industry], ix (Wrocław, Warsaw and Kraków, 1970), pp. 7–139

A. Kąsinowski: *Podstawowe zasady murarstwa gotyckiego na Pomorzu Zachodnim* [Basic principles of Gothic brickwork in Western Pomerania], Studia z dziejów rzemiosła i przemysłu [Studies of the history of craft and industry], x (Wrocław, Warsaw and Kraków, 1970), pp. 47–131

G. Ionesco: *Histoire de l'architecture en Roumanie* (Bucharest, 1972)

J. Białostocki: *The Art of the Renaissance in Eastern Europe: Hungary, Bohemia, Poland* (Oxford, 1976)

V. A. Chanturiya: *Istoriya arkhitektury Byelorussii* [History of the architecture of Belarus'] (Minsk, 1977), pp. 30, 58–93

P. A. Rappoport: *Russkaya arkhitektura, X–XIII vv: Katalog pamyatnikov* [Russian architecture, 10th–13th centuries: catalogue of monuments] (Leningrad, 1982)

P. Crossley: *Gothic Architecture in the Reign of Kasimir the Great* (Kraków, 1985)

J. Minkevicius, ed.: *Lietuvos architekturos istorija* [Architectural history of Lithuania] (Vilnius, 1987), pp. 46–8, 91, 112, 128–58

H. J. Boker: *Die mittelalterliche Backsteinarchitektur Norddeutschlands* (Darmstadt, 1988)

A. Miłobędzki: *Zarys dziejów architektury w Polsce* [Outline history of architecture in Poland] (Warsaw, 1988), pp. 41–118

MARIA BRYKOWSKA

(h) Spain and Portugal. Although of minor importance in Roman Spain, brick remained in use under the Visigoths and was well established by the time of the Arab conquest (8th century AD). It continued to be employed throughout the Middle Ages, mainly in the Mediterranean kingdoms of Spain, but was rarely used in Portugal. The brick industry in Valencia is well documented from 1393, and there are also significant brick buildings in New Castile and Andalusia.

Brick was used for mosques and synagogues. The Mezquita (begun 785) at Córdoba (*see* CÓRDOBA (i), §3(i)(a)) has two tiers of horseshoe arches in alternating bands of red brick and white stone. An exception to the general practice between the 14th and 16th centuries of rebuilding mosques is at Mertola (Portugal), which retains its square plan and 13th-century vault. In Seville the brick minaret, known as the Giralda (see fig. 13), was preserved as the cathedral bell-tower. The lower part is stone, built in 1184 by Ahmad ibn Baso. Ali de Gómera completed the major part in 1198, using diapering panels (*ajaracas*) to frame the balconied central part of each face. Hernán Ruiz II added the upper stages with an open belfry (1558–68). In Toledo the Ibn Shoshan synagogue (rebuilt 1250; now S María la Blanca) has five aisles, separated by arcades of octagonal brick piers, now covered with white plaster. The Sinagoga del Tránsito (1366), also in Toledo, built for Samuel Halevi (*fl* 1350s–1360s), Treasurer to Peter the Cruel, King of Aragon (*reg* 1350–79), has rich Moorish friezes applied to the brick walls.

Some stone churches have brick towers: there are several examples in Saragossa, including the twin towers of the cathedral, and also at S Tomé (rebuilt 1300–20), Toledo, and S Nicolás de Bari, Madrigal de las Altas Torres (Valladolid). Santiago del Arrabal, Toledo, has a *Mudéjar* tower (1179) and a recessed brick façade (13th century); the interior brick vaulting is unusual. The 16th-century parish church at Villaverde de Medina (Valladolid) is one

13. The Giralda, Seville Cathedral, 1184–98; upper stages by Hernán Ruiz II, 1558–68

of the few Spanish churches wholly in brick. Conventual buildings in brick include the cloister (16th century) of S Domingo, Pamplona. The two-storey brick cloister (1402–12) at GUADALUPE, built in the *Mudéjar* style, has at its centre a fountain pavilion with a three-stage octagonal brick spire with brick blind arcading beneath each gable.

The use of brick in secular architecture was concentrated in Andalusia and the Castilian heartland between the rivers Douro and Tagus. High-level patronage was important for major castles. In 1440 John II, King of Castile and León (*reg* 1406–54), commissioned Fernando Carreño to rebuild LA MOTA CASTLE at Medina del Campo with round corner turrets and machicolation. From 1454 La Mota belonged to Alonso de Fonseca, Archbishop of Seville (1418–73), who built the pink brick COCA CASTLE. The donjon has four octagonal turrets, of which the upper parts and the connecting battlements have distinctive columns of semicircular cut headers. In Islamic palaces, for example in the Torre de Comares, built for Yusuf I (*reg* 1333–54) at the Alhambra, Granada, and in the Alcázar at Seville (for illustration *see* MUDÉJAR; *see also* SEVILLE, §IV, 2)), there is an extreme contrast between the simple use of brick and the finery of the decoration. Plain brick private houses, of which the Casa del Greco, Toledo, is typical, also survive.

BIBLIOGRAPHY
G. K. Kuebler and M. Soria: *Art and Architecture in Spain and Portugal and their American Dominions, 1500–1800*, Pelican Hist. A. (Harmondsworth, 1959), pp. 1–119
G. Goodwin: *Islamic Spain*, Architectural Guides for Travellers (Harmondsworth, 1990)

DAVID H. KENNETT

(ii) 1600 and after.

(a) 17th century. (b) 18th century. (c) 19th century. (d) 20th century.

(a) 17th century. The use of brick had spread through much of Europe by 1600, when it was relatively inexpensive, as prices had remained fairly stable during the 16th-century inflation. Manufacture remained mostly small-scale and local, much as it had been during the Middle Ages. During the 17th century, however, coal replaced wood and turf as fuel. With this came new kiln types, although brickmakers in some regions, for example parts of Flanders and around the Thames, east of London, continued to fire without kilns, stacking the bricks in clamps with fuel intermixed. The earliest patent for a pug-mill was issued in England in 1609. This was horse-driven and produced more consistent raw material, resulting in bricks of a more uniform quality. Sizes varied, with English bricks (*c.* 60 mm) rather thicker than other European examples (*c.* 40 mm); this could affect the overall appearance of wall faces.

Choice of bond also affected the appearance of walls. In the early 17th century the most popular were English bond (see fig. 2a above) and its variant Cross bond, in which the perpends (vertical joints) in a stretcher course are placed over the centre of the bricks in the next stretcher course below: this gives a muted diagonal grid over the wallface. During the mid-17th century, however, Flemish bond (see fig. 2c above) was adopted in England, beginning with Kew Palace (1631), London. In Flanders and the rest of northern Europe, however, English and Cross bond remained the norm.

The new library (1623–8; see fig. 14) built for St John's College, Cambridge, was still Gothic, although with some classical elements in its stone decoration. Generally, however, classical styles had displaced Gothic in brick architecture by this time. A series of sober, even severe, English mansions was built in red brick with stone dressings, large windows and parapets masking rooflines. Stone strapwork decoration was much used, and main entrances were sometimes wholly of stone. Hatfield House (1607–12), Herts, is the grandest example, but smaller versions occur, for example Charlton House (1607), Greenwich, London.

Continental buildings were less severe: the Place des Vosges (1605), Paris, is of red brick with rusticated stone window surrounds and pilaster strips, creating a busy effect. Later examples include the earliest portion of the château at Versailles (1624), but after *c.* 1630 brick was abandoned for French public buildings until the mid-19th century, although it continued to be used for smaller houses. A similar style was adopted in Belgium at, for example, Thoricourt Castle (17th century), near Ath.

14. Library of St John's College, Cambridge, 1623–8

In the northern Netherlands brick was the dominant material for large public buildings and for houses. Most adopted Renaissance stone detailing, notably strapwork and finials, although the continued use of gables of basically triangular form, and of spires for churches, continued to give a 'Gothic' appearance: Hendrick de Keyser's Westerkerk (1620), Amsterdam, for example, has a gabled east end, transepts and porches topped by classical pediments. Actual Gothic details (buttresses and traceried windows) were still used in the smaller towns, for example in Vrouwenpolder church (1624), Zeeland. Houses were normally built end-on to the street, enabling gables to be developed, and some towns, notably Amsterdam, Bruges, Arras and Gdańsk, retain whole series of them. The simplest are the stepped gable, which rises in a series of steps, each with a flat coping-stone, and spout-gables, shaped like an inverted funnel, the square top section capped with a flat coping-stone. In rural areas this top section was sometimes replaced by a short chimney-stack. The straight gable sides were often constructed with tumbling-in (triangular sections of brickwork with courses at right angles to the gable slopes), with and without stone copings. Reducing the number of steps to two, enlarging them and filling the re-entrants with stone scrolls led to the elevated neck-gable, which was popular in the mid-17th century and often topped by a pediment. Neck-gables proper, in which there is a single pair of steps, again filled with scrolls, and with a pediment, became popular before the mid-17th century and continued into the 18th. A little later scrolled gables were introduced, with curving sides giving a bell-like outline, often with a pediment (*see* GABLE, DECORATIVE); they can be highly developed, particularly on such public buildings as town halls. Copings and trim are normally in stone, although rural examples might be more crudely fashioned from brick, as at the Toegangspoort, Beers, Friesland. This Netherlandish brick architecture was widely influential in northern France, Germany, Denmark, Sweden and as far east as Gdańsk; sometimes Dutch architects were involved, for example Antonis van Obberghen, who worked on the Gdańsk Arsenal (1601–9; for illustration *see* OBBERGHEN, ANTONIS VAN), while the Trinity Church (1617–28), Kristianstad, Sweden, has been attributed to Lourens van Steenwinckel and Hans van Steenwinckel.

The situation in England was more complex. Spout-gables occur on the small brick church of St Peter (1614–26), Buntingford, Herts, and the library (?*c*. 1600) at Trinity Hall, Cambridge, has stepped gables with flat copings: English examples normally have tentlike copings of inclined bricks. English gables are simpler in shape than Netherlandish types, and are usually without stone trim; they are often simple compass-gables formed of quarter-circles. Some may be the work of immigrants from the Low Countries. Most larger houses, however, such as Kew Palace and Broome Park (*c*. 1635), Kent, seem to derive more from pattern books. In their turn they influenced the design of smaller brick houses in eastern England, which are sometimes dated by numerals in wrought iron or raised or black bricks. The best brickwork, as at Kew Palace, incorporated gauged brickwork, in which fairly soft bricks were sawn to shape and rubbed to a precise size using a harder brick; they were laid with fine joints of lime putty. Many architectural features were constructed in this way. In southern Europe thin bricks were used in no regular bond since they were plastered to imitate stone. Borromini's unfinished S Andrea delle Fratte (begun 1653), Rome, shows how intricate classical features were constructed from brick before plastering.

During the 17th century brickwork was taken to America. German, Swedish and French settlers built mostly in wood; the French, however, sometimes used brick infilling for the timber frames (*briqueté entre poteaux*). In Spanish areas adobe was traditional, but in mass form; the Spaniards introduced large adobe bricks (*c*. 460×250×130 mm). The Dutch and English had the greatest impact: illustrations of New Amsterdam (later New York) show a town indistinguishable from those of the Netherlands. English and Cross bond predominated at first, although the Old Brick Church (*c*. 1660), Isle of Wight County, VA, was already in Flemish bond; it has Gothic buttresses and traceried windows and a stepped gable with brick copings of English type, but there is a classical round-headed west door and triangular pediment. Other early American brick churches include the Roman Catholic chapel (1634–8) in St Mary's City, VA. Most are towerless, although a tower was added to the first brick church (1639–44) at Jamestown, VA, at the end of the 17th century. Houses also followed European styles: Bacon's Castle (1664–5), Surrey County, VA, designed by Arthur Allen, has compass-gables of English form. Most of the houses (destr.) of New Amsterdam had stepped gables of Dutch form, with flat stone copings. The Dutch also introduced coloured and glazed bricks for elaborate patterns. Some early bricks were imported, but brickyards were set up as early as 1628 at New Amsterdam and 1629 at Salem, MA, while brick was later exported to Bermuda in exchange for limestone.

More strictly classical styles were adopted in Europe in the mid- and late 17th century. Giant pilasters of brick or stone articulated otherwise simple façades; Pieter Post and Jacob van Campen's Mauritshuis (1638–44) in The Hague (for illustration *see* CAMPEN, JACOB VAN) was an important influence on Hugh May's Eltham Lodge (1663–4), Kent, and on houses elsewhere, including John Foster's House (1689–92), Boston, MA. In England, Christopher Wren introduced more elaboration, as in the chequer brickwork, stone swags and rustication of St Benet (1677–83), Paul's Wharf, London, and similar work at Hampton Court Palace (1690–96; see WREN, CHRISTOPHER, fig. 3). His greatest work in brick, however, is hidden from view: a vast brickwork cone (1675–1710) that does the structural work within the dome of St Paul's Cathedral, London (see DOME, §1).

(b) 18th century. The more restrained style of the late 17th century set the trend for the 18th century in Europe, America and Australasia. In mainland Europe this often involved a return to stone, although for town houses a simple brick façade with large windows was often adopted, topped by a deep cornice in elaborate Louis XIV style stonework. Such detailing might also be added to door surrounds. Simpler, shallower cornices were introduced later. Houses of these types are common in the Netherlands and were introduced in other countries. Johann Boumann built low-corniced houses (1738–42) in the Mittelstrasse, Potsdam, with simple pilasters and Louis XIV style doorcases, placing them next to buildings with more traditionally shaped gables in the city's Dutch Quarter (*see* POTSDAM, §1). The force of tradition was particularly strong in Bruges, where stepped and shaped gables continued to be used.

In Britain the less mannered Georgian style employed brick façades with well-proportioned windows, cornices or parapets and minimal ornament, although cut-brick decoration was sometimes added: there are good examples of carved capitals at 14 and 15 Tooks Court, London. Larger façades were sometimes articulated by giant order pilasters. The style was used for private dwellings, typically in long terraces, as well as for public buildings and churches. It was exported to America and, later, to Australia. Among free-standing houses, the MacPheadris–Warner House (1718–23) in Portsmouth, NH, and Westover, Charles City County, VA (1730–35; *see* UNITED STATES OF AMERICA, fig. 4), are outstanding. The terrace house was also introduced into America, the most ambitious example being Tontine Crescent (1793; destr.), Boston, designed by Charles Bulfinch. Wren's influence is seen in many churches, including the small St James (1713), Goose Creek, SC, and the larger St Philip (1711–23; destr. 1835), Charleston, SC. Christ Church (1727), Philadelphia, PA, owes more to Wren's younger contemporary James Gibbs: it has two tiers of brick-built pilasters framing round-headed windows and a square tower.

As some British architects in the second quarter of the century encouraged a return to Palladian principles, buildings were often in stone or stuccoed brick, but some have exposed brickwork. Isaac Ware dismissed red brick as 'fiery': 'there is something disagreeable in the transition from red brick to stone' (*A Complete Body of Architecture*, London, 1756). Accordingly, when exposed brick was employed it tended to be 'white' (usually yellowish or grey). The exterior of Holkham Hall (1734–64), Norfolk, designed by Thomas Coke, 1st Earl of Leicester, is of greenish-cream bricks that resemble stone from a distance, although the courtyard is of cheaper red bricks. Palladian architects did not always follow their own precepts: James Leoni's Clandon Park (?1731–3), Surrey, is in red brick. Red brick was more acceptable in America. Drayton Hall (1738–42), Charleston, SC, for example, with its block form and portico, is firmly Palladian yet is of red brick, as was the early version (1771–80) of Thomas Jefferson's MONTICELLO, VA, and his buildings for the University of Virginia (1823–7), Charlottesville. For the stuccoed Palladian Government House (1788–9), Sydney, Australia, 5000 bricks were shipped from England, the rest locally produced at Brickfield Hill.

The most refined Georgian brickwork employed rubbed bricks of precise shape laid with fine lime putty joints. This was expensive, however, and more usually such rubbed and gauged brickwork was reserved for window surrounds, arched panels, rusticated angles and 'aprons' beneath windows, all usually in differently coloured bricks. Similarly, in arch construction, each voussoir had to be sawn and rubbed to a precise shape. Fine lime putty joints were used, or occasionally the bricks were joined with mastic, almost eliminating visual joints. The horizontal joints in arches did not always occur in aesthetically desirable places; they were therefore filled with mortar coloured to match the bricks; bastard joints were chiselled at the 'correct' places and filled with lime putty. The lower edges of flat arches were sometimes cut to a wavy form.

The appearance of an overall gauged brickwork façade could be simulated at relatively low cost by tuck-pointing. Bricks were laid normally, but the joints were raked and filled with mortar coloured to match the bricks. This was finished flush, and narrow grooves (w. 3–6 mm) were formed in it before it dried and filled with lime putty. Instead of following the mortar joints, perpends could be chiselled into the bricks if this resulted in greater regularity.

An interesting English practice was the use of flanged mathematical tiles (brick tiles) that gave the appearance of brickwork when hung on a wall. They were available in normal brick colours and with black glaze, which was much used in Brighton and Lewes, E. Sussex. They usually simulated Flemish bond, although header bond was usual with the black-glazed tiles. Their main purpose was for modernizing timber buildings, although they were sometimes used from the outset on new framed structures and occasionally to change a red brick façade into a more up-to-date 'white' façade. Although found occasionally elsewhere in England (and in one case in Wales), they belong predominantly to south-east England. They do not appear to have been used in other parts of Europe, America or Australia, nor, contrary to a long-held belief, were they introduced to circumvent the British Brick Tax (1784–1850).

The predominant use of Cross bond in continental Europe continued to give wallfaces a muted diagonal mesh pattern. Where Flemish bond was used, a chequer pattern was sometimes created by using lighter stretchers and darker headers. Christ Church (1727), Philadelphia, shows this, as does the basement storey of Stratford Hall (c. 1725–

30), VA. It was often used in England and was occasionally copied in mathematical tiles.

(c) 19th century. During the 19th century there was a tremendous increase in the use of and demand for brick, partly owing to burgeoning populations. The railways were also important, as their engineering works required enormous quantities of brick, while the spreading network made transport of brick easier and cheaper. Mechanization was only gradually introduced in the brickmaking industry, but the invention of the Hoffmann kiln (1858), allowing continuous firing, was a great advance and was rapidly adopted (*see* §I, 1(ii) above) in most areas. Brickmaking machines, including those for producing wirecut bricks, were also developed; machine-made bricks were harder, smoother and more uniform than handmade examples.

In countries where Flemish bond had become dominant there was often a return to English bond: it was stronger than Flemish bond for engineering works and represented a return to medieval methods for ecclesiastical and some other public buildings. Engineering works were regarded as functional, although massed brickwork, as in the piers of viaducts, is particularly compelling to modern taste: 13 million bricks were required for the viaduct (1848–50) built by Lewis Cubitt (*b* 1799) at Digswell, near Welwyn, Herts.

Nineteenth-century revival styles were used for brick as well as stone buildings. Some Greek Revival buildings were in stuccoed brickwork, while the Doric portico of St Andrew (1831), Niagara-on-the-Lake, Ont., was placed before a Georgian-style red brick nave. Karl Friedrich Schinkel was an outstanding creator of heavy classical buildings in brick, notably the Bauakademie (1831–5; destr. 1961; *see* SCHINKEL, KARL FRIEDRICH, fig. 2) in Berlin. Exposed brickwork was well suited to Gothic or Byzantine Revival styles, although some Romanesque Revival examples were constructed: at St Botolph (1837–8), Colchester, Essex, for example, William Mason (ii) recreated Norman architecture using moulded white brick units. Hermann Friedrich Waesemann (1813–79) introduced Lombardy Gothic to Berlin with his so-called 'Rotes Rathaus' (1861–9), while Conrad Wilhelm Hase turned to native forms and erected several *Backsteingotik* buildings in Hannover (e.g. Christuskirche, 1859–64) and influenced the work of others in Hamburg, Lübeck, Gdańsk and elsewhere.

In the *Seven Lamps of Architecture* (London, 1849) and the *Stones of Venice* (London, 1851–3), John Ruskin urged the employment of polychrome brickwork drawing on medieval Italian examples; G. E. Street and George Gilbert Scott I also advocated polychrome brickwork in their publications. 'Structural polychromy' was developed particularly by William Butterfield, whose design for All Saints' (1849–54), Margaret Street, London, became the model for other churches and secular buildings. Butterfield also used it for Keble College (1867–83) in the traditionally stone-built Oxford (*see* BUTTERFIELD, WILLIAM, §§2 and 4 and figs 1 and 2; *see* POLYCHROMY, colour pl. I, fig. 2). At Girton College (begun 1872), Cambridge, Alfred Waterhouse employed red brick and terracotta, with fine black mortar joints. Red, yellow, buff, black and white bricks could all be combined with stone and tiles to give a rich carpet-like pattern: appropriately, the finest example in Scotland is the Italianate façade (1889) built by William Leiper for Templeton's Carpet Factory, Glasgow. Polychromy was applied to terraced houses and continued in use into the early 20th century. For large public buildings, however, it was already out of favour by the completion of Keble College.

In mainland Europe, polychromy was used for much longer on public buildings. It had been employed in the *brique et fer* technique, using an exposed cast-iron frame infilled with decorative brickwork panels, at Les Halles (1854–6; destr.), Paris, and the Menier Chocolate Factory (1871), Noisiel-sur-Marne. Les Halles was illustrated by Lacroux together with numerous other examples of polychrome brickwork. Viollet-le-Duc also urged its use in *Entretiens sur l'architecture* (Paris, 1863–72). Polychrome brickwork is especially striking when combined with projecting bricks, as on the St Vincentiusgesticht (1873), Antwerp. The technique survived long enough to be combined with early 20th-century Art Nouveau patterning, as in the Huis 'De Slag van Waterloo' in Berchem, near Antwerp.

The use of polychrome brickwork also crossed the Atlantic. Leopold Eidlitz's Holy Trinity Episcopal Church (1870–75; destr. 1901), New York, was in the style advocated by Ruskin with much use of diapering and other patterns. The Memorial Hall (1865–78) designed by Ware & Van Brunt for Harvard University, Cambridge, MA, is in an eclectic style, again using polychromy. It was also applied to houses, and a local polychrome style developed in southern Ontario was much used for farmhouses. As in continental Europe, the fashion persisted longer than in Britain. In Australia polychrome brickwork at first followed an Elizabethan tradition revived by S. S. Teulon and others in England. In the 1860s this was superseded by a heavy Italianate style, as at Rippon Lea, Melbourne. The polychromy, although not the style, was adopted for suburban housing, especially in Melbourne, but was abandoned for plain red brickwork after the economic depression of 1893.

In the late 19th century in Britain there was a return to plainer brickwork, especially in the work of Richard Norman Shaw (*see* QUEEN ANNE REVIVAL). The earliest example is Philip Webb's Red House (1858–60), Bexleyheath. Other revivals included the well-wrought Dutch style used by Basil Champneys, for example at Newnham College (1878–94), Cambridge. Westminster Cathedral (1895–1902), London, designed by J. F. BENTLEY, combines red brick with bands of white stone in the 'Italo-Byzantine' style: the slim campanile is striking.

During the 19th century and early 20th experiments were made, especially in the USA, Italy and Switzerland, with hollow and perforated bricks, larger than standard bricks. They have been fairly extensively used in those countries and in Germany; many buildings of this type were intended to be rendered. The development of calcium silicate bricks, which are not fired like clay bricks and are available in many colours and textures, often simulating clay bricks, was also important. Production began in Germany in 1894 and had spread to Britain by 1904.

Cavity-walling was advocated as early as 1805 in William Atkinson's *Views of Picturesque Cottages with Plans* (London, 1805), which recommended a cavity of 150 mm with brick ties at intervals, citing cheapness of construction and thermal insulation. Later, Thomas Downes Wilmot Dearn (1777–1853) suggested two leaves of 110 mm with a cavity of 50 mm (*Hints on Improved Method of Building*, London, 1821), and others also advocated this type of construction, suggesting different cavity widths and adding protection from damp penetration as a reason. From the 1860s larger numbers of houses were erected with cavity walls in Britain, particularly in the south. In North America cavity-walling was apparently introduced by Ithiel Town at New Haven, CT; in Australia it was used from *c.* 1870 and was normal for suburban houses by 1900.

(d) 20th century.

Style and construction. In the 20th century there was much experiment in brick techniques. Frank Lloyd Wright made dramatic use of brickwork planes at the Larkin Building (1902–6), Buffalo, NY, and continued to employ the material throughout his career. His influence may be seen in W. M. Dudok's work in the Netherlands, for example at the Hilversum Raadhuis (1927–31; for illustration *see* DUDOK, W. M.), where plain blocks of brickwork are tellingly juxtaposed, together with a high, slim brick tower. Dudok also built several schools in a similar style in Hilversum, and his influence may be seen in France (Cachan-sur-Seine) and England, for example at Hornsey Town Hall (1933) by Reginald Uren and Greenwich Town Hall (1939) by Clifford Culpin. In the Netherlands H. P. Berlage's Beursgebouw (1896–1903; *see* NETHERLANDS, THE, fig. 11), Amsterdam, was highly influential on Michel de Klerk, P. L. Kramer and other architects of the AMSTERDAM SCHOOL, who used brick in a more Expressionist mode. Other Expressionist brick buildings are P. V. Jensen-Klint's Grundtvig church (1921–40), Copenhagen (see fig. 15), echoing the *Backsteingotik* of the Middle Ages, the Planetarium (1922–4), Düsseldorf, by Wilhelm Kreis and the Milch Chemical Factory (1911–12) at Luban (for illustration *see* POELZIG, HANS). Although architects of the Modern Movement favoured reinforced concrete, one of the most important buildings, the Fagus Factory (1911–13), Alfeld an der Leine, designed by Walter Gropius and Adolf Meyer, used brickwork and glass, as did Mies van der Rohe's Wolf House (1926; destr.) at Guben and others in Krefeld. Some buildings that appear to be of concrete are actually of rendered brickwork: Erich Mendelsohn's Einsteinturm (1920–24), Potsdam, and Gerrit Rietveld's Schröder House (1924), Utrecht.

Until the late 19th century brick buildings employed load-bearing walls even when rising through several storeys. This ended with the advent of steel frames (and, later, reinforced concrete); the last load-bearing, high-rise brick building in the old manner is Burnham & Root's elegant Monadnock Building (1889–92), Chicago, the walls of which are 2 m thick at the base. Thereafter, frame construction was widely adopted. Brick might be added as external 'skin', for example for Louis Sullivan's Wainwright Building (1890–91), St Louis, which has a steel skeleton clothed in brick piers (*see* UNITED STATES OF AMERICA,

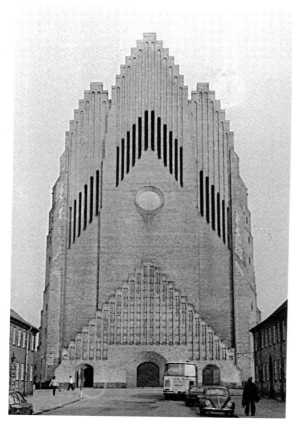

15. Grundtvig church, Copenhagen, by P. V. Jensen-Klint, 1921–40

fig. 7); the logical expression of the frame through brick cladding is well exemplified by Sigurd Frosterus's Stockmann department store (1924–31), Helsinki. Alternatively, brick panels might be placed within the framework, for example at Albert Kahn's factory (1908; most destr.) for Henry Ford at Highland Park, Detroit. On the Johnson Wax Tower (1950), Racine, WI, Frank Lloyd Wright swept the brickwork round the corners, while on the Kline Science Center (1962–5), New Haven, CT, Philip Johnson & Richard Foster neatly wrapped the brickwork around the reinforced concrete frame.

Experiments in Switzerland after World War II, for example at Zurich, demonstrated that load-bearing, high-rise brick walls could be much thinner than those built according to earlier methods. This type of construction is cheaper than frame-building and was revived in other European countries, including Britain, and in the USA and Australia, where it has been found to withstand well the effects of earthquakes. David Krantz's ten-storey Tower Ridge, Perth, has staggered windows that strengthen shear-resistance while providing decorative façades. In England the William Stone Building (1963–4) at Peterhouse College, Cambridge, by Sir Leslie Martin and Colin St John Wilson has varying façades. In such work it is essential to include fully bonded T- and L-junctions so that walls brace each other against buckling. Walls themselves may be of cavity construction.

The use of cavity-walling increased rapidly in the inter-war period, with larger building firms often giving the lead. Twisted-wire ties became common. In Europe low-rise cavity-walling is largely restricted to the north-western countries, with Belgium favouring a 100 mm outer leaf and a 200 mm inner leaf, in contrast to the commoner scheme of two 100 mm leaves. Solid-wall construction, although often using hollow bricks, has generally been retained in France, south Germany and southern Europe. From World War II the inner leaf has normally been of building blocks, allowing faster construction and improving thermal insulation. Cavities are sometimes filled with insulating material. An interesting Australian variant has been 'brick veneer' construction, in which a half-brick outer leaf protects a timber-stud frame. Apparently introduced in Melbourne in 1915, it developed rapidly from the 1930s and was employed for about half the houses built in Victoria in the 1960s.

Decorative brickwork. In the 20th century the use of brick sculpture was revived. In early decades Expressionist architects sometimes treated buildings as large-scale sculpture, whether Cubist, for example Mies van der Rohe's Karl Liebknecht and Rosa Luxemburg Monument to the November Revolution (1926; destr.) at Friedrichsfelde, Berlin, or more plastic, such as the buildings of the Amsterdam school. Antoni Gaudí's chapel (commissioned 1898; 1908–15) for the Colonia Güell, near Barcelona, uses brick and stone columns with brick vaulting in a typically fanciful manner. The cavernous interior of Peter Behrens's I. G.-Farben dye-works (1920–24) at Hoechst is more like applied sculpture, built from plain bricks. Bernhard Hoetger's Pavla-Modersohn-Becker-Haus (1926–7), Bremen, uses the same technique to create wild, sculptural façades; his own house, Brunnenhof (1915–27), in Worpswede, combines this with timber-framed vernacular.

An early example of low-relief brick sculpture, carved *in situ*, is Eric Gill's tribute to Lord Rutherford (1871–1937), known as *The Crocodile*, on the Mond Laboratory (1933), Cambridge. Walter Ritchie, a master of low relief and intaglio, received commissions from Britain, Argentina, Germany, Switzerland and the USA. His birds and animals are finely delineated, his nudes often tenderly beautiful, notably the *Mother and Child* at Bristol Eye Hospital, England. A similar technique, although with a deliberately coarser finish, was used by John Rothwell at County Hall, Morpeth, Northumb., for a coat of arms and a series of historical figures. Others preferred to carve bricks before firing, with careful numbering to aid bricklaying: Mara Smith's *Reflections*, celebrating American commercial and industrial development, on the American Bank, Reading, PA, is a powerful example; more wistful is James Marshall's depiction of a Blackfoot myth at Medicine Hat, Alberta.

An altogether different appearance can be imparted by sand-blasting finished brickwork: William Mitchell Design Consultants produced examples in Britain, including a robust *Canterbury Tales* (1971) in the library at Grays, Essex. Other artists prefer moulding in slightly higher relief: Judith Bluck's historical scenes at Sheffield, S. Yorks, and Lowestoft, Suffolk, are fine examples. For much bolder relief, brickwork blocks may be built into a wall and carved *in situ*, for example the characteristically abstract–organic forms (1955) by Henry Moore on the Bouwcentrum, Rotterdam. Related to sculpture is the use of plain and shaped bricks to produce boldly projecting letters or numerals, such as the words CLYDE REGIONAL CENTRE at that complex in Glasgow.

Bricks of a single contrasting colour may be used to form letters or informative pictures: figures on a public convenience or sports hall, a teapot and cup on a refreshment kiosk, buses at a bus station entrance or crosses on a church. Street names can also be indicated in brick. More complex pictures may be created using standard bricks of several colours, a celebrated example being Paul Waplington's huge *Steelworker* (1984) at Sheffield. Such bricks may be slightly projected, as in van der Bijl's *Noah's Ark* (1965), with dove and olive branch, on the A. C. W. Schefferschool, Harlingen, in the Netherlands; Dutch work inspired Peter Roberts's logo for the MENCAP organization, in cut coloured bricks, at Lincoln. A related development was the creation of carpet-like, polychrome brick pavings, such as that by Adrian Fisher at Kentwell Hall, Long Melford, Suffolk, and that by Tess Jaray at Centenary Square, Birmingham.

Coloured bricks are not essential for bold patterns, which may be achieved by variations in mortar colour alone, most strikingly at Quintin Kynaston School (1958), St John's Wood, London, designed by Edward David Mills (*b* 1915), where large coloured lozenges and hexagons are formed in this way. Mortar colour affects overall appearance, depending on whether it matches or contrasts with the bricks. Overall texture is affected by the joints, whether flush or recessed, and it is possible to provide variation by combining flush horizontal joints with recessed perpends (or vice versa).

In the 20th century there was also much experiment in bricklaying techniques. Even a change of bond influences general appearance, especially by adopting Cross bond, traditional in the Low Countries and used by some 20th-century architects: the muted diagonal mesh across the surface is well exploited on sweeping curves at Ralph Erskine's Pulp Factory (1950–53) at Fors, Sweden. Monk bond (see fig. 2e above) was used by a number of architects, including Dudok and Alvar Aalto. It was adopted by Edward Maufe for Guildford Cathedral (1936–61), Surrey. Howell, Killick, Partridge & Amis returned to using Rat-trap bond (see fig. 2g above) at Darwin College (1965–70) and Blundell Court (1967–9), Sidney Sussex College, both in Cambridge. Walls with this type of bond resemble those built with large hollow bricks (Flem. *snelbouw*; 'quickbuild') that were first introduced for external façades in Belgium *c*. 1970 and also much used in France, Italy, Portugal and Spain. Some types of unusual bond employed in the early 20th century by Amsterdam school architects, such as Stack bond (bricks on end), Basket-weave bond (square blocks of horizontally and vertically laid bricks), Flemish bond laid vertically and others, including bricks with their large faces showing, were revived by architects in the late 20th century. Bricks may even be laid on edge with their frogs showing to give a textured effect.

More complex textures have been achieved by different arrangements of projecting or recessed bricks, for example at the Carlsberg Brewery (founded 1866), Copenhagen, at Århus University (from 1934), on the Provinciehuis (1954), Arnhem, and on Werner Moser's clergy house (1941) beside the Altstetten reformed church in Zurich. A honeycomb pattern using Flemish bond with the headers omitted occurs in a deep screen wall at the top of Ignazio Gardella's Dispensario Antitubercolare (1936) at Alessandria, Italy. Header bond remains in use for smooth curves, but more interest can be created by using Stretcher bond so that each brick projects slightly, as in the stairwell of Julio Lafuente's Santuario dell'Amore Misericordioso at Colvalenza, near Todi, where the courses are raked and the effect enhanced by the thin bricks. In his circular interdenominational chapel (1952–4) for the Massachusetts Institute of Technology at Cambridge, MA, Eero Saarinen incorporated deformed bricks at random to give a rough texture. Overburnt bricks ('clinkers') were much in vogue for textural effects in Sydney after World War II.

Brick has played a part in architectural jokes, such as van Impe's quirky shop and dwelling in Ghent and the formless tower and house of Het Zandkasteel, Utrecht. The buildings for Best Products by SITE and James Wines (*b* 1932) in the USA, such as Indeterminate Façade (1974–5), Houston, TX, which has a cascade of bricks falling from an apparently collapsed wall-top, achieve their effect by undermining architectonic expectations. Post-modern architects often used bricks of many colours, textures and shapes in eclectic, often playful, ways, as in London's Docklands development. Others employed more traditional modes, as in the Zilverpand precinct, Bruges, or the Hillingdon Civic Centre (1975–7), London, by Robert Matthew, Johnson-Marshall & Partners. Others again preferred bold geometrical forms in plain brickwork, as in Aalto's Technical College (1964) at Otaniemi or Harry Weese's First Baptist Church (1965), Columbus, IN. Modern cosmopolitan culture has sometimes produced welcome exotica, such as mosques drawing on Muslim brickwork traditions, a fine example of which is at Luton, Beds.

BIBLIOGRAPHY

J. Lacroux: *La Brique ordinaire au point de vue décoratif* (1878), i of *Constructions en briques* (Paris, 1878–84); Eng. trans., ed. D. Jenkins, as *Architectural Brickwork* (London, 1990) [excellent colour pls of 19th-century French polychrome brickwork]

L. Lefèvre: *La Céramique du bâtiment* (Paris, 1897; Eng. trans., London, 1900)

S. R. Jones: *Old Houses in Holland* (London, 1912/*R* 1986)

B. Butterworth and D. Foster: 'The Development of the Fired-earth Brick', *Trans. Brit. Cer. Soc.*, iv/7 (1956), pp. 457–505

J. G. Van Derpool: 'The Restoration of St Luke's, Smithfield, Virginia', *J. Soc. Archit. Hist.*, xvii/2 (1958), pp. 12–18

Early American Brick Masonry and Restoration of Exterior Brick Walls: National Park Service Historic Training Conference: Philadelphia, 1963

C. W. Condit: *American Building: Materials and Techniques from the First Colonial Settlements to the Present* (Chicago, 1968, 2/1982)

W. Pehnt: *Expressionist Architecture* (London, 1973)

C. C. Handisyde and B. A. Haseltine: *Bricks and Brickwork* (London, [1974])

A. Whittick: *European Architecture in the Twentieth Century* (Aylesbury, 1974)

J. De Visser and H. Kalman: *Pioneer Churches* (Toronto, 1976) [North America]

C. C. Handisyde: *Hard Landscape in Brick* (London, 1976)

J. Woodforde: *Bricks to Build a House* (London, 1976) [mostly Britain]

H.-R. Hitchcock: *Netherlandish Scrolled Gables of the Sixteenth and Early Seventeenth Centuries* (New York, 1978)

G. Peirs: *Uit klei gebouwd: Baksteen architectuur van 1200 tot 1940* [Built from clay: brick architecture from 1200 to 1940] (Tielt and Amsterdam, 1979) [Belgium]

M. Whiffen and F. Koeper: *American Architecture, 1607–1976* (London and Henley, 1981)

G. Peirs and P. Aerschot: *Uit klei gebouwd: Baksteen architectuur na 1945* [Built from clay: brick architecture after 1945] (Tielt and Bussum, 1982) [Belgium]

W. de Wit, ed.: *The Amsterdam School: Dutch Expressionist Architecture, 1915–1930* (New York and Cambridge, MA, 1983)

Decorative Brickwork: The Development of Terracotta in Contemporary Architecture, Ibstock Building Products Ltd (London, 1985)

R. Irving: 'Mostly about Walls', *The History and Design of the Australian House*, ed. R. Irving (Melbourne, 1985), pp. 188–211

T. P. Smith: 'Brick Tiles (Mathematical Tiles) in Eighteenth- and Early Nineteenth-century England', *J. Brit. Archaeol. Assoc.*, cxxxviii (1985), pp. 132–64

D. Krantz: 'Structural Brickwork for Multistorey Buildings', *Brickwork Yesterday and Tomorrow*, ed. T. A. Merefield and others (Perth, [mid-1980s]) [mostly Australia]

R. W. Brunskill: *Brick Building in Britain* (London, 1990)

W. Pohl: 'Der Einfluss der historischen Architekturstile auf die Anwendung des Ziegels/The Influence of Historical Architectural Styles on the Use of Brick', *Ziegelindustrie International* (July 1991), pp. 352–60 [bilingual text]

TERENCE PAUL SMITH

4. ISLAMIC LANDS. Since antiquity, brick has been the primary construction material for all types of buildings—mosques, minarets, mausolea, palaces, baths and city walls—in the enormous region stretching from the Euphrates to Afghanistan, as good building stone was rarely available. There was little timber in the eastern Islamic lands for scaffolding, superstructures or centring, and ingenious techniques of brick vaulting were developed. Brick was also used as a secondary material in the western Islamic lands, where antique masonry traditions were largely maintained for public construction, although brick was often used for vernacular construction. Only occasionally was brick the primary material in the West.

Both mud-brick and baked brick were common. Mud-brick is cheap and practical in areas of low rainfall, a characteristic of much of the region, and its fragile surface can be protected with more durable revetments of plaster or stucco, which, when carved or painted, can also enliven the plainness of brick. The scarcity of fuel for firing makes baked brick more expensive, but its lasting qualities make it preferable in those areas with higher rainfall or more extreme climates. Baked brick can also be plastered, particularly on interiors, but it was frequently left uncovered on exteriors, which were ornamented with decorative bonds and the addition of carved (terracotta) and glazed elements. Magnificent exteriors in glazed brick and tile typified much of the architecture in the eastern Islamic world after *c.* 1250. By contrast, particularly in the western Islamic lands, much indifferent brick construction was intended from the outset to be covered with plaster or some other rendering.

Brick was also used in combination with other materials. The Byzantine technique of alternating courses of brick and stone was used sporadically in Islamic lands, particularly in Syria and Anatolia but also in Spain. The arches of the great mosque of Córdoba (AD 785) have voussoirs of several bricks alternating with limestone blocks, and later additions to the mosque exploited the decorative potential of this device (*see* ISLAMIC ART, fig. 45). The origin of this technique remains unexplained: it may have been a Syrian technique carried to Spain or, alternatively, a local technique invented for structural, economic or decorative reasons.

The use of brick vaults in Syrian architecture of the Umayyad period, as at the 8th-century palace of MSHATTA in Jordan, is thought to have been the product of increased contact with Iran rather than the result of revived Roman techniques. Under the Abbasid caliphs (*reg* 749–1258), whose empire was centred on Mesopotamia, both unbaked and baked brick were used widely for construction. At Samarra', the Abbasid capital for much of the 9th century, immense mosques and palaces were constructed of brick and rendered with plaster, often painted or carved in a variety of styles (*see* BEVELLED STYLE and STUCCO AND PLASTERWORK, §III, 4), but comparatively few spaces were vaulted. Due to the esteem in which the practices of the Abbasid court were held, construction in brick was introduced to the Mediterranean Islamic lands for public architecture. For example in Cairo, the mosque of 'Amr ibn al-'As, founded in the 7th century, had masonry walls and reused marble columns supporting a flat wooden roof; in contrast, the mosque of Ibn Tulun (completed 879; *see* ISLAMIC ART, fig. 24) followed Abbasid precedents by having brick piers and arcades rendered with plaster. Construction of the Azhar Mosque (begun 970) was mixed, with marble columns supporting brick arcades covered with plaster, and that of the Hakim Mosque (completed 1013; *see* ISLAMIC ART, fig. 36) had brick piers and arcades within an enclosure of small stones treated like bricks (*see* CAIRO, §III, 1–4). Later construction in Egypt tended to use fine stone masonry over a rubble core, and vaulting was normally done in stone.

The finest brick construction was practised in Iran and adjacent areas (*see* ISLAMIC ART, §II, 5(i)(b)). The interior and exterior decoration of the tomb of the Samanids, Bukhara (920s; *see* ISLAMIC ART, fig. 27), in which bricks are laid in complex bonds resembling textile patterns, presupposes a long tradition. This sophisticated construction replaced the alternating courses of stretcher and soldier bricks covered in plaster that had been common in the early Islamic period, seen at UKHAYDIR (late 8th century) in Iraq, the Tarik-Khana Mosque at DAMGHAN (9th century; *see* ISLAMIC ART, fig. 23) in northern Iran and even in the octagonal pavilion (998–9) at NATANZ in central Iran. The trend was from large square bricks towards small rectangular ones: those used at Natanz (290×240×50 mm) are considerably smaller than typical Sasanian bricks, and those used in the new style of brick decoration are smaller still. The courtyard of the mosque at NA'IN, for example, was redecorated in the late 10th century with small rectangular bricks (100×150×30 mm) laid in complex bonds to form relief patterns. This style became extremely popular in the 11th century, as at Damghan (e.g. Pir-i 'Alamdar, 1026–7, and Chihil Dukhtaran, 1054–5) and the tomb towers at Kharraqan (1067–8 and 1093–4), where intricate patterns and inscriptions are worked in shaped and cut bricks. The use of cornices of corbelled bricks on such buildings can be linked with the development of MUQARNAS, the stalactite corbelling typical of much later Islamic architecture, as a decorative device. While the use of intricate brick patterns was largely associated with Iran, a rare example from the opposite end of the Islamic lands is the mosque of Bab Mardum (999–1000) at Toledo, the façade of which is elaborately patterned and inscribed in cut brick.

Some brick decoration was elaborately painted, while in other cases, such as the North Dome (1088–9; *see* ISLAMIC ART, fig. 31) of the Friday Mosque at Isfahan, the natural variations in the colour of fired brick were exploited and set off against other materials. The second tomb tower at Kharraqan may have had glazed plugs inset between bricks, and the use of colour expanded in the 12th century. At MARAGHA, for example, the Gunbad-i Surkh (1147–8) has restrained decoration in light blue that complements the reddish brick, an anonymous cylindrical tomb tower (1167) shows a more extensive use of light-blue tile, and the Gunbad-i Kabud (1196–7) is almost enveloped in a glazed web. The exploitation of colour in brick buildings followed two directions: one was the revetment of entire surfaces with glazed tiles or tile mosaic, while the other was the *bannā'ī* technique, in which an entire structure or wall was decorated, often with inscriptions, formed by glazed bricks set between plain ones (*see* ISLAMIC ART, fig. 72).

The attention given to enlivening brick walls (*see* IS-LAMIC ART, §II, 6(i)(a)) was matched by the attention lavished on brick vaults, where structural necessities were transformed into a *tour de force* of decoration. The pitched-brick barrel vault common in early Islamic times (*see*

VAULT: PITCHED BRICK) was gradually replaced by more complex coverings created by combining segments of pitched-brick vaults to form decorative patterns. This development is seen most clearly in the myriad ribbed vaults at the Friday Mosque in Isfahan (*see* ISFAHAN, §3(i)), which were constructed, repaired and renewed over the centuries. The greatest ancient brick vault, that of the Sasanian palace at KTESIPHON, was often seen as a model to be surpassed: the mosque of 'Alishah (*c.* 1310) at Tabriz retains massive brick walls 25 m high; the monumental vault they once supported collapsed soon after construction.

BIBLIOGRAPHY
G. King: 'The Mosque Bāb Mardūm in Toledo and the Influences Acting upon it', *A. & Archaeol. Res. Pap.*, ii (1972), pp. 29–40
E. Galdieri: *Isfahān: Masğid-i Ğuma'a*, 3 vols (Rome, 1972–84)
S. S. Blair: 'The Octagonal Pavilion at Natanz', *Muqarnas*, i (1983), pp. 69–94
L. Bier: *Sarvistan: A Study in Early Islamic Architecture* (University Park, PA, 1986)

SHEILA S. BLAIR, JONATHAN M. BLOOM

5. AFRICA. The earliest surviving brick buildings in Africa are the royal tombs (mastabas) of the Early Dynastic Period (*c.* 2925–*c.* 2575 BC) in Egypt. Tomb paintings and reliefs show the technique used to make bricks, whereby a wooden rectangular frame was filled with either puddled mud alone or mud with straw or dung added to bind the mixture. (This technique continues to be used in Egypt and such other African countries as Zambia to make both

16. Part-built brick house with bricks drying in the sun, Ndasa village, Bemba country, Northern Province, Zambia; from a photograph by Margret Carey, 1972

sun-dried and burnt bricks.) Bricks, often plastered and painted, were the usual material for building palaces, walls, temple annexes and houses, but few of these structures have survived. Nevertheless, it is known that the dome and barrel vault were in use from the Old Kingdom (*c.* 2575–*c.* 2150 BC). Barrel vaults were constructed by arranging each course so that it sloped backward slightly, the first course being only two or three bricks high. Burnt bricks were not used in Egypt until Roman times and were probably fired in the manner still seen in the Near East: stacked, with air vents, around fuel, then covered over and fired.

In Islamic North Africa stone was reserved for important structures, and brick was frequently used for domestic and commercial buildings. Decorative effects were obtained through the use of ornamental chevron patterns, sometimes in an open form as air vents, coloured bricks, glazed bricks and tiles and carved or moulded bricks. South of the Sahara, brick is a traditional building material in such places as Mauritania, southern Mali and Niger, the northern parts of Côte d'Ivoire, Ghana, Nigeria and Chad. Especially in the towns, the rectangular buildings are made of mud or sun-dried bricks (see fig. 16), although burnt bricks and even stone are also used. A mud-built structure will be built up in puddled-mud or mud-and-straw courses that are about 500 mm high, with only one course completed per day. Building with bricks is faster, since the chief part of the material has already dried, although the mortar is the same, i.e. wet puddled mud. The typical Hausa sun-dried brick of this area is 'pear-shaped' (*see* HAUSA). It has a cylindrical base, tapering slightly at the top, and is *c.* 250–300 mm high. Both mud-built and brick-built structures have exterior plastering of mud mixed with potash, vegetable butter or an infusion of locust beans. Roofs may be flat, domed or barrel-vaulted and made of mud reinforced with wood or palm-fronds.

Bricks have other advantages besides enabling buildings to be erected quickly: mud-brick buildings may be two storeys high; they have thick walls and are usually clustered together, thus reducing the effect of the sun's heat; in urban areas, the use of mud-brick reduces the risk of fire, since brick is not combustible.

Islam has generated such striking brick-built buildings as the mosques (14th century; rebuilt *c.* 1950) at Mopti and Djenné, both in Mali. The old brick-built Hausa town walls of, for example, Kano, northern Nigeria, date back to the 13th century. One of the oldest brick buildings in Sub-Saharan Africa is the Great Mosque of Timbuktu, Mali, dated to 1327. Here, the architectural style is distinctive, with vertical buttresses reinforcing outer walls that are crowned with tapering pinnacles.

See also AFRICA, §VI, 1(ii)(c).

BIBLIOGRAPHY
P. Oliver: *African Shelter* (London, 1975)
S. Denyer: *African Traditional Architecture: An Historical and Geographical Perspective* (London, 1978)

MARGRET CAREY

6. INDIAN SUBCONTINENT. Brick has been used continuously in the Indian subcontinent for at least four millennia. The early cities of the Indus Valley, such as HARAPPA and MOHENJO-DARO (*c.* 2550–*c.* 2000 BC), were

17. Brick temple podium mouldings and wall, Tahdauli, Uttar Pradesh, late 9th century or early 10th

built almost exclusively of fired brick notable for its uniformity and durability. These bricks, produced in great quantity, were rectangular in shape and devoid of decoration. As the Indus civilization declined (perhaps due in part to deforestation caused by centuries of using brick kilns), nomadic people of Indo-European ancestry entered the upper reaches of the Indus Valley and settled in northern India. While having no substantial architecture in brick or other materials, these people nonetheless had a sophisticated religion, as is documented by the Vedic texts (*see* INDIAN SUBCONTINENT, §I, 2 and 7), which indicate that brick altars of various shapes and sizes were employed for ritual purposes. These altars were invested with cosmic meaning and at times consisted of complex trapezoidal brickwork. Thus, the two early cultures of the Indian subcontinent about which there is detailed information both employed brick, one using it as a mass-produced building material, while the other used it for limited ritual activities. These applications also characterize the subsequent history of brick production in the Indian subcontinent.

The first cities of the Gangetic plain (from *c.* 8th century BC) incorporated substantial quantities of brick. An example is KAUSAMBI, where the massive rampart was provided with a sloping brick face that has survived to a height of 154 courses. Brick was also a staple building material elsewhere in the major alluvial plains. Unfired brick was used particularly for domestic architecture. Literary references and archaeological evidence of contemporary practice indicate that brick was usually faced with plaster and whitewashed. As Vedic rituals were never

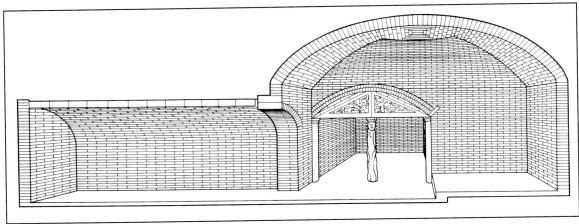

18. Hollow baked bricks (*zhuan*) used to line a Chinese tomb chamber, Luoyang, Henan Province, Warring States period (403–221 BC)

abandoned, there was, in addition, a continuing demand for altar brick. Vedic rites can continue for a year or more; when the performance has been completed, the makeshift buildings are set alight and the site abandoned. One such ritual site, dating from the 4th century AD and having bricks with incised Sanskrit verses, was excavated near Dehra Dun in the Himalayan foothills.

Due to its association with ancient ritual, brick was regarded as an ideal material for sacred monuments. The earliest stupas were made of brick, BHARHUT being a well-known example (*see* STUPA, §1). Temples were also constructed of brick from an early period, but only the foundations have survived. More complete examples from the 5th century AD and later were built of rectangular bricks of great density and hardness. In some cases relief decoration was incised into the bricks before firing, a practice elaborated after the 8th century. Details were also cut into fired brick (see fig. 17). Terracotta plaques were fitted into temple walls, a custom that continued until the 19th century in Bengal.

While temple architecture in brick was often overtaken by subsequent achievements in stone, brick was never displaced as a building material. Stone was occasionally dressed to resemble it, and in southern India brick superstructures were often placed on stone foundations and walls. Although the Islamic conquest (from *c.* AD 1000) radically altered building styles, the material continued to be used in those regions with established brick architecture. In the colonial period an unprecedented variety of new building materials was introduced, but many regions and rural localities maintained the time-honoured preference for brick and plaster.

For further discussions of brick architecture in the Indian subcontinent *see* INDIAN SUBCONTINENT, §III, 3, 4, 5(i)(a) and (e), and 7(ii)(e).

BIBLIOGRAPHY
V. S. Agrawala: 'Mathura Terracottas', *J. United Prov. Hist. Soc.*, ix (1936), pp. 6–38
S. R. Rao: 'A Śātavāhana Brick Temple', *Lalit Kala*, xv (1972), pp. 17–18 [excavated pillar temple at Pattadakal]
J. Harle: *Gupta Sculpture* (Oxford, 1974)

MICHAEL D. WILLIS

7. CENTRAL AND EAST ASIA. Sun-dried mud bricks (and later baked clay bricks) were a common building material in eastern Central Asia (*see* CENTRAL ASIA, §II, 2), where they were used for such early buildings as Temple Y in Khocho (Chin. Gaochang), Xinjiang Uygur Autonomous Region. In Mongolia, fired bricks were used to build massive free-standing structures, such as the Violet Tower of Kublai Khan (*reg* 1260–94) in Kaiping (later Shangdu; *see* MONGOLIA, §III). In China, the preferred materials for domestic architecture were wood or stone; bricks were used for building terraces, walls, pagodas, bridges and particularly for tombs (*see* CHINA, §II, 1(iv) and 6). Brick construction was unknown in Japan until the Meiji period (1868–1912). The size and shape of bricks vary from tile-shaped (150×130×30 mm) to block-shaped (300×240×150 mm). Several methods of construction were used, ranging from Box bond (placing several layers of vertical stretchers between layers of horizontal ones) to Cross bond (placing stretchers in groups of three).

The rammed-earth (Chin. *hangtu*) walls of Chinese cities of the Shang (*c.* 1600–*c.* 1050 BC) and Zhou (*c.* 1050–256 BC) periods were probably faced with mud bricks. Hollow baked bricks (*zhuan*) were used to build tomb chambers during the Warring States period (403–221 BC; see fig. 18). Brick tombs of the Qin period (221–206 BC) with impressed and incised bricks up to 470 mm long have been found in the ruins of Xianyang (Shaanxi Province) and various sites in the Wei Valley. In the Han period (206 BC–AD 220), large hollow terracotta bricks (up to 550 mm long) were fired, often stamped with patterns and scenes from daily life, to line tomb chambers. Many tomb bricks were fired in particular shapes—wedges and dovetails, for example—depending on their placement in the tomb. Brick arches became more common in the Eastern Han period (AD 25–220), and arches and corbelled vaults were later used in the construction of pagodas, the earliest extant example of which is the Songyue Pagoda (AD 523; Henan Province). From the Tang period (AD 618–907) terraces were frequently faced with brick, as in the palace buildings in Chang'an (now Xi'an, Shaanxi Province). Brick balustrades and staircases came into use during the

Yuan period (1279–1368). By the Ming (1368–1644) and Qing (1644–1911) periods, when a factory operated near Beijing, brick construction was widespread, especially for walls and terraces, which had previously been made of rammed earth. Most of Beijing's walls were faced with up to eight layers of brick during the Ming period, and a new north wall of brick was constructed; large sections of the Great Wall of China were paved with a triple layer of brick to form a thoroughfare. In domestic architecture, residential compounds were often surrounded by brick walls; these were covered in a red wash in Beijing and whitewashed in Anhui Province.

Brick construction was rarer in Korea than in China, but it was used for palaces, monasteries and tombs (*see* KOREA, §II, 3(i) and (ii)) during the Paekche period (18 BC–AD 660). One of the finest examples is the tomb of King Munyŏng (*reg* AD 501–23; Kongju, South Ch'ungch'ŏng Province; *see* KOREA, fig. 13), in which four layers of bricks with geometric patterns alternate with one layer of upright bricks. The relief lotus pattern on the upright bricks is formed by the juxtaposition of two bricks. During the Silla period (57 BC–AD 668) andesite bricks were used to imitate clay brick, as in the Punhwang Temple pagoda (7th century; Kyŏngju, North Kyŏngsan Province). For a brief period during the Unified Silla period (AD 668–918) brick pagodas were built in Andong (North Kyŏngsan Province), including one at Chot'ap-dong (8th

century). After this, brick was only used very occasionally, as in the Koryŏ-period (918–1392) pagoda at Silluk Temple (Kyŏnggi Province).

BIBLIOGRAPHY
Guide to Korea's Kyŏngju (Kyŏngju, n.d.)
J. Needham: *Science and Civilization in China*, iv (Cambridge, 1971)
Kim Won-yong [Kim Wŏn-yong], Han Byong-sam [Han Pyŏng-sam] and Chin Hong Sup [Chin Hong-sŏp]: *Ancient Art* (1979), i of *The Arts of Korea* (Seoul, 1979), p. 195
5000 Years of Korean Art (exh. cat., ed. R.-Y. Lefebvre d'Argencé and D. Turner; San Francisco, CA, Asian A. Mus.; Seattle, WA, A. Mus.; Chicago, IL, A. Inst.; and elsewhere; 1979–81), p. 158
J. Rawson: *Ancient China: Art and Archaeology* (London, 1980)
A. Cotterell: *The First Emperor of China* (London, 1981)
W. Watson: *Art of Dynastic China* (London, 1981), pp. 537–8
Along the Ancient Silk Routes: Central Asian Art from the West Berlin State Museums (exh. cat. by H. Hartel and M. Yaldiz, New York, Met., 1982), p. 55

8. SOUTH-EAST ASIA. Throughout South-east Asia the use of brick, together with stone, was almost exclusively confined to such religious structures as temples, monastic buildings and stupas. The earliest brick remains in South-east Asia are the vaulted brick tombs in Vietnam dating from the Eastern Han period (AD 25–220). Some of the baked ceramic bricks used in these tombs are glazed and stamped with geometric reliefs. However, depictions of buildings on Dong Son drums, some of which date from *c.* 600 BC, suggest that the tradition of building with brick is far older. Both the Chams and the Khmers used baked

19. Brick tower sanctuaries (*prasat*) on laterite bases, Prasat Yai Ngao (Don Ngao), Sangkhla District, Surin Province, Thailand, 12th century; view from the east

bricks for tower sanctuaries (see fig. 19), stupas and other Hindu and Buddhist monuments. Flat, rectangular bricks were fired to a high quality, rubbed smooth, ground together and closely bonded with a strong vegetal mortar so that the joinery is almost imperceptible. After the bricks were laid they were sometimes carved; they were then covered with a thin layer of stucco that permitted finely chiselled decoration. Before the 9th century most Khmer temples were built entirely of brick, and sandstone was only used for those parts, such as lintels, that required elaborate decoration (see DOOR, §VI); after c. 900, however, sandstone and laterite were increasingly employed both for the construction of the bases on which the temples were built and for the temples themselves. The bricks were laid without mortar by means of a flexible substance of vegetal origin. They were occasionally carved in relief and then painted or stuccoed. Outstanding examples of Khmer brick reliefs are the early 10th-century carvings of Vishnu and Lakshmi at Prasat Kravan, Angkor (see CAMBODIA, fig. 17).

In the Mon kingdom of Duaravati (7th–13th century) in Thailand, clay bricks of poor quality (c. 400×200×100 mm) tempered with rice-chaff and bonded with unbaked clay were used. In the Thai kingdom of Sukhothai (13th–15th centuries) and its successor Ayutthaya (1351–1767), stuccoed brick was also widely used in temple architecture, usually in conjunction with laterite, and from the 15th century palace buildings as well as temples were often constructed in stuccoed brick, for example Phra Narai Ratchaniwet, the enormous palace at Lopburi built for King Narai of Ayutthaya (reg 1656–88), and the nearby palace of Constantin Phaulkon, the Greek adventurer who became Narai's chief minister. Brick was rarely used in northern Thailand, although in the kingdom of Lan Na (11th–18th centuries) wooden temples were usually supported on brick bases, and raised brick shrines were placed inside them.

Brick was widely used from an early period in Burma. Pyu cities (1st–9th centuries) were enclosed by glazed brick walls, and large baked bricks were used for Pyu vaulted temples and shrines. Some bricks are marked with Pyu lettering. Pagan (9th–13th centuries) is the largest complex of ancient brick buildings in South-east Asia. Large baked clay bricks of various sizes (usually c. 360×180×50 mm) were used for temples, stupas and, less commonly, ancillary religious buildings. They were cemented with a thin layer of clay. Sometimes the bricks were manufactured locally, and sometimes they were brought in from elsewhere, as is shown by the names of the sources stamped on many of them. Broken or half-bricks were occasionally used for minor monuments. Baked clay bricks were also sometimes used for temples in Indonesia, notably at such sites in Sumatra as Padang Lawas and Muara Takus. Few of these brick temples survive, since they were constructed without mortar. Some of the bricks were carved with reliefs. In Central Java brick was less commonly used, although some minor Hindu temples were constructed in brick after about AD 850, and fortified brick walls were built round palaces (kraton). Brick is more commonly found in East Java, where it was widely used for building Hindu temples throughout the

Singhasari (1222–92) and Majapahit (1292–c. 1500) periods. Thomas Stamford Raffles described a flourishing brick-making industry in Java in the early 19th century. Made from baked clay 'obtained from the decomposition of basaltic stones' mixed with earth, bricks were used for the construction of grander houses. Baked bricks have also been widely used in the construction of mosques since the first introduction of Islam into the islands of Indonesia and in Hindu temples in Bali, where it is generally employed in association with a soft, grey stone called paras, which lends itself well to carved decoration and creates a striking colour contrast with the red brick (see INDONESIA, fig. 10).

BIBLIOGRAPHY
J. Dumarçay: The Temples of Java (Oxford, 1986)
P. Strachan: Pagan: Art and Architecture of Old Burma (Arran, 1989)
S. Siribhadra and E. Moore: Palaces of the Gods: Khmer Art and Architecture in Thailand (Bangkok, 1992)

SIAN E. JAY

9. PRE-COLUMBIAN AMERICAS. Adobe brick (see §I, 1(i) above) was used throughout Mesoamerica from the Early Pre-Classic period (c. 2000–c. 1000 BC) and in the Central Andean area from the Initial period (c. 1800–c. 900 BC). Adobe bricks, both handmade and moulded, and larger solid masses were used on their own or in combination with stone for vast complexes of apartments, storerooms, enclosures, palaces, tombs and platforms and for internal partitions and upper floors. Andean architects used unbonded blocks of adobe bricks as both the cores and cladding of pyramidal platforms and hillside terracing and to encase natural hills. Bricks from at least the Early Intermediate period (c. 200 BC–c. AD 600) at northern Andean Moche sites have special marks thought to be makers' marks.

Fired bricks (see §I, 1(ii) above) were used extremely rarely in Mesoamerica and were unknown in the Andes. The Mesoamerican examples are scattered widely. At Late Classic-period (c. AD 600–c. 900) Maya COMALCALCO (Tabasco, Mexico), the corbel-vaulted palace and tomb with stucco reliefs were built of bricks (190×250×240 mm) laid in lime mortar of burnt oyster shells and covered in thick stucco. In one wall the mortar binding is thicker than the bricks. Pebble-tempered clay bricks were used at Late Classic Maya SANTA RITA COROZAL (Belize), and fired bricks were also found at Late Classic–Early Post-Classic (c. AD 600–c. 1200) Maya Zacualpa (Guatemalan highlands). The use of fired bricks at Early Post-Classic (c. AD 900–c. 1200) Toltec TULA (Hidalgo) is disputed, as the firing may have resulted from conflagration at the time of the site's destruction. At Late Post-Classic (c. AD 1200–1521) Tizatlán (Tlaxcala) bricks measuring 560×300×60 mm were used for walls, stairs, altar tables and benches.

BIBLIOGRAPHY
G. Kubler: The Art and Architecture of Ancient America, Pelican Hist. A. (Harmondsworth, 1962, rev. 3/1984)
M. P. Weaver: The Aztecs, Maya and their Predecessors: Archaeology of Mesoamerica (New York, 1972, rev. 3/1993)
R. W. Keatinge, ed.: Peruvian Prehistory: An Overview of Pre-Inca and Inca Society (Cambridge, 1988)
M. E. Moseley: The Incas and their Ancestors: The Archaeology of Peru (London, 1992)

DAVID M. JONES

III. Conservation.

From Roman times brick has been considered more resistant than marble, but nonetheless it is susceptible to deterioration. This can be caused by several factors and diverse mechanisms, resulting in different decay patterns. The main causes of deterioration are salt crystallization and frost; such other factors as air pollution and biological action play a lesser role.

The presence of soluble salts, either in the brick or mortar or in the foundations on which the bricks are laid, in an environment with alternating wet and dry cycles can cause rapid deterioration in a very short time. The deterioration is caused by the pressure exerted by the crystallizing salts as the water that carried them into the porous body evaporates. The damage produced will be proportional to the amount of salt that crystallizes and the number of wetting and drying cycles to which the masonry is exposed (see both Lewin and Pühringer). This deterioration is compounded if, during fluctuations of temperature and relative humidity, the crystallizing salts form hydrates. Transitions between the two forms can then take place, and the secondary crystallization process can be far more destructive than the simple crystallization of a non-hydrate-forming salt. When several salts are present, a distribution pattern can be observed in the masonry: the most soluble salts will tend to migrate up the wall, while the less soluble ones will crystallize closer to the ground. The relative porosity of brick and mortar will determine which material will deteriorate first, since crystallization will take place preferentially in the more porous.

The deterioration produced by frost cannot be totally attributed to the volume increase that water undergoes when freezing. Several arguments have been put forward to explain the development of pressures large enough to disrupt the matrix of the brick mechanically: the main ones attribute these pressures to ice crystal growth (a process similar to salt crystallization) or to liquid water trapped between a frozen core and an advancing freezing front (see Binda, Baronio and Charola; also Nägele). The susceptibility of brick to frost damage will depend upon its porosity and pore-size distribution. The extent of the deterioration will depend on the degree of water saturation, the number of freeze–thaw cycles, the length of the freezing period and the rate at which the temperature changes take place.

The deterioration caused by air pollution alone is negligible, but because it can produce soluble salts upon reaction with lime mortar, it can eventually cause damage to the masonry (see Binda and Baronio). Biological action cannot be considered a major agent of deterioration, except when plants grow in a masonry structure and destroy it mechanically.

As the deterioration of brick is caused either directly or indirectly by the action of water, the main conservation concern is that of keeping the masonry dry. The source of water infiltration has to be identified and stopped before any protective measures can be applied successfully to the masonry. The best protection is provided by hydrophobization agents, the most successful being those based on alkyl alkoxy silanes, siloxanes or silicone resins (see Charola and Lazzarini). Attempts at pre-treating bricks with these agents before they are used in masonry have not been successful. The conservation of brick cannot be undertaken independently of the masonry of which it forms part. When bricks are replaced or an old masonry structure is repointed, care must be taken that the porosity of the new materials matches that of the old. As with new masonry, the correct setting of the bricks in the mortar is important to ensure an effective bond between the two materials. This will diminish water penetration, thus increasing the durability of the masonry.

BIBLIOGRAPHY

T. C. Powers: 'Basic Considerations Pertaining to Freezing–Thawing Tests', *Amer. Soc. Testing & Mat. Proc.*, lv (1955), pp. 1132–55
D. H. Everett: 'The Thermodynamics of Frost Damage to Porous Solids', *Trans. Faraday Soc.*, lvii/9 (1961), pp. 1541–51
J. Iñiguez Herrero: *Alteración de calizas y areniscas como materiales de construcción* (Madrid, 1961)
——: *Altération des calcaires et des grès utilisés dans la construction* (Paris, 1967)
G. G. Litvan: 'Freeze–thaw Durability of Porous Building Materials', *Durability of Building Materials and Components*, American Society for Testing and Materials: Special Technical Publication, 691 (Philadelphia, 1980), pp. 455–63
G. Torraca: *Porous Building Materials* (Rome, 1981)
A. Arnold: 'Rising Damp and Saline Minerals', *Proceedings of the IVth International Congress on the Deterioration and Preservation of Stone Objects: Louisville, KY, 1982*, pp. 11–28
S. Z. Lewin: 'The Mechanism of Masonry Decay through Crystallization', *Conservation of Historic Stone Buildings and Monuments* (Washington, DC, 1982), pp. 120–44
J. Pühringer: *Salt Disintegration: Salt Migration and Degradation by Salt— A Hypothesis*, Swedish Council for Building Research; Document D15:1983 (Stockholm, 1983)
H. Weber: *Mauerfeuchtigkeit* (Sindelfingen, 1984)
L. Binda and G. Baronio: 'Alteration of the Mechanical Properties of Masonry Prisms due to Aging', *Proceedings of the 7th International Brick Masonry Conference: Melbourne, 1985*, pp. 605–16
L. Binda, G. Baronio and A. E. Charola: 'Deterioration of Porous Materials due to Salt Crystallization under Different Thermohygrometric Conditions. I. Brick', *Proceedings of the Vth International Congress on Deterioration and Conservation of Stone: Lausanne, 1985*, pp. 279–88
C. T. Grimm: 'Durability of Brick Masonry: A Review of the Literature', *Masonry: Research, Application, and Problems*, American Society for Testing and Materials: Special Technical Publication, 871 (Philadelphia, 1985), pp. 202–34
E. Nägele: 'Hydrophobierung von Baustoffen: Theorie und Praxis', *Bautenschutz + Bausanierung*, viii/4 (1985), pp. 163–72
A. E. Charola and L. Lazzarini: 'Deterioration of Brick Masonry due to Acid Rain', *Materials Degradation caused by Acid Rain* (Washington, DC, 1986), pp. 250–58

A. ELENA CHAROLA

Brickdale, Eleanor Fortescue. *See* FORTESCUE-BRICK-DALE, ELEANOR.

Brickell, Barry (*b* New Plymouth, New Zealand, 26 Oct 1935). New Zealand potter. In 1960 he obtained a Bachelor of Science degree from the University of Auckland and in 1961 became a full-time studio potter. His interest in historical methods of potting and firing and in the relationship between the arts and industry led to his construction of small-scale railways and a variety of firing kilns. A particular interest was in using coal-fired kilns to achieve a salt-glaze finish to his work, as can be seen in his 'Thinso' jug (*see* NEW ZEALAND, §VII, 2 and fig. 13). Brickell is best known for his sculptural terracotta work, many examples of which are held in New Zealand institutions and museums. A relief tile mural by Brickell is on display in the offices of Waitaki Refrigeration Ltd, London. In 1987 Brickell published *A New Zealand Potter's Dictionary*, a guide to the materials and techniques of pottery for New Zealand and South Pacific Island potters.

WRITINGS

A New Zealand Potter's Dictionary (1987)

PETER GIBBS

Bridan. French family of sculptors.

(1) Charles-Antoine Bridan (*b* Ravières, Burgundy, 31 July 1730; *d* Paris, 28 April 1805). He was a pupil of Jean-Joseph Vinache and won the Prix de Rome in 1754. Following a period in Paris at the Ecole Royale des Elèves Protégés, he was in Rome at the Académie de France from 1757 to 1762. On his return to France he was accepted (*agréé*) by the Académie Royale in 1764 and received (*reçu*) as an academician in 1772 on presentation of the group the *Martyrdom of St Bartholomew* (marble; Paris, Louvre). The somewhat flaccid quality of this work is also apparent in the statue *Vulcan Presenting Venus with the Arms of Aeneas* (marble, exh. Salon 1781; Paris, Luxembourg Gardens) and in his marble statues of *Sébastien Leprestre de Vauban* (exh. Salon 1785) and *Bayard* (1790; both now Versailles, Château), commissioned for the Crown by Charles-Claude de Flahaut de la Billarderie, Comte d'Angiviller, director of the Bâtiments du Roi, for the series of 'Illustrious Frenchmen'.

Bridan's portrait busts include that of *François César le Tellier, Marquis de Courtanvaux* (marble, exh. Salon 1775; Paris, Bib. Ste–Geneviève), for whom he executed a funerary monument (fragments, 1785; Tonnerre, Hôp.); he also provided a funerary monument for *Jean-Baptiste Boyer* (marble, 1775; Aix-en-Provence, Mus. Granet). He was, however, principally known for his pleasingly modelled and widely reproduced statuettes on allegorical themes, such as *Fidelity* (plaster painted as terracotta, Chartres, Mus. B.-A.), which were a pretext for the execution of charmingly erotic female nudes. He also executed matched pairs with libidinous overtones, such as the *Little Girl with a Nest* and the *Little Boy with a Bird*, commissioned in marble by Victor, Duc de Luynes (terracotta versions *c.* 1784; Chartres, Mus. B.-A.).

Bridan's monumental masterpiece was the sculptural decoration for the choir of Chartres Cathedral to designs by the architect Victor Louis. The marble group of the *Assumption of the Virgin* on the high altar (marble, 1767–73; *in situ*) is an astonishingly theatrical Baroque ensemble and one of the last manifestations of its kind in the religious art of 18th-century France. The eight low reliefs surrounding it representing *Scenes from the Life of the Virgin* (marble, 1786–8; *in situ*) have a more classicizing style, with clear and symmetrical compositions and measured movement. Together they illustrate some of the stylistic contradictions in late 18th-century French sculpture.

BIBLIOGRAPHY

Lami

F. Benoit: 'Le Conflit de styles dans la cathédrale de Chartres au XVIIIème siècle', *Rev. Hist. Mod. & Contemp.*, ii (1901), pp. 45–57

M. Furcy-Raynaud: *Inventaire des sculptures exécutées au XVIIIème siècle pour la direction des Bâtiments du Roi* (Paris, 1927), pp. 62–73

M. Jusselin: 'Projets pour la transformation du choeur de la cathédrale de Chartres au XVIIIème siècle', *Bull. Mnmtl* (1929), pp. 503–8

GUILHEM SCHERF

(2) Pierre-Charles Bridan (*b* Paris, 10 Nov 1766; *d* Versailles, 4 Aug 1836). Son of (1) Charles-Antoine Bridan. He studied with his father; in 1791 he won the Académie Royale's first prize for sculpture and in 1793 went to Italy as a *pensionnaire*. He remained in Rome until 1799, when he returned to Paris. He contributed to Napoleon I's monumental projects in Paris, notably providing 12 sections of bronze low relief for the Colonne de la Grande Armée (1806–10) in the Place Vendôme and a statue of a cannonier for the Arc de Triomphe du Carrousel (1807–8). In 1813 he was commissioned by the imperial administration to produce an enormous elephant as the central feature of a fountain for the Place de la Bastille. Never cast in bronze, it remained in the square in its plaster version until after 1830. During the Bourbon Restoration (1815–30) he produced the statue of *Bertrand Duguesclin* (marble, 1824) for the Pont de la Concorde in Paris. In 1831 the work was removed from the bridge and in 1966 sent to the military academy at Coëtquidan. Bridan also executed the tomb of *Margaret of Burgundy, Queen of Sicily* (1826; Tonnerre, Hôp.). These two works adopt the same costume medievalism found in his father's statue of *Bayard*.

BIBLIOGRAPHY

Lami

PHILIP WARD-JACKSON

Bridell, Frederick (Lee) (*b* Southampton, 5 Dec 1830; *d* London, 20 Aug 1863). English painter. His early works were portraits, but in 1848 the picture-dealer Edwin Holder gave him a five-year contract to copy Old Masters. He specialized in landscape and first exhibited at the Royal Academy in 1851 (*A Bit in Berkshire*). In 1853 he travelled to Munich, where his enthusiasm for Alpine scenery began (*Kaiserspitze*, exh. London, RA, 1856). On returning to England he settled in Southampton, where he received a number of commissions from a shipping magnate, J. H. Wolff. Wolff's 'Bridell Gallery' in his Southampton home was intended to house the artist's masterpiece, the *Colosseum by Moonlight* (1858–9), now in Southampton City Art Gallery with many other Bridells from the W. Burrough Hill collection.

Bridell continued to work on continental landscapes, visiting the Rhine and Italy in 1858–9 and the Como region in 1860. Between 1851 and 1863 he showed six pictures at the Royal Academy, eleven at the British Institution and two at the Society of British Artists. When he died his reputation was high. His friend Henry Rose reports Charles Lock Eastlake's admiration, and Sir Theodore Martin's obituary claims his skies as 'only second to Turner'. The National Gallery, London, acquired his *Woods of Sweet Chestnut above Varenna* in 1887 (now London, Tate). His best work combines deep interest in light, a feeling for ruins influenced by German painting and a particularly rich paint texture.

BIBLIOGRAPHY

DNB

[Sir Theodore Martin]: Obituary, *A. J.* [London] (Jan 1864), p. 12

H. Rose: *Southampton Times*, 14 Jan 1888 [letter]

J. Sweetman: *F. L. Bridell 1830–1863*, Southampton, C.A.G. cat. (1970)

——: 'F. L. Bridell and Romantic Landscape', *Apollo* (1974), pp. 142–5

JOHN SWEETMAN

Bridge. Raised structure for passage over a declivity or obstacle. Until the advent of railways most important bridges spanned rivers, canals or sea inlets.

1. Types. 2. History and development. 3. Writings.

1. TYPES. Bridges are classified by the traffic they serve (*see also* AQUEDUCT; VIADUCT) and by structural type. There follows an alphabetical listing and descriptions of bridge types. Cross-references within this article to this list are in the form '*see Arch bridge*'; cross-references to other sections of this article and to other articles in the Dictionary are in the usual form '*see* ARCH'.

Arch bridge. Each span is an arch, a structure that thrusts horizontally as well as vertically on its supports (see fig. 1(top); *see* ARCH, §§1 and 2). The common types of arch are as follows:

Bow-string arch. An alternative term for a tied arch (see below).

Open-spandrel arch. Commonly built of timber, metal or reinforced concrete and bearing columns that support a deck (for road, rail etc) above the crown of the arch (see fig. 1(top)d). An example is the Garabit Viaduct (*see* §2(iii)(c) below).

Tied arch [bow-string]. Commonly built of timber, metal or reinforced concrete, with the deck suspended from the arch at a low level. By tying the ends of the arch, the deck relieves the supports of horizontal thrust. An example is Alsea Bay Bridge at Waldport, OR (*see* §2(iii)(d) below).

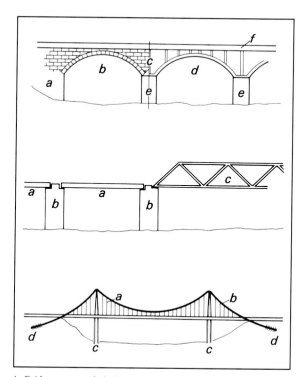

1. Bridge types and their constituent parts: (top) arch bridge: (a) abutment; (b) voussoir arch; (c) spandrel; (d) open-spandrel arch; (e) pier; (f) parapet; (middle) beam or girder bridge: (a) beam; (b) pier; (c) girders; (bottom) suspension bridge: (a) hangers; (b) cables; (c) tower; (d) anchorage

Voussoir arch. Built of wedge-shaped stone voussoirs with all the joints perpendicular to the arch curve (see figs 1(top)b and 2), or less perfectly of bricks, blocks or irregular stones with tapered mortar joints (*see* MASONRY, §III, 2(ii)). The road is formed on solid filling between the spandrel walls.

Beam bridge. Each span comprises several parallel beams spanning between two supports, and the deck is laid directly on the beams (see fig. 1(middle)a).

Cable-stayed bridge. The deck is a beam or girder supported at a number of points by inclined cables strung from one or more towers (see fig. 4 below).

Cantilever bridge. A bridge in which the main spanning members are beams or girders that overhang their supports.

Balanced cantilever. A beam or girder that overhangs its supports equally at both ends, for example in the Forth Bridge (1883–90; *see* §2(iii)(c) below).

Floating bridge. A bridge formed of a sequence of planks or beams spanning from one to another along a line of floats extending across a waterway.

Bridge of boats. The floats are low-decked boats.

Pontoon bridge. The floats are hollow boxes called 'pontoons'; modern examples are usually of iron or steel.

Girder bridge. 'Girder' was originally applied to large solid timber beams but, since the mid-19th century, usually denotes a fabricated framework, most commonly a lattice of short members of iron, steel or timber (see fig. 1(middle)c), making possible much longer spans than those of beam bridges. Examples are the Tay Bridge (1870–78; destr. 1879; *see* §2(iii)(c) below) and its replacement (1882–7).

Bow-string girder. A hybrid similar to the bow-string or tied arch (see *Arch bridge*) but with diagonal members that enable it to span as both girder and arch.

Box girder. A girder of closed tubular form, such as the Conwy Rail Bridge (1848; *see* §2(iii)(c) below).

Truss. A girder of open framework.

Opening bridge. A bridge in which one or more beam or girder spans can be opened to allow passage of craft or for purposes of defence.

Bascule. A counter-balanced lever by which one span or half-span is raised, pivoting at its support, most commonly to provide a large opening for ships, for example Tower Bridge (1886–94), London, by John Wolfe Barry and Horace Jones.

Drawbridge. A simple bridge with the span or half-spans pivoting at the support or supports and the free ends lifted by ropes, commonly used at medieval castle gates.

Swing bridge. Bridge in which a span or half-span pivots horizontally to open a water passage, for example the Swing Bridge (1876), Newcastle upon Tyne, by J. F. Ure.

Vertical lift. A whole span is raised vertically by cables, for example the Tees (Newport) Bridge (1934), Middlesbrough, Cleveland, by Mott, Hay and Anderson.

Suspension bridge. A bridge, generally of iron or steel, in which the deck is suspended by hangers from main chains or cables draped between the tops of towers and extended beyond them to anchorages in the ground (see fig. 1(bottom)). The line of the cables is called a 'catenary', from its similarity to the shape adopted by a freely hanging chain.

Transporter bridge. Bridge in which vehicles are carried on a platform suspended from a trolley running on high-level girders under which vessels can pass; for example the Transporter Bridge (1911), Middlesbrough, by Cleveland Bridge and Engineering Ltd.

Truss bridge. See *Girder bridge* above.

2. HISTORY AND DEVELOPMENT.

(i) Before *c.* 1500. (ii) *c.* 1500–*c.* 1790. (iii) After *c.* 1790.

(i) Before c. *1500.* To make durable foundations was always the greatest test of a bridge-builder's art. Some dispensed with foundations by building bridges of boats: for crossings of the Danube by both the Greek and Achaemenid Persian armies *c.* 510 BC; two crossings of the Bosporus by the army of Darius I in 493 BC; and one of the Dardanelles by that of Xerxes I in 480 BC, the latter bridge laid on two strings of boats 674 in number. In China bridges of boats were used from the 8th century BC until the mid-20th century.

For bridges of stone or brick, the foundations were always laid on bedrock if possible, up to the 18th century. On softer ground wooden piles were driven with mauls, from the third millennium BC; and the 'piling gin', with a weight repeatedly raised and dropped on the pile head by a team of men hauling on ropes, was well known by medieval times. Laying foundations 'in the dry' could be achieved by temporary diversion of rivers, as in Babylon *c.* 2000 BC for a major bridge of stone piers and timber deck, and by cofferdams devised by the Romans and the

Chinese, both using walls of wooden piles sealed with clay. In shallow waters banks of earth were used to form cofferdams in many parts of the world; this technique was still in use in the late 20th century.

Julius Caesar described a bridge of piles and beams built from trees cut near by across the Rhine by the Roman army in 55 BC and destroyed when the army had crossed (*Conquest of Gaul*, IV.vii). For permanent bridges the Romans used stone piers with either wooden beams or semicircular stone arches. From the 2nd century BC they raised arches in one, two or three tiers for the spectacular aqueducts that supplied water to their cities, such as those at Segovia (mid-1st century AD; for illustration *see* AQUEDUCT) and the Pont du Gard (?early 1st century AD; *see* NÎMES, §2). These and the provincial road bridges at Salamanca (rebuilt *c.* AD 89) and Mérida (*see* AUGUSTA EMERITA) are plain structures, but ornament and sculpture were added to bridges at Rome, such as the Ponte Sant'Angelo (AD 134; sculptures renewed 1527–1669), Rimini (AD 20) and elsewhere. The voussoirs of these bridges were so well hewn that they could be laid in perfect contact without mortar, a practice without parallel except in some Chinese arch bridges built on different principles.

The voussoirs of these Chinese bridges were long thin stones that could pivot a little at the dry contacts to adjust to movements of the foundations. The bridges might be of one or of many arches, which were generally semicircular. A notable example of the multi-arched bridges at Luguo (1189) near Beijing; it was admired by Marco Polo and boasts 283 stone lions, all different, on carved pedestals along the parapets. The most remarkable and also the oldest arch bridge in use in China is the Anji Bridge (see fig. 2), near Xhao xian, Hebei Province, built (605–17) by Li Chun during the Sui dynasty (581–618). It is a circular segment of 37.5 m span with two arched voids through each spandrel—a device not seen in Europe until seven centuries later at Céret (see below) and then forgotten until used at Pontypridd in 1756 (*see* §(ii) below). The Anji arch is composed of 28 individual arches side by side (a feature also of the Pont du Gard (for illustration *see* CENTERING), which has four arches in its width, and other Roman bridges), allowing the supporting centering on which the arch was formed to be of narrow width and reused for each of the parallel arches. From the 11th century to the 13th in the coastal province of Fujian, massive beam bridges of stone, with spans up to 21 m, were common. The individual beams, weighing up to 200 tonnes, must have been placed from pontoons by the falling tide.

Throughout Europe, Roman bridges became accepted models of good structure and architecture, but the skill of the Romans in underwater work was not sustained. They had added a natural volcanic ash called 'pozzolana' to lime to make mortar that would harden under water; and for lack of such material and inability to seal deep cofferdams, medieval bridges in deep or tidal rivers had to be founded on 'starlings'. A starling was made by dumping rough stones into the water within a wall of wooden piles and paving the top above low-water level to form a base for a masonry pier. Starlings, such as those of Old London Bridge (1176–1209; destr. 1831–2), built by Peter of Colechurch (*fl* 1163; *d* 1205), and Rochester Bridge (1383–97;

2. Anji Bridge, Hebei Province, by Li Chun, early 7th century

destr. 1857) by Henry Yevele, greatly impeded navigation and the flow of the tides and required frequent repairs.

Civil governments in medieval times generally lacked funds, stability and the will to build large bridges. Churchmen became the frequent patrons of bridges, assisted sometimes by lay 'brotherhoods of bridge-builders' whose origins are shrouded in legend but who, from motives of piety and charity, provided money, designs and labour. Old London Bridge, the Pont St Bénézet (1177–87) at Avignon and the Pont St Esprit (1265–97; destr. 1953) at Lyon were all accomplished by such cooperation. Bridges in both Europe and Asia tended to become the local focus of commercial or social life, which resulted in extensive building on city bridges such as Old London Bridge and serious constriction of the roadway. The old wooden Rialto Bridge in Venice continued, through repeated reconstructions, to be the city's financial centre.

Pointed arches were introduced in bridges of short spans and a few of larger spans, such as at the Pont Valentré (1308–55; spans 16.5 m; see CAHORS, §2) and the Brig o' Balgownie (1320; span 21.3 m) at Old Aberdeen. Ribbed arches also became common. At Céret (Pyrénées-Orientales) an arch of the longest span to date (45.3 m) was built in the early 14th century with arched voids through its high spandrels like those of the early Chinese Anji Bridge. A change from semicircular arches to lower segmental and similar shapes, suitable for longer spans, appeared at Avignon and later in Italy in the Ponte Vecchio (1345), Florence, the Ponte Coperto (1351–6; rebuilt), Pavia, and the Ponte Scaligero (1355–8; cut during World War II, repaired), Verona. Newton Cap Bridge (1388–1405), Bishop Auckland, Co. Durham, has similar arches.

Bridges in the Middle East were often rebuilt on Roman or Sasanian foundations. The piers of some stone bridges built in northern Mesopotamia (now Turkey) in the 12th and 13th centuries are decorated with relief sculpture, including *Signs of the Zodiac* at Cizre and figures in Turkish military dress at Hasankeyf. This tradition was also adopted in Egypt, for example in the north face of a bridge (1226–7) over the canal of Abu'l-Munagga, near Cairo, which is decorated with 40 lions passant. Islamic traditions of bridge-building were introduced to India from c. 1200.

(ii) c. 1500–c. 1790. Perhaps the finest bridge of the Ottoman empire was the large single arch (1566; destr. 1993) at Mostar, Bosnia. In Iran, brick was the common material of bridges, with stone foundations. Roman methods had been planted in Iran by the 3rd century AD and applied to the needs of the hot, dry country. The paragon of the resulting bridges is the Pul-i-Khwaju (1642–67; see ISLAMIC ART, fig. 69) at Isfahan, comprising 24 arches and covered arcades on two storeys, separate lanes for pedestrians and caravans and steps down to the water on the lower side of every pier—a place of rest and social intercourse for tired travellers.

In spite of the emphasis on Roman models in the treatises of Alberti and Palladio (see §3 below), European designers tried new forms of arch: semi-elliptical in the Pont Neuf (1543–1632), Toulouse, by Jacques Le Mercier and Pierre Souffron, and the Pont Henri IV (1576–1611), Châtellerault, by Laurent Joguet and Gaschon Belle; and chamfered edges (called *cornes de vâche*) on the arches for

easier flow of water at Châtellerault and the Pont Neuf (1578–1607; part rebuilt 1848), Paris, by Jacques Androuet Du Cerceau. The most beautiful elevation of the 16th century was that of the Ponte Santa Trinita (1567–9; destr. 1944; rebuilt), Florence, by BARTOLOMEO AMMANATI, with low arches of a unique shape, obtusely pointed but with the point covered by a cartouche.

The excellent French writings on bridges in the 18th century were mostly penned by practising engineers (see §3 below) in government service. Their chief, JEAN-RODOLPHE PERRONET, was the first to allow the thrust of each arch to be transmitted by other arches to the abutments of a bridge, so reducing the required thickness of piers to one-tenth of the arch span in his five-arch bridge at Neuilly-sur-Seine (1768–74; destr. 1939). This and others of the best French bridges were built with perfectly horizontal roads and no added ornament.

British designers used ornament, influenced by Palladio's illustration of the Roman bridge at Rimini and 'triumphal bridge' designs made in Rome about 1740–50. Blackfriars Bridge (1760–70; destr. 1864), London, by Robert Mylne, had twin Ionic columns forming a 'tabernacle' for sculpture (though never occupied) over every pier. These details derived from an extravagant 'triumphal' design by GIOVANNI BATTISTA PIRANESI (*Opera varie de architettura, prospettiva, grotteschi, antichità*, Rome, 1750, pl. VIII), and the motif was repeated by JOHN RENNIE, among others, in his Kelso Bridge (1800–04), Borders, and Waterloo Bridge (1811–17; destr. 1938), London. A fine late example is Kirklee Bridge (1899–1901), Glasgow, by Charles Forman. Spandrel voids, similar to those used in the bridges of Anji and Céret (see §(i) above), were adopted in 1756 by William Edwards at Pontypridd, Mid Glamorgan, without knowledge of the precedents, to balance the loads on his very slim segmental arch (42.7 m span) after it had collapsed twice under filled spandrels.

In estates and gardens bridges were mainly *objets d'art*. The garden bridge at Wilton House (1736–7), Wilts, by Henry Herbert, 9th Earl of Pembroke, with Roger Morris, was a jewel-sized copy of a rejected design by Palladio for the Rialto Bridge, Venice (*Quattro libri*, iii.13, pls ix–x), with balustrades, colonnade and roof. Three other copies followed at Stowe (Bucks), Prior Park (Avon) and Hagley Park (Hereford and Worcs). Robert Adam and others designed ruined bridges for romantic effect, while some wooden bridges were built in rustic or Chinese style. The first iron arched footbridge (1769; destr. c. 1840) was erected by Michael Tobin, blacksmith, in Kirklees Park, W. Yorks. Other iron bridges followed, the largest number in the Royal Gardens of Tsarskoye Selo, Russia (see PUSHKIN), for which Catherine II, Empress of Russia, after first commissioning a copy of the Earl of Pembroke's bridge in Siberian marble, ordered eight wrought iron arch bridges, which were forged at the state arms works in 1783–90.

Timber truss bridge designs spread from the forested countries of central and northern Europe. They provided low-cost bridges of long span that served to avoid damage by floating ice. Trussed arches were briefly popular in Britain from 1735–55 but quickly decayed. Hans Ulrich Grubenmann (see GRUBENMANN) prevented decay of trusses by giving his bridges walls and roofs of boards, a common Swiss practice. He bridged the Rhine at Schaffhausen (1755–7; destr. 1799) with two trusses, 52 and 59 m long, and, with his brother Johannes Grubenmann, bridged the Limmat at Wettingen (1764; destr. 1799) in a single 61-m span of arch ribs formed of timbers bent to gentle curves and clamped together with iron straps, presaging the laminated arches used in Europe and America in the early years of railways (*see* §(iii) below). Both bridges were destroyed by Napoleon's army in retreat.

(iii) After c. 1790. Since 1790 the continuous increase in the weight and speed of vehicles, especially on railways and motor roads, has required gentler bends and often skew (i.e. oblique) bridges. Construction methods have also changed as steam, motor and electric machinery have been developed (*see* CONSTRUCTION MACHINERY). For bridges of increasing scale and bridges of iron the traditional architectural styles soon became meaningless and, as early as 1812, THOMAS TELFORD advised in the *Edinburgh Encyclopaedia* that in bridges 'the utmost simplicity ... should be preserved; ... all decorations should be kept perfectly subservient to, and in unison with, the essential parts.'

(a) Wood. The abundant forests of North America provided the material for almost all the bridges built there up to 1840. Many ingenious types of truss were patented from 1790 on. Most large bridges were enclosed and several hundreds of them survive, such as the Cornish-to-Windsor bridge (1866, by James F. Tasker), NH/VT, of two 62.4 m spans. The longest span reached 104 m in the trussed arch of the Upper Ferry Bridge (1812; destr. 1842), Philadelphia, built by Lewis Wernwag (1769–1843). The horizontal profile of trusses was ideal for the early railroads, with the patent trusses greatly strengthened. In Europe laminated wooden arch bridges were used for economy on early railways from about 1830.

(b) Masonry. Stone was chosen for many city bridges before 1900, and most early railway viaducts in Europe were strings of arches of stone or brick. The longest spans in stone extended to 61 m in the Grosvenor Bridge (1827–33, by THOMAS HARRISON) at Chester, and 66.5 m in the

Cabin John Bridge (1864, by MONTGOMERY MEIGS), a pipe aqueduct at Washington, DC. These spans were overtaken only when a few open-spandrel arches were built of masonry in Europe, including the Pont Adolphe (1907, by Paul Séjourné) in Luxembourg.

(c) Iron and steel. Cast iron, strong in compression but weak in tension, was used early in this period for large arches. After the first large arch was built (now Ironbridge, Salop; *see* IRON AND STEEL, fig. 3) in 1779, of 30.5 m span, there were exciting projects, such as a design of 183 m span to bridge the Thames at London proposed to a parliamentary committee by Telford and James Douglass in 1800 but not executed; good bridges, such as John Rennie's three-arch Southwark Bridge (1814–19; destr. 1913–21) with middle span of 73.2 m; and fine canal aqueducts, including the astounding Pont Cyssylte (1805–9), near Llangollen, Clwyd, by Telford and William Jessop (1745–1814), which has 19 arched spans of 13.7 m over a wide, deep valley. Cast-iron girders trussed with bars of wrought-iron and up to 30 m long were developed for railway bridges, but after the fracture of such a girder near Chester in 1847, with five deaths and many injuries, cast-iron beams were used only for short spans, seldom exceeding 10 m.

Wrought-iron is strong in tension and compression. By the 1840s it was being rolled into bars of L-shaped cross-section as well as long flat plates, and the two could be assembled with rivets to form members of large cross-section, including I shapes and hollow rectangles, and such members in turn were assembled to form the much larger open-frame girders of the next generation of railway bridges. ISAMBARD KINGDOM BRUNEL spanned the Thames at Windsor (1849) with a wrought-iron bowstring girder bridge of 61.6 m and followed it with a span (1851–3; replaced 1962) of 91.5 m at Chepstow, Gwent. His Royal Albert Bridge (completed 1859; see fig. 3) at Saltash, Devon, has two spans of 139 m, each truss having an arched tubular top boom combined with suspension chains of flat bars to carry the horizontal track. In contrast, Robert Stephenson (1803–59) designed bridges in which the tracks ran through tubular girders. His Britannia Bridge (1846–50; replaced 1970–74) across the Menai Straits, Gwynedd, had four spans, two of them measuring 140 m; Conwy Bridge (1848), Gwynedd, has one span of 126 m; and Victoria Bridge (1854–9; replaced 1897–8) at Montreal crossed the St Lawrence River on 25 spans of total length 1.87 km.

A feverish trade in patent iron girder bridges developed in the USA and Canada, repeated Ws or Ns being the commonest truss patterns; but hurried construction contributed to failures, of which the worst in America, at Ashtabula, OH, in 1876, caused 80 deaths. The collapse of 13 spans of the world's longest bridge, the Tay Bridge (1870–78, by Thomas Bouch), Tayside, in 1879 with the loss of 75 lives led to the introduction of a new bridge form, the balanced cantilever, and a new material, steel (*see* IRON AND STEEL, §II, 1), in bridging the neighbouring estuary of the Forth. The Forth Bridge (1883–90), designed by John Fowler (1817–98) and Benjamin Baker (1840–1907), has three balanced cantilevers, standing splay-legged for lateral stability, 104 m high and making two

3. Royal Albert Bridge, Saltash, Devon, by Isambard Kingdom Brunel, completed 1859

522-m spans. In the latter years of the 19th century steel quickly overtook wrought-irons in the range of shapes and size of cross-sections available to bridge-builders. The bridge over the St Lawrence River at Quebec, the profile of which closely follows that of the Forth Bridge, was designed by P. L. Szlapka and Theodore Cooper and completed in 1917 after partial collapses during erection in 1907 and 1916. Later variants of the cantilever type span many bays and harbours including Oakland (1934–6), CA, Charleston (three separate bridges), SC, Auckland (1959), New Zealand, and Tenmon (1966), Japan.

Many long-span steel arches have been erected as twin cantilevers from the supports until joined at mid-span with a horizontal deck then suspended from the arch. The large depth of cantilever structure at the supports was made permanent in Hell Gate Bridge (1916; span 305 m), New York, by Gustav Lindenthal (1850–1935) and Sydney Harbour Bridge (1925–32; span 503 m) by Ralph Freeman (1880–1950). By using temporary structures to tie back the cantilevers, a lighter, crescent-shaped profile is achieved, as in the Volta Bridge (1955–6; span 246 m), Ghana, by Gilbert Roberts of Freeman Fox with Halcrow & Partners. The most graceful crescent, however, is the wrought-iron arch of the Garabit Viaduct (1879–84; span 165 m) by GUSTAVE EIFFEL with the horizontal railway girder touching its crown at a height of 122 m.

For much of the 19th century, and again since 1931, the longest spans in the world have been suspension bridges. The first to be built with iron chains and stiff road deck in any western country were designed by James Finley (1762–1828), a judge in Pennsylvania. A series of his bridges, of maximum span 74.4 m, were built in 1801–10. Catenary chains were adopted for experiments in England in 1814; and between 1816 and 1820 at least four small bridges of wire and two larger chain bridges had been erected in southern Scotland, including Union Bridge (1820; span 133 m) by Samuel Brown over the Tweed at Paxton. It was surpassed by Telford's Menai Straits Bridge (1819–26) in Wales, which spanned 176 m at 30 m above high-water. Like other early suspension bridges, it suffered oscillation in high winds until stiffening girders were added to the deck.

John Augustus Roebling devised the technique of 'spinning' many parallel wires to form the main cables (for illustration and discussion *see* ROEBLING, (1)). With his son Washington Augustus Roebling he designed and built Brooklyn Bridge (1869–93; span 486 m), New York, which is stiffened by trusses and fanning radial stays. It was the last large suspension bridge with stone towers and the first with steel cables and trusses. Spun steel cables have been used worldwide ever since.

From 1900 to 1940 US designers refined their designs structurally and aesthetically. George Washington Bridge (1927–31), New York, designed by Othmar Hermann Ammann (1879–1965), spanned 1.07 km without deck trusses, and the Golden Gate Bridge (1933–7), San Francisco, by Joseph Baermann Strauss (1870–1938), reached 1.28 km with slimmer towers. But slimness of deck spelled disaster in 1940 when the new Tacoma Narrows Bridge (1938–40; span 854 m), Seattle, by Leon S. Moisseiff (1872–1943) suffered resonant twisting oscillations in a brisk wind and tore itself to pieces. Stiffening trusses

returned in subsequent bridges, until the Severn Bridge (1963–8), by Gilbert Roberts of Freeman Fox & Partners, was built with its deck a steel box girder of streamlined shape only 3 m deep on a span of 988 m and resonant oscillation inhibited by a vertically-elongated zigzag pattern of deck suspenders. The same engineers bridged the Bosporus at Istanbul (1973; span 1.07 km) and the Humber estuary (1980; span 1.41 km). These bridges were surpassed in bulk by the Seto Ohashi Bridge (1988) in Japan, which has three double-deck spans each more than 989 m, but stiffened in the old way by heavy trusses.

(d) Concrete. Being strong in compression but weak in tension, concrete was first used as a cheap substitute for masonry in arch bridges of short span, including railway bridges from about 1875. An outstanding group in Scotland on the line from Fort William to Mallaig, Highland, includes the 21-arch Glenfinnan Viaduct (1901, by Simpson & Wilson). Reinforcement with steel for tensile strength made possible open-spandrel bridges of longer spans (*see* CONCRETE, §II, 1(iii)), early examples being the three-arched Pont Neuf (1899, by François Hennebique), Châtellerault, and Connecticut Avenue Bridge (1904), Washington, DC, by George Shattuck Morison (1842–1903), a high viaduct with five arches of 45.7 m. The concrete of the latter was 'bush-hammered', the first of many treatments intended to improve the often blotchy appearance of plain concrete.

Reinforced concrete has been used for structures of all shapes for which moulds, or 'formwork', can be made. Its economy was proved in 1910–12 when EUGÈNE FREYSSINET undertook to build three three-arch concrete bridges over the River Allier in central France for the cost of one masonry bridge. In building them he introduced 'prestressing': the application of external forces to induce stress and strain opposite to (and therefore partly neutralising) the stresses and strains caused by the weight of bridge and traffic. Prestressing is now used in virtually all long concrete spans; for example Gladesville Bridge (1964, by G. Maunsell & Partners), Sydney, an arch of 305 m span formed of tubular 'voussoirs' stressed together. Two concrete arches of 244 and 390 m span (1976–80) join Krk to mainland Croatia.

The bridges in Switzerland by Robert Maillart are noted for their beauty and invention rather than their size. He chose novel forms to exploit the intrinsic properties of reinforced concrete. In refining his three-hinged arch designs from Zuoz (1901) to Garstatt (1940), he produced the Salginatobel Bridge (1930), which leaps 90 m across a sheer-sided valley in deep forest, its silhouette becoming one of the icons of Modern architecture. In another series of 'deck-stiffened' bridges, the arches are very thin and the decks stiffened by deep parapet walls, the best example being at Schwandbach (1933; span 37.5 m); for illustration *see* MAILLART, ROBERT).

Between 1927 and 1936 Conde B. McCullough built a series of large concrete bridges along the Oregon coast, using open-spandrel arches, tied arches (e.g. Alsea Bridge, Waldport, 1936) and beam-and-slab spans. He used decorative obelisks and fluted textures with good judgement, in contrast to the excessive ornament that has often marred concrete bridges in American parks.

4. Helgeland Bridge, by Elljarn Jordet and Holger S. Svensson, 1991

(e) Mixed and synthetic materials. In the first suspension bridges in Scotland (*see* §(c) above) the decks were supported partly or wholly by inclined straight wires from the heads of the towers, and the Roeblings combined straight stays with catenary cables in their bridges. Similar stays are used in modern cable-stayed (girder) bridges (*see* §1 above), of which early development was centred in West Germany in the 1950s. The arrangement of stays varies widely, including single thick cables, as at Erskine Bridge (1974, by Freeman Fox), Strathclyde, 'harps', as at the Brotonne Bridge (1977) across the Seine near Saint-Wandrille, and 'fans', as in Norway at Helgeland Bridge (1991, by Elljarn Jordet and Holger S. Svensson; see fig. 4). The last is a bridge of concrete deck and towers with steel cables. It spans 425 m with a deck only 1.2 m deep and cables 200 mm thick, giving it a high degree of transparency, which is necessary in modern bridges at sites of great beauty. The first substantial bridge built entirely of synthetic materials is a footbridge (1992; span 63 m, by Maunsell Structural Plastics) spanning the Tay at Aberfeldy, Tayside, which is also cable-stayed, the cables of aramid fibre and the deck and towers of glass-reinforced polyester. A unique bridge crossing an Alpine valley at Ganter (1980, by Christian Menn) has steel stays encased in concrete that allow it to be curved in plan and of striking shapes, but notably non-transparent.

3. WRITINGS. Specific descriptions of bridges, such as those of Julius Caesar (*see* §2(i) above) and SEXTUS JULIUS FRONTINUS, are very rare in early centuries and most of our knowledge of early bridges is derived from general historical chronicles. Amongst the early printed architectural treatises, Alberti gave advice on construction and proportions of bridges (*De re aedificatoria*, iv.6), and Palladio was the first to emphasise style (*Quattro libri*, iii). Many of the 18th-century pattern books included bridge designs. Advice on timber bridges was given by Palladio, Mathurin Jousse and Jacob Leupold.

Henri Gautier's monograph (1716) was the first to cover the whole field of design and construction from personal experience. In 1729 Bernard Forest de Bélidor produced the first scientific treatise on bridge design. Other French texts followed, including Perronet's detailed

record of his own bridge-building, and were followed by compendia of the work of Smeaton (1812) and Telford (1838) in Britain. From *c.* 1800, encyclopaedias in Britain included articles, both theoretical and practical, on bridges and related topics, and some of them were soon republished in the USA. By 1840 engineering journals, and especially those of professional institutions in European countries and the USA, were the prime organs of information and debate, and by 1850 textbooks were available in most European languages.

BIBLIOGRAPHY

TREATISES AND MEMOIRS

Sextus Julius Frontinus: *De aquis urbis Romae* (*c.* AD 100); ed. and Eng. trans. by C. E. Bennett, Loeb Class. Lib. (London, 1925)

L. B. Alberti: *De re aedificatoria* (Florence, 1485); Eng. trans. by J. Leoni as *The Architecture of Leon Battista Alberti*, 3 vols (London, 1726, 3/1755), ed. J. Rykwert as *Ten Books on Architecture by Leone Battista Alberti* (London, 1955/*R* 1965); further Eng. trans. of orig. text by J. Rykwert, N. Leach and R. Tavernor as *On the Art of Building in Ten Books* (Cambridge, MA, 1988, 2/1991)

A. Palladio: *I quattro libri dell'architettura* (Venice, 1570, 3/1601/*R* Newcastle upon Tyne, 1971); Eng. trans. by I. Ware (London, 1738/*R* New York, 1965)

M. Jousse: *Le Théâtre de l'art de charpentier* (La Flèche, 1627); ed. M. De La Hire as *L'Art de charpenterie* (Paris, 1702, 3/1751/*R* 1978)

H. Gautier: *Traité des ponts* (Paris, 1716, rev. 3/1728/*R* 1765)

——: *Dissertation sur les culées, voussoirs, piles et poussées des ponts* (Paris, 1717/*R* 1765)

J. Leupold: *Theatrum pontificiale* (Leipzig, 1726, 2/1774)

B. Forest de Bélidor: *La Science des ingénieurs*, 6 vols (Paris, 1729, rev. 1813/*R* 1830)

——: *Architecture hydraulique*, 4 vols (Paris, 1737–53)

J.-R. Perronet: *Description des projets et de la construction des Ponts de Neuilly, de Mantes, d'Orléans et autres*, 2 vols (Paris, 1782–3, 2/1788)

E.-M. Gauthey: *Traité de la construction des ponts*, 2 vols (Paris, 1809–13, 3/Mons, 1843)

J. Smeaton: *Reports of the Late John Smeaton FRS*, 3 vols (London, 1812/*R* 1837)

T. Telford: *Life of Thomas Telford Written by Himself*, ed. J. Rickman (London, 1838) [with an atlas of plates]

J. Weale, ed.: *The Theory, Practice and Architecture of Bridges of Stone, Iron, Timber and Wire*, 3 vols (London, 1843)

P. Sejourné: *Grandes Voûtes*, 6 vols (Bourges, 1913–16)

STUDIES

T. Telford and A. Nimmo: 'Bridge', *The Edinburgh Encyclopaedia*, iv (Edinburgh, 1812), pp. 479–545

W. A. Provis: *An Historical and Descriptive Account of the Suspension Bridge over the Menai Straits in North Wales* (London, 1828)

S. Smiles: *Lives of the Engineers*, 3 vols (London, 1861–2/*R* Newton Abbot, 1968)

W. Westhofen: 'The Forth Bridge', *Engineering*, xlix (28 Feb 1890), pp. 213–83, pls i–xix; as book (London, 1890, 2/1990)

F. de Dartein: *Etudes sur les ponts en pierre remarquables par leurs décorations antérieurs au XIXe siècle*, 4 vols (Paris, 1907–12)

W. J. Watson: *Bridge Architecture* (New York, 1927)

C. S. Whitney: *Bridges* (New York, 1929)

G. C. Home: *Old London Bridge* (London, 1931)

H. Fugl-Meyer: *Chinese Bridges* (Shanghai, 1937)

A. U. Pope and P. Ackerman, eds: *Survey of Persian Art*, 7 vols (London, 1938–58), pp. 570–72, 1226–41

W. B. Parsons: *Engineers and Engineering in the Renaissance* (Baltimore, 1939, rev. Cambridge, MA, and London, 2/1968)

D. B. Steinman and S. R. Watson: *Bridges and their Builders* (New York, 1941, rev. 2/1957)

M. Bill: *Robert Maillart: Bridges and Constructions* (Zurich, 1949, 3/1969)

H. S. Smith: *The World's Great Bridges* (London, 1953, 2/1964)

P. S. A. Berridge: *The Girder Bridge* (London, 1969)

H. J. Hopkins: *A Span of Bridges* (Newton Abbot, 1970)

J. Needham and others: *Science and Civilization in China*, iv/3 (Cambridge, 1971), pp. 145–210

D. Plowden: *Bridges: The Spans of North America* (New York, 1974)

M. N. Boyer: *Medieval French Bridges* (Cambridge, MA, 1976)

Mao Yi-Sheng: *Bridges in China Old and New* (Beijing, 1978)

D. P. Billington: *Robert Maillart's Bridges: The Art of Engineering* (Princeton, 1979)

T. Ruddock: *Arch Bridges and their Builders, 1735–1835* (Cambridge, 1979)

J. G. James: 'The Evolution of Iron Bridge Trusses to 1850', *Newcomen Soc. Trans.*, lii (1980–81), pp. 67–102

——: 'The Evolution of Wooden Bridge Trusses to 1850', *J. Inst. Wood Sci.*, ix (1982), pp. 116–35, 168–93

F. Leonhardt: *Brücken-Bridges: Aesthetics and Design* (Stuttgart, 1982)

J. G. James: 'Russian Iron Bridges to 1850', *Newcomen Soc. Trans.*, liv (1982–3), pp. 79–104

D. P. Billington: *The Tower and the Bridge* (New York, 1983, Princeton, 1985)

H. Luschey: 'The Pul-i Khwājū in Isfahan: A Combination of Bridge, Dam and Water Art', *Iran*, xxiii (1985), pp. 143–51

N. A. F. Smith: 'The Pont du Gard and the Aqueduct of Nimes', *Newcomen Soc. Trans.*, lxii (1990–91), pp. 53–80

J. Deloche: *Land Transport* (1993), i of *Transport and Communications in India Prior to Steam Locomotion* (New Delhi and Oxford, 1993–), pp. 125–43

C. O'Connor: *Roman Bridges* (Cambridge, 1993)

TED RUDDOCK

Bridge, John. *See under* RUNDELL, BRIDGE & RUNDELL.

Bridgeman, Charles (*d* London, 19 July 1738). English landscape gardener. His origins and education are obscure, but his father may have been gardener to the Harley family at Wimpole Hall, Cambs. Bridgeman is first recorded at BLENHEIM PALACE, Oxon, working for Henry Wise, the Royal Gardener, under the general supervision of John Vanbrugh. A plan of the estate drawn by Bridgeman in 1709 reveals him to have been an accomplished surveyor, and he may well have worked for Wise and his partner George London previously.

Bridgeman's contribution at Blenheim during this period is unknown, but it may be assumed that Vanbrugh was pleased with his work, for the two men collaborated at STOWE, Bucks, for Richard Temple, 1st Viscount Cobham (from 1716); at Eastbury (destr.), Dorset, for George Bubb Dodington, 1st Baron Melcombe (1691–1762), in 1718; and at Claremont, Surrey, for Thomas Pelham-Holles, 1st Duke of Newcastle (1693–1768), in the 1720s. By the mid-1720s he was established as the most successful, influential and fashionable gardener of his day and had begun a long association with Edward Harley, 2nd Earl of Oxford, at Wimpole and, from 1719, at Marylebone, London. For the development of the Marylebone estate Harley employed the architect James Gibbs; Bridgeman, who had already collaborated with Gibbs at King's College (1724), Cambridge, designed the layout of Cavendish Square, the central feature of the enterprise, in 1729, purchasing the lease of 8 Henrietta Street (destr. 1956). Through Harley, Bridgeman became intimate with James Thornhill, John Wootton, Alexander Pope and Matthew Prior, for the latter of whom he designed the grounds of Down Hall, Essex, in 1721.

In 1723 Bridgeman purchased 19 Broad Street, Westminster, built by his brother-in-law John Mist (*d* 1737), with whom he collaborated on a number of commissions. The following year he received his first royal commission, that of improving the gardens of Marble Hill House, London, for George Augustus, Prince of Wales, later George II (*reg* 1727–60). This work may have contributed to Bridgeman's appointment as Wise's partner in managing the royal gardens on the death of Joseph Carpenter in

1726. Wise and Bridgeman jointly wrote a report, *A State of the Royal Gardens, from the Revolution, to the Year 1727* (London, PRO), which showed a marked increase in expenditure and probably hastened Wise's retirement in 1728. In that year Bridgeman assumed sole control for an annual fee of £2220 (based on the acreage of land at Hampton Court, Kensington, St James's Park and Richmond) and a grace-and-favour residence at Hampton Court. Also in 1728 he resumed work for Sarah, Duchess of Marlborough (1660–1744), at Blenheim and in 1731 at Wimbledon House (destr.), Surrey, which was to result in an acrimonious lawsuit between his widow and the Duchess. His appointment as Royal Gardener brought him a close and privileged relationship with the Board of Works, leading to a profitable collaboration with Henry Flitcroft in the late 1720s and with William Kent in the early 1730s.

Bridgeman was considered by his contemporaries to be a man of taste and distinction, described by Pope in 1724, in a letter to Prior, as 'A man of virtuosa class as well as I'. In 1726 he was elected to the exclusive and prestigious St Luke's Club of Artists and is among those portrayed by Gawen Hamilton in a *Club of Artists* (1735; London, N.P.G.); he also appears, rather more ambiguously, in William Hogarth's engraving *The Levee* (1735), from the series *A Rake's Progress* (1734–5; London, Soane Mus.), signifying fashionable extravagance on gardens.

Bridgeman's importance lies in his pivotal role in the transition from the formal French tradition of gardening, established from 1652 by the French Royal Gardener André Le Notre at the château of Versailles, to the natural landscape garden or *jardin anglais*. He was fortunate to be working at a time when gardening was a topic of great intellectual and artistic interest and was seen as having a moral and symbolic purpose derived from Classical antecedents, particularly Virgil and Ovid. Perhaps for the first time in England, house and garden were seen as aesthetically inseparable, as Bridgeman's friend Stephen Switzer realized, writing in his *Ichnographia* (1718): 'When you first begin to build and make gardens the gardener and builder ought to go Hand in Hand and to consult together.' The great interest in gardening and its elevation by contemporary poets to equality with art and poetry coincided with a period of prosperity, building and enclosure, and several of Bridgeman's commissions were carried out for directors of the South Sea Company, made rich by speculation.

At Stowe (see fig.), his most famous work, Bridgeman retained formal parterres, kitchen gardens, straight avenues and rides and geometric ponds and lakes, but within this framework he introduced asymmetry, partly dictated by the shape of the estate, and irregularity. His most important innovation was the introduction of the ha-ha, a concealed ditch that divided garden from countryside while retaining an uninterrupted vista. An import from France, the ha-ha was described by Antoine Joseph Dezallier d'Argenville in *La Théorie et la pratique du jardinage* (1709), translated into English in 1712 by John James. Its introduction at Stowe may have been Vanbrugh's idea, but Horace Walpole, 4th Earl of Oxford, credited it to Bridgeman in his *History of Modern Taste in Gardening* (1780). After Vanbrugh's death, Bridgeman extended the gardens to the west in 1726, virtually doubling them in size between 1727

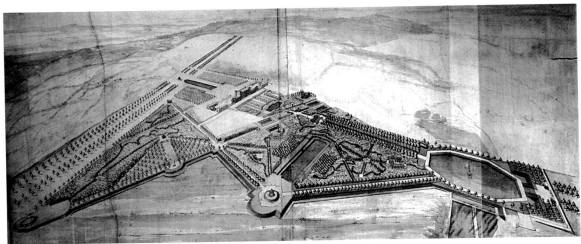

Charles Bridgeman: bird's-eye view of Stowe, Buckinghamshire, 1720 (Oxford, Bodleian Library, MS. Gough Drawings a.4, fol. 46)

and 1732 and incorporating semi-natural features and a large, irregular lake.

Water features largely in Bridgeman's work and in some cases is all that remains, as at Chicheley Hall, Bucks, where he designed a U-shaped canal for Sir John Chester in 1722. At Claremont, the grass amphitheatre above elaborate waterworks by Switzer is one of the few remaining examples of his work; an engraving of it was published by Switzer in *An Introduction to a General System of Hydrostaticks and Hydraulicks* (1729). Water predominated at Boughton House, Northants, designed for John Montagu, 2nd Duke of Montagu (1688–1749), in the late 1720s, as well as in his most celebrated urban scheme, the design of St James's Square, London (1727), which comprises an octagonal walk surrounding a large, circular central lake (destr. 1854). The Round Pond (1728) and Serpentine River (1731) in Kensington Gardens, London, remain much as he designed them.

The prosperity of Bridgeman's patrons that had enriched him in life proved unfortunate after his death, for with sufficient means to follow fashion, they soon obliterated his work with later alterations. Changes at Stowe began during his lifetime with the creation of the Elysian Fields 'after Mr. Kent's notion' in 1735; nevertheless, a record of Bridgeman's work there exists, for he had invited the French artist Jacques Rigaud (*c.* 1681–1754) to make drawings of the gardens in 1733; these were published by his widow Sarah Bridgeman (*d* 1743/4) in 1739. Kent had also altered Claremont in the 1730s, while Richmond Gardens (now part of the Royal Botanic Gardens, Kew), Blenheim and Wimbledon were remodelled by Lancelot 'Capability' Brown in 1760, 1764 and 1765 respectively; the gardens at Woburn Abbey, Beds, designed by Bridgeman in 1733, were 'improved' by Humphry Repton in 1804.

BIBLIOGRAPHY

S. Switzer: *Ichnographia, or the Nobleman, Gentleman and Gardener's Recreation* (1718)
H. Walpole: *History of Modern Taste in Gardening*, iv of *Anecdotes of Painting in England* (1771)
J. D. Hunt and P. Willis, eds: *The Genius of the Place: The English Landscape Garden, 1620–1820* (London, 1975)
J. D. Hunt: *The Figure in the Landscape: Poetry, Painting and Gardening during the Eighteenth Century* (London, 1977)
P. Willis: *Charles Bridgeman and the English Landscape Garden* (London, 1977) [substantial bibliog., with reproductions of all known designs by Bridgeman]

See also GARDEN, §VIII, 4(iv).

DAVID RODGERS

Bridgens, Richard (Hicks) (*b* ?Sheffield, 1785; *d* Port of Spain, Trinidad, Nov 1846). English sculptor, designer and architect. In 1810 he exhibited at the first Liverpool Academy Exhibition and showed models and drawings there in 1811, 1812 and 1814. These included designs for the restoration of the screen in Sefton church, Merseyside, and for a chimney-piece for Speke Hall, Liverpool, and two drawings of Joseph Ridgway's house at Ridgmont, Horwich, Lancs. Bridgens designed furniture and furnishings in Gothic and Elizabethan styles for GEORGE BULLOCK. In 1814 he moved to London with Bullock, using his address at 4 Tenterden Street, Hanover Square, and prepared designs for Sir Godfrey Vassal Webster (1789–1836) for improvements to Battle Abbey, E. Sussex, and similarly for Sir Walter Scott's home, Abbotsford House, at Melrose on the Borders. Two chair designs for Battle Abbey were published in Rudolph Ackermann's *Repository of Arts* in September 1817, and Bridgens was also involved in the design of chairs supplied to Abbotsford House in 1818. Following Bullock's death in 1818 Bridgens moved to 10 Tenterden Street and later attempted to set up an architectural practice in Birmingham. From 1819 he was employed by James Watt (1769–1848) to produce designs for the restoration and furnishing of Aston Hall in Birmingham. Examples of designs for Jacobean-style furniture and furnishings are dated 1819–24 and 1834–7. While in Birmingham Bridgens also published a folio volume of engravings of Sefton church. By 1825 he had closed the Birmingham practice, as it had attracted insufficient clients, and moved to Trinidad, where his wife had inherited a sugar plantation. He was in England soon after April 1831 and published 58 plates dated September 1825 to October 1826 under the title *Furniture with Candelabra and Interior Decoration Applicable to the Embellishment of Modern and Old English Mansions* (London, 1833;

rev. 1838). The important designs in this publication are those in the Elizabethan and Jacobean styles, and the book greatly influenced early Victorian design and helped to promote the styles that were then becoming fashionable.

BIBLIOGRAPHY
V. Glenn: 'George Bullock, Richard Bridgens and James Watt's Regency Furnishing Schemes', *Furn. Hist.*, xv (1979), pp. 54–67
George Bullock: Cabinet-maker (exh. cat. by C. Wainwright and others, London, Blairman & Sons, 1988)

BRIAN AUSTEN

Bridgewater, 3rd Duke of. *See* EGERTON, (1).

Bridgwater, Henry (Scott) (*b* 1864; *d* 1946). English mezzotint engraver. He lived in Bushey, Herts, and worked for most of the leading London print publishers and dealers. He first exhibited at the Royal Academy, London, in 1889, with *A Schoolgirl* after Luke Fildes, and continued to show there until his death in 1946, when his only exhibited original work, *On the Welsh Border*, was included. He was a prolific engraver with a catholic range of subjects including portraits, genre and landscape, and he copied a wide variety of artists from Elisabeth Vigée-Lebrun and George Romney to Gustave Courbet (e.g. *The Storm*, exh. RA 1933) and Hubert von Herkomer. His engraving of the *Soul's Awakening* (exh. RA 1890) after the painting by James Sant is in the Victoria and Albert Museum, London.

BIBLIOGRAPHY
H. Beck: *Victorian Engravings* (London, 1973)
R. K. Engen: *Dictionary of Victorian Engravers, Print Publishers and their Works* (Cambridge and Teaneck, NJ, 1979)

Briem, Jóhann (*b* Stóri-Núpur, southwest Iceland, 17 July 1907; *d* Reykjavík, Feb 1991). Icelandic painter. During the summer of 1929 he painted in the towns, on farms and on islands in Skagen and North Jutland, Denmark, before studying at private schools (1929–31) and the Staatliche Kunstakademie (1931–4) in Dresden. During the period 1934–40 he ran a private school in Reykjavík, together with the painter Finnur Jónsson and the sculptor Ásmundur Sveinsson. Among his students were the painters Nína Tryggvadóttir and Kristján Davíðsson. Briem was the president of the Icelandic Artists' Society (Félag íslenskra myndlistarmanna) in 1941–3, and as such he defended the views of progressive artists in a public dispute that ended in 1943 with the founding of the first public exhibition hall for Icelandic artists.

Briem was an independent figurative painter. He underwent no noticeable stylistic influences in Germany, although German Existentialist philosophy of art had a permanent influence on his subject-matter. He dealt mostly with depictions of rural life in the 1930s and at that time developed a simple formal structure and composition, together with a dark, thick and warm handling of colour. After 1941 his subject-matter became more symbolic and fantastic, with bright colours reminiscent of Fauvism. About 1950 Briem abandoned fantastic subjects and simplified his painting gradually until it became almost disembodied. He began to improvise Existentialist paintings of one or two shadow figures in a landscape, for which he used broad brushes and palette knives to create a rich protruding surface, reminiscent of coarse textile.

BIBLIOGRAPHY
B. Th. Björnsson: *Íslensk myndlist á 19. og 20. öld* [Icelandic art in the 19th and 20th centuries], 2 vols (Reykjavík, 1964–73)
H. B. Runólfsson: *Jóhann Briem* (Reykjavík, 1983)
Aldarspegill [The century in retrospect] (exh. cat., ed. K. Kristjánsdóttir, essay H. B. Runólfsson; Reykjavík, N.G., 1988) [incl. Eng. trans.]

HALLDÓR BJÖRN RUNÓLFSSON

Brienne, Comte de [Loménie, Louis-Henri de] (*b* Paris, 13 Jan 1635; *d* Château-Landon, Seine-et-Marne, 16 April 1698). French secretary of state, collector and writer. The son of a secretary of state, he spent three years touring Europe as far north as Lapland, after which he published his first work, the *Itinerarium* (1655). He then began a career in government, rising to the highest offices, during which he formed one of the finest art collections in Paris, which included medals, books, prints and drawings. (He sold the collection of medals to Louis XIV in 1668.)

About 30 of Brienne's finest pictures are described in his small published volume of Latin verses, *De pinacotheca sua* (1662), which he dedicated to the Dutch diplomat and courtier Constantijn Huygens (i). Italian paintings, particularly of the Venetian and Bolognese schools, formed an important part of his collection, of which the masterpiece was the small *Holy Family* (Paris, Louvre), now attributed to Giulio Romano but which Brienne believed was by Raphael, an attribution contested at the time by various collectors and critics. In 1662 it was bought by the King—the only picture he obtained directly from Brienne. Others that eventually joined the French royal collection include the *bozzetto* (Paris, Louvre, inv. no. 141) for Veronese's *Raising of Jairus's Daughter* (untraced), owned for a time by the collector Everard Jabach, Annibale Carracci's *Village Wedding* (Marseille, Mus. B.-A.), sold to Louis XIV in 1668 by Gaspard Marsy, and Domenichino's *Landscape with the Flight into Egypt* (Paris, Louvre). Brienne was a keen collector of works by Nicolas Poussin: *Moses Trampling the Crown of Pharaoh* (Woburn Abbey, Beds) and the early version of the *Arcadian Shepherds* ('*Et in Arcadia Ego*'; Chatsworth, Derbys) were in Brienne's possession.

Brienne's fall *c.* 1663, the causes of which are not clear, was as sudden as his rise to power. His collection (catalogued in 1662) was presumably dispersed soon after. Following the death of his wife in 1664 he retired to the Paris Oratory. The next year he was ordained as a subdeacon, but following his involvement in a scandalous incident while in the German duchy of Mecklenburg his family caused him to be imprisoned in St Lazare, Paris, from where he corresponded with the writers Gilles Ménage (1613–92) and Charles Perrault.

While in prison Briene wrote his *Mémoires*, in which he gave an account of the small circle of collectors active in Paris in the mid-17th century, as well as an ambitious dissertation on painting, part of which survives (Paris, Bib. N.). It also contains a commentary on *De arte graphica* (1668) by Charles-Alfonse Dufresnoy and a study of Poussin, in which Brienne supplied some interesting observations despite his extensive copyings from André Félibien's *Entretiens* (1666–88). In 1693 Brienne was transferred to the abbey of Château-Landon, where he remained until his death.

UNPUBLISHED SOURCES
Paris, Bib. N., MS. facs. 16986 [diss. on ptg]

WRITINGS
De pinacotheca sua (Paris, 1662)
Mémoires de Louis-Henri de Loménie, Comte de Brienne, ed. P. Bonnefon, 3 vols (Paris, 1916–19)

BIBLIOGRAPHY
Le Catalogue de Brienne (Paris, 1662), ed. E. Bonnaffé (Paris, 1873)
L. Hourticq: 'Un Amateur de curiosité sous Louis XIV: Louis-Henri de Loménie, Comte de Brienne, d'après un manuscrit inédit', *Gaz. B.-A.*, n.s. 2, xxxiii (1905), pp. 57–71, 237–51, 326–40
J. Thuillier: 'Pour un corpus Pussinianum', *Nicolas Poussin: Colloques internationaux sciences humaines: Paris, 1958*, ii, pp. 49–238

M.-A. DUPUY

Brière, Gaston (*b* Paris, 1 Dec 1871; *d* Paris, 22 June 1962). French art historian and museum curator. Educated at the Sorbonne, he joined the Musée National du Château de Versailles as a curator in 1903. He spent almost his entire career at Versailles until his retirement in 1938 and was involved in the reorganization of the historical collections. He brought back from the Musée du Louvre to Versailles some of the decorative works that had been moved at the beginning of the 19th century, including paintings by Gabriel Blanchard and Charles de La Fosse for the Salon de Diane, those by Noël Coypel for the Salle des Gardes de la Reine and those for the dining-room of the Petit Trianon.

Brière was president of many historical societies, a joint editor of the *Répertoire d'histoire moderne et contemporaine de la France* (1898–1906) and of the *Revue d'histoire moderne et contemporaine* (1899–1914) and a professor at the Ecole du Louvre (1911–38). His research concentrated in the main on French painting from the 16th to 18th centuries. He produced numerous books and articles; his complete bibliography consists of 187 items.

WRITINGS
Le Château de Versailles: Architecture et décoration, 2 vols (Paris, 1909)
Le Parc de Versailles: Sculpture décorative (Paris, 1911)
'L'Architecture en France et la peinture sous le règne de Henri IV et pendant les deux premières années du règne de Louis XIII', *Histoire de l'art: Depuis les premiers temps chrétiens jusqu'à nos jours*, ed. A. Michel, v/2 (Paris, 1913), pp. 701–34, 777–92
with E. Fleury: *Catalogue des pastels de M.-Q. De la Tour* (Paris, 1920, rev. 2/1932, 3/1954)
L'Ecole française (1924), i of *Musée national du Louvre: Catalogue des peintures exposées dans les galeries* (Paris, 1924–6)
with A. Pérate: *Compositions historiques* (1931), i of *Musée national du château de Versailles* (Paris, 1931–80)
L'Art de Versailles (exh. cat., Paris, Mus. Orangerie, 1932)

BIBLIOGRAPHY
'Hommage à Gaston Brière', *Archvs A. Fr.*, n. s. xxii (1959) [whole issue; complete bibliog.]

SIMONE HOOG

Bright, Henry (*b* Saxmundham, Suffolk, ?5 June 1810; *d* Ipswich, 21 Sept 1873). English painter and draughtsman. He was the son of Jerome Bright, a Suffolk clockmaker. He may have taken lessons in Norwich from John Berney Crome (1794–1842) and was apprenticed to Alfred Stannard (1806–89) for a short period. In 1836 he moved to London where he remained for some 20 years.

Bright became a member of the New Society of Painters in Water-Colours in 1839, where he exhibited until 1844. Although his obituarist in the *Art Journal* (Nov 1873, p. 327) states that he did not exhibit oils until the Royal Academy exhibition of 1845, this is not certain. During this period he developed friendships with leading artists, including Samuel Prout and James Duffield Harding. Bright was influenced by Harding's oil and pencil technique and, like him, he issued a number of drawing-books in the 1840s.

Bright's name was also associated with the manufacture of coloured crayons. He established a profitable career teaching the titled and well-to-do, many of whom became his patrons. In 1844 Queen Victoria purchased Bright's *Entrance to an Old Prussian Town* (Brit. Royal Col.) from the New Society of Painters in Water-Colours. His professional success extended to producing works jointly with other artists, including John Frederick Herring and William Shayer. Bright's contribution was usually the landscape background.

Bright maintained links with the Norwich artists. His use of chalk and stump on buff paper is similar to that of Robert Leman (1799–1863), while John Middleton strongly influenced his use of watercolour, particularly in 1847. Bright had to leave London in 1858 due to illness, and the last of his subsequent moves was to Ipswich in 1868.

BIBLIOGRAPHY
W. F. Dickes: *The Norwich School of Painting* (Norwich, 1905)
M. Allthorpe-Guyton: *Henry Bright 1810–1873: A Catalogue of Paintings and Drawings in the Collection of Norwich Castle Museum* (Norwich, 1973, rev. 1986) [fully illus.]
For further bibliography see NORWICH, §2.

ANDREW W. MOORE

Brightness [brilliance]. The psychological perception of intensity. The perception of brightness results from both the luminance of a given surface and the relationship of that surface to others in the visual field. *See* LIGHT.   □

Brighton. Town and seaside resort in West Sussex, England. It originated in the medieval fishing village of Brighthelmstone, becoming a fashionable resort from the 1750s. The town achieved its greatest artistic significance under the patronage of the Prince Regent (later King George IV; *reg* 1820–30) from the late 18th century. Brighton contains several outstanding Victorian churches and, with the contiguous town of Hove, has some fine streets of 19th-century houses. The University of Sussex, designed by Basil Spence, was founded at Falmer, north of the town, in 1961.

The remnants of the original village survive in the twisting alleys of the Lanes, where the walls of many buildings are patterned in local flint and cobblestones. The 14th-century parish church of St Nicholas (altered 1850s by R. C. Carpenter) is situated above the old town on a hill that once commanded views across the English Channel and the South Downs. East of this area is the Old Steine, an open garden space.

Fashionable society was first attracted to Brighton in the 1750s by the curative treatment of drinking and bathing in sea-water, devised by Dr Richard Russell (1687–1759). By the turn of the 19th century, all the pleasurable trappings of Georgian life—assembly rooms, ballrooms, circulating libraries, a theatre, swimming baths and a race-course (most destr.)—had been established; but it was the annual residence of George, Prince of Wales, that confirmed Brighton as the country's most favoured resort. In 1785, the Prince commissioned HENRY HOLLAND to design the Royal Pavilion, a small and restrained villa overlooking the Old Steine. Its elegant proportions and tall bay windows were to set the prevailing image for much of Brighton's architecture. The Picturesque, however, was soon to touch the Prince's imagination: Holland and the decorating firm of John Crace and Frederick Crace (*see* CRACE) refashioned the interior in a luxurious Chinese taste *c.* 1801. In the grounds, a magnificent stable building (now the Dome concert hall) dominated by a great laminated timber-rib and glass dome was erected between 1803 and 1808 to the designs of William Porden. The stable, decorated in an Islamic style, prefigured the dramatic transformation by John Nash (i) of the Royal Pavilion (see fig.) into a fantasy of Eastern domes, minarets, Islamic crenellations and arches (1815–22). Within, Frederick Crace, Robert Jones and later in the century J. D. Crace designed an oriental extravaganza (for illustration *see* OVERDOOR). The banqueting room, music-room and saloon are exotic displays of dragon-encrusted chandeliers, chinoiserie decoration, rich furnishings, gilded walls and murals.

Brighton's housing boom was in full swing when in 1823 construction began on the Kemp Town Estate, *c.* 1.5 km east of the town centre. The local landowner Thomas Read Kemp (1782–1844) empowered architects Charles Augustin Busby (1786–1834) and Amon Henry Wilds (1784–1857) to collaborate with the builder Thomas Cubitt in erecting long avenues of terraced houses faced with stucco and adorned with decorative balconies. At the heart of the estate is Lewes Crescent (wider than the Royal Crescent in Bath), which leads away from the sea to the seclusion of Sussex Square. Busby was solely responsible for the other great estate of the period, Brunswick Town in Hove (also begun in 1823); surrounded by streets of terraces running down to the pebbly beach, Brunswick Square is an expanse of garden flanked by undulating façades and the imposing Corinthian front of Brunswick Terrace facing out to sea. More Victorian in its Italianate manner is the adjoining Adelaide Crescent (begun 1830), an austere development by Decimus Burton.

The Regency style continued in Brighton and Hove well into the Victorian period. In 1833 Wilds built as his own residence the Western Pavilion, a stuccoed villa modelled on the Royal Pavilion, complete with an oriental dome and minarets. Wilds was also responsible for the elegance of Montpelier Crescent, where he used ammonite-shell capitals as a pun on his Christian name.

The Victorian period in Brighton is best displayed in its fine churches. An exemplary lead had been given by Charles Barry's design for St Peter's (1824–8, enlarged 1898–1902), which was erected in the Gothic Revival style on the prominent site of the Level. The judges who awarded this commission included the Rev. Henry Mitchell Wagner (1792–1870), Vicar of Brighton. He and his eldest son, the Rev. Arthur Douglas Wagner (1824–1902), were vigorous sponsors, both spiritually and financially, of many

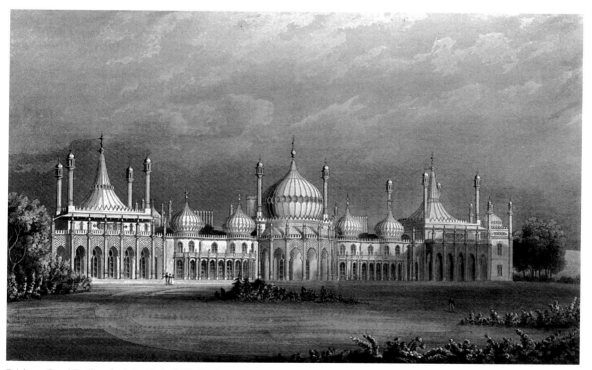

Brighton, Royal Pavilion, by John Nash, 1815–22; from an engraving by Augustus Charles Pugin, 1826

of the town's great churches. Three churches built under their auspices are exceptionally fine: St Paul's on West Street, with its massive timber tower and spire, was raised in 1846–8 to the designs of R. C. Carpenter; St Bartholomew's (1872–4), by the local architect Edmund Evan Scott (*fl* 1851; *d* 1896), has a soaring, aisleless nave with some rich furnishings of *c.* 1898 by the Arts and Crafts designer Henry Wilson; and St Martin's was built in 1872–5 by the local architect G. Somers Clarke jr (1841–1926). Independently, the chapel of St Michael and All Angels was the outcome of a double campaign of building: the nave was raised to the design of William Burges *c.* 1868, after his death, as an addition to the original church (1858–62) by G. F. Bodley. Some of the fine stained glass is by William Morris, who with Philip Webb was also responsible for the painting on the sanctuary roof.

With the arrival of the railway in 1841, day-trippers from London had begun to visit in large numbers. The fun of the Victorian seaside found its architectural counterpart in such buildings as Eugenius Birch's West Pier (1863–6), R. St Moore's Palace Pier (1899; replacing the Chain Pier, built 1823; destr. 1896) and the latticed arches and terrace of Madeira Drive, which stretches for *c.* 1.5 km.

Brighton and Hove boast several noteworthy examples of Modern Movement architecture. Along the coast, the sleek, streamlined curves of Embassy Court (1936), the block of flats by Wells Coates, and Burnet, Tait and Lorne's St Dunstan's Institute of the Blind (1937–9) illustrate the growing influence of continental and Scandinavian architectural sources, while the concrete structure and zigzag decoration of the Brighton, Hove & Worthing Airport at Shoreham (1934–8, by R. Stavers Tiltman) show the influence of American Art Deco. St Wilfred's Church (1932–4, by H. S. Goodhart-Rendel) is a studied example of brick Gothic Revival.

Brighton's combination of sea views and society inevitably attracted visiting artists. John Constable, although disliking the town, stayed almost every year between 1824 and 1830; his seascapes include the *Chain Pier, Brighton* (London, Tate), which records what was once one of Brighton's favourite attractions. Walter Sickert kept a studio in Sussex Square, organizing the influential exhibition *Work of English Post-Impressionists, Cubists and Others* at the Brighton Art Gallery in December 1913. The gallery houses one of the country's finest collections of decorative arts and furniture of the late 19th century and early 20th.

BIBLIOGRAPHY

The Rape of Lewes (1940), vii of *The Victoria County History of the County of Sussex*, Victoria Hist. Co. England (Oxford), pp. 244–63
A. Dale: *Fashionable Brighton, 1820–1860* (London, 2/1967)
C. Musgrave: *Life in Brighton* (London, 1970, rev. 2/1981)
A Guide to the Buildings of Brighton (Brighton, 1987)
N. R. Bingham: *C. A. Busby: The Regency Architect of Brighton and Hove* (London, 1991)

NEIL R. BINGHAM

Brigittine Order [Order of the Holy Saviour]. Religious order named after its foundress, St Bridget of Sweden (*c.* 1303–73; *can* 1391), a devout woman with Swedish court connections. In 1346 she founded VADSTENA ABBEY in Sweden, which she intended to be an influential spiritual centre reflecting the original group of the faithful with the Virgin at its head. Vadstena became the model for other Brigittine houses. Bridget went to Rome in 1349 to seek approval for her Order, dying there after returning from a pilgrimage to the Holy Land. Her body was returned to Vadstena in 1374.

The Brigittine Rule, the *Regula Sancti Salvatoris*, supposedly was revealed to Bridget by Christ. With the Augustinian Rule (*see* AUGUSTINIAN CANONS, §1), it formed the constitution of the Order, which was finally recognized by Pope Urban VI (*reg* 1378–89) in a bull of 1378. The Order flourished mainly in northern Europe in the later Middle Ages. Intended primarily for women, it had double houses with separate but adjacent convents for men and women, sharing a church. Monks were superior in spiritual matters, the abbess in all else. Monasteries were large by contemporary standards, the rule stipulating that they should have 85 members. Convents were consecrated at Vadstena in 1384, with sisters, priests and lay brothers.

The earliest daughter houses date from the 1390s, with foundations in Florence (1392) and Danzig (now Gdańsk; 1394–6). In the early 15th century there were foundations at Revel, Lublin, Lübeck, Stralsund, Maribo, Bergen and Syon (England), with further expansion after 1435 in Scandinavia, Germany and the Netherlands. By the Reformation there were about 80 houses. In 1595 Vadstena was confiscated and the Order banished from Sweden; houses elsewhere were suppressed. A version of the Order was revived in the 20th century, and four houses in England, the Netherlands and Germany follow the Rule.

St Bridget received about 700 revelations, concerning not only the Passion of Christ but also political and religious events of her day. A Latin compilation of these, *Liber celestis revelationum*, was prepared in the 1370s to support her canonization process, and numerous vernacular versions were circulated in the later Middle Ages. The Brigittines did much to promote the spread of printing with an early printing press established at Vadstena. They were also important promoters of textiles, especially in Finland (*see* FINLAND, §XI).

St Bridget is usually depicted in the Brigittine habit with a cross on her forehead; she is often shown writing or receiving revelations. A full-page miniature in the Boucicaut Hours (15th century; Paris, Mus. Jacquemart-André, MS. 2, fol. 42*v*) shows her in a white veil with praying hands, ascending to heaven in the arms of an angel.

BIBLIOGRAPHY

St Bridget of Sweden: *Liber celestis revelationum*; ed. R. Ellis as *The Liber Celestis of St Bridget of Sweden*, Early English Texts Society (Oxford, 1987–)
——: *Revelationes*; (Lübeck, 1492) [Lat. trans.; with woodcuts]
M. J. Heimbucher: *Die Orden und Kongregationen der katholischen Kirche*, i (Paderborn, 1896, 3/1933), pp. 620–25
A. Lindblom: *Den heliga Birgitta: Bildwerk i skulptur och maleri fran Sveriges medeltid* [St Bridget: imagery in sculpture and painting from the Middle Ages in Sweden] (Stockholm, 1918)
J. Jorgensen: *Den hellige Birgitta af Vadstena* [St Bridget of Vadstena], 2 vols (Copenhagen, 1941; Eng. trans., New York, 1954)
B. Berthelson: 'Studier i Birgittinerordens byggnadsskick' [Studies in the building style of the Brigittine Order], *Kun. Vitt., Hist. & Ant. Akad. Hand.*, lxiii (1947) [whole issue]
C. Nordenfalk: 'Saint Bridget of Sweden as Represented in Illuminated Manuscripts', *De artibus opuscula XL: Essays in Honor of Erwin Panofsky*, i (New York, 1961), pp. 371–93
H. Cnattingius: *The Crisis in the 1420s*, Studies in the Order of St Bridget of Sweden, i (Stockholm, 1963)

Birgitta van Zweden, 1303–1373: 600 jaar kunst en cultuur van haar kloosterorde (exh. cat., ed. L. van Liebergen; Uden, Mus. Relig. Kst, 1986)

VIRGINIA DAVIS

Brignole and Brignole-Sale. Italian family of collectors and patrons. The Brignole settled in Genoa in the 14th century and achieved noble status in the 16th century. During the 17th and 18th centuries several members of the family held high public office. Giacomo Maria Brignole (1724–1801) was the last doge of Genoa.

Giovanni Francesco Brignole di Antonio (*b* Genoa, *c.* 1582; *d* Genoa, 15 July 1637) was the founder of the Brignole-Sale branch of the family by his marriage (25 July 1603) to Geronima Sale, whose father Giulio (*d* 1606), having no male heirs, bequeathed his fortune and marquisate of Groppoli in Tuscany to her children on condition that they assumed his name. Giovanni Francesco, who served as Doge of Genoa from 1635 to 1637, was a patron of the Savonese poet Gabriello Chiabrera (1552–1638) and of the local painter Andrea Ansaldo, from whom he commissioned (*c.* 1628–33) decorations in the family palazzo in Piazza Embriaci, close to the church of S Maria di Castello. The family chapel in S Maria di Castello was decorated with paintings by Ansaldo and Luciano Borzone and an altarpiece by Giovanni Battista Paggi. Giovanni Francesco's son and heir was Anton Giulio Brignole-Sale (*b* Genoa, 23 June 1606; *d* Genoa, 1665), Marchese di Groppoli, who made his name as a poet and politician and became a Jesuit in 1652. Brignole-Sale played a central part in Genoese cultural life. He was largely responsible for reviving the Accademia degli Addormentati as a focus for philosophical debate in the 1630s, while his praise of the painter Domenico Fiasella in his poem *Le instabilità dell'ingegno* (Bologna, 1635) testified to his interest in Genoese art. He is best remembered, however, as a patron in Genoa of Anthony van Dyck, who *c.* 1626–7 painted the portraits of *Anton Giulio Brignole-Sale*, of his mother, *Geronima Brignole-Sale with her Daughter Aurelia*, and of his wife, *Paola Adorno* (all Genoa, Gal. Pal. Rosso). Giovanni Francesco's nephew was Emanuele Brignole (*b* Genoa, 1617; *d* Genoa, 1678). He became a wealthy financier and public benefactor, on whose initiative was founded in 1656 the great Albergo dei Poveri (2 Piazza E. Brignole), one of the major Genoese public building projects of the 17th century.

On the death of Anton Giulio Brignole-Sale in 1665 the rights of primogeniture were shared by his eldest sons, Ridolfo Maria (*d* Genoa, 1683) and Giovanni Francesco the younger (*b* Genoa, 11 April 1643; *d* Genoa, Oct 1693), who on 22 May 1671 obtained from the Genoese senate permission to use part of their protected inheritance to build a new palace in the Strada Nuova (the Palazzo Rosso, Via Garibaldi 18; 1671–7), designed by Matteo Lagomaggiore to include two *piani nobili* of equal dignity. On the second of these they commissioned fresco decoration (1679–*c.* 1694) from Gregorio de' Ferrari, Domenico and Paolo Girolamo Piola, Giovanni Andrea Carlone (i), Carlo Antonio Tavella (1668–1738) and Bartolomeo Guidobono. The magnificence of the new residence was further enhanced with tapestries designed by Rubens, mirrors and candelabra by Filippo Parodi and many precious fitments, such as the large silver chandelier designed by Gregorio de' Ferrari.

The Palazzo Rosso became the principal home of the family and of their growing art collection, which at this time already included such notable works as Rubens's *Venus and Mars* and van Dyck's *Christ with a Coin* (1623–4; both Genoa, Pal. Bianco). The quality and quantity of the collection was greatly enriched by the bequest of Giuseppe M. Durazzo, the father-in-law of Giovanni Francesco the younger. This included Veronese's *Judith* (*c.* 1580–85) and Bonifazio de' Pitati's *Adoration of the Magi* (both Genoa, Gal. Pal. Rosso). The magnificence of the collection was the subject of comment in diaries of travellers such as Charles de Brosses and Charles-Nicholas Cochin (1715–90). From 1711 the family also owned the building on the opposite side of the street, known as the Palazzo Bianco (Via Garibaldi 11). This was purchased by Maria Durazzo, widow of Giovanni Francesco Brignole-Sale the younger, from the de Franci family and subsequently remodelled by Giacomo Viano.

On the death of the last member of the family, Antonio Brignole-Sale (1786–1863), the family properties passed to his daughter Maria (*b* Genoa, 5 April 1811; *d* Paris, 9 Dec 1888), the wife of the financier Raffaele de Ferrari, Duca di Galliera (*d* 1876), and a generous benefactress of the poor and sick of Genoa and of the Genoese Commune; in 1874 she donated the Palazzo Rosso and its art collection to the Commune and bequeathed the Palazzo Bianco for use as a public art gallery. It was she who bought Zurburán's *St Euphemia*, *St Ursula* (both 1635–40) and the *Communion of St Bonaventura* (?1639) and Murillo's *Flight into Egypt* (*c.* 1645; all Genoa, Gal. Pal. Rosso) at the auction of the Soult collection in Paris (1852).

DBI

BIBLIOGRAPHY
A. Cappellini: *Tre insigni benefattori genovesi: E. Vernazza, E. Brignole, la duchessa di Galliera* (Rome, n.d.)
N. Battilana: *Genealogie delle famiglie nobili di Genova* (Genoa, 1825)
O. Grosso: *Catalogo del Palazzo Rosso* (Genoa, 1931)
C. Marcenaro: 'Una fonte barocca per l'architettura organica: Il Palazzo Rosso di Genova', *Paragone*, xii/134 (1961), pp. 24–49
——: *Gli affreschi del Palazzo Rosso di Genova* (Genoa, 1965)
E. Poleggi: *Strada Nuova: Una lottizzazione del cinquecento a Genova* (Genoa, 1968)
E. Gavazza: *La grande decorazione a Genova* (Genoa, 1974), pp. 85–91, 337, n. 4)
R. Gallo: 'Anton Giulio Brignole-Sale', *Dibattito politico e problemi di governo a Genova nella prima metà del seicento* (Genoa, 1975), pp. 177–208
G. Doria: 'Investimenti della nobiltà genovese nell'edilizia di prestigio', *Stud. Stor.*, i (1986), pp. 5–55

JANET SOUTHORN, LAURA TAGLIAFERRO

Brik, Osip (Maksimovich) (*b* Moscow, 16 Jan 1888; *d* Moscow, 22 Feb 1945). Russian theorist and critic. He trained as a lawyer at Moscow University but never practised law, devoting himself instead to art and literature. Prior to the October Revolution of 1917 his apartment was a meeting-place for Futurist poets and he was an active member of the Formalist group OPOYAZ (the Society for the Study of Poetical Language). After the Revolution he worked in the Fine Arts department (IZO) of NARKOMPROS and as a commissar of the Petrograd (now St Petersburg) Svomas (Free Art Studios) in 1919.

In 1918 he established the group IMO (Iskusstvo Molo-dykh: Art of the Young). Gaining Anatoly Lunacharsky's support and a subsidy from Narkompros, this group was able to publish its views through the radical newspaper *Iskusstvo kommuny* ('Art of the Commune') (1918–19). Brik promoted Russian Futurism as a revolutionary Communist art and actively participated in the setting up of Kom-Fut, a Communist Futurist collective in Petrograd in 1919. Failing to win the support of the Party for Kom-Fut's ideas about a new Communist cultural ideology, Brik eventually abandoned the organization in 1921 and in the following year took over from Vasily Kandinsky as head of the Moscow INKHUK. Brik had argued for the creation of an organization where artists were to be trained to design and make prototypes of new objects for proletarian use as early as 1918. As head of Inkhuk, he presided over its rejection in a formal declaration of easel painting and, with the encouragement of the theorists Boris Arvatov and BORIS KUSHNER, established a materialist Marxist approach to production that promoted industrial Constructivism (*see* CONSTRUCTIVISM, §1). These ideas were set out in *Iskusstvo v proizvodstve* ('Art in production'), published in 1921. Brik was also closely associated with Vladimir Mayakovsky, whom he met in 1915 and with whom he collaborated on many publications and enterprises, not least the journals *Lef* (1923–5), for which he wrote extensively on photography and design, and *Novyy lef* (New Lef, 1927–8). Increasingly, Brik's interests focused on literature and the 'factography' promoted by NIKOLAY CHUZHAK. After Mayakovsky's death in 1930 he concentrated on promoting the poet's memory. He edited various editions of his works and wrote about 200 articles on them. He also wrote a number of film scripts and opera librettos.

WRITINGS
'Drenazh iskusstva' [The drainage of art], *Isk. Komm.*, 1 (1918), p. 1
'Khudozhnik i kommuna' [The artist and the commune], *Izobrazitel'noye Isk.*, 1 (1919), pp. 25–6
with S. Filippov and D. Shterenberg: *Iskusstvo v proizvodstve* [Art in production] (Moscow, 1921)
'My-futuristy' [We are the Futurists], *Novyy lef*, 8–9 (1927), pp. 49–52
'Ne teoriya a lozung' ['Not a theory but a slogan'], *Pechat & Revolyutsiya*, 1 (1929)

BIBLIOGRAPHY
V. D. Barooshian: *Brik and Mayakovsky* (The Hague, 1978)
B. Jangfeldt: 'Osip Brik: A Bibliography with an Introduction and a Post Scriptum', *Rus. Lit.*, viii (1980), pp. 579–604
H. Stephan: '*Lef* and the Left Front of the Arts', *Slav. Beitr.*, cxlii (1981) [whole issue]

JEREMY HOWARD

Bril [Brill]. Flemish family of artists. (1) Matthijs Bril and (2) Paul Bril were the sons of the painter Matthijs Bril the elder (*b* ?Breda; *fl* ?Antwerp, *c.* 1550) and presumably began their artistic training with their father in Antwerp before settling in Rome in the last quarter of the 16th century. There, specializing in landscapes in various media, they became the most important northern landscape artists in Italy. Their art contributed to the rapid growth of landscape painting, both imaginary and topographical, in the 17th century.

(1) Matthijs [Mattheus] **Bril** the younger (*b* Antwerp, 1550; *d* Rome, 8 June 1583). Painter and draughtsman. He arrived in Rome *c.* 1575, where, according to Baglione,

he painted landscapes in the Vatican Palace, initially under Lorenzo Sabatini, superintendent of works for Pope Gregory XIII (*reg* 1572–85). The first of Bril's two major commissions in the Vatican Palace was the fresco series in the Galleria Geografica of topographical *Views of Rome with the Translation of the Remains of St Gregory Nazianzus*, executed soon after the event in June 1580. Van Mander attributed the views to Bril and Mancini wrote that Antonio Tempesta painted the figures. Bril's second major project was in the Torre dei Venti, a papal apartment suite in the Vatican Palace that was designed by Ottaviano Mascherino to commemorate the Gregorian calendar reform in 1582. Part of a larger programme created by the papal cosmographer, Ignazio Danti, the four rooms painted by Bril depict biblical cycles in landscape friezes and two contain wall-sized paintings placing topographical views of Rome and imaginary *vedute* in an illusionistic framework. (The surrounding allegorical figures were executed by Niccolò Pomarancio and his studio.)

It is unlikely that the large-scale illusionistic views were by Paul Bril, as Baer first suggested, for Matthijs was more renowned for his topographical renderings than his brother (cf. such drawings as the *View of the Castel Sant'Angelo* executed for the *Translation* frescoes and the *Arch of Septimius Severus*; both Paris, Louvre). Several of Matthijs's drawings of ancient Roman sites were preserved by Paul and copied by contemporaries, notably Jan Breughel the elder. Characteristic of Matthijs's novel rendition of topography is the coupling of extraordinary detail with an emphasis on the structures' monumentality, achieved by means of a viewpoint from below and dynamic recession into the distance. His other imaginary landscapes observe nature less closely and can thus be considered more typically Mannerist; they have dramatic contrasts of light and dark, a predominance of acid blues and greens in the palette and bravura impressionistic brushwork. These also served as models for the later work of Paul and others. Simon Frisius issued two series of prints, both entitled *Topographia variarum regionum* (1611 and 1613–14), after a group of Matthijs's imaginary landscapes.

(2) Paul Bril (*b* Antwerp, *c.* 1554; *d* Rome, 7 Oct 1626). Painter, printmaker and draughtsman, brother of (1) Matthijs Bril. According to van Mander, Paul studied in Antwerp with Damiaan Wortelmans (1545–after 1588/9) before travelling to Rome, via Lyon, *c.* 1574, to join his brother, whom, according to Baglione, he assisted on Vatican commissions after 1576. However, no document places Paul in Rome before 1582, and in any case Matthijs was probably not there until *c.* 1575. Paul's first known independent works are monumental frescoes dating from the late 1580s. They include a dramatic rendering of *Jonah and the Whale* (1588) in the Scala Santa in the Vatican (based on a drawing by Matthijs; Paris, Louvre) and a series of landscape lunettes (*c.* 1589) in the Lateran Palace.

One of Paul Bril's most important early commissions was his fresco cycle (*c.* 1599) in S Cecilia in Trastevere, Rome, depicting hermit saints praying in lush, wooded landscapes. He executed another major work in this period, a monumental seascape, the *Martyrdom of St Clement*

Paul Bril: *Hunting Scene*, 1621 (Rome, Galleria Doria-Pamphili)

(*c.* 1600–02/3), painted with the brothers Giovanni and Cherubino Alberti in the Vatican Palace's Sala Clementina for Pope Clement VIII (*reg* 1592–1605). In 1601 Paul received a third major commission, to paint a series of large canvases featuring properties of the Mattei family (four examples in Rome, Pal. Barberini). In the 1590s Bril began painting small landscapes on panel and copper, often depicting subjects that he and his brother had rendered earlier in large scale, such as tempestuous sea-scapes, hermits in the wilderness, travelling pilgrims, peasants among ancient ruins, as well as hunters and fishermen (e.g. the *Rabbit Hunt*, 1595, Florence, Pitti; *Landscape with Travellers*, Milan, Ambrosiana; and *Land-scape with Roman Ruins*, 1600, Dresden, Gemäldegal. Alte Meister).

Paul Bril's contemporaries Baglione and Mancini noted that his style changed distinctly during his Roman sojourn. The landscapes from his early period derive their vocabulary largely from the Flemish tradition inaugurated by Joachim Patinir and Pieter Bruegel the elder and developed by his own brother. The paintings feature strong contrasts of forms that engender a sense of dramatic motion. Bril juxtaposed precipitous cliffs with chasms or dark, twisting trees grow from rising mounds next to flat, sunlit pastures. The compositions, sharply divided by light and dark strips, recede rapidly into the distance. Around 1605 his style changed to a calmer, classicizing mode, perhaps influenced by Annibale Carracci and Adam Elsheimer. Works from this period have lower horizons and flatter, less abrupt transitions from foreground to background through gently rising diagonals and a more subtle rendition of light. They often contain pastoral or bucolic figures and settings, and also explicit mythological subjects. Excellent examples of this change are Bril's frescoes of the *Four Seasons*, painted for Cardinal Scipione Borghese in the Casino Aurora (1611; Rome, Pal. Rospigliosi–Pallavicini), the *Hunting Scene* (Rome, Gal. Doria-Pamphili; see fig.) and the *Land-scape with a Dancing Satyr* (1623; Oberlin Coll., OH, Allen Mem. A. Mus.) with figures by Pietro Paolo Bonzi.

Bril's active membership of the Roman Accademia di S Luca culminated in the post of principal in 1620. He was renowned throughout Italy, for his work was avidly collected by such patrons as Cardinal Federico Borromeo in Milan, Cardinal Carlo de' Medici in Florence and Duke Ferdinando Gonzaga in Mantua. Bril's art was appreciated in the Netherlands as well, and the drawings he sent back to Antwerp (e.g. *Italian Farmhouse by a Stream*; Amster-dam, Rijksmus.) were engraved by a variety of artists. In addition to the effect on his immediate followers such as Willem van Nieulandt, Bril's art influenced the develop-ment of the idealizing landscape in Italy, as practised by the DUTCH ITALIANATES Cornelis Poelenburgh and Bartholomäus Breenbergh and by Agostino Tassi and Claude Lorrain.

BIBLIOGRAPHY

Hollstein: *Dut. & Flem.*
K. van Mander: *Schilder-boek* ([1603]–1604)
G. Mancini: *Considerazioni. . .sulla pittura* (*c.* 1621); ed. A. Marucchi, 2 vols, Fonti e documenti per la storia dell'arte, i (Rome, 1956–7)
G. Baglione: *Vite* (1642); ed. V. Mariani (Rome, 1935), pp. 19, 59, 92, 197, 296
A. Bertolotti: *Artisti belgi ed olandesi a Roma nei secoli XVI e XVII* (Florence, 1880/*R* 1974)
A. Mayer: *Das Leben und die Werke der Brüder Matthäus und Paul Brill* (Leipzig, 1910)
J. A. F. Orbaan and G. J. Hoogewerff: *Bescheiden in Italië omtrent Nederlandsche kunstenaars en geleerden* (The Hague, 1913)
R. Baer: *Paul Bril: Studien zur Entwicklungsgeschichte der Landschaftsmalerei um 1600* (Freiburg, 1930)
M. Vaes: 'Matthieu Bril: 1550–1583', *Bull. Inst. Hist. Belge Rome*, vii (1938), pp. 283–331
F. Lugt: *Inventaire général des dessins des écoles du nord: Ecole flamande*, Paris, Louvre cat., i (Paris, 1949), pp. 16–28
L. Salerno: *Landscape Painters of the Seventeenth Century in Rome*, i (Rome, 1977)
D. Burnett: 'The Drawing Styles of Matthew Bril', *Ksthist. Tidskr.*, xlvii (1978), pp. 103–10
N. Courtwright: *Gregory XIII's Tower of the Winds in the Vatican* (diss., New York, Inst. F.A., 1990)

NICOLA COURTWRIGHT

Brinckmann, Philipp Hieronymus (*b* Speyer, 1709; *bur* Mannheim, 21 Dec 1760). German painter, draughtsman and etcher. Trained by Johann Georg Dathan (1703–*c.* 1748) in Speyer, he was a court painter in Mannheim from 1733 until his death, from 1755 gallery director and from 1757 a privy councillor. Of the religious works that, as a court painter, he was obliged to produce, the only ones that survive are frescoes (spandrel paintings) depicting the *Four Quarters of the World* (after 1748; Mannheim, former Jesuit church of SS Ignaz und Franz Xavier) and ceiling paintings in Electress Elizabeth Augusta's library in Schloss Mannheim.

Brinckmann's landscapes show two opposing trends. On the one hand, there are small, detailed picturesque landscapes in courtly or rural settings with suitable accessories, often with many figures. According to the terms of his contract, he had to produce two such paintings each year; typical examples are the *Court Gardens at Mannheim* (1745) and *Wolfbrunnens near Heidelberg* (1739; both Augsburg, Schaezlerpal.), which depict precise locations with unusual clarity. On the other hand, there are wider, more painterly, freer landscapes, often without figures, in which the influence of Christian Hilfgott Brand has been seen. They are better understood, however, as impressions of a trip to Switzerland in 1745. Brinckmann's most important picture, *Rheinfall near Schaffhausen* (1745; Augsburg, Schaezlerpal.), shows the resulting heightened awareness of nature.

In 1760 Brinckmann travelled to Paris and visited the engraver Jean-Georges Wille, a key influence on his subsequent style. He produced over 50 etchings of varied quality, only a small proportion being landscapes. The most interesting are book illustrations based on designs by Paul Egell. The quality of Brinckmann's drawings is often remarkable, particularly the *Images from the Life of Christ* (Munich, Staatl. Graph. Samml.), which are surprisingly close to Bavarian Rococo art.

BIBLIOGRAPHY

G. Jacob: *Philipp Hieronymus Brinckmann: Ein Beitrag zur Kunstgeschichte des 18. Jahrhunderts mit besonderer Berücksichtigung der Entwicklung der Landschaftskunst* (diss; U. Würzburg, 1923)
Deutsche Barockgalerie, Augsburg, Städt. Kstsammlungen, ii (Augsburg, 1970), pp. 40, 41 [with bibliog.]

GODE KRÄMER

Brindaban. *See* VRINDAVAN.

Brinkman. Dutch family of architects. (1) M. Brinkman and his son (2) J. A. Brinkman, who carried on his firm, are regarded respectively as the pioneer and the leading exponent of the Dutch Modernist architectural movement known as Nieuwe Bouwen. Associated partnerships formed after the death of M. Brinkman were Brinkman & Van der Vlugt (1925–36), Brinkman & Van den Broek (1937–48) and VAN DEN BROEK & BAKEMA (from 1948). These firms were particularly influential on the development of public housing in Rotterdam.

(1) M(ichiel) Brinkman (*b* Rotterdam, 16 March 1873; *d* Rotterdam, 19 Feb 1925). He studied at the Academie voor Beeldende Kunsten en Technische Wetenschappen in Rotterdam. After a long collaboration with the architect Bernard Hooykaas (*b* 1908) in Rotterdam, he set up as an independent architect in 1910. His first commissions were for offices and factory buildings, for example the De Maas Flour Factory (1913) and a grain silo in Rotterdam. His pioneering reputation, however, derives from the design for 273 workers' flats (1919–22) in Spangen, previously one of Rotterdam's grimmest districts. His experimental urban design consisted of three-storey blocks enclosing an interior space, on to which the flats faced. The most innovative aspect was the wide concrete gallery that encircles the inward side of the blocks at the third-floor level, providing the traditional functions of the street. In the spacious, grassed interior he designed smaller housing blocks and a central building with social facilities. The carefully detailed, sober brick architecture harmonizes with the concrete construction of the gallery. There is also a stark contrast between the stern, rhythmical street façades and the lively treatment of those facing the inner space, while the structural conception of the plan and design recall the work of Charles Rennie Mackintosh and Frank Lloyd Wright. In particular the addition of a gallery to a residential building had a great impact on Dutch architecture. Brinkman was also responsible for the Konigin Wilhelmina and Konigin Emma schools (both 1920) and several town houses (1920–24), all in Rotterdam. Through such works as these he established a reputation as one of the leading Rationalist architects of the early 20th century in the Netherlands. At the time of his death he was working on a plan for the Van Nelle Tobacco Factory, Rotterdam.

BIBLIOGRAPHY

H. P. Berlage, A. Keppler and J. Wils: *Arbeiderswoningen in Nederland* (Rotterdam, 1921)
L. Hilbersheimer: *Gross-stadt Architektur* (Stuttgart, 1927)
J. B. Bakema: 'Een huis in Spangen voor 270 families', *Forum*, v (1960–61), pp. 161–71
M. Bock: 'Hoe nieuw en wat is het Nieuwe Bouwen?', *Het Nieuwe Bouwen: Voorgeschiedenis* (Delft, 1982), pp. 6–22

(2) J(ohannes) A(ndreas) Brinkman (*b* Rotterdam, 22 March 1902; *d* Rotterdam, 6 April 1949). Son of (1)

M. Brinkman. He studied road and waterworks construction at the Technische Hogeschool, Delft. He joined his father's firm in 1921 and became head of it following the latter's death. At the instigation of his client and friend C. H. van der Leeuw, a director of the Van Nelle concern, Brinkman employed in 1925 the more experienced Leendert Cornelis van der Vlugt (1894–1936) to assist in the ongoing project for the Van Nelle Factory (1925–31) in Rotterdam. Van der Vlugt and Brinkman were both members of the avant-garde group DE OPBOUW, and the project was marked by an unusual amount of collaboration between client and architects. Van der Vlugt, who had studied at the Academie voor Beeldende Kunsten en Technische Wetenschappen, Rotterdam, had already designed a technical school in Groningen (1922; with Jan Wiebenga (1886–1974)), with an early use of glass curtain-walls. His design for the Van Nelle Factory (see fig.), on which Mart Stam also collaborated, came to be regarded as one of the most representative of its age for its combination of specific functional role, progressive building technology and unified aesthetic image. Van der Leeuw's requests for provision of hygiene, recreation and open-plan work areas were translated by the architects into basic, functionally defined forms, in which van der Vlugt sought to harmonize the contrasts between horizontal and vertical, open and closed, round and rectangular. The curved office building, the round tea-room on the roof and the transport bridges between the dispatch section and the factory are the salient elements of the composition. The non-structural glass façades serve to maximize natural lighting and visibility of the workspace and to reveal the reinforced-concrete pillars that form the constructional system. The design united a number of sources of inspiration: most notably De Stijl, in its use of primary colours, and the works of Johaness Duiker and Le Corbusier, who saw the factory in 1932 and approvingly called it 'a creation of the modern age'.

The firm of Brinkman & Van der Vlugt continued to be mainly active in Rotterdam, where their projects had a strong determining influence on the development of Nieuwe Bouwen through their advocacy of a Functionalist and Rationalist approach. Brinkman maintained the business contacts of the partnership and led the technical research; van der Vlugt was the chief designer. Through van der Leeuw, they also obtained new commissions from the Theosophical movement, to which both van der Leeuw and van der Vlugt belonged. These were for pavilions (1925–9) at Ommen and a meeting hall and administration building (1925–9) in Amsterdam. In collaboration with Willem van Tijen, they also built the Bergpolder Flats (1932), Rotterdam, an experimental nine-storey workers' residential block. Here constructional economies, linked to standardization and prefabrication, enabled the provision of natural light, air and social facilities, combined with cheap rents. Other designs from the early 1930s include a standard form for a telephone kiosk (1930–32), which appeared throughout the Netherlands. By 1936, however, when van der Vlugt died, they had developed a more expressive design vocabulary in such works as the Clubhouse Rotterdam golfclub (1933), Rotterdam, and the

J. A. Brinkman, Leendert Cornelis van der Vlugt and Mart Stam: Van Nelle Factory, Rotterdam, 1925–31

Airport Ypenburg (1935–7), Rijswijk, which nevertheless continued to be realized through functional means.

After van der Vlugt's death Brinkman went into partnership with J. H. van den Broek. The new firm produced a large number of designs, largely in the spirit of the former partnership and continuing to show a clear functionalism at a time when traditionalism was gaining ground. Notable examples include several workers' housing projects in Rotterdam, the Van Ommeren Office Building (1937–40), Antwerp, and extensions (1942–3) to the Van Nelle Factory. Brinkman became seriously ill during the 1940s, and van den Broek gradually took over the office.

WRITINGS
'In Memoriam Van der Vlugt', *De 8 & Opbouw*, x (1936), p. 109

BIBLIOGRAPHY
Bouwen voor een open samenleving: Brinkman, Brinkman, Van der Vlugt, Van den Broek, Bakema (Rotterdam, 1962)
J. Molenaar: *Van Nelle's Fabrieken: Bureau Brinkman en Van der Vlugt, 1925–1931* (Amsterdam, 1963)
G. Fanelli: *Architettura Moderna* (1968)
N. Luning Prak: 'De Van Nelle Fabriek te Rotterdam', *Bull. Kon. Ned. Oudhdknd. Bond*, iv (1970), pp. 123–6
W. J. R. Curtis: *Modern Architecture since 1900* (Oxford, 1982, 2/1987)
J. Geurst and J. Molenaar: *Van der Vlugt: Architect, 1894–1936* (Delft, 1983)

S. J. DOORMAN

Brioloto (*fl* Verona, 1189–1226). Italian sculptor. He is mentioned in an inscription now on the interior south wall of S Zeno Maggiore, Verona, and in various Veronese documents between 1189 and 1226. He completed the upper part of the façade of S Zeno, where he was responsible for the rose window and the six figures surrounding the *Wheel of Fortune*. Although the inscription associates him directly only with the window, he may also have remodelled the portal beneath, adding new framing figures and friezes (*see* VERONA, §3(ii)). Brioloto's figure style, in which rich, sweeping drapery folds cover elongated, classicizing figures gesturing theatrically, is related to the work of the Campionesi and to Nicholaus, rather than to Benedetto Antelami. Several other works in Verona have been attributed to Brioloto and to his contemporary, Adamino da San Giorgio (*fl* 1217–25; responsible for the animal frieze of the choir-screen of S Zeno), such as the font for the baptistery of S Giovanni in Fonte, which bears scenes from the *Infancy of Christ* and employs Byzantine iconographical details. Other dated works attributed to Brioloto are the tomb effigy of *Pope Lucius III* (1185) in Verona Cathedral and the sarcophagus of *SS Sergius and Bacchus* (Verona, Castelvecchio), commissioned by Abbot Gherardo in 1185, with scenes of the saints' lives and martyrdom. It is possible that Brioloto or his followers were also responsible for two large caryatid figures (de Francovich, 1943), the 12 monumental *Apostles* from the choir-screen of S Zeno and the figure of *St Zeno* (all in Verona, Castelvecchio), four large versions of the *Virgin Suckling the Infant Christ* (Verona, Pal. Vescovile; Brussels, Stoclet priv. col.; Aquileia Cathedral; Berlin, Kaiser-Friedrich Mus., destr.) and some figural reliefs, now set inside Treviso Cathedral.

BIBLIOGRAPHY
L. Simeoni: *La Basilica di San Zeno in Verona: Studi con nuovi documenti* (Verona, 1909)
A. K. Porter: *Lombard Architecture*, iii (New Haven, 1917), pp. 526–7
W. Arslan: *L'architettura romanica veronese* (Verona, 1939)

——: 'Appunto su Brioloto', *Arti: Rass. Bimest. A. Ant. & Mod.*, iv (1941–2), pp. 128–30
——: *La pittura e scultura veronese del secolo VIII al secolo XIII* (Milan, 1943)
G. de Francovich: 'Contributi alla scultura romanica veronese', *Riv. Reale Ist. Archeol. & Stor. A.*, ix (1943), pp. 103–47
R. Jullian: *L'Eveil de la sculpture italienne: La Sculpture romane dans l'Italie du nord* (Paris, 1945–9), pp. 277–8
G. H. Crichton: *Romanesque Sculpture in Italy* (London, 1954), p. 43
E. Kain: 'The Marble Relief on the Façade of S Zeno, Verona', *A. Bull.*, lxiii (1981), pp. 358–74

CHRISTINE B. VERZAR

Brion, Gustave (*b* Rothau, Vosges, 24 Oct 1824; *d* Paris, 5 Nov 1877). French painter and illustrator. His family settled in Strasbourg in 1831 and placed him in the studio of the portrait and history painter Gabriel-Christophe Guérin (1790–1846) in 1840. He then earned his living mainly by teaching drawing and copying paintings. In 1847 he successfully submitted his first work to the Salon: *Farmhouse Interior at Dambach* (untraced). In the summer of 1850 he moved to Paris, where he took a studio in a house shared by Realist artists. Brion exhibited regularly at the Salon: in 1852 *The Towpath* (untraced) was bought by the de Goncourt brothers; and in 1853 he showed the *Potato Harvest during the Flooding of the Rhine in 1852* (Nantes, Mus. B.-A.), in which the influence of Gustave Courbet and Jean-François Millet (ii) can be seen in the Alsatian peasant figures.

During the 1850s Brion produced landscape, rustic and historical genre subjects and portraits, but later in the decade he concentrated on subjects from Alsace, which he regularly visited. Their success, and Napoleon III's campaign to foster Alsatian culture, led him to produce such historical pieces as *Vosges Peasants Fleeing before the Invasion* (1867; St Louis, MO, Washington U., Gal. A.), combining the idealized peasant types of Jules Breton with the techniques of academic history painting. Local detail became increasingly important in his works, earning him the reputation of leading painter of Alsatian folklore.

In 1862 Brion produced the designs for the first illustrated version of Victor Hugo's *Les Misérables* (Paris, 1865), which contain 100 wood-engravings. Following its enormous commercial success, he made studies for Hugo's *Notre-Dame de Paris* (Paris, 1867).

The loss of Alsace Lorraine after the Franco-Prussian War in 1870 was a crushing personal and professional blow to Brion. He did not see Alsace again and led a very secluded life until his premature death from apoplexy.

BIBLIOGRAPHY
H. Haug: 'Un Peintre alsacien sous le second empire: Gustave Brion, 1824–1877', *Vie Alsace* (March 1925), p. 45
R. Heitz: *La Peinture en Alsace, 1050–1950* (Strasbourg, 1975)
The Realist Tradition (exh. cat., ed. G. Weisberg; Cleveland, OH, Mus. A., 1982), p. 276

MICHÈLE LAVALLÉE

Briosco, Andrea. *See* RICCIO, ANDREA.

Briosco, Benedetto (*b* Milan, *c.* 1460; *d* ?Milan, after April 1514). Italian sculptor. The first notice of his activity dates from 1477, when he and his brother-in-law Francesco Cazzaniga were employed as sculptors on the monument to *Giovanni Borromeo and Vitaliano Borromeo* (Isola Bella, Palazzo Borromeo, chapel), which was executed for S Francesco Grande, Milan. By 1482 he had begun employment for the Works of Milan Cathedral and in 1483 was paid for carving a figure of *S Apollonia* (untraced). Although he was a master figure sculptor at the cathedral until the middle of 1485, the other work he did there remains unknown. During 1483–4 it is likely that he assisted Francesco and Tommaso Cazzaniga in the execution of the tomb of *Cristoforo and Giacomo Antonio della Torre* (Milan, S Maria delle Grazie). In 1484 he and the Cazzaniga brothers began work on the tomb of *Pietro Francesco Visconti di Saliceto* destined for the Milanese church of S Maria del Carmine (destr.; reliefs in Cleveland, OH, Mus. A.; Kansas City, MO, Nelson-Atkins Mus. A.; and Washington, DC, N.G.A.; architectural elements in Paris, Louvre). This project was completed by Briosco and Tommaso Cazzaniga following Francesco Cazzaniga's death at the beginning of 1486. In the same year Benedetto and Tommaso were commissioned to finish the tomb of *Giovanni Francesco Brivio* (Milan, S Eustorgio), designed and begun by Francesco. Briosco's hand is virtually impossible to distinguish in these collaborative works. In 1489 the Apostolic Prothonotary and ducal councillor Ambrogio Griffo engaged Briosco to execute his funerary monument, to be installed in the church of S Pietro in Gessate, Milan. This tomb, which in its original form consisted of an effigy mounted on a high rectangular sarcophagus, appears to be Briosco's first major independent work and represents a significant break with Lombard tradition; although its design may to some extent have been influenced by Giovanni Antonio Amadeo's tomb to *Medea Colleoni* (Bergamo, Colleoni Chapel), it was freestanding and entirely secular in content. In 1490 Briosco returned to Milan Cathedral, where he was engaged to carve four life-size statues each year until he or his employers should cancel the arrangement. Although he worked at the cathedral until mid-1492, only a figure of *St Agnes* (Milan, Mus. Duomo) is documented from this period.

In July 1492 Briosco was hired by Amadeo as his assistant at the Certosa di Pavia, and was probably at first chiefly occupied with decorations for the façade of the church. By 1494 or 1495 he was working there with Gian Cristoforo Romano on the monument to *Gian Galeazzo Visconti, 1st Duke of Milan* in the right transept. Briosco's signed statue of the *Virgin and Child* on the upper register of this monument is in the full Roman Classical style imported by Romano; at considerable variance with the *St Agnes*, it may well have been designed by Gian Cristoforo. Towards the end of the 1490s Amadeo and Briosco began work on the main portal of the church of the Certosa. Amadeo relinquished all responsibility for the façade in 1499, and the portal was completed by Briosco and assistants. The reliefs that encrust the portal have a liveliness and, at times, an almost foppish elegance that distinguishes them from Amadeo's more sober contribution.

In late 1495 Briosco undertook, on behalf of Giovannina Porro (*d* 1504), to complete the monument to her husband *Ambrosino Longignana* (Isola Bella, Pal. Borromeo, chapel), barely begun by Francesco Cazzaniga for the family chapel in S Pietro in Gessate, Milan; he probably executed most of it in 1496–8, although the commission had been entrusted to him some years earlier. Some

elements may be related to the *Gian Galeazzo* monument, on which he was at work contemporaneously. In 1506 Briosco was engaged by officials of the church of S Tommaso, Cremona, to execute a large reliquary to house the remains of the martyr saints Peter and Marcellino. Although work proceeded intermittently until 1513, the project was never finished; the reliefs carved by Briosco are installed in the recomposed monument in the crypt of Cremona Cathedral.

In 1508 Briosco and Antonio della Porta took over responsibility for the construction and decoration of the façade of the Certosa di Pavia. Benedetto was partially occupied with this project until at least 1513. In 1508 he began a profitable commercial association with Margarita de Foix, mother and guardian of the young Marchese, Michelantonio di Saluzzo (1495–1528). At some time between 1508 and 1512 he executed the tomb (Saluzzo, S Giovanni) of *Lodovico II of Saluzzo* (1438–1504); his last major work, it is, in terms of its design, essentially a reprise of the *Griffo* monument. Much of the carving is the work of assistants, but the effigy, certainly autograph, is a figure of exceptional power and beauty. The latest notarial act in which Briosco is named is dated April 1514; he probably died shortly thereafter.

Briosco is a transitional figure. Formed in the Cazzaniga workshop and influenced by Amadeo, he nonetheless absorbed some of the lessons offered by Gian Cristoforo Romano, Cristoforo Solari and other sculptors of the younger generation. His son Francesco and his probable apprentice Agostino Busti emerged during the second decade of the 16th century as exponents of the 'modern', Romanizing style.

BIBLIOGRAPHY
R. Bossaglia: 'La scultura', *La Certosa di Pavia* (Milan, 1968), pp. 41–80
C. Mandelli: 'I primordi di Benedetto Briosco', *Crit. A.*, xix (1972), no. 124, pp. 41–57; no. 126, pp. 39–53
C. R. Morscheck: *Relief Sculpture for the Façade of the Certosa di Pavia, 1473–1499* (New York and London, 1978)
A. Roth: 'The Lombard Sculptor Benedetto Briosco: Works of the 1490s', *Burl. Mag.*, cxxii (1980), pp. 7–22
A. Viganò: 'Briosco, scultori', *Dizionario della chiesa ambrosiana*, i (Milan, 1987), pp. 507–9

JANICE SHELL

Briot, François (*b* Damblain, Lorraine, *c.* 1550; *d* ?Montbéliard, *c.* 1612). French metalworker and medallist. He was born of Huguenot parents and moved in 1579 to Montbéliard (Mömpelgard), then in Germany, to escape religious persecution. In 1585 he was appointed Graveur de son Excellence to Duke Frederick I of Württemburg-Mömpelgard (*d* 1608) and specialized in cutting dies for coins and medals. It is also likely that he worked as a *Bildschnitzer* or *Formschneider*, making models for goldsmiths' work, although there is no firm evidence for this. He is best known for his fine pewter vessels decorated in relief with densely packed Mannerist ornament (e.g. ewer, *c.* 1600; Paris, Louvre). Because of the softness of the metal these would not have been suitable for practical use and were intended as a cheap, decorative substitute for fine plate. The Temperantia dish (so-called from its ornament, *c.* 1585; Dresden, Mus. Ksthandwerk; *see* PEWTER, fig. 2) and accompanying ewer are in the same style as goldsmiths' work of the Fontainebleau school. It has been suggested that the sharply defined surface of Briot's vessels indicates that the ornament may have been struck by steel dies, although whether the vessels were formed from assembled struck components or cast and then struck is not clear. His vessels were widely imitated, especially by the Nuremberg pewterer Caspar Enderlein and in ceramics by Bernard Palissy.

BIBLIOGRAPHY
H. Demiani: *François Briot, Caspar Enderlein* (Leipzig, 1897)
J. F. Hayward: *Virtuoso Goldsmiths and the Triumph of Mannerism, 1540–1620* (London, 1976)

TIMOTHY SCHRODER

Briot, Nicolas (*b c*.1579; *d* London, 1646). French medallist, also active in England and Scotland. Briot succeeded Philippe Danfrie (i) as Engraver-General of French coinage in 1606. His tenure of the office was stormy, partly because of his frequent absences while working at the mints of Nancy, Charleville and Sedan and partly because of his scheming to gain control of all the mints in France through the introduction of his own mechanized system of coin production. His invention was, however, both a mechanical and a financial failure, forcing him to flee to London in 1625. He was appointed engraver at the Royal Mint and in 1635 became Master of the Scottish Mint.

Briot was responsible for the coronation medal of *Louis XIII* (1610; e.g. London, BM), whose portrait is probably from a wax by Guillaume Dupré, and a series of small, jetton-like struck medals made to commemorate events in England during the reign of Charles I. His other works include a large cast medal of the King's physician *Theodore de Mayerne* (1625; e.g. London, BM), a highly detailed view of London on his struck medal celebrating Charles I's return to London in 1633 (e.g. London, BM) and the *Dominion of the Seas* (*c*. 1630; e.g. London, BM), his best-known medal. Royalist in sympathy and responsible for the *Peace or War* medal (1643), Briot remained in London during the Civil War and was ejected from his lodgings in the Tower by Parliament before his death.

BIBLIOGRAPHY
A. Dauban: *Nicolas Briot* (Paris, 1857)
F. Mazerolle: 'Nicolas Briot, médailleur et mécanicien', *Congrès international de numismatique: Bruxelles, 1891*, pp. 507–9
J. Rouyer: *L'Oeuvre du médailleur Nicolas Briot en ce qui concerne les jetons* (Nancy, 1895)
F. Mazerolle: *Les Médailleurs français du XVe siècle au milieu du XVIIe* (Paris, 1902–4), i, pp. cix–cxxx, 298–485; ii, pp. 552–622
H. Farquhar: 'Portraiture of our Stuart Monarchs on their Coins and Medals', *Brit. Numi. J.*, (1908), pp. 145–262
——: 'Nicolas Briot and the Civil War', *Numi. Chron.*, n. s. 3, xiv (1914), pp. 169–235
M. Jones: *A Catalogue of French Medals in the British Museum*, ii (London, 1988), pp. 143–76

MARK JONES

Brisbane. Australian city and capital of the state of Queensland. It is situated on the banks of the Brisbane River on the eastern coastal plain of the continent, *c*. 400 km south of the Tropic of Capricorn, and it is Australia's third largest city (population *c*. 1.25 million). Brisbane was founded in 1825, when a convict settlement established in 1824 at Redcliffe, Moreton Bay, was moved *c*. 20 km up-river to the present site in a deep S-bend of the river. By the time the penal settlement was closed (1839) there were only two streets of any importance, one

of which later became Queen Street, the city's principal retail thoroughfare. In 1842 Brisbane was opened to free settlement and the first land sale held; several plans drawn in 1840–43 by Henry Wade show the adoption of a rectangular grid, although Governor George Gipps ordered the streets to be made narrower than initially planned. The first official residence was Newstead House (1846), Breakfast Creek, which was bought and enlarged in 1847 by Captain John Wickham, Police Magistrate and later Government Resident (1853–9).

By 1859, when Queensland became a separate colony and Brisbane its capital, the city had a population of *c*. 5000. Its subsequent growth was stimulated by the development of pastoral agriculture in the surrounding region, notably in the Darling Downs, and by the discovery of gold to the north. Large-scale construction phases took place in the 1860s, 1880s and 1900s, when several important public buildings were erected: South Brisbane Town Hall (1862; by John Hall), a florid, Italianate brick building; the classical Government House (1860–62; now part of the University of Queensland) and the French Renaissance Parliament House (1865–8, 1878–80), both by Charles Tiffin; the huge Treasury Building (1889–1922; by J. J. Clark), in Italian Renaissance Revival style; and the Anglican cathedral of St John (begun 1906; by J. L. Pearson) in French Gothic Revival style. A simpler approach was adopted for St Andrew's Presbyterian Church (1907; by G. D. PAYNE; *see* AUSTRALIA, fig. 4), with plain brickwork and bold arches. Suburban expansion in the 19th century was marked by the evolution of a distinctive vernacular domestic architecture, related to the sub-tropical climate and available resources: the 'Queenslander', generally built of timber and elevated on wooden stumps, is characterized by a galvanized corrugated iron roof, fairly steeply pitched to provide insulation space, and wide verandahs shaded with lattice screens; opening fanlights over internal doors permit cross-ventilation. Such houses may still be found in many Brisbane suburbs, including Paddington, Red Hill, Ascot, Kelvin Grove and Clayfield; in the early years of the 20th century the 'Queenslander' was reinterpreted in the domestic work of ROBIN DODS.

In 1925 several local authority areas were amalgamated to form Greater Brisbane, beginning a period of urban consolidation and infrastructure development; a new city hall (1930; by Hall & Prentice) in King George Square was designed with a temple front and tall tower. After World War II three decades of sustained growth supported by the state's mining and tourism booms (1960s and 1980s) were accompanied by extensive suburban expansion and the development of large regional retail centres. At the same time the city skyline (see fig.) was dramatically altered by commercial construction cycles and the development of several skyscrapers, notably the mirror-glass AMP Place (1978; by Peddle, Thorp & Harvey); Riverside Centre (1983–6; by Harry Seidler), with an extensive riverfront plaza; and the aluminium-clad Central Plaza towers (1988 and 1989; by Kishō Kurokawa and Peddle, Thorp & Walker). The hosting of the Commonwealth Games (1982) and World Expo (1988) provided the impetus for airport upgrading, new hotels and urban improvements, while the subsequent development of the

Expo site along the riverbank opposite the city centre provided further opportunities for urban consolidation.

The early development of art life in Brisbane was greatly stimulated by Walter Jenner (1836–1902), Oscar Frestrom (1856–1918) and L. W. K. Wirth (1858–1950), who were involved in establishing the Queensland Art Society (1887), and by Godfrey Rivers (1859–89), who helped found the Queensland Art Gallery (1895), taught at the Technical College and was President of the Art Society. Other important advocates for art in Brisbane included Vida Lahey (1882–1968) and Daphne Mayo (1895–1982), who were leading figures in establishing the Queensland Art Fund (1929) for the Queensland Art Gallery. Geographical isolation was a problem for the arts in Brisbane, but change was accelerated by World War II and improvements in transportation, and by the 1950s a volatile art community had formed, with ideas and influences evident from interstate and overseas; the Marodian Gallery (Johnstone Gallery) founded by Brian Johnstone was the art community's meeting-place at this time. Several important art galleries were subsequently established, notably the Institute of Modern Art (1975), dedicated to advanced and experimental contemporary art, and the Brisbane Civic Art Gallery (1977), based on the Brisbane City Council's historical collections. In 1976 the University of Queensland Art Museum was opened; its collection, the first university collection in Australia, was begun in the 1940s. In 1982 the Queensland Art Gallery moved to a new building in the Queensland Cultural Centre (begun 1980; by Robin Gibson), South Brisbane, which also houses the Queensland Museum (founded 1855), State Library (1896) and Performing Arts Centre.

See also AUSTRALIA, especially §§II, III and XI–XIII.

BIBLIOGRAPHY
J. Sheldon: 'Art in Brisbane', *A. Australia*, 3rd ser., lxxvi (1939), pp. 30–32
J. Hogan: *Building Queensland's Heritage,* The National Trust of Queensland (Richmond, Victoria, 1978)
Retrospect and Prospect (exh. cat., Brisbane, Queensland A.G., 1983)
A Survey of 80 Painters, Queensland: Works, 1950–1985 (exh. cat., Brisbane, Queensland A.G., 1985)
G. De Gruchy: *Architecture in Brisbane* (Brisbane, 1988)

CHRISTINE CLARK

Brise-soleil [Fr.: 'sun-break']. In modern architecture, a feature consisting of a slatted or louvred screen incorporated into the façade of a building, first used by Le Corbusier in 1933 to reduce glare (for illustration *see* ROBERTO, M. M. M.).

Briseux, Charles-Etienne (*b* Baume-les-Dames, Doubs, 1680; *d* 1754). French writer and architect. His family appears to have been of modest means, and little is known of his career as an architect. Numerous châteaux are attributed to him, but without any evidence; his only known building is a town house built for the Sieur Daugny in the Faubourg Poissonnière, now the town hall for the 9e Arrondissement in Paris and much altered. Briseux left an important body of written work, dealing with both practice and theory of architecture. In two collections of designs for domestic dwellings (1728 and 1743) he revived the idea behind Pierre Le Muet's *Manière de bâtir pour*

Brisbane, aerial view of the city centre, 1994

toutes sortes de personnes (Paris, 1623), proposing different ground-plans and layouts for the construction of town houses on urban sites and for châteaux of increasing sizes. He added one complicating factor to the exercise as practised by Le Muet: irregularity in the shape of the ground plots, which was often inevitable in Paris and some large provincial cities. For both town houses and country residences, he increased the number of circulation spaces, entrances and service stairs, as well as facilities for comfort and hygiene. He clearly separated public areas (the business and reception rooms) from the private apartments, which became intimate living quarters (*petits appartements*). In the areas set aside for public life he graded the effects carefully, from the cold bareness of the entrance hall to the rich magnificence of the reception rooms. He remained a faithful exponent of the use of projecting pavilions on façades. Briseux's other major work was a treatise on aesthetics, the *Traité du beau essentiel dans les arts* (1752). Basing his theories on an analysis of Palladio's villas and palaces, he restated the Platonic value of proportions and denounced as pernicious the influence of Claude Perrault. He accused Perrault of having freed architects unduly from the rules of harmonic proportion (here he referred to music) and of having thus given rise to the anarchic development of ornament. The last part of the work was devoted to types of panelling and ironwork for architecture, which remained very faithful to the forms of the French Rococo.

WRITINGS
L'Architecture moderne ou l'art de bien bâtir pour toutes sortes de personnes (Paris, 1728)
L'Art de bâtir des maisons de campagne (Paris, 1743/*R* Farnborough, 1966) [plates by J.-F. Blondel]
Traité du beau essentiel dans les arts appliqué à l'architecture et démontré physiquement et par l'expérience (Paris, 1752)

BIBLIOGRAPHY
W. G. Kalnein and M. Levey: *Art and Architecture of the Eighteenth Century in France*, Pelican Hist. A. (Harmondsworth, 1972)

FRANÇOISE HAMON

Brisley, Stuart (*b* Haslemere, 19 Oct 1933). English artist and sculptor. He studied at Guildford School of Art (1949–54) and the Royal College of Art in London (1956–9), as well as at the Akademie der Bildenden Künste in Munich (1959–60) and Florida State University in Tallahassee (1960–62). Influenced by Marxist counter-cultural politics in the 1960s, he adopted performance as the democratic basis for a new relationship between artist and audience. Working solely within public spaces in the 1970s, Brisley developed a series of solo and collaborative works, such as *ZL 65 63 95C* (1972; *see* PERFORMANCE ART, fig. 2), *Ten Days* (1978; London, ICA) and *Between* (1979; London, ICA), that pushed the body through various extended tasks or rituals. Vulnerable, exposed, Brisley's 'body in struggle' dramatized the conflict between human autonomy and the instrumental forces of bureaucratic and state power. In the 1980s, in the face of both changing conceptions of the political in art and the increasing implausibility of performance as avant-garde interventionist activity, Brisley moved from performance to installations, tape–slide work and object-making. His critical motivations remained unchanged: the production of a political art that in its richness of metaphor and range of expressive resources is capable of capturing the 'morbid symptoms' of capitalist culture.

BIBLIOGRAPHY
Stuart Brisley: A Retrospective (exh. cat., ed. S. Nairne; London, ICA, 1981) [texts by P. Overy, J. Roberts and S. Hood]
The British Show (exh. cat., ed. W. Wright and A. Bond; Sydney, A.G. NSW, 1985)
The Georgiana Collection (exh. cat., text by M. Archer; Glasgow, Third Eye Cent.; Londonderry, Orchard Gal.; 1986)

JOHN ROBERTS

Bristol. English city and seaport, the county town of Avon, with a population of *c.* 400,000. Sited near the junction of the River Avon and the River Frome, the city subsequently developed around a bridge over the Avon *c.* 10 km from the estuary of the River Severn (see fig. 1). The accessibility of Bristol's port to the Midlands, southwest England and Wales encouraged the city's development, and the rivers and docks mean that water and

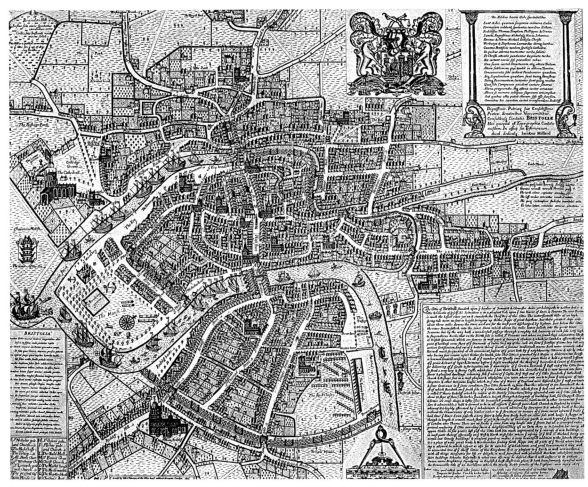

1. Early map of Bristol (detail); from an engraving by Jacob Millerd, 1673 (Bristol City Museum)

reflections play an important part in its appearance. Bristol has access to abundant supplies of building stone, favouring Dundry stone, Pennant sandstone and Dolomitic Conglomerate, but from the 18th century onwards brick has been widely used. Diversions of the courses of the Frome (*c.* 1247) and the Avon (1804–9) freed land for building and improved the river harbour. Bristol enjoyed particular prosperity in the 14th century as a centre for the manufacture and export of woollen cloth and again in the 18th century, when it became a leading centre of porcelain, pottery, metalwork and glass production (*see* §3 below), and fostered a distinctive school of landscape painting (*see* §2 below). The city suffered extensive bomb damage in World War II.

1. History and urban development. 2. Art life and organization. 3. Centre of production. 4. Cathedral.

1. HISTORY AND URBAN DEVELOPMENT.

(i) Before c. *1700.* The earliest surviving buildings are Romanesque and cannot be linked stylistically with other buildings in the district. Remains can be seen of the donjon (*c.* 1120) of Bristol Castle (mostly destr.). St James's Priory, founded in 1129, was the earliest monastery in Bristol; its mid-12th-century church nave has simple arcades, and the west front features interlaced arches below an unusual wheel window. The chapter house and lower section of the gate-house of St Augustine's Abbey (founded *c.* 1140; now the cathedral; *see* §4 below) both date from *c.* 1150 and have richly chiselled decoration. The church of the Knights Templar, who settled in Bristol *c.* 1150, still stands, as does the dormitory, complete with original roof, of the Blackfriars' or Dominicans' priory (founded before 1230). The Early Gothic period is represented by shafted lancets in the tower of the church of SS Philip and Jacob (*c.* 1200; possibly the church of a Benedictine priory) and by foliate and figure carving in the cathedral's Elder Lady Chapel (1216–34). All that survives of St Bartholomew's Hospital (founded in the early 13th century) is the deeply moulded entrance arch, which leads to trefoil-headed arcading (*c.* 1250). It contains a fine though mutilated statue of a seated *Virgin*, which is stylistically akin to statues on the west front at Wells Cathedral. Other medieval religious houses that have completely disappeared (although some are remembered in street names) include the Whitefriars or Carmelites, the Greyfriars or Franciscans, and the Augustinian Canons.

Cloth exports boomed in the 14th century, and Bristol's wealth led to increased building. Rebuilding at St Mary Redcliffe acknowledged the ambitious nature of earlier plans, as revealed by the inner north porch (*c.* 1200–30) and traces of a nave vault of *c.* 1200, and inspired the creation of a 'mini-cathedral'-style church with aisled transepts, complete stone vaulting, flying buttresses and an eastern Lady Chapel (14th-century; lengthened 15th century). The figure carving (*c.* 1325; now kept inside the church) from the hexagonal outer north porch and the stellate edging of some tomb recesses resemble similar work in the contemporary choir of the cathedral, suggesting a local school of masons influenced by those of Wells. After the interruption of the Black Death in 1348, St Mary

Redcliffe was finished *c.* 1400 in a splendid early Perpendicular style. Other Bristol churches were also rebuilt about this time. From *c.* 1398 the Temple Church replaced the earlier oval church; now gutted, its upper storey (*c.* 1460) and the impressive 114 ft tower lean alarmingly because of inadequate foundations. In 1520 the Poyntz Chapel was added to the Lord Mayor's Chapel (originally the chapel of St Mark's Hospital, founded 1220) and has Bristol's only medieval specimen of fan vaulting.

When Henry VIII created the diocese of Bristol in 1542, the city had a population of between 12,000 and 15,000. Growth was slow during the rest of the 16th century, and cloth exports were badly affected by the war with Spain (1587–8). Mostly domestic in character, as also in the 17th century, urban development was largely confined to the sites of dissolved religious houses, and of the castle. For example, the Red Lodge (*c.* 1585–95; now part of Bristol Art Gallery) was built on land formerly owned by the Carmelites. Its interior is one of the few surviving examples of Elizabethan architecture in the city, with a typically ornate stone chimney-piece and original panelling and plaster ceilings. Such timber-frame houses as the Llandoger Trow (1669) retained jetties and bays. Almshouses tended to be less conservative, notably the Colston Almshouses of 1691, which have a hipped roof and cross-windows and form an open courtyard.

(ii) After c. *1700.* As Atlantic trade flourished, new growth occurred, and Bristol soon became England's second largest city. Corporation leases allowed building on new sites: Queen Square, for example, was begun *c.* 1700, and the houses, with vernacular Baroque detail, were among the first in Bristol to use brick. In the square is John Michael Rysbrack's bronze equestrian statue of *William III* (1736). New houses were often designed and built by masons or 'house carpenters', using softwood building timber and bar iron for railings imported from the Baltic and Scandinavia. The Palladian style of Queen Square was also used for public buildings, as at the Exchange (1743; see fig. 2), which has an imposing front block before a colonnaded courtyard, by John Wood I of Bath. The creation of new urban areas in the old city and towards Clifton continued in the prosperous 18th century. Georgian and Regency Bristol spread along wooded valleys and up towards the open Downs, ending abruptly in the jagged drama of the Avon Gorge. The city's early Georgian merchants accepted current notions of taste in architecture and the decorative arts. Thanks to its neighbouring coalfield Bristol was a pioneering industrial city as well as a centre of commerce, shipping and distribution.

Unlike Bath, Bristol has many buildings in the Georgian Gothic Revival style. As well as the Palladian mansion of the Royal Fort (1761), James Bridges designed the Gothick exterior of Arnos Court (*c.* 1760–65) for the copper smelter William Reeves. Its stable block and offices (*c.* 1765; known as Arnos Castle), built in black slag blocks from Reeves's copper furnaces, with white stone dressings, were described by Horace Walpole as 'the Devil's cathedral' (Ison, p. 182). The plasterwork at both the Royal Fort and Arnos Court was by William Stocking. Further examples of Georgian Gothic include Blaise Castle (1766) by William Paty (*d* 1800), with its triangular plan and three

2. Bristol, the Exchange, Corn Street, by John Wood I, 1743

cylindrical towers, and the grotto (1739), orangery (refaced 1933), terrace (1753–4) and Gothick tower (1757) at Goldney House in Clifton. Late Georgian developments at the top of Park Street (1761–*c.* 1790), and other nearby ranges by Thomas Paty (?1712–89) and his successors were mostly faced with Bath stone. Eastward expansion included the varied elevations of Brunswick Square (1766–84) and the stone-faced Neo-classical Portland Square (*c.* 1790–1820), which ranks among England's best late Georgian squares. In Clifton development involved the building of individual mansions, for example the unadorned Clifton Hill House (1746–50; now part of the university) by Isaac Ware, followed by such Greek Revival terraced groupings as Royal York Crescent (*c.* 1810–20) and Charles Underwood's Worcester Terrace (1851).

In 1804–9 drastic topographical change occurred when the river harbour was made non-tidal by a channel, the New Cut, which carried the tidal flow of the Avon along a line south of St Mary Redcliffe. Around 1810 John Nash (i) created the romantic idyll of Blaise Hamlet, together with the orangery and dairy, in contrast to the development of Bedminster, south of the New Cut, as an industrial centre with coal mines and factories that eventually housed

the tobacco industry. However, for various reasons, including the inability of the inner harbour to accommodate large modern ships, 19th-century Bristol entered a period of relative decline. Nevertheless, a variety of Victorian villas accounted for much suburban expansion, and the port's problem was eventually solved by the building of river-mouth docks at Avonmouth and Portishead. A considerable revival soon started, with suburban growth towards Avonmouth and as far as the city's northern boundary.

Architects prominent in the Greek Revival designed public buildings and churches, for instance St George's Church (1823) on Brandon Hill with its Doric portico, and the five-bay Old Council House (1822–7), both by Robert Smirke (ii). Charles Robert Cockerell brought new elements to a strictly Grecian style at Holy Trinity (1829–30; interior destr.), Hotwells, which was influenced by Wren, and at the Bank of England (1844–7). By and large, however, the Greek Revival buildings are somewhat scattered and, built at a time of economic decline, served to supplement an architectural pattern established in the more prosperous 18th century.

Bristol's most distinctive Victorian buildings were in the Byzantine Revival style, based on medieval buildings in central Italy, the finest being the Welsh Back Granary (1869) in rich multicoloured brickwork by W. V. Ponton (1842–1918) and A. Gough (*d*?1880). Bristol's best-known 19th-century structure is the Clifton Suspension Bridge by ISAMBARD KINGDOM BRUNEL, which spans the Avon Gorge. The project was initiated in 1752 by a bequest, but work did not begin until 1836. Brunel's Egyptian design of the 1830s had been modified by the time the bridge was completed in 1864 after his death.

Charles Holden's Municipal Library (1906) is in Tudor Revival style. Sir G. A. Wills (1854–1928) and W. H. Wills (1830–1911), who made their fortune from Bristol's tobacco industry, gave Bristol University the Arts and Crafts Gothic style building (completed 1925), by Sir George Oatley (1863–1950), the octagonal lantern tower of which dominates the skyline of central Bristol. Bristol's Edwardian Baroque, though not without such interesting buildings as the City Museum and Art Gallery (1899–1904), by Frank Wills (1852–1932), is, however, less spectacular than that in more prosperous commercial cities such as Liverpool and London.

Since 1918 urban growth has largely taken the form of municipal housing estates, with a final extension of the city's boundary on its extreme southern side. Once-separate villages, including Westbury-on-Trym, Brislington and Henbury, with the Blaise estate, are now within the city. Bristol's post-war architecture started unpromisingly, with chunky office blocks jarring with the historical character of the centre. Since 1970, however, sympathetic architecture, as evidenced by the brick-faced Scottish Life Building (1975) by Burnet, Tate & Powell in the Welsh Back, has improved matters. The new offices of the Central Electricity Generating Board, by Arup Associates, are noteworthy for the respect paid to the semi-rural landscape of the south-western outskirts. The Roman Catholic cathedral in Clifton (completed 1975) by the Percy Thomas Partnership was planned as an elongated hexagon and is almost all in concrete.

BIBLIOGRAPHY

W. Ison: *The Georgian Buildings of Bristol* (Bristol, 1952)
B. Little: *The City and County of Bristol: A Study in Atlantic Civilisation* (London, 1954, 2/1967)
Modern Buildings in Bristol, Bristol Civic Society (Bristol, 1975)
T. Aldous: *Changing Bristol: New Architecture and Conservation, 1960–1980* (Bristol, 1979)
A. Gomme, M. Jenner and B. Little: *Bristol: An Architectural History* (London, 1979)
B. Little: *Bristol: A Public View (Public Buildings and Statues)* (Bristol, 1982)

BRYAN LITTLE

2. ART LIFE AND ORGANIZATION. It is remarkable that centuries of wealth and cosmopolitanism in Bristol failed to nurture artists; the only notable painter with a strong local connection was Sir Thomas Lawrence, fourth president of the Royal Academy, but even he left Bristol as a child. Before the 19th century aspiring Bristol artists had lacked a focus for their work, but that began to change with the spread of Romanticism. Amid the growing fascination with landscape, local artists set out in informal sketching parties to explore the cityscapes and countryside around them, which produced perfect subjects. Across the breathtaking ravine of the Avon Gorge is the arcadian setting of Leigh Woods, and further west are huge views

of the Severn estuary with the pale outlines of the Welsh mountains beyond.

In 1824 came a turning-point, with the first exhibition of Bristol artists. This was held at the newly opened headquarters of the Bristol Literary and Philosophical Institution in Park Street. What is now known as the Bristol school of artists had come together with leading members FRANCIS DANBY and Samuel Jackson (1794–1869) and disciples including WILLIAM JAMES MÜLLER, all outstanding landscape painters with a particular taste for the sort of scenery that Bristol offers. The founding of the Royal West of England Academy in the mid-19th century and the creation of the City of Bristol Museum and Art Gallery in the early 20th gave the city the necessary status symbols of an important provincial centre; from the late 1960s the City Art Gallery led the revival of the reputations of Danby and Jackson and established the national importance of the Bristol school. Another key event of the 1960s was the foundation by Jeremy Rees of the Arnolfini Gallery, which was intended to attract artists of international reputation and also to accommodate the performance arts, film, jewellery and an art bookshop. It became a model for similar ventures not just in Britain but also in Europe.

The continuing importance of landscape to local artists was emphasized by the experimental Brotherhood of Ruralists, who came together in 1975 and had strong connections with Bristol. Peter Blake chose the City of Bristol Museum and Art Gallery for his first major retrospective, and leading member David Inshaw lived in Bristol during one of his most creative periods, working alongside Alfred Stockham, later head of fine art in the faculty of art at Bristol Polytechnic (now the University of the West of England) and a painter who found some of his most powerful images in the landscape of the Avon Gorge. The Brotherhood's most successful exhibition was staged at the Arnolfini in 1981. The inspiration of Bristol's landscape continues to play an important role. The city's most celebrated late 20th-century artist, Richard Long, son of a local school teacher, who spent his boyhood walking the Downs above Clifton and exploring the Avon Gorge and the woods beyond, was inspired by them, just as Jackson and Danby were.

BIBLIOGRAPHY

The Bristol School of Artists: Francis Danby and Painting in Bristol, 1810–1840 (exh. cat., ed. F. Greenacre; Bristol, Mus. & A.G., 1973)
The Brotherhood of Ruralists: Ann Arnold, Graham Arnold, Peter Blake, Jann Haworth, David Inshaw, Annie Ovenden, Graham Ovenden (exh. cat. by N. Usherwood, Bristol, Arnolfini Gal., 1981)
F. Greenacre and S. Stoddard: *The Bristol Landscape: The Watercolours of Samuel Jackson, 1794–1869* (Bristol, 1986)
F. Danby, 1793–1861 (exh. cat. by F. Greenacre, Bristol, Mus. & A.G., 1988)

JAMES BELSEY

3. CENTRE OF PRODUCTION.

(i) *Ceramics.* A number of potteries were producing tin-glazed earthenware in Bristol from *c.* 1650 until the late 18th century. The principal potters were Richard Frank and Joseph Flower. Tableware dominated production, in particular blue-dash chargers, which were decorated in maiolica colours with portraits of notables, including the monarchs Charles II and William III. Chinoiserie decoration dominated from *c*. 1720, and wares included punchbowls and posset-pots. From 1755 wares were often decorated with *bianco-sopra-bianco*. By 1770 the production of tin-glazed earthenware had virtually ceased; it was superseded by cream-coloured earthenware.

Soft-paste porcelain was made in Bristol (1749–52) by Benjamin Lund, who used soapstone (steatite) from the Lizard, Cornwall, and employed a formula he developed with William Cookworthy. Wares produced included cream jugs and sauceboats decorated with chinoiseries in underglaze blue or polychrome enamels. Dr Wall's Worcester Porcelain Factory acquired Lund's establishment in 1752. Cookworthy was a chemist who worked in Plymouth and introduced hard-paste porcelain to Bristol. About 1768 he obtained a patent to exploit the kaolin (china clay) deposits in Cornwall. In the same year he founded the porcelain factory at Plymouth, which in 1770 he transferred to Bristol. The production concentrated on everyday utilitarian wares, and the decoration shows influences from the porcelain factories of Sèvres and Derby. In 1774 Cookworthy's patent was taken over by Richard Champion (1743–91). Fine, elaborately decorated, armorial dinner services, vases and figure groups were produced under Champion's direction, and later he became the proprietor. Pierre Stephan was a modeller at Derby (1770–73) and then became an independent modeller at Bristol. In 1780, after financial difficulties, the factory was forced to close, and the patent was sold to the New Hall Porcelain Factory in Shelton, Staffs.

(ii) Glass. The first recorded glasshouse in Bristol was established *c*. 1651 by a branch of the Dagnia family from Italy, who were brought to England *c*. 1630 by Robert Mansell (1573–1656). Some members later moved to Newcastle upon Tyne to establish a glasshouse. The earliest production was dominated by window glass and bottles. However, during the 1760s Bristol became a centre for high-quality, enamelled wine-glasses with opaque-twist stems. These glasses, with waisted bucket-bowls, often recorded the privateers based at Bristol during the Seven Years War and are decorated with diamond- and wheel-engraved ships.

Bristol is especially noted for its opaque white glass, said to have been first made *c*. 1757 at the Redcliff Backs Glasshouse. It was made to emulate porcelain and was often decorated with chinoiseries by Michael Edkins (1734–1811). In 1785 Edkins was employed by Lazarus Jacobs (*d* 1796) at the Temple Street Glasshouse as a gilder and enameller. In 1788 the Nailsea Glasshouse was established about seven miles outside Bristol by John Robert Lucas (1754–1828) with William Chance. At first it made crown glass for windows and then sheet glass and bottles; later it made cheap domestic wares such as jugs, vases, friggers (objects such as rolling-pins and tobacco pipes) and bowls in various shades of green, flecked with red and white glass. In 1805 Lazarus Jacobs's son, Isaac Jacobs (*fl* 1790–1835), set up the Non-Such Flint Glassworks, where he decorated blue-glass wine coolers, decanters and finger bowls with gilt, key-fret borders.

BIBLIOGRAPHY

W. J. Pountney: *Old Bristol Potteries* (Bristol, 1920/*R* Wakefield, 1972)
W. A. Thorpe: *A History of English and Irish Glass* (London, 1929)
F. S. Mackenna: *Cookworthy's Plymouth and Bristol Porcelain* (Leigh-on-Sea, 1946)
F. H. Garner: *English Delftware* (London, 1948, rev. 2/1972)
R. J. Charleston: *English Glass and the Glass Used in England, c. 400–1940* (London, 1984)
C. Witt, C. Weedon and A. Palmer Schwind: *Bristol Glass*, Mus. & A.G. (Bristol, 1984)

K. SOMERVELL

(iii) Metalwork. Silver was made in Bristol on a limited scale from the Middle Ages until the 18th century. A charter for silversmiths, dating from 1462, established a town mark consisting of a bull's head, although no objects with this mark are known. More than 100 silversmiths active in Bristol before 1700 have been recorded, and an assay office operated between 1720 and 1740. Silversmithing, however, was never as important as the manufacture of pewter and brass.

The first ordinances for the Pewterers' Guild were established in 1456–7, but the manufacture of pewter was at its peak in the late 17th century and early 18th, with pewterers such as Richard Going (*fl* 1715; *d* 1764). His shop is portrayed in an oil painting in the City of Bristol Museum and Art Gallery. The success of pewter was based on local demand as well as on exports and depended on the supply of tin from Cornwall. In the 17th century there were between 30 and 60 pewterers in Bristol, more than in any other English city except London. Most Bristol pewterers concentrated on flat or sadware. A good collection of plates, including some by the Edgar family who traded *c*. 1776–1852, are housed at Blaise Castle House Museum, Bristol. Large quantities of pewter were exported to the USA in the late 18th century and early 19th, but as elsewhere, the industry was in decline after 1830.

The availability of copper from Cornwall, calamine (zinc carbonate) from the Mendip Hills, Somerset, and the abundance of coal from the Forest of Dean, Glos, and Radstock, Avon, led to the establishment of the first brass manufacturing works in the area of Bristol *c*. 1700. The Bristol Brass Wire Co. was also established in 1702. Until 1770 there was large-scale development of brassmaking, and the manufacture of finished brass goods increased in the valley of the Avon and those of its tributaries. The first brass mills were in Keynsham, Avon, and these were followed by others along the valleys. In 1729, for example, there were 36 furnaces operating in the area. The works in Warmley, Avon, were opened in 1741, and soon after 17 copper furnaces, 12 brassmaking furnaces and 4 calamine zinc furnaces were operating, employing over 800 men at the peak of production. The gradual development of Birmingham as a centre of brassworking, however, led to a decline in the importance of Bristol, and after 1800 the industry there was of relatively little importance.

BIBLIOGRAPHY

J. Day: *Brass in Bristol: A History of the Industry* (London, 1973)
G. E. P. Haw: 'The Goldsmiths of Bristol', *Connoisseur* (Aug 1974), p. 252

PETER HORNSBY

4. CATHEDRAL.

(i) Architecture. St Augustine's Abbey (the cathedral since 1542) was founded *c*. 1140 by Robert Fitzharding, an ancestor of the Berkeley family, for the Augustinian

Canons of the Order of St Victor. A late Saxon carving depicting the *Harrowing of Hell*, now in the south transept, was discovered under the chapter house floor in 1831 and pre-dates the abbey. Only parts of the transepts survive from the first church, and little else is known about it. The main Romanesque survival is the chapter house (*c.* 1150), richly decorated in the fashion of other Augustinian chapter houses, such as Kenilworth Priory, Warwicks. The ornaments include chevron, cable pattern and intersecting arcading, and both chapter house and vestibule are rib-vaulted. Other 12th-century remains include the lower parts of the outer gatehouse (rest.). Under Abbot David (1216–34) the Elder Lady Chapel was added to the north transept. The details resemble the western parts of Wells Cathedral (*c.* 1220), a link corroborated by a contemporary letter (London, BL, Cotton Charter IV, 58 A971W, letter no. 56) from Abbot David to the Dean of Wells asking for his servant 'L' to work on the chapel; perhaps Adam Lock, master mason at Wells until 1229.

The architectural fame of St Augustine's lies in the imaginative rebuilding of its east end in the Decorated style (see fig. 3). Abbot Newland's roll, compiled *c.* 1490, attributes this work to Edmund Knowle, begun in 1298 and continued during his abbacy (1306–32). A reference to the burial of Joan, Lady Berkeley, in the south choir aisle in 1309 and a doubtful argument that the great east window was glazed by 1322 have encouraged the view that construction advanced rapidly after 1298. Stylistic comparison with other related buildings, however, indicates that the main architectural features were designed *c.* 1315 or later. Neither Knowle nor his successor was buried in the east end; this implies that the work of fitting out was not finished until *c.* 1350, which is the more

convincing date argued for the east window (Sabin). Abbot Asshe (1341–53) was the first to be buried in the new choir.

Preparation for the rebuilding is suggested by the provision of the Elder Lady Chapel with a new vault and east window, datable to 1290–1300. Presumably it was used extensively while the east end was unavailable. The foundations and lower walls of the new east end, including the southern vestry (Berkeley Chapel), were laid out directly after 1298. The only clue that a hall church might have been intended from the start lies perhaps in the deeply projecting buttresses. The arcades, aisle bridges (see fig. 3) and vaults were erected in phases between *c.* 1315 and *c.* 1340, a dating confirmed by the petal and reticulated patterns of the window tracery. The earliest high vaults are those of the south transept chapel (Newton Chapel) and the south choir aisle, west bay; only afterwards were lierne vaults introduced. One addition to the plan was the ante-chapel (sacristy), creating a new entrance to the Berkeley Chapel. The original entrance was then converted into a tomb recess, connected with Thomas, 1st Baron Berkeley (*d* 1321), rather than his wife, Joan (*d* 1309). Features of the ante-chapel indicate the hand of WILLIAM JOY and suggest that he may have been responsible for the details of the upper parts of the main church, especially the choir vault, which is related to vaulting experiments at Wells Cathedral (from 1323). The new work is notable for its hall church elevation, combined with a spatial playfulness expressed in the aisle bridges and the flying ribs of the ante-chapel. The rarity of the hall church in England suggests inspiration from Europe, possibly western France (Bony), and it was probably deployed here to increase the grandeur of a relatively small architectural space. The aisle bridges mimic timber-roof construction and may be a conscious reflection of the architecture of secular halls, together with the window transoms, which represent the first consistent use of this feature in ecclesiastical architecture. These ideas are to be associated with the tombs of the secular patrons, the Berkeleys, that line the choir aisles.

No further major architectural work was undertaken until the 15th century: the crossing and tower are attributed to Abbot Newbury (1428–73), and the lierne vaults of the transepts and crossing to Abbots Hunt (1473–81) and Newland (1481–1515). Newland also largely rebuilt the outer gatehouse and began a new nave, but this had reached only window-sill level at the Dissolution of the Monasteries in 1539. The present nave is by G. E. Street (from 1868), and Street's west towers were completed by J. L. Pearson (1888), who restored the medieval arrangement of the eastern arm.

BIBLIOGRAPHY

I. H. Jeayes: 'Abbot Newland's Roll of the Abbots of St Augustine's Abbey by Bristol', *Trans. Bristol & Glos Archaeol. Soc.*, xiv (1889–90), pp. 117–30
N. Pevsner: 'Bristol-Troyes-Gloucester: The Character of the Early 14th Century in Architecture', *Archit. Rev.* [London], cxiii (1953), pp. 88–98
A. Sabin: 'The 14th-century Heraldic Glass in the Eastern Lady Chapel of Bristol Cathedral', *Antiqua. J.*, xxxvii (1957), pp. 54–70
H. Bock: 'Bristol Cathedral and its Place in European Architecture', *Bristol Cathedral: 800th Anniversary, 1165–1965* (Bristol, 1965), pp. 18–27
J. Bony: *The English Decorated Style* (Oxford, 1979)

3. Bristol Cathedral, interior of choir and presbytery looking east, *c.* 1298–*c.* 1350

N. Pevsner and P. Metcalf: *The Cathedrals of England: Southern England* (Harmondsworth, 1985), pp. 34–48

R. K. MORRIS

(ii) Stained glass. The Lady Chapel glazing is a significant example of the Victorian treatment of fragmentary medieval glass. Records by the antiquary Samuel Lysons (1763–1819) and others indicate how dismembered the glass had become. Joseph Bell (1810–95) of Bristol, in consultation with Charles Winston (1814–64), many of whose detailed drawings survive (London, BL, Add. MS. 33846–9; 3511(G)), was responsible for the restoration carried out in 1847–8 and 1852–3.

Excellent heraldic glass survives in the tracery of the great east window (for dating *see* §(i) above), comprising 17 shields of local families, especially the Berkeleys. The main lights are filled with a *Tree of Jesse*, one of a group including those at St Peter's, Lowick (Northants), St Laurence, Ludlow (Salop), and St Mary's, Shrewsbury (Salop). The central *Virgin and Child* is mainly original glass, but most of the rest was replaced by copies; several fine original fragments are reset in the cloister windows. Further 14th-century glass survives in the two south windows of the chapel, especially a *St Stephen* and the *Martyrdom of St Edmund*, interpreted as a reference to Abbot Edmund Knowle.

All the glass of the northern windows, apart from fragments, is Victorian. In the lower parts of the southern windows are figures including Berkeleys and other knights, 19th-century versions of muddled original glass that was probably earlier than the Despenser glass at Tewkesbury Abbey (Glos). Other windows include one of *c.* 1515, some 17th-century glass, late Victorian work by Hardman (founded 1839) and Kempe and Tower (founded mid-19th century), a war memorial series (1947–9) by Arnold Robinson and an abstract *Pentecost* of 1965 by Keith New.

BIBLIOGRAPHY
S. Lysons: *A Collection of Gloucestershire Antiquities*, 2 vols (London, 1803)
M. Q. Smith: *The Stained Glass of Bristol Cathedral* (Bristol, 1983) [with comprehensive bibliog.]

M. Q. SMITH

Bristol, 4th Earl of. *See* HERVEY, (1).

Britannia metal. *See under* PEWTER.

Brite & Bacon. *See under* BACON, HENRY.

British Guiana. *See* GUYANA.

British Nyasaland. *See* MALAWI.

British Somaliland Protectorate. *See* SOMALIA.

Brito, Luis (*b* Río, Sucre, 20 March 1945). Venezuelan photographer. He took courses in cinema at the Ateneo in Caracas, where his interest in photography began. After winning second prize in the National Salon of Photography, he went to Rome on a scholarship to study at the Centro de Adiestramiento Profesional 'Don Orione'. His black-and-white photographic work is distinctive in its capturing of physical details and gestures of people in the street, such as their hands, feet and faces, obliging the spectator to complete the figure with his imagination.

Among these photographs are *The Exiles*, *Level with the Ground*, *The Mask* and *Parallel Relations*. He exhibited in Rome, Cairo, Bilbao, London, Barcelona, New York and Lyon.

CRUZ BARCELÓ CEDEÑO

Brito (Avellana), María (*b* Havana, 10 Oct 1947). Cuban sculptor, active in the USA. She arrived in the USA during the 1960s. In 1979 she obtained an MFA at the University of Miami. She worked primarily in three formats: wall-hanging constructions, free-standing sculpture and installations situated in corners like stage props. Using mixed media, often wood and found objects, she focused on the objective representation of personal dreamed images, reminiscent of the assemblages of Joseph Cornell and Marisol (e.g. *Next Room (Homage to R.B.)*, mixed media, 1986; see 1987–8 exh. cat., p. 259). Brito exhibited widely throughout the USA, in both one-woman and group exhibitions.

BIBLIOGRAPHY
P. Plagens: 'Report from Florida: Miami Slice', *A. America*, lxxiv/11 (Nov 1986), pp. 26–39
R. Pau-Llosa: 'The Dreamt Objectivities of María Brito Avellana', *Dreamworks*, v/2 (1986–7), pp. 98–104
Outside Cuba (exh. cat. by I. Fuentes-Perez, G. Cruz-Taura and R. Pau-Llosa, New Brunswick, NJ, Rutgers U., Zimmerli A. Mus.; New York, Mus. Contemp. Hisp. A.; Oxford, OH, Miami U., A. Mus.; and elsewhere; 1987–9), pp. 258–61
C. S. Rubenstein: *American Women Sculptors: History of Women Working in Three Dimensions* (Boston, 1990), pp. 564–5

RICARDO PAU-LLOSA

Brittain, Miller (Gore) (*b* Saint John, NB, 12 Jan 1912; *d* Saint John, 21 Jan 1968). Canadian painter. He studied from 1930 to 1932 at the Art Students' League, New York. While there he was particularly influenced by the personality and teaching of Harry Wickey (1892–1968), who encouraged him to abandon his original intention of becoming a commercial artist and to concentrate instead on fine art, although Brittain did not begin to work in oil or tempera–oil mixed media until 1938. Mixed media painting was much studied at the Art Students' League and elsewhere in North America during the 1930s, in the hope that an emphasis on sound craftsmanship would form the basis of a reintegration of art into society as a whole. This concern was also reflected in the city-oriented subjects of the American Scene painters and others. Brittain's work prior to World War II relied heavily on such subjects, as in his *Longshoremen* (1940; Ottawa, N.G.). Whether this was due more to an interest in active social reform than to a passive recognition of the results of economic stagnation in Saint John is debatable.

After serving in the Royal Canadian Air Force in England during World War II, Brittain became an official war artist (1945–6) and produced conté drawings and two paintings (all Ottawa, Can. War Mus.). However, most of his 1940s drawings and paintings are of biblical subjects, and those of the 1950s and 1960s exhibit a Surrealist style based on Freudian themes, anthropomorphic objects and images from the poetry of Blake. Profoundly depressed by his wife's death in 1958, he later became something of a recluse.

BIBLIOGRAPHY
Drawings and Pastels, c. 1930–1967, by Miller Gore Brittain (exh. cat. by D. F. P. Andrus, Fredericton, U. NB, Creative A. Centre, 1968)

Miller Brittain—Painter (exh. cat. by J. R. Harper, Sackville, NB, Mount Allison U., Owens A.G., 1981)

B. Foss: *Spirituality and Social Consciousness in the Art and Thought of Miller Gore Brittain, c. 1930–1945* (diss., Montreal, Concordia U., 1985)

BRIAN FOSS

Brittany, House of. Dynasty of rulers, collectors and patrons. The dynasty originated with Peter I of Dreux, Count of Richemont and, through his marriage to Alix, eldest daughter of Guy de Thouars, Count of Brittany (*reg* 1213–37). The ducal title was formally recognized by King Philip IV in 1297 when John II (*reg* 1286–1305) was created peer of the realm. The main patrons of the family were the 15th-century dukes: (1) Francis I was succeeded by his brother Peter II (*reg* 1450–57) and then by their uncle (2) Arthur III. After the death of the latter's nephew (3) Francis II, the duchy was incorporated into the kingdom of France through the marriages of Francis's daughter, Anne, Duchess of Brittany (*see* VALOIS, (12)), first to Charles VIII and then to Louis XII.

BIBLIOGRAPHY

G. A. Lobineau: *Histoire de Bretagne*, 2 vols (Paris, 1707)

H. Morice: *Mémoires pour servir de preuves à l'histoire ecclésiastique et civile de Bretagne*, 2 vols (Paris, 1742–6)

La Bretagne au temps des ducs (exh. cat., Daoulas Abbey, 1991)

(1) Francis I, 7th Duke of Brittany [Count of Montfort and Richemont] (*b* Vannes, 11 May 1414; *reg* 1442–50; *d* Vannes, 17 July 1450). He was the son of John V (*reg* 1399–1442) and Joanna of France. Although he supported the policies of Charles VII, he concurrently affirmed the independence of his duchy, minting different coins known as *cavaliers d'or* or *bretons d'or*. In 1431 he married Yolande of Anjou (*d* 1440). In 1439, before acceding to the duchy, Francis commissioned a manuscript of Aegidius Colonna's *Livre du gouvernement des princes* (Paris, Bib. N., MS. fr. 12254), illuminated by a follower of the Boucicaut Master. He was also a benefactor of the Franciscan church in Nantes, where he and his second wife, Isabella Stuart (*d c.* 1495), were depicted as donors in a stained-glass window (destr.) recorded in a drawing (Paris, Bib. N.) made for Roger de Gaignières and in an engraving (Montfaucon). Also in Nantes the Duke founded and endowed a Charterhouse (1445) and established a Carmelite convent (1448; both destr.). Duchess Isabella, whose arms appear on a silver-gilt chalice (Séné, Morbihan, St-Patern) made in Nantes by Jean Pigeon, owned several illuminated devotional books. These included a Book of Hours (Cambridge, Fitzwilliam, MS. 63) with miniatures of *c.* 1417–18 by the Master of the Rohan Hours and his workshop, and with the addition of Isabella's arms and portrait (fols 20 and 28). The manuscript probably came into her possession after her marriage since Francis I's first wife was the daughter of Yolande of Aragon, thought to be the artist's patron. Around 1455–65 Isabella, by then Dowager Duchess, commissioned two Books of Hours (Paris, Bib. N., MSS lat. 1369 and nouv. acq. lat. 588) and a *Somme le roi* (Paris, Bib. N., MS. fr. 958), which was recorded as copied in 1464 by Jean Hubert; all have miniatures by followers active in Nantes of the Master of the Rohan Hours. The same workshop, probably commissioned by the Duchess, produced a Missal (Princeton U., NJ, Lib., MS. Garnet 40) for the Carmelite church of St Jean, Nantes; it includes miniatures in the Temporal

depicting the dukes of Brittany. Francis I created the chivalric Order *de l'Epi* in 1445. He was buried in the choir of St Sauveur, Redon. Architectural fragments of his tomb, in Flamboyant style, survive *in situ*.

BIBLIOGRAPHY

B. de Montfaucon: *Les Monumens de la monarchie françoise qui comprennent l'histoire de France, avec les figures de chaque règne que l'injure des tems a épargnées*, iii (Paris, 1733)

H. Bouchot: *Inventaire des dessins exécutés pour Roger de Gaignières*, 2 vols (Paris, 1891)

E. Caron: 'Un demi-cavalier d'or de François, duc de Bretagne', *Gaz. Numi. Fr.*, ii (1898), pp. 56–60

M. R. Toynbee: 'The Portraiture of Isabella Stuart, Duchess of Brittany', *Burl. Mag.*, lxxxviii (1946), pp. 300, 302–6

M. Meiss: *The Limbourgs and their Contemporaries* (1974), ii of *French Painting in the Time of Jean, Duc de Berry* (London and New York, 1967–74)

(2) Arthur III, 9th Duke of Brittany [Constable of Richemont and Count of Richemont, Dreux, Estampes and Montfort] (*b* Sucinio, 25 Aug 1393; *reg* 1457–8; *d* Nantes, 26 Dec 1458). Uncle of (1) Francis I. Jean Fouquet probably painted a bust-length portrait of *Arthur, Duke of Brittany* that is recorded in a 16th-century drawing (Paris, Bib. N., Cab. Est., Oa14, fol. 48); he is depicted as an older man in armour wearing a fur-brimmed hat. He was also shown riding as victor of the Battle of Formigny in a 15th-century tapestry of royal commission, which was recorded in the château of Blois in 1501 and was extant until the 17th century at the château of Fontainebleau; drawings (Paris, Bib. N., MS. nouv. acq. fr. 5174) record two scenes from the tapestry. Arthur owned an illuminated copy of Honoré Bonet's *Arbre des batailles* (Paris, Bib. Arsenal, MS. 2695), which was produced *c.* 1460 in Angers. The joint cenotaph (destr. 1792) of Arthur and his third wife, Catherine of Luxembourg (*d* 1489) was in the choir of the charterhouse of Nantes, of which he had been a principal benefactor. A drawing (Oxford, Bodleian Lib.) made for de Gaignières shows the monument with Renaissance-style pilasters that suggest a date later than 1458. The tomb was probably commissioned by Catherine.

BIBLIOGRAPHY

P. de Lisle du Dreneuc: 'Les Tombeaux des ducs de Bretagne', *Bull. Archéol. Assoc. Bret.*, 3rd ser., ix (1891), pp. 54–69

E. Cosneau: *Le Connétable de Richemont: Arthur de Bretagne, 1393–1458* (Paris, 1896)

J. B. de Vaivre: 'Une Enseigne du XVe siècle: L'Etendart du Connétable de Richemont', *Archv Herald.*, xxv (1979), pp. 10–17

Les Dossiers du Louvre: Jean Fouquet (exh. cat., Paris, Louvre, 1981)

(3) Francis II, 10th Duke of Brittany (*b* 23 June 1435; *reg* 1458–88; *d* Coiron, 9 Sept 1488). Nephew of (2) Arthur III. He served under Charles VII and Louis XI of France. He officially founded the university of Nantes, confirmed by a papal bull in 1460, and in 1462 he promulgated a new constitution of the Parliament of Brittany. In 1466 the Duke began to enlarge the château at NANTES. As a result of the continuous encroachments of Louis XI and Anne of France, Francis II openly joined forces with rebels against the French crown, but was kept in check until finally defeated by Charles VIII in 1488. To rival the splendour of the French court, Francis II employed goldsmiths to expand the ducal collection of plate and ordered a sumptuous crown (destr.) that he was later forced to pawn. He was a benefactor of the Franciscan foundations at Vannes and Nantes (both destr.). In 1480 he and his second wife, Marguerite of Foix (*d* 1486), founded a Charterhouse (destr. *c.* 1790) at Auray. A later 15th-century statue in Loire style of the Virgin, known as *La Vièrge au duc* (Rennes, Carmelite Convent of St Melaine), is thought to have been originally part of his personal chapel. The Book of Hours of Marguerite of Foix (London, V&A, MS. Salting 1222) was illuminated *c.* 1470–80 by a follower of Jean Fouquet active in Rennes. Marguerite is held to have presented a silver arms reliquary to the church of Paimpont (Ille-et-Vilaine) and her will lists a collection of precious goldwork. Francis and Marguerite were buried in the Carmelite church of St Jean, Nantes, before the main altar; their daughter, Anne, Duchess of Brittany, commissioned a monumental tomb (1497–1507; now Nantes Cathedral) designed by Jean Perréal and carved by Michel Colombe (*see* COLOMBE, (1)) and assistants.

BIBLIOGRAPHY
M. Elder: *Le Château des ducs de Bretagne* (Nantes, 1935)
A. Mussat: 'Michel Colombe: L'Art de la Loire et la Bretagne', *An. Bretagne*, lxi (1954), pp. 54–64

PATRICK M. DE WINTER

Britto, Giovanni [Breit, Johannes; Brit, Johannes] (*fl* Venice, 1530–50). Woodcutter of German origin, active in Italy. His first work in Venice was the illustration of *Petrarca spirituale* by Girolamo Malipiero, published by Francesco Marcolini in 1536. In 1543 the inscription *In Vinegia per Giovanni Britto Intagliatore*. . . appears in the colophon of *La congiuratione de Gheldresi contro la città Danversa* by Joannes Servilius (Florence, Bib. N. Cent.), an unillustrated book printed by Marcolini, but there is no documentary evidence that Britto designed the fount, and his relationship with Marcolini is unclear. Among his works are several woodcuts derived from works by Titian, for example the *Adoration of the Shepherds* (see 1976 exh. cat., no. 44), two portraits of the *Holy Roman Emperor Charles V* (1976 exh. cat., nos 46; inspired by a model drawn by Titian) and 47 (known only from a copy in the British Museum, London, MS. 1866-7-14-31)) and a *Self-portrait of Titian* (1976 exh. cat., no. 45) signed *In Venetia per Gioanni Britto Intagliatore* datable to 1550 on account of Pietro Aretino's laudatory sonnet addressed 'to the German engraver'. A portrait of *Süleyman I* (1976 exh. cat., no. 48) has been attributed to Britto as well as a group of woodcuts after Titian previously thought to be the work of Niccolò Boldrini: the *Landscape with a Milkmaid* (1976 exh cat., no. 21), *St Jerome in the Wilderness* (1976 exh. cat., no. 22) and *The Stigmatization of St Francis* (1976 exh. cat., no. 23). In 1550 Britto signed the *Descrittione di Bologna Maritima*. . ., a wood-engraved plan of the siege of Boulogne-sur-Mer by Henry II, King of France, in 1549 (reproduced in, for example, the *Lafréry Atlas*). Stylistically Britto's work is marked by two phases. The first is still close in style to the German tradition, while the next, more individual, is clearly inspired by the technique of copper-engraving. The monogram ⯑·, once considered the seal of Boldrini, is now generally accepted as belonging to Britto.

DBI

BIBLIOGRAPHY
K. Oberhuber: 'Titian Woodcuts and Drawings: Some Problems', *Tiziano e Venezia: Convegno internazionale di studi: Venice, 1976*, pp. 523–8

Titian and the Venetian Woodcut (exh. cat. by M. Muraro and D. Rosand, Washington, DC, N.G.A. and Int. Exh. Found., 1976)
M. A. Chiari: *Incisioni da Tiziano: Catalogo del fondo grafico a stampa del Museo Correr*, Venice, Correr cat. (Venice, 1982), pp. 35–6 [pubd as suppl. of *Boll. Mus. Civ. Ven.*, 1982]
D. Landau: 'Printmaking in Venice and the Veneto', *The Genius of Venice* (exh. cat., ed. J. Martineau and C. Hope; London, RA, 1983), pp. 303–54 (333, 339–40)
W. R. Rearick: 'Titien: La Fortune du dessinateur', *Le Siècle de Titien* (exh. cat., Paris, Grand Pal., 1993), pp. 554, 563–4 and pls 210–11

FELICIANO BENVENUTI

Britton, Alison (*b* Harrow, Middx, 4 May 1948). English potter. After a foundation year at Leeds College of Art (1966–7), she studied ceramics at the Central School of Art, London (1967–70), and then at the Royal College of Art (1970–73) under Hans Coper. She is well known as a teacher and writer as well as a potter. She began her career decorating tiles. Her first solo exhibition was at the Amalgam Gallery, London, in 1976. In 1979 the Crafts Council, London, held an important show of her colourfully glazed and painted jugs, decorated with naive, figural motifs. The jugs gained her fast recognition and with hindsight were regarded as a breakthrough for British ceramics. She hand-built her pieces from slabs of earthenware that were rolled flat, painted and then cut and used to construct asymmetrical vessels. The early naive motifs of 1976 to 1979 (jugs, 1978; London, V&A) gave way in the 1980s to abstract patterns, and her forms became tougher and more complex (green vessels set, 1983; London, V&A). The pots made in the late 1980s have an architectural feel, consisting of overhanging upper and lower storeys; she also worked on large, headless, ceramic torsos. She exhibited regularly in Britain, America and Japan, and in 1984 began to teach part-time at the Royal College of Art.

BIBLIOGRAPHY
The Work of Alison Britton (exh. cat. by J. Houston and others, London, Crafts Council Gal., 1979)
P. Dormer and D. Cripps: *Alison Britton in the Studio* (London, 1985)
A. Suttie: 'Alison Britton', *Cer. Rev.*, 107 (1987), pp. 6–8
O. Watson: *British Studio Pottery: The Victoria and Albert Museum Collection* (London, 1990)

☐

Britton, John (*b* Kington St Michael, nr Chippenham, Wilts, 7 July 1771; *d* London, 1 Jan 1857). English art historian. He began work as an apprentice publican in Clerkenwell in London. From an early age he supplemented his income by writing ballads, although his main scholarly interest was in the topography and architectural history of Great Britain. In 1801 he published the first volume of *The Beauties of Wiltshire*, the success of which enabled him to engage in the more ambitious *The Beauties of England and Wales*. He wrote this jointly with Edward Wedlake Brayley (1773–1854), and the first volume appeared in 1801. Although most of Britton's publications were concerned with architecture, he also had a strong interest in painting, producing *The Fine Arts of the English School* in 1812. He published many other authoritative and illustrative works, including *The Architectural Antiquities of Great Britain* (1807–26), *The Cathedral Antiquities of England* (1814–35), *Illustrations of the Public Buildings of London* (1825–8) and, with Augustus Charles Pugin, *Specimens of Gothic Architecture* (1821–3). These volumes, which incorporate ground-plans, elevations and scrupulously drawn details as well as intelligent and informative texts, transformed the study of medieval architecture. Britton's serious-minded archaeological approach to medieval architecture proved invaluable as a model for both amateurs and architects of the Gothic Revival, and their appreciation of his efforts was reflected by the formation of the Britton Club in December 1845.

WRITINGS

with E. W. Brayley: *The Beauties of England and Wales*, 18 vols (London 1801–16)
The Beauties of Wiltshire, 3 vols (London, 1801–25)
with others: *The Architectural Antiquities of Great Britain*, 5 vols (London, 1807–26)
The Fine Arts of the English School (London, 1812)
with others: *The Cathedral Antiquities of England*, 3 vols (London, 1814–35)
with A. C. Pugin: *Illustrations of the Public Buildings of London*, 2 vols (London, 1825–8) [drgs by A. C. Pugin, suppl. 45 by W. H. Leeds, 1838]
Autobiography, 3 vols (London, 1850)

BIBLIOGRAPHY

DNB
A. C. Pugin and E. J. Willson: *Specimens of Gothic Architecture*, 2 vols (London, 1821–3)
P. Ferriday: 'John Britton', *Archit. Rev.* [London], cxxii (1957), pp. 367–9
J. M. Crook: 'John Britton and the Genesis of the Gothic Revival', *Concerning Architecture*, ed. J. Summerson (London, 1968), pp. 98–119

MARTIN POSTLE

Brixia. *See* BRESCIA.

Brixworth, All Saints' Church. Church of the former Benedictine monastery in Northamptonshire, England. It is one of the most substantial Anglo-Saxon buildings to remain largely intact above ground-level. The present structure is not necessarily the first to be built on the site: results of excavations carried out in 1981–2 suggest an 8th-century date. It is referred to in the early 12th-century Peterborough chronicle of Hugo Candidus, which implies that a monastery was founded there after *c.* 675. The first monks probably came from Peterborough, as in the case of the parallel foundation at Breedon on the Hill in Leicestershire, which other documents confirm was established by 690. Brixworth may have been identical with Clofesho, an otherwise unidentified Mercian royal monastery at which councils were held in the 8th and 9th centuries. At Domesday the manor belonged to the king and one priest is recorded, which may imply that the church had declined to parochial status. Nevertheless its former rank and the survival of its endowments are suggested by the fact that it was given as a prebend by Henry I to the Chancellor of Sarum in the early 12th century. A 14th-century stone reliquary with its relic have survived in the church and have been associated with a cult of St Boniface, attested from 1253, but presumably established in the pre-Conquest period.

Alterations and additions to the church in the Middle Ages were not extensive, and, following antiquarian-minded restorations in 1864–6, the fabric gives a substantial impression of the Anglo-Saxon building. In size, layout, style and building materials it contrasts with other surviving pre-Conquest churches in Northamptonshire (and, to a large extent, elsewhere in England). Elements of the oldest surviving building can be recognized in the existing fabric

and many minor investigations made over the past hundred and fifty years have supplemented the evidence (see fig.).

The church was entered through a narthex at the west end. This was a structure of at least two storeys, consisting on the ground-floor of five compartments of varying size. The central compartment survives as the base of the present tower. The great west door (now blocked by the later stair-turret) led into this vestibule and a slightly smaller door gave access to the nave; on either side much smaller doors led into flanking compartments to the north and south. The upper floor may have consisted of a single long north–south gallery, and there was access to the nave at this level by a round-headed door on the axis of the church. The rectangular nave (*c.* 20×10 m) is heavily restored but retains its original form. The side walls consist of blocked arcades of four round-headed arches on rectangular rubble piers, surmounted by a three-bay clerestory. The arches originally led into a range of flanking chambers on either side of the nave; each range consisted of five separate rooms, or *porticus*, and overlapped the choir by one bay. The excavations of 1981–2 failed to establish either the function of these *porticus* or whether the dividing walls between them were ever removed to convert the rows of chambers into conventional aisles. To the east of the nave, the choir (*c.* 10×10 m) retains little of its original walling. Nave and choir appear to have been separated by a triple arcade, but by the 14th century this

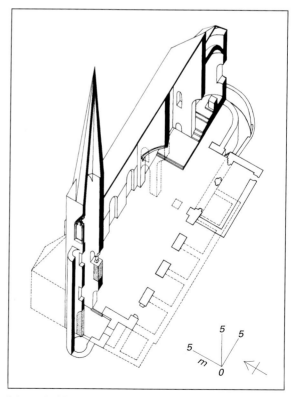

Brixworth, All Saints' Church, 8th century onwards; axonometric projection showing extent of existing fabric (solid line) and reconstructed pre-Conquest building (broken line)

had been replaced by a broad double-chamfered Gothic arch. In the east wall of the choir is the tall rebuilt sanctuary arch, with flanking splayed windows high in the wall. Directly below these windows, just above the present floor-level, are the heads of doorways leading down into an ambulatory, a partly underground passage of stilted, semicircular plan surrounding the apse. Now open to the sky, it was originally barrel-vaulted and roofed, and led presumably to a relic chamber at the crown of the apse. The ambulatory may belong to the first phase of the building but owing to modern work this cannot be proved.

In the later Anglo-Saxon period, probably in the mid-11th century, the church was drastically altered and its capacity reduced, perhaps because it was no longer monastic. The *porticus* were demolished and the arcades blocked. The narthex was reduced to a single compartment on which a tower was erected, with a triple window giving on to the nave. To the west of the tower was built a semicircular turret with a helical barrel-vaulted staircase. The apse, of which two panels survive on the north side, was rebuilt in polygonal form. In the late 12th century a south door was inserted into the west arcade arch, and *c.* 1300 a three-bay chapel was added to the south-east (reduced to two bays in 1864–6). A belfry and spire were added in the 14th century.

The Anglo-Saxon fabric is a mixture of igneous rocks from Leicestershire and limestone from Blisworth (Northants). It consists largely of reused masonry, which in the earliest phase is Roman, including the bricks of which the arch heads are formed. Three fragments of Anglo-Saxon cross sculpture survive: a section of shaft inside the church, and two arms built into the fabric of the nave.

BIBLIOGRAPHY

H. M. Taylor: *Anglo-Saxon Architecture*, 2 vols (Cambridge, 1965), pp. 108–14
[E. G. M.] Fletcher: 'Brixworth: Was There a Crypt?', *J. Brit. Archaeol. Assoc.*, 3rd ser., xxxvii (1974), pp. 88–96
D. Parsons: 'Past History and Present Research at All Saints' Church, Brixworth', *Northants Past & Present*, vi/2 (1979), pp. 61–71
M. Audouy and others: 'Excavations at the Church of All Saints, Brixworth, Northamptonshire (1981–2)', *J. Brit. Archaeol. Assoc.*, cxxxvii (1984), pp. 1–44
D. S. Sutherland and D. Parsons: 'The Petrological Contribution to the Survey of All Saints' Church, Brixworth, Northamptonshire: An Interim Study', *J. Brit. Archaeol. Assoc.*, cxxxvii (1984), pp. 45–64

DAVID PARSONS

Brizguz y Bru, Athanasio Genaro [Zaragoza y Ebri, Agustín Bruno] (*b* Alcalá de Chisvert, Castellón, 5 Oct 1713). Spanish mathematician and architectural theorist. Athanasio Genaro Brizguz y Bru was the anagrammatic pseudonym under which, aged 25, the Valencian priest and mathematician Agustín Bruno Zaragoza y Ebri published his treatise on civil architecture. It was probably connected with the proposed foundation in Valencia of a mathematical academy, to include the teaching of architecture, with Brizguz y Bru as a founder-member. The book should be seen in the context of the classicizing trend away from the vernacular Baroque tradition encouraged by Valencian mathematicians at the end of the 17th century and related to the ideals of artistic academicism in Spain in the second half of the 18th century. It comprises an introduction on the definition, origin and development of architecture, followed by three parts dealing with

geometry and the architectural orders, ecclesiastical and civil buildings and aspects of construction. It refers to Spanish authors as diverse as Caramuel de Lobkowitz, Fr Lorenzo de San Nicolas and Tomás Vicente Tosca (1651–1723) as well as to French writers such as Augustin Charles D'Aviler, Pierre Le Muet, François Blondel, Claude Perrault and Sébastien Leclerc, from whose treatises illustrations were borrowed. An important aspect of this French influence, which was peculiar to the architecture of the Mediterranean coast of Spain, is the inclusion of a section devoted to secular buildings and their internal arrangement. An indication of the success of Brizguz y Bru's treatise was its republication as late as 1804.

WRITINGS
Escuela de arquitectura civil en que se contienen los cinco órdones de arquitectura, la distribución de los templos y casas y el conocimiento de los materiales (Valencia, 1738)

BIBLIOGRAPHY
V. Ximeno: *Escritores del Reyno de Valencia*, ii (Valencia, 1749)
G. Kubler: *Arquitectura de los siglos XVII y XVIII*, A. Hisp. (Madrid, 1957)
J. Bérchez: 'La difusión de Vitruvio en el marco del Neoclasicismo español', *Cl. Perralt, Compendio de los diez libros de arquitectura de Vitruvio . . . Madrid, 1761* (Murcia, 1981)
D. Wiebenson, ed.: *Los tratados de arquitectura: De Alberti a Ledoux* (Madrid, 1988)

JOAQUÍN BÉRCHEZ

Brizio, Francesco (*b* Bologna, *c.* 1574; *d* Bologna, 1623). Italian painter, draughtsman and engraver. He studied with Bartolomeo Passerotti and afterwards at the Accademia degli Incamminati, founded by the Carracci, where he participated in group projects supervised by Ludovico Carracci. These included frescoes (*c.* 1598–1600) in the Palazzo Fava in Bologna depicting scenes from the *Aeneid* (here it seems that he worked on the last room, in collaboration with Leonello Spada); decorations (*c.* 1600) in the oratory of S Maria dell'Orazione annexed to the oratory of S Colombano, Bologna (*Road to Calvary*); and others (1604–05; almost invisible) in the octagonal cloister of the monastery of S Michele in Bosco, Bologna (*Three Stories of St Benedict*). He was left in charge of the workshop while Ludovico made a brief visit to Rome in 1602, suggesting that he held a prestigious position (although the best pupils had by then already left). Brizio continued to work with Leonello Spada and Lucio Massari, more gifted painters whose work has elements in common with his. They collaborated on frescoes in the Palazzo Bonfioli-Rossi in Bologna (1604–5) and the oratory of the Trinity at Pieve di Cento (*c.* 1605). His loyalty to Ludovico Carracci's style is evident in numerous altarpieces that remain in Bolognese churches, such as S Domenico, S Martino and S Salvatore, and in paintings in the Pinacoteca Nazionale, Bologna, and the Pinacoteca di Brera, Milan. Malvasia praised his ability to organize large-scale compositions with many figures, as in the *Coronation of the Virgin of St Luke* (1618; Bologna, S Petronio). Not a highly gifted painter, but noted for his witty narratives, he occupied a secondary role in the figurative Bolognese tradition. His work as a draughtsman and engraver is also noteworthy.

BIBLIOGRAPHY
DBI [with bibliog.]
C. C. Malvasia: *Felsina pittrice* (1678); ed. G. Zanotti (1841), i, pp. 379–84
—— : *Le pitture di Bologna* (Bologna, 1686)

F. Arcangeli: 'Una "gloriosa gara"', *A. Ant. & Mod.*, iii (1958), pp. 246–7

F. Frisoni: 'Per Francesco Brizio', *Paragone*, xxviii/323 (1977), pp. 72–84

V. Birke: *Italian Masters of the Sixteenth and Seventeenth Centuries, Commentary* (1987), 40 [XVIII/ii] of *The Illustrated Bartsch*, ed. W. Strauss (New York, 1978–)

E. Hermann-Atorino: *Francesco Brizio, bolognese, 1574–1623* (Worms, 1989)

A. Brogi: 'Francesco Brizio', *Disegni emiliani del sei-settento: Dipinti da stanza e da altare*, ed. D. Benati (Milan, 1991), pp. 86–8

DANIELE BENATI

Brizzi, Ary (*b* Avellaneda, nr Buenos Aires, 11 May 1930). Argentine painter and sculptor. He studied in Buenos Aires at the Escuela Nacional de Bellas Artes Manuel Belgrano and at the Escuela Superior de Bellas Artes Ernesto de la Cárcova, leaving in 1951, and then worked as a researcher for the Centro de Investigaciones de Comunicación Masiva, Arte y Tecnología in Buenos Aires. He played a leading role in the second wave of artists using geometric abstraction in Argentina, painting asymmetric compositions from 1957 and later making reliefs of plastic, painted wood and aluminium. As a sculptor he often worked with repeated elements, such as plastic or metal rods with which he created a continuous rhythm describing an apparently curved space. He also used sheets of transparent acrylic to make monumental parallelepipeds and boxes over which he placed bands of colour to create superpositions, coincidences and dissonances that produce an effect of criss-crossing forces in movement as the observer changes his or her position, as in *Kinetic Expansion* (1967; Buenos Aires, Mus. A. Mod.). In other works he explored the possibilities of bending or moulding plastic by heating it, or used its transparency to create ambiguous spaces.

Brizzi returned to painting in order to explore the unlimited possibilities of imaginary space, using progressively gradated bands of colour in dynamic serial formations whose energy and impact create an almost mystical effect, as in *Krypton III* (1978; Buenos Aires, Mus. N. B.A.). He was made a full member of the Academia Nacional de Bellas Artes in 1976 and won numerous prizes, including the first prize for painting at the Salón Nacional de Artes Plásticas in 1970 and the Premio Rosario of the Academia Nacional de Bellas Artes in 1980.

BIBLIOGRAPHY

Ary Brizzi: Retrospectiva (exh. cat. by N. Perazzo, Buenos Aires, Fund. S Telmo, 1986)

NELLY PERAZZO

Brno [Ger. Brünn]. City in the Czech Republic. Capital of the Southern Moravian administrative region, it is situated at the confluence of the rivers Svratka and Svitava and has a population of *c.* 395,000. Brno is notable for its wealth of historic buildings of all periods and its pioneering modern architecture.

1. BEFORE *c.* 1800. Permanent settlement in the area of Brno occurred at the turn of the 10th century, either on the low-lying land by the ford across the River Svratka ('Old Brno'), hence the name Brno (Old Slav.: moorland or mud), or around a castle (destr. beginning 13th century) built on the higher ground (Celtic brynn: hill town). The area around the castle was occupied later by a town called Petrov-Petersberg (founded after 1021), a settlement that included the parish church of St Michael in the castle precincts. Other villages also existed on the present site of the city: a Czech settlement around SS Peter and Paul, an aisleless church with a very lofty nave (founded 1222); a German settlement near the church of St James; and one established by Flemish and Walloon merchants near the church of St Nicholas. To the south of Brno (Brno-Komárov) the Benedictine monastery was founded (*c.* 1195), to the east (Brno-Zábrdovice) the Premonstratensian monastery (from 1200). All these areas together constituted an urban entity that was probably consolidated into a town in the 1330s, by which time the Dominican Order (*c.* 1228) and the Franciscan Order (after 1231) had also been incorporated. In the 1340s the town was fortified. Augustinian nuns moved in under the patronage of the Dominican Friary, and the Knights Hospitaller took up residence in the castle precincts. A number of architectural fragments survive from this period, e.g. the remains of Lokat Manor with its chapel (*c.* 1240), which today forms the core of the Old Town Hall, and the western wing of the Dominican Friary (before 1250). Only one of the original gates of Brno has been preserved, the Měnínská Gate, restored during the Baroque period.

Around the mid-13th century Přemysl Ottakar II built the Špilberk fortress (to replace the original castle) on a hill 288 m high outside the town: this, together with the church of SS Peter and Paul, gives Brno its characteristic silhouette (see fig. 1). Špilberk Castle was used mainly for provincial administration, but during the reign of the House of Luxembourg (1310–1437) it served as the residence of the Moravian margraves, although OLOMOUC, the rival town to Brno, was the capital of Moravia. In 1498 the castle was mortgaged to the secular feudal lords and subsequently fell into disrepair, and in 1560 it was acquired by the municipality.

From the 14th century to the 16th Brno became an important centre of commerce and culture. Between 1315 and 1320 the Dominicans converted the church of St Michael into a three-aisled hall church. Cloisters were added (completed 1493), and these, together with the refectory, acquired an important political function: the provincial court was held there, and the Estates met there for ceremonial receptions of the ruling margraves of Moravia, starting with Charles IV, Holy Roman Emperor; purpose-built construction for the Provincial Estates was initiated in 1582. The Franciscans erected the new church of St John the Baptist and St John the Evangelist at the end of the 13th century and rebuilt it *c.* 1320. In the 14th century three important royal monasteries were established near the town. The oldest, the convent Aula Sanctae Mariae, was founded by the widowed Queen Elizabeth (*d* 1335) in 1323 and given to the Cistercian Order in Old Brno. The conventual church has a strikingly complex ground-plan: a double nave with transept and a choir with two chapels placed at angles to it. It is a brick building, notable for the richness of its window tracery. Elizabeth presented the convent with a set of eight illuminated manuscripts (Brno, State Archvs). The second monastery (given to the Augustinian hermits), with its church of St Thomas, was built in the mid-14th century (completed 1397) but has only a few Gothic fragments in its exterior, which was reconstructed in the Baroque period. Inside the

1. Brno, view of the city showing SS Peter and Paul and, in the distance, Špilberk Castle

church is a medieval *Pietà*, possibly the work of Heinrich (Parler) von Gmünd. The Carthusian monastery and church (Cella Trinitatis, 1375) in Králové Pole retain their original layout with monks' cells (rest. in the Baroque period) and bear some resemblance to the courtyard buildings typical in Prague in that period. The parish church of St James has a very long history, beginning in 1314. Work on it resumed at the end of the 14th century, probably under the direction of Peter Parler's workshop in Prague. The presbytery was finished by 1473, and work advanced under the local architect and sculptor Anton Pilgram until 1514, when Mert Hübel continued in a Late Gothic style. The building was finally completed in 1592. St James is a hall church ending in a single great apse lit by six windows; the nave is roofed with net vaulting. Pilgram also created the remarkable statuary on the 'Jewish Gate', fragments of which survive (Brno, Mus. City), and the decorative main portal of the Old Town Hall (1511; see fig. 2).

In the second half of the 16th century various artists from northern Italy came to live and work in Brno and were responsible for much of the Renaissance sculpture and architecture there. Giorgio Gialdi (*d* 1623) sculpted the portal of the Christoph Schwanz House (1589), Antonio Silva built the lantern on the tower of the Old Town Hall (1577), and Elia Canevale created the stonework at the Provincial Estates House (the New Town Hall). The architects Antonio Gabri and Pietro Gabri completed the Provincial Estates House (from 1585) above the refectory of the Dominican monastery and built the arcaded courtyard of the Bishop's Palace (1593), the tower (1592) of St James's church and the house (1593) of the Lípá family. The Italians in Brno formed a large community that supported the Counter-Reformation and the artistic endeavours of the Jesuit Order (in Brno since 1572); they built the church of the Assumption (1598–1602) to plans supplied by the Order. During the Thirty Years War (1618–48) Brno successfully withstood the Swedish siege of 1645 and obtained great privileges from Ferdinand III, Holy Roman Emperor, shortly afterwards becoming the new capital of Moravia. Among the many fine works belonging to the early Baroque period (from the mid-17th century) are the loggias (1630) at the Bishop's Palace, the restoration of St Thomas's church (1634) and the church of St Mary Magdalene (1651–4) by the master mason Andrea Erna; buildings by Paul Weinberger (*fl* 1650–68) include St Joseph's church (1651–8), the choir of SS Peter and Paul (1651–2) and the Premonstratensian church at Brno-Zábrdovice, designed by Giovanni Pietro Tencala in 1661–9. From his arrival in the town in

2. Brno, Old Town Hall, Gothic portal by Anton Pilgram, 1511

1704, the enterprising builder Mauriz Grimm (*see* GRIMM, (1)) undertook an increasing workload: he completed the New Town Hall (1717–19; façade 1726–33) and built the Schrattenbach Palace (from 1730). One of his finest creations is the Loreto Chapel (1716–26), the adjoining façades of which provide an undulating Baroque townscape of ingenious liveliness. In the second half of the 17th century a new ring of fortifications was added to Špilberk Castle, and in 1725–9 the castle itself was thoroughly modernized by Giovanni Pieroni da Galiano, Pierre Philippe de Rochepine and others. Towards the end of the 18th century Špilberk Castle was increasingly used as a much-feared gaol (the Habsburg monarchy's 'prison of the nations').

2. *c*. 1800 AND AFTER. In the early 19th century industrial production in Brno grew to the extent that the town became known as the 'Austrian Manchester'. New buildings were needed to contain the increasing industrialization, particularly after the mid-19th century. At first Brno was modernized in accordance with the orderly plans of Ludwig von Förster and Johann Lorenz, who used ideas taken from the Ringstrasse, Vienna. The experts responsible for the new buildings erected in place of the old fortifications were mainly Viennese, including Ludwig von Förster (Augarten casino, 1846; Palais Klein, 1848), Theophilius Hansen (St Anna Hospital, 1868; Czech Meeting House, 1872; Palais Pražák, 1872) and Heinrich

von Ferstel (Protestant Church, 1863–5; Palais Bergl, 1863–9). At the close of the 19th century a further wave of modernization occurred, during which a number of medieval and Baroque buildings were ruthlessly destroyed, despite strong opposition from the respected art historian Max Dvořák in Vienna.

Brno is particularly noted for its 20th-century buildings. The ideas of ADOLF LOOS helped to shape the architectural development of the city from the turn of the century onwards. His efforts to achieve unity of style were continued by Arnošt Wiesner, Emil Králík and others. The concept of the English garden city (*see* URBAN PLANNING, §V) was applied in the administrative district. In the winter of 1924–5 Le Corbusier gave a series of lectures that further inspired local architects: traditionalists such as Josef Polášek continued to work alongside such representatives of the modern International Style as Bohuslav Fuchs, whose Hotel Avion (1927–8) is one of the best examples of this trend. In 1928 an Exhibition of Contemporary Culture in Czechoslovakia took place in Brno. An area was set aside for buildings that would be examples of the International Style both in the town itself and in Czechoslovakia. In 1928–30 Ludwig Mies van der Rohe produced one of his most influential European creations, the Villa Tugendhat (*see* CZECH REPUBLIC, fig. 6) at Brno. The Brno Technika was an important artistic and engineering centre; among those lecturing here were Emil Králík, a representative of Loos's purism trend, and from 1925 Jiří Kroha, one of the most original figures in Czech modern architecture. After World War II new building was mainly restricted to the creation of surburban housing and the gradual renovation of the historic centre. The museums and galleries in Brno have a long-standing tradition: the Moravian Museum (1817–18) is one of the oldest museums in Central Europe. Its art collections were moved in 1961 to the newly established Moravian Gallery. The art collections of special significance to Brno are kept at Špilberk Castle (Brno, Mus. City).

BIBLIOGRAPHY

C. d'Elvert: *Versuch einer Geschichte Brünns* (Brno, 1828)

——: *Neu-Brünn* (Brno, 1888)

G. Trautenberger: *Die Chronik der Landeshauptstadt Brünn*, 5 vols (Brno, 1891–7)

B. Bretholz: *Die Pfarrkirche St Jakob in Brünn* (Brno, 1901)

W. Schram: *Ein Buch für jeden Brünner*, 5 vols (Brno, 1901–05)

A. Prokop: *Die Markgrafschaft Mähren in kunstgeschichtlicher Beziehung*, 4 vols (Brno, 1904)

F. Šujan: *Dějepis Brna* [History of Brno], 2nd edn (Brno, 1928)

J. Leisching: *Kunstgeschichte Mährens* (Brno, n.d.)

V. Richter: *Nejstarší plán jezuitského kostela v Brně* [Earliest plan for Jesuit church at Brno] (Brno, 1936)

——: 'Z počátků města Brna' [Brno's beginnings], *Časop. Matice Morav.*, lx (1936), pp. 257–314

B. Bretholz: *Brünn: Geschichte und Kultur* (Brno, 1938)

C. Hálová-Jahodová: *Brno: Stavební a umělecký vývoj města* [Architectural and artistic development of Brno] (Prague, 1947)

V. Hrubý: *Pravěk Brna* [Prehistoric Brno] (Brno, 1955)

Brno v minulosti a dnes: Sborník příspěvků k dějinám a výstavbě Brna [Brno, past and present: A collection of articles on the history and architecture of Brno], 7 vols (Brno, 1959–65)

Dějiny města Brna [History of Brno], 2 vols (Prague, 1969–73)

V. Richter and Z. Kudělka: 'Die Architektur des 17. und 18. Jahrhunderts in Mähren', *Sborn. Prac. Filoz. Fak. Brn. U.*, xvi (1972), pp. 91–130

C. Hálová-Jahodová: *Brno: Dílo přírody, člověka a dějin* [Brno: The work of nature, man and history], 2nd edn (Brno, 1975)

I. Crhonek and others: *Brno v architektuře a výtvarném umění* [Brno: architecture and fine arts] (Prague, 1981)

J. Bílek: *Brněnské kostely* [Brno's churches] (Brno, 1988)

JIŘÍ KROUPA

Broach. *See* BHARUCH.

Broadhead, Caroline (*b* Leeds, W. Yorks, 28 June 1950). English jewellery and textile designer. She trained at Leicester School of Art (1968–9) and at the Central School of Art and Design, London (1969–72). In her early pieces she employed flexible nylon monofilament structures that could be collapsed to form a neckpiece, pulled up to form a ruff effect or even expanded to cover the face and head (e.g. neckpiece/veil, 1983; see Dormer and Turner, pl. 161). She also used multi-coloured woven flax for broad hooped necklaces and bracelets (e.g. tufted necklace, 1979; see Houston, pl. 12). The range of plain and coloured acrylic jewellery produced by C&N Buttons & Jewellery Production, a company she formed in London in 1978 with Nuala Jamison (*b* 1 Oct 1948), had a broader appeal. In her work Broadhead proposed new functions for materials and techniques, going beyond the idea of a unique item of value, to fuse clothing and decorative accessories in a complete and imaginative ensemble. In the 1980s she created a new mood with elusive body garments: *Cocoon*, *Seam* (both 1986) and *Web* (1989; all London, Crafts Council Gal.) are cotton and nylon fabrics that, once wrapped, form surreal patterns that play on an ambiguity between clothing and personality. Broadhead has been recognized as a leading innovator in the New Tradition tendency in Europe, a generation of designers who, over two decades into the 1980s, revised many of jewellery's conventions.

BIBLIOGRAPHY

P. Dormer and R. Turner: *The New Jewellery: Trends and Traditions* (London, 1985)

G. Dale: 'Caroline Broadhead', *Ornament*, ix (1986), pp. 43–5

J. Houston: *Caroline Broadhead: Jewellery in Studio* (London, 1990)

D. Norton: 'Caroline Broadhead: Jewellery and Beyond', *Metalsmith*, ii (1991)

Broadside [Fr. *canard*]. Single sheet of unfolded paper printed on one side only, with text and usually either woodcut or, later, wood-engraved illustrations. Broadsides were popular in Europe (especially Germany) from the 16th century and were sold by local booksellers, roaming hawkers or 'colporteurs'. They carried official announcements, news bulletins, the latest songs (slip ballads), lurid crime reports and other information, often sensational, of short-lived and general interest to the public. Cheap, quickly produced and ephemeral, they were the newspapers, magazines, fliers and posters of their day. Relatively few survive. The term 'broadsheet' is frequently regarded as synonymous, but strictly speaking it should be applied to an unfolded sheet with printing on both sides.

See also POPULAR PRINTS.

Broc, Jean (*b* Montignac, Dordogne, 16 Dec 1771; *d* Poland, 1850). French painter and designer. He came from a family of shopkeepers and tailors and he served in the Republican army during the wars of the Vendée. By 1798 he was a student of Jacques-Louis David, who provided a small apartment in the Louvre where Broc often lived. With a group of David's students and some writers, Broc formed a dissenting sect called LES PRIMITIFS, Barbus (bearded ones), Méditateurs or Penseurs. Broc was typical of the Primitifs in finding inspiration in Greek vase painting and Italian 15th-century art.

The *School of Apelles* (1800; Paris, Louvre) was Broc's first Salon entry and the first exhibited work by a member of the Primitifs. The picture represents Apelles speaking to his students about his unfinished allegory of *Calumny*. The composition derives from Raphael's *School of Athens* (Rome, Vatican, Stanza Segnatura), and the picture on the easel is based on a drawing of *Calumny* then attributed to Raphael (Paris, Louvre). The *School of Apelles* has been interpreted as a statement on the isolation of the artist and his subjection to the injustices of the ruling class, a theme relevant to the Primitifs' own ideals. In the 1801 Salon Broc exhibited the *Death of Hyacinth* (Poitiers, Mus. B.-A.); its subtle pastel colour scheme, for which Broc was often criticized, and the attenuated figure proportions recall the art of Botticelli and Perugino, and it anticipates the stylistic mannerism of Ingres's early work. Broc's *Shipwreck of Virginie*, known only from a sketch of it by Antoine Monsaldy (1768–1816), was also exhibited in the Salon of 1801 and received more critical acclaim.

Broc was the first to leave the Primitifs; he abandoned primitivism and pursued more conventional Napoleonic history painting and portraiture, for example his full-length portrait of *Maréchal Soult* for the Salle de Concert in the Palais des Tuileries (1805; destr.; copy at Versailles, Château). In the Salon of 1806 he exhibited the *Death of General Desaix* (Versailles, Château), which was indebted to Benjamin West's *Death of General Wolfe* (1771; Ottawa, N.G.). Broc continued to exhibit at the Salon until 1833, but received little notice. He accepted students into his studio and created designs for a wallpaper manufacturer. These have been noted for their early use of Oriental landscape motifs.

BIBLIOGRAPHY

E.-J. Delécluze: *David, son école et son temps: Souvenirs* (Paris, 1855)

G. Levitine: 'The "Primitifs" and their Critics in the Year 1800', *Stud. Romanticism*, i/4 (1962), pp. 209–19

——: '"L'Ecole d'Apelle" de Jean Broc: Un "Primitif" au Salon de l'an VIII', *Gaz. B.-A.*, lxxx (1972), pp. 285–94

J. H. Rubin: 'New Documents on the Méditateurs: Baron Gerard, Mantegna and French Romanticism circa 1800', *Burl. Mag.*, cxvii (1975), pp. 785–90

Search for Innocence: Primitive and Primitivistic Art of the 19th Century (exh. cat. by M. Curtis, College Park, U. MD, A.G., 1975)

G. Levitine: *The Dawn of Bohemianism: The Barbus Rebellion and Primitivism in Neo-classical France* (University Park, PA, 1978)

NADIA TSCHERNY

Brocandel, Hipólito Rovira y. *See* ROVIRA Y BROCANDEL, HIPÓLITO.

Brocas. Irish family of painters and engravers. Active from the 1780s to the 1860s, the Brocas family included five landscape painters who worked on a small scale, largely in the media of watercolour and engraving. Views of Dublin and other Irish towns and paintings of animals and antiquities predominate, together with engraved portraiture. Henry Brocas sr (1762–1837) was a prolific engraver and an occasional landscape painter. His achievements in landscape were recognized in 1801, when he was appointed Master of the Landscape and Ornament School of the [Royal] Dublin Society. As an engraver, he is memorable for his many portraits of Dublin figures of the late 18th century. Many of these were published in the *Hibernian Magazine*. He had four sons who became artists, of whom James Henry Brocas (*c.* 1790–1846) is remembered chiefly as an animal painter. Like his father and brothers, he exhibited at the Society of Artists of Ireland in Dublin between 1804 and 1810. On at least one occasion James Henry and his brother Samuel Frederick (1792–1847) shared the same patron: in 1809, at the Society of Artists exhibition, they exhibited a number of paintings of the prize cattle of the Hon. Thomas Newcomen, Bart. Although Samuel Frederick was an occasional painter of animal scenes, he is best remembered for his views of Dublin. He worked closely with his youngest brother, Henry Brocas jr (*c.* 1798–1873), in producing a set of 12 views of Dublin in 1820; Samuel Frederick did the drawings, Henry the engravings. William Brocas (1794–1868) was alone among his family in becoming a Royal Hibernian Academician. He specialized in portraits and figure subjects, particularly scenes from Irish rural life. The wide range of their activities suggests that the Brocas family ran a successful art business in Dublin in the early decades of the 19th century.

Strickland   BIBLIOGRAPHY
A. Crookshank and the Knight of Glin: *The Painters of Ireland, c. 1660–1960* (London, 1979), pp. 198–9

FINTAN CULLEN

Brock, Sir **Thomas** (*b* Worcester, 1 March 1847; *d* London, 22 Aug 1922). English sculptor. He trained under J. H. Foley from 1866 and the following year entered the Royal Academy Schools, winning the gold medal for sculpture in 1869. After Foley's death in 1874 Brock completed his stone and bronze *O'Connell Monument* (1866–83; Dublin, O'Connell Street) and most of his other unfinished works. Many commissions for public monuments followed, and by 1890 Brock led the field in official sculpture.

Brock's statues combine realist historical accuracy with a vigorous sense of composition and silhouette. These qualities are evident in the equestrian *Black Prince* (bronze, 1902; Leeds, City Square). Brock's figures strike characteristic, active poses, conveying piety, for example in the marble monument to Bishop Henry Philpott (1896; Worcester Cathedral), or drama, as in the statue of *Henry Irving* (London, Charing Cross Rd). His ideal works include a *Moment of Peril* (bronze, 1880; London, Tate, on loan to Leighton House) and *Eve* (marble version, 1898; London, Tate). Eve's meditative pose and naturalness indicate Brock's assimilation of the stylistic precepts of the New SCULPTURE, as does his bronze and marble monument to *Frederic Leighton* (1900; London, St Paul's Cathedral).

Brock's crowning achievement is the *Queen Victoria Memorial* (stone, marble and bronze, 1901–24; London, The Mall; *see* STATUE, fig. 8), executed in collaboration with the architect Aston Webb, a magnificent demonstration of his eclecticism and intelligent approach to symbolism. The surmounting gilded Victory and the marble statue of the Queen owe much to Alfred Gilbert, the allegorical marble statues of Courage and Constancy to Alfred George Stevens, and Motherhood to Jules-Aimé Dalou. After the unveiling of the statue of Queen Victoria in 1911, Brock was knighted; his other honours included membership of the Royal Academy (ARA, 1883; RA, 1891) and founding presidency of the Royal Society of British Sculptors (1905).

DNB   BIBLIOGRAPHY
M. H. Spielmann: *British Sculpture and Sculptors of To-day* (London, 1901), pp. 25–33
E. Darby and M. Darby: 'The Nation's Monument to Victoria', *Country Life*, clxiv (9 March 1978), pp. 647–50
B. Read: *Victorian Sculpture* (London and New Haven, 1982), pp. 72–3, 75, 289, 291, 371–9
S. Beattie: *The New Sculpture* (London and New Haven, 1983), pp. 175–7, 223, 228–30
J. A. Sankey: 'London's Forgotten Sculptor', *Illus. London News* (Christmas 1985), pp. 61–4

MARK STOCKER

Brockhurst, Gerald Leslie (*b* Birmingham, 31 Oct 1890; *d* Franklin Lakes, NJ, 4 May 1978). English painter and printmaker. He attended the Birmingham School of Art, where he showed a prodigious talent for drawing. In 1907 he entered the Royal Academy Schools, London, attaining, among other awards, the Gold Medal and Travelling Scholarship in 1913; the latter took him to Paris and Italy, where he studied the works of the Italian 15th-century painters. Piero della Francesca and Leonardo remained important influences. From 1915 to 1919 Brockhurst and his first wife, Anaïs, lived in Ireland, where he was introduced by Oliver St John Gogarty to Augustus John and his circle. In 1919 the Chenil Galleries, London, held the first significant exhibition of Brockhurst's work, and the artist returned to England.

During the 1920s Brockhurst embarked on a career as an etcher, achieving an exceptionally high degree of technical virtuosity in a competitive field. His subjects were almost exclusively female portraits, with Anaïs as his model (e.g. *The Dancer*, 1925). By 1930 he had returned to painting, and, working with a new model, Dorette, who became his second wife, he proceeded to establish himself as one of the most fashionable and successful British portrait painters active in the inter-war period. His sitters included *Merle Oberon* (exh. RA 1937; USA, priv. col.), *Marlene Dietrich* (exh. RA 1939; London, priv. col.) and the *Duchess of Windsor* (1939; Paris, priv. col.). In 1939, at the height of his success, Brockhurst moved to America, where he lived and worked for the rest of his life. The best of his work of the 1920s and 1930s, such as the etching *Adolescence* (1933), is marked by an uncompromising technical perfection and overt classicism informed by a highly personal intensity.

BIBLIOGRAPHY
H. Stokes: 'The Etchings of G. L. Brockhurst', *Prt Colr Q.*, xi (1924), pp. 409–43
H. J. L. Wright: 'Catalogue of the Etchings of G. L. Brockhurst', *Prt. Colr Q.*, xxii (1935), pp. 62–77
Gerald Brockhurst (exh. cat. by A. Goodchild, S. Wildman and M. Symmes, Sheffield, Graves, A.G.; Birmingham, Mus. & A.G.; London, N.P.G.; 1986–7)

ANNE L. GOODCHILD

Brocky, Károly [Charles] (*b* Temesvár, Hungary [now Timisoara, Romania], 22 May 1807; *d* London, 8 July 1855). Hungarian painter, active in England. Between 1823 and 1832 he studied at the Akademie der Bildenden Künste in Vienna and painted mainly miniatures on ivory and portraits in the Viennese Biedermeier style. On study trips to Italy and Paris (1837) he copied Old Master paintings in the galleries and was particularly influenced by Italian Renaissance and Baroque art. In Paris he became acquainted with Hugh Andrew Johnstone Munro, a Scottish aristocrat who in 1838 invited him to visit London. In 1839, having received the support of the art dealer Dominic Colnaghi (1790–1879), he exhibited at the Royal Academy and in 1840 at the British Institution; over the next several years he was to show frequently with both of them. He became a favourite portrait painter of the British aristocracy and the wealthy bourgeoisie, rendering his sitters much in the manner of van Dyck and Gainsborough (e.g. *Sir Dominic Colnaghi, c.* 1840; untraced). An eclectic painter, he was most influenced by William Etty of all his English contemporaries. In the 1840s he painted mainly portraits of women and children (e.g. *Mrs Norman Wilkinson*, after 1847; Budapest, N.G.) and scenes from the novels of Walter Scott (e.g. *Lucy Ashton and Ravenswood Visiting Blind Alice*, 1843; Budapest, priv. col., see Lajta, pl. 11). He visited Germany and made a second trip to Italy, where he did studies, in brilliant and fiery colours, of models in Italian dress. In 1845–6 he again stayed in Vienna and then moved permanently to London. He also painted watercolours, which have a lightness of touch (e.g. *Girl Reading by a Window, c.* 1850; London, V&A).

In 1850 Brocky was at the height of his career. Around this time he painted a *Self-portrait* dressed in red (after 1850; Budapest, N.G.) and the grand mythological composition *The Nymph* (1850; Budapest, N.G.), the iconography of which was borrowed from the Italian late Renaissance. Between 1850 and 1855 he painted a series of nude torsos of women (e.g. *Sleeping Maenad*, 1850–55; Budapest, priv. col., see Lajta, pl. 31). In 1854 he was elected a member of the New Society of Painters in Watercolours. Although he was little known in Hungary, he kept in close contact with Hungarian émigrés living in London and painted portraits of two of them: *Lázár Mészáros*, a former minister of war, and *General György Kmetty* (both 1851; Budapest, N. Mus.). His only history painting, *Granting a Charter to Hungary* (*c.* 1851; destr.), represents a subject from Hungary's past. His first posthumous exhibition in Hungary was held in 1896, during the country's millennium celebrations.

BIBLIOGRAPHY

N. Wilkinson: *Sketch of the Life of Charles Brocky the Artist* (London, 1870)
J. Szentkláray: *Brocky Károly festőmüvész élete* [The life of the painter Károly Brocky] (Temesvár, 1907)
S. Nyári: *Brocky Károly festőmüvész élete és müvei* [The life and works of the painter Károly Brocky] (Budapest, 1910)
Catalogue of Water Colour Paintings by British Artists and Foreigners Working in Great Britain (exh. cat., London, V&A, 1927), pp. 52–3
Brocky Károly, 1808–1855 [sic] (exh. cat. by E. Lajta, Budapest, Mus. F.A., 1955)
E. Lajta: *Brocky Károly, 1807–1855* (Budapest, 1957, 2/1984)

KATALIN GELLÉR

Brocquy, Louis le. *See* LE BROCQUY, LOUIS

Brodovitch, Alexey (*b* Ogolitchi, nr St Petersburg, 1898; *d* Le Thor, Vaucluse, 15 April 1971). American typographic designer, art director and photographer. After settling in the USA in 1930, he established a reputation as one of the most influential art directors of the 20th century. He was best known for his 24-year career (1934–1958) at the American magazine *Harper's Bazaar* and for his Design Laboratory, operated first under the auspices of the Philadelphia Museum School (1936–40) and then (1941–59) of the New School for Social Research and the American Institute of Graphic Arts, both in New York. Through his work at *Harper's*, Brodovitch revolutionized modern magazine design by forging a greater integration of typography, text and photography. His innovative layouts and numerous cover illustrations for the magazine popularized the techniques of montage, full-bleed paging and strategic sequencing of photographs that fostered interactive readership. In 1945 Brodovitch published *Ballet*, an influential book featuring his own photographs of the Ballets Russes de Monte Carlo taken between 1935 and 1939. The book's blurred, fast-paced, almost Surrealist photographs suggest Brodovitch's preference for unconventional framing and juxtaposition, while its sequencing demonstrated for many the fundamental principles underlying his art direction and instruction. During his years teaching the Design Laboratory courses in New York, Brodovitch directly affected the careers of several important photographers, including Diane Arbus, Richard Avedon, Irving Penn and Lisette Model. His influence on graphic design and photography continued to be manifest in magazine and book publishing at the end of the 20th century.

PHOTOGRAPHIC PUBLICATIONS
Ballet (New York, 1945)

BIBLIOGRAPHY
A. Grundberg: *Brodovitch* (New York, 1989)
J. Livingston: *The New York School: Photographs, 1936–63* (New York, 1992), pp. 36–51

JAMES CRUMP

Brodowski, Antoni (Stanisław) (*bapt* Warsaw, 26 Dec 1784; *d* Warsaw, 31 March 1832). Polish painter and teacher. He studied for a short time under Jean-Baptiste Augustin in Paris between 1805 and 1808, returning later to Paris at the end of 1809 and remaining until the autumn of 1814 as a bursar of the Chamber of Public Education of the Duchy of Warsaw. He wished to study under Jacques-Louis David but was able to do so only on a part-time basis. After a brief period of study under Anne-Louis Girodet, he became a pupil of François Gérard in 1811. At this time Brodowski painted his first oil portraits, one of the best being his *Self-portrait* (1813; Warsaw, N. Mus.). He also started work on a large composition suggested by Gérard, *Saul's Anger at David* (1812–19; Warsaw, N. Mus.), which was exhibited after his return to Warsaw at the first public fine arts exhibition in 1819, where it won first prize. The painting clearly shows the influence of David and Brodowski's commitment to the strict canons of the French Empire style; it became a model for Neoclassical painting in Warsaw.

Brodowski considered his principal task to be the composition of large-scale scenes with many figures, based on themes from Antiquity. Such works include *Hector Reproaching Paris for his Sloth in front of Helen* (1821; destr., see Sroczyńska, no. 32), inspired by David's painting the *Courtship of Paris and Helen* (1788; Paris, Louvre), and *Oedipus and Antigone* (1828; Warsaw, N. Mus.), a painting that is close to Gérard's *Belisarius* (exh. 1795) and reflects Brodowski's other leading principle, the observation of nature. His only painting based on contemporary events was the *Conferring of the Diploma for the Institution of a University in Warsaw by Alexander I* (ex-U. Warsaw, untraced, see Sroczyńska, no. 40; oil sketches, Warsaw, N. Mus.), commissioned by the government. He was also active as a portrait painter, chiefly of people from university and literary circles, the Warsaw intelligentsia, political activists and members of the aristocracy. Among his most notable portraits are those of his brother *Karol Brodowski* (1815; Warsaw, N. Mus.), which has a striking Romantic air, the teacher and writer *Ludwik Osiński* (*c.* 1820; Warsaw, N. Mus.) and the Primate of the Kingdom of Poland, *Szczepan Hołowczyc* (1828; Poznań, N. Mus.). In this last portrait Brodowski's emerging realistic tendency finds its fullest expression. He frequently painted posthumous portraits but rarely painted portraits of women, and those that exist are generally inferior to his depictions of men. His colour range is subdued, with a tendency towards warmer tones. There is a frequent use of various shades of brown with reddish and gold tinges, along with soft reds and olive greens.

Brodowski was one of the artists who contributed designs in 1826 for the unrealized painted decorations for the interior of Antoni Corazzi's Teatr Wielki (Grand Theatre) in Warsaw. The designs (destr. except for one watercolour, Warsaw, N. Mus.) indicate strong links with the decorative paintings of palaces in Paris during the First Empire. During the 1820s Brodowski was active as a lithographer but, unfortunately, nearly all of these works have been destroyed. In 1820 he was appointed Professor of Painting in the Faculty of Education and Fine Art at the University of Warsaw. He radically transformed the teaching methods, introducing the study of sculptures from Antiquity through copying and the practice of figure drawing from life, while also strongly recommending the imitation of nature. In 1824 Brodowski published his treatise *Co stanowi szkołę malarską* ['What constitutes a school of painting'] as the theoretical grounding for the changes he had introduced. No outstanding artists emerged from his circle of students, but his influence on the development of portrait painting in Poland was remarkable. He also played an active role in Warsaw's intellectual and artistic life and took part in the fine art exhibitions of the period 1819–28, in 1821 being appointed a member of the exhibition jury. Two of Brodowski's sons, Tadeusz (1823–48) and Józef (1828–1900), were also painters.

WRITINGS
Co stanowi szkołę malarską [What constitutes a school of painting] (Warsaw, 1824)

SAP

BIBLIOGRAPHY
S. Kozakiewicz and K. Sroczyńska, eds: *Malarstwo polskie od XVI do początku XX wieku* [Polish painting from the sixteenth century to the beginning of the twentieth century], Warsaw, N. Mus. cat. (Warsaw, 1975)
S. Kozakiewicz: *Malarstwo Polskie: Oświecenie, Klasycyzm, Romantyzm* [Polish painting: the Enlightenment, Classicism, Romanticism] (Warsaw, 1976), pp. 281–2, 284
K. Sroczyńska: *Antoni Brodowski: Życie i dzieło* [Antoni Brodowski: life and work] (Warsaw, 1985)

KRYSTYNA SROCZYŃSKA

Brodrick, Cuthbert (*b* Hull, 1 Dec 1821; *d* Jersey, 2 March 1905). English architect. He was articled in Hull from 1837 to 1843 to Henry Francis Lockwood (1811–78). He set up practice there in 1845 after a European tour, during which he was greatly impressed by Parisian architecture. The Royal Institution, Hull (1852; destr.), shows the influence of the east front of the Louvre and may be regarded as a first essay for his best-known and greatly influential building, Leeds Town Hall, won in open competition in 1853. A noble colonnaded structure, in which both St George's Hall, Liverpool (1841–54), and the Bourse des Valeurs, Paris (1808–15), can be identified as sources, its original design was revised to incorporate a massive domed tower. As the first complete municipal palace, opened in 1858, the Town Hall influenced later public buildings in the British Empire. His most original design, Leeds Corn Exchange (1860–62; *see* IRON AND STEEL, fig. 4), owes something to the Halle au Blé, Paris; in its bold detailing and ingenious roof construction it represents Brodrick at the height of his brief career. The Leeds Institution (1860–66) and Hull Town Hall (1861–2; destr.) are less successful, but in the monumental Grand Hotel, Scarborough (1862–7), with its brick and terracotta façades reminiscent of the work of Jean-Nicolas-Louis Durand and Second Empire roof-line, Brodrick displayed again the influence of France.

Brodrick took part in national competitions including those for the Government Offices, Whitehall (1857), the extension of the National Gallery, London (1866), and Manchester Town Hall (1866), and was commissioned to design a Custom House in Bombay (1866; unexecuted). All his executed designs are or were in Yorkshire; they include Wells House in Ilkley (1853) and, in Leeds, Headingley Congregational Church (1864–6), Oriental Baths (1866; destr.) and King Street warehouses (1867; destr.). In 1869 Brodrick retired to France and later moved to Jersey.

BIBLIOGRAPHY
D. Harbron: 'Cabbages at Salona', *Archit. Rev.* [London], lxxix (1936), pp. 33–4
T. Wilson: *Two Leeds Architects* (Leeds, 1937)
D. Linstrum: 'Cuthbert Brodrick: An Interpretation of a Victorian Architect', *J. Royal Soc. A.*, cxix (1971), pp. 72–88

DEREK LINSTRUM

Brodsky, Isaak (Izrailevich) (*b* Sofiyevka, nr Dnepropetrovsk, Ukraine, 6 Jan 1884; *d* Leningrad [now St Petersburg], 14 Aug 1939). Russian painter, graphic artist and collector, of Ukrainian birth. He studied at the School of Art in Odessa (1896–1902) under Kiriak Kostandi (1852–1921) and at the Academy of Arts in St Petersburg (1902–8) under Il'ya Repin, who remained an important influence throughout his life. During the revolutionary years 1905 to 1907 Brodsky became famous as a political caricaturist and for his painting *Red Funeral: The Funeral* *of the Victims of the Armed Attack on the Peaceful Demonstration in St Petersburg on 9 Jan 1905* (1906; St Petersburg, Acad. A., Mus.). From 1909 to 1911 he worked in Germany, France, Italy, Spain and Austria on a scholarship from the Academy. Brodsky's landscapes and portraits of the period are generally traditional and academic in style.

In 1917 Brodsky drew a series of portraits of the members of the Provisional Government and in 1919 received first prize in the 'Great Russian Revolution' competition for his painting *Lenin and the Demonstration* (Moscow, Cent. Lenin Mus.). Subsequently he painted a number of large canvases devoted to events during the October Revolution (e.g. *The Execution of the 26 Commissars of Baku*, 1925; Baku, Mus. Revolution), and to revolutionary leaders, particularly Lenin and Stalin. Brodsky's works were used as historical illustrations; he based his paintings on detailed research and made a great many preparatory sketches and studies, often from life (e.g. *Lenin*, pencil, 1920; Moscow, Cent. Lenin Mus.), and he made extensive use of photographs. During the 1930s he continued to paint portraits of Soviet leaders, Joseph Stalin in particular, and his works were regarded as classic examples of Socialist Realism. In 1934 he became Rector of the Academy of Art in Leningrad and, being strongly opposed to post-revolutionary avant-garde experiments, he favoured conservative traditionalism.

A collection of Brodsky's work is in the Art Museum at Berdyansk in the Ukraine (1932). He was also known as a collector; with other works by Brodsky, the Brodsky Apartment Museum in Leningrad (1949) contains what remains of his collection. The latter, consisting mainly of the works of Russian painters of the 19th and 20th centuries, among them several early paintings by Marc Chagall, is not dogmatically conservative.

WRITINGS
Moy tvorcheskiy put' [My creative journey] (Leningrad, 1940)
Stat'i. Pis'ma. Dokumenty [Essays, letters, documents] (Moscow, 1956)

BIBLIOGRAPHY
I. A. Brodsky: *I. I. Brodsky* (Moscow, 1956)
I. I. Brodsky. 1884–1939 (exh. cat., St Petersburg, Rus. Mus., 1984)

V. RAKITIN

Brodszky, Sándor (*b* Tóalmás, 20 June 1819; *d* Budapest, 23 Jan 1901). Hungarian painter. He studied medicine in Pest, before moving on in 1841 to the Akademie der Bildenden Künste in Vienna, where he studied painting under Josef Mössmer (1780–1845) and Franz Steinfeld (1787–1868). In 1845 he went to Munich, where he spent ten years, during which time he studied at the Akademie der Bildenden Künste under Albert Zimmermann (1808–88) and Friedrich Voltz (1817–86). His ideal landscape painter, however, was Karl Rottmann. In 1847 he exhibited his painting *Solitary Mill* (ex-Kstver., Munich) at the Kunstverein in Munich. He subsequently became a well-known landscape painter. As well as many successful exhibitions in Germany, from 1842 he regularly exhibited landscapes and still-lifes in the annual exhibitions of the Artists' Association of Pest (Pesti Műegylet) and he settled in the capital in 1856. In the same year he painted a view of the *Margaret Island* (Laxenburg, Royal Col.) for the Emperor Francis Joseph. In 1857 the Hungarian National

Museum in Budapest bought three of his newly painted landscapes: *Balaton in Storm, Ruins of Saskő* and *Esztergom and its Surroundings* (all Budapest, N.G.). Brodszky's main interest was stormy landscapes and landscapes with ruins. Sometimes he painted Hungarian landscapes with details that were more typical of the Campagna of Rome. His landscapes also included small staffage figures and popular genre scenes, often painted in a Romantic style. After 1870 he was one of the conservative landscape painters in Hungary who preserved the traditions of the artists in Vienna and Munich during the 1840s and 1850s.

BIBLIOGRAPHY
Thieme–Becker
J. Szabó: *Painting in Nineteenth Century Hungary* (Budapest, 1988), pp. 234–5, pl. 215

JULIA SZABÓ

Broeck, van den [Paledaen; Palidamus; Paludanus]. Flemish family of artists. The painter Jan van den Broeck (*d* 1551 or after) of Mechelen had three sons who became artists. All three moved to Antwerp, where (1) Willem van den Broeck was active as a sculptor, as was his son Raphael van den Broeck (*fl* 1585–99). Willem's two brothers (2) Crispin van den Broeck and (3) Hendrik van den Broeck were probably both trained as painters by their father and then, according to Guicciardini, by Frans Floris in Antwerp. Hendrik's career was subsequently spent entirely in Italy, while Crispin, except for a short visit to Middelburg in 1564, remained in Antwerp, where he also designed and made prints. He taught engraving to his daughter Barbara van den Broeck (*b c.* 1558–60), who was also active as an engraver in Antwerp.

BIBLIOGRAPHY
L. Guicciardini: *Descrittione di. . . tutti i Paesi Bassi* (1567), p. 99

CARL VAN DE VELDE

(1) Willem [Guillaume] **van den Broeck** (*b* Mechelen, *c.* 1520; *d* Antwerp, 11 March 1579). Sculptor. He began his training in his native town and continued it on a subsequent journey to Italy. In 1557 he was admitted as a master to the Guild of St Luke in Antwerp, where he became a citizen in 1559. He is documented in 1566–7 as receiving payment for three statues for Antwerp Cathedral. In 1571 he executed a base for the life-size bronze statue (destr. 1577) of *Don Fernando Alvárez de Toledo, Duque de Alba*, in the citadel of Antwerp. He seems also to have been in demand with foreign patrons. Possibly through the mediation of his friend Abraham de Hel (1534–98), a painter from Antwerp residing in Augsburg, he was commissioned in 1560 to produce five alabaster reliefs, showing scenes from the Old and New Testaments, for an altar in the Dominikanerkirche, Augsburg (now Röm. Mus.). An alabaster relief of the *Crucifixion* (1560), signed G. P. F. (*Guilelgmus Paludanus fecit*), is in the collections of the Maximilianmuseum, Augsburg. Van den Broeck produced in Antwerp other sculptures in marble and alabaster for export, including relief panels (*c.* 1563) for the palace chapel in Schwerin of the dukes of Mecklenburg-Schwerin and three chancel screens (1571; destr.), sent to Spain. Together with Cornelis Floris II he is named as the architect of the Stadhuis in Antwerp and is especially noted for his work on the gables. Van den Broeck's artistry, his sensitive, not too linear surface treatment of alabaster (the preferred material in the Netherlands in the mid-16th century) combined with especially fine detail work, is best seen in his small-scale sculptures—statuettes, reliefs and small groups—which were much sought after by private collectors. Some of these, such as a marble group of *Venus and Cupid* (1559) at the manor house of Hamal in Tongeren, Belgium, mark the transition to the Baroque.

See also ANTWERP, §IV, 2.

BIBLIOGRAPHY
N. Lieb: *Führer durch die Städtischen Kunstsammlungen Augsburg* (Augsburg, 1953)
G. van der Osten and H. Vey: *Painting and Sculpture in Germany and the Netherlands, 1500–1600*, Pelican Hist. A. (Harmondsworth, 1969)
Antwerpen in de XVI de eeuw, Genootschap voor Antwerpse geschiedenis (Antwerp, 1975)

ELISABETH GUROCK

(2) Crispin [Crispijn; Crispiaen] **van den Broeck** (*b* Mechelen, 1523; *d* Antwerp, between 1589 and 6 Feb 1591). Painter, draughtsman and engraver, brother of (1) Willem van den Broeck. His date of birth can be deduced from his age of 34 years inscribed on a *Self-portrait* dated 1557 and his own declaration of being 60 years old on 4 August 1584. Probably trained by his father, he first worked in his native town, where he still lived in 1557, although he had been enlisted as a master in the Antwerp Guild of St Luke in 1555–6. On 27 July 1558 he rented a house in Antwerp, where he became a citizen in 1559. In 1561 he bought a piece of land in the Gasthuisbeemden, in a newly developed quarter of Antwerp where shortly afterwards Frans Floris and Hieronymus Cock became his neighbours. On his arrival in Antwerp, Crispin probably went to work in the studio of Floris, whose trusted collaborator he remained until the master's death in 1570. According to van Mander, an altarpiece for the Grand-Prior of Spain left incomplete at the time of Floris's death was completed by Crispin van den Broeck and Frans Pourbus the elder.

Besides the *Self-portrait* of 1557, there is a *Last Judgement* (1560; Brussels, Mus. A. Anc.) that dates from his early period, but in general, van den Broeck's independent career seems to have begun only after 1570. In that year he signed a contract for an altarpiece (untraced) for the convent of the Carmelites at Schoonhoven. The first dated book illustrations for the publisher Christoph Plantin are from 1571, but it is possible that he worked for him as early as 1566. Crispin van den Broeck was commissioned by the Guild of St Sebastian (the young crossbowmen) to paint an altarpiece for them (wings, 1573; Lier, St Gummarus), and in 1582 he collaborated on the decorations for the State Entry into Antwerp of Francis of Anjou (later Francis II, Duke of Lorraine) and contributed a painting of the *Judgement of Solomon* (untraced) to the redecoration of the Stadhuis after its destruction in the 'Spanish Fury' of 1576. His drawings for engravings, including the illustrations for Plantin, are numerous and are mostly dated from the 1570s onwards (e.g. drawings for the *Sacrarum antiquitatum monumenta*, Windsor Castle, Royal Lib., pubd by Plantin, 1577; see fig.).

In 1584, accused of leaving Antwerp during the siege by Alessandro Farnese, Duke of Parma, van den Broeck stated that he was temporarily residing in Middelburg, in

Crispin van den Broeck: *Sacrifice of Abraham*, pen and brown ink, with grey wash, 120×83 mm, *c.* 1577 (Windsor, Windsor Castle, Royal Library)

order to execute a commission. On 3 August 1588 he was godfather to a child of Gillis Mostaert, who may have been his pupil. The last record of his guild dues being paid was for the year 1588–9. Van den Broeck was, as van Mander called him, 'a good inventor', as the impressive number of engravings after his compositions prove. In his rather limited production of paintings, he followed the Romanist style of Frans Floris, without attaining the latter's level of sophistication.

BIBLIOGRAPHY
G. J. Lugard: 'Een schilderscontract met den Antwerpschen meester Crispiaen van den Broeck anno 1570', *Oud-Holland*, lxi (1946), pp. 106–10
E. Greindl: 'Le *Jugement dernier* de Crispin van den Broeck', *Mus. Royaux B.-A. Belgique: Bull.*, xv (1964), pp. 159–68
H. Vlieghe: 'Het altaar van de Jonge Handboog in de Onze-Lieve-Vrouwekerk te Antwerpen', *Album Amicorum J. G. van Gelder* (The Hague, 1973), pp. 342–6
P. Wescher: 'Crispin van den Broeck as Painter', *Jb.: Kon. Mus. S. Kst.* (1974), pp. 171–85
M. Díaz Padrón: 'Algunas pinturas inéditas de Crispin van den Broeck en España', *El Greco: Italy and Spain, Stud. Hist. A.*, xiii (Washington, Hannover and London, 1984), pp. 77–82
I. M. Veldman: 'The Sons of Jacob: The Twelve Patriarchs in Sixteenth-century Netherlandish Prints and Popular Literature', *Simiolus*, xv (1985), pp. 176–96

(3) Hendrik van den Broeck [?Arrigo Fiammingo, Arrigo Paludano; Hennequin de Meecle, Henricus Malinis, Henricus van Mechelen] (*b* Mechelen, *c.* 1530; *d* Rome, 28 Sept 1597). Painter and draughtsman, brother of (1)

Hendrik van den Broeck: *Resurrection* (1571–2 or 1573–5), fresco, east wall of the Sistine Chapel, the Vatican, Rome

Willem van den Broeck and (2) Crispin van den Broeck. He probably travelled to Italy sometime in the 1550s, and, despite his presumed early training in Antwerp with Frans Floris, his work shows little influence of either Floris or other Netherlandish painters and belongs instead to the Roman Mannerist school around Vasari. Guicciardini mentioned that Hendrik, whom he describes as a promising young man, had worked for the Duke of Florence (probably Cosimo de' Medici). From 1561 onwards Hendrik is recorded in several Italian cities, and in that year he was commissioned to paint the *Miracles of Christ* for Orvieto Cathedral, though he left the execution to Niccolò Pomarancio, with whom he signed a formal contract of partnership in 1564. Hendrik's main work during the 1560s was carried out in Perugia, where he produced an *Adoration of the Magi* (1561; Perugia, G. N. Umbria), signed *Henricus Malinis*, for the church for S Francesco and also designed stained-glass windows for the cathedral.

According to Hoogewerff, in 1565 Hendrik van den Broeck became a member of the confraternity of S Maria in Campo Santo, a group of Netherlandish artists living in Rome. It is unlikely (*pace* Bombe) that he is identical with the 'Errico de Errico' from Mechelen who worked in S Gaudioso in Naples in 1567, since his father's name was Jan; nor is it certain that the 'Arrigo Fiammingo' listed among the members of the confraternity of S Barbara in Florence in 1572 and again in 1580 was the same man. Indeed, during that period, Hendrik van den Broeck lived in Rome rather than in Florence and is mentioned by Vasari in a letter of 5 February 1573 as one of his collaborators in the Sala Regia in the Vatican. Hendrik's best surviving work in Rome is the fresco of the *Resurrection* (see fig.) on the east wall of the Sistine Chapel in the Vatican, which was painted to replace Domenico Ghirlandaio's work of the same subject, ruined by the collapse of the entrance door in 1522. It was painted either under Pope Gregory XIII, between 1573 and 1575, or under Pope Pius V, between June 1571 and November 1572 (see Stassny).

In 1581 Hendrik was again active in Perugia, painting an altarpiece for the chapel of S Lorenzo in S Agostino, and between 1582 and 1585 he executed frescoes in the church of Mongiovino near Città della Pieve in Umbria. His last important undertaking was the commission by Pope Sixtus V, between 1585 and 1590, of a fresco in the Biblioteca Vaticana of the *Third Council of Constantinople*, for which there survives an example of his preparatory drawings (Stockholm, Nmus.). According to Baglione, he died in poverty.

BIBLIOGRAPHY
W. Bombe: 'Arrigo Fiammingo', *Rev. Belge Archéol. Hist. A./Belge Tijdschr. Oudhdknde & Kstgesch.*, v (1935), pp. 231–44
N. Dacos: *Les Peintres belges à Rome au seizième siècle* (Brussels and Rome, 1964), p. 94
F. Stassny: 'A Note on Two Frescoes in the Sistine Chapel', *Burl. Mag.*, cxxi (1979), pp. 777–83
B. Magnusson: 'A Drawing by Hendrick van den Broeck for a Fresco in the Vatican Library', *Master Drgs*, xix (1981), pp. 160–63

CARL VAN DE VELDE

Broederlam, Melchior (*b* Ypres, *c.* 1355; *d* Ypres, *c.* 1411). South Netherlandish painter. Broederlam's family, long-established in Ypres, provided three aldermen for the city and sided with the French Counts of Flanders against the Flemish populace. After a training that may have included contact with Jan Boudolf in Bruges before 1368 or Paris after 1370 and an extended visit to Italy, the artist became, by 1381, an official painter of the reigning count, Louis de Mâle (*reg.* 1346–84), painting leather chairs, pennons and banners. On 13 May 1384, directly after Louis's death, he was appointed a *valet de chambre* to the count's heir, Philip the Bold, Duke of Burgundy, and in 1385 was sent to live in the castle at Hesdin, Artois, in order to supervise the rebuilding of its galleries of entertainment and to paint the walls according to a plan devised by Philip himself.

In the spring of 1386 Broederlam began painting scenes, perhaps of the *Trojan War*, in one of the galleries, but he was ordered to Sluis, the port of Bruges, in the late summer to help with preparations for a French armada against England. Although the invasion was finally abandoned, Broederlam supervised the embroidery and painting of banners, pennons and the awnings, poop and mainsail of the Duke's ship, executing some of the work himself. He returned to Hesdin in the autumn and spent two more years painting in the galleries and two adjacent rooms. For one of these he almost certainly designed the weather machine and painted the cycle of the *Golden Fleece* that the English printer William Caxton (*c.* 1422–91) later admired. Although the paintings were destroyed with the castle, the compositions are preserved on a parchment roll of drawings attributed to Dreux Jean (Berlin, Kupferstichkab.).

After he had finished the paintings in 1388 Broederlam stayed on at Hesdin, designing floor tiles for the galleries, supervising the decoration of a tower room in the Duke's apartment and probably repainting the gallery pictures after they were damaged in a storm. He decorated chairs

for a meeting of the ducal council and painted jousting caparisons, trumpet banners, standards and pennons for Philip the Bold to use in Dijon, Paris and Brittany; he probably also designed the cartoons for a tapestry of sheep for the duchess Margaret of Flanders.

In 1392 Broederlam certified the expenses of the sculptor Jacques de Baerze for sending two partially finished carved triptychs to the charterhouse of Champmol, near Dijon. In December these were sent to Hesdin and then on to Ypres, where the painter returned at the New Year. On 28 February 1393 Broederlam signed a contract to gild and paint the carvings and to paint scenes on the exterior of the wings. Work was under way when Philip the Bold visited his shop a year later, but the triptychs remained unfinished until the sculptor completed his part in the spring of 1398. It was August 1399 before Broederlam could accompany them to Burgundy and supervise their installation in the monastery church. Both triptychs survive (Dijon, Mus. B.-A.), but only one has retained its exterior scenes.

Meanwhile, Broederlam was occupied by assignments in Ypres. His work for Philip the Bold in 1393 may have been in the ducal residence, where in the following year he painted metal banners and a roof crest and designed stained-glass windows for the chapel. He painted banners for the Duke's expedition to Friesland in 1396, joined Hue de Boulogne and Jean Malouel in making the decorations for the wedding of Philip's second son, Antoine, in 1401 and spent six weeks painting in Burgundy in 1403. After Philip's death in 1404, Broederlam worked for his widow,

Melchior Broederlam: scenes from the *Infancy of Christ*, oil on panel, 1.62×2.60 m, *c.* 1393–9 (Dijon, Musée des Beaux-Arts)

Margaret, among other things decorating her litter. Broederlam's last assignment for the ducal family was to add full-length portraits of Philip and Margaret to the series of Flemish counts in the chapel of the residence in Kortrijk in 1407. For the city of Ypres he designed the aldermen's robes in 1406 and made models of a lily, a lion and a rose for goldsmiths to execute in silver as rhetoricians' prizes in 1409 and 1410.

Broederlam's style is seen indirectly through the *Golden Fleece* drawings and directly in the triptych exterior with scenes of the *Infancy of Christ* (see fig.): in both, the foreground figures propel the narrative to the right before a continuous rocky landscape. Both rely on Italian models. Two of the *Golden Fleece* scenes follow Venetian manuscripts of the *Historia destructionis Troiae* (Milan, Bib. Ambrosiana, MS. H86 super; London, BL, MS. Add. 15477). The triptych's *Presentation of Christ* is the only known imitation outside Tuscany of Ambrogio Lorenzetti's influential work (Florence, Uffizi), and the angel kneeling outside the porch of the *Annunciation* is also Sienese in inspiration. The forbidding empty landscape, meditative introversion of the figures and Joseph's peasant humour express a piety appropriate to the Carthusian monastery for which the scenes were destined. The other panels that have been attributed to Broederlam's milieu can hardly have been designed, much less executed, by the same artist.

Broederlam's brilliant, oil-based colours are unusually mixed and subtly modelled for the period; in the underdrawing, long curved strokes are gathered along the contours with loose cross-hatching in the shadows. This technique was taken up by the next generation. Broederlam is known to have trained younger artists such as Hue de Boulogne; the Master of Flémalle and Jan van Eyck carried on his depiction of solidly modelled figures in spatially coherent rooms and his occasional use of genre objects as religious symbols. Broederlam's works also furnished designs for later artists. Parts of the *Golden Fleece* compositions reappear in Philip the Good's first Alexander romance, attributed to Dreux Jean (Paris, Bib. N., MS. 9342), and in Lieven van Lathem's *Histoire de Jason* (Paris, Bib. N., MS. 331). The Dijon *Flight into Egypt* is imitated in manuscripts of 1400–25 (London, BL, Add. MS. 11575; Baltimore, MD, Walters A.G., MS. 265; Rouen, Bib. Mun., MS. 3024) and in German stained glass of *c.* 1470 (New York, Cloisters).

BIBLIOGRAPHY

C. Dehaines: 'Le Peintre Melchior Broederlam', *An. Cté. Flam. France* (1887), pp. 165–82
C. Monget: *La Chartreuse de Dijon*, i (Montreuil-sur-Mer, 1898), pp. 201–9
E. Panofsky: *Early Netherlandish Painting*, i (Cambridge, MA, 1953), pp. 86–9, 111–15
C. I. Minott: 'A Group of Stained Glass Roundels at the Cloisters', *A. Bull.*, xliii (1961), pp. 237–9
G. Troescher: *Burgundische Malerei*, i (Berlin, 1966), pp. 96–102
A. H. van Buren: 'The Model Roll of the Golden Fleece', *A. Bull.*, lxi (1979), pp. 359–76
M. Smeyers and B. Cardon: 'Vier eeuwen Vlaamse miniatuurkunst in handschriften uit het Grootseminarie te Brugge' [Four centuries of Flemish illumination in miniatures from the Grootseminarie of Bruges], *De Duinenabdij en het Grootseminarie te Brugge* (Tielt, 1984), no. 29
M. Comblem-Sonkes: *Le Musée des Beaux-arts de Dijon*, Les Primitifs flamands, i (Brussels, 1986)
A. H. van Buren: *Melchior Broederlam* (in preparation)
ANNE HAGOPIAN VAN BUREN

Broek, J. H. van den. *See under* VAN DEN BROEK & BAKEMA.

Broggi, Luigi (*b* Milan, 6 May 1851; *d* Milan, 4 Oct 1926). Italian architect, teacher and writer. He studied at the Accademia di Brera, Milan, under Camillo Boito, and his career began in 1879 with the Ossario della Bicocca, a commemorative pyramid in Novara. His early works are eclectic in style, employing many High Renaissance features (a style known as *Cinquecentismo*) in such works as the Società d'Assicurazioni d'Italia (1889; rebuilt 1945) in the Via Meravigli, Milan, and the unsuccessful competition entry (1890) for the new Palazzo del Parlamento Nazionale in Rome, both joint works with his former pupil Giuseppe Sommaruga. Other important projects included the Grand Hotel delle Terme (1898) at Salsomaggiore and the former Palazzo della Borsa (1898–1901; interior destr.), Via Orefici, Milan. In his most significant work, the Magazzino Contratti (1902–3; now part of the adjacent Palazzo del Credito Italiano (1901), also by Broggi), Via Tommaso Grossi, Milan, Broggi makes expressive use of new materials: the cast-iron structure is boldly displayed on the exterior, while windows and the entrance canopy are covered with intricate and highly naturalistic floral designs in wrought iron. Broggi may have been inspired by the Palazzo Castiglioni (1901–3), Milan, by Sommaruga, which is one of Italy's most important examples of the *Stile floreale*. Broggi returned to eclecticism, however, in two later commercial buildings: the Banca d'Italia (1907–12; jointly with Cesare Nava (1861–1933)) in the Via Armorari, Milan, and the Cassa di Risparmio (1909) in Alessandria. Broggi taught for most of his career at the Accademia di Brera and wrote several books on individual buildings and on theory. He retired *c.* 1915.

WRITINGS

L'edificio del Teatro della Scala in Milano (Milan, 1878)
Reale Accademia di Belle Arti in Milano: Le Accademie e gli artisti (Milan, 1894)

BIBLIOGRAPHY

DBI; *Macmillan Enc. Architects*
C. L. V. Meeks: *Italian Architecture, 1750–1914* (New Haven and London, 1966), pp. 236, 356, 418
R. Bossaglia: *Il Liberty in Italia* (Milan, 1968)
P. Mezzanotte and B. Mezzanotte: *Milano nell'arte e nella storia* (Milan, 1968)

Brogi, Giacomo (*b* Florence, 6 April 1822; *d* Florence, 29 Nov 1881). Italian photographer and engraver. He began *c.* 1855 to deal in photographic prints, after working for some years as a copper engraver with the engraver (and later photographer) Achille Paris (1820–84). Brogi had also worked with the print publisher Batelli from the age of 11, and as the copper engraver and publisher Giuseppe Bardi's print retoucher. He also attended, on a private basis, the school run by the engraver Perfetti. He probably learnt photography from the scientist Tito Puliti, whose photographic work at the Istituto di Fisica of the university from 1839 had pioneered the medium in Florence.

In 1860 Brogi set up his own photographic laboratory at Lungarno delle Grazie 15. He concentrated mainly on portraits, competing with the Alinari family whose studio was already flourishing but was devoted mainly to the reproduction of works of art, a field in which Brogi was less interested. He successfully exhibited a series of 'natural and coloured artistic photographs' at the first Esposizione Italiana, Agraria, Industriale, Artistica held in Florence in 1861 as part of the celebrations for the Unification of Italy under the reign of King Victor Emanuel II. In 1863 he published his first catalogue, which he later expanded to include a series of views of Palestine and Egypt. It is not known whether these photographs were actually taken by Brogi himself, or whether they were commissioned from other photographers and then purchased. Brogi presented one of these albums of sacred sites to Pope Pius XI in 1869. Brogi had studios and associates throughout Italy, considerably widening his scope in every sector of photography, although his speciality remained portraiture. His son Carlo (c. 1850–1925) followed him in this work and was also the author of an important photographic manual, *Il ritratto in fotografia* (Florence, 1895).

BIBLIOGRAPHY

G. Gamberucci da Prato: *Di Giacomo Brogi e delle sue opere, commentario* (Florence, 1882)
Fotografia italiana dell'ottocento (Milan, 1979)
P. Becchetti: *La fotografia a Roma* (Rome, 1983)
I. Zannier: *Storia della fotografia italiana* (Bari, 1986)
N. N. Perez: *Focus East* (New York, 1989)

ITALO ZANNIER

Broken pediment. Term applied to a pediment where the sloping sides stop short of the apex.

☐

Brokof. Bohemian family of sculptors. (1) Jan Brokof was a successful sculptor based in Prague, whose statue of *St John Nepomuk* on the Charles Bridge was the model for numerous similar works throughout the territories of the Austro-Hungarian monarchy in the late 17th century and the 18th. His sons Michal Jan Josef Brokof (1686–1721) and (2) Ferdinand Maximilián Brokof trained in the family workshop. Ferdinand Maximilián became, with Matyáš Bernard Braun, the foremost Baroque sculptor in Bohemia. He also worked in Breslau, Silesia (now Wrocław, Poland).

(1) Jan [Johann] **Brokof** (*b* St Georgenberg, Upper Hungary [now Spišska Sobota, Slovakia], 1652; *d* Prague, 18 Dec 1718). He went to Prague in 1675 and in 1682 made a full-size model for a bronze statue of *St John Nepomuk* after a *bozzetto* by the Viennese sculptor Mathias Rauchmiller. The statue, on the Charles Bridge in Prague, is the first monument of the victorious Counter-Reformation in Bohemia. During work on this project Brokof converted from Lutheranism to Catholicism. He went on to produce a considerable number of other sculptures in western Bohemia, returning to Prague in 1692. His figures are typical of Baroque sculpture in Central Europe, though sometimes weak in their treatment of the anatomy underlying their heavy draperies. Among the apprentices in his workshop were Jan Jerzy Urbansky and his own sons.

(2) Ferdinand Maximilián Brokof (*b* Červený Hrádek [Ger. Rothenhaus], nr Chomutov, Bohemia (now in the Czech Republic), 12 Sept 1688; *d* Prague, 8 March 1731). Son of (1) Jan Brokof. He trained with his father, and it is assumed that he was in Vienna before 1710. There he would have seen the work of the sculptors Paul Strudel and Giovanni Giuliani and of the architect Johann Bernhard Fischer von Erlach. In Prague he came under the influence of the realism of the sculpture of Jan Jiří Bendl and the paintings of Karel Škréta. His earliest work is thought to be a stone statue of *St Elizabeth* from a group of three female saints on the Charles Bridge, Prague, supplied by his father's workshop in 1707. In 1709 he made a statue of *St Adalbert*, also for the Charles Bridge. A wooden model for this survives (Prague, N. Mus.).

Ferdinand Maximilián went on to supply a number of the most important stone sculptural groups on the Charles Bridge. In 1710, the year in which Matyáš Bernard Braun made his group of the *Vision of St Lutgard* for the bridge, Brokof carved his first independent work, a group of *St Francis Borgia between Two Angels*, which impresses by its quiet dignity. As early as 1709 he received a commission from the Jesuits of Prague to make pendant statues for the bridge representing *St Ignatius Loyola* and *St Francis Xavier* (both completed 1711). The *St Ignatius* group (Prague, Lapidarium Hist. Mus.) comprises female personifications of the four continents lifting a globe on which stands the saint holding up the superscription. The *St Francis Xavier* group has male personifications of the continents raising a slab on which stands the saint holding a Cross before a kneeling oriental king. The face of one of the king's pages is a self-portrait of Brokof.

The group of *SS Vincent Ferrer and Procopius* (1712), also on the Charles Bridge, is generally considered to be Brokof's masterpiece: on a high base, with busts of a Turk, a rabbi and a demon, St Vincent stands on the lid of a coffin, which is lifted by a skeleton that he has brought to life; beside him St Procopius stands on the back of the Devil. The exceptional composition of the two main figures and the delicacy of the base give the impression that the saints are hovering in the air. Further works for the bridge are a statue of *St Vitus* (1713–14), probably made in conjunction with Michal Brokof, and another big narrative group of *SS John of Matha, Felix of Valois and Ivan* (1714; see fig.). The latter is composed as a rock-built jail in which poor Christians are being guarded by a Turk with a dog: the two Trinitarian saints bring liberty to the slaves, while St Ivan prays.

Brokof began to emulate the achievement of Braun with his sculptural decoration (1714) for the Morzin Palace, Prague, where the magnificent stone portal with figures of *Moors* serving as atlantids (see CZECH REPUBLIC, fig. 10) and his lyrical busts of *Day* and *Night* are contemporaneous with Braun's work at the Clam-Gallas Palace. Brokof was most clearly influenced by Braun in his marble tomb of *Count Vratislav Mitrovic* (1714–16) in St James's church, Prague, to a design by Fischer von Erlach. The effigy of the deceased is lifted by a figure of *Glory*, while a personification of *Fame* records the Count's achievements on an obelisk. In particular the statues of *Time* and *Contemplation* are close in conception to works by Braun.

Ferdinand Maximilián Brokof: *SS John of Matha, Felix of Valois and Ivan*, stone group, over-life-size, 1714 (Prague, Charles Bridge)

A *Calvary* and the *Stations of the Cross* (1716) in St Castulus, Prague, are examples of Brokof's output of wood-carvings, though done with the participation of his workshop. The culmination of his activity in this field is the decoration of a chapel in St Gall, Prague, with a *Calvary* and niche statues of the *Evangelists* (1719–20). There he achieved the expression of deep inward emotion through relatively restrained gesture. He achieved this even more successfully in a *Crucifix* now in Prague Cathedral.

The esteem that Brokof enjoyed in Central Europe by around 1720 is demonstrated by a commission to decorate the Chapel of Electors in the cathedral at Breslau, Silesia (now Wrocław, Poland), where he worked to designs by Fischer von Erlach in the period up to 1722. For the altar he made two over-life-size marble statues of *Moses* and *Aaron*, which are indebted to works by Michelangelo and Nicolas Cordier respectively. These are among Brokof's best works. In addition, the decoration of the chapel includes seated personifications of the *Old Testament* and the *New Testament*. Also in Wrocław, in St Elizabeth's, is Brokof's stucco and marble funerary monument to *Johann*

Georg Wolf, with the design of the architectural component once again coming from Fischer von Erlach's office. It consists of a reserved but monumental figure of a mourning angel leaning on an obelisk above a magnificently realistic bust of the deceased.

Brokof made a number of stone statues of *St John Nepomuk* for various sites in Bohemia, most after his father's model. Among them *St John Nepomuk Giving Alms* (*c.* 1725), in the church of the Holy Spirit, Prague, is outstanding. It is similar in style to the statues of the Lady column in Old Town Square, Prague, which dates from 1724–6, but the share of the carving given to workshop assistants in the latter is clearly greater. This is also the case with such works as the stucco and marble funerary monument to *Johann Leopold Trautson* (before 1727) in the Michaelerkirche, Vienna, which is notably inferior to the Wolf monument, and the large stone statues of *Moses* and *St Gregory* (1729–30) flanking the portal of the monastery church at Krzeszów, Poland (formerly Grüssau, Silesia), which are workshop productions. Brokof's wooden sculpture (*c.* 1730) for the high altar of St Castulus, Prague, is of high quality, but in general there seems to have been a decline in the vitality of his late work, perhaps the result of the progression of his tuberculosis and of religious and social oppression in Bohemia during the reign of Emperor Charles VI.

BIBLIOGRAPHY
Thieme–Becker
O. J. Blažíček: *Sochařství baroku v Čechách* [Baroque sculpture in Bohemia] (Prague, 1958), pp. 97–9, 122–33 [with Fr. and Ger. summary]
——: *Ferdinand Brokof* (Prague, 1986)
I. Kořán, M. Suchomel and K. Neubert: *Charles Bridge* (Prague, 1991), pp. 46–121

IVO KOŘÁN

Bromberg, Paul (*b* Amsterdam, 12 July 1893; *d* Amsterdam, 11 May 1949). Dutch interior designer, furniture designer and writer. He was the son of a furniture dealer and was involved with the profession from an early age. He took lessons with the architect J. L. van Ishoven (1870–1931) and gained work experience in Germany. After operating independently for a few years he became the leading designer of the Amsterdam firm Metz & Co. His work displayed a rational concept of form and became well known through exhibitions and publications. At the firm of Hendrik Pander & Zonen in The Hague, where he was employed from 1924 to 1933, he specialized in using different types of wood that gave his taut, functional, batch-produced furniture a distinctive decorative character. On account of their plastic shapes his designs were considered to be related to those of the Amsterdam school architects. For Bromberg functionalism in interiors was a vital starting-point. He created various model rooms and homes in order to illustrate new ideas about the arrangement of domestic interiors. He also taught and wrote manuals, children's books and many articles in periodicals and trade journals promoting contemporary applied art. He was particularly active within the Dutch Association of Trade and Industrial Art and the Good Living foundation. At home and abroad he organized exhibitions of colleagues' work.

BIBLIOGRAPHY

C. Brandes: 'Beschouwingen over binnenhuisarchitectuur en het werk van Paul Bromberg' [Observations on interior architecture and the work of Paul Bromberg], *Levende Kst*, i (1918), pp. 137–46

H. Salmonson: 'Ter herdenking van Paul Bromberg' [In memory of Paul Bromberg], *Goed Wonen*, ii (1949), p. 64

M. Teunissen: *Paul Bromberg (1893–1949): Binnenhuisarchitect en publicist* [Paul Bromberg (1893–1949): Interior designer and publicist] (Rotterdam, 1987)

MONIQUE D. J. M. TEUNISSEN

Bromide print. *See under* PHOTOGRAPHY, §I.

Bromley. English family of artists. William Bromley (*b* Carisbrooke, Isle of Wight, 1769; *d* 24 Nov 1842) exhibited paintings as a young man and engraved plates for Thomas Macklin's Bible (1800). He is best known for his engraved portraits, of which there are more than 50. He was commissioned by the print-seller John Boydell to engrave (1812) for £800 Arthur William Devis's *Death of Nelson* (exh. RA 1809; London, N. Mar. Mus.). In 1818 he engraved a fine full-length portrait after Lawrence of *Arthur Wellesley, 1st Duke of Wellington* (1814–15; Windsor Castle, Berks, Royal Col.), which was admired by the painter, and in 1819 became an associate engraver of the Royal Academy. He spent several years making engravings (exh. RA 1822–35) of the Elgin Marbles, after drawings by George Corbould, for the trustees of the British Museum, London. His son John Charles Bromley (*b* 1795; *d* 3 April 1839) executed some large plates, notably one (1830) after George Hayter's *Trial of Lord William Russell* (1825; Woburn Abbey, Beds) and another (1837) after Benjamin Robert Haydon's *Reform Banquet* (London, N.P.G.), which he published himself. James Bromley (*b* 1800; *d* London, 12 Dec 1838), son of William Bromley, engraved portraits and some large plates, including that after Hayter's *Trial of Queen Caroline* (London, N.P.G.). Frederick Bromley (*fl* 1832–70), son of William Bromley, engraved mezzotints of sporting subjects and portraits, executing some ambitious group portraits that include *Peninsular Heroes* (1847), a mixed media print after John Prescott Knight (1803–81).

BIBLIOGRAPHY

DNB; O'Donoghue

A. Graves: *The Royal Academy of Arts: A Complete Dictionary of Contributors and their Work*, i (London, 1905), pp. 295–8

R. Engen: *Dictionary of Victorian Engravers* (Cambridge, 1979), pp. 34–5

DAVID ALEXANDER

Bromley, Walter Davenport. *See* DAVENPORT BROMLEY, WALTER.

Bromoil print. *See under* PHOTOGRAPHY, §I.

Brompton, Richard (*b c.* 1734; *d* St Petersburg, 1783). English painter. He trained in London with Benjamin Wilson before going to Rome in 1757, where he studied with Anton Raphael Mengs. In Rome he met Charles Compton, 7th Earl of Northampton, who paid him an allowance and in Venice in 1763 introduced him to Edward Augustus, Duke of York. The Duke commissioned a conversation piece of himself and his travelling companions (version, 1764; London, Kew Pal., Royal Col.). The figures are awkwardly posed, but the polished elegance of each shows the influence of Mengs. In 1765 Brompton returned to London with Nathaniel Dance and established a good practice with small-scale works in the manner of Johann Zoffany, such as *William Pitt, 1st Earl of Chatham* (1772; Chevening, Kent), which exists in several versions. He also produced portraits on a larger scale, including the enormous *Henry Dawkins with his Family* (1773; Over Norton Hall, Oxon). He was also active as a restorer, doing some poor work in 1773–4 on Anthony van Dyck's *Earl of Pembroke with his Family* (Wilton House, Wilts).

Brompton exhibited at the Society of Artists between 1767 and 1777 and again in 1780 (when he was elected its President). He also exhibited at the Free Society in 1767–8 and at the Royal Academy in 1772, when he showed companion portraits of *George, Prince of Wales* (later George IV) and *Frederick, Duke of York* (1771; both British Royal Col.); despite their formal dress and pose, the royal children are depicted with freshness and charm. In 1780 Brompton was imprisoned for debt but was released when Catherine II of Russia invited him to St Petersburg, where he was employed as a court portrait painter.

BIBLIOGRAPHY

Waterhouse: *18th C.*

W. T. Whitley: *Artists and their Friends in England*, 2 vols (London, 1928)

HUGH BELSEY

Bromwich, Thomas K. (*d* 1787). English paper-stainer and upholsterer. He traded in London at the sign of the Golden Lion, Ludgate Hill. His trade card dated 1748 indicates that he supplied upholstery materials ('Chints's, Callicoes, Cottons, Needlework & Damasks'), screens, window-blinds, table-covers and wallpapers. Later commissions include papier-mâché, gilding and the supply of mirrors and girandoles. Bromwich took partners, and the business is described as Thomas Bromwich & Leonard Leigh (1758–65), Bromwich & Isherwood (1766) and Bromwich, Isherwood & Bradley (1770–88). He became Master of the Painter-Stainers' Company in 1761 and two years later received a royal appointment as Paper-hanging Maker in Ordinary to the Great Wardrobe. Horace William Walpole, 4th Earl of Orford, obtained 'new furniture wallpapers' from Bromwich in 1754. Between July 1766 and September 1768 goods including wallpaper and papier-mâché were supplied for the decoration of Shelburne House, Berkeley Square, London. Outside London, Bromwich worked for John Bligh, 3rd Earl of Darnley (*d* 1781), at Cobham Hall, Kent, where the Chinese paper he supplied in 1773 is *in situ*. A papier-mâché ceiling supplied by Bromwich for Dunster Castle, Somerset, still exists. Other clients included Sir Matthew Fetherstonhaugh of Uppark, W. Sussex (1748–54), James West of Alscot Park, Warwicks (1762), Charles Long of Saxmundham, Suffolk (1769), Paul Methuen of Corsham Court, Wilts (1770–73), Edward Morant of Brockenhurst Park, Hants (1773), and Sir Edward Knatchbull (1704–89) of Mersham-le-Hatch, Kent. Bromwich's name appears in the accounts for Holkham Hall, Norfolk, and as a supplier to the London designer and cabinetmaker John Linnell (i).

BIBLIOGRAPHY

A. Heal: *London Furniture Makers from the Restoration to the Victorian Era, 1660–1840* (London, 1953)

E. A. Entwisle: *The Book of Wallpaper* (London, 1954)

G. Beard and C. Gilbert, eds: *Dictionary of English Furniture Makers, 1660–1840* (London, 1986)

BRIAN AUSTEN

Bronchorst [Bronckhorst], van. Dutch family of artists.

(1) Jan (Gerritsz.) van Bronchorst (*b* Utrecht, *c.* 1603; *d* Amsterdam, before 22 Dec 1661). Glass painter, etcher and painter. Son of a gardener, he was apprenticed aged 11 to the Utrecht glass painter Jan Verburch (*fl* early 17th century). He also studied in Arras with the otherwise unidentified Pieter Mathys. From Arras he went to Paris to work with Chamu (*fl* 1585–early 17th century), one of the leading glass painters there. After his return to the Netherlands he became a citizen of Utrecht and worked both as a glass painter and as a designer of coats of arms for tapestries and seals. In 1622 he married Catalijntje van Noort. By this time he was taking lessons in the workshop of Gerrit van Honthorst, a leading member of the UTRECHT CARAVAGGISTI. In the 1630s he produced etchings after Cornelis van Poelenburch and later also after his own designs. The *Siege of Breda* (1637), printed from six plates, is a high point of his graphic work.

Van Bronchorst subsequently concentrated on oil painting, though continuing to work as a glass painter, and in 1639 he became a member of the Utrecht Guild of St Luke. His earliest dated oil painting, the *Idolatry of Solomon* (1642; Greenville, SC, Bob Jones U. Gal. Sacred A.), is notable for combining Flemish and Utrecht sources. The theatrical composition clearly relies on martyrdom scenes in the tradition of Veronese and Peter Paul Rubens, while the combination of contrasting areas of shadow and light with cool colouring is reminiscent of the work of van Honthorst as well as that of Hendrick ter Brugghen, whose painterly approach and fluent brushwork seem to have served as an example for van Bronchorst. A compositional type exploited by van Bronchorst throughout his career is that of the *Music-making Party on a Balcony* (e.g. 1646; Utrecht, Cent. Mus.), in which the figures are seen illusionistically from below, set against a classicizing architectural background; the result is a friezelike decorative composition, unlike the rough genre scenes of the Utrecht Caravaggisti. He did, however, follow his fellow Utrecht painters in incorporating life-size figures in pastoral costumes into his history paintings and genre scenes. The plump proportions and round faces of these figures give the pictures a provincial charm. There are only a few known portraits, painted in a style indebted to van Honthorst and Paulus Moreelse.

From 1647 van Bronchorst received major commissions for monumental glass windows in Amsterdam. The fame of his four windows in the Nieuwe Kerk was widespread, but the only surviving part is a section from the north transept window depicting the *Donation of the Amsterdam City Coat of Arms by Count Willem IV*. In its illusionistic portrayals and the modelling of the figures by means of an accentuated chiaroscuro, this window resembles the style of his oil paintings. One drawing survives for a window (destr.) in the Amsterdam Oude Kerk (1656; Amsterdam, Gemeente Archf). Due to the increasing number of such commissions he moved, *c.* 1650, to Amsterdam, where he became a citizen in 1652.

In Amsterdam, van Bronchorst continued to be successful and was involved in the most important contemporary decorative painting schemes. In 1655 he decorated the shutters of the new organ in the Nieuwe Kerk with scenes from the *Life of King David*. His experience in mastering monumental picture areas in his glass paintings was put to good use in these exceptionally large works. The main scene, the *Anointment of David* (1655), despite its impressive size and magnificent colouring is an incoherent composition, consisting of figural motifs taken largely from works by Veronese and Titian. His works for the Amsterdam Stadhuis (now the Royal Palace) show a similarly eclectic classicism. In 1659 he signed his last major work, *Moses Appointing Judges over the People of Israel*, which was installed above one of the fireplaces in the council chamber (*raadzaal*). In 1660 he was asked by the civic commissioners to improve this enormous work but by then was suffering from a severe illness that probably prevented him from doing so.

(2) Johannes (Jansz.) van Bronchorst (*b* Utrecht, *bapt* 21 Aug 1627; *d* Amsterdam, *bur* 16 Oct 1656). Painter, son of (1) Jan (Gerritsz.) van Bronchorst. Johannes and his younger brother Gerrit (Jansz.) van Bronchorst (*b* Utrecht, *c.* 1636; *bur* Utrecht, 1 April 1673), who later worked in the style of Cornelis van Poelenburch, travelled together to Rome, where Johannes is documented between 1648 and 1650. There he developed a cool, academic style, which he combined with Caravaggesque light effects. Closest to the work of Caravaggio is his *St Bartholomew* (1652; Vaduz, Samml. Liechtenstein). The influence of his father is perhaps most obvious in *Bathsheba with David's Letter* (Rome, Pal. Barberini). Its composition of figures seen from below was inspired by Jan Gerritsz.'s balcony scenes, but the darker colouring, the elegantly elongated proportions and the contemplative air of his figures distinguish the work from that of his father, as does the different style of his signature. In Rome and later in Amsterdam, he was regarded as the creator of particularly refined portraits, in which the sitters are so stylized as to be lifeless (e.g. *Nicolaes Oetgens van Waveren*; 1656; Amsterdam, Hist. Mus.).

Johannes returned to the Netherlands *c.* 1652 and collaborated with his father on larger projects, including the decoration of the Amsterdam Stadhuis, where he painted the ceiling of the Burgomaster's chamber with *Allegories of the Powers of the Burgomaster* (1655–6). The magnificent *Allegory of Dawn and Night* (Hartford, CT, Wadsworth Atheneum), long considered the work of his father, must be regarded as Johannes's masterpiece. Strongly influenced by contemporary Italian sources and by van Poelenburch, the two-tiered composition depicts Aurora and her attendants hovering in a dark cloud above the bearded figure of Tithonus and two river gods, who are seated in a hazy golden landscape reminiscent of those painted by Dutch Italianate artists. Johannes left a small oeuvre of impressive quality, which anticipated the endeavours of the following generation of Dutch classicists, such as Gérard de Lairesse. By the 18th century, however, he had been forgotten, and until the mid-1980s his works were wrongly attributed to his father.

BIBLIOGRAPHY

Hollstein: *Dut. & Flem.*

S. Colvin: 'Drie brieven van Jan Gerritsz. van Bronchorst', *Oud-Holland*, iv (1886), pp. 212–13

A. van der Boom: 'Monumentale glasschilderkunst in Zuid- en Noord Nederland in de zeventiende eeuw', *Kunstgeschiedenis der Nederlanden*, iii, ed. J. Duverger (Utrecht, 1956), pp. 239–47

G. J. Hoogewerff: 'Jan Gerritsz. en Jan Jansz. van Bronchorst: Schilders van Utrecht', *Oud-Holland*, lxxiv (1959), pp. 139–60

J. R. Judson: 'Allegory of Dawn and Night', *Wadsworth Atheneum Bull.*, vi/2 (1966), pp. 1–11

B. J. Buchbinder-Green: *The Painted Decorations of the Town Hall of Amsterdam* (diss., Evanston, Northwestern U., 1974, microfilm, Ann Arbor, 1975), pp. 92–3, 112, 125–6, 132–4

Holländische Malerei in neuem Licht: Hendrick ter Brugghen und seine Zeitgenossen (exh. cat., ed. A. Blankert and L. J. Slatkes; Utrecht, Cent. Mus.; Brunswick, Herzog Anton Ulrich-Mus.; 1986–7), pp. 236–44

T. Döring: 'Caravaggeske Aspekte im Werk Johannes van Bronchorsts', *Hendrik ter Brugghen und die Nachfolger Caravaggios in Holland: Beiträge eines Symposions im Herzog Anton Ulrich-Museum Braunschweig 1987*, ed. R. Klessmann (Brunswick, 1988), pp. 155–65

——: 'Between Caravaggism and Classicism: Bathsheba by Jan Gerritsz. and Johannes van Bronchorst', *Hoogsteder-Naumann Mercury*, vii (1988), pp. 51–67

——: *Studien zur Künstlerfamilie van Bronchorst* (Alfter, 1993)

THOMAS DÖRING

Bronckorst [Bronckhorst; van Bronckhorst; van Brounckhorst; van Brounckhurst], **Arnold** [Arthur] (*fl* 1566–86). Netherlandish painter, active in England and Scotland. He was one of the first painters to introduce a relatively sophisticated, European mode of portraiture into Scotland. His early career in England is only vaguely known, beginning with a reference to a portrait of *Sir Henry Sidney* (1529–86) in 1566. Also from his English years is his one fully signed and dated work, a portrait of *Oliver, 1st Baron St John of Bletso* (1578; priv. col.; see 1975 exh. cat., no. 7). Bronckorst was an associate and friend of the miniaturist Nicholas Hilliard, and this portrait in particular bears some resemblance to the latter's work, especially in the sensitivity to the nuances of personality. Bronckorst first travelled to Scotland as Hilliard's agent in order to prospect for gold. This endeavour was carried out in association with another painter, Cornelius de Vos (or Devosse), about whom nothing else is known. Although Bronckorst had some success in the search, he was prevented by the Regent, James, 4th Earl of Morton, from exporting the gold. As a result, he was forced to enter the royal service as a painter and is recorded in April 1580 as having painted a number of unspecified portraits for the Scottish king James VI.

The work expected of Bronckorst encompassed both miniatures and life-size portraits. In September 1580 he was paid for three recently completed portraits: one of the King's tutor George Buchanan (*c.* 1506–82), a full-length of the King and another of the King 'fram the belt upward'. This last is probably the small half-length portrait (*James VI Holding a Hawk*, Edinburgh, N.P.G.), formerly in the collection of King Charles I. The King, who carries a sparrow-hawk on his wrist, has a childlike appearance that has led some writers to date it to the early 1570s, thus implying an earlier visit by Bronckorst to Scotland, and this possibility cannot be entirely ruled out. A portrait of *James, 2nd Earl of Arran* (priv. col.) that is similar to the portrait of the King in a number of respects, although on a larger scale, is dated 1578 and does seem to suggest activity in Scotland before the first documentary reference to his presence. There is also a portrait of about the same date (and certainly no later than 1581, when the sitter was executed) of the *Earl of Morton* (Edinburgh, N.P.G.), with whom he had negotiated, unsuccessfully, for the removal of his gold. It is close in style to these works, with elements of Netherlandish Mannerism both in its drawing and in its elaborate interior setting with a landscape beyond. In 1581 Bronckorst was granted an official post at the court. He seems to have returned to London late in 1583 when, described as a 'Dutch painter', he is recorded as living in the city. Confusingly, his name is given as 'Arthur', which is also the name used in the near-contemporaneous description of his gold-prospecting activities. The name 'Arnold', however, is regularly used in the Scottish Treasurer's records and is likely to be the correct one. A child by his wife Sara was born in 1586, but there is no further evidence of his work as a painter.

BIBLIOGRAPHY

E. Auerbach: *Tudor Artists* (London, 1954), pp. 151–2

R. Strong: *The English Icon* (London, 1969), pp. 135–8

The Elizabethan Image (exh. cat. by R. Strong, London, Tate, 1969), pp. 136–7

Painting in Scotland, 1570–1650 (exh. cat. by D. Thomson, Edinburgh, N.P.G., 1975), pp. 22–4

M. Edmund: *Hilliard and Oliver* (London, 1983), pp. 55–7

DUNCAN THOMSON

Brongniart, Alexandre-Théodore (*b* Paris, 15 Feb 1739; *d* Paris, 6 June 1813). French architect. He was educated at the Collège de Beauvais and at the Ecole des Beaux-Arts, Paris, where he studied (*c.* 1760) under Jacques-François Blondel and Etienne-Louis Boullée. He never won the Prix de Rome, however, nor did he study in Italy, but in the 1770s he became one of the most fashionable architects of town houses (*hôtels particuliers*) in Paris, particularly in the northern part of the Chaussée d'Antin quarter and south of Les Invalides, which he helped develop as smart residential areas. His success was largely the result of the patronage of Louis-Philippe I, 4th Duc d'Orléans (1725–85), and Louis-Philippe's rival the Prince de Condé; this patronage began after the Marquise de Montesson, mistress to the Duc d'Orléans (after 1773 his wife), inherited the Marquis's fortune in 1769 and commissioned Brongniart to build her a house (destr.; drawing, Paris, Carnavalet). The result was a relatively modest hôtel just east of the Rue de la Chaussée d'Antin, recalling the early work of Boullée.

In 1773 Brongniart designed a large house in the Rue de Provence, adjacent to the Hôtel de Montesson, for the Duke of Orléans; it was executed, with major modifications, by Henri Piètre, architect to the Orléans family. The building was not unlike a country house in character and scale: Brongniart's design was organized around a large oval courtyard leading to a theatre on one side and the house on the other, the latter with a circular salon and curved galleries overlooking a formal garden. In the later 1770s Brongniart built a series of large stable blocks opposite the entrance to the duke's house. During the same period he built several other houses in the northeast of Paris, including one in the Rue de Richelieu for Taillepied de Bondy, the Receveur des Finances for Auch. In 1775 he began work on the Hôtel Massais, Rue de la

Chaussée d'Antin, and the hôtel owned by Claude-Pierre-Maximilien Radix de Saint-Foix, which had a square plan divided into nine compartments. A pair of side wings loosely abutted the *corps de logis*.

The Hôtel de Monaco (1774–7), in the Rue St Dominique, was commissioned by the Prince de Condé for his mistress, Mary Catherine Grimaldi (*d* 1813), Princess of Monaco. The building was articulated inside and out by an order of pilasters with a central curved portico, but it has been severely impaired by 19th-century embellishments. For Louise de Condé, the Prince's daughter, Brongniart was commissioned to design an hôtel (1781) in Rue Monsieur, south-east of Les Invalides; this is a building of great simplicity, the façades of which are ornamented only with rustication.

One of Brongniart's best-known buildings is the Capuchin monastery of St Louis d'Antin (1779–82; now the Lycée Condorcet) in the Rue des Capuchins, Chaussée d'Antin, the first of his larger buildings in Paris. Its stark Neo-classicism, reflecting the influence of Boullée as well as the austerity of the Order, contrasts with the more ornate classicism of his earlier works. The rusticated street elevation is bare save for a few niches and a central portico flanked by Tuscan columns. Pedimented end pavilions front the church and conventual buildings. Inside, a central courtyard is surrounded by cloister walks with baseless Tuscan columns. In 1785 Brongniart took over from Boullée the work on the stables and observatory of Anges-Jacques Gabriel's Ecole Militaire, which he finished the following year. He also took over as architect and supervisor at Les Invalides, although his practice continued to be mainly in town houses. His subsequent work in Paris included the Archives of the Chevaliers de St Lazare (1787), Rue Monsieur; the Maison Chamblin (1789) in the Rue Plumet; and the Théâtre Louvois (1791; destr.), which had a brick façade of Neo-classical severity, with identical frameless arched windows articulating the first and second floors above a balcony resting on eight Tuscan columns.

With the outbreak of the French Revolution, Brongniart lost his posts at the Ecole Militaire and Les Invalides and took refuge in Bordeaux, where he supervised the décor for revolutionary festivals. He returned to Paris in 1795 and was rapidly elected to the Conseil des Bâtiments Civils and appointed consultant to the Panthéon, but after losing these posts he turned in 1800 to designing porcelain and furniture. He was employed by the Sèvres porcelain factory and designed the 'Table des Maréchaux' (1808; London, Buckingham Pal., Royal Col.), made for Napoleon. In 1804, he was appointed Chief of Public Works, Paris, in which capacity he designed the layout of Père-Lachaise Cemetery (1805; for illustration *see* CEMETERY) and the Bourse (1808–13; much altered). The Bourse, which is his most famous work in Paris, is again different in style from his earlier works. The revolutionary simplicity of the Capuchin monastery and the Théâtre Louvois was replaced by the decorative pomp of a Corinthian peristyle in a manner that conformed to Napoleon's taste for Classical temples. Inside, a top-lit central hall is surrounded by two tiers of arcaded galleries giving on to offices and reception rooms. Brongniart was buried in the cemetery that he had helped to create as a public park as well as a necropolis.

WRITINGS
Plans du Palais de la Bourse de Paris et du cimetière Mont-Louis (Paris, 1814)

BIBLIOGRAPHY
J. S. de Sacy: *Alexandre Théodore Brongniart* (Paris, 1940)
R. Rosenblum: *Transformations in Late Eighteenth Century Art* (Princeton, 1967)
W. G. Kalnein and M. Levey: *Art and Architecture of the Eighteenth Century in France*, Pelican Hist. A. (Harmondsworth, 1972)
S. Eriksen: *Early Neoclassicism in France* (1974)
A. Braham: *The Architecture of the French Enlightenment* (London, 1980, 2/1989)
D. D. Egbert: *The Beaux-art Tradition in French Architecture* (Princeton, 1980)
Alexandre-Théodore Brongniart, 1739–1813: Architecture et décor (exh. cat., Paris, Carnavalet, 1986)

Bronze. Alloy of copper and tin. In the West bronze was largely superseded by BRASS, the alloy of copper and zinc, by the 5th century AD; many brass artworks, however, are commonly described as 'bronze'. In early times most languages had just one term for copper and copper alloys, thus for example the Chinese had the word *tang*, the Tibetans *li*, the Greeks *khalkos* and the Romans *aes*. (For copper–zinc alloys produced by cementation (*see* BRASS, §II) the Greeks had the term *oreikhalkos* and the Romans the related term *aurichalcum*, but these were not often used in general literature.) The equivalent Anglo-Saxon general term was 'brass', and up to the 17th century this simply meant copper or one of its alloys. Various terms for copper–zinc alloys, such as *latten* and *maslin*, were in use in the late medieval and early post-medieval periods (see Blair and Blair, pp. 81–106). At about this time the term *bronzo* came into use in Italy, specifically for the copper alloys used in the ancient world. In particular, it was applied to the corroded, copper-base metals of the antiquities that were being dug up in Italy. These had an attractive patina, which was held to be due to some lost alloy. Much of this Classical metalwork was of copper alloyed with tin, whereas in Renaissance Italy copper alloyed with zinc was prevalent. Thus, the quite accidental association of bronze with patinated metal and of brass with a bright, clean finish was established.

By the time the word 'bronze' entered the English language, sometime in the late 17th century or the early 18th, it was associated with decorative or art metalwork, especially ancient metalwork and thus, by implication, with copper–tin alloys, while the term 'brass' continued to be used for everyday metalwork, which tended to be of copper and zinc. However, as late as the mid-18th century Samuel Johnson still regarded the two words as synonymous when he compiled his *Dictionary*. Only in the 19th century did engineers and metallurgists (and the *Oxford English Dictionary*) specify that bronze was an alloy of copper and tin, and brass an alloy of copper and zinc.

Popular usage, however, continued to apply the terms quite loosely. Bronze still tends to be the slightly more prestigious word, used for copper-based metals that are obviously old, patinated or decorative; whereas brass tends to be used for bright, shiny, utilitarian, obviously new items, regardless of composition. In truth, without analysis it is impossible to tell which has been used, so there is perhaps a strong case for retaining the more general usage of the term bronze.

This article discusses the early history of copper alloys and bronze in the West, and its development elsewhere. Further information on the use of bronze is given in the metalwork sections of individual country and regional surveys in this dictionary. *See also* COPPER, §2(ii), for the use of bronze in architecture.

BIBLIOGRAPHY
C. Blair and L. Blair: 'Copper Alloys', *English Medieval Industries*, ed. J. Blair and N. Ramsay (London, 1991), pp. 81–106

I. Properties. II. Technical history.

I. Properties.

The colour of bronze depends on the tin content. It ranges from an attractive golden shade with *c.* 5% tin, to a steely grey when the tin exceeds 20%. The metal is easy to cast but suffers from problems of segregation and sweating (*see* METAL, §III). The hardness of the alloy increases with the tin content. With up to *c.* 10% tin the metal may be safely cold-worked, with periodic annealing, hence the popularity of this alloy range for hammered bronzes in antiquity. As the tin content increases, so the danger of cracking increases, and with more than 15% tin it is not possible to carry out cold work. When the tin content exceeds 20% the metal becomes extremely brittle. However, bronzes containing 20–25% tin may be satisfactorily hot-worked (*see* §II below).

BIBLIOGRAPHY
R. Chadwick: 'The Effect of Composition and Constitution on the Working and on Some Physical Properties of Tin Bronzes', *J. Inst. Metals*, lxiv (1939), pp. 331–47
D. Hanson and W. T. Pell-Walpole: *Chill Cast Bronzes* (London, 1951)
A. R. Bailey: *A Textbook of Metallurgy* (London, 1964)

II. Technical history.

1. Early history. 2. The Classical world. 3. China and South-east Asia. 4. Indian subcontinent. 5. West Africa. 6. Special bronzes.

1. EARLY HISTORY. Copper and lead had been used on a limited scale from the inception of the Neolithic period in the 8th millennium BC. However, for almost the first half of this immensely long era, metal was insignificant both economically and artistically, limited to what has been called 'trinket technology' (Moorey, 1988). It was not until the later 4th millennium BC that metal tools, weapons and ceremonial items rapidly became common throughout the eastern Mediterranean and the Middle East. An important reason for this may well have been the introduction of alloying.

Copper, which is rather viscous when molten, is quite difficult to cast satisfactorily, and it is rather soft, making it unlikely to retain an edge (*see* COPPER, §1), but these properties can be improved by the addition of arsenic. Smelting of copper ores rich in arsenic may have resulted in a natural alloy, and certainly from the end of the 4th millennium BC arsenical copper became quite common. The attractive silvery colour of the arsenical copper may also have been desirable.

Although arsenical copper was eventually supplanted by tin bronze, it is by no means certain that it pre-dates bronze: the use of both metals seems to have begun in the later 4th millennium BC. Around 3000 BC copper–lead alloys were briefly in vogue for castings, and it is likely that it was the adoption of the concept of alloying, rather than any one alloy, that caused the rapid expansion of

metal usage. Tin bronze held obvious advantages over arsenical copper, which was made from smelting arsenic-rich copper ores or by adding arsenic minerals to molten copper. Since it was impossible to prepare metallic arsenic, and because of the great volatility of arsenic in the molten copper, it was difficult to effect any sort of quality control. These problems were further compounded by the great variation in the properties of the alloy over a small composition range. Finally, there was the toxicity of the arsenic fumes. By contrast, metallic tin was easy to smelt from its ores, and precise alloys could be easily formed by mixing two weighed quantities of the two metals.

Why then was arsenical copper more prevalent until at least the 2nd millennium BC? The answer is simple: copper ores are frequently associated with arsenic minerals but rarely with tin, and exploitable tin deposits are quite rare. There are no significant sources within the Mediterranean region or the Middle East; the nearest are in south-west Britain, Central Europe, east Asia, South-east Asia and Nigeria, all far too distant to have played any part in the inception of Middle Eastern bronze metallurgy. Indeed, the vexed question of the source of the tin in the earliest Middle Eastern bronzes was only resolved in the 1980s with the discovery of tin deposits in Afghanistan and, even more important, the discovery of a tin mine at Kestel in central Turkey, dating from the 3rd millennium BC. By the mid-3rd millennium BC tin bronze was becoming quite common from the Aegean and the Troad through to Mesopotamia, notably at Ur and Iran. The tin must have come from such sources as Kestel, within the region where metallurgy was already practised.

By the end of the 3rd millennium BC metallurgy had developed through much of Europe and also in China and South-east Asia, and therefore the major tin fields were potentially available. In these areas, tin bronze rapidly became prevalent: in Britain, for example, after a very brief 'copper age', bronze became almost universal from *c.* 2000 BC. By contrast, in the Mediterranean region and the Middle East, which lacked major indigenous tin sources, the change from arsenical copper to tin bronze was much more gradual, extending through the 2nd millennium BC.

Occasionally the availability of the two distinct metals, silvery arsenical copper and golden bronze, was used to create polychromy. The superb lions from the temple at Tell al-Ubaid (mid-3rd millennium BC; London, BM) have heads wrought from arsenical copper and bodies of bronze hammered over bitumen cores. Unfortunately, the metal is totally corroded, but the original polychromy, together with the eyes inlaid with stone, must have been striking.

By the mid-2nd millennium BC, bronze metallurgy was well developed in southern China and South-east Asia (*see* §3 below). Excavations carried out at Ban Chiang and other sites in north-east Thailand in the 1960s and 1970s revealed bronze artefacts in association with highly sophisticated ceramics, including spear points, socketed tools, bracelets, pins and other ornaments.

At this time, in both Mycenaean Greece and China, lead began to be added to bronze casting alloys. The lead lowered the melting point of the alloy and made the molten metal more fluid. This was a great advantage in casting, as the metal flowed more easily through the mould, filling all the details and enabling quite intricate patterning—for example that worked on the moulds of the early Chinese bronzes—to be picked up accurately. Through the 1st millennium BC leaded bronze became quite prevalent for cast-bronze work, especially when large supplies of cheap lead became available in Greece and the Middle East as a by-product of smelting silver for coinage.

Together with the developments in alloying, rapid improvements in casting, joining and metalworking techniques took place from about the 4th millennium BC. Thus, the sophisticated technique of lost-wax casting seems to have originated at that time, as demonstrated by an unused clay mould for making a lost-wax casting of an axehead from Poliochni, on the Aegean island of Lemnos. Of similar date is the extraordinary hoard of metalwork found at Nahal Mishmar in the hills above the Dead Sea. It contained several hundred maceheads, sceptres and crowns (Jerusalem, Israel Mus.; see SYRIA-PALESTINE, fig. 3), which were mainly lost-wax castings of a complex copper–antimony–arsenic alloy. Even more extraordinary than the number of objects and the weight of metal is the advanced nature of the technique: many of the sceptre shafts were hollow castings, and the maceheads were cast around clay cores. Clearly, the technique of hollow casting around a core supported from the walls of the outer mould by chaplets (see METAL, §III) was fully understood by this date. The quantity of cast decorative and ritual metalwork in the Nahal Mishmar hoard is exceptional, but it is clear from other finds that arsenical copper and bronze had always been cast for decorative fittings, ritual items, jewellery and small sculpture, as well as for tools and weapons. In addition, there is evidence of major work in sheet-metal hammered over wooden or bitumen formers. The spectacular finds from the Royal Graves at Alaca Höyük in central Anatolia, dating from the mid-3rd millennium BC, include complex bronze standards (for illustration see ALACA HÖYÜK) and finely modelled figures of deer, inlaid with precious metals (see ANATOLIA, ANCIENT, fig. 8), which are accomplished works by any standard.

This was the period of the rise of the great civilizations in Mesopotamia. The grave goods from the Royal Cemetery at Ur contain a comprehensive range of bronze and copper tools, weapons, vessels and ornaments, and contemporary Early Dynastic copper figurines made by the lost-wax technique are known from elsewhere in Mesopotamia. Towards the end of the 3rd millennium BC the Akkadians produced some excellent hollow lost-wax castings, including the material from Diyala region and the male head from Nineveh known as the 'Head of Sargon' (Baghdad, Iraq Mus.; see AKKADIAN, fig. 2). The detail on this head is very fine: there is evidence of tool marks left by finishing work after casting, but most of the detail was crisply reproduced from the mould.

Other techniques of working bronze were also developed in this period. Quite proficient bronze vessels were raised by hammering, and some even had handles or lugs attached by tin solder. Thus, by the end of the 3rd millennium BC, bronze was firmly established throughout the Middle East, the eastern Mediterranean and beyond, utilizing such sophisticated processes as lost-wax and hollow casting, polychromy, raising and soldering to produce artefacts that rival those of later civilizations.

Ornaments and tools of copper, bronze and other alloys also formed a significant part of New World technology in the high civilizations of the Andean areas from the 1st millennium BC (although goldworking dates from the 2nd millennium BC) and of Mesoamerica from the 9th century AD (see SOUTH AMERICA, PRE-COLUMBIAN, §VIII, 5, and MESOAMERICA, PRE-COLUMBIAN, §IX, 5).

See also MESOPOTAMIA, §IV, and PREHISTORIC EUROPE, §§V, 3, and VI, 3(ii).

BIBLIOGRAPHY

F. Heger: *Alte Metalltrommeln aus Südostasien* (Leipzig, 1902)
S. Lloyd: *Early Highland Peoples of Anatolia* (London, 1967)
K. Branigan: *Aegean Metalwork of the Early and Middle Bronze Age* (Oxford, 1974)
P. T. Craddock: 'Deliberate Alloying in the Atlantic Bronze Age', *The Origins of Metallurgy in Atlantic Europe*, ed. M. Ryan (Dublin, 1978), pp. 369–85
H. McKerrell: 'Non-Dispersive XRF Applied to Ancient Metalworking in Copper and Tin Bronze', *PACT*, i (1978), pp. 138–73
P. Bar-Adon: *The Cave of the Treasure* (Jerusalem, 1980)
E. A. Braun-Holzinger: 'Figürliche Bronzen aus Mesopotamien', *Prähistorische Bronzefunde*, IV/i (Munich, 1984)
P. R. S. Moorey: *Materials and Manufacture in Ancient Mesopotamia*, Brit. Archaeol. Rep., Int. Ser., no. 237 (Oxford, 1985)
——: 'Early Metallurgy in Mesopotamia', *The Beginning of the Use of Metals and Alloys*, ed. R. Maddin (Cambridge, MA, 1988), pp. 28–33
J. D. Muhly: 'The Beginnings of Metallurgy in the Old World', *The Beginning of the Use of Metals and Alloys*, ed. R. Maddin (Cambridge, MA, 1988), pp. 2–20
K. A. Yenner and others: 'Kestel: An Early Bronze Age Source of Tin Ore in the Taurus Mountains, Turkey', *Science*, ccxliv (1989), pp. 200–03

2. THE CLASSICAL WORLD. The Minoans and Mycenaeans produced a wide range of bronzework on a considerable scale, as attested by the discovery of shipwrecks, for example those off southern Turkey at Cape Gelidonya and at Kaş, with cargoes that included several tonnes of copper and tin ingots. The range of Minoan bronzework included beaten bronze vessels and small statuettes for votive and probably purely ornamental use. The latter were usually solid cast by the lost-wax process and are rarely more than about 100 mm in their maximum dimension. These small figures, typically depicting bulls or humans (see MINOAN, fig. 18), seem to have been especially common in the Late Minoan period, but, following the collapse of the Minoan civilization, their production ceased in the Aegean world for several centuries, in common with that of other luxury items.

With the return of stability and prosperity in the 1st millennium BC the production of bronze decorative items was resumed, notably the elaborate bronze brooches and figurines of the Geometric period (see GREECE, ANCIENT, fig. 49). These were also solid lost-wax castings. The small quadrupeds often have their bodies hollowed out and open on the underside. It seems the craftsman modelled the wax around a wedge of clay, which remained exposed beneath. The wax and clay would then be invested with more clay, and the usual procedure of lost-wax casting followed. After the casting had cooled, the mould was broken away, and the clay wedge dug out. In the succeeding Archaic period of the 6th and 7th centuries BC, true hollow castings were made in which the clay core was totally encased inside the modelled wax and supported by chaplets.

From the Minoan period the Greeks had been skilled in hammered metalwork for vessels or even armour, as the extraordinary example from Dendra testifies (late 2nd millennium BC; see fig. 1). In the Geometric period large statuettes were made from sheet bronze riveted together on a wooden support. This technique was known by the Greeks as *sphyrelaton*, meaning 'wrought by hammering'. The first person to make major statues of bronze was said to be Daidalos of Crete. He may well be a mythical figure, but several large works dating from the 8th century BC have been found, for example at the Cretan shrine of Dreros (Herakleion, Archaeol. Mus.; for illustration *see* CULT STATUE). The body of the Dreros statue is very simplified, which possibly suggests the work of an armourer.

By the 7th century BC the technique of true hollow casting had been developed by the Greeks for life-size statues of both humans and animals. It is true that life-size statues had been made before, but not on a regular basis: such early examples as the statue of Pepy I of Egypt (*reg c.* 2289–*c.* 2256 BC; Cairo, Egypt. Mus.) are more famous for their early date and rarity than for any technical or artistic accomplishment. The popularity of bronze statuary among the Greeks gave rise to a level of technical excellence that has rarely been matched since, the greater naturalism and detail of depiction calling for extreme skill in both casting and finishing. Detailed studies of such masterpieces as the two 5th-century BC life-size warriors (Reggio Calabria, Mus. N.; *see* GREECE, ANCIENT, fig. 58) found in the sea off Riace, Calabria, and the excavation of workshops with casting pits in the Athenian Agora and at Olympia have shown in considerable detail exactly how the Greeks set about the casting of a large statue.

The technique of indirect lost-wax casting (*see* METAL, §III) was perfected by the Greeks and later adopted by the Romans; it changed very little until the late 20th century. A plaster cast was taken from the clay or wax original, and the plaster cut into sizes convenient for the production of moulds for casting by the lost-wax process. Such details and extremities as hands, long curls and even toes were often cast separately: a life-size statue could easily be made up of 30 or more components, but so carefully joined and finished afterwards that they appear as one casting. The sections seem to have been joined by pouring on bronze of a similar composition to the statue itself, so fusing the components together. The join would then have been carefully scraped, filed and polished on the outside, but the pours of metal remain visible on the inside. Casting faults in the main castings, for example where the metal failed to flow or where the mould was damaged, were cut out, and a rectangular patch inserted. Careful examination of Classical statuary can sometimes reveal dozens of these minor repairs, but they are so well worked and finished as to be almost invisible.

Classical bronzes are now usually covered by a uniform brown or green PATINA, but originally the bronze would have had more polychromy. The bronze itself would have been kept polished, and perhaps oiled to give it a lustrous hue, but such details as the lips and nipples were usually of red copper, and the teeth might be of silver, as on the

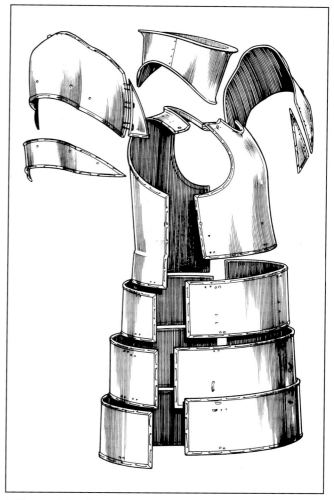

1. Hammered sheet-bronze suit of armour, Mycenaean, from Dendra, Greece, late 2nd millennium BC (Navplion, Archaeological Museum); reconstruction drawing

Riace bronzes. The eyes would have been made up of shell or stone, as for example on the life-size head of Augustus (late 1st century BC; London, BM) from Meroë in the Sudan, where even the inner corners of the eye are depicted with inlays of tiny fragments of red garnet.

Greek statues were, in general, never gilt, though a few were covered with gold foil, as evidenced by the grooves in the bronze into which the edges of the foils were hammered (e.g. the small head of Nike; late 5th century BC; Athens, Agora Mus.). According to Pliny (*Natural History* XXXIV.lxiii), even as late as the time of Nero (54–68 AD) gilded statues were not popular. However, in the later Roman Empire the taste for gilding grew, and statues were regularly gilt; the superb late Roman life-size statues of the four horses of S Marco, Venice, for example, were cast from almost pure copper to aid the process of mercury gilding (*see* GILDING, §I, 3). The date of the horses has long been the subject of debate, with suggestions that they could be Hellenistic. However, the fact that they were made of an alloy specifically to be gilded has helped to confirm that they are late Roman in date. After adorning the portico of S Marco for almost 800 years, the horses are now in the S Marco Museum, Venice.

The practice of adding lead to the bronze alloy became steadily more prevalent through the 1st millennium BC. The early Greek statues had been of unleaded bronze, but during the Hellenistic period lead began to be included, and the Romans almost universally added considerable quantities, typically 10–30%. This made the molten metal more fluid, enabling it to flow through narrow spaces, and the bronze in some Roman statues is as little as 20 mm thick. Although brass became steadily more common through the Roman period, largely superseding bronze by the 5th century, it was never used for statuary, an interesting example of artistic conservatism.

See also GREECE, ANCIENT, §IV, 1(iii), and ROME, ANCIENT, §IV, 1(iii).

BIBLIOGRAPHY

H. Maryon: 'Fine Metalwork', *A History of Technology*, ed. C. S. Singer and H. J. Plenderleits, i (Oxford, 1954, rev. 3/1957), pp. 623–62
J. Boardman: *The Cretan Collection in Oxford* (Oxford, 1961)
A. M. Snodgrass: *Greek Arms and Armour* (Edinburgh, 1964)
G. F. Bass: 'Cape Gelidonya: A Bronze Age Shipwreck', *Trans. Amer. Philos. Soc.*, vii (1967) [whole issue]
P. T. Craddock: 'The Composition of Copper Alloys Used by the Greek, Etruscan and Roman Civilisations', I', *J. Archaeol. Sci.*, iii (1976), pp. 93–113
W. A. Oddy, L. Borrelli Vlad and N. D. Meeks: 'The Gilding of Bronze Statues in the Greek and Roman World', *The Horses of San Marco*, ed. G. Perocco (London, 1979), pp. 182–6
C. C. Mattusch: *Bronzeworkers in the Athenian Agora* (Princeton, 1982)
E. Formigli: 'Due bronzi da Riace', *Boll. A.*, special ser., iii/1 (1984), pp. 107–42
G. F. Bass: 'Oldest Known Shipwreck Reveals Bronze Age Splendors', *N. Geog.*, clxxii (1987), pp. 693–734
W.-D. Heilmeyer and G. Zimmer: 'Die Bronzegiesserei unter der Werkstatt des Phidias in Olympia', *Olympiabericht*, ii (in preparation)

3. CHINA AND SOUTH-EAST ASIA. Research in northern China since the mid-1970s has revealed the slow development of metallurgy from the 4th millennium BC. Shortly after 2000 BC there arose in that region the remarkable Shang bronze-founding tradition, which was to shape the course of Chinese bronzeworking for millennia to come. The typical products of this industry were ornate and highly decorated ritual vessels cast in piece-moulds. The bronzes themselves have been extensively studied to discover how they were made, and from the 1930s bronze foundries were excavated at such ancient Shang-period settlements as Erlitou, Zhengzhou, Panlongcheng (Hubei Province) and, in particular, Anyang in northern China. The bronze alloy frequently contained considerable quantities of lead, which would have enabled the molten bronze to pick up the intricate detail on the moulds. The moulds were of fine loessic clay, which occurs all over northern China and may be said to be partially responsible for the development of the piece-moulding industry. This clay has the invaluable property that it does not distort or shrink on firing, which is essential if the assembled components of the piece-mould are to remain in accurate location after firing.

The basic form of the vessel was first made in wood or clay. Prepared clay was pressed against this to make a mould and then cut up and pulled away in sections (*see*

CHINA, figs 139 and 142). The intricate designs would be incised into the mould surface before the pieces were reassembled, fitting tightly together to form the moulds for the inside and outside of the vessel. The inner and outer moulds were separated by bronze or clay pegs. Pouring channels, risers and sprues were added, and the completed mould fired. Then, while the mould was still hot, the bronze was poured in. The resulting casting came from the mould virtually finished, complete with handles and all the decoration, requiring only a little cleaning up and polishing. Where the mould sections met there are sometimes seams into which the molten metal ran, and there is sometimes evidence of slight misalignment of two mould pieces on running or repeating patterns. The high tin and lead content of the bronze rendered it too brittle for extensive chiselling, and if the bronzes receive a sharp blow they tend to break rather than bend.

Lost-wax casting was introduced only during the 6th century BC. At first the technique appears to have been used in combination with the piece-mould method; sometimes precast appendages (e.g. handles) were produced by the lost-wax method and then soldered on to the main body. Large, flamboyant, openwork pieces (*see* CHINA, fig. 164) were produced in the state of Chu, south China, by this means. Later, during the 2nd century BC, complex three-dimensional scenes of figures, animals and architecture were similarly cast on the lids of large, drum-shaped containers in the kingdom of Dian in south-west China (*see* DIAN, fig. 1).

About 500 BC the bronze- and iron-using Dong Son culture developed in Yunnan and the Red River Valley area of northern Vietnam, which was then subject to the Chinese Han dynasty. The most characteristic products of this culture are single-ended, waisted drums in a bronze alloy containing a high proportion of lead and generally also a small quantity of iron, which are claimed to have been cast either in a stone mould or by the lost-wax method. Most of them have elaborate incised decoration. Dong Son drums and other bronze artefacts have been found throughout South-east Asia and were traded as far as New Guinea (*see also* SOUTH-EAST ASIA, §III).

In China bronze ritual vessels had lost their function as symbols of political authority by the Han period (206 BC–AD 220), and thereafter much of the production relied on the shapes and styles of earlier ages. However, production continued on a considerable scale, and with their superb furnace and mould technology the Chinese were able to produce bronze castings of a size and complexity that were not attained in Europe until the 18th and 19th centuries.

The early bronzes had relied extensively on cast detail for their decoration, but from the 6th century BC vessels were frequently inlaid with silver foil, or gilded and silvered to create polychrome work. During the Song (AD 960–1279) and Ming (1368–1644) periods archaistic bronzes were made with superb, chemically induced patinas, in imitation of those on the ancient bronzes recovered from subterranean tombs. Inlays of malachite and jade were also frequently added.

The alloys continued to be of leaded bronze apparently through to the end of the Ming period. They were then rapidly supplanted by brass, following the introduction of zinc smelting in China at the end of the 15th century (*see* BRASS, §II).

See also CHINA, §VI, 2.

BIBLIOGRAPHY
O. R. T. Janse: *The Ancient Dwelling Site of Dong-so'n (Thanh Hoa-Annam)*, iii of *Archaeological Research in Indo-China* (Bruges, 1958)
A. J. Bernet Kempers: *The Kettledrums of Southeast Asia: A Bronze Age World and its Aftermath* (Rotterdam, 1988)

For further bibliography *see* CHINA, §VI, 2.

4. INDIAN SUBCONTINENT. The use of copper can be traced back to the pre-Harappan settlements in Pakistan dating to the 4th–3rd millennia BC. Small but well-observed naturalistic statuettes in bronze (e.g. *Dancing Girl*; New Delhi, N. Mus.; *see* INDIAN SUBCONTINENT, fig. 130) made by the lost-wax method have been found at Mohenjo-daro and other sites of the Harappan civilization of 2500–1700 BC. Copper weapons dating from *c.* 1000 BC (e.g. New Delhi, N. Mus.) have been recovered from various sites in north India, but bronze sculptures are rare for a period of some 1000 years following the collapse of the Harappan civilization. Isolated finds include the cast figurines of an elephant, a rhinoceros, a buffalo and a chariot, all mounted on wheels, from Daimabad (Archaeol. Survey of India, on loan to Bombay, Prince of Wales Mus.). Together they weigh about 60 kg, and they are apparently prehistoric. Bronze statuettes seem to have become common again only in the early 1st millennium AD. They were produced in the north-west region of Gandhara, where a hellenizing influence can be seen in the style, and in other parts of India, where the style is purely Indian. By the Gupta period (4th–6th century AD) brass was already becoming the dominant alloy. The surviving pieces are mainly small, but examples such as the life-size statue of the Buddha (*c.* 7th century AD; Birmingham, Mus. & A.G.) found in the ruins of a monastery at Sultanganj in Bihar show that major castings could be performed. It is a lost-wax hollow casting of impure copper that was apparently cast in one piece and mercury gilded. The Chinese Buddhist monk Xuan Zang in his travels through north India in the 7th century AD recorded other monumental castings, including a statue of Buddha 31.5 m high at the monastery of Nalanda in Bihar.

The origins of bronzeworking in south India are not known, but by the mid-1st millennium BC quite sophisticated small decorative bronzes were being produced, as attested by the finds from Nagpur-culture burials at Adichanallur in the Tirunelveli District of Tamil Nadu. By the 1st millennium AD major castings existed of the full pantheon of Hindu deities. Many of these statues are of copper, which, as noted above, is rather viscous when molten, and perhaps for this reason the pieces were often solid cast and thus of enormous weight. The art of fine bronze-casting developed during the Chola period (9th–13th centuries), and from the 10th century many great masterpieces of near life-size figures were produced for Hindu temples.

The Chola bronzes were usually of leaded tin bronze, and the major figures were hollow castings. Although the aesthetic quality of the bronzes may have declined since the Chola period, the production of major pieces has continued apparently without interruption to the present day at such centres as Swamimalai in Tamil Nadu (see fig. 2), and government-sponsored schools of traditional image casting have been established at Mahabalaipuram,

2. Making the wax model for a bronze statue at Swamimalai, Tamil Nadu, South India, 1985

near Madras. The image is sculpted from a mixture of wax and a natural resin, *kunguliyam*. This has similar properties to wax alone, but is rather harder and stronger. The model is covered with a fine clay slip, and around that a stronger layer of clay, heavily tempered with rice husks, is built up. Even quite major figures are usually cast in one piece in a casting pit, with the metal poured from a series of crucibles in a carefully orchestrated sequence. After casting, the surface of the bronze is extensively worked with scraper and chisel, a process that sometimes lasts over a period of weeks, before the final polish is applied. The methods used at Swamimalai are close to those of the Chola period, though a little zinc is added to the bronze to help deoxidize the metal.

By contrast, the tradition in north India, Nepal and Tibet has always favoured brass. This difference is due to the proximity of the zinc sources in north India and the strong contacts between south India and the tin-producing lands in South-east Asia.

BIBLIOGRAPHY
P. Ray: *History of Chemistry in Ancient and Medieval India* (Calcutta, 1956)
C. Sivaramamurti: *South Indian Bronzes* (New Delhi, 1963)
M. V. Krishnan: *Cire Perdu Casting in India* (New Delhi, 1976)
P. T. Craddock: 'The Copper Alloys of Tibet and their Background', *Aspects of Tibetan Metallurgy*, ed. W. A. Oddy and W. Zwalf (London, 1981), pp. 1–36
D. P. Agrawal: *The Archaeology of India* (London, 1982)
B. Allchin and R. Allchin: *The Rise of Civilisation in India and Pakistan* (Cambridge, 1982)
B. A. Rathnasabapathy: *The Divine Bronzes* (Thanjavur, 1982)

5. WEST AFRICA. Although the bronzes of West Africa have been studied since the early 20th century, relatively

3. Bronze bowl, diam. 264 mm, cast by lost-wax process, complete with handles and decoration, excavated at Igbo-Ukwu, Nigeria, 10th century AD (Lagos, National Museum)

little is known of the origins and cultural affiliations of the various bronze- and brass-casting traditions. There was a proficient ironworking industry in West Africa from the late 1st millennium BC, but little evidence exists for copper- or bronzeworking, much less for a tradition of casting tools and weapons out of which a major art medium could grow. Yet the earliest dated pieces of art bronzework are among the most accomplished. These are the hundreds of ritual vessels and regalia found with a burial at Igbo-Ukwu in south-east Nigeria, dated by radiocarbon analysis to the 10th century AD (*see* IGBO-UKWU and figs 1 and 2). The vast majority are lost-wax (or, more probably, lost-latex) castings of bronze or leaded bronze. They are among the most inventive and technically accomplished bronzes ever made. Great vessels of 250–400 mm in diameter were cast in one, with walls never more than 1 or 2 mm thick, complete with handles and with each detail of the complex decorative scheme on the mould perfectly picked up by the metal (e.g. bronze bowl; Lagos, N. Mus.; see fig. 3). The apparent absence of a bronzeworking tradition leading up to this level of achievement, coupled with the mistaken belief that copper was not available in Nigeria, led many to believe that the metalworking skills, if not the metal itself, must have come from across the Sahara. Recent careful study of the Igbo bronzes has shown that the range of metalworking skills was actually very limited, and that the usual metalworking techniques of raising, soldering, riveting and wire-making were unknown to the Igbo smiths. Also, at the period when the Igbo bronzes were made, all the civilizations to the north of the Sahara were using brass. However, in the 1980s copper and lead sources with signs of early exploitation were identified in south-east Nigeria, and of course Nigeria is one of the world's major sources of tin. Thus the craft of bronze-casting is likely to be an indigenous development within West Africa.

The Igbo bronzes remain an isolated phenomenon at present, but several centuries later other major bronze-casting traditions were developing elsewhere in Nigeria, as exemplified by the hollow-cast, half life-size figure of a man (of unknown date; Lagos, N. Mus.) from Tada in central Nigeria made of impure copper. Although part of an isolated find, this too must stand at the head of a long tradition of casting technology. From Benin City in the Kingdom of Benin, west of the Niger River, a whole series of life-size, naturalistic bronze heads are known (also referred to as brass; *see* BENIN). The majority of the pieces are likely to predate 1600. These are lost-wax hollow castings with uniform thin walls, the clay cores held in place by iron chaplets, evidencing great technical skill.

These bronzes may well have been made from local metal (although not from the same source as the Igbo bronzes as the trace-element composition is different), but from the 12th century Arab caravans began to cross the Sahara bringing brass, which was certainly in use by the 15th century at Ife in southern Nigeria to cast the famous life-size heads found there (*see* IFE). At the end of the 15th century the first European vessels reached the West African coast, and within a short time enormous quantities of copper and brass were being imported into the hinterland of West Africa. This new supply of metal triggered a huge increase in the production of copper-alloy art metalwork all over West Africa, especially at

Benin, but at the expense of the local copper and lead industry, which seems to have died out completely, though tin production continued.

BIBLIOGRAPHY

T. Shaw: *Igbo-Ukwu* (London, 1970)

P. T. Craddock and J. Picton: 'Medieval Copper Alloy Production and West African Bronze Analyses, II', *Archaeometry*, xxviii (1986), pp. 3–32

V. E. Chikwendu and others: 'Nigerian Sources of Copper, Lead and Tin for the Igbo-Ukwu Bronzes', *Archaeometry*, xxxi (1989), pp. 27–36

6. SPECIAL BRONZES. In addition to what may be termed the 'usual' bronzes discussed above, made either by cold hammering or casting, there were a number of uses for which special fabrication methods and specific alloys, usually containing much more tin, were employed. These special bronzes often continued in use long after ordinary bronze had been supplanted by brass.

Early mirrors in the West tended to be made of bronze with *c.* 10% tin, which gave a rather golden reflection. In China, however, from the Shang period in the 2nd millennium BC, mirrors were always made of a bronze alloy with *c.* 20–25% tin and a little lead. This was a silvery and extremely hard alloy that was capable of taking a high polish as well as being resistant to scratches and deformation. A similar alloy began to be used for mirrors in the Hellenistic world at the end of the 1st millennium BC; it was also the usual composition for Roman mirrors. Although silvered glass became increasingly popular, bronze continued to be used for Byzantine mirrors and for those in the Islamic and medieval periods long after brass had replaced bronze for most other uses.

The resonant properties of high-tin bronze made it specially suitable for bells. Large bells seem always to have been made of an alloy containing *c.* 20% tin. They seem to have originated in late antiquity and to have first been cast by the smiths who made large statues. The earliest specific mention of a campanile to hold large church bells would seem to be in Italy in the 8th century AD. An excellent account of medieval bell casting is given by Theophilus. As the bells were so large they were often cast on site, and casting pits containing the fragments of the crucibles and moulds are frequently encountered during the excavation of medieval churches.

Bronze containing *c.* 20% tin is extremely brittle when cold but can be beaten out quite readily at red heat. High-tin bronze vessels were hammered out and then quenched from red heat in Thailand in the late 1st millennium BC. The resulting metal is very attractive, with a bright silver or golden surface; it was also used for vessels in the Nilgiri Hills of south India. The same metal was used by the Sasanians and, later, in the Islamic world. Metalworkers in Kirman refer to it as *haftjūsh* (meaning 'boiled or heated seven times') and claim that it contains copper, silver, tin, antimony, lead, gold and iron, though analysis shows it to be copper with *c.* 20% tin. The special quality of vessels made from it lies in the alloy and the hot working they receive.

This same alloy, made resonant and strong by hammering and quenching, is the traditional material for cymbals and gongs. The traditional gongs of South-east Asia have been hammered out of high-tin bronze at high temperature for centuries, and it is tempting to link that technology

with the similar process used to make the bronze bowls in Thailand.

Apart from these specialized uses outlined above, simple bronzes are now very rarely used: brass is both cheaper and easier to work. Even statuary bronze usually contains *c.* 5% each of tin, lead and zinc with the copper.

BIBLIOGRAPHY

Theophilus, also called Rugerus: *De diversis artibus* (?1110–40); Eng. trans. by J. G. Hawthorne and C. S. Smith as *On Divers Arts* (Chicago and London, 1963), pp. 167–76

A. S. Melikian-Chirvani: 'The White Bronzes of Early Islamic Iran', *Met. Mus. J.*, ix (1974), pp. 123–51

P. T. Craddock: 'The Copper Alloys of the Medieval Islamic World', *World Archaeol.*, xi (1979), pp. 68–79

W. Rajpitak and N. J. Seeley: 'The Bronze Bowls from Ban Don Ta Phet, Thailand', *World Archaeol.*, xi (1979), pp. 26–31

M. Goodway and H. C. Conklin: 'Quenched High-tin Bronzes from the Philippines', *Archaeomaterials*, ii (1987), pp. 1–27

W. Rodwell: *Church Archaeology* (London, 1989)

P. T. CRADDOCK

Bronzino, Agnolo [Agniolo di Cosimo di Mariano Tori] (*b* Monticelli, nr Florence, 17 Nov 1503; *d* Florence, 23 Nov 1572). Italian painter and poet. He dominated Florentine painting from the 1530s to the 1560s. He was court artist to Cosimo I de' Medici, and his sophisticated style and extraordinary technical ability were ideally suited to the needs and ideals of his ducal patron. He was a leading decorator, and his religious subjects and mythological scenes epitomize the grace of the high *maniera* style; his cool and highly disciplined portraits perfectly convey the atmosphere of the Medici court and of an intellectual élite.

1. Life and work. 2. Working methods and technique. 3. Critical reception and posthumous reputation.

1. LIFE AND WORK.

(i) Early work: Florence and Pesaro, 1522–40/45. (ii) Court artist to Duke Cosimo I de' Medici, 1539–60. (iii) Last works, after *c.* 1560.

(i) *Early work: Florence and Pesaro, 1522–40/45.* Bronzino was the pupil first of the conservative Raffaellino del Garbo and then of Jacopo Pontormo, who portrayed him *c.* 1518 in the foreground of *Joseph in Egypt* (London, N.G.). Pontormo's Mannerism was the major formative influence on Bronzino's art. He worked with Pontormo in 1523–6 in the cloister at the Certosa di Galluzzo, near Florence, where he painted lunettes (damaged) of the *Martyrdom of St Lawrence* (oil) and the *Man of Sorrows with Two Angels* (fresco). In 1526–8, he painted tondi of *St Luke* and *St Mark* for the pendentives of the vault opposite Pontormo's *Lamentation* in the Cappella Capponi in S Felicità, Florence. There are also a number of Pontormesque pictures (some collaborative; all of disputed attribution) from *c.* 1525–30: the *Virgin Enthroned with SS Jerome and Francis*, the *Legend of the Ten Thousand Martyrs* and *Pygmalion and Galatea* (all Florence, Uffizi); the *Madonna with St John* (Florence, Gal. Corsini); and the *Holy Family with St John* (after a drawing by Pontormo; St Petersburg, Hermitage). In the *Holy Family with SS Elizabeth and John* (Washington, DC, N.G.A.), the most successful of these works and long attributed to Pontormo, Bronzino attempted to accommodate his master's style, but his manner is less fluent, his vision more literal and his response to the subject-matter less sensitive.

Bronzino also painted works in a more individual style in the late 1520s: they include *St Benedict Tempted in the Wilderness* (fresco trans. to canvas; Florence, S Salvi), the *Dead Christ with the Virgin and the Magdalene* (Florence, Uffizi) and the *Noli me tangere* (destr. fresco, ex-S Girolamo delle Poverine, Florence).

In 1530 Bronzino went to Pesaro. There he worked, together with Raffaellino dal Colle, as an assistant on Girolamo Genga's fresco decoration of the Villa Imperiale, Pesaro, where Smyth (1956) has identified work by his hand. He came into contact with the classicism of the post-Raphael Roman school. Bronzino also painted for Guidobaldo II della Rovere a harpsichord cover of *Apollo and Marsyas*, which is strikingly Pontormesque in style (1531–2; St Petersburg, Hermitage); his portrait of *Guidobaldo* (1532; Florence, Pitti) is his first essay in the state portrait.

Bronzino returned in 1532 to Florence, where he painted a number of small altarpieces, which demonstrate a new individuality and independence of style. The surfaces of his panels are opaque and smooth in contrast to the transparency and luminous vibrancy of Pontormo's paintings; and his immobile forms are seen almost as elements of still-life, as opposed to the rhythmic fluidity of Pontormo's compositions. Among these pictures are *St Sebastian* (c. 1533; Madrid, Mus. Thyssen-Bornemisza), the *Adoration of the Shepherds* (c. 1539; Budapest, Mus. F.A.) and the *Virgin with SS Elizabeth and John* (c. 1540; London, N.G.). The major work of this group is the *Holy Family with St John* (c. 1540; Florence, Uffizi), painted for the Florentine aristocrat, poet and epigrammatist Bartolomeo Panciatichi (1507–72), wherein virtuoso draughtsmanship is joined with sculptural forms polished to enamel-like smoothness. These figures demonstrate Bronzino's penchant for antique sculpture, especially the Virgin, who is based on a Classical Venus. Later, but related stylistically, is the *Holy Family with SS Elizabeth and John* (c. 1545–50; Vienna, Ksthist. Mus.). If this work is the second *Holy Family* mentioned by Vasari as painted for Panciatichi, as Smith (1982) suggested, it may date closer to 1540.

Bronzino also worked on decorative schemes and executed a number of works now lost, damaged or destroyed: lunettes with half-length figures of *Dante*, *Petrarch* and *Boccaccio* (1533–4) for a room in the house of Bartolomeo Bettini, the ruined *Pietà with Angels* (c. 1535–9; Mercatale, S Casciano) in a tabernacle at the Villa of Matteo Strozzi and the allegorical fresco decorations (1535–43) at the Medici villas of Careggi and Castello, where he assisted Pontormo.

Bronzino achieved his greatest distinction in these years as a portrait painter, and by the early 1540s he had become the leading exponent in Florence. Examples of the early 1530s include the *Portrait of Lorenzo Lenzi* (Milan, Castello Sforzesco) and the *Portrait of a Man with a Lute* (Florence, Uffizi). *Andrea Doria as Neptune* (c. 1533; Milan, Brera), an unusual allegorical portrait resembling a painted sculpture, was made for Doria's friend, Paolo Giovio. More mature examples of Bronzino's *maniera* portraiture towards the mid-century are the portraits of the poet *Ugolino Martelli* (1540; Berlin, Gemäldegal.), the *Portrait of an Unknown Man* (c. 1540–45; New York, Met.), the *Portrait of a Woman with her Son* (c. 1540–46; Washington, DC,

N.G.A.) and the pair of portraits of *Bartolomeo Panciatichi* and his wife *Lucrezia Panciatichi* (both c. 1540; Florence, Uffizi). In these three-quarter-length frontal images Bronzino evolved a formula for aristocratic portraiture in which the emphasis is on the social or intellectual status of the sitter rather than on human communication. Elegance of design is combined with an objective detachment from the sitter, who, in turn, exhibits a masklike impenetrability. Elaborate, ambiguous and claustrophobic architectural settings set up a tension with the oppressive fixity of the images.

Many of Bronzino's portraits are of poets, musicians and men of letters. He was himself a poet, author of many sonnets, songs and burlesque rhymes; his first publication was *Del pennello* (1538). Bronzino was one of a small intellectual élite and a founder-member of the Accademia degli Umidi (later Fiorentina) in 1540. In 1547 (owing to new regulations) Bronzino and other artists were expelled from the academy, but he rejoined in 1566. In 1546 Benedetto Varchi, an eminent intellectual, asked a number of artists to express their views on the PARAGONE (debate) on the primacy of painting or sculpture. Bronzino's reply was published in Varchi's *Due lezioni* (1549). In 1537 he became a member of the Painters' Company of St Luke.

(ii) Court artist to Duke Cosimo I de' Medici, 1539–60. In 1539 Bronzino contributed to the sumptuous decorations for Duke Cosimo's marriage to Eleonora of Toledo. This marked the beginning of a long period as court artist, a role that ensured his dominant position in Florentine painting until 1555, when ducal favour shifted increasingly to Giorgio Vasari.

(a) Figure paintings and designs for tapestries. Bronzino's first commission from the Duke was the decoration of a chapel for Duchess Eleonora (the Cappella di Eleonora), which is the major painted decorative ensemble of his career (1540–45; Florence, Pal. Vecchio). The vault of the chapel is frescoed with *St Michael, St John the Evangelist, St Jerome* and *St Francis*; on the walls are frescoes of stories of Moses (the *Brazen Serpent, Moses Striking the Rock and the Gathering of Manna* and the *Crossing of the Red Sea and Moses Appointing Joshua*). There Bronzino embraced an idealizing sculptural style suggesting the influence of the Antique and Michelangelo, which co-exists with passages of naturalism recalling his own earlier style. These frescoes—completely covering the walls of the small chapel (4 m sq.)—are one of the earliest examples of a characteristic type of *maniera* decoration in which all the wall surfaces are painted with complex, densely interwoven figural and decorative motifs, giving the impression of a jewelled ornament. The chapel's altarpiece of the *Lamentation* (1545; Besançon, Mus. B.-A. & Archéol.; see fig. 1), which was partly based on a lost drawing by Baccio Bandinelli, is one of the key religious paintings of the Florentine *maniera*. It represents Bronzino at the height of his powers. With its controlled line, gleaming marmoreal forms and lavish use of the expensive lapis lazuli paint, it is an opulent, precious object, even more jewel-like than the frescoes in which it was set. The altarpiece, justly called 'a most rare object' by Vasari, was sent by the Duke to Cardinal Nicholas Granvelle (1484–1550) as a diplomatic

1. Agnolo Bronzino: *Lamentation*, oil on panel, 2.68×1.73 m, 1545 (Besançon, Musée des Beaux-Arts et d'Archéologie)

see fig. 2) for the Duke, who gave it to François I, King of France, as a diplomatic gift. The work, stylistically the secular counterpart to the *Lamentation* in the Cappella di Eleonora, is Bronzino's masterpiece in the genre of mythological painting. It is an allegory of the Triumph of Venus, but the identity of some of its characters and the details of its iconography have been the subject of much debate. In these years Bronzino also worked for other Florentine patrons, mainly in the Medici court circle. Two large altarpieces for major Florentine churches, both highly elaborate compositions of idealized nudes, continue the 'bella maniera' of his religious works of the 1540s. The *Christ in Limbo* (1552; Florence, Mus. Opera Santa Croce) was painted for the chapel of Giovanni Zanchini in Santa Croce. It contains numerous portraits of Bronzino's friends in Florentine literary and artistic circles. The *Resurrection* (1552; Florence, SS Annunziata) was commissioned for the Cappella Guadagni. His mythological themes were developed in two further allegories of Venus: *Venus, Cupid, and Jealousy* (c. 1550; Budapest, Mus. F.A.), which is a simplified and less subtle variant on the *Venus, Cupid, Folly and Time* of 1544–5, and *Venus, Cupid, and a Satyr* (c. 1555; Venus' drapery added later; Rome, Gal. Colonna), painted for Alamanno Salviati. In 1557–8 he completed frescoes left unfinished at the death of Pontormo in 1556: *The Deluge*, the *Resurrection of the Dead* and the *Martyrdom of St Lawrence* in the choir of S Lorenzo (destr. 1738).

(b) *Portraits.* Bronzino was court portrait painter to Duke Cosimo, producing (with his workshop) dozens of portraits of the Duke, the Duchess Eleonora and their

gift. Bronzino's darker and more sombre replica of 1553 replaced it, and its original wings, *St John the Baptist* (Malibu, CA, Getty Mus.) and *St Cosmas* (untraced), were replaced in 1564 by Bronzino's *Annunciation.*

In the 1540s Bronzino made important designs for tapestries. His numerous tapestries designed for the ducal palace (1545–53) were executed by the Flemish weavers Giovanni Rost and Nicholas Karcher. The earliest series of tapestries (1545; all Florence, Pitti) included an *Abundance* (inv. no. 540), a *Primavera* (inv. no. 541; *see* TAPESTRY, fig. 8) and the *Vindication of Innocence.* There followed his most important work in this medium: 16 cartoons for an ambitious series, on which he collaborated with Pontormo and Francesco Salviati, of the *Story of Joseph* (divided between Rome, Pal. Quirinale, and Florence, Pal. Vecchio), an allegory of the life and rule of Cosimo which was to hang in the Sala de' Dugento of the Palazzo Vecchio. In 1549 he designed the cartoon for the *Allegory with the Arms of the Medici and Toledo* (Florence, Pitti); and in 1555–7 cartoons followed for a tapestry series of the *Metamorphoses,* of which only *Apollo and Marsyas* survives (Parma, G.N.).

Bronzino also painted the famous allegory known as *Venus, Cupid, Folly and Time* (c. 1544–5; London, N.G.;

2. Agnolo Bronzino: *Venus, Cupid, Folly and Time*, oil on panel, 1.46×1.16 m, c. 1544–5 (London, National Gallery)

children Maria (*b* 1540), Francesco (*b* 1541), Isabella (*b* 1542), Giovanni (*b* 1543), Lucrezia (*b* 1545), Garzia (*b* 1547), Ferdinando (*b* 1549) and Pietro (*b* 1554). The state portraits of Cosimo are propagandist images of Medici rule, which combine an idealized type with a convincing surface realism. There are three Bronzino prototypes: a half-length portrait of *Cosimo in Armour* (1543; Florence, Uffizi, dep. 28), of which there is a three-quarter-length version painted for Paolo Giovio in 1544–5 (priv. col., see Simon, 1982, cat. A19a), a portrait of *Cosimo at Age Thirty-six* (1555–6; no extant original; a copy, ex-Gal. Erhardt, Berlin, is inscribed ANNI XXXVI; replica in Turin, Gal. Sabauda) and a portrait of *Grand Duke Cosimo* (1569; no extant original), painted in the year when he had been granted the title of Grand Duke of Tuscany. Bronzino also painted *Cosimo de' Medici as Orpheus* in 1539 (Philadelphia, PA, Mus. A.).

Bronzino's portraits of Duchess Eleonora are also of several types, which, like those of Cosimo, were often replicated. The earliest is a bust-length portrait (1543; Prague, N.G., Šternberk Pal.). In 1545 Bronzino painted the state portrait of *Eleonora of Toledo and her Son Giovanni* (Florence, Uffizi; see fig. 3). In this work, which is his most important Medici portrait and is technically a *tour de force*, the elaborate brocaded gown seems as much the subject of the portrait as Eleonora herself. He also painted Eleonora with Francesco (1549–50; workshop versions, Pisa, Mus. N. & Civ. S Matteo). As a pendant to the contemporaneous portrait of the Duke, Bronzino painted Eleonora in 1555–6 (no extant original; bust-length workshop version, Berlin, Gemäldegal.; three quarter-length workshop version, Washington, DC, N.G.A.).

4. Agnolo Bronzino: *Ludovico Capponi*, oil on panel, 1.16×0.86 m, *c.* 1550 (New York, Frick Collection)

The sequence of Bronzino's portraits of the Medici children begins with a posthumous portrait of Cosimo's illegitimate daughter Bia, who died in 1542 (Florence, Uffizi). In 1545 Bronzino painted *Giovanni with a Goldfinch* (Florence, Uffizi). There followed in 1551 portraits of Maria (Florence, Uffizi), Francesco (Florence, Uffizi), Giovanni (Oxford, Ashmolean) and Garzia (Lucca, Mus. & Pin. N.). Giovanni was portrayed again *c.* 1552 (Bowood House, Wilts) and in 1560–62 he was represented by Bronzino as *St John the Baptist* (Rome, Gal. Borghese). Ferdinando was painted by Bronzino in 1559 (Lucca, Mus. & Pin. N.), and there is also a workshop portrait of Isabella (*c.* 1552; Stockholm, Nmus.).

According to Vasari, Bronzino also painted portraits of Cosimo's mother, Maria Salviati, and a dwarf–servant, Morgante. The unusual double-sided full-length portrait of the *Dwarf Morgante* (Florence, Uffizi; the front heavily repainted) was probably painted in response to Benedetto Varchi's *Paragone* and was completed before 1553.

During the 1540s Bronzino painted a few portraits of other sitters, which are stylistically related to his Medici portraits of this decade, although decidedly more individualistic. They include *Portrait of a Girl with a Missal* (*c.* 1545; Florence, Uffizi), the *Portrait of a Young Man with a Statuette* (*c.* 1545; Paris, Louvre), the portrait of Cosimo's general, *Stefano Colonna* (1546; Rome, Pal. Barberini) and the *Giannettino Doria* (1546–7; Rome, Gal. Doria-Pamphili). An impressive series of later portraits, dating from the 1550s, includes some of his masterpieces in the genre: the *Portrait of a Boy with a Statuette of Bacchus*

3. Agnolo Bronzino: *Eleonora of Toledo and her Son Giovanni*, oil on panel, 1.15×0.96 m, 1545 (Florence, Galleria degli Uffizi)

(*c*. 1550; London, N.G.) and the magnificent *Ludovico Capponi* (*c*. 1550; New York, Frick; see fig. 4). In these works there is a new daring in colour, as in the bright pink of the curtain behind the boy, and Ludovico's black-and-white costume (the colours of the Capponi family arms) set against an acid green curtain. Other portraits of *c*. 1550–55 are: the *Portrait of an Unknown Woman* (Cleveland, OH, Mus. A., and Turin, Gal. Sabauda), the *Portrait of a Man with a Statuette of Venus* (Ottawa, N.G.), possibly a pendant to the Turin *Woman*, the *Portrait of a Youth with a Plumed Cap* (Kansas City, MO, Nelson–Atkins Mus. A.) and *Luca Martini* (Florence, Pitti). Bronzino's last major portrait, dating from *c*. 1560, is of the poet *Laura Battiferi* (Florence, Pal. Vecchio). The stylization of appearance and personality in the abstracting profile of his friend seems to carry *maniera* to an extreme.

(iii) Last works, after c. *1560.* The *Noli me tangere* (1561; Paris, Louvre), which was painted for the Cappella Cavalcanti in Santo Spirito, is Bronzino's last purely *maniera* painting. In the 1560s his art was affected by the reaction against Mannerism in Italian painting. He seemed to renounce the beauty and artificiality of the *maniera* in paintings in which the rarefied abstraction of his earlier style gives way to a greater descriptiveness. In these works there is a new involvement of the spectator, which, as a response to a demand for narrative clarity, suggests the influence of the Counter-Reformation.

In the early 1560s Bronzino painted major altarpieces for Cosimo. The *Deposition from the Cross with Saints* (1561; Florence, Accad.) was commissioned for the convent of the Zoccolanti, Portoferraio (Elba), and the *Adoration of the Shepherds* (1564) was painted for the church of S Stefano dei Cavalieri, Pisa. His last commission from the Duke was the *Martyrdom of St Lawrence* (1565), an enormous Michelangelesque fresco which occupies a large section of the left nave wall of S Lorenzo, Florence. At about the same time he displayed his virtuosity in painting works of completely contrasting scales by executing a miniature-like (420×300 mm) *Pietà* on copper (Florence, Uffizi), probably for Cosimo's son, Francesco I de' Medici. In 1565 he contributed to the wedding decorations for Francesco's marriage to Joanna of Austria, and in 1567 painted for him a small jewel-like work on copper, the *Allegory of Happiness* (Florence, Uffizi). Bronzino's final works were a *Pietà* for a pilaster in Santa Croce, Florence (*c*. 1569), and an altarpiece, the *Raising of the Daughter of Jairus* (*c*. 1571–2; Florence, S Maria Novella). This was mentioned by Borghini as Bronzino's last painting: probably completed with the assistance of his pupil Alessandro Allori, it strives for a new clarity of expression and gesture.

In 1572 Bronzino became consul of the Accademia del Disegno, in which he had been active since 1566; on his death he was buried in the church of S Cristoforo.

2. WORKING METHODS AND TECHNIQUE.

(i) Drawings. Bronzino's highly disciplined compositions and polished forms evolved through careful preparatory drawings; he was heir to the Florentine tradition of the most detailed preparation for a painting. However, he was not a prolific draughtsman, and only about 50 preparatory drawings have survived. In black (less often red) chalk he

investigated ideal form with a pure line less yielding than Pontormo's. He combined pen and wash with rich colouristic effect in finished composition drawings, such as a modello for the vault of the Cappella di Eleonora (*c*. 1540; Frankfurt am Main, Städel. Kstinst.) in pen and wash with touches of white heightening on blue paper, and a drawing in the same medium for the borders of his tapestries (London, BM). He also made studies from life of individual figures, whose formal beauty suggests the influence of antique sculpture. However, two life studies for the Cappella di Eleonora, the *Young Man Seen from the Back* (Florence, Uffizi, 6704F), in black chalk on yellow paper, and a study for *St Michael* (Paris, Louvre, 6356), in black chalk on blue paper, reveal how even the most elaborate poses began with a study from nature. The later drawings are less softly lit and more schematic, the outlines are sharp and clear and the figures highly finished and precisely modelled.

(ii) Workshop practice. After 1548 Raffaello dal Colle assisted Bronzino with the tapestries; Lorenzo di Bastiano Zucchetti and Alessandro Allori assisted him in the border cartoons. Allori, Bronzino's ward and pupil, was his only real follower. He combined his master's idealizing, sculptural style with a personal inclination to naturalism. Santi di Tito, who may have been Bronzino's pupil, modelled his paintings after 1564 on Bronzino's, but later turned towards naturalism and luminism. Giovan Maria Butteri began as Bronzino's pupil but became a follower of Allori.

Bronzino's workshop produced many replicas and variants of his most famous Medici portraits. Among such works is a series of miniature historical portraits of the Medici, based on originals by Bronzino and other artists and inscribed with the names of the subjects (Florence, Uffizi). The set was begun in 1551, and by 1553 the portraits of Cosimo I, Lorenzo the Magnificent, Giuliano di Piero, Pope Leo X, Pope Clement VII, Lorenzo (Duke of Urbino) and Cosimo's children Maria, Francesco and Garzia (the children are after the Bronzino portraits of 1551 noted above) were finished. The remainder of the series was completed before 1568. The portrait of Duke Cosimo is by Bronzino himself, after the *Cosimo in Armour* of 1543.

3. CRITICAL RECEPTION AND POSTHUMOUS REPUTATION. During his lifetime Bronzino enjoyed a high reputation in the court circle of the Medici and among the intellectual élite of Florence. Vasari began his chapter on living artists with the life of Bronzino—'the most important and oldest'—and unconditionally praised Bronzino's works in painting and poetry. However, after Bronzino's death, it was Vasari's own more fluent variant on *maniera* that attracted the larger following; and when the general reaction against *maniera* set in after about 1580, Bronzino's reputation began to decline until, eventually, his place as the last major master of the Florentine Renaissance rested largely on his portraits. Only since World War II has Bronzino been recognized as the most sophisticated and technically accomplished Italian painter to embody the ideals of the *maniera*, the last great representative of the Florentine tradition of *disegno* and sculptural form. Only

since 1979 have the later religious works begun to be rehabilitated.

Bronzino's reputation was spread through engravings: the Budapest *Adoration of the Shepherds* by Giorgio Ghisi (1553) and Giovanni Battista de Cavalieri (1565); the *Crossing of the Red Sea and Moses Appointing Joshua* by Hieronymous Cock; and the portrait of *Andrea Doria as Neptune* in Paolo Giovio's *Elogia virorum bellica virtute illustrium* (1577).

WRITINGS
F. Petrucci Nardelli, ed.: *Agnolo Bronzino: Rima in burla* (Rome, 1988)

BIBLIOGRAPHY

EARLY SOURCES
B. Varchi: *Due lezioni* (Florence, 1549)
G. Vasari: *Vite* (1550, rev. 2/1568); ed. G. Milanesi (1878–85), vii, pp. 593–605
R. Borghini: *Il riposo di Raffaello Borghini* (Florence, 1584); ed. M. Rosci, 2 vols (Milan, 1967)
J. W. Gaye: *Carteggio* (1839–40)
A. Furno: *La vita e le rime di Agnolo Bronzino* (Pistoia, 1902)

GENERAL WORKS
F. Goldschmidt: *Pontormo, Rosso, und Bronzino* (Leipzig, 1911)
Mostra di disegni dei fondatori dell'Accademia delle Arti del Disegno (exh. cat. by P. Barocchi and others, Florence, Uffizi, 1963) [entries on Bronzino by A. Forlani]
M. B. Hall: *Renovation and Counter-Reformation: Vasari and Duke Cosimo in Sta Maria Novella and Sta Croce, 1565–1577* (Oxford, 1979)
K. Langedijk: *The Portraits of the Medici: 15th to 18th Centuries*, 3 vols (Florence, 1981–7)
C. Adelson: 'Cosimo I de' Medici and the Foundation of Tapestry Production in Florence', *Firenze e la Toscana dei Medici nell'Europa del '500*, iii (Florence, 1983), pp. 900–24

MONOGRAPHS
H. Schulze: *Die Werke Angelo Bronzinos* (Strasbourg, 1911)
A. McComb: *Agnolo Bronzino, his Life and Works* (Cambridge, MA, 1928)
C. H. Smyth: *Bronzino Studies* (diss., Princeton U., NJ, 1955; 2 vols, Ann Arbor, 1956)
A. Emiliani: *Il Bronzino* (Busto Arsizio, 1960) [incl. an anthol. of his poetry]
——: *Bronzino*, Maestri Colore (Milan, 1966) [good colour pls]
M. Levey: *Bronzino*, The Masters, no. 82 (London, 1967) [good illus.]
C. H. Smyth: *Bronzino as Draughtsman* (Locust Valley, NY, 1971)
E. Baccheschi: *L'opera completa del Bronzino* (Milan, 1972) [good colour pls]
C. McCorquodale: *Bronzino* (New York, 1981) [bibliog. to 1980; colour pls]

SPECIALIST STUDIES
E. Panofsky: 'Father Time', *Studies in Iconology: Humanistic Themes in the Art of the Renaissance* (New York, 1944), pp. 69–94
C. H. Smyth: 'The Earliest Works of Bronzino', *A. Bull.*, xxxi (1949), pp. 184–211
D. Heikamp: 'Agnolo Bronzinos Kinderbildnisse aus dem Jahre 1551', *Mitt. Ksthist. Inst. Florenz*, vii (1955), pp. 133–8
J. Cox-Rearick: 'Some Early Drawings by Bronzino', *Master Drgs*, ii (1963), pp. 363–82
M. Levey: 'Sacred and Profane Significance in Two Paintings by Bronzino', *Studies in Renaissance and Baroque Art and Architecture Presented to Anthony Blunt on his 60th Birthday*, ed. M. Kitson and J. Shearman (London, 1967), pp. 30–33
J. Cox-Rearick: 'Les Dessins de Bronzino pour la Chapelle d'Eleonora au Palazzo Vecchio', *Rev. A.*, xiv (1971), pp. 7–22
K. W. Forster: 'Metaphors of Rule: Political Ideology and History in the Portraits of Cosimo I de' Medici', *Mitt. Ksthist. Inst. Florenz*, xv (1971), pp. 65–105
J. Beck: 'Bronzino nell'inventario medico del 1560', *Ant. Viva*, ii (1972), pp. 10–12
J. Cox-Rearick: 'Two Studies for Bronzino's Lost *Noli me tangere*', *Master Drgs*, xix (1981), pp. 289–93
G. Smith: 'Jealousy, Pleasure and Pain in the *Allegory of Venus and Cupid*', *Pantheon*, xxxix (1981), pp. 250–58
J. Cox-Rearick: 'Bronzino's *Young Woman with her Little Boy*', *Stud. Hist. A.*, xii (1982), pp. 67–79

R. B. Simon: *Bronzino's Portraits of Cosimo I de' Medici* (diss., New York, Columbia U., 1982; Ann Arbor, 1984)
G. Smith: 'Bronzino's *Holy Family* in Vienna: A Note on the Identity of its Patron', *Source*, ii (1982), pp. 21–5
R. W. Gaston: 'Iconography and Portraiture in Bronzino's *Christ in Limbo*', *Mitt. Ksthist. Inst. Florenz*, xxvii (1983), pp. 41–72
G. Smith: 'Bronzino's *Allegory of Happiness*', *A. Bull.*, lxvi (1984), pp. 390–99
R. B. Simon: 'Bronzino's *Cosimo I de' Medici as Orpheus*', *Bull.: Philadelphia Mus. A.*, lxxxi (1985), pp. 17–27
E. Pilliod: 'Bronzino's S Croce *Pietà*', *Burl. Mag.*, cxxviii (1986), pp. 577–9
J. Cox-Rearick: 'Bronzino's *Crossing of the Red Sea and Moses Appointing Joshua*: Prolegomena to the Chapel of Eleonora di Toledo', *A. Bull.*, lxix (1987), pp. 44–67
——: 'A *Saint Sebastian* by Bronzino', *Burl. Mag.*, cxxix (1987), pp. 155–62
——: 'From Bandinelli to Bronzino: The Genesis of the *Lamentation* from the Cappella di Eleonora', *Mitt. Ksthist. Inst. Florenz*, xxxiii (1989), pp. 37–84
——: 'Deux dessins de Bronzino (1503–1572) découverts au Louvre', *Rev. Louvre*, 5–6 (1991), pp. 35–47
R. W. Gaston: 'Love's Sweet Poison: A New Reading of Bronzino's London *Allegory*', *I Tatti Stud.*, Essays in the Renaissance, 4 (1991), pp. 249–88
E. Pilliod: 'Le *Noli me tangere* de Bronzino et la décoration de la chapelle Cavalcanti de l'église Santo Spirito à Florence', *Rev. Louvre*, 5–6 (1991), pp. 33ff
——: 'Bronzino's Household', *Burl. Mag.*, cxxxiv (1992), pp. 92–100
J. Cox-Rearick: *Bronzino's Chapel for Eleonora di Toledo in the Palazzo Vecchio* (California, 1993)

JANET COX-REARICK

Broodthaers, Marcel (*b* Brussels, 28 Jan 1924; *d* Cologne, 28 Jan 1976). Belgian painter, sculptor, printmaker, draughtsman, film maker and poet. He lived in poverty for 20 years as a bohemian poet in Brussels; with no artistic training he turned to visual art in 1964 as an ironic gesture, with an exhibition at the Galerie St Laurent in Brussels. He launched himself caustically into the art market with a brief text printed on the invitation: 'I too wondered if I could not sell something and succeed in life . . . Finally the idea of inventing something insincere finally crossed my mind and I set to work straightaway' (quoted in 1980 exh. cat., p. 13). In the 11 years that remained to him he established himself, in more than 70 one-man exhibitions, as an artist of considerable influence in terms not of style or sensibility but of attitude and approach.

Broodthaers regarded his art as a defence of European high cultural traditions in the face of barbarian threats and especially of western commercialism. His strategy allowed him to appropriate techniques and media from Nouveau Réalisme, Pop art, conceptual art and performance art so as to subvert them to his own aims; he emphasized the craftsmanship of his art but without any trace of academic technique or dexterity, as his work was often executed by others. At its most personal his work employed techniques associated with poetry but applied by him not only to words but to images and symbols, with a particular emphasis on irony, metonymy, tautology and synecdoche.

Broodthaers associated with other artists, including Magritte and Piero Manzoni, before he became an artist himself and he adapted from their work particular devices and improbable conjunctions of images. In *Magritte's Curse* (wooden relief with objects, 1966; see 1980 exh. cat., p. 33, no. 32), for example, he conjoined painted and printed images of a clouded blue sky. He expressed his resistance to American Pop art in sculptures such as

Casserole and Closed Mussels (1965; London, Tate; see fig.), assembled from found materials such as eggshells, mussels and European household goods that spoke of simplicity and poverty in the face of big business, banality and mass production. From his first exhibition he conceived of the temporary installation as a medium in itself, involving not only the objects and their display but the catalogue, titles of works and the private view as an event. From 1966 he began to use film (a medium that he had used in the 1950s) and photography as an integral part of installations, which presaged later developments in conceptual art. He went on to create his own peripatetic imaginary museum, which he inaugurated in his Brussels apartment-studio in 1968 as the *Museum of Modern Art, Eagle Department, 19th-century Section* and to which he continued to add ironically titled sections.

Broodthaers spent his last years in Germany and England as well as in Brussels, creating during this period a series of exhibitions collectively titled *Décors*, which were his definitive achievement. These temporary installations included *Catalogue* (1974; Brussels, Pal. B.-A.), *Eulogy of the Subject* (1974; Basle, Kstmus.), *Invitation to a Bourgeois Exhibition* (1975; Berlin, Tiergarten N.G.), the *Privilege of Art* (1975; Oxford, MOMA) and the *Angelus of Daumier* (1975; Paris, Mus. N. A. Mod.). To a greater extent than before individual works were brought together in different combinations according to the 'laws' of a personal syntax and poetics involving the transposition of media as well as of objects: paintings with printed inscriptions such as *Painting* (1973; London, Tate), a series of nine stretched canvases bearing descriptive phrases concerning various English-speaking writers; reproductions of paintings as photographs such as *Mademoiselle Rivière and Monsieur Bertin* (1975; London, Tate), after Ingres; hand-painted

Marcel Broodthaers: *Casserole and Closed Mussels*, metal and mixed media, 305×279×248 mm, 1965 (London, Tate Gallery)

prints (e.g. *Didactic Model [Mr X]*, 1973–4; see 1980 exh. cat., p. 38, no. 119); films as objects; and objects as films. His work became increasingly complex and technically ambitious in all his chosen media, including paintings, drawings, films, photographs, performances, books, exhibition catalogues, prints, plastic reliefs, sound tapes, slide projections, collages, assemblages and installations. He conceived of his inclusive medium, however, as art and culture in the broadest sense, and it is in this respect that his influence has been most lasting.

BIBLIOGRAPHY

N. Calas: 'Marcel Broodthaers' Throw of the Dice', *Artforum*, xiv/9 (1976), pp. 34–7

B. Marcellis: 'Marcel Broodthaers: L'opera, le opere', *Domus*, 588 (1978), pp. 46–9

B. Buchloch: 'Marcel Broodthaers: Allegories of the Avant-garde', *Artforum*, xviii/9 (1980), pp. 52–9

Marcel Broodthaers (exh. cat. by M. Compton and B. Reise, London, Tate, 1980) [incl. reprints of texts by Broodthaers and a list of his principal pubns and films]

Marcel Broodthaers (exh. cat. by M. Compton and others, Los Angeles, CA, Mus. Contemp. A.; Pittsburgh, PA, Carnegie Mus. A.; Brussels, Pal. B.-A.; 1990)

MICHAEL COMPTON

Brooke, Earls of. *See* GREVILLE.

Brooker, Bertram (Richard) (*b* Croydon, London, 31 March 1888; *d* Toronto, 21 March 1955). Canadian painter, critic and writer of English birth. He emigrated in 1905 to Portage la Prairie, Manitoba. In 1921 he moved to Toronto to work as an editor and publisher. He is best known as a pioneer of abstract painting in Canada. His show (1927) at Toronto's Arts & Letters Club was the first solo exhibition of abstract art by a Canadian artist. His early work is characterized by the bold non-objective imagery seen in the complex *Sounds Assembling* (1928; Winnipeg, A.G.). After 1930 he reassessed his artistic direction: he turned first to figurative imagery (e.g. *Torso*, 1937; Ottawa, N.G.) and then looking to Cubism he re-examined the nature of abstraction in his painting, without returning to the non-objectivity of his earlier work. Between 1926 and 1930 Brooker wrote 'The Seven Arts', a syndicated column of art criticism for the Southam Press. In addition, he edited *The Yearbook of the Arts in Canada* (1928–9; 1936) and, under the pseudonym of Richard Surrey, he wrote three books on advertising. His novel *Think of the Earth* won the first Governor General's Prize for Literature in 1936; he later published two other novels. Throughout his life he was an active participant in the Canadian cultural scene and he continued to paint and exhibit his art.

BIBLIOGRAPHY

D. Reid: *Bertram Brooker* (Ottawa, 1973)

B. Sproxton, ed.: *Sounds Assembling: The Poetry of Bertram Brooker* (Winnipeg, 1980)

J. Oille Sinclair, ed.: *Bertram Brooker and Emergent Modernism: Provincial Essays* (Toronto, 1989)

JOYCE ZEMANS

Brooking, Charles (*b* ?London, *c*. 1723; *d* London, ?March 1759). English painter. According to Edwards, Brooking was 'bred in some department of the dockyard at Deptford'. His father was possibly the Charles Brooking who was employed as a painter and decorator at Greenwich Hospital, London, between 1729 and 1736. From the period before 1750 there are two small marine paintings inscribed 'C. Brooking aged 17 years' (USA, priv. col.), and it is recorded that he worked for a picture dealer in Leicester Square, London. In 1752 he worked as a botanical draughtsman for John Ellis (?1710–76), providing the illustrations for the latter's *Natural History of the Corallines* (London, 1755), in which he was referred to in the introduction as 'a celebrated painter of sea-pieces'. His reputation as a marine artist was well established by 1755: four of his paintings portraying the recent exploits of a squadron of ships, the 'Royal Family' privateers, were engraved and published in 1753, and in 1754 he completed a commission from the Foundling Hospital (London) for the large sea-piece *Flagship before the Wind under Easy Sail* (London, Foundling Hosp.), possibly intended as a pendant to an earlier work by Peter Monamy. In June 1754 he was elected as one of the hospital's governors and guardians.

Although few are dated, most of Brooking's extant paintings seem to belong to the last six years of his career. They are almost exclusively of marine subject-matter, but their stylistic range is considerable; Brooking could imitate the manner of (and even particular paintings by) Simon de Vlieger and Willem van de Velde II with an ease unparalleled in the work of his contemporaries, yet elsewhere his approach was uncompromisingly individualistic. His direct but imaginative response to natural effects at sea and his evidently informed knowledge of maritime practice and naval architecture combined to create images that are at once scrupulously accurate and powerfully evocative. His widow and children were allocated 10 guineas from the profits of the Society of Artists' exhibition of 1761.

BIBLIOGRAPHY
E. Edwards: *Anecdotes of Painters* (London, 1805)
Charles Brooking, 1723–1759 (exh. cat., ed. B. Taylor and C. Sorensen; Bristol, Mus. & A.G., 1966)

STEPHEN DEUCHAR

Brooks, James (i) (*b* Hatford, Wantage, Berks, 30 March 1825; *d* London, 7 Oct 1901). English architect and designer. Along with G. F. Bodley and J. L. Pearson he was the major designer of Gothic Revival churches in the later Victorian period. He began his training in London in 1847 and entered the Royal Academy Schools two years later, but his contacts in Oxfordshire with important High Church patrons such as John Butler, the vicar of Wantage, and key architect members of the Ecclesiological Society, including G. E. Street and William White, are of greater significance. As was the case with Street and White, secular commissions were to occupy only a minor part in Brooks's career.

Brooks set up as an independent architect in London in 1852. Little happened, however, until 1860, when he began rapidly to gain prominence through a sequence of town churches. The issue of building large churches for the working-class poor in the unfashionable new districts of London was a major concern at this time among the Ecclesiologists, particularly A. J. B. Hope (ii), and even provoked debates in Parliament; a 'model town church' was then provided by Pearson with his London church of St Peter (begun 1860), Vauxhall. As a result of the

campaign to improve conditions (for which the businessman Richard Foster contributed large sums), Brooks designed five major churches for Shoreditch and the surrounding area in east London in the 1860s. Their layout followed the broad recommendations of Hope in his *The English Cathedral in the 19th Century* (1861): a town church should have a high clerestory and so be spacious and lofty, and its general outline should be simple; those for the capital should be built in red brick and not the yellowish London Stock brick (which the Ecclesiologists particularly disliked). Further characteristics of these churches were derived from continental examples, particularly from what was then called 'Early French'. This term was meant to imply the simplicity and 'muscularity' of 12th-century French Gothic, though the sheer brick walls Brooks often used came from Italian medieval prototypes, to which both Street and John Ruskin had drawn attention. The windows in these churches by Brooks have sometimes the rudimentary plate tracery of the 'Early French' style but frequently no tracery at all. Brooks, as was the case with most other church architects of the time, designed the fittings of his churches in a correspondingly massive style. Perhaps the most extreme example of this is found at his Ascension Church (1876), Lavender Hill, Battersea, in south London, which has a vast apse that is an undisturbed semicircle. In many cases he also designed the subsidiary buildings, such as vicarages or schools, which adhere to a similarly severe brick style. These buildings excel in the way their elevations strike a balance between the functional accentuations (e.g. sizes of windows) that A. W. N. Pugin had popularized and the overall unity of the complete group. Perhaps the outstanding example of this is Brooks's St Columba, Kingsland, in north London: schools (1865), church (1868–9) and parsonage (1873–4).

Brooks continued to build town churches for the rest of his career, though the earlier political and social implications became gradually less pressing, and it became a matter of serving the ever-growing suburbs. The formal treatment of these buildings changed into a more gentle Late Victorian mode. He cannot be said to have cultivated an intensely personal style during his later career, at least not to the extent that Bodley or Pearson did. Even so, in his last major church, All Hallows (1892–1914), Gospel Oak, in north London, he made another powerful and austere statement, this time in rough Kentish ragstone.

BIBLIOGRAPHY
C .L. Eastlake: *A History of the Gothic Revival* (London, 1872)
H. Muthesius: *Die neuere kirchliche Baukunst in England* (Berlin, 1901)
S. Muthesius: *The High Victorian Movement in England* (London, 1972)
R. Dixon: *The Life and Works of James Brooks* (diss., U. London, 1976)
R. Dixon and S. Muthesius: *Victorian Architecture*, World A. (London, 1978)

STEFAN MUTHESIUS

Brooks, James (ii) (*b* St Louis, MO, 18 Oct 1906; *d* Long Island, New York, 9 March 1992). American painter. He moved in 1916 to Dallas, TX, where he studied at Southern Methodist University from 1923 to 1925, majoring in art, and from 1925 to 1926 at the Dallas Art Institute. In 1926 he moved to New York, where he studied at the Art Students League from 1927–30 while earning his living as a commercial artist. In the 1930s he painted in the prevailing social realist style, usually taking the rural West and Midwest as his subject-matter. From 1936 to 1942 he participated in the Works Progress Administration's Federal Art Project, executing murals in public buildings; the most important of these, including the *Acquisition of Long Island* (1937–8; New York, Woodside Lib.; destr. 1963, with few remaining fragments) and the vast *Flight* (3.65×99 m, 1938–42; for detail, see I. Sandler, *Abstract Expressionism: The Triumph of American Painting*, New York, 1970, p. 234) at La Guardia Airport in New York, were later destroyed. Even in these representational works, with their meticulously organized spaces, a tendency to formal and abstract concerns is in evidence.

After serving as an artist correspondent during World War II, Brooks returned to painting, evolving a style characterized by freer and looser forms through variations on Cubism. Influenced first by the work of Picasso, by the late 1940s he developed a preference for fluid colours as used by Jackson Pollock, with whom he became close friends from 1946. In this mature period, during which he became associated with Abstract Expressionism, he demonstrated his mastery and control of colour and gesture, allowing the paint to whirl and blot freely in paintings such as *Boon* (oil on canvas, 1.8×1.73 m, 1957; London, Tate), with colour and space in harmonious balance. His preference for subtle tonalities and calm, lyrical moods distinguished his work from the more aggressive tone of the branch of Abstract Expressionism sometimes referred to as action painting. In later paintings such as *Cooba* (2.03×1.88 m, 1963; Buffalo, NY, Albright–Knox A.G.) he introduced elegant linear elements as a decorative counterpoint to the flat irregular shapes against which they were placed.

BIBLIOGRAPHY
Twelve Americans (exh. cat., ed. D. C. Miller, New York, MOMA, 1956)
James Brooks (exh. cat., foreword J. I. H. Baur, essay S. Hunter; New York, Whitney, 1963)
Recent Paintings by James Brooks (exh. cat., New York, Martha Jackson Gal., 1968)
James Brooks (exh. cat., New York, Martha Jackson Gal., 1971)
James Brooks (exh. cat., intro. M. Rueppel; Dallas, TX, Mus. F.A., 1972)
James Brooks: Paintings 1952–1975, Works on Paper 1950–1975 (exh. cat., New York, Martha Jackson Gal., 1975)

ALBERTO CERNUSCHI

Brooks, Romaine (*b* Rome, 1 May 1874; *d* Nice, 7 Dec 1970). American painter and draughtswoman. She grew up in various European and American cities, including Paris, Rome, Geneva and New York, living in a disturbing family atmosphere. When she was seven, her mother abandoned her in New York, and her Irish laundress, Mrs Hickey, took her into her home, where they lived in severe poverty until Brooks's grandfather's secretary collected her. Brooks was allowed and encouraged to draw by Mrs Hickey. In 1896–7 Brooks went to Rome, studying at the Scuola Nazionale by day and the Circolo Artistico by night. The only woman at the Scuola, she was one of the first to be allowed to draw from a nude male model. In summer 1899 she studied at the Académie Colarossi, Paris. A substantial fortune inherited from her grandfather (1902) markedly altered the quality of her life. Brooks moved to London (1902–4), made her earliest mature portrait paintings of young women, and returned to Paris.

Her first one-person exhibition was at the Galerie Durand-Ruel (1910), of 13 portraits, including those of noted members of Parisian society. These and later works for which she is renowned (e.g. *Ida Rubenstein*, 1917; Washington, DC, Smithsonian Inst.) have a characteristic boldness that sets the figures apart from their environments. Her drawings are more imaginary, exploring personal and fanciful themes. Brooks's style suggests an interest in Symbolism and Art Nouveau. Interest in Brooks was reawakened by a major exhibition at the National Collection of Fine Arts, Washington, DC, in 1971.

BIBLIOGRAPHY
A. Breeskin: *Romaine Brooks, Thief of Souls* (Washington, DC, 1971)
M. Secresst: *Between me and my Life: A Biography of Romaine Brooks* (London, 1976)

□

Broome, Isaac (*b* Valcartier, Qué., 16 May 1836; *d* Trenton, NJ, 4 May 1922). American sculptor, ceramic modeller and teacher of Canadian birth. He received his artistic training at the Pennsylvania Academy of Fine Arts in Philadelphia, where he was elected an Academician in 1860 and taught (1860–63) in the Life and Antique department. In 1854 he assisted Thomas Crawford with the statues on the pediment of the Senate wing of the US Capitol in Washington, DC, and tried unsuccessfully to establish a firm for architectural terracotta and garden ornaments in Pittsburgh and New York.

From 1875 Broome was employed as a modeller by the firm of Ott & Brewer in Trenton, NJ. The parian porcelain sculpture he created for their display at the Centennial International Exhibition of 1876 in Philadelphia won him medals for ceramic arts (*see* UNITED STATES OF AMERICA, fig. 41). Following his success at the Exhibition and at the Exposition Universelle of 1878 in Paris, for which he was Special Commissioner from the USA, he was active as a teacher and lecturer and was keenly interested in educational, political and industrial reforms. He also continued as a modeller for potters in Ohio and Trenton, including the Trent Tile Co. and the Providential Tile Co., producing major work as late as 1917, when he modelled a parian portrait bust of Walter Scott Lenox (Lawrenceville, NJ, Lenox Inc.).

BIBLIOGRAPHY
Who Was Who in America, i (Chicago, 1943)

ELLEN PAUL DENKER

Brosamer, Hans (*b* ?Fulda, *c*. 1500; *d* ?Erfurt, 1554 or after). German painter, draughtsman, engraver and woodcut designer. He worked in Fulda from *c*. 1520 to the mid-1540s, as is known from a series of dated paintings and copper engravings, including portraits of distinguished citizens of Fulda. Of the few surviving portraits, mainly from the 1520s, only one, that of *Chancellor Johannes von Othera* (1536; Switzerland, priv. col.), is signed with his full name. All have brownish flesh tones and a green background and are typified by rather angular faces, a certain stiffness and an interest in fine materials. A group of portraits bearing the monogram HB and a griffin's head and also dating from the 1520s, which has been associated with this series, cannot be attributed to Brosamer with certainty; they mostly represent leading citizens of Nuremberg and are closer to Lucas Cranach (i) in character.

Hans Brosamer: *David and Bathsheba*, woodcut, 800×976 mm, 1554 (London, British Museum)

Brosamer was specifically described as *Johannes Brosamer Fuldae degens*, on an engraving of the *Crucifixion* (1542; Hollstein, no. 7) and on one of *Samson and Delilah* (1545; Hollstein, no. 2), but his subsequent move to Erfurt is confirmed by the inscription *Hans Brosamer Formschneider zu Erffordt* on the woodcut portrait of *Landgrave Philip of Hesse* (*c.* 1546; Hollstein, no. 598). By then, like many other not very successful German painters of his day, he was devoting himself exclusively to graphic work for printing, both copper-engravings and woodcuts, either as single prints or as book illustrations. Over 30 copper engravings reveal his rather slight repertory of designs but a well thought-out technique, which he acquired by studying north German contemporaries such as Heinrich Aldegrever and Jakob Binck, as well as the Mannerists of the Netherlands. He also achieved a characteristic dense texture by using very closely hatched lines. He engraved Christian, mythological and Classical themes as well as a few genre scenes. Three plates that must have formed part of a larger set devoted to Old Testament subjects (then currently popular) are particularly successful: *Samson and Delilah*, *Samson Worshipping Idols* and *Bathsheba Bathing* (all 1545; Hollstein, nos 2–4); they are all the same size and have ambitious architectural backgrounds incorporating groups of figures, following Netherlandish models.

In contrast to the engravings, which have a certain unity of style, Brosamer's woodcuts present a more confused picture. Single prints are notably outnumbered by book illustrations, but of the many illustrations with the initials HB that appeared in Protestant works published in Frankfurt am Main, Wittenberg and Magdeburg, many must be the work of other artists, such as Hans Baldung. However, illustrations in Martin Luther's Bible, printed in Wittenberg (1550) by Hans Lufft (1495–1584), were the work of Hans Brosamer, some dated 1549 and 1550 (particularly those for the Old Testament, the epistles of St Paul and Revelations), as well as those for Luther's *Catechism* (1550), published by Weygand in Frankfurt am Main.

Despite many uncertainties as to the extent of his woodcut oeuvre, Brosamer must be ranked alongside Georg Lemberger as one of the most important masters who helped raise the standard of German Protestant book illustration, though both were overshadowed by Lucas Cranach (i).

According to a comment on the register of holders of a master's degree in Erfurt, Brosamer died of the plague in 1552, but this must be wrong: his large woodcut of *David and Bathsheba* (see fig.), which was published in Erfurt, is dated 1554. The monogram MB that appears alongside his on the woodcut probably stands for Martin Brosamer (*fl* 1554), presumably his son, who in later years was a publisher in Erfurt.

BIBLIOGRAPHY
Hollstein: *Ger.*; *NDB*; Thieme–Becker
A. von Bartsch: *Le Peintre-graveur* (1803–21), viii, pp. 455–70
J. D. Passavant: *Le Peintre-graveur* (Leipzig, 1860–64), iv, pp. 32–9
H. Röttinger: *Beiträge zur Geschichte des sächsischen Holzschnittes* (Strasbourg, 1921), pp. 16–65
H. Zimmermann: *Beiträge zur Bibelillustration des 16. Jahrhunderts* (Strasbourg, 1924), pp. 69–83
I. Kunze: 'Der Meister mit dem Greifenkopf: Ein Beitrag zur Brosamer Forschung', *Z. Dt. Ver. Kstwiss.*, viii (1941), pp. 209–38
P. Strieder: *Ger. Nmus. [Nürnberg]: Jber.*, xciv (Nuremberg, 1949), pp. 9–16
Die Welt des Hans Sachs: 400 Holzschnitte des 16. Jahrhunderts (exh. cat., Nuremberg, Stadtgesch. Museen, 1976)
R. A. Koch: *Early German Masters* (1981), 17 [VIII/iv] of *The Illustrated Bartsch*, ed. W. Strauss (New York, 1978–), pp. 9–78
JANEZ HÖFLER

Brosse, Salomon de (*b* Verneuil-sur-Oise, *c.* 1571; *d* Paris, 8 Dec 1626). French architect. He was one of the most important architects of the early 17th century in France. His rational, monumental approach marked a move away from late Mannerism and was a precursor to the subsequent development of French classicism by such architects as François Mansart.

1. Training and early works, before 1615. 2. Palais du Luxembourg and late works, 1615 and after.

1. TRAINING AND EARLY WORKS, BEFORE 1615. He was the son of Jean de Brosse, an architect who settled at Verneuil-sur-Oise in the late 1560s and worked on the château there; his mother, Julienne de Brosse, was a daughter of the engraver Jacques Androuet Du Cerceau (i). Both families were Protestant. Salomon de Brosse was probably first trained at Verneuil, a Protestant centre, by his father and, after his father's death (before 1585), by his uncle Jacques Androuet Du Cerceau (ii). In 1592 he married Florence Métivier, an architect's daughter, and their one son, Paul de Brosse (*fl* 1615–44), also became an architect. Salomon de Brosse is not known to have travelled abroad; he remained at Verneuil at least until the mid-1590s and is first heard of professionally in 1598, working with Jacques Du Cerceau (ii) at the château of Montceaux, near Meaux. The late start of his career is probably explained by the Wars of Religion.

In 1601 de Brosse was commissioned to complete the château de Verneuil (after its acquisition by Henriette d'Entragues) and the château de Montceaux (for Marie de' Medici, Henry IV's queen); in the same year he signed documents as 'Ingénieur de la Reyne'. Verneuil was destroyed in 1734, but plans and elevations made after its completion (1608) show that de Brosse modified and completed the entrance pavilion and built a rusticated forecourt with massive gates and square-domed pavilions. At Montceaux (destr. French Revolution), some buildings remain that are certainly by de Brosse: the ruins of the entrance pavilion, part of a habitable wing, and the forecourt gateway and chapel. The plans of Verneuil and the remains at Montceaux illustrate de Brosse's impressive use of restricted centralized spaces. The entrance pavilions to both châteaux were domed, with a giant order of Corinthian columns and a centrally planned chapel on the upper floor. At Verneuil, the entrance pavilion and chapel were both circular: at Montceaux, an oval chapel (probably c. 1615) was built in a basically square pavilion (probably begun c. 1601). Such centralized plans were related to designs by Sebastiano Serlio and Du Cerceau (i), to Philibert de L'Orme's chapels at the châteaux of Anet (1549–52) and Saint-Léger-en-Yvelines (c. 1555) and to Jean Bullant's Valois Chapel (begun 1572; destr.) at Saint-Denis Abbey, Paris. The composition of the façade of the forecourt chapel at Montceaux, articulated by Doric pilasters supporting a triangular pediment, combines an engraving by Serlio with the façade of Jacopo Vignola's S Maria del Piano (1559–65) at Capranica di Sutri, Italy, which de Brosse must have known from a drawing.

In 1608 Henry IV's chief minister, the Duc de Sully, commissioned de Brosse to build the new town of Henrichemont (Cher), of which some of the original houses survive (see SULLY). In Paris, de Brosse enlarged the Hôtel de Soissons (1611–12), Hôtel de Bouillon (1612), which he largely rebuilt, Hôtel de Bullion (1614) and Hôtel Bégnine-Bernard (1614), all now destroyed. Another Paris building by de Brosse was the Hôtel de Liancourt (see Marot), begun in 1613 for the Duc de Bouillon and named after the marquis who purchased it in 1623. On the death of Jacques Androuet Du Cerceau (ii) in 1614 de Brosse inherited the position of Architecte du Roi and was given a royal pension. In the same period he designed two important châteaux: Blérancourt (Aisne) and Coulommiers, near Meaux, which were both executed by de Brosse's relative Charles Du Ry. Of Blérancourt (begun 1612; destr. World War I; see CHÂTEAU, fig. 2), two detached pavilions, several gates and a rebuilt fragment of the château remain. The building was constructed entirely of stone and had no wings; it marked an important step in the development of the free-standing château, begun in France in the previous century. The corps-de-logis and its angle pavilions had the same number of storeys, and the pavilions were covered by low domes on a rectangular plan so that the roof-line was nowhere abruptly broken. The façades were articulated by superimposed orders of pilasters and in treatment were indebted to Pierre Lescot's façade in the Cour Carrée of the Louvre. The surviving moat pavilions and gates show the traditions of the Du Cerceau workshop, modified to a marked degree by the influence of Vignola's work engraved in his *Architettura* (Rome, 1562) and by the suite of Mannerist gateway designs appended to that treatise. Blérancourt was built for Bernard Potier, whose wife, Charlotte de Vieuxpont, was an active and learned patron. She had travelled in

Italy, collected architectural drawings and admired Vignola's work, and she stipulated in the contracts that there should be correct classical detail at Blérancourt.

The château of Coulommiers was begun in 1613 for Catherine de Gonzague, Duchesse de Longueville. It was built on a badly chosen site and was an over-ambitious project; financial mismanagement led to the demolition of the unfinished building in 1738, and almost nothing designed by de Brosse remains. Drawings of Coulommiers survive, made overly classical in Jean Marot's engravings of 1655 (for illustration see MAROT, (1)). At Coulommiers, de Brosse returned to the traditional courtyard château of brick and stone exemplified by Verneuil and Montceaux. His original design for doubled angle pavilions was later modified, presumably by Du Ry; four of them were heightened, which destroyed de Brosse's horizontal emphasis. The exterior, with its superimposed rusticated pilasters, was comparatively severe. In contrast, the courtyard façades had superimposed full columns and an abundance of relief sculptures, busts and statues, the principal theme of which—the female as hero—reflected the preoccupations of the patron. From this court survive ruined quadrant arcades that linked the corps-de-logis to the wings. A similar motif was used by de Brosse at the Hôtel de Bouillon in Paris and was later adopted by François Mansart at Berny and Blois. De Brosse's design for the entrance screen and pavilion at Coulommiers was later abandoned (1630) in favour of a much-reduced scheme by Mansart, but the design was taken up again at the Palais du Luxembourg for Marie de' Medici, of whose circle Mme de Longueville was a member.

2. PALAIS DU LUXEMBOURG AND LATE WORKS, 1615 AND AFTER. The commission for the Palais du Luxembourg (begun 1615; see PARIS, §V, 8), the most important of his career, was won by de Brosse in open competition. The site of the palace was originally on the outskirts of Paris, and it was conceived as a courtyard château. It was built of stone, and the Queen's wish for a building reminiscent of her former home, the Palazzo Pitti in Florence, was fulfilled by de Brosse in the rustication of the whole building and the incorporation of certain details from Bartolomeo Ammanati's elevations at the Palazzo Pitti. The corps-de-logis at the Palais du Luxembourg was on the plan of Blérancourt, flanked by wings terminating in single pavilions that were linked by a screen (now an open arcade but originally closed) to the entrance pavilion. In the corps-de-logis the unusual combination of the central staircase with an exedra containing a chapel beyond it (both destr. 19th century) may reflect the arrangement of the château of Nantouillet (1515), near Meaux. The roof-lines, courtyard levels and other parts of the building were later altered and the interior drastically changed, but the engravings of Marot and Jean-François Blondel allow an appreciation of the outstanding merit of de Brosse's work: his ability to compose in mass, although he was sometimes less sure in detail. The least-altered parts remained the entrance pavilion (see fig. 1) and the structures flanking the screen.

In 1616 de Brosse designed the west front of the Late Gothic church of St Gervais in Paris (see FRANCE, fig. 8). Here he faced the problem of how to combine a classical

1. Salomon de Brosse: entrance pavilion of the Palais du Luxembourg, Paris, begun 1615

façade with a tall Gothic nave. Several experiments with three-storey façades were made in France in the early 17th century. De Brosse's solution was to adapt the three-storey château frontispiece with superimposed orders, as exemplified in de L'Orme's *corps-de-logis* at Anet, and the result—with its three orders of fluted columns, Doric portico and bold, segmental pediment—was highly original if somewhat stark. Although Mansart borrowed freely from de Brosse's design for his own two-storey façade at the church of the Feuillants, Paris (1623), the arrival in France of the Roman type of church interior and two-storey façade (of which St Joseph-des-Carmes (1615–20), Paris, is an early example) lessened the impact of St Gervais on future church designs.

In 1618 de Brosse designed a new Salle des Pas Perdus (public hall) for the Palais de Justice in Paris and in the same year travelled to Rennes to provide plans (executed by Germain Gaultier (1571–1624)) for the completion of the Palais du Parlement of Brittany (now the Palais de Justice); both buildings survive in altered form. His hall in the Palais de Justice, Paris (see fig. 2), with its Doric arcades and barrel vault, goes back to designs based on the Antique by Du Cerceau. There is a hall of similar type in the Palais de Justice at Rennes, but without arcades; de Brosse's most important contribution here, however, was the principal façade, which consists of a two-storey central block with flanking pavilions contained under the same roof-line. Above the rusticated lower storey, the first floor is articulated by coupled Doric pilasters with, in the central block, arched windows modelled on those by Vignola at the Villa Farnese, Caprarola. The composition was spoilt by the removal of de Brosse's exterior staircase, which greatly

weakens its horizontal character. The Rennes façade was influenced by Francesco Primaticcio's Aile de la Belle Cheminée (1568) at Fontainebleau, particularly in its roof-line, and was later recalled by Mansart at Blois (1635–8).

A new Protestant 'Temple' (destr.) was begun to de Brosse's design in 1623 at Charenton, near Paris, the interior of which is known from Marot's engravings. Its plan and elevation were based on Vitruvius's description of the Roman basilica at Fano and on similarly derived Palladian prototypes. In its turn the Temple exerted considerable influence on Protestant church planning in Europe and on synagogue architecture, particularly in Holland. De Brosse was dismissed from the Luxembourg in 1624 for faults of mismanagement similar to those at Coulommiers, which were exacerbated by his being contractor as well as architect and left him financially embarrassed. Because of failing health, he often retired to the house he built at Verneuil from 1622 (which partially survives); he undertook no more work of significance. Engravings and a few drawings, none certainly attributable to de Brosse, provide all that is known of many of his buildings; an album of drawings in the Louvre formerly attributed to him is probably the work of Du Ry.

By birth and training de Brosse was closely linked to the Du Cerceau workshop, with its tradition of late 16th-century architectural and decorative design and the polychromatic use of brick and stone. Equally important was his study of Vignola, whose *Architettura*, in print for 50 years, had hitherto had a negligible impact in France; he was also indebted to de L'Orme, Lescot and Serlio. His synthesis of all these influences enabled him to develop a highly individual style but not a consistent one. Each building was an experiment in manner, in which he sought suitably to reflect the status and character of the patron or to deal with a specific problem, as at St Gervais. Clearly he preferred the designing to the execution and supervision of his projects, but despite the consequences of this practice his prestige as the architect of the Queen's palace in Paris was high. His work had a direct influence on Mansart, Pierre Le Muet and others, but he remains a somewhat enigmatic figure; his buildings were so varied that if no documentary evidence existed there would scarcely be reason to attribute any two of them to the same architect.

BIBLIOGRAPHY

J. Marot: *Recueil des plans, profils, et elevations de plusiers palais, chasteaux, églises, sepultures, grotes et hostels bâtis dans Paris* (Paris, c. 1660–70/R Farnborough, 1969) [known as the *Petit Marot*; engrs]
——: *L'Architecture françoise* (Paris, c. 1670, rev. 1727 as vol. iv of J. Mariette: *L'Architecture française/R* 1927–9) [known as the *Grand Marot*; engrs]
H. Sauval: *Histoire et recherches des antiquités de Paris* (Paris, 1724)
A. Blunt: *Art and Architecture in France, 1500–1700*, Pelican Hist. A. (Harmondsworth, 1953, rev. 1982), pp. 170–76
R. Coope: 'The Château of Montceaux-en-Brie', *J. Warb. & Court. Inst.*, xxii (1959), pp. 71–87
H. Derottleur: *Le Château Neuf de Coulommiers, 1613–1738* (diss., U. Paris, 1959) [with comprehensive transcriptions of source docs incl. the *procès-verbal* (description and estimate for repairs to the château) dated 17–22 Oct 1714]
R. Coope: 'History and Architecture of the Château of Verneuil-sur-Oise', *Gaz. B.-A.*, lxxiv (1962), pp. 291–318
——: *Salomon de Brosse and the Development of the Classical Style in French Architecture from 1565–1630* (London, 1972) [somewhat outdated in approach to 'classical style'; reliable for bldgs, cat., doc. etc]

2. Salomon de Brosse: interior of the Salle des Pas Perdus, Palais de Justice, Paris, 1618

C. Mignot: 'Travaux récents sur l'architecture française: Du maniérisme au classicisme', *Rev. A.* [Paris], xxii (1976), pp. 78–85

J. Sartre: *Châteaux 'brique et pierre' en France* (Paris, 1981)

ROSALYS COOPE

Brosses, Charles de (*b* Dijon, 7 Feb 1709; *d* Paris, 7 May 1777). French magistrate and writer. He was successively Conseiller (1730), Président à Mortier (1740) and Premier Président (1775) of the Parlement of Burgundy. For his fierce defence of the independence of this institution against the French monarchy he was twice disgraced and exiled, in 1744 and 1771–2. In addition to his official duties he devoted himself to works of historical, literary, linguistic and geographical scholarship, becoming a member of the Académie des Inscriptions et Belles Lettres (1746) and also of the Académies of Dijon and Lyon. He published works on Herculaneum (1750), Australasia (1756) and the religious cults of ancient Egypt (1760), as well as a translation of Sallust (1777). It was probably research for this last work, conceived many years earlier, that prompted his tour of Italy in 1739–40. His year-long travels were the occasion for the composition of the first version of the literary work for which de Brosses is best remembered, the *Lettres familières*, which he addressed to his friends in Burgundian society.

De Brosses set out for Italy on 30 May 1739. He had several travelling companions, and they visited successively Genoa, Milan, Padua, Venice, Bologna, Florence, Livorno, Pisa, Siena, Rome, Naples and then returned to Rome, where they stayed for four months. De Brosses moved in the highest social circles and was received at the court of Charles III (*reg* 1734–59) in Naples, at that of Charles-Emmanuel III of Savoy in Turin and in Rome by Pope Clement XII. His insatiable curiosity led him to visit methodically all artistic sites and monuments and to attend many theatrical performances and concerts. He returned from Italy in April 1740 to find the success of his letters such that they were already in circulation in copies. At the request of his friends de Brosses augmented and corrected the text in the years 1745–55. The first, posthumous, edition was not, however, published until 1799, while the first reliable transcription of the manuscripts did not appear until 1836.

In matters of art, de Brosses evinced a taste substantially reflecting the spirit of his times and that propagated by the Académie Royale de Peinture et de Sculpture, with history painting in the Grand Style at the peak of the hierarchy of genres. He preferred the works of Raphael and Correggio and of such artists of the Bolognese school as the Carracci, Domenichino, Guercino, Francesco Albani and Guido Reni to the art of the early Renaissance or medieval periods. Paintings that were classicizing in style and that reflected the ideas of the Counter-Reformation in subject matter pleased him more than the realism of Caravaggio or the Dutch school. The value of the *Lettres familières* lies in their presentation of the aesthetic taste of French classicism, as codified at the end of the 17th century by Roger de Piles, with the charm, spontaneity and freshness of a private correspondence.

WRITINGS

R. Colomb, ed.: *L'Italie il y a cent ans ou lettres écrites d'Italie en 1739 et 1740* (Paris, 1836); 2nd edn as *Le Président de Brosses en Italie: Lettres familières écrites d'Italie en 1739 et 1740* (Paris, 1858)
Y. Bézard, ed.: *Lettres familières sur l'Italie publiées d'après les manuscrits, avec une introduction et des notes* (Paris, 1931)
F. d'Agay, ed.: *Lettres d'Italie du Président de Brosses* (Paris, 1986)

BIBLIOGRAPHY

T. Foisset: *Le Président de Brosses: Histoire des lettres et des parlements au XVIIIe siècle* (Paris, 1842)
M. Sandoz: 'Le Président Charles de Brosses et la peinture d'histoire', *Actes du colloque Charles de Brosses, 1777–1977: Dijon, 1977*, pp. 81–95
——: 'Remarques de Charles de Brosses sur les peintures et tableaux vus en Italie d'après ses *Lettres familières*', *Nouv. Répub. Lett.*, 1 (1983), pp. 65–112

ALEXANDRA SKLIAR-PIGUET

Brosterhuisen [Brosterhuysen], **Jan** [Johannes] **(van)** (*b* Leiden, *c.* 1596; *d* Breda, 13 Sept 1650). Dutch etcher, painter, poet, musician and botanist. As early as 1610 he enrolled as a student at Leiden University. He was a member of the Muiderkring, a society to which such people as Caspar Barlaeus (1584–1648) and Constantijn Huygens belonged. Although he was a versatile artist, he seems to have been less successful on a social level. Much is known about his life from his correspondence with Huygens. In 1639 he became secretary to the innkeeper in Heusden, near 's Hertogenbosch, and by 1642 had moved to Amersfoort. At this time he was in close contact with the architect Jacob van Campen, for whom he translated the treatises of Vitruvius and Palladio. In 1646 Huygens found him a job at Breda University, where he taught Greek and botany. But his private life gave rise to criticism: Rivet, the university curator, condemned Brosterhuisen for living with his housekeeper, and on Huygens's insistence he finally married her. In 1662–3 the poet P. C. Hooft, Barlaeus and Huygens managed to get him an appointment as '*hortulanus*' (botanist) at Amsterdam's Atheneum Illustre.

Although he produced paintings, Brosterhuisen concentrated mainly on etching. His themes were views of Amersfoort and landscapes (e.g. Amsterdam, Rijksmus.), the latter notable for the artist's interest in trees as the principal subject-matter (e.g. *Landscape with Avenue of Trees*, Hollstein, p. 237), perhaps a consequence of his professional training. He also made several etchings after drawings of Brazilian subjects by Frans Post for Barlaeus's book on the history of the Dutch occupation of Brazil, which was published by Johannes Blaeu.

UNPUBLISHED SOURCES

Leiden, Bib. Rijksuniv. [correspondence: 50 letters]

PRINTS

C. Barlaeus: *Rerum per octennium in Brasília gestarum historia* (Amsterdam, 1647)

BIBLIOGRAPHY

Hollstein: *Dut. & Flem.*; Thieme–Becker
C. Kramm: *De levens en werken der Hollandsche en Vlaamsche kunstschilders, beeldhouwers, graveurs en bouwmeesters* (Amsterdam, 1857–64/R 1974), i, p. 169
Constantijn Huygens, zijn plaats in geleerd Europa (Amsterdam, 1973), pp. 217–24
I. de Groot: *Landscape Etchings by the Dutch Masters of the Seventeenth Century* (London, 1979), pp. 90–95
D. Freedberg: *Dutch Landscape Prints of the Seventeenth Century* (London, 1980)

TRUDY VAN ZADELHOFF

Brostoloni, Giambattista. *See* BRUSTOLON, GIAMBATTISTA.

Brotherhood of St Luke. *See* FELLOWSHIP OF ST LUKE.

Brotherhood of the Linked Ring. *See* LINKED RING.

Brothers Dalziel [Dalziel Brothers]. English wood-engraving firm founded in 1839 by George Dalziel (*b* Wooler, Northumb. [now Tyne and Wear], 1 Dec 1815; *d* London, 4 Aug 1902). In 1835 he came to London, where he was later joined by his brothers Edward Dalziel (*b* Wooler, 5 Dec 1817; *d* London, 25 March 1905), John Dalziel (*b* Wooler, 1 Jan 1822; *d* Drigg, Cumberland [now Cumbria], 21 May 1869) and Thomas Dalziel (*b* Wooler, 9 May 1823; *d* Herne Bay, Kent, 17 March 1906) and his sister Margaret Dalziel (*b* Wooler, 3 Nov 1819; *d* London, 12 July 1894). George acquired his engraving skill from Charles Gray (*d* 1847) during the 1830s and then trained his siblings. Their family firm—the Brothers Dalziel—was the most influential wood-engraving firm in the 1860s and 1870s.

The exact number of engravers employed at any one time by the Dalziels is not known, although it was commonly considered a big firm. They had journeyman-engravers and apprentices but also contracted out work to others. Their apparent domination of Victorian wood-engraving is due as much to their role as arbiters of taste—exercised through their activities both as art editors of books and magazines and as publishers and printers in their own right—as it is to the vast amount of illustrative work that carried their distinctively engraved name.

As reproductive engravers on wood, their task was to interpret the original artwork of others. They knew many of the leading artists and writers of the period, a fact emphasized in George Dalziel's *The Brothers Dalziel: A Record of Fifty Years' Work* (1901), and persuaded some of the best draughtsmen to draw for them, including Myles Birket Foster, George Du Maurier, John Gilbert, Frederic Leighton, John Everett Millais and John Tenniel. They also discovered and promoted unknown talent; Fred Walker, G. J. Pinwell, Arthur Boyd Houghton and John Dawson Watson (1832–92) were just a few of the well-known illustrators of the 19th century who benefited early in their careers from the Dalziels' commissions.

The Dalziels' best work was for the magazines and books of the 1860s. They produced the engravings for the popular *Cornhill* magazine, and both engraved and commissioned the illustrations to *Good Words* and the *Sunday Magazine*. They contributed work to many books, but considered their highest achievements to be such sumptuous 'fine art' books as *Pictures of English Landscape* (1863; illustrated by Birket Foster), *Parables of Our Lord* (1864; illustrated by Millais), *Don Quixote* (1866; illustrated by Arthur Boyd Houghton) and Lewis Carroll's *Alice* stories (1865, 1871; illustrated by Tenniel).

Dante Gabriel Rossetti wrote a polemical parody in verse ('O woodman spare that block') implying a tradesman's indifference on the Dalziels' part when engraving from his original drawings on the block. However, Rossetti had failed to understand the limitations of the process and provided the Dalziels with designs in a style singularly inappropriate to their medium. Nevertheless writers have quoted the short poem in implicit, if not explicit, criticism of the Dalziels in particular and commercial engraving on wood in general, and the Dalziels' reputation (and that of 19th-century commercial wood-engraving as a whole) has yet to be fully cleared of Rossetti's charge of carelessness.

The importance of the Dalziel Brothers is diverse. Although they were not innovators, they set high standards of engraving that others were obliged to meet. During the 1860s many famous illustrations passed through their hands for engraving, and as art editors and patrons they were partly responsible for the growth and popularity of both book and magazine illustration in the Victorian period (see BOOK ILLUSTRATION, §IV). The British Museum, London, has the largest collection of their work, including 49 albums containing 54,000 impressions.

WRITINGS

G. Dalziel: *The Brothers Dalziel: A Record of Fifty Years' Work* (London, 1901, R/1978)

BIBLIOGRAPHY

G. White: *English Illustration: 'The Sixties', 1855–70* (London, 1897, R/Bath, 1970)

G. N. Ray: *The Illustrator and the Book in England from 1790 to 1914* (Oxford, 1976), pp. 90–96

The Dalziel Family: Engravers and Illustrators (sale cat., London, Sotheby's, 16 May 1978)

LEO JOHN DE FREITAS

Brou, priory church. Former Benedictine priory church, dedicated to St Nicholas of Tolentino, near Bourg-en-Bresse, Burgundy, France. Situated on an important road linking the northern provinces with Italy, the church was built by Margaret of Austria (see HABSBURG, §I(4)) after the death of her third husband Philibert the Fair, Duke of Savoy, in 1504. Earlier, in 1480, Margaret's mother-in-law Margaret of Bourbon had undertaken to transform the small priory of Brou into a larger monastery if her husband Philippe, Comte de Bresse, survived a hunting accident, but despite his recovery the vow was not fulfilled. Margaret of Austria saw Philibert's death, the result of another hunting accident, as divine retribution, and she immediately decided to initiate the work, securing the services of artists from the south Netherlands, Burgundy, Italy and France. She spared no expense on the church's embellishment, realizing that the monastery was fast becoming, in the eyes of her contemporaries, a testimony to her economic and political power and wishing to rival her sister-in-law Louise of Savoy (1476–1531), the mother of Francis I. Although Brou has traditionally been seen as a symbol of conjugal love, it seems to be more a monument to Margaret of Austria's glory.

The church was built from 1513 to 1532 by Loys van Bodeghem (c. 1470–1540). The architecture is relatively simple, but the furnishings are sumptuous. The most notable feature of the exterior is the richly carved west portal. On the tympanum, set beneath a basket arch, are the kneeling figures of Margaret of Austria and Philibert with their patron saints; between them, in the centre, *Christ* is flanked by angels holding shields. *St Nicholas of Tolentino* (on whose feast day Philibert had died) is

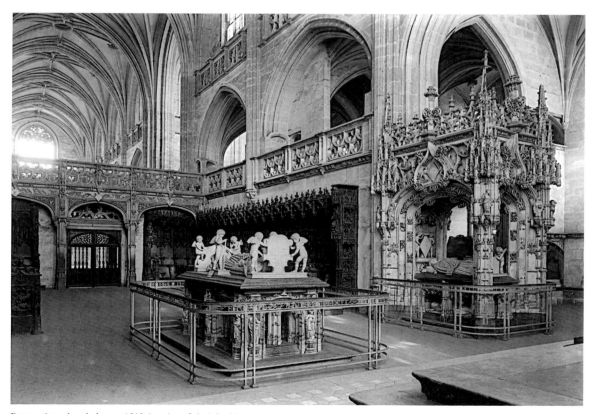

Brou, priory church, begun 1513, interior of choir looking west

represented on the trumeau, with *SS Peter and Paul* on the embrasures and *St Andrew* at the apex of the arch above the portal. The rich decoration of foliage, flowers and fruit (laurel, vine, acanthus, palms and daisies) shows both Flamboyant and Renaissance inspiration, and the whole is strewn with the initials of Philibert and Margaret united by 'love knots', small cords festooned between two letters.

Inside, the church has a four-bay, aisled nave, a slightly projecting transept and a choir with a five-sided apse, flanked by staggered, rectangular chapels. The pier mouldings continue into the arches and vaults without capitals, and the only ornamentation of the nave is the traceried Flamboyant balustrade in front of the triforium passage. The vault, typical of the period, has liernes and tiercerons of simple profile, with carved bosses. A rare survival in France is the rood screen, delicately carved with ornamental motifs and statues of Christ and saints. The exceptionally well-lit choir, shielded from the nave by the screen (see fig.), retains much of its stained glass, executed between 1525 and 1531 by a workshop from Lyon. The axial window contains glass representing *Noli me tangere* (upper part) and the *Appearance of Christ to his Mother* (lower part), after engravings by Albrecht Dürer; to the left and right are Philibert and Margaret kneeling with their patron saints, their coats of arms above. Further stained-glass windows in Margaret of Austria's chapel on the north side of the choir depict the *Assumption of the Virgin*, with Margaret and Philibert, and the *Triumph of Faith*. The chapel also contains a monumental altarpiece of white marble, with representations of the *Seven Joys of the Virgin*.

The richly carved choir-stalls (1530–32), executed by Pierre Berchod (called Terrasson), a carpenter from Bresse, depict biblical scenes, the *Old Testament* on the south side and the *New Testament* on the north. Margaret of Austria's main attention, however, was focused on the tombs, for which she may have received advice from PIETRO TORRIGIANI. The effigies were designed by Jan van Roome, Jean Perréal and Michel Colombe but executed by CONRAT MEIT. The tomb of *Margaret of Bourbon* is related to a widespread late medieval type: her effigy, watched by angels, lies on a sarcophagus decorated with weepers, with a greyhound (symbol of fidelity) at her feet, the whole fitted into a recess in the south wall of the choir screen. The tomb of *Philibert the Fair*, in the centre of the choir, is in a more up-to-date style, modelled on such tombs as those of *Francis II, Duke of Brittany*, and *Marguerite de Foix* in Nantes Cathedral and of *Louis XII* at Saint-Denis Abbey. On the upper part, Philibert's effigy is dressed in clothes of state, a lion (symbol of power) at his feet, while below lies a representation of his naked corpse. Statuettes, of south Netherlandish workmanship, surround the tomb under carved canopies; *St Mary Magdalen* is outstanding in its grace and elegance. Although not in the place of honour, the tomb of *Margaret of Austria*, set against the cloister wall of the choir, is the most sumptuous of the three tombs, its magnificent canopy overrun with sculptural decoration. The tomb itself, however, is quite simple. Margaret's features are respectfully treated, although not idealized, and the depiction of her corpse on the lower level of the tomb shows the gangrenous foot wound from which she died.

BIBLIOGRAPHY
A.-N. Didron: *Monographie de Notre-Dame de Brou* (Lyon, 1842)
J. Baux: *Recherches historiques et archéologiques sur l'église de Brou* (Bourg, 1844)
C. Jarrin: *Brou: Sa reconstruction, ses architectes* (Bourg, 1888)
V. Nodet: *L'Eglise de Brou* (Paris, 1925)
F. Mathey: *Brou* (Paris, 1967, 2/1978)
A. Bidet: *Brou: Temple de la fidélité* (Paris, 1973)

CATHERINE LEGROS

Brough, Robert (*b* Invergordon, Highland, 20 March 1872; *d* Sheffield, 21 Jan 1905). Scottish painter. He studied in the early 1890s at Aberdeen School of Art, at the Royal Scottish Academy of Art and in Paris under Benjamin Constant. He returned in 1894 to Aberdeen, where he produced numerous portraits before moving to London in 1897, the year in which he exhibited *Fantaisie en folie* (London, Tate). Thereafter he exhibited with the Royal Society of Arts and with the Royal Academy from 1901. In 1900 he won the Silver Medal at the Exposition Universelle in Paris, and in 1904 he was elected an Associate of the Royal Scottish Academy.

Brough is best known for portraits such as *John Donald Esquire* (1903; Aberdeen A.G.), which shows a three-quarter-length seated figure in a black frock coat, his left hand resting on his umbrella handle, and *Rev. Alexander Ogilvie LLD of Robert Gordon's College, Aberdeen* (1903; Aberdeen, A.G.), again a three-quarter length, life-size figure seated as if to write at a table strewn with books and documents, the tones of his face subtly contrasted with the light-grey tones of the wall. He was influenced above all by traditions of portraiture in Great Britain as represented by Henry Raeburn, Joshua Reynolds and Thomas Lawrence or by contemporaries such as James Abbott McNeill Whistler and John Singer Sargent. In addition to these portraits in oil he produced Scottish landscapes and pictures using African, Breton and Spanish motifs in a variety of media including watercolour, pastel, chalk and charcoal. Two years after his death following a railway accident near Sheffield, a memorial exhibition was organized with the help of Sargent.

BIBLIOGRAPHY
Thieme–Becker
Exhibition of Pictures & Sketches by Robert Brough A.R.S.A. (exh. cat., London, Burlington F.A. Club, 1907)

KENNETH G. HAY

Brouwer, Adriaen [Adriaan] (*b* ?Oudenaarde, 1605–6; *bur* Antwerp, 1 Feb 1638). Flemish painter and draughtsman, active also in the northern Netherlands. His date of birth, although unrecorded, can be deduced from Bullaert's biography, which states that he was 32 years old when he died. He is first documented in March 1625, when he was staying at an inn in Amsterdam run by the painter Barent van Someren (*c.* 1572–1632). Brouwer is also recorded on 23 July 1626 as a notary's witness at a sale of pictures in Amsterdam. He must have been living in Haarlem then, as he is mentioned in 1626 in connection with the rhetoricians' chamber De Wijngaertranken, an amateur literary society whose motto was 'In Liefde Boven Al' (Love above all). According to Houbraken, Brouwer was a pupil of Frans Hals in Haarlem, but there is no evidence of Hals's direct influence in his work. (Brouwer may also have studied with his father (*d* 1621/2), a designer of tapestry cartoons in Oudenaarde in Flanders.) When exactly Adriaen Brouwer left Haarlem is not known, but in 1631–2 he was enrolled in the Antwerp Guild of St Luke as an independent master and is regularly mentioned in documents in that city in subsequent years, mainly in connection with debts. He was imprisoned in 1633, possibly for tax debt though probably for political reasons. By April 1634 he had been released and was living in the house of the engraver Paulus Pontius. The same year he joined the Antwerp rhetoricians' chamber known as De Violieren. His only recorded pupil was a Jan Dandoy in 1635, of whom nothing is now known, although Houbraken and de Bie cite Joos van Craesbeeck too, who must have been attached to him unofficially rather than through the Guild; his early work certainly reveals Brouwer's influence. Brouwer's burial in the Carmelite church suggests that he died in poverty.

Brouwer made a significant contribution to peasant genre painting in the first part of the 17th century. His interior settings and unsentimental representations of coarse facial expressions and strong emotions were important thematic innovations. (This was decades before art theory began to focus on the expressive potential of emotions.) Brouwer's works, moreover, contain deliberate references to moralizing literature, which elevated low-life genre painting to a new intellectual level. His paintings were highly regarded in his lifetime, not least by Rembrandt and Rubens, who, according to contemporary inventories, owned six and seventeen of his works respectively.

1. PAINTINGS. The chronology of Brouwer's painted work is speculative as none of the pictures is dated. Only two pictures, *The Smokers* (New York, Met.) and the *Peasants' Feast* (Zurich, Ksthaus), are signed in full; various pictures bear the monogram AB or B, but many of them are generally acknowledged as not being his, so that scarcely 60 paintings can be attributed to Brouwer with certainty. Except for one on copper, *The Innkeeper* (Munich, Alte Pin., 2014; see fig. 1), all his surviving paintings are on mainly small wooden panels; the 480×670 mm format of the *Tavern Scene* (London, N.G.) is exceptional. The paintings are notable for their thin, partly transparent layers of paint on a light-coloured ground. The figures, subtly differentiated by shading in the colour, are completely integrated with the interiors in order to convey a sense of atmosphere. Drapery is modelled with a pointed brush in short parallel strokes. Glazes with fine gradations of colour, often lost as a result of cleaning, unify the areas of colour. The accomplished use of these means distinguishes Brouwer's own works from the many imitations and copies, some very good, that were in circulation even in his own lifetime.

Brouwer's stylistic development can be described only tentatively. Pictures in bright natural colours, which are closest to the work produced *c.* 1610–30 by such Haarlem painters as Willem Buytewech or Esaias van de Velde, are always ascribed to the beginning of his career. Examples in which Bode (1924, pp. 36–94) recognized the Haarlem influence are no longer considered to be by Brouwer, whereas the following authentic pictures do reveal this style: the *Peasants' Feast* (Zurich, Ksthaus), the *Pancake Man* (Philadelphia, PA, Mus. A.), the *Fight over Cards*

1. Adriaen Brouwer: *The Innkeeper*, oil on copper, 310×240 mm, before *c.* 1631 (Munich, Alte Pinakothek)

(The Hague, Mauritshuis), the *Tavern Interior* (Rotterdam, Mus. Boymans–van Beuningen) and the *Slaughter Feast* (Schwerin, Staatl. Mus.). They are distinguished by larger, strongly coloured areas that are built up with a thin brush in the gentlest of small strokes, yet sharply contoured to stand out from one another. The scenes are enlivened by bright highlights on the faces, light sections of drapery and utensil handles. Two other paintings (both Munich, Alte Pin.), the *Village Barber Performing a Foot Operation* (561; see fig. 2) and the *Fight over Cards* (562), have special, enamel-like detailing and a whitish creamy tone. This tone is also evident in the first paintings of the Haarlem painter Adriaen van Ostade, made in the early 1630s, suggesting that Brouwer had adopted this manner before leaving Haarlem for Antwerp.

In Antwerp, Brouwer may have first painted a group of pictures notable for their sparing colours: dark, grey–green tones next to green–blue on a grey ground, interspersed with small dabs of white or red, such as *Two Peasants Fighting* or the *Allegory of Smell* (both Munich, Alte Pin., 2112 and 2095). David Teniers (ii) used the same tones *c.* 1633, no doubt influenced by Brouwer. No other paintings can be related to dated works by other artists. *The Smokers* includes a figure generally identified as Jan Davidsz. de Heem, who arrived in Antwerp in 1636, so the painting must have been created after that date. The main figures are still in dark colours, some emphasized by the lighting. Cuffs, collars, scarves or frills in gleaming white or glowing red are the only accents. Other pictures with these features belong to the same period, such as *Soldiers Gambling* and the *Innkeeper and his Wife Sampling*

2. Adriaen Brouwer: *Village Barber Performing a Foot Operation*, oil on panel, 314×396 mm, 1631/2 (Munich, Alte Pinakothek)

(both Munich, Alte Pin., 242 and 1281); they share a certain generosity of scale and focus on essentials. Comparable tones, a tender, atmospheric mood and a rapid brush technique are also found in Brouwer's few surviving landscapes, for example *Dune Landscape* (Vienna, Gemäldegal. Akad. Bild. Kst.), the *Ball Players* and the *Landscape with a Full Moon* (both Berlin, Gemäldegal.); these date from the later 1630s.

Landscapes, including a much earlier version of the *Ball Players* (Brussels, Mus. A. Anc.), are exceptions in Brouwer's work. His true theme was the representation of the everyday world of peasants and simple folk, not at work, but mainly relaxing at the inn. These peasant genre scenes link him to the older literary and pictorial tradition that reached a highpoint with Pieter Bruegel the elder. But whereas Bruegel and his immediate followers depicted peasant activities mainly out of doors, Brouwer transferred the scene, except in a few cases, to the interior. He exploited the Dutch tradition of filling the space with large figures, presenting the subjects drinking, card-playing, throwing dice and engaged in the quarrels and fights that often arose from these activities. In this, he was deliberately referring to the medieval tradition in which gambling, drinking, profligacy and quarrelling were judged in accordance with the Christian canon of vices as the deadly sins

of gluttony and anger. In such early pictures as the *Fight over Cards* (The Hague), *The Innkeeper* (Munich, Alte Pin.; see fig. 1 above) and the *Tavern Interior*, Brouwer used the same symbols and attributes as occur in 16th-century representations of the vices and made direct pictorial references to them, thereby communicating the same moral message: a warning against excessive drinking, which leads to nausea, quarrels and sloth.

In the course of his career Brouwer moved away from the narrow field of Christian morality, turning more to ethical themes and problems with a general application. The simplistic symbols of the vices became less evident as his interest concentrated increasingly on the faces that reflected pain, anger and joy. Several paintings of tavern brawls, such as the *Fight over Cards* or the *Fight Scene* (both Munich, Alte Pin., 562 and 861), are particularly memorable examples of this; they show open rage in varying degrees on morose, roaring faces, fierce anger in the wry looks, then suddenly great pain.

Brouwer was the first artist to make these elements central in the genre of tavern interiors, endowing the figures in his compositions with distinctive individuality. The outbreaks of bad temper or anger are no longer denounced as a Christian sin but are judged as an expression of lack of self-control, a reference to the ethical ideas of Seneca and to Justus Lipsius's Neo-Stoicism, which would have been familiar to Brouwer through Antwerp's humanist circle.

The ways that mental agitation, mood, passion and physical well-being are mirrored in the face became Brouwer's principal preoccupation. He therefore presented his peasants not only in fights but also smoking and undergoing operations. In the operation scenes of the *Village Barber* (see fig. 2 above), the *Allegory of Touch* (both Munich, Alte Pin., 561 and 581), the *Back Operation* and the *Foot Operation* (both Frankfurt am Main, Städel. Kstinst. & Städt. Gal.), he addressed another traditional theme, for which there were precedents in medical tracts and 16th-century paintings, but he brought a new dimension to them: the event is not simply narrated, the faces reveal the interrelationship between the doctor and the patient. The dogged enjoyment at carrying out the operation on the one hand and the pain borne with faltering breath and cowed eyes on the other are acutely portrayed. Brouwer's extraordinary new contribution to genre painting lies in this emphasis on caricature. Probably because of this interest, which was then unparalleled, he turned to a new theme that had only recently emerged, in the early 17th century, the smoking of tobacco. *The Smokers* includes a self-portrait, in the pose of a smoker with rolling eyes and a rounded, wide-open mouth. In other pictures, including *Two Cavaliers* (London, Apsley House), the *Tobacco Inn* (Paris, Louvre) and the *Allegory of Taste* and the *Allegory of Smell* (both Munich, Alte Pin., 581 and 2095), he depicted the enjoyment of smoking in various stages of preparation and gratification. Energetic drawing and puffing and pleasurable inhaling provided the opportunity to introduce different physical states. Brouwer's interest in caricature culminated in *Bitter Medicine* (Frankfurt am Main, Städel. Kstinst. & Städt. Gal.), a study of a single face, which does not refer to a larger narrative. There is nothing in Dutch or Flemish art to compare with the graphic vividness with which the expression is depicted, except Rembrandt's studies of faces in etchings and paintings of the early 1630s. It is conceivable that there was some interchange between the two artists during Brouwer's time in the northern Netherlands.

2. DRAWINGS AND PRINTS. None of the drawings traditionally ascribed to Brouwer can be linked to any of his paintings, none is signed and only a few have old inscriptions with Brouwer's name. The question of their attribution is thus even more vexed than for the paintings. One group, consisting of studies of single figures and small groups, possibly originally all from the same sketchbook but now widely scattered, is closest to Brouwer's paintings in the figure types, gestures and expressions. Only outlines of the figures have been drawn, quickly, in pen and ink over a pencil underdrawing; the touch is sure and catches the gestures and facial expressions, almost caricaturing them. The figures are then modelled with crosshatching in pen or pencil, and wash is applied to convey light and shade. As well as ten drawings of high quality (Berlin, Kupferstichkab., 1374, 2299, 5391, 7539; Besançon, Mus. B.-A., D 63 and 62; Dresden, Kupferstichkab.; Hamburg, Ksthalle, 34130; Heino, Hannema-

De Stuers Fund.; and London, V&A), there are many weaker drawings under Brouwer's name that cannot be by him. The better ones might be by Philips Koninck or Egbert van Heemskerck, but most, especially those of complete compositions, remain anonymous.

A special problem is posed by a group of five studies of heads in Stockholm (Nmus., H 2103, H 2105, H 2106, H 2107, H 2109): they, too, are of unequal quality and are linked to Brouwer through old inscriptions. Again, they portray faces that are similar in character to those in Brouwer's paintings, but they are built up in dense layers of strokes and lack the economy and penetration of the sketchbook pages. The most impressive in quality is the full-face *Study of a Peasant* (116×89, H 2103), in which the layers of confident, energetic strokes give the face a roguish look and a remarkably eloquent expression. Though it could well be by Brouwer, the attribution of the remaining drawings is uncertain.

Three etchings, *Peasant with a Pipe before a Fireplace* (see Scholz, no. 8), *Four Peasants Sitting around a Cask* (s 9), *Two Peasants and a Country Woman Playing the Flute* (s 10), and twelve etchings of *Heads of Peasants and Country Women* (s 136–47) are inscribed *Brouwer fecit*. They are accordingly still occasionally ascribed to Brouwer, but as Bode pointed out as early as 1884, their quality compared with the paintings is too poor for them to be accepted. These false signatures and the appearance in the 17th century of another 132 prints with genuine or Brouwer-like compositions is evidence of his renown soon after his death and of the enduring popularity of his themes.

BIBLIOGRAPHY

C. de Bie: *Het gulden cabinet* (1661), pp. 91–5
I. Bullaert: *Academie des sciences et des arts*, ii (Amsterdam, 1682), pp. 487–9
A. Houbraken: *De groote schouburgh* (1718–21), i, pp. 318–33
F. J. Van den Branden: 'Adriaan de Brouwer en Joos van Craesbeeck', *Ned. Ksthode*, iii (1881), pp. 156–7
W. von Bode: 'Adriaen Brouwer: Ein Bild seines Lebens und seines Schaffens', *Graph. Kst.*, vi (1884), pp. 21–72
J. H. W. Unger: 'Adriaan Brouwer te Haarlem', *Oud-Holland*, ii (1884), pp. 161–9
C. Hofstede de Groot: *Holländischen Maler* (1907–28), iii, pp. 585–701
F. Schmidt-Degener: *Adriaen Brouver et son évolution artistique* (Brussels, 1908)
W. von Bode: *Adriaen Brouwer: Sein Leben und seine Werke* (Berlin, 1924)
G. Knuttel: *Adriaen Brouwer: The Master and his Work* (The Hague, 1962)
H. Scholz: *Brouwer invenit: Druckgraphische Reproduktionen des 17.–19. Jahrhunderts nach Gemälden und Zeichnungen Adriaen Brouwers* (Marburg, 1985) [s]
Adriaen Brouwer und das niederländische Bauerngenre, 1600–1660 (exh. cat. by K. Renger, Munich, Alte Pin., 1986)
H.-J. Raupp: 'Adriaen Brouwer als Satiriker', *Holländische Genremalerei im 17. Jahrhundert*, ed. H. Bock and T. Gaehtgens (Berlin, 1987), pp. 225–51
K. Renger: 'Adriaen Brouwer: Seine Auseinandersetzung mit der Tradition des 16. Jahrhunderts', *Holländische Genremalerei im 17. Jahrhundert*, ed. H. Bock and T. Gaehtgens (Berlin, 1987), pp. 253–82
Von Bruegel bis Rubens: Das goldene Jahrhundert der flämischen Malerei (exh. cat., ed. E. Mai and H. Vlieghe; Cologne, Wallraf-Richartz-Mus.; Antwerp, Kon. Mus. S. Kst.; Vienna, Ksthist. Mus.; 1992–3), pp. 415–18
The Age of Rubens (exh. cat. by P. C. Sutton and others, Boston, MA, Mus. F.A.; Toledo, OH, Mus. A.; 1993–4), pp. 406–16

KONRAD RENGER

Brouwer, Willem C(oenraad) (*b* Leiden, 19 Oct 1877; *d* Zoeterwoude, 23 Oct 1933). Dutch potter and sculptor.

He trained as a drawing teacher but took a particular interest in bookbinding, decorative woodcuts and household pottery. From the example of the Arts and Crafts Movement he learnt the value of traditional techniques and craftsmanship. In 1898 he settled in Gouda in order to perfect his technical knowledge of pottery-making. Three years later he started his own ceramics firm in Leiderdorp. His ceramics are characterized by their intentionally plain shapes, combined with mostly geometric linear ornament and frequently with sculptural decoration applied in low relief. His work attracted international attention and gained awards at several exhibitions, including the Esposizione Internazionale d'Arte Decorativa in Turin (1902) and the Exposition Universelle et Internationale in Brussels (1910). Around 1907 Brouwer began to experiment with large-scale ceramic decoration. His terracotta ornaments and façade sculptures were greatly admired by contemporary architects, who secured him important commissions in this field, for example the Vredespaleis in The Hague, the Scheepvaarthuis in Rotterdam, and the railway stations at Maastricht and Zandvoort. His architectural sculptures survive in large numbers on buildings throughout the Netherlands. In the course of his career he gradually moved towards monumental sculpture, yet he never entirely relinquished the link with architectural decoration.

BIBLIOGRAPHY

E. Ebbinge: 'W. C. Brouwer (1877–1933): Aarden vaatwerk, tuinaardewerk, bouwaardewerk', *Mededbl. Ned. Ver. Vrienden Cer.*, xcvii–xcviii (1980), pp. 1–2

E. EBBINGE

Brown. English family of gem-engravers. Nothing is known of the early training and apprenticeships of the brothers William Brown (*b* 1748; *d* London, 20 July 1825) and Charles Brown (*b* 1749; *d* 1 June 1795), although their address in 1769 was that of the seal- and gem-engraver John Frewin, who had won a premium for intaglio-engraving offered by the Society of Arts, London, in 1762. William competed the following year but was disqualified, having cheated in the drawing competition two years before. Despite this early setback he exhibited at the Society of Arts from 1766 until 1770, when both brothers began to show annually at the Royal Academy, London (until 1785). William offered a large number of subjects from the Antique (e.g. *Head of Hygeia*, cornelian intaglio, before 1705; St Petersburg, Hermitage) and portraits of contemporaries, which were his forte; Charles rarely showed more than one gem at a time, among them the animal subjects for which he became famous (e.g. *Horse Frightened by Lion*, before 1782, after George Stubbs's painting; St Petersburg, Hermitage).

In 1786 the Brown brothers ceased to exhibit, having received the first of many lavish orders from the Russian court, which they supplied from London with almost 200 gems during the lifetime of Catherine II, Empress of Russia. Although their total output was large, amounting to perhaps twice that number, their work for other patrons has been dispersed, while their work sent to Russia has been preserved in the collections of the Hermitage Museum, St Petersburg. Among these gems, the many-figured intaglio scenes from Classical mythology, some depicting figures in violent movement (e.g. *Rape of Proserpina*, before 1794), others in Classical repose, show a remarkable mastery in composition and the recession of planes, while the most delicate engraving is shown in such jugate busts as *Mars and Bellona* (before 1785, signed C. BROWN, INVT) or William's *Muse of Tragedy* (before 1772). Their Russian commissions were only briefly interrupted by a successful excursion to the court of Louis XVI in 1788, from which they returned to London the following year. In subsequent years they worked in the new genre of historical allegory, perhaps inspired by the intaglios of Jacques Guay in France: such commissions as the large cameo medallions *Catherine II Crowning Potemkin* (1789) and the *Allegory of the Victory of Russia over Turkey* (before 1794) are allegories of contemporary Russian history. Many of their gems are signed BROWN and may have been worked in collaboration. Their last joint production for Catherine before Charles's early death in 1795 was a comprehensive cameo series of the *Kings of England*, followed by the early numbers of the *Kings of France*, which show a considerable decline in quality. Thereafter William occasionally exhibited at the Royal Academy, showing portraits of such contemporaries as *Sir Walter Scott* and *George Gordon, 6th Baron Byron* (both untraced) and especially of 'political characters', which he advertised in the *Monthly Magazine* (no. 185, 1809). A cameo portrait of *George III* is in the British Museum, London.

BIBLIOGRAPHY

Reznye kamni Vil'yama i Charlza Braunov [The engraved gems of William and Charles Brown] (exh. cat., ed. I. O. Kagan; St Petersburg, Hermitage, 1976)

L. Dukelskaya, ed.: *The Hermitage: English Art, Sixteenth to Nineteenth Century* (Leningrad, 1979), nos 220–28

GERTRUD SEIDMANN

Brown, Arthur, jr. *See under* BAKEWELL & BROWN.

Brown, (Lancelot) 'Capability' (*bapt* Kirkharle, Northumb., 30 Aug 1716; *d* London, 6 Feb 1783). English landscape gardener and architect.

1. EARLY CAREER, BEFORE *c*. 1754. Following his schooling at the nearby village of Cambo, Brown was first employed *c*. 1732 by Sir William Loraine of Kirkharle, who was then extending his grounds and remodelling the house. Here Brown learnt the rudiments of building and land management and in time was entrusted with laying out extensions to the garden. At Kirkharle, Loraine rebuilt the village on a new and more distant site and, with Brown's assistance, laid out extensive lawns, flanking them with massive plantations in which several thousand trees of contrasting foliage were introduced. Scarcely a trace remains of this transformation, but a descendant of Loraine recorded that it was Brown's 'first landscape work' and led to him being consulted on other gardens in the area towards the end of the decade.

In about 1739 Brown decided to make a career for himself further south, and his first known commission (*c*. 1740) was the formation of a lake at Kiddington Park, Oxon. Within a few months he came to the notice of Sir Richard Temple, Lord Cobham, and was taken on at Stowe, Bucks, in March 1741. Brown's nominal position was Head Gardener, but after a few weeks he was acting as paymaster and had assumed responsibility for some 40 workmen, including masons, carpenters, carters, plasterers and under-gardeners. The Stowe gardens at that time were being remade, largely to William Kent's designs, but the execution was delegated to Brown, giving him ample opportunity to study and absorb Kent's style while developing his own. Kent was not the sole influence at this time however; several of Brown's later designs for Gothick-style garden buildings reflect the type of decorative detailing found on James Gibbs's triangular Gothic Temple at Stowe (1741–4), the construction of which certainly involved Brown. Projects also carried out under his supervision in the 1740s included the replacement in 1743 of an earlier parterre to the south of the house, the opening up of cross views through the main avenues, alterations to the outlines of the lakes, the landscaping of the Grecian Valley and the planting of large quantities of trees.

While never making any claim to great skill as a draughtsman, it is clear that Brown was influenced by examples of Kent's designs for gardens and temples, which he saw in the course of his years at Stowe. His earliest known plans and drawings (1751; for Packington, Warwicks) include details for a grotto and cascade flanked by trees; although somewhat crudely drawn, these are unmistakably after Kent's manner. Within a short time, however, he evolved a simpler and more precise style, with conifers and deciduous trees defined and with an accompanying key to the principal features. Characteristic elements in these designs are sinuous outlines of water (Brown's lakes were usually contrived from nearby springs or were adaptations of existing streams); the encircling ride or shelter belt; plantations flanking the house to screen domestic quarters and stables; a winding drive offering glimpses of the house between trees; and small scattered groups of trees or single specimens on lawns before or behind the house. Critics later in the century, who were to object to what they called the 'belting, clumping and dotting' apparent in Brown's designs, failed to realize that these outlines represented only the initial planting. Once the protective and quick-growing 'nurse' trees were removed and the slow-growing hardwoods began spreading their branches, the outlining would gradually become less distinct.

By 1750 Brown had begun to practise as an independent designer, receiving commissions to transform the parks at Warwick Castle and Petworth, Sussex. In 1751 Horace Walpole considered the new grounds at Warwick 'well laid out by one Brown who has set up on a few ideas of Kent and Mr Southcote'. Brown was to continue working there for many years, during which time he remodelled a number of new rooms within the castle itself.

In the autumn of 1751 Brown moved with his family from Stowe (where he had married in 1744) to a house in Hammersmith, then a village near west London. From then on his commissions increasingly involved architectural design. By 1750 he had begun a major commission, undertaking (with Sanderson Miller's assistance) the design and construction of Croome Court, Worcs, a Palladian mansion for George, Lord Deerhurst (later the 6th Earl of Coventry) in a landscape setting made by Brown from a marshy tract of ground. In 1753 he designed a new

Classical façade and remodelled several rooms at Newnham Paddox, Warwicks, and the same year he began a long programme of work at Burghley House, Northants, which included alterations to the south front and the provision of new stables and garden buildings in an extensive landscape. William Mason (i) was later to attribute Brown's first ventures into architecture to the 'great difficulty . . . in forming a picturesque whole where the previous building had been ill-placed or of improper dimensions'— certainly the case both at Newnham Paddox and Burghley.

2. LATER WORK AND ROYAL APPOINTMENT, AFTER *c.* 1754. A measure of Brown's rapid success at this time is indicated by his nickname 'Capability', current by 1760. Said to have derived from his habit of referring to the capabilities of the places about which he was consulted, it may nevertheless have been meant to indicate his skill in dealing with the unpromising terrain with which he was frequently confronted. Yet an attempt by several influential clients in 1758 to obtain a royal appointment for him was unsuccessful. The list of their names establishes that in addition to the places already mentioned above, he had by then carried out designs for grounds at Moor Park, Herts; Ashburnham, Sussex; Syon Hill and Syon House, Middx; Peper Harow, Surrey; Enville, Staffs; Grimsthorpe, Lincs; Wotton, Bucks; Ragley, Warwicks; and Alnwick Castle, Northumb. A second application in 1764 was successful: Brown was appointed Master Gardener for Richmond, Surrey, and Hampton Court, Middx. At Richmond Old Park, now part of the Royal Botanic Gardens at Kew, he removed the more fanciful features, including Merlin's Cave, which had been devised by Kent for Queen Caroline. At Hampton Court, however, he is said to have declined George III's suggestion that he sweep away the late 17th-century embroidered parterre; instead he confined his activities to routine maintenance and planting, including the Black Hamburg vine, which continues to produce an impressive annual crop.

In the same year that Brown received his royal appointment he was given three major landscaping commissions, of which Blenheim, Oxon (for plan of gardens and park *see* GARDEN, fig. 4), is the best known, and for the next 20 years he continued to dominate his profession. A handful of emulators of his style appeared, including Richard Woods (?1716–93), William Emes (1729–1803) and Thomas White the elder (1736–1811), but Brown's one surviving account book (dating from the 1760s) shows no decline in commissions, all of which involved a considerable amount of travelling before designs could be prepared and even more if he undertook also to supervise their execution. Notable examples for this period include the parks at Wimbledon, Surrey (from 1764), Weston Park, Staffs (from 1765), Sandbeck, S. Yorks (from 1766), Compton Verney, Warwicks (from 1768) and Brocklesby, Lincs (from 1771).

By the end of the 1760s Brown, realizing that none of his three sons were interested in following his profession, took on Henry Holland as his assistant. Holland's first assignment was to help decorate the interior of Claremont, Surrey, designed by Brown for Robert, Lord Clive, in 1770; their collaboration continued for the building of

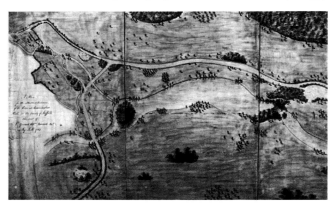

'Capability' Brown: Heveningham, Suffolk, plan for the further part of the park, 1782 (London, Department of the Environment)

Mount Clare, Surrey, for Clive's cousin in 1772. The next year Holland married Brown's elder daughter and assisted his new father-in-law with the building of Benham, Berks. Cadland, Hants, followed as a joint work in 1775, and although Holland set up an independent practice in 1776, he continued to assist in such projects until Brown's death.

Several prominent Tories were among Brown's clients, but his personal political allegiance, perhaps influenced by his patrons Lord Cobham at Stowe and William Pitt, 1st Earl of Chatham, lay with the Whigs. In 1772 he served as High Sheriff for Huntingdonshire, the county in which he was nominally resident by virtue of his purchase some years earlier of the manor of Fenstanton. However, he and his wife continued to reside mainly at his official residence, Wilderness House at Hampton Court. Although he suffered from asthma for many years, Brown continued to travel extensively through England and Wales in the course of his work. Many of his contracts involved periodic visits to the numerous estates for which he was responsible; there were also new contracts for buildings and landscape designs, such as Nuneham Courtenay, Oxon (from 1778), and Heveningham, Suffolk (from 1781; see fig.), where Brown provided a lake and garden buildings to complement Sir Robert Taylor's newly-built house for Sir Gerard Vanneck. Brown continued to work right up to his sudden death in 1783; the following year François de la Rochefoucauld, on a visit to England, recorded a fitting testimony to Brown's energy and skill in his *Mélanges sur Angleterre*: 'on riding around a park for an hour he could conceive a design for the whole place, and that afterwards half a day sufficed for him to mark it out on the ground'. Brown's name is connected with around 200 estates in England; he remains the most celebrated of landscape designers.

BIBLIOGRAPHY
D. Stroud: *Capability Brown* (London, 1950, rev. 1975)
P. Willis: 'Capability Brown in Northumberland', *Gn Hist.*, ix (1981), pp. 157–83
D. Jacques: *Georgian Gardens: The Reign of Nature* (London, 1983)
R. Williams: 'Making Places: Garden-mastery and English Brown', *J. Gn Hist.*, iii (1983), pp. 382–5
P. Willis: 'Capability Brown's Account with Drummond's Bank, 1753–83', *Archit. Hist.*, xxvii (1984), pp. 382–91

T. Hinde: *Capability Brown: The Story of a Master Gardener* (London, 1986)
DOROTHY STROUD

Brown, Deborah (*b* Belfast, 1927). Irish painter and sculptor. She studied painting in 1946 at Belfast College of Art, and from 1947 to 1950 at the National College of Art, Dublin, and in Paris. Her early landscapes, inspired by the coastline of Antrim, gave way to pure abstraction *c.* 1958, when she became aware of Abstract Expressionism and particularly of Jackson Pollock. To pale broad sweeps of colour, she gradually added brown paper collage. In *White on Canvas with Inlay of Brown Paper* (1962; artist's priv. col., see 1982 exh. cat., no. 19) she cut a hole in the canvas, the rough line of the circular edge adding tension to the work. This was followed by three-dimensional paintings such as *Papier-mâché Form on Canvas* (1964; Dublin, A.C. Ireland), in which the painted ground is extended into a sculptural form; in later works such additions were made of fibreglass with a background of strong colour.

Brown's first major commission was for a series of eight canvases for the interior of the new Ferranti building at Hollinwood, near Manchester, England, in 1965. In the early 1970s she freed her fibreglass forms from the canvas, turning them into opaque or translucent, white or neutral-coloured sculptures, once with political connotations, in the *Barbed Wire* series (1972; for example see 1982 exh. cat., no. 64), but otherwise they were purely abstract, as in *Glass Fibre Form in Box* (1974; Dublin, Bank of Ireland Col.). From 1977 she turned to a figurative naturalistic sculptural idiom, modelling sheep, cattle and seated people in wire and paper, or papier-mâché, on a large or miniature scale, describing these works as encounters. More recently she has used bronze, the most striking piece being *Sheep on the Road* (1993; Belfast, A. C. N. Ireland).

BIBLIOGRAPHY
Deborah Brown: A Selected Exhibition of Works Completed between 1947 and 1982 (exh. cat., intro. by A. Crookshank; Belfast, A.C.N. Ireland, 1982)
HILARY PYLE

Brown, Everald (*b* St Ann, Jamaica, 1917). Jamaican painter and sculptor. He was self-taught, and not discovered until the late 1960s. A mystic and visionary, he drew his artistic inspiration from very personal interpretation of two Afro-Christian Jamaican cults, Rastafarianism and Revivalism. His imagery developed through meditation and techniques similar to the automatism of the Surrealists. The curious limestone formations found in his environment frequently served as a source of inspiration, as in *Bush Have Ears* (1976; Kingston, N.G.). He also made ritual objects for his cult, such as carved wooden staffs and decorated musical instruments. During the 1970s he worked in close collaboration with his son Clinton Brown (*b* 1954), who also received substantial critical acclaim.

BIBLIOGRAPHY
V. Poupeye-Rammelaere: 'The Rainbow Valley: The Life and Work of Brother Everald Brown', *Jamaica J.*, xxi/2 (May–June 1988), pp. 2–14
VEERLE POUPEYE

Brown, Ford Madox (*b* Calais, 16 April 1821; *d* London, 6 Oct 1893). English painter and designer.

1. Early career, to 1847. 2. Pre-Raphaelite period, 1848–64. 3. Later career, 1865–93.

1. EARLY CAREER, TO 1847. The son of a retired ship's purser who had settled at Calais, Brown received an academic training under Albert Gregorius (1774–1853) at Bruges, under Pieter van Hanselaere (1786–1862) at Ghent and under Baron Gustaf Wappers at the Academie in Antwerp (1837–9). He moved to Paris in 1840, married the following year and studied independently of the ateliers, concentrating on works by Rembrandt and the Spanish masters in the Orléans Collection, then in the Louvre.

Among contemporary French painters Brown particularly admired Eugène Delacroix and Paul Delaroche. He experimented with an eclectic style marked by strong chiaroscuro and dark tones created with bitumen. His primary concern for dramatic gesture and facial expressiveness characterized all later changes of style and received most criticism. His subjects included romantic themes from English history, for example *Mary Queen of Scots* (exh. Salon 1842; untraced, sketch in U. Manchester, Whitworth A.G.), and several from Byron including *Manfred on the Jungfrau* (1841; Manchester, C.A.G.). Painted in Paris, this work was Brown's first experiment with outdoor lighting. His ruggedly outlined pen designs (e.g. U. Manchester, Whitworth A.G.) based on Shakespeare's *King Lear* served as the foundation of some later paintings.

In 1844 and 1845 Brown entered three ambitious cartoons for the competitions to decorate the new Houses of Parliament, but without success. He turned from the influence of Delacroix in the *Body of Harold Brought before William the Conqueror* (London, S. London A.G.) to the formal German architectural style in the *Spirit of Justice* (1845; fragments and a photograph exist), which was admired by Benjamin Robert Haydon. Also in 1844 Brown settled in London, where he associated with Charles Lucy and W. Cave Thomas (1820–after 1884). The paintings of Daniel Maclise, who had helped to introduce the German style to England, were a particular influence on this circle, and they inspired Brown to abandon his Rembrandtesque style in favour of 'more luxurient [sic] & attractive materials' (*Diary*, p. 1).

In 1845 Brown travelled via Basle (where he saw works by Hans Holbein (ii)) to Rome for his wife's health (she died in 1846). While there he was impressed by both the Italian masters and the German Nazarenes. The result was his *Chaucer at the Court of Edward III* (1846–51; Sydney, A.G. NSW; smaller version, 1867–8; London, Tate), already planned in London to glorify English literature in the spirit of the cartoon competition. In Rome he designed it as a triptych (oil study; Oxford, Ashmolean), but he abandoned this format when he returned to the picture in London in 1847. It owed its clear-cut, delicate detail to Holbein and initially had a pale, fresco-like tonality in a scheme noteworthy for its informal naturalness and outdoor lighting. The diary Brown began in September 1847

1. Ford Madox Brown: *Work*, oil on canvas, 1.37×1.97 m, 1852, 1856–63 (Manchester, City Art Gallery)

charts his emerging career and records in detail his work on *Chaucer* and on subsequent pictures, in particular *Wycliffe* (1848; Bradford, Cartwright Hall) and *Cordelia at the Bedside of Lear* (1849; London, Tate), shown at the Free Exhibition in 1848 and 1849 respectively.

2. PRE-RAPHAELITE PERIOD, 1848–64. Brown's exhibited works attracted Dante Gabriel Rossetti, who became his pupil in 1848, and their influence is apparent in Rossetti's first oil painting, the *Girlhood of Mary Virgin* (1848–9; London, Tate). Through Rossetti, Brown met William Holman Hunt and John Everett Millais, whose radical reconsideration of the direction of English art resulted in the formation of the Pre-Raphaelite Brotherhood (*see* PRE-RAPHAELITISM) that autumn. The older Brown was not invited to join but was a close associate of the group and contributed to their journal, *The Germ* (1850). Their example inspired him to retouch *Chaucer* in a brighter key, to produce landscape studies and to portray his sitters with the individuality of friends. *Chaucer* was well received at the Royal Academy in 1851, though the Pre-Raphaelites were pilloried. Nevertheless, Brown found it difficult to sell his work, and he depended on a small private income.

Brown explored the brilliant palette and minute technique of the Pre-Raphaelites and, like Millais and Hunt, he turned to landscape. He settled in Stockwell, south London, in 1851, with his model Emma (whom he married in 1853) and their child Catherine, and he painted them in the cabinet-sized *Pretty Baa-lambs* (exh. RA 1852; Birmingham, Mus. & A.G.). It is a study of glowing summer heat, going beyond Pre-Raphaelite practice to place the figures outside in the atmospheric envelope of the landscape. While still half a 'costume-piece', its deliberate lack of literary content made it enigmatic to the contemporary eye. Brown emulated Pre-Raphaelite religious themes in *Jesus Washing Peter's Feet* (exh. RA 1852; London, Tate), but on the monumental scale of the Renaissance and with a humanist approach of close-up realism. He attempted the Pre-Raphaelite technique of painting on a wet white ground for greater luminosity and paralleled Hunt in studying the effect of artificial light in the small *Waiting* (1851; finished study, Liverpool, Walker A.G.). This domestic subject, replacing Victorian sentiment with objective realism, was his first work representing modern life, a field in which he was to excel. Reviewers turned on Brown as a convert to Pre-Raphaelitism, and he persistently lacked the support of John Ruskin.

Brown's admiration for Thomas Carlyle's works encouraged him to explore social subjects, thereby anticipating the Pre-Raphaelites. In a period of semi-isolation in lodgings at Hampstead between 1852 and 1854, 'most of the time intensely miserable very hard up & a little mad' (*Diary*, p. 78), he designed his three finest, most closely considered and highly finished paintings: *Work* (1852, 1856–63; Manchester, C.A.G.; see fig. 1), *The Last of England* (1852–5; Birmingham, Mus. & A.G.; see fig. 2) and an *English Autumn Afternoon* (1852–5; Birmingham, Mus. & A.G.). Executed in minute brushwork and brilliant atmospheric colour, each commented objectively on an aspect of modern life that closely concerned Brown; respectively, they celebrated labour in all its forms, the dilemma of the respectable middle class forced into emigration, and the idyllic semi-rural simplicity of a landscape seen casually from a window on the very edge of the city turmoil. The largest, *Work*, aspired to the stature of a grand exhibition piece, and its intensive detail required an extensive written explanation in the catalogue of the one-man show he organized in 1865. In contrast, *The Last of England*, with its dour portrait of the artist himself with Emma, is a poignantly direct image. Brown never achieved popularity through engravings. He failed to get the prominent dealer Ernest Gambart to publish *Work*, but *The Last of England* appeared in the *Art Journal* in 1870.

Fully awake to the bright spectrum of colour in nature and partly inspired by Millais's work, Brown turned again to painting landscapes with a heightened palette. Small fresh studies were made near his homes at Finchley and Kentish Town: *The Cornfield*, *The Hayfield* and the *Brent at Hendon* (1854–5; all London, Tate), *Hampstead from my Window* (1857; Wilmington, DE A. Mus.) and *Walton-on-the-Naze* (1859–60; Birmingham, Mus. & A.G.). He advised Thomas Seddon and completed his unfinished landscapes after the latter's premature death. Perceptive portrait studies of his family were frequently introduced into his pictures. From 1858 to 1860 Brown taught at the Working Men's College, London, following Rossetti, and provided a systematic foundation in draughtsmanship.

In the late 1850s Brown turned against the Royal Academy, enraged at the poor hanging and several refusals that deprived him of an important outlet. However, he continued to exhibit in the provinces; at the Liverpool Academy he gained the useful £50 prize in 1856 and 1858

2. Ford Madox Brown: *The Last of England*, oil on panel, 825×750 mm, 1852–5 (Birmingham, City of Birmingham Museum and Art Gallery)

and met local Pre-Raphaelite followers, including W. L. Windus, William Davis and their patron John Miller. He depended on dealer D. T. White, who paid poorly. Rossetti introduced Brown to T. E. Plint of Leeds, who commissioned the completion of *Work*, while George Rae of Birkenhead and James Leathart of Newcastle were his closest sympathizers. For each of them he retouched earlier works and began new commissions.

In need of simply constructed furniture for his own use, Brown became increasingly interested in design in the 1850s and was a founder-member of Morris, Marshall, Faulkner & Co. in 1861. He produced many stained-glass cartoons that combined vigorous movement within a two-dimensional framework and a consciousness of the Gothic tradition that inspired the Morris company. With Rossetti in the 1860s he also designed patterns for carved, gilt oak frames to enhance their own pictures. In his limited commissions for wood-engravings he applied the same vigorous originality, notably in the *Prisoner of Chillon* for Willmott's *Poets of the Nineteenth Century* (London, 1857) and for *Dalziels' Bible Gallery* (London, 1863–4).

3. LATER CAREER, 1865–93. Brown's stained-glass cartoons were the basis of his later approach to painting, which as a result developed a more linear and decorative style, becoming also more sensuous under Rossetti's influence. His colouring in the later 1860s increasingly lightened, and his palette became more earthy. Commissioned replicas in various media became an important source of income; for example, the dramatic *Entombment* (1865 and later) was produced in stained glass, watercolour and oil. He returned again to the historical and literary compositions of his youth as the inspiration for the decorative *Cordelia's Portion* (1865) and the brooding *Cromwell on his Farm at St Ives* (1874; both Port Sunlight, Lady Lever A.G.). The sensuous *Don Juan* coincided with an illustration (1870), while the contorted imagery of the newly designed *Romeo and Juliet* (oil, 1869–70; Wilmington, DE A. Mus.) was later admired by French critics and the French government, which in 1892 unsuccessfully negotiated for its purchase. He had a few portrait commissions, lectured occasionally in the provinces and attempted to gain the Slade professorship at Cambridge (1872–3). Brown was aware of the importance of photography and circulated photographs of his later drawings privately. In the 1870s *Cordelia's Portion* was the first of a small group of autotype reproductions, and three later works were etched by George Woolliscroft Rhead (1855–1920).

A period of limited prosperity continued into the mid-1870s, when his house in Fitzroy Square became a centre for artistic and literary gatherings; the death in 1874 of his son Oliver, a promising writer and painter, virtually marked its end. In 1878, through the goodwill of Frederic Shields and Charles Rowley of Manchester, Brown gained the commission for the wall paintings in the Great Hall, Manchester Town Hall. He lived in Manchester from 1881 to 1887. This rare instance of public patronage, though poorly remunerated, proved his last and greatest opportunity to display the full vigour of a lively historical style in subjects illustrating Manchester history. The 12 panels embody Brown's love of incident and contorted gesture

and combine movement and depth with an overall decorative presentation, balancing their elaborate Gothic surroundings. He used at first the Gambier-Parry fresco technique (*see* GAMBIER-PARRY, THOMAS) directly on the wall, but the last five scenes were painted in oil on canvas in the studio and then glued to the walls. Increasing attacks of gout impeded his progress and severely affected his style; the mixed reception in Manchester of the last of the series clouded his remaining years.

Albert Goodwin was a studio assistant in the mid-1860s. Closest to Brown were his three children, Lucy (1843–94), who married W. M. Rossetti, Catherine (1850–1927), who married the author and music critic Francis Hueffer (1843–89), and Oliver (1855–74). They worked in his studio in the 1860s and acted as assistants. Marie Spartali was also a pupil with them. They all exhibited watercolours and oils for a few years at the Dudley Gallery, London, and sometimes at the Royal Academy, in a decorative style close to Brown's and merging into Aestheticism.

For illustration *see also* ASSYRIAN REVIVAL.

WRITINGS
V. Surtees, ed.: *The Diary of Ford Madox Brown* (New Haven, 1981)

BIBLIOGRAPHY
F. M. Hueffer: *Ford Madox Brown: A Record of his Life and Work* (London, 1896)
Ford Madox Brown (exh. cat. by M. Bennett, Liverpool, Walker A.G., 1964)
W. D. Paden: 'The Ancestry and Families of Ford Madox Brown', *Bull. John Rylands Lib.*, l/1 (1967–8), pp. 124–35
W. E. Fredeman: 'Pre-Raphaelite Novelist Manqué: Oliver Maddox [sic] Brown', *Bull. John Rylands Lib.*, li/2 (1968), pp. 27–72
A. C. Sewter: 'A Check-list of Designs for Stained Glass by Ford Madox Brown', *J. Morris Soc.*, ii (1968), pp. 19–29
M. Bennett: 'Ford Madox Brown at Southend in 1846', *Burl. Mag.*, cxv/839 (1973), pp. 74–8
A. Staley: *The Pre-Raphaelite Landscape* (Oxford, 1973), pp. 31–44
H. O. Borowitz: '*King Lear* in the Art of Ford Madox Brown', *Vict. Stud.*, xxi (1978), pp. 309–34
L. Rabin: *Ford Madox Brown and the Pre-Raphaelite History Picture* (New York, 1978)
E. D. Johnson: 'The Making of Ford Madox Brown's *Work*', *Victorian Artists and the City: A Collection of Critical Essays*, ed. I. B. Nadel and F. S. Schwarzbach (New York, 1980), pp. 142–51
A. S. Marks: 'Ford Madox Brown's *Take your Son Sir*', *A. Mag.*, liv (Jan 1980), pp. 135–41
A. Boime: 'F. M. Brown, Thomas Carlyle and Karl Marx: Meaning and Mystification of Work in the Nineteenth Century', *A. Mag.*, lvi (Sept 1981), pp. 116–25
H. B. Bryant: 'Two Unfinished Pre-Raphaelite Paintings: Rossetti's *Found* and F. M. Brown's *Take your Son Sir*', *J. Pre-Raphaelite Stud.*, iii/1 (1982), pp. 56–65
J. Butler: 'A Pre-Raphaelite Shibboleth: *Joseph*', *J. Pre-Raphaelite Stud.*, iii/1 (1982), pp. 78–90
J. Carman: 'Ford Madox Brown and *Cromwell on his Farm at St. Ives*: A Debt to Thomas Carlyle', *J. Pre-Raphaelite Stud.*, iv/1 (1983), pp. 121–31
M. Bennett: 'The Price of *Work*: The Background to its First Exhibition, 1865', *Pre-Raphaelite Papers*, ed. L. Parris (London, 1984), pp. 143–52
J. R. Elkan: 'Ford Madox Brown's *Chaucer at the Court of Edward III*', *J. Pre-Raphaelite Stud.*, iv/2 (1984), pp. 87–92
The Pre-Raphaelites (exh. cat., ed L. Parris; London, Tate 1984)
M. Bennett: 'Family Portraits of Ford Madox Brown', *NACF Rev.* (1985), pp. 128–32
J. Treuherz: 'Ford Madox Brown and the Manchester Murals', *Art and Architecture in Victorian Manchester*, ed. J. H. G. Archer (Manchester, 1985), pp. 162–207
T. Newman and R. Watkinson: *Ford Madox Brown and the Pre-Raphaelite Circle* (London, 1991)
G. Curtis: 'Ford Madox Brown's *Work*: An Iconographic Analysis', *A. Bull.*, lxxiv/4 (Dec 1992), pp. 623–36

K. Bendiner: 'Brown and Wilkie', *Gaz. B.-A.*, n. s., cxxi (May–June 1993), pp. 227–30

For further bibliography see W. E. Fredeman: *Pre-Raphaelitism: A Bibliocritical Study* (Cambridge, MA, 1965)

MARY BENNETT

Brown, Frederick (*b* Chelmsford, Essex, 14 March 1851; *d* Richmond, Surrey, 8 Jan 1941). English teacher and painter. From 1868 to 1877 he studied at the National Art Training School, London (later the Royal College of Art), where he grew to detest the inept, mechanical teaching methods then prevalent in Britain. As headmaster of the Westminster School of Art (1877–92), Brown, inspired by Alphonse Legros's reforms at the Slade School, taught his students basic observational and analytical skills while encouraging them to develop individual styles. In 1883 he studied at the Académie Julian, Paris; his work for several years thereafter, notably *Hard Times* (1886; Liverpool, Walker A.G.) and *Marketing* (1887; Manchester, C.A.G.), shows the influence of the French realist Jules Bastien-Lepage. Shortly before 1890 Brown took up portraiture in a style strongly influenced by Whistler; he was also drawn to Impressionist landscape painting by his friend Philip Wilson Steer, whose influence is noticeable in the *Horse-shoe Bend of the Severn* (1909; Dublin, Hugh Lane Mun. Gal.). A founder of the New English Art Club in 1886 and author of its constitution, he belonged to the 'Impressionist clique' that won control of the club in the early 1890s. As Slade Professor of Art (1893–1918), he consolidated and expanded Legros's reforms and ensured the school's progressive character by appointing Steer and Henry Tonks to teaching positions early in his tenure. Among the artists who benefited from his liberal and enlightened instruction were Tonks and Beardsley at the Westminster School, and Augustus John, William Orpen and Wyndham Lewis at the Slade. Brown's 'Recollections' are published in the journal *Artwork* (vi, 1930, pp. 149–60, 269–78).

BIBLIOGRAPHY

D. S. MacColl: 'Professor Brown: Teacher and Painter', *Mag. A.* (1894), pp. 403–9
R. Schwabe: 'Three Teachers: Brown, Tonks and Steer', *Burl. Mag.*, lxxxii (1943), pp. 141–6

KENNETH NEAL

Brown, George Loring (*b* Boston, MA, 2 Feb 1814; *d* Malden, MA, 25 June 1889). American painter and illustrator. He was apprenticed at about 14 to the Boston wood-engraver Alonzo Hartwell and had produced scores of illustrations by 1832, when he turned to painting and sailed to Europe for further training. After brief stays in Antwerp and London, he settled in Paris, where he was admitted to the atelier of Eugène Louis Gabriel Isabey. Returning to America in 1834, Brown produced illustrations, portraits and landscapes. He travelled throughout the north-eastern USA, sketching in watercolour and in oil. His work was admired by Washington Allston, who assisted him in a second visit to Europe.

Brown and his wife settled in Florence from 1841 to 1846. At first he painted copies from Old Masters for American and British tourists, but gradually, as his technique and composition improved, he began to create original Italian landscapes with strong chiaroscuro and impasto. He became closely involved with American expatriates and many artists and writers. He moved to Rome in 1847 and for the next 12 years produced colourful and attractive landscapes such as a *View of Amalfi* (1857; New York, Met.).

When American tourism waned during the financial crisis in 1859, Brown returned home. His bold, colourful style shocked American eyes, but he determined to 'fight with my brush' to revitalize American art. At first he succeeded, selling Italian and American scenes, such as a *View of Norwalk Islands* (1864; Andover, MA, Phillips Acad., Addison Gal.), for high prices, but the Civil War intervened and tastes altered to embrace Ruskinian idealism and the Barbizon school. Brown's popularity gradually declined.

BIBLIOGRAPHY

H. T. Tuckerman: *Artist-life, or Sketches of American Painters* (New York, 1847), pp. 229–31
George Loring Brown: Landscapes of Europe and America, 1834–1880 (exh. cat. by W. C. Lipke, Burlington, U. VT, Robert Hull Fleming Mus., 1973)
T. W. Leavitt: 'Let the Dogs Bark: George Loring Brown and the Critics', *Amer. A. Rev.*, i/2 (1974), pp. 87–99

THOMAS W. LEAVITT

Brown, John (i) (*d* London; *bur* St Vedast, Foster Lane, 1532). English painter. He was employed on decorative and heraldic work by the Crown at least as early as 1502. He was appointed King's Painter for life in 1511 and in 1527 became SERJEANT PAINTER. His documented work (none of which survives) included decorations for Henry VIII's ship *Henry Grace à Dieu* and other vessels, as well as ephemeral work for the Field of the Cloth of Gold when Henry met Francis I at Guisnes in 1520. In 1523 Brown acknowledged receipt of £24 for heraldic work for the army sent to France under Charles Brandon, Duke of Suffolk (BL, Lansdowne MS. 858, fol. 12v); in the same year he became an alderman of the City of London. He died a wealthy man and left a property in Little Trinity Lane near St Paul's Cathedral, London, to the Painter-Stainers' Company. Their halls have been on the site ever since.

BIBLIOGRAPHY

E. Auerbach: *Tudor Artists* (London, 1954), pp. 7–8, 11–15, 54, 81, 144
M. Edmond: 'Limners and Picturemakers', *Walpole Soc.*, xlvii (1980), pp. 177, 212

MARY EDMOND

Brown, John (ii) (*b* Edinburgh, 1749; *d* Leith, 5 Sept 1787). Scottish draughtsman and printmaker. He was the son of a goldsmith and watchmaker, and studied at the Trustees' Academy, Edinburgh, before moving to Rome in 1769 to join his friend Alexander Runciman. He produced small-scale or miniature works, using pencil, pen and wash. For his Scottish employers, William Townley and Sir William Young, he drew antiquities, landscapes and archaeological ruins in Italy and Sicily, such as the *Basilica of Constantine and Maxentius* (*c.* 1774–6; Edinburgh, N.G.). Among the more personal works that survive from his 11 years in Italy are a number of strange little genre scenes, such as *Two Men in Conversation* (*c.* 1775–80; U. London, Courtauld Inst. Gals), which clearly show the influence of another friend, Henry Fuseli. Brown's reputation rests principally on his great skill as a portrait draughtsman. He returned to Scotland in 1780, and spent his later years executing fine pencil and pen portraits of various dignitaries, such as *David Steuart Erskine, 11th Earl of Buchan* (1780; Edinburgh, N.P.G.). After a period in London in 1786–7, ill-health forced him to return to spend his last days in Scotland.

BIBLIOGRAPHY

J. L. Caw: *Scottish Painting: Past and Present, 1620–1908* (Edinburgh, 1908), p. 44

D. Irwin and F. Irwin: *Scottish Painters at Home and Abroad, 1700–1900* (London, 1975), pp. 79–80, 112–13

D. Macmillan: *Painting in Scotland: The Golden Age* (Oxford, 1986), pp. 61–2

Brown, John George (*b* Durham, England, 11 Nov 1831; *d* New York, 8 Feb 1913). American painter. A popular painter of rural and urban genre scenes, he spent his youth in England, where he served an apprenticeship as a glasscutter. By 1853 he was employed in Brooklyn, NY. After serious study he became, in 1860, a fully fledged member of the New York artistic community, with a studio in the Tenth Street Studio Building and participating regularly in National Academy of Design exhibitions.

Brown's first genre scenes focused on rural children out of doors. Often sentimental, these exhibited a clarity of light and drawing attributable to his early interest in the Pre-Raphaelite painters. The *Music Lesson* (1870; New York, Met.), a courtship scene set in a Victorian parlour, reveals his debt to English painting. In 1879 Brown painted the *Longshoreman's Noon* (Washington, DC, Corcoran Gal. A.), an affectionate but sober rendering of the variety of ages and physical types in the urban working class. About 1880 he found a new type for his genre scenes in the urban street-boys in such occupations as newsboy, bootblack and fruit vendor. *Tuckered out—the Shoeshine Boy* (*c*. 1890; Boston, MA, Mus. F. A.) is characteristic; the boy is scrubbed, his clothes patched and ragged but clean, and he appeals to the viewer's sympathy. The motif, which perhaps served as a palliative to the urban poverty and numbers of abandoned children on the streets, was enormously popular, and Brown had many patrons.

BIBLIOGRAPHY

John George Brown, 1831–1913: A Reappraisal (exh. cat., Burlington, U. VT, Robert Hull Fleming Mus., 1976)

N. Spassky, ed.: *American Paintings in the Metropolitan Museum of Art*, ii (Princeton, 1985)

Country Paths and City Sidewalks: The Art of J. G. Brown (exh. cat., Springfield, MA, Smith A. Mus., 1989)

ELIZABETH JOHNS

Brown, John-Lewis (*b* Bordeaux, 16 Aug 1829; *d* Paris, 14 Nov 1890). French painter and lithographer of Scottish descent. He spent his childhood in Bordeaux, where he developed a love of horses. In 1841 the family moved to Paris, where Brown taught himself to paint by studying works in museums, especially the Louvre. He first exhibited at the Salon in 1848, with a number of equestrian paintings. In 1852 he received a commission from the State to make a copy (Tours, Mus. B.-A.) of Rembrandt's *Christ at Emmaus* (Copenhagen, Stat. Mus. Kst). In 1859, after a five-year stay in Bordeaux, he returned to the Salon, again showing equestrian works. During the Franco-Prussian War (1870–71) Brown was in the front line painting battle scenes that often concentrate on the tragic

aspects of the conflict. For some years after this he continued to work on military subjects, as in *Episode from the Life of Marshal Conflans* (1876; Tours, Mus. B.-A.). He then returned to equestrian and sporting subjects, producing such works as the *Fox Hunters* (1886; New York, Met.). The content of his later work was influenced by Edgar Degas and the Impressionists and includes scenes from the racetrack, as in *Before the Start* (1890; Paris, Louvre). His style was most strongly influenced by Ernest Meissonier and the academic artist Eugène Lami.

The subject-matter of Brown's graphic work was also dominated by equestrian and military scenes, as in the lithograph *Dragoon on a Horse* (1861; Paris, Bib. N.). He often produced coloured lithographs—a late example is *Cavalryman on a Grey Horse* (1884; Paris, Bib. N.)—and was an important figure in the revival of interest in this medium during the Second Empire.

DBF   BIBLIOGRAPHY

G. Hediard: *Les Maîtres de la lithographie: John-Lewis Brown* (Paris, 1897)

L. Bénédite: *John-Lewis Brown: Etude biographique et critique suivie du catalogue de l'oeuvre lithographique et gravé de cet artiste exposé au Musée du Luxembourg* (Paris, 1903)

J. Laran: *Inventaire du fonds français après 1800*, Paris, Bib. N., Cab. Est. cat., iii (Paris, 1942), pp. 459–61

□

Brown, Joseph (i) (*b* Providence, RI, 3 Dec 1733; *d* Providence, 3 Dec 1785). American architect. He was from one of the leading families of Providence. Primarily a mathematician and astronomer, he became Professor of Experimental Philosophy at Rhode Island College (now Brown University). In 1770 he served, with Robert Smith (i), on the building committee for the College Edifice (now University Hall), which is modelled on Nassau Hall at Princeton University, NJ (architects Robert Smith (i) and William Shippen, 1754).

Brown was an amateur architect who never developed a personal style. The Providence Market House, built to his design in 1772–7, was of a plainness that makes all the more surprising the Baroque swagger of the curved pediment crowning the façade of his own house in South Main Street, Providence (1774). The design of his biggest building, the First Baptist Meeting House (1774–5), Providence, was assembled from plates in James Gibbs's *Book of Architecture* (1728); its beautiful spire is from one of the alternative designs for the spire of St Martin-in-the-Fields, London, while the underscaled portico comes from the Oxford Chapel (now St Peter's) in Vere Street, London. The substantial house of his brother John in Power Street, Providence, begun in 1786 after Brown's death but nonetheless attributed to him, is in a mid-18th-century style, updated with a projecting porch with columns.

BIBLIOGRAPHY

Macmillan Enc. Architects

A. F. Downing: *Early Homes of Rhode Island* (Richmond, VA, 1937)

H. R. Hitchcock: *Rhode Island Architecture* (Providence, 1939/*R* New York, 1968)

J. H. Cady: *The Civic and Architectural Development of Providence, 1636–1950* (Providence, 1957)

MARCUS WHIFFEN

Brown, Joseph (ii) (*b* Łódź, Poland, 30 March 1918). Australian collector and dealer. He settled in Australia with his Polish Jewish family in 1933. He won a scholarship to the Brunswick Technical Art School, Melboune, but his studies were curtailed by the depression of the 1930s, and he was obliged to seek work. After a successful business career in the fashion industry, Brown opened an art gallery in Melbourne in 1963, where he held one-man exhibitions and published important catalogues of Australian art. He became an authority on the subject and a consultant to museums, libraries, galleries and universities throughout the country. He was best known for his large collection of Australian art, assembled over a 40-year period and ranging from colonial, Victorian and Impressionist works to 20th-century abstract and contemporary art. He bought many of the works at small cost, at a time when Australian art was thought to be beneath consideration by most Australian collectors. The collection, housed at Caroline House in Melbourne, is unique in presenting a chronological history of Australian art, beginning with examples of Aboriginal bark painting and the heroic landscapes of such early colonial painters as John Glover, Conrad Martens, Eugene von Guérard, Tom Roberts and Nicholas Chevalier (e.g. *Mount Arapiles and the Mitre Rock*, 1863). Brown's enthusiasm for 20th-century art is exemplified in his acquisition of works by Roy de Maistre, Russell Drysdale (e.g. *Tree Form*, 1945), Sidney Nolan, Arthur Boyd (e.g. *Bride and Groom by a Creek*, c.1960) and Clement Meadmore (*Bent*, steel, h. 889 mm, 1966).

BIBLIOGRAPHY
D. Thomas: *Outlines of Australian Art: The Joseph Brown Collection* (Melbourne, 1973, 2/1980, 3/1989)
Australian Paintings from the Joseph Brown Collection (exh. cat. by B. Pearce, Sydney, A.G. NSW, 1989)

Brown, Mather (*b* Boston, 7 Oct 1761; *d* London, 25 May 1831). American painter, active in England. He was descended from four generations of New England religious leaders; John Copley painted portraits of his mother (New Haven, CT, Yale U., A.G.) and his maternal grandfather (Worcester, MA, Amer. Antiqua. Soc.; Halifax, NS, U. King's Coll.). John Trumbull was his friend and Gilbert Stuart 'learnt me to draw' at age 12. At 16 he walked 640 km to Peekskill, NY, and back selling wine and painting miniature portraits; from these pursuits he earned enough to pay for three years of study in Europe. In London, on Benjamin Franklin's recommendation, Benjamin West accepted him as a free student. Brown was admitted as a student to the Royal Academy in January 1782 and exhibited four paintings the following year. He showed 80 paintings there in all. In 1785–6 he painted much admired portraits of *Thomas Jefferson* (Charles Francis Adams priv. col., see Meschutt, p. 48) and *John Adams* (untraced; second version, 1788; Boston, MA, Athenaeum) and several of his family. He painted two full-length portraits of *Frederick Augustus, Duke of York* (Waddesdon Manor, Bucks, NT) and the *Prince of Wales*, later George IV (London, Buckingham Pal., Royal Col.), in 1788, and in the same year he was appointed historical and portrait painter to the Duke of York.

Brown's portrait style was influenced by that of Gilbert Stuart, under whom he worked in West's studio, with the result that his unsigned portraits have often been confused with those of Stuart. Evans, however, revealed an impressive body of portraiture in which Brown relied on superior drawing and developed his own freer techniques of high colouring and longer, sweeping brushstrokes. Despite his phenomenal early success, Brown fell on hard times. He was disinherited by his father, and an obsession drove him to concentrate on large unsaleable religious and historical subjects. Typical of these works are *Richard II Resigning his Crown to Bolingbroke* (London, BM), the *Baptism of Henry VIII* (1.83×2.70 m; Bristol, Mus. & A.G.), *Lord Cornwallis Receiving as Hostages the Sons of Tippo Sahib* (2.75×2.14 m; London, Stratford House [Oriental Club]) and *Lord Howe on the Deck of the 'Queen Charlotte'* (London, N. Mar. Mus.). In 1809 Brown left London to live and work in Bath, Bristol and Lancashire. He returned to London in 1824 and died there in poverty, in a room crowded with unsold paintings.

BIBLIOGRAPHY
W. Dunlap: *A History of the Rise and Progress of the Arts of Design in the United States* (New York, 1834/*R* 1969), i, pp. 228–9
F. A. Coburn: 'Mather Brown', *A. Amer.*, xi (1923), pp. 252–60
W. T. Whitley: *Artists and their Friends in England, 1700–1799* (London, 1928), ii, pp. 97–100
D. Evans: 'Twenty-six Drawings Attributed to Mather Brown', *Burl. Mag.*, cxiv (1972), pp. 534–41
——: *Benjamin West and his American Students* (Washington, DC, 1980)
——: *Mather Brown: Early American Artist in England* (Middletown, CT, 1982)
D. Meschutt: 'The Adams-Jefferson Portrait Exchange', *Amer. A. J.*, xiv/2 (1982), pp. 47–54
ROBERT C. ALBERTS

Brown, Mike [Michael] **(Gordon Challis)** (*b* Sydney, 8 May 1938). Australian painter and sculptor. He studied art at the East Sydney Technical College (1956–8) but left dissatisfied before completing the course. An important stage in his development was his discovery in 1959 of Australian Aboriginal art and the art of Melanesia and Polynesia, which he saw in New Zealand and on a visit to New Guinea in 1960 while working with the Australian Commonwealth Film Unit. In 1961–2 he lived in the Sydney suburb of Annandale with fellow artist Ross Crothall (*b* 1934) producing the first of his significant work. With Colin Lanceley the artists held two influential exhibitions in 1962 of painting, collages and assemblage, in Melbourne at the Museum of Modern Art and Design and in Sydney at the Rudy Komon Art Gallery, using the name ANNANDALE IMITATION REALISTS. They exploited discarded materials and disdained finish in a raw and irreverent art that mixed painting and sculpture, often collaborating on work. Imitation Realism was the first full expression of Dada in Australian art, more than 40 years after its inception in Europe. In addition to non-Western art, key influences were the art of Jean Dubuffet and *art brut* rather than American neo-Dada. A major work was Brown's *Mary Lou* (1962; destr., see Hughes, p. 308): part satire on Hollywood glamour, part icon and part fertility fetish, later reworked for a 1964 version, *Mary Lou as Miss Universe* (see Smith, p. 397).

During the 1960s Brown's work ranged from Pop to abstract art, and he used exhibitions as opportunities to attack the condition of Australian modernism and the wider censorship that prevailed in Australian society. One consequence was a conviction in 1966 for exhibiting obscene painting. From 1970 Brown lived in Melbourne. In his work he continued earlier themes and preoccupations: in particular murals, assemblages and the need for a public and accessible art.

BIBLIOGRAPHY

R. Hughes: *The Art of Australia* (Harmondsworth, 1966)
B. Smith: *Australian Painting, 1788–1970* (London, 2/1971)
Mike Brown: A Survey of Work, 1961 to 1977 (exh. cat., Melbourne, N.G. Victoria, 1977)
G. Catalano: *The Years of Hope: Australian Art and Criticism, 1959–1968* (Melbourne, 1981), pp. 122–35, 139, 156–7, 160, 201
Power to the People: A Retrospective Exhibition of the Work of Mike Brown, 1958 to 1995 (exh. cat., Melbourne, N.G. Victoria, 1995)

RICHARD HAESE

Brown, Percy (*b* 1872; *d* Srinagar, 1955). English art historian, museum curator, educationalist, painter and collector. In 1899, after a short period of training as an archaeologist in Egypt, Brown went to India, where he served as curator of Lahore Museum and principal of the Mayo School of Art, Lahore. While working in these posts, he was also assistant director of the Delhi Exhibition of 1902–3 (*see* DELHI, §II), under George Watt. In 1909 he took up employment in Calcutta as principal of the Government School of Art and curator of the art section of the Indian Museum. In 1927 he retired from the Indian Educational Service to take up an appointment as secretary and curator of the Victoria Memorial Hall in Calcutta, where he remained until 1947. After this he lived on a houseboat on the Dal Lake in Srinagar, Kashmir.

Brown's earliest publications included a contribution to the catalogue of the Delhi Exhibition and a descriptive guide to the Department of Industrial Art at Lahore Museum in 1909. After moving to Calcutta, he concentrated his attention on the history of Indian painting. Published in 1924, *Indian Painting under the Mughals* was the first major connected account of Mughal painting and presented a comprehensive history of the school together with fine photographic plates. Turning his attention to Nepal, Brown then wrote a book and a number of articles on Nepalese art and architecture and in the early 1940s published *Indian Architecture*. In addition to carrying out his professional duties and research, he was a gifted painter. He supervised the painting of murals in the Council Room of the Viceroy's House in New Delhi in about 1930 and designed Indian coinage. He also travelled widely, including to North America, and was an Associate of the Royal College of Art, London. His collection of Tibetan *tangka*s is in the Indian Department of the Victoria and Albert Museum, London.

WRITINGS

Indian Painting (Calcutta, 1918)
Indian Painting under the Mughals, AD 1550–1750 (Oxford, 1924)
Indian Architecture (?Bombay [1941–2], rev. Bombay, 1956 with add. phot.)

BIBLIOGRAPHY

H. G. Rawlinson: Obituary, *A. & Lett.*, xxix/1 (1955), p. 35

S. J. VERNOIT

Brown, Richard (*fl* 1804–45). English architect, designer and drawing-master. He appears to have had strong connections during his early life with South Devon: his earliest known design, exhibited at the Royal Academy in 1804, was of a *Villa with a Distant View of the Catwater,*

Plymouth, and other designs (1807–12) also relate to this county. However, Brown may have been living in London during this period as he ran an architectural academy at 4 Wells Street. There the importance of perspective drawing was taught, and in 1815 he published the *Principles of Practical Perspective.* He also became increasingly interested in furniture design, and in the need for designers in this discipline to master the art of perspective. Drawing is one of the main themes in his work the *Rudiments of Drawing Cabinet Furniture* (1820), which consists of 24 coloured plates, each accompanied by commentary. The designs are in the Classical style and acknowledge the work of Thomas Hope (ii), George Smith and Charles Percier. Brown also praised the quality of George Bullock's cabinetmaking, and the plates appear to have been derived from Bullock's designs. One plate depicts a sofa made in 1815 by Bullock for the exiled Napoleon Bonaparte on the instructions of the Prince Regent (later George IV). Brown produced architectural designs throughout this period including *Regency Park* (1812), *A Military Chapel and Officer's Apartments . . . at Cape Castle, on the Gold Coast* (1818), *Gaol and House of Correction, St Giles Gates, Norwich* (1823) and *A Market House, Great Yarmouth* (1827). The only buildings known to have been executed from his designs are a lodge (1831) for Holland House, Kensington, London, and the Independent Chapel, Topsham, Devon, near where he was probably living by 1839. His later books *Domestic Architecture* (1842; *see* PATTERN BOOK, fig. 4) and *Sacred Architecture* (1845) are dated at Topsham and Exeter respectively.

WRITINGS

Principles of Practical Perspective (London, 1815)
Rudiments of Drawing Cabinet Furniture (London, 1820)
Domestic Architecture (Topsham, 1842)
Sacred Architecture (Exeter, 1845)

BIBLIOGRAPHY

Colvin
F. Collard: *Regency Furniture* (Woodbridge, 1985)
George Bullock: Cabinet-Maker (exh. cat. by C. Wainwright and others, London, Blairman & Sons, 1988)

BRIAN AUSTEN

Brown, Vernon [Akitt] (*b* London, 23 March 1905; *d* Auckland, 28 Jan 1965). New Zealand architect of English birth. He was educated at Highgate School, London, and arrived in New Zealand in 1927. After working for several architectural firms in Auckland, he began his own practice in 1937. From 1945 he taught at the School of Architecture, University of Auckland. During the 1940s and 1950s he designed a series of simple, austere timber-frame houses clad in dark-stained weatherboards with low-pitched roofs, for example Redwood House (1943), Orakei, and Melville House (1947), Epsom. The plans of these houses were economical and rigorously organized, while construction techniques and details were those commonly available. Brown was one of the first New Zealand architects to discover in the principles of the Modern Movement the key to an authentic architectural idiom for his own time and place. Through his example as a practising architect and as a teacher, he exerted a strong influence on a generation of post-World War II New Zealand architects, encouraging them to find their own identity rather than relying on imported concepts and styles.

BIBLIOGRAPHY

D. Mitchell and G. Chaplin: *The Elegant Shed: New Zealand Architecture since 1945* (Auckland, 1984)

IAN J. LOCHHEAD

Browne, Alexander (*fl* 1660–83). English miniature painter, writer, printmaker and print publisher. In 1665 he taught limning to Elizabeth Pepys, wife of Samuel Pepys, probably on the recommendation of Pepys's superior, Sir William Penn, whose daughter he had previously taught. Pepys, finding Browne over-familiar, terminated the acquaintance the following year. In 1669 Browne published *Ars Pictoria, or an Academy Treating of Drawing, Painting, Limning and Etching*, with 31 plates etched by himself after Old Master painters. It was published with Browne's portrait by Jacob Huysmans, engraved by Arnold de Jode (*b* 1638; *fl* 1658–66), as its frontispiece. Six years later Browne added *An Appendix to the Art of Painting in Miniture* [*sic*] *or Limning, etc* and in 1677 published *A Commodious Drawing Book* with 40 plates after modern masters. In 1683, according to Horace Walpole, Browne obtained a 14-year patent to publish 100 mezzotint prints from works by Anthony van Dyck and Peter Lely. Chaloner Smith records 44 of these, 24 of which are in the British Museum, London. Redgrave and other authorities have credited Browne with miniatures of *Charles II*, *William, Prince of Orange* and the *Countess Stuart*, but without naming owners or locations.

PRINTS

A Commodious Drawing Book (London, 1677)

WRITINGS

Ars Pictoria, or an Academy Treating of Drawing, Painting, Limning and Etching (London, 1669)
An Appendix to the Art of Painting in Miniture or Limning, etc (London, 1675)

BIBLIOGRAPHY

DNB; Redgrave; Waterhouse: *16th & 17th C.*
J. C. Smith: *British Mezzotinto Portraits*, i (London, 1878), pp. 105–23
D. Foskett: *Dictionary of British Miniature Painters*, i (London, 1972)

DAVID RODGERS

Browne, George (*b* Belfast, 5 Nov 1811; *d* Montreal, 19 Nov 1885). Canadian architect of Irish origin. The son of an architect of the same name, he arrived in Quebec City in 1830. He established a practice there in 1831 and designed houses, including a Gothic Revival villa for the provincial secretary Dominick Daly (1798–1868), who may have been responsible for Browne's appointment as Chief Architect for the Board of Works. He designed many public buildings in Kingston and Montreal; the former became capital of the Province of Canada in 1841, and Browne was commissioned to modify, add to and erect various government buildings. His masterpiece in Kingston is the City Hall (1843–4; then known as the Town Hall and Market Building), the commission he won in a competition held in 1841. The City Hall shows his characteristic massing of volumes and contrasting textures, using a varied vocabulary and a strong sculptural sense. Facing the waterfront, the main entrance to the T-shaped City Hall has a pediment supported by four columns, surmounted by a tall dome capped by a cupola. He was also responsible for many commercial and domestic commissions in Kingston, notably the houses known as St Andrew's Manse for St Andrew's Presbyterian Church

and Rockwood for John Solomon Cartwright (both 1841). His commercial buildings include Commercial Mart (additions 1841), which has pedimented dormers in the attic storey, and Wilson's Buildings (1841–3); both are on sites at the intersection of two streets and have round corners and arcades on the street level.

Browne moved to Montreal when it became capital of the Province of Canada in 1844, again to modify buildings for the government. That year he made additions and alterations to the James Monk house, known as Monklands (built 1803–4), to transform it into the governor-general's residence. As at Kingston, however, he became better known for his commercial buildings, particularly the head office for Molson's Bank (1864–6; now Bank of Montreal), on the corner of Rue St-Jacques and Rue St-François. Here Browne used the Second Empire style, contrasting twisted rustication for the basement with channelled rustication on the ground level; the smooth ashlar on the two upper storeys is juxtaposed with details such as swags, Corinthian capitals, bosses and paired capitals, pilasters and volutes. Other noteworthy buildings in Montreal are the Merchant's Exchange (1866; now the offices of *Le Devoir* newspaper), the Urquhart Building (1855), the Law, Young & Co. Building (1857) and the Frotingham & Workman Hardware Store (1871). Browne went to Quebec City in 1851–2 to supervise the alterations to the Parliament Buildings and Spencer Wood, the governor-general's residence. Many of his buildings have been designated historic monuments.

DCB

BIBLIOGRAPHY

J. D. Borthwick: *Biographical Sketches* (Montreal, 1875)
M. Angus: *The Old Stones of Kingston* (Toronto, 1966)
A. J. H. Richardson: 'Biographical Dictionary of [Quebec City] Architects and Builders', *Bull. Assoc. Preserv. Technol.*, ii (1970), pp. 76–7
N. Mika and H. Mika: *Kingston City Hall* (Kingston, 1973)

DONNA MCGEE

Browne, Sir George Washington (*b* Glasgow, 21 Sept 1853; *d* Sambrook, Salop, 15 June 1939). Scottish architect and writer. He was apprenticed to the Glasgow firm of Salmon, Son & Richie before joining Douglas & Sellars, also of Glasgow, in 1873. He worked in London (1875–8) for both J. J. Stevenson and Arthur William Blomfield (1829–99) and won the Pugin Travelling Scholarship, which enabled him to study in Paris and Belgium. In 1879 he returned to Scotland as chief assistant to Rowand Anderson, working as his junior partner (1881–5) after another brief spell in London with W. E. Nesfield, whose work influenced him profoundly. In 1887 Browne won the competition for Edinburgh Central Library with a scholarly and sophisticated early French Renaissance Revival design that launched his career. Early major commissions were the Flemish Late Gothic Revival Redfern's Building (Messrs Radfern; 1891–2; destr.), 31–2 Princes Street, Edinburgh (a ladies' fashion department store, and the Netherlandish Renaissance Revival Cranston's Tearooms (1895–6; interior destr.; now Clydesdale Bank), 91 Buchanan Street, Glasgow. Also at this time he adopted an accomplished Jacobean Revival style at the Sick Children's Hospital (1891–5; altered) in Edinburgh. From the mid 1890s until *c.* 1905 Browne was in partnership with J. M. Dick Peddie in the firm Peddie & Kinnear, with whom he designed a series of provincial branch banks in revival styles for the Royal Bank of Scotland and the British Linen Bank, and the latter's office (1905), 69 George Street, Edinburgh, which is in an early French Renaissance Revival style. His masterpiece was the North British and Mercantile Building (1903–4; destr.) in Princes Street, Edinburgh, a neo-Georgian structure with central European Baroque-style details. In his domestic work, notably at Johnsburn, Lothian (*c.* 1900), Browne adopted a picturesque Scottish idiom with northern French touches. After 1914 he devoted himself to teaching, from which he retired in 1922. He remained a powerful figure in architectural circles as President of the Royal Scottish Academy (1924–33).

WRITINGS
The Planning of Public Libraries (London, 1893)

BIBLIOGRAPHY
J. Wilson: Obituary, *RIBA J.*, xlvi (1939), pp. 141–3
Obituary, *The Times* (16 June 1939); *The Scotsman* (16 June 1939)
D. C. Mays: 'A Profile of Sir George Washington Browne', *The Age of Mackintosh*, Architectural Heritage, iii (Edinburgh, 1992), pp. 52-63

DAVID WALKER

Browne, Hablot Knight [Phiz] (*b* London, 12 July 1815; *d* Hove, W. Sussex, 8 July 1882). English illustrator, etcher and painter. Browne's only formal education consisted of sporadic attendance at the St Martin's Lane Academy life class and apprenticeship to the line-engraver William Finden. In 1834 he cancelled his indenture and established an illustrators' workshop with fellow apprentice Robert Young, producing etchings and watercolours in preference to the more laborious line-engravings. He won the Silver Isis medal of the Society of Arts in 1833 for his etching, *John Gilpin's Ride*. He also produced illustrations for *Sunday under Three Heads* (1836), an anti-Sabbatarian pamphlet published pseudonymously by Charles Dickens, who later preferred Browne to Thackeray as collaborator in the production of *The Posthumous Papers of the Pickwick Club*. Initially *The Pickwick Papers* was merely meant to accompany etchings of pastimes of contemporary London by Robert Seymour (1798–1836), but after Seymour's suicide took charge and made them a narrative with illustrations in monthly parts. Symptomatic of this accommodation of image to prose is Browne signing himself first 'Nemo' and then 'Phiz' (a depicter of physiognomies) to harmonize with Dickens's 'Boz'. Browne played an important part, for instance, in the portrayal of Sam Weller, whom he made less wiry, less an example of what Dickens called 'loutish humour', but more resilient and knowingly ironical.

To aid his depiction of the schoolmaster Squeers in *Nicholas Nickleby*, Browne went to Yorkshire in 1837 to gather evidence of moral and physical disease by means of surreptitious sketching of likely-looking teachers. The results were curious: the hero, an elegant paragon of social and familial virtue, is portrayed in a completely different style from the parade of grotesques that surround him. For *Master Humphrey's Clock*, in which *The Old Curiosity Shop* (1840) and *Barnaby Rudge* (1841) were published in weekly instalments, Dickens employed George Cattermole as well as Browne, trying to marry narrative and image as intimately as possible. Cattermole was occupied with the antiquities of the old curiosity shop and with Nell's serene countenance, while Browne elaborated the contemporary elements. Quilp, the deformed and deforming villain, incarnation of a monstrous historical inheritance which threatens to absorb all virtue, is nonetheless both grotesque and witty in Browne's memorable images.

Following the example of Honoré Daumier, Browne's etchings for *Martin Chuzzlewit* (1843–4) and *Dombey and Son* (1846–8) were executed in a more precise and coherent visual style (e.g. details, often pictures, of domestic interiors in ironical counterpart to the main action). This subtler form not only facilitated the more intricate rendering of the anxious fireside in *David Copperfield* (1849–50) but also encouraged Browne to produce *Home Sketches* (1851), 16 etchings exemplifying Victorian bourgeois virtue. His late work for Dickens avoided this strain of homily. The dark-plate etchings for *Bleak House* (1853), notably an image of a woman lying at the gate of a graveyard (see fig.), provide not only narrative fascination but also a visual drama unprecedented in his previous work.

Browne's long career as an illustrator, including less memorable work for Charles Lever, William Ainsworth and Anthony Trollope, dwindled after he was passed over in favour of Marcus Stone (1840–1921) for *Our Mutual Friend* (1864–5). Partially paralyzed in 1867, he worked less and less, but his earlier achievements as an illustrator were recognized by the award of a Royal Academy pension.

Hablot Knight Browne: *The Morning*, dark-plate etching from Charles Dickens: *Bleak House* (London, 1853), opposite p. 576

BIBLIOGRAPHY

F. G. Kitton: *Phiz: a Memoir* (London, 1882)
D. C. Thomson: *Life and Labours of Hablot Knight Browne, Phiz* (London, 1884)
E. Browne: *Phiz and Dickens* (London, 1913)
A. Johannsen: *Phiz: Illustrations from the Novels of Charles Dickens* (Chicago, 1956)
J. R. Harvey: *Victorian Novelists and their Illustrators* (London, 1970)
M. Steig: *Dickens and Phiz* (Bloomington, 1978)
J. R. Cohen: *Charles Dickens and his Original Illustrators* (Columbus, 1980), pp. 61–122

LEWIS JOHNSON

Browne, John (*b* Finchingfield, Essex, 26 April 1741; *d* London, 2 Oct 1801). English engraver. He was apprenticed to the engraver John Tinney (*d* 1761), who was also the master of William Woollett, to whom Browne transferred his apprenticeship in 1761–3. He remained with Woollett until 1766, and Woollett found in him the ideal assistant for his system of preliminary etching. According to Blake, 'Woollett's best works...all that are called Woolletts were Etchd by Jack Brown' (*William Blake's Writings*, ed. G. E. Bentley jr, Oxford, 1977, ii, p. 1035); in fairness to Woollett, however, Browne's contribution was acknowledged on the prints and in advertisements. Browne engraved many plates of his own and made his name with a number of large prints of pictures by Claude Lorrain, Meindert Hobbema, Peter Paul Rubens and Salvator Rosa, which he engraved for John Boydell in the late 1760s. In 1770 he was one of the first Associate Engravers elected to the Royal Academy. Browne was a specialist engraver and all his prints, which include four after his own drawings (published in the late 1790s), have a landscape element.

BIBLIOGRAPHY

DNB; Redgrave; Thieme–Becker
Catalogue of the Prints and Copper-Plates of John Browne, Associate, London, King's: 16 January 1802
C. Le Blanc: *Manuel de l'amateur d'estampes* (Paris, 1854–89), i, p. 529
A. Graves: *The Royal Academy of Arts: A Complete Dictionary of Contributors from 1769 to 1904* (London, 1905–6/*R* 1970), i
——: *The Society of Artists of Great Britain, 1760–1791 [and] The Free Society of Artists, 1761–1783* (London, 1907), p. 42
I. Maxted: *The London Book Trades, 1775–1800* (Folkestone, 1977), p. 31

DAVID ALEXANDER

Browne, Lyde (*d* 10 Sept 1787). English collector, businessman and banker. Elected a Fellow of the Royal Society in 1752, he assumed a leading role in antiquarian circles in London, and his house at Wimbledon was famous for its large and ever-changing collection. It included the statue that has been attributed to Michelangelo of a *Crouching Youth* (St Petersburg, Hermitage), as well as gems, Old Master paintings and other curiosities, but it was as a collector of ancient marbles that he was best known. From around 1760 until his death he purchased extensively from Thomas Jenkins in Rome, becoming one of his major clients. Browne published two catalogues of his collection, the first, in Latin, appearing in 1768, and the second, in Italian, in 1779, with 236 items arranged typologically. These catalogues give many provenance details noting acquisitions not only from prominent princely collections in Rome and elsewhere—most notably the Giustiniani, Verospi, Barberini, Mattei, Negroni and Albani—but also from contemporary excavations in and around Rome. Browne is recorded in Italy in 1776, scouring dealers' shops in Venice, Florence, Naples and especially Rome,

where he purchased mainly minor items from Jenkins, Gavin Hamilton, Bartolomeo Cavaceppi and Giovanni Battista Piranesi. In England Browne sold groups of statues, mainly busts, to Charles Wyndham, 2nd Earl of Egremont, Charles Watson-Wentworth, 2nd Marquess of Rockingham, and Charles Townley. The sale from Houghton Hall, Norfolk, in 1779 of the collection of pictures that had belonged to Robert Walpole, 1st Earl of Orford, to Catherine II, Empress of Russia, encouraged Browne to offer her his collection of marbles. Agreement was struck in 1784, and it appears that his collection was dispatched to St Petersburg in 1785. As a result of the bankruptcy of his Russian agent, Browne only received one payment of £10,000, and this devastating loss is said to have hastened his death. The majority of the ancient marbles now in the Hermitage, St Petersburg, and at Pavlovsk Palace, Pavlovsk, can be identified as coming from Browne's collection. The process of identification has been assisted by two groups of drawings of busts and statues in Browne's collection. The first group is by Jenkins and was presented by Browne to the Society of Antiquaries of London in the 1760s; the second is a bound volume in the British Museum, London, of 23 drawings of busts by Giovanni Battista Cipriani, almost certainly intended to be engraved.

WRITINGS

Catalogus veteris aevi varii generis monumentorum quae cimelarchio Lyde Browne (London, 1768)
Catologo dei piu scelti e preziosi marmi che si conservano nella galleria del Sgr Lyde Browne (London, 1779)

BIBLIOGRAPHY

DNB
X. Gorbunova: 'Classical Sculptures from the Lyde Browne Collection', *Apollo*, c (1974), pp. 460–67
O. Neverov: 'The Lyde Browne Collection and the History of Ancient Sculpture in the Hermitage Museum', *Amer. J. Archaeol.*, lxxxviii (1984), pp. 33–42
S. Rowland Pierce: 'Thomas Jenkins in Rome, in the Light of Letters, Records and Drawings at the Society of Antiquaries of London', *Antiqua. J.*, xlv (1965), pp. 200–29

GERARD VAUGHAN

Brownlow, Emma [King, Mrs E. B.] (*b* London, 1832; *d* Kent, 1 Jan 1905). English painter. Although she had no formal training, she began drawing at an early age and exhibited regularly at the Royal Academy (1852–67) and the British Institution, London, and sent works as far as Manchester, Liverpool and Glasgow. She painted domestic genre scenes, many based on her travels to Brittany, Switzerland and Belgium in the 1850s and 1860s.

Brownlow's father was secretary of the Foundling Hospital, London, and her exposure to hospital life inspired a number of her paintings. Her scenes of life at the Hospital contain portraits of administrators, doctors and children living there at the time. *The Foundling Restored to its Mother* (1858; London, Foundling Hosp.) includes a portrait of her father. Brownlow's awareness of Hogarth led her to adopt his method of using paintings in the background to comment on the foreground action, and the hospital's rich picture collection allowed her to do so while faithfully representing interior settings. Thus *The Christening* (1863; London, Foundling Hosp.) takes place in front of Benjamin West's *Christ Presenting a Little Child* (1801; also London, Foundling Hosp.), which hung in the chapel (destr.) where Sunday christenings were conducted.

Unlike Hogarth's, Brownlow's intentions were not satirical: her concern was more with a depiction of hospital life that reflected the benevolence of its administrators and courteous behaviour of its foundlings.

Brownlow married in 1867 and ceased exhibiting in 1877. Health problems induced her to travel to New Zealand (1888) and Ceylon (1901).

BIBLIOGRAPHY

C. Wood: *Victorian Panorama: Paintings of Victorian Life* (London, 1976), pp. 69–71
P. Gerrish Nunn: *Victorian Women Artists* (London, 1987), pp. 158–74

SHEARER WEST

Brožík, Václav (*b* Železný Hamr u Třemošné, western Bohemia, 5 May 1851; *d* Paris, 15 April 1901). Czech painter. He was one of the leading official painters of Austria–Hungary and probably the most celebrated Bohemian artist working in Europe during the last quarter of the 19th century. From 1868 to 1875 he studied at the Prague Academy of Fine Arts under Antonín Lhota (1812–1905) and Emil Lauffer (1837–1909), moving from there to the Dresden Hochschule der Bildenden Künste and then to Munich. He completed his studies under Léon Bonnat in Paris, where he lived from 1876.

Brožík's most notable successes were colossal history paintings with broad popular appeal; these either did the rounds of the most prestigious exhibitions of Europe, or were exhibited independently. They include the *Nuptial Deputation of Ladislav, King of Bohemia, to Charles VII, King of France* (1877; Prague, Hradčany Castle), the *Condemnation of Jan Hus at the Council of Constance* and the *Election of Jiří of Poděbrady as King of Bohemia* (1883 and 1898; both Prague, N.G., Staré Město Old Town Hall). Apart from these whole-heartedly historical paintings he also produced historicized, 'fancy-dress' portraits, such as the *Actress Julie Šamberková in the Role of Messalina* (1876; Prague, N.G., Convent of St Agnes), and historical genre paintings (e.g. *Bible Reading among Protestants*, 1888; sketch at Prague, N.G., Convent of St Agnes).

Apart from his late phase of conventional historicism, Brožík's work enhanced the role of Czech history painting as part of a national culture striving for greater political self-affirmation; though its general political stance is inevitably one of loyalty to the Habsburg dynasty and the Austro-Hungarian monarchy (for instance, *Tu Felix Austria Nube*, 1897; sketches, Prague, N.G., Convent of St Agnes). In his genre painting he specialized in interiors from salon society. Brožík also painted village genre scenes in the tradition of Jules Breton (e.g. *The Meadow*; Prague, N.G., Convent of St Agnes). His fresh *plein-air* sketches, along with some of his portraits and portrait studies, testify to his feeling for unpretending Realism, which explains his success as a teacher at the Prague Academy of Fine Arts, where he was professor of history painting from 1893. He always saw his work in a Czech context, and he was generally inspired by Central Europeans, including Jaroslav Čermák, Gabriel Max, Karl Theodor von Piloty, Mihály von Munkácsy and Jan Matejko.

BIBLIOGRAPHY

J. Neumann: *Modern Czech Painting and the Classical Tradition* (Prague, 1958), pp. 31–7
Václav Brožík (exh. cat., ed. M. Mrázová; Prague, N.G., 1976)
M. Nováková: 'Václav Brožík', *Die tschechische Malerei des XIX. Jahrhunderts* (exh. cat., ed. J. Kotalík; Vienna, Belvedere, 1984)

ROMAN PRAHL

Bruand [Bruant]. French family of architects. Sébastien Bruand (*d* 1670), an architect active in Paris, became Maître Général des Bâtiments et des Ponts et Chaussées and Maître Général des Oeuvres de Charpenterie du Roi. Of his sons, (1) Jacques Bruand was architect to Gaston, Duc d'Orléans and Architecte du Roi, while (2) Libéral Bruand inherited Sébastien's positions. One of Libéral's sons, François Bruand (1679–1732), became a member of the Académie Royale d'Architecture in 1706.

BIBLIOGRAPHY

L. Hautecoeur: *Architecture classique* (1943–57)
A. Blunt: *Art and Architecture in France, 1500–1700*, Pelican Hist. A. (Harmondsworth, 1953, rev. 4/1980/*R* 1982)

(1) Jacques Bruand (*b* ?Paris, *c.* 1620; *d* Paris, 7 Sept 1664). In 1644 he was made architect to Gaston, Duc d'Orléans (1608–60), and was appointed Architecte du Roi two years later. In 1646–7 Bruand worked in Paris as master-builder to Antoine Le Pautre on the Hôtel de Fontenay-Mareuil in the Rue Coq Héron. In partnership with his brother (2) Libéral Bruand, he extended the Hôtel Catelan (1659–61), 18 Rue Vivienne. Further works in Paris in the 1650s include the façade of the Bureau des Marchands-Drapiers (now Musée Carnavalet) at 11 Rue des Déchargeurs, which was designed as the background to an ornamental sculpture, and the Château du Fayel (1653–60) for the Maréchal de la Mothe Houdancourt. This château is in a 'brick-and-stone' style unfashionable in the mid-17th century, but it has several innovative features: Italianate ceilings, peristyles at the entrance and no moat. Bruand's designs for the Hôtel Jabach (*c.* 1650) somewhat prefigure the high classical style of French Baroque architecture. Towards the end of his career he appears to have supervised work on the Hôtel de Guéménée.

MYRIAM TEITELBAUM

(2) Libéral Bruand (*b* ?Paris, *c.* 1635; *d* Paris, 22 Nov 1697). Brother of (1) Jacques Bruand. With his appointment as Architecte du Roi in 1663, he inherited the positions his father, Sébastien, had held, giving him administrative responsibility for the maintenance of bridges, highways and other civil engineering works throughout France. He also undertook residential commissions, such as the remodelling (1666) of the Hôtel Vendôme (destr. *c.* 1686), Paris, and possibly the unexecuted design for a house (*c.* 1662) in England for James Stuart, Duke of York (later James II) at Richmond near London. In 1669 he succeeded Pierre Le Muet as director of works at the Hôpital de la Salpêtrière, which had been founded by Cardinal Jules Mazarin in 1656 on the outskirts of Paris to house mendicants and others. The following year Bruand began construction of its domed, centrally planned chapel—St Louis de la Salpêtrière. Four rectangular naves forming a Greek cross radiate from its octagonal crossing—a plan that provided discrete areas, from which the various categories of inmates could follow the services conducted at the central altar. Between the naves are four octagonal chapels. Both exterior and interior elevations are composed of simply detailed, broad expanses of ashlar masonry punctuated by arches. The overall solemn and monumental effect of this church (completed 1677) befits a royal institution devoted to charity.

Bruand's work at the Salpêtrière brought him to the attention of Michel Le Tellier, Marquis de Louvois (1641–91), who in 1670 invited him to submit a design for a veterans' hospital and home to be built in Paris. Louvois had more than humanitarian concerns in mind for this, the Hôtel des Invalides (*see* PARIS, §V, 7). He envisioned it as a monument to Louis XIV, one symbolizing the monarch's commitment to the welfare of his armies. Construction began in 1671 and proceeded rapidly; by 1674 the Invalides was sufficiently complete for it to be dedicated and partially occupied. Unfortunately, the relationship between Louvois and Bruand deteriorated amid allegations of falsified accounts and Bruand's alleged orders for unauthorized changes, and after 1675 Jules Hardouin Mansart effectively displaced Bruand as principal architect. Hardouin Mansart supervised the construction of the Eglise des Soldats (begun 1676) as well as providing the definitive designs for the domed Eglise St Louis des Invalides (built 1676–1706). For his own plan of the Invalides, Bruand had drawn upon traditional schemes of organizing hospitals and monastic foundations around courtyards. His hierarchic arrangement of a chapel at the head of a central courtyard flanked symmetrically by smaller ones appears to have been inspired by the Escorial, Madrid. Bruand treated the exterior elevations simply and limited ornament to dormers and entrance pavilions. For the central courtyard he used an ashlar wall and arcade, as he had done at the Salpêtrière and as he later employed for the façade of his own house (1685) on the Rue de la Perle in Paris. Except for a portal (1677; destr.) for the monastery of the Feuillants, Paris, Bruand received no further major commissions after 1675. Nevertheless, he maintained an active private practice building residences for wealthy patrons. In the 1670s and 1680s he speculated on the Paris property market and built a number of hôtels in Versailles and Paris, including the Hôtel Libéral-Bruant (1685; rest.), Rue de la Perle.

BIBLIOGRAPHY

P. Jarry: *Les Vieux Hôtels de Paris: Le Quartier Saint-Antoine; Architecture et décorations intérieures* (Paris, 1929)
P. Reutersward: 'A French Project for a Castle at Richmond', *Burl. Mag.*, civ (1962), pp. 533–5
——: *The Two Churches of the Hôtel des Invalides: A History of their Design* (Stockholm, 1965)
R. Strandberg: 'Libéral Bruand et les problèmes que soulèvent l'Eglise des Soldats et le Dôme des Invalides', *Ksthist. Tidskr.*, xxxv (1966), pp. 1–22

RICHARD CLEARY

Bruandet, Lazare (*b* Paris, 3 July 1755; *d* Paris, 26 March 1804). French painter and etcher. A pupil of Martin Roeser (1757–1804) and Jean-Philippe Sarazin (*d* ?1795), Bruandet was a wild and dissolute character who achieved posthumous fame as a precursor of the Barbizon School of landscape painters. Inspired by the Dutch masters of the 17th century, he favoured a naturalistic depiction of landscape and painted extensively in the open air. His most frequent subjects were the forests of the Ile-de-France, notably that of Fontainebleau, where he became a familiar if solitary figure: Louis XVI noted in his diary on

14 July 1789 that, while out hunting in the forest of Fontainebleau, he had encountered nothing but boars and Bruandet. Bruandet exhibited a *View in the Forest of Fontainebleau* (untraced) at the Salon of 1789, but, though he continued to exhibit regularly until his death, he met with no great critical acclaim. He was a good friend of his contemporary Georges Michel, and, like Michel, he often called on other artists to paint the figures in his landscapes, especially Jean-Louis Demarne and Jacques-François Swebach. The *Monks in the Forest* (exh. Salon 1793; Grenoble, Mus. Grenoble) is one such collaboration, the brooding forest landscape by Bruandet and the monks by Swebach. Bruandet also made a number of etchings (Roux attributes seven to him), all small in size and of similar subjects to his paintings.

BIBLIOGRAPHY

A. Sensier: 'Conférence sur le paysage', suppl. to *Souvenirs sur Théodore Rousseau* (Paris, 1872), p. x
M. Roux: *Inventaire du fonds français: Graveurs du dix-huitième siècle*, Paris, Bib. N., Cab. Est. cat., iii (Paris, 1934), pp. 379–81

□

Bruce, Patrick Henry (*b* Long Island, VA, 25 March 1881; *d* New York, 12 Nov 1936). American painter. He studied in New York under William Merritt Chase (1901) and Robert Henri (1903). In 1903 he went to Paris and was organizer, with Sarah Stein, of Matisse's school. From 1912 he was closely associated with Sonia Delaunay and Robert Delaunay. He remained in Paris until 1936, when he returned to New York, committing suicide a few months later.

Bruce destroyed much of his own work: only *c*. 100 of his paintings remain. His oeuvre can be divided into four periods. The first, lasting until *c*. 1907, reflects the influence of Henri in the bravura brushwork and deep tonalities of such portraits as *Littleton Maclurg Wickham* (1903; Julia Wickham Porter priv. col., see Agee and Rose, p. 14). In the second period, from 1907 to 1912, Bruce painted a few landscapes and portraits, but predominant in this period are still-lifes in a style reflecting an interest in Cézanne and his study with Matisse. In these works, for example *Still-life of Red-cheeked Pears* (1912; B. F. Garber priv. col., see Agee and Rose, p. 16), Bruce combined the bright colours of Fauvism with the structure of Cubism. From his third phase, which lasted until *c*. 1920, several Orphist-like, hard-edged Compositions remain, including *Composition II* (1916; New Haven, CT, Yale U. A.G.) in which colours are unmodulated and angled forms are flat and unmodelled. In the final phase of his oeuvre Bruce produced geometric Cubist still-lifes based on architectural themes, such as *Painting/Still-life* (*c*. 1925–6; Washington, DC, Hirshhorn).

Although Bruce never identified himself with any school, he has often been labelled a Synchromist. His works became more widely known in the USA through an exhibition on Synchromism organized by William C. Agee at M. Knoedler and Co., Inc. in 1965.

BIBLIOGRAPHY

W. D. Judson III: *Patrick Henry Bruce, 1881–1936* (diss., Oberlin Coll., OH, 1968)
T. M. Wolf: 'Patrick Henry Bruce', *Marsyas*, xv (1970–72), pp. 73–85
W. C. Agee and B. Rose, eds: *Patrick Henry Bruce: American Modernist* (New York, 1979) [cat. rais.; also used as catalogue for exhibitions at New York, MOMA, and Houston, TX, Mus. F.A., 1979]

A. A. Davidson: *Early American Modernist Painting, 1910–1935* (New York, 1981)

M. SUE KENDALL

Bruce, Thomas, 7th Earl of Elgin and 11th Earl of Kincardine (*b* Broomhall, Fife, 20 July 1766; *d* Paris, 14 Nov 1841). Scottish landowner, soldier, politician, diplomat and collector. Having only a modest income, he turned to the only careers open to an 18th-century nobleman: the army, politics and diplomacy. His innate talent and excellent education brought him early success in all three, but he is chiefly remembered for his appointment in 1798 as Ambassador Extraordinary and Minister Plenipotentiary to the Ottoman Court at Constantinople (now Istanbul), which then controlled Greece, and the opportunity this gave him to acquire a large collection of antiquities (now London, BM), including sculptures and architectural fragments from the Parthenon and the Erechtheion in Athens (*see* ATHENS, §II, 1(ii) and GREECE, ANCIENT, fig. 60).

Thomas Harrison, the architect of Elgin's new house (1796–9) at Broomhall, Fife, encouraged him to commission drawings and moulds of sculptures and architectural details of the buildings on the Acropolis to improve the knowledge of Greek art and architecture in Britain. Having failed to recruit British artists, Elgin enlisted the Italian landscape painter Giovanni Battista Lusieri (*d* 1821), who gathered a team of artists and moulders. They reached Athens in August 1800, but the reluctance of the Turkish authorities to admit them to the Acropolis compelled Elgin to seek a firman (permit) from the government in Constantinople. Advised by his chaplain the Rev. Philip Hunt that the antiquities were at risk from vandalism and neglect, Elgin also sought permission to remove sculptures and inscriptions. In appreciation of recent British military successes in Egypt, the Turkish Government granted the firman promptly.

Armed with this authority, the artists and moulders were able to accomplish their tasks, and Lusieri began to collect sculptures and inscriptions, even obtaining permission to remove metopes, slabs of the frieze and pedimental figures from the Parthenon itself. When Elgin first visited Athens in 1802, much of this material had already been crated and shipped. One consignment on Elgin's brig *Mentor* was shipwrecked off Kythera in September 1802. Its salvage continued until October 1804, costing Elgin about £5000 at the time.

Elgin's embassy ended in January 1803. On the way home he visited Athens, took most of the artists with him and left behind only Lusieri, who continued to collect until October 1805. Dispatch of the remaining crates was delayed by war, but permission to ship them was granted in 1809, and the last consignment left in 1811. After returning to London in 1806, Elgin exhibited his collection and allowed such artists as John Flaxman, Benjamin Robert Haydon, Benjamin West and John Henning the elder to draw the marbles.

Elgin's embassy had proved very expensive, leaving him deeply in debt. In 1811 he offered his collection to the government for £62,000 but was refused, and in 1815 his second offer left the price to the judgement of a Select Committee of the House of Commons. After taking evidence from Elgin himself, from his secretary, William Richard Hamilton, from such connoisseurs as George Gordon, 4th Earl of Aberdeen, and Richard Payne Knight and from artists familiar with the marbles, the committee concluded that Elgin had acquired the collection legally but in his private capacity and recommended its acquisition for the nation at Lord Aberdeen's valuation of £35,000. This figure fell many thousands of pounds short of what the collection had actually cost Elgin in wages, presents, transport costs and interest, but his financial straits left him no choice but to accept. Controversy over the marbles barred him from further office, and he spent the rest of his life in financial difficulties, mainly abroad.

See also ART LEGISLATION, §2.

DNB

BIBLIOGRAPHY

A. H. Smith: 'Lord Elgin and his Collection', *J. Hell. Stud.*, xxxvi (1916), pp. 163–372
W. St Clair: *Lord Elgin and the Marbles* (London, 1967, rev. Oxford and New York, 1983)
S. Checkland: *The Elgins, 1766–1917* (Aberdeen, 1988)

B. F. COOK

Bruce, Sir William (*b* Perthshire, ?1625; *d* 1710). Scottish architect and garden designer. He was the younger son of Robert Bruce of Blairhall, Perthshire, and probably attended St Salvator's College, St Andrews, in 1637–8. Bruce was interested in the arts and was reputed to be well versed in languages, but it was as a politician that he first achieved recognition. He played a significant role in General Monk's conversion to the Royalist cause in 1659 and was a confidential messenger between the Scottish Lords and Charles II in the months preceding the Restoration. Shortly after 1660 he was knighted, and through John Maitland, 2nd Earl and 1st Duke of Lauderdale—whose second wife was a full cousin of Bruce's—he obtained various minor though lucrative employments before his appointment in 1671 as Surveyor-General of the Royal Works in Scotland (the ancient post of Master of the Royal Works, which had been re-created specifically for the rebuilding of the Palace of Holyroodhouse in Edinburgh), which he held until 1678.

Bruce was granted a baronetcy in 1668 and was a Justice of the Peace, a Parliamentary commissioner and a Privy Councillor, but his good fortune failed on the death of Charles II; distrusted by James VII of Scotland (James II of England) and subsequently suspected (not without cause) of Jacobite sympathies, he was more than once placed under confinement.

It is probable that Bruce developed an interest in architecture through theoretical studies and travel (see 1970 exh. cat.). When necessary he employed English, German and Dutch craftsmen; journeys to the Low Countries and England are documented (he knew London particularly well) and he almost certainly visited France in 1663.

Holyroodhouse (*see* EDINBURGH, §4) has traditionally been ascribed to Bruce, but a set of drawings of the Palace by the King's Master Mason Robert Mylne (i), whose name is inscribed on the building itself, suggests that much of the design was by Mylne, with Bruce as adviser and administrator. Bruce's principal contribution to the Mylne design was the grand Baroque state apartments; this was his only work for the crown, apart from minor fortifications.

Bruce's chance to combine his twin interests of architecture and garden design came when he purchased Balcaskie House, Fife. He remodelled the existing house in 1668–74, duplicating a crow-stepped tower house to produce a regular and symmetrical composition with angle pavilions that was almost vernacular, though it followed the arrangement for Panmure House, Tayside, as designed in 1668 by John Mylne. Bruce's interior decoration, however, was of the style then fashionable in England, carried out by the English plasterer Dunsterfield, who had been brought north to work at Holyroodhouse and was also active at Thirlstane Castle (1670–77), Borders, one of three houses remodelled by Bruce for Lauderdale, his greatest patron.

Though stylistically dissimilar, Bruce's houses bear comparison with those of Pratt and May in England. Dunkeld House (c. 1676–84; destr. 1830), Tayside, and Moncrieffe House (1679; destr. 1957), Perthshire, which is attributed to Bruce, have deep tripartite plans with plain elevations, clean roof-lines and attics suppressed below eaves. For Bruce, house and garden were interrelated, and at Balcaskie he exploited in his formal layout the house's alignment on the Bass Rock, a formula he repeated at Kinross House (1686–93), Tayside, which he aligned on the ruined Lochleven Castle. Kinross was built on the 'double-pile' formula with a giant order and has a monumental dignity, though Bruce's changed fortunes meant that it was completed only with difficulty. At Hopetoun House (1699–1703), Lothian, he adopted a centralized plan with rooms on two axes about a central stair, an arrangement perhaps unlike any other house of its time south of the border but with parallels in some of James Smith's 'Palladian' drawings. At Craigie Hall (c. 1695–9) he again arranged the rooms about a central stair.

Bruce was essentially a gentleman architect who, apart from his royal and public works, produced designs for fellow members of the Scottish aristocracy. He achieved a great reputation as an arbiter of architectural taste. Leading by example and through the 'indirect ascendancy that he was able to establish over the works of other designers' (see 1970 exh. cat.), he exerted an enormous influence on Scottish architecture. Five years after Bruce's death, Colen Campbell recorded that he was 'justly esteemed the best Architect of his time in (Scotland)', and this reputation has survived, although as more buildings associated with him have been studied his precise architectural role has been brought into question. It is unclear how much his draughtsmen contributed to his work—Alexander Edward (1651–1708) and Alexander McGill (?1679–1734) both became significant figures in their own right—but the result was the erection of several houses of considerable quality, which, together with those of James Smith, brought Scotland into the mainstream of European architecture.

BIBLIOGRAPHY

Colvin

H. Fenwick: *Architect Royal: The Life and Works of Sir William Bruce, 1630–1710* (Kineton, 1970)

Sir William Bruce, 1630–1710 (exh. cat., ed. J. G. Dunbar; Edinburgh, Scot. A.C., 1970)

AONGHUS MACKECHNIE

Bruchsal, Schloss. German palace in the town of Bruchsal, situated *c.* 25 km south of Speyer between Heidelberg and Karlsruhe, Baden-Württemberg. When Damian Hugo Schönborn was elected Prince–Bishop of Speyer in 1719, he initially intended to rebuild the destroyed bishop's palace that was attached to the north flank of Speyer Cathedral, but the project brought him into conflict with the Protestant municipal authorities. He then decided to construct a new Residenz on the northern edge of Bruchsal, which had been part of the bishopric of Speyer since the 11th century. As war could be expected at any time in the area, the Residenz complex was to consist of individual buildings separated from one another and grouped around courtyards, an arrangement that would help to control the spread of fire. Plans were procured from Maximilian von Welsch, the architect of Damian Hugo's uncle, Lothar Franz, Elector of Mainz. Von Welsch's scheme for Schloss Bruchsal is lost, but his ability to arrange larger groups of buildings effectively on a site suggests that he devised the layout of free-standing buildings and interlocked axes. The tall, rectangular block of the palace was placed on an axis formed by a tree-lined avenue and gardens on one side and on the other by a symmetrical arrangement of buildings and a large courtyard that extended over the adjoining Bergstrasse (now Schönbornstrasse). The street was straddled by the Damian Gate at one end, and at the other it was bracketed by long rows of buildings. Work began first on the flanking blocks, to the designs of von Welsch, but Damian Hugo, who paid close attention to bishopric finances, began building without hiring an architect to supervise the work. He subsequently employed Johann Michael Ludwig Rohrer, court architect to Electoress Sibylla Augusta of the neighbouring state of Baden-Baden, for five years. In 1728 Johann Georg Stahl (1687–1755) was appointed architect for the Speyer bishopric, and he continued to oversee building operations on the site until his death. The central block of Schloss Bruchsal was designed in 1725 by Anselm F. Ritter zu Groenesteyn, a young architect also in Lothar Franz's service. During the summer of 1726 Damian Hugo decided that a mezzanine should be inserted between the ground and main floors. This created insurmountable problems for Ritter zu Groenesteyn, who was unable to make his circular staircase (for which the foundations were already in place) accommodate the extra height, and he soon resigned from the project.

Ritter zu Groenesteyn was replaced by Balthasar Neumann, who was consulted on all major design decisions. From 1728 he took over such utilitarian structures as the riding hall, arsenal and water system, but his most important contributions were the court and garden façades of the palace and its staircase with adjoining spaces and formal rooms (*see* NEUMANN, BALTHASAR, fig. 1). Neumann articulated the middle sections of the palace façades with pilasters and string courses that framed large windows and glazed doors, giving the impression of a masonry frame containing large sheets of glass. Behind these transparent centres he orchestrated one of his grandest sequences of spaces. The court entrance in the centre of the *corps de logis* opens on to a rectangular vestibule in which paired columns support a coved vault, giving the sense of a space within a space. The far side of the vestibule

Schloss Bruchsal, stair hall (*Treppenhaus*) by Balthasar Neumann, 1728–50

presents three openings that lead through from darkness to light. The central opening passes into an oval vaulted room, painted with rocks to resemble a grotto, and continues on to a garden room beyond. The other two give access to the stair hall (*Treppenhaus*) and the arms of a circular staircase that rise between curved walls, the inside ones arcaded. At the lower levels of the flights a view of the dim grotto room is afforded through these arcades, which diminish in height with the ascent, while the amount of light that filters down progressively increases, until at the top an oval platform is reached, the size of the grotto room below, surmounted by a voluminous dome lit by many windows. The platform appears to float like an island within the confines of the outer oval walls, tethered by bridges to the two great salons that open off it, their entrance doors surmounted by exuberant Rococo cartouches (see fig.).

In 1743 Damian Hugo was succeeded by Franz Christoph von Hutten, who completed the building and the décor of many of the interiors at Schloss Bruchsal. The vaults of the Fürstensaal (prince's hall) and marble hall, and the stair dome were frescoed by Johann Zick and his son Januarius Zick between 1751 and 1754. Later in the century, the formal garden was remodelled according to the English style. After the secularization of the bishopric in the early 19th century, Schloss Bruchsal was used by government officials. Restorations in the early 1900s and

1930s provided detailed documentation of the existing complex; when the buildings were extensively destroyed in World War II, these records were available for the rebuilding project, which began in the 1960s.

BIBLIOGRAPHY
F. Hirsch: *Das Bruchsaler Schloss im 19. Jahrhundert* (Heidelberg, 1906)
—: 'Eine Treppenstudie', *Archit.: Z. Gesch. Archit.*, ii (1908–9), pp. 155–63
—: *Das Bruchsaler Schloss* (Heidelberg, 1910)
H. Rott: 'Bruchsal, Quellen zur Kunstgeschichte des Schlosses und der bischöflichen Residenzstadt', *Archit.: Z. Gesch. Archit.* (1914) [supplement xi, whole issue]
J. Gamer: 'Fürstbischöflich-speyerisches Residenzschloss St Damiansburg', *Balthasar Neumann in Baden-Württemberg* (exh. cat., ed. G. Thiem; Stuttgart, Staatsgal., 1975), pp. 9-59

CHRISTIAN F. OTTO

Brücke, Die [Ger.: 'the bridge']. German group of painters and printmakers active from 1905 to 1913 and closely associated with the development of Expressionism (*see* EXPRESSIONISM, §1).

1. FOUNDING OF THE GROUP. The Künstlergruppe Brücke was founded on 7 June 1905 in Dresden by four architecture students: Fritz Bleyl (1880–1966), Erich Heckel, Ernst Ludwig Kirchner and Karl Schmidt (later Schmidt-Rottluff). They were joined by other German and European artists, including Max Pechstein, Cuno Amiet and Lambertus Zijl in 1906, Akseli Gallen-Kallela

in 1907, Kees van Dongen and Franz Nölken in 1908, Bohumil Kubišta and Otto Mueller in 1910; Emil Nolde was a temporary member (1906–7). Kirchner and Bleyl had become friends in 1901 as architecture students at the Technische Hochschule in Dresden. Heckel and Schmidt-Rottluff had met while at school in Chemnitz. Through Heckel's brother Manfred they met Kirchner while studying architecture in Dresden c. 1904. They were united by a common aim to break new boundaries in art.

The four founder-members were self-taught as artists, their only training from private drawing lessons. They nevertheless acted as a group immediately, seeing themselves as pioneers who would change the world from its very basis and revive art. In their first manifesto, which they called a *Programm* (1906), they named the impulses behind their work: faith in the future, the strength of youth, the value of directness and authenticity, and the rejection of the older forces of the establishment. Although the use of pure colour and a more two-dimensional treatment of subject-matter had obvious similarities with Fauvist art, and in particular that of Henri Matisse, whose work the group saw at an exhibition in Berlin in 1908, the artists of Die Brücke aimed to encompass all life, rather than just the field of art, with their radical stance.

The art of Die Brücke was accompanied by a philosophical demand for totality. The writings of Friedrich Nietzsche were important, and both their name and the stylized imagery of the bridge motif were linked to the writer's *Also sprach Zarathustra*. The idea for the name was later attributed to Schmidt-Rottluff, who considered it appropriate as signifying leading from one shore to another; the group as a whole felt that it stood for the image of the bridge leading to new worlds, a representation that appeared in vignettes, on invitation cards or other printed matter produced by the group in 1905 and 1906.

2. HISTORY AND DEVELOPMENT. In the early years of the group's existence much discussion took place on the various positions of international art, based on the influences that the young artists had come under in Germany, particularly the graphic art of *Jugendstil* and the work of various Post-Impressionist artists including Paul Gauguin, Vincent van Gogh and the Pointillists Georges Seurat and Paul Signac, as well as Edvard Munch and Matisse. Another influence was African and Oceanic sculpture, which they saw in the Völkerkundemuseum in Dresden. In 1905 some of the artists exhibited woodcuts and watercolours in Leipzig, and in 1906 Die Brücke held their first group exhibition in the showrooms of a lamp factory in Dresden. They quickly won access to the leading modern art galleries of Dresden and were able to exhibit their works annually: from 1907 until 1909 in Emil Richter's Kunstsalon; and in 1910 in the Galerie Ernst Arnold. They were soon able to exhibit throughout Germany.

The formation of Die Brücke can be seen from two angles: they not only associated for reasons of principle, to create a new sort of art within the group, but also for practical reasons such as better organization, particularly in exhibitions. Collaboration, which sometimes led to very close stylistic similarities, occurred through communal drawing and painting and the exchange of technical processes in their graphic works. They did not, however, live together in a commune, nor did they all always work together. On the contrary, they often worked in pairs on communal projects. The actual interrelation of their lives was small. They met in their studios with girlfriends and models, whom they painted as they moved about freely. In summer they went into the countryside to paint models in natural surroundings. Among their most famous outings were the periods spent by Heckel, Kirchner and Pechstein at the Moritzburger lakes near Dresden (see Heckel's *Bathers by a Pond (Moritzburg)*, 1910; Cambridge, MA, Busch-Reisinger Mus.), individual periods spent by Kirchner and Heckel on the Baltic island of Fehmarn and Heckel's and Schmidt-Rottluff's time spent in Dangast on the North Sea. Heckel had an especially key role as a communicator within the group and was also in charge of the group's business activities.

The connection that Die Brücke sought to make between art and life was expressed in a number of ways, including the organization of their own studio apartments. Kirchner and Heckel decorated their studios, which were shops in a working-class district of Dresden, with furniture and sculpture they had carved themselves and painted wall decorations. These studios are documented in many paintings and drawings. The peak of their association, both in terms of communal development and group exhibitions, occurred between 1909 and 1911, when their characteristic style of painting became very two-dimensional and employed luminous colours, as in Schmidt-Rottluff's *Estate in Dangast* (1910; Berlin, Neue N.G.). After this the members began to develop very individual styles. After Pechstein moved to Berlin in 1908, over the course of 1911 Heckel, Kirchner and Schmidt-Rottluff followed him. The association became looser; Pechstein was excluded from the group in 1912, after contravening an agreement between the members by showing at an exhibition of the Berlin Secession, which had become highly conservative. In Berlin in 1913 the group was formally dissolved as a result of Kirchner's account of the history of the group in the *Chronik der Künstlergemeinschaft Brücke* (Berlin, 1913), in which he portrayed himself as leader. The style associated with Die Brücke, however, was sustained by its originators for many years to come.

3. GROUP MEMBERSHIP, PORTFOLIOS AND GRAPHIC WORK. Die Brücke was organized along the lines of a German artists' association. As well as the 'active members' or artists, there were 'passive members' or friends and supporters, including important figures such as the collector Gustav Schiefler (1857–1935) and the art historian Rosa Schapiro (1874–1954). Between 1906 and 1912 the artists annually made a gift of a portfolio of graphic work for these passive members. The first three contained a single work by each of the artists, and from 1909 each was devoted to a single artist. After the *Programm* of 1906, the group published annual reports from 1907 until 1912, as well as various woodcut membership cards (see fig.).

Although painting was central to the work of all the members of the group, they also devoted themselves with great vigour to graphic work as an important step on the way to the discovery of form and the composition of surfaces. On the other hand, they gave the print an

Erich Heckel: *Membership Card for Passive Members of Die Brücke*, four-colour woodcut, 97×75 mm, 1912 (Berlin, Brücke-Museum)

independence from other artistic forms that it had not previously enjoyed. They saw themselves as reviving a specifically German late medieval tradition to which they referred in woodcuts, engravings and lithographs of elemental force, such as Heckel's *Two Seated Women* (colour woodcut, 1912; Berlin, Brücke-Mus.). They transformed the very foundations of these media and set new standards for them (*see* WOODCUT, §II, 6).

4. FINAL YEARS AND HISTORICAL IMPORTANCE. The group Die Brücke came to epitomize what is understood by the term Expressionism, sowing the seeds of the movement in Germany. It was not until 1909 that the NEUE KÜNSTLERVEREINIGUNG MÜNCHEN, later BLAUE REITER, was formed as the second cornerstone of German Expressionism. Through Die Brücke, artists completed the step towards overcoming Impressionism and Post-Impressionism that had begun in France under Matisse and the Fauves, a step towards two-dimensionality in painting, pure colour and unrestrained independence of style. Die Brücke exemplified the striving among modern artists for a rebirth of artistic activity, communal ways of working and the unity of art with life. The group became synonymous with the call of youth for a revolution and a complete overhaul of the foundations of artistic thought.

5. THE BRÜCKE-MUSEUM. The Brücke-Museum originated in 1964 with the donation by Schmidt-Rottluff of his art collection, later supplemented by the bequest of his entire fortune. It was also supported by extensive contributions from Erich Heckel. Based in Berlin from 1967, its principal concerns have been collecting and documenting the art of Die Brücke, so that it contains the most extensive collection of paintings, drawings and prints by all the members of the group.

For further illustrations *see* PECHSTEIN, MAX and SCHMIDT-ROTT-LUFF, KARL.

BIBLIOGRAPHY
U. Appollonio: *'Die Brücke' e la cultura dell'Espressionismo* (Venice, 1952)
L.-G. Buchheim: *Die Künstlergemeinschaft Brücke: Gemälde, Zeichnungen, Graphik, Plastik, Dokumente* (Feldafing, 1956)
P. Selz: *German Expressionist Painting* (Berkeley and Los Angeles, 1957)
Ausstellung Künstlergruppe Brücke: Jahresmappen, 1906–1912 (exh. cat. by H. Bolliger and E. W. Kornfeld, Berne, Klipstein & Kornfeld, 1958) [incl. complete cat. of membership cards, annual reports, exh. cats and posters]
L.-G. Buchheim: *Die Künstlergruppe 'Brücke' und der deutsche Expressionismus*, 2 vols (Feldafing, 1973)
L. Reidemeister: *Künstlergruppe Brücke* (Berlin, 1975)
Unmittelbar und unverfälscht: Frühe Graphik des Expressionismus (exh. cat., ed. H. Robels and D. Ronte; Cologne, Wallraf-Richartz-Mus., 1976)
G. Reinhardt: 'Die frühe Brücke: Beiträge zur Geschichte und zum Werk der Dresdner Künstlergruppe Brücke der Jahre 1905 bis 1908', *Brücke-Archv*, ix/10 (1977–8)
W.-D. Dube: 'The Artists' Group Die Brücke', *Expressionism: A German Intuition* (exh. cat., ed. P. Vogt; New York, Guggenheim; San Francisco, CA, MOMA; 1980), pp. 90–102
B. Martensen-Larsen: 'Primitive Kunst als Inspirationsquelle der Brücke', *Hafnia*, vii (1980), pp. 90–118
Künstler der Brücke: Heckel, Kirchner, Müller, Pechstein, Schmidt-Rottluff: Gemälde, Aquarelle, Zeichnungen, Druckgraphik, 1909–1930 (exh. cat. by G. W. Költzch, Saarbrücken, Saarland-Mus., 1980)
Die Künstlergruppe 'Brücke' (exh. cat., ed. B. Holeczek; Hannover, Sprengel Mus., 1983)
H. Jähner: *Künstlergruppe Brücke: Geschichte einer Gemeinschaft und das Lebenswerk ihrer Repräsentanten* (Berlin, 1984) [incl. comprehensive bibliog.]
The Print in Germany, 1880–1933: The Age of Expressionism (exh. cat. by F. Carey and A. Griffiths, London, BM, 1984)

LUCIUS GRISEBACH

Brucker [Bruckher]**, Nikolaus.** *See* PRUGGER, NIKOLAUS.

Brudenell. English family of patrons and collectors. George Brudenell, 4th Earl of Cardigan and 1st Duke of Montagu of the second creation (*b* London, 26 July 1712; *d* London, 23 May 1790), succeeded his father as Earl of Cardigan in 1732. In 1730 he married Mary, heiress of John Montagu, 2nd Duke of Montagu (?1688–1749), and granddaughter of Ralph Montagu, 1st Duke of Montagu (*see* MONTAGU, (1)), and in 1766 the dukedom was revived in his favour. Both he and his wife were collectors on a considerable scale, sometimes buying in partnership. The pictures they acquired for Montagu House, Whitehall, London, built by Henry Flitcroft for Mary's father, transformed the character of the Montagu family collection. In the 1750s theirs was one of the most distinguished collections in London and included not only conventional purchases, such as Murillo's *St John the Baptist* (Duke of Buccleuch priv. col.), bought by Lady Cardigan in 1757, and cabinet pictures by such artists as Aert van der Neer, but unconventional ones for the time, such as El Greco's *Adoration of the Shepherds* (Duke of Buccleuch priv. col.). Cardigan's other acquisitions included the late Mantegna grisaille, *Esther and Mordecai* (Cincinnati, OH, A. Mus.), Rubens's *Watering Place* (London, N.G.) and three major Rembrandts, *Saskia as Flora* (1635; London, N.G.), an *Old Woman Reading* (1655; Duke of Buccleuch priv. col.) and a *Self-portrait* (1659; Washington, DC, N.G.A.). Lady Cardigan was also the subject of penetrating portraits by

Joshua Reynolds (c. 1767–9; Deene Park, Northants) and Thomas Gainsborough (c. 1768; Duke of Buccleuch priv. col.).

John Brudenell, Lord Brudenell and Marquess of Monthermer [Baron Montagu] (b 18 March 1735; d 11 April 1770), son of the 4th Earl, was, like his father, a discerning collector. He made an extensive Grand Tour (1754–60) with his tutor Henry Lyte; this resulted in his commissioning from Antonio Joli no fewer than 38 views, mostly of the Kingdom of the Two Sicilies, which Brudenell had explored with unusual thoroughness. Brudenell acquired landscapes from Carlo Bonavia at Naples in 1757 and sat in 1758 to Pompeo Batoni and to Anton Raphael Mengs (Duke of Buccleuch priv. col.). He also collected antiquities and in 1758 spent over £2000 in Rome through the agency of Thomas Jenkins. After his return to England Lord Brudenell continued to add to his collection, and in 1761 he was elected as a member of the Society of Dilettanti. As he died without issue the collection was inherited by his sister Elizabeth, Duchess of Buccleuch, and for the most part remains in the possession of the family.

BIBLIOGRAPHY

J. Fleming: 'Lord Brudenell and his Bear-leader', *Eng. Misc.*, ix (1958), pp. 127–41

The Treasure Houses of Britain: Five Hundred Years of Private Patronage and Art Collecting (exh. cat., ed. G. Jackson-Stops; Washington, DC, N.G.A., 1985), nos 173–5, 262, 292, 306, 472

M. Jaffé: *The Paintings and Drawings in Boughton House: The English Versailles* (London, 1992), pp. 74–89

FRANCIS RUSSELL

Bruegel [Breughel; Brueghel]. South Netherlandish family of artists. They were active for four generations and were closely related to several other Netherlandish artists' families (see fig.). The first important member of the family, (1) Pieter Bruegel I, was one of the greatest artists in 16th-century northern Europe. The influence of his work, particularly his allegories and landscapes (some of which were disseminated through engravings), was widespread and long-lasting. Bruegel's art combines religion, folklore and humanism and falls between the last elements of medieval mysticism of Bosch and the Baroque exuberance of Rubens. His son (2) Pieter Brueghel II is known primarily as his father's copyist, his works often providing the only evidence of lost compositions by Pieter the elder. Pieter the younger's son Pieter Brueghel III (1589–c. 1640) became a painter in 1608 and, like his father (although a lesser artist), was known as a copyist, mainly of his grandfather's work. (3) Jan Breughel I was also a son of Pieter the elder; his work, however, was more individual than that of his brother, and he became a noted artist in his own right, specializing in flower-pieces and paradise scenes. Jan the elder was renowned for his ability to convey textures through the medium of oil paint (hence his nickname 'Velvet Breughel'). Two of Jan's sons were reputable artists: (4) Jan Breughel II took over his father's studio and, in general, followed in his footsteps, while the work of (5) Ambrosius Breughel, who also painted flower-pieces, is difficult to separate from that of other members of the family and still awaits closer study. In the next generation, three of Jan the younger's sons were also painters in the style of their father, uncle and grandfather:

Jan Pieter Breughel (b Antwerp, bapt 29 Aug 1628; d after 1682); Abraham Breughel (1631–?1680); and Jan Baptist Breughel (1647–1710); Jan van Kessel II and David Teniers III (1638–85) were also grandsons of Jan Breughel the elder.

BIBLIOGRAPHY

Hollstein: *Dut. & Flem.*; Thieme–Becker

K. van Mander: *Schilder-boeck* ([1603]–1604)

P. Rombouts and T. van Lerius: *Die liggeren en andere historische archieven der Antwerpsche Sint-Lucasgilde*, i (Antwerp and The Hague, 1864/*R* Amsterdam, 1961)

Brueghel: Een dynastie van schilders (exh. cat., Brussels, Mus. Royaux B.-A., 1980)

(1) Pieter Bruegel I [the elder] (b ?Breda, ?c. 1525–30; d Brussels, 1569). Painter and draughtsman. Although heir to the early Netherlandish painters, particularly Hieronymus Bosch, Bruegel brought a new humanizing spirit and breadth of vision to the traditional subjects he depicted while creating many new ones. His style and subject-matter were adopted but rarely surpassed by the many artists of the later 16th century and the 17th who were influenced by his work, especially the landscape and genre artists of the northern provinces of the Netherlands. Today, thanks to modern techniques of reproduction, Bruegel's paintings are immensely popular, while as a draughtsman he is scarcely known except to specialists. Yet in the 16th century and the early 17th it was drawings attributed to him, especially those issued by Hieronymus Cock as engravings, that made him famous as a 'second Bosch', a term used by Vasari as early as 1568. Many of the drawings traditionally ascribed to him, however, including some 20 alpine landscapes and village scenes, have now been reattributed to Jacques Savery and Roelandt Savery. It is unclear whether the Saverys made these drawings, which bear 'signatures' and dates ranging from 1559 to 1562, as deliberate forgeries or as virtuoso emulations of a famous old master whose work enjoyed a tremendous revival of interest c. 1595–c. 1610.

I. Life and intellectual background. II. Work. III. Critical reception and posthumous reputation.

I. Life and intellectual background.

The sources for Bruegel's biography are surprisingly scanty: there is, in fact, nothing beyond van Mander's work of 1604, which is lively and anecdotal but not always accurate. Still more surprisingly, Bruegel left no writings, as might be expected from an artist of that period with a humanistic background. The portrait of him in Hendrick Hondius's *Pictorum aliquot celebrium Germaniae inferioris effigies*, published in 1572 by Hieronymus Cock, shows the profile of a bearded man with refined, intelligent, civilized, 'modern' features.

1. EARLY LIFE, TRAINING AND APPRENTICESHIP, BEFORE 1551. According to van Mander, Bruegel was born in the village of Breughel near Breda; however, none of the three Flemish villages of that name is close to Breda. Probably van Mander's statement is a biographer's commonplace, and he assumed that Bruegel was of peasant origin because he painted peasants. There is, in fact, every reason to think that Pieter Bruegel was a townsman and a highly educated one, on friendly terms with the humanists of his time. Guicciardini, an Italian contemporary of

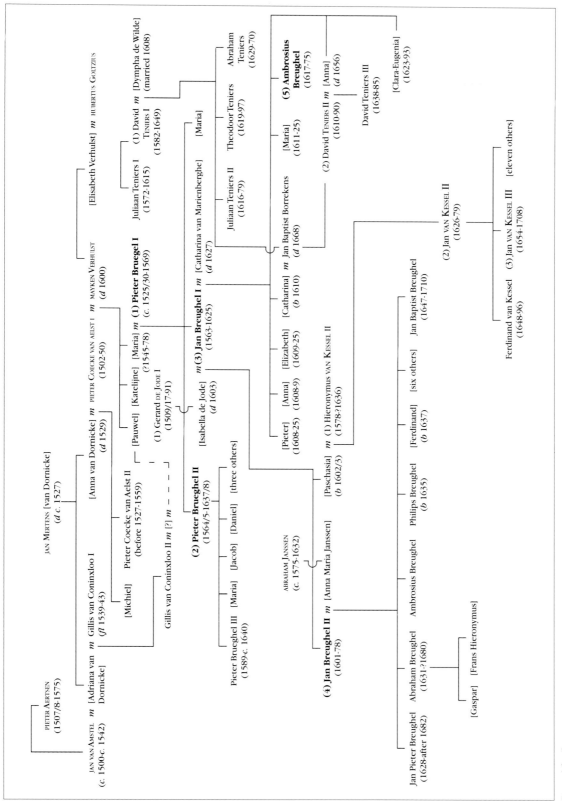

Bruegel family tree

Bruegel's who lived in Antwerp, was probably more correct when he wrote that the artist came from Breda. Auner (1956) has also argued for Breda as his birthplace, adducing several historical references to support this view. In the register of the Antwerp Guild of St Luke, the painter's name appears as 'Brueghels': the 's' is a regular patronymic suffix in Dutch, whereas a place of origin would be indicated by 'van'. It may be, however, that an ancestor of Bruegel's was, after all, born in a village of the same name, which then became the family's surname.

The year of Bruegel's birth is equally uncertain. Various scholars have suggested that it was between 1525 and 1530, or between 1520 and 1522; the latter two dates, however, are incorrect (Grossmann, 1955). Bruegel became a master in the Guild of St Luke in Antwerp between October 1551 and October 1552, which makes it likely that he was born between 1525 and 1530.

Van Mander claimed that Bruegel learnt painting in Antwerp from Pieter Coecke van Aelst, and although there is very little affinity between the art of the Romanist Pieter Coecke and the later work of Bruegel, there is no reason in this case to doubt van Mander. In his time Coecke was one of the most admired painters in the country: he was court painter to Emperor Charles V and was moreover active as a sculptor, architect and designer of tapestries, stained glass and festal decorations. Another important early influence on Bruegel was no doubt the Brunswick Monogrammist, who is now generally identified with Jan van Amstel. The elder brother of Pieter Aertsen, van Amstel was brother-in-law to Pieter Coecke and thus close to him on both artistic and family grounds. He provided Bruegel with a stimulus in both landscape and figure painting. As van Mander observed, van Amstel practised the interesting technique of allowing the underpainting to show through as part of the tonality of the final picture; this, as well as the practice of painting in diluted colours, is not found in any of Jan van Amstel's contemporaries but reappears in the work of Pieter Bruegel. According to van Mander, after leaving Coecke's studio, Bruegel went to work for the print publisher Hieronymus Cock, who was also based in Antwerp.

Bruegel seems to have left Antwerp in 1550 at the latest, as between September 1550 and October 1551 he was in Mechelen in the studio of Claude Dorizi, working with Peeter Baltens on an altarpiece (untraced) for the glovemakers' guild; Baltens painted the central panel, Bruegel the grisaille wings. Although this first attested work by Bruegel is lost, the documented commission confirms the connection postulated by Glück between Bruegel and Mechelen, where there were about 150 workshops for *waterschilderen* (an unusual technique involving opaque watercolour or tempera on canvas, which was used for making wall hangings as a substitute for tapestries). This technique was employed by Bruegel in some paintings, such as the *Adoration of the Magi* (Brussels, Mus. A. Anc.), the *Parable of the Blind* (see fig. 6 below) and *The Misanthrope* (both Naples, Capodimonte). Mechelen was not, however, the only place where this technique was practised in the 16th century: others who used it were Jan van Eyck, Rogier van der Weyden, Joachim Patinir, Lucas van Leyden, Jan van Scorel and Hieronymus Bosch.

2. VISIT TO ITALY, 1551–*c.* 1554. Soon after becoming a master in 1551, Bruegel set out for Italy. He travelled by way of Lyon and the Mt Cenis Pass and may have been accompanied by the painter Marten de Vos (as has been supposed from a letter to the cartographer and scholar Abraham Ortelius from the geographer Scipio Fabius in Bologna, enquiring after de Vos and 'Petro Bruochl', who appear to have stayed with him as his guests). Bruegel did not content himself, as was usual, with travelling as far as Rome: in 1552 he continued to Calabria in southern Italy, as can be inferred from his drawing of *Reggio in Flames* (Rotterdam, Mus. Boymans–van Beuningen) resulting from the attack by the Turks in that year. The sheet is neither signed nor dated and is much altered and disfigured by 17th-century wash additions in the foreground. However, the engraving by Frans Huys after Bruegel, entitled *Sea Battle in the Straits of Messina*, clearly shows the town to be Reggio. From Reggio, Bruegel must have crossed to Messina, a view of which is incorporated in the engraving. Grossmann suggested that he went as far as Palermo, since Bruegel's *Triumph of Death* (Madrid, Prado; see fig. 3 below) is clearly reminiscent of the famous fresco of the subject in the Palazzo Sclàfani there. What are still considered by many scholars to be Bruegel's earliest dated works, both drawings of 1552—*Mountain Landscape with Italian-style Cloister* (Paris, Louvre) and *River Valley with Mountain in the Background* (Berlin, Küpferstichkab.)— may also have originated in southern Italy. The painted *Harbour at Naples* (Rome, Gal. Doria-Pamphili) is further evidence of Bruegel's journey to southern Italy.

By 1553 Bruegel was back in Rome, as is known from two etchings by Joris Hoefnagel, inscribed '*Petrus Bruegel Fecit Romae Ao 1553*'. Bruegel's stay in Rome is also attested by the formerly disputed drawing of the *Ripa Grande* (Chatsworth, Derbys) and by the estate inventory of the Roman illuminator Giulio Clovio, which mentions 'a small miniature painted half by himself and half by Pieter Bruegel', as well as other works by Bruegel: a small picture of the *Tower of Babel* on ivory, a *View of Lyon* in gouache, two other landscapes and a gouache with a study of trees. All these works are untraced, but Tolnay (1965 and later) attributed to Bruegel several miniatures in the margin of works by Clovio, including his major work, the Towneley Lectionary (New York, Pub. Lib. MS 91).

Bruegel set out for the north in 1554 at the latest. The route he took has been a matter of dispute: the Mt Cenis Pass, Switzerland and Lyon or the eastern route via Munich? The question arose from attempts to localize the drawings he was thought to have made of alpine subjects. The tradition attached to these alpine views, all of which are now rejected (*see* §II, 2 below), goes back to an often quoted passage in van Mander, who claimed that 'when Bruegel was in the Alps he swallowed all the mountains and rocks and spat them out again, after his return, on to his canvases and panels'.

3. THE SOUTHERN NETHERLANDS, 1555–69. Bruegel must have been back in Antwerp by 1555, as in that year Hieronymus Cock published the series of 12 prints known as the *Large Landscapes*. Bruegel's first dated paintings appear from 1557, and this seems to have been a period of great creativity. By the mid-16th century

Antwerp was one of the richest and most flourishing towns in Europe. Bruegel's circle of friends and acquaintances included some of the most eminent humanists of the Netherlands, such as Ortelius and the publisher Christoph Plantin. From 1559 Bruegel altered his signature from the Gothic minuscule *brueghel* to the Roman capitals BRVEGEL (the omission of the H may have signified an intention to Latinize his name according to humanist custom).

In 1563 Bruegel married Maria or Mayken Coecke (*b* ?1545; *d* 1578), the youngest daughter of Pieter Coecke van Aelst and his second wife, the illuminator and watercolour painter MAYKEN VERHULST. The wedding took place in Brussels, and at the same time Bruegel moved to that city, where his most famous pictures and other major works were created. Pieter and Maria's children, Pieter II, Jan I and a daughter, of whom nothing is known, were born in Brussels. According to van Mander, Jan I was taught to paint watercolours by his grandmother, by whom no painting has ever been identified (though in 1567 Guicciardini described her as one of the four principal female painters in the Netherlands).

Shortly before his death, according to van Mander, Bruegel had his wife burn certain drawings 'which were too sharp or sarcastic. . .either out of remorse or for fear that she might come to harm or in some way be held responsible for them'. This statement has led to much speculation concerning Bruegel's political and religious views: whether he was an Anabaptist, for instance, or a political satirist. The latter is certainly not the case; but, as a keen observer of social reality, he was certainly not indifferent to the atrocities of the Spanish occupation under the Duke of Alba from 1566 onwards. What danger the destroyed drawings might have represented to a painter who was admired by Cardinal Granvelle, Archbishop of Mechelen and President of the Council of State, and a close friend of Abraham Ortelius, the geographer to Philip II of Spain, is unclear. On the other hand, Bruegel is seen as an adherent of the Neo-Stoic philosophy, acquainted with Erasmus of Rotterdam and Thomas More and with the ethical writings of the humanist Dirck Volckertsz. Coornhert (considered an important source especially by Stridbeck, 1956). Ortelius's role was emphasized especially by Müller-Hofstede (in Simson and Winner, p. 75), who stated that 'given his close relations with Bruegel, [Ortelius] is the only reliable authority for the contemporary intellectual background of the latter's art. Any of Ortelius's statements afford a trustworthy basis for examining which of the ideas current in the Netherlands between about 1555 and 1575 can be validly applied to Bruegel's position.' However, it seems most likely that Bruegel, as an educated individualist, was not close to any particular party or religious group, nor indoctrinated with any one philosophy. His humanistic sentiments were a matter of experience rather than reading; his view of the world was artistic and intuitive rather than philosophical. His work is imbued with a spirit of independence and impartiality towards the phenomena of his time, akin to such minds as Rabelais, Montaigne or Shakespeare.

II. Work.

1. Paintings. 2 Drawings and prints.

1. PAINTINGS. About 40 pictures by Bruegel are known, 12 of which are in the Kunsthistorisches Museum in Vienna. Acquired by Archduke Ernst (1594) and Emperor Rudolf II, they belong to the original core of the Habsburg imperial collections. Not included in this total are lost works or those preserved only in copies, for Bruegel's oeuvre is known to have been a good deal more extensive than it now appears.

According to an old description, Bruegel was a 'second Bosch'. But only two of his paintings bear any relation to Bosch's demonology: the *Fall of the Rebel Angels* (Brussels, Mus. A. Anc.) and *Dulle Griet* ('Mad Meg'; Antwerp, Mus. Meyer van der Bergh; see fig. 2 below). The two painters' mentalities were, in fact, distinctly different: Bruegel's work is Bosch secularized. Bosch is late medieval, the last 'primitive'; Bruegel, by contrast, is the first 'modern'. Bosch's pandemonium is poised within a bottomless world of pious fear, with innumerable trap-doors leading to Hell; Bruegel's spirits and goblins play their tricks on the firm ground of humanist *ratio*. In Bosch they were still perceived as real creatures; in Bruegel they are only allusions, often with ironical overtones, and in the drawing of the *Fall of the Magician Hermogenes* (1564; Amsterdam, Rijksmus.) Bruegel finally took leave of these spirits.

But Bosch was not the only source of Bruegel's art. The whole Flemish tradition was important: Joachim Patinir and his followers, but especially Bruegel's immediate predecessors Jan van Amstel and Cornelis Massys. On the other hand, the influence of Italian art (e.g. Titian's landscape drawings, or prints after them) is limited or well concealed; scholars' attempts to identify such influences have arguably had little success. Bruegel assimilated the Italian Renaissance in his own sovereign way. He lacked interest in the nude, and the depiction of sensual nakedness is alien to his work. His figures are rotund, heavy and swathed in thick materials. Rhetoric and declamation were also foreign to him. He was interested in human physiognomy but not in the individual portrait as a genre. There is only one very small self-portrait in the *Road to Calvary* (Vienna, Ksthist. Mus.), where he can be seen, wearing a cap, on the extreme right, close to the pole surmounted by a wheel.

(i) Early period, 1553–60. (ii) Middle period, 1561–4. (iii) Late period, 1565–9.

(i) Early period, 1553–60. The earliest known painting is the *Landscape with Christ Appearing to the Apostles* (c. 1553; priv. col.), in which the figures may be the work of Marten de Vos. Another painting generally regarded as a youthful work is the original *Fall of Icarus*, of which there are two versions, both probably copies (Brussels, Mus. A. Anc., and Brussels, van Buren, priv. col.). The *Netherlandish Proverbs* (1559; Berlin, Gemäldegal.), of which at least 16 copies are known, is the first painting to show the characteristic marks of Bruegel's style. It is also the first of three great works of this period, all of which have many small figures scattered in a novel and ingenious manner over a large space. The composition of the *Netherlandish Proverbs* has no direct precedent. Over 100 proverbs have

1. Pieter Bruegel I: *Battle between Carnival and Lent*, oil on panel, 1.18×1.65 m, 1559 (Vienna, Kunsthistorisches Museum)

been identified: the most complete and convincing interpretations are those by Fraenger (1923), Grauls (1938) and Glück with Borms (1951). The general theme is that of 'the world turned upside-down', as is indicated iconographically by the precise blue shade of the inverted globe, the blue cloak (denoting deceit) and so on. The work is a catalogue without condemnation, a kaleidoscope of the Netherlandish vocabulary and the lively wit of the common people. 'The moralist's lament over the sinfulness and corruption of mankind is opposed by the smiling understanding of popular wisdom' (Huizinga). This was certainly Bruegel's view. His method in this early work was to express the figurative language of proverbs literally in pictorial form. The effect is enhanced by the pseudo-logic of village architecture and the everyday setting, which create the impression of an open-air lunatic asylum.

Bruegel adopted the same method in another great early work, the *Children's Games* (1560; Vienna, Ksthist. Mus.). Flemish folklore also figures in a third masterpiece, the *Battle between Carnival and Lent* (1559; Vienna, Ksthist. Mus.; see fig. 1). The theme is an old one and occurs in 13th-century Burgundy, but the pictorial treatment is Bruegel's own and unprecedented. Frans Hogenberg's engraving of the subject, published by Cock in 1558, is only a thematic suggestion and not a direct model. Bruegel's picture represents the kind of tournament that actually occurred in carnival processions, with a contest between the allegorical figures of Shrovetide (a portly male

character) and Lent (a skinny female one). The left half of the picture belongs to Carnival, the right half to Lent. The tavern and the church confront each other, while in between is an encyclopedic collection of customs proper to the season of festivities and that of penance, depicted as though contemporaneous. The illustrations are as exhaustive as possible, recalling the completeness of the *Proverbs* and *Children's Games*. There has been a vast amount of detailed research into this picture, resulting in the most varied interpretations. It should be emphasized, as Demus pointed out (1981, p. 63), that the picture does not constitute 'a key to allegorical, moral, religious, political or any such "deeper meaning"'; it reveals no particular partisanship on Bruegel's part. The bird's-eye perspective is not mathematical, as has been proposed, but 'extended' (Novotny), in order to accommodate more scenes: the mass of figures forms a large ellipse around the centre and a smaller one around the house in the background. Only real motifs are depicted, and they have been identified in great detail by folklorists (e.g. Demus, pp. 61ff).

Certain customs and motifs featured in the *Battle between Carnival and Lent* also form the subject of separate, later works: the two carnival games 'Orson and Valentine' and the 'Dirty Bride' (or the 'Wedding of Mopsus and Nisa') on the left of the picture appear in woodcuts (Bastelaer, nos 215–16), while in 1568 Bruegel made a painting of *The Cripples* (Paris, Louvre), with figures similar to those at the centre left of the 1559 painting. Related in theme are the *Three Heads* (Copenhagen, Stat. Mus. Kst) generally believed to be by Pieter Bruegel I and the compositions of *Fat Cooking* and *Lean Cooking* (or the *Rich Kitchen* and the *Poor Kitchen*), preserved only in two etchings.

(ii) Middle period, 1561–4. No dated painting of 1561 is known. For 1562 there are five, including another three tremendous works: the *Fall of the Rebel Angels* (Brussels, Mus. A. Anc.), *Dulle Griet* ('Mad Meg'; Antwerp, Mus. Meyer van den Bergh; see fig. 2) and the *Triumph of Death* (Madrid, Prado; see fig. 3). The last is not dated, but the similarity of its theme suggests that it belongs to nearly the same time as the other two. The three works were perhaps executed for a patron who wanted something in the style of Bosch (Auner, 1956). They represent both a culmination and a turning-point, the prelude to a departure from Bosch's style. The Fall of the Rebel Angels was also depicted by Bosch but only as a small, incidental scene in some representations of Paradise. From him comes the idea that the angels, while still falling, were transformed into hellish vermin. Bruegel developed this scene into an almost inextricable tangle of overlapping figures. In an easily won battle the angels, led by the Archangel Michael in golden armour, drive the loathsome brood, glittering with many colours, down into the chaotic abyss of Hell. In this painting Bruegel ventured to adopt an extremely complicated—almost Baroque—treatment of space. The colouring is the most varied of any of his works, with a subtle rhythmic cycle of yellows, reds, greens and blues in all their tones (Jedlicka, 1938). Yellow, especially, undergoes a palpable development from the most spiritual connotation to the most material. It begins, at the top of the picture, as immaterial light and then materializes in the garments of some of the angels and in their trumpets; it is still more tangible in the glittering gold of the archangel's armour in the centre of the scene and reappears as a ghostly hue, 'much broken, turbid and jelly-like. . .in the amorphous yet precise mass of the hellish creatures' (Jedlicka). No less masterly is the contrast in the adversaries' external appearance: above, the garments of inviolable purity; below, the nakedness of animal bodies, slimy, hairy and prickly. The picture may have been suggested by the central panel of Frans Floris's altarpiece of the *Fall of the Rebel Angels* (1554; Antwerp, Kon. Mus. S. Kst.) in the chapel of St Michael in Antwerp Cathedral and perhaps by Dürer's woodcuts of the *Apocalypse* (1498).

Dulle Griet (see fig. 2) is one of Bruegel's most intricate compositions and the literature concerning it extensive. The central figure is a tragi-comic, witchlike character from folklore, also connected with the proverbial saying: 'The best Margaret [Griet] ever found was the one that tied the Devil to a cushion.' In Bruegel's work she is on a plundering expedition to the mouth of Hell. The painting, at first confusing in its complexity, has been interpreted in many ways. The simplest is Grossmann's view that

2. Pieter Bruegel I: *Dulle Griet* ('Mad Meg'; detail), oil on panel, 1.15×1.61 m, 1562 (Antwerp, Museum Mayer van den Bergh)

'Mad Meg' represents the deadly sin of avarice: the painting can thus be seen as an enormously enlarged and elaborated version of the drawing in the series of *Deadly Sins* (1558; London, BM).

The *Triumph of Death* (see fig. 3) is perhaps the richest of all Bruegel's compositions with small figures. In contrast to the fantastic and devilish motifs of the *Fall of the Rebel Angels* and *Dulle Griet*, it consists of a profusion of lifelike human scenes and is easier to read and understand. Van Mander spoke of it as a picture 'in which all means are adopted to ward off death'. As Tolnay pointed out, Bruegel combined two iconographic traditions: the Italian 'Triumph of Death' (e.g. Buffalmacco's work in the Camposanto, Pisa, and the fresco in the Palazzo Sclàfani in Palermo) and the northern 'Dance of Death' (as found in Hans Holbein the younger's *Dance of Death* woodcuts). In the former, Death appears on horseback as a skeleton with a sickle, meting out death to all; in the latter, the individual death of a member of any class or estate is shown, with Death personified as a rickety, bony figure who comes to fetch one and all in accordance with the saying 'mors certa, hora incerta' ('Death is certain, though the hour is not'). Bruegel's combination is further enriched by the motif of the 'battalions of death' (Tolnay) fighting against the living. As in *Dulle Griet*, the multiple horrors are presented in a hellish landscape such as that depicted by Bosch and his followers. Bruegel, with his usual completeness and lively sense of fantasy, offered a catalogue of the ways in which death may overtake humans. All try to escape, but no one succeeds. The 'Dance of Death' motif is represented by five forceful examples in the foreground. In one, on the extreme left, the emperor has fallen back helplessly and Death mockingly shows him an hour-glass to indicate that his time has come. The maliciousness of death is emphasized and is indeed part of the main theme.

The composition illustrates Bruegel's powers of organizing both content and form. As is frequently the case, the right and left halves of the picture are differently constructed, each intensifying the other. They are linked by the foreground, in which the five scenes are placed at equal intervals from left to right: the emperor, the cardinal, a pilgrim, a warrior and a loving couple. This is a classical form of Renaissance symmetry, which Bruegel skilfully conceals. Earthly power and love, in the two corners, represent opposite extremes; in the centre is the man who has renounced both, the pilgrim, in the white garb of a penitent. All four corners of the painting are marked by distinctive accents. The forms of the emperor and the lovers are bent so as to fit into them; above on the left are the big funeral bells, on the right the wheel. It has been suggested that this painting alludes to the deaths caused by the political oppression of Spanish rule.

Other works from 1562 are the *Two Monkeys* (Berlin, Gemäldegal.) and the *Suicide of Saul* (Vienna, Ksthist. Mus.). These were followed by two masterpieces of 1563, the *Flight into Egypt* (U. London, Courtauld Inst. Gals), which is a landscape like the *Suicide of Saul*, and the *Tower of Babel* (Vienna, Ksthist. Mus.; see fig. 4), the undated variant of which (Rotterdam, Mus. Boymans–van Beuningen) is usually thought to have been painted *c.* 1567–8. The theme of the Tower of Babel does not occur on panel

before Bruegel, except for a lost work by Patinir that is said to have been in Cardinal Grimani's palace in Venice. Bruegel's eerie architectural Utopia is modelled on the ruins of the Colosseum in Rome, which he must have studied while in Italy. He conceived the vision of a Roman monstrosity, the fearful scale of which far exceeded all architectural megalomanias of the past. The Tower of Babylon, described in the Bible and by Josephus Flavius, symbolizes the fact that all the works of mankind are doomed to imperfection. According to Demus, the tower could not be completed because the hubristic design of its builders had reached the limits of possibility. Bruegel's intent is to make evident this frustration: the scene typifies 'a glaring want of coordination', 'a muddled conception doomed from the outset', 'an absurd state of helplessness before the grandiose mockery of a nightmarish bankruptcy of reason'. The impression that it is built on a slant

> . . . is not to be explained by an intention to show it as likely to collapse. On the contrary, Bruegel's decision, with spurious logic, to make the main axis and all other up-and-down lines vertical in relation to the 'horizontal' approach ramps gives an impression of massive compactness and immovability. The fact that the whole thing is out of true despite this apparent observance of the laws of statics is a crowning demonstration of the radical flaw in its conception (Demus, p. 78).

The *Road to Calvary* (1564; Vienna, Ksthist. Mus.) is Bruegel's largest picture. Its composition is based on a long Flemish tradition going back to Jan van Eyck. Immediate predecessors were works by Jan van Amstel and Pieter Aertsen, which clearly show the extent of Bruegel's imaginative genius. Each of the 200 or so figures is full of rich and lively observation. The intentional playing-down of the main scene (the figure of Christ is quite small but is placed exactly in the centre) expresses a stoical attitude *vis-à-vis* the generality of mankind, indifferent and eternally blind to the significance of great events.

(iii) Late period, 1565–9. In these last four years of his life Bruegel synthesized all his accumulated experience of landscape, figure painting and composition. In 1565 he painted the great series of *The Seasons*; several winter landscapes with religious subjects; the *St John the Baptist Preaching* (Budapest, Mus. F.A.); and a *Peasant Wedding in the Open Air* (Detroit, MI, Inst. A.). Also typical of this last phase are compositions with large figures in the foreground (e.g. the *Peasant Dance*; see BELGIUM, fig. 15, and the *Peasant Wedding*; see fig. 7 below; both Vienna, Ksthist. Mus.) and others with a few monumental figures (*Land of Cockaigne*, Munich, Alte Pin.; *The Cripples*, Paris, Louvre; the *Parable of the Blind*, Naples, Capodimonte; see fig. 6 below) or a single figure (the *Unfaithful Shepherd*, Philadelphia, PA, priv. col.). Bruegel must have worked like a man possessed: apart from two or three early works, his whole output of about 40 paintings was produced in a mere 12 years (1557–69), and the last six years in Brussels alone account for nearly two-thirds of the total—about 30 masterpieces, not counting those that are lost or survive only in copies.

The Seasons are unique in 16th-century landscape painting: they achieve a rare combination of nature and vision, idea and reality, visual exploration and the recognition of

3. Pieter Bruegel I: *Triumph of Death*, oil on panel, 1.17×1.62 m, *c.* 1562 (Madrid, Museo del Prado)

4. Pieter Bruegel I: *Tower of Babel*, oil on panel, 1.14×1.55 m, 1563 (Vienna, Kunsthistorisches Museum)

form—a resounding diapason of everything in nature, and a cycle in which human beings, especially peasants, form an integral part. Compared to this universality of Bruegel's, all later landscapes (except those of Rubens and Rembrandt) are mere fragments of what he conceived and depicted as a unity. Originally *The Seasons* formed a frieze decorating a room in Nicolaas Jonghelinck's house in Antwerp. They were completed in 1565, having probably taken a year to execute. In 1566, along with other paintings by Bruegel (and a picture by Dürer and 22 by Frans Floris), they were used by Jonghelinck as surety for a debt of 16,000 guilders; the surety was forefeited, and in 1594 the city presented *The Seasons* to the stadholder, Archduke Ernst. The long and complicated dispute as to whether there were six or twelve pictures has been resolved. There were only six (Demus, p. 86), five of which survive: the *Gloomy Day*, the *Return of the Herd* (see fig. 5) and *Hunters in the Snow* (all Vienna, Ksthist. Mus.), as well as *Haymaking* (Prague, N.G.) and the *Corn Harvest* (New York, Met.). The sixth, a picture of spring, is lost. The division of the year into six parts, although rare, was not uncommon in the Netherlands. Besides the four main seasons were 'early spring' (*kleinlente* as opposed to *grootlente*) and 'late autumn'. The pictures thus do not have to be assigned to

particular months (a point that previously caused confusion). The cycle begins with early spring (the *Gloomy Day*) and ends with winter (*Hunters in the Snow*). Unlike the older tradition of calendar scenes, Bruegel's emphasis is not on seasonal labours but on the transformation of the landscape itself. Novotny (1948, p. 26) drew attention to the basic tonality of the landscapes, and Mössner (no. 86) observed that the six paintings (including the lost one of spring) form a chromatic order: brownish-black for early spring (blue for spring), green for haymaking, yellow for the corn harvest, yellow ochre for autumn and white for winter. Although the paintings do not depict identifiable locations, the cycle is the end product of a long 'incubation' of observations and sketches, which were then transformed into an elaborate imaginative work. Also in 1565 Bruegel painted the small *Winter Landscape with a Bird-trap* (Brussels, Mus. A. Anc.). This extremely popular work was copied over 100 times, more often than any other of the artist's works.

Among the major late works of a monumental character, the *Parable of the Blind* (1568; Naples, Capodimonte; see fig. 6) is one of the most profound and fascinating. It is based on the text in Matthew 15:14: 'If the blind lead the blind, both shall fall into the ditch.' The phenomenon of

5. Pieter Bruegel I: *Return of the Herd*, oil on panel, 1.17×1.59 m, 1565 (Vienna, Kunsthistorisches Museum)

6. Pieter Bruegel I: *Parable of the Blind*, opaque watercolour on canvas, 860×1540 mm, 1568 (Naples, Museo e Gallerie Nazionali di Capodimonte)

blindness finds its ultimate and fullest expression here, from bodily disability to the symbol of the spiritual blindness of all mankind. The line of straggling, stumbling blind folk illustrates the parable in terms of a parabola, a curve in the mathematical sense. The monumental power of Bruegel's brilliant composition, its complexity and sureness of organization and the interlocking of its many levels of significance were analysed by Sedlmayr (1959, p. 319), who pointed out three associations: with the Wheel of Fortune (the theme of fatality), the grotesque and uncanny Dance of Death and the suggestion of damnation, especially in the countenance of the second man from the right. It remains an open question why Bruegel entrusted one of his most important paintings to the perishable medium of watercolour on canvas.

Even though the *Peasant Wedding* (*c.*1568) and the *Peasant Dance* have both been overinterpreted iconologically in terms of greed, anger etc, Demus (1981) has shown that the wedding (see fig. 7) is depicted exactly according to custom. The table is set up on a threshing-floor, the bride sits alone in the centre of the table, wearing her wreath and with downcast eyes and folded hands; she is not allowed to speak or eat. To the right are the notary, a Franciscan friar and the lord of the manor. The man pouring out beer may be the bridegroom or one of the lord's servants; in any case, the groom, as was customary, is not at the table. According to Demus (pp. 110–11):

> Not one of the lifelike, individual types is caricatured so as to appear comic, coarse or ugly; though unembellished, all the

proceedings are natural and orderly. . .all [previous] iconological consideration of the picture has ignored two facts. In the first place, it exhibits the full classical unity in which the object, theme and content are one. Secondly, the artistic form developed in and with the objective approach has attained a classical purity that wholly excludes any negative or even humorous intent, implying undue prepossession with the theme.

While it is certainly true that earlier etchings, such as those of Cornelis Massys and, above all, the *Peasant Kermis* and *Peasant Wedding* of Pieter van der Borcht, have a moralizing tone associated with the depiction of riotous excess, this is plainly not the case with Bruegel's two pictures.

The diagonal arrangement of the marriage table is foreshadowed, albeit remotely, in Jan van Amstel's *Feeding of the Poor* (Brunswick, Herzog Anton Ulrich-Mus.) and looks forward to Tintoretto's *Last Supper* (1592–4; Venice, S Giorgio Maggiore). Bruegel's *Peasant Wedding* and *Peasant Dance* are so similar in style and content that they have been regarded as pendants or even parts of a planned series on peasant life. Throughout his career Bruegel showed masterly skill in depicting physical movement. In the *Peasant Wedding in the Open Air* (1566) the dance itself is the dominant motif. In the Vienna *Peasant Dance* it is displaced into the middle distance; the couple in the foreground are not yet dancing but are running to join in. The man's leg poised in the air is both distinctive and definitive in form, like the unforgettable pose of the red-capped serving-man in the *Peasant Wedding*. The groups

7. Pieter Bruegel I: *Peasant Wedding*, oil on panel, 1.14×1.63 m, *c.* 1568 (Vienna, Kunsthistorisches Museum)

of figures and their relationship to each other are subtly and rhythmically conceived. This painting is neither an allegory nor a genre scene in the 17th-century sense. Instead, Bruegel articulated for the first time, and in individual fashion, what was reduced only later to a pictorial type and a commonplace humorous genre scene. The picture is also a mine of information on folklore.

The riddle of the *Peasant and the Birdnester* (1568; Vienna, Ksthist. Mus.) is still unsolved, as is the meaning of the drawing of the *The Beekeepers* (*see* §2 below). Also mysterious and much interpreted is the *Magpie on the Gallows* (1568; Darmstadt, Hess. Landesmus.), which, according to van Mander, Bruegel bequeathed to his wife, signifying thereby 'the gossips whom he would deliver to the gallows'. (There is a Netherlandish saying that treasonous talk can bring one to the gallows.) Particular motifs remain unexplained, above all the strange contrast between the lyrical, sun-drenched landscape, the dancing couples and the sombre gallows motif. The *Storm at Sea* (Vienna, Ksthist. Mus.), long regarded as a late work by Bruegel, has now been shown (Demus) to be by Josse de Momper II. The stylistic conclusion was corroborated by a dendrochronological examination of the oak panel by Dr P. Klein of Hamburg, which showed that the tree was felled in 1580 at the earliest, at least 11 years after Bruegel's death. Nothing has survived of the series of pictures, which according to van Mander, the magistrates of Brussels commissioned from Bruegel to commemorate the digging of the Brussels–Antwerp canal (completed in 1565). Apparently the work was interrupted by Bruegel's death.

2. DRAWINGS AND PRINTS. By 1907 Bastelaer had already enumerated 104 original drawings, and in 1908 he was the first critic to compile a list of prints by Bruegel. The basic critical catalogues of the drawings were compiled by Tolnay in 1925 and 1952 and, on the basis of his work, by Münz in 1961. Since then, however, research has drastically reduced the number of drawings attributed to Bruegel.

In 1970 van Leeuwen and Spicer independently recognized that the *c.* 80 figure studies carried out *naer het leven* ('from life'), until then given to Bruegel (Münz, nos 51–88 and 91–125), were the work of Roelandt Savery. The second major reassessment came as more of a shock. In 1986 the whole series of 'small landscapes' (M 27–45), the series of three sheets depicting the *Gates and Towers of Amsterdam* (M 47–9) and the *Parable of the Blind* (M 46)—a total of 23 sheets on which scholars had previously relied as authentic (except for one or two that were occasionally called in question)—were shown by Mielke to be forgeries by Roelandt's brother Jacob Savery (see also 1986–7 exh. cat., nos 97–100). It was subsequently recognized by Mielke (1991) and P. Dreyer (lecture at College Art Association, 1993) that even the large alpine landscape drawings could not be by Bruegel. The *Upper Rhine Landscape* (New York, Pierpont Morgan Lib.), until then considered the largest, most beautiful and attractive of Bruegel's landscape drawings, was found to be on paper with a watermark dating to *c.* 1585–8. It was reattributed to Roelandt Savery. The rejection of this drawing effectively eliminated most but not all of the other landscape drawings from Bruegel's oeuvre. Some areas, however,

remain debated: the Italianate landscapes of 1552 were still accepted by Mielke but rejected by Dreyer. Mielke also accepted those surviving drawings (London, BM, and Paris, Louvre) related to Cock's series of 12 etchings known as the *Large Landscapes*, all composite alpine landscapes except for *Pagus nemorosus*, which depicts an idyllic Flemish village beside a wood. When published by Cock *c.* 1555, these prints mentioned Bruegel as the designer, but other prints (and designs) traditionally associated with him, such as Cock's two series of prints of *Views of Villages near Antwerp* (1559 and 1561), do not carry Bruegel's name until later editions (e.g. that published by C. J. Visscher in 1612).

Even after the loss of these major groups of drawings, it is clear that Bruegel was a draughtsman of extraordinary range, importance and innovative power, who was responsible for an important group of allegorical and satirical compositions with small or numerous figures. In 1556–8 he made the preliminary drawings for etchings published by Cock that established his reputation as a 'second Bosch': the *Temptation of St Anthony*, *Big Fishes Eat Little Ones*, the *Ass in the School* (M 127–9), the allegories of the *Seven Deadly Sins* (M 130–36), the *Last Judgement*, *Elck* ('Everyman') and *The Alchemist* (M 137–9). In 1559–60 followed the allegories of the *Seven Virtues* (M 142–8); in 1561 *Christ in Limbo* (Vienna, Albertina); and in 1564 the *Fall of the Magician Hermogenes* (M 150), Bruegel's last work with a demonological theme. There are also two non-allegorical scenes of popular life: *Skaters before the Gate of St George, Antwerp* (1558; M 140) and the *Kermis at Hoboken* (1554; M 141).

The theme of the *Seven Deadly Sins* and the *Seven Virtues*, a series that appeared two years later, come from the *Psychomachia* of Prudentius: the battle between virtues and vices for the human soul. The virtues and vices first began to be depicted as female figures with characteristic attributes during the Middle Ages. However, Bosch (in the tabletop in the Prado, Madrid) had already renounced animal attributes and expressed the allegories as scenes of everyday life. Bruegel consciously reverted to the older schema, showing the sins at work in a world dominated by hellish creatures and using animal attributes in an archaic style (see 1975 exh. cat., nos 64–74). The complicated iconography of his allegories is significant on several levels (see Stridbeck, 1956). However, the drawings again confirm Bruegel's critical detachment, his ironical attitude expressed in conscious archaism and the inexhaustible fantasy of his often malicious humour. Bruegel is not an austere moralist. The satirical intention of the whole cycle of Virtues is clear from the buffoonish slaughter of *Fortitude* (Rotterdam, Mus. Boymans–van Beuningen) and the horrors of *Justice* (Brussels, Bib. Royale Albert 1er; see fig. 8): the scenes are a sarcastic travesty in which each virtue turns into its opposite. The world may be topsy-turvy and behave accordingly, but it is described exactly as it is—big fishes do eat little ones. The picturesque accumulation of all possible examples already foreshadows the encyclopedic quality that is fully apparent in the first three big paintings of 1559–60: the *Netherlandish Proverbs*, the *Children's Games* and the *Battle between Carnival and Lent*.

8. Pieter Bruegel I: *Justice*, pen and brown ink, 223×295 mm, 1559 (Brussels, Bibliothèque Royale Albert 1er)

The elaborate and disquieting *Elck* (London, BM) is doubtless drawn from contemporary moral philosophy and has been interpreted as an allegory of human egoism. The inscription, in three languages, comprises three different sayings: 'Everyone seeks himself', 'Everyone tugs for the longest end' and 'No one knows himself'. Elck is the eternal unsatisfied seeker, entangled by his own cupidity; the accumulated objects take on a *vanitas* character. His restlessness makes him a victim as well as a doer. The drawing exemplifies the many-sidedness and multiple significance of Bruegel's inventions. Among the humorous details is an empty, broken chest on which Bruegel has depicted the emblem of Hieronymus Cock's firm; just above it, two old men tug at a twisted piece of cloth—perhaps an allusion to Bruegel's business connection with Cock?

In the delicate drawing of *The Alchemist* (1558; Berlin, Kupferstichkab.), the moral appears to be that the alchemist's promises are illusory: they will not make the family rich but bring them instead to the poor-house. The *Resurrection* (Rotterdam, Mus. Boymans–van Beuningen), dated 1562 by Grossmann (1966, no 30), is a grisaille-like brush drawing in a vertical format unusual for Bruegel (see also 1975 exh. cat., no. 85). The drawing is much damaged and has been questioned because of the unusual technique, but Grossmann's convincing analysis has removed lingering doubts as to the authenticity of this striking composition, which combines the gospels of St

Mark (16:1–7) and St Matthew (28:1–8). Bruegel chose a different point in the traditional biblical account, in order to depict the women at the sepulchre and the angel seated beside it. Bruegel's vivid narrative sense is expressed in the massive size of the stone beside the grave, enhancing the effect of the miracle. Although not originally so intended, an engraving was made of the sheet, probably by Philip Galle—the gesture of blessing thus appearing the wrong way round.

Between 1560 and his death in 1569 Bruegel was fully occupied with the large paintings, so that his professional graphic work for Cock declined in quantity. Nonetheless, he executed some particularly fine compositions on paper, reduced to a few monumental single figures, which in some cases merge into the landscape—an evolution of style that is also found in his paintings from 1565 onwards. *The Shepherd* (Dresden, Kupferstichkab.), of which there is an exact copy in Vienna (Albertina), probably dates to *c.* 1560–63. The '*Painter and his Patron*' (*c.* 1565; Vienna, Albertina), also regarded as a late work, has been interpreted in very different ways but may express the artist's somewhat hostile attitude towards a pedantic layman. The painter with his expressive countenance has been regarded by some as a self-portrait and by others as an idealized portrait of Bosch; both conjectures are likely to be wrong. Contemporary admiration of the drawing, which was probably conceived as an independent piece, is attested by four good copies (M A 45–8).

In 1563 Bruegel executed the two delightful allegories, preserved only as prints, the *Fat Kitchen* and the *Lean Kitchen*; in 1565 both *Spring* (Vienna, Albertina) and the allegorical *Calumny of Apelles* (London, BM); in 1566 the designs for woodcuts (Bastelaer, nos 215–16) with figures from a carnival farce, *Orson and Valentine* and the *Dirty Bride* (M 153); and in 1568 *Summer* (Hamburg, Ksthalle) and *The Beekeepers* (Berlin, Kupferstichkab.). Religious themes do not occur in any of these drawings. Although *Spring* and *Summer* are separated by three years, they are part of a planned series of the *Four Seasons*, which was interrupted by Bruegel's death. Cock completed the series with *Autumn* and *Winter* by Hans Bol and published them as prints in 1570. Unlike the large paintings of *The Seasons* of 1565, which were really a depiction of the transformations of nature, Bruegel's designs for engravings emphasize typical seasonal activities in the traditional way of calendar illustrations. Here again he went to work in a very novel and personal manner. *Spring* combines the months of March, April and May; here, even more clearly than in *Summer*, the activities of each month are arranged spatially one after the other. While *Elck*, for instance, is imbued with deep unrest, the atmosphere here is one of quiet and calm, despite busy activity. The silently organized labour of the workers is expressed by the repetition of movement and emphasized by the hiding of their faces, their round caps and eyes fixed on the ground. The maid on the right also looks downwards. (This self-absorption of the figures

is brought to its logical conclusion in the complete anonymity of *The Beekeepers*.) Bruegel's stipple-like technique of drawing is developed to the full and achieves an inimitable delicacy in the gradation of volume, which is lost in reproduction. The gravitas of the figures has, not without reason, been compared to Michelangelo; but suggestions as to particular models are not really convincing. Direct borrowings in Bruegel are not known; nor does he ever repeat himself. Despite the similarity of theme in the drawing of *Summer* and the painting of the *Corn Harvest* of 1565, no single motif is repeated literally. In *Summer* three months are again combined, but two (June, haymaking, and July or August, the fruit and vegetable harvest) are thrust to either side by the main motif of reaping (July or August). The whole scene is bathed in shimmering summer heat. Bruegel needs no shadow to represent light; however, the scene is not only full of light, but sweltering as well. The bodies are heavy, and so is their toil in the summer sun. This is emphasized by the drinking labourer whose thrown-back head expresses the ecstasy of quenching his thirst. The effect of facelessness can be seen here even more clearly than in *Spring*, 'the artist displaying his virtuosity by showing most of the figures as turned away' (see 1975 exh. cat., p. 91). As is clear from the figure of the mower who appears left-handed, this drawing too is in reverse for the engraving.

The impressive drawing of *The Beekeepers* is generally regarded as a late work. The date MDLXV... is cut off on

9. Pieter Bruegel I: *Rabbit Hunters*, etching, 223×294 mm, 1560 (London, British Museum)

the right and should certainly be read as 1568. It may have been Bruegel's last work and is undoubtedly one of the most mysterious, with its disguised figures and their circumspect movements. Its presumed meaning can be elucidated from the contemporary proverb on the right, which reads: *dye den nest Weet dyen Weeten/dyen Roft dy heeten* ('He who knows where the nest is has the knowledge; he who steals it has the nest'); the boy in the tree is, in fact, plundering a bird's nest. But this proverb has, in turn, led to all kinds of divergent interpretations, none of which is totally convincing. (This sheet has always been discussed together with the equally enigmatic painting of the *Peasant and the Birdnester*.) The *double entendre* of the proverb is that a bold wooer will fare better than a shy one. While the words are inscribed in the same ink as the drawing, opinions differ as to whether they are in Bruegel's hand.

Altogether Bruegel published 64 etchings with Cock, but there is only one by his own hand, the *Rabbit Hunters* (see fig. 9). Also published by Cock, it is signed at the lower left BRVEGEL with the date 1560. This has previously been read as 1566, but on stylistic grounds the work must be earlier; moreover, the correct date, 1560, appears on a reversed copy after the preliminary drawing (Paris, Fond. Custodia, Inst. Néer.). The composition recalls that of the *Large Landscapes*. Bruegel used the etching needle as a drawing tool, rather than fully exploiting the new medium (see White, in Simson and Winner, p. 190); this is perhaps why he did not try further experiments in etching. Philipp Fehl (see 1975 exh. cat., nos 75 and 75a) has pointed out that the sportsman is aiming at two rabbits at once and thus will miss them both. The drawing (though not the etching) shows a third hare in the foreground, probably to indicate that the hunter could easily hit it were he able to be content with one only. Fehl cited Erasmus of Rotterdam's proverb 'Duos insequens lepores neutrum capit' ('He who chases two hares will catch neither'). The man with the spear, according to Fehl, is a marauding soldier who is about to turn the tables by hunting the hunter. This is plausible, but as an example of Bruegel's humour rather than his 'cosmic pessimism'.

III. Critical reception and posthumous reputation.

Among the first to collect Bruegel's work were Cardinal Granvelle and the rich, highly respected Nicolaas Jonghelinck of Antwerp. Which or how many pictures Granvelle owned is not known. The only one whose provenance can be traced back to him with certainty is the *Flight into Egypt*. Jonghelinck possessed no fewer than 16 paintings by Bruegel, including *The Seasons*, a *Tower of Babel* and the *Road to Calvary*. The number of works by Bruegel owned by Abraham Ortelius is also unknown, but he certainly possessed the *Death of the Virgin* (Upton House, Warwicks, NT), a grisaille that he had engraved.

The 17th, 18th and even the 19th century had no real understanding of Bruegel and regarded his son Jan as a superior artist. For a long period Pieter the elder was appreciated merely for the 'drollness' of his peasant figures. 'His field of enquiry is certainly not of the most extensive; his ambition, too, is modest. He confines himself to a knowledge of mankind and the most immediate objects.'

This view, expressed in 1890 by Hymans, the 'rediscoverer' of Bruegel, is questionable in many respects; it is typical of a classicist misconception that for 300 years prevented a true understanding and appreciation of Bruegel's art. It must be said, however, that his work was then known chiefly from engravings, crude replicas and imitations. His masterpieces were removed from public gaze, reposing in aristocratic collections; no fewer than 14 belonged to the Habsburgs. Only from the beginning of the 20th century did his greatness begin gradually to be recognized by art historians such as Hulin de Loo and van Bastelaer, Romdahl, Baldass, Glück, Tolnay, Friedländer and Dvořák. His work as a draughtsman was radically reassessed in the last quarter of the century, and his contribution to the development of landscape drawing, in particular, was reconsidered.

BIBLIOGRAPHY

EWA; Thieme–Becker

EARLY SOURCES

G. Vasari: *Vite* (1550, rev. 2/1568); ed. G. Milanesi (1878–85)
L. Guicciardini: *Descrittione di tutti i Paesi Bassi* (Antwerp, 1567)
D. Lampsonius: *Pictorum aliquot celebrium Germaniae inferioris effigies* (Antwerp, 1572; ed. J. Puraye; *Les Effigies des peintres célèbres de Pays-Bas* (Bruges, 1956)
A. Ortelius: *Album amicorum* (MS., Antwerp, 1574–96; Cambridge, Pembroke Coll.); trans by F. Grossmann in W. Stechow: *Northern Renaissance Art, 1400–1600: Sources and Documents* (Englewood Cliffs, NJ, 1966), pp. 37–8
K. van Mander: *Schilder-boeck* ([1603]–1604)
J. Denucé: *De Antwerpsche 'konstkamers': Inventarissen van kunstverzamelingen te Antwerpen in de 16e en 17e eeuwen* (Amsterdam, 1932; Ger. trans., Antwerp, 1932)

GENERAL

L. v. Baldass: 'Die niederländische Landschaftsmalerei von Patinir bis Bruegel', *Jb. Ksthist. Samml. Allerhöch. Kserhaus.*, xxxiv (1918), pp. 111–57
J. Huizinga: *The Waning of the Middle Ages* (London, 1924)
O. Benesch: *The Art of the Renaissance in Northern Europe* (London, 1945, rev. 3/1965)
G. T. Faggin: *La pittura ad Anversa nel cinquecento* (Florence, 1968)
H. G. Franz: *Niederländische Landschaftsmalerei im Zeitalter des Manierismus*, 2 vols (Graz, 1969)
J. Białostocki: 'Die Geburt der modernen Landschaftsmalerei', *Bull. Mus. N. Varsovie/Biul. Muz. Warszaw.*, xiv/1–4 (1973), pp. 6–13 [issue devoted to *La Peinture de paysage en Europe, 1550–1650*]
K. Demus, F. Klauner and K. Schutz: *Flämishe Malerei von Jan van Eyck bis Pieter Bruegel d. Ä.*, Vienna, Ksthist. Mus. Cat. (Vienna, 1981)

MONOGRAPHIC STUDIES

H. Hymans: 'Pierre Brueghel le vieux', *Gaz. B.-A.*, xxxii (1890), no. 1, pp. 361–75; no. 2, pp. 361–73; xxxiii (1891), no. 1, pp. 20–40
A. L. Romdahl: 'Pieter Brueghel der Ältere und sein Kunstschaffen', *Jb. Ksthist. Samml. Allerhöch. Kserhaus.*, xxv (1905), pp. 85–169
R. van Bastelaer and G. Hulin de Loo: *Peter Bruegel l'ancien: Son oeuvre et son temps* (Brussels, 1907)
V. Barker: *Peter Bruegel the Elder: A Study of his Paintings* (New York, 1926, rev. 2 London, 1927)
E. Michel: *Bruegel* (Paris, 1931)
G. Glück: *Bruegels Gemälde* (Vienna, 1932)
C. de Tolnay: *Pieter Bruegel l'ancien* (Brussels, 1935)
M. J. Friedländer: *Die altniederländische Malerei*, xiv (Berlin, 1937); Eng. trans. as *Early Netherlandish Painting*, xiv (Leiden, 1976)
G. Jedlicka: *Pieter Bruegel: Der Maler in seiner Zeit* (Erlenbach and Zurich, 1938)
M. Dvořák: *Die Gemälde Pieter Bruegels d.Ä.* (Vienna, 1941)
J. B. Knipping: *Pieter Bruegel de oude* (Amsterdam, 1945)
A. L. Romdahl: *Pieter Bruegel den äldre* (Stockholm, 1947)
G. Glück: *Das grosse Bruegel-Werk* (Vienna, 1951)
V. Denis: *Tutta la pittura di Pieter Bruegel* (Milan, 1952)
F. Grossmann: *Bruegel: The Paintings* (London, 1955, rev. 2/1966, rev. 3/1973)
M. Auner: 'Pieter Bruegel: Umrisse eines Lebensbildes', *Jb. Ksthist. Samml. Wien*, lii (1956), pp. 51–122

C. G. Stridbeck: *Bruegelstudien* (Stockholm, 1956)

M. Fryns: *Pierre Brueghel l'ancien* (Brussels, 1964)

G. W. Menzel: *Pieter Bruegel der Ältere* (Leipzig, 1966)

G. Arpino and P. Bianconi: *L'opera completa di Bruegel*, Class. A., vii (Milan, 1967)

H. A. Klein and M. C. Klein: *Pieter Bruegel the Elder* (New York, 1968)

B. Claessens and J. Rousseau: *Unser Bruegel* (Antwerp, 1969)

R.-H. Marijnissen: *Bruegel* (Stuttgart, 1969)

W. Stechow: *Pieter Bruegel the Elder* (New York, 1970)

E. G. Grimme: *Pieter Bruegel d.Ä.: Leben und Werk* (Cologne, 1973)

C. Brown: *Bruegel* (London, 1975)

W. S. Gibson: *Bruegel* (London, 1977; Fr. trans., Paris, 1980)

O. von Simson and M. Winner, eds: *Pieter Bruegel und seine Welt: Ein Colloquium* (Berlin, 1979)

A. Wied: *Bruegel* (Milan, 1979; Eng. trans., Sydney, 1980; Fr. trans., Paris, 1980)

R.-H. Marijnissen and others: *Bruegel: Tout l'oeuvre peint et dessiné* (Antwerp, 1988)

EXHIBITION CATALOGUES

Le Siècle de Bruegel: La Peinture en Belgique au XVIe siècle (exh. cat., Brussels, Mus. Royaux B.-A., 1963)

Die Kunst der Graphik, IV: Zwischen Renaissance und Barock, Das Zeitalter von Bruegel und Bellange (exh. cat. by K. Oberhuber, Vienna, Albertina, 1967)

Bruegel: De schilder en zijn wereld (exh. cat., Brussels, Mus. Royaux B.-A., 1969)

Pieter Bruegel d.Ä. als Zeichner (exh. cat., Berlin, Kupferstichkab., 1975)

L'Epoque de Lucas van Leyde et Pierre Bruegel: Dessins des anciens Pays-Bas dans la Collection Frits Lugt, Institut Néerlandais, Paris (exh. cat. by K. G. Boon, Florence, Inst. Univ. Oland. Stor. A.; Paris, Fond. Custodia, Inst. Néer.; 1980–81)

The Age of Bruegel: Netherlandish Drawings in the Sixteenth Century (exh. cat. by J. O. Hand and others, Washington, DC, N.G.A.; New York, Pierpont Morgan Lib.; 1986–7)

DRAWINGS

L. Burchard: 'Pieter Bruegel im Kupferstichkabinett zu Berlin', *Amtl. Ber. Kön. Kstsamml.*, xxxiv/11 (1913), pp. 223–34

K. Tolnai: *Die Zeichnungen Pieter Bruegels* (Munich, 1925)

——: 'Beiträge zu Bruegels Zeichnungen', *Jb. Preuss. Kstsamml.*, l (1929), pp. 195–216

J. G. van Gelder and J. Borms: *Brueghels deugden en hoofdzonden* (Amsterdam, 1939)

A. E. Popham: 'Two Landscape Drawings by Pieter Bruegel the Elder', *Burl. Mag.*, xci (1949), pp. 319–20

H. Gerson: 'De Ripa Grande te Rome', *Oud-Holland*, lxvi (1951), p. 65

C. de Tolnay: *Die Zeichnungen Pieter Bruegels* (Zurich, 1952); rev. by O. Benesch in *Kstchronik*, vi (1953), pp. 76–82

F. Grossmann: 'The Drawings of Pieter Bruegel the Elder in the Museum Boymans', *Bull.: Mus. Boymans*, v/2 (1954), pp. 41–63

O. Benesch: 'Zur Frage der Kopien nach Pieter Bruegel', *Mus. Royaux B.-A. Belgique: Bull.*, viii (1959), pp. 35–42

C. de Tolnay: 'Remarques sur quelques dessins de Bruegel l'ancien sur un dessin de Bosch récemment réapparu', *Mus. Royaux B.-A. Belgique: Bull.*, ix (1960), pp. 3ff

L. Münz: *Bruegel Drawings* (London, 1961; Ger. trans., Cologne, 1962) [M]

K. Arndt: 'Unbekannte Handzeichnungen von Pieter Bruegel d.Ae.', *Pantheon*, xxiv (1966), pp. 207–16

I. L. Zupnick: 'The Meaning of Bruegel's *Nobody* and *Everyman*', *Gaz. B.-A.*, lxvii/1 (1966), pp. 257–70

K. Arndt: 'Frühe Landschaftszeichnungen von Pieter Bruegel d.Ae.', *Pantheon*, xxv (1967), pp. 97–104

C. de Tolnay: 'A Contribution to Pieter Bruegel the Elder as Draughtsman', *Miscellanea I.Q. van Regteren Altena* (Amsterdam, 1969), pp. 61–3

F. van Leeuwen: 'Iets over het handschrift van de "naar het leven"-tekenaar', *Oud-Holland*, lxxxv (1970), pp. 25–32

J. A. Spicer: 'The "Naer het Leven" Drawings: Pieter Bruegel or Roelandt Savery?', *Master Drgs*, viii/1 (1970), pp. 3–30

——: 'Roelandt Savery's Studies in Bohemia', *Uměni*, xviii (1970), pp. 270–75

F. van Leeuwen: 'Figuurstudies van "P. Bruegel"', *Simiolus*, v/3–4 (1971), pp. 139–49

K. Arndt: 'Pieter Bruegel d. Ä. und die Geschichte der Waldlandschaft', *Jb. Berlin. Mus.*, xiv (1972), pp. 69–121

H. Mielke: [review of 1980–81 exh. cat. by K. G. Boon], *Master Drgs*, xxiii–xxiv (1986), pp. 75–90

——: 'Pieter Bruegel d. Ä.: Probleme seines zeichnerischen Oeuvres', *Jb. Berlin. Mus.*, n. s., xxxiii (1991), pp. 124–34

——: *Die Zeichnungen Pieter Bruegels* (in preparation)

PRINTS

R. van Bastelaer: *Les Estampes de Peter Bruegel l'ancien* (Brussels, 1908)

H. A. Klein: *Graphic Worlds of Peter Bruegel the Elder* (New York, 1963)

J. Lavalleye: *Lucas van Leyden, Peter Bruegel d. Ä.: Das gesamte graphische Werk* (Vienna and Munich, 1966; Eng. trans., New York, 1967)

L. Lebeer: *Bruegel: Le stampe* (Florence, 1967)

T. A. Riggs: *Hieronymus Cock (1510–1570): Printmaker and Publisher in Antwerp at the Sign of the Four Winds* (diss., New Haven, CT, Yale U., 1971)

SPECIALIST STUDIES

W. Fraenger: *Der Bauern-Bruegel und das deutsche Sprichwort* (Erlenbach and Zurich, 1923)

F. Lugt: 'Pieter Bruegel und Italien', *Festschrift für Max Friedländer* (Leipzig, 1927), pp. 111–29

A. Haberlandt: 'Volkskundliches zur *Bauernhochzeit* P. Brueghels d.Ä.', *Z. Vlksknd.*, n. s. 2, xl/1–2 (1930), pp. 10–16

E. Michel: 'Pierre Bruegel le vieux et Pieter Coecke d'Alost', *Mélanges Hulin de Loo* (Brussels, 1931), pp. 266–71

A. Haberlandt: 'Das Faschingsbild des Pieter Bruegel d.Ä.', *Z. Vlksknd.*, n. s. 5, xliii/3 (1933), pp. 237–50

H. Sedlmayr: 'Die "macchia" Bruegels', *Jb. Ksthist. Samml. Wien*, n. s., viii (1934), pp. 137–59

E. Tietze-Conrat: 'Pieter Bruegels Kinderspiele', *Oudhdknd. Jb.*, ii (1934), pp. 127–30

K. von Tolnai: 'Studien zu Gemälden Pieter Bruegels d. Ä.', *Jb. Ksthist. Samml. Wien*, n. s., viii (1934), pp. 105–35

G. Glück: 'Über einige Landschaftsgemälde Pieter Bruegels des Älteren', *Jb. Ksthist. Samml. Wien*, n. s., ix (1935), pp. 151–65

E. Michel: 'Bruegel le vieux: A-t-il passé par Genève?', *Gaz. B.-A.*, lxxviii/1 (1936), pp. 105–8

J. Grauls: *De spreekworden van P. Bruegel den oude verklaard* (Antwerp, 1938)

E. Michel: 'Bruegel et la critique moderne', *Gaz. B.-A.*, lxxx/1 (1938), pp. 27–46

C. de Tolnay: 'La Seconde *Tour de Babel* de Pierre Bruegel l'ancien', *Ann. Mus. Royaux B.-A. Belgique* (1938), pp. 113–21

F. Würtenberger: 'Zu Bruegels Kunstform, besonders ihr Verhältnis zur Renaissancekomposition', *Z. Kstgesch.*, ix (1939), pp. 30–48

V. De Meyere: *De kinderspelen van Pieter Bruegel den oude verklaard* (Antwerp, 1941)

C. Terlinden: 'Pierre Bruegel le vieux et l'histoire', *Rev. Belge Arch. & Hist. A.*, xii (1942), pp. 229–57

D. Bax: 'Over allerhand bisschopen en Bruegels kreupelen in het Louvre', *Historia* [Utrecht], ix (1943), pp. 241–8

G. Glück: 'Peter Brueghel the Elder and Classical Antiquity', *A. Q.* [Detroit], vi (1943), pp. 167–86

F. Baumgart: 'Zusammenhänge der niederländischen mit der italienischen Malerei der zweiten Hälfte des 16. Jahrhunderts', *Marburg. Jb. Kstwiss.*, xiii (1944), pp. 187–250

J. Bakker: 'De humor van Pieter Brueghel den ouden', *Historia* [Utrecht], x (1944–5), pp. 277–83

L. Baldass: 'Les Paysanneries de Pierre Bruegel', *A. Plast.*, xi–xii (1948), pp. 471–84

F. Novotny: *Die Monatsbilder Pieter Bruegels des Älteren* (Vienna, 1948)

D. Bax: 'Pieter Bruegel: *De jongen met het vogelnest*', *Historia* [Utrecht], xiv (1949), pp. 55–7

K. Boström: 'Das Sprichwort vom Vogelnest', *Ksthist. Tidskr.*, xviii/2–3 (1949), pp. 77–98

B. Lagercrantz: 'Pieter Bruegel und Olaus Magnus', *Ksthist. Tidskr.*, xviii/2–3 (1949), pp. 71–6

G. Glück: 'Peter Bruegel the Elder and the Legend of St Christopher in Early Flemish Painting', *A. Q.* [Detroit], xiii (1950), pp. 37–47

F. Novotny: 'Volkskundliche und kunstgeschichtliche Betrachtungsweise, zu Pieter Bruegels *Heimkehr der Herde*', *Österreichische Z. Vlkskd.*, n. s., iv/1–2 (1950), pp. 42–53

H. Swarzenski: '*The Battle between Carnival and Lent*', *Bull. Mus. F.A., Boston*, xlix (1951), pp. 2–11

C. de Tolnay: 'Bruegel et l'Italie', *A. Plast.* (Sept 1951), pp. 121–30

A. Haberlandt: 'Volksbrauch im Jahreslauf auf den *Monatsbildern* Pieter Bruegels d. Ä.', *Österreichische Z. Vlkskd.*, n. s., vi (1952), pp. 43ff

C. Linfert: 'Die Vermummung, eine Figuration der Angst (in Bildern von Bosch, Bruegel und Max Beckmann)', *Atti del II congresso internazionale di studi umanistici a cura di E. Castelli: Milano-Roma, 1953*, pp. 263–8

O. Buyssens: '*De schepen* by Pieter Bruegel de oude, proeve van identificatie', *Meded. Acad. Marine België*, viii (1954), pp. 159–91

J. Avalon: '*Bataille de Carnaval et de Carême*', *Aesculape*, xxxvii (1955), pp. 67–71

K. C. Lindsay and B. Huppé: 'Meaning and Method in Brueghel's Painting', *J. Aesth. & A. Crit.*, xiv (1956), pp. 376–86

C. G. Stridbeck: '*Combat between Carnival and Lent* by Pieter Bruegel the Elder: An Allegorical Picture of the Sixteenth Century', *J. Warb. & Court. Inst.*, xix (1956), pp. 96–109

F. Anzelewsky: 'Besprechung von Grossmann 1955', *Kunstchronik*, x (1957), pp. 19ff

H. Bauer: 'Besprechung von Stridbeck 1956 und Würtenberger 1957', *Kunstchronik*, x (1957), pp. 235–40

J. Grauls: *Volkstaal en volksleven in het werk van Pieter Bruegel* (Antwerp and Amsterdam, 1957)

J. Hills: *Das Kinderspielbild von Pieter Bruegel d. Ä.: Eine volkskundliche Untersuchung*, Veröff. Österreich. Mus. Vlksknd., x (Vienna, 1957)

H. Sedlmayr: 'Pieter Bruegel: *Der Sturz der Blinden*, Paradigma einer Strukturanalyse', *Hft. Ksthist. Semin. U. München*, ii (1957); also in *Epochen und Werke*, i (Vienna and Munich, 1959), pp. 319–57

F. Würtenberger: *Pieter Bruegel d. Ä. und die deutsche Kunst* (Wiesbaden, 1957)

P. J. Vinken: 'De betekenis van Pieter Bruegels *Nestrover*' [The meaning of Pieter Bruegel's *Birdnester*], *Het Boek*, xxxiii/2 (1958), pp. 106–15

F. Grossmann: 'New Light on Bruegel', *Burl. Mag.*, ci (1959), pp. 341–6

J. Briels: 'Amator pictoriae artis: De Antwerpse kunsthandelaar Peeter Stevens (1590–1668) en zijn Constkamer', *Jb.: Kon. Mus. S. Kst.* (1960), pp. 137–226

F. Grossmann: 'Bruegels Verhältnis zu Raffael und zur Raffael-Nachfolge', *Festschrift Kurt Badt* (Berlin, 1961), pp. 135–43

P. Portmann: '*Die Kinderspiele* Pieter Bruegels d. Ä.' (Berne, 1961)

H. Bartlett Wells: 'Arms in Bruegel's *Slaughter of the Innocents*', *J. Arms & Armour Soc.*, iv/10 (1964), pp. 193–209

E. Brochhagen: 'Besprechung der Ausstellung *Le Siècle de Bruegel*', *Kunstchronik*, xvii (1964), pp. 1–7

I. L. Zupnick: 'Bruegel and the Revolt of the Netherlands', *A. J.* [London], xxiii (1964), pp. 283–9

W. S. Gibson: 'Some Notes on Pieter Bruegel the Elder's *Peasant Wedding Feast*', *A. Q.* [Detroit], xxviii (1965), pp. 194–208

J. van Lennep: 'L'Alchimie et Pierre Brueghel l'ancien', *Mus. Royaux B.-A. Belgique: Bull.*, xiv (1965), pp. 105–26

G. Marlier: 'Peeter Balten, copiste ou créateur?', *Mus. Royaux B.-A. Belgique: Bull.*, xiv (1965), pp. 127–41

C. de Tolnay: 'Newly Discovered Miniatures by Pieter Bruegel the Elder', *Burl. Mag.*, cvii (1965), pp. 110ff

S. Ferber: 'Pieter Bruegel and the Duke of Alba', *Ren. News*, xix/3 (1966), pp. 205–19

V. Dene: 'Une Paysage de Pieter Brueghel le jeune d'après celui de Pieter Bruegel le vieux dans la collection du Musée d'Art de Bucarest', *Miscellanea Jozef Duverger* (Ghent, 1968), i, pp. 269–74

P. Thon: 'Bruegel's *The Triumph of Death* Reconsidered', *Ren. Q.*, xxi/3 (1968), pp. 289–97

A. Deblaere: 'Erasmus, Bruegel en de humanistische visie', *Vlaanderen*, 103 (1969)

G. Marlier: *Pierre Brueghel le jeune*; rev. and annotated by J. Folie (Brussels, 1969)

C. de Tolnay: 'Pierre Bruegel l'ancien', *Actes du XXIIe congrès international d'histoire de l'art: Budapest, 1969*, i, pp. 31–44

J. Weyns: 'Bij Bruegel in de leer voor honderd-en-een dagelijkse dingen' [Bruegel as a source for learning 101 things about daily life in the 16th century], *Tijdschrift van het Verbond voor Heemkunde*, xxiii/3 (1969), pp. 97–113

K. Renger: 'Bettler und Bauern bei Pieter Bruegel d. Ä.', *Kstgesch. Ges. Berlin*, n. s. 20 (1971–2), pp. 9–16

C. Gaignebet: 'Le Combat de Carnaval et de Carême de P. Bruegel', *An., Econ., Soc., Civilis.*, xxvii (1972), pp. 313–45

S. Alpers: 'Bruegel's Festive Peasants', *Simiolus*, iv (1972–3), pp. 163–76

F. Grossmann: 'Notes on Some Sources of Bruegel's Art', *Album amicorum J. G. van Gelder* (The Hague, 1973), pp. 147–58

J. B. Bedaux and A. van Gool: 'Bruegel's Birthyear: Motive of an *ars of natura* Transmutation', *Simiolus*, vii (1974), pp. 133–56

A. Monballieu: 'De *Kermis van Hoboken* bij P. Bruegel, J. Grimmer en G. Mostaert', *Jb.: Kon. Mus. S. Kst.* (1974), pp. 139–69

W. Mössner: *Studien zur Farbe bei Pieter Brueghel d.Ä.* (diss., U. Würzburg, 1975)

S. Karling: '*The Attack* by Pieter Bruegel the Elder in the Collection of the Stockholm University', *Ksthist. Tidskr.*, xv (1976), pp. 1–18

D. Mattioli: 'Nuove ipotesi su i quadri di "Bruol Vecchio" appartenuti ai Gonzaga', *Civil. Mant.*, 10 (1976), pp. 32–43

Y. Mori: 'The Influence of German and Flemish Prints on the Works of Pieter Bruegel', *Bull. Tama A. Sch.*, ii (1976), pp. 17–60

P. Dreyer: 'Bruegels *Alchimist* von 1568: Versuch einer Deutung *ad usum mysticum*', *Jb. Berlin. Mus.*, xix (1977), pp. 69–113

D. Kunzle: 'Bruegel's Proverb Painting and the *World Upside Down*', *A. Bull.*, lix (1977), pp. 197–202

M. A. Sullivan: 'Madness and Folly: Pieter Bruegel the Elder's *Dulle Griet*', *A. Bull.*, lix (1977), pp. 55–66

F. Klauner: *Die Gemäldegalerie des Kunsthistorischen Museums in Wien* (Salzburg and Vienna, 1978)

H. D. Brumble III: 'Peter Bruegel the Elder: The Allegory of Landscape', *A. Q.*, n. s. 2 (1979), pp. 125–39

A. Monballieu: 'De *Hand als teken op het kleed* bij Bruegel en Baltens', *Jb.: Kon. Mus. S. Kst.* (1979), pp. 197–209

M. Walder: '*Die Heimkehr der Herde*', *Terra Plana*, 3 (1979), pp. 5–6

R. Genaille: '*La Montée au Calvaire* de Bruegel l'ancien', *Jb.: Kon. Mus. S. Kst.* (1980), pp. 61–97

C. de Tolnay: 'Further Miniatures by Pieter Bruegel the Elder', *Burl. Mag.*, cxxii (1980), pp. 616–23

H.-J. Raupp: *Bauernsatiren: Entstehung und Entwicklung des bäuerlichen Genres in der deutschen und niederländischen Kunst c. 1470–1570* (Niederzier, 1986)

L. S. Milne: *Dreams and Popular Beliefs in the Imagery of Pieter Bruegel the Elder* (diss., U. Boston, 1990)

M. Sullivan: *Bruegel's Peasants: Art and Audience in the Northern Renaissance* (Cambridge, 1994)

ALEXANDER WIED

(2) Pieter Brueghel [Breughel] **II** [the younger] [Hell Brueghel] (*b* Brussels, 1564/5; *d* Antwerp, 1637–8). Painter, son of (1) Pieter Bruegel I. Van Mander was the only contemporary author to mention Pieter II and suggested that he received his first training from Gillis van Coninxloo III, a claim that is not generally accepted. It is also possible that, like his younger brother (3) Jan Breughel I, he was trained in watercolour painting by his talented grandmother Mayken Verhulst, reputedly an accomplished miniature and watercolour painter. Pieter II became a master in the Antwerp painters' corporation in 1584–5. On 5 November 1588 he married Elisabeth Godelet, by whom he had seven children. Archival evidence indicates that Pieter II never enjoyed anything like his brother Jan's financial success, for documents mention arrears of several months on house rent owed in 1597. From 1588 to 1626 Pieter II had at least eight apprentices, including Frans Snyders in 1593. Many more people must have been involved in the Breughel enterprise, however, for he ran a thriving atelier, and, to judge from contemporary Antwerp inventories, such as those of the affluent Antwerp art dealer family Forchoudt, his paintings were in popular demand and evidently sold cheaply since they were recognized and accepted as copies and imitations of his father's most famous compositions. Pieter II's work did not have the depth of his father's nor the refinement of that of his younger brother Jan. His original compositions are energetic translations of his father's style into a bold, bright and admittedly often rather loud 17th-century idiom. Many copies have the same composition, format and size. In the 18th and 19th centuries his name and oeuvre were neglected. Only in 1934 did Glück draw attention to his paintings. After the posthumous publication of Marlier's monograph in 1969, Pieter II was finally rediscovered.

Among the most frequently copied prototypes by Pieter Bruegel the elder was the *Winter Landscape with Skaters and a Bird-trap* (1565; Brussels, Mus. A. Anc., 8724).

Pieter II and his atelier produced at least 60 copies of this composition, of which 10 are signed and 4 are dated (1601, 1603, 1616 and 1626). In addition, they made at least 30 copies after Pieter the elder's *Adoration of the Magi in the Snow* (1567; Winterthur, Samml. Oskar Reinhart), some of which (e.g. Prague, N.G., Šternberk Pal., O–42) show less snow than in his father's original, while in other versions the snow is deleted altogether and facial features are rendered in more caricatural detail (e.g. Brussels, Mus. A. Anc., no. 9132, see fig. 1; Amsterdam, Rijksmus., A 731).

No less than 25 copies of Pieter the elder's *St John the Baptist Preaching* (1565; Budapest, Mus. F.A.) have survived, considered by many as a reflection of the clandestine Protestant preaching in the 16th century. A significant detail, however, is deliberately deleted in many versions (e.g. priv. col.; see 1980 exh. cat., no. 70): an unidentified figure of a bearded man in black, turned towards the spectator. The blatant omission seems to confirm earlier suggestions that his prominent presence in the original composition was less than accidental and that Pieter II added or omitted elements to alter the meaning. Changes and omissions are also noticeable in no less than 17 copies of Pieter Bruegel the elder's *Netherlandish Proverbs* (1559; Berlin, Gemäldegal., 1720), the oldest version of which is probably that of 1607 (Lier, Stedel. Mus. Wuyts-van Campen, 62). There are about 25 changes, with only 100 proverbs illustrated instead of the original 115.

Before its discovery in 1952, a small grisaille panel (241×343 mm) with *Christ and the Woman Taken in Adultery*, painted by Pieter the elder in 1565 (London, Courtauld Inst. Gals), was known only through an engraving of 1579 by Pierre Perret and through six copies by Pieter II and his atelier. Intriguingly, Pieter II did not copy his father's painting but used Perret's engraving as a model, despite the fact that the original was in his brother Jan's possession until his death in 1625, when he bequeathed it to Federigo Borromeo. Perhaps Pieter II made his copies after 1628, as the date on one version indicates (priv. col.; see 1980 exh. cat, no. 83). The use of engravings as intermediaries between original compositions by Pieter the elder and copies by Pieter II can also be observed in a small tondo (diam. 195 mm) with the *Parable of the Blind* (Prague, N.G., Šternberk Pal., O–7924), not made after his father's version (1568; Naples, Capodimonte; *see* (1), fig. 6 above) but copied from an engraving generally attributed to Pieter van der Heyden. The same applies to *The Misanthrope* (1594; Antwerp, Kon. Mus. S. Kst., 872/2), possibly one of the earliest known paintings by Pieter II and likewise not painted after his father's tondo (1568; Naples, Capodimonte) but imitated from an engraving by Jan Wierix.

1. Pieter Brueghel II: *Adoration of the Magi in the Snow*, panel, 360×560 mm (Brussels, Musée d'Art Ancien)

2. Pieter Brueghel II: *Whitsun Bride*, tempera and oil on panel, 508×784 mm (New York, Metropolitan Museum of Art)

Some of Pieter II's paintings provide additional information concerning lost compositions by Pieter the elder. Several versions of the so-called *Visit to the Farm* are known, some attributed to Pieter II (e.g. priv. col., 400×570 mm; see 1980 exh. cat., no. 90) and some to his brother Jan. Yet not a single work by their father corresponds to this small composition. Perhaps the original *Visit to the Farm* was also a grisaille similar to Bruegel's *Christ and the Woman Taken in Adultery*. The same applies to the *Drunk Thrown out of the Inn* (Montreal, Mus. F.A., 955.1122), which some consider a copy after a lost composition by Pieter the elder, either that in distemper on linen mentioned in the 1696 inventory of the collection of Evrard Jabach or that on panel formerly in the Koenigs collection in Haarlem and lost in a fire.

The *Brawl between Peasants* (priv. col.; see 1980 exh. cat., no. 91) may reflect another lost original by Pieter I. Possibly it is based on an engraving of 1621 by Lucas Vorsterman, which is accompanied by a Latin poem glorifying the composition as a major work by Pieter the elder. This is corroborated by a letter from Lord Arundel written shortly after 1625 to his Antwerp agent Lionel Wake, instructing him to buy a panel depicting a *Brawl between Peasants*, begun by Brueghel and completed by Gillis Mostaert; the letter also mentions the engraving by Vorsterman, and the 1640 inventory of Rubens's collection also describes a composition of fighting peasants by the elder Bruegel, without specifying, however, whether it was a drawing or painting. Other paintings by Pieter II confirm the original shapes and compositions of his father's works;

thus, for instance, the copy of Pieter the elder's *Adoration of the Magi* (1564; London, N.G., 3556) previously in the convent of the Poor Clares in Tongeren (Brussels, Baron F. Cogels priv. col.; see 1980 exh. cat., no. 82) confirms earlier suggestions that the original was cut down slightly at some point.

Some paintings by Pieter II, such as the *Inn of St Michael* (priv. col.; see 1980 exh. cat., no. 102) or a fragment of a *Procession* (Brussels, Mus. A. Anc., 671), are freely inspired by his father's compositions and motifs. The *Crucifixion* (Budapest, Mus. F.A.) and several variants made between 1605 and 1618 also seem to be based on a lost composition by Pieter I, to which Pieter II added his own landscape in the background. Occasionally, Pieter II was capable of creating his own original compositions, such as the *Whitsun Bride* (New York, Met.; see fig. 2), which is known in at least five autograph versions, or four small tondos (diam. 16.5 cm) with the *Four Stages of the River* (each diam. 165 mm; all Prague, N.G., Šternberk Pal., 077–80). Pieter II's style never evolved. He remained close to the manner he adopted in his early career, and the only criterion sometimes proposed to date his work is the spelling of his name as 'Brueghel' before 1600 and 'Breughel' after 1600.

BIBLIOGRAPHY

Thieme–Becker

K. van Mander: *Schilder-boeck* ([1603]–1604), fol. 234

G. Glück: 'Peter Brueghel der Jüngere', *De Helsche en de Fluwelen Breughel en hun invloed op de kunst in de Nederlanden* (exh. cat., Amsterdam, Ksthandel P. de Boer, 1934), pp. 6–9

G. Marlier: *Pieter Brueghel le Jeune* (Brussels, 1969) [posth. pubn annotated by J. Folie]

J. Folie: 'Pieter Brueghel de Jongere', *Bruegel: Een dynastie van schilders* (exh. cat., Brussels, Mus. A. Anc., 1980), pp. 137–42
W. Liedtke: *Flemish Paintings in the Metropolitan Museum of Art* (New York, 1984), pp. 25–8

(3) Jan Breughel I [Velvet Breughel; Paradise Breughel; Flower Breughel] (*b* Brussels, 1568; *d* Antwerp, 13 Jan 1625). Painter and draughtsman, son of (1) Pieter Bruegel I. Jan is famous for his small-scale history paintings, some of which were executed on copper, exquisite flower still-lifes, allegorical and mythological scenes and various types of landscapes, including imaginary mountain landscapes, forest interiors, villages and country roads, ports, river views, seascapes, hunting pieces, battles and scenes of Hell and the underworld.

1. Life. 2. Work. 3. Workshop and collaboration. 4. Critical reception and posthumous reputation.

1. LIFE. Because of the early death of his father, Jan received his first training in watercolour painting from his maternal grandmother, Mayken Verhulst. According to van Mander, Pieter Goetkindt (*d* 1583) taught Jan to paint in oils. In 1589 Jan travelled to Italy via Cologne. He was in Naples in 1590, and from 1592 to 1594 he lived in Rome under the patronage of Cardinal Ascanio Colonna. In 1595 and 1596 Jan visited Milan at the insistence of his lifelong patron, Cardinal Federico Borromeo. He returned to Antwerp by October 1596, and the following year he became a master in the Antwerp painters' corporation. He married Isabella de Jode (*d* Antwerp, 1603), daughter of the engraver Gerard de Jode, on 23 January 1599, and on 13 September 1601 their first son, (4) Jan Breughel the younger, was born. Jan received his Antwerp citizenship in the same year and became subdeacon of the painters' guild, of which he eventually served as dean in 1602. His wife Isabella died suddenly in 1603, possibly caused by the birth of their second child, a daughter named Paschasia, who later married the artist Hieronymus van Kessel II.

In 1604 Jan purchased a house called 'De Meerminne' (The Mermaid) in the Lange Nieuwestraat in Antwerp, travelled to Prague and returned to Antwerp by the end of the same year. He married Catharina van Marienberghe (*d* Namur, 1627) in April 1605, who gave him eight children. In 1606 he went to Nuremberg, and two years later, in 1608, he was mentioned in Brussels as court painter of the Archdukes Albert and Isabella, the Habsburg regents of the Netherlands, a function he kept until his death. He also received commissions from Emperor Rudolf II and King Sigismund III of Poland.

Around 1613 Jan travelled to the northern Netherlands on official business in the company of Rubens and Hendrick van Balen. On 27 August 1615 the Antwerp magistrates presented four paintings by Jan Breughel to the Archdukes Albert and Isabella. In 1618 the city magistrates commissioned the 12 major painters of Antwerp to produce a representative sample of their painterly abilities for the Archdukes. But instead of each working on a separate painting, artists such as Rubens, Frans Snyders, Josse de Momper the younger, Hendrick van Balen, Frans Francken the younger and Sebastiaen Vrancx all collaborated on one single project, the *Allegory of the Five Senses*, under the direction of Jan Breughel. Unfortunately, these paintings were destroyed by fire in 1713. In

1619 Jan purchased a house called 'Den Bock' (The Billy-goat) in the Arembergstraat in Antwerp. Jan died from a cholera epidemic, which also claimed the lives of three of his children, Pieter, Elizabeth and Maria. On 3 June and 23 June 1627 Jan's estate was divided among his widow and all his surviving children from his first and second marriages. Executors of Jan's will were Rubens, Pauwel van Halmale, Hendrick van Balen and Cornelis Schut.

2. WORK. Unlike his brother Pieter the younger, Jan did not merely imitate his father. His early compositions show transformations of his father's style into his own delicate miniaturistic idiom. Jan Breughel's landscapes contain numerous figures, either in everyday dress or representing biblical, mythological or allegorical subjects. An early *Wooded Landscape with a Deer Hunt* (*c*. 1593; Vienna, Ksthist. Mus., 458; on dep., Innsbruck, Schloss Ambras) as well as one of the several wooded landscapes that Jan painted *c.* 1597 (Milan, Pin. Ambrosiana, 74.d–18) provide evidence for the debate that concerns Jan's artistic debt to the famous landscapist Gillis van Coninxloo III. Many of Jan's early landscapes are painted from a high vantage-point (bird's eye perspective) with a panoramic and far-reaching horizon in the *Weltlandschaft* tradition of Joachim Patinir, Herri met de Bles and Cornelis van Dalem. His early style is exemplified, for instance, in the *Departure of St Paul to Caesarea* (1596; Raleigh, NC Mus. A., 52.9.92; see fig. 1) as well as in the *Crucifixion* (1598; Munich, Alte Pin., 823) and in several versions of the *Adoration of the Magi* (e.g. London, N.G., 3547; Vienna, Ksthist. Mus., 617; St Petersburg, Hermitage, no. 3090), all datable between 1598 and 1600. (Intriguingly, after 1600 Jan no longer painted the latter subject, although he frequently drew on ideas or compositions by his father and freely adapted motifs from such predecessors as Albrecht Dürer, Nikolas Manuel Deutsch, Jacopo Zucchi, Rosso Fiorentino, Luca Signorelli and Jacopo Tintoretto.)

Jan Breughel the elder also copied some of the Roman townscapes of the Flemings Paul and Matthijs Bril, with whose art he must have become familiar during his sojourn in Rome (*see also* ROME, ANCIENT, fig. 33). There he also met the German Hans Rottenhammer, with whom he collaborated for a short period on several paintings, such as two small paintings on copper, the *Rest on the Flight into Egypt* (*c.* 1595; The Hague, Mauritshuis, 283) and the *Descent into Limbo* (1597; The Hague, Mauritshuis, 265). Around and shortly after 1600 he occasionally painted hallucinatory scenes of Hell, such as *Juno in the Underworld* (Dresden, Gemäldegal. Alte Meister, 877), several versions of the *Temptation of St Anthony* (e.g. Karlsruhe, Ksthalle, 808; Vienna, Ksthist. Mus., 667; Dresden, Gemäldegal. Alte Meister, 878) and several versions of *Aeneas and the Sibyl in Hell* (e.g. Budapest, Mus. F.A., 551 and 553; Vienna, Ksthist. Mus., 817). These compositions are reminiscent of those of Hieronymus Bosch and Jan Mandijn. An equally fantastic *Triumph of Death* (1597; Graz, Alte Gal., 58) was clearly based on a prototype by his father, Pieter Bruegel the elder.

Both the subject-matter and the style of six small landscape paintings on copper (Milan, Pin. Ambrosiana, 74, a–15; 74, e–17; 74, b–16; 74, d–18; 74, e–19; 74, f–20), possibly commissioned by Cardinal Federico Borromeo

1. Jan Breughel I: *Departure of St Paul to Caesarea*, oil on copper, 358×546 mm, 1596 (Raleigh, NC, North Carolina Museum of Art)

and dating from Jan's Milanese period (1595–6), give an accurate insight into Jan's own individual interests, possibilities and stylistic idiosyncrasies towards the turn of the century. The paintings are all framed together and include a *Scene of Hell*, followed by a *Mountainous Landscape with a Monk Reading*, a *Rocky Landscape with a Hermit*, *Christ in a Storm at Sea*, a *Clearing in a Forest* and, finally, an *Allegory of the Elements*, of which the figures were probably painted by Hendrick van Balen. After the turn of the century Jan continued to paint panoramic landscapes with a wide horizon, high vantage-point and many figures. Examples include the *Harbour with the Preaching of Christ* (Munich, Alte Pin., 187), the crowded *Fish Market* (1603; Munich, Alte Pin., 1889), the *Fish Market at the Border of a River* (1605; Munich, Alte Pin., 1883), the *Calling of SS Peter and Andrew* (1608; Dresden, Gemäldegal. Alte Meister, 883) and another, equally crowded harbour scene, with the *Continence of Scipio* (c. 1609; Munich, Alte Pin., 827), the latter three all on copper.

No less than 106 paradise landscapes are attributed to Jan Breughel the elder, most of which are probably by his hand, including several versions of *Noah's Ark* (e.g. Budapest, Mus. F.A.; London, Apsley House, WM 1637, 1948) and an *Adam and Eve in Paradise* (The Hague, Mauritshuis, 253), of which Breughel painted the landscape and animals, while Rubens painted the figures. The theme was varied in several exotic paradise landscapes (e.g. Berlin, Gemäldegal., 742; Rome, Gal. Doria-Pamphili, 341) with Adam and Eve in the background.

The allegorical series of five canvases with the *Five Senses*, as well as two pendants, one with the *Allegory of Sight and Smell* and the other the *Allegory of Touch, Hearing and Taste* (all 1617–18; Madrid, Prado, 1394–8, 1403–4), are probably related in composition and iconography to the lost commission of 1618 from the Antwerp city magistrates. Jan also painted allegorical landscapes, such as four paintings on copper of *The Seasons* (1616; Bayreuth, Neues Schloss, 13709–12). Jan's multifigured allegorical paintings are collaborative works, such as the *Allegory of the Elements* (Vienna, Ksthist. Mus., 815), with figures by Hendrick van Balen.

Flower-pieces with a distinct *vanitas* connotation also formed an important part of Jan Breughel's oeuvre. They include bouquets in various types of vases (e.g. Antwerp, Kon. Mus. S. Kst., 643; Vienna, Ksthist. Mus., 558) and wooden vessels (e.g. Vienna, Ksthist. Mus., 570), floral garlands with *vanitas* still-lifes (e.g. Brussels, Mus. A. Anc., 1015), baskets and dishes of flowers (e.g. Madrid, Prado, 1422) and garlands of flowers surrounding sacred figures or scenes, which were usually painted by others (e.g. Madrid, Prado, 1418). The floral bouquets, in particular, are quite numerous. The elaborate vases often contain flowers that do not bloom at the same time of the year, and though they appear to be realistic, they are, in fact, a careful combination of drawn models, with the blossoms always at their height of perfection. This cumulative practice is elucidated, among other sources, in Jan's letter of April 1606 to Cardinal Federico Borromeo in Milan, in which he explained to the Cardinal that he had begun a

2. Jan Breughel I: *Bouquet with Irises*, oil on panel, 510×400 mm, after 1599 (Vienna, Kunsthistorisches Museum)

bouquet of flowers for him, many of which were unknown and extremely rare and that he even went to Brussels to draw some flowers from life not to be found in Antwerp. His earliest flower-piece (Milan, Pin. Ambrosiana, 66) was possibly painted that same year. The earlier assumption that the *Bouquet with Irises* (Vienna, Ksthist. Mus., 548; see fig. 2) should be dated 1599 is no longer generally accepted.

Many drawings by Jan Breughel the elder have survived. Most represent landscapes such as appear in his paintings, but they also include a few still-lifes and history subjects and several vigorously sketched study sheets. He seems to have drawn exclusively with the pen and brush, occasionally combining brown and blue washes in a manner also practised by many of his contemporaries, such as David Vinckboons or Paulus van Vianen.

3. WORKSHOP AND COLLABORATION. It is possible that Jan Breughel operated a workshop comparable in size to that of Rubens, which would explain the more than 3000 paintings that were formerly ascribed to him. In reality, however, no more than *c.* 450 can be correctly attributed to Jan, of which at least 58 are the result of his collaboration with Josse de Momper. Among the other artists with whom he collaborated were Rubens, van Balen, Frans Snyders, Vrancx, Hendrik de Clerck, Frans Francken the younger, Pieter van Avont and Tobias Verhaecht. The Antwerp still-life painter and priest Daniel Seghers was one of Jan's most famous pupils.

4. CRITICAL RECEPTION AND POSTHUMOUS REPUTATION. His reputation as 'Velvet Breughel', 'Paradise Breughel' or 'Flower Breughel' was firmly established in his day, and he was mentioned in leading 17th- and 18th-century biographies, such as Karel van Mander's *Schilder-boeck* ([1603]–1604), Cornelis de Bie's *Het gulden cabinet van de edel vry schilder const* (Lier, 1661), André Félibien's *Entretiens sur la vie et sur les ouvrages des plus excellents peintres* (Paris, 1666–88), Arnold van Houbraken's *De groote schouburgh der Nederlantse konstschilders en schilderessen* (Amsterdam, 1718–21) and Jan Campo Weyerman's *De levens-beschryvingen der Nederlandsche kunstschilders en schilderessen* (The Hague, 1729). Moreover, when Duke John Ernest of Saxony visited Antwerp in 1614, the chronicler Johann Wilhelm Neumayr described Jan Breughel the elder and Rubens as the two most prominent painters of the city—an assessment confirmed by the city's choice of Breughel to coordinate the commissions for the Archdukes (*see* §1 above).

BIBLIOGRAPHY

K. van Mander: *Schilder-boeck* ([1603]–1604)

M. Winner: 'Zeichnungen des älteren Jan Breughel', *Jb. Berlin. Mus.*, iii (1961), pp. 190–241

M. Eemans: *Breughel de Velours* (Brussels, 1964)

M. Winner: 'Neubestimmtes und Unbestimmtes im zeichnerischen Werk von Jan Breughel der Ältere', *Jb. Berlin. Mus.*, xiv (1972), pp. 122–60

K. Ertz: *Jan Breughel der Ältere* (Cologne, 1979, rev., without cat., Cologne 1981)

——: 'Jan Breughel de oudere', *Bruegel: Een dynastie van schilders* (exh. cat., Brussels, Mus. A. Anc., 1980), pp. 165–209, nos 106–47

S. Bedoni: *Jan Breughel in Italia e il collezionismo del seicento* (Florence and Milan, 1983)

M.-L. Hairs: *Les Peintres flamands de fleurs au XVIIe siècle* (Brussels and Paris, 1985), pp. 35–115

P. M. Jones: *Federico Borromeo and the Ambrosiana: Art Patronage and Reform in Seventeenth-century Milan* (Cambridge and New York, 1993) [with complete cat. of original col.]

(4) Jan Breughel II [the younger] (*b* Antwerp, 13 Sept 1601; *d* Antwerp, 1 Sept 1678). Painter, son of (3) Jan Breughel I. He probably trained in the studio of his father and then went to Milan to meet his father's patron, Cardinal Federico Borromeo. In the spring of 1624 Jan the younger travelled to Palermo, Sicily, with his childhood friend Anthony van Dyck. After the sudden death of his father in a cholera epidemic in Antwerp, Jan returned to the Netherlands, and by early August 1625 he was back in Antwerp, where he took over his father's studio. He sold the pictures left by his father and successfully completed half-finished works. In 1625 Jan II joined the Antwerp Guild of St Luke, and in 1626 he married Anna Maria, the daughter of Abraham Janssen; they had eleven children. Jan the younger headed a large studio with students and assistants, and in 1630–31 he became the dean of the Antwerp guild. The same year he was commissioned to paint an *Adam Cycle* for the French court. Thereafter, the studio declined and he produced a number of small paintings in his father's manner that no longer fetched high prices. According to an inscription attributed to one of his sons on the last page of Jan's journal, which ends in 1651, Jan II was also in France in the 1650s, working in Paris, although no information has yet emerged to indicate how long he stayed there and what he painted. In 1651 he worked for the Austrian court. He is mentioned again in Antwerp in 1657, and various sources indicate that he remained there until his death.

Like his father, Jan II worked with Rubens and Hendrick van Balen, and his journal also indicates that he collaborated with such artists as his father-in-law, Abraham Janssen, Pieter de Lierner, Adriaen Stalbemt, Lucas van Uden and David Teniers the younger (his brother-in-law). Jan tried to stay close to his father's model. Although the general quality of his work never surpassed that of his father, the distinction between his father's late work and his own juvenilia remains problematic. The painted oeuvre of *c.* 340 pictures by Jan the younger includes landscapes, religious, allegorical and mythological themes, still-lifes and a new picture category, animals in a landscape (see fig.). His landscapes can be subdivided according to subject-matter: wooded landscapes, 'near-and-far' landscapes, wide landscapes, water landscapes, village landscapes, landscapes with the Archdukes Albert and Isabella, Hell landscapes and, finally, landscapes with the Holy Family.

The wooded landscapes include forest scenes, forest roads vanishing in the distance and close-up compositions of trees, such as *Forest Road with Travellers* (Florence, Uffizi, 1890), *Wooded Landscape with Riders* (Maastricht, Bonnefantenmus., 541) and *River Crossing* (Warsaw, N. Mus., A. 13). A typical example of the 'near-and-far' landscapes, all of which appear to be composed in a two-dimensional mosaic style, is the *Wooded River Valley with*

Road (Basle, Kunstmus., 1089). In the wide landscapes, with or without a mill, Jan repeated the compositions of his father, though with a different palette, as can be seen in the *Attack on a Baggage Train* (Madrid, Prado, 1884) or in the *Landscape with Mills* (The Hague, Dienst Verspreide Rijkscol., NK 2688). His water landscapes, such as the *Harbour Scene in Antwerp* (Antwerp, Mus. Mayer van den Bergh, 492) or *River Landscape with Wharf* (Sarasota, FL, Ringling Mus., A. 765), also rely on his father's example. In the village landscapes Jan began in his father's idiom but developed his own style in the 1640s. Examples are a *Village Street with Dancing Peasants* (Prague, N.G., Šternberk Pal., O–148) and a *Village Street with Canal* (Aschaffenburg, Schloss Johannisburg Staatsgal., 1897). Of the landscapes with the Archdukes Albert and Isabella, one, of the *Royal Castle in Brussels* (Madrid, Prado, 1857), was executed in collaboration with Sebastiaen Vrancx. Some of the paradise landscapes, which again emulated his father's creations, were also collaborative efforts; for example, the *Paradise Landscape with the Fall of Man* (Madrid, Prado, 1408) was carried out with Denijs van Alsloot and Hendrik de Clerck. Examples of the much rarer Hell landscapes include the *Temptation of St Anthony* (Karlsruhe, Staatl. Ksthalle, 808), *Christ in Purgatory* (The Hague, Mauritshuis, 285) and *Aeneas and the Cumaean Sibyl in the Underworld* (Brussels, Mus. A. Anc., 6249).

Jan Breughel II: *Concert of Birds*, oil on copper, 205×280 mm, 1640s (Brunswick, Herzog Anton Ulrich-Museum)

Finally, landscapes with the Holy Family were for the most part executed after his return from Italy in 1625 and are the result of his collaboration with Hendrick van Balen. The landscape backgrounds were among Jan's best, while van Balen painted the figures. The *Rest on the Flight into Egypt* recurs frequently (e.g. Amsterdam, Rijksmus., A69). Religious scenes, such as a *Noli me tangere* (Paris, Mus. A. Déc., GR 837), reveal less influence of Jan I.

Most of the allegories of the Senses, the Elements, the Seasons and Abundance were executed in the 1620s, while most of Jan II's mythological themes are joint productions, for example the *Rape of Europa* (Vienna, Ksthist. Mus., 814), with van Balen, or the *Banquet of Achelous* (New York, Met., 45.141), painted with Rubens and his studio. Jan II's flower paintings and still-lifes either follow his father's models or are variations on them. His flowers are usually less dense, thinner and less exact in detail, while the picture format is often narrower or reduced in size. In his cartouche paintings, Jan is indebted to Daniel Seghers.

BIBLIOGRAPHY
M. Vaes: 'Le Journal de Jean Breughel II', *Bull. Inst. Hist. Belge Rome*, vii (1926–7), pp. 152–223
J. Denucé: *Brieven en documenten betreffende Jan Breughel I en II* (Antwerp, 1934)
M.-L. Hairs: 'Jan Breughel de jongere', *Bruegel: Een dynastie van schilders* (exh. cat., Brussels, Mus. A. Anc., 1980), pp. 226–30, 238–43, nos 170–78
K. Ertz: *Jan Breughel der Jüngere* (Freren, 1984)
M.-L. Hairs: *Les Peintres flamands de fleurs au XVIIe siècle* (Brussels and Paris, 1985), pp. 223–36

(5) Ambrosius Breughel (*b* Antwerp, *bapt* 10 Aug 1617; *d* Antwerp, 9 Feb 1675). Painter, son of (3) Jan Breughel I. After the death of his father, Ambrosius was placed under the guardianship of Rubens, Hendrick van Balen, Cornelis Schut and Pieter de Jode (i). It is possible that Ambrosius studied under his half-brother Jan the younger. On 10 September 1639 Ambrosius drew up his will in the presence of a witness, the still-life painter Jacob van Hulsdonck (1582–1647), which has been interpreted as proof that he travelled south. At this occasion, he bequeathed a *Crucifixion* by his father and a case of drawings to his brother-in-law David Teniers (ii), who was married to his sister Anna, and Rubens's *Portrait of his Parents* to Jan-Baptist Borrekens (*d* 1668), a painter and art dealer, who was married to his other sister Catherina. In 1645 Ambrosius became a master together with his nephew Jan Pieter Breughel. Ambrosius married Anna-Clara van Triest (*d* Antwerp, 28 Aug 1682) on 20 February 1649. The couple and their four children lived in a house called 'De Fontein' (The Fountain) in the Antwerp Hoogstraat, given as dowry by Michiel van Triest. Ambrosius became dean of the painters' guild in 1653 and 1671 and was also a town official.

An assessment of Ambrosius's oeuvre is still problematic: several flower still-lifes have been attributed to him, as well as a *Vanitas Still-life with Mask and Flowers* (sold London, Sotheby's, 10 July 1974, lot 124; see fig.). However, the attribution of a *Decorated Vase with Flowers* (Prague, N.G., Šternberk Pal., DO 4153) to Ambrosius remains questionable. The same applies to two versions of a *Still-life with Fruit and Flowers* (both Turin, Gal. Sabauda), sometimes attributed to Ambrosius but in reality the work of his nephew Abraham Breughel. The notion

Ambrosius Breughel (attrib.): *Vanitas Still-life with Mask and Flowers*, panel, 1.24×0.77 m (sold London, Sotheby's, 10 July 1974, lot 124)

that Ambrosius was exclusively a landscape painter is largely based on testimony from the 19th century, for example a *Landscape* signed and dated *Ambrosius Breughel fecit 1653* seen in 1876 in the collection of J. Lenglart, Lille, while another *Landscape*, allegedly with figures by David Teniers the younger, signed *Ambrosius Broeghel*, was in the Fahnenburg near Düsseldorf in 1894. A *Landscape with Satan Seeding the Grass* is signed and dated *A. Breughel fecit 1661* (priv. col.; see 1980 exh. cat., no. 179). A similar landscape was previously in Paris (see 1935 exh. cat., p. 18), but its present whereabouts are unknown. Paintings by Ambrosius were also mentioned in the Hendrick van Balen inventory and the inventory drawn up after the death of Jan Baptist Borrekens in 1668. Another *Village View* by Ambrosius was sold twice in 1905 (Brussels, Gal. Sainte-Gudule, 12–13 July, lot 118; Berlin, Mersch, Keller & Reiner, 27–28 Nov, lot 127). Unfortunately, no trace has been found of any of these paintings.

BIBLIOGRAPHY
Die jüngeren Breughel und ihr Kreis (exh. cat., Vienna, Gal. St Lucas, 1935)
E. Greindl: *Les Peintres flamands de nature morte au 17e siècle* (Brussels, 1956)
M.-L. Hairs: 'Ambrosius Breughel', *Bruegel: Een dynastie van schilders* (exh. cat., Brussels, Mus. A. Anc., 1980), pp. 230–34, 244–6, nos 179–82

——: *Les Peintres flamands de fleurs au XVIIe siècle* (Brussels and Paris, 1985), pp. 237–43

HANS J. VAN MIEGROET

Bruehl, Anton (*b* Hawker, Port Augusta, S. Australia, 11 March 1900; *d* San Francisco, CA, 10 Aug 1983). American photographer of Australian birth. He trained as an electrical engineer in Melbourne, but in 1919 he emigrated to the USA. He developed his interest in photography while working for the Western Electric Company, New York. In 1923 he attended an exhibition by students of Clarence H. White, who was then considered America's most prominent Pictorialist photographer. White agreed to teach him privately, but by 1924 Bruehl had become both a regular student at White's New York school and a member of his summer faculty in Canaan, CT. White encouraged the individualism shown by his students. Among them, Bruehl, Paul Outerbridge and Ralph Steiner (*b* 1899) became known for a crisp, graphic style that would distinguish the best commercial photography in the 1920s and 1930s.

In 1927 Bruehl opened his own studio, which prospered in New York until 1966. The photograph *Untitled* (Riverside, U. CA, Mus. Phot., see 1985 exh. cat., no. 20) of an apple, camera and lamp exemplifies his use of high contrast with black background and is an example of the table-top still-lifes that appeared in such magazines as *Vanity Fair*, *House and Garden* and *Vogue* along with his glamorous portraits of international society figures and stars, including *Peter Lorre* (1935; see 1985 exh. cat., no. 18). Bruehl's appointment as chief of colour photography at Condé Nast publishers in the early 1930s led to his most influential work. In collaboration with Fernand Bourges, a French colour technician, he set the standard for commercially printed colour work of the period. Bruehl did not, however, give up working in black and white, as seen in his most important publication *Mexico* (1933), a collection of 25 sensitive portraits of Mexican villagers.

PHOTOGRAPHIC PUBLICATIONS
Mexico (New York, 1933)

BIBLIOGRAPHY
J. Deal: 'Anton Bruehl', *Image*, xix/2 (1976), pp. 1–9
N. Hall-Duncan: *The History of Fashion Photography* (New York, 1979), pp. 99, 120–21, 225
Photography Rediscovered (exh. cat. by D. Travis, New York, Whitney, 1979)
A Collective Vision: Clarence H. White and his Students (exh. cat., ed. L. Barnes, J. Bledsoe and C. Glenn; Long Beach, CA State U., A. Mus., 1985)

CONSTANCE W. GLENN

Bruges [Flem. Brugge]. Belgian city in western Flanders on the River Reie, *c.* 12 km inland from Zeebrugge. It flourished particularly from the 13th to the 15th century, when it was an international port and centre of the cloth trade. Under the patronage of the Dukes of Burgundy, from 1384 the arts flourished in the city, drawing to Bruges such painters as Jan van Eyck, Hans Memling and Gerard David (*see* §II below). With the silting of the outlets to the sea and the withdrawal of the leading merchant houses to Antwerp, the city's prosperity was reduced in the 16th century. Now with a population of *c.* 120,000, Bruges survives as one of the best-preserved medieval cities in Europe.

I. History and urban development. II. Art life and organization. III. Centre of production. IV. Buildings.

I. History and urban development.

The medieval core of Bruges is contained within the line of the 14th-century walls (destr.), *c.* 8 km in circumference, and almost entirely encircled by canals. The urban plan is centred on two squares, Burg (see fig. 1a), the site of the former castle, surrounded by the River Reie, and the adjacent Markt (1b), where the market halls were built (*see* §IV, 1 below). Although Stone Age implements and traces of a Gallo-Roman villa have been found, permanent settlement began only in the 9th century AD, when Count Baldwin Iron-Arm (*reg* 862–79) established a stronghold on the irregular, polygonal site that became the Burg. Inside it were several scattered buildings, including the collegiate church of St Donatien (the first cathedral; destr. 1799), the design of which was based on the Palatine Chapel at Aachen. The first port facilities, which bordered the sea, lay to the north in the present district of St Gillis (1c); but the sea rapidly retreated leaving only a channel. A chapel of St Walburga (1d) was founded near by, and the first churches of St Salvator (1e) and the Onze Lieve Vrouwe (1f) were also built. The first walls had been erected before 1089, the urban area comprising 86 ha.

In 1128 Count Charles the Good (*reg* 1119–28) was assassinated and Bruges won a measure of civic independence. A coastal inundation in 1134 created the Zwin estuary linking Bruges with the sea, and the city's trade developed strongly, although in 1180 the steady silting of the Zwin compelled Count Philip (*reg* 1168–91) to build Damme as an outer harbour *c.* 5 km north of Bruges. As other ports liked to supply their own hinterlands the Bruges merchants switched to international markets based on the cloth trade. A fair was established in 1200, and a Hanse of merchants from 17 cities formed a ruling oligarchy. The population greatly increased, with the creation of new parishes (1239, St Walburga; 1240, St Jakob (1g) and St Gillis, which was at first a chapel of ease to the Onze Lieve Vrouwe and achieved full parochial status in 1311). The Franciscans, Dominicans and Augustinians became established in the city. The cathedral of St Salvator and the churches of St Donatien (the former cathedral) and the Onze Lieve Vrouwe were rebuilt, and the Waterhalle (destr. 1786) was built on the east side of Markt where merchandise could be unloaded directly from the Reie. In the late 13th century a new outer harbour, L'Ecluse, was built on the Zwin. The first Genoese galley arrived via the Straits of Gibraltar in 1277, and in 1294 Edward I, King of England, chose Bruges as the wool staple, through which all continental purchases of English wool had to be conducted. Bruges was caught up in the Anglo-French conflicts of the 1290s and the Hundred Years War (1338–1453) from 1336; the fortifications, ordered to be dismantled in 1305, had to be rebuilt. The new ramparts covered a much larger area, including the new district east of the Reie that became the parish of St Anna (1h), but the population never expanded to fill it. These walls were destroyed in 1782 on the orders of Emperor Joseph II (*reg* 1765–90); four towered gates (altered) and the Minnewater (an inner harbour; 1i) survive.

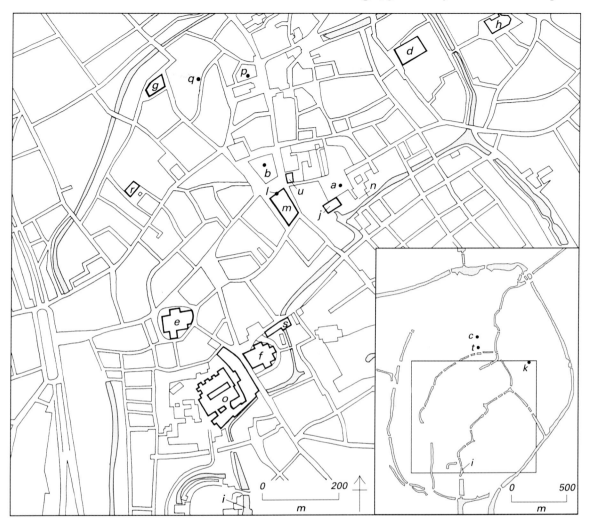

1. Bruges, plan: (a) Burg; (b) Markt; (c) St Gillis; (d) St Walburga; (e) St Salvator; (f) Onze Lieve Vrouwe; (g) St Jacob; (h) St Anna; (i) Minnewater; (j) basilica of the Heilig Bloed; (k) Jerusalem Church; (l) belfry; (m) town hall; (n) Oude Griffie; (o) hospital of St Jan; (p) Genoese trading house; (q) Bladelinhof; (r) Prinsenhof; (s) Gruuthusehof; (t) Oosterlingenhuis; (u) post office

The earliest surviving church in Bruges is the two-storey basilica of the Heilig Bloed (Holy Blood; 1j), built on Burg in 1139–40; the Romanesque lower church has massive columnar piers (the upper church was rebuilt in the 15th century; rest.). In their present state St Salvator and the Onze Lieve Vrouwe are 13th-century vaulted basilicas with tall triforia. St Salvator was restored in the 14th century after a fire, and its radiating chapels with Flamboyant tracery were added from 1482 by Jan van den Poele (*fl* 1478–1520). Its west tower was begun in the 12th century, but the upper part was completed only in 1846. The outer aisles of the Onze Lieve Vrouwe were added in the 14th and 15th centuries, and its tall brick tower, completed 1297, was restored 1853–8. The Jerusalem Church (1k), based on the church of the Holy Sepulchre in Jerusalem, with a tomb of Christ in its crypt, was built as a private church by members of the Bruges branch of the Genoese mercantile Adorno family in 1428.

Bruges is built mostly of brick and timber, with some stone buildings, notably the belfry (1l) and town hall (1m) and the Oude Griffie (1n), the municipal records office, built 1535–7 by Jean Wallot in a style that combines Late Gothic with Renaissance decorative motifs. In addition to the brick hospital of St Jan (now the Memlingmuseum; 1o), which retains its large 13th-century aisled hall, Bruges has a collection of incomparable houses. In the Middle Ages they were timbered, with shutters that could be opened to display merchandise. From 1417, to alleviate fire risks, the authorities subsidized tile roofs, and from 1467 these became obligatory in the main streets. Thatch was forbidden completely in 1535, and from 1616 there was even a tendency to prohibit building in wood.

Vaulted cellars survive from the 13th and 14th centuries, and the earliest small houses date from the 15th. The most important houses were gabled, either fronting a pitched roof (the Genoese trading house, 1399; 1p) or as crenellated screen walls. The earliest date from the 14th century. Houses had towers and were built round galleried courtyards (Bladelinhof, 1451; 1q). The Prinsenhof (1r), the palace of the dukes of Burgundy, no longer exists, but it is known from records, including the engraved plan of the city published by Marcus Gheeraerts (i) in 1562. The distinctive Bruges bay system, whereby several storeys of windows are recessed within a single, tall containing arch, was perhaps derived from the elongated arches of such south Netherlandish churches as S Bertinus, Poperinge. It was adumbrated in the town hall (*see* §IV, 2 below), whence it influenced such houses as the Gruuthusehof (1425, rest.; now Gruuthusemuseum; 1s), Bouchoutehof on Markt and the house of the German Hanse (1478; see fig. 1t and 2), built by Jan van den Poele.

The civic conflicts exacerbated by the Hundred Years War and the more monarchical government of the dukes of Burgundy contributed to the city's decline, but its fortunes were also adversely affected by the decline of the cloth industry and the silting of the Zwin and by changes in international trade. With new industries, however, it did not wholly decline until the Industrial Revolution: fine Baroque buildings include the Jesuit church of St Walburga, built from 1619 by Peter Huyssens in the style of Il Gesù in Rome. In the 1720s the Neo-classical Courts of Justice were built on the east side of Burg, partly on the site of the government centre for the Brugse Vrije, the Liberty of Bruges, the area beyond the city itself. The gabled style of the houses was adapted to the curves and counter-curves of the Baroque, although there was a tendency to stress horizontals by extending cornices.

After the Industrial Revolution, which bypassed Bruges, the city became a museum town. The first signs of antiquarian interest appeared with the Gothic Revival in the 1840s. Buildings in this style contributed to the sense of cohesion in the city, although some restorations, under the direction of LOUIS DELA CENSERIE, were drastic. The public buildings on the site of the Waterhalle on Markt are in the style of Flemish Late Gothic: Dela Censerie's post office (completed 1891; see fig. 1u) and the provincial governor's residence, built 1920–21 by Jules Coomans (1871–1937). Restorations in Post-modern styles are in keeping with the general character of the city.

BIBLIOGRAPHY

E. Gilliat-Smith: *The Story of Bruges* (London, 1901)
A. Duclos: *Bruges: Histoire et souvenirs* (Bruges, 1910)
T. Luykx and J. L. Broekx: *Brugge* (Antwerp, 1943)
J. de Vincennes: *Églises de Bruges* (Bruges, 1950)
R. Mullie: *Monuments de Bruges*, 4 vols (Woluwe-Saint-Lambert, 1960–61)
J. A. Van Houtte: *Bruges: Essai d'histoire urbaine* (Brussels, 1967)
L. Devliegher: *De huizen te Brugge* (Liège, 1968)

JACQUES THIEBAUT

II. Art life and organization.

Before the 15th century, the art of Bruges was produced principally for major civic and ecclesiastical institutions. Following the establishment of the city as a major site of Burgundian court activity in the early 15th century, the art produced there gradually found an international audience, particularly as a result of the accomplishments of the painters Jan van Eyck, Petrus Christus, Hans Memling and Gerard David. Although none was a native of Bruges, each was drawn to the community because of its wealth, court activity and an increasingly sophisticated community of potential patrons. Indeed, 15th-century travellers to Bruges reported that Bruges was 'a large and beautiful city rich in merchandise' (Leo of Rozmital) and noted its many 'fine houses and streets … very beautiful churches and monasteries, and excellent inns' (Pero Tafor). In 1520–21 Albrecht Dürer, on his journey through the Netherlands, noted in his diary that the Emperor's house, the former Prinsenhof, was 'large and splendid'; its chapel had been painted by Rogier van der Weyden and contained other pictures by a 'great old master'. Dürer was also impressed with the great quantities of paintings that were displayed in the many churches of the city and mentioned in particular works by Hugo van der Goes and Jan van Eyck. He also noted having seen Michelangelo's sculpted *Virgin and Child* (1503–05) in the church of Onze Lieve Vrouw.

The demand for painting in Bruges was linked to the city's expanding population and its prosperous merchant communities and urban patriciate (see fig. 3), who embellished their own houses and founded private family chapels in the parish churches, furnishing them with liturgical objects and altarpieces, such as the private chapel of TOMMASO PORTINARI in St Jakob. Increasing numbers of painters came to Bruges for their professional advancement, particularly in the second half of the 15th century and into the first three decades of the 16th. In order to practise the art of painting an individual had to be a citizen of the town and join the painters' guild, an institution that had been founded in the 14th century and became increasingly important throughout the 15th. Its statutes were renewed in 1444, and records of inscribed masters and apprentices were begun in 1454. In addition to the

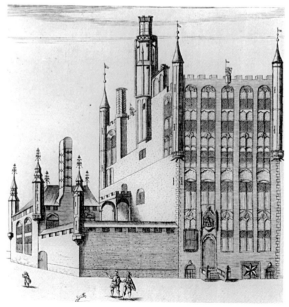

2. Bruges, house of the German Hanse by Jan van den Poele, 1478; from A. Sanderus: *Flandria illustrata* (Amsterdam, 1641)

individual painters cited above, other Bruges master painters of note include: Jan Provoost, Aelbrecht Cornelis, Adriaen Isenbrandt, Ambrosius Benson, Lancelot Blondeel and Pieter Pourbus. The work of such painters as the Master of the Legend of St Lucy and the Master of the Holy Blood was apparently also highly regarded.

Painters who had not trained in Bruges were required to present to the guild proof that their level of craftsmanship was adequate and presumably did so with an example of their work. These individuals, who were noted as 'foreign' (*vreemde*) in the guild inscription lists after 1468, were also required to pay somewhat higher entrance fees to the guild than were paid by painters native to Bruges. The statutes of the painters' guild provide a glimpse into their concerns. Master painters were permitted to have apprentices, provided that they registered them with the guild and did not endeavour to train more than one apprentice at a time. The period of apprenticeship was two years, but between 1479 and 1497 the guild extended it to four years, undoubtedly in response to the rapidly expanding profession during this period. All work accomplished by an apprentice was undertaken under the master's name.

Master painters had workshops, usually within their homes, and sold their paintings from the ground-floor areas fitted with windows opening on to the street. Workshops were staffed by the members of the master's shop, and the skills of individual family members were no doubt also employed when appropriate: there is evidence that painters' wives may have been responsible for the sale of their husbands' works. Wives also inherited their husbands' free-master status in the guild and were responsible for the continuation of the workshop. The few surviving contracts for paintings suggest that the patron may have had considerable control over the production of an artefact. Painters were responsible for arranging the woodworking involved in the project, including both panel and frame, and for paying the woodworker. A patron might stipulate that the master alone be responsible for painting certain portions of the commissioned work, suggesting that assistants' participation in the execution of a work was essentially expected but was, perhaps, to be restricted to the less significant portions of the work. Painters were held responsible for their works even after their completion.

Manuscript illumination was also important in 15th-century Bruges; the relationship between the painters and manuscript illuminators was, however, complex and often strained. Their disputes over the importation of single-leaf miniatures as well as the illuminators' use of certain materials, such as gold, silver and an oil medium, were heard in the civic courts and were frequently decided in favour of the painters. In addition, illuminators were required to register their signature marks with the painters' guild even after they had been permitted to form their own Guild of SS John and Luke in 1454. Among the major manuscript illuminators active in Bruges, Willem Vrelant, Dreux Jean, Loyset Liédet, David Aubert (*fl* 1435; *d* 1482) and Simon Bening were perhaps the most important.

3. *Jan de Leeuw*, a goldsmith of Bruges, by Jan van Eyck, oil on panel, 245×190 mm, 1436 (Vienna, Kunsthistorisches Museum, Gemäldegalerie)

Bruges was also a centre of printing in the second half of the 15th century. Colard Mansion (*fl* 1475–84) produced several luxurious printed editions of popular religious and didactic manuscripts, which he had apparently borrowed from the extensive library of one of his principal patrons, LOUIS DE GRUUTHUSE (see fig. 4). The renowned English printer William Caxton may have learnt much about the printing process from Mansion in Bruges before moving on to Westminster in 1476.

Although the patrons of painting were initially the city's churches and civic institutions, this audience expanded in the 15th century to include guilds, foreign merchants and increasing numbers of private citizens. In 1482 a special market-place—the *pandt*—was constructed in a district south of Markt on the grounds of the Franciscan cloister. This market-place specialized in the display and sale of such luxury commodities as sculpture, goldsmiths' work and painting. During the biannual trade fairs craftsmen rented stalls in the *pandt*, and many appear to have had considerable success with this method of marketing. The practice of selling works from display areas in the home, however, continued throughout the 16th century, although during this period independent shops specializing in the sale of art objects became established, together with the profession of art dealer.

Although the most renowned art of Bruges is principally late medieval, some later work deserves notice. The

4. *Louis de Gruuthuse*, attributed to the Master of the Portraits of Princes, oil on panel, 342×228 mm, 1472–80 (Bruges, Groeningemuseum)

monumental chimney-piece in the palace of the Brugse Vrije is a complex sculpted ensemble of wood, marble and alabaster, designed by Lancelot Blondeel and executed by numerous sculptors. In addition to coats of arms and nearly life-size figures of *Charles V* and his ancestors—*Maximilian I, Mary, Duchess of Burgundy, Ferdinand of Aragon* and *Isabella of Castile*—the chimney contains numerous Renaissance decorative motifs, such as garlands, putti and medallions. Baroque monuments include the rood-screen in St Salvator and the elaborate late 17th-century pulpit in St Jakob.

Many paintings have been moved from the city's churches to the Groeningemuseum, but tombs (*in situ*) include those of *Mary, Duchess of Burgundy* (1495–1502; see HERALDRY, fig. 18) and *Charles the Bold, Duke of Burgundy* (1559–62) in the Onze Lieve Vrouwe, *Anselmo Adorno* (1424–83) and his wife (*d* 1463) in the Jerusalem Church and the tomb of *Ferry de Gros* (*d* 1544), Treasurer of the Order of the Golden Fleece, in St Jakob. In the building restorations of the 19th century, the work of Dela Censerie was complemented by Gothic Revival painting and stained glass by such artists as Jean-Baptiste Charles François Bethune (e.g. in St Salvator and the Onze Lieve Vrouwe).

The major museums of Bruges include the Groeningemuseum (Flemish paintings) and the Memlingmuseum at the hospital of St Jan, which contains several of the master's important works. The Gruuthusemuseum houses an important archaeological collection, including prehistoric artefacts and extensive collections of late medieval wood sculptures, particularly devotional figures, as well as porcelain, coins and lace.

BIBLIOGRAPHY

EARLY SOURCES

Pero Tafur: *Andanças é viajes de Pero Tafur por diversas partes del mundo avidos* (U. Salamanca, Bib. Patrm., Sala 2a. j. pl. 4; 1435–9); ed. D. Marcos Jimenez de la Espada (Madrid, 1874); ed. and Eng. trans. by M. Letts (New York and London, 1926)

Leo of Rozmital: *Travels* (MSS; 1465–7); ed. and Eng. trans. by M. Letts as *The Travels of Leo of Rozmital through Germany, Flanders, England, France, Spain, Portugal and Italy, 1465–1467*, Hakluyt Soc. (Cambridge, 1957)

A. Dürer: *Tagebuch der Reise in die Niederlande* (MS.; 1520–21); Eng. trans., ed. J.-A. Goris and G. Marlier (Greenwich, CT, 1971)

GENERAL WORKS

A. Michiels: *Les Peintres brugeois* (Brussels, 1846)

H. Fierens-Gevaert: *La Peinture à Bruges* (Brussels and Paris, 1922)

F. Winkler: *Die flämische Buchmalerei des XV. und XVI. Jahrhunderts* (Leipzig, 1925)

G. Marlier: *Ambrosius Benson et la peinture à Bruges au temps de Charles-Quint* (Damme, 1957)

F. Cali: *Bruges: The Cradle of Flemish Painting* (Chicago, 1964)

V. Vermeersch: *Brugges kunstbezit* (Bruges and Utrecht, 1969)

H. Stalpaert: *Volkskunde van Brugge* (Bruges, 1974)

V. Vermeersch: *Bruges, mille ans d'art: De l'époque carolingienne au néo-gothique, 875–1975* (Antwerp, 1981)

J. A. Van Houtte: *De geschiedenis van Brugge* (Tielt and Bussum, 1982)

E. J. Mundy: *Painting in Bruges, 1470–1550: An Annotated Bibliography*, Ref. Pubns A. Hist. (Boston, MA, 1985)

G. Dogaer: *Flemish Miniature Painting in the 15th and 16th Centuries* (Amsterdam, 1987)

PAINTERS, ILLUMINATORS AND GUILDS

W. H. J. Weale: 'Inventaire des chartes et documents appartenant aux archives de la corporation de Saint Luc et Saint Éloi, à Bruges', *Le Beffroi*, i (1863), pp. 112–18, 145–52, 201–22, 290–95; ii (1864–5), pp. 241–63

——: 'Documents inédits sur les enlumineurs de Bruges', *Le Beffroi*, ii (1864–5), pp. 298–319; iv (1872–3), pp. 111–19, 238–337

D. Van de Casteele: 'Documents divers de la Société S. Luc à Bruges', *Hand. Genoot. Gesch. 'Soc. Emul.' Brugge*, xviii (1866), pp. 1–430

W. H. J. Weale: 'Documents inédits sur les peintres brugeois', *Le Beffroi*, iii (1866–70), pp. 231–45

D. Van de Casteele: *Keuren (1441–1774): Livres d'admission (1453–1547) et autres documents concernant la Ghilde de St Luc à Bruges* (Bruges, 1867)

C. Van den Haute: *La Corporation des peintres de Bruges* (Bruges and Courtrai, 1913)

J. P. Sosson: 'Une Approche des structures économiques d'un métier d'art: La Corporation des peintres et selliers de Bruges', *Rev. Archéologues & Historiens A. Louvain*, iii (1970), pp. 91–100

J. D. Farquhar: 'Identity in an Anonymous Age: Bruges Manuscript Illuminators and their Signs', *Viator*, xi (1980), pp. 371–84

WORKSHOPS, PRODUCTION PRACTICES AND THE ART MARKET

P. Saenger: 'Colard Mansion and the Evolution of the Printed Book', *Lib. Q.*, 45 (1975), pp. 405–18

L. Campbell: 'The Art Market in the Southern Netherlands in the Fifteenth Century', *Burl. Mag.*, cxviii (1976), pp. 188–98

——: 'The Early Netherlandish Painters and their Workshops', *Le Dessin sous-jacent dans la peinture, Colloque III, 7–9 septembre 1979: Le Problème Maître de Flémalle—van der Weyden* (Leuven, 1981), pp. 43–61

J. C. Wilson: 'The Participation of Painters in the Bruges 'pandt' Market, 1512–1550', *Burl. Mag.*, cxxv (1983), pp. 476–9

——: 'Marketing Paintings in Late Medieval Flanders and Brabant', *Artistes, artisans et production artistique au moyen âge*, ed. X. Barral I Altet, iii (Paris, 1990), pp. 621–7

——: 'Workshop Patterns and the Production of Paintings in Sixteenth-century Bruges', *Burl. Mag.*, cxxxii (1990), pp. 523–7

JEAN C. WILSON

III. Centre of production.

1. TAPESTRY. Tapestry-weavers in Bruges were probably united with the ticking-weavers in a single guild and are recorded as early as 1302. From the last quarter of the 14th century a few painters can be identified as having supplied designs or cartoons for tapestries, including Gillis de Stichele (*fl* 1429–30) and Jan Fabiaan, who it has been suggested is the Master of the Legend of St Lucy. Fabiaan was born in Bethune and settled in Bruges in 1469. In 1478–9, and again in 1480, he was paid for cartoons for tapestries intended to decorate the Great Judgement Chamber of the Bruges Parliament. One of these portrayed a *Wild Man and Wild Woman* (untraced), and the figures carried between them the arms of the Bruges Parliament. There are no extant examples of 15th-century or earlier tapestries, although some pieces have been ascribed to Bruges. At this time tapestry was produced for the most part for daily use and was thus exposed to normal wear and tear.

Late medieval Bruges was an important centre of trade, where, in addition to local work, foreign work was also bought and sold. An ordinance of 1506 relating to the tapestry industry and trade in Bruges suggests that, for the most part, it was very similar to other cities. Such trade undoubtedly had a positive effect on the quality of the work being produced. Several 16th-century tapestry-workers are known by name, and numerous wall hangings are preserved.

By the beginning of the 16th century a series depicting the *Life of St Anatolius* (1502–6; Paris, Louvre) had been woven for the church in Salins in the Franche-Comté. At about the same time pieces depicting coats of arms with intertwining branches filled with flowers and leaves and a distinctive border were also being produced. The principal motif was a blazon surrounded by a laurel wreath. Experienced masters of this time sometimes produced highly finished work, intended for export, such as the illustrated example (see fig. 5), which bears the arms of Paolo Giovio of Como (second quarter of the 16th century; London,

V&A). The work was, however, often rather provincial in character. Traditional motifs can sometimes be found that had been discarded in Brussels years earlier. In Bruges grotesque tapestries, large-leaved *verdures* and pieces with historical and religious scenes were all produced. The *Story of Gombaut and Macée*, a series that was produced several times *c.* 1600, showed links with the past. In a landscape filled with flowers, shrubbery and birds, scenes from pastoral life were portrayed. The exceptional success of this series was due to more than the ribald verses written on the tapestry. Both well- and lesser-known painters contributed cartoons for the tapestry industry at this time. The most important of them was probably Lancelot Blondeel; others included Frans Floris, Marten de Vos (1532–1603) and Joannes Stradanus.

During the 17th century, and possibly as late as the early 18th, many tapestries were produced, some in local monastic workshops, others in private workshops. Several signed pieces of above-average quality dating from this period have survived. A late 17th-century account by a tapestry-worker from Paris notes that Bruges should be considered one of the oldest centres of tapestry production in the region, and that it was famous above all others in earlier times for the rich colours of its wall hangings. Some of the best work was of a quality equal to that of Brussels, but it could not compete with the enormous output of Oudenaarde. The range of subjects displayed in Bruges tapestries at this time is almost equal to that of the major tapestry centres, although the cartoons that were used did not always reflect contemporary artistic developments and would have been considered outdated in other cities. The charmingly coloured borders are noticeably less crowded than tapestries from other towns; in this way they could be completed more rapidly. Although very little is known of the cartoon painters who were active during this period, some can be identified: for example, Cornelis Schut I painted the cartoons *c.* 1640 for a repeatedly utilized series of the *Seven Liberal Arts*, and Pauwels Ricx (*c.* 1610–68) may have contributed the designs for the *Story of Astrée*. Nevertheless, it is certain that the primary source for Bruges tapestry designs was—with a few alterations—drawings and engravings after masters from Antwerp and elsewhere. The Bruges workshops also made use of

5. *Verdure* tapestry with the arms of Paolo Giovio of Como, wool and silk, 2.21×6.83 m, made in Bruges, second quarter of the 16th century (London, Victoria and Albert Museum)

cartoons from the preceding century, including the Renaissance cartoons by Lukas van Nevele (*fl* 1548–65) of the *Months of Luke*; these were altered only slightly, betraying the advent of the Baroque style. There were still a reasonable number of Bruges tapestries in 18th-century collections, for example Prince Karel Alexander of Lotharingen's estate lists (16 Oct 1780) a costly series of tapestries with small figures, woven after Teniers; however, no names of weavers from this period survive.

BIBLIOGRAPHY

J. Versyp: *De geschiedenis van de tapijkunst te Brugge* [The history of Bruges tapestry] (Brussels, 1954)
G. Delmarcel and E. Duverger: *Bruges et la tapisserie* (Bruges, 1987)

ERIK DUVERGER

2. GOLD AND SILVER. Until the 15th century, when Bruges declined as an international trading centre, the gold- and silversmiths of the city, who had been organized as a group from 1302, enjoyed a flourishing reputation. Although their production was still considerable in the 17th and 18th centuries, the influence of the local style remained limited to the area of the ancient bishopric of Bruges. The city mark was derived from the coat of arms: a crowned lion's head looking to the left. A red copper plate (Bruges, Gruuthusemus.) engraved with the names and makers' marks of 186 gold- and silversmiths from 1568 to 1638 survives.

See also BELGIUM, §IX, 1(i) and (ii).

BIBLIOGRAPHY

C.-A. Wauters, ed.: 'De Brugse edelsmeedkunst' [The art of gold- and silversmithing in Bruges], *Vlaanderen*, xxxvi (1987), pp. 1–41
Meesterwerken van de Brugse edelsmeedkunst, (exh. cat. by D. Marechal, Bruges, Memlingmus., and Branwynmus., 1993)

LEO DE REN

IV. Buildings.

1. BELFRY. Covered markets, probably built of brick and stone, existed in Bruges from the beginning of the 13th century. Before 1280 a new building, 84×43 m, was begun on the south side of Markt, built of *moeffen*, large bricks *c.* 300 mm long, with Tournai stone used for the corner shafts and heads of openings. An arch in the north façade led through to the galleries; eight large windows with pointed arches were pierced in the north façade. The market building has a central courtyard, with galleries along the first floors of the short sides. Interior alterations were made in the 16th century.

The belfry (see fig. 6) was built in the centre of the north side. At first it consisted of two square stages, presumably with a wooden superstructure containing the communal bell. The lower storey had bartizans, with their linking galleries; the upper storey had turrets, although these had no spires, nor were there any galleries. A fire in 1280 destroyed the city charter that was kept in a chamber below the bell. The tower was presumably repaired, and after storm damage *c.* 1380 double windows were inserted in each face of the upper storey and spires added to the turrets. A record of restoration in 1413 is evidence that above the entrance portal there was a bay window from which proclamations were made. A clock was installed at the base of the upper storey *c.* 1450 and later in the same

6. Bruges, Belfry, begun *c.* 1280

century openings were made for musicians. The appearance of the belfry at this time is recorded in several paintings, including two works by the Master of the Legend of St Ursula: the *Departure from Brittany* in the *Legend of St Ursula* (Bruges, Groeningemus.) and the *Virgin Enthroned with the Christ Child and Two Angels* (U. Rochester, NY, Mem. A.G.).

Between 1482 and 1486 the silhouette of the belfry was transformed by the addition of the tall octagonal storey, by Pieter Roelins and Joos Roelins. Blind at top and bottom and crowned by a parapet with pinnacles, the deep middle stage has pointed openings (the lower parts later subdivided). Small flying buttresses connect the octagon to the turrets of the upper tower.

2. TOWN HALL. Until the 14th century the aldermen held their meetings in the principal market, but between 1376 and 1420 a town hall (Stadhuis) was built on Burg by the architect Pieter van Oost. Its façade (see fig. 7) measures only *c.* 30 m in length, while its depth is 19 m. The building comprises a single storey over an undercroft, but it is topped by a steeply pitched roof pierced by dormer windows, and its small dimensions are further belied by the overhanging turrets crowned by spires at the corners and centres of the long sides. All the emphasis is

on the vertical, with six tall windows in the form of the Bruges bay (*see* §I above) rising from dado to cornice alternating with tiers of paired niches for statues of the *Virgin*, the *Prophets*, *David* and *Solomon*, and the *Counts of Flanders* from Baldwin Iron-Arm onwards. In the windows are 24 coats of arms of cities in the Liberty of Bruges. The original sculptures were made from 1379 by Jean de Valenciennes and his workshop. According to the records, they were painted in gold, vermilion, blue, 'Spanish' green and ochre, but the originals were destroyed in 1792.

The undercroft of the town hall has a wooden roof supported on four stone columns, but the great hall on the first floor has a fine wooden vault by Jean de Valenciennes, with two rows of quadripartite rib-vaulted bays, divided by deep pendants. Its richly sculpted ribs are supported on stone corbels carved by Pieter van Oost, representing the 12 months of the year. Figures of saints and Old Testament subjects are represented on the pendant bosses, and the vault was painted by Jacques Averechte (*d c.* 1420) and Jacques Zwine. Gerard David was commissioned to decorate the walls with biblical subjects. Over the fireplace, Jan Coene (*fl* 1387; *d* 1408) provided the lion couchant of Flanders supporting a standard with the arms of the house of Burgundy. In 1390–91 Jan Hanoot sculpted the entrance portal of the hall. The town hall was heavily restored in the 19th century, both inside and out.

At the end of the 14th century Bruges, like other cities in the Netherlands, was on the verge of losing its autonomy. The wealth of the middle classes allowed them to compensate for the loss of effective power with the politics of prestige. The Bruges town hall served as a model for the other great buildings of this kind in the late Middle Ages. The association of the main façade with the arcading system of the market and the belfry attained the happy synthesis that constituted such great town halls as those of Brussels, Arras and Oudenaarde.

BIBLIOGRAPHY

C. Dehaisnes: *Histoire de l'art dans la Flandre, l'Artois & le Hainaut avant le XVe siècle* (Lille, 1886)
M. Battard: *Beffrois, halles, hôtels de ville dans le nord de la France et la Belgique* (Arras, 1948)
F.-L. Ganshof: 'Les Halles et le beffroi de Bruges', *Congr. Archéol. France*, cxx (1962), pp. 16–28

For further bibliography *see* §I above.

JACQUES THIEBAUT

Brüggemann, Hans (*b* Walsrode, Lower Saxony, 1480–90). German wood-carver. His place of origin is mentioned in a contract of 1523. From the style of his work it can be deduced that his apprenticeship in Lower Saxony was followed by travels in the Lower Rhine area (Xanten and Kalkar) and in the Netherlands (Utrecht and 's-Hertogenbosch). Important models were provided by Albrecht Dürer's *Small Woodcut Passion* series (1510–11)

7. Bruges, Town Hall, 1376–1420; restored 19th century

and the paintings of Hieronymus Bosch. Between 1514 and 1523 Brüggemann worked in Schleswig-Holstein, where he produced a tabernacle (1520) for the former Marienkirche in Husum: the surviving fragments depict an angel with a lute (Berlin, Skulpgal.) and the Virgin (Copenhagen, Kon. Saml.). He also produced a huge altarpiece (1521), originally in the monastery church of the Augustinian Canons at Bordesholm but moved in 1666 to Schleswig Cathedral. Brüggemann is credited with these works in chronicles. Other works attributed to him are the figure of *St Christopher* (Schleswig Cathedral), the *St George* group (ex-Marienkirche, Husum; Copenhagen, Nmus.) and a small altarpiece showing the *Holy Family* (Schleswig, Schleswig-Holsteinisches Landesmus.) from the Goschhof hospital and almshouse chapel (destr. 1879) in Eckernförde. None of these works is dated. In Schleswig-Holstein Brüggemann's style had no precursors and only a few successors: with the beginnings of the Reformation carved altarpieces and figures of saints were no longer required.

BIBLIOGRAPHY

D. Ellger: *Der Dom und der ehemalige Dombezirk*, ii of *Die Kunstdenkmäler der Stadt Schleswig*, x of Die Kunstdenkmäler des Landes Schleswig-Holstein (Munich and Berlin, 1966), pp. 316–37
H. Appuhn: *Der Bordesholmer Altar und die anderen Werke von Hans Brüggemann* (Königstein, 2/1987)

HORST APPUHN

Illustration Acknowledgements

We are grateful to those listed below for permission to reproduce copyright illustrative material and to those contributors who supplied photographs or helped us to obtain them. The word 'Photo:' precedes the names of large commercial or archival sources who have provided us with photographs, as well as the names of individual photographers (where known). It has generally not been used before the names of owners of works of art, such as museums and civic bodies. Every effort has been made to contact copyright holders and to credit them appropriately; we apologize to anyone who may have been omitted from the acknowledgements or cited incorrectly. Any error brought to our attention will be corrected in subsequent editions. Where illustrations have been taken from books, publication details are provided in the acknowledgements below.

Line drawings, maps, plans, chronological tables and family trees commissioned by the *Dictionary of Art* are not included in the list below. All of the maps in the dictionary were produced by Oxford Illustrators Ltd, who were also responsible for some of the line drawings. Most of the line drawings and plans, however, were drawn by the following artists: Diane Fortenberry, Lorraine Hodghton, Chris Miners, Amanda Patton, Mike Pringle, Jo Richards, Miranda Schofield, John Tiernan, John Wilson and Philip Winton. The chronological tables and family trees were prepared initially by Kate Boatfield and finalized by John Johnson.

Bible *1, 5, 9* Bildarchiv, Österreichische Nationalbibliothek, Vienna; *2* Ecole des Hautes Etudes en Sciences Sociales, Paris; *3* British Library, London (no. 10546, fol. 25*v*); *4* His Grace the Archbishop of Canterbury and the Trustees of Lambeth Palace Library/Photo: Conway Library, Courtauld Institute of Art, London; *6* Pierpont Morgan Library, New York; *7* British Library, London (no. L102.1.5); *8* British Library, London (Harley MS. 1527); *10* Bibliothèque Nationale de France, Paris; *11, 13–14* Photo: Mendel Metzger; *12* Staatliche Museen zu Berlin, Preussischer Kulturbesitz

Bible of Borso d'Este Soprintendenza per i Beni Artistici e Storici di Modena e Reggio Emilia/Photo: Studio Fotografico Roncaglia, Modena

Biccherna Staatliche Museen zu Berlin, Preussischer Kulturbesitz

Bicci di Lorenzo *1* Photo: Archivi Alinari, Florence; *2* Soprintendenza per i Beni Ambientali, Architettonici, Artistici e Storici, Arezzo

Bichvinta Photo: VAAP, Moscow

Biedermeier Graphische Sammlung Albertina, Vienna (inv. no. 28336)

Bierstadt, Albert Metropolitan Museum of Art, New York (Rogers Fund, 1907; no. 07.123)

Bihzad National Library, Cairo

Bijapur Photo: Robert Harding Picture Library, London

Bijlert, Jan van Photo: Ali Meyer, Fine Art Photography, Vienna

Bijogo Photo: Danielle Gallois Duquette

Bijvoet & Duiker Photo: Jan Derwig, Architectuur Fotografie, Amsterdam

Bilivert, Giovanni Photo: Collezione Piero Bigongiari, Florence

Bill, Max Bauhaus-Archiv, Berlin

Binbirkilise Photo: Gertrude Bell Photographic Archive, University of Newcastle upon Tyne

Binck, Jakob Photo: AKG Ltd, London

Bindesbøll: (1) Gottlieb Bindesbøll Photo: Ole Woldbye, Copenhagen

Bingham, George Caleb National Gallery of Art, Washington, DC

Birch, Thomas Pennsylvania Academy of the Fine Arts, Philadelphia, PA (Bequest of Charles Graff)

Bird, Francis Photo: Conway Library, Courtauld Institute of Art, London

Bird's-eye view *1* Guildhall Library, Corporation of London; *2* Amon Carter Museum of Western Art, Fort Worth, TX

Birmingham *1* Reference Library, Local Studies and History Service, Birmingham Central Library; *2* Birmingham Museums and Art Gallery

Biscaino, Bartolomeo Trustees of the British Museum, London

Bishan Das Staatliche Museen zu Berlin, Preussischer Kulturbesitz

Bishapur Werner Forman Archive, London/Photo: Edgar Knobloch

Bisschop, Jan de Archivio Fotografico, Soprintendenza per i Beni Artistici e Storici del Piemonte, Turin

Bistolfi, Leonardo Photo: Studio Fotolinea, Casale Monferrato

Black Sea colonies *1* Hermitage Museum, St Petersburg; *2* Photo: Mira Adanja-Polak

Blaeser, Gustav Staatliche Museen zu Berlin, Preussischer Kulturbesitz

Blake, Peter Whitworth Art Gallery, University of Manchester/© Peter Blake/DACS, 1996

Blake, William *1* Syndics of the Fitzwilliam Museum, Cambridge; *2–4* Tate Gallery, London

Blanchard: (1) Jacques Blanchard Courtauld Institute Galleries, London

Blanchet, Thomas Musée des Beaux-Arts, Lyon

Blaue Reiter Städtische Galerie im Lenbachhaus, Munich

Blechen, Karl *1* Gemäldegalerie Alte Meister, Dresden/Photo: Sächsische Landesbibliothek, Dresden; *2* Stiftung Preussischer Schlösser und Gärten Berlin-Brandenburg

Blenheim Palace Photo: Conway Library, Courtauld Institute of Art, London

Bles, Herri met de Photo: © ACL Brussels

Blind arcade © Maurice H. Ridgway/Photo: Fred H. Crossley

Block-book *1* Art Museum, Princeton University, Princeton, NJ (Museum purchase, Laura P. Hall Memorial Fund); *2* British Library, London (no. I.B.18); *3* British Library, London (no. G.11784)

Blocke: (1) Willem van den Blocke Institute of Art PAN, Warsaw

Blocke: (2) Izaak van den Blocke Institute of Art PAN, Warsaw

Blocklandt, Anthonie Photo: Rheinische Bildarchiv, Cologne

Bloemaert: (1) Abraham Bloemaert *1* Statens Museum for Kunst, Copenhagen; *2* Rijksmuseum, Amsterdam

Bloemen: (2) Jan Frans van Bloemen Photo: Archivi Alinari, Florence

Blois Photo: Anthony Kersting, London

Blomfield, Reginald Drawing: Cyril Farey/Photo: Sydney Newbery

Blondeel, Lanceloot Photo: © ACL Brussels

Blondel: (1) Jacques-François Blondel *1* British Architectural Library, RIBA, London; *2* Photo: Arch. Phot. Paris/© DACS, 1996

Bloomsbury Group National Portrait Gallery, London (Duncan Grant Estate, 1978, by courtesy of Henrietta Garnett)

Blue-and-white ceramic *1* Ashmolean Museum, Oxford; *2* Photo: William R. Sargent; *3* Ho-am Art Museum, Seoul; *4* Schloss Charlottenburg, Berlin/Photo: Bridgeman Art Library, London

Böblinger: (1) Hans von Böblingen I Bayerisches Nationalmuseum, Munich

Böblinger: (3) Matthäus Böblinger Stadtarchiv, Ulm

Hans von Böblingen III Kupferstichkabinett, Akademie der Bildenden Künste, Vienna

Bobo Photo: Christopher D. Roy

Boccaccino: (1) Boccaccio Boccaccino Photo: Archivi Alinari, Florence

Boccaccio, Giovanni Biblioteca Nazionale Centrale, Florence

Boccioni, Umberto *1* Museum of Modern Art, New York (Gift of Vico Baer); *2* Museum of Modern Art, New York

Böcklin, Arnold *1* Bayerische Staatsgemäldesammlungen, Munich; *2* Kunstmuseum, Basle/Photo: Martin Bühler

Bourbon, §II: (2) Elizabeth Museo del Prado, Madrid/Photo: Bridgeman Art Library, London

Bourbon, §II: (4) Charles III Museo del Prado, Madrid

Bourdelle, Emile-Antoine Musée Bourdelle, Paris/© DACS, 1996

Bourdichon, Jean *1–2* Bibliothèque Nationale de France, Paris

Bourdon, Sébastien Photo: © RMN, Paris

Bourges *1–2* Photo: Conway Library, Courtauld Institute of Art, London; *3* Photo: Zodiaque, St-Léger-Vauban; *4, 6* Photo: Arch. Phot. Paris/© DACS, 1996; *5* Photo: Stephen K. Scher

Bouts: (1) Dieric Bouts I *1* Photo: © ACL Brussels; *2* Musées Royaux des Beaux-Arts de Belgique, Brussels; *3–4* Trustees of the National Gallery, London; *5* Bayerische Staatsgemäldesammlungen, Munich

Bouts: (2) Albrecht Bouts Musées Royaux des Beaux-Arts de Belgique, Brussels

Bove, Osip Photo: VAAP, Moscow

Box, gold Metropolitan Museum of Art, New York

Boyd: (2) Arthur Boyd National Gallery of Victoria, Melbourne

Boyle: (2) Boyle, Richard *1* British Architectural Library, RIBA, London; *2* National Portrait Gallery, London; *3* Yale University Press Photo Library, London; *4* Devonshire Collection, Chatsworth, Derbys. By permission of the Duke of Devonshire and the Trustees of the Chatsworth Settlement

Boys, Thomas Shotter Board of Trustees of the Victoria and Albert Museum, London

Boznańska, Olga National Museum, Kraków

Braccesco, Carlo Photo: © RMN, Paris

Bracci, Pietro Photo: Archivi Alinari, Florence

Bracquemond: (1) Félix Bracquemond Bibliothèque Nationale de France, Paris

Braga Photo: Cesar Valenca

Braganza: (7) John V Photo: Conway Library, Courtauld Institute of Art, London

Braganza: (13) Ferdinand II *3* Museu-Biblioteca da Casa de Bragança/Paço Ducal de Vila Viçosa

Brak, Tell Trustees of the British Museum, London

Bramante, Donato *1* Courtauld Institute Galleries, London; *2* Photo: Bibliotheca Hertziana, Rome; *3–4* Photo: Archivi Alinari, Florence; *5* Photo: Conway Library, Courtauld Institute of Art, London; *6* Photo: Overseas Agenzia Fotografica, Milan

Bramantino Trustees of the National Gallery, London

Bramer, Leonard Museo del Prado, Madrid

Brancusi, Constantin *1* Philadelphia Museum of Art, Philadelphia, PA/© ADAGP, Paris, and DACS, London, 1996; *2* Muzuel Naţional de Artă al României, Bucharest/© ADAGP, Paris, and DACS, London, 1996; *3* Musée National d'Art Moderne, Paris/© ADAGP, Paris, and DACS, London, 1996; *4* © ADAGP, Paris, and DACS, London, 1996

Brand: (2) Johann Christian Brand Germanisches Nationalmuseum, Nuremberg

Brandenburg Photo: Ernst Ullman

Brandl, Petr National Gallery, Prague

Brandt, Bill Board of Trustees of the Victoria and Albert Museum, London

Braque, Georges *1, 3* Museum of Modern Art, New York/© ADAGP, Paris, and DACS, London, 1996; *2* Kunstmuseum, Basle (Gift of Dr H.C. Raoul La Roche, 1952)/Photo: Martin Bühler/© ADAGP, Paris, and DACS, London, 1996; *4* © ADAGP, Paris, and DACS, London, 1996

Brass *2, 6, 9* Photo: Dr P.T. Craddock; *7, 10* Photo: Joan Day, Bristol; *8* Trustees of the British Museum, London

Brassaï © Estate Brassaï/Photographie Brassaï/International Museum of Photography at George Eastman House, Rochester, NY

Brasses, monumental Photo: Wilhelm Castelli, Lübeck

Bratislava *1* Hutchison Library, London/Photo: Liba Taylor; *2* Photo: Peter Paul, Bratislava

Braun, Matyáš Bernard National Gallery, Prague

Brauner, Victor Musée National d'Art Moderne, Paris/© ADAGP, Paris, and DACS, London, 1996

Bray, de: (1) Salomon de Bray Provinciale Atlas Noord-Holland, Rijksarchief in Noord-Holland, Haarlem

Bray, de: (2) Jan de Bray J.B. Speed Art Museum, Louisville, KY

Brazil *2* Trustees of the British Museum, London; *3* Collection João Marino, São Paulo; *4* Bridgeman Art Library, London; *5, 7* South American Pictures, Woodbridge, Suffolk/Photo: Tony Morrison; *6* Photo: G.E. Kidder Smith, New York; *8* Photo: Antonio Fernando Batista dos Santos; *9* Photo: Museu Nacional de Belas Artes, Rio de Janeiro; *10* Photo: Brazilian Embassy, London/© DACS, 1996; *11* Instituto Lina Bo e P.M. Bardi/Photo: F. Albuquerque, 1948; *12* Museu de Arte de São Paulo

Bréa, Louis Archivio Fotografico del Servizio Beni Culturali, Genoa

Breenbergh, Bartholomeus *1* Governing Body, Christ Church, Oxford; *2* Photo: Gabinetto Fotografico Nazionale, Istituto Centrale per il Catalogo e la Documentazione, Rome

Bregno: (1) Antonio Bregno I Photo: Osvaldo Böhm, Venice

Bregno: (2) Andrea Bregno Photo: Archivi Alinari, Florence

Bregno: (3) Giovanni Battista Bregno Reale Fotografia Giacomelli, Venice/Photo: Anne Markham Schulz

Bregno: (4) Lorenzo Bregno Photo: Reale Fotografia Giacomelli, Venice

Bremen Board of Trustees of the Victoria and Albert Museum, London

Brenet, Nicolas-Guy Photo: © RMN, Paris

Brescia Photo: Archivi Alinari, Florence

Bresdin, Rodolphe Trustees of the British Museum, London

Breton, Jules Photo: © RMN, Paris

Brett, John Birmingham Museums and Art Gallery

Breu: (1) Jörg Breu (i) Stift Melk/Photo: P. Jeremia

Breu: (2) Jörg Breu (ii) Pierpont Morgan Library, New York (acc. no. 1978.38)

Breuer, Marcel Museum of Modern Art, New York (Purchase)

Breviary British Library, London (MS. 2897, fol. 188)

Brick *1* Redland Bricks Ltd, Newcastle under Lyme; *3* Photo: RCHME/© Crown Copyright; *4, 11* Photo: Nicholas J. Moore; *6* Photo: Yves Calvet; *7* Photo: Robert Ousterhout; *8* Photo: Archivi Alinari, Florence; *9* Museum für Kunst und Kulturgeschichte, Lübeck; *10* Rijksdienst voor de Monumentenzorg, Zeist; *12* Institute of Art PAN, Warsaw; *13* Photo: Ampliaciones y Reproducciones MAS, Barcelona; *14* Master and Fellows of St John's College, Cambridge; *15* Photo: Bildarchiv Foto Marburg; *16* Photo: Margaret Carey; *17* Photo: Dr Michael Willis; *19* Photo: © Michael Freeman, London

Bridge *2–4* Photo: E.C. Ruddock

Bridgeman, Charles Bodleian Library, Oxford (MS. Gough Drawings a.4, fol. 46)

Brighton British Architectural Library, RIBA, London

Bril: (2) Paul Bril Photo: Archivi Alinari, Florence

Brinkman: (2) J. A. Brinkman Tentoonstellingsraad Archive/Nederlands Architectuurinstituut, Rotterdam

Brisbane Photo: Jones Lang Wootton, Australia

Bristol *1* City of Bristol Museum and Art Gallery; *2* Photo: John Trelawney-Ross; *3* Photo: RCHME/© Crown Copyright

Brno *1* Robert Harding Picture Library, London/Photo: © Gavin Heller; *2* Moravian Museum, Brno

Broeck, van den: (2) Crispin van den Broeck Royal Collection, Windsor Castle/© Her Majesty Queen Elizabeth II

Broeck, van den: (3) Hendrik van den Broeck Photo: Scala, Florence

Broederlam, Melchior Photo: © ACL Brussels

Brokof: (2) Ferdinand Maximilián Brokof Photo: Josef Ehm, Prague

Bronze *2* Photo: P.T. Craddock; *3* Photo: Werner Forman Archive, London

Bronzino, Agnolo *1* Photo: Giraudon, Paris; *2* Trustees of the National Gallery, London; *3* Photo: Archivi Alinari, Florence; *4* Frick Collection, New York

Broodthaers, Marcel Tate Gallery, London

Brosamer, Hans Trustees of the British Museum, London

Brosse, Salomon de *1–2* Photo: Arch. Phot. Paris/© DACS, 1996

Brou, priory church Photo: Conway Library, Courtauld Institute of Art, London

Brouwer, Adriaen *1–2* Bayerische Staatsgemäldesammlungen, Munich

Brown, 'Capability' London Library, London

Brown, Ford Madox *1* Manchester City Art Galleries; *2* Birmingham Museums and Art Gallery

Browne, Hablot Knight British Library, London (no. C.58, fol. 21)

Bruchsal, Schloss Photo: Bildarchiv Foto Marburg

Brücke, Die Erich Heckel Estate, Hemmenhofen/© DACS, 1996

Bruegel: (1) Pieter Bruegel I *1, 4* Akademie der Bildenden Künste, Vienna/Photo: AKG Ltd, London; *2* Photo: © ACL Brussels; *3* Museo del Prado, Madrid; *5* Kunsthistorisches Museum, Vienna; *6* Soprintendenza per i Beni Artistici e Storici, Naples; *7* Kunsthistorisches Museum, Vienna/Photo: Bridgeman Art Library, London; *8* Bibliothèque Royale Albert 1er, Brussels; *9* Trustees of the British Museum, London

Bruegel: (2) Pieter Brueghel II *1* Photo: © ACL Brussels; *2* Metropolitan Museum of Art, New York (Gift of the Estate of George Quackenbush, in his memory, 1939; no. 39.16)